FAIRBAIRN'S CRESTS.

ABBREVIATIONS.

Pl.	plate.	Beds.........	Bedfordshire.	Linc.........	Lincolnshire.
cr.	crest.	Berks.........	Berkshire.	Middx.......	Middlesex.
fig.	figure.	Bucks.........	Buckinghamshire.	Monm.......	Monmouthshire.
		Cambs........	Cambridgeshire.	Norf.........	Norfolk.
or.........	gold.	Chesh........	Cheshire.	Northamp..	Northamptonshire.
ar.........	argent.	Cornw........	Cornwall.	Northumb..	Northumberland.
gu.........	gules.	Cumb.........	Cumberland.	Notts........	Nottinghamshire.
az.........	azure.	Derbs........	Derbyshire.	Oxon........	Oxfordshire.
purp.......	purpure.	Devons......	Devonshire.	Ruts.........	Rutlandshire.
sa.........	sable.	Dors.........	Dorsetshire.	Salop........	Shropshire.
vert.......	green.	Durh.........	Durham.	Somers......	Somersetshire.
ppr........	proper.	Ess...........	Essex.	Staffs.......	Staffordshire.
erm........	ermine.	Glamorg.....	Glamorganshire.	Suff.........	Suffolk.
		Glouc........	Gloucestershire.	Surr.........	Surrey.
Eng........	English.	Hants........	Hampshire.	Suss.........	Sussex.
Sco........	Scotch.	Heref........	Herefordshire.	Warw.......	Warwickshire.
Iri.........	Irish.	Herts........	Hertfordshire.	Westm......	Westmoreland.
Lond.......	London.	Hunts........	Huntingdonshire.	Wilts........	Wiltshire.
Wel........	Welsh.	Lanc.........	Lancashire.	Worc........	Worcestershire.
co.........	County.	Leic.........	Leicestershire.	Yorks.......	Yorkshire.

NOTE.—It will occasionally be found that reference is made to crests which do not exactly agree with the description; where this occurs, the deficiencies are either marked by parentheses, or correct representations are referred to. Heraldic Painters, Engravers, Chasers, and others, for whose benefit this has been done, will appreciate its value.

CONTENTS OF VOL. I.

ARMS OF BRITAIN	TITLE
INDEX	1
GLOSSARY	523
MOTTOES	531

FAIRBAIRN'S CRESTS
OF THE FAMILIES OF
Great Britain and Ireland

Compiled from the best Authorities by James Fairbairn,

AND REVISED BY

LAURENCE BUTTERS

Seal Engraver in ordinary to the Queen for Scotland.

VOLUME FIRST.

EDINBURGH.

INGLIS & JACK, 20 Cockburn Street.

Drawn & Engraved by James Fairbairn Edin.

Printed and bound by Antony Rowe Ltd, Eastbourne

INDEX

TO

FAIRBAIRN'S CRESTS

OF THE FAMILIES OF

Great Britain and Ireland.

AAR *ABE*

AARON, and AARONS, Eng., a lady's arm from elbow, in pale, ppr. *Plate* 91, *crest* 8.
AAROONS, same crest.
ABADAIN, or ABAUDAIN, a savage, wreathed about head and middle with laurel leaves, holding over shoulder a club, all ppr. *Pl.* 14, *cr.* 11.
ABADAM, Eng., in dexter hand a broken spear, all ppr. *Pl.* 66, *cr.* 4.
ABADAM, EDWARD, Esq., of Middleton Hall, Carmarthen, out of a ducal coronet, or, a demi-lion, gardant, gu. *Aspire—Persevere—*and—*Indulge not. Pl.* 35, *cr.* 4, (coronet, *pl.* 128, *fig.* 3.)
ABARLE, Eng., a flute, in pale, ppr. *Pl.* 15, *cr.* 1.
ABAROUGH, or ABARON, Somers., a ferret, ar., collared, or, lined, az. *Pl.* 12, *cr.* 2.
ABBAT, Eng., a unicorn's head, issuing, ppr. *Pl.* 20, *cr.* 1.
ABBEFORD, Leic., on a chapeau, ppr., a water-bouget, sa. *Pl.* 56, *cr.* 9.
ABBERBURY, Oxon. and Suff., a hawk, wings expanded, resting dexter on a mount, ppr. *Pl.* 49, *cr.* 1.
ABBERBURY, Oxon. and Suff., a camel's head, sa. *Pl.* 109, *cr.* 9.
ABBETOT, Warw., in dexter hand a cutlass, in pale, ppr., hilted, or. *Pl.* 66, *cr.* 6.
ABBETT, Eng., a unicorn's head, ppr., collared, az. *Pl.* 73, *cr.* 1.
ABBEY, Lond., an eagle's head, erased, ppr. *Pl.* 20, *cr.* 7.
ABBEY, Eng., a leopard, rampant, ppr. *Pl.* 73, *cr.* 2.
ABBIS, ABBISS, ABIS, or ABYS, Norf., a spur, az., leather, sa., buckle, of the first. *Pl.* 15, *cr.* 3.
ABBORNE, a dexter arm, ppr., vested, az., cuffed, or, in hand, of the first, a baton, in bend sinister, gu., tipped with gold. *Pl.* 18, *cr.* 1.
ABBOT, Baron Colchester of Colchester, Ess., out of a ducal coronet, or, a unicorn's head, erm., maned and tufted, of the first, (between six ostrich-feathers, ar., quilled, or.) *Deo patriæ amicus. Pl.* 110, *cr.* 1.
ABBOT, or ABBOTT, Iri., in hand a dagger, point downward, dropping blood. *Pl.* 18, *cr.* 3.

ABBOT, a fox, passant, ppr., charged on shoulder with a water-bouget, ar. *Labore. Pl.* 126, *cr.* 5; *pl.* 14, *cr.* 12.
ABBOT, a snail, ppr. *Pl.* 105, *cr.* 8.
ABBOT, out of a ducal coronet, a unicorn's head, or, between two ostrich-feathers, ar. *Pl.* 110, *cr.* 1.
ABBOT, Lincoln, a unicorn's head, erased, ar., attired and crined, or, (charged with a bar-gemelle.) *Pl.* 67, *cr.* 1.
ABBOT, out of a ducal coronet, a horse's head. *Pl.* 50, *cr.* 13.
ABBOT, Eng., a demi-unicorn, erm., armed and maned, ar., collared, az., studded, or. *Pl.* 21, *cr.* 1.
ABBOT, a cubit arm, erect, vested, az., cuffed, erm., in hand, ppr., a crescent, ar. *Pl.* 110, *cr.* 7.
ABBOT of Castleacre, Norf., or ABOAT, a griffin, sejant, or. *Pl.* 100, *cr.* 11.
ABBOT, Eng., a griffin, sejant, az., bezantée. *Pl.* 100, *cr.* 11, (bezant, *pl.* 141.)
ABBS, Durh., the sun in splendour. *Noli irritare leonem. Pl.* 68, *cr.* 14.
ABBY, Eng., a cross crosslet, az. *Pl.* 66, *cr.* 8.
ABCOT, or ABCOTT, a rose, per pale, or and az., barbed, counterchanged. *Pl.* 20, *cr.* 2.
ABDAY, Eng., an eagle's head, erased, ppr. *Pl.* 20, *cr.* 7.
ABDEN, Eng., a swan's head, ppr., between wings, az. *Pl.* 54, *cr.* 6.
ABDEY, Lond., Felix Hall, Bart., Ess.; and Albins, Bart., Ess.; an eagle's head, erased, ppr., beaked, or. *Pl.* 20, *cr.* 7.
ABDY, and ABDEY, Ess., an eagle's head, erased, ppr. *Pl.* 20, *cr.* 7.
ABDY, Lond.; Stapleford-Abbot, Ess.; and Cobham Place, Bart., Surr.; same crest.
ABDY of Felix Hall, Bart., Ess., an eagle's head, ppr., couped, or. *Tenax et fidelis. Pl.* 100, *cr.* 10.
ABDY, Bart., an eagle's head, erased, ppr. *Tenax et fidelis. Pl.* 20, *cr.* 7.
ABECK, or HABECK, Eng., out of a mural coronet, an arm from elbow, vested, az., cuffed, ar., in hand, ppr., a mullet, gu. *Pl.* 34, *cr.* 1.

A

A'BECKETT, Eng., a Cornish chough, ppr. *Pl.* 100, *cr.* 13.

ABEL, and ABELL, Ess. and Kent, an arm, in armour, embowed, ppr., hand grasping a sword, ar., hilted, or, arm enfiled with a wreath, ar. and gu. *Pl.* 21, *cr.* 4.

ABEL, Ess., an arm, in armour, embowed, hand grasping a couteau, all ppr. *Pl.* 81, *cr.* 11.

ABELEYN, Eng., a peacock, passant, ppr. *Pl.* 54, *cr.* 13.

ABELHALL, or ABLEHALL, Eng., a lion's head, erased, sa., between wings, or. *Pl.* 73, *cr.* 3.

ABELL, Kent, a boar's head, erect, sa., couped, armed, or, (transpierced by an arrow, in bend sinister, shaft, ar., pheon, az.) *Pl.* 108, *cr.* 1, (without feathers.)

ABELL, Cork, same crest. *Invicta veritate.*

ABELINE, or ABLIN, a sword, in pale, enfiled with a savage's head, ppr. *Pl.* 27, *cr.* 3.

ABELON, or ABILON, Eng., a mitre, ppr., ribbons, gu. *Pl.* 12, *cr.* 10.

ABELYN, or ABELYNE, Eng., on a globe, ppr., an eagle, wings expanded and inverted, gu. *Pl.* 34, *cr.* 2.

ABENHALL, or ABLEHALL, Eng., two branches of laurel, issuing, cheveron-ways, vert. *Pl.* 21, *cr.* 2.

ABENY, in hand, ppr., vested, gu., cuffed, or, a mill-rind, ppr. *Pl.* 34, *cr.* 3.

ABER, Eng., a demi-talbot, rampant, ar., ducally gorged, gu. *Pl.* 15, *cr.* 2.

ABERBURY, Oxon., a hawk, wings expanded, resting dexter on a mount, ppr. *Pl.* 49, *cr.* 1.

ABERBUTHNET, merchant, Montrose, a dove, with an adder in a circle, ppr. *Innocue ac provide.* *Pl.* 92, *cr.* 6.

ABERBUTHNET of Fiddes, a peacock, passant, ppr. *Tam interna, quam externa.* *Pl.* 54, *cr.* 13.

ABERBUTHNET of Findowrie, a peacock, issuing. *Interna præstant.* *Pl.* 24, *cr.* 1.

ABERBUTHNOT, Sco., a peacock. *Pl.* 92, *cr.* 11.

ABERBUTHNOT, ALEXANDER, Sco., a peacock's head, ppr., beaked, or. *Laus Deo.* *Pl.* 100, *cr.* 5.

ABERBUTHNOT, Sco., same crest and motto, but head erased, ppr. *Pl.* 86, *cr.* 4.

ABERCORN, Marquess of, and Visc., Eng.; Earl of, and Baron Paisley, Abercorn, Hamilton, Mountcastle, and Kilpatrick, Sco.; Visc. and Baron Strabane, and Baron Mountcastle, Iri., (Hamilton ;) out of a ducal coronet, or, an oak, fructed, penetrated transversely in main stem by a frame-saw, ppr., frame, or. *Through*—and—*Sola nobilitas virtus.* *Pl.* 100, *cr.* 2.

ABERCORNE, Sco., a boar's head, couped, ppr. *Pl.* 48, *cr.* 2.

ABERCORNE, Sco., two daggers, in saltier, ppr. *Pl.* 24, *cr.* 2.

ABERCROMBIE, Sir Robert, Sco.; of Tullibody and Glasshaugh; and Baroness, Sco.; a bee, volant, ppr. *Vive ut vivas.* *Pl.* 100, *cr.* 3.

ABERCROMBIE, of Birckenbog, Bart., a hawk, rising, ppr., belled, or. *Mercy is my desire* —and—*Petit alta.* *Pl.* 105, *cr.* 4.

ABERCROMBIE of that Ilk, Sco., on a mount, an oak-tree, acorned, all ppr. *Tace.* *Pl.* 48, *cr.* 4.

ABERCROMBIE in Carolina, a cross on grieces, gu. *In cruce salus.* *Pl.* 49, *cr.* 2.

ABERCROMBIE of Fetternier, a cross crosslet, fitched, gu. *In cruce salus.* *Pl.* 16, *cr.* 10.

ABERCROMBY, a bee, volant, ppr. *Vive ut vivas.* *Pl.* 100, *cr.* 3.

ABERCROMBY, Baron, of Aboukir and Tullibody, (Abercromby;) a bee, ppr. *Vive ut vivas.* *Pl.* 107, *cr.* 13.

ABERCROMBY, Banff, on a mount, an oak-tree, acorned, all ppr. *Tace.* *Pl.* 48, *cr.* 4.

ABERDEEN, Sco., in dexter hand an annulet, ppr. *Intemerata fides.* *Pl.* 24, *cr.* 3.

ABERDEEN, Marischal College, the sun in splendour. *Luceo.* *Pl.* 68, *cr.* 14.

ABERDEEN, Earl of, Sco.; Visc. Gordon, Eng., (Hamilton-Gordon;) a sinister arm and dexter hand, with bow, and arrow ready to fly, ppr. *Ne nimium.* *Pl.* 100, *cr.* 4.

ABERDOUR, an anchor with cable, and a sword, in saltier, all ppr. *Hinc spes effulget.* *Pl.* 25, *cr.* 1.

ABERDWELL, or ABREDROBELL, Eng., a greyhound, ar., current towards a tree, vert. *Pl.* 27, *cr.* 2.

ABERGAVENNY, Earl of, and Baron, Visc. Neville, (Noville;) a bull, ar., pied, sa., armed, or, (charged on neck with a rose, barbed and seeded, ppr.) *Ne vile velis.* *Pl.* 66, *cr.* 11.

ABERKERDOUR, and ABERKIRDOR, Sco., a sword, in pale, ppr. *Pro rege et patria.* *Pl.* 105, *cr.* 1.

ABERKIRDOR, Sco., within horns of a crescent, ar., a buckle, az. *Pl.* 25, *cr.* 3.

ABERKIRDOR, and ABERKIRDOUR, Sco., on the point of a sword, in pale, a garland, all ppr. *Pro rege.* *Pl.* 15, *cr.* 6.

ABERNEATHY, Sco., a ship under sail, ppr. *Salus per Christum.* *Pl.* 109, *cr.* 8.

ABERNETHY, Lord, Sco., and of Rothmay, a parrot feeding on a bunch of cherries, all ppr. *Salus per Christum.* *Pl.* 49, *cr.* 3.

ABERNETHY, Sco., a cross crosslet, fitched, gu. *In Christo salus.* *Pl.* 16, *cr.* 10.

ABERNETHY of Corskie, in the sea a ship in distress. *Salus per Christum.* *Pl.* 21, *cr.* 11.

ABERNETHY of Auchinloich, a parrot, ppr. *In Christo salus.* *Pl.* 25, *cr.* 2.

ABERNETHY, Sco., a ship under sail, ppr. *Salus per Christum.* *Pl.* 109, *cr.* 8.

ARERTON, Eng., on a human heart, gu., an eagle's foot, erased, ppr. *Pl.* 27, *cr.* 1.

ABETT, Eng., a unicorn's head, gu., collared, or. *Pl.* 73, *cr.* 1.

ABILEM, a man's head, in profile, issuing, ppr. *Pl.* 36, *cr.* 3.

ABINGDON, or ABINGTON, of Dowdeswell, Glouc., an arm, in armour, embowed, in fess, couped at shoulder, garnished, or, in hand an ancient mace, handled, sa., headed and studded, gold, girt near shoulder with a sash, tied in a bow, ar., fringed, of the first. *Pl.* 28, *cr.* 2.

ABINGDON, a dexter arm, in armour, embowed, ppr., in hand a sword by the blade, point downward. *Pl.* 65, *cr.* 8.

ABINGDON, a bull, rampant. *Pl.* 18, *cr.* 4.

ABINGDON, Worc. and Heref., an eagle, displayed, or, crowned, az. *Pl.* 85, *cr.* 11, (not charged.)

ABINGDON, Earl of (Bertie;) a Saracen's head, couped, ppr., ducally crowned, or (charged on chest with a fret, az.) *Virtus ariete fortior.* *Pl.* 28, *cr.* 3.

ABINGER, Baron, (Scarlet;) a Tuscan column, chequy, or and gu., supported on either side by a lion's gamb, erm., erased, of the second. *Sine stet viribus.* *Pl.* 77, *cr.* 4.

ABLE, Eng., an arm, in armour, embowed, hand grasping a sword, all ppr. *Pl.* 2, *cr.* 8.

ABLYN, Eng., a sword, in pale, enfiled with a savage's head, ppr. *Pl.* 27, *cr.* 3.

ABNEY, WILLIAM-WOTTON, Esq. of Measham Hall, Derby, a demi-lion, rampant, or, between paws a pellet, sa. *Fortiter et honeste.* *Pl.* 126, *cr.* 12.

ABORIL, and ABROL, Worc., a lion's head, ppr., vomiting flames, gu. *Pl.* 20, *cr.* 3.

ABOT, Eng., a unicorn's head, erased, ppr. *Pl.* 67, *cr.* 1.

ABRAHALL, Heref., a hedgehog, ppr. *Pl.* 32, *cr.* 9.

ABRAHAM, Eng., the sun, or. *Pl.* 68, *cr.* 14.

ABRAHAMS, Eng., a chapeau, with plume of ostrich-feathers, all ppr. *Pl.* 28, *cr.* 1.

ABRAM, Eng., the sun rising from a cloud, ppr. *Pl.* 67, *cr.* 9.

ABRAM, Lorraine, a bee, or. *Pl.* 107, *cr.* 13.

ABREY, Eng., a chevalier on horseback, at full speed, holding a broken spear, all ppr. *Pl.* 43, *cr.* 2.

ABRISCOURT, Oxon., a hare, close, among grass, ppr. *Pl.* 29, *cr.* 1.

ABROOK, and ABROOKE, Eng., a wolf's head, erased, sa. *Pl.* 14, *cr.* 6.

ABSALEM, ABSOLOM, ABSOLON, and ABSOLUM, Eng., a fleur-de-lis, or. *Pl.* 68, *cr.* 12.

ABTOT, a bear, couchant, ar., collared, muzzled, and langued, or. *Pl.* 76, *cr.* 5.

ABURTON, Eng., on a human heart, gu., an eagle's foot, erased, ppr. *Pl.* 27, *cr.* 1.

ABUSCOURT, Eng., a hare, close, among grass, ppr. *Pl.* 29, *cr.* 1.

ABUSTOURT, Eng., same crest.

ACCORNE, Sco., an oak-tree, vert. *Stabo.* *Pl.* 16, *cr.* 8.

ACECK, ACBICHE, or HACKBECK, a cross pattée, erm. *Pl.* 15, *cr.* 8.

ACFORD, a horse's head, sa., bridled, or. *Pl.* 92, *cr.* 1.

ACGUILLUM, in dexter hand a holly-branch, ppr. *Pl.* 55, *cr.* 6.

ACHALON, (a flower-pot, eared,) or, filled with roses, gu. *Pl.* 23, *cr.* 2.

ACHAM, Plenyth, Cornw., a lion, sejant, or, collared and lined, sa. *Pl.* 21, *cr.* 3.

ACHAM, a demi-lion, ar., holding a maunch, gu. *Pl.* 67, *cr.* 10, (maunch, *pl.* 78, *cr.* 1.)

ACHANY, Sco., out of a crescent, a cross crosslet, fitched, sa. *Per ardua ad alta.* *Pl.* 43, *cr.* 3.

ACHARD, a crescent inflamed, ppr. *Pl.* 29, *cr.* 2.

ACHELEY, Lond. and Salop, an eagle's head, gu., winged, or, in beak a branch of lilies, ar., leaved, vert. *Pl.* 81, *cr.* 10, (lily, *same plate, cr.* 9.)

ACHELEY, Eng., a griffin's head, erased, ppr. *Pl.* 48, *cr.* 6.

ACHELEY, Eng., a griffin's head, ppr. *Pl.* 38, *cr.* 3.

ACHELEY, Lord Mayor of London, 1512, a demi-swan, gu., winged, or, (in mouth a flower, ar., stalked and leaved, vert.) *Pl.* 54, *cr.* 4.

ACHELEY, Lond., same crest, collared, or.

ACHER, Kent, a bull's head, erased, gu. *Pl.* 19, *cr.* 3.

ACHESON, Earl of Gosford, Iri., a cock, gu., standing on a trumpet, ppr. *Vigilantibus.* *Pl.* 2, *cr.* 1.

ACHESON, Eng., a sandglass, ppr. *Pl.* 43, *cr.* 1.

ACHESON, Sco. and Iri., a cock, ppr. *Pl.* 67, *cr.* 14.

ACHESON, Sco., an eagle, displayed. *Pl.* 48, *cr.* 11.

ACHESON, Sco., an astrolabe, ppr. *Observe.* *Pl.* 26, *cr.* 2.

ACHILLES, Eng., a savage's head, affrontée, ducally crowned, ppr. *Pl.* 28, *cr.* 3.

ACHILLIS, Eng., same crest.

ACHYEM, Eng., a crescent, or. *Pl.* 18, *cr.* 14.

ACHYM, or ACKLAME, a lion, sejant, (gardant,) or, collared and chained, sa. *Pl.* 21, *cr.* 3.

ACKELOM, a sagittarius, shooting, ppr. *Pl.* 70, *cr.* 13.

ACKERMAN, or ACKERMANN, Eng., out of a palisado coronet, or, an arm embowed, ppr., vested, gu., cuffed, ar., in hand an oak-branch, vert., acorned, of the first. *Pl.* 2, *cr.* 2, (coronet, *pl.* 128, *fig.* 21.)

ACKERS, Eng., a Doric column, or. *Pl.* 33, *cr.* 1.

ACKERS, GEORGE-HOLLAND, Esq., of Moreton Hall, Chester, a dove, (rising,) in mouth an olive-branch, all ppr. *La liberté.* *Pl.* 48, *cr.* 15.

ACKHURST, a demi-lion, ar., in dexter, an acorn, slipped, vert, fructed, or. *Pl.* 39, *cr.* 14, (acorn, *pl.* 81, *cr.* 7.)

ACKLAM, or ACLOME, Yorks., a demi-lion, ar., holding a maunch, gu. *Pl.* 84, *cr.* 7, (maunch, *pl.* 78, *cr.* 1.)

ACKLAME, a lion, sejant, or, collared, sa. *Pl.* 21, *cr.* 3.

ACKLAND of Columb-John, Bart., Devons., on a sinister arm, in fess, vested, az., in a glove, ar., a hawk, perched, of the last, beaked and belled, or. *Inébranlable.* *Pl.* 83, *cr.* 13.

ACKROYD, or ACKEROYD, Eng., a dog, sleeping, ppr. *Pl.* 29, *cr.* 3.

ACKWORTH, Eng., a griffin's head, erased, ppr. *Pl.* 48, *cr.* 6.

ACKWORTH, Kent, a griffin, segreant, per fess, az. and purp., armed, or. *Vincit qui patitur.* *Pl.* 67, *cr.* 13.

ACLAND, Bart., Killerton, Devons., and Holnicote, Somers., on a man's hand, in fess, gloved, a falcon, perched, all ppr. *Inébranlable.* *Pl.* 83, *cr.* 13.

ACLAND, PALMER-FULLER, Somers., Bart.;
1. For *Acland*, on a sinister arm, in fess, vested, az., gloved, ar., a hawk, perched, gold, beaked and belled, or. *Pl.* 83, *cr.* 13.
2. For *Palmer*, a demi-panther, gardant, ar., spotted, gu., vert, or, and az. alternately, flames issuing out of mouth and ears, holding a palm-branch, ppr. *Pl.* 76, *cr.* 1.
3. For *Fuller*, on a ducal coronet, gu., a lion's head, ar. *Palma virtuti.* *Pl.* 90, *cr.* 9.

ACLAND, in dexter hand, couped, in fess, a rose-branch. *Pl.* 46, *cr.* 12, (rose, *pl.* 105, *cr.* 7.)

ACLE, Devons., an annulet, or, stoned, sa. *Pl.* 35, *cr.* 3.

ACLEHUM, a (demi)-lion, vert, holding an escutcheon, gu. *Pl.* 22, *cr.* 13.

ACOCK, out of a mural coronet, a swan, issuing, ppr. *Pl.* 100, *cr.* 7, (coronet, *pl.* 128, *fig.* 18.)
ACOTTS, or ACOTTIS, Eng., a lion, rampant, gu., supporting a standard, ppr., flag, az., charged with a saltier, ar. *Pl.* 99, *cr.* 2.
ACOTTS, or ACOTIS, a lion, rampant, supporting the standard of Scotland, ppr. *Pl.* 99, *cr.* 2.
A'COURT, Bart., an eagle, displayed, sa., (charged with two cheveronels, ar.,) beaked, and legged, gu., in beak a lily, slipped, ppr. *Grandescunt aucta labore*. *Pl.* 48, *cr.* 11, (lily, *pl.* 81, *cr.* 9.)
A'COURT, Eng., a lion's head, erased, regardant, gu. *Pl.* 35, *cr.* 2.
ACRAMAN, Eng., out of a vallary coronet, or, an arm, embowed, ppr., vested, gu., cuffed, gold, in hand an oak-branch, vert, acorns, of the second. *Pl.* 2, *cr.* 2, (coronet, *pl.* 128, *fig.* 21.)
ACRE, Westm., a triangular harrow, ppr. *Pl.* 7, *cr.* 2.
ACRES, Northumb., an eagle, displayed, ppr., charged on breast with a torteau, sa. *Pl.* 12, *cr.* 7.
ACRIS, Westm., same crest.
ACTON, Bart., Salop, within a wreath, ar. and gu., a leg and thigh, in armour, ppr., garnished, or, couped, and dropping blood. *Pl.* 76, *cr.* 4.
ACTON, EDWARD-FARRER, Esq., of Gatacre Park, Salop, same crest.
ACTON, THOMAS, Esq., of West Aston, co. Wicklow, same crest. *Adjuvante Deo.*
ACTON, Chesh., a demi-lion, rampant, regardant, ar., grasping a spear, or, enfiled with a boar's head, sa., couped, gu. *Pl.* 33, *cr.* 2.
ACTON, Worc., an arm, in armour, embowed, ppr., hand grasping a sword, ar., hilt, or, enfiled with a boar's head, couped, sa., dropping blood. *Pl.* 2, *cr.* 8, (head, *pl.* 10, *cr.* 2.)
ACTON, WILLIAM-JOSEPH, Esq., of Wolverton, Worcester, same crest. *Vaillance avance l'homme.*
ACTON, Eng., a pine-tree, leaved, vert, fructed, or. *Pl.* 26, *cr.* 10.
ACTON, Iri., a torteau, sa., between wings, gu. *Pl.* 2, *cr.* 3.
ACTON, a demi-lion, regardant, supporting a spear, enfiled with a savage's head. *Pl.* 33, *cr.* 2.
ACWORTH, Eng., a griffin's head, erased, ppr. *Pl.* 48, *cr.* 6.
ADAIR, of Kinghilt, Bart., Hinhilt, and Renkelt, a man's head, couped, and bloody, ppr. *Loyal au mort*. *Pl.* 23, *cr.* 1.
ADAIR, GEORGE, Esq., of Bellegrove and Rath, Queen's co., Iri., same crest and motto.
ADAIR, ALEXANDER, Esq., of Heatherton Park, Somerset, and Colehouse, Devon, same crest. *Loyal à mort.*
ADAIR, Maryport, Cumb., and Sco., a Saracen's head, couped, and impaled with a spear, ppr. *I dare*. *Pl.* 7, *cr.* 3.
ADAIR, Bart., of Flixton Hall, Suff., a man's head, affrontée, couped at neck, (bloody,) ppr. *Loyal au mort*. *Pl.* 19, *cr.* 1.
ADAIR, THOMAS-BENJAMIN, Esq., of Loughanmore, co. Antrim, a man's head, couped at neck, ppr. *Loyal au mort*. *Pl.* 81, *cr.* 15.

ADAIR, Sco., on a sword, in pale, a Saracen's head, affrontée, dropping blood, all ppr. *Arte et marte*. *Pl.* 42, *cr.* 6.
ADAM, Christ-church, Hants., a crescent, ar. *Pl.* 18, *cr.* 14.
ADAM, Culross, N.B., a cross crosslet, and sword, in saltier, ppr. *Crux mihi grata quies*. *Pl.* 89, *cr.* 14.
ADAM, or ADAMS, Eng., a griffin's head, gu., between wings, or, pellettée, beaked, az. *Pl.* 22, *cr.* 2.
ADAM, an eagle, volant, ppr. *Pl.* 114, *cr.* 10.
ADAM, of Runcorn, two swords, in saltier, and a cross crosslet, fitched, in pale. *Dominus ipse faciet*. *Pl.* 42, *cr.* 5.
ADAM, Sco., in hand a cross crosslet, fitched, gu. *Crux mihi grata quies*. *Pl.* 99, *cr.* 1.
ADAM, Walden, Ess., a talbot, passant, az., semée of bezants, collared, ar. *Pl.* 65, *cr.* 2, (bezants, *pl.* 141.)
ADAM, WILLIAM-PATRICK, Esq., of Blairadam, Kinross, a cross crosslet, fitched, gu., and sword, in saltier, ppr., hilt and pommel, or. *Crux mihi grata quies*. *Pl.* 89, *cr.* 14.
ADAMS, HENRY-WILLIAM, Esq., of Ansty Hall, Warwick, and Morton Pinkney, Northampton, a talbot, passant, az., semée of bezants, collared, ar. *Sub cruce veritas*. *Pl.* 65, *cr.* 2, (bezant, *pl.* 141.)
ADAMS, WILLIAM-DACRES, Esq., of Bowdon, Devon, a dexter arm, (in armour, embowed,) in hand a cross crosslet, fitched, charged on elbow with a torteau. *Libertas et natale solum*. *Pl.* 99, *cr.* 1, (torteau, *pl.* 141; arm, *pl.* 120, *cr.* 11.)
ADAMS, JOHN, of Holyland, Pembroke, a martlet, ar. *Certior in cœlo domus*. *Pl.* 111, *cr.* 5.
ADAMS, The Very Rev. SAMUEL, A.M., of Northlands, co. Cavan, on a mount, vert, a cross crosslet, fitched, or, (charged with a bleeding heart, gu.) *In cruce salus*. *Pl.* 58, *cr.* 6, (without sun.)
ADAMS, THOMAS-TRAVERS, Esq., of Ahavagurrah, co. Limerick, a griffin's head, erased, az. *Malo mori quam fœdari*. *Pl.* 48, *cr.* 6.
ADAMS, Bart., a greyhound's head, couped. *Pl.* 14, *cr.* 4.
ADAMS, Devons., out of a ducal coronet, a demi-lion, gardant. *Pl.* 35, *cr.* 4, (coronet, *pl.* 128, *fig.* 3.)
ADAMS, Camb., a griffin's head, gu., between wings, or. *Pl.* 22, *cr.* 2.
ADAMS, Linc., a griffin's head, between wings, gu., beaked, az., on each wing three bezants. *Pl.* 22, *cr.* 2, (bezant, *pl.* 141.)
ADAMS, Lond. and Iri., a boar's head, ar., (another, or,) couped, gu. *Pl.* 48, *cr.* 2.
ADAMS, Lond., a lion, rampant, or. *Pl.* 67, *cr.* 5.
ADAMS, Eng., on a bezant, a demi-eagle, sa. *Pl.* 7, *cr.* 6, (eagle, *pl.* 52, *cr.* 8.)
ADAMS, Middx., an eagle, volant, regardant. *Pl.* 114, *cr.* 10.
ADAMS, Salop, a greyhound's head, erased, erm. *Pl.* 89, *cr.* 2.
ADAMS, Cheaton, Salop, a griffin's head, erased, erm., beaked, gu., (charged with a cheveron vair, or and az.) *Pl.* 48, *cr.* 6.
ADAMS, Eng., a griffin's head, between wings, addorsed, vert, (charged on breast with a cross, or.) *Pl.* 22, *cr.* 2.

ADAMS, Eng., a raven, sa. *Pl.* 123, *cr.* 2.
ADAMS, Iri., an arm, couped at shoulder, embowed, ppr., vested, gu., in hand a flag, sa., charged with a bee. *Pl.* 99, *cr.* 3.
ADAMS, a dexter arm, in armour, embowed, in hand a cross crosslet. *Pl.* 45, *cr.* 10, (cross, *pl.* 99, *cr.* 1.)
ADAMS of Anstey, Warw., same crest. *Sub cruce veritas.*
ADAMS, Lond., a wolf's head, erased, erm. *Pl.* 14, *cr.* 6.
ADAMS, on a mount, vert, an eagle, reverse and regardant, wings expanded, ppr., beak and legs, or, in beak a mullet, sa., sinister resting on a crescent, reversed, gold.
ADAMS, a greyhound's head, couped, ermines, (charged on neck with two bars-gemelle.) *Pl.* 14, *cr.* 4.
ADAMSON, Newcastle-upon-Tyne, a cross crosslet, gu. *Pl.* 66, *cr.* 8.
ADAMSON, a lion, passant, in dexter a cross crosslet, fitched, gu. *Pl.* 48, *cr.* 8, (cross, *pl.* 141.)
ADAMSON, Westm., a talbot, passant, az., collared, or, bezantée. *Pl.* 65, *cr.* 2, (bezant, *pl.* 141.)
ADAMSON, Sco., a cross crosslet, fitched, and sword, in saltier, ppr., hilt and pommel, or. *Pl.* 89, *cr.* 14.
ADAMSON, Eng., a tilting-spear, broken in three pieces, two in saltier, head-piece in pale, pointed, or banded, gu. *Pl.* 33, *cr.* 3.
ADCANE, Eng., a griffin's head, ppr. *Pl.* 38, *cr.* 3.
ADCOCK, Eng., a fox's head, issuing, ar. *Pl.* 91, *cr.* 9.
ADDAGH, a lion, rampant. *Mea gloria fides.* *Pl.* 67, *cr.* 5.
ADDAMS, Eng., a griffin's head, between wings, gu. *Pl.* 22, *cr.* 2.
ADDCOCK, Eng., a fox's head, ppr. *Pl.* 91, *cr.* 9.
ADDERBURY, Suss., an embattled tower, ppr. *Pl.* 12, *cr.* 5.
ADDERLEY, Weddington, Warw., and Staffs., on a chapeau, gu., turned up, erm., a stork, ar. *Pl.* 106, *cr.* 6.
ADDERLEY, CHARLES-BOWYER, Esq., of Hams Hall, Warwick, same crest.
ADDERLEY, The Rev. GEORGE-WILLIAM-BOWYER, of Fillongley Hall, Warwick, same crest.
ADDERLY, Staffs. and Sco., a rose, gu. *Pl.* 105, *cr.* 7.
ADDERSTONE, ADERSTON, or ADDRESTON, Eng., a martlet, sa. *Pl.* 111, *cr.* 5.
ADDERTON, Eng., a hand grasping a scimitar, ppr. *Pl.* 29, *cr.* 8.
ADDEY, Kent, on a mount, a stag, lodged, ppr. *Pl.* 22, *cr.* 5.
ADDINGTON, Viscount Sidmouth, a leopard, sejant, gardant, ppr., resting dexter on a shield, or. *Libertas sub rege pio.*
ADDINGTON, a cat, passant, ppr. *Pl.* 119, *cr.* 7.
ADDIS, or ADES, Eng., out of a tower, ppr., a demi-lion, az. *Pl.* 42, *cr.* 4.
ADDISON, a pair of wings, erect, ppr. *Pl.* 63, *cr.* 12.
ADDISON, a unicorn's head, erased, (transpierced by an arrow, in bend sinister, guttée.) *Let the deed shaw.* *Pl.* 67, *cr.* 1.
ADDLINGTON, Devons. and Linc., a goat's head, erased, ppr. *Pl.* 29, *cr.* 13.

ADDRESTON, Eng., a martlet, gu. *Pl.* 111, *cr.* 5.
ADDURSTON, a swan's neck and wings, ar., beaked, gu., gorged with a ducal coronet, or. *Pl.* 54, *cr.* 6, (gorging, *pl.* 30, *cr.* 10.)
ADDY, Kent, on a mount, a stag lodged, all ppr. *Pl.* 22, *cr.* 5.
ADEAN, Eng., a stag's head, cabossed, ppr. *Pl.* 36, *cr.* 1.
ADEANE, HENRY-JOHN, Esq., of Babraham, Cambridge, a griffin's head, between wings, (collared.) *Pl.* 22, *cr.* 2.
ADELIN, a chevalier on horseback, at full speed, brandishing a sword, all ppr. *Pl.* 118, *cr.* 14.
ADELMARE, (the sea, vert,) thereon a dolphin, embowed, ppr. *Pl.* 48, *cr.* 9.
ADELSORF, two wings, elevated, sa. *Pl.* 39, *cr.* 12.
ADELSTON, or ADESTON, an escutcheon, ar., charged with a cinquefoil, gu. *Pl.* 36, *cr.* 11, (cinquefoil, *pl.* 141.)
ADENSTOUN, ADINGSTOUN, or ADINSTON, Sco., in dexter hand a cross pattée, fitched. *Pl.* 99, *cr.* 15.
ADERLEY, Blackhall, Staffs., a leopard's head, couped, or, (pierced through mouth with a sword blade, broken, ar.) *Pl.* 92, *cr.* 13.
ADERSON, Eng., a cup, or, with three branches of laurel, issuing, vert. *Pl.* 35, *cr.* 1.
ADERTON, Eng., a hand grasping a scimitar, ppr. *Pl.* 29, *cr.* 8.
ADERSTONE, Eng., a martlet, sa. *Pl.* 111, *cr.* 5.
ADEY, ADREY, ADY, on a mount, vert, a stag lodged, ar., attired and (ducally crowned,) or. *Pl.* 22, *cr.* 5.
ADGER, Eng., a swan, wings addorsed, regardant, ar., murally crowned, gu., resting dexter on an escallop, or. *Pl.* 44, *cr.* 15.
ADIE, Crieff, a dagger, ppr., and cross crosslet, fitch-d, gu., in saltier. *Crux mihi grata quies.* *Pl.* 89, *cr.* 14.
ADIE, AEDIE, and ADDIE, Crieff, and Sco., a cross crosslet, and sword in saltier, ppr. *Crux mihi grata quies.* *Pl.* 89, *cr.* 14.
ADIS, Eng., out of a tower, ppr., a demi-lion, az. *Pl.* 42, *cr.* 4.
ADKINS, Eng., a lion, rampant, gu., supporting a flag-staff with ropes, ppr., flag, ar., charged with a cross, of the first. *Pl.* 99, *cr.* 2.
ADLAM, Eng., in hand, gu., a hawk's lure, or. *Pl.* 44, *cr.* 2.
ADLAM, Somers., on a mount, vert, in front, rays of the sun, an eagle, ppr., collared, sa. *Tyme proveth truth.*
ADLARD, a cubit arm, in hand a dagger, erect, all ppr. *Pl.* 23, *cr.* 15.
ADLER, Haverstoke, Ess., a demi-eagle, wings displayed, sa., charged on breast with an etoile, or. *Pl.* 44, *cr.* 14.
ADLINGTON, Eng., a goat's head, erased. *Pl.* 29, *cr.* 13.
ADLINGTON, a heraldic antelope's head, erased, ar. *Pl.* 76, *cr.* 3.
ADLYN, on a mount, vert, a martlet, or. *Pl.* 36, *cr.* 5.
ADNEY, Eng., an eagle's head, in beak an acorn, slipped and leaved, ppr. *Pl.* 22, *cr.* 1.
ADSHEAD, and ADSHADE, Eng., an antelope, passant, ppr. *Pl.* 63, *cr.* 10.
ADSON, Sco., an oak-tree. *Stand sure.* *Pl.* 16, *cr.* 8.

ADVENTURERS, Merchant, or Hambro' Merchants of London, a pegasus, current, wings addorsed, or. *Dieu nous adventure donne bonne*. *Pl.* 28, *cr.* 9.

ADY, or ADRY, Eng., a leopard's face, or, jessant-de-lis, gu. *Pl.* 123, *cr.* 9.

ADYE, Kent, a cherub's head, ppr. *Pl.* 67, *cr.* 11.

ADYER, Kent and Durh., a cherub's head, ppr. *Pl.* 67, *cr.* 11.

ADYN, Dorchester, a lion's head, ppr. *Pl.* 126, *cr.* 1.

AERMINE, Eng., on a mount, vert, an ermine, ar., tip of tail, sa. *Pl.* 87, *cr.* 3.

AETH, Eng., a demi-griffin, or, in dexter a battle-axe, gu. *Pl.* 44, *cr.* 3.

AFFLECK, Bart., Dalham Hall, Suss., an ear of rye, ppr. *Pretiosum quod utile*. *Pl.* 41, *cr.* 3.

AFFLECK of that Ilk, Sco., same crest and motto.

AFFLECK of Balmanno, Sco., two wings, issuing. *Rerum sapientia custos*. *Pl.* 63, *cr.* 12.

AFFLECK, Bart., an ear of wheat, bearded, ppr. *Pretiosum quod utile*. *Pl.* 85, *cr.* 6.

AFFORDBIE, of Afordby, Linc., a horse's head, erased, sa., bridled, or. *Pl.* 92, *cr.* 1.

AFFORDBY, same crest.

AFRICAN COMPANY OF SCOTLAND, the rising sun, ppr. *Qua panditur orbis*. *Pl.* 67, *cr.* 9.

AGAD, a heraldic antelope's head, issuing. *Pl.* 76, *cr.* 3.

AGAN, out of a ducal coronet, or, a stag's head, cabossed, ppr. *Pl.* 29, *cr.* 7.

AGAR, Iri., a demi-lion, rampant, ar. *Vita trita via tuta*. *Pl.* 67, *cr.* 10.

AGAR, Lord Clifden and Lord Callan, Iri. and Ess., a demi-lion, rampant, or. *Spectemur agendo*. *Pl.* 67, *cr.* 10.

AGARD, Lanc., a bugle-horn, ar., garnished, or, stringed, sa. *Pl.* 48, *cr.* 12.

AGARD, Lanc., an ibex's head, or, charged with hurts, maned, tufted, horned, and collared, az. *Pl.* 105, *cr.* 12.

AGAS, Wymondham, Norf., a moor's head, sa., wreathed, ar. and gu. *Pl.* 48, *cr.* 7.

AGBURY, Kent, a bird, supporting a flag, charged with a cross. *Pl.* 65, *cr.* 3.

AGER, or AUGER, Bishopbourn, Kent and Glouc., a bull's head, erased, gu., attired, or. *Pl.* 19, *cr.* 3.

AGG, or AUGE, Eng., a moor's head, couped, sa., banded, ar. and az. *Pl.* 48, *cr.* 7.

AGGS, or AGALL, on a chapeau, ppr., a bull, statant, sa. *Pl.* 65. *cr.* 11.

AGLIONBY, Cumb., a demi-eagle, displayed, or. *Pl.* 22, *cr.* 11.

AGMONDESHAM, Horsley, Surr., a stag, or. *Pl.* 81, *cr.* 8.

AGMONDISHAM, or AGMUNDESHAM, Surr., a stag, lodged, ppr. *Pl.* 67, *cr.* 2.

AGNEW, Eng., the sun shining on stump of tree, ppr. *Pl.* 123, *cr.* 3.

AGNEW, or AGNEU, Sheuchan and Lothian, Sco., an eagle, issuant and regardant, ppr. *Consilio non impetu*. *Pl.* 27, *cr.* 15.

AGNEW, and AGNEU, Lochryan and Creach, an eagle, regardant, in dexter a sword, ppr. *Consilio et impetu*. *Pl.* 87, *cr.* 5.

AGNEW of Castle Wiger, an eagle, rising, regardant, ppr. *Consilio non impetu*. *Pl.* 35, *cr.* 8.

AGNEW, a crow, statant, wings expanded, transfixed with an arrow, all ppr. *Pl.* 110, *cr.* 13.

AGNEW of Lochnaw, Bart, an eagle, issuing, regardant, ppr. *Consilio non impetu*. *Pl.* 27, *cr.* 15.

AGNEW-VANS, ROBERT, Esq., of Barnbarroch, Wigton, Sco.: 1. For *Agnew*, an eagle, issuant, regardant, ppr. *Consilio non impetu*. *Pl.* 27, *cr.* 15. 2. For *Vans*, a lion, rampant, in dexter a pair of scales. *Be faithful*. *Pl.* 67, *cr.* 5, (scales, *pl.* 26, *cr.* 8.)

AGREVELL, Eng., a bezant, or. *Pl.* 7, *cr.* 6.

AGRUALL, Eng., a lion's head, gardant, between wings, ppr. *Pl.* 87, *cr.* 2.

AGUILAR, and AGUILLAR, Eng., an eagle's head, erased, in beak a fleur-de-lis, ppr. *Pl.* 121, *cr.* 7.

AGUILLON, Yorks., a pelican, vulning, ppr. *Pl.* 109, *cr.* 15.

AGWORTH, Eng., a torteau, gu. *Pl.* 7, *cr.* 6.

AHANNY, AHANY, HANNAY, or HANNEY, Sco., out of a crescent, a cross crosslet, fitched, sa. *Per ardua ad alta*. *Pl.* 43, *cr.* 3.

AHEM, Iri., a vine, ppr. *Pl.* 89, *cr.* 1.

AHER, Iri., a sand-glass, sa., winged, gu. *Pl.* 32, *cr.* 11.

AHRENDS, Eng., an eagle, ppr. *Post nubila phœbus*. *Pl.* 7, *cr.* 11.

AICKEN, Eng., a fountain, ppr. *Pl.* 95, *cr.* 15.

AICKIN, Eng., same crest.

AICKINSON, and AITKENSON, Eng., a demi-lady, in dexter a tower, in sinister a palm-branch. *Pl.* 20, *cr.* 6.

AIDGMAN, a demi-eagle, or, (charged on breast with a thistle, ppr.) *Pl.* 22, *cr.* 11.

AIFLER, two wings, in lure. *Pl.* 87, *cr.* 1.

AIGHTON, Lanc., a snake, coiled, ppr. *Pl.* 79, *cr.* 7.

AIGLER, or AYLER, two wings, in lure. *Pl.* 87, *cr.* 1.

AIGLES, Northumb., a hunting-horn, ppr. *Pl.* 89, *cr.* 3.

AIKEN, a fountain throwing up water, ppr. *Pl.* 49, *cr.* 5.

AIKEN, Sco., a cross crosslet, fitched, gu. *In cruce salus*. *Pl.* 16, *cr.* 10.

AIKEN, Iri., an ox-yoke, az., stapled, or. *Pl.* 35, *cr.* 11.

AIKENHEAD, Sco., a demi-savage, in dexter three laurel-sprigs, fructed, ppr. *Rupto robore nati*. *Pl.* 35, *cr.* 12.

AIKENHEAD, Sco., an oak-tree, fructed, ppr. *Annoso robore quercus*. *Pl.* 16, *cr.* 8.

AIKMAN, a man, ppr., holding a standard, gu., vested, ar., coat, az. *Pl.* 79, *cr.* 5.

AIKMAN of Cairnie and Brambleton, an oak-tree, ppr. *Sub robore virtus*. *Pl.* 16, *cr.* 8.

AIKMAN of Bromlinton, an oak-tree, acorned, ppr. *Sub robore virtus*. *Pl.* 16, *cr.* 8.

AILE, and AILES, Eng., a dexter arm, embowed, fist clenched, ppr. *Pl.* 87, *cr.* 7.

AILESBURY, a sea-horse, naiant, ppr. *Think and thank*. *Pl.* 100, *cr.* 1.

AILESBURY, Marquess and Earl of, Earl Bruce, and Viscount Savernake, (Brudenell-Bruce): 1. For *Ailesbury*, a sea-horse, naiant, ppr. *Think and thank*. *Pl.* 100, *cr.* 1. 2. For *Bruce*, a lion, passant, az. *Fuimus*. *Pl.* 48, *cr.* 8.

AILLEN, Edinr., a pelican, in nest, feeding her young, ppr. *Non sibi*. *Pl.* 44, *cr.* 1.

AILMER, or AYLMER, Lond., a goat, passant, or, (attired with one horn.) *Pl.* 66, *cr.* 1.
AILSA, Marquess of, and Baron Ailsa, Eng.; Earl of Cassilis and Lord Kennedy, Sco., (Kennedy;) a dolphin, naiant, ppr. *Avis la fin. Pl.* 48, *cr.* 9.
AIME, and AINE, Eng., a pillar, barry of four, gu. and or, winged, ppr. *Pl.* 33, *cr.* 12.
AIMGEVYNE, Theshelthorpe, Linc., a vine, or, bearing three bunches of grapes, ppr. *Pl.* 89, *cr.* 1.
AINES, AINGER, AITKEN, a common boat, ppr. *Pl.* 42, *cr.* 11.
AINGE, Eng., a boat, ppr. *Pl.* 42, *cr.* 11.
AINGE, Lond., a cross formée, fitched, or, between wings, az. *Pl.* 29, *cr.* 14, (fitched, *pl.* 27, *cr.* 14.)
AINLIE, an arm, in hand a laurel chaplet, ensigned with a bird. *Pl.* 44, *cr.* 13.
AINSLEY, Sir ROBERT, Bart., Eng., an arm, embowed, brandishing a scimitar, ppr. *Pro rege et patria. Pl.* 92, *cr.* 5.
AINSLEY, or AINSLIE, of Blackhill, a pelican's head, erased, ppr. *Pietas tutissima virtus. Pl.* 26, *cr.* 1.
AINSLEY, and AINSLIE, Sco., an arm, embowed, issuing, hand grasping a scimitar, all ppr. *Pro rege et patria. Pl.* 92, *cr.* 5.
AINSLIE, of Pilton, Bart., and Colonel, same crest and motto.
AINSLIE, Bart., Linc., a dexter arm, hand grasping a scimitar, ppr. *Pro rege et patria. Pl.* 92, *cr.* 5.
AINSLIE, Eng., an arm, from elbow, vested, az., cuffed, indented, ar., in hand two branches of laurel, in orle, ensigned with a bird. *Pl.* 44, *cr.* 13.
AINSLIE, Eng., a hand grasping a scimitar, ppr. *Pl.* 29, *cr.* 8.
AINSLIE, Quebec, an eagle's head, erased, ppr. *Pietas tutissima virtus. Pl.* 20, *cr.* 7.
AINSWORTH, PETER, of Smithills Hall, Lancaster, a man in armour, in dexter a battle-axe, ppr. *Mea gloria fides. Pl.* 60, *cr.* 2, (axe, *pl.* 121, *cr.* 14.)
AINSWORTH, Lanc., same crest.
AINSWORTH, and ANESWORTH, Eng., a falcon, wings expanded and inverted, belled, ppr. *Courage sans peur. Pl.* 105, *cr.* 4.
AIR, Sco., stump of oak-tree, branches sprouting, ppr. *Pl.* 92, *cr.* 8.
AIRD, Sco., a cock, ppr. *Vigilantia. Pl.* 67, *cr.* 14.
AIRD, Eng., in hand a hawk's lure, ppr. *Pl.* 44, *cr.* 2.
AIREY, a cinquefoil, gu. *Pl.* 91, *cr.* 12.
AIRLIE, Alyth, and Lintrathen, Earl of, and Baron Ogilvy, Sco., (Ogilvy;) a lady, from waist, holding a portcullis. *A fin. Pl.* 101, *cr.* 2.
AIRMINE of Osgodsby, Bart., on a mount, vert, an ermine, passant, ar. *Pl.* 87, *cr.* 3.
AIRTH, Sco., a cock crowing, ppr. *Pl.* 67, *cr.* 14.
AIRTH, Sco., a stag's head, (erased,) at gaze, ppr. *Pl.* 111, *cr.* 13.
AISCOUGH, Eng., a cross crosslet, fitched, az. *In hoc signo vinces. Pl.* 16, *cr.* 10.
AISELBIE, or AISLABIE, Yorks., a lion's head, erased, gu., (gorged with three lozenges, conjoined in fess, ar.) *Pl.* 81, *cr.* 4.

AISINCOURT, Eng., a demi-eagle, displayed, with two heads. *Pl.* 4, *cr.* 6, (no escutcheon.)
AISKELL, AISKILL, and ASKILL, Eng., in the sea an anchor, in pale, ppr. *Pl.* 62, *cr.* 10.
AITCHESON, Sco., a cock, ppr., wattled and combed. *Vigilantibus. Pl.* 67, *cr.* 14.
AITCHISON of Rochsolloch, same crest and motto.
AITCHISON of Glengarsie, a cock, standing on a trumpet, ppr. *Pl.* 2, *cr.* 1.
AITCHISON of Clancairny, Bart., N.S., a cock, standing on a trumpet, ppr. *Vigilantibus. Pl.* 2, *cr.* 1.
AITCHISON, Earl of Gosford, same crest and motto.
AITCHISON of Pittenweem, an astrolabe, ppr. *Observe. Pl.* 26, *cr.* 2.
AITKEN of Aitkenside, a cross crosslet, fitched, gu. *In cruce salus. Pl.* 16, *cr.* 10.
AITKEN, AITKIN, and ATKIN, Eng., a boat, ppr. *Pl.* 42, *cr.* 11.
AITKENHEAD, Advocate, Sco., a demi-savage, in dexter three laurel sprigs, fructed, ppr. *Pl.* 35, *cr.* 12.
AITKENHEAD, Sco., an oak-tree, ppr. *Rupto robore nati. Pl.* 16, *cr.* 8.
AITKENS, a dexter arm, in armour, embowed, in hand, ppr., a cross crosslet, fitched, erect, ar. *Pl.* 88, *cr.* 7, (armour, *pl.* 65, *cr.* 13.)
AITKENSON, Eng., a demi-lady, in dexter a tower, in sinister a palm-branch. *Pl.* 20, *cr.* 6.
AITKENSON, Eng., and Sco., a cock, ppr. *Pl.* 67, *cr.* 14.
AITKINE, Sco., a cross crosslet, fitched, gu. *In cruce salus. Pl.* 16, *cr.* 10.
AITKINSON, Sco., a cock, ppr. *Pl.* 67, *cr.* 14.
AITO, or AUITO, Devons., out of a cloud, an arm, ppr., grasping a sword, erect, ar., hilt, or, on blade a Moor's head, sa. *Pl.* 76, *cr.* 6.
AITON of that Ilk, Sco., Bart., a dexter hand pulling a rose, ppr. *Et decerptæ dabunt odorem. Pl.* 48, *cr.* 1.
AITON of Dunmure, same crest and motto.
AITON, a rose, gu. *Virtute orta occidunt rarjus. Pl.* 105, *cr.* 7.
AITON of Kippo, a rose-tree, vert, flowered, gu. *Et decerptæ dabunt odorem. Pl.* 23, *cr.* 2.
AITON of Kinaldie, same crest.
AITOUNE of Inchdairnie, same crest and motto.
AKARYS, AKERS, AKERIS, or AKYRIS, a griffin's head, gu. *Pl.* 38, *cr.* 3.
AKARYS, Eng., a demi-griffin, or. *Pl.* 18, *cr.* 6.
AKASTER, Eng., same crest.
AKELAND, Devons., on a sinister arm, vested, az., gloved, a hawk, perched, ar., belled, or. *Pl.* 83, *cr.* 13.
AKELITZ, AKELITS, or HAKELUT, Eng., a halbert, issuing, ppr. *Pl.* 16, *cr.* 3.
AKELOND, Eng., a hawk, perched and belled, ppr. *Pl.* 67, *cr.* 3.
AKENHEAD, Sco., an oak-tree, ppr. *Pl.* 16, *cr.* 8.
AKENHEAD, Eng., a cock, ppr. *Pl.* 67, *cr.* 14.
AKENSIDE, Sco., a harrow, ppr. *Pl.* 7, *cr.* 2.
AKER, or ACRE, a triangular harrow. *Pl.* 7, *cr.* 2.

AKERIS, Eng., a griffin's head, gu. *Pl.* 38, *cr.* 3.

AKERMAN, or ACKERMAN, Lond. and Surr., out of a pallisado coronet, or, an arm, embowed, vested, gu., cuffed, ar., in hand, ppr., an oak-branch, leaved, vert, fructed, or. *Pl.* 2, *cr.* 2, (coronet, *pl.* 128, *fig.* 21.)

AKEROYD, and AKROYD, Eng., a dog sleeping, ppr. *Pl.* 29, *cr.* 3.

AKERS, ARETAS, Esq., of Malling Abbey, Kent, an arm, vested, bendy, az. and or, in hand a pennon, bendy, az. and gold, charged with a Saracen's head, ppr., between eight crosses crosslet, counterchanged. *Je vive en esperance.*

AKERS, Eng., a Doric column, or. *Pl.* 33, *cr.* 1.

AKIRIS, or AKYRIS, Eng., a griffin's head, gu. *Pl.* 38, *cr.* 3.

AKLAND, Eng., on a sinister hand, couped, in fess, gloved, a hawk, hooded and belled. *Pl.* 83, *cr.* 13.

ALABASTER, and ALLEBASTER, Eng., a feather, ar., enfiled with a ducal coronet, or. *Pl.* 8, *cr.* 9.

ALAND, Iri., a leopard, passant, gardant, or. *Pl.* 51, *cr.* 7.

ALAND, Lord Fortescue, same crest. *Forte scrutum salus ducem.*

ALANSON, Eng., on a mount, a lion, rampant, gardant, gu., supporting a long cross, or. *Pl.* 82, *cr.* 4.

ALATE, Eng., a unicorn's head, ar., collared, sa. *Pl.* 73, *cr.* 1.

ALBALANDA, Eng., a boar, passant, gu., armed, bristled and membered, or. *Pl.* 48, *cr.* 14.

ALBAN, a lion's head, erased, pierced in breast with an arrow. *Pl.* 113, *cr.* 15, (one arrow.)

ALBANY, Lond., Salop, and Beds., out of a ducal coronet, gu., a demi-dolphin, haurient, or. *Pl.* 94, *cr.* 14, (haurient, *pl.* 14, *cr.* 10.)

ALBANY, Salop, Lond., Beds., and Middx., a dolphin, haurient, or. *Pl.* 14, *cr.* 10.

ALBASTER, Staffs., a feather, in pale, enfiled with a ducal coronet. *Pl.* 8, *cr.* 9.

ALBEMARLE, Earl of, Viscount Bury, and Baron Ashford, (Keppel,) out of a ducal coronet, or, a demi-swan, close, ppr. *Ne cede malis.*

ALBENEY, Eng., a yoke, in bend, ppr. *Pl.* 35, *cr.* 11.

ALBENEY, Berks., a stock-dove, az., in beak a branch, vert, fructed, gu. *Pl.* 48, *cr.* 15.

ALBEROUGH, or ALBROUGH, Eng., a castle, at sinister base, a thistle-bush, ppr. *Pl.* 8, *cr.* 7.

ALBERRY of Wickingham, Berks., a stock-dove, az., in beak a branch, vert, fructed, gu. *Pl.* 48, *cr.* 15.

ALBERT, a demi-savage (wreathed about middle with leaves), over shoulder a sledge-hammer, all ppr. *Pl.* 51, *cr.* 14.

ALBERTON, a pennon, in bend, gu., staff-headed, sa., (and tasseled, or.) *Pl.* 8, *cr.* 8.

ALBERTUS, Poland, the hull of a ship, with only main-mast, and top without tackling, or. *Deus dabit vela.*

ALBON, ALBONE, ALLEBONE, and ALLIBONE, Eng., a bull's head, affrontée. *Pl.* 18, *cr.* 15.

ALBOROUGH, Somers., a fox, ar., (collared and lined, or.) *Pl.* 80, *cr.* 5.

ALBRECHT, or ALBREGHT, in dexter hand, ppr., a fleur-de-lis, or. *Pl.* 46, *cr.* 12.

ALBYN, in lion's gamb, issuing, sa., a spear, or, on top a flag, gu. *Pl.* 85, *cr.* 13.

ALCHORN, Kent, a human heart, gu., ducally crowned, or, between wings, ar. *Pl.* 52, *cr.* 2.

ALCHORNE, Suss., same crest.

ALCOCK, HARRY, Esq., of Wilton Castle, co. Wexford, a cock, ar., standing on a globe, armed, combed, and gilled, or. *Vigilate. Pl.* 34, *cr.* 2, (cock, *pl.* 67, *cr.* 14.)

ALCOCK, Kent, out of a ducal coronet, az., a demi-swan, erm., wings expanded, and ducally crowned, or. *Pl.* 100, *cr.* 7, (crown, *pl.* 128, *fig.* 3.)

ALCOCK of Silvertost, Northamp., a cock, erm., beaked, membered, crested, and wattled, or. *Pl.* 67, *cr.* 14.

ALCOCK, Staffs., a cock, gu. *Pl.* 67, *cr.* 14.

ALCOCK, Bishop of Ely, on a crown, a cock.

ALCOCK, Iri., on a globe, a cock, armed and combed, ar. *Vigilate. Pl.* 34, *cr.* 2, (cock, *pl.* 67, *cr.* 14.)

ALDAM, Eng., out of a ducal coronet, a plume of five ostrich-feathers, banded. *Pl.* 100, *cr.* 12.

ALDANE, Eng., same crest.

ALDBOROUGH, or ALDEBURGHE, York, an ibex, passant, or. *Pl.* 115, *cr.* 13.

ALDBOROUGH, Earl of, Viscount Amiens, and Baron Baltinglass, (Stratford,) Iri., a dexter arm, in armour, embowed, in hand, ppr., a scimitar, az., hilted and pommelled, or. *Virtuti nihil obstat et armis. Pl.* 81, *cr.* 11.

ALDE, Eng., a torteau, sa. *Pl.* 7, *cr.* 6.

ALDEBOROUGH, an escallop, or, between wings, az. *Pl.* 62, *cr.* 4.

ALDEN, Herts. and Lond., out of a ducal coronet, per pale, gu. and sa., a demi-lion, or. *Pl.* 45, *cr.* 7.

ALDEN, out of a coronet, ar., two wings, gu. and az. *Pl.* 17, *cr.* 9.

ALDEN, or ALDON, Herts. and Middx., out of a ducal coronet, or, a demi-lion, gu. *Pl.* 45, *cr.* 7.

ALDER, Eng., a griffin's head, gu. *Pl.* 38. *cr.* 3.

ALDERFORD, Norf., a rat, ppr. *Pl.* 121, *cr.* 10.

ALDERINGTON, Eng., in dexter hand a hawk's lure, ppr. *Pl.* 44, *cr.* 2.

ALDERSEY, Chesh., Lond., and Kent, out of a plume of ostrich-feathers, or, a demi-griffin, segreant, gu., beaked and armed, gold. *Pl.* 11, *cr.* 6.

ALDERSEY, SAMUEL, Esq., of Aldersey Hall and Spurstow, Chester, same crest.

ALDERSON, from behind a mount, vert, thereon a branch of alder, the sun rising, ppr. *Pl.* 38, *cr.* 6.

ALDERSON, Eng., a pillar, ppr. *Pl.* 33, *cr.* 1.

ALDERSON, Norf., from a plume of feathers, ar., a griffin, rising, of the same. *Pl.* 11, *cr.* 6.

ALDERSON-LLOYD, Middx.: 1. For *Alderson*, a dove, in mouth an olive-branch, ppr. *Pl.* 48, *cr.* 15. 2. For *Lloyd*, a boar's head, couped, or. *Pl.* 48, *cr.* 2.

ALDERTON, Suff., a crescent, ar. *Pl.* 18, *cr.* 14.

ALDEWINCLE, ALDEWINCLE, ALDEWINKELL, ALDWINCKLE, and ALDWINKLE, Eng., a wyvern, wings addorsed, ducally crowned, vomiting fire. *Pl.* 51, *cr.* 2.

ALDHAM, Shrimpling, Norf., a talbot's head, erased, or, collared, sa., (lined, gu.) *Pl.* 2, *cr.* 15.

ALDIRFORD, a monkey's head, ppr. *Pl.* 11, *cr.* 7.

ALDRED, Eng., an arm from elbow, in armour, in hand a cross crosslet, fitched, in pale. *Pl.* 71, *cr.* 13.

ALDRIDGE, Eng., a phœnix in flames, ppr., (on breast and each wing a bezant.) *Pl.* 44, *cr.* 8.

ALDRIDGE, or ALDRIGE, Eng., a phœnix in flames, ppr. *Pl.* 44, *cr.* 8.

ALDRINGTON, and ALEWRINGTON, Eng., in dexter hand a hawk's lure, ppr. *Pl.* 44, *cr.* 2.

ALDWORTH, RICHARD-OLIVER, Esq., of Newmarket, co. Cork, a dexter arm in armour, embowed, hand grasping a straight sword, all ppr. *Nec temere, nec timide. Pl.* 2, *cr.* 8.

ALDWORTH, Sco., a torteau, gu. *Pl.* 7, *cr.* 6.

ALDWORTH, Sco. and Iri., a sand-glass, az., winged, or. *Pl.* 32, *cr.* 11.

ALEN, Iri., a heraldic tiger, quarterly, or and gu., (holding a rose.) *Pl.* 119, *cr.* 9.

ALENÇON, France, a greyhound, ar. *Pl.* 66, *cr.* 15.

ALEPHE, Lond., a cock's head, erased, quarterly, sa. and ar., combed and wattled, or. *Pl.* 92, *cr.* 3.

ALESTON, or ALSTON, a lion, passant, regardant, gu., ducally gorged and chained, or. *Pl.* 121, *cr.* 4.

ALEXANDER, Bart., Dublin, a dexter arm, embowed, hand grasping a sword, ppr., charged on wrist with a mullet, or. *Pl.* 34, *cr.* 7, (mullet, *pl.* 141.)

ALEXANDER, Summer-hill, Kent, a cubit arm, erect, hand grasping a sword, ppr., pommel and hilt, or. *Pl.* 21, *cr.* 10.

ALEXANDER, Hants, a talbot's head, erased, ar., collared, gu. *Pl.* 2, *cr.* 15.

ALEXANDER of Auchmull, in hand a pair of scales equally poised, ppr. *Quod tibi ne alteri. Pl.* 26, *cr.* 8.

ALEXANDER of Kinglassie, a horse's head, couped, gu., bridled, ar. *Ducitur non trahitur. Pl.* 92, *cr.* 1.

ALEXANDER, Eng., a cock, ar., beaked and membered, gu. *Pl.* 67, *cr.* 14.

ALEXANDER of Boghall, in hand a quill. *Fidem servo. Pl.* 26, *cr.* 13.

ALEXANDER, Earl of Caledon, a dexter hand, in armour, grasping a sword, all ppr. *Per mare, per terras. Pl.* 63, *cr.* 5.

ALEXANDER, Earl of Stirling, a bear, sejant, erect, ppr. *Per mare, per terras. Pl.* 1, *cr.* 1.

ALEXANDER, Lond., of Scottish descent, an arm, in armour, embowed, hand grasping a sword, all ppr. *Pl.* 2, *cr.* 8.

ALEXANDER, Eng., a horse's head, ar., bridled, sa. *Ducitur non trahitur. Pl.* 92, *cr.* 1.

ALEXANDER, a bear, rampant, ppr. *Pl.* 1, *cr.* 3, (without staff.)

ALEXANDER, Porydstone, Ayr, a bear, sejant. *Per mare, per terras. Pl.* 1, *cr.* 1.

ALEXANDER, Stirling, a beaver, ppr. *Per mare, per terras. Pl.* 49, *cr.* 5.

ALEXANDER, Sir JAMES-EDWARD, of Powis, same crest and motto.

ALEXANDER, Sco., a serpent, waved, in fess, ppr. *Ingenium vires superat. Pl.* 51, *cr.* 3.

ALEXANDER, Halifax, Yorks., a demi-lion, gardant, wielding with dexter a battle-axe, ppr., (sinister resting on a cross, fleury, gorged with a collar, az., charged with two bezants.) *Pl.* 26, *cr.* 7.

ALEXANDER of Pitskellie, two dexter hands conjoined, ppr. *Ora et labora. Pl.* 1, *cr.* 2.

ALEXANDER, M.D., Sco., a serpent, coiled, in fess, ppr. *Ingenium vires superat. Pl.* 79, *cr.* 7.

ALFORD, Berks. and Suss., a boar's head, ar., broken spear in mouth, handle thrust down throat, or. *Pl.* 11, *cr.* 9.

ALFORD, Surr., Yorks., and Salop, a boar's head, ar., in mouth three feathers of a pheasant's tail, ppr. *Pl.* 108, *cr.* 1.

ALFORD, Suff., a hind's head, ppr. *Pl.* 21, *cr.* 9.

ALFOUNDER, Ess., an arm, couped at elbow, and erect, vested, gu., cuffed, ar., in hand, ppr., three nails, or, all between wings, ar. *Pl.* 11, *cr.* 11.

ALFREY, and ALLFREY, Suss., an ostrich-head and neck, between two ostrich-feathers, ar. *Pl.* 50, *cr.* 1.

ALFREY, and ALLFREY, Suss., an ostrich-head and neck, between two ostrich-feathers, ar., gorged with a ducal coronet, or. *Pl.* 108, *cr.* 2.

ALGAR, and ALGER, Eng., a greyhound's head, sa., charged with four bezants, or. *Pl.* 14, *cr.* 4.

ALGIE, ALGEO, and ALGOE, Eng., a bear, rampant, supporting a staff, raguly. *Pl.* 1, *cr.* 3.

ALGIST, Eng., a dexter and sinister arm from shoulder, couped, in saltier, ppr., vested, dexter, az., sinister, gu., cuffed, or, each brandishing a scimitar, ar., hilted, gold. *Pl.* 52, *cr.* 1.

ALGLOVAL, a goat, statant, ar. *Pl.* 66, *cr.* 1.

ALGOE, Sco., a bear, sejant, on hind legs, supporting a staff. *Pl.* 78, *cr.* 11.

ALGOOD, and ALLGOOD, Northumb. and Devons., two arms, in armour, embowed, ppr., in hands, of the last, a human heart, gu., inflamed, or, (charged with a tower tripletowered, ar.) *Age omne bonum. Pl.* 36, *cr.* 4.

ALGOOD, and ALLGOOD, Northumb., two arms, in armour, embowed, holding up a flaming heart, all ppr. *Pl.* 36, *cr.* 4.

ALICOCK, Northamp., a cock, erm., combed and wattled, or. *Pl.* 67, *cr.* 14.

ALIE, or ALLY, a dexter hand holding up the sun, ppr.

ALINGTON, GEORGE-MARMADUKE, Esq., of Swinhope, Lincoln, a talbot, passant, erm. *Pl.* 120, *cr.* 8.

ALISON, Sco., a tree, ppr., with a bell hung on each side. *Crescit sub pondere virtus. Pl.* 50, *cr.* 3.

ALISON, Sco., an eagle's head, erased, ppr. *Vincit veritas. Pl.* 20, *cr.* 7.

ALISON, Rev. A., Sco., a falcon's head, erased, ppr. *Vincit veritas. Pl.* 34, *cr.* 11.

ALISON, Sir ARCHIBALD, Possil House, Lanarkshire, same crest and motto.

ALJOY, Sco., stump of oak-tree, new branches sprouting. *Non deficit alter. Pl.* 92, *cr.* 8.

ALKENE, ASKUE, or AYSKEW, a man's head, affrontée, couped at shoulders, ppr. *Pl.* 19, *cr.* 1.

ALLAN, W. S., Sco., a comet, ppr. *Luceo et terreo.* Pl. 39, cr. 9.

ALLAN, Durh., a demi-lion, rampant, ppr., holding up a rudder, gu. *Fortiter gerit crucem.* Pl. 102, cr. 4.

ALLAN, Sco. and Rotterdam, a cross crosslet, fitched, gu. *Fide et labore.* Pl. 16, cr. 10.

ALLAN of Errol, Sco., and Middx., an eagle, rising, ppr. *Fortiter.* Pl. 67, cr. 4.

ALLAN, Eastwood, Mid-Lothian, same crest and motto.

ALLAN, WILLIAM, Esq., of Blackwell Grange, Durham, a demi-lion, rampant, ar., ducally crowned, gu., in dexter a cross-potent, or, in sinister a rudder, of the second. *Fortiter gerit crucem.* Pl. 66, cr. 2.

ALLAN, ROBERT-HENRY, Esq., of Blackwell Hall, Durham, and of Barton, York, same crest and motto.

ALLAND, a bear's paw, erect, ppr. Pl. 126, cr. 2.

ALLANSON, a demi-eagle, wings expanded, *Virtute et labore.* Pl. 22, cr. 11.

ALLANSON, and ALLENSON, Eng., on a mount, vert, a lion, rampant, gardant, or, supporting a long cross, gu. Pl. 82, cr. 4.

ALLARDAS, ALLARDES, ALLARDICE, ALLERDYCE, and ALLERDES, Sco., a torteau, between wings, az. Pl. 2, cr. 3.

ALLARDICE, Wel., a dove and olive-branch. *Amicitia sine fraude.* Pl. 48, cr. 15.

ALLARDICE, and ALLERDICE, of that Ilk, a naked man from middle, grasping in dexter a scimitar, all ppr. *In defence of the distressed*—and—*My defence.* Pl. 82, cr. 2.

ALLARDICE of Dunninald, an ear of wheat, and palm-branch, in saltier, ppr. *Bene qui pacifici.* Pl. 63, cr. 3.

ALLATT, Eng., a unicorn's head, ar., collared, sa. Pl. 73, cr. 1.

ALLATT, on a demi-bezant, issuing, a beehive, bees swarming, ppr. Pl. 64, cr. 10.

ALLAUNSON, Durh., a pheon, ar., shaft broken, or. Pl. 27, cr. 12.

ALLAUNSON, Eng., on a mount, a lion, rampant, gardant, gu., supporting a long cross, or. Pl. 82, cr. 4.

ALLAWAY, and ALLOWAY, Eng. and Sco., an anchor, in pale, ppr. Pl. 25, cr. 15.

ALLAWAY, and ALLOWAY, on an anchor a dove, with olive-branch, all ppr. Pl. 3, cr. 10.

ALLCARD, Lanc., a demi-swan, wings elevated, ar., (semée of mullets, az.), in mouth a bulrush, ppr. *Semel et semper.* Pl. 54, cr. 4.

ALLCOCK, a cock, ppr. Pl. 67, cr. 14.

ALLDEN, ALLDIN, and ALLDON, Eng., a scimitar and caduceus, in saltier, ensigned with a round hat. Pl. 17, cr. 13, (without head above hat.)

ALLEN, Viscount ALLEN, Iri., a bezant, charged with a talbot's head, erased, sa. *Triumpho morte tam vitâ.* Pl. 38, cr. 2.

ALLEN, Bath, a bird, wings elevated. Pl. 108, cr. 5.

ALLEN, Chelsea, a talbot's head, erased, per pale, indented, ar. and gu., collared and (chained, sa.) Pl. 2, cr. 15.

ALLEN, Devons., a mullet, gu., pierced, or. Pl. 45, cr. 1.

ALLEN, Thaxted, Ess., Bart., and Fenchurch. Middx., a demi-lion, az., holding a rudder, or. Pl. 102, cr. 4.

ALLEN, or ALLEYN, Chesh., Suff., and Wilts., a martlet, ar., winged, in beak an acorn, or, leaved, vert. Pl. 111, cr. 5, (acorn, pl. 31, cr. 7.)

ALLEN, Derbys., Lon., and Staffs., out of a ducal coronet, or, a horse's head, ar. Pl. 50, cr. 13.

ALLEN, Grove, near Maidstone, Kent, on a coronet, or, lined, erm., a bloodhound, passant, sa., collared, gold, armed, gu. Pl. 3, cr. 8.

ALLEN, Kent, a talbot, passant, or, collared, gu. Pl. 65, cr. 2.

ALLEN, Kent, on a mount, vert, paled round, or, a hound, sa., collared, of the last.

ALLEN, Lond., a demi-griffin, (holding a branch, vert, fructed, or.) Pl. 44, cr. 3.

ALLEN, Lond., a griffin's head, erased, per fess, ar. and gu. Pl. 48, cr. 6.

ALLEN, SEYMOUR-PHILIPS, Esq., of Cressolly Pembroke, a dove and olive-branch. *Amicitia sine fraude.* Pl. 48, cr. 15.

ALLEN, Surr., an arm, couped at elbow, erect, in hand a human heart, out of flames of fire, all ppr. Pl. 64, cr. 12.

ALLEN, a demi-greyhound, rampant, paly of six, ar. and sa., (collared. gu., between paws a crescent, or.) Pl. 6, cr. 9.

ALLEN, Somers., a partridge, wings elevated. Pl. 108, cr. 5.

ALLEN, Eng., a cock, or, combed, wattled, and legged, gu. Pl. 67, cr. 14.

ALLEN, Middx., an eagle, rising, ppr. *Fortiter.* Pl. 67, cr. 4.

ALLEN, a snake, coiled, supporting two pennons, in saltier. Pl. 108, cr. 3.

ALLEN, Errol, an eagle, perched, wings expanded. *Fortiter.* Pl. 67, cr. 4.

ALLEN, Sco., a demi-lion, gu. *Remember.* Pl. 67, cr. 10.

ALLENSON, and ALLESON, a talbot's head, or, collared, (and ringed, az.,) between wings expanded, of the last. Pl. 2, cr. 5, (wings, pl. 94, cr. 2.)

ALLENSON, Eng., a demi-lion, rampant, gardant, or, holding a cross, gu. Pl. 119, cr. 3.

ALLERTON, a lion's head, gu., collared, sa. Pl. 42, cr. 14.

ALLESTOWE, or HALLESTOWE, in hand the butt-end of a broken spear. Pl. 66, cr. 4.

ALLESTRY, Eng., a demi-lion, rampant, az., brandishing a scimitar, ar., hilted, or. Pl. 126 a, cr. 1.

ALLETT of Iwood, Somers., a unicorn's head, ar., collared, sa. Pl. 73, cr. 1.

ALLEY, Eng., a lion's head, cabossed, or, between wings, ppr. Pl. 87, cr. 2.

ALLEY, Iri., out of a ducal coronet, or, a mullet, gu., between two laurel-branches, vert. Pl. 82, cr. 6.

ALLEYN, and ALLYN, Devons., a demi-lion, rampant, az., fretty, ar., holding a rudder, gu. Pl. 102, cr. 4.

ALLEYN, Eng., a demi-lion, gu., supporting a rudder, sa. Pl. 102, cr. 4.

ALLEYNE, Bart., Ess., out of a ducal coronet, or, a unicorn's head, ar. *Non tua, te, moveant sed publica vota.* Pl. 45, cr. 14.

ALLFREY, Eng., an ostrich-head, between two ostrich-feathers, ar. Pl. 50, cr. 1.

ALLFREY, ROBERT, Esq., of Wokefield Park, Berks., an ostrich-head and neck, gorged with a crown, (and lined,) or, between ostrich-feathers, ar. Pl. 108, cr. 2.

ALLGOOD, LANCELOT-JOHN-HUNTER, Esq., of Nunwick, Northumb., two arms, in armour, embowed, ppr., in hands a human heart, gu., inflamed, or, (charged with a tower, triple-towered, ar.) *Age omne bonum.* *Pl.* 36. *cr.* 4.

ALLICOCK, and ALLICOCKE, Eng., a cock, ppr. *Pl.* 67, *cr.* 14.

ALLIESON, or ALLISON, Eng., a demi-savage brandishing a scimitar, ppr. *Pl.* 82, *cr.* 2.

ALLIN, Suff., a snake coiled up, (and environed with flags or rushes, ppr.) *Pl.* 79, *cr.* 7.

ALLIN, a partridge, wings expanded. *Pl.* 108, *cr.* 5.

ALLINGHAM, Eng., a church and spire, environed with trees, ppr. *Pl.* 110, *cr.* 5.

ALLINGRIDGE, Eng., a castle, triple-towered, flag displayed. *Pl.* 123, *cr.* 14.

ALLINGRIDGE, a castle, triple-towered, ppr., flag displayed, ar., charged with a cross, sa. *Pl.* 123, *cr.* 14.

ALLINGTON, out of a ducal coronet, or, a buck's head, ppr., attired, of the first, pierced through neck with an arrow, gold, barbed and flighted, ar. *Pl.* 56, *cr.* 11, (head, *pl.* 66, *cr.* 9.)

ALLINGTON, Horse Heath, Camb., a talbot, passant, erm. *Pl.* 120, *cr.* 8.

ALLINGTON, Eng., a talbot, or, langued, gu. *Pl.* 120, *cr.* 8.

ALLINGTON, a talbot, bezantée. *Pl.* 120, *cr.* 8, (bezant, *pl.* 141.)

ALLISON, Sco., a falcon's head, erased. *Vincit veritas.* *Pl.* 34, *cr.* 11.

ALLISON, a peacock, ppr. *Pl.* 54, *cr.* 13.

ALLISON, a pheasant, in dexter a key, in beak an ear of barley, ppr. *Pl.* 64, *cr.* 14.

ALLISON, Sco., an eagle's head, erased, ppr. *Vincit veritas.* *Pl.* 20, *cr.* 7.

ALLIX, Linc., a wolf's head, erased. *Pl.* 14, *cr.* 6.

ALLIX, CHARLES, Esq., of Willoughby Hall, Linc., a wolf's head, erased, at neck, ppr. *Pl.* 14, *cr.* 6.

ALLMACK, Sco., a tower, ppr. *Pl.* 12, *cr.* 5.

ALLMAN, Suss., a leg, in armour, couped above knee, ppr., spurred, or. *Pl.* 81, *cr.* 5.

ALLNETT, and ALLNUTT, Eng., a thunderbolt, ppr. *Pl.* 110, *cr.* 3.

ALLOT, and ALLOTT, Lanc. and Linc., an arm, couped at shoulder, embowed, ppr., vested, gu., resting elbow on the wreath, grasping a sword, enfiled with a leopard's head. *Pl.* 102, *cr.* 5.

ALLOTT, South Kirkby, Yorks., a cubit arm, erect, (vested, or, charged with a fess, between four barrulets, cuffed, ar.), in hand, pyr., a mullet, or. *Pl.* 62, *cr.* 13.

ALLOTT, The Rev. JOHN, of Hague Hall, Yorks., a dexter arm, couped at elbow, vested, or, charged with a fess, double cotised, wavy, az., cuff, ar., in hand, ppr., a mullet, gold. *Fortiter et recte.* *Pl.* 110, *cr.* 7, (mullet, *pl.* 62, *cr.* 13.)

ALLPORT, Cannock, Staffs., a demi-lion, erm., gorged with a mural coronet, gu. *Pl.* 87, *cr.* 15, (coronet, *pl.* 128, *fig.* 18.)

ALLSOP, ALLSUP, and ALSOPE, Eng., a dove, in mouth an olive-branch, ppr. *Pl.* 48, *cr.* 15.

ALLVEY, and ALVEY, Eng., a plough, ppr. *Pl.* 28, *cr.* 15.

ALLWRIGHT, or ALWRIGHT, Eng., on a chapeau, a greyhound, statant, all ppr. *Pl.* 104, *cr.* 1.

ALLYE, Tewkesbury, Glouc., a leopard's head, or, between wings, sa. *Pl.* 92, *cr.* 13, (wings, *pl.* 87, *cr.* 2.)

ALLYE, Dors., a stag's head, erased, per pale, ar. and or, attired, of the first, (gorged with a collar, double embattled, gu., charged with three escallops, or.) *Pl.* 66, *cr.* 9.

ALLYN, a tree eradicated, vert, fructed with branches of berries, gu.

ALMACK, Suff., a tower, ar., with a flag, (inscribed, *Pax.*) *Pl.* 8, *cr.* 13.

ALMAN, Pearnsey, Suss., a leg, in armour, spurred, or, couped in middle of thigh. *Pl.* 81, *cr.* 5.

ALMANERLAVAL, a tower, ppr. *Pl.* 12, *cr.* 5.

ALMARD, Eng., a stag, trippant, ppr. *Pl.* 68, *cr.* 2.

ALMAYNE, on a ducal coronet, or, a cinquefoil, gu. *Pl.* 83, *cr.* 3, (cinquefoil, *pl.* 141.)

ALMEARS, or ALMEERS, Eng., a long cross, crossed, on three grieces, ar. *Pl.* 23, *cr.* 12.

ALMER, and ALMOR, a palmer's staff, erect, or.

ALMERIOUS, a nag's head, erased, ar., ducally gorged, or. *Pl.* 46, *cr.* 4, (coronet, *pl.* 128, *fig.* 3.)

ALMEWAKE, and ALNWICK, Eng., on a chapeau, a cock, ppr. *Pl.* 104, *cr.* 3.

ALMIGER, on a ducal coronet, ppr., a tiger, sejant, gu. *Pl.* 86, *cr.* 8.

ALMOND, Eng., three cinquefoils, az., stalked and leaved, vert. *Pl.* 72, *cr.* 12, (cinquefoils, *pl.* 141.)

ALMOT, ALNOT, and ALNEOT, Eng., a thunderbolt, ppr. *Pl.* 110, *cr.* 3.

ALMS, a stag's head, erased, or. *Pl.* 66, *cr.* 9.

ALPHE, Hants., out of a ducal coronet, ar., a hawk's head, or. *Pl.* 24, *cr.* 10.

ALPHE, Hants., out of a ducal coronet, an eagle's head, ppr. *Pl.* 20, *cr.* 12, (without pellet in beak.)

ALPIN, Sco., a man's head, couped, affrontée, ppr., crined, gu. *Cuinich bas alpin*—and—*Virtutis regia merces.* *Pl.* 19, *cr.* 1.

ALRED, Holderness, Yorks., a griffin's head, ppr. *Pl.* 38, *cr.* 3.

ALSOP, Derbs. and Leic., a dove, wings expanded, in mouth an ear of wheat.

ALSOP, Eng., a dove, in mouth an ear of corn, all ppr., and in dexter a key, erect, sa. *Pl.* 108, *cr.* 8.

ALSOPPE, Lond., a dove, ar., legged, gu., between two ostrich-feathers, sa.

ALSTANTAN, out of a mural coronet, or, an arm, in armour, embowed, grasping a dagger, all ppr. *Pl.* 115, *cr.* 14.

ALSTON, Odell, Beds., Bart., a crescent, ar., charged with an etoile, or. *Immotus.* *Pl.* 18, *cr.* 14, (etoile, *pl.* 141.)

ALSTON, or ALSTONE, of Chelsea, Bart., and of Mile-end, Bart., same crest.

ALSTON, WILLIAM-CHARLES, Esq., of Elmdon Hall, Warwick, a demi-eagle, wings displayed, or, (on each wing a crescent, reversed, gu.) *In altum.* *Pl.* 52, *cr.* 8.

ALSTON, Eng., a star, ppr. *E tenebris lux.* Pl. 21, cr. 6.
ALSTON, Westerton, an eagle, issuing, wings expanded, ppr. *Sursum.* Pl. 52, cr. 8.
ALSTONE, Sco., same crest.
ALSTONE of Newton, Suff.; Assington; and Marleford; an etoile, or, in a crescent, ar. Pl. 111, cr. 15.
ALSTONE, Colonel, Sco., a demi-eagle, wings expanded and inverted, ppr., on each wing a crescent, reversed, gu. *In altum.* Pl. 22, cr. 11, (crescent, pl. 141.)
ALTHAM, and ALLTHAM, Lond. and Ess., a demi-lion, gu., supporting a rudder, sa. Pl. 102, cr. 4.
ALTHAN, or ALTHAUN, a demi-archer shooting, ppr., vested, vert, cap, sa. Pl. 60, cr. 5.
ALTHOUN, Eng., a dexter hand, apaumée, ppr. Pl. 32, cr. 14.
ALVANLEY, Baron, (Arden,) out of a ducal coronet, or, five ostrich-feathers, ar., charged with a crescent, gu. *Patentiâ vinces.* Pl. 100, cr. 12.
ALVARES, a demi-lion, rampant, ppr., in dexter paw a mascle, az. Pl. 89, cr. 10, (mascle, pl. 141.)
ALVAS, and ALVES, Sco., a garb, or. *Deo favente.* Pl. 48, cr. 10.
ALVENSLEBEN, Baron DE, out of a marquess's coronet, a staff raguly, per pale, gu. and or, couped, (surmounted by a rose.) Pl. 78, cr. 15, (coronet, pl. 127, cr. 4.)
ALVERD, or ALURED, Eng., a mill-rind, or. Pl. 54, cr. 3.
ALVARDE, Ipswich, same crest.
ALWAYE, Streetley, Beds., a hind's head, ar., (between two holly-branches, vert, fructed with berries, gu.) Pl. 13, cr. 9.
ALWOOD, and ALLWOOD, a demi-stag, salient, ppr., attired, or. Pl. 55, cr. 9, (without rose.)
ALWYN, Ess., a lion's gamb, erect and erased, sa., enfiled with a mural coronet, or. Pl. 93, cr. 9, (coronet, pl. 128, fig. 18.)
ALYE, a lion's head, cabossed, between wings. Pl. 87, cr. 2.
ALYE, Glouc., a lion's head, cabossed, between wings. Pl. 87, cr. 2.
ALYSON, Kent, a pheon, ar., with part of broken shaft, or. Pl. 27, cr. 12.
AMAND, AMANE, or AMARME, Eng., a pomegranate, ppr. Pl. 67, cr. 8.
AMARLE, or ARMARLE, a lion, passant, or, resting fore dexter on a mullet, gu. Pl. 78, cr. 4, (mullet, pl. 141.)
AMARY, Ess., a cat's head, issuing, affrontée, ar., in mouth a rat, sa. Pl. 108, cr. 4.
AMBESACE, and AMBORAES, out of a ducal coronet, or, a man's head, in profile, ppr. Pl. 81, cr. 15, (coronet, pl. 128, fig. 3.)
AMBLER, Eng., a mascle, or. Pl. 54, cr. 1.
AMBLER, and ANBLER, two dexter hands conjoined, supporting a royal crown. Pl. 1, cr. 2, (crown, pl. 127, fig. 2.)
AMBLER, Kirkton, Linc., a demi-leopard, ar., holding a laurel crown, ppr. Pl. 12, cr. 14, (laurel, pl. 128, cr. 6.)
AMBOROW, ANBURY, or ANBOROW, a bear's head, erased, sa., muzzled, or. Pl. 71, cr. 6.
AMBRIDGE, Eng., a cross crosslet, fitched, in pale, gu., and two swords, in saltier, ppr. Pl. 42, cr. 5.

AMBROS, AMBROSE, and AMBROSS, Eng., in hand a billet, ar. Pl. 28, cr. 8.
AMBROSE, a cherub's head, between wings. Pl. 126, cr. 10.
AMBRY, or AMBREY, a wolf's head, erm., in mouth a rose-branch, vert, bearing a rose, ar. Pl. 92, cr. 15.
AMCOT, a squirrel, sejant, gu., cracking a nut, or. Pl. 16, cr. 9.
AMCOTES, and AMCOTTS, Kittlethorpe Park; Astrop and Writtenby, Linc.; a squirrel, sejant, gu., cracking a nut, or. Pl. 16, cr. 9.
AMCOTS, a squirrel, gu., cracking a nut, or. Pl. 16, cr. 9.
AMCOTTS, Eng., a squirrel, sejant, gu., collared, or. Pl. 85, cr. 3.
AMEERS, Eng., a long cross, crossed on three grieces. Pl. 23, cr. 12.
AMENTON, Eng., an antelope's head, ppr. Pl. 24, cr. 7.
AMERANCE, Eng., a mascle, ar. Pl. 54, cr. 1.
AMERDLEY, a heart inflamed, gu., winged, or. Pl. 64, cr. 13.
AMEREDITH, or AMERIDETH, of Marston, Devons., a demi-lion, sa., ducally gorged (and lined), or. Pl. 87, cr. 15.
AMEREDITH of Tamerton, same crest.
AMEREX, and AMERICE, Eng., a torteau, gu., charged with a talbot's head, ar., erased, or. Pl. 38, cr. 2.
AMERIE, Eng., in dexter hand, ppr., a fleur-de-lis, in pale, or. Pl. 95, cr. 9.
AMERY, JOHN, Esq., F.S.A., of Park House, Stourbridge, Worc., out of a mural coronet, a talbot's head. *Tu ne cede malis.* Pl. 91, cr. 15.
AMES, LIONEL, Esq., of The Hyde, Bedford, a rose, ar., stalked and leaved, vert. Pl. 105, cr. 7.
AMES, and AMOS, Eng., a square collegiate cap, sa. Pl. 126, cr. 3.
AMHERST, Earl and Baron, Visc. Holmesdale, on a mount, vert, three tilting-spears, or, headed, ar., one in pale, and two in saltier, environed with a chaplet of laurel, vert. *Victoria concordia crescit*—and—*Constantia et virtute.* Pl. 64, cr. 15.
AMHERST, The Rev. FRANCIS-KERRIL, of Fieldgate House, Warwick, same crest.
AMHERST, Kent and Suss., same crest.
AMHERST, or AMHURST, Kent, on a mount, vert, three lances, or, pointed, ar., with a chaplet of laurel, vert. Pl. 64, cr. 15.
AMIAS, Norf., a buck's head, erased, ar., horned, or, neck wreathed, sa. Pl. 38, cr. 1.
AMIDAS, Lond., a branch of oak, ppr. acorned, or. Pl. 32, cr. 13.
AMIEL, Eng., a hunting-horn, unstrung, sa., (another, gu.) Pl. 89, cr. 3.
AMITESLY, Glouc., a bezant, or, charged with a pale, indented, gu. Pl. 63, cr. 7.
AMO, a negress's head from breast, affrontée, smiling, ppr., with ear-rings, or. Pl. 108, cr. 11.
AMOCK, Eng., a man's head, from shoulders, in profile, ppr., vested, gu., wreathed, ar. and sa. Pl. 126, cr. 8.
AMOND, or ST. AMOND, Sco., three cinque-foils, az., stalked and leaved, vert. Pl. 72, cr. 12, (cinquefoil, pl. 141.)
AMOND, Sco., out of a mural coronet, a griffin's head, ducally gorged. Pl. 101, cr. 6.

AMOND, Sco., an arm, in armour, embowed, brandishing a scimitar, all ppr. *Pl.* 81, *cr.* 11.

AMORIE, or D'AMORIE, Glouc., out of a mural coronet, or, a talbot's head, az., eared, gold. *Pl.* 91, *cr.* 15.

AMORY, out of a ducal coronet, or, a plume of seven ostrich-feathers, ar., four and three. *Pl.* 114, *cr.* 8, (without under-plume.)

AMOS, ANDREW, Esq., of St Ibbs, Hertford, a stag's head. *Sapere aude. Pl.* 91, *cr.* 14.

AMOSLEY, a horse at full speed, sa. *Pl.* 8, *cr.* 2.

AMOUTH, a battle-axe and the top of a javelin, in saltier, ppr. *Pl.* 52, *cr.* 10, (javelin, *pl.* 19, *cr.* 7.

AMPHLET, Staffs., a dromedary, ppr. *Pl.* 17, *cr.* 2.

AMPHLETT, JOHN, Esq., of Clent House, Worc., a dromedary, ppr. *Pl.* 17, *cr.* 2.

AMRAS, Norf., a stag's head, erased, gorged with a wreath, (tied in a bow.) *Pl.* 38, *cr.* 1.

AMSDEN, and AMSDON, Eng., a cross-fleury, fitched, or, fleury, gu., between wings, ppr. *Pl.* 71, *cr.* 2.

AMSON, Lees, Chesh., a cock-blackbird, ppr., between two ostrich-feathers, ar. *Pl.* 98, *cr.* 8, (feathers, *pl.* 13, *cr.* 7.)

AMSON, Eng., a crane, ppr. *Pl.* 111, *cr.* 9.

AMY, or AMYE, Camb., out of a ducal coronet, or, an eagle's head, ppr., (in beak a sprig, vert.) *Pl.* 20, *cr.* 12.

AMYAND, Lond., a naked arm, embowed, ppr., in hand three ears of corn, bladed, all or. *La vie durante. Pl.* 89, *cr.* 4.

AMYAND, an arm, embowed, (vested, or,) in hand, ppr., three stalks of wheat, gold. *Pl.* 89, *cr.* 4.

AMYAND of Moreas Court, Heref., Bart., a crow, ppr. *Pl.* 23, *cr.* 8.

AMYAS, Norf., a stag's head, erased, or, gorged with a wreath, ar. and sa., (tied in a bow.) *Pl.* 38, *cr.* 1.

AMYAS, Tilbury, Ess., a hind, ppr., (collared, gu.) *Pl.* 20, *cr.* 14.

AMYAT, and AMYATT, Eng., a ram, passant, ppr. *Pl.* 109, *cr.* 2.

AMYATT, Southampton, a ram, passant, ar. *Pl.* 109, *cr.* 2.

AMYS, Ess., a hind, passant, ar., (collared, gu.) *Pl.* 20, *cr.* 14.

ANBY, AUBLY, and AUBLEY, in dexter hand, ppr., a cross pattée, fitched, in pale, gu. *Pl.* 99, *cr.* 15.

ANCHER, and ANCHOR, Kent, a bull's head, erased, gu. *Pl.* 19, *cr.* 3.

ANCRAM, Hill House Frome, Somers., an anchor, erect, sa. *Hold fast. Pl.* 25, *cr.* 15.

ANDBY, ANDY, or ANDEY, Devons., on stump of tree, a crane, statant, ppr. *Pl.* 23, *cr.* 5.

ANDEGARVIA, Eng., an escarbuncle, sa. *Pl.* 51, *cr.* 10.

ANDELBY, an escutcheon, gu., charged with a cross moline, or. *Pl.* 36, *cr.* 11, (cross, *pl.* 141.)

ANDERDON, Hants., a dexter arm, in armour, embowed, ppr., garnished, or, hand apaumée, also ppr. *Pl.* 97, *cr.* 1.

ANDERLEY, Eng., a dolphin, haurient, devouring a fish, ppr. *Pl.* 71, *cr.* 1.

ANDERSON, THOMAS, Esq., of Jesmond House, Northumb., and Wallington Lodge, Surr., on a mount, vert, a stag, couchant, (wounded in breast by an arrow, in mouth an ear of wheat, all ppr., charged on side with a bugle-horn, or.) *Nil desperandum, auspice Deo. Pl.* 22, *cr.* 5.

ANDERSON, The Rev. JOSHUA, A.M., an oak-tree, ppr. Over crest, *Stand sure;* under arms, *Dum spiro spero. Pl.* 16, *cr.* 8.

ANDERSON, Bart., of Fermoy, Cork, a tree, ppr., (surmounted of a saltier humettée, sa.) *Stand sure. Pl.* 100, *cr.* 14.

ANDERSON, Bart., Yorks., a water-spaniel, passant, or. *Guaviter. Pl.* 58, *cr.* 9.

ANDERSON, Aberdeen, a cross staff, erect, marked with the degrees of latitude. *Per mare.*

ANDERSON, banker, Lond. and Sco., a phœnix in flames, ppr. *Providentia. Pl.* 44, *cr.* 8.

ANDERSON of Lea, Bart., and Broughton, Bart., Linc.; St Ives, Bart., Hunts.; and Eyemouth, Bart., Beds.; a talbot, passant. *Pl.* 120, *cr.* 8.

ANDERSON, Edinr., an eagle, issuing, in dexter an olive-branch, ppr. *Qui honeste fortiter. Pl.* 37, *cr.* 2.

ANDERSON of Wester Airdbreck and Winter-field, an oak-tree, ppr. *Stand sure. Pl.* 16, *cr.* 8.

ANDERSON, W.S., Sco., a crescent, or. *Gradatim. Pl.* 18, *cr.* 14.

ANDERSON, Edinr., an eagle, issuing. *Qui honeste fortiter. Pl.* 52, *cr.* 8.

ANDERSON, Glasgow, a cloud, ppr. *Recte quod honeste. Pl.* 124, *cr.* 12.

ANDERSON, Penley, Herts., a spaniel dog, passant. *Pl.* 58, *cr.* 9.

ANDERSON, Lond., out of a ducal coronet, ar., a hind's head, or, pierced through neck with an arrow, sa., feathered, ar. *Pl.* 56, *cr.* 11.

ANDERSON, Mill Hill, Middx., three ostrich-feathers, (encircled with a chain, or, on centre one a crescent.) *Pl.* 12, *cr.* 9.

ANDERSON, Newcastle, an eagle's head, erased, ar., (in beak, in pale, an arrow, gu., headed and feathered, or.) *Pl.* 20, *cr.* 7.

ANDERSON of Newbigging, a mullet, az. *Nil conscire sibi. Pl.* 41, *cr.* 1.

ANDERSON of Whiteburgh, a crescent, ar. *Ut se crescit clarescit. Pl.* 18, *cr.* 14.

ANDERSON, Glasgow, an elephant's head, couped, ppr. *Pl.* 35, *cr.* 13.

ANDERSON of Nethertarvit, a mullet, or. *Give and forgive. Pl.* 41, *cr.* 1.

ANDERSON, out of a ducal coronet, or, a stag's head, affrontée, (in mouth a dart, ppr.) *Pl.* 29, *cr.* 7.

ANDERSON, merchant, Lond., a phœnix in flames, ppr. *Dominus providebit. Pl.* 44, *cr.* 8.

ANDERSON, a stag, lodged, ppr. *Pl.* 67, *cr.* 2.

ANDERSON, an eagle, (issuing, wings expanded and inverted, ppr.,) gazing at the sun, gu. *Pl.* 43, *cr.* 5.

ANDERSON, a ship in full sail, ppr. *Pl.* 109, *cr.* 8.

ANDERSON, a blazing star. gu. *Pl.* 39, *cr.* 9.

ANDERSON, Iri., on a mount, vert, a leopard, couchant, gardant, with antique crown. *Pl.* 9, *cr.* 14.

ANDERSON of Linkwood, in hand a pen, ppr. *Honesty is the best policy. Pl.* 26, *cr.* 13.

ANDERSON, Dalkeith, same crest and motto.

ANDERSON, Samuel, Sco., a crescent, ppr. *Gradatim.* *Pl.* 18, *cr.* 14.

ANDERSON, Kingsbarns, Fife, a sword, in pale, between two branches of laurel, in orle, ppr. *Pro bello vel pace.* *Pl.* 71, *cr.* 3.

ANDERSON, Bradley, Durh., on a chapeau, gu., turned up, erm., a griffin's head, erased, ar., (charged on neck with fetterlock, sa.) *Pl.* 122, *cr.* 11, (head, *pl.* 48, *cr.* 6.)

ANDERSON, Alnwick, Newcastle, a stag, lodged, (amidst rushes, neck pierced with an arrow, or, headed, ar.) *Pl.* 22, *cr.* 5.

ANDERTON, Chesh. and Lanc., a dexter arm, in armour, embowed, hand apaumée, ppr. *Pl.* 97, *cr.* 1.

ANDERTON of Tushielaw, a sword, in pale, between two branches of laurel, in orle, ppr. *Pro bello vel pace.* *Pl.* 71, *cr.* 3.

ANDERTON, Lanc., a curlew, ar. *Pl.* 52, *cr.* 12.

ANDERTON, WILLIAM-INCE, Esq., of Euxton and Ince, Lancaster, a curlew, ppr. *We stoop not.* *Pl.* 52, *cr.* 12.

ANDESLEY, Eng., a sword, ppr., and cross crosslet, sa., in saltier. *Pl.* 89, *cr.* 14.

ANDLAW, an eagle's head, sa. *Pl.* 100, *cr.* 10.

ANDRADE, a wolf's head, or. *Pl.* 14, *cr.* 6.

ANDRE, or ANDREE, Eng., a mill-rind, az. *Pl.* 54, *cr.* 3.

ANDREA, or ST ANDREW, Eng., a cinquefoil, ar. *Pl.* 91, *cr.* 12.

ANDREA, Eng., a bezant, az., charged with lion's head, erased, collared, gu. *Pl.* 121, *cr.* 12.

ANDREW, Backhould and Plymouth, Devons., a stag's head, erased, sa., attired, or. *Pl.* 66, *cr.* 9.

ANDREW of Denton and Norton, Bart., a moor's head, couped. *Pl.* 120, *cr.* 3.

ANDREW of Nethertarvit, a star, or. *Give and forgive.* *Pl.* 21, *cr.* 6.

ANDREWES, Ruts., a demi-lion, or, ducally crowned, ar., in dexter a human heart, gu. *Pl.* 61, *cr.* 4, (heart, *pl.* 54, *cr.* 13.)

ANDREWES, Eng., a moor's head, in profile, sa., banded, ar. *Pl.* 48, *cr.* 7.

ANDREWES, Bart., Carlisle, a moor's head, couped, ppr. *Pl.* 120, *cr.* 3.

ANDREWES, Northamp., a moor's head, ppr. *Pl.* 120, *cr.* 3.

ANDREWES, Suff., a stag's head, ar., erased, charged with a crescent. *Pl.* 61, *cr.* 9.

ANDREWES, Lond., an arm erect, vested, vert, cuffed, ar., (sleeve charged with a quatrefoil, or,) in hand, ppr., a branch, vert, (with three quatrefoils.) *Pl.* 101, *cr.* 3.

ANDREWES of Lathbury, Bucks., Bart., a stag's head, ar. *Pl.* 66, *cr.* 9.

ANDREWES of Shaw Place, Bart., out of an eastern coronet, a moor's head, in profile, ppr. *Pl.* 57, *cr.* 5.

ANDREWES, Eng., a moor's head, in profile, couped at shoulders, ppr. *Pl.* 120, *cr.* 3.

ANDREWS, Bart., Denton, Northamp., a blackamoor's head, in profile, couped at shoulders, wreathed. *Pl.* 48, *cr.* 7.

ANDREWS, Bart., Shaw, Berks., out of an eastern crown, or, a blackamoor's head, couped, (in ear, a pendant, or.) *Victrix fortunæ sapientia.* *Pl.* 57, *cr.* 5.

ANDREWS, Middx., above a naval coronet, or, a dove, volant, in mouth an olive-branch, all ppr. *Pl.* 25, *cr.* 6, (coronet, *pl.* 128, *fig.* 19.)

ANDREWS, Suff., a stag's head, erased, ar. *Pl.* 66, *cr.* 9.

ANDREWS, Bishop of Winchester, same crest.

ANDREW, and ANDREWS, of Clockmill, in dexter hand a laurel-branch, ppr. *Virtute et fortuna.* *Pl.* 43, *cr.* 6.

ANDREWS, Suff., an acorn, vert. *Pl.* 81. *cr.* 7.

ANDREWS, Sco., in hand a branch of laurel, ppr. *Virtute et fortuna.* *Pl.* 43, *cr.* 6.

ANDREWS, Eng., a moor's head, couped, ppr. *Pl.* 120, *cr.* 3.

ANDREWS of Norton, Bart., a moor's head, in profile, sa., banded, ar. *Pl.* 48, *cr.* 7.

ANDREWS, Berks., out of an eastern crown, or, a moor's head, couped. *Pl.* 57, *cr.* 5.

ANDREWS, Hants., a greyhound's head, per pale, or and sa., (charged on neck with a saltier humettée, between two roundles, in fess, all counterchanged). *Pl.* 89, *cr.* 2.

ANDREWS, Lathbury, Bucks., of Norf. and Suff.: 1. A stag's head, ar. *Pl.* 66, *cr.* 9. 2. For the Suff. branch, a stag's head, erased, ar., charged with a crescent for difference. *Pl.* 61, *cr.* 9.

ANDREWS, Suff., a bird, wings expanded, az, in beak a laurel-branch, (another, an acorn,) vert. *Pl.* 108, *cr.* 5, (laurel, *pl.* 123, *cr.* 5; acorn, *pl.* 81, *cr.* 7.)

ANDREWS, a dexter arm, vested, vert, cuffed, ar., in hand a branch. *Pl.* 113, *cr.* 5.

ANDREWS, a greyhound's head, couped, per pale, or and sa., (on neck a saltier, counterchanged.) *Pl.* 14, *cr.* 4.

ANDREWS, ROBERT, Esq., of Little Lever and Rivington, Lanc., a moor's head, in profile, couped at shoulders, ppr., in ear a pendant, ar. *Fortiter defendit.* *Pl.* 120, *cr.* 3.

ANDROS, on a tower, a lion, rampant, sa. *Pl.* 121, *cr.* 5.

ANDSON, Angus, a fir-tree, seeded, ppr. *Stand sure.* *Pl.* 26, *cr.* 10.

ANELCHE, Eng., an eagle, wings expanded, ppr. *Pl.* 67, *cr.* 4.

ANELSHEY, Glouc., a bezant, or, charged with a pale, indented, gu. *Pl.* 63, *cr.* 7.

ANEYS, Eng., a sword, in bend, ppr. *Pl.* 22, *cr.* 7.

ANGAS, or ANGES, an ostrich-head, erased, ar., in mouth a horse-shoe, ppr. *Pl.* 99, *cr.* 12, (without feathers.)

ANGE, a cross-formée, fitched, or, between wings, az. *Pl.* 29, *cr.* 14, (fitched, *pl.* 27, *cr.* 14.)

ANGEL, ANGLE, ANEGALL, or ANEGAL, on a chapeau, a tower, ppr. *Pl.* 12, *cr.* 5, (chapeau, *pl.* 127, *fig.* 13.)

ANGELDON, Lond., a knot, sa., between wings, or.

ANGELL, Lond., out of a ducal coronet, or, a demi-pegasus, ar., crined, gu. *Pl.* 76, *cr.* 2, (coronet, *pl.* 128, *fig.* 3.)

ANGELL, Lond., on a mount, vert, a swan, ar., (ducally gorged, or,) beaked, gu., legged, sa. *Pl.* 122, *cr.* 13.

ANGELL, a swan, ar., ducally gorged, or. *Pl.* 111, *cr.* 10, (without crown.)

ANGELLIS, or ANGLES, a lion's gamb, issuing, holding a cross pattée, fitched, or. *Pl.* 46, *cr.* 7.

ANGER, and ANGIER, Kent, a martlet, flying over a castle, (sinister tower ruined, ppr.) *Pl.* 37, *cr.* 1.

ANGER, an escarbuncle, or. *Pl.* 51, *cr.* 10.
ANGERSTEEN, a lion's head, erased, gu., in mouth a quatrefoil, vert. *Pl.* 95, *cr.* 6, (quatrefoil, *pl.* 141.)
ANGERSTEIN, Eng., a lion's head, erased, gu., in mouth a trefoil, vert. *Pl.* 95, *cr.* 6, (trefoil, *pl.* 141.)
ANGESTEEN, a crane, ppr., in dexter a mullet, ar. *Pl.* 26, *cr.* 11, (mullet, *pl.* 141.)
ANGEVILLE, and ANGEVINE, of Thethelthorpe, Linc., a branch of three roses, ar., stalked and leaved, vert. *Pl.* 23, *cr.* 2.
ANGEVYNE, Linc., same crest.
ANGLESEY, Marquess of, Earl of Uxbridge, and Baron Paget (Paget); a demi-heraldic tiger, salient, sa., armed, ducally gorged, and tufted, ar. *Per il suo contrario.* *Pl.* 57, *cr.* 13.
ANGOLESME, Eng., the sail of a ship, ppr. *Pl.* 22, *cr.* 12.
ANGOLISME, Eng., a lion's gamb, sa. *Pl.* 68, *cr.* 3.
ANGUILLA, Eng., a bezant, charged with talbot's head, erased, sa. *Pl.* 38, *cr.* 2.
ANGUISH, Norwich, a snake, nowed, ppr., between two branches of fern, vert. *Latet anguis in herba.* *Pl.* 1, *cr.* 9, (fern, *pl.* 80, *cr.* 1.)
ANGUISHE, Norf., a snake, nowed, ppr., between two branches of fern, vert. *Pl.* 1, *cr.* 9, (fern, *pl.* 80, *cr.* 1.)
ANGUS, Eng., a quadrangular castle. *Pl.* 28, *cr.* 11.
ANGUS, Sco., a lion, with antique crown, or. *Fortis est veritas.* *Pl.* 98, *cr.* 1, (crown. *pl.* 128, *fig.* 2.)
ANHELET, Eng., a gem ring, or, stoned, gu. *Pl.* 35, *cr.* 3.
ANKE, or ANKOR, Eng., a bull's head, erased, gu. *Pl.* 19, *cr.* 3.
ANKETEL, Eng., a rose, gu. *Pl.* 105, *cr.* 7.
ANKETELL of Shaftesbury, on a mount, vert, an oak-tree, ppr. *Pl.* 48, *cr.* 4.
ANKETELL, Eng., stump of oak-tree, erased, branches sprouting, ppr., acorned, or. *Pl.* 92, *cr.* 8.
ANKETELL, WILLIAM, Esq., of Anketell Grove, Monaghan, an oak-tree, ppr. *Vade ad formicam.* *Pl.* 16, *cr.* 8.
ANKYRSLEY, Eng., a hunting-horn, without strings, veruled, ar. *Pl.* 89, *cr.* 3.
ANLABY, or HANLABY, on a mount, an oak-tree, ppr. *Pl.* 48, *cr.* 4.
ANLEBY, and ANSELBY, Eaton, Yorks., an arrow in pale, enfiled with a ducal coronet, or. *Pl.* 55, *cr.* 1.
ANLET, and ANLETT, Yorks., on a rock, a fire-beacon, ppr. *Pl.* 89, *cr.* 9.
ANLEY, Eng., a dexter arm, in hand, (gloved,) a hawk's lure, ppr. *Pl.* 44, *cr.* 2.
ANMERS, or ANNERS, Chesh., a lion's head, erased, ppr. *Pl.* 81, *cr.* 4.
ANMETESLEY, Eng., a bezant, or, charged with a pale, indented, gu. *Pl.* 63, *cr.* 7.
ANNA, DE, Eng., a bezant, or. *Pl.* 7, *cr.* 6.
ANNABELL, ANNABLE, and ANNABLES, Eng., a stag at gaze, ppr. *Pl.* 81, *cr.* 8.
ANNAND, Surr., a griffin, segreant. *Sperabo.* *Pl.* 67, *cr.* 13.
ANNAND, Annandale, a rose, stalked and leaved, ppr. *Quod honestum utile.* *Pl.* 105, *cr.* 7.
ANNANDALE, Sco., same crest and motto.
ANNANDALE, a spur, erect, or, winged, ar. *Pl.* 59, *cr.* 1.

ANNAT, Sco., a boar, sa., transfixed with an arrow. *Pl.* 36, *cr.* 2.
ANNCELL, Eng., a stag's head, affrontée, ducally gorged. *Pl.* 55, *cr.* 2.
ANNCEY, Eng., on a mural coronet, a stag, sejant, ppr. *Pl.* 101, *cr.* 3.
ANNE, Oxon. and Northamp., a woman's head, couped at breasts, ppr., hair dishevelled, or. *Pl.* 45, *cr.* 5.
ANNE, Northamp. and Oxon., a woman's head, couped at breasts, face, ppr., vested, ar., hair dishevelled, or. *Pl.* 45, *cr.* 5.
ANNE of Trickley, Yorks., a buck's head, cabossed, ar. *Pl.* 36, *cr.* 1.
ANNELES, a mermaid, ppr., tail, vert. *Pl.* 48, *cr.* 5.
ANNELSHIE, a bezant, or, charged with a pale, indented, gu. *Pl.* 63, *cr.* 7.
ANNESLEY, Earl Annesley, Iri., a moor's head, couped, ppr., wreathed, ar. and sa. *Pl.* 48, *cr.* 7.
ANNESLEY, Iri., a demi-lady supporting a portcullis. *Pl.* 126, *cr.* 6.
ANNESLEY, Oxon., moor's head couped, sa., wreathed, ar. and az. *Virtutis amore.* *Pl.* 48, *cr.* 7.
ANNESLEY, Earl Mountmorris, Iri., moor's head, issuing, sa., wreathed, ar. and az. *Virtutis amore.* *Pl.* 48, *cr.* 7.
ANNESLEY, Earl of Anglesey, Eng., same crest.
ANNESLEY, Earl of, and Baron, Viscount Glerawley, (Annesley,) Iri., moor's head, in profile, sa., wreathed, ar. and az. *Virtutis amore.* *Pl.* 48, *cr.* 7.
ANNESLEY, Viscount Valentis, Iri., moor's head, in profile, couped, ppr., wreathed, ar. and az. *Virtutis amore.* *Pl.* 48, *cr.* 7.
ANNESLEY, ARTHUR-LYTTLETON, Esq. of Arley Castle, Stafford, same crest and motto.
ANNESLEY, Bucks. and Oxon., a Saracen's head, in profile, wreathed, ar. and az. *Pl.* 36, *cr.* 3.
ANNESLEY, Eng., a buck's head, or. *Pl.* 66, *cr.* 9.
ANNES, ANNESS, and ANNIS, Eng., a mascle, or. *Pl.* 54, *cr.* 1.
ANNGELL, Kent, out of a ducal coronet, or, a demi-pegasus, ar. *Pl.* 76, *cr.* 2, (coronet, *pl.* 128, *fig.* 3.)
ANNOT, ANNOTT, or ANNAT, Eng., a boar, passant, sa., transfixed with an arrow, ppr. *Pl.* 36, *cr.* 2.
ANNYSLAY, Eng., moor's head, couped, sa. *Pl.* 120, *cr.* 3.
ANSCELL, or ANSTRELL, of Barford, Beds., a demi-lion, az., ducally gorged, (and lined,) or. *Pl.* 87, *cr.* 15.
ANSDELL, in dexter hand, ppr., a buckle, or. *Pl.* 38, *cr.* 9.
ANSELBIE, and Anselby, Eng., an arrow, in pale, enfiled with a ducal coronet, or. *Pl.* 55, *cr.* 1.
ANSELL, Eng., a demi-lion, ppr., ducally gorged, (and chained.) *Pl.* 87, *cr.* 15.
ANSERT, Eng., a demi-lion, rampant, imperially crowned, in dexter a sword, wavy, ppr. *Pl.* 54, *cr.* 2.
ANSON, Bart., Lanc., out of a ducal coronet, or, a spear, erect, staff, purp., headed, ppr. *Nil desperandum.* *Pl.* 97, *cr.* 4, (coronet, *pl.* 128, *fig.* 3.)

ANSON, Viscount: 1. Out of a ducal coronet, or, a spear-head, ppr., staff, purp. *Pl.* 97, *cr.* 4, (coronet, *pl.* 128, *fig.* 3.) 2. A greyhound's head, couped, erm., charged on neck with two bars-gemelle, or. *Nil desperandum. Pl.* 14, *cr.* 4, (instead of bezants, bars.)

ANSON, a crow, ppr., between two ostrich-feathers, ar. *Pl.* 23, *cr.* 8, (feathers, *pl.* 13, *cr.* 7.)

ANSON, a dove, ppr., between two ostrich-feathers, or. *Pl.* 66, *cr.* 12, (feathers, *pl.* 13, *cr.* 7.)

ANSTAVILL, Eng., a castle, triple-towered, a demi-lion, rampant, out of the middle tower. *Pl.* 101, *cr.* 1.

ANSTAY, ANSTEE, ANSTEY, and ANSTIE, Eng., a martlet, or. *Pl.* 111, *cr.* 5.

ANSTEAD, ANSTED, or ANTISHED, a cross formée, or, charged with five torteaux. *Pl.* 15, *cr.* 8, (torteaux, *pl.* 141.)

ANNTIE, Eng., a leopard's head, ppr., jessant-de-lis, gu. *Pl.* 123, *cr.* 9.

ANSTIS, Cornw., out of a ducal coronet, five ostrich-feathers, ppr. *Pl.* 100, *cr.* 12, (no charge.)

ANSTIS, or ANSTICE, a dexter arm, vested, per pale, embattled, in hand a griffin's head, erased. *Pl.* 94, *cr.* 6.

ANSTON, a martlet, issuing, ppr. *Pl.* 111, *cr.* 5.

ANSTROTHER, out of a ducal coronet, or, a demi-man, in armour, ppr., in hand a spear, sa., headed, a*l. Pl.* 58, *cr.* 2, (without wings.)

ANSTRUTHER, Bart., Staffs., two arms, in armour, gauntlets, ppr., garnished, or, grasping a battle-axe, of the first. *Periissem ni perissem. Pl.* 41, *cr.* 2.

ANSTRUTHER of that Ilk, Bart., N.S., two arms, in armour, embowed, grasping a battle-axe, all ppr. *Periissem ni perissem. Pl.* 41, *cr.* 2.

ANSTRUTHER, Sir RALPH ABERCROMBIE, Bart., of Balcaskie, Fife, same crest and motto.

ANSTRUTHER, JAMES-HAMILTON-LLOYD, Esq., of Hintlesham Hall, Suffolk, same crest and motto.

ANSTRUTHER, Inverkeithing, same crest and motto.

ANSTRUTHER, Airdrie, same crest.

ANSTRUTHER-CARMICHAEL, Bart., Sco.: 1. For *Anstruther*, same crest and motto as above. *Pl.* 41, *cr.* 2. 2. For *Carmichael*, an arm, in armour, erect, grasping a broken spear, ppr. *Toujours prêt. Pl.* 23, *cr.* 9.

ANSTY, Cumb. and Camb., a martlet, or. *Pl.* 111, *cr.* 5.

ANTESBEY, and ANTESLEY, Eng., a bezant, or, charged with a pale, indented, gu. *Pl.* 63, *cr.* 7.

ANTHONY, and ANTONIE, Lond., a goat's head, ar. *Pl.* 105, *cr.* 14.

ANTHONY, a goat's head, or. *Pl.* 105, *cr.* 14.

ANTON of Stoatfield, Linc.; Middx.; Lond.; and Iri.; out of a mural coronet, a lion's head, ar. *Pl.* 45, *cr.* 9.

ANTONY, or ANTONIE, Suff., a goat's head, gu. *Pl.* 105, *cr.* 14.

ANTONY, Lond., a demi-antelope, salient, ppr. *Pl.* 34, *cr.* 8, (without collar.)

ANTRAM, Dors., a demi-griffin, az., winged, beaked, and membered, or. *Prudentia et animo. Pl.* 18, *cr.* 6.

ANTRIM, Earl of, and Viscount Dunluce, Iri., (Seymour-M'Donnell,) a dexter arm, vested, couped at shoulder, embowed, in fess, in hand a cross crosslet, fitched, gu. *Pl.* 88, *cr.* 7.

ANTROBUS, Bart., Chesh., a unicorn's head, couped, ar., horned and maned, or, (gorged with a wreath of laurel, vert,) out of rays, ppr. *Dei memor, gratus amicis. Pl.* 20, *cr.* 1, (rays, *pl.* 116, *cr.* 13.)

ANTROBUS, GIBBS-CRAWFURD, Esq., of Eaton Hall, Chester, same crest and motto.

ANTROBUS, Lond., a unicorn's head, ar., crined and armed, or, out of rays, of the second, (gorged with a chaplet of leaves, vert.) *Pl.* 20, *cr.* 1, (rays, *pl.* 116, *cr.* 13.)

ANTWISEL, or ANTISELL, an eagle, wings expanded and inverted, ppr. *Pl.* 67, *cr.* 4.

ANVERS, Chesh., a branch with three roses, ppr. *Pl.* 23, *cr.* 2.

ANVERS, DE, Eng., a wyvern, sa. *Pl.* 63, *cr.* 13.

ANWILL, and ANWYL, Wel., a dexter and sinister hand out of clouds, in chief, pulling an anchor out of the sea, ppr. *Pl.* 94, *cr.* 4.

ANVORY, in dexter hand a holly-branch, ppr. *Pl.* 55, *cr.* 6.

ANWELL, ANWYL, and ANWYLL, Eng., and Parkin, Merionethshire, on astrolabe, ppr. *Pl.* 26, *cr.* 2.

ANWICK, Lond., a dexter arm, gu., hand, ppr., grasping a broken tilting-spear, or. *Pl.* 66, *cr.* 4.

ANWYT, an eagle, displayed, ppr. *Pl.* 48, *cr.* 11.

AOLUITE, on a chapeau, a lion, (statant, tail extended, ppr., collared, gu.) *Pl.* 107. *cr.* 1.

APEELE, a fleur-de-lis, or, between wings, ar. *Pl.* 21, *cr.* 13, (wreath instead of chapeau.)

APESLEY, Surr. and Suss., same crest.

AP-EYNIONS, Eng., a sheaf of arrows, ppr., banded, gu. *Virtuti fido. Pl.* 43, *cr.* 14.

AP-GRIFFITH, out of a cloud, a dexter and sinister arm shooting an arrow, all ppr. *Pl.* 100, *cr.* 4, (cloud, *pl.* 124, *cr.* 12.)

APHE, Hants, out of a ducal coronet, ar., a parrot's head, or. *Pl.* 24, *cr.* 10, (head, *pl.* 94, *cr.* 2.)

APHERY, Eng., a trefoil, slipped, vert. *Pl.* 82, *cr.* 1.

AP-HOWELL, in gauntlet, erect, a sword, ppr. *Pl.* 125, *cr.* 5.

APIFER, in hand a spiked club, ppr. *Pl.* 28. *cr.* 6.

APILIARD, APPLEYARD, or APPULYARD, East Carlton, Norf., a demi-tiger, quarterly, gu. and az., tail, of the last, tufted, or, (in mouth a rose, gu., stalked and leaved, vert.) *Pl.* 53, *cr.* 10.

APILSTON, in nest a pelican, wings displayed, feeding her young, or, vulned, ppr. *Pl.* 44, *cr.* 1.

APLEGATH, or APLEGARTH, Rapley, Hants, a demi-tiger, gu., bezantée, armed and tufted, or, (charged with a bend, of the last.) *Pl.* 53, *cr.* 10.

APLETREE, Hants, a goat, passant, ar. *Pl.* 66, *cr.* 1.

APLEYARD, Norw. and Yorks., an owl, ar. *Pl.* 27, *cr.* 9.

APPLEBEE, a martlet, or. *Pl.* 111, *cr.* 5.

APPELTON, and APPOLTON, Eng., a camel, couchant, ppr., trappings, gu., fringed, or. *Pl.* 70, *cr.* 2.

APPLEBY, Leic., an apple, or, stalked and leaved, vert.

APPLEFORD, Eng., a demi-savage, in dexter a sword, in sinister a baton, ensigned with a royal crown. *Pl.* 121, *cr.* 8.

APPLETON, or APLETON, Suff., an elephant's head, couped, sa., eared, or, (in mouth a snake, vert, wreathed about trunk.) *Pl.* 35, *cr.* 13.

APPLEWHAITE, Stoke Ask, Suff., a cubit arm erect, in hand an open book, clasped, all ppr. *Pl.* 82, *cr.* 5, (without clouds.)

APPLEYARD, Shotsham, Norf., an owl, ar. *Pl.* 27, *cr.* 9.

APPLEYARD, a demi-dragon, ppr., (in dexter a scimitar, ar.) *Pl.* 82, *cr.* 10.

APPLEYARD, Norf., a demi-tiger, gu. and az., (in mouth a rose, slipped, ppr.) *Pl.* 53, *cr.* 10.

APRECE, Bucks. and Hants., an otter, ppr., collared and lined, or. *Pl.* 9, *cr.* 9.

APRECE, Bucks. and Hants., a spear, erect, ar. *Labora ut æternum vivas. Pl.* 97, *cr.* 4.

APREECE, Bart., Washingley, Hunts., and Honington, Linc., a spear-head, erect, ppr. *Vix labora ut in æternum vivas. Pl.* 82, *cr.* 9.

APREECE, a civet cat, ppr., pierced through middle with a spear-head, erect.

APRICE, Heref, a cock, wings expanded, gu., (in beak a rose, ppr., leaved and stalked, vert.) *Pl.* 76, *cr.* 7, (without mount.)

AP-RICE, a boar's head, erect, ar., pellettée, between two oak-branches, vert, fructed, or. *Pl.* 19, *cr.* 8, (erect, *pl.* 60, *cr.* 7.)

APRIL, or APRILL, a boar's head, erect, ppr., between two olive-branches, vert. *Pl.* 21, *cr.* 7, (branches, *pl.* 128, *fig.* 15.)

APSEY, Eng., a dove, olive-branch in mouth, volant over water, all ppr. *Pl.* 46, *cr.* 13.

APSLEY, Suss., a fleur-de-lis, or, between wings, ar. *Pl.* 21, *cr.* 13, (wreath instead of chapeau.)

AQUITAR, Lond., a demi-lion, rampant, or, murally crowned, az., in dexter a laurel-branch, slipped, ppr. *Pl.* 67, *cr.* 10, (laurel, *pl.* 123, *cr.* 5; crown, *pl.* 128, *fig.* 18.)

ARABIN, Eng., the sun rising behind a mountain, ppr. *Pl.* 38, *cr.* 6.

ARABIN, RICHARD, Esq., of Beech Hill Park, Ess., and Drayton House, Middx., an eagle's head, erased, between wings, sa., ducally crowned, or. *Nec temere, nec timide. Pl.* 81, *cr.* 10, (crown, *pl.* 128, *fig.* 3.)

ARABIN, an eagle's head, erased, between wings, sa., ducally crowned, or. *Pl.* 81, *cr.* 10, (crown, *pl.* 128, *fig.* 18.)

ARABYN, a griffin's head, erased, ppr., ducally crowned, or, between wings, ar. *Pl.* 65, *cr.* 1, (crown, *pl.* 128, *fig.* 3.)

ARBLASTER, or ALLEBASTER, Staffs., a feather, in pale, enfiled with a ducal coronet. *Pl.* 8, *cr.* 9.

ARBLESTER, AREBLASTER, and ARABLESTER, Eng., out of a ducal coronet, a greyhound's head, sa. *Pl.* 70, *cr.* 5.

ARBUCKLE, Sco., a ram, ppr. *Pl.* 109, *cr.* 2.

ARBURTHNET, Findoury, Sco., a peacock, issuing, ppr. *Interna præstant. Pl.* 24, *cr.* 1.

ARBURTHNET of Catherlan, a peacock's head, couped, ppr., charged with a mullet, or. *Sit laus Deo. Pl.* 100, *cr.* 5, (mullet, *pl.* 141.)

ARBURTHNET, same crest. *Tam interna, quam externa.*

ARBUTHNOT, Montrose, a dove, within an adder, in orle, ppr. *Innocue ac provide. Pl.* 92, *cr.* 6.

ARBUTHNOT, Sco., a peacock's head, couped, ppr., beaked, or. *Laus Deo. Pl.* 100, *cr.* 5.

ARBUTHNOT, Bart., Edinr., a peacock's head, ppr. *Innocent and true. Pl.* 100, *cr.* 5.

ARBUTHNOT, Weymouth, a ship under sail, ppr. *Fluctuo sed affluo. Pl.* 109, *cr.* 8.

ARBUTHNOT, a cross pattée, or. *Pl.* 15, *cr.* 8.

ARBUTHNOT of Arbuthnothaugh, a peacock's head, couped, gu. *Deus me sustinet. Pl.* 100, *cr.* 5.

ARBUTHNOT of Fiddes, a peacock, passant, ppr. *Tam interna, quam externa. Pl.* 54, *cr.* 13.

ARBUTHNOT, Viscount, Sco., a peacock's head, erased, ppr. *Laus Deo. Pl.* 86, *cr.* 4.

ARCEDECKNE, or ARCHDECKNE, a dexter arm, in armour, embowed, hand grasping a scimitar, ppr. *Pl.* 81, *cr.* 11.

ARCEDECKNE, ANDREW, Esq., of Glevering Hall, Suffolk, a dexter arm, in hand a sword. *Pl.* 21, *cr.* 10.

ARCESTER, Glouc., on a bezant, an escarbuncle, sa. *Pl.* 7, *cr.* 6, (escarbuncle, *pl.* 141.)

ARCHARD, Kent, out of a ducal coronet, a demi-fish, ppr. *Pl.* 36, *cr.* 13.

ARCHBALD, and ARCHIBALD, of Blackhall, a decrescent, ar. *Ut reficiar. Pl.* 16, *cr.* 15.

ARCHBALD, and ARCHIBALD, Sco., a palm-branch, erect, ppr. *Ditat servata fides. Pl.* 123, *cr.* 1.

ARCHDALE, and ARCHEDALE, Lond., out of a ducal coronet, a tiger's head, ar., maned and tufted, sa. *Pl.* 36, *cr.* 15.

ARCHDALL, WILLIAM, Esq., of Castle Archdall, co. Fermanagh; and Trillic, co. Tyrone, Iri.: 1. For *Archdall*, out of a ducal coronet, a heraldic tiger's head, ppr. *Data fata secutus. Pl.* 98, *cr.* 4. 2. For *Montgomery*, on a chapeau, ppr. a hand, (vested, az.), grasping a sword, ppr., hilt and pommel, or. *Honneur sans repos. Pl.* 21, *cr.* 10, (chapeau, *pl.* 127, *fig.* 13.) 3. For *Mervyn*, a squirrel, sejant, ppr. *De Dieu tout. Pl.* 85, *cr.* 3, (without collar.)

ARCHDALL, Iri., a cross pattée, erm. *Pl.* 15, *cr.* 8.

ARCHDALL, or ARCHDELL, out of a ducal coronet, or, a griffin's head. *Pl.* 54, *cr.* 14.

ARCHDEACON, Cornw., a martlet flying over a tower, ppr. *Pl.* 37, *cr.* 1.

ARCHEBOLD, or ARCHBOLD, Staffs., a lion's head, erased, ar., collared, gu. *Pl.* 7, *cr.* 10.

ARCHER, EDWARD, Esq., of Trelaske House, Cornw., a quiver, in fess, ppr. *Pl.* 19, *cr.* 4.

ARCHER of Bourne, Kent, a bull's head, erased, gu., armed, or. *Pl.* 19, *cr.* 3.

ARCHER, Ess., a griffin's head, erased, ar., (pierced through neck by a spear, in bend sinister, point downward.) *Pl.* 48, *cr.* 6.

ARCHER, Cornw., on a quiver full of arrows, in fess, a serpent. *Pl.* 19, *cr.* 4, (serpent, *pl.* 1, *cr.* 9.)

ARCHER, Ess. and Kent, a bull's head, erased, gu. *Pl.* 19, *cr.* 3.

B

ARCHER, Chelmsford, Ess., a griffin's head, erased, ar., (pierced by a spear, in bend sinister, point downward, collared, gu., charged with two crosses pattée, of the first, in beak a slip of oak, fructed, ppr.) *Pl.* 48, *cr.* 6.

ARCHER, Linc., a dragon's head, per pale, gu. and az., wings expanded, sinister wing, or, dexter, ar., out of a mural coronet, per pale, of the last and third. *Pl.* 101, *cr.* 4, (wings, *pl.* 105, *cr.* 11.)

ARCHER, Baron, of Umberslade, Warw., out of a mural coronet, gu., a dragon's head, ar. *Sola bona quæ honesta.* *Pl.* 101, *cr.* 4.

ARCHER, a demi-dragon, (in dexter a dart.) *Pl.* 82, *cr.* 10.

ARCHER, Eng., a palm-branch, ppr. *Ditat servata fides.* *Pl.* 26, *cr.* 3.

ARCHER, Iri., a mound, az., banded and crossed, or. *Pl.* 37, *cr.* 3.

ARCHER, Sco., a dexter hand, and sinister arm, issuing, drawing an arrow to the head, ppr. *Pl.* 100, *cr.* 4.

ARCHER, an archer, vested, vert, (in dexter a bugle-horn, ar., raised to mouth, in sinister, a bow erect,) across shoulders a quiver full of arrows. *Pl.* 90, *cr.* 3.

ARCHER-DE BOYS, Ess.: 1. A wyvern, ar. *Pl.* 63, *cr.* 13. 2. A leg couped at thigh, embowed at knee, quarterly, sa. and ar., spur and leather, or. *Pl.* 38, *cr.* 14.

ARCHEVER, Sco., two arms drawing arrow to the head, ppr. *Ready.* *Pl.* 100, *cr.* 4.

ARCHIBALD, CHARLES-DICKSON, Esq., of Rusland Hall, Lancaster. *Palma non sine pulvere.*

ARCHIDECKNIE, a dexter arm in armour, embowed, ppr., in hand a dagger, also ppr. *Pl.* 120, *cr.* 11.

ARCY, DE, Iri., a tilting-spear broken in three pieces, ppr., head in pale, other two in saltier, banded, gu. *Pl.* 33, *cr.* 3.

ARD, Eng., a cock, ppr. *Vigilantia.* *Pl.* 67, *cr.* 14.

ARDEM, Eng., a cross, az., on three grieces, *Pl.* 49, *cr.* 2.

ARDEN, Baron Alvenley, of Alvenley, Chester, out of a ducal coronet, or, a plume of five feathers, ar., charged with a crescent, gu. *Patientiâ vinces.* *Pl.* 100, *cr.* 12.

ARDEN, or ADERNE, Beds. and Warw., a plume of feathers, ar., charged with a martlet, or. *Pl.* 12, *cr.* 9, (martlet, *pl.* 111, *cr.* 5.)

ARDEN, Middx., on a mount, vert, a boar, passant, ar., (semée-de-lis, az., langued, gu., armed and unguled, or.) *Doluére dente lacessiti.* *Pl.* 108, *cr.* 9.

ARDEN, Eng., on a chapeau, gu., turned up, erm., a boar, passant, or. *Pl.* 22, *cr.* 8.

ARDERNE, Staffs., same crest.

ARDEN, Baron, (Perceval,) out of a ducal coronet, or, a boar's head, sa. (muzzled, or.) *Sub cruce candida.* *Pl.* 102, *cr.* 14.

ARDEN, Norf. and Suff., on a chapeau, purp., turned up, erm. a wild boar, passant, or *Quo me cunque vocat patria.* *Pl.* 22, *cr.* 8.

ARDEN, The Rev. FRANCIS-EDWARD, of Gresham, Norf., same crest and motto.

ARDEN, Warw., on a chapeau, gu., turned up, gold, a boar, passant, or. *Pl.* 22, *cr.* 8.

ARDERES, Meriden, Warw., a demi-lion, az., gorged with a collar, or, (charged with three mullets, of the first.) *Pl.* 18, *cr.* 13.

ARDERN, Eng., in a coronet, or, a pyramid of leaves, vert. *Pl.* 61, *cr.* 13, (coronet, *pl.* 128, *fig.* 3.)

ARDERNE, Staffs., on a chapeau, gu., turned up, erm., a boar, passant, or. *Pl.* 22, *cr.* 8.

ARDERNE, Chesh. and Lanc., out of a ducal coronet, or, a plume of (five) feathers, three or, and two az. *Pl.* 64, *cr.* 5.

ARDERNE, Chesh. and Lanc., out of a ducal coronet, or, a plume of seven feathers, ar., tipped, gu. *Pl.* 114, *cr.* 8, (without under plume.)

ARDERNE, Warw., on a chapeau, az., turned up, erm., a boar, passant, or. *Pl.* 22, *cr.* 8.

ARDERNE, Warw., a boar, passant, or. *Pl.* 48, *cr.* 14.

ARDERNE, (out of a case or bandage,) or, a plume of feathers, ar. *Pl.* 12, *cr.* 9.

ARDERNE, Eng., a plume of feathers, ppr. *Pl.* 12, *cr.* 9.

ARDERNE, a plume of feathers, ar., (banded, or.) *Pl.* 12, *cr.* 9.

ARDES, Sharington, Bucks., within a Catharine-wheel, sa., (ducally crowned, or, the sun in splendour.) *Pl.* 1, *cr.* 7.

ARDES, a Catharine-wheel, or, pierced, sa., (ducally crowned, of the first.) *Pl.* 1, *cr.* 7.

ARDINGTON, or ARTHINGTON, Yorks., a dove with olive-branch in mouth, ppr. *Pl.* 48, *cr.* 15.

ARDIS, a demi-lion, rampant, gu., in dexter a rose, or, leaved, vert. *Pl.* 39, *cr.* 14.

ARDYN, a cross, az., on three grieces. *Pl.* 49, *cr.* 2.

ARDYN, Eng., on a chapeau, gu., turned up, erm., a boar, passant, or. *Pl.* 22, *cr.* 8.

AREL, French and Eng., a boar's head, between two ostrich-feathers, ppr. *Pl.* 60, *cr.* 7.

ARESKIN, in dexter hand an escutcheon. *Pl.* 21, *cr.* 12, (not charged.)

ARESKINE, Sco., in dexter hand a sword, erect, between two laurel-branches, all ppr. *Pl.* 23, *cr.* 15, (branches, *pl.* 79, *cr.* 14.)

ARESKINE, Captain, Sco., a demi-griffin, in dexter a sword, ppr. *Ausim et confido.* *Pl.* 49, *cr.* 4.

ARESKINE of Alva, Bart., an arm, in armour, embowed, gauntleted, grasping a sword, all ppr. *Je pense plus.* *Pl.* 2, *cr.* 8.

ARESKINE, of Dun, a griffin's head, erased, in beak a sword, in bend, ppr., on blade—*In Domino confido.* *Pl.* 35, *cr.* 15.

ARFECE, ARFOIS, or ARFORCE, Eng., a scaling-ladder, az. *Pl.* 98, *cr.* 15.

ARGAHAST, a Doric column, ppr. *Pl.* 33, *cr.* 1.

ARGAL, Eng., a lion's head, erased, gu. *Pl.* 81, *cr.* 4.

ARGALL, of Low-hall, and Much-baddow, Ess., a sphinx, wings expanded, ppr. *Pl.* 91, *cr.* 11.

ARGALL, an arm, in armour, embowed, grasping a battle-axe, all ppr. *Pl.* 121, *cr.* 14.

ARGALL, ARGELL, or ARGILL, a lion's head, erased, ppr. *Pl.* 81, *cr.* 4.

ARGALL, Eng., a sphinx, or, winged, ar. *Pl.* 91, *cr.* 11.

ARGALL, Ess. and Sco., a sphinx, ppr. *Pl.* 91, *cr.* 11.

ARGENTE, Camb., a demi-lion, gu., holding a covered cup, ar. *Pl.* 89, *cr.* 10, (cup, *pl.* 75, *cr.* 13.)

ARGENTON, Eng., a martlet, sa. *Pl.* 111, *cr.* 5.

ARGENTRE, Eng., an eagle's head, erased, gu. *Pl.* 20, *cr.* 7.

ARGENTREE, France, an eagle's head, erased, gu. *Pl.* 20, *cr.* 7.

ARGUILLA, on a bezant, a talbot's head, erased, sa. *Pl.* 38, *cr.* 2.

ARGUM, ARGUN, or ARGUNE, Eng., in hand, erect, out of a cloud, an open book, ppr. *Pl.* 82, *cr.* 5.

ARGYLL, Duke, Marquess, and Earl of, Sco.; Baron Sundridge, and Lord Hamilton, Eng.; (Campbell;) a boar's head, in fess, couped, or. *Vix ea nostra voco*—and—*Ne obliviscaris.* *Pl.* 48, *cr.* 2.

ARIEL, and ARIELL, Eng., an anchor, cabled, and sword, in saltier. *Pl.* 25, *cr.* 1.

ARIES, Iri., a satyr, in dexter a sword, in sinister a partizan, all ppr.

ARKELL, or ARKLE, a griffin, sejant, ar., in dexter a garland of laurel, vert. *Pl.* 56, *cr.* 10.

ARKINSTALL, Camb., on a mount, vert, a greyhound, sejant, erm. *Pl.* 5, *cr.* 2.

ARKLEY, Sco., two thistles, in orle, flowered, ppr., in centre a rose. *Bene qui sedulo.* *Pl.* 23, *cr.* 10, (rose, *pl.* 117, *cr.* 10.)

ARKROYD, Eng., a dog, sleeping. *Pl.* 29, *cr.* 3.

ARKWRIGHT, ROBERT, Esq., of Sutton Scarsdale and Willersley, Derby, an eagle, rising, or, (in beak an escutcheon, pendant by a ribbon, gu., charged with a hank of cotton, ar.) *Multa tuli fecique.* *Pl.* 67, *cr.* 4.

ARKYBUS, a lion's head, erased, ar. *Pl.* 81, *cr.* 4.

ARLE, Eng., a boar's head, erect, between two ostrich-feathers. *Pl.* 60, *cr.* 7.

ARLOTE, or ARLOTT, on a chapeau, a leopard, passant, (gardant, three blades of rushes on each side, all ppr.) *Pl.* 110, *cr.* 8.

ARMESBURY, Ess., two hands conjoined, out of clouds, ppr. *Pl.* 53, *cr.* 11.

ARMESTON, Burbage, Leic., a dragon's head, erased, vert, scaled, or, (charged with a crescent, of the same, for difference.) *Pl.* 87, *cr.* 12.

ARMESTONE, Leic., a dragon's head, erased, ppr. *Pl.* 87, *cr.* 12.

ARMESTRANG, or ARMSTRONG, of Whittock, Sco., an arm, embowed, ppr. *Invictus maneo.* *Pl.* 87, *cr.* 7.

ARMESTRANG, ARMSTRANG, or ARMSTRONG, of Parknow, Sco., in hand, out of a cloud, a club, all ppr. *Invicta labore.* *Pl.* 37, *cr.* 13.

ARMIGER, or ARMEIER, North Creake, Norf., on a ducal coronet, or, a tiger, sejant, gu., crined and tufted, gold. *Pl.* 86, *cr.* 8.

ARMINE, Osgodby, Linc., on a mount, vert, an ermine, ppr. *Pl.* 87, *cr.* 3.

ARMISTEAD, a dexter arm, in armour, embowed, ppr., hand grasping butt of a broken spear, or. *Suivez la raison.* *Pl.* 44, *cr.* 9.

ARMIT, and ARMITT, Eng., on a mount, vert, a bull, passant, ppr. *Pl.* 39, *cr.* 5.

ARMITAGE, WHALEY, Esq., of Atherdee, Coole, and Drumim, co. Louth. *Fractum non abjicio ensem.*

ARMITAGE, Kirklees, Bart., Yorks., a dexter arm, embowed, vested, or, cuff, ar., grasping in hand, ppr., a sword by the blade, also ppr., hilt, gold, point downward. *Pl.* 65, *cr.* 8, (vesting, *pl.* 120, *cr.* 1.)

ARMITAGE, an arm, embowed, vested, in hand a sword, ppr. *Pl.* 120, *cr.* 1.

ARMITAGE, JOSEPH, Esq., of Milnsbridge House, Yorks., a dexter arm, embowed, couped at shoulder, vested, or, cuffed, ar., (in hand, ppr., a staff, gu., headed and pointed, gold.) *Semper paratus.* *Pl.* 120, *cr.* 1.

ARMO, three passion-nails, ppr., one in pale and two in saltier. *Pl.* 47, *cr.* 10, (saltier, *pl.* 7, *cr.* 9.)

ARMONY, a stag, gu. *Pl.* 68, *cr.* 2.

ARMORY COMPANY, Kerry, Iri., an eagle's head, or. *Pl.* 100, *cr.* 10.

ARMOUR, Sco., a dexter hand holding up an esquire's helmet, all ppr. *Cassis tutissima virtus.* *Pl.* 37, *cr.* 15.

ARMSTRANG, an armed arm, ppr. *Pl.* 97, *cr.* 1.

ARMSTRANG, an arm, gu. *Pl.* 87, *cr.* 7.

ARMSTRANG of Mangerton, an arm, in armour, from shoulder, embowed, ppr. *Pl.* 97, *cr.* 1.

ARMSTRONG, an arm, in armour, issuing, grasping a sword, az., hilted and pommelled, or. *Invictus maneo.* *Pl.* 2, *cr.* 8.

ARMSTRONG, Lond., a dexter arm, in armour, embowed, couped at elbow, hand apaumée, ppr. *Pl.* 97, *cr.* 1.

ARMSTRONG, Bart., Iri., an arm, in armour, embowed, in hand trunk of oak-tree, eradicated, all ppr. *Invictus maneo.* *Pl.* 97, *cr.* 1.

ARMSTRONG of Whittock, an arm, embowed, ppr. *Invictus maneo.* *Pl.* 87, *cr.* 7.

ARMSTRONG, Linc. and Notts., a dexter arm, vambraced in armour, hand, ppr. *Pl.* 97, *cr.* 1.

ARMSTRONG, Sco., an arm, embowed, couped, vested, gu., cuffed, ar., hand grasping a sword, all ppr. *Strength.* *Pl.* 120, *cr.* 1.

ARMSTRONG, WILLIAM-EDWARD, Esq., of New Hall and Kilkee, Clare, in (armed) hand and arm, a leg and foot, in rich armour, couped at thigh. *Vi et armis.* *Pl.* 39, *cr.* 6.

ARMSTRONG, GEORGE-DE LA POER, Esq., of Mealiffe, co. Tipperary; and Chaffpoole, co. Sligo; same crest and motto.

ARMSTRONG, EDMUND-JOHN, Esq., of Willow Bank, co. Clare; and Adzar House, co. Dublin; an arm, in armour. *In Deo robur meus.* *Pl.* 97, *cr.* 1.

ARMSTRONG, JOHN-WARNEFORD, Esq., of Ballycumber, King's County, a dexter arm, in armour, ar., hand, ppr. *Vi et armis.* *Pl.* 97, *cr.* 1.

ARMSTRONG, Harkness Rig, Canobie, same crest and motto.

ARMSTRONG, THOMAS-ST. GEORGE, Esq., of Garry Castle House, King's County, same crest and motto.

ARMSTRONG, WILLIAM-JONES, Esq., of Batleagh Lodge, Tynan, co. Armagh, same crest. *Invictus maneo.*

ARMSTRONG, an arm, in armour, couped at shoulder, embowed, in fess. *Pl.* 107, *cr.* 15, (without scimitar.)

ARMSTRONG, The Rev. CHARLES-EDWARD, M.A., of Hemsworth, York, an arm, in armour. *Vi et armis. Pl.* 97, *cr.* 1.

ARMYTAGE, Bart., Kirklees, Yorks., a dexter arm, embowed, couped at shoulder, vested, or, cuff, ar., in hand, ppr., a sword, gu., garnished, gold. *Pl.* 120, *cr.* 1.

ARMYTAGE, Lond. and Yorks., a demi-lion, ar., in dexter a cross botonnée, gu. *Pl.* 65, *cr.* 6, (cross, *pl.* 141.)

ARNALD, or ARNAULD, Eng., a demi-cat, gardant, ppr. *Pl.* 80, *cr.* 7.

ARNEEL, ARNIED, or ARNEIL, Sco., an eel, naiant, vert. *Sans peur. Pl.* 25, *cr.* 13.

ARNET, Eng., on a mount, vert, a bull, passant, ppr. *Pl.* 39, *cr.* 5.

ARNET, Sco., a crescent, or. *Speratum et completum. Pl.* 18, *cr.* 14.

ARNET, Bart., Lond. and Yorks., a demi-lion, ar., in dexter a cross. *Pl.* 65, *cr.* 6.

ARNETT, ARNOT, and ARNOTT, Eng., on a tower, ppr., a flag displayed, az. *Pl.* 8, *cr.* 13.

ARNEWAY, ARNAWAY, and ARNOLD, Bucks. and Linc., a crosier, or. *Pl.* 7, *cr.* 15.

ARNEWOOD, Hants., out of a ducal coronet, a demi-leopard. *Pl.* 12, *cr.* 14, (coronet, *pl.* 128, *fig.* 3.)

ARNEY, Chamberry, Dors., on a mural coronet, or, three arrows, ar., through a human heart, gu., two in saltier, and one in pale, of the second. *Pl.* 106, *cr.* 14.

ARNOLD, Lond., in hand, ppr., a bunch of grapes, purp., leaved, vert. *Pl.* 37, *cr.* 4.

ARNOLD, Glouc., a demi-tiger, ar., (pellettée.) *Pl.* 53, *cr.* 10.

ARNOLD, Devons., out of a ducal coronet, an antelope's head. *Pl.* 24, *cr.* 7, (coronet, same plate, *cr.* 10.)

ARNOLD, Cromer, Norf.; and Bellesford, Suff.; a dolphin, embowed, ar. *Pl.* 48, *cr.* 9.

ARNOLD, Chilwick, Herts., an eagle's head, erased, gu., gorged with a mural coronet, ar., in beak an acorn, slipped, leaved, vert. *Pl.* 22, *cr.* 1, (coronet, *pl.* 128, *fig.* 18.)

ARNOLD, Lond., a demi-tiger, sa., bezantée, maned and tufted, or, (holding a broad arrow, stick, gu., feathers and pheon, ar.) *Pl.* 53, *cr.* 10, (bezant, *pl.* 141.)

ARNOLD, The Rev. EDWARD-GLADWIN, of Little Missenden Abbey, Bucks., same crest. *Nil desperandum.*

ARNOLD, a demi-tiger, ar., pellettée, between paws a fireball, sa. *Pl.* 53, *cr.* 10, (fireball, *pl.* 70, *cr.* 12.)

ARNOLD, Iri., a feather and sword, in saltire. *Pl.* 106, *cr.* 9.

ARNOT, ARRAT, and ARROT, Sco., in hand a dagger, erect, ppr. *Pax armis acquiritur. Pl.* 23, *cr.* 15.

ARNOT, Dr, Edinr., same crest and motto.

ARNOT of Balcormo, a crescent, or. *Speratum et completum. Pl.* 18, *cr.* 14.

ARNOTT of Arlary, a crescent, or. *Speratum et completum. Pl.* 18, *cr.* 14.

ARNUT, Sco., a crescent, gu. *Speratum et completum. Pl.* 18, *cr.* 14.

ARNWAY, Linc., a crosier, or. *Pl.* 7, *cr.* 15.

ARON, Eng., a lady's arm, from elbow, in pale. *Pl.* 91, *cr.* 8.

ARPIN, arm in armour, in hand a holly-branch, all ppr. *Pl.* 55, *cr.* 6.

ARRAN, Earl of, and Visc. Sudley, Iri., (Gore;) a wolf, salient, ar., (collared, gu.) *In hoc signo vinces. Pl.* 10, *cr.* 3.

ARRAS, in a tower, gu., embattled, or, a lion's head, gold. *Pl.* 42, *cr.* 4.

ARRAT, Sco., in dexter a dagger, in pale. *Pax armis acquiritur. Pl.* 23, *cr.* 15.

ARRIS, a satyr, in dexter a partizan.

ARROL, Sco., a demi-lion, rampant, in dexter a scimitar. *Courage. Pl.* 126 *a, cr.* 1.

ARROT of that Ilk, Sco., in dexter a sword, in pale, ppr. *Antiquum assero decus. Pl.* 23, *cr.* 15.

ARROT, Lieut.-Col., same crest and motto.

ARROT, Sco., in hand a dagger, in pale, ppr. *Pax armis acquiritur. Pl.* 23, *cr.* 15.

ARROWOOD, or ARWOOD, Lanc., a savage, in dexter a club, resting on the wreath, ppr.

ARROWSMYTH, Huntingfield Hall, Suff., seven arrows, ppr., enfiled with a ducal coronet, or. *Pl.* 37, *cr.* 5, (add two.)

ARSCOT, Devons., a demi-man, affrontée, in Turkish habit, looking forward, in dexter a scimitar held over head, sinister resting on a tiger's head, issuing. *Pl.* 62, *cr.* 2.

ARSCOTT, Eng., same crest.

ARSICK, ARSIKE, ARSYCKE, and ARSYKE, Eng., a talbot, sejant, ppr., dexter on a shield, gu. *Pl.* 19, *cr.* 2.

ARSKING of Ava, (ERSKINE of Alva,) a dexter arm, from shoulder, brandishing a scimitar, ppr. *Je pense plus. Pl.* 92, *cr.* 5.

ARTHER, and ARTHUR, Eng., a mullet of six points, gu. *Pl.* 45, *cr.* 1.

ARTHINGTON, Yorks., a dove, in mouth an olive-branch, ppr. *Pl.* 48, *cr.* 15.

ARTHUR, Dublin, a falcon, volant, ppr., jessed and belled, or. *Pl.* 94, *cr.* 1.

ARTHUR, Springfield, Ess., a pelican, sa., in nest, or, breast vulned, gu. *Pl.* 44, *cr.* 1.

ARTHUR, an eagle, sa., in nest, or, feeding her young, of the first, (on breast a crescent.) *Pl.* 44, *cr.* 1.

ARTHUR, THOMAS, Esq., of Glanomera, co. Clare, a falcon, rising, ppr., jessed and belled, or. *Impelle obstantia. Pl.* 105, *cr.* 4.

ARTHUR, Sco., a pelican in nest, vulning. *Fac et spera. Pl.* 44, *cr.* 1.

ARTHURE, Iri., a demi-savage, regardant, ppr. *Pl.* 16, *cr.* 4.

ARTKED, a dexter arm, from shoulder, couped, resting on elbow, ppr., in hand a cross-crosslet, fitched, in pale, sa. *Pl.* 88, *cr.* 7.

ARTON, a candlestick, or.

ARTUS, an eagle's head, in beak a quill, ppr. *Pl.* 22, *cr.* 1, (quill, *pl.* 86, *cr.* 7.)

ARUNDEL, Baron, of Wardour, Wilts., a wolf, passant, ar. *Deo data. Pl.* 46, *cr.* 6.

ARUNDEL, Lord Arundel, Eng., same crest.

ARUNDEL, Iri., on a chapeau, sa., turned up, erm., a swallow, ar. *Cruce dum spiro fido. Pl.* 89, *cr.* 7.

ARUNDEL, Viscount Galway, Iri., a martlet, or. *Pl.* 111, *cr.* 5.

ARUNDEL-Harris, Devons. and Cornw.: 1. For *Arundel*, a stag's head, ppr., horned, or. *De Hirundine. Pl.* 66, *cr.* 9. 2. On a chapeau, sa., turned up, ar., a martlet, of the last. *Nulli præda. Pl.* 89, *cr.* 7. 3. For *Harris*, an eagle, rising, erm., beaked and spurred, or. *Kar Deu*—and—*Res. pub. tra. Pl.* 67, *cr.* 4.

ARUNDEL, and ARUNDELL of Trerice, and Lord Trevise, Cornw., on a chapeau, gu., a martlet, ar. *Pl.* 89, *cr.* 7.

ARUNDELL, Cornw., (on a mount,) a horse, passant, ar., (against a tree, ppr.) *Pl.* 15, *cr.* 14.

ARUNDELL, Lord Wardure, Eng., a wolf, passant, ar. *Pl.* 46, *cr.* 6.

ARWEIL, or ARWELL, Sco. and Eng., in hand a helmet, ppr. *Pl.* 37, *cr.* 15.

ASADAM, Eng., a rook, feeding, sa. *Pl.* 51, *cr.* 8.

ASBORNE, Eng., in lion's paw a flag, ar., charged with eagle, displayed, sa. *Pl.* 7, *cr.* 7.

ASBURNER, Eng., an ash-tree, ppr. *Pl.* 18, *cr.* 10.

ASCHE, ASCHEY, or ASCHER, Eng., in the sea, a ship in full sail, ppr. *Pl.* 109, *cr.* 8.

ASCON, Eng., a mascle, ar. *Pl.* 54, *cr.* 1.

ASCOUGH of Sailing-Borough and Blibers, Linc., an ass, ar. *Pl.* 42, *cr.* 2.

ASCOUGH, Linc., Yorks., and Bucks., an ass's head, erased, ar. *Pl.* 91, *cr.* 7.

ASCOUGH, Linc., an ass, passant, sa. *Pl.* 42, *cr.* 2.

ASCUE, Eng., an ass's head, erased, ar. *Pl.* 91, *cr.* 7.

ASCUM, Eng., a fleur-de-lis, sa., (another, ar.) *Pl.* 68, *cr.* 12.

ASELOCK, Suff., a talbot's head, erased, or, guttée, ar. *Pl.* 90, *cr.* 6.

ASELOCK, or ASLAKE, Suff., a talbot's head, sa., guttée d'eau. *Pl.* 123, *cr.* 15.

ASEN, Eng., a martlet, gu. *Pl.* 111, *cr.* 5.

ASERBURNE, Eng., an ash-tree, ppr. *Quicquid crescit, in cinere perit.* *Pl.* 18, *cr.* 10.

ASGILE, Bart., Lond., a sphinx, gardant, wings addorsed, ar., crined, or. *Sui oblitus commodi.* *Pl.* 91, *cr.* 11.

ASGIL, Lond., same crest and motto.

ASGILL, Lond. and Hants, on a mural coronet, or, a sphinx, couchant, (gardant,) body brown, face and breasts, ppr., winged, or. *Sui oblitus commodi.* *Pl.* 116, *cr.* 5, (coronet, *pl.* 128, *fig.* 18,) (without trefoil.)

ASH, Eng., an old man's head, in profile, ppr., wreathed and stringed, or and az. *Pl.* 23, *cr.* 3.

ASH, Stalsted, Kent, on a rock, a goose, wings addorsed, ppr. *Pl.* 94, *cr.* 3.

ASH, a cockatrice's head, erased. *Pl.* 76, *cr.* 9.

ASH, WILLIAM-HAMILTON, Esq., of Ashbrook, co. Londonderry, a squirrel. *Non nobis sed omnibus.* *Pl.* 16, *cr.* 9.

ASHAWE, Lanc., an arm, embowed, vested with green leaves, out of a mural coronet, or, in hand a cross pattée, fitched, ar. *Pl.* 57, *cr.* 2.

ASHBERTON, on a chapeau, ppr., a communion cup, or. *Pl.* 127, *fig.* 13, (cup, *pl.* 42, *cr.* 1.)

ASHBORNE, or ASHBURNE, Iri., a tower, triple-towered, ppr. *Pl.* 123, *cr.* 14.

ASHBORNE, or ASHBURY, Worc., in lion's paw a flag, ar., charged with eagle, displayed, sa. *Pl.* 7, *cr.* 7.

ASHBROOK, Iri., a raven, ppr., in beak an ermine-spot. *Mens conscia recti.* *Pl.* 123, *cr.* 2, (ermine, *pl.* 141.)

ASHBURNHAM, Earl and Baron, and Viscount St Asaph, (Ashburnham;) out of a ducal coronet, or, an ash-tree, ppr. *Le roi et l'estat.* *Pl.* 94, *cr.* 5.

ASHBURNHAM, Bart., Bromham, Suss., same crest.

ASHBURNHAM, or ASHBRENHAM, a griffin's head, ppr., (collared, ar.) *Pl.* 38, *cr.* 3.

ASHBURNHAM, Suss. and Suff., out of a ducal coronet, ar., an ash-tree, fructed, ppr. *Will God, and I shall.* *Pl.* 94, *cr.* 5.

ASHBURNHAM of Ashburnham, Suss., out of a ducal coronet, or, an ash-tree, fructed, ppr. *Will God, and I shall.* *Pl.* 94, *cr.* 5.

ASHBURNHAM, Lord Ashburnham, Eng., out of a ducal coronet, or, an ash-tree, vert. *Le roi et l'estat.* *Pl.* 94, *cr.* 5.

ASHBURTON, a mullet of six points, pierced, or, between wings displayed, ar. *Pl.* 1, *cr.* 15.

ASHBURY, Eng., in lion's paw a flag, charged with eagle, displayed. *Pl.* 7, *cr.* 7.

ASHBY, GEORGE-ASHBY, Esq., of Naseby, Northampton, and of Greenfields, Salop:
1. For *Maddock*, a demi-lion, rampant, in dexter a sword, (erect.) *Pl.* 41, *cr.* 13.
2. For *Ashby*, on a mural coronet, ar., a leopard's head, or. *Pl.* 46, *cr.* 11, (without gorging.) *Be just, and fear not.*

ASHBY, WILLIAM-ASHBY, Esq., of Quenby Hall, Leic., out of a mural coronet, ar., a leopard's head, (affrontée,) or. *Be just, and fear not.* *Pl.* 46, *cr.* 11, (without gorging.)

ASHBY, Leic., a ram's head, ar., attired, or. *Pl.* 34, *cr.* 12.

ASHBY, Leic., an eagle, close, ar., ducally crowned, or. *Pl.* 7, *cr.* 11, (crown, *pl.* 128, *fig.* 3.)

ASHBY, Middx., an eagle, wings expanded, ar., ducally crowned, or. *Pl.* 85, *cr.* 11, (not charged.)

ASHCOMB, or AISHCOMB, Berks., on a chapeau, a demi-eagle, displayed, sa., ducally crowned, or. *Pl.* 96. *cr.* 9, (crown, *same plate, cr.* 7.)

ASHDOUN, or ASHDOWN, a lion's head, gu., collared, or, (bezantée, sa.) *Pl.* 42, *cr.* 14.

ASHE, Twickenham, Middx., Bart., a cockatrice, or, combed and wattled, gu. *Pl.* 63, *cr.* 15.

ASHE, WILLIAM-WELLESLEY, Esq., of Ashfield, co. Meath, a cockatrice, or, crested, wattled, and armed, gu. Above shield— *Fight;* below—*Non nobis sed omnibus.* *Pl.* 63, *cr.* 15.

ASHE, or ESHE, Devons., a cockatrice, ar., charged on breast with a trefoil, slipped, gu. *Pl.* 63, *cr.* 15, (trefoil, *pl.* 141.)

ASHE, Iri., and Wilts., a cockatrice, or, crested and armed, gu. *Non nobis sed omnibus.* *Pl.* 63, *cr.* 15.

ASHENDEN, Eng., a lion's gamb, erased, gu., holding up hilt of broken sword, ppr. *Pl.* 49, *cr.* 10.

ASHENDEN, Eng., a lion, rampant, supporting an arrow, erect, point downward. *Pl.* 22, *cr.* 15.

ASHENHURST, Beardhall, Derb., a cockatrice, or, tail, nowed, (serpent's head, sa., comb, wattles, and head, gu., in beak a trefoil, vert.) *Pl.* 63, *cr.* 15.

ASHER, Eng., a ship in full sail, ppr. *Pl.* 109, *cr.* 8.

ASHERBURNE, and ASHBURNER, of Cockermouth, Cumb., an ash-tree, ppr. *Quicquid crescit, in cinere perit.* *Pl.* 18, *cr.* 10.

ASHERST, Lanc., a fox, passant, ppr. *Pl.* 126, *cr.* 5.

ASHETON, Great Lever and Whalley, Lanc., a boar's head, couped, ar., armed, langued, and bristled, gu. *In domino confido.* *Pl.* 48, *cr.* 2.

ASHETON, or ASSHETON, a mower, vested, ar. and sa., paleways, counterchanged, scythe, ppr.

ASHETON, or ASHTON, a demi-angel, wings expanded, hands closed as in prayer, vested, ar., face and hands, ppr., hair, wings, and girdle, or. *Pl.* 94, *cr.* 11, (without laurel.)

ASHFIELD, Warw. and Bucks., a wolf, passant, or. *Pl.* 46, *cr.* 6.

ASHFIELD, Bucks. and Warw., a wolf, current, erm. *Pl.* 111, *cr.* 1.

ASHFIELD, Norf. a griffin, passant, ar. *Pl.* 61, *cr.* 14, (without collar.)

ASHFORD of Ashford, Devons., and Cornw., a moor's head, in profile, sa., wreathed, ar., out of a chaplet of oak-leaves, vert. *Pl.* 48, *cr.* 7, (chaplet, *pl.* 128, *fig.* 7.)

ASHFORDBY, Wilts., an ass's head, (erased, or, gorged with a collar, sa., charged with three mullets, gold.) *Pl.* 91, *cr.* 7.

ASHINGHURST, a cockatrice, (close, sa., wattled and legged, gu., tail, nowed, ending with serpent's head, in mouth of cockatrice a sprig, vert.) *Pl.* 63, *cr.* 15.

ASHLEY, Somers., on a chapeau, gu., turned up, erm., a bull, sa., ducally gorged, or. *Pl.* 65, *cr.* 11, (coronet, *same plate.*)

ASHLEY, Eng., on a chapeau, ppr., a bull, passant, sa., murally gorged, or. *Pl.* 65, *cr.* 11, (coronet, *pl.* 128, *fig.* 18.)

ASHLEY, Dors., a plume of feathers, ppr. *Pl.* 12. *cr.* 9.

ASHLEY, Dors., a harpy, ppr. *Pl.* 32, *cr.* 3.

ASHLEY, on a chapeau, gu., turned up, erm., a plume of five ostrich-feathers, ar., out of a ducal coronet, or. *Pl.* 106, *cr.* 11.

ASHLEY of Winborn, Dors., on a chapeau, gu., turned up, erm., a bull, passant, sa., gorged with a mural coronet, armed, or. *Pl.* 65, *cr.* 11, (coronet, *pl.* 128, *fig.* 18.)

ASHLEY, Chesh., a bear's head, muzzled, ppr. *Pl.* 2, *cr.* 9.

ASHLEY-COOPER, Earl of Shaftesbury, Baron Ashley, and a Bart., on a chapeau, gu., turned up, erm., a bull, passant, sa., gorged with a ducal coronet, or, attired and hoofed, ar. *Love, serve.* *Pl.* 65, *cr.* 11, (coronet, *same plate.*)

ASHLIN, a fir-tree. ppr. *Pl.* 26, *cr.* 10.

ASHMAN, Lymmington, Wilts., a hautboy, in pale. *Pl.* 12, *cr.* 1.

ASHMOLE, Staffs., a greyhound, current, sa. *Pl.* 28, *cr.* 7, (without charge.)

ASHMORE, Iri., a demi-eagle, displayed, two heads, or, each royally crowned, ppr. *Pl.* 63, *cr.* 2.

ASHOE, a hawk, ppr., belled, or. *Pl.* 67, *cr.* 3.

ASHONDON, Eng., a lion, rampant, supporting an arrow, erect, point downward. *Pl.* 22, *cr.* 15.

ASHTON, Chester, and Leic., a boar's head, couped, ar. *Pl.* 48, *cr.* 2.

ASHTON, or ASHETON, Chesh. and Lanc., a boar's head, couped, ar. *In domino confido.* *Pl.* 48, *cr.* 2.

ASHTON, a stag, statant, regardant, ar., attired and unguled, or, gorged with chaplet of laurel, ppr. *Pl.* 81, *cr.* 8, (laurel, *pl.* 128, *fig.* 16.)

ASHTON of Middleton, Bart., Lanc., a boar's head, couped, ppr. *In Domino confido.* *Pl.* 48, *cr.* 2.

ASHTON of Spalding, Lanc., Linc., Lond., Ashton-under-Line, and Sheering, Ess., out of a mural coronet, ar., a griffin's head, gu., ducally gorged and beaked, or. *Pl.* 101, *cr.* 6.

ASHTON, Shepley and Lanc., a mower with scythe, face and hands, ppr., habit and cap, counterchanged, ar. and sa., handle of scythe, or blade, ar., as in action.

ASHTON, Lanc., the same, but on a chapeau, gu., turned up, erm.

ASHTON, or ASHETON, Crofton, Lanc., (out of clouds,) ppr., a demi-angel, wings expanded, vested, ar., face and hands, ppr., hair, wings, and girdle, or. *Pl.* 94, *cr.* 11, (without laurel.)

ASHTON, Chesh., Lanc., and Leic., a boar's head, couped, ar. *Pl.* 48, *cr.* 2.

ASHTON, Dumfries, a lion's head, erased, ppr. *Pl.* 81, *cr.* 4.

ASHTOWN, Baron, Iri., (Trench,) an arm, in armour, embowed, hand grasping a sword, all ppr. *Virtutis fortuna comes.* *Pl.* 2, *cr.* 8.

ASHURST, Oxon., a wolf, ppr. *Pl.* 46, *cr.* 6.

ASHURST, Eng., a wolf, passant, ppr. *Pl.* 46, *cr.* 6.

ASHURST, a fox, ppr. *Pl.* 126, *cr.* 5.

ASHURST, JOHN-HENRY, Esq., of Waterstock, Oxford, a fox, statant, ppr. *Vincit qui patitur.* *Pl.* 126, *cr.* 5.

ASHWOOD, on a chapeau, the sun, all ppr. *Pl.* 127, *cr.* 13, (the sun, *pl.* 68, *cr.* 14.)

ASHWORTH, Heyford, Oxon., (on a mount, vert,) a fox, ppr. *Pl.* 126, *cr.* 5.

ASHWORTH, Eng., a savage's head, affrontée, ppr. *Pl.* 19, *cr.* 1.

ASHWORTH, (on a mount, vert,) an ash-tree, ppr. *Pl*, 18, *cr.* 10.

ASHWORTH, Iri., on a chapeau, a garb, ppr. *Pl.* 62, *cr.* 1.

ASHWORTH, Hants.; (on a mount, vert,) a fox, ppr. *Cœlum non animum.* *Pl.* 126, *cr.* 5.

ASKE of Aske and Chowbent, Lanc.; and Auchton, and Aske, Yorks.; an old man's head, in profile, ppr., wreathed, or and az., and tied with a bow, of the colours. *Pl.* 23, *cr.* 3.

ASKE, Eng., a dragon's head, couped, ar. *Pl.* 87, *cr.* 12.

ASKEAM, ASKEHAM, or ASKHAM, a dolphin, az. *Pl.* 48, *cr.* 9.

ASKEBY, ASKELY, ASKLABY, ASKLAKBY, or ASKLAKEBY, Eng., a sun-dial on pedestal, ppr. *Pl.* 97, *cr.* 6.

ASKEN, or ASKENE, Eng., an ass's head, sa. *Pl.* 91, *cr.* 7.

ASKETINE, or ASKENTINE, of West Peckham, Kent, two lions' gambs, erect, sa., supporting a crescent, or. *Pl.* 62, *cr.* 3.

ASKEW, or ASCOUGH, Newcastle-upon-Tyne, and Sco., a naked arm, ppr., grasping a sword, ar., hilt and pommel, or, enfiled with a Saracen's head, couped, ppr., wreathed, or and sa., blood issuing, gu. *Fac et spera.* *Pl.* 102, *cr.* 11.

ASKEW, RICHARD-CRASTER, Esq., of Pallinsburn, Northumb., same crest. *Patientia casus exuperat omnes.*

ASKEW, HENRY-WILLIAM, Esq., of Redheugh; Conishead Priory, Lanc.; and of Glenridding, Camb.; same crest.

ASKEW, or ASKUE, Lond., an ass's head, ppr. (gorged with three bars, or,) between wings, or and ar. *Pl.* 91, *cr.* 7, (wings, *pl.* 1, *cr.* 15.)

ASKEW, Linc., an ass, ar. *Pl.* 42, *cr.* 2.

ASKILL, Eng., in the sea, an anchor, in pale, ppr. *Pl.* 62, *cr.* 10.

ASKHAM, a dolphin, az. *Pl.* 48, *cr.* 9.

ASKWITH, York, a mascle, gu. *Pl.* 54, *cr.* 1.

ASLACK, ASLAKE, and ASLOKE, of Holme, Norf., and Suff., a talbot's head, sa., guttée, ar. *Pl.* 123, *cr.* 15.

ASLAKBY, or ASLAKEBY, a sun-dial on pedestal, ppr. *Pl.* 97, *cr.* 6.

ASLIN, Lond., a demi-horse, ppr. *Pl.* 96, *cr.* 2, (without wings and gorging.)

ASLIN, ASLYN, or ASSLAN, an escutcheon, (charged with a rose, gu.) *Pl.* 36, *cr.* 11.

ASLOUM, Sco., a spur, ppr. *Pl.* 15, *cr.* 3.

ASLOUM, Eng., a spear, ppr. *Pl.* 97, *cr.* 4.

ASPALL, Suff., a dragon's head, couped, or. *Pl.* 87, *cr.* 12.

ASPATH, two spears, in saltier. *Pl.* 125, *cr.* 8, (without flags and wreath.)

ASPIN, Bucks., a dragon's head, or, (between two aspin-branches,) ppr. *Pl.* 87, *cr.* 12.

ASPINALL, Preston, Lanc., a demi-griffin, erased, sa., beaked, legged, (and collared,) or. *Pl.* 18, *cr.* 6.

ASPINWALL, Manchester, same crest.

ASPINALL, JOHN, Esq., of Standen Hall, Lanc., a demi-griffin, erased, sa., collared, winged, and beaked, or. *Ægis fortissima virtus. Pl.* 18, *cr.* 6.

ASSCOTI, or ASCOTTI, Eng., a spread eagle, ppr., (imperially) crowned, or. *Dum spiro spero. Pl.* 63, *cr.* 2.

ASSENT, out of a ducal coronet, a horse's head, ar., (bridled, gu.) *Pl.* 50, *cr.* 13.

ASSHETON, Sco., a boar's head, couped, gu. *Pl.* 48, *cr.* 2.

ASSHETTON, Eng., same crest.

ASTEL, or ASTLE, Staffs., a sea-horse couchant, (ducally gorged.) *Pl.* 103, *cr.* 3, (coronet, *pl.* 128, *fig.* 3.)

ASTELL, RICHARD-WILLIAM, Esq., of Everton House, Huntingdon: 1. A cross crosslet, or, entwined with a serpent, vert. *Pl.* 106, *cr.* 7. 2. A lion's head, erased, purp., gorged with a coronet, or. *Sub cruce glorior. Pl.* 81, *cr.* 4, (coronet, *pl.* 128, *fig.* 3.)

ASTELL, Beds., Hunts., Lond., and Middx., a cross crosslet, or, entwined with a serpent, vert. *Pl.* 106, *cr.* 7.

ASTELL, Hunts., a lion's head, erased, purp., gorged with a coronet, or. *Sub cruce glorior. Pl.* 81, *cr.* 4, (coronet, *pl.* 128, *fig.* 3.)

ASTERBY, Linc., an oak-tree, ppr. *Pl.* 16, *cr.* 8.

ASTERY, ASTERLLEY, or ESTERLEY, an etoile, between wings, ppr. *Pl.* 1, *cr.* 15, (etoile, *pl.* 141.)

ASTLEY of Melton Constable, Bart., Norf. and Kent, out of a ducal coronet, or, a plume of feathers in a case, ar. *Pl.* 106, *cr.* 11, (without chapeau.)

ASTLEY, FRANCIS-DUNKINFIELD-PALMER, Esq., of Felfoot, Lanc.; and Dunkinfield Lodge, Chester; out of a ducal coronet, or, a plume of seven ostrich-feathers, gu. *Pl.* 114, *cr.* 8, (without under row.)

ASTLEY, out of a ducal coronet, or, a harpy, ar. *Pl.* 128, *fig.* 3, (harpy, *pl.* 32, *cr.* 3.)

ASTLEY, Bart., Warw., Norf., and Northumb., on a chapeau, gu., turned up, erm., a demi-pillar, of the first, environed with a ducal coronet, or, out of which issues a plume of feathers, ar.

ASTLEY, Bart., Wilts., out of a ducal coronet, three ostrich-feathers. *Pl.* 44, *cr.* 12, (one less.)

ASTLEY, Ess., on a chapeau, a plume of feathers, ar., banded, gu., environed with a ducal coronet, or. *Pl.* 106, *cr.* 11.

ASTLEY, Patishull, Salop, out of a ducal coronet, ar., a double plume of feathers, gu. and or. *Pl.* 64, *cr.* 5.

ASTLEY, out of a ducal coronet, or, a harpy, ar., ducally gorged and crined, gold. *Pl.* 32, *cr.* 3, (coronet, *pl.* 128, *fig.* 3.)

ASTLEY, Bart., Wilts., out of a ducal coronet, or, a plume of seven ostrich-feathers, gu. *Fide, sed cui vide. Pl.* 114, *cr.* 8, (without under row.)

ASTON, SIR ARTHUR, G.C.B., of Aston, Chester, an ass's head, ppr. *Prêt d'accomplir. Pl.* 191, *cr.* 7.

ASTON of Fairnham, Bart., Hants., an ass's head. *Pl.* 91, *cr.* 7.

ASTON, Eng., a bull's head, couped, or, armed, sa. *Pl.* 120, *cr.* 7.

ASTON, Baron Aston, of Forfar, a bull's head, couped, sa. *Numine et patria asto. Pl.* 120, *cr.* 7.

ASTON, a fox's head, ppr. *Pl.* 91, *cr.* 9.

ASTON, Staffs., Chesh., and Lanc., an ass's head, per pale, ar. and sa. *Prêt d'accomplir. Pl.* 91, *cr.* 7.

ASTON, Chesh., an ass's head, per cheveron, ar. and sa. *Pl.* 91, *cr.* 7.

ASTON, Iri., Lord Aston, and Staffs., a bull's head, or, the horns, ar., tipped, sa. *Pl.* 120, *cr.* 7.

ASTON, Eng., a bull's head, or, horned, per fess, sa. and ar. *Pl.* 120, *cr.* 7.

ASTON, a chapeau, gu., turned up, erm., (on each side of cap, within the ermines, a horn, ppr.) *Pl.* 127, *cr.* 13.

ASTON, Eng., an etoile, ppr. *E tenebris lux. Pl.* 63, *cr.* 9.

ASTONNE, Eng., an ass's head, gu. *Pl.* 91, *cr.* 7.

ASTRIE, Henbury, and Astry, Wood-end, Beds., a stag's head, erased, gu., attired, or. *Pl.* 66, *cr.* 9.

ASTROVEL, Eng., a buckle, or. *Pl.* 73, *cr.* 10.

ASWELL, or ASHWELL, Eng., on a chapeau, a garb, ppr. *Pl.* 62, *cr.* 1.

ATBAROUGH, or ATBOROUGH, Somers., a martin or weasel, ar., collared and lined, or. *Pl.* 12, *cr.* 2.

ATCHERLEY, a demi-bustard, couped, gu., wings elevated, or, in beak a lily, ar., slipped, vert. *Spe posteri temporis.*

ATCHERLEY, DAVID-FRANCIS, Esq., of Marton, Salop, a demi-bustard, couped, gu., wings elevated, or, in mouth a lily, ar., slipped, vert. *Spe posteri temporis.*

ATCHESON of Pittenween, an astrolabe, ppr. *Observe. Pl.* 26, *cr.* 2.

ATCHESON, Sco., a cock standing on a trumpet, ppr. *Vigilantibus. Pl.* 2, *cr.* 1.

ATCHISON, Sco. and Eng., a cock, ppr. *Vigilantibus.* *Pl.* 67, *cr.* 14.
ATCLIFF, ATCLIFFE, ATCLYFF, or ATCLYFFE, Eng., a cross crosslet, ar. *Pl.* 66, *cr.* 8.
ATETSE, Eng., a Cornish chough, ppr. *Pl.* 100, *cr.* 13.
ATFIELD, an arm, embowed, throwing an arrow, in fess. *Pl.* 92, *cr.* 14.
ATFOE, Eng., on a chapeau, a lion's head, erased, ppr. *Pl.* 99, *cr.* 9.
ATHANRAY, Iri., out of a ducal coronet, a goat's head, horns bent backward and twisted. *Pl.* 72, *cr.* 2.
ATHELL, Eng., a dog, sleeping, ppr. *Pl.* 29, *cr.* 3.
ATHELL, Sco. and Suff., a castle, ar., masoned, sa. *Pl.* 123, *cr.* 14.
ATHELSTAN, or ATHELSTON, Eng., a hand holding a sword, in pale, enfiled with a savage's head, couped and wreathed. *Pl.* 118, *cr.* 3.
ATHELSTANE, Eng., a mound, gu., banded and crossed, or. *Pl.* 37. *cr.* 3.
ATHERLEY, Eng., a lion's head, erased, sa. *Pl.* 81, *cr.* 4.
ATHERLEY, on a chapeau, a stork, ppr. *Pl.* 106, *cr.* 6.
ATHERTON, or ATTERTON, Lanc., a hawk, ppr., legged and beaked, or. *Pl.* 67, *cr.* 3.
ATHERTON, Lanc., a swan, az., ducally gorged and lined, or. *Pl.* 111, *cr.* 10, (without crown and charging.)
ATHERTON of Atherton, Yorks., a demi-swan, ar., beaked, gu., enfiled with a ducal coronet, or. *Pl.* 54, *cr.* 4, (coronet, *pl.* 128, *fig.* 3.)
ATHIL, ATHILL, and ATHYLL, Eng. and Sco., an arm, in armour, embowed, brandishing a scimitar, all ppr. *Pl.* 81, *cr.* 11.
ATHILL, and ATHYLL, Eng., an arm in armour, embowed, hand grasping a sword, all ppr. *Pl.* 2, *cr.* 8.
ATHLONE, Earl of, Iri., (De Ginkell,) a pair of wings, erect, ar., (charged with two bars dancettée.) *Malo mori quam fœdari.* *Pl.* 39, *cr.* 12.
ATHOL, Sco., an arm, in armour, brandishing a scimitar, ppr. *Pl.* 81, *cr.* 11.
ATHOLL, Duke, Marquess, and Earl of, Sco.; Earl and Baron Strange, and Baron Murray, Eng., (Murray ;) a demi-savage, ppr., (wreathed about head,) and waist, vert, in dexter a dagger, also ppr., pommel and hilt, or, in sinister a key, of the last. *Furth fortune, and fill the fetters.* *Pl.* 88, *cr.* 10.
ATHORPE, a hawk, ppr. *Pl.* 67, *cr.* 3.
ATHOWE of Bryseley, Norf., a bird, ar. *Pl.* 52, *cr.* 12.
ATHURTON, Eng., a swan, ar., ducally gorged and lined, or. *Pl.* 111, *cr.* 10, (without crown.)
ATHWAT, a horse's head, erm., out of a plume of five ostrich-feathers, gu. *Pl.* 106, *cr.* 4.
ATHYLL, Eng., an arm, in armour, embowed, hand grasping a sword, all ppr. *Pl.* 2, *cr.* 8.
ATKIN, and ATKINS, Eng., a boat, ppr. *Pl.* 42. *cr.* 11.
ATKIN, Iri., an ox yoke, az., stapled, or. *Pl.* 35, *cr.* 11.
ATKINS, Yelverton, Norf., a demi-tiger, erm., (collared and lined, or.) *Pl.* 53, *cr.* 10.

ATKINS, Lond., an etoile. *Pl.* 63, *cr.* 9.
ATKINS, Somers., two greyhounds' heads, addorsed, collar dovetailed, per pale, or and az., counterchanged, erased, gu. *Pl.* 62, *cr.* 5.
ATKINS, or ATKYNS, Totteridge, Herts., and Glouc., two greyhounds' heads, erased, addorsed, collared and ringed, counterchanged, ar. and sa. *Vincunt cum legibus arma.* *Pl.* 62, *cr.* 5.
ATKINS of Yelverton, Norf., a demi-lion, rampant, erm., langued, gu., armed and ducally gorged, or, (with chain affixed to coronet, pending down breast, between feet, thence over back, gold.) *Pl.* 87, *cr.* 15.
ATKINS, ROBERT, Esq., of Waterpark, co. Cork, a pelican, vulning, ppr. *Be just, and fear not.* *Pl.* 109, *cr.* 15.
ATKINS, Cork, a demi-heraldic tiger, ppr., erminée, ducally gorged (and chained), or. *Honor et virtus.* *Pl.* 57, *cr.* 13.
ATKINSON, Newcastle-upon-Tyne, a pheon, between two rose-sprigs. *Pl.* 26, *cr.* 12; *pl.* 125, *cr.* 6.
ATKINSON, a lion's head, erased, ppr. *Pl.* 81, *cr.* 4.
ATKINSON, Eng., a swan, wings addorsed, swallowing a fish, ppr. *Pl.* 103, *cr.* 1.
ATKINSON, Newcastle, a pheon, az. *Pl.* 26, *cr.* 12.
ATKINSON, or ATCHINSON, Newark and Yorks., a pheon, or. *Pl.* 26, *cr.* 12.
ATKINSON, ADAM, Esq., of Lorbottle, Northumb., a pheon, or. *Pl.* 26, *cr.* 12.
ATKINSON, CHARLES, Esq., of Rehins, co. Mayo, an eagle with two heads, displayed, ar. *Est pii Deum et patriam diligere.* *Pl.* 87, *cr.* 11, (without flames.)
ATKINSON, CHARLES, Sheffield, a pheon, or. *Aut homo aut nullus.* *Pl.* 26, *cr.* 12.
ATKINSON, GUY, Esq., of Cangort, King's County, an eagle, with two heads, displayed, az., beaked and legged, gu. *Deo et regi fidelis.* *Pl.* 87, *cr.* 11, (without flames.)
ATKINSON, GEORGE-GUY, Esq., of Ashley Park, co. Tipperary, same crest and motto.
ATKINSON, JAMES-HENRY-HOLLIS, Esq., of Angerton, Northumb., (on a mount,) a pheon, az., between two roses, stalked and leaved, ppr. *Crede Deo.* *Pl.* 26, *cr.* 12, (roses, *pl.* 125, *cr.* 6.)
ATKINSON, FRANCIS-BARING, Esq., of Rampsbeck Lodge, Cumb.; and Moreland, Westm.; a falcon, wings expanded. *Pl.* 105, *cr.* 4.
ATKINSON, Lond., Northumb., and Somers., an eagle, wings expanded, ar., beaked and legged, gu. *Pl.* 126, *cr.* 7.
ATKINSON, Camb., a sea-lion, sejant, ar., in dexter an escallop, or. *Pl.* 80, *cr.* 13, (escallop, *pl.* 141.)
ATKINSON, Notts., a demi-eagle, displayed, or., (collared, sa.) *Pl.* 22, *cr.* 11.
ATKINSON, Lond., Newcastle, and Somers., an eagle, wings expanded, ar., beaked and legged, gu. *Pl.* 126, *cr.* 7.
ATKYN, an arm, in armour, embowed, ppr., in gauntlet a cross formée, fitched, az., flory, or. *Pl.* 96, *cr.* 4, (cross, *pl.* 27, *cr.* 14.)
ATKYNS of Saperton, Glouc., two greyhounds' heads, addorsed, ar. and sa., collared and ringed, counterchanged. *Vincet cum legibus arma.* *Pl.* 62, *cr.* 5.

ATKYNS, Herts., a stork, ar., wings and tail, sa., beaked and. legged, gu., preying on a dragon, vert. *Pl.* 121, *cr.* 13, (dragon, *pl.* 90, *cr.* 10.)

ATLEE, and ATLEY, Suss., two lions' heads, addorsed, ppr. *Pl.* 28, *cr.* 10.

ATLEY, on an escutcheon, ar., a pheon, az. *Pl.* 36, *cr.* 11, (pheon, *pl.* 141.)

ATMORE, and ATTEMORE, Eng., a mermaid, ppr., crined, or, comb and mirror, gold. *Pl.* 48, *cr.* 5.

ATSLEY, a leopard's head, erased, or; spotted, sa., and ducally gorged, gold. *Pl.* 116, *cr.* 8.

ATSOE, or ATFOE, Eng., on a chapeau, a lion's head, erased, gu. *Pl.* 99, *cr.* 9.

ATTELOUND, or ATTELOUNDE, a hound, couchant, gardant, ar. *Pl.* 106, *cr.* 8.

ATTERTON, Lanc., a hawk, ppr., beaked and legged, or. *Pl.* 67, *cr.* 3.

ATTERTON, Lanc., a swan, ar., ducally gorged and lined, or. *Pl.* 111, *cr.* 10, (without crown.)

ATTFIELD, an arm, embowed, throwing an arrow, in fess. *Pl.* 92, *cr.* 14.

ATTHILL, The Rev. WILLIAM, of Brandiston Hall, Norf., A.M.: 1. Demi-griffin, segreant. *Honorantes me honorabo*. *Pl.* 18, *cr.* 6. 2. A falcon, or, ducally gorged, az., belled and leashed, gold. *Monte de alto*. *Pl.* 67, *cr.* 3, (coronet, *pl.* 128, *fig.* 3.)

ATTON, or ATTONE, Eng., out of a ducal coronet, or, two lions' paws, in saltier, sa. *Pl.* 110, *cr.* 2.

ATTWOOD, a demi-lady, in dexter a pair of scales, ppr. *Pl.* 57, *cr.* 1.

ATTY, on a ducal coronet, or, a fox, passant, ppr. *Pl.* 128, *fig.* 3 ; *pl.* 126, *cr.* 5.

ATTY, JAMES, Esq., of Penley Hall; Rugby, Warwick; and Pinchbeck, Linc.; on a ducal coronet, an ermine, passant. *Eamus quo ducit fortuna*. *Pl.* 9, *cr.* 5 ; (coronet, same plate.)

ATTYE, ROBERT-JAMES, Esq., of Ingon Grange, Warw., same crest and motto.

ATWATER, Eng., between attires of stag, fixed to scalp, or, a rose, gu. *Pl.* 50, *cr.* 14.

ATWELL, Devons., a lion, rampant, erminois, in paws an annulet. *Pl.* 67, *cr.* 5; (annulet, *pl.* 141.)

ATWOOD, an antelope's head, ppr. *Pl.* 24, *cr.* 7.

ATWOOD, Iri., an arm, couped at elbow, in fess, in hand a cross crosslet, fitched, erect. *Pl.* 88, *cr.* 7.

ATWOOD of Broomfield, Ess., and Gray's Inn, Middx., trunk of tree, in fess, or, between two branches, vert, a fleur-de-lis, ar. *Pl.* 14, *cr.* 14.

ATYE, or ATTYE, Eng., an ermine, passant, ppr. *Pl.* 9, *cr.* 14.

ATYE of Newington, Middx., same crest.

AUBEMARLE, Eng., an ear of wheat, bladed, and palm-branch, in saltier, ppr. *Pl.* 63, *cr.* 3.

AUBERT, Lond., a talbot, passant, ppr., with broken collar between fore legs as if fallen from neck, a line affixed to collar, reflexing over back, passing between hind legs, with a double bow at end, all or. *Fide et fortitudine*. *Pl.* 104, *cr.* 2.

AUBIN, and ST. AUBIN, on a rock, a Cornish chough, ppr. *Pl.* 34, *cr.* 13.

AUBIN, Cornw., on a rock, an eagle, rising, ar. *Pl.* 79, *cr.* 2.

AUBLEY, or AUBLY, in dexter hand, ppr., a cross pattée, fitched, gu., erect. *Pl.* 99, *cr.* 15.

AUBREY, Llantrithried, Glamorgans., Bart., an eagle's head, erased, or. *Solem fero*. *Pl.* 20, *cr.* 7.

AUBREY, Brecknocks., same crest.

AUBREY of Derton, Bart., Bucks., an eagle's head. *Pl.* 100, *cr.* 10.

AUBYN, ST., Somers., a squirrel, sejant, erm., collared, (and lined,) or. *Pl.* 85, *cr.* 3.

AUBYN, Eng., an eagle, wings displayed, ppr. *Pl.* 126, *cr.* 7.

AUCHER, or ACHER, of Bourne and Bishopbourne, Kent, Bart., a bull's head, erased, gu., attired, or. *Pl.* 19, *cr.* 3.

AUCHER, Eng., a bull's head, erased, gu., horned, ar. *Pl.* 19, *cr.* 3.

AUCHER, and AUCHERR, Eng., a bull's head, ppr. *Pl.* 63, *cr.* 11.

AUCHINLECK of that Ilk, Sco., an ear of rye, ppr. *Pretiosum quod utile*. *Pl.* 41, *cr.* 3.

AUCHINLECK of Balmano, Sco., two wings, issuing, ppr. *Rerum sapientia custos*. *Pl.* 63, *cr.* 12. (Formerly this family carried a decrescent, ar. *Ut deficiar*. *Pl.* 16. *cr.* 15.)

AUCHMUTY, Sco., an arm, in armour, embowed, in hand a spear, all ppr. *Pl.* 44, *cr.* 9, (not broken.)

AUCHMUTY, Iri., an arm, in armour, embowed, ppr., in hand part of a spear. *Dum spiro spero*. *Pl.* 44, *cr.* 9.

AUCHTERLONIE, Sco., an eagle, displayed, ppr. *Deus mihi adjutor*. *Pl.* 48. *cr.* 11.

AUCHTERLONY of Guynd, same crest.

AUCHTERLONY, Sco., a lion's head, erased, sa., collared, or. *Pl.* 7, *cr.* 10.

AUCKLAND, Baron, (Eden,) an arm, in armour, embowed, ppr., in hand a garb, or. *Si sit prudentia*. *Pl.* 45, *cr.* 10 ; (garb, *pl.* 3, *cr.* 3.)

AUDBOROUGH, Eng., an escallop, or, between wings, az. *Pl.* 62, *cr.* 4.

AUDELEY, Eng., a mullet of six points, or, between wings, az. *Pl.* 1, *cr.* 15.

AUDIN, a lion, passant, or, in dexter a banner, gu., thereon a cross, ar. *Pl.* 106, *cr.* 5.

AUDIN, a lion, rampant, ar., in dexter an ancient battle-axe, of the same. *Pl.* 26, *cr.* 7.

AUDLEY of Waldon, Ess., on a chapeau, gu., turned up, erm., a wyvern, wings addorsed, quarterly, or and az. *Pl.* 104, *cr.* 5, (not crowned.)

AUDLEY, Eng., a Saracen's head, couped, ppr., wreathed, ar. and purp. *Pl.* 36, *cr.* 3.

AUDLEY, or AUDLY, Eng., a martlet, sa. *Pl.*, 111 *cr.* 5.

AUDLEY, Baron, (Thicknesse-Touchet :) 1. For *Thicknesse*, a cubit arm, erect, vested, paly of six, or and gu., in hand a scythe, ppr., blade downward. *Pl.* 106, *cr.* 2. 2. For *Touchet*, out of a ducal coronet, or, a swan, rising, ar., ducally gorged, of the first, *Je le tiens*. *Pl.* 100, *cr.* 7.

AUDLEY, Boston, Linc., a man's head, couped at shoulders, sa., with cap, or, turned up, erm. *Pl.* 38, *cr.* 13.

AUDRY, Wilts., a stag, trippant, ppr. *Pl.* 68, *cr.* 2.

AUDYN, Dorchester, a lion, passant, (crowned, or,) bearing on shoulder a paschal banner, disvelloped, ar., staff and cross, gu. *Pl.* 106, *cr.* 5.

AUDYN, Dorchester, a lion, passant, (tail extended, or,) bearing a banner, ar., charged with a cross, gu. *Pl.* 106, *cr.* 5.

AUFFRICK, two arms, in armour, embowed, in hands a gem ring, all ppr. *Pl.* 6, *cr.* 8, (ring, *pl.* 35, *cr.* 3.)

AUFORUS, Eng., a mullet, or. *Pl.* 41, *cr.* 1.

AUFRERE, GEORGE-ANTHONY, Esq., of Foulsham Old Hall, Norf. *Esto quod esse videris.*

AUGE, Eng., a savage's head, couped, wreathed, ar. and sa. *Pl.* 36, *cr.* 3.

AUGER of Bourne, Kent, a bull's head, erased, gu., attired, or. *Pl.* 19, *cr.* 3.

AUGHTERLONY, Eng., an eagle, displayed, ppr. *Deus mihi adjutor.* *Pl.* 48, *cr.* 11.

AULD, Sco., the sun rising out of a cloud, ppr. *Major virtus quam splendor.* *Pl.* 67, *cr.* 9.

AULD, a lion's head, erased, ppr. *Pl.* 81, *cr.* 4.

AULD, or AULDE, Sco., a cherub's head, ppr., wings in saltier. *Virtute et constantia.* *Pl.* 67, *cr.* 11.

AULD, Sco., the rising sun, ppr. *Major virtus quam splendor.* *Pl.* 67, *cr.* 9.

AULDJO, stump of tree, leaves sprouting, all ppr. *Pl.* 92, *cr.* 8.

AUMARLE, AUMERLE, and AMERLE, Eng., an arrow, in pale, ppr. *Pl.* 56, *cr.* 13.

AUNCELL, Eng., a lion, passant, ppr. *Pl.* 48, *cr.* 8.

AUNCELL, Eng., a stag's head, affrontée, ppr., ducally gorged, or. *Pl.* 55, *cr.* 2.

AUNDELIGH, Eng., a sceptre, in pale, or. *Pl.* 82, *cr.* 3.

AUNGATE, on a torteau, an etoile, or. *Pl.* 7, *cr.* 6, (etoile, *pl.* 141.)

AUNGER, Eng., an escarbuncle, or. *Pl.* 51, *cr.* 10.

AUNGER, Lond., a demi-griffin, or. *Pl.* 18, *cr.* 6.

AUNSHAM, Eng., an escallop, or, between two palm-branches, vert. *Pl.* 86, *cr.* 9.

AURD, a buck's head, erased, ppr. *Pl.* 66, *cr.* 9.

AURELIS, a demi-youth, ppr., vested, ar., coat, az., buttoned, or.

AURIOL, Lond.; and Brussels, Flanders; an eagle, rising, right wing erect, (left close.) (See *Pl.* 126, *cr.* 7.)

AUSTE, Eng., a garb, ppr. *Pl.* 48, *cr.* 10.

AUSTEN, Tynterden, Kent; and Guildford, Surr.; a three-quarter spread eagle, three annulets on breast. *Pl.* 4, *cr.* 6.

AUSTEN, Sir HENRY-EDMUND, Knt., of Shalford House, Surr., on a leopard's head, az., a falcon, rising, or. *Ne quid nimis.* *Pl.* 92, *cr.* 13; *pl.* 105, *cr.* 4.

AUSTEN, or AUSTIN, Fairfield Cottage, and of Bexley, Kent, Bart.; and Hants.; on a mura coronet, or, a stag, sejant, ar., attired, gold. *Pl.* 101, *cr.* 3.

AUSTIN, Dr, Eng., a lion's paw, erased, ppr. *Pl.* 68, *cr.* 3.

AUSTIN, Sco., an arm, couped at shoulder, embowed, ppr., vested, vert, cuffed, or, resting elbow on wreath, in hand a cross crosslet, fitched, gu. *Pl.* 88, *cr.* 7.

AUSTIN, Lond., a long cross, or, between wings, sa. *Pl.* 71, *cr.* 2, (cross, *pl.* 141.)

AUSTIN, a paschal lamb, ar. *Pl.* 48, *cr.* 13.

AUSTIN, a demi-eagle, displayed, erminois, in beak, pendant, an annulet, sa. (See *pl.* 22, *cr.* 11; and annulet, *pl.* 141.)

AUSTON, or AUSTIN, Sco., an arm, embowed, vested, vert, cuffed, or, couped, resting on elbow, in hand, ppr., a cross crosslet, fitched, gu. *Pl.* 88, *cr.* 7.

AUSTON, Sco., a mullet, pierced. *Pl.* 45, *cr.* 1.

AUSTREY, Hartington, Beds., a demi-ostrich, ar., wings, gu. *Pl.* 29, *cr.* 9.

AUSTREY, of Sommerton, Hunts.; and of Yorks.; an ostrich-head, erased, ar., (between ostrich-wings, gu.,) in beak a horseshoe. (See *Pl.* 28, *cr.* 13.)

AUSTYN, Eng., out of a ducal coronet, or, a stag's head at gaze, ppr. *Pl.* 29, *cr.* 7.

AUVERQUERQUE, on a chapeau, az., turned up, erm., a lion, rampant, gardant, or. (See *pl.* 127, *fig.* 13; and *pl.* 92, *cr.* 7.

AUVERQUERQUE, Eng., a griffin's head, sa. *Pl.* 38, *cr.* 3.

AUVRAY, France, a demi-savage, with club over dexter shoulder, all ppr. *Pl.* 14, *cr.* 11.

AVAGOUR, or AVAUGOUR, and AVOUGOUR, Eng. and French, a parrot's head, between wings, ppr. *Pl.* 94, *cr.* 2.

AVELIN, or EVELIN, Long Ditton, Surr., a demi-hind, erm., vulned in shoulder, gu.

AVELINE, Windsor and Frogmore, Berks., a lion's head, erased, ar., in mouth, in pale, a sword, ar., hilt and pommel, or.

AVELINE, France, a griffin's head, erased, or. *Pl.* 48, *cr.* 6.

AVELINE, France, a demi-griffin, ppr. *Pl.* 18, *cr.* 6.

AVENAYNE, or AVENAR, a buck's head, cabossed, ppr. *Pl.* 36, *cr.* 1.

AVENEL, or AVENETT, Camb. and Sco., out of a baron's coronet a hand, grasping a scimitar, ppr. (See *pl.* 127, *fig.* 11; and *pl.* 29, *cr.* 8.)

AVENEL, or AVENYLE, a buck's head, cabossed, ppr. *Pl.* 36, *cr.* 1.

AVENET, or AVENETT, Eng., a torteau, gu., charged with a lion's head, erased, or. *Pl.* 50, *cr.* 10.

AVENEYLE, Eng., a buck's head, cabossed, ppr. *Pl.* 36, *cr.* 1.

AVERINGES, a raven, sa. *Pl.* 123, *cr.* 2.

AVERN, Warw., a horse's head, erm. *Pl.* 92, *cr.* 1.

AVERY, or AVEREY, Tillingly, Warw., a leopard, couchant, ar., bezantée, ducally gorged, or. (See *pl.* 111, *cr.* 11; and coronet, *pl.* 128, *fig.* 3.)

AVERY, Huwish, Somers.; and Enfield, Middx.; two lions' gambs, or, supporting a bezant. *Pl.* 42, *cr.* 3.

AVERY, a leopard, couchant. *Pl.* 111, *cr.* 11.

AVISON, a dexter hand, vested and cuffed, holding an anchor. *Pl.* 53, *cr.* 13.

AVISON, Eng., a hand, out of a cloud, holding an anchor. *Pl.* 41, *cr.* 5.

AVONMORE, Viscount, and Baron Yelverton, Iri., (Yelverton,) a lion, passant, regardant, gu. *Renascentur.* *Pl.* 121, *cr.* 4, (without collar or chain.)

AWBORN, a unicorn, passant, or, gorged with a ducal coronet, and chained, sa. *Pl.* 106, *cr.* 3.

AWBREY, Eng., an eagle's head, erased, or. *Pl.* 20, *cr.* 7.

AWDREY, Oxon., on a lion's gamb, ppr., a cheveron, or, charged with a mullet, sa. *Pl.* 88, *cr.* 3.

AWDRY, AMBROSE, Esq., of Seend, Wilts., out of a ducal coronet, a lion's head, az. *Nil sine Deo. Pl.* 90, *cr.* 9.

AWDRY, Sir JOHN-WITHER, Knt., of Notton House, Wilts., same crest.

AWGER, or AGER, Kent and Glouc., a bull's head, erased, gu., attired, ar. *Pl.* 19, *cr.* 3.

AWING, on a quatrefoil, party, per cross, gu. and vert, a lion's head, ar. *Pl.* 65, *cr.* 7, (head, *pl.* 126, *cr.* 1.)

AWMACK, or ALLMACK, a tower, ppr. *Cavendo tutus. Pl.* 8, *cr.* 13.

AWNDYE, Devons., on a lion's gamb, ppr., a cheveron, or, charged with a mullet, sa. *Pl.* 88, *cr.* 3.

AWNSAM, an escallop, or, between two palm-branches, vert. *Pl.* 86, *cr.* 9.

AYDE, Norf., a demi-lion, rampant, gardant, or, supporting a battle-axe, ar. *Pl.* 26, *cr.* 7.

AYERS, a dove, wings expanded, (dexter resting on a branch.) *Pl.* 27, *cr.* 5.

AYGLE, a bugle-horn, ar. *Pl.* 89, *cr.* 3.

AYLEMER, and AYLENER, Iri., on a ducal coronet, a sea aylet, wings displayed, sa. *Pl.* 8, *cr.* 5.

AYLES, Eng., a dexter arm, embowed, fist clenched, ppr. *Pl.* 87, *cr.* 7.

AYLESBURY: 1. A staff, in pale, raguly, or. *Pl.* 78, *cr.* 15, (wreath instead of coronet.) 2. A dragon's head, or, (gorged with three bars, gu.) *Pl.* 87, *cr.* 12.

AYLESFORD, Earl of, and Baron Guernsey, (Heneage-Finch,) a griffin, passant, sa. *Aperto vivere voto. Pl.* 66, *cr.* 13.

AYLET, Ess., an arm, gu., grasping a sword, hilted, or, blade, ar. *Not in vain. Pl.* 34, *cr.* 7.

AYLETT, Braintree, Ess., a demi-unicorn, regardant, ar., crined and armed, or. *Pl.* 106, *cr.* 1.

AYLEWARD, AYLWARD, and AYLWARDE, Norf., between the horns of a crescent, or, a cross pattée, gu. *Pl.* 37, *cr.* 10.

AYLFORD, and AYLNFORD, Eng., a fire between two branches of palm, in orle, both ppr. *Pl.* 62, *cr.* 6.

AYLIFFE, Lond.; and Brinksworth, Wilts.; out of a ducal coronet, or, an oak-tree, ppr., fructed, gold. *Pl.* 94, *cr.* 5.

AYLMER, Lord, (Whitworth-Aylmer,) Iri.: 1. For *Whitworth*, out of a ducal coronet, or, a garb, gu. *Pl.* 48, *cr.* 10, (coronet, *pl.* 128, *fig.* 3.) 2. For *Aylmer*, out of a ducal coronet, or, a demi-Cornish chough, rising, ppr. *Steady—and—Dum spiro spero. Pl.* 8, *cr.* 5.

AYLMER, Lord AYLEND, on a ducal coronet, or, a Cornish chough, wings displayed, sa. *Steady. Pl.* 8, *cr.* 5.

AYLMER, MICHAEL-VALENTYNE, Esq., of Lyons; Derry House, co. Tipperary; out of a ducal coronet, a Cornish chough, rising, all ppr. *Hallelujah. Pl.* 8, *cr.* 5.

AYLMER, Bart., Iri., same crest and motto.

AYLMER, Durh., same crest and motto.

AYLMER, JOHN-HARRISON, Esq., of Walworth Castle, Durh., same crest and motto.

AYLMER, Lord AYLMER, same crest.

AYLMER, Iri., same crest.

AYLMER, Ess., on a marquess' coronet, or, a Cornish chough's head, erased, sa., beaked, gu., between eagles' wings, expanded, gold.

AYLOFFE, Braxted Magna, Ess.; and Framfield, Suss.; a demi-lion, or, collared, gu. *Pl.* 18, *cr.* 13.

AYLOFFE, Eng., a demi-lion, rampant, or. *Pl.* 67, *cr.* 10.

AYLWARD, JAMES-KEARNEY, Esq., of Shankill Castle, co. Kilkenny, out of a ducal coronet, a dexter arm, in armour, embowed, couped at shoulder, ppr., in hand an anchor, ar. *Verus et fidelis semper. Pl.* 122, *cr.* 8.

AYLWIN, or ALWIN, Suss., a lion's gamb, erect (and erased,) sa., enfiled with a mural coronet, or. *Pl.* 93, *cr.* 9, (coronet, *pl.* 128, *fig.* 18.)

AYLWORTH, Somers., Glouc., Kent, and Devons., an arm, vested, sa., out of rays, or, in hand, ppr., a human skull, ar. *Pl.* 37, *cr.* 6.

AYNCOTES, a covered cup, or, between wings, sa.

AYNCOTTS, a squirrel, sejant, gu., collared, or. *Pl.* 85, *cr.* 3.

AYNESWORTH, and AYNEWORTH, Lanc., two battle-axes, in saltier, ppr. *Courage sans peur. Pl.* 52, *cr.* 10.

AYNESWORTH, or AYNSWORTH, Eng., a falcon, wings expanded and inverted, ppr., belled, or. *Courage sans peur. Pl.* 105, *cr.* 4.

AYNESWORTH, Lanc., a demi-man, in armour, ar., over dexter shoulder a sash tied on sinister, gu., in dexter a battle-axe, in pale, of the first.

AYNSCOMB, Mayfield, Suss.; and Cowdon, Kent; an arm, couped at elbow, erect, ppr., in hand a fleur-de-lis, sa. *Pl.* 95, *cr.* 9.

AYNSCOMB, and AYNISCAMP, Suss., same crest.

AYNSLEY, Northumb., a man in armour, (in dexter a sword, erect, ppr., hilted and pommelled, or, in sinister a shield, gu., charged with a bend, ar., thereon three mullets of six points.) *Furth fortune, and fill the fetters. Pl.* 60, *cr.* 2.

AYNWORTH, two battle-axes, in saltier, ppr. *Pl.* 52, *cr.* 10.

AYPE, an antelope, passant, ar., (collared, sa.) *Pl.* 63, *cr.* 10.

AYRE, Notts., on a ducal coronet, or, a wyvern, vert. *Pl.* 104, *cr.* 11.

AYSCOUGH, Durh., an ass's head, erased, ar. *Pl.* 91, *cr.* 7.

AYSCOUGH, D. D., Eng., an ass, erm. *Pl.* 42, *cr.* 2.

AYSCOUGH, Newcastle-upon-Tyne, a naked arm, ppr., hand grasping a sword, ar., hilt and pommel, or, enfiled with a Saracen's head, couped, of the first, wreathed, or and sa., dropping blood, gu. *Fac et spera. Pl.* 97, *cr.* 3.

AYSINGCOURT, or AYSYNGCOURT, Eng., an eagle's head, between wings, ppr. *Pl.* 81, *cr.* 10.

AYSKEY, and AYSKEW, a man's head, affrontée, couped at shoulders, ppr. *Pl.* 19, *cr.* 1.

AYSON, Lond. and Ess., out of a mural coronet, ar., a griffin's head, gu., ducally gorged, or. *Pl.* 101, *cr.* 6.

AYSSCOUGH, Eng., an ass, passant, ppr. *Pl.* 42, *cr.* 2.

AYTON, Eng., in hand, (gauntleted,) a hawk's lure, ppr. *Pl.* 44, *cr.* 2.

B

BAAD, or BAD, Sco., in dexter hand, ppr., a trident, az. *Pl.* 12, *cr.* 3.

BABB, or BABE, Dors., a dexter hand, erect, pointing with two fingers to the sun, ppr. *Pl.* 15, *cr.* 4.

BABBWELL, or BABWELL, Middx., a gate, or. *Pl.* 73, *cr.* 4.

BABEHAM, or BABEHAW, Lond., a demi-man, ppr., head wreathed with a knot, gu., in dexter a wing, sa., guttée d'or. *Pl.* 20, *cr.* 4.

BABER, Middx. and Somers., on a mount, vert, a cock, wings expanded, ar., combed, wattled, and legged, gu. *Pl.* 76, *cr.* 7.

BABINGTON, Dethickin, Oxon.; and Derbs.; a demi-bat, displayed, gu. *Pl.* 108, *cr.* 6.

BABINGTON, Dethickin, Oxon.; and Derbs.; a dragon's head, between wings, gu., (out of mouth a scroll.) *Pl.* 105, *cr.* 11.

BABINGTON, Oxon. and Derbs., a dragon's head, erased, between wings, gu. *Pl.* 105, *cr.* 11.

BABINGTON, THOMAS-GISBORNE, Esq., A.M., of Rotheley Temple, Leic., a dragon's head, between wings, gu. *Foy est tout*. *Pl.* 105, *cr.* 11.

BABINGTON, Lodley, Leic., Dors., and Staffs., a fox's head, ppr. *Pl.* 91, *cr.* 9.

BABINGTON, Eng., out of a ducal coronet, a demi-eagle, displayed, ppr. *In solitos docuere nisus*. *Pl.* 9, *cr.* 6.

BABTHORP, Yorks., a cockatrice's head, erased, ar., beaked, combed, and wattled, or. *Pl.* 76, *cr.* 9.

BACCHE, or BACHE, Somers., a savage's head, affrontée, between two branches of laurel, in orle, ppr. *Pl.* 90, *cr.* 8.

BACCHE, Stanton, a demi-lion, rampant, regardant, in paws a bezant. *Pl.* 33, *cr.* 2, (bezant, *pl.* 141.)

BACHELER, Berks., a dragon's head, erased, or, vulned in neck, gu. *Pl.* 107, *cr.* 10, (without collar.)

BACHELER, BACHELOR, and BACHELOUR, a leg, erased, above knee, ppr. *Pl.* 73, *cr.* 5.

BACKHOUSE, Lond., out of a ducal coronet, an arm, in armour, brandishing a scimitar. *Pl.* 15, *cr.* 5.

BACKHOUSE, Durh., Cumb., and Kent, on a snake, embowed, tail, nowed, an eagle, displayed. *Confido in Deo*. *Pl.* 75, *cr.* 11.

BACKHOUSE, Lond., out of a ducal coronet, an arm from elbow, in armour, brandishing a scimitar, in bend sinister. *Pl.* 15, *cr.* 5.

BACKIE, a sword and cross crosslet, fitched, in saltier, ppr. *Pl.* 89, *cr.* 14.

BACKIE, or BAIKIE, Tankerness, Orkney, a flame of fire, ppr. *Commodum non damnum*. *Pl.* 16, *cr.* 12.

BACKWELL, Lond., out of a mural coronet, or, a demi-bull, sa. *Pl.* 63, *cr.* 6, (coronet, *pl.* 128, *fig.* 18.)

BACON, Hants, a tiger, sejant, gu., (pierced through breast with broken spear, or,) headed, ar. *Pl.* 26, *cr.* 9.

BACON, Twyhouse, Somers., a greyhound's head, erased, sa., in mouth a stag's foot, or. *Pl.* 66, *cr.* 7.

BACON, Bart., Premier, Redgrave, Suff., a boar, passant, erm. *Mediocria firma*. *Pl.* 48, *cr.* 14.

BACON, Gillingham, Norf.; and Redgrave, Suff.; a boar, passant, erm., armed and hoofed, or. *Pl.* 48, *cr.* 14.

BACON, a boar's head, couped, or, (in mouth a griffin's head, erased, az.) *Pl.* 2, *cr.* 7.

BACON, Bart., Suff., a boar, statant, erm. *Mediocria firma*. *Pl.* 48, *cr.* 14.

BACON, Hesset, Norf., a talbot's head, sa., erased, gu., (in mouth a deer's leg, or.) *Pl.* 90, *cr.* 6.

BACON, Notts, on a mount, vert, a boar, statant, ar., bristled and tusked, or, semée of mullets, sa., in mouth a ragged staff, vert. *Mediocria firma*. *Pl.* 108, *cr.* 9.

BACON, Harlston, Norf., a demi-boar, or, armed and bristled, az. *Pl.* 20, *cr.* 5.

BACON, Newton Cup, Durh.; and Stewart Pile, Northumb.; a demi-wild boar, rampant, gardant, az., bristled, armed, and unguled, or, langued, gu., in mouth a tilting spear, ar., stricken in shoulder, and vulned, ppr. *Pl.* 115, *cr.* 2.

BADBY, Lond., a sphinx, passant, gardant, ppr., wings addorsed. *Pl.* 91, *cr.* 11.

BADCOCK, Kensington, Ess.; and Middx.; a stag lodged, gardant, between two branches of laurel, in orle, all ppr. *Pl.* 24, *cr.* 4.

BADD, Fareham, Hants., a lion's head, erased, gardant, ar., ducally crowned, az. *Pl.* 1, *cr.* 5.

BADDER, on stump of tree, in fess, couped and eradicated, a lion, sejant. *Pl.* 76, *cr.* 11.

BADDIFORD, Dartmouth, Devons., an eagle's head, or, crowned with a coronet flory, sa., between two branches of lily, ar., stalked and leaved, vert. *Pl.* 72, *cr.* 3.

BADDIFORD, an eagle's head, or, crowned with a cross crosslet, sa., between two branches of thistle, ppr. *Pl.* 72, *cr.* 3.

BADELEY, Ess. and Suff., a boar's head and neck, couped, ar. *Pl.* 2, *cr.* 7.

BADELISMERE, or BADELSMERE, Yorks., in lion's gamb, erased, sa., a laurel-branch, vert. *Pl.* 68, *cr.* 10.

BADGER, Eng., a badger, ppr. *Pl.* 34, *cr.* 4.

BADGER, Camb., Glouc., and Leic., a boar's head, cabossed, sa., between attires a greyhound, current, ar., collared, gu. *Pl.* 115, *cr.* 1.

BADHAM, an eagle, displayed, with two heads, charged on breast with a saltier. *Pl.* 25, *cr.* 5.

BAETT, or BATT, a demi-lion, or, guttée-de-sang. *Pl.* 67, *cr.* 10.

BAGELEY, or BAGLEY, Eng., on top of spear, issuing a wyvern, sans legs, tail nowed. *Pl.* 25, *cr.* 4.

BAGENHALL, Staff., a dragon's head, erased, gu., gorged with a bar-gemelle, or. *Pl.* 107, *cr.* 10.

BAGENHOLT, a horse, current, bridled, ppr. *Pl.* 8, *cr.* 2.

BAGGE, WILLIAM, Esq., of Stradsett Hall, Norf., two wings, addorsed, or, semée of annulets, gu. *Spes est in Deo*. *Pl.* 63, *cr.* 12.

BAGGE, on point of sword, in pale, a garland of laurel, ppr. *Pl.* 15, *cr.* 6.

BAGGE, or BAGG, Plymouth, Devons., a cinquefoil, az., between wings, addorsed, dexter, gu, sinister, ar. *Pl.* 4, *cr.* 10, (cinquefoil, *pl.* 141.)

BAGGELEY, Chesh., a ram's head, az., attired, ar, charged with three lozenges, gold. *Pl.* 34, *cr.* 12, (lozenge, *pl.* 141.)

BAGGELEY, Chesh., a ram's head, az., attired, or. *Pl.* 34, *cr.* 12.

BAGGS, a rose, charged with a thistle, ppr. *Pl.* 73, *cr.* 6.

BAGHOTT, on a ducal coronet, or, a leopard, sejant, gardant, ppr. *Pl.* 86, *cr.* 8.

BAGLEY, an arm, in armour, embowed, in hand a sword. *Pl.* 2, *cr.* 8.

BAGNALL, Kent, a dragon's head, erased, gu., gorged with two bars, or. *Pl.* 107, *cr.* 10.

BAGNALL, Staffs. and Wales, an antelope, sejant, ar., billettée, sa., ducally gorged, lined, armed, and tufted, or. *Pl.* 115, *cr.* 3.

BAGNE, and BAGUE, on a chapeau, a pelican vulning, ppr. *Pl.* 21, *cr.* 5.

BAGNEL, BAGNELL, BAGNILL, or BAGNOLL, a galley, sails furled, ppr. *Pl.* 24, *cr.* 5.

BAGNELL, a goat, rampant, ducally gorged, and staked to the ground. *Pl.* 72, *cr.* 1.

BAGOT, Baron Bagot, of Blithfield, Staffs., and a Bart., out of a ducal coronet, or, a goat's head, ar., attired, gold. *Antiquum obtinens. Pl.* 72, *cr.* 2.

BAGOT, Dublin, same crest.

BAGOT, CHARLES, Esq., of Kilcoursey, King's co., same crest and motto.

BAGOT, The Rev. EGERTON-ARDEN, of Pype Hall, Staffs., same crest and motto.

BAGOT, JOHN-JAMES, Esq., of Castle Bagot, co. Dublin, same crest. *Pour Dieu et mon roi.*

BAGOT, THOMAS NEVILLE, Esq., of Hamlet Cottage, near Ballymoe, co. Galway, same crest.

BAGSHAW, South Okendon, Ess., a bugle-horn, or. *Pl.* 89, *cr.* 3.

BAGSHAW, Delaridge, Derb., an arm, couped at elbow, erect, ppr., in hand a bugle-horn, sa., (stringed, vert.) *Pl.* 109, *cr.* 3.

BAGSHAWE, (out of clouds,) an arm, erect, ppr., in hand a bugle horn, sa. *Pl.* 109, *cr.* 3.

BAGSHAWE, FRANCIS-WESTBY, Esq., of The Oaks, in Norton, near Sheffield; and Wormhill Hall, near Buxton; (out of clouds,) a dexter cubit arm, in hand, ppr., a bugle-horn, or, handle, sa., (within the strings a rose, gu.) *Forma flos ; fama, flatus. Pl.* 109, *cr.* 3.

BAGSHOLE, an acorn, slipped and leaved, ppr. *Pl.* 81, *cr.* 7.

BAGSHOTE, an acorn, slipped and leaved, ppr. *Pl.* 81, *cr.* 7.

BAGWELL, out of a mural coronet, a demi-bull, rampant. *Pl.* 63, *cr.* 6, (coronet, *pl.* 128, *fig.* 18.)

BAGWELL, JOHN, Esq., of Marlfield, near Clonmel; and Eastgrove, Queenstown; out of a mural coronet, a demi-bull, all ppr. *In fide et in bello fortes. Pl.* 63, *cr.* 6, (coronet, *pl.* 128, *fig.* 18.)

BAIGHTON, a heron's head, erased, in mouth an eel, ppr. *Pl.* 41, *cr.* 6.

BAIKIE, a flame of fire, ppr. *Commodum non damnum. Pl.* 16, *cr.* 12.

BAILEY, CRAWSHAY, Esq., of Aberaman, near Pontyprydd, Wel., a griffin, sejant, ar., seméе of annulets, gu. *Libertas. Pl.* 100, *cr.* 11, (annulet, *pl.* 141.)

BAILEY, a cat, salient, gardant. *Pl.* 70, *cr.* 15.

BAILEY, a demi-lady, in dexter a tower, in sinister a laurel-branch, vert. *Pl.* 20, *cr.* 6.

BAILLIE of Walston, a dove, volant, in mouth an olive-branch. *Patior et spero. Pl.* 25, *cr.* 6.

BAILLIE of Jerviswood, a crescent, or. *Major virtus quam splendor. Pl.* 18, *cr.* 14.

BAILLIE, Inshaughy, Iri., a star of eight points, or, out of a cloud, ppr. *Nil clarius astris. Pl.* 16, *cr.* 13.

BAILLIE of Balmudyside, the morning star, ppr. *Vertitur in lucem. Pl.* 21, *cr.* 6.

BAILLIE of Hoperig, East Lothian, a boar's head, couped. *Quid clarius astris? Pl.* 48, *cr.* 2.

BAILLIE, Bart., Polkenet, Linlithgow, an etoile of eight points, or, out of a cloud, ppr. *In caligine lucit. Pl.* 16, *cr.* 13.

BAILLIE, GEORGE, Esq., of Jerviswood, and Mellerstain, Berwick, a crescent, or, (surmounted of a sun.) *Major virtus quam splendor. Pl.* 111, *cr.* 15.

BAILLIE, EVAN, Esq., of Douchfour, Inverness, a boar's head, couped. *Quid clarius astris? Pl.* 48, *cr.* 2.

BAILLIE of Lamington and Carphin, Sco., a boar's head, erased, ppr. *Quid clarius astris? Pl.* 16, *cr.* 11.

BAILLIE of Rosehall, Sco., a cat, sejant, ppr. *Spero meliora. Pl.* 24, *cr.* 6.

BAILLIE of Carnbrae, on point of sword, in pale, ppr., hilt and pommel, or, a laurel wreath, fructed, of the first. *Perseverantia. Pl.* 15, *cr.* 6.

BAILLIE of Corstorphine, a crow, ppr. *Be not wanting. Pl.* 23, *cr.* 8.

BAILLIE, Sco., a cockatrice, wings expanded. *Pl.* 63, *cr.* 15.

BAILLIE of Hardington, Sco., in hand a pen, ppr. *Fides servata ditat. Pl.* 26, *cr.* 13.

BAILWOOD, a bull's head, couped, sa. *Pl.* 120, *cr.* 7.

BAILY, out of a ducal coronet, a wyvern's head, ppr. *Pl.* 87, *cr.* 12, (coronet, *pl.* 128, *fig.* 3.)

BAILY, THOMAS-FARMER, Esq., of Hall Place, Leigh, Kent, a goat's head, erased, az., bezantée, attired, or. *Vestigia nulla restrorsum. Pl.* 29, *cr.* 13, (bezant, *pl.* 141.)

BAIN, Northumb., in hand a scroll. *Virtute. Pl.* 27, *cr.* 4.

BAIN, Berwick, same crest.

BAIN, or BAINE, Eng., a lion, rampant, gu., between wings, or. *Pl.* 29, *cr.* 5.

BAIN, a dexter arm, in armour, embowed, ppr., garnished, or, hand grasping a dagger, also ppr. *Et marte, et arte. Pl.* 21, *cr.* 4.

BAIN, Sco., an arm embowed, in hand a dagger, ppr. *Et arte, et marte. Pl.* 21, *cr.* 4.

BAINBRIDGE, or BAINBRIGGE, Derb., on a mount, vert, a goat, passant, sa., horned, and unguled, or, collar and bell, ar. *Pl.* 11, *cr.* 14.

BAINBRIDGE, Eng., an arm, from shoulder, out of the sea, in hand an anchor, corded, all ppr. *Pl.* 27, *cr.* 6.

BAINBRIGG, or BAMBRIDGE, Leic., on a mount, vert, a goat, sa., collared, ar. *Pl.* 11, *cr.* 14.

BAINBRIGGE, THOMAS-PARKER, Esq., Hill House, Derby, on a mount, vert, a goat, sa., horned, unguled, and collared, ar. *Pl.* 11, *cr.* 14.

BAINES, Peteonly, Sco., in dexter hand a dagger, ppr. *Vel arte vel marte. Pl.* 28, *cr.* 4.

BAINES, a bone and palm-branch, in saltier, ppr. *Pl.* 25, *cr.* 11.

BAINES, a wild duck among flags, ppr. *Pl.* 34, *cr.* 6.
BAINES, Bell Hall, near York, a cubit arm, erect, in hand a leg-bone, in bend sinister, ar. *Pl.* 28, *cr.* 14, (bone, *pl.* 25, *cr.* 11.)
BAIRD, Auchmedden, Sco., a griffin's head, erased, ppr. *Dominus fecit. Pl.* 48, *cr.* 6.
BAIRD, Bart., of Yardleybury, Herts; Fernton, Perthshire; and Newbyth, East Lothian: 1. A mamaluke on horseback, in dexter a scimitar, all ppr. *Pl.* 115, *cr.* 5. 2. A boar's head, erased, or. *Pl.* 16, *cr.* 11. *Vi et virtute.*
BAIRD, JAMES, Esq., of Cambusdoon, Ayr, an eagle's head, erased. *Dominus fecit. Pl.* 20, *cr.* 7.
BAIRD, a cockatrice, wings addorsed, gu. *Pl.* 63, *cr.* 15.
BAIRD, Sco., a dove, wings expanded, ppr. *Virtute et honore. Pl.* 27, *cr.* 5.
BAIRD of Saughton Hall, Sco., a boar's head, erased, or. *Vi et virtute. Pl.* 16, *cr.* 11.
BAIRD, Newbaith, same crest and motto.
BAIRD, Sco., a boar's head, erased, ppr., charged with a crescent. *Pl.* 16, *cr.* 11, (crescent, *pl.* 141.)
BAIRD, of Frankfield, Sco., an eagle's head, ppr. *Vi et virtute. Pl.* 100, *cr.* 10.
BAIRD, an eagle's head, erased, ppr. *Dominus fecit. Pl.* 20, *cr.* 7.
BAIRD of Craigton, Sco., a ship in full sail, ppr. *Adsit Deus non demovebor. Pl.* 109, *cr.* 8.
BAIRNSFATHER, or BARNESFATHER, Sco., a boar's head, couped, or. *Pl.* 48, *cr.* 2.
BAIRSTOW, out of a crescent, a demi-eagle, displayed. *Pl.* 11, *cr.* 10.
BAKE, a demi-man, in armour, in dexter a sword, all ppr. *Pl.* 23, *cr.* 4.
BAKER, Bart., Nicholshayne and Loventor, Devons., a dexter arm, embowed, (vested, az., cuffed, ar.,) in hand, ppr., an arrow, of the last. *Pl.* 92, *cr.* 14.
BAKER, Sisinghurst, Kent, a dexter arm, ppr., in hand a swan's head, erased, ar., beaked, gu. *Pl.* 29, *cr.* 4.
BAKER, Bart., Upper Dunstable-House, Surr., a demi-lion, rampant, per fess, indented, erminois and ermines, in paws an escallop, ar., charged with an ermine spot. *Pl.* 126 *a*, *cr.* 13.
BAKER, Bart., late Littlehales, of Ranston, Dors.; and Ashcombe, Suss.: 1. For *Baker*, a horse's head, erased, ar., charged on neck with a cross formée, fitched, in mouth a trefoil, slipped, vert. *Pl.* 11, *cr.* 12. 2. For *Littlehales*, between wings elevated, or, an arm, in armour, embowed, ppr., garnished, or, hand gauntleted, grasping an arrow, entwined with an olive-branch, vert. *Finis coronat opus. Pl.* 115, *cr.* 4.
BAKER, Chester and Shrewsbury, out of a ducal coronet, a dexter arm, embowed, vested, or, in hand, gauntleted, of the same, a tilting spear, in bend, on shaft a ring, gold, enfiled with a garland, vert.
BAKER, Kent, an arm, embowed, vested with green leaves, in hand, ppr., a swan's head, erased, or. *Pl.* 29, *cr.* 4, (arm, *pl.* 57, *cr.* 2.)
BAKER, an ostrich-head, erased, or, in mouth a horse-shoe, ar. *Pl.* 28, *cr.* 13, (without wings.)

BAKER, Bart., Surr., out of an antique crown, a demi-lion, rampant, per fess, indented, erminois and pean, between paws an escallop, ar., charged with an ermine spot. *Fidei coticula crux.*
BAKER, out of a cloud, a dexter arm, in fess, raising a garb, all ppr. *Pl.* 43, *cr.* 4.
BAKER, a boar's head, couped, or. *Pl.* 48, *cr.* 2.
BAKER, a rose-tree, vert, flowered, or. *Pl.* 23, *cr.* 2.
BAKER, Kent and Suss., a musk-rose branch, vert, flowered, ar., seeded, or. *Pl.* 23, *cr.* 2.
BAKER, Linc.; and Smallborough, Norf.; a demi-unicorn, (erased,) ar., armed and maned, or. *Pl.* 26, *cr.* 14.
BAKER, in dexter hand, gu., a club, sa. *Pl.* 28, *cr.* 6.
BAKER, Lond. and Worc., a cockatrice, erm., combed and wattled, gu. *Pl.* 63, *cr.* 15.
BAKER, a tower, ar., between two laurel branches, ppr. *Pl.* 72, *cr.* 15.
BAKER, Walton, Norf., a stag's head, cabossed, or, on a chapeau, az., turned up, erm. *Pl.* 108, *cr.* 14.
BAKER, a naked dexter arm, embowed, in hand an arrow, ppr. *Pl.* 92, *cr.* 14.
BAKER, a naked dexter arm, in hand a purse. *Pl.* 11, *cr.* 13.
BAKER, a dexter arm, in armour, embowed, in hand an arrow, ppr. *Pl.* 96, *cr.* 6.
BAKER, Radnorshire, a hawk's head, ar., between wings, gu., in beak three ears of wheat, of the last. *Pl.* 99, *cr.* 10, (wheat, *pl.* 89, *cr.* 4.)
BAKER, a greyhound's head, erased, ar., gorged with a fess, engrailed, sa., fimbriated, or, charged with three fleurs-de-lis, gold *Pl.* 89, *cr.* 2, (fleur-de-lis, *pl.* 141.)
BAKER, Lond., (on a mount, vert,) a tower, ar., between two laurel branches, ppr. *Pl.* 72, *cr.* 15.
BAKER, Lond. and Worc., in hand, out of clouds, ppr., a cross potent, sa. *Nemo sine cruce beatus. Pl.* 26, *cr.* 4, (cross, *pl.* 141.)
BAKER, ROBERT, Esq., of West Hay, in the parish of Wrington, Somerset, a dexter arm, in armour, the under vest seen at elbow, vert, in hand, ppr., a swan's neck, or, beaked, gu. *Pl.* 29, *cr.* 4, (arm, *pl.* 51, *cr.* 1.)
BAKER, HENRY-JOHN-BAKER, Esq., of Elemore Hall and Crook Hall, Durh.: 1. For *Baker*, a lion, rampant, ar., (charged on shoulder with a saltier, az., between paws a shield, of the last, thereon a maunch, or.) *Pl.* 67, *cr.* 5. (shield, *pl.* 22, *cr.* 13.) 2: For *Tower*, a griffin, passant, per pale, or. and erm., dexter resting on a shield, sa., charged with a tower, gold. *Love and dread. Pl.* 39, *cr.* 8, (shield, *pl.* 42, *cr.* 8.)
BAKER, WILLIAM-ROBERT, Esq., of Bayfordbury, Herts, a cockatrice, per fess, indented, erminois and pean, combed and wattled, gu., (collared, az.,) in beak a quatrefoil, slipped, vert. *So run that you may obtain. Pl.* 63, *cr.* 15, (quatrefoil, *pl.* 141.)
BAKER, RICHARD-WESTBROOK, Esq., of Cottesmore, and Langham, Rutland, a greyhound's head, erased, ppr., (charged with a fess, invecked, between six ears of wheat, or.) *Non sibi sed patriæ. Pl.* 89, *cr.* 2.

BAKER, WILLIAM, Esq., of Orsett Hall, Ess.: 1. For *Baker*, a cockatrice, erm., combed and wattled, gu. *Pl.* 63, *cr.* 15. 2. A griffin, passant, vert. *Pl.* 66, *cr.* 13.
BAKER, THOMAS-BARWICK-LLOYD, Esq., of Hardwicke Court, near Gloucester, a naked dexter arm, ppr., in hand a swan's head, erased, ar. *Pl.* 29, *cr.* 4.
BAKER, Dur., a lion, rampant, ar. *Pl.* 67, *cr.* 5.
BAKER, an ostrich-head, erased, or, in mouth a horse-shoe, ar. *Pl.* 28, *cr.* 13, (without wings.)
BAKER, Mayfield, Suss., on a tower, sa., an arm, in mail, embowed, ppr., (in hand a piece of plate-iron, az.) *Pl.* 116, *cr.* 12.
BAKER-CRESSWELL of Cresswell, Northumb.: 1. A goat's head, erased, ar., attired, or. *Pl.* 29, *cr.* 13. 2. On a mount, vert, a torteau, charged with a squirrel, sejant, ar. *Pl.* 117, *cr.* 6, (squirrel, *pl.* 85, *cr.* 3.)
BALAM, Norf. and Suff., a lion's head, erased, gu., collared, (and lined), or, charged on neck with a cinquefoil, ar. *Pl.* 7, *cr.* 10, (cinquefoil, *pl.* 141.)
BALAM, Walstoken, Marsland, Bewford Hall, Norf.; and Barton, Suff.; out of a ducal coronet, or, a demi-cock, gu., wings displayed, combed, and wattled, or. *Pl.* 115, *cr.* 8.
BALABYSE, a lion, couchant, gardant, or. *Pl.* 101, *cr.* 8.
BALBERNEY, Sco., a stag, lodged, ppr. *Pl.* 67, *cr.* 2.
BALCARRES, Earl of, Sco.; Baron Wigan, Eng., (Lindsay;) a tent, az., semée of stars, or, canopy and fringes, of the same, on top a pennon, gu. *Astra, castra; numen, lumen, munimen.* *Pl.* 111, *cr.* 14.
BALDBERNEY, or BALBIRNEY, Sco., a steel cap, ppr. *Pl.* 18, *cr.* 9.
BALDERSTON, or BALDERSTONES, Sco., in hand a lancet, ppr. *Vulnere sano.* *Pl.* 29, *cr.* 6.
BALDERSTONE, Sco., out of a cloud, a dexter arm, in fess, ppr., in hand a cross pattée, fitched, az. *Pl.* 26, *cr.* 4.
BALDOCK, Petham, Kent., on a mount, vert, a greyhound, sejant, dexter resting on an escallop, ar. *Pl.* 108, *cr.* 10.
BALDOCK, Cauleston, Norf., an eagle, close, gazing at the sun. *Pl.* 43, *cr.* 5.
BALDRIE, or BALDRY, a trefoil, slipped, vert. *Pl.* 82, *cr.* 1.
BALDRY, out of a gillyflower, vert, the flower gu., a demi-man, habited, per pale, indented, sa. and or, the arms counterchanged, face, ppr.
BALDWID, a squirrel, sejant, or. *Pl.* 16, *cr.* 9.
BALDWIN, a squirrel, sejant, or, holding a sprig of hazel, vert. *Pl.* 2, *cr.* 4.
BALDWIN, Diddlebery, Salow and Warw., on a mount, vert, a cockatrice, ar., beaked, combed and wattled, or, ducally gorged and lined, of the last. *Pl.* 72, *cr.* 5.
BALDWIN, Stede Hill, Kent, a lion, rampant, az., in paws a cross crosslet, fitched, or. *Pl.* 125, *cr.* 2, (cross, *pl.* 141.)
BALDWIN, HERBERT, Esq., M.D., of Clohina. co. Cork, a dove, in mouth an olive-branch, ppr. *Est voluntas Dei.* *Pl.* 48, *cr.* 15.
BALE, Carleton-Curlew, Leic., a (demi-)lion, gu., supporting a broken spear, or. *Pl.* 60, *cr.* 4.
BALES, NORTON, Northamp., a lion, sejant, gu., resting dexter on a cross pattée, fitched, or. *Pl.* 109, *cr.* 7, (cross, *pl.* 27, *cr.* 14.)

BALES, WILBY, Suff., a tiger's head, erased, sa., armed, or, (gorged with a fess, wavy, az.) *Pl.* 94, *cr.* 10.
BALES, WILBY, Suff., on a mount, vert, a lion sejant, erm. *Pl.* 108, *cr.* 12.
BALES, JAMES, same crest.
BALFOUR, Sir PATRICK, N.S., Bart., Denmilne, Fifeshire, a crescent, or. *God gives increase.* *Pl.* 18, *cr.* 14.
BALFOUR of Pilrig, Sco., in dexter hand an ivy-branch, ppr. *Adsit Deus.* *Pl.* 43, *cr.* 6.
BALFOUR of Randerston, a crescent. *Pl.* 18, *cr.* 14.
BALFOUR of Dunbog, a mermaid, ppr., in dexter a boar's head, erased, sa. *Omne solum forti patria.* *Pl.* 2, *cr.* 5.
BALFOUR, DAVID, Esq., of Balfour Castle, and Noltland Castle, Orkney, a dexter arm, ppr., couped at elbow, in hand a baton, ar. *Forward.* *Pl.* 18, *cr.* 1.
BALFOUR, JOHN, Esq., of Balbirnie, Markinch, Fife, a palm-tree, ppr. *Virtus ad æthera tendit.* *Pl.* 18, *cr.* 12.
BALFOUR, JAMES MAITLAND, Esq., of Whittinghame, East Lothian, and Strathconan, Ross, same crest and motto.
BALFOUR, BLAYNEY-TOWNLEY, Esq., of Townley Hall, near Drogheda, co. Louth: 1. A lady standing on a rock, in dexter an otter's head, in sinister a swan's head. 2. On a perch, or, a hawk, close, ppr., beaked and belled, gold, round neck a ribbon, gu. *Omne solum forti patria.* *Pl.* 38, *cr.* 12.
BALFOUR of Forret, an eagle, rising, ppr. *Dieu aidant.* *Pl.* 67, *cr.* 4.
BALFOUR, Sco., a heraldic tiger, passant, sa. *Pl.* 7, *cr.* 5.
BALFOUR, Sco., in hand, in armour, a truncheon, ppr. *Forward.* *Pl.* 33, *cr.* 4.
BALFOUR, a mermaid, in dexter an otter's head, erased, all ppr. *Pl.* 2, *cr.* 5, (otter's head, *pl.* 68, *cr.* 8.)
BALFOUR of Grange, on battlements of castle, ar., a woman standing, attired, gu., in dexter an otter's head. *Nil temere.* *Pl.* 26, *cr.* 5.
BALFOUR, Lord, of Burleigh, a woman standing on a rock, in dexter an otter's head, in sinister a swan's head. *Omne solum forti patria.*
BALFOUR of Balmouth, an otter's head, couped. *Forward, non temere.* *Pl.* 97, *cr.* 11.
BALGUY, JOHN, Esq., of Duffield, Derby, a bear, passant, ppr., collared and chained, or. *Pl.* 61, *cr.* 5.
BALIOL, Sco., a decrescent and increscent, ar. *Pl.* 99, *cr.* 4.
BALL, Northamp., (out of clouds, ppr.,) a demi-lion, rampant, sa., powdered with etoiles, ar., holding a globe, or. *Pl.* 126, *cr.* 12, (etoile, *pl.* 141.)
BALL, Bart., Blofield, Norf., out of a naval coronet, a cubit arm erect, (in naval uniform,) in hand a grenade bursting, ppr. *Pl.* 93, *cr.* 1, (*pl.* 70, *cr.* 12.)
BALL, a demi-lion, rampant, in paws a ball. *Pl.* 126, *cr.* 12.
BALL, Chesh., out of a ducal coronet, an arm, in armour, embowed, in hand a fire-ball, all ppr. *Pl.* 122, *cr.* 8, (*pl.* 70, *cr.* 12.)
BALL, Lanc., a turtle-dove, ppr. *Pl.* 66, *cr.* 12.

BALL, an arm, erect, or, in hand, a fire-ball, all ppr. *Pl.* 2, *cr.* 6.
BALL, Lincoln's Inn, Lond., a caltrap, az., upper point bloody. *Pl.* 7, *cr.* 4.
BALL of Scotto, Norf., a demi-lion, rampant, gardant, sa. *Pl.* 35, *cr.* 4.
BALLANTYNE, JAMES, Esq., of Holylee, Sco., a demi-griffin, in dexter a sword, erect, ppr. *Nec cito, nec tarde. Pl.* 49, *cr.* 4.
BALLANTYNE, Sco., a demi-griffin, wings expanded. *Pl.* 18, *cr.* 6.
BALLARD, a demi-griffin, wings addorsed, erm., beaked and legged, or. *Pl.* 18, *cr.* 6.
BALLARD, a griffin's head, erased, erm. *Pl.* 48, *cr.* 6.
BALLARD, a griffin's head and wings, erm., beaked, gu. *Pl.* 65, *cr.* 1.
BALLARD, a griffin's head, between wings, erm., beaked, gu. *Pl.* 22, *cr.* 2.
BALLARD, or BALLORD, Heref., a demi-griffin, erm., supporting a broken tilting spear, ppr. *Pl.* 44, *cr.* 3, (spear, *same plate, cr.* 9.)
BALLENDEN of Broughton, a hart's head, couped, ppr., attired, or, between attires a cross crosslet, fitched, gold. *Sic itur ad astra. Pl.* 24, *cr.* 9.
BALLENGER, a dragon's head, wings addorsed, ppr. *Pl.* 82, *cr.* 10.
BALLENTINE, a demi-griffin, sa., wings addorsed, erm., in dexter a sword, erect, ar., hilt and pommel, or. *Pl.* 49, *cr.* 4.
BALLETT, Hatfield, Ess., out of a mural coronet, or, a demi-eagle, displayed, sa. *Pl.* 33, *cr.* 5.
BALLOW, Westminster, two arms, embowed, vested, sa., cuffed, turned up, ar., in hands, ppr., conjoined, an etoile of eight points, or. *Pl.* 6, *cr.* 8, (*pl.* 45, *cr.* 2; *pl.* 141.)
BALLWARD, and BALVAIRD, in dexter hand a hunting horn. *Pl.* 109, *cr.* 3.
BALM, and BALME, a hat, turned up, with three ostrich-feathers, ar. *Pl.* 28, *cr.* 1.
BALMANNO of Affleck, Sco., in dexter hand a scimitar, ppr. *Fortiter. Pl.* 29, *cr.* 8.
BALMANNO, or BALMANO, Sco., an eagle, displayed, gu., in each claw a sword, ppr. *Pl.* 99, *cr.* 5.
BALNAVES of Carnbody, in dexter hand a football, ppr. *Hinc origo. Pl.* 33, *cr.* 6.
BALNAVES, or BALNEAVES, in dexter hand, ppr., a cannon-ball, sa. *Fortitudine et velocitate. Pl.* 33, *cr.* 6.
BALSCOTT, on a ducal coronet, or, a lion, passant, gardant, ar. *Pl.* 107, *cr.* 11.
BALSILLIE, Sco., in dexter hand, ppr., a cross crosslet, fitched, gu. *Pl.* 99, *cr.* 1.
BALTREY, out of a mural coronet, or, a goat's head, erased, quarterly, ar., and ermines. *Pl.* 72, *cr.* 2, (coronet, *pl.* 128, *fig.* 18.)
BAMBELL, out of a ducal coronet, or, a pelican vulning, sa. *Pl.* 64, *cr.* 1, (coronet, *pl.* 128, *fig.* 3.)
BAMBROUGH, Rendlesham, Suff., a skull-cap, ar. *Pl.* 18, *cr.* 9.
BAMBURY, Yorks. and Suff., a skull-cap, ar. *Pl.* 18, *cr.* 9.
BAMFIELD, or BAMFYLDE, a lion's head, erased, sa., crowned, or. *Pl.* 90, *cr.* 4.
BAMFIELD, or BAUMFIELD, a lion's head, erased, sa., ducally crowned, gu., charged on neck with an annulet, or. *Pl.* 90, *cr.* 4, (annulet, *pl.* 141.)

BAMFIELD, Devons., a lion's head, erased, ducally crowned. *Pl.* 90, *cr.* 4.
BAMFIELD, Cornw. and Devons., a lion, statant, gardant, in dexter an anchor, flukes resting on the wreath. *Pl.* 35, *cr.* 6.
BAMFIELD, Poltmore, Devons., a lion's head, erased, sa., ducally crowned, gu. *Pl.* 90, *cr.* 4.
BAMFORD of Bamford, Derbs., on a chapeau, a serpent, nowed. *Pl.* 123, *cr.* 4.
BAMFORD, BAUMFORD, or BAUNFORD, Staffs., a lion's head, erased, ppr. *Pl.* 81, *cr.* 4.
BAMME, or BAUM, out of a ducal coronet, a griffin's head, in beak a key, ppr. *Pl.* 89, *cr.* 5.
BAMPFYLDE, Bart., Poltimore, Devons., a lion's head, erased, sa., ducally crowned, or. *Delectare in domino. Pl.* 90, *cr.* 4.
BANARD, or BANYARD, Stakey, Norf., on a lion's gamb, erased, sa., a martlet, or. *Pl.* 126, *cr.* 9, (martlet, *pl.* 111, *cr.* 8.)
BANBURY, or BANDBURY, Oxon., a falcon, regardant, in dexter a garland of laurel, all ppr. *Pl.* 42, *cr.* 7.
BANCE, Lond.; and Callow, Berks.; out of a ducal coronet, or, in lion's paw, a cross crosslet, fitched, sa. *Pl.* 65, *cr.* 5.
BANCROFT, Lond., a garb, between wings expanded, or. *Pl.* 108, *cr.* 13.
BAND, EDWARD-WRIGHT, Esq., of Wookey House, Somers., an eagle, or. *Dieu est mon aide. Pl.* 7, *cr.* 11.
BAND, Ess., on a chapeau, an owl, ppr., wings expanded, or. *Pl.* 123, *cr.* 6.
BANDENELL, Netherbury, a griffin, statant, ppr. *Pl.* 66, *cr.* 13.
BANDON, Earl of. *See* BERNARD.
BANESTER, or BANASTER, Lanc., a peacock in pride, body and wings, or, tail, ppr. *Pl.* 92, *cr.* 11.
BANESTER, a lobster, or. *Pl.* 18, *cr.* 2.
BANESTER, Surr., a peacock, ppr. *Pl.* 54, *cr.* 13.
BANESTER, Leic. and Staffs., a peacock sitting, ppr., collared, gu., charged with three bezants. *Pl.* 54, *cr.* 13, (bezant, *pl.* 141.)
BANGER, a greyhound's head, erased, per fess, gu. and or. *Pl.* 89, *cr.* 2.
BANGOR, Viscount and Baron, South-well-Warde, Iri., a Saracen's head, affrontée, couped, ppr. *Sub cruce salus. Pl.* 19, *cr.* 1.
BANISTER, a torteau, gu. *Pl.* 7, *cr.* 6.
BANKE, or BANCK, Lond. and Yorks., on stump of tree, couped, a stork, close, all ppr. *Pl.* 23, *cr.* 5.
BANKE, or BANCKES, Glouc. and Lanc., a griffin, segreant, ar., holding a cross formée, fitched, gu. *Pl.* 67, *cr.* 13, (cross, *pl.* 141.)
BANKES, Lond. and Middx., a man's head, couped at shoulders, sa., on head a chapeau, gu., turned up, erm. *Pl.* 19, *cr.* 1, (chapeau, *pl.* 127, *fig.* 13.)
BANKES, WILLIAM-JOHN, Esq., M.A., of Kingston Lucy, Dors., a moor's head, affrontée, couped at shoulders, ppr., on head a chapeau, gu., turned up, erm., (adorned with a crescent, whence issues a fleur-de-lis.) *Pl.* 38, *cr.* 13.
BANKES, MEYRICK, Esq., of Winstanley Hall, near Wigan, on stump of tree, a stork, statant, ppr., ducally gorged, gu. *Pl.* 23, *cr.* 5, (coronet, *pl.* 128, *fig.* 3.)
BANKS, Yorks., an eagle's head, erased, sa., between two fleurs-de-lis, ar. *Pl.* 108, *cr.* 15.

BANKS, Revesby-Abbey, Linc., on stump of oak-tree, couped, sprouting, a stork, ar., beaked, or. *Nullius in verba.* Pl. 23, cr. 5.

BANKS, Yorks., on a mount, vert, a dragon, rampant, ar., supporting a cross pattée, or. Pl. 82, cr. 10, (cross, pl. 141.)

BANKS, Yorks., an eagle's head, couped, ar. Pl. 100, cr. 10.

BANKS, Middx., a blackamoor's head, affrontée, couped at shoulders, ppr., in ears, ear-rings, or, on head, a chapeau, gu., turned up, erm. Pl. 38, cr. 13.

BANKS, Dors., a blackamoor's head, affrontée, couped at shoulders, ppr., in ears, ear-rings, or, on head, a chapeau, gu., turned up, erm., (charged with a crescent, issuing therefrom, a fleur-de-lis, or.) Pl. 38, cr. 13.

BANKS, Aylesford, Kent, a dragon's head, erased, ar. Pl. 107, cr. 10.

BANKS, Lond., an arm, in armour, embowed, ar., garnished, or, out of clouds, ppr., in hand, a falchion, ar., hilt and pommel, or, on falchion, a chaplet, vert. Pl. 30, cr. 6, (chaplet, pl. 128, fig. 16.)

BANNATYNE, Sco., a demi-griffin. Pl. 18, cr. 6.

BANNATYNE of Corhouse, a demi-griffin, in dexter a sword, erect, all ppr. *Nec cito, nec tarde.* Pl. 49, cr. 4.

BANNATYNE, Sco., a griffin's head, erased. Pl. 48, cr. 6.

BANNATYNE of Newhall, a demi-griffin, in dexter a sword. *Dum spiro spero.* Pl. 49, cr. 4.

BANNATYNE of Kames, a demi-griffin, in dexter a sword. *Nec cito, nec tarde.* Pl. 49, cr. 4.

BANNER, Lond., an arm, in armour, embowed, in hand, ppr., a banner, gu., fringe and staff, ar., charged with a fleur-de-lis, or. Pl. 6, cr. 5, (fleur-de-lis, pl. 141.)

BANNER, Lond., a demi-wolf, ppr., ducally gorged and chained, or, between paws a mullet of six points, gold. Pl. 65, cr. 4.

BANNERMAN, Bart., Sco., a demi-man, in armour, dexter grasping a sword, all ppr. *Pro patria.* Pl. 23, cr. 4.

BANNERMAN, Edinr., same crest and motto.

BANNERMAN, Elsick, a demi-priest, vested, ppr., in the act of prayer. Pl. 90, cr. 5.

BANNERMAN, Elsick, Sco., a demi-man, in armour, grasping in dexter a sword, ppr. Pl. 23, cr. 4.

BANNESTER, and BANNISTER, an arm, in armour, couped, in fess, hand grasping a scimitar, ar., in pale, enfiled with a boar's head, couped, ppr. Pl. 107, cr. 15, (head, pl. 48, cr. 2.)

BANNING, Lond., (on a mount, vert,) an ostrich, ar., in mouth a key, or. Pl. 16, cr. 2.

BANTRY, Earl of, Viscount and Baron, and Viscount Bearhaven, (White,) Iri., an ostrich, ar., beaked and legged, or. *The noblest motive is the public good.* Pl. 16, cr. 2, (without horse-shoe or gorging.)

BANWORTH, on a ducal coronet, a griffin, sejant, resting dexter on an escutcheon. Pl. 42, cr. 8.

BAPTISTA, Castile, out of a ducal coronet, or, a dragon's head, vert, in flames of fire, ppr. Pl. 93, cr. 15.

BAPTIST-BROWNE, Italy, a dragon's head between wings, sa., (gorged with a bar-gemelle, or,) dexter ear, gu., sinister, ar., wings purfled, gold. Pl. 105, cr. 11.

BARATTY, an eagle, regardant, wings expanded, in dexter a sword. Pl. 87, cr. 5.

BARBAN, or BARBON, a leopard's head and neck, ppr. Pl. 92, cr. 13.

BARBE, ST., Lymington, Hants., a wyvern, sa., Pl. 63, cr. 13.

BARBER, Sco., in dexter hand a cross crosslet, fitched, gu. Pl. 99, cr. 1.

BARBER, Sco., in dexter hand a cross pattée, fitched, gu. Pl. 99, cr. 15.

BARBER, Herts., out of a ducal coronet, or, a bull's head, per pale, ar. and gu. Pl. 43, cr. 9.

BARBER, out of a ducal coronet, a bull's head, gu. Pl. 43, cr. 9.

BARBER, Suff., out of a ducal coronet, gu., a bull's head, ar. Pl. 43, cr. 9.

BARBERIE, or BARBERRIE, in dexter hand an arrow, point downward, all ppr. *Suivez-raison.* Pl. 43, cr. 13.

BARBON, Lond., a leopard's head, issuing, ar., spotted, sa. Pl. 92, cr. 13.

BARBOR, on a staff raguly, in fess, an eagle, displayed, with two heads, az., ducally crowned, or, inside of legs and wings, or. Pl. 5, cr. 8; pl. 63, cr. 2.

BARBOUR, Staffs., a passion cross on three grieces, gu. *Nihilo nisi cruce.* Pl. 49, cr. 2.

BARBY, Devons. and Northamp., a heraldic tiger, statant, ar., (attired with four horns, turned round like those of a ram, or.) Pl. 7, cr. 5.

BARCLAY, Sir ROBERT S., Bart., of Pierston, a sword, in pale, ar., hilt and pommel, or. *Crux Christi nostra corona.* Pl. 105, cr. 1.

BARCLAY, Lond., same crest and motto.

BARCLAY, Sco., a dove, in mouth an olive-branch, ppr. *Cedant arma.* Pl. 48, cr. 15.

BARCLAY, Sco., in hand a dagger, in pale, ppr. *Crux Christi nostra corona.* Pl. 23, cr. 15.

BARCLAY, an arm, couped and embowed, resting elbow on wreath, in hand three ears of wheat, all ppr. Pl. 89, cr. 4.

BARCLAY, a demi-griffin, regardant, az., supporting a flag, erect, charged with a crescent. Pl. 46, cr. 1.

BARCLAY of Johnston, Sco., the sun out of a cloud, ppr. *Servabit me semper Jehovah.* Pl. 67, cr. 9.

BARCLAY, Sco., a mitre, ppr. *In cruce spero.* Pl. 12, cr. 10.

BARCLAY, CHARLES, Esq., of Bury Hill, Dorking, Surr., same crest and motto.

BARCLAY-ALLARDICE, ROBERT, Esq., of Allardice, Kincardine. For *Allardice*, a naked arm from middle, in hand a scimitar, all ppr. *In the defence of the distressed.* Pl. 29, cr. 8.

BARCLAY, THOMAS-BROCKHURST, Esq., of Wavertree Lodge, near Liverpool, a cross pattée, gu., surmounted by a Moorish crown, or. *Mieux être que paroître.* Pl. 15, cr. 8, (crown, pl. 128, fig. 2.)

BARCLAY, Burford Lodge, Surr., a cross pattée, gu., ensigned by an eastern crown, or. Pl. 15, cr. 8, (crown, pl. 128, fig. 2.)

BARCLAY of Touch, Sco., a cross pattée, gu. *Crux salutim confert.* Pl. 15, cr. 8.

BARCLAY, Balmakenan, Sco., a cross pattée, gu. *Sola cruce salus.* Pl. 15, cr. 8.

BARCROFT, Worc., a wolf, rampant, gu. Pl. 10, cr. 3.

c

BARD, Caversfield, Bucks., in lion's gamb, couped and erect, or, a horse's leg, erased, sa. *Pl.* 11, *cr.* 15.

BARDIN, Dublin, a demi-youth, ppr., (over shoulder a broken axe.) *Pl.* 122, *cr.* 1.

BARDOLFE, or BARDOLPH, out of a ducal coronet, or, a dragon's head, gold, wings expanded, gu. *Pl.* 59, *cr.* 14.

BARDOLPH, Lond., out of a mural coronet, gu., a dragon's head, between wings, of the last, each charged with a mascle, ar. *Pl.* 101, *cr.* 4, (wings, *pl.* 105, *cr.* 11.)

BARDWELL, an arm, in armour, in hand a broken spear, pieces in saltier. *Pl.* 88, *cr.* 4.

BARE, Iri., a wolf's head, sa. *Pl.* 14, *cr.* 6.

BARENTINE, or BARRENTINE, an eagle, displayed, ar., between attires and over scalp of a stag, or. *Pl.* 48, *cr.* 11, (attires, *pl.* 33, *cr.* 15.)

BARETT, a demi-leopard, gardant, ppr. *Pl.* 77, *cr.* 1, (without anchor.)

BAREU, or BAREW, a holly-branch, vert. *Pl.* 99, *cr.* 6.

BARFOOT, or BARFORD, out of a ducal coronet, an arm from elbow, in armour, hand grasping a sword, in bend sinister, ppr. *Pl.* 63, *cr.* 5, (coronet, *pl.* 128, *fig.* 3.)

BARFOOT, Eng., a stag, statant, gorged with a ducal coronet. *Pl.* 68, *cr.* 2, (coronet, *pl.* 128, *fig.* 3.)

BARFORD, or BERFORD, Ruts., a bear, passant, sa. *Pl.* 61, *cr.* 5.

BARGRAVE, or BARGROVE, Kent, (on a mount, vert,) a pheon, gu., between two laurel-branches, of the first. *Pl.* 56, *cr.* 15, (branches, *pl.* 79, *cr.* 14.)

BARHAM, Baron, (Noel), a buck at gaze, ar., attired, or. *Tout bien ou rien.* *Pl.* 81, *cr.* 8.

BARHAM, or BRAHAM, Suff. and Surr., a wolf's head, ar. *Pl.* 14, *cr.* 6.

BARHAM, Staines, Middx., a stork among bullrushes, all ppr. *Pl.* 124, *cr.* 1.

BARING, Bart., Larkbeer, Devons., a mullet, erminois, between wings, ar. *Pl.* 1, *cr.* 15.

BARING, Eng., a dexter arm, in armour, in hand a caltrap, all ppr. *Pl.* 22, *cr.* 4.

BARING, Baron, Ashburton. *See* ASHBURTON.

BARKAS, or BARCAS, Newcastle, an arm, in hand a roll of bark, ppr. *Fari quæ sentiat.* *Pl.* 27, *cr.* 4.

BARKE, an arm, from shoulder, in hand a spade, ppr. *Pl.* 89, *cr.* 6.

BARKELEY, Somers., a unicorn, (statant,) gu., armed, or. *Pl.* 106, *cr.* 3, (without gorging or line.)

BARKELEY, a mitre, gu., charged with a cheveron, between ten crosses formée, ar. *Pl.* 12, *cr.* 10, (cross, *pl.* 141.)

BARKELEY, Okenbury, Cornw., on a mount, vert, a stag, lodged, ppr. *Pl.* 22, *cr.* 5.

BARKEMAN, Lond., two arms, in armour, embowed, or, between hands, ppr., a bundle of arrows, ar., banded, gu. *Pl.* 124, *cr.* 2.

BARKER, Bart., Bocking Hall, Ess., a bear, sejant, or, (collared, sa.) *Pl.* 1, *cr.* 1.

BARKER, Ipswich, Suff., same crest.

BARKER, PONSONBY-WILLIAM, Esq., of Kilcooly Abbey, co. Tipperary: 1. For *Barker*, a bear, sejant, or, (collared, sa.) *Pl.* 1, *cr.* 1. 2. For *Ponsonby*, in a ducal coronet, az., three arrows, one in pale and two in saltier, points downward, enveloped with a snake, ppr. *Pl.* 86, *cr.* 12.

BARKER-RAYMOND, JOHN-RAYMOND, Esq., of Fairford Park, Glouc.: 1. For *Barker*, on a rock, ar., a hawk, close, or. *Pl.* 99, *cr.* 14. 2. Out of a mural coronet, a demi-eagle, displayed. *Virtus tutissima cassis.* *Pl.* 33, *cr.* 5.

BARKER, Newbury, a bear's head, erased, per pale, or and az., muzzled, of the first, between wings, dexter, az., sinister, gold. *Pl.* 44, *cr.* 5.

BARKER, a bear's head, sa., muzzled, or. *Pl.* 111, *cr.* 4.

BARKER, Wollerton, Salop, on a rock, ar., a hawk, close, or. *Pl.* 99, *cr.* 14.

BARKER, Hurst., Berks., and Warw., a naked boy, ppr., holding an arrow. *Pl.* 17, *cr.* 5.

BARKER, Berks., a naked man, holding a spear, in pale, ppr.

BARKER, Berks., a demi-moor, ppr., in dexter an arrow, or, feathered and headed, ar., (on sinister arm a shield, gold, over his shoulder a sash, gu.) *Pl.* 119, *cr.* 2.

BARKER, Chelsum, Bucks., a turtle-dove, ppr., (in mouth a rose, gu., stalked and leaved, vert.) *Pl.* 48, *cr.* 15.

BARKER, Ipswich, Suff., a greyhound, sejant, ar., (collared, ringed, and lined, or, line held by hind dexter.) *Pl.* 66, *cr.* 15.

BARKER, Bockenhall, Ess., an ostrich-head, (erased,) or, in mouth a horse-shoe, ar. *Pl.* 28, *cr.* 13, (without wings.)

BARKER, Middx., Kent, and Surr., out of a ducal coronet, or, an eagle, displayed, sa., beaked and legged, gu. *Pl.* 9, *cr.* 6.

BARKER, Norf., a bear's head, erased, gu., muzzled, or. *Pl.* 71, *cr.* 6.

BARKER, Holbeach, Norf., out of a ducal coronet, or, a griffin's head, ppr. *Pl.* 54, *cr.* 14.

BARKESWORTH, or BARKSWORTH, Yorks., out of a ducal coronet, two arms, dexter and sinister, vested, embowed, in each hand an ostrich-feather. *Pl.* 45, *cr.* 2.

BARKHAM, an arm, couped at shoulder, in a maunch, embowed, in fess, elbow on the wreath. *Pl.* 8, *cr.* 11.

BARKHAM, Lond., two arms, in armour, embowed, ppr., garnished, or, in hands a sheaf of arrows, or, feathered, ar., banded *Pl.* 124. *cr.* 2.

BARKSTEADE, Lond., out of a ducal coronet, or, an arm, in armour, embowed, ppr., grasping a sword, ar., hilt and pommel, gold. *Pl.* 115, *cr.* 14, (coronet, *pl.* 128, *fig.* 3.)

BARLANDE, a lion, rampant, gu., supporting a garb., ppr. *Pl.* 63, *cr.* 14.

BARLAY, or BARLEY, a boar's head, or, tusked, az., charged on breast with a mullet. *Pl.* 44, *cr.* 6.

BARLEY, Lond., a dexter arm, vested, charged with a fess vair, cottised, cuff, ar., in hand, ppr., a staff, in pale. *Pl.* 18, *cr.* 1.

BARLEY, a demi-stag, (per pale, charged with three bars wavy, counterchanged.) *Pl.* 55, *cr.* 9, (without rose.)

BARLEY, Derbs., a boar's head, erased, or, in mouth a quatrefoil, az. *Pl.* 16, *cr.* 11, (quatrefoil, *pl.* 141.)

BARLOSS, a cock, or, combed, legged, and wattled, gu. *Pl.* 67, *cr.* 14.

BARLOW, Sheffield, on Mercury's cap, or, wings, ar., an eagle's head, erased, ppr., collared, erm. *Pl.* 124, *cr.* 3.

BARLOW, Sir GEORGE-HILARE, Bart., East Indies, out of an eastern coronet, or, a demi-lion, ar., in paws a cross crosslet, fitched, az. *Sis pius in primo. Pl.* 119, *cr.* 3, (coronet, *pl.* 128, *fig.* 2.)

BARLOW, a spread eagle's head, couped at neck, ppr.

BARLOW, Slebege, Pembrokeshire, a demi-lion, ar., in dexter a cross crosslet, fitched, sa. *Pl.* 65, *cr.* 6.

BARLOW, an eagle's head, erased, ppr., in beak an escallop. *Pl.* 22, *cr.* 1, (escallop, *pl.* 141.)

BARLOW, Somers., two eagles' heads, erased, ar. *Pl.* 94, *cr.* 12.

BARLOW, a demi-lion, rampant, gardant, ar., (collared, gu., thereon three bezants, between paws a cross moline, gu., charged with a bezant.) *Pl.* 35, *cr.* 4.

BARNABY, a demi-moor, ppr., in dexter a rose, gu. *Pl.* 35, *cr.* 12.

BARNABY, a boar's head, erased, (per fess, nebulée, sa. and or.) *Pl.* 16, *cr.* 11.

BARNABY, a demi-greyhound, gu., (between paws a branch of laurel, ppr.) *Pl.* 6, *cr.* 9.

BARNABY, Worc., a lion, sejant, (gardant,) sa. *Pl.* 21, *cr.* 3, (without collar or line.)

BARNABY, a lion, couchant, gardant, sa. *Pl.* 101, *cr.* 8.

BARNABY, Colchester, Ess., a demi-greyhound, gu., (collared and ringed, ar., holding a branch of laurel, vert.) *Pl.* 48, *cr.* 3.

BARNABY, Worc., an escallop, sa. *Pl.* 117, *cr.* 4.

BARNABY, Salop, a leopard, couchant, sa. *Pl.* 111, *cr.* 11.

BARNACK, or BARNAKE, a bear's head, sa., muzzled, or, between wings, gold. *Pl.* 44, *cr.* 5.

BARNARD, Norf. and Yorks., a demi-lion, rampant, ar., charged on shoulder with a mullet within an annulet, in paws a snake, entwined, az. *Pl.* 124, *cr.* 5.

BARNARD, HENRY-GEE, Esq., of Cave Castle, Yorks. : 1. For *Barnard*, a bear, rampant, sa., muzzled, or. *Pl.* 1, *cr.* 1. 2. For *Boldero*, a greyhound, current. *Pl.* 28, *cr.* 7.

BARNARD, THOMAS, Esq., of Bartlow, Camb., a demi-bear, rampant, sa., muzzled, or. *Pl.* 104, *cr.* 10.

BARNARD, Yorks., same crest.

BARNARD, Lond., out of a ducal coronet, or, a demi-bear, rampant, sa., muzzled, or. *Pl.* 56, *cr.* 2.

BARNARD, Linc., a dragon's head, erased, ar., collared, (and lined, or, gorged with three bars, gu.) *Pl.* 107, *cr.* 10.

BARNARD, Lond., an escallop, ar. *Pl.* 117, *cr.* 4.

BARNARDISTON, NATHANIEL-CLARKE, Esq., of The Ryes, near Sudbury, an ass's head, ar. *Pl.* 91, *cr.* 7.

BARNARDISTON, Kiddington, Suff., an ass's head, ar. *Je trouve bien. Pl.* 91, *cr.* 7.

BARNARDISTON, Great Cotes, Linc., among rushes, ppr., a stork, or. *Pl.* 124, *cr.* 1.

BARNBY, Yorks., a bear's head, couped, sa., muzzled, or. *Pl.* 111, *cr.* 4.

BARNE, FREDERICK, Esq., of Dunwich and Sotterley Park, Suff., and May Place, Kent, an eagle, displayed, sa. *Nec timide, nec temere. Pl.* 48, *cr.* 11.

BARNE, Lond., out of a ducal coronet, on a mount, vert, a stag, statant, ppr. *Pl.* 19, *cr.* 14.

BARNEBY, JOHN HABINGTON, Esq., of Brockhampton, Heref., a lion, couchant, gardant, sa. *Virtute non vi. Pl.* 101, *cr.* 8.

BARNEBY, Heref., a lion, couchant, gardant, purfled, or. *Pl.* 101, *cr.* 8.

BARNELL - PEGGE : 1. For *Barnell*, a lion's gamb, erect and erased, sa., (in paw a bunch of violets, ppr.) *Pl.* 60, *cr.* 14. 2. For *Pegge*, the sun in splendour, rays alternately, sa., or, and ar. *Pl.* 68, *cr.* 14.

BARNES, Berks., a demi-unicorn, erm., horned, collared, (and lined,) or. *Pl.* 21, *cr.* 1.

BARNES, a demi-lion, or. *Pl.* 67, *cr.* 10.

BARNES, a demi-greyhound, ppr., (in paws a garb, or.) *Pl.* 48, *cr.* 3.

BARNES, out of a cloud, ppr., issuing rays, in pale, or, an arm erect, vested, gold, in hand a broken sword, ar., hilt, of the third. *Pl.* 44, *cr.* 4.

BARNES, Lond., in rushes, ppr., a duck, ar. *Pl.* 34, *cr.* 6.

BARNES, a falcon, wings expanded, ar., ducally gorged, beaked, and legged, or. *Pl.* 61, *cr.* 12.

BARNES, Herts. and Lanc., an etoile, pierced, or. *Pl.* 45, *cr.* 1.

BARNES, Kent, on a mount, vert, a falcon, wings expanded, ar., ducally gorged, beaked, and legged, or. *Pl.* 61, *cr.* 12.

BARNES, Cambs., a leopard, passant, ar., spotted, sa., (collared and lined, or.) *Pl.* 86, *cr.* 2.

BARNES, Eng., a demi-savage, wreathed about head and middle, holding a club, in pale, all ppr. *Pl.* 87, *cr.* 13.

BARNESDALE, out of rays, or, a crane's head, ar., beaked, gu. *Pl.* 20, *cr.* 9, (rays, *pl.* 116, *cr.* 13.)

BARNESFATHER, Sco., a boar's head, couped. *Pl.* 48, *cr.* 2.

BARNESLEY, Staffs. and Surr., an old man's head, affrontée, couped at breast, ppr., charged with a mullet for difference. *Pl.* 31, *cr.* 2, (mullet, *pl.* 141.)

BARNET, a holly-branch, ppr. *Pl.* 99, *cr.* 6.

BARNETT, out of a ducal coronet, or, a demi-bear, rampant, ar., muzzled, sa. *Pl.* 56, *cr.* 2.

BARNETT, CHARLES, Esq., of Stratton Park, Biggleswade, Beds., a trefoil. *Pl.* 82, *cr.* 1.

BARNEVELT, a demi-buck, gu. *Pl.* 55, *cr.* 9, (without rose.)

BARNEWALL, Viscount and Baron, and a Bart., Iri., from a plume of ostrich-feathers, or, gu., az., vert, and ar., a falcon, rising, of the last. *Malo mori quam fœdari. Pl.* 54, *cr.* 8.

BARNAWELL, Baron Trimlestown, Iri., same crest and motto.

BARNEWELL, or BARNAWELLE, Stamford, Linc.; and Cranesley, Northamp.; a boar's head, erased, ar., gorged with a collar, (embattled, gu., charged with three bezants, in front a double ring, or.) *Pl.* 36, *cr.* 9.

BARNEWELL, Iri., an arm, from elbow, vested, in hand two branches of laurel, in orle, with martlet perched between. *Pl.* 44, *cr.* 13.

BARNEWELL, a wolf's head, erased, (gorged with three bezants, in front a double ring, or.) *Pl.* 14, *cr.* 6.

BARNEY, or BERNEY, Norf., a garb, or. *Pl.* 48, *cr.* 10.
BARNEY, in hand, in armour, a pheon, in pale, ppr. *Pl.* 123, *cr.* 12.
BARNEY, Park Hall, Norf., on a wreath a plume of seven feathers, az. and gu., four at bottom, three at top. *Pl.* 114, *cr.* 8, (without coronet or bottom row.)
BARNFIELD, Newport, Salop; and Devons. ; a lion's head, erased, sa., ducally crowned, gu. *Pl.* 90, *cr.* 4, (without charge.)
BARNHAM, a crescent, gu. between two branches of laurel, in orle, ppr. *Pl.* 82, *cr.* 13.
BARNHAM, Kent, a dragon's head, pellettée, ar., between wings, bezantée, sa. *Pl.* 105, *cr.* 11, (pellet and bezant, *pl*, 141.)
BARNS, Glasgow, a garb, or. *Peace and plenty.* *Pl.* 48, *cr.* 10.
BARNS, a torteau, sa. *Pl.* 7, *cr.* 6.
BARNSLEY, a dragon, passant, ar., (charged on breast with a rose, gu.) *Pl.* 90, *cr.* 10.
BARNWELL, The Rev. CHARLES-BARNWELL, of Mileham Hall, Norf., a wolf's head, erased, ar., (gorged with collar, embattled, gu., studded, or, chained, gold.) *Loyal au mort.* *Pl.* 14, *cr.* 6.
BARNWELL, on a mount, vert, a wolf, statant, regardant, ppr.
BAROBY, a squirrel, sejant, gu., cracking a nut, ppr., (charged on body with a cheveron, or.) *Pl.* 16, *cr.* 9.
BARON, a demi-lion, rampant, ppr. *Pl.* 67, *cr.* 10.
BARON, a demi-unicorn, erm., armed, sa., crined, collared, (and chained,) or. *Pl.* 21, *cr.* 1.
BARON of Bradwell and Skirnby, Ess., a garb, vert, eared, or. *Pl.* 48, *cr.* 10.
BARON of Preston, Sco., a demi-eagle, displayed, sa. *Ipse amicus.* *Pl.* 22, *cr.* 11.
BARON, Cornw., a talbot's head, couped, or. *Pl.* 123, *cr.* 15.
BARON, or BARRON, Sco., on a mount, vert, a pyramid, ppr., environed with ivy, of the first. *Pl.* 8, *cr.* 10.
BARONSDALE, Lond., out of an antique crown, or, a stork's head, ar., beaked, gu. *Pl.* 79, *cr.* 12, (head, *pl.* 32, *cr.* 5.)
BAROUGH, or BARROW, a lion, passant, az., (resting dexter on a ball, or.) *Pl.* 48, *cr.* 8.
BARR, a branch of laurel, fructed, ppr. *Pl.* 123, *cr.* 5.
BARR, a lion's head, erased, gu., collared, or. *Fortitudine.* *Pl.* 7, *cr.* 10.
BARR, an arm, couped at shoulder, vested, gu., in fess, elbow on wreath, in hand a bow, ppr. *Pl.* 51, *cr.* 5.
BARR, a demi-savage, head and loins, wreathed. *Pl.* 87, *cr.* 13, (without club.)
BARRAT, or BARRATT, a galley, oars, in saltier, sa., flags, gu. *Pl.* 77, *cr.* 11.
BARRATT, a wyvern, ppr., the wing, barry of four, ar. and gu., per pale, counterchanged, (collared, of the third, and chained, or.) *Pl.* 63, *cr.* 13.
BARRATT, a wyvern, ppr., (collared, gu., chained, or.) *Pl.* 63, *cr.* 13.
BARRE, or BARREY, an arm, (in armour,) couped at elbow, in fess, in hand a sword, in pale, ensigned with a Saracen's head, affrontée. *Pl.* 97, *cr.* 3.

BARREL, or BARRELL, Heref. and Kent, a talbot's head, couped, ar., eared, gu. *Pl.* 123, *cr.* 15.
BARRET, a demi-unicorn, ar., collared, sa. *Pl.* 21, *cr.* 1.
BARRETT, a wyvern, (collared and lined.) *Pl.* 63, *cr.* 13.
BARRETT, Castle Barrett, Cork, a human heart, or, between wings, az., semée of etoiles. *Pl.* 39, *cr.* 7, (etoiles, *pl.* 141.)
BARRETT, Bellhouse, Aveley, Ess., a hydra with seven heads, wings addorsed, vert, scaled, or. *Pl.* 38, *cr.* 5.
BARRETT, on a globe, a hawk, wings expanded, ppr. *Pl.* 34, *cr.* 2.
BARRETT, Cambs., a griffin, segreant, (regardant,) or, beaked, legged, and winged, gu. *Pl.* 67, *cr.* 13.
BARRETT, Suff., a helmet, ar., garnished and plumed with feathers, or. *Pl.* 8, *cr.* 12.
BARRETT, D.D., Attleborough, Norf., a wyvern, erm., (collared and chained, sa., charged on neck with an escallop, of the last,) wings displayed, barry of four, per pale, counterchanged, ar. and gu. *Pl.* 63, *cr.* 13.
BARRETT, JOHN BASIL, Esq., of Milton House, Berks., a wyvern, wings erect, or, (collared and chained, az.) *Honor, virtus, probitas.* *Pl.* 63, *cr.* 13.
BARRETT, Suff., a demi-greyhound, ar., (collared and lined, sa.) *Pl.* 48, *cr.* 3.
BARRETT, Heref., a lion, rampant, (or, between paws an escallop, sa.) *Pl.* 67, *cr.* 5.
BARRETT, Lea Priory, Kent, a lion, couchant, ar., (dexter resting on a mullet, sa.) *Pl.* 101, *cr.* 8.
BARRETT, Shortney, Notts., a nag's head, erased, per pale, gu. and az., (gorged with two bars, ar.) *Pl.* 46, *cr.* 4.
BARRETT, Warw., a griffin, segreant, (regardant,) gu., wings elevated, or. *Pl.* 67, *cr.* 13.
BARRETTO, Lond., out of a count's coronet, a demi-tiger, ppr., collared, with three barrulets, and holding a star pagoda, also ppr.
BARRIE, Sco., a demi-otter, sa. *Pl.* 9, *cr.* 9.
BARRIFFE. *See* BERIFFE.
BARRIFF, Northamp., on a mount, vert, a beaver, passant, ppr., gorged with a plain collar and ring, or. *Pl.* 3, *cr.* 11.
BARRINGTON, Bart., Barrington Hall, Ess. ; and Swaynton, Isle of Wight, Hants. ; a hermit's bust, with cowl, vested, paly, ar. and gu. *Ung durant ma vie.* *Pl.* 51, *cr.* 4.
BARRINGTON, Sir FITZWILLIAM, Bart., Barrington Hall, Ess., a capuchin friar, affrontée, ppr., couped below shoulders, vested, paly of six, ar. and gu., on head a cap, or. *Tont ung durant ma vie.* *Pl.* 31, *cr.* 2.
BARRINGTON, Viscount and Baron, Iri., (Barrington;) a capuchin friar, couped at breast, black hair, vested, paly of six, ar. and gu., on head a cap, or cowl, hanging behind, of the last. *Honesta quam splendida.* *Pl.* 51, *cr.* 4.
BARRINGTON, Ess., same crest and motto.
BARRINGTON, Bart., Iri., out of a vallery crown, or, a hermit's bust, with cowl, vested, paly of six, ar. and gu. *Ung durant ma vie.* *Pl.* 51, *cr.* 4, (crown, *pl.* 128, *fig.* 17.)
BARRITT, Jamaica, a talbot's head, per fess, ar. and erm., collared, or, eared, sa. *Pl.* 2, *cr.* 15.
BARRON, Norf., a garb, ppr. *Pl.* 48, *cr.* 10.

BARRON, an eagle, regardant, wings expanded, in dexter a sword, all ppr. *Pl.* 87, *cr.* 5.
BARRON of Belmont House, Kilkenny; and Glenanra, Waterford, Iri.; a boar, passant, az. *Fortuna audaces juvat. Pl.* 48, *cr.* 14.
BARRON, or BARON, Bart., Iri., same crest and motto.
BARRON, PIERSE-MARCUS, Esq., of Glenview and Killoen, co. Waterford, on a chapeau, ppr., a boar, passant, az. *Audaces fortuna juvat. Pl.* 22, *cr.* 8.
BARROTT, a hydra with seven heads, wings addorsed, vert, scaled, or. *Pl.* 38, *cr.* 5.
BARROW, Northamp., a demi-boar, rampant, or, (charged with three billets, between two bendlets, sa.) *Pl.* 20, *cr.* 5.
BARROW, Suff., a hind's head, ar. *Pl.* 21, *cr.* 9.
BARROW, Bart., Lanc., on a mount, vert, a squirrel, sejant, cracking a nut, all ppr., (charged on shoulder with an anchor.) *Pl.* 16, *cr.* 9.
BARROW, Winthorpe, Norf., a deer's head, couped, ar. *Pl.* 91, *cr.* 14.
BARROW, a horse's head, (charged with three bezants, or.) *Pl.* 92, *cr.* 1.
BARROW, Cambs., an ostrich-head, (erased, ar., in beak a key, or.) *Pl.* 50, *cr.* 1, (without feathers.)
BARROW, Glouc., an Amazonian woman, ppr.
BARROW, WILLIAM HODGSON, Esq., of Southwell, Linc., on a perch, ppr., a squirrel, sejant, or, collared, (and chained, cracking a nut, all ppr.) *Non frustra. Pl.* 85, *cr.* 3.
BARROWE, a demi-lion, rampant, ar., in dexter a cross crosslet, fitched, sa. *Pl.* 65, *cr.* 6.
BARROWMAN, Sco., a demi-huntsman, shooting, ppr. *Pl.* 51, *cr.* 6.
BARRY, Earl, Viscount and Baron, out of a castle, ar., a wolf's head, sa. *Poussez en avant. Pl.* 101, *cr.* 1, (head, *pl.* 8, *cr.* 4.)
BARRY, a lion's head, erased, gu., collared, or. *Fortitudine. Pl.* 42, *cr.* 14.
BARRY, Winscot, Devons., a wolf's head, erased, sa. *Pl.* 14, *cr.* 6.
BARRY, Devons, a wolf's head, sa., (charged with a crescent, or.) *Pl.* 14, *cr.* 6.
BARRY, JAMES, Esq., of Ballyclough, co. Cork, out of a castle, ar., a wolf's head, sa. *Boutez en avant. Pl.* 101, *cr.* 1, (head, *pl.* 8, *cr.* 4.)
BARRY, PENDOCK-BARRY, Esq., of Roclaveston Manor, Notts., the embattlement of a tower, gu., (charged with three roses, in fess, ar.) *A rege et victoriâ. Pl.* 12, *cr.* 5.
BARRY-SMITH, JAMES HUGH, Esq., of Marbury Hall, Chesh.; and Foaty Island, co. Cork; out of a castle, ar., a wolf's head, sa. *Boutez en avant. Pl.* 101, *cr.* 1, (head, *pl.* 8, *cr.* 4.)
BARRY, Sir WALTER, Bart., Iri., same crest and motto.
BARRY-GARRETT-STANDISH of Lemlara, Cork, Iri., out of a castle, ar., a wolf's head, sa. *Boutez en avant. Pl.* 101, *cr.* 1, (head, *pl.* 8, *cr.* 4.)
BARSANE, or BARTANE, Edinr., a raven, rising, ppr. *His securitas. Pl.* 50, *cr.* 5.
BARSHAM, Norf., a garb, in fess. *Pl.* 12, *cr.* 15.
BARSTOW, Yorks., a horse's head, couped, ar. *Pl.* 92, *cr.* 1.
BARTAN, BARTANE, or BARTAIN, Sco., a tent, az., flag, gu. *Pl.* 111, *cr.* 14.
BARTELOTT, a peacock, ar. *Pl.* 54, *cr.* 13.
BARTELOTT-SMYTH, Suss., a swan, couchant, ar., wings expanded. *Pl.* 114, *cr.* 3.

BARTLET, or BARTLETT, Stopham, Suss.; and Suff.; a swan, couchant, ar., wings expanded and addorsed. *Pl.* 114, *cr.* 3.
BARTLET, Lond., out of a ducal coronet, or, two demi-dragons, without wings, vert. *Pl.* 6, *cr.* 4.
BARTLEY, a lion, passant, tail extended, ppr. *Pl.* 118, *cr.* 10.
BARTOLOMEW, or BARTHOLEMEW, Rochester, a demi-goat, ar., (gorged with a chaplet of laurel, vert.) *Pl.* 90, *cr.* 12.
BARTON, Kent, an owl, ppr. *Pl.* 27, *cr.* 9.
BARTON, Lanc., an acorn, or, leaved, vert. *Pl.* 81, *cr.* 7.
BARTON, a wolf's head, erased, erm. *Pl.* 14, *cr.* 6.
BARTON, a wolf's head, erased, or. *Pl.* 14, *cr.* 6.
BARTON of Barton, Lanc., a boar's head, couped, gu. *Pl.* 48, *cr.* 2.
BARTON, Swithills, Manchester, and Lanc., an oak-branch, vert, acorned, or. *Pl.* 32, *cr.* 13.
BARTON, Sco. *See* BARTAN.
BARTON, an owl, ar., (ducally gorged, or.) *Pl.* 27, *cr.* 9.
BARTON, a dragon's head, couped, or, (crowned, gold.) *Pl.* 87, *cr.* 12.
BARTON, THOMAS-EDWARD-WALTER, Esq., of Threxton House, near Watton, Norf., a griffin's head, erased, ppr. *Fortis est veritas. Pl.* 48, *cr.* 6.
BARTON, Norf., a dragon's head, couped, or. *Pl.* 87, *cr.* 12.
BARTON, JOHN HOPE, Esq., of Stapleton Park, near Pontefract, an acorn, or, leaved, vert. *Cresitur cultu. Pl.* 81, *cr.* 7.
BARTON, WILLIAM, Esq., of Grove, near Fethard, co. Tipperary, a boar's head, gu. *Quod cro spero*—ancient motto—*Vis fortibus armæ. Pl.* 48, *cr.* 2.
BARTON, FOLLIOT-WARREN, Esq., of Clonelly, co. Fermanagh, Iri., same crest and motto.
BARTON, SAMUEL-WILLIAM, Esq., of Rochestown, Caher, co. Tipperary, same crest and motto.
BARTON, HUGH-WILLIAM, Esq., of The Waterfoot, co. Fermanagh, same crest and motto.
BARTON, NATHANIEL, Esq., of Straffan, co. Kildare, same crest. *Fide et fortitudine.*
BARTON, THOMAS-JOHNSTON, Esq., of Glendalough House, co. Wicklow, same crest. *Fide et fortitudine.*
BARTON, Edinr., a raven, rising, sa. *His securitas. Pl.* 50, *cr.* 5.
BARTRAM, Cumb., an arm, embowed, in hand a scimitar, all ppr. *Pl.* 92, *cr.* 5.
BARTRAM, Sco., out of an antique crown, or, a ram's head, ar. *J'avance. Pl.* 124, *cr.* 8.
BARTTELOT, GEORGE, Esq., of Stopham House, Petworth, Suss.: 1. A swan, couched, ar., wings expanded and addorsed. *Pl.* 114, *cr.* 3. 2. A castle, ppr. *Mature. Pl.* 123, *cr.* 14.
BARWELL, a talbot, passant. *Pl.* 120, *cr.* 8.
BARWELL, a demi-wolf, salient, erm. *Pl.* 56, *cr.* 8, (without spear.)
BARWELL, a demi-lady, in dexter a garland of laurel, ppr. *Pl.* 87, *cr.* 14.
BARWICK, Northumb., on a mount, vert, a stag, or, attired, sa. *Pl.* 50, *cr.* 6.
BARWICKE, Ess., an escarbuncle, centre, az., rays, ar. *Pl.* 51, *cr.* 10.

BARWIS, Yorks., a bear, muzzled. *Bear and forbear.* Pl. 61, cr. 5.
BARWIS, The Rev. WILLIAM-CUTHBERT, M.A., Langrigg Hall, Cumb., a bear, muzzled. *Bear and forbear.* Pl. 61, cr. 5.
BARWIS, Cumb., a hand, issuing, in bend, cutting an ostrich-feather with scimitar. Pl. 59, cr. 9.
BARZEY, Shrewsbury, a squirrel, sejant, ppr., cracking a nut, or. Pl. 16, cr. 9.
BASCEILLY, a torteau, gu., charged with a pale, indented, or. Pl. 63, cr. 7.
BASHE, Herts., and Heref., a griffin, segreant, per pale, ar. and sa., in beak a broken spear. Pl. 74, cr. 10.
BASIER, or BASIRE, in hand, ppr., a buckle, or. Pl. 38, cr. 9.
BASKENFORD, Sco., a sword and ear of wheat, bladed, in saltier, all ppr. *Armis et diligentia.* Pl. 50, cr. 4.
BASKERNILL, or BASKIRNELL, a lion's head, erased, (thrust through with an arrow.) Pl. 113, cr. 15.
BASKERVILE, Heref. and Warw., a lion's head, (pierced through mouth with a spear.) Pl. 113, cr. 15.
BASKERVILLE, Wilts., a wolf's head, erased, or, (in mouth a broken spear, gold, headed, ppr., embrued, gu.) Pl. 14, cr. 6.
BASKERVILLE, Heref. and Warw., a wolf's head, erased, ar., (in mouth an arrow, the feathers upward.) Pl. 14, cr. 6.
BASKERVILLE, Heref. and Warw., a sheaf of rosemary, ppr. Pl. 13, cr. 2.
BASKERVILLE, Chesh., a forester, vested, vert, edgings, or, over dexter shoulder a crossbow, gold, in other hand, in leash, a hound, passant, ar.
BASKERVILLE-MYNORS, THOMAS BASKERVILLE, Esq., of Clyrow Court, co. Radnor, Wel., a wolf's head, erased, ar., (in mouth a broken spear, staff, or, head, of the first, embrued, gu.) *Spero ut fidelis.* Pl. 14, cr. 6.
BASKERVILLE, HENRY, Esq., of Woolley House, parish of Bradford, Wilts.; and Crowsley Park, Henley-on-Thames, Oxon.; same crest and motto.
BASKETT, or BASKET, Dors., a demi-lion, or. Pl. 67, cr. 10.
BASKIN, Sco., same as BASKENFORD.
BASKIN, Sco., a sword and stalk of wheat, in saltier. *Armis et diligentia.* Pl. 50, cr. 4.
BASNET, on a mount, covered with long grass, an oak-tree, all ppr. Pl. 48, cr. 4.
BASNETT, an arm, in armour, embowed, hand grasping a cutlass, ppr. Pl. 81, cr. 11.
BASPOOLE, Beston, Norf., out of a ducal coronet, or, a stag's head, erm., attired, of the first, (wreathed about neck, ar. and sa., and tied behind with two bows.) Pl. 29, cr. 7.
BASQUER, Isle of Wight, Hants., out of a mural coronet, gu., a griffin's head, or. Pl. 101, cr. 6, (without gorging.)
BASS, out of a ducal coronet, two wings, ppr. Pl. 17, cr. 9.
BASSE, a demi-lion, gu., (resting dexter on an oval shield, in cartouch, or, charged with a fleur-de-lis, az.) Pl. 96, cr. 3.
BASSE, a demi-lion, gu., (resting paws on an oval shield, or.) Pl. 40, cr. 6.
BASSET, Devons., same crest and motto.

BASSET, FRANCIS, Baron de Dunstanville, of Tehidy, Cornw., a unicorn's head, couped, ar., armed and maned, or, (charged with two bars, dancettée, gu.) *Pro rege et populo.* Pl. 20, cr. 1.
BASSET, JOHN, Esq., of Tehidy, Cornw., same crest and motto.
BASSET, Devons., same crest and motto.
BASSET, and BASSETT, a griffin, segreant, sa., (semée-de-lis, or, collared and chained, gold.) Pl. 67, cr. 13.
BASSET, a unicorn's head, couped. Pl. 20, cr. 1.
BASSET, and BASSETT, Glouc., a falcon, displayed, ar. Pl. 48, cr. 11.
BASSET, a boar's head, erm., armed, or. Pl. 48, cr. 2.
BASSET, RICHARD, Esq., of Beaupré, Glam., Wel., a stag's head, cabossed, between attires a cross crosslet, fitched. *Gwell angau na chywilydd.* Pl. 36, cr. 1, (cross, pl. 141.)
BASSETT, RICHARD, Esq., of Bonvilstone House, Cardiff, same crest and motto.
BASSETT, or BASSET, Langley, Derbs., out of a ducal coronet, or, a boar's head, gu. Pl. 102, cr. 14.
BASSETT, Womberly, Devons., a unicorn's head, ar., (charged with two bars, dancettée, gu.) *Pro rege et populo.* Pl. 20, cr. 1.
BASSETT, or BASSET, a horse's head, erased. Pl. 81, cr. 6.
BASSETT, Warw., a boar's head, ar., couped, gu. Pl. 48, cr. 2.
BASSET, ARTHUR-DAVIE, Esq., of Watermouth, in the parish of Ilfracombe; and Umberleigh, near Exeter: 1. For *Basset*, a unicorn's head, couped, ar., mane, beard, and horn, or, (on neck two bars, indented, gu.) Pl. 20, cr. 1. 2. For *Davie*, on a mount, vert, a lamb, passant, ar., (in mouth a sprig of cinquefoil, gu., slipped, vert.) Pl. 101, cr. 9, (without flag.)
BASSINGBORNE, out of a ducal coronet, or, a bull's head, gu., (ducally crowned, of the first.) Pl. 43, cr. 9.
BASSINGES, three roses, gu., stalked and leaved, vert, issuing. Pl. 79, cr. 3.
BASTARD, Aslington, Norf., an elephant's head, per cheveron, or and sa., eared, of the second. Pl. 35, cr. 13.
BASTARD, an arm, in armour, embowed, in hand a dagger, ppr. Pl. 21, cr. 4.
BASTARD, EDMUND-RODNEY-POLLEXFEN, Esq., Kitley, near Yealmpton, and Buckland Court, near Ashburton, Devons., a dexter arm, in plate armour, embowed, ppr., garnished, or, hand, gauntleted, grasping a sword, in bend sinister, point downward, also ppr., hilt and pommel, of the second. *Pax potior bello.* Pl. 65, cr. 8.
BASTARD, THOMAS-HORLOCK, Esq., of Charlton Marshall, Dors., a griffin's head, (collared and armed, or.) Pl. 38, cr. 3.
BASTO, a horse's head, couped, ar. Pl. 92, cr. 1.
BATCHELOR, or BATCHELLOR, a leg, erased, above knee, ppr. Pl. 73, cr. 5.
BATE, Yorks., a stag's head, ar., attired, or, (vulned through neck with an arrow, of the second, feathered and headed, of the first.) Pl. 66, cr. 9.

BATE, a bull's head, couped, erm., armed, or. *Pl.* 120, *cr.* 7.
BATEMAN, RICHARD-THOMAS, ESQ., of Hartington Hall, Derby, out of a crescent, or, an etoile, gu., between wings, gold. *Sidus adsit amicum.* *Pl.* 124, *cr.* 11.
BATEMAN, THOMAS, Esq., of Middleton Hall, Derby, same crest.
BATEMAN, The Rev. EDMUND-HAZELRIGG, M.A., of Guilsborough, Northamp., same crest and motto.
BATEMAN, Lond., Herts., and Heref., a Muscovy duck's head, couped, between wings, erect, expanded, all ppr. *Nec prece, nec pretio.*
BATEMAN, Derbs., out of a crescent, or, an etoile, gu. *Pl.* 111, *cr.* 15.
BATEMAN, Whitechapel, Middx., out of a mural coronet, ar., an eagle, rising, (with a garland in beak, ppr.) *Pl.* 33, *cr.* 5.
BATEMAN, an increscent, ar., between wings, dexter, ar., sinister, gu. *Pl.* 62, *cr.* 4, (increscent, *pl.* 141.)
BATEMAN, JOHN, Esq., of Knypersley Hall, Stafford; and Tolson Hall, Westm.; a tower, ar., issuant, a demi-eagle, (wings elevated, sa., charged on breast with the chemical character of Mars, or, in beak a wreath of oak, ppr.) *Pl.* 112, *cr.* 4.
BATEMAN, Baron, U. K., (Bateman-Hanbury:) 1. For *Hanbury*, out of a mural coronet, sa., a demi-lion, or, in paws a battle-axe, of the first, handle, gold. *Pl.* 120, *cr.* 14. 2. For *Bateman*, a duck's head and neck, between wings, ppr. *Nec prece, nec pretio.*
BATEMAN, JOHN, Esq., of Oak Park, Killeen and Ardravale, co. Kerry, Iri., a pheasant, ppr. *Nec prece, nec pretio.* *Pl.* 82, *cr.* 12.
BATEMAN, COLTHURST, Esq., of Bartholey House, Monm., same crest and motto.
BATES, a lion's head, erased, gu. *Pl.* 81, *cr.* 4.
BATES, HENRY-WILLIAM, Esq., of Denton, Suss., an arm, in armour, embowed, in hand a truncheon. *Manu et corde.* *Pl.* 33, *cr.* 4.
BATES, NATHANIEL, Esq., Milbourne Hall, Northumb., a naked man, (in dexter a willow-wand, ppr.) *Et manu et corde.* *Pl.* 35, *cr.* 12.
BATES, Yorks., a demi-lion, rampant, in dexter a thistle, in sinister a fleur-de-lis, ppr. *Pl.* 45, *cr.* 15.
BATES, Northumb., a naked boy, (in dexter a willow-wand, ppr.) *Pl.* 17, *cr.* 5.
BATESON, Bart., Iri., of Killoguin, co. Antrim, a bat's wing, sa. *Probitas verus honos.* *Pl.* 1, *cr.* 6.
BATESON, Bart., Iri., of Belvoir, and Moria Parks, co. Down, same crest and motto.
BATH, a wolf's head, sa., in mouth a rose, slipped, ppr. *Pl.* 92, *cr.* 15.
BATH, Marquess of, Viscount Weymouth; Baron Thynne, a Bart., K.G., &c.; (Thynne;) a rein-deer, statant, or. *J'ai bonne cause.* *Pl.* 12, *cr.* 8.
BATHERNE, Penhow, Monm., out of rushes, a demi-swan, rising, ppr. *Pl.* 66, *cr.* 10.
BATHGATE, Sco., a bee, volant, ppr. *Vive ut vivas.* *Pl.* 100, *cr.* 3.
BATHURST, Bart., Leachlade, Glouc., (on a mount, vert,) a bay-horse, statant. *Pl.* 15, *cr.* 14.
BATHURST, a horse, passant. *Pl.* 15, *cr.* 14.

BATHURST, Earl and Baron, and Baron Apsley, a dexter arm, in armour, embowed, ppr., in hand a spiked club, or. *Tien ta foy.* *Pl.* 45, *cr.* 10.
BATHURST, CHARLES, Esq., of Lydney Park, Glouc., same crest and motto.
BATHURST, Lond., Kent, Hants., Suss., and Glouc., same crest.
BATHURST, Isle of Wight, a dexter arm, in armour, embowed, ppr., charged with an annulet, or. *Pl.* 97, *cr.* 1, (annulet, *pl.* 141.)
BATHURST, a tiger, (in dexter a fleur-de-lis, ppr.) *Pl.* 67, *cr.* 15.
BATLEY, Yorks., a demi-lion, rampant, gu., between paws a bezant. *Pl.* 126, *cr.* 12.
BATLEY, BATTLEY, BATTALEY, or BATTELEY, a castle, double-towered, (weeds growing round sinister tower, ppr.) *Pl.* 96, *cr.* 5, (without lion.)
BATNYMERSH, a dexter arm, in armour, in hand, ppr., a baton, sa., tipped, ar. *Pl.* 33, *cr.* 4.
BATSON, a lion, passant, gardant, ar. *Pl.* 120, *cr.* 5.
BATSON, a bat's wing, erect, ar. *Pl.* 1, *cr.* 6.
BATT, ROBERT, Esq., of Purdysburn, co. Down; and Ozier-Hill, Wexford; a crescent, ar., charged with an escallop, gu. *Virtute et valore.* *Pl.* 18, *cr.* 14, (escallop, *pl.* 141.)
BATT, Hackney, Middx., a wolf, passant, ppr. *Pl.* 46, *cr.* 6.
BATT, Kensington, Middx., a demi-lion, guttée-de-sang, (between paws a marshal's staff, in pale, or, tipped, sa.) *Pl.* 47, *cr.* 4.
BATTAYLL, or BATTAILLE, out of an antique crown, or, a dexter arm, ppr., in hand a cross crosslet, fitched, in pale, gu. *Pl.* 99, *cr.* 1, (crown, *pl.* 128, *fig.* 2.)
BATTEN, a hand, couped, in fess, charged with an eye. *Pl.* 10, *cr.* 14.
BATTEN, JOHN, Esq., of Thorn Faulcon and Yeovil, Somers.: 1. Trunk of oak-tree, couped at top, sprouting, all ppr. *Pl.* 92, *cr.* 8. 2. A sea-lion, erect, (in paws an anchor, all ppr.) *Pl.* 25, *cr.* 12.
BATTERSBEE, and BATTERSBY, a ram, passant, erm., armed, and unguled, or. *Pl.* 109, *cr.* 2.
BATTERSBY, ROBERT, Esq., M.D., of Ashgrove and Lislin, co. Cavan, a ram, passant, armed, and unguled, gold. *Ante honorem humilitas.* *Pl.* 109, *cr.* 2.
BATTERSBY, GEORGE, Esq., of Lough Bane, Collinstown, Westmeath, same crest and motto.
BATTIE, a kingfisher, ppr., chained, or.
BATTIE, Wadsworth, Yorks., a stork, (with fish in mouth, all ppr.) *Pl.* 33, *cr.* 9.
BATTIE, Wadsworth, Yorks., a kingfisher, ppr., ducally gorged and chained, or, in mouth a fish, ar.
BAUD, and BAUDE, a lion's head, gardant, erased, gu., ducally crowned, or. *Pl.* 1, *cr.* 5.
BAUDERSTONE, BAUDERSTON, BALDERSTON, and BALDERSTOUN, Sco., in dexter hand, in fess, out of a cloud, ppr., a cross pattée, fitched, az. *Pl.* 26, *cr.* 4.
BAUGH, Glouc., on a ducal coronet, or, a talbot, sejant, sa. *Pl.* 107, *cr.* 7, (coronet, *pl.* 128, *fig.* 3.)

BAUMFORD, or BAUNFORD, Donington, Linc., on a chapeau, a serpent, nowed. *Pl.* 123, *cr.* 4.

BAUNCEFORD, a lion, rampant. *Pl.* 67, *cr.* 5.

BAUSEFIELD, out of a ducal coronet, or, a griffin's head, ppr. *Pl.* 54, *cr.* 14.

BAVENT, Norf., a sheaf of six arrows, in saltier, sa., feathered, ar., bearded, or, banded, gu. *Pl.* 101, *cr.* 13, (without cap.)

BAWDE, Curringham, Ess. and Beds., a satyr's head, in profile, sa., with wings, or, tongue hanging out, gu.

BAWDEWYN, or BAWDWEN, a sceptre, in pale, or. *Pl.* 82, *cr.* 3.

BAWLE, an arm, embowed, vested, gu., cuffed, or, in hand, ppr., a branch of laurel, vert. *Pl.* 120, *cr.* 1, (laurel, *pl.* 123, *cr.* 5.)

BAWTRE, or BAWTREE, Cambs., a lion's head, erased, gu. *Pl.* 81, *cr.* 4.

BAWTRE, Yorks., a goat's head, erased, ar. *Pl.* 29, *cr.* 13.

BAXTER, a falcon, belled and jessed, or. *Virtute non verbis.* *Pl.* 67, *cr.* 3.

BAXTER, Sco., an escarbuncle, sa. *Pl.* 51, *cr.* 10.

BAXTER, Stannow, Norf., a lion's gamb, erased, or, in paw a spear, sa., head, ar., stringed and tasselled, of the first. *Pl.* 1, *cr.* 4.

BAXTER, an eagle's head, couped. *Pl.* 100, *cr.* 10.

BAY, Lond. and Hants., a dexter wing, sa., charged with an escallop, or. *Pl.* 39, *cr.* 12, (escallop, *pl.* 141.)

BAYARD, a demi-horse. *Pl.* 91, *cr.* 12, (without wings or coronet.)

BAYEN, Eng., a poplar-tree, vert. *Pl.* 95, *cr.* 2.

BAYFORD, Eng., an owl, ar. *Pl.* 27, *cr.* 9.

BAYLEE, BAILIE, or BAILEY, Eng., a demi-lady, in dexter a tower, in sinister a branch of laurel. *Pl.* 20, *cr.* 6.

BAYLEY, Eng., a boar's head, erased, ppr. *Pl.* 16, *cr.* 11.

BAYLEY, Lond., a dexter arm, embowed, vested, az., (on arm a fess, vair, in hand, ppr., a staff, or.) *Pl.* 120, *cr.* 1.

BAYLEY, Middle Temple, a demi-lion, rampant, gardant, or, (in dexter a branch, vert.) *Pl.* 35, *cr.* 4.

BAYLEY, Bart., Lond., (on a mount, vert, behind a wall, ar.,) a lion, rampant, of the second. *Pl.* 77, *cr.* 5.

BAYLEY, Eng., a griffin, sejant, erm., wings and fore-legs, or. *Pl.* 100, *cr.* 11.

BAYLEY, Hoddesdon, Herts., out of a ducal coronet, or, a nag's head, ar. *Pl.* 50, *cr.* 13.

BAYLEY, a lion, rampant, ppr. *Pl.* 67, *cr.* 5.

BAYLIE, Eng., within seven mullets, or, in orle, a cross pattée, gu. *Pl.* 33, *cr.* 10.

BAYLIS, Glouc., out of an eastern coronet, or, charged on band with auricula flower, a bay-tree, fructed, ppr.

BAYLIS, Lond., a demi-antelope, ppr., collared and buckled, or. *Pl.* 34, *cr.* 8.

BAYLOL, Sco., an increscent and decrescent, ar. *Pl.* 99, *cr.* 4.

BAYLOLL, Eng., on a mount, vert, a lion, rampant, (collared,) in dexter an arrow, all ppr. *Pl.* 59, *cr.* 5.

BAYLY, Lond., an arm, couped at elbow and erect, (vested, gu., charged with a fess, vair, cuff, ar.,) in hand, ppr., a mullet of six points, or. *Pl.* 62, *cr.* 13.

BAYLY, EDWARD-SYMES, Esq., of Ballyarthur, co. Wicklow, a boar's head, erased, ppr. *Quid clarius astris?* *Pl.* 16, *cr.* 11.

BAYLY, Somers., a goat's head, az., bezantée, attired, or. *Pl.* 105, *cr.* 14, (bezant, *pl.* 141.)

BAYN, Sco., a dexter hand grasping a dagger, in pale, or. *Et marte, et arte.* *Pl.* 23, *cr.* 15.

BAYN, Eng., a Saracen's head, in profile, az., wreathed and stringed behind, ar. and az. *Pl.* 23, *cr.* 3.

BAYNARD, Blagdon, Somers., a demi-unicorn, rampant, or, armed, ppr., crined, sa. *Pl.* 26, *cr.* 14.

BAYNARD, Stukey, Norf., a bear's paw, erased, sa., (charged with a martlet, or.) *Pl.* 126, *cr.* 2.

BAYNBRIDGE, or BAYNBRIGGE, a stag's head, erased, ar., attired, or. *Pl.* 66, *cr.* 9.

BAYNBRIDGE-BUCKERIDGE, Grand Chester, Cambs., a dexter arm, erect, couped at elbow, vested, per pale, indented, az. and vert, charged with three bars, erminois, in gauntlet, ppr., a cross crosslet, fitched, sa. *Pl.* 51, *cr.* 1.

BAYNE, Tulloch, Sco.; and Pitcarlie; a dexter hand grasping a dirk, ppr. *Et marte, et arte.* *Pl.* 28, *cr.* 4.

BAYNE, Eng., a pellet, between wings, ar. *Pl.* 2, *cr.* 3.

BAYNE, Sco., in hand a scroll of paper, ppr. *Virtute.* *Pl.* 27, *cr.* 4.

BAYNE, Lanc., an etoile, or. *Pl.* 63, *cr.* 9.

BAYNES, Cumb., Ess., and Lond., an arm, couped, vested, az., in hand, ppr., (a jaw-bone, ar.) *Pl.* 18, *cr.* 1.

BAYNES, JOHN, Richmond Terrace, Blackburn, a cubit arm, erect, ppr., vested, ar., hand grasping a shuttle, or, all within a wreath of the cotton plant, flowered and fructed, ppr. *Arte et Industriâ.* *Pl.* 126 a, *cr.* 14.

BAYNES, Bart., Middx., a cubit arm, vested, az., cuffed, erminois, (in hand a jaw-bone,) ar. *Furor arma ministrat.* *Pl.* 34, *cr.* 3.

BAYNES, or BAINES, Surr., a dove, volant, (regardant,) or, in mouth a myrtle-branch, ppr. *Pl.* 25, *cr.* 6.

BAYNHAM, Kent and Glouc., a bull's head, couped at neck, cr. *Pl.* 120, *cr.* 7.

BAYNHAM, Glouc., out of a mural coronet, gu., a bull's head, ar. *Pl.* 19, *cr.* 3, (coronet, *pl.* 128, *fig.* 18.)

BAYNING, Baron, (Powlett,) a buck, statant, sa., attired, or, charged on body with mullet, ar. *Stare super vias antiquos.* *Pl.* 88, *cr.* 9, (mullet, *pl.* 141.)

BAYNTON, an eagle's head, erased. *Pl.* 20, *cr.* 7.

BAYNTON, and BAYNTUN, Wilts., a griffin's head, erased, sa. *Pl.* 48, *cr.* 6.

BAYNTON, a goat, (passant,) ppr. *Pl.* 66, *cr.* 1.

BAYNTUN-ROLT, Bart., Seacombe-Park, Herts.; and Spye-Park, Wilts.; a griffin's head, erased, sa., beaked, or. *Pl.* 48, *cr.* 6.

BAYONS, and BAYOS, Eng., a horse, at full speed, in mouth a spear-head, ppr. *Pl.* 107, *cr.* 5.

BAZELEY, or BAZLEY, in hand a chapeau, between two branches of laurel, in orle. *Pl.* 59, *cr.* 4.

BAZILIE, or BAZELY, a crow, sa. *Be not wanting.* *Pl.* 23, *cr.* 8.

BEACH, WILLIAM, Esq., of Oakley Hall, Hants, a demi-lion, rampant, ar., in paws an escutcheon, az., charged with a pile, or. *Pl.* 67, *cr.* 10, (escutcheon, *pl.* 22, *cr.* 13.)

BEACH, Beds. and Kent, out of a ducal coronet, or, a demi-lion, ar. *Pl.* 45, *cr.* 7.

BEACHCROFT, a beech-tree, ppr., behind six park pales, ar. *Pl.* 100, *cr.* 14, (pales, *pl.* 13, *cr.* 12.)

BEACHER, Lond., out of a ducal coronet, a demi-lion, rampant, ppr. *Pl.* 45, *cr.* 7.

BEADLE, JOHN, Esq., of South Ella, East Riding, Yorks., a stag's head, erased, ppr., ducally gorged, or. *Pl.* 66, *cr.* 9, (coronet, *pl.* 128, *fig.* 3.)

BEADNELL, out of a ducal coronet, a grey-hound's head, (gorged with a rosary and a bell, or.) *Nec timide, nec temere. Pl.* 70, *cr.* 5.

BEAGHAN, a pellet between wings, ar. *Pl.* 2, *cr.* 3.

BEAGHAN, a pellet between wings, (paly of six, per fess, counterchanged, gu. and sa.) *Pl.* 2, *cr.* 3.

BEAGHAN, Iri., two swords, in saltier, (points downward.) *Pl.* 75, *cr.* 13, (without cup.)

BEAK, out of a ducal coronet, horns, scalp, and ears of an ox. *Pl.* 111, *cr.* 6, (coronet, *pl.* 128, *fig.* 3.)

BEAKE, or BEEKE, Dors., an ostrich-head, ar., in mouth a horse-shoe, or. *Pl.* 28, *cr.* 13, (without wings.)

BEAL, a lion's head, erased. *Pl.* 81, *cr.* 4.

BEAL, or BEALL, Eng., a demi-wolf, sa., holding a spear-head, in pale, tasselled, ppr. *Pl.* 56, *cr.* 8.

BEALE, Surr., a unicorn's head, sa., erased, gu., armed and crined, or. *Pl.* 67, *cr.* 1.

BEALE, Cork, Iri., and Lond., a unicorn's head, erased, or, charged with an etoile, gu. *Malo mori quam fœdari. Pl.* 67, *cr.* 1, (etoile, *pl.* 141.)

BEALE, THOMAS, Esq., of The Heath House, Salop, a unicorn's head, erased, ar., charged on neck with three etoiles, gu. *Pl.* 67, *cr.* 1. (etoiles, *pl.* 141.)

BEAMISH-BERNARD, ARTHUR, Esq., of Raheroon, Palace Anne, co. Cork, a demi-lion, rampant, gu. *Virtus insignit audentes. Pl.* 67, *cr.* 10.

BEAMISH, THOMAS, Esq., of Kilmalooda House, co. Cork, same crest and motto.

BEAMISH, BENJAMIN-SWAYNE, Esq., of Mount Beamish, co. Cork, same crest and motto.

BEAMISH of Willsgrove, ROBERT-DELACOUR, Esq., Ditchley, co. Cork, same crest and motto.

BEAMISH, or BEMISH, Eng., a pair of scales, ppr. *Pl.* 12, *cr.* 11.

BEAMONT, or BEAUMONT, Lond., a bull's head, quarterly, ar. and gu. *Pl.* 120, *cr.* 7.

BEAN, or BEANE, a lion, rampant, between paws a plumb-rule, sa. *Pl.* 50, *cr.* 8.

BEARCROFT, a demi-bear, rampant, muzzled. *Pl.* 104, *cr.* 10.

BEARD, Linc., a lion's gamb, couped, or, grasping a horse's leg, erased above knee, sa. *Pl.* 11, *cr.* 15.

BEARD, around the point of a pillar, (a snake, environed, ppr.) *Pl.* 33, *cr.* 1.

BEARD, Aberton and Cowfold, Suss., on a chapeau, gu., turned up, erm., a tiger, couchant, or, maned, armed, and tufted, sa. *Pl.* 114, *cr.* 11, (chapeau, *cr.* 13.)

BEARDMORE, or BERDMORE, on a mitre, sa., semée of crosses pattée, ar., a cheveron, of the last. *Pl.* 12, *cr.* 10, (crosses, *pl.* 141.)

BEARDMORE, JOHN, Esq., of Uplands, Hants, a griffin's head, erased. *Providentiæ me committo. Pl.* 48, *cr.* 6.

BEARDMORE, a wolf, erect, standing on hind dexter. *Pl.* 10, *cr.* 3.

BEARDOE, and BEARDOR, Lanc., a demi-bear, (in dexter a bundle of six arrows, in saltier, ppr., headed, or, flighted, ar.) *Pl.* 104, *cr.* 10.

BEARE, or BEERE, Kent, on a garb, in fess, or, a raven, sa. *Pl.* 112, *cr.* 10.

BEASLEY, Eng., a demi-leopard, in dexter a sprig of laurel, ppr. *Pl.* 97, *cr.* 5.

BEATH, or BEITH, Sco., a dragon's head, vomiting fire, ppr. *Fortuna virtute. Pl.* 37, *cr.* 9.

BEATH, or BIETH, Sco., a dragon's head, couped, ppr. *Fortuna virtute. Pl.* 87, *cr.* 12.

BEATH, Sco., a wolf's head, erased. *Fortuna virtute. Pl.* 14, *cr.* 6.

BEATHELL: 1. Out of a ducal coronet, a boar's head, couped. *Pl.* 102, *cr.* 14. 2. An eagle, between wings displayed, az., on neck an etoile, or. *Pl.* 52, *cr.* 8, (etoile, *pl.* 141.)

BEATIE, or BEATTIE, Sco., a star issuing from a crescent, or. *Lumen cœleste sequamur. Pl.* 111, *cr.* 15.

BEATIE, or BEATTY, Sco. and Eng., a castle, sa. *Pl.* 28, *cr.* 11.

BEATLEYS, a star issuing from a crescent, or. *Lumen cœleste sequamur. Pl.* 111, *cr.* 15.

BEATON, a lion, passant, sa. *Fortis in arduis. Pl.* 48, *cr.* 8.

BEATSON, Knowle Farm, Suss., a bee, volant, ppr. *Pl.* 100, *cr.* 3.

BEATSON, ALEXANDER-JOHN, Esq., of Rossend, Fife, Sco., a bee, erect, wings expanded, ppr. *Cum prudentia sedulus. Pl.* 100, *cr.* 3.

BEATTY, Iri., on a ducal coronet, a lion, passant, gardant, ducally crowned. *Pl.* 34, *cr.* 15.

BEATY, (two) keys, in saltier, ppr. *Pl.* 54, *cr.* 12.

BEAUCHAMP, Earl and Baron, and Viscount Elmley, (Pyndar;) a lion's head, erased, ar., ducally crowned, or. *Ex fide fortis. Pl.* 90, *cr.* 4, (not charged.)

BEAUCHAMP, on a mount, vert, a greyhound. sejant. *Pl.* 5, *cr.* 2.

BEAUCHAMP, Hoult, Ess., a swan's head and neck, ar., beaked, gu., between wings, sa. *Pl.* 54, *cr.* 6.

BEAUCHAMP, Earl of Warwick, out of a ducal coronet, or, a demi-swan, ar. *Pl.* 10, *cr.* 11, (without arrow.)

BEAUCHAMP, POWYCKE, Glouc., a tiger, passant, or, (vulned in shoulder, gu.) *Pl.* 67, *cr.* 15.

BEAUCHAMPE, a plume of feathers, or. *Pl.* 12, *cr.* 9.

BEAUCHAMPE, Glouc. and Warw., out of a coronet, gu., a swan's head and neck, ar., billed, of the first. *Pl.* 83, *cr.* 1.

BEAUCHATT, Eng., a cat's head, erased, gardant, gu. *Pl.* 97, *cr.* 7.

BEAUCLERK, AUBREY-DE VERE, Esq., of Ardglass Castle, co. Down. *See* ST ALBANS.

BEAUFEY, or BEAUFOY, Eng., a demi-griffin, between paws a close helmet. *Pl.* 19, *cr.* 15.

BEAUFORD, or BEAUFORT, a portcullis, or, nailed, az., chains, gold. *Mutare vel timere sperno. Pl.* 51, *cr.* 12.

BEAUFORT, Duke of, and Baron, Marquess and Earl of Worcester, Earl of Glamorgan, &c., (Somerset,) a portcullis, or, nailed, az., with chains, gold. *Mutare vel timere sperno.* *Pl.* 51, *cr.* 12.

BEAUMAN, of Hyde Park, Wexford, Iri., an arm, in armour, embowed, in hand a sabre. *Fortiter.* *Pl.* 81, *cr.* 11.

BEAUMONT, Sir GEO. HOWLAND WILLOUGHBY, Bart., Leic., on a chapeau, az., semée of fleur-de-lis, or, turned up, erm., a lion, passant, gold. *Erectus non electus.* *Pl.* 107, *cr.* 1.

BEAUMONT, Devons., a stork or heron, wings expanded, ar. *Pl.* 6, *cr.* 13.

BEAUMONT, Buckland, Surr., on a chapeau, gu., turned up, erm., a lion, passant, or. *Pl.* 107, *cr.* 1.

BEAUMONT, Suff., a bear's head, erased, ppr. *Pl.* 71, *cr.* 6.

BEAUMONT, of Whitley-Beaumont, Yorks., a bull's head, erased, quarterly. *Fide sed cui vide.* *Pl.* 19, *cr.* 3.

BEAUMONT, WENTWORTH, of Bretton Hall, Yorks., and Hexam Abbey, Northumb., same crest and motto.

BEAUMONT, Derbs., on a chapeau, az., turned up, erm., (charged with three fleurs-de-lis, or,) a lion, passant, gold, (tail extended.) *Pl.* 107, *cr.* 1.

BEAUMONT, JOHN, Esq., of Barrow-upon-Trent, Derby, on a chapeau, gu., turned up, erm., a lion, passant, or. *Erectus non electus.* *Pl.* 107, *cr.* 1.

BEAUMONT, RICHARD-HENRY, Esq., of Whitley Beaumont, York, a bull's head, erased, quarterly. *Fide sed cui vide.* *Pl.* 19, *cr.* 3.

BEAUMONT, WENTWORTH-BLACKETT, Esq., of Bretton Hall, York, same crest and motto.

BEAUMONT, DE, Eng., a demi-lion, gardant, sa. *Pl.* 35, *cr.* 4.

BEAUMONT, Leic. and Suff., a lion, passant, or. *Pl.* 48, *cr.* 8.

BEAUMONT, Leic., and Beaumont Hall, Suff., an elephant, on back a tower, triple-towered, ar., garnished, or. *Pl.* 114, *cr.* 14.

BEAURAIN, a lion's head, erased, ar., pellettée. *Pl.* 81, *cr.* 4, (pellet, *pl.* 141.)

BEAUVALE, Baron, (LAMB,) a demi-lion, rampant, gu., between paws a mullet, sa. *Virtute et fide.* *Pl.* 89, *cr.* 10.

BEAUVOIR, Eng., a griffin's head, between wings, ppr. *Pl.* 65, *cr.* 1.

BEAUVOIR, Lond., a demi-dragon, wings addorsed, ppr. *Pl.* 82, *cr.* 10.

BEAUVONS, Eng., a bull's head, sa. *Pl.* 120, *cr.* 7.

BEAVAN, or BEVAN, a dove, hovering, ppr., (in mouth a gem-ring, or,) over a mount, vert. *Semper virtute constans.* *Pl.* 25, *cr.* 6.

BEAVAN, a lion's head, erased, az., in mouth a rose, gu. *Pl.* 95, *cr.* 6.

BEAVER, a beaver, ppr. *Pl.* 49, *cr.* 5.

BEAVER, a leopard, ppr. *Pl.* 86, *cr.* 2.

BEAVER, Eng., a leopard, rampant, ppr. *Pl.* 73, *cr.* 2.

BEAVIS, Devons., a pheon, ar., (another, or.) *Pl.* 26, *cr.* 12.

BEAWFICE, Eng., a holy lamb supporting a flag. *Pl.* 48, *cr.* 13.

BEAWPELL, Eng., out of a mural coronet, in hand, ppr., vested, gu., a sword, wavy, az. *Pl.* 79, *cr.* 4, (sword, *pl.* 71, *cr.* 7.)

BEBB, Eng., a torteau, az., charged with a pale indented, gu. *Pl.* 63, *cr.* 7.

BEBINGTON, Bebington, Chesh., out of a ducal coronet, a demi-eagle, displayed, sa., bezantée. *Pl.* 9, *cr.* 6.

BEC, or BECK, Eng., on a chapeau, gu., turned up, erm., a lion's head, erased, of the first. *Pl.* 99, *cr.* 9.

BECCLES, a dexter arm, in armour, embowed, in hand a cross pattée, all ppr. *Pl.* 24, *cr.* 14, (cross, *pl.* 99, *cr.* 15.)

BECHE, Berks., in hand, ppr., vested, or, cuffed, gu., an escarbuncle, of the last. *Pl.* 114, *cr.* 4.

BECHER, Chancellor-House, Tunbridge-Wells, Kent, a demi-lion, rampant, gu., (body encircled with a ducal coronet,) or. *Pl.* 87, *cr.* 15.

BECHER, or BEACH, Kent and Beds., out of a ducal coronet, or, a demi-lion, ar. *Pl.* 45, *cr.* 7.

BECHER, or BEACH, Beds., and Kent, a demi-lion, rampant, ar., (enfiled round body with a ducal coronet,) or. *Pl.* 87, *cr.* 15.

BECHER-WRIXON, Bart., Iri., out of a ducal coronet, or, a demi-lion, erm., (gorged with a plain collar, vert.) *Bis vivit qui bene.* *Pl.* 45, *cr.* 7.

BECK, Norf., out of the sea, ppr., a sea-wolf, ar., finned, or, between paws a cross pattée, gu.

BECK, Suff., a peacock, ppr. *Pl.* 54, *cr.* 13.

BECK, Wel., (on a mount, vert,) a pelican, ar., vulning, gu. *Pl.* 109, *cr.* 15.

BECK, Lond., a raven, ppr., between wings, or. *Pl.* 123, *cr.* 2, (wings, *pl.* 39.)

BECK, or BEC, on a chapeau, gu,, turned up, erm., a lion's head, erased, of the first. *Pl.* 99, *cr.* 9.

BECKERING, and BEKERING, Yorks., a crow, perched on an oak-tree. *Pl.* 71, *cr.* 5.

BECKET, Courthither, Cornw., a Cornish chough, wings expanded, sa., beaked and legged, gu., ducally gorged, or. *Pl.* 44, *cr.* 11.

BECKET, Iri., a Cornish chough, ppr. *Pl.* 100, *cr.* 13.

BECKETT, Bart., Leeds, Yorks.; and Somerby-Park, Linc.; a boar's head, couped, or, pierced by a cross pattée, fitched, erect, sa. *Prodesse civibus.* *Pl.* 48, *cr.* 2, (cross, *pl.* 27, *cr.* 14.)

BECKETT, an ostrich-head, erased, ducally gorged, or. *Pl.* 108, *cr.* 2, (without feathers.)

BECKETT, Wilts., a Cornish chough, ppr. *Pl.* 100, *cr.* 13.

BECKETT, a boar's head, couped, or, ensigned with a cross formée, fitched, between ears, sa. *Pl.* 48, *cr.* 2, (cross, *pl.* 27, *cr.* 14.)

BECKETT, JOHN STANIFORTH, Esq., of The Knoll, Torquay, Devons., a boar's head, couped, or, pierced by a cross pattée, fitched, erect, sa. *Prodesse civibus.* *Pl.* 48, *cr.* 2, (cross, *pl.* 27, *cr.* 14.)

BECKFORD, Baron RIVERS. *See* RIVERS.

BECKFORD, Lond., Wilts., and Leic., a stork's head, (erased,) in mouth a fish, all ppr. *Pl.* 41, *cr.* 6.

BECKFORD, WILLIAM, Esq., of Ruxley Lodge, Surr., a heron's head, erased, or, collared flory-counterflory, gu.,) in mouth a fish, ar. *De Dieu tout.* *Pl.* 41, *cr.*

BECKFORD-LOVE, of Basing Park, Hants, a heron's head, (erased,) or, in beak a fish, ppr. *Pl.* 41, *cr.* 6.

BECKFORD, Fonthill-Gifford, Wilts. : 1. A heron's head, (erased, or, collared, flory, counter-flory, gu.,) in mouth a fish, ar. *Pl.* 41, *cr.* 6. 2. [Granted in consequence of the descent of Mr Beckford from the families of Hamilton and Latimer.] Out of a ducal coronet, or, an oak-tree, fructed, ppr., stem penetrated transversely by a frame saw, also ppr., (differenced with a shield pendant from a branch of the tree, charged with a cross flory, or.) *De Dieu tout*—and—*Through.* *Pl.* 100, *cr.* 2.

BECKHAM, a horse's head, ar., (pierced through neck with a broken tilting spear, or, in mouth top of spear, embrued, gu.) *Pl.* 46, *cr.* 4.

BECKINGHAM, Hoe, Norf., a demi-griffin, ar., legs and beak, sa., wings addorsed, gu., in dexter a cutlass, ar., hilt, or. *Pl.* 49, *cr.* 4.

BECKINGHAM, Tolshunt-Beckingham, Ess., a demi-griffin, sa., in dexter a cutlass, ar., hilt and pommel, or. *Pl.* 49, *cr.* 4.

BECKLEY, BECKLY, or BICKLEY, Devons., a cross pattée, gu., between wings, or. *Pl.* 29, *cr.* 14.

BECKMAN, Lond., an ostrich-head, couped, ar., gorged with a fess dancettée, sa., between two palm-branches, ppr. *Pl.* 49, *cr.* 7.

BECKWELL, or BEKEWELL, Eng., a horse-shoe, ppr. *Pl.* 52, *cr.* 4.

BECKWITH, or BICKWITH, a stag's head, erased. *Pl.* 66, *cr.* 9.

BECKWITH, an antelope, ppr. *Pl.* 63, *cr.* 10.

BECKWITH, WILLIAM, Esq., of Thurcroft, York; and of Trimdon, Durh., an antelope, ppr., (in mouth a branch, vert.) *Jouir en bien.* *Pl.* 63, *cr.* 10.

BECKWITH, Bart., Aldborough, Yorks., same crest and motto.

BECKWITH, a dove, (in mouth three ears of wheat, all ppr.) *Pl.* 48, *cr.* 15.

BECKWITH, Durh., a roebuck's head, couped, sa. *Pl.* 91, *cr.* 14.

BECKWITH, Aldborough, Yorks.; and Durh.; a stag's head, couped, sa. *Pl.* 91, *cr.* 14.

BECKWITH, Yorks., a stag's head, quarterly, per fess, indented, or and gu., (another, or and az.) *Pl.* 91, *cr.* 14.

BECKWORTH, and BECKWITH, Yorks., an eagle's head, or, depressed with two bends, vert, wings, one, ar., the other, sa., beaked, gu. *Pl.* 81, *cr.* 10.

BECTON, a demi-heraldic tiger, ducally gorged (and chained,) or. *Pl.* 57, *cr.* 13.

BECTON, a demi-heraldic tiger, ducally gorged (and chained, between feet a mullet of six points.) *Pl.* 57, *cr.* 13.

BEDALL, Ess., a buck's head, gu., attired, or, (between attires a bough of a tree, leaved, ppr.) *Pl.* 9, *cr.* 10.

BEDELL, Rumford, Ess., an arm, in armour, couped at elbow, ppr., hand grasping a cutlass by blade, ar., hilted, or. *Pl.* 65, *cr.* 8.

BEDELL, and BEDOLFE, Staff. and Ess., an arm, embowed, vested, az., in hand, ppr., a sword, ar., hilt and pommel, or, pierced into the side of a squirrel, sejant, regardant, or, side of squirrel, guttée-de-sang.

BEDELL, Hamerton, Hunts., out of a palisado coronet, a buck's head, or, attired, az. *Pl.* 128, *fig.* 21, (head, *pl.* 91, *cr.* 14.)

BEDELL, a stag's head, couped, gu., attired, or, branches, az., between attires a thistle, gold, stalked and leaved, vert. *Pl.* 91, *cr.* 14, (thistle, *pl.* 100, *cr.* 9.)

BEDEWELL, or BEDWELL, Eng., (on a rock,) a fort in flames, ppr. *Pl.* 118, *cr.* 15.

BEDFORD, in hand, ppr., a sphere, erect, or. *Pl.* 33, *cr.* 6, (sphere, *pl.* 14, *cr.* 1.)

BEDFORD, Henloc, Beds.; and Lond.; a demi-lion, sa., ducally crowned, or, between paws a sphere, gold. *Pl.* 61, *cr.* 4, (sphere, *pl.* 14, *cr.* 1.)

BEDFORD, Duke and Earl of, Marquess of Tavistock, Baron Russell, &c., (Russell ;) a goat, passant, ar., armed, or. *Che sara sara.* *Pl.* 66, *cr.* 1.

BEDFORD, Eng., a demi-lion, rampant, az., in dexter a fleur-de-lis, or. *Pl.* 91, *cr.* 13.

BEDFORD, a demi-lion, rampant, ppr., (in dexter a trefoil, slipped, vert.) *Pl.* 39, *cr.* 14.

BEDINGFIELD, Oxborough and Beckhall, Norf., an eagle, displayed, or. *Despicio terrena.* *Pl.* 48, *cr.* 11.

BEDINGFELD, Sir RICHARD, Bart., Oxburgh, Norf., a demi-eagle, wings expanded, gu. *Solem contemplor despicio terram.* *Pl.* 52, *cr.* 8.

BEDINGFELD, JOHN-LONGUEVILLE, Esq., of Ditchingham Hall, Norf., a demi-eagle, gu. *Aquila non capit muscas;* or, *Despicio terrena.* *Pl.* 52, *cr.* 8.

BEDINGFIELD, a unicorn's head, erased, sa., horn wreathed, or and ar. *Pl.* 67, *cr.* 1.

BEDINGFIELD, a demi-eagle, wings elevated, or. *Despicio terrena.* *Pl.* 52, *cr.* 8.

BEDLE, or BEDELL, Lond., a stag's head, (erased, or,) attired and ducally gorged, gu., *Pl.* 55, *cr.* 2.

BEDO, and BEDON, Putney, Surr., a boar's head, (couped,) and erect, gu. *Pl.* 21, *cr.* 7.

BEDWIN, Wilts., a griffin, passant, or. *Pl.* 61, *cr.* 14, (without gorging.)

BEE, Basingstoke, Staffs., a dragon's head, gu., (pierced through with an arrow, ar.) *Pl.* 121, *cr.* 9.

BEEBY, Eng., a mullet, or. *Pl.* 41, *cr.* 1.

BEECH, JAMES, Esq., of Brandon Lodge, Warwick; and The Shawe, Stafford; a stag's head, cabossed. *Sub tegmine fagi.* *Pl.* 36, *cr.* 1.

BEECHEY, and BEECHY, Eng., a torteau, az. *Pl.* 7, *cr.* 6.

BEECROFT, Bp.-Wearmouth, Durh., two arms, dexter and sinister, in armour, ppr., embowed, between fingers an annulet, gu. *Pl.* 6, *cr.* 8, (annulet, *pl.* 141.)

BEEKENSHALL, Lanc., an arm, erect, ppr., couped below elbow, in hand a garland, gu. *Pl.* 41, *cr.* 7.

BEER, Eng., on a garb, or, a raven, sa. *Pl.* 112, *cr.* 10.

BEERS, JOHN, Esq., Leslie Hill, co. Donegal, on a garb, or, a raven, sa. *In Deo spes mea.* *Pl.* 112, *cr.* 10.

BEESLEY, or BEESLY, Eng., out of a mural coronet, two branches of palm, in saltier, ppr., surmounting a spear, in pale. *Pl.* 97, *cr.* 8.

BEESTON, BEESTONE, or BEISTON, Eng., a heart, gu., within a fetterlock, sa. *Pl.* 59, *cr.* 6.

BEESTON, Chesh., (on a mount, vert,) a castle, or, issuant therefrom an arm, in armour, embowed, ppr., garnished, gold, brandishing a sword, ppr., hilted, of the first. *Pl.* 161, *cr.* 12.

BEEVOR, Sir THOMAS-BRANTHWAYT, Bart., Bethel, Norf., a beaver, passant, ppr. *Pl.* 49, *cr.* 5.
BEG, or BEGG, Sco., a cross crosslet, fitched, between two branches of palm, in orle, ppr. *Pl.* 37, *cr.* 14, (branches, *pl.* 87, *cr.* 8.)
BEGBIE, Sco., out of a ducal coronet, in lion's paw, a spear head. *Pl.* 120, *cr.* 6.
BEGBIE, Eng., a cross moline, lozenge-pierced, az. *Pl.* 91, *cr.* 10.
BEGGAR, or BEGGER, a pelican's head and neck, erased, vulning. *Pl.* 26, *cr.* 1.
BEHETHLAND, Eng., from a cloud, in sinister, in dexter hand, in fess, a club, in pale, all ppr. *Pl.* 68, *cr.* 7.
BEHEVENS, Lond., a demi-bear. *Pl.* 104, *cr.* 10.
BEIGHTON, Werkswerth, out of a mural coronet, or, a greyhound, erm., collared, gold. *Pl.* 113, *cr.* 6.
BEILBY, Warw., a leopard's head. *Pl.* 92, *cr.* 13.
BEILBY, Eng., a hawk, close, ppr. *Pl.* 67, *cr.* 3.
BEIST, or BIEST, Salop, a sinister arm, couped above elbow, (vested, sa., cuffed, ar.,) in hand, ppr., a bow, stringed, also ppr. *Pl.* 3, *cr.* 12.
BEITH, or BIETH, Sco., a dragon's head, couped, vert. *Fortuna virtute. Pl.* 87, *cr.* 12.
BEKE, BEEKE, or BEACK, Durh., out of a ducal coronet, gu., two bull's horns, erm. *Pl.* 9, *cr.* 6, (horns, *same plate, cr.* 15.)
BEKE, or BECK, Berks.; and Beck, Linc.; a peacock's head, (erased, or, gorged with two bars, dancéttée, sa.,) between wings, az., each charged with three bezants, in pale. *Pl.* 50, *cr.* 9, (bezant, *pl.* 141.)
BEKE, or BECK, Berks. and Linc., a hare's head.
BEKE, Norf., a dragon's head, erased, or collared, vair. *Pl.* 107, *cr.* 10.
BEKETT, on a wreath, or and vert, (garnished with laurel-leaves,) of the second, a falcon, rising, ar., legged and beaked, gu., and ducally gorged, or. *Pl.* 61, *cr.* 12.
BELASIS, a stag's head, erased, ar. *Bonne et belle assez. Pl.* 66, *cr.* 9.
BELASYSE, Newborough, Yorks., Viscount Fauconburgh, and a Bart.; a stag's head, erased, ppr., attired, or, in mouth an acorn, of the first, leaved, vert. *Bonne et belle assez. Pl.* 66, *cr.* 9, (acorn, *pl.* 81, *cr.* 7.)
BELCHER, Northampton, a demi-hawk, or, wings expanded, sa., (another, ar.) *Pl.* 99, *cr.* 10.
BELCHER, Gilsborough, Northamp.; Staffs.; and Warw.; a greyhound's head, (erased,) erm., collared, gu., rimmed and ringed, or. *Pl.* 43, *cr.* 11.
BELCHES, Sco., a horse's head, ar., bridled, gu. *Keep tryst. Pl.* 92, *cr.* 1.
BELCHES, or BELSCHES, of Tofts, Sco., stump of oak-tree, eradicated, shooting branches, ppr. *Revirescit. Pl.* 92, *cr.* 8.
BELCHES, and BELSCHES, Sco., a greyhound's head, couped, ar., collared, az. *Fulget virtus intaminata. Pl.* 43, *cr.* 11.
BELDERO, Suff., a greyhound, current, gu., (collared and ringed,) or. *Pl.* 28, *cr.* 7.
BELEW, or BELLOW, Devons., an arm, embowed, vested, vert, in hand, ppr., a bell, or. *Pl.* 39, *cr.* 1, (bell, *pl.* 73, *cr.* 15.)
BELFARGE, or BELFRAGE, Sco., on a ducal coronet, or, a hawk, belled, ppr. *Pl.* 41, *cr.* 10.

BELFIELD, Lond. and Hertford, a demi-tiger, ar., armed and tufted, or, (pierced through body with broken staff of a flag, flag hanging between fore-legs, party per fess, wavy, ar. and az.) *Pl.* 53, *cr.* 10.
BELFOUR, BELFORE, BELFOURE, and BALFOUR, a hautboy, in pale, ppr. *Pl.* 12, *cr.* 1.
BELGRAVE, North Kilworth and Belgrave, Leic., a ram's head, ar. *Pl.* 14, *cr.* 12.
BELGRAVE, The Rev. WILLIAM, M.A., of Preston Hall, Rutland, a ram's head. *Pl.* 34, *cr.* 12.
BELHAVEN and STENTON, Baron, Sco.; Baron Hamilton, Eng., (Hamilton;) a nag's head, couped, ar., bridled, gu. *Ride through. Pl.* 92, *cr.* 1.
BELHOUSE, a squirrel, sejant, per pale, ar. and az., tailed, or, fore feet against an oak-branch, acorned, or, leaved, vert. *Pl.* 2, *cr.* 4.
BELHOUSE, Eng., a wolf's head, party per pale, or and az. *Pl.* 8, *cr.* 4.
BELIALD, Thorpe, Northamp., a lion's head, couped, gu., billettée, ar. *Pl.* 126, *cr.* 1, (billet, *pl.* 141.)
BELL, Glouc., an arm, embowed, vested, gu., in hand, ppr., a battle-axe, staff, gu., head, ar. *Pl.* 39, *cr.* 1, (axe, *pl.* 121, *cr.* 14.)
BELL, Berks. and Bucks., a hawk, wings expanded, ar., beaked and belled, or, (a string flotant from bells, gu.) *Pl.* 105, *cr.* 4.
BELL, Lond., a human heart, between wings. *Forward, kind heart. Pl.* 39, *cr.* 7.
BELL, Newcastle and Cumb., a hawk, close, ppr., beaked and belled, or. *Perseverantia. Pl.* 67, *cr.* 3.
BELL, Middx., a portcullis, ppr. *Pl.* 51, *cr.* 12.
BELL, Sunderland, Durh., a hawk, close, ppr., beaked and belled, or. *Pl.* 67, *cr.* 3.
BELL, on a mount, an eagle, rising, ppr. *Viam affectat Olympo. Pl.* 61, *cr.* 1.
BELL, MATHEW, Esq., of Woolsington, Not-thumb., a hawk, belled. *Pl.* 67, *cr.* 3.
BELL, Ess., a talbot, passant, erm. *Pl.* 120, *cr.* 8.
BELL, Sco., an arm, in armour, hand grasping a scimitar, all ppr. *Pro rege et patria. Pl.* 81, *cr.* 11.
BELL, by the side of a tree, ppr., a bear, resting fore dexter on a bell. *Pl.* 18, *cr.* 10, (bear, *pl.* 61, *cr.* 5.)
BELL, a falcon, close, belled, or. *Prend moi tel que je suis. Pl.* 67, *cr.* 3.
BELL, Provosthaugh, Sco., on a mount, vert, a roebuck, feeding, ppr. *Signum pacis amor. Pl.* 37, *cr.* 8.
BELL, Sco., a bell, or. *Pl.* 73, *cr.* 15.
BELL, Sco., a demi-lion, rampant. *Dextra fideque. Pl.* 67, *cr.* 10.
BELL, Jamaica, a stag's head, erased, gu., attired, ar. *Fulget virtus. Pl.* 66, *cr.* 9.
BELL, a stag's head, ppr. *Signum pacis amor. Pl.* 91, *cr.* 14.
BELL, a hawk's bell, stringed, ppr. *Pl.* 141.
BELL, Leith, a dexter hand, with two last fingers folded down, ppr. *Confido. Pl.* 67, *cr.* 6.
BELL, Eng., on a rock, ppr., a martlet, erminois. *Pl.* 36, *cr.* 5.
BELL, a garb, ppr. *Quid utilius. Pl.* 48, *cr.* 10.
BELLAIRS, Rev. HENRY, A.M., of Kirby Bellars, a lion's gamb, erased, gu. *In cruce mea fides. Pl.* 126, *cr.* 9.

BELLAM, BALLAM, and BELLOME, out of a ducal coronet, or, a cock's head, between wings, gu., combed and wattled, gold. *Pl.* 97, *cr.* 15, (wings, *same plate, cr.* 13.)

BELLAMY, an arm, couped, vested, sa., cuffed, ar., in hand, ppr., a sceptre, or, surmounted by a crescent, ar.

BELLARS, New Lodge, Berthampstead, Herts., a lion's gamb, ppr. *Pl.* 126, *cr.* 9.

BELLAS, a stag's head, erased, per fess, indented, ar. and gu., attired, or, in mouth, a fleur-de-lis, az. *Pl.* 66, *cr.* 9, (fleur-de-lis, *pl.* 141.)

BELLASIS, or BELLASSES, Sco. and Eng., on a mount, a palm-tree, ppr. *Pl.* 52, *cr.* 6.

BELLASIS, MORTON, Durh., a stag's head, erased, ppr., attired, or. *Pl.* 66, *cr.* 9.

BELLASIS, or BELLASSIS, Yorks., a lion, couchant, gardant, az. *Pl.* 101, *cr.* 8.

BELLASIS, Yorks., a stag's head, erased, (in mouth an oak-branch, acorned, ppr.) *Pl.* 66, *cr.* 9.

BELLERBY, Yorks., a dexter hand, couped at wrist, (pierced through the palm with an arrow, in bend sinister,) all ppr. *Pl.* 32, *cr.* 14.

BELLERE, Eng., a spur rowel, az. *Pl.* 54, *cr.* 5.

BELLET, Chesh., a fox's head, erased, sa. *Pl.* 71, *cr.* 4.

BELLETT, Norf. and Wilts., an arm, in armour, couped at elbow and erect, ppr., in gauntlet, a baton, or, tipped at both ends, sa. *Pl.* 33, *cr.* 4.

BELLEW, JOHN-PRESTWOOD, Esq., of Stockleigh Court, Devons., an arm, embowed, vested, hand, ppr., grasping a chalice pouring water (*belle eau*, in allusion to the name) into a basin, also ppr. *Tout d'en haut.*

BELLEW, Eng., a boar, passant, sa. *Pl.* 48, *cr.* 14.

BELLEW, Sir PATRICK, Bart., Iri., an arm, in armour, embowed, in hand a sword, ppr. *Tout d'en haut. Pl.* 2, *cr.* 8.

BELLEW, an arm, in armour, embowed, in hand a dagger, point downwards. *Pl.* 120, *cr.* 11.

BELLEW-DILLON, Bart., of Mount Bellew, co. Galway, an arm, in armour, embowed, ppr., charged with a crescent for difference, in hand a sword, of the first, hilt and pommel, or. *Tout d'en haut. Pl.* 2, *cr.* 8, (crescent, *pl.* 141.)

BELLEWE, Newstead, Linc., a buck's head, erased, or, guttée, az., dexter horn, ar., sinister, az., guttée counterchanged. *Pl.* 66, *cr.* 9.

BELLINGHAM, Linc. and Yorks., a buck's head, couped, ar., on a branch twisted, or and az., leaved, vert. *Pl.* 91, *cr.* 14.

BELLINGHAM, Iri., a stag's head, erased, sa., attired, or, charged with a fleur-de-lis, gold. *Pl.* 66, *cr.* 9, (fleur-de-lis, *pl.* 141.)

BELLINGHAM, Orston, St George, Wilts., a demi-buck, (supporting a banner charged with the family arms.) *Pl.* 55, *cr.* 9, (without rose.)

BELLINGHAM, Sir ALAN, Bart., Castle-Bellingham, Iri., a buck's head, couped, or. *Amicus amico. Pl.* 91, *cr.* 14.

BELLINGHAM, Brumby, Linc.; and Suss.; a stag's head, ar., attired, or, gorged with a chaplet, vert. *Pl.* 38, *cr.* 1.

BELLINGHAM, Cumb., a stag's head, erased, az., attired, or. *Pl.* 66, *cr.* 9.

BELLINGHAM of Hissington, a bugle-horn, ar. *Pl.* 89, *cr.* 3.

BELLIS, in hand, in armour, a holly-branch, all ppr. *Pl.* 55, *cr.* 6.

BELLISMO, out of water, top of spear, in pale, sustaining a dolphin, naiant. *Pl.* 116, *cr.* 4.

BELLOMONT, a cross moline, lozenge-pierced, gu. *Pl.* 91, *cr.* 10.

BELMORE, Earl of, Viscount and Baron, (Corry,) Iri., a cock, ppr. *Virtus semper viridis. Pl.* 67, *cr.* 14.

BELMOUR, a griffin's head. *Pl.* 38, *cr.* 3.

BELSHES, Invermay, a horse's head, ar., bridle, gu. *Keep tryst*—and—*Reverescit. Pl.* 92, *cr.* 1.

BELSON, Eng., in hand, a key, in bend sinister. *Pl.* 41, *cr.* 11.

BELTEAD, BELSTEDE, BELSTED, or BELSTIDE, Eng., a seax, az., hilted, or. *Pl.* 27, *cr.* 10.

BELTOFT, or BELTOFTS, Eng., a cock, sa., beaked, combed, and wattled, gu. *Pl.* 67, *cr.* 14.

BELTOFT, or BELTOFTS, Linc., out of a ducal coronet, in hand a sword, ppr. *Pl.* 103, *cr.* 2.

BELVALE, Eng., two arms, in armour, embowed, in hands a heart inflamed, ppr. *Pl.* 36, *cr.* 4.

BELWARD, a pheon, sa. *Pl.* 26, *cr.* 12.

BELYN, Chesh., a unicorn's head, erased, ar., armed, or, (charged on neck with four bars, gu.) *Pl.* 67, *cr.* 1.

BEMPDE, a winged spur. *Pl.* 59, *cr.* 1.

BEN, and BENNE, Newport-Cranley, Surr., a tiger, passant, erm., ducally gorged, or. *Pl.* 120, *cr.* 9.

BENBOW, Newport, Salop, a harpy, close, or, face, ppr., head wreathed with a chaplet of flowers, gu. *Pl.* 126, *cr.* 11.

BENCE, Aldborough, Benhall, and Kingsfield, Suff., a tower, ar., (charged with a fret, gu.) *Pl.* 12, *cr.* 5.

BENCE, HENRY-BENCE, Esq., of Thorington Hall, Suff., a castle, triple-towered. *Virtus castellum meum. Pl.* 123, *cr.* 14.

BENCLER, a stag's head, cabossed, between attires, a bugle-horn, strung, ar. *Pl.* 115, *cr.* 1, (horn, *pl.* 48, *cr.* 12.)

BENDALL, Middx., a demi-lion, (double-queued,) az., holding an anchor, ppr. *Pl.* 19, *cr.* 6.

BENDISH, Steeple-Bamstead, Ess., out of an earl's coronet, a talbot's head, all or. *Pl.* 80, *cr.* 11, (head, *pl.* 123, *cr.* 15.)

BENDLOWES, Ess., a centaur, with bow and arrow, all or. *Pl.* 70, *cr.* 13.

BENDYSHE, JOHN, Esq., of Barrington, Cambridge, out of a ducal coronet, or, a talbot's head. *Utráque Pallade. Pl.* 99, *cr.* 7.

BENE, a buck's head, erased, per pale, embattled, in mouth a rose slip, ppr., thereon three roses, ar. *Pl.* 66, *cr.* 9, (roses, *pl.* 23, *cr.* 2.)

BENEGALL, a battering ram, per fess.

BENETT, Wilts., out of a mural coronet, or, a lion's head, ar., charged with a mullet, or. *Pl.* 45, *cr.* 9, (mullet, *pl.* 141.)

BENGE, an eagle, displayed, ppr. *Pl.* 48, *cr.* 11.

BENGER, Lond. and Kent, a cockatrice, per pale, or and vert, wings expanded, counterchanged. *Pl.* 63, *cr.* 15.

BENHAN, BENGHAM, or BENHAM, Eng., a chart, ppr. *Pl.* 59, *cr.* 3.

BENJAMIN, Eng., on a chapeau, a flame of fire, all ppr. *Pl.* 71, *cr.* 11.

BENLEY, Eng., a sand-glass, gu. *Pl.* 43, *cr.* 1.

BENNET, Eng., a ship in full sail, ppr. *Pl.* 109, *cr.* 8.

BENNET, in dexter hand a cross pattée, fitched, gu. *Benedictus qui tollit crucem. Pl.* 99, *cr.* 15.
BENNET, Sco., a demi-lion, in dexter a cross crosslet, fitched. *Benedictus qui tollit crucem. Pl.* 65, *cr.* 6.
BENNET, Iri., an arm, couped at elbow, in hand a thistle, slipped, all ppr. *Pl.* 36, *cr.* 6.
BENNET, Eng., a Cornish chough, ppr. *Pl.* 100, *cr.* 13.
BENNET, Lond., out of a mural coronet, or, a lion's head, gu., charged with a bezant, gold. *Pl.* 45, *cr.* 9, (bezant, *pl.* 141.)
BENNET, of Abbington, out of a mural coronet, ar., a lion's head, gu., charged with a bezant, or. *Pl.* 45, *cr.* 9, (bezant, *pl.* 141.)
BENNET, Lond., out of a mural coronet, or, a lion's head, ar., charged with a bezant, or. *Deo gloria. Pl.* 59, *cr.* 9, (bezant, *pl.* 141.)
BENNET, Earl of Tankerville, *see* TANKERVILLE.
BENNET, Lond., a double scaling ladder, or. *Pl.* 59, *cr.* 7.
BENNET, Sco., a demi-lion, in dexter a cross pattée, gu. *Pl.* 65, *cr.* 6, (cross, *pl.* 141.)
BENNET, Surr., out of a mural coronet, a lion's head, ar., charged on neck with a bezant. *Pl.* 45, *cr.* 9, (bezant, *pl.* 141.)
BENNET, JOHN WICK, Esq., or Laleston, Glamorg., Wel., a goat's head, erased, sa., barbed and double armed, or, langued, gu. *Aut nunquam tentes, aut perfice. Pl.* 29, *cr.* 13.
BENNET, PHILIP, Esq., of Tollesbury, Ess.; and Rougham Hall, Suff.; out of a mural coronet, or, a lion's head, couped, charged on neck with a bezant. *Bene tenax. Pl.* 45, *cr.* 9, (bezant, *pl.* 141.)
BENNET, of Grubet, Bart., in hand, out of a cloud, ppr., a cross pattée, fitched, gu. *Benedictus qui tollit crucem. Pl.* 26, *cr.* 4.
BENNET, Lond., on a mount, vert, a martin, ppr. *Pl.* 36, *cr.* 5.
BENNET, Newcastle, Northumb., a tower, triple-towered. *Pl.* 123, *cr.* 14.
BENNET, Norf., two dolphins, one, or, other, ar., in saltier, erect on tails. *Pl.* 125, *cr.* 1.
BENNET, Steeple-Ashton, Wilts., a demi-lion, rampant, ar., crowned, or, supporting a tower, ppr. *Pl.* 61, *cr.* 4, (tower, *pl.* 12, *cr.* 5.)
BENNET, Wel., a goat's head, erased, sa. *Pl.* 29, *cr.* 13.
BENNETT, Dublin, an arm, couped at elbow, in hand a thistle, all ppr. *Pl.* 36, *cr.* 6.
BENNETT, The Rev. HENRY-LEIGH, of Thorpe Place, Surr., out of a mural coronet, a lion's head. *Dux vitæ ratio. Pl.* 45, *cr.* 9.
BENNETT, DANIEL, Esq., of Faringdon House, Berks., a lion's head, charged with a bezant. *De bon valoir servir le roi. Pl.* 126, *cr.* 1, (bezant, *pl.* 141.)
BENNETT, WILLIAM, Esq., of Stourton Hall, near Stourbridge, (on a mount, vert,) a horse's head, couped, ar., (pierced through neck by an arrow, in bend sinister, point downward, ppr.) *Irrevocabile. Pl.* 100, *cr.* 6.
BENNETT, JOSEPH-HENRY, Esq., of Bennett's Court, co. Cork, out of a mural coronet, or, a demi-lion, rampant, ar., in dexter a bezant. *Serve the king. Pl.* 17, *cr.* 7, (bezant, *pl.* 141.)

BENNETT, Finsbury, a demi-lion, rampant, or, in paws a bezant. *Pl.* 126, *cr.* 12.
BENNETT, Pitehouse, Wilts., on a whilk-shell, or, a bird, sa., beaked and legged, gu. *Pl.* 10, *cr.* 12, (shell, *pl.* 117, *cr.* 13.)
BENNETT, Surr. and Berks., out of a mural coronet, or, a lion's head, gu., charged on neck with a bezant. *Pl.* 59, *cr.* 9, (bezant, *pl.* 141.)
BENNIE, BENNY, BENZIE, or BINNIE, Sco., a horse's head, bridled, ppr. *Virtute et opera. Pl.* 92, *cr.* 1.
BENNING, a demi-horse, saddled and bridled.
BENNINGHAM, Iri., a horse at full speed, with point of broken spear in mouth. *Pl.* 107, *cr.* 5.
BENNS, a tiger, passant, erm., ducally gorged, or. *Pl.* 120, *cr.* 9.
BENOLT, a stag, (current,) ppr. *Pl.* 68, *cr.* 2.
BENON, Aldington, Suss., (on a mount, vert,) a griffin, segreant, wings elevated, ar. *Pl.* 67, *cr.* 13.
BENSE, or BENST, Eng., a sea-lion, holding a cross patonce. *Pl.* 59, *cr.* 2.
BENSLEY, MORES DE BONN, in dexter hand a (plume) of ostrich-feathers. *Pl.* 69, *cr.* 1.
BENSLEY, or BENSLY, Eng., a sand-glass, gu. *Pl.* 43, *cr.* 1.
BENSON, a horse, passant, saddled and bridled. *Pl.* 99, *cr.* 11.
BENSON, the sun, surmounted by a rainbow, each end of the latter out of clouds, all ppr. *Pl.* 68, *cr.* 14, (rainbow, *pl.* 79, *cr.* 1.)
BENSON, a bear's head, erased, ppr., muzzled and collared, or. *Pl.* 71, *cr.* 6.
BENSON, Eng., a talbot's head, erased, ar., ducally crowned, or. *Pl.* 25, *cr.* 10.
BENSON, The Rev. HENRY, A.M., of Utterby House, Lincoln, a bear's head, erased, ar., muzzled, gu. *Inconcussa virtus. Pl.* 71, *cr.* 6.
BENSON, MOSES-GEORGE, Esq., of Lutwyche Hall, Salop, a horse, passant, caparisoned, ppr. *Leges arma tenent sanctas. Pl.* 99, *cr.* 11.
BENSTED, BENSTEAD, BENST, or BENSE, a sea-lion holding a cross patonce. *Pl.* 59, *cr.* 2.
BENT of Batsford House, Staffs., a demi-lion, az., holding a bezant. *Nec temerè, nec timidè. Pl.* 126, *cr.* 12.
BENT, JOHN, Esq., of Wexham Lodge, Bucks., a demi-lion, rampant, per fess, az. and gu., collared, indented, between paws a bull's head, cabossed, or. *Tutamen deus. Pl.* 67, *cr.* 10, (head, *pl.* 111, *cr.* 6.)
BENT, a demi-lion, az., between paws a bezant. *Pl.* 126, *cr.* 12.
BENT, a demi-lion, az., holding a lozenge, ar. *Pl.* 39, *cr.* 14, (lozenge, *pl.* 141.)
BENTALL of Bentall, Salop, on a ducal coronet, or, a leopard, ar., spotted, sa. *Pl.* 86, *cr.* 8.
BENTHAM, a lion, rampant, ar. *Pl.* 67, *cr.* 5.
BENTHAM, Eng., on a cross flory, fitched, quarterly, gu., and ar., the sun, or, between wings expanded, of the second, each charged with a rose, of the first, seeded, gold, barbed, vert. *Pl.* 26, *cr.* 6.
BENTICK, Eng., a chevalier standing beside his horse, with a hold of the bridle, all ppr. *Pl.* 37, *cr.* 11.
BENTINCK. *See* PORTLAND, Duke of.

BENTINCK, GEORGE-WILLIAM-PIERREPONT, Esq., of Terrington St Clement, Norf., out of a marquess's coronet, ppr., two arms, counter-embowed, vested, gu., on hands gloves, or, in each an ostrich-feather, ar. *Pl.* 45, *cr.* 2, (coronet, *pl.* 127, *fig.* 4.)

BENTLEY, JOHN, Esq., of Birch House, Lancaster, a wolf, rampant, erm., ducally gorged, or. *Benigno numine. Pl.* 126, *cr.* 13, (coronet, *pl.* 128, *fig.* 3.)

BENTLEY, on a chapeau, a spaniel dog, statant. *Pl.* 127, *fig.* 13, (dog, *pl.* 58, *cr.* 9.)

BENTLEY, Staffs. and Derbs., a spaniel dog, passant, ar. *Pl.* 58, *cr.* 9.

BENTLEY, a demi-lion, rampant. *Pl.* 67, *cr.* 5.

BENTLEY, a demi-lion, rampant, grasping a thunderbolt, or. *Pl.* 113, *cr.* 2, (bolt, *pl.* 110, *cr.* 3.)

BENTON, Wilts., on a mount, vert, a lamb with flag, az. *Pl.* 101, *cr.* 9.

BENTON, a griffin's head, erased, ar. *Pl.* 48, *cr.* 6.

BENVIL, or BENVILL, Eng., a demi-swan, rising, ppr. *Pl.* 54, *cr.* 4.

BENWEIL, or BENWELL, Eng., a greyhound, sejant, collared, wings addorsed. *Pl.* 101, *cr.* 7.

BENWELL, Lond. and Oxon., a garb, or, (entwined by a serpent, ppr., head issuing through the ears of corn to sinister.) *Pl.* 36, *cr.* 14.

BENWIN, out of a ducal coronet, gu., a boar's head, erect, ar., langued, of the first. *Pl.* 102, *cr.* 14.

BENYNGTON, Ess., a lion's head, erased, ar., semée of torteaux, gu., ducally crowned, or. *Pl.* 90, *cr.* 4.

BENYON, Horton Hall, Salop, a griffin, segreant, wings elevated, ar. *Pl.* 67, *cr.* 13.

BENYON, Suff., (on a mount, vert,) a griffin, sejant, ar. *Pl.* 100, *cr.* 11.

BENYON, Salop, (on a mount, vert,) a griffin, sejant, ar., (charged with a canton, az.) *Pl.* 100, *cr.* 11.

BENYON, RICHARD, Esq., of Englefield House, Berks., a griffin, sejant, or, (collared with an eastern crown, gu., in beak a Guernsey lily, ppr. *Vincam vel moriar. Pl.* 100, *cr.* 11.

BENZIE, Sco., a horse's head, bridled, ppr., *Virtute et opera. Pl.* 92, *cr.* 1.

BERBLOCK, Lond., in a gauntlet, in fess, ppr., garnished, or, lined, gu., the lower part of a spear, in pale, gold.

BERE, Kent; and Oakenham, Berks.; on a garb, in fess, oz, a bird, sa. *Pl.* 112, *cr.* 10.

BERE, Huncham, Devons., a bear's head, erased, sa., muzzled, or. *Pl.* 71, *cr.* 6.

BERE, a tiger, sejant, az., bezantée, maned and tufted, or. *Pl.* 26, *cr.* 9.

BEREARLY, Lond. a cross potent, fitched, between wings, expanded. *Pl.* 71, *cr.* 2, (cross, *pl.* 141.)

BEREFORD, Staffs., an ostrich-head, between two palm-branches. *Pl.* 49, *cr.* 7.

BERENGER, and BERANGER, Eng. and French, on a mount, a tree, vert. *Pl.* 48, *cr.* 9.

BERENS, Kent, a demi-bear, salient, sa. *Pl.* 104, *cr.* 10.

BERESETH, a griffin's head, erased, ppr., (collared, or.) *Pl.* 48, *cr.* 6.

BERESFORD, Baron DECIES, Iri. *See* DECIES.

BERESFORD, Baron, a dragon's head, (erased, az., wounded with broken spear through neck, or, broken point, ar., thrust through upper jaw.) *Nil nisi cruce. Pl.* 121, *cr.* 9.

BERESFORD, WILLIAM-CARR, Viscount and Baron, out of mural coronet, or, a dragon's head, (per fess, wavy, az. and gu., pierced in neck with broken tilting-lance, in bend, gold, upper part of spear in mouth.) *Nil nisi cruce. Pl.* 101, *cr.* 4.

BERESFORD, Bart., same crest and motto.

BERESFORD, Kent; and Bentley, Derbs.; a dragon's head, (erased, az., pierced through neck with broken spear, or, part of same in mouth, headed, ar.) *Pl.* 121, *cr.* 9.

BERESFORD, a dolphin, haurient on its tail. *Pl.* 14, *cr.* 10.

BERESFORD, a dragon's head, couped, az., (pierced through neck with broken sword, or, part of same in mouth.) *Pl.* 121, *cr.* 9.

BERESFORD, Marquess of Waterford. *See* WATERFORD.

BEREY of Croston, Lanc., between wings, erm., an eagle's head, couped, or. *Pl.* 81, *cr.* 10.

BERGAIGNE, or BERGAINE, a demi-lion, in dexter a sword, ar. *Pl.* 41, *cr.* 13.

BERGER, Eng., in lion's paw, erased, sa., a dagger, ppr. *Pl.* 56, *cr.* 3.

BERIFFE, Colchester, Ess., out of a mural coronet, gu., a demi-lion, rampant, or, (ducally crowned, of the first, in dexter a trefoil, slipped, vert.) *Pl.* 17, *cr.* 7.

BERIFFE, Ess., in grass, vert, a beaver, passant, ppr., collared, or. *Pl.* 3, *cr.* 11.

BERINGER, Bucks., a stem of holly-tree, reguled and trunked, jacent, sprouting out a branch, in pale, leaved and fructed, all ppr. *Pl.* 25, *cr.* 9.

BERINGHAM, or BERRINGHAM, Worc., a cross moline, az. *Pl.* 89, *cr.* 8.

BERINGHAM, an arm, in armour, embowed, in hand a spiked club, ppr. *Pl.* 45, *cr.* 10, (club, *pl.* 83, *cr.* 2.)

BERINGTON, a lion, sejant, (crowned.) *Pl.* 126, *cr.* 15.

BERINGTON, CHARLES-MICHAEL, Esq., of Little Malvern Court, Worcester, a greyhound's head, couped, ar., gorged, or. *Pl.* 43, *cr.* 11.

BERINGTON, Bradwell, Chesh., out of a ducal coronet, or, a greyhound's head, ar., (collared, gu., charged with three plates.) *Pl.* 70, *cr.* 5.

BERKELEY, WILLIAM, Esq., of Cotheridge Court, Worc., a bear's head, couped, ar., muzzled, gu. *Dieu avec nous. Pl.* 111, *cr.* 4.

BERKELEY, ROBERT, Esq., of Spetchley, Worc., same crest and motto.

BERKELEY, on a mitre, gu., a cheveron, between eight crosslets, ar. *Virtute, non vi. Pl.* 49, *cr.* 15, (cross, *pl.* 141.)

BERKELEY, Earl of, and Baron; Viscount Dursley; a mitre, gu., labelled and garnished, or, charged with a cheveron, between ten crosses pattée, ar. *Dieu avec nous. Pl.* 12, *cr.* 10.

BERKELEY, Eng., a bishop's mitre, ppr. *Pl.* 12, *cr.* 10.

BERKENHEAD, Eng., out of a ducal coronet, in hand a sheaf of arrows, points downward, all ppr. *Pl.* 9, *cr.* 4.

BERKHEAD, Crestwhite, Cumb., a goat's head, erased, party per fess, or and gu., attired, sa. *Pl.* 29, *cr.* 13.

BERKHEAD, or BERKENHEAD, a goat, salient, ar., attired, or, resting fore dexter on a garb, gold. *Pl.* 32, *cr.* 10, (garb, *pl.* 48, *cr.* 10.)

BERKLEY, a unicorn, passant, gu., armed and crined, or. *Pl.* 106, *cr.* 3, (without collar or line.)

BERKLEY, a bear's head, couped, ar., muzzled, gu. *Pl.* 111, *cr.* 4.

BIRMINGHAM, Warw., two lions' gambs, in saltier, sa. *Pl.* 20, *cr.* 13.

BERNALL, a demi-lion, rampant, gu. *Pl.* 67, *cr.* 10.

BERNARD, Nettleham, Linc.; and Nether-Winchendon, Bucks.; a demi-bear, muzzled and (collared,) or. *Bear and forbear. Pl.* 104, *cr.* 10.

BERNARD, Earl of Bandon, Viscount Bernard, and Baron Bandon, Iri., a demi-lion, ar., in paws a snake, ppr. *Virtus probata florebit. Pl.* 124, *cr.* 5, (without charging.)

BERNARD, Huntingdon, a demi-bear, muzzled and (collared,) or. *Nisi paret imparat. Pl.* 104, *cr.* 10.

BERNARD-BEAMISH, ARTHUR, Esq., of Palace Anne, co. Cork, a demi-lion, ar., between paws a snake, ppr. *Virtus probata floresbit. Pl.* 124, *cr.* 5, (without charging.)

BERNERS, Tharfield, Herts., a monkey, ppr., covered about loins, and lined, or. *Pl.* 101, *cr.* 11.

BERNERS, JOHN, Esq., of Woolverstone Park, Suff., a monkey, ppr., environed about loins, and lined, or, holding a scroll with motto— *Del fugo I avola. Pl.* 101, *cr.* 11.

BERNEY, Norf., a garb, or. *Pl.* 48, *cr.* 10.

BERNEY, Sir HANSON, Bart., Parkhall, in Reedham, Norf., a plume of (six) ostrich-feathers, per pale, az. and gu., alternately. *Nil temere, neque timore. Pl.* 12, *cr.* 9.

BERNEY, an eagle's head, ppr., (gorged with an eastern coronet, or, in mouth a palm-branch, vert,) between wings, erm. *Pl.* 81, *cr.* 10.

BERNEY, Norf., a sheaf of reeds, or. *Pl.* 13, *cr.* 2.

BERNEY, Kirkbedoe, Norf., a plume of ostrich-feathers, per pale, az. and gu. *Nil temere, neque timore. Pl.* 12, *cr.* 9.

BERNEY, Norf., out of a ducal coronet, or, a plume of five ostrich-feathers, alternately, ar. and az. *Pl.* 100, *cr.* 12, (without charging.)

BERNHEIM, a fleur-de-lis, ar. *Pl.* 68, *cr.* 12.

BERNIL, and BIRNALL, a greyhound's head, between two roses, stalked and leaved. *Pl.* 84, *cr.* 13.

BERNS, Soham, Camb., an ounce, ar., (collared and chained, or.) *Pl.* 120, *cr.* 9.

BERONDON, and BERONDOWNE, Northumb., a unicorn, rampant, ppr. *Pl.* 37, *cr.* 7.

BEROWE, and BEREW, Glouc., a sea-horse's head, erased, sa., bezantée, maned and finned, or. *Pl.* 58, *cr.* 15.

BERRETON, out of a ducal coronet, a bear's head and neck, muzzled. *Pl.* 6, *cr.* 6.

BERREY, Eng., in hand a dagger. *Pl.* 28, *cr.* 4.

BERRING, out of a ducal coronet, or, a greyhound's head, ppr. *Pl.* 70, *cr.* 5.

BERRY, or BERRIE, Westerbogie, Sco., a demi-lion, gu., in dexter, a cross crosslet, fitched, az. *In hoc signo vinces. Pl.* 65, *cr.* 4.

BERRY, JAMES-WILLIAM-MIDDLETON, Esq., of Ballynegall, Westmeath : 1. A griffin's head and neck, per pale, indented, gu. and ar., charged with a trefoil, counterchanged. *Pl.* 38, *cr.* 3, (trefoil, *pl.* 141.) 2. A demi-lion, rampant, az., in paws an escallop, or. *Nihil sine labore. Pl.* 47, *cr.* 4, (escallop, *pl.* 141.)

BERRYMAN, Devons., a horse's head, erased, sa. *Pl.* 81, *cr.* 6.

BERTIE, Bart., Nether Hall, Dedham, Ess., a man's head, affrontée, couped at shoulders, ppr., ducally crowned, or, (charged on breast with a bandlet wavy sinister gobony, ar. and az.) *Loyaute m'oblige. Pl.* 28, *cr.* 3.

BERTIE, Eng., a tree, fructed with pears, ppr. *Pl.* 105, *cr.* 13.

BERTIE, Earl of Lindsey. *See* LINDSEY.

BERTIE, Earl of Abingdon. *See* ABINGDON.

BERTLES, or BERTLEYS, Chesh., a lion, rampant, az., (holding a tree, erased at root, ppr.) *Pl.* 67, *cr.* 5.

BERTRAM, a bull's head, erased, ppr., ducally gorged, or. *Pl.* 68, *cr.* 6.

BERTRAND, Eng., in hand a pistol, ppr. *Pl.* 101, *cr.* 12.

BERTUE, a savage's head, couped at shoulders, ppr., ducally crowned, or. *Loyaute m'oblige. Pl.* 28, *cr.* 3.

BERTWHISTLE, Eng., a dolphin, naiant, ppr. *Pl.* 48, *cr.* 9.

BERVY, Devons., a griffin's head, erased, per pale, indented, ar. and gu. *Pl.* 48, *cr.* 6.

BERVY, Sir EDWARD, Bart., Catton, Norf., between wings, elevated, erm., an eagle's head, couped, ppr., (gorged with an eastern crown, or, in beak a palm-branch, vert.) *Per ardua. Pl.* 81, *cr.* 10.

BERVY, out of an eastern coronet, or, a demi-talbot, rampant, ppr. *Pl.* 25, *cr.* 8, (talbot, *pl.* 5, *cr.* 13, without collar or line.)

BERVY, Eng., between horns of a crescent, or, a cross pattée, gu. *Pl.* 37, *cr.* 10.

BERVY, an eagle's head, ppr., (gorged with an eastern coronet, or, in beak a laurel-slip, vert.) *Pl.* 100, *cr.* 10.

BERWICK, Baron, (Hill ;) on the battlements of a demi-tower, ar., a fawn, statant, ppr., collared and chained, or. *Qui uti scit, ei bona. Pl.* 90, *cr.* 7.

BERWICK, Lanc., two ears of wheat, in saltier, ppr. *Pl.* 9, *cr.* 8.

BERY of Bury, Devons., a griffin's head, erased, party per pale, dancettée, ar. and gu. *Pl.* 48, *cr.* 6.

BERY, or BARRY, Winscot and Bendon, Devons., a wolf's head, erased, sa. *Pl.* 14, *cr.* 6.

BESBOROUGH, Earl of, and Baron ; Viscount Duncannon, Iri.; Baron Ponsonby, Eng., (Ponsonby ;) in a ducal coronet, az., three arrows, one in pale, and two in saltier, points downward, environed by a snake, ppr. *Pro rege, lege, et grege. Pl.* 86, *cr.* 12.

BESELEY, Lanc. and Yorks., an arm, in armour, embowed, per fess, couped at shoulder, resting on elbow, in hand a club, all ppr. *Pl.* 65, *cr.* 13.

BESELEY, Yorks., a castle, triple-towered, ar., on centre tower a standard floating to sinister, sa., charged with a saltier, of the first. *Pl.* 123, *cr.* 14.

BESELEY, BESLEY, or BESLY, Eng., a lion, rampant, between paws a ducal coronet. *Pl.* 9, *cr.* 7.

BESELEY, BESLEY, or BESLY, out of a mural coronet, two branches of palm, in saltier, surmounted by a spear, in pale, ppr. *Pl.* 97, *cr.* 8.

BESILES, or BESILLS, Yorks., in hand a bunch of grapes, all ppr. *Pl.* 37, *cr.* 4.

BESOOK, on a mural coronet, a beaver, passant, ppr. *Pl.* 49, *cr.* 5, (coronet, *pl.* 128, *fig.* 18.)

BESSELL, a (demi)-lion, affrontée, (in each paw a slip of columbine, ppr., flowered, purp.) *Pl.* 120, *cr.* 2.

BEST, South Dalton, near Beverley, Yorks., a cubit arm, vested and cuffed, in hand a falchion, ppr. *Pl.* 21, *cr.* 10.

BEST, out of a mural coronet, or, an ostrich-head, ar., in mouth a cross crosslet, gold. *Pl.* 50, *cr.* 1, (coronet, *pl.* 128, *fig.* 18 ; cross, *pl.* 141.)

BEST, Kent, out of a ducal coronet, or, an ostrich-head, between wings, ar., in mouth a cross crosslet, gold. *Pl.* 28, *cr.* 13, (coronet, *pl.* 128, *fig.* 3 ; cross, *pl.* 141.)

BEST, a griffin's head, erased. *Pl.* 48, *cr.* 6.

BEST, Glouc. ; and Greenwich, Kent, out of a ducal coronet, or, an ostrich-head, between wings, ar. *Pl.* 28, *cr.* 13, (coronet, *pl.* 128, *fig.* 3.)

BEST, Lond. and Kent, out of a ducal coronet, gu., a demi-peacock, wings displayed, or, in mouth a snake, ppr., entwined round body. *Pl.* 53, *cr.* 12, (coronet, *pl.* 128, *fig.* 3.)

BEST, Lond., a peacock, wings elevated, or, in beak a serpent, reflexed over back, az. *Pl.* 53, *cr.* 12.

BEST, Baron WYNFORD. *See* WYNFORD.

BEST, HEAD-POTTINGER, Esq., of Donnington, Berks., a cubit arm (vested, gu., cuff, ar.,) in hand a falchion, ppr. *Optimus est qui optime facit.* *Pl.* 21, *cr.* 10.

BEST, GEORGE, Esq., of Eastbury House, Compton, Surr., a griffin's head, erased, sa. *Haud nomine tantum.* *Pl.* 48, *cr.* 6.

BEST, (The late) THOMAS-FAIRFAX, Esq., of Chilston ; and of Wierton, Kent; out of a (mural) coronet, or, a demi-ostrich, ar., in beak a cross crosslet, fitched, gold. *Pl.* 29, *cr.* 9, (cross, *pl.* 141.)

BEST, JAMES, Esq., of Park House, Kent, same crest.

BESTE, Middleton-Quernhow, Richmond, Yorks., the sinister arm of an archer, couped and embowed, in fess, gu., in hand a bow, in pale, ppr., strung, ar. *Pl.* 52, *cr.* 5.

BESTNEY, Herts., out of a ducal coronet, a demi-griffin, ar. *Pl.* 39, *cr.* 2.

BESTON, a demi-talbot in mouth an arrow. *Pl.* 97, *cr.* 9.

BESTORICKE, or BESTORIKE, a demi-talbot, in mouth an arrow. *Pl.* 97, *cr.* 9.

BESTOW, Eng., a crescent, ar. *Pl.* 18, *cr.* 14.

BESTROE, and BESTROW, an elephant's head, erased, per cheveron, or and sa., armed, of the last. *Pl.* 68, *cr.* 4.

BESVILLE, a dragon's head, erased, gu. *Pl.* 107, *cr.* 10, (without collar.)

BESWICK, Lond. and Kent, a demi-lion, ppr., between paws a bezant. *Pl.* 126, *cr.* 12.

BESWICK of Beswick, Kent, a demi-lion, ppr., double-queued, between paws a bezant. *Pl.* 126, *cr.* 12, (double-queued, *pl.* 120, *cr.* 10.)

BESWICK, WILLIAM, Esq., of Gristhorpe, Yorks.: 1. *Ancient,* a dexter hand, couped at wrist, ppr., surmounted by an etoile, radiated, or. *Pl.* 68, *cr.* 5, (etoile, *pl.* 141.) 2. *Ordinary,* a demi-lion, rampant, or, between paws a bezant. *Denique cœlum.* *Pl.* 126, *cr.* 12.

BESWICK of Winnington, Chesh., a demi-lion, or, between paws a bezant. *Pl.* 126, *cr.* 12.

BETAGH, Iri., two anchors, in saltier. *Pl.* 37, *cr.* 12.

BETENHAM, or BETNAM, Kent, a bear's head, erased, sa., muzzled and bellittée, or. *Pl.* 71, *cr.* 6.

BETENSON, BETTENSON, or BETTERSON, Kent, a lion's head, erased, sa., collared, ar. *Qui sera sera.* *Pl.* 7, *cr.* 10.

BETENSON, Devons., a griffin's head, couped, ppr. *Pl.* 38, *cr.* 3.

BETHAM, Bucks., out of a ducal coronet, or, an elephant's head, ar. *Pl.* 93, *cr.* 13.

BETHELL, Dors., a demi-eagle, wings displayed, az., charged on body with an etoile of six points, or. *Pl.* 44, *cr.* 14.

BETHELL, York and Hants., out of a ducal coronet, or, a boar's head, couped, sa. *Pl.* 102, *cr.* 14.

BETHELL, Heref. and Yorks., between wings, displayed, az., an eagle's head, couped, of the same, charged on neck with an etoile, or. *Pl.* 44, *cr.* 14.

BETHELL, or BYTHELL, Winchester and Glouc., out of a ducal coronet, or, a boar's head and neck, couped, ar. *Pl.* 102, *cr.* 14.

BETHUNE, Bart., Sco., an otter's head, erased, ppr. *Debonnair.* *Pl.* 126, *cr.* 14.

BETHUNE, an otter's head, couped, ppr. *Urbane.* *Pl.* 126, *cr.* 14.

BETHUNE of Blebo, Sco., an otter, issuing, ar. *Debonnair.* *Pl.* 9, *cr.* 9.

BETHUNE of Nethertarvit, a physician's squadrangular cap, sa. *Resolutio cauta.* *Pl.* 39, *cr.* 3.

BETHUNE, Sco., an otter's head, couped, ar. *Debonnair.* *Pl.* 126, *cr.* 14.

BETHWATER, a fawn's head, cabossed, or. *Pl.* 36, *cr.* 1, (without horns.)

BETON, BEATON, BETTON, and BETUNE, a lion, passant, sa. *Fortis in arduis.* *Pl.* 48, *cr.* 8.

BETRAY, an arm, embowed, vested, gu., cuffed, ar., in hand, ppr., a torteau. *Pl.* 39, *cr.* 1, (torteau, *pl.* 141.)

BETSON of Glassermount and Kilrie, Sco., a bee, volant, in pale, ppr. *Cum prudentia sedulus.* *Pl.* 100, *cr.* 3.

BETSON of Contle, Sco., a bridge of three arches, ppr. *Pro patria.* *Pl.* 38, *cr.* 4.

BETSWORTH, out of a tower, ar., a demi-lion, or, (ducally crowned, in dexter a battle-axe, az.) *Pl.* 42, *cr.* 4.

BETTENSON, or BETTINSON, Seven Oaks, Kent, a lion's head, erased, sa., collared, ar. *Qui sera sera.* *Pl.* 7, *cr.* 10.

BETTES, out of a ducal coronet, or, a buck's head, gu., attired, gold, (collared, ar., charged with three cinquefoils, of the second.) *Pl.* 29, *cr.* 7.

BETTES, Hants., out of a ducal coronet, or, a bull's head, ar. *Pl.* 68, *cr.* 6.

BETTESWORTH, Tyning, Suss., on stump of tree, vert, a lion, sejant, per fess, or and ar., (in dexter a battle-axe, gu., headed, of the third.) *Pl.* 76, *cr.* 11.

D

BETTIE, or BETTY, Eng., a goat's head, erased, (collared,) ppr. *Pl.* 29, *cr.* 13.
BETTISON, Warw., a lion's head, erased, sa., collared, ar. *Qui sera sera. Pl.* 7, *cr.* 10.
BETTON, RICHARD, Esq., of Overton House, Salop, a demi-lion, rampant. *Nunquam non paratus. Pl.* 67, *cr.* 10.
BETTON, Eng., a demi-bear, rampant, ppr. *Pl.* 104, *cr.* 10.
BETTS, Eng., a leopard, passant, gardant, ppr. *Pl.* 51, *cr.* 7.
BETTS, EDWARD-LADD, Esq., of Preston Hall, Kent, out of the battlements of a tower, ppr., a stag's head, ar., charged with a cinquefoil, ppr. *Ostendo non ostento. Pl.* 90, *cr.* 7, (head, *pl.* 91, *cr.* 14; cinquefoil, *pl.* 141.)
BETTS, The Rev. THOMAS D'EYE, of Wortham Hall, Suff., out of a ducal coronet, or, a buck's head, gu., attired, gold. *Pl.* 29, *cr.* 7.
BETTSWORTH, out of a tower, ar., a demi-lion, rampant, per fess, or and ar., crowned, az., in paws a battle-axe, handle, or, headed, ar. *Pl.* 42, *cr.* 4.
BETTY, a demi-lion, in dexter a crescent, ar. *Pl.* 89, *cr.* 10, (crescent, *pl.* 141.)
BETUNE, Eng., a demi-bear, rampant. *Pl.* 104, *cr.* 10.
BEUFO, a beech-tree, with a saw through it, ppr. *Pl.* 100, *cr.* 2, (without coronet.)
BEUGO, an arm, in armour, embowed, wielding a scimitar, turned to dexter, all ppr. *Qui nos vincet?—*and—*Pro Deo, patria, et rege. Pl.* 81, *cr.* 11.
BEUZEVILL, a lion's head, ppr., (semée-de-plates.) *Pl.* 126, *cr.* 1.
BEVAN, or BEVIN, Cornw., a griffin, passant, or. *Pl.* 61, *cr.* 14, (without gorging.)
BEVAN, on a mural coronet, a griffin, passant. *Pl.* 61, *cr.* 14, (coronet, *pl.* 128, *fig.* 18.)
BEVAN, ROBERT-COOPER-LEE, Esq., of Fosbury House, Wilts.; and Trent Park, East Barnet, Herts.; on a mural coronet, ar., a griffin, passant, or, gorged with an eastern coronet, gu. *Pl.* 61, *cr.* 14, (coronet, *pl.* 128, *fig.* 18.)
BEVANS, or BEVAINS, Eng., a weaver's shuttle, in pale, threaded, ppr. *Pl.* 102, *cr.* 10.
BEVELEY, a bull's head, sa., ducally (crowned,) or. *Pl.* 68, *cr.* 6.
BEVEREHAM, Iri., out of a coronet, or, an arm, in armour, in hand a sword, ppr. *Pl.* 115, *cr.* 14.
BEVERIDGE, Kent, Chichester, Normandy, and Sco., out of a ducal coronet, or, a demi-beaver, ppr.
BEVERLEY, between wings, expanded, a nail, erect. *Pl.* 47, *cr.* 10, (wings, *pl.* 39, *cr.* 12.)
BEVERLEY, ROBERT-MACKENZIE, Esq., of Beverley, York, a bull's head, erased, ar. *Ubi libertas, ibi patria. Pl.* 19, *cr.* 3.
BEVERLEY, Earl of, and Baron Louvaine, (Percy,) on a chapeau, gu., turned up, erm., a lion, (statant, az., tail extended, charged on shoulder with a crescent, ar.) *Esperance en Dieu. Pl.* 107, *cr.* 1.
BEVERLEY, (on a mount, vert,) a wolf, passant, ar., (pierced through neck with an arrow, ppr.) *Pl.* 46, *cr.* 6.
BEVERS, a demi-wyvern, vert, armed, gu. *Pl.* 116, *cr.* 15.
BEVERSHAM, Holbrook-Hall, Suff., out of a tower, ar., a demi-lion, gu. *Pl.* 42, *cr.* 4.

BEVIL, Eng., a bull's head, gu., horned, or. *Pl.* 120, *cr.* 7.
BEVILE, Suff., a dove, volant, with olive-branch, ppr. *Pl.* 25, *cr.* 6.
BEVILL, or BEVILLE, Cornw., a griffin, passant, gu. *Pl.* 61, *cr.* 14.
BEVILL, Cornw., a griffin, passant, or, collared, sa. *Pl.* 61, *cr.* 14.
BEVILLE, Cornw., a griffin, passant, or. *Pl.* 61, *cr.* 14.
BEVILLE, Killegarth, a griffin, or. *Futurum invisibile. Pl.* 66, *cr.* 13.
BEVIS, a pheon, az. *Pl.* 56, *cr.* 15.
BEW, Eng., a peacock's head, couped and erect, ppr. *Pl.* 100, *cr.* 5.
BEWEHAM, or BEWCHAM, Eng., a hand, issuing, pruning a vine, ppr. *Pl.* 83, *cr.* 4.
BEWES, Cornw., on a chapeau, crimson, turned up, erm., a pegasus, rearing, of a bay colour, mane and tail, sa., wings, or, in mouth a sprig of laurel, ppr. *Pl.* 57, *cr.* 15, (chapeau, same plate, *cr.* 14.)
BEWICKE, Northumb., a goat's head, erased, ar., gorged, with a mural coronet, gu. *In cœlo quies. Pl.* 29, *cr.* 13, (coronet, *pl.* 128, *fig.* 18.)
BEWLEY, Suff., an ibex's head, or, out of the centre of a rose, gu., barbed, vert. *Pl.* 72, *cr.* 9, (rose, *pl.* 69, *cr.* 6.)
BEWLEY, Linc., a moor's head, affrontée, vested in a cowl, all ppr. *Pl.* 38, *cr.* 13.
BEWRIS, or BEWRYS, a lion's head, ar., (charged with two cheverons, sa.,) ducally crowned, or. *Pl.* 90, *cr.* 4.
BEWSHIN, out of a ducal coronet, or, in lion's paw a palm-branch, ppr. *Pl.* 88, *cr.* 8.
BEXLEY, Baron, (Vansittart,) upon two crosses, pattée, ar., a demi-eagle, couped, sa., wings elevated. *Grata quies. Pl.* 117, *cr.* 15.
BEYARD, Eng., on a tower, ar., loopholes and door, sa., a lion, rampant, gu. *Pl.* 121, *cr.* 5.
BEYKLE, Eng., a cross pattée, gu., between wings, or. *Pl.* 29, *cr.* 14.
BEYNHAM, Heref., a beaver, ppr. *Pl.* 49, *cr.* 5.
BEYNHAM, Hunts., a raven, ppr. *Pl.* 123, *cr.* 2.
BEYNON of Bath, a lion, rampant, ppr., between paws a rose, or, barbed, vert. *Pl.* 125, *cr.* 2, (rose, *pl.* 141.)
BEYNON, The Rev. EDMUND-TURNER, A.M., of Carshalton, Surr.: 1. For *Beynon*, a lion, rampant, ar., (semée of cross crosslets, vert, between paws an escutcheon, of the first, charged with a griffin's head, erased, pean.) *Pl.* 125, *cr.* 2. 2. For *Batley*, a griffin's head, erased, pean, in beak a mill-rind. *Pl.* 9, *cr.* 12, (mill-rind, *pl.* 141.)
BEYNTON, Eng., a griffin's head, erased, sa. *Pl.* 48, *cr.* 6.
BICKERSTAFFE, Kent and Lanc., the sun surmounted of a unicorn, rampant, ppr. *Pl.* 114, *cr.* 1.
BICKERTON, Sir RICHARD HUSSEY, Bart., Upwood, Hunts.: 1. For *Bickerton*, a dexter arm, in armour, embowed, in hand a dagger, all ppr., (suspended from arm by a crimson ribbon, an escutcheon, charged with a mullet and increscent, ar.) *Pl.* 120, *cr.* 11. 2. For *Hussey*, a hind, passant, ppr., (ducally gorged and chained, or.) *Pro Deo et rege. Pl.* 20, *cr.* 14.

BICKERTON, Bart., Upwood, Hunts. and Heref., an arm, in armour, embowed, in hand a dagger, all ppr. *Pl.* 120, *cr.* 11.

BICKERTON, Ess.; and Beeby, Leic.; a martlet, or. *Pl.* 111, *cr.* 5.

BICKLEY, Attleborough, Norf., a hind's head, ppr., (collared,) ar. *Pl.* 21, *cr.* 9.

BICKLIFE, Lond., a hind's head, ppr., (collared, ar.) *Pl.* 21, *cr.* 9.

BICKNALL, or BICKNELL, Eng., an angel praying, between two branches of laurel, in orle. *Pl.* 94, *cr.* 11.

BICKNALL, or BICKNELL, Spring-Garden Terrace, a dragon's head, (couped,) collared. *Pl.* 107, *cr.* 10.

BICKNOLL, a dragon's head, erased, vert. *Pl.* 107, *cr.* 10, (without collar.)

BICKNOR, BICKENOR, or BYKENORE, a pheon, erm. *Pl.* 56, *cr.* 15.

BICKWITH, Yorks., a stag's head, quarterly, per fess, indented, or and az. *Pl.* 91, *cr.* 14.

BIDDELL, BIDDLE, or BIDDELLE, Glouc., a demi-heraldic tiger, rampant, gu., ducally gorged, or. *Deus clypeus meus. Pl.* 57, *cr.* 13.

BIDDULPH, ROBERT-MYDDELTON, Esq., of Chirk Castle, Denbigh; and Burghill, Heref.: 1. For *Biddulph*, a wolf, salient, ar., (charged on shoulder with a trefoil, slipped, vert.) *Pl.* 126, *cr.* 13. 2. For *Myddelton*, out of a ducal coronet, or, a bloody hand, ppr. *In veritate triumpho. Pl.* 79, *cr.* 6, (without wings.)

BIDDULPH, ROBERT, Esq., of Ledbury, Heref.; 1. A wolf, salient, ar., (charged on shoulder with a trefoil, slipped, vert.) *Pl.* 126, *cr.* 13. 2. A wolf, sejant, (regardant, ar., vulned on shoulder, gu.) *Sublimiora petimus. Pl.* 110, *cr.* 4.

BIDDULPH, Bart., Westcombe, Kent, a wolf, sejant, ar., (vulned in shoulder, ppr.) *Pl.* 110, *cr.* 4.

BIDDULPH-WRIGHT, ANTHONY-JOHN, Esq., of Burton Park, Suss.; 1. A wolf, salient, ar. *Pl.* 126, *cr.* 13. 2. Out of a ducal coronet, or, a dragon's head, ppr. *Pl.* 59, *cr.* 14.

BIDDULPH, Cleve Court and Brockley, Somers., a wolf, salient, ar. *Pl.* 126, *cr.* 13, (without collar.)

BIDGOOD, Exeter, Devons., in dexter hand, erect, (in armour,) or, an adder, ppr. *Pl.* 91, *cr.* 6.

BIDLAKE, Somers., a cock, in beak a trefoil, all ppr. *Pl.* 55, *cr.* 12.

BIDON, Eng., between wings, a lion, rampant. *Pl.* 29, *cr.* 5.

BIDULPH, East Greenwich, Kent, a wolf, salient, ar., (vulned on shoulder, gu.) *Pl.* 126, *cr.* 13.

BIDWELL, or BYDEWELL, Devons., in hand, couped, in fess, a curling-stone. *Pl.* 104, *cr.* 6.

BIDWELL, a martlet. *Pl.* 111, *cr.* 5.

BIE, two oak-branches, in saltier, ppr. *Pl.* 19, *cr.* 12.

BIELBY, a hawk, close, ppr. *Pl.* 67, *cr.* 3.

BIEST, Eng., a fetterlock, ppr. *Pl.* 122, *cr.* 12.

BIFIELD, or BYFIELD, Lond., a cross crosslet, fitched, gu., between two palm-branches, vert. *Pl.* 37, *cr.* 14, (branches, *pl.* 87, *cr.* 8.)

BIG, BIGG, or BIGGE, three savages' heads conjoined in one neck, one looking to sinister, one to dexter, and one upward, wreathed, vert. *Pl.* 32, *cr.* 2.

BIG, BIGG, or BIGGE, Ridgewell and Stambourn, Ess., a cockatrice's head, couped, beaked, and (crowned, or,) wings, displayed, vert. *Pl.* 77, *cr.* 5, (without coronet.)

BIGBERY, Ess., in hand a leg, in armour, couped above knee, and spurred, all ppr. *Pl.* 39, *cr.* 6.

BIGG, Hants., a rhinoceros, ppr. *Pl.* 4, *cr.* 11.

BIGG, an arm, embowed, vested, couped at shoulder, in hand a serpent, ppr., tail environing arm. *Pl.* 91, *cr.* 6, (arm, *pl.* 120, *cr.* 1.)

BIGG, Iping, Suss.; and Arnwood, Hants.; an eagle's head, couped, ducally crowned, between wings, elevated. *Pl.* 81, *cr.* 10, (coronet, *pl.* 128, *fig.* 3.)

BIGG, Eng., out of a mural coronet, seven Lochaber axes, ppr. *Pl.* 62, *cr.* 8.

BIGGAR, or BIGGER, Sco., a pelican's head, couped, ppr. *Giving and forgiving. Pl.* 41, *cr.* 4.

BIGGAR, or BIGGER, a pelican's head, vulning, ppr. *Pl.* 41, *cr.* 4.

BIGGE of Linden, Northumb., a cockatrice's head, turreted, or, wings erect, az. *Pl.* 106, *cr.* 15, (without gorging.)

BIGGE, an eagle's head, erm., murally crowned, between wings, of the last. *Pl.* 81, *cr.* 10, (coronet, *pl.* 128, *fig.* 18.)

BIGGE, or BIGGS, an eagle's head, erm., ducally crowned, or, between wings, ar. *Pl.* 81, *cr.* 10, (coronet, *pl.* 128, *fig.* 3.)

BIGGS, HARRY, Esq., of Stockton, Wilts., a leopard's face, ppr. *Pl.* 66, *cr.* 14.

BIGGS, a griffin's head, erased. *Pl.* 48, *cr.* 6.

BIGGS, Lond., a lamb, (couchant,) ar. *Pl.* 116, *cr.* 1.

BIGGS, Lond., a leopard's face, gu. *Pl.* 66, *cr.* 14.

BIGGS, Eng., in dexter hand, charged with a bendlet, ar., a serpent, vert. *Pl.* 91, *cr.* 6.

BIGLAND, Suff., a lion, passant, (holding an arrow.) *Pl.* 48, *cr.* 8.

BIGNELL, Salisbury, Wilts., Norf., and Lond., a wyvern, gu., wings elevated and addorsed, or, (dexter on an anchor, gold.) *Pl.* 63, *cr.* 13.

BIGOT, or BIGOTT, Eng., a martlet, sa. *Pl.* 111, *cr.* 5.

BIGWOOD, Eng., in hand, erect, issuing from a cloud, a club, in bend sinister. *Pl.* 37, *cr.* 13.

BILESBY of Bilesby, Linc., a lion's head, erased, ar. *Pl.* 81, *cr.* 4.

BILL, Eng., a stork's head, erased, ppr. *Pl.* 32, *cr.* 5.

BILLAM, FRANCIS, Esq., of Newall Hall, Yorks., a dexter arm, in hand an arrow, ppr. *Azincourt. Pl.* 43, *cr.* 13.

BILLCLIFFE, Targanby, Kent, a naked arm, couped at elbow and erect, in hand a battle-axe, all ppr. *Pl.* 73, *cr.* 7.

BILLERS, Lond., a snail in its shell, ppr. *Pl.* 105, *cr.* 8.

BILLESWORTH, a squirrel, sejant, cracking a nut, all ppr., collared, or. *Pl.* 16, *cr.* 9.

BILLET, BILLOT, or BELLET, Devons. and Norf., a hand and arm, couped at elbow, in armour, and gauntleted, ppr., holding a baton, or. *Pl.* 33, *cr.* 4.

BILLICH, a rat, (salient,) sa. *Pl.* 121, *cr.* 10.

BILLING, Norf., a dexter arm, vambraced, ppr., in hand an anchor. *Pl.* 122, *cr.* 8, (without coronet.)

BILLING, and BILLINGE, Deding, Oxon.; and Billinge, Lanc.; an arm, couped at shoulder, in fess, elbow on wreath, in hand a spear, in pale. *Pl.* 107, *cr.* 3.

BILLING, a mount, semée of quaterfoils. *Pl.* 62, *cr.* 11.

BILLING, or BILLINGE, a buck, passant, ppr. *Pl.* 68, *cr.* 2.

BILLINGHAM, Eng., a lion, rampant, ppr. *Pl.* 67, *cr.* 5.

BILLINGHAM, a lion, rampant, double-queued, ar. *Pl.* 41, *cr.* 15.

BILLINGHURST, Suss., issuant from a human heart a bunch of roses, ppr. *Pl.* 55, *cr.* 13, (roses, *pl.* 23, *cr.* 2.)

BILLINGHURST, Newport, Isle of Wight, an eagle, displayed, or, in beak a cross crosslet, fitched, ar. *Pl.* 48, *cr.* 11, (cross, *pl.* 141.)

BILLINGS, Beds., an arm, embowed, vested, in hand a covered cup. *Pl.* 39, *cr.* 1.

BILLINGSLEY, Lond. and Salop, (on a mount, vert,) a leopard, couchant, or, spotted, sa. *Pl.* 111, *cr.* 11.

BILNEY, Norf., a demi-griffin, ar., between paws a buckle, sa. *Pl.* 18, *cr.* 6, (buckle, *pl.* 73, *cr.* 10.)

BILSDON, Eng., a ram's head, couped, or *Pl.* 34, *cr.* 12.

BILSON, or BILLSON, Hants., a bugle-horn, or, stringed, ar., and tasselled, gold. *Pl.* 48, *cr.* 12.

BINCKES, BINCKS, or BINKS, a winged column, gu. *Pl.* 33, *cr.* 12.

BINDLEY, or BINDLY, out of a mural coronet, a dexter arm, embowed, wielding a sword, ppr. *Pl.* 115, *cr.* 14.

BINDLOSS, a demi-horse, ar. *Pl.* 91, *cr.* 2, (without wings or coronet.)

BINDLOSSE, Borwick, Lanc.; and Westm.; a demi-horse, ar., ducally gorged, az. *Pl.* 91, *cr.* 2, (without wings.)

BINDON, Iri., on a mount, vert, a bull, passant, ar. *Pl.* 39, *cr.* 5.

BING, Kent, a demi-pegasus, regardant, winged, or, holding in pale a flag, gu. *Pl.* 32, *cr.* 1.

BING, Middx. *See* BYNG.

BINGE, Kent, an antelope, erm., attired, or. *Pl.* 63, *cr.* 10.

BINGHAM, Lord Clanmorris, Baron Clanmorris of Newbrook; an eagle, wings addorsed, ppr. *Spes mea Christus.* *Pl.* 121, *cr.* 3, (without arrow.)

BINGHAM, RICHARD-HIPPISLEY, Esq., of Bingham's Melcombe, Dorset, on a rock, ppr., an eagle, rising, or. *Spes mea Christus.* *Pl.* 61, *cr.* 1.

BINGHAM, Bingham-Melcombe, Dors., an arm, couped at elbow, erect, ppr., (vested, az., charged on sleeve with a cross formée, ar., cuffed, of the same,) in hand, ppr., a laurel-branch, vert. *Pl.* 43, *cr.* 6.

BINGHAM, Dors., on a rock, ppr., an eagle, rising, or. *Pl.* 61, *cr.* 1.

BINGHAM. *See* LUCAN, Earl of.

BINGLEY, Yorks., a bear's head, erased, ar., muzzled, (and collared, gu., studded and ringed, or.) *Pl.* 71, *cr.* 6.

BINGLEY, Lond. and Ess., a bear's head, erased, ar., muzzled, sa., (collared, gu., studded and ringed, or.) *Pl.* 71, *cr.* 6.

BINGLEY, Middx. and Flintshire, a pheon, ar., between wings, or, backed by a pellet.

BINGLEY, Notts., on a pellet a cross formée, ar. *Pl.* 15, *cr.* 8, (pellet, *pl.* 141.)

BINGLEY, Notts., on a pellet a cross formée, ar., charged with an annulet, gu., between wings, or.

BINGLEY, a phœnix in flames, ppr. *Pl.* 44, *cr.* 8.

BINKS, Durh., a lion's head, erased, between wings, all or. *Pl.* 73, *cr.* 3.

BINKS, Eng., an eagle's head, erased, ducally gorged, in beak a pheon. *Pl.* 39, *cr.* 4.

BINNING of Wallifoord, Sco., a demi-horse, furnished for a waggon, ppr. *Christo duce felicite.* *Pl.* 49, *cr.* 6.

BINNING of Carloury Hall, Sco., a horse's head, furnished for a waggon, ppr. *Virtute dologue.* *Pl.* 49, *cr.* 6.

BINNS, Worc., a martlet. *Labore et diligentia.* *Pl.* 111, *cr.* 5.

BINNS, a mortar, mounted, ppr. *Pl.* 55, *cr.* 14.

BINNS, Iri., in hand a close helmet, az. *Pl.* 37, *cr.* 15.

BINNY, or BINNEY, Eng., in dexter hand, ppr., a sword, in pale, az., hilt and pommel, or. *Pl.* 23, *cr.* 15.

BINNY of Fearn, Sco., a horse's head, ar., bridled, gu. *Virtute et opera.* *Pl.* 92, *cr.* 1.

BINNY, or BINNIE, Sco., a horse's head, bridled, ppr. *Virtute et opera.* *Pl.* 92, *cr.* 1.

BIRCH, Bart., Lanc., on a mount, vert, a hare, salient, collared, ar. *Libertas.*

BIRCH, a hare, current, sa., collared, or.

BIRCH, Birch-Hall, Lanc.; Linc.; and Lond.; a fleur-de-lis, ar., entwined by a serpent, ppr. *Pl.* 15, *cr.* 13.

BIRCH, Lanc. and Salop, a demi-bird, wings displayed, sa. *Pl.* 22, *cr.* 11.

BIRCH, WYRLEY, Esq., of Wretham Hall, Norf., a fleur-de-lis, (with shamrock,) and serpent entwined, ppr. *Prudentia et simplicitate.* *Pl.* 15, *cr.* 13.

BIRCH-NEWELL, JOHN-WILLIAM, Esq., of Henley Park, Oxford, same crest and motto.

BIRCHETT, Rye, Suss., a tiger, sejant, vert, ducally gorged and maned, or. *Pl.* 26, *cr.* 9, (coronet, *pl.* 128, *fig.* 3.)

BIRCHILL of Birchill, Chesh., a lion, rampant, az., (supporting a tree, vert.) *Pl.* 67, *cr.* 5.

BIRD, The Rev. CHARLES-JOHN, A.M., and F.A.S., of Drybridge House, Hereford, a martlet, gu. *Cruce spes mea.* *Pl.* 111, *cr.* 5.

BIRD, Chesh., a martlet, ppr. *Pl.* 111, *cr.* 5.

BIRD, on a dolphin, ppr., an eagle, or, wings expanded. *Pl.* 34, *cr.* 2, (dolphin, *pl.* 48, *cr.* 9.)

BIRD, Drybridge, Heref., a martlet, (wings expanded,) gu., charged on breast with a mullet, or. *Pl.* 111, *cr.* 5, (mullet, *pl.* 141.)

BIRD, Westminster, a ring-dove, ppr., (resting dexter on a rose, or.) *Pl.* 66, *cr.* 12.

BIRD, Lond. and Warw., a greyhound's head, vert, erased, gu., (gorged with a dove-tailed collar, or.) *Pl.* 89, *cr.* 2.

BIRD, Derb., on a mount, vert, stump of tree, couped and eradicated, thereon a (falcon,) (wings addorsed,) all ppr. *Pl.* 55, *cr.* 11.

BIRD, out of an eastern coronet, a demi-lion, in dexter a cross crosslet. *Pl.* 65, *cr.* 6, (coronet, *pl.* 128, *fig.* 2.)

BIRKBECK, Lond.: 1. A bow, erect, entwined by oak-branch, ppr., acorned, or. 2. An oak-branch, ppr., acorned, or, and a rose-branch, of the first, flowered, gu., entertwined and erected. *Fide, sed cui vide.*

BIRKBERKE, a nut-branch, vert, fructed, or. *Pl.* 81, *cr.* 7.

BIRKBY, or BUCKBY, on a chapeau, gu., turned up, erm., a garb, or, banded, ar. *Pl.* 62, *cr.* 1.

BIRKENHEAD, Backford, Chesh., a goat, salient, ar., attired, or, resting fore-feet on a garb, gold. *Pl.* 32, *cr.* 10, (garb, *pl.* 48, *cr.* 10.)

BIRKENHEAD, Chesh., out of a ducal coronet, or, an arm, embowed, ppr., in hand three arrows, gold. *Pl.* 9, *cr.* 4, (arm, *pl.* 123, *cr.* 10.)

BIRKES, an ear of wheat and palm-branch, in saltier, ppr. *Pl.* 63, *cr.* 3.

BIRKET, and BIRKETT, Eng., on a hand, couped at wrist, an eagle, rising, ppr. *Pl.* 104, *cr.* 14.

BIRLE, Ess., an arm, couped at shoulder, in fess, vested, ar., cuff, sa., in hand, ppr., a cross formée, fitched, or, an arm three torteaux. *Pl.* 88, *cr.* 7, (cross, *pl.* 27, *cr.* 14.)

BIRLEY, JOHN, Esq., of Woodend, Cumb.; and Lanc.; a demi-boar, sa., (collared, az., chain reflexed over back, or,) supporting a branch of wild teazle, ppr., charged on shoulder with a mill-rind, ar. *Omni liber metu.* *Pl.* 20, *cr.* 5, (teazle, *pl.* 74, *cr.* 9.)

BIRLEY of Manchester, same crest and motto.

BIRLEY, The Rev. JOHN-SHEPHERD, M.A., of Halliwell Hall and Kirkham, Lancaster, same crest and motto.

BIRMINGHAM, Norf., two lion's paws, in saltier, sa. *Pl.* 20, *cr.* 13.

BIRMINGHAM, a goat's head, erased. *Pl.* 29, *cr.* 13.

BIRN, or BRIN, Iri., a dexter hand, couped, gu. *Pl.* 32, *cr.* 14.

BIRNAL, or BIRNALL, a greyhound's head, between two roses, stalked and leaved. *Pl.* 84, *cr.* 13.

BIRNEY, Broomhill, Sco., a lion's head, erased, gu. *Sapere aude, incipe.* *Pl.* 81, *cr.* 4.

BIRNEY, Sco., in dexter hand, ppr., an anchor, erect, or, environed with clouds, ppr. *Arcus, artes, astra.* *Pl.* 41, *cr.* 5.

BIRNEY, and BIRNIE, in dexter hand an anchor, erect. *Pl.* 41, *cr.* 5, (without clouds.)

BIRNIE, a demi-lion, rampant. *Pl.* 67, *cr.* 10.

BIRON, Eng., a mermaid, with glass and comb, ppr. *Crede Byron.* *Pl.* 48, *cr.* 5.

BIRREL, and BIRRELL, Eng., an arm, in armour, embowed, brandishing scimitar, all ppr. *Pl.* 81, *cr.* 11.

BIRT, a flounder.

BIRTE, Devons., a dexter arm, embowed, in fess, issuing from a cloud, in sinister, in hand a garland of laurel, all ppr. *Pl.* 80, *cr.* 3.

BIRTLES of Birtles, Chesh., (on sinister side of a tree, vert,) a lion, rampant, az. *Pl.* 67, *cr.* 5.

BISCHOFF, Basle, in Switzerland, a demi-lion, rampant, or. *Pl.* 67, *cr.* 10.

BISCHOFF, Basle, in Switzerland, a crosier, erect, or. *Pl.* 7, *cr.* 15.

BISCHOFF, Basle, in Switzerland, a crosier, erect, or, between wings of an imperial eagle, dexter, ar., sinister, sa. *Pl.* 7, *cr.* 15, (wings, *pl.* 69, *cr.* 7.)

BISET, Sco., stump of oak-tree shooting branches, ppr. *Exitus acta probat.* *Pl.* 92, *cr.* 8.

BISH, Eng., on a chapeau, a demi-lion, rampant. *Pl.* 46, *cr.* 8.

BISHOP, Dors. and Somers., an eagle's head, erased, party per fess, or and gu., beaked, gold. *Pl.* 20, *cr.* 7.

BISHOP, Sco., on a chapeau, a lion, passant, gardant, ducally crowned. *Pl.* 7, *cr.* 14.

BISHOP, a griffin's head, erased, sa., between two laurel-branches, vert. *Pl.* 48, *cr.* 6, (branches, *pl.* 79, *cr.* 14.)

BISHOP, Devons., an eagle's head, erased, gu. and or, counterchanged. *Pl.* 20, *cr.* 7.

BISHOP of Holway, an eagle's head, erased. *Pl.* 20, *cr.* 7.

BISHOP, Dors. and Somers., an eagle's head, erased, party per pale, or and gu., beaked, gold. *Pl.* 20, *cr.* 7.

BISHOP, Evesham, Worc., out of a mural coronet, ar., a griffin's head, sa., beaked, or. *Pl.* 101, *cr.* 6, (without gorging.)

BISHOP, Bart., Suss., on a ducal coronet, or, a griffin, sejant, resting dexter on an escutcheon, ar. *Pl.* 42, *cr.* 8.

BISHOPPE, Bristol, Somers., a griffin, sejant, ar., (resting dexter on an escutcheon.) *Pl.* 42, *cr.* 8, (without coronet.)

BISHOPSTON, and BISHOPSTONE, Warw., an arm, issuing from a cloud, in fess, in hand a terrestrial globe. *Pl.* 104, *cr.* 4.

BISPHAM, Lanc., on a chapeau, gu., turned up, erm., a lion, passant, ar., resting dexter on an escutcheon, of the first. *Pl.* 107, *cr.* 1, (escutcheon, *pl.* 42, *cr.* 8.)

BISPLEAM, Eng., a stag's head, cabossed, erm., attired, or. *Pl.* 36, *cr.* 1.

BISS, Eng., an eagle, preying on a partridge, all ppr. *Pl.* 61, *cr.* 7.

BISS, Durh., two serpents entwined, erect, or, on a mount, vert, looking at each other, ppr. *Ayez prudence—and—Nil conscire sibi.*

BISS, Somers. and Iri., two serpents entwined, in saltier, or, looking at each other.

BISSE, Iri., on a mount, vert, two snakes or, interlaced, respecting each other, ppr.

BISSELL, a demi-eagle, wings, displayed, sa., charged on neck with an escallop, or. *Pl.* 22, *cr.* 11, (escallop, *pl.* 146.)

BISSET, Eng., trunk of oak-tree, sprouting, ppr. *Revivesco.* *Pl.* 92, *cr.* 8.

BISSET, stump of tree, eradicated and erased, a branch sprouting, ppr. *Repullulat.* *Pl.* 92, *cr.* 8.

BISSET, in hand, couped, in fess, a sword, in pale, on point a garland of laurel, all ppr. *Pl.* 56, *cr.* 6.

BISSET, Sco., trunk of tree, ppr., a shield, ar., pendent from branches. *Revirescit.* *Pl.* 23, *cr.* 6.

BISSHOPP, The Rev. Sir GEORGE, Bart., Parham Park, Suss., on a ducal coronet, or, a griffin, sejant, ar., resting dexter on an escutcheon, of the last. *Pro Deo et ecclesia.* *Pl.* 42, *cr.* 8.

BISSHE, Ess., a hind, trippant, ar. *Pl.* 20, *cr.* 14.

BISSHOPP, Baron DE LA ZOUCHE, of Harringworth, and a Bart.: 1. On a ducal coronet, or, a griffin, sejant, ar., resting fore-dexter on an escutcheon, of the last. *Pl.* 42, *cr.* 8. 2. (On a flag folded round a halberd, in fess,) a falcon, ar. *Pro Deo et ecclesia. Pl.* 38, *cr.* 12.

BISSLAND, BILSLAND, or BULLSLAND, Renfrewshire, a bull's head. *Certum pete finem. Pl.* 120, *cr.* 7.

BISTLEY, Eng., a doric column, or. *Pl.* 33, *cr.* 1.

BISTLEY, a cross pattée, gu., between wings, or. *Pl.* 29, *cr.* 14.

BITSON, a bridge of three arches, ppr. *Pl.* 38, *cr.* 4.

BITFIELD, a demi-wolf, rampant, (pierced through shoulder and transfixed by a flagstaff.) *Pl.* 56, *cr.* 8.

BITTERLEY, Cowdrey, Suss., out of a ducal coronet, in hand, vested, the sun, ppr. *Pl.* 89, *cr.* 11.

BLAAUW, Suss., a demi-lion, rampant, ar. *Festina lente. Pl.* 67, *cr.* 10.

BLABLEY, Devons., a tiger's head, erased, ar., out of rays, or. *Pl.* 94, *cr.* 10, (rays, *pl.* 116, *cr.* 13.)

BLACHFORD, or BLACKFORD, Lond. and Dors., a demi-swan, springing, ar., guttée, sa. *Pl.* 54, *cr.* 4.

BLACHFORD, Lond. and Dors., a demi-swan, rising, wings expanded, ar., guttée, az. *Pl.* 54, *cr.* 4.

BLACK, Sco., a demi-lion, ppr. *Non crux, sed lux. Pl.* 67, *cr.* 10.

BLACK, Eng., a reindeer's head, ppr., collared. *Pl.* 2, *cr.* 13.

BLACK, Lond., an arm, in armour, embowed, ppr., in hand, also ppr., a scimitar, ar. *Spe vires augentur. Pl.* 81, *cr.* 11.

BLACK, Eng., an arm, embowed, vested, purfled at shoulder, the part above elbow, in fess, in hand, in pale, a branch of palm, ppr. *Pl.* 62, *cr.* 7.

BLACKADER of Blackader, Sco., an adder, sa., in pale, in mouth a rose, gu., leaved and stalked, vert. *Vise a la fine. Pl.* 104, *cr.* 9.

BLACKALL, Devons., a tiger's head, erased, ar., out of rays, or. *Pl.* 94, *cr.* 10, (rays, *pl.* 116, *cr.* 13.)

BLACKALL, two arms, embowed, (vested,) between hands, ppr., a greyhound's head, erased. *Pl.* 36, *cr.* 4, (head, *pl.* 89, *cr.* 2.)

BLACKBORN, BLACKBORNE, BLACKEBORNE, or BLACKBURN, Yorks., out of a cloud, shedding forth rays, an arm from elbow, erect, vested, gu., in hand a broken sword, ppr. *Pl.* 22, *cr.* 6.

BLACKBURN, Orford Hall, Lanc., an antelope's head, erased, ar. *Pl.* 24, *cr.* 7.

BLACKBURN, Sco., an arm, couped at shoulder, resting elbow on wreath, in hand a bombshell, fired, ppr. *Pl.* 62, *cr.* 9.

BLACKBURN, Wavertree Hall, Lanc.; and Hawford Lodge, near Worc.; on a trumpet, or, a cock, statant, ppr. *Pl.* 2, *cr.* 1.

BLACKBURNE, JOHN-IRELAND, Esq., of Orford and Hale, Lanc., a cock, ppr., standing on a trumpet, or. *Pl.* 2, *cr.* 1.

BLACKE, Suff. and Ess., a hand, couped, in fess, ppr. *Pl.* 32, *cr.* 4.

BLACKENSTEINER, out of a crown, or, a plume of three feathers, the centre, ar., the others, gu. *Pl.* 69, *cr.* 11, (without wings.)

BLACKER, WILLIAM, Esq., of Carrick Blacker, co. Armagh: 1. *Ancient*, a Danish battleaxe. *Pl.* 14, *cr.* 8. 2. *Ordinary*, an arm, in armour, in hand a Danish battle-axe, ppr. *Pro Deo et rege. Pl.* 121, *cr.* 14.

BLACKER, a nag's head, couped, az., bridled, or. *Pl.* 92, *cr.* 1.

BLACKER, Bucks. and Wilts., two lions' heads, erased, (collared,) and addorsed. *Pl.* 28, *cr.* 10.

BLACKER, Bucks., a horse's head, couped, az., bridled, or. *Pl.* 92, *cr.* 1.

BLACKESTON, or BLACKISTON, Durh., a cock, or. *Pl.* 67, *cr.* 14.

BLACKET, Bart., Matfen, Northumb., a hawk's head, erased, ppr. *Nous travaillerons en l'espérance. Pl.* 34, *cr.* 11.

BLACKET, a hawk's head, couped, ppr. *Pl.* 99, *cr.* 10.

BLACKET, or BLACKETT, Newcastle, Northumb.; and Calverly, Yorks.; a falcon's head, erased, ppr. *Nous travaillerons en l'espérance. Pl.* 34, *cr.* 11.

BLACKETT, JOHN-FENWICK-BURGOYNE, Esq., of Wylam, Northumb., a hawk's head, erased, ppr. *Nous travaillerons dans l'espérance. Pl.* 34, *cr.* 11.

BLACKHALL, Sco., an annulet, or, stoned, vert. *Pl.* 35, *cr.* 3.

BLACKIE, and BLACKLEY, Lanc., a dragon's head, vert, ducally gorged, or. *Pl.* 36, *cr.* 7.

BLACKIE, Edinr., a tiger, (salient,) ppr. *Spero in Deo. Pl.* 73, *cr.* 2.

BLACKIE, Sco., a wolf's head, erased, ppr. *Virtute et fidelitate. Pl.* 14, *cr.* 6.

BLACKISTON, Lond., a cock, or. *Pl.* 67, *cr.* 14.

BLACKLEY, or BLAKEY, Blackley Hall, Lanc., a dragon's head, vert, ducally gorged, or. *Pl.* 36, *cr.* 7.

BLACKMAN, a demi-moor, in fetters, crowned with an eastern coronet. *Pl.* 98, *cr.* 10, (coronet, *pl.* 128, *fig.* 2.)

BLACKMAN, Lond. and East Indies, a griffin, erm. *Pl.* 66, *cr.* 13.

BLACKMAN, and BLACKMANE, East Indies and Lond., a demi-griffin, segreant, erm. *Pl.* 18, *cr.* 6.

BLACKMAN, a demi-griffin, vert, (semée of crescents, ar., collared, gu.) *Fide et fiducia. Pl.* 74, *cr.* 15, (without anchor.)

BLACKMORE, Lond., out of a mural coronet, or, a dexter arm, in armour, ppr., purfled, or. *Pl.* 115, *cr.* 14, (without sword.)

BLACKMORE, Devons., a moor's head in profile, (erased at neck,) sa., round neck a chaplet of roses, or leaved, vert. *Pl.* 36, *cr.* 3, (chaplet, *pl.* 41, *cr.* 7.)

BLACKMORE, an arm, in armour, embowed, ppr., garnished, or, supporting a standard-banner, gold, staff of the first, pointed, ar. *Pl.* 6, *cr.* 5.

BLACKMORE, out of a mural coronet, an arm, in armour, embowed, ppr., garnished, or. *Pl.* 115, *cr.* 14, (without sword.)

BLACKMORE, Eng., a demi-griffin, segreant, erm. *Pl.* 18, *cr.* 6.

BLACKNELL, Warw. and Berks., an arm, embowed, vested, gu., cuff, ar., in hand, ppr., four feathers, per pale, ar. and gu. *Pl.* 39, *cr.* 1, (feathers, *pl.* 44, *cr.* 12.)
BLACKNEY, or BLACKENEY, a harpy, gardant, ppr. *Pl.* 126, *cr.* 11.
BLACKNOLL, and BLAKENHALL, out of a cloud, az., in hand, fesswise, ppr., a plume of six feathers, ar. and gu., counterchanged. *Pl.* 26, *cr.* 4, (feathers, *pl.* 106, *cr.* 11.)
BLACKSHAME, Eng., an acorn, or, stalked and leaved, vert. *Pl.* 81, *cr.* 7.
BLACKSTONE, and BLACKSTON, Eng., a cock, gu. *Pl.* 67, *cr.* 14.
BLACKWALL, Lond., in dexter hand, gauntleted, a pheon, all ppr. *Pl.* 123, *cr.* 12.
BLACKWELL, Ampney Park, Glouc., two arms, (in scale armour,) embowed, between hands, ppr., a greyhound's head, couped at neck, gu., collared, sa. *Pl.* 36, *cr.* 4, (head, *pl.* 89, *cr.* 2.)
BLACKWELL, a martlet. *Pl.* 111, *cr.* 5.
BLACKWELL, Sprouston-Hall, Norf., a swan's head and neck, (erased,) ar., ducally gorged, or. *Pl.* 30, *cr.* 10.
BLACKWELL, a dove, (issuing.) *Pl.* 27, *cr.* 5.
BLACKWELL, or BLACKWALL, two arms, in mail, embowed, ppr., between hands, ar., a greyhound's head, couped, sa., collared, checky, or and gu. *Pl.* 36, *cr.* 4, (head, *pl.* 43, *cr.* 11.)
BLACKWELL of Blackwell, Derbs., a griffin's head, erased, sa., beaked, or, charged on neck with a bar gemelle, ar., and a trefoil, slipped, erm. *Pl.* 48, *cr.* 6.
BLACKWILL, a demi-lion, between paws an anchor, ppr. *Pl.* 19, *cr.* 6.
BLACKWOOD, Bart., the sun rising from behind a cloud, all ppr. *Per vias rectas. Pl.* 67, *cr.* 9.
BLACKWOOD, Iri., Baron, the sun in splendour. *Per vias rectas. Pl.* 68, *cr.* 14.
BLACKWOOD, Sco., in hand a couteau sword, ppr. *Virtute parta tuemini. Pl.* 29, *cr.* 8.
BLACKWOOD, (on a mount, vert,) an escutcheon, ar., between two laurel-branches, ppr. *Pl.* 14, *cr.* 7.
BLACKWOOD, a half-moon, ar. *Pl.* 43, *cr.* 8.
BLACKWOOD, Baron Dufferin and Claneboye. *See* DUFFERIN.
BLADEN, Glastonny, Somers., a greyhound's head, erased, ppr. *Toujours fidele. Pl.* 89, *cr.* 2.
BLADERIKE, a lion's head, erased, (struck through mouth with a sword, in fess,) all ppr. *Pl.* 113, *cr.* 15.
BLADES, Broxwell Hall, Surr., a demi-tiger, rampant, gardant, ppr., supporting a staff with banner, az., fringed, or. *Pl.* 53, *cr.* 10, (staff, *pl.* 2, *cr.* 14.)
BLADES, Yorks., a talbot's head, erased, sa. *Pl.* 90, *cr.* 6.
BLADEWELL, or BLADWELL, Staffs. and Norf., a demi-lion, per pale, indented, ar. and gu. *Pl.* 67, *cr.* 10.
BLADFORD, Dors., in dexter hand a pistol, ppr. *Pl.* 101, *cr.* 12.
BLAGE, Eng., on a chapeau, gu., turned up, erm., a martlet, ar. *Pl.* 89, *cr.* 7.
BLAGE, (on a broken tilting-spear, or,) a lion, passant, ar., crowned, gold. *Pl.* 48, *cr.* 8.
BLAGRAVE, Eng., a falcon, ppr. *Pl.* 67, *cr.* 3.

BLAGRAVE, Bullnash-Court, Berks., an oak-tree, eradicated, vert. *Pl.* 92, *cr.* 8.
BLAGROVE, a palm-tree, fructed, ppr. *Pl.* 18, *cr.* 12.
BLAGRAVE, JOHN, Esq., of Colcot Park, Berks.:
1. A falcon, ppr., belled, or. *Pl.* 67, *cr.* 3.
2. An oak-tree, eradicated, ppr. *Pl.* 92, *cr.* 8.
3. (Three) palm-branches, ppr. *Pl.* 87, *cr.* 8. *Pro marte et arte.*
BLAIKIE, or BLACKIE, Sco., a wolf's head, erased, ppr. *Virtute et fidelitate. Pl.* 14, *cr.* 6.
BLAIKIE of Craigiebuckler, Sco., a moor's head, ppr. *Fidelis. Pl.* 120, *cr.* 3.
BLAIN, BLAINE, or BLEAN, Sco. and Liverpool, a sword, in pale, az., hilt and pommell, or. *Pax aut bellum. Pl.* 105, *cr.* 1.
BLAIR, Sir DAVID HUNTER, Dunskey, Wigtownshire, Bart., a stag's head, cabossed, ppr. *Vigilantia, robur, voluptas. Pl.* 36, *cr.* 1.
BLAIR, WILLIAM-FORDYCE, Esq., of Blair, Ayr, a stag, lodged, ppr. *Amo probos. Pl.* 67, *cr.* 2.
BLAIR, NEIL-JAMES-FERGUSSON, Esq., of Balthayock, Perth, a dove, wings expanded, ppr. *Virtute tutus. Pl.* 27, *cr.* 5.
BLAIR, Aberdeen. *Non crux, sed lux.*
BLAIR, Sco., a garb, ppr. *Virtute tutus. Pl.* 48, *cr.* 10.
BLAIR, Balmill, Sco., a Roman head, armed, ppr. *Facies qualis mens talis. Pl.* 33, *cr.* 14.
BLAIR, Sco., a crescent, ar. *God be my guide. Pl.* 18, *cr.* 14.
BLAIR, Sco., an eagle, rising, ppr. *Virtute tutus. Pl.* 67, *cr.* 4.
BLAIR, Lethendy, Sco., a garb, ppr. *Nec temere, nec timide. Pl.* 48, *cr.* 10.
BLAIR, Iri., a stag, lodged, ppr. *Pl.* 67, *cr.* 2.
BLAIR, a boar's head, couped. *Pl.* 48, *cr.* 2.
BLAIR of Borgue, Sco., a dove, wings expanded, ppr. *Virtute et honore. Pl.* 27, *cr.* 5.
BLAIR of Dunsky, a boar's head, couped, ppr. *Virtute et honore. Pl.* 48, *cr.* 2.
BLAKE, Wilts., on a chapeau, gu., turned up, erm., a martlet, sa. *Pl.* 89, *cr.* 7.
BLAKE, HENRY, Esq., of Renvyle, co. Galway, a mountain-cat, passant, ppr. *Virtus sola nobilitat. Pl.* 119, *cr.* 7.
BLAKE, MARTIN-JOSEPH, Esq., of Blallyglunin Park, co. Galway, same crest and motto.
BLAKE, VALENTINE-O'CONNOR, Esq., of Towerhill, co. Mayo, same crest and motto.
BLAKE, FRANCIS, Esq., of Cregg Castle, co. Galway, same crest and motto.
BLAKE, ANDREW-WILLIAM, Esq., of Furbough, co. Galway, same crest and motto.
BLAKE, CHARLES, Esq., late of Merlin Park, co. Galway, same crest and motto.
BLAKE, THEOBALD-MICHAEL, Esq., of Kiltullagh and Frenchfort, co. Galway, same crest and motto.
BLAKE, Bart., Durh., a martlet, ar., charged on breast with a fret, gu. *Pl.* 111, *cr.* 5, (fret, *pl.* 82, *cr.* 7.)
BLAKE, Baron. *See* WILLISCOURT.
BLAKE, a bear's head, sa., (gorged with a collar, ar., in mouth a lion's gamb, erased, or.) *Pl.* 2, *cr.* 9.
BLAKE, Bart., Langham, Suff., a leopard, passant, ppr. *Pl.* 86, *cr.* 2.

BLAKE, SIR JOHN, Bart., of Ireland, a cat, passant, gardant, ppr. *Virtus sola nobilitas.* Pl. 119, cr. 7.
BLAKE, Ess., a dragon's head, erased, ar., pellettée. Pl. 107, cr. 10.
BLAKE, Wilts., on a chapeau, gu., turned up, erm., a martlet, sa. Pl. 89, cr. 7.
BLAKE, Suff., a mountain-cat, passant, gardant, ppr. Pl. 119, cr. 7.
BLAKE, a mountain-cat, passant, ppr. *Virtus sola nobilitat.* Pl. 119, cr. 7.
BLAKE-JEX, Norf.: 1. A horse's head, erased, ar., maned, or, in mouth a broken spear, gold. Pl. 110, cr. 6. 2. On a morion, a martlet, all ppr. *Bene præparatum pectus.* Pl. 18, cr. 9, (martlet, pl. 111, cr. 5.)
BLAKEBORNE, Yorks., out of a cloud, shedding forth rays, an arm, from elbow, erect, vested, gu., in hand a broken sword, ppr. Pl. 22, cr. 6.
BLAKENEY, JOHN-HENRY, Esq., of Albert, Castle Blakeney, co. Galway, out of a ducal coronet, an arm, erect, couped at elbow, vested, gu., cuffed, ar., in hand a sword, ppr., hilt and pommel, or. *Auxilium meum ab alto.* Pl. 89, cr. 11, (sword, pl. 21, cr. 10.)
BLAKENEY, an arm, erect, couped at elbow, vested, gu., cuffed, ar., in hand a sword, ppr., hilt and pommel, or. *Auxilium meum ab alto.* Pl. 21, cr. 10.
BLAKENEY, Iri., out of a plume of three ostrich-feathers, an eagle, rising, ppr. Pl. 54, cr. 8.
BLAKENHALL, or BLACKNOLL, in hand, ppr., out of a cloud, az., in fess, a plume of six feathers, two, two, and two, ar. and gu., all counterchanged. Pl. 26, cr. 4, (feathers, pl. 12, cr. 9.)
BLAKENY, or BLACKNEY, Norf., a harpy, gardant, ppr. Pl. 126, cr. 11.
BLAKER, Salisbury, Wilts., a demi-horse, sa., ducally gorged, or. Pl. 91, cr. 2, (without wings.)
BLAKER, Portslade, Suss., a horse's head, sa., maned and bridled, or. Pl. 92, cr. 1.
BLAKES, Bart., Iri., a mountain-cat passant, gardant, ppr. *Virtus sola nobilitas.* Pl. 119, cr. 7.
BLAKESTON, or BLAKISTON, Durh., a cock, or, (collared,) combed, and wattled, gu. Pl. 67, cr. 14.
BLAKISTON, Bart., Lond. and Hants., a cock, gu. *Do well, and doubt not.* Pl. 67, cr. 14.
BLAKISTON, Bart., Lond., same crest.
BLAKISTON, or BLAKSTON, Eng., a cock, or. Pl. 67, cr. 14.
BLAKIT, Eng., a falcon's head, erased, ppr. Pl. 34, cr. 11.
BLAMIRE, WILLIAM, Esq., Cumb., a wolf, sejant, ppr., (chained, or.) *Faire sans dire.* Pl. 110, cr. 4.
BLAMIRE of Thackwood, Cumb., a tiger, sejant, Pl. 26, cr. 9.
BLAMORE, Eng., a trout, naiant, ppr. Pl. 85, cr. 7.
BLANCHARD, Lanc., on a chapeau, an arm, in armour, embowed, in hand a battle-axe. Pl. 121, cr. 14, (chapeau, pl. 27, cr. 3.)
BLANCHARD, Wilts. and Somers., on point of sword, in pale, a mullet. Pl. 55, cr. 15.

BLANCKAGAM, a dove and olive-branch, ppr. Pl. 48, cr. 15.
BLANCKHARDEN, or BLANCHARDEN, Kent, (a cock's) leg, gu., armed with a spur, collar, or, spur, sa., erased at thigh, issuing therefrom a plume of five ostrich-feathers, counterchanged, or. and az. Pl. 83, cr. 7, (plume, pl. 106, cr. 11.)
BLANCKHARDON, a falcon's claw, erased, conjoined to a plume of five ostrich-feathers. Pl. 83, cr. 7, (plume, pl. 106, cr. 11.)
BLANCKMAYNES, or BLANCHMAYNES, a leopard's head, gardant, erased, or. Pl. 94, cr. 10.
BLAND, LOFTUS-HENRY, Esq., of Blandsfort, Queen's County, out of a ducal coronet, a lion's head, ppr., (charged with a crescent,) gu. *Quo fata vocant.* Pl. 90, cr. 9.
BLAND, a holly-branch, vert. Pl. 99, cr. 6.
BLAND, a cock, gu. Pl. 67, cr. 14.
BLAND-DAVISON, THOMAS, Esq. of Kippax Park, Yorks., out of a ducal coronet, or, a lion's head, ppr. Pl. 90, cr. 9.
BLANDFORD, Dors., in hand a pistol, ppr. Pl. 101, cr. 12.
BLANE, Bart., Blanefield, Arysh.; and Culverlands, Berks.; a sword, in pale, ppr. *Pax aut bellum.* Pl. 105, cr. 1.
BLANE, or BLAIN, Sco., same crest and motto.
BLANE, and BELEAN, Sco., a sword, in pale, ppr. *Pax aut bellum.* Pl. 105, cr. 1.
BLANE, Bart., Berks., a sword, erect, ppr., hilt and pommel, or. *Paritur pax bello.* Pl. 105, cr. 1.
BLANEY, or BLAYNEY, Lond., a horse's head, couped, ar., in complete armour, ppr., bridled, az. Pl. 7, cr. 12.
BLANEY, Heref., a nag's head, couped, ar., maned and tufted, sa., bridled, gu. Pl. 92, cr. 1.
BLANEY, Heref., a fox, passant, ar. Pl. 126, cr. 5.
BLANK, Lond., a dragon's head, erased, vert, collared, (and chained,) ar., in mouth a firebrand, ppr. Pl. 107, cr. 10, (torch, pl. 70, cr. 14.)
BLANTYRE, Baron, (Stewart,) Sco., a dove with olive-leaf, ppr. *Sola juvat virtus.* Pl. 48, cr. 15.
BLAQUIER, Baron and a Bart., a garb, ppr., banded, or. *Tiens á la vérité.* Pl. 48, cr. 10.
BLASHFORD, a swan, issuant, wings expanded. Pl. 54, cr. 4.
BLATCHFORD, a swan's head and neck, (erased,) sa., between wings, ar. Pl. 54, cr. 6.
BLATHWAITE, on a rock, ppr., an eagle, rising, ar. Pl. 79, cr. 2.
BLATHWAYT, GEORGE-WILLIAM, Esq., of Dyrham Park, Gloucester; and of Langridge and Porlock, Somerset; on a rock, ppr., an eagle, rising, ar., wings, az. *Virtute et veritate.* Pl. 79, cr. 2.
BLAUMESTER, Eng., a demi-savage, holding a club over shoulder, all ppr. Pl. 14, cr. 11.
BLAUMIRE, Thackwood, Cumb., a tiger, sejant, gu. Pl. 26, cr. 9.
BLAVERHASSET, Eng., in dexter hand a hunting horn, sans strings, ppr., veruled, or. Pl. 109, cr. 3.
BLAW, Castle Hill, Sco., in armed hand a sword, in pale, ppr. Pl. 125, cr. 5.
BLAW, a demi-lion, rampant, ar. *Festina lente.* Pl. 67, cr. 10.

BLAXTON, Eng., a goat, (passant,) or. *Pl.* 66, *cr.* 1.
BLAYDES, CHARLES-BENJAMIN, Esq., of Ranby Hall, Notts., a talbot's head, erased, and erect, sa. *Pro Deo, rege, et patria. Pl.* 90, *cr.* 6.
BLAYDES, Eng., a thistle, vert, flowered, gu. *Pl.* 100, *cr.* 9.
BLAYDES, a demi-leopard, salient, ppr., in dexter a sword, ar., hilt and pommel, or. *Pl.* 97, *cr.* 5.
BLAYDES, Oulton House, near Leeds, Yorks., a demi-leopard, collared and (chained, or, in dexter a sword, erect, ppr.) *Pl.* 125, *cr.* 4.
BLAYDES-MARVEL, Yorks., a talbot's head, erased and erect, sa. *Pro Deo, rege, et patria. Pl.* 90, *cr.* 6.
BLAYKESTON of Blaykeston, Durh., a cock, or, crested and wattled, gu. *Pl.* 67, *cr.* 14.
BLAYNE, Berks., a greyhound's head, ar., collared, az. *Pl.* 43, *cr.* 11.
BLAYNEY, Lond., a horse's head, couped, ar., in complete armour, ppr., bridle, az. *Pl.* 7, *cr.* 12.
BLAYNEY, ROBERT, Esq., M.A., of The Lodge, Evesham, Worc., a fox, ar. *I rest to rise. Pl.* 126, *cr.* 5.
BLAYNEY, Kensham, Heref., an ermine, passant, ar. *Pl.* 9, *cr.* 5.
BLAYNEY, Lord Blaney, Baron, of Moraghan, Iri., a nag's head, couped, ar., bridled, gu., on forehead a plate of armour, in centre of which a spike, all ppr. *Integra mens augustissima possessio. Pl.* 7, *cr.* 12.
BLEAYMIRE, an heraldic tiger, sejant, (collared and chained.) *Pl.* 111, *cr.* 7.
BLEDDYN, or BLEEDDYN, Wel. and Eng., a boar, passant, sa., bristled, ar. *Pl.* 48, *cr.* 14.
BLEDLOW, Lond., in the sea an anchor, ppr. *Pl.* 62, *cr.* 10.
BLENCOWE, Marston Hall, Oxon., a sword, in pale, handle upwards, pierced through a human heart, all ppr., between wings, ar. *Pl.* 39, *cr.* 7, (sword, *pl.* 21, *cr.* 15.)
BLENCOWE, JOHN-JACKSON, Esq., of Marston St Lawrence, Northamp., same crest.
BLENCOWE, ROBERT-WILLIS, Esq., M.A., of The Hook, Suss., same crest and motto.
BLENERHASSET, Suff., a fox, sejant, gu. *Pl.* 87, *cr.* 4.
BLENERHASSET, Suff., a wolf, sejant, gu., tail flected over back, langued, az. *Pl.* 110, *cr.* 4.
BLENKINSOPP, GEORGE-THOMAS LEATON, Esq., of Hoppyland Castle, Durh.; and Humbleton Hall, Northumb.: 1. For *Blenkinsopp*, a lion, rampant, or. *Pl.* 67, *cr.* 5. 2. For *Leaton*, out of a mural coronet, two wings, expanded, ar., (each charged with a cross crosslet, fitched, sa.) *Dieu defende le droit. Pl.* 39, *cr.* 12, (coronet, *pl.* 128, *fig.* 18; cross, *pl.* 141.)
BLENMAN, Croscombe, Somers., a dexter arm, couped at elbow, ppr., vested, sa., ruffle, ar., at wrist a diamond button, in hand a roll of parchment, ppr. *Pl.* 32, *cr.* 6.
BLENNERHASSET, Iri., in the sea a pillar, ppr. *Pl.* 14, *cr.* 3.
BLENNERHASSET, Sir ROBERT, Bart., Iri., a wolf, sejant, ppr. *Fortis fortuna juvat. Pl.* 110, *cr.* 4.

BLENNERHASSETT, CHARLES-JOHN, Esq., of Ballyseedy, a wolf, sejant, ppr. *Fortis fortuna juvat. Pl.* 110, *cr.* 4.
BLENSHELL, or BLINSHALL, Aberdeen, a hollyleaf, vert. *Deo favente florebo. Pl.* 99, *cr.* 6.
BLESBY, or BLESBIE, Linc., a griffin's head, erased, or. *Pl.* 48, *cr.* 6.
BLESET, or BLESSET, Eng., an eagle, displayed, ppr. *Pl.* 48, *cr.* 11.
BLESSONE, Eng., a martlet, ar., or russet colour. *Pl.* 111, *cr.* 5.
BLETSHO, Winington, Beds., a wolf's head, or., semée of hurts, murally gorged, az. *Pl.* 8, *cr.* 4.
BLEVERHASSET, or BLENERHASSET, Lowdham, Suff., a fox, sejant, gu. *Pl.* 87, *cr.* 4.
BLEVERHASSET, Norf., a wolf, sejant, gu. *Pl.* 110, *cr.* 4.
BLEWET, BLEWETT, and BLUET, Cornw. and Devons., a squirrel, sejant, or, collared and lined, gu., in paws an acorn, gold, leaved, vert. *Pl.* 85, *cr.* 3.
BLEWET, BLEWETT, BLEWITT, and BLEUETT, Glouc., and Grenham, Somers., a mort head, ppr. *Pl.* 62, *cr.* 12.
BLEWITT, Lond., Somers., and Monm., a squirrel, sejant, ppr., eating an acorn, fructed, or. *Spes mea in Deo. Pl.* 16, *cr.* 9.
BLICK, Bucks., a leopard, passant, ar., semée of mullets, sa. *Pl.* 86, *cr.* 2.
BLICK, and BLICKE, Eng., a hawk's lure, az., ringed, or. *Pl.* 97, *cr.* 14.
BLIGH, or BLIGHE, Cornw., a dexter arm, or and az., couped at elbow, in hand a battleaxe, of the second and first. *Pl.* 73, *cr.* 7.
BLIGH, a griffin's head, erased, or. *Pl.* 48, *cr.* 6.
BLIGH, Iri., a griffin's head, erased, or. *Finem respice. Pl.* 48, *cr.* 6.
BLIGH, Earl of Darnley, Viscount and Baron, Iri., a griffin's head, erased, or. *Finem respice. Pl.* 48, *cr.* 6.
BLINCKARNE, or BLINCARNE, Kent, a demi-lion, in dexter a cross, (engrailed,) gu. *Pl.* 65, *cr.* 6.
BLISS, Eng., an arm from elbow, in hand a bundle of four arrows, points downward. *Pl.* 56, *cr.* 4.
BLISSETT, a sword in pale, enfiled with a (thistle,) ppr. *Pl.* 15, *cr.* 6.
BLITHE, Lond. and Linc., on top of tower, a lion, all ar. *Pl.* 121, *cr.* 5.
BLITHE, Lond., a lion, sejant, gu. *Pl.* 126, *cr.* 15.
BLITHE, Derb., a peacock, or, in mouth a serpent, reflexed over neck, ppr. *Pl.* 53, *cr.* 12.
BLITHMAN, a demi-bear, ar., muzzled, gu., between paws a battle-axe, of the last. *Pl.* 104, *cr.* 10, (axe, *pl.* 14, *cr.* 8.)
BLIZARD, a fleur-de-lis, az. *Pl.* 68, *cr.* 12.
BLIZARD, or BLIZZARD, Eng., a lady's arm, erect, round wrist a bracelet. *Pl.* 85, *cr.* 10.
BLOCKLEY, (the sun shining) on a spread eagle, in flames, ppr. *Pl.* 44, *cr.* 8.
BLOCKLEY, Eng., (the sun shining) on a demi-eagle, with two heads, in flames, ppr. *Pl.* 87, *cr.* 11.
BLOCKNEY, Iri., out of a ducal coronet, az., a boar's head and neck, or, collared, gu. *Pl.* 102, *cr.* 14.

BLODLOW, a lion, rampant, sa. *Pl.* 67, *cr.* 5.
BLODLOW, a lion, rampant, sa., (charged on neck with three bezants.) *Pl.* 67, *cr.* 5.
BLODWELL, Suff., a demi-lion, per pale, indented, ar. and gu. *Pl.* 67, *cr.* 10.
BLOER, Lond., a cubit arm, vested, vert, in hand, ppr., a pomme. *Pl.* 114, *cr.* 4, (pomme, *pl.* 141.)
BLOFELD, of Hoverton House, Norf., three ostrich-feathers, ar. *Domino quid reddam.* *Pl.* 12, *cr.* 9.
BLOIS, Bart., Grundisburgh Hall, Suff., (in a gauntlet, ppr.,) a fleur-de-lis, ar. *Je me fie en Dieu.* *Pl.* 95, *cr.* 9.
BLOIS, DE, and BLOYS, a lion, rampant, gardant, gu. *Pl.* 92, *cr.* 7.
BLOMBERG, Eng., two eagles' wings, addorsed, ppr. *Pl.* 63, *cr.* 12.
BLOMBERG, out of a ducal coronet, a demi-lion, rampant, double-queued. *Pl.* 120, *cr.* 10, (coronet, *pl.* 45, *cr.* 7.)
BLOME, Seven Oaks, Kent, a peacock's tail, erect, or. *Post virtutum curro.* *Pl.* 120, *cr.* 13, (without coronet.)
BLOMEFIELD, Bart., Attleborough, Norf., out of a mural coronet, ar., a demi-heraldic tiger, az., armed and tufted, or, (collared, of the first, holding a broken sword, ppr.) *Pl.* 57, *cr.* 13, (coronet, *pl.* 128, *fig.* 18.)
BLOMER, or BLOOMER, Hagthorpe, Glouc., Lond., and Warw.; a tiger, sejant, vert, ducally gorged, lined, tufted, and crined, or. *Pl.* 26, *cr.* 9.
BLOMFEILD, BLOMEFIELD, BLOMFIELD, or BLOOMFIELD, two wings displayed, ppr. *Pl.* 39, *cr.* 12.
BLOMMART, an arm, couped and embowed, elbow on wreath, in hand a sword, in pale, enfiled with a savage's head, couped. *Pl.* 102, *cr.* 11.
BLOND, and BLOUNT, (behind the rays of the sun, or,) a bull's head, sa. *Pl.* 63, *cr.* 11.
BLOND, LE, Iri., on a chapeau, gu., turned up, erm., a game-cock, ppr. *Pl.* 104, *cr.* 3.
BLONDELL, Eng., in dexter hand a battle-axe, all ppr. *Pl.* 73, *cr.* 7.
BLONDEVILL, or BLONVILLE, Eng., a Cornish chough, ppr. *Pl.* 100, *cr.* 13.
BLOOD, a buck's head, erased, ppr., attired, or, (in mouth an arrow, gold.) *Pl.* 66, *cr.* 9.
BLOOD, Iri., a talbot's head, sa., collared, or. *Pl.* 2, *cr.* 15.
BLOODWORTH, Eng., in dexter hand, couped, in fess, gu., a cross crosslet, fitched, in pale, sa. *Pl.* 78, *cr.* 9.
BLOOM, a cubit arm, erect, vested, az., cuffed, ar., in hand, ppr., some slips of broom, stalked, vert, blossomed, or. *Pl.* 94, *cr.* 15.
BLOOMFIELD, Baron, Iri., out of a mural coronet, or, charged with two cinquefoils, in fess, az., a bull's head, ppr. *Fortes fortuna juvat.* *Pl.* 120, *cr.* 7, (coronet, *same plate, cr.* 14; cinquefoil, *pl.* 141.)
BLOOMFIELD, a fox's head, ppr. *Pl.* 91, *cr.* 9.
BLOOMFIELD, a bull's head, ppr. *Pl.* 120, *cr.* 7.
BLOOMFIELD, Eng., two wings, issuing, ppr. *Pl.* 63, *cr.* 12.
BLOOR, or BLOORE, Eng., an arm, in armour, embowed, in hand a cutlass, all ppr. *Pl.* 81, *cr.* 11.

BLOSS, Ipswich, Suff., a demi-angel, in dexter a griffin's head, erased. *Pl.* 24, *cr.* 11.
BLOSSE-LYNCH, Bart., Iri., a wolf, passant, coward, ar. *Nec temere, nec timide.* *Pl.* 46, *cr.* 6.
BLOSSOM, or BLOSSOME, Eng., out of a ducal coronet, in hand a swan's head and neck, erased. *Pl.* 65, *cr.* 12.
BLOSSOME, or BLOSSUN, Eng., a ram, passant, ppr. *Pl.* 109, *cr.* 2.
BLOUNDELL, or BLUNDELL, a squirrel, sejant, or, cracking a nut, ppr. *Pl.* 16, *cr.* 9.
BLOUNDELL, Carlington, Beds., a squirrel, sejant, gu., collared, holding a nut, or. *Pl.* 85, *cr.* 3.
BLOUNT, Lord Montjoye, on a ducal coronet, or, a wolf, passant, sa. *Pl.* 46, *cr.* 6, (coronet, *pl.* 128, *fig.* 3.)
BLOUNT, Lond. and Glouc., a sea-lion, erm., rampant, ducally crowned, or. *Pl.* 80, *cr.* 13, (coronet, *pl.* 128, *fig.* 3.)
BLOUNT, the sun, or, charged with a gauntlet, sa. *Pl.* 68, *cr.* 14, (gauntlet, *pl.* 15, *cr.* 15.)
BLOUNT, Bart., Soddington, Worc., an armed foot in the sun, ppr. *Lux tua vita mea.* *Pl.* 68, *cr.* 14, (foot, *pl.* 118, *cr.* 6.)
BLOUNT, in a crescent, az., two swans' heads, reversed, ar., the one crossing the other, in mouth of each an annulet, gu.
BLOUYLE, Suff., a demi-lion, rampant, per pale, indented, ar. and gu. *Pl.* 67, *cr.* 10.
BLOWER, Eng., out of a mural coronet, or, a demi-eagle, displayed, vert, vulned in breast by an arrow, of the first, feathered, ar. *Pl.* 85, *cr.* 5.
BLOXAM, Oxon. and Warw., an anchor, in bend, sinister, or, cabled, az. *Pl.* 37, *cr.* 12.
BLOXHOLMEDAX, a tree, vert, and boar, passant, ar. *Pl.* 57, *cr.* 11.
BLOYAM, and BLOXHAM, Eng., a shuttle, az. *Pl.* 102, *cr.* 10.
BLOYE, a mullet, gu., between two branches of plam, in orle, vert. *Pl.* 3, *cr.* 9.
BLOYS, Ipswich, Suff., (in gauntlet, ppr., purfled, or,) a fleur-de-lis, gold. *Pl.* 95, *cr.* 9.
BLUCK, a bull's head, erased, gu., armed, or. *Pl.* 19, *cr.* 3.
BLUDDER, or BLUDER, Linc. and Middx., a lion's head, erased, ar., (pierced through neck with a broken spear, of the same, the wound, gu.) *Pl.* 113, *cr.* 15.
BLUDDER, BLUDER, BLUTHER, Lond., a lion's head, erased, ar., (pierced through neck with the blade of a sword, ar., the wound, gu.) *Pl.* 113, *cr.* 15.
BLUDWORTH, a naked arm, embowed, ppr., guttée-de-sang, in hand a wreath of laurel, vert. *Pl.* 118, *cr.* 4.
BLUET, Holcolm-Regis, Devons., a squirrel, sejant, or, collared, lined, and cracking a nut. *Pl.* 85, *cr.* 3.
BLUETT, PETER, Esq., of Holcombe Court, Devons., a squirrel, sejant, or, in dexter an acorn, vert, fructed, gold. *In Deo omnia.* *Pl.* 2, *cr.* 4, (acorn, *pl.* 81, *cr.* 7.)
BLUETT, Eng., a squirrel, sejant, cracking a nut, ppr. *Pl.* 16, *cr.* 9.
BLUFIELD, a demi-greyhound, (wounded on breast with an arrow, ppr.) *Pl.* 48, *cr.* 3.

BLUND, Eng., a cock's head, erased, gu. *Pl.* 92, *cr.* 3.
BLUNDELL, Iri., on a tower, an eagle, rising, ppr. *Pl.* 84, *cr.* 3, (eagle, *same plate.*)
BLUNDELL, a unicorn's horn, ppr. *Pl.* 73, *cr.* 1.
BLUNDELL, Hants, the sun in glory, charged on the centre with an eye, issuing tears, all ppr. *Inter lachrymas micat. Pl.* 68, *cr.* 14 and 15.
BLUNDELL, Eng., a hawk, in dexter an ear of wheat, ppr. *Pl.* 94, *cr.* 7.
BLUNDELL, a squirrel, sejant, ppr., collared, cracking a nut, or. *Pl.* 85, *cr.* 3.
BLUNDEN, Iri., on the point of a spear, a dolphin, naiant, ppr. *Pl.* 49, *cr.* 14.
BLUNDEN, Bishop's Castle, Salop, a demi-griffin, or, (gorged with a fess, erm.) *Pl.* 18, *cr.* 6.
BLUNDESTONE, and BLUNSTONE, Suff., the sun rising, ppr. *Post nubes lux. Pl.* 67, *cr.* 9.
BLUNT, The Rev. WALTER, of Waldop House, Hants, the sun in glory, charged on centre with an eye, issuing tears, all ppr. *Inter lachrymas micat. Pl.* 68, *cr.* 14 and 15.
BLUNT, Eng., within a coronet, or, a bull's head, (couped near shoulders,) sa. *Pl.* 68, *cr.* 6.
BLUNT, Notts., a wolf, passant, sa. *Pl.* 46, *cr.* 6.
BLUNT, Bart., Lond., the sun in glory, charged on the centre with an eye, issuing tears, all ppr. *Lux tua vita mea. Pl.* 68, *cr.* 14 and 15.
BLUNT, Eng., the sun in splendour, or. *Pl.* 68, *cr.* 14.
BLUNT, Notts., (a slipper in) the sun. *Pl.* 68, *cr.* 14.
BLYTH, Sco., an arm, in armour, embowed, holding by the middle a drawn sword, point downward, all ppr. *Pl.* 65, *cr.* 8.
BLYTH, Eng., a buck's head, ppr. *Spero meliora. Pl.* 91, *cr.* 14.
BLYTHE, Bodmyn, Cornw., a griffin's head, erased, or. *Pl.* 48, *cr.* 6.
BLYTHE, Cornw., an arm, embowed, ppr., vested, per pale, or and az., in hand a battle-axe, of the last, headed, ar. *Pl.* 120, *cr.* 1, (axe, *same plate, cr.* 14.)
BLYTHE, Yorks., a buck's head, erased, or, attired, of the same, (collared, az.) *Pl.* 66, *cr.* 9.
BLYTHE, Norf., a stag's head, couped, gu., gorged with a chaplet of laurel, ppr. *Pl.* 38, *cr.* 1.
BLYTHE, Yorks., on wreath, erm. and gu., a roebuck's head, erased, of the second, attired, or, gorged, with a chaplet, vert. *Pl.* 38, *cr.* 1.
BLYTHE, Derbs. and Yorks., a stag's head, erased, gu., gorged with a chaplet, vert, and also a wreath, erm. and gu. *Pl.* 38, *cr.* 1.
BLYTHE, on the top of a tower, ppr., a lion, (statant.) *Pl.* 121, *cr.* 5.
BOADE, a ram's head, (gorged with a fess, indented, sa.,) charged with three escallops, ar. *Pl.* 34, *cr.* 12, (escallop, *pl.* 141.)
BOAG, BOG, or BOGG, a sand-glass, ppr. *Pl.* 43, *cr.* 1.
BOAK, Eng., a beacon, fired, ppr. *Pl.* 88, *cr.* 6.
BOARD, Bordhill, Suss., and Lindfield, a stag, erm. *Pl.* 81, *cr.* 8.

BOARDMAN, Eng., a lion, sejant, collared and lined, or. *Pl.* 21, *cr.* 3.
BOASE, Cornw., a demi-lion, (charged with three bezants on shoulder, and a star on hip, in paws five arrows, four in saltier, and one in fess at top.) *Pl.* 67, *cr.* 10.
BOATFIELD, Eng., five arrows, sa., enfiled with a ducal coronet, or. *Pl.* 37, *cr.* 5.
BOCK, a hawk's leg and wing, conjoined, the first belled and jessed, all ppr. *Pl.* 101, *cr.* 15.
BOCK, Eng., a hawk's leg and wing, conjoined, jessed and belled, all ppr. *Pl.* 101, *cr.* 15.
BOCKET, Eng., a horse's head, in profile, between wings, addorsed. *Pl.* 19, *cr.* 13.
BOCKETT, on a wreath entwined with laurel, vert, a falcon, wings expanded and ducally gorged, or, beaked and legged, gu. *Pl.* 61, *cr.* 12.
BOCKING, Suff., on a chapeau, gu., turned up, erm., a leopard, passant, ppr. *Pl.* 110, *cr.* 8.
BOCKINGHAM, Suff., on a chapeau, a lion, statant, gardant, collared and ducally crowned, *Pl.* 120, *cr.* 15.
BOCKLAND, or BOCKLANDE, a bull's head, erased, ar., ducally gorged, sa. *Pl.* 68, *cr.* 6.
BOCKLAND, a hawk, close, regardant, ar., beaked and belled, or. *Pl.* 42, *cr.* 7, (without garland.)
BOCKLEY, (the sun shining) on a demi-eagle, with two heads, in flames, ppr. *Pl.* 87, *cr.* 11.
BODDAM, Enfield, Middx. and Ess., a stag, trippant, ppr. *Pl.* 68, *cr.* 2.
BODDICOTT, BODICOTE, or BODYCOAT, Lond., a weaver's shuttle, in pale, az., threaded, ar. *Pl.* 102, *cr.* 10.
BODDIE, or BODY, Ess., on the middle of a staff, raguly, gu., a ducal coronet, or. *Pl.* 78, *cr.* 15.
BODDIE, or BODDY, Ess., out of a ducal coronet, or, a staff, raguly, gu. *Pl.* 78, *cr.* 15.
BODDINGTON, or BODINGTON, Eng., a lion's paw, grasping a scimitar, all ppr. *Pl.* 18, *cr.* 8.
BODDINGTON, or BODDINTON, a demi-lion, gu., in dexter, a cross crosslet, fitched, ar. *Pl.* 65, *cr.* 6.
BODE, Feversham, Kent, a greyhound's head, couped, ar., collared and ringed, sa., (charged with three escallops, of the first.) *Pl.* 43, *cr.* 11.
BODELL, a dexter arm, embowed, vested, stabbing with a sword, a squirrel, sejant, regardant, ppr.
BODELSGATE, Cornw., a horse's head, erased, ar. *Pl.* 81, *cr.* 6.
BODENFIELD, an eagle's head, erased, between wings, ar., ducally crowned, or. *Pl.* 61, *cr.* 10, (coronet, *pl.* 128, *fig.* 3.)
BODENHAM of Rotherwas, Heref., a dragon's head, erased, sa. *Veritas liberabit. Pl.* 107, *cr.* 10.
BODENHAM, Heref., out of a ducal coronet, or, a wing, sa. *Pl.* 80, *cr.* 4.
BODENHAM, Heref., a dragon's head, ppr. *Pl.* 87, *cr.* 12.
BODENHAM, Heref., a dragon's head, erased, sa. *Pl.* 107, *cr.* 10.
BODENHAM, CHARLES-THOMAS, Esq., of Rotherwas, Heref., a dragon's head, erased, sa. *Veritas liberabit. Pl.* 107, *cr.* 10.

BODINGTON, a demi-lion, rampant, gu., in dexter, a cross crosslet, fitched, ar. *Pl.* 65, *cr.* 6.

BODKIN, ROBERT, Esq., of Annagh, co. Galway, a wild boar, ppr. *Crom-a-boo*. *Pl.* 48, *cr.* 14.

BODKIN, Eng., a pillar, sa. *Pl.* 33, *cr.* 1.

BODLEY, or BODLEGH, Duncombe, Devons., on a ball, az., encircled with rays, or, a ducal coronet, of the second.

BODLEY, Streatham, Surr., a bull's head, or. *Pl.* 120, *cr.* 7.

BODLEY, a demi-wolf, between paws a ducal coronet, all ppr. *Pl.* 65, *cr.* 4.

BODRIGAN, a dexter hand, erect, round wrist a ribbon. *Pl.* 44, *cr.* 7.

BODWIDA, a dexter arm, in armour, embowed, ppr., in hand a fleur-de-lis, or. *Pl.* 24, *cr.* 14.

BODYHAM, Eng., a pegasus at speed, wings addorsed (and ducally gorged.) *Pl.* 28, *cr.* 9.

BOEHM, BOHEM, and BOEHAM, between two elephants' trunks, per fess, ar. and sa., a horseshoe, of the first. *Pl.* 96, *cr.* 1, (shoe, *pl.* 52, *cr.* 4.)

BOEVY-CRAWLEY, Bart., Glouc., (on a mount, vert.,) a heron, ppr., collared, or, in dexter, a saltier, gold. *Esse quam videri*. *Pl.* 26, *cr.* 11.

BOGER, Eng., an eagle, wings expanded, supporting a flag. *Pl.* 65, *cr.* 3.

BOGG, Sutterin, Linc., a bat, displayed, ar., armed, ppr. *Pl.* 94, *cr.* 9.

BOGGIS, or BOGGS, the sail of a ship, ppr. *Pl.* 22, *cr.* 12.

BOGIE, and BOGGIE, Eng., a lamb, supporting a flag. *Deus pastor meus*. *Pl.* 48, *cr.* 13.

BOGLE, Sco., a rose, slipped and leaved, ppr. *Dulcedine*. *Pl.* 105, *cr.* 7.

BOGLE, Sco., a rose, stalked and leaved, ppr., thereon a bee feeding, sa. *E labore dulce do*. *Pl.* 109, *cr.* 6.

BOGLE, a ship in full sail, ppr. *Spe meliore vehor*. *Pl.* 109, *cr.* 8.

BOGLE, same crest.

BOGLE, Eng., a tower, ppr. *Pl.* 12, *cr.* 5.

BOGLEY, Eng., a cross, sa., on three grieces, gu. *Pl.* 49, *cr.* 2.

BOHUN, DE, a wolf, current, ppr. *Pl.* 111, *cr.* 1.

BOHUN, Tressingfield, Suff., on a chapeau, a quatrefoil, pierced, erm., in centre, a bezant. *Pl.* 13, *cr.* 14, (quatrefoil, *pl.* 65, *cr.* 7.)

BOHUN, or BOONE, Lincoln, out of a ducal coronet, gu., a cap, ar., between two elephants' tusks, or.

BOIDELL, Eng., a greyhound's head, erased, az. *Pl.* 89, *cr.* 2.

BOILEAU, Eng., a heart inflamed, ppr. *Pl.* 68, *cr.* 13.

BOILEAU, Bart., of Tacolnstone Hall, Norf., in a nest, or, a pelican in her piety, ppr., (charged on breast with a saltier, gu.) *De tout mon cœur*. *Pl.* 44, *cr.* 1.

BOIS, a stag's head, ar., attired, gu., between attires a mound, or. *Pl.* 66, *cr.* 9, (mound, *pl.* 37, *cr.* 3.)

BOIS, Eng., a lion, rampant, gu. *Pl.* 67, *cr.* 5.

BOKELAND, a lion, rampant, between paws a pair of scales, ppr. *Pl.* 67, *cr.* 5, (scales, *pl.* 12, *cr.* 11.)

BOKELAND, Eng., an eagle's head, couped, gu., between wings, chequey, or and vert. *Pl.* 81, *cr.* 10.

BOKENHAM, Norf., three mullets, two at bottom, one at top. *Pl.* 46, *cr.* 15.

BOKENHAM, Norf., a lion, rampant, gu. *Pl.* 67, *cr.* 5.

BOKINGE, or BOKING, Suff., a man's head, couped at shoulders, ar., hair, vert. *Pl.* 121, *cr.* 2.

BOLAINE, or BOLOINE, Lond., a bull's head, couped, ar. *Pl.* 120, *cr.* 7.

BOLAND, Devons., out of a ducal coronet, or, an arm from elbow, in hand a bunch of three arrows, in bend, sinister. *Pl.* 9, *cr.* 4.

BOLBECK, or BOLEBECK, a lion, sejant, supporting with dexter a broken lance, all ppr. *Pl.* 60, *cr.* 4.

BOLCOLE, a (demi)-reindeer, ppr., collared, traced, and (charged on shoulder with an etoile, or.) *Pl.* 2, *cr.* 13.

BOLD, or BOLDE, Eng., out of a ducal coronet, gu., a griffin's head, sa., between wings, or. *Pl.* 97, *cr.* 13, (without charging.)

BOLD of Bold, Lanc., a griffin, segreant, sa., beaked and legged, or. *Pl.* 67, *cr.* 13.

BOLD of Bold, Lanc., out of a ducal coronet, gu., a demi-eagle, sa., winged, or. *Pl.* 19, *cr.* 9.

BOLDEN, JOHN, Esq., of Hyning, Lancaster: 1. Out of a ducal coronet, or, a tiger's head, ar. *Pl.* 36, *cr.* 15. 2. A swan, or. *Pour bien désirer*. *Pl.* 122, *cr.* 13, (without mount.)

BOLDERO, and BOLDEROWE, Eng., a torteau, vert. *Pl.* 7, *cr.* 6.

BOLDERO, Suff., a greyhound, sejant. *Audax ero*. *Pl.* 66, *cr.* 15.

BOLDERS, a greyhound, current, ar., (collared, or.) *Pl.* 28, *cr.* 7, (without charge.)

BOLDORNE, and BOLDRON, Eng., a greyhound, current, gu., collared, or. *Pl.* 28, *cr.* 7, (without charge.)

BOLDROWE, Suff., in lion's gamb, ar., a saltier, az. *Pl.* 89, *cr.* 15, (saltier, *pl.* 82, *cr.* 7.)

BOLEBEC, or BOLEBECK, Eng., a lion, sejant, in dexter a broken lance, all ppr. *Pl.* 60, *cr.* 4.

BOLEINE, a bull's head, couped, ar., langued, gu., charged on neck with a crescent, or. *Pl.* 120, *cr.* 7, (crescent, *pl.* 141.)

BOLES, Eng., out of a mural coronet, az., a lion's head, ar. *Pl.* 45, *cr.* 9.

BOLEYN, BOLLEYN, BOLEYNE, BOLLENS, or BOLLIN, Eng., two branches of thorn, in orle, ppr. *Pl.* 110, *cr.* 10.

BOLGER, Eng., a dexter arm, couped and embowed, ppr., in hand three ears of rye, leaved, or. *Pl.* 89, *cr.* 4.

BOLGER, St Austins, near Arklow, Iri., an escallop reversed, or. *Deus nobis hæc otio fecit*. *Pl.* 53, *cr.* 3.

BOLHALTH, Eng., from top of tower, an arm, embowed, in hand a spear, in fess. *Pl.* 3, *cr.* 7.

BOLINGBROKE, and ST JOHN, Viscount and Baron, (St John,) on a mount, ppr., a falcon, rising, belled, or, ducally gorged, gu. *Nec quærere, nec spernere honorem*. *Pl.* 61, *cr.* 12.

BOLLAND, Clapham, Surr., an eagle's head, erased, ppr., (gorged with a collar, erm., in beak a peg, sa.) *Pl.* 74, *cr.* 1.

BOLLAND, Eng., a hart, trippant, ppr., armed, or. *Pl.* 68, *cr.* 2.

BOLLEN, Eng., a talbot, gu., collared and leashed, or. *Pl.* 65, *cr.* 2.

BOLLERS, Eng., an arm, vested, couped, and embowed, in fess, elbow on wreath, in hand a cross crosslet, fitched. *Pl.* 88, *cr.* 7.

BOLLES, Middx.; and Scampton, Linc.; a buck's head, ar., attired, or. *Pl.* 91, *cr.* 14.

BOLLES, Suff., a cock crowing, or, combed, wattled, and armed, gu. *Pl.* 67, *cr.* 14.

BOLLINGBROKE, BOLLINGBROOK, and BOLLINSBROOK, a Spanish hat, az., turned up, ar., in front three feathers, of the last. *Pl.* 28, *cr.* 1.

BOLLS, Eng., a cock crowing, or, combed, armed, beaked, legged, and wattled, gu. *Pl.* 67, *cr.* 14.

BOLNEY, Berks. and Suss., a skeleton's head, couped at shoulders, ppr., (in mouth a firebrand, or, flammant at ends, ppr.) *Pl.* 62, *cr.* 12, (brand, *pl.* 70, *cr.* 14.)

BOLOURD, Eng., out of a ducal coronet, or, a demi-eagle, gu. *Pl.* 19, *cr.* 9.

BOLRON, a dove, volant, sa. *Pl.* 25, *cr.* 6.

BOLRON, Eng., an arm, in fess, couped at shoulder, elbow on wreath, in hand a sword, in pale, enfiled with a savage's head. *Pl.* 102, *cr.* 11.

BOLSTRED, a bull's head and neck, (erased,) gu., attired, ar., between wings expanded, of the last. *Pl.* 60, *cr.* 9.

BOLSTRODE, Eng., a bull's head, couped, gu., armed, or. *Pl.* 120, *cr.* 7.

BOLT, or BOULT, a stork, ppr. *Pl.* 33, *cr.* 9.

BOLTER, Eng., a lion's head, erased, sa., imperially crowned, or. *Pl.* 123, *cr.* 13.

BOLTHORPE, a demi-tiger, salient, or, ducally gorged, ar. *Pl.* 53, *cr.* 10.

BOLTON, Iri., a stag's head, erased, ar., (pierced through nose with an arrow.) *Pl.* 66, *cr.* 9.

BOLTON, RICHARD, Esq., of Bective Abbey, co. Meath, a hawk, belled, ar. *Pl.* 67, *cr.* 3.

BOLTON, JANE, of Mount Bolton, co. Waterford, a buck's head, erased, attired, or, gorged with a chaplet, vert, (pierced through neck with an arrow, of the second.) *Vi et virtute.* *Pl.* 38, *cr.* 1.

BOLTON, Baron, (Powlett,) a falcon, wings expanded, and belled, or, (charged on breast and wings with three etoiles, in fess, gu., gorged with a ducal coronet, az., in beak a salmon, ppr.) *Aymez loyaulte.* *Pl.* 105, *cr.* 4.

BOLTON, (a bolt, gu.,) in a tun, or. *Pl.* 124, *cr.* 9.

BOLTON, a tun, erect, ppr., (transpierced by an arrow, in fess,) or. *Pl.* 6, *cr.* 15.

BOLTON, Suff., a falcon, close, ar., (charged on breast with a trefoil, slipped, vert,) beaked and belled, or. *Pl.* 67, *cr.* 3.

BOLTON, BOLTONE, or BOLTOUN, a horse, current, saddled and bridled. *Pl.* 8, *cr.* 2.

BOLTON, Lanc., a hawk, ar., belled, or. *Pl.* 67, *cr.* 3.

BOLTON, or BOULTON, Lanc. and York., a buck's head, erased, ar., attired, or, gorged with chaplet, vert, (pierced through neck with an arrow,) gold. *Pl.* 38, *cr.* 1.

BOLTON, a falcon, ar., wings expanded, or. *Pl.* 105, *cr.* 4.

BOMFORD, Iri., an eagle, displayed, in dexter a dagger. *Pl.* 107, *cr.* 4.

BOMONT, an ostrich, wings expanded, ar. *Pl.* 9, *cr.* 3.

BON, LE, Eng., out of a ducal coronet, or, a plume of ostrich-feathers, ar. *Confido.* *Pl.* 100, *cr.* 12.

BONAR, Lond.; and Chiselhurst, Kent; a sword, in pale, blade, ppr., hilt and pommel, or, *Pl.* 105, *cr.* 1.

BONAR, JOHN, Esq., Kimmerghame, a sword, in pale, ppr. *Denique cœlum.* *Pl.* 105, *cr.* 1.

BONAR, JAMES, Esq., of Kimmerghame, Berwick; and Warriston, in Mid-Lothian: 1. For *Bonar, ancient,* two swords. *Pl.* 75, *cr.* 13, (without cup.) 2. For *Bonar, modern,* a crusader's sword. *Pl.* 22, *cr.* 7. 3. As honourable augmentation, granted to the family by the King of France, two banners, crossed. *Pl.* 53, *cr.* 14.

BOND, Peckham, Surr.; and Cornw.; a demi-pegasus, az., semée of etoiles, or. *Pl.* 91, *cr.* 2, (without coronet.)

BOND, a lion, sejant, erm. *Pl.* 126, *cr.* 15.

BOND, or BONDE, Eng., an old man's head, in profile, ppr., hair, sa. *Pl.* 81, *cr.* 15.

BOND, Saltash, Cornw., out of a ducal coronet, or, a cubit arm, erect, in armour, sa., garnished, gold, in hand a sword, ppr., hilt and pommel, of the first. *Pl.* 15, *cr.* 5.

BOND, Iri., an ostrich-head between two branches of palm, in orle. *Pl.* 49, *cr.* 7.

BOND, Sir THOMAS, Bart., Iri., a lion, sejant, ar. *Pl.* 126, *cr.* 15.

BOND, HENRY-COOTE, Esq., of Bondville, co. Armagh, a lion, sejant, ar. *Pl.* 126, *cr.* 15.

BONDE, Dorchester, a demi-pegasus, az., winged and guttée d'or. *Pl.* 91, *cr.* 2, (without coronet.)

BONDE, Dorchester, a lion, sejant, ar. *Pl.* 126, *cr.* 15.

BONDIVILLE, Yorks., a stag's head, ppr. *Pl.* 91, *cr.* 14.

BONE, Sco., a goat, statant, in mouth a branch of oak, all ppr. *Pl.* 15, *cr.* 9.

BONE, a bone and palm-branch, in saltier, ppr. *Pl.* 25, *cr.* 11.

BONE, or BOUN, Eng., a sword and key, in saltier, ppr. *Pl.* 54, *cr.* 12.

BONEHAM, and BONHAM, Eng., a pheon, in pale, point downward, with part of broken shaft. *Pl.* 27, *cr.* 12.

BONEKILL, Sco., a demi-man, in armour, in dexter a sword, all ppr. *Pl.* 23, *cr.* 4.

BONEKILL, Sco., in dexter hand, ppr., a buckle, or. *Pl.* 38, *cr.* 9.

BONELL, Derby, a demi-lion, rampant, sa. *Pl.* 67, *cr.* 10.

BONEST, Lond., a talbot's head, couped, ar. *Pl.* 123, *cr.* 15.

BONFOY, or BUNFOY, Hease, Middx., an arm, couped and erect, in armour, ppr., in hand a cross calvary, gu. *Pl.* 51, *cr.* 1, (cross, *pl.* 141.)

BONHAM, Wilts., stump of tree, in fess, sprouting, ensigned with a fleur-de-lis. *Pl.* 14, *cr.* 14.

BONHAM, Ess., a mermaid, ppr. *Pl.* 48, *cr.* 5.

BONHAM, Petersfield, Hants, a dragon's head, ar., guttée-de-sang. *Pl.* 87, *cr.* 12.

BONIFACE, Lond. and Suss., a talbot, passant, sa. *Pl.* 120, *cr.* 8.

BONNELL, Norf., a lion, rampant, or, between paws a cross crosslet, az. *Pl.* 125, *cr.* 2, (cross, *pl.* 141.)

BONNELL, Lond., a demi-lion, (erased, or, pellettée, tail-forked and interlaced, supporting a spear.) *Pl.* 67, *cr.* 10.

BONNER, a unicorn's head, couped, between wings, in mouth a trefoil. *Pl.* 20, *cr.* 1, (trefoil, *pl.* 141.)
BONNER, Oxon., a talbot's head, ar., collared, az., studded, edged, and ringed, or. *Pl.* 2, *cr.* 15.
BONNET, Lond., a unicorn's head, couped, vert, purfled and crined, or. *Rara bonitas. Pl.* 20, *cr.* 1.
BONNETT, Eng., an arm from elbow, in armour, in fess, in hand a cross crosslet, fitched, az. *Pl.* 71, *cr.* 13.
BONNEY, Eng., a square padlock, ppr. *Pl.* 18, *cr.* 7.
BONNIMAN, Sco., a spur, between wings, ppr. *Pl.* 109, *cr.* 12.
BONSHAW, in dexter hand, issuing from a cloud, in fess, a sword, in pale, on point a garland of laurel, all ppr. *Mente manuque. Pl.* 73, *cr.* 11.
BONSOR, Lond. and Surr., on a staff raguly, or, in fess, a wolf, passant, sa., collared, chain reflexed over back, gold, (dexter resting on a rose, gu., barbed and seeded, ppr.) *Pl.* 5, *cr.* 8.
BONTEIN, Sco., an arm, in hand a sword, ppr. *Fortiter et fide. Pl.* 34, *cr.* 7.
BONTEIN, Eng., a cross crosslet and two palm-branches, in saltier. *Pl.* 66, *cr.* 8, (palm, *pl.* 63, *cr.* 3.)
BONTEIN, and BONTEINE, Sco., an armillary sphere, ppr. *Soli Deo gloria. Pl.* 114, *cr.* 6.
BONTEN, a griffin, segreant, in dexter, (a sword, in pale.) *Pl.* 67, *cr.* 13.
BONTIEN, out of a ducal coronet, or, an eagle, rising, purp. *Pl.* 19, *cr.* 9.
BONTON, Eng., an arm from elbow, in hand a mill-rind, ppr. *Pl.* 34, *cr.* 3.
BONUS, and BONEST, Lond., a talbot's head, couped, ar. *Pl.* 123, *cr.* 15.
BONVILE, Devons., a stag's head, ppr. *Pl.* 91, *cr.* 14.
BONVILL, a demi-lion, rampant, supporting an anchor, ppr. *Pl.* 19, *cr.* 6.
BONWICK, Surr., a lion's head, erased, gu., charged with an etoile, or, a crescent for difference. *Pl.* 81, *cr.* 4, (chargings, *pl.* 141.)
BOODAM, Eng., an etoile of eight rays, or. *Pl.* 83, *cr.* 3, (without coronet.)
BOODLE, Eng., a horse's head, neck transpierced with spear, in bend, ppr. *Pl.* 110, *cr.* 6.
BOOER, Eng., a wolf's head, erased, erm. *Pl.* 14, *cr.* 6.
BOOKER, Iri., a crow feeding, ppr. *Pl.* 51, *cr.* 8.
BOOKER, Lond. and Notts., a swan, collared and lined, ppr. *Pl.* 73, *cr.* 14.
BOOKER, THOMAS-WILLIAM, Esq., of The Leys, and Cobrey Park, Heref.; and Velindra House, Glamorgan; a demi-eagle, displayed. *Pl.* 22, *cr.* 11.
BOOKEY, a dove, volant, ar., in mouth a sprig, vert. *Pl.* 25, *cr.* 6.
BOON, or BOONE, Eng., a bell, ppr. *Pl.* 73, *cr.* 15.
BOON, or BOONE, in hand a sheaf of arrows, points downward, ppr. *Pl.* 56, *cr.* 4.
BOORNE, Lond. and Ess., a tiger, segant, gu., maned, tufted, and tailed, or. *Pl.* 26, *cr.* 9.
BOORNE, out of a ducal coronet, a stag's head, ar. *Pl.* 29, *cr.* 7.

BOORNE, Battle, Suss., a stag's head, erased, gu., attired and guttée, ar. *Pl.* 66, *cr.* 9.
BOORS, Eng., an eel, naiant, az. *Pl.* 25, *cr.* 13.
BOOT, or BOOTE, a greyhound, couchant, between two branches of laurel, in orle. *Pl.* 102, *cr.* 13.
BOOTH, Derbs., a demi-St Catherine, ppr., couped at knees, vested, ar., crowned, or, in dexter a catherine wheel, in sinister a sword, point downward.
BOOTH, Salford, Lanc., two laurel-branches, vert, in orle, thereon a lion, passant, ar. *Non mihi, sed Deo et regi. Pl.* 60, *cr.* 6.
BOOTH, Bart., Ess., a lion, passant, ar., (gorged with a bar-gemelle, in dexter a chaplet of laurel, vert.) *Deus adjuvat nos. Pl.* 60, *cr.* 6.
BOOTH, GORE, Bart., Iri.: 1. A lion, rampant, ar. *Quod ero spero. Pl.* 67, *cr.* 5. 2. A wolf, rampant, ar. *In hoc signo vinces*—and —*Genti æquus utrique. Pl.* 10, *cr.* 3.
BOOTH, RICHARD, Esq., of Glendon Hall, Northamp., a lion, passant, ar. *Quod ero spero. Pl.* 48, *cr.* 8.
BOOTH, a lictor's rod, ppr. *Pl.* 65, *cr.* 15.
BOOTH, or BOOTHE, Chesh., a lion, passant, ar. (Another, or.) *Pl.* 48, *cr.* 8.
BOOTH, Twemlow, Chesh., a lion, passant, (per pale, wavy, ar., and erm., charged on shoulder with a hank of cotton, ppr.) *Pl.* 48, *cr.* 8.
BOOTH, Berks., a porcupine's head, erased. *Pl.* 55, *cr.* 10.
BOOTH, Eng., a boar's head, erased, erect, sa. *Pl.* 21, *cr.* 7.
BOOTH, a demi-leopard, rampant. *Pl.* 12, *cr.* 14.
BOOTH, Kellingham, Linc., a boar's head, erased and erect, sa., armed, or, (in mouth a spear-head, ar.) *Pl.* 108, *cr.* 1.
BOOTH, Chesh., on a chaplet, vert, a lion, passant, ar. *Pl.* 60, *cr.* 6.
BOOTH, Chesh., Linc., Lanc., Lond. and Warw., on a chaplet, vert, a lion, passant, ar. *Non mihi, sed Deo et regi. Pl.* 60, *cr.* 6.
BOOTH, a boar's head, couped, sa. *Pl.* 48, *cr.* 2.
BOOTHBY, Bart., Broadlow Ash, Derbs., a lion's paw, erased, erect, or. *Mors Christi, mors mortis mihi. Pl.* 126, *cr.* 9.
BOOTLE, Eng., a leopard, couchant, or, spotted, gu. *Pl.* 111, *cr.* 11.
BOOTLE, Wilbraham. *See* SKELMERSDALE.
BOOTLE, a demi-lion, rampant, regardant, ppr., (between paws an antique oval shield, gu., rimmed, or, charged with a cross patonce, crossed, ar.) *Pl.* 33, *cr.* 2, (without spear or head.)
BOOTY, Suff., (on a mount, vert,) in hand, ppr., couped at wrist, a sword, ar., hilted, or. *Pl.* 21, *cr.* 10.
BORASTER, Heref., Worc., and Berks., out of a mural coronet, sa., a griffin's head, or, (gorged with a fess between two bars-gemelle, gu.) *Pl.* 101, *cr.* 6.
BORDELAYS, BORDELEYS, BORDELEY, or BORDELOYS, Camb., an Indian goat, salient, (in mouth a branch of trefoil.) *Pl.* 32, *cr.* 10, (without tree.)
BOREHAM, or BORHAM, Eng., on a mural coronet, ppr., a serpent, nowed, vert. *Pl.* 103, *cr.* 11.
BOREHONT, Hants., on a mural coronet, ppr., a serpent, nowed, vert. *Pl.* 103, *cr.* 11.

BORELACE, a boar's head, couped at neck, bendy of six, or and sa., (in mouth a rose, per pale, gu., and of the second, leaved, vert.) *Pl.* 2, *cr.* 7.
BORELANDS, Edinr., a broken lance, ppr. *Press through. Pl.* 3, *cr.* 6.
BORELL, or BURRELL, Heref.; and Brommer Park, near Alnwick, Northumb.; a naked arm, embowed, ppr., charged with three pellets, (in hand a bunch of leaves, vert, fructed, or.) *Pl.* 87, *cr.* 7, (pellet, *pl.* 141.)
BORLEY, and BORSELEY, Wilts., in front of a rock a Cornish chough, ppr. *Pl.* 70, *cr.* 11.
BOREMAN, Eng., on stump of tree, an eagle, rising, ppr. *Pl.* 1, *cr.* 11.
BORESTON, or BORRESTON, Eng., a parrot, vert, breasted, gu. *Pl.* 25, *cr.* 2.
BORGOINE, Eng., a marigold, on top a bee, all ppr. *Pl.* 109, *cr.* 6, (marigold, *pl.* 105, *cr.* 15.)
BORLACE, Treluddro, Cornw., a boar's head, couped at neck, bendy of four, or and sa., erased, gu., between two roses, of the last, stalked and leaved, vert. *Pl.* 2, *cr.* 7, (roses, *pl.* 125, *cr.* 6.)
BORLAND, and BORLANDS, Sco., a broken lance, ppr. *Press through. Pl.* 3, *cr.* 6.
BORLAND, Eng., a bull's head, erased, ar., ducally gorged, sa. *Pl.* 68, *cr.* 6.
BORLAND, a (broken) sword, ppr. *Pl.* 22, *cr.* 7.
BORLASE, Bockmer, Bucks., a wolf, passant, regardant, ar., struck in shoulder with an arrow, or, held in mouth. *Pl.* 77, *cr.* 14.
BORMAN, Devons. and Somers., a bull's head, erased, or, attired, sa. *Pl.* 19, *cr.* 3.
BORMINGHALL, Eng., a wolf's head, erased, gu. *Pl.* 14, *cr.* 6.
BORMINGHALL, Eng., a wolf's head, gu. *Pl.* 8, *cr.* 4.
BORNE, Kent, a lion, sejant, or, collared, az., resting fore-dexter on a pellet. *Pl.* 21, *cr.* 3, (pellet, *pl.* 141.)
BORODAILE, a dragon's head, erased, ppr. *Pl.* 107, *cr.* 10.
BORODAILE, a dragon's head, ppr. *Pl.* 87, *cr.* 12.
BORON, a dragon's head, and wings, sa., (collared,) or. *Pl.* 105, *cr.* 11.
BOROUGH, Linc.; and Richmond, Yorks.; a swan's head and neck, ar., beaked, gu. *Pl.* 54, *cr.* 6, (without wings.)
BOROUGH, Bart., Baseldon Park, Berks., three plates surmounted by a plume of five ostrich-feathers, ar. *Survez moi. Pl.* 106, *cr.* 11, (plate, *pl.* 141.)
BOROUGH, Sandwich, Kent, a dove, standing on a snake, ppr. *Pl.* 3, *cr.* 4.
BOROUGH, or BURGH, Eng., a falcon, rising, erm., billed, and ducally gorged, or. *Pl.* 61, *cr.* 12, (without mount.)
BOROUGH, Northamp., Devons., and Kent, two wings, addorsed, erm. *Pl.* 63, *cr.* 12.
BORRADAILE, BORRODAILE, or BORADAILE, out of a tower, a demi-greyhound, between paws a branch of laurel, all ppr. *Pl.* 73, *cr.* 13.
BORRER, WILLIAM, Esq., of Henfield, Suss., a buck's head, ppr., erased, (fretty, ar., in mouth an auger, of the first.) *Fide laboro. Pl.* 66, *cr.* 9.
BORRETT, Lond. and Westm., a boar's head and neck, erased, gu., bristled, or, neck transpierced with broken spear, gold, end held in mouth. *Pl.* 115, *cr.* 2.
BORRETT, Yorks., a lion, passant, ppr. *Pl.* 48, *cr.* 8.

BORROW, Derbs., (on a mount,) an eagle, regardant, wings expanded, all ppr., (supporting with dexter the shield of Pallas, or.) *Pl.* 35, *cr.* 8,
BORROWES, Bart., Iri., a lion, sejant, ar., ducally crowned, or. *Et vi et virtute. Pl.* 126, *cr.* 15, (crown, *pl.* 98, *cr.* 1.)
BORROWES, or BORROWS, Iri., a boar's head, erased, in fess, with sword thrust through under jaw, in pale, and issuing out of mouth. *Pl.* 28, *cr.* 14.
BORROWES, or BORROWS, Eng., a crane, supporting with dexter an anchor. *Pl.* 61, *cr.* 10.
BORROWMAN, Sco., a demi-man, in armour, brandishing a sword, ppr. *Pro patria. Pl.* 23, *cr.* 4.
BORSELLE, Eng., over stump of oak-tree an eagle, volant, ppr. *Pl.* 114, *cr.* 10, (stump, *pl.* 92, *cr.* 8.)
BORSTON, Eng., a dagger, in pale, az., pommel, or. *Pl.* 73, *cr.* 9.
BORTHWICK, a withered rose-bush, sprouting anew from root. *Virtus post facta. Pl.* 23, *cr.* 2.
BORTHWICK, JOHN, Esq., of Crookston; and Borthwick Castle, Edinr., a moor's head, couped, ppr. *Qui conducit*—and—*Fide et spe. Pl.* 120, *cr.* 3.
BORTHWICK, Sco., a dexter hand, couped apaumée, charged with an eye, ppr. *Mente manuque. Pl.* 99, *cr.* 13.
BORTHWICK, Hartside, Sco., a hart's head, erased, gu., attired, or, devouring a serpent, ppr. *Cœlitus datum. Pl.* 54, *cr.* 7.
BORTHWICK, Muirhouse, Sco., a pelican, wings expanded, or, vulning breast, ppr. *Ex vulnere salus. Pl.* 109, *cr.* 15.
BORTHWICK, Sco., a Saracen's head, affrontée, ppr. *Qui conducit. Pl.* 19, *cr.* 1.
BORTHWICK, Sco., a negro's head, sa. *Qui conducit. Pl.* 120, *cr.* 3.
BORTHWICK, Sco., a savage's head, ppr. *Qui conducit. Pl.* 19, *cr.* 1.
BORTHWICK, Sco., an eagle, displayed, sa., charged on breast with a saltier. *Fide et spe. Pl.* 25, *cr.* 5.
BORTHWICK, Mayshiels, Sco., an eagle, rising, ppr. *Nec deerit operi dextra. Pl.* 67, *cr.* 4.
BORTON, Stapleford, a boar's head, couped, or, in mouth a branch of laurel, vert. *Pl.* 125, *cr.* 7, (laurel, *pl.* 123, *cr.* 5.)
BORTON, Suff., a boar's head, ppr. *Pl.* 48, *cr.* 2.
BOSANQUET, Eng., out of a tower, ppr., a lady, in hand a cross, gu. *Pl.* 26, *cr.* 5.
BOSANQUET, SAMUEL-RICHARD, Esq., of The Forest House, Epping Forest, Ess.; and of Dingeston Court, Monmouth; a demi-lion, rampant, couped, gu. *Pl.* 67, *cr.* 10.
BOSANQUET, GEORGE-JACOB, Esq., of Broxbournbury, Herts., same crest.
BOSCAWEN, Cornw., a falcon, ppr. *Pl.* 67, *cr.* 3.
BOSCAWEN, Cornw., a boar, passant, gu., armed and membered, or. *Pl.* 48, *cr.* 14.
BOSCOWEN, a boar, passant, or, (collared and lined.) *Pl.* 48, *cr.* 14.
BOSCOWEN, EDWARD, Earl of Falmouth, Viscount Falmouth, and Baron Boscowen-Rose, Cornw.: 1. A boar, passant, gu., armed, bristled, and unguled, or. *In cœlo quies. Pl.* 48, *cr.* 14. 2. A falcon, close, ppr., belled, or. *Patience passe science. Pl.* 67, *cr.* 3.

BOSGRAVE, Eng., a boar's head, erased, ar., between two oak-branches, vert, fructed, or. *Pl.* 19, *cr.* 8.

BOSNE, and BOSNEY, Eng., a cockatrice, displayed. *Pl.* 102, *cr.* 15.

BOSOM, BOSOME, and BOSSUM, Cornw., a tree growing out of a mount, ppr. *Pl.* 48, *cr.* 4.

BOSS, Durh., out of a naval coronet, an arm, in hand a billet, all ppr. *Cada uno eshijo de sub obras. Pl.* 93, *cr.* 1, (billet, *pl.* 28, *cr.* 8.)

BOSTOCK, Abingdon, Berks., an antelope, ar., attired, or. *Pl.* 63, *cr.* 10.

BOSTOCK, Salop, a martlet, ar. *Pl.* 111, *cr.* 5.

BOSTOCK, Chesh., on stump of tree, erect, ar., a bear's head, erased, sa., muzzled, or. *Pl.* 71, *cr.* 6, (stump, *pl.* 10, *cr.* 6.)

BOSTOCK, Chesh., an antelope, or. *Pl.* 63, *cr.* 10.

BOSTON, Baron and a Bart., Linc., (Irby,) on a wreath, ar. and sa., a Saracen's head, ppr. *Honor fidelitatis præmium. Pl.* 19, *cr.* 1.

BOSTON, Sco., a dove, between two branches of laurel, in orle, ppr. *Pl.* 2, *cr.* 11.

BOSTON, Eng., a horse's head, in armour, ppr. *Pl.* 7, *cr.* 12.

BOSTRADEPONS, Sco., an etoile of eight points, radiated, or. *Pl.* 83, *cr.* 3, (without coronet.)

BOSUM, Norf., a talbot's head, erased, ar., eared, and ducally crowned, or. *Pl.* 25, *cr.* 10.

BOSVILE, or BOSVILLE, Iri., a bull, (statant, hinder part behind a clump of oak-trees, ppr.) *Pl.* 66, *cr.* 11.

BOSVILLE, Eng., a cock's head, erased. *Pl.* 92, *cr.* 3.

BOSVILLE, and BOSSEVILLE, (behind an oak-tree,) a ram, passant, all ppr. *Pl.* 109, *cr.* 2.

BOSWELL, Bart., Auchinleck, Ayrs., a falcon, ppr., hooded, gu., belled, or. *Vraye foy. Pl.* 38, *cr.* 12.

BOSWELL, Sco., same crest and motto.

BOSWELL, Sco., a falcon's head, couped, ppr. *Pl.* 99, *cr.* 10, (without wings.)

BOSWELL, Yorks., (out of a wood, ppr.,) a bull, passant, ar. *Pl.* 66, *cr.* 11.

BOSWELL, Yorks. and Kent, a lion's head. *Pl.* 126, *cr.* 1.

BOSWELL, Glassmount, Sco., a lark, volant, ppr. *Nothing venture, nothing have. Pl.* 87, *cr.* 10.

BOSWELL, Dowen, Sco., same crest. *I hope for better.*

BOSWELL, Balmuto, Sco., in hand a scimitar, ppr. *Fortiter. Pl.* 29, *cr.* 8.

BOSWORTH, Eng., a lily, slipped and leaved, ppr. *Pl.* 81, *cr.* 9.

BOSWORTH, Rev. JOSEPH, D.D., F.R.S., of Trinity College, Camb.; British chaplain at Rotterdam; a demi-lion, rampant, ppr. *Animus valet. Pl.* 67, *cr.* 10.

BOTATORT, or BOTETOURT, Norf., out of a mural coronet, six spears, in saltire, ppr. *Pl.* 95, *cr.* 8.

BOTELER, Teston, Kent, two eagles supporting a vine, ppr. *Aquilæ vitem pocula.*

BOTELER, Hatfield-Woodhall, Herts., an arm, in armour, embowed, in hand a sword, ppr. *Pl.* 21, *cr.* 4.

BOTELL, and BOTHELL, Ess., a marigold, ppr. *Pl.* 105, *cr.* 15.

BOTELLER, Eng., a covered cup, or. *Pl.* 113, *cr.* 9, (without swords.)

BOTERWIKE, a hawk, in dexter an ear of wheat, ppr. *Pl.* 94, *cr.* 7.

BOTESHED, Eng., a stag's head, ar. *Pl.* 91, *cr.* 14.

BOTEVILE, BOTEVILLE, or BONTEVILLE, Salop, a reindeer, or. *J'ay bonne cause. Pl.* 12, *cr.* 8.

BOTFIELD, BERIAH, Esq., of Norton Hall, Northamp., and Decker Hill, Salop., a reindeer, (statant,) or. *J'ay bonne cause. Pl.* 12, *cr.* 8.

BOTFIELD, a buck, statant, ppr. *Pl.* 88, *cr.* 9. (without arrow.)

BOTH, or BOTHE, Eng., on a tower, embattled, a flag, displayed. *Pl.* 8, *cr.* 13.

BOTHWELL, Sco., a naked boy pulling down top of a green pine-tree. *Obduram adversus urgentia. Pl.* 94, *cr.* 8.

BOTILER, and BOTTILER, a cinquefoil, gu. *Pl.* 91, *cr.* 12.

BOTOCKSHED, Eng., a stag's head, ar. *Pl.* 91, *cr.* 14.

BOTREAULX, or BOTREAUX, Devons.; and Cockermouth, Cumb.; a dove, standing on a hill, ppr. *Pl.* 104, *cr.* 8.

BOTREAUX, a man, vested, gu., cap, ppr., legs, ar., holding a flail, handle, of the last, other part, or.

BOTREULX, or BOTREUX, Cornw., two laurel-branches, in saltire, ppr. *Pl.* 82, *cr.* 11, (without axe.)

BOTT, Staffs., on a glove, a falcon, ppr. *Pl.* 1, *cr.* 13.

BOTTELER, Iri., a cock's head and neck, vert, combed, wattled, beaked, and (ducally gorged, or, the coronet round the throat, between two dragons' wings, expanded, ar.) *Pl.* 92, *cr.* 3.

BOTTELEY, BOTILLY, or BOTLEY, a boar's head and neck, sa., ducally gorged, or. *Pl.* 36, *cr.* 9.

BOTTELL, Eng., an escallop, az. *Pl.* 117, *cr.* 4.

BOTTILER, Eng., a cinquefoil, vert. *Pl.* 91, *cr.* 12.

BOTTLESHAM, Eng., an escallop, between wings. *Pl.* 62, *cr.* 4.

BOTTOMLEY, Yorks., out of a tower, a demi-lion, ppr. *Fortiter fideliter et feliciter. Pl.* 42, *cr.* 4.

BOTTONLEY, a hawk, standing on a fish, ppr. *Pl.* 29, *cr.* 11.

BOUCHE, Eng., a Saracen's head, couped at shoulders, affrontée, ppr., wreathed, ar. and sa. *Pl.* 97, *cr.* 2.

BOUCHER, an owl, ppr. *Non vi sed voluntate. Pl.* 27, *cr.* 9.

BOUCHER, Salisbury, Wilts., a greyhound, sejant, ar., (collared and lined, or.) *Pl.* 66, *cr.* 15.

BOUCHER, Eng., an old man's head, in profile, couped at shoulders, ppr., on head a cap, turned down in front. *Pl.* 51, *cr.* 4.

BOUCHER, or BOUCHIER, Lond., an owl, ppr. *Pl.* 27, *cr.* 9.

BOUCHERETT, AYSCOGHE, Esq., of Willingham and Stallingborough, Lincoln, a cockatrice, or. *Primâ voce salutat. Pl.* 63, *cr.* 15.

BOUCHIER, Little Stainbridge, Ess., a greyhound, sejant, ar., ducally gorged, or. *Pl.* 66, *cr.* 15, (coronet, *same plate.*)

BOUGE, Thurcaston, Leic., a bat, displayed, ar. *Pl.* 94, *cr.* 9.

BOUGH, Sco., stump of oak-tree, sprouting branches, ppr. *Quod ero spero. Pl.* 92, *cr.* 8.

BOUGHEY, Cotton, Staffs., an angel praying, between two branches of laurel, in orle, ppr. *Pl.* 94, *cr.* 11.

BOUGHEY-FLETCHER, Sir THOMAS FENTON, Bart., Betley Court, Staffs.: 1. For *Fletcher*, a plate, charged with a pheon, per pale, erm. and sa., point downward. See *pl.* 141. 2. For *Boughey*, out of an eastern crown, gold, points alternately or and ar., a buck's head, ermines, attired and (collared,) of the first. *Nec quærere, nec spernere, honorem. Pl.* 91, *cr.* 14, (crown, *pl.* 128, *fig.* 2.)

BOUGHS, stump of tree, sprouting, ppr., from one of the branches pendent a shield, gu. *Pl.* 23, *cr.* 6.

BOUGHTON, Eng., a stork's head, erased, in beak an eel. *Pl.* 41, *cr.* 6.

BOUGHTON, Warw., a lion's head, couped, or. *Pl.* 126, *cr.* 1.

BOUGHTON, Eng., a goat's head, couped, per pale, ar. and gu., (the first charged with pellets, the second with bezants, attired, or.) *Pl.* 105, *cr.* 14.

BOUGHTON-ROUSE, Sir WILLIAM-EDWARD, Bart., Warw., Worc., Salop., and Middx.: 1. For *Boughton*, a stork's head, erased, per cheveron, of four, sa. and ar., in beak a snake, ppr. *Pl.* 32, *cr.* 5. 2. For *Rouse*, a man's head, ppr., beard, hair, and whiskers, sa., head surrounded and crossed by a ribbon, knotted at top, and flowing from sides, ar. *Omne bonum Dei donum. Pl.* 23, *cr.* 3.

BOULBY, or BOWLBY, two branches of thorn, in orle. *Pl.* 110, *cr.* 10.

BOULD, and BOULDE, of Bould, Lanc., out of a ducal coronet, or, a griffin's head, sa., beaked, gu., between wings, gold. *Pl.* 97, *cr.* 13.

BOULING, Eng., a garb, or. *Pl.* 48, *cr.* 10.

BOULSTED, and BOULSTRED, Devons., a bull's head, gu., between wings. *Pl.* 60, *cr.* 9.

BOULT, Eng., a morion cap, ppr. *Pl.* 18, *cr.* 9.

BOULTBEE, Norf. and Ely, a stag's head, erased, ppr. *Pl.* 66, *cr.* 9.

BOULTBEE, or BOULTBIE, Eng., out of a ducal coronet, a demi-boar, ppr. *Pl.* 102, *cr.* 14.

BOULTON, Norf. and Yorks., on a holly-bush, vert, fructed, a hawk, rising, ppr. *Pl.* 99, *cr.* 6, (hawk, *pl.* 105, *cr.* 4.)

BOULTON, Gibbon Grove, Surr., a hawk, ar., collared, legged, and belled, gu., wings expanded, dexter supporting a shield, of the first, (charged with a fleur-de-lis, or.) *Pl.* 4, *cr.* 1.

BOULTON, Eng., a horse, at full speed, saddled and bridled. *Pl.* 8, *cr.* 2.

BOUND, Eng., on top of tower, a lion, rampant. *Pl.* 121, *cr.* 5.

BOUNN, or BOUN, Eng, a sword and key, in saltier, ppr. *Pl.* 54, *cr.* 12.

BOURCH, Iri., a demi-lion, rampant, gu., in dexter a fleur-de-lis, or. *Pl.* 91, *cr.* 13.

BOURCHER, BOURCHIR, or BOURCHIER, Eng., an old man's head, in profile, ppr., couped at shoulders, vested, vert, collar, or, crowned with a ducal coronet, gold, and issuing therefrom a cap, tasselled, turned forward, gu. *Pl.* 78, *cr.* 14.

BOURCHER, Worc., on a mount, vert, a greyhound, sejant, ar., (ducally gorged and lined, or.) *Pl.* 5, *cr.* 2.

BOURCHIER, a greyhound, salient, ar. *Pl.* 48, *cr.* 3.

BOURCHIER, Ess. and Lond., a greyhound, sejant, ar., ducally gorged, or. *Pl.* 66, *cr.* 15, (coronet, *same plate.*)

BOURCHIER, Eng., a mullet of six points. *Pl.* 45, *cr.* 1.

BOURDELAIN, and BOURDILLON, on a chapeau, a martlet, (wings addorsed, ppr.) *Pl.* 89, *cr.* 7.

BOURDEN, Eng., a bunch of grapes, ppr. *Pl.* 77, *cr.* 7.

BOURDON, Eng., a gilliflower, ppr. *Pl.* 22, *cr.* 9.

BOURDON, Sco., a lion, rampant, ar., holding a battle-axe, ppr. *Pl.* 125, *cr.* 2, (axe, *pl.* 14, *cr.* 8.)

BOURGES, Somers., a camel's head, erased, ppr., bezantée. *Pl.* 109, *cr.* 9.

BOURK, Iri., a demi-cat, sa. *Pl.* 80, *cr.* 7.

BOURK, on a ducal coronet, or, a cat, sejant, ppr. *Pl.* 24, *cr.* 6, (coronet, *pl.* 128, *fig.* 3.)

BOURKE, on a chapeau, a lion, sejant, gardant. *Pl.* 113, *cr.* 8.

BOURKE, Earl of Mayo. See MAYO.

BOURKE, St Andrews, Holborn, Middx., a lion, couchant, gardant, tail issuing from between hind legs, or, charged on shoulder with a fleur-de-lis, az. *Chacun le sien. Pl.* 77, *cr.* 10.

BOURKE, General Sir RICHARD, K.C.B., of Thornfield, co. Limerick, a mountain-cat, sejant, gardant, ppr., (collared and chained,) or. *In cruce salus. Pl.* 24, *cr.* 6.

BOURNE, Iri., between wings, a peacock's head, in mouth a serpent, tail coiled round neck. *Pl.* 50, *cr.* 9.

BOURNE, Lond., out of clouds, ppr., an arm, erect, vested, or, cuffed, ar., in hand, ppr., a pheon by the point, sa. *Pl.* 22, *cr.* 6, (pheon, *pl.* 141.)

BOURNE, Wells, Somers., a demi-tiger, ar., armed, maned, and tufted, sa., (gorged with a collar, erminois.) *Pl.* 53, *cr.* 10.

BOURNE, Chesterton, Oxon., a pegasus, current, wings addorsed, gu., (semée of etoiles, or., in mouth a rose, of the first, stalked and leaved, ppr., seeded, gold.) *Pl.* 28, *cr.* 9.

BOURNE, JAMES, Esq., of Hilderstone Hall, Staffs., (on a mount, vert,) a pegasus, salient, wings or, per fess, or and gu., charged on body with two fountains, ppr., in mouth a trefoil, slipped, vert. *Hæc omnia transeunt. Pl.* 57, *cr.* 15, (chargings, *pl.* 141.)

BOURNE, CORNELIUS, Esq., of Stalmine Hall, Lancaster, an heraldic-tiger, sejant, or, guttée-de-sang, (resting dexter on a cross pattée, gu.) *Esse quam videri. Pl.* 111, *cr.* 7, (without coronet.)

BOURNE, JAMES, Esq., of Hackinsall, Lancaster, same crest and motto.

BOURNE, Lanc., same crest, *Semper vigilans.*

BOUSFIELD, Lond. and Yorks., out of a ducal coronet, an eagle's head, ppr. *Pl.* 20, *cr.* 12, (without pellet.)

BOUSTEAD, Eng., on a lion's head, erased, a chapeau, all ppr. *Pl.* 99, *cr.* 9.

BOUTFLEUR, a fleur-de-lis, az. *Pl.* 68, *cr.* 12.

E

BOUVERIE, DES, a demi-eagle, displayed, with two heads, sa., (gorged with a ducal coronet, or, charged on breast with a cross crosslet, ar.) *Pl.* 4, *cr.* 6.

BOUVERIE, JACOB PLEYDELL, Earl of Radnor. *See* RADNOR.

BOUVERIE, EDWARD, Esq., of Delapré Abbey, Northamp., a demi-eagle, with two heads, displayed, sa., (ducally gorged, or, on breast a cross crosslet, ar.) *Patria cara, carior libertas*. *Pl.* 4, *cr.* 6.

BOUVIER, Eng., an eagle, wings expanded and inverted, ppr. *Pl.* 67, *cr.* 4.

BOUWEN, Eng., a tent, gu., garnished, or. *Pl.* 111, *cr.* 14.

BOVER, Eng., a goat's head, ppr. *Pl.* 105, *cr.* 14.

BOVER, Appleton, Chesh., a goat's head, couped, sa., horned and charged with a fleur-de-lis, or. *Pl.* 105, *cr.* 14, (charge, *pl.* 141.)

BOVEY, Wordon Abbey, Beds.; and Stow, Cambs., in lion's paw, erect and erased, per fess, or and gu., a bow, of the second, stringed, gold. *Pl.* 85, *cr.* 15, (bow, *pl.* 3, *cr.* 12.)

BOVIL, and BOLVILE, Eng., a demi-friar, (in dexter) a crucifix. *Pl.* 90, *cr.* 5.

BOVILE, and BOVYLE, Eng., a bull, passant. *Pl.* 66, *cr.* 11.

BOVILE, BOVYLE, and BOVYLL, Eng., a bull, passant, quarterly, sa. and or. *Pl.* 66, *cr.* 11.

Bow, Sco., a lion's head, erased, ppr. *Fideliter*. *Pl.* 81, *cr.* 4.

BOWATER, Lond., out of clouds, a rainbow, ppr. *Pl.* 79, *cr.* 1, (without globe.)

BOWCHER, out of a ducal coronet, or, a demi-pelican, vulning, ar.

BOWDAN, and BOWDEN, Eng., a bezant, charged with a lion's head, erased, gu., collared, ar. *Pl.* 50, *cr.* 10.

BOWDEN, Derbs., a heron's head, erased, or. *Pl.* 32, *cr.* 5.

BOWDEN, Surr., in front of a battle-axe and tilting-spear, in saltier, or, a heron's head, erased, sa.

BOWDITCH of Bowditch, Dors., seven arrows, or, barbed and feathered, ar., six in saltier, one in pale. *Pl.* 110, *cr.* 11.

BOWDLER, a dexter arm, embowed, in hand an arrow, all ppr. *Pl.* 92, *cr.* 14.

BOWDON, on a chapeau, a fox, sejant. *Pl.* 57, *cr.* 14.

BOWDON, Staffs., out of a ducal coronet, a demi-eagle, displayed, (with a cross formée over its head.) *Pl.* 9, *cr.* 6, (cross, *pl.* 141.)

BOWDON, HENRY, Esq., of Southgate House and Beightonfields, Derby: 1. A heron's head, erased, ppr., beaked (and charged on neck with three ermine spots,) sa. *Pl.* 32, *cr.* 5. 2. Out of a ducal coronet, or, a demi-eagle, displayed, ppr. *Vanus est honor*. *Pl.* 9, *cr.* 6.

BOWDON-BUTLER, JOHN, Esq., of Pleasington Hall, Lanc.: 1. For *Bowdon*, a lion, passant, ar., langued, gu. *Pl.* 48, *cr.* 8. 2. For *Butler*, a covered cup, or. *Comme je trouve*. *Pl.* 75, *cr.* 13, (without swords.)

BOWELL, Berry-Court, Hants, a lion's head, erased, barry of six, ar. and gu. *Pl.* 52, *cr.* 7.

BOWEN, Iri., in hand, issuing from a cloud, in fess, a sphere. *Pl.* 104, *cr.* 4.

BOWEN, Kittle Hill and Swansea, Glamorganshire, a stag, statant, vulned in back with an arrow, all ppr. *Pl.* 88, *cr.* 9.

BOWEN-WEBB, CHARLES-WHEELER-TOWNSEND, Esq., of Camrose House, Pembroke, a lion, rampant, sa. *Pl.* 67, *cr.* 5.

BOWEN, The Rev. THOMAS, of Troedyrawr, co. Cardigan, a nag's head, bridled. *Pl.* 92, *cr.* 1.

BOWEN, Oxon., an arm, couped at elbow, and erect, (vested, sa., cuffed, erm.,) in hand, ppr., a chaplet of laurel, vert. *Pl.* 86, *cr.* 1.

BOWEN, a stag, trippant, ppr. *Cautus a futuro*. *Pl.* 68, *cr.* 2.

BOWER, or BOOER, Lond., a wolf's head, erased, erm. *Pl.* 14, *cr.* 6.

BOWER, Dors., a talbot's head, erased, or. *Pl.* 90, *cr.* 6.

BOWER, Oxenfield, Durh., a human leg, couped at thigh, ppr., (charged above knee with a plate, dropping blood, ppr.) *Pl.* 38, *cr.* 14.

BOWER, THOMAS-BOWYER, Esq., of Iwerne House, Dors., a talbot's head, ar. *Hope well and have well*. *Pl.* 123, *cr.* 15.

BOWER, ROBERT, Esq., of Wellham, Yorks., a human leg, couped at thigh, (transpierced by a broken spear, in bend, ppr.) *Esse quam videri*. *Pl.* 38, *cr.* 14.

BOWER, Eng., a demi-moor, ppr., holding a drawn bow and arrow, or. *Pl.* 80, *cr.* 9.

BOWER, a talbot's head, sa. *Pl.* 123, *cr.* 15.

BOWER, Sco., a dexter and sinister arm shooting an arrow from a bow, all ppr. *Ad metam*. *Pl.* 100, *cr.* 4.

BOWER, Cloughton and Bridlington, Yorks., an escallop, ar. *Pl.* 117, *cr.* 4.

BOWER, a bow, in bend, and a sheaf of arrows, in saltier, all ppr. *Ad metam*. *Pl.* 12, *cr.* 12.

BOWER, Kellerby, Yorks., a human leg, couped at thigh, (transpierced above knee by a broken spear, in bend, ppr.) *Pl.* 38, *cr.* 14.

BOWER, Lond., a wolf's head, erased, erm. *Pl.* 14, *cr.* 6.

BOWERBANK, Eng., a demi-savage, ppr., wreathed about head and middle with leaves, vert. *Pl.* 14, *cr.* 11.

BOWERMAN, Eng., a goat's head, erased, or. *Pl.* 29, *cr.* 13.

BOWERMAN, or BOWREMAN, Devons. and Wilts., a goat's head, erased, or, horns twisted, or and sa. *Pl.* 29, *cr.* 13. (Another crest,) a bull's head, erased, or, horns twisted, or and sa. *Pl.* 19, *cr.* 3.

BOWERS, Chichester, Suss., a lion, passant, ar., collared and chained, or, (in dexter, a bow, bent, of the second, stringed, gold.) *Pl.* 121, *cr.* 4.

BOWES, Streatlam, Durh., nine arrows, or, one in pale, (eight) in saltier, feathered and headed, ar., banded, az. *Pl.* 110, *cr.* 11.

BOWES, Iri., a hawk, ppr. *Pl.* 67, *cr.* 3.

BOWES, Durh. and Northumb., (eight) arrows interlaced, in saltier, pointed, ar., barbed, or, bound by a ribbon, gu., tasselled, gold. *Pl.* 110, *cr.* 11.

BOWES, a demi-leopard, rampant, gardant, gu. *Pl.* 77, *cr.* 1, (without anchor.)

BOWES, two bundles of arrows, in saltier, flighted and headed, ppr., banded, gu. *Pl.* 101, *cr.* 13, (without cap.)

BOWES, Durh. and Yorks., five arrows, four in saltier and one in pale, or, headed and feathered, ar., banded, az. *Pl.* 54, *cr.* 15.

Bowes, Durh., a sheaf of arrows, or, bound in a girdle, az. *Sans variance et mon droit*—and—*In multis in magnis, in bonis expertus.* *Pl.* 54, *cr.* 15.
Bowes, a demi-leopard, rampant, gardant, gu., (holding a bundle of arrows, feathered, ar., headed, or, banded, vert.) *Pl.* 77, *cr.* 1, (without anchor.)
Bowes, Yorks. and Durh., five arrows, four in saltier, and one in pale, or, feathered and headed, ar., tied, az. *Pl.* 54, *cr.* 15.
Bowes, Earl of Strathmore and Kinghorn. *See* Strathmore.
Bowet, or Bewet, Yorks., on a chapeau, gu., turned up, erm., a leopard, ar., ducally gorged, or. *Pl.* 120, *cr.* 9, (coronet, *same plate, cr.* 13.)
Bowida, Eng., a dexter arm, in armour, embowed, ppr., in hand a fleur-de-lis, or. *Pl.* 24, *cr.* 14.
Bowie, Sco., a demi-lion, az., in dexter a dagger, ppr. *Quod non pro patriâ. Pl.* 41, *cr.* 13.
Bowker, Eng., on a tower, a lion, rampant. *Pl.* 121, *cr.* 5.
Bowland, Ess. and Lond., out of a ducal coronet, an arm, in armour, couped at elbow, or, in hand a (sword,) ar., pommel, gold. *Pl.* 15, *cr.* 5.
Bowland, Ess. and Lond., an arm, in armour, couped at elbow, in hand a sword, or, on point a laurel-branch, vert. *Pl.* 125, *cr.* 5, (laurel, *pl.* 15, *cr.* 6.)
Bowland, two demi-ducks, wings displayed and inverted, respecting each other, the dexter, ar., sinister, sa., beaked, or.
Bowlby, a Catherine-wheel, or. *Pl.* 1, *cr.* 7.
Bowlby, Eng., two branches of thorn, in orle. *Pl.* 110, *cr.* 10.
Bowle, Eng., a (demi)-bittern, regardant. *Pl.* 77, *cr.* 15.
Bowler, a boar's head, couped, per pale, az. and gu., bezantée. *Pl.* 48, *cr.* 2, (bezant, *pl.* 141.)
Bowles, Charles-Oldfield, Esq., of North Aston, Oxford, a demi-boar, wounded in breast with broken spear. *Pl.* 115, *cr.* 2.
Bowles, Heref. and Herts., out of a ducal coronet, or, a boar's head, couped, sa., between wings, gu., billettée, gold. *Pl.* 102, *cr.* 14, (wings, *pl.* 17, *cr.* 9.)
Bowles, (on straw,) ppr., an owl, wings expanded. *Pl.* 123, *cr.* 6, (without chapeau.)
Bowles, out of a ducal coronet, or, a demi-boar, sa., pierced through neck by an arrow. *Pl.* 102, *cr.* 14, (demi, *pl.* 20, *cr.* 5.)
Bowles, Wilts., a griffin's head, erased, or. *Pl.* 48, *cr.* 6.
Bowles, Shaftesbury, Wilts., out of a ducal coronet, a griffin's head, erased, or. *Pl.* 54, *cr.* 14.
Bowles, Lond., out of a ducal coronet, or, a griffin's head, sa., beaked, and between wings, gold. *Pl.* 97, *cr.* 13, (without charge.)
Bowles, Inner Temple, Lond., a demi-boar, erect, erminois, (sinister shoulder pierced with an arrow, ar.) *Ut tibi sic alteri. Pl.* 20, *cr.* 5.
Bowles, Herts., on a ducal coronet, or, a boar's head, ar., between wings, gu., in mouth, a bezant. *Pl.* 102, *cr.* 14, (wings, *pl.* 17, *cr.* 9.)
Bowles, Gosberkirk, Linc., a demi-boar, az., armed, hoofed, and bristled, or, pierced through chest with an (arrow, gold, headed, ar.) *Pl.* 115, *cr.* 2.

Bowles, Lond., a buck's head, ar., attired, or. *Pl.* 91, *cr.* 14.
Bowley, a mullet of five points, pierced, through perforation a sword.
Bowley, Eng., a sword, in pale, between two branches of laurel, in orle. *Pl.* 71, *cr.* 3.
Bowly, Glouc., a garb, ppr. *Pl.* 48, *cr.* 10.
Bowman, Sco., a demi-blackamoor, shooting an arrow, all ppr. *Pl.* 80, *cr.* 9.
Bowman, a stag, (trippant,) pierced on shoulder with an arrow, all ppr. *Pl.* 88, *cr.* 9.
Bowman of Ashinyards, Sco., a quiver of arrows, (in pale,) ppr. *Sublimia cures. Pl.* 19, *cr.* 4.
Bowman, on stump of tree, ppr., a quiver, vert, of arrows, gu., headed, az., suspended by a belt, sa. *Pl.* 23, *cr.* 6, (quiver, *pl.* 19, *cr.* 4.)
Bowman, Norf., a sword, in pale, ar., hilt and pommel, or, on each side of blade a demi-annulet, indented, gold. *Pl.* 105, *cr.* 1, (annulet, *pl.* 141.)
Bowman, Hethleton, Dors., on a staff, ruguled, couped, and erect, ar., a quiver of arrows, gu., heads, of the first, buckled on staff with a belt, sa. *Pl.* 78, *cr.* 15, (quiver, *pl.* 19, *cr.* 4.)
Bown, Eng., in hand, an escutcheon, charged with a (rose.) *Pl.* 21, *cr.* 12.
Bownas, Eng., out of a ducal coronet, a sceptre, environed by two serpents, all between wings, ppr. *Pl.* 27, *cr.* 8.
Bownas, on a mount, vert, a swan, (wings displayed, erm., each charged with a lozenge, gu., in mouth an arrow, ppr.) *Pl.* 122, *cr.* 13.
Bowne, and Bowyn, Eng., on top of tower, issuing, an eagle, wings addorsed, ppr., in beak an acorn, slipped and leaved, vert. *Pl.* 60, *cr.* 8.
Bownell, Eng., a savage's head, from shoulders, helmeted, all ppr. *Pl.* 53, *cr.* 8.
Bownes, Eng., an oak-tree, ppr., an escutcheon pendent, gu. *Pl.* 23, *cr.* 6.
Bownes, Eng., out of a ducal coronet, a cock's head, ppr. *Pl.* 97, *cr.* 15.
Bowre, Dunhead, St Andrews, Dors., a talbot's head, sa. *Pl.* 123, *cr.* 15.
Bowrie, Sco., a demi-lion, az., in dexter a dagger, ppr. *Quod non pro patriâ. Pl.* 41, *cr.* 13.
Bowring, Eng., a parrot, vert, feeding on a bunch of cherries, ppr. *Pl.* 49, *cr.* 3.
Bowssar, Eng., a demi-talbot, gu., gorged with a collar, chequey, or and az., charged on body with three guttées-d'or. *Pl.* 15, *cr.* 2.
Bowth, Linc., on a chaplet, vert, a lion, passant, ar. *Pl.* 60, *cr.* 6.
Bowyer, Bart., Bucks. and Berks., on a ducal coronet, or, an heraldic-tiger, sejant, ar. *Contentement passe richesse. Pl.* 111, *cr.* 7.
Bowyer, Charlwood, Surr. and Lond., an arm, couped and erect, ppr., (vested, gu., cuffed and charged with three bends, or,) in hand a dragon's head, erased. *Pl.* 94, *cr.* 6.
Bowyer, Suss. and Linc., a demi-man, shooting an arrow, all ppr. *Pl.* 41, *cr.* 8.
Bowyer, Bart., Denham Court, Bucks., a falcon, rising, ppr., belled, or. *Contentement passe richesse. Pl.* 105, *cr.* 4.
Bowyer, an eagle's head, erased, ar., in mouth an anchor, gu., by middle of shank, flukes downward. *Pl.* 22, *cr.* 1, (anchor, *pl.* 25, *cr.* 15.)

BOWYER, Lond., an eagle, wings addorsed, or, beaked and legged, sa. *Pl.* 61, *cr.* 1.

BOWYER, Knipersley, Staffs.; Linc.; and Suss.; out of a tower, gu., a demi-dragon, rampant, or. *Pl.* 68, *cr.* 11, (dragon, *pl.* 82, *cr.* 10.)

BOWYER, Hants., a cubit arm, erect, in hand a serpent coiled round arm, all ppr. *Pl.* 91, *cr.* 6.

BOWYER, an arm, couped and embowed, vested, in hand a dragon's head, erased. *Pl.* 94, *cr.* 6, (arm, *pl.* 120, *cr.* 1.)

BOWYER, Bucks. and Suss., a falcon, rising, ppr., belled, or. *Pl.* 105, *cr.* 4.

BOWYER, a falcon, wings expanded, ppr. *Pl.* 105, *cr.* 4.

BOWYER, Camberwell, Surr., on a ducal coronet, a tiger, sejant, or. *Pl.* 86, *cr.* 8.

BOWYER, Linc., from top of castle, gu., a demi-griffin, issuant, or. *Pl.* 68, *cr.* 11.

BOWYER, an arm, couped at shoulder, embowed, vested, in hand a serpent. *Pl.* 120, *cr.* 1, (serpent, *pl.* 91, *cr.* 6.)

BOWYER, on a mount, vert, a tower, triple-towered, gu., thereon a demi-dragon, or. *Pl.* 151, *cr.* 1, (dragon, *pl.* 82, *cr.* 10.)

BOWYER, an arm, couped at elbow and erect, vested, gu., cuffed, ar., in hand a fish. *Pl.* 105, *cr.* 9, (vesting, *pl.* 18, *cr.* 1.)

BOYES, a dog, sejant, ppr. *Pl.* 77, *cr.* 8.

Box, a demi-griffin, or, winged, ar., between claws a fire-ball, ppr. *Pl.* 18, *cr.* 6, (fire-ball, *pl.* 70, *cr.* 12.)

Box, Oxon., an arm, couped at elbow, in fess, vested, gu., cuffed, ar., in hand, ppr., a branch of box, vert, at elbow, another branch.

Box, a demi-griffin, or, winged, az., the first feather, gold, between claws a fire-ball, of the first, flames, gu. *Pl.* 18, *cr.* 6, (fire-ball, *pl.* 70, *cr.* 15.)

BOXALL, and BOXEL, Eng., a gad-fly, ppr.

BOXALL, and BOXELL, Eng., an eagle's leg, erased, in fess, holding a feather, in pale. *Pl.* 60, *cr.* 15.

BOXHALL, and BOXMELL, Suss., two anchors, in saltier, az. *Pl.* 37, *cr.* 12.

BOXSTED, and BOXSTEAD, Eng., a hand, issuing, pulling a thistle. *Pl.* 54, *cr.* 11.

BOYCE, Iri., out of a tower, a demi-lion, rampant. *Pl.* 42, *cr.* 4.

BOYCE, or BOYSE, Eng., Sco., and Iri., a lion, rampant. *Pl.* 67, *cr.* 5.

BOYCE, and BOYSE, Eng. and Sco., a star of six points, or, within a crescent, ar. *Pl.* 111, *cr.* 15.

BOYCE, or BOYSE, Iri., a castle, triple-towered, out of middle tower a demi-lion, rampant. *Pl.* 101, *cr.* 1.

BOYCOAT, and BODYCOAT, an arm, (in armour,) couped at elbow, in hand a fire-ball, all ppr. *Pl.* 2, *cr.* 6.

BOYD, Trochrig, a sun-dial. *Eternitatem cogita. Pl.* 97, *cr.* 6.

BOYD, Bart., Danson, Kent, three ostrich-feathers, sa. *Confido. Pl.* 12, *cr.* 9.

BOYD, JAMES, Esq., of Rosslare, co. Wexford, a dexter hand, couped at wrist, erect, third and fourth fingers turned down, ppr. *Confido. Pl.* 67, *cr.* 6.

BOYD, Kilmarnock and Edinr., a dexter hand, pointing with thumb and two fore-fingers, ppr. *Confido. Pl.* 67, *cr.* 6.

BOYD, Pitcon, a dexter hand, pointing with thumb and two fore-fingers to the sun, ppr. *Spes mea in cœlis. Pl.* 15, *cr.* 4.

BOYD, Pinkell, Sco., a cross moline, sa. *Prudentia me sustinet. Pl.* 89, *cr.* 8.

BOYD, Sco., a star of five points, or. *Virtus nobilitat. Pl.* 41, *cr.* 1.

BOYD, a mullet of (five) points, pierced. *Pl.* 45, *cr.* 1.

BOYD, or BOYDE, Eng., a plume of three feathers, sa. *Pl.* 12, *cr.* 9.

BOYDELL, Chesh., a stag, statant, pierced in side with an arrow, in bend sinister. *Pl.* 88, *cr.* 9.

BOYER, Eng., a lady's arm, from elbow, erect, enfiled with a bracelet, sa. *Pl.* 85, *cr.* 10.

BOYER, a demi-griffin, segreant. *Pl.* 18, *cr.* 6.

BOYER, an arm, from elbow, erect, vested, cuffed, in hand, ppr., three (trefoils) slipped. *Pl.* 101, *cr.* 5, (without charge.)

BOYES, Eng., in hand a cross pattée, fitched, ppr. *Pl.* 99, *cr.* 15.

BOYES, and BOYS, Sco., a dog, sejant, ppr. *Attendez vous. Pl.* 77, *cr.* 8.

BOYLE, Eng., a griffin's head, erased, or, gorged with a ducal coronet, az., in beak a branch of laurel, fructed, ppr. *Pl.* 42, *cr.* 9.

BOYLE, Heref., a lion's head, erased, ppr., per pale, embattled, ar. and gu. *Pl.* 81, *cr.* 4.

BOYLE, and BOYLEY, Middx., out of a ducal coronet, or, a lion's head, erased, per pale, embattled, ar. and gu. *Pl.* 90, *cr.* 9.

BOYLE, EDMUND, Earl of Cork and Orrery, Viscount and Baron; out of a ducal coronet, or, a lion's head, erased, per pale, crenellée, ar. and gu. *Honor virtutis præmium. Pl.* 90, *cr.* 9.

BOYLE, Earl of Shannon. *See* SHANNON.

BOYLE, Earl of Glasgow, Viscount Kelburn, and Lord Boyle of Stewarton, Baron Ross, U.K.; an eagle, displayed, with two heads, per pale, embattled, ar. and gu. *Dominus providebit. Pl.* 67, *cr.* 11, (without flames.)

BOYLE, PATRICK, of Shewalton, Esq., M.A., Oriel College, Oxon., an eagle, displayed, with two heads, per pale, embattled, ar. and gu. *Dominus providebit. Pl.* 87, *cr.* 11, (without flames.)

BOYLEY, on a ducal coronet, or, a lion's head, erased, gu. *Pl.* 90, *cr.* 9.

BOYMEN, BOYNAM, BONHAM, and BOYNAN, trunk of tree, in fess, between branches a fleur-de-lis. *Pl.* 14, *cr.* 14.

BOYNE, Viscount, Baron Hamilton, (Hamilton,) Iri., in a ducal coronet, or, an oak, ppr., fructed, gold, penetrated transversely in main stem by a frame-saw, ppr., frame, of the first. *Nec timeo, nec sperno. Pl.* 100, *cr.* 2.

BOYNELL, and BOYVILLE, Eng., a boy pulling a branch from a tree. *Pl.* 94, *cr.* 8.

BOYNTON, Bart., Barmston, Yorks., a goat, (passant,) sa., guttée d'eau, beard, horns, and hoofs, or. *Il tempo passa. Pl.* 66, *cr.* 1.

BOYNTON, on a cinquefoil, gu., a talbot's head, erased, sa., guttée d'or. *Pl.* 90, *cr.* 6, (cinquefoil, *pl.* 91, *cr.* 12.)

BOYNTON, a goat, (passant,) sa., attired, or, ducally gorged, ar. *Pl.* 66, *cr.* 1.

BOYNTON, an arm, from elbow, in hand a mill-rind. *Pl.* 34, *cr.* 3.

BOYS, DE, Ess., a wyvern, ar. *Pl.* 63, *cr.* 13.

Boys, Kent, a demi-dog, gobonated, sa. and or, holding an oak-branch, leaved and fructed, gold. *Pl.* 6, *cr.* 9, (branch, *pl.* 123, *cr.* 1.)

Boys, Linc., a stag's head, couped, ar., attired, gu., between attires a mound and cross, or. *Pl.* 9, *cr.* 10, (mound, *pl.* 37, *cr.* 3.)

Boys, Norf., an owl, ducally crowned, or, (in a holly-bush, ppr.) *Pl.* 27, *cr.* 9, (crown, *same plate.*)

Boys, Kent, on a chapeau, az., turned up, erm., a demi-lion, ar., ducally crowned, or. *Pl.* 46, *cr.* 8, (coronet, *same plate, cr.* 2.)

Boys, Botshanger, Kent, a demi-lion, ar., ducally crowned, or. *Pl.* 61, *cr.* 4, (without branch.)

Boyse, a buck's head, erased, attired, gu. *Pl.* 66, *cr.* 9.

Boyton, Eng., a crow transfixed with an arrow, wings expanded, ppr. *Pl.* 110, *cr.* 13.

Boyville, Eng., a demi-eagle, displayed, with two heads, or. *Pl.* 4, *cr.* 6, (without charge.)

Boyzell, a talbot's head, sa., (in mouth a stag's horn, or.) *Pl.* 123, *cr.* 15.

Brabant, Devons., a rose, gu., slipped and leaved, vert, and a pointed lance, or, in saltier. *Pl.* 104, *cr.* 7.

Brabantine, a dog, passant, ar., collared, or, (collar charged with three leopards' heads, sa.) *Pl.* 65, *cr.* 2.

Brabazon, Leic., (over a mount,) vert, a falcon, volant, or. *Pl.* 94, *cr.* 1.

Brabazon, Eng., a falcon, wings expanded and inverted, belled, ppr. *Pl.* 105, *cr.* 4.

Brabazon, Earl of Meath. *See* Meath.

Brabon, and Brabourne, Lond. and Devons., a mewed hawk, ppr., armed, az., jessed and belled, or. *Pl.* 38, *cr.* 12.

Bracays, and Brakes, a demi-leopard, rampant, gardant, ppr. *Pl.* 77, *cr.* 1, (without anchor.)

Bracciano, Rome, on a ducal coronet, an eagle, displayed, sa., gazing at a comet to the sinister, ppr.

Braccinano, a dexter arm, vested, az., cuff, ar., in hand a sprig of roses, ppr. *Pl.* 64, *cr.* 7, (roses, *pl.* 69, *cr.* 10.)

Brace, a lion's face, ppr., ducally crowned, or, within two laurel-branches, in orle, vert. *Pl.* 92, *cr.* 4, (crown, *pl.* 128, *fig.* 3.)

Brace, an arm, ppr. *Pl.* 87, *cr.* 7.

Brace, Worc., an arm, in armour, embowed, ppr., in hand a sword, ar., hilted, or. *Pl.* 2, *cr.* 8.

Bracebridge, Suff., (on a mount, vert,) a wolf, passant, ar. *Pl.* 46, *cr.* 6.

Bracebridge, and Brasbridge, Linc., stump of tree, ppr., raguled, or. *Pl.* 92, *cr.* 8.

Bracegirdle, Chesh., two augers, erect and addorsed, conjoined with a girdle, gu.

Bracester, Eng., on a cloud, a mullet of six points. *Pl.* 16, *cr.* 13.

Bracey, a unicorn, sejant, resting dexter on an oak-tree, ppr. *Pl.* 110, *cr.* 15.

Bracey, or Brassy, a unicorn, sejant, resting dexter against an oak-tree, ppr. *Pl.* 110, *cr.* 15.

Bracken, Eng., a Catherine-wheel. *Pl.* 1, *cr.* 7.

Brackenbury, Eng., a savage's head, couped, ppr. *Pl.* 81, *cr.* 15.

Brackenbury, an old man's head, couped. *Pl.* 19, *cr.* 1.

Brackenbury, Sir Edward, Knt., of Skendleby House, Lincoln, a lion, couchant, sa., at foot of oak-tree, ppr. *Sans reculla j'amais.* *Pl.* 101, *cr.* 8, (oak, *pl.* 16, *cr.* 8.)

Brackesby, a boar's head and neck, couped, gu., bristled, or. *Pl.* 2, *cr.* 7.

Brackley, Northamp.: 1. A lion, rampant, gu., supporting an arrow, ppr., barbed and feathered, ar. *Pl.* 22, *cr.* 15. 2. On a chapeau, ppr., an eagle, wings addorsed, or, preying on a child, of the first, swaddled, gu., banded, ar. *Pl.* 121, *cr.* 6.

Bracy, Maddresfield, a human heart, pierced, sa. *Pl.* 16, *cr.* 14.

Bracy, or Bracey, Eng., a garb, environed by two snakes, ppr. *Pl.* 36, *cr.* 14.

Brad, a griffin, sejant, erect, between foreclaws a battle-axe. *Pl.* 44, *cr.* 3.

Bradbridge, Bredbridge, or Brodbridge, a leopard's head, erased, ar., pellettée, ducally gorged, or, between two spears, ppr., headed, of the first. *Pl.* 116, *cr.* 8, (spears, *pl.* 69, *cr.* 14.)

Bradburne, and Bradbourne, Lond., a pine-tree, vert, fructed, or. *Pl.* 26, *cr.* 10.

Bradbury, Derb. and Lond., a dove, volant, ar., fretty, gu., in mouth a slip of barberry, vert, fructed, gu. *Pl.* 25, *cr.* 6.

Bradbury, Ess. and Suff., a boar's head, erect, between two ostrich-feathers. *Pl.* 60, *cr.* 7.

Bradby, Eng., a serpent, half erect and nowed, in its mouth a garland of laurel, ppr. *Pl.* 104, *cr.* 9.

Braddyll, Eng., an anchor, in pale, surmounted by a fleur-de-lis. *Pl.* 51, *cr.* 15.

Brade, a bee-hive, with bees, volant, ppr. *Pl.* 81, *cr.* 14.

Brade, a griffin, sejant, resting dexter on an escutcheon. *Pl.* 42, *cr.* 8, (without coronet.)

Bradestone, Bradstone, and Bradston, Eng., out of a ducal coronet, two lions' paws, in saltier, ppr. *Pl.* 110, *cr.* 2.

Bradfield, Norf., an arm, from elbow, erect, in hand two branches of palm, in orle. *Pl.* 16, *cr.* 5.

Bradfoot, Braidfoot, and Bradfute, Sco., a demi-griffin, rampant, or, armed, gu. *Pl.* 18, *cr.* 6.

Bradford, Yorks., a peacock's head, ppr., in mouth a snake, entwined round neck, vert. *Pl.* 50, *cr.* 9.

Bradford, Baron, Eng., a lion, rampant, ar., between paws a garland of roses. *Nec temere, nec timide.* *Pl.* 9, *cr.* 7, (garland, *pl.* 41, *cr.* 7.)

Bradford, Earl of. *See* Bridgeman.

Bradford, Swindon, Wilts., a stag's head, erased, or. *Pl.* 66, *cr.* 9.

Bradford, Iri., a camel's head, sa. *Pl.* 109, *cr.* 9.

Bradgate, Leic., an arm, in armour, ppr., (banded with a ribbon,) vert, couped below elbow, in bend, in hand, ppr., upper part of broken spear, gu., point downward, ar. *Pl.* 44, *cr.* 9.

Bradhull, Lanc., a badger, passant, or. *Pl.* 34, *cr.* 4.

Bradley, and Bradeley, Eng., a boar, sa., bristled and hoofed, or, gorged with a garland, vert. *Pl.* 29, *cr.* 10.

Bradley, Iri., a bull's head, cabossed, ppr. *Pl.* 111, *cr.* 6.

BRADLEY, on a thorn-bush, a nightingale, ppr. *Pl.* 13, *cr.* 4.

BRADLEY, Lanc. and Lond., a boar's head, couped, gu. *Pl.* 48, *cr.* 2.

BRADLING, Eng., an arm, in armour, couped at shoulder, embowed, in fess, elbow on wreath, in hand a (sword,) ppr. *Pl.* 107, *cr.* 15.

BRADNEY, a hawk, ppr., belled and jessed, or. *Pl.* 67, *cr.* 3.

BRADSAY, and BRADSEY, a demi-greyhound, (collared.) *Pl.* 48, *cr.* 3.

BRADSHAGH, BRADSHAIGH, and BRADSHAW, Chesh., Lanc., and Leic., on a mount, vert, a stag, at gaze, ppr., under a vine-tree, also ppr., fructed, purp. *Qui vit content tient assez.* *Pl.* 85, *cr.* 2.

BRADSHAGH, on a mount, a stag, at gaze, under a vine-tree, fructed, all ppr. *Pl.* 85, *cr.* 2.

BRADSHAW, FRANCIS, Esq., of Barton Blount, Derby, a hart, gu., standing under a vine-branch, vert. *Qui vit content tient assez.* *Pl.* 85, *cr.* 2.

BRADSHAW, Lanc., on a mount, a stag, ducally gorged, standing under a vine, all ppr. *Non nobis solum nati sumus.* *Pl.* 85, *cr.* 2.

BRADSHAW, Salop, a wolf's head, erased, ar., (collared and lined.) *Pl.* 14, *cr.* 6.

BRADSTON, Eng., a dove, with olive-branch in mouth, ppr. *Pl.* 48, *cr.* 15.

BRADSTON, and BRADESTON, Glouc., out of a ducal coronet, or, a boar's head, sa. *Pl.* 102, *cr.* 14.

BRADSTREET, Bart., Iri., a unicorn's head, between two laurel-branches, in orle. *Pl.* 54, *cr.* 9.

BRADWARDEN, Eng., a demi-otter, rampant. *Pl.* 9, *cr.* 9.

BRADWAY, Glouc., on a coronet, a greyhound, sejant, (erect.) *Pl.* 66, *cr.* 15, (coronet, *same plate.*)

BRADWELL, Chesh., a rock, ppr. *Pl.* 73, *cr.* 12.

BRADY, Cambs., (on a mount, vert,) a griffin, sejant, or, beaked, gu. *Pl.* 100, *cr.* 11.

BRADY, Iri., in hand a scimitar, cutting at a feather, ppr. *Pl.* 59, *cr.* 9.

BRADY, Iri., a cherub, ppr. *Pl.* 126, *cr.* 10.

BRADY, Lond., Devons., and Hants., an arm, in armour, embowed, in hand an (olive-branch,) fructed, all ppr. *Pl.* 68, *cr.* 1.

BRADY, (on a mount, vert,) a griffin, sejant, or, beaked, sa., supporting with dexter an escutcheon, ar. *Pl.* 42, *cr.* 8, (without coronet.)

BRAGDEN, and BRAGDON, Lond., a boar, issuant (out of a rock.) *Pl.* 57, *cr.* 12.

BRAGE, or BRAGGE, Lond. and Ess., out of a ducal coronet, per pale, ar. and or, a bull's head, sa., attired, gold. *Pl.* 68, *cr.* 6.

BRAGE, or BRAGGE, Surr., a bull's head, sa., attired, or. *Pl.* 120, *cr.* 7.

BRAGES, and BRUGES, Lond., on an anchor, or, a scroll. *Mihi cœlum portus.* *Pl.* 42, *cr.* 12.

BRAGG, Somers., a bull, passant, gu. *Pl.* 66, *cr.* 11.

BRAGG, or BRAGGE, Sco. and Surr., out of a ducal coronet, or, a bull's head, sa. *Pl.* 68, *cr.* 6.

BRAGG, Somers., a lion's head, erased, ar., collared, vairé, or and az. *Pl.* 7, *cr.* 10.

BRAGGE, Sco., in hand a sword. *Honorat mors.* *Pl.* 21, *cr.* 10.

BRAHAM, Lond.; and Finchley, Middx.; (on a bar, dancettée, ar.,) a phœnix, erm., winged, az., fire, ppr., (in mouth, a lyre, or.) *Pl.* 44, *cr.* 8.

BRAHAM, Windsor and Berks., four ostrich-feathers, sa., enfiled with a ducal coronet, or. *Pl.* 44, *cr.* 12.

BRAHAM, Lond. and Berks., out of a ducal coronet, or, a plume of five ostrich-feathers, sa. *Pl.* 100, *cr.* 12, (without charge.)

BRAHAM, Lond. and Bucks., a cubit arm, erect, (vested, bendy, wavy, of four, az. and gu.,) in hand, ppr., a fish, ar. *Pl.* 105, *cr.* 9.

BRAHAM, a wolf's head, couped. *Pl.* 8, *cr.* 4.

BRAHAN, Eng., a lion, rampant, gardant. *Pl.* 92, *cr.* 7.

BRAID, Eng. and Sco., a demi-lion, gu. *Floreat majestas.* *Pl.* 67, *cr.* 10.

BRAIDFOOT, Sco., a demi-griffin, or. *Pl.* 18, *cr.* 6.

BRAIDWOOD, Sco., an oak-tree, acorned, ppr. *Vigueur de dessus.* *Pl.* 16, *cr.* 8.

BRAIMOR, Sco., an arm, in armour, embowed, throwing a pheon, hafted. *Pl.* 47, *cr.* 15.

BRAIKENRIDGE, Somers., a bee-hive, or, between two rose-branches, ppr. *Bello ac pace paratus.* *Pl.* 81, *cr.* 14, (roses, *pl.* 125, *cr.* 6.)

BRAILSFORD, out of a ducal coronet a dragon's head. *Pl.* 59, *cr.* 14.

BRAIN, or BRAINE, Eng., a torteau, az., charged with a talbot's head, erased, or. *Pl.* 38, *cr.* 2.

BRAINE, or BRAYNE, Glouc., a leopard's head, ar. *Pl.* 92, *cr.* 13.

BRAITHWAIT, Yorks., a greyhound, couchant, ar., (collared and lined, gu.) *Pl.* 6, *cr.* 7.

BRAITHWAIT, on a mount, vert, a greyhound, couchant. *Pl.* 5, *cr.* 2.

BRAKSDALL, a sheaf of arrows, ppr., feathered and banded, gu. *Pl.* 54, *cr.* 15.

BRAKYN, Cambs., a demi-fish, erect, az., (charged with three bezants, in bend, between two cottises, or.) *Pl.* 122, *cr.* 6.

BRAKYN, Chesterton, Cambs., a hawk's head, erased, ar., ducally gorged, or. *Pl.* 34, *cr.* 11, (coronet, *same plate, cr.* 15.)

BRAKYN, a whale's head, erect, between two cinquefoils, or, stalked and leaved, vert.

BRAMFELL, out of a ducal coronet, an arm, embowed, wielding a scimitar. *Pl.* 92, *cr.* 5, (coronet, *pl.* 128, *fig.* 3.)

BRAMHALL, Chesh., a lion, passant, or. *Pl.* 48, *cr.* 8.

BRAMHALL, Chester and Lond., a lion, passant, or, on shoulder a crescent upon a crescent, for difference. *Pl.* 48, *cr.* 8, (crescent, *pl.* 141.)

BRAMLEY, Eng., a pheasant, ppr. *Pl.* 82, *cr.* 12.

BRAMPSTON, Eng., a fetterlock, az. *Pl.* 122, *cr.* 12.

BRAMPTON, a demi-marine, vested, ppr., (in sinister an anchor, in dexter a spear.) *Pl.* 2, *cr.* 12.

BRAMPTON, Norf., a lion, rampant, or. *Pl.* 67, *cr.* 5.

BRAMPTON, Norf., out of a mural coronet, a talbot's head, gu., eared, ar. *Pl.* 91, *cr.* 15.

BRAMPTON, Norf., on a tiger, ar., bridled, a naked man astride, ppr., wreathed about the temples, of the first and gu.

BRAMPTON, Lond., on a tun, or, a dove, ppr., in mouth a branch, vert, fructed, gu. *Pl.* 124, *cr.* 9, (dove, *pl.* 48, *cr.* 15.)

BRAMSON, and BRANSON, Eng., an arm, from elbow, in hand a scorpion, erect. *Pl.* 110, *cr.* 14.

BRAMSTON, THOMAS-WILLIAM, Esq., of Skreens, Ess., a lion, sejant, or, collared, sa., (charged with three plates, ar.) *Pl.* 21, *cr.* 3.

BRAMWELL, Eng., out of a ducal coronet, or, two lions' paws, in saltier, ppr. *Pl.* 110, *cr.* 2.

BRANCH, out of a ducal coronet, or, a cock's head, az., combed, gu., (in beak a branch, vert.) *Pl.* 97, *cr.* 15.

BRAND, Baron Dacre. *See* DACRE.

BRAND of Laurieston, Sco., a vol, ppr. *Pl.* 15, *cr.* 10.

BRAND, Sco., a vol, with a baton, in pale. *Pl.* 15, *cr.* 10, (baton, *pl.* 33, *cr.* 4.)

BRAND, Suff. and Lond., out of a ducal coronet, or, a leopard's head, ar., (semée of roundles, of the colours.) *Pl.* 36, *cr.* 15.

BRAND, Eng., in hand a battle-axe, ppr. *Pl.* 73, *cr.* 7.

BRAND, Sco., two elephants' proboscess, ar., (the dexter charged with three mascles, the sinister with three spur-rowels, sa.) *Aye forward.* *Pl.* 24, *cr.* 8.

BRAND, beside a tree, a stag, statant, ppr. *Pl.* 118, *cr.* 13.

BRAND, on stump of tree, in fess, erased, shooting a branch, an eagle, statant, regardant. *Pl.* 77, *cr.* 13, (tree, *pl.* 14, *cr.* 14.)

BRAND, Lond., a leopard's head and neck, erased, gardant, (quarterly, ar. and or, semée of roundles, sa., vert, and gu.) *Pl.* 56, *cr.* 7.

BRAND, Surr., out of a ducal coronet, or, a cockatrice's head, gu., between wings, ppr. *Pl.* 77, *cr.* 5.

BRANDEETH, and BRANDRETH, Staffs., a lamb, couchant, ar.

BRANDER, Eng., an elephant, passant, ar. *Pl.* 56, *cr.* 14.

BRANDER, Eng., an arm, from elbow, ppr., (vested, chequey, or and az., in hand a branch of palm, of the first.) *Pl.* 23, *cr.* 7.

BRANDER, Hants., a phœnix in flames, ppr. *Pl.* 44, *cr.* 8.

BRANDER, Surr., and Sco., a dove, regardant, in mouth an olive-branch, ppr. *Silentio et spe.* *Pl.* 77, *cr.* 2.

BRANDER, Sco., a dove, with olive-branch, ppr. *Silentio et spe.* *Pl.* 48, *cr.* 15.

BRANDESTON, Eng., a dexter hand, couped, in fess, gu. *Pl.* 32, *cr.* 4.

BRANDFORD, Lond., an eagle, rising, or, in beak a sprig of oak, fructed, vert. *Pl.* 60, *cr.* 8, (without tower.)

BRANDLING, Northumb., stump of tree, couped and erased, from top issuing flames, from sinister side sprig, acorned and leaved, all ppr. *Fide et virtute.* *Pl.* 96, *cr.* 12.

BRANDON, Suff., a lion's head, erased, or, guttée, sa., ducally crowned, party, per fess, ar. and gu. *Pl.* 90, *cr.* 4.

BRANDON, a dove, regardant, in mouth an olive-branch, ppr. *Pl.* 77, *cr.* 2.

BRANDON, Lond., a lion's head, erased, ar., (charged with two bars, gu., on each of which three bezants.) *Pl.* 81, *cr.* 4.

BRANDON and HAMILTON, Duke of. *See* HAMILTON.

BRANDRAM, Lond., a bee, volant, or. *Pl.* 100, *cr.* 3.

BRANDRAM, Lond., a lamb, passant, ar., (charged with a pile, wavy, between two fer-de-moline, sa.; on a pile, a bee, volant, or.) *Pl.* 116, *cr.* 1.

BRANDRAM, a lamb, passant, ar. *Pl.* 116, *cr.* 1, (without charge.)

BRANDRETH, an escallop, or. *Pl.* 117, *cr.* 4.

BRANFILL, BENJAMIN-AYLETT, Esq., of Upminster Hall, Ess., out of a cloud, ppr., a naked arm, in hand a sword. *Not in vain.* *Pl.* 93, *cr.* 7.

BRANDT, Eng., a stag, rising out of a bush, ppr. *Pl.* 82, *cr.* 8.

BRANDWOOD, Durh., a yew-tree, ppr. *Pl.* 49, *cr.* 13.

BRANFELL, Ess., a lion's head, erased. *Pl.* 81, *cr.* 4.

BRANSCOMB, BRANSCOMBE, and BRONSCOMB, Eng., a lion, passant, regardant, ducally gorged and chained, ppr. *Pl.* 121, *cr.* 4.

BRANSON, or BRAUNSON, an arm, from elbow, in hand a scorpion, ppr. *Pl.* 110, *cr.* 14.

BRANT, Eng., a lion, passant, or. *Pl.* 48, *cr.* 8.

BRANTHWAITE, and BRAITHWAITE, Lond., on a rock, ppr., an eagle, rising, ar. *Pl.* 61, *cr.* 1.

BRANTINGHAM, Devons., an oak-tree, ppr. *Pl.* 16, *cr.* 8.

BRANTWAYTE, on a rock, ppr., an eagle, rising, ar. *Pl.* 79, *cr.* 2.

BRASBRIDGE, Warw., a staff, raguly, ar. *Pl.* 78, *cr.* 15, (without coronet.)

BRASH, Sco., in hand, erect, issuing from a cloud, an anchor, in pale, pp. *Pl.* 41, *cr.* 5.

BRASHIER, or BRASIER, Londonderry, a demi-lion, rampant, party, per pale, or and sa. *Pl.* 67, *cr.* 10.

BRASIER, or BRAZIER, Eng., a dove, with olive-branch, ppr. *Pl.* 48, *cr.* 15.

BRASSEY, Eng., a hand throwing a dart., ppr. *Pl.* 42, *cr.* 13.

BRASY, a bird, ar., legged, gu. *Pl.* 52, *cr.* 12.

BRATHWAIT-BOUGHTON, Poston Court, Heref., a stork's head, erased, in beak a snake, ppr. *Pl.* 41, *cr.* 6.

BRATHWAYTE, Westm., a greyhound, couchant, ar., (collared and lined, gu., studded and ringed, or.) *Pl.* 6, *cr.* 7.

BRATT, Staffs., two greyhounds' heads, erased, collared and addorsed, ppr. *Pl.* 62, *cr.* 5.

BRATTLE, Eng., between a laurel and a myrtle branch, in saltier, a battle-axe, all ppr. *Pl.* 82, *cr.* 11.

BRAUNCH, out of a ducal coronet, or, a demi-lion, rampant, (pierced in breast with an arrow) *Pl.* 45, *cr.* 7.

BRAUNCH and BRAUNCHE, Eng., on a garb, or, a bird, sa. *Pl.* 112, *cr.* 10.

BRAVING, Wilts, a demi-talbot, gu., guttée-d'or, ducally (crowned,) ar. *Pl.* 15, *cr.* 2.

BRAWNE, Lond. and Surr., out of a mural coronet, or, a dragon's head, sa. *Pl.* 101, *cr.* 4.

BRAY, or BRAYE, Cornw., out of a ducal coronet, az., a griffin's head, or. *Pl.* 54, *cr.* 14.

BRAY, EDWARD, Esq., of Shere, Surr., a flax-breaker, or.

BRAY, CECIL-NICHOLAS, Esq., of Langford Hill, Cornw., out of a ducal coronet, az., a griffin's head, erm., beaked, or. *Pl.* 54, *cr.* 14.

BRAY, an ounce, ppr. *Pl.* 67, *cr.* 15.

BRAY, an arm, erect, (vested, az.,) in hand, ppr., a chaplet, vert. *Pl.* 41, *cr.* 7.

BRAY, Beds., and Suss., a lion, passant, gardant, or, (between wings, addorsed, vaire, of the first, and az.) *Pl.* 120, *cr.* 5.

BRAYBROKE, and BRAYBROOK, Suff., a maiden's head, ppr., hair, or, wreathed with a garland of violets and leaves, of the first. *Pl.* 114, *cr.* 2.

BRAYBROOK, Baron, (Neville-Griffin:) 1. For *Griffin*, a talbot's head, erased, sa. *Pl.* 90, *cr.* 6. 2. For *Neville*, a bull, ar., pied, sa., armed, or, (charged on neck with a rose, barbed and seeded. ppr.) *Ne vile velis*. *Pl.* 66, *cr.* 11.

BRAYBROOKE, Eng., a Minerva's head, affrontée, all ppr. *Pl.* 92, *cr.* 12.

BRAYE, out of a ducal coronet, or, a plume of five ostrich-feathers, three, ar., two, az., on top a griffin's head, gu. *Pl.* 100, *cr.* 12, (head, *pl.* 54, *cr.* 14.)

BRAYLESFORD, and BRAYFORD, Derbs., out of a ducal coronet, or, a stag's head, affrontée, ppr. *Pl.* 29, *cr.* 7.

BRAYNE, Glouc., from behind a mount, vert, the sun, rising, ppr. *Pl.* 38, *cr.* 6.

BRAYNTON, Eng., a griffin's head, erased, ppr. *Pl.* 48, *cr.* 6.

BRAYTOFT, Linc., a demi-lion, rampant, gu., crusily, ar. *Pl.* 67, *cr.* 10.

BREACH, Eng., an escarbuncle, gu. *Pl.* 51, *cr.* 10.

BREACH, Cirencester, Glouc., an antelope, sejant, ppr. *Pl.* 115, *cr.* 3, (without charging, collar, or line.)

BREADALBANE, Marquess of, and Baron; Earl of Ormelie, Breadalbane, and Holland; Viscount Campbell, &c., (Campbell,) Sco.; a boar's head, erased, ppr. *Follow me*. *Pl.* 16, *cr.* 11.

BREAM, Lond., an arm, couped at elbow, and erect, (vested, bendy of six, or and az., cuffed, gold,) in hand a fish, ppr. *God is my defender*. *Pl.* 105, *cr.* 9.

BREANON, Sco., an arm, in armour, embowed, in hand a sword. *Pl.* 2, *cr.* 8.

BREANT, Eng., a demi-griffin, regardant, holding a flag, (charged with a saltier.) *Pl.* 46, *cr.* 1.

BREAREY, or BREARY, the bust of a nun, couped at shoulders, affrontée, (veiled,) ppr. *Jesu sel bon e lel*. *Pl.* 45, *cr.* 5.

BREARLY, a cross potent, gu., between wings, ar. *Pl.* 71, *cr.* 2, (cross potent, *pl.* 7, *cr.* 13.)

BREAWSE, Eng., a human heart transfixed with a sword, in bend, sinister, all ppr. *Pl.* 21, *cr.* 15.

BREBNER, of Lairney, Sco., a cock's head, erased, gu. *Pl.* 92, *cr.* 3.

BRECHE, Eng., out of a cup, ar., three roses, stalked and leaved, ppr. *Pl.* 102, *cr.* 12.

BRECK, or BREEK, a demi-lion, ppr. *Firmus maneo*. *Pl.* 67, *cr.* 10.

BRECKNOCK, and BRECKNOY, Eng., an arm, from elbow, erect, issuing from clouds, in hand an anchor, in pale. *Pl.* 41, *cr.* 5.

BRECKNOCK, Baron. *See* CAMDEN.

BREDEL, Lond., an owl, ppr. *Nitor in adversum*. *Pl.* 27, *cr.* 9.

BREE, Eng., a hand, couped, in fess. *Pl.* 32, *cr.* 4.

BREEDON, Berks. and Northamp., a demi-lion, ar., holding a cross pattée, fitched, gu. *Pl.* 65, *cr.* 6, (cross, *pl.* 27, *cr.* 14.)

BREES, and BREEZE, Eng., a stag at gaze, or. *Pl.* 81, *cr.* 8.

BREETON, Eng., a naked arm, embowed, in hand, ppr., a wreath of laurel, vert. *Pl.* 118, *cr.* 4.

BREMBER, Lond., two arms, in armour, embowed, in hands a battle-axe, all ppr. *Pl.* 41, *cr.* 2.

BREMER, Devons, out of a naval coronet, or, sails, ar., a dexter cubit arm, in armour, in hand, gauntleted, gold, a sword, ppr., hilt and pommel, of the first, between two branches of oak, gold, arm charged with an anchor, erect, sa. *A la vérité*.

BREMNER, Eng. and Sco., a dexter arm, vambraced, in gauntlet a pheon, erect. *Per tela, per hostes*. *Pl.* 123, *cr.* 12.

BREMNER, Eng., a cock's head, erased. *Pl.* 92, *cr.* 3.

BRENAN, Iri., out of a mural coronet, a demi-eagle, displayed. *Pl.* 33, *cr.* 5.

BRENAN, and BRENNAN, Iri., a wheel, gu. *Pl.* 32, *cr.* 15.

BRENCHESLEY, and BRENCHLEY, Eng., an annulet, or, within it an escutcheon, az., charged with a cross, patonce, gold. *Pl.* 77, *cr.* 9.

BRENCHLEY, Kent, a dexter arm, couped near elbow, erect, in hand a laurel-branch, all ppr. *Pl.* 43, *cr.* 6.

BRENDE, Norf., a lion, rampant, gardant, ar. *Pl.* 92, *cr.* 7.

BRENDE, Suff., the fore-part of a lion, gu., united to hind-part of a dragon, vert, sejant.

BRENDON, an eagle, displayed. *Pl.* 48, *cr.* 11.

BRENT, Glouc., Kent, and Somers., a dragon's head, between wings, expanded, ar. *Pl.* 105, *cr.* 11.

BRENT, a lion, rampant. *Pl.* 67, *cr.* 5.

BRENT, a wyvern's head, between wings, ar., charged on breast with three ermine spots, one and two. *Pl.* 105, *cr.* 11, (ermine, *pl.* 141.)

BRENTINGHAM, Eng., an oak-tree, ppr. *Pl.* 16, *cr.* 8.

BRENTON, Bart., out of a naval coronet, or, on circle, "Spartan," a swan, ar., guttée-de-sang. *Go through*. *Pl.* 128, *fig.* 19, (swan, *pl.* 122, *cr.* 13.)

BRENTON, a swan, ar. *Pl.* 122, *cr.* 13.

BRENTON, Eng., a demi-savage, affrontée, hand-cuffed, ppr. *Pl.* 98, *cr.* 10.

BREOS, DE, Eng., an eagle, rising, regardant, ppr. *Pl.* 35, *cr.* 8.

BRERES, Lanc., a stag's head, erminois. *Pl.* 91, *cr.* 14.

BRERES, Lanc., a nag's head, erminois. *Pl.* 81, *cr.* 6.

BRERETON, on a chapeau, gu., turned up, or, a griffin, statant, wings elevated, of the first. *Pl.* 122, *cr.* 11.

BRERETON, JOHN, Esq., of Brinton, Norf., a bear, ppr., muzzled, or. *Opitulante Deo*. *Pl.* 61, *cr.* 5.

BRERETON, or BREWERTON, a bear's head and neck, or, muzzled, sa. *Pl.* 2, *cr.* 9.
BRERETON, Iri., a demi-unicorn, collared. *Pl.* 21, *cr.* 1.
BRERETON, Chesh. and Norf., a bear's head and neck, erased, sa., muzzled, gu., studded, or. *Pl.* 71, *cr.* 6.
BRERETON, on a chapeau, az., turned up, erm., a dragon, wings expanded. *Pl.* 90, *cr.* 10, (chapeau, *pl.* 127, *fig.* 13.)
BRERETON, Chesh., out of a ducal coronet, or, a bear's head, ppr. *Pl.* 6, *cr.* 6.
BRERWOOD, or BRIERWOOD, Chester, two swords, in saltier, pommels and hilts, or, enfiled with an earl's coronet, ppr. *Pl.* 13, *cr.* 8, (coronet, *pl.* 127, *fig.* 8.)
BRESIER, out of a crown vallary, a lion's head. *Pl.* 126, *cr.* 1, (crown, *pl.* 2, *cr.* 2.)
BRESINGHAM, on a chapeau, ppr., a demi-lion, rampant, gardant, or. *Pl.* 35, *cr.* 4, (chapeau, *pl.* 46, *cr.* 8.)
BRESSEY, on a mount, vert, a teal, ar. *Pl.* 94, *cr.* 3.
BREST, an arm, ppr., vested, sa., in hand a bow, ar. *Pl.* 52, *cr.* 5.
BRETARGH, Lanc., in lion's paw, an ostrich-feather. *Fari qui sentient. Pl.* 58, *cr.* 7.
BRETON, on a lion's gamb, az., a cheveron, or, between three billets, ar., charged with a mullet, sa. *Pl.* 88, *cr.* 3.
BRETON, Leic., Lond., Island of Jersey, and Staffs., a lion's gamb, erased, az., charged with a cheveron, or, between three billets, ar. *Pl.* 88, *cr.* 3.
BRETON, or BRETTON, Lond., Ess., Staff., and Leic., on a lion's gamb, az., a cheveron, or, charged with a mullet, sa. *Pl.* 88, *cr.* 3.
BRETON, Norf., a demi-talbot, gu., eared, (collared and lined, or, in feet line coiled up.) *Pl.* 15, *cr.* 2.
BRETON, Northamp., on a mural coronet, gu., a boar's head, couped, sa. *Pl.* 6, *cr.* 2, (without sword.)
BRETON, Eng., a wolf, paly of eight, or and az. *Pl.* 46, *cr.* 6.
BRETON, or BRETTON, Eng., on a lion's gamb, az., a cheveron, or. *Pl.* 88, *cr.* 3.
BRETROOK, Eng., a horse, saddled and bridled, at full speed. *Pl.* 8, *cr.* 2.
BRETT, a sphinx, passant. *Pl.* 91, *cr.* 11.
BRETT, Iri., a crane, regardant, wings addorsed, resting dexter on a stone. *Pl.* 77, *cr.* 15.
BRETT, Glouc. and Leic., on a tower, ar., a man's head, ppr. *Pl.* 12, *cr.* 5, (head, *pl.* 19, *cr.* 1.)
BRETT, Staffs., a lion's gamb, erect and erased, ar., grasping a wolf's head, erased, ppr. *Pl.* 60, *cr.* 14, (head, *pl.* 14, *cr.* 6.)
BRETT, Staffs., a lion's gamb, erect and erased, ar., grasping a dragon's head, vert. *Pl.* 126, *cr.* 9, (head, *pl.* 87, *cr.* 12.)
BRETT, Kent and Devons., a lion, passant, gu. (Another, or.) *Pl.* 48, *cr.* 8.
BRETT, Kent, a griffin's head, between wings, az., beaked, or. *Pl.* 65, *cr.* 1.
BRETT, Eng., a demi-lion, tail forked, ar., langued and armed, gu. *Pl.* 67, *cr.* 10.
BRETTLE, a griffin's head, erased, ppr. *Pl.* 48, *cr.* 6.
BREW, Eng., a park gate, gu. *Pl.* 73, *cr.* 4.
BREWDNELL, Eng., from an old castle in ruins, a martlet, rising, sa. *Pl.* 107, *cr.* 6.

BREWER, or BREUER, Kent, out of a mural coronet, an arm, from elbow, erect, vested, gu., billettée, or, in hand, ppr., a battle-axe, az. *Pl.* 79, *cr.* 4, (axe, *pl.* 73, *cr.* 7.)
BREWER, or BREUER, Devons., a mermaid, with mirror and comb, ppr. *Pl.* 48, *cr.* 5.
BREWER, Lond. and Somers., a syren, human part, ppr., tail scaled, or and gu., divided by parallel lines, wavy, charged with a mullet for difference. *Pl.* 48, *cr.* 5.
BREWES, DE, Eng., out of a ducal coronet, gu., a lion's gamb. *Pl.* 67, *cr.* 7.
BREWIN, two eagles' wings, addorsed, ppr., semée of trefoils, slipped, vert. *Pl.* 39, *cr.* 12.
BREWLEY, a lion, rampant, ppr., (semée of roundles, ar., holding in paws a shield, erm., thereon a bend, gu., charged with three cheverons, or.) *Pl.* 67, *cr.* 5.
BREWS, or BREWIS, Eng., out of a ducal coronet, a cock's head, ppr. *Pl.* 97, *cr.* 15.
BREWS, BREWSE, and BREWES, Eng., a lion, passant, az. *Pl.* 48, *cr.* 8.
BREWS, or BREWSE, a demi-Hercules, clothed with a skin, holding over shoulder a club, ppr. *Pl.* 49, *cr.* 11.
BREWS, or BREWES, Eng., out of a ducal coronet, gu., a lion's gamb, ppr. *Pl.* 67, *cr.* 7.
BREWSTER, and BREWSTED, Sco., a leopard's head, erased, az. *Pl.* 94, *cr.* 10.
BREWSTER, Whitfield, Ess., a demi-lion, in dexter (a club.) *Pl.* 11, *cr.* 2.
BREWSTER, Northamp. a leopard's head, erased, sa. *Pl.* 94, *cr.* 10.
BREWSTER, Northamp., a leopard's head, erased, az., (bezantée.) *Pl.* 94, *cr.* 10.
BREWSTER, Suff., a bear's head, erased, az. *Pl.* 71, *cr.* 6.
BREY, Eng., a hill, ppr. *By degrees. Pl.* 62, *cr.* 11.
BREYTON, on a mount, vert, a wild duck, ppr. *Pl.* 94, *cr.* 3.
BRIAN, Eng., a demi-savage, ppr. *Pl.* 14, *cr.* 11.
BRIAN, Eng., a beacon, flammant, or. *Pl.* 89, *cr.* 9.
BRIAND, and BRIANT, Eng., out of a mural coronet, a bundle of (seven) arrows, banded. *Pl.* 19, *cr.* 7, (arrows, *pl.* 54, *cr.* 15.)
BRICE, a stag, passant. *Pl.* 68, *cr.* 2.
BRICE, Somers., a lion's head, erased, erm., pierced through with an arrow, or, headed and feathered, ar. *Pl.* 113, *cr.* 15.
BRICE, Iri., a cubit arm, erect, ppr., in hand a scimitar, ar., hilt and pommel, or. *Pl.* 29, *cr.* 8.
BRICE, Iri., in hand a cutlass, all ppr. *Do well, and doubt not. Pl.* 29, *cr.* 8.
BRICHEN, Sco., an arm, in fess, out of clouds, ppr., in hand a club. *Pl.* 68, *cr.* 7.
BRICKDALE, Eng., on a ducal coronet, or, a dolphin, naiant, az. *Pl.* 49, *cr.* 14.
BRICKENDEN, in lion's gamb, erased, a rose-branch, slipped, ppr. *Pl.* 60, *cr.* 14.
BRICKENDEN, Eng., a demi-dragon, vert. *Pl.* 82, *cr.* 10.
BRICKENDEN, a demi-wyvern, vert. *Pl.* 116, *cr.* 15.
BRICKHURST, Linc., out of a mural coronet, or, a tiger's head and neck, ar. *Pl.* 5, *cr.* 15, (without gorging.)

BRICKWOOD, a demi-savage, affrontée, ppr., wreathed about (head) and middle with leaves, vert, in dexter a slip of oak, of the last. *Pl.* 35, *cr.* 12.

BRID, Lond., an eagle's head, (bendy of eight, ar. and sa.,) ducally gorged, or. *Pl.* 39, *cr.* 4, (without pheon.)

BRIDE, Eng., two eagles' heads, erased and addorsed, ppr. *Pl.* 94, *cr.* 12.

BRIDGE, Heref. and Ess., two wings, addorsed, ar., (on each a cheveron, engrailed, sa., charged with a chaplet, or.) *Pl.* 39, *cr.* 12.

BRIDGEMAN, Coney-Weston Hall, Norf., a trefoil, slipped, vert. *Pl.* 82, *cr.* 1.

BRIDGEMAN, Lanc., Warw., and Salop, a fox, sejant, ppr. *Pl.* 87, *cr.* 4.

BRIDGEMAN, GEORGE - AUGUSTUS - FREDERIC-HENRY, Earl of Bradford, Viscount and Baron, and a Bart., Warw. and Staffs., a demi-lion, ar., (between paws a garland of laurel, or.) *Nec temere, nec timide. Pl.* 47, *cr.* 4, (laurel, *pl.* 56, *cr.* 10.)

BRIDGEN, a demi-mariner, ppr., vested, in russet, round waist a sash, on head a cap, gu., in dexter a sphere, or, sinister resting on an anchor, gold.

BRIDGER, or BRIGER, Glouc., a dragon's head, vert, transfixed with end of spear, ppr., in bend sinister. *Pl.* 121, *cr.* 9.

BRIDGER, Kent, out of a ducal coronet, or, a crab, gu. *Pl.* 116, *cr.* 14, (coronet, *same plate.*)

BRIDGER, HARRY-COLVILL, Esq., of Buckingham House, Old Shoreham, Suss., a crab, gu. *Pl.* 116, *cr.* 14.

BRIDGES, Bart., Kent, out of a ducal coronet, or, a moor's head, in profile, sa., banded, ar. *Pl.* 120, *cr.* 3, (coronet, *same plate.*)

BRIDGES, Edinr., a demi-lion, gu. *Maintien le droit. Pl.* 67, *cr.* 10.

BRIDGES, on a tower, (a hawk,) wings displayed, all ppr. *Pl.* 8, *cr.* 15.

BRIDGES, an anchor, in pale, ppr. *Pl.* 25, *cr.* 15.

BRIDGES, or BRYDGES, Ess., a boar, passant, ar., (pierced through neck with broken spear, headed, of the first, embrued, gu.) *Pl.* 36, *cr.* 2.

BRIDGES, Glouc., a man's head, from shoulder, in profile, ppr., verted, paly of six, ar., semée of torteaux, wreathed, of the last, and az. *Pl.* 126, *cr.* 8.

BRIDGES, same crest. *Maintien le droit.*

BRIDGES, Eng., on a tower, ar., masoned, sa., a dove, rising, ppr. *Pl.* 8, *cr.* 15.

BRIDGET, Salop, a fox, sejant, ppr. *Pl.* 87, *cr.* 4.

BRIDGEWATER, a demi-stag, or, attired, sa. *Pl.* 55, *cr.* 9, (without rose.)

BRIDGMAN, Eng., a fox, sejant, ppr. *Nec temere, nec timide. Pl.* 87, *cr.* 4.

BRIDGMAN, Warw., a demi-lion, rampant, ar., between paws a garland of laurel, ppr. *Pl.* 67, *cr.* 10, (laurel, *pl.* 56, *cr.* 10.)

BRIDGSTOCK, a raven, sa., in dexter an escallop, *Pl.* 123, *cr.* 2, (escallop, *pl.* 141.)

BRIDON, Suff., a hawk's head, erased, sa., charged with three bezants, one and two. *Pl.* 34, *cr.* 11, (bezant, *pl.* 141.)

BRIEN, Iri., a cross pattée, gu., between horns of a crescent, or. *Pl.* 37, *cr.* 10.

BRIERLY, Eng., a fox., sejant, ppr. *Pl.* 87, *cr.* 4.

BRIERLY, Lond., a cross, potent, fitched, gu., between wings, ar. *Pl.* 71, *cr.* 2, (cross, *pl.* 7, *cr.* 13.)

BRIERS, Beds., a demi-leopard, rampant, gardant, erased, az., gorged with a collar, ar., charged with three mullets, pierced, gu. *Pl.* 125, *cr.* 4.

BRIERWOOD, two swords, in saltier, enfiled with an earl's coronet. *Pl.* 13, *cr.* 8, (coronet, *pl.* 127, *fig.* 8.)

BRIG, an arm, in armour, embowed, in hand a dagger, ppr. *Pl.* 21, *cr.* 4.

BRIGGES, Westm., a fox, ppr. *Pl.* 126, *cr.* 5.

BRIGGS, Bart., Salop, on stump of tree, a pelican, or, vulning, ppr. *Virtus est Dei. Pl.* 1, *cr.* 11, (pelican, *pl.* 109, *cr.* 15.)

BRIGGS, a tiger's head, (couped,) affrontée. *Pl.* 56, *cr.* 7.

BRIGGS, Salop, an arm, embowed, covered with leaves, vert, in hand, ppr., a bow, gu., strung, sa., and an arrow, ar. *Pl.* 76, *cr.* 10, (leaves, *pl.* 83, *cr.* 2.)

BRIGGS, Brecknockshire, an arm, vambraced, in hand a bow and arrow, ppr. *Pl.* 76, *cr.* 10.

BRIGGS, Yorks., (on a mount, vert,) a laurelbranch, erect, ppr., in front a lion, passant, erm., dexter resting on a pheon, sa. *Fortiter et fideliter. Pl.* 4, *cr.* 14, (laurel, *pl.* 123, *cr.* 5; pheon, *pl.* 141.)

BRIGHAM, Yorks., on a cloud, a crescent, between two branches of palm, in orle. *Pl.* 118, *cr.* 2.

BRIGHAM, or BRIGGAM, Yorks., a boar's head, in bend, couped, sa. *Pl.* 2, *cr.* 7.

BRIGHAM, WILLIAM, Esq., of Foxley House, Lymrn, Chester, out of a ducal coronet, a plume of feathers. *In cruce salus. Pl.* 44, *cr.* 12.

BRIGHOUSE, Linc., out of a mural coronet, or, a tiger's head, ar. *Pl.* 5, *cr.* 15, (without gorging.)

BRIGHT, Iri., in hand, erect, ppr., vested, sa., out of a cloud shedding forth rays, a morthead, of the first. *Pl.* 37, *cr.* 6.

BRIGHT, Eng., a dragon's head. *Pl.* 78, *cr.* 12.

BRIGHT, Eng., the sun in glory, or, in clouds, ppr. *Pl.* 67, *cr.* 9.

BRIGHT, Sir CHARLES, Harrow-weald, a mass of clouds, and therefrom a sun, issuant, all ppr. *Pl.* 67, *cr.* 9.

BRIGHT, Chesh., a demi-griffin, in dexter a mullet, sa. *Pl.* 49, *cr.* 4, (mullet, *pl.* 141.)

BRIGHT, Suff., a dragon's head, gu., vomiting fire, ppr., collared and lined, or. *Pl.* 37, *cr.* 9.

BRIGHTMAN, or BRITZMAN, Surrey, out of rays, or, an arm, in armour, embowed, ppr., garnished, gold, in gauntlet a sword, ar., hilted, gold, tied round arm with a sash, or and purp. *Pl.* 40, *cr.* 14.

BRIGID, Iri., out of a cloud, ppr., an etoile of eight rays. *Pl.* 16, *cr.* 13.

BRIGNAC, Eng., a reindeer's-head, cabossed. *Pl.* 114, *cr.* 7.

BRIGNALL, an eagle, with two heads, displayed, charged on breast with a saltier. *Pl.* 25, *cr.* 5.

BRIGWOOD, a demi-savage, affrontée, wreathed about head and middle with leaves, in dexter a slip of oak, all ppr. *Pl.* 35, *cr.* 12.

BRIN, Iri., a dexter hand, couped, gu. *Pl.* 32, *cr.* 14.

BRINDLEY, and BRINLEY, Eng., a wyvern, in mouth a hand, ppr. *Pl.* 61, *cr.* 8.

BRINE, Eng., two swords, in saltier, ppr., surmounted by a cross crosslet, fitched, gu. *Pl.* 42, *cr.* 5.
BRINGBORNE, Kent, on a wolf's head, erased, sa., (a pile, or.) *Pl.* 14, *cr.* 6.
BRINGHAM, Eng., a cat, salient, gardant, ppr. *Pl.* 70, *cr.* 15.
BRINGHURST, Leic., an arm, in armour, embowed, ar., in hand a club, sa., spiked, or. *Pl.* 45, *cr.* 10, (club, *pl.* 83, *cr.* 2.)
BRINKHURST, a demi-lion, ar., ducally crowned, or, in each paw a bezant. *Pl.* 61, *cr.* 4, (bezants, *pl.* 141.)
BRINKLOW, or BRINGLOW, a demi-lion, or, supporting a flaming sword, gu., hilt, gold. *Pl.* 41, *cr.* 13, (sword, *pl.* 58, *cr.* 11.)
BRINKWORTH, Bath, (on a mount, vert,) a willow-tree, ppr. *Pl.* 18, *cr.* 10.
BRINS, a talbot's head, collared, (swallowing a bird, wings expanded.) *Pl.* 2, *cr.* 15.
BRISAC, Eng., an arm, embowed, ppr., vested, gu., in hand a covered cup, or. *Pl.* 39, *cr.* 1.
BRISBAN, or BRISBANE, Sco., an anchor, in pale, with serpent wreathed, all ppr. *Animum prudentia firmat. Pl.* 64, *cr.* 9.
BRISBANE, M'DOUGALL, Bart., Sco., a stork's head, (erased,) in beak a serpent, nowed, all ppr. *Certamine summo. Pl.* 41, *cr.* 6.
BRISBANE-M'DOUGALL, Sco., same crest. *Dabit otia Deus.*
BRISBANE, Sco., an ant-hillock, (semée of ants,) ppr. *Virtuti damnosa quies. Pl.* 62, *cr.* 11.
BRISBANE, Eng., a demi-savage, holding over shoulder a club, ppr. *Pl.* 14, *cr.* 11.
BRISBANE, and BRISBON, Sco., a heron's head, erased, in mouth an eel, all ppr. *Certamine summo. Pl.* 41, *cr.* 6.
BRISBON, or BRISBONE, on a chapeau, a lion, rampant, holding an arrow, point downward. *Pl.* 22, *cr.* 15, (chapeau, *same plate, cr.* 8.)
BRISCO, Bart., Cumb., a greyhound, current, sa., seizing a hare, ppr.
BRISCOA, Eng., a pennon, gu., charged with a crescent, ar., staff in bend, sa., headed, or. *Pl.* 8, *cr.* 8, (crescent, *pl.* 141.)
BRISCOE, and BRISCOWE, Eng., a pheon, between two arms, in armour, embowed, supporting a Saracen's head, affrontée. *Pl.* 83, *cr.* 11.
BRISCOE, and BRISCOWE, Iri., a Saracen's head, affrontée, ppr. *Pl.* 19, *cr.* 1.
BRISE-RUGGLES, Ess. and Suff., a tower, or, transpierced with four darts, in saltier, inflamed, ppr. *Struggle.*
BRISLAY, a cock-pheasant, ppr., (standing among flowers, az., leaved, vert.) *Pl.* 82, *cr.* 12.
BRISTED, Eng., in dexter hand, a spur, ppr. *Pl.* 34, *cr.* 9.
BRISTOL, Marquess and Earl of, Earl Jermyn, and Baron Hervey, (Hervey;) a leopard, passant, sa., bezantée, ducally gorged and chained, or, in dexter a trefoil, slipped, vert. *Je n'oublierai jamais. Pl.* 86, *cr.* 2, (bezant and trefoil, *pl.* 141.)
BRISTOW, Herts., out of a crescent, or, a demi-eagle, displayed, az. *Pl.* 11, *cr.* 10.
BRISTOW, ROBERT, Esq., of Broxmore Park, Wilts., out of a crescent, or, a demi-eagle, displayed, az. *Vigilantibus non dormientibus. Pl.* 11, *cr.* 10.

BRISTOWE, SAMUEL-ELLIS, Esq., of Beesthorpe Hall, Nottingham, and of Twyford, Derbs., same crest and motto.
BRITAIN, Eng., in dexter hand, ppr., a key, or. *Pl.* 41, *cr.* 11.
BRITAIN, BRITON, BRITTEN, and BRITTON, out of a naval coronet, a mermaid, in dexter a purse, in sinister a comb, ppr. *Pl.* 32, *cr.* 8.
BRITLEY, on a chapeau, a demi-lion, in dexter a mullet. *Pl.* 46, *cr.* 8, (mullet, *pl.* 141.)
BRITTAIN, or BRITTAINE, Eng., in eagle's claw, erased, in fess, a quill. *Pl.* 60, *cr.* 15.
BRITTEN, Eng., an ear of wheat and palm-branch, in saltier, ppr. *Pl.* 63, *cr.* 3.
BRITWEESIL, Eng., a salmon, naiant, ppr. *Pl.* 85, *cr.* 7.
BRITWEESIL, a turbot, ar. *Pl.* 85, *cr.* 7.
BRIWER, or BRIWERE, Eng., out of a cloud, a dexter arm, in hand an open book, ppr. *Pl.* 82, *cr.* 5.
BRIXTON, or BRIXTONE, a demi-horse, rampant, ar. *Pl.* 91, *cr.* 2, (without wings or gorging.)
BROAD, on a chapeau, gu., turned up, erm., a leopard's face, ar. *Pl.* 66, *cr.* 14, (chapeau, *pl.* 110, *cr.* 8.)
BROAD, on a chapeau, a tiger's head, ducally crowned.
BROAD, Eng., a demi-savage, in dexter three arrows, pointing with sinister to an imperial crown. *Pl.* 86, *cr.* 3.
BROADBELT, an eagle displayed, ppr. *Pl.* 48, *cr.* 11.
BROADBENT, or BRODBENT, a pheon, ar., point, guttée-de-sang, staff broken near point, or. *Pl.* 27, *cr.* 12.
BROADBENT, Eng., a dexter arm, ppr., in hand a covered cup, or. *Pl.* 88, *cr.* 5.
BROADHEAD, Bart., Yorks., a demi-lion, rampant, collared and chained, or, supporting a shield, erm., charged with an eagle, displayed, gu. *Perseverando.*
BROADHEAD, Eng., on a chapeau, a garb, ppr. *Pl.* 62, *cr.* 1.
BROADHURST, Eng., a mermaid, in dexter a dagger, ppr. *Pl.* 88, *cr.* 12.
BROADHURST, in water, a swan, swimming, ppr., wings expanded, or, fretty, raguly, az., charged on breast with an etoile, sa. *Pl.* 66, *cr.* 10, (charge, *pl.* 141.)
BROADLEY, Eng., a stag's head, erased, ppr. *Mitis sed fortis. Pl.* 66, *cr.* 19.
BROADLEY, Lond., a talbot, passant, ppr. *Non immemor beneficii. Pl.* 120, *cr.* 8.
BROADLEY, Lond., a stag's head, erased, ppr. *Non immemor beneficii. Pl.* 66, *cr.* 9.
BROADMEAD, Somers., on a fret, az., a stag's head, erased, in mouth an acorn, slipped, ppr. *Semper fidelis. Pl.* 82, *cr.* 7, (head, *pl.* 100, *cr.* 8.)
BROADOCKSHAW, and BRODOCKSHAW, Eng., a stag's head. ar. *Pl.* 91, *cr.* 14.
BROADSTONE, Eng., in a cloud, a crescent, between two palm-branches. *Pl.* 118, *cr.* 2, (without star.)
BROADWOOD, Lond. and Suss., a yew-tree, (leaved and eradicated, ppr., on trunk an annulet, or, transfixed by three arrows, one in fess, two in saltier, of the last.) *Semper virens. Pl.* 49, *cr.* 13.
BROCAS, Lond., a man's head, couped at shoulders, radiated, ppr. *Pl.* 19, *cr.* 1.

BROCAS, Wokefield House, Mortimer, Bucks., a negro's head, in profile, ppr., couped at shoulder, crowned with an eastern coronet, or. *Pl.* 120, *cr.* 3, (coronet, *pl.* 57, *cr.* 5.)

BROCK, Sco., on a chapeau, gu., a dove, rising, ppr. *Pl.* 109, *cr.* 10.

BROCK, Ess., a pegasus, az. *Pl.* 28, *cr.* 9.

BROCK, or BROCKE, Chesh., a demi-lion, rampant, gu., in dexter a (dart,) or, feathered, of the first. *Pl.* 41, *cr.* 13.

BROCK, an escallop, or. *Pl.* 117, *cr.* 4.

BROCK, Guernsey, out of a mural coronet, ar., a demi-Canadian Indian, dexter supporting a tomahawk, erect, ppr. *Canada.*

BROCKAS, or BROKAS, Hants, a lion, sejant, in dexter a cross pattée, fitched, resting sinister against a pyramid. *Pl.* 56, *cr.* 12.

BROCKDON, Devons., a stag's head, erased, per cheveron, ar. and gu., attired, or. *Pl.* 66, *cr.* 9.

BROCKET, STANES, Esq., of The Ryes, Ess., a stag, lodged, sa. (ducally gorged and lined, or.) *Pl.* 67, *cr.* 2.

BROCKET, a stag's head, erased, pierced through neck with an arrow. *Pl.* 66, *cr.* 9.

BROCKET, or BROCKHILL, Kent, a badger, sa. *Pl.* 34, *cr.* 4.

BROCKET, a brocket, or young deer, lodged, ppr. *Pl.* 67, *cr.* 2.

BROCKHOLES, Eng., a fret, ar. *Pl.* 82, *cr.* 7.

BROCKHOLES, Lanc., a brock or badger, passant, sa. *Pl.* 34, *cr.* 4.

BROCKHOLES-FITZHERBERT, THOMAS, Esq., of Claughton Hall, Lancaster, a brock or badger, passant, sa. *Pl.* 34, *cr.* 4.

BROCKLEHURST, a brock, ppr. *Veritas me dirigit.* *Pl.* 34, *cr.* 4.

BROCKMAN, the Rev. TATTON, of Beachborough, Kent, on a sword, erect, ar., hilt and pommel, or, a stag's head, cabossed, ppr., attired, gold, blade through head, bloody at point. *Pl.* 105, *cr.* 1, (head, *pl.* 36, *cr.* 1.)

BROCKUS, a moor's head, couped at shoulders, wreathed about temples, ppr. *Pl.* 36, *cr.* 3.

BROCTON, Salop, a hand holding up a ducal coronet, couped and tasselled, between two branches of laurel, in orle. *Pl.* 95, *cr.* 11.

BRODERIP, BRODREPP, or BRODRIBB, Eng., in a cup, or, three roses, gu., slipped and leaved, vert. *Pl.* 102, *cr.* 12.

BRODIE, WILLIAM, Esq., of Brodie, in Morayshire, in dexter hand a bunch of arrows, all ppr. *Pl.* 56, *cr.* 4.

BRODIE, JAMES-CAMPBELL, Esq., of Lethen and Coulmony, Nairn, same crest. *Be mindful to unite.*

BRODIE of Lethem, in dexter hand a sheaf of (four arrows, points upward, ppr.) *Be mindful to unite.* *Pl.* 56, *cr.* 4.

BRODIE, Bart., Suff., a dexter cubit arm, erect, in hand (three arrows, ar., encircled by a civic wreath.) *Unite.* *Pl.* 56, *cr.* 4.

BRODIE, or BRODY, Suss. and Sco., in hand a sheaf of arrows, ppr. *Unite.* *Pl.* 56, *cr.* 4.

BRODIE, Eng., in lion's paw, erased, sa., a palm-branch, ppr. *Pl.* 70, *cr.* 9.

BRODLEY, Lond. and Lanc., a boar's head, couped, gu. *Pl.* 48, *cr.* 2.

BRODNAX, Kent and Chesh., out of a mural coronet, a demi-eagle, or, winged, gu., (gorged with a collar, gold, charged with three cinquefoils, ar.) *Pl.* 33, *cr.* 5.

BRODOCKSHAW, Eng., a stag's head, ar. *Pl.* 91, *cr.* 14.

BRODRICK, Surr., a spear-head, ar., embrued, gu. *Pl.* 82, *cr.* 9.

BRODRICK, Baron. *See* MIDDLETON.

BROESE, Eng., a crane, in claw a stone, ppr. *Pl.* 26, *cr.* 11.

BROGDEN, Eng., out of a ducal coronet, in hand a rose, gu., slipped and leaved, vert. *Pl.* 60, *cr.* 1.

BROGE, BROGG, BROIGE, and BRAGGE, Sco., in dexter hand, a sword, ppr. *Honorat mors.* *Pl.* 21, *cr.* 10.

BROGRAVE, Bart., Norf., an eagle, displayed, erm., ducally crowned, beaked and membered, or. *Finis dat esse.* *Pl.* 85, *cr.* 11, (without charge.)

BROGRAVE, Norf. and Warw., an eagle, displayed, ppr. *Pl.* 48, *cr.* 11.

BROGRAVE, Lond., Herts., and Lanc., an eagle, displayed, with two heads, erm., each ducally crowned, or. *Pl.* 63, *cr.* 2.

BROHIER, or BROHEIR, Eng., in a crescent, an arrow, in pale. *Pl.* 82, *cr.* 15.

BROKE, Eng., a fox's head, ppr. *Pl.* 91, *cr.* 9.

BROKE, a demi-horse. *Pl.* 91, *cr.* 2, (without wings or coronet.)

BROKE, Bart., Suff., family crest, a brock or badger, passant, ppr. *Pl.* 34, *cr.* 4. And, *as an honourable augmentation*, out of a naval coronet, or, a dexter arm, embowed, encircled with a wreath of laurel, ppr., hand grasping a trident, gold. *Saevumque tridentem servamus.* *Pl.* 93, *cr.* 1.

BROKELSBEY, Linc., a brock or badger, ppr. *Pl.* 34, *cr.* 4.

BROKER, Northamp., a demi-seahorse, or. *Pl.* 58, *cr.* 15.

BROKESBY, Leic., a boar's head, couped, gu. *Pl.* 48, *cr.* 2.

BROMAGE, Worc., out of a ducal coronet, an armed arm, in gauntlet, (a sword,) ppr. *Pl.* 15, *cr.* 5.

BROMALL, a Bacchus's head, couped at shoulders, gu. *Pl.* 19, *cr.* 1.

BROMBOROUGH, out of a ducal coronet, or, a cubit arm, az., cuffed, ar., in hand an oak-branch, ppr., fructed, gold. *Pl.* 2, *cr.* 2, (coronet, *pl.* 128, *fig.* 3.)

BROMBY, and BROMLEY, Yorks., out of a ducal coronet, or, a demi-lion, rampant, ar., (sustaining a standard, sa., flag, gu., charged with a lion, passant, gardant, of the first.) *Pl.* 45, *cr.* 7.

BROME, BROOM, and BROOME, Oxon., an arm, couped at elbow, and erect, vested, bendy of six, or and gu., in hand, ppr., a bunch of broom, vert, seeded, gold. *Pl.* 94, *cr.* 15.

BROME, CHARLES-JOHN-BYTHESEA, Esq., of West Malling, Kent; and of Salop and Herts., an arm, vested, gu., turned up, ar., in hand, ppr., a slip of broom, vert, flowered, or. *Domine, dirige nos.* *Pl.* 94, *cr.* 15.

BROMEALL, a demi-lion, rampant, double-queued, ppr. *Pl.* 120, *cr.* 10.

BROMELEY, Cambs., out of a mural coronet, or, a demi-lion, rampant, sa., holding a standard, vert, charged with a griffin, passant, of the second. *Pl.* 86, *cr.* 11.

BROMELL, Eng., a demi-eagle, displayed, with two heads, each ducally crowned. *Pl.* 63, *cr.* 2.

BROMEWICH, and BROMWICH, Glouc. and Heref., out of a mural coronet, or, a unicorn's head, sa. *Pl.* 45, *cr.* 14, (coronet, *same plate.*)

BROMEWICH, and BROMWICH, Glouc., Heref., and Herts., out of a ducal coronet, or, a unicorn's head, sa. (Another, guttée-d'or.) *Pl.* 45, *cr.* 14.

BROMFIELD, Kent and Chesh., a demi-tiger, az., armed, maned, and tufted, or, (holding erect a broken sword, ar., handle, gu., hilt and pommel, gold.) *Pl.* 53, *cr.* 10.

BROMFIELD, Staffs., a lion, passant, gardant, (gorged with a wreath, or and az.) *Pl.* 120, *cr.* 5.

BROMFLET, or BRONSLET, Lanc., on a chapeau, sa., turned up, ar., a wyvern, vert, ducally crowned, or. *Pl.* 104, *cr.* 5.

BROMFLETE, in a ducal coronet, or, a wolf's head, gu. *Pl.* 14, *cr.* 6, (coronet, *pl.* 128, *fig.* 3.)

BROMHALL, Beds., a demi-lion, or, (between paws) a cross crosslet, fitched, sa. *Pl.* 65, *cr.* 6.

BROMHALL, Lond. and Chesh., a lion, passant, or. *Pl.* 48, *cr.* 8.

BROMHEAD, Bart., Linc., out of a mural coronet, gu., a unicorn's head, ar., armed and crined, or, (in mouth a rose, gu.,) slipped and leaved, ppr. *Concordia res crescunt. Pl.* 46, *cr.* 14, (coronet, *same plate.*)

BROMHEAD, Iri., a pelican, vulning, ppr. *Pl.* 109, *cr.* 15.

BROMLEY, Baron Montford. *See* MONTFORD.

BROMLEY, Chesh., Staffs., and Yorks., out of a ducal coronet, or, a demi-lion, ar., (supporting a banner, gu., charged with a lion, passant, gold staff, of the last.) *Pl.* 45, *cr.* 7.

BROMLEY, Salop, a lion's gamb, erect, ar. *Pl.* 126, *cr.* 9.

BROMLEY, Sir ROBERT HOWE, Bart., Eaststoke, Notts., a pheasant, sitting, ppr. *Pensez forte. Pl.* 72, *cr.* 6, (without hawk's leg.)

BROMLEY, Salop, same crest.

BROMPTON, Eng., a lion, rampant, or. *Pl.* 67, *cr.* 5.

BROMWICH, out of a ducal coronet, a unicorn's head, sa., guttée-d'or. *Pl.* 45, *cr.* 14.

BROND, or BROUNDE, Lond. and Suff., a demi-griffin, or, in dexter a battle-axe, in bend, ar., handle, gu. *Pl.* 49, *cr.* 4.

BRONKER, Kent and Middx., a talbot, passant, gu., (under dexter a garland of flowers, ppr.) *Pl.* 120, *cr.* 8.

BRONKER, Wilts., a cubit arm, erect, (vested, sa., cuffed, ar.,) in hand, ppr., a lozenge, of the first. *Pl.* 41, *cr.* 9.

BRONSCOMB, or BRANSCOMB, a lion, regardant, ducally gorged and chained. *Pl.* 121, *cr.* 4.

BRONSCOMB, Eng., a lion, regardant, ducally gorged and chained. *Pl.* 121, *cr.* 4.

BROOK, Chesh., a badger, passant, ppr. *Pl.* 34, *cr.* 4.

BROOK, Lond., on a mount, vert, in front of an oak-tree, a badger or brock, passant, ppr., (fore-dexter resting on a chaplet, or.) *Pl.* 48, *cr.* 4, (badger, *pl.* 34, *cr.* 4.)

BROOK, Yorks., a sword, erect, ar., hilted, or, thereon two serpents entwined, respecting each other ppr. *Æst necastu.*

BROOK, or BROOKE, Bucks., a hawk's lure, with line formed into a bow-knot, between wings, all ppr. *Pl.* 4, *cr.* 4.

BROOK, a fleur-de-lis, ar., around it a serpent entwined, ppr. *Pl.* 15, *cr.* 13.

BROOK, or BROOKE, Suff. and Kent, on a chapeau, turned up, erm., a wing, displayed, gu., charged with a cheveron, ar., and thereon a lion, rampant, sa., crowned, or. *Pl.* 83, *cr.* 8.

BROOKE, Knt., Rajah of Sarawak, on an eastern crown, a brock, ppr., (ducally gorged, or.) *Dum spiro, spero. Pl.* 34, *cr.* 4.

BROOKE, THOMAS-JOHN-LANGFORD, Esq., of Mere Hall, Chester, a badger, passant, ppr. *Vis unita fortior. Pl.* 34, *cr.* 4.

BROOKE, RICHARD, Esq., of Handford, Chester, and of Liverpool, same crest. *Pro avitâ fide.*

BROOKE, The Rev. JOHN, of Haughton Hall, Salop, same crest. *Virtus est Dei.*

BROOKE, FRANCIS-CAPPER, of Ufford Place, Suff., on a chapeau, gu., turned up, erm., a wing, erect, of the first, cheveron, ar., thereon a lion, rampant, sa., crowned, gold. *Pl.* 83, *cr.* 8.

BROOKE, and WARWICK, Earl of, and Baron Brooke, (Greville) : 1. Out of a ducal coronet, gu., a swan, wings expanded, ar., beaked, of the first. *Pl.* 83, *cr.* 1. 2. A bear, erect, ar., muzzled, gu., collared and chained, or, supporting a ragged staff, of the first. *Vix ea nostra voco. Pl.* 1, *cr.* 3.

BROOKE, DE CAPEL, Bart., Northamp., a demi-sea-horse, ar., maned and finned, or. *Spes mea in Deo. Pl.* 58, *cr.* 15.

BROOKE, Hants, a lion, rampant, or. *Pl.* 67, *cr.* 5.

BROOKE, Staffs., a stork or crane, or. *Pl.* 33, *cr.* 9.

BROOKE, Salop, (on a mount, vert,) a badger, passant, ppr. *Pl.* 34, *cr.* 4.

BROOKE, a goat's head, erased, sa., horned and bearded, or. *Pl.* 29, *cr.* 13.

BROOKE, Bart., Chester, a man, in armour, in dexter a spear, on sinister arm a shield, all ppr. *Pl.* 90, *cr.* 1.

BROOKE, an Indian goat's head, bendy of six, gu. and az., erased, per fess, or, eared and armed, gold. *Pl.* 105, *cr.* 14.

BROOKE, Bart., Chesh. and Iri., a brock or badger, ppr. *Pl.* 34, *cr.* 4.

BROOKE, Bucks., out of a coronet, or, a plume of (six) ostrich-feathers, or and sa., counterchanged. *Pl.* 44, *cr.* 12.

BROOKE, a demi-lion, gu., between paws a (broad arrow, or, feathered and headed, ar.) *Pl.* 47, *cr.* 4.

BROOKE, on a ducal coronet, a cock, ppr., combed and wattled, gu. *Pl.* 104, *cr.* 3, (coronet, *same plate.*)

BROOKE, a griffin's head, erased, (charged with a fess dancettée, and in base a crosslet, fitched, gu.) *Pl.* 48, *cr.* 6.

BROOKES, or BROOKS, Eng., three organ pipes, (two in saltier, one in pale,) or, enfiled with a garland of laurel, vert. *Pl.* 50, *cr.* 12.

BROOKESBY, Eng., a boar's head, couped, gu., bristled, or. *Pl.* 2, *cr.* 7.

BROOKING, Eng., a sword, in pale, enfiled with a savage's head, couped, ppr. *Pl.* 42, *cr.* 6.

BROOKMAN, or BROCKMAN, Kent, on a sword, erect, ar., hilt and pommel, or, a stag's head, cabossed, ppr., attired, of the second, blade through head, and bloody at point.

BROOKMAN, Eng., a crane, in dexter a stone. *Pl.* 26, *cr.* 11.
BROOKS, Bedford, on a mural coronet, an otter, ppr. *Ut amnis vita labitur. Pl.* 9, *cr.* 5, (coronet, *pl.* 128, *fig.* 18.)
BROOKS, or BROOKES, Sco., a beaver, passant. *Perseverando. Pl.* 49, *cr.* 5.
BROOKS, a bear, ppr., muzzled and lined. *Pl.* 61, *cr.* 5.
BROOKS, Eng., a badger, ppr. *Pl.* 34, *cr.* 4.
BROOKS, a lion, passant. *Pl.* 48, *cr.* 8.
BROOKSBANK, Yorks. and Middx., a hart's head, couped, ppr., attired, or, (gorged with two bars, wavy, az.) *Pl.* 91, *cr.* 14.
BROOME, Heref., a demi-eagle, or, winged, sa., (in beak a slip of broom, vert.) *Pl.* 52, *cr.* 8.
BROOMFIELD, Eng., a hand, issuing from a cloud, in fess, pointing to a serpent, head erect, ppr. *Pl.* 19, *cr.* 11.
BROOMFIELD, a demi-heraldic tiger, (in dexter a broken sword.) *Pl.* 57, *cr.* 13, (without gorging.)
BROOMHEAD, Eng., a cockatrice, displayed, gu. *Pl.* 102, *cr.* 15.
BROON, Eng., a branch of holly, and a cross crosslet, fitched, in saltier. *Pl.* 102, *cr.* 3.
BROSTER, Chester, in dexter hand, ppr., (vested, barry of five, ar. and gu.,) a palm-branch, vert. *Pl.* 23, *cr.* 7.
BROTHERS, a demi-greyhound, sa., (in feet a dart, gu., feathered, ar.) *Pl.* 58, *cr.* 3.
BROTHERTON, Eng., in hand, a club, in pale, ppr. *Pl.* 28, *cr.* 6.
BROTHERTON, Stubbing's House, Maidenhead: 1. An eagle, displayed, ppr. *Pl.* 48, *cr.* 11. 2. A bear's head, erased at neck, ar., in (mouth an arrow, or, pheoned and feathered, of the first.) *Pl.* 71, *cr.* 6.
BROUGH, Linc., a lion, sejant, collared and lined, or. *Pl.* 21, *cr.* 3.
BROUGH, Sco., a buffalo's head, sa. *Pl.* 57, *cr.* 7.
BROUGHAM and VAUX, Baron, (Brougham,) Brougham-Hall, Penrith, an arm, in armour, embowed, in gauntlet a lucy, ar., on elbow a rose, gu. *Pro rege, lege, grege.*
BROUGHAM, BROUGHAN, BRONHAN, and BROUCHAN, Wel., out of a ducal coronet, gu., in dexter hand (a sword, ppr.) *Pl.* 103, *cr.* 2.
BROUGHTON, Ess. and Beds., an eagle's head, erased, sa., (in mouth a snake, ar., charged on breast with two cheverons, of the last.) *Pl.* 20, *cr.* 7.
BROUGHTON, Berks., out of a ducal coronet, or, a boar's head, sa., bristled, gold, (gorged with a collar, az., charged with three escallops, ar.) *Pl.* 102, *cr.* 14.
BROUGHTON, Bart., Staffs. and Chesh., a sea-dog's head, gu., erased and finned, ar. *Pl.* 68, *cr.* 8.
BROUGHTON, Salop, a talbot, passant, gu. *Pl.* 120, *cr.* 8.
BROUGHTON, three ostrich-feathers. *Pl.* 12, *cr.* 9.
BROUGHTON, Staffs., a squirrel, sejant, gu. *Pl.* 16, *cr.* 9.
BROUGHTON, Salop, an owl, ar., (charged on breast with three snakes, in fret, vert.) *Pl.* 27, *cr.* 9.

BROUGHTON, a savage's head, affrontée, ppr. temples wreathed, rising therefrom three ostrich-feathers. *Pl.* 105, *cr.* 2.
BROUGHTON, Eng., a crane's head and neck, erased, in mouth a serpent, ppr. *Pl.* 41, *cr.* 6.
BROUGHTON, a badger, ppr. *Pl.* 34, *cr.* 4.
BROUGHTON, Somers., on a mount, vert, a spaniel, couchant, erm.
BROUGHTON, Baron, Hobhouse, out of a mural coronet, per pale, az. and gu., a crescent and etoile. *Spes vitæ melioris. Pl.* 111, *cr.* 15, (coronet, *pl.* 128, *fig.* 18.)
BROUN, Bart., Sco., a lion, rampant, in dexter a fleur-de-lis, or. *Floreat majestas. Pl.* 87, *cr.* 6.
BROUN, a dexter arm, from elbow, erect, in hand, ppr., a book. *Pl.* 45, *cr.* 3.
BROUNCKER, Iri. and Suss., an arm, in armour, embowed, in gauntlet a sword, ppr. *Pl.* 2, *cr.* 8.
BROUND, or BROUNDE, Lond. and Suff., a demi-griffin, or, in dexter a battle-axe, ar., handle, gu. *Pl.* 44, *cr.* 3.
BROUNKER, Iri., the Roman fasces, ppr. *Pl.* 65, *cr.* 15.
BROUNKER, Eng., in lion's paw, erased, ppr., a bezant, or. *Pl.* 97, *cr.* 10.
BROUNLEE, a demi-peacock, issuing, ppr. *Pl.* 24, *cr.* 1.
BROWELL, Eng., in dexter hand a scimitar, ppr. *Pl.* 29, *cr.* 8.
BROWKER, Lond. and Southwark, a talbot, passant, gu., (supporting with dexter a chaplet, vert.) *Pl.* 120, *cr.* 8.
BROWN, Norf., on a mount, vert, an ostrich, ar., winged, beaked, legged, and collared, or. *Pl.* 16, *cr.* 2.
BROWN, Sco., a lion, rampant, per pale, az. and gu., charged with a cinquefoil, between two fleurs-de-lis, ar, *Si sit prudentia. Pl.* 67, *cr.* 5.
BROWN, JOHN, Esq., of Clonboy, co. Clare, an eagle, displayed. *Virtus dabit, cura servabit. Pl.* 48, *cr.* 11.
BROWN, a lion, rampant, in dexter a fleur-de-lis, or. *Floreat majestas. Pl.* 87, *cr.* 6.
BROWN, Sco., a demi-lion, gu., in dexter a fleur-de-lis, or. *Floreat majestas. Pl.* 91, *cr.* 13.
BROWN, Eng., same crest. *Gaudeo.*
BROWN, same crest. *Tandem licet sero.*
BROWN, or BROUN, Sco., a vine-tree, ppr. *Præmium virtutis honor. Pl.* 89, *cr.* 1.
BROWN, German and Sco., a dolphin, naiant, ppr. *Virtus dedit, cura servabit. Pl.* 48, *cr.* 9.
BROWN, Sco., a ship in full sail, in the sea, all ppr. *Deus adesto. Pl.* 109, *cr.* 8.
BROWN, an eagle's head, erased, ppr. *Vi et virtute. Pl.* 20, *cr.* 7.
BROWN, Herts., a griffin's head, erased, sa., beaked and eared, or, (charged on neck with a bar-gemelle, ar., and a trefoil slipped, erm.) *Si sit prudentia. Pl.* 48, *cr.* 6.
BROWN, Herts., a buck's head, sa., attired, or, issuing from a crown, paly, gold. *Si sit prudentia. Pl.* 29, *cr.* 7.
BROWN, a demi-lion, rampant, in dexter (a trefoil,) vert. *Pl.* 39, *cr.* 14.
BROWN, and BROWNE, Eng., a griffin's head, erased, or. *Pl.* 48, *cr.* 6.
BROWN, a lion, passant. *Pl.* 48, *cr.* 8.

BROWN, a lion's gamb, erased and erect, gu., (holding a wing, ar.) *Pl.* 126, *cr.* 9.
BROWN, a hare, current, ppr.
BROWN, and BROWNE, Eng., an eagle, displayed, vert. *Suivez la raison. Pl.* 48, *cr.* 11.
BROWN, Bart., Westminster and Sco., a demi-lion, gu., in dexter a fleur-de-lis, or. *Pl.* 91, *cr.* 13.
BROWN, and BROWNE, Durh., a stork's head, couped at neck, nowed, ppr., between wings, ar., (another, az.)
BROWN, Sco., a ship under sail, ppr. *Caute et sedulo*—and—*Deus adesto. Pl.* 109, *cr.* 8.
BROWN, Sco., a rose, gu., stalked and leaved, ppr. *Armat et ornat. Pl.* 105, *cr.* 7.
BROWN, Sco., a lion, rampant, ppr. *Famæ studiosus honestæ. Pl.* 67, *cr.* 5.
BROWN, Sco., a dolphin, naiant, ppr. *Labor omnia vincit. Pl.* 48, *cr.* 9.
BROWN, Sco., in hand an open book, ppr. *Deus evehit pios. Pl.* 82, *cr.* 5.
BROWN, Colston, Sco., a lion, rampant, in dexter a fleur-de-lis, or. *Floreat majestas. Pl.* 87, *cr.* 6.
BROWN, Glasgow, Sco., same crest and motto.
BROWN, out of a crown vallary, or, a buck's head, sa., attired, gold. *Pl.* 91, *cr.* 14, (crown, *pl.* 2, *cr.* 2.)
BROWN, Bart., Sco.; and BROWN of Thornydikes, a lion, rampant, in dexter a fleur-de-lis, or. *Pl.* 87, *cr.* 6.
BROWN, Sco., a cock, ppr. *Docendo disco. Pl.* 67, *cr.* 14.
BROWN, Sco., a lion, rampant. *Spero. Pl.* 67, *cr.* 5.
BROWN, Edinr., in hand a closed book, ppr. *Delectat et ornat. Pl.* 45, *cr.* 3.
BROWN, Sco., an eagle's head, erased, ppr. *Pl.* 20, *cr.* 7.
BROWN, or BROWNE, Sco. and Iri., an arm, in armour, embowed, couped at shoulder, resting elbow on the wreath, in hand a (sword,) ppr. *Pl.* 107, *cr.* 15.
BROWN, on a lure, a falcon, rising ppr. *Pl.* 10, *cr.* 7.
BROWNE, Marquess of Sligo. *See* SLIGO.
BROWNE, Sir JOHN-EDMUND, Bart., Johnstown, Dublin, an eagle, displayed, vert. *Suivez la raison. Pl.* 48, *cr.* 11.
BROWNE, ROBERT, Esq., of Kilskeagh, co. Galway, same crest and motto.
BROWNE, HUGH-JOHN-HENRY, Esq., of Raheens, co. Mayo, same crest and motto.
BROWNE, Liverpool, Lanc., an eagle, displayed, with two heads, per pale, az. and gu., wings, or, each wing charged with a fleur-de-lis, sa. *Pl.* 87, *cr.* 11, (without flames.)
BROWNE, Derbs., a lion, rampant, ar., ducally crowned, or, supporting a tilting-spear, ppr., headed, of the first. *Pl.* 98, *cr.* 1.
BROWNE, Derbs., a griffin's head, erased, vert, eared, beaked, and (collared, or, charged on neck with a trefoil, erm.) *Pl.* 48, *cr.* 6.
BROWNE, Suss., a stag, ppr., attired, (ducally gorged, and lined, or.) *Pl.* 68, *cr.* 2.
BROWNE, Baron Kilmaine. *See* KILMAINE.
BROWNE, Notts., a cock-pheasant, az., combed and beaked, gu., collared, or. *Pl.* 82, *cr.* 12.
BROWNE, Dors., on a mount, vert, a hare, current, ar.
BROWNE, a demi-lion, ducally gorged and chained, or. *Pl.* 87, *cr.* 15.

BROWNE, Devons. and Heref., a demi-man, sa., (wreathed about middle and temples,) in dexter a hammer, or. *Pl.* 51, *cr.* 14.
BROWNE, Lanc., an eagle, displayed, ar., on wings two bars, sa. *Pl.* 48, *cr.* 11.
BROWNE, Bucks., a tiger, az., maned, tufted, and armed, or. *Pl.* 67, *cr.* 15.
BROWNE, Kent, a vulture, wings addorsed, displuming a mallard's wing, all ppr. *Pl.* 114, *cr.* 5.
BROWNE, Eng., in bear's paw, couped and erect, or, a falchion, ar. *Pl.* 47, *cr.* 14.
BROWNE, a pewit, ar., in nest, or.
BROWNE, Islington, a crane, az., beaked and legged, or, crown of head, gu., (in mouth an ear of wheat, gold.) *Pl.* 46, *cr.* 9.
BROWNE, Herts., a dragon's head, ar., guttée-de-poix, between wings, expanded, sa., guttée-de-larmes. *Pl.* 105, *cr.* 11.
BROWNE, Earl of Kenmare. *See* KENMARE.
BROWNE, out of a mural coronet, gu., a crane's head, erased, erm., (charged on neck with an escallop, az.) *Verum atque deceus. Pl.* 40, *cr.* 8, (without scroll.)
BROWNE, a stork's head, in mouth an acorn, slipped, vert, fructed, or, between wings expanded, az., each charged with an escallop, gold.
BROWNE, a mullet, suspended between stags' horns, all sa. *Pl.* 71, *cr.* 8, (mullet, *pl.* 141.)
BROWNE, Wymondham, Norf.: 1. An escallop, ar., charged with a cross moline, gu., between four pellets. *Pl.* 117, *cr.* 4, (cross, *pl.* 141.) 2. A demi-talbot, rampant, ar., pellettée, (holding a spear erect, or.) *Pl.* 97, *cr.* 9.
BROWNE, PETER-RUTLEDGE-MONTAGUE, Esq., of Janeville, co. Down, an eagle, displayed, vert. *Suivez la raison. Pl.* 48, *cr.* 11.
BROWNE, JOHN-WILLIAM, Esq., of Mount Kelly, co. Galway, same crest and motto.
BROWNE, Lieutenant-General Sir THOMAS-HENRY, Knt., K.C.H., of Bronwylfa, co. Flint, an eagle, displayed, vert. *Spectemur agendo. Pl.* 48, *cr.* 11.
BROWNE, Suss. and Berks., same crest and motto.
BROWNE, ROBERT-CLAYTON, Esq., of Browne's Hill, co. Carlow, an eagle, displayed, with two heads, sa. *Fortiter et fideliter. Pl.* 87, *cr.* 11, (without flames.)
BROWNE, MICHAEL-JOSEPH, Esq., of Moyne, co. Galway, a griffin's head, erased. *Fortiter et fideliter. Pl.* 48, *cr.* 6.
BROWNE, JOHN-FRANCIS, Esq., of Greenville and Tuam, co. Galway, same crest and motto.
BROWNE, Ess., an eagle, displayed, with two heads, sa. *Pl.* 87, *cr.* 11, (without flames.)
BROWNE, an eagle, displayed, with two heads, sa., per az. and gu., winged, or. *Ib.*
BROWNE, Heref., a demi-griffin, vert, winged and legged, or. *Pl.* 18, *cr.* 6.
BROWNE, Suff., a demi-stork, wings expanded, ppr., neck nowed.
BROWNE, Leic., a boar's head, erased, sa., pierced through neck with a (broken spear,) or, headed, ar. *Pl.* 11, *cr.* 9.
BROWNE, Middx., a buck's head, erased, ppr., attired, or. *Pl.* 66, *cr.* 9.
BROWNE, Lond., a bee-hive, with bees volant, ppr. *Virtus et industria. Pl.* 81, *cr.* 14.

BROWNE, Salop, out of a mural coronet, gu., a stork's head, erm. *Pl.* 40, *cr.* 8, (without scroll.)
BROWNE, Lond., (a cubit arm,) vested, gu., cuffed, ar., in hand, ppr., a sword, erect, also ppr., hilted, or, enfiled with a leopard's head, of the second. *Virtus curâ servabit.* *Pl.* 102, *cr.* 5, (arm, *pl.* 118, *cr.* 3.)
BROWNE, an arm, couped and erect, (vested, az., cuffed, erm.,) in hand, ppr., a caltrap, or. *Pl.* 22, *cr.* 4.
BROWNE, a griffin's head, erased, or, collared, ar. *Pl.* 69, *cr.* 13.
BROWNE, an eagle's head, erased, ar., (in beak an arrow, ppr.) *Pl.* 20, *cr.* 7.
BROWNE, Somerset House, a lion, rampant, ppr. *Pl.* 67, *cr.* 5.
BROWNE, Weymouth, Dors., a griffin's head, erased, sa., beaked, or. *Pl.* 48, *cr.* 6.
BROWNE, Durham, a sword, erect, ar., (embrued at point, gu.) *Pl.* 105, *cr.* 1.
BROWNE, a lion, sejant, sa., resting dexter on a shield, ar., (charged with a mullet,) of the first. *Pl.* 126, *cr.* 15, (shield, *pl.* 19, *cr.* 2.)
BROWNE, a crane's head and neck, erased, az., (ducally gorged, or, in mouth a bezant.) *Pl.* 20, *cr.* 9.
BROWNE, a demi-griffin, vert, wings elevated, or. *Pl.* 18, *cr.* 6.
BROWNE, WILLIAM, Esq., of Tallantire Hall, Cumb., a griffin's head, vert, between wings. *Traducere ævum leniter.* *Pl.* 22, *cr.* 2.
BROWNE, Bart., Suss., an eagle, displayed, vert. *Pl.* 48, *cr.* 11.
BROWNE, JAMES-ARTHUR, Esq., of Browne Hall, co. Mayo, a griffin's head, erased, ar., langued, gu. *Fortiter et fideliter.* *Pl.* 48, *cr.* 6.
BROWNE-WILLIAM, the Rev. P., of Rathbane, co. Limerick, on a marquess's coronet, ppr., an eagle, displayed, gu., winged and membered, or. *Suivez la raison.* *Pl.* 48, *cr.* 11, (coronet, *pl.* 127, *fig.* 4.)
BROWNELL, Yorks., an escallop, ar. *Pl.* 117, *cr.* 4.
BROWNELL, Derbs., out of a ducal coronet, a triple-plume of twelve ostrich-feathers, ar., five, four, and three. *Pl.* 114, *cr.* 8.
BROWNHILL, Sco., the sun rising from behind a mountain, ppr. *Radii omnia lustrant.* *Pl.* 38, *cr.* 6.
BROWNING, Comley, Glouc., on a chapeau, gu., turned up, erm., a pair of wings, erect, in bend sinister. *Pl.* 80, *cr.* 15.
BROWNING, out of a ducal coronet, a cockatrice's head. *Pl.* 77, *cr.* 5.
BROWNING, Iri., a dexter arm, (embowed,) in hand a battle-axe, ppr. *Pl.* 73, *cr.* 7.
BROWNING, Eng., a sinister arm, from elbow, issuing from a cloud in sinister, hand above a serpent's head, erect from middle, and looking toward the sinister, ppr. *Pl.* 121, *cr.* 1.
BROWNLEE, and BROWNLIE, Sco., an arm, in armour, in hand a sword. *Pl.* 2, *cr.* 8.
BROWNLEE, and BRONLIE, Eng., a demi-peacock, issuing, ppr. *Pl.* 24, *cr.* 1.
BROWNLEE, and BROWNLIE, Sco., an eagle, displayed, charged on breast with an annulet. *Pl.* 48, *cr.* 11, (annulet, *pl.* 141.)
BROWNLOW, Iri., a goat's head, erased, ar. *Pl.* 29, *cr.* 13.

BROWNLOW, Iri., a goat's head, erased, ar., collared, gu. *Pl.* 29, *cr.* 13.
BROWNLOW, Earl and Baron, Viscount Alford, and a Bart., (Cust ;) a lion's head, erased, sa., gorged with a collar, paly, wavy of six, ar. and az. *Opera illius mea sunt.* *Pl.* 7, *cr.* 10.
BROWNLOW, Lond. and Linc., on a chapeau, gu., turned up, erm., a greyhound, (passant,) or, collared of the first. *Pl.* 104, *cr.* 1.
BROWNRIG, or BROWNRIGG, Eng., a lion, rampant, in dexter a fleur-de-lis, ppr. *Pl.* 87, *cr.* 6.
BROWNRIGG, a sword, in pale, environed with a snake, all ppr. *Pl.* 105, *cr.* 1, (snake, *pl.* 30, *cr.* 3.)
BROWNRIGG, Bart., Iri., out of a mural coronet, or, a sword, erect, ppr., pommel and hilt, or, entwined by a serpent, vert. *Virescit vulnere virtus.* And as an honourable augmentation, a demi-Kandian, in dexter a sword, in sinister, the crown of Kandy.
BROWNSMITH, (in a frame, lozenge-shaped,) five arrows, points downward, one in pale, four in saltier. *Pl.* 54, *cr.* 15.
BROWNSWORD, Eng., a pegasus, current, ppr. *Pl.* 28, *cr.* 9.
BROXHOLME, Linc., a bear, statant, against an elm-tree, all ppr. *Pl.* 61, *cr.* 5, (elm, *pl.* 18, *cr.* 10.)
BROYN, two lions' paws, sa., holding up a shield, ar. *Pl.* 43, *cr.* 12.
BRUCE, Bart., Iri., a lion, passant, az., in dexter (a trefoil, slipped, ppr.) *Pl.* 4, *cr.* 14.
BRUCE, CHARLES-BRUCE-BRUDENELL, Marquess of Ailesbury. *See* AILESBURY.
BRUCE, Earl of Elgin and Kincardine. *See* ELGIN.
BRUCE, ROBERT, Esq., of Kennet, Clackmannan; and Dunnogot, Perth; in hand, a sceptre, ppr. *Fuimus.* *Pl.* 17, *cr.* 12, (sceptre, *pl.* 82, *cr.* 3.)
BRUCE, EDWARD, Esq., of Scoutbush and Killroot, co. Antrim, a cubit arm, couped at elbow, erect, in hand a scimitar, ppr. *Do well, doubt nought.* *Pl.* 29, *cr.* 8.
BRUCE, Sco., a horse's head, bridled, ppr. *Be true.* *Pl.* 91, *cr.* 1.
BRUCE, Sir WILLIAM, N.S. Bart., Stenhouse, Stirling, on a chapeau, an arm, from shoulder, couped, fesswise, in hand a (sceptre, ensigned on point with an open crown, as that worn by Robert I. of Scotland.) *Fuimus.* *Pl.* 57, *cr.* 3.
BRUCE, Newton, Sco., an eagle's head, couped, ppr. *Spes mea supernè.* *Pl.* 100, *cr.* 10.
BRUCE, Mowance, Sco., in dexter hand a heart, ppr. *Omnia vincit amor.* *Pl.* 59, *cr.* 12.
BRUCE, Sco., a naked arm flexed, (out of a cloud,) in hand a human heart, ppr. *Semper fidelis.* *Pl.* 64, *cr.* 12.
BRUCE, Sco. and Eng., a lion, passant, az. (Another, or.) *Pl.* 48, *cr.* 8.
BRUCE, Balcaskie, Sco., the setting sun, ppr. *Irrevocabile.* *Pl.* 38, *cr.* 6.
BRUCE, Sco., a lion, rampant. *Fuimus.* *Pl.* 67, *cr.* 5.
BRUCE, of Wester Kinlock, Sco., a star, or. *Ad summa virtus.* *Pl.* 21, *cr.* 6.
BRUCE, Pittarthie, Sco., a horse's head, couped and furnished, ppr. *True.* *Pl.* 92, *cr.* 1.
BRUCE, Garvet, Sco., in hand a sword, ppr. *Venture forward.* *Pl.* 21, *cr.* 10.

BRUCE, Sco., an arm, embowed, in hand a cutlass, ppr. *Do well, doubt nought*. *Pl.* 92, *cr.* 5.
BRUCE of Arnot, Sco., the sun rising from a cloud, ppr. *Nec me qui cœtera vincit*. *Pl.* 67, *cr.* 9.
BRUCE, Sco., an arm, in hand a cutlass, ppr. *Do well, doubt nought*. *Pl.* 92, *cr.* 5.
BRUCKSHAW, or BRUCKSHOW, Eng., a sea-chart, ppr. *Pl.* 59, *cr.* 3.
BRUDENAL, and BRUDENELL, Eng., a battle-axe, in pale, surmounted by a branch of laurel and a branch of rue, in saltier, ppr. *Pl.* 119, *cr.* 8.
BRUDENELL, Earl of Cardigan. *See* CARDIGAN.
BRUDENELL, Leic. and Northamp. : 1. An arm, embowed, covered with leaves, vert, in hand, ppr., a spiked club, or, slung to arm with a line, gold. *Pl.* 83, *cr.* 2. 2. A talbot, ar., (ducally) gorged, gu. *Pl.* 65, *cr.* 2. 3. A sea-horse, ar. *En grace affie*. *Pl.* 103, *cr.* 3.
BRUDENELL, a sea-horse, ar. *En grace affie*. *Pl.* 103, *cr.* 3.
BRUEN, or BRUIN, a pedlar, passant, ar., with a crutch in dexter, and a pack on back, or.
BRUEN, Chesh., a fisherman, vested, per pale, ar. and sa., counterchanged, in dexter a fisherman's staff, in sinister a landing net over the shoulder, or.
BRUER, a mermaid, ppr. *Pl.* 48, *cr.* 5.
BRUGES, DE, Eng., a calvary cross, on three grieces, gu. *Pl.* 49, *cr.* 2.
BRUGES, Lond., on an anchor, or, a scroll. *Mihi cœlum portus*. *Pl.* 42, *cr.* 12.
BRUCES, Glouc., Wilts., and Ess., a Saracen's head, in profile, couped at shoulder, ppr., vested, ar., semée of torteaux, and wreathed, of the second, and sa. *Pl.* 126, *cr.* 8.
BRUGET, Eng., out of a ducal coronet, or, a swan's head and neck, between wings, ar. *Pl.* 83, *cr.* 1.
BRUMFIELD, Eng., a pheon, az. *Pl.* 56, *cr.* 15.
BRUMHERD, Eng., a mermaid, ppr. *Pl.* 48, *cr.* 5.
BRUMIN, a lion's head, erased, or, fretty, sa. *Pl.* 81, *cr.* 4.
BRUMMEL, or BRUMMELL, a dove with an olive-branch, ppr. *Pl.* 48, *cr.* 15.
BRUMSTEAD, a demi-griffin, ar., wings expanded, or, in dexter a cross formée, fitched, gu. *Pl.* 18, *cr.* 6, (cross, *pl.* 27, *cr.* 14.)
BRUN, Kent and Dors., a stag, lodged, sa. *Pl.* 67, *cr.* 2.
BRUNE, a goat, (passant), ar., horned, or. *Pl.* 66, *cr.* 1.
BRUNE-PRIDEAUX, Cornw. and Dors., a man's head, in profile, couped at shoulders, on head a chapeau, az., turned up, ar. *Pl.* 51, *cr.* 4.
BRUNECK, Eng., an eagle's head, erased, sa. *Pl.* 20, *cr.* 7.
BRUNET, Eng., a cockatrice, displayed, gu. *Pl.* 102, *cr.* 15.
BRUNSELL, Notts., in lion's gamb, erased, a rose, ar., stalked and leaved, vert. *Pl.* 60, *cr.* 14.
BRUNSFIELD, and BRUNSFIELDS, Sco., a demi-chevalier, brandishing a sword, ppr. *Pl.* 23, *cr.* 4.
BRUNTON, Sco., a beacon in flames, ppr. *Fax mentis incendium gloriœ*. *Pl.* 89, *cr.* 9.
BRUNTON, a beacon in flames, sa. *Pl.* 89, *cr.* 9.
BRUNTON, Eng., an anchor, sa. *Pl.* 25, *cr.* 15.

BRUSE, out of a ducal coronet, gu., a lion's head, or. *Pl.* 90, *cr.* 9.
BRUSE, Norf., a Saracen's head, in profile, ppr., wreathed, ar. and gu. *Pl.* 36, *cr.* 3.
BRUSE, an eagle, rising, regardant, ppr. *Pl.* 35, *cr.* 8.
BRUSE, out of a ducal coronet, or, a demi-lion, az. *Pl.* 45, *cr.* 7.
BRUSELL, a lion's head, erased, gu. *Pl.* 81, *cr.* 4.
BRUSKETT, out of a ducal coronet, or, a demi-lion, az. *Pl.* 45, *cr.* 7.
BRUTON, or BRUTYN, Exeter, a demi-wolf, ducally (crowned,) between paws a mullet, ppr. *Pl.* 65, *cr.* 4.
BRUTTON, a cat, sejant, gardant, ppr. *Pl.* 24, *cr.* 6.
BRUTTON, Eng., a sphere, ppr. *Pl.* 114, *cr.* 6.
BRUYER, and BRUYERES, Eng., a bear's paw, (erased.) *Pl.* 126, *cr.* 2.
BRUYIN, or BRUYN, Surr. and Ess., a goat, ar., attired, or. *Pl.* 66, *cr.* 1.
BRUYN, and BRUYNE, on a chapeau, an ibex, gu. *Pl.* 115, *cr.* 13, (chapeau, *pl.* 127, *fig.* 13.)
BRUZEAD, Eng., a cat, sejant, sa. *Pl.* 24, *cr.* 6.
BRYAN, Upton, Wexford, on a mural coronet, ppr., a lion, rampant, gu., collared, gemelle, or, (charged on shoulder with a cinquefoil, ar.) *Pl.* 88, *cr.* 1, (coronet, *pl.* 128, *fig.* 18.)
BRYAN, Kent, a greyhound, current, regardant, collared.
BRYAN, Kent, on a garb, in fess, a bird. *Pl.* 112, *cr.* 10.
BRYAN, Iri., a demi-savage, ppr. *Pl.* 14, *cr.* 11.
BRYAN, Linc., a greyhound, current, regardant, eared and collared, or. *Pl.* 28, *cr.* 7, (without charge.)
BRYAN, on a dexter hand, couped, in fess, a hawk, close, ppr. *Pl.* 83, *cr.* 13.
BRYAN, on a chapeau, gu., turned up, erm., a bugle-horn, unstrung, or, tipped and garnished, sa. *Pl.* 89, *cr.* 3, (chapeau, *same plate*.)
BRYAN, Iri., a Saracen's head, (erased at neck,) sa. *Pl.* 19, *cr.* 1.
BRYAN, DE, Iri., a dexter hand, ppr., holding an escallop, or. *Pl.* 57, *cr.* 6.
BRYANT, Eng., a flag, az., charged with a sal-tier, ar. *Pl.* 8, *cr.* 3.
BRYCE, a cock, ppr., in beak an (ear of corn.) *Pl.* 55, *cr.* 12.
BRYCE, Eng., a griffin's head, erased, or. *Pl.* 48, *cr.* 6.
BRYCE, Sco., a dexter arm, in hand a cutlass, ppr. *Do well, doubt nought*. *Pl.* 92, *cr.* 5.
BRYCE, Sco., out of a cloud, in sinister, in dexter hand, a pair of scales, ppr. *Fiat justitia*. *Pl.* 43, *cr.* 4, (scales, *pl.* 12, *cr.* 11.)
BRYDALL, Middx., in lion's gamb, erect and erased, az., a broken lance, ar., headed, or. *Pl.* 85, *cr.* 15.
BRYDEN, Berwicks., a hawk's head, erased, ppr., (charged with three bezants, one and two.) *Keep watch*. *Pl.* 34, *cr.* 11.
BRYDEN, Sco., a lion, passant, az. *Pl.* 48, *cr.* 8.
BRYDGES, Kent, the bust of an old man, in profile, ppr., vested, paly, of six, ar. and gu., and semée of roundles, counterchanged, wreathed round temples, of the first and az. *Maintien le droit*. *Pl.* 126, *cr.* 8.

F

BRYDGES, Bart., Heref., two wings, addorsed, ar., (charged with a bend, engrailed, sa.) *Pl.* 63, *cr.* 12.

BRYDGES, Bart., Kent, a Saracen's head, in profile, ppr., vested, paly, of the first and gu., (and semée of roundles, counterchanged,) on head a cap, or, lined with fur, ar., cap and breast charged with a pheon, sa. *Maintien le droit. Pl.* 51, *cr.* 4, (chargings, *pl.* 141.)

BRYDGES-JONES, Sir HARFORD, Bart., K.C., Boultibrook, Heref.: 1. For *Bridges*, two wings, addorsed, ar., (charged with a bend, engrailed, sa.) 2. For *Jones*, a cushion, gu., garnished and tasselled, or, a representation of the royal arms of Persia. 3. A crow, sa., resting dexter on the star of the Order of the Crescent. *Deus pascit corvos.*

BRYEN, or BRIAN: 1. A beacon in flames, or. *Pl.* 89, *cr.* 9. 2. An heraldic tiger, (current,) ar., bezantée. *Pl.* 7, *cr.* 5.

BRYKES, a wolf's head, (erased,) pierced with an arrow, ppr. *Pl.* 40, *cr.* 12.

BRYKES, or BYRKES, a wolf's head, (erased,) per pale, or and az., in mouth an arrow, gold, feathered, gu. *Pl.* 14, *cr.* 6.

BRYMER, Sco., in hand, gauntleted, a pheon, ppr. *Per tela, per hostes. Pl.* 123, *cr.* 12.

BRYMTON, BRYMPTON, and BRUMPTON, out of a ducal coronet, ppr., a lion's paw (charged with a bezant.) *Pl.* 67, *cr.* 7.

BRYNE, in lion's paw, a hawk's lure, ppr. *Pl.* 68, *cr.* 10, (lure, *pl.* 97, *cr.* 14.)

BRYNE, Iri., a mermaid, with mirror and comb, ppr. *Pl.* 48, *cr.* 5.

BRYSILLY, Eng., a cock-pheasant, purp. *Pl.* 82, *cr.* 12.

BRYSON, BRYSOUN, BRYSSAN, or BRYSSONE, Sco., a spur-rowel, ppr. *Pl.* 54, *cr.* 5.

BRYSON of Craigton, in hand a horn, ppr. *Ever ready. Pl.* 109, *cr.* 3.

BRYSON, Eng., a ship under sail. *God, with my right. Pl.* 109, *cr.* 8.

BUBB, Carlisle, Cumb., (on a mount, vert,) a unicorn, sejant, ar., crined and armed, or, dexter on a shield, per pale, gold and erm. *Pl.* 100, *cr.* 15, (shield, *pl.* 19, *cr.* 2.)

BUCCLEUCH and QUEENSBERY, Duke of, Baron Douglas, &c., Sco.; Earl of Doncaster and Baron Tyndale, Eng., (Scott-Douglas,) a stag, trippant, ppr., attired and unguled, or. *Amo. Pl.* 68, *cr.* 2.

BUCHAN, Earl of, Lord Cardross, (Erskine,) Sco., a dexter arm, in hand a baton, raguled, ppr. *Judge nought. Pl.* 123, *cr.* 10.

BUCHAN, Sco., a demi-lion, rampant, between paws a laurel-branch, ppr. *Fortior qui melior. Pl.* 47, *cr.* 4, (branch, *pl.* 123, *cr.* 5.)

BUCHAN, Sco., a lion's head, erased, gu. *Pl.* 81, *cr.* 4.

BUCHAN, Iri., a wolf, sejant, sa. *Pl.* 110, *cr.* 4.

BUCHANAN, Sco., a dexter hand, holding up a ducal cap, ppr., tufted with a rose, gu., all within two laurel-branches, vert. *Clarior hinc honos. Pl.* 95, *cr.* 11.

BUCHANAN, Sco., same crest. *Audaces juvo.*

BUCHANAN, Sco., a lion's paw, erased and erect, ppr. *Nobilis est ira leonis. Pl.* 126, *cr.* 9.

BUCHANAN, Sco., a dagger, erect, ppr. *Nobilis est ira leonis. Pl.* 73, *cr.* 9.

BUCHANAN, Sco., in hand a sword, ppr. *God, with my right. Pl.* 21, *cr.* 10.

BUCHANAN, Sco., in hand a sabre, in bend, ppr. *Audacia et industria. Pl.* 29, *cr.* 8.

BUCHANAN, Sco., a sinister arm, embowed, in fess, vested, in hand a bent bow, or. *Par sit fortuna labori. Pl.* 52, *cr.* 5.

BUCHANAN, Sco. and Eng., two hands, conjoined and couped, in fess. *Pl.* 1, *cr.* 2.

BUCHANAN, Sco., a dove and olive-branch, ppr. *Nuncia pacis. Pl.* 48, *cr.* 15.

BUCHANAN, Sco., a hand pointing a lance, in bend, ppr. *Secundo curo. Pl.* 99, *cr.* 8.

BUCHANAN, a cubit arm, erect, ppr., couped below wrist, in hand a sword, of the last, hilt and pommel, or. *Pl.* 21, *cr.* 10.

BUCHANAN, ANDREW, Esq., of Auchintorlie, Dumbarton, in hand, couped, a duke's coronet, with two laurel-branches wreathed under it. *Clarior hinc honos. Pl.* 95, *cr.* 11.

BUCHANAN, Iri., a demi-unicorn, or. *Pl.* 26, *cr.* 14.

BUCHANAN, Sco., a rose, slipped, gu. *Ducitur hinc honos. Pl.* 105, *cr.* 7.

BUCHANAN, JOHN, Esq., of Ardoch, Dumbarton, two hands grasping a two-handed sword, ppr. *Clariora sequor. Pl.* 3, *cr.* 5.

BUCHANNAN, Sco., in (dexter) hand a bow, in bend, ppr. *Pl.* 3, *cr.* 12.

BUCHE, out of a ducal coronet, or, a demi-boar, sa., pierced in neck with an arrow, ppr.

BUCK, a demi-lion, rampant, ppr., ducally crowned, or, in paws a bow, gold. *Pl.* 47, *cr.* 4, (bowl, *pl.* 12, *cr.* 12.)

BUCK, Norf., a buck, lodged, ppr. *Pl.* 67, *cr.* 2.

BUCK, WILLIAM, Esq., of Denholme, Yorks., and Glenarbeth, co. Cardigan, a portcullis. *Nosce teipsum. Pl.* 51, *cr.* 12.

BUCK, Hants, an arm, in armour, embowed, ppr., garnished, or, in hand a scimitar, ar., hilted, gold. *Pl.* 81, *cr.* 11.

BUCK, a buck's head, couped, ppr. *Pl.* 91, *cr.* 14.

BUCK, Glouc. and Worc., a buck's attires, ar., fixed to scalp, or. *Pl.* 33, *cr.* 15, (without head.)

BUCK, Linc., a Saracen's head, in profile, ppr., wreathed, or and az., on head a cap, neck charged with two bars-gemelle, of the second, vested, of the third. *Pl.* 51, *cr.* 4.

BUCK, Linc., a portcullis, az., garnished and chained, or. *Pl.* 51, *cr.* 12.

BUCKBY, Eng., on a chapeau, gu., turned up, erm., a garb, or, banded, ar. *Pl.* 62, *cr.* 1.

BUCKE, Camb., a buck, at gaze, erm., against an olive-tree, ppr. *Pl.* 118, *cr.* 13.

BUCKE, Kent, an arm, in armour, embowed, ppr., garnished, or, in hand a cutlass, ar., hilt, gold. *Pl.* 81, *cr.* 11.

BUCKERIDGE, Middx., a stag, current, ppr. *Pl.* 3, *cr.* 2.

BUCKET, Eng., a lily and a holly-branch, in saltier, ppr. *Pl.* 60, *cr.* 11.

BUCKFIELD, BUCKFOLD, and BUCKFOULD, a buck, ppr., attired, or, in a field, vert, paled around, of the first. *Pl.* 13, *cr.* 12.

BUCKINGHAM, a lion, rampant, gu. *Pl.* 67, *cr.* 5.

BUCKINGHAM, Lond., on a chapeau, az., turned up, erm., a demi-swan, wings expanded, ppr., membered, or, ducally gorged, gu. *Pl.* 80, *cr.* 15, (swan, *pl.* 30, *cr.* 10.)

BUCKINGHAM and CHANDOS, Duke and Marquess of, Earl Temple, Viscount and Baron Cobham, K.G., Eng.; Earl Nugent, Iri., (Temple - Nugent - Brydges - Chandos - Grenville): 1. For *Grenville*, a garb, vert. *Pl.* 48, *cr.* 10. 2. For *Temple*, on a ducal coronet, a martlet, or. *Pl.* 98, *cr.* 14. 3. For *Brydges*, an old man's head, in profile, ppr., vested, paly, of the first and gu., (semée of roundles, counterchanged, on head a cap, or, lined with fur, ar., cap and breast charged with a pheon, sa.) *Templa quam dilecta.* *Pl.* 126, *cr.* 8.

BUCKINGHAMSHIRE, Earl of, Baron Hobart, and a Bart., (Hobart - Hampden): 1. For *Hampden*, a talbot, statant, erm., collared, ringed, and lined, gu., (end of line tied in a knot over back.) *Pl.* 65, *cr.* 2. 2. For *Hobart*, a bull, passant, per pale, sa. and gu., (bezantée, in nose a ring, or.) *Auctor pretiosa facit.* *Pl.* 66, *cr.* 11.

BUCKLAND, Bucks., on a mount, vert, a stag, lodged, ppr. *Pl.* 22, *cr.* 5.

BUCKLAND, and BUCKLE, Somers., on a chapeau, gu., turned up, erm., a talbot, sejant, or. *Pl.* 107, *cr.* 7, (chapeau, *same plate*.)

BUCKLE, Suss., out of a ducal coronet, or, a demi-ounce, ar. *Nil temerè tenta nil timidè.*

BUCKLE, a lion's head, erased. *Pl.* 81, *cr.* 4.

BUCKLE, or BUCKEL, Lond., out of a ducal coronet, or, a bull's head, ar. *Pl.* 68, *cr.* 6.

BUCKLE, out of a ducal coronet, or, a demi-leopard, ar. *Pl.* 12, *cr.* 14, (coronet, *pl.* 128, *fig.* 3.)

BUCKLER, or BUCLER, Dors., a dragon's head, erased, sa., (charged with two bars, or, between three bezants.) *Pl.* 107, *cr.* 10, (without collar.)

BUCKLER, Oxon. and Dors., a dragon's head, erased, sa., guttée-d'or. *Pl.* 107, *cr.* 10, (without collar.)

BUCKLEY, Wilts., out of a ducal coronet, or, a bull's head, ar., armed, gold. *Nec temere, nec timide.* *Pl.* 68, *cr.* 6.

BUCKLEY, Kent, a demi-eagle, rising, ppr. *Pl.* 52, *cr.* 8.

BUCKLEY, Chesh., a griffin's head, gu., between wings, of the same, bezantée. *Pl.* 65, *cr.* 1.

BUCKLEY, Eng., a stag's head. *Pl.* 91, *cr.* 14.

BUCKMASTER, Linc., Devons., and Northamp., a demi-lion, sa., in dexter a fleur-de-lis, or, charged on shoulder with three annulets, of the same. *Pl.* 91, *cr.* 13, (annulet, *pl.* 141.)

BUCKMINSTER, Northamp., a demi-lion, rampant, sa., supporting a battle-axe, erect, or, headed, ar. *Pl.* 101, *cr.* 14, (without charge.)

BUCKNALL, Eng., a buck's head, cabossed, sa. *Pl.* 36, *cr.* 1.

BUCKNALL, JOHN-CHARLES LINDSEY, Esq., of Turin Castle, co. Mayo, a buck's head, cabossed, sa., attired, or. *Pl.* 36, *cr.* 1.

BUCKNELL, or BUCKNEL, Eng., in dexter hand, issuing from a cloud, in fess, a ball, ppr. *Pl.* 104, *cr.* 4.

BUCKNER, a fleur-de-lis, gu., with adder entwined, head issuing from centre leaf, ppr. *Pl.* 15, *cr.* 13.

BUCKSTON, Derby, a pelican, vulning, or. *Fructum habet caritas.* *Pl.* 109, *cr.* 15.

BUCKSTON, the Rev. GERMAN, of Bradborne, Derby, a pelican, vulning, or. *Fructum habet caritas.* *Pl.* 109, *cr.* 15.

BUCKTON, Yorks., a goat's head, erased. *Pl.* 29, *cr.* 13.

BUCKTON, Northumb., a goat's head, erased, per fess, indented, ar. and sa., attired, or. *Pl.* 29, *cr.* 13.

BUCKTON, or BUKETON, Yorks., a demi-shark, issuing, regardant, gorging a negro, ppr. *Pl.* 16, *cr.* 6.

BUCKTON, DE, a goat's head, couped, per fess, ar. and sa., armed, or and vert. *Pl.* 105, *cr.* 14.

BUCKWORTH, Surr., a demi-lion, in dexter a cross crosslet, fitched. *Pl.* 65, *cr.* 6.

BUCKWORTH, Bart., Surr., a man's head and shoulders, affrontée, armed and helmeted, beaver up, all ppr. *Pl.* 53, *cr.* 8.

BUCTON, a hand, issuing from a cloud, in fess, reaching to a garland of laurel, ppr. *Pl.* 73, *cr.* 11.

BUDD, Iri., an heraldic tiger, passant, gu. *Pl.* 7, *cr.* 5.

BUDD, Eng., a dragon's head, neck transpierced with a spear. *Pl.* 121, *cr.* 9.

BUDD, Willesley, Devons., a hurt, charged with a star of seven points, or.

BUDDEN, Eng., a bull's head, ppr., (charged with a cross batonée, or.) *Pl.* 63, *cr.* 11.

BUDDS, Eng., a ram, passant, ar. (Another, or.) *Pl.* 109, *cr.* 2.

BUDGEN, Eng., in lion's paw, sa., a spear, tasselled, in bend sinister. *Pl.* 1, *cr.* 4.

BUDORSHIDE, and BUDOXHEAD, Cornw., a stag's head, erased, ar. *Pl.* 66, *cr.* 9.

BUDWORTH, Eng., a sinister arm, couped, ppr., vested, az., in hand a bent bow, of the first. *Pl.* 52, *cr.* 5.

BUDWORTH, Ess., a wolf's head, erased, ppr. *Pl.* 14, *cr.* 6.

BUGGE, Ess., out of a ducal coronet, or, a moor's head, in profile, sa., wreathed, gold and az. *Pl.* 36, *cr.* 3, (coronet, *same plate.*)

BUGGEN, and BUGGIN, Kent and Lond., a cockatrice, displayed, ar. *Pl.* 102, *cr.* 15.

BUGGEN, BUGGIN, and BUGGENS, a Doric column, ar., entwined with laurel, vert. *Pl.* 14, *cr.* 15.

BUGGINE, Kent and Lond., a cockatrice, displayed, ar., crested, membered, and jelloped, gu. *Pl.* 102, *cr.* 15.

BUGGINE, an antelope, sejant, ar., armed, tufted, and unguled, sa. *Pl.* 115, *cr.* 3.

BUIST, Perth, a swan, naiant, wings addorsed, devouring a perch, all ppr. *Assiduitate.* *Pl.* 103, *cr.* 1.

BUKETON, or BUCKTON, Yorks., a demi-shark, issuing, swallowing a negro, ppr. *Pl.* 16, *cr.* 6.

BUKHILL, Eng., a talbot's head, ar. *Pl.* 123, *cr.* 15.

BULBEC, and BULBECK, Ess., a lion's head, regardant, ppr. *Pl.* 35, *cr.* 2.

BULBEC, and BULBECK, in hand a sealed letter, ppr. *Pl.* 33, *cr.* 8.

BULBECK, Kingston, a bull, passant, vert, hoofed, maned, and armed, or. *Pl.* 66, *cr.* 11.

BULCOCK, Lond. and Devons., a lion's head, gu., within a chain, in orle, issuing, or. *Pl.* 28, *cr.* 12.

BULIMORE, Eng., a demi-lion, rampant, sa. *Pl.* 67, *cr.* 10.

BULKALEEL, Eng., out of a ducal coronet, or, a bull's head, ar., armed, gold. *Pl.* 68, *cr.* 6.

BULKELEY-WILLIAMS, Bart., Wel.: 1. For *Bulkeley*, out of a ducal coronet, or, a bull's head, ar., horned, gold, and charged with a cheveron, sa. *Pl.* 68, *cr.* 6. 2. For *Williams*, a Saracen's head, couped at shoulders, ppr. *Nec temere, nec timide*. *Pl.* 19, *cr.* 1.

BULKELEY, Iri., Bucks. and Chesh., out of a ducal coronet, or, a bull's head, ar., armed, gold. *Nec temere, nec timide*. *Pl.* 68, *cr.* 6.

BULKELEY, Eng., a bull's head and neck, erased, per pale, ar. and sa. *Pl.* 19, *cr.* 3.

BULKELEY, Eng., a bull's head and neck, couped, per pale, ar. and sa., armed, or and ar. *Pl.* 63, *cr.* 11.

BULKELEY, or BULKELY, Iri., a bull's head, couped at neck, sa. *Pl.* 120, *cr.* 7.

BULL, Lond. and Yorks., on a cloud, ppr., a celestial sphere, az., the circles, or, and on the Zodiac the signs aries, taurus, gemini, and cancer. *Sol, mi, re, fa*. *Pl.* 110, *cr.* 9.

BULL, a bull's head and neck, erased, sa. *Pl.* 19, *cr.* 3.

BULL, Iri., a rose, gu. *Pl.* 52, *cr.* 11.

BULL, Lond., Yorks., and Norf., a bull's head, erased, sa., charged with six annulets. *Pl.* 19, *cr.* 3, (annulet, *pl.* 141.)

BULL, Oxon., a bull's head, cabossed, gu., between wings, or. *Pl.* 111, *cr.* 6, (wings, *pl.* 60, *cr.* 9.)

BULL, Ess., a bull's head, cabossed, gu., horned, or, between wings, gold. *Ib.*

BULL, Lond., a lion's head, erased, sa., ducally crowned, or. *Pl.* 90, *cr.* 4.

BULLEN, Linc., a bull's head, couped, sa., armed, or. *Pl.* 120, *cr.* 7.

BULLER, Bart., Cornw., Devons., and Somers., an old man's head, affrontée, (wreathed,) ppr. *Pl.* 19, *cr.* 1.

BULLER, Cornw.: 1. An eagle, (on a rock,) supporting a banner. *Pl.* 65, *cr.* 3. 2. A Saracen's head, ppr. *Aquila non captat muscas*. *Pl.* 19, *cr.* 1.

BULLER, Somers. and Cornw., an old man's head, affrontée, ppr. *Pl.* 19, *cr.* 1.

BULLER, Cornw. and Somers., a moor's head, affrontée, couped, ppr., wreathed, ar. and az. *Pl.* 97, *cr.* 2.

BULLER, Sir FRANCIS, Bart., Lupton, Devons., a Saracen's head, couped, ppr. *Pl.* 81, *cr.* 15.

BULLER, JAMES-WENTWORTH, Esq., of Downes, Devon, a Saracen's head, couped, ppr. *Aquila non cupit muscas*. *Pl.* 81, *cr.* 15.

BULLEY, Eng., a heart, inflamed, ppr. *Pl.* 68, *cr.* 13.

BULLINGHAM, Linc., an escallop, ar., between two palm-branches, vert. *Pl.* 86, *cr.* 9.

BULLIVANT, a demi-lion, or, (charged on breast with a fleur-de-lis, vert), between gambs a tower, sa. *Pl.* 47, *cr.* 4, (tower, *pl.* 12, *cr.* 5.)

BULLMAN, and BULMAN, out of a ducal coronet, a bull's head, ppr. *Pro patria*. *Pl.* 68, *cr.* 6.

BULLO, and BULOW, Eng., an arm., embowed, hand clenched, ppr. *Pl.* 87, *cr.* 7.

BULLOCK, seven arrows, six in saltier, and one in base, gu., feathered and headed, ar., enfiled with a mural coronet, of the last. *Pl.* 110, *cr.* 11, (coronet, *pl.* 128, *fig.* 18.)

BULLOCK, five triple-pointed spears, staves, or, headed, ar., tied together with a knot, gu.

BULLOCK, Lond., (on a mount, vert,) a bee-hive, or, thereon a bee, displayed, ppr. *Pl.* 81, *cr.* 14, (bee, *pl.* 100, *cr.* 3.)

BULLOCK, Hants, five pole-axes, ppr., encircled by a ribbon, az.

BULLOCK, Ess., five battle-axes, staves, or, heads, sa., tied together with a bow knot, gu.

BULLOCK, Ess., five bills, az., bound with a line, or.

BULLOCK-WATSON, Ess.: 1. For *Bullock*, five antique halberds, blades, ppr., handles, or, encircled with a ribbon, gold, the cord tied in a knot, gu. *Nil conscire sibi*. 2. For *Watson*, a dexter arm, in armour, embowed, in gauntlet a palm-branch, ppr. *Esperance en Dieu*. *Pl.* 68, *cr.* 1, (palm, *pl.* 62, *cr.* 7.)

BULMAN, or BULLMAN, out of a ducal coronet, a bull's head, ppr. *Pro patria*. *Pl.* 68, *cr.* 6.

BULMAN, Northumb., (on a mount, vert,) a bull, passant, ar., dexter on a roundle, az. *Pl.* 66, *cr.* 11.

BULMAR, a demi-lion, rampant, holding an escallop. *Pl.* 126 *a*, *cr.* 13.

BULMER, a demi-bull, rampant, gu., armed, or, thereon an escallop, between two billets, in pale, gold. *Pl.* 63, *cr.* 6, (chargings, *pl.* 141.)

BULMER, or BULLMER, Ess. and Yorks., a bull, passant, gu., armed and unguled, or. *Pl.* 66, *cr.* 11.

BULMER, a demi-bull, rampant, gu., armed, or. *Pl.* 63, *cr.* 6.

BULSTREE, and BOULSTREE, out of a mural coronet, a stag's head. *Pl.* 91, *cr.* 14, (coronet, *same plate.*)

BULSTRODE, Beds. and Bucks., a bull's head and neck, gu., attired, ar., between wings, of the first. (Another, the wings ar.) *Pl.* 60, *cr.* 9.

BULT, Eng., an arm, in armour, couped, embowed, resting elbow on the wreath, ppr., a sash at shoulders, gu., in hand a club. *Pl.* 28, *cr.* 2.

BULTEEL, JOHN, Esq., of Flete, Devons., out of a ducal coronet, gu., a pair of wings, ar., billettée, of the first. *Pl.* 17, *cr.* 9.

BULTEEL, and BULTELL, Somers., a bull's head, gu., between wings, or. *Pl.* 60, *cr.* 9.

BULWER, Norf., a horned wolf. *Adversis major, par secundis*.

BULWER-LYTTON, Bart., M.P., of Knebworth, Herts.: 1. For *Bulwer*, an ibex's head, erased, erm., armed and crined, or. *Pl.* 72, *cr.* 9. 2. For *Wiggett*, a dove, regardant, in beak a laurel-branch, all ppr. *Adversis major, par secundis*. *Pl.* 77, *cr.* 2.

BULWORTH, out of a ducal coronet, or, a stag's head, between two branches of palm, ppr. *Pl.* 29, *cr.* 7, (palm, *pl.* 87, *cr.* 8.)

BULWORTH, a stag's head, erased, ppr. *Pl.* 66, *cr.* 9.

BUMSTEAD, and BUMSTED, Suff., out of a cloud a dexter hand, erect, pointing to a star, all ppr. *Pl.* 77, *cr.* 6.

BUNBURY, Bart., K.C.B., Chesh., two swords, in saltier, through the mouth of a leopard's face, or, the blades, ppr., hilts and pommels, gold. *Firmum in vitâ nihil.*
BUNBURY, Iri., a hand, in fess, issuing from a cloud, and reaching to a garland of laurel, all ppr. *Pl.* 73, *cr.* 11.
BUNBURY-RICHARDSON, Bart., Iri.: 1. For *Bunbury*, in front of a tree, ppr., on a mount, vert, a leopard's head, paly of six, ar. and sa., transfixed by two arrows, in saltier, also ppr. 2. For *Richardson*, a lion, rampant, erm., (in mouth a trefoil, slipped, vert, the four paws semée of torteaux, and charged on breast with a cross crosslet, or.) *Virtus paret robur. Pl.* 67, *cr.* 5.
BUNCE, Lond. and Kent, a demi-boar, az., pierced through neck with a broken spear, gu., headed, ar. *Sic vivere, vivetis. Pl.* 115, *cr.* 2.
BUNCH, Sco., a stork, ppr. *Pl.* 33, *cr.* 9.
BUND, Worc., an eagle's head, erased, or. *Pl.* 20, *cr.* 7.
BUNDY, Worc., a cubit arm, erect, in hand an eagle's leg, erased, all ppr. *Certum pete finem. Pl.* 103, *cr.* 4.
BUNFORD, Eng., out of a ducal coronet, a demi-lion, gu. *Pl.* 45, *cr.* 7.
BUNGEY, Kent, Surr., Norf., and Durh., an eagle, wings addorsed, ar., standing on a (laurel-branch,) vert, fructed, or. *Pl.* 61, *cr.* 1.
BUNHILL, in bear's paw, erased, sa., a rose, slipped and leaved, ppr. *Pl.* 60, *cr.* 14.
BUNN, Eng., an ostrich-head, ar., collared, gu., between two branches, vert. *Pl.* 49, *cr.* 7.
BUNNELL, Eng., on a ducal coronet, a Cornish chough, rising, ppr. *Pl.* 8, *cr.* 5.
BUNNEY, and BUNNY, Yorks. and Durh., a goat's head, erased, sa., attired, or, (charged on one of the horns with two annulets conjoined, of the last.) *Monte dessus. Pl.* 29, *cr.* 13.
BUNNY, Ryton, Durh., a goat's head, erased, sa., charged with a mullet. *Monte dessus. Pl.* 29, *cr.* 13, (mullet, *pl.* 141.)
BUNTEN, Sco., a hand grasping a sword, ppr. *Fortiter et fide. Pl.* 21, *cr.* 10.
BUNTEN, and BUNTING, Sco., a bantam, on a garb, ppr. *Copiose et opportune. Pl.* 122, *cr.* 3.
BUNTING, Eng., in hand, issuing from a cloud, erect, two branches of laurel, in orle. *Pl.* 88, *cr.* 13.
BUNTING, Eng., an armillary sphere, ppr. *Pl.* 114, *cr.* 6.
BUNTON, Eng., on a ducal coronet, a talbot, passant, collared and lined. *Pl.* 3, *cr.* 8.
BURARD, Eng., on a ducal coronet, or, an etoile of eight points, ppr. *Pl.* 83, *cr.* 3.
BURBAGE, a boar's head, erased, ar., between two branches, vert. *Pl.* 19, *cr.* 8.
BURBIDGE, Eng., between the attires of a stag, or, erect and erased, a boar's head, sa. *Pl.* 33, *cr.* 15.
BURBRIDGE, Eng., out of a ducal coronet, az., two arms, embowed, vested, gu., gloved, or, in each an ostrich-feather, ar. *Pl.* 45, *cr.* 2.
BURBYCHE, Middx. and Heref., a boar's head and neck, erased, ar., bristled, or, between two oak-branches, vert, fructed, of the second. *Pl.* 19, *cr.* 8.

BURCETRE, Eng., a comet star, ppr. *Pl.* 39, *cr.* 9.
BURCHALL, Heref., a lion, rampant, az., (supporting a tree, vert.) *Pl.* 22, *cr.* 15.
BURCHALL, and BURCHILL, Eng., out of a ducal coronet, two hands, dexter and sinister, in saltier, each grasping a scimitar, ppr. *Pl.* 57, *cr.* 8.
BURCHALL, and BURCHAM, Eng., a greyhound, sejant, collared and lined, ar. *Pl.* 66, *cr.* 15.
BURCHAR, Lond. and Ess., a greyhound, sejant, ar., ducally gorged, or. *Pl.* 66, *cr.* 15, (gorging, *same plate.*)
BURCHE, Eng., an eagle, wings expanded, gu. *Pl.* 126, *cr.* 7.
BURCHETT, Eng., a winged spur, ppr. *Pl.* 59, *cr.* 1.
BURCKHEAD, and BURKETT, a goat, rampant, ar., between paws, a garb, of the same, armed, or.
BURD, and BYRDE, Lond., an eagle's head, erased, bendy of eight, ar. and sa., ducally gorged, or. *Pl.* 74, *cr.* 1, (coronet, *same plate.*)
BURDEN, Eng., a heart, transfixed by a sword in bend, sinister. *Pl.* 61, *cr.* 15.
BURDENBROKE, a boar's head, erased, gu. *Pl.* 16, *cr.* 11.
BURDENBROKE, Eng., an otter's head, erased, sa. *Pl.* 126, *cr.* 14.
BURDET, or BURDETT, Bart., Yorks., on a tower, ar., a martlet, wings displayed, or. *Pl.* 107, *cr.* 6.
BURDETT, GEORGE, Esq., of Ballymany, co. Kildare, and Ballywater, co. Tipperary, a lion's head, erased, sa. *Pl.* 81, *cr.* 4.
BURDETT, JOHN HEAD, Esq., of Hunstanton, King's County, same crest.
BURDETT, Bart., Derbs., a lion's head, erased, sa., langued, gu. *Pl.* 81, *cr.* 4.
BURDETT, Eng., a lion's head, couped, sa. *Pl.* 126, *cr.* 1.
BURDETT, Warw. and Yorks., a thistle, ppr. *Pl.* 68, *cr.* 9.
BURDETT, Sir WILLIAM-BAGANEL, Bart., Iri., a lion's head, erased, sa. *Pl.* 81, *cr.* 4.
BURDON, Durh., a lion, rampant, (supporting himself by a pilgrim's staff, or.) *Pl.* 99, *cr.* 2.
BURDON, Eng., a gilliflower, or. *Pl.* 22, *cr.* 9.
BURDUS, or BURDUSS, Middx., an elephant, erm., on a mount, vert, under a tree, ppr. *Pl.* 56, *cr.* 14, (tree, *pl.* 52, *cr.* 6.)
BURE, Eng., an eagle, ppr. *Pl.* 7, *cr.* 11.
BURFOOT, Lond., on a wreath an eastern crown, thereon a pine-apple, leaved, and crowned with leaves which grow from the top, all or.
BURG, a falcon, standing on a serpent, nowed, ppr. *Pl.* 83, *cr.* 5.
BURGACE, BURGASS, BURGAS, and BURGASE, Eng., two pigeons, billing, ppr. *Pl.* 60, *cr.* 13.
BURGE, Eng., a branch of olive, ppr. *Pl.* 98, *cr.* 8.
BURGES, Ess., a Saracen's head, in profile, ppr., wreathed, ar. and sa., vested over shoulders, of the first, in stripes, palewise, ar., semée of torteaux, gu. *Pl.* 126, *cr.* 8.
BURGES, Linc., on a mural coronet, chequy, or and sa., a round buckle, gold, tongue erect. *Pl.* 73, *cr.* 10, (coronet, *pl.* 112, *cr.* 5.)

BURGESS, Suss. and Berks., a camel's head, ppr., (erased,) gu., bezantée. *Levius fit patientiâ.* *Pl.* 109, *cr.* 9.

BURGESS, a lion, rampant. *Pl.* 67, *cr.* 5.

BURGESS, a griffin's head, erased. *Pl.* 48, *cr.* 6.

BURGESS, Eng., a greyhound's head, ppr., bezantée, or. *Pl.* 89, *cr.* 2.

BURGESS, a lion, rampant, gu., (in dexter an annulet enclosing a fleur-de-lis, ar.) *Pl.* 87, *cr.* 6.

BURGH, ULYSSES, Baron Downes. *See* DOWNES.

BURGH, K.C.B., Iri., a mountain-cat, sejant, ppr., (collared and chained, or.) *Pl.* 24, *cr.* 6.

BURGH, an arm, in armour, couped, fesswise, elbow on the wreath, hand apaumée, ppr., ribboned and bowed. *Pl.* 28, *cr.* 2, (without mace.)

BURGH, Eng., a falcon, rising, erm. belled and ducally gorged, or. *Pl.* 61, *cr.* 12.

BURGH, a fleur-de-lis, ar., environed with a serpent, vert. *Pl.* 15, *cr.* 13.

BURGHALL, Iri., a wolf's head, erased, sa. *Pl.* 14, *cr.* 6.

BURGHEP, or BURGHEPE, a friar's head, in profile, ppr., couped at shoulders, vested, grey. *Pl.* 51, *cr.* 4.

BURGHERSH, Baron. *See* WESTMORELAND.

BURGHERSH, Devons. and Norf., on a mural coronet, gu., a demi-lion, double-queued, ar. *Pl.* 120, *cr.* 10, (coronet, *same plate*, *cr.* 14.)

BURGHERSH, Eng., two stumps of trees, couped and raguly, in saltier, ppr., banded, vert. *Pl.* 60, *cr.* 12.

BURGHILL, Suff. and Well., a lion's head, erased, ar. *Pl.* 81, *cr.* 4.

BURGHILL, a lion's head, ar., crowned with a Saxon crown, or. *Pl.* 90, *cr.* 4.

BURGHLEY, and BURGLY, Eng., a winged greyhound, sejant. *Pl.* 101, *cr.* 7.

BURGIN, Eng., a sword and key, in saltier, ppr. *Pl.* 54, *cr.* 12.

BURGIS, Eng., a camel's head, ppr. *Pl.* 109, *cr.* 9.

BURGOIGNE, or BURGOYNE, Cambs. and Devons., an antelope, sejant, ar., attired, tufted, and maned, sa. *Pl.* 115, *cr.* 3.

BURGON, Eng., a cock, crowing, or. *Pl.* 67, *cr.* 14.

BURGON, Longstanton, Herts., a tiger, sejant, ar., maned and tufted, sa. *Pl.* 26, *cr.* 9.

BURGONE, and BURGOYNE, Oxon., on a ducal coronet, or, a lion, passant, gu. *Pl.* 107, *cr.* 11.

BURGOYNE, Bart., Beds., a talbot, sejant, ar. *Pl.* 107, *cr.* 7.

BURGOYNE, Sir JOHN MONTAGU, Bart., Sutton Park, Beds., a talbot, sejant, or, ears, sa., gorged with a plain collar, gu. *Pl.* 107, *cr.* 7.

BURK, under the shade of (two) trees, a stag, lodged, ppr. *Pl.* 95, *cr.* 10.

BURKE, a demi-bull, rampant, armed and unguled, or, gorged with a chaplet, vert. *Pl.* 73, *cr.* 8.

BURKE, Sir JOHN, Bart., Iri., a mountain-cat, sejant, gardant, ppr., (collared and chained, or.) *Ung roy, ung foy, ung loy.* *Pl.* 24, *cr.* 6.

BURKE, Iri., a cat, sejant, ppr. *A cruce salus.* *Pl.* 24, *cr.* 6.

BURKE, Sir JOHN IGNATIUS, Bart., Iri., out of a ducal coronet, or, a plume of ostrich-feathers, ar. *In hoc signo vinces.* *Pl.* 44, *cr.* 12.

BURKET, and BURKETT, Eng., a garb, or. *Impendam, expendar.* *Pl.* 48, *cr.* 10.

BURKET, BURKETT, and BURKITT, Eng., a dexter arm, embowed, in hand a club. *Pl.* 123, *cr.* 10.

BURKIN, Suff., a crab, ppr. *Pl.* 116, *cr.* 14.

BURLAND, Eng., a demi-savage, brandishing a scimitar, ppr. *Pl.* 82, *cr.* 2.

BURLAND, a griffin's head, erased, (collared.) *Pl.* 48, *cr.* 6.

BURLEIGH, Eng., a stag's head, erased, gu. *Pl.* 66, *cr.* 9.

BURLES, a squirrel, sejant, cracking a nut, all ppr. *Pl.* 16, *cr.* 9.

BURLEY, Leic. and Wilts., a demi-boar, ppr., armed, hoofed, and bristled, or, (and gorged with a chain, gold, supporting a thistle, ppr.) *Pl.* 20, *cr.* 5.

BURLINGTON, Earl of, Baron Cavendish, (Cavendish,) a snake, nowed, ppr. *Cavendo tutus.* *Pl.* 1, *cr.* 9.

BURLINSON, Durh., a demi-lion, (between paws) a rose, ar., barbed, vert. *Pl.* 39, *cr.* 14.

BURLTON, a dexter and sinister arm, vested, holding up a cross crosslet, fitched. *Pl.* 113, *cr.* 12, (cross, *pl.* 141.)

BURLY, or BURLEY, Suff., a squirrel, sejant, supporting a ragged staff, or. *Pl.* 85, *cr.* 3, (staff, *pl.* 103, *cr.* 12.)

BURMAN, Eng., a demi-peacock, az. *Pl.* 24, *cr.* 1.

BURMESTER, Eng., a cross pattée, az., within six mullets, in a circle, or. *Pl.* 33, *cr.* 10.

BURMESTER, a cross pattée, az., within six mullets, in orle, or. *Pl.* 33, *cr.* 10.

BURMEY, Eng., in dexter hand, ppr., an anchor, erect, or, environed with clouds, ar. *Arcus, artes, astra.* *Pl.* 41, *cr.* 5.

BURN, Sco. and Lisbon, in hand, ppr., a cross crosslet, fitched, az. *Vincit veritas.* *Pl.* 99, *cr.* 1.

BURN, or BURNE, Iri., a torteau, az. *Pl.* 7, *cr.* 6.

BURN, an arm, erect, vested, sa., cuffed, ar., in hand, ppr., a fleur-de-lis, or. *Pl.* 95, *cr.* 9.

BURN, Sco. and Lond., in dexter hand a horn, ppr. *Ever ready.* *Pl.* 109, *cr.* 3.

BURN, Perthshire, two daggers, in saltier, ppr. *Tendit ad astra fides.* *Pl.* 24, *cr.* 2.

BURN, or BURNE, Eng., a heart, gu. *Pl.* 55, *cr.* 13.

BURN, in hand, ppr., a cross crosslet, fitched, az. *Vincit veritas.* *Pl.* 99, *cr.* 1.

BURNABY, Bart., Oxon., out of a naval coronet, a demi-lion, rampant, gardant, or, in dexter a staff, ppr., thereon a flag, gu. *Pro rege.*

BURNABY, and BURNEBY, Middx., a demi-man, sa., in dexter a bunch of columbine flowers, ppr., (and round neck a rope, or.) *Pl.* 35, *cr.* 12.

BURNBY, and BURNEBY, Middx., (on a mount,) a stag rising from under a tree, ppr. *Pl.* 95, *cr.* 10.

BURNELL, Lond., a greyhound, sejant, ar. *Pl.* 66, *cr.* 15.

BURNELL, in lion's gamb, erased, sa., a rosebranch, gu., leaved, vert. *Pl.* 60, *cr.* 14.

BURNELL, Norf., a tower, in flames, ppr. *Pl.* 118, *cr.* 15.

BURNELL, in lion's gamb, (erased, sa., a sprig of woodbine,) ppr. *Pl.* 68, *cr.* 10.

BURNELL, or BURNEL, in lion's gamb, erased, sa., three flowers, az., leaved, vert. *Pl.* 86, *cr.* 15.

BURNES, Montrose: 1. *By augmentation, on dexter side*, out of a mural coronet, per pale, vert and gu., inscribed "Cabool," letters, ar., a demi-eagle, displayed, transfixed, by a (javelin) in bend, sinister, ppr. *Pl.* 85, *cr.* 5. 2. *On sinister side*, out of an Eastern crown, or, an oak-tree, withered, renewing its foliage, ppr. *Ob patriam vulnera passi. Pl.* 92, *cr.* 8, (crown, *pl.* 128, *fig.* 3.)

BURNESS, Sco., a pegasus-head, ar., crined, between wings, or, (gorged with a bay-branch, ppr.) *Perseverantia vincit. Pl.* 19, *cr.* 13.

BURNET, a dexter hand (out of a cloud) grasping a pruning-knife, within a vine, fructed, all ppr. *Pl.* 83, *cr.* 4.

BURNET, Aberdeen, Sco., a hand with a cutlass, cutting through a vine-branch, ppr. *Tandam fit surculus arbor. Pl.* 83, *cr.* 4.

BURNET, Sco., a branch of holly, slipped, ppr. *Nec fluctu, nec flato. Pl.* 99, *cr.* 6.

BURNET, Sco., a holly-branch, slipped, ppr. *Nec fluctu, nec flatu. Pl.* 99, *cr.* 6.

BURNET, or BURNETT, Northumb., a holly-bush, vert, fructed. gu. *Virtute cresco. Pl.* 124, *cr.* 10.

BURNET, Sco., a boar's head, erased, ar. *Quidni pro sodali. Pl.* 16, *cr.* 11.

BURNET, Wilts., a vine, couped, ppr. *Virescit, vulnere virtus. Pl.* 89, *cr.* 1.

BURNET of Craigmyle, Sco., in dexter hand a palm-branch, ppr. *Quæ vernant crescent. Pl.* 23, *cr.* 7.

BURNET, Sco., a holly-branch, ppr. *Virtute cresco. Pl.* 99, *cr.* 6.

BURNET, Peebles, Sco., a vine-branch, slipped, ppr. *Tandem fit surculus arbor. Pl.* 89, *cr.* 1.

BURNET, BARNIS, Sco., in hand a knife, pruning a vine-tree, ppr. *Virescit vulnere virtus. Pl.* 83, *cr.* 4.

BURNET, LEES, Sco., same crest and motto.

BURNET, Sir ROBERT, N.S. Bart, Leys, Aberdeen, same crest and motto.

BURNETT, (on a mount, a vine; out of clouds,) in the sinister, a man's hand, grasping a knife, in the act of pruning, all ppr.; the whole on a mural coronet, or. *Pl.* 83, *cr.* 4, (coronet, *pl.* 128, *fig.* 18.)

BURNETT, Sco., (out of a cloud, in sinister,) a hand, in fess, grasping a pruning-knife, ppr. *Pl.* 83, *cr.* 4.

BURNETT, Iri., a holy lamb, regardant, ar., holding the standard of St Patrick, ppr. *Pl.* 48, *cr.* 13.

BURNETT, a bull's head, ducally gorged (and crowned.) *Pl.* 68, *cr.* 6.

BURNETT, a lion's head, erased, gu. *Pl.* 81, *cr.* 4.

BURNETT, Bart., Sco., in hand a knife, pruning a vine, ppr. *Virescit vulnere virtus. Pl.* 83, *cr.* 4.

BURNEY, Kent, an arm in a maunch, in fess, in hand a cross pattée, fitched. *Omne bonum desuper. Pl.* 22, *cr.* 14, (cross, *pl.* 99, *cr.* 15.)

BURNEY, or BURNIE, Sco., a lion's head, erased, gu. *Sapere aude incipie. Pl.* 81, *cr.* 4.

BURNEY, or BURNIE, Eng., a bull's head, ducally gorged and crowned. *Pl.* 86, *cr.* 6.

BURNHAM, Linc., out of a ducal coronet, in hand a dagger, in pale, blade, wavy. *Pl.* 65, *cr.* 10.

BURNHAM, Eng., a leopard's head, erased, ppr. *Pl.* 94, *cr.* 10.

BURNHAM, Linc., out of a ducal coronet, in hand a dagger, in pale, blade, wavy. *Pl.* 65, *cr.* 10.

BURNMAN, Devons., a bull's head, erased, or, horned, gobony, or and sa. *Pl.* 19, *cr.* 3.

BURNS, Sco., two hands issuing from clouds, conjoined in fess, ppr., holding up a laurel-branch, vert. *Pl.* 102, *cr.* 2, (laurel, *pl.* 21, *cr.* 2.)

BURNS, Sco. and Eng., a dove, wings expanded, az. *Pl.* 27, *cr.* 5.

BURNSIDE, Sco., a crescent, ar. *Gradatim plena. Pl.* 18, *cr.* 14.

BURNSIDE, Eng., a branch of oak, ppr. *Pl.* 32, *cr.* 13.

BURR, Eng., a lion's head, ppr., collared, or. *Pl.* 42, *cr.* 14.

BURRARD, Bart., Hants., out of a mural coronet, per pale, or and ar., an arm, embowed, hand grasping a sword, (about arm a wreath of laurel, all ppr.) *Pl.* 115, *cr.* 14.

BURRARD, Isle of Wight, out of a mural coronet, or, a cubit arm, erect, ppr., (charged with a cross pattée, gu.,) in hand a trident, in bend sinister, point downward, gold. *Pl.* 93, *cr.* 1, (coronet, *pl.* 115, *cr.* 14.)

BURRARD, Hants., a dexter arm, embowed, hand grasping a sword, ppr. *Pl.* 34, *cr.* 7.

BURRELL, Baron Gwydyr, and a Bart.: 1. A naked arm, embowed, in hand a (branch) of laurel, all ppr. *Pl.* 118, *cr.* 4. 2. On a ducal coronet, a talbot, passant. *Animus non afficit æquus. Pl.* 3, *cr.* 8.

BURRELL, BOREEL, BURELL, or BEREEL, Kent and Suss., an arm, embowed, ppr., in hand a branch of laurel, vert. *Pl.* 118, *cr.* 4.

BURRELL, Earl Willoughby D'Eresby. *See* WILLOUGHBY.

BURRELL, Bart., Ess. and Suss., a naked arm, embowed, in hand a branch of laurel, both ppr. *Sub libertate quietem. Pl.* 118, *cr.* 4.

BURRIDGE, Devons., a demi-mariner, ppr., waistcoat, gu., cap, az., neckerchief, ar., supporting a rudder, sa.

BURRISH, out of a tower, per pale, ar. and gu., a demi-lion, rampant. *Pl.* 42, *cr.* 4.

BURROUGH, or BOROUGH, Linc., an eagle, wings expanded, erm. *Pl.* 126, *cr.* 7.

BURROUGHS, Bart., Iri., on an Eastern crown, or, a lion, passant, gu. *Audaces fortuna juvat. Pl.* 48, *cr.* 8, (crown, *pl.* 128, *fig.* 3.)

BURROUGHS, Norf., a griffin's head, erased, charged (with two chevronels, vert.) *Pl.* 48, *cr.* 6.

BURROW, Sco. and Eng., a lion, passant, gardant, ar. *Deus nobis hæc otia fecit. Pl.* 120, *cr.* 5.

BURROW, a falcon, erm., wings expanded. *Pl.* 105, *cr.* 4.

BURROWES, and BURROWS, a lion, sejant, ar., (ducally crowned, or.) *Pl.* 126, *cr.* 15.

BURROWES, and BURROWS, an eagle, wings displayed, erm., (ducally gorged, or.) *Pl.* 126, *cr.* 7.

BURROWES, and BURROWS, Eng., an ostrich-feather, enfiled with a ducal coronet. *Pl.* 8, *cr.* 9.

BURROWES, and BURROWS, Eng., two wings, addorsed, erm. *Pl.* 63, *cr.* 12.
BURROWES, and BURROWS, Iri., a stag, passant. *Pl.* 68, *cr.* 2.
BURRS, Eng., a demi-antelope, collared. *Pl.* 34, *cr.* 8.
BURRY, a fox's head, couped, ppr. *Pl.* 91, *cr.* 9.
BURSLAM, or BURSLEM, a pestle and mortar. *Pl.* 83, *cr.* 6.
BURSTED, Eng., a wyvern, gu. *Pl.* 63, *cr.* 13.
BURT, or BURTT, Eng., a demi-leopard, gardant, supporting an anchor, ppr. *Pl.* 77, *cr.* 1.
BURT, a bugle-horn, sa., stringed, gu. *Pl.* 48, *cr.* 12.
BURT, Sco., a stag, ppr. *Pl.* 81, *cr.* 8.
BURTHOGGE, Devons., a demi-wolf, or, gorged with a bar-gemelle, az. *Pl.* 56, *cr.* 8, (without spear.)
BURTON, ROBERT, Esq., of Longner Hall, Salop, a dexter gauntlet, ppr., couped at wrist. *Dominus providebit*, *Pl.* 15, *cr.* 15.
BURTON, Sir CHARLES, Bart, Iri., on a ducal coronet, a dexter gauntlet, palm inward, all ppr. *Deus providebit.*
BURTON, Staffs. and Warw., out of a ducal coronet, or, a tree, vert. *Pl.* 94, *cr.* 5.
BURTON, Bart., Leic., an owl, ar., (crowned, or.) *Pl.* 27, *cr.* 9.
BURTON, Yorks. and Salop, a gauntlet, ar. *Pl.* 61, *cr.* 11.
BURTON, Derbs., (on a mount, vert,) a tower, ar., triple-towered, or. *Pl.* 123, *cr.* 14.
BURTON, Derbs., a tower, triple-towered, ar. *Pl.* 123, *cr.* 14.
BURTON, Ess. and Suss., over a castle in (ruins,) ar., a falcon, volant, or. *Pl.* 94, *cr.* 1, (castle, *pl.* 37, *cr.* 1.)
BURTON, Salop, out of a ducal coronet, or, a sinister gauntlet, erect, ppr., charged with a lozenge, gu. *Deus providebit.*
BURTON, Yorks., an arm, couped and erect, vested, per pale, ar. and gu., cuffed, of the first, in hand, ppr., a walking staff, of the second, headed, rimmed, and veruled, or. *Pl.* 18, *cr.* 1.
BURTON, Lond., a boar's head, erased, in fess, or, (in mouth a laurel-branch, vert.) *Pl.* 125, *cr.* 7.
BURTON, Leic. and Warw., (on a mount, vert,) a beacon, ar., fired, ppr., ladder, or. *Pl.* 88, *cr.* 6.
BURTON, Lond., on a ducal coronet, or, a wyvern, vert. *Pl.* 104, *cr.* 11.
BURTON, an esquire's helmet, ppr. *Timet pudorem.* *Pl.* 109, *cr.* 5.
BURTON, Derbs., on a ducal coronet, or, a wyvern, wings addorsed, az., collared, gold. *Pl.* 104, *cr.* 11.
BURTON, Sco., a beacon, fired, ppr. *Pl.* 89, *cr.* 9.
BURTON, an owl, az., (ducally crowned, or.) *Pl.* 27, *cr.* 9.
BURTON, a boar's head, couped, erect. (Another, erased.) *Pl.* 21, *cr.* 7.
BURTON, Logner Hall, Salop: 1. For *Burton*, out of a ducal coronet, or, a sinister gauntlet, erect, ppr., charged with a lozenge, gu. 2. For *Ligen*, five leeks, erect, ppr., encircled with a ducal coronet, or. *Dominus providebit.*

BURTON, an owl, ar. *Pl.* 1, *cr.* 8.
BURTZ, a squirrel, sejant, resting fore-paws on a staff, raguly. *Pl.* 85, *cr.* 3, (staff, *pl.* 103, *cr.* 12.)
BURWASCH, BURWASCHE, or BURWASH, Eng., the helm of a ship, ppr. *Pl.* 60, *cr.* 10.
BURWELL, a Saracen's head, couped at shoulders, ppr. *Pl.* 19, *cr.* 1.
BURWELL, Suff., in lion's gamb, erect and erased, or, (three bur-leaves, vert.) *Pl.* 126, *cr.* 9.
BURWOOD, a boar's head, ppr. *Pl.* 2, *cr.* 7.
BURY, Linc. and Somers., a demi-dragon, ar., wings, ears, and claws, sa. *Pl.* 82, *cr.* 10.
BURY, CHARLES-WILLIAM, Earl of, and Viscount Charleville, and Baron Tullimore, Iri., a boar's head, couped, transpierced through mouth with an arrow, ppr. *Virtus sub cruce crescit.* *Pl.* 8, *cr.* 14.
BURY, Viscount. See ALBEMARLE.
BURY. See BERRY.
BURY, Devons., a griffin's head, erased, party per pale, or and gu. *Pl.* 48, *cr.* 6.
BURY, Devons., a tiger's head, erased, erm., crined, sa., gorged with a collar, az., charged with a bezant, between two fleur-de-lis, or. *Pl.* 86, *cr.* 13.
BURYE, Eng., a dove, regardant, in mouth an olive-branch, ppr. *Pl.* 77, *cr.* 2.
BUSBIE, a bee, erect, (head downward,) wings expanded, ppr. *Pl.* 100, *cr.* 3.
BUSBRIDGE, Ess., an arm, in mail, erect, in hand a cutlass, ppr. *Pl.* 81, *cr.* 11.
BUSBY, and BUSHBY, a stag's head, ar., erased, gu., (pierced through back of neck with an arrow, sa., headed and barbed, of the first.) *Pl.* 66, *cr.* 9.
BUSFIELD, Yorks., an arm, in armour, erect, ppr., in hand a fleur-de-lis, ar. *Medio tutissimus ibis.* *Pl.* 24, *cr.* 14.
BUSFIELD, Yorks., an eagle's head, erased. *Pl.* 20, *cr.* 7.
BUSH, BUSHE, or BUSSCHE, Eng., trunk of tree, with branches, ppr., pendent an escutcheon, ar. *Pl.* 23, *cr.* 6.
BUSH, a goat's head, erased, ar., armed, or. *Pl.* 29, *cr.* 13.
BUSH, a stag, statant. *Pl.* 81, *cr.* 8.
BUSHBY, Suss. and Cumb., a crow, picking, ppr. *Pl.* 51, *cr.* 8.
BUSHE, Wilts., a goat's head, ar., attired, sa., (charged on neck with a crescent.) *Pl.* 105, *cr.* 14.
BUSHE, and BUSSE, Linc., a dragon, sans legs and wings, paly-wavy of ten, ar. and sa.
BUSHE, GERVASE-PARKER, Esq., of Glencairn Abbey, co. Waterford, a goat's head, ar. *Moderata durant.* *Pl.* 105, *cr.* 14.
BUSHE, Iri., a cross pattée, fitched, ar., between two ears of wheat, in orle. *Pl.* 23, *cr.* 14, (cross, *pl.* 27, *cr.* 14.)
BUSHELL, Warw., an arm, from elbow, in armour, in hand a caltrap. *Pl.* 22, *cr.* 4.
BUSHELL, or BUSSHELL, Chesh., a cherub's head, ppr. *Pl.* 126, *cr.* 10.
BUSHMAN, and BUSHNAN, Lond., (a sinister arm,) embowed, vested, sa., cuffed, ar., in hand a roll of paper, ppr. *Pl.* 39, *cr.* 1, (roll, *pl.* 27, *cr.* 4.)
BUSHNELL, Eng., on a ducal coronet, or, a wyvern, sans foot. *Pl.* 104, *cr.* 11.

BUSHRUDD, Dors., a tiger's head, ar., crined and tufted, sa., collared, gu. *Pl.* 86, *cr.* 13.
BUSHY, or BUSHEY, Eng., a boar's head, erased, sa. *Pl.* 16, *cr.* 11.
BUSK, EDWARD-THOMAS, Esq., of Ford's Grove, Middx., a stag, at gaze, ppr. *Suaviter sed fortiter. Pl.* 81, *cr.* 8.
BUSK, and BUSKE, Eng., out of a ducal coronet, or, a fish's head, az. *Pl.* 36, *cr.* 13.
BUSSELL, Warw., a cherub's head, between wings, ppr. *Pl.* 126, *cr.* 10.
BUSSELL, issuing from clouds, two dexter hands, conjoined, holding up an olive-branch, all ppr. *Pl.* 102, *cr.* 2.
BUSSELL, Eng., a crane's head, erased, ar. *Pl.* 20, *cr.* 9.
BUSSEY, Linc. and Camb., a sea-dragon, (sans wings and legs,) tail coiled and terminating in a second head, all barry, ar. and sa. *Pl.* 109, *cr.* 13.
BUSSIE, Eng., an eagle, displayed, az. *Pl.* 48, *cr.* 11.
BUSTARD, Devons., a bustard's head, ar., between wings, gu., between neck and wings, two ears of wheat, erect, or.
BUSTEED, Eng., an eagle, rising, ppr. *Pl.* 67, *cr.* 4.
BUSTERD, Iri., a cannon, mounted, ppr. *Pl.* 111, *cr.* 3.
BUSTIN, Eng., an escallop, between two branches of palm, ppr. *Pl.* 86, *cr.* 9.
BUSVARGUS, or BOSVARGUS, Cornw., a Cornish chough, ppr. *Pl.* 100, *cr.* 13.
BUSWELL, Northamp., out of a wood, vert, a bull, passant, ar. *Pl.* 66, *cr.* 11.
BUTCHER, Eng., a lion, passant, gu., in dexter a crescent, ar. *Pl.* 77, *cr.* 3.
BUTCHER, an oak-slip, acorned, ppr. *Pl.* 32, *cr.* 13.
BUTE, Marquess of, Earl of Windsor, &c., Eng.; Earl of Dumfries, of Bute, &c., Sco., (Crichton-Stuart): 1. For *Stuart,* a demi-lion, rampant, gu. *Nobilis ira. Pl.* 67, *cr.* 10. 2. For *Crichton,* a wyvern, wings elevated and addorsed, fire issuant from mouth, all ppr. *Avito viret honore. Pl.* 51, *cr.* 2.
BUTHALL, a wyvern, ppr., (charged on breast with a hand, couped at wrist, gu.) *Pl.* 63, *cr.* 13.
BUTLER, Earl of Carrick. *See* CARRICK.
BUTLER, Earl of Lanesborough. *See* LANESBOROUGH.
BUTLER, Marquess of Ormonde. *See* ORMONDE.
BUTLER, Earl of Kilkenny. *See* KILKENNY.
BUTLER, Earl of Glengall. *See* GLENGALL.
BUTLER, Iri., on a plume of feathers, or and vert, an eagle, rising, ar. *Comme je trouve. Pl.* 54, *cr.* 8.
BUTLER, Iri., (on a row of five leaves, vert,) a demi-eagle, displayed. *Pl.* 22, *cr.* 11.
BUTLER, or BOTELER, Kent and Lincoln's Inn, two eagles, wings addorsed, ar., supporting a vine, fructed, ppr.
BUTLER, a covered cup, or, banded, sa., and a ball on the top, of the second. *Pl.* 75, *cr.* 13, (without swords.)
BUTLER, two arms, in armour, embowed, ppr., purfled, or, in hand, ppr., a round buckle, gold. *Pl.* 6, *cr.* 8, (buckle, *pl.* 73, *cr.* 10.)
BUTLER, out of a ducal coronet, five ostrich-feathers, therefrom a demi-eagle, rising. *Pl.* 100, *cr.* 12, (eagle, *pl.* 52, *cr.* 8.)

BUTLER, Derbs., an arm, embowed, vested, az., cuffed, ar., in hand a bunch of grapes, ppr. *Pl.* 39, *cr.* 1, (grapes, *pl.* 37, *cr.* 4.)
BUTLER, Lanc., a unicorn, (salient,) ar., armed, or, gorged with a sash, gold. *Pl.* 37, *cr.* 7.
BUTLER, or BOTELER, Kent, a covered cup, or, between wings, dexter, gold, sinister, az.
BUTLER, Lond., a boar's head, per pale, gu. and az., guttée, counterchanged. *Pl.* 2, *cr.* 7.
BUTLER, Devons., in lion's gamb, erased, gu., a (covered) cup, or. *Pl.* 30, *cr.* 4.
BUTLER, Marquess of Ormondy. *See* ORMONDY.
BUTLER, Baron Dunboyne. *See* DUNBOYNE.
BUTLER, GARRET, Viscount Galmoye, Iri., a falcon, rising out of a plume of feathers, ar. *Comme je trouve. Pl.* 54, *cr.* 8, (falcon, *pl.* 103, *cr.* 6.)
BUTLER, Iri., from a plume of ostrich-feathers, an eagle, rising, ar. *Comme je trouve. Pl.* 54, *cr.* 8.
BUTLER, Middx., a greyhound, sejant, or, (collared, gu., ringed, gold.) *Pl.* 66, *cr.* 15.
BUTLER, Cotes, Linc., a horse's head, erased, quarterly, ar. and sa. *Pl.* 46, *cr.* 4.
BUTLER, Lond., an eagle, wings addorsed, in dexter, a vine-branch, all ppr. *Pl.* 61, *cr.* 1, (branch, *pl.* 89, *cr.* 1.)
BUTLER, an arm, in armour, embowed, in gauntlet, a sword, all ppr. *Pl.* 2, *cr.* 8.
BUTLER, a ram, statant, ar., armed and hoofed, or, (collared, gu., with a bell to collar, of the second.) *Pl.* 109, *cr.* 2.
BUTLER, an arm, embowed, vested, az., ruffle of indented lace, ar., in hand, ppr., a covered cup, erect. *Pl.* 39, *cr.* 1.
BUTLER, Chesh., Lanc., Durh., and Northumb., a horse, passant, ar., pellettée, and bridled, sa. *Pl.* 99, *cr.* 11.
BUTLER, Lond., Durh., and Sco., a covered cup, or. *Sapienter uti bonis. Pl.* 75, *cr.* 13, (without swords.)
BUTLER, Sco., an uncovered cup, or. *Sapienter uti bonis. Pl.* 42, *cr.* 1.
BUTLER, Beds., out of a mural coronet, a boar's head and neck, ar. *Pl.* 2, *cr.* 7, (coronet, *pl.* 128, *fig.* 18.)
BUTLER, or BOTTELER, Cambs., a cockatrice's head and wings, head, vert, wings, ar., ducally gorged, combed and wattled, or. *Pl.* 106, *cr.* 15.
BUTLER, Herts., a dexter arm, in armour, gauntleted, az., garnished, or, in hand a sword, sa., hilted, of the second. *Pl.* 2, *cr.* 8.
BUTLER-DANVERS, Leic.: 1. For *Danvers,* a wyvern, or. *Pl.* 63, *cr.* 13. 2. For *Butler,* a demi-cockatrice, couped, vert, combed, beaked, wattled, and ducally gorged, or. *Liberté toute entiére. Pl.* 106, *cr.* 15.
BUTLER, EDMUND, Earl of Kilkenny. *See* KILKENNY.
BUTT, Lond. and Kent, a lion, sejant, in dexter a broken spear. *Pl.* 60, *cr.* 4.
BUTTER, Eng., a camel's head, couped, ppr. *Pl.* 109, *cr.* 9.
BUTTERFIELD, Hants., out of a ducal coronet, or, a dragon's head, wings elevated, vert. *Pl.* 59, *cr.* 14.
BUTTERFIELD, Surr., out of a ducal coronet, or, a demi-dragon, wings elevated, ar., (on each wing a butterfly, volant, az.) *Pl.* 59, *cr.* 14.

BUTTERS, Sco., two naked arms, issuing, shooting an arrow from a bow, ppr. *Pl.* 100, *cr.* 4.

BUTTERWORTH, Sco., a hand, issuing from a cloud, in fess, pointing to a serpent, nowed, head erect, ppr. *Pl.* 19, *cr.* 11.

BUTTERWORTH, Eng., a sphere, resting on a cloud, ppr. *Pl.* 110, *cr.* 9.

BUTTERWORTH, an eagle, wings elevated, erminois, supporting with dexter an escutcheon, az., (charged with a cross crosslet, or.) *Pl.* 61, *cr.* 1, (escutcheon, *pl.* 103, *cr.* 5.)

BUTTERY, Northamp., a tiger, passant, ar., tufted and maned, or, (supporting with dexter an escutcheon.) *Pl.* 67, *cr.* 15.

BUTTLER, an uncovered cup, or. *Pl.* 42, *cr.* 1.

BUTTON, Herts., a branch of cotton-tree, fructed, all ppr.

BUTTON, a ram, (statant, ar., armed and hoofed, or, collared, gu., pendent thereto, a bell, gold.) *Pl.* 109, *cr.* 2.

BUTTON, a ram (statant,) ar., armed and hoofed, or. *Pl.* 109, *cr.* 2.

BUTTON, Wilts., a wyvern, sa. *Pl.* 63, *cr.* 13.

BUTTON, or BUDDEN, Eng., a bull's head, ppr., charged with a cross botonée, or. *Pl.* 120, *cr.* 7, (cross, *pl.* 141.)

BUTTON, Wilts., on each side of a chapeau, gu., turned up, erm., a horn, or.

BUTTS, Suff., a horse's head, caparisoned, all ppr., from top of head, issuant, (two) feathers, dexter, or, sinister, sa. *Pl.* 55, *cr.* 7.

BUTTS, Norf., a horse's head, ar., armed and bridled, or, on head a plume of three feathers, of the first and gold. *Pl.* 55, *cr.* 7.

BUTTS, DE, Eng., a ferret, passant, ppr. *Pl.* 119, *cr.* 15.

BUTTS, Norf., a horse's head, the mane and sorrel plaited, ar. and or., on head a skull-plate, az., and two feathers, gold, and of the third. *Pl.* 55, *cr.* 7.

BUTTS, Surr., an arm, couped at elbow, and erect, ppr., in hand a fish, ar. *Pl.* 105, *cr.* 9.

BUXTON, a stag's head, ppr. *Pl.* 91, *cr.* 14.

BUXTON, Bart., Norf., a buck's head, couped, gu., attired, or. *Pl.* 91, *cr.* 14.

BUXTON, a demi-doe, ppr.

BUXTON, Norf. and Derbs., a pelican, or, wings expanded, vulning, gu. *Pl.* 109, *cr.* 15.

BUXTON, a stag's head, cabossed. *Pl.* 36, *cr.* 1.

BY, Suss., a demi-lion, or, in dexter a fleur-de-lis, ppr. *Pl.* 91, *cr.* 13.

BY, and BYE, Eng., two oak-branches, in saltier. *Pl.* 19, *cr.* 12.

BYAM, Suss. and Somers.: 1. A wolf, passant, or, collared and lined, vert. *Pl.* 5, *cr.* 8, (without staff.) 2. A dragon's head, erased, ppr., in mouth a sinister hand, couped, gu., dropping blood. *Pl.* 106, *cr.* 13.

BY-DE, Herts., an arm, erect, ppr., vested, az., cuffed, ar., in hand an anchor, sa., fluke, or. *Pl.* 53, *cr.* 13.

BY-DE, a demi-griffin, az., armed and winged, or, holding a garb, gold. *Pl.* 18, *cr.* 6, (garb, *pl.* 48, *cr.* 10.)

BYDEWELL, or BIDWELL, Eng., in hand, couped at wrist, in fess, a curling-stone. *Pl.* 104, *cr.* 6.

BYEING, Eng., an angel, (pointing upward,) ppr. *Pl.* 25, *cr.* 7.

BYER, and BYERS, Northamp., a griffin's head, party per pale, gu. and az., charged with a pheon, ar. *Pl.* 38, *cr.* 3, (pheon, *pl.* 141.)

BYERLEY, Midridge, Grange, Durham, on an esquire's helmet, a cross crosslet. *Pl.* 109, *cr.* 5, (cross, *pl.* 141.)

BYERLY, BYERLEY, and BYORLEY, Lond. and Yorks., two lions' gambs, ppr., holding a cross crosslet, or. *Pl.* 106, *cr.* 12.

BYERS, Sco., a cock, regardant, ppr. *Marte suo tutus.* *Pl.* 19, *cr.* 10.

BYFELD, or BYFIELD, Lond., a cross crosslet, fitched, sa., between two palm-branches, vert. *Pl.* 37, *cr.* 14, (palm, *pl.* 87, *cr.* 8.)

BYFIELD, on a man's head, affrontée, a chapeau, ppr. *Pl.* 38, *cr.* 13.

BYFIELD, Lond., an antelope, passant, ppr. *Pl.* 63, *cr.* 10.

BYFLEET, Cambs., a Saracen's head, (affrontée, ppr.,) wreathed with a ribbon, ar., tied in a bow-knot, *Pl.* 23, *cr.* 3.

BYFORD, and BYFFORD, Heref., in lion's gamb, erect, or, an eagle's leg, erased at thigh, sa. *Pl.* 89, *cr.* 13.

BYFORD, or BAYFORD, Eng., an owl, ar. *Pl.* 27, *cr.* 9.

BYGAN, Yorks, an ermine, ppr. *Pl.* 9, *cr.* 5.

BYGBERY, Devons., in hand a leg, in armour, couped above knee, and spurred, ppr. *Pl.* 39, *cr.* 6.

BYGOD, or BYGODE, Yorks., on a chapeau, ar., turned up, gu., charged with two bars, az., a dolphin devouring the cap, or.

BYGOT, Eng., seven arrows, or, one in pale, and six in saltier. *Pl.* 110, *cr.* 11.

BYIRLEY, Eng., in lion's gamb, a human heart, all ppr. *Pl.* 23, *cr.* 13.

BYKENOR, and BICKNOR, Kent, an antelope's head, gu., armed, ar., (collared, or.) *Pl.* 24, *cr.* 7.

BYKENOR, Eng., a pheon, erm. *Pl.* 26, *cr.* 12.

BYLES, out of a ducal coronet, or, a lion's head, per bend, embattled, ar. and gu. *Pl.* 90, *cr.* 9.

BYLNEY, Norf., out of a tower, a demi-griffin, sa. *Pl.* 68, *cr.* 11.

BYNE, Eng., a hind, regardant, or, resting foot on a ball, sa. *Pl.* 106, *cr.* 10.

BYNE, Eng., a hind, regardant, or, collared, gu., resting dexter on a ball, sa. *Pl.* 106, *cr.* 10.

BYNG, Viscount Torrington. *See* TORRINGTON.

BYNG, Middx., an heraldic antelope, statant, erm., horned, tusked, maned, and hoofed, or. *Tuebor.* *Pl.* 115, *cr.* 13.

BYNGHAM, in hand, ppr., three branches of cinquefoil, gu., leaved, vert, and charged on sleeve, sa., with a cross, ar. *Pl.* 101, *cr.* 5.

BYNGLEY, or BYNLEY, a harp, or. *Pl.* 104, *cr.* 15.

BYRCH, Ess., on a mount, a birch-tree, ppr. *Pl.* 50, *cr.* 3, (without bells.)

BYRCH, Beds., a hare, current, sa., collared, or.

BYRCH, Kent and Suss., an eagle, rising, ppr., in dexter a banner, az., charged with a cross clechée, or, staff, point, and tassels, of the same. *Pl.* 65, *cr.* 3.

BYRCH, Ess., a squirrel, sejant, bendy-wavy of six, or and az., (eating an apple, in sinister a branch of birch, vert.) *Pl.* 2, *cr.* 4.

BYRCHE, Ess., a squirrel, sejant, bendy-wavy of six, or and az., holding a branch of birch, vert. *Pl.* 2, *cr.* 4.

BYRCHETT, a tiger, vert, gorged with a ducal coronet, or. *Pl.* 67, *cr.* 15.

BYRDALL, a stag's head, erased, ppr. *Pl.* 66, *cr.* 9.
BYRDE, Kent, a stag's head, cabossed, ar., between attires a bird, or. *Pl.* 58, *cr.* 13.
BYRDE, Linc., a demi-lion, sa., guttée-de-sang. *Pl.* 67, *cr.* 10.
BYRDE, on a dolphin, embowed, ppr., an eagle, wings addorsed, or. *Pl.* 48, *cr.* 9, (eagle, *pl.* 114, *cr.* 13.)
BYRES, of Coates, a bee, volant, or. *Rule be ours. Pl.* 100, *cr.* 3.
BYRES, Sco., a Catherine wheel. *Pl.* 1, *cr.* 7.
BYRMYNCHAM, a cap, per pale, indented, ar. and sa., between wings, expanded, or.
BYRN, Iri. and Eng., a mermaid, ppr. *Pl.* 48, *cr.* 5.
BYRNE, Iri., a mermaid, ppr., (charged with escallops, or, in dexter a mirror, in sinister a dart.) *Pl.* 48, *cr.* 5.
BYRNE, and BYRN, Eng., in hand, issuing from a cloud, in pale, a garb. *Pl.* 43, *cr.* 4.
BYRNE, GEORGIANA-MARY, of Cabineteely, co. Dublin, a mermaid, in dexter a mirror, in sinister a comb, all ppr. *Certavi et vici. Pl.* 48, *cr.* 5.

BYROM, Eng., out of a ducal coronet, or, a tree, vert. *Pl.* 94, *cr.* 5.
BYRON of Rochdale, Lanc., a mermaid, with comb and mirror, ppr. *Crede Byron. Pl.* 48, *cr.* 5.
BYRON, Herts. and Surr., a mermaid, ppr., in dexter an escutcheon, suspended by a ribbon, az., in sinister a mirror. *Pl.* 88, *cr.* 12.
BYRTWHYSELL, Lanc., a dolphin, ppr. *Pl.* 48, *cr.* 9.
BYSHE, Eng., on a chapeau, gu., turned up, erm., a demi-lion, or. *Pl.* 46, *cr.* 8.
BYSHE, Eng., a mule, passant, ar.
BYSSE, on a mount, vert, two snakes interwoven and erect, respecting each other, or.
BYSTLEY, a cross pattée, gu., between wings, or. *Pl.* 29, *cr.* 14.
BYTHESEA, Kent, an eagle, displayed, ppr. *Pl.* 48, *cr.* 11.
BYTHESEA, Kent and Sco., out of a mural coronet, ar., masoned, sa., a griffin's head, ducally gorged, ppr. *Pl.* 101, *cr.* 6.
BYWATER, Eng., out of a ducal coronet, in hand, in armour, a scimitar, ppr. *Pl.* 15, *cr.* 5.

C

CABELL, Eng., a square padlock, or. *Pl.* 18, *cr.* 7.
CABOURNE, and CABRONE, Linc., out of a ducal coronet, or, a lozenge, ar., charged with a martlet, sa. *Pl.* 76, *cr.* 14.
CABYTOTT, Norf., a greyhound, current, az., collared and ringed, or. *Pl.* 28, *cr.* 7, (without charge.)
CACHER, Lond., out of a ducal coronet, or, a demi-leopard, ar., spotted and collared, gold. *Pl.* 12, *cr.* 14, (coronet, *pl.* 128, *fig.* 3.)
CADDEL, Sco., a tower, gu., windows and doors, or. *Pl.* 12, *cr.* 5.
CADDELL, and CADELL, Sco., a stag's head, ppr. *Vigilantiá non cadet. Pl.* 91, *cr.* 14.
CADDEY, (a pile,) charged with a cross pattée, fitched, or. *Pl.* 27, *cr.* 14.
CADDON, an arm, in armour, embowed, in hand an arrow, in pale, surmounted by a bow, stringed, in fess, cord crossing in saltier over arrow. *Pl.* 76, *cr.* 10.
CADDY, Eng., a cross crosslet, vert. *Pl.* 66, *cr.* 8.
CADE, Kent, a demi-cockatrice, winged, gu., combed, or. *Pl.* 106, *cr.* 15.
CADE, Derbs., a demi-lion, rampant, gu. *Pl.* 67, *cr.* 10.
CADE, Derbs. and Ess., a demi-lion, gu., in dexter a fleur-de-lis, charged with a bezant, or. *Pl.* 91, *cr.* 13, (bezant, *pl.* 141.)
CADICOTT, in dexter hand, per fess, gu. and ar., a battle-axe, ppr. *Pl.* 73, *cr.* 7.
CADICOTT, a demi-ape, ppr. *Pl.* 24, *cr.* 12, (without coronet.)
CADIMAN, Lond., and Norf., a rock, ppr., surmounted by a fleur-de-lis, or. *Pl.* 76, *cr.* 12.
CADMAN, a stork's head, royally crowned, ppr. *Pl.* 49, *cr.* 9.

CADOGAN, Earl, and Baron, Viscount Chelsea, and Baron Oakley, (Cadogan,) out of a ducal coronet, or, a dragon's head, vert. *Qui invidet minor est. Pl.* 59, *cr.* 14.
CADURCIS, a griffin's head, erased, gu., in beak a trefoil, vert, gorged with a ducal coronet, or. *Pl.* 42, *cr.* 9, (trefoil, *pl.* 141.)
CADWOODLEY, Eng., an antelope, passant, per pale, gu. and or, armed, of the last. *Pl.* 63, *cr.* 10.
CADYE, and KADYE, Glouc., on a mount, vert, a cockatrice, ar., combed and wattled, gu., ducally gorged and chained, or. *Pl.* 72, *cr.* 5.
CÆSAR, Hunts., a cross-pattée, per pale, or and gu. *Pl.* 15, *cr.* 8.
CAGE, Kent, a stag, passant, erm., attired, or, charged on shoulder with an annulet, gu. *Pl.* 15, *cr.* 7.
CAHAN, and CAHANE, Iri., an arm, embowed, in hand a sword, ppr. *Pl.* 34, *cr.* 7.
CAHILL, Iri. and Eng., in lion's paw a scimitar, ppr. *Pl.* 18, *cr.* 8.
CAHILL, and CAHIL, Iri., a demi-bull, rampant, sa., gorged with a chaplet, vert. *Pl.* 73, *cr.* 8.
CAHN, and CAHUN, Sco., a stag's head, erased. *Si je puis. Pl.* 66, *cr.* 9.
CAHURTA, a stag, erm., attired, or. *Pl.* 68, *cr.* 2.
CAIN, and CAINE, a demi-antelope, per fess, ar. and az., collared and armed, or. *Pl.* 34, *cr.* 8.
CAIRD, a demi-friar, in hand a staff, ppr. *Pl.* 72, *cr.* 8.
CAIRLEON, Eng., a cross moline, lozenge-pierced, erm. *Pl.* 91, *cr.* 10.
CAIRNCROSS, Sco., a dagger, in pale. *Certamine parata. Pl.* 73, *cr.* 9.
CAIRNE, Sco., in hand a fish, ppr. *Pl.* 105, *cr.* 9.

CAIRNES, Sco., a fleur-de-lis. *Effloresco.* Pl. 68, cr. 12.
CAIRNES, Sco., a cinquefoil, ppr. *Effloresco.* Pl. 91, cr. 12.
CAIRNES, on a tower, a martlet, statant, ppr. Pl. 107, cr. 6.
CAIRNIE, Sco., a ship under sail, ppr. Pl. 109, cr. 8.
CAIRNIE, on a cinquefoil, vert, a martin, statant, sa. *Ad alta.* Pl. 91, cr. 12, (martin, pl. 111, cr. 5.)
CAIRNS, Sco., a bell, az. *Sub spe.* Pl. 73, cr. 15.
CAIRNS, Sco., a palm-tree, ppr. *Virtus ad æthera tendit.* Pl. 18, cr. 12.
CAIRNS of Pilmor, a cinquefoil, ppr. *Effloresco.* Pl. 91, cr. 12.
CAIRNS, Sco., a stag's head, erased, ppr., between attires, a cross crosslet, fitched. *Semper fidelis.* Pl. 24, cr. 9.
CAITHNESS, Earl. of, (Sinclair,) a cock, ppr. *Commit thy work to God.* Pl. 67, cr. 14.
CALAMY, a hedgehog, ppr. Pl. 32, cr. 9.
CALAMOUNT, Eng., an antelope's head, erased, erm., armed, ar. Pl. 24, cr. 7.
CALANDRINE, Eng., a demi-eagle, displayed, ar., in beak a scroll. *Sursum.* Pl. 27, cr. 7.
CALCOTT-BERKELEY, GEORGE, Esq., of Caynham Court, Salop: 1. A demi-lion, or, between paws a crescent. Pl. 47, cr. 4, (crescent, pl. 141.) 2. A bear's head, couped, ar., muzzled, gu. *Dieu avec nous.* Pl. 111, cr. 4.
CALCRAFT, Lond., Kent, and Dors., a greyhound, current, sa., (collared and ringed, ar., on body a pellet, wavy, or.) Pl. 28, cr. 7.
CALCRAFT, Lond., Kent, and Lincoln, a greyhound, current, sa., charged with a cross crosslet, or. Pl. 28, cr. 7.
CALCRAFT, on a chapeau, a greyhound, current. Pl. 47, cr. 2.
CALDECOT, HENRY, Esq., of Holton Hall, Lincoln, a martlet. Pl. 111, cr. 5.
CALDECOT, Oxon., a demi-tiger, or, tufted, maned, and (attired with two straight horns.) Pl. 53, cr. 10.
CALDECOT, Chesh., an ostrich, ppr. Pl. 16, cr. 2.
CALDECOTT, Chesh., a demi-lion, rampant, or, charged with a cinquefoil, gu. Pl. 67, cr. 10, (cinquefoil, pl. 141.)
CALDECOTT, Warw., Leic., and Ruts., a demi-lion, rampant, gu., charged on shoulder with a cinquefoil, ar. Pl. 67, cr. 10.
CALDER, a stag's head, cabossed, ppr. Pl. 36, 12, cr. 1.
CALDER, Eng., within a serpent, disposed in orle, a boar's head, erased and erect. Pl. 12, cr. 6.
CALDER of Lynegar, a stag's head, cabossed, ppr. *Vigilans non cadit.* Pl. 36, cr. 1.
CALDER, a swan, ppr., crowned, or. *Be mindful.* Pl. 33, cr. 7.
CALDER, Bart., Sco., a swan, swimming in a loch, bordered with flags, ppr. *Vigilans non cadet.* Pl. 66, cr. 10.
CALDER, in water, a duck, swimming, ppr. Pl. 47, cr. 1.
CALDERWOOD of Pittedy, in dexter hand a palm-branch, ppr. *Veritas premitur non opprimitur.* Pl. 23, cr. 7.

CALDERWOOD of Polton, a phœnix, in flames ppr. *Virtus sibi præmium.* Pl. 44, cr. 8.
CALDERWOOD, Sco., a bee-hive, ppr., with bees, volant. Pl. 81, cr. 14.
CALDERWOOD, Sco., a dove, in mouth a (palm)-branch, ppr. *Spero.* Pl. 48, cr. 15.
CALDMORE, a demi-Turk, vested, in dexter a staff, headed with a crescent. Pl. 72, cr. 8.
CALDRON, Eng., in dexter hand a palm-branch, slipped, ppr. Pl. 23, cr. 7.
CALDWELL, Staffs., Lond., and Worc., a cock's head, between wings, expanded, ar., combed and wattled, gu., in beak a cross formée, fitched, or. Pl. 47, cr. 3.
CALDWELL, Bart., Iri., out of a ducal coronet, a sceptre, or, entwined with two serpents, vert, between wings, ppr. Pl. 27, cr. 8.
CALDWELL, Sco., a fountain, throwing up water, ppr. Pl. 49, cr. 8.
CALDWELL, a demi-lion, grasping a (broken scimitar.) Pl. 41, cr. 13.
CALDWELL, Norf., a demi-cock, rising. Pl. 72, cr. 4.
CALDWELL, a cock's head, winged, sa., crested, gu., in beak a cross pattée, fitched, or. Pl. 47, cr. 3.
CALDWELL, a cockatrice's head, couped, between wings, ppr., in beak a cross pattée, fitched. Pl. 47, cr. 3, (cockatrice, pl. 106, cr. 15.)
CALDWOOD, and CALWOOD, in dexter hand a palm-branch, slipped, ppr. Pl. 23, cr. 7.
CALDWOODLEY, Devons., an antelope, passant, per pale, gu. and or, armed, gole. Pl. 63, cr. 10.
CALEBOT, Norf., a greyhound, current, az., (collared and ringed, or.) Pl. 28, cr. 7.
CALEDON, Earl and Baron, Viscount Alexander, (Dupré-Alexander,) Iri., a cubit arm, in armour, ppr., in hand a sword, of the last, hilt and pommel, or. *Per mare, per terras.* Pl. 63, cr. 5.
CALENDER, and CALLANDER, Sco. and Iri., out of an Eastern coronet, or, in dexter hand a billet, ppr. Pl. 25, cr. 8.
CALIBUT, a stag's head, at gaze, az. Pl. 111, cr. 13.
CALL, Bart., Cornw., a demi-lion, rampant, in paws a trumpet, in pale, ar. *Grata manu.* Pl. 47, cr. 4.
CALLAGAN, and O'CALLAGAN, Iri., a naked arm, embowed, in hand a sword, with snake entwined round blade, head towards hand, all ppr. Pl. 116, cr. 11.
CALLAGAN, a morion, ppr. Pl. 18, cr. 9.
CALLAGHAM, Iri., a morion, ppr. Pl. 18, cr. 9.
CALLANDAR, and CALLENDER, Sco. and Iri., in dexter hand, a billet, ppr. *I mean well.* Pl. 28, cr. 8.
CALLANDER, Bart., Stirlingshire, out of an Eastern crown, gold, a cubit arm, ppr., in hand a billet. *Et domi et foris.* Pl. 25, cr. 8.
CALLANDER, and CALLENDAR, Eng., two elephants' proboscess, addorsed, per fess, gu. and or. Pl. 24, cr. 8.
CALLEY, HENRY, Esq., of Blunsdon St Andrew, Wilts., a demi-lion, ar., charged with a bend, gu., thereon three mullets, of the first, in dexter a battle-axe, handle, of the second, head, of the first. *Callide et honeste.* Pl. 101, cr. 14.

CALLEY, and CALEY, Yorks. and Wilts., a demi-lion, in dexter a battle-axe, ar., handle, gu., on shoulder a bend, of the last, charged with three mullets, of the first. *Pl.* 101, *cr.* 14.

CALLIS, out of a ducal coronet, a cockatrice's head, between wings. *Pl.* 77, *cr.* 5.

CALLORE, on a ducal coronet, a sheaf of arrows, environed by a serpent. *Pl.* 86, *cr.* 12.

CALLOW, Eng., on a ducal coronet, a peacock, ppr. *Pl.* 43, *cr.* 7.

CALMADY, Devons., a pegasus, current, or. *Pl.* 28, *cr.* 9.

CALMADY, Devons., a pegasus, ar. *Pl.* 57, *cr.* 15.

CALMADY, CHARLES-BIGGS, Esq., of Langdon Hall, Devon, a pegasus, ar. *Similis frondescit virga metallo. Pl.* 57, *cr.* 15.

CALSHILL, Eng., a (dexter)-wing, erect, or. *Pl.* 39, *cr.* 10.

CALSTON, Eng., the moon in her compliment. *Pl.* 44, *cr.* 8.

CALTHORP, and CALTHROP, Suff. and Norf., a boar's head and neck, az., armed and bristled, or. *Pl.* 2, *cr.* 7.

CALTHORPE, Bart., Eng., a boar's head and neck, couped, vert. *Pl.* 2, *cr.* 7.

CALTHORPE, Baron, (Gough-Calthorpe,) a boar's head, couped at neck, az., bristled and tusked, or, between two woodmen, with clubs over shoulders, all ppr. *Gradu diverso via una.*

CALTHROP, Norf., on a mount, vert, a hawk, close, ar., beaked and belled, or. *Pl.* 111, *cr.* 8.

CALTHROP, JOHN, Esq., of Stanhoe Hall, Norf., a salamander, or, in flames, ppr. *Victrix fortunæ sapientia. Pl.* 20, *cr.* 15.

CALTHROP, the Rev. JOHN, of Gosherton, Linc., same crest and motto.

CALTOFT, Linc., a rose, gu., between two laurel-branches, vert. *Pl.* 3, *cr.* 13.

CALTON, Hunts., a talbot, passant, ar., collared and lined, or. *Pl.* 65, *cr.* 2.

CALTON, Cambs., a boar, passant, ar. *Pl.* 48, *cr.* 14.

CALVERLEY, and CALVELEY, Chesh. and Yorks., out of a ducal coronet, a calf's head, affrontée, sa. *Pl.* 43, *cr.* 9.

CALVERLEY, Suss. and Surr., a horned owl, ar. *En caligine veritas. Pl.* 1, *cr.* 8.

CALVERLEY, JOHN, Esq., of Oulton Hall, Yorks., a horned owl, ar. *Pl.* 1, *cr.* 8.

CALVERLY-BLACKETT, Bart., Yorks. and Northumb., an owl, ar. *Pl.* 27, *cr.* 9.

CALVERT, out of a mural coronet, or, two forked pennons flowing to dexter, one gold, the other pean, staves, gu.

CALVERT, Lanc., an owl, ar., guttée, sa. *Pl.* 27, *cr.* 9.

CALWOOD, in dexter hand a palm-branch, vert. *Pl.* 23, *cr.* 7.

CAM, and CAMM, a dove, between two laurel-branches, in orle. *Pl.* 2, *cr.* 11.

CAMAC, and CAMIC, Eng., a martlet, sa. *Pl.* 111, *cr.* 5.

CAMBELL, Ess., a bear's head, couped, per fess, or and az., muzzled, gu. *Pl.* 111, *cr.* 4.

CAMBELL, a swan, ppr., ducally crowned, or, between two laurel-branches, vert. *Pl.* 33, *cr.* 7, (laurel, *pl.* 79, *cr.* 14.)

CAMBELL, a lion's head, affrontée. *Pl.* 47, *cr.* 6.

CAMBELL, a swan, ppr., crowned, or. *Pl.* 33, *cr.* 7.

CAMBELL, a boar's head, couped. *Pl.* 48, *cr.* 2.

CAMBER, Ess., a Saxon crown, per pale, sa. and ar., between wings, counterchanged. *Pl.* 115, *cr.* 6.

CAMBORNE, Cornw., three broken spears, or, tied together with a band, gu., two in saltier, one in pale. *Pl.* 33, *cr.* 3.

CAMBRIDGE, and CAMBRIGE, Eng., a lion, passant, gardant, ppr. *Pl.* 120, *cr.* 5.

CAMBRIDGE, a griffin's head, erased, or, in beak a cross crosslet, fitched, of the same. *Pl.* 9, *cr.* 12, (cross, *pl.* 141.)

CAMDEN, Marquess, Earl, and Baron; Earl of Brecknock, Viscount Bayham, &c., (John-Jeffreys-Pratt,) an elephant's head, erased, ar. *Judicium parium, aut leges terræ. Pl.* 68, *cr.* 4.

CAMDEN, Eng., a cross pattée, per pale, sa. and ar., between wings, counterchanged. *Pl.* 29, *cr.* 14.

CAMEL, Eng., a camel's head. *Pl.* 109, *cr.* 9.

CAMERON, DONALD, Esq., of Lochiel, Inverness, a dexter arm, in armour, embowed, in hand a sword, all ppr. *Pro rege et patria. Pl.* 2, *cr.* 8.

CAMERON, Sco., an arm, in armour, in hand a sword, ppr. *Pro rege et patria. Pl.* 2, *cr.* 8.

CAMERON, Eng., in lion's paw, sa., a flag, ar., charged with an eagle, with two heads, displayed, sa. *Pl.* 7, *cr.* 7.

CAMERON of Glendessary, an arm, in armour, in hand a sword, ppr. *Hinc orior. Pl.* 2, *cr.* 8.

CAMERON, Bart., Sco.: 1. Out of a mural coronet, or, a dexter arm, in armour, embowed, in hand a sword, all ppr. *Pl.* 115, *cr.* 14. 2. By honourable augmentation, a Highlander of the 92nd regiment, wading through water, in dexter a broadsword, and in sinister a banner, thereon the number 92, within a wreath of laurel, all ppr. *Arriverette.*

CAMERON, Hants, a dexter arm, in armour, embowed, ppr., garnished, or, in hand a sword, also ppr., hilt and pommel, or. *Pl.* 2, *cr.* 8.

CAMFIELD, and CAMFYLD, Norf., out of a tower, a demi-lady, ppr. *Pl.* 26, *cr.* 5, (without head.)

CAMFIELD, an arm, erect, couped at elbow, vested, in hand, (three) wheat-ears, ppr. *Pl.* 63, *cr.* 1.

CAMOYS, Baron. See STONOR, of Stonor Park, Oxon.

CAMOYS, or CAMAYS, a lion's head, erased, az., in mouth a trefoil, slipped, ppr. *Pl.* 95, *cr.* 6, (trefoil, *pl.* 141.)

CAMP, Eng., a griffin's head, erased, ducally gorged, in mouth a branch of laurel, all ppr. *Pl.* 42, *cr.* 9.

CAMPBELL, ROBERT-NUTTER, Esq., of Ormidale, Argyll, a boar's head, couped, or. *Ne obliviscaris. Pl.* 48, *cr.* 2.

CAMPBELL, WILLIAM-GUNNING, Esq., of Fairfield, Ayr, an eagle's head, erased, ppr. *Constanter et prudentiâ. Pl.* 20, *cr.* 7.

CAMPBELL, ALEXANDER, Esq., of Monzie Castle, Perth, and Inveraw, Argyll, a boar's head, erased, ppr. *Follow me. Pl.* 16, *cr.* 11.

CAMPBELL, Sco., an eagle's head, couped, ppr. *Constanter et prudentiâ. Pl.* 100, *cr.* 10.

CAMPBELL of Lawers, a boar's head, erect and erased, az. *Fac et spera.* Pl. 21, cr. 7.
CAMPBELL, GEORGE-JAMES, Esq., of Treesbank, Ayr, a phœnix-head, erased, or. *Constanter et prudentiâ.* Pl. 20, cr. 7.
CAMPBELL, JOHN, Esq., of Sornbeg, Ayr, same crest and motto.
CAMPBELL of Asnish, a boar's head, couped, or. *Nunquam obliviscar.* Pl. 48, cr. 2.
CAMPBELL, ARCHIBALD, Esq., of Lochnell, Argyll, in dexter hand, a spear, in bend, ppr. *Audaces juvo—*and—*Arma parata fero.* Pl. 99, cr. 8.
CAMPBELL of Gargunnock, a stork, ppr. *Refero.* Pl. 33, cr. 9.
CAMPBELL, Bart., of Succoth, Sco., a camel's head, couped, ppr. *Labor omnia superat.* Pl. 109, cr. 9.
CAMPBELL, JANE-ELIZABETH-MARY, of Ardchattan Priory, Argyll, a swan, ppr., crowned, or. Pl. 33, cr. 7.
CAMPBELL, COLIN, Esq., of Colgrain, Dumbarton, a boar's head, erect and erased, or, armed and langued, ar. *Fac et spera.* Pl. 21, cr. 7.
CAMPBELL, WILLIAM-JOHN-LAMB, Esq., of Glenfalloch, Perth, a man's heart, pierced through with a dart, ppr. *Thus far.* Pl. 16, cr. 14.
CAMPBELL of Calder, a swan, ppr., crowned, or. *Be mindful.* Pl. 33, cr. 7.
CAMPBELL, Bart., of Ardnamurchan and Airds, Sco., same crest and motto.
CAMPBELL, WALTER-WILLIAM-THOMAS-BEAUJOLOIS, Esq., of Skipness Castle, Argyll, two oars, in saltier. *Terrâ marique fides.* Pl. 7, cr. 9.
CAMPBELL, ROBERT, Esq., of Skerrington, Ayr, a dexter arm, in armour, in hand a garland of laurel, all ppr. *Campi fero prœmia, belli.* Pl. 68, cr. 1.
CAMPBELL, COLIN, Esq., of Jura and Craignish, Argylls., in hand a spear, ppr. *Audaces juvo.* Pl. 99, cr. 8.
CAMPBELL, Sir JAMES, Knt., of Stracathro, Forfars., a boar's head, erased. *Ne obliviscarsis.* Pl. 16, cr. 11.
CAMPBELL, Sir GUY, Bart., Sco., a boar's head, in fess, couped, ppr. *Follow me.* Pl. 48, cr. 2.
CAMPBELL, Sir DONALD, Bart., Sco., same crest and motto.
CAMPBELL, a boar's head, couped, sa. *Usque ad aras.* Pl. 48, cr. 2.
CAMPBELL, W.S., Sco., a swan, ppr., crowned, or. *Be ever mindful.* Pl. 33, cr. 7.
CAMPBELL, a dove with olive-branch, ppr. *Gaudium adfero.* Pl. 48, cr. 15.
CAMPBELL of Morechaster, a boar's head, erased, chequey, or and sa. *Sequor.* Pl. 16, cr. 11.
CAMPBELL of Ardkiulis, a galley, her oars in action, sa. *Set on.* Pl. 34, cr. 5.
CAMPBELL of Craignish, a boar's head, erased, ppr. *Fit via vi.* Pl. 16, cr. 11.
CAMPBELL of Auchinbreck, Bart., in dexter hand, ppr., a spear, or. *Forget not.* Pl. 99, cr. 8.
CAMPBELL of Auchawilling, two oars of a galley, in saltier. *Armis et fide.* Pl. 7, cr. 9.
CAMPBELL, same crest. *Vi et fide.*
CAMPBELL, same crest. *Terra marique fide.*

CAMPBELL of Inveraw, a hart's head, ppr. *Pro aris et focis.* Pl. 91, cr. 14.
CAMPBELL of Lochdochart, a boar's head, erased, ppr. *Recte sequor.* Pl. 16, cr. 11.
CAMPBELL, Earl of Islay, a boar's head, couped. *Memini.* Pl. 48, cr. 2.
CAMPBELL of Glenfeacher, a goat, standing, az., armed and hoofed, or, in mouth a sprig of ivy, ppr. *Marbu mhiann leon.* Pl. 15, cr. 9.
CAMPBELL of Netherplace, in hand, issuing from a cloud, a signet letter, ppr. *Optime quod opportune.* Pl. 23, cr. 8.
CAMPBELL, HUME-PURVES, Bart., of Berwick, in dexter hand, issuing from a heart, a scimitar, all ppr. *True to the end.* Pl. 35, cr. 7.
CAMPBELL, Port-Glasgow, a boar's head, erased, ppr. *Deo volente.* Pl. 16, cr. 11.
CAMPBELL of Park, a boar's head, erased and erect, or, langued, az. *Fac et spera.* Pl. 21, cr. 7.
CAMPBELL of Skerrington, an eagle's head. *Constans et prudens.* Pl. 100, cr. 10.
CAMPBELL, Bart., of Barcaldine, Sco., a man in full highland garb, in dexter a broadsword, on sinister arm a shield, all ppr. *Paratus sum.*
CAMPBELL, Sco., an arm, in armour, embowed, in hand a dagger. *Paratus sum.* Pl. 120, cr. 11.
CAMPBELL, a lion, sejant, affrontée and erect, in dexter a sword, in sinister a crown of laurel. *Victoriam coronat Christus.* Pl. 120, cr. 2, (laurel, pl. 128, fig. 6.)
CAMPBELL, Sco., an arm, issuant, ppr., in hand a spur, or. *Memor esto.* Pl. 34, cr. 9.
CAMPBELL, in water, a demi-eagle, displayed, with two heads, above it the sun shining, ppr. Pl. 115, cr. 7.
CAMPBELL, Baron, a boar's head, erased, gyronné of eight, or and sa. *Audacter et aperte.* Pl. 16, cr. 11.
CAMPBELL, Sir JAMES, N.S. Bart., Aberuchill, Perthshire, a lion, rampant, gardant, (in dexter a sword, in sinister a laurel crown.) *Sequitur victoria forteis.* Pl. 92, cr. 7.
CAMPBELL, Lord Clyde, a boar's head, erased, or. *Nil tibi.* Pl. 16, cr. 11.
CAMPBELL, Duke of Argyll. *See* ARGYLL.
CAMPBELL, Earl of Loudoun. *See* LOUDOUN.
CAMPBELL, Marquess of Breadalbane. *See* BREADALBANE.
CAMPBELL, Earl Cawdor. *See* CAWDOR.
CAMPBELL, WALTER-FREDERICK, Esq., of Woodhall, Lanark, a griffin, erect, between forefeet the sun, ppr. *Fidus amicus.* Pl. 13, cr. 10.
CAMPBELL-COCKBURN, Bart., of Gartsford, Sco.:
1. For *Campbell*, a cubit arm, erect, in hand, a scimitar, ppr. *Without fear.* Pl. 29, cr. 8.
2. For *Cockburn*, a cock, ppr. *Vigilans et audax.* Pl. 67, cr. 14.
CAMPBELL, Bart., Sco.: 1. On a mount, vert, a Burmese warrior on horseback, armed and accoutred, ppr. Pl. 115, cr. 5. 2. Out of an Eastern crown, or, a demi-lion, ppr., in dexter, a crowned heart, gu.
CAMPBELL, Iri., the wings of an eagle conjoined, ppr. *Ulterius et melius.* Pl. 15, cr. 10.
CAMPBELL, Sco., a human heart, gu., transfixed with an arrow, in bend, ppr. *Thus far.* Pl. 16, cr. 14.

CAMPBELL, Bart., Iri., an Eastern crown, surmounted by a boar's head, erased, ppr. *Ne obliviscaris. Pl.* 16, *cr.* 11, (crown, *pl.* 182, *fig.* 2.)

CAMPBELL, Suff., a lion's head, affrontée. *I beare in minde. Pl.* 47, *cr.* 6.

CAMPBELL, Sco., a ship at anchor. *Vincit labor. Pl.* 115, *cr.* 9.

CAMPBELL, Lond., a demi-hound, az., gorged with a ducal coronet, or. *Fœstina lente. Pl.* 48, *cr.* 3.

CAMPBELL, Sco., in dexter hand a horseman's lance, in bend sinister. *Arma parata fero. Pl.* 99, *cr.* 8.

CAMPBELL, Sco., a demi-man in a coat of mail, in dexter a sword, (on sinister arm a shield, charged with a unicorn's head and neck.) *Quid non pro patria. Pl.* 23, *cr.* 4.

CAMPE, Eng., a griffin's head, erased, ducally gorged, in mouth a branch of laurel, ppr. *Pl.* 42, *cr.* 9.

CAMPER, an anchor, between wings. *Pl.* 115, *cr.* 10.

CAMPERDOWN, Earl of, Viscount Dundas, (Dundas-Haldane-Duncan,) a dismasted ship, ppr. *Secundis dubiisque rectus. Pl.* 21, *cr.* 11.

CAMPION, Lond. and Ess., out of a ducal coronet, or, a talbot's head, sa. *Pl.* 99, *cr.* 7.

CAMPION, and CAMPYON, a turkey in pride, ppr., combed and wattled, gu.

CAMPION, and CAMPYON, a bear's head and neck, per pale, erm. and sa., muzzled, or. *Pl.* 2, *cr.* 9.

CAMVILLE, Eng., on a mount, a leopard, sejant, ppr. *Pl.* 123, *cr.* 8.

CANBY, (a mount, sa.,) ensigned with a cross pattée. *Pl.* 15, *cr.* 8.

CANCELLER, and CANCELLOR, Eng., an arm, couped at shoulder, in fess, elbow on the wreath, supporting a flag, displayed, az., charged with a crescent, ar. *Pl.* 87, *cr.* 9.

CANCELOR, and CANDISHELER, Eng., in dexter hand, ppr., a covered cup, or. *Pl.* 35, *cr.* 9.

CANDISH, Suff., an ostrich-head, az., (gorged with a collar, sa., rimmed, or, and charged with three bezants. *Pl.* 50, *cr.* 1, (without feathers.)

CANDISHE, Eng., a wolf's head, couped, az., collared, or. *Pl.* 8, *cr.* 4.

CANDLER, Norf., a shark's head, erased, ppr. *Pl.* 17, *cr.* 15, (without coronet.)

CANDLER, Worc., an angel, ppr., vested, ar., in dexter (a sword, blade wavy, of the first, hilt and pommel, or.) *Ad mortem fidelis. Pl.* 25, *cr.* 7.

CANDLER, a goat's head, couped, sa., armed and maned, ar. *Pl.* 105, *cr.* 14.

CANDLER, Suff., an eagle, rising, regardant, ppr. *Pl.* 35, *cr.* 8.

CANDLISH, an ostrich-head, (collared and ringed.) *Pl.* 108, *cr.* 2, (without feathers.)

CANDLISH, or M'CANDLISH, a snake, nowed, ppr. *Cavendo tutus. Pl.* 1, *cr.* 9.

CANE, Eng. and Iri., a human heart, gu., charged with a cinquefoil, or. *Pl.* 123, *cr.* 7.

CANE, a leopard, rampant, (gorged with a mural coronet.) *Pl.* 73, *cr.* 2.

CANHAM, Eng., two palm-branches, in orle, ppr. *Pl.* 87, *cr.* 8.

CANING, Eng., a quatrefoil, ppr. *Pl.* 65, *cr.* 7.

CANKNIER, out of a mural coronet, a demi-lion, (holding up a garland of laurel, all ppr.) *Pl.* 17, *cr.* 7.

CANKRIEN, Yorks., a demi-lion, rampant, between paws a plummet. *Pl.* 29, *cr.* 12, (plumb, *pl.* 50, *cr.* 8.)

CANKRIEN, Yorks., a demi-lion, rampant, erminois, (between paws a palmer's scrip, sa.,) strap and tassels, or. *Pl.* 12, *cr.* 12.

CANKRIEN, Germany, out of a ducal coronet, or, two crabs' claws, between wings, erect, ppr. *Pl.* 17, *cr.* 9, (claws, *pl.* 116, *cr.* 6.)

CANN, Devons., a leopard, statant, ppr. *Pl.* 86, *cr.* 2.

CANN, Cornw., a cross crosslet, fitched, between wings, conjoined. *Pl.* 34, *cr.* 14.

CANN, and CAN, Glouc., out of a mural coronet, or, a plume of five ostrich-feathers, ar. *Pl.* 125, *cr.* 11, (feathers, *pl.* 100, *cr.* 12.)

CANNING, Viscount, (Canning,) a demi-griffin, az., guttée-d'or. *Ne cede malis, sed contra. Pl.* 18, *cr.* 6.

CANNING, a demi-lion, rampant, in dexter (a dart.) *Pl.* 41, *cr.* 13.

CANNING, a demi-griffin, az. *Pl.* 18, *cr.* 6.

CANNING, a demi-lion, rampant, erm., supporting a battle-axe, ppr. *Pl.* 101, *cr.* 14, (without charge.)

CANNOCK, Linc., a demi-buck, couped, ar., attired and (ducally gorged, or, one foot resting on the wreath.) *Pl.* 55, *cr.* 9, (without rose.)

CANNON, Sco., between horns of a crescent, a buckle, az. *Pl.* 25, *cr.* 3.

CANNON, Wel., a cannon, sa., mounted on a carriage, or. *Pl.* 111, *cr.* 3.

CANNYNGS, Eng., two dexter hands, conjoined, (gauntleted,) issuing from clouds, holding up a heart, inflamed, all ppr. *Pl.* 20, *cr.* 8.

CANT of Dryburnford, a dove, ppr. *Ales reposita. Pl.* 66, *cr.* 12.

CANTELOW, Heref., and Cantelupe, Eng., a leopard's face, gu., jessant-de-lis, or. *Pl.* 123, *cr.* 9.

CANTELOW, Iri., a demi-bull, per pale, or and az. *Pl.* 63, *cr.* 6.

CANTERBURY, Viscount, Baron Bottlesford, (Manners-Sutton,) on a chapeau, gu., turned up, erm., a peacock in pride, ppr. *Pour y parvenir. Pl.* 50, *cr.* 15.

CANTILLION, Iri., an arm, embowed, in hand a dagger, ppr. *Pl.* 120, *cr.* 11.

CANTILON, Iri., in hand an arrow, point downward. *Pl.* 43, *cr.* 13.

CANTIS, Kent, a hart's head, erased, ppr., attired, or, gorged with a collar, ar., charged with three roses, gu., barbed and seeded, ppr. *Pl.* 125, *cr.* 6, (without roses.)

CANTLOW, Eng., a boar, passant, quarterly, or and gu. *Pl.* 48, *cr.* 14.

CANTON, Iri., on a chapeau, ppr., a boar, passant, per pale, ar. and vert. *Pl.* 22, *cr.* 8.

CANTON, Kent, on a chapeau, a lion's head, erased, ppr. *Pl.* 99, *cr.* 9.

CANTRELL, Eng., an arm, in armour, embowed, in hand a sword by the middle, in fess, all ppr. *Pl.* 65, *cr.* 8.

CANTRELL, Lanc., and Cantrell, Suff., a tower, ar., port, sa. *Pl.* 12, *cr.* 5.

CANTWELL, Eng., in hand, ppr., an annulet, or. *Pl.* 24, *cr.* 3.

CAPE, a lion, passant, gu., (in fore-dexter a sword, in pale, ppr., hilt and pommel, or.) *Pl.* 48, *cr.* 8.

CAPEL, WILLIAM, Esq., of The Grove, Painswick, Glouc., a plume of three ostrich-feathers, two ar., and one gu. *Sic vita humana. Pl.* 12, *cr.* 9.

CAPEL-CONINGSBY, Earl of Essex. *See* ESSEX.

CAPELL, Heref., a plume of three ostrich-feathers, two ar., the other gu. *Pl.* 12, *cr.* 9.

CAPELL, Eng., an anchor, bezantée, corded, gu. *Pl.* 42, *cr.* 12.

CAPELL, Glouc., a demi-lion, rampant, ar. *Pl.* 67, *cr.* 10.

CAPELL, Glouc., a plume of three ostrich-feathers, the centre one, ar., the others, or. *Pl.* 12, *cr.* 9.

CAPES, Eng., a cross fleury, fitched, gu., flowered, or. *Pl.* 65, *cr.* 9.

CAPLING, Lond., out of the centre tower of a castle, triple-towered, a demi-lion, rampant, (between paws an anchor, in pale,) all ppr. *Pl.* 101, *cr.* 1.

CAPON, Eng., a demi-lion, gu. *Pl.* 67, *cr.* 10.

CAPP, Eng., a spur, winged, or. *Pl.* 59, *cr.* 1.

CAPPER, Lond., Middx., and Herts., a ram's head and neck, couped, charged on neck with a rose. *Pl.* 34, *cr.* 12, (rose, *pl.* 141.)

CAPPER, Warw. and Staffs., a dexter arm, couped at shoulder, embowed, vested, gu., cuffed, ar., in hand a banner, az., staff, or, charged with a bee, volant, gold. *Pl.* 99, *cr.* 3.

CAPPER, a ram's head, erased. *Pl.* 1, *cr.* 12.

CAPPS, Norf., a demi-antelope, or. *Pl.* 34, *cr.* 8.

CAPRON, a demi-man, in armour, (with lance and shield, all ppr.) *Pl.* 23, *cr.* 4.

CAPSAL, or CAPSALL, a castle, triple-towered, ppr., ensigned with a flag, gu., charged with a cross, ar. *Pl.* 123, *cr.* 14.

CAPSAL, Eng., a hand, holding a military sash, ppr. *Pl.* 44, *cr.* 7.

CARBERY, Baron, (Evans-Freke), Iri.: 1. For *Evans*, a demi-lion, rampant, regardant, or, (between paws) a boar's head, couped, sa. *Pl.* 33, *cr.* 2. 2. For *Freke*, a bull's head, couped. *Libertas. Pl.* 120, *cr.* 7.

CARBINELL, out of a ducal coronet, an arm, in armour, in hand a scimitar, ppr. *Pl.* 15, *cr.* 5.

CARBONEL, CARBONELL, or CARBONELLE, Eng., a demi-lion, az., crowned, gu. *Pl.* 61, *cr.* 4, (without branch.)

CARBONEL, or CARBONELL, a sword, in bend, ppr. *Pl.* 22, *cr.* 7.

CARD, Lond., out of a cloud, in hand a letter, ppr. *Pl.* 33, *cr.* 8.

CARDALE, Lond., a linnet, ppr. *Studendo et contemplando inde fessus. Pl.* 52, *cr.* 12.

CARDEN, Bart., Iri., a pheon, sa. *Fide et amore. Pl.* 26, *cr.* 12.

CARDEN, a wolf, statant, sa., (in mouth an arrow, in pale, ppr.) *Pl.* 46, *cr.* 6.

CARDEN, Sco., a cross moline, gu. *Pl.* 89, *cr.* 8.

CARDEN, Eng., a tower, per pale, or and gu. *Pl.* 12, *cr.* 5.

CARDEN, Bucks., a wolf's head, (erased,) sa., pierced with an arrow, ar. *Pl.* 40, *cr.* 12.

CARDEW, Eng., out of a ducal coronet, a plume of four feathers. *Pl.* 44, *cr.* 12.

CARDIFFE, Eng., on a chapeau, gu., turned up, or, a martlet, sa. *Pl.* 89, *cr.* 7.

CARDIFF, Iri., a gilliflower, slipped and leaved, ppr. *Pl.* 22, *cr.* 9.

CARDIGAN, Earl of, Baron Brudenell, and a Bart., (Brudenell,) a sea-horse, ppr. *En grace affie. Pl.* 103, *cr.* 3.

CARDIGAN, in lion's gamb, erect and erased, or, an antique mace, az. *Pl.* 124, *cr.* 4.

CARDINAL, Ess., a dromedary, ppr. *Pl.* 17, *cr.* 2.

CARDINGTON, Eng., a bull, passant, per fess, ar. and sa. *Pl.* 66, *cr.* 11.

CARDONNEL, DE, Eng., a dove, ppr. *L'esperance me console. Pl.* 66, *cr.* 12.

CARDONNEL, Northumb., a goldfinch, ppr., on breast a trefoil, vert. *Pl.* 10, *cr.* 12, (trefoil, *pl.* 141.)

CARDOZO, Lond., a demi-savage, affrontée, ppr., in dexter a stalk of tobacco, (sinister resting on a triangle,) or. *Pl.* 35, *cr.* 12.

CARDWELL, a knight, in complete armour, ppr., visor up, on top of helmet a plume of feathers, gu., (in dexter a battle-axe, of the first.) *Pl.* 60, *cr.* 2.

CARDWELL, Eng., a tower, ppr., domed, or, with a flag thereon, sa. *Pl.* 42, *cr.* 10.

CAREW, Baron, Iri., (Shapland-Carew), an antelope, passant, gu. *Nil admirari. Pl.* 63, *cr.* 10.

CAREW, Bart., Devons., a mainmast, the roundtop environed with a ducal coronet, set off with palisadoes, or, and a demi-lion, issuant, sa. *Nil conscire sibi.*

CAREW, ROBERT, Esq., of Ballinamona, co. Waterford, an antelope, passant, gu. *Pl.* 63, *cr.* 10.

CAREY, THOMAS, Esq., of Rozel, Guernsey, a swan, ppr. *Pl.* 122, *cr.* 13.

CAREY, Viscount Falkland, Sco., a swan, ppr. *In utroque fidelis. Pl.* 122, *cr.* 13.

CAREY, a swan, ar., wings addorsed. *Pl.* 46, *cr.* 5.

CAREY, a wolf, passant, regardant, per pale, ar. and gu., in mouth a rose-branch, flowered, of the second, leaved and stalked, vert.

CAREY, a horse's head and neck, bendy of six, ar. and sa., armed with a shield plate and bridled, or. *Pl.* 52, *cr.* 9.

CAREY, Iri., on a mount, a fire-beacon, ppr. *Pl.* 89, *cr.* 9.

CAREY, or CARY, a maiden's head, ppr. *Pl.* 45, *cr.* 5.

CARFRAE, Sco., a tower, embattled, ar. *Fortis et fide. Pl.* 12, *cr.* 5.

CARFRAE, Sco., a wyvern, ppr. *Vigilantia. Pl.* 63, *cr.* 13.

CARGILL, Sco., a demi-angel, ppr., on head (a cross pattée.) *Pl.* 90, *cr.* 11.

CARGILL, Sco., a martlet, ppr. *Pl.* 111, *cr.* 5.

CARGILL, Eng., a martlet, ar. *In Domino confido. Pl.* 111, *cr.* 5.

CARINGTON, Eng., out of a coronet, ar., a unicorn's head, sa., maned and horned, of the first. *Pl.* 45, *cr.* 14.

CARKETTLE, Sco., a griffin's head, erased, ppr. *Pl.* 48, *cr.* 6.

CARLEILL, WILLIAM, Esq., of Sewerby, Yorks., a moor's head, in profile, couped at shoulders, ppr. *Pl.* 81, *cr.* 15.

CARLETON, Lond., Surr., Beds., and Cambs., out of a ducal coronet, or, a unicorn's head, sa., the horn twisted, of the first and second. *Pl.* 45, *cr.* 14.

CARLETON, Viscount Carleton, Iri., a unicorn's head. *Quærere verum.* *Pl.* 20, *cr.* 1.
CARLIFE, a martlet, or, (in mouth a sprig of two roses, gu., leaved and stalked, vert.) *Pl.* 111, *cr.* 5.
CARLILL, Cumb. and Westm., an arm, in armour, embowed, in hand, ppr., a spear, ar. *Pl.* 44, *cr.* 9.
CARLILL, Cumb. and Kent, an arm in armour, embowed, or, garnished, gu., in hand, ppr., a baton, gold. *Pl.* 44, *cr.* 9, (baton. *pl.* 33, *cr.* 4.)
CARLING, Bristol, a buck's head, erased, ppr. *Tout droit.* *Pl.* 66, *cr.* 9.
CARLISLE, Earl of, Viscount Morpeth, (Howard,) on a chapeau, gu., turned up, erm., a lion, statant, gardant, tail extended, or, ducally crowned, ar., and gorged with a label of three points, of the last. *Volo non valeo.* *Pl.* 120, *cr.* 15.
CARLOS, two swords, in saltier, between two branches of laurel, in orle. *Pl.* 71, *cr.* 3, (swords, *pl.* 75, *cr.* 13.)
CARLOS, a sword, ar., hilt and pommel, or, and a sceptre, of the last, in saltier, enfiled with a civic crown, vert. *Pl.* 124, *cr.* 6.
CARLTON, an arm, embowed, ppr., in hand an arrow. *Pl.* 96, *cr.* 6.
CARLYON, a demi-lion, (collared,) between paws a bezant. *Turris tutissima virtus.* *Pl.* 126, *cr.* 12.
CARLYON, Eng., in the sea, a pillar, ppr. *Pl.* 14, *cr.* 3.
CARMALT, Cumb., a dragon's head, erased, per pale, or and vert, gorged with a collar, charged with three escallops, counterchanged. *Pl.* 107, *cr.* 10.
CARMARDEN, and CARMARTHEN, Lond. and Kent, a lion's gamb, erased, or. *Pl.* 126, *cr.* 9.
CARMICHAEL-GIBSON, Bart., of Skirling, an arm, embowed, in hand a broken lance, top pendent, ppr. *Toujours prest.* *Pl.* 44, *cr.* 9.
CARMICHAEL, of Balmblae, a woman's head and neck, issuing. *Fortune helps the forward.* *Pl.* 45, *cr.* 5.
CARMICHAEL, Iri., an arm from elbow, in armour, in hand a pheon, ppr. *Pl.* 123, *cr.* 12.
CARMICHAEL of Maulslei, an arm, in armour, in hand a broken spear, ppr., and charged with a mullet, or. *Toujours prest.* *Pl.* 44, *cr.* 9, (mullet, *pl.* 141.)
CARMICHAEL, Sco., an arm, in armour, in hand a tilting-spear, ppr. *Toujours prest.* *Pl.* 44, *cr.* 9, (spear, *pl.* 97, *cr.* 4.)
CARMINOW, CARMYNOW, or CARMENOW, Eng., a dolphin, naiant, or. *Pl.* 48, *cr.* 9.
CARNABY, Eng., a bull's head, per cheveron, or and gu. *Pl.* 63, *cr.* 11.
CARNABY, a lion's head, issuing, sa., (charged with a cheveron, ar.) *Pl.* 126, *cr.* 1.
CARNAC, on a crescent, per pale, gu. and erm., a sword, ppr., hilt and pommel, or, point upward. *Pl.* 93, *cr.* 12.
CARNAC-RIVETT, Bart., Derbs. and Lond., out of a crescent, erm., interior, or, a sword, erect, ppr., hilt and pommel, gold. *Sic itur ad astra.* *Pl,* 93, *cr.* 12.
CARNAGHI, or CARNAGIE, in dexter hand, gu., a thunderbolt, winged, or. *Dread God.* *Pl.* 21, *cr.* 8.

CARNAGIE, Sco., a star, ppr. *Alis aspicit astra.* *Pl.* 21, *cr.* 6.
CARNAGIE, Sco., out of a cloud, two dexter hands gauntleted, supporting a flaming heart, all ppr. *Armis et animis.* *Pl.* 20, *cr.* 8.
CARNARVON, Earl of, Baron Porchester, (Herbert,) a wyvern, wings elevated, vert, in mouth a sinister hand, couped at wrist, gu. *Ung je serviray.* *Pl.* 61, *cr.* 8.
CARNEGIE of Kenraird, Angus; and Castle of Leuchars, Fifeshire; in dexter hand a thunderbolt, ppr. *Deum timete.* *Pl.* 21, *cr.* 8.
CARNEGIE, Earl of Northesk. *See* NORTHESK.
CARNEGIE of Pitarow, Bart., a demi-eagle, displayed, az. *Video alta sequorque.* *Pl.* 22, *cr.* 11.
CARNEGIE of Craigo, a star, ppr. *Alis aspicet astra.* *Pl.* 21, *cr.* 6.
CARNEGIE of Lour, a leopard's head, erased, ppr. *Armis et animis.* *Pl.* 94, *cr.* 10.
CARNEGIE, Sir JAMES, Bart., of Southesk, a dexter hand holding a thunderbolt, ppr. *Dread God.* *Pl.* 21, *cr.* 8.
CARNEGY, JOHN-ALLAN, Esq., Lond., a demi-leopard, ppr. *Tache sans tache.* *Pl.* 12, *cr.* 14.
CARNEGY, Sco., in dexter hand a thunderbolt, gu., winged, or. *Dread God.* *Pl.* 21, *cr.* 8.
CARNEGY-LINDSAY, of Spynie and Boysack, and Kinblethmont: 1. An ostrich-head, issuing, ar., in mouth a horse-shoe, az. *Pl.* 99, *cr.* 12, (without feathers.) 2. A demi-leopard, ppr. *Tache sans tache—and—Endure furth.* *Pl.* 12, *cr.* 14.
CARNEGY-WATSON: 1. For *Carnegy*, a demi-leopard, ppr. *Tache sans tache.* *Pl.* 12, *cr.* 14. 2. For *Watson*, a lily of the Nile, ppr. *Sine injuriâ.* *Pl.* 22, *cr.* 9.
CARNELL, Yorks., an arm, in armour, embowed, in hand a sword, ppr. *Pl.* 2, *cr.* 8.
CARNEY, a swan's head and neck, (erased, in mouth an annulet.) *Pl.* 30, *cr.* 10, (without gorging.)
CARNIE, Sco., on a rock, sa., weeds, vert. *Pl.* 73, *cr.* 12.
CARNIE, Eng., out of a cloud, a hand, in fess, pointing to a crosier, in pale, all ppr. *Pl.* 45, *cr.* 4.
CARNIQUET, Sco., a swan, wings addorsed, ar., ducally gorged and chained, or. *Pl.* 111, *cr.* 10, (without charge.)
CARNOCK, Sco., in hand, ppr., a fleur-de-lis, az. *Pl.* 95, *cr.* 9.
CARNWATH, Earl of, and Baron Dalzell, Sco., (Dalzell,) a dagger, erect, ppr., pommel and hilt, or. *I dare.* *Pl.* 73, *cr.* 9.
CARPENTER, Eng., on a stand, a globe, ppr. *Per acuta belli.* *Pl.* 81, *cr.* 1.
CARPENTER, a stag's head, ar., with wings addorsed, az. *Pl.* 91, *cr.* 14, (wings, *pl.* 63, *cr.* 12.)
CARPENTER, a demi-lion, rampant, gu., ducally crowned, or, collared, sa. *Pl.* 18, *cr.* 13, (crown, *same plate.*)
CARPENTER, Worc., a coney, sejant, ar. *Pl.* 70, *cr.* 1.
CARPENTER, Eng., a church, ppr. *Pl.* 45, *cr.* 6.
CARPENTER, Somers., a snail, passant, ppr., shell, ar. *Pl.* 105, *cr.* 8.
CARPENTER, Surr., a greyhound's head, erased, per fess, sa. and ar. *Pl.* 89, *cr.* 2.
CARPENTER, Earl of Tyrconnel. *See* TYRCONNEL.

CARPENTER, Eng., a falcon, wings expanded, ar., beaked, legged, and belled, or. *Pl.* 105, *cr.* 4.
CARPENTER, Cornw., a plume of ostrich-feathers. *Pl.* 12, *cr.* 9.
CARPENTER, an arm, in armour, embowed, in hand, ppr., a hammer, or. *Pl.* 97, *cr.* 1, (hammer, *pl.* 51, *cr.* 14.)
CARPENTER, an arm, in armour, embowed, in hand a passion nail. *Pl.* 120, *cr.* 11, (nail, *pl.* 47, *cr.* 10.)
CARPENTER, an arm, in armour, embowed, (in hand, ppr., a musket, in bend sinister.) *Pl.* 96, *cr.* 4.
CARR, Lanc. and Linc., a stag's head, ar., charged with two bars-gemelle, gu., attired, or. *Pl.* 91, *cr.* 14.
CARR, Sco., a buck's head, erased, or. *Friendship.* *Pl.* 66, *cr.* 9.
CARR, Northumb. and Durh., a stag's head, erased, ppr. *Nil desperandum.* *Pl.* 66, *cr.* 9.
CARR, Northumb. and Durh., a stag's head, couped, ppr. *Nil desperandum.* *Pl.* 91, *cr.* 14.
CARR, a lion's head, erased, or. *Pl.* 81, *cr.* 4.
CARR, a dexter arm, erect, couped below wrist, ppr., in hand a dagger, ar., hilt and pommel, or. *Pl.* 23, *cr.* 15.
CARR-HAY, Earl of Errol. *See* ERROL.
CARR-STANDISH of Cocken Hall, Derbs., a lion's head, erased. *Est nulla fallacia.* *Pl.* 81, *cr.* 4.
CARRANT, Somers., a bull's head, cabossed, per pale, gu. and ar., armed, counterchanged. *Pl.* 111, *cr.* 6.
CARRE, Sco., a stag's head, erased, or. *Tout droit.* *Pl.* 66, *cr.* 9.
CARRELL, Suss., on a mount, vert, a stag, lodged, regardant, ar., attired, or. *Pl.* 22, *cr.* 5.
CARRELL, Suss., (on a mount, vert,) an ibex, ar., maned and horned, or. *Pl.* 115, *cr.* 13.
CARRELL, Suss. and Kent, a lion's head, erased, vert, between wings, ar. and sa., on neck two bends, or. *Pl.* 73, *cr.* 3.
CARRELL, a tiger, sejant, vert, maned and tufted, or. *Pl.* 26, *cr.* 9.
CARRICK, Earl of, and Viscount Ikerrin, Iri., (Butler,) out of a ducal coronet, a plume of five ostrich-feathers, ar., thereupon a falcon, rising, of the last. *Soyez ferme.* *Pl.* 103, *cr.* 6, (feathers, *pl.* 100, *cr.* 12.)
CARRICK, Sco., a demi-lion, or, in dexter a thistle, ppr., in sinister a fleur-de-lis, gu. *Pl.* 45, *cr.* 15.
CARRICK, Glouc., an ostrich, ar., beaked and legged, or, (in mouth a staff, of the same, with flag, gu.) *Garde bien.* *Pl.* 16, *cr.* 2.
CARRIE, Iri., an arm, in armour, embowed, in hand, ppr., a dart in bend, point downward. *Pl.* 96, *cr.* 6.
CARRIER, Hants., out of a ducal coronet, or, a dragon's head, vert. *Pl.* 59, *cr.* 14.
CARRINGTON, Baron, Eng. and Iri., (Smith,) an elephant's head, erased, or, eared, gu., charged on neck with three fleurs-de-lis, two and one, az. *Tenax et fidelis.* *Pl.* 68, *cr.* 4, (charge, *pl.* 141.)
CARRINGTON, Lond. and Yorks., out of a ducal coronet, or, a unicorn's head, sa. *Pl.* 45, *cr.* 14.

CARRINGTON, Chesh., a unicorn's head, ar., armed and crested, or. *Pl.* 20, *cr.* 1.
CARRINGTON, an eagle, close. *Pl.* 7, *cr.* 11.
CARRINGTON, Oxon., out of a ducal coronet, or, a unicorn's head, sa., crined, ar., horn twisted, of the last and second. *Pl.* 45, *cr.* 14.
CARRINGTON, Warw., a peacock's head, erased, ppr., ducally gorged, or. *Pl.* 69, *cr.* 5.
CARROL, or CARROLL, Iri., a tent, gu. *Pl.* 111, *cr.* 14.
CARROL, or CARROLL, Iri., on stump of oak, sprouting, a hawk, ppr., belled, or. *Pl.* 78, *cr.* 8.
CARROL, or CARROLL, Eng., a bear's head, sa., muzzled, or, between wings, of the last. *Pl.* 44, *cr.* 5.
CARROLL, HENRY, Esq., of Ballynure, co. Wicklow, on stump of oak, sprouting, a hawk, ppr., belled, or. *In fide et in bello fortes.* *Pl.* 78, *cr.* 8.
CARROL, Knt., Lond., on a mount, vert, a stag, lodged, regardant, ar., attired, or. *Semper eadem.* *Pl.* 51, *cr.* 9.
CARRON, Sco., a camel's head, per fess, ar. and az. *Pl.* 109, *cr.* 9.
CARRUTHERS of Howmains, a seraphim, volant, ppr. *Promptus et fidelis.* *Pl.* 46, *cr.* 3.
CARRUTHERS, Annandale, a seraphim, standing, vested, ppr. *Pl.* 25, *cr.* 7.
CARRUTHERS, a cherub's head, (between three pairs of wings,) ppr. *Pl.* 126, *cr.* 10.
CARRUTHERS of the Isle of Annandale, a cherub, ppr. *Paratus et fidelis.* *Pl.* 126, *cr.* 10.
CARRY, Eng., a cross Calvary, ppr. *Pl.* 7, *cr.* 13.
CARRYNGTON, Eng., out of a coronet, or, a unicorn's head, sa. *Pl.* 45, *cr.* 14.
CARSAIN, Sco., in dexter hand, a scimitar, ppr. *Ne m'oubliez.* *Pl.* 29, *cr.* 8.
CARSE, Sco., a falcon's head. *Velocitate.* *Pl.* 34, *cr.* 11.
CARSE, or CARSS, Sco., between horns of a crescent, a cross crosslet, fitched, or. *In cruce salus.* *Pl.* 43, *cr.* 3.
CARSEY, Norf., a hand and arm, couped at elbow, and erect, vested, az., purfled and cuffed, ar., in hand a bunch of gilliflowers, all ppr. *Pl.* 64, *cr.* 7.
CARSEWELL, and CARSWELL, Sco., a lion's head, within a fetterlock. *Pl.* 90, *cr.* 14.
CARSTAIRS, Sco., the sun shining on a primrose, ppr. *Te splendente.* *Pl.* 45, *cr.* 13.
CARSEWELL, Eng., a lion, passant, tail extended, ppr. *Pl.* 118, *cr.* 10.
CART, Eng. and Sco., a stag's head, in mouth a serpent, all ppr. *Pl.* 54, *cr.* 7.
CART, Sco. and Eng., in hand, a club, in pale, all ppr. *Pl.* 28, *cr.* 6.
CARTARET, a squirrel, sejant, gu., cracking a nut, ppr., in dexter a branch of laurel. *Pl.* 2, *cr.* 4.
CARTELL, a tower, triple-towered, ar., masoned, sa. *Pl.* 123, *cr.* 14.
CARTER, a talbot, sejant, resting dexter on a Catherine-wheel, per pale, ar. and az. *Pl.* 19, *cr.* 2, (wheel, *pl.* 1, *cr.* 7.)
CARTER, a lion's head, in mouth a (comet-star,) ppr. *Pl.* 95, *cr.* 6.
CARTER, Yorks., out of a mural coronet, or, a demi-monkey, ppr. *Pl.* 24, *cr.* 12.
CARTER, Northamp., a talbot's head, ar. *Pl.* 123, *cr.* 15.

CARTER, Northamp., a talbot's head, ar., charged with a mullet, gu. *Pl.* 123, *cr.* 15, (mullet, *pl.* 141.)

CARTER, Cornw., a lion's head, erased, or. *Pl.* 81, *cr.* 4.

CARTER, Cornw., on a mural coronet, sa., a talbot, passant, ar. *Pl.* 120, *cr.* 8, (coronet, *same plate, cr.* 14.)

CARTER, Kent, a dexter arm, in armour, embowed, ppr., in hand a roll of paper. *Pl.* 97, *cr.* 1, (roll, *pl.* 27, *cr.* 4.)

CARTERET, Baron, (Thynne,) a reindeer, (statant,) or. *Loyal devoir. Pl.* 12, *cr.* 8.

CARTHEW, Sco., a wild duck, ppr. *Pl.* 90, *cr.* 15.

CARTHEW, a falcon, rising, ducally gorged and belled, ppr. *Pl.* 61, *cr.* 12.

CARTILES, Northumb., a talbot, passant, per pale, indented, or and vert. *Pl.* 120, *cr.* 8.

CARTLAND, Iri., a demi-eagle, rising, ppr. *Pl.* 52, *cr.* 8.

CARTLITCH, two hands, wielding a two-handed sword, ppr. *Pl.* 3, *cr.* 5.

CARTWRIGHT, Lond. and Glouc., a griffin's head, erased, or, (pierced through neck with a lance, broken, ppr., vulned,) gu. *Pl.* 48, *cr.* 6.

CARTWRIGHT, Lond. and Notts., a wolf's head, (erased,) or, pierced through neck with an arrow, gu. *Pl.* 40, *cr.* 12.

CARTWRIGHT, a lion's head, ar., charged on neck with a Catherine-wheel, sa. *Pl.* 81, *cr.* 4, (charge, *pl.* 1, *cr.* 7.)

CARTWRIGHT, Linc., a wolf's head, erased, or, pierced through neck with a (spear,) ar. *Defend the fold. Pl.* 40, *cr.* 12.

CARUS, Westm., an eagle, wings expanded, sa., beaked and legged, or, charged with a cinque-foil, ar. *Pl.* 126, *cr.* 7.

CARVELT, Eng., a leopard's head, erased, gardant. *Pl.* 56, *cr.* 7.

CARVER, Eng., between wings, a peacock's head, in beak a snake, tail coiled round neck, all ppr. *Pl.* 50, *cr.* 9.

CARVER, out of a ducal coronet, or, a Saracen's head, couped at shoulders, ppr. *Pl.* 19, *cr.* 1, (coronet, *same plate, cr.* 9.)

CARVILE, Northumb., an arm, in armour, embowed, ppr., garnished, or, in hand, ppr., a sword, ar., hilt and pommel, of the second. *Solas virtus triumphat. Pl.* 2, *cr.* 8.

CARVILL, Eng., a goat, (passant,) sa., attired, or. *Pl.* 66, *cr.* 1.

CARWARDINE, Herts., a wolf, passant, ar., (in mouth an arrow, sa., embrued, gu.) *Pl.* 46, *cr.* 6.

CARWELL, Eng., a leopard's head, erased, gardant, ppr. *Pl.* 56, *cr.* 7.

CARY, ROBERT-SHEDDEN-SALYARDE, Esq., of Torr Abbey, Devons., a swan, ppr. *Virtute excerptæ. Pl.* 122, *cr.* 13.

CARY, GEORGE-STANLEY, Esq., of Follaton Park, Devons.: 1. For *Cary*, a swan, ppr. *Pl.* 122, *cr.* 13. 2. For *Fleming*, in dexter hand, in armour, a sword, all ppr. *Virtute excerptæ. Pl.* 125, *cr.* 5.

CARY, GEORGE, Esq., of White Castle, co. Donegal, a swan, ppr. *Sine maculâ. Pl.* 122, *cr.* 13.

CARY, Eng., a horse's head, bendy of six, ar. and sa., armed with a shield plate, bridled, or. *Pl.* 52, *cr.* 9.

CARY, Iri., two hands, couped and conjoined, ppr., supporting a cross crosslet, fitched, az. *Pl.* 52, *cr.* 15.

CARY, Lond., a lion, couchant, gardant, ppr. *Pl.* 101, *cr.* 8.

CARY, Lond., a swan, ppr., wings erect, on breast a rose, sa. *Pl.* 111, *cr.* 10.

CARYER, Kent, a dove, wings elevated, ar., membered, gu., within a circle of glory, rayonné, or. *Pl.* 124, *cr.* 7.

CARYSFORT, Earl and Baron, Eng. and Iri., (Proby,) an ostrich-head, erased, ar., ducally gorged, or, in mouth a key, of the last. *Manus hæc inimica tyrannis. Pl.* 108, *cr.* 2, (key, *pl.* 9, *cr.* 12.)

CASAER, or CEASER, Sco., a dolphin. *Pl.* 48, *cr.* 9.

CASAER, Sco., a dolphin, haurient. *Pl.* 14, *cr.* 10.

CASE, and CASSE, Eng., on a winged globe, a dove, rising, ppr. *Pl.* 50, *cr.* 7.

CASE, Sco., a cubit arm, in armour, or, in hand, gauntleted, a sword, ar., hilt and pommel, of the first, (round the arm a scarf, tied in a bow, ar. and gu.) *Pl.* 125, *cr.* 5.

CASE, Lanc. and Staffs., a cubit arm, vested, ermines, cuffed, ar., in hand, ppr., a round buckle, or. *Pl.* 38, *cr.* 9.

CASEY, Eng., a demi-talbot, per fess, or and gu. *Pl.* 97, *cr.* 9, (without arrow.)

CASEY, Eng., out of a ducal coronet, two branches of laurel, in orle. *Pl.* 114, *cr.* 15.

CASEY, Iri., out of a cloud, in hand, in fess, a garb. *Pl.* 43, *cr.* 4.

CASH, Eng., out of a mural coronet, or, on a garb, ppr., a bird. *Pl.* 14, *cr.* 5.

CASHALL, Eng., a lion, rampant, supporting a plumb-rule, ar. *Pl.* 50, *cr.* 8.

CASHEN, Berks., a rose-sprig, with leaves and buds. *Rosam ne rode. Pl.* 23, *cr.* 2.

CASLON, a spear-head, ppr. *Pl.* 82, *cr.* 7.

CASMAJOR, a lion, rampant. *Pl.* 67, *cr.* 5.

CASON, Cambs. and Herts., a cubit arm, (vested, purp., cuffed, ar.,) in hand a firelock, all ppr. *Pl.* 101, *cr.* 12.

CASS, Sco., a pair of scales, ppr. *Pl.* 12, *cr.* 11.

CASSAN, Iri., on a chapeau, a fleur-de-lis, between wings, ppr. *Pl.* 21, *cr.* 13.

CASSAN, MATTHEW-SHEFFIELD, Esq., of Sheffield House, Queen's County, issuant from an earl's coronet, ppr., a boar's head and neck, erased, or, langued, gu. *Juvant arva parentum. Pl.* 2, *cr.* 7, (coronet, *pl.* 80, *cr.* 11.)

CASSEL, or CASSELL, a hawk, regardant, supporting with dexter a garland of laurel, all ppr. *Pl.* 42, *cr.* 7.

CASSELS, a castle, ppr. *Galea spes salutis. Pl.* 28, *cr.* 11.

CASSIDY, Eng., a spear, broken in three pieces, two in saltier, the head in pale, banded, gu. *Pl.* 33, *cr.* 3.

CASSIE, Eng., a hind's head. *Pl.* 21, *cr.* 9.

CASSILIS, Earl. See AILSA, Marquess of.

CASSILS, Sco., an arm, in armour, embowed, in hand a fleur-de-lis. *Pl.* 24, *cr.* 14.

CASSON, from a tower, a dove, rising, az. *Pl.* 8, *cr.* 15.

CASSTLE, out of a castle, triple-towered, a griffin, issuant. *Pl.* 68, *cr.* 11, (castle, *pl.* 101, *cr.* 1.)

CASSY, a crow, feeding, ppr. *Pl.* 51, *cr.* 8.

CASSY, an eagle, displayed, with two heads, vert. *Pl.* 87, *cr.* 11, (without flame.)

CASTELL, Norf., a dragon's head, couped, gu. *Pl.* 87, *cr.* 12.

CASTELL, Cambs., a tower, triple-towered, sa., purfled, or. *Pl.* 123, *cr.* 14.

CASTELL, Iri., a cross fleury, fitched, vert, flowered, or. *Pl.* 65, *cr.* 9.

CASTELL, a tower, ar., in flames at top, ppr. *Pl.* 118, *cr.* 15.

CASTELL, Iri., on a tower, triple-towered, ar., an arm, in armour, erect, in hand a roundle, all ppr. *Pl.* 116, *cr.* 12, (roundles, *pl.* 141.)

CASTELYON, Linc., on a tower, a lion, (passant, or.) *Pl.* 101, *cr.* 1.

CASTER, Norf., a savage, standing on a serpent, ppr. *Pl.* 109, *cr.* 1.

CASTILLON, Berks., a lion's head, erased, gardant, ducally crowned. *Pl.* 1, *cr.* 5.

CASTLE, Lond., a tower, in flames, ppr. *Pl.* 118, *cr.* 15.

CASTLE, Lond., a dexter arm, couped and embowed, in fess, ppr., vested, gu., cuffed, or, in hand a pennon, of the second, charged with a bee, volant, gold, staff, of the first. *Pl.* 99, *cr.* 3.

CASTLE-STEUART, Earl and Baron, Viscount Steuart, (Steuart,) Iri., a unicorn's head, ar., armed, or, between two branches of laurel, vert. *Forward. Pl.* 54, *cr.* 9.

CASTLECOMB, an arm, in armour, embowed, ppr., garnished, or, in hand a pistol, ppr. *Pl.* 96, *cr.* 4.

CASTLELOCK, Kent, out of a mural coronet, or, a demi-griffin, segreant, in talon a cross crosslet, fitched, of the last.

CASTLEMAINE, Viscount and Baron, (Handcock,) Iri., a demi-lion, rampant, az., between paws a fusil, ar., (charged with a cock, gu.) *Vigilate et orate. Pl.* 126, *cr.* 12, (fusil, *pl.* 141.)

CASTLEMAN, Eng., a lion, rampant, between wings. *Pl.* 29, *cr.* 5.

CASTLEMAN, a demi-man, in armour, in hand a flag of defiance, displayed over head, sinister on the pommel of his sword, all ppr.

CASTLETON, Surr., Suff., and Linc., a dragon's head, between wings, gu. *Pl.* 105, *cr.* 11.

CASTLETON, Suff., a dragon, passant, wings addorsed, vert. *Pl.* 90, *cr.* 10.

CASTLETON, Surr., a demi-dragon, wings addorsed, gu. *Pl.* 82, *cr.* 10.

CASTLYN, a tower, ppr., with flag, gu. *Pl.* 8, *cr.* 13.

CASTON, Eng., in lion's paw, erased, sa., a cross pattée, fitched, erm. *Pl.* 46, *cr.* 7.

CASWELL, Middx., a dexter arm, couped at shoulder, in mail, in hand, ppr., a cross crosslet, fitched, or. *Pl.* 96, *cr.* 4, (cross, *pl.* 99, *cr.* 1.)

CASWELL, Middx., an arm, in armour, embowed, in hand a broken spear, all ppr. *Pl.* 44, *cr.* 9.

CATCHER, Eng., a garb, or, banded, vert. *Pl.* 48, *cr.* 10.

CATER, Berks., Hunts., and Leic., a demi-griffin, ar., beaked and legged, gu. *Pl.* 18, *cr.* 6.

CATER, Lond., a demi-griffin, gu. *Pl.* 18, *cr.* 6.

CATER, Lond. and Berks., a lion's head, erased, barry of six, or and az. *Pl.* 52, *cr.* 7.

CATERALL, Lanc. and Chesh., a cat, passant, gardant, ppr. *Pl.* 119, *cr.* 7.

CATERALL, Chesh., on a chapeau, az., turned up, erm., a cat, passant, ppr. *Pl.* 119, *cr.* 7, (chapeau, *same plate*, *cr.* 11.)

CATESBY, a leopard, passant, ppr. *Pl.* 86, *cr.* 2.

CATESBY, Northamp., an antelope's head, (couped,) ar., between attires, or, two battle-axes, erect, ppr. *Pl.* 24, *cr.* 7, (axes, *pl.* 52, *cr.* 10.)

CATESBY, or CATTESBYE, Bucks., a lion, passant, sa., crowned, or. *Pl.* 120, *cr.* 5, (coronet, *same plate*.)

CATESBY, Northamp. and Bucks., a leopard, passant, gardant, ar., pellettée. *Pl.* 51, *cr.* 7.

CATESNELBOGE, Eng., an anchor, ppr. *Pl.* 42, *cr.* 12.

CATHCART, Earl and Viscount, Baron Greenock, Eng. and Sco., (Schaw-Cathcart,) a dexter hand, couped above wrist, and erect, ppr., grasping a crescent, ar. *I hope to speed. Pl.* 38, *cr.* 7.

CATHCART, Bart., Sco., a dexter hand, holding up a heart, royally crowned, all ppr. *By faith we are saved. Pl.* 59, *cr.* 12, (crown, *pl.* 127, *fig.* 2.)

CATHCART, Eng., a pyramid, ar., environed by a vine, vert. *Pl.* 8, *cr.* 10.

CATHCART, TAYLOR, Esq., of Carbiston, Ayrs., in dexter hand, couped at wrist, a crescent, ar. *I hope to speed. Pl.* 38, *cr.* 7.

CATHCART, ALEXANDER, Esq., of Knockdolian Castle, Ayrs., same crest and motto.

CATHERENS, CATHERNS, and CATHARINES, Eng., a griffin, or, pellettée. *Pl.* 66, *cr.* 13.

CATHERY, a boar's head, couped, sa., in mouth three arrows. *Pl.* 8, *cr.* 14.

CATHIE, Sco., a stag's head, couped, ppr. *Pl.* 91, *cr.* 14.

CATHROPE, on a mount, a stag, current. *Pl.* 3, *cr.* 2.

CATLEY, in hand, erect, a sealed letter, ppr. *Pl.* 33, *cr.* 8, (without clouds.)

CATLIN, or CATLYN, Beds. and Northamp., a lion's head, erased, ar., collared and lined, or. *Pl.* 7, *cr.* 10.

CATLIN, Kent, a lion, sejant, gardant, or, between wings, addorsed, (barry of six, of the first, and az.) *Pl.* 113, *cr.* 8, (wings, *pl.* 29, *cr.* 5.)

CATOR, JOHN, Esq., of Beckingham Place, Kent, and Woodbastwick Hall, Norf., a lion's head, erased, or, collared with a bar-gemelle, az. *Nihil sine labore. Pl.* 7, *cr.* 10.

CATT, a horned owl, ppr. *Pl.* 1, *cr.* 8.

CATTELIN, a demi-leopard, rampant, gardant, ar., pellettée, ducally gorged, vert, between wings, of the last.

CATTLE, Lanc., a wolf's head, az. *Pl.* 8, *cr.* 4.

CATTLEY, a demi-cat, rampant, gardant, supporting an anchor. *Pl.* 80, *cr.* 7, (anchor, *pl.* 19, *cr.* 6.)

CATTON, a horned owl, ar. *Pl.* 1, *cr.* 8.

CATTY, a goat's head, erased, ar. *Pl.* 29, *cr.* 13.

CATZNELLAGE, Eng., the attires of a stag, or. *Ne supra. Pl.* 71, *cr.* 8.

CAULDWELL, a cock's head, couped, ar., combed and wattled, gu., between wings, in beak a cross pattée, fitched. *Pl.* 47, *cr.* 3.

CAULEY, Eng., from a plume of three ostrich-feathers, an eagle, rising, ppr. *Pl.* 54, *cr.* 8.

CAULFEILD, EDWARD-HOUSTON, Esq., of Drumcairne, co. Tyrone, a dragon's head, erased, gu., gorged with bar-gemelle, ar. *Deo duce, ferro comitante.* *Pl.* 107, *cr.* 10.

CAULFEILD, EDWIN-SOBY, Esq., R.N., of Raheenduff, Queen's County, same crest and motto.

CAULFEILD, Lieutenant-Colonel JOHN, of Bloomfield, co. Westmeath, same crest and motto.

CAULFEILD, ST GEORGE-FRANCIS, Esq., of Donamon Castle, co. Roscommon, same crest and motto.

CAULFIELD, Eng., out of a mural coronet, in hand, a sword, wavy. *Pl.* 65, *cr.* 10, (coronet, *pl.* 128, *fig.* 18.)

CAULFIELD, Earl of Charlemont. *See* CHARLEMONT.

CAUNDIS, out of an antique crown, or, a lion's head, gu. *Pl.* 126, *cr.* 1, (crown, *pl.* 79, *cr.* 12.)

CAUNTER, a naked arm, erect, couped at elbow, in hand a branch, ppr. *Pl.* 23, *cr.* 7.

CAUS, Eng., a cinquefoil, per pale, ar. and az. *Pl.* 91, *cr.* 12.

CAUSTON, Surr., a demi-leopard, (with a lion's tail, ar.,) collared, per pale, az. and gu. *Pl.* 12, *cr.* 14.

CAUSTON, Ess., a cubit arm, erect, (vested, gu., charged with two bends, wavy, sa., cuffed, ar.,) in hand, ppr., a round buckle, or. *Pl.* 38, *cr.* 9.

CAUSTON, Eng., a wolf's head, erased, or. *Pl.* 14, *cr.* 6.

CAUTY, Eng., a Catherine-wheel, az. *Pl.* 1, *cr.* 7.

CAUVIN, Sco., in dexter hand, a dagger, point downward. *Pl.* 18, *cr.* 3.

CAVALIER, Eng., a horse's head, couped, sa., armed and bridled, or, on head a plume of feathers, ar. and gu., on forehead a spiked plate, of the last. *Pl.* 55, *cr.* 7.

CAVALL, a naked man, holding a palm-tree, ppr.

CAVAN, Earl and Baron, Viscount Kilcoursie, and Lord Lambart, (Lambart,) Iri., (on a mount, vert,) a centaur, ppr., drawing a bow, gu., arrow, or. *Ut quocunque paratus.* *Pl.* 70, *cr.* 13.

CAVANAGH, Iri., a stag, lodged, between two branches of laurel. *Pl.* 24, *cr.* 4.

CAVE, Bart., Northamp., a greyhound, current, sa., (in mouth a scroll.) *Gardez.* *Pl.* 28, *cr.* 7.

CAVE, Linc. and Leic., a greyhound, current, ar. *Ib.*

CAVE, Eng., a greyhound, current, sa., collared, ar. *Ib.*

CAVE, a greyhound, current, sa., collared, or. *Cave, Deus videt.* *Ib.*

CAVENAGH, Eng., out of clouds, two dexter hands, grasping an oak-stump, sprouting anew, ppr. *Pl.* 126, *cr.* 4.

CAVENDISH, Suss., a wolf's head, or, collared, gu. *Pl.* 8, *cr.* 4.

CAVENDISH, a serpent, nowed, vert. *Pl.* 1, *cr.* 9.

CAVENDISH, on a ducal coronet, a snake, nowed, ppr. *Pl.* 116, *cr.* 2.

CAVENDISH, Duke of Devonshire. *See* DEVONSHIRE.

CAVENDISH, Baron Waterpark. *See* WATERPARK.

CAVENDISH, a stag, trippant. *Pl.* 68, *cr.* 2.

CAW, Sco., a stag's head, in mouth a serpent, ppr. *Pl.* 54, *cr.* 7.

CAWDOR, Earl and Baron, Viscount Emlyn, (Campbell,) a swan, ar., ducally crowned, or. *Be mindful.* *Pl.* 33, *cr.* 7.

CAWDOR, Eng., a sheaf of arrows, sa., shods and feathers, or, banded, gu. *Pl.* 54, *cr.* 15.

CAWLEY, Eng., out of a plume of three ostrich-feathers, an eagle, rising, ppr. *Pl.* 54, *cr.* 8.

CAWODLY, Eng., a falcon's leg and wing conjoined, ar., belled, or. *Pl.* 101, *cr.* 15.

CAWOODLEY, Devons., a hawk's leg, az., joined at knee to a wing, or, belled, of the same. *Pl.* 101, *cr.* 15.

CAWSON, Lond., out of a ducal coronet, or, a unicorn's head, ar., (ducally gorged, lined, and winged, sa.) *Pl.* 45, *cr.* 14.

CAWTHORNE, Eng., a raven. *Pl.* 123, *cr.* 2.

CAWTHORNE, Yorks., an arm, embowed, ppr., in hand a cross patonce, or. *Pl.* 47, *cr.* 13, (cross, *pl.* 141.)

CAWTON, Eng., a dromedary, sa., bezantée. *Pl.* 17, *cr.* 2.

CAY, Durh., a griffin's head, erased, az. *Patria cara carior libertas.* *Pl.* 48, *cr.* 6.

CAY, Northumb., a hawk, ppr. *Pl.* 67, *cr.* 3.

CAY, Northumb., a royal eagle, (gorged with a collar and banner, vert, bearing a rose, ar.) *Sit sine spinâ.* *Pl.* 7, *cr.* 11.

CAYLE, Iri., a demi-stag, in mouth a rose, slipped and leaved. *Pl.* 55, *cr.* 9.

CAYLE, and CAYLY, Eng., a mascle, vert. *Pl.* 54, *cr.* 1.

CAYLEY, Bart., Yorks., a lion, rampant, or, charged with a bend, gu., thereon three mullets, ar., in paws a battle-axe, ppr. *Pl.* 101, *cr.* 14, (lion, *pl.* 67, *cr.* 5.)

CAYLEY, and CEYLEY, a demi-lion, holding a battle-axe, ppr. *Pl.* 101, *cr.* 14, (without charge.)

CAYLEY, Wilts., a demi-lion, ar., charged with a bend, gu., thereon three mullets, in dexter a battle-axe of the first, handled, of the second. *Pl.* 101, *cr.* 14.

CAYLEY, EDWARD-STILLINGFLEET, Esq., of Wydale and Low Hall, Yorks., a demi-lion, rampant, or, charged with a bend, gu., thereon three mullets, ar., in paws a battle-axe, ppr. *Pl.* 101, *cr.* 14.

CAZENOVE, Eng., a sword, in pale, az., hilted, or. *Pl.* 105, *cr.* 1.

CECIL, Marquess of Salisbury and Exeter. *See* those titles.

CECILL, Eng., a garb, or, supported by two lions, rampant, the one, az., the other, ar. *Pl.* 36, *cr.* 8, (without chapeau.)

CEELY, Cornw., a tiger, sejant, ar. *Pl.* 26, *cr.* 9.

CEILY, or CEELY, an arm, in armour, in hand, a pheon, point upward, all ppr. *Pl.* 123, *cr.* 12.

CELY, or CEELY, Ess., a bundle of quills, ppr. *Pl.* 86, *cr.* 7.

CENINO, Eng., an escallop, between two palm-branches, ppr. *Pl.* 86, *cr.* 9.

CERVINGTON, Devons., a tun, or, out of the bung-hole five roses, of the same, stalked and leaved, ppr. *Pl.* 124, *cr.* 9.

CEVILIOC, Eng., an arm, in armour, embowed, round shoulder a ribbon tied in a bow, in hand a knotted club. *Pl.* 28, *cr.* 2.

CHABNOR, Herts., a pheon, or. *Pl.* 26, *cr.* 12.

CHACE, a lion, rampant, or, between feet a cross patonce, gu. *Pl.* 125, *cr.* 2, (cross, *pl.* 141.)

CHAD, Bart., Norf., a falcon, wings expanded, ppr., beaked, legged, and membered, or, supporting in dexter a cross potent, per pale, gu. and ar. *Pl.* 94, *cr.* 7, (cross, *pl.* 141.)

CHADBORN, Glouc., a demi-griffin, az. *Pl.* 18, *cr.* 6.

CHADERTON, a griffin's head, couped, gu. *Pl.* 38, *cr.* 3.

CHADOCK, a martlet, ar. *Pl.* 111, *cr.* 5.

CHADOCK, Eng., on a ducal coronet, or, a martlet, gu. *Pl.* 98, *cr.* 14.

CHADS, a unicorn's head, couped, between two laurel-branches, ppr. *Pl.* 54, *cr.* 9.

CHADWELL, out of a ducal coronet, in dexter hand a swan's head, erased, ppr. *Pl.* 65, *cr.* 12.

CHADWICK, ELIAS, Esq., of Puddleston Court, Leominster, a white lily, stalked and leaved, in pale, ppr., surmounted by two crosses, crosslet, fitched, in saltier. *In candore decus. Pl.* 126 A, *cr.* 15.

CHADWICK, Lanc., a talbot's head, gu., (pierced through neck with an arrow, or, and gorged with a collar charged with the arms of Hansacre, erm., three chess rooks, gu.) *Juxta Salopiam. Pl.* 123, *cr.* 15.

CHADWICK, Staffs., a martlet, ar. *Pl.* 111, *cr.* 5.

CHADWICK, Notts., Staffs., and Lanc., a lily, ar., stalked and leaved, vert. *In candore decus. Pl.* 22, *cr.* 9.

CHADWICK, on a ducal coronet, or, a martlet, gu. *Pl.* 98, *cr.* 14.

CHAFFY, a peacock in pride, pp. *Pl.* 92, *cr.* 11.

CHAFIN, or CHAFFIN, Dors., a talbot, or. *Pl.* 120, *cr.* 3.

CHAIGNEAU, Iri., a lion's head, erased, gu. *Pl.* 81, *cr.* 4.

CHALBOTS, Eng., two anchors, in saltier, ppr. *Pl.* 37, *cr.* 12.

CHALIE, in water, a swan, wings addorsed. *Pl.* 66, *cr.* 10.

CHALKHILL, Middx., out of a ducal coronet, or, a horse's head, erm., maned, gold. *Pl.* 50, *cr.* 13.

CHALKLEN, on a mural coronet, a sheaf of seven arrows, points upward.

CHALLENG, Glouc., an eagle's head, sa. *Pl.* 100, *cr.* 10.

CHALLENOR, Suss., a tiger, ar., biting a broken javelin, or, struck through his back, the butt erect against his side.

CHALLON, a mermaid, ppr. *Pl.* 48, *cr.* 5.

CHALLONER, Northumb., a demi-sea-wolf, rampant, or. *Sicut quercus.*

CHALMERS, JOHN-INGLIS, Esq., of Aldbar Castle, Forfars., an eagle, rising, ppr. *Spero. Pl.* 67, *cr.* 4.

CHALMERS, Balnecraig, Sco., same crest and motto.

CHALMERS, Sco., a demi-lion, in dexter a fleur-de-lis, gu. *Quid non Deo juvante. Pl.* 91, *cr.* 13.

CHALMERS, Sco., a lion's head, erased, sa. *Avancez. Pl.* 81, *cr.* 4.

CHALMERS, Sco., a hawk, rising, ppr., belled, or. *Promptus et fidelis. Pl.* 105, *cr.* 4.

CHAMBER, a demi-eagle, with two heads, displayed, per pale, sa. and ar., counterchanged, the heads (imperially) crowned, or. *Pl.* 63, *cr.* 2.

CHAMBER, Middx., Cornw., and Ess., a bear, passant, sa., muzzled, collared, and lined, or. *Pl.* 61, *cr.* 5.

CHAMBERLAIN, Bart., Lond., an eagle, displayed, ppr., dexter resting on an armillary sphere, or. *Spes et fides. Pl.* 48, *cr.* 11, (sphere, *pl.* 114, *cr.* 6.)

CHAMBERLAIN, an ass's head, erased, ar., ducally crowned, or. *Pl.* 91, *cr.* 7, (crown, *pl.* 128, *fig.* 3.)

CHAMBERLAIN, and CHAMBERLAYN, Camb., an ape's head, erased, ppr., ducally gorged, or. *Pl.* 11, *cr.* 7, (gorging, *pl.* 128, *fig.* 3.)

CHAMBERLAIN, out of a ducal coronet, or, a camel's head, ar. *Pl.* 55, *cr.* 5, (without crown or collar.)

CHAMBERLAIN, and CHAMBERLAYNE, Eng., a swan, wings addorsed, crowned, ppr. *Pl.* 33, *cr.* 7.

CHAMBERLAIN, out of a mural coronet, gu., a demi-lion, rampant, or, in dexter a key, ar. *Pl.* 120, *cr.* 11, (key, *pl.* 54, *cr.* 12.)

CHAMBERLAIN, a bear's head, erased, ar. *Pl.* 71, *cr.* 6.

CHAMBERLAIN, and CHAMBERLAN, Eng., a pheon, with part of broken shaft, ppr. *Pl.* 27, *cr.* 12.

CHAMBERLAIN, or CHAMBERLAYN, Eng., an ass's head, couped, ar. *Pl.* 91, *cr.* 7.

CHAMBERLAINE, Glouc., Oxon., and Yorks., out of a ducal coronet, an ass's head, ar. *Pl.* 80, *cr.* 6.

CHAMBERLAYNE, JOSEPH-CHAMBERLAYNE, Esq., of Maugersbury House, Glouc.: 1. Out of a ducal coronet, an ass's head. *Pl.* 80, *cr.* 6. 2. A lion's head, erased, charged with three trefoils. *Virtuti nihil invium. Pl.* 81, *cr.* 4, (trefoil, *pl.* 141.)

CHAMBERLAYNE, HENRY-THOMAS, Esq., of Stoney Thorpe, Warw., out of a ducal coronet, or, an ass's head. *Prodesse quam conspici. Pl.* 80, *cr.* 6.

CHAMBERLAYNE, THOMAS, Esq., of Cranbury Park, and Weston Grove, Hants, out of a ducal coronet, or, an ass's head, ar. *Mors potior maculâ. Pl.* 80, *cr.* 6.

CHAMBERLEN, Lond., a dexter arm, couped and embowed, in hand a grenade, fired, all ppr. *Pl.* 62, *cr.* 9.

CHAMBERS, JOHN, Esq., of Fox Hall, co. Donegal, a falcon, close, belled, ppr. *Spero dum spiro. Pl.* 67, *cr.* 3.

CHAMBERS, Iri., on a mount, a tree, ppr. *Pl.* 48, *cr.* 4.

CHAMBERS, Eng., an arm, in armour, embowed, ppr., charged with a cross, couped, gu., in hand of the first, a scimitar, ar., hilt and pommel, or. *Pl.* 81, *cr.* 11.

CHAMBERS, Sco., a lion's head, sa., langued, gu. *Pl.* 126, *cr.* 1.

CHAMBERS, Sco., a lion's head, erased, sa. *Avancez. Pl.* 81, *cr.* 4.

CHAMBERS, Sco., in dexter hand a pair of scales, ppr. *Lux mihi laurus. Pl.* 26, *cr.* 8.

CHAMBERS, an eagle's head and neck, erased, ppr., vulning, gu. *Pl.* 41, *cr.* 4.

CHAMBERS, a falcon, belled, ppr. *Non præda, sed victoria. Pl.* 67, *cr.* 3.

CHAMBERS, a bear, passant, sa., muzzled, collared, and chained, or. *Pl.* 61, *cr.* 5.

CHAMBERS, Kent, a bear, passant. *Pl.* 61, *cr.* 5.

CHAMBERS, Lond., within a mountain, vert, a man working in a copper mine, in hand a pick-axe, elevated, ppr., his cap, shirt, drawers, and hose, ar., shoes, sa., the planet Venus rising behind the mountain, or.

CHAMBERS, Lond. and Herts., a bear, passant, ppr., collared and chained, or. *Pl.* 61, *cr.* 5.

CHAMBLEY, and CHAMBLY, Eng., above a globe, a ship, ppr. *Pl.* 41, *cr.* 12.

CHAMBRE, Lond., a cock, gu., holding three wheat-ears, or. *Pl.* 55, *cr.* 12, (wheat, *pl.* 9, *cr.* 8.)

CHAMBRE, Eng., a rose-branch, ppr. *Pl.* 23, *cr.* 2.

CHAMIERE, a ducal helmet, ppr. *Pl.* 38, *cr.* 15.

CHAMOND, Cornw., a lion, sejant. *Pl.* 126, *cr.* 15.

CHAMOND, Eng., on a chapeau, ppr., a fleur-de-lis, gu., between wings, of the first. *Pl.* 21, *cr.* 13.

CHAMP, a stag, ppr. *Pl.* 68, *cr.* 2.

CHAMPAGNE, Eng., a cluster of grapes, slipped and leaved, vert. *Pl.* 89, *cr.* 1.

CHAMPAYN, Sco., a bear's head, couped, sa. *Pl.* 111, *cr.* 4.

CHAMPERNON, a lion's head, erased, ar., semée of roundles, sa., ducally crowned, or. *Pl.* 90, *cr.* 4.

CHAMPERNONNE, out of a ducal coronet, an ostrich, rising, (in mouth a horse-shoe, all ppr.) *Pl.* 29, *cr.* 9.

CHAMPEROUN, Eng., in dexter hand, a rose-branch, ppr. *Pl.* 118, *cr.* 9.

CHAMPION, Berks. and Ess., an arm, in armour, embowed, ppr., garnished, or, in gauntlet a chaplet of laurel, vert. *Pl.* 68, *cr.* 1.

CHAMPION, Kent, an arm, in (armour,) erect, couped below elbow, in hand a chaplet of laurel. *Pl.* 86, *cr.* 1.

CHAMPION, an arm, erect, vested, ar., cuffed, gu., holding the same.

CHAMPION, an arm, vested, gu., in hand a rose-branch, ppr. *Pl.* 64, *cr.* 7, (rose, *pl.* 118, *cr.* 9.)

CHAMPION, Kent and Suss., a turkey-cock, ppr.

CHAMPNEY, Lond., a leopard's head, erased, gardant, or, ducally gorged, sa. *Pl.* 116, *cr.* 8.

CHAMPNEY, Eng., a lion's gamb, erased, supporting a torteau, gu. *Pl.* 97, *cr.* 10.

CHAMPNEYS, and CHAMPNEIS, Eng., a demi-man, in profile, ppr., wreathed, ar. and sa., waistcoat, gu., sleeves, or, cuffs, gold, in dexter a gem-ring, of the fifth, stoned, az. *Pl.* 9, *cr.* 11.

CHAMPREYS, Eng., same crest. *Pro patria non timidus perire.*

CHAMPNEYS-MOSTYN, Bart., Somers. : 1. Out of a ducal coronet, or, a sword, gu., between wings, ar. *Pl.* 17, *cr.* 9, (sword, *pl.* 105, *cr.* 1.) 2. A demi-moor, full-faced, ppr., in dexter hand a diamond ring. *Pro patria non timidus perire.*

CHANCE, Warw., a demi-lion, rampant, (in paws a sword, erect,) ppr. *Pl.* 67, *cr.* 10.

CHANCELOR, or CHANCELLOR, Sco., an eagle, displayed, sa. *Que je surmonte. Pl.* 48, *cr.* 11.

CHANCEY, Herts., out of a ducal coronet, or, a griffin's head, gu., (charged with a pale, az.,) between wings, displayed, of the last, inner part of wings, of the second. *Pl.* 97, *cr.* 13.

CHANCEY, Ess. and Norf., and Chauncey, Herts., out of a ducal coronet, or, a griffin's head, wings addorsed, bendy, gu. and az., beaked, gold. *Pl.* 39, *cr.* 2.

CHANDEW, a pelican's nest, with three young birds, ppr. *Pl.* 44, *cr.* 1.

CHANDLER, Lond., a bull's head, sa., attired, ar. *Pl.* 63, *cr.* 11.

CHANDLER, a pelican, sa., in nest, vert. *Pl.* 44, *cr.* 1.

CHANDOIS, and CHANDOS, Eng., a stag's head, gu., between horns a cross pattée, az. *Pl.* 9, *cr.* 10.

CHANDOS, Eng., out of a ducal coronet, or, a dragon's head, sa. *Pl.* 59, *cr.* 14.

CHANDOS, Herts., an old man's head, in profile, ppr., hair gray, wreathed. *Pl.* 36, *cr.* 3.

CHANNY, Herts., out of a ducal coronet, a demi-eagle, displayed, or. *Pl.* 9, *cr.* 6.

CHANNSY, or CHANSEY, a griffin's head, erased, in beak a key. *Pl.* 9, *cr.* 12.

CHANTRELL, a tower, ar., (in portal a boar's head, sa.) *Pl.* 12, *cr.* 5.

CHANTRY, Eng., a lion, rampant, gu., supporting a pillar, sa. *Pl.* 67, *cr.* 5, (pillar, *pl.* 33, *cr.* 1.)

CHAPE, or CHAPPE, Norf., in dexter hand, gauntleted, a pheon, point upward, ppr. *Pl.* 123, *cr.* 12.

CHAPLAIN, a griffin's head, erased, murally gorged. *Pl.* 48, *cr.* 6, (coronet, *pl.* 128, *fig.* 18.)

CHAPLIN of Coliston, Sco., a griffin's head, erased, gu. *Labor omnia vincit. Pl.* 48, *cr.* 6.

CHAPLIN, CHARLES, Esq., of Blankney and Tathwell, Linc., a griffin's head, erased, or, murally gorged, vert. *Ib.*

CHAPLIN, Lond. and Hants., a griffin's head, erased, ar., ducally gorged, or. *Pl.* 42, *cr.* 9, (without laurel.)

CHAPMAN, Sir THOMAS, Bart., Iri., an arm, in armour, embowed, in hand a broken spear, (encircled with a wreath of laurel, all ppr.) *Crescit sub pondere virtus. Pl.* 44, *cr.* 9.

CHAPMAN, Middx., a dexter arm, in armour, embowed, in hand a broken tilting-spear, ppr., (enfiled with a chaplet, vert.) *Pl.* 44, *cr.* 9.

CHAPMAN, Linc., a fleur-de-lis, or, between two olive-branches, vert. *Pl.* 68, *cr.* 12, (branches, *pl.* 128, *fig.* 15.)

CHAPMAN, a dragon's head, couped, vert, the butt of broken spear thrust through neck, point in mouth, ppr. *Pl.* 121, *cr.* 9.

CHAPMAN, Lond. and Yorks., a buck's head, per cheveron, ar. and gu. *Pl.* 91, *cr.* 14.

CHAPMAN, Lond., an heraldic antelope's head, (erased, sa., horned, armed, and crined, or, pierced in neck by an arrow, of the last, headed, ar., embrued, gu.) *Pl.* 76, *cr.* 3.

CHAPMAN, Somers., a buck's head, cabossed, sa., attired, or, between attires two arrows, in saltier, of the last, feathered, ar. *Pl.* 124, *cr.* 14.

CHAPMAN, Iri., out of a cloud, in hand, erect, a sword, wavy, all ppr. *Pl.* 71, *cr.* 7.

CHAPMAN, Sco., a hawk, regardant, ppr., in dexter a garland of laurel. *Pl.* 42, *cr.* 7.

CHAPMAN, Sco., in hand a sword, in pale, thrust through a boar's head, erased, ppr. *Pl.* 71, *cr.* 9.

CHAPMAN, Lond., out of a crescent, per pale, or and gu., a unicorn's head, of the last, maned, horned, and guttée, gold. *Pl.* 18, *cr.* 14, (head, *pl.* 20, *cr.* 1.)

CHAPPEACE, an eagle, close, ppr. *Pl.* 7, *cr.* 11.

CHAPPELL, Lond., an arm, vested, in hand a viper, ppr. *Pl.* 58, *cr.* 4.

CHAPPES, Eng., in hand, gauntleted, a pheon, point upward, ppr. *Pl.* 123, *cr.* 12.

CHAPPLE, on stump of a tree, couped, a falcon, hooded, ppr. *Pl.* 78, *cr.* 8.

CHARD, Somers., an eagle, rising, ar., (dexter resting on an escutcheon, az., charged with a bugle-horn, stringed, or, gorged with a collar, gemelle, sa., in beak an oak-branch, slipped, ppr. *Nil desperandum. Pl.* 60, *cr.* 8.

CHARDIN, Leic., a lion, rampant. *Pl.* 67, *cr.* 5.

CHARDIN, Eng., a dove, ppr. *Pl.* 66, *cr.* 12.

CHARINGWORTH, Eng., a naked arm, embowed, in hand a cutlass, ppr. *Pl.* 92, *cr.* 5.

CHARLEMONT, Earl of, Viscount and Baron, U.K., (Caulfield,) Iri., a dragon's head, erased, gu., gorged with a bar-gemelle, ar. *Deo duce, ferro comitante. Pl.* 107, *cr.* 10.

CHARLES, Devons., a demi-eagle, displayed, with two heads, per pale, or and erm. *Pl.* 4, *cr.* 6, (without escutcheon.)

CHARLES, Lond., a demi-wolf, erm., holding a (halberd,) ar., tasselled, or. *Pl.* 56, *cr.* 8.

CHARLESWORTH, out of a ducal coronet, a cock's head, ppr. *Pl.* 97, *cr.* 15.

CHARLETON, or CHARLTON, Eng., a leopard's head, or. *Pl.* 92, *cr.* 13.

CHARLEVILLE, Earl of, and Viscount, and Baron Tullamore, Iri. *See* BURY.

CHARLEVILLE, a boar's head, couped, (pierced through back of neck with a broken dart.) *Pl.* 2, *cr.* 7.

CHARLEWOOD, or CHARLWOOD, Eng., a Saracen's head, ppr. *Pl.* 19, *cr.* 1.

CHARLEWOOD, an arrow, in pale, enfiled with a ducal coronet, all ppr. *Pl.* 55, *cr.* 1.

CHARLEY, WILLIAM, Esq., of Lisburn, Iri., on a chapeau, gu., turned up, erm., a falcon's head, erased, ppr. *Justus esto et non metu. Pl.* 126 A, *cr.* 7.

CHARLEY, and CHARNLEY, a griffin, passant, in dexter a buckle. *Pl.* 39, *cr.* 8.

CHARLTON, Ess., out of a ducal coronet, or, a demi-eagle, displayed, sa., (in beak a heart's-ease flower, ppr.) *Pl.* 9, *cr.* 8.

CHARLTON, Oxon., out of a ducal coronet, or, a unicorn's head, sa., crined, ar., horn twisted, of the last and second. *Pl.* 45, *cr.* 14.

CHARLTON, a leopard's head, cabossed. *Pl.* 66, *cr.* 14.

CHARLTON, Northumb. and Salop, two lions' gambs, erect, gu. *Pl.*42,*cr.*3,(without bezant.)

CHARLTON, Heref., a lion's face, affrontée, gu. *Sans varier. Pl.* 47, *cr.* 6.

CHARLTON, Suss., an arm, embowed, (vested, gu., cuffed, erm.,) in hand a broad arrow, ppr. *Pl.* 96, *cr.* 6.

CHARLTON, WILLIAM-HENRY, Esq., of Hesley-side, Northumb., a demi-lion, rampant. *Sans varier. Pl.* 67, *cr.* 10.

CHARLTON-LECHMERE, FRANCIS, Esq., of Ludford, Heref.: 1. For *Charlton*, a leopard's head, cabossed, gu. *Pl.* 66, *cr.* 14. 2. For *Lechmere*, out of a ducal coronet, a pelican, vulning, ppr. *Pl.* 64, *cr.* 1, (coronet, *same plate, cr.* 5.)

CHARLTON, on a chapeau, a leopard, statant, ppr. *Pl.* 110, *cr.* 8.

CHARNELL, Warw. and Leic., out of a ducal coronet, or, a demi-eagle, displayed. *Pl.* 9, *cr.* 6.

CHARNELL, a peacock, close, or. *Pl.* 54, *cr.* 13.

CHARNEY, Eng., on a rock, a dove, with olive-branch, ppr. *Pl.* 85, *cr.* 14.

CHARNOCK, Lanc., a dove, ppr. *Pl.* 66, *cr.* 12.

CHARNOCK, Beds., a lapwing, ppr. *Pl.* 10, *cr.* 12.

CHARPENTIER, Eng., in dexter hand a fleur-de-lis, gu. *Pl.* 46, *cr.* 12.

CHARRINGTON, Eng., out of a cloud, a dexter hand pointing to a star, all ppr. *Pl.* 77, *cr.* 6.

CHARTER, an ass, passant, ppr. *Pl.* 42, *cr.* 2.

CHARTERIS. *See* WEMYSS, Earl of.

CHARTERIS, Sco., a dexter hand, grasping a dagger, ppr. *This is our chart. Pl.* 28, *cr.* 4.

CHARTERIS, CHARTERS, and CHARTRES, Eng., a demi-cat, rampant, gardant, ppr. *Pl.* 80, *cr.* 7.

CHARTNAY, or CHARTNEY, Eng., two arms, in armour, embowed, vambraced, wielding a battle-axe, ppr. *Pl.* 41, *cr.* 2.

CHARTSEY, Eng., a dexter arm, embowed, holding up two (olive)-branches, in orle, ppr. *Pl.* 118, *cr.* 4.

CHARTSEY, a wolf, passant, sa., (devouring a fish, ppr.) *Pl.* 46, *cr.* 6.

CHASE, Eng., a griffin's head, erased, in beak a key. *Pl.* 9, *cr.* 12.

CHASE, Herts., a lion, rampant, sa., between paws a cross flory, or. *Pl.* 125, *cr.* 2, (cross, *pl.* 141.)

CHASSEREAU, a demi-chevalier, in armour, brandishing a sword, ppr. *Pl.* 23, *cr.* 4.

CHASTELIN, Eng., a fleur-de-lis, or. *Pl.* 68, *cr.* 12.

CHASTELON, on the point of a sword, in pale, a maunch. *Pl.* 78, *cr.* 1.

CHATER, a demi-lion, double queued, ppr. *Pl.* 120, *cr.* 10.

CHATER, Yorks., an ass, passant, ppr. *Pl.* 42, *cr.* 2.

CHATFIELD, a demi-moor, with a quiver on back, shooting an arrow, all ppr. *Pl.* 30, *cr.* 9.

CHATFIELD, or CHATFEILD, Suss., an antelope's head, erased, ar., horned, and ducally gorged, gu. *Che sara sara. Pl.* 24, *cr.* 7, (coronet, *pl.* 128, *fig.* 3.)

CHATFIELD, an heraldic antelope's head, (erased, ar.,) ducally gorged, or. *Pl.* 76, *cr.* 3, (coronet, *same plate, cr.* 8.)

CHATTERTON, Bart., Iri., an antelope's head, erased, ar., (pierced through back of neck by an arrow, ppr.) *Loyal à mort. Pl.* 79, *cr.* 9.

CHATTERTON, Cambs., a demi-griffin, gu., beaked, legged, and winged, or. *Pl.* 18, *cr.* 6.

CHATTING, Eng., a human heart, gu., transpierced by a sword, in bend sinister, point downward, ppr. *Pl.* 21, *cr.* 15.

CHATTOCK, Eng., in dexter hand a lion's paw, ppr. *Pl.* 94, *cr.* 13.

CHAUCER, two lions' gambs, ar. and gu., supporting a shield, party, per pale, counter-changed. *Pl.* 78, *cr.* 13.

CHAUCER, CHAUSER, and CHAWCER, Eng., a tortoise, passant, ppr. *Pl.* 12, *cr.* 13.

CHAUMOND, Eng., on a chapeau, ppr., a fleur-de-lis, az., between wings, of the first. *Pl.* 21, *cr.* 13.

CHAUNCEY, a savage's arm, embowed, in hand a club, ppr. *Pl.* 123, *cr.* 10.

CHAUNCEY, a dexter hand, striking with a dagger, ppr. *Pl.* 18, *cr.* 3.

CHAUNCY, CHARLES-SNELL, Esq., of Munden Parva, Herts., out of a ducal coronet, or, a griffin's head, gu., between wings, az., inward parts of wings, gu. *Pl.* 97, *cr.* 13, (without charge.)

CHAUSTER, stag's horns, ppr. *Pl.* 71, *cr.* 8.

CHAUSY, out of a ducal coronet, or, a griffin's head, paly of four, az. and gu., beaked, ar., between wings, the dexter, az., quill feathers, gu., the sinister, gu., feathered, az. *Pl.* 97, *cr.* 13, (without charge.)

CHAWNER, Eng., an ermine, passant, ppr. *Pl.* 9, *cr.* 5.

CHAWNER, EDWARD-HORE, Esq., of Newton Manor House, Hants., a sea-wolf's head, erased, sa. *Nil desperandum. Pl.* 113, *cr.* 3.

CHAWORTH, a tower, ppr., on top five ostrich-feathers, ar. *Pl.* 12, *cr.* 5, (feathers, *pl.* 100, *cr.* 12.)

CHAWORTH, a tower, ppr., on top seven ostrich-feathers, ar. *Pl.* 12, *cr.* 5, (feathers, *pl.* 114, *cr.* 8.)

CHAWORTH, a tower, ppr., (on top six laurel-leaves.) *Pl.* 72, *cr.* 15.

CHAWORTH, Eng., (a dagger, az., hilt and pommel, or,) and cross crosslet, fitched, sa., in saltier. *Pl.* 89, *cr.* 14.

CHAWREY, and CHAWSEY, Eng., an arm, from elbow, erect, ppr., (vested, per pale, ar. and sa.,) in hand a covered cup, ar. *Pl.* 35, *cr.* 9.

CHAYTOR, Bart., Yorks., a stag's head, erased, lozengy, ar. and az., dexter horn, of the first, sinister, of the second. *Fortune le veut. Pl.* 66, *cr.* 9.

CHAYTOR-CLERVEAUX, of Spennithorne Hall, Yorks.: 1. For *Chaytor*, a stag's head, erased, lozengy, ar. and az., dexter horn, of the first, sinister, of the second, *Pl.* 66, *cr.* 9. 2. For *Clerveaux*, an eagle, displayed. *Pl.* 48, *cr.* 11. 3. A heron, ppr. *Pl.* 6, *cr.* 13.

CHEALES, an eagle's head, erased, or, ducally crowned, ar. *Pl.* 20, *cr.* 7, (coronet, *pl.* 141.)

CHEAP, Sco., a garb, or, banded, vert. *Pl.* 48, *cr.* 10.

CHEDDER, and CHEDER, Eng., on a chapeau, gu., turned up, ar., a lion, passant, gardant, az., ducally crowned, ppr. *Pl.* 120, *cr.* 15.

CHEDWORTH, Devons., a wolf's head, sa., collared, or. *Pl.* 8, *cr.* 4.

CHEDWORTH, Devons., a demi-lion, rampant, gardant, az., in dexter a battle-axe, ppr. *Pl.* 26, *cr.* 7.

CHEEKE, on a chapeau, a lion, passant, ppr. *Pl.* 107, *cr.* 1.

CHEEKE, Somers. and Suff., a sword, in pale, ensigned with a cross pattée. *Pl.* 56, *cr.* 1.

CHEEKE, Suff., out of a naval coronet, or, a demi-mermaid, ppr. *Pl.* 32, *cr.* 8.

CHEESE, Eng., a talbot, passant, az., collared, or. *Pl.* 65, *cr.* 2.

CHEESE, a talbot, passant. *Pl.* 120, *cr.* 8.

CHEESE, JAMES, Esq., of Huntington Court, Heref., a lion's head, erased, or. *Omnia fert ætas. Pl.* 81, *cr.* 4.

CHEESEMAN, and CHESMAN, Eng., a dexter hand holding up a royal crown, ppr. *Pl.* 97, *cr.* 12.

CHEFFIELD, Ruts., an arm, in armour, couped, resting on elbow, in hand a (sword,) all ppr. *Pl.* 107, *cr.* 15.

CHEIN, and CHEINE, Eng., on a chapeau, two lions supporting a garb, ppr. *Pl.* 36, *cr.* 8.

CHEIN, and CHEINE, Sco., a cross pattée, fitched, ar. *Patientia vincit. Pl.* 27, *cr.* 14.

CHEISLY, or CHESLY, Sco., a rose, ppr. slipped and leaved, vert. *Fragrat post funera virtus. Pl.* 105, *cr.* 7.

CHELLEY, Eng., a leg, in armour, couped below knee, and spurred, all ppr. *Pl.* 81, *cr.* 5.

CHELMSFORD, Baron, a cornucopia, (in fess,) the horn, or, fruit, ppr., thereon a dove, in mouth a sprig of laurel, ppr. *Spes et fortuna. Pl.* 91, *cr.* 4, (dove, *pl.* 48, *cr.* 15.)

CHELSUM, a garb, or. *Pl.* 48, *cr.* 10.

CHELSUM, Eng., a greyhound, current, ar. *Pl.* 28, *cr.* 7, (without charge.)

CHELTENHAM, a demi-eagle, displayed, ppr. *Pl.* 22, *cr.* 11.

CHEMERE, a peer's helmet, or. *Pl.* 8, *cr.* 12.

CHENELL, Eng., an arm, ppr., vested, sa., cuffed, or., in hand a covered cup, ar. *Pl.* 39, *cr.* 1.

CHENEY, Eng., two bulls' horns, ar. *Pl.* 9, *cr.* 15.

CHENEY, ROBERT-HENRY, Esq., of Badger Hall, Salop, a bull's scalp, ar. *Fato prudentia major. Pl.* 9, *cr.* 15.

CHENY, a demi-lion, ar., (holding a gem ring, or, enriched with a precious stone, ppr.) *Pl.* 113, *cr.* 2.

CHEOKE, a bird's head, sa. *Pl.* 100, *cr.* 10.

CHEPSTOW, Eng., an arm, vambraced, az., studded and garnished, or, in hand a sword, ppr. *Pl.* 2, *cr.* 8.

CHERBRON, in lion's gamb, erect, gu., a griffin's head, erased, or. *Pl.* 126, *cr.* 9, (head, *pl.* 38, *cr.* 3.)

CHERE, Eng., a talbot, passant, az., collared and ringed, or. *Præmium virtutis honor. Pl.* 65, *cr.* 2.

CHERLEY, Eng., a cross patonce, between two stalks of wheat, or, leaved, ppr. *Pl.* 9, *cr.* 13.

CHERNOCK, a martlet, sa. *Pl.* 111, *cr.* 5.

CHERWOOD, Eng., a unicorn's head, or, between two laurel-branches, vert. *Pl.* 54, *cr.* 9.

CHESBROUGH, a demi-lion, rampant, gu., between paws a cross pattée, or. *Pl.* 126, *cr.* 12, (cross, *pl.* 141.)

CHESELDON, and CHESELDYNE, Ruts., a talbot, couchant, ar., spotted, sa. *Pl.* 32, *cr.* 7.

CHESELDON, and CHESELDYNE, Ruts., a talbot, passant, ar., spotted, sa., collared and lined, or. *Pl.* 65, *cr.* 2.

CHESHAM, Lanc., out of a ducal coronet, a lion's gamb, erect, or. *Pl.* 67, *cr.* 7.

CHESHAM, Lanc., a falcon, wings expanded, ppr. *Pl.* 105, *cr.* 4.

CHESHIRE, a talbot, sejant, supporting with paws a shield, (charged with a garb.) *Pl.* 19, *cr.* 2.

CHESHIRE, or CHESSHYRE, Eng., a hawk's lure, purp. *Pl.* 97, *cr.* 14.

CHESLIE, CHIESLY, and CHISLIE, Sco., an eagle, displayed, ppr. *Credo et videbo.* Pl. 48, cr. 11.

CHESLIN, Lond., a tower, ar. Pl. 12, cr. 5.

CHESLIN, Lond., a fleur-de-lis, per pale, vert and az. Pl. 68, cr. 12.

CHESNEY, a man's head, bearded and wreathed, ppr. Pl. 36, cr. 3.

CHESTER, CHARLES, Esq., Bush Hall, Herts., a demi-griffin, rampant, erm., beak, tongue, talons, and eyes, ppr. *Vincit qui patitur.* Pl. 18, cr. 6.

CHESTER, the Rev. ANTHONY, of Chichley Hall, Bucks., a ram's head, couped, ar., attired, or. Pl. 34, cr. 12.

CHESTER, Glouc., in lion's gamb, erased, gu., a broken sword, ar., hilted, or. Pl. 49, cr. 10.

CHESTER, Bucks., a ram's head, erased, ar., armed, or. Pl. 1, cr. 12.

CHESTER, Leic., a dragon, passant, ar. Pl. 90, cr. 10.

CHESTER, Ess., a (cutlass,) ar., hilt and pommel, or, between two branches of laurel, ppr. Pl. 71, cr. 3.

CHESTER, Glouc., a griffin, (passant.) Pl. 66, cr. 13.

CHESTERFIELD, Earl of, and Baron Stanhope, (Stanhope,) from battlements of tower, az., a demi-lion, issuant, or, ducally crowned, gu., between paws a grenade, fired, ppr. *A Deo et rege.* Pl. 53, cr. 2.

CHESTERFIELD, Eng., on a chapeau, a greyhound, statant, ppr. Pl. 104, cr. 1.

CHESTERTON, a tiger's head, erased. Pl. 94, cr. 10.

CHESTON, Suff., in dexter, gauntleted, in fess, ppr., a sword, ar., hilt and pommel, or, on blade a Saracen's head, couped, (dropping blood, gu.) *Ex merito.* Pl. 36, cr. 10.

CHETHAM, Eng., in the sea, a rock, ppr. Pl. 91, cr. 5.

CHETHAM, Suff., a griffin, passant, regardant, ar., wings addorsed, or, charged with a crescent, gu. Pl. 4, cr. 9, (crescent, pl. 141.)

CHETITOR, Durh., a stag's head, erased, lozengy, ar. and az., dexter horn, ar., sinister, az. Pl. 66, cr. 9.

CHETTLE, Eng., on a rock, a wyvern, wings addorsed, ppr. Pl. 73, cr. 12, (wyvern, pl. 122, cr. 2.)

CHETUM, Lanc., a demi-griffin, gu., charged with a cross potent, az. Pl. 18, cr. 6, (cross, pl. 141.)

CHETWODE, Bart., Bucks. and Staffs., out of a ducal coronet, or, a demi-lion, rampant, gu. *Corona mea Christus.* Pl. 45, cr. 7.

CHETWODE, a sea-lion, sejant. Pl. 80, cr. 13.

CHETWODE-LUDFORD, Warw.: 1. For *Chetwode*, out of a ducal coronet, a demi-lion, rampant, gu. Pl. 45, cr. 7. 2. For *Ludford*, a boar's head, couped, erminois, in mouth a cross pattée, gu. Pl. 125, cr. 7, (cross, pl. 141.)

CHETWYN, Eng., a human heart, pierced with a passion nail, ppr. Pl. 81, cr. 3.

CHETWYND, Viscount, and Baron Rathdowne, (Chetwynd,) Iri., a goat's head, erased, ar., armed, or. *Probitas verus honos.* Pl. 29, cr. 13.

CHETWYND, Sir GEORGE, Bart., Staffs., a goat's head, erased, ar., armed, or. *Quod Deus vult fiet.* Pl. 29, cr. 13.

CHEUREUSE, an eagle, displayed, or, winged, ar. Pl. 48, cr. 11.

CHEVALIER, Eng., a demi-chevalier, in armour, brandishing a scimitar. Pl. 27, cr. 11.

CHEVERELL, and CHEVERILL, Eng., two dexter hands, conjoined, holding a sword, in pale, all ppr. Pl. 75, cr. 8.

CHEVERS, Eng., an arm, in armour, embowed, couped at shoulder, part above elbow, in fess, in hand, in pale, a close helmet, ppr. Pl. 114, cr. 9.

CHEVIL, Eng., an arm, in armour, embowed, in hand a sword, all ppr. Pl. 2, cr. 8.

CHEW, Lond. and Beds., a griffin, sejant, ar., guttée-de-sang, beaked, legged, and winged, sa., dexter resting on a Catherine-wheel, gu. Pl. 56, cr. 13, (wheel, pl. 1, cr. 7.)

CHEYN, and CHEYNE, Eng., in dexter hand an escallop, ppr. Pl. 57, cr. 6.

CHEYNE, Eng. and Sco., a cross pattée, or. *Patientia vincit.* Pl. 15, cr. 8.

CHEYNE, of Esselmont, a cross pattée, fitched, or. *Patientia vincit.* Pl. 27, cr. 14.

CHEYNE, of Straloch, a capuchin's cap. *Fear God.* Pl. 55, cr. 3.

CHEYNE, a buck's head, erased. Pl. 66, cr. 9.

CHEYNE, Sco., a cross crosslet, fitched. Pl. 16, cr. 10.

CHEYNEY, Kent, Beds., and Berks., a bull's scalp, or, attired, ar. Pl. 9, cr. 15.

CHEYNEY, Cambs., a cap, or, turned up, az., on each side a feather, erect, ppr. Pl. 6, cr. 12.

CHEYNEY, a wolf, passant, vert, ducally gorged and lined, or. Pl. 46, cr. 6, (coronet, *same plate,* cr. 2.)

CHEYNEY, Bucks., a bear's head, erased, gu., (chained, ar., ringed, or.) Pl. 71, cr. 6.

CHEYNEY, Beds., a bull's scalp, or, attired, ar. Pl. 9, cr. 16.

CHEYTER, and CHEYTOR, Durh., a bull's head, erased, lozengy, ar. and az., attired, counterchanged. Pl. 91, cr. 14.

CHIBNALL, Northamp., Bucks., and Beds., a wolf's head, ppr. Pl. 14, cr. 6.

CHIBNALL, Beds. and Northamp., a dragon's head, (erased,) sa., ducally gorged and lined, or. Pl. 36, cr. 7.

CHICHELEY, Cambs., a tiger, passant, ar. Pl. 67, cr. 15.

CHICHESTER, ROBERT, Esq., of Hall, Devons., a heron, rising, with eel in mouth, ppr. *Ferme en foy.* Pl. 59, cr. 11.

CHICHESTER, Marquess of Donegal. See DONEGALL.

CHICHESTER, Earl of, and Baron Pelham, (Pelham:) 1. A peacock in pride, ar. Pl. 92, cr. 11. 2. A buckle, ar. *Vincet amor patriæ.* Pl. 73, cr. 10.

CHICHESTER, Bart., Devons., a bittern, rising, in beak an eel, ppr. Pl. 59, cr. 11.

CHICHESTER, Devons. and Dors., a (stork,) wings addorsed, ppr., in beak a snake, vert. Pl. 59, cr. 11.

CHICK, a demi-pegasus, rampant, sa., enfiled round body with a ducal coronet. Pl. 91, cr. 2.

CHICKLEY, Eng., a demi-pegasus, rampant, sa., enfiled round body with a ducal coronet, or. Pl. 91, cr. 2.

CHIEFLY, a lion's head, erased, or. Pl. 81, cr. 4.

CHIENE, on a chapeau, two lions supporting a garb, ppr. *Pl.* 36, *cr.* 8.

CHIESLY, Sco., a rose, gu., stalked, vert. *Fragrat post funera virtus.* *Pl.* 105, *cr.* 7.

CHIESLY, Sco., an eagle, displayed, ppr. *Credo et videbo.* *Pl.* 48, *cr.* 11.

CHILBORNE, Ess., a hawk's head, erased, az., (in beak a ring, or, to which is attached an etoile, gold.) *Pl.* 34, *cr.* 11, (ring and etoile, *pl.* 141.)

CHILCOTE, and CHILCOTT, out of a ducal coronet, a mount, thereon a stag, statant, gu. *Pl.* 46, *cr.* 2.

CHILD, Lond. and Worc., on a rock, ppr., an eagle, rising, wings addorsed, ar., (gorged with a ducal coronet, or, round neck a snake entwined, ppr.) *Pl.* 61, *cr.* 1.

CHILD, Ess., a leopard's face, or, between two laurel-branches, ppr. *Spes alit.* *Pl.* 31, *cr.* 7, (branches, *same plate, cr.* 5.)

CHILD, on a mount, an eagle, rising, (in mouth a snake, all ppr.) *Pl.* 61, *cr.* 1.

CHILD, Hants and Salop, an eagle, wings expanded, ar., round the neck a snake entwined, ppr. *Imitare quam invidere.* *Pl.* 67, *cr.* 4, (snake, *pl.* 119, *cr.* 1.)

CHILD, an eagle, wings expanded, erm., in beak a trefoil, slipped, vert. *Pl.* 67, *cr.* 4, (trefoil, *pl.* 141.)

CHILD, Surr., an eagle, wings expanded, between two ears of big wheat, in beak a serpent, entwined round neck, all ppr. *Imitare quam invidere.* *Pl.* 67, *cr.* 4, (wheat, *pl.* 9; serpent, *pl.* 50, *cr.* 9.)

CHILDERS, Yorks., an arm, (in armour,) erect, ppr., in hand a buckle, az. *Pl.* 38, *cr.* 9.

CHILDERS-WALBANKE, JOHN, Esq., of Cantley, Yorks., in dexter hand a round buckle. *Pl.* 38, *cr.* 9.

CHILMICK, Salop, a lion, sejant, gardant, or, supporting with dexter an escutcheon, vert. *Pl.* 113, *cr.* 8, (escutcheon, *pl.* 19, *cr.* 2.)

CHILTON, a boar's head, couped at neck, or, (in mouth two roses, one ar., the other gu., leaved and stalked, ppr.) *Pl.* 125, *cr.* 7.

CHILTON, Kent, a griffin, passant, sa., bezantée, or. *Pl.* 66, *cr.* 13, (bezants, *pl.* 141.)

CHILWORTH, Devons., a boar's head and neck, erased, sa., ducally gorged, or. *Pl.* 36, *cr.* 9.

CHINEY, Eng., an arm, in armour, embowed, in gauntlet a sabre, ppr. *Pl.* 81, *cr.* 11.

CHINN, Glouc., on a ducal coronet, or, a greyhound, sejant, ar. *Pl.* 66, *cr.* 15, (coronet, *pl.* 128, *fig.* 3.)

CHINNERY, Sir BRODERICK, Bart., Iri., a falcon, rising from the top of a bezant, all ppr., (collared, or.) *Nec temere, nec timide.* *Pl.* 105, *cr.* 4, (bezant, *pl.* 141.)

CHIPCHASE, or CHIPEHASE, Eng., a demi-eagle, in dexter a laurel-branch, ppr. *Pl.* 59, *cr.* 13.

CHIPMAN, Somers., a leopard, sejant, ar.; murally crowned, gu. *Pl.* 86, *cr.* 8, without coronet; (crown, *same plate, cr.* 11.)

CHIPNAN, Heref., a dexter and sinister arm shooting an arrow, ppr. *Pl.* 100, *cr.* 4.

CHIPPENDALE, in lion's gamb, erect, ar., a fleur-de-lis, or. *Pl.* 60, *cr.* 14, (fleur-de-lis, *pl.* 141.)

CHIPPENDALL, Lond., in lion's gamb, erased, a fleur-de-lis, or. *Firmor ad fidem.* *Pl.* 60, *cr.* 14, (fleur-de-lis, *pl.* 141.)

CHIRBROND, Eng., a winged heart, ppr. *Pl.* 39, *cr.* 7.

CHIRNSIDE, Sco., a hawk, wings expanded, ppr. *Pl.* 105, *cr.* 4.

CHISALME, Sco., a boar's head, erased, ppr. *Pl.* 16, *cr.* 11.

CHISELDINE, a talbot, couchant, ar., spotted, sa., eared, and (collared, gu., chained, or, end of chain in a bow-knot, gold.) *Pl.* 32, *cr.* 7.

CHISENAL, and CHISENHALL, Lanc., a griffin, segreant, gu. *Pl.* 67, *cr.* 13.

CHISHOLM, Lond. and Northumb., in dexter hand a sword, erect, ppr., on point a boar's head, couped, gu. *Vi et arte.* *Pl.* 71, *cr.* 9.

CHISHOLM, Kent and Sco., in hand, couped below wrist, a dagger, erect, all ppr., on point a boar's head, erased, or, langued, gu. *Pl.* 71, *cr.* 9.

CHISHOLM, The, DUNCAN-MACDONELL CHISHOLM, of Erchless Castle, Inverness, in dexter hand a dagger, erect, ppr., on point a boar's head, couped, gu. *Feros ferio.* *Pl.* 71, *cr.* 9.

CHISHOLME, Eng., out of a ducal coronet, a dragon's head, wings addorsed. *Pl.* 59, *cr.* 14.

CHISHOLME, Sco., a boar's head, erased. *Pl.* 16, *cr.* 11.

CHISHOLME, Sco., of Comer, in dexter hand a dagger, in pale, ppr. *Vi et virtute.* *Pl.* 23, *cr.* 15.

CHISWELL, Lond., a mermaid, ppr. *Pl.* 48, *cr.* 5.

CHISWELL, Lond., a dove with olive-branch, ppr., on a bezant. *Pl.* 48, *cr.* 15, (bezant, *pl.* 141.)

CHITTOCK, a demi-stag, ppr., attired, or. *Pl.* 55, *cr.* 9, (without rose.)

CHITTOCK, Eng., an antelope, trippant, ppr. *Pl.* 63, *cr.* 10.

CHITTY, Lond., a talbot's head, couped, or. *Pl.* 123, *cr.* 15.

CHITWOOD, Eng., on a mount, vert, a crow, sa. *Pl.* 34, *cr.* 13.

CHITWYNDE, a sword, in pale, ppr., on point a boar's head, erased. *Pl.* 10, *cr.* 2.

CHIVERS, a comet star, tail towards sinister, ppr. *Pl.* 39, *cr.* 9.

CHOARE, on top of a tower, ar., port, sa., a row of five feathers, or. *Pl.* 12, *cr.* 5, (feathers, *pl.* 106, *cr.* 11.)

CHOISEUL, Iri., a dexter and sinister hand supporting a two-edged sword, in pale, all ppr. *Pl.* 75, *cr.* 8.

CHOKE, out of a ducal coronet, a demi-stork, ppr.

CHOKE, Berks., a stork's head, ppr., beaked, gu. *Pl.* 32, *cr.* 5.

CHOLMELEY, Bart., Linc., a garb, or. *Pl.* 48, *cr.* 10.

CHOLMELEY, and CHOLMONDLEY, Eng., a demi-griffin, segreant, sa., winged and beaked, or, in claws a helmet, ppr. *Pl.* 19, *cr.* 15.

CHOLMELEY, a royal helmet, ar., (another, or.) *Pl.* 38, *cr.* 15.

CHOLMLEY, GEORGE, Esq., of Whitby and Howsham, Yorks., a demi-griffin, segreant, sa., beaked, or, in dexter a helmet, ar. *Pl.* 19, *cr.* 15.

CHOLMELEY, FRANCIS, Esq., of Bransby Hall, Yorks., same crest.

CHOLMONDELEY, Marquess and Earl of, Earl of Rocksavage, Viscount Malpas, &c., (Cholmondeley,) a demi-griffin, segreant, sa., beaked, winged, and membered, or, between claws a helmet, ppr., garnished, gold. *Cassis tutissima virtus.* Pl. 19, cr. 15.

CHOLMONDELEY, Yorks., a garb, or. Pl. 48, cr. 10.

CHOLMONLY, Lond., a helmet, ar., garnished, or, charged with three torteaux, one and two. Pl. 109, cr. 5, (torteau, pl. 141.)

CHOLWELL, a leopard's face, az. Pl. 66, cr. 14.

CHOLWICH, and CHOLWICK, a lion's gamb, sa., supporting an ancient shield, or. Pl. 43, cr. 12.

CHOLWICH, and CHOLWICK, a fox's head, couped, sa. Pl. 91, cr. 9.

CHOLWILL, or CHOLVILLE, Devons., a linnet, ppr. Pl. 52, cr. 12.

CHOOKE, an ibex's head, erased, ar., (gorged with a crown, gu.,) double-horned, or. Pl. 72, cr. 9.

CHOPINGE, Lond., a tree, vert, fructed, or, stem, ar., charged with two bends, wavy, gu., on sinister side of stem a woodpecker, ppr. Pl. 13, cr. 4.

CHORLEY, Lanc. and Staffs., on a chapeau, gu., turned up, erm., a hawk's head, erased, ar. Pl. 34, cr. 11, (chapeau, *same plate*, cr. 10.)

CHOUGH, a demi-lion, rampant, sa., collared, ar., (in paws a halberd, in pale, or.) Pl. 18, cr. 13.

CHOWNE, Kent, in (gauntlet, ar.,) a broad arrow, sa., feathered, of the first. Pl. 43, cr. 13.

CHRIGHTON, or CRIGHTON, a dragon's head, vomiting fire, ppr. Pl. 37, cr. 9.

CHRISOPE, an antelope, passant, ppr., (collared and chained, or.) Pl. 63, cr. 10.

CHRISOPE, Eng., a bear's head, muzzled. Pl. 111, cr. 4.

CHRISTALL, Sco., a fir-tree, ppr. *Per augusta ad augusta.* Pl. 26, cr. 10.

CHRISTIAN, Iri., a lion, couchant, gardant, ppr. Pl. 101, cr. 8.

CHRISTIAN, a unicorn's head, erased, ar., maned and armed, or. Pl. 67, cr. 1.

CHRISTIAN, Eng., a lion, sejant, gardant, on its hind legs, in dexter a cross, resting sinister on a pyramid, sa. Pl. 56, cr. 12.

CHRISTIAN, the figure of Hope, ppr., robed, ar., leaning on an anchor, or. Pl. 107, cr. 2, (without man's head.)

CHRISTIAN, a greyhound, current, ppr. Pl. 28, cr. 7, (without charge.)

CHRISTIAN, out of a naval coronet, a unicorn's head. Pl. 20, cr. 1, (coronet, pl. 128, fig. 19.)

CHRISTIAN, JOHN, Esq., M.A., of Ewanrigg Hall, Cumb., and Milntown, Isle of Man, a unicorn's head, erased, ar., armed, and gorged with a collar, invecked, or. *Salus per Christum.* Pl. 73, cr. 1.

CHRISTIE, a cross Calvary, on three grieces, gu. *Sit vita nomini congrua.* Pl. 49, cr. 2.

CHRISTIE, of Craigton, a holly-branch, withered, with leaves sprouting anew, ppr. *Sic viresco.* Pl. 25, cr. 9.

CHRISTIE, Iri., out of an earl's coronet, a moor's head, from shoulders, ppr. Pl. 80, cr. 11.

CHRISTIE, a holly-slip, leaved and fructed, ppr. Pl. 99, cr. 6.

CHRISTIE, CHARLES-MAITLAND, Esq., of Durie, Fife, in dexter hand a missive letter, ppr. *Pro rege.* Pl. 28, cr. 8.

CHRISTIE, a laurel-branch, ppr. Pl. 123, cr. 5.

CHRISTIE, Sco., a holly-bush, ppr. *Sic viresco.* Pl. 124, cr. 10.

CHRISTIE, a phoenix in flames, ppr. Pl. 44, cr. 8.

CHRISTMAS, an arm, embowed, ppr., vested, or, covered with leaves, vert, supporting a staff, couped and raguly, ar. Pl. 83, cr. 2, (staff, pl. 78, cr. 15.)

CHRISTMAS, an arm, ppr., charged with two bars, or and gu., holding a double branch of roses, flowered, gold, leaved, vert.

CHRISTOPHER, Norf., a unicorn's head, erased, ar. Pl. 67, cr. 1.

CHRISTOPHER, Lond., two arms, embowed, vested, az., hands, ppr., supporting an anchor, sa., cable, ar.

CHRISTOPHER, Eng., a stag's head, cabossed, ppr. Pl. 36, cr. 1.

CHRYSTIE, in lion's paw, erased, a dagger, ppr. Pl. 56, cr. 3.

CHUBBE, a demi-lion, az., holding a bezant. Pl. 126, cr. 12.

CHUDLEIGH, a savage, ppr., wreathed about loins and temples, vert, in dexter a club, spiked, or.

CHUDLEIGH, a savage, ppr., in profile, in dexter a spiked club, or, a bugle-horn hung over left shoulder, wreathed about loins and temples, vert.

CHUN, a boar, passant, regardant, pierced in shoulder by an arrow, end in mouth, all ppr.

CHURCH, Ess., an arm, in armour, ppr., garnished, or, in hand a baton, gold. Pl. 33, cr. 4.

CHURCH, in hand a sword, erect, between two branches of laurel, entwined round blade, all ppr. *Virtute.* Pl. 23, cr. 15, (laurel, pl. 71, cr. 3.)

CHURCH, Middx. and Wel., in hand a sword, erect, between two branches of laurel entwined round blade, all ppr. Pl. 23, cr. 15, (laurel, pl. 71, cr. 3.)

CHURCH, Iri., a talbot, collared, ppr. Pl. 65, cr. 2.

CHURCH, Eng., a cloud, ppr. Pl. 124, cr. 12.

CHURCH, a greyhound's head, (erased, sa.,) collared, or, charged with eight bezants, ar. Pl. 43, cr. 11, (bezant, pl. 141.)

CHURCHAR, Suss., a tiger, passant, ar., maned and tufted, or. Pl. 67, cr. 15.

CHURCHE, Ess., a demi-greyhound, sa., (collared, or, charged with three lozenges, gu., holding a trefoil, of the second.) Pl. 48, cr. 3, (chargings, pl. 141.)

CHURCHE, Salop, a greyhound's head, (erased,) erm., collared and ringed, or. Pl. 43, cr. 11.

CHURCHEY, Wel., a greyhound's head, (erased,) sa., collared, or. Pl. 43, cr. 11.

CHURCHILL, Baron, (Spencer,) out of a ducal coronet, or, a griffin's head, between wings, expanded, ar., (gorged with a bar-gemelle, gu.,) armed, of the first. *Dieu defend le droit.* Pl. 97, cr. 13, (without charge.)

CHURCHILL, Eng., a savage's head, affrontée, ducally crowned, ppr. Pl. 28, cr. 3.

CHURCHILL, Duke of Marlborough. *See* MARLBOROUGH.

CHURCHILL, a lion, couchant, gardant, ar., (holding a banner, of the last, charged with a hand, erect, gu.) *Pl.* 101, *cr.* 8.

CHURCHILL, Dors., Devons., and Somers., out of a ducal coronet, or, a demi-lion, rampant, ar. *Pl.* 45, *cr.* 7.

CHURCHMAN, Lond., on a garb, in fess, or, a cock, ar., beaked, legged, and wattled, gu. *Pl.* 122, *cr.* 3.

CHURCHMAN, Salop, out of a ducal coronet, or, a demi-lion, rampant, ar. *Pl.* 45, *cr.* 7.

CHURCHYARD, an arm, in armour, embowed, in hand a baton, and thereon suspended a laurel crown, ppr.

CHURSTON, Lord. *See* BULLER.

CHUTE, Hants and Kent, in gauntlet, ppr., a (broken sword,) ar., hilt and pommel, or. *Pl.* 125, *cr.* 5.

CHUTER, in dexter hand a spur. *Pl.* 34, *cr.* 9.

CHUTZ, an arm, in armour, in gauntlet a (broken sword,) all ppr. *Pl.* 125, *cr.* 5.

CHYNER, an antelope's head, erased, erm. *Pl.* 24, *cr.* 7.

CIDDEROWE, out of a tower, ar., a demi-lion, rampant, sa. *Pl.* 42, *cr.* 4.

CIELY, Cornw., a tiger, sejant, ar. *Pl.* 26, *cr.* 9.

CINSALLAGH, Iri., a lion's head, erased, ppr. *Pl.* 81, *cr.* 4.

CIPRIANI, an eagle, displayed, sa., crowned, gu. *Pl.* 85, *cr.* 11, (without charge.)

CLABROCK, Middx. and Kent, out of a ducal coronet, or, a demi-ostrich, ar., wings displayed, erm., (in mouth a horse-shoe, sa.) *Pl.* 29, *cr.* 9.

CLACK, Eng., on a mount, a holy lamb and flag, ppr. *Pl.* 101, *cr.* 9.

CLACK, Eng., an old man's head, couped at shoulder, vested, gu., wreathed, ar. *Pl.* 126, *cr.* 8.

CLACK, Heref. and Berks., a demi-eagle, or, winged, erm. *Pl.* 52, *cr.* 8.

CLAGETT, Lond., Kent, and Surr., an eagle's head, erased, erm., ducally crowned, or, between wings, sa. *Pl.* 20, *cr.* 7, (crown, *same plate, cr.* 12.)

CLAGSTONE, a falcon, rising, ppr. *Pl.* 105, *cr.* 4.

CLAMOND, Cornw., a griffin, sejant, or. *Pl.* 100, *cr.* 11.

CLANBRASIL, Baron. *See* RODEN, Earl of.

CLANCARTY, Earl of, Viscount Dunlo, and Baron Kilconnel, Iri.; Viscount Clancarty and Baron Trench, Eng., (*Le Poer*-Trench): 1. An arm, in armour, embowed, in hand a sword, all ppr. *Pl.* 2, *cr.* 8. 2. A lion, rampant, or, (imperially crowned, in dexter a sword, ar., hilt and pommel, gold, in sinister a sheaf of arrows, of the last.) *Pl.* 98, *cr.* 1.) 3. A stag's head cabossed, ar., attired, or, between attires a crucifix. *Consilio et prudentiâ*. *Pl.* 36, *cr.* 1, (cross, *pl.* 141.)

CLANCY, Iri.; and CLANNY, Durh., in hand, gauntleted, a dagger, in pale, on point a wolf's head, couped, dropping blood, gu. *Pl.* 96, *cr.* 11.

CLANDINEN, Iri., a demi-lion, holding a mullet of (six) points. *Pl.* 89, *cr.* 10.

CLANMORRIS, Baron, (Bingham,) Iri., on a rock, an eagle, rising, ppr. *Spes mea Christus*. *Pl.* 61, *cr.* 1.

CLANRICARDE, Marquess and Earl of, Baron Dunkellin, Iri.; Baron Somerhill, Eng., (De Burgh,) a mountain-cat, sejant, gardant, ppr., (collared and chained, or.) *Une roy, une foy, une loy*. *Pl.* 24, *cr.* 6.

CLANWILLIAM, Earl of, and Viscount, Iri.; Baron Clanwilliam, U.K., (Meade,) an eagle, displayed, with two heads, sa., armed, or. *Toujours prêt*. *Pl.* 87, *cr.* 11, (without flames.)

CLAPCOTT, a buck's head, couped, sa., armed, or. *Pl.* 91, *cr.* 14.

CLAPHAM, Lond., Northamp., and Devons., a lion, rampant, sa., collared, ar., (holding a sword, of the last, hilted, or.) *Pl.* 88, *cr.* 1.

CLAPHAM, Sco., in dexter hand a helmet, ppr. *Pl.* 37, *cr.* 15.

CLAPHAM, JOHN-PEELE, Esq., of Burley Grange, Yorks., a lion, rampant. *Post est occasio calva*. *Pl.* 67, *cr.* 5.

CLAPP, Eng., a pike, naiant, ppr. *Pl.* 39, *cr.* 11.

CLAPPERTON, Sco., a talbot, passant, ar. *Fides præstantior auro*. *Pl.* 120, *cr.* 8.

CLAPTON, Hants, a dolphin, erect, (head downwards.) *Pl.* 14, *cr.* 10.

CLARE, Earl of, Viscount and Baron Fitzgibbon, Iri.; Baron Fitzgibbon, U. K., (Fitzgibbon,) a boar, passant, gu., bristled, or, charged on body with three annulets, gold. *Nil admirari*. *Pl.* 48, *cr.* 14, (annulet, *pl.* 141.)

CLARE, Salop and Worc., a stag's head, cabossed, ppr. *Pl.* 36, *cr.* 1.

CLARENDON, Earl of, and Baron Hyde, (Villiers,) a lion, rampant, ar., ducally crowned, or. *Fidei coticula crux*. *Pl.* 98, *cr.* 1.

CLAREUX, Yorks., a chatter, ppr., top of head, gu. *Pl.* 10, *cr.* 12.

CLARGE, a ram's head, (with two straight and two bent horns, or.) *Pl.* 34, *cr.* 12.

CLARGES, out of a ducal coronet, a ram's head, armed with four horns, or. *Pl.* 124, *cr.* 8, (coronet, *pl.* 128, *fig.* 3.)

CLARINA, Baron, (Massey,) Iri., out of a ducal coronet, or, a bull's head, gu., armed, sa. *Pro libertate patriæ*. *Pl.* 68, *cr.* 6.

CLARK, GEORGE T., Esq., Dowlais House, Merthyr Tydvil, a lion, rampant, supporting a shield, gyronny of eight. *Try and tryst*. *Pl.* 126 B., *cr.* 5.

CLARK, Bucks. and Beds., a goat, ar., against a tree, ppr. *Pl.* 32, *cr.* 10.

CLARK, or CLARKE, Derbs., in a gem ring, or, set with a diamond, sa., a pheon, ar. *Pl.* 75, *cr.* 15.

CLARK, Eng., a fox's head, gu. *Pl.* 91, *cr.* 9.

CLARK, Eng. and Sco., a demi-huntsman, winding a horn, ppr. *Free for a blast*. *Pl.* 38, *cr.* 8.

CLARK, a falcon, rising. *Pl.* 105, *cr.* 4.

CLARK, in hand a dagger, in bend sinister. *Pl.* 28, *cr.* 4.

CLARK, a pheon, ppr. *Pl.* 26, *cr.* 12.

CLARK, Iri., on a mural coronet, az., a stag, sejant, or. *Pl.* 101, *cr.* 3.

CLARK, a talbot's head, (couped,) or, collared, az., charged with a plate. *Pl.* 2, *cr.* 15.

CLARK, a demi-griffin, ducally gorged. *Pl.* 18, *cr.* 6, (coronet, *pl.* 128, *fig.* 3.)

CLARK, a talbot's head, erased, or. *Pl.* 90, *cr.* 6.

CLARK, Norf., an eagle's leg, gu., joined to a wing, or. *Pl.* 101, *cr.* 15, (without bell.)

CLARK, a lion, rampant, (supporting an oval shield.) *Pl.* 67, *cr.* 5.

CLARK, a griffin's head, erased. *Pl.* 48, *cr.* 6.
CLARKE, Bart., Notts., an arm, couped near wrist, ppr., in hand a sword, in pale, ar., hilted, or. *Pl.* 23, *cr.* 15.
CLARKE, Bart., Durh., out of a ducal coronet, or, a demi-lion, az. *Pl.* 45, *cr.* 7.
CLARKE, Suff., an elephant's head, quarterly, gu. and or. *Pl.* 35, *cr.* 13.
CLARKE, Eng., a demi-lion, rampant, or. *Pl.* 67, *cr.* 10.
CLARKE, Berks., a cross formée, or, between wings, az. *Pl.* 29, *cr.* 14.
CLARKE, Lond. and Yorks., a demi-lion, rampant, or, holding a cross crosslet, fitched, az. *Pl.* 65, *cr.* 6.
CLARKE, Lond. and Glouc., out of a ducal coronet, or, a demi-lion, ppr. *Pl.* 45, *cr.* 7.
CLARKE, Bart., Norf., on a mount, vert, a dove, wings elevated, or, in mouth an ear of wheat, ppr., dexter resting on an annulet, sa.
CLARKE, Sir WILLIAM HENRY ST LAWRENCE, Bart., Iri., out of an Eastern crown, gu., a demi-dragon, wings elevated, or. *Pl.* 59, *cr.* 14, (coronet, *pl.* 128, *fig.* 2.)
CLARKE, on stump of tree, a lark, wings expanded, ppr., in mouth two ears of wheat, or.
CLARKE, Linc., a sinister wing, or. *Pl.* 39, *cr.* 10.
CLARKE, NATHANIEL-RICHARD, of Handsworth, Staffs., a wing, or. *Pl.* 39, *cr.* 10.
CLARKE, EDWARD-HYDE, Esq., of Hyde Hall, Chesh.: 1. A pheon, ppr. *Pl.* 26, *cr.* 12. 2. An eagle, wings expanded, sa., beaked and membered, or. *Pl.* 126, *cr.* 7.
CLARKE, out of a mural coronet, a demi-lion, rampant, holding a pennon, gu. *Pl.* 86, *cr.* 11.
CLARKE, out of a mural coronet, a demi-lion, rampant, in dexter a pennon, (resting sinister on an escutcheon.) *Pl.* 86, *cr.* 11.
CLARKE, Heref., an escallop, quarterly, gu. and or. *Pl.* 117, *cr.* 4.
CLARKE, of Arlington, Berks., on a wreath, sa. and ar., a cross pattée, or, between eagles' wings, erect, az. *Absit ut glorier nisi in cruce. Pl.* 29, *cr.* 14.
CLARKE, Surr., on a ducal coronet, or, a cross pattée, gold, between phœnix's wings, sa. *Pl.* 17, *cr.* 9, (cross, *pl.* 25, *cr.* 8.)
CLARKE, Suff., a conger-eel's head, erect and erased, gu., collared with a bar-gemelle, or.
CLARKE, Surr., a bear, sejant, ar., (supporting a battle-axe, erect, az.) *Pl.* 1, *cr.* 1.
CLARKE, Kent and Ess., a greyhound's head, couped, or, charged with a cinquefoil, az. *Pl.* 84, *cr.* 13, (without roses; cinquefoil, *pl.* 141.)
CLARKE, Kent, a unicorn's head, erased, ar., crined and armed, or, gorged with a collar, gu., charged with three plates. *Pl.* 73, *cr.* 1.
CLARKE, Suff., a nag's head, erased, sa. *Pl.* 81, *cr.* 6.
CLARKE, Kent, a fleur-de-lis, per pale, ar. and sa. *Pl.* 68, *cr.* 12.
CLARKE, out of a ducal coronet, or, a demi-bull, rampant. *Pl.* 63, *cr.* 6, (coronet, *pl.* 128, *fig.* 3.)
CLARKE, Iri., a sea-horse, vert. *Pl.* 103, *cr.* 3.
CLARKE, Heref., a lion, rampant, vert, (holding a pen, ar.) *Pl.* 67, *cr.* 5.
CLARKE, an eagle, wings expanded, sa., beaked and membered, or. *Pl.* 126, *cr.* 7.

CLARKE, Durh., and Iri., a swan, ppr., (dexter on an ogress.) *Pl.* 122, *cr.* 13.
CLARKE, a dove, wings expanded, (in mouth an ear of wheat, all ppr.) *Pl.* 27, *cr.* 5.
CLARKESON, an arm, in armour, ppr., in hand a sword, ar., hilt and pommel, sa., (on blade a pennon, flotant, gu.) *Pl.* 2, *cr.* 8.
CLARKSON, an arm, in armour, embowed, in hand a couteau-sword, all ppr. *Per ardua. Pl.* 81, *cr.* 11.
CLARKSON, Yorks., an arm, in armour, ppr., in fess, wreathed, ar. and sa., in hand a couteau-sword, erect, ar., (garnished with a pennon, flotant, gu.) *Per ardua. Pl.* 107, *cr.* 15.
CLASON, and CLASSON, Sco., a rose-branch, ppr. *Pl.* 23, *cr.* 2.
CLATER, Eng., in dexter hand a crescent. *Pl.* 38, *cr.* 7.
CLAUDE, Eng., a demi-unicorn, rampant, collared, ppr. *Pl.* 21, *cr.* 1.
CLAUS, Eng., on point of a sword, in pale, a cross pattée. *Pl.* 56, *cr.* 1.
CLAVEDON, Eng., a pelican, vulning, ppr. *Pl.* 109, *cr.* 15.
CLAVEL, and CLAVELL, Eng., a human heart, in flames, ppr. *Pl.* 68, *cr.* 13.
CLAVER, Bucks., in lion's gamb, (couped) and erect, or, a key, sa. *Pl.* 5, *cr.* 5.
CLAVERING, Bart., Durh., out of a ducal coronet, or, a demi-lion, az. *Pl.* 45, *cr.* 7.
CLAVERING, EDWARD-JOHN, Esq., of Callaly Castle, Northumb., a man's head, affrontée, couped at shoulders, between wings, ppr. *Ad cœlos volans. Pl.* 12, *cr.* 4, (wings, *pl.* 4, *cr.* 4.)
CLAVERING, Northumb., out of a ducal coronet, or, a demi-lion, rampant, sa. *Pl.* 45, *cr.* 7.
CLAVERING, Northumb., a cherub's head, wings erect. *Ad cœlos volans. Pl.* 126, *cr.* 10.
CLAVERING, out of a ducal coronet, or, a demi-lion, rampant, sa. *Pl.* 45, *cr.* 7.
CLAXSON, Glouc., on a mount, vert, a stag, lodged, az., attired and unguled, or, (supporting with dexter an escutcheon, gu., charged with a porcupine, ar.) *Sapere aude, incipe. Pl.* 22, *cr.* 15.
CLAXTON, Durh., Norf., and Yorks., a hedgehog, ar. *Pl.* 32, *cr.* 9.
CLAXTON, Suff., a hedgehog, sa., (bezantée.) *Pl.* 32, *cr.* 9.
CLAXTON, Durh., on a ducal coronet, or, a hedgehog, ar. *Pl.* 18, *cr.* 11.
CLAY, CLAYE, and CLEY, Derbs., two wings, expanded, ar., semée of trefoils, slipped, sa. *Pl.* 39, *cr.* 12.
CLAY, or CLAYE, Lond. and Salop, a lion's head, per pale, vert and sa., charged with an escallop, ar. *Pl.* 81, *cr.* 4.
CLAYDAN, Eng., an arm, in armour, brandishing a sword, ppr. *Probitatem quam divitias. Pl.* 2, *cr.* 8.
CLAYDON, Ess. and Lond., a demi-lion, rampant, az., vulned on shoulder, gu., murally crowned, ar., in paws a cross flory, fitched, of the second.
CLAYFIELD, Eng., a moor's head, couped, sa. *Pl.* 19, *cr.* 1.
CLAYHILLS, Sco., in hand an imperial crown, ppr. *Corde et animo. Pl.* 97, *cr.* 12.
CLAYLEY, a greyhound's head, ar., between two rose slips, flowered, gu., stalked and leaved, vert. *Pl.* 84, *cr.* 13.

CLAYTON, Bart., Surr., in leopard's paw, erect, ar., a pellet. *Virtus in actione consistit*—and—*Quid leone fortius? Pl.* 97, *cr.* 10.

CLAYTON, Bart., Lanc., a dexter arm, embowed, in hand a dagger, ppr. *Probitatem quam divitias. Pl.* 34, *cr.* 7.

CLAYTON, an arm, in armour, embowed, in hand a sword, point downward, ppr. *Pl.* 120, *cr.* 11.

CLAYTON, RICE-RICHARD, Esq., of Hedgerley Park, Bucks., a leopard's gamb, erased and erect, grasping a pellet. *Virtus in actione consistit*—and—*Quid leone fortius? Pl.* 97, *cr.* 10.

CLAYTON, the Rev. JOHN-HENRY, Esq., of Enfield Old Park, Middx., a dove, with olive-branch, all ppr. *Quod sors, fert, ferimus. Pl.* 48, *cr.* 15.

CLAYTON, out of a mural coronet, or, in leopard's paw, ar., a pellet. *Pl.* 97, *cr.* 10, (coronet, *same plate, cr.* 8.)

CLAYTON, Lond., in a lion's gamb, ppr., a torteau, sa. *Pl.* 97, *cr.* 10.

CLAYTON, Norf., a unicorn, couchant, ar., maned, armed, and unguled, or, under dexter a bezant.

CLEALAND, on a sinister gauntlet, in fess, a falcon, all ppr. *Pl.* 83, *cr.* 13.

CLEATHER, Cornw., a cubit arm, vambraced, in hand, gauntleted, erect, a dagger. *Pl.* 125, *cr.* 5.

CLEATHER, a sand-glass, gu., winged, ar. *Pl.* 43, *cr.* 1.

CLEAVER, an arm, erect, vested, ar., in hand, ppr., a chaplet of thorns, vert. *Pl.* 18, *cr.* 1, (chaplet, *pl.* 78, *cr.* 7.)

CLEAVER, in lion's gamb, couped, or, a key, sa. *Pl.* 5, *cr.* 5.

CLEAVLAND, Eng., a greyhound's head, sa., charged with three bezants, one and two, or. *Pl.* 14, *cr.* 4.

CLEDEROW, Lond., out of a tower, ar., a demi-lion, sa. *Pl.* 42, *cr.* 4.

CLEEVE, a fox's head, erased, sa. *Pl.* 71, *cr.* 4.

CLEEVE, Eng., in hand a buckle. *Pl.* 38, *cr.* 9.

CLEG, or CLEGG, Eng., out of a ducal coronet, or, a demi-lion, rampant, imperially crowned, all ppr. *Pl.* 54, *cr.* 2, (coronet, *same plate, cr.* 14.)

CLEGAT, an eagle's head, erm., ducally crowned and beaked, or, between wings, sa. *Pl.* 81, *cr.* 10, (crown, *pl.* 128, *fig.* 3.)

CLEGHORN, Eng., an arm, from elbow, erect, in hand a balance and scales, equally poised, ppr. *Pl.* 26, *cr.* 8.

CLEGHORN, in dexter hand, issuing from a cloud in sinister, a laurel-branch, all ppr. *Insperata floruit. Pl.* 43, *cr.* 4, (branch, *pl.* 123, *cr.* 5.)

CLEGHORN, an arm, in armour, embowed, throwing a dart, ppr. *Sublime petimus. Pl.* 96, *cr.* 6.

CLEILAND, or CLEILLAND, Sco., on a sinister hand, couped and gloved, ppr., a falcon, statant. *For sport. Pl.* 83, *cr.* 13.

CLELAND-ROSE, JAMES BLACKWOOD, Esq., of Rath-Gael House, co. Down: 1. For *Cleland*, on a sinister glove, a hawk, ppr. *Pl.* 1, *cr.* 13. 2. For *Rose*, a rose, gu., seeded and slipped, ppr., between wings, erm. *For sport*—and—*Je pense à qui pense plus. Pl.* 105, *cr.* 7, (wings, *same plate, cr.* 6.)

CLELAND, Sco., a falcon, rising, ppr. *Si je pouvois. Pl.* 105, *cr.* 4.

CLELAND, on a sinister hand, gloved, a falcon, belled, ppr. *Non sibi. Pl.* 83, *cr.* 13.

CLELAND, Eng., a moor's head, sa., wreathed, ar. *Pl.* 36, *cr.* 3.

CLELLAND, a rose, gu., leaved and stalked, vert. *Fragrat, delectat, et sanat. Pl.* 105, *cr.* 7.

CLELLAND, Sco., a buck, at gaze, ppr. *Ne cadem insidiis. Pl.* 81, *cr.* 8.

CLEMENT, Norf., a lion, passant, ar., guttée-de-sang. *Pl.* 48, *cr.* 8.

CLEMENT, Iri., a cross moline, or. *Pl.* 89, *cr.* 8.

CLEMENTS, HENRY-THEOPHILUS, Esq., of Ashfield Lodge, co. Cavan, a hawk, statant, ppr. *Patriis virtutibus. Pl.* 67, *cr.* 3.

CLEMENTS, THEOPHILUS, Esq., of Rathkenny, co. Cavan, same crest.

CLEMENTS, Baron. See LEITRIM, Earl of.

CLEMENTS, CAVAN, a fawn's head, erased, ppr. *Pl.* 6, *cr.* 1.

CLEMENTS, a falcon, close. *Pl.* 67, *cr.* 3.

CLEMENTS, Eng., a leopard, gardant, per pale, gu. and erm., ducally gorged, or. *Pl.* 120, *cr.* 9.

CLEMENTS, Iri., out of a ducal coronet, or, in lion's paw, sa., a cross crosslet, fitched, gold. *Pl.* 65, *cr.* 5.

CLEMENTSON, an arm, from elbow, ppr., vested, paly gu. and or, cuffed, counterchanged, in hand a palm-branch, of the first. *Pl.* 113, *cr.* 5, (branch, *pl.* 123, *cr.* 1.)

CLEMSBY, Eng., a tower, ppr. *Pl.* 12, *cr.* 5.

CLENCH, or CLENCHE, Eng., a reindeer's head, cabossed, ppr. *Pl.* 114, *cr.* 7.

CLENCH, Suff., out of a Saxon crown, or, an arm, erect, vested, gu., cuffed, ar., in hand, ppr., a club, vert, spiked, of the first.

CLENDON, Eng., a stag's head, ppr., between attires, a cross pattée, ar. *Pl.* 9, *cr.* 10.

CLENT, Worc., two lions' gambs, erect, sa., holding a chaplet, vert, flowered, or. *Pl.* 62, *cr.* 3, (chaplet, *pl.* 41, *cr.* 7.)

CLEPAN, and CLEPHAN, Sco., in dexter hand a helmet, ppr. *Ut sim pariatior. Pl.* 37, *cr.* 15.

CLEPOLE, Notts., a fleur-de-lis, ar., enfiled with a ducal coronet, or. *Pl.* 47, *cr.* 7.

CLERE, Norf., the sun, or, between wings, az., on each a crescent, of the first. *Pl.* 75, *cr.* 9.

CLERE, Norf., out of a ducal coronet, or, a plume of ostrich-feathers, ar. *Pl.* 44, *cr.* 12.

CLERE, Norf., a camel's head, ducally gorged, ppr., bridled, gu. *Pl.* 120, *cr.* 12.

CLERK, Bart., of Pennycuick, Sco., a demi-huntsman, winding a horn, ppr. *Free for a blast. Pl.* 38, *cr.* 8.

CLERK, M.D., Sco., an Esculapius' rod, ppr. *Sat cito, si sat tuto. Pl.* 49, *cr.* 11.

CLERK, Norf., a demi-forester, ppr., (on breast a star, ar.) *Amat victoria curam. Pl.* 121, *cr.* 1.

CLERK, around a spiked club, in pale, ppr., a serpent, coiled, vert.

CLERKE, Bart., Bucks., a ram's head, couped, ppr. *Pl.* 34, *cr.* 12.

CLERKE, on a partridge, ppr., an eagle's leg, gu., winged at thigh, or.

CLERKE, a pheon, ar. *Pl.* 26, *cr.* 12.

CLERKE, a swan, ppr. *Pl.* 122, *cr.* 13.

CLERKE, an eagle's head, erased, ar., in beak a branch of laurel, vert. *Pl.* 20, *cr.* 7, (branch, *pl.* 123, *cr.* 5.)

CLERKE, Eng., an arm, in hand an arrow, ar., feathered, or. *Pl.* 92, *cr.* 14.

CLERKE, Eng., a boar's head, gu., in mouth a sword, in bend, ppr. *Pl.* 28, *cr.* 14.

CLERKE, out of a naval coronet, or, a moor's head, ppr. *Pl.* 19, *cr.* 1, (coronet, *pl.* 128, *fig.* 19.)

CLERKE, out of clouds, in hand, ar., a branch, vert. *Pl.* 88, *cr.* 13.

CLERKE, JENNINGS, Salop and Hants, a wolf's head, erased, per pale, ar., and vert. *Ut prosim aliis.* *Pl.* 14, *cr.* 6.

CLERMONT, Baron Fortescue, an heraldic tiger, ppr., (supporting with fore-paw a plain shield, ar.) *Forte scutum salus ducum.* *Pl.* 119, *cr.* 9.

CLERMONT, Eng., a savage, ppr., wreathed about head and middle with leaves, vert, standing on a serpent, of the last. *Pl.* 109, *cr.* 1.

CLERMONT, a pole-cat, ppr. *Pl.* 119, *cr.* 7.

CLESBY, Yorks., a reindeer, passant, ppr. *Pl.* 12, *cr.* 8.

CLESBY, Eng., an ensign, ppr., coat, gu., holding a banner, of the last. *Pl.* 79, *cr.* 5.

CLETHEROW, and CLYDEROWE, a Roman soldier, in armour, ppr., holding a spear. *Pl.* 92, *cr.* 2.

CLEVE, Lond., Middx., and Chesh., a griffin, passant, wings addorsed, ducally gorged, or. *Pl.* 61, *cr.* 14.

CLEVE, and CLIVE, Lond. and Salop, a wolf's head, per pale, dançettée, ar. and sa. *Pl.* 8, *cr.* 4.

CLEVELAND, Duke and Marquess of, Earl of Darlington, Viscount and Baron Barnard, &c., (Vane:) 1. A dexter gauntlet, ppr., bossed and ringed, or, brandishing a sword, also ppr. *Pl.* 63, *cr.* 5. 2. On a chapeau, gu., turned up, erm., a lion, passant, gardant, or, gorged with a collar, componée, of the second and az., and crowned with a five-leaved ducal coronet, of the last. *Nec temere, nec timide.* *Pl.* 120, *cr.* 15.

CLEVELAND, a demi-old man, ppr., vested, az., with cap, gu., turned up, with a hair front, in dexter a spear, headed, ar., on top thereof a line, ppr., passing behind him, and coiled up in sinister hand.

CLEVELAND, Eng., a demi-man, affrontée, ppr., in a military habit, gu., with belt and sash, holding the union flag, ppr. *Pl.* 2, *cr.* 12.

CLEVELAND, Eng., a bishop's mitre, ppr. *Pl.* 12, *cr.* 10.

CLEVES, two elephants' probosces, addorsed, sa. *Pl.* 24, *cr.* 8.

CLEVLAND, ARCHIBALD, Esq., of Tapeley Park, in hand a sword, hilted and pommelled, or. *Fortuna audaces juvat.* *Pl.* 21, *cr.* 10.

CLEYPOLE, out of a ducal coronet, or, a fleur-de-lis, ar. *Pl.* 68, *cr.* 12, (coronet, *same plate.*)

CLIFDEN, Viscount and Lord, Iri., Baron Mendip, U.K., (Agar-Ellis,) a demi-lion, rampant, or. *Non hæc sine numine.* *Pl.* 67, *cr.* 10.

CLIFF, a lion, rampant, ar. *Pl.* 67, *cr.* 5.

CLIFFE, a griffin, passant, wings addorsed, ar., ducally gorged, or. *Pl.* 61, *cr.* 14.

CLIFFE, ANTHONY, Esq., of Bellevue, co. Wexford, a wolf's head, erased, quarterly, per pale, indented, or and sa. *In cruce glorior.* *Pl.* 14, *cr.* 6.

CLIFFE, Ess. and Devons., an archer, ppr., coat, vert, shooting an arrow, of the first. *Pl.* 60, *cr.* 5.

CLIFFE, CLYFF, and CLYFFE, Eng., two lions' paws, in saltier, erased, each holding a seax, all ppr. *Pl.* 32, *cr.* 12.

CLIFFORD, HENRY-CLIFFORD, Esq., of Frampton, Glouc., a hand, ppr., holding a fleur-de-lis, or. *Dulcis amor patriæ.* *Pl.* 46, *cr.* 12.

CLIFFORD, HENRY-MORGAN, Esq., of Perristone, Heref., and Llantilio, Monmouth, a griffin, segreant, sa. *Semper paratus.* *Pl.* 67, *cr.* 13.

CLIFFORD, EDWARD, Esq., of Castle Annesley, co. Wexford, in hand, in fess, ppr., a fleur-de-lis. *Dulcis amor patriæ.* *Pl.* 46, *cr.* 12.

CLIFFORD, Baron, (Clifford,) out of a ducal coronet, or, a wyvern, rising, gu. *Semper paratus.* *Pl.* 59, *cr.* 14.

CLIFFORD, Cumb.; Brecon, Linc.; and Devons., same crest.

CLIFFORD, Glouc., in dexter hand, couped, in fess, a fleur-de-lis. *Dulcis amor patriæ.* *Pl.* 46, *cr.* 12.

CLIFFORD, Iri., a dexter hand, apaumée, gu. *Pl.* 32, *cr.* 14.

CLIFFORD, a talbot's head, erased, gu., eared, or. *Pl.* 90, *cr.* 6.

CLIFFORD, out of clouds, the sun rising, ppr., surmounted by a fleur-de-lis, ar. *Pl.* 67, *cr.* 9, (fleur-de-lis, *pl.* 141.)

CLIFFORD, a tiger, passant, gardant, (in dexter, head of a broken spear.) *Pl.* 67, *cr.* 15.

CLIFTON, Bart., Notts., out of a ducal coronet, a demi-peacock, per pale, ar. and sa., wings expanded, counterchanged. *Tenez le droit.* *Pl.* 50, *cr.* 9, (coronet, *same plate*, *cr.* 13.)

CLIFTON, Lanc. and Yorks., an arm, in armour, embowed, ppr., garnished, or, in gauntlet, a sword, ar., hilted, of the second. *Pl.* 2, *cr.* 8.

CLIFTON, an arm, in fess, vested, az., in hand, ppr., a hawk, ar. *Pl.* 83, *cr.* 13.

CLIFTON, JOHN TALBOT. Esq., of Clifton, and Lytham, Lanc., a dexter arm in armour, embowed, in hand a sword, ppr. *Mortem aut triumphum.* *Pl.* 2, *cr.* 8.

CLIFTON, Baron. *See* DARNLEY, Earl.

CLINCH, or CLYNCH, on a hand, couped, in fess, gauntleted, an eagle, rising, ppr. *Pl.* 104, *cr.* 14.

CLINTON, Baron, (Trefusis,) a griffin, segreant, or, (resting dexter on a shield, ar.) *Tout vient de Dieu.* *Pl.* 67, *cr.* 13.

CLINTON, Lond., Herts., and Sco., out of a ducal coronet, gu., five ostrich-feathers, ar., banded by a ribbon, az. *Pl.* 106, *cr.* 11, (without chapeau.)

CLINTON, DE, Eng., on a mount, a stag, feeding, ppr. *Pl.* 37, *cr.* 8.

CLINTON, Duke of Newcastle. *See* NEWCASTLE.

CLIPSHAM, Eng., a boar's head, couped, sa. *Fortiter.* *Pl.* 48, *cr.* 2.

CLITHEROW, out of a tower, ar., a demi-lion, rampant, sa. *Pl.* 42, *cr.* 4.

CLIVE, the Rev. ARCHER, of Whitfield, Heref., a griffin, passant, ar., ducally gorged, gu. *Audacter et sincere.* *Pl.* 61, *cr.* 14.

CLIVE, Lord Clive, Iri., same crest and motto.

CLIVE, Eng., a horse's head, sa., between wings, ar. *Pl.* 19, *cr.* 13.
CLIVE, Baron. *See* POWIS, Earl.
CLIVE, Lond., Chesh., and Middx., a griffin, wings addorsed, ar., ducally gorged, or. *Pl.* 61, *cr.* 14.
CLIVE, Eng., in hand a buckle, or. *Pl.* 38, *cr.* 9.
CLIVE, Chesh. and Salop, a griffin, passant, wings addorsed, ar., langued, gu., ducally gorged, or. *Credo, ama et regna.* *Pl.* 61, *cr.* 14.
CLIVE, Chess. and Salop, a boar's head, erased at neck, sa., same motto. *Pl.* 16, *cr.* 11.
CLOAKE, Eng., out of a plume of (five) ostrich-feathers, an eagle, rising, all ppr. *Pl.* 54, *cr.* 8.
CLOBERY, Devons., a goat's head, erased, sa., attired, or. *Pl.* 29, *cr.* 13.
CLOCK, or CLOKE, Eng., a demi-bear, rampant, sa. *Pl.* 104, *cr.* 10.
CLOCKMAKERS, COMPANY OF, a sphere, or. *Tempus rerum imperator.* *Pl.* 114, *cr.* 6.
CLODE, a demi-lion, holding a lozenge, pierced, ar. *Pl.* 91, *cr.* 13, (lozenge, *pl.* 141.)
CLOGSTON, an eagle, wings expanded. *Pl.* 126, *cr.* 7.
CLONBROCK, Baron, (Dillon,) Iri., on a chapeau, gu., turned up, erm., a falcon, rising, ppr., belled, or. *Auxilium ab alto.* *Pl.* 105, *cr.* 4, (chapeau, *same plate, cr.* 5.)
CLONCURRY, Baron, (Browne-Lawless,) Eng. and Iri., a demi-man, in armour, in hand an (arrow,) all ppr. *Virtute et numine.* *Pl.* 23, *cr.* 4.
CLONMEL, Earl of, and Viscount, (Scott,) Iri., a buck, trippant, ppr. *Fear to transgress.* *Pl.* 68, *cr.* 2.
CLOPTON, Suff., a wolf's head, party, per pale, or and az. *Pl.* 14, *cr.* 6.
CLOPTON, Durh., on a tun, a falcon. *Pl.* 1, *cr.* 13, (tun, *pl.* 124, *cr.* 9.)
CLOSE, Colonel MAXWELL, of Drumbanagher, Armagh, a demi-lion, vert, holding a battle-axe, or, headed, ar. *Fortis et fidelis.* *Pl.* 126 D, *cr.* 6.
CLOSE, or CLOSS, Eng., a boar, sa., among weeds, vert. *Pl.* 104, *cr.* 12.
CLOTWORTHY, Devons,, a stag's head, erased, sa., attired, (and charged on neck with two mullets, in pale, ar., pierced by an arrow, or, feathered and headed, of the second, vulned, gu.) *Pl.* 66, *cr.* 9.
CLOTWORTHY, Iri., a boar, passant, or. *Pl.* 48, *cr.* 14.
CLOUGH, Yorks., a demi-lion, rampant, erm., holding a battle-axe, sa., handle, ar. *Pl.* 101, *cr.* 14, (without charge.)
CLOUGH, HARRIETT-ELLEN, of Plâs Clough, Denbighs., a demi-lion, rampant, az., in dexter, a sword, ar., handled, or. *Sine maculâ macla.* *Pl.* 41, *cr.* 13.
CLOUGH-BUTLER, Wel., an arm, embowed, vested, az., ruffle of point lace, ar., in hand, ppr., a cup, or. *Pl.* 39, *cr.* 1.
CLOUGH-LLOYD, Wel. : 1. For *Clough*, a demi-lion, rampant, az., in dexter a sword, erect, ar., hilt and pommel, or. *Pl.* 41, *cr.* 13. 2. For *Lloyd*, a hart, passant, ar., attired, or, in mouth a snake, vert. *Pl.* 68, *cr.* 2, (snake, *pl.* 54, *cr.* 7.)
CLOUN, and CLUN, Eng., a chevalier, in armour, ppr., in dexter a marshal's baton, ar., tipped, sa. *Pl.* 60, *cr.* 2.

CLOUN, and CLUNE, Eng., a wolf, collared and lined, in dexter a trefoil, all ppr. *Pl.* 5, *cr.* 8, (trefoil, *pl.* 141.)
CLOVE, a camel's head, couped, or. *Pl.* 109, *cr.* 9.
CLOVEL, or CLOVELL, Eng., a bull, passant, gu. *Pl.* 66, *cr.* 11.
CLOWBERRY, a goat's head, erased, ar., attired, or. *Pl.* 29, *cr.* 13.
CLOWES, Lond., Staffs., and Warw., a demi-lion, vert, ducally crowned, or, holding a battle-axe, of the last, headed, ar. *Pl.* 61, *cr.* 4, (axe, *pl.* 26, *cr.* 7.)
CLUBB, a demi-unicorn. *Pl.* 26, *cr.* 14.
CLUD, and CLUDDE, a bull's head, per cheveron, gu. and erm. *Pl.* 63, *cr.* 11.
CLUDDE, ANNA-MARIA, of Orleton, Salop, an eagle, wings expanded, ppr., preying on a cony, ar. *Pl.* 61, *cr.* 3.
CLULOW, Yorks., on a garb, in fess, a lion, passant, gardant. *Pl.* 59, *cr.* 15.
CLUNES, Sco., a demi-lion, rampant, ducally gorged, ppr. *Pl.* 87, *cr.* 15.
CLUNES, Sco., a demi-leopard, rampant, ducally gorged, ppr. *Pl.* 125, *cr.* 4.
CLUNIE, Sco., a sand-glass, winged. *Pl.* 32, *cr.* 11.
CLUNIE, Sco., a tree, ppr. *Pl.* 100, *cr.* 14.
CLUTTERBUCK, Lond. and Glouc., out of a ducal coronet, in hand a rose, slipped and leaved, ppr. *Pl.* 60, *cr.* 1.
CLUTTERBUCK, Lond., Middx., and Wilts., a buck, sejant, gu., between two laurel-branches, ppr. *Pl.* 24, *cr.* 4.
CLUTTON, Heref., on a mount, vert, on stump of tree, an owl, all ppr. *Pl.* 27, *cr.* 13, (stump, *pl.* 55, *cr.* 11.)
CLUTTON, THOMAS-CHARLTON, Esq., of Charlton Hall, Chester, a cock, or. *Pl.* 67, *cr.* 14.
CLYNCH, Eng., a camel's head, per fess, or and az. *Pl.* 109, *cr.* 9.
CLYNCKE, Eng., a lion's head, royally crowned, ppr. *Pl.* 123, *cr.* 13.
CLYPLESBY, and CLYPSBY, a bull, passant, sa., bezantée, ar. *Pl.* 66, *cr.* 11.
COACH, a stag, sejant, gu., attired, or, between two laurel-branches, vert. *Pl.* 24, *cr.* 4.
COACHMAN, Lond., a demi-lion, rampant, sa., crusily, between paws a cinquefoil, ar. *Pl.* 126, *cr.* 12, (cinquefoil, *pl.* 141.)
COAKLEY, a lion, passant, or, in dexter an eagle's leg, erased, gu. *Pl.* 48, *cr.* 8, (leg, *pl.* 89, *cr.* 13.)
COANE, Sco., a lily, ppr. *Pl.* 81, *cr.* 9.
COAPE, in dexter hand, a sword, erect, ppr. *Pl.* 23, *cr.* 15.
COATES, or COATS, Eng., a swan's head, between wings, ar. *Pl.* 54, *cr.* 6.
COATS, or COTES, Yorks. and Salop, a cock, ppr., combed, wattled, and legged, gu. *Pl.* 67, *cr.* 14.
COATS, or COTES, an arm, erect, vested, paly of six, or and az., cuffed, ar., in hand a covered cup, or. *Pl.* 39, *cr.* 1.
COATS, or COTES, Sco., an anchor, ppr. *Be firm.* *Pl.* 42, *cr.* 12.
COATS, or COTES, Iri., two lions' paws, erased, supporting a crescent. *Pl.* 62, *cr.* 2.
COATS, or COTES, Iri., a cock, ppr. *Watchful and bold.* *Pl.* 67, *cr.* 14.
COBB, Oxon., Norf., and Yorks., an elephant, or. *Pl.* 56, *cr.* 14.

H

COBB, Kent, out of a ducal coronet, or, a demi-leopard, rampant, ppr. *Pl.* 12, *cr.* 14, (coronet, *pl.* 128, *fig.* 3.)
COBB, Norf., a swan's (head,) or, in beak a fish, ar. *Pl.* 103, *cr.* 1.
COBB, a shoveller, sa., beaked and legged, or. *Pl.* 52, *cr.* 12.
COBB, and COBBE, Iri., a dexter hand, per fess, gu. and or, brandishing a scimitar, ppr. *Pl.* 29, *cr.* 8.
COBBEN, COBBIN, COBBYN, COBENN, and COBYN, on a garb, in fess, a lion, passant, gardant. *Pl.* 59, *cr.* 15.
COBBES, a shoveller, sa. *Pl.* 52, *cr.* 12.
COBBETT, Middx., a bird, (rising,) or, pellettée, in beak a sprig of laurel, ppr. *Pl.* 25, *cr.* 6.
COBBOLD, Eng., a thunderbolt, ppr. *Pl.* 110, *cr.* 3.
COBHAM, Kent, an old man's head, in profile, couped at shoulders, ppr., with long cap, gu., turned up, ar., fretty and sa., a button at top, or. *Pl.* 78, *cr.* 15.
COBHAM, a man's head, in profile, helmeted, ppr. *Pl.* 33, *cr.* 14.
COBHAM, Eng., in dexter hand a dagger, point downward, ppr. *Pl.* 18, *cr.* 3.
COBHAM, a hind's head, ar., crowned with a palisado crown, or. *Pl.* 21, *cr.* 9, (crown, *pl.* 128, *fig.* 21.)
COBHAM, Herts., a demi-lion, rampant, or. *Pl.* 67, *cr.* 10.
COBLEGH, COBLEIGH, and COBLEY, an arm, in armour, embowed, in fess, elbow on the wreath, in hand a sceptre, all ppr. *Pl.* 104, *cr.* 13.
COBLEGH, or COBLEIGH, a cock's head, erased, gu., combed, wattled, and guttée, or, (in beak a laurel-branch, ar.) *Pl.* 92, *cr.* 3.
COBURN, a demi-dragon, wings addorsed, (between claws an escutcheon, charged with a roundle.) *Pl.* 116, *cr.* 15.
COBURN, Sco., a cock, ppr. *Pl.* 67, *cr.* 14.
COCHER, a lion, couchant, erm. *Pl.* 101, *cr.* 8.
COCHET, Eng., a talbot, passant, sa., spotted, ar. *Pl.* 120, *cr.* 8.
COCHRANE, Earl of Dundonald. *See* DUNDONALD.
COCHRANE, or COCHRAN, Sco., a horse, passant, ar. *Pl.* 15, *cr.* 14.
COCHRANE, or COCHRAN, a hand, issuing from a cloud, raising a garb. *Pl.* 43, *cr.* 4.
COCHRANE, or COCHRAN, Sco., in dexter hand a human heart, ppr. *Concordia vincit.* *Pl.* 59, *cr.* 12.
COCHRANE, or COCHRAN, Sco., a stag at gaze, ppr., attired, gu. *Vigilante salus.* *Pl.* 81, *cr.* 8.
COCHRANE, or COCHRAN, Sco., a greyhound, current, ar. *Virtute et labore.* *Pl.* 28, *cr.* 7, (without charge.)
COCK, Norf., an ostrich, gu., ducally gorged, in mouth a horse-shoe, or. *Pl.* 16, *cr.* 2.
COCK, on stump of tree, ppr., a cock, gu. *Pl.* 2, *cr.* 1, (stump, *pl.* 30, *cr.* 5.)
COCK, or COCKS, Eng., a chevalier on horseback, brandishing a sword, all ppr. *Pl.* 28, *cr.* 5.
COCK, Northumb. and Sco., a cock, ppr. *Pl.* 67, *cr.* 14.
COCK, Herts., an ostrich, in mouth a horse-shoe, ppr. *Pl.* 16, *cr.* 2.
COCKAIN, COKAINE, and COKAYNE, a cock's head, erased, gu., crested and jelloped, sa. *Virtus in arduis.* *Pl.* 92, *cr.* 3.

COCKAYN, or COCKAYNE, a cock's head, gu. *Pl.* 92, *cr.* 3.
COCKBURN, Bart., (Berwick,) Sco., a cock, crowing. *Accendit cantu.* *Pl.* 67, *cr.* 14.
COCKBURN, Sco., a dexter arm, in hand a broken spear, in bend, ppr. *Press through.* *Pl.* 66, *cr.* 4.
COCKBURN, Bart., of that Ilk, Sco., a cock, crowing. *Accendit cantu*—and—*Vigilans et audax.* *Pl.* 67, *cr.* 14.
COCKBURN, Eng., a cock, ppr. *Pl.* 67, *cr.* 14.
COCKBURN, Sco., a cock's head, ppr. *I rise with the morning.* *Pl.* 92, *cr.* 3.
COCKBURN, Eng., (on a rock, ppr.,) a leopard, sejant, per fess, or and gu. *Pl.* 26, *cr.* 9.
COCKBURN, or COCKBURNE, Sco., a cock, gu. *In dubiis constans.* *Pl.* 67, *cr.* 14.
COCKE, Eng., in dexter hand, couped, a dagger, in pale, all ppr. *Pl.* 23, *cr.* 15.
COCKE, Sco., in lion's paw, a sceptre, in pale, all ppr. *Pl.* 16, *cr.* 1.
COCKE, a bear's head, ar., (crowned, or.) *Pl.* 2, *cr.* 9.
COCKEINE, Kent, on a mural coronet, ar., a cock, of the same, beaked, barbed, and membered, gu. *Pl.* 2, *cr.* 1, (coronet, *pl.* 128, *fig.* 18.)
COCKELL, on a mural coronet, or, a cock, gu., (semée of roundles, resting dexter on an escallop, in beak a sprig of laurel, ppr.) *Pl.* 55, *cr.* 12, (coronet, *pl.* 128, *fig.* 18.)
COCKER, Linc., a lion, couchant, gardant, erm. *Pl.* 101, *cr.* 8.
COCKERELL, Glouc., within a crescent, az., a tiger's face, ppr., crowned with an Eastern crown. *Pl.* 84, *cr.* 1.
COCKERELL, between wings, a lion's head, ppr. *Pl.* 87, *cr.* 2.
COCKERITH, Eng., a fire beacon, ppr. *Pl.* 89, *cr.* 9.
COCKES, in hand, a lion's paw, erased, ppr. *Pl.* 94, *cr.* 13.
COCKET, Herts., Norf., and Suff., a man's head, in profile, couped at shoulders, ppr., vested, vert, collar, or, on head a cap, bendy, wavy, of the last, and az., turned up, indented, sa. *Pl.* 51, *cr.* 4.
COCKETT, Eng., a poplar-tree, ppr. *Pl.* 95, *cr.* 2.
COCKFIELD, Eng., an eagle, wings addorsed, preying on a tortoise. *Pl.* 70, *cr.* 8.
COCKFIELD, or COKEFIELD, on stump of tree, an eagle, wings addorsed, ppr. *Pl.* 1, *cr.* 11.
COCKLE, Eng., a talbot, passant, gu., collared, ar. *Pl.* 65, *cr.* 2.
COCKMAN, a demi-eagle, displayed, sa. *Pl.* 22, *cr.* 11.
COCKRAM, out of clouds, an arm, in hand an anchor, erect, fluke upward, ppr. *Pl.* 41, *cr.* 5.
COCKRELL, Eng., a leopard's face, ppr. *Pl.* 66, *cr.* 14.
COCKRIDGE, a cock, ppr. *Pl.* 67, *cr.* 14.
COCKRIDGE, a cock crowing, ppr. *Pl.* 67, *cr.* 14.
COCKS, a hind's head, erased, (collared.) *Pl.* 6, *cr.* 1.
COCKS, Glouc. and Suff., on a mount, vert, a stag, lodged, ar., attired, sa.
COCKS, a cock, ppr. *Pl.* 67, *cr.* 14.
COCKS, Worc., a buck, couchant, ppr. *Pl.* 67, *cr.* 2.
COCKS-SOMERS, Earl Somers. *See* SOMERS.

COCKSEDGE, a cock, gu., in beak, a (violet,) ppr. *Pl.* 55, *cr.* 12.
COCKSEY, a tiger's head, couped, sa., (charged on neck with a cinquefoil, between two bars, or.) *Pl.* 92, *cr.* 13.
COCKSEY, Eng., a bishop's mitre, ppr. *Pl.* 12, *cr.* 10.
COCKSEY, on a garb, in fess, a cock, ppr. *Pl.* 122, *cr.* 3.
COCKSHUTT, Lanc. and Salop, a demi-griffin, sa. *Pl.* 18, *cr.* 6.
COCKSHUTT, Herts., a demi-griffin, ar., collared, gu., guttée, of the first. *Pl.* 74, *cr.* 15, (without anchor.)
COCKWORTHY, and COOKWORTHY, a cock, gu. *Pl.* 67, *cr.* 14.
CODD, Norf., a heron's head, erased, ppr. *Pl.* 32, *cr.* 5.
CODD, or CODDE, Eng. and Iri., a hawk's leg, erased, belled, ppr. *Pl.* 83, *cr.* 7.
CODD, a physician's cap, sa., tufted, or. *Pl.* 39, *cr.* 3.
CODD, or CODDE, Eng., a square fort, with four towers, ppr. *Pl.* 28, *cr.* 11.
CODD, a lion, rampant, gorged with a mural coronet, and charged with two torteaux. *Pl.* 88, *cr.* 1, (coronet, *pl.* 128, *fig.* 18.)
CODD, or CODDE, Iri., a lion's head, erased, in mouth a hand, ppr. *Pl.* 107, *cr.* 9.
CODDINGTON, and CODINTON, Eng., on a chapeau, an eagle, wings expanded and inverted, all ppr. *Pl.* 114, *cr.* 13.
CODDINGTON, Iri., in hand a sword, ppr. *Pl.* 21, *cr.* 10.
CODDINGTON, HENRY-BARRY, Esq., of Oldbridge, co. Meath, a wolf's head, erased, or. *Nil desperandum*—or—*Nec metuas nec optes.* *Pl.* 14, *cr.* 6.
CODENHAM, a lion's head, erased, or, langued, az., (charged on neck with three trefoils, slipped, vert.) *Pl.* 81, *cr.* 4, (trefoil, *pl.* 141.)
CODHAM, a lion's head, erased, or, (charged with three trefoils, slipped, vert, two and one.) *Pl.* 81, *cr.* 4, (trefoil, *pl.* 141.)
CODRINGTON, Sir WILLIAM-RAIMOND, Bart., Glouc., a dragon's head, couped, gu., between wings, chequy, or and az. *Pl.* 105, *cr.* 11.
CODRINGTON, out of a ducal coronet, or, a dragon's head, gu., between wings, chequy, or and az. *Pl.* 59, *cr.* 14, (dragon, *pl.* 105, *cr.* 11.)
CODRINGTON, Glouc., Somers., and Wilts., out of a ducal coronet, or, a dragon's head, couped, gu., between wings, chequy, or and az. *Pl.* 105, *cr.* 11, (dragon, *pl.* 59, *cr.* 14.)
CODRINGTON, WILLIAM-WYNDHAM, Esq., of Wroughton, Wilts., out of a ducal coronet, a dragon's head, gu., between wings, chequy, or and az. *Immersabilis est vera virtus.* *Pl.* 105, *cr.* 11.
COE, two swords, in saltier, ppr., surmounted by a cross crosslet, fitched, sa. *Pl.* 42, *cr.* 5.
COE, Eng., a martlet, sa. *Præsto et persto.* *Pl.* 111, *cr.* 5.
COE, Norf., an arm, in armour, embowed, ppr., in hand a chaplet, vert. *Pl.* 68, *cr.* 1.
COE, Eng., a crane, supporting with dexter an anchor, ppr. *Pl.* 61, *cr.* 10.
COE, a demi-eagle, with two heads, displayed. *Pl.* 4, *cr.* 6, (without charge.)

COFFIELD, Eng., on a cross fleury, fitched, gu., between wings, or, (a crescent,) gold. *Pl.* 71, *cr.* 2.
COFFIN, a camel's head, erased, or, bridled, lined, ringed, and gorged with a ducal coronet, sa. *In tempestate floresco.* *Pl.* 120, *cr.* 12.
COFFIN, Bart., on stern of a ship, a pigeon, wings addorsed, or, in beak a laurel-sprig, vert. *Extant recte factis præmia.* *Pl.* 55, *cr.* 11, (stern, *pl.* 128, *fig.* 19.)
COFFIN, Eng., a long cross, sa. *Pl.* 7, *cr.* 13.
COFFIN-PINE, the Rev. JOHN-THOMAS, of Portledge, Devons.: 1. A martlet, az., charged on breast with two bezants. *Pl.* 111, *cr.* 5, (bezants, *pl.* 141.) 2. A pine-tree, ppr. For PINE, *In tempestate floresco.* *Pl.* 26, *cr.* 10.
COFFYN, a martlet, or, between two cinquefoils, ar., stalked and leaved, ppr. *Pl.* 111, *cr.* 5, (cinquefoil, *pl.* 141.)
COGAN, or COGGAN, a talbot, passant, collared and lined. *Constans fidei.* *Pl.* 65, *cr.* 2.
COGAN, a lion's head, erased, gu., (semée of mullets, or.) *Pl.* 81, *cr.* 4.
COGAN, Iri., a pine-tree, ppr. *Pl.* 26, *cr.* 10.
COGGER, Eng., an arm, in armour, embowed, in hand a club, ppr. *Pl.* 45, *cr.* 10.
COGGESHALL, Suff., a stag, lodged, sa., attired, or. *Pl.* 67, *cr.* 2.
COGHILL, Lond., Yorks., Oxon., and Herts., a cock, wings addorsed, erm. *Pl.* 76, *cr.* 7.
COGHILL, Lond., Yorks., Oxon., and Herts., a cock, sa., wings expanded, or. *Pl.* 76, *cr.* 7.
COGHILL, Bart., Yorks., on a mount, vert, a cock, wings expanded, or, ducally crowned, gu. *Non dormit qui custodit.* *Pl.* 76, *cr.* 7, (coronet, *same plate*, *cr.* 14.)
COGHLAN, Iri., a demi-lion, rampant, ducally crowned, in dexter a sword, all ppr. *Pl.* 41, *cr.* 13, (coronet, *pl.* 128, *fig.* 3.)
COGHLAN, or COGHLEN, Eng., a fret, or. *Pl.* 82, *cr.* 7.
COHAM, Devons., out of a ducal coronet, a plume of straight ostrich-feathers. *Fuimus, et sub Deo erimus.* *Pl.* 44, *cr.* 12.
COHEN, Eng., a bear's head, couped, sa., muzzled, gu. *Pl.* 111, *cr.* 4.
COIN, Eng., two wings, expanded. *Pl.* 39, *cr.* 12.
COKE, Eng., in dexter hand, couped, a dagger, in pale, ppr. *Pl.* 23, *cr.* 15.
COKE, Eng., the sun, ppr. *Pl.* 68, *cr.* 14.
COKE, Earl of Leicester. *See* LEICESTER.
COKE, D'EWES, Esq., of Brookhill Hall, Derbs., the sun in splendour, or. *Non aliunde pendere.* *Pl.* 68, *cr.* 14.
COKE, the Rev. GEORGE, of Lower Moor House, Heref., same crest and motto.
COKE, Norf., on a chapeau, az., an ostrich, ppr., in mouth a horse-shoe, or. *Pl.* 16, *cr.* 2, (chapeau, *pl.* 127, *fig.* 13.)
COKENINGHAM, Yorks., a goat's head, erased, ar. *Pl.* 29, *cr.* 13.
COKER, Dors., a moor's head, affrontée, ppr., wreathed, ar. and gu. *Pl.* 97, *cr.* 2.
COKER, Dors., a moor's head, in profile, sa., wreathed, ar. and gu. *Pl.* 36, *cr.* 3.
COKER, LEWIS, Esq., of Bicester, Oxon., a moor's head, in profile, wreathed, ar. and gu. *Fiat justitia.* *Pl.* 36, *cr.* 3.

COKERELL, Eng., the lictor's rod and axe, ppr. *Pl.* 65, *cr.* 15.

COKFELD, Eng., out of a ducal coronet, a lion's paw. *Pl.* 67, *cr.* 7.

COLAMORE, Warw., a moor's head, couped, sa., wreathed, ar. and gu. *Semper eadem.* *Pl.* 36, *cr.* 3.

COLBATCH, Middx., a dexter arm, embowed, per pale, dancettée, vert and az., cuffed, erm., in hand a pine-apple, ppr. *Pl.* 47, *cr.* 13, (pine, *pl.* 84, *cr.* 12.)

COLBECK, Beds., on a chapeau, gu., turned up, erm., a lion's head, erased, or, pellettée. *Pl.* 99, *cr.* 9.

COLBORNE, Baron, (Ridley-Colbourne :) 1. For *Colborne*, a stag's head, couped, ppr., gorged with a ducal coronet, (pendent therefrom a bugle, stringed, gu.) *Pl.* 55, *cr.* 2. 2. For *Ridley*, a bull, passant, gu. *Constans fidei.* *Pl.* 66, *cr.* 11.

COLBORNE, Somers., out of a ducal coronet, or, a reindeer's head, ar., attired, or. *Pl.* 60, *cr.* 3.

COLBRAND, Suss., a tiger, sejant, ar., maned, or. *Pl.* 26, *cr.* 9.

COLBROKE, COLEBROOK, and COLEBROCK, a spear, in pale, ppr. *Pl.* 97, *cr.* 4.

COLBURN, out of a ducal coronet, an antelope's head, erased. *Pl.* 24, *cr.* 7, (coronet, *same plate, cr.* 10.)

COLBY, Middx., Norf., and Suff., an arm, in armour, embowed, ppr., garnished, or, in gauntlet a dagger, ppr., hilt and pommel, or. *Pl.* 120, *cr.* 11.

COLBY, Middx., Norf., and Suff., an arm, in armour, embowed, ppr., garnished, or, in gauntlet a scimitar, all ppr. *Pl.* 81, *cr.* 11.

COLBY, or COLEBY, Middx., Norf., and Suff., an arm, in armour, embowed, ppr., garnished, or, in gauntlet a broken sword, ar., hilt and pommel, gu., embrued, ppr. *Pl.* 2, *cr.* 8, (sword, *pl.* 44, *cr.* 4.)

COLBY, a dexter arm, embowed, ppr., vested, az., in hand a dagger, of the first, hilt and pommel, or. *Pl.* 34, *cr.* 7.

COLCHESTER, Baron, (Abbot,) out of a ducal coronet, or, a unicorn's head, erm., maned and tufted, gold, between (six) ostrich-feathers, ar., quilted, of the first. *Perseverando.* *Pl.* 110, *cr.* 1.

COLCHESTER, Lond. and Warw., a demi-lion, ppr., holding an etoile, gu. *Pl.* 89, *cr.* 10, (etoile, *pl.* 141.)

COLCLEUGH, Eng., a lion, passant, gardant, or, (collared, gu.,) holding an anchor, sa. *Pl.* 120, *cr.* 5, (anchor, *pl.* 19, *cr.* 6.)

COLCLOUGH, or COLCLOUGHE, a hind's head, ppr., vulned, gu. *Pl.* 21, *cr.* 9.

COLCLOUGH, Staff., a demi-eagle, displayed, sa., (ducally gorged, or.) *Pl.* 22, *cr.* 11, (gorging, *pl.* 128, *fig.* 3.)

COLDE, and COLFE, (in flames of fire, ppr.,) a ram, ar., attired, or. *Pl.* 109, *cr.* 2.

COLDHAM, Suss., a dragon's head, gu., pierced with a spear, or, headed, ar. *Pl.* 121, *cr.* 9.

COLDHAM, Norf., a griffin's head, erased, gu., (transfixed with an arrow, ar.) *Pl.* 48, *cr.* 6.

COLDICOTT, in dexter hand, ppr., a billet, gu. *Sum quod sum.* *Pl.* 28, *cr.* 8.

COLDSTREAM, Sco., a swan, swimming, wings addorsed. *Pl.* 66, *cr.* 10.

COLE, a bull's head, erased. *Pl.* 19, *cr.* 3.

COLE, a bull, current, winged.

COLE, ROBERT, Esq., of Holybourne Lodge, Hants., a naked arm, in hand a scorpion, ppr., armed, or. *Deum cole, regem serva—or—Esto quod esse videris.* *Pl.* 110, *cr.* 14.

COLE, Earl of Enniskillen. *See* ENNISKILLEN.

COLE, Lond., a bull's head, couped, sa. *Pl.* 120, *cr.* 7.

COLE, out of a ducal coronet, or, a bull's head, gu., armed, of the first. *Pl.* 68, *cr.* 6.

COLE, Oxon., a bundle of arrows, ar., belted and buckled, or. *Pl.* 54, *cr.* 15.

COLE, Herts., a demi-dragon, az., winged, or., holding a chaplet, vert. *Pl.* 116, *cr.* 15, (chaplet, *pl.* 128, *fig.* 16.)

COLE, Northumb., an arm, erect, ppr., in hand a scorpion, sa. *Pl.* 110, *cr.* 14.

COLE, Hants, a falcon, wings expanded, ar., guttée, sa., preying on a fish, or. *Pl.* 29, *cr.* 11, (falcon, *pl.* 61, *cr.* 7.)

COLE, Somers., an eagle, displayed, ar. *Pl.* 48, *cr.* 11.

COLE, Somers., an eagle, ducally gorged, or. *Pl.* 7, *cr.* 11.

COLE, Cornw., a demi-dragon, holding an arrow, or, headed and feathered, ar. *Pl.* 82, *cr.* 10.

COLE, Ess., a leopard's head, (erased,) ar., collared and chained, or, in mouth an oakslip, vert. *Pl.* 40, *cr.* 10, (oak, *pl.* 81, *cr.* 7.)

COLEBROOKE, Bart., Surr., a wyvern, wings expanded, or, resting dexter on an escutcheon, gu. *Sola bona quæ honesta.* *Pl.* 63, *cr.* 13, (escutcheon, *pl.* 42, *cr.* 8.)

COLEGRAVE, on a mural coronet, two arrows, in saltier, banded. *Pl.* 43, *cr.* 14, (coronet, *pl.* 128, *fig.* 18.)

COLEMAN, Lond. and Leic., a nag's head, erased, sa., maned and bridled, ar., tasselled, or. *Pl.* 92, *cr.* 1.

COLEMAN, a demi-greyhound, sa., (collared, ar.,) holding a mullet, of the first.) *Pl.* 6, *cr.* 9.

COLEMAN, a horse's head, erased, ppr. *Pl.* 81, *cr.* 6.

COLEMAN, out of a ducal coronet, a greyhound's head, ppr. *Pl.* 70, *cr.* 5.

COLEMERE, and COLMORE, Eng., a harpy, wings expanded, ppr. *Pl.* 32, *cr.* 3.

COLEMERE, COLLMORE, and COLLYMORE, a moor's head, in profile, ppr., wreathed, or and gu. *Pl.* 36, *cr.* 3.

COLEN, a sword (and pastoral staff,) in saltier, ppr. *Pl.* 54, *cr.* 12.

COLEPEPER, Eng., a falcon, belled, ppr. *Pl.* 67, *cr.* 3.

COLERIDGE, Eng., a griffin's head, ppr., between wings, or. *Pl.* 65, *cr.* 1.

COLES, Eng., on a tower, a lion, rampant, ppr. *Pl.* 121, *cr.* 5.

COLES, Iri., a horse, trotting, ar., saddled and bridled, sa. *Pl.* 99, *cr.* 11.

COLES, out of a ducal coronet, or, a demi-dragon, vert, (in dexter a dart,) ppr. *Pl.* 59, *cr.* 14.

COLES, Eng., in hand a sword, in pale, enfiled with a boar's head, couped, ppr. *Pl.* 10, *cr.* 2.

COLES, around a marble pillar, ppr., garnished, or, (a snake entwined, vert.) *Pl.* 14, *cr.* 15.

COLES, an arm, (in armour, embowed,) ppr., in hand a serpent, entwined round arm, vert. *Pl.* 91, *cr.* 6.
COLET, Eng., in hand a battle-axe, ppr. *Pl.* 73, *cr.* 7.
COLEY, a dexter arm, in armour, ppr., in hand a scimitar, ar., hilt and pommel, or. *Pl.* 81, *cr.* 11.
COLFOX, out of a ducal coronet, or, a demi-wolf, gu., devouring a hand, ar.
COLFOX, Eng., out of a tower, ppr., a demi-greyhound, az., holding a branch, vert. *Pl.* 73, *cr.* 13.
COLING, a demi-griffin, segreant, ppr., between paws a fusil, gu., charged with a crescent, ar. *Pl.* 18, *cr.* 6, (fusil and crescent, *pl.* 141.)
COLLADON, Eng., out of the sea, a dexter arm, ppr., in hand an anchor, with cable, sa. *Pl.* 27, *cr.* 6.
COLLAND, a fish-wheel, or. *Pl.* 32, *cr.* 15.
COLLAR, a tiger's head, erased, or. *Pl.* 94, *cr.* 10.
COLLARD, Ess., a demi-lion, rampant, (supporting a cross-bow, or.) *Pl.* 67, *cr.* 10.
COLLARD, Devons., a demi-lion, rampant, holding a scaling ladder, or. *Pl.* 29, *cr.* 12, (ladder, *pl.* 98, *cr.* 15.)
COLLAY, Chesh., Herts., Warw., an elephant's head, gu., between wings, sa. *Pl.* 35, *cr.* 13, (wings, *pl.* 39, *cr.* 12.)
COLLE, Northumb., in dexter hand a scorpion, ppr. *Pl.* 110, *cr.* 14.
COLLEE, a griffin, segreant, ar., armed and beaked, or. *Pl.* 100, *cr.* 11.
COLLEGE OF ARMS, Lond., on a ducal coronet, or, a dove, rising, az. *Pl.* 55, *cr.* 11, (coronet, *same plate*, *cr.* 1.)
COLLEN, or COLLIN, Ess., a griffin's head, erased, vert, (collared, or.) *Pl.* 48, *cr.* 6.
COLLEN, or COLLIN, Ess., a griffin's head, erased, or, (collared, erm.) *Pl.* 48, *cr.* 6.
COLLEN, or COLLIN, a demi-griffin, or, (collared, ar.) *Pl.* 18, *cr.* 6.
COLLENS, or COLLINS, Dors., a dove, ar. *Volabo ut requiescam.* *Pl.* 66, *cr.* 12.
COLLES, Somers., on a mount, vert, an eagle, displayed, ar., ducally gorged and membered, or. *Pl.* 84, *cr.* 14, (coronet, *same plate*.)
COLLES, a griffin's head, couped, or, between two oak-branches, vert, fructed of the first. *Pl.* 38, *cr.* 3, (branches, *pl.* 74, *cr.* 7.)
COLLES, Iri., out of a cloud, in dexter hand a sword, wavy, all ppr. *Pl.* 71, *cr.* 7.
COLLES, on a dolphin, lying on its back, a sea-pie, standing, wings expanded, or, guttée, sa.
COLLES, Devons., a falcon, wings expanded, ppr., guttée, or, preying on a fish, of the first. *Pl.* 61, *cr.* 7, (fish, *pl.* 29, *cr.* 11.)
COLLET, Lond. and Suff., a hind, trippant, ar. *Pl.* 12, *cr.* 8.
COLLETON, Bart., Herts., a stag's head, couped, ppr. *Pl.* 91, *cr.* 14.
COLLETON, Devons., same crest.
COLLETON, Devons., a roebuck's head, couped, ppr., collared, ar. *Pl.* 91, *cr.* 14.
COLLETT, Suff., a hind's head, erased at neck, ar., gorged with a mural crown, sa. *Pl.* 6, *cr.* 1, (crown, *same plate*, *cr.* 2.)
COLLETT, Lond. and Herts., a stag, ppr., (supporting with dexter an escutcheon, sa.) *Pl.* 68, *cr.* 2.

COLLEY, a griffin, segreant, ar., beaked and legged, or. *Pl.* 67, *cr.* 13.
COLLEY, Iri., in sinister hand a bow, ppr. *Pl.* 3, *cr.* 12.
COLLEY, an arm, erect, in hand a spear, in bend, (with the banner of St George appended,) ppr. *Unica virtus necessaria.* *Pl.* 99, *cr.* 8.
COLLIAR, or COLLYAR, Staffs., a demi-negro, ppr., with pearls in ears, ar., in dexter an acorn-branch, fructed, or. *Pl.* 35, *cr.* 12.
COLLICK, a lion, passant, in dexter a cross crosslet, fitched. *Pl.* 48, *cr.* 8, (cross, *pl.* 16, *cr.* 10.)
COLLIER, out of a naval coronet, or, on the circle the words "St Sebastian," a cross pattée, (fitched,) or, between wings, pean. *Pl.* 29, *cr.* 14, (coronet, *pl.* 32, *cr.* 8.)
COLLIER, a cross pattée, fitched, between wings, or. *Pl.* 29, *cr.* 14, (fitched, *pl.* 27, *cr.* 14.)
COLLIER, a unicorn, rampant, ar., armed, or. *Pl.* 37, *cr.* 7.
COLLIER, Dors., a wyvern, wings addorsed, ar. *Pl.* 63, *cr.* 13.
COLLIER, a unicorn's head, ar., erased and armed, or. *Pl.* 67, *cr.* 1.
COLLIMORE, Lond., a demi-man, in profile, vested, gu., collar turned over, and billettée, ar., on head a cap, gu., wreathed and ensigned with a crescent, of the second, in dexter a sceptre, or, on top a crescent, ar. *Pl.* 72, *cr.* 8.
COLLIN, Eng., a griffin, passant, gu. *Pl.* 61, *cr.* 14.
COLLIN, Notts., a talbot's head, erased, per fess, indented, or and ar., eared, and (charged on neck with a cross formée, gu.) *Pl.* 90, *cr.* 6.
COLLIN, on a chapeau, gu., turned up, erm., a griffin, passant, per pale, sa. and gu. *Pl.* 122, *cr.* 11.
COLLINGBORNE, Northumb., on a torteau, quarterly, or and az., a cross pattée, counterchanged. *Pl.* 116, *cr.* 7, (cross, *pl.* 141.)
COLLINGBORNE, Devons. and Wilts., a demi-woman, ppr., hair dishevelled, or, vested, erm., sleeves, gu., in dexter a covered cup, or. *Pl.* 2, *cr.* 10, (cup, *pl.* 35, *cr.* 9.)
COLLINGS, Eng., a sphere, ppr. *Pl.* 114, *cr.* 6.
COLLINGWOOD, Norf., a buck's head, ar., attired, or. *Pl.* 91, *cr.* 14.
COLLINGWOOD, Northumb., a buck's head, erased, sa. *Feror unus et idem.* *Pl.* 66, *cr.* 9.
COLLINGWOOD, Northumb., a stag at gaze, in a holly-bush, ppr. *Nil conscire sibi.* *Pl.* 118, *cr.* 13.
COLLINGWOOD, Durh. and Northumb., in front of trees, a stag, statant, ppr. *Pl.* 85, *cr.* 2.
COLLINS, the Rev. JOHN FERDINANDO, of Betterton, Berks., a griffin's head, erased, vert, crowned, or. *Per callem collem.* *Pl.* 100, *cr.* 15.
COLLINS, EDWARD, Esq., of Truthan and Newton-Ferrars, Cornw., a dove, wings expanded, ppr. *Volabo ut requiescam.* *Pl.* 27, *cr.* 5.
COLLINS, Devons., a camel's head, (erased,) ppr. *Sermoni consona facta.* *Pl.* 109, *cr.* 9.
COLLINS, a demi-griffin, or, armed, gu. *Pl.* 18, *cr.* 6.
COLLINS, Kent, a demi-griffin, or, beaked, legged, and ducally gorged, ar. *Pl.* 18, *cr.* 6, (gorging, *pl.* 128, *fig.* 3.)

COLLINS, Iri., a human heart, transpierced by a passion nail, in pale, ppr. *Pl.* 81, *cr.* 3.
COLLINS, a griffin's head, couped. *Pl.* 38, *cr.* 3.
COLLINS, Somers., a demi-griffin, or, collared, erm. *Pl.* 74, *cr.* 15, (without anchor.)
COLLINS, Somers., a demi-griffin, or, collared, ar. *Deum et regem. Ib.*
COLLINS, Devons., a cubit-arm, erect, in hand a lighted torch, ppr. *Pl.* 27, *cr.* 4, (torch, *pl.* 70, *cr.* 14.)
COLLINS, Ess., on a chapeau, gu., turned up, or, a griffin, statant, per pale, ar. and gu. *Pl.* 122, *cr.* 11.
COLLINS, Lond., Kent, and Suss., a demi-griffin, or, beaked and legged, gu., collared, erm. *Pl.* 74, *cr.* 15, (without anchor.)
COLLINSON, Eng., a rose, gu., between two branches of laurel, in orle, ppr. *Pl.* 3, *cr.* 13.
COLLIRAY, Eng., a martlet, flying over a tower, ppr. *Pl.* 37, *cr.* 1.
COLLIS, Iri., a dexter arm, throwing a dart, ppr. *Pl.* 92, *cr.* 14.
COLLIS, Eng., an eagle, preying on a fish, ppr. *Mens conscia recti. Pl.* 3, *cr.* 15.
COLLISON, East Bilney, Norf., a demi-lion, rampant, ppr., between paws a cinquefoil, or, centre leaf, gu. *Pl.* 126, *cr.* 12, (cinquefoil, *pl.* 141.)
COLLISON, Eng., a bomb-shell, fired, ppr. *Pl.* 70, *cr.* 12.
COLLISON, and COLLISONE, Sco., a falcon's head, erased, ppr. *Hoc virtutis opus. Pl.* 34, *cr.* 11.
COLLIVER, Eng., in hand a club, ppr. *Pl.* 28, *cr.* 6.
COLLIVER, Eng., a dexter hand, couped, in fess, gu. *Pl.* 32, *cr.* 4.
COLLOW, Sco., in hand a dagger, in pale, ppr. *Pro patriâ semper. Pl.* 23, *cr.* 15.
COLLS, Eng., on a ducal coronet, a griffin, sejant, wings addorsed, ppr., supporting an escutcheon, ar. *Pl.* 42, *cr.* 8.
COLLUMBEL, Linc., on a chapeau, gu., turned up, erm., a dove, (close, ppr., in mouth an ear of wheat, or.) *Pl.* 109, *cr.* 10.
COLLVILE, Sco., a bull's head, couped. *Nil obliviscar. Pl.* 120, *cr.* 7.
COLLVILE, Iri., a hind's head, ar., (charged with a cross formée, sa.) *Pl.* 21, *cr.* 9.
COLLWELL, Camb., on a chapeau, gu., turned up, erm., a lion, passant, ar., (gorged with a label of three points, gu.) *Pl.* 107, *cr.* 1.
COLLYEAR, in dexter hand, ppr., a key, az. *Pl.* 41, *cr.* 11.
COLLYEAR, a unicorn, rampant, ar., armed and unguled, or. *Pl.* 37, *cr.* 7.
COLLYER, Eng., a wyvern, wings addorsed, sa. *Pl.* 63, *cr.* 13.
COLLYER, a cross pattée, fitched, or, between eagle's wings, sa. *Pl.* 29, *cr.* 14, (fitched, *pl.* 27, *cr.* 14.)
COLLYER, Dors., a demi-unicorn, ar., armed, hoofed and maned, or. *Pl.* 26, *cr.* 14.
COLLYER, the Ven. JOHN-BEDINGFELD, M.A., of Hackford Hall, Norf., a unicorn's head, ppr. *Avance. Pl.* 20, *cr.* 1.
COLLYNGS, Suff., a nag's head, sa., bridled, or. *Pl.* 92, *cr.* 1.
COLMAN, Kent, a greyhound's head, sa., gorged with a collar and ring, ar., charged with three mullets, sa. *Pl.* 43, *cr.* 11, (mullets, *pl.* 141.)

COLNE, or COLNEY, a talbot, sejant, per pale, sa. and erm., collared, ar. *Pl.* 107, *cr.* 7.
COLNET, Hants, a dragon's head, ducally gorged and chained, ppr. *Pl.* 36, *cr.* 7.
COLPEPPER, a martlet, gu., between attires of an ox. *Pl.* 9, *cr.* 15, (martlet, *pl.* 111, *cr.* 5.)
COLPOYS, out of a naval coronet, a dexter hand, apaumée. *Pl.* 32, *cr.* 14, (coronet, *same plate, cr.* 8.)
COLQUHON, Sco., a hart's head, couped, gu., attired, ar. *Si je puis. Pl.* 91, *cr.* 14.
COLQUHON, of Drumpelder, a branch of laurel, slipped, ppr. *Dum spiro spero. Pl.* 123, *cr.* 5.
COLQUHOUN, JOHN-CAMPBELL, Esq., of Killermont, Dumbarton, a stag's head, erased, ppr. *If I can. Pl.* 66, *cr.* 9.
COLQUHOUN, (of London,) Sco.: 1. A hart's head, couped, ppr. *Pl.* 91, *cr.* 14. 2. In hand a buckle. *Pl.* 38, *cr.* 9.
COLQUHOUN, Bart., of Colquhoun, Sco., a hart's head, erased, gu. *Si je puis. Pl.* 66, *cr.* 9.
COLQUHOUN, Bart., of Tilliquhoun, Sco., a stag's head, erased, ppr. *Si je puis. Pl.* 66, *cr.* 9.
COLQUHOUN, of Kennuoir, Sco., a buck's head, erased, ppr. *Si je puis. Pl.* 66, *cr.* 9.
COLQUHOUN, Bart., of Luss, a hart's head, gu., attired, ar. *Si je puis. Pl.* 91, *cr.* 14.
COLQUHOUN, of Dunyelder, a laurel-branch, slipped, ppr. *Dum spiro spero. Pl.* 123, *cr.* 5.
COLQUHOUN, of Kilmardony, a stag's head, erased, ppr. *Festina lente. Pl.* 66, *cr.* 9.
COLQUHOUN, of Garscadden, in dexter hand a buckle, ppr. *Omnia firmat. Pl.* 38, *cr.* 9.
COLQUHOUN, Eng., an arm, from elbow, ppr., verted, gu., cuff, indented, or, in hand a baton, of the first, veruled, gold. *Pl.* 18, *cr.* 1.
COLQUITT, Eng., a hawk, rising, ducally gorged and belled, ppr. *Pl.* 61, *cr.* 12.
COLSHILL, and COLSILL, Ess. and Cornw., an arm, in armour, garnished, or, in hand a gauntlet, all ppr. *Pl.* 97, *cr.* 1, (gauntlet, *pl.* 61, *cr.* 11.)
COLSHULL, Eng., an arrow, in pale. *Pl.* 56, *cr.* 13.
COLSON, two arms, couped at elbow, vested, in hands, ppr., an escutcheon, or. *Pl.* 113, *cr.* 12.
COLSTON, Eng., a ship's boat, ppr. *Pl.* 42, *cr.* 11.
COLSTON, Eng., a dolphin, naiant, ppr. *Pl.* 48, *cr.* 9.
COLSTON, EDWARD, Esq., of Filkins Hall, Oxon.; and Roundway Park, Wilts.; a dolphin, naiant, ppr. *Go thou and do likewise. Pl.* 48, *cr.* 9.
COLSTON, a dolphin, naiant, sa. *Pl.* 48, *cr.* 9.
COLT, Bart., Heref., a colt, at full speed, sa. *Vincit qui patitur. Pl.* 107, *cr.* 5, (without spear.)
COLT, Kent, (in fire, ppr.,) a ram, ar., attired, or. *Pl.* 109, *cr.* 2.
COLT, Sco., a hand, throwing a dart, ppr. *Transfigam. Pl.* 42, *cr.* 13.
COLT, Suff., a nag's head, erm. *Pl.* 81, *cr.* 6.
COLT, Ess., a colt, at full speed, sa., in mouth part of a broken tilting-spear, or, headed, az., the remainder lying between hind legs. *Pl.* 107, *cr.* 5.

COLT, Suff., a colt, passant, ar. *Pl.* 15, *cr.* 14.
COLTER, and COULTER, Sco., a harpy, gardant, ppr. *Pl.* 126, *cr.* 11.
COLTHURST, Bart., Iri., a colt, (statant,) sa. *Justum et tenacem. Pl.* 15, *cr.* 14.
COLTHURST, Somers., a demi-lion, rampant, gardant, ar. *Pl.* 35, *cr.* 4.
COLTHURST, a greyhound's head, sa., between two roses, gu., leaved and slipped, ppr. *Pl.* 84, *cr.* 13.
COLTHURST, Iri., on stump of tree, a crane, perched, ppr. *Pl.* 23, *cr.* 5.
COLTMAN, Lond. and Leic., a nag's head, erased, sa., maned and bridled, ar., tasselled, or. *Pl.* 92, *cr.* 1.
COLTMAN, Yorks., a horse's head, erased, sa., bridled, ppr. *Pl.* 92, *cr.* 1.
COLTON, Eng., a spear-head, in pale, enfiled with a savage's head, couped, ppr. *Pl.* 88, *cr.* 15.
COLTON, Chesh., a boar, passant, ar., armed and bristled, or, vulned in shoulder, gu. *Pl.* 36, *cr.* 2.
COLUMBALL, a camel's head, ppr. *Pacem amo. Pl.* 109, *cr.* 9.
COLVIL, and COLVILLE, a demi-hind, ppr.
COLVIL, and COLVILLE, in hand, in pale, issuing from a cloud, a dagger, wavy. *Pl.* 71, *cr.* 7.
COLVIL, and COLVILLE, Sco., a talbot's head, ar. *Ad finem fidelis. Pl.* 123, *cr.* 15.
COLVIL, and COLVILLE, Linc. and Cambs., on a chapeau, az., turned up, erm., a lion, passant, ar., (charged on shoulder with a label of three points, gu.) *Pl.* 107, *cr.* 1.
COLVIL, and COLVILLE, Eng., a demi-stag, in mouth a rose, ppr. *Pl.* 55, *cr.* 9.
COLVIL, and COLVILLE, Sco., a hind's head, couped, ppr. *Obliviscar. Pl.* 21, *cr.* 9.
COLVIL, and COLVILLE, Sco., a hind's head, couped, ar. *Non obliviscar. Pl.* 21, *cr.* 9.
COLVIL, and COLVILLE, Sco., a hind's head, ar., charged with a cross pattée, sa. *Pl.* 21, *cr.* 9, (cross, *pl.* 141.)
COLVIL, and COLVILLE, Sco., a demi-Hercules, with a lion's skin and a club, all ppr. *Oublier ne puis. Pl.* 49, *cr.* 11.
COLVIL, and COLVILLE, Sco., a bull's head. *Ne obliviscaris. Pl.* 120, *cr.* 7.
COLVILE, and COLWALL, Kent, a bird, rising, ppr., in mouth a sprig, vert. *Pl.* 48, *cr.* 15.
COLVILLE, Baron, (Colville,) Sco., a hind's head, couped, ar. *Oublier ne puis. Pl.* 21, *cr.* 9.
COLVILLE, Linc., a cock-pheasant, (wings elevated,) ppr., in mouth a hawk's bell, or. *Pl.* 82, *cr.* 12, (bell, *pl.* 141.)
COLWELL, Eng., a talbot, (statant,) ar., spotted, gu. and sa., collared, az. *Pl.* 120, *cr.* 8.
COLWICH, Eng., a bat, displayed, ppr. *Pl.* 94, *cr.* 9.
COLWICK, and COLWYKE, Eng., issuing from a cloud, in hand, in pale, holding a sealed letter. *Pl.* 33, *cr.* 8.
COLWICK, and COLWYKE, Eng., in the sea, an anchor, in pale, ensigned with a dove and olive-branch, all ppr. *Pl.* 3, *cr.* 10.
COLYEAR, a lion, rampant. *Pl.* 67, *cr.* 5.
COLYEAR, Iri., a unicorn, rampant, ar., armed and maned, or. *Pl.* 37, *cr.* 7.
COLYEAR, a unicorn's head. *Pl.* 20, *cr.* 1.

COMB, or COMBE, Somers., a demi-lion, sa., ducally gorged, ar. *Pl.* 87, *cr.* 15.
COMB, or COMBE, Sco., a crane, in mouth a bunch of clover, ppr. *Pl.* 46, *cr.* 9.
COMBER, Suff., a greyhound's head, sa., charged with three bezants, two and one, or. *Pl.* 14, *cr.* 4.
COMBERFORD, Iri., a peacock, in pride, ppr. *Pl.* 92, *cr.* 11.
COMBERFORD, a dove, volant, in mouth an olive-branch, ppr. *Pl.* 25, *cr.* 6.
COMBERFORD, and CUMBERFORD, Warw., a crow, (wings addorsed,) ppr. *Pl.* 50, *cr.* 5.
COMBERMERE, Viscount and Baron, and a Bart., G.C.B., &c., (Stapleton-Cotton: 1. A falcon, ppr., wings expanded and belled, or, (in dexter a belt, az., buckled, of the second.) *Pl.* 105, *cr.* 4. 2. Of augmentation, on a mount, vert, a soldier of the 3d Regiment Light Dragoons, mounted, ppr., in the attitude of charging the enemy, and over this crest, on a scroll, az., the word "Salamanca," in letters of gold. *In utrámque fortunam paratus.*
COMBERTON, two lions' paws, sa., supporting a Doric pillar, ar. *Pl.* 77, *cr.* 4.
COMBERTON, a demi-savage, a hammer over shoulder, ppr. *Pl.* 51, *cr.* 14.
COMBES, of Cotham, Bristol, an arm, in armour, embowed, in hand a broken tilting-spear. *Pl.* 44, *cr.* 9.
COMBREY, Sco., a sheaf of arrows, (points upward,) ppr. *Pl.* 54, *cr.* 15.
COMBERFORD, Iri., a pestle and mortar, sa. *Pl.* 83, *cr.* 6.
COMES, Lond., out of a ducal coronet, or, a lion's gamb, ar., holding a staff, raguly, sa., slipped at each end, gu. *Pl.* 120, *cr.* 6, (staff, *pl.* 11, *cr.* 2.)
COMMERELL, JOHN, Esq., of Strood, Suss., a dexter arm, in hand a laurel-branch, all ppr. *Pl.* 118, *cr.* 4.
COMMOLIN, Eng., a fir-tree, ppr. *Pl.* 26, *cr.* 10.
COMPERE, Lond., a demi-lion, rampant, holding a roundle. *Pl.* 126, *cr.* 12.
COMPIGNE, Eng., in dexter hand, per fess, ar. and az., a covered cup, or. *Pl.* 35, *cr.* 9.
COMPION, Eng., a demi-talbot, vert. *Pl.* 97, *cr.* 9, (without arrow.)
COMPORT, Kent, a demi-lion, ar., charged with a quartrefoil, gu., holding a torteau. *Pl.* 126, *cr.* 12, (cinquefoil, *pl.* 141.)
COMPTON, Marquess of Northampton. See NORTHAMPTON.
COMPTON, Glouc. and Northamp., a beacon, ppr., (round the frame a scroll,) with the motto, *Je ne cherche que ung. Pl.* 88, *cr.* 6.
COMPTON, HENRY-COMBE, Esq., of the Manor House, Minestead, Hants, a demi-dragon, erased, wings elevated, body enfiled with a ducal coronet. *Pl.* 82, *cr.* 10, (coronet, *pl.* 91, *cr.* 2.)
COMPTON, Northamp., on a mount, vert, a beacon, or, inflamed, ppr., (round the support a scroll) with this motto, *Nisi Dominus. Pl.* 89, *cr.* 9.
COMPTON, Glouc., a beacon, ppr. *Nisi Dominus. Pl.* 88, *cr.* 6.
COMPTON, a beacon, inflamed, ppr. *Dum spiro spero. Pl.* 89, *cr.* 9.

COMRIE, or COMRY, Sco., a demi-archer, shooting an arrow, ppr. *Ad metam.* Pl. 60, cr. 5.

COMRIES, Sco., a cross crosslet, on three grieces. Pl. 23, cr. 12.

COMYN, Ess. and Durh., two arms, embowed, vested, erm., between hands, ppr., a garb, or.

COMYN, Durh., a sheaf of cumin, or. Pl. 13, cr. 2.

COMYNS, Eng., on a chapeau, gu., turned up, erm., a bloodhound, sejant, ppr. Pl. 102, cr. 9.

CONANT, on a mount, vert, a stag, statant, (resting dexter on an escutcheon.) Pl. 50, cr. 6.

CONARTON, Cornw., a talbot's head, erased, per pale, or and gu., collared, counterchanged. Pl. 2, cr. 15.

CONCANON, EDMOND-JOHN, Esq., of Waterloo, co. Galway, an elephant, statant, ppr., tusked, or. *Sagesse sans tache.* Pl. 56, cr. 14.

CONDIE, on a ducal coronet, or, a lion, passant, az. Pl. 107, cr. 11.

CONDUITT, Lond., two caducei, in fess, or, thereon a peacock's head, erased, ppr.

CONELEY, or CONELLY, a talbot, couchant, ppr. Pl. 32, cr. 7.

CONESBY, Eng., a cony, sejant, ar. Pl. 70, cr. 1.

CONGALTON, and CONGILTON, Sco., a bee, ppr. *Magnum in parvo*—and—*Multum in parvo.* Pl. 100, cr. 3.

CONGLETON, Baron. See PARNELL, Bart.

CONGRAVE, Berks. and Kent, a falcon, wings expanded, ppr., belled, or. Pl. 105, cr. 4.

CONGREVE, Bart., Staffs., a falcon, wings expanded, ppr. *Persevere*—and—*Non moritur cujus fama vivit.* Pl. 105, cr. 4.

CONGREVE, Berks., a falcon, rising, ppr. *Non moritur cujus fama vivit.* Pl. 105, cr. 4.

CONGREVE, WILLIAM, Esq., of Congreve, Staffs., a falcon, rising, wings expanded. *Non moritur cujus fama vivit.* Pl. 105, cr. 4.

CONINGESBY, CONINGSBY, and CONISBIE, a cony, sejant, ar. Pl. 70, cr. 1.

CONINGHAM, on a ducal coronet, or, a mount, vert, thereon a stork, gold, (in mouth a snake, between two cinquefoils, stalked and leaved, ppr.) Pl. 46, cr. 2, (stork, pl. 33, cr. 9.)

CONINGHAM, Iri., an anchor and sword in saltier. Pl. 25, cr. 1.

CONINGSBY, out of a ducal coronet, or, a plume of ostrich-feathers, thereon a cony, sejant, all ppr. Pl. 44, cr. 12, (cony, pl. 70, cr. 1.)

CONINGSBY-CAPEL, a demi-lion, in dexter a cross crosslet. Pl. 65, cr. 6.

CONMELL, Sco., a stag's head, erased, ar., charged with a trefoil, vert. Pl. 61, cr. 9, (trefoil, pl. 141.)

CONNACK, out of a ducal coronet, a demi-eagle, ppr. Pl. 19, cr. 9.

CONNEL, a stag's head, erased, charged with a trefoil. Pl. 61, cr. 9, (trefoil, pl. 141.)

CONNEL, or CONNELL, Sco., a bee, volant, ppr. *Non sibi.* Pl. 100, cr. 3.

CONNEL, or CONNELL, Eng., a goat, current towards a tree, ppr. Pl. 70, cr. 3.

CONNELL, Eng., on a dexter hand, apaumée, in fess, a bird, perched. Pl. 104, cr. 14.

CONNELL, Iri., out of a tower, a demi-griffin, rampant, ppr. Pl. 68, cr. 11.

CONNELLEY, CONELLY, and CONOLLY, Eng. and Iri., a female, in dexter an anchor, in sinister a Saracen's head. Pl. 107, cr. 2.

CONNELLEY, CONNELLY, CONNELY, CONNOLLY, and CONOLLY, Eng., a talbot, couchant, ppr. Pl. 32, cr. 7.

CONNER, Eng., an arm, in armour, embowed, in hand a dagger. Pl. 120, cr. 11.

CONNER, DANIEL, Esq., of Manch House, co. Cork, a dexter arm, in armour, embowed, ppr., garnished, or, in hand a short sword, ppr., hilt and pommel, of the last. *Min, sicker, reag.* Pl. 2, cr. 8.

CONNOCKE, Cornw., out of a ducal coronet, a demi-griffin, segreant, or. Pl. 39, cr. 2.

CONNOP, out of horns of a crescent, ar., an arm, erect, vested, az., cuffed, of the first, in hand a branch of oak, ppr.

CONNOR, Eng., in hand a hawk's lure. Pl. 44, cr. 2.

CONNOR, Corcamroe, a hand, gauntleted, (holding a javelin, in bend, sinister, point downward.) Pl. 23, cr. 9.

CONNOUR, CONNOR, and CONOR, Eng. and Iri., an arm, in armour, embowed, in hand a sword, all ppr. Pl. 2, cr. 8.

CONOLLY, Iri., an arm, (in armour,) erect, in hand, ppr., an annulet, ar. *En Dieu est tout.* Pl. 24, cr. 3.

CONOLLY, Somers., an arm, erect, vested, sa., cuffed, ar., in hand a chaplet of roses, ppr. Pl. 126 A, cr. 7.

CONOLLY, in hand a chaplet, ppr. Pl. 41, cr. 7.

CONQUEROR, a spear-head, ppr. *Victoria.* Pl. 82, cr. 9.

CONQUEST, Beds., a holly-tree, fructed, ppr. Pl. 22, cr. 10.

CONRADUS, a unicorn's head, erased, studded, or. Pl. 67, cr. 1.

CONRAN, Sco., a flame of fire, between two palm-branches, in orle, ppr. Pl. 62, cr. 6.

CONRAN, a demi-stork, wings expanded, in mouth a cross pattée, fitched.

CONRAN, Eng., two doves, billing, ppr. Pl. 60, cr. 13.

CONRAN, Iri., a pillar, entwined with woodbine, ppr. Pl. 14, cr. 15.

CONROY, Bart., a cubit arm, vested, or, cuffed, erm., in hand a wreath of laurel, vert. *L'antiquité ne peut pas l'abolir.* Pl. 44, cr. 13, (without bird.)

CONROY, Iri., a lion, rampant, vert, supporting a pennon, gu. Pl. 99, cr. 2.

CONROY, Knt., Iri., a wreath of laurel. *L'antiquité ne peut pas l'abolir.* Pl. 79, cr. 14.

CONSIDINE, Eng., a hand, issuing, plucking a thistle, ppr. Pl. 54, cr. 11.

CONSTABLE, Eng., a dragon's head, couped, or, (charged with four barulets, az.) Pl. 87, cr. 12.

CONSTABLE, Yorks., a ship in full sail, or. Pl. 109, cr. 8.

CONSTABLE, Sco., a greyhound, (passant, ar., collared.) Pl. 104, cr. 1.

CONSTABLE, Surr., a ship to the sinister, sails furled, all or. Pl. 115, cr. 9.

CONSTABLE, of Wassand, Yorks.: 1. A ship, with tackle, guns, and apparel, all or. Pl. 109, cr. 8. 2. A stork, in mouth an eel. Pl. 33, cr. 9, (eel, pl. 41, cr. 6.)

CONSTABLE, Sco., out of a cloud, in the sinister, a hand, pointing to a crosier, on the dexter, ppr. *Præclarior, quo propinquior.* Pl. 45, cr. 4.
CONSTABLE, Iri., an arm, from shoulder, hand clenched, ppr. Pl. 87, cr. 7.
CONSTABLE-CLIFFORD, Bart., late Clifford of Tixal, Staffs.; and Burton Castle, Yorks: 1. For *Constable,* a dragon's head, ar., charged with three bars, gu., on each as many mascles, or. Pl. 87, cr. 12. 2. For *Clifford,* out of a ducal coronet, or, a wyvern, rising, gu. Pl. 59, cr. 14. 3. *Another crest,* from behind dark clouds, the sun rising, from the rays, (issuant in chief, a lily of France, all ppr., surmounted by an escallop, inscribed,) "Surgit post nubila Phœbus." *Semper paratus.* Pl. 67, cr. 9.
CONSTANTINE, Eng., in lion's gamb, erased, a broken sword, ppr. Pl. 49, cr. 10.
CONSTANTYNE, Lond., Chesh., and Salop., a sword, in bend sinister, ppr., surmounted by a cross crosslet, az. Pl. 89, cr. 14.
CONWY, WILLIAM-SHIPLEY, Esq., of Bodrhyddan, Flints., a moor's head, in profile, couped, ppr., wreathed, ar. and az. *Fide et amore.* Pl. 36, cr. 3.
CONWAY, and KILLULTAGH, Baron. *See* HERTFORD, Marquess of.
CONWAY, Lond., out of a ducal coronet, a demicock, wings expanded, gu., beaked, and wattled, az. Pl. 72, cr. 4, (coronet, *same plate, cr.* 2.)
CONWAY, Glouc., Bucks., Warw., and Iri., a moor's head, in profile, ppr., banded, ar. and az. Pl. 36, cr. 3.
CONWAY, a griffin's head, couped. Pl. 38, cr. 3.
CONY, Cumb., a talbot's head, or, (tongue hanging out, dropping blood,) ppr. Pl. 123, cr. 15.
CONY, or CONEY, a cony, sejant, ar. Pl. 70, cr. 1.
CONY, or CONEY, Herts. and Hunts., on a mount, vert, a cony, or. Pl. 10, cr. 4.
CONYERS, Ess., Northamp., and Durh., a trefoil, slipped, ppr. Pl. 82, cr. 1.
CONYERS, Yorks. and Durh., a sinister wing, gu. Pl. 39, cr. 10.
CONYERS, Ess., a bull's head, erased, or, armed, sa., pierced through (neck) with an arrow, of the last, barbed and feathered, ar., vulned, gu. Pl. 64, cr. 4.
CONYERS, Eng., a moor's head, sa., wreathed and stringed, ar. and az. Pl. 23, cr. 3.
CONYERS, Eng., a spear, broken in three, headed, ar., banded together by a ribbon, gu. Pl. 33, cr. 3.
CONYERS, Lord D'Arcy, on a chapeau, ar., turned up, erm., a bull, (statant,) sa. Pl. 65, cr. 11.
CONYNGHAM, WILLIAM-LENOX, Esq., of Spring Hill, co. Londonderry: For *Conyngham,* a unicorn's head, couped, ar., maned and horned, or. *Over, fork over.* Pl. 20, cr. 1.
CONYNGHAM, Marquess, Earl, Viscount, and Baron, Earl Mountcharles, &c., Iri.; Baron Minster, U.K., (Conyngham,) a unicorn's head, erased, ar., armed and maned, or. *Over, fork over.* Pl. 67, cr. 1.
CONYNGHAM, Eng., a dexter arm, in armour, vambraced, in hand a sword, ppr. Pl. 2, cr. 8.

CONYSTON, Eng., out of a ducal coronet, or, a peacock's tail, ppr. Pl. 120, cr. 13.
COO, a crane, supporting an anchor, ppr. Pl. 61, cr. 10.
COOCK, or COOK, a talbot, sejant, resting dexter on an escutcheon, or. Pl. 19, cr. 2.
COOK, or COOKE, Hants., a dexter arm, embowed, ppr., in hand a chaplet of laurel, vert, (surmounted by an etoile, ar.) Pl. 118, cr. 4.
COOK, Yorks. and Northumb., a demi-lion, gardant, sa., ducally gorged, or. Pl. 35, cr. 4, (coronet, *pl.* 128, *fig.* 3.)
COOK, Lond., a demi-lion, gu., in dexter an etoile, or. Pl. 89, cr. 10, (etoile, *pl.* 141.)
COOK, a horse's head and neck, couped. Pl. 92, cr. 1.
COOK, Beds., an ostrich, in mouth a horseshoe, ar. Pl. 16, cr. 2.
COOK, or COOKE, Hants., a dexter arm, embowed, ppr., (encircled with a wreath of laurel, vert,) in hand an etoile, or. Pl. 118, cr. 4, (etoile, *pl.* 141.)
COOK, Sco., a sea-chart, ppr. *Tutum monstrat iter.* Pl. 59, cr. 3.
COOKE, Derb., the sun in splendour, or. Pl. 68, cr. 14.
COOKE, JOSEPH, Esq., of Cordangen, co. Tipperary, a demi-lion, rampant, gu., between paws a mullet, or. *Tu ne cede malis, sed contra audentior ito.* Pl. 89, cr. 10.
COOKE, Ess., a bear's head, erased, (in mouth a trefoil, slipped.) Pl. 71, cr. 6.
COOKE, of Peak and Stowbrow, Yorks., a lion's head, ar. Pl. 126, cr. 1.
COOKE, Kent and Suss., on a mount, vert, a beaver, passant, or. Pl. 3, cr. 11.
COOKE, Devons. and Cornw., a demi-cat, rampant, gardant, or, (holding an oakbranch, vert, fructed, of the first.) Pl. 80, cr. 7.
COOKE, a demi-lion, rampant, (erased,) between paws a bezant. Pl. 126, cr. 12.
COOKE, Ess. and Glouc., a unicorn's head, or, between wings, addorsed, az. Pl. 54, cr. 9, (wings, *same plate.*)
COOKE, Lond., out of a ducal coronet, or, a dragon's head, ar. Pl. 59, cr. 14.
COOKE, Ess. and Suss., a wolf's head, erased, erm., in mouth a trefoil, slipped, per pale, or and az. Pl. 14, cr. 6, (trefoil, *pl.* 141.)
COOKE, Camb., a greyhound's head, couped, per pale, or and gu., gorged with two bars, counterchanged. Pl. 43, cr. 11.
COOKE, Suff., a lion's head and neck, erased, affrontée, ar. Pl. 1, cr. 5, (without crown.)
COOKE, Suff., on a chapeau, sa., turned up, erm., an ostrich, ar., in mouth a horse-shoe, of the last. Pl. 16, cr. 2.
COOKE, (a demi-eagle,) per pale, gu. and sa., wings displayed, ducally crowned, or. Pl. 52, cr. 8, (crown, *same plate, cr.* 2.)
COOKE, Yorks., out of a mural coronet, ar., a demi-lion, rampant, gardant, sa., ducally gorged, or. Pl. 35, cr. 4, (coronets, *pl.* 128, *figs.* 3 and 18.)
COOKE, Suff., a wolf's head, ar., ducally gorged, gu. Pl. 8, cr. 4, (coronet, *same plate.*)
COOKE, Iri., a leopard's head, erased, pean. Pl. 94, cr. 10.
COOKE, a cockatrice, wings (expanded.) Pl. 63, cr. 15.

COOKE, Norf., out of a mural coronet, or, two wings expanded, per pale, gold and sa. *Pl.* 17, *cr.* 9, (coronet, *same plate, cr.* 7.)

COOKE, Suff., a lion's head, erased, gardant, ar. *Pl.* 1, *cr.* 5, (without coronet.)

COOKE, Warw., a wolf's head, per pale, gu. and or, (gorged with two bars, counterchanged.) *Pl.* 8, *cr.* 4.

COOKE, Suff., a demi-cockatrice, wings addorsed, ppr. *Pl.* 106, *cr.* 15, (without gorging.)

COOKE, Worc., out of a mural coronet, or, an arm, in armour, embowed, ppr., garnished, of the first, in hand a sword, ar., hilt, gold, on arm two cheverons, gu. *Pl.* 115, *cr.* 14.

COOKE, Middx., on a mount, vert, a unicorn, sejant, or, resting dexter on a cross potent, gu. *Pl.* 110, *cr.* 15, (cross, *pl.* 141.)

COOKE, Suff., an antelope's head, erased, or, tusked, horned, and tufted, gu. *Pl.* 24, *cr.* 7.

COOKE, an arm, erect, vested, paly of six, or and gu., in hand (a bunch of columbines and roses,) ar., cuffed, ppr. *Pl.* 64, *cr.* 7.

COOKE, Sco., a griffin's head, ar. *Pl.* 38, *cr.* 3.

COOKE, Suff., a griffin, segreant, sa. *Pl.* 67, *cr.* 13.

COOKE, an ostrich, in mouth a horse-shoe, or. *Pl.* 16, *cr.* 2.

COOKE, out of a mural coronet, or, an eagle's head, ar. *Pl.* 121, *cr.* 11.

COOKER, Devons., within the horns of a crescent, gu., an etoile, or. *Pl.* 111, *cr.* 15.

COOKES, Worc., in hand a dagger, ppr. *Pl.* 101, *cr.* 10.

COOKES, out of a ducal coronet, or, a negress' head, affrontée, sa., with ear-rings, wreathed. *Pl.* 80, *cr.* 11, (coronet, *same plate.*)

COOKES, THOMAS-HENRY, Esq., of Bentley, Worc., out of a mural coronet, an arm, in hand a short sword. *Deo, Regi, Vicino. Pl.* 115, *cr.* 14.

COOKESEY, and COOKSEY, Eng., on a garb, in fess, a cock, standing, ppr. *Pl.* 122, *cr.* 3.

COOKMAN, a griffin's head, between wings, expanded, or, ducally gorged, az. *Pl.* 65, *cr.* 1, (coronet, *same plate.*)

COOKSON, Cumb., a demi-lion. *Nil desperandum. Pl.* 67, *cr.* 10.

COOKSON, Linc., a demi-lion, rampant, sa., ducally crowned, or. *Pl.* 61, *cr.* 4, (without branch.)

COOKSON, a demi-lion, rampant, supporting a staff, raguly. *Pl.* 11, *cr.* 2.

COOKSON, JOHN, Esq., of Whitehill, Durh., a demi-lion, rampant, bearing a staff, raguly, ppr. *Nil desperandum. Pl.* 11, *cr.* 2.

COOKSON, JOHN, Esq., of Meldon Park, Northumb., same crest and motto.

COOLEY, Eng., a leopard's head, jessant-de-lis, or. *Pl.* 123, *cr.* 9.

COOLING, Eng., a griffin, segreant, ar., beaked and legged, or. *Pl.* 67, *cr.* 13.

COOMBES, or COOMBS, Eng., in dexter hand, a cushion. *Pl.* 83, *cr.* 9.

COOP, or COOPE, Eng., a demi-eagle, with two heads, displayed *Pl.* 4, *cr.* 6, (without escutcheon.)

COOPER, Sco., a dexter arm, embowed, in hand a battle-axe, ppr. *Pour ma patrie. Pl.* 87, *cr.* 7, (axe, *pl.* 73, *cr.* 7.)

COOPER, Bart., Herts., out of a mural coronet, ar., a spear, erect, ppr., tasselled, gu., surmounted by two palm-branches, in saltier, vert. *Nil magnum, nisi bonum. Pl.* 97, *cr.* 8.

COOPER, Iri., a demi-leopard, gardant, (in dexter a rose, all ppr.) *Pl.* 77, *cr.* 1.

COOPER, East Dereham, Norf., a falcon, close, ppr. *Pl.* 67, *cr.* 3.

COOPER, Rev. Sir WILLIAM HENRY, Bart., in hand a garland, ppr. *Virtute. Pl.* 41, *cr.* 7.

COOPER, an arm, erect, ppr., in hand a chaplet, vert. *Pl.* 41, *cr.* 7.

COOPER, a phœnix in flames. *Pl.* 44, *cr.* 8.

COOPER, a sand-glass, ppr. *Pl.* 43, *cr.* 1.

COOPER, Sco., between horns of a crescent, an etoile of six points, ppr. *Pl.* 111, *cr.* 15.

COOPER, a lion's head, ar., erased, gu., gorged with a chaplet of laurel, ppr. *Pl.* 22, *cr.* 3.

COOPER, a greyhound, sejant, sa. *Pl.* 66, *cr.* 15.

COOPER, Northumb., a cock's head, erased, or. *Pl.* 92, *cr.* 3.

COOPER, Yorks., a lion, sejant, ar., supporting a battle-axe, sa., headed, of the first. *Pl.* 109, *cr.* 7.

COOPER, a dove, with olive-branch, ppr. *Pl.* 48, *cr.* 15.

COOPER, Kent, Suss., and Herts., in lion's gamb, (erased,) or, a branch, vert, fructed, gu. *Pl.* 68, *cr.* 10.

COOPER, Glouc., on a mural coronet, ar., a pelican, vulning, ppr. *Pl.* 64, *cr.* 1.

COOPER, Durh., on a tower, a moorish king's head, in profile, ppr.

COOPER, an oak-tree, a branch thereof borne down by a weight, ppr. *Inclinata resurgo. Pl.* 50, *cr.* 3.

COOPER, Dors., on a chapeau, gu., turned up, erm., a bull, passant, sa., ducally gorged, or. *Pl.* 65, *cr.* 11.

COOPER, Berks., on a garb, or, a pelican, vulning, ppr. *Pl.* 12, *cr.* 15, (pelican, *pl.* 109, *cr.* 15.)

COOPER, Notts., on a mount, vert, a unicorn, sejant, ar., armed and crined, or, (supporting a broken tilting-spear, gold.) *Pl.* 110, *cr.* 15.

COOPER, Eng., a demi-lion, rampant, between paws a battle-axe, all ppr. *Fide et fortitudine. Pl.* 101, *cr.* 14, (without charge.)

COOPER, Durh., a bull, passant. *Pl.* 66, *cr.* 11.

COOPER, Wilts., a demi-leopard, (gardant, ppr., ducally crowned, ar., in dexter a hollybranch, fructed, ppr.) *Pl.* 97, *cr.* 5.

COOPER, a demi-leopard, gardant, in dexter a rose-branch, slipped, ppr. *Pl.* 97, *cr.* 5.

COOPER, a demi-leopard, rampant, in dexter (a rose,) all ppr. *Pl.* 16, *cr.* 7.

COOPER, WILLIAM, Esq., of Failford, Ayrshire; and Solsgirth, Dumbarton: 1. On dexter, in dexter hand a garland of laurel, both ppr. *Virtute. Pl.* 86, *cr.* 1. 2. On sinister, an oak-tree, with a branch borne down by a weight, both ppr. *Resurge. Pl.* 50, *cr.* 3.

COOPER-ASHLEY, Baron Shaftesbury. See SHAFTESBURY.

COORE, HENRY, Esq., of Scruton Hall, Yorks., a unicorn's head, or. *Qui semina vertu raccoglia fama. Pl.* 20, *cr.* 1.

COORE, Eng., a tower, triple-towered. *Pl.* 123, *cr.* 14.

COOTE, Bart., Donnybrook, Iri., a coot, ppr. *Pl.* 90, *cr.* 15.
COOTE, Eng., same crest.
COOTE, CHARLES-CHIDLEY, Esq., of Mount Coote, co. Limerick, same crest.
COOTE, Bart, (Ballyfin,) Iri., a coot, close, ppr. *Vincit veritas. Pl.* 90, *cr.* 15.
COOTE, Linc., Norf., and Ess., a coot's head, erased, sa. *Pl.* 70, *cr.* 6.
COOTES, a cubit arm, erect, (vested, paly of four, or and az.,) in hand, ppr., a covered cup, of the first. *Pl.* 35, *cr.* 9.
COPE, Bart., Hants, a fleur-de-lis, or, issuing from the top thereof a dragon's head, gu. *Æque adeste animo. Pl.* 68, *cr.* 12, (head, *pl.* 87, *cr.* 12.)
COPE, ANNA GARLAND, of Drummilly, co. Armagh, same crest and motto.
COPE, Middx., Ess., Northamp., Northumb., Oxon., and Staffs., a fleur-de-lis, party, per pale, or and ar. *Pl.* 68, *cr.* 12.
COPE, Iri., a harp, gu. *Pl.* 104, *cr.* 15.
COPELAND, a lion, passant, ppr. *Pl.* 48, *cr.* 8.
COPEN, in dexter hand a pair of compasses. *Vivitur ingenio. Pl.* 69, *cr.* 3.
COPENGER, Norf., a falcon's leg, belled, and wing conjoined, ppr. *Pl.* 101, *cr.* 15.
COPENGER, Lond., a buck's head, ar. *Pl.* 91, *cr.* 14.
COPILDIKE, COPLEDIKE, and COPLEDYKE, Kent, a wyvern, wings addorsed, statant, on a wheel, ppr. *Pl.* 122, *cr.* 2.
COPINGER, Suff., a chamois-deer's head, sa. *Pl.* 70, *cr.* 4.
COPINGER, Kent, a ram's head, sa. *Pl.* 34, *cr.* 12.
COPINGER, a parrot's head, between wings, vert, in mouth, gu., a sprig of three marigolds, ppr., leaved, or. *Pl.* 94, *cr.* 2, (marigolds, *pl.* 64, *cr.* 7.)
COPLAND, COPELAND, COPPLAND, and COWPLAND, Eng., in hand a military sash. *Pl.* 44, *cr.* 7.
COPLAND, COPELAND, COPPLAND, and COWPLAND, Eng., a castle, triple-towered, ppr., ensigned with a flag, gu., charged with a cross, ar. *Pl.* 123, *cr.* 14.
COPLAND, a horse's head and neck, couped, bridled, (and decked with oak-slips, fructed, ppr.) *Pl.* 92, *cr.* 1.
COPLAND, a lion, rampant, winged. *Pl.* 75, *cr.* 4.
COPLAND, a chevalier, in armour, on horseback, in dexter a sword. *Pl.* 118, *cr.* 14.
COPLAND, out of a ducal coronet, a swan's head. *Pl.* 30, *cr.* 10.
COPLAND, Aberdeen, a swan, wings addorsed, neck embowed, ppr., gorged with a ducal coronet, sa. *Æquo adeste animo. Pl.* 11, *cr.* 10.
COPLESTONE, Dors. and Devons., a wolf, passant, az. *Pl.* 46, *cr.* 6.
COPLESTONE, Dors. and Devons., a demi-tiger, gu., maned and tufted, or. *Pl.* 53, *cr.* 10.
COPLESTONE, a demi-lion, rampant. *Pl.* 67, *cr.* 10.
COPLEY, Baron Lyndhurst. *See* LYNDHURST.
COPLEY, Sir JOSEPH, Bart., Yorks., a griffin's head, erased. *Pl.* 48, *cr.* 6.
COPLEY, a dexter arm, in armour, embowed, (wreathed with laurel, and charged with an escallop,) in hand a sword. *Pl.* 21, *cr.* 4.

COPLEY, Yorks., a covered cup, or. *Pl.* 35, *cr.* 9, (without hand.)
COPLEY, Yorks., on a goat's head, quarterly, ar. and sa., attired, or, (four crescents, counterchanged.) *Pl.* 105, *cr.* 14.
COPLEY, Suff., a griffin, sejant, regardant, wings expanded, ar. *Pl.* 100, *cr.* 11, (regardant, *pl.* 4, *cr.* 9.)
COPLEY, Surr. and Yorks., a griffin, sejant, ar., ducally gorged and lined, or. *Pl.* 100, *cr.* 11, (gorging, *pl.* 61, *cr.* 14.)
COPLEY, Yorks., out of a ducal coronet, or, (eight ostrich-feathers, ar., three and five.) *In cruce vinco. Pl.* 114, *cr.* 8.
COPOLDYKE, Linc., a goat's head, erased, ar., armed and ducally gorged, or. *Pl.* 29, *cr.* 13, (gorging, *same plate, cr.* 15.)
COPPARD, Suss., a stag, regardant, ar., attired and unguled, or, (collared, gu., in mouth two ears of barley, ppr.) *Pl.* 3, *cr.* 2.
COPPEN, out of an earl's coronet, or, a demi-griffin, gold, armed, sa., (ducally gorged, az.) *Pl.* 18, *cr.* 6, (crowned, *pl.* 80, *cr.* 11.)
COPPENDALE, Middx., a stag, at gaze, ppr., attired, or. *Pl.* 81, *cr.* 8.
COPPIN, Norf., out of a ducal coronet, or, a demi-griffin, az., beaked and legged, gold. *Pl.* 39, *cr.* 2.
COPPINGER, or COPPENGER, a demi-lion, rampant. *Pl.* 67, *cr.* 10.
COPPINGER, WILLIAM, Esq., of Ballyvolane and Barryscourt, co. Cork, a demi-lion, rampant. *Virtute non vi. Pl.* 67, *cr.* 10.
COPPINGER, THOMAS-STEPHEN, Esq., of Midleton, co. Cork, same crest and motto.
COPPINGER, STEPHEN, Esq., of Leemount, Cork, same crest and motto.
COPPINGER, or COPPENGER, Iri., in dexter hand, ppr., vested, or, a holly-branch, vert. *Pl.* 64, *cr.* 7, (holly, *pl.* 4, *cr.* 15.)
COPPULL, Lanc., a lion's head, erased, erm., (charged with three guttée, two and one, or.) *Pl.* 81, *cr.* 4.
COPSON, Eng., stump of tree, couped at each end, in fess, ppr., shooting forth a branch spreading to dexter and sinister, vert, ensigned with a fleur-de-lis, or. *Pl.* 14, *cr.* 14.
COPWOOD, Herts., an eagle, displayed, vert. *Pl.* 48, *cr.* 11.
COPWOOD, Herts., an eagle, wings addorsed, or. *Pl.* 61, *cr.* 1.
COR, Sco., an increscent and decrescent, or. *Pl.* 99, *cr.* 4.
CORAM, and CORHAM, Devons., a beaver, passant, or. *Pl.* 49, *cr.* 5.
CORBALLY, Iri., a trout, naiant, ppr. *Pl.* 85, *cr.* 7.
CORBEN, CORBIN, and CORBYN, in dexter hand, ppr., a cross pattée, fitched, az. *Pl.* 99, *cr.* 15.
CORBET, Sco., a raven's head, erased, sa. *Save me, Lord! Pl.* 27, *cr.* 13.
CORBET, Salop, a raven, (in mouth a holly-branch, fructed, all ppr.) *Pl.* 123, *cr.* 2.
CORBET, Herts., Heref., and Salop, an elephant, ar., armed, or, on back a tower, of the first, the trappings, gu. and gold. (Another, the tower, or, trappings, sa.) *Pl.* 114, *cr.* 14.
CORBET, Lond., (on a mount, vert,) a squirrel, sejant, cracking a nut, or, leaved, ppr. *Pl.* 16, *cr.* 9.

CORBET, Norf. and Suff., a squirrel, sejant, or. *Pl.* 2, *cr.* 4.
CORBET, or CORBETT, Sco. and Iri., a crow, sa. *Pl.* 23, *cr.* 8.
CORBET, Bart., Salop, an elephant and castle, ppr. *Deus pascit corvos. Pl.* 114, *cr.* 14.
CORBET, ANDREW-WILLIAM, Esq., of Sundorne Castle, Salop, same crest and motto.
CORBETT, THOMAS-GEORGE, Esq., of Elsham, Linc.; and Darnhall, Chesh., same crest and motto.
CORBETT, a wolf, sejant, collared and lined, ppr. *Pl.* 110, *cr.* 4.
CORBOT, an elephant, on back a tower, all ppr. *Pl.* 114, *cr.* 14.
CORBREAKE, and CORBREYKE, Eng., in dexter hand a roll of paper, ppr. *Pl.* 27, *cr.* 4.
CORBREAKE, a cross crosslet, gu. *Pl.* 66, *cr.* 8.
CORBY, on a chapeau, a dove, wings addorsed, ppr. *Pl.* 109, *cr.* 10.
CORBY, in the sea, ppr., a pillar, ar. *Pl.* 14, *cr.* 3.
CORBYN, two arms, in armour, embowed, in saltier, in dexter a sword, on point a boar's head, couped, in sinister a human heart, all ppr. *Pl.* 93, *cr.* 14.
CORDALL, Suss., a cockatrice, vert, beaked, combed, jelloped, and crowned, gu. *Pl.* 63, *cr.* 15.
CORDALL, Norf. and Suff., a cockatrice, vert, combed, and wattled, gu. *Pl.* 63, *cr.* 15.
CORDALL, Lond., a cockatrice, vert, (collared,) combed, wattled, and legged, sa. *Pl.* 63, *cr.* 15.
CORDEL, CORDELL, and CORDELLE, Eng., a demi-savage, in dexter a scimitar, in sinister a constable's baton, ppr. *Pl.* 121, *cr.* 8.
CORDERAY, and CORDEROY, a human heart, gu., ducally crowned, or. *Pl.* 52, *cr.* 2, (without wings.)
CORDIN, a boar's head, couped, between (two) serpents, in orle, nowed at top, and respecting each other. *Pl.* 12, *cr.* 6.
CORDINGLEY, Eng., out of a crown vallery, or, an arm, embowed, vested, az., in hand an oak-branch, fructed, ppr. *Pl.* 2, *cr.* 2.
CORE, and COREY, Lond. and Norf., out of a ducal coronet, a griffin's head, between wings, or, (each wing charged with three etoiles, in pale, gu.) *Pl.* 97, *cr.* 13.
CORFIELD, Eng., in hand two palm-branches, in orle, ppr. *Pl.* 16, *cr.* 5.
CORIE, or CORY, Eng., a griffin's head, gu., between wings, or, each charged with a mullet, of the first. *Pl.* 65, *cr.* 1, (mullet, *pl.* 141.)
CORINGHAM, or CORYNGHAM, a rook, ppr. *Pl.* 123, *cr.* 2.
CORITON, or CORYTON, a lion, passant, gardant, gu. *Dum spiro spero. Pl.* 120, *cr.* 5.
CORK and ORRERY, Earl of. See BOYLE.
CORK, (by a tree, vert,) a holy lamb, passant, with staff and banner, ppr. *Pl.* 48, *cr.* 13.
CORKE, Eng., out of a cloud, a hand, erect, pointing to a star, ppr. *Pl.* 77, *cr.* 6.
CORKER, Iri., a demi-lion, rampant, erm, holding an etoile, or. *Pl.* 89, *cr.* 10, (etoile, *pl.* 141.)
CORMAC, or CORMACK, on a rock, a martlet, ppr. *Sine timore. Pl.* 36, *cr.* 5.
CORMICK, Iri., in hand, in fess, a sword, in pale, on point a garland of laurel, ppr. *Pl.* 56, *cr.* 6.

CORNACK, a sword, in pale, ppr., hilt and pommel, or. *Pl.* 105, *cr.* 1.
CORNELIUS, Eng., out of a cloud, in sinister, in dexter hand, in fess, ppr., a cross pattée, fitched, az. *Pl.* 26, *cr.* 4.
CORNER, in lion's gamb, erased, an eagle's leg, erased. *Pl.* 89, *cr.* 13.
CORNEWALL, Bart., Lond. and Herts.: 1. A Cornish chough, ppr. *Pl.* 100, *cr.* 13. 2. A demi-lion, rampant, gu., ducally crowned, or. *La vie durante. Pl.* 61, *cr.* 4, (without branch.)
CORNEY, a lion's head, erased, per pale, ar. and gu., (on neck a rose, counterchanged.) *Pl.* 81, *cr.* 4.
CORNEY, Lond., a bugle-horn, ar., stringed, gu. *Fac recte, nil time. Pl.* 48, *cr.* 12.
CORNINGHAM, Eng., a rock, ppr. *Pl.* 73, *cr.* 12.
CORNISH, Kent and Ess., on branch of tree, couped at each end, in fess, ppr., with one sprig at dexter end, vert, a Cornish chough, sa., wings addorsed, beaked and legged, gu. *Pl.* 6, *cr.* 11, (branch, *pl.* 10, *cr.* 1.)
CORNISH, JAMES, Esq., of Black Hall, Devons., a Cornish chough, ppr. *Pl.* 100, *cr.* 13.
CORNISH, WILLIAM, Esq., of Marazion, Cornw., a Cornish chough, sa., wings addorsed, beaked and legged, gu., standing on branch of olive, ppr. *Pl.* 6, *cr.* 11, (branch, *pl.* 98, *cr.* 8.)
CORNISH, Beds., out of a ducal coronet, or, a demi-eagle, displayed, sa. *Pl.* 9, *cr.* 6.
CORNISH, an eagle, displayed. *Pl.* 48, *cr.* 11.
CORNSLEY, Eng., in lion's gamb, a sabre, in pale, ppr. *Pl.* 18, *cr.* 8.
CORNWALL, on a chapeau, gu., turned up, erm., a lion, statant, ppr. *Pl.* 107, *cr.* 1.
CORNWALL, Salop, a Cornish chough, ppr. *Pl.* 100, *cr.* 13.
CORNWALL, Sco., a Cornish chough, hatching in the face of a rock, ppr. *We big, you see, warily. Pl.* 70, *cr.* 11.
CORNWALL, Dors., a boar's head, couped, or, in bend, blade of broken sword thrust down throat, ppr. *Pl.* 28, *cr.* 14.
CORNWALL, Berks., a demi-lion, rampant, gu., ducally crowned, or. *Pl.* 61, *cr.* 4, (without branch.)
CORNWALLIS, Earl and Baron, Viscount Brome, (Mann:) 1. For *Mann*, a demi-dragon, sa., guttée-d'eau. *Pl.* 82, *cr.* 10. 2. For *Cornwallis*, on a mount, vert, a stag, lodged, regardant, ar., attired and unguled, or, (gorged with a chaplet of laurel, vert, vulned in shoulder, ppr.) *Virtus vincit invidiam. Pl.* 51, *cr.* 9.
CORNWALLIS, a lion, rampant, (gardant,) between paws a ducal coronet, the whole between two standards. *Pl.* 9, *cr.* 7, (standards, *pl.* 53, *cr.* 14.)
CORNWALLIS, Iri., on a mount, a hind, statant, ppr. *Pl.* 122, *cr.* 5.
CORP, Eng., a yew-tree, ppr. *Pl.* 49, *cr.* 13.
CORRANCE, FREDERICK, Esq., of Parham Hall, Suff., a raven, in dexter an escutcheon, sa., charged with a leopard's face, or. *Pl.* 6, *cr.* 11.
CORREY, out of a ducal coronet, or, a demi-griffin, ppr., wings, semée of trefoils, sa. *Pl.* 39, *cr.* 2.

CORRIE, or CORRY, a demi-cupid, holding a hymenial torch, in pale, or, flamed, gu. *Pl.* 70, *cr.* 14.
CORRIE, or CORRY, Sco. and Iri., a cock, ppr. *Vigilans et audax. Pl.* 67, *cr.* 14.
CORRIE, or CORRY, Sco., a demi-lion, ppr. *Courage. Pl.* 67, *cr.* 10.
CORRY, Iri., a griffin's head, couped. *Pl.* 38, *cr.* 3.
CORRY, Iri., in hand, ppr., vested, az., cuffed, or, a mill-rind, sa. *Pl.* 34, *cr.* 3.
CORRY, Earl of Belmore. *See* BELMORE.
CORRY, ISAAC, Esq., of Abbey Yard, Newry, co. Down, out of a ducal coronet, a dragon's head, between wings. *Gripe fast. Pl.* 105, *cr.* 11, (coronet, *pl.* 128, *fig.* 3.)
CORSANE, Sco., an eagle, close, (crowned with an antique crown,) gazing at the sun, all ppr. *Præmium virtutis gloria. Pl.* 43, *cr.* 5.
CORSAR, or CORSER, Sco., a pegasus, ppr. *Recto cursu. Pl.* 28, *cr.* 9.
CORSE, Sco., a cross crosslet, fitched, az. *Certum pete finem. Pl.* 16, *cr.* 10.
CORTHINE, Yorks., a demi-lion, couped, in dexter an etoile, sinister resting on a torteau. *Pl.* 91, *cr.* 13, (etoile and torteau, *pl.* 141.)
CORYTON, Eng., a marigold, ppr. *Pl.* 105, *cr.* 15.
CORYTON, AUGUSTUS, Esq., of Pentillie Castle, Cornw., a lion, passant, gu. *Pl.* 48, *cr.* 8.
COSARD, Hants, a lion's head, erased, gu., ducally crowned, or. *Pl.* 90, *cr.* 4.
COSARS, a buffalo's head, erased, ppr. *Pl.* 57, *cr.* 7.
COSARS, Eng., from a castle, triple-towered, a demi-lion, rampant, ppr. *Pl.* 101, *cr.* 1.
COSBY, Eng., an arm, from elbow, in armour, in hand two pieces of broken spear, all ppr. *Pl.* 88, *cr.* 4.
COSBY, Iri., a griffin, segreant, gu., supporting broken spear, or, the head, ar. *Pl.* 67, *cr.* 13, (spear, *pl.* 60, *cr.* 4.)
COSEN, Norf., on a chapeau, az., turned up, erm., a tiger, sejant, or. *Pl.* 86, *cr.* 8, (chapeau, *same plate, cr.* 14.)
COSEN, Norf., on a ducal coronet, az., lined, erm., a tiger, sejant, or. *Pl.* 86, *cr.* 8.
COSENS, Eng., a demi-griffin, in paws a battle-axe, ppr. *Pl.* 44, *cr.* 3.
COSGRAVE, a tiger's head, erased, affrontée. *Pl.* 65, *cr.* 7.
COSGRAVE, a stag's head, erased, affrontée. *Pl.* 8, *cr.* 6.
COSINS, or COSYNS, Leic., a demi-lion, rampant, or, guttée-de-sang. *Pl.* 67, *cr.* 10.
COSSAR, or COSSER, a horse, tenné, passant, saddled and bridled, ar. *Pl.* 99, *cr.* 11.
COSSAR, or COSSER, on a thistle, a bee, ppr. *Pl.* 68, *cr.* 9.
COSSENS, a Doric pillar, gu. *Pl.* 33, *cr.* 1.
COSSON, and COSSEN, Lond. and Cornw., a lion, rampant, or, guttée-de-sang, and ducally crowned, gold. *Pl.* 98, *cr.* 1.
COSTELLO, a falcon, ppr., close, billed, or. *Audaces fortuna juvat. Pl.* 67, *cr.* 3.
COSTERTON, Norf., on a mount, vert, a lion, (statant,) erminois, in front of a beacon, or, inflamed, ppr. *Pro patriâ uro. Pl.* 89, *cr.* 9, (lion, *pl.* 48, *cr.* 8.)
COSTLEY, Eng., in hand, erect, ppr., a cross crosslet, fitched. *Pl.* 99, *cr.* 1.

COSWAY, a moor's head, couped at shoulders, ppr. *Pl.* 19, *cr.* 1.
COSYN, on a mount, vert, a hare, sejant, sa., (holding a bunch of flowers, ppr.) *Pl.* 70, *cr.* 1.
COSYN, Durh., an eagle. *Pl.* 7, *cr.* 11.
COSYN, Eng., an anchor, sa., environed by a serpent, vert. *Pl.* 35, *cr.* 14.
COTELL, on a ducal coronet, or, a leopard, sejant, ppr. *Pl.* 86, *cr.* 8.
COTES, JOHN, Esq., of Woodcote, Salop, a cock, ppr., combed, wattled, and legged, or. *Pl.* 67, *cr.* 14.
COTES, Bucks. and Leic., a cock, or, combed and wattled, gu. *Pl.* 67, *cr.* 14.
COTGRAVE, COTGREVE, and COTGRIEVE, Eng., a comet-star, towards the sinister, ppr. *Pl.* 39, *cr.* 9.
COTGRAVE, out of a ducal coronet, or, a demi-peacock, ppr. *Pl.* 24, *cr.* 1, (coronet, *same plate, cr.* 10.)
COTGREAVE, Knt., Chesh., a demi-peacock, ar., charged on breast with a fess, indented, gu., wings elevated, or, each charged with an ermine spot. *Antiquam obtinens. Pl.* 53, *cr.* 12, (without snake.)
COTHER, Eng., a pegasus' head, between wings, ar. *Pl.* 19, *cr.* 13.
COTHER, a dexter arm, in armour, embowed, ppr., garnished, or, in hand, also ppr., a chaplet, vert. *Pl.* 68, *cr.* 1.
COTON, Norf., an eagle, rising, or. *Pl.* 67, *cr.* 4.
COTREL, COTRELL, and COTTRELL, a talbot's head, erased, sa., collared and lined, ar., collar charged with three torteaux. *Pl.* 2, *cr.* 15, (torteau, *pl.* 141.)
COTRELL, and COTRELL, a demi-savage, in dexter a club, round sinister arm a serpent entwined, all ppr. *Pl.* 92, *cr.* 10.
COTSFORD, out of a ducal coronet, a griffin's head, ppr. *Pl.* 54, *cr.* 14.
COTTELL, Devons. and Somers., on a ducal coronet, or, a leopard, sejant, ppr., charged with a crescent. *Pl.* 86, *cr.* 8, (crescent, *pl.* 141.)
COTTENHAM, Baron. *See* PEPYS.
COTTER, Iri., a lion, passant, regardant. *Pl.* 100, *cr.* 6.
COTTER, Eng., two lions' paws, sa., supporting a pillar, ar. *Pl.* 77, *cr.* 4.
COTTERALL, COTTERELL, and COTTERILL, a hand holding a glove, ppr. *Pl.* 42, *cr.* 15.
COTTERELL, Bart., Herefs., an arm, in armour, embowed, ppr., holding by the top an escutcheon, ar., charged with a talbot's head, sa., collared and chained, or. *Non rapui, sed recepi.*
COTTERELL, Yorks., a talbot's head, couped, ar., eared and collared, or. *Pl.* 2, *cr.* 15.
COTTESFORD, Oxon. and Devons., a bear, couchant, sa., muzzled and collared, or. *Pl.* 76, *cr.* 5.
COTTESMORE, Eng., an arm, in armour, in hand two pieces of broken spear, ppr. *Pl.* 88, *cr.* 4.
COTTINGHAM, Eng., on a chapeau, ppr., a greyhound, sejant, ar. *Pl.* 66, *cr.* 15, (chapeau, *pl.* 127, *cr.* 13.)
COTTINGTON, Glouc. and Wilts., a stag's head, ar., attired, or, gorged with a collar, az., charged with three (roses,) of the second. *Pl.* 125, *cr.* 6, (without roses.)

COTTON, Lord Combermere. *See* COMBERMERE.
COTTON, Bart., Cambs., a griffin's head, erased, ar. *Fidelitas vincit.* *Pl.* 48, *cr.* 6.
COTTON, a hawk's head, erased. *Pl.* 34, *cr.* 11.
COTTON, a griffin's head, erased, in mouth a gauntlet, ppr. *Pl.* 48, *cr.* 6, (gauntlet, *pl.* 61, *cr.* 8.)
COTTON, a hawk, ppr., beaked and belled, or, (in foot a demi-garter, sa., buckled, of the second.) *Pl.* 94, *cr.* 7.
COTTON, Suff., a griffin's head, erased, ar. *Pl.* 48, *cr.* 6.
COTTON, a Cornish chough, (in mouth a cotton-hank, all ppr.) *Pl.* 100, *cr.* 13.
COTTON, Glouc., five snakes tied together, ppr. *Pl.* 119, *cr.* 13.
COTTON, Staffs. and Worc., a hawk, ppr., beaked and legged, ar. (Another, beaked, or.) *Pl.* 67, *cr.* 3.
COTTON, Hunts., out of a ducal coronet, a demi-eagle, displayed, ar. *Pl.* 9, *cr.* 6.
COTTON, Leic. and Staffs., an eagle displayed, ar. *Pl.* 48, *cr.* 11.
COTTON, Hants and Salop, an eagle, wings expanded, ar., beaked and legged, or, (in dexter a belt, az., buckle, of the second.) *Pl.* 67, *cr.* 4.
COUCH, and COUCHE, Eng., a demi-bear, rampant. *Pl.* 104, *cr.* 10.
COUCHER, and COWCHER, Eng., a well, ppr. *Pl.* 70, *cr.* 10.
COUCHMAN, a demi-lion, rampant, sa., (semée of cross crosslets, ar.,) between paws a cinquefoil, of the last. *Pl.* 126, *cr.* 12, (cinquefoil, *pl.* 141.)
COUCHTREE, a hawk's head, between wings. *Pl.* 99, *cr.* 10.
COUDRAY, COUDREY, and COUDRY, in lion's paw, erased, az., a battle-axe, or. *Pl.* 51, *cr.* 13.
COULCHER, Yorks., out of a vallery crown, a buck's head, all ppr. *Pl.* 91, *cr.* 14, (crown, *pl.* 2, *cr.* 2.)
COULDWELL, Eng., a sea-lion, rampant, vert. *Pl.* 25, *cr.* 12.
COULSON, Northumb., in nest, ppr., a pelican feeding her young, ar., vulning, ppr. *Pl.* 44, *cr.* 1.
COULSON, and COULSTON, Eng., a dolphin, naiant, sa. *Pl.* 48, *cr.* 9.
COULSON, and COULSTON, Hants, an eagle, wings addorsed, ar., preying on a dolphin, ppr. *Pl.* 61, *cr.* 3, (dolphin, *pl.* 48, *cr.* 9.)
COULSON, JOHN-BLENKINSOPP, Esq., of Blenkinsopp Castle, Northumb., a pelican feeding her young. *Je mourrai pour ceux que j'aime.* *Pl.* 44, *cr.* 1.
COULT, Sco., an arm, embowed, hand grasping a dart, ppr. *Transfigam.* *Pl.* 92, *cr.* 14.
COULTHAND, Cumb., a demi-lion, rampant, gu. *Pl.* 67, *cr.* 10.
COULTHART, JOHN-ROSS, Esq., of Coulthart, Wigtown; Collyn, Dumfries; and Croft House, Ashton-under-Lyne, Lanc.; a war-horse's head and neck, couped, ar., armed and bridled, ppr., garnished, or. *Virtute non verbis.* *Pl.* 7, *cr.* 12.
COULTHURST, Eng., issuing from clouds, two hands grasping the stump of a tree. *Pl.* 126, *cr.* 4.
COULTNAN, Eng., three ears of wheat, ppr. *Pl.* 102, *cr.* 1.

COULTON, a lion's paw, supporting an escutcheon. *Pl.* 43, *cr.* 12.
COULTS, Sco., a demi-moor, shooting an arrow, ppr. *Pl.* 80, *cr.* 9.
COUPER, Bart., out of a mural coronet, a hand grasping a garland, ppr. *Virtute.* *Pl.* 41, *cr.* 7, (coronet, *pl.* 128, *fig.* 18.)
COUPER, on a mural coronet, ar., a pelican, wings addorsed, erm., beaked and legged, or, vulned, gu. *Pl.* 64, *cr.* 1.
COUPER, Eng., a dexter arm, erect, hand clenched, gu. *Pl.* 87, *cr.* 7.
COUPER, Sco., in hand a garland, ppr. *Virtute.* *Pl.* 41, *cr.* 7.
COUPER, an arm, in hand a cutlass, ppr. *Pl.* 92, *cr.* 5.
COUPER, or COUPIR, Eng., a cock's head, gu. *Pl.* 92, *cr.* 3.
COUPLAND, Eng., a salmon, naiant, ppr. *Pl.* 85, *cr.* 7.
COURCY, DE, Lord Courcy, on a ducal coronet, or, an eagle, displayed, az. *Vincit omnia veritas.* *Pl.* 48, *cr.* 11, (coronet, *pl.* 128, *fig.* 3.)
COURCY, DE, Eng., out of a mural coronet, in hand a mullet, ppr. *Pl.* 34, *cr.* 1.
COURT, and COWRT, Eng., out of a ducal coronet, or, a unicorn's head, ar., armed and crined, gold, charged with a mullet, gu. *Pl.* 45, *cr.* 14, (mullet, *pl.* 141.)
COURT, a stag's head, erased, ppr. *Pl.* 66, *cr.* 9.
COURT, A', Eng., a lion's head, erased, regardant. *Pl.* 35, *cr.* 2.
COURTEENE, Worc., a demi-talbot, sa. *Pl.* 97, *cr.* 9, (without arrow.)
COURTEIS, Eng., a demi-husbandman, over shoulder a ploughshare. *Pl.* 122, *cr.* 1.
COURTEIS, and COURTEYS, a wolf's head, couped, ar., collared and spiked, sa., chained, or. *Pl.* 8, *cr.* 4.
COURTENAY, a dolphin, naiant, ppr. *Pl.* 48, *cr.* 9.
COURTENAY, a dolphin, naiant, ar., charged with four torteaux, (devouring a ducal cap, gu., in a coronet, or.) *Pl.* 48, *cr.* 9.
COURTENAY, WILLIAM, Viscount, of Powdenham Castle, Devons., and Bart., of Ireland, a dolphin, naiant, ppr. *Ubi lapsus? Quid feci?* *Pl.* 48, *cr.* 9.
COURTNEY, Iri., a cherub, wings in saltier, ppr. *Pl.* 67, *cr.* 11.
COURTNEY, Iri., a cherub, ppr. *Pl.* 126, *cr.* 10.
COURTNEY, Devons., out of a ducal coronet, or, a plume of feathers, ar., charged with a crescent, sa. *Pl.* 100, *cr.* 12.
COURTHOPE, Kent, a camel's head, or, (vulned, gu.) *Pl.* 109, *cr.* 9.
COURTHOPE, Suff., a demi-stag, gu., semée of etoiles, and attired, or. *Pl.* 55, *cr.* 9, (without rose.)
COURTHORP, Suss., an arm, erect, ppr., in hand an anchor, az., fluke and ring, or. *Pl.* 27, *cr.* 6.
COURTIS, Eng., a phœnix in flames, ppr. *Pl.* 44, *cr.* 8.
COURTOIS, and COURTOYS, a mount, vert. *Pl.* 62, *cr.* 11.
COURTOIS, and COURTOYS, a castle, triple-towered. *Pl.* 123, *cr.* 14.
COURTOWN, Earl of, and Baron, Viscount Stopford, Iri., Baron Saltersford, U.K., (Stopford,) a wyvern, wings addorsed, vert. *Patriæ infelici fidelis.* *Pl.* 63, *cr.* 13.

COURTRY, Kent, a falcon's head, or, between wings, az., each charged with a fleur-de-lis, or. *Pl.* 99, *cr.* 10, (fleur-de-lis, *pl.* 141.)

COUSEN, Eng., a ram's head, erased, gu. *Pl.* 1, *cr.* 12.

COUSMAKER, and COUSSMAKER, Eng., an etoile, or. *Pl.* 63, *cr.* 9.

COUSTON, Sco. and Eng., a sword and garb, in saltier, ppr. *Pl.* 70, *cr.* 7.

COUTS, Sco., a stag's head, erased. *Esse quam videri.* *Pl.* 66, *cr.* 9.

COUTTS, Eng., a demi-moor, shooting a bow, ppr. *Pl.* 41, *cr.* 8.

COUTTS, a demi-centaur, ppr. *Pl.* 70, *cr.* 13.

COVE, Eng., in lion's paw a palm-branch, ppr. *Pl.* 70, *cr.* 9.

COVE, Heref., out of a ducal coronet, or, a dexter arm, in armour, embowed, in gauntlet a battle-axe, ppr. *Pl.* 70, *cr.* 9.

COVELL, Lond., on a chapeau, gu., turned up, erm., a lion, passant, ar., (charged with a file of three lambeaux, gu.) *Pl.* 107, *cr.* 1.

COVENTRY, Earl of, Viscount Deerhurst, (Coventry,) on a garb, in fess, or, a cock, gu., combed, wattled, and legged, gold. *Candide et constanter.* *Pl.* 122, *cr.* 3.

COVENTRY, Lord Alesburgh, same crest.

COVENTRY, on a chapeau, gu., turned up, ar., a cock-pheasant, ppr., beaked and membered, of the first. *Pl.* 82, *cr.* 12, (chapeau, *pl.* 127, *fig.* 13.)

COVENTRY, Town of, Warw., a leopard, passant, ppr. *Pl.* 86, *cr.* 2.

COVERDALE, and COVERDALL, Eng., a lion, rampant, per fess, or and gu. *Pl.* 67, *cr.* 5.

COVERT, Suss., a leopard's head, or. *Pl.* 92, *cr.* 13.

COVERT, Kent and Surr., a leopard's face, or. *Pl.* 66, *cr.* 14.

COVERT, Kent and Surr., a lion's face, or. *Pl.* 47, *cr.* 6.

COVERT, Somers., out of a ducal coronet, or, a unicorn's head, ar., armed and crined, gold, (charged with a mullet, gu.) *Pl.* 45, *cr.* 14.

COVILL, and COVILLE, an arm, in armour, embowed, ppr., bound with a shoulder ribbon, gu., in hand a club, of the first. *Pl.* 28, *cr.* 2.

COW, COWE, COWEE, COWEY, and COWIE, Eng., a feather, in pale, ppr. *Pl.* 105, *cr.* 3.

COWAN, Bo'ness, an escallop, or. *Sic itur in altum.* *Pl.* 117, *cr.* 4.

COWAN, a demi-lion, double-queued, ppr. *Pl.* 120, *cr.* 10.

COWAN, Iri., a lion, rampant, sa., ducally crowned, or. *Pl.* 98, *cr.* 1.

COWAN, (out of clouds, ppr.,) a cubit arm, erect, also ppr., in hand a heart, gu. *Pl.* 64, *cr.* 12.

COWAN, a fret, gu. *Pl.* 82, *cr.* 7.

COWARD, a demi-greyhound, sa., (between feet a stag's head, cabossed, ar., attired, or.) *Pl.* 6, *cr.* 9.

COWBROUGH, and COWBRUGH, Sco., a griffin's head, between wings, ppr. *Pl.* 22, *cr.* 2.

COWCEY, COWCIE, and COWEY, Eng., out of a ducal coronet, an arm, in armour, embowed, in hand an anchor, corded, all ppr. *Pl.* 122, *cr.* 8.

COWDEN, Eng., a demi-lion, sa., charged with annulets, or. *Pl.* 67, *cr.* 10, (annulet, *pl.* 141.)

COWDREY, Hants, out of a ducal coronet, or, an arm, in armour, embowed, ppr., garnished, gold, in gauntlet, an anchor, gu., stock, sa., cordage entwined round arm, of the last. *Pl.* 122, *cr.* 8.

COWEY, DE, Eng., a nag's head, ar., bridled, gu. *Pl.* 92, *cr.* 1.

COWELL, Eng., on a chapeau, gu., turned up, erm., a lion, passant, or, gorged with a label, of the first. *Pl.* 107, *cr.* 1.

COWELL, Sco., out of a bush, a lion's face, ppr. *Pl.* 111, *cr.* 2.

COWEN, Eng., on a winged globe, an eagle, rising, ppr. *Pl.* 34, *cr.* 2, (globe, *pl.* 50, *cr.* 7.)

COWIE, Sco., a fleur-de-lis, az. *Per cœli favorem.* *Pl.* 68, *cr.* 12.

COWIE, Surr., on stump of tree, sprouting new branches, a falcon, (wings expanded, ppr.) *Pl.* 78, *cr.* 8, (falcon, *pl.* 105, *cr.* 4.)

COWLEY, Baron, (Wellesley,) out of a ducal coronet, or, a demi-lion, rampant, gu., holding a forked pennon, of the last, flowing to sinister, one third per pale, from the staff, ar., charged with the cross of St George. *Porro unum est necessarium.*

COWLEY, Lond., out of a ducal coronet, or, a demi-lion, ermines. *Pl.* 45, *cr.* 7.

COWLEY, on a mural coronet, az., a leopard's head, ar., jessant-de-lis, or. *Pl.* 123, *cr.* 9, (coronet, *pl.* 128, *fig.* 18.)

COWLING, on a lion's head, erased, az., a chapeau. *Pl.* 122, *cr.* 10.

COWMEADOW, a demi-lion, rampant, ar., in dexter a trefoil, slipped, vert. *Pl.* 89, *cr.* 10, (trefoil, *pl.* 141.)

COWPER, Earl and Baron, Viscount Fordwich, (Cooper,) in lion's gamb, erect, (and erased,) or, a branch, vert, fretted, gu. *Tuum est.* *Pl.* 68, *cr.* 10.

COWPER, Yorks., on a castle, the head of a Saracen king, ppr., wreathed, ar. and az., and crowned with a Saxon coronet, or. *Pl.* 28, *cr.* 11, (head, *same plate, cr.* 3.)

COWPER, Sco., in hand, a wreath of laurel, ppr. *Pl.* 86, *cr.* 4.

COWPER, Chesh., out of a mural coronet, gu., a demi-wolf, ar., supporting a gauntlet, or.

COWPER, Kent and Herts., in lion's gamb, erased, or, a branch, vert, fructed, gu. *Pl.* 68, *cr.* 10.

COWPER, Suss., in a pheon, ar., a laurel sprig, ppr., between wings, gu.

COWPER, Glouc., in hand, a cutlass, ppr. *Pl.* 29, *cr.* 8.

COWSFIELD, out of a ducal coronet, a camel's head. *Pl.* 55, *cr.* 5.

COX, WILLIAM, Esq., of Ballynoe, co. Limerick, an antelope's head, erased, ar., attired, or, transfixed through neck by a broken spear, ppr. *Fortiter et fideliter.* *Pl.* 79, *cr.* 9.

COX, Col. Sir WILLIAM, of Coolcliffe, co. Wexford, a goat's head, erased, sa. *Fide et fortitudine.* *Pl.* 29, *cr.* 13.

COX, RICHARD-SNEAD, Esq., of Broxwood and Eaton Bishop, Heref.; and Souldern, Oxon.; an antelope's head, erased, ppr., pierced through neck by a spear. *Pl.* 79, *cr.* 9.

COX, Lond., a goat's head, erased, ar. *Pl.* 29, *cr.* 13.

COX, Iri., two hands conjoined, in fess, supporting a heart, gu. *Pl.* 43, *cr.* 15.

Cox, Sir John, Bart., Iri., a goat's head, erased, az., armed, or. *Fide et fortitudine.* Pl. 29, cr. 13.
Cox, Herts., an antelope's head, erased, sa., pierced through neck by a broken spear and vulned, gu. Pl. 79, cr. 9.
Cox, Suss., a griffin's head, erased, sa., (pierced through neck by an arrow, gu., headed and feathered, ar.) Pl. 48, cr. 6.
Cox, Lond., an arm, in armour, ppr., garnished, or, in hand a battle-axe, ar., handle, gu. Pl. 121, cr. 14.
Cox, Sco., out of the sea, an arm, in hand an anchor, cabled, ppr. Pl. 27, cr. 6.
Cox, an arm, ar., in hand a triple bunch of (pinks,) leaved, ppr. Pl. 47, cr. 13.
Cox, Lond. and Glouc., a goat's head, ar., attired, or, in mouth an oak-leaf, az. Pl. 105, cr. 14.
Cox, Herts., a goat's head, erased, sa., horned, bearded, (and pierced through neck by an arrow, or, the wound guttée-de-sang.) Pl. 29, cr. 13.
Cox, Lond., a cock, gu., ducally crowned, or. Pl. 67, cr. 14, (crown, *same plate.*)
Cox, Kent, a demi-horse, salient, ar., (charged on neck with a thunderbolt, ppr.) Pl. 91, cr. 2, (without wings or coronet.)
Cox, Norf., out of a ducal coronet, a griffin's head, between wings. Pl. 97, cr. 13.
Coxan, or Coxen, a lion, rampant, or, in dexter a fleur-de-lis, az. Pl. 87, cr. 6.
Coxe, Lond., a demi-lion, rampant, ar., collared, sa., (in dexter a spear-head, or.) Pl. 18, cr. 13.
Coxed, Oxon., out of an Eastern crown, or, a griffin's head, vert, langued, ppr. Pl. 54, cr. 14, (crown, pl. 128, fig. 2.)
Coxhead, a lion, passant, paly of six, or and gu. Pl. 48, cr. 8.
Coxon, or Coxson, a cock, ar., combed, wattled, and legged, gu. Pl. 67, cr. 14.
Coxon, Yorks., a demi-lion, rampant, or, supporting a staff, raguly, ar. Pl. 11, cr. 2.
Coxs, Linc., on a mount, a stag, lodged, regardant, ppr. *Prodesse quam conspici.* Pl. 51, cr. 9.
Coxton, Eng., an antelope, passant, ppr. Pl. 63, cr. 10.
Coxwell, Glouc., a dragon's head, ar., between wings, gu. Pl. 105, cr. 11.
Coyle, Iri., a hind's head, erased, or. Pl. 6, cr. 1.
Coyne, Staff., an arm, erect, vested, sa., slashed and cuffed, or, in hand, ppr., (a cutlass, ar.,) embowed, gu., hilt and pommel, or. Pl. 120, cr. 1.
Coyne, Iri., a sea-horse, ppr. Pl. 103, cr. 3.
Coyners, Eng., a sinister wing, gu. Pl. 39, cr. 10.
Coyney, or Coyny, Eng., an oak-branch, ppr. Pl. 32, cr. 13.
Coys, Ess., (out of clouds, ppr., issuing rays, or,) an arm, erect, hand grasping a snake, entwined round arm, all ppr. Pl. 91, cr. 6.
Coytmore, a dagger, in pale, ppr. Pl. 56, cr. 13.
Cozens, Eng., a lion, rampant, sa., in dexter a battle-axe, az., hafted, gu. Pl. 67, cr. 5, (axe, pl. 26, cr. 7.)
Crab, Sco., a salmon, naiant, ppr. Pl. 85, cr. 7.

Crab, or Crabbe, a shield, az., charged with a fleur-de-lis, or. Pl. 26, cr. 11, (fleur-de-lis, pl. 141.)
Crab, or Crabbe, in lion's gamb, erased, a dagger, ppr. Pl. 56, cr. 3.
Crabtree, Eng., in hand, erect, a dagger, in pale, ppr. Pl. 23, cr. 15.
Cracherode, a demi-boar, salient, regardant, or, wounded in shoulder with an arrow, ppr., held in mouth. Pl. 115, cr. 2.
Cracklow, Eng., out of a crescent, a flame of fire, ppr. Pl. 29, cr. 2.
Cracroft, now Amcotts, Robert, Esq., of Hackthorn, Linc., a stork, ppr., supporting a battle-axe, staff, or, headed, ar. Pl. 61, cr. 10, (axe, pl. 14, cr. 8.)
Craddock, or Cradock, Somers. and Wilts., a bear's head, erased, sa., billettée, and muzzled, or. Pl. 71, cr. 6.
Craddock, or Cradock, out of a ducal coronet, or, a lion's paw holding a spear, tasselled, ppr. Pl. 120, cr. 6.
Craddock, or Cradock, Iri., a lion, rampant, between paws a ducal coronet. Pl. 9, cr. 7.
Craddock, or Cradock, stump of oak-tree, sprouting a branch on sinister side, ppr. Pl. 92, cr. 8.
Craddock, or Cradock, Eng. and Wel., a horse, passant, sa. Pl. 15, cr. 14.
Craddock, or Cradock, a bear's head, couped, ar., muzzled, gu. Pl. 2, cr. 9.
Cradock, or Carodoc, Baron Howden. *See* Howden.
Crackanthorpe, William, Esq., of Newbiggin Hall, Westmoreland, a holly-tree, ppr. Pl. 22, cr. 10.
Crafford, a falcon's head, or. Pl. 34, cr. 11.
Craford, Kent and Ess., a hawk's head, or. Pl. 34, cr. 11.
Craford, Northumb., an eagle's head, between wings, ar. Pl. 81, cr. 10.
Craford, Berks., a deer's head, ppr., between attires, a cross. Pl. 24, cr. 9.
Crafton, Eng., a dolphin, haurient, swallowing a fish, ppr. Pl. 71, cr. 1.
Crag, or Cragg, Eng., in a chapeau, gu., turned up, erm., a fleur-de-lis, between wings, az. Pl. 21, cr. 13.
Craggs, two arms embowed, on each hand a scimitar, ppr. Pl. 52, cr. 1.
Craick, Sco., an anchor, ppr. *Providence.* Pl. 42, cr. 12.
Craig, Sco., a chevalier on horseback, in dexter a broken spear, all ppr. *J'ai bonne esperance.* Pl. 43, cr. 2.
Craig-Gibson, Bart., Sco., a chevalier on horseback, in dexter a broken spear, all ppr. *Vive Deo ut vivas.* Pl. 43, cr. 2.
Craig, Iri., a demi-lion, gu., in dexter a mullet, or. Pl. 89, cr. 10.
Craig, or Craige, Sco., a chevalier on horseback, holding a broken lance, in bend, all ppr. *Vive ut vivas.* Pl. 43, cr. 2.
Craig, Eng., a lion's head, vert, collared, or. Pl. 42, cr. 14.
Craig, Sco., a pillar, ar. Pl. 33, cr. 1.
Craigdallie, Sco., a dexter hand, pulling a thistle, ppr. Pl. 54, cr. 11.
Craigdallie, Sco., a lion, rampant, holding a battle-axe, ppr. Pl. 67, cr. 5, (axe, pl. 26, cr. 7.)
Craigdallie, a pillar, ar.. Pl. 33, cr. 1.

CRAIGG, Sco., a cornucopia. *Honeste vivo.* Pl. 91, cr. 4.
CRAIGG, CRAIGGE, or CRAIGE, a boar, passant, ar. Pl. 48, cr. 14.
CRAIGIE, Sco., a pillar, ppr. Pl. 33, cr. 1.
CRAIGIE, Sir WILLIAM, Bart., Gairsay, Orkney, a boar, passant, ar., armed, az. *Timor omnes abesto.* Pl. 48, cr. 14.
CRAIGY, Sco., a boar, passant, ar., armed and langued, gu. *Timor omnes abesto.* Pl. 48, cr. 14.
CRAIK, an eagle's leg, erased at thigh, ppr. Pl. 83, cr. 7, (without bell.)
CRAIK, Iri., a goat's head, ar., armed, gu. Pl. 29, cr. 13.
CRAISTER, Northumb., a raven, ppr. Pl. 123, cr. 2.
CRAKE, on a chapeau, ppr., a talbot, sejant, or. Pl. 102, cr. 9.
CRAKENTHORP, Eng., three ears of wheat, or. Pl. 102, cr. 1.
CRAKENTHORPE, a pillar, ensigned with a heart. Pl. 122, cr. 4.
CRAMER, or CRAMMER, Eng., a gauntlet, ppr. Pl. 15, cr. 15.
CRAMER, on a mount, a cock, wings expanded, ppr. *Non dormit qui custodit.* Pl. 76, cr. 7.
CRAMER, Iri., out of a ducal coronet, or, a talbot's head, sa., eared, ar. Pl. 99, cr. 7.
CRAMMOND, Sco., a tower, ar., masoned, sa. *My hope is constant in thee.* Pl. 12, cr. 5.
CRAMPHORNE, Herts., a talbot's head, erased, erm., eared, sa., gorged with a collar, gu. (charged with three cross crosslets, fitched, or.) Pl. 2, cr. 15.
CRAMPTON, Iri., a Roman fasces, in pale, ppr. Pl. 65, cr. 15.
CRANAGE, Chesh., out of a mural coronet, a demi-monkey, ppr. Pl. 24, cr. 12.
CRANAGE, Chesh., out of a ducal coronet, a demi-stork, wings expanded, ppr. Pl. 29, cr. 9, (stork, pl. 33, cr. 9.)
CRANBER, Suff., out of a ducal coronet, in hand a sheaf of arrows, ppr. Pl. 9, cr. 4.
CRANE, Suff., a crane, ppr. Pl. 111, cr. 9.
CRANE, Iri., a wheel, sa. Pl. 32, cr. 15.
CRANE, a demi-hind, or, ducally gorged, az.
CRANFIELD, on a ducal coronet, or, a fleur-de-lis between two ostrich-feathers, ar. Pl. 110, cr. 1, (fleur-de-lis, pl. 68, cr. 12.)
CRANFORD, Eng., an eagle, wings expanded, ppr., supporting a flag, az. Pl. 65, cr. 3.
CRANFORD, Eng., a cross moline, sa. Pl. 89, cr. 8.
CRANMER, Notts., a crane's head, erased, az., (pierced through neck by an arrow, ppr., barbed and plumed, ar., neck vulned, gu.) Pl. 20, cr. 9.
CRANMORE, a crane's head, erased, ar., beaked, gu., (pierced through by an arrow, ppr., barbed and plumed, ar., neck vulned, gu.) Pl. 20, cr. 9.
CRANSTON, Eng., a column, ar., entwined with woodbine, vert. Pl. 14, cr. 15.
CRANSTON, Sco., a crane's head, erased, ppr. *I desire not to want.* Pl. 20, cr. 9.
CRANSTOUN, JAMES-EDWARD, Baron, (Cranstoun,) Sco., a crane, (roosting with head under wings,) and holding up a stone with dexter foot, all ppr. *Thou shalt want ere I want.* Pl. 26, cr. 11.

CRANSTOUN, Sco., a crane's head, erect, ppr. *I desire not to want.* Pl. 20, cr. 9.
CRANWELL, Linc., a crane, ar. Pl. 111, cr. 9.
CRANWELL, on a mount, vert, a hare, current, ar.
CRANWORTH, Baron Rolfe, a dove, ar., in mouth a sprig of olive, ppr., (ducally gorged, gu.,) dexter resting on three annulets, interlaced, or. *Post nubila Phœbus.* Pl. 48, cr. 15, (annulets, pl. 119, cr. 10.)
CRASTEIN, a Cornish chough, ppr., between wings, gu. Pl. 100, cr. 13, (wings, pl. 2, cr. 3.)
CRASTER, Northumb., a raven, ppr. Pl. 123, cr. 2.
CRASTER, on a ducal coronet, or, a cock, ppr. Pl. 104, cr. 3, (coronet, *same plate,* cr. 11.)
CRATFORD, Worc., a demi-lion, rampant, gardant, erminois, ducally gorged, az. Pl. 87, cr. 15.
CRATHORNE, Linc., on a thorn-bush, a bird, ppr. Pl. 13, cr. 4.
CRATHORNE, Yorks., on a mount, vert, a bird, sa. Pl. 31, cr. 3.
CRAUFORD, or CRAUFURD, Eng., in hand a lancet. Pl. 29, cr. 6.
CRAUFUIRD, THOMAS-MACMIKEN, Esq., of Grange House, Ayrshire, a game-hawk, hooded and belled, ppr. *Durum patientiâ frango.* Pl. 38, cr. 12.
CRAUFURD-HOWISON, WILLIAM, Esq., of Craufurdland, Ayrshire, and Braehead, Mid-Lothian : 1. For *Craufurd,* a marble pillar, supporting a man's heart, ppr. *Stant innixa Deo.* Pl. 122, cr. 4. 2. For *Howison,* a dexter hand, erect, couped at wrist. *Sursum corda.* Pl. 32, cr. 14.
CRAUFURD, JOHN, Esq., of Auchinames and Crosbie, Ayrshire : 1. A stag's head, erased, gu., between attires, a cross crosslet, fitched. Pl. 24, cr. 9. 2. A phœnix, ppr., in flames. *Tutum te robore reddam*—and—*God show the right.* Pl. 44, cr. 8.
CRAUFURD, Bart., Sco., a buck's head, erased, gu., between attires a cross crosslet, fitched, of the same. Pl. 24, cr. 9.
CRAUSE, out of a ducal coronet, in hand a rose, slipped and leaved, ppr. Pl. 60, cr. 1.
CRAVEN, CHARLES-COOLEY, Esq., of Richardstown, co. Louth, on a chapeau, gu., turned up, erm., a griffin, sa., wings addorsed, beaked, and semée of fleurs-de-lis, or. *Fortitudine crevi.* Pl. 122, cr. 11.
CRAVEN, Earl of, and Baron, Viscount Uffington, (Craven,) on a chapeau, purp., turned up, erm., a griffin, statant, wings elevated and addorsed, of the last, beaked, or. *Virtus in actione consistet.* Pl. 122, cr. 11.
CRAVEN, on a pedestal, sa., a falcon, az., (wings expanded,) beaked and legged, gu. Pl. 10, cr. 7.
CRAVEN, Warw. and Berks., on a chapeau, gu., turned up, erm., a griffin, (passant,) of the last. Pl. 122, cr. 11.
CRAVEN, Berks., a griffin, statant, erm. Pl. 66, cr. 13.
CRAVEN-FULWAR, Esq., of Brock Hampton Park, Glouc. ; and Draycott Fitzpaine, Wilts. ; on a chapeau, gu., turned up, erm., a griffin, statant, of the second, beaked, or. *Virtus in actione consistit.* Pl. 122, cr. 11.
CRAW, of East Reston, a crow, sa. *Cui debeo fidus.* Pl. 23, cr. 8.

I

CRAW, of Netherbyer, a crow, sa. *God is my safety.* Pl. 23, cr. 8.
CRAW, of Heughead, on a garb, a crow, sa. *Nec careo, nec curo.* Pl. 112, cr. 10.
CRAWE, Eng., a hawk, wings expanded, ar., (charged on breast with a cinquefoil, az.) Pl. 105, cr. 4.
CRAWFIELD, a lion, rampant. Pl. 67, cr. 5.
CRAWFORD, Berks., a deer's head, ppr., between attires a cross, or. Pl. 24, cr. 9.
CRAWFORD, of Comlarg, a dexter hand, out of a cloud, grasping a hart by the horns, and bearing him to the ground, all ppr. *Tutum te robore reddam.* Pl. 46, cr. 10.
CRAWFORD, Carsburn, and Crawfurd, Hamilton, a crescent, ar., (charged with a star.) *Sine labe lucebit.* Pl. 18, cr. 14.
CRAWFORD, Drumsey, a stag's head, erased, gu., between attires a cross crosslet, fitched, of the same. *Tutum te robore reddam.* Pl. 24, cr. 9.
CRAWFORD, a griffin's head, erased, between wings. Pl. 65, cr. 1.
CRAWFORD, Jardinhill, a pair of balances, on point of a dagger, in pale. *God save the right.* Pl. 44, cr. 10.
CRAWFORD, of Crawfordburn, on point of a dagger, ar., hilted, or, a pair of balances, suspended, gold, stringed, gu. *Quod tibi, hoc alteri.* Pl. 44, cr. 10.
CRAWFORD, of Haining, a hart's head, couped, ppr. *Hactenus invictus.* Pl. 91, cr. 14.
CRAWFORD, of Easter Seaton, an increscent, (chequey, ar. and az.) *Fide et diligentiâ.* Pl. 122, cr. 15.
CRAWFORD, of Cloverhill, a garb, ppr. *God feeds the crows.* Pl. 48, cr. 10.
CRAWFORD, of Crawfordsland, on the top of a marble pillar, a man's heart, ppr. *Stant innixa Deo.* Pl. 122, cr. 4.
CRAWFORD, on point of dagger, erect, a pair of balances, all ppr. *God shaw the right.* Pl. 44, cr. 10.
CRAWFORD, of Ardmillan and Crawfuird, Sco., a falcon, hooded and belled, ppr. *Durum patientiâ frango.* Pl. 38, cr. 12.
CRAWFORD, of Kilbirney and Crawfuird, Sco., an ermine, passant, ppr. *Sine laba nota.* Pl. 9, cr. 5.
CRAWFORD, Sco., a palm-branch, ppr. *Calcar honeste.* Pl. 26, cr. 3.
CRAWFORD, Sco., a castle, ppr. Pl. 123, cr. 14.
CRAWFORD, Sco., a phœnix in flames, ppr. *God shaw the right.* Pl. 44, cr. 8.
CRAWFORD, or CRAWFORDE, Eng., in hand a lancet, ppr. Pl. 29, cr. 6.
CRAWFORD, Sco., a decrescent. *Sine labe lucebit.* Pl. 16, cr. 15.
CRAWFURD, ROBERT, Esq., of Saint Hill, Suss., a hawk, hooded and belled, ppr. *Durum patientiâ frango.* Pl. 38, cr. 12.
CRAWFURD, Eng., a goat's head, gu. Pl. 105, cr. 14.
CRAWFURD, Sco., a cinquefoil, slipped, vert. *Feliciter floret.* Pl. 91, cr. 12.
CRAWFURD-POLLOCK, Bart., Jordan Hill, Renfrew, a castle, triple-towered, ppr. *Expugnare.* Pl. 123, cr. 14.
CRAWFURD-STIRLING, WILLIAM-STUART, Esq., of Milton, Lanark, a crescent, ar. Pl. 18, cr. 14.

CRAWHALL, a crow, supporting in dexter a battle-axe. *Præsto et persto.* Pl. 23, cr. 8, (axe, pl. 14, cr. 8.)
CRAWLEY, Dors., a lion's head, erased, (semée-de-hurts,) gorged with a ducal coronet. Pl. 1, cr. 5.
CRAWLEY, Suss., a stork, ppr., in dexter a fleur-de-lis, az. Pl. 61, cr. 10, (fleur-de-lis, pl. 141.)
CRAWLEY, Beds., a crane, ppr., in dexter a fleur-de-lis, or. Pl. 26, cr. 11, (fleur-de-lis, pl. 141.)
CRAWLEY, Iri., a triangular harrow. Pl. 7, cr. 2.
CRAWSHAW, Eng., a greyhound, current, ar., (collared, gu.) Pl. 28, cr. 7.
CRAWSHAY, Eng., a greyhound, current, sa. Pl. 28, cr. 7.
CRAWSHAY, Norf., a dog, sa., standing over a heap of olives, ppr. Pl. 117, cr. 8.
CRAY, Kent, a chevalier on horseback, holding a sword, in pale, ppr. Pl. 118, cr. 14.
CRAYCRAFT, or CRECROFT, a stork, (in dexter a battle-axe, ppr.) Pl. 61, cr. 10.
CREAGH, Iri., an arm, in hand a dagger, point downward. Pl. 18, cr. 3.
CREAGH, a horse's head, bridled, (decked with a slip of laurel, all ppr.) Pl. 92, cr. 1.
CREAGH, Iri., a nag's head, erased, bridled, ppr. Pl. 92, cr. 1.
CREAKE, Eng., a stag, passant, gu. Pl. 68, cr. 2.
CREAN, Iri., a hand plucking a thistle, ppr. Pl. 54, cr. 11.
CREASY, Eng., a greyhound's head, sa., collared, ar. Pl. 43, cr. 11.
CRECK, Eng., a swan, ar. Pl. 122, cr. 13.
CREE, Sco., an arm, in armour, embowed, wielding a scimitar, ppr. Pl. 81, cr. 11.
CREECK, Sco., in hand a crown of laurel, ppr. *Volenti nil difficile.* Pl. 86, cr. 1.
CREED, on an oak-branch, vert, a dove, ar., (in mouth a sprig, ppr.,) charged on breast with a cross pattée, gu. Pl. 15, cr. 11, (cross, pl. 141.)
CREED, a dove and olive-branch, ppr. Pl. 48, cr. 15.
CREED, a demi-wolf, (regardant, erminois, in dexter an etoile, gu.) Pl. 65, cr. 4.
CREED, Eng., a dragon's head, gu. Pl. 87, cr. 1.
CREETON, a dragon, passant, (vomiting fire, ppr.) Pl. 90, cr. 10.
CREEVEY, or CREVY, a griffin, sejant, per pale, ar. and sa., winged, or. Pl. 100, cr. 11.
CREIGHTON, Eng., a bomb-shell, fired, ppr. Pl. 70, cr. 12.
CREIGHTON, Earl of Erne. *See* ERNE.
CREKE, Cambs., in a crescent, ar., a bundle of five arrows, or, headed and barbed, ar., tied with a ribbon, gu. Pl. 82, cr. 15, (arrows, pl. 54, cr. 15.)
CREKETOT, Eng., a stag's head, erased, or. Pl. 66, cr. 9.
CREMER, Lond. and Norf., a ram's head, erased, paly of six, ar. and gu., attired, of the first. Pl. 1, cr. 12.
CREMORE, Baron, (Dawson,) Iri., an etoile of six points, or. Pl. 63, cr. 9.
CRENAGE, or CRENIDGE, out of a mural coronet, a demi-monkey, ppr. Pl. 24, cr. 12.
CRENWAY, Eng., on a chapeau, gu., a boar, passant, or. Pl. 22, cr. 8.

CREPPING, or CREPING, Linc., a lion, passant, ppr., in dexter a crescent, ar. *Pl.* 77, *cr.* 3.

CRESPIGNY, on a chapeau, gu., turned up, erm., in gauntlet, ppr., a cutlass, ar., hilt and pommel, or.

CRESPINE, CRESPIN, or CRISPIN, a hydra, with seven heads, vert. *Pl.* 38, *cr.* 5.

CRESS, or CRESSE, Notts., a griffin's head, couped, sa. *Pl.* 38, *cr.* 3.

CRESSALL, Eng., two lions' paws, erased, supporting a bezant, or. *Pl.* 42, *cr.* 3.

CRESSENOR, or CRESSNER, a dexter arm, couped and embowed, in hand three wheat-stalks, ppr. *Pl.* 89, *cr.* 4.

CRESSET, Salop, a demi-lion, rampant, gardant, ar., ducally crowned, or, holding a beacon, of the first, fired, ppr.

CRESSWELL, Iri., a savage's head, ppr., wreathed, vert. *Pl.* 36, *cr.* 3.

CRESSWELL, Suff., a squirrel, sejant, cracking a nut, ppr. *Pl.* 16, *cr.* 9.

CRESSWELL, Eng., a lion, passant, gardant, ar., in dexter a mill-rind. *Pl.* 120, *cr.* 5, (mill-rind, *pl.* 141.)

CRESSWELL, a dexter arm, embowed, (vested,) slashed, in hand, ppr., a mace. *Pl.* 28, *cr.* 2.

CRESSWELL, Lond. and Northumb., on a mount, vert, a torteau, charged with a squirrel, sejant, ar.

CRESSWELL, Lond. and Northumb., a goat's head, erased, ar., attired, or. *Pl.* 29, *cr.* 13.

CRESSY, Linc., out of a ducal coronet, or, a demi-eagle, displayed, ppr. *Pl.* 9, *cr.* 6.

CRESTON, a lion, passant, resting dexter on a torteau. *Pl.* 48, *cr.* 8, (torteau, *pl.* 141.)

CRESWELL, WILLIAM-HENRY, Esq. of Pinkney Park, Wilts., and Sidbury, Salop, a Saracen's head, ppr., wreathed, vert and ar. *Aut nunquam tentes, aut perfice.* *Pl.* 36, *cr.* 3.

CRESWELL, Northamp., on branch of tree, barwise, vert, a squirrel, sejant, gu., cracking a nut, or, between two hazel-twigs, fructed, ppr. *Pl.* 5, *cr.* 6.

CRESWELL, Northamp., a Saracen's head, ppr. *Pl.* 19, *cr.* 1.

CRESWELL, Hants., a sinister arm, in chain armour, in hand, ppr., a cross botonnée, fitched, or. *Pl.* 51, *cr.* 1.

CRESWICK, out of a ducal coronet, or, an arm, in armour, embowed, in hand a dagger, ppr. *Pl.* 120, *cr.* 11, (coronet, *same plate, cr.* 4.)

CRETING, Kent, and CRETINGE, Suff., a bear, (passant, transpierced by an arrow, in bend sinister.) *Pl.* 82, *cr.* 14.

CREVEGUER, or CREVERGUERE, Eng., a mountain in flames, ppr. *Pl.* 92, *cr.* 9.

CREW, Chesh., out of a ducal coronet, or, a lion's gamb., ar. *Pl.* 67, *cr.* 7.

CREW, Durh., a ferret, collared and lined. *Pl.* 12, *cr.* 2.

CREW, (on a mount, vert,) a doe, lodged, ppr. *Pl.* 1, *cr.* 14, (without bee-hive.)

CREWE, Baron, (Crewe,) out of a ducal coronet, or, a lion's gamb, erect, ar. *Sequor nec inferior.* *Pl.* 67, *cr.* 7.

CREWE, Iri., in dexter hand an open book, ppr. *Pl.* 82, *cr.* 5, (without clouds.)

CREWE, a boar, passant, sa. *Pl.* 48, *cr.* 14.

CREWKER, an arm, in armour, embowed, brandishing a scimitar. *Pl.* 81, *cr.* 11.

CREWS, CREWSE, or CRUSE, Devons., on a mount, vert, a stork, ppr., in dexter an escallop, ar. *Pl.* 122, *cr.* 7.

CREYKE, RALPH, Esq., of Marton and Rawcliffe, Yorks., on a garb, or, a raven, ppr. *Pl.* 112, *cr.* 10.

CREYKE, Yorks., on a garb, in fess, or, an eagle, wings addorsed, ar. *Pl.* 61, *cr.* 1, (garb, *pl.* 12, *cr.* 15.)

CREYKE, Yorks., a crow, wings addorsed, sa. *Pl.* 6, *cr.* 11, (without escutcheon.)

CRIALL, out of a mural coronet, a demi-lion, rampant, gardant, gu., between paws a key, or. *Pl.* 17, *cr.* 7, (key, *pl.* 54, *cr.* 12.)

CRICHE, Lond. and Oxon., a demi-lion, erm., crowned, or, holding a cross formée, fitched, gold. *Pl.* 61, *cr.* 4, (cross, *pl.* 27, *cr.* 14.)

CRICHTON, Eng., a galley, oars in saltier, sa. *Pl.* 77, *cr.* 11.

CRICHTON, Sco., a dragon's head, vert, vomiting fire, ppr. *God send grace.* *Pl.* 37, *cr.* 9.

CRICHTON, a dragon's head, erased, ppr. *Perseverantia.* *Pl.* 107, *cr.* 10.

CRICHTON, Sco., a pillar, ar. *Stand sure.* *Pl.* 33, *cr.* 1.

CRICHTON-STUART, Marquess of Bute. *See* BUTE.

CRICKET, or CRICKITT, Eng., a lion, passant, gardant, az. *Pl.* 120, *cr.* 5.

CRICKET, or CRICKITT, Ess., a drake's head, erased, ppr. *Pl.* 70, *cr.* 6.

CRICKMAN, Eng., a stag, lodged, ppr. *Pl.* 67, *cr.* 2.

CRIDLAND, Somers., issuing from clouds, two dexter hands, conjoined, ppr. *Pl.* 53, *cr.* 11.

CRIGAN, Iri., a harp, ppr., ensigned with a human heart, gu. *Pl.* 104, *cr.* 15, (heart, *pl.* 55, *cr.* 15.)

CRIKTOFT, a demi-unicorn, az. *Pl.* 26, *cr.* 14.

CRIMES, Dors., a martlet, sa. *Pl.* 111, *cr.* 5.

CRIOLL, Eng., environed with clouds, ppr., a mullet, or. *Pl.* 16, *cr.* 13, (mullet, *pl.* 141.)

CRIPPS, and CRIPS, Eng., an arm, in armour, embowed, in hand a scimitar, ppr. *Pl.* 81, *cr.* 11.

CRISIE, Sco., a bee-hive, sa., with bees, volant, or. *Industria.* *Pl.* 81, *cr.* 14.

CRISP, Eng., out of a ducal coronet, or, the attires and scalp of a stag, all ppr. *Pl.* 86, *cr.* 10.

CRISP, or CRISPE, Kent, a camel-leopard, ar., pellettée, attired, collared, and lined, or.

CRISP, or CRISPE, Middx., a camel-leopard, or, attired and collared, or, lined, ar.

CRISPIE, a lion, passant, gu., dexter resting on a bezant, or. *Pl.* 48, *cr.* 8, (bezant, *pl.* 141.)

CRISPIN, a chevalier on horseback, at full speed, tilting with a lance, all ppr. *Pl.* 43, *cr.* 2.

CRITCHLEY, or CRITCHLOW, Eng., a harp, vert. *Pl.* 104, *cr.* 15.

CROACHROD, a wolf, regardant, pierced through body by a spear, end in mouth. *Pl.* 77, *cr.* 14.

CROAD, or CROADE, Eng., on a cloud a celestial sphere, ppr. *Pl.* 110, *cr.* 9.

CROASDAILE, Eng., a demi-man, in armour, in hand a sword, ppr. *Pl.* 23, *cr.* 4.

CROBBER, Eng., on a winged globe, an eagle, wings expanded, ppr. *Pl.* 34, *cr.* 2, (globe, *pl.* 50, *cr.* 7.)

CROCHROD, Ess. and Suff., a demi-boar, rampant, regardant, gu., armed, or, transpierced by a broken spear, ar., grasped in mouth. *Pl.* 115, *cr.* 2.

CROCKAT, or CROCKETT, on a rock, a swan, ppr. *Pl.* 122, *cr.* 13.
CROCKAT, or CROCKETT, a solan goose, ppr. *Pl.* 90, *cr.* 15.
CROCKAT, or CROCKETT, Sco., a dog, sleeping, sa., spotted, ar. *Tak tent. Pl.* 29, *cr.* 3.
CROCKER, Devons., a cup, or. *Pl.* 42, *cr.* 1.
CROCKFORD, Eng., in dexter hand a roll of parchment. *Pl.* 27, *cr.* 4.
CROFT, Sir THOMAS ELMSLEY, Bart., Heref., a griffin, sejant, ppr. *Esse quam videri. Pl.* 100, *cr.* 11.
CROFT, Bart., Yorks. and Kent.: 1. A lion, passant, gardant, or, (supporting a shield charged with the arms of St George.) *Pl.* 120, *cr.* 5. *Esse quam videri.* 2. A lion, passant, gardant, per pale, indented, gu. and erminois, fore-dexter resting on an escutcheon, ar., charged with a representation of the star of the Order of the Tower and Sword, ppr. *Valor e lealdade. Pl.* 120, *cr.* 5, (escutcheon, *pl.* 42, *cr.* 8.)
CROFT, Yorks., a lion, passant, gardant, sa., supporting with dexter an escutcheon, pean, charged with a lion, passant, gardant, or. *Pl.* 120, *cr.* 5, (escutcheon, *pl.* 42, *cr.* 8.)
CROFT, a wyvern, vert. *Pl.* 63, *cr.* 13.
CROFT, a dragon's head, couped, vert. *Pl.* 87, *cr.* 12.
CROFT, a talbot, sejant. *Pl.* 107, *cr.* 7.
CROFTON, EDWARD, Baron, and Bart., (Crofton,) Iri., (seven) stalks of wheat, or. *Dat Deus incrementum. Pl.* 102, *cr.* 1.
CROFTON, Bart., of Leitrim, a wheat-stalk, ppr. *Pl.* 35, *cr.* 6.
CROFTON, an eagle's head, erased, ducally gorged, in beak, a pheon, all ppr. *Pl.* 39, *cr.* 4.
CROFTON, Iri., an ear of wheat, ppr. *Pl.* 85, *cr.* 6.
CROFTON, Iri., a savage's head, ppr. *Pl.* 19, *cr.* 1.
CROFTON, out of a mount, vert, (six) ears of wheat, or, bladed, ppr. *Pl.* 4, *cr.* 5.
CROFTS, the Rev. WILLIAM, Esq., of Velvetstown, co. Cork, a bull's head, cabossed, sa. *Virtute et fidelitate. Pl.* 111, *cr.* 6.
CROFTS, FREEMAN, Esq., of Cloheen House, co. Cork, same crest and motto.
CROFTS, a dragon's head, vert, (charged with three ermine spots.) *Pl.* 87, *cr.* 12.
CROFTS, Heref. and Salop, a wyvern, wings addorsed, az. *Pl.* 63, *cr.* 13.
CROFTS, Salop and Heref., a lion, passant, gardant, or. *Pl.* 120, *cr.* 5.
CROFTS, Norf. and Suff., a bull's head, couped, sa., armed, or. *Pl.* 120, *cr.* 7.
CROFTS, Norf. and Suff., a bull's head, cabossed, ar., armed, or. *Pl.* 111, *cr.* 6.
CROFTS, on a chapeau, az., turned up, erm., an eagle's neck, with two heads, erased, sa., gorged with an Eastern crown, or.
CROFTS, a talbot, sejant, erm. *Pl.* 107, *cr.* 7.
CROG, or CROGG, a crescent, gu. (charged with an etoile, ar.) *Pl.* 111, *cr.* 15.
CROG, or CROGG, Eng., a cross moline, or, between two ears of wheat, gold. *Pl.* 23, *cr.* 14.
CROKE, Knt., D.C.L., Oxon., two swans' necks, addorsed and interlaced, issuing from a crescent, all ar. *Pl.* 30, *cr.* 10, (crescent, *pl.* 118, *cr.* 12.)

CROKE, Bucks., two swans' necks, addorsed, conjoined in base, and erased, ar., in each beak an annulet, issuing from between the horns of a crescent, az.
CROKE, or CROOK, Eng., a celestial and terrestrial sphere, ppr. *Pl.* 85, *cr.* 9.
CROKER, Iri., a demi-wyvern, wings expanded, sa. *Pl.* 116, *cr.* 15.
CROKER, Devons., in a vase, a bouquet, ppr. *Pl.* 102, *cr.* 12.
CROKER, Lond. and Glouc., an arm, in armour, embowed, garnished, or, in hand an anchor, ppr. *Pl.* 122, *cr.* 8, (without coronet.)
CROKER, Oxon., a raven, ppr., (ducally gorged, or,) in mouth an ear of wheat, gold. *Pl.* 112, *cr.* 10, (without garb.)
CROKER, the Right Hon. JOHN WILSON, of West Molesey, Sur., a drinking-cup, or, with three fleurs-de-lis above it, ppr., on centre a rose, gu. *Deus alit eos*—and—*J'ay ma foi tenu à ma puissance. Pl.* 102, *cr.* 12, (fleur-de-lis, *pl.* 141.)
CROKEY, Yorks., a lion's head, sa., erased, gu. *Pl.* 81, *cr.* 4.
CROLE, a unicorn's head, erased, ar., armed and crined, or, between two elephants' trunks, sa. *Pl.* 67, *cr.* 1, (trunks, *pl.* 24, *cr.* 8.)
CROLLY, Eng., a wolf, passant, sa. *Pl.* 46, *cr.* 6.
CROMBIE, Eng., a demi-lion, rampant, gardant, or, in dexter fleur-de-lis, gu. *Pl.* 35, *cr.* 4, (fleur-de-lis, *pl.* 141.)
CROMBIE, an eagle, displayed, gu. *Pl.* 48, *cr.* 11.
CROMBIE, of Phesdo, Sco., an eagle, displayed, gu. *Fear God. Pl.* 48, *cr.* 8.
CROME, Berks. and Middx., out of a mural coronet, or, a demi-lion, sa., in dexter a fleur-de-lis, ar. *Pl.* 17, *cr.* 7, (fleur-de-lis, *pl.* 141.)
CROMER, on a ram's head, couped, gu., two pales, ar. *Pl.* 34, *cr.* 12.
CROMER, Norf., a crow, sa. *Pl.* 23, *cr.* 8.
CROMER, Eng., a demi-lion, ar., armed and langued, gu. *Pl.* 67, *cr.* 10.
CROMER, Eng., a chevalier, in full armour, standing beside a war-horse, holding bridle, all ppr. *Pl.* 37, *cr.* 11.
CROMIE, Bart., Iri.: 1. A centaur, with bow and arrow, ppr., the equestrian part, grey. *Pl.* 70, *cr.* 13. 2. A dexter hand, apaumée, ppr. *Labor omnia vincit. Pl.* 32, *cr.* 14.
CROMIE, Iri., in dexter hand, erect, a cross crosslet, fitched. *Pl.* 99, *cr.* 1.
CROMLYN, a fawn's head, cabossed, or.
CROMMELIN—DE LA CHEROIS, NICHOLAS, Esq., Carrowdore Castle, co. Down: 1. For *Crommelin*, out of a ducal coronet, or, a swan, rising, ppr. *Pl.* 100, *cr.* 7. 2. For *De la Cherois*, an anchor, az. *Fac et spera. Pl.* 42, *cr.* 12.
CROMPE, Suss., three quatrefoils, erect, or, stalked and leaved, ppr. *Pl.* 72, *cr.* 12.
CROMPE, a cat, rampant, sa. *Pl.* 126 A, *cr.* 10.
CROMPTON, Staff. and Lanc., a talbot, sejant, or, (in dexter a coil of rope, gold.) *Pl.* 19, *cr.* 2.
CROMPTON, Staffs., out of a mural coronet, or, a sea-horse's head, ar. *Pl.* 58, *cr.* 15, (coronet, *pl.* 141.)
CROMPTON, Lond., out of a mural coronet, vert, a sea-horse's head, or. *Pl.* 58, *cr.* 15, (coronet, *pl.* 141.)

CROMPTON, Derb., a demi-horse, sa., vulned in chest by an arrow, ppr.
CROMPTON, Yorks., a demi-horse, sa., maned or, vulned in chest by an arrow, ar.
CROMUEL, Hants., an eagle, displayed, in dexter a sword. *Pl.* 107, *cr.* 4.
CROMWELL, Surr., on a chapeau, gu., turned up, erm., a pelican, or, guttée, az., vulned, gu. *Pl.* 21, *cr.* 5.
CROMWELL, Hants., a demi-lion, rampant, ar., guttée, sa., (holding a spear, or, headed, az.) *Pl.* 41, *cr.* 13.
CROMWELL, ELIZABETH-OLIVERIA, of Chesnut Park, Herts., a demi-lion, rampant, ar., in dexter, (a gem-ring, or.) *Pax quæritur bello.* *Pl.* 113, *cr.* 2.
CROMWELL, Iri., in dexter hand an (olive)-branch, ppr. *Pl.* 43, *cr.* 6.
CROMWELL, a demi-lion, rampant, or, (holding a gem-ring, or, stone, gu.) *Pl.* 113, *cr.* 2.
CROMWELL, in lion's gamb, (a gem-ring, or, stone, gu.) *Pl.* 97, *cr.* 10.
CRON, or CRONE, seven arrows, six in saltier, and one in pale, or. *Pl.* 110, *cr.* 11.
CRON, or CRONE, Eng., a demi-fish, az. *Pl.* 122, *cr.* 6.
CROOK, Eng., a (sinister hand issuing from a cloud in the dexter,) pointing towards a serpent, head erected, ppr. *Pl.* 19, *cr.* 11.
CROOK, an eagle, displayed, or. *Pl.* 48, *cr.* 11.
CROOK, Sco., an arm, in armour, embowed, ppr., in hand a fleur-de-lis, or. *Pl.* 24, *cr.* 14.
CROOK, a raven, ppr. *Pl.* 123, *cr.* 2.
CROOKE, Hants., a fleur-de-lis, or, environed by a snake, vert, its head issuing through it. *Pl.* 15, *cr.* 13.
CROOKS, Sco., a demi-leopard, ppr. *Pl.* 12, *cr.* 14.
CROOKS, an elephant, quarterly, or and gu. *Pl.* 56, *cr.* 14.
CROOKSHANK, Iri., a wyvern, wings addorsed, vomiting fire at both ends, ppr. *Pl.* 109, *cr.* 11.
CROOKSHANK, Eng., in dexter hand an ear of wheat, ppr. *Pl.* 71, *cr.* 15.
CROOKSHANK, a demi-negro, in dexter a cocoanut, ppr.
CROONE, a lion's gamb, erect and erased, holding a snake, all ppr. *Pl.* 112, *cr.* 13.
CROPLEY, Lond. and Middx., a lynx, passant, gardant, ppr. *Pl.* 122, *cr.* 14.
CROPLEY, Cambs. and Hunts., a mountain-cat, passant, erm. *Pl.* 119, *cr.* 7.
CROPPER, Eng., a triangular harrow, ppr. *Pl.* 7, *cr.* 2.
CROSBEE, or CROSBIE, Sco., stump of oak-tree, shooting new branches. *Resurgam.* *Pl.* 92, *cr.* 8.
CROSBIE, Bart., Iri., and CROSBIE, Sco., three swords, handles upwards, one in pale, two in saltier, environed by a snake, all ppr.
CROSBIE, or CROSBEY, Sco., a quill and sword, in saltier, ppr. *Pl.* 49, *cr.* 12.
CROSBIE, or CROSBY, Sco., a holy lamb, ppr., standard, gu. *Nil desperandum.* *Pl.* 48, *cr.* 13.
CROSBY, Iri., a lion, passant, gardant, ar. *Pl.* 120, *cr.* 5.
CROSBY, between horns of a crescent, per pale, ar. and gu., a cross flory, or. *Te duce libertas!* *Pl.* 37, *cr.* 10, (cross, *pl.* 141.)

CROSBY, Eng., a dexter and sinister arm, couped, in saltier, ppr., vested, dexter, gu., sinister, az., each brandishing a scimitar, of the first. *Pl.* 52, *cr.* 1.
CROSELL, Eng., a stag's head, at gaze, gu., armed, ar. *Pl.* 111, *cr.* 13.
CROSIER, an arm, erect, (vested, gu., cuffed, ar.,) in hand a crosier, or. *Pl.* 17, *cr.* 12.
CROSLEY, Berks., a dragon's head, sa., collared, or, charged with a cinquefoil, gu. *Pl.* 107, *cr.* 10.
CROSS, Chesh., on a mount, vert, a stork, erm., beaked and membered, gu., resting dexter on a cross crosslet, of the last, (in mouth a plummet, sa.) *Pl.* 122, *cr.* 7, (cross, *pl.* 141.)
CROSS, Iri., two hands, couped, and conjoined, in fess, holding a (scimitar,) in pale, ar. *Pl.* 75, *cr.* 8.
CROSS, Norf., a griffin, passant, ar. *Pl.* 61, *cr.* 14, (without gorging.)
CROSS, a dragon's head, couped, vert. *Pl.* 87, *cr.* 12.
CROSS, Eng., a lion, passant, gardant, supporting an anchor, ppr. *Pl.* 120, *cr.* 5, (anchor, *pl.* 19, *cr.* 6.)
CROSS, Sco., a griffin, segreant, per fess, gu. and sa., winged, ar., tips, or. *Pl.* 67, *cr.* 13.
CROSS, a dragon's head, erased. *Pl.* 107, *cr.* 10.
CROSSDELL, out of a mural coronet, a cross patonée, charged with a leopard's face, behind cross two swords, in saltier, points upward.
CROSSE, Yorks., a stork, ppr., supporting with dexter a crescent, ar. *Pl.* 61, *cr.* 10, (crescent, *pl.* 141.)
CROSSE, Sco., a cross crosslet, az. *Certum pete finem.* *Pl.* 66, *cr.* 8.
CROSSE, Sco., a cross crosslet, fitched, gu. *Certum pete finem.* *Pl.* 16, *cr.* 10.
CROSSE, Lanc., a stork, ppr., in mouth a cross pomée, ar. *Pl.* 33, *cr.* 9, (cross, *pl.* 141.)
CROSSE, Somers., from the top of a tower, ar., flames issuing, ppr. *Pl.* 118, *cr.* 15.
CROSSE, Lond., on a chapeau, gu., turned up, erm., a stork, az., resting dexter on a cross-moline, ar. *Pl.* 106, *cr.* 6, (cross, *pl.* 141.)
CROSSE, Eng., a hand plucking a thistle, ppr. *Pl.* 54, *cr.* 11.
CROSSFIELD, a lion, rampant. *Pl.* 67, *cr.* 5.
CROSSLEY, Eng., on a rock, a swan, ppr. *Pl.* 122, *cr.* 13.
CROSSMAN, Somers., a demi-lion, ermines, holding an escallop, sa. *Pl.* 126, *cr.* 12, (escallop, *pl.* 141.)
CROSSWELL, an arm, erect, (vested,) in hand a club, ppr. *Pl.* 28, *cr.* 6.
CROST, Eng., out of a ducal coronet, or, a swan's head, between wings, ppr. *Pl.* 83, *cr.* 1.
CROSTE, Leic., a griffin's head, ar. *Pl.* 38, *cr.* 3.
CROSTHWAITE, Iri., a fox, sejant, or. *Pl.* 87, *cr.* 4.
CROTTY, Eng., in hand, a scorpion, ppr. *Pl.* 110, *cr.* 14.
CROTTY, Iri., a hind, trippant, gu. *Pl.* 20, *cr.* 14.
CROUCH, or CROWCH, Herts. and Lond., on a mount, vert, a lamb, couchant, ppr.
CROUCH, Eng., a sword, in pale, between two palm-branches, in orle, ppr. *Pl.* 71, *cr.* 3, (palm, *pl.* 87, *cr.* 8.)

CROUCHFIELD, on a mount, a palm-tree, ppr. *Pl.* 52, *cr.* 6.
CROUCHLEY, Eng., a leopard's face, ppr. *Pl.* 56, *cr.* 14.
CROUDACE, Durh., an angel, hands clasped on breast, vested, ppr. *Pl.* 25, *cr.* 7.
CROUGHTON, Eng., a leopard's head, erased, affrontée, ducally gorged. *Pl.* 116, *cr.* 8.
CROUGHTON, a dragon's head, (couped,) in mouth a glove. *Pl.* 106, *cr.* 13.
CROW, Iri., a goat, (passant,) ar., armed and hoofed, sa. *Pl.* 66, *cr.* 1.
CROW, Wel., a cock, ar., combed, wattled, and membered, or. *Pl.* 67, *cr.* 14.
CROW, Norf., five arrows, sa., feathered, ar., four in saltier, one in pale, banded, gu. *Pl.* 54, *cr.* 15.
CROW, or CROWE, a camel's head, or, (vulned, gu.) *Pl.* 109, *cr.* 9.
CROWCHER, a lion, couchant, ppr., charged with a cross pattée, or. *Pl.* 77, *cr.* 10, (cross, *pl.* 141.)
CROWDER, Eng., an escallop, ar., charged with a mullet, gu. *Pl.* 109, *cr.* 14.
CROWDER, Surr., (on broken shaft of a tilting-spear, gu.,) an heraldic tiger, passant, ar. *Pl.* 119, *cr.* 9.
CROWE, Eng., out of a mural coronet, an arm, vested, in hand a mullet. *Pl.* 34, *cr.* 1.
CROWGAY, or CROWGIE, an arm, from elbow, in hand a key, ppr. *Pl.* 41, *cr.* 11.
CROWGEY, Eng., a greyhound, current, ar. *Pl.* 28, *cr.* 7, (without charge.)
CROWHALL, on a garb, a crow, ppr. *Pl.* 112, *cr.* 10.
CROWHALL, Eng., on a rock, a crow, ppr. *Nec cupias, nec metuas. Pl.* 38, *cr.* 10.
CROWN, or CROWNE, a lion's head, erased, sa., ducally crowned, ar. *Pl.* 90, *cr.* 4, (without chargings.)
CROWNALL, Eng., a bull's horns and scalp, ppr. *Pl.* 9, *cr.* 15.
CROWNALL, Eng., in dexter hand a dagger, point downward, all ppr. *Pl.* 18, *cr.* 3.
CROWTHER, Lond. and Salop, (on a tilting-spear, gu.,) a tiger, passant, or. *Pl.* 86, *cr.* 2.
CROWTON, Eng., a stag's head, or. *Pl.* 91, *cr.* 14.
CROZIER, Eng., a stag's head, cabossed, ppr. *Pl.* 36, *cr.* 1.
CRUCK, Eng., a demi-greyhound, sa. *Pl.* 48, *cr.* 3.
CRUCKS, Sco., a demi-leopard, ppr. *Pl.* 12, *cr.* 14.
CRUCKS, Sco., a fetterlock, az. *Pl.* 122, *cr.* 12.
CRUDEN, Eng., a griffin's head, couped. *Pl.* 38, *cr.* 3.
CRUDINGTON, a boar, passant. *Pl.* 48, *cr.* 14.
CRUELL, or CRULL, Eng., a centaur, shooting an arrow, ppr. *Pl.* 70, *cr.* 13.
CRUGG, a falcon's head, couped, ar., (collared, gu.,) wings addorsed, bendy of four, or and sa. *Pl.* 103, *cr.* 10.
CRUICE, or CRUISE, Eng., a demi-lion, rampant, or. *Pl.* 67, *cr.* 10.
CRUICE, or CRUISE, Iri., a greyhound's head, erased, or. *Pl.* 89, *cr.* 2.
CRUICKSHANK, Lond., a hawk's head, erased, ppr. *Audito et gradito. Pl.* 34, *cr.* 11.
CRUIKSHANK, an arm, in armour, in hand a sword, ppr. *Pl.* 2, *cr.* 8.

CRUIKSHANK, of Stracathro, Sco., a dexter hand, in armour, grasping a dagger, in pale, ppr. *Cavendo tutus. Pl.* 125, *cr.* 5.
CRUIKSHANKS, a boar's head, erased, ppr. *Vis fortibus arma. Pl.* 16, *cr.* 11.
CRUIKSHANKS, Sco., a boar's head, couped, armed, and langued, az. *Pl.* 48, *cr.* 2.
CRUIKSHANKS, Sco., an arm, in armour, in hand a dagger, in pale, on point a boar's head, all ppr. *Pl.* 125, *cr.* 5, (head, *pl.* 10, *cr.* 2.)
CRUKES, on a garb, in fess, an eagle, wings addorsed, vulning. *Pl.* 61, *cr.* 1, (garb, *pl.* 122, *cr.* 3.)
CRULL, or CRULLE, an arm, in armour, in fess, couped at elbow, holding, in pale, a broken lance, ppr., head falling to sinister.
CRUMB, Sco., an eagle, displayed, ppr. *Fear God. Pl.* 48, *cr.* 11.
CRUMBIE, Sco., an eagle, with two heads, displayed, ppr. *Pl.* 87, *cr.* 11, (without flames.)
CRUMP, or CRUMPE, Eng., a cat, salient, gardant, sa. *Pl.* 70, *cr.* 15.
CRUMPTON, Eng., a fire-beacon, ppr. *Pl.* 88, *cr.* 6.
CRUTCHFIELD, on a mount, vert, a palm-tree, ppr. *Pl.* 52, *cr.* 6.
CRUTCHLEY, Eng., on a chapeau, a lion, passant, gardant, ducally crowned. *Pl.* 120, *cr.* 15, (without chapeau.)
CRUTCHLEY, or CRUCHLEY, a talbot, sejant, ar. *Pl.* 107, *cr.* 7.
CRUTTENDON, a goat's head, erased, ppr. *Pl.* 29, *cr.* 13.
CRUTTENDON, an elk's head, ppr. *Pl.* 70, *cr.* 4.
CRUTWELL, Eng., in hand a key, ppr. *Pl.* 41, *cr.* 11.
CRUX, Kent, a demi eagle, wings expanded, ar., in mouth a cross formée, fitched, sa. *Pl.* 52, *cr.* 8, (cross, *pl.* 27, *cr.* 14.)
CRYMES, Surr. and Devons., a martlet, vert. *Pl.* 111, *cr.* 5.
CRYMES, an arm, embowed, in fess, vested, or, in hand a chaplet of laurel, ppr. *Pl.* 58, *cr.* 4, (chaplet, *pl.* 118, *cr.* 4.)
CRYNES, Eng., a lion's head, erased. *Pl.* 81, *cr.* 4.
CUBIT, or CUBITT, Eng., out of clouds, a dexter and sinister hand, combating with scimitars, ppr. *Pl.* 122, *cr.* 9.
CUBIT, or CUBITT, Norf., an arm, in armour, embowed, throwing an arrow. *Pl.* 96, *cr.* 6.
CUCKBORNE, Eng., on a chapeau, gu., turned up, erm., a fire, ppr. *Pl.* 71, *cr.* 11.
CUDDEN, Eng., a wolf, sejant, az. *Pl.* 110, *cr.* 4.
CUDMORE, and CUDNOR, Ess. and Suff., a griffin, passant, or. *Pl.* 61, *cr.* 14, (without gorging.)
CUDMORE, and CUDNOR, Ess. and Suff., a griffin's head, erased, sa. *Pl.* 38, *cr.* 3.
CUDWORTH, Lanc., on a mount, vert, an arm, erect, vested, erminois, in hand a battle-axe, head, sa., handle, or.
CUE, a demi-lion, rampant, or, between paws, a garb, az. *Pl.* 84, *cr.* 7.
CUERDEN, and CURETON, a stag's head, quarterly, per fess, indented, or and az., attired, counterchanged. *Pl.* 91, *cr.* 14.
CUFF, Eng., a demi-griffin, ppr. *Pl.* 18, *cr.* 6.
CUFFE, Earl of Desart. *See* DESART.

CUFFE, an arm, erect, (vested, az., cuffed, erm.,) in hand a battle-axe, ppr. *Pl.* 73, *cr.* 7.
CUFFE-WHEELER, Sir JONAH DENNY, Bart., Iri., an arm, in armour, embowed, az., in hand a baton, gu. *Animus tamen idem. Pl.* 33, *cr.* 4, (arm, *pl.* 97, *cr.* 1.)
CUILER, Eng., a broken spear, in pale, top falling to sinister, ppr. *Pl.* 3, *cr.* 6.
CUILLEN, Iri., a mermaid, with comb and mirror, ppr. *Pl.* 48, *cr.* 5.
CULCHECH, or CULEHECH, an ox-yoke, in bend, sa. *Pl.* 35, *cr.* 11.
CULCHECH, and CULCHETH, out of clouds, two hands, pulling an anchor from the sea, all ppr. *Pl.* 94, *cr.* 4.
CULEY, an arm, embowed, (vested,) in hand a scimitar, ppr., hilted, or. *Pl.* 92, *cr.* 5.
CULLAMORE, Lond., a demi-Turk, in profile, vested, gu., billettée, or, turban, ar., cap, of the first, on top a crescent, of the third, in dexter a Turkish sceptre, of the second. *Pl.* 72, *cr.* 8.
CULLEN, Surr., an eagle, displayed, gu. *Pl.* 48, *cr.* 11.
CULLEN, Sco., a pelican, in nest, ppr. *Non sibi. Pl.* 44, *cr.* 1.
CULLEN, CAIRNCROSS-THOMAS, Esq., of Glenade, co. Leitrim, a pelican, in nest, feeding her young, ppr. *Carpe diem. Pl.* 44, *cr.* 1.
CULLIFORD, two elephants' probosces, addorsed, ppr. *Pl.* 24, *cr.* 8.
CULLING, Eng., a griffin, segreant, ar. *Pl.* 67, *cr.* 13.
CULLOWE, Eng., a unicorn's head, ar. *Pl.* 20, *cr.* 1.
CULLUM, Suff., a demi-lion, ppr., supporting a column, or. *Pl.* 102, *cr.* 4, (column, *pl.* 33, *cr.* 1.)
CULLUM, Bart., a lion, sejant, or, between paws a column, ar., capital and base, gold. *Sustineatur. Pl.* 109, *cr.* 7, (column, *pl.* 33, *cr.* 1.)
CULME, Devons., a lion, sejant, or, supporting a pillar, ar. *Pl.* 109, *cr.* 7, (pillar, *pl.* 33, *cr.* 1.)
CULMER, Devons., a leopard, rampant, ppr. *Pl.* 73, *cr.* 2.
CULPEPER, a falcon, ar., belled, or. *Pl.* 67, *cr.* 3.
CULVERTON, a pelican, vulning, ppr. *Pl.* 109, *cr.* 15.
CULY, Eng., a wolf's head, erased, erm. *Pl.* 14, *cr.* 6.
CUMBER, Suss., a lynx's head, or, charged with three pellets.
CUMBERLAND, Eng., a hunting-horn, gu., between wings, ppr. *Pl.* 98, *cr.* 2.
CUMBERLAND, a demi-wolf, salient, sa. *Pl.* 56, *cr.* 8, (without spear.)
CUMBERLEGE, or CUMBERDEDGE, Staffs., a unicorn's head, erased, az. *Pl.* 67, *cr.* 1.
CUMBY, Eng., a griffin's head, erased, gu. *Pl.* 48, *cr.* 6.
CUMINE, CUMING, or CUMMIN, Sco., a garb, or. *Courage. Pl.* 48, *cr.* 10.
CUMINE, or CUMMING, Sco. and Eng., in a maunch, gu., an arm, ppr. *Pl.* 22, *cr.* 14.
CUMINE, or CUMMING, Sco., in dexter hand, a sword, ppr. *Pl.* 21, *cr.* 10.
CUMINE, or CUMMING, Sco., in dexter hand, a sickle, ppr. *Hinc garbe nostra. Pl.* 36, *cr.* 12.

CUMING, Sco., a lion, rampant, gu., in dexter (a dagger,) ppr. *Courage. Pl.* 87, *cr.* 6.
CUMMING, Sco., an eagle, rising, ppr. *Nil arduum. Pl.* 67, *cr.* 4.
CUMMING, Sir JOHN, a lion, rampant, ppr., armed and langued, gu. *Courage. Pl.* 67, *cr.* 5.
CUMMING, Bart., N.S., a garb, or. *Courage. Pl.* 48, *cr.* 10.
CUMMING, or CUMMYNG, two swords, in saltier, ppr. *Courage. Pl.* 75, *cr.* 13.
CUMMINGS, in dexter hand, ppr., vested, az., a roll of paper, ar. *Pl.* 32, *cr.* 6.
CUNDALL, CUNDILL, or CUNDY, Eng., two ears of wheat, in saltier, ppr. *Pl.* 9, *cr.* 8.
CUNINGHAM, Sco., in hand a lozenge, or. *Pl.* 41, *cr.* 9.
CUNINGHAME, ARCHIBALD, Esq., of Caddell and Thornton, Ayrs., a unicorn's head, erect, couped. *Over, fork over. Pl.* 20, *cr.* 1.
CUNLIFFE, Bart., Lanc., a greyhound, sejant, ar., collared, sa. *Pl.* 66, *cr.* 15.
CUNLIFFE, a hawk, rising, ppr. *Pl.* 105, *cr.* 4.
CUNLIFFE, Kent and Lanc., a greyhound, sejant, ar., (collared, or.) *Pl.* 66, *cr.* 9.
CUNNINGHAM, Sco., a unicorn's head, ar., maned and horned, or. *Over, fork over. Pl.* 20, *cr.* 1.
CUNNINGHAM, of Bedland, a unicorn's head, couped, ar., horned and maned, or. *Virtute et labore. Pl.* 20, *cr.* 1.
CUNNINGHAM, W.S., Edinr., trunk of oak-tree, with (one) sprig, vert. *Tandem. Pl.* 92, *cr.* 8.
CUNNINGHAM, Bart., N.S., in dexter hand, ppr., a lozenge, or. *Curâ et candore. Pl.* 41, *cr.* 9.
CUNNINGHAM, on a ducal coronet, or, a mount, vert, thereon a stork, statant, in mouth a snake, tail coiled, body, ppr. *Pl.* 46, *cr.* 2, (stork, *pl.* 33, *cr.* 9; snake, *pl.* 41, *cr.* 6.)
CUNNINGHAM, of Baquhan, a boar's head, couped, az. *Cura et constantia. Pl.* 48, *cr.* 2.
CUNNINGHAM, of Lainshaw, Sco., stump of oak-tree, ppr., with (one) sprig, vert. *Non obstante Deo. Pl.* 92, *cr.* 8.
CUNNINGHAM, of Robertland, Sco., a unicorn's head. *Fortitudine. Pl.* 20, *cr.* 1.
CUNNINGHAM, of Bonintoun, a demi-lady, holding a pair of scales. *Præstat auro virtus. Pl.* 57, *cr.* 1.
CUNNINGHAM, Iri., a lion's head, erased, or, semée of torteaux, gu., ducally crowned, az. *Pl.* 90, *cr.* 4.
CUNNINGHAM, a cubit arm, erect, vested, per pale, or and az., cuffed, ar., in hand a pineapple, ppr.
CUNNINGHAM, Eng., a demi-unicorn, or. *Pl.* 26, *cr.* 14.
CUNNINGHAM, out of a ducal coronet, or, a dragon's head, (collared and chained,) wings addorsed. *Pl.* 59, *cr.* 14.
CUNNINGHAM, on a mount, vert, a unicorn, couchant.
CUNNINGHAM, a dexter hand holding up the ring of an anchor. *Pl.* 24, *cr.* 3.
CUNNINGHAM, of Balgonie, an oak-tree, ppr. *Tandem. Pl.* 16, *cr.* 8.
CUNNINGHAM-FAIRLIE, Bart., Sco., a unicorn's head, ar., horned, or, (point of horn charged with a rose, gu.) *Fortitudine. Pl.* 20, *cr.* 1.

CUNNINGHAM, a unicorn's head, erased, ppr. Sans varier. *Pl.* 67, *cr.* 1.
CUNNINGHAM, Edin., a unicorn's head, erased, ar. *Over, fork over. Pl.* 67, *cr.* 1.
CUNNINGHAME, Stockholm, a martlet, volant. *Prospere qui sedulo. Pl.* 40, *cr.* 4.
CUNNINGHAME, Sir JAMES MONTGOMERY, Bart., Ayrshire, a unicorn's head, erased, ppr. *Over, fork over. Pl.* 67, *cr.* 1.
CUNNINGHAME, Durh., stump of oak-tree, sprouting, ppr. *Pl.* 92, *cr.* 8.
CUNNINGHAME, Eng., an arm, in armour, in hand a sword, ppr. *Pl.* 2, *cr.* 8.
CUNNINGTON, a demi-lion, rampant, gu. *Pl.* 67, *cr.* 10.
CUNYNGHAME, Bart., of Milncraig, Sco., a unicorn's head, armed and crined, or. *Over, fork over. Pl.* 20, *cr.* 1.
CUPHOLME, Linc., a ram's head, erased, gu., attired, or. *Pl.* 1, *cr.* 12.
CUPPAGE, Eng., a sun-dial, ar. *Pl.* 97, *cr.* 6.
CUPPLADE, Lanc., a lion's head, erased, erm., (charged with three guttées, or, two and one.) *Pl.* 81, *cr.* 4.
CUPPLES, Eng., a demi-man, in military costume, ppr., holding a banner, az. *Pl.* 2, *cr.* 12.
CURE, Lond., out of a ducal coronet, ar., a griffin's head, wings expanded, of the first, charged on neck with a rose, gu. *Pl.* 97, *cr.* 13.
CURE, Middx., a griffin's head, erased. *Pl.* 48, *cr.* 6.
CURL, and CURRELL, Sco., a bugle-horn, stringed and knotted. *Forward. Pl.* 48, *cr.* 12.
CORLE, Hants., an eagle, wings expanded, ppr., beaked and legged, or. *Pl.* 126, *cr.* 7.
CURLE, (on a mount, vert), a hedge-hog, or. *Un Dieu, un roy, un foy. Pl.* 32, *cr.* 9.
CURLE, on a mount, vert, a hedge-hog, ppr. *Un Dieu, un roy, un foy. Pl.* 32, *cr.* 9.
CURLEY, and CURLING, Kent., on a mural coronet, or, a dragon's head, erased, vert, ducally gorged and lined, of the first, from the mouth issuing flames of fire, ppr. *Pl.* 101, *cr.* 4, (flames, *pl.* 37, *cr.* 9; gorging, *same plate.*)
CURLING, Eng., a savage's head, in profile, ppr., wreathed, vert. *Pl.* 36, *cr.* 3.
CURRAN, and CURREN, Iri., a parrot's head, between wings. *Pl.* 94, *cr.* 2.
CURRELL, Devons., a peacock's head, couped, ppr. *Pl.* 100, *cr.* 5.
CURRER, Yorks., a lion's head, erased, ar., collared, sa., rimmed and studded, or. *Mérite. Pl.* 7, *cr.* 10.
CURRER, a sword, erect, ppr. *Pl.* 105, *cr.* 1.
CURRER, Clifton House, Yorks.: 1. For *Currer*, a lion's head, erased, ar., gorged with a collar, sa., (charged with three bezants.) *Pl.* 7, *cr.* 10. 2. For *Roundell*, a sword, erect, ppr. *Pl.* 105, *cr.* 1.
CURREY, CURRIE, or CURREY, Eng., a golden fleece, ppr. *Pl.* 77, *cr.* 12.
CURREY, CURRIE, or CURREY, a rose, ar., barbed and seeded, vert. *Pl.* 52, *cr.* 11.
CURRIE, Sco., a demi-lion, ppr. *Courage. Pl.* 67, *cr.* 10.
CURRIE, ISAAC-GEORGE, Esq., of Bush Hill, Middx., same crest.
CURRIE, Sco., a cock crowing, ppr. *Vigilans et audax. Pl.* 67, *cr.* 14.

CURRY, Herts., a cock, gu. *Pl.* 67, *cr.* 14.
CURRY, a demi-lion, ar. *Fortis et lenis. Pl.* 67, *cr.* 10.
CURRY, a cock, gu. *Pl.* 67, *cr.* 14.
CURRYER, Lond., a cinquefoil, vert. *Pl.* 91, *cr.* 12.
CURSON, Derb., a popinjay, wings expanded, or, beaked, legged, and collared, gu.
CURSON, Derb., a cockatrice, wings addorsed, tail nowed, gu. *Pl.* 63, *cr.* 15.
CURSON, an eagle, wings displayed. *Let Curson hold what Curson held. Pl.* 126, *cr.* 7.
CURTAYNE, on a rock, a leopard, sejant, ppr. *Pl.* 123, *cr.* 8.
CURTEIS, HERBERT-MASCALL, Esq., of Windmill Hill, Suss., a unicorn, passant, or, between four trees, ppr. *Pl.* 106, *cr.* 3, (trees, *pl.* 125, *cr.* 14.)
CURTEIS, a wolf's head, couped, ar., collared, (and spiked, sa., chained, or.) *Pl.* 8, *cr.* 4.
CURTEIS, CURTESS, CURTEYS, CURTOIS, or CURTOYS, Eng., a demi-husbandman, vested, az., over shoulder an ox-yoke, ppr. *Pl.* 122, *cr.* 1.
CURTIS, Bart., Middx., a ram's head, couped, ar., (surmounted by two oak-branches, in saltier, ppr.) *Gradatione vincimus. Pl.* 34, *cr.* 12, (branches, *pl.* 19, *cr.* 12.)
CURTIS, Bart., Hants., out of a naval coronet, an arm, embowed, vested, az., cuffed, ar., supporting a flag-staff, ppr., thereon a flag, of the second, charged with a wolf's head, or, and a canton gyronné of four, gu. and az., thereon a cross, of the third, within a bordure, of the first. *Per ardua.*
CURTIS, Kent., an arm, in armour, embowed, in hand a sword, ppr., garnished, ar. *Pl.* 2, *cr.* 8.
CURTIS, a greyhound's head, between two roses. *Pl.* 84, *cr.* 13.
CURTIS, Suff., a lion, sejant, ppr., in dexter a shield. *Pl.* 22, *cr.* 13.
CURTIS, Iri., in hand (four) arrows, points downward. *Pl.* 56, *cr.* 4.
CURTIS, an arm, erect, in mail, ppr., garnished, ar., in hand, also ppr., a sword, of the last, hilt and pommel, or. *Pl.* 2, *cr.* 8.
CURTIS, FRANCIS-SAVAGE, Esq., of East Cliffe House, Devons., an arm, in armour, embowed, in hand, ppr., a scimitar, ar., hilt and pommel, or. *Pl.* 81, *cr.* 11. (*Another crest*, an arm, in armour, erect, in hand a sword, all ppr., hilt and pommel, or. *Velle bene facere. Pl.* 2, *cr.* 8.)
CURTOYS, Eng., a triton, in sinister, a trident. *Pl.* 35, *cr.* 10.
CURWAN, a nag's head, erased, ppr. *Pl.* 81, *cr.* 6.
CURWEN, Eng., a demi-savage, regardant, wreathed about head and middle with leaves, all ppr. *Pl.* 16, *cr.* 4.
CURWEN, HENRY, Esq., of Workington Hall, Cumb., a unicorn's head, erased, ar., armed, or. *Si je n'estoy. Pl.* 67, *cr.* 1.
CURZON, a griffin, sejant, resting dexter on an escutcheon. *Pl.* 42, *cr.* 8, (without coronet.)
CURZON, Earl Howe, and Barons Scarsdale and Teynham. *See those titles.*
CUSACH, CUSACK, and CUSACKE, a spear, enfiled with a savage's head, couped, ppr. *Pl.* 88, *cr.* 15.

CUSACKE, Eng., in dexter hand a couteau-sword, indented on back, cutting at a quill, all ppr. *Pl.* 39, *cr.* 13.

CUSAKE, Iri., a mermaid, with comb and mirror, ppr. *Pl.* 48, *cr.* 5.

CUSH, or CUSHE, Eng., a cock, sa., combed and wattled, gu. *Pl.* 67, *cr.* 14.

CUSHNEY, Sco., an anchor, ppr., surmounted by a fleur-de-lis. *Spes meum solatium. Pl.* 51, *cr.* 15.

CUSSANS, Eng., a dexter hand holding a boar's head, in pale, erased, ppr. *Pl.* 86, *cr.* 6.

CUSSANS, or CUSSONS, an eagle, displayed, gu., armed and langued, az., (on breast a bend, ar., charged with three fleurs-de-lis, sa.) *Dum spiro spero. Pl.* 48, *cr.* 11.

CUST, Earl Brownlow. See BROWNLOW.

CUST, Linc., a lion's head, erased, sa., collared, gobonée, ar. and az. *Pl.* 7, *cr.* 10.

CUSTANCE, Eng., a covered cup. *Pl.* 75, *cr.* 1, (without swords.)

CUSTANCE, Norf., out of a ducal coronet, or, a phœnix, gu., in flames, ppr. *Pl.* 53, *cr.* 6.

CUSTANCE, HAMBLETON-FRANCIS, Esq., of Weston House, Norf., a demi-eagle displayed, gu., charged on breast with a star of (six) points, or. *Appetitus rationi pareat. Pl.* 44, *cr.* 14.

CUTBERD, CUTHBERD, CUTHBERT, and CUTBERT, a lion's head, erased, ar., collared, gu., charged with three cross crosslets, fitched, of the first. *Pl.* 7, *cr.* 10, (crosslet, *pl.* 141.)

CUTHBERT, or CUTHBURT, Eng., on a heart, gu., an eagle's claw, erased at thigh, ppr. *Pl.* 27, *cr.* 1.

CUTHBERT, Sco., in hand, (gauntleted,) a dart. *Nec minus fortiter. Pl.* 42, *cr.* 13.

CUTHBERT, an arm, in armour, embowed, in hand a broken spear, all ppr. *Pl.* 44, *cr.* 9.

CUTHBERT, Iri., a demi-lion, az., (between paws,) a battle-axe, ppr. *Pl.* 101, *cr.* 14, (without charge.)

CUTHBERTSON, Sco., a (gauntleted hand) throwing a dart. *Nec minus fortiter. Pl.* 42, *cr.* 13.

CUTHELL, or CUTHILL, on a ducal coronet, a leopard, sejant. *Pl.* 86, *cr.* 8.

CUTLER, GEORGE-HENRY, Esq., of Upton, Devons., same crest.

CUTLER, Suff., a demi-lion, gu., holding a battle-axe, ppr., handle, ar. *Pl.* 101, *cr.* 14, (without charge.)

CUTLER, Suff., a dragon's head, erased, or, ducally gorged, gu. *Pl.* 36, *cr.* 7.

CUTLER, Yorks., a dragon's head, erased, or, ducally gorged, az. *Pl.* 36, *cr.* 7.

CUTLER, a dragon's head, erased, gu. *Pl.* 107, *cr.* 10.

CUTLER, a dragon's head, erased, az., gorged with a mural coronet, or, in mouth a laurel-branch, vert. *Pl.* 107, *cr.* 10, (coronet, *pl.* 128, *fig.* 18.)

CUTTES, an eagle, displayed, ar., beaked and membered, gu. *Pl.* 48, *cr.* 11.

CUTTING, a demi-griffin, ar., collared, az., between claws, an escallop, or. *Pl.* 18, *cr.* 6, (escallop, *pl.* 141.)

CUTTS, a greyhound's head, (erased,) ar., collared, gu., ringed, or. *Pl.* 43, *cr.* 11.

CUYET, Eng., a goat's head, erased, sa. *Pl.* 29, *cr.* 13.

CUYLER, Bart., Herts., on a mural coronet, ppr., a battle-axe, erect, surmounted by two arrows, in saltier, or, flighted, ar., points upward.

CYFER, Eng., a griffin's head, ppr. *Pl.* 38, *cr.* 3.

D

DABBINS, out of a mural coronet, chequy, ar. and sa., an acorn, ppr. *Pl.* 20, *cr.* 10.

DABERNON, Devons., in a maunch, gu., a hand, apaumée, ppr. *Pl.* 8, *cr.* 11.

DABETOT, or DABITOT, a dove with olive-branch, ppr. *Pl.* 48, *cr.* 15.

DABRIDGCOURT, out of a ducal coronet, or, four feathers, ar. *Pl.* 44, *cr.* 12.

DACASTA, a reindeer, trippant, ppr. *Pl.* 12, *cr.* 8.

DACCOMB, a pair of wings conjoined. *Pl.* 15, *cr.* 10.

DACKCOMBE, Dors., an oak-tree, ppr., fructed, or. *Virtutis robore robor. Pl.* 16, *cr.* 8.

DA COSTA, a reindeer, passant, ppr. *Pl.* 12, *cr.* 8.

DACRE, an eagle, rising, sa. *Pl.* 67, *cr.* 4.

DACRE, Baron (Brand;) out of a ducal coronet, or, a leopard's head, ar., spotted, of the colours. *Pour bien desirer. Pl.* 36, *cr.* 15.

DACRE, a bull, (statant, tail extended,) gu. *Pl.* 66, *cr.* 11.

DACRE, a bull, passant, collared and lined. *Forte en loyauté.*

DACRE, a demi-tiger, ducally gorged and chained, ppr. *Pl.* 125, *cr.* 4.

DACRES, Heref., a buckle. *Pl.* 73, *cr.* 10.

DACRES, a dove, az., charged on neck with an escallop, or, between two oak-branches, vert, fructed, gold. *Pl.* 15, *cr.* 11.

DADE, Norf. and Suff., a garb, or, enfiled with a ducal coronet, per pale, az. and gu. *Pl.* 76, *cr.* 13.

DADLEY, an arm, embowed, in hand (two slips of columbine,) all ppr. *In malos cornu. Pl.* 47, *cr.* 13.

D'AETH, a griffin's head, erased, or. *Pl.* 48, *cr.* 6.

D'AETH, a griffin's head, couped, or, in mouth a trefoil, slipped, vert. *Pl.* 38, *cr.* 3, (trefoil, *pl.* 141.)

DAGGET, an eagle, displayed, gu., charged with a bezant. *Pl.* 12, *cr.* 7.

DAGGET, Sco., a demi-talbot, sa., collared, or. *Pl.* 15, *cr.* 2.

DAGLEY, Eng., a Minerva's head, from shoulders, affrontée. *Pl.* 92, *cr.* 12.

DAGWORTH, in lion's paw, erased, hilt of broken sword, ppr. *Pl.* 49, *cr.* 10.

DAILE, Sco., a swan's head and neck, couped, ppr. *Laudes cano heroum. Pl.* 54, *cr.* 6, (without wings.)

DAINTRY, Eng., a bull's head and neck, ducally gorged, ppr. *Pl.* 68, *cr.* 6.

DAISIE, Sco., a hawk's head, erased, ppr. *Pl.* 34, *cr.* 11.

DAKEHAM, Linc. and Salop, a dove, or. *Pl.* 66, *cr.* 12.
DAKEYN, and DEAKIN, Derb., out of a naval coronet, or, an arm, embowed, ppr., in hand a'battle-axe, on wrist a ribbon, az.
DAKYNS, Derbs. and Yorks., a dexter arm., embowed, ppr., in hand a battle-axe, ar. *Strike, Dakyns, the Devil's in the hempe.* *Pl.* 121, *cr.* 14.
DALAVALL, Northumb., a ram's head, ar., attired, or. *Pl.* 34, *cr.* 12.
DALBIAC, Yorks., a dove, wings expanded, in mouth an olive-branch. *Pl.* 79, *cr.* 8, (without globe.)
DALBIE, and DALBY, a crane, regardant, resting foot on a stone. *Pl.* 77, *cr.* 15.
DALBY, Eng., a demi-Hercules, with lion's skin and club, ppr. *Pl.* 49, *cr.* 11.
DALE, Sco., an arm, brandishing a scimitar, ppr. *Pl.* 92, *cr.* 5.
DALE, an arm, in hand a sword, in bend, ppr. *Pl.* 34, *cr.* 7.
DALE, JAMES-CHARLES, Esq., M.A., of Glanville's Wootton, and Newton-Montague, Dors., a garb, ppr. *Pl.* 48, *cr.* 10.
DALE, HELEN-KATHARINE, and FRANCES-ELIZABETH, (on a mount, vert,) three Danish battle-axes, one in pale, and two in saltire, ppr., the staves, az., encompassed by a chaplet of roses, alternately, gu. and az., banded, by a riband, or. *Non arbitrio popularis auræ.* *Pl.* 20, *cr.* 11.
DALE, Northumb., a stork, ppr. *Pl.* 33, *cr.* 9.
DALE, Ruts., three battle-axes, one in pale, and two in saltire, handles, or, heads, ar., enfiled with a chaplet of roses, gold. *Pl.* 20, *cr.* 11.
DALE, Lond. and Northamp., a stork, ar., beaked, legged, and ducally gorged, or. *Pl.* 33, *cr.* 9, (coronet, *pl.* 128, *fig.* 3.)
DALE, on a chapeau, a stork, ppr. *Pl.* 106, *cr.* 6.
DALES, Eng., a demi-lion, rampant, or, collared, gu. *Pl.* 18, *cr.* 13.
DALGETY, or DALGETTY, Eng., a lion, rampant, gardant, az. *Pl.* 35, *cr.* 4.
DALGLISH, Sco., a book, expanded, ppr. *Deliciæ mei.* *Pl.* 15, *cr.* 12.
DALGLEISH, Sco., trunk of oak-tree, sprouting new branches. *Revirescam.* *Pl.* 92, *cr.* 8.
DALHOUSIE, Earl of, Lord Ramsay, Sco., Baron Dalhousie, U.K., (Ramsay,) a unicorn's head, couped, ar., armed and crined, or. *Ora et labora.* *Pl.* 20, *cr.* 1.
DALHURST, a crescent, ar. *Pl.* 18, *cr.* 14.
DALINGRUGGE, Eng., a demi-lion, ppr. *Pl.* 67, *cr.* 10.
DALISON, Kent and Linc., a man, in armour, ppr., in dexter a battle-axe, ar., handle, gu. *Pl.* 60, *cr.* 2, (axe, *pl.* 14, *cr.* 8.)
DALL, Eng., a sword and pen, in saltire, ppr. *Pl.* 49, *cr.* 12.
DALL, a lion, passant, gardant, ducally gorged, and royally crowned. *Coronat fides.* *Pl.* 120, *cr.* 5, (gorging, *same plate,* and crown, *pl.* 127, *fig.* 2.)
DALLAS, Sco., a crescent. *Gradatim.* *Pl.* 18, *cr.* 14.
DALLAS, Bart., Staff., a crescent, party, per cross, or and gu. *Lux venit ab alto.* *Pl.* 40, *cr.* 15.
DALLAS, Sco., an open lancet, ppr. *Semper paratus.* *Pl.* 10, *cr.* 10.

DALLAS, a crescent, per pale, ar. and gu. *Pl.* 18, *cr.* 14.
DALLENDER, Suff. and Surr., an eagle's head, vairy, ar. and gu. *Pl.* 100, *cr.* 10.
DALLES, a demi-lion, or, collared, gu. *Pl.* 18, *cr.* 13.
DALLEY, Iri., a ferret, collared and lined, ppr. *Pl.* 12, *cr.* 2.
DALLING, Bart., Surr., a cubit arm, erect, in hand a (branch of oak, fructed, ppr.) *Pl.* 43, *cr.* 6.
DALLY, a horse's head, armed. *Pl.* 7, *cr.* 12.
DALLYSON, Middx., the sun rising from a cloud, ppr. *Pl.* 67, *cr.* 9.
DALRYMPLE, HORN-ELPHINSTON, Sir ROBERT, Bart., Sco., in the centre a rock, ppr. *Pl.* 73, *cr.* 12. *Firme.* On the dexter, two horns of a bull, issuing, per fess, or and sa., counterchanged. *Pl.* 9, *cr.* 15. On the sinister, an arm in (armour,) in hand an ostrich-feather, in pale, all ppr. Under arms, *Moneo et munio.* *Pl.* 69, *cr.* 1.
DALLEY, and DALLY, Eng., a demi-angel, in dexter a griffin's head, erased, ppr. *Pl.* 24, *cr.* 11.
DALLING, a cannon, arched over with a chain, within the arch a lion's head, erased, ppr. *Pl.* 115, *cr.* 12.
DALLYSON, a man, in complete armour, ppr., visor open, striking with a battle-axe, which he wields with both hands.
DALMAHOY, of that Ilk, in dexter hand a sword, both ppr. *Absque metu.* *Pl.* 21, *cr.* 10.
DALMER, Eng., on a chapeau, a lion's head, erased, ducally crowned. *Pl.* 34, *cr.* 10.
DALMER, a demi-lion, rampant, erminois, (between paws, a mullet of six points, ar., pierced,) vert. *Pl.* 89, *cr.* 10.
DALRYMPLE, Earl of Stair. *See* STAIR.
DALRYMPLE, Sco., a hart's head, ppr. *Pl.* 91, *cr.* 14.
DALRYMPLE, Eng., a lion's head, erased, or. *Pl.* 81, *cr.* 4.
DALRYMPLE, Sco., a rock, ppr. *Quiescam.* *Pl.* 73, *cr.* 12.
DALRYMPLE, Bart., Iri., a rock, ppr. *Firm.* *Pl.* 73, *cr.* 12.
DALRYMPLE, Bart., Sco., out of a viscount's coronet, a rock, ppr. *Firm.* *Pl.* 72, *cr.* 11.
DALRYMPLE, Sco., a rock, ppr. *Atavis.* *Pl.* 73, *cr.* 12.
DALRYMPLE, Sco., a rock, ppr. *Firm.* *Pl.* 73, *cr.* 12.
DALRYMPLE, Sco., a rock, ppr. *Steady.* *Pl.* 73, *cr.* 12.
DALSIEL, Lond., a demi-man, in armour, in dexter a scimitar, brandished aloft, ppr. *I dare.* *Pl.* 27, *cr.* 11.
DALSTON, Cumb., out of a ducal coronet, or, a falcon's head, ppr. *Pl.* 24, *cr.* 10.
DALSTON, Cumb., a blackbird's head, ppr., beaked, or. *Pl.* 27, *cr.* 13.
DALSTON, out of a ducal coronet, or, an eagle's head, ppr., in beak a pellet. *Pl.* 20, *cr.* 12.
DALTON, Lanc., a dragon's head, vert, between wings, or. *Pl.* 105, *cr.* 11.
DALTON, Eng., a ram's head, couped, ar., attired, or. *Pl.* 34, *cr.* 12.
DALTON, Yorks. and Linc., a dragon's head, wings displayed, vert, (gorged with a collar, nebulée, ar.) *Pl.* 105, *cr.* 11.
DALTON, Iri., a seax, ppr. *Pl.* 27, *cr.* 10.

DALYELL, Sco., a demi-man, in armour, in hand a scimitar. *Pl.* 27, *cr.* 11.
DALZELL, Eng., a dagger, in pale, ppr. *Pl.* 73, *cr.* 9.
DALZIEL, a naked man, ppr. *I dare.*
DALZIELL, Bart., Sco., in dexter hand a scimitar, ppr. *I dare. Pl.* 59, *cr.* 8.
DALTON, of Thurnham, a dragon's head, vert, between wings, or. *Pl.* 105, *cr.* 11.
DALTON, EDWARD, Esq., of Dunkirk Manor House, Glouc., a demi-dragon, vert, wings ouvert. *Inter cruces triumphans in cruce. Pl.* 105, *cr.* 11.
DALY, a demi-angel, in hand a griffin's head, erased, ppr. *Pl.* 24, *cr.* 11.
DALY, Iri., a ferret, collared and lined, ppr. *Pl.* 12, *cr.* 2.
DALZELL, Earl of Carnwath. *See* CARNWATH.
DALZELL, in dexter hand a scimitar, both ppr. *Pl.* 29, *cr.* 8.
DALZIEL, Lond., a demi-man, in armour, in dexter a scimitar, ppr. *I dare. Pl.* 27, *cr.* 11.
DALZIEL, Sco., a sword, in pale, ppr. *I dare. Pl.* 105, *cr.* 1.
DALZIEL, in dexter hand a scimitar. *I dare. Pl.* 29, *cr.* 8.
DALZIEL, Eng., a branch of laurel and a thistle, issuing from two hands, couped and conjoined, one armed, the other nude. *Pl.* 23, *cr.* 10.
DAMANT, Eng., two lions' heads, addorsed. *Pl.* 28, *cr.* 10.
DAMBOYS, Eng., a rook, sa. *Pl.* 123, *cr.* 2.
DAMER, Earl of Dorchester, out of a mural coronet, or, a talbot's head, az., eared, gold. *Tu ne cede malis. Pl.* 91, *cr.* 15.
DAMER, Dors., out of a mural coronet, or, a talbot's head, az., eared, gold. *Pl.* 91, *cr.* 15.
DAMERLEY, Eng., in dexter hand a scimitar, both ppr. *Pl.* 29, *cr.* 8.
DAMERLEY, Eng., a lion's head, erased, within a chain, or, in orle. *Pl.* 28, *cr.* 12.
DAMMANT, Eng., in dexter hand a scimitar, ppr. *Pl.* 29, *cr.* 8.
D'AMORIE, Glouc., out of a mural coronet, or, a talbot's head, az., eared, gold. *Pl.* 91, *cr.* 15.
DAMORY, Iri., a demi-lion, rampant, gardant, sa. *Pl.* 35, *cr.* 4.
DALMORY, a wolf, current. *Pl.* 111, *cr.* 1.
DAMPORT, Chesh., a lion, passant, erm., (ducally crowned, or, resting dexter on an escutcheon, gold.) *Pl.* 48, *cr.* 8.
DAMPORT, Lanc. and Somers., a man's head, in profile, ppr., (with halter round neck, or.) *Pl.* 81, *cr.* 15.
DAN, or DANN, out of a mural coronet, a demi-monkey, rampant. *Pl.* 24, *cr.* 12.
DANA, Eng., a bull's head, affrontée. *Pl.* 18, *cr.* 15.
DANBY, Yorks., a crab, erect, or. *Pl.* 116, *cr.* 14.
DANCASTER, Berks., a stag's head, ar., attired, or, (vulned in neck, ppr.) *Pl.* 91, *cr.* 14.
DANCE, HOLLAND, Berks. and Hants., a horse's head, az., caparisoned, or, (charged on neck with an escutcheon, ar., thereon a lion's head, erased, gu.) *Pl.* 92, *cr.* 1.
DANCE, Eng., out of a ducal coronet, a stag's head, affrontée. *Pl.* 29, *cr.* 7.
DANCE, a horse's head, couped, az., bridled, gu., *Pl.* 92, *cr.* 1.

DANCE, a horse's head, ar. *Pl.* 81, *cr.* 6.
DANCE, Herts., a horse's head, couped, sa., (wreathed round neck with oak, vert,) bit, or, bridle, of the first. *Pl.* 92, *cr.* 1.
DANCER, Bart., Iri., an arm, in armour, embowed, in hand a broken spear, broken part hanging down, ppr. *Pl.* 44, *cr.* 9.
DANCER, Eng., a pheon, with part of broken shaft. *Pl.* 27, *cr.* 12.
DANCEY, Wilts., a horse's head, couped, gu., bezantée, maned and bridled, or. *Pl.* 92, *cr.* 1.
DAND, Notts., on a mount, vert, a swan, ar. *Pl.* 122, *cr.* 13.
DANDERN, out of a ducal coronet, or, a demi-ostrich, wings addorsed, ar. *Pl.* 29, *cr.* 9.
DANDRIDGE, Worc., a lion's head, erased, charged with a mascle, ar. *Pl.* 81, *cr.* 4, (mascle, *pl.* 141.)
DANDY, Suff., on a garb, or, a dove, close, ar. *Pl.* 12, *cr.* 15, (dove, *pl.* 66, *cr.* 12.)
DANE, Somers., out of a ducal coronet, or, a demi-lizard, vert.
DANE, Iri., out of a ducal coronet, or, a demi-lizard, salient, ppr.
DANES, or DANEYS, Eng., a quadrangular castle. *Pl.* 28, *cr.* 11.
DANET, Eng., a greyhound's head, couped, ar., collared, gu., studded and buckled, or. *Pl.* 43, *cr.* 11.
DANFORD, Eng., a man in military costume, ppr., in dexter a flag, displayed, az. *Pl.* 79, *cr.* 5.
DANGERFIELD, a savage's head, wreathed with laurel-leaves, ppr. *Pl.* 118, *cr.* 7.
DANGERFIELD, Worc., a griffin's head, erased, ppr. *Pl.* 48, *cr.* 6.
DANHECK, Lond., a rose, ppr. *Pl.* 52, *cr.* 11.
DANIEL, Wilts. and Yorks., a unicorn's head, erased, or. *Pl.* 67, *cr.* 1.
DANIEL, a dexter arm, enfiled with a ducal coronet, in hand a sabre. *Pl.* 47, *cr.* 8, (sabre, *pl.* 29, *cr.* 8.)
DANIEL, a pelican, encircled with two branches of laurel, all ppr. *Pl.* 109, *cr.* 15, (laurel, *pl.* 79, *cr.* 14.)
DANIEL, Eng., a unicorn's head, couped, ar., attired, or. *Pl.* 20, *cr.* 1.
DANIEL, Eng., a galley, oars in saltier. *Pl.* 77, *cr.* 11.
DANIEL, Iri., a bull, passant, ppr. *Pl.* 66, *cr.* 11.
DANIELL, Cornw., and DANIELS, Hants., on two oak-branches, vert, fructed, or, meeting saltierwise in base, a pelican, erm., in nest, feeding her young, ppr. *Pl.* 76, *cr.* 15.
DANIELL, Somers., Chesh., and Suff., a tiger, passant, regardant, ar. *Pl.* 67, *cr.* 15.
DANIELL, Staffs., a wolf, (statant,) regardant, gu. *Pl.* 77, *cr.* 14, (without spear.)
DANIELL, Sco., a unicorn's head, ar. *Pl.* 20, *cr.* 1.
DANIELL, Herts., Yorks., and Wilts., a unicorn's head, erased, or. *Pl.* 67, *cr.* 1.
DANIELL, Dors., an arm, couped, in fess, vested, az., cuffed, or, in hand a cross crosslet, fitched, in pale, gu. *Pl.* 88, *cr.* 7.
DANIELL, Somers. and Chesh., a unicorn's head, couped, ar. *Pl.* 20, *cr.* 1.
DANIELS, Hants., a dove, with olive-branch, ppr. *Pl.* 48, *cr.* 15.
DANKYRSLEY, Yorks., a demi-woman, vested, ar., playing on a harp, or. *Pl.* 72, *cr.* 14.

DANMARE, Eng., a lion's gamb, sa., supporting an escutcheon, gu. *Pl.* 43, *cr.* 12.

DANNAT, or DANNANT, a greyhound's head, erased, ar., collared, or, the ring gu., charged with three torteaux. *Pl.* 43, *cr.* 11.

DANSEY, DANSEY-RICHARD, Esq., of Easton Court, Heref., a lion's head, erased, ar., collared, gu. *Pl.* 7, *cr.* 10.

DANNCEY, or DAUNCEY, Heref., a lion's head, erased, ar., collared, gu. *Pl.* 7, *cr.* 10.

DANNSEY, a nag's head, gu., bezantée, maned and bridled, or. *Pl.* 92, *cr.* 1.

DANNSEY, a dragon's head, erased, vert. *Pl.* 107, *cr.* 10.

DANREY, Cornw., a horse, passant, saddled and bridled. *Pl.* 99, *cr.* 11.

DANSEY, Eng., a demi-savage, wreathed round middle, in dexter a slip of myrtle, all ppr. *Pl.* 35, *cr.* 12.

DANSEY, Heref., a lion, rampant, per fess, or and gu. *Pl.* 67, *cr.* 5.

DANSIE, a sea-horse, ppr. *Pl.* 103, *cr.* 3.

DANSON, a garb, quarterly, or and gu. *Pl.* 48, *cr.* 10.

DANT, a chough's head, erased, sa., beaked, gu. *Pl.* 27, *cr.* 13.

DANVERS, Lond. and Bucks., a fleur-de-lis, erm., enfiled with a ducal coronet, or. *Pl.* 47, *cr.* 7.

DANVERS, a water-wyvern, or. *Pl.* 63, *cr.* 13.

DANVERS, a wyvern, or. *Pl.* 63, *cr.* 13.

DANVERS, Leic., a parrot, close, (in mouth an oak-branch, fructed, all ppr.) *Pl.* 25, *cr.* 2, (oak, *pl.* 32, *cr.* 13.)

DANVERS, Oxon. and Northamp., a parrot, vert, in mouth an annulet, or. *Pl.* 33, *cr.* 11.

DANVERS, Leic. and Oxon., a parrot, vert, winged, gu., in mouth a round buckle, or. *Pl.* 33, *cr.* 11, (buckle, *same plate, cr.* 3.)

DANVERS, Warw., Oxon., and Northamp., a wyvern, wings addorsed, or. *Pl.* 63, *cr.* 13.

DANYERS, a parrot, ppr. *Pl.* 25, *cr.* 2.

DAPIPER, an eagle, az. *Pl.* 7, *cr.* 11.

DARBY, Iri., a yew-tree, ppr. *Pl.* 49, *cr.* 13.

DARBY, Linc., an antelope's head, erased, gu., maned, tufted, armed, and double attired in fret, or. *Pl.* 24, *cr.* 7.

DARBY, Lond. and Dors., out of a tower, ar., two wings, the dexter or, sinister, az. *Pl.* 47, *cr.* 9.

DARBY, Suff., a garb, ar., banded, or. *Pl.* 48, *cr.* 10.

DARBY, Middx. and Dorc., an eagle's head, erased, ar. *Pl.* 20, *cr.* 7.

DARCEY, Ess., a lady, attired, hair dishevelled, ppr., in hand a branch of three cinquefoils, vert. *Pl.* 2, *cr.* 10.

DARCIE, Linc. and Durh., a woman's head, couped at breasts, ppr., hair flowing, or, wreathed about head with cinquefoils, gu., pierced, or. *Pl.* 81, *cr.* 13.

DARCY, or D'ARCY, Eng. and Iri., a tilting-spear, broken in three pieces, head in pale, the other two, in saltier, ppr., banded, gu. *Pl.* 33, *cr.* 3.

D'ARCY, a bull, ppr. *Un Dieu, un roi. Pl.* 66, *cr.* 11.

D'ARCY, Northumb., on a chapeau, ar., turned up, erm., a bull, passant, sa. *Pl.* 65, *cr.* 11.

D'ARCY, Eng. and Iri., on a chapeau, ppr., a bull, (statant,) sa. *Pl.* 65, *cr.* 11.

D'ARCY, Ess., a demi-virgin, in dexter a branch of cinquefoils, all ppr. *Pl.* 2, *cr.* 10.

D'ARCY, GEORGE-JAMES-NORMAN, Esq., of Hyde Park, co. Westmeath, on a chapeau, a bull, sa., armed, or. *Un Dieu, un roi. Pl.* 65, *cr.* 11.

D'ARCY, RICHARD, Esq., of New Forest, co. Galway; and Fisher Hill, co. Mayo; on a chapeau, gu., turned up, erm., a bull, sa., armed, or. *Un Dieu, un roi. Pl.* 65, *cr.* 11.

D'ARCY, the Rev. HYACINTH, co. Galway, a spear, broken in three pieces, or, headed, ar., banded together in middle by a ribbon, gu. *Un Dieu, un roi. Pl.* 33, *cr.* 3.

DARCYE, Eng., a lion's head, issuing, ar., collared, sa. *Pl.* 42, *cr.* 14.

DARE, Ess., a demi-lion, rampant, az., semée of bezants, charged on shoulder with a cross crosslet, or, between paws a lozenge, of the same, charged with an increscent, gu. *Loyauté sans tache. Pl.* 126, *cr.* 12, (chargings, *pl.* 141.)

DARE, on a chapeau, a demi-lion, ppr., between paws an increscent, ar. *Pl.* 47, *cr.* 11.

DARE, an arm, couped and embowed, in fess, elbow on the wreath, girt above elbow with a ribbon, in hand a slip of laurel, all ppr. *Pl.* 89, *cr.* 4, (laurel, *pl.* 43, *cr.* 6.)

DARELL, Cornw., a wolf, passant, ppr. *Pl.* 46, *cr.* 6.

DARELL, Kent, out of a ducal coronet, or, a Saracen's head, couped below shoulders, ppr., wreathed, ar. and az., on head a cap, of the last, fretty, ar., turned up, erm. *Pl.* 38, *cr.* 13, (coronet, *same plate, cr.* 11.)

DARK, an arm, embowed, purp., in hand a streamer, az., on flag, an escutcheon, ar., charged with a cross, sa. *Pl.* 6, *cr.* 5, (escutcheon, *same plate.*)

DARKER, an arm, embowed, in hand a bunch of hop-vine, all ppr. *Pl.* 47, *cr.* 13.

DARLEY, HENRY-BREWSTER, Esq., of Aldby Park, Yorks., a horse's head, couped, gu., accoutred in armour and bridled, or. *Vivitur ingenio. Pl.* 52, *cr.* 9.

DARLEY, a garb, ar., banded, or, charged with an anchor, sa. *Pl.* 48, *cr.* 10, (anchor, *pl.* 42, *cr.* 12.)

DARLEY, Iri., out of a ducal coronet, or, a demi-lion, vert. *Pl.* 45, *cr.* 7.

DARLEY, a garb, ar., banded, or. *Pl.* 48, *cr.* 10.

DARLEY, a horse's head, ar., bridled, gu. *Dare. Pl.* 92, *cr.* 1.

DARLEY, Yorks., a horse's head, couped, gu., accoutred in armour, ar., bridled, or. *Pl.* 7, *cr.* 12.

DARLEY, Yorks., on an esquire's helmet, out of a mural coronet, a lion, rampant, holding a staff. *Pl.* 109, *cr.* 5. (coronet, *pl.* 128, *fig.* 18; lion, *pl.* 93, *cr.* 10.)

DARLING, Eng., in hand, gauntleted, a pheon, erect, point upward. *Pl.* 123, *cr.* 12.

DARLING, Lond., a lady, ppr., vested in a loose robe, ar., body pink, flowing round her a robe, gu., in dexter a cross crosslet, fitched, gu., in sinister a book, ppr. *Pl.* 107, *cr.* 14, (cross, *pl.* 141; book, *pl.* 45, *cr.* 3.)

DARLING, out of a mural coronet, or, an arm, in armour, embowed, ppr., (in hand an escutcheon, charged with two swords, in saltier.) *Pl.* 115, *cr.* 14.

DARLING, Sco., in hand, a heart, ppr. *Dei donum.* *Pl.* 59, *cr.* 12.
DARLINGTON, Eng., a winged pillar. *Pl.* 33, *cr.* 12.
DARLSTON, Worc., a hawk's head, between wings, barry of four, ar. and sa., beaked, or. *Pl.* 99, *cr.* 10.
DARNALL, DARNEL, or DARNOL, Middx., a lion's head, erased, ar., between wings, or. *Pl.* 73, *cr.* 3.
DARNELL, Durh., on a cock-pheasant, sitting, ppr., a falcon's leg, erased and belled. *Pl.* 72, *cr.* 6.
DARNLEY, Earl of, Iri. *See* BLIGH.
DARNLEY, on a ducal coronet, a martlet, ppr. *Pl.* 98, *cr.* 14.
DAROCH, a demi-negro, in dexter a dagger, ppr. *Pl.* 41, *cr.* 8.
DARRELL, Bart., Surr., out of a ducal coronet, or, a Saracen's head, couped at shoulders, ppr., bearded, sa., wreathed, ar. and az., on head a cap, of the last, fretty of the fourth, tasselled, gold, turned up, erm. *Pl.* 51, *cr.* 4, (coronet, *same plate.*)
DARRELL, an eagle, preying on a child, swaddled, ppr. *Pl.* 123, *cr.* 11.
DARRELL, Bucks., Yorks., Wilts., and Linc., a goat's head, erased, ar., attired, or. *Pl.* 29, *cr.* 13.
DART, or DARTE, Devons. and Cornw., a flame of fire, ppr. *Pl.* 16, *cr.* 12.
DARTMOUTH, Earl of, Baron, Viscount Lewisham, (Legge,) out of a ducal coronet, or, a plume of five ostrich-feathers, three ar., two az. *Gaudet tentamine virtus.* *Pl.* 100, *cr.* 12.
DARVALL, or DARWALL, a lion's head, gorged with a collar, charged with three bezants. *Pl.* 42, *cr.* 14, (bezant, *pl.* 141.)
DARWELL, Eng., a lion's head, erased, **or**, ducally crowned, gu. *Pl.* 90, *cr.* 4.
DARWEN, or DARWIN, a camel's head, couped, ppr. *Pl.* 109, *cr.* 9.
DARWIN, Sir FRANCIS-SACHEVEREL, of Breadsall Priory, Derbs., a demi-griffin, vert, between claws an escallop, or. *Pl.* 18, *cr.* 6, (escallop, *pl.* 141.)
DASHWOOD, Bart., Oxon., a griffin's head, erased, per fess, erminois and gu. *Pl.* 48, *cr.* 6.
DASHWOOD, Lond., a griffin's head, erased, per fess, or and gu. *Pro Magnâ Chartâ.* *Pl.* 48, *cr.* 6.
DASHWOOD, the Rev. SAMUEL-VERE, of Stanford Park, Notts., a griffin's head, erased, erm. *Pl.* 48, *cr.* 6.
DAST, a flame of fire, ppr. *Pl.* 16, *cr.* 12.
DASTIN, Worc., a reindeer's head, ar., couped, gu., (pierced through neck by a broad arrow.) *Pl.* 2, *cr.* 13.
DATMER, an eagle's head, erased, ppr. *Pl.* 20, *cr.* 7.
DAUBENEY, GEORGE-MATTHEWS, Esq., of Cote, Glouc., a pair of wings, sa. *Pl.* 63, *cr.* 12.
DAUBENY, Glouc., two dragons' wings displayed, ar. *Pl.* 105, *cr.* 11, (without head.)
DAUBUZ, a griffin's head, wings addorsed, ppr. *Pl.* 18, *cr.* 6.
DAUDIE, Cornw., a horse, passant, saddled and bridled. *Pl.* 99, *cr.* 11.
DAULBENY, an eagle, wings expanded, or. *Pl.* 126, *cr.* 7.

DAUNCEY, Heref., a lion's head, erased, ar., collared, gu. *Pl.* 7, *cr.* 10.
DAUNSCOURT, a negro's head, couped at shoulders, vested, paly of six, erm. and ermines, pendents at ears, or, wreathed on forehead, and with bats' wings to head, expanded, sa. *Pl.* 115, *cr.* 11.
DAUNT, MARY, of Owlpen, Glouc.; and Gortigrenane, co. Cork, a bugle-horn, or, stringed, sa. *Vigilo et spero.* *Pl.* 48, *cr.* 12.
DAUNT, a bugle-horn, or, strung. *Pl.* 48, *cr.* 12.
DAUNT, Eng., a cockatrice, displayed, ppr. *Pl.* 102, *cr.* 15.
DAUNTSEY, out of a ducal coronet; in dexter hand a fleur-de-lis. *Pl.* 120, *cr.* 4.
DAUVERGEUE, Eng., a horse's head, sa., bridled, or. *Pl.* 92, *cr.* 1.
DAVALL, or DAVELL, Yorks., a terrestrial globe, ppr. *Pl.* 14, *cr.* 1.
DAVELL, Yorks., a dexter hand, apaumée, charged with an eye, ppr. *Pl.* 99, *cr.* 13.
DAVENANT, Ess., a (sinister) arm, embowed, in hand a chaplet of wheat, or. *Pl.* 89, *cr.* 4.
DAVENPORT, a friar's head, in profile, ppr., hooded, sa., (round neck a rope, of the first.) *Pl.* 51, *cr.* 4.
DAVENPORT, a Saracen's head, in profile, ppr., wreathed, (and round neck a rope.) *Pl.* 36, *cr.* 3.
DAVERNETT, a woodpecker, close, ppr. *Pl.* 52, *cr.* 12.
DAVERPORT, a lion, passant, erm., ducally crowned, or, resting dexter on an escutcheon, gold. *Pl.* 48, *cr.* 8, (crown, *pl.* 128, *fig.* 3; escutcheon, *pl.* 42, *cr.* 4.)
DAVERS, Eng., a demi-savage, in dexter a club, in sinister a serpent, nowed, ppr. *Pl.* 92, *cr.* 10.
DAVERS, a talbot, passant, ar. *Pl.* 120, *cr.* 8.
DAVERS, Suff., a jay, ppr., in beak an annulet, or. *Pl.* 33, *cr.* 11.
DAVEY, an ostrich's head, in mouth a horse-shoe, between two feathers. *Pl.* 99, *cr.* 12.
DAVID, Wel., a lion's head, erased, quarterly, ar. and sa. *Pl.* 81, *cr.* 4.
DAVID, a lamb, passant, ar., (in mouth a sprig, vert, fructed, gu.) *Pl.* 116, *cr.* 1, (without charge.)
DAVIDGE, Somers., a demi-lion, ar., gorged with a collar, gu., charged with three lions, passant, of the same. *Pl.* 18, *cr.* 13, (lion, *pl.* 48, *cr.* 8.)
DAVIDSON, Sco., a falcon's head, couped, ppr. *Viget in cinere virtus.* *Pl.* 99, *cr.* 10, (without wings.)
DAVIDSON, Eng., out of a mural coronet, az., a lion's head, gu. *Pl.* 45, *cr.* 9.
DAVIDSON, Sco., a pheon. *Pl.* 26, *cr.* 12.
DAVIDSON, Sco., in dexter hand a human heart, ppr. *Sapienter si sincere.* *Pl.* 59, *cr.* 12.
DAVIE, Bart., Devons., a holy lamb, ppr. *Auspice Christo.* *Pl.* 48, *cr.* 13.
DAVIE, on a chapeau, vert, turned up, erm., a boar, ar., armed and crined, or, (gorged with a bough, ppr.) *Pl.* 22, *cr.* 8.
DAVIE, Sco., an eagle's head, couped, ppr. *Sedulitate.* *Pl.* 100, *cr.* 10.
DAVIE, Devons. and Sco., a paschal lamb, ar., bearing banner, gu., charged with a cross. *Auspice Christo.* *Pl.* 48, *cr.* 13.

DAVIES, JOHN, Esq., of Marrington Hall, Salop, a lion's head, couped, quarterly, ar. and sa. *Heb ddûn heb ddym ddûwadygan. Pl.* 126, *cr.* 1.

DAVIES, DAVID-ARTHUR-SAUNDERS, Esq., of Pentre, Pembroke: 1. For *Davies*, a wolf, salient, ar. *Pl.* 126, *cr.* 13. 2. For *Saunders*, a demi-bull, salient, couped at loins, ar. *Solem ferre possum. Pl.* 63, *cr.* 6.

DAVIES, Lond., on a cap, sa., turned up, or, a demi-lion, rampant, gold. *Pl.* 46, *cr.* 8.

DAVIES, Salop, on a mount, vert, a goat, (lodged,) ar., against a tree, ppr. *Pl.* 70, *cr.* 3, (mount, *pl.* 11, *cr.* 14.)

DAVIES, in lion's paw, erased, a mullet of five points. *Pl.* 97, *cr.* 10, (mullet, *pl.* 141.)

DAVIES, Iri., a nag's head, ar., charged with a caltrap, sa. *Pl.* 46, *cr.* 4.

DAVIES, JAMES, Esq., of Moor Court, Heref., a griffin, segreant, or. *Pl.* 67, *cr.* 13.

DAVIES, a mullet of (five) points, pierced, between wings. *Pl.* 1, *cr.* 15.

DAVIES, Somers., a fawn, couchant, ppr. *Pl.* 1, *cr.* 14, (without hive.)

DAVIES, Lond., a lion, rampant. *Nisi dominus frustra. Pl.* 67, *cr.* 5.

DAVIES, Lond. and Salop, two lions' gambs, erased, the dexter ermines, sinister, erm., holding a buckle, or. *Pl.* 42, *cr.* 3, (buckle, *pl.* 73, *cr.* 10.)

DAVIES, Hants, a dove, wings addorsed, ar., in mouth a sprig, vert, bearing three roses, or. *Pl.* 79, *cr.* 8, (without globe.)

DAVIES, Kent, a boar's head, couped and erect, or. *Pl.* 48, *cr.* 2.

DAVIES, Kent, a demi-lion, rampant, sa. *Pl.* 67, *cr.* 10.

DAVIES, Suss., on a ducal coronet, or, a boar's head, couped, sa. *Pl.* 102, *cr.* 14.

DAVIES, on a chapeau, sa., turned up, or, a demi-lion, rampant, gold, in dexter a mullet. *Pl.* 89, *cr.* 10, (chapeau, *same plate, cr.* 7.)

DAVIES-BOWEN, DAVID-THOMAS, Esq., of Maesy-Crygie, Carmarthen; and Glanrhocca, Cardigan; an eagle, displayed. *Virtus sine dote. Pl.* 48, *cr.* 11.

DAVIS, Eng., a lion's head, erased, or, ducally crowned, gu. *Pl.* 90, *cr.* 4, (without charge.)

DAVIS, Kent, a wolf, passant, erm. *Pl.* 46, *cr.* 6.

DAVIS, Hants, an arm, in armour, embowed, in hand a scimitar, all ppr. *Pl.* 81, *cr.* 11.

DAVIS, Lond. and Westm., a demi-wolf, rampant, (regardant, erased, az.,) ducally gorged and chained, or, in paws a mullet of six points, ar. *Pl.* 65, *cr.* 4.

DAVIS, Somers., two arms, embowed, (vested, erm., cuffed, az.,) in hands, ppr., a mound, or. *Pl.* 6, *cr.* 8, (mound, *pl.* 37, *cr.* 3.)

DAVIS, Iri., an arm, from shoulder, embowed, in hand a club, ppr. *Pl.* 123, *cr.* 10.

DAVIS, a lion, rampant. *Pl.* 67, *cr.* 5.

DAVIS, Heref., out of a mural coronet, a demi-wolf, salient, ar., holding a cinquefoil, gu.

DAVIS, a lamb, couchant.

DAVIS, Lond., a lion's head, erased, ppr. *Ne tentes, aut perfice. Pl.* 81, *cr.* 4.

DAVIS, a leopard's head, (erased,) ppr. *Pl.* 92, *cr.* 13.

DAVIS, three arrows, one in pale, two in saltier, ppr. *Pl.* 43, *cr.* 14.

DAVIS, a boar's head, erased, ppr. *Pl.* 16, *cr.* 11.

DAVISON, a dove, issuing, wings addorsed, in beak three wheat-ears.

DAVISON, out of an earl's coronet, or, a dove, rising, ar., in mouth a wheat-stalk, bladed and eared, all ppr. *Pl.* 79, *cr.* 8, (coronet, *pl.* 127, *fig.* 8.)

DAVISON, Durh., out of a crown vallery, or, a dove, wings addorsed, in mouth three wheatears. *Pl.* 79, *cr.* 8, (crown, *pl.* 2, *cr.* 8.)

DAVISON, out of a mural coronet, a stag's head, affrontée, ppr.. *Pl.* 29, *cr.* 7, (crown, *pl.* 128, *fig.* 8.)

DAVISON, a stag's head, couped, between wings, or. *Pl.* 91, *cr.* 14, (wings, *pl.* 1, *cr.* 15.)

DAVISON, Salop, an eagle, displayed, ar., collared, gu., in beak an ear of wheat, or. *Pl.* 48, *cr.* 11.

DAVISS, Eng., out of a ducal coronet, in hand a sword, waved, in pale, ppr. *Pl.* 65, *cr.* 10.

DAVISS, out of a ducal coronet, in hand a sword, wavy, in pale. *Pl.* 65, *cr.* 10.

DAVORON, a hind, ppr. *Pl.* 20, *cr.* 14.

DAVY, Devons., a paschal lamb, (regardant,) ar., holding a pennon, of the last, staff, or. *Pl.* 48, *cr.* 13.

DAVY, Devons., Norf., and Suff., out of a ducal coronet, or, an elephant's head, sa., armed, ar. *Pl.* 93, *cr.* 13.

DAVY, an elephant's head, ppr. *Pl.* 35, *cr.* 13.

DAVY, Devons., a bird, wings addorsed, ppr., (in beak a sprig, vert, thereon three roses, or.) *Pl.* 79, *cr.* 8, (without globe.)

DAVY, Suss., Suff., and Wilts., a lion, sejant, ar., supporting a column, or. *Pl.* 22, *cr.* 13, (column, *pl.* 33, *cr.* 1.)

DAVY, Devons., a dove and olive-branch, ppr. *Pl.* 48, *cr.* 15.

DAVY, JOHN, Esq., of Ingoldsthorpe, Norf., out of a ducal coronet, or, an elephant's head, sa., armed, ar., (in front of coronet, a ring, thereto a line and ring, gold, turned over trunk.) *Pl.* 93, *cr.* 13.

DAVY, Sco., a talbot's head, erased, or, ducally crowned. *Pl.* 25, *cr.* 10.

DAVY, Sco., a talbot's head, erased, ar., crowned, (collared,) and eared, or. *Pl.* 25, *cr.* 10.

DAVYE, an elephant's head, ppr., charged on shoulder with a mullet, sa. *Pl.* 35, *cr.* 13, (mullet, *pl.* 141.)

DAVYS, an ostrich, in mouth a horse-shoe, ppr. *Pl.* 16, *cr.* 2.

DAW, Eng., an eagle, wings expanded, looking at the sun, ppr. *Pl.* 126, *cr.* 7, (sun, *pl.* 43, *cr.* 5.)

DAWBENCY, Worc., a holly-tree, vert, fructed, gu. *Pl.* 124, *cr.* 10.

DAWBENEY, and DAWBNEY, a cross pattée, ar., within an orle of seven mullets, or. *Pl.* 33, *cr.* 10.

DAWBENEY, Eng., a leopard's face, or, jessant-de-lis, gu. *Pl.* 123, *cr.* 9.

DAWBENEY, Eng., two lions' paws, erased, holding up a crescent, or. *Pl.* 62, *cr.* 3.

DAWBENEY, Eng,, an elephant's head, erased, per fess, or and vert. *Pl.* 68, *cr.* 4.

DAWBIN, a Triton, in sinister a trident, ppr. *Pl.* 35, *cr.* 10.

DAWE, Somers., out of a ducal coronet, a dexter arm, in hand a swan's head and neck, erased, all ppr. *Pl.* 65, *cr.* 12.

DAWE, Dors., in lion's gamb, erased and erect, ar., a fleur-de-lis, or. *Pl.* 60, *cr.* 14, (fleur-de-lis, *pl.* 68, *cr.* 12.)

DAWES, Lond., Salop, Suff., Staffs., and Leic., on point of a halberd, erect, or, a wyvern, tail nowed, sans legs, sa., bezantée, or, vulned, gu. *Pl.* 25, *cr.* 4.

DAWES, Middx., a dexter arm, embowed, vested, gu., cuffed, ar., in hand, ppr., an oak-slip, vert, fructed with three acorns, or. *Pl.* 120, *cr.* 1, (oak, *pl.* 69, *cr.* 12.)

DAWES, Staffs. and Lanc., a wyvern, sa., bezantée, in dexter a battle-axe, erect, az. *En Dieu est tout. Pl.* 63, *cr.* 13, (axe, *pl.* 14, *cr.* 8.)

DAWKER, out of a palisado coronet, an arm, embowed, vested, in hand a battle-axe, in fess, ppr. *Pl.* 128, *cr.* 1, (axe, *pl.* 73, *cr.* 7.)

DAWKINS, a dexter arm, couped at shoulder, ppr., in hand a battle-axe, of the last, in bend, on blade a rose, gu. *Pl.* 118, *cr.* 4, (axe, *pl.* 73, *cr.* 7.)

DAWN, and DAWNE, a crane, in mouth an oak-branch, ppr. *Pl.* 46, *cr.* 9.

DAWNAY, Baron. *See* DOWNE, Viscount.

DAWNEY, and DAWNY, Eng., a (dexter) wing, or. *Pl.* 39, *cr.* 10.

DAWNSEY, a nag's head, couped, az., bezantée, bridled, or. *Pl.* 92, *cr.* 1.

DAWS, Surr., on a demi-battle-axe, handled, or, headed, ar., a dragon, sans legs, wings addorsed, bezantée. *Pl.* 25, *cr.* 4.

DAWSON, Linc., an arm, in armour, embowed, ppr., garnished, or, in gauntlet a battle-axe, gold. *Pl.* 121, *cr.* 14.

DAWSON, CHARLES, Esq., of Edwardston Hall, Suff., a tabby cat's head, gardant, erased, in mouth a rat, ppr. *Vitæ via virtus. Pl.* 108, *cr.* 4.

DAWSON, the Right Honourable GEORGE-ROBERT, of Castle Dawson, co. Londonderry, an etoile of six points, or. *Toujours propice. Pl.* 63, *cr.* 9.

DAWSON, Earl of Portarlington, and Viscount Cremorne. *See those titles.*

DAWSON, a cat's head, erased, affrontée, in mouth a mouse. *Pl.* 108, *cr.* 1.

DAWSON, Yorks., on a mount, vert, a hound, sa. *Pl.* 117, *cr.* 8.

DAWSON, Yorks. and Lanc., a leopard's head, erased, gardant. *Pl.* 56, *cr.* 7.

DAWSON, Lond., an etoile, or. *Pl.* 63, *cr.* 9.

DAWSON, Eng., a hand, erect, charged with an eye, ppr. *Pl.* 99, *cr.* 13.

DAWSON, Cumb., a demi-talbot, erm., eared, az., holding an arrow, or, flighted and pointed, ar. *Pl.* 97, *cr.* 9.

DAWSON, Northumb., a talbot, passant, ppr. *Vitæ via virtus. Pl.* 120, *cr.* 8.

DAWTREY, Suss., a unicorn, ar. *Pl.* 106, *cr.* 3.

DAX, between horns of a crescent, a cross pattée. *Pl.* 37, *cr.* 10.

DAY, the Rev. EDWARD, of Beaufort, co. Kerry, two hands clasping each other, couped at wrist, conjoined to a pair of wings, ppr. *Sic itur ad astra. Pl.* 14, *cr.* 9.

DAY, Cambs., Suss., Berks., and Bucks., two hands conjoined, ppr., affixed to two wings, expanded, the dexter, or, sinister, az., each charged with a mullet, counterchanged. *Pl.* 14, *cr.* 9, (mullet, *pl.* 141.)

DAY, Berks., Suss., Cambs., Bucks., and Norf., two wings, expanded, or and az. *Pl.* 39, *cr.* 12.

DAY, a demi-cockatrice, wings expanded. *Pl.* 63, *cr.* 15.

DAY, a greyhound's head, (erased,) ar., collared, ringed, and lined, gu., the end nowed. *Pl.* 43, *cr.* 11.

DAYRELL, Bucks., a goat's head, ar. *Pl.* 105, *cr.* 14.

DAYRELL, Bucks., a goat's head, erased, ar., attired, or. *Pl.* 29, *cr.* 13.

DAYRELL, EDMUND-FRANCIS, Esq., of Lillingston Dayrell, Bucks., a goat's head, erased, ppr. *Securè vivere mors est. Pl.* 29, *cr.* 13.

DAYRELL, the Rev. THOMAS, Esq., of Shudy Camps Park, Cambs., out of a ducal coronet, a goat's head, erased, ppr. *Virtus mille scuta. Pl.* 72, *cr.* 2.

DAYROLLES, Surr., a mullet of six points, or. *Pl.* 21, *cr.* 6.

DEA, an arm, couped below wrist, in fess, vested, gu., cuff dancettée, ar., in hand, ppr., a broken sword, of the last, hilt and pommel, or. *Pl.* 22, *cr.* 6, (in fess, *pl.* 46, *cr.* 12.)

DEACLE, out of a mural coronet, ar., an eagle, or, in beak a rose, gu. *Pl.* 7, *cr.* 11, (coronet, *pl.* 128, *fig.* 18; rose, *pl.* 117, *cr.* 10.)

DEACON, Eng., a nag's head, ar. *Pl.* 81, *cr.* 6.

DEACON, Eng., a nag's head, per fess, or and gu. *In utroque paratus. Pl.* 81, *cr.* 6.

DEACON, a nag's head, per fess, erased, or and az. *Pl.* 81, *cr.* 6.

DEACONS, Beds., Bucks., and Warw., a demi-eagle, displayed, ar., winged, sa. *Pl.* 22, *cr.* 11.

DEACONS, Bucks., Beds., and Warw., an eagle's head, erased, ar., between wings, sa. *Pl.* 81, *cr.* 10.

DE AGUILAR, a lion, rampant, charged with a plate. *Pl.* 67, *cr.* 5.

DEAKEN, or DEAKIN, Eng., out of a mural coronet, gu., a leopard's head, or, ducally gorged, gold. *Pl.* 46, *cr.* 11.

DEALBENEY, an ox-yoke, in bend, sa. *Pl.* 35, *cr.* 11.

DEALE, Kent, within a snake, coiled up, ppr., a dove, ar., beaked and legged, gu. *Pl.* 92, *cr.* 6.

DEALTRY, out of a cloud, a hand holding a stag by the horns. *Pl.* 46, *cr.* 10.

DEALTRY, a fleur-de-lis, ar. *Pl.* 68, *cr.* 12.

DEALTRY, an escallop, erect. *Pl.* 117, *cr.* 4.

DEAN, Lond., a griffin's head, erased, ar. *Pl.* 48, *cr.* 6.

DEAN, Eng., a winged pillar, ppr. *Pl.* 33, *cr.* 12.

DEANE, Baron Muskerry. *See* MUSKERRY.

DEANE, a demi-lion, rampant, or, in dexter a crescent, gu. *Pl.* 89, *cr.* 10, (crescent, *pl.* 18, *cr.* 14.)

DEANE, Iri., a lion's gamb, erased, gu. *Pl.* 126, *cr.* 9.

DEANE, Ess. and Lanc., a bear's head, couped, ar., muzzled, or. *Pl.* 111, *cr.* 4.

DEANE, or DEAN, Eng., in hand, couped, in fess, ppr., a fleur-de-lis, or. *Pl.* 46, *cr.* 12.

DEANE, or DANE, Hants, a griffin's head, erased, or. *Pl.* 48, *cr.* 6.

DEANE, (on a mount, vert,) a tortoise, or. *Pl.* 12, *cr.* 13.

DE ANGOLESME, Eng., a boat's sail affixed to a mast, ppr. *Pl.* 22, *cr.* 12.

DEANS, Eng. and Sco., a sword, in pale, ppr., ensigned on top with a cross pattée. *Arte vel marte. Pl.* 56, *cr.* 1.

DEANS, Sco., a sword, in pale, point upward, ppr., hilt and pommel, or. *Pl.* 105, *cr.* 1.

DEAR, and DEARE, Eng., a horse at full speed, saddled and bridled. *Pl.* 8, *cr.* 2.

DEAR, a deer's head, ppr. *Pl.* 91, *cr.* 14.

DEAR, a deer's head, erased, ppr. *Pl.* 66, *cr.* 9.

DEARDEN, Lanc., a stag, trippant, (regardant.) *Dum spiro spero. Pl.* 68, *cr.* 2.

DEARMAN, out of a ducal coronet, or, five cinquefoils, gu., stalked and leaved, ppr.

DEARDS, a Catherine-wheel, ducally-crowned, or. *Pl.* 1, *cr.* 7, (coronet, *same plate, cr.* 5.)

DEAS, Sco., on a daisy, a bee feeding, ppr. *Industria. Pl.* 109, *cr.* 6.

DEASE, Iri., out of a ducal coronet, a demi-ostrich, wings addorsed, ppr. *Pl.* 29, *cr.* 9.

DEASIE, Sco., a hawk's head, erased, ppr. *Pl.* 34, *cr.* 11.

DEATH, Kent, a griffin's head, or, in beak a trefoil, vert. *Pl.* 38, *cr.* 3, (trefoil, *pl.* 141.)

DEAVES, Eng., in lion's paw, erased, gu., a dagger, or. *Pl.* 56, *cr.* 3.

DEBENHAM, Eng., a dexter hand, apaumée, ppr., in a maunch, or, cuffed, gu. *Pl.* 8, *cr.* 11.

DE BATHE, Bart., Iri., a lion, rampant, ar., supporting in paws a dagger, of the first, hilt and pommel, or. *Nec parvis sisto. Pl.* 125, *cr.* 2, (dagger, *pl.* 73, *cr.* 9.)

DE BEAUVOIR, Bart., Iri.: 1. A griffin's head and neck, wings addorsed, ar., (in beak a branch of woodbine, ppr.) *Pl.* 18, *cr.* 6. 2. An eagle, displayed, vert. *Conduct is Fate. Pl.* 48, *cr.* 11.

DE BELLOMONT, Eng., a cross moline, lozenge-pierced, gu. *Pl.* 91, *cr.* 10.

DE BEST, Lond., on a mural coronet, or, a fleur-de-lis, party, per pale, of the first and az., between two laurel-branches, vert. *Pl.* 21, *cr.* 13, (coronet, *pl.* 141.)

DE BETUM, Eng., an elephant, ppr. *Pl.* 56, *cr.* 14.

DE BLAQUIERE, Baron, Iri., a garb, or. *Tiens à la verité. Pl.* 48, *cr.* 10.

DE BLOIS, Eng., a lion, rampant, gardant, gu. *Pl.* 92, *cr.* 7.

DEBNAM, a bear, transfixed by a broken spear, ppr. *Pl.* 82, *cr.* 14.

DE BOHUN, Eng., a wolf, current, ppr. *Pl.* 111, *cr.* 1.

DE BOUCHE, Eng., a cloud, ppr. *Pl.* 124, *cr.* 12.

DE BOYS, Ess. a wyvern, gu. *Pl.* 63, *cr.* 13.

DE BOYS, Ess., a leg, in armour, embowed, couped, ar. and sa., spur and leather, or. *Pl.* 81, *cr.* 5.

DEBRAM, a wheel, between wings. *Pl.* 2, *cr.* 3, (wheel, *pl.* 32, *cr.* 15.)

DE BRETEVILLE, Eng., a staff, raguly, in pale, sa., surmounted by an eagle, displayed, gu. *Pl.* 8, *cr.* 1.

DE BREVILL, Eng., in hand a sheaf of arrows, ppr. *Pl.* 56, *cr.* 4.

DE BURG, a bull's head, between wings. *Pl.* 60, *cr.* 9.

DE BRUGES, Eng., a cross Calvary, on three grieces, gu. *Pl.* 49, *cr.* 2.

DE BURGH, Middx., an arm, in armour, embowed, couped at shoulder, gauntlet, apaumée, ppr., stringed as a bugle-horn, az., tassels, gold. *Nec parvis sisto. Pl.* 97, *cr.* 1.

DE BURGH, Eng., a water-bouget, az. *Pl.* 14, *cr.* 12.

DE BURGO, Bart., Iri., a mountain-cat, sejant, gardant, ppr., (collared and chained, or.) *Ung roy, ung foy, ung loy. Pl.* 24, *cr.* 6.

DE BURGO, Marquess Clanricarde. See CLANRICARDE.

DE CARDONNEL, Eng., a dove, az. *L'esperance me console. Pl.* 66, *cr.* 12.

DE CARTERET, Eng., a reindeer's head, cabossed. *Pl.* 114, *cr.* 7.

DE CHANDEW, a nest of young birds, ppr. *Pl.* 56, *cr.* 5.

DECIES, Baron, Iri., (Beresford,) a dragon's head, erased, az., transfixed in neck by a broken tilting-spear, or, point, ar., (thrust through upper jaw.) *Nil nisi cruce. Pl.* 121, *cr.* 9.

DECKER, Eng., a mountain-cat, current, regardant, ppr. *Pl.* 114, *cr.* 12.

DE CLARE, Eng., the standard of St George, ppr. *Pl.* 8, *cr.* 3.

DE CLIFFORD, Baron, a demi-Indian goat, ar., armed, eared, and ducally gorged, gu., charged on body with three annulets, in pale, of the last. *Pl.* 90, *cr.* 12.

DE CLINTON, Eng., on a mount, vert, a stag, feeding, ppr. *Pl.* 37, *cr.* 8.

DE COSTA, Eng., a plume of ostrich-feathers, or. *Pl.* 12, *cr.* 9.

DE COURCY, Baron Kingsale. See KINGSALE.

DE COURCY, Eng., a demi-leopard, or, spotted, gu. *Pl.* 12, *cr.* 14.

DE COURCY, Iri., a horse's head, (issuing,) gu. *Pl.* 81, *cr.* 6.

DE COWCY, Eng., a horse's head, couped, ar., bridled, gu. *Pl.* 92, *cr.* 1.

DE CRESPIGNY, Bart., Surr., on a chapeau, gu., turned up, erm., a cubit arm, erect, in hand, a broadsword, ppr. *Mens sibi conscia recti. Pl.* 21, *cr.* 10, (chapeau, *same plate.*)

DE DEN, and DE DENA, in dexter hand, in fess, couped, a sword, in pale, on point a garland, all ppr. *Pl.* 56, *cr.* 6.

DE DREUX, a ram's head, erased, ar., horned, or. *Pl.* 1, *cr.* 12.

DEE, Surr., a lion, sejant, gardant, or, in dexter a cross formée, fitched, az., on cross a label, with motto– *Hic labor*—sinister, on a pyramid, ar., on it a label with this motto—*Hoc opus. Pl.* 56, *cr.* 12.

DEEDES, WILLIAM, Esq., of Sandling Park, Kent, an eagle's head, erased, per fess, nebulée, gu. and ar., between wings, sa. *Facta, non verba. Pl.* 81, *cr.* 10.

DEEDES, an eagle's head, erased, per fess, nebulée, gu. and ar., between wings, sa. *Pl.* 81, *cr.* 10.

DEERHAM, Norf., a bear, sejant, rampant, sa., muzzled, lined, and ringed, or. *Pl.* 1, *cr.* 1.

DEERING, Kent, in a ducal coronet, or, (a mount, vert,) thereon a horse, passant, sa. *Pl.* 76, *cr.* 8.

DEERING, out of a ducal coronet, az., a dragon's head, or. *Pl.* 59, *cr.* 14.

DEEVES, Eng., out of a ducal coronet, or, a unicorn's head, gu., armed and crined, or. *Pl.* 45, *cr.* 14.

DE FERRARS, on a chapeau, an eagle, preying on a child, swaddled, all ppr. *Pl.* 121, *cr.* 6.
DE FERRERS, Eng., a pheon, az. *Pl.* 26, *cr.* 12.
DE FORTIBUS, Eng., an escarbuncle, or. *Pl.* 51, *cr.* 10.
DE FREYNE, Baron, (Trench,) a dolphin, naiant, ppr. *Malo mori quam fœdari. Pl.* 48, *cr.* 9.
DE GAUNT, Eng., a cross pattée, fitched, sa. *Pl.* 27, *cr.* 14.
DEGGE, Derbs. and Staffs., on a ducal coronet, or, a falcon, close, ar., jessed and belled, of the last. *Pl.* 41, *cr.* 10.
DE GINKELL. See ATHLONE, Earl.
DEGON, Eng., on a ducal coronet, a dolphin, haurient. *Pl.* 94, *cr.* 14, (dolphin, *pl.* 14, *cr.* 10.)
DEGON, Eng., a portcullis, az. *Pl.* 51, *cr.* 12.
DE GRAY, Eng., a dart and palm-branch, in saltier, ppr. *Pl.* 50, *cr.* 11.
DE GREY, Baron Walsingham. See WALSINGHAM.
DE GREY, Earl, Baron Lucas and Grantham, (De Grey :) 1. On a chapeau, gu., turned up, erm., a cockatrice, wings erect, or. *Pl.* 103, *cr.* 9. 2. Out of a ducal coronet, or, a mount, vert, thereon a stag at gaze, gold. *Qualis ab incepto. Pl.* 19, *cr.* 14.
DEHANEY, Iri., a demi-bear, rampant, ppr. *Pl.* 104, *cr.* 10.
DE HARCLA, Eng., a fret, az. *Pl.* 82, *cr.* 7.
DE HATFIELD, Eng., on stump of tree, sprouting branches, an eagle, wings addorsed and inverted, all ppr. *Pl.* 1, *cr.* 11.
DEINSTON, Sco., a tree, ppr., fructed, gu. *Pl.* 16, *cr.* 8.
DEKENER, Middx., out of a tower, vert, a tiger's head, ppr., collared, or. *Pl.* 51, *cr.* 11.
DELABER, Eng., a greyhound, sejant, sa. *Pl.* 66, *cr.* 15.
DE LA CHAMBRE, Suss., an ass's head (erased,) ar. *Pl.* 91, *cr.* 7.
DE LA CHEROIS, DANIEL, Esq., of Donaghadee, co. Down, an anchor, erect, ppr. *Fac et spera. Pl.* 25, *cr.* 15.
DELADOWNE, an arm, vested, az., cuffed, or, in hand, ppr., a cup, of the first, flames issuing, ppr. *Pl.* 39, *cr.* 1, (cup, *pl.* 40, *cr.* 9.)
DELAFELD, and DELAFIELD, Eng., an ox's foot, couped, sa. *Pl.* 91, *cr.* 3.
DELAFIELD, Eng., a cross pattée, gu., between wings, or. *Pl.* 29, *cr.* 14.
DELAFIELD, Middx., a dove, wings expanded, (in mouth an olive-branch,) all ppr. *Insignia fortunæ paria—and—Fest. Pl.* 27, *cr.* 5.
DE LA FONS, Eng., a wolf, sejant, or. *Pl.* 110, *cr.* 4.
DE LA FOSSE, a cock, or. *Pl.* 67, *cr.* 14.
DE LA FOUNTAINE, Ess., (on a mount, vert,) a griffin, sejant, or, in dexter an Eastern crown, ar. *Pl.* 56, *cr.* 10, (crown, *pl.* 128, *fig.* 2.)
DELAHAY, on a torteau, vert, a lion's head, erased, ar., collared, az. *Pl.* 50, *cr.* 10.
DELAHEY, Heref., a wolf's head. *Pl.* 14, *cr.* 6.
DELAHILL, Eng., a caltrap, az. *Pl.* 7, *cr.* 4.
DELAITE, a cock, or. *Pl.* 67, *cr.* 14.
DELALAUD, Eng., two dexter hands conjoined, supporting a human heart, ppr. *Pl.* 43, *cr.* 15.

DELALAUD, Eng., a leopard's head, issuing from a tower, ppr. *Pl.* 105, *cr.* 10.
DELALEIGH, out of a crescent, or, a cross crosslet, fitched, sa. *Pl.* 43, *cr.* 3.
DELALYND, Eng., in the sea, ppr., an anchor. *Pl.* 62, *cr.* 10.
DELALYND, and DELALYNDE, Eng., an escallop, gu., between eagles' wings, or. *Pl.* 62, *cr.* 4.
DELAMAINE, Eng., a man in military uniform, az., holding a flag in bend, gu. *Pl.* 2, *cr.* 12.
DELAMARE, Eng., an eel, naiant, ppr. *Pl.* 25, *cr.* 13.
DELAMARE, Eng., a ship under sail, in the sea, ppr. *Pl.* 109, *cr.* 8.
DELAMAYNE, same crest.
DELAMERE, Baron, (Cholmondeley,) a demi-griffin, segreant, sa., beaked, winged, and membered, or, (ducally gorged and chained, between claws a helmet, ppr., garnished, or.) *Cassis tutissima virtus. Pl.* 19, *cr.* 15.
DELAMERE, Chesh., same crest.
DELAMERE, a pheasant, ppr. *Pl.* 82, *cr.* 12.
DELAMOTE, and DELAMOTTE, Eng., an ostrich's head, in mouth a horse's shoe, between two feathers, ppr. *Pl.* 99, *cr.* 2.
DELAMOTE, a lion, passant, gardant, (collared,) vair. *Pl.* 120, *cr.* 5.
DELANCEY, and DELANCY, Eng., a demi-leopard, gardant, supporting an anchor, ppr. *Pl.* 1, *cr.* 10.
DELANCEY, a sinister arm, in armour, embowed, in hand a standard, with flag. *Pl.* 6, *cr.* 5.
DELAND, Eng., a leopard's head, issuing from a tower, ppr. *Pl.* 105, *cr.* 10.
DELANE, Eng., an eagle, displayed, or, charged with a mullet, sa. *Pl.* 44, *cr.* 14.
DELANEY, and DELANY, Eng., an antelope, trippant, ppr. *Pl.* 63, *cr.* 10.
DELANEY, and DELANY, between wings, a swan, statant, ppr. *Pl.* 122, *cr.* 13, (wings, *pl.* 1, *cr.* 15.)
DELANEY, Iri., a buffalo's head, erased, gu. *Pl.* 57, *cr.* 7.
DELAP, Surr., two arms, embowed, dexter, ppr., in hand, a rose, gu., sinister in armour, and holding a sword, ppr., hilt and pommel, or. *Merito. Pl.* 93, *cr.* 14, (rose, *pl.* 118, *cr.* 9.)
DELAP, Eng., a rose-branch, with three roses, ppr. *Pl.* 23, *cr.* 2.
DELAP, Lond. and Surr., a cubit arm, in armour, per pale, embattled, or and az., hand grasping a sword, ppr., hilt and pommel, gold. *Pl.* 125, *cr.* 5.
DELAPINDE, in lion's gamb, erased, ar., three (pines,) or, leaved, vert. *Pl.* 86, *cr.* 15.
DELAPIPE, Eng., three organ pipes, or, enfiled with a garland of laurel, vert. *Pl.* 50, *cr.* 12.
DELAPLAUNCH, Eng., a cross moline, erm. *Pl.* 89, *cr.* 8.
DELAPLAUNCH, Eng., a hunting-horn, sans strings, sa., garnished, or. *Pl.* 89, *cr.* 3.
DE LA POER-BERESFORD. See WATERFORD, Marquess; and DECIES, Baron.
DELAPOOL, DELAPOOLE, and DE LA POOLE, Eng., a crosier, gu. *Pl.* 7, *cr.* 15.
DELAPOOLE, Eng., on a chapeau, a leopard, statant, ppr. *Pl.* 110, *cr.* 8.
DE LA RIVER, and DELARIVER, Yorks., in lion's paw a broken spear, ppr. *Pl.* 85, *cr.* 15.

K

DE LA RIVER, and DELARIVER, a shepherd's flute, or. *Pl.* 12, *cr.* 1.
DELAROUS, an armed arm, in hand a sword, ppr. *Pl.* 2, *cr.* 8.
DELATUNE, Hants., an antelope, passant, or. *Pl.* 63, *cr.* 10.
DELAUNE, the lion of St Mark, sejant, wings elevated, round head a glory, all ppr., dexter on the Gospel, close, or, covered, gu., garnished, of the second. *Pl.* 88, *cr.* 14, (Bible, *pl.* 117, *cr.* 7.)
DE LA VACH, and DELAVACHE, Eng., a cow's tail, ppr. *Pl.* 3, *cr.* 1.
DELAVACHE, Eng., an ox-yoke, in pale, sa. *Pl.* 35, *cr.* 11.
DELAVAL, Northumb., out of a ducal coronet, or, a goat's head, ar., attired, gold. *Dieu me conduise.* *Pl.* 72, *cr.* 2.
DELAVAL, a salamander in flames, ppr. *Pl.* 20, *cr.* 15.
DELAVALL, Northumb., a ram's head, erased, ar., attired, or. *Pl.* 1, *cr.* 12.
DELAVERE, a stag, salient, ppr. *Pl.* 65, *cr.* 14.
DELAVERE, a Catherine wheel, (dropping blood,) all gu. *Pl.* 1, *cr.* 7.
DELAWAR, a bird's head, couped, ar., beaked, gu. *Pl.* 100, *cr.* 10.
DELAWARR, Earl and Baron, Viscount Cantalupe, (West,) out of a ducal coronet, or, a griffin's head, az., beaked and eared, gold. *Jour de ma vie!* *Pl.* 54, *cr.* 14.
DELECHAMBER, Suss., an ass's head, (erased,) ar. *Pl.* 91, *cr.* 7.
DELEGH, out of a crescent, or, a cross crosslet, fitched, sa. *Pl.* 43, *cr.* 3.
DELEVAL, Eng., on a chapeau, a lion's head, erased, ducally crowned, all ppr. *Pl.* 34, *cr.* 10.
DELGARNO, Eng., a sea-lion, statant, in dexter a (cross-moline.) *Pl.* 59, *cr.* 2.
DELILERS, Lond., a demi-lion, rampant, az., ducally crowned, gu. *Pl.* 61, *cr.* 4, (without branch.)
DELINE, Eng., a rock, ppr. *Esse quam videri.* *Pl.* 73, *cr.* 12.
DE LISLE and DUDLEY, Baron, (Sydney:) 1. For *Sidney*, a porcupine, statant, az., quills, (collar and chain, or.) *Quo fata vocant.* *Pl.* 55, *cr.* 10. 2. For *Shelley*, a griffin's head, erased, ar., ducally gorged, or. *Pl.* 42, *cr.* 9, (without branch.)
DE LISLE, a lion, passant, gardant. *Pl.* 120, *cr.* 5.
DELL, Eng., issuing from a cloud, in hand, erect, a garb. *Pl.* 67, *cr.* 12.
DELLABER, Eng., a tower, ppr., flagged, ar., (charged with a saltier, sa.) *Pl.* 8, *cr.* 13.
DELLABER, a greyhound, sejant, sa. *Pl.* 66, *cr.* 15.
DELLABERE, Glouc., out of a ducal coronet, or, a plume of feathers, party, per pale, ar. and az. *Pl.* 44, *cr.* 12.
DELLEE, Eng., on a mount, a dove, ppr. *Pl.* 104, *cr.* 8.
DELLYNE, Eng., on a ducal coronet, a Cornish chough, ppr. *Pl.* 8, *cr.* 5.
DELMAR, a lion, sejant, gu., collared, dancettée, dexter resting on a fleur-de-lis. *Pl.* 126, *cr.* 15, (fleur-de-lis, *pl.* 4, *cr.* 14.)
DELME, and DELMIE, a lion, passant, gu., against an anchor, sa. *Pl.* 48, *cr.* 8, (anchor, *pl.* 42, *cr.* 12.)

DELSUME, Eng., a pegasus' head, ar., between wings, or. *Pl.* 19, *cr.* 13.
DELVES, Sco. and Eng., out of a ducal coronet, or, a demi-eagle, displayed, ar. *Je ne puis.* *Pl.* 9, *cr.* 6.
DELVES, Eng., a dolphin, embowed, az. *Pl.* 48, *cr.* 9.
DE MANDEVILE, Eng., on a mount, vert, a stag, current, regardant, ppr. *Pl.* 3, *cr.* 2.
DE MARDESTON, Eng., a cross fleury, fitched, gu., fleury, or. *Pl.* 65, *cr.* 9.
DE MARDESTON, Suff., out of a mural coronet, a lion's head. *Pl.* 45, *cr.* 9.
DE MAULEY, Baron, (Spencer-Ponsonby,) out of a ducal coronet, three arrows, points downward, one in pale, two in saltier, crowned at the intersection by a snake, all ppr. *Pro rege, lege, grege.* *Pl.* 86, *cr.* 12.
DEMESCHINES, Eng., in hand, a cutlass, ppr. *Pl.* 29, *cr.* 8.
DE MENBURGH, a cinquefoil. *Pl.* 91, *cr.* 12.
DE MOHUN, Eng., a lion's head, regardant, ppr. *Pl.* 35, *cr.* 2.
DE MONTACUTE, Eng., a griffin's head, gu., between wings, or. *Pl.* 65, *cr.* 1.
DE MONTGOMERY, Eng., a demi-savage, in dexter a sword, in sinister a marshal's baton, ppr. *Pl.* 121, *cr.* 8.
DE MONTMORENCY, a peacock in pride, ppr. *Pl.* 92, *cr.* 11.
DE MONTMORENCY, HARVEY, Esq., of Castle Morres, co. Kilkenny, a peacock in pride, ppr. *Dieu ayde.* *Pl.* 92, *cr.* 11.
DE MORTON, Eng., a griffin, segreant, sa. *Pl.* 67, *cr.* 13.
DE MOWBRAY, Eng., a fox, current, ppr. *Pl.* 80, *cr.* 5.
DEMPSEY, Eng., a sphinx, wings addorsed, ppr. *Pl.* 91, *cr.* 11.
DEMPSEY, Iri., out of a mural coronet, seven battle-axes, erect, ppr. *Pl.* 62, *cr.* 8.
DEMPSTER, GEORGE, of Skibo Castle, Sutherland, a leg-bone and palm-branch, in saltier, ppr. *Mors aut vita decora.* *Pl.* 25, *cr.* 11.
DEMPSTER, a demi-lion, gu., in dexter a sword, in pale, ppr. *Fortiter et strenue.* *Pl.* 41, *cr.* 13.
DEN, and DENA, Eng., a black's head, sa., banded, ar. *Pl.* 48, *cr.* 7.
DEN, and DENNE, Kent, on a staff, raguly, vert, a stag, lodged, ppr., attired, or. *Pl.* 67, *cr.* 2, (staff, *pl.* 5, *cr.* 8.)
DEN, and DENNE, on a mount, vert, a stag, lodged, regardant, ar. *Pl.* 51, *cr.* 9.
DENBIGH, Earl of, Viscount Fielding, Eng.; Earl of Desmond, Viscount Callan, and Baron Fielding, Iri., (Percy-Fielding,) a nuthatch, with a hazel-branch, fructed, all ppr. *Virtutis præmium honor.* *Pl.* 2, *cr.* 4.
DENBY, Eng., an antelope, passant, gu., (collared, ar.) *Pl.* 63, *cr.* 10.
DENCH, Eng., a unicorn's head, between two branches of laurel, in orle, ppr. *Pl.* 54, *cr.* 9.
DENE, Devons., in dexter hand, a cross crosslet, fitched. *Pl.* 99, *cr.* 1.
DENESTON, Eng., a cross fleury, fitched, gu., fleury, or. *Pl.* 65, *cr.* 9.
DE NEWBURG, Eng., a quatrefoil, vert. *Pl.* 65, *cr.* 7.
DENGAINE, on a mount, a stag, feeding, ppr. *Pl.* 37, *cr.* 8.

D'ENGAINE, on a mount, a stag, feeding, ppr. *Pl.* 37, *cr.* 8.
DENGAYNE, Eng., a tower, sa., with a cupola, gu., surmounted by a flag, also gu. *Pl.* 42, *cr.* 10.
DENHAM, Sco., a thistle and rose slip, in saltier, all ppr. *Juvant aspera probum. Pl.* 57, *cr.* 10.
DENHAM, Sco., a crane, in dexter a stone, ppr. *Cura dat victoriam. Pl.* 26, *cr.* 11.
DENHAM, Lond., Bucks., and Surr., a lion's head, erased, erminois. *Pl.* 81, *cr.* 4.
DENHANY, a demi-bear, salient, ar. *Pl.* 104, *cr.* 10.
DENHOLM, Sco., a stag, lodged, ppr. *Pl.* 67, *cr.* 2.
DENIS, Eng., out of a ducal coronet, a plume of five ostrich-feathers, ppr. *Pl.* 100, *cr.* 12, (without charge.)
DENISON, Eng., out of a naval coronet, a demi-mermaid, in dexter a mirror, in sinister a comb, ppr. *Pl.* 32, *cr.* 8.
DENISON, Yorks., a dexter arm, embowed, vested, az., cuffed, or, hand, ppr., pointing to a mullet of six points, of the second. *Pl.* 39, *cr.* 1, (mullet, *pl.* 77, *cr.* 6.)
DENISON, Lanc., a dexter arm, (in bend, sleeved, vert,) hand, ppr., pointing to a star, or. *Pl.* 77, *cr.* 6.
DENISON, Lond. and Surr., a cubit-arm, in bend, (vested, az., cuffed, ar.,) hand, ppr., pointing with forefinger to a star, or. *Pl.* 77, *cr.* 6, (hand in bend, *pl.* 59, *cr.* 9.)
DENISTOUN, in dexter hand an antique shield, sa., charged with a star, or. *Pl.* 21, *cr.* 12.
DENMAN, Baron, (Denman,) a raven, rising, ppr., in beak, an annulet, or. *Prudentia et constantia. Pl.* 50, *cr.* 5, (annulet, *pl.* 141.)
DENMAN, Eng., a demi-greyfriar, vested, ppr., in dexter a lash. *Pl.* 83, *cr.* 1.
DENN, Suss., out of a ducal coronet, a camel's head, or. *Pl.* 55, *cr.* 5.
DENNE, Kent, on a chapeau, vert, turned up, erm., a peacock in pride, ppr. *Pl.* 50, *cr.* 15.
DENNESTOUN, Lord, Sco., in dexter hand, ppr., an antique shield, sa., charged with a star, or. *Adversa virtute repello. Pl.* 21, *cr.* 12.
DENNET, Lond., a boar's head, erased, az. *Pl.* 16, *cr.* 11.
DENNETT, Eng., in hand an escallop, ppr. *Pl.* 57, *cr.* 6.
DENNETT, a demi-wolf, sa., (collared, indented, ar.) *Pl.* 65, *cr.* 4, (without mullet.)
DENNEY, and DENNY, Ess. and Norf., a cubit arm, erect, ppr., in hand a bunch of barley, or. *Pl.* 71, *cr.* 15.
DENNIE, and DENNY, Sco., a hand, erect, pointing with two fingers to the sun. *Pl.* 15, *cr.* 4.
DENNIS, Glouc., a demi-lion, rampant, az., bezantée. *Pl.* 67, *cr.* 10.
DENNIS, a leopard's head and neck, couped, ppr. *Pl.* 92, *cr.* 13.
DENNIS, Iri., out of a ducal coronet, in hand a sheaf of arrows, ppr. *Pl.* 9, *cr.* 4.
DENNIS, Cornw., a dragon's head and neck, couped. *Pl.* 87, *cr.* 12.
DENNIS, Cornw., Devons., and Hants., a tiger's head, erased, erm. *Pl.* 94, *cr.* 10.
DENNIS, Cornw., Devons., and Hants., a tiger's head, erased, ar. *Pl.* 94, *cr.* 10.

DENNISTOUN, Eng., a squirrel, sejant, or. *Pl.* 16, *cr.* 9.
DENNY, Bart., Iri., a cubit arm, vested, az., cuffed, ar., in hand five wheat-ears, or. *Et mea messis erit. Pl.* 63, *cr.* 1.
DENNY, Iri., a garb, in fess, ppr. *Pl.* 12, *cr.* 15.
DENNY, Eng., a buck's head, couped at neck. *Pl.* 91, *cr.* 14.
DENNYS, Eng., out of a ducal coronet, a plume of five ostrich-feathers, ppr. *Pl.* 100, *cr.* 12.
DENOUAC, Eng., between wings a globe, thereon an eagle, wings expanded, ppr. *Pl.* 34, *cr.* 2, (wings, *same plate, cr.* 14.)
DENOVAN, Sco., a stag, trippant, gu. *Pl.* 68, *cr.* 2.
DENSHIRE, Eng., a lion, regardant, holding with both paws an anchor, all ppr. *Pl.* 100, *cr.* 6, (anchor, *pl.* 42, *cr.* 12.)
DENSTON, Eng., out of a ducal coronet, or; in dexter hand a sword, blade wavy, per pale, ppr. *Pl.* 65, *cr.* 10.
DENSY, Eng., on a chapeau, a stag, passant, ppr. *Pl.* 63, *cr.* 8.
DENT, a demi-wolf. *Pl.* 56, *cr.* 8, (without spear.)
DENT, a demi-wolf, salient, sa., (charged on neck with a collar, dancettée, ar.) *Pl.* 56, *cr.* 8, (without spear.)
DENT, Northumb., a tiger's head, (erased,) erm., maned, sa., vomiting fire, ppr. *Pl.* 112, *cr.* 9.
DENT, Surr., a tiger's head, couped, ar. *Pl.* 92, *cr.* 13.
DENTON, a stork, ppr. *Pl.* 33, *cr.* 9.
DENTON, Cumb., a martlet, sa. *Pl.* 111, *cr.* 5.
DENTON, Camb., a lion, couchant, or. *Pl.* 101, *cr.* 8.
DENYS, Bart., Northamp., a demi-lion, erminois, collared, gu., between paws a French lily, slipped, ppr. *Hora e sempre. Pl.* 18, *cr.* 13, (lily, *pl.* 81, *cr.* 9.)
DENYS, by a tree, vert, an antelope, passant, ppr. *Pl.* 63, *cr.* 10, (tree, *pl.* 95, *cr.* 10.)
DEPDEN, Eng., an anchor, or, surmounted by a fleur-de-lis. *Pl.* 51, *cr.* 15.
DEPDEN, a dexter and sinister hand, wielding a two-handed sword, ppr. *Pl.* 3, *cr.* 5.
DEPHAM, Eng., a church, ppr. *Pl.* 45, *cr.* 6.
DEPHAM, Eng., a lion, passant, ppr. *Pl.* 48, *cr.* 8.
DE PLACETES, a lion's head, ppr., collared, or. *Pl.* 42, *cr.* 14.
DE PONTHIEU, a tree, vert. *Pl.* 100, *cr.* 14.
DEPTUN, Eng., an anchor, or, enfiled by a fleur-de-lis, sa. *Pl.* 51, *cr.* 15.
DE PUDSEY, Eng., an eagle's head, gu., in beak an acorn, slipped and leaved, vert. *Pl.* 22, *cr.* 1.
DERAM, Eng., in hand, in fess, couped, a fleur-de-lis, ppr. *Pl.* 46, *cr.* 12.
DERAM, a pyramid, entwined by a vine, ppr. *Pl.* 8, *cr.* 10.
DERAW, Eng., a bundle of quills, ar. *Pl.* 86, *cr.* 7.
DERBY, Earl of, and Baron STANLEY, (Smith, Stanley,) on a chapeau, gu., turned up, erm., an eagle, wings addorsed, or, (feeding an infant in its nest, ppr.,) swaddled, az., banded, of the third. *Sans changer. Pl.* 121, *cr.* 6.

DERBY, a garb, ar., banded, or. *Pl.* 48, *cr.* 10.
DERBY, a dromedary, ppr. *Pl.* 17, *cr.* 2.
DEREHAM, Norf., a bear, rampant, sejant, sa., muzzled, (lined and ringed, or,) charged on shoulders with an annulet, ar. *Pl.* 1, *cr.* 1, (annulet, *pl.* 141.)
DERHAM, Iri., a demi-wolf, per pale, or and sa. *Pl.* 56, *cr.* 8, (without spear.)
DERHAM, Eng., two hands, winged and clasped. *Pl.* 14, *cr.* 9.
DERHAUGH, Suff., a tiger, passant, or, tufted and maned, sa. *Pl.* 86, *cr.* 2.
DERING, Bart., Kent, on a ducal coronet, or, a horse, passant, sa., maned, gold. *Terrere nolo, timere nescio. Pl.* 76, *cr.* 8.
DE RINZY, MATTHEU-SCANDERBEG, Esq., of Clobewan Hall, co. Wexford, a sword, erect, ppr., hilted, or. *Facta, non verba. Pl.* 105, *cr.* 1.
DE RIVERS, and DE RYVERS, Eng., a tortoise, passant, ppr. *Pl.* 12, *cr.* 13.
DERMOTT, Iri., a griffin's head, erased, or. *Pl.* 48, *cr.* 6.
DERMOT, or DERMOTT, Eng., a demi-lion, holding a spear, in pale, thrust through a bear's head, all ppr. *Pl.* 69, *cr.* 14, (bear's head, *pl.* 111, *cr.* 4.)
DERNFORD, Eng., a cross crosslet, fitched, az., and sword, ppr., in saltier. *Pl.* 89, *cr.* 14.
DERNFORD, Eng., a sphinx, passant, gardant, wings addorsed, ppr. *Pl.* 91, *cr.* 11.
DE ROMARA, Eng., a stag's head, at gaze, ppr. *Pl.* 111, *cr.* 13.
DE ROS, Baron, (Fitzgerald De Ros,) crest and motto same as those of the Duke of Leinster.
DE ROUILLON, Norf., a dolphin, haurient, sa. *Pl.* 14, *cr.* 10.
DERRICK, on a spear-head, a savage's head, couped, (dropping blood, ppr.) *Virtute, non viribus. Pl.* 88, *cr.* 15.
DERULE, Eng., a demi-wolf, gu. *Pl.* 56, *cr.* 8, (without spear.)
DERWELL, Eng., a harp, or. *Pl.* 104, *cr.* 15.
DERWIN, a demi-griffin, in claws an escallop. *Pl.* 18, *cr.* 6, (escallop, *pl.* 141.)
DE SALLIS, out of a ducal coronet, a demi-harpy, displayed, ducally crowned. *Pl.* 32, *cr.* 3, (coronet, *pl.* 128, *fig.* 3.)
DESANGES, a cherub's head, or. *Pl.* 126, *cr.* 10.
DESART, Earl of, Viscount Castle Cuffe, (Otway-O'Connor-Cuffe,) Iri., a cubit arm, erect, (vested, or, charged with two bendlets undée, az., cuffed, erm.,) in hand, ppr., a pole-axe, of the first, staff, of the second. *Virtus repulsæ nescia sordidæ. Pl.* 73, *cr.* 7.
DE SAUMAREZ, Baron, K.C.B., &c., (Saumarez,) a falcon, wings expanded, ppr. *In Deo spero. Pl.* 105, *cr.* 4.
DESBARRES, Eng., an arm, couped at shoulder, embowed, resting elbow on wreath, in hand a spear, in pale, all ppr. *Pl.* 19, *cr.* 5.
DESBOROUGH, and DESBROWE, a bear's head, couped, sa., muzzled, or. *Pl.* 111, *cr.* 4.
DESBOUVERIE, Eng., a demi-eagle, with two heads, displayed, sa., ducally gorged, charged with a cross crosslet. *Pl.* 31, *cr.* 9, (gorging, *pl.* 128, *fig.* 3.)
DESBRISAY, Eng., a bell, or. *Pl.* 73, *cr.* 15.

DESBROWE, a talbot's head, erased. *Pl.* 90, *cr.* 6.
DESCHAMPS, Eng., the golden fleece, girt round middle with a collar, or. *Pl.* 77, *cr.* 12.
DE SENLIZE, Eng., a lion, passant, gardant, tail extended, gu. *Pl.* 120, *cr.* 5.
DE SILVA, a lion, rampant, gu. *Pl.* 67, *cr.* 5.
DESLAND, Iri., two hands, couped and conjoined, supporting a heart. *Pl.* 43, *cr.* 15.
DESMOND, a lion, passant, gardant, or, (grasping a saltier, gu.) *Pl.* 120, *cr.* 5.
DESMOND, Earl of, Iri. See Denbigh, Earl of.
DESNAY, Eng., on a chapeau, ar., turned up, gu., charged with fleur-de-lis, or, a lion, passant, gu. *Pl.* 107, *cr.* 1, (fleur-de-lis, *pl.* 141.)
DESNE, a leopard's face, affrontée, (breaking with its mouth a sword.) *Pl.* 66, *cr.* 14.
DESNEY, a wyvern, sans legs, vert. *Pl.* 80, *cr.* 8, (without chapeau.)
DESPARD, Iri., in hand a broken spear. *Pl.* 66, *cr.* 4.
DESPARD, Eng., on a ducal coronet, or, a star of (twelve) rays, ar. *Pl.* 30, *cr.* 13, (coronet, *pl.* 128, *fig.* 3.)
DESPENCER, LE, Eng., a griffin's head, ppr. *Pl.* 38, *cr.* 3.
DESPENCER, Eng., two wings conjoined, ppr. *Pl.* 15, *cr.* 10.
DESS, on a chapeau, gu., turned up, erm., an owl, close, or. *Pl.* 27, *cr.* 9, (chapeau, *pl.* 123, *cr.* 6.)
DESSBON, a marquess's coronet, ppr. *Pl.* 127, *fig.* 4.
DESSE, on a chapeau, gu., turned up, erm., an owl, wings expanded, or. *Vigilo. Pl.* 123, *cr.* 6.
DESSEN, a porcupine, sa., spines, tipped, or. *Pl.* 55, *cr.* 10.
DES VOEUX, Bart., Iri., a squirrel, sejant, ppr. *Altiora in votis. Pl.* 16, *cr.* 9.
DE TABLEY, Baron, (Warren,) a swan's neck, couped, ar., guttée-de-sang. *Pro rege et patriâ. Pl.* 30, *cr.* 10, (without gorging.)
DETHICK, Derbs. and Norf., a nag's head, erased, ar. *Pl.* 81, *cr.* 6.
DETHICK, Durh., a horse's head, (couped,) ar., charged on neck with a mullet, on a crescent. *Pl.* 81, *cr.* 6, (charging, *pl.* 141.)
DETHICKE, Eng., an eagle, regardant, wings expanded and inverted, ppr. *Pl.* 35, *cr.* 8.
DETON, and DETTON, Eng., a goat's head, erased, ar., (collared, gu.) *Pl.* 29, *cr.* 13.
DETON, Eng., on a tower, ar., a crescent, gu. *Pl.* 85, *cr.* 1.
DEUCHAR, Sco., a boar's head, erased, between two branches of laurel, ppr. *Verus ad finem. Pl.* 19, *cr.* 8, (laurel, *pl.* 79, *cr.* 14.)
DEUCHAR, Sco., a boar's head, couped, between (two alder-branches.) *Pl.* 19, *cr.* 8.
DEUCHAR, Sco., out of a mural coronet, an arm, in armour, embowed, in hand a sword, all ppr. *Pl.* 115, *cr.* 14.
DE UFFORD, Eng., a demi-eagle, displayed, sa. *Pl.* 22, *cr.* 11.
D'EUREUX, Eng., five arrows, gu., headed, or, feathered, ar., bound by a belt, of the first, buckled, gold. *Pl.* 54, *cr.* 15.
D'EUREUX, Eng., out of a ducal coronet, or, a talbot's head. *Pl.* 99, *cr.* 7.
DEVALL, Eng., on a chapeau, a greyhound, sejant. *Pl.* 66, *cr.* 15, (chapeau, *pl.* 57, *cr.* 14.)

DE VALLANCE, Eng., a greyhound's head, gu. *Pl.* 89, *cr.* 2.

DEVAYNES, Eng., a lion, rampant, between paws a battle-axe. *Pl.* 125, *cr.* 2, (axe, *pl.* 14, *cr.* 8.)

DEVAYNES, out of a baron's coronet, a demi-dragon, in dexter a sword.

DEVEN, a lion, rampant, ar., (ducally gorged,) or. *Pl.* 98, *cr.* 1.

DEVENDALE, Eng., a long cross, az. *Pl.* 7, *cr.* 13.

DEVANISH, Suss., a demi-tiger, salient, vert, in dexter a cross crosslet, fitched, ar. *Pl.* 53, *cr.* 10, (cross, *pl.* 16, *cr.* 10.)

DEVENPORT, a savage's head, affrontée, (round head a snake.) *Pl.* 19, *cr.* 1.

DEVENPORT, on a mount, vert, a hound, sejant, ppr., resting dexter on a stag's head, cabossed. *Pl.* 66, *cr.* 15, (stag, *pl.* 36, *cr.* 1.)

DEVENSHIRE, Cornw., an eagle, ppr. *Pl.* 7, *cr.* 11.

DEVERAL, and DEVEREL, Eng., the rays of the sun issuing from behind a cloud, ppr. *Pl.* 25, *cr.* 14.

DEVERE, Bart., Iri.: 1. On a chapeau, turned up, erm., a boar, passant, az., bristled and tusked, or. *Pl.* 22, *cr.* 8. 2. The Castle of Limerick, ppr. *Vero nihil verius. Pl.* 123, *cr.* 14.

DEVERE, Eng., the sun shining on a sun-flower, ppr. *Pl.* 45, *cr.* 13, (sun-flower, *pl.* 84, *cr.* 6.)

DEVEREAUX, and DEVEREUX, Iri., a stag, trippant, ppr. *Pl.* 68, *cr.* 2.

DEVEREULX, a talbot's head, ar., ducally crowned, or. *Pl.* 25, *cr.* 10.

DEVEREUX, Heref. and Warw., out of a ducal coronet, or, a talbot's head, ar., eared, gu. *Pl.* 99, *cr.* 7.

DEVEREUX, a tower, ppr. *Pl.* 12, *cr.* 5.

DEVEREUX, Viscount Hereford, out of a ducal coronet, or, a talbot's head, ar., eared, gu. *Virtutis comes invidia. Pl.* 99, *cr.* 7.

DEVERSON, a lion's head, gardant and erased, gu., (collared, or.) *Pl.* 1, *cr.* 5, (without coronet.)

DE VESCI, Viscount and Baron Knapton, (Vesey,) Iri., in hand, in armour, a laurel-branch, all ppr. *Sub hoc signo vinces. Pl.* 55, *cr.* 6, (laurel, *pl.* 43, *cr.* 6.)

DEVESTON, Eng., a cross fleury, fitched, gu. *Pl.* 65, *cr.* 9.

DEVETTS, issuing from clouds, a cubit arm, in fess, in hand a sword, erect, enfiled with a boar's head, erased. *Pl.* 93, *cr.* 8, (head, *pl.* 71, *cr.* 9.)

DEVEY, Eng., a dexter arm, embowed, in fess, couped, ppr., vested, sa., in hand a cross crosslet, fitched, gu. *Pl.* 88, *cr.* 7.

DE VISME, an eagle, displayed, ppr. *Pl.* 48, *cr.* 11.

DE VISME, an eagle, displayed, (sans legs, ppr.) *Pl.* 44, *cr.* 14, (without charge.)

DEVOIKE, a dexter hand throwing an arrow, ppr. *Pl.* 42, *cr.* 13.

DEVON, Eng., a horse's head, ar., thrust through by a spear, sa., head, or. *Pl.* 110, *cr.* 6.

DEVON, Earl of, (Courtenay,) a dolphin, naiant, ppr. *Ubi lapsus? quid feci? Pl.* 48, *cr.* 9.

DEVONSHIRE, Eng., a cross moline, or. *Pl.* 89, *cr.* 8.

DEVONSHIRE, Duke of, Marquess of Hartington, Earl of Devonshire, Baron Cavendish and Clifford, K. G., &c., (Spence-Cavendish,) a snake, nowed, ppr. *Cavendo tutus. Pl.* 1, *cr.* 9.

DE WAETOR, WAGER, Eng., the attires of a stag fixed to scalp, or. *Pl.* 33, *cr.* 15, (without boar.)

DEWAR, Northumb., a holy lamb bearing the banner of St Andrew, ppr. *Pl.* 48, *cr.* 13.

DEWAR, Sco., a cock, crowing, ppr. *Gloria patri. Pl.* 67, *cr.* 14.

DE WARREN, Eng., a lion, passant, gardant, az. *Pl.* 120, *cr.* 5.

DEWELL, and DEWELLE, Eng., on a mount, vert, a horse, current, ar., bridled, sa. *Pl.* 57, *cr.* 9.

DEWELLES, an ostrich's head and wings, ar., ducally gorged, gu., in mouth a horse-shoe, az. *Pl.* 28, *cr.* 13, (gorging, *plate* 128, *fig.* 3.)

DEWERS, an anchor, with cable, ppr. *Pl.* 42, *cr.* 12.

DEWES, Warw., a wolf's head, (erased,) or, collared, vair, in mouth a quatrefoil, pierced, gu., slipped, ppr. *Pl.* 8, *cr.* 4, (quatrefoil, *pl.* 141.)

DEWHURST, Lanc., a wolf's head, erminois. *Spes mea in Deo. Pl.* 14, *cr.* 6.

DEWHURST, Lanc., a wolf's head, (erased,) erminois, collared, az. *Spes mea in Deo. Pl.* 8, *cr.* 4.

DEWING, Norf., a greyhound's head, (erased,) ar., collared and ringed, gu. *Pl.* 43, *cr.* 11.

DE WINTON, WALTER THOMPSON, Esq., of Clifton, Glouc., a wyvern, ppr. *Syn ar dy Hûn. Pl.* 63, *cr.* 13.

DEWSBURY, Glouc., on a mount, vert, a martlet, or. *Pl.* 36, *cr.* 5.

DEXTER, Eng., a tree, pendent therefrom two weights. *Pl.* 50, *cr.* 3.

DEYCOURT, Eng., a sword, in pale, enfiled with a leopard's face. *Pl.* 24, *cr.* 13.

DEYNCOURT, Eng., the standard of St George, ppr. *Pl.* 8, *cr.* 3.

DEYNES, Suff., out of a mural coronet, gold, a dragon's head, sa., gorged with two bars, or. *Pl.* 59, *cr.* 14.

DEYVELLE, DEYVILL, and DAVELL, Eng., an arm, in fess, ppr., (vested,) in hand a fleur-de-lis, or. *Pl.* 46, *cr.* 12.

DEYVIL, Eng., a fleur-de-lis, gu. *Pl.* 68, *cr.* 12.

D'EYVILL, Eng., an arm, in armour, embowed, ppr., in hand a club, sa., spiked, or. *Pl.* 45, *cr.* 10.

DIAMONT, a demi-lion, or, in dexter a fusil, gu., charged with a fleur-de-lis, gold. *Pl.* 91, *cr.* 13, (fusil, *pl.* 141.)

DIAS, Eng., on a garland of laurel, a lion, passant, ppr. *Pl.* 60, *cr.* 6.

DIBBLE, DIABLE, and DIBLE, Eng., on a chapeau, a lion, statant, gardant, ducally gorged, tail extended. *Pl.* 7, *cr.* 14.

DIBDIN, Eng., a talbot, passant, collared, ppr. *Pl.* 65, *cr.* 2.

DIBLE, and DIBLEY, Eng., a demi-Hercules, holding over shoulder a club, ppr. *Pl.* 49, *cr.* 11.

DICCONSON, Eng., a hind's head, or. *Pl.* 21, *cr.* 9.

DICEY, a demi-lion, or. *Fide et amore. Pl.* 67, *cr.* 10.

DICEY, Eng., a lion, sejant, gu., supporting between paws a shield, ar. *Pl.* 22, *cr.* 13.

DICHER, Salop, a bear, passant, ar. *Pl.* 61, *cr.* 5.

DICK, QUINTIN, Esq., of Layer Tower, Ess., a cat, sejant. *Semper fidelis. Pl.* 24, *cr.* 6.

DICK, Bart., of Braid, Sco., a stag's head, erased, ppr., attired, or. *Virtute*—and—*Publica salus mea merces. Pl.* 66, *cr.* 9.

DICK, Bart., of Prestonfield, Sco., in dexter hand a plumb rule, ppr. *Over, fork over. Pl.* 43, *cr.* 13, (rule, *pl.* 13, *cr.* 3.)

DICK, Sco., a ship in distress, ppr. *At spes infracta. Pl.* 21, *cr.* 11.

DICK, Iri., a horse's head, armed, ppr., bridled, gu. *Pl.* 7, *cr.* 12.

DICK, a leopard, sejant, ppr. *Pl.* 10, *cr.* 13, (without flag.)

DICK, Eng., a dagger and sword, in saltier, ppr. *Pl.* 24, *cr.* 2, (sword, *pl.* 106, *cr.* 9.)

DICKENS, a hind's head. *Pl.* 21, *cr.* 9.

DICKENS, Suff., a lion, rampant, ppr., holding a cross flory, sa. *Pl.* 125, *cr.* 2, (cross, *pl.* 141.)

DICKENS, Eng., an arm, in armour, couped in fess, from elbow, in pale, holding up an esquire's helmet, all ppr. *Pl.* 114, *cr.* 9.

DICKENS, on trunk of tree, entwined by a serpent, a falcon, wings expanded. *Pl.* 105, *cr.* 4, (serpent, *pl.* 84, *cr.* 4.)

DICKENS, a lion, couchant, or, in dexter a cross patonce, sa. *Pl.* 101, *cr.* 8, (cross, *pl.* 141.)

DICKENS, a demi-leopard, ppr. *Hostis honori invidia. Pl.* 12, *cr.* 14.

DICKENSON, Wilts., out of a ducal coronet, or, a dexter arm, ppr., in hand a fleur-de-lis, gold. *Pl.* 120, *cr.* 4.

DICKENSON, out of a ducal coronet, a phœnix in flames, ppr. *Pl.* 53, *cr.* 6.

DICKENSON, out of clouds, a cubit arm, erect, in hand a (branch) of laurel, all ppr. *Pl.* 88, *cr.* 13.

DICKENSON, Lond., in hand an ox-yoke, ppr. *Pl.* 83, *cr.* 14.

DICKENSON, a tiger, sejant, erm., (ducally gorged, or, in gamb a broad arrow, gold, feathered, ar.) *Pl.* 26, *cr.* 9.

DICKENSON, and DICONSON, Linc., Yorks., and Staff., a demi-lion, rampant, per pale, erminois and az. *Pl.* 67, *cr.* 10.

DICKENSON, a greyhound's head, between two roses, slipped and leaved, ppr. *Pl.* 84, *cr.* 13.

DICKENSON, Iri., in hand, ppr., vested, gu., an escarbuncle, ar. *Pl.* 114, *cr.* 4.

DICKENSON, out of clouds, a cubit arm, erect, in hand three wheat-ears, all ppr. *Pl.* 69, *cr.* 10, (wheat, *pl.* 89, *cr.* 4.)

DICKESON, Eng., a boar's head, couped, in mouth (four) arrows, all ppr. *Pl.* 8, *cr.* 14.

DICKESON, or DICKINSON, a camel's head, ppr., bridled, gu., (on top of head a plume of ostrich-feathers, and under throat a bell, or.) *Pl.* 120, *cr.* 12.

DICKEY, and DICKIE, Eng., a ferret, ppr. *Pl.* 12, *cr.* 2.

DICKIE, Sco., on a rock, an alder-tree, growing, ppr. *Pl.* 98, *cr.* 13.

DICKIN, Salop, a lion, sejant, or, in dexter a cross crosslet, gold. *Vincit veritas. Pl.* 109, *cr.* 7, (cross, *pl.* 141.)

DICKINS, Suss.: 1. A lion, sejant, sa., holding a cross flory, or. *Pl.* 109, *cr.* 7, (cross, *pl.* 141.) 2. On stump of tree, entwined by a serpent, ppr., a falcon, also ppr., beaked, membered, and belled, or. *Pl.* 78, *cr.* 8, (serpent, *pl.* 84, *cr.* 4.)

DICKINS, Kent, a lion, sejant, or, holding a cross flory, sa. *In hoc signo vinces. Pl.* 109, *cr.* 7, (cross, *pl.* 141.)

DICKMAN, Eng., an ostrich, ar., in mouth a (key), az. *Diligentia. Pl.* 16, *cr.* 2.

DICKMAN, a demi-horse, rampant. *Pl.* 91, *cr.* 2, (without wings and coronet.)

DICKSON, Bart., Norf., over an arm, in armour, brandishing a falchion, ppr., (a trident and spear in saltier, or.) *Fortes fortuna juvat. Pl.* 2, *cr.* 8.

DICKSON, JAMES R., Esq., Woodville, Arbroath, in dexter hand a sword, in bend, ppr., hilt and pommel, or. *Fortes fortuna juvat. Pl.* 21, *cr.* 10.

DICKSON, Sco., in dexter hand a sword, in bend, ppr. *Fortes fortuna juvat. Pl.* 21, *cr.* 10.

DICKSON, Iri., out of a tower, a lion's head, ppr. *Pl.* 42, *cr.* 4.

DICKSON, Sco., a winged heart, ppr. *Cœlum versus. Pl.* 39, *cr.* 7.

DICKSON, Sco., a hart, couchant, gardant, ppr., attired, or, within two branches of laurel, in orle, vert. *Cubo sed curo. Pl.* 24, *cr.* 4.

DICOM, and DICONS, Beds., a cock's head, az., beaked, or, combed, and wattled, gu. *Pl.* 92, *cr.* 3.

DICOME, Linc., a unicorn's head, erased, quarterly, erm. and gu., crined, or, the horn gobony, of the last and ar. *Pl.* 67, *cr.* 1.

DIDDIER, or DIDEAR, a demi-griffin, wings expanded, ppr. *Pl.* 18, *cr.* 6.

DIETZ, out of a ducal coronet, a pair of stag's horns. *Pl.* 118, *cr.* 11.

DIFFORD, and DITFORD, a lion's head, erased, or, ducally crowned, gu. *Pl.* 90, *cr.* 4, (without charging.)

DIGBY, Earl and Baron, Viscount Coleshill, Eng.; Lord Digby, and Baron Geashill, Iri., (Digby,) an ostrich, ar., in mouth a horseshoe, or. *Deo, non fortund. Pl.* 16, *cr.* 2.

DIGBY, an ostrich, ar., in mouth a horse-shoe, ppr. *Pl.* 16, *cr.* 2.

DIGBY, SIMON, Esq., of Osbertstown, co. Kildare, an ostrich, ar., in mouth a horse-shoe, or. *Deo, non fortunâ. Pl.* 16, *cr.* 2, (without gorging.)

DIGGES, an eagle's leg, ppr., thigh plumed with three feathers, sa. *Pl.* 83, *cr.* 7, (without bell.)

DIGGS, and DYGES, Kent, Surr., and Wilts., an eagle's leg, couped from thigh, sa., plumed with three ostrich-feathers, ar.

DIGGS, and DYGES, Kent, Surr., and Wilts., an eagle's head, sa. *Pl.* 100, *cr.* 10.

DIGHTON, Herts., in lion's gamb, erased, or, a cross formée, fitched, gu. *Pl.* 46, *cr.* 7.

DIGHTON, Linc., a squirrel, sejant, per pale, ar. and gu., collared, cracking a nut, or. *Pl.* 85, *cr.* 3.

DIGHTON, Lond., Linc., and Worc., on a ducal coronet, or, a hawk, close, ar., beaked and legged, gu., belled, gold. *Pl.* 41, *cr.* 10.

DIKENS, a bird's head, neck, az., top of head, gu., beaked, or. *Pl.* 100, *cr.* 10.

DIKENS, Eng., a lion's head, erased, gu., ducally crowned, or. *Pl.* 90, *cr.* 4.

DIKES, and DYKES, a lobster, vert. *Pl.* 18, *cr.* 2.
DILKE, Lond., Leic., Staffs., and Warw., a dove, close, ar., beaked and legged, gu. *Pl.* 66, *cr.* 12.
DILKES, Eng., a mill-rind, gu. *Pl.* 54, *cr.* 3.
DILLINGTON, Norf., on a perch, ar., a hawk, close, ppr., beaked, belled, and legged, or. *Pl.* 10, *cr.* 7.
DILLON, Viscount, (Dillon-Lee,) Iri. : 1. For Lee, out of a ducal coronet, or, a pillar, ar., thereon a falcon, az. *Pl.* 41, *cr.* 10, (pillar, *pl.* 33, *cr.* 1.) 2. For *Dillon*, a demi-lion, rampant, gu., between paws an etoile, ar. *Dum spiro, spero.* *Pl.* 126, *cr.* 12, (etoile, *pl.* 141.)
DILLON, Bart., Iri. : 1. On a chapeau, gu., turned up, erm., a falcon, rising, ar., beaked, legged, and belled, or. *Pl.* 105, *cr.* 4, (chapeau, *same plate, cr.* 5.) 2. A demi-lion, rampant, gu. *Auxilium ab alto.* *Pl.* 67, *cr.* 10.
DILLON, Devons., out of a crescent, gu., a demi-lion, in dexter an etoile, of the same. *Pl.* 89, *cr.* 10, (etoile and crescent, *pl.* 141.)
DILLON, Iri., out of a marquess's coronet, or, a falcon, wings expanded, ar., beaked and legged, or, between the wings an imperial eagle, sa. *Auxilium ab alto.*
DILLON, Eng., a demi-lion, in dexter a mullet. *Dum spiro, spero.* *Pl.* 89, *cr.* 10.
DILLON, Earl of Roscommon, and Baron Clonbrock. *See those titles.*
DILLWYN, LEWIS-WESTON, Esq., of Borough Lodge, and Sketty Hall, Glams., a stag's head, couped, ppr. *Craignez honte.* *Pl.* 91, *cr.* 14.
DIMMOCK, Eng., a boar's head, couped, ppr. between two laurel-branches, vert. *Pl.* 19, *cr.* 8, (laurel, *pl.* 79, *cr.* 14.)
DIMOND, Eng., a cross crosslet, in pale, surmounted by a sword, in bend sinister, point downward. *Pl.* 42, *cr.* 5.
DIMOND, a demi-lion, or, between paws, a fusil, of the same, charged with a fleur-de-lis, az. *Pl.* 91, *cr.* 13, (fusil, *pl.* 141.)
DIMSDALE, Herts., (out of a Russian baron's coronet,) a griffin's head, erm. *Pl.* 38, *cr.* 3.
DIMSDALE, a griffin's head, erased, ar. *Magnus Hippocrates ! tu nobis major.* *Pl.* 48, *cr.* 6.
DINE, Beds., a wyvern, statant, ppr. *J'ay espere mieux avoir.* *Pl.* 63, *cr.* 13.
DINELEY, on a ducal coronet, or, three darts, two in saltier, one in pale, with a serpent entwined, ppr. *Pl.* 86, *cr.* 12.
DINES, a griffin, passant. *Pl.* 61, *cr.* 14, (without gorging.)
DINGDALE, Lanc., a griffin's head, between wings, or. *Pl.* 22, *cr.* 2.
DINGHAM, Eng., a dexter hand, erect, pointing with the two fore-fingers to the sun in splendour, ppr. *Pl.* 15, *cr.* 4.
DINGHAM, in a round top, or, six spears, in the centre a pennon, ar., thereon a cross, gu.
DINGLEY, and DINLEY, Yorks., a Roman head, with a helmet, couped at neck, ppr. *Pl.* 33, *cr.* 14.
DINGWALL, a human heart, ppr. *Pl.* 55, *cr.* 13.
DINNET, a bull's head, gu. *Pl.* 63, *cr.* 11.
DINORBEN, Baron, (Hughes,) out of a crown valley, a demi-lion, rampant, ar., between paws a pike head, ppr.

DINWIDDIE, an eagle, wings addorsed and inverted, (in dexter a guinea-pig.) *Ubi libertas ibi patria.* *Pl.* 61, *cr.* 1.
DINWORDY, a cubit arm, erect, hand grasping a spear, all ppr. *Pl.* 99, *cr.* 8.
DIROM, Sco., a stag's head, erased. *Pl.* 66, *cr.* 9.
DIROM, JOHN PASLEY, Esq., of Mount Annan, Dumfries, a stag's head. *Pl.* 91, *cr.* 14.
DIRWYN, Eng., a peacock's head, erased, ppr. *Pl.* 86, *cr.* 4.
DISHINGTON, Sco., a man, in armour, kneeling. *Unica spes mea Christus.*
DISHINGTON, Sco., an escallop. *Unica spes mea Christus.* *Pl.* 117, *cr.* 4.
DISKENS, on a chapeau, a lion, couchant. *Pl.* 75, *cr.* 5.
DISKER, and DISKERS, (on a mount, vert,) a centaur, passant, regardant, ppr. and ar., drawing a bow and arrow, or, feathered, of the third. *Pl.* 70, *cr.* 13.
DISNEY, Linc. and Bucks., a lion, passant, gardant, gu. *Pl.* 120, *cr.* 5.
DISS, Eng., a demi-lion, vert. *Pl.* 67, *cr.* 10.
DITFORD, Eng., on a mount, or, a bull, passant, gu. *Pl.* 39, *cr.* 5.
DIVE, Beds. and Northamp., a wyvern, wings addorsed, gu. *J'ay espere mieux avoir.* *Pl.* 63, *cr.* 13.
DIVIE, and DIVVIE, Sco., an eagle's head, couped, ppr. *Sedulitate.* *Pl.* 100, *cr.* 10.
DIX, a greyhound's head, ar., ducally gorged, gu., between wings, or.
DIXIE, Eng., a leopard, sejant. *Pl.* 10, *cr.* 13, (without flag.)
DIXIE, Leic., Derbs., and Northamp., an ounce, sejant, ppr., ducally gorged, or. *Quod dixi, dixi.*
DIXON, Norf., a stag's head, erased, per pale, dancettée, sa. and or, attired, counterchanged. *Pl.* 66, *cr.* 9.
DIXON, Herts., (on a mount, vert,) a tiger, sejant, erm., ducally gorged, or. *Pl.* 26, *cr.* 9, (gorging, *pl.* 128, *fig.* 3.)
DIXON, Berks. and Chesh., a demi-lion, rampant, or. *Pl.* 67, *cr.* 10.
DIXON, Kent., a demi-hind, sa., bezantée.
DIXON, Herts., a sphere, az., charged with a pale, indented, vert. *Pl.* 63, *cr.* 7.
DIXON, Devons., an arm, embowed, vested, erminois, cuffed, ar., in hand a torteau, of the first. *Pl.* 39, *cr.* 1, (torteau, *pl.* 141.)
DIXON, Ess. and Durh., a cubit arm, vested, erminois, cuffed, ar., in hand, ppr., a round, of the first. *Pl.* 24, *cr.* 3, (round, *pl.* 141.)
DIXON, Yorks., a stag's head, erased. *Pl.* 66, *cr.* 9.
DIXON, Yorks., an eagle, displayed, sa. *Quod dixi, dixi.* *Pl.* 48, *cr.* 11.
DIXON, Worc., Brecon, and Salop, a demi-eagle, displayed, ppr., winged, vair. *In recto fides.* *Pl.* 22, *cr.* 11.
DIXON, Sco., a water-bouget, per fess, ar. and az. *Pl.* 14, *cr.* 12.
DIXON, Sheffield, an arm, embowed, vested and cuffed, hand holding up a garland of roses. *Fide et constantia.* *Pl.* 126 A., *cr.* 6.
DIXWELL, Kent. and Warw., in lion's gamb, (couped,) az., an eagle's wing with leg conjoined, sa. *Pl.* 89, *cr.* 13.
DOANE, Chesh., a sheaf of arrows, or, headed and feathered, ar., banded, gu. *Pl.* 54, *cr.* 15.

DOBBIE, and DOBIE, Sco., a cross crosslet, fitched, gu. *Pl.* 16, *cr.* 10.
DOBBIE, and DOBIE, Sco., an eagle, displayed, ppr. *Non minima sed magna prosequor*. *Pl.* 48, *cr.* 11.
DOBBIE, Sco., a crescent, az. *Pl.* 18, *cr.* 14.
DOBBIN, Iri., a demi-lion, or, supporting a long cross, gu. *Pl.* 29, *cr.* 12.
DOBBIN, Eng., in dexter hand a laurel-branch, ppr., fructed, gu. *Pl.* 43, *cr.* 6.
DOBBINS, and DOBINS, Eng., a staff raguly, surmounted by an eagle, displayed, ppr. *Pl.* 8, *cr.* 1.
DOBBS, Eng., a lion, sejant, affrontée, in each paw a dagger, ppr. *Pl.* 89, *cr.* 12.
DOBBS, Iri., a unicorn's head, couped, ar., maned, armed, and tufted, or. *Pl.* 20, *cr.* 1.
DOBBS, Iri., two hands couped and conjoined, in fess, dexter, in armour, supporting a laurel-branch and thistle, in orle. *Pl.* 23, *cr.* 10.
DOBBS, CONWAY-RICHARD, Esq., of Castle Dobbs, co. Antrim, a unicorn's head, erased, ar. *Amor Dei et proximi summa beatitudo*. *Pl.* 67, *cr.* 1.
DOBEDE, Camb., on a mount, vert, a demi-lion, erased, ar., crowned, or, holding an escutcheon. *Droit à chacun*. *Pl.* 62, *cr.* 13, (crown, *same plate*.)
DOBELL, Suss., on a mount, vert, a hart, lodged, (between four bulrushes, ppr.) *Pl.* 22, *cr.* 5.
DOBIE, Eng., in hand a scroll, between two branches of laurel, in orle. *Pl.* 86, *cr.* 5.
DOBLE, Somers., on a mount, vert, a doe, lodged, ar., pierced by four arrows, in saltier, or.
DOBREE, (on a mount, vert,) a thistle, ppr. *Spe vivitur*. *Pl.* 100, *cr.* 9.
DOBREE, Eng., on a ducal coronet, a talbot, passant, collared and lined, or. *Pl.* 3, *cr.* 8.
DOBSON, Westm. and Northumb., two lions' gambs, in saltier, gu. *Pl.* 20, *cr.* 13.
DOBYNS, Lond., out of a ducal coronet, two lions' gambs, in saltier. *Pl.* 110, *cr.* 2.
DOCKENFIELD, and DOKENFIELD, out of a ducal coronet, or, an arm, erect, vested, per pale, gu. and ar., in hand, ppr., the sun in splendour, gold. *Pl.* 89, *cr.* 11.
DOCKER, Eng., a bridge of three arches, ppr. *Pl.* 38, *cr.* 4.
DOCKINGFIELD, a cubit arm, erect, in hand, ppr., the sun, or. *Pl.* 89, *cr.* 11, (without coronet.)
DOCKSEY, on a chapeau, gu., turned up, erm., a lion's head, erased, per pale, az. and ar. *Pl.* 99, *cr.* 9.
DOCKWARE, and DOCKWRAY, Yorks., within a fetterlock, az., a heart, gu. *Pl.* 59, *cr.* 6.
DOCKWRAY, a demi-lion, rampant, between paws a plate, gu. *Pl.* 126, *cr.* 12.
DOCTON, and DOKETON, Eng., a fleur-de-lis, sa. *Pl.* 68, *cr.* 12.
DOD, and DODD, Chesh. and Surr., a garb, or, environed by (a snake,) ppr. (Another, ar.) *Pl.* 36, *cr.* 14.
DOD, Salop, a serpent, vert, issuing from and piercing a garb. *Pl.* 36, *cr.* 14.
DOD, and DODE, Eng., two hands, conjoined, one in armour, ppr., both couped, supporting a branch of palm and a thistle. *Pl.* 23, *cr.* 10.
DOD, and DODD, Iri., a horse, statant, saddled and bridled. *Pl.* 99, *cr.* 11.

DODDS, and DODS, Northumb. and Sco., a ferret, or. *Pl.* 12, *cr.* 2.
DODDS, Eng., out of a ducal coronet, a reindeer's head, ppr. *Pl.* 60, *cr.* 3.
DODERIDGE, Devons., a lion's head, erased, gu., murally gorged, or. *Pl.* 7, *cr.* 10, (coronet, *pl.* 128, *fig.* 18.)
DODGE, Kent, Chesh., and Norf., a demi-sea-dog, az., collared, finned, and purfled, or.
DODGIN, Eng., an arm, from shoulder, vested, or, cuffed, az., embowed, in fess, elbow on the wreath, in hand a sword, enfiled with a leopard's face, ppr. *Pl.* 102, *cr.* 5.
DODINGSELLS, Eng., a wolf, passant, gu. *Pl.* 46, *cr.* 6.
DODINGTON, Salop, a lion's gamb, erect, or. *Pl.* 126, *cr.* 9.
DODINGTON, Somers., in lion's gamb, ppr., a flag, gu., (charged with a cheveron, or.) *Pl.* 85, *cr.* 13.
DODINGTON, Wilts., a stag, lodged, regardant, ar., in mouth an acorn, or, stalked and leaved, vert. *Pl.* 51, *cr.* 9, (acorn, *pl.* 100, *cr.* 8.)
DODMER, and DODMORE, an arm, party per cross, gu. and sa., in hand, ppr., two arrows, vert. *Pl.* 31, *cr.* 10.
DODSON, Westm., two lions' gambs, in saltier, gu. *Pl.* 20, *cr.* 13.
DODSON, a demi-griffin, segreant. *Pl.* 18, *cr.* 6.
DODSON, three faces, two male and one female, conjoined in one neck, male face on top, and male and female to sinister and dexter. *Pl.* 32, *cr.* 2.
DODSWALL, and DODSWELL, a lion's head, erased, ppr. *Pl.* 81, *cr.* 4.
DODSWORTH, Bart., Yorks.: 1. For *Dodsworth*, a cubit arm, in chain mail, or, hand, ppr., grasping a broken tilting-spear, gold. *Pl.* 23, *cr.* 9. 2. For *Smith*, out of a ducal coronet, or, a boar's head, couped at neck, az. *Pl.* 102, *cr.* 14.
DODSWORTH, Eng., a demi-lion, supporting a long cross. *Pl.* 29, *cr.* 12.
DODWELL, JAMES-CROFTON, Esq., of Shankill House, co. Dublin; and Glenmore, co. Sligo, a demi-lion, ar., pellettée, armed and langued, az. *Pl.* 67, *cr.* 10.
DOE, Eng., a demi-lion, supporting a ship's rudder, ppr. *Pl.* 102, *cr.* 4.
DOE, Lanc., a garb, or, (with a coulter stuck within the band, in bend sinister, sa.) *Pl.* 48, *cr.* 10.
DOEG, in hand a thistle. *Pl.* 36, *cr.* 6.
DOGET, and DOGETT, Kent, on a chapeau, a bull, (collared, to collar a bell, pendent, ppr.) *Pl.* 65, *cr.* 11.
DOGGET, Norf., a lion's head, or, murally gorged, sa. *Pl.* 126, *cr.* 1, (gorging, *pl.* 128, *fig.* 18.)
DOGHERTY, and DOHERTY, Eng. and Iri., a wolf, current, erm. *Pl.* 111, *cr.* 1.
DOGHERTY, and DOHERTY, Iri., a boar, (regardant,) transfixed by an arrow. *Pl.* 36, *cr.* 2.
DOGHERTY, and DOHERTY, Iri., in hand a sword. *Pl.* 21, *cr.* 10.
DOIG, a falcon, wings expanded and inverted, belled, ppr. *Pl.* 105, *cr.* 4.
D'OILEY, and D'OYLEY, Eng., a demi-wyvern, vert, winged, or. *Pl.* 116, *cr.* 15.
DOILY, out of a ducal coronet, or, an etoile, ar., between wings, gu. *Pl.* 17, *cr.* 9, (etoile, *pl.* 141.)

DOLAN, Eng., a decrescent, gu. *Pl.* 16, *cr.* 15.
DOLBEN, Bart., Northamp., a griffin, sejant, wings addorsed, ppr. *Pl.* 100, *cr.* 11.
DOLBEN, Eng., a demi-bull, ar., gorged with (laurel-leaves,) vert. *Pl.* 73, *cr.* 8.
DOLBY, Ess. and Leic., a demi-griffin, ar., winged and beaked, or. *Pl.* 18, *cr.* 6.
DOLEMAN, Eng., an elephant's head, erased, sa. *Pl.* 68, *cr.* 4.
DOLINE, a fleur-de-lis, az., between wings, ar. *Pl.* 21, *cr.* 13, (without chapeau.)
DOLING, Eng., a buck's head, ppr., (gorged with a bar, dancettée, ar. and sa.) *Pl.* 91, *cr.* 14.
DOLING, a stag's head, erased, ppr. *Pl.* 66, *cr.* 9.
DOLLAR, an arm, embowed, in hand a falchion, ppr., hilt and pommel, or. *Pl.* 34, *cr.* 7.
DOLLING, a buck's head, ppr., attired, or. *Pl.* 91, *cr.* 14.
DOLMAN, Berks., a garb, ar., eared and banded, or. *Pl.* 48, *cr.* 10.
DOLPHIN, OLIVER, Esq., of Turoe, co. Galway, a dolphin, haurient, ppr. *Firmum in vitâ nihil.* *Pl.* 14, *cr.* 10.
DOLPHIN, a swan, ppr. *Pl.* 122, *cr.* 13.
DOLPHIN, Northumb., a swan's head and neck, between wings, ppr. *Pl.* 54, *cr.* 6.
DOLPHIN, and DOLPHINE, a lion, passant, gardant, or, in dexter, a mill-rind, sa. *Pl.* 102, *cr.* 6.
DOLSEBY, a demi-griffin, ar. winged, or. *Pl.* 18, *cr.* 6.
DOLTON, Eng., a demi-lion. *Pl.* 67, *cr.* 10.
DOMERE, Eng., a castle, sa., masoned, ar. *Pl.* 28, *cr.* 11.
DOMINICK, Bucks., a stag, sejant, or, attired, gu., gorged with a naval coronet, of the last, resting dexter on an antique shield, vert.
DOMVILE, and DOMVILLE, Salop, issuing from a cloud, a hand, in fess, stretching towards a garland of laurel in dexter. *Pl.* 73, *cr.* 11.
DOMVILLE, Bart., Iri., a lion's head, erased, ducally crowned. *Pl.* 90, *cr.* 4, (without charging.)
DOMVILLE, Bart., Herts., out of a mural coronet, gu., a demi-lion, ar., (supporting between paws an escutcheon, az., charged with three Oriental crowns, the points alternately radiated, or.) *Pl.* 17, *cr.* 7.
DOMVILLE, TAYLOR, MASCIE-DOMVILLE, Esq., of Lymme Hall, and Moss Hall, Chester, a buck's head, cabossed, ppr. *Pl.* 36, *cr.* 1.
DOMVILLE, Chesh., two lions' gambs, (erased,) in saltier, ar. *Pl.* 20, *cr.* 13.
DON, Bart., Sco., a pomegranate, ppr. *Non deerit alter aureus.* *Pl.* 67, *cr.* 8.
DON, Sco., in dexter hand a pen, ppr. *Suum cuique.* *Pl.* 26, *cr.* 13.
DON, and DONN, Eng., out of a ducal coronet; on a mount, a stag at gaze, all ppr. *Pl.* 19, *cr.* 14.
DONALD, Eng., out of a cloud; in dexter hand, in fess, ppr., a cross pattée, fitched, sa. *Pl.* 26, *cr.* 4.
DONALD, Sco., an arm, in armour, embowed, in hand a sword, all ppr. *Toujours prêt.* *Pl.* 2, *cr.* 8.
DONALD, Sco., an arm, in armour, embowed, in hand a scimitar, all ppr. *Toujours prêt.* *Pl.* 81, *cr.* 11.

DONALD, Sco., a garb, ppr. *Fac et spera.* *Pl.* 48, *cr.* 10.
DONALDSON, Sco., the rudder of a ship, ppr. *Steer steady.* *Pl.* 60, *cr.* 10.
DONALDSON, Lond., in dexter hand a sword, ppr. *My hope is constant in thee.* *Pl.* 21, *cr.* 10.
DONALDSON, Sco., on a rock, az., a raven, sa. *My hope is constant in thee.* *Pl.* 38, *cr.* 10.
DONALDSON, a garb, vert. *Nulli inimicus ero.* *Pl.* 48, *cr.* 10.
DONALDSON, Sco., in hand a sword, ppr. *Aut pax, aut bellum.* *Pl.* 21, *cr.* 10.
DONALDSON, a cock, crowing, ppr., within two adders, in orle. *Prudenter vigilo.* *Pl.* 18, *cr.* 5.
DONALDSON, in dexter hand a dagger, in pale, ppr., hilted, or, pommelled, ar. *Promptus.* *Pl.* 23, *cr.* 15.
DONAND, Eng., on the front of a rock, a Cornish chough, ppr. *Pl.* 70, *cr.* 11.
DONAND, a savage, wreathed about middle with leaves, ppr. *Pl.* 14, *cr.* 11.
DONAVAN, a hawk, wings displayed, ppr. *Pl.* 105, *cr.* 4.
DONCASTELL, Berks., a buck's head, couped, or, (vulned in neck, gu.) *Pl.* 91, *cr.* 14.
DONE, Eng., a bugle-horn. *Pl.* 89, *cr.* 3.
DONE, a bundle of arrows, ar., barbed, az., banded, gu. *Pl.* 54, *cr.* 15.
DONE, Chesh. : 1. A buck's head, couped at shoulders, ppr. *Pl.* 91, *cr.* 14. 2. Two sheaves of arrows, in saltier, or, banded, gu. *Pl.* 54, *cr.* 15.
DONEGAL, Marquess and Earl of, Earl of and Baron Belfast, and Viscount Chichester, Iri., Baron Fisherwick, G. B., (Chichester,) a stork, ppr., wings expanded, (in mouth a snake, ar., headed, or.) *Invitum sequitur honor*—or—*Honor sequitur fugientem.* *Pl.* 33, *cr.* 9, (snake, *pl.* 41, *cr.* 6.)
DONELAN, Eng., in a lion's paw, erased, a sceptre, in pale, ppr. *Pl.* 16, *cr.* 1.
DONELAN, EDMOND-HYACINTH, Esq., of Hillswood, co. Galway, a lion, rampant. *Omni violentiâ major.* *Pl.* 67, *cr.* 5.
DONELAN, and DONNELAN, a greyhound, sejant, ar. *Pl.* 66, *cr.* 15.
DONELLY, and DONNELLY, Iri., a church and spire, ppr. *Pl.* 45, *cr.* 6.
DONERAILE, Viscount and Baron, (Hayes St Leger,) Iri., a griffin, passant, or. *Haut et bon.* *Pl.* 61, *cr.* 14, (without gorging.)
DONGAN, a lion, passant, or, in dexter a helmet, ppr. *Pl.* 48, *cr.* 8, (helmet, *pl.* 19, *cr.* 15.)
DONHAULT, Northamp. and Oxon., a cherub, or. *Pl.* 126, *cr.* 10.
DONITHORN, Cornw., a swan, wings addorsed, naiant in a lake, ppr. *Pl.* 66, *cr.* 10.
DONKIN, a ship in distress, ppr. *Pl.* 21, *cr.* 11.
DONKIN, Eng., a leopard, couchant, ppr. *Pl.* 111, *cr.* 11.
DONNAR, an arm, in armour, embowed, ppr., garnished, or, in hand a truncheon, ar. *Pl.* 96, *cr* 4, (truncheon, *pl.* 33, *cr.* 4.)
DONNE, Chesh., a bundle of arrows, or, headed and feathered, ar., banded, gu. *Pl.* 54, *cr.* 15.
DONNE, a wolf's head, erased, or. *Pl.* 14, *cr.* 6.

DONOUGHMORE, Earl of, and Baron, Viscount Suirdale, Iri., Viscount Hutchinson, U.K., (Hely-Hutchinson,) a cockatrice, wings expanded, az., combed, wattled, and membered, or. *Pl.* 63, *cr.* 15.

DONOVAN, Iri., a cross fleury, fitched, ar. *Pl.* 65, *cr.* 9.

DONOVAN, Suss. and Surr., a hawk, wings displayed, ppr. *Adjuvante Deo in hostes.* *Pl.* 105, *cr.* 4.

DONNIKE, Eng., in dexter hand a tilting-spear, all ppr. *Pl.* 99, *cr.* 8.

DOOLAN, Iri., a demi-lion, rampant, gardant, in dexter a battle-axe, ppr. *Pl.* 101, *cr.* 14, (without charge.)

DOOLMAN, Iri., a wolf, passant, az. *Pl.* 46, *cr.* 6.

DOORE, a demi-tiger, az., crined and tufted, or, holding an escallop, of the last. *Pl.* 53, *cr.* 10, (escallop, *pl.* 141.)

DOPPING, Eng., a dove, volant, az. *Pl.* 25, *cr.* 6.

DOPPING, Iri., a demi-eagle, displayed, sa. *Pl.* 22, *cr.* 11.

DORAN, Eng., in lion's paw, sa., a battle-axe. *Pl.* 51, *cr.* 13.

DORAN, Iri., a bear's head, couped, in fess, between two branches of laurel, in orle, vert. *Pl.* 83, *cr.* 10.

DORAN, Iri., out of a ducal coronet, or, a lion's head, ppr. *Pl.* 90, *cr.* 9.

DORANNAN, Iri., an eagle, rising, ppr. *Pl.* 67, *cr.* 4.

DORCHESTER, Baron, (Guy-Carleton,) a dexter arm, embowed, in hand an arrow, ppr., arm naked to elbow, (the shirt folded above it, ar., and vested above, gu.) *Quondam his vicimus armis.* *Pl.* 92, *cr.* 14.

DORE, Eng., between the horns of a crescent, ar., a cross pattée, or. *Pl.* 37, *cr.* 10.

DORE, Wilts., on a mural coronet, ar., an eagle, rising, purp., in beak an antique shield. *Pl.* 67, *cr.* 4, (coronet, *pl.* 128, *fig.* 18; shield, *pl.* 36, *cr.* 11.)

DORIEN, a demi-savage, holding over dexter shoulder a hammer. *Pl.* 51, *cr.* 14.

DORINGTON, and DORRINGTON, Eng., in lion's gamb, ppr., a flag, gu., charged with a cheveron, or. *Pl.* 85, *cr.* 13.

DORMAN, in lion's paw a tilting-spear. *Pl.* 1, *cr.* 4.

DORMER, Earl of Carnarvon. *See* CARNARVON.

DORMER, Baron, (Dormer,) a (dexter) hand gloved, ppr., surmounted by a falcon, ar. *Cio che Dio vuole is voglio.* *Pl.* 1, *cr.* 13.

DORN, Lond., a stag's head, erased, ppr. *Pl.* 66, *cr.* 9.

DORN, round two battle-axes, addorsed, in pale, a serpent entwined, ppr. *Pl.* 14, *cr.* 13.

DORNFORD, Eng., two battle-axes, in saltier, addorsed, ppr. *Pl.* 52, *cr.* 10.

DORRELL, Bucks., Yorks., Wilts., and Linc., a goat's head, erased, ar., attired, or. *Pl.* 29, *cr.* 13.

DORRELL, an antelope's head, (couped,) ar., attired, or. *Pl.* 24, *cr.* 7.

DORRIEN, Herts., a cubit arm, erect, ppr., in hand a trefoil, slipped, vert. *Pl.* 78, *cr.* 6.

DORSET, Duke of, Earl of Dorset and Middlesex, Viscount Sackville, Baron Buckhurst, Craufield, and Bolebrooke, (Sackville-Germain,) out of a coronet, (composed of eight fleurs-de-lis,) or, an etoile, of eight points, ar. *Aut nunquam tentes, aut perfice.* *Pl.* 83, *cr.* 3.

DORVILLE, Eng., a rose, per fess, gu. and ar. *Pl.* 52, *cr.* 11.

DORWARD, Sco., a cross pattée, fitched, ar. *This I'll defend.* *Pl.* 27, *cr.* 14.

DOTCHEN, Worc., a stork's head, erased, ar., between wings, sa. *Pl.* 32, *cr.* 5, (wings, *pl.* 1, *cr.* 15.)

DOTSON, Cornw., in hand a sword, ppr. *Pl.* 21, *cr.* 10.

DOTTIN, Hants., a doe, trippant, ppr., charged on body with three torteaux, in fess. *Pl.* 20, *cr.* 14, (torteaux, *pl.* 141.)

DOUBLEDAY, Middx., an arm, in armour, or, resting gauntlet on a shield, az., thereon a mullet, pierced, gold.

DOUCE, AUGUSTUS-THOMAS, Esq., of Debtling, Kent, an antelope's head, per pale, ar. and sa. *Celer et vigilans.* *Pl.* 24, *cr.* 7.

DOUGAL, Sco., a bull's head, cabossed, ppr. *Pl.* 111, *cr.* 6.

DOUGAN, Lond., a lion, passant, (dexter cut off at the joint.) *Pl.* 48, *cr.* 8.

DOUGHTY, or DOUTY, a cubit-arm, erect, (vested, per pale, crenellée, or and ar., cuffed, gold,) in hand, ppr., a mullet of six points, sa. *Pl.* 62, *cr.* 13.

DOUGHTY, a dove, rising, in mouth an olive-branch, ppr. *Pl.* 79, *cr.* 8, (without globe.)

DOUGHTY, a mullet, gu. *Pl.* 41, *cr.* 1.

DOUGHTY, HENRY-MONTAGU, Esq., of Theberton Hall, Suff., a mullet, sa. *Palma non sine pulvere.* *Pl.* 41, *cr.* 1.

DOUGLAS, Baron, (Douglas,) Sco., on a chapeau, a salamander, vert, in fire, ppr. *Jamais arriére.* *Pl.* 86, *cr.* 14.

DOUGLAS, Bart., of Glenbervie, Sco., a salamander in flames, ppr. *Jamais arriére.* *Pl.* 20, *cr.* 15.

DOUGLAS, Bart., of Carr, Sco., an arm, in armour, embowed, in hand a dagger, all ppr. *Lock sicker.* *Pl.* 120, *cr.* 11.

DOUGLAS, of Kinglassie, a sanglier between the clefts of an oak-tree, with a chain and lock binding them together, all ppr. *Lock sicker.* *Pl.* 57, *cr.* 12.

DOUGLAS, of Killhead, Bart., a human heart, gu., bezantée, imperially crowned, and winged, or. *Forward.* *Pl.* 52, *cr.* 2, (crown, *pl.* 142, *fig.* 1.)

DOUGLAS, of Cruxton, on a chapeau, gu., turned up, erm., a salamander in flames, ppr. *Forward.* *Pl.* 86, *cr.* 14.

DOUGLAS, of Cavers, in dexter hand a broken lance, in bend, ppr. *Do or die.* *Pl.* 66, *cr.* 4.

DOUGLAS, of Bridgeford, a dexter hand grasping a sword, erect, all ppr. *Petit ardua virtus.* *Pl.* 23, *cr.* 15.

DOUGLAS, of Castle-Douglas, Bart., a heart, gu., imperially crowned, or, winged, ar., on each wing a mullet, sa. *Audax et promptus.* *Pl.* 52, *cr.* 2, (crown, *pl.* 142, *fig.* 1.)

DOUGLAS, of Tympindean, a plume of ostrich-feathers, ppr. *Pl.* 12, *cr.* 9.

DOUGLAS, of Kelhead, a heart, winged, ppr. *Jamais arriére.* *Pl.* 39, *cr.* 7.

DOUGLAS, Eng., a heart, bezantée, royally crowned, between wings, ppr. *Pl.* 52, *cr.* 2, (crown, *pl.* 127, *fig.* 2.)

DOUGLAS, Kent, an arm, in armour, embowed, ppr., garnished, or, hand grasping a dagger, also ppr., hilt and pommel, gold. *Pl.* 120, *cr.* 11.

DOUGLAS, Sco., a human heart, gu., winged and crowned, or, charged with a crescent, chequy, gu. and ar. *Forward.* *Pl.* 52, *cr.* 2.

DOUGLAS, Sco., a martlet, sa. *Sursum.* *Pl.* 111, *cr.* 5.

DOUGLAS, Sco., a peacock, ppr. *Pl.* 54, *cr.* 13.

DOUGLAS, in hand a human heart, ppr., ensigned with a crescent, ar. *Meliora sperando.* *Pl.* 59, *cr.* 12, (crescent, *pl.* 18, *cr.* 14.)

DOUGLAS, out of a bush, in dexter hand an oak-leaf, ppr. *Tandem fit surculus arbor.*

DOUGLAS, an oak-tree, ppr., with a lock hanging from one of the branches. *Quæ serata secura.* *Pl.* 16, *cr.* 8, (lock, *pl.* 18, *cr.* 7.)

DOUGLAS, out of a cloud, in dexter hand a sword, erect, ppr. *God for us.* *Pl.* 93, *cr.* 8.

DOUGLAS, a demi-savage, wreathed about head and middle with leaves, holding a club, ppr. *Pl.* 14, *cr.* 11.

DOUGLAS, on stump of tree, a falcon, wings expanded, ppr., belled, or, charged on breast with a mullet, az. *Sursum.* *Pl.* 78, *cr.* 8, (falcon, *pl.* 105, *cr.* 4.)

DOUGLAS, a heart, gu. *Fortis et fidelis.* *Pl.* 55, *cr.* 13.

DOUGLAS, a greyhound's head, sa. *Pl.* 14, *cr.* 4, (without charging.)

DOUGLAS, a griffin's head, couped. *Pl.* 38, *cr.* 3.

DOUGLAS, (out of a cloud,) in dexter hand a broken tilting-spear. *Pl.* 66, *cr.* 4.

DOUGLAS, SCOTT, Bart.: 1. A lion's head, erased, in mouth a thistle, ppr. *Pl.* 95, *cr.* 6, (thistle, *pl.* 100, *cr.* 9.) 2. A cubit-arm, vert, hand grasping a broken tilting-spear, all ppr. For *Douglas—Do or die*—and for *Scott—Pro patriâ.* *Pl.* 66, *cr.* 4.

DOUGLAS, Duke of BUCCLEUGH, Earl of MORTON, Marquess of QUEENSBERRY, Earl of WEMYSS, and Earl of SELKIRK. *See those titles respectively.*

DOUGLASS, CHARLES-MATHEW, Esq., of Grace Hall, co. Down, a dexter cubit arm, erect, in hand a human heart, all ppr. *Forward.* *Pl.* 59, *cr.* 12.

DOUNIE, and DOWNIE, Sco., a cock, ppr. *Courage.* *Pl.* 67, *cr.* 14.

DOUNIES, Eng., a wolf's head. *Pl.* 14, *cr.* 6.

DOUTHWAITE, on a rock, ppr., a fleur-de-lis, counterchanged, or and gu. *Pl.* 76, *cr.* 12.

DOVE, Sco., a pegasus, salient, wings addorsed, and ducally gorged, all ppr. *Pl.* 57, *cr.* 15.

DOVE, Surr., in a chaplet, vert, banded, or, a dove, ppr. *Pl.* 2, *cr.* 11.

DOVE, on a tower, a dove, rising, ppr. *Pl.* 84, *cr.* 3.

DOVE, Suff., on a tower, ar., a dove, wings expanded, ppr. *Pl.* 8, *cr.* 15.

DOVE, a dove, wings expanded, ppr., (in mouth a sprig, vert.) *Pl.* 27, *cr.* 5.

DOVER, Hants, on a demi-tower, triple-towered, ar., a demi-cockatrice, wings expanded, vert.

DOVER, Eng., an owl, ar. *Pl.* 27, *cr.* 9.

DOVOR, Baron, (Agar-Ellis,) a demi-lion, rampant, or. *Non hæc sine numine.* *Pl.* 67, *cr.* 10.

Dow, Sco., a dove, ar. *Pl.* 66, *cr.* 12.

Dow, Sco., a dove, ppr. *Patience.* *Pl.* 66, *cr.* 12.

DOWBIGGIN, a reindeer's head, cabossed, ppr. *Pl.* 114, *cr.* 7.

DOWD, Iri., a bird, ppr. *Pl.* 52, *cr.* 12.

DOWDAL, and DOWDALL, Eng., out of a ducal coronet, a boar's head and neck, collared, or. *Pl.* 102, *cr.* 14.

DOWDAL, and DOWDALL, a dove, ducally crowned, ppr. *Pl.* 66, *cr.* 12, (crown, *same plate.*)

DOWDAL, and DOWDALL, Iri., a holy lamb, ppr. *Pl.* 48, *cr.* 13.

DOWDE, Iri., a mailed arm, in hand a spear, all ppr., headed, ar. *Pl.* 44, *cr.* 9, (spear, *pl.* 99, *cr.* 8.)

DOWDESWELL, Ess., issuing from clouds, two hands, wrenching asunder the trunk of a tree, ppr. *Pl.* 55, *cr.* 8.

DOWDING, Eng., a Catherine-wheel, az. *Pl.* 1, *cr.* 7.

DOWDS, Iri., a dove, gu. *Pl.* 66, *cr.* 12.

DOWELL, Eng., a lion's head, erased, sa. *Pl.* 81, *cr.* 4.

DOWELL, two lions' gambs, (erased,) in saltier, enfiled with a wreath of laurel. *Pl.* 20, *cr.* 13, (laurel, *pl.* 79, *cr.* 14.)

DOWGLAS, Sco., a dexter arm, in armour, embowed, in hand a sword, all ppr. *Pl.* 2, *cr.* 8.

DOWGLAS, Sco., in hand a scimitar. *Honor et amor.* *Pl.* 29, *cr.* 8.

DOWGLAS, Sco., in dexter hand a couteau-sword, ppr. *Pl.* 29, *cr.* 8.

DOWIE, Sco., a dove, volant, in mouth an olive-branch, ppr. *Patience.* *Pl.* 25, *cr.* 6.

DOWIES, Norf., a wolf's head, erm., charged with a mullet. *Pl.* 14, *cr.* 6, (mullet, *pl.* 141.)

DOWINE, Sco., in dexter hand a dagger, ppr. *Hold fast.* *Pl.* 28, *cr.* 4.

DOWKER, out of a ducal coronet, sa., a plume of five ostrich-feathers, ar. *Pl.* 100, *cr.* 12, (without charge.)

DOWKER, Iri., two dexter hands, couped and conjoined, supporting a human heart, ppr. *Pl.* 43, *cr.* 15.

DOWLAND, Eng., a tiger, passant, gardant, or. *Pl.* 67, *cr.* 15.

DOWLER, Eng., a hand, erect, plucking a thistle, ppr. *Pl.* 54, *cr.* 11.

DOWLEY, Eng., a demi-heraldic-tiger, gu., ducally gorged, or. *Pl.* 57, *cr.* 13.

DOWLING, Iri., a lion's head, erased, az., gorged with two bars, or. *Pl.* 7, *cr.* 10.

DOWLING, Eng., out of a mural coronet, a dexter arm, vested, in hand a sword, wavy. *Pl.* 65, *cr.* 10, (coronet, *pl.* 128, *fig.* 18.)

DOWMAN, Yorks., out of a mural coronet, a bundle of (seven) arrows, banded. *Pl.* 54, *cr.* 15, (coronet, *pl.* 128, *fig.* 18.)

DOWN, and DOWNS, Eng., an arm, from elbow, in hand a broken hammer. *Pl.* 93, *cr.* 5.

DOWNE, Viscount, Iri., and a Bart., Eng., (Dawnay,) a demi-Saracen, in armour, couped at thighs, wreathed about temples, ppr., in dexter a ring, or, stoned, az., in sinister a lion's gamb, erased, of the second, armed, gu. *Timet pudorem.*

DOWNE, Surr., a sea-lion, erect, gu., guttée, or. *Pl.* 25, *cr.* 12.

DOWNE, an arm, ar., cuffed, or, in hand, ppr., a crescent, of the second, (flammant, ppr.) *Pl.* 110, *cr.* 7.

DOWNER, Eng., two hands conjoined, in fess, winged at wrists. *Pl.* 14, *cr.* 9.

DOWNES, Baron, (Ulysses Burgh,) Iri.: 1. For *Burgh*, a mountain-cat, sejant, ppr., (collared and chain reflexed over back, or.) *Pl.* 24, *cr.* 6. 2. For *Downes*, a wolf's head, erased, ppr., charged on neck with a mullet, or. *A cruce salus. Pl.* 14, *cr.* 6, (mullet, *pl.* 141.)

DOWNES, Ess., a stag, lodged, ar. *Pl.* 67, *cr.* 2.

DOWNES, Chesh., a buck, couchant, ar. *Pl.* 67, *cr.* 2.

DOWNES, Suff. and Norf., a wolf's head, ar., charged with a mullet. *Pl.* 14, *cr.* 6, (mullet, *pl.* 141.)

DOWNES, a buck's head, erased, ppr. *Pl.* 66, *cr.* 9.

DOWNES, Suff., a wolf's head, erased, ppr., charged on neck with a mullet, ar. *Pl.* 14, *cr.* 6, (mullet, *pl.* 141.)

DOWNFIELD, a cock, ppr. *Virtute et labore. Pl.* 67, *cr.* 14.

DOWNHAM, Iri., a dexter arm, embowed, ppr., in hand a club, vert. *Pl.* 123, *cr.* 10.

DOWNIE, Sco., a ship under sail, (with a plough on deck,) all ppr. *Ex undis aratra. Pl.* 109, *cr.* 8.

DOWNIE, Eng., a dagger and a cross crosslet, fitched, in saltier. *Pl.* 89, *cr.* 14.

DOWNIE, a boar's head, erased, or. *Pl.* 16, *cr.* 11.

DOWNIE, Sco., out of a ducal coronet, a cock's head. *Pl.* 97, *cr.* 15.

DOWNING, Cambs. and Norf., an arm, in armour, embowed, ar., in hand, ppr., a broad arrow, or, headed and feathered, of the first. *Pl.* 96, *cr.* 6.

DOWNING, Norf., a bear's head, couped, in fess. *Pl.* 111, *cr.* 4.

DOWNING, Iri., a boar's head, couped, gu. *Pl.* 48, *cr.* 2.

DOWNING, Ess., out of a ducal coronet, a swan, or. *Pl.* 100, *cr.* 7.

DOWNMAN, Eng., in a hand, a lancet, ppr. *Pl.* 29, *cr.* 6.

DOWNS, out of a tower, ar., a demi-lion, rampant, gu., (holding a battle-axe, ppr.) *Pl.* 42, *cr.* 4.

DOWNSHIRE, Marquess of, Earl and Viscount Hillsborough, &c., Iri., Earl of Hillsborough, Viscount Fairford, and Baron Harwich, Eng., (Blundell - Sandys - Trumbull - Hill,) a reindeer's head, couped, gu., attired and collared, or. *Ne tentes, aut perfice. Pl.* 2, *cr.* 13.

DOWNTON, Salop, in dexter hand a sword, in pale, enfiled with a savage's head, all ppr. *Pl.* 118, *cr.* 3.

DOWSE, Eng., issuing from clouds, two dexter hands, brandishing scimitars, ppr. *Pl.* 122, *cr.* 9.

DOWSING, Norf., a squirrel, sejant, cracking a nut, ppr. *Pl.* 16, *cr.* 9.

DOWSON, Eng., a lion, rampant, per fess, or and gu. *Pl.* 67, *cr.* 5.

DOWSON, Suff., a dove, ppr. *Pl.* 66, *cr.* 12.

DOX, and DOXEY, Eng., a demi-savage, with a quiver of arrows on back, in dexter three arrows, in pale, sinister pointing to an imperial crown, all ppr. *Pl.* 86, *cr.* 3.

DOYLE, and DOYLEY, Norf., out of a mural coronet, ar., an arm, embowed, ppr., (vested, sa., cuffed, of the first,) in hand a spear, of the second. *Pl.* 115, *cr.* 14, (spear, *pl.* 99, *cr.* 8.)

DOYLE, Bart., Lond., out of a ducal coronet, or, a buck's head, erased, ppr. *Fortitudine vincit. Pl.* 29, *cr.* 7.

DOYLE, Iri., a stag's head, couped, gu., ducally gorged, ppr. *Pl.* 91, *cr.* 14, (gorging, *pl.* 128, *fig.* 3.)

DOYLE, G.C.B., a Mameluke on horseback, at full speed, (in the act of throwing a djirid,) all ppr. *Fortitudine vincit. Pl.* 115, *cr.* 5.

D'OYLEY, or D'OYLY, Bart., Norf., out of a ducal coronet, or, two eagles' wings, (addorsed) and erect, sa., bezantée. *Do no yll, quoth D'Oyle. Pl.* 17, *cr.* 9.

D'OYLEY, Bart., a demi-dragon, wings addorsed, in claws a fleur-de-lis. *Pl.* 82, *cr.* 10, (fleur-de-lis, *pl.* 141.)

D'OYLEY, a buck's head, cabossed, ar. *Pl.* 36, *cr.* 1.

D'OYLEY, Oxon., a demi-dragon, wings addorsed, or. *Pl.* 82, *cr.* 10.

DOYNE, Iri., a holly-tree, vert. *Pl.* 22, *cr.* 10.

DRACELOW, and DRAKELOW, a demi-husbandman, in dexter an ox-yoke, ppr. *Pl.* 122, *cr.* 1.

DRAGHORN, and DREGHORN, on rye-grass, a horse, feeding, ppr. *Utitur ante quæsitis.*

DRAGO, Cambs., a demi-eagle, displayed, per pale, or and gu., dexter wing charged with a fleur-de-lis, of the last, sinister with one, gold. *Invidiâ major. Pl.* 22, *cr.* 11.

DRAGONER, Middx., a pheon, sa. *Pl.* 26, *cr.* 12.

DRAKE, a hand out of clouds drawing a ship round a globe. *Perseverando. Pl.* 26, *cr.* 15.

DRAKE, CHARLES CUTCLIFFE, Esq., of Springfield, Devons.: 1. A dexter arm, erect, couped at elbow, ppr., in hand, a battle-axe, sa., headed, ar. *Pl.* 73, *cr.* 7. 2. An eagle, displayed, gu. *Aquila non captat muscas. Pl.* 48, *cr.* 11.

DRAKE, COLUMBUS-PATRICK, Esq., of Roriston, co. Meath, a wyvern, wings displayed, tail nowed, gu. *Pl.* 63, *cr.* 13.

DRAKE, Bart., of Buckland, Devons., a ship under reef, drawn round a globe with a cable rope, by a hand out of clouds, all ppr. *Auxilio divino* — and — *Sic parvis magna. Pl.* 26, *cr.* 15.

DRAKE, an arm, embowed, ar., thereon two bendlets, wavy, gu., supporting a battle-axe, staff, sa., headed, of the first. *Pl.* 121, *cr.* 14.

DRAKE, a reindeer's head, erased, or, ducally gorged and attired, sa. *Pl.* 2, *cr.* 13, (gorging, *pl.* 128, *fig.* 3.)

DRAKE, ELLIOTT-FULLER, Bart., Devons.: 1. For *Drake*, a ship under reef, drawn round a globe with a cable rope, by a hand out of clouds, all ppr. *Auxilio divino*—and—*Sic parvis magna. Pl.* 26, *cr.* 15. 2. For *Elliott*, a dexter hand, in armour, couped above wrist, grasping a scimitar, all ppr., wrist charged with a key, sa. *Fortiter et recte. Pl.* 125, *cr.* 5. 3. For *Fuller*, out of a ducal coronet, gu., a lion's head, ar. *Sic parvis magna*—and—*Per ardua. Pl.* 90, *cr.* 9.

DRAKE, Norf., Devons., Suss., Bucks., and Iri., a dexter arm, erect, ppr., in hand a battle-axe, sa., headed, ar. *Pl.* 73, *cr.* 7.

DRAKE, Iri. and Eng., a wyvern, wings addorsed, ar. *Pl.* 63, *cr.* 13.

DRAKE, Chesh., a dexter arm, erect, ppr., in hand a battle-axe, sa., headed, or. *Pl.* 73, *cr.* 7.

DRAKE, Norf., a reindeer's head, couped, ar. Pl. 2, cr. 13, (without collar or chain.)
DRAKE, Bucks., a savage, wreathed about waist and temples, vert, holding over dexter shoulder a club, or. Pl. 14, cr. 11.
DRAKE, Bucks., a cubit arm, in hand a battle-axe, erect, all ppr. Pl. 73, cr. 7.
DRAKE-TYRWHITT, Bucks. and Linc. : 1. For Drake, a naked dexter arm, erect, in hand a battle-axe, ar., headed, sa. Pl. 73, cr. 7. 2. For Tyrwhitt, a savage, ppr., wreathed, vert, (holding in both hands a club.) Pl. 14, cr. 11.
DRAKENFORD, an anchor and cable, ppr. Pl. 42, cr. 12.
DRANE, a demi-lion, rampant, ppr. Pl. 67, cr. 10.
DRANSFIELD, Ess. and Yorks., a sword, in pale, enfiled with a Turk's head, all ppr. Pl. 27, cr. 3.
DRAPER, Eng., a stag's head, gu., attired, or, (charged on neck with a fess, between three annulets, of the last.) Vicit, pepercit. Pl. 91, cr. 14.
DRAPER, Northumb., a cubit arm, vert, (vested, erminois,) in hand, ppr., a mullet, of six points, or. Pl. 17, cr. 10.
DRAPER, Iri., a galley, oars in action, ppr. Pl. 34, cr. 5.
DRAPER, Middx., Beds., and Oxon., a tiger's head, vert, tufted, or, pierced through neck by an arrow, gold. Pl. 94, cr. 10.
DRAPER, Leic. and Notts., a cubit arm, erect, (vested, vert, cuffed and puffed, ar.,) in hand, ppr., a covered cup, or. Pl. 35, cr. 9.
DRAPER, Bucks., a camel's head, erm., bridled, or, maned, sa. Pl. 120, cr. 12, (without gorging.)
DRAPER, Lond., a stag's head, erased, gu., (gorged with a fess between two gemelles, ar., and charged with a fleur-de-lis, sa.) Pl. 66, cr. 9.
DRAX, a demi-dragon, wings addorsed, or. Pl. 82, cr. 10.
DRAX, out of a ducal coronet, or, an eagle's head, ppr. Pl. 20, cr. 12, (without pellet.)
DRAYCOTE, Derbs., a dragon's head, erased, gu., scaled, or. Pl. 107, cr. 10, (without collar.)
DRAYCOT, or DRAYCOTT, a dragon's head, couped, vert. Pl. 87, cr. 12.
DRAYCOT, or DRAYCOTT, a dragon's head, erased, gu. Pl. 107, cr. 10, (without collar.)
DRAYNER, Kent, a lion, sejant, in paws a broken tilting-spear, all ar. Pl. 60, cr. 4.
DRAYNER, Middx., a pheon, or. Pl. 26, cr. 12.
DRAYTON, Lond., the sun, or. Non nobis solum. Pl. 68, cr. 14.
DRAYTON, Eng., in dexter hand, couped, ppr., a cross crosslet, fitched, gu. Pl. 99, cr. 1.
DRAYTON, an eagle's leg, couped, or, thigh, az.
DREUX, Eng., a ram's head, ar., armed, or. Pl. 34, cr. 12.
DREW, Iri., in dexter hand a chapeau, all ppr., between two laurel-branches, vert. Pl. 59, cr. 4.
DREW, Wilts., a lion's head, erased, gu., collared, gobony, or and az. Pl. 7, cr. 10.
DREW, Wilts., Devons., and Herts., a bull's head, erased, sa., armed, or, in mouth three wheat-ears, gold. Pl. 19, cr. 3, (wheat, pl. 89, cr. 4.)

DREW, on a mount, vert, a roebuck, current, or. Pl. 84, cr. 5, (without laurel or gorging.)
DREW, Sco., a cup, or. Pl. 42, cr. 1.
DREWE, Eng., two arms, from shoulder, couped, in saltier, ppr., vested, ar., each holding a scimitar, in pale, of the first. Pl. 52, cr. 1.
DREWELL, Bucks., a dexter arm, embowed, ppr., vested, or, cuffed, gu., in hand a covered cup, of the second. Pl. 39, cr. 1.
DREWRY, Suss., a greyhound, current, sa., (collared, or.) Pl. 28, cr. 7, (without charge.)
DREWRY, Ess., Norf., and Suff., a greyhound, current, ar. Pl. 28, cr. 7, (without charge.)
DRING, Eng., on a chapeau, a phœnix in flames, ppr. Pl. 83, cr. 12.
DRINKWATER, three ears of wheat, two in saltier and one in pale, enfiled with a ducal coronet, all or. Pl. 102, cr. 1, (coronet, pl. 8, cr. 9.)
DRISDALE, Iri., within a chaplet, or, a thistle, slipped and leaved, ppr. Pl. 72, cr. 7, (thistle, pl. 68, cr. 9.)
DRIVER, Eng., a heart, gu., winged, or. Pl. 39, cr. 7.
DROGHEDA, Marquess and Earl of, Viscount and Baron Moore, Iri., Baron Moore, U.K., (Moore,) out of a ducal coronet, or, a moor's head, ppr., (wreathed, ar. and az.) Fortis cadere, cedere non potest. Pl. 120, cr. 3, (coronet, same plate, cr. 6.)
DROUGHT, Eng., under a tree, a stag at gaze, ppr. Pl. 118, cr. 13.
DROUGHT, Iri., a sceptre, or. Pl. 82, cr. 3.
DROUGHT, JOHN-HEAD, Esq., of Lettybrook, King's County, a rainbow, ppr. Semper sitiens. Pl. 79, cr. 1, (without globe.)
DRUCE, Eng., two arms, couped, in saltier, gu., each hand holding a scimitar, in pale, ppr. Pl. 52, cr. 1.
DRUCE, an arm, in armour, embowed, hand grasping a scimitar, ppr. Pl. 81, cr. 11.
DRUITT, Eng., out of a ducal coronet, a plume of five ostrich-feathers, banded. Pl. 106, cr. 11, (without chapeau.)
DRUMMOND, Eng. and Sco., two arms drawing a bow and arrow, ppr. Arte et marte. Pl. 100, cr. 4.
DRUMMOND, Bart., of Hawthornden, Sco., a demi-pegasus, ar., winged, or. Hos gloria reddit honores. Pl. 91, cr. 2, (without gorging.)
DRUMMOND, JOHN, Esq., of The Boyce, Glouc., two arms drawing an arrow to head, ppr. Marte et arte. Pl. 100, cr. 4.
DRUMMOND, ANDREW-ROBERT, Esq., of Cadland, Hants., a goshawk, wings expanded, ppr. Pl. 105, cr. 4.
DRUMMOND, Earl of Kinnoul, and Viscount Strathallan. See KINNOUL and STRATHALLAN.
DRUMMOND, a pegasus, ppr., maned and winged, or. Hos gloria reddit honores. Pl. 28, cr. 9.
DRUMMOND, a demi-pegasus, armed and winged, or. Pl. 91, cr. 2, (without coronet.)
DRUMMOND, a falcon, rising, ppr. Pl. 105, cr. 4.
DRUMMOND, of Riccarton, a lion, rampant, az., armed and langued, gu. Dum spiro, spero. Pl. 67, cr. 5.
DRUMMOND, of Cargill, an eagle, volant. Pl. 114, cr. 10.
DRUMMOND, of Arncraig, two arms, ppr., shooting an arrow from a bow, or. Marte et arte. Pl. 100, cr. 4.

DRUMMOND, Earl of Perth, on a ducal coronet, a sloth-hound, standing, ppr., collared and leashed, gu. *Gang warily. Pl.* 3, *cr.* 8.

DRUMMOND, of Blair, a nest of young ravens, ppr. *Deus providebit. Pl.* 56, *cr.* 5.

DRUMMOND, of Invermay, in dexter hand a flaming heart, ppr. *Pl.* 59, *cr.* 12, (heart, *pl.* 68, *cr.* 13.)

DRUMMOND, of Machany, a falcon, hooded, jessed, and belled, ppr. *Prius mori quam fidem fallere. Pl.* 38, *cr.* 12.

DRUMMOND, of Logie Almond, a dexter arm, from shoulder, in hand a broadsword, ppr. *Nil timeo. Pl.* 34, *cr.* 7.

DRUMMOND, of Colnhalzie, on a rock, a turtle-dove, ppr. *Stomobolis. Pl.* 85, *cr.* 14.

DRUMMOND, of Pitkellanie, a sword and garb, in saltier, both ppr. *Et marte, et arte. Pl.* 70, *cr.* 7.

DRUMMOND, of Cultmalundy, in hand a heart, ppr. *Cum corde. Pl.* 59, *cr.* 12.

DRUMMOND, of Carlowrie, a dexter hand holding a curling-stone. *Have at all. Pl.* 104, *cr.* 6.

DRUMMOND, of Midhope, three stars, in a cheveron, or. *Ad astra per ardua. Pl.* 71, *cr.* 12.

DRUMMOND, of Kildees, a garland of laurel, ppr. *Si recte facias. Pl.* 54, *cr.* 10.

DRUMMOND, of Madderty, a falcon, ppr., armed, jessed, and belled, or. *Lord, have mercy. Pl.* 67, *cr.* 3.

DRUMMOND, of Monedie, a dove, standing on an anchor, in pale, ppr. *Spes mea, res mea. Pl.* 3, *cr.* 10.

DRUMMOND, a ship in distress, ppr. *Pl.* 21, *cr.* 11.

DRUMMOND, a demi-lion, az. *Dum spiro, spero. Pl.* 67, *cr.* 10.

DRUMMOND, a goshawk, wings displayed, ppr. *Pl.* 105, *cr.* 4.

DRUMMOND, in hand a spear, ppr. *Per mare, per terras. Pl.* 99, *cr.* 8.

DRUMMOND, a pheon, or. *Consequitur quodcunque petit. Pl.* 26, *cr.* 12.

DRUMMOND, a garland of laurel, ppr. *Si recti facies. Pl.* 54, *cr.* 10.

DRUMMOND, on a (dexter hand, gloved, a hooded hawk,) ppr. *Prius mori quam fidem fallere. Pl.* 83, *cr.* 13.

DRUMMOND, an eagle, rising from a globe, ppr. *Altiora peto. Pl.* 34, *cr.* 2.

DRUMMOND, on a ducal coronet, or, a greyhound, statant, ar. *Pl.* 104, *cr.* 1, (coronet, *same plate.*)

DRUMMOND, a falcon, close, regardant, in dexter a garland of laurel, all ppr. *Pl.* 42, *cr.* 7.

DRUMMOND, on a ducal coronet, or, a talbot, statant, ar., collared and lined, gu. *Pl.* 3, *cr.* 8.

DRUMMOND, an eagle, rising, (to sinister, head in the sun.) *Pl.* 67, *cr.* 4.

DRUMSON, in dexter hand a battle-axe, ppr. *Spectemur agendo. Pl.* 73, *cr.* 7.

DRURY, Eng., a greyhound's head, erased, ppr. *Pl.* 89, *cr.* 2.

DRURY, a greyhound, current, ppr., collared, or. *Pl.* 28, *cr.* 7, (without charge.)

DRURY, Iri., a battle-axe, in pale, ppr. *Pl.* 14, *cr.* 8.

DRY, Lond., on a ducal coronet, a lion, passant, gardant, ducally crowned, ppr. *Pl.* 120, *cr.* 15, (coronet, *same plate.*)

DRYDEN, Bart., Northamp., a demi-lion, az., sustaining in dexter a sphere, or. *Pl.* 113, *cr.* 2, (sphere, *pl.* 114, *cr.* 6.)

DRYLAND, Norf., a demi-man, in military costume, holding a banner, displayed, gu., charged with a cross, ar. *Pl.* 2, *cr.* 12.

DRYSDALE, Sco., an anchor, with cable, ppr. *Non sine anchord. Pl.* 42, *cr.* 12.

DRYSDALE, Eng., a crane's head, crowned, ppr. *Pl.* 71, *cr.* 10.

DRYSDALE, Sco., a martlet, sa. *Per varios casus. Pl.* 111, *cr.* 5.

DRYWOOD, Ess., a greyhound's head, per pale, or and gu., collared, az., between wings, counterchanged. *Pl.* 43, *cr.* 11, (wings, *pl.* 1, *cr.* 15.)

DRYWOOD, Ess., an oak-branch, fructed, ppr. *Pl.* 32, *cr.* 13.

DUANE, Eng. and Iri., a wolf's head, erased, ppr. *Pl.* 14, *cr.* 6.

DUBBER, Surr., out of a mural coronet, gu., two wings expanded, ar., each charged with a bend, of the first, and thereon three crescents, of the second. *Pl.* 80, *cr.* 15, (coronet, *pl.* 128, *fig.* 18 ; crescent, *pl.* 141.)

DUBERLEY, JAMES, Esq., of Gaines Hall, Hunts., a dexter arm, embowed, ppr., in hand three ears of wheat, or. *Res, non verba. Pl.* 89, *cr.* 4.

DUBERLEY, and DUBERLY, a cock, in beak a trefoil, ppr. *Pl.* 55, *cr.* 12.

DUBERLEY, and DUBERLY, Wel., a dexter arm, embowed, ppr., in hand, also ppr., three wheat-ears, or. *Pl.* 89, *cr.* 4.

DUBISSON, a cannet, sa. *Nil impossibile. Pl.* 90, *cr.* 15.

DUBISSON, on a chapeau, a cannet, sa. *Nil impossibile. Pl.* 90, *cr.* 15, (chapeau, *pl.* 127, *fig.* 13.)

DU BOIS, a falcon, close, ppr., belled, or. *Pl.* 67, *cr.* 3.

DU BOYS, Lond., a wheel, or. *Pl.* 32, *cr.* 15.

DU CANE, Lond. and Ess., a demi-lion, rampant, sa., ducally crowned, or, supporting an anchor, erect, gold. *Pl.* 19, *cr.* 6, (crown, *same plate, cr.* 9.)

DUCAREL, Surr., a cock, gu. *Pl.* 67, *cr.* 14.

DUCAT, and DUCHET. Sco. and Eng., issuing from clouds, two hands conjoined, in fess, holding a palm-branch, all ppr. *Pl.* 102, *cr.* 2.

DUCIE, Earl of, and Baron Moreton, (Reynolds-Morton,) a demi-moorcock, displayed, ppr., combed and wattled, gu. *Perseverando. Pl.* 90, *cr.* 13.

DUCIE, Staffs., a sea-lion, per fess, or and ppr., holding an anchor, of the second. *Pl.* 25, *cr.* 13, (anchor, *pl.* 42, *cr.* 12.)

DUCIE, Eng., two palm-branches, in orle, vert. *Pl.* 87, *cr.* 8.

DUCIE, a sea-lion, fore-part, or, tail, ar., supporting with dexter an anchor, az., fluke, of the first. *Pl.* 80, *cr.* 13, (anchor, *pl.* 42, *cr.* 12.)

DUCK, Norf. and Devons., on a mount, vert, a falcon, az., wings expanded, beaked and legged, or. *Pl.* 61, *cr.* 12, (without gorging.)

DUCK, on an anchor, erect, a snake, entwined, ppr. *Pl.* 35, *cr.* 14.

DUCKENFIELD, a demi-husbandman, holding over dexter shoulder a ploughshare, all ppr. *Pl.* 122, *cr.* 1.

DUCKENSFIELD, Eng., on a tower, embattled, a flag, displayed, or. *Pl.* 8, *cr.* 13.

DUCKET, Lond. and Wilts., a garb of lavender, vert, flowered, az., banded, or. *Pl.* 13, *cr.* 2.

DUCKET, a sheldrake, ppr. *Pl.* 90, *cr.* 15.

DUCKET, Eng., three wheat-ears, ppr. *Pl.* 102, *cr.* 1.

DUCKETT, Bart., Wilts.: 1. For *Jackson*, a sheldrake, ppr., (charged on breast with a saltier, gu.) *Malo pati quam fœdari. Pl.* 90, *cr.* 15. 2. For *Duckett*, a garb of lavender, vert. *Je veux le droit. Pl.* 13, *cr.* 2.

DUCKETT, Wilts., out of a ducal coronet, or, a plume of (six) ostrich-feathers, ar. *Je veux le droit. Pl.* 100, *cr.* 12, (without charge.)

DUCKETT, Eng., a cockatrice, displayed, ppr. *Pl.* 102, *cr.* 15.

DUCKINFIELD, and DUCKINGFIELD, out of a ducal coronet, or, a dexter arm, vested, gu., cuffed, ar., in hand the sun in splendour, gold. *Pl.* 89, *cr.* 11.

DUCKWORTH, Bart., Devons., a tower, the battlements partly demolished, from the top flames issuant, ppr., on sinister side a sea-lion, erect, az., paws against the tower. *Disciplinâ, fide, perseverantiâ. Pl.* 118, *cr.* 15, (lion, *pl.* 25, *cr.* 12.)

DUCKWORTH, on a garb, in fess, or, a wild duck, ppr. *Pl.* 122, *cr.* 3, (duck, *pl.* 90, *cr.* 15.)

DUCKWORTH, a female, in dexter, the sun, in sinister, the moon, ppr. *Pl.* 107, *cr.* 14.

DU COIN, Eng., three mullets, one and two. *Pl.* 46, *cr.* 15.

DUDDINGSTON, and DUDINGSTOUN, Sco., a greyhound's head, couped, ppr. *Pl.* 14, *cr.* 4, (without charge.)

DUDGEON, Eng., a holly-branch, vert, and a cross crosslet, fitched, az., in saltier. *Pl.* 102, *cr.* 3.

DUDGEON, Sco., issuing from a human heart, a hand, grasping a scimitar, all ppr. *Pl.* 35, *cr.* 7.

DUDGEON, Sco., issuing from a human heart, a hand, holding a (sword.) *Pl.* 35, *cr.* 7.

DUDLEY, Cambs., a buck's head, erased, ar., attired, sa., (neck pierced by an arrow, barbed and flighted, ppr., and gorged with a collar, gu., therefrom pendent an escutcheon, of the second, charged with a hand, in bend, or.) *Pl.* 66, *cr.* 9.

DUDLEY, a unicorn, passant. *Pl.* 106, *cr.* 3.

DUDLEY, out of a viscount's coronet, or, a lion's head, az., collared and ringed, gold. *Pl.* 42, *cr.* 14, (coronet, *pl.* 72, *cr.* 11.)

DUDLEY, Eng., an eagle, wings expanded, sa. *Pl.* 126, *cr.* 7.

DUDLY, out of a ducal coronet, or, a lion's head, az., (collared and ringed, gold.) *Pl.* 90, *cr.* 9.

DUDMAN, Eng., a salmon, naiant, ppr. *Pl.* 85, *cr.* 7.

DUER, Eng., a branch of laurel, vert. *Pl.* 123, *cr.* 5.

DUFF, Sco., in hand an escallop. *Omnia fortunæ committo. Pl.* 57, *cr.* 6.

DUFF, Eng., a lion's head, erased, within a fetterlock, ppr. *Pl.* 90, *cr.* 14.

DUFF, a demi-lion, ppr., in dexter a sword, erect, ar., hilt and pommel, or, (in sinister a human heart, gu., with one wing to it.) *Pl.* 41, *cr.* 13.

DUFF, Earl of Fife. *See* FIFE.

DUFF, ROBERT, Esq., of Fetteresso Castle, Kincardine; and Culter House, Aberdeen, a demi-lion, rampant, gu., in dexter a dagger, ppr. *Virtute et operâ. Pl.* 41, *cr.* 13.

DUFF, a winged heart, ppr. *Kind heart. Pl.* 39, *cr.* 7.

DUFF, a demi-lion, gu., in dexter a broadsword, ppr., hilt and pommel, or. *Deus juvat. Pl.* 41, *cr.* 13.

DUFF, a demi-lion, gu., in dexter a scimitar, ppr. *Virtute et operâ. Pl.* 126 A, *cr.* 1.

DUFF, Sco., a stag's head, ppr. *Virtute et operâ. Pl.* 91, *cr.* 14.

DUFFERIN, and CLANEBOYE, Baron, and a Bart., (Blackwood,) Iri., the sun in splendour, or. *Per vias rectas. Pl.* 68, *cr.* 14.

DUFFIELD-DAWSON, Yorks: 1. For *Duffield*, a dove, with olive-branch, ppr. *Pl.* 48, *cr.* 15. 2. For *Dawson*, a greyhound, (passant,) sa. *Pl.* 11, *cr.* 1, (without trees.)

DUFFIELD, a bear's head, couped, sa., muzzled and (collared.) *Pl.* 2, *cr.* 9.

DUFFIELD, Lond., a talbot, passant, or, eared, gorged with a plain collar, and ringed, sa. *Pl.* 65, *cr.* 2.

DUFFIN, Eng., a griffin, rampant, ppr. *Pl.* 67, *cr.* 13.

DUFFUS, Baron, (Dunbar,) Sco., a sword and key, in saltier, ppr. *Sub spe. Pl.* 54, *cr.* 12.

DUFFY, Eng., an angel, ppr. *Pl.* 25, *cr.* 7.

DUFFY, Iri., two palm-branches, in orle, ppr. *Pl.* 87, *cr.* 8.

DU FOU, Eng., a pole-cat, passant, ppr.

DUFRENE, a tree, ppr. *Pl.* 16, *cr.* 8.

DUGAN, and DUGGAN, Eng., a talbot, statant, ppr., collared, ar. *Pl.* 65, *cr.* 2.

DUGDALE, Eng., a demi-griffin. *Pl.* 18, *cr.* 6.

DUGDALE, Lanc. and Warw., a griffin's head, between wings, or. *Pestis patriæ pigrities. Pl.* 22, *cr.* 2.

DUGGAN, a demi-lion, between paws a sword, environed by a snake. *Pl.* 47, *cr.* 4, (sword, *pl.* 116, *cr.* 11.)

DUGMORE, Norf., an eagle, rising, ppr. *Pl.* 67, *cr.* 4.

DUGNALL, Eng., a cross pattée, per pale, or and gu., between wings, counterchanged. *Pl.* 29, *cr.* 14.

DUGUID, Sco., a dove, with olive-branch, ppr. *Patientiâ et spe. Pl.* 48, *cr.* 15.

DU HALGOET, Eng., a moor's head, couped at neck, ppr. *Pl.* 120, *cr.* 3.

DUINE, Iri., a dexter hand, ppr. *Celer atque fidelis. Pl.* 32, *cr.* 14.

DUKE, Surr., Kent, Wilts., and Devons., a demi-griffin, or, holding a chaplet, az. *Pl.* 18, *cr.* 6, (chaplet, *pl.* 56, *cr.* 10.)

DUKE, Suff., on a plume of five ostrich-feathers, three az., two ar., a sword, of the second, hilted, or.

DUKE, Salop, an arm, in armour, embowed to the sinister, garnished, or, in gauntlet a tilting-lance, ppr., thereon a forked pennon, (flowing to the sinister, per fess, ar. and sa., fringed and tasselled, of the first, and charged with an escutcheon, bearing the arms of the Holy Trinity.) *Pl.* 6, *cr.* 5.

DUKENFIELD, of Dukenfield, Bart., Chesh., out of a ducal coronet, or, a dexter arm, erect, gu., cuffed, ar., in hand, ppr., the sun in splendour. *Ubi amor, ibi fides. Pl.* 89, *cr.* 11.

DUKES, Eng., a tent, ppr. *Pl.* 111, *cr.* 14.
DULANEY, a winged bull, sejant, resting dexter on a book, open.
DUMAR, on a foreign helmet, ppr., two elephants' trunks, sa., each charged with a fess, ar.
DUMARESQ, and DUMARESQUE, Eng., out of a mural coronet, a demi-lion holding a flag. *Pl.* 86, *cr.* 11.
DUMAS, a lion's gamb, erased, gu. *Pl.* 126, *cr.* 9.
DUMBAIS, an arm, in armour, embowed, in fess, the shoulder on the wreath, in hand a cross crosslet, fitched. *Pl.* 114, *cr.* 9, (cross, *pl.* 99, *cr.* 1.)
DUMBAR, Sco., a lion's head, erased, (crowned with an open crown, or.) *Fortis et fidelis. Pl.* 81, *cr.* 4.
DUMBLANE, Viscount. *See* LEEDS, Duke of.
DUMBLETON, Eng., an eagle, displayed, per pale, ermine and erminois. *Pl.* 48, *cr.* 11.
DUMBRECK, Sco., in dexter hand a sword, in pale, on point a boar's head, couped, ppr. *Nocentes prosequor. Pl.* 71, *cr.* 9.
DUMMER, Hants., a demi-lion, az., in dexter a fleur-de-lis, or. *Pl.* 91, *cr.* 13.
DU MOULINE, Eng., an eagle, wings addorsed, preying on an infant, swaddled. *Pl.* 123, *cr.* 11.
DUN, five snakes, erect on tails, bound in middle by one snake, in fess, or.
DUN, Somers., three snakes, erect, gu., tied in middle in a knot, ppr.
DUN, Somers., out of a ducal coronet, a bear's paw, erect, or, grasping a snake, ppr.
DUN, Sco., in dexter hand a key, ppr. *Mecum habita. Pl.* 41, *cr.* 11.
DUN, and DUNN, Eng., within a serpent, in orle a boar's head, erased and erect, snout upward. *Pl.* 12, *cr.* 6.
DUNALLEY, Baron, (Prittie,) Iri., a wolf's head, erased, ar. *In omnia paratus. Pl.* 14, *cr.* 6.
DUNBAR, Baron Duffus. *See* DUFFUS.
DUNBAR, Bart., of Mochrum, Sco., a horse's head, bridled, (a dexter hand, couped, ppr., holding the bridle.) *In promptu—and—Sub spe. Pl.* 92, *cr.* 1.
DUNBAR, Bart., of Durn, Sco., two laurel-sprigs, in saltier, ppr. *Spes dabit auxilium.*
DUNBAR, Bart., of Boath, Sco., a dexter hand apaumée, reaching to two earls' coronets tied together. *Sub spe.*
DUNBAR, of Grange, a wreath of laurel, ppr. *Sub spe. Pl.* 79, *cr.* 14.
DUNBAR, of Hempriggs, a demi-lion, in dexter a rose, gu., slipped and leaved, vert. *Ornat fortem prudentia. Pl.* 39, *cr.* 14.
DUNBAR, Eng., a griffin's head, erased, ducally gorged, in beak a pheon, ppr. *Pl.* 29, *cr.* 15, (pheon, *pl.* 39, *cr.* 4.)
DUNBAR, of Baldóon, Sco., a horse's head, ar., bridled, gu. *Firmior quo paratior. Pl.* 92, *cr.* 1.
DUNBAR, of Inchbreck, in hand an' ear of wheat, ppr. *Sapiens non eget. Pl.* 71, *cr.* 15.
DUNBAR, of Leuchit, Sco., a dexter hand holding a glove, ppr. *Sapit qui laborat. Pl.* 42, *cr.* 15.
DUNBAR, of Machermore, Sco., a lion's head, erased ar., crowned with an (antique crown, or.) *Fortis et fidelis. Pl.* 123, *cr.* 13.

DUNBAR, of Hillhead, a rose, slipped, gu. *Olet et sanat. Pl.* 105, *cr.* 7.
DUNBAR, Iri., a demi-eagle, displayed, with two heads, imperially crowned. *Pl.* 63, *cr.* 2.
DUNBAR, Sco., a sword and key in saltier, ppr. *Sub spe. Pl.* 54, *cr.* 12.
DUNBAR, Sco., a dexter hand, couped, ppr. *Pl.* 32, *cr.* 14.
DUNBAR, a horse's head. *Pl.* 81, *cr.* 6.
DUNBAR, two branches of laurel, in orle. *Pl.* 79, *cr.* 14.
DUNBOYNE, Baron, Iri., (Butler;) in a ducal coronet, or, a plume of five ostrich-feathers, therefrom rising a demi-hawk, ar. *Timor Domini fons vitæ. Pl.* 100, *cr.* 12, (hawk, *pl.* 103, *cr.* 10.)
DUNCAN, a hunting-horn, ppr. *Pl.* 89, *cr.* 3.
DUNCAN, Eng. and Sco., a ship under sail. *Disce pati. Pl.* 109, *cr.* 8.
DUNCAN, Viscount. *See* CAMPERDOWN, Earl of.
DUNCOMBE, Earl of Feversham. *See* FEVERSHAM.
DUNCAN, of Mairdrum, a boar's head, erased, ppr. *Pl.* 16, *cr.* 11.
DUNCANNON, Baron, (Ponsonby,) Viscount Duncannon, Iri., in a ducal coronet, az., three arrows, one in pale, two in saltier, points downward, environed by a snake, ppr. *Pro rege, lege, grege. Pl.* 86, *cr.* 12.
DUNCOMBE, Eng. and Iri., out of a ducal coronet, or, a horse's leg, ppr. *Pl.* 38, *cr.* 11.
DUNCAN, a ship in distress, ppr. *Disce pati. Pl.* 21, *cr.* 11.
DUNCAN, Sco., a greyhound, ppr., (collared, or.) *Pl.* 66, *cr.* 15.
DUNCAN, of Ardounie, a demi-greyhound, ppr., (collared, or.) *Vivat veritas. Pl.* 48, *cr.* 3.
DUNCANSON, a dexter hand, apaumée, ppr. *Mens et manus. Pl.* 32, *cr.* 14.
DUNCH, Berks., out of a ducal coronet, or, an antelope's head, maned, armed, and attired, gold. *Pl.* 24, *cr.* 7, (coronet, *same plate, cr.* 10.)
DUNCH, Berks., a demi-antelope, az., bezantée, armed, maned, and attired, or. *Pl.* 34, *cr.* 8, (without collar.)
DUNCOMBE, Bucks., a talbot's head, erased, gu., eared, sa., collared, ar. *Non fecimus ipsi. Pl.* 2, *cr.* 15.
DUNCOMBE, out of a ducal coronet, or, in lion's gamb, sa., a horse-shoe, ar. *Pl.* 67, *cr.* 7, (shoe, *pl.* 52, *cr.* 4.)
DUNCOMBE, Sco., a demi-lion, ppr. *Pl.* 67, *cr.* 10.
DUNDAS, Baron, (Dundas,) a lion's head, affrontée, ppr., (crowned with an antique crown, or,) struggling through an oak-bush, also ppr., fructed, or. *Essayez. Pl.* 119, *cr.* 5.
DUNDAS, Bart., Surr. and Wel., a dexter arm, erect, couped below elbow, in hand, ppr., a mullet, az. *Essayez. Pl.* 62, *cr.* 13.
DUNDAS, Bart., Sco., a lion's face, in a bush, ppr. *Pl.* 111, *cr.* 2.
DUNDAS, of Duddingston, in dexter hand a star, az. *Essayez. Pl.* 62, *cr.* 13.
DUNDAS, of Kinkevel, a lion's gamb, erect, ppr. *Essayez hardiment. Pl.* 126, *cr.* 9.
DUNDAS, of Dundas, a lion's head, affrontée, looking through a bush of oak, ppr. *Essayez. Pl.* 111, *cr.* 2.
DUNDAS, of Arniston, same crest and motto.

DUNDAS, Sco., a salamander in flames, ppr. *Extinguo.* Pl. 20, cr. 15.
DUNDAS, Eng., on a chapeau, a flame, ppr. Pl. 71, cr. 11.
DUNDAS, a lion's head, couped, or. *Essayez.* Pl. 126, cr. 1.
DUNDAS, Viscount Melville. *See* MELVILLE.
DUNDAS, RICHARD-LESLIE, Esq., of Blair Castle, Perth, a lion's head, affrontée, gu., looking through a bush of oak, ppr. *Essayez.* Pl. 111, cr. 2.
DUNDAS-WHITLEY-DEANS, Sir JAMES, G.C.B., of Barton Court, Berks.: 1. For *Dundas*, a lion's head, affrontée, looking through a bush of oak, ppr. *Essayez.* Pl. 111, cr. 2. 2. For *Whitley*, a stag's head, ar., attired, or, in mouth the end of a scroll, bearing motto, "Live to live." *Arte vel Marte*, for DEANS. Pl. 91, cr. 14.
DUNDAS-HAMILTON, GABRIEL, Esq., of Duddingston: 1. For *Dundas*, in hand, a mullet, az. *Essayez.* Pl. 62, cr. 13. 2. For *Hamilton*, in hand a spear, ppr. *Et arma, et virtus.* Pl. 99, cr. 8.
DUNDEE, Town of, a lily, ar. Pl. 81, cr. 9.
DUNDONALD, Earl of, Baron Cochrane, (Cochrane,) Sco., a horse, passant, ar. *Virtute et labore.* Pl. 15, cr. 14.
DUNE, Eng., a mullet, quarterly, or and sa. Pl. 41, cr. 1.
DUNFERMLINE, Baron, (Abercromby,) a bee, erect, ppr. Pl. 100, cr. 3.
DUNFORD, Eng., a wheat-ear, slipped, or. Pl. 85, cr. 6.
DUNFORD, a lion's head, erased, ar., in mouth, a dexter hand, couped at wrist, ppr. Pl. 107, cr. 9.
DUNCAN, Iri., a lion, passant, or, supporting with dexter a close helmet, ar., garnished, gold. Pl. 48, cr. 8, (helmet, pl. 114, cr. 9.)
DUNGANNON, Viscount, and Baron Hill, (Hill-Trevor,) Iri., a wyvern, sa. *Quid verum atque decens.* Pl. 63, cr. 13.
DUNHAM, Linc., a martin, passant, or, between two spears, erect, ppr. Pl. 119, cr. 15, (spears, pl. 69, cr. 14.)
DUNIES, Sco. and Eng., two palm-branches, in orle, ppr. Pl. 87, cr. 8.
DUNIGUID, Sco., a dove, in mouth a (laurel-branch,) ppr. *Patientiâ et spe.* Pl. 48, cr. 15.
DUNK, Eng., a lion's head, collared, or. Pl. 42, cr. 14.
DUNKIN, Eng., an arm, in armour, couped at elbow, in fess, in hand a cross crosslet, fitched. Pl. 71, cr. 13.
DUNKIN, Iri., an eel, naiant, ppr. Pl. 25, cr. 13.
DUNKLEY, Eng., a falcon's leg, erased at thigh, belled and lined, ppr. Pl. 83, cr. 7.
DUNLOP, between the horns of a stag, az., a cross pattée, ar. Pl. 9, cr. 10.
DUNLOP, Sco., a rose, ppr. *E spinis.* Pl. 105, cr. 7.
DUNLOP, Sco., in dexter hand a dagger, ppr. *Merito.* Pl. 28, cr. 4.
DUNLOP, Sco., in dexter hand a sword, ppr. *Merito.* Pl. 21, cr. 10.
DUNLUCE, Viscount. *See* ANTRIM, Earl of.
DUNMORE, Earl of, Viscount Fincastle and Baron Murray, Sco.; Baron Dunmore, U.K., (Murray,) a demi-savage, wreathed about head and loins with oak, in dexter a sword, erect, ppr., hilt and pommel, or, in sinister a key, gold. *Furth fortune and fill the fetters.* Pl. 88, cr. 10.

DUNMURE, an anchor, ppr. *Spes anchorâ tuta.* Pl. 42, cr. 12.
DUNN, Durh., five snakes, erect, on tails, tied together round middle by one snake, in fess, or.
DUNN, Sco., on point of a sword, in pale, a garland of laurel, ppr. Pl. 15, cr. 6.
DUNN, and DUNNE, two lions' paws supporting a pillar, ppr. Pl. 77, cr. 4.
DUNN, and DUNNE, two swords, in saltier, ppr., entwined by a ribbon, az., thereto a key, pendent, sa. Pl. 13, cr. 8.
DUNN, and DUNNE, Iri., three holly-leaves, ppr., banded, gu. Pl. 78, cr. 12.
DUNN, Heref., six snakes, erect, contrary posed, three and three, encircled by a ribbon.
DUNN, Iri., in front of a tree, a lizard, passant, all ppr. *Vigilans et audax.* Pl. 93, cr. 4.
DUNNAGE, a parrot, in beak a branch of cherry-tree, all ppr. Pl. 49, cr. 3.
DUNNAGE, Eng., a sword, in pale, enfiled with a leopard's head, cabossed. Pl. 24, cr. 13.
DUNNET, Sco., (on a rock,) a fox, ppr. *Non terrâ, sed aquis.* Pl. 126, cr. 5.
DUNNING, Sco. and Eng., a demi-talbot, rampant, in mouth an arrow. Pl. 91, cr. 7.
DUNRAVEN, and MOUNTEARL, Earl of, Viscount Mountearl and Adare, and Baron Adare, (Wyndham-Quin,) Iri.: 1. For *Wyndham*, a lion's head, erased, within a fetterlock and chain, or. Pl. 90, cr. 14. 2. For *Quin*, a wolf's head, couped, ar. *Quod sursum volo videre.* Pl. 91, cr. 9.
DUNSANY, Baron, (Wadding-Plunkett,) a horse, passant, ar. *Festina lente.* Pl. 15, cr. 14.
DUNSBORD, Devons., out of a ducal coronet, a demi-lion, rampant. Pl. 45, cr. 7.
DUNSFORD, Eng., out of a mural coronet, an eagle's head, ppr. Pl. 121, cr. 11.
DUNSTABLE, Eng., a swan's head, ar., between wings, sa. Pl. 54, cr. 6.
DUNSTAVILLE, and DUNSTAVILE, a demi-friar, holding a lash. Pl. 83, cr. 15.
DUNSTER, Eng., out of the top of a tower, ar., an arm, embowed, vested, gu., cuffed, of the first, in hand a tilting-spear, sa. Pl. 5, cr. 1.
DUNSTON, or DUSTON, Eng., a man's head, in profile, ppr. Pl. 81, cr. 15.
DUNTZE, Bart., Devons., between wings a mullet. Pl. 1, cr. 5.
DUPA, or DUPPA, Eng., an acorn, slipped and leaved, ppr. Pl. 81, cr. 7.
DUPERON, on a chapeau, a martlet, ppr. Pl. 89, cr. 7.
DUPONT, a flag, or, staff, ppr. Pl. 52, cr. 14.
DU PORT, on a rock, ppr., guttée-de-sang, a falcon, also ppr., beaked and legged, gu. Pl. 99, cr. 14.
DUPPA, Kent, an arm, (in armour,) in hand a lion's paw, erased, or. Pl. 94, cr. 13.
DUPRE, a rose, per fess, or and gu. Pl. 52, cr. 11.
DUPREE, a lion, rampant, ar. Pl. 67, cr. 5.
DUPREE, a lion, rampant, ar., resting hind-dexter on a fleur-de-lis, gu. Pl. 67, cr. 5, (fleur-de-lis, pl. 141.)
DUPUY, a demi-griffin. Pl. 18, cr. 6.

L

DURAND, Eng., a yew-tree, ppr. *Pl.* 49, *cr.* 13.

DURANT, Middx., a dragon, passant, gu., in dexter a sword, erect, ar., point bloody, hilt and pommel, or, on blade a ducal coronet, of the last. *Pl.* 90, *cr.* 10, (sword and coronet, *pl.* 119, *cr.* 4.)

DURANT, Eng., out of a ducal coronet, or, a greyhound's head, sa., charged with an etoile, of the first. *Pl.* 78, *cr.* 2.

DURANT, a boar, ar., bristled, armed, and unguled, or, pierced in side with a broken (spear,) ppr., vulned, gu. *Pl.* 36, *cr.* 2.

DURBAN, Eng., the sun shining on stump of tree, ppr. *Pl.* 123, *cr.* 3.

DURBAN, Somers., a talbot, passant, regardant, liver-coloured, charged on shoulder with a bezant, dexter supporting a lance, or, headed, ppr., thereon a banner, displayed, gu., charged with a gauntlet, ar.

DURBAN, and DURBIN, issuing from a cloud, in sinister, a dexter arm, in hand a club, all ppr. *Pl.* 68, *cr.* 7.

DURBOROUGH, Eng., a demi-chevalier, in dexter a sword, ppr. *Pl.* 23, *cr.* 4.

DURELL, Lond., a Saracen's head, affrontée, ppr., on head a cap, az., fretty, ar., tufted, or, doubled, erm., wreathed about temples, or and az. *Pl.* 38, *cr.* 13.

DURHAM, Earl of, and Baron, Viscount Lambton, (Lambton :) 1. For *Lambton*, a ram's head, cabossed, ar., attired, sa. 2. For *Hedworth*, a woman's head, affrontée, couped at breasts, ppr., hair flowing, or, (wreathed about temples with a garland of cinquefoils, gu., pierced, of the second.) *Pl.* 45, *cr.* 5. 3. For *D'Arcy*, out of a ducal coronet, or, an antelope'a head, winged, ar., attired and barbed, gold. *Le jour viendra. Pl.* 24, *cr.* 7, (coronet, *same plate*.)

DURHAM, Eng., a cannon, mounted, ppr. *Pl.* 111, *cr.* 3.

DURHAM, Sco., a hand pulling a thistle, ppr. *Vive Deo. Pl.* 54, *cr.* 11.

DURHAM, of Largo, Sco., on a baron's coronet, a dolphin, ppr. *Victoria non præda. Pl.* 48, *cr.* 9, (coronet, *pl.* 127, *fig.* 11.)

DURHAM, Sco., an increscent. *Augeor dum progredior. Pl.* 122, *cr.* 15.

DURHAM, of Ardownie, Sco., a dolphin, naiant, ppr. *Ulterius. Pl.* 48, *cr.* 9.

DURHAM, of Grange, Sco., two dolphins, haurient, addorsed, ppr. *Ultra fert animus. Pl.* 81, *cr.* 2.

DURHAM, a dolphin, haurient. *Pl.* 14, *cr.* 10.

DURIE, and DURY, Sco., a dove, with olive-branch, volant, ppr. *Pl.* 25, *cr.* 6.

DURIE, and DURY, a dove, with olive-branch, regardant, ppr. *Pl.* 77, *cr.* 2.

DURING, Eng., in hand, in fess, couped at wrist and gauntleted, a dagger, and thereon a savage's head, couped, affrontée. *Pl.* 36, *cr.* 10.

DURLEY, a horse's head, (couped,) az., gorged with an Eastern crown, or. *Pl.* 81, *cr.* 6, (crown, *pl.* 128, *fig.* 2.)

DURNARD, Sco., a cross pattée, fitched, ar. *This I'll defend. Pl.* 27, *cr.* 14.

DURNFORD, Eng., a dagger, in pale, ppr. *Pl.* 73, *cr.* 9.

DURNING, Lanc., a demi-antelope, erased, az. *Pl.* 34, *cr.* 8.

DURNO, Sco., in hand a sword, in pale. *Ex recto decus. Pl.* 23, *cr.* 15.

DURNO, Sco., a dexter arm, in hand a sword, ppr. *Ex recto decus. Pl.* 21, *cr.* 10.

DURRANT, Bart., Norf., a boar, ar., bristled, armed, and langued, or, pierced in side by an arrow, sa. *Labes pejor morte. Pl.* 36, *cr.* 2.

DURRANT, Norf., a boar, passant, per fess, wavy, ar. and gu., bristled and tusked, az., pierced through body by (a broken lance, in bend, sa., head downward, or.) *Pl.* 36, *cr.* 2.

DURRANT, Iri., on a ducal coronet, a peacock, ppr. *Pl.* 43, *cr.* 7.

DURRANT, Derbs., a lion, rampant, ar., in dexter a fleur-de-lis, or, (in mouth a sword, ppr., hilt and pommel, of the second, point downward.) *Pl.* 87, *cr.* 6.

DURWARD, Sco., a demi-man, ppr., vested, gu., holding a gem-ring. *Pl.* 9, *cr.* 11.

DURWARD, Eng., in dexter hand a scimitar, indented on back, cutting at a pen, all ppr. *Pl.* 39, *cr.* 13.

DUSAUTOY, Eng., in hand a sickle, ppr. *Pl.* 36, *cr.* 12.

DUSSEAUX, Eng., a ram's head, erased, ar., armed, or. *Pl.* 1, *cr.* 12.

DUSTON, and DUSTONE, Eng., a man's head, couped, ppr. *Pl.* 19, *cr.* 1.

DUTHIE, Sco., in hand a sword, erect. *Pl.* 21, *cr.* 10.

DUTTON, JOSEPH, Esq., of Burland Hall, Chester, out of a ducal coronet, a plume of five ostrich-feathers, ar., az., or, vert, and gu. *Servabo fidem. Pl.* 100, *cr.* 12, (without charge.)

DUTTON, Baron Sherborne. *See* SHERBORNE.

DUTTON, a plume of five ostrich-feathers, ar. *Pl.* 100, *cr.* 12, (without coronet or charge.)

DUTTON, Chesh., out of a ducal coronet, a plume of five ostrich-feathers, gu., az., or, vert, and tené. *Pl.* 100, *cr.* 12, (without charge.)

DUVAL, and DUVALL, a lion, sejant, per pale, ar. and gu., supporting a shield. *Pl.* 22, *cr.* 13.

DUVAL, Lond., on a globe, a monkey, sejant, in fore-dexter a slip of palm, all ppr.

DUVAL, and DUVALL, Eng., a dexter arm, couped and embowed, in hand a hunting spear, ppr. *Pl.* 39, *cr.* 15.

DUVERNET, or DUVERNETTE, Eng., a stag, passant, ppr. *Pl.* 68, *cr.* 2.

DUXBURY, Eng., on stump of tree, growing out of a mount, vert, a dove, rising, ppr. *Pl.* 124, *cr.* 13.

DWARIS, Lond., a demi-lion, rampant, ar., pellettée, in (paws) a battle-axe, or. *Pl.* 101, *cr.* 14.

DWIGWID, of Archenheuf, a dove and olive-branch, ppr. *Patientiâ et spe. Pl.* 48, *cr.* 15.

DWIRE, Iri., in hand a sword, in bend sinister, *Pl.* 21, *cr.* 10.

DWYRE, Eng., out of a mural coronet, a lion's head, charged with a torteau, gu. *Pl.* 45, *cr.* 9, (torteau, *pl.* 141.)

DWYRE, Iri., two lions' heads, erased and addorsed, ppr. *Pl.* 28, *cr.* 10.

DY or DYE, Eng., on a ducal coronet, or, a swan, wings addorsed, (ducally) gorged, ppr. *Pl.* 100, *cr.* 7.

DYAS, Eng., out of a ducal coronet, in hand a swan's head, erased. *Pl.* 65, *cr.* 12.

DYCE, Eng., an escutcheon, gu. *Decide and dare. Pl.* 36, *cr.* 11.

DYCHFIELD, Ess., Oxon., and Lanc., and porcupine. *Pl.* 55, *cr.* 10.
DYER-SWINNERTON, Middx., out of a ducal coronet, or, a goat's head, sa., armed, gold. *Pl.* 72, *cr.* 2.
DYER, Herts., a goat's head, erased, ppr., in mouth, a rose, ar. *Pl.* 29, *cr.* 13, (rose, *pl.* 95, *cr.* 6.)
DYER, a Saracen's head, in profile, ppr., on head a cap, or, verged round temples, chequy, ar. and az. *Pl.* 51, *cr.* 4.
DYER, Eng., an old man's head, in profile, couped at shoulders, ppr., hair, ar., beard, sa., cap, or, turned up, chequy, ar. and az. *Pl.* 51, *cr.* 4.
DYKE, Bart., Kent and Suss., a cubit-arm, in armour, ppr., garnished, or, in hand a cinquefoil, slipped, sa. *Pl.* 53, *cr.* 15.
DYKES, Wilts., Kent, and Surr., an eagle's head, sa. *Pl.* 100, *cr.* 10.
DYKES-BALLANTINE, Cambs., a lobster, vert, *Prius frangitur quam flectitur. Pl.* 18, *cr.* 2.
DYMOKE, Linc.: 1. A sword, erect, ar., hilt and pommel, or. *Pl.* 105, *cr.* 1. 2. A lion, passant, ar., (crowned, or.) *Pl.* 48, *cr.* 8. 3. The scalp of a (hare,) ears erect, ppr. *Pro rege Dimico. Pl.* 124, *cr.* 15.
DYMOKE, or DYMOCK, out of a ducal coronet, or, a rod, raguly, vert. *Pl.* 78, *cr.* 15.
DYMOKE, and DYMOCK, Warw., an arm, in armour, ppr., in hand a tilting-spear, sa., headed, ar., embrued, gu. *Pl.* 44, *cr.* 9.
DYMOKE, or DYMOCK, Staffs., a demi-negro, ppr., with pearls in ears, ar., in dexter an acornbranch, fructed, or. *Pl.* 35, *cr.* 12, (branch, *pl.* 81, *cr.* 7.)
DYMOKE, or DYMOCK, two ass's ears, ppr. *Pl.* 124, *cr.* 15.
DYMON, a demi-lion, in dexter a fusil, gu., charged with a fleur-de-lis, or. *Pl.* 91, *cr.* 13, (fusil, *pl.* 141.)
DYMOND, Devons., a female's arm, from elbow, enfiled with a bracelet. *Pl.* 85, *cr.* 10.
DYNDY, a dragon's head, erased, vert. *Pl.* 107, *cr.* 10, (without collar.)
DYNE, or DYNNE, Norf., a plume of feathers, or. *Pl.* 12, *cr.* 9.
DYNE, and DYNNE, Norf., out of a ducal coronet, a marlin's sinister wing, ar. *Pl.* 80, *cr.* 4.
DYNEVOR, Baron, (Talbot-Rice,) a crow, ppr. *Nihil alienum. Pl.* 23, *cr.* 8.
DYNHAM, a bell, az. *Pl.* 73, *cr.* 15.
DYNHAM, (in a round top, or,) six spears, in the centre a pennon, ar., thereon a cross, gu. *Pl.* 95, *cr.* 8, (pennon, *pl.* 53, *cr.* 14.)
DYON, on an escallop, or, the point in base, a lion, passant, sa. *Pl.* 53, *cr.* 3, (lion, *pl.* 48, *cr.* 8.)
DYOT, Staffs., a tiger, passant, ar., armed, or, (collared, lined, and winged, gu.) *Pl.* 67, *cr.* 15.
DYRWARD, DYRWARNE, and DYRRWARNE, Eng., a cup, or. *Pl.* 42, *cr.* 1.
DYSART, Irl., a griffin's head, between wings. *Confido, conquiesco. Pl.* 65, *cr.* 1.
DYSON, Staffs., on a mount, vert, a paschal lamb, ar., with banner, ppr. *Pl.* 101, *cr.* 9.
DYXTON, a palm-tree, fructed and leaved, ppr. *Pl.* 18, *cr.* 12.
DYVE, between bats' wings, gu., a horse's head, reversed, vert. *Pl.* 19, *cr.* 13, (wings, *pl.* 94, *cr.* 9.)
DYXON, a demi-hind, sa., bezantée.

E

EADES, Middx. and Suff., a leopard's face, ar. *Pl.* 66, *cr.* 14.
EADON, a mitre, bezantée, charged with a cheveron, gu. *Pl.* 12, *cr.* 10.
EADY, Eng., a fleur-de-lis, environed with a serpent. *Pl.* 15, *cr.* 13.
EAENS, on a mount, vert, a Cornish chough. *Pl.* 34, *cr.* 13.
EAGAR, Eng., a quill, in pale, ppr. *Pl.* 105, *cr.* 3.
EAGLE, Suff., in lion's gamb, erect and erased, or, an eagle's leg, erased at thigh, gu. *Pl.* 89, *cr.* 13.
EAGLES, Eng., two lions' paws, in saltier, ppr. *Pl.* 20, *cr.* 13.
EAGLESFIELD, and EGLESFIELD, out of a tower, a demi-greyhound, in dexter a branch of palm, ppr. *Pl.* 73, *cr.* 13.
EALAND, Yorks., an arrow, in pale, ar. *Pl.* 56, *cr.* 13.
EALES, Eng., in lion's gamb, a human heart, ppr. *Pl.* 23, *cr.* 13.
EALES, Lond. and Bucks., on an eel, embowed, vert, an eagle, displayed, ppr. *Pl.* 119, *cr.* 1.
EAM, Lond. and Berks., a demi-lion, rampant, sa. *Pl.* 67, *cr.* 10.
EAMER, Eng., a hind, trippant, az. *Pl.* 20, *cr.* 14.
EARDLEY, Eng., a sword, in pale, ppr., enfiled with a leopard's head, cabossed, gu. *Pl.* 24, *cr.* 13.
EARL, Berks., a lion's head, erased, or, pierced by a (broken dart,) ppr. *Pl.* 113, *cr.* 15.
EARL, a nag's head, erased, sa., maned, or. *Pl.* 81, *cr.* 6.
EARL, Eng., on point of tilting-spear, ppr., headed, ar., a dolphin, naiant, of the first. *Pl.* 49, *cr.* 14.
EARLE, Linc., a lion's head, erased, or, pierced through head by a (broken spear,) ar., point embrued, gu. *Pl.* 113, *cr.* 15.
EARLE, Sco., a nag's head. *Pl.* 81, *cr.* 6.
EARLES, a cross, gu., between wings, erm. *Pl.* 34, *cr.* 14.
EARNLEY, Suss., a savage's head, affrontée, round temples a wreath, issuing therefrom a plume of three ostrich-feathers. *Pl.* 105, *cr.* 2.
EARNSHAW, a cross pattée, fitched, or, bordered, gu. *Pl.* 27, *cr.* 14.
EAST, Bart., a horse, erm., supporting with fore-leg a pilgrim's cross, sa. *Æquo pede propera. Pl.* 4, *cr.* 2.
EAST, Bucks. and Berks., a horse, passant, sa. *J'avance. Pl.* 15, *cr.* 14.

EASTCHURCH, Eng., the sun rising from behind a cloud, ppr. *Pl.* 67, *cr.* 9.

EAST-CLAYTON, Bart., of Hall Place, Berks., 1. For *East*, on a mount, vert, a horse, passant, sa., fore-dexter resting on a horse-shoe, or, in mouth a palm-branch, vert. *Pl.* 15, *cr.* 14, (branch, *pl.* 26, *cr.* 3.) 2. For *Clayton*, a (leopard's) gamb, erased and erect, ar., charged with a crescent, and grasping a pellet. *J'avance.* *Pl.* 97, *cr.* 10, (crescent, *pl.* 141.)

EASTDAY, Kent., on a mount, vert, a hind, lodged, ppr. *Pl.* 1, *cr.* 14, (without beehive.)

EASTHOPE, Surr., out of a vallery crown, or, a horse's head, ar., maned, gold, (charged on neck with two bendlets,) engrailed, az. *Pl.* 81, *cr.* 6, (crown, *pl.* 128, *fig.* 17.)

EASTLAND, Eng., an arm, in armour, embowed, ppr., in hand a fleur-de-lis, or. *Pl.* 24, *cr.* 14.

EASTMAN, Eng., a swan, collared and lined, ppr. *Pl.* 73, *cr.* 14.

EASTOFT, Eng., a dagger and pen, in saltier, ppr. *Pl.* 49, *cr.* 12.

EASTON, Devons., a yew-tree, ppr. *Pl.* 49, *cr.* 13.

EASTON, Sco., a demi-chevalier, in armour, brandishing a sword, ppr. *Pl.* 23, *cr.* 4.

EASTWOOD, on a ducal coronet, per pale, or and gu., a lion, passant, gardant, of the same, crowned, ppr. *Pl.* 34, *cr.* 15.

EASTWOOD, a boar, passant, ppr. *Pl.* 48, *cr.* 14.

EASUM, on a mount, five wheat-ears, ppr. *Pl.* 4, *cr.* 5.

EATEN, and EATON, Eng., a crow's head, erased, ppr. *Pl.* 27, *cr.* 13.

EATON, Notts., an eagle's head, erased, sa., in beak a sprig, vert. *Vincit omnia veritas.* *Pl.* 22, *cr.* 1.

EATON, Iri., a beaver, passant, ar. *Pl.* 49, *cr.* 5.

EATON, out of a ducal coronet, or, a bull's head, sa., armed, ar. *Pl.* 68, *cr.* 6.

EATON, Eng., a boar's head, erased, in mouth a sword. *Pl.* 28, *cr.* 14.

EBERSTEIN, Eng., a peacock's head, ppr. *Pl.* 86, *cr.* 4.

EBHERT, Eng., a salamander in flames, ppr. *Pl.* 20, *cr.* 15.

EBSWORTH, a demi-wolf, erm., supporting a spear, tasselled. *Pl.* 56, *cr.* 8.

EBURY, Baron Grosvenor. *See* WESTMINSTER, Marquess.

ECCLES, Eng., a gauntlet, ppr. *Pl.* 15, *cr.* 15.

ECCLES, ECLES, and EKLES, Sco. and Iri., a broken halberd. *Se defendendo.* *Pl.* 24, *cr.* 15.

ECCLESTON, or ECLESTONE, Eng., in dexter hand a dagger, in pale, ppr. *Pl.* 23, *cr.* 15.

ECCLESTON, or ECLESTONE, a magpie, ppr. *Pl.* 10, *cr.* 12.

ECHARD, Suff., an ostrich, wings expanded, (in mouth a key.) *Pl.* 16, *cr.* 2.

ECHLIN, the Rev. JOHN ROBERT, M.A., co. Down, a talbot, passant, ar., spotted, sa., langued, gu. *Non sine prædâ.* *Pl.* 120, *cr.* 8.

ECHLIN, Bart., Iri., a talbot, passant, ppr. *Rumor acerbe, tace.* *Pl.* 120, *cr.* 8.

ECKERSALL, and ECKERSDALE, Middx., a dexter arm, in armour, embowed, ppr., and inverted, charged with a lozenge, ar., in hand an esquire's helmet, of the first, garnished, or. *Pl.* 114, *cr.* 9, (lozenge, *pl.* 141.)

ECKFORD, Sco., a griffin, statant, or. *Pl.* 66, *cr.* 13.

ECKINGHAM, Eng., a bell, ppr. *Pl.* 73, *cr.* 15.

ECKLEY, America, in hand a battle-axe, in bend, all ppr. *Pl.* 73, *cr.* 7.

ECLES, Sco., in hand a battle-axe, ppr. *Pl.* 73, *cr.* 7.

ECLESTON, Linc., a cock-pheasant, ppr. *Pl.* 82, *cr.* 12, (without collar.)

ECTON, Eng., in hand a branch of palm, ppr. *Pl.* 23, *cr.* 7.

EDDINGTON, Eng., a phœnix, in flames, ppr. *Pl.* 44, *cr.* 8.

EDDISBURY, Baron, on a chapeau, gu., turned up., erm., an eagle, wings expanded, or, preying on an infant, ppr., swaddled, of the first, banded, ar. *Sans changer.* *Pl.* 121, *cr.* 6.

EDDOWES, Eng., a mitre, semée of bezants, charged with a cheveron. *Pl.* 49, *cr.* 15.

EDDOWS, a man's head, within a helmet, ppr., beaver open. *Pl.* 33, *cr.* 14.

EDE, a cross moline, az., between two ears of wheat, in orle, ppr. *Pl.* 23, *cr.* 14.

EDEN, Durh., an arm, embowed, vested, barry of four, az. and gu., in hand, ppr., a bunch of wheat, vert. *Pl.* 89, *cr.* 4, (vesting, *pl.* 120, *cr.* 1.)

EDEN, Kent and Suff., a plume of feathers, ar. *Pl.* 12, *cr.* 9.

EDEN, an ostrich, in mouth a horse-shoe, ppr. *Pl.* 16, *cr.* 2.

EDEN, Ess. and Suff., a demi-dragon, sans wings, vert, holding a rose-branch, flowered, ar., stalked and leaved, ppr. *Pl.* 87, *cr.* 12, (branch, *pl.* 118, *cr.* 9.)

EDEN, an eagle, volant, ppr. *Pl.* 94, *cr.* 1.

EDEN, Baron Auckland. *See* AUCKLAND.

EDEN-JOHNSON, Bart., Durh., a dexter arm, in armour, embowed, couped at shoulder, ppr., hand grasping a garb, in bend, or, banded, vert. *Si sit prudentia.* *Pl.* 68, *cr.* 1, (garb, *pl.* 3, *cr.* 3.)

EDGAR, Suff., a demi-ostrich, rising, in mouth a horse-shoe. *Pl.* 28, *cr.* 13.

EDGAR, Sco., a dagger and quill, in saltier, ppr. *Potius ingenio quam vi.* *Pl.* 49, *cr.* 12.

EDGAR, Sco., a withered oak-branch, sprouting afresh, ppr. *Apparet quod.* *Pl.* 32, *cr.* 13.

EDGAR, Suff., an ostrich's head, between wings, expanded, or, each charged with two bends, az., in mouth a horse-shoe, ar. *Pl.* 28, *cr.* 13.

EDGAR, Sco., in hand a dagger, point downward, ppr. *Man do it.* *Pl.* 18, *cr.* 3.

EDGCUMBE, Earl of Mount-Edgcumbe. *See* MOUNT-EDGCUMBE.

EDGCUMBE, Devons. and Cornw., a boar, passant, ar., armed, bristled, and membered, or, gorged with a chaplet of oak, vert, fructed, gold. *Au plaisir fort de Dieu.* *Pl.* 29, *cr.* 10.

EDGE, Lond. and Staffs., a (demi)-sea-lion, ppr. *Pl.* 25, *cr.* 12.

EDGE, an ostrich's head, (erased,) between wings. *Pl.* 28, *cr.* 13.

EDGE, Notts., a reindeer's head, couped, ppr., collared and chained, or. *Pl.* 2, *cr.* 13.

EDGELL, HARRY-EDMUND, Esq., of Standerwick Court, Somers., a falcon, rising, belled, ar., guttée-de-sang, resting dexter on an antique shield, of the first, charged with a cinquefoil, gu. *Qui sera sera.* *Pl.* 4, *cr.* 1.

EDGELL, Eng., on a chapeau, ppr., a dove, wings addorsed, az. *Pl.* 109, *cr.* 10.

EDGEMOUTH, out of a ducal coronet, an eagle, wings addorsed, vulning. *Pl.* 109, *cr.* 15, (coronet, *pl.* 128, *fig.* 3.)

EDGEWORTH, Eng., a lion's head, erased, ar. *Pl.* 81, *cr.* 4.

EDGEWORTH, CHARLES-SNEYD, Esq., of Edgeworthstown, co. Longford, on a ducal coronet, a pelican, feeding her young, or. *Constans contraria spernit. Pl.* 44, *cr.* 1, (coronet, *same plate.*)

EDGHILL, a falcon, wings addorsed and inverted, supporting with dexter a carved shield, charged with a cinquefoil. *Pl.* 4, *cr.* 1.

EDGILL, a demi-lion, rampant, in dexter a cinquefoil, gu., slipped and leaved, vert. *Pl.* 39, *cr.* 14, (cinquefoil, *pl.* 141.)

EDIE, Sco., a cross crosslet, fitched, and a skean, in saltier. *Pl.* 89, *cr.* 14.

EDIEOK, and EGIOK, Worc., a demi-griffin, erm., beaked and legged, or, holding a broken tilting-spear, ppr. *Pl.* 18, *cr.* 6, (spear, *pl.* 23, *cr.* 9.)

EDINBURGH, City of, an anchor and cable, ppr. *Nisi Dominus frustra. Pl.* 42, *cr.* 12.

EDINGTON, Eng., a savage's head, couped, dropping blood, ppr. *Pl.* 23, *cr.* 1.

EDINGTON, or EDINGTOUN, an arm, in armour, embowed, wreathed with laurel, in hand a standard, erect, all ppr., flag, (charged with the sun,) or. *Pl.* 6, *cr.* 5.

EDINGTON, Sco., a stag's head, erased, or. *Labor omnia vincit. Pl.* 66, *cr.* 9.

EDINGTON, a Saracen's head, couped at shoulders, ppr., wreathed, ar. and gu. *Pl.* 36, *cr.* 3.

EDINGTOUN, an arm, in armour, embowed, wreathed above elbow with laurel, sustaining a standard, (charged with the rising sun.) *Pl.* 6, *cr.* 5.

EDLIN, Eng., a swan's head, between wings, ar. *Pl.* 54, *cr.* 6.

EDMANDS, Surr. and Middx., a griffin's head, erased, ar., in beak a cross crosslet, fitched, az., between wings, also ar., (each charged with a thistle, ppr.) *Pl.* 65, *cr.* 1, (cross, *pl.* 16, *cr.* 10.)

EDMERSTON, Eng., a dexter hand throwing a dart, ppr. *Pl.* 42, *cr.* 13.

EDMISTON, or EDMISTONE, Sco., a camel's head and neck. *Pl.* 109, *cr.* 9.

EDMOND, Eng., a demi-lion, ppr., supporting a long cross, gu. *Pl.* 29, *cr.* 12.

EDMOND, on a chapeau, a fleur-de-lis. *Pl.* 21, *cr.* 13, (without wings.)

EDMONDES, Hants and Suss., a dragon's head, erased, quarterly, vert and ar., (semée of roundles, charged with a crescent.) *Pl.* 107, *cr.* 10.

EDMONDES, Suss., a dragon's head, erased, ar., (charged on breast with three pellets.) *Pl.* 107, *cr.* 10.

EDMONDS, Cambs., a greyhound, sejant, sa., bezantée, (collared,) or. *Pl.* 66, *cr.* 15.

EDMONDS, within a wreath, ar. and sa., a lion, rampant, per fess, of the same. *Pl.* 72, *cr.* 7.

EDMONDS, Bucks. and Cornw., between wings, a lion, couchant, gardant, all or. *Pl.* 101, *cr.* 8, (wings, *pl.* 1, *cr.* 15.)

EDMONDS, Lond. and Suff., a wing, erect, per pale, or and ar. *Pl.* 39, *cr.* 10.

EDMONDS, Oxon., a griffin's head, erased, gu., in beak a cross crosslet, fitched, or. *Pl.* 35, *cr.* 15, (cross, *pl.* 141.)

EDMONDS, Devons., on a chapeau, gu., turned up, erm., a fleur-de-lis, or, between wings, az. *Pl.* 21, *cr.* 13.

EDMONDS, Yorks., a three-masted ship in full sail, ppr. *Pl.* 109, *cr.* 8.

EDMONDS, an arm, in armour, embowed, ppr., throwing a pheon, az., handle, of the first. *Pl.* 47, *cr.* 15.

EDMONDSON, Lond., a lion, rampant, or, gorged with a bar-gemelle, gu., supporting a pennon, az., staff, gu., headed, ar. *Pl.* 2, *cr.* 14.

EDMONDSON, Yorks., a demi-lion, sa., holding an escallop, ar. *Pl.* 126 A, *cr.* 13.

EDMONSTONE, Bart., Sco., out of a ducal coronet, or, a swan's head and neck, ppr. *Virtus auget honorem. Pl.* 83, *cr.* 1.

EDMONSTONE, Sco., a demi-lion, rampant, gu., armed and langued, az., in paws a battle-axe, ppr. *Be hardie. Pl.* 101, *cr.* 14, (without charge.)

EDMONSTONE, a squirrel, sejant, or. *Pl.* 16, *cr.* 9.

EDMUND, Eng., on a chapeau, gu., turned up, ar., a lion, passant, gardant, az., ducally gorged, or. *Pl.* 7, *cr.* 14.

EDMUNDS, Yorks., in the sea, an ancient ship of three masts under sail, all ppr. *Votis tune velis. Pl.* 109, *cr.* 8.

EDMUNDS, Hants, a (winged) lion, couchant, gardant, or. *Pl.* 101, *cr.* 8.

EDMUNDS, Eng., two hands, in fess, couped and conjoined, supporting a human heart, all ppr. *Pl.* 43, *cr.* 15.

EDNOR, Eng., a griffin's head, erased, gu., beaked, or. *Pl.* 48, *cr.* 6.

EDNOWAIN, Wel., a boar's head, couped, sa., langued, gu., tusked, or, transfixed by a (dagger,) ppr. *Pl.* 28, *cr.* 14.

EDOLPHE, Kent, an ibex's head, erased, sa., maned, armed, and attired, or. *Pl.* 72, *cr.* 9.

EDON, Kent and Suff., a plume of feathers, ar. *Pl.* 12, *cr.* 9.

EDRIDGE, a hawk, standing on a fish, ppr. *Pl.* 29, *cr.* 11.

EDRIDGE, Lond. and Norf., a lion's head, erased, gu. *Pl.* 81, *cr.* 4.

EDRIDGE, Wilts., a lion, rampant, ar. *Pl.* 67, *cr.* 5.

EDRINGTON, a goat's head, ppr., (collared,) erm. *Pl.* 105, *cr.* 14.

EDWARD, Eng., a torteau, ppr. *Nec flatu, nec fluctu. Pl.* 7, *cr.* 6.

EDWARD, a buck's head, couped, or. *Pl.* 91, *cr.* 14.

EDWARDES, Bart., Salop, a man's head, in profile, within a helmet, ppr., garnished, or. *Gratia naturam vincit. Pl.* 33, *cr.* 14.

EDWARDES-TUCKER, WILLIAM, Esq., of Sealy Ham, Pembroke, in bear's paw a battle-axe, ar. *Vigilate—*and*—Gardez la foy. Pl.* 51, *cr.* 13.

EDWARDES, Baron Kensington. See KENSINGTON.

EDWARDES, Carmarthen, a demi-lion, or, between paws a bowens-knot. *Aspera ad virtutem est via. Pl.* 67, *cr.* 10, (knot, *pl.* 11, *cr.* 5.)

EDWARDES, Eng. and Wel., a lion's head, erased, per bend sinister, erm. and ermines. *Pl.* 81, *cr.* 4.

EDWARDS, Eng. and Wel., a lion's head, erased, charged with four fleurs-de-lis. *Pl.* 81, *cr.* 4, (fleur-de-lis, *pl.* 141.)

EDWARDS, Somers., an eagle, displayed, az. *Pl.* 48, *cr.* 11.

EDWARDS, Beds., three ostrich-feathers, ar. *Pl.* 12, *cr.* 9.

EDWARDS, Heref., out of a ducal coronet, or, a demi-lion, rampant, gu., in dexter a sword, ppr. *Pl.* 41, *cr.* 13, (coronet, *same plate.*)

EDWARDS, Cornw., an antelope, rampant, sa., bezantée, attired, or. *Pl.* 72, *cr.* 10.

EDWARDS, Iri., a crosier, in pale, or. *Pl.* 7, *cr.* 15.

EDWARDS, GEORGE ROWLAND, Esq., of Ness Strange, Salop, a lion, rampant, counterchanged. *Pl.* 67, *cr.* 5.

EDWARDS, JOHN KYNASTON, Esq., of Old Court, co. Wicklow: 1. For *Edwards*, a lion's head, erased, ermines, between two palm-branches, issuing, ppr., mantled, gu., doubled, ar. *Heb Dduw, heb ddim, Dduw a digon.* *Pl.* 11, *cr.* 3, (without collar or flames.) 2. For *Kynaston*, an arm, in armour, in hand a sword, within a sun, ppr. *Honor potestate honorantis.* *Pl.* 40, *cr.* 14.

EDWARDS, Lond. and Beds., on a wreath, a helmet, ppr., garnished, or, on top, another wreath, with a plume of feathers issuing, ar. *Pl.* 38, *cr.* 15.

EDWARDS, Wel., a boar's head, erased, ar. *Pl.* 16, *cr.* 11.

EDWARDS, Cambs. and Suss., on a ducal coronet, ar., a tiger, passant, or. *Pl.* 67, *cr.* 15, (coronet, *same plate.*)

EDWARDS, Wel., an oak-tree, ppr., in dexter a gate, also ppr., on sinister a lion, rampant, against the tree, gu.

EDWARDS, Lond., on a ducal coronet, ar., a tiger, passant, sa., maned, of the first. *Pl.* 67, *cr.* 15, (coronet, *same plate.*)

EDWARDS, Devons., Hunts., and Salop, an ibex, passant, sa., bezantée, maned, armed, and attired, with two straight horns, or. *Pl.* 115, *cr.* 13.

EDWARDS, Kent and Salop, a unicorn, sa., (double horned,) or. *Pl.* 106, *cr.* 3.

EDWARDS, Warw., a talbot, passant, ppr. *Pl.* 120, *cr.* 8.

EDWARDS, Eng. and Wel., (on a mount, vert,) a horse's head, erased, or, (charged on neck with a cheveron,) gu., between two oakbranches, ppr. *Duw vde ein cryfden.* *Pl.* 81, *cr.* 6, (branches, *pl.* 74, *cr.* 7.)

EDWARDS, a turtle-dove, in mouth an olivebranch, ppr. *Pl.* 48, *cr.* 15.

EDWARDS, Glouc., a demi-lion, rampant, or, (holding a castle,) ar. *Pl.* 67, *cr.* 10.

EDWARDS, an eagle's head, erased, sa., ducally gorged, or. *Pl.* 39, *cr.* 4, (without pheon.)

EDWARDS, out of a marquess's coronet, a talbot's head. *Pl.* 123, *cr.* 15, (coronet, *pl.* 127, *fig.* 4.)

EDWARDS, on a mount, vert, a wyvern, ar. *Pl.* 33, *cr.* 13.

EDWARDS, Iri., a lion's head, erased, erm., between two palm-branches, ppr. *Pl.* 81, *cr.* 4, (branches, *pl.* 11, *cr.* 3.)

EDWARDS, Lond., in hand, gu., a cross pattée, fitched, or. *Pl.* 99, *cr.* 15.

EDWARDS, an antelope, passant, ppr. *Pl.* 63, *cr.* 10.

EDWARDS, a lion, passant, gardant, or. *Pl.* 120, *cr.* 5.

EDWARDS, Bart., of Garth, Montgomery, a lion, gardant, per pale, or and gu., (resting dexter on an escutcheon, of the second, charged with a nag's head,) erased, ar. *Y Gwir yn erbyn y byd.* *Pl.* 120, *cr.* 5.

EDWARDS, Norf., a martlet, sa., (charged on breast with a cinquefoil,) or. *Pl.* 111, *cr.* 5.

EDWARDS, Beds.: 1. The Prince of Wales's feathers, (surmounted by a heron plume.) *Pl.* 12, *cr.* 9. 2. An esquire's helmet, ppr. *Pl.* 109, *cr.* 5.

EDWIN, Eng., a lion, sejant, between paws an escutcheon, both party, per cheveron, gu. and or. *Pl.* 22, *cr.* 13.

EEL, Eng., a boar's head, couped, or. *Pl.* 48, *cr.* 2.

EELES, a dexter arm, in armour, in fess, couped, in hand a cutlass, enfiled with a boar's head, all ppr. *Pl.* 85, *cr.* 12.

EFFINGHAM, Earl, (Howard,) on a chapeau, gu., turned up, erm., a lion, statant, gardant, tail extended, or, gorged with a ducal coronet, ar. *Virtus mille scuta.* *Pl.* 7, *cr.* 14.

EGAN, Eng., a long cross, gu. *Pl.* 7, *cr.* 13.

EGAN, Iri., a demi-eagle, regardant. *Pl.* 27, *cr.* 15.

EGERTON, on a chapeau, gu., turned up, erm., a lion, rampant, of the first, supporting a broad arrow, sa. *Sic donec.* *Pl.* 22, *cr.* 15, (chapeau, *same plate.*)

EGERTON, Iri., a lion, sejant, gu., supporting in dexter a battle-axe, ar., staff, of the first, in sinister a laurel-branch, ppr. *Pl.* 115, *cr.* 15.

EGERTON, five arrows, one in pale, and four in saltier. *Pl.* 54, *cr.* 15.

EGERTON, Eng., a buck's head, erased, sa., attired, or. *Pl.* 66, *cr.* 9.

EGERTON, Chesh. and Salop, a lion, rampant, gu., supporting an arrow, ppr., headed and feathered, ar. *Pl.* 22, *cr.* 15.

EGERTON, Chesh., in lion's gamb, gu., a sword, ar., hilt and pommel, or. *Pl.* 47, *cr.* 14.

EGERTON, a lion, rampant, ppr. *Pl.* 67, *cr.* 5.

EGERTON, Chesh., Wilts., and Salop, three arrows, ar., headed and feathered, sa., banded, or. *Pl.* 43, *cr.* 14.

EGERTON, Chesh., a plume of feathers, erm. *Pl.* 12, *cr.* 9.

EGERTON, Eng., an arm, gu., in hand, ppr., a sword, ar. *Pl.* 34, *cr.* 7.

EGERTON, Earl of Wilton. *See* WILTON.

EGERTON-GREY, Bart., Chesh.: 1. Three broad arrows, one in pale, and two in saltier, or, pheoned and feathered, sa., banded by a ribbon, gu. *Pl.* 43, *cr.* 14. 2. On a hand, a falcon (rising.) *Virtuti, non armis fido.* *Pl.* 83, *cr.* 13.

EGG, out of a ducal coronet, a pair of stag's horns. *Pl.* 118, *cr.* 11.

EGGERLY, Eng., a Cornish chough, ducally gorged, ppr. *Pl.* 44, *cr.* 11.

EGGINGTON, Yorks., a talbot, sejant, ar., eared, sa., gorged with a collar, per fess, nebulée, or and az., dexter resting on a sphere, ppr. *Pl.* 107, *cr.* 7, (sphere, *pl.* 114, *cr.* 6.)

EGISKE, Eng., a griffin, passant, per pale, or and az. *Pl.* 61, *cr.* 14, (without gorging.)

EGLEBY, and EGLIONBY, Warw., a demi-eagle, wings expanded, or, charged with a mullet. *Pl.* 44, *cr.* 14.

EGLEFELDE, and EGLEFIELD, a dexter hand, apaumée, charged with an eye, ppr. *Pl.* 99, *cr.* 13.

EGLESTON, Eng., a talbot's head, erased, sa., collared, ar. *Pl.* 2, *cr.* 15.

ECLIN, Eng., on a mount, vert, an eagle, rising, or, (surmounted by an anchor and cable, in bend sinister, sa., in dexter a rose, gu., slipped, vert.) *Pl.* 61, *cr.* 1.

EGLINTON, Earl of, and Lord Montgomerie, Sco.; Baron Ardrossan, U.K., (Montgomerie,) a female figure, ppr., antiquely attired, ar., in dexter an anchor, or, in sinister a savage's head, couped, of the first. *Gardez bien.* *Pl.* 107, *cr.* 2.

EGMANTON, Lanc., in hand a cross pattée, fitched, gu. *Pl.* 99, *cr.* 15.

EGMONT, Earl of, Viscount and Baron Perceval, Iri.; Lord Lovel and Holland, Eng., (Perceval,) a thistle, erect, leaved, ppr. *Yvery*—and—*Sub cruce candida.* *Pl.* 68, *cr.* 9.

EGREMOND, Eng., a lion's head, gu., imperially crowned, or. *Pl.* 123, *cr.* 13.

EGREMONT, Earl of, Baron Cockermouth, (Windham,) a lion's head, erased, or, within a fetterlock, of the same, the arch compony counter-compony, or and az. *Au bon droit.* *Pl.* 90, *cr.* 14.

EISTON, Sco., out of a cloud, the sun rising, ppr. *Veritas.* *Pl.* 67, *cr.* 9.

EKENEY, on a chapeau, ppr., a pheon, az. *Pl.* 26, *cr.* 12, (chapeau, *pl.* 127, *fig.* 13.)

EKINS, a lion's gamb, sa., holding up a lozenge, ar., charged with a cross crosslet, fitched, of the first. *Pl.* 89, *cr.* 15.

EKINS, in lion's gamb, sa., a cross crosslet, fitched, in bend, gu. *Pl.* 46, *cr.* 7, (cross, *pl.* 141.)

EKINTON, and EKINGTON, a sand-glass, gu. *Pl.* 43, *cr.* 1.

ELAM, Kent, between attires of stag, attached to scalp, a boar's head, erased and erect, ppr. *Pl.* 33, *cr.* 15.

ELAND, and ELLAND, Eng., on a chapeau, az., turned up, or, a martlet, gu. *Pl.* 89, *cr.* 7.

ELAND, and ELLAND, Eng., a demi-female, in dexter a garland of laurel. *Pl.* 87, *cr.* 14.

ELCOCK, Eng., a stag, salient, ppr. *Pl.* 65, *cr.* 14.

ELCOCKE, Chesh., out of a mural coronet, or, a demi-cock, az., (in beak a wheat-ear, ppr.) *Pl.* 72, *cr.* 4, (coronet, *pl.* 128, *fig.* 18.)

ELCOCKS, Chesh., out of a mural coronet, or, a cock's head, gu., (in beak a wheat-ear.) *Pl.* 97, *cr.* 15, (coronet, *same plate.*)

ELD, Lond. and Staffs., a falcon, rising, or, beaked, membered, jessed, and belled, gu., beak embrued, ppr. *Pl.* 105, *cr.* 4.

ELDECUR, ELERCUR, and ELLERCUR, Eng., a cock, sa., combed, gu., beaked, or. *Pl.* 67, *cr.* 14.

ELDER, Eng., a demi-unicorn, rampant. *Pl.* 26, *cr.* 14.

ELDER, Sco., in dexter hand a palm-branch, ppr. *Virtute duce.* *Pl.* 23, *cr.* 7.

ELDERSHAW, Sco., a demi-lion, rampant, gu., ducally gorged, or. *Pl.* 87, *cr.* 15.

ELDERTON, Eng., a fox's head, ppr. *Pl.* 91, *cr.* 9.

ELDON, Earl of, and Baron, Viscount Encombe, (Scott,) a lion's head, erased, gu., charged on neck with a portcullis, chained, or, and a mullet for difference. *Sed sine tabe decus.* *Pl.* 81, *cr.* 4, (portcullis, *pl.* 51, *cr.* 12.)

ELDRED, Eng., a dexter hand, couped, in fess, reaching to a laurel-crown, all ppr. *Pl.* 73, *cr.* 11.

ELDRED, Ess., a Triton, ppr., holding an escallop, or. *Pl.* 35, *cr.* 10, (escallop, *pl.* 141.)

ELDRES, Eng., a camel's head, couped, ppr. *Pl.* 109, *cr.* 9.

ELDRES, a winged globe, ppr. *Pl.* 50, *cr.* 7.

ELDRIDGE, Eng., out of a ducal coronet, a peacock's tail, ppr. *Pl.* 120, *cr.* 13.

ELDRINGTON, Ess., a heron, sa. *Pl.* 6, *cr.* 13.

ELERKAR, two dolphins, haurient, az. and or. *Pl.* 81, *cr.* 2.

ELEY, Linc., an arm, erect, vested, ar., in hand a fleur-de-lis, sa. *Pl.* 95, *cr.* 9.

ELEY, Yorks., an arm, (in armour,) in hand a hawk's lure, ppr. *Pl.* 44, *cr.* 6.

ELFE, or ELPHE, an eagle's head, couped. *Pl.* 100, *cr.* 10.

ELFORD, Bart., Devons., a demi-lion, rampant, erased, ducally crowned. *Difficilia quæ pulchra.* *Pl.* 61, *cr.* 4, (without branch.)

ELFORD, Cornw., a demi-lion, rampant, crowned, or. *Difficilia quæ pulchra.* *Pl.* 61, *cr.* 4, (without palm-branch.)

ELFRED, Suss., on a mount, vert, a lamb, couchant, ar., between two olive-branches, ppr.

ELGIE, on a ducal coronet, a swan, wings addorsed, (ducally crowned.) *Pl.* 100, *cr.* 7.

ELGIN and KINCARDINE, Earl of, and Baron Bruce, (Bruce,) Sco., a lion, passant, gu. *Fuimus.* *Pl.* 48, *cr.* 8.

ELHAM, out of a mural coronet, a fire-beacon, between wings, ppr. *Pl.* 119, *cr.* 14.

ELIBANK, Baron, (Murray,) Sco., a lion, rampant, gardant, gu., holding a Lochaber-axe, ppr. *Virtute fideque.* *Pl.* 92, *cr.* 7, (axe, *pl.* 26, *cr.* 7.)

ELINGHAM, an eagle's head, couped, ppr. *Pl.* 100, *cr.* 10.

ELIOT, of Borthwickbrae, Sco., in dexter hand, erect, a horseman's lance, in bend, ppr., headed, ar. *Hoc majorum opus.* *Pl.* 99, *cr.* 8.

ELIOT, Eng., an elephant's head, sa., armed and eared, ar. *Pl.* 35, *cr.* 13.

ELIOT, (out of clouds,) a dexter arm, embowed, throwing a dart, ppr. *Pl.* 92, *cr.* 14.

ELIOT, Baron, Earl St Germans. *See* ST GERMANS.

ELIOT, Surr., a griffin's head, couped, wings addorsed, sa., (collared,) ar. *Pl.* 18, *cr.* 6.

ELIOTT, Bart., Sco., a dexter arm, in hand a cutlass, ppr. *Peradventure.* *Pl.* 92, *cr.* 5.

ELKIN, a demi-heraldic-antelope, or, armed and tufted, sa.

ELKINGTON, Lond. and Leic., on a mural coronet, chequy, or and sa., embattled, of the first, a demi-griffin, ar., winged, gu., (in dexter a gem-ring,) gold, gem, of the second. *Pl.* 39, *cr.* 2.

ELKINS, Eng., on a castle, triple-towered, ppr., a flag, displayed, gu. *Pl.* 123, *cr.* 14.

ELLAMES, Lanc., an elm-tree, ppr. *Nec sperno, nec timeo.* *Pl.* 18, *cr.* 10.

ELLARD, Eng., a torteau, gu., charged with a stag, or, standing on a mount, vert. *Pl.* 45, *cr.* 11.

ELLARD, on a mount, vert, a stag, or. *Pl.* 50, *cr.* 6.
ELLAWAY, five arrows, one in pale, four in saltier, points downward, environed with a serpent, all ppr. *Pl.* 21, *cr.* 14.
ELLENBOROUGH, Baron (Law,) a cock, gu., (chained round neck, charged on breast with a mitre,) or. *Compositum jus fasque animi. Pl.* 67, *cr.* 14.
ELLERKER, Yorks., a talbot's head, ar. *Pl.* 123, *cr.* 15.
ELLERKER, Yorks., a talbot's head, erased, sa. *Pl.* 90, *cr.* 6.
ELLERKER, Yorks., two dolphins, haurient and addorsed, az. and or, (enfiled with a ducal coronet,) per pale, counterchanged. *Pl.* 81, *cr.* 2.
ELLESTON, a demi-heraldic-tiger, between paws a naval crown. *Pl.* 57, *cr.* 13, (crown, *pl.* 128, *fig.* 19.)
ELLESWORTH, Eng., a dexter arm, in armour, embowed, couped, in hand a club, ppr. *Pl.* 45, *cr.* 10.
ELLEY, Eng., an anchor, in pale, az., entwined by a serpent, vert. *Pl.* 35, *cr.* 14.
ELLICE, Middx. and Herts., an arm, erect, couped below elbow, in armour, in gauntlet a snake, entwined round arm, all ppr. *Pl.* 91, *cr.* 6.
ELLICE, a mermaid, with mirror and comb, ppr. *Pl.* 48, *cr.* 5.
ELLICK, a wolf's head, erased, sa. *Pl.* 14, *cr.* 6.
ELLICOMB, a buck's head, erased, murally gorged and (chained.) *Pl.* 55, *cr.* 2.
ELLICOMBE, Devons., a dexter arm, in armour, embowed, in hand a sword, all ppr. *Pl.* 2, *cr.* 8.
ELLICOMBE, or ELLACOMBE, Glouc. and Devons., a stag's head, (erased,) murally gorged and chained. *Nullis fraus tuta latebris. Pl.* 55, *cr.* 2.
ELLICOTT, a hawk, wings expanded, belled, ppr. *Pl.* 105, *cr.* 4.
ELLICOTT, or ELLACOTT, Eng., in a maunch, or, cuffed, gu., a hand clenched, ppr. *Pl.* 22, *cr.* 14.
ELLIES, Sco., a lily, (close in the flower,) ppr. *Sub sole patebit. Pl.* 81, *cr.* 9.
ELLINGTON, Eng., in lion's paw, a cross pattée, fitched, sa. *Pl.* 46, *cr.* 7.
ELLIOT-FOGG, Durh.: 1. For *Elliot,* a dexter arm, in hand a cutlass, ppr. *Pl.* 92, *cr.* 5. 2. For *Fogg,* a unicorn's head, couped, ar. *Peradventure. Pl.* 20, *cr.* 1.
ELLIOT, or ELLIOTT, a demi-sea-horse, az., scaled, or. *Pl.* 58, *cr.* 15.
ELLIOT, or ELLIOTT, Suff., an elephant's head, or, eared and armed, gu. *Pl.* 35, *cr.* 13.
ELLIOT, or ELLIOTT, Lond., a demi-sea-horse, az., finned, or. *Pl.* 58, *cr.* 15.
ELLIOT, or ELLIOTT, Cornw., an elephant's head, ar., (collared,) gu. *Pl.* 35, *cr.* 13.
ELLIOT, or ELLIOTT, a boar's head, couped, (pierced through dexter eye) by a broken spear. *Pl.* 11, *cr.* 9.
ELLIOT, or ELLIOTT, in dexter hand, ppr., a crescent, sa. *Pl.* 38, *cr.* 7.
ELLIOT, or ELLIOTT, a nail, erect, ppr. *Pl.* 47, *cr.* 10.
ELLIOT, or ELLIOTT, a ram, ppr. *Vellera fertis oves. Pl.* 109, *cr.* 2.

ELLIOT, or ELLIOTT, an oak-tree, ppr. *Fortiter. Pl.* 16, *cr.* 8.
ELLIOT, or ELLIOTT, an anchor and cable, in pale, ppr. *Candide et caute. Pl.* 42, *cr.* 12.
ELLIOT, or ELLIOTT, a dexter arm, in hand a dart, point downward, ppr. *Suaviter sed fortiter. Pl.* 43, *cr.* 13.
ELLIOT, or ELLIOTT, out of a mural coronet, an elephant's head, (collared.) *Pl.* 35, *cr.* 13, (coronet, *pl.* 128, *fig.* 18.)
ELLIOT, of Laurieston, same crest. *Apto cum lare.*
ELLIOT, or ELLIOTT, issuing from a cloud, a dexter hand throwing a dart. *Non eget arcu. Pl.* 45, *cr.* 12.
ELLIOT, or ELLIOTT, a dexter arm, in hand a cutlass, ppr. *Peradventure. Pl.* 92, *cr.* 6.
ELLIOT, GEORGE-HENRY, Esq., of Binfield Park, Berks.; and Stonehouse, Glouc.: 1. For *Elliot,* an elephant's head, ar., erased, gu., (about neck two barrulets, inverted, vert.) *Pl.* 68, *cr.* 4. 2. For *Glasse,* a mermaid, with glass and comb, ppr. *Pl.* 48, *cr.* 5.
ELLIOT, Earl of Minto. *See* MINTO.
ELLIOT, or ELLIOTT, in dexter hand a flute, ppr. *Inest jucunditas. Pl.* 46, *cr.* 14.
ELLIOT, or ELLIOTT, a demi-man, in armour, ppr. *Pro rege et limite. Pl.* 23, *cr.* 4.
ELLIOT, Iri., over the sea, a dove, volant, in mouth an olive-branch, ppr. *Pl.* 46, *cr.* 13.
ELLIOT, or ELLIOTT, Surr., a griffin's head, couped, wings addorsed, sa. *Pl.* 18, *cr.* 6.
ELLIS, the Rev. JOHN-WILLIAMS, M.A., of Glasfryn, Carnarvon: 1. A mermaid, gu., crined, or, in dexter a mirror, in sinister a comb. *Pl.* 48, *cr.* 5. 2. An arm, in armour, embowed, in hand a broken spear-head, all ppr. *Wrth ein ffrwythau yn hadna byddir. Pl.* 44, *cr.* 9.
ELLIS, Baron Seaford. *See* SEAFORD.
ELLIS, Baron Howard de Walden. *See* HOWARD.
ELLIS, Viscount Clifden, and Baron Dovor. *See* CLIFDEN.
ELLIS, Herts., out of a ducal coronet, or, a lion's head, gu., (crowned,) gold. *Fort et fidèle. Pl.* 90, *cr.* 9.
ELLIS, Yorks. and Kent, a naked woman, hair dishevelled, ppr.
ELLIS, Sco., an eel, ppr. *Sperans. Pl.* 25, *cr.* 13.
ELLIS, Cornw., a mermaid, with mirror and comb, ppr. *Pl.* 48, *cr.* 5.
ELLIS, Lond., (out of grass,) ppr., a goat's head, ar., horned, of the first. *Pl.* 105, *cr.* 14.
ELLIS, Linc., in a crescent, gu., an escallop, or. *Pl.* 47, *cr.* 12.
ELLIS, Eng., a garb, per fess, or and vert. *Pl.* 48, *cr.* 10.
ELLIS, Wel., on a chapeau, az., turned up, erm., a lion, passant, gu. *Pl.* 107, *cr.* 1.
ELLIS, between the horns of a crescent, a stag's head, cabossed. *Pl.* 74, *cr.* 2.
ELLISON, Durh., an eagle's head, erased, or. *Pl.* 20, *cr.* 7.
ELLISON, Sco., a cross crosslet, fitched, gu. *Pl.* 16, *cr.* 10.
ELLISON, Eng., a lion, passant, gardant, in dexter an anchor. *Pl.* 120, *cr.* 5, (anchor, *pl.* 42, *cr.* 12.)
ELLISON, a greyhound, sa. *Pl.* 104, *cr.* 1, (without chapeau.)

ELLISON, an eagle's head, erased, per fess, or and gu., murally gorged, az. *Pl.* 74, *cr.* 1.

ELLISTON, Lond., an eagle's head, erased, ppr., ducally gorged, ar. *Pl.* 39, *cr.* 4, (without pheon.)

ELLISTON, Eng., three mullets, az., one and two. *Pl.* 46, *cr.* 15.

ELLISWORTH, Eng., between attires of stag, ppr., a rose, gu. *Pl.* 50, *cr.* 14.

ELLNOR, out of a ducal coronet, or, an eagle's head, between wings, sa., beaked, gu., charged with a bezant. *Pl.* 66, *cr.* 5, (bezant, *pl.* 141.)

ELLOWAY, a dragon's head, gu. *Pl.* 87, *cr.* 12.

ELLWOOD, Yorks., on a mural coronet, a stag, sejant, ppr. *Pl.* 101, *cr.* 3.

ELLY, an arm, erect, vested, ar., in hand, ppr., a fleur-de-lis, sa. *Pl.* 95, *cr.* 9.

ELLYOT, and ELLYOTT, Eng., an elephant's head, couped, ar. *Pl.* 35, *cr.* 13.

ELMSLEY, Viscount. See BEAUCHAMP, Earl.

ELLYOTT, Lond., a demi-pegasus, ar., maned, winged, and hoofed, or. *Pl.* 91, *cr.* 2, (without coronet.)

ELMEET, Holland, a horse's head, bridled. *Pl.* 92, *cr.* 1.

ELMEN, on a ducal coronet, a wyvern. *Pl.* 104, *cr.* 11.

ELMES, Lanc. and Northamp., out of a ducal coronet, or, a woman's head and neck, couped below breasts, ppr., hair, gold. *Pl.* 74, *cr.* 5.

ELMHURST, Linc., a clump of elms, ppr. *Pl.* 125, *cr.* 14, (without lion.)

ELMORE, the top of a halberd, ppr. *Pl.* 24, *cr.* 15.

ELMORE, a Cornish chough, ppr. *Pl.* 100, *cr.* 13.

ELMSALL-GREAVES, Yorks.: 1. For *Elmsall*, an elm-tree, trunk entwined with a vine-branch, ppr., fructed. *Pl.* 74, *cr.* 4. 2. For *Greaves*, on a mount, vert, a stag, trippant, or, (in mouth a slip of oak, ppr.) *Amicta vitibus ulmus.* *Pl.* 50, *cr.* 6, (oak-slip, *pl.* 32, *cr.* 13.)

ELMSEY, a falcon's head, erased, ppr. *Pl.* 34, *cr.* 11.

ELMSLIE, Eng., a demi-wolf, holding a spear, in pale, tasselled, all ppr. *Pl.* 56, *cr.* 8.

ELMSLY, Sco., a thistle, leaved, ppr. *Prenez garde.* *Pl.* 68, *cr.* 9, (without bee.)

ELMY, and ELNEY, on a chapeau, a tower, ppr. *Pl.* 12, *cr.* 5, (chapeau, *pl.* 127, *fig.* 13.)

ELPHINGSTON, Sco., a dove, ar., holding a snake, ppr. *Pl.* 74, *cr.* 3.

ELPHINGSTON, Sco., a griffin, sejant, sa., in dexter a laurel wreath, vert. *Pl.* 56, *cr.* 10.

ELPHINGSTON, Sco., a griffin, sejant, sa., holding a sword, in pale, on point a Saracen's head, all ppr. *Do well, and let them say.* *Pl.* 41, *cr.* 14.

ELPHINGSTON, Sco., a demi-lady, richly attired, in dexter a garland, ppr. *Merito.* *Pl.* 87, *cr.* 14.

ELPHINGSTON, two arms, in saltier, (in dexter a sword, in sinister, a branch of laurel,) all ppr. *In utroque paratus.* *Pl.* 52, *cr.* 1.

ELPHINGSTON, Sco., in dexter hand a pen. *Fidelitate.* *Pl.* 26, *cr.* 13.

ELPHINGSTON, Sco., a demi-greyhound, ar. *Pl.* 48, *cr.* 3.

ELPHINSTONE, Baron, (Elphinstone,) Sco., a demi-female, from the girdle, richly attired, ar. and gu., in dexter a tower, of the first, masoned, sa., and in sinister a branch of laurel, ppr. *Cause caused it.* *Pl.* 20, *cr.* 6.

ELPHINSTONE, Baroness Keith. See KEITH.

ELPHINSTONE, Bart., Cumb., out of a mural coronet, gu., a demi-woman, affrontée, vested, (in dexter a sword,) ppr., hilt and pommel, or, in sinister an olive-branch, vert. *Semper paratus.* *Pl.* 20, *cr.* 6, (coronet, *same plate*, *cr.* 10.)

ELPHINSTONE-HORN-DALRYMPLE, Bart., Sco., two stags' horns, erect, per fess, or and sa. *Moneo et munio.* *Pl.* 71, *cr.* 8.

ELRICK, Sco., out of a ducal coronet, a horse's head, ppr. *Dum spiro, spero.* *Pl.* 50, *cr.* 13.

ELRINGTON, Eng., the Roman fasces, in pale, ppr. *Pl.* 65, *cr.* 15.

ELSLEY, a saggittarius, per fess, ppr. and ar., bow and arrow, of the first, (horse charged with a rose, gu.) *Pl.* 70, *cr.* 13.

ELSON, Suss., a demi-eagle, displayed, ar., billettée, sa. *Pl.* 22, *cr.* 11.

ELSTOB, Durh., a demi-lion, in dexter a mullet, ar. *Pl.* 89, *cr.* 10.

ELSTON, Eng., on a chapeau, an escallop, between wings, ppr. *Pl.* 17, *cr.* 14.

ELSWELL, on a bezant, a cross pattée, gu. *Pl.* 7, *cr.* 6, (cross, *pl.* 15, *cr.* 8.)

ELSWORTH, a heart, winged and crowned, ppr. *Pl.* 52, *cr.* 2.

ELTON, Bart., Somers., an arm, in armour, embowed, ppr., in gauntlet a scimitar, ar., hilt and pommel, or, (tied round arm with a scarf, vert.) *Pl.* 81, *cr.* 11.

ELTON, Oxon., same crest.

ELTON, Lond. and Berks., out of a mural coronet, gu., an arm, vested, or, turned up, ar., in hand, ppr., a mullet, of the second. *Pl.* 34, *cr.* 1.

ELTON, Heref., a lion's head, erased and affrontée, collared, az. *Pl.* 1, *cr.* 5.

ELTON-MARWOOD, Bart., of Widworthy Court, Devons., an arm, in armour, embowed, ppr., garnished, or, charged with two etoiles, gu., adorned (with a scarf about the wrist, vert,) in gauntlet a falchion, ppr., hilt and pommel, or. *Pl.* 2, *cr.* 8, (etoile, *pl.* 141.)

ELVEN, a lion's head, erased, collared. *Pl.* 7, *cr.* 10.

ELVEN, a stag's head, couped. *Pl.* 91, *cr.* 14.

ELVES, and ELWES, Wilts., Linc., Notts., Suff., and Northamp., five arrows, or, entwined by a snake, ppr. *Pl.* 21, *cr.* 14.

ELVET, a lion, sejant, or. *Pl.* 126, *cr.* 15.

ELVIN, Norf., a demi-lion, rampant, or, issuing from the summit of a rock, holding a vine-branch, ppr. *Elvenaca floreat vitis.* *Pl.* 72, *cr.* 13, (branch, *pl.* 89, *cr.* 1.)

ELWAS, (three) arrows, one in pale, and two in saltier, or, flighted, ar., headed, ppr., environed by a serpent, vert. *Pl.* 21, *cr.* 14.

ELWELL, a dart, erect, point downward. *Pl.* 56, *cr.* 13.

ELWICK, an armed arm, or, bound with a scarf, az., holding a staff, raguly, of the first, raguled, of the second. *Pl.* 21, *cr.* 4, (staff, *pl.* 78, *cr.* 15.)

ELWILL, Linc., an arm, erect, vested, sa., cuffed, ar., in hand, ppr., a fleece, or. *Pl.* 74, *cr.* 6.

ELWIN, ELWYN, and ELWYNN, Eng., a demi-savage, over dexter shoulder a hammer, ppr. *Pl.* 51, *cr.* 14.

ELWOOD, an arm, in armour, embowed, in hand a pick-axe, all ppr. *Vide et sedulitate.* *Pl.* 2, *cr.* 8, (axe, *pl.* 113, *cr.* 10.)

ELWORTH, on a mount, an ermine, passant, ppr. *Pl.* 87, *cr.* 3.

ELWORTHY, Eng., a steel cap, ppr.

ELY, Marquess and Earl of, Viscount and Baron Loftus, Iri.; Baron Loftus, U.K., and a Bart., (Loftus,) a boar's head, (couped) and erect, ar., langued, gu. *Prend moi tel que je suis*—and—*Loyal à mort.* *Pl.* 21, *cr.* 7.

ELY, Iri., a pheon, point upward, gu. *Pl.* 56, *cr.* 15.

ELYARD, Eng., an arm, in armour, embowed, in hand a scimitar. *Pl.* 81, *cr.* 11.

ELYE, Eng., an arm, (in armour,) in hand a hawk's lure, ppr. *Pl.* 44, *cr.* 2.

EMAN, a lion, sejant, (regardant,) purp. *Pl.* 126, *cr.* 15.

EMBERY, Eng., a dexter arm, embowed, in hand a sword, in pale, enfiled with a Saracen's head, (in profile,) all ppr. *Pl.* 102, *cr.* 11.

EMBERY, a pillar, az., environed by a serpent, ppr., masonry of the base, ar. *Pl.* 14, *cr.* 15, (serpent, *pl.* 21, *cr.* 14.)

EMENFIELD, Eng., a hand holding an escutcheon, or, charged with a martlet, ppr. *Pl.* 21, *cr.* 12, (martlet, *pl.* 111, *cr.* 5.)

EMER, out of a ducal coronet, or, a demi-lion, rampant, gardant, ppr., (in dexter a sword,) also ppr., hilt and pommel, gold. *Pl.* 26, *cr.* 7, (coronet, *pl.* 128, *fig.* 3.)

EMERSON, Northumb., a sinister hand, (charged with a bend,) and thereon three bezants. *Pl.* 74, *cr.* 8, (bezant, *pl.* 141.)

EMERSON, Durh., a lion, rampant, vert, bezantée, holding a battle-axe, gu., headed, ar. *Pl.* 125, *cr.* 2, (axe, *pl.* 26, *cr.* 7.)

EMERSON, Linc. and Norf., issuing from a cloud, rays of the sun, all ppr. *Pl.* 25, *cr.* 14.

EMERY, Kent, a demi-unicorn, rampant, (erased,) gu., hoofed and armed, or, crined, sa. *Pl.* 26, *cr.* 14.

EMERY, Somers., out of a mural coronet, a demi-horse, collared. *Fidelis et suavis.*

EMERYKE, out of a ducal coronet, or, a boar's head and neck, sa., (collared,) ar. *Pl.* 102, *cr.* 14.

EMES, and EMME, Lond. and Berks., a demi-lion, rampant, sa. *Pl.* 67, *cr.* 10.

EMLINE, or EMLYN, a demi-savage, wreathed, holding a club, all ppr. *Honestum prætulit utili.* *Pl.* 14, *cr.* 11.

EMLY, Iri., in lion's gamb a battle-axe, ppr. *Pl.* 51, *cr.* 13.

EMMERSON, Eng., a cock, ppr. *Pl.* 67, *cr.* 14.

EMMET, or EMMETT, Eng., on a chapeau, a unicorn's head, erased, ppr. *Pl.* 102, *cr.* 7.

EMMOT, or EMMOTT, Eng., a hind, (sejant, regardant,) resting dexter on a bee-hive, ppr. *Pl.* 1, *cr.* 14.

EMPSON, Yorks., a tent, ar., adorned, or, lined, az., charged with a cross pattée, of the first. *Pl.* 111, *cr.* 14, (cross, *pl.* 141.)

EMPSON, Eng., a lion, sejant, gardant, or, in dexter a long cross, gu., sinister resting on a triangle, pierced, sa. *Pl.* 56, *cr.* 12.

EMSLIE, or EMSLY, Sco., a thistle, leaved, ppr. *Prenez garde.* *Pl.* 68, *cr.* 9, (without bee.)

ENDAS, or ENEUS, a castle, triple-towered, ppr., domed, gu. *Pl.* 123, *cr.* 14, (domed, *pl.* 42, *cr.* 10.)

ENDERBIE, and ENDERBY, a swan, sa. *Pl.* 122, *cr.* 13.

ENDERBY, or ENDERBIE, in a maunch, a hand, clenched. *Pl.* 22, *cr.* 14.

ENDERBY, or ENDERBIE, a harpooner, in the act of striking a whale, ppr.

ENDSORE, Staffs., a cubit arm, (vested,) gu., in hand a sword, ar., hilt and pommel, or. *Pl.* 21, *cr.* 10.

ENELL, Eng., a mermaid, with comb and glass, ppr. *Pl.* 48, *cr.* 5.

ENERY, WILLIAM-HAMILTON, Esq., of Ballyconnell House, co. Cavan, a falcon, close, ppr. *Sans changer.* *Pl.* 67, *cr.* 3.

ENFIELD, Ess., in hand, an escutcheon, or, charged with a martlet, ppr. *Pl.* 21, *cr.* 12, (martlet, *pl.* 111, *cr.* 5.)

ENGAINE, a tower, sa., cupola and flag, gu. *Pl.* 42, *cr.* 10.

ENGHAM, Kent, two lions' paws, or, holding up a fire-ball, gu. *Pl.* 42, *cr.* 3, (fire-ball, *pl.* 70, *cr.* 12.)

ENGHAM, an arm, embowed, vested, az., turned up and indented, ar., hand grasping a snake, entwined, vert. *Pl.* 58, *cr.* 4, (snake, *pl.* 91, *cr.* 6.)

ENGLAND, Eng., a cherub, ppr. *Pl.* 126, *cr.* 10.

ENGLEBERT, Dors., two wings addorsed, (charged with two bends.) *Pl.* 63, *cr.* 12.

ENGLEDUE, a greyhound's head, erased, sa., collared, ar. *Pl.* 30, *cr.* 7, (without leg.)

ENGLEFIELD, Wilts., an eagle, displayed, per pale, az. and gu. *Pl.* 48, *cr.* 11.

ENGLEFIELD, Wilts., a sinister arm, vested, per pale, az. and gu., cuffed, ar., in hand, ppr., a branch, vert. *Pl.* 52, *cr.* 5, (branch, *pl.* 23, *cr.* 7.)

ENGLEHEART, an armed arm, embowed, in gauntlet a sword, ppr. *Pl.* 2, *cr.* 8.

ENGLISH, a greyhound's head, between two roses, slipped and leaved. *Pl.* 84, *cr.* 13.

ENGLISH, a rose-branch, ppr., flowered, gu. *Pl.* 23, *cr.* 2.

ENGLISH, a demi-lion. *Pl.* 67, *cr.* 10.

ENGLISH, in hand, ppr., a covered cap, ar. *Pl.* 35, *cr.* 9.

ENGLISH, Iri., a pyramid, entwined with woodbine. *Pl.* 8, *cr.* 10.

ENGOLISME, Eng., a torteau, ppr. *Pl.* 7, *cr.* 6.

ENNEW, Ess., a lion's head, erased, gu. *Pl.* 81, *cr.* 4.

ENNIS, Eng., an anchor, az., surmounted by a fleur-de-lis. *Pl.* 51, *cr.* 15.

ENNIS, Iri., an ox-yoke, in bend. *Pl.* 35, *cr.* 11.

ENNISHOWEN, and CARRICKFERGUS, Baron, (Chichester,) a stork, in mouth a snake, ppr. *Famæ vestigia retinens.* *Pl.* 33, *cr.* 9, (snake, *pl.* 41, *cr.* 6.)

ENNISKILLEN, Earl of, and Viscount, Baron Mountflorence, Iri.; Baron Grinstead, U.K., (Willoughby-Cole,) Iri., a demi-dragon, vert, langued, gu., (in dexter a dart, ppr., in sinister an escutcheon, or.) *Deum cole, regem serva,* *Pl.* 82, *cr.* 10.

ENNYS, Cornw., in hand a sheaf, ppr. *Pl.* 3, *cr.* 3.

ENOKE, Worc., a demi-lion, in paws a serpent, nowed, ppr. *Pl.* 124, *cr.* 5, (without charge.)

ENSON, Staffs., an arm, in armour, ppr., garnished, or, in hand a sword, ar., hilt and pommel, gold. *Pl.* 2, *cr.* 8.
ENSOR, Eng., a lion, rampant, per fess, or and sa., in dexter a fleur-de-lis, gu. *Pl.* 87, *cr.* 6.
ENSOR, Norf., a unicorn's head, ar., horned and maned, or. *Pl.* 20, *cr.* 1.
ENSWELL, and ENTWISSELL, Lanc., on a mount, vert, a hind, ppr., collared, ar. *Pl.* 75, *cr.* 6.
ENSWELL, and ENTWISSELL, a human heart, gu. *Pl.* 55, *cr.* 13.
ENTWICK, a dexter hand, couped, in fess, (pointing with the forefinger,) and sustaining a fleur-de-lis. *Pl.* 46, *cr.* 12.
ENTWISLE, Lanc.: 1. A hand, couped, in fess, ppr., holding a fleur-de-lis, erect, or. *Pl.* 46, *cr.* 12. 2. A dexter arm, in armour, embowed, holding by the hair a Saracen's head, erased, and affrontée, all ppr. *Pl.* 104, *cr.* 13, (Saracen's head, *pl.* 19, *cr.* 1.)
ENYS, JOHN-SAMUEL, Esq., of Enys, Cornw., three white feathers, erect. *Serpentes velut et columbæ.* *Pl.* 12, *cr.* 9.
EPITRE, a cinquefoil, pierced, gu. *Pl.* 91, *cr.* 12.
EPPS, Kent, on a chaplet, vert, flowered, or, a falcon, rising, gold. *Pl.* 105, *cr.* 4, (chaplet, *pl.* 128, *fig.* 16.)
ERCALL, Eng., in dexter hand, ppr., a mullet of six points, or, charged with a crescent, sa. *Pl.* 17, *cr.* 10.
ERDESWIKE, Staffs., out of a ducal coronet, gu., a boar's head, per pale, ar. and sa., langued, of the first. *Pl.* 102, *cr.* 14.
ERDINGTON, Eng., in hand a ball, sa. *Pl.* 33, *cr.* 6.
EREDY, Lond., out of a coronet, two wings, ppr. *Pl.* 17, *cr.* 9.
ERESEY, on a sinister glove, a falcon, ppr. *Pl.* 1, *cr.* 13.
ERINGTON, or ERRINGTON, Northumb. and Wilts., a cock, gu., combed and wattled, sa. *Pl.* 67, *cr.* 14.
ERINGTON, Northumb., a unicorn's head, erased, quarterly, ar. and gu. *Pl.* 67, *cr.* 1.
ERISBY, Eng., a broken halberd, ppr. *Auxilio Dei.* *Pl.* 24, *cr.* 15.
ERISEY, Cornw., a cinquefoil, erm. *Pl.* 91, *cr.* 12.
ERISEY, Cornw., a stag, trippant, ppr. *Pl.* 68, *cr.* 2.
ERLE, Dors., a lion's head, erased, or, transpierced by a (spear,) ar., embrued, gu. *Pl.* 113, *cr.* 15.
ERLEY, or ERLY, Eng., in hand, erect, ppr., a gem-ring, or, stone, gu. *Pl.* 24, *cr.* 3, (ring, *pl.* 35, *cr.* 3.)
ERMINE, Eng., an ermine, ppr. *Pl.* 9, *cr.* 5.
ERMINGLAND, Norf., out of antique crown, a demi-lion, gu. *Pl.* 67, *cr.* 10, (crown, *pl.* 79, *cr.* 12.)
ERNE, Earl of, Viscount and Baron, Iri., (Creighton,) a dragon's head, couped, vert, fire issuing from mouth (and ears,) ppr. *God send grace.* *Pl.* 37, *cr.* 9.
ERNLEY, and ERNLY, Eng., an eagle, displayed, or. *Pl.* 48, *cr.* 11.
ERNLEY, Wilts., a man's head, in profile, ppr., wearing a long cap, barry of six, or and sa., stringed and tasselled, of the second. *Pl.* 51, *cr.* 4.
ERNST, Eng., an eagle, gazing at the sun, ppr. *Pl.* 43, *cr.* 5.

ERRINGTON, Northumb. and Ess., a unicorn's head, erased, per pale, ar. and gu. *Pl.* 67, *cr.* 1.
ERRINGTON, a cock, gu., combed and wattled, sa. *Pl.* 67, *cr.* 14.
ERROL, Earl of, and Baron Hay, Sco.; Baron Kilmarnock, U.K., (Hay-Carr,) Sco., a falcon, rising, ppr. *Serva jugum.* *Pl.* 105, *cr.* 4.
ERSKINE, Baron, a dexter arm, embowed, couped below elbow, hand grasping a club, all ppr. *Trial by jury.* *Pl.* 123, *cr.* 10.
ERSKINE, Bart., of Torrie, Sco., a cubit arm, erect, hand grasping a sword, ppr., hilt and pommel, or. *Fortitudine.* *Pl.* 21, *cr.* 10.
ERSKINE, Earl of Buchan, Earl of Rosslyn, Lord Cardross, and Earl of Marr, and Kellie. *See* BUCHAN, ROSSLYN, and MARR.
ERSKINE, Bart., of Cambo., Sco., a garb, in fess, or, thereon, a cock, ppr., wings expanded, (charged with a bend, wavy,) sinister, az. *Vellient et vaillant.* *Pl.* 122, *cr.* 3, (cock, *pl.* 76, *cr.* 7.)
ERSKINE, Sco., a dexter arm, in armour, in hand a sword, ppr. *Je pense plus.* *Pl.* 2, *cr.* 8.
ERSKINE, Sco., a griffin's head, erased, in beak a sword, in bend. *In Domino confido.* *Pl.* 35, *cr.* 15.
ERSKINE, Sco., a dexter arm, ppr., in hand a cross crosslet, or. *Think well.* *Pl.* 39, *cr.* 1, (cross, *pl.* 66, *cr.* 8.)
ERSKINE, Sco., a demi-lion, rampant, gu. *Pl.* 67, *cr.* 10.
ERSKINE, Sco., a dexter hand holding a dagger, in pale, ppr., within an orle of laurel, vert. *Je pense plus*—and—*Perspicax, audax.* *Pl.* 23, *cr.* 15, (laurel, *pl.* 95, *cr.* 11.)
ERSKINE, Sco., a cubit arm, erect, hand grasping a sword, ppr., hilted, or. *Pl.* 21, *cr.* 10.
ERSKINE, Sco., in dexter hand a club, raguly, ppr. *Judge nought.* *Pl.* 28, *cr.* 6.
ERSKINE, THOMAS, Esq., of Linlathen, same crest and motto.
ERSKINE, Sco., a dexter arm, embowed, in hand a scimitar. *Je pense plus.* *Pl.* 92, *cr.* 5.
ERSKINE, Lord Erskine, a dexter hand, grasping a club, or. *Fortitudine.* *Pl.* 28, *cr.* 6.
ERSKINE, Sco., a demi-griffin, in dexter a sword, all ppr. *Ausim et confido.* *Pl.* 49, *cr.* 4.
ERSKINE, Sco., a demi-lion, rampant, gu., in dexter a thistle, ppr., in sinister a fleur-de-lis, az. *Pl.* 45, *cr.* 15.
ERSKINE, Sco., a dexter arm, in armour, embowed, in hand a dagger, (erect.) *Pl.* 120, *cr.* 11.
ERTHE, Sco., a cock crowing. *Audax.* *Pl.* 67, *cr.* 14.
ERVING, Eng., in hand a mill-rind. *Pl.* 34, *cr.* 3.
ERVING, on a torteau, ar., a cross, sa. *Pl.* 7, *cr.* 6, (cross, *pl.* 141.)
ERWIN, Sco., on a mount, vert, a tree, ppr., thereto chained a boar, passant, or, collar, chain, and padlock, az. *Lock sick.* *Pl.* 57, *cr.* 12.
ESCALES, out of a ducal coronet, gu., (seven) ostrich-feathers, ar. *Pl.* 44, *cr.* 12.
ESCLABOR, Eng., a galley, with sails furled, sa., flags, gu. *Pl.* 24, *cr.* 5.
ESCOT, or ESSCOT, Cornw., a lion, passant, per pale, ar. and sa. *Pl.* 48, *cr.* 8.
ESCOTT, Eng., an ostrich, gu., in mouth a horse-shoe, or. *Pl.* 16, *cr.* 2.

ESCUDAMORE, Eng., on a chapeau, a peacock in pride, all ppr. *Pl.* 50, *cr.* 15.
ESDAILE, Lond., a demi-lion, rampant, in paws a mullet of (six) points, or. *Pl.* 89, *cr.* 10.
ESDAILE, Eng., a flag, issuant, sa. *Pl.* 52, *cr.* 14.
ESHARTON, Eng., a demi-lion, per cheveron, or and vert. *Pl.* 67, *cr.* 10.
ESINGOLD, Eng., a chevalier, on horseback, brandishing a sword, ppr. *Pl.* 118, *cr.* 14.
ESMOND, Iri., a horned owl, sa. *Pl.* 1, *cr.* 8.
ESMONDE, Bart., Iri., out of a mural coronet, gu., a head, in profile, helmeted, all ppr. *Pl.* 33, *cr.* 14, (coronet, *same plate*.)
ESPEKE, Eng., an ostrich's head, between wings, ar., in mouth a horse-shoe, az. *Pl.* 28, *cr.* 13, (without charging.)
ESPINASSE, a boar's head, in fess, couped, pierced by a broken spear, in bend. *Pl.* 11, *cr.* 9.
ESPINASSE, issuing from clouds, two hands conjoined, in fess, supporting a heart inflamed, ppr. *Pl.* 52, *cr.* 13.
ESSE, Eng., a cockatrice, or, beaked, gu. *Pl.* 63, *cr.* 15.
ESSE, Devons., a mortar-piece, ppr. *Pl.* 55, *cr.* 14.
ESSEX, Lond., out of a mural coronet, erm., a griffin's head, or. *Pl.* 101, *cr.* 6, (without gorging.)
ESSEX, Earl of, Viscount Malden, and Baron Capel, (Capel-Coningsby:) 1. For *Capel*, a demi-lion, rampant, or, in dexter a cross crosslet, fitched, gu. *Pl.* 65, *cr.* 6. 2. For *Coningsby*, a cony, sejant, ar. *Fide et fortitudine.* *Pl.* 70, *cr.* 1.
ESSEX, in a mural coronet, erm., a demi-eagle, or, wings, vair. *Pl.* 33, *cr.* 5.
ESSEX, an eagle's head, or, gorged with a ducal coronet, per pale, az. and sa. *Pl.* 39, *cr.* 4, (without pheon.)
ESSEX, Berks., an eagle's head, or, in mouth a hawk's leg, erased at thigh, gu. *Pl.* 20, *cr.* 7, (leg, *pl.* 83, *cr.* 7.)
ESSINGTON, Linc., a horse's head, erased, ar. *Pl.* 81, *cr.* 6.
ESSINGTON, Glouc., in hand, ppr., a fusil, or. *Pl.* 41, *cr.* 9.
ESTANTON, Eng., a wyvern, or. *Pl.* 63, *cr.* 13.
ESTATFORD, a dexter hand holding a sword, (by the blade,) in bend, point upward, all ppr. *Pl.* 21, *cr.* 10.
ESTCOURT, Norf.: 1. Out of a mural coronet, a demi-eagle, displayed. *Pl.* 33, *cr.* 5. 2. A stag's head, affrontée. *Pl.* 111, *cr.* 13.
ESTCOURT, Eng., out of a mural coronet, az., a demi-eagle, displayed, ppr., beaked, or. *Pl.* 33, *cr.* 5.
ESTDAY, Kent, on a mount, vert, a hind, lodged, ar. *Pl.* 22, *cr.* 5, (hind, *pl.* 1, *cr.* 14.)
ESTE, Eng., a garb, or, banded, gu. *Pl.* 48, *cr.* 10.
ESTELEY, and ESTLEY, on a ducal coronet, three daggers, one in pale, and two in saltier, or. *Pl.* 86, *cr.* 12, (daggers, *pl.* 24, *cr.* 2.)
ESTERCOMBE, Somers., out of a ducal coronet, or, a griffin's head, az., beaked, gold. *Pl.* 54, *cr.* 14.
ESTERLEY, Linc., a (mastiff,) passant, ar. *Pl.* 120, *cr.* 8.
ESTLAND, and ESTLIN, an arm, in armour, embowed, ppr., in hand a fleur-de-lis, or. *Pl.* 24, *cr.* 14.
ESTMERTON, Eng., two dexter hands, in fess, couped and conjoined, ppr., supporting a cross crosslet, fitched, sa. *Pl.* 52, *cr.* 15.

ESTOFT, Linc., in lion's gamb, quarterly, gu. and ar., a crescent, or. *Pl.* 91, *cr.* 1.
ESTON, Devons., on a mount, vert, five ears of wheat, erect, or, stalked and leaved, ppr. *Pl.* 4, *cr.* 5.
ESTOTE, Eng., a fleur-de-lis, gu. *Pl.* 68, *cr.* 12.
ESTOWER, and ESTEWER, a goat, ar. *Pl.* 66, *cr.* 1.
ESTRANGE, Glouc., a chevalier on horseback, at full speed, holding a broken lance, ppr. *Pl.* 43, *cr.* 2.
ESTWOOD, Eng., a lion's head, erased and crowned, or. *Pl.* 123, *cr.* 13.
ETELUM, a talbot's head, ducally crowned, or. *Pl.* 25, *cr.* 10.
ETHELSTAN, Lanc., an eagle, displayed, purp. *Pl.* 48, *cr.* 11.
ETHELSTAN, and ETHELSTON, Eng., a broken spear. *Pl.* 3, *cr.* 6.
ETHELSTON, Chesh., a ram's head, couped, sa., charged with three cross crosslets, in cheveron, or. *Dat et sumit Deus.* *Pl.* 34, *cr.* 12, (crosslets, *pl.* 141.)
ETHERIDGE, Eng., a crescent, (charged) with an etoile of six points. *Pl.* 111, *cr.* 15.
ETHERINGTON, Yorks., a tower, (decayed on sinister side,) on a battlement thereof a leopard's face, ppr. *Pl.* 105, *cr.* 10.
ETON, Eng., a crow's head, erased, ppr. *Pl.* 27, *cr.* 13.
ETTON, Chesh., a hand holding a dagger, in pale, thrust through a boar's head, couped, ppr. *Pl.* 71, *cr.* 9.
ETTRICK, ANTHONY E., Esq., High Barnes, Durham, a demi-lion, rampant, gu., holding in dexter paw a marshal's baton, sa., tipped at each end, or. *Pl.* 126 c, *cr.* 10.
ETTRICK, Durh., *same crest.*
ETTY, Eng., a lion, rampant, gardant. *Pl.* 92, *cr.* 7.
ETY, Yorks., a husbandman, (mowing) with a scythe, ppr. *Pl.* 122, *cr.* 1, (scythe, *pl.* 106, *cr.* 2.)
EUEN, Sco., a demi-lion, in dexter a mullet, gu. *Audaciter.* *Pl.* 89, *cr.* 10.
EURE, Eng., a stag's head, erased, az., attired, ar., charged with the sun, or. *Pl.* 62, *cr.* 14.
EURE, Eng., a horse's head, ar. *Artis vel Martis.* *Pl.* 81, *cr.* 6.
EURE, a talbot, passant, or. *Pl.* 120, *cr.* 8.
EUREUX, Eng., five arrows, one in pale, four in saltier, gu., headed, or, feathered, ar., bound by a belt, of the first, buckled, gold. *Pl.* 54, *cr.* 15.
EUSTACE, Eng., in hand a close helmet, ppr. *Pl.* 37, *cr.* 15.
EUSTACE, Iri., a stag, statant, ppr. *Pl.* 88, *cr.* 9, (without charge.)
EUSTON, Eng., a boar, passant, sa., armed, bristled, and hoofed, ar. *Pl.* 48, *cr.* 14.
EVANS, FREKE, Baron Carberry. See CARBERRY.
EVANS, Lond. and Salop, an arm, embowed, vested, gu., cuffed, or, in hand a gilliflower, ppr. *Pl.* 39, *cr.* 1, (flower, *pl.* 22, *cr.* 9.)
EVANS, Heref., out of an earl's coronet, an arm, in armour, embowed, in hand a sword, all ppr., point embrued, gu. *Pl.* 2, *cr.* 8, (coronet, *pl.* 80, *cr.* 11.)
EVANS, Norf., a dexter arm, erect, vested, barry-wavy of six, az. and or, cuffed, ar., in hand a parchment-roll, ppr. *Pl.* 32, *cr.* 6.

EVANS, Iri. and Wel., a demi-lion, rampant, regardant, or, between paws a boar's head, couped, sa. *Libertas. Pl.* 33, *cr.* 2, (without spear.)
EVANS, Eng. and Wel., a lion, passant, sa. *Pl.* 48, *cr.* 8.
EVANS, Eng. and Wel., on a ducal coronet, or, a boar's head, in fess, erased, sa. *Pl.* 102, *cr.* 14, (head, *pl.* 16, *cr.* 11.)
EVANS, Bucks., an eagle's head, between wings, sa., in beak a rose, gu., stalked and leaved, ppr. *Pl.* 81, *cr.* 10, (rose, *pl.* 118, *cr.* 9.)
EVANS, Heref., a cubit arm, erect, in hand a torch inflamed, erect, all ppr. *Pl.* 118, *cr.* 9, (torch, *pl.* 70, *cr.* 14.)
EVANS, Eng., a lamb, passant, bearing a banner. *Pl.* 48, *cr.* 13.
EVANS, Derbs., a boar's head, (in a charger,) erased, ar. *Pl.* 16, *cr.* 11.
EVANS-D'ARCY, THOMAS, Esq., of Knockaderry House, co. Limerick, a spear, broken in three pieces, or, two in saltier, one in pale, headed, ppr., banded at middle by a ribbon. *Libertas. Pl.* 33, *cr.* 3.
EVATT, Eng., in lion's paw, erased, a torteau, gu. *Pl.* 97, *cr.* 10.
EVE, Eng., on a chapeau, a fox, sejant, ppr. *Pl.* 57, *cr.* 14.
EVELEIGH, Devons., between two laurel-branches, in orle, a stag, lodged, gardant, ppr. *Pl.* 24, *cr.* 4.
EVELEIGH, Devons., a demi-griffin, per pale, or and sa. *Pl.* 18, *cr.* 6.
EVELICK, Sco., a sword, in pale, on point a pair of scales, all ppr. *Recta vel ardua. Pl.* 44, *cr.* 10.
EVELYN, Bart., Surr., a griffin, passant, or, beak and fore-legs, az., ducally gorged, of the last. *Pl.* 61, *cr.* 14.
EVELYN, a griffin, (passant,) or. *Pl.* 66, *cr.* 13.
EVELYN, WILLIAM-JOHN, of Wotton, Surr., and St Clere, Kent, a griffin, passant, or, ducally gorged. *Durate. Pl.* 61, *cr.* 14.
EVENS, Eng., a demi-lion, rampant, sa. *Pl.* 67, *cr.* 10.
EVERARD, Bart., Much-Waltham and Broomfield Green, Ess., a man's head, couped at shoulders, ppr., on head a long cap, barry-wavy of eight, or and sa., turned up, gold. *Pl.* 38, *cr.* 13.
EVERARD, Leic., Staffs., Ess., Northamp., and Norf., same crest.
EVERARD, Gillingham, Norf., a man's head, in profile, ppr., with cap, or, fretty, sa. *Pl.* 51, *cr.* 4.
EVERARD, Hawkdown, Suff., three annulets, conjoined, or. *Pl.* 119, *cr.* 10.
EVERARD, EDWARD, Esq., of Middleton, Norf., a man's head, couped at shoulders, with cap, bendy wavy of six, ar. and sa. *Say and do. Pl.* 38, *cr.* 13.
EVERARD, a moor's head, couped at shoulders, in profile, ppr., wreathed, ar. and az. *Pl.* 36, *cr.* 3.
EVEREST, Eng., on point of a sword a mullet, ppr. *Pl.* 55, *cr.* 15.
EVERET, or EVERETT, Eng., an arm, in armour, couped and embowed, elbow on a chapeau, in hand a spear. *Pl.* 57, *cr.* 3.
EVERET, or EVERETT, a griffin's head, erased, sa., (collared,) gemelle of three pieces, the middle, or, the others, ar. *Pl.* 48, *cr.* 6.

EVERINGHAM, Yorks. and Linc., a demi-lion, rampant, ar., in dexter a rose-branch, flowered, or, stalked and leaved, vert. *Pl.* 39, *cr.* 14.
EVERIT, or EVERITT, Eng., a demi-lady, in dexter a pair of scales, equally poised, ppr. *Pl.* 57, *cr.* 1.
EVERS, Eng., a dexter arm, ppr., vested, quarterly, or and sa., cuff, indented, gu., holding a roll of paper, ar. *Pl.* 32, *cr.* 6.
EVERSFIELD, Suss., out of a ducal coronet, a camel's head, or. *Pl.* 55, *cr.* 5, (without collar or crown.)
EVERSHEAD, Surr., a mullet of six points, or, between wings, ar. *Pl.* 1, *cr.* 15.
EVERTON, Suff., a buck's head, erased, or, pellettée and attired, sa. *Pl.* 66, *cr.* 9.
EVERY, Bart., Derbs., a demi-unicorn, guttée-de-sang and crined, or. *Suum cuique. Pl.* 26, *cr.* 14.
EVERY, Staffs., Devons., and Dors., a demi-unicorn, gu., crined, attired, and hoofed, or. *Pl.* 26, *cr.* 14.
EVERY, a unicorn's head, ppr. *Pl.* 20, *cr.* 1.
EVES, Eng., three legs in armour, united at thigh, flexed at knee, and spurred, ppr. *Pl.* 71, *cr.* 14.
EVETT, Worc., a demi-dragon, or, holding a cross formée, gu. *Pl.* 82, *cr.* 10, (cross, *pl.* 141.)
EVINGTON, and EVINTON, on a serpent, in orle, a boar's head, erased and erect. *Pl.* 12, *cr.* 6.
EVINGTON, Middx. and Hants, out of a mural coronet, az., a nag's head, in armour, ppr., on head three feathers, one ar., between two, of the first. *Pl.* 55, *cr.* 7, (coronet, *pl.* 128, *fig.* 18.)
EVINGTON, Linc., a horse's head, erased, ar., (collared, az.) *Pl.* 92, *cr.* 1.
EVRE, Eng., a parrot, feeding on a bunch of cherries. *Pl.* 49, *cr.* 3.
EVREUX, Eng., out of a ducal coronet, a talbot's head, sa. *Pl.* 99, *cr.* 7.
EWAN, Sco., a demi-lion, rampant. *Audaciter. Pl.* 67, *cr.* 10.
EWAR, round a broken arrow, in pale, pheoned, or, a snake entwined, ppr. *Pl.* 112, *cr.* 2.
EWARBY, out of a ducal coronet, or, a female's bust, face, ppr., breasts, gu., hair, gold. *Pl.* 74, *cr.* 5.
EWART, Eng., in hand, erect, gauntleted, a cross crosslet, fitched, in pale. *Pl.* 51, *cr.* 1.
EWART, in hand a dagger, ppr. *A best timor. Pl.* 21, *cr.* 10.
EWART, in hand a cutlass, ppr. *Pl.* 29, *cr.* 8.
EWART, a heart, ppr., transfixed by a sword, ar., hilt and pommel, or. *Pl.* 21, *cr.* 15.
EWBANK, Durh., out of a ducal coronet, gu., a dragon's head, or. *Pl.* 59, *cr.* 14.
EWBANK, Eng., out of a ducal coronet, a dexter and sinister hand, each holding an ostrich-feather. *Pl.* 45, *cr.* 2.
EWEN, on a mount, vert, a stork, statant, ppr. *Pl.* 122, *cr.* 7, (without escallop.)
EWEN, a curlew, ppr. *Pl.* 52, *cr.* 12.
EWENS, Dors. and Somers., (on a mount, vert,) a curlew, rising, ppr. *Pl.* 52, *cr.* 12.
EWER, a pheon, ar., mounted on a broken dart, gu., entwined by a serpent, ppr. *Pl.* 30, *cr.* 3.
EWERBY, Eng., an eagle, displayed, per fess, vert and ar. *Pl.* 48, *cr.* 11.
EWERS, a staff, raguly, or. *Pl.* 78, *cr.* 15, (without coronet.)

Ewes, Eng., a quatrefoil, vert. *Pl.* 65, *cr.* 7.
Ewing, Eng., an arm, in armour, couped, and tied at shoulder, embowed, resting elbow on a chapeau, gu., in hand a sceptre. *Pl.* 57, *cr.* 3, (sceptre, *pl.* 104, *cr.* 13.)
Ewing, Sco., a demi-lion, gardant. *Pl.* 35, *cr.* 4.
Ewing, Iri., the moon in her complement, ppr. *Pl.* 43, *cr.* 8.
Ewing, Sco., a demi-lion, gu., in dexter a mullet, az. *Audaciter.* *Pl.* 89, *cr.* 10.
Exall, an eagle's head, erased, sa., charged on neck with three etoiles, in fess, ppr. *Pl.* 20, *cr.* 7, (etoiles, *pl.* 141.)
Exeter, Marquess and Earl of, and Baron Burghley, (Brownlow-Cecil,) on a chapeau, gu., turned up, erm., a garb, or, supported by two lions, dexter, ar., sinister, az. *Cor unum, via una.* *Pl.* 36, *cr.* 8.
Exeter, Eng., out of a ducal coronet, two arms, in saltier, ppr., in each hand a scimitar, in pale. *Pl.* 57, *cr.* 8.
Exmew, a dove, ar., in mouth a text, R, or, by a sprig of laurel, ppr. *Pl.* 66, *cr.* 12, (laurel, *pl.* 123, *cr.* 5.)
Exmouth, Viscount and Baron, (Pellew,) upon waves of the sea, the wreck of the Dutton, East Indiaman, upon a rocky shore, off Plymouth garrison, all ppr. *Deo adjuvante—* and—*Algiers*. *Pl.* 21, *cr.* 11.
Exton, Eng., the sail of a ship, ppr. *Pl.* 22, *cr.* 12.
Eychebald, Yorks., a boar's head, in bend, couped, sa. *Pl.* 2, *cr.* 7.
Eye, on a chapeau, turned up, erm., two wings. *Pl.* 80, *cr.* 15.
Eyer, Eng., a talbot's head, erased, ar., spotted, gu., collared, az. *Pl.* 2, *cr.* 15.
Eyland, Linc., on a chapeau, az., turned up, or, a martlet, gu. *Pl.* 89, *cr.* 7.
Eynes, Salop, Oxon., and Dors., an eagle, displayed, on a tortoise, ppr. *Pl.* 102, *cr.* 8.
Eynes, Salop, Oxon., and Dors., an eagle displayed, az., semée of etoiles, or. *Pl.* 48, *cr.* 11, (etoiles, *pl.* 141.)
Eynford, and Eynsworth, Eng., in hand a wheat-ear, or. *Pl.* 71, *cr.* 15.
Eyre, Earl of Newburgh. *See* Newburgh.
Eyre, Bucks., a phœnix, close, ppr. *Pl.* 112, *cr.* 7.

Eyre, Eng., an armed leg, couped at thigh, quarterly, ar. and sa., counterchanged. spur, or. *Pl.* 81, *cr.* 5.
Eyre, Lord Eyre, Iri., same crest. *Pro rege sæpe, pro patriâ semper.*
Eyre, Eng., an armed leg, couped at thigh, quarterly, vair and sa. *Pl.* 81, *cr.* 5.
Eyre, Eng., an armed leg, couped at thigh, per pale, ar. and sa., spur, or. *Pl.* 81, *cr.* 5.
Eyre, Eng., an armed leg, couped at thigh, per pale, ar. and gu., spurred, or. *Pl.* 81, *cr.* 5.
Eyre, an antelope, sejant, or, ducally gorged and attired, ar. *Pl.* 115, *cr.* 3.
Eyre, an ibex, maned, armed, and ducally gorged, ar. *Pl.* 115, *cr.* 13, (gorging, *same plate.*)
Eyre, Eng., a lion, passant, gardant, tail extended, gu. *Pl.* 120, *cr.* 5.
Eyre, Eng., a dexter gauntlet, ppr. *Pl.* 15, *cr.* 15.
Eyre, Wilts., on a chapeau, a booted leg. *Virtus sola invicta.* *Pl.* 95, *cr.* 13, (chapeau, *pl.* 127, *cr.* 13.)
Eyres, Eng., in lion's gamb, sa., a sceptre, in pale, or. *Pl.* 16, *cr.* 1.
Eyres, Eng., a griffin's head, erased, ducally gorged and lined, in beak a laurel-branch. *Pl.* 42, *cr.* 9.
Eyston, Eng., an etoile of eight points. *Pl.* 83, *cr.* 3, (without coronet.)
Eyston, two arms, embowed, (vested,) holding up an escallop. *Pl.* 6, *cr.* 8, (escallop, *pl.* 117, *cr.* 4.)
Eyston, Charles, Esq., of East Hendred, Berks., a lion, sejant, or. *Pl.* 126, *cr.* 15.
Eyston, Berks., a lion, sejant, or. *Pl.* 126, *cr.* 15.
Eyton, Leic. and Northamp., a demi-dragon, wings addorsed, ppr., (collared,) winged and lined, ar., in dexter a sword, of the last, hilt and pommel, or, the point embrued, gu. *Pl.* 82, *cr.* 10, (sword, *pl.* 105, *cr.* 1.)
Eyton, a lion's head, ar., devouring a tun, or. *Pl.* 126, *cr.* 1, (tun, *pl.* 124, *cr.* 9.)
Eyton, a reindeer's head, or, in mouth an acorn-slip, vert, fructed, gold. *Pl.* 2, *cr.* 13, (acorn-slip, *pl.* 81, *cr.* 7.)
Eyvill, D', Eng., an arm, in armour, embowed, in hand a spiked club, all ppr. *Pl.* 45, *cr.* 10.

F

Faal, Sco., a pair of scales. *Honestas.* *Pl.* 12, *cr.* 11.
Fabian, in lion's gamb, erased, a sceptre, in pale, or. *Pl.* 16, *cr.* 1.
Fabian, on a chapeau, a fleur-de-lis, gu., from between the flowers, two split flags, ar., each charged with a spot, erm. *Pl.* 21, *cr.* 13, (flags, *pl.* 53, *cr.* 14.)
Faconbridge, Eng., a yew-tree, vert. *Pl.* 49, *cr.* 13.
Fagan, Iri., out of a ducal coronet, a swan's head and neck, between wings, ppr. *Pl.* 83, *cr.* 1.
Fagan, or Fargon, Iri., a griffin, segreant, supporting an olive-branch. *Pl.* 67, *cr.* 13, (branch, *pl.* 98, *cr.* 8.)

Fagan, Iri., a griffin, segreant, supporting a branch of laurel, ppr. *Pl.* 67, *cr.* 13, (branch, *pl.* 123, *cr.* 5.)
Fage, Eng., a cross crosslet, surmounted by a sword, in bend sinister, point downwards. *Pl.* 89, *cr.* 14.
Fagg, Bart., Suss., an ostrich, wings expanded, ar., beaked, legged, and ducally gorged, or, in beak a horse-shoe, az. *Pl.* 16, *cr.* 2.
Fahy, Iri., a dexter arm, in hand a hunting spear, point downward. *Pl.* 39, *cr.* 15.
Fair, Eng., a garb, or, environed by two snakes, vert. *Pl.* 36, *cr.* 14.
Fairbairn, Eng., a griffin, passant, sa. *Pl.* 61, *cr.* 14, (without gorging.)

FAIRBAIRN, Sco., the sun in splendour, or. *Semper eadem.* *Pl.* 68, *cr.* 14.
FAIRBORNE, Notts., an arm, (in armour,) couped, fesswise, in hand a sword, erect, enfiled with a Turk's head, affrontée, all ppr. *Tutus si fortis.* *Pl.* 102, *cr.* 11.
FAIRBROTHER, Eng., a cockatrice, displayed, ppr. *Pl.* 102, *cr.* 15.
FAIRCLOUGH, Lond., Herts., Linc., and Lanc., a demi-lion, rampant, sa., (between) paws a fleur-de-lis, az. *Pl.* 91, *cr.* 13.
FAIREBORNE, in hand, vambraced, a sword, in pale, on point a savage's head, affrontée, ppr. *Pl.* 36, *cr.* 10.
FAIRFAX, Yorks., on a chapeau, a lion, passant, gardant, sa. *Je le feray durant ma vie.* *Pl.* 120, *cr.* 5, (lion, *same plate, cr.* 5.)
FAIRFAX, Bart., of The Holmes, Roxburgh, a lion, passant, ppr. *Fari fac.* *Pl.* 48, *cr.* 8.
FAIRFAX, Baron, (Fairfax,) Sco., a lion, passant, gardant, sa. *Fari fac.* *Pl.* 120, *cr.* 5.
FAIRFAX, THOMAS, ESQ., Yorks., same crest and motto.
FAIRFAX, Yorks., a lion, rampant, sa. *Pl.* 67, *cr.* 5.
FAIRFAX, a lion, (statant,) gardant, sa. *Pl.* 120, *cr.* 5.
FAIRFAX, Yorks., a lion, passant, sa. *Pl.* 48, *cr.* 8.
FAIRFAX, Yorks. and Norf., a lion's head, erased, sa., gorged with three bars-gemelle, and ducally crowned, or. *Pl.* 90, *cr.* 4.
FAIRFIELD, Eng., a demi-savage, affrontée, handcuffed, ppr. *Pl.* 98, *cr.* 10.
FAIRFORD, on a chapeau, a talbot, sejant, ppr. *Pl.* 102, *cr.* 9.
FAIRFORD, out of a mural coronet, a spear, surmounted by two laurel-branches, in saltier, all ppr. *Pl.* 57, *cr.* 11.
FAIRFOWL, Sco., a parrot. *Loquendo placet.* *Pl.* 25, *cr.* 2.
FAIRGRAY, Yorks., an anchor, ppr. *Pl.* 42, *cr.* 12.
FAIRHOLM, Sco., a dove, with an olive-branch, ppr. *Spero meliora.* *Pl.* 48, *cr.* 15.
FAIRHOLM, Sco., a spur, winged, or, leathered, gu. *Nunquam non paratus.* *Pl.* 59, *cr.* 1.
FAIRHOLME, Sco., a dove, with an olive-branch, ppr. *Fide et firme.* *Pl.* 48, *cr.* 15.
FAIRLIE, or FAIRLY, Sco., a lion's head, couped, or. *Paratus sum.* *Pl.* 126, *cr.* 1.
FAIRLIE, or FAIRLY, Sco., a unicorn's head, couped, ar. *I am ready.* *Pl.* 20, *cr.* 1.
FAIRN, between two laurel-branches, in orle, an open book, all ppr. *Pl.* 4, *cr.* 3.
FAIRNIE, Sco., a greyhound, current, ppr. *Quiescens et vigilans.* *Pl.* 28, *cr.* 7, (without charge.)
FAIRWEATHER, the sun in splendour, or. *Volvitur et ridet.* *Pl.* 68, *cr.* 14.
FAITH, on stump of tree, a crane, perched, ppr. *Pl.* 23, *cr.* 5.
FAITHFULL, a key, in pale, wards upward, surmounted by a crosier and a sword, in saltier. *Pl.* 4, *cr.* 8.
FAITHFULL, a talbot, (statant,) ppr. *Pl.* 120, *cr.* 8.
FAKENHAM, and FECKENHAM, a square padlock, az. *Pl.* 18, *cr.* 7.
FALCH, three quatrefoils on one branch, stalked and leaved, ppr. *Pl.* 72, *cr.* 12.

FALCON, and FAWCON, Eng., four arrows, points downward, and a bow, in saltier, ppr. *Pl.* 12, *cr.* 12.
FALCONER, Sco., a falcon, rising ppr. *Fortiter sed apte.* *Pl.* 105, *cr.* 4.
FALCONER, Lond., same crest. *Vi et industriâ.*
FALCONER, RANDLE-WILLBRAHAM, Esq., M.D., Wel., a falcon, perched, hooded, and belled, ppr. *Vive ut vivas.* *Pl.* 38, *cr.* 12.
FALCONER, Earl of Kintore. *See* KINTORE.
FALCONER, Sco., between two branches of laurel, a falcon, perched, ppr. *Pl.* 67, *cr.* 3, (laurel, *pl.* 79, *cr.* 14.)
FALCONER, Sco., a falcon, ppr., hooded, gu. *Paratus ad œthera.* *Pl.* 38, *cr.* 12.
FALCONER, Sco., a falcon, rising, ppr. *Pl.* 105, *cr.* 4.
FALCONER, Lond., a trefoil, slipped, or. *Pl.* 82, *cr.* 1.
FALCONER, Sco., an angel, praying, or, within an orle of laurel, ppr. *Vive ut vivas.* *Pl.* 94, *cr.* 11.
FALDO, Beds., (three) arrows, gu., feathered, ar., two in saltier, one in pale, enfiled with a ducal coronet, or. *Pl.* 37, *cr.* 5.
FALKINER, Bart., Iri., a falcon's lure, ppr., between wings, az. *Fortunâ favente.* *Pl.* 4, *cr.* 4.
FALKINER, Iri., out of a ducal coronet, a hand, vested, gu., cuffed, or, holding the sun, ppr. *Pl.* 89, *cr.* 11.
FALKLAND, Viscount, Sco.; Baron Hundsdon, U.K., (Cary,) a swan, ppr. *In utroque fidelis.* *Pl.* 122, *cr.* 13.
FALKNER, Eng., on stump of tree, an escutcheon, pendent, ppr. *Pl.* 23, *cr.* 6.
FALKNOR, Eng., a garb, banded, or. *Pl.* 48, *cr.* 10.
FALL, Sco., a cornucopia, ppr. *Honestas.* *Pl.* 91, *cr.* 4.
FALL, a talbot, passant. *Pl.* 120, *cr.* 8.
FALLESBY, a demi-antelope, ar. *Pl.* 34, *cr.* 8, (without collar.)
FALLESLEY, a dexter arm, from shoulder, extended, ppr., in hand an anchor, az., cabled, sa. *Pl.* 27, *cr.* 6, (without sea.)
FALLON, Eng., in hand a mill-rind. *Pl.* 34, *cr.* 3.
FALLOWFIELD, Cumb., on a chapeau, a lion, gardant, collared and ducally crowned. *Pl.* 105, *cr.* 5.
FALMOUTH, Earl of. *See* BOSCOWEN.
FALSTOFFE, Eng., an oak-tree, vert. *Pl.* 16, *cr.* 8.
FALSTOFFE, Norf. and Suff., a hawk, sa., wings expanded, in mouth an oak-branch, vert, fructed, ar. *Pl.* 105, *or* 4, (branch, *pl.* 32, *cr.* 13.)
FANACOURT, a chevalier, in armour, (wielding a sword, ppr.) *Pl.* 60, *cr.* 2.
FANCOURT, out of a ducal coronet, or, a wyvern, erect, between feet a staff, raguly. *Pl.* 63, *cr.* 13, (coronet and staff, *pl.* 78, *cr.* 15.)
FANCOURT, Eng., two staffs, raguly, banded with (olive,) ppr. *Pl.* 103, *cr.* 12.
FANE, Linc., in gauntlet, or, a sword, ppr., hilt and pommel, gold. *Pl.* 125, *cr.* 5.
FANE, Linc., in gauntlet, or, a broken sword, ar., hilt and pommel, gold. *Pl.* 23, *cr.* 9, (sword, *pl.* 22, *cr.* 6.)
FANE, Earl of Westmoreland. *See* WESTMORELAND.

FANE, Iri., in dexter hand a laurel-branch, ppr. Pl. 43, cr. 6.
FANNELL, a tiger, sejant, sa., ducally gorged, or. Pl. 26, cr. 9, (gorging, pl. 128, fig. 3.)
FANNER, out of a ducal coronet, a buck's head, or. Pl. 29, cr. 7.
FANNING, Eng., in dexter hand, ppr., vested, sa., a mill-rind, az. Pl. 34, cr. 3.
FANSHAW, Derbs., a dragon's head, erased, or, (charged with two cheverons, ermines.) Pl. 107, cr. 10.
FANSHAW, Iri., a greyhound, sejant, gu. Pl. 66, cr. 15.
FANSHAW, Derbs., Ess., and Herts., a dragon's head, (erased,) vert, flames issuant from mouth, ppr. Pl. 37, cr. 9.
FANSHAWE, Eng., on a ducal coronet, az., a wyvern, sa. Pl. 104, cr. 11.
FANSHAWE, a cockatrice's head, ppr. Pl. 76, cr. 9.
FAQUIER, a hand, issuant, pruning a vine, ppr. Pl. 83, cr. 4.
FARBRIDGE, Iri., a parrot, gu. Pl. 25, cr. 2.
FARBY, Kent, a cinquefoil, or. Pl. 91, cr. 12.
FARDELL, Lond. and Linc., a mount, vert, therefrom issuant a demi-lion, or, holding a book, expanded, ppr., charged on shoulder with a rose, gu. Non nobis solum. Pl. 72, cr. 13.
FARELL, Heref. and Warw., a boar's head, couped, sa., collared, ar. Pl. 2, cr. 7.
FAREWELL, Somers., a (tiger,) sa., ducally gorged, armed, and tufted, or. Pl. 120, cr. 9.
FAREY, Eng., a plough, ppr. Pl. 28, cr. 15.
FARINGHAM, and FARNEHAM, out of an earl's coronet, or, a moor's head, from shoulders, ppr. Pl. 80, cr. 11.
FARINGTON, Lanc., a wyvern, statant, ar., (sans wings, tail nowed, ducally gorged, and chain reflexed over back, or.) Pl. 63, cr. 13.
FARINGTON, Lond., a dragon, passant, ppr. Pl. 90, cr. 10.
FARINGTON, Eng., on a chapeau, gu., turned up, or, a fox, sejant, ppr. Pl. 57, cr. 14.
FARLEY, Eng., an antelope's head, erased, pierced through neck by a spear-head, ppr. Pl. 79, cr. 9.
FARLOUGH, Lanc., a demi-lion, rampant, in dexter a fleur-de-lis, sa. Pl. 91, cr. 13.
FARLOW, a dragon's head, ducally gorged and chained. Pl. 36, cr. 7.
FARMER, Bart., Suss., a leopard, passant, gardant, ppr. Pl. 51, cr. 7.
FARMER, Sco., a cross fleury, fitched, between wings, each charged with a crescent. Pl. 71, cr. 2, (crescent, pl. 141.)
FARMER, Leic., out of a ducal coronet, or, a salamander in flames, ppr. Pl. 74, cr. 11.
FARMER, Norf., a cock's head, gu., combed and wattled, or, in beak a rose, of the first, stalked and leaved, vert. Pl. 92, cr. 3, (rose, pl. 117, cr. 10.)
FARMER, WILLIAM-FRANCIS-GAMUL, Esq., of Nonsuch Park, Surr., out of a ducal coronet, or, a cock's head, gu., crested and wattled, gold. Hora e sempre. Pl. 97, cr. 15.
FARMER, Northamp., out of a ducal coronet, or, a cock's head, gu., crested and jelloped, gold. Pl. 97, cr. 15.
FARMER, a tiger's face, affrontée. Pl. 66, cr. 14.

FARMINGHAM, Eng., a sea-lion, rampant, or. Pl. 25, cr. 12.
FARMOUR, a cock's head, erased, gu., combed and wattled, or, in beak a bunch of flowers, ar., leaved, ppr. Pl. 92, cr. 3, (flowers, pl. 23, cr. 2.)
FARNABY, Bart., Kent, a stork, ar. Pl. 33, cr. 9.
FARNABY, Kent, out of a mural coronet, a stork, rising, ppr., charged with two bars-gemelle, ar., in beak a snake, vert. Pl. 59, cr. 11, (coronet, pl. 128, fig. 18.)
FARNABY, Kent, out of a ducal coronet, a stork, rising, ppr., charged with two bars-gemelle, ar., in beak a snake, vert. Pl. 59, cr. 11, (coronet, same plate.)
FARNABY, Kent, out of a mural coronet, a stork, close, ppr. Pl. 33, cr. 9, (coronet, same plate.)
FARNAM, out of a ducal coronet, a griffin's head, in beak a cross crosslet, fitched. Pl. 89, cr. 5, (cross, pl. 141.)
FARNBOROUGH, Baron, (Long,) out of a five-leaved ducal coronet, or, a lion's head, ar., guttée-de-sang. Ingenuas suscipit artes. Pl. 90, cr. 9.
FARNDEN, Suss., on a mural crown, or, a leopard's head, purp. Pl. 46, cr. 11, (without gorging.)
FARNELL, a hawk, wings expanded and inverted, ducally gorged and belled, ppr. Pl. 61, cr. 12, (without mount.)
FARNHAM, Baron, (Maxwell-Barry,) Iri., a buck's head, erased, ppr. Je suis prêt. Pl. 66, cr. 9.
FARNHAM, an eagle, preying on a cony, ppr. Pl. 61, cr. 3.
FARNHAM, Eng., out of ducal coronet, or, a moor's head, from shoulders, ppr. Pl. 80, cr. 11, (coronet, same plate.)
FARNHAM, an eagle, or, preying on a hare, ar. Pl. 61, cr. 3.
FARNHAM, EDWARD-BASIL, Esq., of Quorndon House, Leic., an eagle, or, wings (close,) preying on a rabbit, ar. Pl. 61, cr. 3.
FARQUHAR, Bart., Lond., an eagle, rising, ppr. Mente manuque. Pl. 67, cr. 4.
FARQUHAR-TOWNSHEND, Bart., of Mauritius, same crest and motto.
FARQUHAR, Sco., a lion, rampant. Sto, cado, fide et armis. Pl. 67, cr. 5.
FARQUHAR, and FERQUHAR, Sco., issuing out of a cloud, ppr., a star, ar. Vertitur in diem., Pl. 16, cr. 13.
FARQUHAR, Sco., a dexter hand, apaumée, ppr. Fide et armis. Pl. 32, cr. 14.
FARQUHAR, Sco., a dexter hand, couped, ppr. Sto, cado, fide et armis. Pl. 32, cr. 14.
FARQUHAR-GRAY, Sco., a sinister hand, apaumée, gu. Sto, cado, fide et armis. Pl. 74, cr. 8.
FARQUHARSON, JAMES, Esq., of Invercauld, a demi-lion, gu., in dexter a sword, ppr., pommelled, or. Fide et fortitudine. Pl. 41, cr. 13.
FARQUHARSON, ROBERT-FRANCIS-OGILVIE, Esq., of Haughton, the sun rising from behind a cloud, ppr. Illumino. Pl. 67, cr. 9.
FARQUHARSON, and FARQUHERSON, Eng., a portcullis, gu. Pl. 51, cr. 12.
FARQUHARSON, Sco., a demi-lion, rampant, gu. In memoriam majorum. Pl. 67, cr. 10.

FARQUHARSON, Dors., a demi-lion, rampant, in dexter paw a dagger, erect, ppr., hilt and pommel, or. *Pl.* 41, *cr.* 13.

FARQUHARSON, Eng., the sun in splendour, ppr. *Illumino. Pl.* 68, *cr.* 14.

FARQUHARSON, Sco., out of a cloud, the sun, rising, ppr. *Non semper sub umbrâ. Pl.* 67, *cr.* 9.

FARR, Eng., on the point of a sword, in pale, a maunch, gu. *Pl.* 78, *cr.* 1.

FARRAND, Norf., in front of a garb, or, a pheasant, ppr. *Nullâ pallescere culpâ. Pl.* 82, *cr.* 12, (garb, *pl.* 48, *cr.* 10.)

FARRAND, an arm, in armour, embowed, in hand a battle-axe. *Pl.* 121, *cr.* 14.

FARRANT, Lond. and Kent, a cubit arm, erect, vested, az., cuffed, ar., charged with a cross patonce, vairé, of the last, and gu., the hand grasping an anchor, cabled, ppr. *Pl.* 53, *cr.* 13, (cross, *pl.* 141.)

FARRANT, Kent, out of a ducal coronet, or, a pelican's head, ar., vulning, gu., between wings of the last. *Pl.* 41, *cr.* 4, (coronet, *pl.* 17, *cr.* 9.)

FARRANT, Surr. and Yorks., a cubit-arm, erect, vested, vair, cuffed, ar., in hand, ppr., a battle-axe, of the second. *Pl.* 73, *cr.* 7, (arm, *pl.* 39, *cr.* 1.)

FARRAR, Yorks., a horse-shoe, sa., between wings, ar. *Pl.* 17, *cr.* 3.

FARRAR, Eng., a (thistle) and cross crosslet, fitched, in saltier, ppr. *Pl.* 102, *cr.* 3.

FARREL, and FARRELL, Iri., a bear, transfixed by a spear-head, in bend sinister. *Pl.* 82, *cr.* 14.

FARREL, and FARRELL, Iri., a bear, passant, sa., pierced through shoulder by a hunting-spear, ar. *Pl.* 82, *cr.* 14.

FARRELL, Iri., on a ducal coronet, a greyhound, current, (gorged with a collar, and affixed thereto by a broken chain, a regal crown,) ppr. *Cu re bu. Pl.* 47, *cr.* 2, (coronet, same plate.)

FARRER, and FARROR, Lond., Yorks., and Herts., a horse-shoe, sa., between wings, or. *Pl.* 17, *cr.* 3.

FARRER, Somers., Beds., and Herts., a horse-shoe, ar., between wings, sa. *Pl.* 17, *cr.* 3.

FARRER, and FARROR, Herts., Yorks., and Lond., a horse-shoe, ar., between wings, or. *Pl.* 17, *cr.* 3.

FARRER, JAMES-WILLIAM, Esq., of Ingleborough, Yorks., a horse-shoe, between wings, ppr. *Ferrè va Ferme. Pl.* 17, *cr.* 3.

FARRER, out of a ducal coronet, or, between wings, ar., a crescent, gold. *Pl.* 17, *cr.* 9, (crescent, *pl.* 18, *cr.* 14.)

FARRIER, a horse-shoe. *Pl.* 52, *cr.* 4.

FARRINGTON, Bart., Kent, a dragon, wings elevated, tail nowed, vert, bezantée, (gorged with a mural coronet, ar., and chain reflexed over back, or, charged on body with two caltraps, in fess, gold.) *Le bon temps viendra. Pl.* 90, *cr.* 10.

FARRINGTON, a lamb, passant, ar., bearing a banner, pink, staff, ppr., surmounted by a cross, or. *Pl.* 48, *cr.* 13.

FARRINGTON, Lond., a wyvern, vert. *Pl.* 63, *cr.* 13.

FARRINGTON, Leic., a dragon, passant, (sans wings, ar., murally gorged, gu., chained, or.) *Pl.* 90, *cr.* 10.

FARRINGTON, Lond., a dragon, passant, ppr. *Pl.* 90, *cr.* 10.

FARRINGTON, Lanc., a wyvern, (sans wings, tail extended, vert.) *Pl.* 63, *cr.* 13.

FARRINGTON, Leic., a wyvern, (close,) vert. *Pl.* 63, *cr.* 13.

FARROW, Eng., a lion's paw, holding a thistle, ppr. *Pl.* 109, *cr.* 4.

FARWELL, two oak-branches, in orle, vert, acorned, or. *Pl.* 74, *cr.* 7.

FASANT, a Cornish chough, wings expanded, ppr. *Pl.* 50, *cr.* 5.

FASSETT, Eng., a shark's head, issuant, regardant, swallowing a negro, all ppr. *Pl.* 16, *cr.* 6.

FAUCONBRIDGE, or FAWCONBRIDGE, out of a ducal coronet, or, a plume of (three) ostrich-feathers, banded, ppr. *Pl.* 44, *cr.* 12.

FAUKENNER, Surr., a falcon, ppr., belled, or. *Pl.* 67, *cr.* 3.

FAULDER, on a mountain, a beacon inflamed, all ppr. *Pl.* 89, *cr.* 9.

FAULKNER, Suff., a demi-cockatrice, wings addorsed, ppr. *Pl.* 106, *cr.* 15, (without gorging.)

FAULKNER, Eng., a cross moline, pierced, gu. *Pl.* 91, *cr.* 10.

FAULKNER, a falcon's lure, or, between falcon's wings, ppr. *Pl.* 4, *cr.* 4.

FAULKNER, Middx., a dragon's head and neck, with wings addorsed, couped at shoulders, ppr. *Pl.* 82, *cr.* 10.

FAULKNER, HUGH, Esq., of Castletown, co. Carlow, on a mount, vert, an angel in a praying posture, or, within an orle of laurel, ppr. *Vive ut vivas. Pl.* 94, *cr.* 11.

FAULKS, a boar's head, couped, ppr. *Pl.* 48, *cr.* 2.

FAUNCE, a demi-lion, rampant, sa., langued, gu., ducally gorged, or. *Ne tentes, aut perfice. Pl.* 87, *cr.* 15.

FAUNTAN, FAUNT, and FANT, a naked boy, ppr., in dexter a toy, or. *Pl.* 17, *cr.* 5.

FAUNTLEROY, Cornw., the head of a halberd, issuant, ppr. *Pl.* 16, *cr.* 3.

FAUNTLEROY, Wilts., a fleur-de-lis, or, between wings, az. *Pl.* 21, *cr.* 13, (without chapeau.)

FAUSSET, Kent, a demi-lion, rampant, sa., in paws a Tuscan column, bendwise, gobonée, ar. and gu., the base and capital, or. *Pl.* 29, *cr.* 12, (column, *pl.* 33, *cr.* 1.)

FAUZE, a tower, ppr. *Pl.* 12, *cr.* 5.

FAVELL, Eng., on the point of a sword, in pale, a maunch, all ppr. *Pl.* 78, *cr.* 1.

FAVENC, Lond., on a (bale of Piedmont thrown silk, a falcon, ppr., beaked, membered, and belled, or,) gorged with a collar, and thereupon a chain reflexed over back, gold. *Pl.* 103, *cr.* 5, (without shield.)

FAVILL, Yorks., an esquire's helmet, ppr. *En Dieu et ma foi. Pl.* 109, *cr.* 5.

FAWCET, Eng., a dolphin, naiant, ppr. *Pl.* 48, *cr.* 9.

FAWCETT, Eng., a stag's head. *Pl.* 91, *cr.* 14.

FAWCETT, Iri., a mitre. *Pl.* 12, *cr.* 10.

FAWCONER, and FAWKONER, a tower, sa., masoned, or. *Pl.* 12, *cr.* 5.

FAWETHER, and FAYREWEATHER, a lion's head, erased, gu., (billettée, or.) *Pl.* 81, *cr.* 4.

FAWKES, Yorks., a falcon, ppr. *Pl.* 67, *cr.* 3.

FAWKNE, a hawk's head, erased. *Pl.* 34, *cr.* 11.

FAWKNER, and FAWKENOR, a trefoil, (slipped,) or. *Pl.* 82, *cr.* 1.

FAWLCONER, Hants. and Northamp., a garb, or, banded, gu. *Pl.* 48, *cr.* 10.

M

FAWLDE, Beds., (three) arrows, one in pale, and two in saltier, gu., headed and feathered, ar., issuing through a ducal coronet, or. *Pl.* 37, *cr.* 5.

FAWSET, or FAWSSET, Linc., a stag's head, erased. *Pl.* 66, *cr.* 9.

FAY, Iri., a dexter arm, in gauntlet a dagger, all ppr. *Pl.* 120, *cr.* 11.

FAY, Iri., a cubit arm, vambraced, in gauntlet a dagger, all ppr. *Pl.* 125, *cr.* 5.

FAYT, Eng., a water-bouget, gu. *Pl.* 14, *cr.* 12.

FAZAKERLEY, Lanc., on a mount, vert, a swan, close, ar. *Pl.* 122, *cr.* 13.

FEA, a man, digging, ppr. *Fac et spera.*

FEAD, Eng., the sun, surmounted by a unicorn, rampant. *Pl.* 114, *cr.* 1.

FEAKE, and FEEKE, out of a ducal coronet, or, a demi-ostrich, wings expanded, ar., beaked, gu., in mouth a (horse-shoe,) gold. *Pl.* 29, *cr.* 9.

FEARGUSON, Iri., an arm, in armour, embowed, in hand a broken tilting-spear. *Pl.* 44, *cr.* 9.

FEARNLY, a talbot, passant, ar., (through fern, vert,) collared and lined, or. *Pl.* 65, *cr.* 2.

FEARON, Eng., within an annulet, or, an escutcheon, gu. *Pl.* 77, *cr.* 9.

FEARON, a demi-lion, rampant, ppr., between paws a (shield, gu., surrounded by an annulet, or.) *Pl.* 126, *cr.* 10.

FEARON, Suss., out of a ducal coronet, a falcon's head, ppr. *Pl.* 24, *cr.* 10.

FEAST, Middx., a pheon, point upward, gu. *Pl.* 56, *cr.* 15.

FEATHERSTON, or FEATHERSTONE, Eng., a cross crosslet. *Pl.* 66, *cr.* 8.

FEATHERSTONHAUGH, Durh., a falcon, ppr. *Pl.* 67, *cr.* 3.

FEAULITEAU, Surr., a squirrel, sejant, cracking a nut, all ppr. *Pl.* 16, *cr.* 9.

FECHER, Eng., a spur-rowel, between wings, ppr. *Pl.* 54, *cr.* 5, (wings, *same plate.*)

FEDELOW, an ermine, (statant, ppr., collared and lined, sa.) *Pl.* 9, *cr.* 5.

FEILD, Herts., out of a cloud, an arm, in armour, in fess, in hand, gauntleted, a sphere, all ppr. *Pl.* 98, *cr.* 7.

FEILDEN, Bart., Lond., a nut-hatch, perched on a hazel-branch, ppr., (in mouth a rose, or, slipped, vert.) *Virtutis præmium honor. Pl.* 2, *cr.* 4.

FEILDEN, Derbs. and Lanc., a nut-hatch feeding on a hazel-branch, all ppr. *Pl.* 2, *cr.* 4.

FELBRIDG, a man's heart, imperially crowned, between wings. *Pl.* 52, *cr.* 2.

FELBRIDGE, from a tower, embattled, the sun rising, ppr. *Pl.* 12, *cr.* 5, (sun, *pl.* 67, *cr.* 9.)

FELBRIDGE, Eng., a tower, embattled, thereon a bird, rising. *Pl.* 84, *cr.* 3.

FELD, Sco., an eagle's head, erased, ppr. *Pl.* 20, *cr.* 7.

FELD, and FIELD, Yorks., out of clouds, ppr., a dexter arm, in fess, (vested, gu.,) in hand a sphere, or. *Pl.* 104, *cr.* 4.

FELDING, on a branch, vert, fructed, or, a woodpecker, ppr. *Pl.* 13, *cr.* 4.

FELDINGHAM, or FILLINGHAM, a slip of three teazles, or. *Pl.* 74, *cr.* 9.

FELDON, Leic., a wild man. *Pl.* 14, *cr.* 11.

FELDRIDGE, Worc., a bird, in beak a nutbranch, vert, fructed, ppr. *Pl.* 60, *cr.* 8.

FELFAIR, a gem-ring. *Pl.* 35, *cr.* 3.

FELIX, Eng., a covered cup, gu. *Pl.* 75, *cr.* 13, (without swords.)

FELL, a pelican, wings elevated and addorsed, vulning, ppr. *Pl.* 109, *cr.* 15.

FELL, Northumb., a Catherine wheel, ensigned on the top with a cross pattée, fitched, or. *Pl.* 74, *cr.* 14.

FELL, Lond., a hand holding a clarionet, ppr. *Pl.* 98, *cr.* 9.

FELL, out of a ducal coronet, or, a demi-eagle, displayed, (ducally gorged.) *Pl.* 9, *cr.* 6.

FELL, Lond., out of a mural coronet, gu., a dexter arm, embowed, in armour, ppr., garnished, or, in hand, ppr., a tilting-spear, of the last. *Pl.* 115, *cr.* 14, (spear, *pl.* 99, *cr.* 8.)

FELL, a lion, sejant, ppr. *Pl.* 126, *cr.* 15.

FELLGATE, Suff., a griffin, sejant, salient, ar., pierced through breast by a broken spear, or, the point in mouth. *Pl.* 74, *cr.* 10.

FELLOW, Iri., a lion, sejant, gardant, per fess, gu. and or, resting dexter on an escutcheon, paly, of the first and second. *Pl.* 113, *cr.* 8, (escutcheon, *pl.* 42, *cr.* 3.)

FELLOWES, Eng., out of a cloud, a dexter hand, holding a club, all ppr. *Pl.* 87, *cr.* 13.

FELLOWES, Devons., a lion's head, erased, ducally crowned. *Pl.* 90, *cr.* 4, (without charging.)

FELLOWES, a lion's head, erased, or, murally crowned, ar., (charged with a fess, dancettée, erm.) *Pl.* 81, *cr.* 4, (crown, *pl.* 128, *fig.* 18.)

FELLOWES, or FELLOWS, Devons., a scaling-ladder, ppr., hooked at top. *Pl.* 98, *cr.* 15.

FELT, on a mural coronet, or, a stag, passant, ppr. *Pl.* 68, *cr.* 2, (coronet, *pl.* 128, *fig.* 18.)

FELTER, a dexter hand, ppr., holding a cup, or. *Pl.* 35, *cr.* 9.

FELTHAM, Lond., an arm, in armour, in gauntlet a broken spear, the pieces in saltier, all ppr. *Portanti spolia palmâ. Pl.* 44, *cr.* 9, (spear, *pl.* 88, *cr.* 4.)

FELTON, in a ducal coronet, two wings, or and ar. *Pl.* 17, *cr.* 9.

FELTON, a stag, lodged, gu., (ducally gorged and lined, or, attired, vert, on the top of each branch a bezant.) *Pl.* 67, *cr.* 2.

FENCOURT, Eng., a portcullis, sa., chained, az. *Pl.* 51, *cr.* 12.

FENIS, Eng., a bridge of three arches, ppr. *Pl.* 38, *cr.* 4.

FENKELL, Eng., a mullet, sa. *Pl.* 41, *cr.* 1.

FENN, Suff., a dragon's head, erased, az., collared, ar., on the collar three escallops, of the first. *Pl.* 107, *cr.* 10, (escallop, *pl.* 141.)

FENN, Norf., a dragon's head, erased. *Pl.* 107, *cr.* 10, (without collar.)

FENN, Eng., a talbot's head, erased, or, collared, az. *Pl.* 2, *cr.* 15.

FENNEL, or FENNELL, Eng., a hunting-horn, sans strings. *Pl.* 89, *cr.* 3.

FENNER, two hands, couped and conjoined, in fess, gu., supporting a cross crosslet, fitched, az. *Pl.* 52, *cr.* 15.

FENNER, Eng., an eagle, displayed, or, winged, ar. *Pl.* 48, *cr.* 11.

FENNER, an eagle, displayed, ar., membered, or. *Pl.* 48, *cr.* 11.

FENNING, Eng., a lion, passant, regardant, ducally gorged and lined. *Pl.* 121, *cr.* 4.

FENNISON, Sco., a crane's head, ppr. *Vigilat et orat. Pl.* 20, *cr.* 9.

FENNOR, Eng., a mermaid, in dexter a dagger, all ppr. *Pl.* 88, *cr.* 12.

FENOUILLET, Lond., a demi-pegasus, gardant, or, winged, gu., holding a banner, vert, (charged with a bee-hive, or,) staff, gu. *Industriâ et spe. Pl.* 32, *cr.* 1.

FENROTHER, Lond., a boar's head, couped, between two branches, in orle, ppr. *Pl.* 19, *cr.* 8.

FENTIMAN, Eng., a Cornish chough, (rising,) ducally gorged, ppr. *Pl.* 44, *cr.* 11.

FENTON, Yorks. and Notts., a fleur-de-lis, sa., enfiled with a ducal coronet, or. *Pl.* 47, *cr.* 7.

FENTON, on a ducal coronet, a fleur-de-lis. *Pl.* 68, *cr.* 12, (coronet, *pl.* 128, *fig.* 3.)

FENTON, WILLIAM, Esq., of Underbank Hall, Yorks., out of a ducal coronet, a fleur-de-lis, ppr. *Pl.* 47, *cr.* 7.

FENTON, Sco., out of a rock, a palm-tree, growing, ppr. *Per ardua surgo. Pl.* 52, *cr.* 6.

FENWICK, or FENNWICK, a phœnix in flames. *Virtute sibi præmium. Pl.* 44, *cr.* 8.

FENWICK, Durh., a phœnix in flames, ppr., (murally gorged, or.) *Virtute sibi præmium. Pl.* 44, *cr.* 8.

FENWICK, a beaver, passant, ppr., (in mouth a sugar cane, or.) *Pl.* 49, *cr.* 5.

FENWICK, Leic., a phœnix, az., winged, gu., (ducally gorged, or,) in flames, ppr. *Pl.* 44, *cr.* 8.

FENWICK, Northumb., a phœnix in flames, ppr., (murally gorged, or.) *Perit ut vivat. Pl.* 44, *cr.* 8.

FENWICK, Northumb., a phœnix in flames, ppr., (murally gorged, or.) *Toujours loyal. Pl.* 44, *cr.* 8.

FERBY, Kent, on a mural coronet, or, a plate, between wings, sa. *Pl.* 119, *cr.* 14, (plate, *pl.* 141.)

FERGANT, a cross crosslet, quarterly, or and gu. *Pl.* 66, *cr.* 8.

FERGUS, Sco., a dexter arm, in armour, in hand a sword, in pale, az. *Pl.* 125, *cr.* 5.

FERGUSHILL, Sco., out of a ducal coronet, a cock's head, ppr. *Pl.* 97, *cr.* 15.

FERGUSON, Bart., Iri., on a thistle, leaved and flowered, ppr.; a bee, or. *Dulcius ex asperis. Pl.* 68, *cr.* 9.

FERGUSON, of Craig-darroch, Sco., in dexter hand a spear, in bend, ppr. *Vi et arte. Pl.* 99, *cr.* 8.

FERGUSON, Sco., a thistle, and thereon a bee, ppr. *Industria. Pl.* 68, *cr.* 9.

FERGUSON, Cumb., a demi-lion, in dexter a thistle, ppr. *Marte et arte. Pl.* 45, *cr.* 15.

FERGUSON, Heref. and Sco., out of clouds, ppr., a crescent, ar. *Pl.* 74, *cr.* 12.

FERGUSON, Sco., (issuing from a cloud,) a dexter hand grasping a broken spear, in bend, ppr. *Arte et animo. Pl.* 66, *cr.* 4.

FERGUSON, in hand a dagger, erect. *Arte et marte. Pl.* 23, *cr.* 15.

FERGUSON, a hand grasping a broken spear, ppr. *Vi et arte. Pl.* 66, *cr.* 4.

FERGUSON, Lond., an arm, in armour, in hand a broken spear, all ppr. *True to the last. Pl.* 44, *cr.* 9.

FERGUSON, Eng. and Sco., in a crescent, a cock, ppr. *Pl.* 17, *cr.* 1.

FERGUSON, a demi-lion, ppr., between paws a buckle, gu. *Virtutis fortuna comes. Pl.* 47, *cr.* 4, (buckle, *pl.* 73, *cr.* 10.)

FERGUSON, a demi-lion, in dexter a scimitar. *Pl.* 126 A, *cr.* 1.

FERGUSON, on clouds, a crescent, horns upward, *Virtute. Pl.* 74, *cr.* 12.

FERGUSSON, Bart., Sco., on a thistle, leaved and flowered, ppr., a bee, or. *Dulcius ex asperis. Pl.* 68, *cr.* 9.

FERGUSSON, of Isle, co. Dumfries, an increscent, or. *Growing. Pl.* 122, *cr.* 15.

FERMOR, Earl of Pomfret. *See* POMFRET.

FERMOR, Suss., a tiger, passant, ar. *Pl.* 67, *cr.* 15.

FERMOUR, two oak-branches, in saltier, ppr. *Pl.* 19, *cr.* 12.

FERMOY, Baron, on a rock, ppr., a fish-eagle, wings displayed, ar., membered, or, in dexter a roach. *Mon Dieu est ma roche. Pl.* 84, *cr.* 8.

FERNANDEZ, Eng., on a cloud, a celestial sphere, ppr. *Pl.* 110, *cr.* 9.

FERNE, Linc. and Staffs., (out of fern, ppr.,) a talbot's head, ar., eared and collared, gu., garnished and ringed, or. *Pl.* 2, *cr.* 15.

FERNE, on a mount of fern, ppr., a garb, or, banded, gu. *Pl.* 13, *cr.* 2.

FERNE, Derbs., Linc., and Staffs., a garb, or, between wings expanded, per pale, indented, of the first, and gu. *Pl.* 108, *cr.* 13.

FERNELY, or FERNLEY, (through fern, vert,) a talbot, passant, ar., collared and lined, or. *Pl.* 65, *cr.* 2.

FERNEY, Sco., a crescent, ar. *Pl.* 18, *cr.* 14.

FERNIE, Sco., a greyhound, current. *Quiescens et vigilans. Pl.* 28, *cr.* 7, (without charge.)

FERNS, Iri., out of a cup, az., a bouquet of roses, ppr. *Pl.* 102, *cr.* 12.

FERON, Sco., a cross pattée, erm. *Pl.* 15, *cr.* 8.

FERRALL, Iri., a dagger and a (sword,) in saltier, ppr. *Pl.* 24, *cr.* 2.

FERRAND, Yorks., an arm, in armour, embowed, in hand a battle-axe, ppr. *Justus et propositi tenax. Pl.* 121, *cr.* 14.

FERRANT, Eng., a demi-lion, or, semée of torteaux, az. *Pl.* 95, *cr.* 4.

FERRARD, Viscount, and Baron Oriel, Iri.; Baron Oriel, U.K., (Skeffington-Foster,) a mermaid, with comb and mirror, all ppr. *Renascentur. Pl.* 48, *cr.* 5.

FERRARILS, Eng., a léopard, passant, gardant, ducally gorged, ppr. *Pl.* 120, *cr.* 9.

FERRARS, Eng., on a chapeau, an eagle preying on a child, swaddled, ppr. *Pl.* 121, *cr.* 6.

FERRERS, MARMION-EDWARD, Esq., of Baddesley Clinton, Warw., a unicorn, passant, erm. *Splendeo tritus. Pl.* 106, *cr.* 3.

FERRERS, Earl, Viscount Tamworth, (Washington-Shirley,) the bust of a Saracen in profile, ppr., wreathed about temples, or and az. *Honor virtutis præmium. Pl.* 36, *cr.* 3.

FERRERS, Glouc., an ostrich, ppr., in mouth a horse-shoe, or. *Pl.* 16, *cr.* 2.

FERRERS, Herts., two bees, volant, saltierwise, ppr. *Pl.* 13, *cr.* 1.

FERRERS, Derbs. and Warw., a unicorn, passant, erm. *Pl.* 106, *cr.* 3.

FERRERS, Sco., a leopard, passant, gardant, ducally gorged, ppr. *Pl.* 120, *cr.* 9.

FERRERS, Eng., a pheon, az. *Pl.* 26, *cr.* 12.

FERRIE, Sco., an anchor and cable, ppr. *Be firm. Pl.* 42, *cr.* 12.

FERRIER, Sco., a garb, or, banded, gu. *Diligentia ditat. Pl.* 48, *cr.* 10.

FERRIER, Eng., a horse-shoe, ppr. *Bon fortune. Pl.* 52, *cr.* 4.

FERRIER, Sco., a plumb-rule, or. *Pl.* 13, *cr.* 3.
FERRIER, Sco., a horse-shoe, az., between wings, or. *Advance. Pl.* 17, *cr.* 3.
FERRINGTON, an heraldic-tiger, passant, vert, (tail nowed, ducally gorged and lined, or.) *Pl.* 7, *cr.* 5.
FERRIS, Eng., out of a ducal coronet, a sinister hand, between wings, ppr. *Pl.* 79, *cr.* 6.
FERRON, Eng., out of a ducal coronet, an arm, in armour, in hand a cutlass, ppr. *Pl.* 15, *cr.* 5.
FERRY, or FERREY, a plough, ppr. *Pl.* 28, *cr.* 15.
FESANT, Eng., a demi-antelope, ppr., collared, gu. *Pl.* 34, *cr.* 8.
FESANT, a cock-pheasant, ppr. *Pl.* 82, *cr.* 12, (without collar.)
FESTING, Eng., a fire-beacon inflamed, ppr. *Pl.* 88, *cr.* 6.
FETHERSTON, Bart., Iri., an antelope, (statant,) ar., armed, or. *Volens et valens. Pl.* 63, *cr.* 10.
FETHERSTON, Cambs., an antelope's head, erased, gu. *Pl.* 24, *cr.* 7.
FETHERSTON, an antelope's head, erased, gu., crined and armed, or, charged on neck with an ostrich-feather and an annulet, ar. *Pl.* 24, *cr.* 7, (feather, *pl.* 12, *cr.* 9; annulet, *pl.* 141.)
FETHERSTON, a griffin's head, erased, murally gorged. *Pl.* 48, *cr.* 6, (gorging, *pl.* 128, *fig.* 18.)
FETHERSTON, JOHN, Esq., of Packwood House, Warw., an antelope's head, erased, gu., horned and langued, vert. *Christi pennatus sidera morte peto. Pl.* 24, *cr.* 7.
FETHERSTON, Cumb., an antelope's head, erased, gu., crined and armed, or, (charged on neck with an ostrich-feather and an annulet, ar.) *Pl.* 24, *cr.* 7.
FETHERSTON, or FETHERSTONE, Iri., a cross crosslet, fitched, ar., and a sword, az., in saltier. *Pl.* 89, *cr.* 14.
FETHERSTONEHAUGH, Bart., Eng., an antelope, (statant,) ar., armed, or. *Pl.* 63, *cr.* 10.
FETHERSTONHAUGH, TIMOTHY, Esq., of The College, Kirkoswald, Cumb., an antelope's head, erased, gu., armed, or. *Valens et volens. Pl.* 24, *cr.* 7.
FETHERSTONHAUGH, Iri., an antelope, (statant,) armed, or. *Valens et volens. Pl.* 63, *cr.* 10.
FETON, a chevalier, in complete armour, wielding a scimitar, ppr. *Pl.* 27, *cr.* 11.
FETTES, Bart., Sco., and FETTUS, Sco., a bee, volant, ppr. *Industria. Pl.* 100, *cr.* 3.
FETTEW, a bee, erect, ppr. *Pl.* 100, *cr.* 3.
FETTIPLACE, Berks., a griffin's head, vert, beaked, gu. *Pl.* 38, *cr.* 3.
FETTIPLACE, Berks., a cock's head, erased, gu., crested and wattled, or. *Pl.* 92, *cr.* 3.
FETTYPLACE, a griffin's head, erased, vert, beaked and eared, gu. *Pl.* 48, *cr.* 6.
FEVERSHAM, Baron (Duncombe,) out of a ducal coronet, or, a horse's hind-leg, sa., shod, ar. *Deo, regi, patriæ. Pl.* 38, *cr.* 11.
FEWTRELL, a leopard's head, ppr., gorged with a collar, ar., charged with three mullets, sa. *Pl.* 40, *cr.* 10, (mullet, *pl.* 141.)
FEYREY, and FEYTREY, a cross crosslet, fitched, sa. *Pl.* 16, *cr.* 10.
FEYRY, Beds., a griffin, segreant, in dexter a sword, ppr. *Pl.* 49, *cr.* 4.
FFARRINGTON, Lanc., a dragon, ar., (sans wings, tail nowed, langued and ducally gorged, gu.,) wreathed with a chain, or.) *Domat omnia virtus. Pl.* 90, *cr.* 10.

FFLOKES, Bart., Norf., a dexter arm, embowed, (vested, per pale, vert and gu.,) in hand a spear, ppr. *Pl.* 39, *cr.* 15.
FFOLLIOTT, a lion, rampant, per pale, gu. and ar., double queued, and murally crowned, or. *Quo virtus et fata vocant. Pl.* 41, *cr.* 15, (crown, *pl.* 128, *fig.* 18.)
FFOULKES, JOHN-JOCELYN, Esq., of Eriviatt, Wel., a boar's head, erased, ar. *Jure non dono. Pl.* 16, *cr.* 11.
FFRENCH, Baron and Bart., (Ffrench,) Iri., a dolphin, naiant, ppr. *Malo mori quam fœdari. Pl.* 48, *cr.* 9.
FFYTCHE, a leopard's face, or, pierced by a sword, in bend sinister, ppr., hilt and pommel, gold. *Pl.* 125, *cr.* 9.
FFYTCHE, Linc.: 1. A leopard, passant, ppr., holding an escutcheon, charged with a leopard's face, or. *Pl.* 86, *cr.* 2, (escutcheon, *pl.* 6, *cr.* 11.) 2. A pelican, wings addorsed, vulning. *Esperance. Pl.* 109, *cr.* 15.
FICHET, Somers., a demi-lion, pean, ducally crowned, or. *Pl.* 61, *cr.* 4, (without branch.)
FICKLING, on a chapeau, gu., turned up, erm., an eagle's head, az. *Pl.* 96, *cr.* 9, (head, *pl.* 100, *cr.* 10.)
FIDDES, Eng., a cinquefoil, erm. *Pl.* 91, *cr.* 12.
FIDELOW, a dexter hand, in fess, couped, reaching toward a garland of olive. *Pl.* 73, *cr.* 11.
FIDLER, Eng., a dexter hand holding a palm-branch, ppr. *Pl.* 23, *cr.* 7.
FIELD, a wheatsheaf, or, banded, gu. *Pl.* 48, *cr.* 10.
FIELD, (issuing from clouds,) a dexter arm, in fess, ppr., (vested,) gu., cuffed, az., in hand a javelin, of the first. *Pl.* 39, *cr.* 15.
FIELD, Iri., a lily and a holly-branch, in saltier, ppr. *Pl.* 60, *cr.* 11.
FIELDEN, a bird, on a branch, ppr. *Pl.* 13, *cr.* 4.
FIELDEN, Eng., a lion, rampant, in dexter a fleur-de-lis. *Pl.* 87, *cr.* 6.
FIELDING, Warw.: 1. On dexter, an eagle, displayed. *Pl.* 48, *cr.* 11. 2. In centre, a palm-tree. *Pl.* 18, *cr.* 12. 3. On sinister, a black-bird sitting on an oak-stump, acorned, all ppr. *Pl.* 71, *cr.* 5.
FIELDING, Earl of Denbigh. *See* DENBIGH.
FIELDING, Eng., an eagle, displayed, sa., armed and membered, or, and charged on breast with the family coat. *Honor virtutis præmium. Pl.* 12, *cr.* 7.
FIELDS, issuing from a cloud; in hand, erect, a club, ppr. *Pl.* 37, *cr.* 13.
FIENES, Eng., a wolf, sejant, (collared and lined.) *Pl.* 110, *cr.* 4.
FIENNES, Eng., issuing from clouds, in fess, two hands, supporting a flaming heart, ppr. *Pl.* 52, *cr.* 13.
FIENNES, Baron Say and Sale. *See* SAY.
FIFE, Earl of, Viscount Macduff and Baron Braco, Iri.; Baron Fife, U.K., (Duff:) 1. A horse, in full gallop, ar., covered with a mantling, gu., bestrewed with escutcheons, or, each charged with a lion, rampant, of the second, on his back a knight, in complete armour, with sword drawn, ppr., on sinister arm a shield, charged as the escutcheons, and on his helmet a wreath, of the colours, thereon a demi-lion, rampant, gu. *Pl.* 61, *cr.* 2. 2. A demi-lion, rampant, gu., in dexter a broadsword, ppr., hilt and pommel, or. *Virtute et opere. Pl.* 41, *cr.* 13.

FIFE, or FIFFE, Sco., a demi-lion, rampant, sa. *Pl.* 67, *cr.* 10.
FIFIELD, Kent, a falcon, rising, gu. *Pl.* 105, *cr.* 4.
FIGES, Eng., two anchors, in saltier, az., stocks, gu. *Pl.* 37, *cr.* 12.
FIGGINS, Wilts, a dexter arm, in hand a cross crosslet, fitched, gu. *Pl.* 99, *cr.* 1.
FILBUT, and FILBUTT, Eng., an arm, in armour, in hand a carved shield. *Pl.* 98, *cr.* 5.
FILFED, Eng., a cross crosslet, fitched, between two palm-branches, ppr. *Pl.* 37, *cr.* 14.
FILIOLL, Ess. and Dors., a unicorn's head, couped, sa. *Pl.* 20, *cr.* 1.
FILKIN, and FILKYN, Eng., wings in leure, ppr. *Pl.* 87, *cr.* 1.
FILLINGHAM, Norf., in dexter hand, gauntleted, a pheon, point upward, ppr. *Pl.* 123, *cr.* 12.
FILLINGHAM, Eng., on a chapeau, ar., turned up, gu., a boar, sa. *Pl.* 22, *cr.* 8.
FILMER, Bart., Kent, on a (ruined) castle, or, a falcon, wings expanded, ppr., beaked and legged, gold. *Pl.* 8, *cr.* 15.
FINCH, a griffin, segreant. *Pl.* 67, *cr.* 13.
FINCH, Ruts., a griffin, passant, sa. *Pl.* 61, *cr.* 14, (without gorging.)
FINCH, a lion, rampant, in dexter a gilliflower, slipped, ppr. *Pl.* 64, *cr.* 2, (flower, *pl.* 22, *cr.* 9.)
FINCH, Kent, a griffin, passant, wings addorsed, sa., ducally gorged, or. *Pl.* 61, *cr.* 14.
FINCH, Earl of Aylesford. *See* AYLESFORD.
FINCH, Iri., a griffin, passant, az. *Bono vince malum.* *Pl.* 61, *cr.* 14, (without gorging.)
FINCHAM, Eng., a wolf's head, erased, in mouth a branch of laurel, vert, fructed, gu. *Pl.* 14, *cr.* 6, (laurel, *pl.* 123, *cr.* 5.)
FINCHAM, a hind's head, erased, or, in mouth a branch of laurel, vert, fructed, gu. *Pl.* 6, *cr.* 1, (laurel, *pl.* 123, *cr.* 5.)
FINCHE, Surr., a griffin, passant, sa., ducally gorged, ar. *Pl.* 61, *cr.* 14.
FINCH-HATTON, Earl of Winchilsea. *See* WINCHILSEA.
FINCHINGFIELD, Eng., a dagger and a (sword) in saltier, ppr. *Pl.* 24, *cr.* 2.
FINDERNE, Derbs. and Staffs., an ox-yoke, or. *Pl.* 35, *cr.* 11.
FINDLATER, an eagle, regardant, ppr. *Pl.* 35, *cr.* 8.
FINDLAY, ROBERT, Esq., of Easterhill, Lanark, a boar, passant, ar. *Fortis in arduis.* *Pl.* 48, *cr.* 14.
FINDLEY, Sco., a boar, passant, ar. *Fortis in arduis.* *Pl.* 48, *cr.* 14.
FINEAUX, Kent, an eagle's head, erased, or, ducally crowned, ar. *Pl.* 20, *cr.* 7, (crown, *same plate.*)
FINET, Kent, a tower, ar., round the top, fleurs-de-lis. *Pl.* 12, *cr.* 8, (fleurs-de-lis, *pl.* 141.)
FINGALL, Earl of, and Baron Killeen, Iri., Baron Fingall, U. K., (Plunkett,) a horse, passant, ar. *Festina lente.* *Pl.* 15, *cr.* 14.
FINGLASSE, Iri., a demi-eagle, displayed, with two heads, per pale, or and sa. *Pl.* 4, *cr.* 6, (without charge.)
FINLASON, Sco., a stag's head, erased, ppr. *Cœlitus datum.* *Pl.* 66, *cr.* 9.
FINLAY, ALEXANDER STRUTHERS, Esq., of Castle Toward, Greenock, in hand a dagger, ppr. *I'll be wary.* *Pl.* 28, *cr.* 4.

FINLAY, Sco., a naked arm, in hand a scimitar, ppr. *Fortis in arduis.* *Pl.* 92, *cr.* 5.
FINLAY, Sco., an olive-branch, slipped, ppr. *Beati pacifici.* *Pl.* 98, *cr.* 8.
FINLAYSON, Sco., a stag's head, at gaze, erased, ppr. *Pl.* 8, *cr.* 6.
FINLAYSON, Eng., a spur-rowel. *Pl.* 54, *cr.* 5.
FINLAYSON, Sco., a stag's head, erased, in mouth a serpent. *Cœlitus datum.* *Pl.* 54, *cr.* 7.
FINLAYSON, Sco., same crest. *Haud on.*
FINLEY, Eng., in dexter hand, a sword, ppr. *Pl.* 21, *cr.* 10.
FINN, Eng., a unicorn, sejant, resting dexter against a tree, ppr. *Pl.* 110, *cr.* 15.
FINNAN, a dove, wings expanded, az., in mouth an olive-branch, ppr. *Pl.* 27, *cr.* 5, (branch, *pl.* 98, *cr.* 8.)
FINNCANE, Iri., a vine-branch, leaved, vert, fructed, ppr. *Pl.* 89, *cr.* 1.
FINNES, Eng., a wolf, sejant, ar., (collared, indented, and chained, or.) *Pl.* 110, *cr.* 4.
FINNEY, Eng., a bundle of seven arrows, ppr. *Pl.* 110, *cr.* 11.
FINNIE, Sco., a dove, with a leaf in mouth, ppr. *Tandem.* *Pl.* 48, *cr.* 15.
FINNIS, Eng., a cross crosslet, fitched, gu., and a sword, az., in saltier. *Pl.* 89, *cr.* 14.
FIOTT, a demi-horse, ar., charged on breast with a fleur-de-lis, sa.
FIREBRAE, a flame of fire, ppr. *Fideli quid obstat.* *Pl.* 16, *cr.* 12.
FIRMAGE, Suff., an ermine, (sejant, ppr., collared and lined, or.) *Pl.* 9, *cr.* 5.
FIRMIN, Lond., a demi-dragon, wings addorsed, vert, between feet a garb, or. *Firmus in Christo.* *Pl.* 82, *cr.* 10, (garb, *pl.* 84, *cr.* 7.)
FIRTH, Eng., out of a ducal coronet, a broken battle-axe, head in bend sinister. *Pl.* 24, *cr.* 15, (coronet, *same plate.*)
FIRTH, Chesh., on a mount, vert, a griffin, passant, sa., in front of a hurst of six trees, ppr. *Deus incrementum dabit.* *Pl.* 61, *cr.* 14, (trees, *pl.* 125, *cr.* 14.)
FISCHE, out of a cloud, in dexter hand, (gloved,) a terrestrial globe. *Pl.* 104, *cr.* 4.
FISCHER, a lion, paassnt, tail extended, gu. *Pl.* 118, *cr.* 10.
FISH, a tiger's head, erased, erm., maned and tusked, or. *Pl.* 94, *cr.* 10.
FISH, Middx., on a rock, ppr., a stork, erm., beaked and legged, gu., charged on breast with an increscent, of the last. *Pl.* 122, *cr.* 7, (crescent, *pl.* 141.)
FISHACRE, Devons., issuing from a cloud, in dexter hand, in fess, ppr., a ball, sa. *Pl.* 104, *cr.* 4.
FISHBORNE, Lond. and Middx., a lion's head, ar., collared, sa., charged with three fleurs-de-lis, of the first. *Pl.* 7, *cr.* 10, (fleur-de-lis, *pl.* 141.)
FISHER, a demi-wild boar, regardant, pierced in breast by a spear, end in mouth. *Pl.* 115, *cr.* 2.
FISHER, Middx., a demi-lion, rampant, gardant, (holding a carved shield of arms, the carving or.) *Pl.* 35, *cr.* 4.
FISHER, Lond., Herts., and Staffs., a demi-lion, rampant, gu., between paws a laurel-branch, ppr. *Pl.* 47, *cr.* 4, (branch, *pl.* 123, *cr.* 5.)
FISHER, Wilts., a demi-stag, (collared and lined.) *Pl.* 55, *cr.* 9, (without rose.)

FISHER, Staffs., a demi-lion, rampant, gu., between paws an anchor, az. *Spe et amore.* Pl. 19, cr. 6.

FISHER, Sco., an anchor, cabled, ppr. *Spe et amore.* Pl. 42, cr. 12.

FISHER, out of a ducal coronet, a demi-lion, rampant, between paws a gauntlet. *Virtutem extendere fac.* Pl. 45, cr. 7, (gauntlet, pl. 40, cr. 6.)

FISHER, Kent, on a branch, couped and raguly, in fess, sprouting a branch at each end, a peacock, in pride, all ppr. Pl. 92, cr. 11, (branch, pl. 5, cr. 8.)

FISHER, Iri., a pelican's head, erased, ppr., vulning, gu. Pl. 26, cr. 1.

FISHER, on a branch, trunked and raguly, in fess, sprouting from dexter a honeysuckle, a kingfisher, all ppr., in beak a fish, or.

FISHER, Sco., a garvie, naiant. Pl. 39, cr. 11.

FISHER, Warw., a talbot's head, erased, ar., collared and eared, gu. Pl. 2, cr. 15.

FISHER, on a bezant, charged with three bars, in fess, between bulrushes, ppr., a kingfisher, wings addorsed, in beak a fish.

FISHER, Northamp., a demi-sea-dog, rampant, or.

FISHER, Lond. and Derbs., a kingfisher, ppr., in beak a fish, or.

FISHER, Warw., (a cubit arm, erect,) vairy, ar. and purp., on hand a glove, holding a falcon, tasselled, all of the first. Pl. 83, cr. 13.

FISHER, Leic., a kingfisher, ppr., in dexter a fleur-de-lis, sa.

FISHER, on stump of tree, couped and eradicated, a kingfisher, all ppr.

FISHER, an eagle, displayed, sa., charged on breast with a cross, ar. Pl. 48, cr. 11, (cross, pl. 141.)

FISHER, a demi-sea-dog, per cross, ar. and az.

FISHERWICK, Baron. *See* DONEGAL, Marquess of.

FISKE, Eng., out of a ducal coronet, a reindeer's head. Pl. 60, cr. 3.

FISKE, Suff., a triangle, erected, sa., on vertex an etoile, ppr. Pl. 13, cr. 6.

FITCH, Kent and Ess., a leopard's head, cabossed, or, across mouth a sword, ppr., hilted, gu. Pl. 125, cr. 9.

FITCH, Ess., a leopard, passant, ppr., sustaining an escutcheon, vert, charged with a leopard's head, or. Pl. 86, cr. 2, (escutcheon, pl. 6, cr. 11.)

FITCH, Ess., two swords, in saltier, gu., enfiled with a leopard's head, cabossed, or. Pl. 75, cr. 13, (head, pl. 66, cr. 14.)

FITCHET, Eng., a cubit arm, in hand a dagger, ppr. Pl. 23, cr. 15.

FITCHETT, Eng., a lion, rampant, erminois, ducally crowned, or. Pl. 98, cr. 1.

FITHIE, Sco., a stork's head, erased, ar. Pl. 32, cr. 5.

FITHIER, Eng., a martlet, volant, sa., winged, or. Pl. 40, cr. 4.

FITHIER, an angel, dexter on breast, (sinister pointing to heaven.) Pl. 25, cr. 7.

FITON, a demi-moor, shooting an arrow from a bow, ppr. Pl. 80, cr. 9.

FITTER, an antelope's head, erased, ar. Pl. 24, cr. 7.

FITTON, Heref., Chesh., and Lanc., on a chapeau, a wyvern, sans legs, wings expanded. Pl. 80, cr. 8.

FITTON, Chesh., on a chapeau, az., turned up, erm., a lily, ppr., stalked and leaved, vert. Pl. 81, cr. 9, (chapeau, pl. 127, fig. 13.)

FITTZ, two elephants' probosces, erect. Pl. 24, cr. 8.

FITZ, Devons., an escallop, ar., charged with a centaur, gu. Pl. 117, cr. 4, (centaur, pl. 70, cr. 13.)

FITZ-ALAN, Suss. and Salop, (on a mount,) vert, a horse, passant, ar., in mouth an oak-branch, ppr. Pl. 15, cr. 14, (branch, pl. 32, cr. 13.)

FITZ-ALLAN, or FITZ-ALIN, Salop, a spear, broken in three pieces, one in pale, and two in saltier, ppr., banded, gu. Pl. 33, cr. 3.

FITZ-ALLEN, Eng., a sword, in pale, between two laurel-branches, in orle, ppr. Pl. 71, cr. 3.

FITZ-ALLEN, a dexter arm, ppr., vested, gu., in hand a mill-rind, or. Pl. 34, cr. 3.

FITZ-AMOND, out of a ducal coronet, or, two wings addorsed, ppr. Pl. 17, cr. 9.

FITZ-BARNARD, Eng., a peacock, issuant, az. Pl. 24, cr. 1.

FITZ-BARNARD, and FITZ-BERNARD, a cup, or. Pl. 42, cr. 1.

FITZ-ELLIS, Eng., within a crescent, ar., an arrow, in pale, point upward, ppr. Pl. 82, cr. 15.

FITZ-EUSTACE, on a chapeau, ppr., a cockatrice, sejant, gu. Pl. 103, cr. 9, (without coronet.)

FITZ-GEFFREY, Beds. and Northamp., out of a ducal coronet, or, a demi-bull, rampant, sa., armed, gold. Pl. 73, cr. 8, (coronet, pl. 128, fig. 3.)

FITZ-GEOFFRY, a fox, current, ppr. Pl. 80, cr. 5.

FITZ-GERALD, Bart., Iri., a boar, passant, gu., armed, and bristled, or. *Shanet a Boo.* Pl. 48, cr. 14.

FITZGERALD and VESCI, Baron, Iri., Baron Fitzgerald, U.K., (Vesey-Fitzgerald:) 1. For *Fitzgerald*, a soldier, fully equipped, on horseback, at full speed, and holding a sword, erect, ppr. Pl. 118, cr. 14. 2. For *Vesey*, in dexter hand, (in armour,) a laurel-branch, ppr. *Shanet a Boo.* Pl. 43, cr. 6.

FITZGERALD, Suff. and Northamp., a monkey, passant, gardant, sa., collared and chained round the body, or. Pl. 101, cr. 11.

FITZGERALD, CHARLES-LIONEL, Esq., of Furlough Park, co. Mayo, a boar, passant. *Honor probataque virtus.* Pl. 48, cr. 14.

FITZGERALD, PETER, Knight of Kerry, of Valentia, co. Kerry, an armed knight on horseback, all ppr. *Mallahar a Boo.* Pl. 118, cr. 14.

FITZGERALD, WILLIAM, Esq., of Adelphi, co. Clare, on a chapeau, a boar, passant. *Shanet a Boo.* Pl. 22, cr. 8.

FITZGERALD-JUDKIN, Bart., of Lisheen, Iri., a chevalier, in complete armour, on horseback, at full speed, sword drawn, and beaver up, all ppr. Pl. 118, cr. 14.

FITZGILBERT, in hand a fleur-de-lis, all ppr. Pl. 95, cr. 9.

FITZ-HAMON, in dexter hand a tilting-spear, in bend, ppr. Pl. 99, cr. 8.

FITZ-HARBERT, Eng., a salamander, or, in flames, gu. Pl. 20, cr. 15.

FITZHARDINGE, Earl Berkeley. *See* BERKELEY, Earl of.

FITZ-HARRIS, a hedgehog, passant, ppr. Pl. 32, cr. 9.

FITZ-HARRIS, an eagle, displayed, sa., imperially crowned, or, in dexter a sceptre, in sinister a mound and cross. *Pl.* 107, *cr.* 4, (crown, *pl.* 142; sceptre, *pl.* 82, *cr.* 3; mound, *pl.* 37, *cr.* 3.)

FITZ-HARRY, Eng., a bear's head, erased, ppr., muzzled, gu. *Pl.* 71, *cr.* 6.

FITZ-HENRY, Eng., a wyvern, vomiting fire at both ends. *Pl.* 109, *cr.* 13.

FITZ-HERBERT, Bart., Derbs., a cubit arm, in armour, erect, the hand appearing clenched within a gauntlet, all ppr. *Pl.* 125, *cr.* 5, (without sword.)

FITZ-HERBERT, Derbs. and Staffs., a cubit arm, in armour, erect, the hand appearing clenched within a gauntlet, all ppr. *Ung je serviray*. *Pl.* 125, *cr.* 5, (without sword.)

FITZ-HERBERT, Derbs. and Oxon., a gauntlet, erect, ppr. *Pl.* 15, *cr.* 15.

FITZ-HERBERT, THOMAS, Esq., of Norbury, Derbs.; and Swinnerton, Staffs., a dexter arm, armed, and gauntleted, ppr. *Ung je serviray*. *Pl.* 97, *cr.* 1.

FITZ-HERBERT, Baron St Helens. *See* ST HELENS.

FITZ-HEWE, or FITZ-HUGH, Bucks., a Cornish chough, ppr. *Pl.* 100, *cr.* 13.

FITZHUGH, THOMAS, Esq., of Plas Power, Wel., a martlet, ppr. *In moderation placing all my glory*. *Pl.* 111, *cr.* 5.

FITZ-HUGH, Yorks. and Oxon., on a chapeau, gu., turned up, erm., a wyvern, sans legs, wings expanded, ar. *Pl.* 80, *cr.* 8.

FITZ-HUGH, on a chapeau, crimson, turned up, erm., a demi-griffin, segreant, ar. *Pl.* 18, *cr.* 6, (chapeau, *pl.* 122, *cr.* 11.)

FITZ-HUMFREY, or HUMPHREY, Ess., a dragon's head, vert, in mouth a sinister hand, gu. *Pl.* 106, *cr.* 13.

FITZ-JAMES, a dolphin, ar., devouring (the top of an antique cap, az.,) turned up, erm. *Pl.* 71, *cr.* 1.

FITZ-JAMES, a buffalo, passant.

FITZ-JOHN, Linc., on a chapeau, a salamander in flames, ppr. *Pl.* 86, *cr.* 14.

FITZ-JOHN, a demi-lion, rampant. *Pl.* 67, *cr.* 10.

FITZ-JOHN, Iri., in dexter hand an (olive-) branch, ppr. *Pl.* 23, *cr.* 7.

FITZ-LEWIS, Ess., a bull (statant,) per pale, or. and purp., hoofed and armed, sa. *Pl.* 66, *cr.* 11.

FITZ-MARMADUKE, Eng., a Catherine-wheel, ar. *Pl.* 1, *cr.* 7.

FITZ-MAURICE, Iri., a saggittarius, shooting an arrow from a bow, ppr. *Virtute, non verbis*. *Pl.* 70, *cr.* 13.

FITZ-MAURICE, Marquess of Lansdowne and Earl of Kerry. *See* LANSDOWNE.

FITZ-MAURICE, Iri., in two hands a sword, in pale, ppr. *Pl.* 75, *cr.* 8.

FITZMAURICE, Earl of Orkney. *See* ORKNEY.

FITZMORE, a parrot, issuant. *Pl.* 94, *cr.* 2.

FITZ-NEEL, Bucks., on a chapeau, ppr., a cinquefoil, or. *Pl.* 91, *cr.* 12, (chapeau, *pl.* 127, *fig.* 13.)

FITZ-OSBERN, and FITZ-OSBERNE, a demi-eagle, displayed, with two heads, az. *Pl.* 4, *cr.* 6, (without charge.)

FITZ-OSBERT, a demi-dragon, vert. *Pl.* 82, *cr.* 10.

FITZ-OSBORN, two arms, in armour, embowed, or, wielding a battle-axe, ar. *Pl.* 41, *cr.* 2.

FITZ-OSBORN, a spear-head, az. *Pl.* 82, *cr.* 9.

FITZ-OURSE, an anchor and cable, sa., and a sword, az., hilt, or, in saltier. *Pl.* 25, *cr.* 1.

FITZPAINE, a lion, passant. *Pl.* 48, *cr.* 8.

FITZPATRICK, Iri., a dragon, vert, surmounted by a lion, sa., tail extended. *Fortis sub forte*. *Pl.* 90, *cr.* 10, (lion, *pl.* 118, *cr.* 10.)

FITZ-PEN, Cornw., a bee, volant, erect, or, winged, vert. *Pl.* 100, *cr.* 3.

FITZ-PIERS, Eng., a bell, az. *Pl.* 73, *cr.* 15.

FITZ-POMEROY, around two (hunting-spears) in pale, a serpent entwined, ppr. *Pl.* 14, *cr.* 13.

FITZ-RALPH, Eng., a square padlock, az. *Pl.* 18, *cr.* 7.

FITZ-RAUSE, on a mount, vert, a hind, statant, ppr. *Pl.* 122, *cr.* 5.

FITZ-RAYNARD, and RAYNOLD, Eng., two wings, conjoined, ppr. *Pl.* 15, *cr.* 10.

FITZ-RICHARD, two dolphins, haurient, addorsed, ppr. *Pl.* 81, *cr.* 2.

FITZ-ROANE, same crest.

FITZ-ROGER, an (eagle's) leg, erased, ar. *Pl.* 83, *cr.* 7.

FITZ-RONARD, a dove, standing on a serpent, nowed in a love-knot, ppr. *Pl.* 3, *cr.* 4.

FITZ-ROY, Duke of Grafton. *See* GRAFTON.

FITZ-ROY, Baron Southampton. *See* SOUTHAMPTON.

FITZ-SIMMONS, Eng., an eagle, wings expanded, looking towards the sun, all ppr. *Pl.* 43, *cr.* 5, (eagle, *pl.* 126, *cr.* 7.)

FITZ-SIMON, a griffin's head, in beak a palm-branch, between wings, all ppr. *Pl.* 65, *cr.* 1, (branch, *pl.* 26, *cr.* 3.)

FITZ-SIMONS, Iri., a boar, passant, regardant, pulling from his shoulder an arrow. *Pl.* 36, *cr.* 2; and *pl.* 115, *cr.* 2.

FITZ-SYMON, Iri., a demi-parrot, close, vert, gorged with a collar, gu., beaked, of the last.

FITZ-SYMON, Eng., a dexter and sinister hand wielding a two-handed sword, ppr. *Pl.* 3, *cr.* 5.

FITZ-SYMOND, Eng., issuing from a cloud, in hand a club, all ppr. *Pl.* 37, *cr.* 13.

FITZ-THOMAS, Ess., a dragon's head, pierced through neck by a spear, in bend sinister, ppr. *Pl.* 121, *cr.* 9.

FITZ-THOMAS, Iri., out of a ducal coronet, or, a sceptre, environed by a serpent, between wings, ppr. *Pl.* 27, *cr.* 8.

FITZ-URSE, out of top of a tower, an arm, in armour, in hand a scimitar, all ppr. *Pl.* 116, *cr.* 12.

FITZ-VRIAN, two battle-axes, in saltier, gu., between tops, a bird, sa. *Pl.* 52, *cr.* 10, (bird, *same plate*.)

FITZ-WALTER, a winged heart, ppr. *Pl.* 39, *cr.* 7.

FITZ-WALTER, Eng., a heart, gu., winged, or. *Pl.* 39, *cr.* 7.

FITZ-WARREN, Somers., a holy lamb, (regardant,) ppr., with banner, sa. *Pl.* 48, *cr.* 13.

FITZ-WARYN, a wyvern, wings expanded, gu. *Pl.* 63, *cr.* 13.

FITZ-WATER, Eng., a lion, rampant, or. *Pl.* 67, *cr.* 5.

FITZ-WATER, Eng., issuing from a cloud, in hand a club, ppr. *Pl.* 37, *cr.* 13.

FITZ-WIGHT, on a chapeau, ppr., a lion, passant, gardant. *Pl.* 7, *cr.* 14, (without gorging.)

FITZ-WILLIAM, Linc., out of a ducal coronet, or, a double plume of ostrich-feathers, ar. *Pl.* 44, *cr.* 12.

FITZ-WILLIAM, Earl, Viscount Milton, and Lord Fitzwilliam, Eng.; Earl and Baron Fitzwilliam, and Viscount Milton, Iri., (Wentworth-Fitzwilliam,) out of a ducal coronet, or, a triple plume of ostrich-feathers, ar. *Appetitus rationi pareat.* Pl. 114, cr. 8.

FITZ-WILLIAM, Surr., a tiger, passant, sa., ducally gorged and lined, ar. Pl. 120, cr. 9.

FITZ-WILLIAM, a trefoil, (stalked, raguly, and slipped,) ar. Pl. 82, cr. 1.

FITZ-WILLIAM, Eng., a phœnix, az., beaked, or, in flames, gu. Pl. 44, cr. 8.

FITZ-WYGRAM, Bart., Ess., (on a mount, vert, a hand, in armour,) couped at wrist, in fess, ppr., charged with an escallop, and holding a fleur-de-lis, erect, or. *Dulcis amor patriæ.* Pl. 46, cr. 12, (escallop, pl. 141.)

FITZ-ZIMON, or ZYMON, a monkey, ppr., banded about middle. Pl. 101, cr. 11.

FLACKE, a covered cup. Pl. 75, cr. 13, (without swords.)

FLAMANK, and FLAMOCK, Cornw., a Saracen's head, ppr., banded, or. Pl. 36, cr. 3.

FLAMSTED, Northamp., a talbot's head, ar., erased, gu., eared and gorged with a bar-gemelle, or. Pl. 2, cr. 15.

FLAMVILE, Leic., two battle-axes, addorsed, in saltire, ensigned by a dove, all ppr. Pl. 52, cr. 10, (dove, pl. 85, cr. 14.)

FLANAGAN, Iri., in lion's paw a crescent. Pl. 91, cr. 1.

FLANAGAN, JOHN-WOULFE, Esq., of Drum be, co. Roscommon, in hand a dagger. *Audaces fortuna juvat.* Pl. 28, cr. 4.

FLANDERS, Eng., a harp, gu. Pl. 104, cr. 15.

FLASHMAN, Eng., out of a ducal coronet, two arms, in saltire, in each hand a scimitar, in pale, all ppr. Pl. 57, cr. 8.

FLATTESBURY, Eng., on a mural coronet, or, a stag, sejant, erm. Pl. 101, cr. 3.

FLAXNEY, Oxon., (on a mount,) vert, a talbot, sa., collared and lined, or, end of line tied in a knot. Pl. 65, cr. 2.

FLEEMING, Sco., a palm-tree, ppr. *Sub pondere cresco.* Pl. 18, cr. 12.

FLEEMING, Sco., a goat's head, erased, ar., armed and (collared,) az., the last charged with three cinquefoils, ar. *Let the deed shaw.* Pl. 29, cr. 13, (cinquefoils, pl. 141.)

FLEEMING, Sco., on a mural coronet, or, a stag, sejant, erm. Pl. 101, cr. 3.

FLEEMING, Staffs., (on a mount,) vert, a cross pattée, fitched, or, thereon perched a Cornish chough, ppr. Pl. 27, cr. 14, (chough, pl. 100, cr. 13.)

FLEEMING, a goat's head, erased, ppr. Pl. 29, cr. 13.

FLEEMING, of Moness, a goat's head, erased, ar., horned, or. *Let the deed shaw.* Pl. 29, cr. 13.

FLEET, Lond., (a sinister arm, embowed, vested, sa., puffed, ar.,) in hand, ppr., a club, of the second. Pl. 45, cr. 10.

FLEET, a goat, in mouth a trefoil, ppr. Pl. 15, cr. 9.

FLEETE, Lond., a sea-lion, (gardant,) erect, upper part, or, holding an escallop, gu., lower part, az. Pl. 59, cr. 2, (escallop, pl. 141.)

FLEETWOOD, Lond., Bucks., Lanc., Northamp., and Staffs., a wolf, passant, regardant, ar., vulned in shoulder, ppr. Pl. 77, cr. 14.

FLEETWOOD-HESKETH, Bart., of Rossall Hall, Lanc.: 1. For *Fleetwood*, a wolf, regardant, ar., charged on breast with a trefoil, vert. Pl. 77, cr. 14, (trefoil, pl. 141.) 2. For *Hesketh*, a garb, erect, or, in front of an eagle, displayed, with two heads, ppr. *Quod tibi, hoc alteri.* Pl. 87, cr. 11, (garb, pl. 48, cr. 10.)

FLEGG, two lions' gambs, in saltire, sa., enfiled with laurel, in orle, vert. Pl. 20, cr. 13, (garland, pl. 125, cr. 8.)

FLEMING, Bart., Westm., a serpent, nowed, in mouth a garland of olives and vines, all ppr. *Pax, copia, sapientia.* Pl. 104, cr. 9.

FLEMING, Iri., a demi-lion, rampant, ducally gorged. Pl. 87, cr. 15.

FLEMING, Hants., an eagle, displayed, sa., beaked, legged, and ducally (gorged,) or. Pl. 85, cr. 11.

FLEMING, Eng. and Wel., in hand, gauntleted, a sword, ppr. Pl. 125, cr. 5.

FLEMING, a snake, ppr. Pl. 1, cr. 9.

FLEMING, ELPHINSTONE, JOHN, Esq., of Cumbernauld House, Dumbarton, a goat's head, erased, ar., armed, or. *Let the deed shaw.* Pl. 29, cr. 13.

FLEMMING, Middx., a goat's head. Pl. 105, cr. 14.

FLEMMING, Eng., a goat's head, erased, ar., armed, or, (collared, az., charged with three cinquefoils, of the first.) *Let the deed shaw.* Pl. 29, cr. 13.

FLEMYNG, Eng., and FLEMYNGE, Sco., a hand, issuant, plucking a rose. Pl. 48, cr. 1.

FLESHER, Eng., a squirrel, sejant, per fess, or and gu. Pl. 16, cr. 9.

FLETCHER, Bart., Cumb., a horse's head, ar., charged with a trefoil, gu. *Martis non cupidinis.* Pl. 11, cr. 12.

FLETCHER, Bart., Iri., out of a mural coronet, or, a horse's head, erm., gorged with a wreath of laurel, vert. Pl. 81, cr. 6, (crown and wreath, pl. 128, figs. 6 and 18.)

FLETCHER, Suss., a talbot, passant, ar., pellettée. Pl. 120, cr. 8.

FLETCHER, Lond. and Oxon., a fleur-de-lis, semée of roundles. Pl. 68, cr. 12.

FLETCHER, Worc. and Derbs., a horse's head, ar., erased, sa., (gorged with a collar) of the second, charged with pheons, points downward, in mouth a rose, gu., slipped and leaved, ppr. *Sub cruce salus.* Pl. 81, cr. 6, (rose, pl. 117, cr. 10; pheon, pl. 141.)

FLETCHER, Glouc., a demi-bloodhound, az., langued, gu., ducally gorged, or. *Dieu pour nous.* Pl. 15, cr. 2.

FLETCHER, EDWARD-CHARLES, Esq., of Corsock, Kirkcudbright, a horse's head, ar. *Martis non cupidinis.* Pl. 81, cr. 6.

FLETCHER, Sco., a demi-lion, az., in dexter a cross crosslet, fitched, gu. *Libertate extinctâ, nulla virtus.* Pl. 65, cr. 6.

FLETCHER, Monm. and Lanc., a dexter arm, embowed, (encircled above elbow by a wreath of yew, ppr.,) in hand, a bow, or, stringed, sa. *Sperans pergo.* Pl. 51, cr. 5.

FLETCHER, Eng. and Sco., a horse's head, erased, ar. Pl. 81, cr. 6.

FLETCHER, Leic. and Warw., a demi-talbot, rampant, az., eared, or. Pl. 97, cr. 9, (without arrow.)

FLETCHER, Chesh., a pheon, point upward, per pale, erm. and sa. Pl. 56, cr. 15.

FLETCHER, a dexter arm, in armour, embowed, in hand an arrow, (in fess,) behind the arm, an anchor, erect, all ppr. *Pl.* 96, *cr.* 6, (anchor, *pl.* 42, *cr.* 12.)
FLETCHER, two arms shooting an arrow from a bow. *Recta pete. Pl.* 100, *cr.* 4.
FLETCHER, Sco., a demi-lion, az., in dexter a cross crosslet, fitched, gu. *Fortis in arduis. Pl.* 65, *cr.* 6.
FLETCHER, Sco. and Iri., out of a ducal coronet, or, a plume of three ostrich-feathers, az., (banded, gold.) *Dieu pour nous. Pl.* 69, *cr.* 11, (without wings.)
FLETCHER, a talbot, sejant. *Pl.* 107, *cr.* 7.
FLETCHER, Leic. and Warw., a demi-talbot, rampant, or. *Pl.* 97, *cr.* 9, (without arrow.)
FLETCHER, Leic. and Warw., a demi-talbot, rampant, az., ducally gorged, or. *Pl.* 15, *cr.* 2.
FLETEWIKES, an arm, embowed, vested and cuffed, ar., in hand, ppr., an arrow, sa., headed and feathered, of the first. *Pl.* 112, *cr.* 1.
FLETEWOOD, Eng., an heraldic-tiger, sa. *Pl.* 7, *cr.* 5.
FLETWICK, Beds., two lions' gambs, supporting an escutcheon, ar. *Pl.* 78, *cr.* 13.
FLEURY, Iri., a lion, passant, in dexter a crescent. *Pl.* 77, *cr.* 3.
FLEXNEY, Eng., a dexter and sinister arm shooting an arrow from a bow, ppr. *Pl.* 100, *cr.* 4.
FLIGHT, a savage's head, from shoulders, ducally crowned, and issuant therefrom a long cap, top turned toward the front. *Pl.* 78, *cr.* 14.
FLIN, and FLINN, Iri., two dexter hands, conjoined, ppr., attached to the wrists, two wings, or. *Pl.* 14, *cr.* 9.
FLINN, Dublin, a lion, passant, in dexter a laurel-branch. *Pl.* 48, *cr.* 8, (laurel, *pl.* 123, *cr.* 5.)
FLINT, out of a cloud, az., an etoile, ar. *Pl.* 16, *cr.* 13, (etoile, *pl.* 141.)
FLINT, out of a cloud, az., a flint, ppr., thereon an etoile, or. *Ib.*
FLINT, Eng., a lion's gamb, erect, sa., holding a laurel-branch, ppr. *Pl.* 68, *cr.* 10.
FLINT, Sco., an etoile. *Sine maculâ. Pl.* 63, *cr.* 9.
FLITT, on a mount, a dove, ppr. *Pl.* 104, *cr.* 8.
FLOCKHART, Sco., on a mount, vert, two harts, one couchant, the other statant, at gaze, ppr. *Pl.* 126 A, *cr.* 8.
FLOOD, Iri., a wolf's head, erased, ar. *Vis unita fortior. Pl.* 14, *cr.* 6.
FLOOD, Devons., a demi-lion, rampant, az., crowned, or, holding a cinquefoil, gold. *Pl.* 61, *cr.* 4, (cinquefoil, *pl.* 141.)
FLOOD, Eng., a chevalier on horseback, in complete armour, visor up. *Pl.* 118, *cr.* 14.
FLOOD, Iri., a heart, crowned, between wings, ppr. *Pl.* 52, *cr.* 2.
FLORIO, Eng., the sun, or. *Pl.* 68, *cr.* 14.
FLOTE, Eng., out of a ducal coronet, a reindeer's head, ppr. *Pl.* 60, *cr.* 3.
FLOUNDERS, Salop and Yorks., a demi-eagle, displayed, vert. *Aquila non captat muscas. Pl.* 22, *cr.* 11.
FLOWER, Iri. *See* ASHBROOK, Viscount.
FLOWER, Surr., out of clouds, a cubit arm, erect, in hand a rose and lily, each slipped, ppr. *Flores curat Deus. Pl.* 69, *cr.* 10, (lily, *pl.* 81, *cr.* 9.)
FLOWER, Wilts., a unicorn's head, couped, or. *Pl.* 20, *cr.* 1.

FLOWER, Bart., Oxon., a demi-lion, per pale, erm. and ermines, (gorged with a chain, within a collar, gemelle, or,) in dexter a gilliflower, ppr. *Perseverando. Pl.* 87, *cr.* 15, (gilliflower, *pl.* 22, *cr.* 9.)
FLOWER, a lion's head, erased, ar., charged with a mullet, gu. *Pl.* 81, *cr.* 4, (mullet, *pl.* 141.)
FLOWER, and FLOWRE, Kent, Northamp., and Yorks., a lion's head, erased, sa. *Pl.* 81, *cr.* 4.
FLOWER, Cambs., a stork, wings (elevated,) ppr., beaked and legged, gu. *Pl.* 33, *cr.* 9.
FLOWERDEW, and FLOWERDUE, Eng., in a maunch, an arm, elbow on the wreath. *Pl.* 8, *cr.* 11.
FLOYD, Bart., a lion, rampant, (regardant, ar., murally crowned, gu., bearing a flag representing the standard of Tippoo Sultaun,) flowing to the sinister, ppr. *Pl.* 99, *cr.* 2, (crown, *pl.* 128, *fig.* 18.)
FLOYD, Eng., a griffin, sejant, az., in dexter a garland of laurel, ppr. *Pl.* 56, *cr.* 10.
FLOYER, Devons. and Somers., out of a ducal coronet, in dexter hand a sword, wavy, in pale, all ppr. *Pl.* 65, *cr.* 10.
FLOYER, Dors., a buck's head, erased, or, (in mouth an arrow,) ar. *Floret virtus vulnerata. Pl.* 66, *cr.* 9.
FLUDD, out of a ducal coronet, or, an ounce's head, ar.
FLUDE, an arm, couped and embowed, elbow on the wreath, in hand a sword, in pale, enfiled with a savage's head, couped, all ppr. *Pl.* 102, *cr.* 11.
FLUDYER, Bart., Lond., an escallop, ar., charged with a cross patonce, between wings, of the first. *Pl.* 80, *cr.* 2, (cross, *pl.* 141.)
FLUDYER, Eng., an escallop, ar., charged with a cross fleury, sa., between wings, of the first. *Pl.* 80, *cr.* 2, (cross, *pl.* 141.)
FLUDYER, Eng., an escallop, between wings. *Pl.* 62, *cr.* 4.
FLY, Hants, an arm, in armour, erect, ppr., in gauntlet a hawk's lure, or, stringed, gu. *Pl.* 97, *cr.* 1, (lure, *same plate, cr.* 14.)
FLYNT, a human heart, purp., winged, or. *Pl.* 39, *cr.* 7.
FODON, Staffs., out of a ducal coronet, or, a pike's head, az. *Pl.* 36, *cr.* 13.
FODRINGAY, Eng., a crane, ar., in mouth a bunch of (clover,) ppr. *Pl.* 46, *cr.* 9.
FODRINGHAM, Yorks., a buck, ppr. *Pl.* 68, *cr.* 2.
FOGG, and FOGGE, Kent, a unicorn's head, ar. *Pl.* 20, *cr.* 1.
FOGG, and FOGGE, Kent, a unicorn's head, couped, ar. *Pl.* 20, *cr.* 1.
FOGG, and FOGGE, Kent, a unicorn's head, couped, ar., powdered with mullets, sa. *Pl.* 20, *cr.* 1, (mullet, *pl.* 141.)
FOGGO, or FOGO, Sco., a cherub's head, ppr. *Pl.* 126, *cr.* 10.
FOGO, Eng., a unicorn's head and neck. *Pl.* 20, *cr.* 1.
FOKERAM, Berks., a long cross, vert. *Pl.* 7, *cr.* 13.
FOKKE, in lion's paw, or, a cross pattée, fitched, gu. *Pl.* 46, *cr.* 7.
FOLBORNE, a (sinister) hand, couped, in fess. *Pl.* 32, *cr.* 4.
FOLCY, Worc., a lion, sejant, ar., between paws a ducal coronet, or. *Pl.* 22, *cr.* 13, (coronet, *pl.* 128, *fig.* 3.)

FOLEBORNE, a branch of fir, vert, fructed, or. *Pl.* 80, *cr.* 1.

FOLEBORNE, Eng., three holly-leaves, vert, banded, gu. *Pl.* 78, *cr.* 12.

FOLET, on a chapeau, ppr., an escallop, or. *Pl.* 17, *cr.* 14 (without wings.)

FOLEY, Baron, (Foley,) a lion, sejant, rampant, or, between paws an escutcheon, charged with the family arms. *Ut prosim. Pl.* 22, *cr.* 13.

FOLEY, Surr., a lion, rampant, ar., holding the same. *Pl.* 67, *cr.* 5.

FOLEY, Iri., a griffin, segreant, gu., winged, legged, and beaked, or. *Pl.* 67, *cr.* 13.

FOLEY, Worc., a lion, sejant, ar., between paws a ducal coronet, or. *Pl.* 22, *cr.* 13, (coronet, *pl.* 128, *fig.* 3.)

FOLIAMB, an armed leg, party per pale, or and sa., gartered with a (wreath,) gold and az., couped at thigh. *Pl.* 81, *cr.* 5.

FOLIAMB, a stag, quarterly, or and sa., attired, gold, and ar. *Pl.* 68, *cr.* 2.

FOLIAMBE, Staffs., a leg, couped at thigh, quarterly, or and sa., spurred, gold, on thigh a fess, gu. *Pl.* 81, *cr.* 5.

FOLIOT, and FOLIOTT, a battle-axe, ppr. *Hope to come. Pl.* 14, *cr.* 8.

FOLJAMBE, Yorks., an armed leg, couped at thigh, quarterly, or and sa., spurred, gold. *Pl.* 81, *cr.* 5.

FOLKENORTH, an ostrich, in mouth a (broken tilting-spear.) *Pl.* 16, *cr.* 2.

FOLKES, Middx., a dexter arm, erect, vested, per pale, vert and gu., cuff turned up, erm., in hand a spear, ppr. *Pl.* 39, *cr.* 1, (spear, same plate, *cr.* 15.)

FOLKES, Norf., a dexter arm., embowed, vested, per pale, vert and gu., cuffed, erm., in hand a spear, ppr. *Qui sera sera*—and—*Principiis obsta. Ib.*

FOLLER, a garb, or. *Pl.* 48, *cr.* 10.

FOLLET, FOLLETT, and FOLLOTT, a wolf, passant, regardant, transfixed by an (arrow.) *Pl.* 77, *cr.* 14.

FOLLETT, Devons., a demi-griffin, segreant, *Quo virtus ducit scando. Pl.* 18, *cr.* 6.

FOLLIOT, and FOLLIOTT, on a chapeau, ppr., a wyvern, sejant, vert. *Pl.* 104, *cr.* 5, (without crown.)

FOLMAN, Eng., a wolf, current, per pale, ar. and erm. *Pl.* 111, *cr.* 1.

FOLSHURST, Chesh., a unicorn's head, couped, or. *Pl.* 20, *cr.* 1.

FOLTON: 1. On a ducal coronet, a pair of wings, or and ar. *Pl.* 17, *cr.* 9. 2. A stag, lodged, gu., (ducally gorged and lined,) or, attired, vert, at top of each branch a bezant. *Pl.* 67, *cr.* 2, (bezant, *pl.* 141.)

FOLVILL, Chesh., a garb, per pale, or and vert, banded, counterchanged. *Pl.* 48, *cr.* 10.

FOLVILL, and FOLLEVILLE, a griffin's head, erased, in beak a sword, ppr. *Pl.* 35, *cr.* 15.

FONCE, a demi-lion, rampant, ducally gorged, between wings. *Pl.* 87, *cr.* 15, (wings, same plate, *cr.* 2.)

FONCEUX, a demi-lioness, ppr.

FONDRE, a moor's head, ppr. *Pl.* 120, *cr.* 3.

FONNEREAU, Lond. and Middx., the sun, or. *Pl.* 68, *cr.* 14.

FONNEREAU, Eng., a lion, rampant, supporting a garb, ppr. *Pl.* 63, *cr.* 14.

FONTAIN, and FONTAINE, a raven's nest, with young birds, ppr. *Pl.* 56, *cr.* 5.

FONTAIN, and FONTAINE, an eagle's head, erased, ppr. *Pl.* 20, *cr.* 7.

FOORD, Eng., a flag, displayed, gu. *Pl.* 52, *cr.* 14.

FOOT, HENRY-BALDWIN, Esq., of Carrigacunna Castle, co. Cork, a pelican in nest, feeding her young, ppr. *Virescit vulnere, virtus. Pl.* 44, *cr.* 1.

FOOT, Eng., a demi-griffin, regardant, gu., winged, or, holding a flag, displayed, of the first, charged with a crescent, ar. *Pl.* 46, *cr.* 1.

FOOTE, Iri., a greyhound's head, per fess, ar. and sa., collared, gu. *Pl.* 43, *cr.* 11.

FOOTE, Kent and Cornw., a lion's head, erased, ar., charged with an ermine spot, sa. *Pl.* 81, *cr.* 4.

FOOTE, Kent, a lion's head, erased, ar. *Pedetentim. Pl.* 81, *cr.* 4.

FOOTE, Devons., a (naked) arm, erect, ppr., in hand a trefoil, slipped, sa. *Pl.* 78, *cr.* 6.

FOOTE, Lond., an arm, erect, vested, sa., cuffed, ar., in hand, ppr., a trefoil, slipped, sa. *Pl.* 78, *cr.* 6.

FOQUETT, Eng., a horse's head, ar., in mail, az., bridled, or, on head a plume of ostrich-feathers, of the first. *Pl.* 55, *cr.* 7.

FORBES, Lord, and Bart., (Forbes,) Sco., a stag's head, ppr. *Grace me guide. Pl.* 91, *cr.* 14.

FORBES, Bart., of Craigievar, Sco., a cock, ppr. *Watch and pray. Pl.* 67, *cr.* 14.

FORBES, Bart., of Pitsligo, Sco.: 1. A heart, between wings. *Pl.* 52, *cr.* 2, (without coronet.) 2. Out of a baron's coronet, in hand a scimitar, all ppr. *Pl.* 103, *cr.* 2, (coronet, *pl.* 127, *fig.* 11.) 3. A dexter arm in hand a sword. *Nec timide, nec temere. Pl.* 34, *cr.* 7.

FORBES, Bart., of Edinglassie, Sco., a dexter arm, in armour, embowed, ppr., garnished, or, in hand a Highland broadsword, also ppr. *Nec timide, nec temere*—and—*Altius ibunt qui ad summa nituntur. Pl.* 2, *cr.* 8.

FORBES, CHARLES-HENRY, of Kingerlock, Argyle, a stag's head, attired, ppr. *Solus inter plurimos. Pl.* 91, *cr.* 14.

FORBES, HENRY-DAVID, Esq., of Balgownie, Aberdeen, a cock, ppr. *Watch. Pl.* 67, *cr.* 14.

FORBES, Earl of Granard. *See* GRANARD.

FORBES, Sco., a griffin's head, erased. *Pl.* 48, *cr.* 6.

FORBES, Sco., a dexter hand holding a battle-axe, ppr. *Salus mea Christus*—and—*Dinna waken sleepin' dogs. Pl.* 73, *cr.* 7.

FORBES, Sco., the sun in splendour. *Spero. Pl.* 68, *cr.* 14.

FORBES, Sco., in hand a dagger, in pale, ppr. *Spero. Pl.* 23, *cr.* 15.

FORBES, of Jolly-how, a stag's head, erased, ppr. *Salus per Christum. Pl.* 66, *cr.* 9.

FORBES, of Newe, an arm, in armour, in hand a broadsword, ppr. *Non temere. Pl.* 2, *cr.* 8.

FORBES, of Brux, an eagle's head, erased, ppr. *Nec mons nec substrahit aer. Pl.* 20, *cr.* 7.

FORBES, an eagle, displayed, ppr. *Spernit humum. Pl.* 48, *cr.* 11.

FORBES, of Corsindae, a bear's head. *Spe expecto. Pl.* 2, *cr.* 9.

FORBES, of Foveran, a cross pattée, ar. *Salus per Christum. Pl.* 15, *cr.* 8.

FORBES, of Polquhor, a stag's head, attired, with ten tynes, ppr. *Salus per Christum. Pl.* 91, *cr.* 14.

FORBES, of Corse, a wreath or crown of thorns, *Rosas coronat spina. Pl.* 78, *cr.* 7.
FORBES, of Watertown, an eagle, displayed, sa. *Virtuti inimica quies. Pl.* 48, *cr.* 11.
FORBES, of Colecden, an eagle, displayed, or. *Salus per Christum. Pl.* 48, *cr.* 11.
FORBES, of Balling, a skean, piercing a man's heart, ppr. *Non deest spes. Pl.* 21, *cr.* 15.
FORBES, of Robslaw, a dove, ppr. *Virtute cresco. Pl.* 66, *cr.* 12.
FORBES, of Echt, a sand-glass, ppr. *Fugit hora. Pl.* 43, *cr.* 1.
FORBES, of Allford, Eng., in hand, out of a cloud, an anchor, ppr. *Non deest spes. Pl.* 41, *cr.* 5.
FORBES, of Monymusk, Bart., a man's heart, ppr., winged, or. *Spe expecto. Pl.* 39, *cr.* 7.
FORBES, of Ardo, a stag's head, couped, gu., attired, ar. *Cura et candore. Pl.* 91, *cr.* 14.
FORBES, of Auchreddy, a sword, in bend, ppr. *Scieniter utor. Pl.* 22, *cr.* 7.
FORBES, of Ballogie, a sheaf of arrows, ppr. *Concordia præsto. Pl.* 43, *cr.* 14.
FORBES, of Milbuy, a bear's head, muzzled. *Virtute, non ferocia. Pl.* 2, *cr.* 9.
FORBES, of Culloden, an eagle, rising. *Salus per Christum—*or*—Spernit humum. Pl.* 67, *cr.* 4.
FORBES, a greyhound, (passant,) ppr. *Delectatio. Pl.* 11, *cr.* 1, (without trees or mount.)
FORBES-LEITH, of Whitehaugh, Aberdeens.: 1. A pelican, vulning, ppr. *I die for those I love. Pl.* 109, *cr.* 15. 2. A stag's head. *Salus per Christum. Pl.* 91, *cr.* 14. 3. A dove and olive-branch, ppr. *Fidus ad extremum. Pl.* 48, *cr.* 15.
FORBISHER, on a chapeau, the sun in splendour. *Pl.* 68, *cr.* 14, (chapeau, *pl.* 127, *fig.* 13.)
FORBS, a bear's head, muzzled. *Pl.* 2, *cr.* 9.
FORCER, Durh., a fox, sejant, ppr., (pierced by an arrow, or, feathered, ar.) *Pl.* 87, *cr.* 4.
FORD, WILLIAM, Esq., of Ellell Hall, Lanc., a lion, rampant, bearing a coronet. *Excitat. Pl.* 9, *cr.* 7.
FORD, CHARLES-INGRAM, Esq., of Abbeyfield, Chesh., a lion's head, erased, az. *Pl.* 81, *cr.* 4.
FORD, Bart., Surr., a greyhound's head, sa., erased, gu., (muzzled,) or. *Omnium rerum vicissitudo. Pl.* 89, *cr.* 2.
FORD, Eng., a greyhound's head, erased, ar. *Pl.* 89, *cr.* 2.
FORD, a greyhound's head, issuant, ppr. *Pl.* 43, *cr.* 11, (without collar.)
FORD, Iri., a greyhound's head, issuant, sa. *Ib.*
FORD, Sco., a demi-greyhound, ar. *Fortis in arduis. Pl.* 48, *cr.* 3.
FORD, a demi-lion, rampant. *Pl.* 67, *cr.* 10.
FORD, a demi-lion, rampant, crowned, or. *Pl.* 61, *cr.* 4, (without branch.)
FORD, a lion, rampant. *Pl.* 67, *cr.* 5.
FORD, Glouc., Kent, and Suff., out of a naval coronet, a bear's head, sa., muzzled. *Pl.* 2, *cr.* 9, (coronet, *pl.* 128, *fig.* 19.)
FORDAM, and FORDHAM, on a mount, vert, a peacock, ppr. *Pl.* 9, *cr.* 1.
FORDE, a tiger, sejant, ppr. *Pl.* 26, *cr.* 9.
FORDE, Iri., a greyhound's head, issuant, sa. *Pl.* 43, *cr.* 11, (without collar.)
FORDE, WILLIAM-BROWNLOW, Esq., of Seaford, co. Down, a martlet, or. *Incorrupta fides nudaque veritas. Pl.* 111, *cr.* 5.

FORDER, Surr., a Hawthorn-tree, vert. *Pl.* 18, *cr.* 10.
FORDYCE, Sco., a camel's head, couped at neck, ppr. *Persevere. Pl.* 109, *cr.* 9.
FORDYCE, Sco., an eagle, volant, ppr., (in its claws an escroll, with the motto—*Altius ibunt qui ad summa nituntur.*) *Pl.* 114, *cr.* 10.
FORDYCE-DINGWALL, ALEXANDER, Esq., of Brucklay Castle, Aberdeens.: 1. An eagle, displayed. *Pl.* 48, *cr.* 11. 2. A stag, couchant. *Altius ibunt qui ad summa nituntur—*and*—In arduis fortis. Pl.* 67, *cr.* 2.
FORDYCE, a stag, lodged, ppr. *In arduis fortis. Pl.* 67, *cr.* 2.
FOREMAN, and FORMAN, Sco., in hand a short scimitar, ppr. *True to the end. Pl.* 29, *cr.* 8.
FORESIGHT, Sco., two wings, expanded, ppr. *Sum quod sum. Pl.* 39, *cr.* 12.
FOREST, Eng., a grenade, fired, ppr. *Pl.* 70, *cr.* 12.
FOREST, a squirrel, sejant, cracking a nut, ppr. *Pl.* 16, *cr.* 9.
FORESTER, Baron, (Weld-Forester): 1. For *Forester,* a talbot, passant, ar., collared, sa., and line reflexed, or. *Pl.* 65, *cr.* 2. 2. For *Weld,* a wyvern, sa., guttée-d'or, (collared,) and interior of the wings, of the last. *Semper eadem. Pl.* 63, *cr.* 13.
FORESTER, a talbot, passant, ar., collared and chained, or. *Pl.* 65, *cr.* 2.
FORESTER, a marigold, slipped and leaved, ppr. *Pl.* 105, *cr.* 15.
FORICAN, Eng., an elephant's head, erased, sa., eared and armed, ar. *Pl.* 68, *cr.* 4.
FORINGTON, a dragon, (sans wings, tail extended,) per fess, or and vert. *Pl.* 90, *cr.* 10.
FORKINGTON, a demi-greyhound, sa., collared, or. *Pl.* 5, *cr.* 10, (without wings.)
FORMAN, Lond. and Leic., a demi-dragon, vert. *Pl.* 82, *cr.* 10.
FORMAN, Eng., a demi-griffin, holding a ducal coronet. *Pl.* 18, *cr.* 6, (coronet, *same plate, cr.* 11.)
FORMBY, a dove, ppr. *Semper fidelis. Pl.* 66, *cr.* 12.
FORNERS, and FORNEYS, a wheel, az. *Pl.* 32, *cr.* 15.
FORREST, Bart., on a mount, vert, an oak-tree, ppr. *Vivant dum virent. Pl.* 48, *cr.* 4.
FORREST, Eng. and Sco., an oak-tree, ppr. *Vivant dum virent. Pl.* 16, *cr.* 8.
FORREST, Sco., in hand, couped, in fess, a cross crosslet, fitched. *Pl.* 78, *cr.* 9.
FORRESTER, Eng., a fountain, ppr. *Pl.* 95, *cr.* 15.
FORRESTER, Baron, Sco. See VERULAM, Earl of.
FORRESTER, Sco., a hunting-horn. *Blow, hunter, the horn. Pl.* 89, *cr.* 3.
FORRESTER, a stag's head, erased. *Pl.* 66, *cr.* 9.
FORRESTER, Sco., a lily, growing through a thorn-bush, ppr. *Spernit pericula virtus. Pl.* 112, *cr.* 3.
FORRESTER, a talbot, (statant,) ar., collared, lined and ringed, or. *Pl.* 65, *cr.* 2.
FORRESTER, Sco., a greyhound (in a leash,) ppr. *Recreation. Pl.* 104, *cr.* 1, (without chapeau.)
FORRESTER, Sco., in dexter-hand a hunting-horn, ppr. *It is good to be blown. Pl.* 109, *cr.* 3.
FORREST-OGLE, a hunting-horn, sa., stringed, gu. *I hope. Pl.* 48, *cr.* 12.
FORSAN, Eng., a griffin's head, per fess, az. and or. *Pl.* 38, *cr.* 3.

FORSER, Durh., a fox, sejant, ppr., (wounded in neck by an arrow, or, feathered, ar.) *Pl.* 87, *cr.* 4.

FORSET, and FORSETT, Middx., a demi-lion, sa., supporting a column, gobony, ar. and gu., the capital and base, or. *Pl.* 29, *cr.* 12, (column, *pl.* 33, *cr.* 1.)

FORSHAM, a talbot's head, ar., eared and spotted, gu. and sa. *Pl.* 123, *cr.* 15.

FORSTER, Lond. and Camb., an arm, in armour, embowed, ar., braced, or, in hand a broken tilting-spear, of the last. *Pl.* 44, *cr.* 9.

FORSTER, Lond., a buck, sa., attired, or. *Pl.* 68, *cr.* 2.

FORSTER, an arm, embowed, vested, sa., charged with a pheon, or, between two bezants, in pale, in hand a bow and arrow, ar. *Pl.* 112, *cr.* 1.

FORSTER, Lond., a dexter arm, in armour, embowed, ar., purfled and braced, or, round the arm a sash, vert, in hand, ppr., an arrow, of the third, broken off at the head, barbed, of the second. *Pl.* 96, *cr.* 6, (sash, *pl.* 28, *cr.* 2.)

FORSTER, Middx. and Suss., a stag at gaze, sa., attired, or. *Pl.* 81, *cr.* 8.

FORSTER, Northumb., an arm, in armour, ppr., in hand a broken tilting-spear, or. *Pl.* 44, *cr.* 9.

FORSTER, Northumb., a stag, sa., attired and guttée, or. *Pl.* 68, *cr.* 2.

FORSTER, Suss., a talbot's head, erased, or, collared and ringed, gu. *Pl.* 2, *cr.* 15.

FORSTER, Northumb., a buck, trippant, ppr. *Pl.* 68, *cr.* 2.

FORSTER, Salop, a talbot, passant, ar., collared and lined, or, the line nowed at the end. *Pl.* 65, *cr.* 2.

FORSTER, Berks., Somers., and Warw., a hind's head, gu., ducally gorged and lined, or. *Pl.* 6, *cr.* 1, (gorging, *same plate*.)

FORSTER, Berks., a stag, (regardant, gu., charged with a martlet,) or, pierced through neck by an arrow, az. *Pl.* 88, *cr.* 9.

FORSTER, Iri., a heart, pierced by a sword in bend sinister, point downward. *Pl.* 21, *cr.* 15.

FORSTER, Suss. and Worc., a stag's head, erased, ar., attired, or, gorged with a collar and line, gold. *Pl.* 125, *cr.* 6, (without roses.)

FORSTER, Suff. and Warw., a stag's head, erased. *Pl.* 66, *cr.* 9.

FORSTER, out of a ducal coronet, or, a stag's head. *Pl.* 29, *cr.* 7.

FORSTER, a demi-boar, az., armed and crined, or. *Pl.* 20, *cr.* 5.

FORSYTH, Sco., a demi-griffin, vert. *Instaurator ruinæ*. *Pl.* 18, *cr.* 6.

FORSYTH, Eng., a cup, gu. *Pl.* 42, *cr.* 1.

FORSYTHE, Sco., a demi-griffin, vert, armed and ducally crowned, or. *Pl.* 18, *cr.* 6, (crown, *same plate*.)

FORT, or FORTE, Eng., a cock, gu., in beak a (daisy,) ppr. *Pl.* 55, *cr.* 12.

FORT, or FORTE, on a rock, a tower, ppr. *Inest clementia forti*. *Pl.* 31, *cr.* 15.

FORT, on a mount, vert, a lion, sejant, (gardant, pellettée, collared,) gu., in dexter a cross crosslet, fitched, of the last. *Pl.* 108, *cr.* 12, (cross, *pl.* 141.)

FORTEATH, GEORGE-ALEXANDER, Esq., of Newton House, Elgin, a buck's head, erased, ppr. *Tam animo quam mente sublimis*. *Pl.* 66, *cr.* 9.

FORTESCUE, Baron Fortescue, Eng., a plain shield, ar. *Forte scutum salus ducum*. *Pl.* 36, *cr.* 11.

FORTESCUE, Baron, Iri., same crest and motto.

FORTESCUE, WILLIAM-BLUNDELL, Esq., of Fallapit, Devons., a tiger, passant, ar., armed and maned, or. *Forte scutum salus ducum*. *Pl.* 67, *cr.* 15.

FORTESCUE, Earl and Baron, Viscount Ebrington, (Fortescue,) an heraldic-tiger, supporting with dexter a plain shield, ar. *Forte scutum salus ducum*. *Pl.* 119, *cr.* 9, (shield, *pl.* 42, *cr.* 8.)

FORTESCUE, Devons., an escutcheon, ar. *Pl.* 36, *cr.* 11.

FORTESCUE, Surr., a tiger, passant, or. *Pl.* 67, *cr.* 15.

FORTESCUE, Lanc. and Bucks., a tiger, passant, ar., maned, armed, and tufted, or. *Pl.* 67, *cr.* 15.

FORTESCUE, Ess. and Iri., a leopard, passant, gardant, ppr. *Pl.* 51, *cr.* 7.

FORTH, Suff., a bear's head, erased, sa., muzzled, or. *Pl.* 71, *cr.* 6.

FORTH, Suff., a bear's head, erased, sa., muzzled, gu. *Pl.* 71, *cr.* 6.

FORTH, Lond., a hind's head, couped, vert, guttée, collared and lined, or. *Pl.* 21, *cr.* 9.

FORTIBUS, DE, Eng., an escarbuncle, or. *Pl.* 51, *cr.* 10.

FORTISCUE, a leopard, passant, resting dexter on a plain shield. *Pl.* 86, *cr.* 2, (shield, *pl.* 42, *cr.* 8.)

FORTRYE, a lion, rampant, holding a (tilting-spear,) ppr. *Pl.* 22, *cr.* 15.

FORTUN, Sco., a dolphin, haurient, az. *Ditat Deus*. *Pl.* 14, *cr.* 10.

FORTUNE, Eng., a demi-lion, gardant, az., in dexter a battle-axe, or. *Pl.* 26, *cr.* 7.

FORTUNE, Sco., on a chapeau, a stag, trippant, ppr. *Pl.* 63, *cr.* 8.

FORTY, Eng., on a ducal coronet, a mullet, between two branches of laurel, in orle, ppr. *Pl.* 82, *cr.* 6.

FORTY, Eng., in lion's paw, erased, sa., a cross pattée, fitched, gu. *Pl.* 46, *cr.* 7.

FOSBROOKE, and FOSBROOKE, Lond. and Derbs., two bears' gambs, sa., supporting a spear, erect, ppr. *Pl.* 77, *cr.* 4, (spear, *pl.* 97, *cr.* 4.)

FOSCOTT, and FOXCOTE, a dove and olive-branch, ppr. *Pl.* 48, *cr.* 15.

FOSKETT, a broken spear, in pale, the end hanging in bend. *Pl.* 3, *cr.* 6.

FOSKETT, Herts., an arm, in armour, embowed, in hand a cross-bow. *Pl.* 76, *cr.* 10, (crossbow, *pl.* 58, *cr.* 3.)

FOSS, Eng., a thistle and rose-branch, in saltier, ppr. *Pl.* 57, *cr.* 10.

FOSTER, Bart., Iri., an arm, in armour, embowed, the hand bare, grasping the butt end of a broken spear, all ppr. *Pl.* 44, *cr.* 9.

FOSTER, out of a mural coronet, chequy, ar. and sa., a buck's head, ppr., attired, or, in mouth an arrow, of the first. *Pl.* 112, *cr.* 5.

FOSTER, JOHN-FREDERICK, Esq., of the Bogue Estates, Jamaica, and of Kempstone, Beds., an arm, in armour, embowed, in hand the head of a broken tilting-spear. *Si fractus fortis*. *Pl.* 44, *cr.* 9.

FOSTER, Viscount Ferrard. *See* FERRARD.

FOSTER, Yorks., an elephant, ppr. *Vix ea nostro voco*. *Pl.* 56, *cr.* 14.

FOSTER, Bart., Norwich, a stag, ppr., (resting dexter on an escutcheon, gu., charged with a tower, ar.) *Pl.* 68, *cr.* 2.
FOSTER, a stag's head. *Redde diem. Pl.* 91, *cr.* 14.
FOSTER, a lion's head, erased, or, collared, gu. *Pl.* 7, *cr.* 10.
FOSTER, a stag's head, quarterly, sa. and ar., attired, or. *Pl.* 91, *cr.* 14.
FOSTER, Bart., Iri., a stag, ppr. *Gloria divina patria. Pl.* 68, *cr.* 2.
FOSTER, Worc., an antelope's head, erased, ar., attired, armed, and (collared, or, from the front of the collar a line and ring flowing, gold.) *Pl.* 24, *cr.* 7.
FOSTER, Berks., a stag's head, erased, ppr. *Pl.* 66, *cr.* 9.
FOSTER, a stag, trippant, ppr. *Pl.* 68, *cr.* 2.
FOSTER-HILL: 1. For *Foster*, an arm, in armour, embowed, in hand, a spear, all ppr. *Pl.* 44, *cr.* 9. 2. For *Hill*, a talbot's head, erased, or, collared, gu. *Pl.* 2, *cr.* 15.
FOSTON, Eng., a gate, az. *Pl.* 73, *cr.* 4.
FOTHERBY, Kent and Linc., a falcon, wings expanded, ppr., beaked, and in mouth an acorn, or, leaved, ppr. *Pl.* 49, *cr.* 1, (acorn, *pl.* 60, *cr.* 8.)
FOTHERGILL, RICHARD, Esq., Aberdare, Glamorg., a talbot, passant, collared. *Pl.* 65, *cr.* 2.
FOTHERGILL, on a rock, a lion, rampant, ppr., collared and chained, or, in dexter an arrow, sa. *Pl.* 121, *cr.* 15.
FOTHERGILL, a stag, ppr. *Pl.* 68, *cr.* 2.
FOTHERINGHAM, a pelican, vulning, feeding her young in a nest. *Pl.* 44, *cr.* 1.
FOTHERINGHAM, a griffin's head, erased, ppr. *Be it fast. Pl.* 48, *cr.* 6.
FOTHERINGHAM, a griffin, sejant. *Be it fast. Pl.* 100, *cr.* 11.
FOTHERINGHAM, Sco., a griffin's head, sa. *Pl.* 38, *cr.* 3.
FOTHERLEY, a lion's gamb, erased, or, grasping a wolf's head, erased, ar. *Pl.* 60, *cr.* 14, (head, *pl.* 14, *cr.* 6.)
FOUK, Eng., a cross pattée, erm. *Pl.* 15, *cr.* 8.
FOULER, Sco., a stag's head, erased, gu., armed, ar. *Pl.* 66, *cr.* 9.
FOULERTON, Eng., a Cornish chough, sa. *Pl.* 100, *cr.* 13.
FOULIS, Bart., Yorks., a cross, fitched, sa. *Pl.* 16, *cr.* 10.
FOULIS, Bart., Sco., in dexter hand, in fess, couped at wrist, a sword in pale, supporting a wreath of laurel, all ppr. *Mente manuque præsto*—and — *Non deficit* — and — *Thure et jure. Pl.* 56, *cr.* 6.
FOULIS, Sco., a flower-pot, with a branch of laurel springing out of it. *Pl.* 35, *cr.* 1.
FOULIS, Yorks., in a crescent, ar., a cross formée, of the same. *Pl.* 37, *cr.* 10.
FOULIS, Sco., a dove, in mouth an olive-leaf, ppr. *Pax. Pl.* 48, *cr.* 15.
FOULIS, of Ravelston, Sco., a dove, volant, in mouth a leaf, ppr. *Thure et jure. Pl.* 25, *cr.* 6.
FOULKE, Worc., a squirrel, sejant, bezantée, collared, or, holding an acorn-branch, vert, fructed, of the second. *Pl.* 2, *cr.* 4.
FOULKES, Eng., a lion's head, erased and collared, per pale, ar. and sa., counterchanged. *Pl.* 7, *cr.* 10.
FOULKES, a boar's head, couped, sa. *Pl.* 48, *cr.* 2.
FOULKES, Eng., a boar's head, couped, in fess. *Pl.* 48, *cr.* 2.

FOULKS, out of a tower, ar., a demi-eagle, sa., beaked, or, in mouth a fleur-de-lis, gu. *Pl.* 112, *cr.* 4.
FOULLER, a greyhound's head, (erased,) sa., collared, or. *Pl.* 43, *cr.* 15.
FOULSHURST, Chesh. and Lanc., a unicorn's head, erminois, attired, or. *Pl.* 20, *cr.* 1.
FOUNDER, and FOUNDOWRE, out of a ducal coronet, a griffin's head, between wings, ppr. *Pl.* 97, *cr.* 13, (without charge.)
FOUNTAIN, Devons., an eagle's head, erased, in beak a snake. *Pl.* 20, *cr.* 7, (snake, *pl.* 41, *cr.* 6.)
FOUNTAIN, of Lochhill, Sco., an eagle, rising, ppr. *Præclarius quo difficilius. Pl.* 67, *cr.* 4.
FOUNTAINE, Norf., an elephant, ppr. *Vix ea nostra voco. Pl.* 56, *cr.* 14.
FOUNTAYNE, Yorks., Norf., and Bucks., an elephant's head, couped, or, armed, ar., (vulned in neck, gu.) *Pl.* 35, *cr.* 13.
FOUNTBERY, a cross pattée, ar., environed by a snake, vert. *Pl.* 112, *cr.* 6.
FOURACRE, New-York, a demi-griffin, or, between paws an escallop, gu. *Pl.* 18, *cr.* 6, (escallop, *pl.* 141.)
FOURBINS, Eng., a sheaf of arrows, ppr., banded, gu. *Pl.* 43, *cr.* 14.
FOURDRINIER, Eng., on a chapeau, a unicorn's head, ppr. *Pl.* 102, *cr.* 7.
FOURNIER, Eng., a martlet, per fess, az. and ar. *Pl.* 111, *cr.* 5.
FOVELL, Chesh., a garb, per pale, or and sa., banded, counterchanged. *Pl.* 48, *cr.* 10.
FOWBERY, Yorks. and Durh., a stag's head, ar., attired, or, charged on neck with three trefoils, vert. *Pl.* 91, *cr.* 14, (trefoil, *pl.* 82, *cr.* 1.)
FOWBERY, Hunts., a stag's head, ar., attired, or, charged on neck with three trefoils, slipped, vert, one and two, in mouth (a rose, gu., stalked and leaved, vert.) *Pl.* 100, *cr.* 8, (trefoil, *pl.* 82, *cr.* 1.)
FOWELL, Devons., out of a mural coronet, an antelope's head, ar., attired, gu. *Pl.* 24, *cr.* 7, (coronet, *same plate, cr.* 12.)
FOWELL, a griffin's head, erased, ar., (pierced through breast by an arrow, ppr.) *Pl.* 48, *cr.* 6.
FOWKE, Bart., Leic., a dexter arm, embowed, vested, vert, cuffed, ar., in hand, ppr., an arrow, or, barbed and flighted, of the second, point downward. *Pl.* 112, *cr.* 1, (without bow.)
FOWKE, Lond., Dors., and Staffs., an Indian goat's head, erased, ar. *Pl.* 72, *cr.* 9.
FOWKE, Iri., an arm, couped at shoulder, embowed, and resting elbow on wreath, in hand a spear, in pale, ppr. *Pl.* 19, *cr.* 5.
FOWKES, Eng., a golden fleece, ppr. *Pl.* 77, *cr.* 12.
FOWKROY, in lion's gamb, an ostrich-feather, ppr. *Pl.* 58, *cr.* 7.
FOWLE, Kent and Suss., a griffin's head, erased, ar., (pierced through neck by an arrow, gu., barbed, of the first, vulned, of the second.) *Pl.* 48, *cr.* 6.
FOWLE, Suss. and Wilts., out of a ducal coronet, or, an arm, in armour, embowed, ppr., garnished, gold, in hand a battle-axe of the same. *Pl.* 122, *cr.* 8, (axe, *pl.* 73, *cr.* 7.)
FOWLE, Norf., an antelope's head, (pierced by an arrow.) *Pl.* 24, *cr.* 7.
FOWLER, Staffs., a cubit arm, (vested,) az., in hand, ppr., a hawk's lure, vert. *Pl.* 44, *cr.* 2.

FOWLER, Beds. and Staffs., an owl, ar., ducally crowned, gu. *Pl.* 27, *cr.* 9, (coronet, *same plate.*)
FOWLER, Surr., an owl, ar., ducally crowned, or. *Ib.*
FOWLER, a stork, ar., membered, gu., in bill a cross formée, fitched, or. *Pl.* 33, *cr.* 9, (cross, *pl.* 27, *cr.* 14.)
FOWLER, Iri., on a chapeau, an owl, rising, gardant, ppr. *Pl.* 123, *cr.* 6.
FOWLER, Glouc. and Sco., an ostrich's head, or, between wings, ar., in beak a horse-shoe, az. *Pl.* 28, *cr.* 13.
FOWLES, Eng., a stag's head, couped, sa. *Pl.* 91, *cr.* 14.
FOWLES, between the horns of a crescent, ar., a cross pattée, fitched, sa. *Pl.* 37, *cr.* 10.
FOWLIS, a sword, in pale, on point a garland. *Pl.* 15, *cr.* 6.
FOWLIS, a dove and olive-branch, ppr. *Pl.* 48, *cr.* 15.
FOWNE, an arm, in armour, embowed, in hand a fleur-de-lis. *Pl.* 24, *cr.* 14.
FOWNES, Eng., a hawk, in dexter an ear of wheat, ppr. *Pl.* 94, *cr.* 7.
FOWNES, Iri., a unicorn's head, erased, gu., armed and bearded, or. *Pl.* 117, *cr.* 3, (without fleur-de-lis.)
FOWNES, out of a ducal coronet, a demi-eagle, wings expanded. *Pl.* 9, *cr.* 6.
FOWTES, a flower-pot, gu., springing thereout an olive-branch, ppr. *Pl.* 35, *cr.* 1.
FOX, Lond., out of a ducal coronet, a greyhound's head, or. *Pl.* 70, *cr.* 5.
FOX, a sceptre, between wings. *Pl.* 82, *cr.* 3, (wings, *pl.* 69, *cr.* 7.)
FOX, an eagle, displayed, sa. *Pl.* 48, *cr.* 11.
FOX, Iri., a fox, sejant, ppr. *Pl.* 87, *cr.* 4.
FOX, Iri., a castle, sa., masoned, ar. *Pl.* 28, *cr.* 11.
FOX, on a chapeau, a fox, passant, between two cross crosslets. *Pl.* 126, *cr.* 5, (cross, *pl.* 66, *cr.* 8; chapeau, *pl.* 128, *fig.* 13.)
FOX, a fox, current, (regardant.) *Pl.* 80, *cr.* 5.
FOX, Lond. and Wilts., on a chapeau, az., turned up, erm., a fox, sejant, or. *Pl.* 57, *cr.* 14.
FOX, Northamp., a fox, passant, (regardant,) per pale, ar. and gu., in mouth a rose-branch, flowered, of the last, stalked and leaved, vert. *Pl.* 126, *cr.* 5, (rose, *pl.* 118, *cr.* 9.)
FOX, Derb., a fox, passant, az. *Pl.* 126, *cr.* 5.
FOX, Heref., Leic., and Salop, a fox, passant, gu. *Pl.* 126, *cr.* 5.
FOX, Eng., on a mount, an oak-tree, growing among grass, ppr. *Pl.* 48, *cr.* 4.
FOX, Lond. and Yorks., a fox's head, erased, ppr. *Pl.* 71, *cr.* 4.
FOX, in hand, gu., a mill-rind, sa. *Pl.* 34, *cr.* 3.
FOX, Bucks., a lion, sejant, gardant, supporting with dexter a book, all or. *Pl.* 113, *cr.* 8, (book, *pl.* 117, *cr.* 7.)
FOX, Durh., on a chapeau, az., turned up, erm., a fox, sejant, or. *Video et taceo. Pl.* 57, *cr.* 14.
FOX, a fox's head, erased, gu., (collared and ringed, or.) *Pl.* 71, *cr.* 4.
FOXALL, Lond., a griffin's head, or, erased and ducally gorged, gu. *Pl.* 42, *cr.* 9, (without laurel.)
FOXALL, out of a ducal coronet, or, a greyhound's head, gold. *Pl.* 70, *cr.* 5.

FOXALL, Iri., two hands couped and conjoined, in fess, supporting a cross crosslet, fitched. *Pl.* 52, *cr.* 15.
FOXE, Iri., a fox, sejant, ppr. *Pl.* 87, *cr.* 4.
FOXFORD, Baron. *See* LIMERICK, Earl of.
FOXLEY, Berks., a hawk's leg, erased at thigh, and belled, ppr. *Pl.* 83, *cr.* 7.
FOX-STRANGWAYS, Earl of Ilchester. *See* ILCHESTER.
FOXTON, Lond. and Cambs., a rose, ar., barbed, vert. *Pl.* 20, *cr.* 2.
FOX-VASSALL, Baron Holland. *See* HOLLAND.
FOXWELL, Eng., a galley, ppr. *Pl.* 34, *cr.* 5.
FOXWEST, Lond., a reindeer's head, erased, ppr. *Pl.* 2, *cr.* 13, (without collar.)
FOY, Eng., an eel, ppr. *Pl.* 25, *cr.* 13.
FOYLE, Hants and Dors., a horse's head, ar., crined, gu., gorged with two bars, compony, or and sa. *Pl.* 81, *cr.* 6.
FOYLE, Hants and Wilts., a cross crosslet, fitched, ar., between (dragon's) wings, chequy, or and az. *Pl.* 34, *cr.* 14.
FOYLER, on a ducal coronet, a fleur-de-lis. *Pl.* 68, *cr.* 12, (coronet, *same plate.*)
FOYSTER, a demi-stag, ppr., attired, or, (collared with a bar-gemelle, gu., sustaining a bugle-horn, gold.) *Pl.* 55, *cr.* 9, (without rose.)
FRAIGNEAU, Lond., a stork, close, ar., beaked and membered, gu., (in beak a slip of ash, ppr.) *Pl.* 33, *cr.* 9.
FRAME, Eng., on a mount, an ermine, ppr. *Pl.* 87, *cr.* 3.
FRAMINGHAM, Eng., a demi-moor, brandishing a scimitar, and therewith attacking a tiger, issuing on the sinister side. *Pl.* 62, *cr.* 2.
FRAMPTON, Dors., a greyhound, sejant, ar., collared and winged, gu. *Pl.* 101, *cr.* 7.
FRAMPTON, out of a mural coronet, a demi-griffin, holding between claws a mullet. *Pl.* 18, *cr.* 6, (coronet, *pl.* 128, *fig.* 18; mullet, *pl.* 141.)
FRAMYNGHAM, Suff., a camel's head, (erased, az., bezantée.) *Pl.* 109, *cr.* 9.
FRANCE, Eng., a stag, springing, ppr. *Pl.* 65, *cr.* 14.
FRANCE, Sco., on a mount, an oak-tree, fructed, ppr. *Pl.* 48, *cr.* 4.
FRANCE, Chester, on a mount, a hurst, ppr., from the centre tree a shield pendent, gu., charged with a fleur-de-lis, or, strap, az. *Virtus semper viridis.*
FRANCES, Sco., stump of oak-tree, shooting a branch from the sinister, vert. *Pl.* 92, *cr.* 8.
FRANCHE, a griffin, segreant, ppr., (collared and lined,) or. *Pl.* 67, *cr.* 13.
FRANCHEVILLE, Eng., two wings, addorsed. *Pl.* 63, *cr.* 12.
FRANCIES, and FRANCES, a lion, resting dexter on an escallop. *Pl.* 48, *cr.* 8, (escallop, *pl.* 141.)
FRANCIES, and FRANCES, issuing from a cloud, a hand seizing a stag by the horns. *Pl.* 46, *cr.* 10.
FRANCIS, out of a ducal coronet, or, a demi-lion, gu. *Pl.* 45, *cr.* 7.
FRANCIS, Staffs., out of a ducal coronet, or, a demi-eagle, displayed, gu. *Pl.* 9, *cr.* 6.
FRANCIS, an eagle, wings addorsed, in dexter a vine-branch, fructed, ppr. *Pl.* 61, *cr.* 1, (vine, *pl.* 89, *cr.* 1.)
FRANCIS, a lamb, passant. *Pl.* 48, *cr.* 13.

FRANCIS, Kent, an eagle, displayed, sa. *Pl.* 48, *cr.* 11.
FRANCIS, Derbs. and Herts., on trunk of a vine-tree, fructed, an eagle, wings elevated, all ppr. *Pl.* 61, *cr.* 1, (vine, *pl.* 96, *cr.* 2.)
FRANCIS, a dove and olive-branch, ppr. *Pl.* 48, *cr.* 15.
FRANCIS, Derbs., an eagle, displayed, erm., beaked and membered, or. *Pl.* 48, *cr.* 11.
FRANCK, out of a mural coronet, or, a lion's head, gu., between wings, erminois. *Pl.* 45, *cr.* 9, (wings, *pl.* 39, *cr.* 12.)
FRANCKLIN, Eng., in dexter hand, ppr., a cross crosslet, fitched, or. *Pl.* 99, *cr.* 1.
FRANCKLIN, JOHN, Esq., of Goralston, Notts., a dolphin's head, or, erased, gu., between two olive-branches, vert. *Sinceritate*. *Pl.* 112, *cr.* 8.
FRANCKLYN, Eng., a dexter hand, in fess, couped, gu., charged with an eye, ppr. *Pl.* 10, *cr.* 14.
FRANCKLYN, Eng., a dexter arm, vested, purp., purfled and diapered, or, cuffed, ar., in hand, ppr., a palm-branch, vert. *Sub pace, copia*. *Pl.* 62, *cr.* 7.
FRANCO, Lond., a dexter arm, vested, purp., purfled and diapered, or, cuffed, ar., in hand, ppr., a palm-branch, vert. *Sub pace, copia*. *Pl.* 62, *cr.* 7.
FRANCOIS, Eng., on stump of tree, shooting branches, a hawk, belled, ppr. *Pl.* 78, *cr.* 8.
FRANCOYS, Eng., a bull's head, erased, sa. *Pl.* 19, *cr.* 3.
FRANK, Yorks. and Norf., a falcon, ppr. *Pl.* 67, *cr.* 3.
FRANK, a lion, salient, the tail forked, ppr. *Pl.* 67, *cr.* 5.
FRANK, Sco., a lion, (salient,) double queued, ppr. *Non omnibus nati*. *Pl.* 41, *cr.* 15.
FRANK, Eng., a goat's head, erased, or, armed, gu. *Pl.* 29, *cr.* 13.
FRANKE, Leic., out of a mural coronet, or, a dexter arm, vambraced, ar., garnished, or, in hand a falchion, ar., hilt and pommel, gold. *Pl.* 115, *cr.* 14.
FRANKFORT-DE-MONTMORENCY, Viscount, Iri., a peacock in its pride, ppr. *Dieu ayde*. *Pl.* 92, *cr.* 11.
FRANKLAND, Bart., Yorks., a dolphin, ar., haurient, and entwined round an anchor, erect, ppr. *Libera terra, liberque animus*. *Pl.* 35, *cr.* 14, (dolphin, *pl.* 14, *cr.* 10.)
FRANKLAND, Herts. and Wilts., an anchor, erect, sa., entwined by a dolphin, ar. *Ib*.
FRANKLAND, Lond., a dexter arm, couped and embowed, in fess, ppr., erect from the elbow, vested, az., cuffed, ar., frilled at shoulder, of the last, in hand a palm-branch, vert. *Pl.* 62, *cr.* 7.
FRANKLIN, a congre-eel's head, erect, or, erased, per fess, gu., between two branches, vert. *Pl.* 58, *cr.* 5, (branches, *pl.* 112, *cr.* 8.)
FRANKLIN, a dolphin's head, in pale, ar., erased, gu., finned, or, between branches, vert. *Pl.* 112, *cr.* 8.
FRANKLIN, Iri., a fox's head, erased. *Pl.* 71, *cr.* 4.
FRANKLYN, Middx. and Herts., a dolphin, naiant, ppr., finned, gu., (pierced through the sides by two fishing-spears, in saltier, or, tied together in a bow-knot, at the top.) *Pl.* 48, *cr.* 9.

FRANKLYN, Suff., a dolphin, ar., haurient, and entwined round an anchor, erect. *Pl.* 35, *cr.* 14, (dolphin, *pl.* 14, *cr.* 10.)
FRANKLYN, Yorks., a fish's head, in pale, or, erased, gu., between two sprigs, vert. *Pl.* 112, *cr.* 8.
FRANKLYN, a hind's head, erased, or, charged with three pellets, between wings, vairé, or and az. *Pl.* 6, *cr.* 1, (wings, *pl.* 1, *cr.* 15; pellet, *pl.* 141.)
FRANKLYN, a greyhound's head, brown, collared, or, between wings, ar. *Pl.* 43, *cr.* 11, (wings, *pl.* 1, *cr.* 15.)
FRANKS, Eng., a demi-lion, rampant, supporting the rudder of a ship. *Pl.* 102, *cr.* 4.
FRANKS, Yorks., a falcon, ppr. *Pl.* 67, *cr.* 3.
FRANKS, a stag's head, erased, ppr. *Pl.* 66, *cr.* 9.
FRANKS, on stump of tree, ppr., a falcon, or. *Pl.* 78, *cr.* 8.
FRANKS, on stump of tree, a hawk, ppr., charged on breast with a torteau. *Pl.* 78, *cr.* 8, (torteau, *pl.* 141.)
FRASER, Baron Saltoun. *See* SALTOUN.
FRASER, Bart., Sco., a buck's head, erased, gu. *Je suis prest*. *Pl.* 66, *cr.* 9.
FRASER, of Inverness, a dexter hand pointing with one finger. *Semper parati*. *Pl.* 35, *cr.* 5.
FRASER, Sco., on a globe, winged, an eagle rising. *In virtute et fortuna*. *Pl.* 50, *cr.* 7, (eagle, *pl.* 34, *cr.* 2.)
FRASER, of Fingask, a stag's head, erased, ppr., charged with an annulet. *Ubique paratus*. *Pl.* 66, *cr.* 9, (annulet, *pl.* 141.)
FRASER, Sco., an eagle, displayed, ppr. *Celas petit*. *Pl.* 48, *cr.* 11.
FRASER, of Auchnagarne, a stag's head, erased, ppr., charged with a crescent. *Pace et bello paratus*. *Pl.* 66, *cr.* 9, (crescent, *pl.* 141.)
FRASER, of Inchculter, a phœnix in flames, ppr. *Ex se ipso renascens*. *Pl.* 44, *cr.* 8.
FRASER, of Poppachie, same crest. *Non exstinquar*.
FRASER, of Inveralochy, a stag's head, ppr. *Je suis prest*. *Pl.* 91, *cr.* 14.
FRASER, Sco., a buck's head, erased. *Ready*. *Pl.* 66, *cr.* 9.
FRASER, Lond., same crest. *Paratus*.
FRASER, of Fyvie, an ostrich, in beak a horseshoe, ppr. *In God is all*. *Pl.* 16, *cr.* 2.
FRASER, of Fraserfield, same crest. *Quam sibi sortem*.
FRASER, of Knock, a rose, gu. *I am ready*. *Pl.* 20, *cr.* 2.
FRASER, of Pitcullain, a stag's head, erased, in ear an annulet. *I am ready*. *Pl.* 66, *cr.* 9, (annulet, *pl.* 141.)
FRASER, a stag's head, erased, or, armed, ar. *I am ready*. *Pl.* 66, *cr.* 9.
FRASER, CHARLES, Esq., of Castle Fraser, Ross: 1. A mount of strawberries, fructed, ppr. *Pl.* 62, *cr.* 11. 2. A stag's head, couped, ppr. *All my hope is in God*—and *Je suis prest*. *Pl.* 91, *cr.* 14.
FRASER, FRANCIS-GARDEN, Esq., of Findrack, Aberdeens., a stag's head, erased, or. *I am ready*. *Pl.* 66, *cr.* 9.
FRASER, Sco., a stag's head, erased, or, attired, ar., between two battle-axes, ppr. *Pl.* 66, *cr.* 9, (axes, *pl.* 52, *cr.* 10.)
FRASER, of Strichen, a stag's head, couped, ar. *Vive ut postea vivas*. *Pl.* 91, *cr.* 14.

FRASER, of Eskdale, a stag's head, erased, ppr., attired, or, charged with an increscent. *Vel pax, vel bellum.* Pl. 66, cr. 9, (increscent, pl. 141.)

FRASER, Sco., a demi-eagle, in flames. Pl. 112, cr. 7.

FRASER, Sco., a sword, and an olive-branch, in saltier, ppr. Pl. 50, cr. 4, (olive, pl. 98, cr. 8.)

FRASER, Sco., a buck's head, erased, ppr. Pl. 66, cr. 9.

FRASER-ALLAN, PATRICK, Esq., of Hospitalfield, Forfar, on a mount, vert, a bush of strawberries, ppr. *Nosce teipsum.* Pl. 62, cr. 11.

FRAUNCEIS, FRAUNCES, and FRAUNCEYS, Eng., a hand issuing out of a cloud, seizing a stag by the horns, ppr. Pl. 46, cr. 10.

FRAY, and FRAYE, Eng., a stag, pierced in side by an arrow. Pl. 88, cr. 9.

FRAZER, Lord Frazer, a mount, full of strawberries, leaved, flowered, and fructed. *All my hope is in God.* Pl. 62, cr. 11.

FREBODY, Suss., a leopard, sejant, (regardant,) ar. Pl. 86, cr. 8, (without coronet.)

FREBY, Eng., a castle, sa., ports and windows, gu. Pl. 28, cr. 11.

FRECHVILLE, Derbs., a demi-angel, affrontée, ppr., crined and winged, or, on the head a cross formée, of the last, (vested in mail, ppr., holding in both hands, an arrow, in bend, of the first, headed and feathered, ar.) Pl. 90, cr. 11.

FRECKELTON, and FRECKLETON, Hunts., a bear's head, ar., muzzled, or. Pl. 71, cr. 6.

FRECKELTON, and FRECKLETON, a camel's head, ar., (bridled,) or. Pl. 109, cr. 9.

FREDERICK, Bart., Surr., on a chapeau, az., turned up, erm., a dove, ar., in mouth an olive-branch, ppr. Pl. 48, cr. 15, (chapeau, pl. 109, cr. 10.)

FREDERICK, Middx., on a chapeau, gu., turned up, erm., a dove, ppr., in mouth a laurelbranch. Pl. 48, cr. 15, (chapeau, pl. 109, cr. 10.)

FREE, Eng., a fox's head, ppr. Pl. 91, cr. 9.

FREEBAIRN, Sco., the sun in splendour. *Always the same.* Pl. 68, cr. 14.

FREEBAIRN, Sco., in dexter hand an eel, ppr. Pl. 91, cr. 6.

FREEFORD, and FREFORD, out of a ducal coronet, an eagle's head. Pl. 20, cr. 12, (without pellet.)

FREELAND, Eng., a leopard, passant, ar., pellettée. Pl. 86, cr. 2.

FREELAND, Eng., a leopard, passant, ppr. *Res, non verba.* Pl. 86, cr. 2.

FREELING, Bart., Suss., a unicorn's head, erased, per pale, indented, erm., and gu., armed, tufted, and crined, or. *Nunquam nisi honorificentissime.* Pl. 67, cr. 1.

FREELING, a unicorn's head, couped, ar., maned, horned and tufted, or. Pl. 20, cr. 1.

FREEMAN, Lond., Wilts., and Yorks., a demilion, rampant, erased, holding a cross fleury. Pl. 29, cr. 12, (cross, pl. 141.)

FREEMAN, out of a ducal coronet, a wolf's head, Pl. 14, cr. 6, (coronet, pl. 128, fig. 3.)

FREEMAN, Northamp., out of a ducal coronet, az., a boar's head, erect, ar. Pl. 102, cr. 14.

FREEMAN, Heref., a demi-lion, rampant, gu., between paws a lozenge, pierced, or. Pl. 126, cr. 12, (lozenge, pl. 141.)

FREEMAN, Ess., Oxon., and Northamp., a demilion, rampant, gu., charged on shoulder with three lozenges, in fess, ar. Pl. 67, cr. 10, (lozenge, pl. 141.)

FREEMAN, Ess., Oxon., and Northamp., a demilion, rampant, gu., charged with a lozenge, ar. Pl. 67, cr. 10, (lozenge, pl. 141.)

FREEMAN-MITFORD, Baron Redesdale. *See* REDESDALE.

FREEMAN-WILLIAMS: 1. For *Freeman*, a demilion, gu., charged with a lozenge, or. Pl. 67, cr. 10, (lozenge, pl. 141.) 2. For *Williams*, a lion, rampant, gorged with a chaplet of oak-leaves, ppr., and crowned with a naval coronet, or. Pl. 112, cr. 11.

FREEMANTLE, Bart., Bucks., out of a mural coronet, or, a demi-lion, rampant, gu., (charged on shoulder with a plate, in paws a standard, flowing to dexter, quarterly, ar. and gold, staff, of the last.) Pl. 86, cr. 11.

FREEMANTLE, out of rays, in dexter hand, vested, a human skull. Pl. 37, cr. 6.

FREER, Eng., a sphere, or. Pl. 114, cr. 6.

FREER, Sco., a swan, ppr. *No sine periculo.* Pl. 122, cr. 13.

FREER, JOHN-BRANSTON, Esq., of Stratfordupon-Avon, Warw., a dolphin, naiant, ppr. Pl. 48, cr. 9.

FREESTON, and FRESTON, Norf., a demi-greyfriar, ppr. Pl. 90, cr. 5.

FREETH, Eng., out of cloud, a hand, in fess, holding a club, in pale, ppr. Pl. 55, cr. 4.

FREEKE, Dors. and Norf., a bull's head, couped, sa., attired, (collared and lined,) or. Pl. 120, cr. 7.

FREEKE, Iri., a dexter arm, in armour, embowed, in hand a sword, all ppr. Pl. 2, cr. 8.

FREKE-EVANS, Baron Carbery. *See* CARBERY.

FREN, and FRENE, Eng., a physician's cap. Pl. 39, cr. 3.

FRENBAND, a demi-lion, gu., in dexter a trefoil, slipped, or. Pl. 39, cr. 14, (trefoil, pl. 141.)

FRENCH, Worc., a fleur-de-lis, sa., seeded, or. Pl. 68, cr. 12.

FRENCH, Sco., a ship, in full sail, ppr. *Par commerce.* Pl. 109, cr. 8.

FRENCH, in a crescent, ar., a fleur-de-lis, sa. Pl. 18, cr. 14, (fleur-de-lis, pl. 141.)

FRENCH, Iri., a fleur-de-lis, or, charged with a trefoil, vert. Pl. 68, cr. 12, (trefoil, pl. 141.)

FRENCH, Sco., a boar's head, couped. *Malo mori quam fœdari.* Pl. 48, cr. 2.

FRENCH, Ess., between horns of a crescent, per pale, ar. and or, a fleur-de-lis, per pale, of the second and first. Pl. 18, cr. 14, (fleurde-lis, pl. 141.)

FRENCH, CHRISTOPHER, Esq., of Cloonyquin, co. Roscommon, a dolphin, naiant, ppr. Pl. 48, cr. 9.

FRENCH, ROBERT, Esq., of Monavie Castle, co. Galway, a dolphin, naiant, ppr. *Malo mori quam fœdari.* Pl. 48, cr. 9.

FRENCH, JAMES, Esq., of Frenchgrove, co. Mayo, same crest and motto.

FRENCH, SAMPSON-TOWGOOD-WYNNE, Esq., of Cuskinny, co. Cork, a dolphin. *Veritas vincit.* Pl. 48, cr. 9.

FRENCH, an heraldic-tiger, rampant. *Spero meliora.* Pl. 57, cr. 13.

FREND, co. Limerick, a buck's head. *Aude e prevalebis.* Pl. 91, cr. 14.

FREND, Eng., a beacon, fired, ppr. *Pl.* 88, *cr.* 6.
FRERE, Norf. and Leic., out of a ducal coronet, gu., an antelope's head, ar., attired, or. *Pl.* 24, *cr.* 7, (coronet, *pl.* 128, *fig.* 3.)
FRESCHEVILLE, Eng., a gem-ring, or, stoned, gu. *Pl.* 35, *cr.* 3.
FRESELL, and FRESILL, a hand, issuant, plucking a rose. *Pl.* 48, *cr.* 1.
FRESH, Eng., out of a ducal coronet, a horse's hind-leg, erect. *Pl.* 38, *cr.* 11.
FRESHACRE, a savage's head, ducally crowned, ppr. *Pl.* 28, *cr.* 3.
FRESHFIELD, Eng., on a mount, vert, a stag, lodged, per fess, or and gu., armed, of the last. *Pl.* 22, *cr.* 5.
FRESHWATER, two tronts, in saltier, heads downward, ppr., enfiled by a ducal coronet, or.
FRESTON, Norf., a demi-greyhound, rampant, sa., collared, or. *Pl.* 5, *cr.* 10, (without wings.)
FRESTON, Suff., a demi-greyhound, rampant, sa., collared, ar., rimmed, or. *Pl.* 5, *cr.* 10, (without wings.)
FRESTON, a talbot's head, gu., eared, ar. *Pl.* 123, *cr.* 15.
FRETON, a unicorn's head, ar., pellettée. *Pl.* 20, *cr.* 1.
FREVILE, on each side of a chapeau, gu., turned up, ar., a wing, addorsed, or. *Pl.* 80, *cr.* 15, (without charging.)
FREVILE, out of a ducal coronet, or, an old man's head, couped below shoulders, ppr., vested, gu., turned back, erm., on head a cap, of the third, tasselled, gold. *Pl.* 51, *cr.* 4, (coronet, *pl.* 128, *fig.* 3.)
FREW, Sco., a demi-lion, or, holding a mullet, az. *Pl.* 89, *cr.* 10.
FREWEN, a demi-lion, rampant, ar., langued and collared, gu., in paws a caltrap, az. *Pl.* 18, *cr.* 13, (caltrap, *pl.* 141.)
FREWIN, a demi-lion, collared, between paws a mullet of (four) points, pierced. *Pl.* 18, *cr.* 13, (mullet, *pl.* 45, *cr.* 1.)
FREWKE, Eng., a goat's head, erased, sa., armed and bearded, ar. *Pl.* 29, *cr.* 13.
FREY, an arm, erect, (vested, vert,) in hand, ppr., a spiked club, of the first. *Pl.* 123, *cr.* 10.
FRIBOURG, Eng., a unicorn's head, erased, erm., maned and armed, or. *Pl.* 67, *cr.* 1.
FRIDAY, out of a ducal coronet, or, a plume of (three) feathers, ar. *Pl.* 44, *cr.* 12.
FRIEND, Eng., a stag's head, cabossed, ppr. *Pl.* 36, *cr.* 1.
FRIER, Linc., out of a ducal coronet, or, an antelope's head, ar. *Pl.* 24, *cr.* 7, (coronet, same plate, *cr.* 10.)
FRIERE, out of leaves, vert, five tulips, or.
FRISEL, Sco., a stag's head, erased, ppr. *Pl.* 66, *cr.* 9.
FRISKENNY, Linc., a plume of five ostrich-feathers, two ar., three az., banded, or and gu. *Pl.* 106, *cr.* 11, (without chapeau or coronet.)
FRISKENNY, or FRISKNAY, a plume of five ostrich-feathers, ar., wreathed, az. *Ib.*
FRODHAM, in dexter hand a fleur-de-lis. *Pl.* 95, *cr.* 9.
FRODSHAM, Chesh., an escallop, or. *Pl.* 117, *cr.* 4. (Another, ar.)
FROELSHAM, Chesh., an escallop, ar. *Pl.* 117, *cr.* 4.

FROGGAT, and FROGGATT, Eng., a parrot, feeding on a bunch of cherries, ppr. *Pl.* 49, *cr.* 3.
FROGMER, Worc., a demi-griffin, wings addorsed, ar., holding a cross crosslet, sa. *Pl.* 18, *cr.* 6, (cross, *pl.* 141.)
FROGMORTON, a falcon, rising, ar., jessed and belled, or. *Pl.* 105, *cr.* 4.
FROHOCK, Lond. and Cambs., a stag, ppr., charged on shoulder with an etoile, ar. *Pl.* 61, *cr.* 15, (etoile, *pl.* 141.)
FROM, a demi-griffin, segreant, or, in dexter a cross crosslet, gu. *Pl.* 18, *cr.* 6, (cross, *pl.* 141.)
FROME, Eng., a greyhound, couchant, between two laurel-branches, in orle, ppr. *Pl.* 102, *cr.* 13.
FROMOND, and FROMONT, in dexter hand an escallop. *Pl.* 57, *cr.* 6.
FROMONDS, Kent and Surr., a tiger, passant. *Pl.* 67, *cr.* 15.
FROST, Yorks., an old man's head, ppr., between two sprigs of laurel, or. *Pl.* 78, *cr.* 5.
FROTHINGHAM, Yorks., a stag, trippant, ppr., attired, gu. *Pl.* 68, *cr.* 2.
FROTHINGHAM, Yorks., a buck, trippant, ppr. *Pl.* 68, *cr.* 2.
FROUD, a Saracen's head, sa., between two ostrich-feathers, ar. *Pl.* 19, *cr.* 1, (feathers, *pl.* 50, *cr.* 1.)
FROUDE, Devons., a stag, regardant, ppr., attired, (collared, and unguled, or, in mouth an oak-sprig, vert, fructed, or.) *Pl.* 3, *cr.* 2.
FROWICKE, and FROWYKE, Middx., two arms, embowed, (vested,) az., in hands, ppr., a leopard's head, or. *Pl.* 6, *cr.* 8, (head, *pl.* 66, *cr.* 14.)
FROYLE, Eng., a demi-lion, per pale, gu. and az., collared, or. *Pl.* 18, *cr.* 13.
FRUEN, Lond., a demi-lion, ar., in paws a caltrap, az. *Pl.* 126, *cr.* 12, (caltrap, *pl.* 141.)
FRY, Dors., a cubit arm, in hand a falchion, ppr., hilted, or. *Pl.* 21, *cr.* 10.
FRY, Dors. and Devons., an arm, in armour, embowed, ppr., in hand a sword, enfiled with a moor's head, all ppr. *Pl.* 2, *cr.* 8, (head, *pl.* 102, *cr.* 11.)
FRY, Devons., a dexter arm, in armour, embowed, in hand, ppr., a sword, of the last, hilt and pommel, or. *Pl.* 2, *cr.* 8.
FRY, a demi-horse, salient, ar. *Pl.* 91, *cr.* 2, (without wings or coronet.)
FRY, a horse's head, bridled. *Pl.* 92, *cr.* 1.
FRYER, Lond., Ess., and Worc., out of a ducal coronet, or, an antelope's head, armed, crined, and tufted, of the first. *Pl.* 24, *cr.* 7, (coronet, *same plate*, *cr.* 10.)
FRYER, on a tower, sa., a cock, or, (the tower environed by a serpent, ar., darting at the cock.) *Pl.* 113, *cr.* 14.
FRYER, Lond., out of a ducal coronet, gu., an antelope's head, ar., armed, crined, and tufted, of the first. *Pl.* 24, *cr.* 7, (coronet, *same plate*, *cr.* 10.)
FRYER, an heraldic-antelope's head, erased, per fess, ar. and gu., gorged with a ducal coronet, or, attired, of the second. *Pl.* 76, *cr.* 3, (coronet, *same plate*, *cr.* 8.)
FRYER, Staffs., a castle, ar., encircled by a branch of oak, fructed, ppr., thereon a cock, sa., combed and wattled, gu. *Mea fides in sapientiâ*. *Pl.* 113, *cr.* 14, (oak, *pl.* 74, *cr.* 7.)

N

FRYTON, an heraldic-tiger's head, ducally gorged and chained, ppr. *Pl.* 113, *cr.* 3, (gorging, *same plate, cr.* 11.)

FULBORN, and FULBORNE, Eng., out of an antique coronet, or, a demi-lion, az. *Pl.* 67, *cr.* 10, (coronet, *pl.* 124, *cr.* 8.)

FULCHER, Eng., a demi-lion, holding an anchor, ppr. *Pl.* 19, *cr.* 6.

FULFORD, Devons. and Dors., a bear's head, erased, ar., muzzled, sa. *Pl.* 71, *cr.* 6.

FULFORD, a bear's head, erased, ar., muzzled, gu. *Pl.* 71, *cr.* 6.

FULFORD, BALDWIN, Esq., of Great Fulford, Devons., a bear's head, erased, sa., muzzled, or. *Bear up. Pl.* 71, *cr.* 6.

FULHAM, Eng., a greyhound's head, ppr. *Pl.* 89, *cr.* 2.

FULHAM, on a mount, vert, a lion, sejant, or, (supporting with dexter an escutcheon, ar., charged with a teazle, ppr.) *Pl.* 108, *cr.* 12.

FULHERST, and FULSHERST, a triangular harrow, ppr. *Pl.* 7, *cr.* 2.

FULKWORTH, a dexter arm, vested, erm., in hand, ppr., a sword, az., headed, or. *Pl.* 120, *cr.* 1.

FULLARTON, Sco., a camel's head. *Lux in tenebris. Pl.* 109, *cr.* 9.

FULLARTON, Sco., an otter's head, erased, gu. *Lux in tenebris. Pl.* 126, *cr.* 14.

FULLARTON, Sco., a tiger's head, per fess, wavy, or and sa., charged with cinquefoils and mullets, ar. *Pl.* 94, *cr.* 10, (charging, *pl.* 141.)

FULLER, AUGUSTUS-ELLIOT, Esq., of Rose Hill, Brightling; and Ashdown House, Suss., a horse, passant, ar. *Currit qui curat. Pl.* 15, *cr.* 14.

FULLER, Hants, a dexter arm, embowed, vested, ar., cuffed, sa., in hand, ppr., a sword, of the first, hilt and pommel, or. *Pl.* 120, *cr.* 1.

FULLER, a greyhound's head, erased, gu. *Pl.* 89, *cr.* 2.

FULLER, Suss., out of a ducal coronet, gu., a lion's head, ar. *Pl.* 90, *cr.* 9.

FULLER, Suss., out of a ducal coronet, or, a lion's head, gu. *Pl.* 90, *cr.* 9.

FULLER, Iri., a horse-shoe, az. *Pl.* 52, *cr.* 4.

FULLESHURST, Chesh., a unicorn's head, erm. *Pl.* 20, *cr.* 1.

FULLWOOD, Eng., two laurel-branches, in orle, vert, fructed, gu. *Pl.* 79, *cr.* 14.

FULLWOOD, Derbs., Staffs., and Warw., a stag, ppr., in mouth an acorn-branch, vert, fructed, or. *Pl.* 68, *cr.* 2, (acorn, *pl.* 81, *cr.* 7.)

FULLWOOD, a demi-man, in armour, ppr., in dexter a broken tilting-spear, or. *Pl.* 60, *cr.* 2, (spear, *pl.* 3, *cr.* 6.)

FULWOOD, a demi-stag, or. *Pl.* 55, *cr.* 9, (without rose.)

FULMESTON, an heraldic-antelope's head, (erased,) gu., pattée, armed, in mouth a rose-branch, ppr. *Pl.* 76, *cr.* 3, (rose, *pl.* 117, *cr.* 10.)

FULRICH, a tower, on top a plume of five ostrich-feathers, ppr. *Pl.* 12, *cr.* 5, (feathers, *pl.* 100, *cr.* 12.)

FULTHORP, and FULTHORPE, Durh. and Yorks., a horse, passant, ar., bridled, az., bit and tassels, or. *Pl.* 99, *cr.* 11.

FULTHORP, an eagle, displayed, ar., charged with a cross moline, sa. *Pl.* 48, *cr.* 11, (cross, *pl.* 141.)

FULTHORP, a horse, passant, ar., bridled, or. *Pl.* 99, *cr.* 11.

FULTON, Sco., on a mount, a stag, lodged, regardant, ppr. *Quæ fecimus ipsi*—and—*Parta labore quies. Pl.* 51, *cr.* 9.

FULTON, Eng., a stag's head, gu., attired, or. *Pl.* 91, *cr.* 14.

FULWAR, Iri., a cushion, ar., tasselled and garnished, or thereon a book, gu. *Pl.* 112, *cr.* 14.

FULWER, Lond., on a mount, vert, a beacon, fired, ppr. *Pl.* 89, *cr.* 9.

FULWOOD, Hants and Warw., a buck, trippant, in mouth an oak-slip, all ppr. *Pl.* 68, *cr.* 2, (oak, *pl.* 32, *cr.* 13.)

FUNEAUX, an arm, in armour, in hand a caltrap, ppr. *Pl.* 22, *cr.* 4, (arm, *pl.* 120, *cr.* 11.)

FURBISHER, out of a ducal coronet, gu., a griffin's head, ar. *Pl.* 54, *cr.* 14.

FURBISHER, and FURBUSHER, a unicorn's head, erased, az., armed, ar., ducally gorged, or. *Pl.* 67, *cr* 1, (gorging, *same plate*.)

FURGUASON, a demi-lion, holding a torteau, semée of etoiles. *Pl.* 126, *cr.* 12, (etoile, *pl.* 141.)

FURLONG, an eagle's head, erased, ppr. *Liberalitas. Pl.* 20, *cr.* 7.

FURNES, FERNESE, and FURNESS, Kent, a talbot, sejant, sa. *Pl.* 107, *cr.* 7, (without collar.)

FURNES, FURNESE, and FURNESS, Eng., out of a ducal coronet, a lion's paw, holding a lance, ppr. *Pl.* 120, *cr.* 6.

FURNIVAL, Baron, U.K., on a chapeau, gu., a lion, passant, tail extended, erminois. *Forte et fidele. Pl.* 107, *cr.* 1.

FURNIVAL, and FURNIVALL, an anchor, cabled, and a sword, in saltier, ppr. *Pl.* 25, *cr.* 1.

FURODON, out of a ducal coronet, a plume of five ostrich-feathers, all ppr. *Pl.* 100, *cr.* 12, (without charge.)

FURSDON, GEORGE, Esq., of Fursdon, Devons., out of a ducal coronet, a plume of five ostrich-feathers, all ppr. *Pl.* 100, *cr.* 12.

FURSE, the Rev. CHARLES-WELLINGTON, of Halsdon, Devons., a castle, ppr. *Nec desit virtus. Pl.* 28, *cr.* 11.

FURSE, Eng., a lion, sejant, affrontée, in dexter a dagger, in sinister a fleur-de-lis. *Pl.* 120, *cr.* 2.

FURSER, and FURZER, on a mount, a stag, lodged, ppr. *Pl.* 22, *cr.* 5.

FURSLAND, a savage's head, affrontée, vested, sa. and ar. *Pl.* 31, *cr.* 2.

FURY, Eng., a demi-lion, rampant. *Pl.* 67, *cr.* 10.

FURY, a demi-lion, rampant, grasping a thunderbolt, or. *Pl.* 113, *cr.* 2, (bolt, *pl.* 110, *cr.* 3.)

FUST, Glouc., a horse at full speed, ar. *Terrena pervices sunt aliena. Pl.* 8, *cr.* 2.

FUTTER, Norf. and Suff., a goat's head, erased, or, attired, sa., in mouth a holly-branch, vert, fructed, gu. *Pl.* 29, *cr.* 13, (branch, *pl.* 99, *cr.* 6.)

FUTTER, Isle of Man, a goat's head, erased, or, attired, sa., in mouth a laurel-branch, slipped, ppr. *Pl.* 29, *cr.* 13, (laurel, *pl.* 123, *cr.* 5.)

FYDELL, Eng., a hind's head, couped, per cheveron, sa. and erm. *Pl.* 21, *cr.* 9.

FYERS, Eng., a goat, (passant,) in mouth a bunch of ivy. *Pl.* 15, *cr.* 9.

FYFE, and FYFFE, Sco., a demi-lion, rampant. *Decens et honestum. Pl.* 67, *cr.* 10.

FYFFE, DAVID, Esq., of Smithfield, Forfar, a demi-lion, gu., armed and langued, az. *Decens et honestum.* Pl. 67, cr. 10.
FYLER, Eng., a fox, sejant, per fess, or and gu. Pl. 87, cr. 4.
FYLER, JAMES-CHAMNESS, Esq., of Woodlands, Surr., a porcupine, ppr. *Volonte de Dieu.* Pl. 55, cr. 10.
FYLKYN, a demi-greyhound, between wings. Pl. 5, cr. 10.
FYLLOLL, Eng., a unicorn's head, erased, sa. Pl. 67, cr. 1.
FYNDERNE, an ox-yoke, or. Pl. 35, cr. 11.
FYNES, Eng., a peacock's head, erased, az., crested, or. Pl. 86, cr. 4.
FYNMORE, Eng., a unicorn, sejant, resting dexter on a tree, ppr. Pl. 110, cr. 15.
FYNMORE, and FINMORE, a bull's head, erased, (charged with two cheveronels, gu.) Pl. 19, cr. 3.
FYNNEY, Staffs., a staff, raguly, or. *Fortem posce animum.* Pl. 78, cr. 15.
FYNTE, a basilisk, or. Pl. 63, cr. 15.
FYRES, in dexter hand, a salamander in flames. *Ardet virtus non urit.* Pl. 32, cr. 14, (salamander, pl. 20, cr. 15.)
FYSHE, Suff. and Herts., a triangle surmounted of an etoile, or. Pl. 13, cr. 6.
FYSHER, Lond., a king-fisher, ppr.
FYSHER, Wilts., a demi-lion, rampant, gardant, gu., holding a gauntlet, ar. Pl. 35, cr. 4, (gauntlet, pl. 15, cr. 15.)
FYSKE, Eng., on a chapeau, a martlet, all ppr. Pl. 89, cr. 7.
FYTCHE, Eng., a tower, triple-towered, ar., masoned, sa. Pl. 123, cr. 14.
FYTHEY, and FYTHIE, Sco., a crane's head, erased. Pl. 20, cr. 9.
FYVIE, Sco., in lion's gamb, a human heart. Pl. 23, cr. 13.

G

GABB, a griffin's head, between wings, in beak a branch of palm, all ppr. Pl. 105, cr. 6.
GABELL, Hants, a boar's head, couped, or. Pl. 48, cr. 2.
GABELL, a savage, wreathed about middle, treading on a serpent, ppr. Pl. 109, cr. 1.
GABRIEL, and GABRYELL, a demi-savage, regardant, ppr. Pl. 16, cr. 4.
GACE, an arm, in armour, embowed, ppr., in hand a (broken) falchion, ar., hilt and pommel, or. Pl. 2, cr. 8.
GADDES, and GADDEZ, a stag's head, ppr. Pl. 91, cr. 14.
GADSBY, a stag, passant, ar. Pl. 68, cr. 2.
GAFF, a demi-antelope, or, collared, gu. Pl. 34, cr. 8.
GAGE, Viscount and Baron, Iri.; Baron Gage, U.K., and a Bart., (Hall-Gage,) a ram, passant, ar., armed and unguled, or. *Courage sans peur.* Pl. 109, cr. 2.
GAGE, Bart., Suff., a ram, passant, ar., armed, or. Pl 109, cr. 2.
GAGE, Herts., a stag, passant, ppr. Pl. 68, cr. 2.
GAEL, a cock, gu. *Vigilate.* Pl. 67, cr. 14.
GAILLE, Eng., out of a mural coronet, a garb, thereon a bird, all ppr. Pl. 14, cr. 5.
GAINE, a demi-lion, rampant. Pl. 67, cr. 10.
GAINSBOROUGH, Earl, (Noel,) a buck, at gaze, ar., attired, or. *Tout bien ou rien.* Pl. 81, cr. 8.
GAINSBOROUGH, Surr., a griffin's head, erased, az., (charged with three cheverons, ar.) Pl. 48, cr. 6.
GAINSBY, out of a mount, a sprig of laurel growing, vert. Pl. 98, cr. 13.
GAINSFORD, Lond., Kent, and Oxon., a demi-woman, vested and crined, or, in dexter a chaplet, vert, in sinister a rose, ppr. Pl. 87, cr. 14, (rose, pl. 117, cr. 10.)
GAIR, Sco., a mill-rind. Pl. 54, cr. 3.
GAIRDEN, Sco., a boar, passant, ar. *Vires animat virtus.* Pl. 48, cr. 14.
GAIRDEN, Sco., in dexter hand two palm-branches, in orle, ppr. *Vive le roi.* Pl. 16, cr. 5.
GAIRDEN, Sco., a rose, slipped, ppr. *Sustine, abstine.* Pl. 105, cr. 7.
GAIRDEN, Sco., two dexter hands, conjoined, ppr., supporting a cross crosslet, fitched, or. Pl. 52, cr. 15.
GAIRDNER, Sco., a demi-leopard, rampant, ppr. Pl. 12, cr. 14.
GAIRDNER, Sco., a dove and olive-branch, ppr. *Jovi confido.* Pl. 48, cr. 15.
GAIRDNER, Sco., a demi-leopard, rampant, ppr. Pl. 12, cr. 14.
GAISFORD, Eng., a boar, passant, per fess, or and gu., hoofed, of the last, bristled, of the first. Pl. 48, cr. 14.
GAITSKILL, on a mountain, an eagle, regardant, (wings expanded, ppr., collared,) az., resting dexter on a pellet. Pl. 79, cr. 2, (pellet, pl. 141.)
GALAAD, Eng., a demi-greyhound, ar. Pl. 48, cr. 3.
GALAY, a snail, horns erect, ppr. Pl. 105, cr. 8.
GALBRAITH, a bear's head, erased, or, muzzled, sa., in mouth a trefoil, slipped, ar. Pl. 71, cr. 6, (trefoil, pl. 141.)
GALBRAITH, Sco., a bear's head, couped, ar., muzzled, or. Pl. 2, cr. 9.
GALBRAITH, a boar's head and neck, per fess, or and gu. Pl. 2, cr. 7.
GALBRAITH, Sco., a lion's head and neck, erased, ppr. *Vigilo et spero.* Pl. 81, cr. 4.
GALE, Cambs., a unicorn's head, az., charged, with an anchor, or, between two pellets, ar. Pl. 20, cr. 1, (anchor, pl. 25, cr. 15; pellet, pl. 141.)
GALE, Eng., a greyhound's head, erased, bendy-wavy of six, or and sa. Pl. 89, cr. 2.
GALE, Yorks., out of a ducal coronet, or, a unicorn's head, paly of six, az. and gold, armed, of the last. Pl. 45, cr. 14.
GALE, Sco., a unicorn's head, sa. Pl. 20, cr. 1.
GALE, a unicorn's head, paly of six, or and az., attired, gold. Pl. 20, cr. 1.
GALE, Dors., a horse's head, bendy-wavy of six, or and sa. Pl. 52, cr. 9.

GALL, Eng., a shank-bone and a palm-branch, in saltier, ppr. *Pl.* 25, *cr.* 11.
GALL, a lion, sejant, gu., holding a banner, ppr. *Pl.* 60, *cr.* 4, (banner, *pl.* 99, *cr.* 1.)
GALL, Sco., a ship, ppr., her flags and pennons flying, gu. *Patientia vincit. Pl.* 109, *cr.* 8.
GALL, Sco., a ship in full sail, ppr. *Patientia vincit. Pl.* 109, *cr.* 8.
GALLAGHER, Iri., in hand a sickle, ppr. *Pl.* 36, *cr.* 12.
GALLAND, a stag, lodged, per pale, or and gu. *Pl.* 67, *cr.* 2.
GALLARD, an arm, embowed, vested, gu., in hand, ppr., a rose, or, slipped and leaved, vert. *Pl.* 39, *cr.* 1, (rose, *pl.* 118, *cr.* 9.)
GALLAWAY, Sco., out of a ducal coronet, or, a dragon's head, wings addorsed, vert. *Pl.* 59, *cr.* 14.
GALLAWAY, or GALLOWAY, Sco., an arm, in hand a dagger, ppr. *Pl.* 34, *cr.* 7.
GALLAY, GALLEY, or GALLE, Somers. and Dors., a stag's head, bendy-wavy of six, ar. and sa. *Pl.* 91, *cr.* 14.
GALLAY, and GALLEY, a nag's head, bendy-wavy of six, ar. and sa. *Pl.* 52, *cr.* 9.
GALLIE, Sco., a horse's head. *Pl.* 81, *cr.* 6.
GALLIERS, an antelope, passant, quarterly, sa. and ar. *Pl.* 63, *cr.* 10.
GALLIEZ, Sco., a savage standing on a serpent, ppr. *Divino robere. Pl.* 109, *cr.* 1.
GALLIGHTLY, a lion's head, issuant, gu., crowned with an antique crown, or. *Hactenus invictus. Pl.* 123, *cr.* 13.
GALLIMORE, a cock, ppr. *Pl.* 67, *cr.* 14.
GALLOP, a boar, passant, sa., pierced by a (broken spear,) ppr. *Pl.* 36, *cr.* 2.
GALLOWAY, Earl of, and Lord Garlies, Sco.; Baron Stewart, G.B. (Stewart,) a pelican, ar., winged, or, in nest feeding her young, ppr. *Virescit vulnere, virtus. Pl.* 44, *cr.* 1.
GALLOWAY, Eng., out of a ducal coronet, or, a dragon's head, wings addorsed, vert. *Pl.* 59, *cr.* 14.
GALLWEY, co. Cork, a cat, sejant, ppr., (collared and chained, or.) *Pl.* 24, *cr.* 6.
GALLWEY-PAYNE, Bart.: 1. For *Gallwey*, a cat, passant, gardant. *Pl.* 119, *cr.* 7. 2. For *Payne*, in lion's gamb, erased, the lower part of a tilting-lance, in bend, ppr. *Pl.* 85, *cr.* 15.
GALLY, a cock, ppr. *Pl.* 67, *cr.* 14.
GALPINE, a plume of feathers, banded, ppr. *Pl.* 116, *cr.* 11, (without coronet or chapeau.)
GALTON, Warw. and Staffs., same crest and motto.
GALTON, a bull's head, erased, gu., ducally gorged, or. *Pl.* 68, *cr.* 6.
GALTON-HOWARD, Worc., on a (mount,) vert, an eagle, erm., looking at the sun, resting dexter on a fleur-de-lis, gu. *Gaudet luce videri. Pl.* 43, *cr.* 5, (fleur-de-lis, *pl.* 141.)
GALWAY, Viscount, and Baron Killard, Iri., (Arundel Monckton:) 1. For *Arundel*, on a chapeau, sa., turned up, erm., a swallow, ar. *Pl.* 89, *cr.* 7. 2. For *Monckton*, a martlet, issuant, or. *Cruci, dum spiro, fido. Pl.* 111, *cr.* 5.
GALWAY, a cat, sejant, ppr., (collared, chain reflexed over back, or.) *Pl.* 24, *cr.* 6.
GAMAGE, Herts., a griffin, segreant, or. *Pl.* 67, *cr.* 13.
GAMAGE, in dexter hand a pen, ppr. *Pl.* 26, *cr.* 13.

GAMBELL, or GAMBLE, a Roman soldier, in full costume, ppr. *Pl.* 90, *cr.* 1.
GAMBELL, or GAMBLE, a crane, in beak a (rose,) stalked and leaved, ppr. *Pl.* 46, *cr.* 9.
GAMELL, or GAMMILL, two lions' heads, addorsed, gu. *Pl.* 28, *cr.* 10.
GAMBIER, Lond., Kent, and Bucks., out of a naval coronet, an eagle, displayed, erminois, charged on breast with an anchor, sa. *Fide non armis. Pl.* 113, *cr.* 4, (eagle, *pl.* 48, *cr.* 11; anchor, *pl.* 25, *cr.* 15.)
GAMBIER, an eagle, displayed. *Pl.* 48, *cr.* 11.
GAMBON, and GAMON, a torteau, gu., between wings, ppr. *Pl.* 2, *cr.* 3.
GAME, Eng., a cross crosslet, fitched, and palm-branch, in saltier, ppr. *Pl.* 102, *cr.* 3, (palm, *pl.* 123, *cr.* 1.)
GAMELL, GAMMEL, or GAMONILL, Sco., a talbot's head, sa. *Pl.* 123, *cr.* 15.
GAMES, Leic., an eagle's head, or, between wings, erm. *Pl.* 81, *cr.* 10.
GAMMELL, Sco., a pelican, vulning, (pierced through breast by an arrow,) ppr. *Moriens, sed invictus. Pl.* 109, *cr.* 15.
GAMMELL, Sco., an eagle, wings addorsed, neck embowed, pierced through breast by an arrow, in bend sinister. *Moriens, sed invictus. Pl.* 121, *cr.* 3.
GAMIN, an arm, in armour, embowed, wreathed with laurel, in hand a sword, all ppr. *Pl.* 21, *cr.* 4.
GAMMON, and GAMON, a boar, passant, charged with a pale. *Pl.* 48, *cr.* 14.
GAMMON, Middx., a boar, passant, ar., (on body a pale, sa., charged with a leopard's face, or.) *Virtus in arduis. Pl.* 48, *cr.* 14.
GAMMON, a boar, passant, ar. *Pl.* 48, *cr.* 14.
GAMOLL, Chesh., a human heart, ppr., crowned, or, between wings, sa., purfled, of the first. *Pl.* 52, *cr.* 2.
GANDER, a demi-talbot, per cheveron, ar. and az. *Pl.* 15, *cr.* 2, (without gorging.)
GANDY, a saltier, gu. *Pl.* 82, *cr.* 7.
GANDY, and GANDEY, a fox, current, per pale, or and sa. *Pl.* 80, *cr.* 5.
GANGE, Glouc., a stork, (drinking out of a horn,) all ppr. *Pl.* 121, *cr.* 13.
GANLARD, in dexter hand a sabre, ppr. *Pl.* 29, *cr.* 8.
GANNOKE, Linc., a stag, sejant, ar., ducally gorged, or. *Pl.* 101, *cr.* 3, (without coronet; gorging, *same plate*, *cr.* 6.)
GANNON, a bull's head, ducally gorged (and crowned.) *Pl.* 68, *cr.* 6.
GANSTIN, Iri., in hand a dagger. *Gladio et virtute. Pl.* 28, *cr.* 4.
GANSTIN, on a ducal coronet, a dexter arm, armed, in hand a dagger. *Gladio et virtute. Pl.* 15, *cr.* 5.
GANT, Eng., a mill-rind, ppr. *Pl.* 54, *cr.* 3.
GANT, Linc., a wolf's head, or, collared, vair. *Pl.* 8, *cr.* 4.
GANUBLE, a lion, passant, tail extended, ppr. *Pl.* 118, *cr.* 10.
GAPE, a lion, passant, regardant, or, pellettée, collared, vair. *Pl.* 121, *cr.* 4.
GAPPER, out of an antique crown, a demi-lion, rampant. *Pl.* 67, *cr.* 10, (crown, *pl.* 79, *cr.* 12.)
GARBET, a demi-spread eagle, with two heads, an escutcheon suspended from neck. *Pl.* 4, *cr.* 6.

GARBRIDGE, Norf., a sheaf of reeds, ppr., banded, ar. and sa. *Pl.* 13, *cr.* 2.

GARD, a tower, ar., between two laurel-branches, vert. *Pl.* 72, *cr.* 15.

GARDE, Irl., an antelope's head, erased, ppr. *Pl.* 24, *cr.* 7.

GARDE, a demi-griffin, sa. *Toujours fidele.* *Pl.* 18, *cr.* 6.

GARDEN, Sco., a boar, passant, sa. *Vires animat virtus.* *Pl.* 48, *cr.* 14.

GARDEN, a rose, gu., slipped and leaved, ppr. *Pl.* 105, *cr.* 7.

GARDEN, Sco., an open book, ppr. *Pl.* 15, *cr.* 12.

GARDEN, a duck amongst flags, ppr. *Pl.* 34, *cr.* 6.

GARDENAR, out of a mural coronet, ppr., an armed arm, ar., in hand a flag, gu., charged with a sword, of the second. *Pl.* 115, *cr.* 14, (flag, *pl.* 6, *cr.* 5.)

GARDENER, Linc., a Turk's head, ppr., turbaned, or and az. *Pl.* 36, *cr.* 3.

GARDENER, Norf., Cambs., and Wilts., a griffin's head, erased, sa. *Pl.* 48, *cr.* 6.

GARDENER, Northumb., on a book, gu., clasped and garnished, a falcon, rising, or. *Pl.* 117, *cr.* 7, (falcon, *pl.* 105, *cr.* 4.)

GARDENOR, a leopard, passant, ar., pellettée, in dexter (a pine-apple, or, stalked and leaved, vert.) *Pl.* 86, *cr.* 2.

GARDIN, Sco., an otter, issuing, devouring a salmon, ppr. *Ad escam et usum.* *Pl.* 74, *cr.* 13.

GARDINER, Berks. and Bucks., a griffin's head, erased, az., charged with three bends, or. *Pl.* 38, *cr.* 3.

GARDINER, Oxon., a stork, ppr. *Pl.* 33, *cr.* 9.

GARDINER, Herts., two halberds, erect, environed by a snake, ppr. *Pl.* 14, *cr.* 13.

GARDINER, Dors., a griffin's head, erased, bendy of six, or and purp. *Pl.* 48, *cr.* 6.

GARDINER, Ess., a griffin, passant, regardant, sa. *Pl.* 4, *cr.* 9.

GARDINER, Worc., out of a mural coronet, or, a dexter arm, in armour, embowed, sa., garnished, of the first, in hand a pennon, gu., charged with a pomegranate, or, staff, ppr., headed, or. *Pl.* 115, *cr.* 14, (pennon, *pl.* 6, *cr.* 5; pomegranate, *pl.* 67, *cr.* 8.)

GARDINER, a moor, weeping, vested, in a sailor's dress, kneeling on one knee, jacket, az., trousers, ar.

GARDINER, a demi-griffin, wings expanded, ppr. *Nil desperandum.* *Pl.* 18, *cr.* 6.

GARDINER, Surr., out of a ducal coronet, or, a goat's head, gu., attired, gold. *Pl.* 72, *cr.* 2.

GARDINER, Sco., in dexter hand a sword, ppr. *My hope is constant in thee.* *Pl.* 21, *cr.* 10.

GARDINER, Lond., a man's head, ppr., thereon a cap, turned up, gu. and az., crined and bearded, sa. *Pl.* 51, *cr.* 4.

GARDINER, a griffin, sejant, (resting dexter on a book, sa.) *Pl.* 100, *cr.* 11.

GARDINER, out of a mural coronet, or, seven battle-axes, ppr. *Omnia superat virtus.* *Pl.* 62, *cr.* 8.

GARDINER, a griffin's head, or, (gorged with a chaplet of laurel, vert,) between wings, az. *Persevere.* *Pl.* 22, *cr.* 2.

GARDINER, Lond. and Norf., a rhinoceros, passant, ar. *Pl.* 4, *cr.* 11.

GARDINER, Oxford, a griffin's head, erased. *Deo, non fortuna.* *Pl.* 38, *cr.* 3.

GARDINER-SMITH-WHALLEY, Bart., a Saracen's head, couped at shoulders, ppr., wreathed, gu. and az., on head a cap, or. *Pl.* 38, *cr.* 13.

GARDNER, of Prestongrange, on a mural coronet, seven battle-axes, ppr., one in pale, three to dexter and sinister. *Omnia superat virtus.* *Pl.* 62, *cr.* 8.

GARDNER, Baron, Eng. and Irl., a demi-griffin, az., collared and lined, supporting an anchor, erect, or. *Valet anchora virtus.* *Pl.* 74, *cr.* 15.

GARDNER, Middx., a reindeer's head, ar., attired, or. *Pl.* 2, *cr.* 13, (without collar.)

GARDNER, Linc., an elphant's head, erm., eared, sa., armed, or. *Pl.* 35, *cr.* 13.

GARDNER, Kent, a griffin's head, erased, gorged with a mural coronet. *Pl.* 48, *cr.* 6, (coronet, *pl.* 128, *fig.* 18.)

GARDNER, Linc. and Suff., an elephant's head, couped, erm. *Pl.* 35, *cr.* 13.

GARDNER, Dors., an elephant's head, bendy, az. and ar. *Pl.* 35, *cr.* 13.

GARDNER, a griffin's head, erased, ppr., charged with a crescent, or. *Virtute et fortund.* *Pl.* 48, *cr.* 6, (crescent, *pl.* 18, *cr.* 14.)

GARDNER, an eagle's head, erased, ppr. *'In virtute et fortund.* *Pl.* 20, *cr.* 7.

GARDNER, Cambs., a griffin's head, erased, ar., gorged with two barrulets, sa., within two laurel-branches, in orle, vert. *Pl.* 48, *cr.* 6, (branches, *pl.* 79, *cr.* 14.)

GARDNER, two swords, in saltier, ppr., hilts and pommels, or, banded, az., pendent from band a key, sa. *Pl.* 13, *cr.* 8.

GARDNER, on a ducal coronet, or, a lion, passant, (gardant,) ar. *Pl.* 107, *cr.* 11.

GARDNER, Surr., a demi-unicorn, erased, or, crined and armed, sa., ducally crowned, ar. *Pl.* 26, *cr.* 14, (crown, *pl.* 128, *fig.* 3.)

GARDNER, Salop, a griffin's head, erased, sa. *Pl.* 48, *cr.* 6.

GARDNER, Sco., on a thistle, a bee, all ppr. *Labore et virtute.* *Pl.* 68, *cr.* 9.

GARDNER, Lond. and Linc., a Saracen's head, full-faced, ppr., erased at neck, gu., wreathed, or and az., on head a cap, gold. *Pl.* 38, *cr.* 13.

GARDYNE, Sco., two dexter hands, couped, conjoined, in fess, supporting a cross crosslet, or. *Cruciata cruci junguntur.* *Pl.* 52, *cr.* 15.

GAREN, a cross crosslet, fitched, gu. *Pl.* 16, *cr.* 10.

GARFIELD, out of a heart, a hand holding a (sword,) ppr. *Pl.* 35, *cr.* 7.

GARFOOT, Ess. and Suff., out of a mural coronet, sa., a goat's head, ar., attired, or. *Pl.* 72, *cr.* 2, (crown, *pl.* 128, *fig.* 18.)

GARFORTH, a wolf, current. *Pl.* 111, *cr.* 1.

GARFORTH, Yorks., out of a ducal coronet, a goat's head, ar. *Pl.* 72, *cr.* 2.

GARGATE, a lion, rampant. *Pl.* 67, *cr.* 5.

GARGINTON, a vine-branch, fructed and leaved, ppr. *Pl.* 89, *cr.* 1.

GARGRAVE, Yorks., a falcon, rising, ppr. *Pl.* 105, *cr.* 4.

GARIOCH, Sco., a dove and olive-branch, ppr. *Pl.* 48, *cr.* 15.

GARIOCHS, and GARIOCK, Sco., a palm-tree, (and a trefoil, slipped,) growing out of a mount, all ppr. *Concussus surgo.* *Pl.* 52, *cr.* 6.

GARIOCK, a palm-tree, ppr. *Concussus surgo.* *Pl.* 18, *cr.* 12.

Garland, Yorks., on a mural coronet, or, a lion, sejant, regardant, ar., supporting with dexter a shield, of the second, charged with a garland, ppr.

Garland, and Garlant, Kent and Suss., in lion's paw, erased, a battle-axe, ppr. *Pl.* 51, *cr.* 13.

Garlick, a dexter arm, in armour, erect, in hand a cutlass, in (pale,) all ppr., hilt and pommel, or. *Pl.* 81, *cr.* 11.

Garling, Eng., a fish's head, erased, in fess, ppr. *Pl.* 79, *cr.* 10.

Garman, and Garmon, an oak-tree, and therefrom two weights, pendent, all ppr. *Pl.* 50, *cr.* 3.

Garmish, Suff., a cubit arm, (erased,) in hand a scimitar, all ppr., hilt and pommel, or. *Pl.* 29, *cr.* 8.

Garmiston, Linc., a shark's head, regardant, ar., swallowing a negro, ppr. *Opera Dei mirifica.* *Pl.* 16, *cr.* 6.

Garnatt, a squirrel, sejant, in paws a branch of hazel, ppr. *Pl.* 2, *cr.* 4.

Garnet, a demi-lion, ducally crowned. *Pl.* 61, *cr.* 4, (without branch.)

Galnett, in dexter hand, a swan's head and neck, erased, ppr. *Pl.* 29, *cr.* 4.

Garnett, Lanc., a demi-lion, ar., (gorged with a wreath of oak, ppr., holding an escutcheon, gu., charged with a bugle-horn, or.) *Diligentiâ et honore.* *Pl.* 126, *cr.* 12.

Garnett, a demi-lion, ar., gorged with a collar, dovetail, gu., between paws an escutcheon, or, charged with a cross pattée, fitched, gu. *Pl.* 18, *cr.* 13, (escutcheon, *pl.* 22, *cr.* 13; cross, *pl.* 141.)

Garnham, a goat's head, erased, sa., armed, or. *Pl.* 29, *cr.* 13.

Garnier, Lond. and Hants, a lion's head, erased, ar. *Pl.* 81, *cr.* 4.

Garnier, a griffin's head, gu., charged with a torteau, between wings, ar. *Pl.* 97, *cr.* 13, (without coronet.)

Garnish, an arm, extended, and (erased,) ar., in hand a falchion, blade, of the first, hilt, or. *Pl.* 34, *cr.* 7.

Garnish, a mermaid with mirror and comb, all ppr. *Pl.* 48, *cr.* 5.

Garnock, Sco., a greyhound, current. *Pl.* 28, *cr.* 7, (without charge.)

Garnon, Suss., a wolf's head, or, collared, gu. *Pl.* 8, *cr.* 4.

Garnons, Wel., a demi-lion, rampant, ducally crowned, and gorged, or. *Nid Cyfoeth, ond Boddlondeb—Not wealth, but contentment.* *Pl.* 87, *cr.* 15, (crown, *pl.* 61, *cr.* 4.)

Garnyl, a mermaid, ppr. *Pl.* 48, *cr.* 5.

Garrard, Lond., Kent, and Bucks., a leopard, sejant, ppr. *Pl.* 10, *cr.* 13, (without flag.)

Garrard, Lond., a wyvern, tail nowed, ppr., pierced through neck by a spear, or, headed, ar. *Pl.* 75, *cr.* 12.

Garrard-Drake, Herts., a leopard, sejant, ppr. *Pl.* 10, *cr.* 13, (without flag.)

Garrard-Drake, Herts., a naked dexter arm, erect, in hand a battle-axe, sa, headed, ar. *Pl.* 73, *cr.* 7.

Garrat, and Garratt, a hind, (sejant, regardant,) resting dexter on a bee-hive, ppr. *Pl.* 1, *cr.* 14.

Garratt, Lond. and Surr., a lion, passant, ermines, resting dexter on a fleur-de-lis, or. *Pl.* 4, *cr.* 14.

Garraway, an escallop, between wings. *Pl.* 62, *cr.* 4.

Garret, a demi-monk, in dexter a lash. *Pl.* 83, *cr.* 15.

Garret, and Garrett, Lond., a lion, passant, erm., resting dexter on a fleur-de-lis. *Pl.* 4, *cr.* 14.

Garrick, Middx., a mullet, or. *Pl.* 41, *cr.* 1.

Garritte, a lion, passant. *Certa cruce salus.* *Pl.* 48, *cr.* 8.

Garrioch, Sco., out of a mount, a tree. *Concussus surgit.* *Pl.* 48, *cr.* 4.

Garrock, Sco., a salmon, haurient. *Pl.* 98, *cr.* 12.

Garrow, Suss., on a mount, vert, a palm-tree, ppr., charged with three torteaux. *Pl.* 18, *cr.* 12, (torteau, *pl.* 141.)

Garroway, Suss. and Herts., a griffin, passant, or. *Pl.* 61, *cr.* 14, (without gorging.)

Garroway, Surr., on a rock, a Cornish chough, ppr., beaked and legged, gu. *Pl.* 38, *cr.* 10.

Garscadden, in hand a buckle, ppr. *Pl.* 38, *cr.* 9.

Garsett, and Garsed, Norf., a bow, erect, gu., stringed, sa., with an arrow, or, headed, az., feathered, ar. *Pl.* 12, *cr.* 12.

Garshore, Sco., an eagle, displayed, ppr. *Pl.* 48, *cr.* 11.

Garside, two daggers, in saltier, ppr. *Pl.* 24, *cr.* 2.

Garstin, the Rev. Anthony, co. Louth, in hand a dagger. *Gladio et virtute.* *Pl.* 28, *cr.* 4.

Garstin, in dexter hand a broken hammer. *Pl.* 93, *cr.* 5.

Garston, on stump of tree, eradicated, a raven, wings expanded, all or. *Pl.* 50, *cr.* 5, (stump, *pl.* 78, *cr.* 8.)

Garston, out of a mural coronet, ar., a wyvern, or, charged on breast with a fire-ball, sa. *Pl.* 63, *cr.* 15, (coronet, *pl.* 128, *fig.* 18; fire-ball, *pl.* 70, *cr.* 12.)

Garstyde, Yorks., a stag, per pale, gu. and sa., attired, and hoofed, or. *Pl.* 68, *cr.* 2.

Garter, Norf. and Northamp., a caltrap, or, embrued, ppr. *Pl.* 7, *cr.* 4.

Garter, a caltrap, per pale, gu. and or. *Pl.* 7, *cr.* 4.

Garter, a caltrap, or, embrued, gu. *Pl.* 7, *cr.* 4.

Garth, Surr., an Indian goat, ar., attired, eared, (collared and lined,) or. *Pl.* 66, *cr.* 1.

Garth, a goat, (passant, ar., collared and chained, or.) *Pl.* 66, *cr.* 1.

Garth, a goat, (passant,) ppr. *Pl.* 66, *cr.* 1.

Garton, Suss., a leopard's head, erased, or, ducally gorged, gu., (on the head two straight horns, of the last.) *Pl.* 116, *cr.* 8.

Garton, an antelope's head, erased, gu., ducally gorged, or. *Pl.* 24, *cr.* 7, (gorging, *same plate*, *cr.* 10.)

Garton, a leopard's head, cabossed. *Pl.* 66, *cr.* 14.

Gartshore, Sco., an eagle, displayed, ppr. *I renew my age.* *Pl.* 48, *cr.* 11.

Gartside, two daggers, in saltier, ppr. *Pl.* 24, *cr.* 2.

Garvagh, Baron, Iri., a demi-griffin, az. *Ne cede malis, sed contra.* *Pl.* 18, *cr.* 6.

Garvey, Iri., a greyhound's head, az., collared, ar. *Pl.* 43, *cr.* 11.

Garvey, co. Mayo, a lion, passant, regardant, gu. *Sis justus nec timeas.* *Pl.* 100, *cr.* 6.

GARVIE, Sco., a dexter hand, pointing with two fingers, gu. *Pl.* 67, *cr.* 6.
GARVIN, Sco., in a dexter hand a dagger, in pale, point downward, ppr. *Pl.* 18, *cr.* 3.
GARVINE, Sco., in hand a fish, ppr. *Always helping. Pl.* 105, *cr.* 9.
GARWAY, a leopard's head, erased, (thrust through neck by an arrow, in fess,) ppr. *Pl.* 56, *cr.* 7.
GARWINTON, Eng., a vine-branch, fructed and leaved, ppr. *Pl.* 89, *cr.* 1.
GASCELYN, an arm, in hand a broken sword, ar., hilted, or. *Pl.* 34, *cr.* 7, (sword, *pl.* 22, *cr.* 6.)
GASCOIGN, out of a ducal coronet, an alligator's head, ppr. *Pl.* 17, *cr.* 15.
GASCOIGNE, Yorks., out of a ducal coronet, or, a demi-lucy, erect, gold, charged with a pellet. *Pl.* 36, *cr.* 13.
GASCOIGNE, Yorks. and Norf., out of a ducal coronet, a demi-lucy, erect, or. *Pl.* 36, *cr.* 13.
GASCOYNE, Beds., a pike's head, erect, or, between two ostrich-feathers, ar. *Pl.* 13, *cr.* 7.
GASELEE, an arm, in armour, embowed, in hand, ppr., a dagger, ar., hilt and pommel, or. *Pl.* 120, *cr.* 11.
GASKELL, Yorks., a stork, ppr., (collared, or, pendent therefrom an escutcheon, sa., charged with an annulet, or,) dexter resting on an escallop, gu. *Pl.* 122, *cr.* 7.
GASKELL, Lanc., out of the sea, a dexter arm, from elbow, in hand an anchor, cabled, all ppr. *Spes. Pl.* 27, *cr.* 6.
GASKELL, and GASKILL, issuing from the sea, an arm, embowed, in hand an anchor, ppr. *Pl.* 27, *cr.* 6.
GASON, Kent, on a chapeau, az., turned up, erm., a goat's head, couped, ar., bearded and attired, or. *Pl.* 105, *cr.* 14, (chapeau, *same plate, cr.* 5.)
GASON, Kent, a goat's head, couped, ar., armed, or, gorged with three mascles, sa. *Pl.* 105, *cr.* 14, (mascle, *pl.* 141.)
GASON, Kent, out of a ducal coronet, az., a goat's head, couped, ar. *Pl.* 72, *cr.* 2.
GASSELYN, and GASSELYNE, Eng., an eagle, displayed, sa. *Pl.* 48, *cr.* 11.
GASTON, an owl, sa. *Pl.* 27, *cr.* 9.
GASTRELL, Glouc., a lion's head, erased, ppr., gorged with a chaplet, vert. *Pl.* 22, *cr.* 3.
GATACRE, a raven, ppr. *Pl.* 123, *cr.* 2.
GATCHELL, Somers., out of a mural coronet, ar., a dexter arm, embowed, vested, az., cuffed, erm., in hand a chaplet of wheat, ppr. *Pl.* 115, *cr.* 14, (wheat, *pl.* 102, *cr.* 1.)
GATEFORD, a demi-antelope, collared. *Pl.* 34, *cr.* 8.
GATES, Ess., Yorks., and Linc., a demi-lion, rampant, gardant, or. *Pl.* 35, *cr.* 4.
GATES, Devons., out of a crescent, flames, ppr. *Pl.* 29, *cr.* 2.
GATESDEN, a dexter arm, embowed, vested, in hand a tilting-spear. *Pl.* 39, *cr.* 1, (spear, *pl.* 97, *cr.* 4.)
GATFIELD, on a ducal coronet, or, a cross, gu. *Pl.* 98, *cr.* 6, (without feathers.)
GATHWAITE, a mastiff, ppr., chained and collared, or. *Pl.* 65, *cr.* 2.
GATORBY, two swords, in saltier, ppr. *Pl.* 75, *cr.* 13, (without cup.)
GATTIE, and GATTY, a stork, sleeping, in dexter a stone. *Pl.* 26, *cr.* 11.

GAUDEN, a peacock's head, ppr. *Pl.* 100, *cr.* 5.
GAUDINE, Sco., a savage's head, couped, ppr. *Pl.* 81, *cr.* 15.
GAULDESBOROUGH, Ess., a pelican, vulning, ppr. *Pl.* 109, *cr.* 15.
GAULER, a hawk, in dexter an ear of wheat, ppr. *Pl.* 94, *cr.* 7.
GAULFIELD, a dexter hand, vested, holding up the sun, or. *Pl.* 89, *cr.* 11, (without coronet.)
GAUNT, Kent and Staffs., a wolf's head, or, collared, vair. *Dum spiro, spero. Pl.* 8, *cr.* 4.
GAUNT, DE, Eng., a cross pattée, fitched, sa. *Pl.* 27, *cr.* 14.
GAUNTLET, Eng., out of a ducal coronet, a bear's head, muzzled, ppr. *Pl.* 6, *cr.* 6.
GAUSEN, and GAUSSEN, a bee-hive, with bees, volant, all ppr. *Pl.* 81, *cr.* 14.
GAUSSEN, a greyhound's head, ar., eared and spotted, sa. *Pl.* 89, *cr.* 2.
GAVELL, Surr., a demi-buck, regardant, or, vulned in shoulder, gu. *Pl.* 55, *cr.* 9, (regardant, *pl.* 51, *cr.* 9.)
GAVEN, and GAWEN, Eng., in dexter hand a ducal coronet, between two laurel-branches, all ppr. *Pl.* 95, *cr.* 11.
GAVEN, a land-tortoise, ppr. *Pl.* 12, *cr.* 13.
GAVIN, Sco., a ship in full sail, ppr. *Remember. Pl.* 109, *cr.* 7.
GAVIN, Sco., in the sea, a (two-)masted ship, in full sail, ppr. *By industry we prosper. Pl.* 109, *cr.* 8.
GAWAINE, and GAWAYNE, a horse-shoe, or. *Pl.* 52, *cr.* 4.
GAWDEN, an arm, in a maunch, gu., hand clenched, ppr. *Pl.* 22, *cr.* 14.
GAWDY, Norf. and Suff., on a chapeau, gu., turned up, erm., (two) swords, erect, ar., hilts and pommels, or. *Pl.* 105, *cr.* 1, (chapeau, *same plate, cr.* 5.)
GAWDY, Norf., a wolf, passant, per pale, ar. and gu. *Pl.* 46, *cr.* 6.
GAWLER, a martlet, sa. *Pl.* 111, *cr.* 5.
GAWLER, a mullet, sa. *Pl.* 41, *cr.* 1.
GAWSWORTH, a savage's head, in profile, ppr. *Pl.* 81, *cr.* 15.
GAY, Somers., a greyhound, current, ppr. *Stat fortuna domus. Pl.* 28, *cr.* 7, (without charge.)
GAY, a demi-greyhound, ppr. *Pl.* 48, *cr.* 3.
GAY, Kent, a demi-greyhound, rampant, sa., collared, or. *Pl.* 5, *cr.* 10, (without wings.)
GAY, in hand a sword, ar., hilt and pommel, or. *Pl.* 21, *cr.* 10.
GAY, Norf., a fleur-de-lis, or. *Pl.* 68, *cr.* 12.
GAY, JAMES, Esq., of Alborough New Hall, Norf., a fleur-de-lis. *Toujours gai. Pl.* 68, *cr.* 12.
GAY, Devons., on a chapeau, gu., turned up, erm., a lion, passant, gardant, or, charged on breast with an escallop, az. *Pl.* 105, *cr.* 5, (without crown or gorging.)
GAYER, a lion, rampant, sa., supporting a spear. *Pl.* 22, *cr.* 15, (spear, *pl.* 97, *cr.* 4.)
GAYLIEN, a hind's head, between two roses, stalked and leaved, ppr. *Pl.* 13, *cr.* 9.
GAYNER, and GAYNOR, Eng., a dexter hand, apaumée, ppr. *Pl.* 32, *cr.* 14.
GAYNES, out of a ducal coronet, a demi-swan, wings expanded, ppr., ducally gorged, sa. *Pl.* 100, *cr.* 7.
GAYNOR, Iri., a lion's head, erased, gu., charged with a trefoil, or. *Pl.* 81, *cr.* 4, (trefoil, *pl.* 141.)

GAYNSFORD, and GAYNSFORTH, a rose, gu., slipped and leaved, vert, and a spear, ppr., in saltier. *Pl.* 104, *cr.* 7.

GAYS, an eagle, with two heads, displayed, ppr. *Pl.* 87, *cr.* 11, (without flame.)

GAYTON, three legs, in armour, conjoined at thigh, flexed at knee, and spurred, ppr. *Pl.* 71, *cr.* 14.

GEACH, an arm, embowed, in hand a battle-axe, enfiled with a garland round elbow, all ppr. *Pl.* 121, *cr.* 14.

GEALE, Iri., out of a ducal coronet, a hand holding a fleur-de-lis. *Pl.* 120, *cr.* 4.

GEAR, and GEARE, Kent and Devons., a leopard's head, az., ducally gorged, or, between wings, gu. *Pl.* 116, *cr.* 8, (wings, *pl.* 115, *cr.* 4.)

GEARY, Bart., Kent, out of a naval crown, a sinister hand and arm, in naval uniform, supporting a flag, ar., charged with a cross, gu. *Chase. Pl.* 93, *cr.* 1, (flag, *pl.* 6, *cr.* 5.)

GEARY, Herts., an antelope's head, erased, quarterly, ar. and sa., (charged with three mascles, counterchanged.) *Pl.* 24, *cr.* 7.

GEARY, Surr., an heraldic-antelope's head, erased, quarterly, ar. and sa., charged with a lozenge, erm. *Pl.* 76, *cr.* 3, (lozenge, *pl.* 141.)

GED, and GEDD, Sco., a pike's head, ppr. *Pl.* 122, *cr.* 6.

GED, Sco., in hand, ppr., an escutcheon, gu. *Pl.* 21, *cr.* 12.

GEDDES, and GEDDIES, Sco., a pike's head, couped, ppr. *Durat, ditat, placet. Pl.* 122, *cr.* 6.

GEDDES, and GEDDIES, Sco., a stag's head, couped, ppr. *Fato prudentia major. Pl.* 91, *cr.* 14.

GEDDES, and GEDDIES, Sco., a stag's head. *Veritas vincit. Pl.* 91, *cr.* 14.

GEDDES, and GEDDIES, Sco., on a mural coronet, a bundle of seven arrows, banded. *Pl.* 106, *cr.* 14, (arrows, *pl.* 54, *cr.* 15.)

GEDDING, and GEDING, a demi-savage, in hand a scimitar, ppr. *Pl.* 82, *cr.* 2.

GEDNEY, a bird, perched on an oak-plant, ppr. *Pl.* 71, *cr.* 5.

GEDNEY, two lucies, in saltier, ppr.

GEE, Lond., Linc., and Yorks., a gauntlet, ar., garnished at wrist, or, in hand a sword, of the first, hilt and pommel, of the second. *Pl.* 125, *cr.* 5.

GEEKIE, Lond., in hand a sickle, ppr. *Pl.* 36, *cr.* 12.

GEERING, Suss., a savage's head, affrontée, ducally crowned, ppr. *Pl.* 28, *cr.* 3.

GEFFRY, Eng., a lion's head, erased, ar., ducally crowned, or. *Pl.* 90, *cr.* 4, (without charging.)

GÆFFRYS, Worc., on a mount, vert, a sea-pie, rising, ppr., beaked and legged, gu. *Pl.* 79, *cr.* 11.

GEIKE, Sco., a boar's head, erased, sa. *Vigilo. Pl.* 16, *cr.* 11.

GEILS, a demi-chevalier, in dexter a sword. *Pl.* 23, *cr.* 4.

GELL, Derbs., a greyhound's head, collared, or. *Pl.* 43, *cr.* 11.

GELLATLY, Sco., a lion's head, gu., crowned with an antique crown, or. *Hactenus invictus. Pl.* 123, *cr.* 13.

GELLIE, or GELLY, Sco., a man standing on a serpent, ppr. *Divino robore. Pl.* 109, *cr.* 1.

GELLING, on a chapeau, a lion, passant, gardant, tail extended, and ducally crowned, ppr. *Pl.* 120, *cr.* 5, (crown, *same plate*.)

GELSTABLE, in dexter hand, a sword, in pale, all ppr. *Pl.* 23, *cr.* 15.

GELSTABLE, Eng., in hand a sword, in pale, ppr. *Pl.* 23, *cr.* 15.

GEM, in dexter hand a gem-ring, ppr., stoned, gu. *Pl.* 24, *cr.* 3.

GEMELL, GEMILL, and GEMMELL, a flame of fire, between two palm-branches, ppr. *Pl.* 62, *cr.* 6.

GEMELL, GEMILL, and GEMMELL, a demi-peacock, ppr. *Pl.* 24, *cr.* 1.

GEMMEL, Sco.: 1. A dexter arm, in hand a dart. *Pl.* 92, *cr.* 14. 2. A laurel-branch and sword, in saltier, ppr. *Pl.* 50, *cr.* 4, (laurel-branch, *pl.* 123, *cr.* 5.)

GENEVILLE, (out of a cloud,) in dexter hand, a broken tilting-spear, all ppr. *Pl.* 23, *cr.* 9.

GENEY, or GENNY, out of a cloud, a hand, in fess, holding a cross-pattée, fitched, ppr. *Pl.* 26, *cr.* 4.

GENN, between two spear-heads, in pale, a Cornish chough, rising, all ppr. *Pl.* 79, *cr.* 13.

GENNETT, a chevalier, on horseback, in hand a scimitar, all ppr. *Pl.* 28, *cr.* 5.

GENNYS, an eagle, per pale, az. and gu., wings raised, (each charged with a bezant, from the beak, a scroll, ar., thereon the words— *Deo gloria. Pl.* 126, *cr.* 7, (scroll, *pl.* 27, *cr.* 7; bezant, *pl.* 141.)

GENOR, in hand a baton, gu., tipped, or. *Pl.* 33, *cr.* 4.

GENT, Northumb., a demi-griffin, gu., wings addorsed, or, holding a gilliflower, of the first, stalked and leaved, ppr. *Pl.* 18, *cr.* 6, (flower, *pl.* 22, *cr.* 9.)

GENT, Ess., out of a ducal coronet, or, a demi-eagle, displayed, erm. *Pl.* 9, *cr.* 6.

GENT, GEORGE, Esq., of Moyns Park, Ess., out of a ducal coronet, an eagle, displayed. *In est clementia forti. Pl.* 9, *cr.* 6.

GENT, Northumb., a griffin, segrent, or, in beak a gilliflower, gu. stalked and leaved, vert. *Pl.* 67, *cr.* 13, (flower, *pl.* 22, *cr.* 9.)

GENT, out of a ducal coronet, a phœnix, or, in flames, ppr. *Pl.* 53, *cr.* 6.

GENT, an eagle, displayed, sa. *Pl.* 48, *cr.* 11.

GENTILL, Sco., two lions' paws, holding a bezant. *Pl.* 42, *cr.* 3.

GENTLE, Sco., a bee, erect, ppr. *Industria. Pl.* 100, *cr.* 3.

GENTLE, on a ducal coronet, an etoile of (twelve) points. *Pl.* 83, *cr.* 3.

GEOGHAM, an arm, in armour, embowed, in hand a dagger. *Manu forti. Pl.* 120, *cr.* 11.

GEOGHEGAN, Eng. and Iri., on a ducal coronet, or, a dolphin, naiant, az. *Pl.* 94, *cr.* 14.

GEORGE, Bart., Middx., a falcon, rising, az., beaked, legged, and belled, or. *Pl.* 105, *cr.* 4.

GEORGE, a demi-talbot, sa., (collared,) indented, and eared, or, between two fir-branches, vert. *Pl.* 15, *cr.* 2, (fir-branch, *pl.* 80, *cr.* 1.)

GEORGE, Iri., a stag's head, erased, ppr. *Pl.* 66, *cr.* 9.

GEORGE, Cornw., a demi-talbot, rampant, sa., (gorged with a collar,) dancettée, and eared, or, between two laurel-branches, vert. *Pl.* 15, *cr.* 2, (laurel-branches, *pl.* 79, *cr.* 14.)

GEORGE, Sco., the sun shining on a sunflower, ppr. *Pl.* 45, *cr.* 13, (sunflower, *pl.* 84, *cr.* 6.)

GEORGE, Middx., a hawk, rising, ppr. *Pl.* 105, *cr.* 4.
GEORGE, Eng., a greyhound's head. *Pl.* 89, *cr.* 2.
GEORGES, Lond. and Middx., a greyhound's head. *Pl.* 89, *cr.* 2.
GEORGES, a demi-talbot, salient, sa., (collared) and eared, or. *Pl.* 15, *cr.* 2.
GEORGES, Glouc., a talbot's head, erased, sa., eared, or. *Pl.* 90, *cr.* 6.
GEORGES, a boar, passant, az., armed and bristled, or. *Pl.* 48, *cr.* 14.
GEPP, a griffin's head (collared,) between wings. *Pl.* 65, *cr.* 1.
GEPP, Ess., on a mount, vert, an eagle, rising, az., wings, erminois, (gorged with a collar, in beak a mascle, or, supporting a sword, in pale, ppr., hilt and pommel, gold.) *Pl.* 61, *cr.* 1.
GERANDOT, a demi-lion, rampant, sa. *Pl.* 67, *cr.* 10.
GERARD, Bart., Lanc., a lion, rampant, erm., crowned, or. *En Dieu est mon espérance.* *Pl.* 98, *cr.* 1.
GERARD, Middx. and Lanc., in lion's gamb, erased, erm., a hawk's lure, gu., garnished and lined, or, tasselled, ar. *Pl.* 126, *cr.* 9, (hawk's lure, *pl.* 97, *cr.* 14.)
GERARD, Kent, a monkey, passant, collared round middle and chained, ppr. *Bono vince malum.* *Pl.* 101, *cr.* 11.
GERARD, Berks., a lion, statant, gardant, ducally crowned, gu. *En Dieu est mon espérance.* *Pl.* 105, *cr.* 5, (without chapeau.)
GERARD, Lanc. and Derbs., two wings, expanded, sa. *Pl.* 39, *cr.* 12.
GERBRIDGE, Eng., in lion's paw, a thistle, ppr. *Pl.* 109, *cr.* 4.
GERCOM, a griffin, segreant, ppr., (collared, gu., in mouth a line and ring, or.) *Pl.* 67, *cr.* 13.
GERDELLEY, and GERDILLY, in hand a sword, ppr. *Pl.* 21, *cr.* 10.
GERDON, on the wreath a human heart, ppr., surmounted by two hands, couped and conjoined, in fess. *Pl.* 13, *cr.* 11.
GERERD, a lion, rampant. *Pl.* 67, *cr.* 5.
GERIDOT, a demi-lion, rampant. *Pl.* 67, *cr.* 10.
GERING, Linc., an antelope's head, erased, quartered, ar. and sa., (charged with four mascles,) counterchanged, attired, or. *Pl.* 24, *cr.* 7.
GERLING, a unicorn's head, erased, ar., collared, sa. *Pl.* 67, *cr.* 1.
GERMAIN, a dexter arm, couped and embowed, in hand a tilting-spear, in pale, ppr. *Pl.* 107, *cr.* 3.
GERMIN, and GERMYN, a lion, rampant, az. *Pl.* 67, *cr.* 5.
GERMIN, and GERMYN, a unicorn's head, between branches of laurel, in orle. *Pl.* 54, *cr.* 9.
GERNEGAN, an allerion, displayed, gu. *Pl.* 48, *cr.* 11.
GERNEY, on a garb, in fess, a cock, statant, ppr. *Pl.* 122, *cr.* 3.
GERNON, GERNOUN, or GERNUN, Eng., in hand, issuing from a cloud, in fess, a club, ppr. *Pl.* 37, *cr.* 13.
GERNON, Iri., a horse, passant, ar. *Parva contemnimus.* *Pl.* 15, *cr.* 14.
GERNON, a wolf's head, couped, az., collared (and ringed,) or. *Pl.* 8, *cr.* 4.

GERNON, Suss., a wolf's head, or, collared, gu. *Pl.* 8, *cr.* 4.
GERNON, a wolf's head, (couped,) on neck two bars-gemelle. *Pl.* 14, *cr.* 6.
GERRE, Herts., a lion's head, gardant, or, gorged with a collar, gu., charged with three mascles, between wings, gold.
GERRY, Lanc., a buck's head, erased, quarterly, ar. and sa., charged with four mascles, counterchanged. *Pl.* 66, *cr.* 9, (mascle, *pl.* 141.)
GERSON, Lanc., an arm, in armour, couped, in fess, in hand a helmet, in pale, ppr. *Pl.* 114, *cr.* 9.
GERVAIS, a lion's head, erased, ar., charged with a fleur-de-lis, of the same. *Sic sustenta crescit.* *Pl.* 81, *cr.* 4, (fleur-de-lis, *pl.* 141.)
GERVIS, Cambs. and Worc., a tiger's head, erased, or. *Pl.* 94, *cr.* 10.
GERVIS, a demi-lion, rampant, gardant, or, (holding a banner, ar., charged with a cross, gu., on the handle, ppr., a mural coronet, gold, and issuing therefrom four small spears, az.) *Pl.* 35, *cr.* 4.
GERWOOD, a cubit arm, ppr., in hand a cross crosslet, fitched, gu. *Pl.* 99, *cr.* 1.
GESSORS, a talbot, sejant, sa., collared, ar. *Pl.* 107, *cr.* 7.
GESSORS, in dexter hand a battle-axe. *Pl.* 73, *cr.* 7.
GETHAM, a bustard, ppr. *Pl.* 30, *cr.* 8.
GETHIN, Bart., Iri., a stag, current, ar., armed, or. *Try.* *Pl.* 3, *cr.* 2.
GETHIN, Iri., Well., Ess., and Wilts., a buck, sejant, ar., attired, or, between wings, of the first. *Pl.* 101, *cr.* 3, (wings, *pl.* 115, *cr.* 6.)
GETHIN, Iri., on a chapeau, gu., turned up, erm., a buck's head, erased, ar., ducally gorged and attired, or. *Pl.* 55, *cr.* 2, (chapeau, *pl.* 127, *fig.* 13.)
GETTENS, a sheldrake, ppr. *Pl.* 90, *cr.* 15.
GEYNES, a griffin's head, erased, in beak a trefoil. *Pl.* 48, *cr.* 6, (trefoil, *pl.* 141.)
GEYNES, out of a cloud, a dexter hand, pointing with fore-finger, ppr. *Pl.* 77, *cr.* 6, (without star.)
GEYNTON, and GEYTON, the sun in splendour, or, at each ray a flame of fire, ppr. *Pl.* 68, *cr.* 14.
GHEST, a swan's head and neck, erased, between two ostrich-feathers, ar. *Pl.* 30, *cr.* 10, (feathers, *pl.* 13, *cr.* 7.)
GHRIMES, a talbot, sejant, sa., collared, ar. *Pl.* 107, *cr.* 7.
GIB, Sco., a mullet, pierced, or. *Spero.* *Pl.* 45, *cr.* 1.
GIB, Sco., a spur, or, between wings, gu. *Pl.* 109, *cr.* 12.
GIBB, Sco., a dagger, in pale, on point a wreath of laurel, ppr. *Pl.* 15, *cr.* 6.
GIBBALL, Iri., a goat, (passant,) ar., hoofed and armed, sa. *Pl.* 66, *cr.* 1.
GIBBARD, an arm, couped, embowed, vested and purfled at shoulder, the part above elbow, in fess, in hand, in pale, a palm-branch, ppr. *Pl.* 62, *cr.* 7.
GIBBE, a Bengal-tiger, passant, gardant, ppr. *Pl.* 67, *cr.* 15.
GIBBENS, and GIBBINS, in hand a fish, ppr. *Pl.* 105, *cr.* 9.
GIBBINES, and GIBBINS, on a ducal coronet, or, the attires of a stag, ppr. *Pl.* 118, *cr.* 11.

GIBBINES, and GIBBINS, a lion, rampant, sa. *Pl.* 67, *cr.* 5.

GIBBON, Kent, on a chapeau, gu., turned up, erm., an escarbuncle, or. *Pl.* 13, *cr.* 14.

GIBBON, Kent, a demi-lion, rampant, gardant, ar., ducally crowned, or, between paws an escallop, gold. *Pl.* 61, *cr.* 4, (escallop, *pl.* 141.)

GIBBON, a stork, wings (expanded,) ppr. *Pl.* 33, *cr.* 9.

GIBBONS, Bart., Middx., in lion's gamb, erased and erect, gu., charged with a bezant, a cross formée, fitched, sa. *Pl.* 46, *cr.* 7, (bezant, *pl.* 141.)

GIBBONS, Wilts., a demi-lion, rampant, sa., holding an escallop, ar. *Pl.* 126 A, *cr.* 13.

GIBBONS, Iri., a dexter and sinister arm, in armour, embowed, hands supporting a heart, inflamed, ppr. *Pl.* 36, *cr.* 4.

GIBBS, Bart., Oxon., an arm, in armour, embowed, garnished, or, and (charged with a cross, couped, gu.,) in hand, ppr., a battle-axe, sa. *Tenax propositi*. *Pl.* 121, *cr.* 14.

GIBBS, an arm, in armour, or, in hand a battle-axe, ar. *Pl.* 121, *cr.* 14.

GIBBS, co. Derry, a griffin's head, erased, ar., (pierced through back of neck by an arrow, or, barbed and feathered, ar.) *Pl.* 48, *cr.* 6.

GIBBS, Kent, an arm, in armour, embowed, in hand a battle-axe, in bend. *Pl.* 121, *cr.* 14.

GIBBS, GEORGE, Esq., of Belmont, Somers., an arm, in armour, embowed, in gauntlet a battle-axe, ar. *Pl.* 121, *cr.* 14.

GIBBS, Kent and Herts., an arm, in armour, embowed, ppr., garnished, or, in gauntlet a (pole-axe,) ar. *Pl.* 121, *cr.* 14.

GIBBS, Devons., a tiger, passant, gardant. *Pl.* 67, *cr.* 15.

GIBBS, Warw., three broken tilting-spears, or, one in pale, two in saltier, enfiled with a wreath, ar. and sa. *Pl.* 33, *cr.* 3.

GIBERNE, a plume of feathers. *Tién ta foi*. *Pl.* 12, *cr.* 9.

GIBERNE, a stag's head, between the horns of a cross pattée. *Pl.* 9, *cr.* 10.

GIBLETT, a demi-stag, in mouth a cinquefoil, slipped. *Pl.* 55, *cr.* 9, (cinquefoil, *pl.* 141.)

GIBON, on a ducal coronet, a lion's head, (couped,) gu., bezantée. *Pl.* 99, *cr.* 9.

GIBON, a demi-wolf, rampant, regardant, ar., (collared,) gu. *Pl.* 10, *cr.* 3.

GIBON, in lion's paw, a cross pattée, or. *Pl.* 46, *cr.* 7.

GIBON, in lion's paw, erased, gu., a cross pattée, fitched, or. *Pl.* 46, *cr.* 7.

GIBSON, Iri., a stork's head, sa., crowned, or. *Pl.* 49, *cr.* 9.

GIBSON, Eng., a stork, (in beak an oak-leaf,) ppr. *Pl.* 33, *cr.* 9.

GIBSON, Lond., Ess., Northumb., and Cumb., out of a ducal coronet, or, in lion's gamb, ppr., a club, gu., spiked, gold. *Pl.* 67, *cr.* 7, (club, *pl.* 83, *cr.* 2.)

GIBSON, a stork, rising, ppr., in beak an olive-branch, vert. *Pl.* 46, *cr.* 9.

GIBSON, Norf., a stork, ar., beaked, legged, and (ducally gorged,) gu. *Pl.* 33, *cr.* 9.

GIBSON, Ess. and Yorks., on a mount, vert, a stork, ar., beaked, membered, and (gorged with a collar, gu., pendent therefrom an escutcheon, az., charged with a barnacle, or.) *Recte et fideliter*. *Pl.* 122, *cr.* 7.

GIBSON, Lond., an arm, in armour, embowed, ppr., garnished, or, in hand a battle-axe, sa. *Pl.* 121, *cr.* 14.

GIBSONE, JOHN-CHARLES-HOPE, Esq., of Pentland, Edinburgh, a pelican in nest, feeding her young. *Pandite, cœlestes portæ*. *Pl.* 44, *cr.* 1.

GIBSON-MAITLAND, Bart., Sco., a lion, sejant, gardant, gu., ducally crowned, in dexter a drawn sword, or, in sinister a fleur-de-lis, az. *Consilio et animis*. *Pl.* 120, *cr.* 2.

GIBTHORP, or GIBTHORPE, a naked arm, embowed, in hand a dagger, ppr. *Pl.* 34, *cr.* 7.

GIDDY, a lion, passant, gu., in dexter a banner, az., charged with a cross, or, the staff and point, ppr. *Pl.* 106, *cr.* 5.

GIDEON, a cock's head, erased, gu. *Pl.* 92, *cr.* 3.

GIDEON, a stag's head, ar., ducally gorged, or. *Pl.* 55, *cr.* 2.

GIDION, Lond., in hand, gu., in fess, an anchor, or, environed with clouds, ppr. *Pl.* 79, *cr.* 15.

GIDION, Lond. and Linc., a stag's head, erased, ar., attired, gu., gorged with a palisado coronet, or, in mouth an acorn-slip, fructed, ppr. *Pl.* 100, *cr.* 8 (coronet, *pl.* 128, *fig.* 21.)

GIDLEY, Devons., a griffin's head, or, wings elevated, sa., bezantée.

GIESQUE, a stag, salient. *Pl.* 65, *cr.* 14.

GIFFARD, Staffs, a demi-archer, ppr., from middle, a short coat, paly, ar. and gu., at his side a quiver of arrows, in hands a bow, arrow drawn, or. *Prenez haleine trez fort*. *Pl.* 60, *cr* 5.

GIFFARD, Staffs., a tiger's head, couped, or, affrontée, fire issuing from mouth, gu. *Prenez haleine trez fort*. *Pl.* 112, *cr.* 9.

GIFFARD, Iri., a sphinx, gardant, wings addorsed, ppr. *Pl.* 91, *cr* 11.

GIFFARD, Sco., a deer's head, couped, ppr. *Spare nought*. *Pl.* 91, *cr.* 14.

GIFFARD, Sco., in dexter hand a thistle, ppr. *Pl.* 36, *cr.* 6.

GIFFARD, co. Wexford, a cock's head, erased, or. *Pl.* 92, *cr.* 3.

GIFFORD, Baron, a panther's head, affrontée, between two branches of oak, ppr. *Non sine numine*.

GIFFORD, Devons., a cock's head, erased, or, (in beak a sprig,) ppr. *Pl.* 92, *cr.* 3.

GIFFORD, an arm, couped, vested, or, (charged with two bars, wavy,) az., cuffed, ar., in hand, ppr., a buck's head, cabossed, gu. *Pl.* 39, *cr.*1, (buck's head, *pl.* 36, *cr.* 1.)

GIFFORD, Sco., a hart's head, ppr. *Spare when you have nought*. *Pl.* 91, *cr.* 14.

GIFFORD, Iri., a cubit dexter arm, in armour, in hand a gilliflower, all ppr. *Potius mori quam fœdari*. *Pl.* 55, *cr.* 6, (flower, *pl.* 22, *cr.* 9.)

GIGON, a dexter arm, in hand a swan's head, erased, ppr. *Pl.* 29, *cr.* 4.

GILBARD, a squarrel, sejant, gu., cracking a nut, ppr. *Pl.* 16, *cr.* 9.

GILBERD, on a chapeau, sa., turned up, erm., a fox, sejant, ppr. *Pl.* 57, *cr.* 14.

GILBERT, Cornw., a squirrel, sejant, on a hill, vert, feeding on a crop of nuts, ppr. *Mallem mori quam mutare*. *Pl.* 2, *cr.* 4.

GILBERT, Norf., a stag's head, or, (on neck a fess, engrailed with plain cottises, gu.) *Tenax propositi*. *Pl.* 91, *cr.* 14.

GILBERT, JOHN-DAVIES, Esq., of Tredrea, Cornw.; and East-Bourn, Suss., a squirrel, sejant, gu., cracking a nut, or. *Teg. Yw. Hedwch.* Pl. 16, cr. 9.

GILBERT, Ess. and Suff., (on a mount, vert,) a demi-eagle, displayed, ar., charged on breast with a mullet, or. Pl. 44, cr. 14.

GILBERT, Suss. and Suff., out of rays, or, an eagle's head, ppr. Pl. 84, cr. 9.

GILBERT, Sco., in hand a fleur-de-lis, or. Pl. 46, cr. 12.

GILBERT, Suss., a squirrel, sejant, gu., cracking a nut, or. Pl. 16, cr. 9.

GILBERT, Norf., out of a ducal coronet, or, a stag's head, erm., attired, gold. Pl. 29, cr. 7.

GILBERT, Leic. and Derbs., an arm, in armour, embowed, ppr., in hand a broken tilting-spear, headed, ar., point downward. Pl. 44, cr. 9.

GILBERT, Herts. and Kent, a griffin's head, az., beaked, or, (collared, erm.) Pl. 48, cr. 6.

GILBERT, out of a ducal coronet, or, a griffin's head, gu., beaked, gold. Pl. 54, cr. 14.

GILBERT, out of a mural coronet, or, a demi-lion, rampant, ducally crowned, gold, holding a battle-axe, sa., headed, ar. Pl. 120, cr. 14, (crown, *same plate.*)

GILBERT, Derbs. and Salop, out of a ducal coronet, an eagle's head, gu., beaked, or. Pl. 20, cr. 12, (without pellet.)

GILBERT, Heref. and Monm., an arm, in armour, embowed, ppr., severed below the wrist, dropping blood, in hand a broken spear, or, headed, ar., point downward. Pl. 44, cr. 9.

GILBERTSON, a snail in its shell, ppr. Pl. 105, cr. 8.

GILBES, a leopard, passant, gardant. Pl. 51, cr. 7.

GILBORNE, Lond. and Kent, a tiger, (salient, ar., lined and collared, or.) Pl. 73, cr. 2.

GILBY, or GILBIE, Linc., a tower, or, (a dragon's head issuing from the top, and the tail out of the door, ar.) Pl. 12, cr. 5.

GILCHRIST, Lond., out of a cloud, the sun rising, ppr. *I hope to speed.* Pl. 67, cr. 9.

GILCHRIST, Sco., a crescent, ar. *Fide et fiduciâ.* Pl. 18, cr. 14.

GILCHRIST, Sco., a lion, rampant, in dexter a (scimitar,) all ppr. *Mea gloria fides.* Pl. 64, cr. 2.

GILDART, Lanc., a demi-lion, rampant, (re-gardant,) crowned, or, in dexter an oak-branch, ppr. Pl. 61, cr. 4.

GILDEA, a wolf's head, erased, ppr., langued, gu. *Re e merito*—and—*Vincit qui patitur.* Pl. 14, cr. 6.

GILDER, an arrow, enfiled with a ducal coronet. Pl. 55, cr. 1.

GILDRIDGE, Suss., a sinister arm, in armour, embowed, ppr., in gauntlet a club, in pale, or, and above gauntlet a dexter hand, ppr., couped, gu., grasping club.

GILES, Lond. and Worc., out of a chalice, or, three pansy-flowers, ppr. Pl. 102, cr. 12.

GILES, a squirrel, sejant, gu., bezantée, in paws an oak-branch, leaved, ppr. Pl. 2, cr. 4.

GILES, Devons., in lion's gamb, erect and erased, an apple-branch, sa., leaved, vert. Pl. 70, cr. 9.

GILES, Sco., a demi-chevalier, in hand a sword. Pl. 23, cr. 4.

GILFILLAN, or GILFILLIAN, Sco. and Iri., an eagle's head, erased, sa., langued, gu. *Armis et animis.* Pl. 20, cr. 7.

GILFORD, an angel, (couped at breast,) ppr. Pl. 25, cr. 7.

GILHAM, and GILLHAM, three savages' heads, conjoined in one neck, one looking to dexter, one to sinister, and one upward, ppr. Pl. 32, cr. 2.

GILL, Herts., a hawk's head, az., between wings, or, fretty, vert. Pl. 99, cr. 10.

GILL, a griffin's head (collared,) wings addorsed. Pl. 38, cr. 3.

GILL, Lond., a salamander in flames, ppr. Pl. 20, cr. 15.

GILL, a demi-eagle, rising, az., wings, or, fretty, vert. Pl. 52, cr. 8.

GILL, Devons., a boar, passant, resting fore-paw on a crescent. *In te, Domine, spes nostra.* Pl. 48, cr. 14, (crescent, *pl.* 141.)

GILLAM, a demi-griffin, vert, winged and beaked, or. Pl. 18, cr. 6.

GILLAM, Ess., out of a ducal coronet, or, a dragon's head, ppr. Pl. 93, cr. 15, (without flames.)

GILLAN, and GILLAND, a dexter arm, embowed, ppr., vested and cuffed, az., in hand a covered cup, ppr. Pl. 39, cr. 1.

GILLANDERS, Sco., in hand a sword, ppr. *Durum sed certissimum.* Pl. 21, cr. 10.

GILLE, Lond. and Warw., a demi-parrot, wings expanded, or. Pl. 94, cr. 2.

GILLEANKS, JACKSON, Esq., of Whitefield House, Cumb., a stag's head, or. *Honore et virtute.* Pl. 91, cr. 14.

GILLIES, in hand an escallop, ppr. Pl. 57, cr. 6.

GILLESPIE, W., Esq., of Torbanehill, a cat, sejant. *Touch not the cat, but a glove.* Pl. 24, cr. 6.

GILLESPIE, Sco., a unicorn's head, ar., armed, or. *Fidelis et in bello fortis.* Pl. 20, cr. 1.

GILLESPIE, Sco., a leopard, sejant, (gardant.) Pl. 10, cr. 13, (without flag.)

GILLESPIE, Sco., an anchor, ppr. *In certâ salutis anchorâ.* Pl. 42, cr. 12.

GILLESPIE, Sco., a demi-cat, ppr. *Touch not the cat, but a glove.* Pl. 80, cr. 7.

GILLET, in hand a dagger, in pale, ppr. Pl. 23, cr. 15.

GILLET, a lion, rampant, in dexter a battle-axe. Pl. 64, cr. 2, (axe, *pl.* 26, *cr.* 7.)

GILLET, Suff., a lucy's head, erased and erect, gu., (collared with a bar-gemelle, or.) Pl.122,cr.6.

GILLET, Suff., a lucy's head, erased and erect, or., (collared with a bar-gemelle, gu.) Pl. 122, cr. 6.

GILLIES, How., ADAM, of Kintrocket, a grey cat, passant, ppr. *Touch not the cat, bot a glove.* Pl. 119, cr. 7.

GILLIES, and GILLIS, Sco., a cat, current, ppr. *Touch not the cat, bot a glove.* Pl. 119, cr. 7.

GILLINGHAM, a dexter arm, couped, and embowed, ppr., vested, sa., cuffed, ar., in hand a sword, in pale, enfiled with a leopard's head, cabossed, ppr. Pl. 102, cr. 5.

GILLOT, a garb, or. Pl. 48, cr. 10.

GILLMAN, co. Cork, a griffin's head, erased, in mouth a bear's paw. *Non cauta sed actu.* Pl. 35, cr. 15, (paw, *pl.* 126, cr. 2.)

GILLON, of Wallhouse, on the face of a rock, a raven, ppr. *Tutum refugium.* Pl. 38, cr. 10.

GILLON, in dexter hand, a bomb, fired, ppr. Pl. 2, cr. 6.

GILLOW, a horse, passant, sa., saddled and bridled, gu. *Pl.* 99, *cr.* 11.

GILLSON, a leopard's head, erased, erm., ducally gorged, az. *Pl.* 116, *cr.* 8.

GILLUM, STEPHEN-FRYER, Esq., of Middleton Hall, Northumb., a dolphin, haurient, ppr. *Pl.* 14, *cr.* 10.

GILMAN, Kent, a man's leg, couped at thigh, in paie, sa., out of rays, or, the foot in chief. *Pl.* 4, *cr.* 12.

GILMAN, Iri., a Bengal tiger, sejant, ppr. *Pl.* 26, *cr.* 9.

GILMER, Suss., a unicorn's head, ar., couped, gu., attired, or. *Pl.* 20, *cr.* 1.

GILMER, and GILMOUR, Sco., in dexter hand, a scroll of paper, within a garland of laurel, ppr. *Nil penna sed usus. Pl.* 86, *cr.* 5.

GILMORE, and GILMOUR, Sco., a dexter arm, from shoulder, vested, gu., in hand a sword, ppr. *Pl.* 120, *cr.* 1.

GILMORE, and GILMOUR, Sco., a dexter arm, from shoulder, vested, az., in hand a sword, ppr. *Pl.* 120, *cr.* 1.

GILMORE, (LITTLE,) of Craigmillar, Bart., Sco., in hand a garland of laurel, ppr. *Perseveranti debetur. Pl.* 86, *cr.* 1.

GILMOUR, Sco., same crest and motto.

GILPIN, Westm. and Cumb., a pine-branch, vert. *Pl.* 80, *cr.* 1.

GILPIN, an arm, in armour, embowed, ppr., in hand a laurel-(sprig,) vert. *Pl.* 68, *cr.* 1.

GILPIN, Suff., three halberds, two in saltier, and one in pale, ppr., (bound with a ribbon, thereon the word *Foy.*) *Pl.* 20, *cr.* 11.

GILPIN, out of a ducal coronet, or, a swan, wings expanded, ppr., collared, and (lined.) *Pl.* 100, *cr.* 7.

GILPIN, three spears, or, (bound with a ribbon, thereon the word *Foy.*) *Une foy mesme. Pl.* 43, *cr.* 14, (spears, *pl.* 95, *cr.* 8.)

GILROY, Sco., a heart, flaming, ppr., winged, or. *Ad finem fidelis. Pl.* 64, *cr.* 13.

GILSLAND, a dexter arm, ppr., vested, ar., cuffed, az., in hand a caltrap, of the first. *Pl.* 39, *cr.* 1, (caltrap, *pl.* 22, *cr.* 4.)

GIMBER, a bear's head, erased, muzzled. *Pl.* 71, *cr.* 6.

GINGER, a savage's head, affrontée, ppr., between two laurel-branches, vert. *Pl.* 12, *cr.* 4.

GIPP, Suff., out of a ducal coronet, or, two wings, expanded, az., (semée of etoiles,) gold. *Pl.* 17, *cr.* 9.

GIPPS, out of a cloud, in dexter hand a wheat-sheaf, all ppr. *Pl.* 67, *cr.* 12.

GIPPS, Kent, out of a mural coronet, or, two wings, elevated, az., (each charged with three etoiles, in pale, gold.) *Pl.* 119, *cr.* 14, (without beacon.)

GIRDLER, Eng., a hand plucking a rose, ppr. *Pl.* 48, *cr.* 1.

GIRDLESTONE, a griffin's head, (gorged with a bar-dancettée, in beak two darts, in saltier.) *Pl.* 35, *cr.* 15.

GIRDWOOD, Sco., a cock's head, between wings *Pl.* 47, *cr.* 3, (without cross.)

GIRFLET, Eng., an arm, in armour, embowed, ppr., bound round shoulder with a sash, gu., in hand a club, sa., spiked, or. *Pl.* 28, *cr.* 2.

GIRLE, Eng., a garb, or. *Pl.* 48, *cr.* 10.

GIRLING, Norf., a demi-griffin, az., between claws, a fleur-de-lis, gu. *Pl.* 18, *cr.* 6, (fleur-de-lis, *pl.* 141.)

GIRLING, Norf., a demi-griffin, az., between paws a fleur-de-lis, per pale, gu. and az. *Pl.* 18, *cr.* 6, (fleur-de-lis, *pl.* 141.)

GIRLING, Norf.: 1. A demi-griffin, az., between paws a fleur-de-lis, per pale, gu. and az. *Pl.* 18, *cr.* 6, (fleur-de-lis, *pl.* 141.) 2. On a ducal coronet, or, a wolf's head, erased, ar. *Pl.* 14, *cr.* 6, (coronet, *pl.* 128, *fig.* 3.)

GIRLINGTON, Lanc. and Yorks., a demi-griffin, wings addorsed, or, holding a bezant. *Pl.* 39, *cr.* 8, (bezant, *pl.* 141.)

GIRON, a horse, ppr. *Pl.* 15, *cr.* 14.

GISBONE, out of a mural coronet, a demi-lion, rampant. *Pl.* 17, *cr.* 7, (without branch.)

GISBORNE, Staffs., out of a mural coronet, ar., a demi-lion, rampant, ermines, gorged with a collar, (dovetailed,) or. *Pl.* 18, *cr.* 13, (coronet, *pl.* 128, *fig.* 18.)

GISBORNE, Iri., a horse's head, az., bridled, gu. *Pl.* 92, *cr.* 1.

GISE, in dexter hand, couped, in fess, a rose, all ppr. *Pl.* 46, *cr.* 12, (rose, *pl.* 118, *cr.* 9.)

GISLAND, a lion's head, ppr. *Pl.* 126, *cr.* 1.

GISSING, and GISSINGE, Eng., an arm, in armour, in hand a sword, ppr. *Pl.* 2, *cr.* 8.

GIST, Glouc., a swan's head and neck, erased, erm., (collared, gu.,) between two palm-branches, vert. *Pl.* 54, *cr.* 6, (palm, *pl.* 87, *cr.* 8.)

GIST, and GEST, a swan's head and neck, erased, between two ostrich-feathers, ar. *Pl.* 54, *cr.* 6, (feathers, *pl.* 13, *cr.* 7.)

GLADHILL, Eng. and Sco., a demi-lion, sa., holding a mullet, or. *Pl.* 89, *cr.* 10.

GLADSTANES, or GLAIDSTANES, Sco., a demi-griffin, in dexter a sword, all ppr. *Fide et virtute. Pl.* 49, *cr* 4.

GLADWIN, Derbs., on a mount, ppr., a lion, sejant, ar., guttée-de-sang, (in dexter a sword, erect, or.) *Pl.* 108, *cr.* 12.

GLANTON, a dexter hand (in armour,) throwing a dart, ppr. *Pl.* 42, *cr.* 13.

GLANVILE, and GLANVILLE, Devons., (on a mount, vert,) a stag, trippant, ppr. *Pl.* 68, *cr.* 2.

GLANVILE, and GLANVILLE, Cornw., a buck, passant, ppr. *Pl.* 68, *cr.* 2.

GLANVILE, and GLANVILLE, a dexter arm, hand clenched, in a maunch, or. *Pl.* 22, *cr.* 14.

GLASBROOK, a demi-lion, gu., ducally crowned, or. *Pl.* 61, *cr.* 4, (without branch.)

GLASCO, Iri., a demi-lion, rampant, or, holding a battle-axe, gu. *Pl.* 101, *cr.* 14, (without charging.)

GLASCOCK, Ess., out of a ducal coronet, or, a dragon's head, per pale, ar. and vert. *Pl.* 93, *cr.* 15, (without flames.)

GLASCOCK, Ess., an antelope's head, ar., attired, or, (gorged with a belt, sa,) beaked and rimmed, gold. *Pl.* 24, *cr.* 7.

GLASFORD, Sco., issuing from clouds, two hands conjoined, grasping a caduceus, ensigned with a cap of liberty, all between two cornucopiæ, all ppr. *Pl.* 52, *cr.* 13, (caduceus and cap, *pl.* 17, *cr.* 13; cornucopia, *pl.* 91, *cr.* 3.)

GLASGOW, City of, a martlet, sa. *Lord, let Glasgow flourish. Pl.* 111, *cr.* 5.

GLASGOW, Sco., a demi-(negro,) in dexter a sugar-cane, all ppr. *Parere subjectus. Pl.* 35, *cr.* 12.

GLASGOW, Earl of. *See* BOYLE.

GLASGOW, Sco., a cubit arm, erect, in hand an imperial crown, all ppr. *Quo fas et gloria.* *Pl.* 97, *cr.* 12.
GLASGOW, co. Cork, an eagle, rising from a rock, ppr. *Dominus providebit.* *Pl.* 61, *cr.* 1.
GLASIER, Chesh., out of a ducal coronet, gu., a dragon's head and neck, wings displayed, or. *Pl.* 105, *cr.* 11, (coronet, *pl.* 128, *fig.* 3.)
GLASIER, and GLAZIER, a man's heart, ppr., charged with a cinquefoil. *Pl.* 123, *cr.* 7.
GLASS, Sco., a mermaid, ppr. *Luctor non mergor.* *Pl.* 48, *cr.* 5.
GLASS, Eng., a unicorn, rampant, ar. *Pl.* 37, *cr.* 7.
GLASSCOTT, an eagle displayed, with two heads, or. *Virtute decoratus.* *Pl.* 87, *cr.* 11, (without flames.)
GLASSE, Eng., a demi-lion, or, maned, gu. *Pl.* 67, *cr.* 10.
GLASTENBURY, Eng., a griffin's head, between wings, (each charged with three bezants.) *Pl.* 22, *cr.* 2.
GLASTINGS, an arm, in armour, embowed, ppr., in hand a baton, sa. *Pl.* 45, *cr.* 10, (baton, *pl.* 33, *cr.* 4.)
GLASTON, an arm, embowed, in hand a laurel crown, ppr. *Pl.* 118, *cr.* 4.
GLAZEBROOK, Lanc., a bear's head, or, muzzled, sa., charged on neck with a fleur-de-lis, in fess, az. *Dum spiro, spero.* *Pl.* 2, *cr.* 9, (fleur-de-lis, *pl.* 141.)
GLEADOW, Yorks. and Salop, a lion's head, erased, az., charged on neck with a cross pattée, or, between wings, gold, each charged with a cross pattée, of the first. *Pl.* 87, *cr.* 2, (cross, *pl.* 141.)
GLEAME, Norf., a Saracen's head, affrontée, ppr., wreathed, ar. and sa. *Pl.* 97, *cr.* 2.
GLEAVE, Eng., Cupid, with bow and arrow, ppr. *Pl.* 17, *cr.* 5.
GLEDSTANES, Sco., an arm, in armour, embowed, in hand a sword, ppr. *Pl.* 2, *cr.* 8.
GLEDSTANES, Upton, a demi-griffin, in dexter a sword. *Fide et virtute.* *Pl.* 49, *cr.* 4.
GLEG, Sco., a falcon, between claws a partridge, ppr. *Qui potest, capere capiat.* *Pl.* 61, *cr.* 7.
GLEG, and GLEGGE, Eng., a demi-eagle, wings expanded, ppr. *Pl.* 52, *cr.* 8.
GLEGG, a hawk, wings expanded, preying on a partridge, all ppr. *Pl.* 61, *cr.* 7.
GLEIG, Sco., in dexter hand a sword, ppr. *Pl.* 21, *cr.* 10.
GLEIO, Sco., a rose, gu., seeded, or, barbed, vert. *Pl.* 20, *cr.* 2.
GLEMHAM, a falcon, volant, ar., beaked and belled, or. *Pl.* 94, *cr.* 1.
GLEN, and GLENN, Eng. and Sco., out of a ducal coronet, a hand holding a swan's head and neck, erased, ppr. *Pl.* 65, *cr.* 12.
GLEN, and GLENN, a ferret, collared and lined. *Pl.* 12, *cr.* 2.
GLEN, and GLENN, Sco., a martlet, sa. *Alta pete.* *Pl.* 111, *cr.* 5.
GLEN, and GLENN, an arm, embowed, vested, sa., in hand, ppr., a heart, gu. *Pl.* 39, *cr.* 1, (heart, *pl.* 55, *cr.* 13.)
GLENDENNING, a sword and wheat-ear, in saltier, ppr. *Pl.* 50, *cr.* 4.
GLENDENNING, and GLENDONWYN, Sco., on point of sword, a maunch, ppr. *Pl.* 78, *cr.* 1.
GLENDOWING, a sword, in pale, on point a maunch. *Have faith in Christ.* *Pl.* 78, *cr.* 1.
GLENEAGLES, Sco., an eagle's head, erased, or. *Suffer.* *Pl.* 20, *cr.* 7.
GLENELG, Baron, a burning mountain, ppr. *Stand suir—and—Revirescimus.* *Pl.* 92, *cr.* 9.
GLENELG, Baron, a banyan-tree, ppr. *Stand suir—and—Revirescimus.* *Pl.* 18, *cr.* 12.
GLENESTER, a boar, passant, sa., (charged with a pale, ar., thereon a leopard's face, ppr.) *Pl.* 48, *cr.* 14.
GLENGALL, Earl of, Viscount and Baron Caher, (Butler,) Iri., out of a ducal coronet, or, a plume of five ostrich-feathers, ar., and therefrom a demi-falcon, rising, of the last. *God be my guide.* *Pl.* 100, *cr.* 12, (demi-falcon, *pl.* 54, *cr.* 8.)
GLENHAM, Suff., a hawk, wings expanded, ar., beaked and legged, gu., belled, or. *Pl.* 105, *cr.* 4.
GLENLYON, Sco., Baron, a demi-savage, wreathed about head and waist with oak-leaves, in dexter a dagger, all ppr., hilt and pommel, or, in sinister a key, erect, gold. *Furth fortune, and fill the fetters.* *Pl.* 88, *cr.* 10.
GLIN, a lion's head, ppr. *Pl.* 126, *cr.* 1.
GLOAG, Sco., an eagle, wings addorsed, ppr. *Nunquam senescit.* *Pl.* 61, *cr.* 1.
GLOAG, Sco., an eagle, wings expanded. *Qui vult capere, capiat.* *Pl.* 126, *cr.* 7.
GLOCESTER, and GLOUCESTER, a swan's head, between wings, ppr. *Pl.* 54, *cr.* 6.
GLODREDD, Wel., a sheaf of arrows, banded, points upward. *Pl.* 75, *cr.* 7, (without mullet.)
GLODRYDD, Wel., an eagle, rising, in beak a trefoil, slipped. *Pl.* 126, *cr.* 7, (trefoil, *pl.* 141.)
GLOVER, Lond., Kent, and Warw., a cross bow, az., between wings, or. *Pl.* 58, *cr.* 3.
GLOVER, Sco., within the horns of a crescent, a cock, ppr. *Surgite, lumen adest.* *Pl.* 17, *cr.* 1.
GLOVER, Lond., Norf., and Kent, an eagle, displayed, ar., charged on breast with three ermine spots. *Pl.* 48, *cr.* 11, (ermine, *pl.* 141.)
GLOVER, Wilts., a talbot, passant, sa., collared, ar. *Pl.* 65, *cr.* 2.
GLOVER, a dragon, passant, az. *Pl.* 90, *cr.* 10.
GLOVER, on a chapeau, sa., turned up, ar., wings expanded, of the first. *Pl.* 17, *cr.* 14, (without escallop.)
GLOVER, a fleur-de-lis, or, between wings, sa. *Pl.* 21, *cr.* 13, (without chapeau.)
GLUBB, a demi-lion, az., bezantée. *Pl.* 67, *cr.* 10, (bezant, *pl.* 141.)
GLYN, Bart., Surr., an eagle's head, erased, sa., guttée-d'or, in beak an escallop, ar. *Pl.* 20, *cr.* 7, (escallop, *pl.* 141.)
GLYN, Cornw., demi-talbot, erm., eared, or. *Pl.* 97, *cr.* 9, (without arrow.)
GLYN, an eagle's head and neck, erased. *Pl.* 20, *cr.* 7.
GLYN, Dors., Bart., an eagle's head, erased, sa., guttée-d'or, in beak an escallop, ar. *Firm to my trust.* *Pl.* 20, *cr.* 7, (escallop, *pl.* 141.)
GLYN, a demi-lion, sa., bezantée. *Pl.* 67, *cr.* 10, (bezant, *pl.* 141.)
GLYNN, Iri., a lion's head, erased, collared, sa. *Pl.* 7, *cr.* 10.

GLYNNE, Bart., Wel., an eagle's head, erased, in beak a brand, raguly, sa., fired, ppr. *Pl.* 20, *cr.* 7, (brand, *pl.* 70, *cr.* 14.)

GOADEFROY, an arm, in armour, embowed, in gauntlet a sword, all ppr. *Pl.* 2, *cr.* 8.

GOAT, and GOATE, a goat, (passant,) ar., armed, or. *Pl.* 66, *cr.* 1.

GOATER, a wolf, sejant, or, grasping a cross crosslet, fitched, gu. *Pl.* 110, *cr.* 4, (cross, *pl.* 141.)

GOATHAM, a hunting-horn, sa., garnished and stringed, gu. *Pl.* 48, *cr.* 12.

GOATLEY, and GOATLY, Kent, a sphinx, couchant, or, winged, ar., face and breasts, ppr. *Pl.* 116, *cr.* 5, (without trefoil.)

GOBAND, Eng., a mermaid, in hand a dagger, ppr. *Pl.* 88, *cr.* 12.

GOBARD, and GOBBARD, Eng., same crest.

GOBEL, Eng., a wyvern, vert. *Pl.* 63, *cr.* 13.

GOBION, in water, a swan, swimming, wings elevated, ppr. *Pl.* 66, *cr.* 10.

GOBLE, a lion, passant, charged on shoulder with a fleur-de-lis. *Pl.* 48, *cr.* 8, (fleur-de-lis, *pl.* 141.)

GOCHE, Lond. and Suff., a talbot, passant, per pale, ar. and sa. *Pl.* 120, *cr.* 8.

GODARD, Hants. and Wilts., a stag's head, couped, and gardant, gu., attired, or. *Pl.* 111, *cr.* 11.

GODARD, Lond., Berks., and Hants., a hawk's head, erased, or, in beak a lure, gu., garnished, gold, stringed, of the second. *Pl.* 34, *cr.* 11, (lure, *pl.* 141.)

GODARD, Norf., an eagle's head, between wings, or. *Pl.* 81, *cr.* 10.

GODBOLD, Surr., an arm, in armour, embowed, in hand an arrow, ppr. *Pl.* 96, *cr.* 6.

GODBOLD, Ess. and Suff., an arm, in armour, ppr., (wreathed, or and az.,) in gauntlet an arrow, sa., feathered, and headed, ar. *Pl.* 96, *cr.* 6.

GODBOW, out of a mural coronet, or, a griffin's head, between wings, gu. *Pl.* 65, *cr.* 1, (coronet, *pl.* 128, *fig.* 18.)

GODBY, a chevalier, on horseback, in complete armour, (visor closed,) ppr. *Pl.* 118, *cr.* 14.

GODDARD, Eng., a salamander in flames, ppr. *Pl.* 20, *cr.* 15.

GODDARD, Wilts., a stag's head, erased at neck, affrontée, ppr. *Pl.* 8, *cr.* 6.

GODDARD, HORATIA-NELSON, Esq., of Cliffe House, Wilts., a stag's head, affrontée, couped at neck, gu., attired, or. *Cervus non servus.* *Pl.* 111, *cr.* 13.

GODDART, Sco., a stag's head, affrontée, couped, gu., attired, or. *Pl.* 111, *cr.* 13.

GODDEN, Kent, on a garb, in fess, a bird, close, in beak a wheat-ear, all or. *Pl.* 112, *cr.* 10.

GODDIN, Eng., a winged heart, ppr. *Pl.* 39, *cr.* 7.

GODESTON, a buffalo's head, sa. *Pl.* 57, *cr.* 7.

GODFREY, Bart., Iri., a griffin, passant, sa., in dexter a sceptre, or. *God friend*—and—*Deus et Libertas.* *Pl.* 61, *cr.* 14, (without gorging; sceptre, *pl.* 82, *cr.* 5.)

GODFREY, Eng., a demi-griffin, or. *Pl.* 18, *cr.* 6.

GODFREY, Kent and Middx., a pelican's head, erased, or, vulning, gu. *Pl.* 26, *cr.* 1.

GODFREY, Eng., an eagle, displayed, sa. *Pl.* 48, *cr.* 11.

GODFREY, Staffs. and Warw., a pelican, wings addorsed, or, gorged with an Eastern coronet, az., in beak a cross crosslet, fitched, gu.

GODFREY, Kent, a demi-negro, ppr., in dexter a cross crosslet, fitched, ar.

GODFREY, a leopard's head, couped, az. *Pl.* 92, *cr.* 13.

GODIN, Eng., an ox-yoke, in bend, sa., stapled, az. *Pl.* 35, *cr.* 11.

GODLEY, co. Leitrim, a unicorn's head, erased, ar., horned, gu., charged with three trefoils, slipped, vert. *Sans Dieu rien.* *Pl.* 67, *cr.* 1, (trefoils, *pl.* 82, *cr.* 1.)

GODLEY, Iri., a demi-lion, (gardant,) or, in dexter a fleur-de-lis, gu. *Pl.* 35, *cr.* 4, (fleur-de-lis, *pl.* 91, *cr.* 13.)

GODMAN, on a mount, vert, a blackcock, wings displayed, ppr. *Cœlum quid quærimus ultra.*

GODMANSTONE, a man's leg, couped at thigh, ppr. *Pl.* 38, *cr.* 14.

GODOLPHIN, Devons. and Cornw., a dolphin, sa., finned, or, *Pl.* 48, *cr.* 9.

GODSAL, PHILIP-LAKE, Esq., of Iscoyd Park, Wel., a griffin's head, erased, paly of six, indented, ar. and sa., beaked, or. *Pl.* 48, *cr.* 6.

GODSALE, Eng., a griffin's head, erased, per pale, ar. and sa., beaked, or. *Pl.* 48, *cr.* 6.

GODSALL, GODSELL, GODSEL, and GODSEEL, an arm, erect, in hand a spade, ppr. *Pl.* 89, *cr.* 6.

GODSALL, and GODSELL, a griffin's head, erased, paly of six, indented, ar. and sa. *Pl.* 48, *cr.* 6.

GODSALOE, Eng., in lion's paw a crescent. *Pl.* 91, *cr.* 1.

GODSALVE, a griffin's head, erased, paly-wavy of four, ar. and sa., in mouth a branch, vert. *Pl.* 29, *cr.* 15, (without coronet.)

GODSCHALL, Eng., in lion's paw a crescent. *Pl.* 91, *cr.* 1.

GODSON, an arm, in armour, embowed, in hand a (broken) sword, enfiled with a crown of thorns, all ppr. *Pl.* 2, *cr.* 8, (crown, *pl.* 78, *cr.* 7.)

GODSTONE, on a chapeau, ppr., a talbot's head, ar. *Pl.* 123, *cr.* 15, (chapeau, *same plate.*)

GODWIN, Somers., a hawk's leg, erased, ppr., belled, or, leashed, gu. *Pl.* 83, *cr.* 7.

GODWYN, a griffin, sejant, or, guttée, sa. *Pl.* 100, *cr.* 1.

GOFF, or GOFFE, Iri., a stag's head, erased, gu., armed, ar. *Pl.* 66, *cr.* 9.

GOFF, or GOFFE, Eng., out of a ducal coronet, or, a rod, raguly, vert. *Pl.* 78, *cr.* 15.

GOFF, Hants, a squirrel, sejant, ppr. *Fier sans tache.* *Pl.* 16, *cr.* 9.

GOFF-DAVIS, STRANGMAN, Esq., of Horetown House, co. Wexford, a squirrel, sejant. *Honestas optima politia.* *Pl.* 16, *cr.* 9:

GOFTON, Surr., on a chapeau, gu., turned up, ar., a rose, or, between wings, expanded, az. *Pl.* 13, *cr.* 14, (rose, *pl.* 20, *cr.* 2.)

GOLBORN, and GOLBORNE, Chesh., a man's leg, couped above knee, vert, spurred, or. *Pl.* 38, *cr.* 14.

GOLBOURN, Eng., a dove and olive-branch, ppr. *Pl.* 48, *cr.* 15.

GOLD, Wilts., a demi-lion, rampant, or. *Pl.* 67, *cr.* 10.

GOLD, Wilts., an eagle's head, erased, az., in beak a (pine,) or. *Pl.* 22, *cr.* 1.

GOLDEN, Linc., a dragon's head, erased, vert, collared and lined, or. *Pl.* 107, *cr.* 10.

GOLDEN, Eng., a cinquefoil, ppr. *Pl.* 91, *cr.* 12.

GOLDESBOROUGH, and GOLDSBROUGH, Eng., a dexter hand, holding a trident, ppr. *Pl.* 12, *cr.* 3.

GOLDESBURGH, Yorks. and Ess., a pelican, wings (addorsed,) vulning, ppr. *Pl.* 109, *cr.* 15.
GOLDESBURGH, Lond., a demi-lion, rampant. *Pl.* 67, *cr.* 10.
GOLDFINCH, Kent, a camel, passant, ppr. *Pl.* 17, *cr.* 2.
GOLDFINCH, a goldfinch, ppr. *Pl.* 10, *cr.* 12.
GOLDFRAP, Eng., a wolf's head, erm. *Pl.* 14, *cr.* 6.
GOLDIE, of Craigmure, Sco., a garb, or. *Quid utilius.* *Pl.* 48, *cr.* 10.
GOLDIE, Sco., a garb, or. *Honestas.* *Pl.* 48, *cr.* 10.
GOLDIE, Sco., an antique crown, or. *Nil solidum.* *Pl.* 79, *cr.* 12.
GOLDIE, Eng., in hand a thistle, ppr. *Pl.* 26, *cr.* 6.
GOLDING, Ess. and Suff., a garb, or. *Pl.* 48, *cr.* 10.
GOLDING, a hind's head, couped, in mouth an acorn-branch, ppr. *Pl.* 21, *cr.* 9, (branch, *pl.* 22, *cr.* 1.)
GOLDINGHAM, Norf. and Suff., a lion's gamb, erect and erased, or. *Pl.* 126, *cr.* 9.
GOLDINGTON, Eng., out of a ducal coronet, or, a cock's head, ppr. *Pl.* 97, *cr.* 15.
GOLDMAN, Sco., a fox, current, ppr. *Pl.* 80, *cr.* 5.
GOLDSMID, Bart., a demi-lion, ar., in paws (a bundle of twigs, erect, or, banded, az.) *Quis similis tui in fortibus, Domine?*—and—*Concordiâ et sedulitate.* *Pl.* 47, *cr.* 4.
GOLDSMIDT, two paws of a lion, (erased,) supporting a crescent, or. *Pl.* 62, *cr.* 3.
GOLDSMIDT, a demi-lion, rampant, between paws, a pillar. *Pl.* 29, *cr.* 12, (pillar, *pl.* 33, *cr.* 1.)
GOLDSMITH, Eng., a bird, close, sa. *Pl.* 52, *cr.* 12.
GOLDSMITH, Hants., a stork, sa., bezantée, or. *Pl.* 33, *cr.* 9.
GOLDSON, Norf., a leopard's head, erased, ar., collared and chained, sa., collar charged with three bezants. *Pl.* 40, *cr.* 10, (bezants, *pl.* 141.)
GOLDSTON, and GOLDSTONE, a Minerva's head, ppr. *Pl.* 92, *cr.* 12.
GOLDSWORTHY, a griffin's head, erased, sa., (in beak, a holly-leaf, vert.) *Pl.* 59, *cr.* 15, (without gorging.)
GOLDSWORTHY, an eagle's head, erased, per pale, or and ar., in beak a holly-leaf, vert. *Ib.*
GOLDTRAP, Kent, in lion's paw, erased, az., a baton, or, between wings, elevated, gold. *Pl.* 112, *cr.* 15.
GOLDWELL, out of a well, or, (a vine, and two columbine branches,) ppr. *Pl.* 70, *cr.* 10.
GOLEVER, Eng., a mermaid, ppr. *Pl.* 48, *cr.* 5.
GOLIGHTLEY, out of an antique crown, a lion's head. *Pl.* 126, *cr.* 1, (crown, *pl.* 79, *cr.* 12.)
GOLLOP, Eng., an antelope, trippant, ppr. *Pl.* 63, *cr.* 10.
GOLLOP-TILLY, Dors., a demi-lion, bendy, or and sa., in dexter a (broken arrow, gu.) *Be bolde, be wyse.* *Pl.* 41, *cr.* 13.
GOLOFER, Eng., an eagle's head, couped, ar. *Pl.* 100, *cr.* 10.
GOLONER, a demi-griffin, ppr., (collared,) holding an anchor, az. *Pl.* 18, *cr.* 5, (anchor, *pl.* 19, *cr.* 6.)
GOLONER, a lion, passant, gardant, ar., ducally crowned, or. *Pl.* 120, *cr.* 15, (without chapeau.)

GOLSTON, Eng., an eagle's head, couped, ar. *Pl.* 100, *cr.* 10.
GOLTSHED, two wings, conjoined, or, thereon a dove, ppr. *Pl.* 87, *cr.* 1, (dove, *pl.* 66, *cr.* 12.)
GOM, (two) scimitars, in saltier, ppr. *Pl.* 52, *cr.* 3.
GOMELDON, (out of a cloud,) an arm, in armour, embowed and gloved, wielding a spiked mace, all ppr. *Pl.* 83, *cr.* 2, (armour, *pl.* 2, *cr.* 8.)
GOMM, Middx. and Bucks., two lions' gambs, in saltier, sa., erased, gu., in each a seax, erect. *Pl.* 32, *cr.* 12.
GONNE, Eng., on a glove, a falcon, ppr. *Pl.* 1, *cr.* 13.
GONOR, a stag's head, ppr., in mouth a (cinquefoil,) or, leaved, vert. *Pl.* 91, *cr.* 14.
GONSTON, Lond. and Ess., an antelope's head, ar., guttée, sa. *Pl.* 24, *cr.* 7.
GONTON, and GUNTON, Eng., out of an earl's coronet, a moor's head, affrontée, ppr. *Pl.* 80, *cr.* 11.
GONVILL, Norf., a dove, ar., beaked and membered, gu., in beak a (flower,) stalked, vert. *Pl.* 48, *cr.* 15.
GOOCH, Bart., Suff., a talbot, passant, per pale, ar. and sa. *Fide et virtute.* *Pl.* 120, *cr.* 8.
GOOCH, out of a ducal coronet, a stag's head, (collared.) *Pl.* 29, *cr.* 7.
GOOCH, Norf., a greyhound, passant, ar., spotted and (collared,) sa. *Pl.* 104, *cr.* 1, (without chapeau.)
GOOCH, Middx., a cubit arm, erect, vested, per pale, embattled, or, in hand a dragon's head, erased, ppr. *Pl.* 94, *cr.* 6, (dragon's head, *pl.* 87, *cr.* 12.)
GOOCHE, Linc., a dexter arm, erect, ppr., vested, per pale, embattled, or and ar., in hand a dragon's head, erased, az. *Pl.* 94, *cr.* 6, (head, *pl.* 107, *cr.* 10.)
GOOCHE, on a ducal coronet, or, a leopard, ar., spotted, sa. *Pl.* 86, *cr.* 8.
GOOD, Eng., on a ducal coronet, or, a leopard, ar., spotted, sa. *Pl.* 86, *cr.* 8.
GOOD, Linc., on a ducal coronet, or, an otter, passant, ar. *Pl.* 9, *cr.* 5, (coronet, *same plate.*)
GOOD, an antelope's head, erased, in mouth a laurel-branch. *Pl.* 24, *cr.* 7, (laurel, *same plate, cr.* 4.)
GOOD, the Holy Bible, closed. *Pl.* 112, *cr.* 14.
GOODACRE, Iri., a unicorn's head, erased, sa., armed and maned, or. *Pl.* 67, *cr.* 1.
GOODALE, and GOODALLE, Sco., a cup, ar. *Good God increase.* *Pl.* 42, *cr.* 1.
GOODALL, Suff., an eagle, displayed, ar., beaked and membered, or, gorged with a chaplet of grass, ppr. *Pl.* 84, *cr.* 14.
GOODALL, a dexter arm, embowed, vested, vert, in hand, ppr., (two) arrows, in saltier, ar., feathered, or. *Pl.* 112, *cr.* 1.
GOODALL, Sco., an eagle, displayed. *Toujours fidelle.* *Pl.* 48, *cr.* 11.
GOODBRIDGE, Devons. and Yorks., a thrush, ppr. *Pl.* 10, *cr.* 12.
GOODCHILD, Eng., a parrot, ppr. *Vincit omnia veritas.* *Pl.* 25, *cr.* 2.
GOODCHILD, a pellet, thereon a parrot, ppr., in beak an annulet, gu. *Pl.* 33, *cr.* 11, (pellet, *pl.* 141.)
GOODDAGE, Ess. and Suff., a greyhound, sejant, erm., (collared and lined, or.) *Pl.* 66, *cr.* 15.

GOODDEN, a griffin's head, erased, or, wings addorsed, vairé, ar. and gu., in beak an olive-branch, ppr. *Jovis omnia plena.* Pl. 105, cr. 6.

GOODE, Lond. and Cornw., a talbot's head, erased, gu., ducally crowned, or. Pl. 25, cr. 10.

GOODE, a lion, passant. Pl. 48, cr. 8.

GOODEAR, and GOODYEAR, a lion's head, erased, imperially crowned, ppr. Pl. 123, cr. 13.

GOODEN, and GOODING, Somers., a dexter arm, ppr., (invested, ar., charged with three bars, gu., in hand a palm-branch, vert.) Pl. 23, cr. 7.

GOODEN, and GOODING, Suff., a griffin, sejant, wings expanded, or, guttée, beaked and clawed, sa. Pl. 100, cr. 11.

GOODENOUGH, a demi-wolf, rampant, ppr., between paws an escallop, ar. Pl. 65, cr. 4, (escallop, pl. 141.)

GOODENOUGH, Eng., in hand a dagger, in pale, ppr. Pl. 23, cr. 15.

GOODENOUGH, on a chapeau, gu., a lion, couchant, or. Pl. 75, cr. 5.

GOODERE, Glouc., a partridge, in beak a wheat-ear, all ppr. *Possunt, quia posse videntur.* Pl. 108, cr. 5, (wheat ear, same plate, cr. 8.)

GOODFELLOW, a horse, (rampant,) gu. Pl. 15, cr. 14.

GOODFORD, Somers., a bear's head, ar., charged on neck with a pellet. Pl. 2, cr. 9, (pellet, pl. 141.)

GOODHALL, Linc., a boar's head, erased and erect, sa., plattée, and ducally gorged, or. Pl. 36, cr. 9.

GOODHAND, Lond. and Linc., an arm, in armour, embowed, ppr., in hand a sword, ar., hilt and pommel, or. Pl. 2, cr. 8.

GOODHARD, or GOODHART, on a ducal coronet, a lion, passant, ppr. Pl. 107, cr. 11.

GOODHART, Kent, a beehive, or, between two bees, all within a rainbow, terminating in clouds, ppr.

GOODING, (on a mount,) vert, a hedgehog, ppr. Pl. 32, cr. 9.

GOODISON, Eng., a peacock's head, ppr. Pl. 100, cr. 5.

GOODLAD, Lond., a wing, ar. Pl. 39, cr. 10.

GOODLAD, Eng., in a frame, a globe, ppr. Pl. 81, cr. 1.

GOODLAKE, a savage, kneeling on left knee, holding over sinister shoulder a club, tied round loins.

GOODLAKE, Berks., on a mount, vert, a woodwift, or wild man, ppr., holding up his club, or. *Omnia bona desuper.*

GOODLAW, Lanc., a griffin, sejant, ar., supporting with dexter a column, az. Pl. 100, cr. 11, (column, pl. 33, cr. 1.)

GOODMAN, Lond., Chesh., and Herts., the battlement and upper part of a tower, ar., thereon a woman, couped at knees, vested, az., hair dishevelled, or, in dexter a (rose,) gu., stalked and leaved, vert. Pl. 2, cr. 10, (tower, pl. 3, cr. 7.)

GOODMAN, an eagle, with two heads, displayed, sa. Pl. 87, cr. 11.

GOODMAN, Wel., out of a ducal coronet, or, a demi-eagle, with two heads, erm., displayed. Pl. 113, cr. 11.

GOODRICH, a lion's head, couped, ppr. Pl. 126, cr. 1.

GOODRICH, Ess., a demi-lion, rampant, couped, ar., in dexter a cross crosslet, or. Pl. 65, cr. 6.

GOODRICK, Middx., Linc., and Camb., a demi-lion, rampant, sa., (collared,) or, supporting a battle-axe, ar., handled, gu. Pl. 101, cr. 14.

GOODRICK, Eng., out of a ducal coronet, or, a demi-lion, erminois, in paws a battle-axe, erect, az., handle, or. Pl. 120, cr. 14, (coronet, same plate.)

GOODRICK, and GOODRICKE, a demi-lion, gu., (collared,) or, in paws a battle-axe, az. Pl. 101, cr. 14.

GOODRICKE, Bart., Yorks., out of a ducal coronet, or, a demi-lion, ermines, armed and langued, gu., between paws a battle-axe, ppr., helved, gold. *Fortior lione justus.* Pl. 120, cr. 14, (coronet, same plate.)

GOODRICKE-HOLY-OAKE, Bart., Yorks. and Warw., on a mount, vert, an oak, fructed, ppr., (around lower part of stem an escroll, and thereon a cross pattée, gu., between the words, *Sacra quercus.*) Pl. 48, cr. 4.

GOODROOD, a unicorn's head, gu., collared, or. Pl. 73, cr. 1.

GOODSIR, Sco., an eagle's head, erased, ppr. *Virtute et fidelitate.* Pl. 20, cr. 7.

GOODSIR, Sco., a cock, in beak a bunch of keys. *Fortiter et fideliter.* Pl. 112, cr. 12.

GOODSON, Eng., a wolf's head, erm., collared, gu. Pl. 8, cr. 4.

GOODWIN, Devons. and Suff., a griffin, sejant, wings expanded, or, guttée-de-poix. Pl. 100, cr. 11.

GOODWIN, a demi-lion, rampant, gardant, sa., holding a bezant. Pl. 35, cr. 4, (bezant, pl. 141.)

GOODWIN, Herts., a griffin's head, ar., wings (addorsed,) vair. Pl. 65, cr. 1.

GOODWIN, a lion, salient, gardant, sa., holding a lozenge, vair. Pl. 35, cr. 4, (lozenge, pl. 141.)

GOODWIN, Camb., out of a ducal coronet, ar., a nag's head, or, maned and (bridled,) of the first. Pl. 50, cr. 13.

GOODWIN, or GOODWYN, Surr. and Suss., an arm, embowed, vested, or, cuffed, ar., in hand, ppr., a lozenge, of the second. Pl. 39, cr. 1, (lozenge, pl. 181.)

GOODWIN, Lond., a lion, sejant, gardant, sa., holding a lozenge, vair. Pl. 35, cr. 4, (lozenge, pl. 141.)

GOODWIN, Derbs., a griffin, sejant. *Fide et virtute.* Pl. 100, cr. 11.

GOODWRIGHT, Eng., a dove and olive-branch, ppr. *Pro bono ad meliora.* Pl. 48, cr. 15.

GOODWYN, a griffin, sejant, or, guttée, sa. Pl. 100, cr. 11.

GOOGE, Eng., a rose, stalked and leaved, ppr. *Audaces juvat.* Pl. 105, cr. 7.

GOOGE, Eng., on a ducal coronet, or, a leopard, passant, ar., spotted, sa. Pl. 110, cr. 8, (coronet, same plate.)

GOOLD, Bart., Iri., a demi-lion, rampant, or. *Deus mihi providebit.* Pl. 67, cr. 10.

GOOLD, Eng., on a mount, vert, an ermine, passant, ppr. Pl. 87, cr. 3.

GOOLD, Sco., within horns of a crescent, ar., a buckle, or. Pl. 25, cr. 3.

GOORICK, a nag's head, erased. Pl. 81, cr. 6.

GOOSELING, in lion's paw, erased, gu., a fleur-de-lis, or. Pl. 5, cr. 5, (fleur-de-lis, pl. 141.)

GOOSTREY, Bucks., a stag's head, erased, or. Pl. 66, cr. 9.

GORDON, of Gordonstone, a cat, salient, armed, az. *Pl.* 70, *cr.* 15.
GORDON, Viscount. *See* ABERDEEN, Earl of.
GORDON, Viscount Kenmure. *See* KENMURE.
GORDON, of Lochinvar, a demi-savage, wreathed about the head and middle. *Dread God. Pl.* 14, *cr.* 11.
GORDON, Sco., out of a cloud, a dexter naked arm, in hand a flaming sword, all ppr. *Dread God. Pl.* 71, *cr.* 7, (sword, *pl.* 58, *cr.* 11.)
GORDON, Sco., a stag, lodged, ppr. *Nunc mihi grata quies. Pl.* 67, *cr.* 2.
GORDON, Sco., a hart, standing at gaze, ppr. *Dum vigilo, paro. Pl.* 81, *cr.* 8.
GORDON, Bart., of Gordonstown, Sco., a stag, at gaze, ppr. *Dum sisto, vigilo. Pl.* 81, *cr.* 8.
GORDON, Bart., of Embo, Sco., a boar's head, erased, or. *Forward, without fear. Pl.* 16, *cr.* 11.
GORDON, Bart., of Lesmore, Sco., a hart's head, couped, ppr. *Bydand. Pl.* 91, *cr.* 14.
GORDON CUMMING, Bart., of Gordonstoun, Sco., a lion, rampant, or, in dexter a (dagger,) ppr. *Sans crainte*—and—*Courage. Pl.* 64, *cr.* 2.
GORDON, Bart., of Earlston, Sco., in dexter hand a sword, ppr. *Dread God. Pl.* 21, *cr.* 10.
GORDON DUFF, Bart., of Halkin, Sco., a demi-lion, gu., charged on breast with a mullet, ar., in dexter a sword, (erect,) ppr., hilt and pommel, or. *Pl.* 41, *cr.* 13, (mullet, *pl.* 141.)
GORDON, WILLOUGHBY, Bart., G.C.B., of Niton, Isle of Wight, out of a mural coronet, a dexter arm, in armour, embowed, ppr., (charged with a mullet, gu.,) garnished, or, in hand a falchion, also ppr., enfiled with a boar's head, erect and erased, gold. *Animo non astutiâ. Pl.* 115, *cr.* 14, (head, *pl.* 71, *cr.* 9.)
GORDON, Bucks. and Notts., a demi-savage, wreathed about head and middle with laurel, holding over shoulder a club, all ppr. *Pl.* 14, *cr.* 11.
GORDON, Wilts., in hand an open book, ppr. *Veritas ingenio. Pl.* 126 A, *cr.* 9.
GORDON, of Beldorny and Wardhouse, a cross crosslet, fitched. *In hoc spes mea. Pl.* 16, *cr.* 10.
GORDON, of Clunie, a dove, volant, ar., with an olive-branch in mouth. *Pax et libertas. Pl.* 25, *cr.* 6.
GORDON, a boar's head, couped, or. *Do well, and let them say. Pl.* 48, *cr.* 2.
GORDON, of Glenbucket, a boar's head, couped and erect, surrounded by an adder, in orle. *Victrix patientia. Pl.* 12, *cr.* 6.
GORDON, of Ardmeally, a boar's head, erased, or. *Byde be. Pl.* 16, *cr.* 11.
GORDON, of Rothemay, a demi-man presenting a gun, all ppr. *Vel pax vel bellum. Pl.* 51, *cr.* 6.
GORDON, of Edinglassie, a boar's head, erased, in mouth a sword, ppr. *Aut mens aut vita Deus. Pl.* 28, *cr.* 14.
GORDON, of Glastirim, a lion's head, erased and langued, ppr. *Divisa conjungo. Pl.* 81, *cr.* 4.
GORDON, of Badenscoth, a hart's head, cabossed, ppr. *Still bydand. Pl.* 36, *cr.* 1.
GORDON, of Birkenburn, a hart's head, (couped,) ppr., charged with a crescent, ar. *Bydand. Pl.* 91, *cr.* 9.
GORDON, of Myrigg, a deer's head, erased, ppr. *Bydand. Pl.* 66, *cr.* 9.

GORDON, of Nethermuir, in dexter hand, out of a cloud, a dart, all ppr. *Majores sequor. Pl.* 45, *cr.* 12.
GORDON, of Denguech, in hand a club, (erect,) ppr. *Manes non fugio. Pl.* 28, *cr.* 6.
GORDON, of Farshank, a stag, lodged, ppr. *Bydand to the last. Pl.* 67, *cr.* 2.
GORDON, of Gight, a buck's head and neck, affrontée, ppr. *Bydand. Pl.* 111, *cr.* 13.
GORDON, of Torquhon, a stag's head, erased, ppr. *Fear God. Pl.* 66, *cr.* 9.
GORDON, Eng. and Sco., a boar's head, gu. *Pl.* 2, *cr.* 7.
GORDON, a cubit arm, erect, in hand a dagger, ppr. *Pl.* 101, *cr.* 10.
GORDON, a buck's head, at gaze, ppr., attired and ducally gorged, or. *Truth prevails. Pl.* 55, *cr.* 2.
GORDON, two arms, drawing a bow and arrow, ppr. *Pl.* 100, *cr.* 4.
GORDON, Sco., in the sea, a ship under sail, ppr. *Fertur discrimine fructus. Pl.* 109, *cr.* 8.
GORDON, Sco., in dexter hand, a scimitar. *Dread God. Pl.* 29, *cr.* 8.
GORDON, Sco., a ship under sail, ppr. *Nil arduum. Pl.* 109, *cr.* 8.
GORDON, Sco., a cross Calvary, gu. *Spero. Pl.* 7, *cr.* 13.
GORDON, Sco., in dexter hand, couped, in fess, a (sword), in pale, enfiled with a boar's head, erased, all ppr. *Aut mors, aut vita decora. Pl.* 85, *cr.* 12.
GORDON, Sco., a crescent, ar. *Gradatim pleno. Pl.* 18, *cr.* 14.
GORDON, Sco., an oak, gu. *Sub tegmine. Pl.* 16, *cr.* 8.
GORDON, Sco., a greyhound, (passant.) *Pl.* 104, *cr.* 1, (without chapeau.)
GORDON, Sco., a cat, (statant,) gardant, ppr. *Pl.* 119, *cr.* 7.
GORDON, Sco., out of a heart, a dexter hand, holding a sword, wavy, ppr. *Pl.* 35, *cr.* 7, (sword, *pl.* 71, *cr.* 7.)
GORDON, Iri., a boar's head, erased and erect, sa., armed and eared, or. *Pl.* 21, *cr.* 7.
GORDON, Sco., a greyhound, (passant,) ar., collared, az. *God with us. Pl.* 104, *cr.* 1, (without chapeau.)
GORDON, Eng., a boar's head, couped, gu., encircled by (two) serpents, internowed, heads respecting each other, in chief, ppr. *Pl.* 12, *cr.* 6.
GORDON, JOHN, Esq., of Cairnfield, Banff, a boar's head, erased, or. *Byde*—and—*Dum vigilo, tutus. Pl.* 16, *cr.* 11.
GORDON, JOHN, Esq., of Cairnbulg, Aberdeens., two naked arms, holding a bow at full stretch, ready to let an arrow fly, all ppr. *Fortuna sequatur. Pl.* 100, *cr.* 4.
GORDON, JAMES-ADAM, Esq., of Knockespock and Terpersie, Aberdeen : 1. A stag's head, erased, ppr., attired, or. *Pl.* 66, *cr.* 9. 2. A stag, at gaze, ppr. *Non fraude sed laude*—and—*Dum vigilo, tutus. Pl.* 81, *cr.* 8.
GORDON-CUMING-SKENE, JOHN, Esq., of Pitlurg and Dyce, Aberdeens., a dove, ar., beaked and membered, gu., in mouth an olive branch, ppr. *I hope. Pl.* 48, *cr.* 15.
GORDON-TAYLOR : 1. For *Gordon*, an oak-tree. *I byde. Pl.* 16, *cr.* 8. 2. For *Taylor*, a stork, ppr., supporting with dexter an anchor, az. *Dum spiro, spero. Pl.* 61, *cr.* 10.

GORE, Bart., Iri., a wolf, (rampant,) ar., collared, gu. *Sola salus servire Deo.* *Pl.* 126, *cr.* 13.
GORE, Eng., a leopard, rampant, ppr. *In hoc signo vinces.* *Pl.* 73, *cr.* 2.
GORE, a lion, rampant. *Pl.* 67, *cr.* 5.
GORE, Iri., (on a mount, vert,) a wolf, salient, ppr., ducally gorged, or. *Pl.* 126, *cr.* 13, (gorging, *pl.* 128, *fig.* 3.)
GORE, a wolf, passant, (collared and lined.) *Pl.* 46, *cr.* 6.
GORE, Wilts., a bull's head, couped, sa. *Pl.* 120, *cr.* 7.
GORE, Middx., Herts., and Surr., a wolf, (rampant,) ppr., ducally gorged, or. *Pl.* 126, *cr.* 13, (gorging, *pl.* 128, *fig.* 3.)
GORE, Lond. and Herts., on a mount, vert, a tiger, salient, ar., tufted and maned, sa., ducally gorged, or.
GORELY, and GORLEY, Eng., in hand, in armour, a cross crosslet, fitched, in pale, ppr. *Pl.* 51, *cr.* 1.
GORE-ORMSBY, Salop : 1. For *Gore,* an heraldic-tiger, rampant, ar., ducally gorged, or. *Pl.* 57, *cr.* 13. 2. An arm, in armour embowed, ppr., charged with a rose, gu., in hand a man's leg, in armour, couped at thigh. *Pl.* 39, *cr.* 6, (arm, *pl.* 120, *cr.* 11.)
GORGE, Eng., a greyhound's head. *Pl.* 89, *cr.* 2.
GORGES, Somers., a greyhound's head, (erased,) ar., collared, gu. *Pl.* 43, *cr.* 11.
GORGES, and GORGIS, Eng., an annulet, or, stoned, az. *Pl.* 35, *cr.* 3.
GORGES, Iri., a salmon, haurient, ppr. *Pl.* 98, *cr.* 12.
GORHAM, Eng., a sword, in pale, on point a garland of laurel, ppr. *Pl.* 15, *cr.* 6.
GORING, Bart., Suss., a lion, rampant, gardant, sa. *Pl.* 92, *cr.* 7.
GORM, Sco., an eagle's head, sa., beaked, or. *Pl.* 100, *cr.* 10.
GORMAN, Eng., a horse, saddled, ppr., at full speed. *Pl.* 8, *cr.* 2.
GORMAN, Iri., a naked arm., in hand a sword, ppr. *Pl.* 34, *cr.* 7.
GORMANSTON, Viscount, Iri., on a chapeau, gu., turned up, erm., a fox, (statant,) ppr. *Sans tache.* *Pl.* 126, *cr.* 5, (chapeau, *pl.* 127, *fig.* 13.)
GORNEY, Lond., Ess., and Devons., on a chapeau, gu., turned up, erm., a lion, passant, ar., resting dexter on a cinquefoil, or. *Pl.* 107, *cr.* 1, (cinquefoil, *pl.* 141.)
GORRIE, and GORREY, Sco., an eagle's head, sa. *Pl.* 100, *cr.* 10.
GORT, Viscount, Iri., out of a mural coronet, gu., a stag's head, ppr. *Vincit veritas.* *Pl.* 29, *cr.* 7.
GORT, Viscount, Iri., a lion's head, couped, ar. *Vincit veritas.* *Pl.* 126, *cr.* 1.
GORT, Viscount, Iri., an antelope, trippant, ppr. *Vincit veritas.* *Pl.* 63, *cr.* 10.
GORTON, Eng., out of an earl's coronet, a moor's head, affrontée, ppr. *Pl.* 80, *cr.* 11.
GORWOOD, and GURWOOD, a unicorn's head, ppr. *Pl.* 20, *cr.* 1.
GOSELL, and GOSSELL, Norf., out of a ducal coronet, or, a talbot's head, erm. *Pl.* 99, *cr.* 2.
GOSFORD, Earl of, a cock, gu., standing on a trumpet, or. *Vigilantibus.* *Pl.* 2, *cr.* 1.

GOSHALL, Eng., out of a ducal coronet, or, in lion's gamb, gu., an (arrow,) gold, headed, of the second. *Pl.* 120, *cr.* 6.
GOSKAR, a Cornish chough, in beak a mullet. *Spes mea in Deo.* *Pl.* 100, *cr.* 13, (mullet, *pl.* 141.).
GOSLETT, Glouc., a stalk of wheat and a palm-branch, in saltier, ppr. *Pl.* 63, *cr.* 3.
GOSLIKE, a griffin's' head, couped, between wings, gu., platée, ar. *Pl.* 65, *cr.* 1.
GOSLING, and GOSOLYN, an eagle's head, erased, sa., charged with a crescent, erm. *Pl.* 20, *cr.* 7, (crescent, *pl.* 141.)
GOSLING, an eagle's head, erased, ermines, charged on neck with a bezant, over it, a cross formée, ar. *Pl.* 20, *cr.* 7, (charging, *pl.* 141.)
GOSNALL, and GOSNOLD, Suff., a bull's head, gardant, per pale, or and az. *Pl.* 18, *cr.* 15.
GOSNALL, and GOSNOLD, Suff., a bull's head, gardant, per pale, or and vert, horns counterchanged. *Pl.* 18, *cr.* 15.
GOSPATRICK, Eng., an antique ship, of one mast, the sail furled, sa., flag, gu. *Pl.* 24, *cr.* 5.
GOSS, or GOSSE, Eng., a falcon, wings expanded and inverted, ppr., ducally gorged, or. *Pl.* 61, *cr.* 12.
GOSSELIN, or GOSSELYN, Eng., an antelope's head, erased, ppr. *Pl.* 24, *cr.* 7.
GOSSELIN, THOMAS LE MARCHANT, Esq., of Bengeo Hall, Herts., a negro's head, ppr. *Pl.* 120, *cr.* 3.
GOSSET, or GOSSETT, Eng., in hand, couped at wrist, a dagger, in pale, ppr. *Pl.* 23, *cr.* 15.
GOSSET, a greyhound's head, (erased,) ar., collared, gu. *Pl.* 43, *cr.* 11.
GOSSIP, a martlet, sa. *Pl.* 111, *cr.* 5.
GOSSIP, Yorks., two goat's heads, erased, and addorsed, dexter, az., sinister, ar.
GOST, Lond., a pheon, or, between wings, ar. *Pl.* 52, *cr.* 4, (pheon, *pl.* 141.)
GOSTLING, Eng., a phœnix in flames, ppr. *Pl.* 44, *cr.* 8.
GOSTWICK, or GOSTWYKE, Beds., a griffin's head, between wings, gu. *Pl.* 65, *cr.* 1.
GOSTWICK, or GOSTWYKE, Beds., a griffin's head, between wings, gu., platée, ar. *Pl.* 65, *cr.* 1.
GOTHAM, Eng., on stump of tree, an eagle, wings addorsed, ppr. *Pl.* 61, *cr.* 1, (stump, *pl.* 5, *cr.* 4.)
GOTHARD, Northumb., out of a ducal coronet, a buck's head, ppr. *Aquila non captat muscas.* *Pl.* 29, *cr.* 7.
GOTOBED, Eng., a pelican, in her piety, gu. *Pl.* 44, *cr.* 1.
GOTT, Lond. and Suss., a griffin's head, erminois, between wings, erm. *Pl.* 22, *cr.* 2.
GOTTES, Camb., a greyhound's head, (erased,) ar., collared and lined, or. *Pl.* 43, *cr.* 11.
GOTTINGTON, Eng., a horned owl, ppr. *Pl.* 1, *cr.* 8.
GOUCELL, a unicorn, passant, or. *Pl.* 106, *cr.* 3.
GOUCH, Eng., a griffin's head, erased, ppr. *Semper eadem.* *Pl.* 48, *cr.* 6.
GOUDIE, Sco., a garb, or. *Honestas.* *Pl.* 48, *cr.* 10.
GOUGH, Viscount, of Goojerat and Limerick : 1. In centre, a boar's head, couped, or. On a scroll, over it, *Faugh-a-Ballagh.* *Pl.* 48, *cr.* 2. 2. Dexter side, on a mural coronet, ar., a lion, passant, gardant, or, (in dexter, two flag-staffs, in bend, sinister, ppr., one

the Union flag, the other a Chinese flag, broken, with device of a dragon, with *China on a scroll*, over.) *Pl.* 120, *cr.* 5, (coronet, *same plate*, *cr.* 14.) 3. Sinister side, a dexter arm, in uniform of 87th Regiment, faced, vert, grasping the colours of same, displayed, and French eagle, reversed and depressed, staff broken, ppr., with *Barrosa*, over.

GOUGH, Somers and Iri., a boar's head, couped, ar. *Pl.* 48, *cr.* 2.

GOUGH, Somers. and Iri., a boar's head, couped, ar., in mouth a broken spear. *Pl.* 11, *cr.* 9.

GOUGHTON, a rose, slipped, gu., leaved and stalked, ppr., between wings. *Pl.* 62, *cr.* 4, (rose, *pl.* 105, *cr.* 7.)

GOULBORNE, Chesh., a stag's head, or, gorged with a chaplet of laurel, ppr. *Pl.* 38, *cr.* 1.

GOULBURN, a dove and olive-branch, ppr. *Pl.* 48, *cr.* 15.

GOULD, Middx., Dors., and Devons., an arm, vested, vert, in hand, ppr., a banner, or, (charged with three bars, wavy, az., and on a canton, ar., a rose, gu.) *Pl.* 99, *cr.* 3.

GOULD, Dors., an arm, embowed, vested, gu., cuffed, or, in hand, ppr., a banner, (paly of six, ar., and of the second, on a canton, ar., a cross, of the first, the staff, or.) *Pl.* 99, *cr.* 3.

GOULD, Iri., a martlet, or. *Pl.* 111, *cr.* 5.

GOULD, a demi-lion, rampant, or, (holding a scroll, ar.) *Pl.* 67, *cr.* 10.

GOULD, Sco., between horns of a crescent, ar., a buckle, or. *Pl.* 25, *cr.* 3.

GOULD, Sco., a stag's head, ppr. *Pl.* 91, *cr.* 14.

GOULD, Devons., a demi-lion, rampant, az., bezantée. *Probitate et labore.* *Pl.* 67, *cr.* 10.

GOULDEN, Eng., a lion's head, erased, ppr. *Pl.* 81, *cr.* 4.

GOULDIE, Sco., a garb, or. *Quid utilius.* *Pl.* 48, *cr.* 10.

GOULDING, Iri., a hawk, jessed, belled, and hooded, ppr. *Pl.* 38, *cr.* 12.

GOULDING, Kent, a lion, sejant, sa., supporting with dexter an escutcheon, or. *Pl.* 126, *cr.* 15, (escutcheon, *pl.* 19, *cr.* 2.)

GOULDINGHAM, Eng., a lion's gamb, erased. *Pl.* 126, *cr.* 9.

GOULDNEY, a quatrefoil, ensigned with a lion's head, erased. *Pl.* 81, *cr.* 4, (quatrefoil, *pl.* 65, *cr.* 7.)

GOULDSMITH, Kent, a Cornish chough, ppr., guttée-d'eau. *Pl.* 100, *cr.* 13.

GOULSTONE, an ostrich's wing of five feathers, alternately, ar. and gu., charged with a bend, sa.

GOULTON, Yorks., a fleur-de-lis, sa. *Pl.* 68, *cr.* 12.

GOURE, a wolf, passant, ar., collared and (lined, or.) *Pl.* 5, *cr.* 8, (without staff.)

GOURING, a lion, rampant. *Pl.* 67, *cr.* 5.

GOURLAY, GOURLEY, and GOURLEE, Eng., a boar's head, erased, ppr. *Pl.* 16, *cr.* 11.

GOURLAY, and GOURLEY, Sco., a mullet of six points, or. *Pl.* 45, *cr.* 1.

GOURLAY, and GOURLEY, Sco., an eagle, issuing. *Profunda cernit.* *Pl.* 52, *cr.* 8.

GOURLIE, Sco., two hands conjoined and couped, in fess, ppr., supporting a cross crosslet, fitched, gu. *Pl.* 52, *cr.* 15.

GOUTON, Eng., out of an earl's coronet, a black's head, affrontée, all ppr. *Pl.* 80, *cr.* 11.

GOVAN, Sco., a sword, in pale, ppr., on point a mullet, ar. *Depechez.* *Pl.* 55, *cr.* 15.

GOVE, Eng., out of a mural coronet, or, a demi-monkey, sa. *Pl.* 24, *cr.* 12.

GOVER, Eng., in a maunch, or, a dexter hand apaumée, ppr. *Pl.* 8, *cr.* 11.

GOVESY, Eng., a demi-woman, ppr., richly attired, az., in dexter a balance, of the first. *Pl.* 57, *cr.* 1.

GOVETT, a demi-savage, in dexter hand a sheaf of arrows, and pointing with sinister to a crown. *Pl.* 86, *cr.* 3.

Gow, Sco., in hand an escallop, ppr. *Pl.* 57, *cr.* 6.

GOWAN, Sco., a lymphad, her oars in action, sa., flag, gu. *Pl.* 34, *cr.* 5.

GOWAN, Sco., a bird, close, ppr. *Pl.* 10, *cr.* 12.

GOWAN, Sco., a sword, in pale, ppr. *Pl.* 105, *cr.* 1.

GOWANS, Sco., a lion's head, erased, ppr., collared, or. *Pl.* 7, *cr.* 10.

GOWCELL, Norf., a unicorn, passant, ar. *Pl.* 106, *cr.* 3.

GOWER, Yorks., a demi-eagle, or. *Pl.* 52, *cr.* 8.

GOWER, Ess. and Worc., a wolf's head, erased, or. *Pl.* 14, *cr.* 6.

GOWER, Iri., two wings, displayed, or. *Pl.* 39, *cr.* 12.

GOWER, Lond., a talbot, sejant. *Pl.* 107, *cr.* 7, (without collar.)

GOWER, Berks. and Yorks., a wolf, passant, ar., collared and lined, or. *Frangas, non flectes.* *Pl.* 65, *cr.* 2.

GOWLAND, Durh., a bezant, charged with a mount, vert, thereon a stag (trippant,) ppr. *Pl.* 45, *cr.* 11.

GOWSHELL, Norf., a bull's head, cabossed, ppr. *Pl.* 111, *cr.* 6.

GOYLIN, a greyhound's head, per pale, ar. and or, between two roses, gu., stalked and leaved, ppr. *Pl.* 84, *cr.* 13.

GRABEN, an eagle, displayed, or, gorged with a chaplet of leaves, vert. *Pl.* 84, *cr.* 14.

GRABHAM, Somers., (on a mount, vert,) a boar's head, erased, or, guttée-de-sang, entwined by a snake, ppr. *L'Esperance du salut.* *Pl.* 12, *cr.* 6.

GRABY, and GREBY, out of a ducal coronet, or, a demi-eagle, displayed, ppr. *Pl.* 9, *cr.* 6.

GRABY, and GREBY, out of a ducal coronet, or, an eagle, displayed, or, armed, gu. *Pl.* 9, *cr.* 6.

GRACE, Bart., Iri., a demi-lion, rampant, ar. *En grace affie*—and—*Concordant nomine facta.* *Pl.* 67, *cr.* 10.

GRACE, Bart., Iri., a boar's head and neck, (erased,) or. *En grace affie*—and—*Concordant nomine facta.* *Pl.* 2, *cr.* 7.

GRACE, Eng., a demi-lion, rampant, ar. *Pl.* 67, *cr.* 10.

GRACE, Wilts., Somers., Hants, and Durh., a lion, passant, per fess, ar. and or. *Pl.* 48, *cr.* 8.

GRACE, Bucks., a lion, rampant, per fess, or and ar. *Pl.* 67, *cr.* 5.

GRACIE, Sco., a fox, current. *Pl.* 80, *cr.* 5.

GRADEN, Sco., a urus's head, erased, ppr. *Pl.* 57, *cr.* 7.

GRADEN, Sco., a demi-otter, erect, sa., devouring a fish, ppr. *Pl.* 74, *cr.* 13.

GRADOCK, and GRADOCKE, a horse-shoe, az., between wings, ppr. *Pl.* 17, *cr.* 3.

GRADWELL, a stag, trippant, ppr., (collared and chained, or,) charged with a rose, gu. *Nil desperandum.* *Pl.* 68, *cr.* 2, (rose, *pl.* 141.)

GRADY, Iri., a horse's head, ar. *Pl.* 81, *cr.* 6.
GRADY, Eng., a demi-lion, rampant, ppr. *Pl.* 67, *cr.* 10.
GRÆME, Perths., an eagle, volant, ppr. *Ardenter prosequor alis.* *Pl.* 114, *cr.* 10.
GRÆME, Perths., a lion, rampant, gu. *Noli me tangere.* *Pl.* 67, *cr.* 5.
GRÆME, GEORGE DRUMMOND, Esq., of Inchbrakie, Perth, in hand a garland, ppr. *A Deo victoria.* *Pl.* 41, *cr.* 7.
GRÆME, Sco., a stag, lodged, ppr. *Cubo ut excubo.* *Pl.* 67, *cr.* 2.
GRÆME, Sco. and Eng., the rising sun, ppr. *Pl.* 67, *cr.* 9.
GRÆME, Durh., a cubit arm, in hand a laurel-chaplet, ppr. *Pl.* 86, *cr.* 1.
GRAFTON, Duke of, on a chapeau, gu., turned up, erm, a lion, statant, gardant, or, ducally crowned, az., and collared, counter-compony, ar., and of the fourth. *Et decus et pretium recti.* *Pl.* 105, *cr.* 5.
GRAFTON, Lond., Bucks., Worc., and Salop., on trunk of tree, couped and eradicated, an eagle, rising, all or. *Pl.* 1, *cr.* 11.
GRAHAM, Bart., of Esk, Cumb., two wings, addorsed, or. *Reason contents me.* *Pl.* 63, *cr.* 12.
GRAHAM, Bart., of Netherby, Cumb., on a wreath, a crown-vallery, or. *Reason contents me.* *Pl.* 128, *fig.* 21.
GRAHAM, Bart., of Norton Conyers, on a wreath, a crown-vallery, or. *Pl.* 128, *fig.* 21.
GRAHAM, Bart., Yorks. and Cumb., out of the battlements of a tower, two arms, in armour, ppr., in hands an escallop, sa. *Fideliter et diligenter.* *Pl.* 12, *cr.* 5, (arms, *pl.* 10, *cr.* 9; escallop, *pl.* 141.)
GRAHAM, Cumb., two wings, conjoined, or. *Pl.* 15, *cr.* 10.
GRAHAM, of Morphie, an eagle, devouring a crane. *Ne oublie.* *Pl.* 17, *cr.* 8.
GRAHAM, of Meiklewood, a stork. *Auxiliante, resurgo.* *Pl.* 33, *cr.* 9.
GRAHAM, of Gartmore, an eagle, displayed, in dexter a sword, in pale, ppr. *For right and reason.* *Pl.* 107, *cr.* 4.
GRAHAM, of Duntroon, a flame of fire, ppr. *Recta sursum.* *Pl.* 16, *cr.* 12.
GRAHAM, of Killern, a falcon, killing a stork, ppr. *Memor esto.* *Pl.* 17, *cr.* 8.
GRAHAM, of Orchill, an eagle, volant, ppr. *Prosequor alis.* *Pl.* 114, *cr.* 10.
GRAHAM, of Braco, two hands, issuing out of a cloud, in each a sword, the dexter flourishing aloft, the sinister in a defensive posture. *Defendendo vinco.* *Pl.* 122, *cr.* 9.
GRAHAM, of Carrock, a lion, rampant, gu. *Noli me tangere.* *Pl.* 67, *cr.* 5.
GRAHAM, of Meikle, a star, ppr. *Auxiliante, resurgo.* *Pl.* 21, *cr.* 6.
GRAHAM, of Dougalstoun, an escallop, or. *Pignus amoris.* *Pl.* 117, *cr.* 4.
GRAHAM, of Balchlave, a stag, lodged, gu. *Cubo ut excubo.* *Pl.* 67, *cr.* 2.
GRAHAM, of Balgowan, a dove, ppr. *Candide et secure.* *Pl.* 66, *cr.* 12.
GRAHAM, of Fintry, a phœnix in flames, ppr. *Bon fin.* *Pl.* 44, *cr.* 8.
GRAHAM, of Drynie, a falcon, ppr., beaked, or, standing on a heron. *Ne oublie.* *Pl.* 17, *cr.* 8.
GRAHAM, of Limekilns, an arm, from shoulder, in hand a tilting-spear, ppr. *Pro rege.* *Pl.* 19, *cr.* 5, (spear, *pl.* 97, *cr.* 4.)

GRAHAM, Sco., in hand a sword, in pale, ppr. *Non immemor.* *Pl.* 23, *cr.* 15.
GRAHAM, of Gorthey, two arms, issuing from a cloud, erect, and holding up a man's skull, encircled with two branches of palm-tree, and over the head a marquess's coronet. *Sepultu viresco.*
GRAHAM, of Grahamshall, Sco., a lion, couchant, under a sword, in pale, ppr. *Nec temere nec timide.* *Pl.* 75, *cr.* 5, (without chapeau; sword, *same plate.*)
GRAHAM, of Inchbraikie, Sco., in hand a garland, ppr. *A Deo victoria.* *Pl.* 41, *cr.* 7.
GRAHAM, of Monargan, Sco., a flame of fire, ppr. *Nunquam deorsum.* *Pl.* 16, *cr.* 12.
GRAHAM, of New Wark, Sco., a pelican's head, couped, ppr. *Pl.* 41, *cr.* 4.
GRAHAM, an oak-branch, erect, ppr., bearing one acorn. *Pl.* 81, *cr.* 7.
GRAHAM, an eagle's head, erased, gu. *Right and reason.* *Pl.* 20, *cr.* 7.
GRAHAM, Sco., a demi-eagle, wings expanded, ppr. *Right and reason.* *Pl.* 52, *cr.* 8.
GRAHAM, WILLIAM, Esq., of Airth Castle, Stirling, in naked hand, a dagger, erect, ppr. *Non immemor.* *Pl.* 23, *cr.* 15.
GRAHAM, WILLIAM, Esq., of Burntshiels, Renfrew, an eagle, devouring a stork, all ppr. *Nes oubliez.* *Pl.* 17, *cr.* 8.
GRAHAM, GEORGE, Esq., of Meiklewood, Stirling, a star, ppr. *Auxiliante, resurgo.* *Pl.* 21, *cr.* 6.
GRAHAM, out of a cloud, in fess, a hand reaching to a garland, all ppr. *Numen et omnia.* *Pl.* 73, *cr.* 11.
GRAHAM, within a wreath of cypress, vert, out of clouds, two arms, embowed, ppr., holding a skull, ar., crowned, or.
GRAHAM, an escallop, or. *Pl.* 117, *cr.* 4.
GRAHAM, Westm., an arm, in armour, embowed, in hand a cutlass, ppr. *Pl.* 81, *cr.* 11.
GRAHAM, Sco., an eagle's head, ppr., beaked, or. *Right and reason.* *Pl.* 100, *cr.* 10.
GRAHAM, Sco., a vol, ppr. *Reason contents me.* *Pl.* 15, *cr.* 10.
GRAHAM, Sco., a falcon, ppr. *Prædæ memor.* *Pl.* 67, *cr.* 3.
GRAHAM, Sco., a dove, ppr. *Candide et secure.* *Pl.* 66, *cr.* 12.
GRAHAM, Iri., in hand, in fess, couped, a fleur-de-lis, or. *Pl.* 46, *cr.* 12.
GRAHAM-MAXWELL, Sco.: 1. An eagle, regardant, rising from the top of a rock, all ppr. *Souvenez.* *Pl.* 79, *cr.* 2. 2. A stag's head, cabossed. *Prospero sed curo.* *Pl.* 36, *cr.* 1.
GRAINGER, Ess., a dexter arm, couped, az., purfled, or, cuffed, ar., in hand, ppr., by the chains, of the second, a portcullis, gu. *Pl.* 39, *cr.* 1, (portcullis, *pl.* 51, *cr.* 12.)
GRAISON, a stag, lodged, regardant, ppr. *Pl.* 51, *cr.* 9.
GRAMMER, Herts., a demi-lion, rampant, az., billettée, or. *Fax mentis incendium gloria.* *Pl.* 95, *cr.* 4.
GRANARD, Earl of, Sco., a bear, passant, ar., guttée-de-sang, and muzzled, gu. *Pl.* 61, *cr.* 5.
GRANCE, a holly-branch, vert, (fructed, gu.) *Pl.* 99, *cr.* 6.
GRANCE, Eng., a demi-bear, rampant, ppr. *Pl.* 104, *cr.* 10.

GRANDFORD, Eng., a hawk, perching on a fish, ppr. *Pl.* 29, *cr.* 11.
GRANDGEORGE, Linc., a stag's head, ar., (gorged with a bar-gemelle, gu.) *Pl.* 91, *cr.* 14.
GRANDGEORGE, Linc., a stag's head, couped, per pale, sa. and or, guttée, counterchanged. *Pl.* 91, *cr.* 14.
GRANDISON, and GRANSON, Eng., a female, supporting a portcullis, ppr. *Pl.* 126, *cr.* 6.
GRANDIVILLE, and GRANVILLE, Eng., a griffin's head, between wings, ppr. *Pl.* 22, *cr.* 2.
GRANDON, and GRANDSON, out of a heart, a hand holding a cutlass, ppr. *Pl.* 35, *cr.* 7.
GRANDORGE, or GRAIN D'ORGE, Yorks.: 1. A hawk, perched, ppr. *Pl.* 67, *cr.* 3. 2. A stag's head, ar., (gorged with a bar-gemelle, gu.) *Pl.* 91, *cr.* 14.
GRANDORGE, Linc., a stag's head, couped, per pale, sa. and or, guttée, counterchanged, in mouth an (ear of barley, vert.) *Pl.* 100, *cr.* 8.
GRANDSON, Eng., out of a heart, gu., a hand holding a scimitar, ppr. *Pl.* 35, *cr.* 7.
GRANDSON, Eng., a poplar-tree, ppr. *Pl.* 95, *cr.* 2.
GRANDVELL, a greyhound's head, sa., collared and ringed, or. *Pl.* 43, *cr.* 11.
GRANDVILLE, a griffin, passant, or. *Pl.* 61, *cr.* 14, (without gorging.)
GRANE, Yorks., a wolf, passant, paly of four, or and sa., in mouth a pen, gold. *Pl.* 46, *cr.* 6, (pen, *pl.* 105, *cr.* 3.)
GRANE, a boar, passant, sa., (collared and lined, or.) *Pl.* 48, *cr.* 14.
GRANELL, round a pheon, shafted, a serpent, entwined, ppr. *Pl.* 93, *cr.* 7.
GRANGE, Lond., in lion's gamb, erect and erased, ppr., a branch of pomegranates, or. *Pl.* 60, *cr.* 14, (pomegranates, *pl.* 67, *cr.* 8.)
GRANGE, Norf. and Cambs., a demi-antelope, or, attired, maned, armed, and hoofed, sa. *Pl.* 75, *cr.* 10, (without escutcheon.)
GRANGER, Staffs., a griffin, passant. *Honestas optima politia.* *Pl.* 61, *cr.* 14, (without gorging.)
GRANGER, a dexter arm, couped and embowed, in hand three wheat-ears, all ppr. *Pl.* 89, *cr.* 4.
GRANT, Iri., a cat, rampant. *Pl.* 126 A, *cr.* 10.
GRANT, Bart., of Dalvey, Sco., on stump of oak-tree, sprouting, the sun shining, all ppr. *Te favente, virebo.* *Pl.* 123, *cr.* 3.
GRANT, Bart., of Monymusk, Sco., a Bible, displayed, ppr. *Jehovah Jireh*—and—*Suum cuique.* *Pl.* 15, *cr.* 12.
GRANT, Sco., a burning-hill, ppr. *Stabit—Stand sure—Stand fast—Craig Elachie.* *Pl.* 92, *cr.* 9.
GRANT, of Ballendalloch, Sco., an oak-tree, ppr. *Suo se robore firmat.* *Pl.* 16, *cr.* 8.
GRANT, of Cullen, a book, expanded. *Suum cuique.* *Pl.* 15, *cr.* 12.
GRANT, of Currimony, Sco., a demi-savage, ppr. *I'll stand sure.* *Pl.* 14, *cr.* 11.
GRANT, of Gartenbeg, Sco., on trunk of oak-tree, sprouting, the sun shining, all ppr. *Wise and harmless.* *Pl.* 123, *cr.* 3.
GRANT, of Kilgraston, Sco., the Roman fasces, ppr. *Leges juraque serva.* *Pl.* 65, *cr.* 15.
GRANT, of Achnanie, Sco., a cock, ppr. *Audacia.* *Pl.* 67, *cr.* 14.

GRANT, JAMES-MURRAY, Esq., of Glenmoriston Inverness; and Moy, Moray, a mountain, in flames, ppr. *Stand firm.* *Pl.* 92, *cr.* 9.
GRANT, of Preston Grange, Sco., a demi-Hercules, with lion's skin, ppr. *Non inferiora secutus.* *Pl.* 49, *cr.* 11.
GRANT, of Rothiemurchas, Sco., an arm, in armour, in hand a broadsword, ppr. *For my Duchess*—and—*In God is all my trust.* *Pl.* 2, *cr.* 8.
GRANT, of Darlway, in dexter hand a branch of (oak,) ppr. *Rudem formant frondes.* *Pl.* 43, *cr.* 6.
GRANT, of Blackburn, an arm, in armour, embowed, in hand a sword, all ppr. *Fortitudine.* *Pl.* 2, *cr.* 8.
GRANT, of Invereshie, a cat, sejant, fore-feet, erected, ppr. *Parcere subjectis.* *Pl.* 53, *cr.* 5.
GRANT, Sco., a rock, ppr. *Immobile.* *Pl.* 73, *cr.* 12.
GRANT, Sco., an oak-tree, ppr. *Suo se robore firmat.* *Pl.* 16, *cr.* 8.
GRANT, Sco., in dexter hand a dagger, in pale, ppr. *Ense et animo.* *Pl.* 23, *cr.* 15.
GRANT, Warw., a fleur-de-lis, az. *Pl.* 68, *cr.* 12.
GRANT, a boar's head, couped. *Pl.* 48, *cr.* 2.
GRANT, Lond. and Hants., a demi-lion, ar. *Tanquam despicatus sum, vinco.* *Pl.* 67, *cr.* 10.
GRANT-MACPHERSON, Bart., Elgin: 1. In dexter hand a dirk, in pale, ppr. *Pl.* 18, *cr.* 3. 2. A cat, sejant, fore-feet erected, gardant, ppr. *Tauch not the cat, bot the glove*—and—*Esne et animo.* *Pl.* 53, *cr.* 5.
GRANTHAM, Linc., a moor's head, couped at shoulders, ppr., crined, or. *Pl.* 19, *cr.* 1.
GRANTHAM, Linc., a demi-griffin, gu. *Pl.* 18, *cr.* 6.
GRANTHAM, in hand, erect, couped at wrist, a dagger, ppr. *Pl.* 101, *cr.* 10.
GRANTHAM, Middx., a mercurial cap, placed above a scimitar, edge downwards, and caduceus, in saltier, thereon a Turk's head, affrontée, erased at shoulders, ensigned with a turban, all ppr. *Pl.* 17, *cr.* 13.
GRANTHAM, CHARLES, Esq., of Ketton Grange, Rutland, a demi-griffin, gu. *Honore et amore.* *Pl.* 18, *cr.* 6.
GRANTLEY, Baron, a moor's head, couped at shoulders, wreathed with ivy, ppr., tied, ar. and az. *Avi numerantur avorum.* *Pl.* 118, *cr.* 7.
GRANVILLE, Earl, a wolf, passant, ar., collared and lined, or. *Frangas non flectus.* *Pl.* 5, *cr.* 8, (without staff.)
GRANVILLE, Warw., on a chapeau, a griffin, or. *Deo, patriæ, amicis.* *Pl.* 122, *cr.* 11.
GRANVILLE, Somers., on a mural coronet, ar., a serpent, nowed, vert. *Pl.* 103, *cr.* 11.
GRANVILLE, a griffin's head, between wings, ppr. *Pl.* 65, *cr.* 1.
GRAPE, Berks., on a mount, vert, a stag, grazing, erminois, (collared,) gu. *Pl.* 37, *cr.* 8.
GRASSAL, and GRASSALL, Eng., an arm, in armour, embowed, in hand a dagger, ppr. *Pl.* 120, *cr.* 11.
GRASSICK, Sco., in dexter hand (three) arrows. *Defend.* *Pl.* 56, *cr.* 4.
GRASSICK, of Buchuam, a lion's head, gu. *Fear God, and spare not.* *Pl.* 126, *cr.* 1.
GRATTAM, a dove, standing on a barrel, in dexter a sceptre, all ppr.

GRATTON, Eng., on a heart, an eagle's leg, ppr. *Pl.* 27, *cr.* 1.

GRATWICK, Suss., an ostrich's head, or, in beak a horse-shoe, ar. *Pl.* 99, *cr.* 12, (without feathers.)

GRAUNDORGE, Linc., a stag's head, ar., (gorged with a bar-gemelle, gu.) *Pl.* 91, *cr.* 14.

GRAUNDORGE, Linc., a stag's head, couped, per pale, sa. and or., guttée, counterchanged. *Pl.* 91, *cr.* 14.

GRAVATT, Eng., a wolf, passant, per pale, erminois and ar. *Pl.* 46, *cr.* 6.

GRAVE, Berks., within an annulet, az., an escutcheon, sa. *Pl.* 77, *cr.* 9, (without cross.)

GRAVE, Iri., a cock, sa., combed and wattled, gu. *Pl.* 67, *cr.* 14.

GRAVE, Suss., Yorks., and Cornw., an eagle. erased, or, beaked, gu., enfiled with a ducal coronet, ar. *Pl.* 52, *cr.* 8, (coronet, *same plate, cr.* 2.)

GRAVE, and GRAVES, Eng., out of a ducal coronet, an eagle, displayed, or, armed, gu. *Pl.* 9, *cr.* 6, (eagle, *pl.* 48, *cr.* 11.)

GRAVES, Eng., out of a ducal coronet, or, a demi-eagle, wings expanded. *Pl.* 9, *cr.* 6.

GRAVES, Eng., a squirrel, sejant, ermines. *Pl.* 16, *cr.* 9.

GRAVES, Baron, Iri., a demi-eagle, displayed and erased, or, encircled round body and below wings with a ducal coronet, ar. *Aquila non captat muscas. Pl.* 52, *cr.* 8, (coronet, *same plate, cr.* 2.)

GRAVES, Glouc., a demi-eagle, erased, or, environed with a ducal coronet, gu., in beak a cross crosslet, fitched, of the last. *Pl.* 52, *cr.* 8, (coronet, *cr.* 2; cross, *cr.* 15, *same pl.*)

GRAVES, a demi-eagle, wings expanded. *Pl.* 52, *cr.* 8.

GRAY, Captain WILLIAM, Wheatfield, upon a rock, ppr., a bear's paw, erect and erased, sa., grasping a snake entwined around it, also ppr. *Pl.* 126 A, *cr.* 9.

GRAY, Baron, Sco., an anchor, in pale, or. *Anchor, fast anchor. Pl.* 25, *cr.* 15.

GRAY, Northumb., on a ducal coronet, or, a phœnix in flames, ppr. *Pl.* 53, *cr.* 6.

GRAY, Northumb., out of a ducal coronet, a demi-swan, ppr. *Pl.* 10, *cr.* 11. (without dart.)

GRAY, Ess., a ram's head, couped, ar. *Pl.* 34, *cr.* 12.

GRAY, Iri., in hand a dagger, in pale, ppr. *Pl.* 23, *cr.* 15.

GRAY, Sco., an anchor, cabled, stuck in the sea, ppr. *Fast. Pl.* 62, *cr.* 10.

GRAY, HAMILTON, Lanark: 1. For *Gray*, an anchor, cabled, stuck in the sea, ppr. *Fast. Pl.* 62, *cr.* 10. 2. For *Hamilton*, out of a ducal coronet, or, an oak-tree, ppr., transversed by a saw. *Through. Pl.* 100, *cr.* 2.

GRAY, a lily, slipped, ppr. *Pl.* 81, *cr.* 9.

GRAY, Sco., a heart, gu. *Constant. Pl.* 55, *cr.* 13.

GRAY, Sco. and Eng., an anchor, the rope waved, ppr. *Anchor, fast anchor. Pl.* 42, *cr.* 12.

GRAY, Durh., in lion's gamb, erased, a serpent. *Pl.* 112, *cr.* 13.

GRAY, a scaling-ladder, ensigned with a ram's head. *De bon vouloir servir le Roy. Pl.* 98, *cr.* 15, (head, *pl.* 34, *cr.* 12.)

GRAY, the sun, or, charged with a unicorn, passant, ar. *Pl.* 114, *cr.* 1, (unicorn, *pl.* 106, *cr.* 3.)

GRAY, of Warriston, a lily, slipped, seeded and bladed, ppr. *Viget in cinere virtus. Pl.* 81, *cr.* 9.

GRAYDON, Eng., two lions' gambs, erect, supporting an escutcheon. *Pl.* 78, *cr.* 13.

GRAYHURST, Eng., a dove, az., with an olive-branch, ppr. *Pl.* 48, *cr.* 15.

GRAYLEY, Ess., in hand a fish, ppr. *Pl.* 105, *cr.* 9.

GRAYSON, Eng., out of a tower, a demi-lion, ducally crowned, holding a ball, fired, ppr. *Pl.* 53, *cr.* 2.

GRAZEBROOK, and GRAZERBROOK, a bear's head, or, muzzled, sa., charged on neck with three fleurs-de-lis, in fess. *Pl.* 2, *cr.* 9, (fleur-de-lis, *pl.* 141.)

GREAM, Yorks., two wings, addorsed, or. *Pl.* 63, *cr.* 12.

GREAT BEDWIN, Town of, Wilts., a griffin, passant, or. *Pl.* 61, *cr.* 14, (without gorging.)

GREATEBROOK, Warw., (on a mount, vert,) a fleur-de-lis, or. *Pl.* 68, *cr.* 12.

GREATHEAD, on a chapeau, gu., turned up, erm., a martlet, wings addorsed, sa. *Pl.* 89, *cr.* 7.

GREATHEAD, Eng., a savage's head, ppr. *Pl.* 19, *cr.* 1.

GREATOREX, Eng., a goat's head, ppr. *Pl.* 105, *cr.* 14.

GREAVES, Staffs., an eagle, displayed, or, winged, gu. *Aquila non captat muscas—Suprema quæro*—and—*Dum spiro, spero. Pl.* 48, *cr.* 11.

GREAVES, Lanc., out of the top of a tower, ppr., a demi-eagle, or, wings expanded, gu., in beak a cross crosslet, fitched, ar., charged on breast with a rose, of the third, leaved, vert. *Spes mea in Deo. Pl.* 112, *cr.* 4, (eagle, *pl.* 52, *cr.* 8; cross and rose, *pl.* 141.)

GREAVES, Warw., an eagle, with two heads, displayed, sa., beaked and membered, or. *Pl.* 87, *cr.* 11, (without flame.)

GREAVES, Derbs., Kent, and Suss., a demi-spread eagle, or, winged, gu. *Pl.* 22, *cr.* 11.

GREAVES, an arm, in armour, embowed, in hand a dagger, ppr. *Pl.* 120, *cr.* 11.

GREAVES, Iri., a cubit arm, in armour, in hand a cross crosslet, fitched, ppr. *Pl.* 51, *cr.* 1.

GREBELL, a greyhound's head, (erased,) ar., pellettée, collared and ringed, or. *Pl.* 43, *cr.* 11.

GREBY, Eng., a demi-eagle, in dexter a branch of laurel, ppr. *Pl.* 59, *cr.* 13.

GREEKE, Lond., trunk of tree, couped at top, and erased at root, ppr., issuing from towards the top two branches, vert, thereon suspended on a belt, gu., a Grecian target, or, (charged with a stag, az.) *Pl.* 23, *cr.* 6.

GREEN, Norf. and Oxon., a stag's head, erased, az., attired, or. *Pl.* 66, *cr.* 9.

GREEN, Oxon., a buck's head, or, charged with a mullet, sa. *Pl.* 61, *cr.* 9, (mullet, *pl.* 141.)

GREEN, Herts., Somers., Berks., and Ess., a buck's head, erased, erm., attired, or. *Pl.* 66, *cr.* 9.

GREEN, Yorks., a griffin's head, erased, sa., langued, gu., (doubly collared, or, between collars a cinquefoil, erm.,) in beak a key, or. *Pl.* 9, *cr.* 12.

GREEN, Bucks., out of a mural coronet, ar., a demi-lion, rampant, purp., in dexter a slip of (laurel,) vert. *Pl.* 17, *cr.* 7.

GREEN, Lond. and Berks., a stag's head, erased and attired, or, charged on neck with a pheon, sa., and under it three guttées-de-sang. *Pl.* 66, *cr.* 9, (pheon, *pl.* 141.)

GREEN, Norf. and Ess., a buck's head, erased, az., attired, or. *Vive valeque. Pl.* 66, *cr.* 9.

GREEN, a griffin's head, erased and (collared,) in beak a key. *Pl.* 9, *cr.* 12.
GREEN, Chesh., a demi-stag, salient, or. *Pl.* 55, *cr.* 9, (without rose.)
GREEN, an antelope's head, (couped,) ppr. *Pl.* 24, *cr.* 7.
GREEN, a stag, trippant, ppr. *Pl.* 68, *cr.* 2.
GREEN, a griffin's head, erased, in mouth a trefoil, slipped, ppr. *Pl.* 48, *cr.* 6, (trefoil, *pl.* 141.)
GREEN, a demi-greyhound. *Pl.* 48, *cr.* 3.
GREEN, Iri., a sinister arm, in armour, embowed, ppr., in hand a shield, or. *Pl.* 98, *cr.* 5.
GREEN, a stag's head, ar., attired, or, gorged with a chaplet of laurel, ppr. *Pl.* 38, *cr.* 1.
GREEN, Kent, out of a mural coronet, gu., a horse's head, ar., maned, or. *Pl.* 50, *cr.* 13, (coronet, *pl.* 128, *fig.* 18.)
GREEN, a cubit arm, erect, (vested, vert, cuffed, or, in hand a holly-branch, fructed, ppr.) *Virtus semper viridis.* *Pl.* 55, *cr.* 6.
GREEN, Ess., a lion, sejant, per pale, or and sa. *Pl.* 126, *cr.* 15.
GREEN, Wilts. and Yorks., a griffin's head, erased, quarterly, or and sa., in beak a trefoil, slipped, of the last. *Pl.* 48, *cr.* 6, (trefoil, *pl.* 141.)
GREEN, Herts., Notts., and Yorks., a woodpecker, pecking at a staff, raguly, couped and erect, ppr.
GREEN, a rose, gu., barbed, vert, seeded, or, environed by two laurel-branches, ppr. *Pl.* 3, *cr.* 13.
GREEN, Herts., a squirrel, sejant, bendy sinister, ar. and sa., in paws an escallop, or. *Pl.* 2, *cr.* 4, (escallop, *pl.* 141.)
GREEN, Herts., (on a mount, vert,) an escallop, az. *Pl.* 117, *cr.* 4.
GREEN, Norf., a dragon, (sans wings,) passant, per fess, or and vert. *Pl.* 90, *cr.* 10.
GREEN, Lond. and Norf., a buck's head, erased, or, attired, murally gorged and chained, ar. *Pl.* 66, *cr.* 9, (gorging, *pl.* 128, *fig.* 18.)
GREEN, Iri., an eagle, displayed, ppr., (charged on breast with a quadrangular lock, ar.) *Memor esto.* *Pl.* 48, *cr.* 11.
GREEN, on a mount, vert, a squirrel, sejant, ppr., holding an escallop, az. *Pl.* 2, *cr.* 4, (escallop, *pl.* 141.)
GREEN, THOMAS-ABBOTT, Esq., of Pavenham Bury, Beds., a buck, trippant, or. *Semper viridis.* *Pl.* 68, *cr.* 2.
GREENALL, out of a mural coronet, a demi-lion, in dexter a palm-branch. *Pl.* 17, *cr.* 7.
GREENAWAY, Eng., a demi-eagle, issuant, wings expanded, ppr. *Pl.* 52, *cr.* 8.
GREENAWAY, a lion, sejant, or, in paws a scaling-ladder, gu. *Pl.* 60, *cr.* 4, (ladder, *pl.* 98, *cr.* 15.)
GREENAWAY, Glouc., a griffin's head, erased, az., in beak an annulet, or. *Pl.* 48, *cr.* 6, (annulet, *pl.* 141.)
GREENE, Iri., a horse's head, sa., between wings, or. *Pl.* 19, *cr.* 13.
GREENE, Eng., a stag, passant, ar. *Pl.* 68, *cr.* 2.
GREENE, Leic., out of park pales, (in a circular form, a stag's head,) ppr., attired, or. *Pl.* 13, *cr.* 12.
GREENE, NUTTALL, Esq., late of Kilmanahan Castle, co. Waterford, out of a ducal coronet, a stag's head. *Nec timeo, nec sperno.* *Pl.* 92, *cr.* 7.

GREENE, Staffs., a stag's head, erased, or. *Pl.* 66, *cr.* 9.
GREENFIELD, Monm., a griffin, passant, wings elevated, or, (resting dexter on a clarion, gu.) *In jus si virescunt.* *Pl.* 39, *cr.* 8.
GREENFIELD, a branch of oak, vert, and a cross crosslet, fitched, in saltier, gu. *Pl.* 98, *cr.* 11.
GREENFIELD, on a chapeau, gu., turned up, arm., a griffin, statant, ar., beaked and membered, or. *Pl.* 122, *cr.* 11.
GREENFIELD, Eng., on a ducal coronet, or, a griffin, sejant, ppr., resting dexter on a shield, ar. *Pl.* 44, *cr.* 8.
GREENHALGH, and GREENHAUGH, Eng., a stork, sa. *Pl.* 33, *cr.* 9.
GREENHILL, Lond. and Middx., a demi-griffin, gu., powdered with thirty-nine mullets, or. *Honos alit artes.* *Pl.* 18, *cr.* 6, (mullet, *pl.* 141.)
GREENHILL, a demi-griffin, segreant, ar. (Another, or.) *Pl.* 18, *cr.* 6.
GREENING, Eng., a nag's head, ar. *Pl.* 81, *cr.* 6.
GREENLAND, Eng., a dexter arm, in hand a bomb, fired, ppr. *Pl.* 2, *cr.* 6.
GREENLAW, Sco., an eagle's head, erased, sa., in beak an acorn-slip, ppr. *Pl.* 22, *cr.* 1.
GREENLAW, on a mount, a cubit arm, in armour, environed by a snake, vert, in hand, ppr., a spear, in bend.
GREENLEES, and GREENLESS, Sco., out of a mount, a sprig growing, ppr. *Viresco.* *Pl.* 98, *cr.* 13.
GREENLOGH, a griffin's head, erased. *Pl.* 48, *cr.* 6.
GREENLY, Heref., a demi-stag, springing, per fess, erm. and erminois, on shoulder an escallop, az. *Fall-y-gallo.* *Pl.* 65, *cr.* 14, (escallop, *pl.* 141.)
GREENOUGH, Lond., the sun in splendour, ppr., within the circumference of a bugle-horn, sa., stringed, gu., rimmed and mounted, or. *Pl.* 68, *cr.* 14, (horn, *pl.* 48, *cr.* 12.)
GREENOUGH, Lond., a stag's head, erased, per fess, indented, ar. and gu., attired, or, in mouth a fleur-de-lis, az. *Pl.* 100, *cr.* 8, (fleur-de-lis, *pl.* 141.)
GREENOUGH, a cock, crowing, between two adders, in orle, their tails in saltier. *Pl.* 18, *cr.* 5.
GREENSMITH, Derb., a dove, close, ar., beaked and legged, gu. *Pl.* 66, *cr.* 12.
GREENSTREET, Kent, a dragon's head, erased, ar., guttée, gu., ducally gorged, az. *Pl.* 36, *cr.* 7.
GREENVILE, Bucks., a garb, vert. *Pl.* 48, *cr.* 10.
GREENVILE, Cornw., out of a ducal coronet, or, a plume of feathers, thereon a dove, rising, ar. *Pl.* 44, *cr.* 12, (dove, *pl.* 124, *cr.* 13.)
GREENVILE, Eng., a griffin's head, wings (addorsed,) or. *Pl.* 65, *cr.* 1.
GREENVILE, a griffin, passant, or, collared, sa. *Pl.* 61, *cr.* 14.
GREENWAY, Surr., a griffin's head. *Pl.* 38, *cr.* 3.
GREENWAY, Warw., a griffin's head, erased, az. *Pl.* 48, *cr.* 6.
GREENWAY, Devons., a griffin's head, erased, az., in mouth an anchor, gu. *Pl.* 9, *cr.* 12, (anchor, *pl.* 25, *cr.* 15.)
GREENWELL, Durh., a stork, ppr., beaked and legged, gu., (round neck a chaplet of laurel, vert.) *Pl.* 33, *cr.* 9.

GREENWELL, Lond. and Durh., an eagle's head, ar., beaked, gu., (gorged with a chaplet of laurel, vert.) *Pl.* 100, *cr.* 10.
GREENWOOD, Hants, a demi-lion, sa., (between paws a saltier, humettée, or.) *Pl.* 47, *cr.* 4.
GREENWOOD, a tiger, sejant, or. *Pl.* 26, *cr.* 9.
GREENWOOD, Derbs. and Yorks., a demi-lion, or, (between paws, a saltier, ar.) *Pl.* 47, *cr.* 4.
GREENWOOD, Suff. and Oxon., a lion, sejant, sa., (holding a saltier, ar.) *Pl.* 22, *cr.* 13.
GREENWOOD, Norf. and Yorks., a mullet, sa., between a pair of ducks' wings, expanded, of the same. *Ut prosim. Pl.* 1, *cr.* 15.
GREER, Eng., in hand, vested, gu., cuffed, or, a trefoil. *Pl.* 78, *cr.* 6.
GREER, a round padlock, ppr. *Pl.* 96, *cr.* 16.
GREERSON, Eng., a fetterlock, ar. *Pl.* 122, *cr.* 12.
GREET, Eng., a cock's head, erased, or. *Pl.* 92, *cr.* 3.
GREETE, a demi-greyhound, ar., collared, az. *Pl.* 5, *cr.* 10, (without wings.)
GREETHAM, Eng., two hands, issuing, holding a two-handed sword, ppr. *Pl.* 3, *cr.* 5.
GREETHEAD, a fleur-de-lis, ar. *Pl.* 68, *cr.* 12.
GREG, an arm, in armour, embowed, in hand a scimitar, az., hilt and pommel, or. *Pl.* 81, *cr.* 11.
GREG, ROBERT-HYDE, Esq., of Norcliffe Hall, Chester, and Cole's Park, Herts., an arm, in armour, embowed, in hand a scimitar, az., hilt and pommel, or. *E'en do and spair not*—and—*S'Rioghal mo Dhream. Pl.* 81, *cr.* 11.
GREGAN, Cornw., a Saracen's head, affrontée, (surmounting a javelin, in bend,) all ppr. *Pl.* 19, *cr.* 1.
GREGG, Middx. and Derbs., out of a ducal coronet, or, an eagle's head, per pale, ar., guttée-de-sang and sa., in beak a trefoil, slipped, of the last. *Pl.* 20, *cr.* 12, (trefoil, *pl.* 141.)
GREGG, Eng., a lion, passant, gardant, az. *Pl.* 120, *cr.* 5.
GREGG, Lond. and Chesh., out of a ducal coronet, or, an eagle's head and neck, per pale, ar. and sa., in beak a trefoil, slipped, of the same. *Pl.* 20, *cr.* 12, (trefoil, *pl.* 141.)
GREGOR, Sco., in hand a dagger, point downward, ppr. *Pro patriâ. Pl.* 18, *cr.* 3.
GREGOR, Eng., a hind's head, erased, gu. *Pl.* 6, *cr.* 1.
GREGOR, Corn., a garb, or. *Pl.* 48, *cr.* 10.
GREGORIE, Notts., a garb, or, banded, gu. *Pl.* 48, *cr.* 10.
GREGORSON, Sco., a lion's head, erased, crowned with an antique crown. *E'en do and spare not. Pl.* 123, *cr.* 13, (crown, *pl.* 79, *cr.* 12.)
GREGORY, Sco., trunk of oak-tree, sprouting. *Nec deficit alter. Pl.* 92, *cr.* 8.
GREGORY, Leic., a demi-boar, rampant, sa., collared, or. *Pl.* 20, *cr.* 5.
GREGORY, Sco., a sphere. *Altius. Pl.* 114, *cr.* 6.
GREGORY, Lanc. and Salop, two lions' heads, addorsed and erased, az. and ar., collared, or. *Pl.* 28, *cr.* 10.
GREGORY, Linc., out of a ducal coronet, or, a maiden's head, ppr., vested, gu. *Pl.* 74, *cr.* 5.
GREGORY, three garbs, or. *Pl.* 96, *cr.* 14.
GREGORY, a demi-boar, (collared) and armed, or. *Pl.* 20, *cr.* 5.
GREGORY, Middx., a demi-boar, salient, ar., armed and crined, or, (collared, az.) *Pl.* 20, *cr.* 5.

GREGORY, Lond., a demi-boar, erect, sa. *Pl.* 20, *cr.* 5.
GREGORY, Lond., a demi-boar, ar., armed and crined, or, (collared,) az., thereon four bezants. *Pl.* 20, *cr.* 4, (bezant, *pl.* 141.)
GREGSON, Durh. and Derbs., an arm, couped at elbow, vested, bendy-wavy of six, ar. and gu., in hand, ppr., a battle-axe, or, handle, sa., (tied round wrist with a ribbon.) *Vigilo. Pl.* 73, *cr.* 7, (vesting, *pl.* 94, *cr.* 15.)
GREGSON, Kent., a cubit arm, (in armour, charged with three bendlets, wavy, sa., in gauntlet,) a battle-axe, of the last, headed, or. *Pl.* 73, *cr.* 7.
GREHAM, Iri., a demi-bull, sa., armed, or. *Pl.* 63, *cr.* 6.
GREIDEN, Sco., a demi-otter, sa., devouring a fish, pp. *Pl.* 74, *cr.* 13.
GREIG, Sco., a boar's head, ppr. *Persevere. Pl.* 2, *cr.* 7.
GREIG, THOMAS, Esq., of Glencarse, a falcon, rising, belled, and ducally gorged, ppr. *Certum pete finem. Pl.* 126 B, *cr.* 3.
GREIG, Eng., a falcon, rising, belled and ducally gorged, ppr., same crest.
GREIG, Sco., an arm, in armour, embowed, in hand a scimitar, ppr. *Strike sure. Pl.* 81, *cr.* 11.
GREIR, and GRIER, Sco., a fetterlock, az. *Hoc securior. Pl.* 122, *cr.* 12.
GREIVE, Sco., an arm, in armour, in hand a scimitar, ppr. *Pl.* 81, *cr.* 11.
GREIVE, Sco., an arm, in armour, in hand a dagger, point downward, ppr. *Quâ fidem servasti. Pl.* 120, *cr.* 11.
GREIVE, Northumb., a martlet, sa. *J'ai la clef. Pl.* 111, *cr.* 5.
GREIVE, Sco., a ram's head, ppr. *Pro rege et grege. Pl.* 34, *cr.* 12.
GRELLEY, Eng., in hand a fish, ppr. *Pl.* 105, *cr.* 9.
GRELLIER, Eng., a demi-eagle, displayed, or. *Pl.* 22, *cr.* 11.
GREMISTON, out of a crescent, ar., a lion's face, sa., crowned with an antique crown, or. *Pl.* 96, *cr.* 13.
GRENDALL, a lion, passant, (gardant,) or, holding a flag, ar., staff, sa. *Pl.* 106, *cr.* 5.
GRENDON, Eng., a decrescent, or. *Pl.* 16, *cr.* 15.
GRENE, JOHN, Esq., of Cappamurra, co. Tipperary, a wolf's head, erased. *Pl.* 14, *cr.* 6.
GRENEHALGH, Notts., a bugle-horn, stringed. *Omnia debeo Deo. Pl.* 48, *cr.* 12.
GRENEWELL, Durh., a stork, close, ppr., beaked and legged, gu., (gorged with a chaplet, vert.) *Pl.* 33, *cr.* 9.
GRENFELL, Bucks., on a chapeau, gu., turned up, erm., a griffin, (passant,) or. *Pl.* 122, *cr.* 11.
GRENFELL, Eng., a griffin, passant, ppr. *Pl.* 61, *cr.* 14, (without gorging.)
GRENFORD, Eng., a hunting-horn, gu., veruled, or. *Pl.* 48, *cr.* 12.
GRENSBY, Eng., in sinister hand, a bow, ppr. *Pl.* 3, *cr.* 12.
GRENTMESNELL, Eng., a plume of ostrich-feathers, ar. *Pl.* 12, *cr.* 9.
GRENVELE, Lond., a sinister arm, couped and embowed, ppr., vested, gu., in hand a bow, bent, sa. *Pl.* 52, *cr.* 5.
GRENVILLE, Lord Grenville, a garb. *Pl.* 48, *cr.* 10.
GRENVILLE, Lord Glastonbury, a garb. *Uno æquus virtute. Pl.* 48, *cr.* 10.

GRESELEY, Eng., an owl, ppr. *Pl.* 27, *cr.* 9.
GRESELEY, Bart., Eng., a lion, passant, ermine. *Meliore fide quam fortunâ. Pl.* 48, *cr.* 8.
GRESHAM, a grasshopper, or.
GRESHAM, on a mount of grass, vert, a grasshopper, or.
GRESLEY, Staffs., a lion, passant, erm, (collared, gu.) *Pl.* 48, *cr.* 8.
GRESOUN, Sco., a fetterlock. *Hoc securior. Pl.* 122, *cr.* 12.
GRESQUE, Linc., a lion, passant, ar., guttée, sa., (collared, gu.) *Pl.* 48, *cr.* 8.
GRESSEY, a talbot, sejant, sa., collared and lined, or. *Pl.* 107, *cr.* 7.
GRESTEY, a lion, passant. *Pl.* 48, *cr.* 8.
GRETTON, Suff., an arm, couped at shoulder, in hand a truncheon. *Pl.* 33, *cr.* 4, (arm, *pl.* 120, *cr.* 11.)
GREVE, Herts., a squirrel, sa., charged with two bends, sinister, ar., holding an escallop, or. *Pl.* 2, *cr.* 4, (escallop, *pl.* 141.)
GREVILE, a greyhound's head, (erased,) sa., collared and ringed, or. *Pl.* 43, *cr.* 11.
GREVILE, Warw., out of a ducal coronet, gu., a demi-swan, wings expanded, ar., beaked, of the first. *Pl.* 100, *cr.* 7, (without collar.)
GREVILLE, Glouc., a greyhound's head, (erased,) sa., collared and ringed, or. *Pl.* 43, *cr.* 11.
GREVIS, Eng., the sun, or. *Pl.* 68, *cr.* 14.
GREVIS, Kent, a squirrel, between paws an escallop, or. *Pl.* 40, *cr.* 5, (escallop, *pl.* 141.)
GREY, Earl, a scaling-ladder, ar. *De bon vouloir server le Roy. Pl.* 98, *cr.* 15.
GREY, THOMAS-ROBINSON, Esq., of Norton, Durh., same crest and motto.
GREY, Beds., Ess., and Herts., a demi-woman, couped at waist, ppr., hair flotant, or, in (each) hand a sprig of laurel, vert. *Pl.* 20, *cr.* 6.
GREY, Northumb., out of a ducal coronet, or, a swan, rising, wings elevated, ar., charged on breast with a trefoil, gu. *De bon vouloir servir le Roy. Pl.* 10, *cr.* 11, (trefoil, *pl.* 141.)
GREY, Sco., a badger, ppr. *Pl.* 34, *cr.* 4.
GREY, out of a ducal coronet, or, a demi-swan, ppr. *Pl.* 100, *cr.* 7, (without collar.)
GREY, Sco., an anchor, entwined with a cable, ppr. *Pl.* 42, *cr.* 12.
GREY, out of a ducal coronet, or, a demi-swan, ar., beaked, gu. *Pl.* 100, *cr.* 7, (without collar.)
GREY, Eng., out of a ducal coronet, gu., a demi-eagle, ppr. *Pl.* 19, *cr.* 9.
GREY, Durh., on a sinister glove, in fess, ar., a falcon, rising, or, (encircled with a branch of honeysuckle, ppr.) *Pl.* 83, *cr.* 13.
GREY, a fox, passant, (regardant,) ppr. *Pl.* 126, *cr.* 5.
GREY, Northumb., a scaling-ladder, ar. *Pl.* 98, *cr.* 15.
GREY, Chesh., in front of the sun, in splendour, ppr., a unicorn, erect, erm., armed, crested, and unguled, or. *Pl.* 114, *cr.* 1.
GREY, Leic., out of a ducal coronet, az., a demi-peacock, in pride, ppr. *Pl.* 92, *cr.* 11, (coronet, *pl.* 120, *cr.* 13.)
GREY, a wyvern, wings addorsed, supporting with dexter a staff, raguly. *Pl.* 63, *cr.* 15, (staff, *pl.* 78, *cr.* 15.)
GREY, Northumb., a ram's head, ar. *Pl.* 34, *cr.* 12.
GREY, Norf. and Yorks., a dragon's head, or. *Pl.* 87, *cr.* 12.

GREY, on a chapeau, gu., turned up, erm., a wyvern, or. *Foy en tout. Pl.* 104, *cr.* 5, (without crown.)
GREY, Heref., (on a mount, vert,) a bear, or. *Pl.* 61, *cr.* 5.
GREY, on a chapeau, gu., turned up, erm., a wyvern, wings elevated and addorsed, or. *A ma puissance. Pl.* 104, *cr.* 5, (without crown.)
GREY, Suff., a unicorn, passant, gu., bezantée, crined, armed, hoofed, and ducally gorged, or. *Pl.* 106, *cr.* 3.
GREY, a demi-lion, rampant, holding a scaling-ladder. *Pl.* 29, *cr.* 12, (ladder, *pl.* 98, *cr.* 15.)
GREYNDOUR, Eng., a squirrel, sejant, cracking a nut, ppr. *Pl.* 16, *cr.* 9.
GREYSTOCK, Eng., a lion, passant, gardant, or. *Volo, non valeo. Pl.* 118, *cr.* 10.
GRICE, Norf., a boar, passant, sa., ducally gorged, or. *Pl.* 48, *cr.* 14, (gorging, *pl.* 128, *fig.* 3.)
GRIERSON, Iri., a demi-lion, rampant, in dexter a rose. *Pl.* 39, *cr.* 14.
GRIERSON, Eng., a dolphin, naiant, az. *Pl.* 48, *cr.* 9.
GRIERSON, Iri., a phœnix, in flames, ppr. *Pl.* 44, *cr.* 8.
GRIERSON, Bart., Sco., a fetterlock, ar. *Hoc securior. Pl.* 122, *cr.* 12.
GRIERSON, Sco., a branch of fir, ppr. *Spem renovat. Pl.* 80, *cr.* 1.
GRIERSON, out of a ducal coronet, or, an arm, erect, ppr., in hand a key, gold. *Pl.* 122, *cr.* 8, (key, *pl.* 41, *cr.* 11.)
GRIESDALE, a dexter hand, in fess, holding a sword, in pale. *Pl.* 93, *cr.* 8, (without cloud.)
GRIEVE, Sco., an anchor, in pale, ppr. *Candide et caute. Pl.* 25, *cr.* 15.
GRIEVE, Eng., an escallop, or, between wings, gu. *Pl.* 62, *cr.* 4.
GRIEVE, Sco., an arm, in armour, in hand a dagger, point downward, ppr. *Hoc securior. Pl.* 120, *cr.* 11.
GRIEVE, Sco., a cock, regardant, ppr. *Pl.* 19, *cr.* 10.
GRIEVES, Eng., a pelican's head, erased, vulning, ppr. *Pl.* 26, *cr.* 1.
GRIFFEN, a unicorn's head, erased, az., bezantée. *Pl.* 67, *cr.* 1, (bezant, *pl.* 141.)
GRIFFETH, Eng., a griffin's head, erased, or. *Non crux, sed lux. Pl.* 48, *cr.* 6.
GRIFFETH, a griffin's head, erased, ppr. *Non crux, sed lux. Pl.* 48, *cr.* 6.
GRIFFIN, Lond., Northamp., and Warw., a talbot's head, erased, sa. *Pl.* 90, *cr.* 6.
GRIFFIN, Staffs., a woman's head, couped at breasts, ppr., hair flotant, or. *Pl.* 45, *cr.* 5.
GRIFFIN, a talbot's head, erased, ar. *Pl.* 90, *cr.* 6.
GRIFFIN, a talbot's head, erased, ppr. *Pl.* 90, *cr.* 6.
GRIFFINHOOFE, a griffin's head, or. *Pl.* 38, *cr.* 3.
GRIFFIS, Eng., a peacock, in pride, ppr. *Pl.* 92, *cr.* 11.
GRIFFITH, Glouc., a woman's head, affrontée. *A fin. Pl.* 45, *cr.* 5.
GRIFFITH, Wel., a buck's head, cabossed, per pale, or and sa. *Pl.* 36, *cr.* 1.
GRIFFITH, Staffs., a woman's head, couped at breasts, ppr., hair flotant, or. *Pl.* 45, *cr.* 5.
GRIFFITH, Somers., a wolf's head, (couped,) sa., semée of etoiles, or. *Pl.* 14, *cr.* 6, (etoiles, *pl.* 141.)

GRIFFITH, a lion, rampant, sa. *Pl.* 67, *cr.* 5.
GRIFFITH, Wel., a lion, passant, sa. *Pl.* 48, *cr.* 8.
GRIFFITH, a stag's head, erased, in mouth a sprig of laurel, ppr. *Pl.* 66, *cr.* 9, (laurel, *pl.* 123, *cr.* 5.)
GRIFFITH, (on a mount, vert,) a squirrel, sejant, gu., holding a hazel-branch, fructed, cracking a nut, ppr. *Pl.* 2, *cr.* 4.
GRIFFITH, Iri., a dexter arm, embowed, in hand a dagger. *Pl.* 34, *cr.* 7.
GRIFFITH, on a ducal coronet, a griffin, sejant. *Pl.* 67, *cr.* 13, (coronet, *same plate.*)
GRIFFITHS, Worc., a demi-lion, rampant, gu. *Pl.* 67, *cr.* 10.
GRIFFITHS, Heref., a wolf's head, (couped,) sa., semée of etoiles, or. *Firmitas et sanitas.* *Pl.* 14, *cr.* 6, (etoile, *pl.* 141.)
GRIFFITHS, a demi-moor, affrontée, (charged on breast with three suns, ppr.,) girt round middle with a band rayonnée, in dexter a spear. *Pl.* 87, *cr.* 13, (spear, *pl.* 97, *cr.* 4.)
GRIFFITHS, a stag's head, cabossed, per pale, gu. and az., between the attires an etoile of eight points, or. *Pl.* 115, *cr.* 1, (etoile, *pl.* 83, *cr.* 3.)
GRIGBY, an ounce's head, (erased,) ppr., collared, ar., charged with two mullets, gu. *Pl.* 40, *cr.* 10, (mullet, *pl.* 141.)
GRIGG, Eng., out of a ducal coronet, in dexter hand a swan's head, all ppr. *Pl.* 65, *cr.* 12.
GRIGGS, Eng., a sword, in pale, enfiled with a leopard's face, ppr. *Pl.* 24, *cr.* 13.
GRIGSON, a ram's head, erased, ppr. *Pl.* 1, *cr.* 12.
GRIGSON, the Rev. WILLIAM, of Saham Toney, Norf., out of a ducal coronet, or, a griffin's head, chequy, ar. and sa. *Pl.* 54, *cr.* 14.
GRILL, Eng., a demi-chevalier, in armour, in hand a scimitar, ppr. *Pl.* 27, *cr.* 11.
GRILLES, Cornw., a porcupine, passant. *Pl.* 55, *cr.* 10.
GRILLS, Devons. and Cornw., a hedgehog, ar. *Pl.* 32, *cr.* 9.
GRIMES, Lond., a martlet, vert. *Pl.* 111, *cr.* 5.
GRIMES, Warw. and Hants, two wings, addorsed, or. *Pl.* 63, *cr.* 12.
GRIMES, a horse's head, couped, or, between wings, ar. *Pl.* 19, *cr.* 13.
GRIMSBIE, and GRIMBSY, Leic., a demi-ram, salient, sa.
GRIMSHAW, JOHN, Esq., of High Bank, Lanc., a demi-griffin, sa. *Tenax propositi, vinco.* *Pl.* 18, *cr.* 6.
GRIMSHAW, Iri., a dexter arm, in armour, ppr., in hand a cross crosslet, fitched, in pale, az. *Pl.* 51, *cr.* 1.
GRIMSHAW, Eng., two lions' heads, erased, (collared,) and addorsed, ppr. *Pl.* 28, *cr.* 10.
GRIMSHAW, Lanc., a griffin, segreant, sa., beaked and membered, or. *Pl.* 67, *cr.* 13.
GRIMSTEAD, and GRIMSTED, a dexter arm, embowed, ppr., elbow on the wreath, in hand a bow. *Pl.* 51, *cr.* 5.
GRIMSTON, a stag's head, (with a ring round neck, ar.) *Faitz proverount.* *Pl.* 91, *cr.* 14.
GRIMSTON, and GRIMSTONE, a stag's head, ar., attired, or. *Pl.* 91, *cr.* 14.
GRIMWOOD, Eng., on the top of a tower, issuing, an eagle, wings addorsed, in beak an acorn, slipped, ppr. *Pl.* 60, *cr.* 8.
GRINDAL, and GRINDALL, Eng., an arm, in armour, embowed, in hand, by the blade, a sword, point downward, ppr. *Pl.* 65, *cr.* 8.

GRINDAL, and GRINDALL, a demi-lion, rampant, per pale, or and az. *Pl.* 67, *cr.* 10.
GRINDLAY, and GRINDLEY, a buffalo's head, erased, gu. *Pl.* 57, *cr.* 7.
GRINDLAY, and GRINDLEY, a dove, ppr. *Pl.* 66, *cr.* 12.
GRINDLAY, and GRINDLEY, a pea-hen, ppr.
GRINGFIELD, Suss., a gauntlet, or. *Pl.* 15, *cr.* 15.
GRISEWOOD, Lond., a demi-lion, (gardant,) ar., environed with laurel, vert, holding a garb, az., banded, or. *Pl.* 84, *cr.* 7, (laurel, *pl.* 79, *cr.* 14.)
GRISLAY, in dexter hand, ppr., a lozenge, or. *Pl.* 41, *cr.* 9.
GRITTON, Eng., a lion's face, between wings, ppr. *Pl.* 87, *cr.* 2.
GRIVE, a martlet, sa. *J'ai lu clef.* *Pl.* 111, *cr.* 5.
GROAT, of Newhall, Sco., an anchor, ppr. *Anchor fast.* *Pl.* 42, *cr.* 12.
GROAT, Middx. and Kent, on a mount, vert, a dexter arm, in armour, embowed, ppr., garnished, or, in hand a javelin, surmounted by two oak-branches, of the second.
GROBHAM, Wilts., a boar's head, couped, or. *Pl.* 48, *cr.* 2.
GROGAN, Iri., a hawk, in dexter a wheat-ear, ppr. *Pl.* 94, *cr.* 7.
GROGAN, Eng., a hind, passant, or. *Pl.* 29, *cr.* 14.
GROME, Suff., an arm, in armour, ppr., garnished, or, in hand a gauntlet, also ppr. *Pl.* 97, *cr.* 1, (gauntlet, *pl.* 42, *cr.* 15.)
GRONOW, a lion, rampant. *Pl.* 67, *cr.* 5.
GRONOW, Rev. THOMAS, M.A., of Ash Hall, Glamorgan; and Gillygudray, Carmarthen, a lion, rampant. *Gronwi hil Gwerninion.* *Pl.* 67, *cr.* 5.
GROOBY, Wilts., out of a ducal coronet, or, an eagle, displayed, ppr., (charged with a label.) *Pl.* 48, *cr.* 11, (coronet, *pl.* 128, *fig.* 3.)
GROOM, GROME, and GROOME, on a torteau, winged, gu., an eagle, wings displayed, or. *Pl.* 80, *cr.* 14.
GROOM, a dexter arm, in armour, embowed, ppr., garnished, or, in hand, of the first, a gauntlet, (suspended from wrist by a pink ribbon, a shield, gold, thereon a pile, gu., charged with a cross pattée, fitched, ar.) *Pl.* 97, *cr.* 1.
GROOMBRIDGE, Eng., out of a mural coronet, a garb, thereon a crow, perched, all ppr. *Pl.* 14, *cr.* 5.
GROSE, Surr., on a mount, vert, a lamb, sa., holding a banner, ar. *Pl.* 101, *cr.* 9.
GROSETH, Sco., in dexter hand a sword, ppr. *Pro patriâ.* *Pl.* 21, *cr.* 10.
GROSS, Eng., on a ducal coronet, a talbot, passant, ppr., collared and lined, or. *Pl.* 3, *cr.* 8.
GROSSE, Eng., out of a ducal coronet, a hand holding (a dagger,) ppr. *Pl.* 65, *cr.* 10.
GROSSET, and GROSSETT, four arrows, points downward, and a strung-bow, in saltier, all ppr. *Pl.* 12, *cr.* 12.
GROSSETT, Wilts., two hands holding a sword, erect, ppr., hilts and pommels, or. *Pl.* 75, *cr.* 8.
GROSVENOR, a talbot, passant. *Pl.* 120, *cr.* 8.
GROSVENOR, Dors., a horse, current, saddled and bridled, ppr. *Pl.* 8, *cr.* 2.

GROTE, Lond. and Surr., between two elephants' proboscies, erect, a pine-tree, all ppr. *Prodesse quam conspici.* *Pl.* 96, *cr.* 1, (pine-tree, *pl.* 26, *cr.* 10.)
GROVE, Dors. and Wilts., a talbot, passant, sa., collared, or. *Pl.* 65, *cr.* 2.
GROVE, Dors. and Wilts., a talbot, passant, sa., collared, ar. *Pl.* 65, *cr.* 2.
GROVE, a talbot, sa., collared, ar. *Pl.* 65, *cr.* 2.
GROVE, Eng., in hand a glove, ppr. *Pl.* 42, *cr.* 15.
GROVE, Eng., a stag, trippant, ppr. *Pl.* 68, *cr.* 2.
GROVE, Eng., in hand a thistle, ppr. *Pl.* 36, *cr.* 6.
GROVE, JOHN, Esq., of Ferne, Wilts., a dog, passant, sa., collared, ar. *Ny dessux ny dessoux.* *Pl.* 65, *cr.* 2.
GROVER, Eng., out of a cloud, from the sinister, an arm, embowed, in hand a garland of flowers, ppr. *Pl.* 80, *cr.* 3.
GROVES, Eng., out of a ducal coronet, or, a cock's head, combed and wattled, gu. *Pl.* 97, *cr.* 15.
GROVES, Staffs., on a mount, vert, a dragon, (statant, ppr., collared and chained, or,) charged on shoulder with an etoile, gu. *Pl.* 90, *cr.* 10, (mount, *pl.* 122, *cr.* 5; etoile, *pl.* 141.)
GROVESNOR, Chesh. and Staffs., a talbot, or. *Pl.* 120, *cr.* 8.
GROWTAGE, or GOUTRIGE, an ostrich's head, in beak a horse-shoe, ppr. *Pl.* 28, *cr.* 13, (without wings.)
GROYN, a bear's head, sa. *Pl.* 2, *cr.* 9.
GROZE, a mullet, or. *Deo juvante.* *Pl.* 41, *cr.* 1.
GRUBB, Sco., a lion's head, erased. *Strength is from heaven.* *Pl.* 81, *cr.* 4.
GRUBB, Herts., a griffin's head, erased, per pale, ar. and gu., charged with a rose, counterchanged. *Pl.* 48, *cr.* 6, (rose, *pl.* 141.)
GRUBB, Wilts., a lion's head, az., ducally crowned, or. *Pl.* 90, *cr.* 4, (without charging.)
GRUBBAM, and GRUBHAM, a cock, ppr. *Pl.* 67, *cr.* 14.
GRUBBE, a lion's head, az., murally crowned, or. *Pl.* 123, *cr.* 13, (crown,*pl.* 128, *fig.* 18.)
GRUBBE, Wilts., in lion's gamb, sa., a rose, gu., stalked and leaved, ppr. *Pl.* 60, *cr.* 14.
GRUBEN, an acorn, slipped and leaved, vert. *Pl.* 81, *cr.* 7.
GRUBHAM, a rose, gu., stalked and leaved, vert. *Pl.* 105, *cr.* 7.
GRUDGFIELD, Suff., a gauntlet, or. *Pl.* 15, *cr.* 15.
GRUFFETH, Staffs. and Warw., a demi-woman, vested, gu., crined, or. *Pl.* 2, *cr.* 10, (without cinquefoil.)
GRUMLEY, Iri., a vine-branch, ppr. *Pl.* 89, *cr.* 1.
GRUMSTEAD, an antelope's head, (couped,) ar., attired, or. *Pl.* 24, *cr.* 7, (without charge.)
GRUNDIE, Notts., a demi-leopard, rampant, gardant, sa., bezantée. *Pl.* 77, *cr.* 1, (without anchor.)
GRUNDIN, Eng., a stag, passant, erm. *Pl.* 68, *cr.* 2.
GRYCE, Norf., a boar, ar., ducally gorged, hoofed, and armed, or. *Pl.* 29, *cr.* 10, (gorging, *same plate.*)
GRYLLS, Cornw., a porcupine, passant, ar. *Vires agematis unus habet.* *Pl.* 55, *cr.* 10.
GRYME, Eng., the Roman fasces, ppr. *Pl.* 65, *cr.* 15.

GRYMES, Eng., out of a cloud, a hand seizing a stag by the horns, all ppr. *Pl.* 46, *cr.* 10.
GRYMSBY, Ess., in sinister hand, a bow, ppr. *Pl.* 3, *cr.* 12.
GRYS, Eng., a lion, sejant, collared and lined. *Pl.* 21, *cr.* 3.
GUBBINS, an arm, from elbow, vested, in hand a branch of holly, vert. *Pl.* 75, *cr.* 3, (branch, *pl.* 55, *cr.* 6.)
GUCHERES, Eng., a water-bouget, sa. *Pl.* 14, *cr.* 12.
GUEST, Sco., a swan, ppr. *Pl.* 122, *cr.* 13.
GUEST, a swan, wings expanded, ppr. *Nec temere, nec timide.* *Pl.* 66, *cr.* 10.
GUEST, Bart., Wel., a swan's head and neck, erased, ppr., gorged with a collar, and charged with a cross moline, sa., between two ostrich-feathers, or.
GUILAMORE, Viscount, Iri., a horse's head, erased. *Pl.* 81, *cr.* 6.
GUILFORD, Earl of, a dragon's head, erased, sa., scaled, ducally gorged and chained, or. *La vertue est la seule noblesse*—and—*Animo et fide.* *Pl.* 36, *cr.* 7.
GUILFORD, Eng., a dragon's head. *Animo et fide.* *Pl.* 87, *cr.* 12.
GUILFORD, Kent, a tree, couped and trunked, or, flammant, gu. *Pl.* 96, *cr.* 12.
GUILFORD, on a chapeau, gu., turned up, erm., an ostrich-feather, erect, or. *Pl.* 125, *cr.* 11, (chapeau, *pl.* 127, *fig.* 13.)
GUILLAM, a dolphin, haurient, ppr. *Pl.* 14, *cr.* 10.
GUILLIM, Glouc., an arm, in armour, embowed, in hand a broken sword, all ppr. *Pl.* 2, *cr.* 8, (sword, *pl.* 22, *cr.* 6.)
GUINNERS, Iri., out of a mural coronet, az., a demi-lion, or, in dexter a palm-branch, vert. *Pl.* 17, *cr.* 7.
GUINNESS, a boar, passant, quarterly, or and gu. *Pl.* 48, *cr.* 14.
GUION, and GUYON, Eng., a cock, az., combed and wattled, or. *Pl.* 67, *cr.* 14.
GUISE, Bart., Glouc., out of a ducal coronet, or, a swan, rising, ppr. *Pl.* 100, *cr.* 7.
GUISE, a leopard's head, affrontée, crowned with an antique crown. *Pl.* 84, *cr.* 1, (without crescent.)
GUISSE, out of a ducal coronet, or, a demi-swan, ar., beaked, sa. *Pl.* 10, *cr.* 11, (without dart.)
GULBY, a naked arm, embowed, (hand thrusting a sword, point downward.) *Pl.* 34, *cr.* 7.
GULDEFORD, a firebrand, flammant, ppr.
GULL, Kent, a dexter arm, in armour, embowed, in fess, elbow on the wreath, in hand a battle-axe, ar., handle, or. *Pl.* 121, *cr.* 14.
GULLAN, Sco., a stag, lodged, ppr. *Pl.* 67, *cr.* 2.
GULLAND, Sco., a dove, within a serpent, in orle, ppr. *Innocence surmounts.* *Pl.* 92, *cr.* 6.
GULLINE, Sco., a dove, ppr. *Pl.* 66, *cr.* 12.
GULLINE, Sco., a falcon, belled, ppr. *Pl.* 67, *cr.* 3.
GULLIVER, a lion, passant, gardant, ar., ducally crowned, or. *Non dormit qui custodit.* *Pl.* 120, *cr.* 5, (crown, *same plate.*)
GULLON, in a cavity of a rock, a blackbird, sitting, all ppr. *Tutum refugium.* *Pl.* 31, *cr.* 3.
GULLY, (two) keys, in saltier. *Nil sine cruce.* *Pl.* 54, *cr.* 12.

GULMAN, a man's leg, in armour, couped and embowed, (the thigh in fess,) the leg in pale, the foot in chief, spurred, all ppr. *Pl.* 4, *cr.* 12, (without rays.)

GULSTON, ALAN-JAMES, Woodland's Castle, Swansea, an ostrich's wing, ppr., charged with a bend, az., thereon three bezants. *Pl.* 126 B, *cr.* 13.

GULSTON, and GULSTONE, Lond., Middx., Surr., Herts.,and Leic., an ostrich's wing,the feathers alternately ar. and gu., charged with a bend, sa.

GUMBLETON, Middx., a demi-griffin, wings addorsed, ar., beaked and legged, gu., holding a mullet, or. *Pl.* 18, *cr.* 6, (mullet, *pl.* 141.)

GUN, co. Kerry, an open dexter hand and wrist, erect, ppr. *Vincit amor patriæ. Pl.* 32, *cr.* 14.

GUN, Sco., a wolf, passant, sa. *Pl.* 46, *cr.* 6.

GUN, a dexter arm, in mail, embowed, in hand a sword, ppr. *Pl.* 2, *cr.* 8.

GUNDRY, Eng., a demi-lion, in dexter a sword, all or. *Pl.* 41, *cr.* 13.

GUNMAN, Kent, out of a naval coronet, ar., an anchor, erect, sa., cabled, or. *Pl.* 42, *cr.* 12, (coronet, *pl.* 128, *fig.* 19.)

GUNN, Eng., on a chapeau, az., a fox, sejant, or. *Pl.* 57, *cr.* 14.

GUNN, Sco., in dexter hand a sword, ppr. *Pl.* 21, *cr.* 10.

GUNN, Sco., in dexter hand, a (musket.) *Pl.* 101, *cr.* 12.

GUNN, Norf., a lion, rampant, gu., holding a bezant. *Pl.* 64, *cr.* 2, (bezant, *pl.* 141.)

GUNNER, Eng., a lion's head, erased, or. *Pl.* 81, *cr.* 4.

GUNNING, Bart., Northamp., a pigeon, in dexter a caduceus, ppr. *Pl.* 66, *cr.* 12, (caduceus, *pl.* 52, *cr.* 3.)

GUNNING, Somers., an ostrich, in beak a horseshoe, ppr., (charged on breast with a cross, pattée.) *Pl.* 16, *cr.* 2, (without gorging.)

GUNSTON, Iri., a tower, triple-towered, ar. *Pl.* 123, *cr.* 14.

GUNTER, Suss., a stag's head, erased, per pale, sa. and gu., attired, or. *Pl.* 66, *cr.* 9.

GUNTER, Suss., a stag's head, couped, gu. and sa., attired, counterchanged. *Pl.* 91, *cr.* 14.

GUNTER, Wel., a stag's head, per pale, gu. and sa. *Pl.* 91, *cr.* 14.

GUNTHORPE, Norf., a lion's head, erased, collared. *Pl.* 7, *cr.* 10.

GUNTHROPE, Eng., a unicorn's head, ar. *Pl.* 20, *cr.* 1.

GUNNING, Kent, on a wreath, of the colours, a dove, az., dexter supporting a sword, wavy, radiated, in bend, ppr., hilt and pommel, or. *Verité sans peur.*

GURDON, Hants, Suff., and Wilts., a goat, ar., attired, or, salient, against a (mountain,) vert. *Pl.* 32, *cr.* 10.

GURDON, Norf. and Suff., a goat climbing up a rock, all ppr. *In arduis viget virtus. Pl.* 11, *cr.* 14.

GURLIN, on a mural coronet, gu., an eagle, wings addorsed, or, in beak an acorn, stalked and leaved, ppr. *Pl.* 60, *cr.* 8, (coronet, *pl.* 128, *fig.* 18.)

GURNEY, a lion's head, erased, or, gorged with a palisado coronet, composed of spear-heads, az. *Pl.* 81, *cr.* 4, (coronet, *pl.* 128, *fig.* 21.)

GURNEY, DANIEL, Esq., of North Runcton, Lynn: 1. On a chapeau, gu., turned up, ermine, a gurnard fish, in pale, head downwards. *Pl.* 126 A, *cr.* 11. 2. On a wreath, ar. and gu., a wrestling collar, or. *Pl.* 126 A, *cr.* 12.

GURNEY, HUDSON, Esq., of Keswick, Norf., same crests.

GURWOOD, out of a mural coronet, a castle, ruined in the centre, and therefrom an arm, in armour, embowed, in hand a scimitar, ppr.

GURWOOD, a unicorn's head. *Pl.* 20, *cr.* 1.

GUSTON, Eng., a demi-wolf, gu. *Pl.* 56, *cr.* 8, (without spear.)

GUTHRIE, Sco., in hand a sword, ppr. *Sto pro veritate. Pl.* 21, *cr.* 10.

GUTHRIE, a salmon, naiant. *Ditat et alit. Pl.* 85, *cr.* 7.

GUTHRIE, Eng., an eagle, displayed, sa., in dexter a sword. *Pl.* 107, *cr.* 4.

GUTHRIE, Sco., a cross crosslet, az. *Ex unitate incrementum. Pl.* 66, *cr.* 8.

GUTHRIE, Sco., a dexter arm, in armour, embowed, brandishing a sword, ppr. *Sto pro veritate. Pl.* 2, *cr.* 8.

GUTHRY, Sco., in lion's paw, a palm-branch, ppr. *Sto pro veritate. Pl.* 70, *cr.* 9.

GUTHRY, Sco., a cross crosslet, fitched, az. *Ex unitate incrementum. Pl.* 16, *cr.* 10.

GUTTERIDGE, or GUTTRIDGE, a swan passant, crowned with an antique crown, or. *Pl.* 33, *cr.* 7.

GUY, Northamp. and Wilts., between wings, or, a lion's head, az., (collared, ar.) *Pl.* 73, *cr.* 3.

GUY, a man's full face, bearded, ppr., crowned with an antique crown, or. *Dare quam accipere. Pl.* 28, *cr.* 3, (crown, *pl.* 79, *cr.* 12.)

GUYAN, Ess., a demi-lion, rampant, or, gorged with a collar, per pale, az. and sa. *Pl.* 18, *cr.* 13.

GUYBYON, an eagle's head, erased, erm. *Pl.* 20, *cr.* 7.

GUYLEMIN, Herts. and Wel., an eagle's head, erased, sa., beaked, gu., in mouth a lion's gamb, or, erased, of the second. *Pl.* 20, *cr.* 7, (gamb, *pl.* 126, *cr.* 9.)

GUYLING, an arm, embowed, ar., in hand a scimitar, of the same, pommelled, or, hand, ppr. *Pl.* 92, *cr.* 5.

GUYLING, Eng., an arm, embowed, ppr., vested, ar., in hand, a (scimitar,) of the last, pommelled, or. *Pl.* 120, *cr.* 1.

GUYOT, Eng., an eagle, displayed, per pale, embattled, or and gu., wings counterchanged. *Pl.* 48, *cr.* 11.

GWATKIN, a garb, or, banded. *Pl.* 48, *cr.* 10.

GWILLAM, a dolphin, haurient, ppr. *Pl.* 14, *cr.* 10.

GWILLANNE, Eng., an eagle, perched, ppr. *Pl.* 7, *cr.* 11.

GWILT, Lond., a cubit arm, couped, ppr., in hand a saltier, or, surmounted by a fleur-de-lis, sa.

GWINNELL, a sinister arm, in fess, couped at shoulder, vested, gu., embowed, resting elbow on the wreath, in hand a bow, ppr. *Pl.* 52, *cr.* 5.

GWINNETT, Glouc., a horse's head, couped, sa., (in mouth a spear, in bend, head downwards, embrued, ppr.) *Pl.* 110, *cr.* 6.

GWYER, Wel., a wolf, passant, ppr. *Pl.* 46, *cr.* 6.

GWYN, Eng., a cannon, mounted, ppr. *Pl.* 111, *cr.* 3.

GWYN, Berks., Lond., and Wel., an arm, in armour, embowed, ppr., in hand a sword, below the hilt, in bend, sinister, ar., hilt and pommel, or. *Pl.* 65, *cr.* 8.

GWYN, two laurel-slips, (in saltier,) ppr. *Pl.* 21, *cr.* 2.

GWYN, ANTHONY, Esq., of Baron's Hall, Fakenham, Norf., a lion, rampant, or. *Pl.* 67, *cr.* 5.

GWYN, Eng., a stag's head, erased, ppr., between attires a cross crosslet, fitched. *Pl.* 24, *cr.* 9.

GWYN, Wel., in gauntlet a sword, ar., pierced through a dragon's head, erased, or, vulned, ppr. *Pl.* 125, *cr.* 5, (head, *pl.* 107, *cr.* 10.)

GWYN, Wel., a sword, in pale, ppr., (point downward,) pierced through a boar's head, sa. *Pl.* 71, *cr.* 9.

GWYN, HOWEL, Esq., of Dyffryn, Wel., in hand, ppr., a dagger, erect, ar., hilted, or, thrust through a boar's head, couped, of the second. *Vim vi repellere licet. Pl.* 71, *cr.* 9.

GWYNNE, Wel., a lion, rampant, regardant, supporting between paws a boar's head, all or. *Pl.* 10, *cr.* 15, (head, *same plate, cr.* 2.)

GWYNNE, Eng. and Iri., a dolphin, naiant, az. *Pl.* 48, *cr.* 9.

GWYNNE, Wel., in hand, (in armour,) couped at wrist, ppr., a dagger, blade, ar., hilt, or, pierced through a boar's head, erased, sa. *Pl.* 71, *cr.* 9.

GWYNNE, Suss. and Lond., a bear and ragged staff. *Pl.* 1, *cr.* 3.

GYBBON, a demi-lion, ar., crowned, or, in dexter, an escallop, of the first. *Pl.* 61, *cr.* 4, (escallop, *pl.* 141.)

GYBBONS, a demi-lion, rampant, sa., charged with three escallops, in pale, ar. *Pl.* 67, *cr.* 10, (escallop, *pl.* 141.)

GYBONS, Oxon., Warw., and Wel., in lion's gamb., erect and erased, gu., a cross formée, fitched, sa. *Pl.* 46, *cr.* 7.

GYFFORD, Eng., a lion's head, erased, gu., collared, or, charged with three roses, of the first. *Pl.* 7, *cr.* 10, (rose, *pl.* 141.)

GYLES, or GYLLS,, in hand a spiked club, ppr., spikes, or. *Pl.* 28, *cr.* 6, (club, *same plate, cr.* 2.)

GYLES, in a nest, a pelican, vulning, ppr. *Pl.* 44, *cr.* 1.

GYLES, Devons., in lion's gamb, erect and erased, gu., (enfiled by a bar-gemelle, or, a branch of apples, of the last, leaved, ppr.) *Pl.* 60, *cr.* 14.

GYLL, Durh. and Yorks., the head of an Eastern king, couped at shoulders, in profile, ppr., crowned and collared, or. *Pl.* 78, *cr.* 14.

GYMBER, Lond., on a garb, a bird, close, az. *Pl.* 112, *cr.* 10.

GYNN, Herts., on a garb, or, a bird, close, az. *Pl.* 112, *cr.* 10.

GYPSES, Eng., a dove and olive-branch, ppr. *Pl.* 48, *cr.* 15.

GYSORS, Eng., a fox's head, erased, gu. *Pl.* 71, *cr.* 4.

GYSSELING, Linc., a lion, rampant, az., winged, or. *Pl.* 75, *cr.* 4.

GYSSINGE, a lion, passant, erm., (collared, gu.) *Pl.* 48, *cr.* 8.

GYTTIES, Kent, an arm, in armour, embowed, ppr., garnished, or, in hand a battle-axe, ar. *Pl.* 121, *cr.* 14.

GYTTINGS, Salop, two tilting spears, in saltier. *Pl.* 125, *cr.* 8, (without pendants and wreath.)

GYVES, a unicorn's head, couped at neck. *Pl.* 20, *cr.* 1.

GYVLIN, Norf., a demi-griffin, az., wings, beak, and legs, or, holding a fleur-de-lis, per pale, of the first and gu. *Pl.* 18, *cr.* 6, (fleur-de-lis, *pl.* 141.)

GYLL, BROOKE-HAMILTON, Esq., of Wyrardisbury House, Bucks., and Leovany Hall, Middx., a hawk's head, az., between wings, fretty, vert. *Virtutis gloria merces. Pl.* 99, *cr.* 10.

GYMBER, Lond., an arm, in armour, ppr., holding a spiked club, or. *Pl.* 28, *cr.* 2.

H

HABGOOD, Eng., a sword and quill, in saltier, ppr. *Pl.* 49, *cr.* 12.

HABINGDON, Worc., an eagle, displayed, or, ducally crowned, az. *Pl.* 85, *cr.* 11, (without charge.)

HABINGDON, a horse's head, erased, ar., (bridled, sa.,) between wings, ppr. *Pl.* 19, *cr.* 13.

HACCOMB, an arm, in hand a bow and arrow, all ppr. *Pl.* 3, *cr.* 12.

HACHET, Warw., a hawk's head, couped, gu. *Pl.* 99, *cr.* 10, (without wings.)

HACHET, Warw., a hawk's head, ppr. 'Ηοέθος 'Ηοεθούμενος. *Ib.*

HACHET, or HACKET, Lond. and Bucks., a demi-panther, ar., spotted, az., or and gu., holding a branch, vert, flowered, of the fourth. *Pl.* 16, *cr.* 7.

HACKER, on trunk of tree, in fess, a moor-cock, ppr. *Pl.* 10, *cr.* 1.

HACKET, Warw., an eagle's head, erased, ppr. *Fides sufficit. Pl.* 20, *cr.* 7.

HACKET, Warw. and Sco., an arm, in armour, embowed, in hand a sword, all ppr. *Pl.* 2, *cr.* 8.

HACKETT, Eng., a demi-eagle, with two heads, displayed, per pale, gu. and or, wings counterchanged, each head ensigned with a crown. *Pl.* 63, *cr.* 2.

HACKFORD, on a trumpet, or, a swan, wings addorsed, ar. *Pl.* 4, *cr.* 7.

HACKLET, Lond., a demi-lion, gu. *Pl.* 67, *cr.* 10.

HACKLET, and HACKLUIT, Sco. and Eng., in hand a hunting-horn, ppr. *Pl.* 109, *cr.* 3.

HACKLET, Lond., a demi-lion, gu. *Pl.* 67, *cr.* 10.

HACKNEY, out of a ducal coronet, a nag's head. *Pl.* 50, *cr.* 13.

HACKOTE, Eng., on a ducal coronet, a martlet, ppr. *Pl.* 98, *cr.* 14.

HACKSHAW, Salop, a heron's head, erased, ar., ducally gorged, gu. *Pl.* 20, *cr.* 9, (gorging, *same plate, cr.* 12.)

HACKVILL, Eng., on a chapeau, a fox, sejant, ppr. *Pl.* 57, *cr.* 14.

HACKWELL, and HAKEWILL, Linc. and Devons., a trefoil, slipped, purp., between wings, displayed, or. *Pl.* 4, *cr.* 10.

HACKWELL, between wings, or, a human heart, gu. *Pl.* 52, *cr.* 2, (without coronet).

HADD, Kent, (on a mount, vert,) a talbot, sejant, ar., eared, sa., ducally gorged, gu. *Pl.* 107, *cr.* 7, (gorging, *same plate, cr.* 11.)

HADDEN, Eng., an arm., embowed, in hand a scimitar, ppr. *Pl.* 92, *cr.* 5.
HADDEN, Sco., an eagle's head, erased, or. *Suffer. Pl.* 20, *cr.* 7.
HADDERWICK, Sco., a dexter arm, from elbow, holding a roll of paper, ppr. *Ne timeas recte faciendo. Pl.* 27, *cr.* 4.
HADDINGTON, Earl of, Sco., Baron Melrose, U.K., (Hamilton,) two dexter hands conjoined, in fess, issuing from clouds, holding a laurel-branch, erect, all ppr. *Præsto et persisto. Pl.* 102, *cr.* 2.
HADDOCK, Eng., in hand a fish, all ppr. *Pl.* 105, *cr.* 9.
HADDON, out of rays, or, a man's leg, couped at thigh, erect, the foot upward, spurred, all ppr. *Pl.* 4, *cr.* 12.
HADDON, Grandholme, Sco., a leg, couped at thigh, foot upward. *Parta tueri. Pl.* 4, *cr.* 12, (without rays.)
HADDOW, Sco., in lion's paw a thistle, all ppr. *Pl.* 109, *cr.* 4.
HADESTOCK, on stump of oak-tree, sprouting, the sun shining, all ppr. *Pl.* 123, *cr.* 3.
HADESWELL, or HADISWELL, Eng., a demi-lion, rampant, gu., in paws a battle-axe, az. *Pl.* 101, *cr.* 14, (without charge.)
HADFIELD, Eng., an escallop, or. *Pl.* 117, *cr.* 4.
HADFIELD, an arm, embowed, vested, az., in hand, ppr., a trefoil, slipped, or. *Pl.* 39, *cr.* 1, (trefoil, *pl.* 78, *cr.* 6.)
HADLEY, Lond. and Heref., a falcon, ar., beaked, legged, and belled, or, in mouth a buckle, of the last. *Pl.* 67, *cr.* 3, (buckle, *pl.* 39, *cr.* 8.)
HADLOW, Sco., in lion's paw, a thistle, all ppr. *Pl.* 109, *cr.* 4.
HADLY, Eng., a falcon. *Pl.* 67, *cr.* 3.
HADOKEES, Eng., a talbot's head, erased, sa., collared, ar. *Pl.* 2, *cr.* 15.
HADSON, on a ducal coronet, or, a lion, rampant, gu. *Pl.* 67, *cr.* 5, (coronet, *same plate, cr.* 7.)
HADSOR, out of a ducal coronet, gu., a dragon's head, or, (in mouth some leaves, ppr.) *Pl.* 87, *cr.* 12, (coronet, *pl.* 128, *fig.* 3.)
HADWEN, the bust of an angel, wings elevated, ensigned with a cross. *Pl.* 90, *cr.* 11.
HADWEN, Lanc., out of a mural coronet, or, an eagle's head, ppr. *Perfero. Pl.* 121, *cr.* 11.
HAFFENDEN, Kent, an eagle's head, couped. *Pl.* 100, *cr.* 10.
HAFFENDEN, ALFRED, Esq., of Homewood, Kent, same crest.
HAFFENDEN, Bloomsbury, a griffin's head, erased, in mouth an arrow. *Pl.* 35, *cr.* 15, (arrow, *pl.* 56, *cr.* 13.)
HAGAR, Eng., a garb, in fess, ppr. *Pl.* 12, *cr.* 15.
HAGART, a lion, rampant, ppr. *Sans peur. Pl.* 67, *cr.* 5.
HAGARTY, Iri., in dexter hand, ppr., an escallop, or. *Pl.* 57, *cr.* 6.
HAGELL, Eng., an olive-branch, slipped, ppr. *Pl.* 98, *cr.* 8.
HAGEN, Eng., a stork's head, erased, ppr. *Pl.* 32, *cr.* 5.
HAGEN, a dove, rising, ar. *Pl.* 27, *cr.* 5.
HAGGAR, Ess. and Cambs., (on a mount, vert,) a talbot, passant, ar., collared and lined, gu. *Pl.* 65, *cr.* 2.
HAGGARD, Eng., a cock's head, erased, ppr. *Pl.* 92, *cr.* 3.

HAGGARD, Kent, a cubit arm, erect, in hand a truncheon. *Dux mihi veritas. Pl.* 18, *cr.* 1.
HAGGARD, Norf.: 1. A mullet of six points, ar. *Pl.* 21, *cr.* 6. 2. Out of a mural coronet, per pale, or and az., a snake, erect, ppr., in mouth a (trefoil, slipped, vert.) *Micat inter omnes. Pl.* 104, *cr.* 9, (coronet, *pl.* 128, *fig.* 18.)
HAGGARTH, a bugle-horn, ar., stringed. *Pl.* 48, *cr.* 12.
HAGGER, Eng., a demi-lion, gu., supporting a long cross, az. *Pl.* 29, *cr.* 12.
HAGGERSTON, Durh., a lion, passant, ar. *Pl.* 48, *cr.* 8.
HAGGERSTON, Bart., Northumb., a lion, rampant, ar. *Pl.* 67, *cr.* 5.
HAGGERSTON, Eng., a talbot, erm. *Pl.* 120, *cr.* 8.
HAGGES, Sco., an arm, in armour, embowed, in hand a scimitar, ppr. *Pl.* 81, *cr.* 11.
HAGLEY, Eng., a dexter arm, in armour, embowed, in hand a battle-axe, all ppr. *Pl.* 121, *cr.* 14.
HAGNE, Eng., issuing from a tower, a leopard's head, (collared, gu.) *Pl.* 105, *cr.* 10.
HAGTHORPE, Durh., in dexter hand, ppr., sleeve striped, in bend, ar. and gu., three leaves, vert. *Pl.* 64, *cr.* 7.
HAHN, on a ducal coronet, a swan, wings addorsed and (ducally) gorged. *Pl.* 100, *cr.* 7.
HAIG, Sco., a rock, ppr. *Tyde what may. Pl.* 73, *cr.* 12.
HAIG, and HAIGH, a demi-savage, over dexter shoulder a hammer. *Pl.* 51, *cr.* 14.
HAIGH, Yorks., a talbot's head, erased, gu. *Pl.* 90, *cr.* 6.
HAILES, Eng., a wheel, or. *Pl.* 32, *cr.* 15.
HAILLY, Sco., a galley, sa., flag, gu. *Pl.* 24, *cr.* 5.
HAILSTONES, Sco., a rose-branch, bearing roses, all ppr. *Pl.* 23, *cr.* 2.
HAINE, a lion, rampant, ar., supporting the Roman fasces, ppr. *In te Domine speravi. Pl.* 67, *cr.* 5, (fasces, *pl.* 65, *cr.* 15.)
HAINES, Eng., on a crescent, an arrow, in pale, ppr. *Pl.* 82, *cr.* 15.
HAINES, an eagle, displayed, az., semée of etoiles, ar. *Pl.* 48, *cr.* 11, (etoile, *pl.* 141.)
HAINS, Eng., an antelope's head, ppr., (collared, sa.) *Pl.* 24, *cr.* 7.
HAIR, Sco., two daggers, in saltier, ppr. *Pl.* 24, *cr.* 2.
HAIR, Eng., a hare, couchant. *Pl.* 29, *cr.* 1.
HAIRSTANES, Sco., a dexter arm, in hand a key, ppr. *Toujours fidele. Pl.* 41, *cr.* 11.
HAITLIE, Eng., in hand (four) arrows, points downward. *Pl.* 56, *cr.* 4.
HAIZE, Lond., a wolf's head, ppr., erased, gu., charged on neck with an escallop, or. *Pl.* 14, *cr.* 6, (escallop, *pl.* 141.)
HAKE, a sword, in pale, ar., hilt and pommel, or, enfiled with a boar's head, couped, in fess, az. *Pl.* 10, *cr.* 2.
HAKE, out of a ducal coronet, (two pot-hooks, addorsed,) between wings. *Pl.* 17, *cr.* 9.
HAKELIOTT, out of a ducal coronet, or, a plume of four ostrich-feathers. *Pl.* 44, *cr.* 12.
HAKEWOOD, Eng., on a chapeau, a garb, ppr. *Pl.* 62, *cr.* 1.
HALBERDYN, a wolf, rampant, regardant, ppr. *Pl.* 10, *cr.* 2.
HALCRO, Sco., two hands holding a sword, in pale, ppr. *Pl.* 75, *cr.* 8.
HALDANE, Eng., a terrestrial globe, ppr. *Pl.* 14, *cr.* 1.

HALDANE, and HALDEN, Sco., an eagle's head, erased, or. *Suffer. Pl.* 20, *cr.* 7.

HALDENBY, Yorks., a swan, close, ar., beaked and legged, gu., (in beak a sprig of laurel, ppr.) *Pl.* 122, *cr.* 13, (without mount.)

HALDERMAN, a dexter arm, embowed, vested, in hand, ppr., a broken spear, in bend. *Pl.* 39, *cr.* 1, (spear, *pl.* 44, *cr.* 9.)

HALDIMAND, Eng., a sea-lion, sejant, ppr. *Pl.* 80, *cr.* 13.

HALE, Eng., a heron's head, erased, ar. *Pl.* 20, *cr.* 9.

HALE, in lion's gamb, erased, az., two arrows, in saltier, or, flighted, ar. *Pl.* 56, *cr.* 3, (arrows, *same plate, cr.* 4.)

HALE, WILLIAM, Esq., of King's Walden, Hertford, a snake, ppr., entwined round five arrows, or, headed, sa., feathered, ar., one in pale, four in saltier. *Pl.* 21, *cr.* 14.

HALES, and HALE, Lond. and Herts., five arrows, one in pale, and four in saltier, or, headed, sa., feathered, ar., environed with a snake, ppr. *Pl.* 21, *cr.* 14.

HALES, a dexter arm, in armour, embowed, in hand an arrow. *Pl.* 96, *cr.* 6.

HALES, Eng., a griffin, sejant, ar. *Pl.* 100, *cr.* 11.

HALES, a dexter arm, in armour, embowed, ppr., garnished, or, in hand an arrow, of the second, (round shoulder a ribbon, tied, gu.) *Pl.* 96, *cr.* 6.

HALEY, Lond. and Middx., a goat's head, erased, ar., (gorged with a chaplet, gu.) *Pl.* 29, *cr.* 13.

HALEY, Suss., on a crescent, ar., a cross patonce, gu. *Pl.* 37, *cr.* 10, (cross, *pl.* 141.)

HALFHEAD, out of a ducal coronet, or, a demi-man, in armour, couped at thighs, ppr., garnished, vizor up, brandishing a pole-axe, gold, between wings, each charged with two decrescents, ar., and three etoiles, pierced, sa. *Pl.* 58, *cr.* 2.

HALFHIDE, a greyhound, sejant, or, (collared, az.,) garnished and ringed, gold. *Pl.* 66, *cr.* 15.

HALFORD, Bart., Leic.: 1. Of *augmentation*, a staff, entwined by a serpent, ppr., and ensigned by a coronet, composed of crosses pattée and fleurs-de-lis. *Pl.* 10, *cr.* 5. 2. A greyhound's head, couped at neck, sa., collared, or. *Mutus inglorius. Pl.* 43, *cr.* 11.

HALFORD, a greyhound's head, erased at neck, sa., collared, or. *Pl.* 89, *cr.* 2.

HALFORD, a demi-greyhound, collared. *Pl.* 5, *cr.* 10, (without wings.)

HALFPENNY, Eng., a lion, sejant, in dexter a cross (crosslet,) fitched, resting sinister on a triangle, gu. *Pl.* 56, *cr.* 12.

HALGOET, Eng., a thistle, ppr. *Pl.* 100, *cr.* 9.

HALHEAD, Eng., a falcon, wings expanded, ar., beaked and belled, or. *Pl.* 105, *cr.* 4.

HALIBURTON, of Pitcur, Sco., a negro's head, couped at shoulders, helmeted. *Pl.* 53, *cr.* 8.

HALIBURTON, Sco., a tree, ppr. *Majora sequor. Pl.* 18, *cr.* 10.

HALIDAY, Sco., a boar's head, couped, ppr. *Virtute parta. Pl.* 48, *cr.* 2.

HALIDAY, ALEXANDER-HENRY, Esq., of Carnmoney, co. Antrim, a boar's head, couped, ar., langued, and tusked, or. *Virtute parta. Pl.* 48, *cr.* 2.

HALIFAD, on stump of a tree, erased at top, and couped at root, in fess, a bird. *Pl.* 10, *cr.* 1.

HALKE, Kent, a dexter arm, in armour, embowed, in hand a battle-axe, all ppr. *Pl.* 121, *cr.* 14.

HALKERSTON, Sco., a hawk's head, erased, gu. *In ardua niter. Pl.* 34, *cr.* 11.

HALKERSTON, Sco., a falcon's head, erased, gu. *Pl.* 34, *cr.* 11.

HALKET, Bart., a falcon's head, erased, ppr. *Fides sufficit. Pl.* 34, *cr.* 11.

HALKET, Eng., a dexter arm, embowed, in hand a scimitar, all ppr. *Pl.* 92, *cr.* 5.

HALKETT, Eng., a lion, passant. *Pl.* 48, *cr.* 8.

HALKETT-CRAIGIE-INGLIS, CHARLES, Esq., of Cramond, Edinr., a falcon's head, erased, ppr. *Fides sufficit* — and — *Honeste vivo. Pl.* 34, *cr.* 11.

HALL, Notts., a crescent, ar., surmounted by a griffin's head, erased, sa., in beak, three ears of wheat, or. *Persevere.*

HALL, Chester, a stag's head, collared, or. *Pl.* 125, *cr.* 6, (without roses.)

HALL, Durh. and Oxon., a talbot's head, erased, sa. *Pl.* 90, *cr.* 6.

HALL, Bart., Monmouth, a palm-branch, in bend sinister, ppr., in front of a griffin's head, erased, or, charged with a gemelle, gu., in beak a hawk's lure, or, tasselled, ar. *Turpiter desperatur.*

HALL, Staffs., a griffin's head, erased, erm. *Pl.* 48, *cr.* 6.

HALL, a bear's head, muzzled, ppr. *Pl.* 111, *cr.* 4.

HALL, ROGER, Esq., of Narrow Water, co. Down, same crest.

HALL, Bart., Sco., a crane, or, (standing on a hill, vert,) in dexter a stone. *Dat cura quietem. Pl.* 26, *cr.* 11.

HALL, Kent, a horse's head, sa., in armour, ppr., bridled and armed, or, on head a plume of two feathers, az. *Pl.* 55, *cr.* 7.

HALL, Wilts., an arm, in armour, embowed, ppr., garnished, or, in hand a battle-axe, ar. *Pl.* 121, *cr.* 14.

HALL, Worc., a dragon's head, az., collared, or. *Pl.* 107, *cr.* 10.

HALL, Leic., a talbot's head, sa., spotted, ar. *Remember and forget not. Pl.* 123, *cr.* 15.

HALL, Kent, a horse's head, in armour, ppr., garnished and bridled, or, on head a plume of feathers, ar. *Pl.* 55, *cr.* 7.

HALL, Worc. and Yorks., a talbot's head, sa. *Pl.* 123, *cr.* 15.

HALL, Durh., a talbot's head, erased, ar., collared, chequy, or and az. *Pl.* 2, *cr.* 15.

HALL, Eng., a griffin's head. *Pl.* 38, *cr.* 3.

HALL, Lond. and Yorks., on a chapeau, gu., turned up, ar., a greyhound, sejant, erm. *Pl.* 66, *cr.* 15, (chapeau, *pl.* 127, *cr.* 13.)

HALL, Lond., in hand, gu., a ball, sa. *Pl.* 33, *cr.* 6.

HALL, a horse's head, between two ostrich-feathers. *Pl.* 58, *cr.* 1.

HALL, Eng., a dove and olive-branch, all ppr. *Pl.* 48, *cr.* 15.

HALL, a demi-wolf, rampant, in dexter a heart, transpierced by two darts, in saltier, the point of one broken off. *Pl.* 56, *cr.* 8, (heart, *pl.* 106, *cr.* 14.)

HALL, Eng., on a mount, vert, a stork, or, in dexter a (flint-stone.) *Pl.* 26, *cr.* 11.

HALL, Iri., a fox's head, paly of six, or and gu. *Pl.* 91, *cr.* 9.
HALL, Sco., a demi-griffin, ppr. *Per ardua ad alta. Pl.* 18, *cr.* 6.
HALL, Sco., a hunting-horn, az., veruled, ar. *Pl.* 89, *cr.* 3.
HALLAM, Eng., on a mount, vert, a bull, gu. *Pl.* 39, *cr.* 5.
HALLES, Herts. and Lond., a snake, ppr., entwined round five arrows, one in pale, and four in saltier, or, headed, sa., feathered, ar. *Pl.* 21, *cr.* 14.
HALLET, Kent, out of a ducal coronet, or, a demi-lion, rampant, ar., between paws a bezant. *Pl.* 45, *cr.* 7, (bezant, *pl.* 141.)
HALLET, Somers., a demi-lion, holding a bezant. *Pl.* 126, *cr.* 12.
HALLETT, Eng., in dexter hand a key, ppr. *Pl.* 41, *cr.* 11.
HALLEWEEL, a boar's head, erect, between two ostrich-feathers, ppr. *Pl.* 60, *cr.* 7.
HALLEY, a boar's head, erased and erect, between two ostrich-feathers, ppr. *Pl.* 60, *cr.* 7.
HALLIBURTON, Sco., a stag at gaze. *Watch well. Pl.* 81, *cr.* 8.
HALLIDAY, JOHN, Esq., of Chapel Cleeve, Somers., a demi-lion, rampant, or, supporting an anchor, az. *Quarta saluti. Pl.* 19, *cr.* 6.
HALLIDAY, an oak-tree, fructed, ppr. *Pl.* 16, *cr.* 8.
HALLIDAY, Sco., a boar's head, couped, ar. *Virtute parta. Pl.* 48, *cr.* 2.
HALLIDAY, Salop and Sco., a dexter arm, in armour, embowed, in fess, in hand a (sword, embrued,) all ppr. *Pl.* 107, *cr.* 15.
HALLIDAY, a boar's head, erased, sa. *Pl.* 16, *cr.* 11.
HALLIFAX, Eng., a mountain, ppr. *Pl.* 98, *cr.* 13.
HALLIFAX, Ess., a moorcock, wings expanded, per bend sinister, sa. and gu., combed and wattled, of the second, ducally gorged, charged on breast with a cross crosslet, or.
HALLINGTON, Eng., out of ducal coronet, or, a greyhound's head, sa. *Pl.* 70, *cr.* 5.
HALLIWELL, Lanc., a griffin, passant. *Pl.* 61, *cr.* 14, (without gorging.)
HALLMAN, or HALMAN, Devons., a crossbow, erect, or, between wings, gu. *Pl.* 58, *cr.* 3.
HALLOM, Eng., a hand, gu., holding a grenade, fired, ppr. *Pl.* 2, *cr.* 6.
HALLOW, an eagle, displayed, regardant, or, in dexter a sword, in pale, ppr. *Pl.* 87, *cr.* 5.
HALLOWAY, Lond., a demi-lion, rampant, gardant, purp. *Pl.* 35, *cr.* 4.
HALLOWTOWN, Eng., out of a ducal coronet, or, a greyhound's head, sa. *Pl.* 70, *cr.* 5.
HALLS, Eng., an arm, vested, gu., cuffed, or, in hand an anchor, ppr. *Pl.* 53, *cr.* 13.
HALLWELL, HALWELL, and HALYWELL, Eng., a hunting-horn, az., stringed, gu., between wings, or. *Pl.* 98, *cr.* 2.
HALLYBURTON, Hon. Lord, Sco., a moor's head, couped, helmeted, ppr. *Watch well. Pl.* 53, *cr.* 8.
HALPIN, on a ducal coronet, an eagle, displayed. *Pl.* 48, *cr.* 11, (coronet, *pl.* 128, *fig.* 3.)
HALPIN, Iri., out of a tower, a demi-griffin, rampant, wings addorsed. *Pl.* 68, *cr.* 11.
HALSBURY, Devons., a demi-lion, rampant, az. *Pl.* 67, *cr.* 10.
HALSE, and HALSEY, Devons. and Norf., a griffin, sejant, wings addorsed, ar. *Pl.* 100, *cr.* 11.

HALSEY, in dexter hand, ppr., (vested sleeve, gu., cuff, ar., a griffin's claw,) erased, or. *Nescit vax missa reverti. Pl.* 103, *cr.* 4.
HALSTEAD, Berks. and Lond., out of a mural coronet, chequy, or and az., a demi-eagle, erm., beaked, or. *Pl.* 33, *cr.* 5.
HALTON, Ess., a lion, sejant, ar., holding a broken lance, ppr. *Pl.* 60, *cr.* 4.
HALY, Iri., a savage's head, in profile, couped, ppr. *Pl.* 81, *cr.* 15.
HALY, Sco., a greyhound, current. *Gang forret. Pl.* 28, *cr.* 7, (without charge.)
HALYBURTON, Sco., a stag at gaze, ppr. *Watch well. Pl.* 81, *cr.* 8.
HALYBURTON, Sco., a boar's head, (couped) and erect, ppr. *Watch well. Pl.* 21, *cr.* 7.
HALYBURTON, Sco., a greyhound's head, couped, ppr. *Fidele. Pl.* 84, *cr.* 13, (without roses.)
HALYBURTON, Sco., a moor's head, sa., banded, ar. *Watch well. Pl.* 36, *cr.* 3.
HALYBURTON, Sco., a boar's head, (couped) and erect, ppr. *Majores sequor. Pl.* 21, *cr.* 7.
HALYS, Eng., a spur rowel, az., between eagles' wings, or. *Pl.* 54, *cr.* 5, (wings, *same plate.*)
HAM, Eng., on a chapeau, a unicorn's head, erased, ppr. *Pl.* 102, *cr.* 7.
HAMBLETON, Eng., a bundle of quills, ppr. *Pl.* 86, *cr.* 7.
HAMBLEY, and HAMBLY, Eng., a dolphin, haurient, az. *Pl.* 14, *cr.* 10.
HAMBROUGH, a horse, at full speed, ppr. *Pl.* 107, *cr.* 5, (without spear.)
HAMBY, Linc., a hawk, volant, ppr., beaked, legged, and winged, or. *Pl.* 94, *cr.* 1.
HAMDEN, Bucks., an eagle's head, erased, az. *Pl.* 20, *cr.* 7.
HAMDEN, Bucks. and Northamp., a talbot, passant, erm., collared and lined, gu., (end of line in a bow knot.) *Pl.* 65, *cr.* 2.
HAMELEN, HAMELIN, and HAMELYN, a hand, pulling a rose from a bush, ppr. *Pl.* 48, *cr.* 1.
HAMER, Eng., on a chapeau, az., turned up, erm., a lion's head, ar. *Pl.* 99, *cr.* 9.
HAMERTON, Eng., in hand a broken hammer, ppr. *Pl.* 93, *cr.* 5.
HAMERTON, JAMES, Esq., of Hellifield-Peel, Yorks., a greyhound, couchant. *Fixus adversa sperno. Pl.* 6, *cr.* 7.
HAMES, Eng., on a ducal coronet, a lion, passant, ppr. *Pl.* 107, *cr.* 11.
HAMIGSTON, Eng., a dragon's head, erased, gu., ducally gorged, ar. *Pl.* 36, *cr.* 7.
HAMILL, Iri., on a ducal coronet, a leopard, sejant, ppr. *Pl.* 86, *cr.* 8.
HAMILL, a palm-tree, fructed, ppr. *Pl.* 18, *cr.* 12.
HAMILL, Iri., a demi-lion, sa., collared, or. *Pl.* 18, *cr.* 13.
HAMILTON, of Broomhill, Sco., a horse's head. *Ride through. Pl.* 81, *cr.* 6.
HHMILTON, Duke and Marquess of, Marquess of Douglas and Clydesdale, Earl of Angus, &c., Sco.; Duke of Brandon, and Baron of Dutton, Eng.; Duke of Chatelherault, Fra., (Hamilton-Douglas,) out of a ducal coronet, or, an oak-tree, fructed, penetrated, transversely in main stem by a frame-saw, ppr., frame, gold. *Through*—for Hamilton ; and —*Jamais arrière*—for Douglas. *Pl.* 100, *cr.* 2.
HAMILTON, WALTER, Esq., of Gilkerscleugh, Lanark, same crest. *Through*—and—*In arduis fortitudo.*

HAMILTON, Bart., of Silverton Hill, Sco., same crest. *Through*—and—*Sola nobilitat virtus.*
HAMILTON-DALRYMPLE, Bart., Sco., a rock, ppr. *Firm.* Pl. 73, cr. 12.
HAMILTON, Bart., of Brecon, Wel., out of a ducal coronet, or, an oak-tree, ppr., fructed, gold, transversed by a frame-saw, also ppr. *Through.* Pl. 100, cr. 2.
HAMILTON, Devons., an oak-tree, ppr., the trunk surmounted by an escutcheon, per pale, gu. and az., charged with a cinquefoil, or. Pl. 75, cr. 2, (cinquefoil, pl. 141.)
HAMILTON, Devons., two spears, in saltier, issuing through an Eastern crown, or, and between spears a bugle-horn, sa.
HAMILTON, JOHN, Esq., of Sundrum, Ayr, out of a ducal coronet, or, an oak-tree, fructed, penetrated transversely in main stem by a frame-saw, ppr. *Through.* Pl. 100, cr. 2.
HAMILTON, Marquess of Abercorn, Earl of Haddington, Baron Belhaven, and Viscount Boyne. *See those titles.*
HAMILTON, of Barnton, Sco., the branch of a tree growing out of an old stock. *Through God revived.* Pl. 92, cr. 8.
HAMILTON, of Byres, Sco., two dexter hands, out of clouds, joined, in fess, holding a branch of laurel, ppr. *Præsto et persto.* Pl. 102, cr. 2, (laurel, *same plate, cr.* 13.)
HAMILTON, of Preston, a man, from middle, brandishing a (sword.) *Pro patriâ.* Pl. 82, cr. 2.
HAMILTON, of Aikenhead, in hand an (oak-slip,) ppr. *Virebo.* Pl. 43, cr. 6.
HAMILTON, of Udstoun, Sco., a boar's head, erased, ppr. *Ubique fidelis.* Pl. 16, cr. 11.
HAMILTON, Sco., same crest. *Non metuo.*
HAMILTON, of Wishaw, Sco., in hand a sword, indented on back like a saw, and a quill, (in saltier,) ppr. *Tam virtus quam honos.* Pl. 39, cr. 13.
HAMILTON, of Orbistown, Sco., an antelope, ppr. *Quis accursabit.* Pl. 63, cr. 10.
HAMILTON, of Barncluith, Sco., a spear, ppr. *Dat Deus originem.* Pl. 97, cr. 4.
HAMILTON, Sco., a ship in distress, ppr. *Littora specto.* Pl. 21, cr. 11.
HAMILTON, Sco., same crest. *Littore sistam.*
HAMILTON, Sco., same crest. *Immersabilis.*
HAMILTON, Sco., same crest. *I gain by hazard.*
HAMILTON, Sco., same crest. *Per varios casus.*
HAMILTON, Sco., within two branches, in orle, two hands, conjoined, out of clouds, all ppr. *Prestando præsto.* Pl. 53, cr. 11, (laurel, pl. 79, cr. 14.)
HAMILTON, Sco., a heart, gu., charged with a cinquefoil, ar. Pl. 123, cr. 7.
HAMILTON, of Caffhes, Sco., the Holy Bible, expanded, ppr. *Ore lego, corde credo.* Pl. 15, cr. 12.
HAMILTON, of Olivestob, Sco., an antelope's head and neck, (gorged with a collar,) and attired, gu. *Invia virtuti pervia.* Pl. 24, cr. 7.
HAMILTON, of Westburn, in hand a lance, in bend, ppr. *Et arma et virtus.* Pl. 99, cr. 8.
HAMILTON, of Neilsland, Sco., an oak-tree, fructed, ppr. *Obsequio non viribus.* Pl. 16, cr. 8.
HAMILTON, of Blanterferm, Sco., trunk of oak-tree, couped, sprouting two branches, ppr. *Non deficit alter.* Pl. 92, cr. 8.

HAMILTON, of Daichmont, Sco., in hand a heart, ppr. *No heart more true.* Pl. 59, cr. 12.
HAMILTON, of Dalziel, Sco., an oak-tree, ppr. *Requiesco sub umbrâ.* Pl. 16, cr. 8.
HAMILTON, of Wessport, Sco., two branches of oak, in saltier, fructed. *Addunt robur.* Pl. 19, cr. 12.
HAMILTON, of Cubardie, a cinquefoil, ar. *Non mutat genus solum.* Pl. 91, cr. 12.
HAMILTON, of Colquot, Sco., a cupid, with bow, quiver, and arrow, ppr. *Quos dedit arcus amor.* Pl. 17, cr. 5.
HAMILTON, Sco., an oak-plant, or. *Tandem fit arbor.* Pl. 32, cr. 13.
HAMILTON, of Presmenaw, in dexter hand a writing-pen, ppr. *Tam virtute quam labore.* Pl. 26, cr. 13.
HAMILTON, Sco., same crest and motto, (but out of clouds.)
HAMILTON, of Smaliston, a mascle, or. *I'll deceive no man.* Pl. 54, cr. 1.
HAMILTON, of Gilkerscleugh, a hand, issuing out of a man's heart, ppr., grasping a (sword.) *In arduis fortitudo.* Pl. 35, cr. 7.
HAMILTON, of Killbrachmonth, a hand pulling up a cinquefoil, ppr. *Et neglecta virescit.* Pl. 53, cr. 15.
HAMILTON, a cubit arm, erect, in hand a scimitar. Pl. 29, cr. 8.
HAMILTON, a cubit arm, erect, in hand a tilting-spear. Pl. 99, cr. 8.
HAMILTON, Sco., in hand an (oak-slip,) ppr. *Virebo.* Pl. 43, cr. 6.
HAMILTON, Sco., in hand a holly-leaf, ppr. *Semper virescens.* Pl. 23, cr. 7, (holly, pl. 78, cr. 12.)
HAMILTON, Sco., an oak-tree, growing out of a torse, and fructed, ppr. *Obsequio non viribus.* Pl. 16, cr. 8.
HAMILTON, Sco., a horse's head, ar., bridled, gu. Pl. 92, cr. 1.
HAMILTON, Sco., a salmon, haurient, ar., an annulet through nose. Pl. 98, cr. 12, (annulet, pl. 141.)
HAMILTON, Sco., a greyhound's head and neck, couped, ppr., collared, gu., garnished, or. Pl. 43, cr. 11.
HAMILTON, Sco., an antelope's head and neck, ppr., (collared,) and attired, gu. *Invia virtuti pervia.* Pl. 24, cr. 7.
HAMILTON, Sco., a demi-goat, affrontée, between the joints of fore-legs, a human heart, all ppr. Pl. 113, cr. 1.
HAMILTON, JAMES, Esq., of Bangour, Ayr, and of Ninewar, East Lothian, a ship in distress, ppr. *Immersabilis.* Pl. 21, cr. 11.
HAMILTON, JOHN, Esq., of St Ernans, co. Donegal, a nag's head, couped, ar., bridled, gu. *Ride through.* Pl. 92, cr. 1.
HAMILTON, Sco., in hand a sword, indented on back like a saw. Pl. 39, cr. 13, (without pen.)
HAMILTON, Sco., in hand a dagger, in pale. Pl. 23, cr. 15.
HAMILTON, Sco., a sword, in pale. Pl. 105, cr. 1.
HAMILTON, Sco., a crescent, ar. Pl. 18, cr. 14.
HAMLEY, Eng., a garb, in fess. Pl. 48, cr. 10.
HAMLIN, Eng., seven arrows, (points upward,) ppr. Pl. 110, cr. 11.
HAMLYN, Eng., a swan, wings addorsed, ppr. Pl. 46, cr. 5.
HAMLYN, Devons., a demi-swan, wings expanded, bezantée. Pl. 54, cr. 4.

P

HAMLYN, Devons., a griffin, gardant. *Caute sed strenue.* Pl. 4, cr. 9.
HAMLYN, a swan, close, (in mouth a baton.) Pl. 122, cr. 13, (without mount.)
HAMLYNG, Eng., a hand pulling a rose from a bush, ppr. Pl. 48, cr. 1.
HAMME, Eng., on a chapeau, a unicorn's head, erased, ppr. Pl. 102, cr. 7.
HAMMERSLEY, Eng., two lions' gambs, holding up a crescent. Pl. 62, cr. 3.
HAMMERSLEY, a demi-griffin, segreant, in dexter a cross crosslet, fitched. Pl. 18, cr. 6, (cross, pl. 141.)
HAMMICK, Bart., Lond., a demi-lion, per pale, or and vert, holding an escarbuncle, gold. Pl. 113, cr. 2.
HAMMILL, Eng., a palm-tree, fructed, ppr. Pl. 18, cr. 12.
HAMMINGTON, Kent, a dragon's head, erased, gu., ducally gorged, ar., (charged on neck with three guttes, in fess, of the last.) Pl. 36, cr. 7.
HAMMOND, Yorks., Herts., Middx., Cambs., and Kent, a wolf's head, erased, quarterly, or and az. Pl. 14, cr. 6.
HAMMOND, an eagle's head, (gorged with a collar, indented.) Pl. 74, cr. 1.
HAMMOND, out of a ducal coronet, an eagle's head, between wings. Pl. 66, cr. 5.
HAMMOND, out of a ducal coronet, or, a demi-eagle, wings expanded, sa., charged on breast with a rose, gu. Pl. 9, cr. 6, (rose, pl. 141.)
HAMMOND, JAMES-WALTHALL, Esq., of Wistaston Hall, Chesh., a boar, passant, ppr. Pl. 48, cr. 14.
HAMMOND, Kent, a hawk's head, (collared, gu.,) rays issuing, or. *Pro rege et patriâ.* Pl. 84, cr. 9.
HAMOND, ANTHONY, Esq., of Westacre, Norf., on a rock, ppr., a dove, ar., in mouth an olive-branch, vert. Pl. 85, cr. 14.
HAMOND, Yorks., Herts., Kent, Middx., and Cambs., a wolf's head, erased, quarterly, or and az. Pl. 14, cr. 6.
HAMOND, Bart., Berks., out of a naval crown, or, an eagle's head, sa. Pl. 113, cr. 4.
HAMPDEN, Eng., a peacock's head, couped, az. Pl. 100, cr. 5.
HAMPDEN, Bucks. and Sco., an eagle's head, erased, az. Pl. 20, cr. 7.
HAMPDEN, Viscount: 1. For *Hampden*, a talbot, (statant,) erm., collared, ringed, and lined, gu., (end of line tied over back.) Pl. 65, cr. 2. 2. For *Trevor*, on a chapeau, gu., turned up, erm., a wyvern, wings addorsed, sa. *Vestigia nulla retrorsum.* Pl. 104, cr. 5, (without crown.)
HAMPDEN, Bucks. and Northamp., a talbot, passant, erm., collared and lined, (the line in a bow-knot over neck, gu.) Pl. 65, cr. 2.
HAMPSON, Bart., Bucks., out of a mural coronet, ar., a greyhound's head, sa., collared, of the first. *Nunc aut nunquam.* Pl. 113, cr. 6.
HAMPSTEAD, and HAMPSTED, Eng., a demi-chevalier, in full armour, brandishing a scimitar, all ppr. Pl. 27, cr. 11.
HAMPTON, Lond., Middx., and Staffs., a wolf's head, erased, sa. Pl. 14, cr. 6.
HAMPTON, Staffs., a wolf's head, ar. Pl. 8, cr. 4, (without collar.)
HAMPTON, Eng., a demi-eagle, displayed, or. Pl. 22, cr. 11.

HANAM, Eng., a demi-griffin, holding a close helmet, ppr. Pl. 19, cr. 15.
HANBURY, Glouc., Worc., and Northamp., out of a mural coronet, sa., a demi-lion, or, in dexter a battle-axe, of the first. Pl. 120, cr. 14.
HANBURY, a lion, holding a pole-axe, ppr. Pl. 109, cr. 7.
HANBY, Eng., two arms, in armour, embowed, holding a heart. Pl. 36, cr. 4, (without flames.)
HANCE, Eng., in hand a sword, in pale, enfiled with a Saracen's head, couped, ppr. Pl. 97, cr. 3.
HANCHETT, Eng., the sun shining on a sunflower, ppr. Pl. 45, cr. 13, (sunflower, pl. 84, cr. 6.)
HANCKFORD, Eng., a demi-cupid, in dexter a torch, ppr. Pl. 70, cr. 14.
HANCOCK, Eng., a cock, ppr. Pl. 67, cr. 14.
HANCOCK, a demi-lion, between paws a lozenge, sa. Pl. 126, cr. 12, (lozenge, pl. 141.)
HANCOCK, an arrow, point downward, ppr. Pl. 56, cr. 13.
HANCOCKE, Devons., a demi-griffin, ar., armed, or. Pl. 18, cr. 6.
HANCOCKS, (on a mount, vert,) a cock, gu., in dexter an ear of wheat, or. *Redeem time.* Pl. 55, cr. 12, (wheat, pl. 85, cr. 6.)
HANCOME, Lond., a lion, sejant, or, collared, gu., charged with two etoiles, of the first. Pl. 21, cr. 3, (etoile, pl. 141.)
HANCOX, Eng., an arrow, point downwards. Pl. 56, cr. 13.
HAND, Eng., an arm, couped at shoulder, in hand three ears of wheat, ppr. Pl. 89, cr. 4.
HAND, Hunts., a dexter hand apaumée, ppr. Pl. 32, cr. 14.
HAND, a stag, trippant, ppr. Pl. 68, cr. 2.
HANDASYD, Hunts., a dexter hand, couped and erect, ppr. Pl. 32, cr. 14.
HANDBY, Eng., a hind's head, per cheveron, az. and ar. Pl. 21, cr. 9.
HANDCOCK, Iri., stump of holly-bush, shooting new leaves, ppr. Pl. 25, cr. 9.
HANDCOCK, a cock, gu. Pl. 67, cr. 14.
HANDCOCK, Eng., out of the sea, an arm, embowed, in hand a bait spade. Pl. 53, cr. 9.
HANDFIELD, Eng., in hand a bomb-shell, fired, ppr. Pl. 2, cr. 6.
HANDFIELD, Cumb., a phœnix's head, ppr., crowned, or. Pl. 44, cr. 8, (crown, *same plate.*)
HANDFORD, Eng., two ears of wheat, in saltier, ppr. Pl. 9, cr. 8.
HANDLEY, Eng., a sceptre, in pale, ppr. Pl. 82, cr. 3.
HANDLEY, a goat, current, sa., bearded, unguled, and armed, or. Pl. 70, cr. 3, (without tree.)
HANDS, Eng., a goat's head, erased, gu. Pl. 29, cr. 13.
HANDY, Eng., two arms, in armour, embowed, holding a battle-axe, ppr. Pl. 41, cr. 2.
HANDYSIDE, Sco., and HANDYSYDE, Lond., a dexter hand, apaumée, ppr. *Munifice et fortiter.* Pl. 32, cr. 14.
HANEY, Eng., a stag's head, ppr., (collared,) or, between attires, a cross pattée, gu. Pl. 9, cr. 10.
HANFORD, Worc., on a chapeau, gu., turned up, erm., a wyvern, of the first, (wings expanded,) ar., beaked and legged, gu. Pl. 104, cr. 5, (without crown.)

HANGER, a griffin, segreant, between fore-feet the sun, or. *Pl.* 13, *cr.* 10.
HANHAM, Bart., Dors., a griffin's head, erased, or. *Pl.* 48, *cr.* 6.
HANHAM, Dors., a griffin's head, erased, ducally gorged, or. *Pl.* 42, *cr.* 9, (without branch.)
HANKEY, Lond., a demi-wolf, erminois. *Pl.* 56, *cr.* 8, (without spear.)
HANKIN, Eng., a boy, pulling a branch from a tree, ppr. *Pl.* 94, *cr.* 8.
HANKLEY, Eng., out of a ducal coronet, or, a triple plume of ostrich-feathers, five, four, and three, ar. *Pl.* 114, *cr.* 8.
HANLEY, Eng., a sceptre, in pale, ppr. *Pl.* 82, *cr.* 3.
HANLY, Iri., three arrows, two in saltier, and one in pale, points downward, banded. *Pl.* 43, *cr.* 14.
HANMAN, a lion, sejant, erm. *Per ardua ad alta.* *Pl.* 126, *cr.* 15.
HANMER, Bart., Wel., on a chapeau, az., turned up, erm., a lion, sejant, gardant, ar. *Gardez l'honneur.* *Pl.* 113, *cr.* 8.
HANMER, Eng., on a ducal coronet, a peacock, close, ppr. *Pl.* 43, *cr.* 7.
HANNA, Eng., a wolf's head, erased, sa. *Pl.* 14, *cr.* 6.
HANNAM, Eng., a demi-griffin, between claws a close helmet, ppr. *Pl.* 19, *cr.* 15.
HANNAY, ROBERT, Esq., of Rusko, Springfield, Ulverston, between the horns of a crescent, a cross crosslet, fitched, in pale, sa. *Per ardua ad alta.* *Pl.* 43, *cr.* 3.
HANNAY, Sco. and Eng., *same crest.*
HANNEY, Eng., a stag's head, ppr., (collared, or,) between attires a cross pattée, gu. *Pl.* 9, *cr.* 10.
HANNING, Eng., a stag's head, erased, or. *Pl.* 66, *cr.* 9.
HANROTT, Lond., an eagle, displayed, with two heads, sa. *Perseverando*—and—*Humani nihil alienum.* *Pl.* 87, *cr.* 11, (without flame.)
HANSARD, Eng., a falcon, volant, az. *Pl.* 94, *cr.* 1.
HANSARD, an arm, in armour, couped at shoulder, embowed, the part from shoulder to elbow in fess, and (bound with a ribbon,) the other part in pale, in hand a broken sword. *Pl.* 114, *cr.* 9, (sword, *pl.* 22, *cr.* 6.)
HANSARD, Eng., an antique crown, or. *Pl.* 79, *cr.* 12.
HANSARD, Lond., a cubit arm, erect, (vested, or, cuffed, ar.,) in hand, ppr., a mullet, of the second. *Probitas verus honos.* *Pl.* 62, *cr.* 13.
HANSARD, Eng., a martlet, sa. *Pl.* 111, *cr.* 5.
HANSBY, Yorks., a pheon, or. *Pl.* 26, *cr.* 12.
HANSFELL, the trunks of two trees, erect, each sprouting a new branch, the two branches in saltier. *Pl.* 75, *cr.* 14.
HANSON, Eng., on a chapeau, a martlet, wings (addorsed,) sa. *Pl.* 89, *cr.* 7.
HANWELL, Eng., in hand a club, (in pale,) ppr. *Pl.* 28, *cr.* 6.
HAPSBURGH, Eng., an eagle, displayed, ar., beaked and membered, gu. *Virtutis premium honor.* *Pl.* 48, *cr.* 11.
HARBER, Eng., in hand (three) arrows, points downward. *Pl.* 56, *cr.* 4.
HARBERT, Eng., two wings, expanded, ppr. *Pl.* 39, *cr.* 12, (without charging.)
HARBERTON, Viscount, and Baron, Iri., (Pomeroy,) a lion, rampant, gu., holding an (apple,) ppr. *Virtutis fortuna comes.* *Pl.* 64, *cr.* 2.

HARBIN, GEORGE, Esq., of Newtown House, Somers., in hand, ppr., a spear, or. *Pl.* 99, *cr.* 8.
HARBIN, Somers., a horned owl, ar. *Pl.* 1, *cr.* 8.
HARBORD, on a chapeau, turned up, erm., a lion, couchant. *Pl.* 75, *cr.* 5.
HARBORNE, Eng., two lions' gambs, sa., holding up a bezant. *Pl.* 42, *cr.* 3.
HARBOROUGH, Earl of, (Sherard,) out of a ducal coronet, or, a peacock's tail, erect, ppr. *Le roi et l'estat*—and—*Hostis honori invidia.* *Pl.* 120, *cr.* 13.
HARBOTTELL, Eng., a goat's head, erased, sa., armed and (collared,) or. *Pl.* 29, *cr.* 13.
HARBOTTLE, Eng., a demi-falcon, or, wings displayed, sa. *Pl.* 103, *cr.* 6, (without coronet.)
HARBOUR, Somers., two hands, couped, holding a cutlass, erect, all ppr. *Pl.* 59, *cr.* 10.
HARCLA, DE, and HARCLE, Eng., a fret, az. *Pl.* 82, *cr.* 7.
HARCLA, and HARCLE, Eng., out of a ducal coronet, or, a reindeer's head, ppr. *Pl.* 60, *cr.* 3.
HARCOURT, Oxon., on a ducal coronet, or, a peacock, close, ppr. *Gesta verbis prævenient.* *Pl.* 43, *cr.* 7.
HARCOURT, GEORGE-SIMON, Esq., of Ankerwycke House, Berks., on a ducal coronet, or, a peacock, close, ppr. *Le bon temps viendra.* *Pl.* 43, *cr.* 7.
HARD, Eng., on a chapeau, a greyhound, ppr. *Pl.* 104, *cr.* 1.
HARDACRE, Eng., on a rock, an eagle, rising, regardant, ppr. *Pl.* 79, *cr.* 2.
HARDCASTLE, Eng., a female, attired, az., in dexter the sun, in sinister the moon, ppr. *Pl.* 107, *cr.* 14.
HARDEL, or HARDELL, Eng., a sheaf of arrows, ppr., banded, gu. *Pl.* 54, *cr.* 15.
HARDEN, Eng., in dexter hand, issuing from a cloud, in fess, an anchor, ppr. *Pl.* 79, *cr.* 15.
HARDGRAVE, and HARDGROVE, Eng., a waterbouget, gu. *Pl.* 14, *cr.* 12.
HARDIE, Eng., a lion, passant, gardant, or, (collared,) az., supporting an anchor, of the last. *Pl.* 35, *cr.* 6.
HARDIE, Sco., in hand a dagger, erect, ppr. *Tout hardie.* *Pl.* 23, *cr.* 15.
HARDIE, Sco., a dexter arm, in hand a dagger, in pale, point downward, ppr. *Pl.* 18, *cr.* 3.
HARDIE, Sco., an arm, in armour, embowed, in hand a scimitar, ppr. *Sera deschormais hardie.* *Pl.* 81, *cr.* 11.
HARDIE, Sco., a spur-rowel. *Pl.* 54, *cr.* 5.
HARDIEMAN, Eng., on a serpent, nowed, a hawk, perched, ppr. *Pl.* 75, *cr.* 11.
HARDIN, Eng., a dexter hand issuing from a cloud, in fess, supporting an anchor, ppr. *Pl.* 79, *cr.* 15.
HARDING, WILLIAM-JUDD, Esq., of Baraset, Warw., on a chapeau, az., turned up, erm., a boar, passant, or. *Pl.* 22, *cr.* 8.
HARDING, Middx. and Derbs., a mitre, gu., banded and stringed, or, charged with a cheveron, ar., fimbriated, or, and thereon three escallops, sa. *Audax omnia perpeti.* *Pl.* 12, *cr.* 10.
HARDING, a falcon, rising, ppr. *Pl.* 105, *cr.* 4.
HARDING, a demi-stag, between fore-feet an anchor. *Pl.* 55, *cr.* 9, (without rose; anchor, *pl.* 35, *cr.* 6.)
HARDING, Iri., an arm, embowed, in fess, couped, in hand a sword, (in pale,) enfiled with a leopard's head, cabossed. *Pl.* 102, *cr.* 5.

HARDINGE, Bart., Iri.: 1. A mitre, gu., charged with a cheveron, ar., fimbriated, or. *Pl.* 49, *cr.* 15. 2. *Of augmentation,* a hand, in fess, couped above wrist, vested in naval uniform, holding a sword, erect, surmounting a Dutch and French flag, in saltier, on the former inscribed *Atalanta,* on the latter, *Piedmontaise,* the blade of the sword passing through a wreath of laurel near the point, and a little below, through another of cypress, with the motto, *Posterâ laude recens.*

HARDINGE, Viscount, of Lahore, &c., a mitre, gu., charged with a cheveron. *Mens æqua rebus in arduis. Pl.* 49, *cr.* 15.

HARDISTY, two hands, issuing from clouds, conjoined, in fess. *Pl.* 53, *cr.* 11.

HARDMAN, a hand, issuant, pulling a rose, ppr. *Pl.* 48, *cr.* 1.

HARDRES, Kent, a stag's head, couped, ppr. *Pl.* 91, *cr.* 14.

HARDRES, a buck's head, couped, or and erm., attired, gu. and az. *Pl.* 91, *cr.* 14.

HARDRESS, a reindeer's head, cabossed, ppr., attired, or. *Pl.* 114, *cr.* 7.

HARDWARE, Chesh., out of a ducal coronet, or, a cubit arm, az., cuff, ar., in hand an oak-branch, ppr., fructed, or. *Pl.* 84, *cr.* 2, (branch, *pl.* 32, *cr.* 13.)

HARDWICK, Salop, on a mount, vert, a stag, current, gorged with a (chaplet of roses,) all ppr. *Pl.* 84, *cr.* 5, (without branches.)

HARDWICKE, a leopard's head, or, jessant-de-lis, gu. *Pl.* 123, *cr.* 9.

HARDWICKE, Earl of, and Baron, Viscount Royston, (Yorke;) a lion's head, erased, ppr., collar, gu., charged with a bezant. *Nec cupias, nec metuas. Pl.* 7, *cr.* 10, (bezant, *pl.* 141.)

HARDY, Bart., Northamp., out of a naval coronet, or, griffin's head, erased, ar., langued, gu. *Pl.* 113, *cr.* 4, (griffin, *pl.* 48, *cr.* 6.)

HARDY, a griffin's head, collared, in beak an olive-branch, between wings. *Pl.* 22, *cr.* 2.

HARDY, Iri., a mitre, gu., banded and stringed, or, charged with a cheveron, ar., and thereon three escallops, sa. *Pl.* 12, *cr.* 10.

HARDYMAN, on a serpent, nowed, a hawk, perched, ppr. *Pl.* 75, *cr.* 11.

HARDYMAN, an arm, in armour, embowed, in hand a boar's head, erased at neck. *Pl.* 75, *cr.* 1.

HARE, HUMPHREY-JOHN, Esq., of Docking Hall, Norf., a demi-lion, rampant, ducally gorged. *Pl.* 87, *cr.* 15.

HARE, Bart., Norf., a demi-lion, rampant, ar., murally gorged, or. *Pl.* 87, *cr.* 15, (gorging, *pl.* 128, *fig.* 18.)

HARE, Norf., a demi-lion, ar. *Pl.* 67, *cr.* 10.

HARE, a demi-lion, ar., holding a cross crosslet, fitched. *Pl.* 65, *cr.* 6.

HARE, Sco., a parrot, gu., in beak an annulet, or. *Pl.* 33, *cr.* 11.

HARESTAINS, Sco., a dexter arm, in hand a key. *Toujours fidele. Pl.* 41, *cr.* 11.

HAREWELL, Suff. and Worc., a hare's head, erased, or.

HAREWOOD, Earl of, and Baron Viscount, Lascelles, (Lascelles;) a bear's head, couped at neck, erm., muzzled, gu., buckled, or, (collared, of the second,) studded, or. *In solo Deo salus. Pl.* 2, *cr.* 9.

HARFETT, Kent, a dolphin, naiant, ppr. *Pl.* 48, *cr.* 9.

HARFLETE, Kent, a dolphin, naiant, ppr. *Pl.* 48, *cr.* 9.

HARFORD, of Blaise Castle, out of a coronet, a griffin's head, or, between wings, az., in flames, and fire issuing from mouth, ppr. *Pl.* 97, *cr.* 13, (flames, *pl.* 53, *cr.* 6.)

HARFORD, out of a ducal coronet, or, two flags, one, gold, other, sa., both staves, gold. *Pl.* 53, *cr.* 14, (coronet, *same plate.*)

HARGIL, Yorks., out of a mural coronet, gu., a lion's head, or. *Pl.* 45, *cr.* 9.

HARGRAVE, Eng., a buck's head, erased, per fess, or and gu., fretty, az., attired, gu., fretty, az. *Pl.* 66, *cr.* 9.

HARGRAVES, Eng., out of a ducal coronet, two branches of laurel, in orle, ppr. *Pl.* 114, *cr.* 15.

HARGREAVES, a buck's head, erased, vert, attired, or, collared, ar., charged with a fret, gu., in mouth a sprig of oak, ppr. *Fortitudine et prudentiâ. Pl.* 110, *cr.* 8, (fret, *pl.* 82, *cr.* 7.)

HARINGTON, Bart., Ruts., a lion's head, erased, or, collared, gu., buckled, gold. *Nodo firmo. Pl.* 7, *cr.* 10.

HARINGTON, Eng., in lion's paw a thistle, ppr. *Pl.* 109, *cr.* 4.

HARKNESS, Sco., a ship in distress, ppr. *Trust in God. Pl.* 21, *cr.* 11.

HARLAND, a demi-sea-horse, ppr., (charged on shoulder with an escallop, gu.,) in claws a buck's head, cabossed, ppr. *Pl.* 58, *cr.* 15, (head, *same plate, cr.* 13.)

HARLAND, Bart., Suff., a sea-lion, sa., supporting an anchor, ppr. *Pl.* 59, *cr.* 2, (anchor, *pl.* 35, *cr.* 6.)

HARLAW, Eng., a moor's head, ppr. *Pl.* 19, *cr.* 1.

HARLEWEN, Eng., a tower, on top a crescent. *Pl.* 85, *cr.* 1.

HARLEY, Earl of Oxford. *See* OXFORD.

HARLEY, Heref., out of a castle, triple-towered, ar., a demi-lion, rampant, gu. *Virtute et fide. Pl.* 101, *cr.* 1.

HARLEY, from top of tower, ar., a demi-lion, issuant, gu. *Pl.* 42, *cr.* 4.

HARLEY, a spear-head, in pale, entwined with an olive-branch. *Pl.* 82, *cr.* 9, (olive-branch, *pl.* 98, *cr.* 8.)

HARLING, Eng., a bomb-shell, inflamed, ppr. *Pl.* 70, *cr.* 12.

HARLINGHAM, a bomb-shell, inflamed, ppr. *Pl.* 70, *cr.* 12.

HARLISTON, Eng., a cannon, mounted, ppr. *Pl.* 111, *cr.* 3.

HARLY, Iri., a demi-lion, gardant, gu., in dexter a battle-axe, ppr. *Pl.* 26, *cr.* 7.

HARMAN, Iri., a water-bouget, or. *Pl.* 14, *cr.* 12.

HARMER, Eng., a book, expanded, ppr. *Pl.* 15, *cr.* 12.

HARNAGE, Bart., Salop: 1. For *Harnage,* out of a ducal coronet, a lion's gamb, holding a torteau. *Deo duce, decrevi. Pl.* 67, *cr.* 7, (torteau, *pl.* 97, *cr.* 10.) 2. For *Blackman,* a demi-griffin, or, semée of crescents, az., collared, gu. *Fide et fiduciâ. Pl.* 74, *cr.* 15, (without anchor.)

HARNAGE, Eng., a lion's paw. *Pl.* 126, *cr.* 9.

HARNAGE, Eng., out of a ducal coronet, a lion's paw, charged with a bezant, ar. *Pl.* 67, *cr.* 7, (bezant, *pl.* 141.)

HARNET, Eng., a hornet-fly, wings elevated, ppr. *Pl.* 107, *cr.* 13.

HARNET, Iri., a demi-lion, gardant, az. *Pl.* 35, *cr* 4.
HARNEYS, and HARNOUS, Beds., a stag's head, sa., guttée and attired, or. *Pl.* 91, *cr.* 14.
HAROKINS, Eng., a griffin's head, chequy, ar. and sa., between wings, gu. *Pl.* 65, *cr.* 1.
HAROLD, and HAROULD, Eng., a hawk's lure, ppr. *Pl.* 97, *cr.* 14.
HAROLD, Iri., a gate, ppr. *Pl.* 73, *cr.* 4.
HARPWAY, and HARPWAYE, an ostrich, wings addorsed, in mouth a horse-shoe, all ppr. *Pl.* 16, *cr.* 2.
HARPDEN, Glouc. a hind's head, or. *Pl.* 21, *cr.* 9.
HARPER, Sco., an old Scottish harp, or, with nine strings, ar. *Te deum laudamus. Pl.* 104, *cr.* 15.
HARPER, Lond., on a crescent, or, charged with a fret, between two martlets, az., an eagle, displayed, of the last.
HARPER, Eng., a lion's head, erased, quarterly, or and gu. *Pl.* 81, *cr.* 4.
HARPER, Sco., a boar, passant, or. *Et suavis et fortis. Pl.* 48, *cr.* 14.
HARPUR, Derbs. and Sco., a boar, passant, or, ducally gorged, gu. *Pl.* 29, *cr.* 10, (gorging, same plate.)
HARPUR, Warw. and Northamp., on battlement of tower, masoned, ppr., a boar's head, erased, in fess. *Pl.* 12, *cr.* 5, (head, *pl.* 16, *cr.* 11.)
HARRIDGE, a lion's head, erased, ppr., langued, gu. *Pl.* 81, *cr.* 4.
HARRIE, Cornw., a demi-sea-dog, rampant, gu., erased and finned, or, between paws a Cornish chough, ppr.
HARRIES, Shrewsbury, a star-fish. *Mot pour mot. Pl.* 63, *cr.* 9.
HARRIES, FRANCIS, Esq., of Cruckton Hall and Broseley Hall, Salop, a hawk, ar., beaked and belled, or, preying on a curlew, of the first. *Pl.* 80, *cr.* 12.
HARRIES, JOHN-HILL, Esq., of Priskelly, Pembroke, Wel., a mullet, pierced, ppr. *Integritas semper tutamen. Pl.* 45, *cr.* 1.
HARRIES, Eng., an oak-tree, growing out of a mount, among long grass, ppr. *Pl.* 48, *cr.* 4.
HARRINGTON, Earl of, and Baron, Viscount Petersham, (Stanhope ;) a tower, ar., issuant from the battlements, a demi-lion, rampant, or, between paws a grenade, fired, ppr. *A Deo et rege. Pl.* 53, *cr.* 2.
HARRINGTON, Lanc., a lion's head, erased, or, gorged with a (belt and buckle, gu.) *Pl.* 7, *cr.* 10.
HARRINGTON, Iri., a talbot's head, gu. *Pl.* 123, *cr.* 15.
HARRINGWORTH, Eng., an antique crown, or. *Pl.* 79, *cr.* 12.
HARRIS, of Hayne, Devons., an eagle, rising, erm., beaked and spurred, or. *Kur Deu res pub trar*, (old Cornish, signifying, *For God and the commonwealth.) Pl.* 67, *cr.* 4.
HARRIS, Leic., (rising from a fern brake, ppr.,) a dove, regardant, az., beaked and membered, gu., in mouth a trefoil, vert. *Virtute et operâ. Pl.* 77, *cr.* 2, (trefoil, *pl.* 141.)
HARRIS, Baron, (Harris;) on a mural coronet, or, a royal tiger, passant, gardant, vert, spotted, gold, (pierced on breast by an arrow, and vulned, ppr., charged on forehead with a Persian character for *Hyder*,) and crowned with an eastern coronet, both of the first. *My prince and my country. Pl.* 67, *cr.* 15, (coronets, *pl.* 128, *figs.* 18 and 2.)

HARRIS, Salop, a hedgehog, az. *Pl.* 32, *cr.* 9.
HARRIS, Salop, a hedgehog, or. *Pl.* 32, *cr.* 9.
HARRIS, Devons., an eagle, displayed, or. *Pl.* 48, *cr.* 11.
HARRIS, Sco., (on a mount, vert,) a crane, in dexter a stone, ppr. *Pl.* 26, *cr.* 11.
HARRIS, Ess., a buck's head, chequy, ar. and az., attired, or. *Pl.* 91, *cr.* 14.
HARRIS, Iri., a monkey, passant, banded round middle. *Pl.* 101, *cr.* 11.
HARRIS, Lond., a winged heart, gu., (imperially) crowned, or. *Pl.* 52, *cr.* 2.
HARRIS, Eng., a buck's head, or, attired with ten tynes, ar. *Dominus dedit. Pl.* 91, *cr.* 14.
HARRIS, Worc., an arm, in hand a dart. *Pl.* 92, *cr.* 14.
HARRIS, Earl of Malmesbury. *See* MALMESBURY, Earl of.
HARRIS, Eng., a hedgehog, ppr., charged with a key, az. *Ubiqui patriam reminisci. Pl.* 32, *cr.* 9. (key, *pl.* 9, *cr.* 12.)
HARRIS, Eng., a demi-antelope, ppr., armed, or. *Pl.* 75, *cr.* 10, (without escutcheon.)
HARRISON, Fiske, a stork, wings expanded, ar., beaked and membered, or. *Ferendo et feriendo. Pl.* 33, *cr.* 9.
HARRISON, Rutland, an ostrich, (in mouth a snake.) *Deo, non fortunâ. Pl.* 64, *cr.* 3, (without coronet.)
HARRISON, Derbs., a demi-lion, or, supporting a chaplet of roses, vert. *Pl.* 39, *cr.* 14, (chaplet, *pl.* 41, *cr.* 7.)
HARRISON, BENSON, Esq., of Greenbank, Westm., a demi-lion, rampant, ar. *Vincit qui patitur. Pl.* 67, *cr.* 10.
HARRISON, JOSEPH, Esq., Galigreare's Hall, Blackburn, within a wreath, or and az., a talbot's head, collared, gold. *Not rashly, nor with fear. Pl.* 126 o, *cr.* 6.
HARRISON, Surr., a demi-lion, rampant, erminois, erased, gu., between paws a garland of laurel, ppr., encircling a mascle, of the second. *Pl.* 39, *cr.* 14, (garland, *pl.* 128, *ig.* 6; mascle, *pl.* 141.)
HARRISON, Lond., on a chapeau, az., turned up and indented, erm., a bird, wings addorsed, sa. *Pl.* 109, *cr.* 10.
HARRISON, out of a ducal coronet, a talbot's head, or, guttée-de-poix. *Pl.* 99, *cr.* 7.
HARRISON, Yorks., a demi-lion, rampant, ar., holding a laurel-branch, vert. *Pl.* 39, *cr.* 14, (branch, *pl.* 123, *cr.* 5.)
HARRISON, Eng., a demi-lion, ar., holding a (branch, vert.) *Pl.* 39, *cr.* 14.
HARRISON, Berks., out of a ducal coronet, a talbot's head, gold, guttée-de-poix. *Pl.* 99, *cr.* 7.
HARRISON, Iri., a cubit arm, in armour, in fess, in hand a scimitar, in pale, enfiled with a boar's head, couped, ppr. *Pl.* 85, *cr.* 12.
HARRISON, out of a ducal coronet, a demi-eagle, wings displayed, (in beak a columbine, ppr.) *Pl.* 9, *cr.* 6.
HARRISON, a griffin's head, erased. *Pl.* 48, *cr.* 6.
HARRISON, Lond., out of a crown, or, a plume of ostrich-feathers, or and sa. *Pl.* 44, *cr.* 12.
HARROLD, Eng., a hawk's lure, ppr. *Pl.* 97, *cr.* 14.
HARROLD, Iri., a gate, ppr. *Pl.* 73, *cr.* 4.
HARROW, Eng., a hand, vested, gu., cuffed, or, holding a baton, az. *Pl.* 18, *cr.* 1.
HARROWBY, Earl of, and Baron, Viscount Sandon, (Dudley-Rider,) out of a mural coronet,

or, a dragon's head, ar., (on neck an ermine-spot, sa.) *Servata fides cineri*. *Pl*. 101, *cr*. 4.

HARROWER, a garb, ppr. *Pl*. 48, *cr*. 10.

HARROWER, Sco., a garb, ppr. *Sedulo numen*. *Pl*. 48, *cr*. 10.

HARRUSE, a bull's head, gorged with a chaplet, ppr. *Pl*. 120, *cr*. 7, (chaplet, *pl*. 73, *cr*. 8.)

HARRY, an angel's head, (couped at breast,) ppr., vested, az., wings expanded. *Pl*. 94, *cr*. 11, (without laurel.)

HARRYSON, Eng., out of a ducal coronet, or, a bull's head. *Pl*. 68, *cr*. 6.

HARRYSON, a serpent, vert, entwined round a broken pillar, or. *Pl*. 112, *cr*. 2, (pillar, *pl*. 33, *cr*. 1.)

HARSNET, a dexter hand holding a sword, blade wavy, ppr. *Pl*. 71, *cr*. 7, (without cloud.)

HART, Iri., on a tower, a flaming heart, ppr. *Cœur fidele*. *Pl*. 12, *cr*. 5, (heart, *pl*. 68, *cr*. 13.)

HART, a hart's head, ppr. *Via una, cor unum*. *Pl*. 91, *cr*. 14.

HART, Linc., a stag's head, erased, in mouth a branch. *Pl*. 100, *cr*. 8.

HART, Iri., a camel, couchant, ppr. *Pl*. 70, *cr*. 2.

HART, Sco., a sun-dial, or, on a pedestal, gu. *Pl*. 97, *cr*. 6.

HART, Kent, a lion's head, (couped,) erm., ducally crowned, or. *Pl*. 90, *cr*. 4, (without charging.)

HART, Middx., a buck, passant, ppr. *Pl*. 68, *cr*. 2.

HARTAGAN, Iri., in hand, gauntleted, a sword, ppr. *Pl*. 125, *cr*. 5.

HARTCUP, a head, in profile, helmeted, between wings. *Pl*. 33, *cr*. 14, (wings, *pl*. 1, *cr*. 15.)

HARTE, or O'HART, Iri., in hand a sword. *Pl*. 21, *cr*. 10.

HARTE, Leic., a stag, ppr. *Pl*. 68, *cr*. 2.

HARTE, Eng., a hart, ppr. *Validus*. *Pl*. 55, *cr*. 13.

HARTE, Kent, a lion's head, erminois, murally crowned, gu. *Pl*. 123, *cr*. 13, (crown, *pl*. 128, *fig*. 18.)

HARTE, Middx. and Norf., a stag's head, (erased,) sa., attired, ar., in mouth a flower, of the last, stalked and leaved, vert. *Pl*. 100, *cr*. 8.

HARTFORD, Eng., a tent, ppr. *Pl*. 111, *cr*. 14.

HARTFORD, Eng., a parrot's head, gu., between wings, vert. *Pl*. 94, *cr*. 2.

HARTGRAVE, a demi-man, in armour, royally crowned, in (sinister,) a scimitar, all ppr. *Pl*. 27, *cr*. 11, (crown, *pl*. 127, *fig*. 2.)

HARTGULE, and HARTGULL, Eng., a buck's head, erased, sa., attired, or. *Pl*. 66, *cr*. 9.

HARTIGAN, an armed hand, erect, holding a sword, ppr. *Pl*. 125, *cr*. 5.

HARTLAND, Baron, (Maurice-Mahon,) Iri., an heraldic-tiger, statant, in dexter, a spear. *Periculum fortitudine evasi*. *Pl*. 119, *cr*. 9.

HARTLEY, Yorks., a stag, couchant, regardant, ar. *Pl*. 51, *cr*. 9, (without mount.)

HARTLEY, Sco., a demi-antelope, collared, sa. *Pl*. 34, *cr*. 8.

HARTLEY, Iri., a dexter arm, in armour, embowed, couped, ppr., in hand a club, sa., spiked, or. *Pl*. 45, *cr*. 10, (club, *pl*. 83, *cr*. 2.)

HARTLEY, Glouc. and Cumb., a martlet, sa., in mouth a cross crosslet, fitched, or. *Pl*. 111, *cr*. 5, (cross, *pl*. 84, *cr*. 10.)

HARTMAN, out of a ducal coronet, or, a demi-man, in armour, couped at thighs, ppr., garnished, or, visor open, brandishing a pole-axe, sa., between wings, each charged with a bend, wavy, thereon, between two decrescents, ar., three etoiles, pierced, sa. *Pl*. 58, *cr*. 2.

HARTMAN, out of a ducal coronet, or, a demi-man, in armour, couped at thighs, ppr., garnished, or, visor up, brandishing a pole-axe, gold, between wings, each charged with two decrescents, ar., and three etoiles, pierced, sa. *Pl*. 58, *cr*. 2.

HARTOP, Leic., out of a ducal coronet, or, a demi-pelican, wings addorsed, ar., vulning, gu. *Pl*. 19, *cr*. 9, (head, *pl*. 41, *cr*. 4.)

HARTOP, Leic., a pelican, or, vulning, gu. *Pl*. 109, *cr*. 15.

HARTOPP, CRADDOCK, Bart., Leic., out of a coronet, or, a pelican, ar., vulning, ppr. *Pl*. 64, *cr*. 1.

HARTOPP, out of a ducal coronet, a swan, wings expanded. *Pl*. 100, *cr*. 7, (without collar.)

HARTRIDGE, Kent and Surr., on a portcullis, sa., lined and studded, ar., a lion, passant, of the last. *Pl*. 13, *cr*. 13.

HARTSHORN, a wolf, passant, collared and lined, ppr. *Pl*. 5, *cr*. 8, (without staff.)

HARTSINK, a demi-lion, (between) paws, a ragged staff. *Pl*. 11, *cr*. 2.

HARTSTONGE, and HARTSTRONGE, Iri., a fleur-de-lis, or, entwined by a serpent, vert. *Pl*. 15, *cr*. 13.

HARTSTRONGE, Iri., a fleur-de-lis, or, entwined by a serpent, vert. *Pl*. 15, *cr*. 13.

HARTWELL, in a park, paled, or, a stag, lodged, ar. *Pl*. 13, *cr*. 12.

HARTWELL, Bart., Ess., on a mount, vert, surrounded with seven pales, the second and fifth charged with a spear-head, sanguinated, ar., a hart, lodged, the dexter foot on a well, of the last, in mouth a sprig of oak, vert. *Sorte suâ contentus*.

HARTWELL, on a mount, vert, paled, or, a hart, current, ppr., attired, of the second.

HARTWELL, Kent, Northumb., and Northamp., a beetle, passant, gu., wings addorsed, sa., horned, ar. *Pl*. 107, *cr*. 13.

HARTY, Iri., a demi-savage, wreathed round head and middle with laurel-leaves, and holding a club over shoulder, all ppr. *Pl*. 14, *cr*. 11.

HARTY, Bart., Iri., an eagle's head, wings expanded. *Malo mori quam fœdari*. *Pl*. 81, *cr*. 10.

HARTY, Kent, a falcon's head, erased, ppr., between wings, expanded, or. *Pl*. 99, *cr*. 10.

HARVEY, C. B., between an oak and a laurel-branch, a cubit arm, erect, ppr., in hand a trident, or, on the staff thereof, a flag, az., and thereon the word *Rosario*, gold.

HARVEY, of Thorpe, Norf., a dexter hand, apaumée, ppr., ensigned by a crescent, reversed, ar., within two branches of laurel, of the first. *Alteri, si tibi*. *Pl*. 68, *cr*. 5, (laurel, *pl*. 86, *cr*. 5.)

HARVEY, JOHN, Esq., of Bargy Castle, and Mount Pleasant, co. Wexford, a dexter arm, in armour, embowed, in hand a sword, ppr., pommel and hilt, or. *Pl*. 2, *cr*. 8.

HARVEY, a cubit arm, in hand a trefoil, ppr. *Pl*. 78, *cr*. 6.

HARVEY, Iri., two wings, in leure, ppr. *Pl*. 87, *cr*. 1.

HARVEY, a cubit arm, in hand a trefoil, ppr., issuant, from a crescent, or. *Pl.* 78, *cr.* 6, (crescent, *pl.* 18, *cr.* 14.)
HARVEY-BATESON, Bucks.: 1. A lion, passant, regardant, supporting with dexter a shield, ar., charged with a bat's wing, sa. *Pl.* 100, *cr.* 6, (shield, *pl.* 19, *cr.* 2; wing, *pl.* 1, *cr.* 6.) 2. A bat's wing, erect, sa. *Pl.* 1, *cr.* 6.
HARVEY, Middx., a leopard, passant, ar., spotted, sa., ducally collared and (chained,) or, on shoulder a trefoil, slipped, of the first. *Pl.* 120, *cr.* 9, (trefoil, *pl.* 141.)
HARVEY, Lond., a lion, passant, ppr., holding a trefoil, vert. *Pl.* 77, *cr.* 3, (trefoil, *pl.* 141.)
HARVEY, Kent, two bear's gambs, ermines, supporting a crescent, erminois. *Pl.* 62, *cr.* 3.
HARVEY, Admiral, G.C.B., Ess., a dexter hand, apaumée, ppr., over it a crescent, reversed, ar. *Temeraire.* *Pl.* 68, *cr.* 5.
HARVEY, PERCY-LORENZO, ESQ., of Kyle, Wexford, same crest. *Semper eadem.*
HARVEY, Lond. and Ess., a leopard, ar., ducally gorged and (lined,) or. *Pl.* 120, *cr.* 9.
HARVEY, Suff. and Devons., a leopard, sa., bezantée, collared and lined, or, in dexter a trefoil, slipped, vert. *Pl.* 120, *cr.* 9, (trefoil, *pl.* 141.)
HARVEY, Ess., Suss., Norf., and Northamp., a sheaf of trefoil, vert, banded, or. *Pl.* 69, *cr.* 4, (trefoil, *pl.* 141.)
HARVEY, Suff., a demi-leopard, sa., bezantée, in dexter a trefoil, vert. *Pl.* 97, *cr.* 5, (trefoil, *pl.* 141.)
HARVEY, Lond. and Ess., two arms, embowed, vested, az., holding up a garb, or.
HARVEY, Cambs. and Suff., a demi-leopard, ar., spotted, sa., holding an increscent, erm. *Pl.* 12, *cr.* 14, (increscent, *pl.* 141.)
HARVEY, Beds., a leopard's head, (couped,) gardant. *Pl.* 56, *cr.* 7.
HARVEY, Hants and Yorks., a leopard, passant, ppr. *Pl.* 86, *cr.* 2.
HARVEY, Yorks., a leopard, passant, ppr., (gorged with a collar, engrailed, gu.) *Pl.* 86, *cr.* 2.
HARVEY-HAWKE. *See* HAWKE, Baron.
HARVIE, Sco., a trefoil, vert. *Delectat et ornat.* *Pl.* 4, *cr.* 10, (without wings.)
HARVIE, Eng., a boar's head and neck, sa. *Pl.* 2, *cr.* 7.
HARVILL, Eng., a goat, (passant,) sa., attired, or. *Pl.* 66, *cr.* 1.
HARVY, Lond., a demi-(tiger,) sa., ducally gorged, or. *Pl.* 125, *cr.* 4.
HARVY, Norf. and Suff., a lion, couchant, gu. *Pl.* 75, *cr.* 5, (without chapeau.)
HARVY, Suff., a leopard, passant, ar., pellettée, (collared and lined, or,) in dexter a trefoil, slipped, vert. *Pl.* 86, *cr.* 2, (trefoil, *pl.* 141.)
HARVYE, Somers., a squirrel, sejant, ar., tail, or, cracking a nut, gold. *Pl.* 16, *cr.* 9.
HARWARD, Surr., a demi-stag, erm., ducally gorged and attired, gu. *Pl.* 55, *cr.* 9, (gorging, *same plate.*)
HARWINE, Lond., a hatchet, ppr. *Pl.* 14, *cr.* 8.
HARWOOD, out of a ducal coronet, or, a triple plume of twelve ostrich-feathers, three, four, and five. *Pl.* 114, *cr.* 8.
HARWOOD, an owl, ar. *Pl.* 27, *cr.* 9.
HASARD, Glouc., a bear's head and neck, sa., muzzled, or. *Pl.* 2, *cr.* 9.

HASE, Norf., a falcon, rising, erm., belled, ar., (charged on breast with an etoile of sixteen points, of the last, in centre an ermine-spot.) *Pl.* 105, *cr.* 4.
HASE, Eng., a falcon, volant, erm., belled, ar., charged on breast with an etoile, of the last. *Pl.* 94, *cr.* 1, (etoile, *pl.* 141.)
HASE, Herts., from a bush, a hare, (current,) all ppr. *Pl.* 29, *cr.* 1.
HASELDEN, Linc., a talbot's head, ar., charged with a mullet, gu. *Pl.* 123, *cr.* 15, (mullet, *pl.* 141.)
HASELDEN, Linc., a talbot's head, ar. *Pl.* 123, *cr.* 15.
HASELERTON, Eng., a sword, in pale, ensigned with a cross pattée, gu. *Pl.* 56, *cr.* 1.
HASELERTON, Eng., a flag, az., charged with a cross, ar. *Pl.* 8, *cr.* 3.
HASELEY, a leopard's face, or. *Pl.* 66, *cr.* 14.
HASELFOOT, or HASSELLFOOT, Lond. and Yorks., a demi-peacock, wings expanded, az., in beak a sneak, ppr., entwined round neck. *Pl.* 53, *cr.* 12.
HASE-LOMBE, two lances, in saltier, or, each charged with a small pennon, gu. *Pl.* 53, *cr.* 14.
HASELRIGGE, Leic., a woman's head, (couped below breasts), ppr., hair, or. *Pl.* 45, *cr.* 5.
HASELRIGGE, Leic., a demi-woman, ppr., crined, or. *Pl.* 2, *cr.* 10, (without branch.)
HASILRIGGE, Bart., Leic., on a chapeau, turned up, erm., a Scot's head, ppr. *Pro aris et focis.* *Pl.* 19, *cr.* 1, (chapeau, *pl.* 127, *fig.* 13.)
HASKELL, Eng., on a mount, an (apple)-tree, fructed, ppr. *Pl.* 48, *cr.* 4.
HASKINS, Surr., a lion's head, erased, ppr. *Pl.* 81, *cr.* 4.
HASKINS, Eng., two hands, issuing from clouds, conjoined, supporting a heart, inflamed, all ppr. *Pl.* 52, *cr.* 13.
HASLAM, Eng., a dragon's head, erased, ducally gorged and lined. *Pl.* 36, *cr.* 7.
HASLAM, Iri., a boar, passant, sa., gorged, with a laurel crown, or. *Pl.* 29, *cr.* 10.
HASLAM, Iri., on a mount, a lamb, couchant, against a hazel-tree, fructed, all ppr.
HASLATINE, a talbot's head, couped, ar. *Pl.* 123, *cr.* 15.
HASLEFOOTE, two wings, addorsed, erm. *Pl.* 63, *cr.* 12.
HASLEN, a squirrel, sejant, cracking a nut, ppr., collared, gemelle, az., between two branches of palm. *Qui nucleum vult, nucem frangat.* *Pl.* 85, *cr.* 3, (branches, *pl.* 87, *cr.* 8.)
HASLEWOOD, Eng., a squirrel, eating a nut, gu. *Pl.* 16, *cr.* 9.
HASLING, Kent, an ostrich, in mouth a broken tilting-spear. *Pl.* 64, *cr.* 3, (without coronet; spear, *pl.* 3, *cr.* 6.)
HASSAL, Chesh., an arm, embowed, vested, or, turned down at wrist, ar., in hand a dart, point downward, gold, feathered, of the second, barbed, sa. *Pl.* 96, *cr.* 6, (vesting, *pl.* 39, *cr.* 1.)
HASSALL, and HASSELL, a hand holding (three) arrows, points downward. *Pl.* 56, *cr.* 4.
HASSALL, and HASSELL, Eng., out of a ducal coronet, a hand, holding three arrows, points downward. *Pl.* 9, *cr.* 4.
HASSARD, Eng., an escallop, or. *Pl.* 117, *cr.* 4.

HASSARD, ALEXANDER-JASON, Esq., of Gardenhill, co. Fermanagh, an escallop, or. *Vive en espoir*—and—*Fortuna viam ducit. Pl.* 117, *cr.* 4.

HASSELL, Cumb., between two oak-branches, a squirrel, sejant, cracking a nut, all ppr. *Pl.* 16, *cr.* 9, (branches, *pl.* 74, *cr.* 7.)

HASSELL, a dexter arm, erect, vested, vert, cuffed, ar., in hand a branch of laurel, ppr. *Pl.* 63, *cr.* 1, (branch, *pl.* 123, *cr.* 5.)

HASSELLWOOD, Northamp., Oxon., and Worc., a squirrel, sejant,az.,collared,or,(charged with three bezants, in pale,) holding a nut-branch, ppr. *Pl.* 85, *cr.* 3, (branch, *pl.* 32, *cr.* 13.)

HAST, Norf., a stag's head, erased, gu., attired, ar., ducally gorged, or. *Pl.* 55, *cr.* 2.

HASTALINE, a talbot's head, couped, ar. *Pl.* 123, *cr.* 15.

HASTDAY, Kent, on a mount, vert, a hare, in grass, ppr. *Pl.* 29, *cr.* 1.

HASTED, Eng., a wheel, ppr. *Pl.* 32, *cr.* 15.

HASTEWOOD, Eng., a squirrel, sejant, az., (collared, ar.,) and charged on side with three bezants, in bend, holding a hazel-branch, vert, fructed, or. *Pl.* 2, *cr.* 4, (bezant, *pl.* 141.)

HASTIE, Sco., a palm branch, vert. *Pro patriâ. Pl.* 123, *cr.* 1.

HASTINGS, Iri., a dexter arm, couped and embowed, in hand a fire-ball, all ppr. *Pl.* 62, *cr.* 9.

HASTINGS, Earl of Huntingdon. See HUNTINGDON.

HASTINGS, Marquess of, Earl of Rawdon, and Viscount Loudoun, U.K. ; Baron Rawdon, G.B. ; Baron Hastings, Hungerford, &c., Eng. ; Earl of Moira, and Baron Rawdon, Iri. ; and a Bart., Eng., (Rawdon, Hastings) : 1. For *Hastings*, a bull's head, erased, sa., armed, ducally gorged, (and crowned,) or. *Pl.* 68, *cr.* 6. 2. For *Rawdon*, on a mural coronet, ar., a pheon, sa., and issuant therefrom a laurel-branch, ppr. *Et nos quoque tela sparsimus.*

HASTINGS, Leic., Dors., and Buck's, a bull's head, erased, sa., attired and ducally gorged, or. *Pl.* 68, *cr.* 6.

HASTINGS, Eng., a bull's head, erased, sa., attired, or, gorged with a ducal coronet, gold. *In veritate victoria. Pl.* 68, *cr.* 6.

HASTINGS, Eng., a bull's head, couped, or, armed, gu. *Pl.* 120, *cr.* 7.

HASTINGS, Eng., a mermaid, gu., mirror and comb, ppr., crined, or. *Pl.* 48, *cr.* 5.

HASTINGS, Northamp., a demi-panther, gardant, ppr., supporting a lozenge, or. *Pl.* 1, *cr.* 10, (lozenge, *pl.* 141.)

HASTINGS-ABNEY, Bart., Derbs., a buffalo's head, erased, erminois, armed and ducally gorged, ar. *In veritate victoria. Pl.* 57, *cr.* 7, (gorging, *same plate.*)

HASWELL, Eng., a talbot's head, erased, az., collared, erm. *Pl.* 2, *cr.* 15.

HATCH, Eng., a flag, in bend. *Pl.* 8, *cr.* 8.

HATCH, Iri., a demi-lion, rampant, or, armed and langued, gu., (charged on breast with a pile of shot,) ppr., holding a staff, ppr., with flag affixed, ar., charged with a (cross,) gu. *Fortis valore et armis. Pl.* 86, *cr.* 11, (without coronet.)

HATCH, Iri., out of a ducal coronet, a hand, holding three arrows, points downward. *Pl.* 9, *cr.* 4.

HATCH, Devons., a lion's head, cabossed, ar. *Pl.* 47, *cr.* 6.

HATCHER, Linc., an arm, embowed, vested, az., (charged with three bars, ar.,) in hand, ppr., a branch of olives, vert. *Pl.* 120, *cr.* 1, (branch, *pl.* 98, *cr.* 8.)

HATCHET, and HATCHETT, Eng., a thunderbolt. *Pl.* 110, *cr.* 3.

HATCHET, the blade of a hatchet, ppr. *Pl.* 16, *cr.* 3.

HATCLIFF, Eng., a lion, rampant, ar., guttée, sa. *Pl.* 67, *cr.* 5.

HATCLIFFE, Linc., a lion, passant, gu., (in dexter a cutlass, ar., hilt and pommel, or.) *Pl.* 48, *cr.* 8.

HATFIELD, Middx., an arm, erect, couped, below elbow, vested, sa., cuffed, ar., in hand, ppr., a cinquefoil, slipped, or. *Pl.* 78, *cr.* 6, (cinquefoil, *pl.* 141.)

HATELY, Sco., an otter's head, erased, sa. *Pl.* 126, *cr.* 14.

HATFIELD, and DE HATFIELD, Eng., on stump of tree, couped, sprouting new branches, an eagle, wings inverted and addorsed, all ppr. *Pl.* 1, *cr.* 11.

HATFIELD, Yorks., a buffalo's head, erased, or. *Pl.* 57, *cr.* 7.

HATFIELD, an ostrich-feather, enfiled with a ducal coronet. *Pl.* 8, *cr.* 9.

HATHAWAY, and HATHEWAY, Eng., a demi-lion, rampant, gu., in dexter a fleur-de-lis. *Pl.* 91, *cr.* 13.

HATHERTON, Baron, (Littleton,) a stag's head, cabossed, sa., attired, or, between attires a bugle-horn, of the second, hanging, and fastened by a bend, gu. *Ung Dieu et ung roy. Pl.* 115, *cr.* 1, (horn, *pl.* 48, *cr.* 12.)

HATHORN, Sco., a lion, rampant, gu., armed and langued, az., grasping a hawthorn-tree, fructed, in dexter a scimitar, ppr.

HATHWAY, Eng., a leopard, sejant, or, (collared, az.,) resting dexter on an escutcheon, sa., charged with the arms. *Pl.* 86, *cr.* 8, (without coronet ; escutcheon, *pl.* 42, *cr.* 8.)

HATLEY, Bucks., Cambs., and Hunts., out of a ducal coronet, an antelope's head, or, armed, tufted, and maned, sa., pierced through neck by a broken spear, gu. *Pl.* 79, *cr.* 9, (coronet, *same plate, cr.* 6.)

HATSELL, Middx., on a mount, a viper's head, both vert, in mouth a branch of rue, ppr. *Pl.* 95, *cr.* 12.

HATT, Ess., Berks., and Lond., a falcon's head, quarterly, ar. and gu., between wings, sa. *Pl.* 99, *cr.* 10.

HATTON, Northamp. and Cambs., a hind, passant, or. *Pl.* 20, *cr.* 14.

HATTON, a hawk, close, ar., in beak an ear of wheat, or. *Pl.* 94, *cr.* 7.

HATTON, Chesh., Cambs., Salop, and Glouc., a hind, trippant, or. *Pl.* 20, *cr.* 14.

HATTON, Lond., a demi-bear, rampant, sa. *Pl.* 104, *cr.* 10.

HATTON, Iri., a demi-griffin, ppr., winged, gu., between paws an esquire's helmet, or. *Pl.* 19, *cr.* 15.

HATWORTH, a hat, sa., charged with a cinquefoil, or. *Pl.* 39, *cr.* 3, (cinquefoil, *pl.* 141.)

HAUGH, Eng., a lion, rampant, per fess, or and az., in dexter a fleur-de-lis, gu. *Pl.* 87, *cr.* 6.

HAUGHTON, Chesh., a bull's head, couped, ar., (charged on neck with three bars, sa.) *Pl.* 120, *cr.* 7.
HAUGHTON, Eng., a pelican's head and neck, vulning, ppr. *Pl.* 41, *cr.* 4.
HAUGHTON, Lond., a bull's head, erased, ar., armed, sa. *Pl.* 19, *cr.* 3.
HAULE, Eng., out of a ducal coronet, gu., a triple plume of ostrich-feathers, or. *Pl.* 114, *cr.* 8.
HAULT, Kent, an ermine, passant, (ducally gorged,) or. *Pl.* 9, *cr.* 5.
HAULTON, Eng., a moon in full, ar. *Pl.* 43, *cr.* 8.
HAULTON, Eng., two hands conjoined. *Pl.* 1, *cr.* 2.
HAULTON, out of clouds, two hands conjoined, all ppr. *Pl.* 53, *cr.* 11.
HAUSSONVILLE, LORRAINE, a tortoise, sa., between two pennons, dexter, or, sinister, az. *Pl.* 12, *cr.* 13, (pennons, *pl.* 53, *cr.* 14.)
HAUSTON, Sco., a sand-glass, winged, ppr. *In time. Pl.* 32, *cr.* 11.
HAUTTEN, and HAUNTON, Oxon., between two sprigs of thistle, ar., stalked and leaved, vert, an ass's head, erased, ppr. *Pl.* 91, *cr.* 7, (thistle, *pl.* 108, *cr.* 7.)
HAVARD, Wel., a bull's head, cabossed, gu. *Pl.* 111, *cr.* 6.
HAVELAND, Eng., a dexter arm, in hand a garland of roses, ppr. *Pl.* 41, *cr.* 7.
HAVELAND, a tower. *Pl.* 12, *cr.* 5.
HAVELOCK, Durh., a lion, rampant, gu., guttée, erm., (charged on shoulder with a castle, ar., sustaining a Danish battle-axe,) ppr. *Pl.* 22, *cr.* 15.
HAVERGAL, Chesh., a greyhound, current, ensigned by an arrow in flight. *Scité citissimé, certé. Pl.* 28, *cr.* 7, (arrow, *pl.* 42, *cr.* 13.)
HAVERING, Eng., a lion, rampant, holding a spear, sa., flagged, gu. *Pl.* 99, *cr.* 2.
HAVERS, Lond. and Norf., a griffin, sejant, ar., beak and fore-legs, or, ducally collared and lined, of the last. *Pl.* 100, *cr.* 11, (collar, *same plate.*)
HAVERS, Lond. and Norf., a griffin, sejant, erm., ducally gorged and chained, gu. *Ib.*
HAVERS, Norf., a griffin, sejant, erm., (crowned and collared.) *Pl.* 100, *cr.* 11.
HAVERSHAM, on a ducal coronet, or, a mullet, sa. *Pl.* 82, *cr.* 6, (without branches.)
HAVILAND, Eng., a sword, in pale, on point a maunch, ppr. *Pl.* 78, *cr.* 1.
HAVILAND, Camb., a cubit arm, (in armour,) or, in hand a battle-axe, ppr. *Dominus fortissima turris. Pl.* 73, *cr.* 7.
HAVILLE, a bull's head, erased, sa. *Pl.* 19, *cr.* 3.
HAW, a poplar-tree, growing out of a mount, ppr. *Pl.* 95, *cr.* 2.
HAWARD, Kent, an arm, (vested, sa., turned up, or,) in hand, ppr., a human heart, gu. *Pl.* 59, *cr.* 12.
HAWARDEN, Viscount, Baron de Montalt, and a Bart., (Cornwallis-Maude,) Iri., a lion's gamb, erased and erect, grasping an oak-branch, ppr., acorned, or. *Virtute securus. Pl.* 60, *cr.* 14, (oak-branch, *pl.* 32, *cr.* 13.)
HAWBERKE, Eng., in hand, a dart, ppr. *Pl.* 43, *cr.* 13.
HAWDEN, Sco., a lion's head, erased, gu. *Ferio, teyo. Pl.* 81, *cr.* 4.

HAWE, Norf., a griffin's head, erased, erm., (collared) and lined, or. *Pl.* 69, *cr.* 13.
HAWES, Suff., Surr., and Lond., out of a mural coronet, az., a lion's head, or. *Pl.* 45, *cr.* 9.
HAWES, a greyhound's head, sa., ducally gorged and lined, or. *Pl.* 43, *cr.* 11, (gorging, *same plate.*)
HAWES, Lond., out of a ducal coronet, or, a stag's head, ppr., in mouth a sprig of (laurel,) vert. *Pl.* 100, *cr.* 8, (coronet, *same plate.*)
HAWES, Dors., a goat's head, sa., in mouth a holly-branch, vert. *Pl.* 105, *cr.* 14, (branch, *pl.* 99, *cr.* 6.)
HAWES, a buck's head, (erased,) ppr., attired, or, in mouth an oak-branch, vert, fructed, gu. *Pl.* 100, *cr.* 8.
HAWK, Eng., a hawk, belled, ppr. *Pl.* 67, *cr.* 3.
HAWKE, Baron, (Harvey-Hawke:) 1. For *Hawke,* a hawk, wings addorsed, erm., beaked, belled, and charged on breast with a fleur-de-lis, or. *Strike.* 2. For *Harvey,* a leopard, statant, ppr., (collared,) gu. *Pl.* 86, *cr.* 2.
HAWKE, a hawk, close, ppr. *Pl.* 67, *cr.* 3.
HAWKE, a falcon, rising, ppr., charged on breast with a fleur-de-lis, or. *Pl.* 105, *cr.* 4, (fleur-de-lis, *pl.* 141.)
HAWKENS, on a hawk's lure, a hawk, statant, (wings addorsed.) *Pl.* 10, *cr.* 7.
HAWKER, Eng., in dexter hand, ppr., a hawk's lure, or. *Pl.* 44, *cr.* 2.
HAWKER, Devons., on stump of tree, (in fess,) a hawk, ppr. *Pl.* 78, *cr.* 8.
HAWKER, Hants., a hawk's head, erased, or. *Accipiter prædam, nos gloriam. Pl.* 34, *cr.* 11.
HAWKES, Eng., a hind's head, erased. *Pl.* 6, *cr.* 1.
HAWKES, Iri., on a chapeau, ppr., an owl, wings expanded, ar. *Pl.* 123, *cr.* 6.
HAWKESFORD, Eng., a griffin, passant, sa. *Pl.* 61, *cr.* 14, (without gorging.)
HAWKESWORTH, and HAWKSWORTH, Eng., (a sinister hand, in fess, issuing from a cloud, in dexter,) and reaching to a serpent, ppr. *Pl.* 121, *cr.* 1.
HAWKEWOOD, a hawk's head, or. *Pl.* 34, *cr.* 11.
HAWKEWORTH, a cubit arm, erect, vested, or, cuffed, ar., in hand, ppr., a cross crosslet, gu. *Pl.* 75, *cr.* 3, (cross, *pl.* 141.)
HAWKEY, Eng., in hand, couped, a curling-stone. *Pl.* 104, *cr.* 6.
HAWKINGS, Eng., a lion's paw, gu., charged with a cheveron, or. *Pl.* 88, *cr.* 3.
HAWKINS, Sco., a falcon, jessed and belled, ppr. *Povidence with adventure. Pl.* 67, *cr.* 3.
HAWKINS, Wel., (on a mount, vert,) a hind, lodged, or. *Toujours pret. Pl.* 1, *cr.* 14, (without hive.)
HAWKINS, Bart., Somers., (on a mount, vert,) a hind, lodged, or. *Pl.* 1, *cr.* 14, (without hive.)
HAWKINS, Herefs. and Glouc., a falcon's head, chequy, ar. and sa., beaked, or, between wings, gu. *Pl.* 99, *cr.* 10.
HAWKINS, Ess. and Devons., a demi-naked man, ppr., (wreathed, ar. and az.,) hands extended, and manacled with a rope passing behind the back. *Pl.* 98, *cr.* 10.

HAWKINS, Cornw., a cubit arm, erect, vested, ar., (charged with two fleurs-de-lis, az., in hand, ppr., a baton, or, tipped, sa. *Pl.* 18, *cr.* 1, (fleur-de-lis, *pl.* 141.)
HAWKINS, Iri., out of a naval coronet, an antelope's head, ppr. *Pl.* 118, *cr.* 5.
HAWKINS, a demi-moor, manacled, ppr. *Pl.* 98, *cr.* 10.
HAWKINS, Berks., a demi-eagle, ar. *Pl.* 52, *cr.* 8.
HAWKINS, Devons., a demi-moor, manacled, ppr., with annulets on arms and ears, or. *Nil desperandum. Pl.* 98, *cr.* 10, (annulet, *pl.* 141.)
HAWKS, Eng., in the sea, a column, ppr. *Pl.* 14, *cr.* 3.
HAWKSHAW, a hawk's head. *Pl.* 34, *cr.* 11.
HAWKSLEY, Eng., a falcon, wings addorsed. *Pl.* 81, *cr.* 12.
HAWKSMORE, Notts., a hawk, preying on a moor-hen, all ppr. *Pl.* 61, *cr.* 7.
HAWKSWORTH, Eng., a hawk, rising. *Pl.* 105, *cr.* 4.
HAWKSWORTH, Eng., a sinister hand, in fess, out of a cloud, reaching to a serpent, ppr. *Pl.* 121, *cr.* 1.
HAWLE, Eng., out of a ducal coronet, or, a mullet, gu., between two laurel-branches, in orle, vert. *Pl.* 82, *cr.* 6.
HAWLES, Hants., a greyhound's head, sa., ducally gorged and lined, or. *Pl.* 43, *cr.* 11, (gorging, *same plate.*)
HAWLEY, WILLIAM-HENRY-TOOVEY, Esq., of West Green House, Hants., a winged thunderbolt, ppr. *Et suivez moy. Pl.* 110, *cr.* 3.
HAWLEY, Bart., Kent, a dexter arm, in armour, embowed, ppr., garnished, or, in hand a spear, in bend, sinister, point downward, also ppr. *Pl.* 44, *cr.* 9.
HAWLEY, Hants., a thunderbolt, ppr. *Pl.* 110, *cr.* 3.
HAWLEY, Eng., an etoile, of (sixteen) points, on a ducal coronet, or. *Pl.* 83, *cr.* 3.
HAWLEY, a falcon, wings addorsed, ppr. *Pl.* 81, *cr.* 12.
HAWLEY, a goat's head, in mouth a slip of oak, ppr. *Pl.* 105, *cr.* 14, (oak, *pl.* 32, *cr.* 13.)
HAWLEYS, Eng., an arm, embowed, throwing a dart, ppr. *Pl.* 96, *cr.* 6.
HAWLING, Eng., an arm, embowed, ppr., in hand a scimitar, ar., pommel, or. *Pl.* 92, *cr.* 5.
HAWORTH, EDMUND, Esq., Churchdale Hall, Derbs., a stag's head, couped, gorged with lozenges, in fess. *Quod ero spero. Pl.* 126 D, *cr.* 1.
HAWORTH, Eng., a wolf, passant, collared, in dexter a trefoil. *Pl.* 5, *cr.* 8, (trefoil, *pl.* 141.)
HAWS, and HAWSE, Eng., a sphinx, (statant, wings expanded.) *Pl.* 91, *cr.* 11.
HAWTHORN, or HAWTHORNE, Eng., a demi-antelope, ppr., collared, gu. *Pl.* 34, *cr.* 8.
HAWTHORN, Sco., in hand a star of (six) points. *Pl.* 62, *cr.* 13.
HAWTON, Lond., a bull's head, erased, ar., armed, sa. *Pl.* 19, *cr.* 3.
HAWTRE, Middx., a lion's head, erased, or, fretty, sa. *Pl.* 81, *cr.* 4.
HAXFORD, a lion, rampant, sustaining an arrow, point downward. *Pl.* 22, *cr.* 15.
HAXTON, Sco., a decrescent. *Resurgo. Pl.* 16, *cr.* 15.
HAY, Bart., of Park, Sco., the yoke of a plough, (in pale,) or, with two bows, gu. *Serva jugum. Pl.* 35, *cr.* 11.

HAY, Earl of Errol. *See* ERROL, Earl of.
HAY, Marquess of Tweeddale. *See* TWEEDDALE.
HAY, Bart., of Smithfield and Hayston, Sco., an ox-yoke, in bend, or, the bows, gu. *Pro patriâ. Pl.* 35, *cr.* 11.
HAY, WILLIAM, Esq., of Dunse Castle, Berwick, a goat's head, erased, ar. *Spare nought. Pl.* 29, *cr.* 13.
HAY, Earl of Kinnoul. *See* KINNOUL.
HAY, Iri., in dexter hand an (olive)-branch, ppr. *Pl.* 43, *cr.* 6.
HAY, Lond., in dexter hand, an ox-yoke, ppr. *Valet et vulnerat. Pl.* 83, *cr.* 14.
HAY, Lond., an ox-yoke, in bend, or. *Pro patriâ. Pl.* 35, *cr.* 11.
HAY, of Mordington, a goat's head, erased, ar., armed, or. *Spare nought. Pl.* 29, *cr.* 13.
HAY, of Spott, a goat's head, erased, ar., horned, or. *Spare nought. Pl.* 29, *cr.* 13.
HAY, of Woodcockdale, a demi-arm, ppr., in hand, an ox-yoke, with bows, gu. *Hinc incrementum. Pl.* 83, *cr.* 14.
HAY, of Balhousie, a demi-man, having a blue cap on his head, and holding over his shoulder the yoke of a plough, gu. *Renovato animo. Pl.* 122, *cr.* 1.
HAY, of Rannes, a goat, (passant,) ppr. *Spare nought. Pl.* 66, *cr.* 1.
HAY, of Cardenie, an ox-yoke, (in pale,) with bows, gu. *Hinc honor et opes. Pl.* 35, *cr.* 11.
HAY, of Linplum, a goat's head, erased, ar., horned, or, and charged with a crescent, az. *Malum bono vince. Pl.* 29, *cr.* 13, (crescent, *pl.* 141.)
HAY, of Drumelzier, a goat's head, erased, ar., armed, or. *Spare nought. Pl.* 29, *cr.* 13.
HAY, of Ranfield and Inchnock, a dexter arm, embowed, in hand an ox-yoke, ppr. *Pl.* 53, *cr.* 7.
HAY, of Newhall, a goat's head and neck, erased, ar., charged with a crescent. *Spare nought. Pl.* 29, *cr.* 13, (crescent, *pl.* 141.)
HAY, Iri., a falcon, ppr. *Pl.* 67, *cr.* 3.
HAY, Eng., the sun in splendour. *Pl.* 68, *cr.* 14.
HAY, in hand an annulet. *Pl.* 24, *cr.* 3.
HAY, Sco., an ox's head, couped, ppr. *Nec abest jugum. Pl.* 120, *cr.* 7.
HAY, Sco., a falcon, perched on stump of tree, sprouting a branch before and behind, in orle, ppr. *Speravi in Domino. Pl.* 78, *cr.* 8.
HAY, of Pitfour, Sco., in dexter hand an ox-yoke, between fingers three ears of wheat. *Diligentia fit ubertas. Pl.* 83, *cr.* 14, (wheat, *pl.* 63, *cr.* 1.)
HAY, JAMES, Esq., of Seggieden, Perth, Sco., a demi-husbandman, ppr., over shoulder an ox-yoke, or, bows, gu. *Diligentia fit ubertas. Pl.* 122, *cr.* 1.
HAY, Sco., the yoke of a plough, (in pale,) with two bows, gu. *Serva jugum sub jugo. Pl.* 35, *cr.* 11.
HAY, Sco., a plough, ppr. *Nil desperandum. Pl.* 28, *cr.* 15.
HAY, Sco., a demi-arm, hand holding aloft an ox-yoke, ppr. *Hoc vince. Pl.* 83, *cr.* 14.
HAY, Sco., a buck's head, cabossed, ppr. *Venture and gain. Pl.* 36, *cr.* 1.
HAY, Sco., an arm, from elbow, in hand an ox-yoke with bows, gu. *Laboranti palma. Pl.* 83, *cr.* 14.

HAY, Sco., an increscent, ppr. *Donec impleat orbem.* *Pl.* 122, *cr.* 15.
HAY, Sco., a falcon, volant, ppr., armed, jessed, and belled, or, (gorged with a label.) *Propter obedientiam.* *Pl.* 94, *cr.* 1.
HAY, Sco., a dove, wings expanded, ppr. *Serva jugum.* *Pl.* 27, *cr.* 5.
HAY, Sco., a goat, (passant,) ar., armed and unguled, or. *Spare nought.* *Pl.* 66, *cr.* 1.
HAY-DALRYMPLE, Bart., Sco., a falcon, ppr., charged on breast with an escutcheon. *Firme* —for Dalrymple. *Serva jugum*—for Hay. *Pl.* 96, *cr.* 10.
HAY-MACDOUGAL, Bart., Mackerston, a lion, passant, gardant, ppr., in dexter a cross crosslet, fitched, gu. *Dread God.* *Pl.* 120, *cr.* 5, (cross, *pl.* 141.)
HAYCOCK, Eng., on a ducal coronet, per pale, or and gu., a lion, passant, per pale, counterchanged. *Pl.* 107, *cr.* 11.
HAYDON, Norf., a talbot, ar., spotted, sa. *Pl.* 120, *cr.* 8.
HAYES, Bart., Iri., a dove, rising, ppr. *Pl.* 27, *cr.* 5.
HAYES, Bart., Lond., on a perch, ppr., a falcon, (wings addorsed,) or, pendent from the beak an escutcheon, gu., charged with a leopard's face, or. *Pl.* 10, *cr.* 7, (escutcheon, *pl.* 6, *cr.* 11.)
HAYES, a falcon, wings addorsed, ppr. *Pl.* 81, *cr.* 12, (without mount or gorging.)
HAYES, Lond., a wolf, passant, erminois. *Pl.* 46, *cr.* 6.
HAYES, Herts., a leopard's head. *Pl.* 92, *cr.* 13.
HAYES, a demi-lion, rampant, holding a flag. *Pl.* 86, *cr.* 11, (without coronet.)
HAYLES, Eng., in hand a torteau. *Pl.* 24, *cr.* 3.
HAYMAN, Eng., a scimitar and caduceus, in saltier, ensigned with a round hat. *Pl.* 17, *cr.* 13, (without head.)
HAYMAN, Iri., a demi-lion, rampant, sa., in dexter a fleur-de-lis. *Virtute non sanguine.* *Pl.* 91, *cr.* 13.
HAYMAN, co. Cork: 1. A demi-moor, affrontée, wreathed round temples, in dexter a rose, slipped and leaved, all ppr. *Pl.* 35; *cr.* 12, (rose, *pl.* 118, *cr.* 9.) 2. A martlet, sa. *Pl.* 111, *cr.* 5.
HAYNE, Dors., an eagle, wings displayed, or, seizing on a tortoise, all ppr. *Pl.* 70, *cr.* 8.
HAYNE, Devons., an eagle, wings displayed, or, charged on each wing with a plate, and the breast with a rose, ar., seizing on a tortoise, all ppr. *Pl.* 70, *cr.* 8, (plate and rose, *pl.* 141.)
HAYNES, Yorks., a stork, wings (displayed,) ppr., in mouth a snake, ar. *Pl.* 59, *cr.* 11.
HAYNES, Eng., an eagle, preying on a tortoise, *Pl.* 70, *cr.* 8.
HAYNES, Iri., a lion, sejant, or, collared, az. *Pl.* 21, *cr.* 3.
HAYNES, a (stork,) rising. *Pl.* 6, *cr.* 13.
HAYNES, a demi-hind, ar.
HAYNES, Eng., three moors' heads, conjoined in one neck, facing the dexter, sinister, and upward. *Pl.* 32, *cr.* 2.
HAYS, Eng., a monkey, passant, ppr., collared round loins, and chained, or. *Pl.* 101, *cr.* 11.
HAYTON, Heref., a cock, gu., combed, wattled, and legged, or, in beak a heart's ease, slipped, ppr. *Pl.* 55, *cr.* 12, (flower, *pl.* 30, *cr.* 1.)
HATTON, Eng., in hand a sickle. *Pl.* 36, *cr.* 12.

HAYWARD, Glouc., out of a mural coronet, or, a demi-lion, rampant, sa., in dexter a fleur-de-lis, gold. *Pl.* 17, *cr.* 7, (fleur-de-lis, *pl.* 141.)
HAYWARD, Surr., a talbot's head, ar., collared and ringed, sa. *Pl.* 2, *cr.* 15.
HAYWARD-CURTIS, JOHN, Esq., of Quedgeley House, Glouc., a demi-lion, rampant, sa., in dexter a fleur-de-lis. *Virtute non sanguine.* *Pl.* 91, *cr.* 13.
HAYWOOD, Eng., a tiger's head, ar., armed and maned, or, (pierced through the neck with a broken spear, sa., headed, of the first, vulned, gu.) *Pl.* 94, *cr.* 10.
HAYWOOD, Eng., on stump of a tree, a falcon, rising, ppr. *Pl.* 78, *cr.* 8.
HAZARD, Eng., on top of anchor, in the sea, a dove, in mouth an olive-branch, ppr. *Pl.* 3, *cr.* 10.
HAZEL, a dexter arm, vested, in hand an (olive)-slip. *Pl.* 43, *cr.* 6.
HAZLEWOOD, Eng., in hand a bunch of grapes, ppr. *Pl.* 37, *cr.* 4.
HEAD, Bart., Kent, a unicorn's head, couped, ermines. *Study quiet.* *Pl.* 20, *cr.* 1.
HEAD, Eng., a unicorn's head, ar. *Pl.* 20, *cr.* 1.
HEAD, Berks. and Lond., a unicorn's head, erased, ar. *Pl.* 67, *cr.* 1.
HEAD-BOND, Bart., Kent, out of an Eastern coronet, or, a plume of three ostrich-feathers, ar. *Pl.* 12, *cr.* 9, (coronet, *pl.* 128, *fig.* 2.)
HEADFORT, Marquess of, and Viscount, Earl Bective, Iri., and a Bart.; Baron Kenlis, U.K., (Taylor); a naked arm, embowed, in hand an arrow, ppr. *Consequitur quodcunque petit.* *Pl.* 92, *cr.* 14.
HEADON, Herts. and Linc., a talbot, passant, or, spotted, sa. *Pl.* 120, *cr.* 8.
HEADLEY, Baron, Iri., (Allanson-Winn,) and a Bart., Eng.: 1. For *Winn*, a demi-eagle, displayed, or. *Pl.* 22, *cr.* 11. 2. For *Allanson*, a demi-lion, rampant, gardant, or, in dexter a cross, gu. *Virtute et labore.* *Pl.* 119, *cr.* 3.
HEADLEY, Hunts., a martlet, or. *Pl.* 111, *cr.* 5.
HEADLEY, on a sphere, a martlet, (wings expanded.) *Pl.* 34, *cr.* 2, (martlet, *pl.* 111, *cr.* 5.)
HEALD, Eng., a sword and key, in saltier, ppr. *Pl.* 54, *cr.* 12.
HEALEY, and HEALY, Eng., on a chapeau, a lion, statant, gardant, ducally gorged. *Pl.* 7, *cr.* 14.
HEALY, Iri., in hand, couped at wrist, a buck's horn. *Pl.* 5, *cr.* 3.
HEALY, Iri., a physician's quadrangular cap. *Pl.* 39, *cr.* 3.
HEAPS, Eng., a cross crosslet, fitched, between two branches of palm, in orle, ppr. *Pl.* 37, *cr.* 14, (palm, *pl.* 87, *cr.* 8.)
HEARD, Somers., a swan, wings elevated, ar., beaked and membered, sa., charged on breast with a rose, gu., barbed and seeded, ppr., ducally crowned, collared and chained, or. *Naufragus in portum.* *Pl.* 111, *cr.* 10.
HEARD, a demi-antelope, collared. *Pl.* 34, *cr.* 8.
HEARLE, Eng., in hand a crosier, in bend sinister. *Pl.* 17, *cr.* 12.
HEARN, and HEARNE, Eng., on a mount, vert, a horse, at full speed, saddled and bridled, ppr. *Pl.* 57, *cr.* 9.
HEARN, Iri., a greyhound, sejant, sa. *Pl.* 66, *cr.* 15.

HEARNE, Iri., a rose-branch, and a spear, in saltier, ppr. *Pl.* 104, *cr.* 7.
HEART, Eng., a leopard, spotted, ppr., passant, gardant. *Pl.* 51, *cr.* 7.
HEART, Sco., in dexter hand, erect, a couteau sword. *Fide et amore. Pl.* 29, *cr.* 8.
HEATH, Norf., Middx., and Durh., a cock's head, erased, or, wattled and combed, gu. *Pl.* 92, *cr.* 3.
HEATH, Middx., a pheasant, ppr. *Pl.* 82, *cr.* 12, (without collar.)
HEATH, a parrot's head, erased, in beak a mullet of five points. *Pl.* 13, *cr.* 15.
HEATH, a tower, in flames. *Pl.* 118, *cr.* 15.
HEATHCOTE, Bart., Ruts., on a mural coronet, az., a pommée, (charged with a cross, or,) between wings, erm. *Deus prosperat justos. Pl.* 2, *cr.* 3, (coronet, *pl.* 128, *fig.* 18.)
HEATHER, Eng., in a lion's paw, sa., a heart, gu. *Pl.* 23, *cr.* 13.
HEATHFIELD, Devons., a greyhound's head, ar., collared, gu. *Pl.* 43, *cr.* 11.
HEATHFIELD, an arm, embowed, ppr., vested and cuffed, vert, in hand a sword, of the first. *Pl.* 120, *cr.* 1.
HEATHFIELD, a garb, or, banded, gu. *Pl.* 48, *cr.* 10.
HEATHORN, Glouc., on a mount, vert, a hawthorn-tree, ppr., pendent therefrom by a ribbon, gu., an escutcheon, az., (charged with a pigeon's head, erased, or.) *Pl.* 75, *cr.* 2.
HEATON, JOHN-RICHARD, Esq., of Plas, Heaton, Denbigh, a buck's head, ar. *Er cordiad y cœra. Pl.* 91, *cr.* 14.
HEATON, a buck's head, cabossed, ar. *Pl.* 36, *cr.* 1.
HEATON, a nag's head, erased, ar. *Pl.* 81, *cr.* 6.
HEBBES, Sco., a lion's head, or, on the neck three roses, sa. *Pl.* 126, *cr.* 1, (rose, *pl.* 141.)
HEBDEN, Eng., a triton, in (dexter) hand a trident, ppr. *Pl.* 35, *cr.* 10.
HEBDEN, (from out of a cave,) a lion, passant, ppr. *Pl.* 48, *cr.* 8.
HEBER, Eng., in lion's gamb, a palm-branch, ppr. *Pl.* 70, *cr.* 9.
HEBER, out of a five-leaved ducal coronet, a female's head, in (profile,) hair dishevelled. *Pl.* 74, *cr.* 5.
HEBERT, Eng., a fish, naiant, ppr. *Pl.* 85, *cr.* 7.
HECTOR, Eng., out of a mural coronet, ar., masoned, sa., a demi-lion, az., in dexter a palm-branch, vert. *Pl.* 17, *cr.* 7.
HEDDLE, a leopard's head, erased. *Virtute et labore. Pl.* 94, *cr.* 10.
HEDDLE, JOHN-GEORGE, Esq., of Melsetter and Hoy, Orkney, a leopard's head, erased. *Virtute et labore. Pl.* 94, *cr.* 10.
HEDGES, Eng., a pomegranate, or, stalked and leaved, vert. *Pl.* 67, *cr.* 8.
HEDLEY, Hunts., a martlet, or. *Pl.* 111, *cr.* 5.
HEEGNIE, Sco., a dove, seated on a rock, in beak a twig of olive, ppr. *Firmé dum fidé. Pl.* 85, *cr.* 14.
HEELEY, and HEELY, Eng., in dexter hand a scimitar, ppr. *Pl.* 29, *cr.* 8.
HEELY, a cockatrice, wattled. *Res, non verbum. Pl.* 63, *cr.* 15.
HEFFERMAN, Iri., in gauntlet a (broken) sword. *Pl.* 125, *cr.* 5.
HEIGHAM, Eng., an escallop, or, charged with a mullet, gu. *Pl.* 109, *cr.* 14.
HEIGHAM, a horse's head, erased, ar. *Pl.* 81, *cr.* 6.

HEIGHAM, JOHN-HENRY, Esq., of Hanston, Suff., a horse's head and neck, erased, ar. *Pl.* 81, *cr.* 6.
HEIGHINGTON, Durh., a demi-(wolf,) erased, erminois, supporting between paws a cross crosslet, fitched, az. *Pl.* 56, *cr.* 9, (cross, *pl.* 141.)
HEIGHINGTON, Durh., a demi-boar, erased, erm., holding a cross crosslet, fitched. *Pl.* 20, *cr.* 5, (cross, *pl.* 141.)
HEISHAM, Eng., a lion, rampant, in dexter a battle-axe, all ppr. *Pl.* 64, *cr.* 2, (axe, *pl.* 104, *cr.* 14.)
HELARD, Eng., a demi-Hercules, ppr. *Pl.* 49, *cr.* 11.
HELIAS, Eng., a leg, in armour, couped at thigh, the knee bent, garnished and spurred. *Pl.* 81, *cr.* 5.
HELLARD, Eng., a demi-Hercules, ppr. *Pl.* 49, *cr.* 11.
HELLEN, Iri., a dolphin, haurient, between wings, ppr. *Pl.* 111, *cr.* 12.
HELLER, Cornw., a Cornish chough, erm. *Pl.* 100, *cr.* 13.
HELLIER, Eng., a cock, ar., guttée-de-sang, combed and wattled, gu. *Pro republicâ semper. Pl.* 67, *cr.* 14.
HELLIS, Eng., in hand an ear of wheat, ppr. *Pl.* 71, *cr.* 15.
HELLY, and HELEY, Eng., an arm, in armour, in hand a broken spear, ppr. *Pl.* 44, *cr.* 9.
HELLORD, Devons., an escarbuncle, ar. *Pl.* 51, *cr.* 10.
HELME, Worc., a pheon. *Pl.* 26, *cr.* 12.
HELWISH, Eng., a lion, sejant, holding a (lance, in pale,) ppr. *Pl.* 60, *cr.* 4.
HELYAR, Somers. and Wilts., a cock, sa., beaked, combed, and wattled, gu., under a cross fleury, fitched. *In labore quies. Pl.* 67, *cr.* 14, (cross, *pl.* 65, *cr.* 9.)
HELYARD, Eng., a cock, sa., combed and wattled, gu. *Pl.* 67, *cr.* 14.
HEMANS, Wel., a lion, passant, gardant. *Verité sans peur. Pl.* 120, *cr.* 5.
HEMENHALL, Eng., a stag's head, erased. *Pl.* 66, *cr.* 9.
HEMING, and HEMMING, Eng., on a chapeau a lion, statant, gardant, collared, and crowned with a ducal coronet. *Pl.* 105, *cr.* 5.
HEMINGTON, HEMINGTONE, and HEMMINGTON, Eng., in hand a sealed letter, ppr. *Pl.* 33, *cr.* 8, (without cloud.)
HEMMING, Worc., an eagle, wings expanded, ar., charged on breast with a pheon, sa., supporting with dexter an escutcheon, erm., thereon a pale, ar., charged with (three) leopards' faces, or. *Pl.* 118, *cr.* 1, (escutcheon, *pl.* 6, *cr.* 11; pheon, *pl.* 141.)
HEMMINGS, out of a ducal coronet, a demi-lion, rampant. *Pl.* 45, *cr.* 7.
HEMPGRAVE, Eng., a young woman's head, affrontée, ppr., couped below breast, vested, az. *Pl.* 74, *cr.* 5, (without coronet.)
HEMSLEY, Eng., on a chapeau, a lion, statant, gorged with a ducal coronet. *Pl.* 7, *cr.* 14.
HEMSTEAD, or HEMSTED, Eng., top of a halberd, issuing. *Pl.* 16, *cr.* 3.
HEMSWORTH, a dexter arm, in armour, embowed, in hand a sword, ppr., hilt and pommel, or, transfixing a leopard's face, sa.
HENCHMAN, Eng., a buffalo's head, erased, gu. *Pl.* 57, *cr.* 7.

HENCKILL, out of a ducal coronet, or, an elephant's proboscis, contrary, embowed. *Pl.* 24, *cr.* 8, (coronet, *same plate, cr.* 10.)
HENDE, Eng., a lion's head, erased, ar. *Pl.* 81, *cr.* 4.
HENDEN, Eng., a greyhound, running against a tree, ppr. *Pl.* 27, *cr.* 2.
HENDER, a sword, wavy, in pale, the blade in flames. *Pl.* 58, *cr.* 11.
HENDERSON, Bart., Sco., in dexter hand, ppr., a star, or, surmounted by a crescent, ar. *Sola virtus nobilitat. Pl.* 17, *cr.* 10.
HENDERSON, Sco., a wheel. *Sic cuncta nobilitat. Pl.* 32, *cr.* 15.
HENDERSON, Stirling, a tilter at the ring. *Practise no fraud. Pl.* 43, *cr.* 2.
HENDERSON, Eng., under a tree, a boar, passant. *Pl.* 57, *cr.* 12.
HENDERSON, Sco., in hand, ppr., a (star,) az. *Virtus nobilitat. Pl.* 62, *cr.* 13.
HENDERSON, in hand, a mullet, surmounted by a crescent. *Sola virtus nobilitat. Pl.* 17, *cr.* 10.
HENDERSON, Sco., an arm, embowed, in hand a mullet, surmounted by a crescent. *Pl.* 88, *cr.* 5, (mullet, *pl.* 17, *cr.* 10.)
HENDEY, Eng., the stump of a holly-bush, shooting out new leaves, ppr. *Pl.* 25, *cr.* 9.
HENDLEY, Kent, a martlet, wings addorsed, or. *Pl.* 107, *cr.* 6, (without tower.)
HENDLEY, Iri., a demi-woman, ppr., attired, az., garnished, or, in dexter a garland, ppr. *Pl.* 87, *cr.* 14.
HENDLEY, Eng., a martlet, rising, or. *Pl.* 107, *cr.* 6, (without tower.)
HENDLY, a column, entwined with woodbine, ppr. *Pl.* 14, *cr.* 15.
HENDMARSH, Eng., an oak-tree, ppr., pendent thereon an escutcheon, gu. *Pl.* 23, *cr.* 6.
HENDRIE, and HENDRY, Eng., a demi-cupid, in dexter a torch, ppr. *Pl.* 70, *cr.* 14.
HENDRY, Eng., a pelican, vulning. *Pl.* 109, *cr.* 15.
HENDRY, a buck's head. *Pl.* 91, *cr.* 14.
HENDY, Eng., the stump of a holly-bush shooting forth new leaves, ppr. *Pl.* 25, *cr.* 9.
HENE, Eng., a demi-lion, rampant, gardant, holding a battle-axe. *Pl.* 26, *cr.* 7.
HENEAGE, Linc., a greyhound, current, sa. *Pl.* 28, *cr.* 7, (without charge.)
HENEAGE, Linc., a greyhound, current, sa. *Toujours ferme. Pl.* 28, *cr.* 7, (without charge.)
HENGHAM, Eng., among clouds, a globe, ppr. *Pl.* 110, *cr.* 9.
HENGRAVE, out of a mural coronet, a leopard's head, ducally gorged. *Pl.* 46, *cr.* 11.
HENGSCOT, Eng., a stag's head, erased and attired, or, (charged on neck with two nails, in saltier, sa., between four pellets.) *Pl.* 66, *cr.* 9.
HENINGHAM, Staffs. and Suff., a savage's head, in profile, ppr., vested round shoulders, gu., on head a cap, or, turned up, erm., and charged with three guttes, of the second. *Pl.* 51, *cr.* 4.
HENLEY, Kent and Surr., a martlet, wings addorsed, or. *Pl.* 107, *cr.* 6, (without tower.)
HENLEY, Eng., a horse's foot, couped, ppr. *Pl.* 17, *cr.* 6.
HENLEY, Hants, a lion's head, erased, ar., torteauxée, az., ducally crowned, or. *Pl.* 90, *cr.* 4.

HENLEY, Oxford, an eagle, wings displayed, or, in dexter an anchor and cable, sa., in beak a trefoil, ppr. *Perseverando. Pl.* 107, *cr.* 4, (anchor, *pl.* 42, *cr.* 12; trefoil, *pl.* 141.)
HENLEY, Baron, (Henley,) Iri., a dexter arm, in armour, couped at shoulder, ppr., (charged above elbow with an annulet, gu., and below with a ribbon, of the same,) in hand a garb, or, banded, vert. *Si sit prudentiâ. Pl.* 21, *cr.* 4, (garb, *pl.* 3, *cr.* 3.)
HENLOCK, Eng., a demi-lion, rampant, gu., maned and armed, or, holding a mullet, az. *Pl.* 89, *cr.* 10.
HENLY, a falcon, wings expanded. *Pl.* 105, *cr.* 4.
HENLY, Eng., a falcon, rising, ppr. *Pl.* 105, *cr.* 4.
HENN, on a mount, vert, a hen-pheasant, ppr. *Gloria Deo.*
HENNADGE, or HENNAGE, Linc. and Ess., a greyhound, current, sa. *Pl.* 28, *cr.* 7, (without charge.)
HENNE, Eng., a demi-lion, rampant, gardant, holding a battle-axe. *Pl.* 26, *cr.* 7.
HENNIDGE, Eng., an eagle's head, erased, ppr. *Deo Duce. Pl.* 20, *cr.* 7.
HENNIKER, Baron, (Henniker-Major,) Iri., and Bart., Eng.: 1. For *Henniker*, an escallop, or, charged with an etoile, gu. *Pl.* 109, *cr.* 14, (etoile, *pl.* 141.) 2. For *Major*, a dexter arm, embowed, vested, gu., cuffed, ar., (charged on elbow, with a plate,) in hand, ppr., a baton, or. *Deus major columna. Pl.* 120, *cr.* 1, (baton, *pl.* 18, *cr.* 1.)
HENNING, Dors., a sea-horse, ar., in paws a plate. *Pl.* 103, *cr.* 3, (plate, *pl.* 141.)
HENRAGHTY, Iri., a dolphin, naiant. *Pl.* 48, *cr.* 9.
HENRIE, Sco., a pelican's head, erased, vulning, ppr. *Fideliter. Pl.* 26, *cr.* 1.
HENRIESON, Sco., in hand a mullet of six points, ensigned on the top with a crescent, all ppr. *Virtus sola nobilitat. Pl.* 17, *cr.* 10.
HENRY, Eng., on a chapeau, gu., turned up, erm., a lion's head, erased, sa., langued, gu. *Pl.* 99, *cr.* 9.
HENRY, Derbs., a dexter arm, in armour, embowed, in hand a scimitar, ppr. *Pl.* 81, *cr.* 12.
HENSHALL, Eng., out of a ducal coronet, or, in hand, vested, ar., cuffed, gu., the sun. *Pl.* 89, *cr.* 11.
HENSHALL, Iri., a cross pattée, az., between wings, or. *Pl.* 29, *cr.* 14.
HENSLEY, Eng., a beech-tree, ppr. *Pl.* 18, *cr.* 10.
HENSLOW, Eng., an eagle, wings expanded, supporting a standard, ppr., flag, gu. *Pl.* 118, *cr.* 1, (standard, *same plate, cr.* 8.)
HENSLOWE, Hants., a cockatrice's head, erased, ppr., enammelled emerald, beaked, combed, and wattled, gu., charged on neck with a trefoil, ar. *Pl.* 76, *cr.* 9, (trefoil, *pl.* 141.)
HENSON, Eng., a holy lamb, (regardant, ar., glory, or,) standard, gu. *Pl.* 48, *cr.* 13.
HENVILL, Eng., a griffin's head, between wings. *Virtus et nobilitas. Pl.* 65, *cr.* 1.
HEPBURN, Sco., a mort head, (overgrown with moss, ppr.) *Virtute et prudentiâ. Pl.* 62, *cr.* 12.
HEPBURN, of Blackcastle, Sco., a horse's head, couped, ppr., garnished, gu. *I keep tryst—* or—*Prudentiâ et virtute. Pl.* 92, *cr.* 1.
HEPBURN, Eng., a rose, surmounted by a thistle, ppr. *Pl.* 73, *cr.* 6.

HEPBURN, Sir JOHN BUCHAN, Bart., Sco.: 1. For *Hepburn*, a horse, ar., furnished, gu., tied to a yew-tree, ppr. *Keep traist*. Pl. 99, cr. 11, (tree, pl. 49, cr. 13.) 2. For *Buchan*, the sun shining on a sun-flower, in full bloom, all ppr. *Non inferiora secutus*. Pl. 45, cr. 13, (sun-flower, pl. 84, cr. 6.)

HEPBURN, of Keith, Sco., an anchor, in pale, ppr. *Expecto*. Pl. 42, cr. 12.

HEPPELL, Northumb., a ship of war, in full sail, ppr. Pl. 109, cr. 8.

HEPWORTH, Eng., out of a mural coronet, a demi-lion, rampant, holding a palm-branch, all ppr. Pl. 17, cr. 7.

HEPWORTH, WILLIAM, Esq., of Ackworth Lodge, Pontefract, Yorks., out of a ducal coronet, or, a wyvern, vert. *Loyal à mort*. Pl. 104, cr. 11.

HERAPATH, Bristol, a demi-lion, or, between paws an (arrow-head,) az. Pl. 47, cr. 4.

HERBERT, Salop, a wyvern, wings addorsed, vert, in mouth a sinister hand, couped, gu. Pl. 61, cr. 8.

HERBERT, Eng., a black-a-moor's head, couped, sa., wreathed and tied, or and gu. Pl. 48, cr. 7.

HERBERT, Iri., in dexter hand an eel, ppr. Pl. 91, cr. 6, (eel, pl. 25, cr. 13.)

HERBERT, Earl of Pembroke. See PEMBROKE.

HERBERT, Earl of Carnarvon. See CARNARVON.

HERBORT, six arrows, in saltier, and one in pale, banded. Pl. 110, cr. 11.

HERBOT, Eng., six arrows, in saltier, and one in pale. Pl. 110, cr. 11.

HERCY, out of a ducal coronet, or, a man's head, ppr., wreathed. Pl. 36, cr. 3, (coronet, same plate.)

HEREFORD, Viscount, and a Bart., (Devereux,) out of a ducal coronet, or, a talbot's head, ar. *Virtutis comes invidia*—and—*Basis virtutum constantia*. Pl. 99, cr. 7.

HEREFORD, Eng., an arm, from elbow, ppr., in hand an annulet, or. Pl. 24, cr. 3.

HEREFORD, an eagle, displayed. Pl. 48, cr. 11.

HEREFORD, RICHARD, Esq., of Sufton Court, Hereford, an eagle, displayed. Pl. 48, cr. 11.

HERIET, Eng., a hind's head, couped, or. Pl. 21, cr. 9.

HERIN, Sco., a demi-lion, rampant. *By valour*. Pl. 67, cr. 10.

HERINGS, Eng., a bull's head, sa., ducally gorged and (crowned,) or. Pl. 68, cr. 6.

HERIOT, Sco., in dexter hand a wreath of laurel, all ppr. *Fortem posce animum*. Pl. 86, cr. 1.

HERIS, Eng., (on a mount, vert,) a crane, in dexter a stone, ppr. Pl. 26, cr. 11.

HERITAGE, Eng., a bear's head muzzled, and parted, per cheveron, ar. and sa., between wings, parted per fess, of the last and first. Pl. 44, cr. 5.

HERIZ, Eng., a demi-female, richly attired, between two laurel-branches, in dexter a rose-branch, all ppr. Pl. 17, cr. 11.

HERLE, Cornw., a lion, passant. Pl. 48, cr. 8.

HERMAN, under a palm-tree, a lion, couchant, gardant. Pl. 101, cr. 8, (tree, pl. 18, cr. 12.)

HERMON, a cubit arm, vested and cuffed, in hand a dagger. Pl. 101, cr. 10, (vesting, same plate.)

HERNS, Sco., a buck's head, or, attired with ten tynes. *Dominus dedit*. Pl. 91, cr. 14.

HERON, a heron, ppr. Pl. 6, cr. 13.

HERON, Bart., Notts., out of a ducal coronet, or, a heron's head, ppr. *Ardua petit ardea*. Pl. 20, cr. 9, (coronet, pl. 36, cr. 13.)

HERON, Sco., a demi-lion, ar. *By valour*. Pl. 67, cr. 10.

HERON, Iri., a dove, volant, in beak an olive-branch, ppr. Pl. 25, cr. 6.

HERON, out of a ducal coronet, a heron's head. Pl. 41, cr. 6, (coronet, same plate, cr. 10.)

HERRICK, Leic., a (bull's head,) couped, ar., horned and eared, sa., gorged with a chaplet of roses, ppr. *Virtus omnia nobilitat*. Pl. 73, cr. 8.

HERRIES, Eng., a cinquefoil, erm. Pl. 91, cr. 12.

HERRIES, Sco., a stag's head, or. *Dominus dedit*. Pl. 91, cr. 14.

HERRING, Eng., a boar's head, couped, in fess, pierced through snout by (four) arrows, ppr. Pl. 8, cr. 14.

HERRING, Sco., a boar's head, couped, sa. Pl. 48, cr. 2.

HERRING, Norf., a lion, passant, ppr., in dexter a trefoil, vert. Pl. 48, cr. 2, (trefoil, pl. 141.)

HERRINGTON, Eng., a horse's head, furnished, ppr. Pl. 49, cr. 6.

HERRIOT, and HERRIOTT, Eng., in a lion's gamb, erect, sa., a crescent, ar. Pl. 91, cr. 1.

HERSAY, Eng., a hedgehog, ppr. Pl. 32, cr. 9.

HERSCHEL, Bart., on a demi-terrestrial sphere, ppr., an eagle, wings elevated, or. *Cœlis exploratis*. Pl. 34, cr. 2.

HERTFORD, Marquess and Earl of, Earl of Yarmouth, Viscount Beauchamp, and Baron Conway, G.B.; Baron Conway, Iri., K.G., &c., (Ingram-Seymour Conway): 1. For *Conway*, a moor's head, in profile, couped, ppr., wreathed, ar. and az. Pl. 36, cr. 3. 2. For *Seymour*, out of a ducal coronet, or, a phœnix in flames, ppr. *Fide et amore*. Pl. 53, cr. 6.

HERTFORD, Eng., a parrot's head, gu., between wings, vert. Pl. 94, cr. 2.

HERTINGTON, Eng., a stag's head, or, (collared,) between attires, a cross pattée. Pl. 9, cr. 10.

HERTOG, Eng., out of a ducal coronet, or, two wings, addorsed, az. Pl. 17, cr. 9.

HERVEY, Iri., a mountain-cat, ppr., in dexter a trefoil, slipped, vert. *Ge n'oublierai jamais*. Pl. 119, cr. 7, (trefoil, pl. 141.)

HERVEY, Cornw. and Somers., a squirrel, sejant, ar., tail, or, cracking nuts, ppr. Pl. 2, cr. 4.

HERVEY, Iri., a lion, rampant, erm., supporting a plumb-rule, ppr. Pl. 50, cr. 8.

HERVEY, and HERVY, Eng., a leopard, passant, sa., bezantée. Pl. 86, cr. 2.

HERVEY, a trefoil, slipped. *Delectat et ornat*. Pl. 4, cr. 10, (without wings.)

HERVEY-BATHURST, Bart., Hants.: 1. For *Hervey*, a leopard, sa., bezantée, (collared and lined, or,) in dexter a trefoil, slipped, vert. Pl. 86, cr. 2, (trefoil, pl. 141.) 2. For *Bathurst*, a dexter arm, embowed, in mail, in hand, ppr., a spiked club, or. Pl. 28, cr. 2.

HERVY, Eng., an ox-yoke, in bend, gu., bows, or. Pl. 35, cr. 11.

HERWORTH, Devons., a cubit arm, erect, ppr., in hand a snake. Pl. 91, cr. 6.

HESDING, Eng., in dexter hand a pistol, ppr. *Pl.* 101, *cr.* 12.
HESELRIDGE, Eng., a man's head, couped at neck, ppr. *Pl.* 81, *cr.* 15.
HESELRIGGE, Eng., on a chapeau, ppr., an escallop, between wings. *Pl.* 17, *cr.* 14.
HESELTINE, Eng., a swan, wings addorsed, ar., crowned with an antique crown, or. *Pl.* 33, *cr.* 7.
HESELTINE, a talbot's head, erased, between wings. *Pl.* 90, *cr.* 6, (wings,*pl.* 1, *cr.* 15.)
HESILL, Eng., on a chapeau, gu., turned up, ar., a flame, ppr. *Pl.* 71, *cr.* 11.
HESILRIGGE, Bart., Leic., on a chapeau, gu., turned up, erm., a man's head, in profile, couped at shoulders, ppr. *Pro aris et focis.* *Pl.* 81, *cr.* 15, (chapeau, *pl.* 127, *fig.* 13.)
HESKETH, Bart., Lanc., a wheat-sheaf, ppr. *Pl.* 48, *cr.* 10.
HESKETH, Eng., a mortar, mounted, ppr. *Pl.* 55, *cr.* 14.
HESKETH, and HESKETT, Eng., a garb, or. *Pl.* 48, *cr.* 10.
HESLOP, Eng., in hand a mill-rind, ppr. *Pl.* 34, *cr.* 3.
HESSE, Middx., on a chapeau, ppr., a cockatrice, vert, ducally crowned, combed, beaked, and wattled, or, charged on breast with the sun, gold. *Supera audi et tace.* *Pl.* 103, *cr.* 9.
HESTER, Eng., a parrot, gu., in beak a ring, or. *Pl.* 33, *cr.* 11.
HETHERFIELD, Eng., a sinister wing, (charged with a cheveron,) gu. *Pl.* 39, *cr.* 10.
HETHERINGTON, Eng., a lion's head, erased, gu., within a chain, ar., both ends issuing from the wreath. *Pl.* 28, *cr.* 12.
HETHERINGTON, out of a ducal coronet, a tower. *Pl.* 12, *cr.* 5, (coronet, *pl.* 128, *fig.* 3.)
HETHERSETE, or HETHERSETTE, Eng., a sinister wing, (charged with a cheveron,) gu. *Pl.* 39, *cr.* 10.
HETHERTON, a lion's head, erased, within a chain, ar., both ends issuing from the wreath. *Pl.* 28, *cr.* 12.
HEUER, or HEVER, Eng., a phœnix in flames, ppr. *Pl.* 44, *cr.* 8.
HEVENINGHAM, Suff. and Staffs., an old man's head, in profile, ppr., vested, gu., on head a cap, or, guttée, or. *Pl.* 51, *cr.* 4.
HEVERINGHAM, Suff. and Staffs., a man's head, in profile, ppr., vested, gu., on head a cap, or, guttée-de-sang, turned up, erm. *Pl.* 51, *cr.* 4.
HEWAT, or HEWATT, the sun rising out of a cloud, ppr. *Post tenebras lux.* *Pl.* 67, *cr.* 9.
HEWES, a peacock's head, erased, az. *Pl.* 86, *cr.* 4.
HEWET, Eng., a cross pattée, between the horns of a crescent, gu. *Pl.* 37, *cr.* 10.
HEWETT, JOHN, Esq., Hants, on stump of tree, sprouting, ppr., a falcon, close, ar., legged and belled, or. *Ne tu quæsiveris extra*—and —*Une pure foy.* *Pl.* 78, *cr.* 8.
HEWETT, Lond., a lapwing, ppr. *Pl.* 10, *cr.* 12.
HEWETT, Eng., a cockatrice, wings (expanded,) or. *Pl.* 63, *cr.* 15.
HEWETT, Bart., Linc., out of a mural coronet, or, the stump of an oak-tree with branches, thereon a hawk, ppr., gorged with an Eastern coronet, and belled, gold. *Pl.* 78, *cr.* 8, (coronets, *pl.* 128, *figs.* 18 and 2.)

HEWETSON, Eng., a serpent, nowed, head in pale, or, in mouth a garland of laurel, vert. *Pl.* 104, *cr.* 9.
HEWETSON, Iri., a demi-friar, vested, ppr., in dexter a lash. *Pl.* 83, *cr.* 15.
HEWGELL, on stump of tree, couped, in fess, (sprouting afresh,) an owl, statant, gardant. *Pl.* 76, *cr.* 11, (owl, *pl.* 27, *cr.* 9.)
HEWGELL, on a staff, raguly, in fess, an eaglet, wings expanded. *Pl.* 5, *cr.* 8, (eagle, *pl.* 126, *cr.* 7.)
HEWGELL, and HEWGILL, Yorks., a horse's head, erased, sa. *Pl.* 81, *cr.* 6.
HEWGILL, HENRY, Esq., of Hornby Grange, Yorks., a nag's head, erased, sa. *Marte et labore.* *Pl.* 81, *cr.* 6.
HEWITT, Eng., a demi-huntsman, ppr., coat, gu., firing a gun, of the first. *Pl.* 51, *cr.* 6.
HEWITT, Eng., on trunk of oak-tree, a falcon, perched, belled, ppr. *Ne tu quæsiveris extra.* *Pl.* 78, *cr.* 8.
HEWITTSON, Northumb., a falcon, gu., belled, or. *Let them talk.* *Pl.* 67, *cr.* 3.
HEWLETT, Eng., on a mount, vert, semée of weeds, an oak-tree, ppr. *Pl.* 48, *cr.* 4.
HEWSHAM, an eagle, wings (addorsed,) sustaining a bannerol, charged with a fleur-de-lis. *Pl.* 65, *cr.* 3, (fleur-de-lis, *pl.* 141.)
HEWSON, Ennismore, co. Kerry; and Castle Hewson, co. Limerick, the sun in splendour. *Num lumen effugio?* *Pl.* 68, *cr.* 14.
HEXMAN, Eng., a yew-tree, ppr. *Pl.* 49, *cr.* 13.
HEXT, Eng., a stag's head, affrontée, ducally gorged, or. *Pl.* 55, *cr.* 2.
HEXT, Cornw., out of a tower, sa., a demi-lion, or, in dexter a battle-axe, of the first. *Pl.* 42, *cr.* 4, (axe, *pl.* 26, *cr.* 7.)
HEYDON, Herts. and Linc., a talbot, passant, ar., spotted, sa. *Pl.* 120, *cr.* 8.
HEYFORD, and HEYFORDE, Eng., out of a ducal coronet, two branches, in orle, ppr. *Pl.* 114, *cr.* 15.
HEYGATE, Bart., Ess., a wolf's head, erased, gu. *Boulogne et Cadiz.* *Pl.* 14, *cr.* 6.
HEYLAND, Eng., on a chapeau, gu., a martlet, sa. *Pl.* 89, *cr.* 7.
HEYLAND, Iri., out of battlements, ppr., (charged with a cross crosslet, gu.,) a nag's head, ppr. *Faveat fortuna. Pl.* 12,*cr.* 5,(head,*pl.* 81,*cr.* 6.)
HEYLEGAIR, a sword, in fess, thrust into a demi-wheel, on the sinister.
HEYLYN, Wel., out of a marquess's coronet, or, a demi-lion, sa. *In utrumque paratus.* *Pl.* 67, *cr.* 10, (coronet, *pl.* 127, *fig.* 4.)
HEYMAN, a demi-negro-boy, wreathed about temples, in dexter a slip of cinquefoils.
HEYNES, Salop, Oxon., and Dors., an eagle, displayed, on a tortoise. *Pl.* 102, *cr.* 8.
HEYRECK, Leic., a (bull's head,) erased, ar., gorged with a chaplet of roses, ppr. *Pl.* 73, *cr.* 8.
HEYSHAM, Eng., a stag's head, affrontée, enfiled with a ducal coronet. *Pl.* 55, *cr.* 2.
HEYTESBURY, Baron, G.C.B., and a Bart., (A'Court,) an eagle, displayed, sa., (charged with two cheveronels,) or, beaked and legged, gu., in beak, a lily, slipped, ppr. *Grandescunt aucta labore.* *Pl.* 48, *cr.* 11, (lily, *pl.* 81, *cr.* 9.)
HEYWARD, a sinister arm, vested and embowed, in hand a battle-axe. *Pl.* 52, *cr.* 5, (axe, *pl.* 73, *cr.* 7.)

HEYWOOD, Bart., of Claremont, Lanc., on a mount, vert, the trunk of a tree, entwined with ivy, therefrom a hawk, rising, all ppr. *Pl.* 55, *cr.* 11.

HEYWOOD, Eng., a tiger's head, ar., armed and maned, or, (pierced through neck by a broken spear, sa., headed, of the first, vulned, gu.) *Pl.* 94, *cr.* 10.

HEYWOOD, Eng., on stump of tree, a falcon, rising, ppr. *Pl.* 78, *cr.* 8.

HIATT, Eng., in lion's paw, erased, a broken spear. *Pl.* 85, *cr.* 15.

HIBBERT, Chesh., an arm, erect, couped below elbow, vested, az., cuff, erm., in hand, ppr., a crescent, ar. *Fidem rectumque colendo.* *Pl.* 110, *cr.* 7.

HIBBERT, Eng., in hand a mill-rind. *Pl.* 34, *cr.* 3.

HICHING, Eng., an anchor, in pale, sa. *Pl.* 25, *cr.* 15.

HICKEY, or HICKIE, a dexter arm, in armour, embowed, ppr., garnished, or, in hand a truncheon, gold. *Pl.* 120, *cr.* 11, (truncheon, *pl.* 33, *cr.* 4.)

HICKEY, Iri., a lamb, (regardant,) holding over dexter shoulder a flag, charged with an imperial crown. *Pl.* 48, *cr.* 13, (crown, *pl.* 127, *fig.* 2.)

HICKEY, Eng., a wyvern, wings expanded, in mouth a human hand, ppr. *Pl.* 61, *cr.* 8.

HICKFORD, Eng., a demi-swan, wings addorsed, ppr. *Pl.* 54, *cr.* 4.

HICKLING, Northamp., a leopard's head, erased, or, pellettée. *Pl.* 94, *cr.* 10.

HICKMAN, a talbot, couchant, (collared and chained.) *Pl.* 32, *cr.* 7.

HICKMAN, a buck's head and neck, couped, at gaze, ppr. *Pl.* 111, *cr.* 13.

HICKS, Lond. and Glouc., a stag's head, or, gorged with a chaplet of (cinquefoils,) of the last, leaved, vert. *Pl.* 38, *cr.* 1.

HICKS, Iri., a lion's gamb, issuing, parted, per cheveron, or and gu. *Pl.* 88, *cr.* 3.

HICKS, Bart., Glouc., a buck's head, couped at shoulders, or, gorged with a chaplet of (roses,) gu. *Tout en bon heure.* *Pl.* 38, *cr.* 1.

HICKS-BEACH, Glouc. and Wilts. : 1. For Beach, a demi-lion, rampant, ar., in paws an escutcheon, az., (charged with a pile, or.) *Pl.* 19, *cr.* 6, (escutcheon, *same plate.*) 2. A stag's head, erased, or, gorged with a wreath of laurel, vert. *Pl.* 38, *cr.* 1.

HICKSON, out of a ducal coronet, a griffin's head, ppr., charged with a trefoil, vert. *Fide et fortitudine.* *Pl.* 54, *cr.* 14, (trefoil, *pl.* 141.)

HIDE, Lanc., an eagle's head, erased, or, beaked, sa. *Pl.* 20, *cr.* 7.

HIDE, Lanc., a hawk's head, erased, or. *Pl.* 34, *cr.* 11.

HIDE, a hawk, close. *Pl.* 67, *cr.* 3.

HIDE, Dors., a martlet, rising, sa., charged with a mullet, or. *Pl.* 107, *cr.* 6, (mullet, *pl.* 141.)

HIDE, Berks., a leopard's head, erased, sa., bezantée. *Pl.* 94, *cr.* 10.

HIDE, Chesh., Herts., Salop, and Wilts., an eagle, wings addorsed, sa., beaked and legged, or. *Pl.* 121, *cr.* 3, (without arrow.)

HIDERS, Eng., a garb, banded. *Pl.* 48, *cr.* 10.

HIGDON, Eng., on a chapeau, gu., a phœnix in flames, ppr. *Pl.* 83, *cr.* 12.

HIGGA, Eng., a dove, in mouth an olive-branch, ppr. *Peace.* *Pl.* 48, *cr.* 15.

HIGGAN, Sco., a dove, in mouth an olive-branch, ppr. *Peace.* *Pl.* 48, *cr.* 15.

HIGGANS, Eng., out of a tower, a demi-lion, rampant. *Fide et fortitudine.* *Pl.* 42, *cr.* 4.

HIGGENBOTTOM, or HIGGINBOTTOM, Eng., a dexter and a sinister arm, shooting an arrow from a bow, all ppr. *Pl.* 100, *cr.* 4.

HIGGENS, Suss., out of a tower, gu., a demi-lion, ar. *Pl.* 42, *cr.* 4.

HIGGINS, co. Mayo, out of a tower, double turreted, sa., a demi-griffin, ar., in dexter a dagger, sa., hilt and pommel, or. *Pro patriâ.* *Pl.* 49, *cr.* 4, (tower, *pl.* 37, *cr.* 1.)

HIGGINS, Beds., a griffin's head, erased, or, (collared, gu.) *Nihil quod obstat virtuti.* *Pl.* 69, *cr.* 13.

HIGGINS, Hereford, a garb, ppr., charged with two crosses pattée, gu. *Patriam hinc sustinet.* *Pl.* 48, *cr.* 10, (cross, *pl.* 141.)

HIGGINS, Yorks., out of a tower, sa., a lion's head, ar. *Pl.* 42, *cr.* 4.

HIGGINS, Eng., a castle. *Tutemus.* *Pl.* 28, *cr.* 11.

HIGGINSON, of Lisburn, out of a tower, ppr., a demi-griffin, segreant, vert, armed and beaked, or. *Malo mori quam fœdari.* *Pl.* 68, *cr.* 11.

HIGGINSON, Eng., a tower. *Pl.* 12, *cr.* 5.

HIGGINSON, Iri., on a chapeau, a dexter arm, in armour, embowed, couped, in hand a tilting-spear, all ppr., (tied at shoulders by a cord and tassels, or.) *Pl.* 57, *cr.* 3.

HIGGINSON, Middx., out of a human heart, a dexter hand, erect, between two wheat-ears, in saltier, all ppr., holding a closed book, sa., garnished, or.

HIGHAM, Suff. and Ess., a talbot, passant, sa., collared and lined, at end of line a coil, knot, or. *Pl.* 65, *cr.* 2.

HIGHGATE, Middx. and Suff., a wolf's head, erased, gu. *Pl.* 14, *cr.* 6.

HIGHLORD, Devons., an escarbuncle, ar. *Pl.* 51, *cr.* 10.

HIGHMORE, Sco., a talbot's head, couped at neck. *Pl.* 123, *cr.* 15.

HIGSON, Eng., a hand, couped, in fess, charged with an eye, ppr. *Pl.* 10, *cr.* 14.

HILDERSHAW, Eng., a swan, devouring a fish, ppr. *Pl.* 103, *cr.* 1.

HILDYARD, the Rev. WILLIAM, Yorks., a cock, sa., beaked, legged, and wattled, gu. *Pl.* 67, *cr.* 14.

HILL, Baron, (ROWLAND-HILL,) G.C.B., &c., a tower, ar., from the battlements, a chaplet of laurel, ppr. *Avancez.* *Pl.* 12, *cr.* 5, (laurel, *pl.* 54, *cr.* 10.)

HILL, Sir ROWLAND, Bart., Salop, same crest and motto.

HILL, Bart., Iri., a talbot's head, (couped,) sa., guttée-d'eau, collared, gu., studded and ringed, or. *Ne tentes, aut perfice.* *Pl.* 2, *cr.* 15.

HILL, Middx. and Worc., a talbot, passant, or, collared, gu. *Pl.* 65, *cr.* 2.

HILL, East Dereham, Norf., a boar's head, erased, ppr., in mouth a trefoil, vert. *Pl.* 125, *cr.* 7, (trefoil, *pl.* 141.)

HILL, a fleur-de-lis. *Pl.* 68, *cr.* 12.

HILL, RICHARD-CLARKE, Esq., of Stallington Hall, Stafford, a hawk, ppr., belled. *Pl.* 67, *cr.* 3.

HILL, Marquess of Downshire. *See* DOWNSHIRE.
HILL, Eng., a buck's head, per pale, gu. and az., the nose, or, collared, gold. *Pl.* 125, *cr.* 6, (without roses.)
HILL, a martlet. *Pl.* 111, *cr.* 5.
HILL, Norf., a boar's head and neck, sa., in mouth a broken spear, ppr., headed, ar. *Pl.* 11, *cr.* 9.
HILL, Somers., a squirrel, sejant, ar., collared and lined, or. *Pl.* 85, *cr.* 3.
HILL, Norf., on a chapeau, gu., turned up, erm., a lion, passant, or, between dragons' wings, of the first. *Pl.* 107, *cr.* 1, (wings, *pl.* 105, *cr.* 11.)
HILL, Staff., a lion, rampant, ar., (pierced through breast by a broken spear,) in bend, ppr., point, guttée-de-sang. *Pl.* 67, *cr.* 5.
HILL, an eagle, wings expanded, ppr., in beak an acorn, slipped, vert, fructed, or. *Pl.* 126, *cr.* 7, (acorn, *pl.* 80, *cr.* 8.)
HILL, (on a mount,) a chalice, with flames issuant therefrom. *Pl.* 40, *cr.* 9.
HILL, Devons., Cornw., and Northamp., a dove, ar., in mouth an olive-branch. *Pl.* 48, *cr.* 15.
HILL, Lond., a talbot's head, erased, between two laurel-branches, vert. *Pl.* 90, *cr.* 6, (branches, *pl.* 79, *cr.* 14.)
HILL, Linc., Cornw., Hants, and Somers., a demi-leopard, ar., spotted, of all colours, ducally gorged, or. *Pl.* 125, *cr.* 4.
HILL, on trunk of tree, (in fess,) or, a falcon, ppr., beaked and belled, gold. *Pl.* 78, *cr.* 8.
HILL, Sco., a stag's head. *Veritas superabit montes.* *Pl.* 91, *cr.* 14.
HILL, a wolf's head, (erased,) az., in mouth a trefoil, slipped, vert. *Pl.* 92, *cr.* 15, (trefoil, *pl.* 141.)
HILL, Sco., the Bible, expanded, ppr. *Veritas superabit montes.* *Pl.* 15, *cr.* 12.
HILL, Kent, a stag's head, (erased,) ppr., in mouth an oak-slip, vert, fructed, or. *Pl.* 100, *cr.* 8.
HILL, Kent, a stag's head, erased, ppr. *Pl.* 66, *cr.* 9.
HILL, Iri., three roses, stalked and leaved, vert. *Pl.* 79, *cr.* 3.
HILL, Iri., a lion, rampant, gardant, gu., (in dexter a sword, ppr.) *Pl.* 92, *cr.* 7.
HILL, Bucks., a goat's head, per pale, indented, gu. and az., (collared,) and armed, or. *Pl.* 105, *cr.* 14.
HILL, Iri., a greyhound, sejant, ar., (collared, az.) *Pl.* 66, *cr.* 15.
HILL, Lond., Middx., and Herts., on a mount, a branch, vert, with three cinquefoils, ar. *Pl.* 98, *cr.* 13, (cinquefoils, *pl.* 2, *cr.* 10.)
HILL, Suff., a boar's head, couped, sa., in mouth an acorn, or, leaved, vert. *Pl.* 125, *cr.* 7.
HILL-NOEL. *See* BERWICK, Baron.
HILLAIRE, Eng., a griffin's head, in beak, a key, ppr. *Pl.* 9, *cr.* 12.
HILLARY, Bart., Ess. and Yorks., out of a mural coronet, gu., a cubit arm, (in armour,) ppr., in hand a caltrap, or. *Virtute nihil invium.* *Pl.* 79, *cr.* 4.
HILLERSDEN, and HILLESDEN, Devons., a squirrel, sejant, ppr., cracking a nut, or. *Pl.* 16, *cr.* 9.
HILLIAR, Eng., a harp, or. *Pl.* 104, *cr.* 15.
HILLIARD, an arm, in armour, embowed, in hand, a (spear,) all ppr. *Pl.* 44, *cr.* 9.

HILLIARD, Yorks. and Durh., a cock, sa., combed, legged, and wattled, gu. *Pl.* 67, *cr.* 14.
HILLIER, Eng., an arm, from elbow, erect, (vested,) in hand a branch of palm. *Pl.* 23, *cr.* 7.
HILLOCKS, Sco., out of a pheon, az., between ostrich-wings, gu., a sprig of laurel, ppr. *Nihil sine cruce.*
HILLS, Eng., a horse, current, gu., in mouth a broken spear-head, sa. *Pl.* 107, *cr.* 5.
HILLS, Kent, a stag's head, (erased,) in mouth an oak-slip, fructed, all ppr. *In cœlo confidemus.* *Pl.* 100, *cr.* 8.
HILLYARD, a cock, ppr. *Pl.* 67, *cr.* 14.
HILTON, Eng., a hand, (vested,) barry, ar. and sa., holding a holly-branch, ppr. *Pl.* 55, *cr.* 6.
HILTON, of Hilton Castle, Durh., on a close helmet, a Moses' head, in profile, glorified and horned, all ppr. *Tant que je puis.*
HINCHLEY, Eng., a leopard, couchant, ppr. *Pl.* 111, *cr.* 11.
HINCHMAN, a demi-lion, in dexter a bugle-horn, stringed. *Pl.* 39, *cr.* 14, (horn, *pl.* 48, *cr.* 12.)
HINCKES, HINCKS, or HINKS, Eng., in hand a scorpion. *Pl.* 110, *cr.* 14.
HINCKLEY, Eng., on a ducal coronet, or, a star of (twelve) points, ppr. *Pl.* 83, *cr.* 3.
HINCKS, Iri., a demi-chevalier, in dexter a scimitar. *Pl.* 27, *cr.* 11.
HINCKS, Yorks., a demi-lion, rampant, gu., guttée-de-larmes, gorged with a collar, dancettée, ar., sinister resting on an annulet, or. *In cruce et lacrymis spes est.* *Pl.* 88, *cr.* 1, (annulet, *pl.* 141.)
HIND, Eng., an ensign, in full dress, with cocked hat, holding the Union standard of Britain. *Pl.* 79, *cr.* 5.
HINDE, Salop, a lion's head, erased, ar. *Pl.* 81, *cr.* 4.
HINDE-HODGSON, JOHN, Esq., Acton House, Northumb., on a rock, a dove, az., wings, or, in mouth an olive-branch, ppr. *Miseris succurrere disco.* *Pl.* 85, *cr.* 14.
HINDLE, a lyre, ppr. *Pl.* 104, *cr.* 15.
HINDMAN, a buck, trippant, ppr. *Pl.* 68, *cr.* 2.
HINDMARSH, Sco., a demi-lion, rampant. *Nil nisi patria.* *Pl.* 67, *cr.* 10.
HINES, Iri., a plough, ppr. *Pl.* 28, *cr.* 15.
HINGHAM, Eng., a horse's head, furnished with cart-harness, ppr. *Pl.* 49, *cr.* 6.
HINGSTON, a hind's head, couped, or, in mouth a holly-slip, ppr. *Pl.* 21, *cr.* 9, (holly, *pl.* 99, *cr.* 6.)
HINSON, Middx., a fleur-de-lis, per pale, erm. and az. *Pl.* 68, *cr.* 12.
HIPKISS, Eng., a sphinx, gardant, wings addorsed, ppr. *Pl.* 91, *cr.* 11.
HIPPISLEY, Bart., Berks., out of a ducal coronet, or, a hind's head, erased, sa., (gorged with a collar of gold.) *Amicitiæ virtutisque fœdus*—and—*Non mihi sed patriæ.* *Pl.* 6, *cr.* 3, (coronet, *same plate, cr.* 4.)
HIRINE, Norf., a talbot, passant, sa., collared and lined, or, (line coiled at end.) *Pl.* 65, *cr.* 2.
HIRST, and HIRSTE, Eng., in hand a scimitar, engrailed on back, cutting at a feather. *Pl.* 59, *cr.* 9.
HISLOP, in dexter hand a mill-rind, ppr. *Pl.* 34, *cr.* 3.
HISLOP, a buck's head, erased. *Pl.* 66, *cr.* 9.
HISLOPE, Sco., in hand a pistol, ppr. *Pl.* 101, *cr.* 12.

Q

HISLOP, Bart., Devons. : 1. *By augmentation*, a soldier of the 22d Light Dragoons, mounted, accoutred, and in the position of attack, ppr. *Deccan.* 2. Out of a mural coronet, a buck's head, couped, ppr. *Pl.* 112, *cr.* 5, (without arrow.)

HITCH, Oxon., an heraldic antelope's head, (erased,) sa., tufted and maned, or, (vulned through neck by a bird-bolt, end in mouth.) *Pl.* 76, *cr.* 3.

HITCHENS, and HITCHINS, Eng., out of a mural coronet, a garb, on the top a bird, perched, ppr. *Pl.* 14, *cr.* 5.

HITCHENS, and HITCHINS, on an heraldic-rose, gu., barbed, vert, a lion's head, erased, or. *Pl.* 69, *cr.* 6.

HITFIELD, Eng., an ostrich-feather, enfiled with a ducal coronet. *Pl.* 8, *cr.* 9.

HOAD, Middx. and Lond., a stag's head, erased, ar. *Pl.* 66, *cr.* 9.

HOADLEY, Eng., on a terrestrial orb, or, a dove, wings expanded, in mouth an olive-branch, ppr. *Pl.* 79, *cr.* 8.

HOAR, Eng., a fox, current, ppr. *Pl.* 80, *cr.* 5.

HOARE, Sir JOSEPH WALLIS, Bart., co. Cork, and Middx., a deer's head, ppr., erased, ar. *Venit hora*—and—*Dum spiro, spero.* *Pl.* 66, *cr.* 9.

HOARE, Iri., a leopard's face, or. *Pl.* 66, *cr.* 14.

HOARE, Middx., a deer's head, erased. *Pl.* 66, *cr.* 9.

HOARE, Iri., a stag's head, gardant, gu., ducally gorged and attired, or. *Pl.* 55, *cr.* 2.

HOARE-COLT, Bart., Wilts., an eagle's head, erased, ar., (charged with an ermine spot.) *Pl.* 20, *cr.* 7.

HOBART, Bucks. and Norf., a bull's head, couped, sa., semée of etoiles, or. *Pl.* 120, *cr.* 7, (etoile, *pl.* 141.)

HOBART, Norf., a bull, passant, sa., semée of etoiles, or. *Quæ supra.* *Pl.* 66, *cr.* 11, (etoile, *pl.* 141.)

HOBBINS, Eng., a stag's head, ppr. *Pl.* 91, *cr.* 14.

HOBBS, Surr., on a (dexter) glove, in fess, ar., a falcon, ppr., beaked, legged, and belled, or. *Pl.* 83, *cr.* 13.

HOBBS, Iri., an arrow, gu., point downward, feathered, or, and a palm-branch, vert, in saltier. *Pl.* 50, *cr.* 11.

HOBERD, and HOBERT, Eng., a demi-lion, gu. *Pl.* 67, *cr.* 10.

HOBERD, and HOBERT, a demi-lion, gu. *Pl.* 67, *cr.* 10.

HOBHOUSE, Somers., a griffin, sejant, ppr. *Pl.* 100, *cr.* 11.

HOBHOUSE-CAM, Bart., Glouc., out of a mural coronet, per pale, an and gu., a crescent, ar., and issuing therefrom an etoile, eradicated, or. *Spes vitæ melioris.* *Pl.* 111, *cr.* 15, (coronet, *pl.* 128, *fig.* 18.)

HOBSON, Surr., a leopard's head, ar., semée of torteaux, gu. *Pl.* 92, *cr.* 13, (torteau, *pl.* 141.)

HOBSON, Eng., a leopard's head, gardant, erased, ar., powdered with torteaux, gu. *Pl.* 56, *cr.* 7, (torteau, *pl.* 141.)

HOBSON, Durh., a griffin's head, couped, ar., between wings, elevated, az. *Fortitudine Dei.* *Pl.* 65, *cr.* 1.

HOBSON, a griffin, segreant, in beak a key, wards upward. *Pl.* 67, *cr.* 13, (key, *pl.* 9, *cr.* 12.)

HOBY, Eng., out of a ducal coronet, a fish's head, ppr. *Pl.* 36, *cr.* 13.

HOBY, on a chapeau, gu., turned up, erm., a tiger, rampant, ar. *Pl.* 73, *cr.* 2, (chapeau, *pl.* 127, *cr.* 13.)

HOCKENHULL, Chesh., a buck's head and neck, erased, per fess, ar. and or, (pierced through nostrils by a dart, in bend, gold, feathered, of the first, barbed, az.) *Pl.* 66, *cr.* 9.

HOCKIN, Devons., on a rock, a sea-gull, rising, all ppr. *Hoc in loco Deus rupes.* *Pl.* 79, *cr.* 11.

HODDAR, and HODDER, Eng., an angel in a praying posture, ppr., between two laurel-branches, vert. *Pl.* 94, *cr.* 11.

HODDENET, and HODDENOT, Eng., in dexter hand (four) arrows, points downward, ppr. *Pl.* 56, *cr.* 4.

HODDER, of Hoddersfield : 1. For *Hodder*, a fire-ship, her courses set, (fire issuing from low rigging,) all ppr. *Pl.* 109, *cr.* 8. 2. For *Moore*, out of a ducal coronet, or, a moor's head, in profile, ppr. *Pl.* 81, *cr.* 15, (coronet, *pl.* 128, *fig.* 3.)

HODDY, a trout, naiant, ppr. *Pl.* 85, *cr.* 7.

HODGE, Sco., a garb, entwined by two serpents, ppr. *Pl.* 36, *cr.* 14.

HODGERS, a crescent. *Pl.* 18, *cr.* 14.

HODGES, Eng., an eagle, rising, looking at the sun, ppr. *Pl.* 43, *cr.* 5.

HODGES, Kent, out of a ducal coronet, or, an antelope's head, ar., horned and tufted, or. *Prævisa mala pereunt.* *Pl.* 24, *cr.* 7, (coronet, *same plate, cr.* 10.)

HODGES, out of a ducal coronet, or, an heraldic-antelope's head, ar., horned and tufted, gold. *Posce teipsum.* *Pl.* 66, *cr.* 3, (coronet, *same plate, cr.* 14.)

HODGES, Eng., a man, ppr., vested, ar., coat, gu., holding a standard, ar., charged with a cross, of the second, on a canton, gu. *Pl.* 79, *cr.* 5.

HODGES, Iri., out of a ducal coronet, a greyhound's head, gu. *Pl.* 70, *cr.* 5.

HODGES, a dove, regardant, in mouth an olive-branch, all ppr. *Pl.* 77, *cr.* 2.

HODGETTS, of Hagley, an eagle, wings expanded, in beak an annulet. *Confido, conquiesco.* *Pl.* 126, *cr.* 7, (annulet, *pl.* 141.)

HODGETTS, Staffs., a horse's head, erm., pierced through neck by a spear, the staff broken, ppr. *Pl.* 110, *cr.* 6.

HODGKINS, Eng., an eagle, rising, looking towards the sun, ppr. *Pl.* 43, *cr.* 5.

HODGSON, Durh., a dove and olive-branch, ppr. *Metuo secundus.* *Pl.* 48, *cr.* 15.

HODGSON, Durh., a martlet, az., winged, or, (in beak an olive-branch, vert.) *Pl.* 107, *cr.* 6.

HODGSON, WILLIAM, Esq., of Houghton House, Cambs., a dove, close, az., in mouth a sprig of laurel, ppr. *Dread God.* *Pl.* 48, *cr.* 15.

HODGSON, Eng., on a tower, ar., a martlet, az., winged, or. *Pl.* 107, *cr.* 6.

HODGSON, Middx., a dove, az., winged, or, beaked and membered, gu., in mouth an olive-branch, ppr. *Pl.* 48, *cr.* 15.

HODGSON, Iri., a salmon, haurient, az. *Pl.* 98, *cr.* 12.

HODGSON, a griffin's head, erased, murally gorged. *Pl.* 74, *cr.* 1, (griffin, *same plate.*)

HODINGTON, Eng., over a tower, ar., a bird, volant, or. *Pl.* 37, *cr.* 1.

HODISWELL, Eng., a well, ppr. *Pl.* 70, *cr.* 10.

HODKINSON, Eng., a shank-bone and palm-branch, in saltier. *Pl.* 25, *cr.* 11.
HODSON, Eng., a dove, on a rock. *Pl.* 85, *cr.* 14.
HODSON, Iri., an antelope's head, erased, gu. *Pl.* 24, *cr.* 7.
HODSON, Bart., Iri., a dove, close, az., in mouth a sprig of laurel, ppr. *Pl.* 48, *cr.* 15.
HODY, Sco., a bull, passant, sa. *Pl.* 66, *cr.* 11.
HODY, Eng., a trout, naiant, ppr. *Pl.* 85, *cr.* 7.
HOE, Eng., in hand a hautboy. *Pl.* 98, *cr.* 9.
HOEY, Iri., a pheasant. *Pl.* 82, *cr.* 12.
HOFFMAN, Eng., out of top of a tower, a demi-woman, ppr., attired, az., in dexter a garland of laurel. *Pl.* 26, *cr.* 5, (garland, *pl.* 87, *cr.* 14.)
HOFFMAN, Lond., a demi-lion, double-queued, az., between two elephants' proboscles, erect, per fess, dexter, gu. and ar., sinister, or and az., (between paws the sun in splendour, ppr.) *Tiens à la verité.* *Pl.* 120, *cr.* 10, (proboscles, *pl.* 96, *cr.* 1.)
HOG, of Blairdrum, Sco., a dexter hand, couped, in fess, ppr. *Dant vires gloriam.* *Pl.* 32, *cr.* 4.
HOG, of Harcars, an oak-tree, ppr. *Dat gloria vires.* *Pl.* 16, *cr.* 8.
HOG, JAMES-MAITLAND, Esq., of Newliston, Linlithgow, an oak-tree, ppr. *Dat gloria vires.* *Pl.* 16, *cr.* 8.
HOGAN, Eng., on a chapeau, gu., an escallop, between wings, ppr. *Pl.* 17, *cr.* 14.
HOGAN, Iri., an ostrich's head, between two feathers, ar. *Pl.* 50, *cr.* 1.
HOGARTH, Sco., a pegasus's head, or, winged, ar. *Candor dat viribus alas.* *Pl.* 91, *cr.* 2, (without coronet.)
HOGG, Devons., a wyvern, vert. *Pl.* 63, *cr.* 13.
HOGG, Sco., a hand, couped, in fess. *Pl.* 32, *cr.* 4.
HOGG, Durh., against an oak-tree, vert, fructed, gu., a boar, statant, ar., pierced in side by an arrow, sa. *Pl.* 36, *cr.* 2, (oak, *pl.* 16, *cr.* 8.)
HOGGESON, a swallow, volant, sa. *Pl.* 40, *cr.* 4.
HOGH, a bull, passant, ar. *Pl.* 66, *cr.* 11.
HOGHTON-BOLD, Bart., Lanc., a bull, passant, ar. *Malgré le tort.* *Pl.* 66, *cr.* 11.
HOGUE, Sco., an oak-tree. *Dat gloria vires.* *Pl.* 16, *cr.* 8.
HOKE, Eng., an escallop, sa, between wings, ar. *Pl.* 62, *cr.* 4.
HOL, six tilting spears, (in pale,) three on the dexter, and three on the sinister. *Pl.* 95, *cr.* 8, (without coronet.)
HOLAND, Eng., an arm, in hand an arrow, ar., feathered, or. *Pl.* 43, *cr.* 13.
HOLBEACH, Eng., an escutcheon, or, pendent from stump of tree. *Pl.* 23, *cr.* 6.
HOLBEAME, Eng., a cross crosslet, gu., between two palm branches. *Pl.* 3, *cr.* 9, (cross, *pl.* 66, *cr.* 8.)
HOLBECH, Warw., a maunch, vert, charged with an escallop, ar. *Pl.* 22, *cr.* 14, (escallop, *pl.* 141.)
HOLBECK, and HOLBECKE, Eng., the sun rising from behind a hill, ppr. *Pl.* 38, *cr.* 6.)
HOLBICKE, Eng., a peacock's head, erased, az. *Pl.* 86, *cr.* 4
HOLBROOK, Eng., a lion, passant, gardant, tail extended, ppr. *Pl.* 120, *cr.* 5.
HOLBROOKE, Suff., a lion's head, erased, sa., (charged with a cheveron), gu. *Pl.* 81, *cr.* 4.

HOLBROW, Glouc., a pair of wings elevated, ar., including three mullets, pierced, in triangle. *Pl.* 39, *cr.* 12, (mullets, *pl.* 141.)
HOLBURNE, Bart., Sco., a demi-lion, in dexter a mullet, ar. *Decus summum virtus.* *Pl.* 89, *cr.* 10.
HOLCOMB, and HOLCOMBE, Eng., a serpent, nowed, in mouth a garland of laurel, ppr. *Pl.* 104, *cr.* 9.
HOLDEN, Lanc., a pheasant, ppr. *Pl.* 82, *cr.* 12.
HOLDEN, Sco., an (eagle's) leg, erased at thigh, ppr. *Pl.* 83, *cr.* 7.
HOLDEN, Sco., a cock, ppr. *Pl.* 67, *cr.* 14.
HOLDEN, Lanc., a moorcock, ppr., charged on breast with a cinquefoil, or. *Nec temere, nec timide.*
HOLDEN, Derby, a moorcock, rising, sa., winged, or.
HOLDER, on a ducal coronet, a lion, sejant. *Pl.* 76, *cr.* 11, (coronet, *same plate*, *cr.* 8.)
HOLDERNESS, Eng., between the horns of a crescent, or, a cross pattée, gu. *Pl.* 37, *cr.* 10.
HOLDICH, and HOLDICHE, Eng., an arm, in armour, embowed, in gauntlet a scimitar, all ppr. *Pl.* 81, *cr.* 11.
HOLDING, Middx., a horn. *Pl.* 89, *cr.* 3.
HOLDICH, Northamp., a martlet, sa., in front of a cross pattée, fitched, between two branches of palm, or. *Pl.* 111, *cr.* 5, (cross, *pl.* 27, *cr.* 14; branches, *pl.* 87, *cr.* 8.)
HOLERTON, Eng., a wyvern, vert. *Pl.* 63, *cr.* 13.
HOLFORD, Lond., a mount, vert, therefrom in front of a greyhound's head, sa., gorged with a collar, gemelle, in mouth a fleur-de-lis, or, the sun rising. *Toujours fidèle.*
HOLFORD, Leic. and Ruts., a greyhound's head, sa., collared and ringed, or. *Pl.* 43, *cr.* 11.
HOLFORD, Ess., a greyhound's head, sa. *Pl.* 89, *cr.* 2.
HOLGATE, out of a mural coronet, a bull's head. *Pl.* 120, *cr.* 7, (coronet, *same plate*, *cr.* 14.)
HOLGRAVE, and HOLGREVE, Eng., a hand holding a thunderbolt, ppr., in pale. *Pl.* 21, *cr.* 8.
HOLHEAD, Eng., a falcon, rising. *Pl.* 105, *cr.* 4.
HOLINSHED, Eng., a bull's head and neck, sa. *Pl.* 63, *cr.* 11.
HOLKER, Eng., a lion, rampant, az. *Pl.* 67, *cr.* 5.
HOLKER, Lond., a lion, rampant, (per cheveron, embattled,) or and az. *Pl.* 67, *cr.* 5.
HOLL, Norf., a sea-lion, sejant, or, guttée-desang. *Pl.* 80, *cr.* 13.
HOLLAND, Baron, on a chapeau, az., turned up, ermn., a fox, sejant, or. *Et vitam impendere vero.* *Pl.* 57, *cr.* 14.
HOLLAND, a horse's head and neck, couped, bridled, (charged with an escutcheon.) *Pl.* 92, *cr.* 1.
HOLLAND, Eng., out of a ducal coronet, or, a plume of ostrich-feathers, ar. *Pl.* 44, *cr.* 12.
HOLLAND, Suss., Cambs., and Linc., out of rays, or, a cubit arm, erect, ppr., in hand a lion's gamb, erased, gold. *Pl.* 94, *cr.* 13, (rays, *pl.* 37, *cr.* 6.)
HOLLAND, Salop, a demi-lion, rampant, gardant, grasping a fleur-de-lis, az. *Pl.* 35, *cr.* 4, (fleur-de-lis, *pl.* 141.)
HOLLAND, out of a ducal coronet, a demi-lion. *Pl.* 45, *cr.* 7.
HOLLAND, out of a ducal coronet, or, a demi-lion, rampant, ar. *Vincit qui se vincit.* *Pl.* 45, *cr.* 7.

HOLLAND, Linc. and Notts., a sinister wing, or. *Pl.* 39, *cr.* 10.
HOLLAND, out of a five-leaved ducal coronet, or, a demi-lion, (tail forked,) ar. *Pl.* 45, *cr.* 7.
HOLLAND, Suss., a wolf, passant, sa. *Pl.* 46, *cr.* 6.
HOLLAND, Norf., Linc., and Cambs., a wolf, passant, sa., charged on breast with a mullet. *Pl.* 46, *cr.* 6, (mullet, *pl.* 141.)
HOLLES, Eng., a moor's head, couped, wreathed, ar. and az. *Pl.* 36, *cr.* 3.
HOLLES, Eng., in a lion's paw, erased, or, a heart, gu. *Pl.* 23, *cr.* 13.
HOLLIDAY, Eng., a grenade, fired, ppr. *Pl.* 70, *cr.* 12.
HOLLIDAY, an esquire's helmet. *Pl.* 109, *cr.* 5.
HOLLIDAY, a demi-pegasus, ar., winged, gu. *Pl.* 91, *cr.* 2, (without coronet.)
HOLLIER, Eng., in dexter hand a fish, ppr. *Pl.* 105, *cr.* 9.
HOLLINGBURY, Eng., a buck's head. *Pl.* 91, *cr.* 14.
HOLLINGS, Eng., a hunting-horn, or, stringed, gu., between wings, az. *Pl.* 48, *cr.* 12.
HOLLINGSHED, Chesh., a bull's head, gorged with a ducal coronet. *Pl.* 68, *cr.* 6.
HOLLINGWORTH, Chesh. and Linc., a stag, couchant, ppr. *Pl.* 67, *cr.* 2.
HOLLINGSWORTH, Durh., a crescent, ar. *Lumen accipe et imperti.* *Pl.* 18, *cr.* 14.
HOLLINS, Eng., a dexter hand pointing with two fingers to a (star,) ppr. *Pl.* 15, *cr.* 4.
HOLLINSWORTH, and HOLLINWORTH, Eng., a mount, ppr., semée of trefoils. *Pl.* 62, *cr.* 11, (trefoil, *pl.* 141.)
HOLLIS, a dexter arm, in armour, embowed, garnished, in hand a branch of holly-berries, all ppr. *Pl.* 97, *cr.* 1, (branch, *pl.* 55, *cr.* 6.)
HOLLIST, a sinister arm, vested and embowed, sa., in hand, ppr., three slips of olive, vert. *Pl.* 52, *cr.* 5, (olive, *pl.* 98, *cr.* 8.)
HOLLOND, the Rev. EDMUND, of Benhall Lodge, Suff., out of a ducal coronet, or, a demi-lion, rampant, ar. *Vincit qui se vincit.* *Pl.* 45, *cr.* 7.
HOLLOWAY, Eng., out of a mural coronet, ar., a lion's head, or, charged with a torteau, gu. *Pl.* 45, *cr.* 9, (torteau, *pl.* 141.)
HOLLOWDAY, Lond., a demi-lion, rampant, gardant, purp. *Pl.* 35, *cr.* 4.
HOLLOWELL, Eng., a goat, (passant,) ar., attired, or. *Pl.* 66, *cr.* 1.
HOLLYLAND, or HOLYLAND, Eng., a demi-savage, handcuffed, ppr. *Pl.* 98, *cr.* 10.
HOLLYNGWORTHE, DE ROBERT, Esq., of Hollyngworthe Hall, Chester, a stag, lodged, ppr. *Disce ferenda pati.* *Pl.* 67, *cr.* 2.
HOLMAN, Lond., a greyhound's head, couped. *Pl.* 14, *cr.* 4, (without charging.)
HOLMDEN, or HOLMEDEN, Surr., an otter's head, erased, or. *Pl.* 126, *cr.* 14.
HOLME, of Paul-Holme: 1. A holly-tree, fructed, ppr. *Pl.* 22, *cr.* 10. 2. Out of a mural coronet, gu., a hound's head, (erased,) or. *Holme semper viret.* *Pl.* 113, *cr.* 6, (without collar.)
HOLME, Chesh., an arm, couped and embowed, vested, barry of six, or and az., cuffed, erm., in hand a rose-branch, ppr. *Pl.* 120, *cr.* 1, (branch, *pl.* 118, *cr.* 9.)
HOLME, a griffin's head, couped, az., between wings, or. *Pl.* 65, *cr.* 1.
HOLME, Eng., on a lion's head, (couped,) or, a chapeau, az., turned up, erm. *Pl.* 122, *cr.* 10.

HOLMES, HERBERT M., Esq., of Derby, on a wreath, ar. and sa., a demi-griffin. *Quod facio valde facio.* *Pl.* 18, *cr.* 6.
HOLMES, the Rev. WILLIAM, M.A., of Scole House, Norf., a lion's head, erased, or. *Ora et labora.* *Pl.* 81, *cr.* 4.
HOLMES, a lion, rampant, or. *Pl.* 67, *cr.* 5.
HOLMES, Yorks., on a lion's head, erased, or, a chapeau, az., turned up, erm. *Pl.* 122, *cr.* 10.
HOLMES, Hants., out of a naval coronet, or, a dexter arm, in armour, embowed, in hand a trident, ppr., headed, gold. *Pl.* 93, *cr.* 1.
HOLMES, Yorks., a demi-griffin. *Pl.* 18, *cr.* 6.
HOLMES, a demi-griffin, segreant. *Pl.* 18, *cr.* 6.
HOLMES, Iri., on point of spear, issuing, a dolphin, naiant, ppr. *Pl.* 49, *cr.* 14.
HOLMES, a lion's head, erased, in mouth a sword. *Pl.* 81, *cr.* 4, (sword, *pl.* 28, *cr.* 14.)
HOLMES, out of a ducal coronet, a stag's head. *Pl.* 29, *cr.* 7.
HOLMESDALE, Baron. *See* AMHERST.
HOLROYD, Earl of Sheffield. *See* SHEFFIELD.
HOLROYD, a demi-griffin, or. *Pl.* 18, *cr.* 6.
HOLROYD, or HOLROYDE, Yorks., a demi-griffin, sa., between paws a coronet, or. *Quem te Deus esse jussit.* *Pl.* 18, *cr.* 6, (coronet, *same plate.*)
HOLT, Camb., a pheon, sa. *Pl.* 26, *cr.* 12.
HOLT, Lond. and Lanc., a dexter arm, in armour, embowed, ppr., garnished, or, in gauntlet a pheon, sa. *Pl.* 47, *cr.* 15.
HOLT, Lond. and Lanc., a dexter arm, erect, (vested, per pale, az. and gu.,) in hand a pheon, sa. *Pl.* 123, *cr.* 12.
HOLT, Warw., a squirrel, sejant, or, holding a hazel-branch, slipped and fructed, all ppr. *Pl.* 2, *cr.* 4.
HOLT, Warw., a squirrel, sejant, or, cracking a nut. *Pl.* 16, *cr.* 9.
HOLT, Middx., a spear-head, ppr. *Ut sanem, vulnero.* *Pl.* 82, *cr.* 9.
HOLT, WILLIAM-HENRY, Esq., M.D., of Enfield and Redbank, Westm., same crest and motto.
HOLT, Middx., a pheon, in pale, sa. *Quod vult, valdé vult.* *Pl.* 26, *cr.* 12.
HOLTON, Eng., a map, ppr. *Pl.* 59, *cr.* 3.
HOLWAY, out of a ducal coronet, or, a greyhound's head, sa. *Pl.* 70, *cr.* 5.
HOLYCOE, Eng., a crescent, ar. *Pl.* 18, *cr.* 14.
HOLYOKE, Eng., a cubit arm, ppr., vested, gu., cuffed, ar., in hand an oak-branch, vert, fructed, or. *Pl.* 32, *cr.* 6, (branch, *same plate,* *cr.* 13.)
HOMAN, Bart., Iri., on a lion's head, erased, or, a chapeau, gu., turned up, erm. *Homo sum.* *Pl.* 122, *cr.* 10.
HOMAN, Iri., in the sea, an anchor, in pale, ppr. *Pl.* 62, *cr.* 10.
HOMAN, Eng., on a lion's head, a chapeau. *Pl.* 122, *cr.* 10.
HOME, Bart., Berks., a unicorn's head and neck, couped, gorged with an Eastern coronet. *Remember.* *Pl.* 20, *cr.* 1, (coronet, *pl.* 128, *fig.* 2.)
HOME, Earl of, and Baron, Baron Dunglas, (Ramey-Home,) Sco., a lion's head, erased, ar., on a chapeau, gu., turned up, erm. *A Home, a Home, a Home*—and—*True to the end.* *Pl.* 99, *cr.* 9.
HOME, of Kaimes, Sco., a pelican's head, couped, ppr. *True to the end*—or—*Semper verus.* *Pl.* 14, *cr.* 4.

HOME, Bart., Sco., an adder, in pale, sa., in mouth a rose, gu., leaved and stalked, vert. *Vise à la fin.* Pl. 119, cr. 12, (without coronet; rose, pl. 118, cr. 9.)
HOME, of Westertoun, Sco., a lion's head, erased, ar., collared, gu., charged with three roses. *True to the end.* Pl. 7, cr. 10, (rose, pl. 141.)
HOME, of Ninewells, Sco., a lion's head, erased, ppr., collared, or, charged with three wells, ppr. *True to the end.* Pl. 7, cr. 10, (wells, pl. 70, cr. 10.)
HOME, of Renton, Sco., a lion's head, erased, gu. *True to the end.* Pl. 81, cr. 4.
HOME, of Kimmerham, a lion's head, erased, ar., collared, gu., charged with roses and fleur-de-lis. *True to the end.* Pl. 81, cr. 4, (roses, and fleur-de-lis, pl. 141.)
HOME, of Blackadder, a lion's head, erased, ar., collared, erm. *True to the end.* Pl. 7, cr. 10.
HOME, of Linhouse, a lion's head, erased, ppr., collared, gu. *True to the end.* Pl. 7, cr. 10.
HOME, of Renton, Sco., a pelican's head, couped, ppr. *True to the end—or—Semper verus.* Pl. 41, cr. 4.
HOME, a boar's head and neck, erased. Pl. 2, cr. 7.
HOME, on a chapeau, a lion's head, erased, Pl. 99, cr. 9.
HOME-EVERARD, Bart., Hants. a lion's head, erased, ppr., (thereon a label of three points, ar., the middle point charged with a fleur-de-lis, az., the other with the Cross of St George, gu.) *True.* Pl. 81, cr. 4.
HOMER, Eng., a lion's gamb, holding up a cross pattée. Pl. 46, cr. 7.
HOMES, Eng., an antelope, passant, ppr. Pl. 63, cr. 10.
HOMFRAY, Yorks., an otter, ppr., (wounded in sinister shoulder.) Pl. 9, cr. 5.
HOMFRAY, Knt., Glam., Wel., an otter, ppr., (wounded in shoulder.) *L'homme vrai aime son pays.* Pl. 9, cr. 5.
HONE, Eng., a sword, in pale, ppr., ensigned, with a cross pattée. Pl. 56, cr. 1.
HONE, Glouc., an arm, in armour, embowed, in hand a scimitar, ppr. Pl. 81, cr. 11.
HONE, Iri., on a mount, overgrown with ryegrass, a birch-tree, ppr. Pl. 18, cr. 10.
HONEYMAN, Bart., Sco., an arrow, in pale, point downward, or, feathered, ar. Pl. 56, cr. 13.
HONEYWILL, a bee-hive, with bees volant, ppr. Pl. 81, cr. 14.
HONNOR, and HONOR, Eng., a serpent, nowed, sa., spotted, or. Pl. 1, cr. 9.
HONNYMAN, or HONYMAN, Sco., an arrow, in pale, ppr., point downward. *Progredere, ne regredere.* Pl. 56, cr. 13.
HONYWOOD, Bart., Kent, a wolf's head, (couped,) erm. *Omne bonum desuper.* Pl. 14, cr. 6.
HOO, a maiden's head, ppr., in a gold ring. Pl. 35, cr. 3, (head, pl. 45, cr. 5.)
HOO, Eng., a bull, passant, quarterly, ar. and sa. Pl. 66, cr. 11.
HOO, Eng., in hand a hautboy. Pl. 98, cr. 9.
HOOD, Lincoln, a hooded crow, (in mouth a Scotch thistle, in dexter a sword.) Pl. 23, cr. 8.
HOOD, Bart., Surr., a Cornish chough, (holding an anchor on the sinister side, in bend sinister,) all ppr. *Zealous.* Pl. 100, cr. 13.
HOOD, of Bardon Park: 1. A demi-talbot, gu., (collared and lined, ar.) Pl. 15, cr. 2. 2. A lion's head, erased, barry of six, ar. and az. Pl. 52, cr. 7.

HOOD, JOHN, Esq., of Stoneridge, Berwick, a demi-archer, accoutred, ppr. *Olim sic erat.* Pl. 60, cr. 5.
HOOD, Viscount and Baron, G.B., and a Bart., Eng.; Baron Hood, Iri., (Hood;) a Cornish chough, ppr. *Ventis secundis.* Pl. 100, cr. 13.
HOOD, a dove, ppr. Pl. 66, cr. 12.
HOOFSTELLER, a talbot, sejant, az., collared, ar. Pl. 107, cr. 7.
HOOK, Eng., a fish, haurient. Pl. 98, cr. 12.
HOOK, an arm, in armour, embowed, (and around it a trumpet,) in hand a pistol. Pl. 96, cr. 4.
HOOKE, Eng., an escallop, sa., between wings, ar. Pl. 62, cr. 4.
HOOKER, Hants., an eagle, displayed, gu., charged on breast with a ducal coronet, or. Pl. 12, cr. 7, (coronet, pl. 128, fig. 3.)
HOOKER, Surr., Suss., Hants., and Glouc., an escallop, sa., between wings, ar. Pl. 62, cr. 4.
HOOKHAM, Eng., a cup, ar. Pl. 42, cr. 1.
HOOLE, Eng., a rose, gu., barbed, vert, seeded, or. Pl. 20, cr. 2.
HOOLEY, Eng., out of a mount, vert, a tree, ppr. Pl. 48, cr. 4.
HOOPER, Somers., a demi-wolf, in dexter an oak-branch, fructed, all ppr. Pl. 56, cr. 8, (branch, pl. 32, cr. 13.)
HOOPER, Cornw., a demi-lion, between paws an annulet. Pl. 126, cr. 12, (annulet, pl. 141.)
HOOPER, Lond., Middx., and Wilts., a boar's head, erased at neck, az., bezantée, armed and crined, or. Pl. 2, cr. 7.
HOORD, Salop, a nag's head, ar., maned, or. Pl. 81, cr. 6.
HOOTON, Eng., a chevalier, holding his horse by the bridle with dexter, ppr. Pl. 37, cr. 11.
HOPCROFT, Eng., a steel cap. Pl. 18, cr. 9.
HOPE, Bart., Sco., a broken globe, ensigned by a rainbow, with clouds at each end, ppr. *At spes non fracta.* Pl. 79, cr. 1.
HOPE, HENRY-THOMAS, Esq., of Deepdene, Surr., and of Trenant Park, Cornw., same crest and motto.
HOPE, Sco., a broken globe, ensigned by a rainbow, ppr. *Spes tamen infracta.* Pl. 79, cr. 1.
HOPE, Derbs., a Cornish chough, wings expanded, ppr. Pl. 8, cr. 5, (without coronet.)
HOPER, Heref. and Suss., a dexter arm, couped at elbow, vested, sa., cuff turned up, ar., in hand a pomegranate, seeded and slipped, or. Pl. 78, cr. 6, (pomegranate, pl. 67, cr. 8.)
HOPETOUN, Earl of, and Baron, Viscount Aithrie, Sco.; Baron Hopetoun, U.K., (Hope;) a globe, fracted at the top, under a rainbow, with clouds at each end, all ppr. *At spes non fracta.* Pl. 79, cr. 1.
HOPKIN, a dove, with an olive-branch. Pl. 48, cr. 15.
HOPKINS, JOHN, Esq., of Tidmarsh House, Berks., a castle in flames, ppr. *Inter primos.* Pl. 118, cr. 15.
HOPKINS, Bart., Iri., a tower, ar., fired, ppr. Pl. 118, cr. 15.
HOPKINS, Eng., a fort in flames, ppr., (charged with two pellets, in fess.) Pl. 59, cr. 8.
HOPKINS, Linc., a demi-lion, rampant, sa. Pl. 67, cr. 10.
HOPKINS, Iri., on an oak-plant, a bird, ppr. Pl. 13, cr. 4.
HOPKINS of Oving House: 1. For *Hopkins*, out of a tower, per bend, indented, ar. and

gu., flames, ppr. *Pl.* 118, *cr.* 15. 2. For *Northey,* a cockatrice, (flames issuing from mouth,) ppr. *Pl.* 63, *cr.* 15.

HOPKIRK, an arm, in armour, pointing with one finger to a crescent, all ppr. *Memorare novissima.*

HOPPARE, Sco., a lion, rampant, gu., in dexter a fleur-de-lis. *Pl.* 87, *cr.* 6.

HOPPE, Eng., a demi-swan, wings addorsed, ppr. *Pl.* 54, *cr.* 4.

HOPPER, of Walworth, Durh.: 1. For *Hopper,* a tower, triple-towered, ar., masoned, sa. *Pl.* 123, *cr.* 14. 2. For *Carles,* a sword, ar., hilt and pommel, or, and a sceptre, gold, in saltier, enfiled with an oaken civic crown, vert, fructed, of the second. *Pl.* 124, *cr.* 6.

HOPPEY, Eng., in dexter hand, ppr., a fleur-de-lis, in pale, az. *Pl.* 95, *cr.* 9.

HOPSON, Eng., a stag, lodged, ppr. *Pl.* 67, *cr.* 2.

HOPSON, of Rochester, Kent, on a mount, vert, a griffin, passant, or, wings elevated, chequy, gold and az., dexter resting on a cinquefoil, of the first. *Vive, ut semper vivas. Pl.* 61, *cr.* 14, (without coronet; cinquefoil, *pl.* 141.)

HOPTON, out of a ducal coronet, a griffin's head, in mouth a bleeding hand. *Pl.* 54, *cr.* 14, (hand, *pl.* 61, *cr.* 8.)

HOPWOOD, out of a ducal coronet, an eagle's head, in beak a trefoil, slipped, all ppr. *Pl.* 20, *cr.* 12, (trefoil, *pl.* 141.)

HOPWOOD, Lanc., in dexter hand, in fess, couped at wrist, ppr., an escallop, or. *Gradatim. Pl.* 57, *cr.* 6, (hand, in fess, *pl.* 46, *cr.* 12.)

HORAN, Iri., in hand a cushion. *Pl.* 83, *cr.* 9.

HORDERN, an ox's head, cabossed, gu., armed, or, surmounting two arrows, in saltier, gold, banded and flighted, ar. *Pl.* 111, *cr.* 6, (arrows, *pl.* 124, *cr.* 14.)

HORE, HERBERT-FRANCIS, Esq., of Pole-Hore, co. Wexford, a demi-eagle, az. *Constanter. Pl.* 52, *cr.* 8.

HORE, and HOREM, Eng., in hand a sickle, ppr. *Pl.* 36, *cr.* 12.

HORN, Durh., a heron, close, ppr., in bill a standard staff, the banner flotant, and thereon the word, "Hastings." *Nil desperandum. Pl.* 46, *cr.* 9.

HORN, Salop, an owl, ppr. *Pl.* 27, *cr.* 9.

HORN, two bulls' horns. *Pl.* 9, *cr.* 15.

HORN, Lond., in hand, gu., a hawk's lure, ar. *Pl.* 44, *cr.* 2.

HORN, and HORNE, Sco., a bugle, az., garnished and stringed, ar. *Monitus, munitus. Pl.* 48, *cr.* 12.

HORNBY, Westm. and Suss., a bugle-horn. *Pl.* 89, *cr.* 3.

HORNBY, of Ribby Hall, a bugle-horn, stringed, sa., (an arrow passing through the knot, in fess, point toward sinister, or.) *Crede cornu. Pl.* 48, *cr.* 12.

HORNBY, Eng., a Roman soldier, in full armour, ppr. *Pl.* 90, *cr.* 1.

HORNBY, EDMUND, Esq., of Dalton Hall, Westm., a bugle-horn. *Pl.* 89, *cr.* 3.

HORNCASTLE, Iri., a unicorn's head, erased, vert, armed and maned, or, charged on neck with a trefoil, gold. *Pl.* 67, *cr.* 1, (trefoil, *pl.* 141.)

HORNCASTLE, Eng., on a chapeau, a serpent, nowed, ppr. *Pl.* 123, *cr.* 4.

HORNE, out of a mural coronet, a tiger's head. *Pl.* 5, *cr.* 15, (without gorging.)

HORNE, a talbot, sejant, ar., collared and lined, or. *Pl.* 107, *cr.* 7.

HORNE, a bull's head, couped, or. *Pl.* 120, *cr.* 7.

HORNE, a unicorn's head, erased, az., semée of mascles, or. *Pl.* 67, *cr.* 1, (mascle, *pl.* 141.)

HORNE, in hand, gu., a hawk's lure, ar. *Pl.* 44, *cr.* 2.

HORNECK, Middx., stump of tree, couped, ppr., a branch sprouting on the sinister. *Pl.* 92, *cr.* 8.

HORNER, Somers., a hound, sejant, ar., (collared and lined, or.) *Pl.* 66, *cr.* 15.

HORNER, Sco., a stag's head, erased, ppr. *Nitor in adversum. Pl.* 66, *cr.* 9.

HORNER, a buck's head, erased, ppr. *Pl.* 66, *cr.* 9.

HORNIOLD, or HORNYOLD, Worc., a demi-unicorn, gu., crined and armed, or. *Pl.* 26, *cr.* 14.

HORNSBY, Eng., a demi-bear, rampant, sa. *Pl.* 104, *cr.* 10.

HORNSEY, Eng., a rock, ppr. *Semper eadem. Pl.* 73, *cr.* 12.

HORNYOLD, THOMAS-CHARLES, Esq., of Blackmore Park and Hanley Castle, Worc., a demi-unicorn, gu., crined and armed, or. *Pl.* 26, *cr.* 14.

HORRELL, Eng., a crow, feeding, ppr. *Pl.* 51, *cr.* 8.

HORROCKS, on a mount, a stag, lodged, regardant, ppr. *Pl.* 51, *cr.* 9.

HORSEBURGH, Sco., a horse's head. *Pl.* 81, *cr.* 6.

HORSEFALL, Yorks., a horse's head, (couped,) erm. *Pl.* 81, *cr.* 6.

HORSEFALL, Eng., on a ducal coronet, or, a swan, wings addorsed, ar., (ducally) gorged, gu. *Pl.* 100, *cr.* 7.

HORSEFORD, Eng., a lion's head, az., between wings, or. *Pl.* 73, *cr.* 3.

HORSEPOOLE, or HORSPOOLE, Kent, out of a ducal coronet, or, a demi-pegasus, rampant, wings expanded, ar. *Pl.* 91, *cr.* 2.

HORSEY, Eng., a horse's head, couped, ar., armed, plumed, and bridled, az. and or. *Pl.* 55, *cr.* 7.

HORSEY, Herts. and Wilts., a horse's head, ar., in armour, bridled, or. *Pl.* 7, *cr.* 12.

HORSFALL, THOMAS B., Esq., Rugeley, a horse's head, issuing, ppr., bridled, or. *Ad finem fidelis. Pl.* 126 O, *cr.* 4.

HORSFALL, or HORSEFALL, a stag's head, couped, around neck a garland. *Pl.* 38, *cr.* 1.

HORSFORD, THOMAS MOOR, Esq., on waves of the sea, ppr., a horse, passant, ar. *Benigno numine. Pl.* 126 B, *cr.* 12.

HORSLEY, a horse's head, furnished, ppr. *Pl.* 49, *cr.* 6.

HORSMAN, a horse's head, in armour, bridled and plumed, ppr. *Pl.* 55, *cr.* 7.

HORSMAN, a castle in flames, ppr. *Pl.* 59, *cr.* 8.

HORT, Bart., Middx., an eagle, regardant, wings expanded, ppr., in beak a chaplet, vert. *Pl.* 35, *cr.* 8, (chaplet, *pl.* 128.)

HORTON, Derbs., issuing from waves of the sea, ppr., a spear-head, in pale, or, headed, ar., on its point a dolphin, of the first. *Pl.* 116, *cr.* 4.

HORTON, Somers. and Wilts., a cubit arm, vested, gu., cuffed, ar., in hand, ppr., an arrow, az., barbed and feathered, or. *Pl.* 43, *cr.* 13, (vesting, *pl.* 74, *cr.* 6.)

HORTON, Lanc., a red rose, seeded and barbed, ppr., between two laurel-branches, in orle. *Pl.* 3, *cr.* 13.

HORTON-WILMOT, Bart., Derbs., an eagle's head, erased, ar., in beak an escallop, gu. *Pl.* 121, *cr.* 7, (escallop, *pl.* 141.)

HORTON, JOSHUA-THOMAS, Esq., of Howroyde, Yorks., same crest. *Pro rege et lege.*
HORWOOD, Eng., a crow, wings expanded, pierced through breast by an arrow, point (upward.) *Pl.* 110, *cr.* 13.
HORWOOD, Eng., a hand issuing from a cloud, in fess, holding a club, ppr. *Pl.* 55, *cr.* 4.
HOSE, Eng., a lion's head, erased. *Pl.* 81, *cr.* 4.
HOSEASON, an eagle, regardant, rising from a rock, ppr. *In recto decus. Pl.* 79, *cr.* 2.
HOSIER, Eng., on a chapeau, az., turned up, or, a talbot, sejant. *Pl.* 102, *cr.* 9.
HOSKEN, Cornw., a lion, rampant, or. *Vis unita fortior. Pl.* 67, *cr.* 5.
HOSKINS, Surr., a cock's head, 'erased, or, pellettée, combed and wattled, gu., between wings, gold. *Pl.* 47, *cr.* 3, (without cross.)
HOSKYNS, Bart., Heref., out of a ducal coronet, a lion's head, erased, or, (flames issuing from mouth, ppr.,) crowned, gold. *Pl.* 90, *cr.* 4, (coronet, *same plate, cr.* 9.)
HOSKYNS, Eng., a lion's head, erased, ppr. *Pl.* 81, *cr.* 4.
HOST, Lond., two wings, addorsed, or, charged with a crescent, gu. *Pl.* 63, *cr.* 12, (crescent, *pl.* 141.)
HOSTE, Suff., two wings, addorsed, or. *Pl.* 63, *cr.* 12.
HOSTE, Bart. : 1. *By augmentation,* Out of a naval coronet, the rim encircled with a branch of laurel, an arm, embowed, vested in naval uniform, hand grasping a flagstaff, flowing therefrom a flag, (inscribed "Cataro.") *Pl.* 76, *cr.* 2, (arm, *pl.* 99, *cr.* 3.) 2. Two wings addorsed, or. *Fortitudine. Pl.* 63, *cr.* 12.
HOTOFT, or HOTOFTE, a lion's gamb, holding up a human heart, ppr. *Pl.* 23, *cr.* 13.
HOTOFT, or HOTOFTE, Eng., in lion's gamb, a human heart, ppr. *Pl.* 23, *cr.* 13.
HOTHAM, Baron, Iri., and a Bart., Eng., (Hotham,) a demi-seaman, out of water, ppr., in dexter a flaming sword, ar., hilt and pommel, or, on sinister a shield of the family arms. *Lead on !*
HOTON, Durh., on an esquire's helmet, a trefoil, slipped. *Pl.* 109, *cr.* 5, (trefoil, *pl.* 141.)
HOTTON, Eng., a martlet, rising, ppr. *Pl.* 107, *cr.* 6, (without tower.)
HOUBLON, Ess. and Berks., in dexter hand a book, expanded, ppr. *Pl.* 82, *cr.* 5, (without cloud.)
HOUBY, Eng., a leopard's head, ppr. *Pl.* 92, *cr.* 13.
HOUELL, Eng., a sea-lion, sejant, erm. *Pl.* 80, *cr.* 13.
HOUGH, Eng., a boar's head, erased, in mouth a sword, in bend sinister. *Pl.* 28, *cr.* 14.
HOUGHTON, Eng., a bull's head, couped, gu., horned, or. *Pl.* 120, *cr.* 7.
HOUGHTON, Lanc., a bull, passant, ar., armed and hoofed, or, tail reflexed over back, tipped, sa. *Malgré le tort. Pl.* 66, *cr.* 12.
HOUGHTON, Eng., a bull, passant, ar. *Malgré le tort. Pl.* 66, *cr.* 12.
HOUGHTON, Iri., a stag's head, or, (collared, gu.,) between attires a cross formée, of the last. *Pl.* 9, *cr.* 10.
HOUGHTON, Eng., a bull, passant. *Malgré le tort. Pl.* 66, *cr.* 11.
HOUGHTON, a scimitar, erect, ar., hilt and pommel, or. *Pl.* 27, *cr.* 10.

HOUISON, Sco., a lion's head, erased, gu. *Pl.* 18, *cr.* 4.
HOULTON, Somers., a ferret, passant, ppr. *Pl.* 119, *cr.* 15.
HOULTON, a talbot's head, erased, az., gorged with a collar, wavy, or, charged with three torteaux. *Semper fidelis. Pl.* 2, *cr.* 15, (torteau, *pl.* 141.)
HOUNDEGART, Eng., a water fountain, in full play, ppr. *Pl.* 49, *cr.* 8.
HOUNHILL, Eng., in lion's gamb, erased, a tilting-spear, in bend, tasselled, all ppr. *Pl.* 1, *cr.* 4.
HOUSE, Eng., two hands, issuing from a cloud, in chief, placing an anchor in the sea, ppr. *Pl.* 94, *cr.* 4.
HOUSTON, Iri., in dexter hand, a dagger, in pale, ppr. *Pl.* 23, *cr.* 15.
HOUSTON, Sco., a sand-glass, ppr. *In time. Pl.* 43, *cr.* 1.
HOUSTON, Sco., a sand-glass, with wings, ppr. *In time. Pl.* 32, *cr.* 11.
HOUSTON, Eng., on a mount, vert, a hind, statant, ppr., collared, or. *Pl.* 122, *cr.* 5.
HOUSTON-BLAKISTON, RICHARD-BAYLY, Esq., of Orangefield and Roddens House, co. Down : 1. A sand-glass, ppr. *Time. Pl.* 43, *cr.* 1. 2. A cock, gu. *Pl.* 67, *cr.* 14.
HOUTON, DE, a fox, current. *Pl.* 80, *cr.* 5.
HOVEDEN, Iri., a dragon's head, vert, out of flames, ppr. *Pl.* 93, *cr.* 15, (without coronet.)
HOVELL, Eng., on a ducal coronet, or, a leopard, sejant, ppr. *Pl.* 86, *cr.* 8.
HOVELL, a leopard, sejant, ppr. *Pl.* 86, *cr.* 8, (without coronet.)
How, or HOWE, Glouc. and Notts., out of a ducal coronet, or, a plume of five ostrich-feathers, az. *Utcunque placuerit Deo. Pl.* 100, *cr.* 12, (without charge.)
How, Lond. and Somers., out of a ducal coronet, or, a demi-wolf, rampant, sa. *Pl.* 56, *cr.* 8, (coronet, *same plate, cr.* 11.)
How, Lond., a wolf's head, erased, pean. *Pl.* 14, *cr.* 6.
How, Ess. and Suff., out of a ducal coronet, or, a unicorn's head, gu., attired and crined, gold. *Pl.* 45, *cr.* 14.
How, Lond., on a chapeau, ppr., a martlet, sa. *Pl.* 89, *cr.* 7.
How, Lond., a wolf's head, sa., in mouth a rose, gu., stalked and leaved, vert. *Pl.* 92, *cr.* 15.
HOWALES, Eng., a griffin, sejant, ppr. *Forward. Pl.* 100, *cr.* 11.
HOWARD, DE WALDEN, Baron, (Ellis,) a lion's head, or. *Non quo, sed quomodo. Pl.* 126, *cr.* 1.
HOWARD, of Effingham, Baron, (Howard ;) on a chapeau, gu., turned up, erm., a lion, statant, gardant, (tail extended,) or, gorged with a ducal coronet, ar. *Virtus mille scuta. Pl.* 7, *cr.* 14.
HOWARD, out of a ducal coronet, a wolf's head. *Pl.* 14, *cr.* 6, (coronet, *pl.* 128, *fig.* 3.)
HOWARD, Eng., on a chapeau, gu., turned up, erm., two wings addorsed, of the first, each charged with a bend, between six cross crosslets, fitched, ar. *Pl.* 80, *cr.* 15.
HOWARD, two wings addorsed, gu., each charged with a bend, between six cross crosslets, fitched, ar. *Pl.* 80, *cr.* 15, (without chapeau.)
HOWARD, Earl of Wicklow, &c. *See* WICKLOW.
HOWARD, Duke of Norfolk. *See* NORFOLK.

HOWARD, out of a ducal coronet, two wings addorsed, gu., each charged with a bend, between six crosslets, fitched, ar. *Pl.* 80, *cr.* 15, (coronet, *same plate, cr.* 6.)

HOWARD, Lond., a lion, couchant, erm., in dexter a cross pommée, fitched, or. *Pl.* 75, *cr.* 5, (without chapeau; cross, *pl.* 141.)

HOWARD, Bart., of Bushy Park, co. Wicklow, on a chapeau, gu., turned up, erm., charged with a crescent, sa., a lion, statant, gardant, or, ducally gorged, gu., (in mouth an arrow, in fess,) ppr. *Inservi Deo, et lætare. Pl.* 7, *cr.* 14, (crescent, *pl.* 141.)

HOWARD, of Corby Castle, Cumb., on a chapeau, gu., turned up, erm., a lion, statant, gardant, tail extended, or, ducally crowned, ar., (gorged with a label of three points, of the last.) *Volo, non valeo. Pl.* 105, *cr.* 5, (without collar.)

HOWARD, Earls of SUFFOLK and CARLISLE. *See those titles.*

HOWARD, Middx., on a chapeau, gu., turned up, erm., a demi-hind, salient, ppr., charged with a cross fleury, ar.

HOWARD, Lanc., a lion, rampant, ar., between paws a cross crosslet, fitched, of the same. *Pl.* 125, *cr.* 2, (cross, *pl.* 141.)

HOWDEN, Baron, Iri. and U.K., (Caradoc;) a man in a coat of mail, crowned with a crown of three points, kneeling upon one knee, and presenting a sword, all ppr. *Traditus, non victus.*

HOWDEN, Sco., a castle, triple-towered, ppr. *Pl.* 123, *cr.* 14.

HOWDON, Eng., a dragon's head, spouting fire, ppr. *Feris tego. Pl.* 37, *cr.* 9.

HOWE, Earl and Baron, Viscount and Baron Curzon, (Pen-Curzon-Howe): 1. For *Howe*, out of a ducal coronet, or, a plume of five feathers, az. *Pl.* 100, *cr.* 12, (without charge.) 2. For *Curzon*, a popinjay, (rising, or, collared, gu.) *Let Curzon holde what Curzon helde. Pl.* 25, *cr.* 2.

HOWE, Wilts. and Notts., a gauntlet, in fess, ppr., lined, gu., holding a falchion, ar., hilted, or, enfiled with a wolf's head, erased, of the first. *Pl.* 96, *cr.* 11.

HOWE, Somers., an arm, erect, ppr., vested, ar., charged with two bends, wavy, gu., in hand a bunch of broom, vert. *Pl.* 94, *cr.* 15.

HOWE, in dexter hand a wheat-ear, ppr. *Pl.* 71, *cr.* 15.

HOWEL, and HOWELL, Eng., a camel, ppr. *Pl.* 17, *cr.* 2.

HOWEL, and HOWELL, a beaver, passant, ppr. *Pl.* 49, *cr.* 5.

HOWELL, Glouc., a stag, lodged, sa., (in mouth a leaf, ppr.) *Pl.* 67, *cr.* 2.

HOWES, or HOWSE, of Morningthorpe, Norf., out of a coronet, a demi-unicorn, ppr. *Stat fortuna domus. Pl.* 26, *cr.* 14, (coronet, *pl.* 128, *fig.* 3.)

HOWETTS, a nail, erect, head (downward,) ppr., enfiled with a mural coronet, ar. *Pl.* 47, *cr.* 10, (coronet, *pl.* 128, *fig.* 18.)

HOWGART, Sco., a horse's head, ppr., between wings, ar. *Candor dat viribus alas. Pl.* 19, *cr.* 13.

HOWISON, Iri., an antelope, passant, gu. *Pl.* 63, *cr.* 10.

HOWLAND, Eng., a leopard, passant, gardant, ducally gorged, ppr. *Pl.* 120, *cr.* 9.

HOWLAND, Baron. *See* BEDFORD, Duke of.

HOWLET, an owl's head, erased, ppr., gorged with a mural coronet, or.

HOWNDHILE, or HOWNDHILL, Eng., a Saracen's head, ppr., wreathed, or and gu. *Pl.* 36, *cr.* 3.

HOWNHILL, Eng., in lion's gamb, erased, a tilting-spear, in bend, tasselled, all ppr. *Pl.* 1, *cr.* 4.

HOWORTH, Lanc., a stag's head, gu., attired, or, gorged with a wreath, ar. *Pl.* 38, *cr.* 1.

HOWSE, Eng., in dexter hand, an ear of wheat, ppr. *Pl.* 71, *cr.* 15.

HOWSON, Eng., a falcon, belled, ppr. *Ad finem fidelis. Pl.* 67, *cr.* 3.

HOWSTON, Sco., on a ducal coronet, a lion, passant. *Pl.* 107, *cr.* 11.

HOWTH, Earl of, and Baron, Viscount St Lawrence (St Lawrence,) Iri., a sea-lion, rampant, per fess, ar. and ppr. *Qui pense. Pl.* 25, *cr.* 12.

HOY, Eng., a demi-lion, gu., supporting a long cross, or. *Pl.* 29, *cr.* 12.

HOY, Iri., a pheasant, ppr. *Pl.* 82, *cr.* 12, (without collar.)

HOYE, Eng., a demi-lion, gu., supporting a passion cross, or. *Pl.* 29, *cr.* 12.

HOYLAND, Eng., a dexter hand, in fess, issuing from a cloud in sinister, pointing towards a crosier, in pale, issuing, ppr. *Pl.* 45, *cr.* 4.

HOYLES, Eng., a youth's head, in a helmet, affrontée, ppr., plumed, ar. *Pl.* 92, *cr.* 12.

HUBAND, GEORGE, Esq., M.A., a wolf, passant, or. *Cave lupum. Pl.* 46, *cr.* 6.

HUBAND, Warw. and Derbs., a wolf, passant, or. *Pl.* 46, *cr.* 6.

HUBBERT, Iri., a boar's head, sa. *Pl.* 48, *cr.* 2.

HUBERT, Middx., on a chapeau, gu., turned up, erm., a lion's head, erased, or, charged with three etoiles, in fess, of the first. *Pl.* 99, *cr.* 9, (etoile, *pl.* 141.)

HUCKMORE, Devons., a falcon, ppr., preying on a moorcock, sa., combed and wattled, gu. *Pl.* 80, *cr.* 12.

HUCKS, between attires of a stag, affixed to scalp, a boar's head, erased and erect. *Pl.* 33, *cr.* 15.

HUDDERSFIELD, Eng., a boar, passant, or. *Pl.* 48, *cr.* 14.

HUDDLESTON, and HUDDLESTONE, Eng., on a ducal coronet, a peacock, ppr. *Pl.* 43, *cr.* 7.

HUDDY, Somers., a bull, passant, sa., attired, or. *Pl.* 66, *cr.* 11.

HUDDLESTON, Camb., two hands holding up a bloody scalp. *Soli Deo honor et gloria.*

HUDDLESTONE, Sco., in dexter hand a writing-pen, ppr. *Ingenio et viribus. Pl.* 26, *cr.* 13.

HUDSON, Lond., a dexter hand, erect, holding with the thumb and first finger a bezant, ppr. *Pl.* 24, *cr.* 3, (bezant, *pl.* 141.)

HUDSON, Norf., a fawn's head, erased, ppr., gorged with a mural coronet, or. *Pl.* 6, *cr.* 1, (coronet, *same plate, cr.* 2.)

HUDSON, Iri., on a chapeau, gu., turned up, or, an owl, wings expanded, ar. *Pl.* 123, *cr.* 6.

HUDSON, Eng., a martlet, az., winged, or. *Pl.* 111, *cr.* 5.

HUDSON, Lond., a martlet, vert, winged, or. *Pl.* 111, *cr.* 5.

HUDSON, out of a ducal coronet, a griffin's head, in mouth a trefoil, slipped. *Pl.* 89, *cr.* 5, (trefoil, *pl.* 141.)

HUDSON-VILLAVINCE, Bart., Leic., a griffin's head, erased, ar., gorged with a mural coronet, gu., charged with three escallops, of the first. *Pl.* 74, *cr.* 1, (griffin, *same plate;* escallop, *pl.* 141.)

HUDSPATH, a griffin, segreant, between claws a tilting-spear, enfiled with a boar's head, erased. *Pl.* 74, *cr.* 10, (head, *pl.* 10, *cr.* 2.)

HUET, a crow, rising, ppr. *Pl.* 50, *cr.* 5.

HUGER, a sprig, thereon a Virginia nightingale, ppr. *Ubi libertas, ibi patria. Pl.* 13, *cr.* 4.

HUGFORD, a lion's paw issuing, and resting upon a shield. *Pl.* 43, *cr.* 12.

HUGGERFORD, Glouc. and Warw., a stag's head, or., gorged with a chaplet of laurel, vert. *Pl.* 38, *cr.* 1.

HUGGESSEN, on a mount, vert, an oak-tree, ppr., between wings, az. *Pl.* 48, *cr.* 4, (wings, *pl.* 1, *cr.* 15.)

HUGGINS, Eng., a sword, in pale, enfiled with a leopard's face. *Pl.* 24, *cr.* 13.

HUGHAM, Eng., a fox's head, ar., semée of torteaux, gu. *Pl.* 91, *cr.* 9, (torteau, *pl.* 141.)

HUGHES, R., Esq., of Kinmel, Invercauld, Braemar, out of a baron's coronet, a demi-lion, rampant, holding between fore-paws a rose. *Heb Dduw heb ddim Duw a digon. Pl.* 126 c, *cr.* 11.

HUGHES, Oxon., a heron, ar. *Pl.* 6, *cr.* 13.

HUGHES, Bart., Suff., a lion, couchant, gardant, or. *Pl.* 101, *cr.* 8.

HUGHES, a lion, rampant, or, holding a thistle, slipped, ppr. *Pl.* 64, *cr.* 2, (thistle, *pl.*109,*cr.*4.)

HUGHES, out of a baron's coronet, a demi-lion, between paws a cinquefoil. *Pl.* 47, *cr.* 4, (coronet, *pl.* 127, *fig.* 11; cinquefoil, *pl.* 141.)

HUGHES, Wel., an eagle's head, erased, sa., in beak a (staff, raguly inflamed,) ppr. *Pl.*22,*cr.*1.

HUGHES, a lion, sejant, (in mouth a dart.) *Pl.* 126, *cr.* 15.

HUGHES, a boar's head, erased, in fess. *Pl.* 16, *cr.* 11.

HUGHES, Iri., a griffin, sejant, gu., winged, armed, and beaked, or, holding a laurel-garland, vert. *Pl.* 56, *cr.* 10.

HUGHES, Sco., out of a ducal coronet, a unicorn's head, ar. *Pl.* 45, *cr.* 14.

HUGHES, Kent, on a chapeau, gu., turned up, erm., a demi-eagle, wings elevated, ppr. *Pl.* 96, *cr.* 9.

HUGHES, a Cornish chough, ppr., in dexter a fleur-de-lis, ar. *Pl.* 100, *cr.* 13, (fleur-de-lis, *pl.* 141.)

HUGHES, out of a ducal coronet, or, a demi-lion, rampant, sa., armed and langued, gu. *Pl.* 45, *cr.* 7.

HUGHES, on a chapeau, gu., turned up, erm., a demi-lion, rampant, in dexter a fleur-de-lis. *Pl.* 46, *cr.* 8, (fleur-de-lis, *pl.* 91, *cr.* 13.)

HUGHES, Wel., in hand, in armour, ppr., couped above wrist, in fess, a fleur-de-lis, ar. *Pl.* 46, *cr.* 12, (armour, *pl.* 85, *cr.* 12.)

HUGHES, Well., (out of a coronet, composed of a plain circle of gold, surmounted by four pearls,) a demi-lion, ar., in paws a rose, gu. *Pl.* 80, *cr.* 11.

HUGHES, ROBERT, Esq., of Ely House, Wexford, a griffin's head, erased, gu. *Verus amor patriæ. Pl.* 38, *cr.* 3.

HUGO, Devons., a lion, rampant, in paws a standard, ar., charged with a cross, gu. *Pl.* 99, *cr.* 2.

HUGWORTH, Eng., a goat, (passant,) ar., armed and hoofed, or. *Pl.* 66, *cr.* 1.

HULBERT, Eng., out of a cloud, a hand, in pale, ppr., holding a garland of laurel. *Pl.* 88, *cr.* 13.

HULBURN, Eng., a lion, issuant, in dexter a mullet, ar. *Pl.* 89, *cr.* 10.

HULGRAVE, Eng., a hand grasping a thunderbolt, ppr. *Pl.* 21, *cr.* 8.

HULL, Durh., a cubit arm, erect, ppr., vested, per pale, az. and gu., cuff, ar., in hand a fleur-de-lis, parted at sleeve. *Pl.* 95, *cr.* 9.

HULL, Eng., a hunting-horn, az., garnished, ar. *Pl.* 89, *cr.* 3.

HULL, Surr., a dragon's head, sa., eared, gu. *Pl.* 87, *cr.* 12.

HULL, Sco., a talbot's head, sa. *Pl.* 123, *cr.* 15.

HULL, Iri., a pigeon, volant, az. *Pl.* 25, *cr.* 6.

HULLEYS, and HULLIES, Eng., out of a ducal coronet, or, a unicorn's head, gu. *Pl.*45, *cr.*14.

HULLY, Iri., a greyhound's head, az., bezantée. *Pl.* 14, *cr.* 4.

HULSE, Bart., Middx., a buck's head, couped, ppr., attired, or, (between attires,) the sun, gold. *Pl.* 62, *cr.* 14.

HULSE, Eng., a buck's head, gorged with a chaplet, ppr. *Pl.* 38, *cr.* 1.

HULTON, a buck's head, cabossed, or. *Pl.* 36, *cr.* 1.

HULTON, out of a tower, ppr., three arrows, sa. *Pl.* 69, *cr.* 9, (arrows, *pl.* 43, *cr.* 14.)

HULTON, out of a mural coronet, a stag's head, in mouth a (branch of hawthorn.) *Mens flecti nescia. Pl.* 112, *cr.* 5.

HULTON, Lanc., out of a crown, or, a hart's head and neck, gardant, ar., horned, gold, between two branches of (hawthorn,) ppr. *Pl.* 29, *cr.* 7, (branches, *pl.* 114, *cr.* 15.)

HULYN, Eng., on a lion's head, (couped,) or, a chapeau, az., turned up, erm. *Pl.*123, *cr.* 13.

HUMBLE, Eng., on a chapeau, an owl, rising. *Pl.* 123, *cr.* 6.

HUMBLE, a stag's head, erased. *Pl.* 66, *cr.* 9.

HUMBLE-NUGENT, Bart., Iri., a demi-stag, ppr., horned, or, charged on breast with a trefoil, vert. *Pl.* 55, *cr.* 9, (without rose; trefoil, *pl.* 141.)

HUMBERSTON, Herts. and Norf., a griffin's head, erased, ar., charged with three pellets, in pale. *Pl.* 48, *cr.* 6, (pellet, *pl.* 141.)

HUME, Bart., Herts., a lion's head, erased, ar. *True to the end. Pl.* 81, *cr.* 4.

HUME, of Humewood, co. Wicklow, same crest and motto.

HUME, of Renton, Sco., a pelican, ppr. *Pl.* 109, *cr.* 15.

HUME, of Crossrigs, Sco., a lion's head, erased, ar., collared, gu. *True to the end. Pl.* 7, *cr.*10.

HUME, of Polwart, Sco., a lion's head, erased, ar., collared, gu., charged with a rose, or. *True to the end. Pl.* 7, *cr.* 10, (rose, *pl.* 141.)

HUME, Sco., a demi-leopard, ppr. *Perseverance. Pl.* 12, *cr.* 14.

HUME, of Coldinghamton, a hand issuing from a human heart, holding a couteau sword, all ppr. *True to the end. Pl.* 35, *cr.* 7.

HUME, of Ninewells, a lion's head, erased, ppr., collared, gu. *True to the end. Pl.* 7, *cr.* 10.

HUME, Sco., a hand holding a scimitar, ppr., issuing from a human heart, or. *Pl.* 35, *cr.* 7.

HUME, Sco., out of a crescent, horns upward, a lion's head. *Pl.* 96, *cr.* 13, (without crown.)

HUMERSTON, Norf., a griffin's head, erased, ar., langued, gu., charged with three pellets, in pale. *Pl.* 48, *cr.* 6, (pellets, *pl.* 141.)

HUMFFREYS, on a chapeau, a boar, passant, ar., fretty, gu. *Pl.* 22, *cr.* 8.

HUMFREY, of Wroxham House: 1. For *Humfrey*, on a ducal coronet, an eagle, wings elevated, in dexter a sceptre, or, charged on breast with a cross crosslet, gu. *Pl.* 118, *cr.* 1, (coronet, *pl.* 128, *fig.* 3; sceptre, *pl.* 82, *cr.* 3; cross, *pl.* 141.) 2. For *Blake*, on a morion, a martlet, ppr. *Pl.* 18, *cr.* 9, (martlet, *pl.* 111, *cr.* 5.)

HUMFREY, co. Cavan, on a ducal coronet, an eagle, wings elevated, in dexter a sceptre, or. *Pl.* 118, *cr.* 1, (coronet, *pl.* 128, *fig.* 3; sceptre, *pl.* 82, *cr.* 3.)

HUMFREY, Northamp., a harpy, ar., eared, ppr., crined, or, wings expanded, gold. *Pl.* 32, *cr.* 3.

HUMFREYS, Dors., a leopard, passant, ar., (embrued at mouth, gu.) *Pl.* 86, *cr.* 2.

HUMPHRESS, a boar's head, couped. *Pl.* 48, *cr.* 2.

HUMPHREY, HUMPHRIE, and HUMPHROY, Eng., a demi-griffin, wings addorsed, between paws a ducal coronet, ppr. *Pl.* 18, *cr.* 6, (coronet, same plate.)

HUMPHREYS, a boar's head, couped, in fess. *Pl.* 48, *cr.* 2.

HUMPHREYS, HUMPHRIES, or HUMPHRYES, Eng., three legs conjoined at thigh, flexed at knees, and spurred, ppr. *Pl.* 71, *cr.* 14.

HUN, Ess., a demi-lion, rampant, ar., ducally gorged, or. *Pl.* 87, *cr.* 15.

HUNCKS, or HUNKES, Bucks., Glouc., Warw., and Worc., a greyhound, current, erm., (collared, sa.) *Pl.* 28, *cr.* 7, (without charge.)

HUNGERFORD, co. Cork, out of a ducal coronet, or, a pepper garb, between two reaping hooks, all ppr. *Et Dieu mon appuy*. *Pl.* 13, *cr.* 10, (coronet, *pl.* 128, *fig.* 3; hook, *pl.* 36, *cr.* 12.)

HUNINGES, Chesh. and Suff., a lion's head, erased, ar., collared, sa. *Pl.* 7, *cr.* 10.

HUNLOKE, Bart., Derbs., on a chapeau, az., turned up, erm., a cockatrice, wings (expanded,) ppr., combed, beaked, and wattled, or. *Pl.* 103, *cr.* 9.

HUNT, LE, Eng., out of a baron's coronet, a hand holding a cutlass, all ppr. *Pl.* 66, *cr.* 6, (coronet, *pl.* 127, *cr.* 11.)

HUNT, LE, Iri., in hand a boar's head, erased and erect, in pale. *Pl.* 86, *cr.* 6.

HUNT, a leopard's face. *Pl.* 66, *cr.* 14.

HUNT, Salop, a talbot, sejant, sa., collared, or, lined, az., line tied to a halberd, in pale, gold, headed, of the third. *Pl.* 107, *cr.* 7, (halberd, *pl.* 14, *cr.* 8.)

HUNT, Bart., Iri., a castle, triple-towered, ar., from the centre tower, of a pyramidal shape, a banner displayed, gu. *Vero nihil verius*. *Pl.* 123, *cr.* 14.

HUNT, (on a mount, vert,) a talbot, sejant, or, collared and lined, gu., the lining fastened by a bow-knot to a halberd, erect, staff, of the second, blade, ar. *Pl.* 107, *cr.* 7, (halberd, *pl.* 14, *cr.* 8.)

HUNT, Derbs., a bugle-horn, sa., stringed, vert. *Pl.* 48, *cr.* 12.

HUNT, between two ostrich-feathers, a boar's head, couped and erect, all ppr. *Pl.* 60, *cr.* 7.

HUNT, Devons. and Worc., a boar's head, erect, between two ostrich-feathers, sa. *Pl.* 60, *cr.* 7.

HUNT, a talbot, sejant, collared. *Pl.* 107, *cr.* 7.

HUNT, Sco., a lion's head, erased, collared, ppr. *Vi et virtute*. *Pl.* 7, *cr.* 10.

HUNTER, Sco., a stag's head, erased, ppr. *Pl.* 66, *cr.* 9.

HUNTER, Sco., an anchor, in pale. *Pl.* 25, *cr.* 15.

HUNTER, Sco., a hunting-horn, vert, stringed, gu. *Spero*—and—*In cornua salutem spero*. *Pl.* 48, *cr.* 12.

HUNTER, Norf., a boar's head, erased, ppr. *Pl.* 16, *cr.* 11.

HUNTER, of Hunter, a greyhound, sejant, ar., (collared, or.) *Cursum perficio*. *Pl.* 66, *cr.* 15.

HUNTER, RICHARD, Esq., of Straadarran, Londonderry, a stag's head, cabossed, ppr. *Arte et Marte*. *Pl.* 36, *cr.* 1.

HUNTER, Bart., Lond., a demi-lion, between paws a cross pattée, fitched, sa. *Pl.* 65, *cr.* 6, (pattée, *pl.* 15, *cr.* 8.)

HUNTER, Sco., a hunting-horn, vert, veruled, or, and stringed, gu. *In cornua salutem spero*. *Pl.* 48, *cr.* 12.

HUNTER, Eng., two lions' heads, addorsed, ppr. *Pl.* 28, *cr.* 10.

HUNTER, Sco., a greyhound's head. *Dum spiro, spero*. *Pl.* 89, *cr.* 2.

HUNTER, Lond., a boar's head, erased. *Pl.* 16, *cr.* 11.

HUNTER, Sco., two hands shooting an arrow from a bow, all ppr. *Fortuna sequatur*. *Pl.* 100, *cr.* 4.

HUNTER, Lond., a fir-tree, ppr. *Fecunditate afficior*. *Pl.* 26, *cr.* 10.

HUNTER, Iri., an urus's head, erased, sa. *Pl.* 57, *cr.* 7.

HUNTER, Sco., a greyhound in full course, ar., (collared,) or. *Expedite*. *Pl.* 28, *cr.* 7.

HUNTER, Sco., a hunting-horn, vert, stringed, gu. *Spero*. *Pl.* 48, *cr.* 12.

HUNTER, a buck's head, erased, or. *Pl.* 66, *cr.* 9.

HUNTER, a greyhound's head and neck, ar. *Pl.* 14, *cr.* 4, (without charge.)

HUNTER, a greyhound's head and neck, erased, ar. *Pl.* 89, *cr.* 2.

HUNTER, Lond., a demi-lion, or. *Pl.* 67, *cr.* 10.

HUNTER, ANDREW, Esq., of Bonnytoun and Doonholm, Ayr, a stag's head, cabossed. *Vigilantia, robur, voluptas*. *Pl.* 36, *cr.* 1.

HUNTER, CHARLES, Esq., of Seaside and Glencarse, Perth, a greyhound's head, ar., collared, gu. *Dum spiro, spero*. *Pl.* 43, *cr.* 11.

HUNTER, MATHEW-DYSERT, Esq., of Durh. and Berwick, a deer's head. *Vigilantia, robur, voluptas*. *Pl.* 91, *cr.* 14.

HUNTER-ARUNDELL, WILLIAM-FRANCIS, Esq., of Barjarg Tower, Dumfries, a stag's head, erased. *Vigilantia, robur, voluptas*. *Pl.* 66, *cr.* 9.

HUNTERCOMB, a sword, in pale, enfiled with a man's head, couped, (wreathed.) *Pl.* 27, *cr.* 3.

HUNTERCOMB, an arm, in armour, issuing from a cloud, hand grasping a sword, ppr. *Pl.* 80, *cr.* 10.

HUNTINGDON, Earl of, (Hastings,) a buffalo's head, erased, sa., crowned and gorged with a ducal coronet, and armed, or. *In veritate*—and—*Honorantes me honorabo*. *Pl.* 57, *cr.* 7, (crown and gorging, *same plate, cr.* 8.)

HUNTINGDON, and HUNTINGTON, Eng., a crosier, ar. *Pl.* 7, *cr.* 15.

HUNTINGFIELD, Baron, Iri., and a Bart., G.B., (Vanneck,) a bugle-horn, gu., stringed, or, between wings, per fess, of the second, and ar. *Droit et loyal.* *Pl.* 98, *cr.* 2.

HUNTINGFIELD, Eng., a dagger and (sword,) in saltier, ppr. *Pl.* 24, *cr.* 2.

HUNTINGTOWER, Lord. See TOLLEMACHE, Bart.

HUNTLEY, Glouc., a talbot, ppr., collared and lined, or. *Pl.* 65, *cr.* 2.

HUNTLY, Eng., a talbot, passant, gu., collared and stringed, or. *Pl.* 65, *cr.* 2.

HURD, Eng., a bear's head, sa., muzzled, gu., between wings. *Pl.* 44, *cr.* 5.

HURD, Worc., a horse's head, (couped,) ar., maned, or. *Pl.* 81, *cr.* 6.

HURELL, and HURLE, a lion, rampant, holding a flag, gu., charged with a cross in the dexter chief. *Pl.* 99, *cr.* 2.

HURLESTONE, Eng., a goat's head, ar., bearded and attired, or, on neck four ermine-spots, in cross. *Pl.* 105, *cr.* 14, (ermine, *pl.* 141.)

HURLEY, Eng., a pillar, ppr. *Pl.* 33, *cr.* 1.

HURLEY, Eng., on a ducal coronet, a peacock, ppr. *Pl.* 43, *cr.* 7.

HURLEY, co. Kerry, out of an antique Irish crown, or, a naked arm, embowed, ppr., in hand a cross crosslet, gold. *Dextra cruce vincit.*

HURLSTON, Lanc., an ermine, passant, ppr. *Pl.* 87, *cr.* 3, (without mount.)

HUROT, Eng., two hands, couped, conjoined, in fess, ppr. *Pl.* 1, *cr.* 2.

HURR, Eng., a harpy, wings expanded, ppr. *Pl.* 32, *cr.* 3.

HURRELL, Eng., a lion, rampant, ppr., holding a flag, displayed, gu., charged with a cross in the dexter chief. *Pl.* 99, *cr.* 2.

HURRY, Sco., a lion's gamb. *Sans tache.* *Pl.* 126, *cr.* 9.

HURSEY, and HURSY, a boot, sa. *Pl.* 95, *cr.* 13.

HURST, Suss., an oak-tree, ppr. *Pl.* 16, *cr.* 8.

HURST, Leic., a dragon, wings elevated, ar., resting dexter on a cross crosslet, or. *Pl.* 90, *cr.* 10, (cross, *pl.* 141.)

HURST, Herts., in a wood, ppr., the sun, or.

HURST, Herts., rising from behind a castle, ppr., standing on a mount, vert, the sun, or. *Pl.* 38, *cr.* 6, (castle, *pl.* 113, *cr.* 7.)

HURT, of Alderwasley, a hart, (passant,) ppr., horned, membered, and pierced in haunch by an arrow, or, feathered, ar. *Mane prædam, vesperi spolium.* *Pl.* 88, *cr.* 9.

HURT, Derb., a stag, trippant, ppr., attired, or, vulned in haunch by an arrow, gold, feathered, ar. *Pl.* 88, *cr.* 9.

HURT, Derbs., Staffs., and Devons., a stag, statant, wounded in buttocks by an arrow. *Pl.* 88, *cr.* 9.

HUSBAND, Eng., a demi-griffin, between paws a ducal coronet, ppr. *Pl.* 18, *cr.* 6, (coronet, same plate.)

HUSDELL, Durh., a demi-lion, ppr. *Trust in God.* *Pl.* 67, *cr.* 10.

HUSE, in dexter hand, ppr., a cross pattée, (in pale,) or. *Pl.* 99, *cr.* 15.

HUSEE, Eng., a leopard, passant, gardant, ppr. *Pl.* 51, *cr.* 7.

HUSKISSON, Suss., an elephant's head, erased, ppr. *Pl.* 68, *cr.* 4.

HUSKISSON, Eng., on a rock, a goose, perched, ppr. *Pl.* 94, *cr.* 3.

HUSON, Eng., a ram's head, erased, ar., horned, or. *Pl.* 1, *cr.* 12.

HUSSEY, on a mount, vert, a hind, passant, ar., under a tree, ppr. *Pl.* 75, *cr.* 6, (tree, *pl.* 95, *cr.* 10.)

HUSSEY, Linc., Dors., and Wilts., on a mount, vert, a hind, couchant, against a hawthorn-tree, ppr.

HUSSEY, Wilts., Ess., Dors., and Salop, a boot, sa., spurred, or, topped, erm. *Pl.* 53, *cr.* 1.

HUSSEY, Linc., Dors., and Wilts., on a mount, vert, a hind, couchant, against a hawthorn-tree, ppr., ducally gorged and lined, or.

HUSSEY, Iri., an arm, in armour, vambraced, az., holding a cross crosslet, fitched, in pale, or. *Pl.* 21, *cr.* 14, (cross, *pl.* 141.)

HUSSEY, a boot, sa., and thereon a human heart, held by two hands, issuing from clouds, fesswise, dexter and sinister. *Pl.* 52, *cr.* 13, (boot, *pl.* 118, *cr.* 6.)

HUSSEY, Kent, a hind, ducally gorged, and chained, couchant, under an oak tree, ppr.

HUSSEY, EDWARD, Esq., Scotney Castle, Suss., a boot, sa., spur, or, turned down, erm. *Ut tibi sic aliis.* *Pl.* 53, *cr.* 1.

HUSTLER, Yorks., a talbot, sejant, gorged with a collar, az., charged with three fleurs-de-lis, or. *Pl.* 107, *cr.* 7, (fleur-de-lis, *pl.* 141.)

HUSTWICK, Yorks., a lion, passant, ppr. *Opera Dei mirifica.* *Pl.* 48, *cr.* 8.

HUTCHENS, a lion's head, erased, or, gorged with a mural coronet, az. *Pl.* 81, *cr.* 4, (coronet, *pl.* 128, *fig.* 18.)

HUTCHESON, Sco., an arm, in armour, throwing a hammer, all ppr. *Sursum.* *Pl.* 96, *cr.* 6, (hammer, *pl.* 51, *cr.* 14.)

HUTCHESON, Sco., an arm, in armour, embowed, az., throwing a dart, pointed, gu., feathered, ar. *Sursum.* *Pl.* 96, *cr.* 6.

HUTCHINGS, Eng., out of a mural coronet, a demi-lion, in dexter a branch of palm, vert. *Pl.* 17, *cr.* 7.

HUTCHINGS, and HUTCHINS, Eng., a lion, passant, gardant, sa. *Pl.* 118, *cr.* 10.

HUTCHINSON, Durh., out of a ducal coronet, a cockatrice, az. *Nihil humani alienum.* *Pl.* 77, *cr.* 5, (cockatrice, *pl.* 63, *cr.* 15.)

HUTCHINSON, Eng., a parrot, gu., in beak an annulet, or. *Pl.* 33, *cr.* 11.

HUTCHINSON, Viscount. See DONOUGHMORE.

HUTCHINSON, Notts., out of a ducal coronet, or, a cockatrice, wings addorsed, az., beaked, combed, and wattled, gu. *Pl.* 77, *cr.* 5, (cockatrice, *pl.* 63, *cr.* 15.)

HUTCHINSON, Durh., a cockatrice, wings (expanded,) az., combed, wattled, and membered, or. *Cunctanter, tamen fortiter.* *Pl.* 63, *cr.* 15.

HUTCHINSON, Durh., a demi-lion, rampant. *Cunctanter, tamen fortiter.* *Pl.* 67, *cr.* 10.

HUTCHINSON, Iri., out of a ducal coronet, a swan's head and neck, between wings, all ppr. *Pl.* 83, *cr.* 1.

HUTCHINSON, Sco., a stag's head, erased, gu., attired, or. *Memor esto.* *Pl.* 66, *cr.* 9.

HUTCHINSON-SYNGE, Bart., Iri.: 1. Out of a ducal coronet, a cockatrice, all ppr. *Pl.* 77, *cr.* 5, (cockatrice, *pl.* 63, *cr.* 15.) 2. Out of a ducal coronet, an eagle's talon, all ppr. *Fortiter gerit crucem.* *Pl.* 96, *cr.* 7.

HUTCHISON, an arm, in armour, throwing a dart, ppr. *Surgam.* *Pl.* 96, *cr.* 6.

HUTCHISON, Eng., a stag, trippant, ppr. *Pl.* 68, *cr.* 2.

HUTCHISON, JAMES, Esq., of Rockend, Dumbarton, a stag's head, erased, gu., attired, or. *Memor esto.* Pl. 66, cr. 9.

HUTCHON, a stag's head, erased, at gaze. *Fortis est veritas.* Pl. 8, cr. 6.

HUTH, Lond., three sprigs of oak, erect, ppr., each bearing an acorn, or. Pl. 69, cr. 12.

HUTHWAIT, a pheon, or. Pl. 26, cr. 12.

HUTTOFT, a whale's head, erect and erased, az., gorged, with a mural coronet, or, thereon three pellets, to the collar a chain and ring, of the second. Pl. 96, cr. 8.

HUTTON, a hind, (statant.) Pl. 60, cr. 14.

HUTTON, JOHN, Esq., Yorks., on a wreath, ar. and gu., a cushion, of the second, (placed lozenge-wise,) thereon an open book, edges gilt, inscribed "Odor," on one side, and "Vitæ," on the other. *Spiritus gladius.* Pl. 112, cr. 14.

HUTTON, TIMOTHY, Esq., Yorks. : 1. Same crest. 2. A stag's head, erased, lozengy, ar. and az. *Spiritus gladius.* Pl. 66, cr. 9, (lozenge, pl. 141.)

HUTTON, WILLIAM, Esq., of Gate Burton, Lincoln, a buck's head, cabossed, or. *Spero.* Pl. 36, cr. 1.

HUTTON, Yorks., (three) broad arrows, two in saltier, and one in pale, sa., enfiled with a ducal coronet, or. Pl. 37, cr. 5.

HUTTON, Cambs. and Cumb., two eagles' heads, erased, (in saltier,) addorsed, sa., enfiled with a coronet, or. Pl. 94, cr. 12, (coronet, *same plate.*)

HUTTON, Durh., an ostrich's head, between wings, ar., in mouth a horse-shoe, or. Pl. 28, cr. 13.

HUTTON, Durh. and Lanc., a man, ppr., banded round waist, ar., in dexter three leaves, vert.

HUTTON, Durh. and Lanc., an American ppr., wreathed round middle, vert, in dexter a tobacco leaf, ppr.

HUTTON, Durh. and Kent, a blackamoor, wreathed about temples and waist, in dexter a trefoil, slipped, vert.

HUTTON, (three double-pointed) darts, sa., feathered and pointed, ar., in a ducal coronet, or. Pl. 37, cr. 5.

HUTTON, Lond., an eagle displayed, or, beaked and legged, sa., between two branches of laurel, vert. Pl. 48, cr. 11, (branches, pl. 79, cr. 14.)

HUTTON, Wilts. and Sco., a serpent, catching at the finger of a man's hand, issuing from a cloud, all ppr. Pl. 121, cr. 1.

HUTTON, Iri., out of a crescent, or, an arrow, in pale, sa. Pl. 82, cr. 15.

HUXHAM, Lond. and Devons., (a demi-lion, rampant,) ermines, in paws an escutcheon, ar., charged with a cross crosslet, gu. Pl. 22, cr. 13, (cross, pl. 141.)

HUXLEY, Middx., out of a ducal coronet, or, a demi-lion, rampant, erm., (collared, gold,) between paws a crescent, of the last. Pl. 47, cr. 11, (coronet, *same plate.*)

HUXLEY, Chesh., a snake, ppr. Pl. 1, cr. 9.

HUXLEY, a wolf's head, (erased,) gorged with a collar, charged with three crescents. Pl. 8, cr. 4, (crescent, pl. 141.)

HUYSHE, an elephant's head, couped, ar., crowned and tusked. Pl. 35, cr. 13, (crown, pl. 128, fig. 3.)

HYATT, out of the battlements of a tower, gu., a demi-lion, rampant, sa. Pl. 42, cr. 4.

HYATT, Eng., a demi-lion, rampant. *Fac et spera.* Pl. 67, cr. 10.

HYDE, of Castle Hyde, a lion's head, erased, sa., bezantée. Pl. 81, cr. 4, (bezant, pl. 90, cr. 4.)

HYDE, Dors., a cock's head, erased, az., crested and jalloped, gu., bezantée, in the mouth a flower, of the last. Pl. 92, cr. 3, (flower, *same plate,* cr. 15.)

HYDE, a cock's head, erased, az., combed, purp., (on neck a lozenge, or, between four bezants,) in beak, a pansy-flower, ppr., stalked and leaved, vert. Pl. 92, cr. 3, (pansy, pl. 30, cr. 1.)

HYDE, Lond., a unicorn's head, erased, ar., armed and maned, or, collared, vair. Pl. 73, cr. 1.

HYDE, Lond., a (dexter) wing, gu. Pl. 39, cr. 10.

HYDE, a unicorn's head, gorged with a collar, compony. Pl. 73, cr. 1.

HYDE, Iri., on a mount, a holy lamb, ppr., standard, az. Pl. 101, cr. 9.

HYDE, a stag's head, ar. Pl. 91, cr. 14.

HYDE, a standard, in pale, with flag and tassels. Pl. 8, cr. 3, (tassels, pl. 1, cr. 4.)

HYETT, in dexter hand, a thistle, in pale, ppr. Pl. 36, cr. 6.

HYETT, Somers., a demi-pegasus, sa., crined, or, wings addorsed, gold. Pl. 91, cr. 2, (without coronet.)

HYETT, of Painwick: 1. For *Hyett,* out of a castle, ppr., charged with four pellets, a lion's head, in mouth a rose, (slipped,) gu. Pl. 28, cr. 11, (head, pl. 95, cr. 6.) 2. For *Adams,* a greyhound's head, erased, erm. Pl. 89, cr. 2.

HYGHLORD, Eng., a ship in the sea, in full sail, all ppr. Pl. 109, cr. 8.

HYGHMORE, Cumb., a moorcock, ppr.

HYLAND, on a mural coronet, a garb, thereon a bird, ppr. Pl. 14, cr. 5.

HYLDEARD, Eng., a cock, ppr. Pl. 67, cr. 14.

HYMAN, Eng., a demi-cupid, in dexter a torch. Pl. 70, cr. 14.

HYND, Lond., in hand, gu., an eagle's claw, ppr. Pl. 103, cr. 4.

HYNDE, Eng., on a griffin's head, az., collared, or, between wings, of the first, guttée, ar., an escallop. Pl. 22, cr. 2, (escallop, pl. 141.)

HYNDE, a hind's head, couped, ppr., (collared, or,) in mouth a rose, gu., leaved, vert. Pl. 21, cr. 9, (rose, pl. 117, cr. 10.)

HYNDE, an ostrich's head, couped, chequy, ar. and sa., in mouth a horse-shoe, az. Pl. 28, cr. 13, (without wings.)

HYNDMAN, the sun, shining on a sun-dial. *True as the dial to the sun.* Pl. 97, cr. 6, (sun, pl. 45, cr. 13.)

HYNELL, an angel, praying. Pl. 94, cr. 11, (without branches.)

HYNES, Iri., an elephant, passant, sa. Pl. 56, cr. 14.

HYRSON, out of a cloud, a dexter hand holding a club. Pl. 37, cr. 13.

I

I'ANSON, a griffin's head, between wings, ppr. *Pl.* 65, *cr.* 1.

IBBETSON, Bart., Yorks., a unicorn's head, erased, per fess, ar. and gu., charged with three escallops, two and one, counterchanged. *Vixi liber, et moriar.* *Pl.* 67, *cr.* 1, (escallop, *pl.* 141.)

IBBETSON, a horse's head, erased. *Pl.* 81, *cr.* 6.

IBBETSON, a horse's head, (charged with a pale, indented,) sa. *Pl.* 81, *cr.* 6.

IBBITSON, or IBBOTSON, Eng., on a ducal coronet, a wyvern, (vomiting flames at end,) ppr. *Pl.* 104, *cr.* 11.

IBETSON, Yorks., a unicorn's head, ar., powdered with escallops, gu., attired, maned, and erased, of the last. *Vixi liber et moriar.* *Pl.* 67, *cr.* 1, (escallop, *pl.* 141.)

IBGRAVE, Herts., a dexter arm, embowed, vested, bendy of six, or and az., cuffed, ar., in hand, ppr., a cross crosslet, fitched, sa. *Pl.* 88, *cr.* 7.

ICHINGHAM, and ILCHINGHAM, Eng., a demi-dragon, wings expanded, vert. *Pl.* 105, *cr.* 11.

IDLE, Eng., a helmet, az., garnished, or. *Pl.* 109, *cr.* 5.

IDLE, a tiger, passant, (under fore-dexter a helmet.) *Pl.* 86, *cr.* 2.

IFIELD, out of a ducal coronet, a dolphin's head, az. *Pl.* 94, *cr.* 14, (head, *pl.* 112, *cr.* 8.)

IHONES, Lond. and Salop, a lion, rampant, or, supporting an anchor, az., timbered, gold. *Pl.* 22, *cr.* 15, (anchor, *pl.* 19, *cr.* 6.)

ILAM, and ILAMY, a peacock's head, or, between wings, in beak a serpent, tail round neck, ppr. *Pl.* 50, *cr.* 9.

ILBERT, Devons., a cock-pheasant, ar., combed and wattled, gu. *Pl.* 82, *cr.* 12, (without collar.)

ILBERT, Devons., a demi-wyvern, vert, (collared, or.) *Pl.* 116, *cr.* 15.

ILCHESTER, Earl of, and Lord, Baron Strangways, (Fox-Strangways,) on a chapeau, az., turned up, erm., a fox, sejant, or. *Faire sans dire.* *Pl.* 57, *cr.* 14.

ILDERTON, Eng., out of a ducal coronet, or, a battle-axe, handle broken, ppr. *Pl.* 24, *cr.* 15, (coronet, *same plate, cr.* 10.)

ILDERTON, Northumb., a dragon. *Pl.* 90, *cr.* 10.

ILE, or LISLE, Durh., a demi-lion, rampant, between paws an escallop. *Pl.* 126 A, *cr.* 13.

ILES, Eng., a wolf, collared and (lined,) ppr. *Pl.* 5, *cr.* 8, (without staff.)

ILEY, a cubit arm, erect, vested, ar., in hand, ppr., a fleur-de-lis, sa. *Pl.* 95, *cr.* 9.

ILEY, ILLEY, and ILNEY, in hand, erect, a cross crosslet, fitched, in pale. *Pl.* 51, *cr.* 1.

ILIFF, out of a ducal coronet, a peacock's tail, ppr. *Pl.* 120, *cr.* 13.

ILINN, Eng., a wolf's head, erased, gu. *Pl.* 14, *cr.* 6.

ILLINGSWORTH, and ILLINGWORTH, within a crescent, ar., a cock, crowing, sa. *Pl.* 17, *cr.* 1.

ILLINGSWORTH, a demi-lion, (charged with three roundles,) between paws a battle-axe. *Pl.* 101, *cr.* 14.

ILLSLEY, or ILSLEY, between two serpents, in orle, tails in saltier, a cock, ppr. *Pl.* 18, *cr.* 5.

IMBRIE, and IMRIE, Sco., a plough, ppr. *Evertendo fœcundat.* *Pl.* 28, *cr.* 15.

IMMANS, and INMANS, a basilisk, ppr. *Pl.* 109, *cr.* 13.

IMMINS, a dragon's head, couped. *Pl.* 87, *cr.* 12.

IMPEY, Eng., an ostrich, wings addorsed, in mouth a horse-shoe, ppr. *Pl.* 16, *cr.* 2.

IMPEY, a tiger's head, affrontée, between wings. *Pl.* 31, *cr.* 7, (wings, *same plate, cr.* 11.)

IMREY, Sco., a plough, ppr. *Nil desperandum.* *Pl.* 28, *cr.* 15.

INCE, on a mount, vert, a horse, sejant, by an oak-tree, ppr. *Pl.* 4, *cr.* 13.

INCE, a goat, salient against a tree, ppr. *Pl.* 32, *cr.* 10.

INCHBOLD, Yorks., a wyvern. *Palladia fama.* *Pl.* 63, *cr.* 13.

INCKPEN, or INKPEN, Eng., in dexter hand a club, ppr. *Pl.* 28, *cr.* 6.

INCLEDEN, Devons., a hand issuing from a cloud, in fess, pointing to a serpent, ppr. *Pl.* 19, *cr.* 11.

INCLEDON, Devons., a falcon, ppr., beaked and belled, or. *Pl.* 67, *cr.* 3.

INERS, a dexter arm, in armour, in hand a scimitar, (in pale,) ppr. *Pl.* 81, *cr.* 11.

INGE, Staffs., two battle-axes, in saltier, ppr., enfiled with a ducal coronet, or. *Pl.* 52, *cr.* 10, (coronet, *same plate, cr.* 2.)

INGE, Eng., in hand a glove, ppr. *Pl.* 42, *cr.* 15.

INGE, Staffs., out of a ducal coronet, two battle-axes, in saltier, ppr. *Pl.* 52, *cr.* 10, (coronet, *pl.* 128, *fig.* 3.)

INGEHAM, or INGHAM, Eng., an arm, in armour, embowed, issuing from a cloud in the sinister, in hand a sword, ppr. *Pl.* 85, *cr.* 4.

INGERLAND, on a plate, a thistle, ppr. *Pl.* 73, *cr.* 6, (plate, *pl.* 141.)

INGHAM, on a chapeau, gu., turned up, erm., an owl, ppr., (sitting in holly-leaves, vert.) *Pl.* 123, *cr.* 6.

INGILBY, Eng., a boar's head, erect and erased, ar. *Pl.* 21, *cr.* 7.

INGILBY-AMCOTTS, Bart., Linc., and Yorks., a boar's head, erect, (couped,) ar., tusked, or. *Pl.* 21, *cr.* 7.

INGLE, Eng., a hand, erect, issuing from a cloud, holding a sword, blade waved, ppr. *Pl.* 71, *cr.* 7.

INGLEBERT, Eng., a greyhound, current towards a tree, vert. *Pl.* 27, *cr.* 2.

INGLEBY, Yorks., a boar's head, ar., tusked, or. *Pl.* 48, *cr.* 2.

INGLEDEW, a dexter arm, embowed, in fess, out of a cloud, in sinister, reaching to a garland of laurel. *Pl.* 73, *cr.* 11.

INGLEDEW, Eng., (on a mount, vert,) an ingle, ppr., issuing therefrom an eagle, wings expanded, ppr. *Ex flamma lux.* *Pl.* 44, *cr.* 8.

INGLEFIELD, Warw., an arm, embowed, vested, per pale, gu. and or, cuff, ar., in hand a branch, vert. *Pl.* 62, *cr.* 7.

INGLETON, Devons., a hand issuing from a cloud, in fess, pointing to a serpent, ppr. *Pl.* 19, *cr.* 11.

INGLES, or INGLIS, Sco., a demi-lion, rampant, ar. *Nobilis est ira leonis.* *Pl.* 67, *cr.* 10.

INGLES, Eng., a fetterlock, az., hasp, or. *Pl.* 122, *cr.* 12.

INGLIS, Bart., Beds., a demi-lion, rampant, ppr., in dexter an etoile, or. *Nobilis est ira leonis*—and—*Recte faciendo securus.* *Pl.* 89, *cr.* 10, (etoile, *pl.* 141.)

INGLIS, Sco., a demi-lion, rampant, in dexter a mullet, or. *Nisi Dominus frustra.* *Pl.* 89, *cr.* 10.

INGLIS, Sco., same crest. *Recte faciendo securus.*

INGLIS, Sco., a demi-lion holding a mullet. *Invictus maneo.* *Pl.* 89, *cr.* 10.

INGLIS, a demi-lion, ar. *Recte faciendo securus.* *Pl.* 67, *cr.* 10.

INGLIS, Sco., a demi-lion, rampant, ppr., in dexter a branch of laurel, vert. *Invictus maneo.* *Pl.* 39, *cr.* 14, (branch, *pl.* 123, *cr.* 5.)

INGLIS, Bart., Beds., a cubit arm, in hand, a scimitar. *Pl.* 29, *cr.* 8.

INGLIS, Sco., a star, environed with clouds, ppr. *In tenebris lucidior.* *Pl.* 16, *cr.* 13.

INGLISH, Eng., an ear of wheat, and a palm-branch, in saltier, ppr. *Pl.* 63, *cr.* 3.

INGO, Ess., out of a ducal coronet, or, a dragon's head, wings addorsed, gu. *Pl.* 59, *cr.* 14.

INGOLDESBY, and INGOLDSBY, Bucks. and Northamp., out of a ducal coronet, or, a demi-lion, gu., charged on shoulder with an etoile, gold. *Pl.* 45, *cr.* 7, (etoile, *pl.* 141.)

INGRAM, Sco., a griffin's head, erased, ppr., (collared,) ar. *Pl.* 69, *cr.* 13.

INGRAM, Eng., a griffin's head, quarterly, gu. and ar. *Pl.* 38, *cr.* 3.

INGRAM, Sco., a cock, ppr. *Magnanimus esto.* *Pl.* 67, *cr.* 14.

INGRAM, Eng., a cock, ppr. *Pl.* 67, *cr.* 14.

INGRAM, Sco., a phœnix, in flames, all ppr. *Pl.* 44, *cr.* 8.

INGRAM, Eng., a bull's head, erased. *Pl.* 19, *cr.* 3.

INKELDON, and INKLEDON, an ibex, passant, or. *Pl.* 115, *cr.* 13.

INKERSALL, Herts. and Middx., a griffin's head, gu., (gorged with a fess, dancettée, erm.,) between wings, or. *Pl.* 65, *cr.* 1.

INMAN, a wyvern, ppr. *Pl.* 63, *cr.* 13.

INMAN, on a mount, vert, a wyvern, ppr., (ducally gorged and lined, or.) *Pl.* 33, *cr.* 13.

INNES, Sco., an arm, embowed, in hand a dagger, ppr. *Sine crimine fiat*—and—*Pro patriâ.* *Pl.* 34, *cr.* 7.

INNES, Middx., a boar's head, erased, or. *Pl.* 16, *cr.* 11.

INNES, of Innes, a boar's head, couped, or. *Be traist.* *Pl.* 48, *cr.* 2.

INNES, of Leighnot, an arm, in hand a sword, ppr. *Honos vitâ clarior.* *Pl.* 34, *cr.* 7.

INNES, of Blairtan, a primrose, ppr., thereon a bee, or. *E labore dulcedo.* *Pl.* 109, *cr.* 6.

INNES, of Balnacraig, a thistle, thereon a bee. *E labore dulcedo.* *Pl.* 68, *cr.* 9.

INNES, of Thurster, a star of (six) rays, environed with clouds, ppr. *Dum spiro, cœlestia spero.* *Pl.* 16, *cr.* 13.

INNES, Sco., a branch of palm, slipped, ppr. *Ornatur radix fronde.* *Pl.* 123, *cr.* 1.

INNES, Eng., on a ducal coronet, or, a wyvern, sejant, gu. *Pl.* 104, *cr.* 11.

INNES, Sco., a bee, volant, ppr. *Non servit sed laborat.* *Pl.* 100, *cr.* 3.

INNES, Sco., a hind's head, erased, ppr. *Fortis et fidus.* *Pl.* 6, *cr.* 1.

INNES, Sco., a mullet, az. *Virtus ad astra.* *Pl.* 41, *cr.* 1.

INNES, Sco., a cock, crowing, ppr. *Prudentiâ et vi.* *Pl.* 67, *cr.* 14.

INNES, Sco., a thistle, ppr., (surmounted by a star, ar.) *E labore dulcedo.* *Pl.* 68, *cr.* 9.

INNES, of Towie, a bee, volant, ppr. *Prodige qui laboriose.* *Pl.* 100, *cr.* 3.

INNES, Sco., a boar's head, erased, sa. *Pl.* 16, *cr.* 11.

INNES, Sco., two hands, joined, in fess, holding a sword, all ppr. *Ditat servata fides.* *Pl.* 75, *cr.* 8.

INNES, Sco., an increscent, ppr. *Je reçois pour donner.* *Pl.* 122, *cr.* 15.

INNES, Sco., an increscent, ar. *Pl.* 122, *cr.* 15.

INNIS, a boar's head, couped. *Pl.* 48, *cr.* 2.

INWARDS, on a chapeau, gu., turned up, erm., an eagle's head, ppr. *Invidiâ major.* *Pl.* 13, *cr.* 5.

INWOOD, Eng., a demi-lion, rampant, or, holding a battle-axe, az. *Pl.* 101, *cr.* 14, (without charging.)

INYS, on a mount, a rabbit, against a tree, both ppr., fructed, or. *Pl.* 10, *cr.* 4.

IPRE, Eng., on a mount, vert, a leopard, couchant, gardant, gu., ducally crowned, or. *Pl.* 111, *cr.* 11, (crown, *same plate.*)

IPRES, Eng., a unicorn's head, or, collared, gu. *Pl.* 73, *cr.* 1.

IRBALL, two halberds, in saltier, addorsed, sa. *Pl.* 52, *cr.* 10.

IRBY, Linc., a wyvern's head, ar., gorged with (two bars-gemelle, gu.) *Pl.* 107, *cr.* 10.

IRBY, Linc., a tiger's head, ar., erased, maned, and collared, gu. *Pl.* 86, *cr.* 13.

IRBY, Linc., a Saracen's head, in profile, couped at shoulders, ppr., wreathed, ar. and sa. *Pl.* 36, *cr.* 3.

IRBY, Baron Boston. *See* BOSTON.

IRBY, of Boyland Hall: 1. For *Irby*, a Saracen's head, ppr. *Pl.* 19, *cr.* 1. 2. For *Garneys*, a cubit arm, erased, in hand a scimitar, (embrued,) all ppr., hilt and pommel, or. *Pl.* 29, *cr.* 8.

IREBY, Eng., an antelope, passant, ppr. *Pl.* 63, *cr.* 10.

IREBY, Eng., a sword, in pale, enfiled with a savage's head, ppr. *Pl.* 27, *cr.* 3.

IRELAND, Herts. and Salop, a fleur-de-lis, ar., entwined with a snake, regardant, vert, perforating the centre leaf. *Pl.* 15, *cr.* 13.

IRELAND, Chesh., Lanc., and Salop, a dove, ar., in mouth a sprig of (laurel,) vert. *Pl.* 48, *cr.* 15.

IRELAND, Sco., a lion, rampant, gardant, gu. *Pl.* 35, *cr.* 4.

IRELAND, Eng., a bird, ar., beaked and legged, gu. *Pl.* 52, *cr.* 12.

IRELAND, THOMAS-JAMES, Esq., of Owsden Hall, Suffs., a dove and olive-branch, ppr. *Pl.* 48, *cr.* 15.

IRELAND, Iri., a dove and olive-branch, ppr. *Amor et pax.* *Pl.* 48, *cr.* 15.

IREMONGER, Eng., a phœnix in flames, ppr. *Pl.* 44, *cr.* 8.

IREMONGER, Lanc. and Salop, a boar's head, ar., (collared, vairé, or and gu.) *Pl.* 36, *cr.* 9.

IREMONGER, Berks. and Notts., a phœnix in flames, ppr. *Pl.* 44, *cr.* 8.

IREMONGER, WILLIAM, Esq., of The Priory, Wherwell, Hants, a phœnix, or, in flames, ppr. *Pl.* 44, *cr.* 8.

IRETON, Derbs. and Staffs., a squirrel. *Pl.* 2, *cr.* 4.

IRETON, Yorks., Hants., Cumb., and Northamp., a demi-lion, sa., (collared, ar.,) in dexter a mullet, gu. *Pl.* 89, *cr.* 10.

IREYS, Dors. and Iri., on an oak-tree, eradicated and erect, ppr., a dragon, or, pierced through breast by a sword, of the first, hilt, gold. *Pl.* 10, *cr.* 6.

IRNYNGE, a child's head, ppr. *Pl.* 126, *cr.* 10.

IRONMONGER, Berks. and Notts., a phœnix, or, in flames, ppr. *Pl.* 44, *cr.* 8.

IRONS, Eng., a cross moline, lozenge-pierced, az. *Pl.* 91, *cr.* 10.

IRONSIDE, Durh., a cross crosslet, fitched, az. *In hoc signo vinces. Pl.* 16, *cr.* 10.

IRONSIDE, a cubit arm, vested, erect, in hand a cross fleury. *Pl.* 75, *cr.* 3.

IRONSIDE, a cubit arm, in armour, erect, in hand a cross crosslet. *Pl.* 51, *cr.* 1.

IRONSIDE, a dexter hand, couped, in fess, holding a sword, in pale, surmounted by a laurel-crown, all ppr. *Pl.* 56, *cr.* 6.

IRTON, SAMUEL, Esq., of Irton Hall, Cumb., a Saracen's head. *Semper constans et fidelis. Pl.* 81, *cr.* 15.

IRTON, of Inverramsey, in hand two holly-branches, of three leaves each, (crossways,) ppr. *Color fidesque perennis. Pl.* 55, *cr.* 6.

IRVINE, a cock, ppr. *Pl.* 67, *cr.* 14.

IRVINE, Sco., a sheaf of holly-leaves, ppr. *Ope solis et umbrâ. Pl.* 78, *cr.* 12.

IRVINE, of Lairnie, a branch of holly and a lily, both slipped, in saltier, ppr. *Candide et constanter. Pl.* 60, *cr.* 11.

IRVINE, Sco., same crest. *Ferendo feres.*

IRVINE, Sco., a cubit arm, in gauntlet a branch of holly, consisting of seven leaves, all ppr. *Haud ullis labentia ventis. Pl.* 55, *cr.* 6.

IRVINE, Sco., same crest. *Moderata durant.*

IRVINE, Sco., same crest. *Sub sole, sub umbrâ virens.*

IRVINE, a lion, rampant, with wings addorsed. *Pl.* 75, *cr.* 4.

IRVINE, a sword and a palm-branch, in saltier. *Pl.* 50, *cr.* 11, (sword, *same plate, cr.* 4.)

IRVINE, Sco., (two) holly-leaves, in saltier, vert. *Pl.* 78, *cr.* 12.

IRVINE, Sco., a sheaf of (seven) holly-leaves, banded, gu. *Pl.* 78, *cr.* 12.

IRVINE, Sco., a holly-branch, gu. *Pl.* 99, *cr.* 6.

IRVINE, Sco., a sheaf of five arrows, banded, ppr. *Sub sole, sub umbrâ virens. Pl.* 54, *cr.* 15.

IRVINE, three holly-leaves, conjoined in one stalk. *Moderata durant. Pl.* 78, *cr.* 12.

IRVINE, Sco., out of a cloud, a hand, gauntleted, holding a thistle, ppr. *Dum memor ipse mei. Pl.* 80, *cr.* 10, (thistle, *pl.* 68, *cr.* 9.)

IRVINE, Sco., a cross crosslet, fitched, gu., and a branch of holly, slipped, vert, in saltier. *Ferendo feres. Pl.* 102, *cr.* 3.

IRVINE, and IRVING, out of a ducal coronet, per pale, ar. and az., a lion's paw, per fess, or and gu., holding a cross crosslet, fitched, of the last. *Pl.* 65, *cr.* 5.

IRVING, Bart., Sco.: 1. A chapeau, gu., turned up, erm., wreathed round the crown with oak, or. *Pl.* 10, *cr.* 8. 2. A dexter arm, in armour, embowed, ppr., garnished, or, in hand two holly-leaves, vert. *Pl.* 68, *cr.* 1, (leaves, *pl.* 78, *cr.* 12.)

IRVING, three arrows, bound by a ribbon, gu. *Pl.* 43, *cr.* 14.

IRVING, Lond. and Sco., a sheaf of three arrows, points upward, banded, charged with a mullet. *Sub sole, sub umbrâ virens. Pl.* 75, *cr.* 7.

IRWIN, THOMAS, Esq., of Justustown, Cumb., a dove and olive-branch, ppr. *Haud ullis labantia ventis. Pl.* 48, *cr.* 15.

IRWIN, or IRWINE, Iri., a mullet, pierced, or. *Pl.* 45, *cr.* 1.

IRWIN, Iri., out of a cloud, a hand grasping a bunch of thistle, ppr. *Nemo me impune lacessit. Pl.* 36, *cr.* 6, (clouds, *pl.* 69, *cr.* 10.)

IRWINE, an arm, in armour, couped above wrist, in fess, in gauntlet, a branch of holly, vert, arm charged with a crescent. *Pl.* 4, *cr.* 15.

ISAAC, a martlet. *Pl.* 111, *cr.* 5.

ISAAC, Worc., a dexter arm, in armour, embowed, in hand a sword, enfiled with a leopard's face, point downward, resting on the wreath, all ppr.

ISAAC, Eng., in the sea, a cross pattée, between two ears of wheat, in orle, ppr. *Pl.* 103, *cr.* 8.

ISAACS, Eng., in hand a mill-rind. *Pl.* 34, *cr.* 3.

ISAACSON, Surr., a demi-lion, rampant, az., between paws an escallop. Θάρσει. *Pl.* 126 A, *cr.* 13.

ISAACSON, Eng., two lions' gambs, sa., holding up a bezant. *Pl.* 42, *cr.* 3.

ISATE, Yorks., a stag's head, erased, per fess, ar. and gu., (pierced by an arrow, ppr.) *Pl.* 66, *cr.* 9.

ISELY, or ISLEY, a hand holding a roll of paper, between two branches of laurel, in orle. *Pl.* 86, *cr.* 5.

ISHAM, Bart., Northamps., a demi-swan, wings addorsed, ppr. *Ostendo non ostento. Pl.* 54, *cr.* 4.

ISHERWOOD, Berks., a wolf's head, per pale, ermines and erminois, erased, gu. *Pl.* 92, *cr.* 15, (without rose.)

ISHERWOOD, a wolf's head. *Pl.* 14, *cr.* 6.

ISHERWOOD, of Marple Hall, Chesh., and Bradshawe Hall, Lanc., a stag at gaze, under a vine-tree, fructed, all ppr. *Pl.* 118, *cr.* 13.

ISRAEL, Eng., the sun rising from behind a cloud, ppr. *Pl.* 67, *cr.* 9.

ISTED, Northamp., a buck's head, erased, ppr., attired and ducally gorged, or. *Pl.* 66, *cr.* 9, (gorging, *same plate.*)

ITHELL, Cambs. and Leic., on a ducal coronet, or, a Cornish chough, wings expanded, sa., beaked and legged, gu. *Pl.* 8, *cr.* 5.

IVAT, or IVATT, Lond., out of a mural coronet, a cubit arm, in armour, in gauntlet, all ppr., a fleur-de-lis, or. *Pl.* 95, *cr.* 9, (coronet, *same plate, cr.* 8.)

IVE, Eng., an arm, in armour, couped and embowed, in hand a (sword,) ppr., elbow resting on the wreath. *Pl.* 107, *cr.* 15.

IVERS, a demi-lion, rampant, or, collared, sa. *Pl.* 18, *cr.* 13.

IVES, Northamp., out of a ducal coronet, gu., an Indian goat's head, ar., guttée-de-sang, attired, or. *Pl.* 72, *cr.* 2.

IVESON, Eng., a moor's head, in profile, (erased) at neck, sa. *Pl.* 81, *cr.* 15.

IVEY, Devons., a demi-lion, rampant, or, supporting a staff, raguly, vert. *Pl.* 11, *cr.* 2.

IVIE, Sco., the attires of a stag, affixed to scalp, ppr. *Pl.* 33, *cr.* 15, (without boar's head.)

IVORY, Eng., a lion, sejant, affrontée, in dexter a sword, in sinister a fleur-de-lis. *Pl.* 120, *cr.* 2.
IVYE, Oxon. and Wilts., a lion, rampant, ar., supporting a staff, raguly, gu. *Pl.* 22, *cr.* 15, (staff, *pl.* 1, *cr.* 3.)
IWARBY, and IWARDBY, Eng., a cock's head, gu. *Pl.* 92, *cr.* 3.
IZACKE, Devons., a leopard's head, (erased,) ducally gorged. *Pl.* 92, *cr.* 13, (gorging, *pl.* 128, *fig.* 3.)
IZOD, Devons., a man's head, in profile, ppr., in armour, or, on head a plume of feathers, gu. and ar. *Pl.* 8, *cr.* 12, (head, *pl.* 33, *cr.* 14.)
IZON, Eng., in dexter hand, in fess, couped, ppr., a cross crosslet, fitched, in pale, sa. *Pl.* 78, *cr.* 9.
IZZARD, a dolphin, naiant, ppr. *Pl.* 48, *cr.* 9.

J

JACK, a pear-tree, vert, fructed, or. *Pl.* 105, *cr.* 13.
JACK, a horse's head, erased, in mouth a broken tilting-spear. *Pl.* 110, *cr.* 6.
JACK, Sco., an arm, in armour, gu., in hand a sword, ppr. *Post nubila. Pl.* 2, *cr.* 8.
JACK, Sco., the sun. *Post nubila Phœbus. Pl.* 68, *cr.* 14.
JACKERELL, on a stand a hawk's lure, and thereon a hawk, perched, ppr. *Pl.* 10, *cr.* 7.
JACKET, out of a cloud, a dexter hand, ppr., holding a cross pattée, fitched, in pale, or. *Pl.* 69, *cr.* 10, (cross, *pl.* 27, *cr.* 14.)
JACKMAN, Eng., a griffin's head, erased, sa., guttée, or. *Pl.* 48, *cr.* 6.
JACKSON, Bart., Iri. and Surr., a shoveller, (tufted on head and breast,) ar., charged with a trefoil, slipped, vert. *Pl.* 90, *cr.* 15, (trefoil, *pl.* 4, *cr.* 10.)
JACKSON, Bart., Beds., a goat's head, couped, ar., guttée-de-sang, armed and bearded, or, (gorged with a collar, gu., charged with three bezants, ringed and lined, reflexed, of the third.) *Pl.* 105, *cr.* 14.
JACKSON, Heref., on a five-leaved coronet, or, a hawk's head and neck, erased, gu., charged on breast with a cross pattée, fitched. *Scuto amoris divini. Pl.* 24, *cr.* 10, (cross, *pl.* 27, *cr.* 14.)
JACKSON, Somers., a dove, close, ppr., in beak an olive-branch, on breast a torteau. *Pl.* 48, *cr.* 15, (torteau, *pl.* 141.)
JACKSON, Middx., a greyhound, (passant, sa., collared,) or, dexter on a pheon, gold. *Pl.* 104, *cr.* 1, (without chapeau; pheon, *pl.* 141.)
JACKSON, Ruts., the sun, rising. *Pl.* 67, *cr.* 9.
JACKSON, Chesh., a goat's head, az., attired, or. *Pl.* 105, *cr.* 14.
JACKSON, Oxon., an eagle, rising, ppr. *Pl.* 67, *cr.* 4.
JACKSON, Cumb. and Oxon., a sun, or, in flames, ppr. *Pl.* 75, *cr.* 9, (without branches.)
JACKSON, Northamp., a demi-horse, ar., guttée-de-sang. *Pl.* 91, *cr.* 2, (without wings or coronet.)
JACKSON, Cumb. and Devons., a horse, current, ar., guttée-de-sang. *Pl.* 107, *cr.* 5, (without spear.)
JACKSON, Lond., in hand, ppr., a boar's head, erased and erect, sa. *Pl.* 86, *cr.* 6.
JACKSON, Durh. and Yorks., a horse at full speed, ar., guttée-de-sang. *Pl.* 107, *cr.* 5, (without spear.)
JACKSON, Kent, a demi-lion, rampant, or, between paws a pheon, az. *Pl.* 126, *cr.* 12, (pheon, *pl.* 141.)
JACKSON, Sco., a holly-(leaf,) ppr. *Virescit virtus. Pl.* 78, *cr.* 12.
JACKSON, Surr., a horse, passant, ar., spotted with cinquefoils, gu. *Pl.* 15, *cr.* 14, (cinquefoils, *pl.* 141.)
JACKSON, Iri., a fleur-de-lis, or, entwined by a serpent, vert. *Pl.* 15, *cr.* 13.
JACKSON, Yorks., the sun, or, between two branches, in orle. *Pl.* 75, *cr.* 9.
JACKSON, Sco., an eagle's head, erased, ppr. *Dominus fecit. Pl.* 20, *cr.* 7.
JACKSON, Sco., same crest. *Sublimiora peto.*
JACKSON, a naked arm, embowed, in hand a poniard, all ppr. *Pl.* 34, *cr.* 7.
JACKSON, Sco., a dexter arm, in armour, embowed, in hand a battle-axe, ppr. *Devant si je puis. Pl.* 121, *cr.* 14.
JACKSON, a horse, current, ar., guttée, gu. *Pl.* 107, *cr.* 5, (without spear.)
JACKSON, a greyhound's head, couped, ar., collared, gu. *Pl.* 43, *cr.* 11.
JACKSON, an arm, in armour, embowed, in hand a battle-axe, all ppr. *Pl.* 121, *cr.* 14.
JACKSON, an eagle, close, ppr. *Pl.* 7, *cr.* 11.
JACKSON, a greyhound, (passant,) ar., resting dexter on a pheon, of the last. *Pl.* 104, *cr.* 1, (without chapeau; pheon, *pl.* 141.)
JACKSON, OLIVER VAUGHAN, Esq., of Carramore, co. Mayo, a horse, passant, ar. *Celer et audax. Pl.* 15, *cr.* 14.
JACOB, Oxon., an heraldic-tiger, passant, ppr., maned and tusked, or. *Tantum in superbos. Pl.* 7, *cr.* 5.
JACOB, a wolf, passant, ppr. *Pl.* 46, *cr.* 6.
JACOB, Dors. and Kent., a lion, rampant, or, supporting a cross botonnée, fitched. *Pl.* 125, *cr.* 2.
JACOB, an heraldic-tiger, passant. *Pl.* 7, *cr.* 5.
JACOB, Wilts., a tiger, passant, sa., resting foredexter on an escutcheon, or. *Pl.* 86, *cr.* 2, (escutcheon, *pl.* 19, *cr.* 2.)
JACOB, Middx., a tiger, passant, ppr. *Parta tuere. Pl.* 67, *cr.* 15.
JACOBS, Eng., an arm, in armour, embowed, in hand a sword, by the blade, ppr. *Pl.* 65, *cr.* 8.
JACOBS, Hull, an heraldic-tiger, passant. *Pl.* 7, *cr.* 5.
JACOMB, a lion's head, erased, barry of six, ar. and az. *Pl.* 52, *cr.* 7.
JACOMB, Eng., in hand two branches of palm, in orle, ppr. *Pl.* 16, *cr.* 5.
JACQUES, Eng., a horse's head, (couped,) and maned, or, struck in breast with a tilting spear, gold. *Pl.* 110, *cr.* 6.
JACQUES, Eng., a bezant, ar., charged with a lion's head, erased and collared. *Pl.* 50, *cr.* 10.
JACSON, Barton Hall, a sheldrake, (rising,) ppr. *Pl.* 90, *cr.* 15.
JAFFRAY, Sco., between two branches of palm, in orle, a mullet, all ppr. *Post nubila Phœbus. Pl.* 3, *cr.* 9.

JAFFRAY, Iri., a demi-leopard, rampant, gu. *Pl.* 12, *cr* 14.

JAFFREY, Sco., the sun shining through a cloud. *Post nubila Phœbus. Pl.* 67, *cr.* 9.

JAGER, Eng., out of a ducal coronet, a hand holding a sword, ppr. *Pl.* 65, *cr.* 10.

JAGO, a talbot, couchant, ppr. *Pl.* 32, *cr.* 7.

JAGO, Eng., out of clouds, two dexter hands, grasping the stump of an old tree, sprouting afresh, all ppr. *Pl.* 126, *cr.* 4.

JAKEMAN, out of a ducal coronet, or, an eagle's head, ppr. *Pl.* 20, *cr.* 12, (without pellet.)

JAKES, Lond., a horse's head, couped, ar., maned, or, struck in breast with a tilting-spear, gold. *Pl.* 110, *cr.* 6.

JALMES, Eng., out of a ducal coronet, or, five ostrich-feathers, three middle ones, sa., two outside ones, ar. *Pl.* 100, *cr.* 12, (without charge.)

JAMES, Bart., Berks., and JAMES, Hants, an ostrich, ar., beaked and legged, or. *J'aime à jamaise. Pl.* 64, *cr.* 3, (without coronet.)

JAMES, Bart., Berks., and JAMES, Hants, on a ducal coronet, or, two laurel-branches, in saltier, vert, (environed with a snake, ppr.) *J'aime à jamaise. Pl.* 114, *cr.* 15.

JAMES, Kent, in a naval coronet, or, a tower, with two port-holes in front, gold, fire issuing from the port-holes and top, ppr., on the tower a flag-staff, of the last, thereon a flag, flotant to the sinister, gu. *Victor.*

JAMES, Cambs., a dove, ar., standing upon two palm-branches, in saltier, vert. *Pl.* 2, *cr.* 11, (palm, *pl.* 87, *cr.* 8.)

JAMES, Kent, an ostrich, ar. *Pl.* 64, *cr.* 3, (without coronet.)

JAMES, Ess. and Kent, a garb, ar., banded, vert. *Pl.* 48, *cr.* 10.

JAMES, Lond., Staffs., and Salop, a demi-lion, rampant, or, holding an escallop, sa. *Pl.* 126 A, *cr.* 13.

JAMES, Ess., Kent, and Surr., out of a ducal coronet, or, a demi-swan, wings expanded, ar., beaked, gu. *Pl.* 100, *cr.* 7.

JAMES, Kent, a buffalo, ar., attired, sa.

JAMES, a demi-lion, rampant, erminois, holding an escallop. *Pl.* 126 A, *cr.* 13.

JAMES, Kent, a buffalo, current, sa., attired, or.

JAMES, Kent, an ostrich, ar. *Pl.* 64, *cr.* 3, (without coronet.)

JAMES, a dexter naked arm, embowed, in hand a sword. *Pl.* 34, *cr.* 7.

JAMES, Somers., a dolphin, naiant. *Pl.* 48, *cr.* 9.

JAMES, a bull, passant. *Pl.* 66, *cr.* 11.

JAMES, Somers., a demi-bull, or, wreathed round middle with a chaplet of laurel, vert. *Pl.* 73, *cr.* 8.

JAMES, a dolphin, naiant, or. *Pl.* 48, *cr.* 9.

JAMES, Cambs. and Cornw., out of a ducal coronet, or, a demi-lion, az., holding an escallop, gu. *Pl.* 45, *cr.* 7, (escallop, *pl.* 141.)

JAMES, Eng., a demi-buffalo, rampant, sa., attired, or. *Pl.* 63, *cr.* 6.

JAMES, a demi-buffalo, salient, horned and unguled, or. *Pl.* 63, *cr.* 6.

JAMES, a demi-lion, rampant, or, between paws an escallop, gu. *Pl.* 126 A, *cr.* 13.

JAMES, out of a ducal coronet, or, a demi-swan, ar. *Pl.* 10, *cr.* 11, (without dart.)

JAMES, Durh., a bull's head, couped, sa., armed, or. *Pl.* 120, *cr.* 7.

JAMES, Worc., out of a mural coronet, az., a demi-lion, rampant, regardant, or, collared, of the first, holding an escallop, sa. *Pl.* 33, *cr.* 2, (coronet, *same plate;* escallop, *pl.* 141.)

JAMES, Otterburn, a buffalo, passant, gu., armed, ppr., resting fore-dexter on an escutcheon, ar., charged with a pheon, sa.

JAMES, Glouc., a garb. *Pl.* 48, *cr.* 10.

JAMES, WILLIAM, Esq., of Barrock, Cumb., a bull, passant, ppr. *Vincit amor patriæ. Pl.* 66, *cr.* 11.

JAMES, JOHN-TAUBMAN-WILLIAM, Esq., of Pantsaison, Pembroke, a demi-bull, rampant, sa., horned and hoofed, or, langued, gu. *Ffyddylon at y gorfin,*—in English, Faithful to the end. *Pl.* 18, *cr.* 4.

JAMES-GREVIS, Igtham Court Lodge, Kent: 1. For *James*, out of a ducal coronet, or, a demi-swan, wings expanded, ar., beaked, gu. *Pl.* 100, *cr.* 7. 2. A squirrel, between paws an escallop, or. *Fide et constantiâ. Pl.* 40, *cr.* 5, (escallop, *pl.* 141.)

JAMES-KINGSTON, Knt. and Bart., Iri., out of a ducal coronet, or, a swan, beaked, gu., in mouth a dart, gold, feathered, ar., point towards the breast. *A jamais. Pl.* 10, *cr.* 11.

JAMESON, an antelope, trippant, or, horned, gu. *Pl.* 63, *cr.* 10.

JAMESON, Sco., a ship in full sail, flag displayed, gu. *Sine metu. Pl.* 109, *cr.* 8.

JAMESON, Galway, a Roman galley, ppr., sail, gu., charged with a lion, passant, gardant, or. *Sine metu. Pl.* 24, *cr.* 5, (lion, *pl.* 120, *cr.* 5.)

JAMESON, or JAMIESON, Iri., a torteau, between wings, gu. *Pl.* 2, *cr.* 3.

JAMIESON, a ship under sail, ppr. *Ad littora tendit. Pl.* 109, *cr.* 8.

JANE, Eng., a swan, wings addorsed, devouring a trout, all ppr. *Pl.* 103, *cr.* 1.

JANES, Cambs. and Cornw., out of a ducal coronet, or, a demi-lion, az., holding an escallop, gu. *Pl.* 45, *cr.* 7, (escallop, *pl.* 141.)

JANES, Kent, out of a naval coronet, or, a tower inflamed on top, ppr. *Pl.* 118, *cr.* 15, (coronet, *same plate, cr.* 5.)

JANSON, an arm, from elbow, (vambraced,) in hand a falcon's lure. *Pl.* 44, *cr.* 2.

JANSON, Eng., on a mount, vert, a hind, ppr., collared, gu. *Pl.* 75, *cr.* 6.

JANSSEN, Eng., the sun, or. *Pl.* 68, *cr.* 14.

JANSSEN, Surr.: 1. A quatrefoil, (stalked and leaved,) vert. *Pl.* 65, *cr.* 7. 2. A trefoil, stalked and leaved, vert. *Pl.* 4, *cr.* 10, (without wings.)

JANSSEN, a rose-slip, with a rose in full bloom, ppr. *Pl.* 105, *cr.* 7.

JAQUES, a horse's head, couped, ar., maned, or, struck in breast by a tilting-spear, gold. *Pl.* 110, *cr.* 6.

JAQUES, Eng., a bezant, or, charged with a lion's head, erased and collared. *Pl.* 50, *cr.* 10.

JARDELAY, a dexter arm, in armour, wielding a scimitar, all ppr. *Pl.* 81, *cr.* 11.

JARDIN, or JARDINE, Sco., a spur-rowel. *Cave, adsum. Pl.* 54, *cr.* 5.

JARDIN, and JARDEN, Sco., in hand a bezant, all ppr. *Ex virtute honos. Pl.* 24, *cr.* 3, (bezant, *pl.* 141.)

JARDIN, Sco., a spur-rowel. *Ex virtute honos. Pl.* 54, *cr.* 5.

JARDINE, an etoile, ppr. *Pl.* 63, *cr.* 9.

R

JARDINE, Bart., Sco., a spur-rowel, of (six) points, ar. *Cave, adsum.* *Pl.* 54, *cr.* 5.

JARDINE, Sco., a dexter hand holding up a spur-rowel. *Pl.* 34, *cr.* 9, (rowel, *pl.* 45, *cr.* 5.)

JARMAN, Eng., an eagle's leg, erased, in bend sinister, holding a feather, in bend dexter. *Pl.* 60, *cr.* 15.

JARRAT, and JARRET, an eagle, wings expanded, ppr. *Pl.* 126, *cr.* 7.

JARRETT, a lion's head, erased, ducally crowned, or, collared, gu. *Pl.* 7, *cr.* 10, (crown, *pl.* 128, *fig.* 3.)

JARRETT, a lion, passant, under fore-dexter a fleur-de-lis. *Pl.* 4, *cr.* 14.

JARRETT, Yorks., in front of a saltier, az., a lion's head, erased, ar., guttée-de-larmes. *Res, non verba.* *Pl.* 81, *cr.* 4, (saltier, *pl.* 25, *cr.* 5.)

JARRETT, Eng., a sword, in pale, on point a garland of laurel, ppr. *Pl.* 15, *cr.* 6.

JARVEIS, out of a naval coronet, or, a demi-pegasus, ar. *Pl.* 76, *cr.* 2.

JARVEIS, and JARVIS, Eng., a lion, rampant, gu. *Pl.* 67, *cr.* 5.

JARVIS, Linc., a unicorn's head, ar., gorged with a collar, charged with three cinquefoils. *Pl.* 73, *cr.* 1, (cinquefoils, *pl.* 141.)

JARY, two arms, in armour, embowed, ppr., holding up a rose, gu. *Pl.* 10, *cr.* 9.

JASON, Wilts., on a chapeau, gu., turned up, erm., a pegasus, salient, wings addorsed, (in mouth a bur, ppr.) *Pl.* 57, *cr.* 15, (chapeau, *same plate, cr.* 14.)

JASPER, Lond., a standard, ar., charged with a cross, gu. *Pl.* 8, *cr.* 3.

JAUDRILL, a demi-antelope, gu., between paws, an escutcheon, or. *Pl.* 75, *cr.* 10.

JAUPIN, Eng., a demi-greyhound, salient, ppr. *Pl.* 48, *cr.* 3.

JAUSSELIN, Lond. and Ess., a falcon's leg, erased at thigh, gu., belled, or. *Pl.* 83, *cr.* 7.

JAVEL, a lion, rampant, in dexter a branch of laurel. *Pl.* 64, *cr.* 2, (branch, *pl.* 123, *cr.* 5.)

JAWDERILL, Eng., an antelope's head, ar., gorged with a belt and buckle. *Pl.* 24, *cr.* 7, (gorging, *pl.* 54, *cr.* 15.)

JAY, Eng., on a ducal coronet, or, a griffin, sejant, az., resting dexter on an escutcheon, gu. *Pl.* 42, *cr.* 8.

JAY, Sco., a lion's paw, holding a thistle, ppr. *Pl.* 109, *cr.* 4.

JAYE, Lond. and Norf., an otter, passant, ppr. *Pl.* 9, *cr.* 5.

JAYE, Surr., out of a ducal coronet, per pale, or and az., a camel's head, sa., bezantée. *Pl.* 55, *cr.* 5, (without collar or crown.)

JEAFFRESON, CHRISTOPHER-WILLIAM, Esq., of Dallingham House, Cambs., a talbot's head, erased, ar., eared, gu. *Pl.* 90, *cr.* 6.

JEANE, Eng., a swan, wings addorsed, devouring a trout, all ppr. *Pl.* 103, *cr.* 1.

JEANES, or JEANS, Eng., a decrescent, or. *Pl.* 16, *cr.* 15.

JEBB, Iri., two rods, raguly, in saltier, banded. *Pl.* 103, *cr.* 12.

JEBB, on a serpent, nowed, a falcon, rising, ppr. *Pl.* 75, *cr.* 11.

JEDDON, a leopard's head. *Pl.* 92, *cr.* 13.

JEEX, a horse's head, couped, ar., maned, or, pierced in breast by a tilting-spear, gold. *Pl.* 110, *cr.* 6.

JEFFCOTT, or JEPHCOTT, Eng. and Iri., a boar, passant. *Pl.* 48, *cr.* 14.

JEFFERAY, Suss., a lion's head, erased, ar., ducally crowned, az. *Pl.* 90, *cr.* 4, (without charge.)

JEFFEREYS, a demi-lion, rampant, or, between paws a chaplet, vert. *Pl.* 47, *cr.* 4, (chaplet, *pl.* 128.)

JEFFERIES, Eng., a lion's head, erased, az., collared, ar., charged with three roses, gu. *Pl.* 7, *cr.* 10, (roses, *pl.* 141.)

JEFFERIS, a lion, rampant, sa. *Pl.* 67, *cr.* 5.

JEFFERSON, Lond. and Yorks., a demi-griffin, az., collared, or, holding a bezant. *Pl.* 74, *cr.* 15, (bezant, *pl.* 141.)

JEFFERSON, a talbot's head, erased, ar., eared, gu. *Pl.* 90, *cr.* 6.

JEFFERSON, a wolf's head, erased. *Pl.* 14, *cr.* 6.

JEFFERY, Eng., a demi-lion, rampant, holding a scimitar, ppr. *Pl.* 126 A, *cr.* 1.

JEFFERYES, Worc. : 1. On a rock, ar., a castle, or, the two end towers, domed. *Pl.* 113, *cr.* 7. 2. On a mount, vert, a castle, ar. *Pl.* 78, *cr.* 10.

JEFFERYES, Worc., on a mount, vert, a dove, wings (addorsed,) ar., beaked and legged, gu. *Pl.* 104, *cr.* 3.

JEFFERYES, Ess., out of a mural coronet, or, a lion's head, az., ducally crowned, gold. *Pl.* 45, *cr.* 9, (crown, *same plate.*)

JEFFERYES, and JEFFRIES, a lily and hollybranch, in saltier, ppr. *Pl.* 60, *cr.* 11.

JEFFERYES, out of a mural coronet, or, a lion's head, az., ducally crowned, gold. *Pl.* 45, *cr.* 9, (crown, *same plate.*)

JEFFERYES, Lond., a lion's head, erased, ar., charged with three billets, sa. *Pl.* 81, *cr.* 4, (billets, *pl.* 141.)

JEFFERYES, or JEFFERYS, Suss., a lion's head, erased, ar. *Pl.* 81, *cr.* 4.

JEFFERYS, Eng., a lion's head, erased. *Pl.* 81, *cr.* 4.

JEFFERYS, Eng., on a hillock, ar., a kingfisher, of the same, beaked and legged, gu. *Pl.* 111, *cr.* 8.

JEFFERYS, by a tree, ppr., a panther, passant, resting fore-dexter on an anchor. *Pl.* 86, *cr.* 2, (anchor, *pl.* 77, *cr.* 1.)

JEFFERYS, a demi-lion, rampant, or, between paws a chaplet, vert. *Pl.* 126, *cr.* 12, (chaplet, *pl.* 128.)

JEFFREY, Eng., on a ducal coronet, a martlet, sa. *Pl.* 98, *cr.* 14.

JEFFREY, Sco., a star of six rays. *Phœbus, lux in tenebris.* *Pl.* 21, *cr.* 6.

JEFFREY, the sun shining through a cloud, ppr. *Post nubila Phœbus.* *Pl.* 67, *cr.* 9.

JEFFREYS, on stump of tree, couped, sprouting new branches, vert, a stork, ar. *Pl.* 23, *cr.* 5.

JEFFREYS, a wolf's head, (couped,) sa. *Pl.* 14, *cr.* 6.

JEFFREYS, a demi-lion, holding a garland of laurel. *Pl.* 39, *cr.* 14, (garland, *pl.* 56, *cr.* 10.)

JEFFREYS, Salop, a lion's head, erased, sa., gorged with a wreath. *Supra spem spero.* *Pl.* 22, *cr.* 3.

JEFFRIES, Eng., a tower, triple-turreted, or. *Pl.* 123, *cr.* 14.

JEFFRY, Lond. and Worc., on a mount, vert, a bird, rising, ar. *Pl.* 61, *cr.* 1.

JEFFS, Eng., a pelican's head, erased, vulning, ppr. *Pl.* 26, *cr.* 1.

JEGGINGS, an eagle, wings expanded, or, beaked, ar. *Pl.* 126, *cr.* 7.

JEGON, Eng., a pelican, or, vulning, gu. *Pl.* 109, *cr.* 15.

JEGON, Eng., an eagle, wings expanded, or, beaked, ar. *Pl.* 126, *cr.* 7.

JEJEEBHOY, Knt., Bombay, on a mount, amidst wheat, a peacock, in beak an ear of wheat, all ppr. *Industry and liberality. Pl.* 9, *cr.* 1, (wheat, *same plate.*)

JEKEN, and JEKIN, Kent, a demi-lion, regardant, erm., semée of crescents, gu., between paws a pheon, sa. *Pl.* 33, *cr.* 2, (pheon and crescents, *pl.* 141.)

JEKLEY, a horse's head, (affrontée,) couped at neck, and bridled, ppr. *Pl.* 92, *cr.* 1.

JEKYL, and JEKYLL, Ess., Middx., Lond., Linc., and Northamp., a horse's head, couped, ar., maned and bridled, sa., studded and tasselled, or. *Pl.* 92, *cr.* 1.

JELF, Glouc. and Lond., a stork, (wings elevated,) ar., beaked and legged, gu., in beak a trefoil, slipped, vert, on breast a cross pattée, of the second, in dexter a fleur-de-lis, or. *Pl.* 33, *cr.* 9, (trefoil, cross, and fleur-de-lis, *pl.* 141.)

JELLEY, and JELLY, Eng., a garb, entwined by two snakes, ppr. *Pl.* 36, *cr.* 14.

JELLICOE, Eng., a cherub. *Pl.* 126, *cr.* 10.

JELTER, a cat, sejant, gardant, or. *Pl.* 24, *cr.* 6.

JEMMET, Kent, a unicorn's head, erased. *Pl.* 67, *cr.* 1.

JENINGS, a dove, volant, az., legged, ar. *Pl.* 25, *cr.* 6.

JENISON, out of a ducal coronet, or, a dragon's head, az. *Pl.* 59, *cr.* 14.

JENKENS, a wyvern, gu., standing on a tilting-spear, without bur or vamplet, and broken off at point, or, in mouth the other part of the shaft, armed, ar. *Pl.* 75, *cr.* 12.

JENKENSON, and JENKINSON, Lond., a sea-horse, assurgent, or, maned, az., supporting a cross pattée, gu. *Pl.* 100, *cr.* 1, (cross, *pl.* 141.)

JENKES, Salop, a dexter arm, embowed, vested, sa., cuffed, ar., enfiled with a ducal coronet, or, in hand, ppr., a sword, of the second, hilt and pommel, gold. *Pl.* 120, *cr.* 1, (coronet, *same plate.*)

JENKIN, Cornw.: 1. A lion, rampant, regardant, sa. *Pl.* 10, *cr.* 15, (without coronet.) 2. On a mural coronet, sa., a lion, passant, regardant, or. *Pl.* 100, *cr.* 6, (coronet, *pl.* 128, *fig.* 18.)

JENKINS, Wel., a battle-axe, handle, or, head, ppr. *Pl.* 14, *cr.* 8.

JENKINS, Iri., on a ducal coronet, or, a talbot, (statant,) ar., collared and lined, gu. *Pl.* 3, *cr.* 8.

JENKINS, in lion's paw, erased, a bezant, or. *Pl.* 97, *cr.* 10.

JENKINS, Salop, on a mural coronet, sa., a lion, passant, regardant, or. *Perge sed caute. Pl.* 100, *cr.* 6, (coronet, *pl.* 128, *fig.* 18.)

JENKINS, seven arrows, one in pale, six in saltier, encircled with an annulet, or. *Pl.* 110, *cr.* 11, (annulet, *pl.* 141.)

JENKINSON, Earl of Liverpool. See LIVERPOOL.

JENKINSON, a horse's head, couped, ar., crined, gu., (gorged with a fess, az.) *Pl.* 2, *cr.* 7.

JENKINSON, Lond. and Linc., a sea-horse, ppr. *Pl.* 103, *cr.* 3.

JENKINSON, Iri., out of a ducal coronet, az., a demi-lion, rampant, holding a palm-branch, vert. *Pl.* 45, *cr.* 7, (branch, *pl.* 61, *cr.* 4.)

JENKINSON, Norf., a sea-horse's (head,) couped, ar., finned and gorged, with two barrulets, or. *Pl.* 58, *cr.* 15.

JENKINSON, a sea-horse, az., (winged, or.) *Pl.* 103, *cr.* 3.

JENKINSON, Norf. and Suff., a bull's head, ar., crined, sa., horns, twisted, or, and of the second. *Pl.* 102, *cr.* 7.

JENKINSON, Norf., a sea-horse, or, finned, gu. *Pl.* 103, *cr.* 3.

JENKS, out of a ducal coronet, or, a griffin's head, ppr. *Pl.* 54, *cr.* 14.

JENKYNS, Yorks., on a ducal coronet, sa., a lion, rampant, gardant, or. *Pl.* 92, *cr.* 7, (coronet, *pl.* 128, *fig.* 3.)

JENNER, Lond., a covered cup, or, between two swords, in saltier, ar., hilts and pommels, gold. *Pl.* 75, *cr.* 13.

JENNER, ROBERT-FRANCIS, Esq., of Wenvoe Castle, Glamorgan, same crest.

JENNER, Ess., a greyhound, sejant, ar. *Pl.* 66, *cr.* 15.

JENNERSON, two swords, in saltier, supporting a scimitar, in fess, ppr., between points of swords, a covered cup, or. *Pl.* 113, *cr.* 9.

JENNESON, Northumb., out of a ducal coronet, or, a dragon's head, az. *Pl.* 59, *cr.* 14.

JENNET, out of a ducal coronet, or, a dexter arm, embowed, in mail, ppr., in hand a (sword,) ar., hilt, gold. *Pl.* 122, *cr.* 8.

JENNET, or JENNETT, Iri., a hind's head, gu. *Pl.* 21, *cr.* 9.

JENNEY, Middx., Linc., and Suff., on a glove, ar., a hawk, or, belled, gold. *Pl.* 1, *cr.* 13.

JENNEY, EDMUND, Esq., of Bredfield House, Suff., same crest.

JENNING, Beds., a hawk, rising, az. *Pl.* 105, *cr.* 4.

JENNINGHAM, Eng., out of a ducal coronet, a demi-eagle, wings expanded, ppr. *Pl.* 9, *cr.* 6.

JENNINGS, Eng., a jay, ppr. *Pl.* 52, *cr.* 12.

JENNINGS, Lond., Yorks., Chesh., and Salop, a wolf's head, erased, per pale, ar. and vert. *Pl.* 14, *cr.* 6.

JENNINGS, Lond., Yorks., Chesh., and Salop, a wolf's head, erased, per pale, ar. and sa. *Pl.* 14, *cr.* 6.

JENNINGS, Iri., out of a mural coronet, az., a garb, or, thereon a sparrow, ppr. *Pl.* 14, *cr.* 5.

JENNINGS, an eagle's head, couped, in beak a plummet, sa. *Pl.* 100, *cr.* 10, (plummet, *pl.* 50, *cr.* 8.)

JENNINGS, Yorks., a griffin's head, couped, between wings, ppr., (in beak a plummet, pendent, sa.) *Pl.* 65, *cr.* 1, (plummet, *pl.* 50, *cr.* 8.)

JENNINGS, a cat's head, erased, gardant, gu., bezantée, in mouth a cross pattée, fitched, ar. *Pl.* 97, *cr.* 9, (cross, *pl.* 27, *cr.* 14.)

JENNINGS, a stag, passant. *Pl.* 68, *cr.* 2.

JENNINGS, a demi-lion, rampant, or, holding the upper part of a spear-shaft, gold. *Pl.* 39, *cr.* 14, (spear, *pl.* 82, *cr.* 9.)

JENNINGS, an eagle's head, (couped,) between wings. *Pl.* 81, *cr.* 10.

JENNINGS, Lond., a demi-dragon, erminois, wings addorsed, gu., erased, of the last, holding a battle-axe, erect, az. *Pl.* 82, *cr.* 10, (axe, *pl.* 26, *cr.* 7.)

JENNINS, a griffin, statant, gu., holding a buckle, or. *Pl.* 39, *cr.* 8.

JENNINS, Hants., a demi-griffin, ppr., in beak a plummet, sa. *Pl.* 18, *cr.* 6, (plummet, *pl.* 50, *cr.* 8.)

JENNOWAY, Eng., a horned owl. *Je pense. Pl.* 1, *cr.* 8.

JENNY, Suff., a falconer's hand within a glove, in fess, ppr., thereon a falcon, perched, or. *Pl.* 83, *cr.* 13.

JENNY, a falcon, rising, belled, or. *Pl.* 105, *cr.* 4.

JENNY, out of a ducal coronet, or, an arm, in armour, in hand a (scimitar,) ppr. *Pl.* 122, *cr.* 8.

JENNYNS, Middx., Worc., and Camb., a leopard's head, erased, and gardant, gu., bezantée, in mouth a cross formée, fitched, ar. *Pl.* 56, *cr.* 7, (cross, *pl.* 27, *cr.* 14.)

JENOURE, and JENOYRE, Ess., a greyhound, sejant. *In pretium persevero. Pl.* 66, *cr.* 15.

JENSSEN, Lond., a quatrefoil, (stalked and leaved,) vert. *Pl.* 65, *cr.* 7.

JENY, a hand, in fess, issuing from a cloud, ppr., holding a cross pattée, fitched, ar. *Pl.* 26, *cr.* 4.

JENYNGE, Hants., a demi-lion, erased and rampant, or, supporting a spear, erect, gold, headed, az. *Pl.* 39, *cr.* 14, (spear, *pl.* 97, *cr.* 4.)

JENYNGES, Suff., a demi-savage, sa., collared, or, wreathed round temples, gold, in dexter a halberd, az., staff, gu. *Pl.* 87, *cr.* 13, (halberd, *pl.* 14, *cr.* 8.)

JENYNGES, a demi-man, vested, sa., cap, vert, in dexter a battle-axe, az. *Pl.* 122, *cr.* 1, (axe, *pl.* 14, *cr.* 8.)

JEPHSON, Bart., Dors., a cubit arm, vested, paly, ar. and az., cuff, of the second, surmounted of a bend, gu., in hand a pansy, or heart's-ease, ppr. *Veritas magna est. Pl.* 113, *cr.* 5.

JEPHSON, and JEFFSON, Lond., an arm, couped at elbow, and erect, vested, paly of four, ar. and az., cuffed, of the first, thereon a bend, gu., in hand a bunch of roses, ppr., stalked and leaved, vert. *Pl.* 113, *cr.* 5, (roses, *pl.* 23, *cr.* 2.)

JEPHSON, Iri., a hind, trippant, or. *Pl.* 20, *cr.* 14.

JEPINE, a lion's head, erased, or, billettée, sa., and ducally crowned, gold. *Pl.* 90, *cr.* 4.

JEPPE, Somers., an eagle, displayed, ppr. *Pl.* 48, *cr.* 11.

JEPSON, Eng., on the top of a tower, an eagle, rising, ppr., in beak an acorn, slipped and leaved, vert. *Pl.* 60, *cr.* 8.

JERARD, or JERRARD, Eng., an eagle, displayed, with two heads, or, charged with a saltier, sa. *Pl.* 25, *cr.* 5.

JERCY, a phœnix in flames, ppr. *Pl.* 44, *cr.* 8.

JEREMY, Eng., an arm, in armour, embowed, gloved, wielding a battle-axe, all ppr. *Pl.* 121, *cr.* 14.

JERMAIN, and JERMAYNE, Eng., a gilliflower, ppr. *Pl.* 22, *cr.* 9.

JERMIN, or JERMYN, Ess., a buck's head, cabossed, sa., between wings, ar. *Pl.* 36, *cr.* 1, (wings, *pl.* 1, *cr.* 15.)

JERMINGHAM, Norf. and Suff., out of a ducal coronet, or, a demi-falcon, displayed, ar. *Pl.* 103, *cr.* 6.

JERMY, a griffin, passant, gu. *Pl.* 61, *cr.* 14, (without gorging.)

JERMY, and JERMYN, Suff. and Norf., a griffin, wings (expanded,) gu. *Pl.* 66, *cr.* 13.

JERMYN, Suss. and Devons., a tiger's head, erased, gu. *Pl.* 94, *cr.* 10.

JERMYN, Saff., a talbot, passant, gorged with a coronet. *Pl.* 120, *cr.* 8, (coronet, *same plate*.)

JERMYN, Suff., out of a ducal coronet, or, a greyhound's head, ppr., collared, gold. *Pl.* 70, *cr.* 5.

JERMYN, Suff., a greyhound's head, sa., gorged with a bar-gemelle, or. *Pl.* 43, *cr.* 11.

JERNEGAN, Suff., a demi-falcon, ar., winged and beaked, or. *Pl.* 103, *cr.* 10.

JERNINGHAM, Baron Stafford. *See* STAFFORD.

JERNINGHAM, Norf., on a ducal coronet, or, a demi-falcon, wings expanded, ppr. *Pl.* 103, *cr.* 6.

JERNINGHAM, out of a ducal coronet, or, a partridge, sa., wings (expanded.) *Pl.* 108, *cr.* 5, (coronet, *pl.* 128, *fig.* 3.)

JERSEY, Earl of, Viscount and Baron Villiers, Eng., Viscount Grandison, Iri., (Child-Villiers,) a lion, rampant, ar., ducally crowned, or. *Fidei coticula crux. Pl.* 98, *cr.* 1.

JERSEY, a phœnix, in flames, ppr. *Pl.* 44, *cr.* 8.

JERVEIS, Worc., a tiger's head, sa. *Pl.* 94, *cr.* 10.

JERVIS, and JERVOIS, Hants., a tiger's head, sa. *Pl.* 94, *cr.* 10.

JERVIS, Leic., a hawk's head, or, between wings, erm. *Pl.* 99, *cr.* 10.

JERVIS-WHITE, Bart., Iri.: 1. An eaglet, close, ar. *Pl.* 7, *cr.* 11. 2. Three arrows, one in pale, two in saltier, (enwreathed.) *Venale nec auro. Pl.* 43, *cr.* 14.

JERVOISE, Herriard: 1. For *Jervoise*, a tiger's head, sa. *Pl.* 94, *cr.* 10. 2. For *Ellis*, a plume of five ostrich-feathers, ar. *Pl.* 100, *cr.* 12, (without coronet or charge.)

JERVOISE-CLARKE, Bart., Hants.: 1. For *Jervoise*, an heraldic-tiger's head, sa. *Pl.* 113, *cr.* 3. 2. For *Clarke*, within a gold ring, set with a diamond, ppr., a roundle, per pale, gu. and az., charged with a pheon, ar. *Pl.* 75, *cr.* 15.

JERVY, Eng., in hand, ppr., an eagle's leg, erased at thigh, gu. *Pl.* 103, *cr.* 4.

JERWORTH, Eng., a crane's head, couped, ppr. *Pl.* 71, *cr.* 10, (without crown.)

JESSE, Eng., a lion, sejant, supporting an escutcheon, gu. *Pl.* 22, *cr.* 13.

JESSE, JOHN, Esq., of Llanbedro Hall, Denbigh, a demi-lion, rampant. *Pl.* 67, *cr.* 10.

JESSON, an arm, erect, vested, paly of six, ar. and az., charged with a (bend,) gu., in hand, ppr., a cinquefoil, purp., leaved, vert. *Pl.* 101, *cr.* 5.

JESSON, Warw., a dexter arm, ppr., vested, gu., charged with a bend, ar., cuffed, or, in hand a rose, of the second, stalked and leaved, vert. *Pl.* 113, *cr.* 5, (rose, *pl.* 118, *cr.* 9.)

JESSOP, a cockatrice's head, erased, purp., combed, gu., winged, ppr. *Pl.* 106, *cr.* 15, (without gorging.)

JESSOP, Iri., a goat's head, erased, sa., armed and (collared,) or. *Pl.* 29, *cr.* 13.

JESSOP, a moorcock, ppr.

JESSOP, FREDERICK-THOMAS, Esq., of Doory Hall, co. Longford, a dove and olive-branch, ppr. *Pax et amor. Pl.* 48, *cr.* 15.

JESSOPE, Dors., a cockatrice, vert, displayed, ppr., combed and wattled, gu. *Pl.* 102, *cr.* 15.

JESSOPE, JESSOPP, or JESSUP, Eng., a man on horseback, at a charge, in hand a broken tilting-spear, ppr. *Pl.* 43, *cr.* 2.

JETT, Lond., (out of rays of the sun, or,) a demi-swan, wings elevated, sa., in mouth an arrow, ar. *Pl.* 10, *cr.* 11, (without coronet.)

JETTER, Suff., out of a ducal coronet, or, a cubit arm, erect, in mail, in hand, all ppr., the blade of a broken sword, ar. *Pl.* 23, *cr.* 9, (sword, *pl.* 22, *cr.* 6.)

JETTER, out of a ducal coronet, an arm, erect, in hand a broken spear, ppr. *Pl.* 23, *cr.* 9, (coronet, *same plate.*)

JEVERS, Eng., a demi-lion, rampant, or, collared, sa. *Pl.* 18, *cr.* 13.

JEWEL, Eng., an oak-branch, bearing acorns, ppr. *Pl.* 32, *cr.* 13.

JEWELL, Devons., a cubit arm, vested, az., cuffed, ar., in hand, ppr., a gilliflower, gu., stalked and leaved, vert. *Pl.* 113, *cr.* 5, (flower, *pl.* 22, *cr.* 9.)

JEWELL, Sco., in dexter hand a gilliflower, ppr. *Pl.* 118, *cr.* 9, (flower, *pl.* 22, *cr.* 7.)

JEWERS, Eng., between horns of a crescent, a buckle, ppr. *Pl.* 25, *cr.* 3.

JEWKES, Lanc. and Warw., a demi-lion, ducally crowned. *Pl.* 61, *cr.* 4, (without branch.)

JEWSSBURY, Glouc., on a mount, vert, a martlet, or. *Pl.* 36, *cr.* 5.

JEYNES, an arm, erect, holding a battle-axe. *Pl.* 73, *cr.* 7.

JEYNOR, Ess., a greyhound, sejant, or. *Pl.* 66, *cr.* 15.

JEYS, Eng., a horse, passant, ar. *Pl.* 15, *cr.* 14.

JOANES, Somers., a tiger's head, erased. *Pl.* 94, *cr.* 10.

JOANES, Lond. and Worc., the sun in splendour, or. *Pl.* 68, *cr.* 14.

JOANES, a greyhound's head, ar., between two roses, gu., slipped and leaved, ppr. *Pl.* 84, *cr.* 13.

JOASS, a sand-glass, winged. *Cogit amor. Pl.* 32, *cr.* 11.

JOB, Lanc., out of a ducal coronet, a bull's head. *Pl.* 68, *cr.* 6.

JOBBER, Eng., a fox, sejant, ppr. *Pl.* 87, *cr.* 4.

JOBLING, a demi-lion, rampant, holding a battle-axe, ppr. *For my country. Pl.* 101, *cr.* 14, (without bend.)

JOBSON, Eng., on a hand, extended, ar., a falcon, close, or. *Pl.* 83, *cr.* 13.

JOBSON, Yorks., on a sinister gauntlet, ar., a bird, close, or. *Pl.* 1, *cr.* 13.

JOCE, Eng., an antelope, passant, ppr. *Pl.* 63, *cr.* 10.

JOCELYN, Earl of Roden. *See* RODEN.

JOCELYN, or JOCELYNE, Herts., a falcon's leg, erased, ppr., belled, or. *Faire mon devoir. Pl.* 83, *cr.* 7.

JOCKEL, Edinr., the mast, gu., and sail of a ship, ar., with pennon flotant at top, az., tackling and yards, ppr. *Fiducid et labore. Pl.* 103, *cr.* 7.

JODDRELL, Bart., Norf., a demi-cock, wings erected, or, combed and wattled, gu., out of a wreath of roses, of the last, seeded, gold. *Non sibi sed patriæ natus. Pl.* 72, *cr.* 4, (wreath, *pl.* 41, *cr.* 7.)

JODDRELL, Eng., on a chapeau, a greyhound, sejant, ppr. *Pl.* 66, *cr.* 15, (chapeau, *pl.* 127, *fig.* 13.)

JODRELL, Chesh., a cock's head and neck, couped, or, wings elevated, ar., combed and wattled, gu. *Pl.* 72, *cr.* 4.

JODRELL, Derbs., a cock's head and neck, couped, wings erect, or, combed and jelloped, gu., issuing from a chaplet of roses, barbed and seeded, ppr. *Pl.* 72, *cr.* 4, (wreath, *pl.* 41, *cr.* 7.)

JOEL, Eng., a hare, lodged among grass, ppr. *Pl.* 29, *cr.* 1.

JOHN, Cornw., an arm, in armour, embowed, in hand a sword. *Pl.* 2, *cr.* 8.

JOHN, on two battle-axes, in saltier, ppr., blades, or, a Cornish chough, sa., beaked and membered, gu. *Pl.* 52, *cr.* 10, (chough, *pl.* 100, *cr.* 13.)

JOHN, Eng., a demi-lion, rampant, ppr. *Pl.* 67, *cr.* 10.)

JOHNES, Monm., two battle-axes, in saltier, ppr., handles, or. *Pl.* 52, *cr.* 10.

JOHNES, Lanc., out of a ducal coronet, a plume of five ostrich-feathers. *Vince malum bono. Pl.* 100, *cr.* 12, (without charge.)

JOHNES, Lond., a lion, rampant, or, supporting an anchor, az., fluke, gold. *Pl.* 22, *cr.* 15, (anchor, *pl.* 19, *cr.* 6.)

JOHNS, Eng., on a mural coronet, a serpent, nowed, vert. *Pl.* 103, *cr.* 11.

JOHNS, Cornw., two battle-axes, in saltier, ppr. *Pl.* 52, *cr.* 10,

JOHNS, Sco., a crow, ppr. *Semper sic. Pl.* 23, *cr.* 8.

JOHNSON, Bart., Middx., an arm, embowed, in hand a sword, ppr. *Deo regique liber. Pl.* 34, *cr.* 7.

JOHNSON, Bart., Bath, a tower, ar., on the battlements, a cock, ppr. *Vicisti et vivimus. Pl.* 113, *cr.* 14.

JOHNSON, Durh., a dexter arm, in armour, embowed, firing a pistol, all ppr. *Pl.* 96, *cr.* 4.

JOHNSON, Chesh., an arm, in armour, in hand, all ppr., an arrow, ar., with a pheon's head, or. *Pl.* 47, *cr.* 5.

JOHNSON, Middx., a triangular harrow, or. *Pl.* 7, *cr.* 2.

JOHNSON, a lion's head, gu., crowned, or, between two ostrich-feathers, ar. *Pl.* 1, *cr.* 5, (feathers, *pl.* 50, *cr.* 1.)

JOHNSON, Northumb., a stalk of wheat, ppr. *Nunquam non paratus. Pl.* 85, *cr.* 6.

JOHNSON, Staffs. and Suff., (on a mount, vert,) an ibex, sejant, erm., ducally gorged, crined and tufted, or, attired, ar. *Pl.* 115, *cr.* 3.

JOHNSON, Lond. and Yorks., a cock, ar., combed and wattled, or, charged on body with three guttes-de-sang, *Pl.* 67, *cr.* 14.

JOHNSON, Ruts. and Notts., a lion's head, erased, gu., ducally crowned, or, between two ostrich-feathers, ar. *Pl.* 1, *cr.* 5, (feathers, *pl.* 50, *cr.* 1.)

JOHNSON, Middx., Norf., and Linc., out of a ducal coronet, per pale, ar. and az., two wings, expanded, counterchanged. *Pl.* 17, *cr.* 9.

JOHNSON, Ruts. and Notts., out of a ducal coronet, ar., a leopard's head, or. *Pl.* 36, *cr.* 15.

JOHNSON, Lond., a spear-head, ar., between two branches of laurel, vert. *Pl.* 71, *cr.* 3, (spear, *pl.* 82, *cr.* 9.)

JOHNSON, (on a mount, vert,) a talbot, couchant, ar., (collared and chained, or.) *Pl.* 32, *cr.* 7.

JOHNSON, Lond., a tiger's head, erminois, maned, ar. *Pl.* 91, *cr.* 10.
JOHNSON, Norf., out of a ducal coronet, or, a leopard's head and neck, gu. *Pl.* 36, *cr.* 15.
JOHNSON, Lond., out of a ducal coronet, a swan's head and neck, or. *Pl.* 82, *cr.* 1.
JOHNSON, a spur, between wings, between the spur an etoile, all ppr. *Pl.* 109, *cr.* 12, (etoile, *pl.* 141.)
JOHNSON, Leic., a demi-griffin, gu., collared, erm., between claws a pheon, or. *Pl.* 74, *cr.* 15, (pheon, *pl.* 141.)
JOHNSON, out of a ducal coronet, per pale, ar. and az., a pair of wings, per pale, counterchanged. *Pl.* 17, *cr.* 9.
JOHNSON, Linc., a leopard, passant, gardant, sa., platée and bezantée. *Pl.* 51, *cr.* 7.
JOHNSON, a man's head, couped at neck, affrontée, bearded, ppr. *Pl.* 19, *cr.* 1.
JOHNSON, Lanc., a spur, or, the strap, gu., between wings, gold. *Pl.* 109, *cr.* 12.
JOHNSON, a lion's head, gardant, erased, per pale, gu. and sa., bezantée, (collared,) or. *Pl.* 1, *cr.* 5, (without crown.)
JOHNSON, Lanc., a tower in flames. *Pl.* 118, *cr.* 15.
JOHNSON, a mermaid, (in dexter a sceptre, in sinister a mirror,) all ppr. *Pl.* 88, *cr.* 12.
JOHNSON, Kent and Glouc., out of a ducal coronet, or, a nag's head, sa. *Pl.* 50, *cr.* 13.
JOHNSON, a wolf, passant, (in mouth, a sprig of woodbine in full blossom,) all ppr. *Pl.* 46, *cr.* 6.
JOHNSON, Chesh., on a ducal coronet, or, an eagle, wings expanded, sa. *Pl.* 9, *cr.* 6.
JOHNSON, a chevalier, in complete armour, on horseback, at speed, in dexter a sabre. *Pl.* 118, *cr.* 14.
JOHNSON, Bucks., a cubit arm, vested, in hand, ppr., a cross fleury, of the first. *Pl.* 75, *cr.* 3.
JOHNSON, out of a ducal coronet, a demi-bear, rampant, muzzled, and ducally crowned, between paws a sword, in pale. *Pl.* 56, *cr.* 2, (sword, *same plate.*)
JOHNSON, Durh., a tiger's head, (couped,) sa., bezantée. *Pl.* 94, *cr.* 10.
JOHNSON, out of a ducal coronet, a griffin's head. *Pl.* 54, *cr.* 14.
JOHNSON, Kent, an arm, erect, vested, per pale, az. and or, in hand, ppr., a cross patonce, gold. *Pl.* 75, *cr.* 3.
JOHNSON, a lion, statant, gardant, royally crowned. *Pl.* 120, *cr.* 5, (crown, *pl.* 127, *fig.* 2.)
JOHNSON, Durh., a leopard's head, sa., bezantée, flames issuing from mouth and ears. *Pl.* 112, *cr.* 9.
JOHNSON, Sco., a winged spur, ppr. *Nunquam non paratus.* *Pl.* 59, *cr.* 1.
JOHNSON, a (sword) and dagger, in saltier, blades, ar., hilts and pommels, or. *Pl.* 24, *cr.* 2.
JOHNSON, Suff., a lion, rampant, in dexter a mullet, under sinister a cross pattée. *Pl.* 87, *cr.* 6, (mullet and cross, *pl.* 141.)
JOHNSON, out of a mural coronet, gu., a cubit arm, erect, vested, or, turned up, ar., in hand, ppr., a scimitar, of the third, hilt, gold. *Pl.* 34, *cr.* 1, (scimitar, *pl.* 29, *cr.* 8.)
JOHNSON, Chesh., out of a crescent, or, a pheon, all between wings, sa. *Servabo fidem.* *Pl.* 31, *cr.* 11, (pheon, *pl.* 141.)

JOHNSON, Ayscough Fee Hall, a ducal coronet. *Onus sub honore.* *Pl.* 128, *fig.* 3.
JOHNSON, Durh., a demi-lion, rampant, regardant, (gorged with a palm-branch,) ar. *Pl.* 33, *cr.* 2, (without spear.)
JOHNSON, Eng., a greyhound's head, couped, vert, collared, or. *Pl.* 43, *cr.* 11.
JOHNSON, Iri., a sword and key, in saltier, ppr. *Pl.* 54, *cr.* 12.
JOHNSON, Lond., an (eagle's) leg, sa. *Pl.* 83, *cr.* 7.
JOHNSON, Bucks., a castle, ppr. *Pl.* 28, *cr.* 11.
JOHNSON, Sco., a bull's head, cabossed, sa., armed, or. *Pl.* 111, *cr.* 6.
JOHNSON, EDWARD, Esq., of Deanery, Chester-le-street, Durh., a savage's head, couped at shoulders, bearded, and wreathed, all ppr. *Nil admirari.* *Pl.* 36, *cr.* 3.
JOHNSOUN, a greyhound's head, couped, vert. *Pl.* 14, *cr.* 4.
JOHNSTON, in hand, an escallop, ppr. *Sine fraude fides.* *Pl.* 57, *cr.* 6.
JOHNSTON, Eng., in hand a bezant, ppr. *Ex solâ virtute honos.* *Pl.* 24, *cr.* 3, (bezant, *pl.* 141.)
JOHNSTON, Sco., a spur-rowel, between two palm-branches, in orle, ppr. *Securior quo paratior:* *Pl.* 103, *cr.* 14.
JOHNSTON, Bart., of Johnston, Sco., a (sword) and a dagger, in saltier, points upward, all pp. *Paratus ad arma*—and—*Vive, ut postea vivas.* *Pl.* 24, *cr.* 2.
JOHNSTON, Bart., Dumfries, a spur, with wings, or, leather, gu. *Nunquam non paratus.* *Pl.* 59, *cr.* 1.
JOHNSTON, of Gartney, a winged spur, or, leathered, gu. *Cave paratus.* *Pl.* 59, *cr.* 1.
JOHNSTON, of Hilltoun, a (sword) and dagger, in saltier, all ppr. *Paratus ad arma.* *Pl.* 24, *cr.* 2.
JOHNSTON, of Poltoun, a winged spur. *Sic paratior.* *Pl.* 59, *cr.* 1.
JOHNSTON, Sco., same crest. *Caute et sedulo.*
JOHNSTON, of Clathrie, a star out of a cloud, or. *Appropinquat Dies.* *Pl.* 16, *cr.* 13.
JOHNSTON, of Caskieben, a phœnix in flames, ppr. *Vive, ut postea vivas.* *Pl.* 44, *cr.* 8.
JOHNSTON, Sco., a phœnix in flames. *Vive, ut vivas.* *Pl.* 44, *cr.* 8.
JOHNSTON, of Corehead or Loch-house, a spur, or. *Ad arma paratus.* *Pl.* 15, *cr.* 3.
JOHNSTON, of Straiton, an arm, in armour, holding in the glove a sword, (erect,) all ppr. *Semper paratus.* *Pl.* 2, *cr.* 8.
JOHNSTON, Sco., a man armed cap-a-pie, on horseback, brandishing a sword. *Cave paratus.* *Pl.* 118, *cr.* 14.
JOHNSTON, Sco. and Eng., a griffin's head, erased, gu. *Pl.* 48, *cr.* 6.
JOHNSTON, Sco., in hand, ppr., an escallop, gu. *Pl.* 57, *cr.* 6.
JOHNSTON, a spur, ppr., between wings, ar. *Pl.* 109, *cr.* 12.
JOHNSTON, a (sword) and dagger, in saltier, points upward, all ppr. *Pl.* 24, *cr.* 2.
JOHNSTON, Sco., a winged spur, or. *Pl.* 59, *cr.* 1.
JOHNSTON, and JOHNSTONE, Iri., a dexter arm, in armour, embowed, hand apaumée, ppr. *Pl.* 97, *cr.* 1.
JOHNSTONE, Sco., an arm, in armour, in hand a sword, (erect,) all ppr. *Semper paratus.* *Pl.* 2, *cr.* 8.

JOHNSTONE, JAMES, Esq., of Alva, Clackmannan, and of Hangingshaw, Selkirk, a spur, with wings, or, leather, gu. *Nunquam non paratus. Pl.* 59, *cr.* 1.

JOHNSTONE, Sco., a spur, or. *Pl.* 15, *cr.* 3.

JOHNSTONE-BEMPDE-VANDEN, Bart., Yorks., a winged spur, erect, or, strapped, gu. *Pl.* 59, *cr.* 1.

JOHNSTONE-HOPE, JOHN JAMES, Esq., of Annandale; of Rachills, Dumfries: 1. For *Johnstone*, a spur, erect, or, winged, ar. *Pl.* 59, *cr.* 1. 2. For *Hope*, a globe, fractured at top, under a rainbow, with clouds at each end, all ppr. *At spes non fracta*—and—*Nunquam non paratus. Pl.* 79, *cr.* 1.

JOHNSTOUN, Eng., a winged spur, or. *Nunquam non paratus. Pl.* 59, *cr.* 1.

JOINER, a greyhound, sejant, sa. *Pl.* 66, *cr.* 15.

JOLLIE, Sco., a fox's head, sa. *Pl.* 91, *cr.* 9.

JOKES, on a ducal coronet, or, a cockatrice, displayed, gu. *Pl.* 77, *cr.* 5, (cockatrice, *pl.* 102, *cr.* 15.)

JOLDIFFE, Bart., Surr., an arm, erect, couped, in armour, in hand a broad-sword, all ppr. *Tant que je puis. Pl.* 125, *cr.* 5.

JOLLES, Lond., out of a mural coronet, a nag's head, or. *Pl.* 50, *cr.* 13, (coronet, *pl.* 128, *fig.* 18.)

JOLLEY, Lanc., a cubit arm, vested, vert, (charged with a pile,) ar., in hand, ppr., a sword, of the second, hilt and pommel, or. *Pl.* 120, *cr.* 2.

JOLLEY, or JOLLY, Lond., a demi-eagle, displayed, or, in beak a sinister hand, ar. *Pl.* 22, *cr.* 11, (hand, *pl.* 61, *cr.* 8.)

JOLLIE, in hand a scimitar, ppr. *Pl.* 29, *cr.* 8.

JOLLIFF, or JOLLEFF, an arm, in hand a dagger. *Pl.* 28, *cr.* 4.

JOLLIFFE, out of a mural coronet, a nag's head. *Pl.* 50, *cr.* 13, (coronet, *pl.* 128, *fig.* 18.)

JOLLIFFE, Somers., a cubit arm, in armour, in hand a (scimitar,) all ppr. *Pl.* 125, *cr.* 5.

JOLLIFFE-TWYFORD, Ammerdown Park, Bath, a cubit arm, erect, (vested and cuffed, sleeve charged with a pile, ar.,) in hand a sword, ppr. *Pl.* 21, *cr.* 10.

JOLLY, Sco., a dove and olive-branch. *Lætavi. Pl.* 48, *cr.* 15.

JOLLYFFE, an eagle's head, erased, sa., beaked, or. *Pl.* 20, *cr.* 7.

JONAS, Eng., on a tower, ppr., a crescent, or. *Pl.* 85, *cr.* 1.

JONES, Bart., Norf., in front of a castle, ar., a lion, couchant, or. *Marte et arte. Pl.* 96, *cr.* 5.

JONES, Beds., on a chapeau, az., turned up, or, an arm, in armour, embowed, tasselled, gu., in hand, ppr., a spear, sheaf, of the fourth, armed, gold. *Pl.* 57, *cr.* 3.

JONES, Lond., out of a ducal coronet, a plume of five ostrich-feathers. *Vince malum bono. Pl.* 100, *cr.* 12, (without charge.)

JONES, Berks., a demi-lion, rampant, or, between paws a mullet, gu. *Pl.* 89, *cr.* 10.

JONES, Heref., a gauntlet, in fess, holding a (spear,) erect, both ppr., enfiled with a boar's head, erased, pean. *Pl.* 85, *cr.* 12.

JONES, MARY-ANNE, of Ystrad, Carmarthen, a stag's head, erased, ppr. *Pl.* 66, *cr.* 9.

JONES, Viscount Ranelagh. See RANELAGH.

JONES, Wel., a boar's head, erased, in fess, or. *Pl.* 16, *cr.* 11.

JONES, WILLIAM-TILSLEY, Esq., of Gwynfryn, Cardigan, a demi-lion, rampant. *Mois mihi lucrum. Pl.* 67, *cr.* 10.

JONES, WYTHEN, Esq., of Rhiewport, Montgomery, a lion, rampant, gu. *Frangas, non flectes. Pl.* 67, *cr.* 5.

JONES, Wel., a boar's head, erect, and erased, or. *Pl.* 21, *cr.* 7.

JONES, a Cornish chough, ppr., in dexter an etoile, ar. *Pl.* 100, *cr.* 13, (etoile, *pl.* 141.)

JONES, Berks., a lion, rampant, or, grasping an anchor, in pale, sa. *Pl.* 22, *cr.* 15, (anchor, *pl.* 19, *cr.* 6.)

JONES, Cornw. and Wilts., a dragon's head, erased, vert. *Pl.* 107, *cr.* 10.

JONES, Wel., the sun, (at the end of each ray a flame of fire,) all ppr. *Pl.* 68, *cr.* 14.

JONES, Wel., a lion's head, erased, per pale, ar. and sa. *Pl.* 81, *cr.* 4.

JONES, a bird's head, sa., in beak a branch, (reversed,) vert. *Pl.* 22, *cr.* 1.

JONES, Heref., a lion, rampant, or. *Pl.* 67, *cr.* 5.

JONES, out of a ducal coronet, or, a goat's head. *Pl.* 72, *cr.* 2.

JONES, Kent, a talbot's head, couped, ar., (with a chain round neck, or.) *Pl.* 123, *cr.* 15.

JONES, Middx. and Heref., a tiger's head, erased, or. *Pl.* 94, *cr.* 10.

JONES, Linc., a cubit arm, erect, vested, purp., cuffed, ar., in hand, ppr., a branch of marigolds, of the third, stalked and leaved, vert. *Pl.* 64, *cr.* 7.

JONES, Lond., a buck's head, erased, sa., attired, or, between horns a bugle-horn, of the first. *Pl.* 115, *cr.* 1, (horn, *pl.* 98, *cr.* 2.)

JONES, Lond., a demi-lion, rampant, ppr. *Pl.* 67, *cr.* 10.

JONES, Wilts., out of a ducal coronet, or, a demi-lion, sa. *Pl.* 45, *cr.* 7.

JONES, Lond., an arm, in pale, (vested,) or, thereon three etoiles, in pale, gu., holding a pheon, erect, ar. *Pl.* 123, *cr.* 12.

JONES, Wilts., out of a ducal coronet, or, a demi-lion, rampant, sa., langued, gu., armed, gold. *Pl.* 45, *cr.* 7.

JONES, Lond., a gaunlet, barwise, or, holding a (sword,) erect, ar., hilt, gold, pierced through a boar's head, erased, vert. *Pl.* 85, *cr.* 12.

JONES, an arm, in fess, couped at elbow, in hand a (sword,) in pale, pierced through a boar's head, couped, ppr. *Pl.* 85, *cr.* 12.

JONES, Norf., a lion, couchant, sa. *Pl.* 75, *cr.* 5, (without chapeau.)

JONES, Wel., a cubit arm, erect, in armour, ppr., in gauntlet a spear, of the first, headed, ar., embrued, gu. *Pl.* 23, *cr.* 9.

JONES, Oxon., a buck, passant, ar. *Pl.* 68, *cr.* 2.

JONES, Salop, the sun in splendour, or. *Pl.* 68, *cr.* 14.

JONES, Norf., a battle-axe and spear, in saltier, handles, gu., heads, ar., mounted, or. *Pl.* 52, *cr.* 10, (spear, *pl.* 97, *cr.* 4.)

JONES, Iri., a talbot's head, couped, ar., (collared and chained, gu.) *Pl.* 123, *cr.* 15.

JONES, Wel., on a chapeau, gu., turned up, erm., a stag, ar., attired, vert. *Pl.* 3, *cr.* 14.

JONES, Iri., a greyhound's head, erased, or, in mouth a stag's foot, erased, gu. *Pl.* 66, *cr.* 7.

JONES, Wel., a lion, rampant, az., holding a shield, or, within a carved bordure. *Pl.* 125, *cr.* 2, (shield, *pl.* 36, *cr.* 11.)

JONES, a dragon's head, erased, vert, ducally gorged, or, in mouth a glove. *Pl.* 106, *cr.* 13, (gorging, *same plate, cr.* 15.)

JONES, a stag, trippant, ar., attired and (collared, or, from collar an escutcheon, pendent, sa., charged with a martlet, gold.) *Pl.* 68, *cr.* 2.

JONES, a nag's head, erased, ar. *Pl.* 81, *cr.* 6.

JONES-TYRWHITT, Bart., Salop, the sun in splendour, rays inflamed, or. *Esto sol testis. Pl.* 75, *cr.* 9, (without branches.)

JONES-WILSON, Esq., of Hartsheath, Flints.; Cefn Coch, and Gelli Gynan, Denbigh; a boar's head, couped, gu. *Heb nevol nerth nid sier saeth—Without help from above the arrow flies in vain. Pl.* 48, *cr.* 2.

JOPE, Cornw., an antelope, sejant, erm., supporting with dexter a shield, per pale, or and ar. *Pl.* 115, *cr.* 3, (shield, *pl.* 19, *cr.* 2.)

JOPLING, or JOPPLING, in dexter hand, ppr., an escallop, or. *Pl.* 57, *cr.* 6.

JOPP, Sco., on a garb, in fess, a cock, crowing, ar. *Sic donec. Pl.* 122, *cr.* 3.

JOPP, Hants., on a garb, in fess, a cock, crowing, all ppr. *Pl.* 122, *cr.* 3.

JORCEY, in hand, ppr., a swan's head and neck, erased, ar., beaked, gu. *Pl.* 29, *cr.* 4.

JORDAN, Somers. and Wilts., a mound, or, surmounted by a scroll, charged with motto— *Percussa resurgo.*

JORDAN, Somers. and Wilts., a foot-ball, ppr. *Pl.* 26, *cr.* 2.

JORDAN, Surr., a lion, sejant, sustaining a cross crosslet, fitched, all or. *Pl.* 109, *cr.* 7, (cross, *pl.* 141.)

JORDAN, Surr., an almond-tree, fructed, or. *Pl.* 105, *cr.* 13.

JORDAN, Surr., a demi-lion, or, resting on sinister foot, in dexter an eagle's head, erased, sa. *Pl.* 96, *cr.* 3.

JORDAYNE, Lond., on a chapeau, gu., turned up, erm., a hawk, or, inside of wings, of the second. *Pl.* 105, *cr.* 4, (chapeau, *same plate, cr.* 5.)

JORDEN, Eng., a demi-talbot, gu. *Pl.* 15, *cr.* 2, (without gorging.)

JORDON, Iri., an arm, embowed, in hand a dagger, ppr. *Pl.* 120, *cr.* 11.

JORDON, Eng., out of a mural coronet, a hand, ppr., (vested,) az., brandishing a sword, waved, of the first. *Pl.* 65, *cr.* 10, (coronet, *pl.* 128, *fig.* 18.)

JORDON, a boar's head, couped, in fess. *Pl.* 48, *cr.* 2.

JORGE, Eng., in hand, ppr., a swan's head and neck, erased, ar., beaked, gu. *Pl.* 29, *cr.* 4.

JOSELIN, or JOSELYN, Eng., a talbot, passant, sa., collared, or. *Pl.* 65, *cr.* 2.

JOSEPH, a garb, or. *Pl.* 48, *cr.* 10.

JOSKIN, or JOSKYN, Eng., an antelope's head, ar., (collared,) gu., armed, sa. *Pl.* 24, *cr.* 7.

JOSSELYNE, JOSELINE, or JOSSELIN, a bear's head and neck, sa., muzzled, or. *Pl.* 2, *cr.* 9.

JOSSEY, Sco., an eye, ppr. *Je voy. Pl.* 68, *cr.* 15.

JOSSEY, Sco., same crest. *Manuque.*

JOUATT, an arm, in armour, ppr., in hand a fleur-de-lis, or. *Pl.* 95, *cr.* 9.

JOULE, Eng., out of a ducal coronet, or, a stag's head, affrontée, ppr. *Pl.* 29, *cr.* 7.

JOURDAN, Eng., two anchors, in saltier, ppr. *Pl.* 37, *cr.* 12.

JOWELES, or JOWLES, Kent and Surr., a tower, gu., surmounted with (eight broad arrows,) falling at top, four and four, fretty, in bend, dexter and sinister. *Pl.* 69, *cr.* 9.

JOWETT, or JOWITT, Eng., a demi-pegasus, regardant, wings addorsed, ar., holding a flag, gu. *Pl.* 32, *cr.* 1.

JOY, Lond. and Wilts., a falcon, standing on a cinquefoil, between two vine-branches, all ppr.

JOY, Iri., in hand an arrow, point downward. *Pl.* 43, *cr.* 13.

JOY, Eng., a demi-lion, rampant. *Pro patriâ ejusque libertate. Pl.* 67, *cr.* 10.

JOYCE, or JOICE, Eng., a demi-chevalier, in armour, brandishing a scimitar, all ppr. *Pl.* 27, *cr.* 11.

JOYE, Wilts., a lion, rampant, ar., supporting a staff, raguly, or. *Pl.* 22, *cr.* 15, (staff, *pl.* 1, *cr.* 3.)

JOYE, Northamp., trunk of vine, with two branches, thereon a dove, all ppr. *Pl.* 96, *cr.* 2.

JOYNER, Lond. and Suss., a dexter arm, in armour, embowed, in gauntlet, a battle-axe, handle, or, headed, ar. *Pl.* 121, *cr.* 14.

JOYNOUR, two battle-axes, in saltier. *Pl.* 52, *cr.* 10.

JUBA, an antelope, sejant, ar., tufted, maned, and armed, or, resting dexter on an escutcheon, per pale, of the second and first. *Pl.* 115, *cr.* 3, (escutcheon, *pl.* 19, *cr.* 2.)

JUCHEN, two wings, expanded, ppr. *Pl.* 39, *cr.* 12.

JUCKES, or JUKES, Eng., a column, ppr. *Pl.* 33, *cr.* 1.

JUDD, and JUDE, Eng., a ferret, passant, ppr., collared and lined, or. *Pl.* 12, *cr.* 2.

JUDGE, Eng., between two laurel-branches, a sword, in pale, all ppr. *Pl.* 71, *cr.* 3.

JUDGSON, and JUDSON, Sco., out of a ducal coronet, two dexter arms, in saltier, vested, ppr., holding two scimitars, in pale. *Pl.* 52, *cr.* 1, (coronet, *pl.* 57, *cr.* 8.)

JUDKIN, Eng., a chevalier on horseback, at full speed, sword in hand. *Pl.* 118, *cr.* 14.

JUDSON, Eng., a wyvern, wings addorsed. *Pl.* 63, *cr.* 13.

JUGE, Leic., two battle-axes, in saltier, handles, gu., headed, ppr., enfiled with a ducal coronet, or. *Pl.* 52, *cr.* 10, (coronet, *pl.* 37, *cr.* 5.)

JUGG, an oak-leaf, vert. *Pl.* 81, *cr.* 7.

JUGLER, two swords, in saltier, ppr., surmounted by a cross crosslet, in pale, sa. *Pl.* 42, *cr.* 1.

JULIAN, and JULION, Eng., on a chapeau, a salamander in flames, ppr. *Pl.* 86, *cr.* 14.

JULIEN, Eng., a lion's paw, erased, holding the hilt of a broken sword, ppr. *Pl.* 49, *cr.* 10.

JUMPER, Eng., a demi-lion, ppr., supporting a long cross, gu. *Pl.* 29, *cr.* 12.

JUPP, Eng., a griffin, passant, in dexter a buckle, ppr. *Pl.* 39, *cr.* 8.

JURY, Eng., a cubit arm, in armour, in hand a caltrap, ppr. *Pl.* 22, *cr.* 4.

JUST, Durh., a swan's head and neck, erased, ar., between two ostrich-feathers, erect, of the first. *Pl.* 54, *cr.* 6, (feathers, *pl.* 108, *cr.* 2.)

JUSTICE, Eng., a cat, sejant, rampant, ppr. *Pl.* 53, *cr.* 5.

JUSTICE, HENRY, Esq., of Hinstock, Salop, a falcon. *Justitiæ soror fides. Pl.* 67, *cr.* 3.

JUSTICE, Sco., a sword, in pale. *Non sine causa.* Pl. 105, cr. 1.
JUSTINE, or JUSTYNE, Eng., a stag's head, erased, affrontée, or. Pl. 8, cr. 6.
JUTTING, a fleur-de-lis, between two elephants' probosces. Pl. 96, cr. 1.
JUXON, an Ionic pillar, on a base, ar. Pl. 33, cr. 1.

K

KADIE, Sco., a lancet, expanded, ppr. Pl. 10, cr. 10.
KADRAD, Eng., two anchors, in saltier, az. Pl. 37, cr. 12.
KADROHARD, Wel., a griffin's head, erased, sa. Pl. 48, cr. 6.
KADWALL, a cock's head, ar., combed, wattled, and beaked, gu. Pl. 92, cr. 3.
KADWELL, Kent, a cock's head, ppr., in beak a cross pattée, fitched, or, all between wings, sa. *Vigilans.* Pl. 47, cr. 3.
KAER, Eng., out of a crescent, two eagles' heads, addorsed. Pl. 118, cr. 12.
KAGG, a falcon, regardant, (resting) dexter on a laurel-crown, ppr. Pl. 42, cr. 7.
KAHL, Eng., a camel's head, ar. Pl. 109, cr. 9.
KAINES, Eng., a wolf, current, gu. Pl. 111, cr. 1.
KANDISHE, Eng., on a chapeau, ppr., a dove, wings addorsed, az. Pl. 109, cr. 10.
KANE, Eng., an arm, in armour, embowed, in hand a sword, ppr. Pl. 2, cr. 8.
KANE, Iri., a roundle, vert, charged with a pale, indented, ar. Pl. 63, cr. 7.
KARABYE, a triton, in (dexter) a trident. Pl. 35, cr. 10.
KARBEN, Eng., out of a ducal coronet, or, an arm, from elbow, vested, gu., cuffed, gold, holding up the sun, ppr. Pl. 89, cr. 11.
KARBYLL, Eng., a stag, lodged, or. Pl. 67, cr. 2.
KARDAILE, and KARDOYLE, an antelope, trippant, erm., armed, gu. Pl. 63, cr. 10.
KARKENTON, and KARKINGTON, out of an antique crown, or, a demi-lion, rampant, gu. Pl. 45, cr. 7, (crown, pl. 79, cr. 12.)
KARR, Sco., in dexter hand a dagger. *Sans peur.* Pl. 28, cr. 4.
KARR, Eng., a stag's head, erased, az. Pl. 66, cr. 9.
KARR, a dexter arm, in pale, couped below wrist, ppr., in hand a dagger, ar., hilt and pommel, or. Pl. 28, cr. 4.
KARRICK, or KARRICKE, Eng., a dexter arm, embowed, ppr., vested, gu., cuffed, or, in hand a covered cup, gold. Pl. 39, cr. 1.
KARVELL, or KARVILL, Eng., on a ducal coronet, or, a wyvern, gu. Pl. 104, cr. 11.
KASSYE, Eng., a dexter hand, pointing with two fingers, gu. Pl. 67, cr. 6.
KATELER, KATELLER, and KATHERLER, on a chapeau, ppr., a lion's head erased, ar., ducally crowned, or. Pl. 34, cr. 10.
KATERLEY, and KATHERLEY, Eng., a hind's head, ppr. Pl. 21, cr. 9.
KATHERAM, an arm, in armour, couped, resting on elbow, in hand a club, ppr. Pl. 65, cr. 13.
KATHRENS, or KATHRINS, Iri., a plume of ostrich-feathers, ar., enfiled with a ducal coronet, or. Pl. 100, cr. 12, (without charge.)
KATING, KATHYNG, KATTING, or KAYTYNG, a demi-angel, in dexter a griffin's head, erased, ppr. Pl. 24, cr. 11.

KAVANAGH, Iri., on point of a sword, erect, a mullet. Pl. 55, cr. 15.
KAVANAGH, Iri., between the horns of a crescent, gu., a garb, or. Pl. 48, cr. 10, (crescent, pl. 74, cr. 2.)
KAWSTON, Eng., out of a mural coronet, a hand, ppr., paly of six, ar. and sa., holding a mullet, of the first. Pl. 34, cr. 1.
KAY, Yorks. and Ruts., a goldfinch, ppr. Pl. 10, cr. 12.
KAY, Hunts., a goldfinch, ppr., charged with a mullet. Pl. 10, cr. 12, (mullet, pl. 141.)
KAY, Sco., a marigold, ppr. Pl. 105, cr. 15.
KAY, Durh. and Northumb., a griffin's head, erased, sa. Pl. 48, cr. 6.
KAY, or KAYE, a falcon, close. Pl. 67, cr. 3.
KAY, Yorks., a griffin's head, erased, ar., beaked, gu., charged with a martlet, sa., in beak a key, or. Pl. 9, cr. 12, (martlet, pl. 69, cr. 15.)
KAY, Manningham : 1. For *Kay*, a griffin's head, (collared.) Pl. 38, cr. 3. 2. For *Linten*, a stag's head, ppr. Pl. 91, cr. 14. 3. For *Cunliffe*, a greyhound, sejant, ar., (collared, sa.) Pl. 66, cr. 15.
KAY, a martlet, volant. *In Deo solo spes mea.* Pl. 40, cr. 4.
KAYBLE, Eng., an arm, from elbow, ppr., vested, erm., cuffed, indented, gu., in hand an escarbuncle, of the last. Pl. 114, cr. 4.
KAYE, Bart., Surr., a griffin's head, erm., (collared,) az., charged with three crescents, in beak a key, or. *Fidem parit integritas.* Pl. 9, cr. 12, (crescent, pl. 141.)
KAYE-LISTER, Bart., Yorks. : 1. For *Kaye*, a goldfinch, charged on breast with a rose, gu. Pl. 10, cr. 12, (rose, pl. 141.) 2. A buck's head, ppr., erased, wavy, or, attired, sa., (in mouth a bird-bolt, in bend, of the third, flighted, ar.) *Kynd kynn knawne kepe.* Pl. 66, cr. 9.
KAYLE, Eng., on a chapeau, gu., turned up, ar., a greyhound, (passant,) of the last. Pl. 104, cr. 1.
KAYLE, Eng., a demi-talbot, ducally gorged. Pl. 15, cr. 2.
KAYNTON, Eng., a mountain, ppr. Pl. 98, cr. 13.
KEAN, Iri., a horse's head, erased. Pl. 81, cr. 6.
KEANE, Bart., Iri., a leopard, sejant, supporting with dexter a flag-staff, thereon hoisted a Union-jack, all ppr. *Virtute.* Pl. 10, cr. 13.
KEANE, Iri., on a chapeau, a stag, trippant, all ppr. Pl. 63, cr. 8.
KEANE, Iri., a wild cat, rampant, gardant, ppr., (gorged with an antique Irish crown, or, charged on shoulder with a trefoil, vert.) Pl. 70, cr. 15.
KEARNEY, Iri., a ruined castle, in flames, ppr. Pl. 118, cr. 15.
KEARNS, Iri., out of a heart, gu., a hand holding a scimitar, ppr. Pl. 35, cr. 7.

KEARSLEY, and KEARSLY, Lond. and Lanc., a demi-eagle, erm., winged, or. *Pl.* 52, *cr.* 8.

KEAT, Eng., a demi-cat, gardant. *Pl.* 80, *cr.* 7.

KEATE, a mountain-cat, passant, sa. *Pl.* 119, *cr.* 7.

KEATING, and KEATINGE, Iri., a Cupid, in dexter an arrow, (in sinister a bow, ppr.) *Pl.* 17, *cr.* 5.

KEATING, and KEEKING, Eng., a boar, passant, or, among nettles, ppr. *Providentiâ divinâ. Pl.* 104, *cr.* 12.

KEATING, (on a mount, vert,) a boar, passant, sa. *Pl.* 48, *cr.* 14.

KEATS, on a naval coronet, or, a tiger, statant, gardant, ppr., (charged on body with an anchor, sa.) *Pl.* 67, *cr.* 15, (coronet, *pl.* 128, *fig.* 19.)

KEATS, Glouc. and Berks., a mountain-cat, passant, sa. *Pl.* 119, *cr.* 7.

KEAY, Eng., an eagle's head, erased, gu. *Fortiter et recte. Pl.* 20, *cr.* 7.

KEAY, and KEY, Sco., a griffin's head, in beak a key, ppr. *Pl.* 9, *cr.* 12.

KEBBLE, Eng., a demi-eagle, wings expanded, ppr. *Illœso lumine solem. Pl.* 52, *cr.* 8.

KEBELL, or KEBYLL, Eng., a demi-eagle, regardant. *Pl.* 27, *cr.* 15.

KEBLE, Suff., a demi-eagle, displayed, ar. *Pl.* 22, *cr.* 11.

KEBLE, Leic., a demi-eagle, displayed, ar., (gorged with a bar-gemelle,) gu., beaked, of the last. *Pl.* 22, *cr.* 11.

KEBLE, an elephant's head. *Pl.* 35, *cr.* 13.

KECK, Lond. and Oxon., out of a ducal coronet, gu., a maiden's head, erm., purfled, or, hair dishevelled, gold, and flotant, (adorned with a chaplet, vert, garnished with roses, ppr,) *Pl.* 45, *cr.* 5, (coronet, *pl.* 45, *cr.* 9.)

KEDDIE, Sco., a lancet, open, ppr. *Opifer per orbem dicor. Pl.* 10, *cr.* 10.

KEDMARSTON, Eng., a demi-lion, rampant, ar. *Pl.* 67, *cr.* 10.

KEDSLIE, an eagle, with two heads, displayed, ppr., on breast a mullet, ar. *Veritas omnia vincit. Pl.* 87, *cr.* 11, (without flames; mullet, *pl.* 141.)

KEEFE, Iri., a lion's gamb, parted, per cheveron, or and gu. *Pl.* 88, *cr.* 3.

KEEGAN, in hand a sheaf of arrows. *Pl.* 56, *cr.* 4.

KEELING, a lion, sejant, or, supporting a scaling-ladder, gu. *Pl.* 109, *cr.* 7, (ladder, *pl.* 98, *cr.* 15.)

KEELING, KELLYNG, KELYNG, and KELYNGE, a sword, erect, enfiled with a Saracen's head, affrontée, all ppr. *Pl.* 42, *cr.* 6.

KEEN, Eng., a bundle of arrows, or, barbed and feathered, ar., banded, gu. *Pl.* 43, *cr.* 14.

KEEN, or KEENE, Suff., a hind's head, erased, sa., bezantée. *Pl.* 6, *cr.* 1.

KEENE, Eng. and Iri., a griffin's head, ppr. *Pl.* 38, *cr.* 3.

KEENE, an eagle's head, couped, ppr. *Pl.* 100, *cr.* 10.

KEENE, Iri., a martlet, or. *Pl.* 111, *cr.* 5.

KEENLYSIDE, a beacon, lighted, ppr. *Pl.* 88, *cr.* 6.

KEEP, Eng., a weaver's shuttle, erect, gu., threaded, ppr. *Pl.* 102, *cr.* 10.

KEET, Kent, a dexter arm, embowed, couped at shoulder, (vested, az., cuff, ar.,) in hand, ppr., a battle-axe, of the second, staff, or, entwined with a serpent, vert. *Pl.* 116, *cr.* 11, (axe, *pl.* 121, *cr.* 14.)

KEETE, Dors., a unicorn's head, erased, ar., collared, gu., buckled and garnished, or, armed, gold. *Pl.* 73, *cr.* 1.

KEIGHLEY, a dragon's head, erased, ar., on breast a mullet, sa. *Pl.* 107, *cr.* 10, (mullet, *pl.* 141.)

KEIGHTLEY, Iri., a griffin's head, erased, ar. *Possunt, quia posse videntur. Pl.* 48, *cr.* 6.

KEIGNES, and KEYNES, Eng., a cross crosslet, fitched, gu., between two (palm)-branches, vert. *Pl.* 37, *cr.* 14.

KEIGNES, Eng., a talbot, passant, sa., collared, ar. *Pl.* 65, *cr.* 2.

KEIGWIN, Cornw., a greyhound's head, couped, or. *Pl.* 14, *cr.* 4, (without charge.)

KEILING, Staffs., a demi-lion, rampant, (supporting an escutcheon, ar., charged with a cross formée, fitched, gu.) *Pl.* 126, *cr.* 12.

KEILY, a male griffin, statant, ppr. *Pl.* 66, *cr.* 13.

KEINSHAM, Eng., a greyhound's head, or, (charged with three bars,) vert, guttée, or. *Pl.* 14, *cr.* 4.

KEIR, Sco., an arm, embowed, vested and cuffed, in hand a sword. *Alterum non lædere. Pl.* 120, *cr.* 1.

KEIR, Sco., an arm, in armour, embowed, in hand a sword, all ppr. *Pl.* 2, *cr.* 8.

KEIR, Sco., a pelican, vulning, ppr. *Deus meum solamen. Pl.* 109, *cr.* 15.

KEIR-SMALL-KEIR: 1. For *Small*, a branch of palm, ppr., erect. *Pl.* 123, *cr.* 1. 2. For *Keir*, in hand a sword, in pale, ppr. *Pl.* 23, *cr.* 15.

KEIRIE, Sco., in hand a rose, ppr. *Virtute viget. Pl.* 118, *cr.* 9.

KEIRLL, a horse's head, erased, ar., in mouth a palm-branch, ppr. *Pl.* 81, *cr.* 5, (branch, *pl.* 123, *cr.* 1.)

KEITH, an ermine, passant, ppr. *Ex candore decus. Pl.* 9, *cr.* 5.

KEITH, a stag's head, erased. *Pl.* 66, *cr.* 9.

KEITH, a demi-lion, rampant, ppr. *Recta sequor. Pl.* 67, *cr.* 10.

KEITH, of Tillygone, a hawk's lure, ppr. *Venit ab astris. Pl.* 97, *cr.* 14.

KEITH, of Craig, Sco.: 1. *Ancient*, a stag at gaze, or, under a bush of holly, all ppr. *Fortiter qui sedulo. Pl.* 118, *cr.* 13. 2. *Modern*, an ermine, ppr. *Ex candore decus. Pl.* 9, *cr.* 5.

KEITH, Earl of Kintore. *See* KINTORE.

KEITH, Sco., a stag's head, ppr. *Veritas vincit. Pl.* 91, *cr.* 14.

KEITH, of Ravelston, a dexter arm, in hand a dagger, ppr. *Pro veritate. Pl.* 34, *cr.* 7.

KEITH, in dexter hand a writing-pen, ppr. *Et loquor et taceo. Pl.* 26, *cr.* 13.

KEITH, of Arthurhouse, in dexter hand a pick, erect, ppr., headed, ar. *Justa sequor. Pl.* 113, *cr.* 10.

KEITH, Sco., a stag's head, couped. *Memento creatorem. Pl.* 91, *cr.* 14.

KEITH, of Bruxie, a stag's head, erased, ar. *Veritas vincit. Pl.* 66, *cr.* 9.

KEITH, of Aquhorsk, in dexter hand a scroll of paper, ppr. *Et loquor et tacco. Pl.* 27, *cr.* 4.

KEITH, Sco., a dexter hand casting an anchor into the water. *Remember thy end. Pl.* 79, *cr.* 15.

KEITH, Sco., an ermine, ppr. *Pl.* 9, *cr.* 5.

KEITH, Sco., in dexter hand a pike, (in pale,) ppr., headed, ar. *Pl.* 12, *cr.* 3.

KEITH, Sco., an arm, in armour, in fess, couped, in hand a (sword, in pale,) ppr. *Pl.* 107, *cr.* 15.

KEKEBOURNE, on a ducal coronet, or, a lion, sejant, holding a (sword,) erect, ppr. *Pl.* 109, *cr.* 7, (coronet, *pl.* 128, *fig.* 3.)

KEKEWICH, Ess., a leopard's head and neck, affrontée. *Pl.* 56, *cr.* 7.

KELE, Lond., a demi-woman, ppr., hair dishevelled, or, (on head a chaplet, vert.) *Pl.* 81, *cr.* 13.

KELHAM, a demi-eagle, displayed, with two heads, az., (semée of ermine spots, or, each wing charged with a covered cup,) gold. *Pl.* 4, *cr.* 6.

KELING, Middx., out of a mural coronet, a demi-lion, or, supporting an escutcheon, ar., charged with a cross pattée, fitched, gu.

KELK, or KELKE, Eng., a wolf, sejant, ppr. *Pl.* 110, *cr.* 4.

KELL, and KELLE, a boar's head, erased, az., ducally gorged, or. *Pl.* 36, *cr.* 9.

KELLAM, and KILLOME, Eng., a cross crosslet, fitched, gu., and a palm-branch, vert, in saltier. *Pl.* 102, *cr.* 3, (palm, *pl.* 5, *cr.* 11.)

KELLAM, or KELLUM, an otter's head, erased, ppr. *Pl.* 126, *cr.* 14.

KELLAM, and KILLOME, Eng., out of a mural coronet, a griffin's head, ducally gorged. *Pl.* 101, *cr.* 6.

KELLAWAYE, Dors., a cock, ar., combed and wattled, az. *Pl.* 67, *cr.* 14.

KELLEHER, Iri., out of a mural coronet, az., a lion's head, or. *Pl.* 45, *cr.* 9.

KELLET, Knt. and Bart., Iri., an arm, in armour, embowed, ppr., garnished, or, in hand a baton, gold. *Feret ad astra virtus.* *Pl.* 120, *cr.* 11, (truncheon, *pl.* 33, *cr.* 4.)

KELLET, Surr., a cubit arm, vested, sa., cuffed and purfled, ar., in hand a roll of parchment, of the last. *Pl.* 32, *cr.* 6.

KELLET, Iri., a demi-wolf, rampant, sa. *Pl.* 56, *cr.* 8, (withour spear.)

KELLEY, Iri., on a mount, an apple-tree, fructed, all ppr. *Pl.* 105, *cr.* 13.

KELLEY, Devons., a sea-horse in water, ppr., (in paws a spiked ball.) *Pl.* 100, *cr.* 1.

KELLEY, KELLY, and KEYLLEY, Eng., a boar, passant, or, wounded by an arrow, ppr. *Pl.* 36, *cr.* 2.

KELLEY, or KELLY, Iri., a hand holding by the horn a bull's head, erased.

KELLOCK, Sco., out of a ducal coronet, a sinister hand between wings, all ppr. *Pl.* 79, *cr.* 6.

KELLOCK, Sco., between wings, or, a heart. *Gloria in excelsis Deo.* *Pl.* 52, *cr.* 2, (without crown.)

KELLOWAY, and KELLAWAY, Devons., a tiger, passant, (regardant,) sa. *Pl.* 67, *cr.* 15.

KELLOWAY, a barnacle-bird, ar. *Pl.* 52, *cr.* 12.

KELLY, on a ducal coronet, or, a greyhound, current, ar. *Pl.* 47, *cr.* 2, (coronet, *same plate.*)

KELLY, Lond., on a chapeau, a dog, (passant.) *Pl.* 104, *cr.* 1.

KELLY, Newton, a griffin, passant. *Pl.* 61, *cr.* 14, (without gorging.)

KELLY, Devons., Suss., and Iri., out of a ducal coronet, gu., an ostrich's head, ar., in beak a horse-shoe, or. *Pl.* 28, *cr.* 13, (coronet, *pl.* 128, *fig.* 3.)

KELSEY, Ess., two cubit arms, in pale, vested, sa., cuffed, or, in hands, ppr., an escutcheon, gold. *Pl.* 113, *cr.* 12.

KELSEY, on a close helmet, an escallop. *Pl.* 109, *cr.* 5, (escallop, *pl.* 141.)

KELSHAW, Eng., a griffin's head, erased. *Pl.* 48, *cr.* 6.

KELSO, Sco., a garb, or. *Otium cum dignitate.* *Pl.* 48, *cr.* 10.

KELSO, EDWARD-JOHN-FRANCIS, Esq., of Kelsoland, of Horkesley Park, Ess., two lions, rampant, gu., (each charged on shoulder with a garb, or.) *Otium cum dignitate.* *Pl.* 36, *cr.* 8, (without chapeau.)

KELTIE, and KELTY, a wheat-sheaf, ppr. *Industria.* *Pl.* 48, *cr.* 10.

KELTON, Salop, a lion, passant, per pale, erm. and ermines. *Pl.* 48, *cr.* 8.

KELVERTON, an eagle's head, couped, ar., gorged with a chaplet of roses, ppr. *Pl.* 100, *cr.* 10, (chaplet, *pl.* 41, *cr.* 7.)

KELWICH, a lion's head, gardant, sa. *Pl.* 47, *cr.* 6.

KEMBLE, between a branch of a laurel on the dexter side, and one of palm on the sinister, ppr., a boar's head and neck, sa., erased, gu., charged with an etoile, ar. *Pl.* 113, *cr.* 13.

KEMBLE, a boar's head, couped, in bend, snout upward. *Pl.* 21, *cr.* 7.

KEMBLE, Eng., a dexter arm, in armour, in hand a broken spear, ppr. *Pl.* 44, *cr.* 9.

KEMEYS, Eng., a unicorn's head, ppr., horned, or. *Pl.* 20, *cr.* 1.

KEMMIS, a unicorn, sejant. *Pl.* 110, *cr.* 15, (without tree.)

KEMOR, a lion's head, erased, or, pierced through by arrows, sa. *Pl.* 113, *cr.* 15.

KEMP, THOMAS-READ, Esq., of Lewes, Suss., a hawk. *Pl.* 67, *cr.* 3.

KEMP, Bart., Norf., on a garb, or, a pelican, vulning, ppr. *Lucem spero.* *Pl.* 109, *cr.* 15, (garb, *pl.* 122, *cr.* 3.)

KEMP, on a mount, vert, a pelican, or, charged on breast with a pomme, picking at a garb, gold.

KEMP, a goat, statant, ar. *Pl.* 66, *cr.* 1.

KEMP, over a garb, an eagle, volant, all or.

KEMP, Surr. and Cornw., a falcon, ppr., beaked and legged, or, hooded, gu. *Pl.* 38, *cr.* 12.

KEMP, Norf. and Suss., on a garb, in fess, or, a falcon, wings addorsed, erm. *Pl.* 81, *cr.* 12, (garb, *pl.* 122, *cr.* 3.)

KEMP, Iri., an antelope, passant, or, (collared,) az. *Pl.* 63, *cr.* 10.

KEMP, and KEMPT, Sco., a demi-lion, in dexter a battle-axe, ppr. *Promptus.* *Pl.* 101, *cr.* 14, (without charge.)

KEMP, and KEMPE, Ess. and Suff., an arm, couped at elbow, vested, ar., charged with two bends, wavy, az., cuffed, of the first, in hand, ppr., a chaplet, vert. *Pl.* 44, *cr.* 13, (without bird.)

KEMPE, Kent, a demi-griffin, or, winged, gu., holding a garb, gold. *Pl.* 44, *cr.* 3, (garb, *pl.* 84, *cr.* 7.)

KEMPE, Suss., Kent, Norf., and Hants., on a garb, in fess, or, a falcon, wings addorsed, ppr. *Pl.* 81, *cr.* 12, (garb, *pl.* 122, *cr.* 3.)

KEMPENFELT, a demi-man, in armour, sinister arm, embowed, dexter holding a sword above his head, all ppr., between wings, erect, vert. *Pl.* 23, *cr.* 4, (wings, *pl.* 1, *cr.* 15.)

KEMPSON, and KEMPSTON, Warw. and Staffs., a demi-lion, az., gorged with a collar, or, charged with three mullets, of the first. *Pl.* 18, *cr.* 13, (mullet, *pl.* 141.)

KEMPSON, a demi-talbot. *Pl.* 15, *cr.* 2, (without gorging.)

KEMPSTER, Eng., in a lion's paw, a thistle, ppr. *Pl.* 109, *cr.* 4.

KEMPSTON, Iri., in hand an olive-branch, ppr. *Pl.* 43, *cr.* 6.

KEMPT, Eng., a hedgehog, or. *Pl.* 32, *cr.* 9.

KEMPTHORNE, a lion, sejant. *Pl.* 126, *cr.* 15.

KEMPTON, Lond., Middx., and Cambs., out of a ducal coronet, or, a garb, ar. *Pl.* 62, *cr.* 1, (coronet, *pl.* 128, *fig.* 3.)

KEMPTON, Eng., a cloud, ppr. *Pl.* 124, *cr.* 12.

KEMPTON, Lond. and Cambs., a goat, erm., horns and hoofs, or, (collared and lined, sa., collar lined with three bezants, with a ring at end of line.) *Pl.* 66, *cr.* 1.

KEMYNG, Eng., a unicorn's head, sa., semée of plates. *Pl.* 20, *cr.* 1.

KEMYS, Somers., (on a mount, vert,) a unicorn, sejant, az., maned and armed, or. *Pl.* 110, *cr.* 15, (without tree.)

KEMYS, Wel., (on a mount, vert,) a unicorn, sejant, ar., armed and crined, or. *Ib.*

KENAN, Sco., a lion, rampant, az. *Pl.* 67, *cr.* 5.

KENDALL, Devons. and Cornw., a lion, passant, gu. *Pl.* 48, *cr.* 8.

KENDALL, in hand a sheaf of arrows, points downward, all ppr. *Pl.* 56, *cr.* 4.

KENDALL, Durh., a wolf's head and neck, erased, gu. *Pl.* 14, *cr.* 6.

KENDALL, out of a ducal coronet, an eagle's head. *Pl.* 20, *cr.* 12, (without pellet.)

KENDALL, EDWARD, Esq., of Austrey, Warw., an eagle, displayed, az. *Aquila petit solem.* *Pl.* 48, *cr.* 11.

KENDRICK, Eng., a hawk's leg, erased, jessed and belled, ppr. *Pl.* 83, *cr.* 7.

KENE, Suff., a hind's head, or, pellettée. *Pl.* 21, *cr.* 9.

KENE, Norf., a hind's head, erased, ar., (gorged with a collar, gu., charged with three bezants, to collar a ring, or.) *Pl.* 6, *cr.* 1.

KENE, Norf. and Suff., a hind's head, erased, ar., pellettée, charged with a trefoil, or. *Pl.* 6, *cr.* 1, (trefoil, *pl.* 141.)

KENERBY, Eng., a wolf's head, erased, erm. *Pl.* 14, *cr.* 6.

KENINGHAM, a man's head, in profile, bearded, ppr., on head a chapeau, turned up, erm. *Pl.* 33, *cr.* 14, (chapeau, *pl.* 127, *fig.* 13.)

KENISHAM, Beds., a greyhound's head, couped, az., charged on neck with three bars, between as many guttes-d'or. *Pl.* 14, *cr.* 4.

KENMARE, Earl of, Viscount and Baron Castlerosse, and a Bart., Iri., (Browne,) a dragon's head, couped, ar., guttée-de-poix, between wings, sa., guttée-d'eau. *Loyal en toute.* *Pl.* 105, *cr.* 11.

KENMURE, Viscount, and Lord Lochinvar, (Gordon,) Sco., a demi-savage, wreathed about head and loins with laurel, ppr. *Dread God.* *Pl.* 14, *cr.* 11.

KENN, Somers., three crescents, interwoven, ar. *Pl.* 119, *cr.* 10, (crescent, *pl.* 141.)

KENNAN, Iri., out of a crescent, az., a cross crosslet, fitched, gu. *Pl.* 43, *cr.* 3.

KENNARD, Eng., a lion's gamb, erased, vert. *Pl.* 126, *cr.* 9.

KENNARD, Iri., in hand, armed, ppr., a broken sword, gu. *Pl.* 125, *cr.* 5, (sword, *pl.* 22, *cr.* 6.)

KENNAWAY, Bart., Devons., an eagle, rising, ppr., (from the beak an escutcheon, pendent, az., charged with the sun in splendour, or.) *Pl.* 67, *cr.* 4.

KENNAWAY, a phoenix in flames, ppr. *Pl.* 44, *cr.* 8.

KENNAWAY, Eng., on a chapeau, a phoenix in flames, all ppr. *Pl.* 83, *cr.* 13.

KENNE, Somers., a unicorn's head, az., bezantée, maned, or, horn twisted, gold, and sa. *Pl.* 20, *cr.* 1.

KENNEDAY, an arm, in pale, in hand a belt, all ppr. *Pl.* 44, *cr.* 7.

KENNEDY, Marquess of Ailsa. *See* AILSA.

KENNEDY, Iri., a greyhound, ar., running against a tree, vert. *Pl.* 27, *cr.* 2.

KENNEDY, of Dunure, in hand a sword. *Fuimus.* *Pl.* 21, *cr.* 10.

KENNEDY, of Clowburn, in dexter hand a military sash. *Vires veritas.* *Pl.* 44, *cr.* 7.

KENNEDY, of Kirkmichael, a palm-branch, slipped, ppr. *Malim esse probus quam haberi.* *Pl.* 26, *cr.* 3.

KENNEDY, of Kirkhill, in hand a dagger, ppr. *Fuimus.* *Pl.* 18, *cr.* 3.

KENNEDY, of Auchterfordle, same crest. *Avise la fine.*

KENNEDY, of Garvin Mains, a dolphin, az. *Avise la fine.* *Pl.* 48, *cr.* 9.

KENNEDY, of Barclanachan, in the sea an anchor, in pale, ppr. *God be guide.* *Pl.* 62, *cr.* 10.

KENNEDY, on a rock, a goose, ppr. *Pl.* 94, *cr.* 3.

KENNEDY, Iri., in hand, ppr., an acorn between two oak-leaves, vert. *Pl.* 118, *cr.* 9, (acorn, *pl.* 81, *cr.* 7.)

KENNEDY, Iri., an arm, in (scale) armour, embowed, in hand a scimitar. *Pl.* 81, *cr.* 11.

KENNEDY, Sco., a dolphin, naiant. *Pl.* 48, *cr.* 9.

KENNEDY, Bennane, out of two oak-leaves, ppr., a fleur-de-lis, or. *Fuimus.* *Pl.* 68, *cr.* 12, (leaves, *pl.* 32, *cr.* 13.)

KENNEDY, Bart., of Johnstown, co. Dublin, a dexter arm, in armour, embowed, in hand an (oak-branch,) all ppr. *Adhæreo virtute.* *Pl.* 68, *cr.* 1.

KENNEDY, Iri., out of a cloud, an arm, in armour, embowed, in fess, in hand, a (dagger,) ppr. *The strongest hand uppermost.* *Pl.* 93, *cr.* 8.

KENNEDY, Iri., in a naked hand, a bloody dagger, ppr. *Laugh ladur an aughtur.* *Pl.* 18, *cr.* 3.

KENNEDY, JOHN, Esq., of Knocknalling, Ayr, a dolphin, naiant, or. *Avise la fin.* *Pl.* 48, *cr.* 9.

KENNEDY, Sco., a palm-branch, slipped, vert. *Pl.* 26, *cr.* 3.

KENNEDY, Sco., a hawk, hooded, ppr. *Pl.* 38, *cr.* 12.

KENNELL, two lions' heads, erased and addorsed, one, or, the other, gu. *Pl.* 28, *cr.* 10.

KENNERLEY, in lion's gamb, a laurel branch, ppr. *Pl.* 68, *cr.* 10.

KENNET, or KENNETT, Norf., two branches of palm, in orle. *Pl.* 87, *cr.* 8.

KENNETT, Lond., an arm, in armour, embowed, in gauntlet a helmet, in pale, all ppr. *Pl.* 114, *cr.* 9.

KENNEY, CHRISTOPHER-FITZGERALD, Esq., of Kilclogher, Galway, out of an earl's coronet, or, pearled, ppr., a demi-arm, erect, sleeved, gules, with a white ruff, in hand a roll of parchment, of the second. *Teneat, luceat, floreat, vi, virtute, et valore.* Pl. 126 B, cr. 9.

KENNEY, NUGENT-THOMAS, Esq., of Correndoo, Galway, same crest.

KENNEY, THOMAS-HENRY, Esq., of Ballyforan, Roscommon, same crest.

KENNEY, C.-LIONEL, Chevalier de France, same crest.

KENNEY, Iri., a greyhound, couchant, between two branches of laurel, in orle, ppr. Pl. 102, cr. 13.

KENNEY, Iri., an arm, in armour, embowed, in hand a baton, all ppr. Pl. 96, cr. 6, (baton, pl. 33, cr. 4.)

KENNICOT, Eng., a griffin's head, erased. Pl. 48, cr. 6.

KENNING, Eng., a yew-tree, (growing out of a mount, semée of trefoils, ppr.) Pl. 49, cr. 13.

KENNISON, Eng., a dove and olive-branch, ppr. Pl. 48, cr. 15.

KENNOWAY, Sco., an arm, embowed, in fess, couped, gu., in hand three stalks of wheat, or. Pl. 89, cr. 4.

KENNOWAY, Sco., a thunderbolt, winged, ppr. Pl. 110, cr. 3.

KENNY, Eng., a demi-lion, rampant, gardant, gu., holding a fleur-de-lis, or. Pl. 35, cr. 4, (fleur-de-lis, pl. 91, cr. 13.)

KENRICK, Lond. and Surr., on a sheaf of arrows, in fess, a hawk, ppr. Pl. 83, cr. 13, (arrows, pl. 19, cr. 4.)

KENRICK, Lond. and Surr., three arrows, one erect, and two in saltier, bound by a ribbon, ppr., charged with a (bird, statant, sa.) Pl. 75, cr. 7.

KENSEY, Herts., a demi-griffin, erased, erm., between paws a mullet, or. Pl. 18, cr. 6, (mullet, pl. 141.)

KENSING, a stag, springing, ppr. Pl. 65, cr. 14.

KENSINGTON, Baron, (Edwardes,) Iri., on a mount, vert, a wyvern, wings expanded, ar. Pl. 33, cr. 13.

KENSINGTON, out of a ducal coronet, a demi-eagle, displayed, ppr. Pl. 9, cr. 6.

KENT, a lion's head, erased, erminois, collared, lined, and ringed, az. Pl. 7, cr. 10.

KENT, a lion's head, erased, or, collared, sa. Pl. 7, cr. 10.

KENT, a wolf's head, (couped.) Pl. 14, cr. 6.

KENT, Iri., a bridge of three arches, ppr. Pl. 38, cr. 4.

KENT, Northamp., a talbot's head, couped, gu., charged on neck with a cinquefoil, erm. Pl. 123, cr. 15, (cinquefoil, pl. 141.)

KENT-EGLETON, Bart., Suff., a lion's head, erased, collared. Pl. 7, cr. 10.

KENTISH, Somers., a (demi-)ostrich, wings addorsed, in beak a horse-shoe. Pl. 16, cr. 2.

KENTON, Eng., on a chapeau, gu., turned up, or, a lion, (passant,) gardant, ar., ducally crowned, ppr. Pl. 120, cr. 15.

KENTON, Eng., in dexter hand, couped, in fess, gu., a fleur-de-lis, or. Pl. 46, cr. 12.

KENWICK, an arm, in armour, in hand an esquire's helmet, ppr. Pl. 114, cr. 9.

KENWRICKE, Berks., Salop, Northamp., and Lanc., on a bundle of arrows, in fess, or, feathered and headed, ar., banded, sa., a hawk, close, of the second, beaked and belled, gold. Pl. 83, cr. 13, (sheaf, pl. 19, cr. 4.)

KENYAN, Lond., a demi-lion, ar., supporting a battle-axe, or, handle, gu. Pl. 101, cr. 14.

KENYON, Lord, and Baron Gredington, (Kenyon,) a lion, sejant, ppr., supporting a cross fleury, ar. *Magnanimiter crucem sustineo.* Pl. 109, cr. 7, (cross, pl. 141.)

KENYON, Eng., on a rock, a dove, in beak an olive-branch, all ppr. Pl. 85, cr. 14.

KEOGH, Iri., an arm, embowed, ppr., vested, az., in hand a covered cup, or. Pl. 39, cr. 1.

KEOGH, Iri., a boar, passant, armed and crined, or. Pl. 48, cr. 14.

KEPPEL, Earl of Albemarle. *See* ALBEMARLE.

KEPPING, a maiden's head, affrontée, hair dishevelled, bust vested. Pl. 45, cr. 5.

KER, of Kerhall, a unicorn's head, erased, ar., maned and horned, or. *Pro Christo et patriâ dulce periculum.* Pl. 67, cr. 1.

KER, of Cevers, a stag's head, erased, or. *Tout droit.* Pl. 66, cr. 9.

KER, of Sutherland-hall, in dexter hand a dagger, ppr. *Abest timor.* Pl. 18, cr. 3.

KER, Sco., the sun, or. *A Deo lumen.* Pl. 68, cr. 14.

KER, of Abbot-rule, the sun rising out of a cloud, ppr. *J'advance.* Pl. 67, cr. 9.

KER, of Caloo, the sun, ppr. *Regulier et vigureux.* Pl. 68, cr. 14.

KER, Sco. and Eng., a stag's head, erased, or. *Deus solamen.* Pl. 66, cr. 9.

KER, of Blackshiels, a unicorn's head, erased, ar. *Virescit vulnere virtus.* Pl. 67, cr. 1.

KER, Sco., a unicorn's head, (couped,) ar., collared, az., charged with three crosses moline, of the first. Pl. 73, cr. 1, (cross, pl. 141.)

KER, Duke of Roxburghe. *See* ROXBURGHE.

KER, Marquess of Lothian. *See* LOTHIAN.

KER, WILLIAM, Esq., of Gateshaw, Roxburgh, a unicorn's head, erased, ar., armed and maned, or. *Pro Christo et patriâ.* Pl. 67, cr. 1.

KER, a stag's head, erased, ppr., with ten tynes, or. Pl. 66, cr. 9.

KERBY, Eng., a hand, in armour, holding a pheon, ppr. Pl. 123, cr. 12.

KERCHER, a cross pommée, az., between wings, (inverted,) or. Pl. 29, cr. 14, (cross, pl. 141.)

KERCHINALL, Northamp., a (demi-)bay-horse, armed and bridled, or, on head three feathers, az., or, and ar. Pl. 55, cr. 7.

KERCY, Eng., a boar's head, couped, or. Pl. 48, cr. 2.

KERDESTON, Eng., on a mountain, ppr., a goshawk, sa. Pl. 99, cr. 14.

KERDIFFE, Eng., out of a tower, ppr., a lion, rampant, or. Pl. 121, cr. 5.

KERDIFFE, Eng., a hind, (sejant, regardant,) resting dexter on a mount, vert. Pl. 1, cr. 14.

KERDISTON, Eng., out of a tower, a demi-griffin, ppr. Pl. 68, cr. 11.

KERDISTON, Eng., a dexter hand, apaumée, couped, in fess. Pl. 32, cr. 4.

KERESFORTH, Yorks., a demi-lion, rampant, gu., in paws a mill-rind, in pale, ar. Pl. 47, cr. 4, (mill-rind, pl. 141.)

KERGOURDENAC, Eng., two dolphins, addorsed, ppr. Pl. 81, cr. 2.

KERIOLL, Eng., a mullet, or, environed with clouds, ppr. Pl. 16, cr. 13.

KERLE, (on a mount, vert,) a hedgehog, or. Pl. 32, cr. 9.

KERNABY, Eng., a cubit arm, ppr., in hand a crescent, sa. *Pl.* 38, *cr.* 7.
KERNE, Cornw., (on a mount, vert,) a greyhound, current, per pale, or and ar., (collared, gu.) *Pl.* 28, *cr.* 7.
KERNEY, a unicorn, sejant, sa., armed and maned, or. *Pl.* 110, *cr.* 15, (without tree.)
KERR, a stag's head, erased, or. (Another, ppr.) *Pl.* 66, *cr.* 9.
KERR, Eng., a chevalier, in full armour, holding a horse by the head, ppr. *Pl.* 37, *cr.* 11.
KERR, Sco., the sun, ppr. *A Deo lumen. Pl.* 68, *cr.* 14.
KERRICK, on a hill, a caltrap, ppr. *Nunquam non paratus. Pl.* 7, *cr.* 4, (hill, *pl.* 62, *cr.* 11.)
KERRISON, Bart., Suff., on a mount, vert, a tiger, passant, ppr., collared and lined, or, fore dexter resting on a caltrap, gold. *Rien sans Dieu.*
KERRY, Salop, a bee-hive, sa., with bees, volant, or. *Pl.* 81, *cr.* 14.
KERRYLL, a lion, rampant, gu., holding a (sword,) erect, ppr. *Pl.* 22, *cr.* 15.
KERS, Sco., a torteau, gu., between wings, or. *Pl.* 2, *cr.* 3.
KERSEY, a boar's head, couped, or. *Pl.* 48, *cr.* 2.
KERSHAW, Eng., a ram, passant, ppr. *Pl.* 109, *cr.* 2.
KERSHAW, Lanc., a cock-pheasant, ppr. *Pl.* 82, *cr.* 12, (without collar.)
KERSLAKE, on trunk of tree, a falcon, close, all ppr. *Pl.* 78, *cr.* 8.
KERSTEMAN, a demi-man, in armour, in dexter an (arrow, in bend dexter.) *Pl.* 27, *cr.* 11.
KERVELL, Eng., on a ducal coronet, or, a wyvern, gu. *Pl.* 104, *cr.* 11.
KERVYLE, Norf., two lions' gambs, in pale, ar., between claws a (cone, reversed, gu.) *Pl.* 78, *cr.* 13.
KERVYLE, Norf., a goat, (passant,) sa., attires and beard, or. *Pl.* 66, *cr.* 1.
KERWELL, Norf., a goat, (passant) sa., armed, or. *Pl.* 66, *cr.* 1.
KERYELL, Eng., an arm, in armour, embowed, couped at shoulder, part above elbow, in fess, resting on the wreath, in hand, erect, a close helmet, all ppr. *Pl.* 114, *cr.* 9.
KESSTELL, Eng., an oak-tree, ppr. *Pl.* 16, *cr.* 8.
KESTELL, Cornw., a demi-bull, erm., attired, unguled, (collared and lined, sa.) *Pl.* 73, *cr.* 8.
KESTELL, Cornw., a tower, ppr. *Pl.* 12, *cr.* 5.
KETCHIN, Sco., a pelican's head, erased, vulning, ppr. *Pl.* 26, *cr.* 1.
KETERIDGE, Lond., out of a mural coronet, a lion's head, or. *Pl.* 45, *cr.* 9.
KETFORD, Eng., a stag's head, erased, affrontée. *Pl.* 8, *cr.* 6.
KETHING, Iri., in dexter hand a (pine)-branch, ppr. *Pl.* 23, *cr.* 7.
KETLAND, a lion, passant, az. *Pl.* 48, *cr.* 8.
KETSON, a lion's head, erased, in mouth a trefoil, slipped, all ppr. *Pl.* 95, *cr.* 6, (trefoil, *pl.* 141.)
KETT, Suff., on a mount, vert, a peacock, ppr. *Rara avis in terris. Pl.* 9, *cr.* 1.
KETT, Norf., a leopard's head, cabossed. *Pl.* 66, *cr.* 14.
KETTLE, Eng., a bundle of five arrows, ppr., banded, gu., buckled, or. *Pl.* 54, *cr.* 15.
KETTLE, a stag's head, erased, (collared and lined.) *Pl.* 66, *cr.* 9.

KETTLEBY, or KETTELBY, Eng., a lion's head, erased, gu., (in mouth an arrow), az., feathered, ar. *Pl.* 113, *cr.* 15.
KETTLEBY, Linc. and Salop, a lion's head, erased, gu. *Pl.* 81, *cr.* 4.
KETTON, Eng., a boar's head, couped, in fess, between two branches of laurel, in orle, ppr. *Pl.* 19, *cr.* 8, (branches, *pl.* 79, *cr.* 14.)
KEUX, Eng., a mound, crossed and banded, ppr. *Pl.* 37, *cr.* 3.
KEVEL, a horse's head, (couped.) *Pl.* 81, *cr.* 6.
KEVEPDON, Lanc., a buck's head, per pale, ar. and az., attired, counterchanged. *Pl.* 91, *cr.* 14.
KEVETT, Warw., a demi-lion, rampant, purp., murally gorged, lined and ringed, or. *Pl.* 87, *cr.* 15, (coronet, *pl.* 128, *fig.* 18.)
KEW, Yorks., a demi-lion, or, (between) paws a garb, az. *Pl.* 84, *cr.* 7.
KEWLEY, Eng., a stag's head, erased, az. *Pl.* 66, *cr.* 9.
KEY, Bart., Glouc., on a mount, vert, a hart, lodged, gardant, ppr., charged on body with three mullets, in fess, sa. *Pl.* 51, *cr.* 9, (mullet, *pl.* 141.)
KEY, Eng., a greyhound's head, ar., charged with three torteaux, sa. *Pl.* 14, *cr.* 4.
KEY, Sco., a bird, volant. *In Deo solo spes mea. Pl.* 87, *cr.* 10.
KEYDON, a dolphin, charged on back with an increscent. *Avise la fin. Pl.* 48, *cr.* 9, (increscent, *pl.* 141.)
KEYE, Oxon., a griffin's head, couped at breast, (wings addorsed, ar.,) in beak a key, or. *Pl.* 9, *cr.* 12.
KEYES, Eng., a griffin's head, between wings, in beak a palm-branch, ppr. *Pl.* 105, *cr.* 6.
KEYLE, Eng., a woman's head and shoulders, az., face, ppr., hair dishevelled, round head a chaplet, or. *Pl.* 81, *cr.* 13.
KEYMER, Eng., an ass, passant, ppr. *Pl.* 42, *cr.* 2.
KEYNE, Suff., six arrows, in saltier, ppr., feathered, ar., barbed, or, banded with a ribbon, sa. *Pl.* 101, *cr.* 13, (without cap.)
KEYNES, Eng., a talbot, passant, sa., collared, ar. *Pl.* 65, *cr.* 2.
KEYNION, Lanc., a lion, sejant, ppr., dexter on a cross fleury, ar. *Pl.* 126, *cr.* 15, (cross, *pl.* 141.)
KEYS, Eng., a Minerva's head, ppr. *Pl.* 92, *cr.* 12.
KEYSALL, a sinister arm, embowed and vested, in hand a slip of lily, flowered. *Pl.* 52, *cr.* 5, (lily, *pl.* 81, *cr.* 9.)
KEYT, Glouc., a kite's head, erased, or. *Pl.* 34, *cr.* 11.
KEYTE, Dors., Worc., and Lond., a unicorn's head, erased, ar., armed and collared, gu. *Pl.* 73, *cr.* 1.
KIBBLE, Sco., an antique crown, az. *Pl.* 79, *cr.* 12.
KIBBLE, Eng., a Roman fasces, erect. *Pl.* 65, *cr.* 15.
KIDD, Eng., a martlet, wings addorsed, ppr. *Pl.* 107, *cr.* 6, (without tower.)
KIDD, Sco., a crescent, ar. *Donec impleat. Pl.* 18, *cr.* 14.
KIDD, Sco., same crest. *Donec impleat orbem.*
KIDDALL, Linc., a goat's head, erased, ar., ducally gorged, attired, and bearded, or. *Pl.* 29, *cr.* 13, (gorging, *same plate.*)

KIDDELL, Glouc., a talbot's head, ar., gorged with a collar, az., studded and rimmed, or. *Pl.* 2, *cr.* 15.

KIDDER, Iri., a cubit arm, erect, vested, az., in hand, ppr., (a packet, thereon the word, *Standard.*) *Boyne. Pl.* 32, *cr.* 6.

KIDDERMINSTER, a greyhound's head, ar., (gorged with a fess, dancettée, az., charged with three bezants.) *Pl.* 14, *cr.* 4.

KIDLEY, a turbot, naiant, az.

KIDNEY, Lond. and Leic., on a mount, vert, an eagle, regardant, rising, ppr., (in beak a kidney, gu.) *Pl.* 79, *cr.* 2.

KIDSON, Durh., a unicorn's head, ar., attired and maned, or, (environed with palisadoes.) *Pro rege et lege. Pl.* 20, *cr.* 1.

KIDWELL, Eng., a peacock's head, couped, ppr. *Pl.* 100, *cr.* 5.

KIER, Sco., on point of a sword, in pale, ppr., a garland, vert. *Pl.* 15, *cr.* 6.

KIERMAN, Iri., a demi-antelope, erm., collared, gu. *Pl.* 34, *cr.* 8.

KIFFIN, on a garland of laurel, in orle, a lion, passant, ppr. *Pl.* 60, *cr.* 6.

KIFT, a lion's head, erased, ducally crowned. *Pl.* 90, *cr.* 4, (without charge.)

KIGHLEY, a dragon's head, erased, sa. *Pl.* 107, *cr.* 10, (without collar.)

KIGHLEY, and KIGHTLEY, Yorks. and Ess., a dragon's head, couped, sa. *Pl.* 87, *cr.* 12.

KILBURNE, Kent. and Lond., a bald coot, ppr. *Pl.* 90, *cr.* 15.

KILBY, Eng., out of a cloud, a hand, in fess, pointing to a crosier, erect, ppr. *Pl.* 45, *cr.* 4.

KILDERBEE, Suff., a demi-cockatrice, or, on breast an escallop, on each wing a cross pattée. *Pl.* 106, *cr.* 15, (escallop and cross, *pl.* 141.)

KILGOUR, Sco., between wings, gu., a mullet, or. *Pl.* 1, *cr.* 15.

KILGOUR, Sco., a wyvern, wings addorsed, the tail terminating with a head. *Pl.* 109, *cr.* 13.

KILGOUR, and KILLGOWR, Sco., a crescent, ar. *Gradatim. Pl.* 18, *cr.* 14.

KILKENNY, Earl of, and Viscount Montgarret, (Butler,) Iri., out of a ducal coronet, or, a plume of five ostrich-feathers, ar., therefrom a falcon, rising, of the last. *Depressus extollor. Pl.* 100, *cr.* 12, (falcon, *pl.* 105, *cr.* 4.)

KILLACH, Sco., a horse, passant, ar. *Pl.* 15, *cr.* 14.

KILLAND, Devons., a demi-tiger, salient, or, maned, ar. *Pl.* 53, *cr.* 10.

KILLEGREW, Cornw., a demi-lion, sa., charged with three bezants, in pale, and one in bend. *Pl.* 95, *cr.* 4.

KILLEGROUE, and KILLIGROUE, in hand a branch of laurel, ppr. *Pl.* 43, *cr.* 6.

KILLEY, Eng., out of a ducal coronet, ar., a bull's head, sa. *Pl.* 68, *cr.* 6.

KILLICKE, a swan, wings addorsed, ar. *Pl.* 46, *cr.* 5.

KILLIKELLEY, Iri., an arm, in armour, throwing a spear, all ppr. *Fortis et stabilis. Pl.* 44, *cr.* 9.

KILLINGWORTH, and KILINGWORTH, Ess. and Northamp., a sea-horse, az., ducally gorged, or, (in mouth a scroll, with motto, *Prate et petago.*) *Pl.* 103, *cr.* 3, (gorging, *same plate, cr.* 9.)

KILLOWE, and KILOH, two hands issuing from clouds, in chief, supporting an anchor, ppr. *Pl.* 94, *cr.* 4.

KILMAINE, Baron, and a Bart., (Cavendish-Browne,) Iri., an eagle, displayed, vert. *Suivez raison. Pl.* 48, *cr.* 11.

KILMARNOCK, Baron. *See* ERROL, Earl of.

KILMORE, Eng., a demi-eagle, with two heads, wings displayed, and ducally gorged. *Pl.* 4, *cr.* 6, (gorging, *pl.* 128, *fig.* 3.)

KILMOREY, Earl of, and Viscount of Newry and Morne, (Needham,) Iri., a phœnix in flames, ppr. *Nunc aut nunquam. Pl.* 44, *cr.* 8.

KILNER, a spread eagle. *Sursum. Pl.* 48, *cr.* 11.

KILPATRICK, in hand a dagger, erect, (dropping blood.) *I make sure. Pl.* 23, *cr.* 15.

KILVINGTON, Eng., a hand, erect, issuing from a cloud, holding a sealed letter, all ppr. *Pl.* 33, *cr.* 8.

KIMBER, Eng., a bull's head, affrontée. *Frangas, non flectes. Pl.* 18, *cr.* 15.

KIMPTON, Eng., a crescent, parted per crescent, or and gu. *Pl.* 40, *cr.* 15.

KINAIRD, Sco., a garland of laurel, vert. *Qui patitur, vincit. Pl.* 54, *cr.* 10.

KINARBY, a flag, gu., flotant to sinister. *Pl.* 8, *cr.* 3.

KINCH, Iri., a demi-lion, ppr., between paws a round buckle, in fess, or. *Pl.* 126, *cr.* 12, (buckle, *pl.* 73, *cr.* 10.)

KINDER, Cambs. and Notts., on a column, or, a Cornish chough, sa., beaked and legged, gu. *Pl.* 33, *cr.* 1, (chough, *pl.* 100, *cr.* 13.)

KINDER, Eng., a crane's head, erased, ppr. *Pl.* 20, *cr.* 9.

KINDON, and KINGDON, Eng., an eagle's head, erased. *Pl.* 20, *cr.* 7.

KINERBY, on a chapeau, gu., turned up, erm., a lion, passant, of the first. *Pl.* 107, *cr.* 1.

KINERSLEY, Salop and Staffs., on a mount, vert, a greyhound, sejant, ar., collared, or, under a holly-tree, of the first, fructed, gu. *Pl.* 5, *cr.* 2, (tree, *pl.* 22, *cr.* 10.)

KINCAID, in dexter hand, a chirurgeon's instrument. *Bis te ici. Pl.* 29, *cr.* 6.

KINCHANT, RICHARD-HENRY, of Park Hall, Salop, out of a ducal coronet, or, a demi-lion, ar. *Virtus pyramidis. Pl.* 45, *cr.* 7.

KING, Earl of Kingston. *See* KINGSTON.

KING, Viscount Lorton. *See* LORTON.

KING, Eng., a lion's paw, erased, charged with a crescent, holding a cross pattée, fitched. *Pl.* 46, *cr.* 7, (crescent, *pl.* 141.)

KING, Iri., out of a ducal coronet, or, a dexter hand. *Medio tutissimus ibis. Pl.* 32, *cr.* 14, (coronet, *pl.* 128, *fig.* 3.)

KING, North Petherton, Somers.: 1. For *King*, on a mount, vert, an arm, in bend dexter, couped at elbow, hand supporting a tilting-spear, erect, head broken, the arm surmounting a branch of oak, in bend sinister, all ppr. 2. For *Meade*, a demi-griffin, ar., wings elevated, erm., in dexter a fleur-de-lis, or. *Pl.* 19, *cr.* 15, (fleur-de-lis, *pl.* 141.)

KING, Staunton Park, Heref., a lion, rampant, bendy, or and az., (supporting two branches, composed of two roses, gu., and three cinque-foils, vert, slipped and leaved, of the last.) *Pl.* 22, *cr.* 15.

KING, Linc., a talbot's head, erased, sa., eared, ar., ringed and collared, gu. *Pl.* 2, *cr.* 15.

KING, EDWARD-BOLTON, Esq., of Umberslade, Warw., out of a ducal-coronet, a demi-lion, rampant. *Pl.* 45, *cr.* 7.

KING, Rev. HENRY, of Ballylin, King's County, an escallop, gu. *Spes tutissima cœlis. Pl.* 117, *cr.* 4.

KING, Baron King, a dexter arm, erect, couped at elbow, vested, az., thereon three ermine-spots, in fess, or, cuffed, ar., in hand, ppr., a truncheon, sa., (top broken off,) bottom couped, of the third. *Labor ipse voluptas. Pl.* 18, *cr.* 1, (ermine, *pl.* 141.)

KING, Bart., Iri., an escallop, gu. *Audaces fortuna juvat. Pl.* 117, *cr.* 4.

KING, Devons. and Northamp., out of a ducal coronet, or, a demi-ostrich, ar., wings ad-dorsed, beak, gold. *Pl.* 29, *cr.* 9.

KING, Devons., out of a mural coronet, ar., a lion's head and neck, sa., (charged with three ducal coronets, or.) *Pl.* 90, *cr.* 9.

KING, out of a ducal coronet, or, a dexter hand, couped at wrist, pointing upward with two fore-fingers. *Pl.* 67, *cr.* 6, (coronet, *same plate*.)

KING, a demi-griffin, or. *Pl.* 18, *cr.* 6.

KING, Leic., a lion, passant, erm., ducally crowned, or. *Pl.* 48, *cr.* 8, (crown, *pl.* 128, *fig.* 3.)

KING, Wilts., a talbot's head, (couped,) sa., collared, or. *Pl.* 2, *cr.* 15.

KING, Hants, an esquire's helmet, ppr., garnished, or, vizor (open.) *Pl.* 109, *cr.* 5.

KING, a lion, sejant, ppr., between paws an escallop, ar. *Pl.* 22, *cr.* 13, (escallop, *pl.* 141.)

KING, Lond., a dog's head, erased, sa., collared and eared, or. *Pl.* 2, *cr.* 15.

KING, a greyhound's head, couped, ducally gorged. *Pl.* 43, *cr.* 11, (gorging, *same plate*.)

KING, Suss., an ostrich-head, ar., ducally gorged, or. *Pl.* 108, *cr.* 2, (without feathers.)

KING, an ostrich-head, erased, gorged with an earl's coronet. *Pl.* 108, *cr.* 2, (coronet, *pl.* 127, *fig.* 8.)

KING, an ostrich-head, erased, ducally gorged, in mouth a key. *Pl.* 108, *cr.* 2, (key, *pl.* 9, *cr.* 12.)

KING, Lond. and Northamp., an arm, couped at elbow, in pale, ppr., in hand a broken spear. *Pl.* 66, *cr.* 4.

KING, a talbot's head, collared and erased, or. *Pl.* 2, *cr.* 15.

KING, Iri., a cubit arm, in hand a dagger, in pale, all ppr. *Pl.* 23, *cr.* 15.

KING, a cock, ppr. *Pl.* 67, *cr.* 14.

KING-BRADLEY, Bart., Iri., a dexter cubit arm, erect, in hand a dagger in pale, all ppr., (surmounted by a scroll, inscribed, "17 *Aug.* 1821.") *Audaces fortuna juvat. Pl.* 23, *cr.* 15.

KING-DASHWOOD, Bart., Bucks., a griffin's head, erased, per fess, erminois and gu. *Pl.* 48, *cr.* 6.

KING-DUCKWORTH, Bart., Kent, in lion's gamb, erased and erect, sa., a cross pattée, fitched, or. *Pl.* 46, *cr.* 7.

KINGDOM, Eng., out of a ducal coronet, a griffin's head, gu., in beak a key, of the first. *Pl.* 89, *cr.* 5.

KINGDOM, a dolphin, naiant, ppr. *Tentando superabis. Pl.* 48, *cr.* 9.

KINGDOM, an eagle, displayed, with two heads and necks. *Pl.* 87, *cr.* 11, (without flame.)

KINGE, Lond., a talbot's head, erased, sa., eared and collared, or. *Pl.* 2, *cr.* 15.

KINGE, an arm, in armour, couped at elbow, ppr., garnished, or, in gauntlet a broken spear, gold, headed, ar., girt round arm with a scarf, of the last. *Pl.* 23, *cr.* 9.

KINGE, Linc., a talbot's head, sa., eared, gu., collared and ringed, or. *Pl.* 2, *cr.* 15.

KINGE, Dors., a lion, sejant, ppr., resting dexter on an escallop, ar. *Pl.* 126, *cr.* 15, (escallop, *pl.* 141.)

KINGESTON, (on a mount, vert,) a goat, ar., horned, or, leaping against a tree, of the first. *Pl.* 32, *cr.* 10.

KINGFORD, Cornw., an eagle, displayed, per fess, gu. and ar., crowned, or, in beak a rose, ar., slipped and barbed, vert, seeded, gold. *Pl.* 85, *cr.* 11, (rose, *pl.* 117, *cr.* 10.)

KINGLEY, Eng., a cross crosslet, fitched, sa., and a sword, ppr., in saltier. *Pl.* 89, *cr.* 14.

KINGLEY, Eng., a cock's head, between wings, ppr. *Pl.* 47, *cr.* 3, (without cross.)

KINGSALE, Lord, Baron Courcy and Kingrove, (Stapleton de Courcy,) Iri., on a ducal coronet, or, an eagle, displayed, ar. *Vincit omnia veritas. Pl.* 9, *cr.* 6, (eagle, *pl.* 48, *cr.* 11.)

KINGSBURY, Iri., a snail issuing from its shell, ppr. *Pl.* 105, *cr.* 8.

KINGSCOTE, THOMAS-HENRY, Esq., of Kingscote, Glouc., an escallop, sa. *Pl.* 117, *cr.* 4.

KINGSDOWN, PEMBERTON-LEIGH, Baron : 1. For Leigh, a demi-lion, rampant, gu., (in paw a lozenge, ar., charged with a rose, of the first.) *Pl.* 126, *cr.* 12. 2. A dragon's head, erm., erased, gu., ducally gorged, or, (transfixed by an arrow, in fess, ppr.) *Ut tibi sic alteri. Pl.* 36, *cr.* 7.

KINGSFORD, Eng., a rose-branch, bearing roses, ppr. *Pl.* 23, *cr.* 2.

KINGSLEY, Herts. and Kent, a goat's head, ar. *Pl.* 105, *cr.* 14.

KINGSLEY, a goat's head, couped, ar. *Pl.* 105, *cr.* 14.

KINGSMILL, Hants., a cubit arm, in pale, vested, ar., cuffed, sa., in hand, ppr., a mill-rind, of the second. *Pl.* 34, *cr.* 3.

KINGSTON, Earl of, and Baron, Viscount Kingsborough, and a Bart., Iri., Baron Kingston, U. K., (King,) Iri., out of a five-leaved ducal coronet, or, a dexter hand, erect, the third and fourth fingers turned down, ppr. *Spes tutissima cœlis. Pl.* 67, *cr.* 6, (coronet, *pl.* 23, *cr.* 11.)

KINGSTON, Lond., out of a mural coronet, counter-componée, or and sa., a unicorn's head, az., crined, ar., horn, gobonée, of the second and first. *Pl.* 67, *cr.* 1, (coronet, *pl.* 128, *fig.* 18.)

KINGSTON, Glouc., a goat, salient, ar., against a tree, vert. *Pl.* 32, *cr.* 10.

KINGSWELL, a parrot, gu., in mouth an annulet, or. *Pl.* 33, *cr.* 11.

KINGTON, Somers., on a crescent, az., five guttes-d'or, between two sprigs of myrtle, ppr. *Pl.* 40, *cr.* 13.

KINLOCH, Bart., Sco., an eagle, rising, ppr. *Altius tendo. Pl.* 67, *cr.* 4.

KINLOCH, Gourdie, Sco., an eagle, soaring aloft. *Yet higher. Pl.* 114, *cr.* 10.

KINLOCH, Sco., a mermaid, in dexter a mirror, in sinister a comb, ppr. *Ut olim. Pl.* 48, *cr.* 5.

KINLOCH, and KINLOCK, Lond., an eagle, rising, ppr. *Non degener. Pl.* 67, *cr.* 4.

KINLOCH, Sco., a young eagle, perching, and looking up to the sun in its splendour. *Non degener.* Pl. 43, cr. 5.
KINLOCH, Sco., an eagle, (regardant, wings addorsed,) sa., armed, gu., looking at the sun, ppr. Pl. 67, cr. 4.
KINLOCH, Sco., an eagle, looking at the sun in splendour. *Altius tendo.* Pl. 43, cr. 5.
KINLOCH, Sco., an eagle, perched, looking at the sun in splendour. *Non degener.* Pl. 43, cr. 5.
KINLOCK, Sco., an eagle, statant, wings extended and addorsed. *Altius tendo.* Pl. 61, cr. 1.
KINNAIRD, Sco., a garland of laurel, vert. *Qui patitur, vincit.* Pl. 54, cr. 10.
KINNAIRD, Baron, Sco., Baron Rossie, U.K., (Kinnaird,) between the horns of a crescent, a mullet, or, out of a cloud, within two branches of palm, in orle, ppr. *Phœbo lux—Qui patitur, vincit—*and*—Certa cruce salus.* Pl. 118, cr. 2.
KINNAIRD, Eng., an otter's head, erased, sa. Pl. 126, cr. 14.
KINNEAR, Sco.: 1. Two anchors, in saltier, cabled, ppr. *I live in hope.* Pl. 37, cr. 12. 2. A crescent, or. *Honesty is the best policy.* Pl. 18, cr. 14.
KINNEAR, Edinr., an anchor, in pale, az. *Spem fortuna alit.* Pl. 25, cr. 15.
KINNEAR, or KINNEIR, two anchors, in saltier, with cables, all ppr. *I live in hope.* Pl. 37, cr. 12.
KINNEDAR, Sco., a greyhound, current, ar. *Gang forret.* Pl. 28, cr. 7.
KINNIMOND, Sco., an oak-tree, vert. *Stabo.* Pl. 16, cr. 8.
KINNOUL, Earl of, Viscount and Baron Hay, Sco., Baron Hay, G.B., (Hay-Drummond,) a countryman, couped at knees, vested in grey, waistcoat, gu., bonnet, az., on shoulder an ox-yoke, ppr. *Renovate animos.* Pl. 122, cr. 1.
KINSMAN, a buck, ppr., lodged in fern, vert. Pl. 22, cr. 5.
KINSEY, Eng., out of the top of a tower, ppr., an arm, embowed, ppr., vested, vert, in hand a spear, in fess. Pl. 95, cr. 14.
KINTORE, Earl of, Lord Keith and Falconer, (Keith-Falconer,) Sco., an angel in a praying posture, or, within an orle of laurel, ppr. *Quæ amissa, salva.* Pl. 94, cr. 11.
KIRBY, and KIRKBY, Eng., an anchor, gu., entwined with a serpent, vert. Pl. 64, cr. 9.
KIRBY, and KIRKBY, Eng., between two branches of palm, in orle, vert, a flaming heart, gu. Pl. 88, cr. 11.
KIRBY, Lond. and Kent, out of a ducal coronet, per pale, or and ar., an elephant's head, gu., eared, of the second, tusked, gold. Pl. 35, cr. 13, (coronet, pl. 128, fig. 3.)
KIRBY, on a chapeau, crimson, turned up, erm., a cross moline, ar., within a wreath, of the last, and gu. Pl. 89, cr. 8, (chapeau, *same plate,* cr. 7.)
KIRCH, on a pillar, ar., a heart, gu. Pl. 122, cr. 4.
KIRCH, Eng., a talbot's head, sa., collared and lined, gu. Pl. 2, cr. 15.
KIRK, Sco., a crosier and dagger, in saltier. *Optimum quod primum.* Pl. 7, cr. 15, (saltier, pl. 24, cr. 2.)

KIRK, Edinr., a church, ppr. *Votis et conamine.* Pl. 45, cr. 6.
KIRK, Sco., a fox, sejant, gu. Pl. 87, cr. 4.
KIRK, Notts., a boar's head, in pale, erased, sa. Pl. 21, cr. 7.
KIRKALDIE, or KIRKALDY, Eng. and Sco., a man's head, face looking upwards, ppr. *Fortissima veritas.* Pl. 121, cr. 2.
KIRKE, Ess., a dexter arm, in armour, embowed, ppr., garnished, or, in hand a cutlass, ar., hilt and pommel, gold. Pl. 81, cr. 12.
KIRKE, WILLIAM, Esq., of Markham Hall, Notts., a boar's head, erect, couped, sa. Pl. 21, cr. 7.
KIRKENTON, a fox, passant, ppr. Pl. 126, cr. 5.
KIRKHAM, Northamp., on a Saracen's head, affrontée, ppr., couped at shoulders, gorged with a ducal coronet, or, wreathed, ar. and sa., a popinjay, vert, beaked and collared, gu. Pl. 19, cr. 1, (coronet, *same plate,* cr. 1; popinjay, pl. 25, cr. 2.)
KIRKHAM, Devons., a lion's head, erased, ar. Pl. 81, cr. 4.
KIRKHAM, Northamp., out of a ducal coronet, or, a moor's head, in profile, ppr., wreathed, ar. and gu. Pl. 118, cr. 7, (coronet, pl. 128, fig. 3.)
KIRKHOVEN, Eng., a beacon, fired, ppr. Pl. 88, cr. 6.
KIRKLAND, and KIRKLEY, a church, environed with trees, ppr. Pl. 110, cr. 5.
KIRKLAND, Sco., a leopard's face, ppr. *Pro aris et focis.* Pl. 66, cr. 14.
KIRKLAND, or KIRKELAND, Eng., on a ducal coronet, a falcon, belled, ppr. Pl. 41, cr. 10.
KIRKLAND, an owl, ar. Pl. 27, cr. 9.
KIRKLEY, or KIRKLY, Eng., two eagles' heads, erased and addorsed, ppr. Pl. 94, cr. 12.
KIRKMAN, a crosier and sword, in saltier, ppr. *In Deo confido.* Pl. 7, cr. 15, (sword, pl. 106, cr. 9.)
KIRKMAN, a demi-lion, rampant, ar. Pl. 67, cr. 10.
KIRKPATRICK, Eng. and Sco., in hand a dagger, erect, (dropping blood.) *I make sure.* Pl. 23, cr. 15.
KIRKPATRICK, a dexter arm, in armour, embowed, in hand a dagger, in fess, ppr. Pl. 120, cr. 11.
KIRKPATRICK, Iri., a mount, in flames, ppr. Pl. 92, cr. 9.
KIRKPATRICK, Eng., a stag's head, ar. Pl. 91, cr. 14.
KIRKTON, and KIRTON, Eng., an arm, couped, resting elbow on the wreath, in hand three ears of wheat, ppr. Pl. 89, cr. 4.
KIRKWOOD, JAMES, Esq., of Woodbrook, co. Roscommon, a pheon, sa. *Spes mea in Deo.* Pl. 26, cr. 12.
KIRKYN, a demi-griffin, ppr., in claws an escallop, or. Pl. 18, cr. 6, (escallop, pl. 141.)
KIRSOPP, on a mount, vert, a crane, ar., (dexter resting on an escutcheon, of the second, charged with the letter *K*, sa.) Pl. 122, cr. 7.
KIRTLAND, two dexter hands, conjoined, supporting a (scimitar,) erect. Pl. 75, cr. 8.
KIRTON, Northamp., a falcon, wings expanded, ar., beaked, (jessed and belled, or, reposing dexter on a hawk's hood, gu.) Pl. 49, cr. 1.
KIRTON, Northamp. and Wilts., a hawk, close, or, hooded, ppr., belled, gold. Pl. 38, cr. 12.

S

KIRWAN, MARTIN-STAUNTON, Esq., of Blindwell, co. Galway, a coot, ppr. *Pl.* 90, *cr.* 15.
KIRWAN, RICHARD-A.-HYACINTH, Esq., of Knockdoe, co. Galway, a Cornish chough, sa. *Mon Dieu, mon roi, et ma patrie. Pl.* 100, *cr.* 13.
KIRWAN, Eng., (out of a cloud,) a hand, in pale, holding a broken spear, ppr. *Pl.* 66, *cr.* 4.
KIRWAN, Iri., a sea-chart, ppr. *Pl.* 59, *cr.* 3.
KIRWAN, a raven, ppr. *Pl.* 123, *cr.* 2.
KISSOCK, Sco., between wings, an arm, erect, vested, az., cuffed, ar., in hand a thistle, ppr.
KITCHEN, Eng., out of a cloud, in sinister, an arm, in armour, embowed, in hand a sword, ppr. *Pl.* 85, *cr.* 4.
KITCHENER, Eng., between two flags, ar., displayed, each charged with a cross, or, a bull's head, cabossed, sa. *Pl.* 118, *cr.* 8.
KITCHIN, Lond., a pelican's head, erased, az., beaked, or, vulned, gu. *Pl.* 26, *cr.* 1.
KITCHINER, a buck's head, erased, (pierced through neck by an arrow, in bend, all ppr.) *Pl.* 66, *cr.* 9.
KITCHING, Heref., on a ducal coronet, or, a wyvern, vert. *Pl.* 104, *cr.* 11.
KITE, or KEYTE, of Ebrington, Glouc., a kite's head, erased, or. *Pl.* 20, *cr.* 7.
KITE, Dors., Lond., and Worc., a unicorn's head, erased, ar., armed and collared, gu. *Pl.* 73, *cr.* 1.
KITSON, of Hengrave, Suff., a unicorn's head, sa., armed and maned, or. *P.* 20, *cr.* 1.
KITSON, or KITTSON, Suff., a unicorn's head, ar., attired and maned, or, (environed by palisadoes, gold.) *Pl.* 20, *cr.* 1.
KITSON, or KITTSON, Suff., (on a mount, or; in flames, ppr.,) a unicorn's head, sa. *Pl.* 20, *cr.* 1.
KITTELBY, or KITTLEBY, Salop, a lion's head, erased, gu. (Another, or.) *Pl.* 81, *cr.* 4.
KITTERMASTEN, on a chapeau, ar., turned up, erm., an eagle, rising, erminois. *Pl.* 114, *cr.* 13.
KITTO, or KITTOE, Eng., a lion, sejant, gu., collared, ar. *Pl.* 21, *cr.* 3.
KIVILIOC, an Indian goat's head, ar. *Pl.* 105, *cr.* 14.
KLEE, Lond., within a serpent, in orle, vert, a boar's head, in pale, erased. *Pl.* 12, *cr.* 6.
KNAPLOCK, Hants, a boar's head, couped, or, mouth embrued. *Pl.* 48, *cr.* 2.
KNAPMAN, Eng., a sword, erect, enfiled with a Saracen's head, couped, ppr. *Pl.* 27, *cr.* 3.
KNAPP, Suff. and Norf., an arm, in armour, embowed, garnished, or, hand, gold, grasping by the blade a (broken) sword, ar., hilt and pommel, of the second, with a branch of laurel, vert. *Pl.* 65, *cr.* 8.
KNAPTON, out of a ducal coronet, two arms, dexter and sinister, in saltier, in each hand a scimitar, erect. *Pl.* 57, *cr.* 8.
KNATCHBULL, Bart., of Mersham-Hatch, Kent, on a chapeau, az., turned up, erm., a leopard, statant, ar., spotted, sa. *In crucifixâ gloria mea. Pl.* 110, *cr.* 8.
KNATCHBULL, Kent and Somers., same crest.
KNELL, Oxon. and Glouc., a demi-lion, or, in dexter a cross crosslet, fitched, az. *Pl.* 65, *cr.* 6.
KNELLER, Wilts., on a mount, vert, a stag, ppr., beside a vine-tree, of the first. *Pl.* 85, *cr.* 2.

KNEVET, Eng., a nest, with young birds, ppr. *Pl.* 56, *cr.* 5.
KNEVET, Eng., in the sea, a ship, in full sail, ppr. *Pl.* 109, *cr.* 8.
KNEVETT, or KNEVIT, Cornw., Norf., and Suff., between wings, sa., a dragon's head. *Pl.* 105, *cr.* 11.
KNEYSWORTH, or KNESWORTH, Eng., a buffalo's head, erased, gu. *Pl.* 57, *cr.* 7.
KNIFE, Eng., a dove, regardant, in beak an olive-branch, ppr. *Pl.* 77, *cr.* 2.
KNIGHT, Leic., between wings, a spur, in pale, (standing on its rowel,) with leather and buckle. *Nunquam non paratus. Pl.* 109, *cr.* 12.
KNIGHT, an arm, couped, vested, bendy of four, or and az., in hand, ppr., the lower half of a fish, couped, of the second.
KNIGHT, out of a ducal coronet, or, an eagle, displayed, erm. *Pl.* 9, *cr.* 6.
KNIGHT, Hants, a griffin's head, gu., beak and dexter ear, ar., the sinister, sa., (gorged with a collar.) *Pl.* 38, *cr.* 3.
KNIGHT, Salop, on a spur, in fess, or, an eagle, per fess, ar. and az., wings expanded, gold, beaked and legged, gu. *Pl.* 126, *cr.* 7, (spur, *pl.* 15, *cr.* 3.)
KNIGHT, Northamp., between wings, gu., a spur, leathered, or. *Pl.* 109, *cr.* 12.
KNIGHT, Kent and Hants, a friar, vested, ppr., in dexter (a cinquefoil, slipped,) ar., in sinister a cross, pendent from wrist, breast charged with a rose, gu. *Pl.* 90, *cr.* 5.
KNIGHT, Kent and Hants, on a mural coronet, or, a buck, sejant, ar., attired, or. *Pl.* 101, *cr.* 3.
KNIGHT, Lond. and Kent, a demi-friar, ppr., vested and (hooded, ar., having an upper mantle, or, in dexter a lantern, purfled, gold,) in sinister a paternoster, gu., with a crucifix hanging at the end. *Pl.* 90, *cr.* 5.
KNIGHT, Hants, on a ducal coronet, gu., an eagle, displayed, or. *Pl.* 9, *cr.* 6.
KNIGHT, Herts. and Notts., a goat's head, or attired and erased, per fess, gu., in mouth a sprig of laurel, vert. *Pl.* 29, *cr.* 13, (laurel, *pl.* 123, *cr.* 5.)
KNIGHT, Hants and Northamp., a dexter arm, in armour, embowed, ppr., in hand a sword, of the last, hilt and pommel, or, point resting on the wreath. *Pl.* 123, *cr.* 5.
KNIGHT, a talbot's head, erased, bezantée. *Pl.* 90, *cr.* 6.
KNIGHT, Hants, a demi-greyfriar, in dexter (a cinquefoil, slipped, ar.,) from sinister wrist a bracelet of beads, pendent, sa. *Pl.* 90, *cr.* 5.
KNIGHT, on a spur, in fess, a hawk, statant. *Pl.* 83, *cr.* 13, (spur, *pl.* 15, *cr.* 3.)
KNIGHT, Iri., on a chapeau, sa., turned up, ar., a serpent, nowed, in a love-knot, or, spotted, vert. *Pl.* 123, *cr.* 4.
KNIGHT, of Ruscombe, Berks., on a ducal coronet, sa., an eagle, displayed, or. *Pl.* 9, *cr.* 6.
KNIGHT, Eng., out of a cloud, a dexter hand, in fess, holding a club, all ppr. *Pl.* 55, *cr.* 4.
KNIGHT, Sco., a winged spur, buckled and strapped, or. *Tu digna sequere. Pl.* 59, *cr.* 1.
KNIGHT, Sco., a ship in full sail, all ppr. *Darcen. Pl.* 109, *cr.* 8.
KNIGHTLEY, Bart., Northamp., a buck's head, couped, ar., attired, or. *Invita fortuna. Pl.* 91, *cr.* 14.

KNIGHTLEY, Eng., a stag's head, erased, ar., attired, or. *Pl.* 66, *cr.* 9.
KNIGHTLEY, Surr., a stag's head, ar., attired, or, charged on neck with a trefoil, vert. *Pl.* 61, *cr.* 9, (trefoil, *pl.* 141.)
KNIGHTLY, Warw. and Northamp., a buck's head, ar., attired, or. *Pl.* 91, *cr.* 14.
KNIGHTLY, Worc., a dragon's head, sa., (having three tongues, gu.) *Pl.* 87, *cr.* 12.
KNIGHTLY, Lanc., a goat's head, ar., charged with a mullet for difference. *Pl.* 105, *cr.* 14, (mullet, *pl.* 141.)
KNIGHTON, Herts. and Suff., out of a ducal coronet, or, two dragons' heads and necks, in saltier, ppr.
KNIGHTON, out of a ducal coronet, gu., two dragons' heads and necks twisted in each other, az.
KNIGHTON, Bart., Dors., out of a ducal coronet, or, two dragons' heads, in saltier, couped at shoulder, the dexter, gu., sinister, or, wreathed with a chain, gold.
KNIPE, Lond. and Lanc., a wolf's head, ar., pierced through breast by a broad arrow, or, feathered and armed, of the first. *Pl.* 40, *cr.* 12.
KNIPELL, between two laurel branches, vert, a tiger's face, or. *Pl.* 31, *cr.* 7, (branches, same plate.)
KNIPHAUSEN, Prussia, out of a coronet with seven pearls on the rim, a demi-lion, rampant, sa., between wings, or. *Pl.* 45, *cr.* 2, (wings, *pl.* 17, *cr.* 9.)
KNIVETON, Devons., between wings, an eagle's head, all ppr. *Pl.* 81, *cr.* 10.
KNOELL, KNOLL, and KNOLLE, Eng., a parrot, feeding on a bunch of cherries, ppr. *Pl.* 49, *cr.* 3.
KNOLAS, a ram's head, couped, ar., horned, or. *Pl.* 34, *cr.* 12.
KNOLLES, Eng., on a cloud, a sphere, ppr. *Pl.* 110, *cr.* 9.
KNOLLES, Hants, a griffin, segreant, or. *Pl.* 67, *cr.* 13.
KNOLLIS, an elephant, statant, ar. *Pl.* 56, *cr.* 14.
KNOLLS, or KNOWLES, Chesh., Lanc., and Norf., a ram's head, ar., attired, or. *Pl.* 34, *cr.* 12.
KNOLLYS, Berks. and Warw., an elephant, ar. *Pl.* 56, *cr.* 14.
KNOT, or KNOTT, a lion's head, erased, gu. *Pl.* 81, *cr.* 4.
KNOTSHULL, Eng., (out of a cloud,) a hand, holding a broken spear, ppr. *Pl.* 66, *cr.* 4.
KNOTT, Eng., a wolf, collared and (chained,) ppr. *Pl.* 5, *cr.* 8, (without staff.)
KNOTT, Suss., a unicorn's head, ar., armed and crined, or. *Pl.* 20, *cr.* 1.
KNOTWOOD, Eng., a boar, (regardant,) sa., seizing an arrow, fixed in shoulder. *Pl.* 36, *cr.* 2.
KNOWELL, Eng., between wings, vert, a parrot's head, gu. *Pl.* 94, *cr.* 2.
KNOWLER, Kent, out of reeds, a demi-heron, ppr., volant.
KNOWLER, Kent, out of a ducal coronet, or, a demi-heron, erm.
KNOWLES, Suff., Northamp., and Sco., out of a ducal coronet, gu., an elephant's head, ar. *Pl.* 93, *cr.* 13.
KNOWLYS, Eng., a unicorn, rampant, ppr. *Pl.* 37, *cr.* 7.

KNOWLES, an elephant, ar. *Pl.* 56, *cr.* 14.
KNOWLES, Sco., a parrot feeding on a bunch of cherries, ppr. *Pl.* 49, *cr.* 3.
KNOWLES, out of a ducal coronet, gu., a ram's head, ar., armed, or. *Pl.* 124, *cr.* 8, (coronet, *pl.* 128, *fig.* 3.)
KNOWLES, Bart., Berks., an elephant, statant, ar. *Semper paratus*. *Pl.* 56, *cr.* 14.
KNOWS, Sco., in hand, erect, ppr., a crescent, or. *Pl.* 38, *cr.* 7.
KNOWSLEY, a leopard's head, couped, collared and lined, a ring at end of line. *Pl.* 40, *cr.* 10.
KNOX, ANNESLEY, Esq., of Rappa Castle, co. Mayo, a falcon, close, on a perch, all ppr. *Pl.* 10, *cr.* 7.
KNOX, JOHN, Esq., of Castlerea, co. Mayo, a falcon, close, perched, ppr. *Pl.* 67, *cr.* 3.
KNOX, JOHN-FREDERIC, Esq., of Mount Falcon, co. Mayo, a falcon, close, on a perch, all ppr. *Moveo et proficio*. *Pl.* 10, *cr.* 7.
KNOX, an eagle, rising. *Pl.* 67, *cr.* 4.
KNOX, Iri., a falcon, perched, ppr. *Moveo et propitior*. *Pl.* 67, *cr.* 3.
KNOX, a demi-lion, ar., in dexter a key, gu. *Pl.* 39, *cr.* 14, (key, *pl.* 54, *cr.* 12.)
KNOX, Eng., a griffin's head, between wings, or, each charged with three torteaux, gu. *Pl.* 65, *cr.* 1, (torteau, *pl.* 141.)
KNOX, Sco., a falcon, close, ppr. *Moveo et proficior*. *Pl.* 67, *cr.* 3.
KNYFTON, THOMAS-TUTTON, Esq., of Uphill, Somers., between wings, sa., an eagle's head, erased, or. *In te Domine confido*. *Pl.* 81, *cr.* 10.
KNYLL, Eng., out of a ducal coronet, a plume of ostrich-feathers, in a case. *Pl.* 106, *cr.* 11.
KNYUET, and KNYVETT, Eng., a demi-dragon, az., langued, gu. *Pl.* 82, *cr.* 10.
KNYVETT, Eng., a sword and an ear of wheat, in saltier, ppr. *Pl.* 50, *cr.* 4.
KNYVETT, a demi-dragon, vert, wings, az. *Pl.* 82, *cr.* 10.
KNYVETT, Eng., out of a cloud, a hand, in pale, pointing to a star of five points. *Pl.* 77, *cr.* 6.
KOEHLER, two coulters, addorsed, in pale, az.
KOGNOSE, Eng., a cock, sa., combed and wattled, gu., beaked and legged, or. *Pl.* 67, *cr.* 14.
KOKE, of Broxbourne, Heref., an ostrich, in mouth a horse-shoe, ar. *Pl.* 16, *cr.* 2.
KOKEFIELD, DE, Eng., out of a ducal coronet, a lion's paw. *Pl.* 67, *cr.* 7.
KOKINGTON, Eng., a unicorn's head, erased, or. *Pl.* 67, *cr.* 1.
KOLLANDS, in dexter hand, in bend, couped, a dagger. *Spes juvet*. *Pl.* 18, *cr.* 3.
KOLON, a bird's head, ar., winged, az., in beak three ears of wheat, or. *Pl.* 99, *cr.* 10, (wheat, *pl.* 63, *cr.* 1.)
KRAG, or KRAGG, in dexter hand, ppr., a garland of laurel, vert. *Pl.* 86, *cr.* 1.
KRAGG, Eng., a cubit arm, in hand a sabre, ppr. *Pl.* 29, *cr.* 8.
KRAMER, Iri., between wings, or, pinioned, ar., a fleur-de-lis. *Pl.* 21, *cr.* 13, (without chapeau.)
KRAMPTON, and KRANTON, Eng., in dexter hand, vested, az., a palm-branch, ppr. *Pl.* 23, *cr.* 7.
KROG, or KROGE, Eng., in hand a garland of roses, leaved, ppr. *Pl.* 41, *cr.* 7.

KROGE, a plough, ppr. *Pl.* 28, *cr.* 15.
KROWTON, an arm, in hand a broken spear, ppr., top pendent. *Pl.* 66, *cr.* 4.
KUCKFIELD, Eng., a demi-lion, rampant, sa., in dexter a sword, or. *Pl.* 41, *cr.* 13.
KUELLEY, or KEWLY, (out of waves,) ppr., the head of a sea-horse. *Pl.* 58, *cr.* 15.
KUKEFIELD, Eng., a demi-lion, rampant, sa., brandishing a scimitar, or. *Pl.* 126 A, *cr.* 1.
KULLINGWIKE, a cubit arm, in pale, vested, sa., cuffed, erm., in hand, ppr., a chaplet of laurel, vert. *Pl.* 44, *cr.* 13, (without bird.)
KUMERSON, Eng., a griffin's head, erased, or. *Pl.* 48, *cr.* 6.
KUTCHIN, Eng., a crane's head, erased, ar. *Pl.* 20, *cr.* 9.
KYAN, a wild cat, salient, ppr., (gorged with an antique Irish crown.) *Pl.* 70, *cr.* 15.
KYCHARD, a wolf's head, or, collared, gu., in mouth a trefoil, vert. *Pl.* 8, *cr.* 4.
KYD, Sco., an increscent, ppr. *Donec impleat orbem.* *Pl.* 122, *cr.* 15.
KYD, or KYDE, Sco., a hunting-horn. *Donec impleat orbem.* *Pl.* 89, *cr.* 3.
KYDD, Sco., a crescent. *Donec impleat.* *Pl.* 18, *cr.* 14.
KYDERMASTER, Suss., on a chapeau, gu., turned up, erm., an eagle, ar., wings addorsed. *Pl.* 114, *cr.* 13.
KYDERMASTER, Warw. and Lond., on a chapeau, az., turned up, erm., a cockatrice, erminois, wings addorsed. *Pl.* 103, *cr.* 9.
KYFFYN, Salop, a lion, rampant, per fess, ar. and sa. *Pl.* 67, *cr.* 10.
KYLE, a deer's head, ppr. *Pl.* 91, *cr.* 14.
KYLE, Sco., an anchor and cable, ppr. *Pl.* 42, *cr.* 12.
KYLE, out of a ducal coronet, or, a bull's head, sa. *Pl.* 68, *cr.* 6.
KYLLE, Eng., a rock, sa. *Pl.* 73, *cr.* 12.
KYLLINGBECK, Eng., on a ducal coronet, a talbot, collared and lined, ppr. *Pl.* 3, *cr.* 8.
KYLOM, a buck's head, couped, gu., attired, or, (on neck a fess, of the second,) between three annulets, ar. *Pl.* 91, *cr.* 14, (annulet, *pl.* 141.)
KYME, DE., Eng., a sagittarius, shooting an arrow from a bow. *Pl.* 70, *cr.* 13.
KYME, Eng., a pole-cat, ppr. *Pl.* 119, *cr.* 7.
KYMER, Dors., a leopard's head, gu. *Pl.* 92, *cr.* 13.
KYMER, Eng., a leopard's head, erased. *Pl.* 94, *cr.* 10.
KYMBERLEE, and KYMBERLEY, Eng., a cock, regardant, gu. *Pl.* 19, *cr.* 10.
KYMES, on a mount, vert, a tortoise, ppr. *Pl.* 12, *cr.* 13.

KYMPTON, Herts., a demi-goat, erm., attired and hoofed, or, (collared and lined, sa.) *Pl.* 90, *cr.* 12.
KYNARDESLEY, Derbs., Somers., Staffs., and Warw., on a mount, vert, a greyhound, sejant, ar., (collared, or,) under a holly-tree, of the first, fructed, gu. *Pl.* 5, *cr.* 2, (holly, *pl.* 22, *cr.* 10.)
KYNARDYSBY, a leopard's head, affrontée, or, (in mouth a sword, ppr.) *Pl.* 125, *cr.* 9.
KYNASTON, Bart., Salop, the sun in splendour, surmounted of a dexter arm, in armour, embowed, in hand a sword, all ppr. *Pl.* 40, *cr.* 14.
KYNASTON, Ess. and Salop, an (eagle's) head, erased, sa., ducally gorged, ar., in beak a laurel-sprig, vert. *Pl.* 29, *cr.* 15.
KYNERBY, on a chapeau, ar., turned up., gu., and charged with four fleurs-de-lis, or, a lion, passant, of the second. *Pl.* 107, *cr.* 1, (fleur-de-lis, *pl.* 141.)
KYNESTON, Eng., a demi-greyhound, az. *Pl.* 48, *cr.* 3.
KYNGESLEY, out of a ducal coronet, gu., a goat's head, ar. *Pl.* 70, *cr.* 5.
KYNN, Eng., an eagle's head, couped, or. *Pl.* 100, *cr.* 10.
KYNNELMARCH, two lions' gambs, united at bottom, guttée, ar. and sa., counterchanged, holding a wolf's head, erased. *Pl.* 62, *cr.* 3, (head, *pl.* 14, *cr.* 6.)
KYNNERSLEY-SNEYD, of Loxley Park, Staffs.: 1. For *Kynnersley*, on a mount, vert, a greyhound, sejant, ar., (collared, or,) under a hawthorn-tree, ppr. *Pl.* 5, *cr.* 2, (tree, *pl.* 10, *cr.* 4.) 2. For *Sneyd*, a lion, (statant,) gardant, tail extended, sa. *Nec opprimere, nec opprimi.* *Pl.* 120, *cr.* 5.
KYNNERTON, between wings, ppr., a chess-rook, sa. *Pl.* 40, *cr.* 11.
KIRBY, out of a ducal coronet, per pale, gold and ar., an elephant's head, gu., eared, of the second, tusked, or. *Pl.* 93, *cr.* 13.
KYRBY, and KYRKBY, Eng., out of a tower, ar., a demi-lion, gu., ducally crowned, between paws a bomb, fired, ppr. *Pl.* 53, *cr.* 2, (crown, *same plate.*)
KYRBY, and KYRKBY, Eng., a demi-savage, affrontée, in hand three leaves, ppr. *Pl.* 35, *cr.* 12.
KYRELL, Kent, a bull's head. *Pl.* 63, *cr.* 11.
KYRELL, Kent, a talbot's head, erased, ar. *Pl.* 90, *cr.* 6.
KYRKLOT, Eng., in dexter hand a sword, erect, all ppr. *Pl.* 23, *cr.* 15.
KYRRELORDE, an antique lamp, or, flammant, ppr. *Pl.* 40, *cr.* 9.

L

LABAN, Iri., an antelope, passant, per pale, or and gu. *Pl.* 63, *cr.* 10.
LABORER, or LABRUER, Eng., a hand, couped, in fess, charged with an eye, both ppr. *Pl.* 10, *cr.* 14.
LACE, Eng., a talbot's head, sa. *Pl.* 123, *cr.* 15.
LACY, Iri., an eagle, wings expanded, ar. *Pl.* 126, *cr.* 7.

LACEY, Eng., in (bear's) paw, erased, a rose-branch, leaved, vert. *Pl.* 63, *cr.* 14.
LACHLAN, Sco., a swan, wings addorsed, ar. *Divina sibi canit.* *Pl.* 46, *cr.* 5.
LACHLAN, Eng., a demi-savage, wreathed about head and middle, in dexter a club, erect, all ppr. *Pl.* 87, *cr.* 13.
LACKE, out of a ducal coronet, a dexter hand,

holding a serpent, entwined round arm. *Pl.* 91, *cr.* 6, (coronet, *pl.* 128, *fig.* 3.)
LACOCK, on a bear's paw, a cock, statant. *Pl.* 126, *cr.* 2, (cock, *pl.* 2, *cr.* 1.)
LACOCK, Notts., a cock, ar., combed, jelloped, and legged, gu., supporting with dexter a gauntlet, sa., purfled, or. *Pl.* 67, *cr.* 14, (gauntlet, *pl.* 106, *cr.* 13.)
LACOCKE, a cock, rising, resting dexter on a gauntlet, sa. *Ib.*
LACON, Ess., Linc., Salop, and Lond., a falcon, ppr., beaked and belled, or. *Pl.* 67, *cr.* 3.
LACON, Bart., Norf., a falcon, ppr., beaked and belled, or. *Probitas verus honos. Pl.* 67, *cr.* 3.
LACON, Sir EDMUND-KNOWLES, Bart., Norf., on a mount, vert, a falcon, ppr., (collared,) charged on breast with a cross patonce, gu. *Probitas verus honos. Pl.* 81, *cr.* 12, (cross, *pl.* 141.)
LACY, Eng., a lion's face, looking out of a bush, ppr. *Pl.* 111, *cr.* 2.
LACY, Linc., a demi-lion, rampant, gu. *Pl.* 67, *cr.* 10.
LACY, Suff. and Norf., out of a ducal coronet, gu., a demi-eagle, wings expanded, or, in beak an arrow, of the first, headed and feathered, ar. *Pl.* 9, *cr.* 6, (arrow, *same plate.*)
LACY, Middx., Oxon., and Somers., on a ducal coronet, or, a lion, sejant, erm. *Pl.* 126, *cr.* 15, (coronet, *pl.* 128, *fig.* 3.)
LACY, Yorks., a buck's head, cabossed, per pale, ar. and or, horns counterchanged. *Pl.* 36, *cr.* 1.
LACY, Leic. and Yorks., a fret-knot, ar. and purp. *Pl.* 82, *cr.* 7.
LACY, Iri., a hawk, close, sa. *Pl.* 67, *cr.* 3.
LADBROKE, Lond., an arm, in pale, couped at elbow, vested, gu., cuffed, ar., in hand, ppr., five quatrefoils, in cross, stalked, of the second, pierced, of the first. *Pl.* 101, *cr.* 5, (quatrefoil, *pl.* 141.)
LADBROOK, or LADBROOKE, Eng., a hawk, rising, ppr., ducally gorged and belled, or. *Pl.* 61, *cr.* 12.
LADBROOKE, a stag's head, erased. *Pl.* 66, *cr.* 9.
LADD, or LADDE, Eng., on a cloud, a crescent, ensigned with a star, all between two palm-branches, in orle. *Pl.* 118, *cr.* 2.
LADE, Kent, Lond., and Suss., a panther's head, gardant, erased, sa., spotted, or. *Pl.* 56, *cr.* 7.
LADE, Bart., Suss., out of a ducal coronet, or, a leopard's head, (regardant,) sa., bezantée. *Pl.* 36, *cr.* 15.
LADE, JOHN-PRYCE, Esq., of Broughton House, Kent, a leopard's head, ppr. *Pl.* 92, *cr.* 13.
LADKIN, Eng., a savage's head, crowned with a garland of laurel, ppr. *Pl.* 118, *cr.* 7.
LAFFAN, Bart., out of a ducal coronet, or, an eagle, displayed, sa., (semée of fleurs-de-lis, gold.) *Vincit omnia veritas. Pl.* 9, *cr.* 6.
LAFFER, Eng., an eagle, rising, resting dexter on a flint-stone, ppr. *Pl.* 118, *cr.* 1.
LA FOREST, and LE FOREST, a unicorn, sejant, ar., armed and tufted, or. *Pl.* 110, *cr.* 15, (without tree.)
LAFOREY, Bart., Devons., a lion, rampant, regardant, in dexter a fire-brand, all ppr. *Loyal à mort. Pl.* 10, *cr.* 15.
LAGENHAM, out of a ducal coronet, or, a serpent, in pale, nowed, vert. *Pl.* 116, *cr.* 2.

LAGFORD, Eng., a dexter arm, gu., in hand a sabre, erect, az., hilted, or. *Pl.* 92, *cr.* 5.
LAIDLAW, Eng. and Sco., a dexter hand holding a (dagger,) in pale, issuing from a heart, all ppr. *Fides probata coronat. Pl.* 35, *cr.* 7.
LAING, Sco., a dove, in mouth a sprig of olive, ppr. *Mercy is my desire. Pl.* 48, *cr.* 15.
LAING, Eng., on a chapeau, az., turned up, ar., a cock, gu. *Pl.* 104, *cr.* 3.
LAING, Sco., a cock, gu. *Vigilant. Pl.* 67, *cr.* 14.
LAING, a cock, ppr. *Vigilance. Pl.* 67, *cr.* 14.
LAING, Sco., a bear's head and neck, ppr., muzzled, ar. *Labor omnia superat. Pl.* 2, *cr.* 9.
LAIRD, Sco., a buck's head, ppr. *Spero meliora. Pl.* 91, *cr.* 14.
LAIRD, Eng., in hand a covered cup. *Pl.* 35, *cr.* 9.
LAKE, Bart., of Edmonston, Middx.: 1. A man in complete armour, on a horse, current, ar., bridle and trappings, all ppr., in dexter a sword, embrued, gu., holding the bridle in his mouth, sinister arm hanging down as useless, round his body a scarf, in bend, of the third. *Pl.* 118, *cr.* 14. 2. A sea-horse's (head, ar., finned, or, gorged with three bars, gu.) *Un Dieu, un roy, un cœur. Pl.* 68, *cr.* 15.
LAKE, a sea-horse's head and neck, couped, ar., in mouth an annulet, or. *Pl.* 58, *cr.* 15, (annulet, *pl.* 141.)
LAKE, Hants, a cannon, mounted, ppr. *Pl.* 111, *cr.* 3.
LAKE, Middx., Yorks., and Somers., a sea-horse's (head,) ar., finned, or, on neck three bars, gu. *Pl.* 58, *cr.* 15.
LAKE, Bucks., Herts., and Staffs., a cross formée, fitched, in a crescent, all within an annulet, or. *Pl.* 77, *cr.* 9, (cross and crescent, *pl.* 141.)
LAKE, Viscount and Baron, (Warwick-Lake,) a horse's head, (couped, ar., charged on neck with a bar-gemelle, gu.) *Pl.* 81, *cr.* 6.
LAKIN, and LAKING, Eng., a dexter arm, ppr., (vested, sa.,) in hand a palm-branch, vert. *Pl.* 23, *cr.* 7.
LAKINGTON, Devons., a pelican, in nest, vulning, ppr. *Pl.* 44, *cr.* 1.
LAKINLEECH, and LAKINLICH, Eng., a harp, or. *Pl.* 104, *cr.* 15.
LALANDE, a dove, (couped at legs, wings addorsed and expanded, ar., in beak three wheat-ears, or.) *Pl.* 108, *cr.* 8.
LALEMAN, Iri., a dexter arm, embowed, in hand a club, all ppr. *Pl.* 123, *cr.* 10.
LALOR, THOMAS, Esq., of Cregg, co. Tipperary, an arm, embowed, vested, gu., cuffed, vert, in hand, ppr., a short sword, also ppr. *Fortis et fidelis. Pl.* 120, *cr.* 1.
LALLY, a buck, passant, ppr. *Pl.* 68, *cr.* 2.
LALYNDE, Eng., a maiden's head, affrontée, couped at breast, ppr., attired, az. *Pl.* 74, *cr.* 5, (without coronet.)
LAMB, Sco., a paschal lamb, ppr. *Pl.* 48, *cr.* 13.
LAMB, Eng., a demi-lion, rampant, erminois, in dexter a mullet, vert. *Pl.* 89, *cr.* 10.
LAMB, same crest. *Per mare, per terras.*
LAMB, Sco., a holy lamb, with staff and flag, charged with a cross. *Pl.* 48, *cr.* 13.
LAMB, Eng., a hand holding a sword, in pale, enfiled with a savage's head, ppr., wreathed, ar. and gu. *Pl.* 97, *cr.* 3.

LAMB, a rhinoceros's head, couped, sa. *Pl.* 116, *cr.* 3.
LAMB, Baron Beauvale. *See* BEAUVALE.
LAMB, Eng., a lion, rampant. *Pl.* 67, *cr.* 5.
LAMB, on a mount, vert, a gate, on the top a paschal lamb, staff of banner entwined with laurel, all ppr. *Pl.* 101, *cr.* 9, (gate, *pl.* 73, *cr.* 4.)
LAMB, Kent and Suff., a demi-lion, gu., (collared, or,) in dexter a mullet, sa. *Pl.* 89, *cr.* 10.
LAMB, Wilts., (on a mount, vert,) a lamb, ar. *Pl.* 116, *cr.* 1, (without charge.)
LAMB, JOSEPH, Esq., of West Denton, Northumb., a paschal lamb, ppr. *Palma non sine pulvere. Pl.* 48, *cr.* 13.
LAMB, MONTOILEU, Bart., Berks., a lamb, passant, sa., charged on body with a bezant, thereon a trefoil, slipped, vert. *Deo et principe. Pl.* 116, *cr.* 1.
LAMBARD, Kent, a reindeer's head, erased, sa. *Deo, patriæ, tibi. Pl.* 2, *cr.* 13, (without collar.)
LAMBARD, Eng., a horse's head, (erased,) or, bridled, gu. *Pl.* 92, *cr.* 1.
LAMBARD, or LAMBARDE, a garb, in fess, ppr. *Pl.* 12, *cr.* 15.
LAMBART, Eng., a hand holding a glove. *Pl.* 42, *cr.* 15.
LAMBART, GUSTAVUS-WILLIAM, Esq., of Beau Parc, co. Meath, a centaur, ppr., drawing his bow, gu., arrow, or. *Ut quocunque paratus. Pl.* 70, *cr.* 13.
LAMBART, Earl of Cavan. *See* CAVAN.
LAMBE, Herts., a demi-lion, rampant, erminois, in dexter a mullet, vert. *Pl.* 89, *cr.* 10.
LAMBE, in lion's paw, (erased,) a palm-branch, vert. *Pl.* 70, *cr.* 9.
LAMBE, a demi-lion, rampant, erm., between paws, a mullet, ar. *Pl.* 126, *cr.* 12, (mullet, *pl.* 141.)
LAMBE, two (bears' paws, erased,) in saltier, ppr. *Pl.* 20, *cr.* 13.
LAMBERBY, on a ducal coronet, a lamb, sejant, ppr.
LAMBERT, Eng., a lion, rampant, ar. *Pl.* 67, *cr.* 5.
LAMBERT, Iri., a centaur, per pale, gu. and or, charged with a trefoil, vert, shooting an arrow from a bow, gold. *Pl.* 70, *cr.* 13, (trefoil, *pl.* 141.)
LAMBERT, Iri., (on a mount, vert,) a centaur, ppr., bow, gu., arrow, or. *Pl.* 70, *cr.* 13.
LAMBERT, a sphinx, couchant, ar., crined, or, in dexter a cinquefoil, of the first, stalked and leaved, vert. *Pl.* 116, *cr.* 5.
LAMBERT, Northumb., a sagittarius, passant, or, head of bow wreathed, az. *Ne mireris homines mirabiliores. Pl.* 70, *cr.* 13.
LAMBERT, two lobsters' claws, in pale, gu., in each a fish, or. *Pl.* 116, *cr.* 6.
LAMBERT, a reindeer's head, az., attired, ar., maned, or. *Pl.* 2, *cr.* 13, (without collar.)
LAMBERT, of Boyton House, Wilts., a demi-pegasus, wings expanded, erm. *Pl.* 91, *cr.* 2, (without coronet.)
LAMBERT, Lond. and Surr., on a mount, vert, a centaur, passant, regardant, the human parts, ppr., the other, erm., girt about loins by a garland of laurel, of the first, drawing a bow and arrow, gu. *Pl.* 29, *cr.* 13.
LAMBERT, Durh., a demi-lamb, rampant, supporting a shield, erminois.

LAMBERT, Kent, a reindeer's head, erased, sa. *Pl.* 2, *cr.* 13, (without collar.)
LAMBERT, Bucks., a lion's head, erased, ar., (gorged with a fess, chequy, or and az.) *Pl.* 81, *cr.* 4.
LAMBERT, Bucks. and Yorks., a sphinx, passant, gardant, or, face, ppr., under dexter a rose, gu., seeded and leaved, vert. *Pl.* 91, *cr.* 11, (rose, *pl.* 141.)
LAMBERT, Bart., Norf., out of a ducal coronet, or, three plumes, ar. *Sequitando si giunge. Pl.* 114, *cr.* 8.
LAMBERT, Eng., a talbot's head, ar. *Pl.* 123, *cr.* 15.
LAMBETH, a badger, or. *Pl.* 34, *cr.* 4.
LAMBFORD, or LAMFORD, in dexter hand, ppr., a scimitar, ar. *Pl.* 29, *cr.* 8.
LAMBORN, or LAMBORNE, a demi-lion, rampant, gu., supporting a ship's rudder, sa. *Pl.* 102, *cr.* 4.
LAMBORNE, Eng., out of a tower, ppr., a lion's head, or, collared, sa. *Pl.* 42, *cr.* 4, (head, *pl.* 7, *cr.* 10.)
LAMBSEY, or LAMESEY, a savage's head, ppr., wreathed, ar. and sa. *Pl.* 36, *cr.* 3.
LAMBTON, Earl of Durham. *See* DURHAM.
LAMBTON, Yorks. and Durh., a ram's head, (cabossed,) ar., attired, sa. *Pl.* 34, *cr.* 12.
LAMBTON, DAWSON, Durh., a torteau, charged with a ram's head, couped at neck, erm., with two branches of oak, or. *Pl.* 116, *cr.* 7, (branches, *pl.* 74, *cr.* 7.)
LAMFORD, Eng., in dexter hand, ppr., a scimitar, ar. *Pl.* 29, *cr.* 8.
LAMMIE, Sco., in hand a crosier, ppr. *Per varios casus.*
LAMOND, a dexter hand, couped, ppr. *Ne parcas, nec spernas. Pl.* 32, *cr.* 14.
LAMOND, Sco., in hand a dagger, in pale, ppr. *Ne parcas, nec spernas. Pl.* 23, *cr.* 15.
LAMOND, and LAMONT, Sco., a hand, couped at wrist, ppr. *Ne parcas, nec spernas. Pl.* 32, *cr.* 14.
LAMONT, in hand a baton, ppr. *Ne parcas, nec spernas. Pl.* 18, *cr.* 1.
LAMONT, ARCHIBALD-JAMES, Esq., of Lamont, Argyll, an open hand, couped, ppr. *Ne parcas, nec spernas. Pl.* 32, *cr.* 14.
LAMORLEY, on a naval coronet, or, a lion, rampant, gu. *Pl.* 67, *cr.* 5, (coronet, *pl.* 128, *fig.* 19.)
LAMPARD, Eng., a cinquefoil, az. *Pl.* 1, *cr.* 12.
LAMPEN, Cornw., a ram's head, (cabossed,) ar., attired, or. *Pl.* 34, *cr.* 12.
LAMPET, and LAMPETH, Eng., a Doric pillar, ar., entwined with a branch of laurel, vert, and surmounted by a flame, ppr. *Pl.* 14, *cr.* 15, (flame, *pl.* 16, *cr.* 12.)
LAMPLOW, of Little Reston, Yorks., and LAMPLUGH, of Lamplugh, Cumb., a goat's head, erased, ar., attired, or. *Pl.* 29, *cr.* 13.
LAMPLOWE, Yorks., Cumb. and Northumb., a goat's head, erased, ar. *Pl.* 29, *cr.* 13.
LAMPLUGH, Cumb., a goat's head, ar., attired and bearded, or. *Providentiâ Dei stabiliuntur familiæ. Pl.* 105, *cr.* 14.
LAMPLUGH, Cumb., a goat's head, erased, ar., attired, or. *Providentiâ Dei stabiliuntur familiæ. Pl.* 29, *cr.* 13.
LAMPREY, Iri., in hand a cross crosslet, fitched, (in pale,) ppr. *Pl.* 99, *cr.* 1.

L'AMY, JOHN-RAMSAY, Esq., of Dunkenny, Forfar, in dexter hand, erect, ppr., a crosier, or. *Per varios casus.* Pl. 17, cr. 12.

LANBURN, two lions' heads, addorsed, ppr., (collared, or.) Pl. 28, cr. 10.

LANCASHIRE, a demi-lion, rampant, ar., (gorged with a chaplet, vert, in paws an escutcheon, charged with two bendlets, or, the uppermost engrailed.) Pl. 47, cr. 4, (escutcheon, pl. 22, cr. 13.)

LANCASTER, Cumb. and Lanc., a lion's head, erased, ar., charged with a crescent, gu. Pl. 81, cr. 4, (crescent, pl. 141.)

LANCASTER, Cumb. and Lanc., a sea-horse, ppr. Pl. 103, cr. 3.

LANCASTER, Iri., in hand a sabre, ppr. Pl. 29, cr. 8.

LANCASTER, DE, a lion, couchant, or. Pl. 75, cr. 5, (without chapeau.)

LANCE, Eng., in hand, ppr., a covered cup, or. Pl. 35, cr. 9.

LANCELOT, Eng., an astrolabe. Pl. 26, cr. 2.

LANCEY, DE, Eng., a demi-leopard, gardant, supporting an anchor, ppr. Pl. 1, cr. 10.

LAND, Eng., a church and spire, environed with trees, ppr. Pl. 110, cr. 5.

LANDAL, LANDEL, and LANDELL, Sco., a dexter arm, embowed, in hand a laurel crown, ppr. Pl. 118, cr. 4.

LANDALE, Sco., a dexter arm, embowed, hand holding up two branches of laurel, in orle, ppr. *Pax aut defensio.* Pl. 118, cr. 4.

LANDEN, Eng., a dexter hand, apaumée, ppr. *Ero quod eram.* Pl. 32, cr. 14.

LANDER, Devons., an elephant's head, sa., armed and ducally crowned, or. Pl. 35, cr. 13, (crown, pl. 128, fig. 3.)

LANDER, Eng., a hand, issuing from a cloud, holding a sword, waved. Pl. 71, cr. 7.

LANDETH, a winged heart, ppr. Pl. 39, cr. 7.

LANDLE, Sco., a cock, crowing, ppr. Pl. 67, cr. 14.

LANDON, Eng., a demi-pegasus, (regardant,) ar., supporting a pennon, gu., tasselled, or. Pl. 32, cr. 1.

LANDOR, Staffs. and Warw., an arm, in pale, vested, bendy of six, or and gu., cuffed, ar., in hand, ppr., a fleur-de-lis, gold. Pl. 95, cr. 9, (bendy, *same plate,* cr. 7.)

LANDOR, WALTER-SAVAGE, Esq., of Ipsley Court, Warw., a dexter arm, gu., banded with two cottises, or, in hand a fleur-de-lis, ar. Pl. 95, cr. 9.

LANDSAY, or LANDSEY, in dexter, a hand, a sword, erect, supporting a pair of scales. Pl. 44, cr. 10, (hand, pl. 23, cr. 15.)

LANDWATH, a demi-pegasus, ar., guttée-de-poix. Pl. 91, cr. 2, (without gorging.)

LANE, Middx., a demi-griffin, ar. Pl. 18, cr. 6.

LANE, of Rosscommon, Iri., out of a ducal coronet, or, a demi-griffin, sa., winged, ar. Pl. 39, cr. 2.

LANE, a dexter arm, vested, ermines, turned up and indented, ar., in hand, ppr., a mullet, az. Pl. 62, cr. 13, (vesting, *same plate,* cr. 7.)

LANE, a bezant, charged with two griffins' heads, erased and addorsed, between two branches, one palm, the other laurel. Pl. 116, cr. 9.

LANE, out of the sea, a spear-head, on point a dolphin, naiant. Pl. 116, cr. 4.

LANE, Suff., a demi-griffin, segreant, gu., bezantée, between claws a bezant. Pl. 18, cr. 6, (bezant, pl. 141.)

LANE, Ess. and Staffs., a strawberry roan-horse, salient, couped at flanks, bridled, sa., bitted and garnished, or, supporting between feet a regal crown, ppr. *Gardez le roy.*

LANE, Bucks., Dors., Heref., Northamp., Somers., and Yorks., out of a crescent, or, two eagles' heads, addorsed, the dexter, gu., the sinister, az. Pl. 118, cr. 12.

LANESBOROUGH, Earl of and Viscount, Baron of Newton-Butler, (Brinsley-Butler,) Iri., a demi-cockatrice, couped, vert, wings elevated, ar., beaked, combed, wattled, and ducally gorged, or. *Liberté toute entière.* Pl. 106, cr. 15, (demi, pl. 18, cr. 6.)

LANFORD, and LANGFORD, an heraldic-tiger, passant, (tail cowered.) Pl. 7, cr. 5.

LANG, Iri., a hand, erect, (issuing from a cloud,) holding a broken spear. Pl. 66, cr. 4.

LANG, Eng., a savage's head, issuing, ppr. Pl. 19, cr. 1.

LANG, Sco., a tower, az., masoned, sa. *Une stay.* Pl. 12, cr. 5.

LANG, Iri., a hand holding a hautboy. Pl. 98, cr. 9.

LANG, three sprigs of oak, bearing acorns. Pl. 69, cr. 12.

LANG, Sco., a dove, in mouth an olive-branch, ppr. *Mercy is my desire.* Pl. 48, cr. 15.

LANG, and LANGAN, Iri., out of a mural coronet, or, a spear, ppr., between two palm-branches, in orle, vert. Pl. 97, cr. 8.

LANGDALE, Yorks., an etoile, ar. (Another, or.) Pl. 63, cr. 9.

LANGDALE, Surr., between two oak-branches, ppr., an etoile, ar. Pl. 103, cr. 14, (branches, pl. 74, cr. 7.)

LANGDALE, Baron, (Bickersteth,) a dexter arm, in armour, embowed, ppr., garnished, or, about the elbow a wreath of oak, vert, in hand a roll of paper, ppr. *Suum cuique.* Pl. 97, cr. 1, (roll, pl. 119, cr. 6.)

LANGDELL, a star, ar. Pl. 21, cr. 6.

LANGDON, Norf., (on a mount, vert,) a lynx, of the same, gorged with two bars, ar. Pl. 122, cr. 14.

LANGEFORD, or LANGFORD, Lond., a demi-shoveller, wings displayed, ar., charged with a crescent.

LANGFORD, Baron, (Langford-Rowley,) Iri., a wolf's head (erased,) sa., collared and langued, gu. *Bear and forbear.* Pl. 8, cr. 4.

LANGFORD, an heraldic-tiger, (statant.) Pl. 7, cr. 5.

LANGFORD, Beds., in a row of partridge-feathers, of different colours, three club-ales, or and ar.

LANGFORD, Derbs., Salop, and Notts., a tiger, passant, (cowered,) gu., maned and tufted, or. Pl. 67, cr. 15.

LANGFORD-NIBBS, a stag's head, cabossed, gu., (pierced in the scalp by an arrow,) or, feathered, ar. Pl. 124, cr. 14.

LANGHAM, Eng., a bear's head and neck, erased, sa., muzzled, or. *Nec sinit esse feros.* Pl. 71, cr. 6.

LANGHAM, out of a coronet, gu., a bear's paw, sa., holding a sword, ar., pommelled, or. Pl. 47, cr. 14, (coronet, *same plate,* cr. 5.)

LANGHAM, and LANGHOLME, Linc., a bear's head, erased, ar. Pl. 71, cr. 6.

LANGHAM, Northamp., Suss., and Lond., a bear's head, erased, sa., muzzled, or. *Pl.* 71, *cr.* 6.

LANGHOLME, Eng., a holy lamb, ppr., standard, gu. *In cruce salus*. *Pl.* 48, *cr.* 13.

LANGHORN, or LANGHORNE, Eng., a bugle-horn, sa., stringed, gu., between wings, ar. *Pl.* 48, *cr.* 12.

LANGLANDS, Sco., in the sea, ppr., an anchor, erect. *Spero*. *Pl.* 62, *cr.* 10.

LANGLEY, Beds., Heref., and Salop, out of a mural coronet, a plume of five ostrich-feathers, three, ar., and two, vert. *Pl.* 100, *cr.* 12, (coronet, *pl.* 125, *cr.* 11.)

LANGLEY, Yorks., Lanc., and Suff., a cock, ar., combed, legged, and wattled, gu. *Pl.* 67, *cr.* 14.

LANGLEY, Lond., Linc., and Salop, a cockatrice, sa., beaked, or, combed and wattled, gu. *Pl.* 63, *cr.* 15.

LANGLEY, Iri., a boar, passant, sa., bristled, hoofed, and tusked, or. *Pl.* 48, *cr.* 14.

LANGLEY, Glouc., in dexter gauntlet, in fess, a sword, in pale, all ppr., blade enfiled with a dragon's head, sa., couped at neck, gu. *Pl.* 96, *cr.* 11, (head *pl.* 107, *cr.* 10.)

LANGLEY, Salop, between two sprigs of laurel, vert, a pheon, or. *Pl.* 30, *cr.* 11, (laurel, *pl.* 79, *cr.* 14.)

LANGLEY, Yorks., out of a ducal coronet, five feathers, ar. *Pl.* 100, *cr.* 12.

LANGLOIS, a rock, ppr. *Pl.* 73, *cr.* 12.

LANGMEAD, Devons., between wings, a spur. *Pl.* 109, *cr.* 12.

LANGMORE, on a chapeau, a greyhound, statant, ppr. *Pl.* 104, *cr.* 1.

LANGRISH, or LANGRISHE, Iri., a dragon's head, gu., vomiting fire, ppr. *Pl*, 37, *cr.* 9.

LANGRISHE, Bart., Iri., a demi-lion, rampant, ppr. *Pl.* 67, *cr.* 10.

LANGSPEAR, a talbot's head, (in mouth a demi-hind, couped.) *Pl.* 123, *cr.* 15.

LANGSTON, or LANGSTONE, Eng., a lion, rampant, gu., supporting a pillar. *Pl.* 22, *cr.* 15, (pillar, *pl.* 33, *cr.* 1.)

LANGTHORNE, a beer-butt, sa., in the bung-hole (three) roses, gu., stalked and leaved, vert. *Pl.* 124, *cr.* 9.

LANGTON, Norf., an eagle and dragon, entwined, ppr.

LANGTON, Middx., out of a ducal coronet, gu., a demi-lion, rampant, or, in paws a battle-axe, ar. *Pl.* 120, *cr.* 14, (coronet, *same plate.*)

LANGTON, a greyhound's head, couped, collared, and (chained.) *Pl.* 43, *cr.* 11.

LANGTON, Eng., a woman's head, couped, ppr., vested, gu., on head a (cap,) or. *Pl.* 81, *cr.* 13.

LANGTON, Lanc., a man's head, in profile, ppr., hair flotant, or, on head a cap, sa., turned up, erminois, couped below shoulders, (in armour,) gu. *Pl.* 51, *cr.* 4.

LANGTON, Lond. and Linc., an eagle, or, and a wyvern, vert, interwoven, and erect on their tails.

LANGTREE, Lanc., an eagle, wings expanded, gu., beaked and legged, or. *Pl.* 126, *cr.* 7.

LANGWORTHY, Somers., a demi-stag, ppr. *Pl.* 55, *cr.* 9, (without rose.)

LANIS, out of a crescent, two eagles' heads, addorsed, ppr. *Pl.* 118, *cr.* 12.

LANKIN, two wings, addorsed, ar., one on each side of a chapeau, ppr., issuing from the rim. *Pl.* 6, *cr.* 12, (wings, *same plate.*)

LANNOY, or LANOY, Eng., a chevalier's head, in a helmet, plumed, all ppr. *Pl.* 33, *cr.* 14.

LANSDOWNE, Marquess and Earl of, Baron Wycombe, &c., G.B., Earl of Kerry, &c., Iri., (Petty-Fitzmaurice,) a centaur, drawing a bow and arrow, ppr., the part from waist, ar. *Pl.* 70, *cr.* 13. 2. A bee-hive, with bees, diversely volant, ppr. *Virtute, non verbis*. *Pl.* 81, *cr.* 14.

LANSFORD, Eng., a savage's head, couped, ppr. *Pl.* 81, *cr.* 15.

LANSLEY, a griffin's head, erased, ppr. *Pl.* 48, *cr.* 6.

LANT, Northamp., on a serpent, nowed, az., a dove, ar., on breast a mullet, of the first. *Prudentiá et simplicitate*. *Pl.* 75, *cr.* 11, (mullet, *pl.* 141.)

LANT, Devons., Northamp., and Staffs., a dove, ar., beaked and legged, gu., standing on a serpent, nowed, ppr. *Pl.* 75, *cr.* 11.

LANT, a swan's head and neck, couped, (bendy of six, ar. and sa., charged with a rose,) between two rose-branches, leaved, vert. *Pl.* 54, *cr.* 6, (branches, *pl.* 125, *cr.* 6.)

LANTE, a serpent, nowed, vert. *Pl.* 1, *cr.* 9.

LANY, Norf., a talbot's head, guttée. *Pl.* 123, *cr.* 15.

LANY, Lond., Leic., and Suff., a merman, ppr., tail, ar., fins and hair, or, (bound round head with two ribbons, ar. and az., in hand a hawk's bell, suspended from two strings, of the second and third.) *Pl.* 35, *cr.* 10.

LANYON, Cornw., a falcon, rising, wings extended, and belled. *Pl.* 105, *cr.* 4.

LANYON, Cornw., on a mount, vert, within a castle with four towers, ar., a falcon, volant, ppr. *Pl.* 90, *cr.* 2.

LAPINGTON, a pelican, in nest, ppr. *Innocue ac provide*. *Pl.* 44, *cr.* 1.

LAPP, Eng., in dexter hand a battle-axe, ppr. *Pl.* 73, *cr.* 7.

LAPP, a demi-mermaid, ppr., in dexter a (purse,) gu., in sinister a comb, or. *Pl.* 48, *cr.* 5.

LAPSLEY, and LAPSLIE, Sco., a long cross, gu. *Corona mea Christus*. *Pl.* 7, *cr.* 13.

LAPTHORNE, a lion's head, erased, or, collared, vair. *Pl.* 7, *cr.* 10.

LAPWORTH, Cambs., a stork, ppr., resting dexter on a fleur-de-lis, or. *Pl.* 61, *cr.* 10, (fleur-de-lis, *pl.* 141.)

LARAYNE, and LAREYN, out of a cloud, a hand holding a garland of laurel, ppr. *Pl.* 88, *cr.* 13.

LARDER, Devons., a woman's head, couped at shoulders, ppr., vested, gu., garnished, or, hair, gold. *Pl.* 74, *cr.* 5, (without coronet.)

LARDNER, Eng., on a chapeau, a bull, ppr. *Pl.* 66, *cr.* 11.

LARGE, Eng., a demi-savage, in dexter a sheaf of arrows, pointing with sinister to a (ducal) coronet, all ppr. *Pl.* 86, *cr.* 3.

LARK, or LARKE, a hand issuing from a cloud, in fess, lifting a garb, ppr. *Pl.* 43, *cr.* 4.

LARKAN, or LARKEN, Eng., a greyhound, sejant, az. *Pl.* 66, *cr.* 15.

LARKIN, and LARKINS, Cambs., Kent, and Heref., a lark, wings addorsed, in beak a columbine, all ppr.

LARKWORTHY, Devons., a demi-stag, ppr. *Perseverando. Pl.* 55, *cr.* 9, (without rose.)
LA ROCHE, Glouc., a crow, ppr. *Pl.* 23, *cr.* 8.
LARPENT, Lond., a unicorn's head, erased, ar., attired, or, charged on neck with a fleur-de-lis, az. *Pl.* 67, *cr.* 1, (fleur-de-lis, *pl.* 141.)
LARPENT, HOCHEPIED, Bart., Surr.: 1. A unicorn's head, couped, ar., attired, or, on neck a fleur-de-lis and four annulets, interlaced, az. *Pl.* 20, *cr.* 1, (annulets and fleur-de-lis, *pl.* 141.) 2. Two military helmets, craticulated, or, open with royal diadems, the one with a crescent, sa., the other with a right hand extended, ppr. *Optivo cognomine crescit.*
LARPING, a unicorn's head, ar., attired, or, charged on neck with a fleur-de-lis, az. *Pl.* 20, *cr.* 1, (fleur-de-lis, *pl.* 141.)
LARRA, an elm-tree, ppr. *Pl.* 18, *cr.* 10.
LASCELLES, or LASCELLS, Yorks., a bear's head, or, muzzled, gu. *Pl.* 2, *cr.* 9.
LASCELLES, Earl Harewood. *See* HAREWOOD.
LASCELLS, Notts. and Yorks., out of a ducal coronet, or, a griffin's head, vert. *Pl.* 54, *cr.* 14.
LASCELLS, a gem-ring, or. *Pl.* 35, *cr.* 3.
LASCELLS, or LASSELLS, Eng., a bear's head, couped, erminois, muzzled, gu. *Pl.* 2, *cr.* 9.
LASHMAR, Eng., a boar's head, erased and erect, sa. *Pl.* 21, *cr.* 7.
LASLETT-EMERSON, Worc.: 1. A demi-lion, rampant, holding a battle-axe. *Pl.* 101, *cr.* 14, (without charge.) 2. A bear's head, couped at neck. *Pl.* 2, *cr.* 9.
LASLEY, a griffin's head, erased, ppr. *Pl.* 48, *cr.* 6.
LASMAN, a squirrel, sejant, or, between paws a branch of laurel, vert. *Pl.* 2, *cr.* 4.
LASSELLS, a bear's head, erm., muzzled, or, collared, gu., ringed, of the second, on collar five bezants. *Pl.* 2, *cr.* 9, (bezants, *pl.* 141.)
LATCH, Leic. and Notts., a lion's head, or, gorged with a fess, wavy, az. *Pl.* 126, *cr.* 1.
LATEWARD, a demi-hawk, wings expanded, sa., (on head two horns, bent, or.) *Pl.* 103, *cr.* 6, (without coronet.)
LATHAM, Ess. and Lanc., an eagle, preying on a child, all ppr., the child in swaddling-clothes, gu., bound, ar., at the head of the child an oak-branch, of the second. *Pl.* 123, *cr.* 11.
LATHAM, Chesh. and Lond., an eagle, wings elevated, erminois, preying on a child, ppr., swaddled, ar. and az., (exposed on a rock, of the second.) *Pl.* 123, *cr.* 11.
LATHUM, (on a hank of cotton,) or, an eagle, regardant, gold, wings expanded. *Pl.* 87, *cr.* 5.
LATIMER, on a mount, vert, a hind, (sejant, ar., collared and chained, or, under a tree, ppr.) *Pl.* 75, *cr.* 6.
LATIMER, Eng., an Eastern crown, gu. *Pl.* 79, *cr.* 12.
LATIMER, a plume of feathers, or. *Pl.* 12, *cr.* 9.
LATON, out of a ducal coronet, or, a stork's head, ar. *Pl.* 32, *cr.* 5, (coronet, *pl.* 128, *fig.* 3.)
LA TOUCH, co. Dublin, a mullet of (five) points, pierced, or. *Pl.* 45, *cr.* 1.
LATOUCHE, or LA TOUCHE, Eng., in hand, in armour, couped, in fess, a scimitar, enfiled with a boar's head, couped. *Pl.* 85, *cr.* 12.

LATOUCHE, Iri., on a heart, gu., an eagle's claw, erased, ppr. *Pl.* 27, *cr.* 1.
LATOUCHE, a mullet of six points, pierced, or. *Pl.* 45, *cr.* 1.
LATOUCHE, Iri., an etoile (pierced,) or. *Pl.* 63, *cr.* 9.
LA TOUCHE, a bezant, charged with a mullet, gu. *Pl.* 7, *cr.* 6, (mullet, *pl.* 141.)
LATTA, Sco., an oak-tree, ppr. *Dum vivo, vireo. Pl.* 16, *cr.* 8.
LATTON, Berks., a cross-bow, or. *Pl.* 58, *cr.* 3, (without wings.)
LAUCHLAN, or LAWCHLAN, Sco., a swan. *Divina sibi canit. Pl.* 122, *cr.* 13.
LAUDER, a hand, couped at wrist, in fess, holding a sword, in pale, on point a leopard's face. *Pl.* 56, *cr.* 6, (face, *pl.* 66, *cr.* 14.)
LAUDER, Sco., on a rock, ppr., a solan goose, (sejant.) *Sub umbrâ alarum tuarum. Pl.* 94, *cr.* 3.
LAUDER, or LAWDER, Eng. and Sco., a tower a demi-griffin issuing from the top, *Strike alike. Pl.* 68, *cr.* 11.
LAUDER, Bart., Sco., a tower, and a sentinel looking from the top thereof, ppr. *Turris prudentia custos. Pl.* 12, *cr.* 5, (sentinel, *pl.* 58, *cr.* 2.)
LAUDERDALE, Earl of, Viscount Lauderdale and Maitland, &c., Sco., Baron Lauderdale, U.K., (Maitland,) a lion, sejant, affrontée, gu., ducally crowned, in dexter a sword, ppr., hilt and pommel, or, in sinister a fleur-de-lis, az. *Consilio et animis. Pl.* 120, *cr.* 2, (coronet, *same plate, cr.* 4.)
LAUGHARNE, Eng., out of a cloud, a hand, in pale, pointing with one finger to the (sun.) *Pl.* 77, *cr.* 6.
LAUGHER, Eng., a plough, ppr. *Pl.* 28, *cr.* 15.
LAUGHLIN, Iri., a talbot, sejant, ar., resting dexter on a shield, gu. *Pl.* 19, *cr.* 2.
LAUGTON, and LAUNGTON, Eng., a dexter arm, in armour, embowed, hand grasping a sword, all ppr. *Pl.* 2, *cr.* 8.
LAUNCE, Suff., in hand, in armour, ppr., in fess, a lance, or, headed, ar. *Pl.* 71, *cr.* 13, (lance, *pl.* 99, *cr.* 8.)
LAUNCE, Cornw., a demi-bull, erm., attired, or, pierced by a broken spear, sa., headed, ar., vulned and guttée-de-sang. *Pl.* 63, *cr.* 6, (spear, *pl.* 74, *cr.* 10.)
LAUNDER, Lanc., a demi-unicorn, sa., attired, unguled and crined, or, body charged with three mullets of six points, in bend, ar. *Pl.* 26, *cr.* 14, (mullet, *pl.* 21, *cr.* 6.)
LAUREL, out of an antique crown, a cubit arm, vested, in hand a bird and a garland of laurel. *Pl.* 44, *cr.* 13, (crown, *pl.* 79, *cr.* 12.)
LAURENCE, Iri., a griffin, sejant, wings addorsed, in dexter a garland of laurel, ppr. *Pl.* 56, *cr.* 10.
LAURENCE, a demi-turbot, tail erect, ar.
LAURENSON, Sco., a dexter arm, in armour, embowed, in hand a scimitar. *Justitia et veritas. Pl.* 81, *cr.* 11.
LAURIE, Eng., a hill, ppr. *Pl.* 62, *cr.* 11.
LAURIE, or LAWRIE, Sco., trunk of oak-tree, sprouting new branches, ppr. *Repullulat. Pl.* 92, *cr.* 8.
LAURIE, Bart., Sco., a garland of laurel, between two branches of the same, ppr. *Virtus semper viridis. Pl.* 79, *cr.* 14, (garland, *pl.* 128, *fig.* 16.)

LAURIE, Lond., an arm, in armour, embowed, ppr., garnished, or, in hand a wreath of laurel, vert. *Pl.* 68, *cr.* 1.

LAURIE, Sco., two branches of laurel, (in saltier,) ppr. *Virtus semper viridis. Pl.* 21, *cr.* 2.

LAURIN, on a chapeau, ppr., an eagle's head, az. *Pl.* 13, *cr.* 5.

LAURISTON, an arm, in armour, embowed, in hand a scimitar, all ppr. *Justitia et veritas. Pl.* 81, *cr.* 11.

LAUTOUR, Herts., an arm, in armour, embowed to (sinister,) ppr., garnished, or, supporting with gauntlet a shield, erminois, charged with a fess, embattled, cottised, gu. *Pl.* 98, *cr.* 5.

LAUTY, Sco., a dexter hand holding a spear, (erect,) ppr. *Pl.* 99, *cr.* 8.

LAUZON, Eng., a mermaid, with mirror and comb, all ppr. *Pl.* 48, *cr.* 5.

LA VACH, a bull's head, reversed, erm. *Pl.* 111, *cr.* 6.

LAVELIS, Cornw., a tower, triple-towered, or. *Pl.* 123, *cr.* 14.

LAVELL, a fox, current, ppr. *Pl.* 80, *cr.* 5.

LAVEN, of Poole, Sco., a buck's head, couped, or. *Pl.* 91, *cr.* 14.

LAVENDER, Lond. and Herts., a demi-horse, ar., gorged with a wreath of lavender.

LAVER, Eng., a talbot's head, erased, gu., ducally crowned, or. *Pl.* 25, *cr.* 10.

LAVERICK, or LAVERIKE, Eng., two lions' gambs, (erased,) sa., supporting a pillar, or. *Pl.* 77, *cr.* 4.

LAVERIN, Eng., a shepherd's flute, erect, ppr. *Pl.* 12, *cr.* 1.

LAVEROCK, Eng., two lions' gambs, (erased,) ppr., supporting a pillar, or. *Pl.* 77, *cr.* 4.

LAVERS, Eng., a hand holding a crosier, in bend sinister. *Pl.* 17, *cr.* 12.

LAVERYE, Eng., a savage's head, affrontée, ppr. *Pl.* 19, *cr.* 1.

LAVIE, Eng., out of a ducal coronet, or, a lion's paw holding a cross crosslet, fitched, az. *Pl.* 65, *cr.* 5.

LAVINGTON, Eng., a covered cup, ar. *Pl.* 75, *cr.* 13, (without swords.)

LAW, Baron Ellenborough. *See* ELLENBOROUGH.

LAW, Iri., in dexter hand a battle-axe, ppr. *Pl.* 73, *cr.* 7.

LAW, Sco., a cock, crowing. *Sat amico, si mihi felix. Pl.* 67, *cr.* 14.

LAW, Sco., a unicorn's head, ppr. *Nec obscura, nec ima. Pl.* 20, *cr.* 1.

LAW, Sco., a cock's head, erased, ppr. *Nec obscura, nec ima. Pl.* 92, *cr.* 3.

LAW, out of a tower, a demi-griffin, segreant. *Pl.* 68, *cr.* 11.

LAW, Middx., a wolf's head, gu., ducally gorged, or. *Pl.* 8, *cr.* 4, (gorging, *same plate.*)

LAW, Kent, a dove and olive-branch, all ppr. *Pl.* 48, *cr.* 15.

LAWARD, LAWARE, and LAWARRE, out of a ducal coronet, or, a griffin's head, az., beaked, gold. *Pl.* 54, *cr.* 14.

LAWARD, a demi-bird, sa., on head two small horns, or, wings expanded, the dexter, outside, gu., inside, ar., the sinister, outside, of the last, inside, of the third. *Pl.* 52, *cr.* 8.

LAWDER, Sco., a balance, ppr. *Mediocria firma. Pl.* 12, *cr.* 11.

LAWDER, Sco., trunk of old tree budding, ppr. *Repullulat. Pl.* 92, *cr.* 8.

LAWES, or LAWSE, Kent and Norf., on a ducal coronet, or, an ermine, passant, ppr. *Pl.* 9, *cr.* 5, (coronet, *pl.* 128, *fig.* 3.)

LAWFORD, a demi-lion, between paws a naval coronet. *Pl.* 126, *cr.* 12, (coronet, *pl.* 128, *fig.* 19.)

LAWFORD, Lond., a lion, rampant, ppr., ducally crowned, or, charged on shoulder with a mullet, ar. *Pl.* 98, *cr.* 1.

LAWFORD, Eng., an arrow, point downward, and a palm-branch, in saltier. *Pl.* 50, *cr.* 11.

LAWFUL, a cornucopia, or, flowers and fruit, ppr., and a trident, az., in saltier. *Pl.* 91, *cr.* 4, (trident, *pl.* 12, *cr.* 3.)

LAWFUL, a helmet, ar., plumed, or. *Pl.* 8, *cr.* 12.

LAWLER, Eng., on a (dexter) hand, couped, in fess, a falcon, rising, ppr. *Pl.* 83, *cr.* 13.

LAWLER, Iri., a bull's head, gu. *Pl.* 120, *cr.* 7.

LAWLESS, Sco., a boar's head, couped, az. *Pl.* 48, *cr.* 2.

LAWLESS, a demi-lion, rampant, ducally crowned. *Pl.* 61, *cr.* 4, (without branch.)

LAWLESS, Baron Cloncurry. *See* CLONCURRY.

LAWLEY, Salop, a wolf, passant, sa. *Pl.* 46, *cr.* 6.

LAWLEY, Bart., Salop, a wolf, passant, sa. *Auspice Christo. Pl.* 46, *cr.* 6.

LAWNDE, Eng., a hand, in armour, couped, holding a cross crosslet, fitched, gu. *Pl.* 51, *cr.* 1.

LAWRENCE, Glouc., a wolf's head, ppr., charged on neck with a crescent, or. *Pl.* 14, *cr.* 6, (crescent, *pl.* 141.)

LAWRENCE, Hants, on a chapeau, gu., turned up, erm., a talbot, sejant, gu. *Pl.* 102, *cr.* 9.

LAWRANCE, Glouc., a wolf's head, ar., on neck a cross crosslet, gu. *Pl.* 14, *cr.* 6, (cross, *pl.* 141.)

LAWRENCE, Eng., two laurel-branches, vert, forming a chaplet. *Pl.* 54, *cr.* 10.

LAWRENCE, Sco., an acorn, slipped and leaved, vert. *Pl.* 81, *cr.* 7.

LAWRENCE, Iri., a griffin, sejant, wings addorsed, in dexter a garland of laurel, ppr. *Pl.* 56, *cr.* 10.

LAWRENCE, Eng., a sea-lion, parted, per fess, ar. and ppr. *Que pensez. Pl.* 25, *cr.* 12.

LAWRENCE, Lond., two trunks of trees, raguly, in saltier, environed with a chaplet, vert. *Pl.* 60, *cr.* 12.

LAWRENCE, Suff., Lanc., Glouc., and Devons., a demi-turbot, ar., tail upward.

LAWRENCE, Suff., Lanc., Glouc., and Devons., a wolf's head, (couped,) ppr. *Pl.* 14, *cr.* 6.

LAWRENCE, Middx., Bucks., and Hunts., a demi-turbot, in pale, gu., tail upward.

LAWRENCE, Bucks. and Hunts., a stag's head, erased, sa., platée, attired, or, ducally gorged, ar. *Pl.* 55, *cr.* 2.

LAWRENCE, Glouc., a griffin's head, erased. *Pl.* 14, *cr.* 6.

LAWRENCE, Glouc., the lower part of a fish, in pale, couped, ppr.

LAWRENCE, Bart., Iri., out of an Eastern crown, or, a cubit arm, entwined by a wreath of laurel, in hand a dagger, all ppr. *Pl.* 93, *cr.* 1, (dagger, *pl.* 28, *cr.* 4.)

LAWRIE, Sco., trunk of oak, in fess, couped and raguly, ppr., ensigned with a cross pattée, fitched, ar., entwined with a laurel-branch, vert, fructed, gu. *Industriâ atque fortunâ. Pl.* 14, *cr.* 14, (cross, *pl.* 27, *cr.* 14; laurel, *pl.* 123, *cr.* 5.)

LAWRIE, Sco., a fox, current, ppr. *Ingenio innumerato habe.* Pl. 80, cr. 5.

LAWRIE, Eng., a monk, in dexter a crucifix, in sinister a rosary. Pl. 90, cr. 5.

LAWRIE, Sco., a dolphin, naiant, behind it a laurel-tree, fructed, ppr. *Industriâ atque fortunâ.* Pl. 48, cr. 9, (tree, pl. 18, cr. 10.)

LAWRIE, Lond. and Kent, trunk of laurel-tree, eradicated, sprouting fresh branches, ppr. Pl. 92, cr. 8.

LAWS, Eng., an elephant, statant, ppr. Pl. 56, cr. 14.

LAWS, Durh. and Sco., a cock, ppr. *Compositum jus fasque animi.* Pl. 67, cr. 14.

LAWSON, of Brayton, Cumb., out of clouds, ppr., two arms, embowed, vested, erm., supporting the sun, ppr. Pl. 107, cr. 8.

LAWSON, Bart., Cumb., two flexed arms, vested, ar., supporting the sun, ppr. *Quod honestum, utile.* Pl. 107, cr. 8.

LAWSON, Sco., a garb, ppr. *Dominus providebit.* Pl. 48, cr. 10.

LAWSON, Sco., a leopard's head, erased, ppr. *Surgo, lumen adest.* Pl. 94, cr. 10.

LAWSON, a demi-lion, rampant, between paws a mullet of six points. Pl. 126, cr. 12, (mullet, pl. 141.)

LAWSON, Staffs., an arm, in armour, embowed, ppr., garnished, or, in gauntlet a battle-axe, handle, gu., head, ar. Pl. 121, cr. 14.

LAWSON, on a chapeau, a martlet. Pl. 89, cr. 7.

LAWSON, a garb, or. Pl. 48, cr. 10.

LAWSON, Iri., an arm, from elbow, vested, gu., cuff, indented, or, in hand a holly-branch, ppr. Pl. 64, cr. 7, (branch, pl. 4, cr. 15.)

LAWSON, Northumb., two arms, embowed, couped at elbow, vested, erm., cuffed, ar., in hands, ppr., (a ring, or, gemmed, gu.,) within the ring the sun in splendour, or. Pl. 107, cr. 8, (without clouds.)

LAWSON, Durh., two arms, embowed, couped at elbow, vested, erm., cuffed, ar., in hands, ppr., (a ring, or, gemmed, ar.,) within the ring the sun in splendour, or. *Rise and shine.* Pl. 107, cr. 8, (without clouds.)

LAWSON, Yorks., a wolf's head, erased, ppr., collared, vert, charged on neck with three bezants. *Loyal secret.* Pl. 8, cr. 4, (bezant, pl. 141.)

LAWSON, Northumb. and Durh., out of clouds, ppr., two arms, embowed, vested, erm., supporting the sun, ppr. *Quod honestum, utile.* Pl. 107, cr. 8.

LAWSON, Northumb. and Durh., same crest. *Rise and shine.*

LAWSON, Northumb. and Durh., two arms, embowed, vested, erm., supporting the sun, ppr. *Quod honestum, utile.* Pl. 107, cr. 8.

LAWSON, Yorks., a hind's head, erased, ar., on neck three pellets, one and two, (collared, vert.) Pl. 6, cr. 1, (pellet, pl. 141.)

LAWSON, MANSFELDT DE CARDONNEL, Cramlington Hall, Northumb.: 1. For *Lawson*, two arms, embowed, vested, erm., supporting the sun, ppr. Pl. 107, cr. 8. 2. For *De Cardonnel*, a goldfinch, ppr., on breast a trefoil, vert. *Rise and shine.* Pl. 10, cr. 12, (trefoil, pl. 141.)

LAWSTON, Iri., a cubit arm, vested, gu., cuff, indented, or, in hand a holly-branch, ppr. Pl. 64, cr. 7, (branch, pl. 4, cr. 15.)

LAWTON, a wolf, passant. Pl. 46, cr. 6.

LAWTON, Chesh., a demi-wolf, salient, regardant, ar., vulned in breast, gu.

LAWTON, a demi-lion, ar., ducally crowned, or. Pl. 61, cr. 4, (without branch.)

LAX, Herts., (on a mount, vert,) a Catherine-wheel, or. Pl. 1, cr. 7.

LAXTON, Eng., out of a tower, ppr., a demi-griffin, or. Pl. 68, cr. 11.

LAY, Eng., an escallop, or, charged with (a saltier,) gu., all between wings, gold. Pl. 80, cr. 2.

LAYARD, Middx., out of a ducal coronet, gold, a mullet of six points, or. *Juvante Deo.* Pl. 83, cr. 3, (mullet, pl. 45, cr. 1.)

LAYER, Eng., a mullet of six points, gu. Pl. 45, cr. 1.

LAYER, Norw. and Norf., a unicorn's head, erased, ar. Pl. 67, cr. 1.

LAYFIELD, a bull's head, cabossed. Pl. 111, cr. 6.

LAYLAND, Eng., on a terrestrial globe, a ship, sailing, ppr. Pl. 41, cr. 12.

LAYMAN, Eng., a demi-bull, rampant, ppr. Pl. 63, cr. 6.

LAYTON, of Delmayne, Cumb., a lion's head, erased, ar., gorged with a collar, sa., charged with three bezants. Pl. 7, cr. 10.

LAYTON, Sco., a demi-lion, rampant. *In omnia paratus.* Pl. 67, cr. 10.

LAYTON, Linc. and Yorks., out of a mural coronet, two wings, expanded, ar., each charged with a cross crosslet, fitched, sa. Pl. 119, cr. 14, (without beacon; cross, pl. 141.)

LAYWORTH, Oxon., a (lapwing, ppr.,) his talon on a fleur-de-lis. Pl. 10, cr. 12, (fleur-de-lis, pl. 141.)

LAZARUS, Eng., in hand, ppr., a dragon's head, erased, vert. Pl. 29, cr. 4, (dragon, pl. 107, cr. 10.)

LEA, Eng., a stag's head, erased, or. Pl. 66, cr. 9.

LEA, Sco., a lion, rampant, or. Pl. 67, cr. 5. (Another, ar.)

LEA, Worc., a beaver, ppr., semée-de-lis, or, in mouth (a branch of willow,) ppr. Pl. 49, cr. 5.

LEA, a stag's head, erased, ar. Pl. 66, cr. 9.

LEACH, and LEACHE, out of a ducal coronet, or, a lion's gamb, holding a cross crosslet, fitched, sa. Pl. 65, cr. 5.

LEACH, a swan, wings expanded, ar., standing on a trumpet. Pl. 4, cr. 7.

LEACH, Cornw., in hand, couped at wrist, a snake. Pl. 91, cr. 6.

LEADBITTER, Durh., out of a mural coronet, gu., a demi-unicorn, erminois, erased, of the first, armed and crined, or. Pl. 26, cr. 14, (coronet, pl. 128, cr. 14.)

LEADER, co. Cork, an arm, embowed, vested, paly of six, vert and gu., in hand, ppr., a branch of leaves, of the second. Pl. 39, cr. 1, (leaves, pl. 43, cr. 6.)

LEADER, Eng., a demi-black, in dexter a arrow, and a quiver of arrows at his back. Pl. 80, cr. 9.

LEAHY, Iri., a demi-savage, over shoulder a club, ppr. Pl. 14, cr. 11.

LEAK, Eng., a hand holding up a heart, all ppr. Pl. 59, cr. 12.

LEAK, Middx. and Ess., a piece of ordnance, mounted on a (ship) gun-carriage, all ppr. Pl. 111, cr. 3.

LEAK, Lond., a cannon, mounted on a carriage, all ppr. *Pl.* 111, *cr.* 3.
LEAK, on each side of a garb, a bird pecking. *Pl.* 14, *cr.* 5, (without coronet.)
LEAKY, Iri., a horse-shoe, ppr. *Pl.* 52, *cr.* 4.
LEALE, LEALL, or LEALLE, out of a ducal coronet, a sceptre, entwined by a serpent, between wings, all ppr. *Pl.* 27, *cr.* 8.
LEAR, Eng., two hands issuing from clouds, grasping the trunk of an oak-tree, ppr. *Pl.* 126, *cr.* 4.
LEARMONT, and LEARMONTH, Sco., a rose, gu., stalked and leaved, vert. *Spero. Pl.* 105, *cr.* 7.
LEARMONTH, Sco., a dove and olive-branch, ppr. *Dum spiro, spero. Pl.* 48, *cr.* 15.
LEARY, Iri., in dexter-hand, ppr., an oak-branch, vert, fructed, or. *Pl.* 43, *cr.* 6, (oak, *pl.* 32, *cr.* 13.)
LEASH, Sco., a demi-lion, rampant, gu., in dexter a thistle, ppr., in sinister a fleur-de-lis, or. *Pl.* 45, *cr.* 15.
LEASK, Sco., a crescent, ar. *Virtute cresco. Pl.* 18, *cr.* 14.
LEATH, out of a mural coronet, a beacon inflamed, between wings. *Pl.* 119, *cr.* 14.
LEATHAM, a dexter arm, in armour, in hand a scimitar. *Maintien le droit. Pl.* 81, *cr.* 11.
LEATHAM, Yorks., on a nest, an eagle, wings elevated, or, the nest and wings, fretty, vert. *Pl.* 44, *cr.* 1.
LEATHER-SELLERS TRADE, Lond., a demi-buck, gu., attired and unguled, sa. *Deo honor et gloria. Pl.* 55, *cr.* 9, (without rose.)
LEATHES: 1. For *Leathes*, a demi-griffin, segreant, armed and langued. *Pl.* 18, *cr.* 6. 2. For *Mussenden*, a dove, in mouth an olive-branch, all ppr. *Pl.* 48, *cr.* 15.
LEATON, Durh.: 1. A lion, rampant, or. *Pl.* 67, *cr.* 5. 2. Out of a mural coronet, ppr., two eagles' wings, expanded, ar., on each a cross crosslet, fitched. *Dieu defend le droit. Pl.* 119, *cr.* 14, (without beacon; (cross, *pl.* 141.)
LEATT, Lond., on a mural coronet, or, a fire-beacon, sa., with fire, ppr., between wings, az. *Pl.* 119, *cr.* 14.
LEAVER, Eng., an arm, embowed, in hand a club, ppr. *Pl.* 123, *cr.* 10.
LE BAREU, Eng., a mullet, ppr. *Pl.* 41, *cr.* 1.
LE BLANC, Lond. and Middx.; and LE BLANC, Rouen, in Normandy, an eagle, displayed, sa., ducally crowned, or, charged on breast with a cinquefoil, gold. *Sans tache. Pl.* 85, *cr.* 11.
LE BON, Eng., out of a ducal coronet, or, a plume of ostrich-feathers, ppr. *Confido. Pl.* 44, *cr.* 12.
LECAUFIELD, Baron, Yorks., a lion's head, erased, or, within a fetterlock, of the same, the arch, compony, counter-compony, gold and az. *Au bon droit. Pl.* 90, *cr.* 14.
LECAWELL, a unicorn, ar., horned, gu. *Pl.* 37, *cr.* 7.
LECHE, Eng., two lions' gambs, erased, sa., holding up a crescent, ar. *Pl.* 45, *cr.* 8.
LECHE, of Carden Park, Chesh.: 1. For *Leche*, a cubit arm, ppr., hand grasping a snake, vert. *Pl.* 91, *cr.* 6. 2. For *Carwarden*, a wolf's head, erased, sa., pierced fesswise, sinister, by an arrow, wavy. *Alla corona fidissimo. Pl.* 40, *cr.* 12.

LECHE, Somers., Derbs., and Chesh., out of a ducal coronet, or, an arm, in pale, ppr., hand grasping a snake, entwined round arm, vert. *Pl.* 91, *cr.* 6, (coronet, *pl.* 128, *fig.* 3.)
LECHFORD, Surr., a leopard's head, per pale, ar. and sa., between wings, counterchanged. *Pl.* 31, *cr.* 7, (wings, *same plate, cr.* 11.)
LECHINGHAM, a ram's head, (cabossed,) or. *Pl.* 34, *cr.* 12.
LECHMERE, of Hanley, a pelican, ppr. *Pl.* 109, *cr.* 15.
LECHMERE, Bart., Worc., a pelican, az., vulning, gu. *Ducit amor patriæ. Pl.* 109, *cr.* 15.
LECHMERE, Middx. and Heref., a pelican, az., vulning, gu. *Pl.* 109, *cr.* 15.
LECHMERE, THOMAS, Esq., of Fownhope Court, Heref., a pelican, az., vulning, ppr. *Ducit amor patriæ.*
LECKIE, Sco., an anchor, in pale, the rope waved round, both ppr. *Deus gubernat navem. Pl.* 42, *cr.* 12.
LECKIE, Sco., a ship, in distress, ppr., in the sea, vert. *At spes non fracta. Pl.* 21, *cr.* 11.
LECKIE, or LECKY, Eng., an arm, embowed, in hand a club, ppr. *Pl.* 123, *cr.* 10.
LECKIE, a dexter and sinister arm, couped at wrist, issuing, holding between them a two-handed sword, all ppr. *Pl.* 59, *cr.* 10.
LECKY, Iri., a fawn, trippant, ppr. *Pl.* 20, *cr.* 14.
LECTON, Eng., a savage's head, couped at shoulders, affrontée, ppr., wreathed round temples, gu. and or. *Pl.* 97, *cr.* 2.
LEDER, Eng., in dexter hand a sheaf of arrows, ppr. *Pl.* 56, *cr.* 4.
LEDER, a cubit arm, vested, bendy sinister of six, gu. and vert, in hand, ppr., a bunch of leaves, of the second. *Pl.* 95, *cr.* 7, (leaves, *pl.* 43, *cr.* 6.)
LE DESPENCER, Eng., a griffin's head, ppr. *Pl.* 38, *cr.* 3.
LE DESPENCER, Baron, (Stapleton,) out of a ducal coronet, or, a Saracen's head, affrontée, ppr., wreathed, ar. and sa. *Pro magna charta* —and—*Ne vile fano. Pl.* 97, *cr.* 2, (coronet, *same plate, cr.* 13.)
LEDGCOMB, Eng., an elephant's head, erased. *Pl.* 68, *cr.* 4.
LEDGER, Eng., an escarbuncle, az. *Pl.* 51, *cr.* 10.
LEDIARD, Glouc., a wolf's head, erased, per pale, pean and gu. *Pl.* 14, *cr.* 6.
LEDLIE, a ram's head, couped, ar., attired, or, behind it a crosier, in bend, sinister, ppr. *Pl.* 34, *cr.* 12, (crosier, *pl.* 4, *cr.* 8.)
LEDSAM, Eng., a bull's head, erased, or. *Pl.* 19, *cr.* 3.
LEDSAM, JOSEPH-FREDERICK, Esq., of Chad Hill, Warw.; and Northfield, Worc., a Cornish chough. *Fac et spera. Pl.* 100, *cr.* 13.
LEE, of Fitchworth, Suss., a stag's head, erased, or. *Pl.* 66, *cr.* 9.
LEE, Viscount Dillon. *See* DILLON.
LEE, Kent and Notts., a demi-moor, ppr., vested, gu., rimmed round collar with two bars, or, tied round waist with a ribbon, ar., wreathed about head, ar. and gu., in dexter a gem-ring, of the third. *Pl.* 9, *cr.* 11.
LEE, Middx., a cock, ar., combed and wattled, or, beaked and legged, gu. *Pl.* 67, *cr.* 14.
LEE, Lond., a dexter hand, in fess, holding a sword, in pale, ppr. *Forte non ignare. Pl.* 56, *cr.* 6, (without garland.)

LEE, THOMAS, Esq., Liverpool, a cubit arm, erect, vested, gu., cuffed, ar., in hand a spear, pointed downwards. *Pl.* 126 c, *cr.* 1.

LEE, Iri., out of a cloud, a hand, erect, holding a sealed letter. *Pl.* 33, *cr.* 8.

LEE, of Ebford, Devons., a bear, sejant, ppr., muzzled and chained, or. *Pl.* 1, *cr.* 1.

LEE, out of a ducal coronet, or, an arm, in armour, embowed, in hand a dart, ppr. *Pl.* 96, *cr.* 6, (coronet, *same plate, cr.* 7.)

LEE, on a ducal coronet, a leopard's face. *Pl.* 66, *cr.* 14, (coronet, *same plate.*)

LEE, out of a ducal coronet, a ram's head, in mouth a branch. *Pl.* 124, *cr.* 8, (coronet, *pl.* 128, *fig.* 3.)

LEE, a falcon, or, wings close, gu. *Pl.* 67, *cr.* 3.

LEE, an eagle, ppr., preying on an (eagle's leg, in fess.) *Pl.* 61, *cr.* 7.

LEE, Lond., a talbot's head, ar., collared, az., to the collar a ring and line, nowed, of the last. *Pl.* 2, *cr.* 15.

LEE, Salop, on a staff, raguly, a squirrel cracking a nut, from the dexter end of the staff, an oak-branch, bearing acorns, all ppr.

LEE, Herts., a dexter arm, in armour, embowed, in hand a sword, ar., hilt and pommel, or, from the blade flames of fire, issuing, ppr. *Pl.* 2, *cr.* 8, (sword, *pl.* 58, *cr.* 11.)

LEE, Lond., a bear, statant, ppr., muzzled, gu., collared and chained, ar., charged on shoulder with a bezant. *Pl.* 61, *cr.* 5, (bezant, *pl.* 141.)

LEE, Durh., an antelope's head, erased, ar., pellettée, maned, tufted, and attired, sa., in mouth a white lily, slipped, ppr. *Pl.* 24, *cr.* 7, (lily, *pl.* 81, *cr.* 9.).

LEE, Somers., a leopard, passant, ppr., (supporting a shield, of the arms, viz., per fess, az. and gu., on a fess, erm., between four cottises, ar., three leopards' faces, sa.) *Pl.* 86, *cr.* 2.

LEE, a leopard, passant, bezantée. *Pl.* 89, *cr.* 2.

LEE, Ess. and Leic., an arm, embowed, vested, in hand, ppr., a sword, in pale, of the second, hilt, or, on the blade a snake, entwined, vert. *Pl.* 116, *cr.* 11, (vesting, *pl.* 39, *cr.* 1.)

LEE, Hants, (on a mount, vert,) a bear, passant, ppr., muzzled and chained, ar. *Pl.* 61, *cr.* 5.

LEE, Cornw. and Wilts., a lion, sejant, or. *Pl.* 126, *cr.* 15.

LEE, on a column, enfiled with a ducal coronet, an eagle, ppr., preying on a bird's leg, erased, az.

LEE, Chesh., out of a ducal coronet, or, a leopard's head, sa. *Pl.* 36, *cr.* 15.

LEECH, or LEECHE, Eng., on a glove, a hawk, ppr. *Pl.* 1, *cr.* 13.

LEECHMAN, and LEESHMAN, Sco., a pelican, ppr. *Industriæ munus.* *Pl.* 109, *cr.* 15.

LEEDS, Eng., a bomb-shell, sa., fired, ppr. *Pl.* 70, *cr.* 12.

LEEDS, Duke of, Marquess of Carmarthen, Earl of Danby, &c., Eng., Viscount Dumblaine, Sco., (Osborne,) an heraldic-tiger, passant, or, maned and tufted, sa. *Pax in bello. Pl.* 7, *cr.* 5.

LEEDS, or LEEDES, Middx., Camb., Linc., and Yorks., on a staff, raguly, vert, a cockatrice, wings addorsed, or, combed and wattled, gu. *Pl.* 63, *cr.* 15.

LEEDS, Bart., Camb., on a staff, raguly, in fess, vert, a cock, gu., wings expanded, combed, wattled, beaked, and legged, ppr., debruised, of the second, by a bendlet, wavy, sinister, erm. *Vigilate.*

LEEDS, on a chapeau, a cock, statant, wings elevated. *Pl.* 104, *cr.* 3, (cock, *pl.* 76, *cr.* 7.)

LEEDS, Town of, an owl. *Pl.* 27, *cr.* 9.

LEEK, Eng., a demi-lion, gardant, in dexter a fleur-de-lis. *Pl.* 91, *cr.* 13.

LEEKE, Salop, a leg, couped at thigh, charged with two fleurs-de-lis. *Pl.* 38, *cr.* 14, (fleur-de-lis, *pl.* 141.)

LEEKE, Notts., a peacock's tail, erect, the plume displayed, ppr., supported by two eagles, with wings expanded, ar.

LEEKE, a leg, couped at thigh, and flexed at knee, (wounded above knee, and dropping blood.) *Pl.* 38, *cr.* 14.

LEEKE, Middx., a leg, couped at thigh, ar., (gartered below knee, az.) *Pl.* 38, *cr.* 14.

LEEKS, a tree, ppr. *Pl.* 16, *cr.* 8.

LEEKY, Iri., in dexter hand a dagger, ppr. *Pl.* 23, *cr.* 15.

LEES, Bart., Eng., in hand a crescent. *Pl.* 38, *cr.* 7.

LEES, Eng., a serpent, erect, tail nowed, in mouth a garland of laurel, vert. *Pl.* 104, *cr.* 9.

LEES, Bart., Iri., a cubit arm, erect, ppr., in hand a crescent, or. *Exegi. Pl.* 38, *cr.* 7.

LEESON, Earl of Miltown. *See* MILTOWN.

LEESON, Eng., on a ducal coronet, three arrows, points downward, wreathed about with a serpent, ppr. *Pl.* 86, *cr.* 12.

LEESON, Eng., on a chapeau, gu., turned up, or, a phœnix in flames, ppr. *Pl.* 83, *cr.* 12.

LEET, or LETE, Cambs., Hunts., and Suff., on a ducal coronet, an antique lamp, or, fire, ppr. *Pl.* 40, *cr.* 7, (coronet, *pl.* 128, *fig.* 3.)

LEETE, Eng., a demi-bull, gu., gorged with a chaplet of laurel, vert. *Pl.* 73, *cr.* 8.

LEETH, a demi-griffin, segreant, gu., winged, az., on body two fleurs-de-lis, or. *Pl.* 18, *cr.* 6, (fleur-de-lis, *pl.* 141.)

LEEVES, of Fortington, Suss., on a mount, vert, a swan, ar., wings elevated, ducally crowned and gorged, or, a chain reflexed over back, gold, charged on breast with three pellets, two and one, beaked and membered, sa. *Pl.* 111, *cr.* 10.

LEFEVER, or LEFEVRE, Eng., trunk of tree, couped and eradicated, in fess, between branches a fleur-de-lis. *Pl.* 14, *cr.* 14.

LEFEVRE, Middx., Hants, and Hunts., six arrows interlaced, in saltier, ppr., points downward, fretting an annulet, or. *Pl.* 101, *cr.* 13, (annulet, *pl.* 141.)

LEFEVRE, Middx., a trefoil, or. *Pl.* 4, *cr.* 10, (without wings.)

LEFEVRE, Hants, a lion, couchant, (tail extended,) or. *Pl.* 75, *cr.* 5, (without chapeau.)

LE FOREST, a unicorn, sejant, ar., armed, crined, and tufted, or. *Pl.* 110, *cr.* 15, (without tree.)

LEFRAY, a demi-wyvern, gu. *Pl.* 116, *cr.* 15.

LEFROY, Eng., a greyhound's head, erased, ar. *Pl.* 89, *cr.* 2.

LEG, Eng., a fountain of (three) raisings, playing, ppr. *Pl.* 49, *cr.* 3.

LEG, or LEGG, Eng., a garden fountain, playing, ppr. *Pl.* 49, *cr.* 8.

LEGARD, Bart., Yorks., a greyhound, or, (collared, sa., ringed and studded, ar.) *Per crucem ad stellas. Pl.* 104, *cr.* 1, (without chapeau.)

LEGARD, Leic. and Yorks., a greyhound, or, collared, gu., charged with three bezants. *Ib.*

LEGAT, or LEGGATT, Sco., a cherub's head, ppr. *Jesus Hominum Salvator.* Pl. 126, cr. 10.
LEGAT, Kent, Ess., and Norf., two lions' gambs, in pale, gu., supporting a mitre, or. Pl. 78, cr. 13, (mitre, pl. 49, cr. 15.)
LEGATT, a lion, sejant, ar. Pl. 126, cr. 15.
LEGER, Eng., a pheon, with part of shaft. Pl. 27, cr. 12.
LEGETT, two lions' paws, supporting the regal crown, all ppr. Pl. 78, cr. 13, (crown, pl. 127, fig. 2.)
LEGGAT, or LEGGATT, Eng., an arm, from elbow, vested, counter-compony, gu. and or, in hand a mill-rind. Pl. 34, cr. 3.
LEGGE, out of a ducal coronet, or, a plume of five ostrich-feathers, three ar., two az. *En parole je vis.* Pl. 100, cr. 12, (without charge.)
LEGGE, Earl of Dartmouth. *See* DARTMOUTH.
LEGGE, Kent and Suss., out of a ducal coronet, or, a plume of five ostrich-feathers, three ar., and two az. *Gaudet tentamine virtus.* Pl. 100, cr. 12, (without charge.)
LEGGE, Cambs., a unicorn's head, erased, ar., crined, armed, and ducally gorged, or. Pl. 67, cr. 1, (coronet, *same plate,* cr. 7.)
LEGGE, Kent, on a triple-tower, a man's leg, couped at thigh, all ppr. Pl. 123, cr. 14, (leg, pl. 38, cr. 14.)
LEGGET, Sco., a mermaid, in dexter a sword, all ppr. Pl. 88, cr. 12.
LEGH, Chesh., a bear, passant, chained, or. Pl. 61, cr. 5.
LEGH, Chesh., a cubit arm, in pale, vested, paly of six, or and sa., cuffed, ar., in hand, ppr., top of a broken tilting-spear, of the third, point downward. Pl. 106, cr. 2, (spear, pl. 66, cr. 4.)
LEGH, Somers. and Devons., a demi-hound, sa., holding a stag's head, ar., attired, or. Pl. 48, cr. 3, (head, pl. 66, cr. 9.)
LEGH, an arm, in armour, embowed, in hand a sword, with a serpent entwined, all ppr. Pl. 116, cr. 11, (armour, pl. 2, cr. 8.)
LEGH, of Norbury Booths Hall, Chesh., an arm, embowed, couped at shoulder, vested, gu., in hand, a sword, erect, ppr., a snake twisted round the same, ar. *Prudens, fidelis et audax.* Pl. 116, cr. 11, (vested, pl. 39, cr. 1.)
LEGH, a cock, gu., head like a ram, ar., attired, or.
LEGH, Chesh., a demi-lion, rampant, gu., collared, or. Pl. 18, cr. 13.
LEGH, GEORGE-CORNWALL, Esq., of High Legh, Chester, a demi-lion, rampant, gu., langued, az., collared, or. *Pour Dieu, pour terre.* Pl. 18, cr. 13.
LEGH, Chesh., out of a ducal coronet, or, a ram's head, ar., attired, gold, in mouth a laurel-sprig, ppr. Pl. 124, cr. 8, (coronet, pl. 128, fig. 3.)
LEGH, Chesh., a unicorn's head, couped, ar., armed and crined, or, charged on neck with a cross patonce, gu. Pl. 20, cr. 1, (cross, pl. 141.)
LEGHAM, and LEIGHAM, Eng., an arm, couped at shoulder, part above elbow in fess, in hand, erect, a bombshell, fired, ppr. Pl. 2, cr. 6, (arm, pl. 62, cr. 7.)
LEGHTON, Eng., a palm-tree, vert. *Per adversa virtus.* Pl. 18, cr. 12.
LE GRICE, Cornw., a boar, passant, sa., (collared, or.) Pl. 48, cr. 14.

LEGROSSE, an arm, embowed, ppr., vested, gu., in hand a sword by the blade, point downward, az., hilted, or. Pl. 65, cr. 8, (vesting, pl. 39, cr. 4.)
LEGRYLE, Norf., a boar, passant, sa. Pl. 48, cr. 14.
LEGUARD, a greyhound, statant, or, (collared and ringed, gu.) Pl. 104, cr. 1, (without chapeau.)
LEHOOP, Eng., a rose, ppr. Pl. 20, cr. 2.
LE HUNT, Linc. and Derbs., on a hill, vert, a goat, sa., collared, horns and hoofs, ar. Pl. 11, cr. 14.
LE HUNT, BAINBRIGGE: 1. For *Le Hunt*, between wings, a leopard's face. Pl. 31, cr. 7, (wings, *same plate.*) 2. For *Bainbrigge*, on a mount, vert, a goat, sa., horned and hoofed, ar., collared. Pl. 11, cr. 14.
LE HUNT, Iri., a demi-chevalier, brandishing a sword, ppr. Pl. 23, cr. 4.
LE HUNT, Eng., out of a baron's coronet, or, pearls, ar., a dexter hand holding a cutlass, all ppr. Pl. 103, cr. 2, (coronet, pl. 127, fig. 11.)
LE HUNTE, GEORGE, Esq., of Artramont, co. Wexford, a lion, sejant. *Parcere prostratis.* Pl. 126, cr. 15.
LE HUNTE, co. Wexford, a lion, sejant. Pl. 126, cr. 15.
LEICESTER, a swan's head and neck, ar. Pl. 30, cr. 10, (without gorging.)
LEICESTER, Salop, a swan's head and neck, (erased,) ar., guttée-de-sang. *Ib.*
LEICESTER, Town of, a wyvern, wings expanded, sans legs, ar., strewed with wounds, gu. Pl. 104, cr. 11, (without coronet.)
LEICESTER, Chesh., a stag's head, per pale, or and gu., attired, of the second, in mouth an oak-branch, vert, fructed, gold. Pl. 100, cr. 8.
LEICESTER, GEORGE, Baron De Tabley, of Tabley House, Chesh.: 1. For *Leicester*, a swan's head and neck, couped, ar., guttée-de-sang. Pl. 30, cr. 10, (without gorging.) 2. For *Byrne*, a mermaid, ppr. *Pro rege et patrid.* Pl. 48, cr. 5.
LEICESTER, Earl of, Viscount Coke, (Coke,) on a chapeau, az., turned up, erm., an ostrich, ar., in mouth a horse-shoe, or. *Prudens qui patiens.* Pl. 16, cr. 2, (chapeau, pl. 127, fig. 13.)
LEICH, out of a ducal coronet, a cubit arm, erect, hand grasping an adder, entwined round arm. Pl. 91, cr. 6, (coronet, pl. 128, fig. 3.)
LEIDS, Eng., an eagle's head, gu., between wings, or. Pl. 81, cr. 10.
LEIGH, a unicorn's head, or. *Tout vient de Dieu.* Pl. 20, cr. 1.
LEIGH, Staffs. and Salop, a unicorn's head, Pl. 20, cr. 1.
LEIGH, Staffs., a unicorn's head, erased, sa., armed, or, crined and collared, ar. Pl. 73, cr. 1.
LEIGH, Glouc. and Warw., a unicorn's head, erased, ar., armed and crined, or. Pl. 67, cr. 1.
LEIGH, Surr., a cockatrice, az., combed and wattled, gu. Pl. 63, cr. 15.
LEIGH, Chesh., a unicorn's head, ar., couped, gu., crined and armed, or. Pl. 20, cr. 1.
LEIGH, a lion, rampant. Pl. 67, cr. 10.

LEIGH, Derbs., a unicorn's head, ar., crined, or, armed gobony, gu. and or. *Pl.* 20, *cr.* 1.

LEIGH, Newport, Isle of Wight, and Hants, a hind, passant, ar. *Pl.* 20, *cr.* 14.

LEIGH, of West Hall, Chesh. : 1. A demi-lion, rampant, gardant, or, holding a banner, az., staff, ppr., headed, ar., (charged in chief with an escutcheon, or, bearing three coats of arms.) *Pl.* 35, *cr.* 4, (banner, *pl.* 99, *cr.* 5.) 2. A lion, rampant, gu., bearing a banner, adorned with scroll-work, or and ar. *Force avec vertu.* *Pl.* 99, *cr.* 2.

LEIGH, a demi-lion, rampant, between paws a lozenge. *Pl.* 126, *cr.* 12, (lozenge, *pl.* 141.)

LEIGH, ROBERT, Esq., of Taunton, a demi-lion, rampant, armed and langued, gu. *Legibus antiquis.* *Pl.* 67, *cr.* 10.

LEIGH, Eng., a unicorn's head, erased, sa., collared, ar., rimmed and studded, gu., armed and tufted, or. *Pl.* 73, *cr.* 1.

LEIGH, Belmont, Chester, a lozenge, gu., charged with a unicorn's head, couped, ar., crined, or. *Pl.* 20, *cr.* 1, (lozenge, *pl.* 141.)

LEIGH, BARDON, Somers., a demi-lion, rampant, ar., armed and langued, gu. *Pl.* 67, *cr.* 10.

LEIGH, Chesh., out of a ducal coronet, or, a ram's head, ar., attired, gold, in mouth a sprig of laurel, vert. *Pl.* 124, *cr.* 8, (coronet, *pl.* 128, *fig.* 3.)

LEIGH, Chesh. and Iri., a demi-lion, or, holding a sceptre, gold. *Pl.* 39, *cr.* 14, (sceptre, *pl.* 39, *cr.* 14.)

LEIGH, a greyhound's head, ar., between two roses, gu., slipped and leaved, ppr. *Pl.* 84, *cr.* 13.

LEIGH, a nag's head, erased. *Pl.* 81, *cr.* 6.

LEIGH, Lanc., a dexter arm, embowed, vested, gu., cuffed, ar., in hand, ppr., a sword, of the second, hilt and pommel, or, environed with a snake, vert. *Pl.* 116, *cr.* 11, (arm, *pl.* 39, *cr.* 1.)

LEIGH, Surr., (on a mount, vert,) a lion, couchant, gardant, ar., charged on breast with an annulet, sa. *Pl.* 101, *cr.* 8, (annulet, *pl.* 141.)

LEIGH, Somers., a demi-greyhound, sa., holding a stag's head, cabossed, ar. *Pl.* 48, *cr.* 3, (head, *pl.* 36, *cr.* 1.)

LEIGH, Berks., Chesh., and Derbs., an arm, in armour, couped at shoulder, or, girt with a scarf, az., hand grasping a halberd, ppr. *Pl.* 28, *cr.* 2, (halberd, *pl.* 121, *cr.* 14.)

LEIGH, Chesh. and Salop, a cubit arm, erect, vested, paly of six, or and sa., cuffed, ar., in hand, ppr., a broken tilting-spear, of the third. *Pl.* 106, *cr.* 2, (spear, *pl.* 66, *cr.* 4.)

LEIGH, Chesh., a demi-lion, rampant, gu. *Pl.* 67, *cr.* 10.

LEIGH, Bart., Lanc., a demi-lion, rampant, gu. *Prodesse quam conspici.* *Pl.* 67, *cr.* 10.

LEIGH, Bart., of South Carolina, a cubit arm, erect, (vested, hand grasping a tilting-spear, in fess, all ppr.) *Pl.* 99, *cr.* 8.

LEIGH-HANBURY, CAPEL, Esq., of Pontypool Park, Monmouth: 1. For *Leigh*, a unicorn's head, erased, ar., armed and crined, or. *Pl.* 67, *cr.* 1. 2. For *Hanbury*, out of a mural coronet, sa., a demi-lion, rampant, or, in paws a battle-axe, of the first, helved, gold. *Pl.* 120, *cr.* 14.

LEIGHAM, Eng., within a fetterlock, az., a human heart, gu. *Pl.* 59, *cr.* 6.

LEIGHAM, Eng., within a fetterlock, az., a human heart, gu. *Pl.* 59, *cr.* 6.

LEIGHT, Hants, a wolf, passant, gu. *Pl.* 46, *cr.* 6.

LEIGHTON, of Shrewsbury, a wyvern, wings expanded, sa. *Dread shame.* *Pl.* 63, *cr.* 13.

LEIGHTON, the Rev. FRANCIS-KNYVETT, of Bausley, Montgomery, same crest and motto.

LEIGHTON, Sco., a lion's head, erased, gu. *Light on*—and—*Dread shame.* *Pl.* 81, *cr.* 4.

LEIGHTON, Bart., Salop, a wyvern, wings expanded, sa. *Dread shame.* *Pl.* 63, *cr.* 13.

LEIGHWOOD, a banyan-tree, ppr. *Pl.* 18, *cr.* 12.

LEINSTER, Duke of, Marquess and Earl of Kildare, &c., Iri., Viscount Leinster, G.B., (Fitzgerald,) a monkey, statant, ppr., environed about middle with a plain collar and chained, or. *Non immemor beneficii*—and—*Crom a boo.* *Pl.* 101, *cr.* 11.

LEIR, Wilts., a demi-unicorn, rampant, between legs a staff, raguly. *Pl.* 26, *cr.* 14, (staff, *pl.* 1, *cr.* 3.)

LEIR, Somers., a quill and sword, in saltier, ppr. *Pl.* 49, *cr.* 12.

LEISHMAN, Eng., a pelican in her piety, ppr. *Industriæ munus.* *Pl.* 76, *cr.* 15.

LEITCH, Sco., a hand holding a serpent, ppr. *Pl.* 91, *cr.* 6.

LEITCH, Sco., a turtle-dove, ppr. *Semper fidus.* *Pl.* 66, *cr.* 12.

LEITH, Norf., a cross crosslet, fitched, sa. *Pl.* 16, *cr.* 10.

LEITH, Sco., a cross crosslet, fitched, sa. *Trusty to the end.* *Pl.* 16, *cr.* 10.

LEITH, Sco., a dove, in mouth an olive-branch, ppr. *Fidus ad extremum.* *Pl.* 48, *cr.* 15.

LEITH, Lieut.-General, K.B. : 1. Out of a mural coronet, a demi-lion, rampant, regardant, ppr. *Pl.* 33, *cr.* 2, (coronet, *same plate, cr.* 5.) 2. A cross crosslet, fitched. *Trusty to the end.* *Pl.* 16, *cr.* 10.

LEITH, a stork, in mouth a staff and banner. *Pl.* 33, *cr.* 9, (banner, *pl.* 32, *cr.* 1.)

LEITH, of Freefield, Sco., a hart at gaze. *Trusty to the end.* *Pl.* 81, *cr.* 8.

LEITH, Bart., Norf., a lion, passant, gu., charged on body with three mullets, in fess, or. *Pl.* 48, *cr.* 8, (annulet, *pl.* 141.)

LEITRIM, Earl of, Viscount and Baron, Iri., Baron Clements, U.K., (Clements,) a fawn's head, erased, ppr. *Patriis virtutibus*—and—*Virtute non astutiâ.* *Pl.* 6, *cr.* 1.

LEIVY, a naked arm, embowed, in hand a sword, all ppr. *Pl.* 34, *cr.* 7.

LEKE, Eng., a garb, or, banded, gu. *Pl.* 48, *cr.* 10.

LEKE, a peacock's tail, erect, the plume displayed, ppr., supported by two eagles, wings expanded, ar.

LEKE, Derbs., two eagles, ar., supporting a garb, or.

LELAM, Northamp. and Yorks., on a mount, vert, a cock, gu., combed, wattled, and legged, or, (on breast a saltier, gold.) *Pl.* 76, *cr.* 7.

LELAND, Eng., a crow, rising, transfixed by an arrow. *Pl.* 110, *cr.* 13.

LELLO, or LELO, Heref., a gem-ring, or, entwined and fretted with two serpents, ppr.

LELLOW, LELOU, and LELOW, Eng., on a rock, a fort, in flames, ppr. *Pl.* 59, *cr.* 8.

LEMAN, Lond., (in a lemon-tree, ppr.,) a pelican in nest, or, feeding her young, ppr. *Pl.* 76, *cr.* 15.
LEMARCH, Eng., an arm, in armour, embowed, striking with a dagger, all ppr. *Pl.* 120, *cr.* 11.
LEMARCHANT, out of a ducal coronet, an (owl's) leg, in pale, or. *Pl.* 96, *cr.* 7.
LE MESURIER, Eng., a demi-savage, wreathed about middle with leaves, in hand (three oak-leaves,) all ppr. *Pl.* 35, *cr.* 12.
LE MESURIER, a hawk, ppr., wings expanded, or. *Pl.* 105, *cr.* 4.
LEMITAIRE, or LEMITARE, Middx., a demi-griffin, sa., holding a Catherine-wheel, ar. *Pl.* 18, *cr.* 6, (wheel, *pl.* 1, *cr.* 7.)
LEMMINGTON, a savage's head, (erased,) affrontée, ppr. *Pl.* 19, *cr.* 1.
LEMMON, or LEMON, Eng., a pelican in nest, feeding her young, or. *Pl.* 44, *cr.* 1.
LEMOINE, a dove with olive-branch. *Pl.* 48, *cr.* 15.
LEMON, Cornw., a lion, passant, gu. *Pl.* 66, *cr.* 8.
LEMPRIERE, Eng., a dove, ppr. *Pl.* 66, *cr.* 12.
LEMPRIERE, a dove, wings expanded, ppr. *Non generant aquilæ columbas. Pl.* 27, *cr.* 5.
LEMSTER, a demi-cupid, (in dexter an arrow, and in sinister a bow, bent, all ppr.) *Pl.* 17, *cr.* 5, (demi, *pl.* 70, *cr.* 14.)
LENAGHAN, Iri., an antelope, passant, or, armed, gu. *Pl.* 63, *cr.* 10.
LENCH, or LENCHE, Eng., a tiger, sejant, or, collared, gu., resting dexter on a shield, per cheveron, gu. and or. *Pl.* 26, *cr.* 9, (shield, *pl.* 22, *cr.* 13.)
LENCHE, Eng., an ounce, couchant, ppr. *Pl.* 111, *cr.* 11.
LENDERICK, (between two elephants' tusks, or,) a lion's head, erased, gu. *Pl.* 81, *cr.* 4.
LENDON, Eng., an eagle, issuing, in dexter a branch of laurel, ppr. *Pl.* 59, *cr.* 13.
LENDRUM, on a mount, vert, a dove, in mouth an olive-branch, all ppr. *Pl.* 104, *cr.* 8.
LE NEVE, Lond., Suff., and Norf., out of a ducal coronet, gold, a lily, ar., stalked and leaved, vert, bladed and seeded, or. *Pl.* 93, *cr.* 3.
LE NEVE, Lond., on a mount, vert, three silver lilies on one stalk, leaved and seeded, all ppr. *Pl.* 98, *cr.* 13, (lily, *pl.* 81, *cr.* 9.)
LENIGAN, co. Tipperary, a lion, rampant, or, leaning on a sword, ar., hilted, gold. *Pl.* 22, *cr.* 15, (sword, *same plate.*)
LENINGTON, or LENNINGTON, Eng., a savage's head, (erased,) affrontée, ppr. *Pl.* 19, *cr.* 1.
LENNARD, Bart., of Bell House, Ess., a hydra, with seven heads. *Pl.* 38, *cr.* 5.
LENNARD, a demi-lion, rampant, ducally gorged, in dexter a rose, gu. *Pl.* 87, *cr.* 15, (rose, *pl.* 60, *cr.* 14.)
LENNARD, Kent and Ess., out of a ducal coronet, or, a tiger's head, ar. *Pl.* 36, *cr.* 15.
LENNARD, a tiger's head, quarterly, or and az. *Pl.* 94, *cr.* 10.
LENNARD-BARRETT, Bart., Ess., out of a ducal coronet, or, on Irish wolf-dog's head, per fess, ar. and erm., charged with an escallop, barwise, nebulée, gu. and sa. *Pour bien desirer. Pl.* 99, *cr.* 7, (escallop, *pl.* 141.)
LENNIE, Sco., a dexter arm, ppr., hand holding up a covered cup, or. *Pl.* 88, *cr.* 5.
LENNOS, or LENOS, Eng., a pennant, parted, per pale, gu. and or, tasselled, gold. *Pl.* 8, *cr.* 8.

LENNOX, Sco., a lion, sejant, collared and lined. *Pl.* 21, *cr.* 3.
LENNOX, Duke of Richmond and Lennox. *See* RICHMOND.
LENT, a horse, passant, ar. *Pl.* 15, *cr.* 14.
LENTHAL, Oxon., a greyhound, current, ppr. *Pl.* 28, *cr.* 7, (without charge.)
LENTHALL, Dors., a greyhound, in full course, sa., collared, or. *Pl.* 28, *cr.* 7, without charge.)
LENTHALL, Wel., same crest. *Azincourt.*
LENTHORP, and LENTHROP, a lady, ppr., richly vested, vert. *Pl.* 107, *cr.* 2, (without anchor and head.)
LENTON, Northamp. and Bucks, a tiger's head, erased, az., tufted, armed, collared, and ringed, or. *Pl.* 94, *cr.* 10.
LENY, Sco., a cubit arm, ppr., hand holding up a covered cup, or. *Pl.* 35, *cr.* 9.
LEONARD, Earl of Sussex, out of a ducal coronet, or, a tiger's head, ar., maned and tufted, gold. *Pour bien desirer. Pl.* 36, *cr.* 15.
LEONARD, out of a ducal coronet, or, a tiger's head, ar. *Pl.* 36, *cr.* 15.
LEPARD, Eng., a fox, current, or. *Pl.* 80, *cr.* 5.
LE POER TRENCH, Earl of Clancarty. *See* CLANCARTY.
LEPTON, Eng., out of a castle, triple-towered, a demi-lion, ppr. *Pl.* 101, *cr.* 1.
LE ROACHE, a rock, ppr. *Pl.* 73, *cr.* 12.
LEROUX, Eng., a plume of feathers, ar. *Pl.* 12, *cr.* 9.
LESCOMB, (on a mount, vert, a greyhound, current,) between two branches of laurel. *Pl.* 102, *cr.* 13.
LE SCOT, Eng., two battle-axes, in saltier, az., hafted, sa. *Pl.* 52, *cr.* 10.
LESLIE, Eng., a demi-lion, rampant, gu., double-queued. *Pl.* 120, *cr.* 10.
LESLIE, Bart., out of a ducal coronet, ar., a griffin's head, gu., beaked, of the first. *Grip fast. Pl.* 54, *cr.* 14.
LESLIE, Sco., an eagle's neck, with two heads, erased, sa. *Hold fast—or—Firma spe. Pl.* 4, *cr.* 6.
LESLIE, Sco., a demi-angel, vested, az., winged, or, in dexter a griffin's head, erased, ppr., beaked, or. *Stat promissa fides. Pl.* 24, *cr.* 11.
LESLIE, Iri., a fox, sejant, or. *Pl.* 87, *cr.* 4.
LESLIE, a griffin's head, erased, ppr. *Firma spe. Pl.* 48, *cr.* 6.
LESLIE, Sco., between the horns of a crescent, a buckle, ar. *Conamine augeam. Pl.* 25, *cr.* 3.
LESLIE, Sco., a crescent, ar. *Crescat, Deo promotore. Pl.* 18, *cr.* 14.
LESLIE, Earl of Rothes, *See* ROTHES.
LESLIE, a cubit arm, erect, in hand a sword, in pale, on point a boar's head, erased, in fess. *Pl.* 71, *cr.* 9.
LESLIE, a cubit arm, erect, in hand a sword, in pale, on point a boar's head, erased, the sword entering the boar's mouth. *Pl.* 71, *cr.* 9.
LESLIE, a chevalier, in complete armour, in dexter a flag-staff, (the pennon flotant over head, and held by sinister hand.) *Pl.* 92, *cr.* 2.
LESLIE, Sco., a demi-griffin. *Pl.* 18, *cr.* 6.
LESLIE, Sco., a demi-griffin, ppr., in claws a buckle, or. *Grip fast. Pl.* 18, *cr.* 6, (buckle, *pl.* 39, *cr.* 8.)
LESLIE, CHARLES-POWELL, Esq., of Glasslough, co. Monaghan, a griffin's head, ppr. *Grip fast. Pl.* 38, *cr.* 3.

LESLIE, Bart., Surr., a camel's head, erased, or, bridled, lined, ringed, and gorged with a ducal coronet, sa. *Mens cujusque is est quisque.* Pl. 120, cr. 12.

LESLIE, Bart., Sco., a demi-griffin, ppr. *Grip fast.* Pl. 18, cr. 6.

LESLIE, WILLIAM, Esq., of Warthill, Aberdeen, a griffin's head, erased, ppr. *Grip fast.* Pl. 48, cr. 6.

LESLIE-MELVILLE, Earl of Leven. See LEVEN.

LESLY, Sco. a griffin, ppr., winged, or, in dexter a buckle, gold. *Probitas et firmitas.* Pl. 39, cr. 8.

LESLY, Sco., a buckle, or. *Keep fast.* Pl. 73, cr. 10.

LESLY, Sco., in hand a writing-pen, ppr. *Soli Deo gloria.* Pl. 26, cr. 13.

LESLY, Sco., a buckle, ar. *Firma durant.* Pl. 73, cr. 10.

LESLY, Sco., a buckle, or. *Hold fast.* Pl. 73, cr. 10.

LESLY, Sir CHARLES-ABRAHAM, Bart., Wardes and Findrassie, Morayshire, a griffin's head, couped, between wings, ppr. *Grip fast.* Pl. 65, cr. 1.

LESLY, Sco., an eagle's neck with two heads, erased, sa. *Hold fast.* Pl. 4, cr. 6.

LESLY, Sco., a griffin's head, erased, ppr. *Grip fast.* Pl. 48, cr. 6.

LESLY, Sco., a griffin's head. *Grip fast.* Pl. 38, cr. 3.

LESLY, Eng., a demi-lion, rampant, gu., double-queued. Pl. 120, cr. 10.

LESLY, Sco., a griffin's head, couped, ppr., charged with a cross crosslet, fitched, ar. Pl. 38, cr. 3, (cross, pl. 141.)

LESLY, Sco., a buckle. Pl. 73, cr. 10.

LESLY, Sco., out of a crescent, ar., a man, in armour, holding a buckle, ar. Pl. 118, cr. 12, (man, pl. 60, cr. 2.)

LESLY, a demi-angel, wings, or, in dexter two greyhounds' heads, erased, ppr. *Stat promissa fides.* Pl. 24, cr. 11, (heads, pl. 62, cr. 5.)

LESON, or LESONE, Northamp., out of a cloud, the sun rising in splendour, all ppr. Pl. 67, cr. 9.

LESSINGHAM, a martlet, sa. Pl. 111, cr. 5.

LESSINGTON, on a baron's coronet, or, a lion, rampant, gu. Pl. 67, cr. 5, (coronet, pl. 127, fig. 11.)

LESSLER, Eng., a Minerva's head, couped at shoulders, ppr. Pl. 92, cr. 12.

LESSLIE, a griffin's head. *Grip fast,* Pl. 38, cr. 3.

LESTER, a demi-griffin, segreant, gu. Pl. 18, cr. 6.

LESTON, a lion, passant, az., ducally gorged and chained, or. Pl. 121, cr. 4, (lion, pl. 48, cr. 8.)

LESTRANGE, Norf., Suff., and Middx., a lion, passant, gardant, or. Pl. 120, cr. 5.

LESTRANGE, two hands couped and conjoined, in fess. Pl. 1, cr. 2.

L'ESTRANGE, Eng., in lion's paw, sa., a dagger, ppr. Pl. 56, cr. 3.

LE STRANGE, STYLEMAN LE STRANGE, of Hunstanton Hall, Norf.; 1. For *Le Strange,* a lion, (statant,) tail extended, or. Pl. 118, cr. 10. 2. For *Styleman,* a camel's head, erased, az., bezantée, muzzled, (collared, lined, and chained, or,) on the collar, three hurts. Pl. 120, cr. 12, (hurts, pl. 141.)

LESTWICHE, Chesh., a still, ar.

LETCH, Eng., a harp, gu. Pl. 104, cr. 15.

LETE, out of a ducal coronet, gold, a lamp of three branches, or, fired, ppr.

LETEMPS, the emblem of Time, passing, with his scythe over shoulder, all ppr.

LETHAM, or LETHEM, Sco. and Eng., a griffin's head, between wings, in beak a feather, ppr. Pl. 65, cr. 1, (feather, pl. 69, cr. 1.)

LETHAM, or LATHEM, Eng. and Sco., on a mount, vert, a peacock, ppr. Pl. 9, cr. 1.

LETHBRIDGE, Sco., out of a mural coronet, a demi-eagle, wings expanded. Pl. 73, cr. 5.

LETHBRIDGE, a bear's paw, erased and erect, holding a spear-head, (point downward,) between wings. Pl. 1, cr. 4, (wings, *same plate,* cr. 15.)

LETHBRIDGE, Devons., a stag's head, erased, per fess, ar. and sa., attired, or, in mouth a rose, of the first, stalked and leaved, vert. Pl. 66, cr. 9, (rose, pl. 55, cr. 9.)

LETHBRIDGE, Bart., Somers., out of a mural coronet, or, a demi-eagle, displayed, ppr. *Spes mea in Deo.* Pl. 33, cr. 5.

LETHIEULLIER, Ess.; and LETHULIER, Middx., a parrot, ppr. Pl. 25, cr. 2.

LETHIM, Sco., a dove, within a serpent, in orle, ppr. Pl. 92, cr. 6.

LETHOOP, a rose, ppr. Pl. 105, cr. 7.

LETT, Eng., three organ-pipes, (two in saltier, surmounted by the third, in pale,) banded, vert. Pl. 50, cr. 12.

LETTON, Eng., a dexter hand, in fess, couped, gu., holding up a cross crosslet, fitched, az. Pl. 78, cr. 9.

LETTON, Herts., a bittern, in flags, seeded, all ppr. Pl. 124, cr. 1, (bittern, pl. 59, cr. 11.)

LEUKENOR, Eng., a unicorn's head, couped, az., platée, horned, or. Pl. 20, cr. 1.

LEUKENOR, Eng., a hawk's lure, az., fringed, or, lined, ar. Pl. 97, cr. 14.

LEVALL, Eng., a Cornish chough, wings expanded, issuing from the top of a tower, all ppr. Pl. 8, cr. 15.

LE VAVASOUR, Yorks., a cock, gu. Pl. 67, cr. 14.

LEVEALE, and LEVEALIS, Cornw., a tower, masoned, sa, Pl. 12, cr. 5.

LEVELAND, in dexter hand a dagger, in pale, with a laurel-wreath pendent therefrom, ppr. Pl. 23, cr. 15.

LEVEN, Earl of, Earl of Melville, Viscount Balgonie, &c., Sco., (Leslie-Melville): 1. For *Melville,* the head of a ratch-hound, erased, sa. *Denique cœlum.* Pl. 89, cr. 2. 2. For *Leslie,* a demi-chevalier, in complete armour, in dexter a dagger, erect, ppr., hilt and pommel, or. *Pro rege et patriâ.* Pl. 23, cr. 4.

LEVENS, Eng., on a chapeau, a wyvern, wings addorsed. Pl. 80, cr. 8.

LEVER, Lanc., a hare, ppr. Pl. 29, cr. 1.

LEVER, Lanc., on a trumpet, nowed, a cock, (wings expanded.) Pl. 2, cr. 1.

LEVER, Lanc., on a trumpet, in fess, a cock, ppr. Pl. 2, cr. 1.

LEVERAGE, Eng., a leopard's head, cabossed, ppr. Pl. 66, cr. 14.

LEVERMORE, Eng., an arm, embowed, in hand a scimitar, (in pale,) ppr. Pl. 92, cr. 5.

LEVERSAGE, Eng., a leopard's head, erased, gardant, ppr. Pl. 56, cr. 7.

LEVERSEDGE, Somers., a leopard's head, jessant-de-lis, or. Pl. 123, cr. 9.

T

LEVERSEDGE, Chesh., a leopard's head, or. Pl. 92, cr. 13.
LEVERSEY, and LEVESEY, Eng., a lion's paw, issuing, ppr., supporting an escutcheon, gu. Pl. 43, cr. 12.
LEVERTON, a hare, sejant, ar. Pl. 70, cr. 1.
LEVERTON, a pelican, ppr. Pl. 109, cr. 15.
LEVERTON, Lond. and Surr., a pelican, vulning, ar. Pl. 109, cr. 15.
LEVESAY, or LEVESEY, Kent, Lanc., and Surr., a lion's gamb, erased, gu., holding four trefoils, slipped, vert. Pl. 86, cr. 15, (trefoil, pl. 4, cr. 10.)
LEVESEY, a lion's paw, gu., holding a cluster of trefoils, of the same. Pl. 86, cr. 15, (trefoil, pl. 4, cr. 10.)
LEVESON, Kent and Salop, a goat's head, erm., attired, or. Pl. 105, cr. 14.
LEVESON, Kent and Salop, a goat's head, erased, erm., attired, or. Pl. 29, cr. 13.
LEVESON, Staffs., an arm, in armour, embowed, ppr., garnished, or, in gauntlet a battle-axe, handle, gu., head, or. Pl. 121, cr. 14.
LEVESQUE, Eng., on a fish, a sparrow-hawk, ppr. Pl. 29, cr. 11.
LEVET, or LEVETT, Eng., a gad-fly, wings addorsed, ppr. Pl. 107, cr. 13.
LEVETT, Suss., a lion, rampant, ar., crowned, or, between paws a cross crosslet, fitched, of the first. Pl. 61, cr. 4, (cross, pl. 141.)
LEVETT, Staffs., a demi-lion, or, (entwined with a sprig of laurel, vert,) supporting a cross crosslet, fitched, sa. Pl. 65, cr. 6.
LEVETT, Wichnor Park, a demi-lion, ar., ducally crowned, or, gorged with a collar, az., in dexter a cross crosslet, fitched, sa., sinister resting on an escutcheon, of the third, charged with a fleur-de-lis, gold. Pl. 66, cr. 2, (cross, pl. 141; escutcheon, pl. 19, cr. 2.)
LEVI, a demi-lion, rampant, gu. Pl. 67, cr. 10.
LEVI, Eng., on a tower, ppr., a flag, ar., charged with a crescent, sa. Pl. 8, cr. 13, (crescent, pl. 141.)
LEVING, Iri., an oak-tree, fructed, ppr. Pl. 16, cr. 8.
LEVING, and LEVINGE, Eng., a sword and garb, in saltier, ppr. Pl. 70, cr. 7.
LEVING, and LEVINGS, within a chaplet, vert, an escallop, ar. Pl. 86, cr. 9.
LEVINGE, Bart., Iri., an escallop, ar., within a garland, ppr. Vestigia nulla retrorsum. Pl. 86, cr. 9.
LEVINGE, Iri., a bell, az. Pl. 73, cr. 15.
LEVINGSTONE, Sco., a demi-savage, over shoulder a club, ppr. Pl. 14, cr. 11.
LEVINS, a bull's head, sa., charged with a crescent, gu. Pl. 120, cr. 7, (crescent, pl. 141.)
LEVINZ, on a torteau, a squirrel, sejant, ppr. Pl. 5, cr. 6, (torteau, pl. 7, cr. 6.)
LEVINZ, Lond., Northamp., and Oxon., on a vine-branch, a squirrel, sejant, all ppr. Pl. 5, cr. 6, (branch, pl. 80, cr. 1.)
LEVY, Eng., an arm, in armour, embowed, hand apaumée, ppr. Pl. 97, cr. 1.
LEW, Eng., a dexter arm, in hand a roll of vellum. Pl. 27, cr. 4.
LEWARD, a demi-lion, rampant, or, (between paws,) a mullet, ar. Pl. 89, cr. 10.
LEWCAS, on a chapeau, an heraldic-tiger, passant, ppr. Pl. 7, cr. 5, (chapeau, same plate, cr. 14.)
LEWELLYN, Eng., a pheon, ppr. Pl. 26, cr. 12.
LEWEN, a full moon, ar. Pl. 43, cr. 8.

LEWES, Eng., a horse's head, bridled, ppr. Pl. 92, cr. 1.
LEWES, Lond., an eagle, displayed, sa., (feet on wreath, in beak,) and entwined round body, a serpent, ppr. Pl. 119, cr. 1.
LEWING, Hartford, a buck, trippant, quarterly, or and az. Pl. 68, cr. 2.
LEWINS, Eng., a demi-lion, rampant, ppr. Pl. 67, cr. 10.
LEWIN, Kent and Suss., a buck, trippant, or, gorged with a chaplet, vert. Pl. 68, cr. 2, (gorging, pl. 38, cr. 1.)
LEWIN, and LEWINS, a demi-lion, rampant, sa., supporting a lozenge, or, on it a trefoil, slipped, vert. Pl. 126, cr. 12, (lozenge and trefoil, pl. 141.)
LEWIN, a buck, trippant, quarterly, or and az. Pl. 68, cr. 2.
LEWIN, Kent, a sea-lion, ppr., the tail nowed, in paws a shield, gu., charged with an escallop, or. Pl. 25, cr. 12, (escallop, pl. 141.)
LEWIN, Horsfall, a demi-lion, between paws a trefoil. Pl. 126, cr. 12, (trefoil, pl. 141.)
LEWIS, Salop, a demi-griffin, ar. Pl. 18, cr. 6.
LEWIS, Yorks., out of a ducal coronet, a plume of five ostrich-feathers, two or, and three sa., (charged with a cheveron, gold.) Spe tutiores armis. Pl. 100, cr. 12.
LEWIS, Sco., a stag's head, erased, affrontée. Pl. 8, cr. 6.
LEWIS, Iri., on top of a spear, issuing, a dolphin, naiant. Pl. 49, cr. 14.
LEWIS, Iri., a lion, rampant, gu. Pl. 67, cr. 5.
LEWIS, a greyhound's head, ar., between two roses, gu., slipped and leaved, ppr. Pl. 84, cr. 13.
LEWIS, a demi-goat, ar., between paws a human heart, gu. Pl. 113, cr. 1.
LEWIS, on a mount, vert, a greyhound, couchant, gu., collared, or. Pl. 6, cr. 7, (mount, pl. 98, cr. 13.)
LEWIS, a demi-wolf, rampant, ar. Pl. 56, cr. 8, (without spear.)
LEWIS, on a chapeau, gu., turned up, erm., a greyhound, sa., (collared, or.) Pl. 104, cr. 1.
LEWIS, FRANKLAND, M.P., &c., Wel., on a chapeau, gu., turned up, erm., a tiger, statant. Expertus fidelem. Pl. 110, cr. 8.
LEWIS, Wel., on a chapeau, gu., turned up, erm., an heraldic-tiger, ppr. Pl. 7, cr. 5, (chapeau, same plate, cr. 14.)
LEWIS, a horse's head, bridled, ppr. Pl. 92, cr. 1.
LEWIS, Lanc., on a chapeau, gu., turned up, erm., an heraldic-tiger, passant. Hæc olim meminisse juvabit. Pl. 7, cr. 5, (chapeau, same plate, cr. 14.)
LEWIS, CHARLES-JAMES, Esq., of St Pierre, Moum., a griffin, segreant, sa. Ha persa la fide, ha perso l'honore. Pl. 67, cr. 13.
LEWIS, Wel., a lion, rampant, sejant, ar. Pl. 60, cr. 4, (without spear.)
LEWIS, Dors. and Somers., an antelope's head, erased, sa., maned, tufted, and ducally gorged, or. Pl. 24, cr. 7, (gorging, same plate, cr. 10.)
LEWIS, Kent, an ermine, passant, ppr. Pl. 9, cr. 5.
LEWIS, Kent, a demi-beaver, ppr. Pl. 9, cr. 9.
LEWIS, Ess., Herts., and Yorks., out of a ducal coronet, or, a plume of five ostrich-feathers, ar. Pl. 100, cr. 12, (without charge.)

LEWIS, LEWIS, Esq., of Gwinfe, Carmarthen, a demi-griffin, segreant, or. *Facta, non verba.* Pl. 18, cr. 6.
LEWIS, Wel., a buck, trippant. Pl. 68, cr. 2.
LEWIS, Wel., an eagle's head, erased, or. Pl. 20, cr. 7.
LEWIS, Hampton, Wel.: 1. For *Lewis*, a Cornish chough, ppr., in dexter a fleur-de-lis, az. Pl. 100, cr. 13, (fleur-de-lis, pl. 141.) 2. For *Hampton*, a wyvern, amidst bulrushes, ppr. Pl. 63, cr. 13, (rushes, pl. 124, cr. 1.)
LEWKENOR, or LEWKNOR, Suff., Suss., and Worc., a greyhound, current, ar., (collared, gu.) Pl. 47, cr. 2, (without chapeau.)
LEWKNOR, Suss. and Worc., a unicorn's head, erased, az., bezantée, horned and maned, or. Pl. 67, cr. 1.
LEWSELL, an antelope's head, gardant, or, attired, sa.
LEWSON, Eng., a goat's head, erased, erm., attired, or. Pl. 29, cr. 13.
LEWTHWAIT, or LEWTHWAITE, an heraldic-tiger's head, (erased,) gu. *Tiens à la verité.* Pl. 113, cr. 3.
LEWTHWAITE, of Broadgate, Cumb., a garb, bound by a serpent, ppr., in mouth a cross crosslet, fitched, gu. *Tendens ad œthera virtus.* Pl. 36, cr. 14, (cross, pl. 141.)
LEWYN, Kent, a buck, party per cross, or and az. Pl. 68, cr. 2.
LEWYS, out of a ducal coronet, a plume of feathers. *Spe tutiores armis.* Pl. 44, cr. 12.
LEXINTON, Eng., a demi-lady, between two branches of palm, in orle, in hand a thistle, ppr. Pl. 17, cr. 11, (palm, pl. 87, cr. 8; thistle, pl. 36, cr. 6.)
LEXTON, out of a castle, triple-towered, a demi-lion, all ppr. P. 101, cr. 1.
LEY, a lion, sejant, or. *Vincendo victus.* Pl. 126, cr. 15.
LEY, Eng., on an escallop, between wings, or, a saltier, gu. Pl. 62, cr. 4.
LEYBORNE, Kent, Westm., and Yorks., an eagle, regardant, wings expanded, az., beaked and legged, or. Pl. 87, cr. 5, (without sword.)
LEYBOURN, a buck's head, erased, ppr. Pl. 66, cr. 9.
LEYBOURNE, Eng., an eagle, volant, regardant, az., beaked and legged, or. Pl. 114, cr. 10.
LEYCESTER, a demi-lion, rampant, in dexter a fleur-de-lis. Pl. 91, cr. 13.
LEYCESTER, of Toft, Chesh., a roebuck, party per pale, or and gu., attired, of the second, in mouth an acorn-branch, ppr. Pl. 68, cr. 2, (acorn, pl. 100, cr. 8.)
LEYCROFT, in hand, ppr., in pale, vested, az., a chaplet, gu. Pl. 44, cr. 13, (without bird.)
LEYE, Eng., an arm in armour, embowed, in gauntlet a battle-axe, all ppr. Pl. 121, cr. 14.
LEYHAW, Eng., a ship, in full sail, ppr. Pl. 109, cr. 8.
LEYLAND, Lanc., a demi-dove, wings addorsed, az., in mouth three ears of wheat, or.
LEYNYS, a hand holding an oak-branch, fructed, or. Pl. 43, cr. 6.
LEYSON, Eng., a goat's head, erased, erm., attired, or. Pl. 29, cr. 13, (oak, pl. 32, cr. 13.)
LEYVER, a leveret, couchant, ppr. Pl. 29, cr. 1.
LIARD, Eng., an antelope, tripping, ppr., (collared, or.) Pl. 63, cr. 10.

LIBBY, out of a paling, or, a dexter arm, ppr., vested, gu., in hand a baton, az., tipped, gold. Pl. 2, cr. 2, (baton, pl. 18, cr. 1.)
LIBERTON, Eng., a stag's head, couped, az. Pl. 91, cr. 14.
LICHFIELD, Eng., on a chapeau, gu., a garb, ppr. Pl. 62, cr. 1.
LICHFIELD, Oxon., an arm, embowed, vested, ar., in hand, ppr., a bow, or, strung, gu. Pl. 51, cr. 5.
LICHFIELD, Earl of, Viscount Anson and Baron Soberton, (Anson:) 1. Out of a ducal coronet, a spear-head, ppr. Pl. 78, cr. 15, (spear, pl. 82, cr. 9.) 2. A greyhound's head, couped, erm., charged on neck with two bars-gemelle, or. *Nil desperandum.* Pl. 43, cr. 11.
LICKIE, Sco., two hands couped below wrist, supporting a sword, ppr., hilt and pommel, or. Pl. 59, cr. 10.
LIDDEL, Sco., a rose, slipped, gu. *Hinc odor et sanitas.* Pl. 105, cr. 7.
LIDDELL, or LIDELL, Sco., a demi-lion, or, in dexter a mullet, gu. Pl. 89, cr. 10.
LIDDELL, Durh. and Northumb., a lion, rampant, sa., billettée, or, crowned with an Eastern crown, gold. *Unus et idem.* Pl. 98, cr. 1, (coronet, pl. 25, cr. 8.)
LIDDELL, Baron Ravensworth. *See* RAVENSWORTH.
LIDDERDALE, Sco., an eagle's head, erased, ppr. *Foresight is all.* Pl. 20, cr. 7.
LIDDERDALE, Lond., same crest. *Per bella qui providet.*
LIDDIARD, Wilts., a demi-lion, rampant, ar., in dexter a mullet, gu. Pl. 89, cr. 10.
LIDDIAT, Staffs. and Worc., a wolf's head, erased, per pale, erminois and gu. Pl. 14, cr. 6.
LIDDLE, Eng., two lions' gambs, erased, supporting a column, ppr. Pl. 77, cr. 4.
LIDEL, Eng., two hands conjoined, in fess, each united to a wing at wrist. Pl. 14, cr. 9.
LIDGBIND, Kent and Suff., in a mural coronet, or, the trunk of a tree, ppr., sprouting, vert, surmounted by a pelican, gold, vulning, of the second, ducally crowned, az.
LIDIARD, Eng., a wolf's head, per pale, erminois and sa. *Guardez vous.* Pl. 14, cr. 6.
LIDSEY, Lond., a demi-griffin, segreant, az., beaked and legged, gu., in dexter a trefoil, slipped, or. Pl. 18, cr. 6, (trefoil, pl. 141.)
LIENIS, and LIENYS, an arm, couped at elbow, in pale, vested, ar., in hand, ppr., a bunch of acorns, vert, fructed, or. Pl. 64, cr. 7, (acorns, pl. 69, cr. 12.)
LIEUBENROOD, Berks., out of an Eastern coronet, gu., two antelopes' horns, ar., round each a ribbon, twisted, vert.
LIEVRE, Surr., a hare, current, ppr. *A ma vie.*
LIFEILDE, or LIFIELD, Surr. and Herts., a bull's head, cabossed, ar., armed, or, charged on forehead with three ermine-spots, one and two. Pl. 111, cr. 8, (ermine, pl. 141.)
LIFFORD, Viscount and Baron, Iri., (Hewitt,) on trunk of tree, in fess, an owl, all ppr. *Be just, and fear not.* Pl. 27, cr. 9, (tree, pl. 10, cr. 1.)
LIGHT, a swan's neck, ar., between wings, gu., behind the neck a plume of three ostrich-feathers, one, ar., between two, gu., all burning over the head. Pl. 54, cr. 6, (feathers, pl. 12, cr. 9.)

LIGH, Chesh., a cubit arm, in pale, (in armour, garnished, or,) in hand a tilting-spear, all ppr., headed, ar. *Pl.* 99, *cr.* 8.

LIGHTBODY, Sco., a star, issuant from a cloud, ppr. *Clarior e tenebris. Pl.* 16, *cr.* 13.

LIGHTBODY, Sco., same crest, *E tenebris lux.*

LIGHTBORNE, or LIGHTBOURNE, Lanc., an eagle, displayed, az., beaked and membered, or. *Pl.* 48, *cr.* 11.

LIGHTBOURNE, Iri., out of a ducal coronet, a cockatrice's head, between wings. *Pl.* 77, *cr.* 5.

LIGHTFOOT, Eng., a human heart, pierced by a passion-nail, in bend. *Pl.* 81, *cr.* 3.

LIGHTFOOT, a griffin's head, erased, gorged with a collar, charged with three escallops. *Pl.* 48, *cr.* 6.

LIGHTON, Sco., an eagle's head, erased, ppr., in beak an acorn, or, stalked and leaved, vert. *Pl.* 22, *cr.* 1.

LIGHTON, Sco., a Minerva's head, affrontée, ppr. *Pl.* 92, *cr.* 12.

LIGHTON, Sco., a palm-tree, vert. *Per adversa virtus. Pl.* 18, *cr.* 12.

LIGHTON, Sco., a lion's head, erased. *Light on. Pl.* 81, *cr.* 4.

LIGHTON, Bart., Iri., a lion's head, (erased, crowned with an Eastern crown, or,) langued, az. *Fortitudine et prudentiâ. Pl.* 123, *cr.* 13.

LIGO, Bucks., on a chapeau, az., turned up, ar., an etoile, between wings, or. *Pl.* 17, *cr.* 14, (etoile, *pl.* 141.)

LIGON, Worc. and Glouc., an old man's head, ppr., hair and beard, sa. *Pl.* 29, *cr.* 1.

LIGON, Glouc. and Worc., a Saracen's head, ppr., wreathed, ar. and gu. *Pl.* 36, *cr.* 3.

LIGONIER, Lond. and Surr., out of a mural coronet, gu., a demi-lion, rampant, erminois, in dexter a branch of palm, vert. *Pl.* 17, *cr.* 7.

LIGONIER, Iri., out of a mural coronet, a demi-lion, erminois, in dexter a palm-branch, vert. *A rege et victoriâ. Pl.* 17, *cr.* 7.

LILBORNE, or LILBOURNE, Eng., a castle, triple-towered, ppr., flagged, sa. *Pl.* 123, *cr.* 14.

LILBORNE, or LILBURNE, an arm, in armour, ppr., in hand a truncheon, or. *Vis viri fragilis. Pl.* 33, *cr.* 4.

LILE, and LILLE, on a chapeau, ppr., a lion, couchant, or. *Pl.* 75, *cr.* 5.

LILFORD, Baron, (Atherton-Powys,) a lion's gamb, erased and erect, gu., grasping a fleur-de-lis, or. *Parta tueri. Pl.* 5, *cr.* 5, (fleur-de-lis, *pl.* 141.)

LILL, Iri., a hand, erect, out of a cloud, holding an anchor, in pale, ppr. *Pl.* 41, *cr.* 5.

LILLAN, Eng., a hand, holding a dagger, on point a moor's head, couped at shoulders. *Pl.* 118, *cr.* 3.

LILLEY, Eng., an oak-tree, ppr. *Pl.* 16, *cr.* 8.

LILLIE, Eng., between the attires of a stag, or, a rose, gu. *Pl.* 50, *cr.* 14.

LILLIE, Sco., out of a cloud, a dexter hand, ppr., grasping a club, all ppr. *Pl.* 37, *cr.* 13.

LILLINGTON-SPOONER, Warw., a demi-dragon, wings expanded, in dexter a battle-axe. *Pl.* 82, *cr.* 10, (axe, *pl.* 44, *cr.* 3.)

LILLY, Iri., a lion, rampant, regally crowned. *Pl.* 98, *cr.* 1.

LILLY, Eng., a dexter hand, apaumée, gu. *Pl.* 32, *cr.* 14.

LIMBERY, and LIMBREY, Dors., a unicorn, passant, gu., crined, armed, and hoofed, or. *Pl.* 106, *cr.* 3.

LIMBORNE, Eng., in dexter hand, a hunting-horn, sans strings, ppr. *Pl.* 109, *cr.* 3.

LIMERICK, a demi-savage, affrontée, in dexter a hatchet, in sinister a club, resting over shoulder. *Pl.* 14, *cr.* 11, (hatchet, *pl.* 44, *cr.* 3.)

LIMERICK, Earl of, and Viscount, Baron Glentworth, Iri., Baron Foxford, U.K., (Pery ;) a fawn's head, erased, ppr. *Virtute non astutiâ. Pl.* 6, *cr.* 1.

LIMESEY, Eng., stump of oak-tree, sprouting new branches, ppr. *Pl.* 92, *cr.* 8.

LIMESIE, Eng., a rose-bush, bearing roses, ppr. *Pl.* 23, *cr.* 2.

LIMSAY, and LIMSEY, Eng., out of a ducal coronet, gu., a dexter arm, in hand a (sword,) ppr. *Pl.* 103, *cr.* 2.

LINACRE, Derbs., a greyhound's head (erased,) quarterly, az. and sa., charged with four escallops, counterchanged. *Pl.* 14, *cr.* 4, (escallop, *pl.* 141.)

LINCH, Kent, a leopard, rampant, ppr. *Pl.* 73, *cr.* 2.

LINCH, a wolf, passant, sa. *Pl.* 46, *cr.* 6.

LINCH, a lynx, passant, ar. *Pl.* 122, *cr.* 14.

LINCOLNE, Eng., out of a ducal coronet, or, a demi-lion, ppr., crowned with an antique crown, gold. *Pl.* 45, *cr.* 7, (crown, *pl.* 79, *cr.* 12.)

LINCOLNE, a lion, rampant, sa. *Pl.* 67, *cr.* 5.

LIND, Sco., two branches of laurel, (in saltier,) ppr. *Semper virescit virtus. Pl.* 20, *cr.* 2.

LINDESAY, co. Tyrone, a swan, ppr., statant, wings close. *Pl.* 122, *cr.* 13, (without mount.)

LINDESEY, Sco., an ostrich, in mouth a horseshoe, ppr. *Patientia vincit. Pl.* 16, *cr.* 2.

LINDON, Iri., an arm, embowed, in hand a scimitar, ppr. *Patria cara, carior libertas. Pl.* 92, *cr.* 5.

LINDON, Iri., a dragon, (statant.) *Pl.* 90, *cr.* 2.

LINDSAY, a cubit arm, ppr., in hand a sword, in pale, ar., hilt and pommel, or, on point a pair of scales, of the last. *Recte vel arduâ. Pl.* 44, *cr.* 10, (hand, *pl.* 23, *cr.* 15.)

LINDSAY, an ostrich's head, erased, ppr., in mouth a horse-shoe, or, about neck a label of three points, ar. *Pl.* 99, *cr.* 12, (without feathers.)

LINDSAY, Sco., a castle, ppr. *Firmus maneo. Pl.* 28, *cr.* 11.

LINDSAY, Sco., an ostrich's head, erased, ppr. *Pl.* 50, *cr.* 1, (without feathers.)

LINDSAY, Sco., a swan, wings addorsed, ppr. *Pl.* 45, *cr.* 5.

LINDSAY, Sco., an otter's head and neck, erased, sa. *Pl.* 126, *cr.* 14.

LINDSAY, Sco., a swan, naiant, ppr. *Live, but dread. Pl.* 66, *cr.* 10.

LINDSAY, Sco., a tower, ppr., ensigned with a crescent, ar. *Firmiter maneo. Pl.* 85, *cr.* 1.

LINDSAY, Sco., two stalks of wheat, in saltier, ppr. *Non solum armis. Pl.* 9, *cr.* 8.

LINDSAY, Sco., a withered branch of oak, sprouting forth green leaves, ppr. *Mortua vivescunt. Pl.* 32, *cr.* 13.

LINDSAY, an ostrich, ppr., in beak a key. *Endure fort. Pl.* 64, *cr.* 3, (key, *pl.* 9, *cr.* 12.)

LINDSAY, Sco., in dexter hand a branch of (olive,) ppr. *Mutus amore cresco. Pl.* 43, *cr.* 6.

LINDSAY, Glenview, Wicklow, a swan, ppr., standing, wings closed. *Live, but dread.* Pl. 126 B, cr. 7. For *Brocas*, a negro's head, in profile, crowned with an eastern crown, or. *Vincit veritas.* Pl. 126 B, cr. 15.
LINDSAY, Earl of Balcarras. *See* BALCARRAS.
LINDSAY, Sco., a sword, in pale, on point a balance and scale, ppr. *Recte vel ardua.* Pl. 44, cr. 10.
LINDSAY, Sco., an ostrich, in mouth a key. *Live, but dread.* Pl. 64, cr. 3, (key, pl. 9, cr. 12.)
LINDSEY, Earl of, (Bertie,) a Saracen's head, couped at breast, ppr., ducally crowned, or. Pl. 28, cr. 3. The paternal crest of *Bertie* is a pine-tree, ppr. *Loyaulte me oblige.* Pl. 26, cr. 10.
LINDSEY, co. Mayo, an eagle, displayed, with two heads. Pl. 87, cr. 11, (without flame.)
LINE, Sco., a griffin's head, erased, gu. Pl. 48, cr. 6.
LINESLEY, Eng., an arm, in armour, embowed, in glove a sabre, all ppr. Pl. 81, cr. 11.
LINFORD, Eng., a talbot, passant, ar. Pl. 120, cr. 8.
LING, and LINGUE, Linc., on a mount, vert, a lion, sejant, gardant, or, resting dexter on a caltrap, az. Pl. 108, cr. 12, (caltrap, pl. 141.)
LINGARD, Eng., a stag's head, affrontée, gorged with a ducal coronet, ppr. Pl. 55, cr. 2.
LINGAYNE, and LINGEN, Derbs., Glouc., Northamp., Salop; and Witton-Lingayne, Worc., out of a ducal coronet, or, a garb, vert. Pl. 62, cr. 1, (coronet, pl. 128, fig. 3.)
LINGEN, Rads., out of a ducal coronet, or, a garb, vert. Pl. 62, cr. 1, (coronet, pl. 127, fig. 3.)
LINGEN, Eng., a dexter arm, in armour, embowed, in hand a scimitar, (fastened to wrist,) all ppr. Pl. 81, cr. 11.
LINGHAM, Eng., two branches of oak, in saltier, ppr. Pl. 19, cr. 12.
LINGHOOKE, Norf., a griffin's head, erased, gu., (gorged with a collar, dancettée, or, in beak a violet, az., stalked and leaved, vert.) Pl. 42, cr. 9.
LINGWOOD, Eng., an antelope's head, erased, erm. Pl. 24, cr. 7.
LINGWOOD, Ess., a talbot's head, or, pellettée, gorged with a mural coronet, gold. Pl. 2, cr. 15, (coronet, pl. 128, fig. 18.)
LINLEY, Sco., out of a ducal coronet, gu., a demi-boar, or. Pl. 102, cr. 14, (demi, pl. 20, cr. 5.)
LINNET, out of a ducal coronet, or, a double plume of ostrich-feathers, ar., five and four. Pl. 64, cr. 5.
LINNING, Sco., a dexter cubit arm, in hand a broad-sword, all ppr. Pl. 21, cr. 10.
LINSEY, a demi-eagle, displayed, on body a quatrefoil. Pl. 44, cr. 14. (quatrefoil, pl. 141.)
LINSKILL, a demi-eagle, displayed, or, in beak a scroll, inscribed "Victor." Pl. 27, cr. 7.
LINT, Eng., a dexter hand, gu., holding a cross crosslet, fitched, sa. Pl. 99, cr. 1.
LINTON, Sco., an eagle's head, erased, in beak an acorn, stalked and leaved, all ppr. Pl. 22, cr. 1.
LINTON, Cambs., a griffin's head, erased. Pl. 48, cr. 6.
LINTOT, two lions' gambs, holding up a garb. Pl. 62, cr. 3, (garb, *same plate, cr.* 1.)
LINWOOD, Eng., a demi-talbot, in mouth an arrow, ppr. Pl. 97, cr. 9.
LIONNEL, Eng., an antique crown. Pl. 79, cr. 12.
LIPPINCOT, out of a mural coronet, gu., five ostrich-feathers, alternately ar. and az. Pl. 125, cr. 11, (feathers, pl. 100, cr. 12.)

LIPSCOMB, Eng., a cubit arm, in armour, in hand an oak-branch, ppr. Pl. 55, cr. 6, (oak, pl. 32, cr. 13.)
LISBONE, and LISBORNE, Eng., a boar, passant, or. Pl. 48, cr. 14.
LISBURNE, Earl of, and Viscount, Lord Vaughan, Iri., (Vaughan;) an arm, in armour, embowed, ppr., in hand a fleur-de-lis, az. *Non revertar inultus.* Pl. 24, cr. 14.
LISLE, Iri., a marigold, slipped and leaved, ppr. Pl. 105, cr. 15.
LISLE, a stag, ar., (collared, chained,) and attired, or. Pl. 68, cr. 2.
LISLE, Hants, a lion's head, couped. Pl. 126, cr. 1.
LISLE, Hants, a stag, trippant, ar., attired, or. Pl. 68, cr. 2.
LISLE, Middx., a lion's gamb, az., holding an escallop, or. Pl. 97, cr. 10, (escallop, pl. 141.)
LISLE, a millstone, ar., charged in the centre with a mill-rind, sa. Pl. 40, cr. 2, (without chapeau.)
LISLE, Baron, Iri., (Lysaght,) an arm, in armour, embowed, in hand a dagger, all ppr. *Bella! horrida bella.* Pl. 120, cr. 11.
LISMORE, Viscount and Baron, Iri., (O'Callaghan,) a dexter arm, embowed, in hand a sword, entwined with a serpent, all ppr. *Fidus et audax.* Pl. 116, cr. 11.
LISTER, Staffs., a buck's head, party, per fess, ppr. and or, charged with a crescent. *Retinens vestigia famæ.* Pl. 61, cr. 9.
LISTER, Sco., a buck's head, erased, ppr. *Malo mori quam fœdari.* Pl. 66, cr. 9.
LISTER, Staffs., on a five-leaved ducal coronet, or, a buck's head, erased, per fess, ar. and gu. Pl. 23, cr. 11, (head, pl. 66, cr. 9.)
LISTER, a stag's head, erased, (collared, pierced through neck with a dart.) Pl. 66, cr. 9.
LISTER, Salop, Derbs., Yorks., and Westm., a stag's head, erased, ppr. Pl. 66, cr. 9.
LISTER, Lond., a stag's head, erased, per fess, ppr. and or, attired, gold. Pl. 66, cr. 9.
LISTER, MATTHEW-HENRY, Esq., of Burwell Park, Linc., a stag's head, erased, ppr. *Est modus.* Pl. 66, cr. 9.
LISTER, Baron Ribblesdale. *See* RIBBLESDALE.
LISTON, Sco., a demi-lion, gu., holding a gilliflower, ppr. Pl. 39, cr. 14, (flower, pl. 22, cr. 9.)
LISTON, Sco., two hands conjoined, couped, ppr. Pl. 1, cr. 2.
LISTOWEL, Earl of, and Viscount, Viscount and Baron Ennismore, Iri., (Hare,) a demi-lion, couped, ar., ducally gorged, or. *Odi profanum.* Pl. 87, cr. 45.
LITCHFIELD, Eng., an arm, in armour, embowed, in hand a sword, ppr. *Semper pugnare paratus.* Pl. 2, cr. 8.
LITCOTT, an old man's head, ppr., vested, sa., ducally crowned, or. Pl. 78, cr. 14.
LITHGOW, Sco., a palm-branch, vert. Pl. 123, cr. 1.
LITLER, or LITTLER, a filbert-tree, ppr., the trunk raguly, (on each side a squirrel, salient, gu.) Pl. 5, cr. 6.
LITSTER, Sco., a deer's head, couped, ppr. *Labore et fiducia.* Pl. 91, cr. 14.
LITSTER, a stag at gaze, ermines, ducally gorged and attired, or. Pl. 81, cr. 8, (gorging, pl. 55, cr. 2.)

LITSTER, Eng., an anchor and cable, sa. *Sine Deo nihil.* Pl. 42, cr. 12.

LITTELL, Eng., two daggers, in saltier, ppr. Pl. 24, cr. 2.

LITTELL, Ess., (on an arrow, or,) a cock, statant, combed and wattled, gu. Pl. 2, cr. 1.

LITTLE, Eng. and Iri., a demi-bull. Pl. 63, cr. 6.

LITTLE, Sco., a leopard's head, or. *Magnum in parvo.* Pl. 92, cr. 13.

LITTLE, a leopard's head, affrontée, erased, or. *Magnum in parvo.* Pl. 56, cr. 7.

LITTLE, WILLIAM-HUNTER, Esq., of Llanvair Grange, Monmouth, a leopard's head, ppr. *Magnum in parvo.* Pl. 92, cr. 13.

LITTLEBOY, Eng., a goat's head, erased, gu. Pl. 29, cr. 13.

LITTLEBURY, Eng., a lion's paw, per fess, gu. and az., holding a spear, sa., point, or. Pl. 1, cr. 4.

LITTLEBURY, Linc., a man's head, couped at shoulders, in mail, all ppr. Pl. 33, cr. 14.

LITTLEDALE, Eng., two lions' paws, in saltier, ppr. Pl. 20, cr. 13.

LITTLEDALE, Bolton Hall, Yorks., a demi-lion, gu., gorged with a collar gemelle, ar., in dexter a cross crosslet, of the same. *Fac et spera.* Pl. 18, cr. 13, (cross, pl. 141.)

LITTLEFIELD, Eng., on a garb, or, a bird, ar., in beak an ear of wheat, vert. Pl. 112, cr. 10.

LITTLEHALES, Suss., between wings, or, an armed arm, embowed, ppr., garnished, gold, in gauntlet, an arrow, entwined with an olive-branch, vert. Pl. 115, cr. 4.

LITTLER, Eng., a squirrel, sejant, cracking a nut, all ppr. Pl. 16, cr. 9.

LITTLETON, Staffs. and Salop, a wyvern's head. Pl. 87, cr. 12.

LITTLETON, Worc., a moor's head, in profile, ppr., wreathed, ar. and sa. Pl. 36, cr. 3.

LITTLETON, Staffs., a stag's head, cabossed, sa., attired, or, between attires a bugle-horn, ar., suspended from a bend, gu. Pl. 115, cr. 1, (horn, pl. 48, cr. 12.)

LITTLETON, Staffs., Salop, Leic., and Cornw., a stag's head, cabossed, sa., attired, or, between attires a bugle-horn, ar., stringed, of the first. Pl. 115, cr. 1, (horn, pl. 98, cr. 2.)

LITTLEWOOD, Eng., on a mount, vert, a peacock, ppr. Pl. 9, cr. 1.

LITTON, Eng., a mountain-cat, current, ppr. Pl. 119, cr. 7.

LITTON, Iri., a goat's head, erased, vert. Pl. 29, cr. 13.

LIVERPOOL, Earl of, Baron Hawkesbury, and a Bart., (Jenkinson,) a sea-horse, assurgent, ar., maned, az., supporting a cross-pattée, gu. *Palma non sine pulvere.* Pl. 100, cr. 1, (cross, pl. 141.)

LIVESAY, and LIVESEY, Eng., a lion's gamb, erased, gu. Pl. 126, cr. 9.

LIVESAY, and LIVESEY, a bear's paw, erect and erased, holding a bunch of trefoils, all ppr. Pl. 60, cr. 14, (trefoil, pl. 141.)

LIVINGSTON, Sco., in dexter hand a sword, ppr. *Ut possim.* Pl. 21, cr. 10.

LIVINGSTON, Sco., a demi-Hercules, wreathed about head and middle, in dexter a club, (erect,) in sinister a serpent, all ppr. *Si je puis.* Pl. 92, cr. 10.

LIVINGSTON, or LIVINGSTONE, Sco., a gilliflower, slipped, ppr. *Nativum retinet decus.* Pl. 22, cr. 9.

LIVINGSTON, Earl of Newburgh. *See* NEWBURGH.

LIVINGSTONE, Sco., a boar's head, couped, in mouth a pair of scales, ppr. *Fortis et æquus.* Pl. 2, cr. 7, (scales, pl. 12, cr. 11.)

LIVINGSTONE, Sco., a savage's head, wreathed with laurel. *Si possim.* Pl. 118, cr. 7.

LIVINGSTONE, Eng., a dexter arm, in hand an (olive)-branch. Pl. 43, cr. 6.

LIVINGSTONE, a demi-man, in hand a baton, in pale, or. Pl. 87, cr. 7.

LIVINGSTONE, of Kinnaird, a moor's head, couped, ppr., banded, gu. and ar., with pendent, ar., at ears. Pl. 48, cr. 7.

LIVINGSTONE, a demi-savage, wreathed about head and middle with laurel, all ppr. *Spe expecto.* Pl. 14, cr. 11.

LIVINGSTONE, in dexter hand a sword, ppr. *Et domi et foris.* Pl. 21, cr. 10.

LIVINGSTONE, Sco., a demi-savage, in dexter a club, (erect,) ppr., round sinister a serpent, vert. *Si je puis.* Pl. 92, cr. 10.

LIVINGSTONE, Sco., a demi-savage, wreathed about head and middle, in dexter a club, all ppr. *Spe expecto.* Pl. 14, cr. 11.

LIVINGSTONE, a demi-savage, holding a club over shoulder, ppr. *Si je puis.* Pl. 14, cr. 11.

LIVINGSTONE, Sir THOMAS, Bart., Stirling, a demi-savage, wreathed about head and middle with laurel leaves, in dexter a baton, (erect,) in sinister a serpent, entwined round arm, all ppr. *Si je puis.* Pl. 92, cr. 10.

LIZARS, Sco., a lion's gamb, ppr. Pl. 68, cr. 3.

LIZARS, Sco., a stag's head, erased, ppr. *Verus ad finem.* Pl. 66, cr. 9.

LIZURS, Eng., in hand a sword, ppr. Pl. 21, cr. 10.

LIZURS, two hands brandishing a sword. Pl. 3, cr. 10.

LLEWELLIN, RICHARD, Esq., of Holm Wood, Glouc., and Tregwynt, Pembroke, a griffin. *Fuimus.* Pl. 66, cr. 13.

LLEWELLYN, a pheon, ppr. Pl. 26, cr. 12.

LLEWELLYN, a demi-lion, rampant, ar. Pl. 67, cr. 10.

LLEWELLYN, a holy lamb. *Vincit qui patitur.* Pl. 48, cr. 13.

LLOYD, Bart., Suss., a lion's head, erased, per bend sinister, erm., and pean, gorged with a wreath of oak, vert. Pl. 22, cr. 3.

LLOYD, Wel., a Saracen's head and neck, (erased,) ppr., wreathed, or and az., (gorged with a collar, engrailed, of the last,) charged with two annulets, of the second. Pl. 126, cr. 8, (annulet, pl. 141.)

LLOYD, an eagle, wings elevated, preying on a pigeon. Pl. 61, cr. 7.

LLOYD, a wolf, rampant, (between fore-paws a dart, erect, point downward, and embrued.) Pl. 10, cr. 3.

LLOYD, Glouc. and Surr., a stag's head, erased, sa., charged on neck with a crescent, erm. Pl. 61, cr. 9.

LLOYD, Hants, on a mount, vert, a lion, sejant, gardant, gu. Pl. 113, cr. 8, (mount, pl. 108, cr. 12.)

LLOYD, Wel., a nag's head, erased, ar. Pl. 81, cr. 6.

LLOYD, Lond. and Wel., out of a ducal coronet, or, a cock's head, between wings, gu., combed, beaked and wattled, gold. Pl. 97, cr. 15, (wings, *same plate*, cr. 13.)

LLOYD, Wel., a horse's head, erased, sa., maned, or. *Pl.* 81, *cr.* 6.

LLOYD, Salop, issuing from a five-leaved coronet, or, a demi-lion, rampant, ar. *Pl.* 45, *cr.* 7, (coronet, *pl.* 23, *cr.* 11.)

LLOYD, Salop, a lion, rampant, gu. *Pl.* 67, *cr.* 5.

LLOYD, Wel., a demi-lion, rampant, gardant, or, holding an arrow, erect, ar. *Pl.* 35, *cr.* 4, (arrow, *pl.* 22, *cr.* 15.)

LLOYD, Bucks., a lion, passant, gu., (with two characters of the planet Venus, one on shoulder, the other on hip.) *Pl.* 48, *cr.* 8.

LLOYD, a stag, trippant, ppr., armed and hoofed, or. *Heb dduw heb ddym dduwadygon. Pl.* 68, *cr.* 2.

LLOYD, Eng., a greyhound's head, erased, sa. *Pl.* 89, *cr.* 2.

LLOYD, Iri., on a mount, a hind, statant, ppr., collared, ar. *Pl.* 75, *cr.* 6.

LLOYD, Eng., a stag's head, couped, ar. *Pl.* 91, *cr.* 14.

LLOYD, Eng., out of a ducal coronet, or, a unicorn's head, ar., crined and armed, gold. *Pl.* 45, *cr.* 14.

LLOYD, a lion, rampant, regardant. *Pl.* 10, *cr.* 15, (without fire-brand.)

LLOYD, a lion, rampant, regardant, in dexter a fleur-de-lis. *Pl.* 10, *cr.* 15, (fleur-de-lis, *pl.* 141.)

LLOYD, Eng., a wolf's head, erased, ar. *Pl.* 14, *cr.* 6.

LLOYD, of Welcomb House, Warw.: 1. A demi-arm, (in scale armour,) arm naked, ppr., cuff, ar., grasping a lizard, vert. *Pl.* 110, *cr.* 14. 2. Two arms in armour, embowed, ppr., supporting a chaplet of oak-branches, vert, fructed, or. *Pl.* 64, *cr.* 11, (chaplet, *pl.* 74, *cr.* 7.)

LLOYD, a cubit arm, (in armour, erect, ppr., garnished, or,) in hand a lizard, gold. *Pl.* 110, *cr.* 14.

LLOYD, Salop, a demi-lion, rampant, or. *Pl.* 67, *cr.* 10.

LLOYD, Wel., a hart, trippant, ar., attired, or, in mouth a snake, vert. *Pl.* 68, *cr.* 2, (snake, *pl.* 54, *cr.* 7.)

LLOYD, Wel. and Kent, a man's head, ppr., in armour, ar., garnished, or, on a label issuing from mouth, and proceeding over head, *Avonno div dervid.*

LLOYD, EDWARD-PRYSE, Esq., of Glansevin, Caermarthen, a lion, rampant. *Fiat justitia, ruat cœlum. Pl.* 67, *cr.* 5.

LLOYD, JOHN-ARTHUR, Esq., of Leaton Knolls, Salop, a demi-lion, rampant, or. *Retinens vestigia famæ. Pl.* 67, *cr.* 10.

LLOYD, ELIZABETH, of Lagues, Carmarthen, an eagle, preying on a bird. *Pl.* 61, *cr.* 7.

LLOYD, Bronwydd, Cardigan, a boar, chained to a holly-bush, ppr. *Pl.* 57, *cr.* 12.

LLOYD, Clochfaen, a lion, rampant, gu. *In te, Domine, speravi. Pl.* 67, *cr.* 5.

LLOYD, Trallwyn, a lion, rampant, ar., guttée-de-sang, surmounting two spears, in saltier, ppr. *Pl.* 67, *cr.* 5, (spears, *pl.* 53, *cr.* 14.)

LLOYD-HARDRESS, Iri., a lion, rampant, ar., between paws a snake. *Respice, prospice. Pl.* 124, *cr.* 5, (lion, *pl.* 67, *cr.* 5.)

LLUELLIN, Herts., a paschal lamb, ppr. *Pl.* 48, *cr.* 13.

LOADER, Eng., on a chapeau, gu., two lions, rampant, supporting a garb, ppr. *Pl.* 36, *cr.* 8.

LOADER, a dragon, passant, ppr. *Pl.* 90, *cr.* 10.

LOADES, Lond., out of a mural coronet, an arm, vested, sa., cuffed, ar., in hand, ppr., a key, or. *Obey and rule. Pl.* 79, *cr.* 4, (key, *pl.* 41, *cr.* 11.)

LOANE, Eng., a demi-lion, rampant, sa., brandishing a scimitar, ppr. *Pl.* 126 A, *cr.* 1.

LOAT, Eng., between wings, a spur-rowel, ppr. *Pl.* 54, *cr.* 5, (wings, *same plate, cr.* 6.)

LOBAN, a dexter arm, in armour, embowed, in hand a tilting-spear, ppr. *Pl.* 44, *cr.* 9, (spear, *pl.* 57, *cr.* 3.)

LOBB, Eng., a lion's head, erased, collared, gu. *Pl.* 7, *cr.* 10.

LOBB, a dexter arm, in armour, embowed, in hand a spear, point downward, sa., headed, ar. *Pl.* 44, *cr.* 9, (spear, *pl.* 57, *cr.* 3.)

LOBERT, a dexter arm, embowed, vested, az., in hand, ppr., a hunting-spear, point downward, sa., headed, ar. *Pl.* 39, *cr.* 1, (spear, *same plate, cr.* 15.)

LOCH, and LOCK, Sco., a swan, wings addorsed, in mouth a fish, both ppr. *Assiduitate, non desidiâ. Pl.* 103, *cr.* 1.

LOCH, Sco., a swan, wings addorsed, swimming in a loch, and devouring a perch, all ppr. *Assiduitate non desidiâ. Pl.* 66, *cr.* 10, (perch, *pl.* 103, *cr.* 1.)

LOCH, Sco., a swan, wings addorsed, devouring a perch, all ppr. *Pl.* 103, *cr.* 1.

LOCHEAD, or LOCHHEAD, Sco., a dexter hand, erect, pointing to the sun with two fingers. *Pl.* 15, *cr.* 4.

LOCHORE, Sco., a fox's head, couped, gu. *Pl.* 91, *cr.* 9.

LOCKE, Lond., a hand, ppr., holding up a cushion, or. *Pl.* 83, *cr.* 9.

LOCKE, a hawk, wings addorsed, in beak a padlock, or. *Pl.* 61, *cr.* 1, (without mount; lock, *pl.* 96, *cr.* 15.)

LOCK, a lion, rampant, between fore-paws a cushion. *Pl.* 125, *cr.* 2, (cushion, *pl.* 83, *cr.* 9.)

LOCK, Hants, a falcon, rising, or, collared, gu., in beak a padlock, sa. *Pl.* 105, *cr.* 4, (padlock, *pl.* 96, *cr.* 15.)

LOCK, Suff., a falcon, rising, or, (ducally crowned,) ar., in beak a padlock, pendent, sa. *Ib.*

LOCK, Surr., a falcon, wings (addorsed,) and belled, in beak a padlock. *Pl.* 105, *cr.* 4, (padlock, *pl.* 96, *cr.* 15.)

LOCKER, a buck's head, erased, ppr. *Pl.* 66, *cr.* 9.

LOCKETT, Chesh., a dexter arm, in armour, embowed, ppr., purfled, in hand a key, (in fess,) or. *Tenuimus. Pl.* 41, *cr.* 11.

LOCKEY, Herts., Yorks., and Wel., an ostrich's head, couped at neck, ar., in beak a key, sa. *Pl.* 99, *cr.* 12, (without feathers, key, *pl.* 9, *cr.* 12.)

LOCKHART, in dexter hand, a boar's head, erased and erect, ppr. *Sine labe fides. Pl.* 86, *cr.* 6.

LOCKHART, Sco., a boar's head, erased, az. *Feroci fortior. Pl.* 16, *cr.* 11.

LOCKHART, Sco., a boar's head, erased, ar. *Sine labe fides. Pl.* 16, *cr.* 11.

LOCKHART, Sco., same crest. *Feroci fortior.*

LOCKHART, Sco., a fetterlock. *Hoc securior. Pl.* 122, *cr.* 12.

LOCKHART, Bart., Sco., a boar's head, erased, ar. *Corda serata pando*—and—*Semper paratus pugnare pro patriâ. Pl.* 16, *cr.* 11.

LOCKHART, Sco., in dexter hand a boar's head, erased, ppr. *Feroci fortior.* Pl. 86, cr. 6.
LOCKHART, three crests: 1. In the centre, two flags, parted, per fees, ar. and gu., flotant to dexter and sinister, placed behind a boar's head, erased. Pl. 53, cr. 14, (head, pl. 16, cr. 11.) 2. On the dexter, on a ducal coronet, an eagle, displayed, regardant. Pl. 48, cr. 11. 3. On the sinister, out of a ducal coronet, a demi-lion, in dexter a sword. *Corda serata pando.* Pl. 41, cr. 13, (coronet, same plate, cr. 10.)
LOCKHART, Sco., a hand holding forth a key, in bend, ppr. *Corda serata pando.* Pl. 41, cr. 11.
LOCKHART, Sco., a boar's head, erased, ppr. *Corda serata pando.* Pl. 16, cr. 11.
LOCKHART, M'DONALD, a boar's head, erased, ar., langued, gu. *Corda serata pando.* Pl. 16, cr. 11.
LOCKHART, Sco., a boar's head, erased. *Sit sine labe fides.* Pl. 16, cr. 11.
LOCKHART-ELLIOTT, ALLAN, Esq., of Borthwickbrae, Selkirk, and Cleghorn, Lanark: 1. A boar's head, erased, ar. Pl. 16, cr. 11. 2. In dexter hand a spear, ppr. *Sine labe fides*—and—*Hoc majorum opus.* Pl. 99, cr. 8.
LOCKSMITH, out of a mural coronet, or, a griffin's head, ppr. Pl. 101, cr. 6, (without gorging.)
LOCKTON, Linc., out of a ducal coronet, or, a griffin's head, az. Pl. 101, cr. 6, (without gorging.)
LOCKWOOD, Eng., a camel's head, couped, sa. Pl. 109, cr. 9.
LOCKWOOD, Ess., Northamp., and Surr., on stump of tree, erased, ppr., a martlet, sa. Pl. 30, cr. 5, (martlet, pl. 111, cr. 5.)
LOCKYER, Eng., an astrolabe, ar. Pl. 26, cr. 2.
LOCKYER, on the sea a ship, (the three topsails hoisted, ppr., the main-topsail charged with a lion, rampant, gu., the fore and mizen topsails each charged with an ant, ppr., a red ensign.) Pl. 115, cr. 9.
LODBROOK, or LODBROOKE, Eng., a unicorn, rampant. Pl. 37, cr. 7.
LODER, Eng., a stag's head, (couped at neck,) between horns a cross crosslet. Pl. 24, cr. 9.
LODGE, Eng., a demi-lion, double-queued, az. Pl. 120, cr. 10.
LODGE, Iri., a talbot's head, erased, az., collared, or. Pl. 2, cr. 15.
LODGE, a demi-lion, rampant, sa., (between paws) a cross pattée, fitched, gu. Pl. 65, cr. 6.
LODGE, a lion, double-queued, az. Pl. 41, cr. 15.
LODGE-ELLERTON, of Bodsilin: 1. For *Ellerton*, a reindeer, trippant, or, attired and hoofed, gu., (gorged with a wreath of oak-leaves, vert.) Pl. 12, cr. 8. 2. A demi-lion, (erased,) sa., semée of fleurs-de-lis, or, supporting a cross pattée, fitched, gu. Pl. 29, cr. 12, (cross, pl. 27, cr. 14; fleur-de-lis, pl. 141.)
LODINGTON, Eng., a demi-lady, ppr., richly attired, az., in dexter a garland, vert. Pl. 87, cr. 14.
LODWICH, and LODWICK, Eng., a cock, ppr. Pl. 67, cr. 14.
LOE, a wolf's head, couped, ar., collared, gu., charged with three bezants. Pl. 8, cr. 4.
LOFT, Linc., a wolf's head, couped, gu., charged on neck with a pheon, (transfixed through mouth by a broken spear, or.) Pl. 40, cr. 12, (pheon, pl. 141.)

LOFTHOUSE, Eng., between wings a spur, ppr. Pl. 109, cr. 12.
LOFTUS, Baron. *See* ELY, Marquess of.
LOFTUS, Iri., a boar's head, in pale, erased, ar., armed, or. Pl. 21, cr. 7.
LOFTUS, Iri., a boar's head, in pale, (couped,) ar., armed, or. Pl. 21, cr. 7.
LOFTUS, Eng., in dexter hand a dagger, both ppr. Pl. 28, cr. 4.
LOFTUS, Norf., a boar's head, erased, ar. Pl. 16, cr. 11.
LOFTUS, of Woolland, Dors., a boar's head, (couped,) and erect, ar., langued, gu. Pl. 21, cr. 7.
LOFTUS, of Kilbride, Iri., a boar's head, (couped,) and erect, ar., langued, gu. *Loyal à la mort.* Pl. 21, cr. 7.
LOFTUS, Bart., Iri., same crest and motto.
LOGAN, Iri., a demi-lion, rampant, vert. Pl. 67, cr. 10.
LOGAN, Sco., a bugle-horn, stringed, ppr. Pl. 48, cr. 12.
LOGAN, Sco., a passion-nail, piercing a man's heart. *Hoc majorum virtus.* Pl. 81, cr. 3.
LOGAN, Eng., a hand, erect, pointing with two fingers to the sun, ppr. Pl. 15, cr. 4.
LOGES, Eng., a swan, collared and lined, ppr. Pl. 73, cr. 14.
LOGGAN, and LOGON, Berks. and. Bucks., a stag's head, erased, gu., attired, collared, and lined, or. Pl. 125, cr. 6, (without roses.)
LOGGIE, Eng., a goat's head, az. Pl. 105, cr. 14.
LOGGIE, Sco., in dexter hand a rose, gu., stalked and leaved, vert. Pl. 118, cr. 9.
LOGHLAN, Sco., a swan. *Divina sibi canat.* Pl. 122, cr. 13.
LOGHLIN, Eng., an anchor and cable, ppr. Pl. 42, cr. 12.
LOGIE, Sco., a leopard's head, affrontée, or. Pl. 56, cr. 7.
LOGY, Sco., in dexter hand a rose, stalked and leaved, all ppr. Pl. 118, cr. 9.
LOMAS, Eng., on a chapeau, a pelican, vulning, ppr. Pl. 21, cr. 5.
LOMAX, Eng., out of a heart, a dexter hand, brandishing a scimitar, all ppr. Pl. 35, cr. 7.
LOMAX, Lanc., out of a mural coronet, a demi-lion, gu., (collared,) holding an escallop. Pl. 17, cr. 7, (escallop, pl. 6, cr. 9.)
LOMAX, Surr., a demi-greyhound, ar., collared, gu. Pl. 5, cr. 10, (without wings.)
LOMB, two spears, in saltier, at the top of each a small pennon. Pl. 53, cr. 14.
LOMELYING, Eng., a demi-lion, rampant, ar. *Fortiter et recte.* Pl. 67, cr. 10.
LOMENER, LOMNEIR, and LOMNYER, between wings, ar., a unicorn's head, sa., armed and crined, or. Pl. 20, cr. 1, (wings, pl. 19, cr. 13.)
LOMNER, a unicorn's head, sa., (winged, ar.,) horned, or, in mouth a rose, ppr. Pl. 20, cr. 1, (rose, pl. 95, cr. 6.)
LOMOND, out of a coronet, or, a tower, ppr. Pl. 12, cr. 5, (coronet, pl. 128, fig. 3.)
LONDETH, Eng., a winged heart, ppr. Pl. 39, cr. 7.
LONDHAM, on a chapeau, ppr., an escallop, sa. Pl. 17, cr. 14, (without wings.)
LONDON, City of, a dragon's sinister wing, expanded, ar., charged with a cross, gu. *Domine, dirige nos.* Pl. 105, cr. 11, (cross, pl. 141.)

LONDON, out of a tower, a demi-man in armour, in profile, holding a sword by the blade, erect.

LONDONDERRY, Marquess and Earl of, Viscount Castlereagh, and Baron Stewart, Iri., Earl Vane, Viscount Seaham, and Baron Stewart, U.K., (Vane-Stewart:) 1. For *Vane,* a dexter gauntlet, erect, holding a sword, ppr., hilt and pommel, or. *Pl.* 125, *cr.* 5. 2. A dragon, (statant,) or. *Metuenda corolla draconis. Pl.* 90, *cr.* 10,

LONDESBOROUGH, Baron: 1. A cubit arm, (in bend, vested, az., cuffed, ar.,) hand, ppr., pointing with the fore-finger to a star, or. *Pl.* 77, *cr.* 6, (without clouds.) 2. A unicorn's head, erased, ar., armed and maned, or. *Adversa virtute repello. Pl.* 20, *cr.* 1.

LONE, Kent, a demi-buck, salient, ar., attired, or. *Pl.* 55, *cr.* 9, (without rose.)

LONE, Lond., a demi-buck, salient. *I am alone. Ib.*

LONESBY, a rabbit, ar. *Pl.* 29, *cr.* 9.

LONEY, Eng., a cubit arm, vested, compony, or and gu., in hand an anchor, ppr., ringed, sa. *Pl.* 53, *cr.* 13.

LONG, Surr. and Herts., out of a ducal coronet, or, a lion's head, ar., guttée-de-sang. *Pieux quoique preux. Pl.* 90, *cr.* 9.

LONG, out of a five-leaved coronet, or, a demi-lion, rampant, ar. *Pl.* 45, *cr.* 7, (coronet, *pl.* 23, *cr.* 11.)

LONG, Wilt., out of a crescent, or, a lion's head, sa., guttée, or. *Pl.* 96, *cr.* 13, (without crown.)

LONG, Wilts., out of a ducal coronet, or, a lion's head, ar., guttée, sa. *Pl.* 90, *cr.* 9.

LONG, Norf., on a mount, vert, a greyhound, current, sa., (collared and lined, erm.) *Pl.* 28, *cr.* 7, (mount, *pl.* 98, *cr.* 13.)

LONG, Lond., a lion's head, erased, per pale, ar. and sa., charged with three guttes, counterchanged, two and one. *Pl.* 81, *cr.* 4.

LONG, Lond., a lion's head, erased, gu. *Iram leonis noli timere. Pl.* 81, *cr.* 4.

LONG, Westm., Devons., Wilts., and Middx., a lion's head, ar., in mouth a sinister hand, erased, ppr. *Pl.* 107, *cr.* 9.

LONG, Herts. and Suff., a lion, rampant, gu., holding a saltier, engrailed, or. *Pl.* 125, *cr.* 2, (saltier, *pl.* 25, *cr.* 5.)

LONG, Beds., out of a ducal coronet, or, a demi-lion, rampant, ar. *Pl.* 45, *cr.* 7.

LONG, Wilts, out of a ducal coronet, or, a demi-lion, ar. *Pl.* 45, *cr.* 7.

LONG, WALTER, Esq., of Rood 'Ashton, Wraxhall and Whaddon, all in Wilts., out of a ducal coronet, or, a demi-lion, rampant, ar. *Pieux quoique preux. Pl.* 45, *cr.* 7.

LONG, Baron Farnborough. *See* FARNBOROUGH.

LONG, Norf., on a chapeau, a (demi-)peacock, wings displayed, ppr. *Pl.* 50, *cr.* 15.

LONG, Lond., on a mount, in front of a tree, ppr., a wyvern, couchant, vert. *Confide recte agens. Pl.* 33, *cr.* 13, (tree, *pl.* 48, *cr.* 4.)

LONGBOTTOM, a horse's head, ppr. *Pl.* 81, *cr.* 6.

LONG-BOW STRING-MAKERS, Eng., an archer, vested, ppr., shooting with a bow and arrow, of the last. *Nec habeo, nec careo, nec curo. Pl.* 90, *cr.* 3.

LONGCHAMP, or LONGCHAMPE, Eng., a tower, triple-towered, ppr. *Pl.* 123, *cr.* 14.

LONGCROFT, Hants, a demi-lion, rampant, ar., between paws, (three annulets, or,) charged on shoulder with a saltier, gu. *Nunc ut olim. Pl.* 126, *cr.* 12, (saltier, *pl.* 25, *cr.* 5.)

LONGDEN, Eng., on a chapeau gu., turned up, or, a dove, wings addorsed, az. *Pl.* 109, *cr.* 10.

LONGE, Eng., in a ducal coronet, a phœnix in flames, ppr. *Pl.* 53, *cr.* 6.

LONGE, Norf., a lion, sejant, gu., holding a saltier, engrailed, or. *Pl.* 22, *cr.* 13, (saltier, *pl.* 25, *cr.* 5.)

LONGEVILE, on a mural coronet, a stag, sejant, ppr. *Pl.* 101, *cr.* 3.

LONGEVILLE, Bucks. and Hants, a talbot's head, gu., eared, ar., gorged with a collar, dancettée, of the last. *Pl.* 2, *cr.* 15.

LONGFIELD, RICHARD, Esq., of Longueville, co. Cork, out of a ducal coronet, a demi-lion, rampant. *Parcere subjectis. Pl.* 45, *cr.* 7.

LONGFIELD, Viscount Longueville, Iri., same crest and motto.

LONGFORD, Eng., a boar's head, erased, az. *Pl.* 16, *cr.* 11.

LONGFORD, Earl of, and Baron, Iri., Baron Silchester, U.K., (Pakenham,) out of a mural coronet, or, a demi-eagle, displayed, with two heads, quarterly, ar. and az. *Gloria virtutis umbra. Pl.* 33, *cr.* 5, (eagle, *pl.* 4, *cr.* 6.)

LONGHAM, Sco., a bear's head, erased, ppr., muzzled, or. *Pl.* 71, *cr.* 6.

LONGHURST, Eng., out of a ducal coronet, or, a griffin's head, in beak a key, ppr. *Pl.* 89, *cr.* 5.

LONGLAND, in the sea an anchor, (in bend sinister.) *Pl.* 62, *cr.* 10.

LONGLAND, an anchor, (in bend dexter,) cabled. *Pl.* 42, *cr.* 12.

LONGLAND, an anchor, in pale. *Pl.* 25, *cr.* 15.

LONGLAND, an arm, couped, or, pellettée, in hand, ppr., a cross crosslet, fitched, gu. *Pl.* 99, *cr.* 1.

LONGLAND, on stump of tree, eradicated and couped, or, a dove, ar. *Pl.* 124, *cr.* 13.

LONGLANDS, Bucks., on a mount, vert, a garb, or. *Pl.* 13, *cr.* 2.

LONGLANDS, Sco., an anchor. *Pl.* 25, *cr.* 15.

LONGLEY, Eng., an arm, couped at shoulder, resting elbow on wreath, in hand a sword, in pale, enfiled with a savage's head, couped, ppr. *Pl.* 102, *cr.* 11.

LONGMAN, Eng., a dexter hand, in fess, holding an anchor, in pale, environed with clouds, all ppr. *Pl.* 79, *cr.* 15.

LONGRIDGE, an arm, embowed, vested, in hand a garb. *Pl.* 39, *cr.* 1, (garb, *pl.* 3, *cr.* 3.)

LONGSDON, Eng., a fox's head, erased, ar. *Pl.* 71, *cr.* 4.

LONGSDON, Eng., an eagle, displayed, with two heads, or. *Pl.* 25, *cr.* 5, (without charging.)

LONGSPEARE, Eng., a talbot's head, couped, paly of four, or and gu., in mouth a demi-hare, erased, az. *Pl.* 123, *cr.* 15, (hare, *pl.* 58, *cr.* 14.)

LONGSPEE, Eng., on a ball, sa., winged, or, an eagle, wings displayed, ppr. *Pl.* 50, *cr.* 7, (eagle, *pl.* 126, *cr.* 1.)

LONGSTAFF, Eng., a stag, at gaze, under a tree, ppr. *Pl.* 118, *cr.* 13.

LONGSTAFF, a demi-lion, rampant, between paws (a quarter-staff,) all ppr. *Pl.* 47, *cr.* 4.

LONGUEVILLE, Bart., Wel., a talbot's head, couped, (on neck a bar-dancettée,) all ar. *Pl.* 123, *cr.* 15.)

LONGWORTH, Eng., a boar's head, couped, in mouth a sword, ppr. *Pl.* 28, *cr.* 14.
LONSDALE, Eng., a bull, passant, gu. *Pl.* 66, *cr.* 11.
LONSDALE, Yorks., a demi-stag, salient, erased, gu., on body a crescent, sa., attired, unguled, (and collared,) of the last, collar charged with three crescents. *Pl.* 55, *cr.* 9, (without rose; crescents, *pl.* 141.)
LONSDALE, Earl of, Viscount and Baron Lowther, and a Bart., (Lowther,) a dragon, passant, ar. *Magistratus indicat virum.* *Pl.* 90, *cr.* 10.
LONYSON, between two ostrich-feathers, or, a swan, ppr. *Pl.* 122, *cr.* 13, (feathers, *pl.* 50, *cr.* 1.)
LOOKER, Eng., a pillar, ensigned with a heart, gu. *Pl.* 122, *cr.* 4.
LOPES, Bart., Devons., a lion, sejant, erminois, gorged with a bar-gemelle, gu., resting dexter on a lozenge, az. *Quod tibi, id alii.* *Pl.* 109, *cr.* 7, (lozenge, *pl.* 141.)
LORAND, on a tower, ar., a martlet, sa. *Pl.* 107, *cr.* 6.
LORD, Eng., in a maunch, az., cuffed, or, a dexter arm, hand clenched. *Pl.* 22, *cr.* 14.
LORD, Iri., a sword and garb, in saltier. *Pl.* 70, *cr.* 7.
LORIMER, Eng., a mascle, gu. *Pl.* 54, *cr.* 1.
LORIMER, Sco., a lion's head, erased. *Pl.* 81, *cr.* 4.
LORIMER, Sco., a lion, rampant, ppr., in dexter a fleur-de-lis, or. *Pl.* 87, *cr.* 6.
LORIMER, a horse, current, ar. *Nulla salus bello.* *Pl.* 107, *cr.* 5, (without spear.)
LORIMER, Sco., out of a cloud, a hand in fess, pointing to a crozier, issuing from the wreath, ppr. *Pl.* 45, *cr.* 4.
LORIMER, Eng., in a maunch, an arm, couped at shoulder, and embowed, elbow resting on the wreath. *Pl.* 22, *cr.* 14.
LORING, and LORINGE, Eng., a hand holding a mill-rind. *Pl.* 34, *cr.* 4.
LORING, and LORINGE, out of a (bowl, or, five) quills, in pale, ar. *Pl.* 86, *cr.* 7.
LORN, Sco., a boar's head, erased. *Ne obliviscaris.* *Pl.* 16, *cr.* 11.
LORRAINE, Bart., Northumb., a laurel-tree, couped, two branches sprouting, ppr., and fixed to the lower part thereof with a belt, gu., edged and buckled, or, an escutcheon, az. *Lauro scutoque resurgo.* *Pl.* 23, *cr.* 6.
LORRAYNE, and LORREYNE, an escutcheon, az., suspended from a palm-tree, all ppr. *Pl.* 23, *cr.* 6, (palm, *pl.* 18, *cr.* 12.)
LORSOR, a wolf, sejant, ppr., in mouth an arrow, erect, or, barbed and feathered, ar. *Pl.* 110, *cr.* 4, (arrow, *same plate.*)
LORT, an Ionic pillar and base, ar. *Pl.* 33, *cr.* 1.
LORTON, Viscount and Baron Erris, Iri., (King:) 1. Out of a ducal coronet, or, a hand, erect, the third and fourth fingers turned down, ar., (charged with a crescent, gu.) *Pl.* 67, *cr.* 6, (coronet, *same plate.*) 2. Out of a ducal coronet, or, an arm, erect, in hand a bunch of roses, ppr. *Spes tutissima cœlis.* *Pl.* 60, *cr.* 1.
LOSACK, Eng., out of a cloud, a dexter hand holding an anchor, in pale, all ppr. *Pl.* 41, *cr.* 5.
LOSCOMBE, Somers., a demi-leopard, ppr., (collared, gu.,) in dexter a cross moline, between two cross crosslets, or. *Pl.* 125, *cr.* 4, (crosses, *pl.* 141.)
LOSH, Eng., a cubit arm, ppr., hand holding up a crescent, or. *Pl.* 38, *cr.* 7.
LOSSE, Suff., a cubit arm, in pale, vested, gu., in hand, ppr., a fleur-de-lis, per pale, ar. and sa. *Pl.* 95, *cr.* 9.
LOSSE, Middx., a lion's head, erased, per saltier, ar. and sa., charged with four guttés, counter-changed. *Pl.* 81, *cr.* 4.
LOTEN, Middx., a gilliflower, ppr., between wings, erect, dexter, or, sinister, vert. *Pl.* 22, *cr.* 9, (wings, *same plate, cr.* 2.)
LOTEREL, Sco., a lion, passant, ppr. *Pl.* 48, *cr.* 8.
LOTH, and LOTHE, an arrow and a bow, in saltier, ppr. *Pl.* 12, *cr.* 12.
LOTHIAN, Sco., a bugle-horn, ar., stringed and veruled, or. *Non dormit, qui custodit.* *Pl.* 48, *cr.* 12.
LOTHIAN, Marquess and Earl of, Earl of Ancrum, Viscount of Brian, Baron Newbattle and Jedburgh, Sco.; Baron Ker, U.K., (Ker,) the sun, in splendour. *Sero sed serio.* *Pl.* 68, *cr.* 14.
LOTYSHAM, Somers, on a ducal coronet, gu., an otter's head, erased, or, in mouth a fish, ppr. *Pl.* 126, *cr.* 14, (coronet, *pl.* 128, *fig.* 3.)
LOUBIS, Devons. and Cornw., a bear, rampant, sa., muzzled and lined, ar. *Pl.* 1, *cr.* 3, (without staff.)
LOUDON, Sco., a bugle-horn. *Non dormit, qui custodit.* *Pl.* 89, *cr.* 3.
LOUDON, Sco., a hand plucking a rose, ppr. *Pl.* 48, *cr.* 1.
LOUDON, Sco., a phœnix, with two heads, in flames, ppr. *I byde my time.* *Pl.* 7, *cr.* 8.
LOUDOUN, Sco., an eagle, displayed, ar., charged with a cinquefoil, gu. *Pl.* 85, *cr.* 11, (without crown.)
LOUGHNAN, Iri., a castle, triple-towered, ppr. *Fortis et fidus.* *Pl.* 123, *cr.* 14.
LOUIS, a wolf, rampant, ar. *Pl.* 10, *cr.* 3.
LOUIS, Sco., in hand a lance, (in bend,) ppr. *Nos aspera juvant.* *Pl.* 29, *cr.* 6.
LOUIS, Bart., Devons., a griffin's head, erased, az., between wings, or, in beak a fleur-de-lis, on breast a trident, erect, or. *In canopo ut ad canopum.* *Pl.* 65, *cr.* 1, (fleur-de-lis, *pl.* 141; trident, *pl.* 12, *cr.* 3.)
LOUNDE, Eng., a hind, (sejant, regardant, ppr., collared, gu.,) resting dexter on a bee-hive, ppr. *Pl.* 1, *cr.* 14.
LOURIS, Devons. and Cornw., a bear, rampant, sa., muzzled and lined, ar. *Pl.* 1, *cr.* 3, (without stuff.)
LOUTH, Baron of, Iri., (Plunkett,) a horse, passant, ar. *Festina lente.* *Pl.* 15, *cr.* 14.
LOUTHFUTTIS, Sco., a swan, naiant, in water, wings addorsed, ppr. *Addicunt aves.* *Pl.* 66, *cr.* 10.
LOUTHIAN, a bugle-horn, pendent, ppr. *Non dormit qui custodit.* *Pl.* 48, *cr.* 12.
LOVAIN, Eng., on a chapeau, gu., turned up, erm., a lion, passant, (tail extended,) az. *Pl.* 107, *cr.* 1.
LOVE, Sco., a buffalo's head, erased, gu., horned, or, eared, ar. *Pl.* 57, *cr.* 7.
LOVE, Hants and Oxon., out of a ducal coronet, or, a cross formée, gu., thereon a bird, ar. *Pl.* 98, *cr.* 6, (bird, *same plate, cr.* 3; cross, *pl.* 141.)

LOVAYNE, and LOVEYNE, Eng., a cross crosslet, fitched, or. *Pl.* 16, *cr.* 10.
LOVAT, Baron, U.K., (Fraser,) a buck's head, erased, or, attired, ar. *Je suis prest. Pl.* 66, *cr.* 9.
LOVE, Norf., an heraldic-tiger's head, erased, vert, maned, ar. *Pl.* 113, *cr.* 3.
LOVE, Kent, a demi-buck. *Pl.* 55, *cr.* 9, (without rose.)
LOVE, Eng., in hand an annulet, ppr. *Pl.* 24, *cr.* 3.
LOVE, on a chapeau, gu., turned up, erm., a lion, passant, ar. *Pl.* 107, *cr.* 1.
LOVE, Northamp., a demi-greyhound, ar., collared and (lined, sa., the end of the line coiled.) *Pl.* 5, *cr.* 10, (without wings.)
LOVEDAY, Suff. and Norf., a squirrel, ppr. *Pl.* 16, *cr.* 9.
LOVEDAY, Oxon., an eagle, displayed, with two heads, counterchanged, armed, membered, and ducally gorged, or. *Pl.* 87, *cr.* 11, (without flame, gorging, *same plate*, *cr.* 15.)
LOVEDEN, a tiger, sejant, or, ducally gorged, ar. *Pl.* 26, *cr.* 9, (coronet, *pl.* 128, *fig.* 3.)
LOVEGROVE, Eng., a staff, raguly, surmounted by an eagle, displayed, ppr. *Pl.* 8, *cr.* 1.
LOVEJOY, Eng., a cubit arm, in armour, in hand a caltrap. *Pl.* 22, *cr.* 4.
LOVELACE, Kent, a staff, raguly, vert, surmounted by an eagle, displayed, ar. *Pl.* 8, *cr.* 1.
LOVELACE, on a staff, raguly, in fess, couped at each end, an eagle, displayed. *Pl.* 48, *cr.* 11, (staff, *pl.* 5, *cr.* 8.)
LOVELACE, Earl of, Viscount and Baron Oakham, Lord King. *See* KING.
LOVELAND, Norf., a boar's head and neck, couped, sa. *Pl.* 2, *cr.* 7.
LOVELASS, Eng., out of a ducal coronet, or, a dexter arm, ppr., vested, purp., cuffed, ar., holding up the sun in splendour. *Pl.* 89, *cr.* 11.
LOVELESS, Eng., a demi-talbot, ppr. *Pl.* 97, *cr.* 9, (without arrow.)
LOVELL, Dors., a wolf, passant, az., bezantée, collared and (lined,) or. *Pl.* 5, *cr.* 8, (without staff.)
LOVELL, Norf., a squirrel, sejant, cracking a nut. *Pl.* 16, *cr.* 9.
LOVELL, Sir LOVELL-BENJAMIN, K.C.B., of Linc. and Bucks., a talbot, passant, ar. *Tempus omnia monstrat. Pl.* 120, *cr.* 8.
LOVELL, a garb, ppr., banded, gu. *Pl.* 48, *cr.* 10.
LOVELL, Yorks, a talbot, (current,) ar. *Pl.* 120, *cr.* 8.
LOVELL, Norf. and Wilts., a squirrel, sejant, ppr., cracking a nut. *Pl.* 16, *cr.* 9.
LOVELL, Norf., a peacock's tail, erect, ppr., (belted, sa., rimmed and buckled, ar., pendent.) *Pl.* 120, *cr.* 13, (without coronet.)
LOVELL, Suff., a greyhound, passant, sa., collared, ringed, and lined, or, a cubit arm, erect, ppr., vested, purp., hand holding the line.
LOVELOCK, Eng., a greyhound, (passant,) sa. *Pl.* 104, *cr.* 1, (without chapeau.)
LOVENEY, Eng., a griffin, sejant, wings addorsed, ppr. *Pl.* 100, *cr.* 11.
LOVET, Hunts., Derbs., Northamp., Ess., and Devons., a wolf's head, erased, sa. *Pl.* 14, *cr.* 6.

LOVET, or LOVETT, a wolf, passant. *Pl.* 46, *cr.* 6.
LOVET, or LOVETT, a demi-wolf, rampant, sa., pierced through breast by an arrow, or, flighted, ar. *Pl.* 40, *cr.* 12.
LOVETOT, and LOVETOFT, Eng., a demi-lady holding a pair of scales. *Pl.* 57, *cr.* 1.
LOVETT, Hants, a griffin, rampant, ppr. *Pl.* 67, *cr.* 13.
LOVETT, of Liscombe and Soulbury, a wolf's head, erased, sa. *Pl.* 14, *cr.* 6.
LOVETT, JOSEPH-VENABLES, Esq., of Belmont, Salop, a wolf, passant, ppr. *Pl.* 46, *cr.* 6.
LOVEYNE, a cross crosslet, fitched, or. *Pl.* 16, *cr.* 10.
LOVIBOND, Bucks., a buck's head. *Pl.* 91, *cr.* 14.
LOVIBOND, Ess., a boar's head, (couped) and erect, gu. *Pl.* 21, *cr.* 7.
LOVIS, a lion's head, erased, gu., on head a chapeau, ar., turned up, erm. *Pl.* 122, *cr.* 10.
LOVISE, Eng., a mound, gu., band and cross, or. *Pl.* 37, *cr.* 3.
Low, Eng., out of a ducal coronet, a peacock's tail, ppr. *Pl.* 120, *cr.* 13.
Low, a wolf's head, erased, sa., charged on neck with a bezant. *Pl.* 14, *cr.* 6, (bezant, *pl.* 141.)
Low, Sco., a leaf, between two (thistles,) stalked and leaved, ppr. *Aspera me juvant. Pl.* 108, *cr.* 7.
Low, a wolf, passant, ar. *Pl.* 46, *cr.* 6.
Low, Eng., a wolf, passant, ppr. *Pl.* 46, *cr.* 6.
Low, Sco., a falcon, regardant, in dexter a laurel crown. *Pl.* 42, *cr.* 7.
LOWDELL, Eng., a sphinx, couchant, (gardant,) wings addorsed. *Pl.* 116, *cr.* 5, (without cinquefoil.)
LOWDEN, Eng., on a ducal coronet, a wyvern, vomiting fire at both ends, all ppr. *Pl.* 109, *cr.* 13, (coronet, *pl.* 128, *fig.* 3.)
LOWDER, Eng., out of a mural coronet, seven halberds, facing outwards. *Pl.* 62, *cr.* 8.
LOWDES, a wyvern, ar. *Pl.* 63, *cr.* 13.
LOWDHAM, Eng., between two palm-branches, an escallop, all ppr. *Pl.* 86, *cr.* 9.
LOWE, Derbs. and Middx., a wolf, passant, ar. (Another, ppr.) *Pl.* 46, *cr.* 6.
LOWE, Wilts., a wolf's head, couped, ar., collared, or. *Pl.* 8, *cr.* 4.
LOWE, the Rev. THOMAS-HILL-PEREGRINE-FURYE, D.D., of Bromsgrove, Worc., a demi-griffin, rampant, or. *Spero meliora. Pl.* 18, *cr.* 6.
LOWE, Locko Park, Derbs.: 1. For *Lowe*, a wolf, passant, ppr. *Pl.* 46, *cr.* 6. 2. For *Drury*, a greyhound, current, sa., collared, and charged on body with two mullets, in fess, or. *Pl.* 28, *cr.* 7, (mullet, *pl.* 141.)
LOWE, Derbs., on a mount, vert, a heathcock, ppr., winged, or.
LOWE, a wolf's head, couped, ppr., collared and ringed, or. *Pl.* 8, *cr.* 4.
LOWE, a wolf, passant, ar., collared and (chained, gu., chain reflexed over back.) *Pl.* 5, *cr.* 8, (without staff.)
LOWE, an ermine, ppr., collared, ringed and lined, gu. *Pl.* 12, *cr.* 2.
LOWE, Kent and Lond., a falcon, wings extended, or. *Pl.* 105, *cr.* 4.
LOWE, Staff., a demi-griffin, segreant, (erased,) ar. *Pl.* 18, *cr.* 6.
LOWE, Bucks., a wolf's head, erased, ar. *Pl.* 14, *cr.* 6.

Lowe, Salop and Wilts., an ermine, passant, ppr., collared, or, lined and ringed, gu. *Pl.* 12, *cr.* 2.

Lowe, Middx., (two) keys in saltier, or, interwoven with a chaplet, ppr. *Pl.* 54, *cr.* 12, (chaplet, *pl.* 124, *cr.* 6.)

Lowe, Worc., a demi-griffin, segreant, or. *Pl.* 18, *cr.* 6.

Lowe, Beds., Middx., and Herts., out of a mural coronet, gu., a wolf's head, ar., transfixed by a spear, or, pointed, of the second. *Pl.* 40, *cr.* 12, (coronet, *pl.* 95, *cr.* 8.)

Lowe, Salop and Wilts., an ermine, passant, ppr., collared, or, lined and ringed, gu. *Pl.* 12, *cr.* 2.

Lowe, Bart., Eng., a boar's head and neck, issuing, sa. *Pl.* 2, *cr.* 7.

Lowe, Eng., a lion's head, erased, regardant. *Pl.* 35, *cr.* 2.

Lowe, a wyvern, wings, vert. *Pl.* 63, *cr.* 13.

Lower, Cornw., a unicorn's head, erased, ar., armed and crined, or. *Pl.* 67, *cr.* 1.

Lower, Cornw., a unicorn's head, erased, ar. *Pl.* 67, *cr.* 1.

Lower, Cornw., a unicorn's head, erased, quarterly, ar. and sa. *Pl.* 67, *cr.* 1.

Lowes, Northumb., a wolf, passant, collared and (lined.) *Dulces ante omnia musæ. Pl.* 5, *cr.* 8, (without staff.)

Lowes, a wolf, passant, collared (and lined.) *Pl.* 5, *cr.* 8, (without staff.)

Lowfield, Eng., a bull's head, erased, sa. *Pl.* 19, *cr.* 3.

Lowis, Sco., a hand holding a spear, (in pale,) ppr. *Nos aspera juvant. Pl.* 99, *cr.* 8.

Lowis, Sco., a hand holding a lance, in bend, ppr. *Nos aspera juvant. Pl.* 99, *cr.* 8.

Lowle, between the horns of a stag's head, cabossed, or, a pheon, az. *Pl.* 124, *cr.* 14, (pheon, *pl.* 141.)

Lowman, Eng., a lion's gamb, erect, erased, sa., holding a battle-axe, or. *Pl.* 51, *cr.* 13.

Lownde, a hind, regardant, ppr., collared, gu., resting dexter on a bee-hive, ppr. *Pl.* 106, *cr.* 10, (hive, *pl.* 1, *cr.* 14.)

Lownde, Cambs., (on a mount,) vert, a griffin, sejant, wings addorsed, or. *Pl.* 100, *cr.* 11.

Lownde, Linc., out of a ducal coronet, or, a hawk, close, gold, beaked and legged, ar. *Pl.* 41, *cr.* 10.

Lowndes, Chesh., a lion's head, erased, or, gorged with a chaplet, vert. *Pl.* 22, *cr.* 3.

Lowndes, or Lownds, Eng. and Sco., a dove, volant, over the waters, in mouth an olive-branch, ppr. *Pl.* 46, *cr.* 13.

Lowndes, Bucks. and Oxon., a leopard's head, erased at neck, gorged with a laurel-branch, ppr. *Pl.* 94, *cr.* 10.

Lowndes, Ess., a lion's head, erased, or. *Pl.* 81, *cr.* 4.

Lowndes-Stone, Bucks. and Oxon.: 1. A leopard's head and neck, erased, or, (gorged,) with laurel, ppr.) *Pl.* 94, *cr.* 10. 2. For Stone, out of a ducal coronet, or, a griffin's head, erm. *Mediocra firma. Pl.* 54, *cr.* 14.

Lownes, Eng., a hydra, with seven heads. *Pl.* 38, *cr.* 5.

Lowrie, or Lowry, Eng., a cat, current, gardant, ppr. *Pl.* 119, *cr.* 7.

Lowrs, Devons. and Cornw., a bear, rampant, sa., muzzled (and lined,) or. *Pl.* 1, *cr.* 3, (without staff.)

Lowry, Iri., a fox's head, couped, gu. *Pl.* 91, *cr.* 9.

Lowry, Cumb., two laurel-sprigs, in orle, ppr. *Pl.* 79, *cr.* 14.

Lowry, Iri., between two branches of laurel, (a garland of the same,) ppr. *Virtus semper viridis*—and—*Floreant lauri. Pl.* 79, *cr.* 14.

Lows, Sco., a lion, rampant, or. *Pl.* 67, *cr.* 5.

Lowste, a dexter hand, ppr., holding up a fleur-de-lis. *Pl.* 46, *cr.* 12.

Lowten, Chesh., a demi-griffin, per fess, indented, erminois and erm., wings elevated, sa., in dexter a cross crosslet, fitched, az. *Pl.* 49, *cr.* 4, (cross, *pl.* 141.)

Lowtham, Eng., an antelope's head, gu., (collared,) erm. *Pl.* 24, *cr.* 7.

Lowthen, a dragon's head, wings addorsed, pierced through breast by a spear. *Pl.* 121, *cr.* 9, (wings, *pl.* 82, *cr.* 10.)

Lowther, Iri., a dexter hand, ppr., holding up an escallop, or. *Pl.* 57, *cr.* 6.

Lowther, Cumb. and Yorks., a dragon, passant, wings displayed, ar. *Pl.* 90, *cr.* 10.

Lowther, Bart., Yorks., a dragon, passant, ar. *Magistratus indicat virum. Pl.* 90, *cr.* 10.

Lowther, Gorges, Esq., of Hampton Hall, Somers., same crest and motto.

Lowther, Earl of Lonsdale. See Lonsdale.

Lowthian, Edinr., a bugle-horn, gu., garnished. *Non dormit qui custodit. Pl.* 89, *cr.* 3.

Lowyn, a crab, sa. *Pl.* 116, *cr.* 14.

Loxam, a stork's head, (couped,) ar., in mouth an escallop, sa. *Pl.* 32, *cr.* 5, (escallop, *pl.* 141.)

Loxdale, Salop, a bull's head, couped, ppr. *Pl.* 120, *cr.* 7.

Loyd, Ess., a stag's head, couped, ppr., attired, or, gorged with a chaplet of laurel, vert. *Pl.* 38, *cr.* 1.

Loyd, a lion, rampant, between paws a boar's head, couped. *Pl.* 9, *cr.* 7, (head, *pl.* 10, *cr.* 2.)

Loyd, Wel., a stag's head, erased, ppr., attired, or. *Pl.* 66, *cr.* 9.

Loyd, or Lloyd, Wel., Salop, and Staffs., a demi-lion, rampant, sa. *Pl.* 67, *cr.* 10.

Loyd, Wel., a wolf, salient, ar., (holding a broken arrow, ppr., point dropping blood.) *Pl.* 126, *cr.* 13.

Luard, Eng., a heart, gu., charged with a rose, ar. *Pl.* 123, *cr.* 7, (rose, *pl.* 141.)

Lubbock, Bart., Norf., a heron, wings addorsed, erm., supporting with dexter (an antique shield, az., bordered, or, charged with a lion, rampant, ar.) *Pl.* 61, *cr.* 10.

Lucan, Earl and Baron of, and a Baronet, N.S., (Bingham,) on a mount, vert, an eagle, wings (expanded,) ppr., armed, or. *Spes mea Christus. Pl.* 61, *cr.* 1.

Lucar, Eng., an arm, per pale, az. and gu., in hand, ppr., a hawk's lure, ar., stringed, of the second. *Pl.* 44, *cr.* 2, (arm, *pl.* 47, *cr.* 13.)

Lucar, Somers., a cubit arm, in pale, (vested, per pale, az. and gu., cuffed, ar.,) in hand a hawk's lure, all ppr. *Pl.* 44, *cr.* 2.

Lucas, Northumb., Ess., and Staffs., out of a ducal coronet, or, a demi-griffin, wings expanded, gu. *Pl.* 18, *cr.* 6, (coronet, *same plate, cr.* 11.)

Lucas, Kent, a cameleopard, passant, sa., attired, or,

LUCAS, Eng., a wyvern, gu. *Pl.* 63, *cr.* 13.
LUCAS, Derbs., an arm, embowed, vested, sa., bezantée, cuffed, ar., in hand, ppr., a cross crosslet, gu., embowed to the sinister. *Pl.* 88, *cr.* 7, (arm, *pl.* 39, *cr.* 1.)
LUCAS, an urn, ar., flammant, gu. *Pl.* 40, *cr.* 9.
LUCAS, out of a ducal coronet, or, a dragon's head, gu., on head a baron's coronet, ppr. *Pl.* 59, *cr.* 14, (coronet, *pl.* 127, *fig.* 11.)
LUCAS, an arm, embowed, ppr., vested, ar., on elbow a quatrefoil, sa., in hand a cross crosslet, fitched, gu. *Pl.* 88, *cr.* 7, (quatrefoil, *pl.* 141.)
LUCAS, out of a ducal coronet, a cockatrice's head, ppr. *Pl.* 77, *cr.* 5.
LUCAS, Ess. and Suff., out of a ducal coronet, or, a dracon's head, gu. *Pl.* 59, *cr.* 14.
LUCAS, Cornw., a lamp, or, lighted, ppr. *Pl.* 40, *cr.* 9.
LUCAS, Linc., an arm, embowed, vested, sa., bezantée, cuffed, ar., in hand, ppr., a cross crosslet, gu. *Pl.* 88, *cr.* 7.
LUCAS, Cornw., a sword, in pale, ar., hilt and pommel, or, between wings, gu. *Pl.* 117, *cr.* 14.
LUCAS, HENRY, Esq., of Uplands, Glamorgan, a wyvern, wings, erect. *Respice finem.* *Pl.* 63, *cr.* 13.
LUCAS, the Right Hon. EDWARD, of Castle Shane, co. Monaghan, out of a ducal coronet, a demi-griffin. *Stat religione parentum.* *Pl.* 39, *cr.* 2.
LUCAS, THOMAS, Esq., of Richfordstown, co. Cork, a unicorn. *Pl.* 106, *cr.* 3.
LUCAS, of Rathealy, out of a ducal coronet, a unicorn. *Pl.* 106, *cr.* 3, (coronet, *pl.* 128, *fig.* 3.)
LUCAS, Shadwell, Suss.: 1. Within an annulet, an escallop. *Pl.* 77, *cr.* 9, (escallop, *pl.* 141.) 2. On a mount, vert, a wyvern, ar., wings elevated, or, charged on body with six annulets, gold. *Pl.* 33, *cr.* 13, (annulet, *pl.* 141.)
LUCE, Eng., an eagle, wings displayed, regardant, in dexter a sword, erect. *Pl.* 87, *cr.* 5.
LUCEY, out of a ducal coronet, a boar's head and neck, between wings. *Pl.* 102, *cr.* 14, (wings, *pl.* 17, *cr.* 9.)
LUCIE, Lond., a crescent, ar. *Pl.* 18, *cr.* 14.
LUCK, Eng., a hawk, (hooded and belled,) perched on stump of tree. *Pl.* 78, *cr.* 8.
LUCKE, Suss., a pelican, wings addorsed, sa., between two branches, in orle, vert. *Pl.* 109, *cr.* 15, (branches, *pl.* 79, *cr.* 14.)
LUCKIN, Ess., out of a tower, paly of six, or and sa., a demi-griffin, or. *Pl.* 68, *cr.* 11.
LUCY, Warw., out of a ducal coronet, a griffin's head, between wings, the head, guttée-de-poix. *Pl.* 97, *cr.* 13.
LUCY, out of a ducal coronet, a boar's head, or, between wings, sa., billettée, gold. *Pl.* 102, *cr.* 14, (wings, *pl.* 17, *cr.* 9.)
LUCY, Hunts., out of a ducal coronet, a griffin's head, between wings, the head, guttée-de-poix. *Non nobis nascimur.* *Pl.* 97, *cr.* 13.
LUCY, out of a ducal coronet, a boar, erm., armed, or. *Pl.* 22, *cr.* 8, (coronet, *pl.* 128, *fig.* 3.)
LUCY, Warw., in a ducal coronet, gu., a boar's head, couped, erm., tusked and crined, or, langued, of the first, between wings, gold. *With truth and diligence.* *Pl.* 102, *cr.* 14, (wings, *pl.* 17, *cr.* 9.)

LUCY, out of a ducal coronet, or, a boar's head and neck, ar., guttée-de-poix, armed, gold, between wings, erect, sa., billettée, gold. *Ib.*
LUDFORD, Warw.: 1. For *Ludford*, a boar's head, couped, erminois, in mouth a cross pattée, gu. *Pl.* 125, *cr.* 7, (cross, *pl.* 141.) 2. For *Newdigate*, a fleur-de-lis, ar. *Pl.* 68, *cr.* 12.
LUDGERSHALL, Eng., a talbot, passant, az., collared, or. *Pl.* 65, *cr.* 2.
LUDHAM, Lond., a [demi-dragon, erm., wings elevated, between paws a key, or, on shoulder a cinquefoil, gu. *Pl.* 82, *cr.* 10, (key, *pl.* 9, *cr.* 12; cinquefoil, *pl.* 141.)
LUDINGTON, a palmer's staff, in pale, sa. *Pl.* 7, *cr.* 15.
LUDKIN, Suff., a bird, wings expanded, az., beaked and legged, or. *Pl.* 126, *cr.* 7.
LUDLOW, Eng., a lion, rampant, sa. *Pl.* 67, *cr.* 5.
LUDLOW, Wilts., a demi-bear, rampant, sa. *Pl.* 104, *cr.* 10.
LUDLOW, Iri., a lion, rampant, sa., bezantée. *Pl.* 87, *cr.* 5.
LUDLOW, Earl and Baron, Viscount Preston, Iri., Baron Ludlow, U.K., (Ludlow,) a lion, rampant, sa., bezantée. *Spero infestis, metuo secundis.* *Pl.* 67, *cr.* 5.
LUDLOW, Heywood House, Wilts.: 1. A lion, rampant. *Pl.* 67, *cr.* 5. 2. A dexter arm, in armour, embowed, in hand a battle-axe, ppr. *Pl.* 121, *cr.* 14.
LUFERS, Eng., a hedgehog, ppr. *Pl.* 32, *cr.* 9.
LUFF, Eng., an elephant, passant, sa. *Pl.* 56, *cr.* 14.
LUFFNAN, a saltier, charged with a crescent. *Pl.* 82, *cr.* 7, (without lozenge; crescent, *pl.* 141.)
LUGDON, a lion's head, (erased,) or, ducally gorged, az. *Pl.* 87, *cr.* 15.
LUGG, Eng., a cherub's head, ppr. *Pl.* 126, *cr.* 10.
LUGG, out of a ducal coronet, or, a pelican's head, vulning, ppr. *Pl.* 41, *cr.* 4, (coronet, same plate, *cr.* 10.)
LUGGAN, Baron, (Brownlow,) on a chapeau, az., turned up, erm., a greyhound, statant, gu. *Pl.* 104, *cr.* 1.
LUKE, Eng., an archer, shooting, ppr. *Pl.* 90, *cr.* 3.
LUKE, Sco., a bull's head, wings (addorsed,) or. *Strenue insequor.* *Pl.* 60, *cr.* 9.
LUKE, Beds., Hunts., and Durh., a bull's head, az., attired, or, wings (addorsed,) gold. *Pl.* 60, *cr.* 9.
LUKE, Cornw., an escallop, ppr. *Pl.* 117, *cr.* 4.
LUKIN, Linc., Kent, and Ess., a demi-lion, ar., collared, gobony, or and az. *Pl.* 18, *cr.* 13.
LUM, Yorks., a moor's head, in profile, ppr., wreathed about temples, or and sa. *Pl.* 36, *cr.* 3.
LUMB, Eng., a sceptre, in pale, or. *Pl.* 82, *cr.* 3.
LUMISDEN, Sco., a heron devouring a salmon, ppr. *Beware in time.* *Pl.* 121, *cr.* 13.
LUMLEY, Linc., a pigeon, ar., in beak a (laurel) sprig, vert. *Pl.* 48, *cr.* 14.
LUMLEY, Yorks. and Middx., a pelican, vulning, in nest, feeding her young, all ppr. *Pl* 44, *cr.* 1.
LUMLEY, an eagle, displayed, with two heads. *Pl.* 87, *cr.* 11, (without flame.)
LUMLEY, Viscount. *See* SCARBOROUGH, Earl of.
LUMSDEAN, Sco., a heron devouring a salmon, ppr. *Beware in time.* *Pl.* 121, *cr.* 13.

LUMSDEAN, and LUMSDEN, a crane, preying on a fish, all ppr. *Pl.* 121, *cr.* 13.

LUMSDEN, Sco., a naked arm, in hand a sword, ppr. *Dei dono sum quod sum*. *Pl.* 34, *cr.* 7.

LUMSDEN, the Rev. HENRY-THOMAS, of Cushnie, Aberdeen, same crest and motto.

LUN, or LUNN, Eng., a greyhound's head, erased, sa., devouring a stag's foot, or, also erased. *Pl.* 66, *cr.* 7.

LUND, and LUNDE, Eng., two laurel-branches, in saltier, vert. *Pl.* 19, *cr.* 12, (laurel, *pl.* 21, *cr.* 2.)

LUNDEN, a cross moline, sa. *Pl.* 89, *cr.* 8.

LUNDEN, Sco., a hand holding a cushion, in pale, ppr. *Tam genus quam virtus*. *Pl.* 83, *cr.* 9.

LUNDIE, Sco., a boar's head, erased and erect, sa. *Pl.* 21, *cr.* 7.

LUNDIN, Sco., a cross moline, gu. *Justitia*. *Pl.* 89, *cr.* 8.

LUNDIN, Sco., out of an open or antique crown, or, a lion, gu. *Dei dono sum quod sum*. *Pl.* 67, *cr.* 5, (crown, *pl.* 79, *cr.* 12.)

LUNDIN, ELIZABETH, (of Auchtermairnie, Fife,) in hand, ppr., a cushion, in pale, or. *Tam genus quam virtus*. *Pl.* 83, *cr.* 9.

LUNDIN, Sco., a dexter hand, apaumée, charged with an eye, ppr. *Certior dum cerno*. *Pl.* 99, *cr.* 13.

LUNDIN, Sco., from an antique crown, a lion, issuing, affrontée, gu., in dexter a sword, erect, in sinister a (thistle,) slipped, all ppr. *Dei dono sum quod sum*. *Pl.* 120, *cr.* 2, (crown, *pl.* 79, *cr.* 12.)

LUNGSFORD, Suss., a boar's head, or, couped, gu. *Pl.* 48, *cr.* 2.

LUNN, a demi-pegasus, regardant. *Pl.* 32, *cr.* 1, (without flag.)

LUNTLEY, a lion's head, or, charged with a martlet, sa. *Pl.* 126, *cr.* 1, (martlet, *pl.* 111, *cr.* 5.)

LUPTON, Oxon. and Yorks., a wolf's head, erased, sa. *Pl.* 14, *cr.* 6.

LUPTON, Eng., out of a mural coronet, a hand, vested, holding a mullet. *Pl.* 34, *cr.* 1.

LUPPINCOTE, on a cross pattée, ar., four hearts, gu. *Pl.* 15, *cr.* 8, (heart, *pl.* 55, *cr.* 13.)

LURFORD, a boar's head, erased at neck. *Pl.* 16, *cr.* 11.

LURTY, Eng., in dexter hand a dagger, in pale, ppr. *Pl.* 23, *cr.* 15.

LUSADO, on a mount, vert, a dove, regardant, ar., in mouth a sprig, ppr., charged on neck with a bar-gemelle, or. *Honour me guide*. *Pl.* 77, *cr.* 2, (mount, *pl.* 104, *cr.* 8.)

LUSCOMBE, a demi-lion, rampant, gardant, crowned, or. *Pl.* 35, *cr.* 4, (crown, *pl.* 1, *cr.* 5.)

LUSHER, Surr. and Lond., a martlet, or. *Pl.* 111, *cr.* 5.

LUSHER, Lond., a demi-lion, gu., laying his paws on a gauntlet, or. *Pl.* 40, *cr.* 6.

LUSHINGTON, of Norton Court, Kent, a lion's head, erased, vert, ducally gorged, or. *Prudens qui patiens*. *Pl.* 81, *cr.* 4, (gorging, *pl.* 128, *fig.* 3.)

LUSHINGTON, Kent, same crest.

LUSHINGTON, Bart., Berks., a lion's head, erased, vert, charged on the erasure with three ermine-spots, or, ducally gorged, ar. *Pl.* 81, *cr.* 4, (gorging, *pl.* 128, *fig.* 3; ermine, *pl.* 141.)

LUSON, Eng., on a ducal coronet, a dolphin, naiant, ppr. *Pl.* 94, *cr.* 14.

LUSY, Eng., out of a ducal coronet, or, a dexter hand holding a rose, stalked and leaved, ppr. *Pl.* 60, *cr.* 1.

LUTEFOOTE, Sco., a swan, ppr., on head a crescent. *Addicunt aves*. *Pl.* 122, *cr.* 13, (crescent, *pl.* 141.)

LUTEFOOTE, Eng., a hand, vested, holding a mill-rind, ppr. *Pl.* 34, *cr.* 3.

LUTEFOOTE, out of a ducal coronet, a dexter and sinister arm, in armour, embowed, supporting a leopard's head, affrontée. *Pl.* 6, *cr.* 8, (coronet, *same plate*; head, *pl.* 66, *cr.* 14.)

LUTHER, Eng., a hand, gauntleted, az., holding a sword, in pale, hilt and pommel, or. *Pl.* 125, *cr.* 5.

LUTHER, Ess., two arms, in armour, embowed, in hand a round buckle. *Pl.* 64, *cr.* 11, (buckle, *pl.* 73, *cr.* 10.)

LUTHER, on a rose, a long cross, gu. *Lætitia per mortem*. *Pl.* 7, *cr.* 13; (rose, *pl.* 141.)

LUTMAN, Hants and Suss., out of a mural coronet, ar., a demi-lion, rampant, az., between paws a mullet, or. *Pl.* 120, *cr.* 14, (mullet, *pl.* 141.)

LUTTELEY, on a plate, an eagle, displayed, sa. *Pl.* 48, *cr.* 11, (plate, *pl.* 141.)

LUTTERELL, or LUTTRELL, Devons. and Somers., a boar, passant, ar., bristled, or, charged on shoulder with a rose, gold. *Pl.* 48, *cr.* 14, (rose, *pl.* 141.)

LUTTERFORD, Staffs., a spear, or, embrued, gu., between wings, sa. *Pl.* 40, *cr.* 3.

LUTTON, Eng., in the sea, a rock, ppr. *Pl.* 91, *cr.* 5.

LUTTRELL, Eng., a dexter hand holding up a garland of roses, all ppr. *Pl.* 41, *cr.* 7.

LUTTRELL, Iri., an otter, (passant,) in mouth a fish, ppr. *En Dieu est ma fiance*. *Pl.* 74, *cr.* 13.

LUTTRELL, Iri., a demi-moor, an armour, ppr., garnished, or, between two branches of laurel, vert, round the temples a wreath, ar. and gu., on breast a fess, counter-embattled, gold. *En Dieu est ma fiance*.

LUTTRELL, an otter, sa., in mouth a fish, ppr. *Pl.* 74, *cr.* 13.

LUTTRELL, Somers. and Devons., out of a ducal coronet, or, a plume of five feathers, ar. *Pl.* 100, *cr.* 12, (without charge.)

LUTWICH, Eng., a dexter arm, in armour, in hand a sword, both ppr. *Pl.* 2, *cr.* 8.

LUTWIDGE, Eng., between two branches of laurel, in orle, a hand holding a scroll of parchment, all ppr. *Pl.* 86, *cr.* 5.

LUTWIDGE, a lion, rampant, gu. *Pl.* 67, *cr.* 5.

LUTWYCHE, Eng., an arm, in armour, in hand a sword, all ppr. *Pl.* 2, *cr.* 8.

LUTWYCHE, Salop, a tiger's head, erased, gu., tufted and maned, or. *Pl.* 94, *cr.* 10.

LUTYENS, a serpent, erect on tail. *Pl.* 119, *cr.* 12, (without gorging.)

LUXFORD, Eng., a dexter arm, embowed, in hand a dagger, both ppr. *Pl.* 34, *cr.* 7.

LUXFORD, Suss., a boar's head, ar., erased at neck, gu., in mouth a spear, or, headed, of the first. *Pl.* 11, *cr.* 9.

LUXFORD, Suss., a wolf, rampant, supporting an arrow, in pale, point downward, or, flighted, ar. *Pl.* 10, *cr.* 3, (arrow, *pl.* 22, *cr.* 15.)

LUXFORD, a boar's head, couped, or. *Pl.* 48, *cr.* 2.
LUXMOORE, or LUXMORE, Eng., a sea-lion, rampant, ppr. *Pl.* 25, *cr.* 12.
LUXMORE, the Rev. CHARLES-THOMAS-CORYNDON, of Witherdon, Devons, a battle-axe. *Securis fecit securum.* *Pl.* 14, *cr.* 8.
LYAL, or LYALL, Sco., a swallow, volant, ppr. *Sedulo et honeste.* *Pl.* 40, *cr.* 4.
LYBB, Oxon., a naked arm, erect, in hand an oak-branch, fructed, all ppr. *Pl.* 47, *cr.* 13, (branch, *pl.* 32, *cr.* 13.)
LYBBE, an arm, in armour, ppr., in hand a spear of three points. *Pl.* 44, *cr.* 9, (spear, *pl.* 12, *cr.* 3.)
LYBBE, Oxon., a dexter arm, in mail, supporting a halberd, ppr. *Pl.* 121, *cr.* 14, (arm, *pl.* 120, *cr.* 11.)
LYCHFELD, an arm, embowed, vested, ar., in hand, ppr., a bow, or, strung, gu. *Pl.* 51, *cr.* 5.
LYCHFIELD, Salop, a boar's head, couped, az. *Pl.* 48, *cr.* 2.
LYCHFORD, Surr., a leopard's head, per pale, ar. and sa., between wings, counterchanged. *Pl.* 66, *cr.* 14, (wings, *pl.* 17, *cr.* 3.)
LYDALL, or LYDDALL, Berks. and Oxon., out of a mural coronet, chequy, or and az., a heron's head, erased, gold, in beak a scroll, with motto—*Et patribus et posteritate.* *Pl.* 40, *cr.* 8.
LYDCOTTE, Bucks., Northamp., and Surr., on a ducal coronet, a boar's head, couped, all or. *Pl.* 102, *cr.* 14.
LYDDEL, Bart., Eng., a lion, rampant, ducally crowned. *Pl.* 98, *cr.* 1.
LYDDEL, a lion, rampant, ar., ducally crowned, or. *Pl.* 98, *cr.* 1.
LYDE, Eng., a stag's head, erased, erminois. *Non sibi.* *Pl.* 66, *cr.* 9.
LYDE, Herts., a buck's head, erased, erminois. *Non sibi.* *Pl.* 66, *cr.* 9.
LYDOWN, Eng., an anchor, in pale, environed with a serpent. *Pl.* 35, *cr.* 14.
LYE, Eng., an antelope's head, ar., armed, or, and collared, gu. *Pl.* 24, *cr.* 7.
LYE, Heref. and Wilts., an eagle, displayed, ar., beaked and legged, gu. *Pl.* 48, *cr.* 11.
LYELL, Sir CHARLES, Knt., of Kinnordy, Angus, in hand, in armour, a sword, ppr., hilt and pommel, or. *Forti non ignavo.* *Pl.* 125, *cr.* 5.
LYELL, or LYLE, Sco., in dexter hand, a (sword,) erect, ppr. *Forti non ignavo.* *Pl.* 23, *cr.* 15.
LYELL, Sco., same crest. *Tutela.*
LYELL, of Kennordy, a dexter hand, gauntleted, holding a broadsword, all ppr. *Forti non ignavo.* *Pl.* 125, *cr.* 5.
LYELL, Sco., a swallow, volant, ppr. *Sedulo et honeste tutela.* *Pl.* 40, *cr.* 4.
LYELL, Sco., a unicorn's head, erased. *At all tymes God me defend.* *Pl.* 67, *cr.* 1.
LYFIELD, Eng., a bull's head, cabossed, ar., guttée, sa. *Pl.* 111, *cr.* 6.
LYFIELD, Surr., a bull's head, cabossed, ar., charged with three guttes, sa. *Pl.* 111, *cr.* 6.
LYFORD, Eng., a fox's head, erased, or. *Pl.* 71, *cr.* 4.
LYGGINS, a greyhound, sejant, ppr. *Pl.* 66, *cr.* 15.
LYGON, a savage's head, affrontée, couped at shoulders. *Ex fide fortis.* *Pl.* 19, *cr.* 1.
LYLE, DE, a cock, or, crested, gu. *An I may.* *Pl.* 67, *cr.* 14.

LYLE, Sco., a cock. *An I may.* *Pl.* 67, *cr.* 14.
LYMESEY, or LYMESY, Eng., a demi-bear, rampant, sa. *Pl.* 104, *cr.* 10.
LYNACRE, or LYNAKER, Eng., a greyhound's head, erased, ar. *Pl.* 89, *cr.* 2.
LYNAM, Iri., a demi-savage, brandishing a scimitar, ppr. *Pl.* 82, *cr.* 2.
LYNAN, Eng., a rose, charged with a thistle. *Pl.* 73, *cr.* 6.
LYNCH, on a ducal coronet, or, a lynx, passant, gardant, ar. *Pl.* 122, *cr.* 14, (coronet, *same plate, cr.* 8.)
LYNCH, Middx., a lynx, passant, (gardant,) ppr. *Pl.* 122, *cr.* 14.
LYNCH, Hants, a fox, (salient,) ppr. *Pl.* 126, *cr.* 5.
LYNCH, Iri., a fox, passant, az., (collared,) or. *Pl.* 126, *cr.* 5.
LYNCH, Iri., two ears of wheat, in saltier, ppr. *Pl.* 9, *cr.* 8.
LYNCH, NICHOLAS, Esq., of Barna, co. Galway, a lynx, passant, gardant, ppr. *Semper fidelis.* *Pl.* 122, *cr.* 14.
LYNDERGREEN, out of a foreign coronet, a sprig. *Pl.* 93, *cr.* 3, (foreign coronet, *pl.* 142.)
LYNDHURST, Baron (Copley,) a dexter arm, in armour, embowed, ppr., charged with an escallop, or, encircled above wrist with a wreath of laurel, vert, in gauntlet a dagger, ppr., hilt and pommel, gold. *Ultra pergere.* *Pl.* 21, *cr.* 4, (escallop, *pl.* 141.)
LYNDON, Eng., five arrows, one in pale, and four in saltier, banded and buckled, ppr. *Pl.* 54, *cr.* 15.
LYNDON, Iri., a sea-dragon, flying, gorged with a mural coronet, or.
LYNDOWN, Eng., on a pillar, a man's heart. *Pl.* 122, *cr.* 4.
LYNDSEY, Eng., an ostrich, in mouth a key. *Pl.* 64, *cr.* 3, (without coronet; key, *pl.* 9, *cr.* 12.)
LYNDSEY, Sco., amidst flames, a heart, transfixed by a dart, all ppr. *Faith and hope.* *Pl.* 40, *cr.* 1.
LYNDSEY, a demi-bear, rampant, sa. *Pl.* 104, *cr.* 10.
LYNDSEY, Lond., an eagle, displayed, sa., beaked and legged, or, on breast a cross pattée, gold. *Pl.* 48, *cr.* 11, (cross, *pl.* 141.)
LYNDSEY, Norf., a unicorn, (sejant, regardant,) ar., armed, hoofed, maned, and ducally gorged, or. *Pl.* 106, *cr.* 3.
LYNDWOOD, a fleur-de-lis, per pale, ar. and sa. *Pl.* 68, *cr.* 12.
LYNE, Hants, Cornw., and Suss., a griffin's head, erased, sa. *Pl.* 48, *cr.* 6.
LYNECAR, or LYNEGAR, Iri., on a mount, a stag, all ppr., charged with a trefoil. *Pl.* 50, *cr.* 6, (trefoil, *pl.* 141.)
LYNEDOCH, Baron, (Graham,) an eagle, or. *Candide et secure.* *Pl.* 7, *cr.* 11.
LYNES, Eng., an elephant's head, erased, purp. *Pl.* 68, *cr.* 4.
LYNES, in front of a fleur-de-lis, ar., a lion, rampant, gu. *Pl.* 67, *cr.* 5, (fleur-de-lis, *pl.* 141.)
LYNGARD, and LYNGHARDE, Northamp., a lion, sejant, gardant, sa., in dexter a key, in pale, or. *Pl.* 113, *cr.* 8, (key, *pl.* 54, *cr.* 12.)
LYNGARD, and LYNGHARDE, Northamp, a lion's gamb, erased and erect, ar., holding three roses, gu., stalked and leaved, vert. *Pl.* 86, *cr.* 15.

LYNGARDE, Warw., a tiger's head, maned and tufted, sa. *Pl.* 94, *cr.* 10.
LYNN, Middx. and Surr., a lion's head, erased, ar. *Pl.* 81, *cr.* 4.
LYNN, a demi-lion. *Pl.* 67, *cr.* 10.
LYNNE, Yorks., a squirrel, sejant, ppr., supporting a cross crosslet, fitched, gu. *Pl.* 40, *cr.* 5.
LYNNE, Northamp., a lion's head, erased, crowned and (collared.) *Pl.* 123, *cr.* 13.
LYNSEY, Lond., a cat's head, ar., spotted, (collared and studded,) or. *Pl.* 97, *cr.* 7.
LYON, Earl of Strathmore. *See* STRATHMORE and KINGHORN, Earl of.
LYON, Iri., a lion's head, erased, sa., (charged with a bar-gemelle, or.) *Pl.* 81, *cr.* 4.
LYON, Iri., out of a ducal coronet, a demi-savage, arms embowed.
LYON, Sco., within two branches of laurel, a lady to the girdle, vested, in dexter the royal thistle. *In te, Domine, speravi.* *Pl.* 17, *cr.* 11, (thistle, *pl.* 36, *cr.* 6.)
LYON, Iri., a hand holding a sword, ppr., enfiled with a boar's head, erased, or. *Pl.* 71, *cr.* 9.
LYON, on a (pink,) flowered, gu., leaved, vert, a lion's head, erased, paly, quarterly, erm. and ermines. *Pl.* 69, *cr.* 6.
LYON, Lond. and Surr., a demi-lady, ppr., vested, ar., stomacher fretty, az., in (dexter a key, or, in sinister a thistle, slipped and leaved,) ppr., within two branches of oak, in orle, fructed, of the last. *Pl.* 17, *cr.* 11, (oak, *pl.* 74, *cr.* 7.)
LYON, THOMAS, Esq., of Appleton Hall, Chesh., a lion's head, erased, ar. *Pro rege et patriâ.* *Pl.* 81, *cr.* 4.
LYON, Iri., out of a ducal coronet, a demi-savage, dexter arm, embowed, pointing with fore-finger, sinister elbow resting on coronet.
LYONS, Baron, Hants, on a chapeau, gu., doubled, erm., a sea-lion's head, erased, ar., gorged with a naval coronet, az., in mouth a flag-staff, in bend sinister, ppr., therefrom a banner, az., inscribed—*Marack gu. Noli irritare leones.*
LYONS, JOHN-CHARLES, Esq., of Ledestown, co. Westmeath, on a chapeau, a lion's head, erased. *Noli irritare leones.* *Pl.* 99, *cr.* 9.

LYSAGHT, Baron Lisle. *See* LISLE.
LYSERS, between wings, or, an anchor, sa. *Pl.* 115, *cr.* 10.
LYSLE, on a chapeau, gu., turned up, erm., a millstone, ar., charged with a mill-rind, or. *Pl.* 40, *cr.* 2.
LYSLEY, out of a ducal coronet, or, a fleur-de-lis, ar. *Pl.* 68, *cr.* 12, (coronet, *same plate, cr.* 6.)
LYSLEY, Yorks., on a chapeau, gu., turned up, erm., a mill-stone, ar., on the centre a mill-rind, sa. *Pl.* 40, *cr.* 2.
LYSLEY, Yorks., a cubit arm, (in armour, erect, in gauntlet, an ancient battle-axe, in bend, attached to the arm by a chain.) *Pl.* 73, *cr.* 7.
LYSONS, Eng., two greyhounds' heads, erased, addorsed and collared. *Pl.* 62, *cr.* 5.
LYSONS, Glouc., the sun rising out of a bank of clouds, ppr. *Valebit.* *Pl.* 67, *cr.* 9.
LYSSERS, Eng., a dolphin, haurient, ppr. *Pl.* 14, *cr.* 10.
LYSTER, Iri., on point of sword, in pale, a garland of laurel. *Pl.* 15, *cr.* 6.
LYSTER, HENRY, Esq., of Rowton Castle, Salop, a stag's head, erased, ppr. *Loyal au mort.* *Pl.* 66, *cr.* 9.
LYSTER, the Very Rev. JAMES, co. Carlow, out of a ducal coronet, a stag's head, all ppr. *Retinens vestigia famæ.* *Pl.* 29, *cr.* 7.
LYSTER, co. Roscommon, out of a ducal coronet, a stag's head, all ppr. *Pl.* 29, *cr.* 7.
LYTE, Eng., a bear, rampant, sa., muzzled, gu., supporting a staff. *Pl.* 1, *cr.* 3.
LYTE, Somers., a swan. *Pl.* 122, *cr.* 13.
LYTE, Somers., a demi-swan, ar., wings extended, gu., against a plume of three ostrich-feathers, the middle one, of the first, the other two, of the second.
LYTTELTON, Lord, Baron of Frankley, G.B.; Baron Westcote, Iri., and an Eng. Bart., (Lyttleton,) a moor's head, in profile, couped at shoulders, wreathed about temples, ar. and sa. *Ung Dieu, ung roy.* *Pl.* 36, *cr.* 3.
LYTTON, Surr., Derbs., and Herts., a bittern, in flags, seeded, all ppr. *Pl.* 124, *cr.* 1.
LYZZERS, Eng., a dolphin, haurient, ppr. *Pl.* 14, *cr.* 10.

M

MABB, Lond., a wyvern, wings addorsed, or, pellettée. *Pl.* 63, *cr.* 13.
MABBALL, and MABBATT, Eng., a wyvern, passant, vert, at tail another head, vomiting flames, ppr. *Pl.* 109, *cr.* 13.
MABERLEY, or MABERLY, Eng., out of a ducal coronet, or, a demi-lion, gu. *Pl.* 45, *cr.* 7.
M'ABEN, Sco., a swallow, ppr. *Nulli præda.* *Pl.* 111, *cr.* 5.
MACADAM, Sco., a cross crosslet, fitched, and sword, in saltier, gu. *Pl.* 89, *cr.* 14.
MACADAM, co. Clare, (on a mount, vert,) a cock, ppr., in bill a cross Calvary. *In hoc signo vinces.* *Pl.* 112, *cr.* 12, (cross, *pl.* 141.)
McADAM, Sco., in dexter hand a hawk's lure. *Pl.* 44, *cr.* 2.
McADAM, or MACADAM, Sco., a stag's head, couped, ppr. *Calm*—and—*Crux mihi grata quies.* *Pl.* 91, *cr.* 14.
M'ADAM, WILLIAM, of Ballochmorrie, Ayrs., a stag's head, erased, ppr. *Calm.* *Pl.* 66, *cr.* 9.
M'ADAM, or MACADAM, Sco., a stag's head, erased, ppr. *Steady.* *Pl.* 66, *cr.* 9.
M'ALASTER, or MACALISTER, Sco., in dexter hand a dirk, in pale, both ppr. *Fortiter.* *Pl.* 18, *cr.* 2.
MACALESTER, C. SOMMERVILLE, of Kennox, a dexter arm, in armour, erect, the hand holding a dagger, in pale, all ppr. *Per mare, per terras.* *Pl.* 126 o, *cr.* 3.
McALISTER, Sco., an arm, in armour, in fess, in hand a cross crosslet, fitched, gu. *Per mare, per terras.* *Pl.* 88, *cr.* 7, (armour, *pl.* 121, *cr.* 14.)
McALLA, or M'AULAY, Sco., a boot, couped at

ancle, ppr., and spurred. *Dulce periculum.* *Pl.* 118, *cr.* 6.
M'ALLISTER, Sco., a dexter arm, in armour, embowed, in hand a dagger, both ppr. *Pl.* 120, *cr.* 11.
M'ALLUM, Sco., a tower, az., masoned, sa. *In ardua tendit. Pl.* 12, *cr.* 5.
MACALPIN, Sco., a Saracen's head, couped at neck, dropping blood, all ppr. *Cuinich bas alpan. Pl.* 23, *cr.* 1.
M'ALPIN, a man's head, bearded, affrontée, crowned with an antique crown, ppr. *Pl.* 19, *cr.* 1, (crown, *pl.* 79, *cr.* 12.)
M'ALPIN, Sco., an old man's head, affrontée, crowned with an antique crown, ppr. *Ib.*
M'ANDREW, Sco., an eagle, wings displayed. *Fear God. Pl.* 126, *cr.* 7.
MACARMICK, Cornw., an arm, in armour, embowed, ppr., in hand a cutlass. *Pl.* 81, *cr.* 11.
McARTHER, or M'ARTHUR, Sco., two laurel-branches, in orle. *Pl.* 79, *cr.* 14.
MACARTHUR, or MACARTHUR, Eng., an escallop, or, charged with a mullet, gu. *Pl.* 109, *cr.* 14.
MACARTHUR, Sco., two wings, addorsed, per pale, indented, erm. and sa. *Pl.* 63, *cr.* 12.
M'ARTHUR, Sco., two laurel-branches, (in saltier.) *Fide et operâ. Pl.* 21, *cr.* 2.
M'ARTHUR, STEWART, Sco., a greyhound, couchant, within two branches of (bay,) ppr. *Fide et operâ. Pl.* 102, *cr.* 13.
MACARTNEY, Eng., a stag, lodged, erm. *Pl.* 67, *cr.* 2.
MACARTNEY, Iri., a hand, in pale, couped above wrist, ppr., holding a rose, gu., stalked and leaved, vert. *Mens conscia recti. Pl.* 118, *cr.* 9.
MACARTNEY, GEORGE, Esq., of Lissanoure, co. Antrim, a cubit arm, erect, in hand a rose-branch, in flower, all ppr. *Mens conscia recti. Pl.* 118, *cr.* 9.
MACARTNEY, Bart., Iri., in hand a slip of three roses, all ppr. *Mens conscia recti. Pl.* 118, *cr.* 9, (roses, *pl.* 25, *cr.* 2.)
MACARTY, Iri., an arm, embowed, vested, in hand a lizard, all ppr. *Pl.* 58, *cr.* 4.
MACAUL, Sco., a fleur-de-lis, ar. *Pour le roi. Pl.* 68, *cr.* 12.
M'AUL, Sco., in hand a sword. *Ferio, tego. Pl.* 21, *cr.* 10.
MACAULAY, Baron, on a rock, a boot, ppr., with spur, or. *Dulce periculum. Pl.* 95, *cr.* 13, (rock, *pl.* 73, *cr.* 12.)
M'AULLY, Sco., in dexter hand a scimitar. *I will. Pl.* 29, *cr.* 8.
MACBAIN, Sco., a wolf's head, ppr. *Vires in arduis. Pl.* 14, *cr.* 6.
MACBEAN, Inverness, a cat, salient, ppr. *Touch not the cat bot a glove. Pl.* 70, *cr.* 15.
MACBEAN, Eng., and M'BEAN, Sco., a demi-cat, rampant, gu. *Pl.* 80, *cr.* 7.
M'BEAN, Sco., a mountain cat, rampant, sa. *Pl.* 126 A, *cr.* 10.
M'BEAN, Sco., a cat, sejant, ppr. *Touch not the cat bot a glove. Pl.* 24, *cr.* 6.
MACBEATH, Sco., a dexter arm, in armour, embowed, resting on elbow, in hand a (sword,) all ppr. *Pl.* 107, *cr.* 15.
M'BEATH, Sco., a dexter arm, in armour, embowed, in hand a broadsword, both ppr. *Pl.* 2, *cr.* 8.
M'BETH, Lond., a serpent's head, couped, ppr. *Conjuncta virtuti fortuna. Pl.* 58, *cr.* 5.

M'BRAID, Sco., in dexter hand, gu., a billet, sa. *Pl.* 28, *cr.* 8.
M'BRAIR, Sco., or M'BRAIRE, Eng., a unicorn's head, erased, ar. *Pl.* 67, *cr.* 1.
M'BREID, Sco., in dexter hand a broadsword, ppr. *I am ever prepared. Pl.* 21, *cr.* 10.
MACBRIDE, Eng., on a chapeau, a salamander in flames, ppr. *Pl.* 86, *cr.* 14.
MACBRIDE, a raven, ppr., wings expanded. *Pl.* 50, *cr.* 5.
M'CAA, Sco., in hand a dagger, erect, ppr. *Manu forti. Pl.* 23, *cr.* 15.
M'CABE, Iri., on a mount, vert, a stag, current, regardant, ppr. *Pl.* 3, *cr.* 2.
M'CALL, Iri., a goat's head, erased, az. *Pl.* 29, *cr.* 13.
M'CALL, Eng. and Sco., a leg, in armour, couped at calf. *Dulce periculum. Pl.* 95, *cr.* 13.
M'CALL, Eng. and Sco., a griffin's head, between wings. *Pl.* 65, *cr.* 1.
M'CALL, Sco., in hand a broadsword, all ppr. *Ferio, tego. Pl.* 21, *cr.* 10.
M'CALLUM, Sco., a castle, ar., masoned, sa. *In ardua tendit. Pl.* 28, *cr.* 14.
M'CALLUM, Eng., a tower, ppr., flag, gu. *Pl.* 8, *cr.* 13.
M'CAN, Iri., a salmon, naiant, ppr. *Pl.* 85, *cr.* 7.
M'CANDLISH, Eng., a demi-lion, vert. *Pl.* 67, *cr.* 10.
M'CANN, Iri., a bull's head, cabossed, sa. *Pl.* 111, *cr.* 6.
M'CARIN, Sco., a swallow, ppr. *Nulli præda. Pl.* 111, *cr.* 5.
M'CARLIE, on dexter side of a mount, vert, a cross crosslet, fitched, sa. *Pl.* 58, *cr.* 6.
M'CARLIE, on dexter side of a mount, vert, the sun, or, shining on a cross crosslet, fitched. *In hoc signo vinces. Pl.* 58, *cr.* 6.
MACCARTHY, Iri., a stag's head, or. *Pl.* 91, *cr.* 14.
M'CARTHY, an arm, erect, in hand a lizard, vert. *Shenichun Erin. Pl.* 110, *cr.* 11, (lizard, *pl.* 58, *cr.* 4.)
M'CARTHY, Eng., a wolf, current, ppr. *Pl.* 111, *cr.* 1.
M'CARTHY, of Cork, a cubit arm, in mail, ar., erect, in hand a newt, ppr. *Forti et fideli nil difficile. Pl.* 33, *cr.* 4, (newt, *pl.* 58, *cr.* 4.)
M'CARTY, Iri., same crest.
M'CARTNAY, or M'CARTNEY, Sco., in dexter hand a slip of a rose-tree, ppr. *Stimulat sed ornat. Pl.* 118, *cr.* 9.
MACCARTNEY, Sco., a griffin, segreant, az., wings, erm., between claws an etoile, or. *Pl.* 67, *cr.* 13, (etoile, *pl.* 141.)
MACCARTNEY, Iri., in dexter hand a branch of laurel, ppr. *Mens conscia recti. Pl.* 43, *cr.* 6.
MACCARTNEY, in hand, erect, couped above wrist, ppr., a rose, gu., stalked and leaved, vert. *Mens conscia recti. Pl.* 118, *cr.* 9.
M'CARTNEY, Sco., same crest. *Sua præmia virtus.*
M'CASKER, Sco., in hand a sword, (erect.) *Manu forti. Pl.* 21, *cr.* 10.
M'CASKILL, Sco., in hand a dagger, erect. *Manu forti. Pl.* 23, *cr.* 15.
MACCAUNACH, Iri., a ferret, passant, ppr. *Pl.* 119, *cr.* 15.
MACCAUSLAND, in hand, couped, a chapeau, between two laurel-branches. *Audaces juvo. Pl.* 59, *cr.* 4.
M'CAUSLAND, Iri., on a chapeau, gu., turned up, erm., a greyhound, sejant, ppr. *Pl.* 66, *cr.* 15.

U

M'CAY, and M'COY, Sco., a talbot's head, erased, or, collared, sa. *Pl.* 2, *cr.* 15.

M'CLAUCHLAN, or M'CLAUGHLAN, Sco., a castle, triple-towered. *Fortis et fidus. Pl.* 123, *cr.* 14.

M'CLEAN, Iri., a bull's head, erased, gu. *Pl.* 19, *cr.* 3.

M'CLEAN, Sco., a tower, embattled, ar. *Virtue mine honour. Pl.* 12, *cr.* 5.

M'CLEAY, a stag's head. *Pl.* 91, *cr.* 14.

M'CLEISH, Sco., a cross crosslet, fitched, gu. *Love. Pl.* 16, *cr.* 10.

M'CLELLAN, Bart., Sco., a moor's head, couped and wreathed, ppr. *Sapit qui reputat. Pl.* 36, *cr.* 3.

M'CLELLAN, Sco., a dexter arm, embowed, in hand a sword, in pale, charged on point with a man's head, couped, all ppr. *Think on. Pl.* 102, *cr.* 11.

M'CLELLAN, Sco., a cubit arm, in hand a sword, both ppr., on point a moor's head, or. *Pl.* 97, *cr.* 3.

M'CLELLAND, Sco., a negro's head, couped, ppr. *Sapit qui reputat. Pl.* 120, *cr.* 3.

M'CLEN, Sco., a castle. *Virtue mine honour. Pl.* 28, *cr.* 11.

M'CLEOD, Sco., the sun, in splendour. *I burn weil, I see. Pl.* 68, *cr.* 14.

M'CLEOD, Sco., a bull's head, cabossed, between two flags, barry of three, gu., az. and ar. *Pl.* 118, *cr.* 8.

MACCLESFIELD, Earl of, Viscount and Baron Parker, (Parker,) a leopard's head, gardant. erased at neck, or, ducally gorged, gu. *Sapere aude. Pl.* 116, *cr.* 8.

M'CLESH, Sco., in dexter hand a cross crosslet, fitched. *Love. Pl.* 99, *cr.* 1.

M'CLEVERTY, Eng., a cross crosslet, fitched, and palm-branch, in saltier. *Pl.* 98, *cr.* 11, (palm, *pl.* 123, *cr.* 1.)

M'CLINTOCK, JOHN, Esq., of Drumcar, co. Louth, a lion, passant, ppr. *Virtute et labore. Pl.* 48, *cr.* 8.

M'CLINTOCK, Sco., a lion, passant, ppr. *Pl.* 48, *cr.* 8.

M'CLOUD, Iri., a fox, current, ppr. *Pl.* 80, *cr.* 5.

M'CLURE, Eng., a domed tower, on top a flag, ppr. *Pl.* 42, *cr.* 10.

M'CLYMONT, out of a mural coronet, a lion's head, charged with a roundle. *Pl.* 45, *cr.* 9, (roundle, *pl.* 141.)

M'COLL, Sco., between the horns of a crescent, an etoile. *Justi ut sidera fulgent. Pl.*111,*cr.*15.

M'COMBIE, a grey cat, sejant, rampant. *Touch not the cat bot a glove. Pl.* 53, *cr.* 5.

MAC CONACH, Sco., a demi-savage, wreathed, ppr., having a loose Clan Donachy tartan plaid hung over sinister shoulder, in dexter a sheaf of arrows, pointing with sinister to a royal crown, (on dexter side of wreath.) *By these we shine*—and—*It is fortified. Pl.* 86, *cr.* 3.

MAC CONACHIE, Aberdeenshire, a demi-savage, wreathed, ppr., having a loose M'Gregor tartan plaid over sinister shoulder, in dexter a sheaf of arrows, ar., pointing with sinister to an antique crown, (on dexter side of wreath,) ppr. *Defend, and spare not*—and—*Ard choille. Pl.* 86, *cr.* 3.

MAC CONCALED, Iri., two trees, couped and raguled, in saltier, ppr., bound by a (garland of leaves,) vert. *Pl.* 60, *cr.* 12.

M'CONNELL, Sco., a dexter arm, in fess, couped, ppr., in hand a cross crosslet, fitched. *Toujours prêt. Pl.* 88, *cr.* 7.

M'CONNEL, DAVID C., Esq., Edinr., and Queensland, Australia, a kangaroo, sejant, erect, regardant, on the ground, under an Australian grass-tree, all ppr. *Vis in vita Deus. Pl.* 126 A, *cr.* 2.

M'CONNEL, HENRY, Esq., Manchester, a stag's head, erased, gu., charged on neck with a shamrock, or. *Victor in arduis. Pl.*126A,*cr.*5.

M'CORDA, Iri., a demi-savage, in dexter a barbed arrow, in sinister a heart. *Via una, cor unum. Pl.* 119, *cr.* 2.

M'CORMACK, and M'CORMICK, Sco., on a rock, ppr., a martlet, sa. *Sine timore. Pl.* 36, *cr.* 5.

M'CORMICK, Iri., in dexter hand a spear, (in pale,) ppr. *Pl.* 99, *cr.* 8.

M'CORQUODALL, Sco., a stag, at gaze, ppr. *Vivat rex. Pl.* 81, *cr.* 8.

M'CORQUODELL, Sco., a stag, at gaze, attired, gu. *Vivat rex. Pl.* 81, *cr.* 8.

M'CORQUODILL, Sco., a stag, at gaze, ppr., attired, sa. *Vivat rex. Pl.* 81, *cr.* 8.

M'COUL, Sco.,a dexter arm, in armour, embowed, in hand a cutlass, ppr. *Vincere. Pl.* 81, *cr.* 11.

M'CRAE, Sco., in hand a sword. *Fortitudine. Pl.* 21, *cr.* 10.

M'CRAE, Sco., an oak-tree, ppr. *Delectat et ornat. Pl.* 16, *cr.* 8.

M'CRACKEN, Sco., a nag's head, bridled, reins broken. *Omnia recte. Pl.* 92, *cr.* 1.

M'CRAW, Sco., a griffin, sejant, per pale, or and gu., wings, gold. *Pl.* 100, *cr.* 11.

M'CRAY, Sco., in hand a sword. *Fortiter. Pl.* 21, *cr.* 10.

M'CREE, or M'CRIE, Sco., an arm, in armour, couped, embowed, in fess, in hand a scimitar. *Delectat et ornat. Pl.* 81, *cr.* 11.

M'CRIRE, a bee-hive, with bees, volant, ppr. *Industria. Pl.* 81, *cr.* 14.

M'CROBIE, Sco., a hawk, rising, ppr. *Despicio terrena. Pl.* 105, *cr.* 4.

M'CRUMMEN, Sco., in hand a shepherd's flute. *Pl.* 46, *cr.* 14.

M'CRUMMEN, or M'CRUMMIN, Sco., a demi-lion, rampant, gu., armed, az., in dexter a thistle, ppr. *Permitte cœtera divis. Pl.* 45, *cr.* 15.

M'CUBBIN, Sco., an arm, in armour, embowed, in hand a scimitar. *Pro rege et patriâ. Pl.* 81, *cr.* 11.

M'CUBBIN, Sco., a martlet, sa. *Pl.* 111, *cr.* 5.

M'CULL, Sco., a leg, in armour, spurred, couped above knee, ppr. *Pl.* 81, *cr.* 5.

M'CULLOCH, Sco., a horse, passant. *Sine maculâ. Pl.* 15, *cr.* 14.

M'CULLOCH, an ermine, ppr. *Sine maculâ. Pl.* 9, *cr.* 5.

M'CULLOCH, DAVID, Esq., of Ardwall, Kirkcudbright, a hand throwing a dart, ppr. *Vi et animo. Pl.* 42, *cr.* 13.

M'CULLOCK, Sco., a naked arm, embowed, throwing a dart. *Pl.* 92, *cr.* 14.

M'CULLOCK, Eng., a triangular harrow, gu. *Pl.* 7, *cr.* 2.

M'CULLUM, Sco., a greyhound's head, or. *Pl.* 14, *cr.* 4, (without charge.)

MACCURDY, Lond. and Iri., a leopard, passant, ppr., resting dexter on an escutcheon, vert, thereon a leopard's face, or. *Pl.* 86, *cr.* 2, (escutcheon, *pl.* 6, *cr.* 11.)

M'DANIEL, Iri., a hand, couped, in fess, holding a cross crosslet, fitched. *Pl.* 78, *cr.* 9.

MacDeargan, Iri., a swallow, ppr. *Pl.* 111, *cr.* 5.

M'Deargan, a swallow, ppr. *Pl.* 111, *cr.* 5.

MacDermot, or MacDermott, Iri., a greyhound, current, sa. *Pl.* 47, *cr.* 2, (without chapeau.)

MacDermot, Coolavin, a demi-lion, gu., in paws a sceptre, (surmounted by a crown,) ppr. *Honore et virtute*. *Pl.* 47, *cr.* 4, (sceptre, *pl.* 82, *cr.* 3.)

M'Dermott, Iri., a greyhound, current, sa. *Pl.* 28, *cr.* 7, (without charge.)

Macdiarmid, Sco., a lion, rampant, ar., between paws a garland of flowers, ppr. *Pl.* 67, *cr.* 5, (garland, *pl.* 41, *cr.* 7.)

M'Diarmid, Sco., a lion, rampant, or. *Pl.* 67, *cr.* 5.

MacDiarmott, Iri., a lion, rampant, or. *Pl.* 67, *cr.* 5.

M'Donagh, Iri., a dexter arm, embowed, in hand a sword, environed with a serpent, all ppr. *Virtutis gloria merces*. *Pl.* 116, *cr.* 11.

MacDonald, a dexter arm, in armour, in fess, couped, ppr., in hand a cross crosslet, fitched, gu. *Per mare, per terras*. *Pl.* 88, *cr.* 7, (armour, *pl.* 121, *cr.* 14.)

MacDonald, of M'Donald, on a rock, az., a raven, sa. *Nec tempore, nec fato*. *Pl.* 38, *cr.* 10.

MacDonald, Sco., on a rock, ppr., a tower. *Sure*. *Pl.* 31, *cr.* 15.

MacDonald, Bart., Surr., a hand, in armour, in fess, holding a cross crosslet, fitched, gu. *Pl.* 71, *cr.* 13.

MacDonald, Baron, Iri., and a Bart., N.S., (Wentworth and Macdonald,) a hand, in armour, in fess, holding a cross crosslet, fitched, gu. *Per mare, per terras*. *Pl.* 71, *cr.* 13.

Macdonald, Durh., in a bush, a lion's head and fore-paws, sa, *Toujours prêt*. *Pl.* 119, *cr.* 5.

Macdonald, Sco., a demi-lion, rampant, ar., regally crowned, ppr., in dexter a sword, wavy, of the last, hilt and pommel, or. *Pro rege in tyrannos*. *Pl.* 54, *cr.* 2.

Macdonald, Sco., in dexter hand a dagger, ppr. *My hope is constant in thee*. *Pl.* 28, *cr.* 4.

Macdonald, William-Bell, of Rammerscales, Dumfries, in hand a dagger, ppr. *I beir the bel*. *Pl.* 28, *cr.* 4.

Macdonald, out of a castle, triple-towered, an arm, in armour, embowed, in hand a scimitar. *Pl.* 116, *cr.* 12.

M'Donald, Eng., a hind, trippant, or. *Pl.* 20, *cr.* 14.

M'Donald, Sco., in hand a cross crosslet, fitched. *My hope is constant in thee*. *Pl.* 99, *cr.* 1.

M'Donald, Iri., a talbot's head, az. *Pl.* 123, *cr.* 15.

M'Donald, Sco., in dexter hand a dirk, erect. *Nec tempore, nec fato*. *Pl.* 23, *cr.* 15.

M'Donald, Sco., the Holy Bible, expanded, ppr. *Cœlestia sequor*. *Pl.* 15, *cr.* 12.

M'Donald, Sco., a castle, ppr. *My hope is constant in thee*. *Pl.* 28, *cr.* 11.

M'Donald, Lockhart, of Lee, a boar's head, erased. *Corda serata pando*. *Pl.* 16, *cr.* 11.

M'Donald, Sco., on a rock, inflamed, a raven, sa. *Nec tempore, nec fato*. *Pl.* 116, *cr.* 10.

M'Donald, Sco., an arm, in armour, embowed, in hand a sword, all ppr. *Per mare, per terras*. *Pl.* 2, *cr.* 8.

M'Donald, Sco., a dexter hand, in armour, couped, in fess, ppr., holding a cross crosslet, fitched, gu. *Nec tempore, nec fato*. *Pl.* 78, *cr.* 9.

M'Donald, Sco., a hand, in armour, holding a cross crosslet, fitched, gu. *Per mare, per terras*. *Pl.* 51, *cr.* 1.

M'Donald, Sco., in hand a dagger, in pale, ppr. *My hope is constant in thee*. *Pl.* 23, *cr.* 15.

M'Donald, Sco., an arm, in armour, gauntleted, in fess, couped, ppr., in hand a cross crosslet, fitched, sa. *Nec tempore, nec fato*. *Pl.* 71, *cr.* 13.

M'Donald, Sco., in hand, couped at wrist, a cross crosslet, fitched, in pale. *Pl.* 99, *cr.* 1.

M'Donall, of Logan, two lions' paws, in saltier, ppr. *Victoria vel mors*. *Pl.* 20, *cr.* 13.

M'Donell, Macdonell, or M'Donnell, in hand, couped, in fess, a fleur-de-lis. *Pl.* 46, *cr.* 12.

MacDonell, Sco., a raven, ppr., perching on a rock, az. *Craggan an fhithich*. *Pl.* 38, *cr.* 10.

MacDonnel, Ann Catherine, Countess of Antrim, and Viscountess Dunluce, Iri., a dexter arm, couped at shoulder, attired, or, turned down, ar., in hand, ppr., a cross crosslet, fitched. *Toujours prest*. *Pl.* 88, *cr.* 7.

MacDonnell, Iri., a dexter arm, in armour, in fess, couped, in hand a cross crosslet, fitched. *Pl.* 71, *cr.* 13.

M'Donnell, Earl of Antrim. *See* Antrim.

M'Donnell, Sco., a raven, ppr., perched on a rock, az. *Pl.* 38, *cr.* 10.

M'Donnell, an arm, in armour, embowed, in fess, in hand a cross crosslet, fitched, in pale. *Pl.* 88, *cr.* 7, (armour, *pl.* 121, *cr.* 14.)

M'Donogh, Iri., an arm, embowed, in hand a sword, environed by a serpent. *Virtutis gloria merces*. *Pl.* 116, *cr.* 11.

M'Dougal, Sco., a lion's paw, erect, and erased, ppr. *Vincere vel mori*. *Pl.* 126, *cr.* 9.

M'Dougal-Hay, Sco., a lion, issuing, (gardant,) ppr., in dexter a cross crosslet, fitched, gu. *Fear God*. *Pl.* 65, *cr.* 6.

MacDougall, Sco., an arm, in armour, embowed, in hand a couteau sword, ppr. *Virtutis laus actio*. *Pl.* 81, *cr.* 11.

Macdougall, Eng., in lion's gamb, erased, sa., a sceptre, in pale, or. *Pl.* 16, *cr.* 1.

M'Dougall, or MacDougall, Sco., in lion's paw, erased and erect, a dagger, ppr. *Fortis in arduis*. *Pl.* 56, *cr.* 3.

M'Dougall, an arm, in armour, embowed, in hand a scimitar. *Pl.* 81, *cr.* 11.

M'Dougall, Eng., a deer's head, erased, ppr *Pl.* 66, *cr.* 9.

M'Dowal, in hand a dagger, in pale. *Virtus in caducis*. *Pl.* 23, *cr.* 15.

M'Dowal, and McDowall, Sco., a lion's paw, erased and erect. *Vincere vel mori*. *Pl.* 126, *cr.* 9.

M'Dowal, Sco., a demi-lion, ppr., in dexter a sword, az., hilted and pommelled, or. *Pl.* 41, *cr.* 13.

M'Dowal, Sco., and M'Dowall, Lond., a lion's paw, erased, a branch of olive, vert. *Vincam vel moriar*. *Pl.* 68, *cr.* 10.

M'Dowal, Sco., a demi-lion, ppr., in dexter a sword, az., hilt and pommel, or. *Pl.* 41, *cr.* 13.

M'Dowall, Hay, Bart., Sco., a lion, passant, gardant, ppr., in dexter a cross crosslet, fitched, gu. *Fear God. Pl.* 120, *cr.* 5, (cross, *pl.* 141.)

M'Dowall, Sco., a demi-lion, ar., crowned with an imperial crown, or, in dexter a flaming sword, all ppr. *Pro rege in tyrannos. Pl.* 54, *cr.* 2.

M'Dowall, Sco., an arm, in armour, embowed, in fess, couped, ppr., in hand a cross crosslet, fitched. *Vincere vel mori. Pl.* 88, *cr.* 7, (armour, *pl.* 121, *cr.* 14.)

M'Dowall, Sco., on a ducal coronet, or, an arm, in armour, embowed, in fess, couped, ppr., in hand a cross crosslet, fitched. *Pl.* 57, *cr.* 3, (coronet, *same plate; cross, pl.* 88, *cr.* 7.)

M'Dowall, Sco., two bears' paws, erased, in saltier. *Pl.* 20, *cr.* 13, (paw, *pl.* 126, *cr.* 2.)

M'Dowall, Sco., a lion's gamb. *Pl.* 126, *cr.* 9.

M'Dowall, Sco., in lion's paw, erased, a dagger. *Pl.* 56, *cr.* 3.

M'Dowall, Sco., a lion's paw, erased and erect, ppr. *Pl.* 126, *cr.* 9.

M'Dowall, Sco., a demi-lion, ar., regally crowned, or. *Pl.* 61, *cr.* 4, (without branch.)

M'Dowell, two bears' paws, in saltier. *Pl.* 20, *cr.* 13.

M'Dowell, Eng., in lion's paw, erased, a dagger, in pale. *Pl.* 56, *cr.* 3.

M'Dowgal, Sco., two lions' paws, in saltier, ppr. *Victoria vel mors. Pl.* 20, *cr.* 13.

Macduff, Sco., a demi-lion, rampant, gu. *Pl.* 67, *cr.* 10.

McDuff, Sco., a demi-lion, gu., holding a dagger. *Deus juvat. Pl.* 31, *cr.* 13.

Mace, Eng., in hand, erect, a scimitar, in pale, ppr. *Pl.* 66, *cr.* 6.

Macelester, Sco., a dexter arm, in armour, couped, in hand a dagger. *Per mare, per terras. Pl.* 120, *cr.* 1.

M'Eniery, and MacEniery, Iri., a falcon, belled, ppr. *Pl.* 67, *cr.* 3.

M'Entire, Sco., in dexter hand a dagger, erect, ppr. *Per ardua. Pl.* 23, *cr.* 15.

M'Evers, a boar's head, couped, in fess. *Pl.* 48, *cr.* 2.

Macevoy, a cubit arm, erect, vested, gu., cuffed, erminois, in hand a sword, ppr. *Bear and forbear. Pl.* 21, *cr.* 10, (vesting, *pl.* 32, *cr.* 6.)

M'Ewan, Sco., trunk of oak-tree, shooting a young branch, ppr. *Reviresco. Pl.* 92, *cr.* 8.

M'Fadyen, and M'Faiden, Sco., a talbot passant, gu. *Pl.* 120, *cr.* 8.

M'Fall, Sco., an eagle's head, erased. *Resurgo. Pl.* 20, *cr.* 7.

Macfarlane, (seven darts, points upward, six in saltier, and one in pale,) enfiled with a ducal coronet. *Pl.* 37, *cr.* 5.

Macfarlane, Sco., an eagle, rising, ppr. *Laboranti numen adest. Pl.* 67, *cr.* 4.

Macfarlane, Eng., a bird, sitting on a tree. *Pl.* 13, *cr.* 4.

Macfarlane, M'Farlane, or M'Farlin, Sco., a demi-savage, in dexter a sheaf of arrows, pointing with sinister to an imperial crown. *This I'll defend. Pl.* 86, *cr.* 3.

M'Farlane, Sco., a naked man, in hand a sheaf of arrows, ppr. *This I'll defend.*

MacFarquhar, Sco., a dexter hand, couped, ppr. *Sto pro fide. Pl.* 32, *cr.* 14.

M'Farquhar, Sco., a demi-lion, rampant, in dexter a sword. *Fide et fortitudine. Pl.* 41, *cr.* 13.

M'Farquhar, Sco., a dexter hand, ppr. *Pl.* 32, *cr.* 14.

M'Farquhar, Eng., on a winged globe, an eagle, rising, ppr. *Pl.* 34, *cr.* 2, (globe, *pl.* 79, *cr.* 8.)

M'Fell, Sco., an eagle's head, erased, ppr. *Aspiro. Pl.* 20, *cr.* 7.

Magfie, Sco., a demi-lion, rampant, gu. *Pro rege. Pl.* 67, *cr.* 10.

M'Fingah, Iri., an arm, in armour, embowed, in hand a tilting-spear. *Pl.* 57, *cr.* 3, (without chapeau.)

M'Gallook Sco., a dove, ppr. *Industriâ et labore. Pl.* 66, *cr.* 12.

MacGan, Iri., a boar's head, couped, az., armed and crined, or. *Pl.* 48, *cr.* 2.

M'Gassook, Sco., a dove, ppr. *Industriâ et labore. Pl.* 66, *cr.* 12.

M'Gavin, Sco., a dragon's head, or, vomiting fire, gu. *Pl.* 37, *cr.* 9.

M'Gee, or M'Ghie, an ostrich, ar., in mouth a horse-shoe, az. *Pl.* 16, *cr.* 2.

M'Gell, Sco., a terrestrial globe. *Honestum utili prefero. Pl.* 14, *cr.* 1.

M'George, Sco., a demi-griffin, ar. *Pl.* 18, *cr.* 6.

M'George, Eng., a greyhound's head, or, collared, gu. *Pl.* 43, *cr.* 11.

M'Gibbon, Sco., two oars, in saltier, sa. *Pl.* 7, *cr.* 9.

M'Gie, a leopard's head, erased, gardant, or. *Pl.* 56, *cr.* 7.

M'Gilevray, Sco., a cat, sejant. *Touch not the cat without a glove. Pl.* 24, *cr.* 6.

M'Gilevray, Sco., a cat, sejant. *Pl.* 24, *cr.* 6.

M'Gill, a phœnix in flames, ppr. *Sine fine. Pl.* 44, *cr.* 8.

M'Gill, Sco., a martlet, ar. *In Domino confido. Pl.* 111, *cr.* 5.

M'Gill, or Macgill, Eng. and Iri., a phœnix in flames, ppr. *Sine fine. Pl.* 44, *cr.* 8.

M'Gill, Sco., a martlet, rising, ppr. *In Deo confido. Pl.* 107, *cr.* 6, (without tower.)

M'Gilleoun, or MacGilleoun, Sco., an arm, embowed, in fess, couped, supporting a spear, issuing in pale, all ppr. *Pl.* 19, *cr.* 5.

M'Gilvray, Sco., a camel's head, sa. *Pl.* 109, *cr.* 9.

M'Glashan, Sco., a long cross, recrossed, gu., on three grieces. *Pl.* 23, *cr.* 12.

M'Gouan, or M'Gowan, Sco., a thistle, ppr. *Juncta arma decori. Pl.* 68, *cr.* 9.

M'Gougan, Sco., an arm, couped at elbow, in fess, in hand a cross crosslet, fitched. *Vincere vel mori. Pl.* 78, *cr.* 9.

M'Gowan, Eng., a galley, with oars in action, ppr. *Pl.* 34, *cr.* 5.

M'Gowan, Sco., a talbot, passant, or, collared, az. *Pl.* 65, *cr.* 2.

McGowran, Iri., an ancient ship or galley. *Pl.* 24, *cr.* 5.

Macgregor, Sco., a lion's head, erased. *Spare not. Pl.* 81, *cr.* 4.

Macgregor, Murray, Sir Evan-John, Bart., C.B., Sco.: 1. Behind two cannons, in saltier, a Highlander, couped above knees, on sinister a shield, ar., thereon a sword and tree, in saltier, in dexter a sword, over this, in the act of striking. *E'en do, and spare not.* 2. Out of a mural coronet, a lion's head, crowned with an antique crown, with points. *Serioghalmo dhream.*

MACGREGOR, Sco., an eagle, perched, wings extended, ppr. *Serioghalmo dhream—and—In libertate sociorum defendenda.* Pl. 126, cr. 7.

MACGREGOR, Gleney, out of a mural coronet, ar., masoned, sa., a lion's head, gu., crowned with an antique crown, or. *Eadhon dean gus na caomhain—and—Virtutis regia merces.* Pl. 45, cr. 9, (crown, pl. 96, cr. 13.)

MACGREGOR, out of a heart, a dexter hand, erect, grasping a scimitar, ppr. *Firrineach gus e chrich.* Pl. 35, cr. 7.

MACGREGOR, Sir WILLIAM, Bart., in hand, couped at wrist, a dagger, erect, ppr., pommel and hilt, gold. *E'en do, and spare not.* Pl. 23, cr. 15.

M'GREGOR, Sco., a lion's head, erased. *E'en do, and spare not.* Pl. 81, cr. 4.

M'GREGOR, Sco., an arm, in armour, ppr., in hand a scimitar, az., hilted and pommelled, or. Pl. 81, cr. 11.

M'GREGOR, Sco., a fir-tree. Pl. 26, cr. 10.

M'GREGOR, Sco., a lion's head, erased, on head an antique crown, ppr. *E'en do, bait spair nocht.* Pl. 90, cr. 4, (crown, pl. 96, cr. 13.)

M'GREGOR, Sco., a naked arm, in hand a sword, blade enfiled with three royal crowns, all ppr. Pl. 119, cr. 4.

M'GRIGOR, Bart., Middx., a lion's head, erased, ppr., crowned with an antique crown, with point, or. Pl. 90, cr. 4, (crown, pl. 96, cr. 13.)

M'GUARIE, Sco., out of an antique crown, an arm, in armour, embowed, in hand a dagger, all ppr. *Turris fortis mihi Deus.* Pl. 120, cr. 11, (crown, pl. 79, cr. 12.)

M'GUARIE, or MACQUARIE, Sco., a nag's head, couped, ar., bridled, gu. *Be true.* Pl. 90, cr. 1.

MACGUFFIE, JAMES, Esq., of Crossmichael, Kirkcudbright, a boar's head, couped, sa. *Arma parata fero.* Pl. 48, cr. 2.

M'GUFFOCK, or MAC GUFFOCK, a dove, ppr. *Industriâ et labore.* Pl. 66, cr. 12.

M'GUIRE, and MACJURE, Iri., a dagger, in pale. Pl. 73, cr. 9.

M'GUIRE, Iri., a buck's head, erased, az. Pl. 66, cr. 9.

M'HADO, and M'HADDO, Sco., in hand a scimitar, ppr. *Vigilo.* Pl. 29, cr. 8.

M'HAFFIE, Sco., a demi-griffin, gu. Pl. 18, cr. 6.

MACHAM, Eng., a greyhound, current, sa. Pl. 47, cr. 2, (without chapeau.)

M'HARDIE, Sco., the sun, or. *Luceo, non uro.* Pl. 68, cr. 14.

M'HARDIE, Sco., an arm, in armour, embowed, in hand a scimitar, all ppr. *Tout hardi.* Pl. 81, cr. 11.

M'HATTIE, Sco., between wings, an escallop, ar., charged with a cross fleury, sa., all ppr. Pl. 80, cr. 2.

MACHELL, a stag's head, erased, ppr. Pl. 66, cr. 9.

MACHELL, Eng., a camel's head, erased, or, ducally gorged, ar. Pl. 120, cr. 12.

MACHEN, EDWARD-TOMKINS, Esq., of Eastbach Court, Glouc., a pelican's head, erased, or. Pl. 26, cr. 1.

MACHEN, or MACHIN, Eng., on a lion's head, erased, sa., a chapeau, or. Pl. 122, cr. 10.

MACHIN, Notts., (on a mount, vert,) a pelican's head, couped, gu., in front of rays of the sun, or. *Auxilium ab alto.* Pl. 116, cr. 13.

M'HUD, Sco., an arm, in armour, embowed, in hand a dagger, ppr. *E'en do.* Pl. 120, cr. 11.

M'HUTCHEON, Sco., a wyvern. *Fortiter gerit crucem.* Pl. 63, cr. 13.

M'ILWHAM, Sco., a parrot, feeding on branch of a cherry-tree, ppr. Pl. 49, cr. 3.

M'INDOE, Sco., a sun-dial, on a stand, ar. Pl. 97, cr. 6.

M'INNES, Eng. and Edinr., a bee, sucking a thistle, ppr. *E labore dulcedo.* Pl. 68, cr. 9.

MACINROY, Sco., a lymphad (in full sail, sa.) *Sequor.* Pl. 24, cr. 5.

M'INROY, Sco., a pelican, in nest. *Fidelitas.* Pl. 44, cr. 1.

M'INTIRE, Eng., out of a tower, a demi-greyhound, rampant, ppr. Pl. 73, cr. 13.

M'INTOSH, Sco., a cat, (rampant.) *Prenez garde.* Pl. 70, cr. 15.

M'INTOSH, Sco., a cat, current, gardant, ppr. Pl. 119, cr. 7.

M'INTOSH, or MACINTOSH, Eng., a demi-cat, salient, sa. *Prenez garde.* Pl. 80, cr. 7.

M'INTOSH, or MACINTOSH, Sco., a cat, salient, ppr. *Touch not the cat bot a glove.* Pl. 70, cr. 15.

M'INTOSH, Sco., a cat, current, gardant. *Touch not the cat bot a glove.* Pl. 119, cr. 7.

M'INTYRE, Sco., in dexter hand a dagger, in pale, both ppr. *Per ardua.* Pl. 23, cr. 15.

M'IVER, a boar's head, couped, or. *Nunquam obliviscar.* Pl. 48, cr. 2.

M'IVER, Eng., a griffin's head, erased, az. Pl. 48, cr. 6.

M'IVER, Lanc., a boar's head, couped, or. *Nunquam obliviscar.* Pl. 48, cr. 2.

MACK, Sco., a water-bouget, sa. *In spe et labore transigo vitam.* Pl. 14, cr. 12.

MACK, a heart, gu., pierced by an arrow, in bend sinister, ar. *Et domi et foris.* Pl. 16, cr. 14.

MACK, Sco., a water-bouget, sa. *En esperanza.* Pl. 14, cr. 12.

M'KAILE, Sco., a cancer, ppr. *Nec ferro, nec igne.* Pl. 116, cr. 14.

M'KALL, Sco., an arm, in armour, in hand a caltrap, ppr. Pl. 22, cr. 4.

MACKARTNEY, in dexter hand a slip of rose-bush, ppr. *Stimulat sed ornat.* Pl. 118, cr. 9.

MACKAULY, a leg, couped at knee, booted and spurred. Pl. 95, cr. 13.

MACKAULY, a boot, couped at ankle, spurred, all ppr. *Dulce periculum.* Pl. 118, cr. 6.

MACKAY, Sco., a dexter cubit arm, erect, in hand a dagger, in pale, all ppr., hilt and pommel, or. *Manu forti.* Pl. 23, cr. 15.

MACKAY, Eng., a lion, passant, or, in dexter a crescent, gu. Pl. 77, cr. 3.

M'KAY, Sco., in hand a scimitar, all ppr. *Manu forti.* Pl. 29, cr. 8.

M'KAY, Eng., a demi-greyhound, vert. Pl. 48, cr. 3. (Another, ppr.)

MACKBEATH, Sco., an arm, in armour, embowed, in fess, in hand a (sword,) all ppr. Pl. 107, cr. 15.

M'KEAN, Sco., a demi-cat, gardant, sa. *Pl.* 80, *cr.* 7.

M'KEAN, a dog, sejant, ppr. *J'ai bonne éspérance. Pl.* 77, *cr.* 8.

M'KEAN, Sco., a talbot, sejant, ppr. *J'ai bonne ésperance. Pl.* 107, *cr.* 7.

M'KECHNIE, Sco., in dexter hand a spur. *Pl.* 34, *cr.* 9.

MACKEILL, Sco., a cross Calvary, gu. *Pl.* 7, *cr.* 13.

M'KELL, Sco., out of clouds, a dexter hand brandishing a scimitar. *Pl.* 29, *cr.* 8, (clouds, *pl.* 71, *cr.* 7.)

M'KELLAR, Sco., out of a castle, triple-towered, a demi-lion, rampant. *Pl.* 101, *cr.* 1.

M'KELLAR, Eng., a cat, (rampant,) gardant, gu. *Pl.* 70, *cr.* 15.

M'KELLAR, and M'KELLOR, Sco., an arm, in armour, embowed, in hand a scimitar, ppr. *Pl.* 81, *cr.* 11.

M'KELLIP, Sco., a demi-talbot. *Non dormit qui custodit. Pl.* 97, *cr.* 9, (without arrow.)

M'KELLIP, Sco., a talbot's head. *Non dormit qui custodit. Pl.* 123, *cr.* 15.

MACKEN, a pelican's head, gu., issuing from rays, or. *Pl.* 116, *cr.* 13.

MACKENAN, and MACKEUAN, or MACKEWAN, Sco., trunk of oak-tree, shooting new branches, ppr. *Revivesco. Pl.* 92, *cr.* 8.

MACKENAY, Iri., an arm, in armour, embowed, in hand a spear, top broken, and pendent, ppr. *Pl.* 44, *cr.* 9.

MACKENNAL, or MACKANNEL, Sco., an eagle's head, erased, ppr. *Intrepidus et benignus. Pl.* 20, *cr.* 7.

M'KENNY, Bart., in hand, in armour, couped at wrist, a roll of parchment. *Pl.* 119, *cr.* 6.

MACKENZIE, JOHN WHITEFOORD, Esq., Edinr., a dexter arm embowed, holding a sword in bend, all ppr. *Fide parta fide aucta. Pl.* 34, *cr.* 7.

MACKENZIE, Sco., a rugged rock, ppr. *Truth will prevail. Pl.* 73, *cr.* 12.

MACKENZIE, on a rock, a stag's head, cabossed. *Pl.* 36, *cr.* 1, (rock, *pl.* 73, *cr.* 12.)

MACKENZIE, Sco., an arm, embowed, in hand a dart, all ppr. *Recte et ardua. Pl.* 92, *cr.* 14.

MACKENZIE, Sco., a man's heart, in flames, within two branches of palm, in orle, all ppr. *Ferendum et sperandum. Pl.* 88, *cr.* 11.

MACKENZIE, an eagle, rising from a (rock,) ppr. *Firma et ardua. Pl.* 61, *cr.* 1.

MACKENZIE, THOMAS, Esq., of Ord, Ross, in hand a dagger, in bend, ppr. *Sic itur ad astra. Pl.* 28, *cr.* 4.

MACKENZIE, Sco., a crescent, ar. *Crescitque virtute. Pl.* 18, *cr.* 14.

MACKENZIE, Sco., the sun in splendour. *Pl.* 68, *cr.* 14.

MACKENZIE, Sco., a mountain, in flames, ppr. *Luceo, non uro. Pl.* 92, *cr.* 9.

MACKENZIE, Middx., a buck's head, cabossed, ar., attired, or. *Pl.* 36, *cr.* 1.

MACKENZIE, Bart., of Kilcoy, Sco., a lady, from waist, with bodice and short sleeves, presenting a rose with dexter, sinister bent outward, and hand resting on side, ringlets loose. *Amore vici. Pl.* 2, *cr.* 10, (rose, *pl.* 118, *cr.* 9.)

MACKENZIE, Sco., a mountain, in flames, ppr. *Pl.* 92, *cr.* 9.

MACKENZIE, Sco., a dexter arm, embowed, in hand, a sword, in bend, all ppr. *Fide parta, fide aucta. Pl.* 34, *cr.* 7.

MACKENZIE, Bart., of Scatwell, Sco.: 1. The sun in splendour, ppr. *Pl.* 68, *cr.* 14. 2. In dexter hand a sword, in bend, ppr. *Pl.* 21, *cr.* 10. *Sine maculâ.*

MACKENZIE, Sco., between the attires of a stag, fixed to the scalp, sa., a boar's head, erect, or. *Pl.* 33, *cr.* 15.

MACKENZIE, or M'KENZIE, Sco., the sun in splendour. *Luceo, non uro. Pl.* 68, *cr.* 14.

MACKENZIE, Bart., of Garlock, a Highlander, wielding a sword, ppr. *Virtute et valore.*

MACKENZIE, Sco., a demi-savage wreathed about head and loins with laurel, in hand a club, all ppr. *Virtute et valore. Pl.* 14, *cr.* 11.

MACKENZIE-MUIR, Bart., Sco.: 1. A palm-branch, in bend dexter, surmounted by a sword, in bend sinister, all ppr. *Pl.* 50, *cr.* 11, (sword, *same plate, cr.* 4.) 2. In dexter hand a dart, ppr. *Pl.* 42, *cr.* 13.

M'KENZIE, Bart., of Coul, a boar's head, erect and erased, or, between the attires of a stag, fixed to the scalp, sa. *Pulchrior ex arduis. Pl.* 33, *cr.* 15.

M'KENZIE, Sco., a dexter arm, throwing a dart, ppr. *Recta et ardua. Pl.* 92, *cr.* 14.

M'KENZIE, Sco., a lion, couchant, gardant, ppr. *Insult me not. Pl.* 101, *cr.* 8.

M'KENZIE, Sco., a dexter arm, in hand a garland of laurel, ppr. *Virtute et amore. Pl.* 118, *cr.* 4.

M'KENZIE, JOHN, Esq., of Glack, Aberdeen, two hands, holding a two-handed sword, in bend, ppr. *Always faithful. Pl.* 3, *cr.* 5.

M'KENZIE, a man's heart, in flames, within two palm-branches, in orle, all ppr. *Ferendum et sperendum. Pl.* 88, *cr.* 11.

M'KENZIE, Sco., in dexter hand a sword, in bend, ppr. *Sic itur ad astra. Pl.* 21, *cr.* 10.

M'KENZIE, or MACKINZIE, Sco. and Eng., a burning mount, ppr. *Luceo, non uro. Pl.* 92, *cr.* 9.

M'KENZIE, Sco., a stag's head, cabossed. *Cuidich in rhi. Pl.* 36, *cr.* 1.

M'KENZIE, or M'KINZIE, Sco., a demi-lady, richly attired, in hand a rose, ppr. *Amore vici. Pl.* 2, *cr.* 10, (rose, *pl.* 118, *cr.* 9.)

M'KENZIE, Sco., in dexter hand, couped and erect, a dagger, both ppr. *Garde. Pl.* 28, *cr.* 4.

M'KENZIE, Sco., a demi-lion, rampant, gu. *Avito viret honore. Pl.* 67, *cr.* 10.

M'KENZIE, Sco., a mountain, in flames, ppr. *Fide parta, fide aucta. Pl.* 92, *cr.* 9.

M'KENZIE, Sco., a dexter cubit arm, in hand a wreath of laural, ppr. *Virtute et valore. Pl.* 86, *cr.* 1.

M'KENZIE, Sco., out of clouds, ppr., two hands, conjoined. *Fides unit. Pl.* 53, *cr.* 11.

M'KENZIE, Sco., a crescent, ar. *Crescitique virtute. Pl.* 18, *cr.* 14.

M'KENZIE, a demi-lady, in dexter a cinquefoil, ppr. *Amore vici. Pl.* 2, *cr.* 10.

M'KENZIE, Sco., a rugged rock, ppr. *Truth will prevail. Pl.* 73, *cr.* 12.

M'KERLIE, Wigtonshire, on dexter side of a mount, a cross crosslet, fitched, sa., with the sun shining from the sinister, or. *In hoc signo vinces. Pl.* 58, *cr.* 6.

M'KERLIE, Sco., on dexter end of a mount, vert, a cross crosslet, fitched, sa. *In hoc signo vinces. Pl.* 58, *cr.* 6.

M'KERRELL, or M'KERREL, Sco., a Roman soldier on his march, with (standard) and utensils, all ppr. *Dulcis pro patriâ labor.* Pl. 90, cr. 1.

M'KERRELL, Sco., an ancient warrior, in armour, with a shield and spear, (over point of the latter, a star.) *Dulcis pro patriâ labor.* Pl. 90, cr. 1.

MACKEY, Eng., a lion's head, erased, ar. Pl. 81, cr. 4.

MACKIE, or M'KIE, Sco., a raven, ppr. *Labora.* Pl. 123, cr. 2.

MACKIE, Eng., two oak-branches, in saltier, acorned, ppr. Pl. 19, cr. 12.

MACKIE, Sco., in hand, couped at wrist, a dagger, all ppr. Pl. 101, cr. 10.

MACKIE, JOHN, Esq., of Bargaly, Kirkcudbright, a raven, ppr. *Labora.* Pl. 123, cr. 2.

MACKIEGAN, Iri., out of a ducal coronet, a griffin's head, in beak a key, all ppr. Pl. 89, cr. 5.

MACKILLOP, or M'KILLOP, Eng., a demi-eagle, regardant, ppr. Pl. 27, cr. 15.

M'KILLOP, Sco., a talbot's head, erased, ppr. *Non dormit qui custodit.* Pl. 90, cr. 6.

M'KILLOP, Sco., a demi-talbot. *Non dormit qui custodit.* Pl. 97, cr. 9, (without arrow.)

M'KIMMIE, Sco., a deer's head, erased, ppr. *Je suis prêt.* Pl. 66, cr. 9.

MACKINDER, or M'KINDER, Eng., an elephant, statant, ppr. Pl. 56, cr. 14.

MACKINDLAY, Sco., a stag, trippant, ppr. *Amo.* Pl. 68, cr. 2.

M'KINDLAY, or MACKINLAY, Sco., an eagle's head, erased, ppr. *Spernit humum.* Pl. 20, cr. 7.

M'KINLAY, Sco., an arm, in armour, in hand a branch of olive, all ppr. *Not too much.* Pl. 68, cr. 1.

M'KINNA, an arm, in armour, embowed, in hand the butt end of a spear, ppr. *Prudentia et honor.* Pl. 44, cr. 9.

MACKINNON, Eng., a spear, in pale, ppr. Pl. 97, cr. 4.

MACKINNON, Hants and Sco., a boar's head, erased, in mouth a shin-bone, all ppr. Pl. 28, cr. 14, (bone, pl. 25, cr. 11.)

MACKINNON, Chief of Clan Kinnon, Sco., a boar's head, erased, ar., (in mouth a deer's shank-bone, ppr.) *Audentes fortuna juvat.* Pl. 28, cr. 14, (bone, pl. 25, cr. 11.)

MACKINTOSH, Eng., a cat's head, cabossed, gu. Pl. 66, cr. 14, (head, pl. 97, cr. 7.)

MACKINTOSH, Sco., a cat, sejant, gardant, sa. *Touch not the cat bot a glove.* Pl. 24, cr. 6.

MACKINTOSH, W.S., a cat, sejant, on hind feet. *Touch not the cat bot a glove.* Pl. 53, cr. 5.

M'KIRDY, Eng. and Sco., a demi-wyvern, or. *Dieu et mon pays.* Pl. 116, cr. 15.

MACKLEANS, a cypress-branch and laurel-slip, in saltier, surmounted of a battle-axe, in pale. Pl. 82, cr. 11.

MACKLELD, an arm, in armour, embowed, in hand a sword, enfiled with a moor's head, all ppr. Pl. 102, cr. 11, (armour, pl. 2, cr. 8.)

MACKLELLAN, or M'LELLAN, Sco., a moor's head and neck, ppr. *Sapit qui reputat.* Pl. 120, cr. 3.

MACKLELLAN, or M'LELLAN, Sco., a naked arm, in hand a sword, on point a moor's head. *Think on.* Pl. 102, cr. 11, (arm, pl. 34, cr. 7.)

MACKLELLAN, Sco., a mortar-piece. *Superba frango.* Pl. 55, cr. 14.

MACKLIN, Eng., an ass's head. Pl. 91, cr. 7.

MACKLIN, Eng., an eagle's head, issuing from rays. Pl. 84, cr. 9.

MACKLOIDE, or M'CLOUD, Sco., a bull's head, cabossed, between two flags. *Hold fast.* Pl. 118, cr. 8.

MACKLOW, a dragon's head, per pale, indented, gu. and ar. guttée, counterchanged, in mouth an eagle's leg, erased, or. Pl. 107, cr. 10, (leg, pl. 89, cr. 13.)

MACKLOW, a sinister arm, in hand a bow, strung. Pl. 3, cr. 12.

MACKMURE, Eng., a dolphin, naiant. Pl. 48, cr. 9.

MACKMORAGH, and MACKMORE, Iri., on a ducal coronet, a griffin, sejant, ppr., resting paw on a shield, ar. Pl. 42, cr. 8.

MACKNIGHT, Sco., an arm, in armour, in hand a spear, (in bend,) ppr. *Fac et spera.* Pl. 44, cr. 9.

MACKNIGHT, or M'KNIGHT, Sco., a tower, sa., masoned, ar. *Justum et tenacem.* Pl. 12, cr. 5.

MACKNIGHT, a lion's head, erased, gu. Pl. 81, cr. 4.

M'KNIGHT, Sco., a lion's head, erased, az. *Omnia fortunæ committo.* Pl. 81, cr. 4.

MACKORDA, a demi-wild Irish savage, in dexter a heart, in sinister a dart, all ppr. Pl. 119, cr. 2.

M'KOWAN, two doves, billing. *Constancy.* Pl. 60, cr. 13.

MACKPHERSON, Sco., a cat, sejant, gardant, ppr. Pl. 24, cr. 6.

MACKRETH, Hants, a phœnix in flames, ppr. Pl. 44, cr. 8.

MACKWILLIAMS, Eng., a phœnix in flames, ppr. Pl. 44, cr. 8.

MACKWORTH, Ruts., a sinister wing, erect, per pale, indented, ar. and sa. Pl. 39, cr. 10.

MACKWORTH, Wel. and Lond., a cock, ppr. *Gwell angua na chywilydd.* Pl. 67, cr. 14.

MACKWORTH, Salop, a cock, beaked, legged, combed, and wattled, all gu. Pl. 67, cr. 14.

MACKWORTH, Ruts. and Norf., a sinister wing, elevated, per pale, intended, erm. and sa. Pl. 39, cr. 10.

MACKWORTH, Bart., Glams., a cock, ppr. Pl. 67, cr. 14.

MACLACHLAN, a castle, triple-towered. Pl. 123, cr. 14.

M'LACHLAN, or MACLAUCHLAN, Sco., a leopard's head, cabossed, ppr. *Fortiter.* Pl. 66, cr. 14.

M'LACHLAN, Sco., out of a ducal coronet, or, a lion's head, gu. *Fortis et fidus.* Pl. 90, cr. 9.

M'LAGAN, Sco., a mortar-piece, or. *Superba frango.* Pl. 55, cr. 14.

M'LAGAN, Sco., a beaver, ppr. *Principiis obsta.* Pl. 49, cr. 5.

M'LAGGAN, Sco., a greyhound, sejant, ar. Pl. 66, cr. 15.

MACLAINE, WILLIAM-OSBORNE, Esq., of Kington House, Thornbury, Glouc., a Lochaber-axe, erect, between branches of laurel and cypress, all ppr. *Altera merces.* Pl. 119, cr. 8.

M'CLAMBROCH, Sco., in hand a dagger. *Fear God, and fight.* Pl. 101, cr. 10.

MACLAREN, Sco., a cannon, mounted, ppr. *Forward.* Pl. 111, cr. 3.

M'LAREN, Sco., a mortar-piece. Pl. 55, cr. 14.

M'LAREN, Sco., a mortar-piece, az. *Frango.* Pl. 55, cr. 14.

M'LAREN, Sco., a mortar, sa. *Frango.* Pl. 55, cr. 14, (without stock.)

M'LARTY, a hand, ppr., holding up a cross crosslet, fitched, in pale, gu. *In te fido.* Pl. 51, cr. 1.

M'LAUCHLAN, Sco., a castle, triple-towered. *Fortis et fidus.* Pl. 123, cr. 14.

MACLAUGHLAN, Sco., a salmon, naiant, ppr. *Fortis et fidus.* Pl. 85, cr. 7.

M'LAUGHLAN, a horse's head, in armour, issuing, on top a plume of ostrich-feathers, all ppr. Pl. 55, cr. 7.

M'LAURANCE, and M'LAURIN, the Virgin and Child, ppr., vested, vert.

MACLAURIN, of Balquhidder and Strathearin, a lion's head, erased, crowned with an Eastern diadem of four points, between two laurel-branches, in orle, ppr. *Ab origine fidus.*

M'LAWS, a garb, or, banded, gu. *Dominus providebit.* Pl. 48, cr. 10.

M'LEA, Sco., two lions' paws, erased, in saltier, ppr. *Vincere vel mori.* Pl. 20, cr. 13.

M'LEA, two arms, dexter and sinister, from shoulders, extended, in saltier, the former holding a pair of compasses, extended, and the latter a sword, in pale, all ppr. *Tam arte quam marte.*

MACLEAN, Bart., Sco., a tower, embattled, ar. Pl. 12, cr. 5.

MACLEAN, ALEXANDER, Esq., of Pennycross, Argyll, a battle-axe, in pale, crossed by a branch of laurel and cypress, in saltier, all ppr. *Altera merces.* Pl. 119, cr. 8.

MACLEAN, a battle-axe, in pale, with two branches, in saltier, laurel to dexter, and cypress to sinister, all ppr. *Sorti æquus utrique.* Pl. 119, cr. 8.

M'LEAN, Sco., a laurel and palm-branch, in saltier, ppr. *Fortiter et strenue.* Pl. 63, cr. 3, (laurel, pl. 21, cr. 2.)

M'LEAN, Sco., a salmon, naiant. Pl. 85, cr. 7.

M'LEAN, Sco., a Lochaber-axe, in pale, crossed by a laurel and cypress-branch, in saltier, all ppr. *Altera merces.* Pl. 119, cr. 8.

M'LEAN, Eng., a dragon's head, vert. Pl. 87, cr. 12.

M'LEAN, Sco., a tower, ar. *Virtue mine honour.* Pl. 12, cr. 5.

MACLEAY, KENNETH, Esq., of Keiss Castle, Caithness, a buck's head, erased, ppr. *Spes anchora vitæ.* Pl. 66, cr. 9.

M'LEAY, Sco., a stag's head, erased. *Spes anchora vitæ.* Pl. 66, cr. 9.

M'LEAY, Sco., a demi-lion, rampant, gardant, or. Pl. 35, cr. 4.

MACLELLAN, a moor's head, on the point of a dagger, all ppr., hilt and pommel, or. *Think on.* Pl. 27, cr. 3.

M'LELLAN, Sco., a mortar-piece. *Superba frango.* Pl. 55, cr. 14.

M'LELLAN, a negro's head, couped, ppr. *Sapit qui reputat.* Pl. 120, cr. 3.

M'LEOD, Sco., the sun in splendour. Pl. 68, cr. 14; and below the arms a mural coronet. Pl. 128, fig. 18. Above the crest, *Loisgim agus soilleirghim;* and below the mural coronet, *Quocunque jeceris, stabit.*

MACLEOD, a urus's head, erased. *Murus aheneus.* Pl. 57, cr. 7.

MACLEOD, Sco., a phœnix in flames, ppr. *Luceo, non uro.* Pl. 44, cr. 8

MACLEOD, Sco., two lions, regardant. *Hold fast*—and—*Murus aheneus.*

M'LEOD, or MACLEOD, Sco., the sun in splendour. *Luceo, non uro.* Pl. 68, cr. 14.

M'LEOD, Sco., a lion's head, erased, ppr. Pl. 81, cr. 4.

M'LEOD, Sco., an eagle's head, ppr. *Murus aheneus.* Pl. 100, cr. 10.

M'LEOD, Sco., an anchor, (the flukes uppermost.) *Vigilando.* Pl. 25, cr. 15.

M'LEOD, or MACLEOD, Sco., a urus's head, cabossed, sa., between two flags, gu., staves, of the first. *Hold fast*—and—*Murus aheneus.* Pl. 118, cr. 8.

M'LEOD, Eng., a lion's head, erased, az. Pl. 81, cr. 4.

M'LEOD, a bull's head, cabossed, gu. *Hold fast.* Pl. 111, cr. 6.

M'LEOD, Sco., the sun in splendour, or. *Quocunque jeceris, stabit.* Pl. 68, cr. 14.

M'LEOD, a lion's head, erased, gu., langued, az. *Hic murus aheneus.* Pl. 81, cr. 4.

M'LEOD, a castle, triple-towered, and embattled, ar., masoned, sa., windows and port, gu. Pl. 123, cr. 14.

M'LEUR, or M'LURE, Sco., an arm, in armour, in hand a falcon's lure, ppr. *Spectemur agendo.* Pl. 44, cr. 2, (armour, pl. 68, cr. 1.)

M'LEURG, Sco., a demi-archer, shooting an arrow from a bow. *Ad metam.* Pl. 60, cr. 5.

M'LIN, Eng., an eagle's head, issuing from rays. Pl. 84, cr. 9.

M'LINTOCK, Iri., a lion, passant, ppr. *Virtute et labore.* Pl. 48, cr. 8.

M'LOWE, Eng., stump of oak-tree, sprouting branches, ppr. Pl. 92, cr. 8.

M'LURE, and MACLURE, Sco., an eagle's head, erased, ppr. *Paratus sum.* Pl. 20, cr. 7.

MACMAHON, Bart., Iri., an arm, in armour, embowed to sinister, in hand a sword, all ppr., surmounted by a portcullis, gu., chained, or. *Sic nos, sic sacra tuemur.*

MACMAHON, Iri., an arm, in armour, embowed, in hand, ppr., a roll, or. Pl. 96, cr. 2, (roll, pl. 119, cr. 6.)

MACMAHON, Bart., an arm, embowed to dexter, in armour, ppr., in hand a sword, wavy, surmounted by a portcullis, gu., chained, or. *Sic nos, sic sacra tuemur.* Pl. 2, cr. 8, (portcullis, pl. 51, cr. 12.)

MACMAHON, an arm, in armour, embowed, in hand a sword. Pl. 2, cr. 8.

M'MAHON, Iri., two dexter hands, in armour, conjoined, environed with clouds, supporting a flaming heart, all ppr. Pl. 20, cr. 8.

MACMAHON, a goat, (passant,) ar., armed and hoofed, or. Pl. 66, cr. 1.

M'MAUGHT, Sco., a dexter hand, in fess, couped, gu., holding a fleur-de-lis, az. *Pro aris et focis.* Pl. 46, cr. 12.

MACMAURE, Iri., between two branches, in orle, ppr., a dexter hand holding a roll of paper. Pl. 86, cr. 5.

MACMICHAEL, Lond. and Sco., a talbot's head, couped, ar., charged with a crescent, or. Pl. 123, cr. 15, (crescent, pl. 141.)

MACMICHAEL, a battle-axe, erect, surmounted by a branch of laurel on dexter, and (oak) on sinister, in saltier, all ppr. *Pl.* 82, *cr.* 11.

M'MICING, M'MICHIN, M'MICKING, or M'MIKIN, Iri., a demi-savage, in dexter an arrow, on his back a quiver, full, ppr. *Pl.* 80, *cr.* 9.

MAC MILLAN, Sco., a dexter and sinister hand, issuing from the wreath, brandishing a two-handed sword, ppr. *Miseris succurrere disco. Pl.* 3, *cr.* 5.

MACMILLAN, Sco., in dexter hand a broadsword, ppr. *Pl.* 28, *cr.* 4.

M'MILLAN, Edinr., a lion, rampant. *Age aut perfice. Pl.* 67, *cr.* 5.

M'MILLAN, Eng., a yew-tree, ppr. *Pl.* 49, *cr.* 13.

M'MILLAN, a mullet, sa. *Pl.* 41, *cr.* 1.

M'MIN, M'MINN, and M'MYNE, Sco., a stag, couchant, ppr. *Nil certum est. Pl.* 67, *cr.* 2.

M'MORE, Iri., a cubit arm, in armour, in hand a sword, ppr. *Pl.* 125, *cr.* 5.

MACMORRAN, Sco., a dexter hand, couped, gu. *Virtus virtutis præmium. Pl.* 32, *cr.* 14.

M'MORRAN, a raven, ppr. *Virtus virtutis præmium. Pl.* 123, *cr.* 2.

M'MORRAN, Sco., a raven, ppr. *Pro lusu et præda. Pl.* 123, *cr.* 2.

M'MORRAN, Sco., a hawk, belled, ppr. *Pro lusu et præda. Pl.* 67, *cr.* 3.

MACMURDOCH, Sco., a lion's head, erased, gu. *Omine secundo. Pl.* 81, *cr.* 4.

M'MURRAY, ROBERT, Esq., Limerick, a demi-lion, rampant, gardant, gu., holding a Lochaber axe, ppr. *Virtute fideque. Pl.* 126 c, *cr.* 12.

M'MURRAY, Sco., a stag's head, ppr. *Pl.* 91, *cr.* 14.

MACNAB, or M'NAB, Sco., a savage's head, affrontée, ppr. *Timor omnis abesto. Pl.* 19, *cr.* 1.

M'NAB, or M'NABB, a savage's head, in profile. *Pl.* 81, *cr.* 15.

M'NAB, Sco., in dexter hand a sword. *Timor omnis abesto. Pl.* 21, *cr.* 10.

M'NABB, Eng., a galley. *Pl.* 24, *cr.* 5.

MACNAGHTON, or M'NAUGTON, Iri., a tower, gu. *I hope in God. Pl.* 12, *cr.* 5.

M'NAIR, a mermaid, ppr., in dexter a mirror, in sinister a comb. *Pl.* 48, *cr.* 5.

M'NAIR, Sco., a demi-negro, (over dexter shoulder a sugar-cane, in sinister a bunch of tobacco-leaves, all ppr.) *Labor omnia vincit. Pl.* 41, *cr.* 8.

MACNAMARA, Eng., a stag's head, or. *Pl.* 91, *cr.* 14.

MACNAMARA, Sco., out of a ducal coronet, or, an arm, embowed, in hand a tilting-spear, ppr. *Pl.* 122, *cr.* 8, (spear, *pl.* 99, *cr.* 8.)

MACNAMARA, a naked arm, embowed, in hand a scimitar, all ppr. *Pl.* 92, *cr.* 5.

MACNAMARA, out of a ducal coronet, or, an arm, embowed, in hand a lance, ppr. *Pl.* 39, *cr.* 15, (coronet, *pl.* 122, *cr.* 8.)

MACNAMARA, an arm, embowed, in hand a dagger, all ppr., hilt and pommel, or. *Pl.* 34, *cr.* 7.

MACNAMARA, Wel., out of a ducal coronet, or, an arm, in hand a sabre, ppr., hilt, gold. *Pl.* 92, *cr.* 5, (coronet, *pl.* 122, *cr.* 8.)

MACNAMARA, PATRICK-JAMES-DILLON, Esq., of Ayle, co. Clare, a naked arm, in hand a scimitar, ppr. *Firmitas in cœlo. Pl.* 92, *cr.* 5.

M'NAMARD, Eng., out of tower, a demi-lion, rampant, ppr. *Pl.* 42, *cr.* 4.

M'NAUGHT, Sco., a lion's head, erased, ar. *Omnia fortunæ committo. Pl.* 81, *cr.* 4.

M'NAUGHT, Sco., a lion's head, erased, ar., langued, gu. *Omnia fortunæ committo. Pl.* 81, *cr.* 4.

M'NAUGHTAN, or M'NAUGHTON, Sco., a tower, embattled, gu. *I hope in God. Pl.* 12, *cr.* 5.

M'NAUGHTAN-WORKMAN, Knt., Iri.: 1. For *M'Naughtan*, a tower, embattled, gu. *Pl.* 12, *cr.* 5. *I hope in God.* 2. For *Workman*, out of a crescent, quarterly, sa. and ar., a lictor's fasces. *Non pas l'ouvrage, mais l'ouvrier. Pl.* 82, *cr.* 15, (fasces, *pl.* 65, *cr.* 15.)

M'NAYR, a mermaid, with mirror and comb, ppr. *Pl.* 48, *cr.* 5.

MACNEIL, Sco., an arm, in armour, from shoulder, issuing, in hand a dagger (point upward,) all ppr. *Vincere vel mori. Pl.* 120, *cr.* 1.

M'NEIL, or MACNEIL, Sco., a rock, ppr. *Per virtutem sciamque. Pl.* 73, *cr.* 12.

M'NEIL, and M'NELLY, Sco., an arm, in armour, embowed, in hand a sword, ppr. *Vincere vel mori. Pl.* 34, *cr.* 7.

M'NEIL, Eng., a lion, rampant, or. *Pl.* 67, *cr.* 5.

MACNEILL, RODERICK, Esq., of Barra, Inverness, a rock, gu. *Vincere vel mori. Pl.* 73, *cr.* 12.

M'NEMARA, Iri., a mermaid, in (dexter) a comb, ppr. *Pl.* 48, *cr.* 5.

MACNICOL, a crescent, gu. *Gradatim. Pl.* 18, *cr.* 14.

M'NICOLL, Sco., a lion's head, erased, ppr. *Nil sistere contra. Pl.* 81, *cr.* 4.

M'NISH, an arm, embowed and couped, in fess, ppr., vested, az., in hand an oak-sprig, vert, fructed, or. *Pl.* 51, *cr.* 5, (oak, *pl.* 32, *cr.* 13.)

M'NISH, Sco., an eagle, rising, ppr. *Animo non astutiâ. Pl.* 67, *cr.* 4.

M'ONALD, Sco., a mountain, in flames. *Pl.* 92, *cr.* 9.

MACONOCHIE, a demi-man, in dexter three arrows, pointing with sinister to an imperial crown, placed on (dexter side of wreath,) head, wreathed, having a loose tartan plaid hung over sinister shoulder, all ppr. *His nitimur et munitur. Pl.* 86, *cr.* 3.

M'ONOGHUY, Sco., a dexter hand, in fess, couped, holding a laurel-branch, ppr. *Certamine summo. Pl.* 46, *cr.* 12, (laurel, *pl.* 123, *cr.* 5.)

M'OUL, an arm, in armour, embowed, in fess, couped, ppr., in hand a cross crosslet, fitched. *Vincere vel mori. Pl.* 114, *cr.* 13, (cross, *pl.* 141.)

M'OWL, in lion's paw, erased, a dagger, all ppr. *Vincere vel mori. Pl.* 56, *cr.* 3.

MACPETER, Sco., out of a mural coronet, ar., masoned, sa., a lion's head, gu., crowned with an antique crown, ppr. *Pour mon Dieu*—and—*E'en do, and spare not. Pl.* 45, *cr.* 9, (crown, *pl.* 79, *cr.* 12.)

M'PHAILL, Sco., a deer's head, erased, ppr. *Memor esto. Pl.* 66, *cr.* 9.

MACPHARLANE, or M'PHARLIN, Sco., a naked arm, in hand a sheaf of arrows, ppr. *This I'll defend. Pl.* 56, *cr.* 4.

MACPHERSON, a cat, sejant, rampant. *Creagn dhubh chloinn Chatain.* Pl. 24, cr. 6.

MACPHERSON, a grey cat, sejant, rampant. *Touch not the cat bot the glove.* Pl. 53, cr. 5.

MACPHERSON, EWEN, of Cluny Macpherson, Inverness, a cat, sejant, ppr. *Touch not the cat bot a glove.* Pl. 24, cr. 6.

MACPHERSON, or M'PHERSON, Eng., a black cat's foot, holding up a crescent, or. Pl. 91, cr. 1.

MACPHERSON, a cat, rampant, ppr. *Qui me tanget pœnitebit.* Pl. 126 A, cr. 10.

M'PHERSON, a cat, current, sa. *Touch not the cat bot a glove.* Pl. 119, cr. 7.

M'PHERSON, Sco., a cat, sejant, ppr. *Touch not the cat bot a glove.* Pl. 24, cr. 6.

M'PHERSON, Iri., a fox's head, erased, gu. Pl. 71, cr. 4.

M'PHIE, Sco., a demi-lion, rampant, gu. *Pro rege.* Pl. 67, cr. 10.

M'QUAID, a lion's head, erased. Pl. 81, cr. 4.

MACQUAIRE, out of a crown, ppr., an arm, in armour, embowed, in hand a dagger, ar. *Turris fortis mihi Deus.* Pl. 115, cr. 14.

MACQUEEN, Sco., a wolf's head, couped, sa. *Vires in arduis.* Pl. 8, cr. 4.

MACQUEEN, Sco., out of a cloud, a dexter arm, in fess, in hand a (laurel) garland, ppr. *Virtus in arduis.* Pl. 80, cr. 3.

MACQUEEN, an heraldic-tiger, rampant, erm., holding an arrow, point downward, ar., pheoned, gu. Pl. 7, cr. 5, (arrow, pl. 22, cr. 15.)

M'QUEEN, a wolf, (rampant,) against a broad arrow, erect on point. Pl. 126, cr. 13, (arrow, pl. 22, cr. 15.)

M'QUEEN, Beds., a wolf's head, erased, ppr. *Quæ sursum volo videre.* Pl. 14, cr. 6.

M'QUEEN, Sco., a wolf's head, couped, ppr. *Virtus in arduis.* Pl. 8, cr. 4.

M'QUEEN, Eng., a boar's head, erect, sa. Pl. 21, cr. 7.

M'QUHAN, Sco., out of a cloud, a dexter arm, from shoulder, in fess, in hand a garland, ppr. Pl. 80, cr. 3.

M'QUIE, Lanc., in dexter hand, couped, a dagger, in pale, all ppr. *Manu forti.* Pl. 23, cr. 15.

M'QUINN, Eng., a wolf's head, ppr. *Que sursum volo.* Pl. 8, cr. 4.

MACQUIRE, or M'QUIRE, Eng. and Iri., a dagger, in pale, ppr. Pl. 73, cr. 9.

M'RACH, Soo., a dexter hand grasping a scimitar, both ppr. *Fortitudine.* Pl. 29, cr. 8.

MACRAE, Sco., in dexter hand a scimitar, both ppr. *Fortitudine.* Pl. 29, cr. 8.

M'RAE, Sco., an arm, embowed, in hand a scimitar, ppr. *Fortitudine.* Pl. 29, cr. 5.

MACREA, Sco., an oak-tree, ppr. *Delectat et ornat.* Pl. 16, cr. 8.

MACREADIE, or MACREADY, in hand, (in bend,) a sword, ppr. *Semper paratus.* Pl. 21, cr. 10.

MACRERY, or MACKRERY, a savage, statant, wreathed round middle with leaves, ppr. Pl. 35, cr. 12.

MACRITCHIE, Sco., a cat, sejant, erect, sa. *Prenez garde.* Pl. 53, cr. 5.

M'RITCHIE, Sco., a lion's paw, charged with a cheveron, and thereon a crescent. Pl. 88, cr. 3, (crescent, pl. 141.)

M'ROBERTSON, Sco., a dexter hand, holding up a royal crown, ppr. *Virtutis gloria merces.* Pl. 97, cr. 12.

MACRORIE, Sco., a lymphad, with sails furled, and oars in action, sa., flagged, gu. *Res, non verba.* Pl. 34, cr. 5.

MACSAGAN, Sco., a greyhound's head, (erased,) ar., collared, sa., ringed, or. *Nec timidé, nec timeré.* Pl. 43, cr. 15.

MACSWEEN, a broadsword, and a bow, in saltier, ppr. *By the providence of God.* Pl. 12, cr. 12, (sword, pl. 22, cr. 7.)

M'TAGGART, a trefoil, ppr. *Ditat Deus.* Pl. 4, cr. 10, (without wings.)

M'TAGGART, Sco., a lion's head, erased, ppr. *Vi et virtute.* Pl. 81, cr. 4.

M'TAGGART, Eng., a greyhound's head, erased, sa. Pl. 89, cr. 2.

M'TAVISH, Sco., a boar's head, erased. *Ne obliviscaris.* Pl. 16, cr. 11.

MACTIER, Sco., an arm, embowed, in hand a battle-axe, ppr. *Hæc manus ob patriam.* Pl. 123, cr. 10, (axe, pl. 73, cr. 7.)

M'TURK, Sco., a ram's head, (cabossed,) ppr. Pl. 34, cr. 12.

M'VEAN, Sco., an arm, in armour, in hand a sword. *Fidelis.* Pl. 2, cr. 8.

M'VICAR, Sco., an eagle, rising, ppr. *Dominus providebit.* Pl. 67, cr. 4.

M'WHIRTER, an antique Scottish harp, or, with nine strings, ar. *Te Deum laudamus.* Pl. 104, cr. 15.

M'WORTH, Eng., a cock. Pl. 67, cr. 14.

MADAM, Lond., Wilts., and Iri., an eagle's head, erased, or. Pl. 20, cr. 7.

MADDEN, Lond. and Iri., out of a ducal coronet, a falcon, rising, or, belled, gu., in beak a cross botonnée, of the second. Pl. 103, cr. 6, (cross, pl. 141.)

MADDEN, Sir FREDERICK, out of a ducal coronet, gu., a falcon, rising, or, belled, of the first, in beak a cross botonnée, of the last. Pl. 103, cr. 6, (cross, pl. 141.)

MADDER, Staffs., on trunk of tree, in fess, vert, a lion, sejant, or. Pl. 76, cr. 11.

MADDISON, Eng., a demi-lion, gu. Pl. 67, cr. 10.

MADDISON, Northumb., out of a crown-flory, an arm, in armour, ppr., garnished, or, in gauntlet a battle-axe, ppr., charged with a cross, gu., staff, sa. Pl. 122, cr. 8, (axe, pl. 73, cr. 7; cross, pl. 141.)

MADDISON, in dexter hand, ppr., (sleeve, erminois,) a battle-axe, sa. Pl. 73, cr. 7.

MADDOCK, a lion, passant. Pl. 48, cr. 8.

MADDOCK, Iri., out of a cloud, a hand, erect, holding a club, ppr. Pl. 37, cr. 13.

MADDOCKS, Eng., an elephant's head, erased, gu. Pl. 68, cr. 4.

MADDOCKS, a demi-lion, in dexter a rose. Pl. 39, cr. 14.

MADDOX, Eng., a Bengal tiger, passant, gardant, ducally gorged, ppr. Pl. 120, cr. 9.

MADELEY, Middx. and Salop, a hawk, ppr., preying on a martlet, sa. Pl. 80, cr. 12, (martlet, pl. 111, cr. 5.)

MADESTON, a cubit arm, in armour, erect, per pale, crenellée, or and ar., in hand a halberd, headed and garnished, of the last. Pl. 73, cr. 7, (armour, pl. 121, cr. 14.)

MADESTON, Eng., an ostrich, (regardant, ducally crowned, resting dexter on a pellet, sa.) Pl. 16, cr. 2.

MADESTON, a cock's head, erm., in beak a trefoil, slipped, vert. *Pl.* 92, *cr.* 3, (trefoil, *pl.* 141.)
MADOCK, Eng., an eagle, displayed, in dexter a sword, in sinister a pistol, all ppr. *Pl.* 99, *cr.* 5, (pistol, *pl.* 101, *cr.* 10.)
MADOCK, Glouc., a lion's head, erased, or, (pierced through neck by a sword, in pale, point issuing from top of head, embrued, ppr., hilted and pommelled, gold.) *Pl.* 10, *cr.* 2, (lion, *pl.* 81, *cr.* 4.)
MADOCKS, JOHN-EDWARD, Esq., of Glanywern, Denbigh, a demi-lion, rampant. *Pl.* 67, *cr.* 10.
MADOX, Eng., in lion's paw, erased, a dagger, both ppr. *Pl.* 56, *cr.* 3.
MADOX, Herts., Salop, and Lond., a lion, sejant, or, in dexter a sword, ar., hilt and pommel, gold. *Pl.* 115, *cr.* 15, (sword, *same plate.*)
MADRESTON, a torteau, charged with the sun, or. *Pl.* 116, *cr.* 7, (sun, *pl.* 68, *cr.* 14.)
MADYSTON, Durh., Linc., and Northumb., a cubit arm, erminois, in hand, ppr., a battleaxe, sa. *Pl.* 73, *cr.* 7.
MAGAN, WILLIAM-HENRY, Esq., of Clonearl, King's County; and Eagle Hill, co. Kildare, a boar's head, az. *Virtute et probitate*. *Pl.* 48, *cr.* 2.
MAGAWLEY, Iri., a horse's head, ar., in a waggon harness, sa. *Pl.* 49, *cr.* 6.
MAGAWLEY, Iri., a swan, wings addorsed, ppr. *Pl.* 46, *cr.* 5.
MAGAWLEY, Iri., a swan, ppr. *Pl.* 122, *cr.* 13.
MAGENIS, RICHARD-WILLIAM, Esq., of Warrington, co. Down, a boar, passant, ppr. *Sola salus servire Deo.* *Pl.* 48, *cr.* 14.
MAGEE, Iri., a lion, sejant, collared. *Pl.* 21, *cr.* 3.
MAGENS, Lond. and Glouc., an arm, erect, ppr., in hand three trefoils, vert. *Pl.* 118, *cr.* 9, (trefoils, *pl.* 141.)
MAGEOGHEGAN, Iri., a blood-hound, passant, collared, indented, ppr. *Pl.* 65, *cr.* 2.
MAGER, or MAJOR, Southampton and Isle of Wight, a greyhound's head, gu., collared, or. *Pl.* 43, *cr.* 11.
MAGILL, Eng., a savage's head, couped, ppr. *Pl.* 81, *cr.* 15.
MAGIN, Eng., a demi-wyvern, vert. *Pl.* 116, *cr.* 15.
MAGINN, Iri., a cockatrice, displayed, vert. *Pl.* 102, *cr.* 15.
MAGINNISE, Iri., a boar, passant, ppr. *Pl.* 48, *cr.* 14.
MAGNALL, Lond. and Linc., on a mount, vert, an eagle, rising, ppr., crowned with an Eastern coronet, or. *Pl.* 61, *cr.* 1, (coronet, *pl.* 79, *cr.* 12.)
MAGNUS, Eng., a lion's gamb, erased, or. *Pl.* 126, *cr.* 9.
MAGOR, a greyhound's head, erased and collared. *Pl.* 43, *cr.* 11.
MAGOUNIS, Iri., a demi-lion, gardant, gu., holding a fleur-de-lis, or. *Pl.* 91, *cr.* 13, (gardant, *pl.* 35, *cr.* 4.)
MAGRATH, Surr., an arm, couped, in fess, ppr. *Salus in fide.* *Pl.* 87, *cr.* 9, (without flag.)
MAGRATH, Eng., on a chapeau, a lion, passant, ppr. *Pl.* 107, *cr.* 1.
MAGRATH, Iri., a crow, sa. *Pl.* 23, *cr.* 8.
MAGUIRE, Iri., an arm, in armour, in hand a sword. *Pl.* 2, *cr.* 8.

MAGUIRE, Eng., on a serpent, in a love-knot, vert, a hawk, statant, ppr. *Pl.* 75, *cr.* 11.
MAGUIRE, Iri., out of a ducal coronet, a demi-eagle, displayed, (in beak a rose, stalked and leaved,) all ppr. *Pl.* 9, *cr.* 6.
MAGUIRE, co. Fermanagh, a stag, statant, ppr., (collared and lined, or.) *Pl.* 88, *cr.* 9, (without arrow.)
MAHEN, co. Tipperary, on a mount, vert, a hawk, rising, belled and hooded, ppr., on each wing a crescent, or. *Pl.* 61, *cr.* 12, (crescent, *pl.* 141.)
MAHER, MARTIN-CHARLES, Esq., of Wilson's Lodge, Somers., an eagle, or, perched on its prey. *In periculis audax*—and—*Firmitas in cœlo*. *Pl.* 61, *cr.* 7.
MAHER, an eagle, wings expanded. *Pl.* 126, *cr.* 7.
MAHER, Iri., a bee, volant, in pale, or. *Pl.* 100, *cr.* 3.
MAHEWE, Cornw., a Cornish chough, erm. *Pl.* 100, *cr.* 13.
MAHEWE, Cornw., an eagle, wings adorsed, or, preying on a snake, nowed, ppr. *Pl.* 61, *cr.* 3, (snake, *pl.* 75, *cr.* 11.)
MAHEWE, Norf., a unicorn's head, erased, ar., maned, gu., the horn twisted, of the first and second, on neck a cheveron, vair. *Pl.* 67, *cr.* 1.
MAHON, Iri., a demi-husbandman, over dexter shoulder, an ox-yoke, ppr. *Pl.* 122, *cr.* 1.
MAHON, Iri., a tiger, (statant, in dexter a broken tilting-spear.) *Pl.* 67, *cr.* 15.
MAHON, Iri., a lion, rampant, in dexter an olive-branch. *Per ardua surgo.* *Pl.* 64, *cr.* 2, (olive, *pl.* 98, *cr.* 8.)
MAHON, Bart., Iri., a dexter arm, in armour, embowed, ppr., garnished, or, in hand a dagger, also ppr., pommel and hilt, gold. *Moniti meliora sequamur.* *Pl.* 120, *cr.* 11.
MAHON, Baron Hartland. See HARTLAND.
MAHONY, out of a coronet, (surmounted on the brim thereof by nine beads or balls,) an armed arm, in hand a sword, ppr., pierced through a fleur-de-lis, or. *Pl.* 115, *cr.* 14, (fleur-de-lis, *pl.* 141.)
MAIDMAN, Eng., a leopard's head, erased, gardant, ducally gorged. *Pl.* 116, *cr.* 8.
MAIDMAN, Hants, an arm, embowed, vested, per pale, indented, az. and or, cuffed, ar., in hand a dove, ppr. *Pl.* 88, *cr.* 5, (dove, *pl.* 66, *cr.* 12.)
MAILLARD, Eng., out of a ducal coronet, a peacock's tail, ppr. *Pl.* 120, *cr.* 13.
MAIN, Sco., an escallop, or, charged with a mullet, gu. *Pl.* 109, *cr.* 14.
MAIN, Eng., a leopard, rampant, ppr. *Pl.* 73, *cr.* 2.
MAIN, Sco., a hand throwing a dart, ppr. *Projeci.* *Pl.* 42, *cr.* 13.
MAIN, a cubit arm, erect and vested, party per cheveron, ar. and sa., in hand, ppr., a cross crosslet, fitched, in pale. *Pl.* 75, *cr.* 3, (cross, *pl.* 141.)
MAIN, Sco., a negro's head, sa., banded, ar. *Pl.* 48, *cr.* 7.
MAINE, out of a mural coronet, per pale, gu. and erm., an arm, in armour, garnished, or, in hand a spear, point downward. *Vincit pericula virtus.* *Pl.* 115, *cr.* 14, (spear, *pl.* 99, *cr.* 5.)
MAINGY, Eng., a wolf's head, erased, erminois. *Pl.* 14, *cr.* 6.

MAINSTONE, Herts. and Lond., a hedgehog, ar. *Pl.* 32, *cr.* 9.

MAINTER, out of a mural coronet, or, a unicorn's head, az., armed and crined, gold. *Pl.* 45, *cr.* 14, (coronet, *same plate.*)

MAINWARING, Bart., Chesh., out of a ducal coronet, or, an ass's head, ppr. *Devant si je puis. Pl.* 80, *cr.* 6.

MAINWARING, of Whitmore, Staffs., out of a ducal coronet, or, an ass's head, (with a hempen halter, all ppr.) *Devant si je puis. Pl.* 80, *cr.* 6.

MAINWARING, Salop, out of a ducal coronet, or, an ass's head, ar. *Pl.* 80, *cr.* 6.

MAINWARING, CHARLES-KYNASTON, Esq., of Oteley Park, Salop; and Brombrough Hall, Chesh.; out of a ducal coronet, an ass's head, couped, ppr. *Devant si je puis. Pl.* 80, *cr.* 6. For *Kynaston,* a lion's head, erased, sa., guttée-d'or. *Pl.* 81, *cr.* 4.

MAIR, Lond. and Sco., a swan, ppr. *Tempore candidior. Pl.* 122, *cr.* 13.

MAIR, Eng., a demi-pegasus, issuing, ar., enfiled round waist with a ducal coronet, gu. *Pl.* 91, *cr.* 2.

MAIR, Sco., a negro's head, issuing from shoulders, sa., banded, ar. *Pl.* 48, *cr.* 7.

MAIRE, a cubit arm, erect, vested, in hand a bugle-horn, stringed. *Pl.* 109, *cr.* 3, (vesting, *pl.* 5, *cr.* 3.)

MAIRIS, Wilts., on a mount, vert, a peacock, in pride, or, in beak, an escroll, inscribed, "Esse quam videre," resting dexter on an escutcheon, az., charged with a cross pattée, fitched, gold. *Si Deus nobiscum, quis contra nos. Pl.* 92, *cr.* 11, (escutcheon, *pl.* 6, *cr.* 11; cross, *pl.* 141.)

MAISTERTON, and MAISTERSON, Chesh., a tiger, passant, ar. *Pl.* 67, *cr.* 15.

MAITLAND, Sco., a rock, in the sea, ppr. *Attamen tranquillus. Pl.* 91, *cr.* 5.

MAITLAND, Earl of Lauderdale. See LAUDERDALE.

MAITLAND, Sco., a demi-monk, vested, grey, in dexter a crucifix, ar., in sinister a rosary, ppr. *Esse quam videri. Pl.* 90, *cr.* 5.

MAITLAND, a rock, placed in the sea, ppr. *Fluctus fluctu. Pl.* 91, *cr.* 5.

MAITLAND, Sco., a lion's head, erased, gu. *Paix et peu. Pl.* 81, *cr.* 4.

MAITLAND, a demi-lion, rampant, gu., langued, and membered, az., in dexter a thistle, ppr., in sinister a fleur-de-lis, of the second. *Fisus et fides. Pl.* 45, *cr.* 15.

MAITLAND, on a ducal coronet, or, a lion, sejant, affrontée, in dexter a sword, ppr., in pale, in sinister a fleur-de-lis, ar. *Deo juvante. Pl.* 120, *cr.* 2, (coronet, *same plate.*)

MAITLAND, a lion, sejant, affrontée, crowned, in dexter a sword, ppr., in pale, in sinister a fleur-de-lis, ar. *Pl.* 120, *cr.* 2, (crown, *same plate.*)

MAITLAND, Sco., in the sea, a rock, ppr. *Pl.* 91, *cr.* 5.

MAITLAND, Sco., a demi-lion, rampant, gu., (couped in all the joints, or, issuing from water, ppr.) *Luctor et emergam. Pl.* 67, *cr.* 10.

MAJENDIE, ASHHURST, Esq., of Hedingham Castle, Ess., an arm, in armour, embowed, in hand a scimitar, ppr. *Qualis ab incepto. Pl.* 81, *cr.* 11.

MAJOR, Iri., an escallop. *Deus major columba. Pl.* 117, *cr.* 4.

MAJOR, Notts., a greyhound, rampant, sa., collared, ar., on collar three mullets, of the first. *Pl.* 5, *cr.* 10, (without wings; mullet, *pl.* 141.)

MAJOR, Suff., an arm, embowed, vested, az., cuffed, ar., charged on arm with a plate, in hand, ppr., a baton, or. *Pl.* 120, *cr.* 1, (baton, *pl.* 18, *cr.* 1; plate, *pl.* 141.)

MAJOREBANKS, MAJORIBANKS, and MARJORIBANKS, Sco., a demi-griffin, rampant. *Et custos et pugnax. Pl.* 18, *cr.* 6.

MAJORIBANKS, or MARJORIBANKS, Sco., a lion's paw, grasping a lance, in bend, ppr. *Advance with courage. Pl.* 1, *cr.* 4.

MAJORIBANKS, a bear's paw, erased, grasping a tilting-spear, in bend sinister. *Pl.* 126, *cr.* 2, (spear, *pl.* 1, *cr.* 4.)

MAKARETH, Lanc., an arm, in armour, embowed, in hand a broken tilting-spear, all ppr. *Pl.* 44, *cr.* 9.

MAKEPEACE, Eng., a unicorn's head, ar., between two laurel-branches, in orle, vert. *Pl.* 54, *cr.* 9.

MAKEPEACE, a dove and olive-branch, all ppr. *Pl.* 48, *cr.* 15.

MAKEPEACE, Lond. and Berks., a leopard, passant, regardant, or, resting dexter on a shield, gu., charged with a cross crosslet, fitched, gold. *Pl.* 86, *cr.* 2, (shield, *pl.* 19, *cr.* 2; cross, *pl.* 141.)

MAKEROTH, or MAKERETH, Eng., an arm, in armour, in hand a broken lance, all ppr. *Pl.* 44, *cr.* 9.

MAKEWE, an eagle, preying on a serpent, nowed. *Pl.* 61, *br.* 7, (serpent, *pl.* 75, *cr.* 11.)

MALBANKE, Eng., on a tortoise, an eagle, perching, ppr. *Pl.* 70, *cr.* 8.

MALBANKE, Lanc., a lion's head, erased, gu., (charged with a bend, erm.) *Pl.* 81, *cr.* 4.

MALBONE, Eng., an eagle, regardant, in dexter a sword, ppr. *Pl.* 87, *cr.* 5.

MALBY, an (Indian) goat, passant, or. *Pl.* 66, *cr.* 1.

MALCOM, on a mount, vert, a pyramid, ar., entwined with ivy, ppr. *Ardua tendo. Pl.* 8, *cr.* 10.

MALCOM, Eng., a demi-swan, rising, ar. *Pl.* 54, *cr.* 4.

MALCOM, Sco., a tower, az., masoned, sa. *In ardua tendit. Pl.* 12, *cr.* 5.

MALCOM, a castle, ar., masoned, sa., portcullis, gu. *In ardua tendit. Pl.* 28, *cr.* 11.

MALCOLM, a demi-swan, rising, ar. *Pl.* 54, *cr.* 4.

MALCOLM, NEILL, Esq., of Pottalloch, Argyll, a tower, ar. *In ardua petit. Pl.* 12, *cr.* 5.

MALCOLM, Bart., Sco., on a mount, vert, a pyramid, encircled by a wreath of laurel, ppr. *Ardua tendo. Pl.* 8, *cr.* 10.

MALE, on a marquess's coronet, a Cornish chough, wings expanded, ppr. *Pl.* 8, *cr.* 5, (coronet, *pl.* 127, *fig.* 4.)

MALEDOCTUS, Eng., a demi-lion, supporting a long cross. *Pl.* 29, *cr.* 12.

MALEFONT, and MALESAUNTS, Eng., a demi-lion, gardant, gu., supporting a spear, enfiled with a boar's head, couped, ppr. *Pl.* 33, *cr* 2.

MALEPHANT, Sco., a demi-lion, rampant, ppr., crowned, or. *Pl.* 61, *cr.* 4, (without branch.)

MALET, Bart., Wilts., out of a ducal coronet, or, a tiger's head, erm. *Ma force d'en haut. Pl.* 36, *cr.* 15.

MALET, out of a ducal coronet, a griffin's head. *Pl.* 54, *cr.* 14.

MALEVERER, Eng., a nag's head, in armour, ppr. *Pl.* 7, *cr.* 12.

MALEVERER, Yorks., a greyhound, (passant,) ar., collared and ringed, or. *Pl.* 104, *cr.* 1, (without chapeau.)

MALFIT, a dexter arm, in armour, in hand a scimitar, (in pale,) all ppr. *Pl.* 81, *cr.* 11.

MALIN, Eng., an elephant, (passant,) or. *Pl.* 56, *cr.* 14.

MALING, Eng., out of a ducal coronet, a plume of five ostrich-feathers, in a case, all ppr. *Pl.* 106, *cr.* 11, (without chapeau.)

MALKIN, Eng., a wolf's head, sa. *Pl.* 14, *cr.* 6.

MALLABAR, a martlet, or. *Pl.* 111, *cr.* 5.

MALLAKE, Devons., on a cubit arm, erect, vested, or, two bends, wavy, sa., in hand, ppr., a (mallet,) of the first. *Pl.* 18, *cr.* 1.

MALLAM, Eng., a dolphin, naiant, or. *Pl.* 48, *cr.* 19.

MALLARD, Eng., on a chapeau, gu., a stag, trippant, ppr. *Pl.* 63, *cr.* 8.

MALLET, Somers., Cornw., and Devons., out of a ducal coronet, or, a tiger's head, erm. *Pl.* 36, *cr.* 15.

MALLET, of Amesbury, Wilts., out of a ducal coronet, a griffin's head, or. *Force d'en haut. Pl.* 54, *cr.* 14.

MALLET, Somers., Devons., and Cornw., a hind's head, ar., ducally gorged, or. *Pl.* 21, *cr.* 9, (gorging, *pl.* 128, *fig.* 3.)

MALLET, Somers., Devons., Cornw., out of a ducal coronet, or, an antelope's head, ar. *Pl.* 24, *cr.* 7, (coronet, *same plate, cr.* 10.)

MALLET, Sco., between two bay-branches, a lion's head. *Cœlitus vires. Pl.* 92, *cr.* 4.

MALLEY, a goat's head, erased, sa., bezantée. *Pl.* 29, *cr.* 13.

MALLEY, a savage, passant, carrying a tree, eradicated, ppr.

MALLEY, a savage, wreathed round temples and loins, with a club resting on shoulder, all ppr. *Pl.* 14, *cr.* 11.

MALLOCK, Sco., between two bay-branches, in orle, a lion's head, crowned with an antique crown, ppr. *Court no friend, dread no foe—and—E'en do, and spare not. Pl.* 96, *cr.* 13, (branches, *pl.* 79, *cr.* 13.)

MALLOM, and MALLON, Norf., an arm, in pale, vested, vert, the cuff turned up, erm., in hand, ppr., a lure, feathered, ar., garnished, or, stringed and tasselled, gu. *Pl.* 44, *cr.* 2, (vesting, *pl.* 32, *cr.* 6.)

MALLORY, Chesh. and Yorks., a nag's head, (couped,) gu. *Pl.* 81, *cr.* 6.

MALLORY, Northamp., a nag's head, or. *Pl.* 81, *cr.* 6.

MALLORY, Northamp., a nag's head, gu., crined, or, charged with a fleur-de-lis, gold. *Pl.* 46, *cr.* 4, (fleur-de-lis, *pl.* 141.)

MALLORY, a horse's head, (couped,) per pale, gu. and az., ducally gorged, or. *Pl.* 81, *cr.* 6, (gorging, *pl.* 116, *cr.* 8.)

MALLOW, on a chapeau, gu., turned up, erm., two sceptres, in saltier, or. *Pl.* 119, *cr.* 11.

MALMAINS, Eng., a lamb, supporting a banner, ar. *Pl.* 48, *cr.* 13.

MALMAYNES, Eng., an arm, in armour, embowed, hand apaumée, ppr. *Pl.* 97, *cr.* 1.

MALMESBURY, Earl and Baron of, and Viscount Fitz-Harris, (Harris,) a hedgehog, or, charged on side with three arrows, one in pale, two in saltier, ar., and across them, barwise, a key, az. *Je maintien drai. Pl.* 32, *cr.* 9, (arrows, *pl.* 43, *cr.* 14; key, *pl.* 54, *cr.* 3.)

MALONE, Eng., on a mount, a lion, rampant, ppr., collared, gu., in dexter an arrow, sa. *Pl.* 121, *cr.* 15.

MALONE, Iri., between wings, ppr., a griffin's head, in beak a palm-branch, vert. *Pl.* 22, *cr.* 2.

MALONE, a man, in complete armour, in dexter a lance, on sinister arm a shield, all ppr. *Fidelis ad urnam. Pl.* 90, *cr.* 1.

MALPAS, Eng., on a ducal coronet, a wyvern, vomiting fire at both ends, ppr. *Pl.* 104, *cr.* 11, (wyvern, *pl.* 109, *cr.* 13.)

MALTBY, Yorks., a garb, or, banded, gu. *Pl.* 48, *cr.* 10.

MALTBY, Ess., a barley-sheaf, erect, and banded, or, (pendent therefrom a bugle-horn, ar.) *Pl.* 48, *cr.* 10, (horn, *pl.* 98, *cr.* 2.)

MALTIWARD, Suff., a demi-griffin, ar., between claws, (a saltier,) sa. *Pl.* 18, *cr.* 6.

MALTON, Eng., a dolphin, haurient, devouring a fish, ppr. *Pl.* 71, *cr.* 1.

MALTON, Iri., on a rock, a dove, in mouth an olive-branch, ppr. *Pl.* 85, *cr.* 14.

MALTON, Devons. and Yorks., a snake, nowed, in pale, ppr., ducally gorged, ar. *Pl.* 119, *cr.* 12.

MALTRAVERS, Baron. *See* NORFOLK, Duke of.

MALTREVERS, Eng., a fountain, ppr. *Pl.* 95, *cr.* 15.

MALY, Iri., a ship. *Pl.* 115, *cr.* 9.

MALY, Kent, an arm, embowed, in hand an anchor, by the middle, in pale, end resting on the wreath. *Pl.* 121, *cr.* 14, (anchor, *pl.* 25, *cr.* 15.)

MALYN, an arm, bent, couped at shoulder, sa., in hand, ppr., an anchor, or. *Pl.* 27, *cr.* 6, (without sea.)

MALYNES, Eng., a reindeer's head, cabossed, ppr. *Pl.* 114, *cr.* 7.

MAN, Eng., on stump of oak-tree, an eagle, perching, ppr. *Pl.* 1, *cr.* 11.

MAN, Sco., a unicorn's head. *Nil time. Pl.* 20, *cr.* 1.

MAN, three legs, in armour, conjoined at thighs, embowed at knees, ppr. *Pl.* 71, *cr.* 14.

MAN, or MANN, Suff., a demi-dragon, wings addorsed, ar., guttée, sa. *Pl.* 82, *cr.* 10.

MANARD, Eng., a stag, passant, or, attired, ppr. *Pl.* 68, *cr.* 2.

MANATON, Cornw., a unicorn's head, erased. *Pl.* 67, *cr.* 1.

MANBY, Linc. and Lond., a cubit arm, couped, erect, (vested, per pale, crenellée, or and ar.,) in gauntlet a sword, az., pommelled, gold. *Pl.* 125, *cr.* 5.

MANCHESTER, Eng., on a mount, an ermine, passant, ppr. *Pl.* 87, *cr.* 3.

MANCHESTER, Duke and Earl of, Viscount Mandeville, and Baron Montagu, (Montagu,) a griffin's head, couped, wings expanded, or, gorged with a collar, ar., charged with three lozenges, gu. *Disponendo me, non mutando me. Pl.* 22, *cr.* 2, (lozenge, *pl.* 141.)

MANDEL, out of a ducal coronet, an eagle's head. *Pl.* 20, *cr.* 12.
MANDER, Eng., a swallow, volant, sa. *Pl.* 40, *cr.* 4,
MANDERNE, Cornw., a lion, rampant, or, guttée-de-sang, crowned, gold. *Pl.* 98, *cr.* 1.
MANDERSON, Eng., an antelope, passant, ar., (collared, gu.) *Pl.* 63, *cr.* 10.
MANDEVILE, Eng., two dexter hands, conjoined, supporting a scimitar, in pale, all ppr. *Pl.* 95, *cr.* 1.
MANDIS, out of a naval coronet, or, an arm, embowed, in hand a couteau sword, ppr. *Pl.* 115, *cr.* 14.
MANDITT, and MANDUYT, a garland of laurel, ppr. *Pl.* 54, *cr.* 10.
MANDUIT, Eng., a demi-lion, rampant, supporting a long cross. *Pl.* 29, *cr.* 12.
MANDUT, MANDUYT, or MANDUIT, Eng., a bezant, ar., charged with a stag, statant, on a mount, ppr. *Pl.* 45, *cr.* 11.
MANEY, Kent, a cubit arm, couped, erect, vested, per pale, ar. and sa., cuff, counterchanged, in hand, ppr., a battle-axe, of the last. *Pl.* 73, *cr.* 7.
MANFIELD, or MANSFIELD, Eng., a griffin's head, erased. *Pl.* 48, *cr.* 6.
MANFIELD, Bucks, a tiger, sejant, or, (ducally gorged, gu.) *Pl.* 26, *cr.* 9.
MANFIELD, Sco., an ostrich's head, between two feathers, ar. *Pl.* 59, *cr.* 1.
MANFORD, three annulets, interlaced, or. *Pl.* 119, *cr.* 10.
MANGIN, Bath, a crane, (in beak a fish,) all ppr. *Pl.* 111, *cr.* 9.
MANGLE, and MANGLES, an arm, in armour, embowed, ppr., charged with two roses, gu., in hand a scimitar, all ppr. *Pl.* 81, *cr.* 11, (roses, *pl.* 141.)
MANICO, a quatrefoil, vert. *Pl.* 65, *cr.* 7.
MANINGHAM, Camb. and Kent, out of a ducal coronet, ar., a talbot's head, or (collared and lined, gu., at end of line a bow-knot.) *Pl.* 99, *cr.* 7.
MANINGTON, Cornw., a demi-unicorn, rampant, sa., armed, hoofed, and maned, ar. *Pl.* 26, *cr.* 14.
MANIOT, a Saracen's head, affrontée, ppr., wreathed, ar. and sa. *Pl.* 97, *cr.* 2.
MANLEY, Eng., a cross pattée, az. *Pl.* 15, *cr.* 8.
MANLEY, a man's head, couped at shoulders, affrontée, ppr., hair, sa., wreathed, vert. *Pl.* 97, *cr.* 2.
MANLEY, Beds. and Chesh., a Saracen's head, affrontée, ppr., wreathed, ar. and sa. *Pl.* 97, *cr.* 2.
MANLOVE, Derbs. and Staffs., out of a mural coronet, gu., a cubit arm, erect, vested, erminois, cuffed, ar., in hand, ppr., a flaming sword, of the third. *Pl.* 79, *cr.* 4, (sword, *pl.* 58, *cr.* 11.)
MANLOVELL, five bell-flowers, in pale, ppr., leaved, vert.
MANLY, Eng., from a terrestrial globe, winged, ppr., an eagle, rising, sa. *Pl.* 34, *cr.* 2, (globe, *pl.* 50, *cr.* 7.)
MANLY, a cross pattée, ar. *Pl.* 15, *cr.* 8.
MANMAKER, two wings, displayed, gu. *Pl.* 39, *cr.* 12, (without charging.)
MANN, Sco., three men's legs, armed, ppr., conjoined in centre of upper part of the thighs, flexed, garnished and spurred. *Pl.* 71, *cr.* 14.

MANN, Lond., a dragon's head, between wings, gu., guttée-d'or. *Pl.* 105, *cr.* 11.
MANN, Ess. and Kent, out of a tower, or, five spears, ppr. *Pl.* 69, *cr.* 9.
MANN, a griffin's head, erased, in beak a sword. *Pl.* 35, *cr.* 15.
MANN, a tower, or, out of the turrets, (five) spears, ppr. *Pl.* 69, *cr.* 9.
MANN, a demi-man, ppr., wreathed about head and middle, vert, holding over dexter shoulder an (arrow,) of the last. *Pl.* 14, *cr.* 11.
MANN, a demi-dragon, wings addorsed, sa., guttée-d'eau, inside of wings and talons, ppr. *Per ardua stabilis*. *Pl.* 82, *cr.* 10.
MANN, Earl of Cornwallis. See CORNWALLIS.
MANNELL, a horse's head, erased, ar. *Pl.* 81, *cr.* 6.
MANNERS, Duke of Rutland. See RUTLAND.
MANNERS, Eng., out of a ducal coronet, or, a bull's head, gu., armed, gold. *Pl.* 68, *cr.* 6.
MANNNERS, Linc. and Leic., on a chapeau, gu., turned up, erm., a peacock, in pride, ppr., (each charged with a bendlet, sinister, wavy, gobony, or and sa.) *Pl.* 50, *cr.* 15.
MANNERS, Baron, (Manners-Sutton :) 1. A wolf's head, erased, gu. *Pl.* 14, *cr.* 6. 2. On a chapeau, gu., turned up, erm., a peacock, in pride, ppr., (charged with a crescent.) *Pour y parvenir*. *Pl.* 50, *cr.* 15.
MANNING, Kent, out of a ducal coronet, or, an eagle's head, sa., between two ostrich-feathers, ar. *Pl.* 110, *cr.* 1, (head, *pl.* 20, *cr.* 7.)
MANNING, Suss., out of a ducal coronet, or, an eagle's head, ar., between wings, sa. *Pl.* 66, *cr.* 5.
MANNOCK, Suff., a tiger's head, erased, quarterly, ar. and gu. *Pl.* 94, *cr.* 10.
MANNOCK, an heraldic-tiger's head, couped, quarterly, ar. and gu. *Pl.* 113, *cr.* 3.
MANNOCK, PATRICK, Esq., of Gifford's Hall, Suff., an heraldic-tiger's head, erased, quarterly, ar. and sa., crined and tufted, or. *Pl.* 76, *cr.* 3.
MANSBRIDGE, Lond., a dexter arm, erect, vested, az., cuffed, ar., in hand, ppr., a demi-eagle, with two heads, gu., ducally gorged, or. *Pl.* 32, *cr.* 6, (eagle, *pl.* 7, *cr.* 8.)
MANSEL, Eng., on a mount, a buck, lodged, ppr. *Pl.* 22, *cr.* 5.
MANSEL, Congrave Hall, Northamp., on a chapeau, gu., turned up, erm., a falcon, rising, ppr. *Pl.* 105, *cr.* 4, (chapeau, *same plate*.)
MANSELL, an eagle, rising, ppr. *Pl.* 71, *cr.* 4.
MANSELL, Eng., and MANSEL, Wel., on a chapeau, gu., turned up, erm., a flame of fire, ppr. *Quod vult, valde vult*. *Pl.* 71, *cr.* 11.
MANSELL, an arm, embowed and vested, in hand a pair of scales, equally poised. *Pl.* 39, *cr.* 1, (scales, *pl.* 26, *cr.* 8.)
MANSERGH, a demi-lion, rampant, ar., gorged with a collar, (raguly, gu., in dexter an arrow, of the last, feathered and barbed, or.) *Pl.* 18, *cr.* 13.
MANSFIELD, Birstall House, Leic., an eagle, rising, wings expanded, in beak an annulet. *Pl.* 126, *cr.* 7, (annulet, *pl.* 141.)
MANSFIELD, Earl of, Eng., Viscount Stormont, and Baron Scone and Balvaird, Sco., (Murray,) a buck's head, couped, ppr., with a cross pattée between antlers, ar. *Una æquus virtute*—and—*Spero meliora*. *Pl.* 9, *cr.* 10.

MANSFIELD, Eng., a cross pattée, fitched, erm. *Pl.* 27, *cr.* 14.

MANSFIELD, GEORGE-PATRICK-LATTIN, ESQ., of Morristown Lattin, co. Kildare, an arm, in armour, embowed, in hand a short sword, all ppr. *Turris fortitudinis. Pl.* 2, *cr.* 8.

MANSH, Gaynes Park, Ess., out of a mural coronet, erm., a griffin's head, az., in beak, or, a rose, slipped, ppr. *Pl.* 101, *cr.* 6, (without gorging; rose, *pl.* 117, *cr.* 10.)

MANSH, Queen's County, a griffin's head, couped, az., gorged with a ducal coronet, or, in beak a rose, ar., seeded, or, slipped and leaved, vert. *Pl.* 42, *cr.* 9, (rose, *pl.* 117, *cr.* 10.)

MANSHAM, Eng., a griffin's head, erased, or, between wings, gu. *Pl.* 65, *cr.* 1.

MANSON, Sco., in dexter hand a thistle. *Meæ memor originis. Pl.* 36, *cr.* 6.

MANSON, Eng., on a chapeau, ppr., a garb, or. *Pl.* 62, *cr.* 1.

MANSTED, an arm, in armour, in hand a holly-branch, fructed, ppr. *Pl.* 55, *cr.* 6.

MANSTON, Eng., a harp, or. *Pl.* 104, *cr.* 15.

MANSUEN, and MANSUER, Westm. and Norf., a pelican's nest, or, young ones, sa., thereon a pelican, sa., vulning, ppr. *Pl.* 44, *cr.* 1.

MANT, Eng., an antelope, passant, or. *Pl.* 63, *cr.* 10.

MANTEBEY, a boar's head, in bend, ar., armed, or, (out of mouth, flames.) *Pl.* 2, *cr.* 7, (flames, *pl.* 20, *cr.* 3.)

MANTELL, or MANTLE, Northamp. and Kent, a stag's head, couped at neck, gardant, ar. *Pl.* 111, *cr.* 13.

MANTON, a unicorn, sejant, or, resting dexter against a tree, vert. *Pl.* 110, *cr.* 15.

MANVERS, Earl, Viscount Newark, and Baron Pierrepont, (Pierrepont,) a lion, rampant, sa., between wings, erect, ar. *Pie repone te. Pl.* 29, *cr.* 5.

MANWAIRING, out of a ducal coronet, or, an ass's head, ar., (haltered, gu.) *Pl.* 80, *cr.* 6.

MANWAIRING, out of a ducal coronet, or an ass's head, ppr. *Devant si je puis. Pl.* 80, *cr.* 6.

MANWAIRING, Chesh., same crest.

MANWAIRING, Whitemore, Staff., an ass's head, ppr., (haltered, ar.,) on neck a mullet for difference. *Pl.* 91, *cr.* 7, (mullet, *pl.* 141.)

MANWARING, Eng., an ass's head, erased, ppr., (bridled,) or. *Pl.* 91, *cr.* 7.

MANWELL, Eng., a ram, passant, gu. *Pl.* 109, *cr.* 2.

MANWIKE, on a hurt, an etoile, or. *Pl.* 7, *cr.* 6, (etoile, *pl.* 141.)

MANWOOD, Kent and Ess., on a ducal coronet, a lion's head, (gardant,) or. *Pl.* 90, *cr.* 9.

MANYNGHAM, Eng., an ostrich, wings addorsed, in beak a horse-shoe, all ppr. *Pl.* 16, *cr.* 2.

MAPES, Norf., an arm, in armour, embowed, or, in hand a spur, ar., leathered, sa. *Pl.* 96, *cr.* 6, (spur, *pl.* 34, *cr.* 9.)

MAPLES, Eng., a tower, or. *Pl.* 12, *cr.* 5.

MAPLESDEN, out of a mural coronet, az., two arms, in armour, embowed, ppr., supporting a flag, gu., flotant to sinister, staff, or. *Pl.* 6, *cr.* 8, (flag and coronet, *same plate*.)

MAPLETOFT, Spring Hall, Stansted, Suff., a demi-lion, rampant, or, holding a cross crosslet, fitched, sa. *Pl.* 65, *cr.* 6.

MAR, Sco., a goat's head, erased. *Pl.* 29, *cr.* 13.

MARBURY, Chesh., a mermaid, ppr. *Pl.* 48, *cr.* 5.

MARBURY, Surr., on a chapeau, gu., turned up and indented, ar., a man's head, in profile, ppr., wreathed, ar. and sa. *Pl.* 36, *cr.* 3, (chapeau, *same plate, cr.* 8.)

MARBURY, on a cap, ar., an old man's head, in profile, of the same, wreathed, ar. and sa., on the cap five gutes-d'or. *Ib.*

MARBURY, a mermaid, ppr., with mirror and comb, or. *Pl.* 48, *cr.* 5.

MARBURY, of Marbury Hall, Chesh., on a chapeau, gu., turned up, ar., and semée of plates, a Saracen's head, in profile, couped, ppr., crined and bearded, sa., wreathed, of the first. *Pl.* 36, *cr.* 3, (chapeau, *same plate, cr.* 8; plate, *pl.* 141.)

MARBURY, Chesh., on a chapeau, gu., turned up, erm., a man's head, in profile, ppr., wreathed, or and az., on chapeau five bezants, in fess. *Ib.*

MARCH, Eng., a griffin, passant, wings addorsed, *Pl.* 61, *cr.* 14, (without gorging.)

MARCH, out of a mural coronet, sa., a nag's head, ar. *Pl.* 50, *cr.* 13, (coronet, *pl.* 128, *fig.* 18.)

MARCH, an arm, bendy wavy sinister, or and purp., in hand, ppr., a flower, gu., leaved, vert, on top a goldfinch, volant, ppr.

MARCH, a demi-lion, rampant, ar. *Pl.* 67, *cr.* 10.

MARCHALL, a mullet, or, between two palm-branches, vert. *Pl.* 3, *cr.* 9.

MARCHANT, out of a ducal coronet, a nag's head, *Pl.* 50, *cr.* 13.

MARCHE, Camb., on a ducal coronet, or, a wolf, passant, ar. *Pl.* 3, *cr.* 8, (wolf, *pl.* 46, *cr.* 6.)

MARCHE, Lond., a griffin's head, erased, az., in beak a rose, gu., stalked and leaved, vert. *Pl.* 9, *cr.* 12, (rose, *pl.* 117, *cr.* 10.)

MARCHMONT, out of a ducal coronet, an eagle's claw, erect. *Pl.* 96, *cr.* 7.

MARCKWICK, Suss., a boar, passant, per pale, ar. and az., (charged with a saltier, counterchanged.) *Pl.* 48, *cr.* 14.

MARCON, Norf., a lion of St Mark.

MARDAKE, an eagle, displayed, or, environed by a serpent, vert, the head turned to dexter, over eagle's head. *Pl.* 119, *cr.* 1.

MARDEN, Heref. and Lond., out of a ducal coronet, or, a unicorn's head, sa., armed and maned, gold. *Pl.* 50, *cr.* 13.

MARE, Eng., a hand, apaumée, gu. *Pl.* 82, *cr.* 14.

MARE, Chesh., a demi-leopard, salient, ar., spotted, sa. *Pl.* 12, *cr.* 14.

MAREWOOD, out of a mural coronet, or, a beacon in flames, ppr., between wings, ar. *Pl.* 119, *cr.* 14.

MARGESSON, Suss. and Surr., on a ducal coronet, or, a lion, passant, gardant, sa., gorged with a ducal coronet, or. *Loyalté me lie. Pl.* 7, *cr.* 14, (coronet, *pl.* 128, *fig.* 3.)

MARGETSON, Eng., on a ducal coronet, or, a lion, passant, gardant, sa. *Pl.* 34, *cr.* 15, (without crown.)

MARGETTS, Eng., the attires of a stag affixed to scalp. *Pl.* 86, *cr.* 10, (without coronet.)

MARGOUTS, Eng., a stag's head, vert. *Pl.* 91, *cr.* 14.

MARIET, a squirrel, sejant, ppr., supporting a staff, raguly, sa. *Pl.* 2, *cr.* 4, (staff, *pl.* 1, *cr.* 3.)

MARISCHALL COLLEGE, Aberdeen, the sun in splendour, ppr. *Luceo. Pl.* 68, *cr.* 14.

MARISHALL, Sco., a trefoil, ppr. *Semper virescit virtus.* Pl. 4, cr. 10, (without wings.)

MARJORIBANKS, ALEXANDER, Esq., of Marjoribanks, Mid-Lothian, a demi-griffin, ppr. Pl. 18, cr. 6.

MARJORIBANKS, Bart., Berw., a lion's gamb, erect and erased, grasping a tilting-lance, in bend sinister, point downward, ppr. *Advance with courage.* Pl. 85, cr. 15.

MARKE, Eng., in lion's gamb, sa., a battle-axe, or. Pl. 51, cr. 13.

MARKE, Cornw., a demi-lion, in dexter a fleur-de-lis. Pl. 91, cr. 13.

MARKER, Eng., an eagle, wings expanded, resting dexter on a mount, ppr. Pl. 118, cr. 1.

MARKER, Devons., a greyhound, statant, ppr. Pl. 104, cr. 1.

MARKHAM, Notts., a lion, sejant, or, winged, and circled round head, ar., resting dexter on a harp, gold. Pl. 88, cr. 14.

MARKHAM, Iri., a falcon's head, erased, erm. Pl. 34, cr. 11.

MARKHAM, Becca Hall, Yorks., the lion of St Mark, sejant, gardant, supporting a harp.

MARKHAM, Yorks., a lion, sejant, gardant, winged, or, the head radiated, ar., supporting the hames of a horse's collar, gold.

MARKHAM, Notts., an ox-goad, or.

MARKHAM, a lion, (couchant,) winged, supporting a lyre, all or. Pl. 88, cr. 14.

MARKHAM, Notts., a lion, sejant, winged and radiated round head, resting dexter on a harp, all or. Pl. 88, cr. 14.

MARKLAND, Eng., a lion's head, erased. Pl. 81, cr. 4.

MARKOE, a demi-lion, gu., ducally gorged, or. Pl. 87, cr. 15.

MARKOE, a demi-lion, gu., ducally gorged, ar. Pl. 87, cr. 15.

MARKS, or MARKES, Suff. and Wilts., a demi-lion, rampant, erm., holding a fleur-de-lis, or. Pl. 91, cr. 13.

MARKS, Middx., a lion, rampant, in dexter a fleur-de-lis, or. Pl. 87, cr. 6.

MARLAY, Iri., on point of spear, issuing, a dolphin, naiant, ppr. Pl. 49, cr. 14.

MARLBOROUGH, Duke and Earl of, Marquess of Blandford, Earl of Sunderland, Baron Spencer and Churchill,(Spencer-Churchill) : 1. For *Churchill*, a lion, couchant, gardant, ar., (supporting with dexter a banner,gu.,charged with a dexter hand, apaumée, of the first, staff, or.) Pl. 101, cr. 8. 2. For *Spencer*, out of a ducal coronet, or, a griffin's head, between wings, ar., gorged with a bar-gemelle, and armed, gu. *Fiel pero desdichado.* Pl. 97, cr. 13.

MARLBOROUGH, Town of, Wilts., a tower, ar. Pl. 12, cr. 5.

MARLER, Lond., on a chapeau, purp., turned up, erm., an eagle, wings addorsed, or, ducally gorged, beaked and legged, gu. Pl. 96, cr. 9.

MARLETON, on a tower, ar., a lion, rampant, ppr. Pl. 121, cr. 5.

MARLEY, Iri., a demi-eagle, rising, ppr. Pl. 52, cr. 8.

MARLEY, and MARLOW, Eng., a cross moline, (square) pierced, erm. Pl. 91, cr. 10.

MARLEY, an eagle, wings expanded. Pl. 126, cr. 7.

MARLION, an ostrich's head and neck, gu., wings (addorsed,) ar. and sa., in mouth a horse-shoe, of the second. Pl. 28, cr. 13.

MARLOTT, Suss., a demi-tiger, rampant, ar., erased, per fess, gu. Pl. 53, cr. 10.

MARLYN, a tower, ar., masoned, sa., on top a cupola, or. Pl. 42, cr. 10.

MARM, Eng., a goat's head, erased. Pl. 29, cr. 13.

MARMADUKE, Eng., three mullets, in cheveron, ar. Pl. 46, cr. 15.

MARMION, Eng., a rose, gu., barbed, vert. Pl. 105, cr. 7.

MARMYON, Eng., a tent, az., garnished. Pl. 111, cr. 14.

MARNELL, Eng., a stag, trippant, or. Pl. 68, cr. 2.

MARNER, Eng., out of a ducal coronet, or, a mullet, az., between two laurel-branches, vert. Pl. 82, cr. 6.

MARNEY, Eng., a grenade, inflamed, ppr. Pl. 70, cr. 12.

MARNEY, Sco., a lion, rampant, sa. Pl. 67, cr. 5.

MARNEY, Cornw., between wings, ar., a chapeau, turned up, erm. Pl. 11, cr. 11, (chapeau, *same plate,* cr. 8.)

MARNHAM, Eng., between two stalks of wheat, in orle, or, a cross moline, gu. Pl. 23, cr. 14.

MARNY, a chapeau, sa., lined, erm., winged on top, ar. Pl. 80, cr. 15.

MARR, Sco., a cross crosslet, fitched, or. *In cruce salus.* Pl. 16, cr. 10.

MARR, Eng., a horse's head, erased and bridled, ppr. Pl. 92, cr. 1.

MARR, Ess., two lions' gambs, erased, in saltier, or, in each a battle axe, handles, gu., blades, ar. Pl. 32, cr. 12, (axes, pl. 52, cr. 10.)

MARR and KELLIE, Earl of, Baron Erskine and Dirleton, Sco., (Erskine,) in dexter hand, couped above wrist, a dagger, erect, ppr., pommel and hilt, or. *Je pense plus.* Pl. 23, cr. 15.

MARRANT, a crane, wings addorsed, regardant, ar., resting dexter on a pellet. Pl. 77, cr. 15.

MARRIOT, or MARRIOTT, Eng., a talbot, passant, sa., collared and lined, or, line coiled at end. Pl. 65, cr. 2.

MARRIOT, out of a ducal coronet, or, a ram's head, ar., attired, gold. Pl. 124, cr. 8, (coronet, pl. 128, *fig.* 3.)

MARRIOT, Norf., on the sun in splendour, or, a ducal coronet, gold, thence issuing a ram's head, ar. Pl. 124, cr. 8, (sun, pl. 68, cr. 14.)

MARRIOTT, THOMAS-BECKETT-FIELDING, Esq., of Avonbank, Worc., a talbot, statant, ppr., chained, or. *Virtute et fide.* Pl. 65, cr. 2.

MARRIOTT, Lond., a talbot, passant, collared, sa., line reflexed over back. Pl. 65, cr. 2.

MARRIS, Yorks., a castle, ppr. Pl. 28, cr. 11.

MARROW, a pillar, ar., base, az. Pl. 33, cr. 1.

MARRYATT, Eng., a lion, rampant, double-queued, ppr. Pl. 41, cr. 15.

MARSDEN, Lanc., a unicorn's head, erased, ar., guttée-de-sang, gorged with a ducal coronet, az. Pl. 67, cr. 1, (coronet, *same plate.*)

MARSH, Middx., a demi-lion, rampant, erased, sa., bezantée, gorged with a ducal coronet, ar. Pl. 87, cr. 15.

MARSH, Middx., a lion's head, erased, gu., ducally crowned, or. *Pl.* 90, *cr.* 4.

MARSH, Kent and Hants, out of a mural coronet, gu., a horse's head, ar., ducally gorged, or. *Pl.* 50, *cr.* 13, (coronet, *pl.* 128, *fig.* 18.)

MARSH, a demi-leopard, rampant. *Pl.* 12, *cr.* 14.

MARSH, Kent, a ram's head, ar., attired and crowned, or. *Pl.* 125, *cr.* 10.

MARSHALL, Sco., a chevalier, in armour, in dexter a marshal's baton, (resting on his side,) ppr. *Deus providebit.* *Pl.* 60, *cr.* 2.

MARSHALL, of Ardwick, Lanc., a man, in armour of a pikeman of the 15th century, in dexter a cross crosslet, fitched, in pale. *Pl.* 60, *cr.* 2, (cross, *pl.* 141.)

MARSHALL, Yorks., a man, in armour, ppr. *Pl.* 60, *cr.* 2.

MARSHALL, Durh. and Hunts., an arrow, ar., headed and feathered, az., enfiled with a ducal coronet, or. *Pl.* 55, *cr.* 1.

MARSHALL, Surr., a greyhound, sejant, ar., gorged with a collar, gu., ringed, or, resting dexter on a buck's head, cabossed, of the second. *Pl.* 66, *cr.* 15, (head, *pl.* 36, *cr.* 1.)

MARSHALL, Somers., an arm, in armour, embowed, ppr., garnished, or, scarf, gold, and az., in hand, ppr., a tilting-spear, gold. *Pl.* 44, *cr.* 9.

MARSHALL, Hants, out of a ducal coronet, a bull's head, all or. *Pl.* 68, *cr.* 6.

MARSHALL, Yorks., a lion, passant, gardant, or. *Pl.* 120, *cr.* 5.

MARSHALL, Hants and Norf., out of a ducal coronet, a stag's head, all or. *Pl.* 27, *cr.* 7.

MARSHALL, Eng. and Sco., a dove and olive-branch. *Pl.* 48, *cr.* 15.

MARSHALL, Surr. and Suss., a demi-man, in armour, ppr., (in dexter a baton, or, tipped, sa., over armour, a sash, az.) *Pl.* 27, *cr.* 11.

MARSHALL, a demi-antelope, (wings addorsed, per pale.) *Pl.* 34, *cr.* 8.

MARSHALL, Sco., a dove, in mouth an olive-branch, ppr. *Virtute tutus.* *Pl.* 48, *cr.* 15.

MARSHALL, Iri., a dove, gu. *Pl.* 66, *cr.* 12.

MARSHALL, Eng., a man's head, couped at shoulder, ppr., temples wreathed, ar. and az. *Pl.* 36, *cr.* 3.

MARSHALL, Yorks., Lond., and Notts., a man, in armour, ppr., in dexter a truncheon, or, (over the armour a sash, gu.) *Pl.* 60, *cr.* 2.

MARSHALL, Sco., a dove, ppr. *Alta petit.* *Pl.* 66, *cr.* 12.

MARSHALL, or MARSHAL, Sco., a trefoil, slipped, ppr. *Semper virescit virtus.* *Pl.* 4, *cr.* 10, (without wings.)

MARSHAM, Eng., a falcon, rising, or, winged, gu. *Pl.* 105, *cr.* 4.

MARSHAM, Kent, a lion's head, erased, gu. *Quod adest.* *Pl.* 81, *cr.* 4.

MARSHAM, Earl of Romney. *See* ROMNEY.

MARSHAM, Ess., a griffin's head, couped, or, between wings, gu. *Pl.* 65, *cr.* 1.

MARSHAM, Norf., a lion's head, erased, gu., charged with three cross crosslets, fitched, or, one and two. *Quod adest.* *Pl.* 81, *cr.* 4, (cross, *pl.* 141.)

MARSHAM, a lion's head, erased, gu. *Pl.* 81, *cr.* 3.

MARSHE, Hants, a griffin's head, sa., in beak a rose, gu., leaved, ppr. *Pl.* 38, *cr.* 3, (rose, *pl.* 117, *cr.* 10.)

MARSHE, of Darkes, Middx., a griffin's head, az., ducally gorged and lined, or, in beak a flower, gu., stalked and leaved, vert. *Pl.* 42, *cr.* 9.

MARSHE, Beds., out of a mural coronet, az., a horse's head, ar., gorged with a chaplet of laurel, ppr. *Pl.* 50, *cr.* 13, (coronet, *pl.* 128, *fig.* 18.)

MARSHE, Hunts., a griffin's head, sa., ducally gorged and lined, or, in beak a rose, gu., stalked and leaved, ppr. *Pl.* 29, *cr.* 15, (rose, *pl.* 117, *cr.* 10.)

MARSKE, Yorks., a lion's head, erased, az., charged with a cinquefoil, or. *Pl.* 81, *cr.* 4, (cinquefoil, *pl.* 141.)

MARSON, a portcullis, az. *Pl.* 51, *cr.* 12.

MARSTON, Eng., the sail of a ship, ppr. *Pl.* 22, *cr.* 12.

MARSTON, a demi-greyhound, ar., gorged with a fess, indented, sa. *Pl.* 5, *cr.* 10, (without wings.)

MARSTON, Salop, a demi-greyhound, sa., (gorged with a collar, dancettée,) erm. *Pl.* 48, *cr.* 3.

MARTAINE, Bowton, Cambs., an etoile, gu. *Pl.* 63, *cr.* 9.

MARTER, on a chapeau, gu., turned up, erm., an eagle, rising, ppr. *Pl.* 114, *cr.* 13.

MARTHAM, Eng., out of a tower, a demi-lion, between paws a bomb, fired, all ppr. *Pl.* 53, *cr.* 2.

MARTIALL, Lond., a greyhound, salient, ppr.

MARTIN, an arm, erect, in hand a scimitar, both ppr., hilt and pommel, or. *Pl.* 92, *cr.* 5.

MARTIN, Yorks., an eagle, displayed, or. *Pl.* 48, *cr.* 11.

MARTIN, Lond., a wood-martin, ppr., collared, ar. *Pl.* 12, *cr.* 2.

MARTIN, Devons. and Wel., a leopard's head, erased, ppr. *Pl.* 94, *cr.* 10.

MARTIN, a Saracen's head, in profile, wreathed about temples, (charged on breast with a saltier.) *Pl.* 126, *cr.* 8.

MARTIN, out of a ducal coronet, a buck's head, couped, between two slips of cypress. *Pl.* 29, *cr.* 7, (cypress, *pl.* 119, *cr.* 8.)

MARTIN, Sco., a lion's dexter paw grasping a crescent, or. *Hinc fortior et clarior.* *Pl.* 91, *cr.* 1.

MARTIN, Iri., a leg, couped above knee, az., spurred, ppr. *Pl.* 38, *cr.* 14.

MARTIN, Sco., a lion, rampant, in dexter a sword, ppr. *Hinc fortior et clarior.* *Pl.* 64, *cr.* 2, (sword, *pl.* 41, *cr.* 13.)

MARTIN, Sco., an adder, with young ones bursting through her side, ppr. *Ingratis servire nefas.* *Pl.* 119, *cr.* 13.

MARTIN, Yorks., a buck's head, couped, ppr. *Pl.* 91, *cr.* 14.

MARTIN, of Anstey, Leic., out of a mural coronet, vert, a talbot's head, ppr., eared and langued, gu., (collared, of the first.) *Sure and steadfast.* *Pl.* 91, *cr.* 15.

MARTIN, Sco., a lion, statant, ppr., in dexter a crescent, or. *Pl.* 77, *cr.* 3.

MARTIN, Suff.: 1. A cockatrice's head between wings. *Pl.* 77, *cr.* 5, (without coronet.) 2. A martin, passant. ppr. *Initium sapientiæ est timor Domini.* *Pl.* 119, *cr.* 15.

MARTIN, a cubit arm, erect, ppr., in hand a scimitar blade, ppr., hilt and pommel, or. *Pl.* 29, *cr.* 8.

X

MARTIN, Eng. and Wel., an etoile, gu. *Pl.* 63, *cr.* 9.
MARTIN, Eng., a tower, triple-towered, chequy, or and az. *Pl.* 123, *cr.* 14.
MARTIN, Eng., a demi-antelope, ar., collared, gu. *Pl.* 34, *cr.* 8.
MARTIN, Sco., a martin, statant, ppr. *Initium sapientiæ est timor Domini. Pl.* 119, *cr.* 15.
MARTIN, Sco., in dexter hand a dagger, ppr. *Pro patriâ. Pl.* 28, *cr.* 4.
MARTIN, Bart., Eng., in dexter hand a scimitar. *Pl.* 29, *cr.* 8.
MARTIN, a greyhound's head, (erased,) ar., collared, sa. *Pl.* 43, *cr.* 11.
MARTIN, a martin, salient against a cannon, erect.
MARTIN, a martin-cat, passant, ppr. *Pl.* 119, *cr.* 7.
MARTIN, Kent and Yorks., a stag's head, sa. *Pl.* 91, *cr.* 14.
MARTIN, Kent, a martin, entwined by a serpent, ppr., in beak a cross crosslet, fitched, or.
MARTIN, Lond. and Herts., a martin, sa., (in beak a buckle, ar.) *Pl.* 111, *cr.* 5.
MARTIN, Bart., Berks., a dexter hand brandishing a sabre, trenchant, ppr., hilt and pommel, or. *Auxilium ab alto. Pl.* 29, *cr.* 8.
MARTIN, Suff., an ape, admiring himself in a looking-glass, ppr.
MARTIN, Hants, in front of a garb, or, a martin-cat, statant, ppr.
MARTIN, ROBERT, Esq., of Ross House, co. Galway, an etoile, of six points, or. *Sic itur ad astra. Pl.* 63, *cr.* 9.
MARTIN, JOSEPH-JOHN, Esq., of Ham Court, Worc., a martin, passant, ppr. *Pejus letho flagitium. Pl.* 119, *cr.* 15.
MARTIN-WYKEHAM, of Leeds Castle, Kent; and Chacombe Priory, Northamp.: 1. For *Martin*, a martin, (entwined by a serpent, ppr., in beak a crosslet, fitched, or.) *Pl.* 111, *cr.* 5. 2. For *Wykeham*, a bull's head, erased, sa., armed, or, (charged with two chevronels, gold.) *Manners makyth man. Pl.* 19, *cr.* 3.
MARTINAL, Eng., three organ-pipes, (two in saltier, one in pale, ppr.) *Pl.* 50, *cr.* 12.
MARTINDALE, Eng., a wolf, current, ppr. *Pl.* 111, *cr.* 1.
MARTINE, Sco., a lion, passant, in dexter a crescent, ppr. *Hinc fortior et clarior. Pl.* 77, *cr.* 3.
MARTINEAN, Eng., a ram's head, erased, gu. *Pl.* 1, *cr.* 12.
MARTINEAU, JOSEPH, Esq., of Basing Park, Hants, a martin, ppr. *Pl.* 111, *cr.* 5.
MARTINIUS, between two elephants' tusks, gu. and sa., a sword, in pale, enfiled with a crown, or.
MARTINSON, Northumb., out of a mural coronet, or, a plume of five ostrich-feathers, ar., (charged) with a martlet, wings expanded, ppr. *We rise. Pl.* 105, *cr.* 11, (feathers, *pl.* 100, *cr.* 12.)
MARTON, Yorks., a stag's head, ppr., attired, or. *Pl.* 91, *cr.* 14.
MARTYN, Berks., out of a ducal coronet, or, a falcon's head, az., beaked, gold. *Pl.* 24, *cr.* 10.
MARTYN, a martlet. *Pl.* 111, *cr.* 5.
MARTYN, Eng., a martin, passant, ppr. *Pl.* 119, *cr.* 15.
MARTYN, Lond., Ess., and Lanc., a wood-martin, ppr., collared, ar. *Pl.* 12, *cr.* 2.

MARTYN, Devons., on a celestial globe, without frame, or, an eagle, wings displayed, ar., (ducally gorged, gold.) *Pl.* 34, *cr.* 2.
MARTYN, Eng., out of a ducal coronet, or, an eagle's head, ar., between wings, gu.' *Pl.* 9, *cr.* 6.
MARTYN, Devons., an etoile of (sixteen points,) gu. *Pl.* 63, *cr.* 9.
MARTYN, or MARTIN, Dors., Somers., and Cornw., on stump of tree, couped and erased, ar., a monkey, sejant, ppr., collared and lined, or, looking in a mirror, framed, gold.
MARTYN, Dors. and Lond., an etoile, or. *Pl.* 63, *cr.* 9.
MARTYN, Durh., an ostrich's head, ar., between ostrich's wings, gu., in mouth a horse-shoe, or. *Pl.* 28, *cr.* 13.
MARTYN, Cambs., a griffin, segreant, per fess, erm. and ar., wings, of the last. *Pl.* 67, *cr.* 13.
MARTYN, Eng., on a celestial globe, an eagle, wings displayed, ar., (ducally gorged, of the first.) *Pl.* 34, *cr.* 2.
MARTYN, Lond., an eagle, displayed, gu. *Pl.* 48, *cr.* 11.
MARTYN, JOHN, Esq., of Tullyra Castle, co. Galway, an etoile of six points, or. *Sic itur ad astra. Pl.* 63, *cr.* 9.
MARTYN, the Rev. THOMAS, of Pertenhall, Beds., a leopard's head, couped, ppr. *Pl.* 92, *cr.* 13.
MARTYR, Eng., an ostrich's head, ar., collared, or, between two palm-branches, vert. *Pl.* 49, *cr.* 7.
MARTYR, a griffin, segreant, or, wings addorsed, ar., holding a rose, gu., stalked and leaved, ppr. *Pl.* 67, *cr.* 13, (rose, *pl.* 117, *cr.* 10.)
MARTYRE, Eng., a demi-lion, rampant, ppr. *Pl.* 67, *cr.* 10.
MARVEL, out of a ducal coronet, or, a plume of ostrich-feathers, ar. *Pl.* 44, *cr.* 12.
MARWICK, a boar, passant, per pale, ar. and az., (charged with a saltier, wavy, counterchanged.) *Pl.* 48, *cr.* 14.
MARWOOD, Yorks. and Durh., a goat's head, erased. *Pl.* 29, *cr.* 13.
MARWOOD, Eng., a goat's head, erased, ar., attired, or, (charged with a cheveron, gu.) *Pl.* 29, *cr.* 13.
MARYET and MARYOT, Suss., Berks., Glouc., and Warw., a talbot, passant, sa., collared and lined, or, line coiled at end. *Pl.* 65, *cr.* 2.
MARYBOROUGH, Baron, (Wellesley-Pole :) 1. For *Pole*, a lion's gamb, erect and erased, gu., armed, or. *Pl.* 126, *cr.* 9. 2. For *Wellesley*, out of a ducal coronet, or, a (demi-)lion, rampant, gu., holding a forked pennon, of the last, flowing to sinister, one-third per pale, from the staff, ar., charged with the cross of St George. *Pl.* 99, *cr.* 2. 3. For *Colley*, a cubit arm, erect, (vested, gu., cuffed, ar.,) in hand a scimitar, ppr., hilt and pommel, or, the arm enfiled with a ducal coronet, gold. *Pollet virtus. Pl.* 29, *cr.* 8.
MASCALL, Eng., a lion's head, erased, ducally crowned, ppr. *Pl.* 90, *cr.* 4, (without plates.)
MASCALL, an elephant, statant. *Pl.* 56, *cr.* 14.
MASOALL, a sea-lion, salient, sa. *Pl.* 15, *cr.* 12.
MASOY, or MASEY, Eng., a lion's head, couped, ar. *Pl.* 126, *cr.* 1.
MASH, out of a mural coronet, a horse's head, ducally gorged. *Pl.* 50, *cr.* 13, (coronet, *pl.* 128, *fig.* 18.)

MASH, issuing from rays, a hand, vested, holding up a skull. *Pl.* 37, *cr.* 6.

MASHAM, Suff., a griffin's head, per pale, or and gu., between wings, az. *Pl.* 65, *cr.* 1.

MASHAM, Ess., a griffin's head, couped, or, between wings, gu. *Pl.* 65, *cr.* 1.

MASHITER, a greyhound, sejant, winged and collared. *Pl.* 101, *cr.* 7.

MASKELL, Eng., a leopard, rampant, ppr. *Pl.* 73, *cr.* 2.

MASKELYNE, a demi-lion, rampant, between paws an escallop. *Pl.* 126 A, *cr.* 13.

MASON, Iri., three moors' heads, conjoined on one neck, wreathed round temples, vert. *Pl.* 95, *cr.* 5.

MASON, Sco., the sun in splendour. *Pl.* 68, *cr.* 14.

MASON, Eng., a deer's head, erased, ppr. *Pl.* 66, *cr.* 9.

MASON, Lond., a lion's head, az., between wings, ar., with a mullet for difference. *Pl.* 73, *cr.* 3, (mullet, *pl.* 141.)

MASON, Norf., a lion's head, (couped,) between wings, az. *Pl.* 73, *cr.* 3.

MASON, Eng., a mermaid, per fess, wavy, ar. and az., the upper part guttée-de-larmes, in dexter a comb, in sinister a mirror, the frame and her hair, sa. *Pl.* 48, *cr.* 5.

MASON, Hants and Salop, a mermaid, ppr. *Pl.* 48, *cr.* 5.

MASON, Sco., a tower, ppr., masoned, sa. *Demeure par la vérité*. *Pl.* 12, *cr.* 5.

MASON, a stag's head, (erased,) sa., attired, or, gorged with a ducal coronet, gold. *Pl.* 55, *cr.* 2.

MASON, Warw., a talbot, passant, (regardant, ar., eared, sa., in mouth a hart's horn, or.) *Pl.* 120, *cr.* 8.

MASON, a lion, rampant, double-headed.

MASON, Berks., a demi-lion, rampant, ar., in dexter a crescent, or. *Pl.* 39, *cr.* 14, (crescent, *pl.* 141.)

MASONS, Trade, Lond., a tower, ar. *In the Lord is all our trust*. *Pl.* 12, *cr.* 5.

MASQUENAY, Iri., a Roman head, with a helmet, couped, ppr. *Pl.* 33, *cr.* 14.

MASSAM, Iri., a demi-griffin, wings addorsed, sa., holding a pole-axe, gu. *Pl.* 44, *cr.* 3.

MASSAREENE, Viscount and Baron Loughneagh, Iri., (Skeffington-Foster,) a mermaid, ppr. *Per angusta ad augusta*. *Pl.* 48, *cr.* 5.

MASSENDEN, Linc., a Cornish chough, sa., beaked and legged, gu., in beak a sprig of laurel, ppr. *Pl.* 100, *cr.* 13, (laurel, *pl.* 42, *cr.* 9.)

MASSEY, Chesh., on a ducal coronet, or, a bull's head, gu. *Pro libertate patriæ*. *Pl.* 68, *cr.* 6.

MASSEY, Camb. and Chesh., an owl, ar. *Pl.* 27, *cr.* 9.

MASSEY, on a chapeau, gu., turned up, erm., a boar, passant, ppr., environed with a net. *Pl.* 64, *cr.* 8.

MASSEY, a demi-pegasus, rampant, ar. *Pl.* 57, *cr.* 15.

MASSEY, Lond., (on a mount, vert,) a lion, current, ar., interlaced with four trees, of the first. *Pl.* 125, *cr.* 14.

MASSEY, or MASSIE, Chesh., a demi-pegasus, wings displayed, quarterly, or and gu. *Pl.* 57, *cr.* 15.

MASSEY, Chesh., on a ducal coronet, or, a bull's head, gu., attired, sa. *Pl.* 68, *cr.* 6.

MASSEY, Bart., Iri., out of a ducal coronet, or, a bull's head, gu., armed, sa. *Pro libertate patriæ*. *Pl.* 68, *cr.* 6.

MASSEY, DUNHAM-MASSEY: 1. For *Massey*, a moorcock, sa., combed and wattled, gu., (charged on breast for distinction with a cross crosslet, or.) *Pl.* 10, *cr.* 1. 2. For *Oliver*, in lion's gamb, erased, a bunch of olive, ppr., pendent therefrom by a chain, a bugle, or. *Pl.* 68, *cr.* 10, (bugle, *pl.* 98, *cr.* 2.)

MASSEY, Chesh., a heathcock, statant, sa., legged, combed, and wattled, gu.

MASSEY, Chesh., out of a ducal coronet, a bull's head, erased, az., armed, or. *Pl.* 68, *cr.* 6.

MASSIE, Eng., a horned owl, ppr. *Pl.* 1, *cr.* 8.

MASSIE, a lion, salient, ar., between two trees.

MASSIE, an owl, attired, ppr. *Pl.* 27, *cr.* 9.

MASSINBERD, Eng., a lion's head, erased, (charged on neck with two darts, in saltier, points downward.) *Pl.* 113, *cr.* 15.

MASSINGBERD, and MASSINBERD, a dragon's head, erased, per pale, or and gu., between wings, az. and sa. *Pl.* 105, *cr.* 11.

MASSINGBERD, of Ormsby, Linc.: 1. A dragon's head, erased, quarterly, or and gu., between wings, az. *Pl.* 105, *cr.* 11. 2. A lion's head, erased, az., charged on neck with two broad arrows, in saltier, ar., barbed, or, between four gutes-d'or. *Est meruisse satis*. *Pl.* 113, *cr.* 15.

MASSINGBERD, of Grunby, Linc., same crest and motto.

MASSINGBIRD, Eng., a laurel-branch, fructed, ppr. *Pl.* 123, *cr.* 5.

MASSINGHAM, Eng., a long cross, on three grieces, recrossed, gu. *Pl.* 23, *cr.* 12.

MASSON, Sco., the sun in splendour. *Pl.* 68, *cr.* 14.

MASSON, Sco., a house, ppr., ensigned on top with a crescent, ar. *Dominus providebit*.

MASSY, Chesh., a lion's head, erased, ar. *Pl.* 84, *cr.* 4.

MASSY, Chesh., an owl, sa., (gorged with a collar, gobony, ar. and az.) *Pl.* 27, *cr.* 9.

MASSY, a lion's head, couped, ar. *Pl.* 126, *cr.* 1.

MASSY, out of a ducal coronet, or, a bull's head, gu., armed, sa. *Pro libertate patriæ*. *Pl.* 68, *cr.* 6.

MASSY, Baron CLARINA. See CLARINA.

MASTER, Wilts., a cubit arm, couped, erect, vested, gu., cuffed, ar., in hand a (bunch of honeysuckles,) all ppr. *Pl.* 113, *cr.* 5.

MASTER, Kent, out of a mural coronet, or, a unicorn's head, ar., crined and armed, ppr. *Pl.* 45, *cr.* 14, (mural coronet, *same plate*.)

MASTER, Kent, within a gem-ring, two snakes, entwined and nowed, ppr. *Pl.* 35, *cr.* 3, (snake, *pl.* 1, *cr.* 9.)

MASTER, Kent, Oxon., and Glouc., within a ring, or, gemmed, ppr., two snakes entwined, erect on their tails, and addorsed, az. *Pl.* 35, *cr.* 3, (snake, *pl.* 116, *cr.* 2.)

MASTERMAN, Yorks., a moor's head, in profile, ppr., wreathed about temples, ar. and gu. *Pl.* 36, *cr.* 3.

MASTERS, (an arrow, erect, sa., barbed and feathered, ar.,) enfiled with a leopard's head, or. *Pl.* 24, *cr.* 13.

MASTERS, an arm, gu., in hand two branches, flowered, ar., leaved, ppr. Pl. 118, cr. 4.

MASTERS, out of a mural coronet, or, a unicorn's head, ar., armed and crined, gold. Pl. 45, cr. 14, (coronet, *same plate*.)

MASTERSON, Eng., a buck, passant, az. Pl. 68, cr. 2.

MASTERTON, and MASTERTOWN, Sco., a dexter hand, issuing, holding a scimitar, ppr. *Pro Deo et rege.* Pl. 29, cr. 8.

MASTERTON, Sco., a stag, running past a fir-tree, ppr. *Per ardua.* Pl. 84, cr. 5, (tree, *pl.* 26, cr. 10.)

MASTERTOUN, Sco., a stag, current, (bearing on his horns an oak-slip, fructed,) ppr. Pl. 84, cr. 5.

MASTON, Eng., the sail of a ship, ppr. Pl. 22, cr. 12.

MATCHAM, an arm, in pale, vested, vert, cuffed, ar., in hand (three) ears of wheat, ppr. Pl. 63, cr. 1.

MATCHELL, Bucks., a camel's head, erased, or, ducally gorged, ar. Pl. 120, cr. 12.

MATCHET, and MATCHETON, Eng., a cross pattée, fitched, gu. Pl. 27, cr. 14.

MATCHETT, Norf., a demi-lion, or, armed and langued, gu. Pl. 67, cr. 10.

MATHER, Sco., a rock, sa. Pl. 73, cr. 12.

MATHER, Eng., out of a cloud, a hand, erect, holding an arrow, point downward. Pl. 45, cr. 12.

MATHER, Sco., an eagle, displayed, ppr. *Fortiter et celeriter.* Pl. 48, cr. 11.

MATHER, a dexter hand, apaumée, charged with an eye. *Deus providebit.* Pl. 99, cr. 13.

MATHER, Wel., a demi-mower, habit and cap, quarterly, ar. and gu., hands and face, ppr., in dexter a bugle-horn, or, in sinister a scythe, ppr. *Mowe warilie.*

MATHESON, Sco., in dexter hand a scimitar, ppr. *Fac et spera.* Pl. 29, cr. 8.

MATHEW, Eng., in dexter hand, ppr., an annulet, or, stoned, gu. Pl. 24, cr. 3.

MATHEW, Sco., an arm, in armour, embowed, in hand a sword, ppr. *Quid non pro patriâ.* Pl. 2, cr. 8.

MATHEW, a cock, close. Pl. 67, cr. 14.

MATHEW, and MATTHEWS, Eng., a stork, ar. Pl. 33, cr. 9.

MATHEW, Norf., a unicorn's head, erased, ar., armed and maned, gu., (on neck a cheveron, vairé, of the first and second.) Pl. 67, cr. 1.

MATHEW, Iri., a heathcock, sa.

MATHEW, Ess., in lion's gamb, erect, a cross crosslet, fitched, in pale, sa. *Cruce non leone fides.* Pl. 46, cr. 7, (cross, *pl.* 141.)

MATHEWS, Iri., an arm, in armour, in hand a sword, ppr. Pl. 2, cr. 8.

MATHEWS, Eng., on an escallop, gu., between wings, az., a cross fleury, or. Pl. 62, cr. 4, (cross, *pl.* 141.)

MATHEWS, Suff., in lion's gamb, a cross pattée, fitched, all sa. Pl. 46, cr. 7.

MATHEWS, a greyhound's head, ar., between two roses, gu., stalked and leaved. Pl. 84, cr. 13.

MATHEWS, a dove, close. Pl. 66, cr. 12.

MATHIAS, Eng., out of a ducal coronet, a broken battle-axe. Pl. 24, cr. 13, (coronet, *same plate*, cr. 10.)

MATHIAS, LEWIS, Esq., of Lamphey Court, and Llangwarren, Pembroke, a stag, trippant, ppr., armed, or. Pl. 68, cr. 2.

MATHIE, Sco., a unicorn's head, erased. *Esse quam videri.* Pl. 67, cr. 1.

MATHIESON, or MATHISON, Sco., a cock, gu. Pl. 67, cr. 14.

MATHILEZ, Eng., a serpent, nowed in a love-knot, vert. Pl. 1, cr. 9.

MATHISON, Sco., a branch of laurel, fructed, ppr. *Viridis semper.* Pl. 123, cr. 5.

MATHISSON, Sco., a lion, rampant. *Vigilans.* Pl. 67, cr. 5.

MATOKE, or MATTICK, Yorks. and Herts., a bear, (salient,) per bend, ar. and sa. Pl. 1, cr. 1.

MATOKE, or MATTOCK, a bear, (salient,) per bend, ar. and sa., muzzled, or. Pl. 1, cr. 1.

MATON, an arm, in armour, embowed, in hand an anchor, by the middle, in fess. Pl. 122, cr. 8, (without coronet.)

MATON, a sheaf of seven arrows, sa., enfiled with a mural coronet, or. Pl. 37, cr. 5, (coronet, *pl.* 128, *fig.* 18.)

MATRAN, a (sinister) arm, hand clenched, ppr. Pl. 87, cr. 7.

MATRAVERS, Eng., two halberds, addorsed, entwined with a serpent, ppr. Pl. 14, cr. 13.

MATREVERS, Eng., a stag's head, cabossed, or. Pl. 36, cr. 1.

MATSON, on a rock, a fort, in flames, ppr. Pl. 59, cr. 8.

MATTHEW, Suss., an eagle, displayed, per fess, ar. and gu. Pl. 48, cr. 11.

MATTHEW, Dors., on a mount, vert, a moor-cock, ppr. Pl. 10, cr. 1, (mount, *pl.* 98, cr. 13.)

MATTHEW, Iri., a heathcock, ppr.

MATTHEWS, Middx. and Ess., a bull's head, between wings. *Omne solum viro patria est.* Pl. 60, cr. 9.

MATTHEWS, Heref., on a mount, vert, a moor-cock, (in mouth a sprig of heather, all ppr.) Pl. 10, cr. 1, (mount, *pl.* 98, cr. 13.)

MATTHEWS, Sco., a cross crosslet, fitched, az., and palm-branch, in saltier, vert. Pl. 102, cr. 3, (palm, *pl.* 123, cr. 1.)

MATTHEWS, a demi-lion, rampant, or. Pl. 67, cr. 10.

MATTHEWS, Middx. and Ess., between wings addorsed, ar., a bull's head, couped, sa. Pl. 60, cr. 9.

MATTHISON, Sco., a demi-lion, ppr., (between paws,) a cross crosslet, gu. Pl. 65, cr. 6.

MAUD, or MAUDE, Eng., a lion's head, erased, gu. Pl. 81, cr. 4.

MAUDE, Iri., in hand two branches of palm, in orle, ppr. Pl. 16, cr. 5.

MAUDE, a lion's head, couped, gu. Pl. 126, cr. 1.

MAUDE, Viscount Hawarden. *See* HAWARDEN.

MAUDE, a lion's head, erased, gu., charged on neck with a cross crosslet, fitched, or. Pl. 81, cr. 4, (cross, *pl.* 141.)

MAUDE, Westm., Durh., and Yorks., a lion's head, couped, gu., charged with a cross crosslet, fitched, or. *De monte alto.* Pl. 126, cr. 1, (cross, *pl.* 141.)

MAUDELE, or MAUDELL, out of a ducal coronet, or, an eagle's head, ar. Pl. 20, cr. 12, (without pellet.)

MAUDIT, Sco., two laurel-branches, in orle, ppr. *Pro rege et lege.* Pl. 79, cr. 14.

MAUDLEY, Somers., out of a ducal coronet, a falcon's head, all ar. *Pl.* 24, *cr.* 10.
MAUDUIT, out of a five-leaved coronet, or, a griffin's head, between wings, ar., beaked, gold. *Pl.* 97, *cr.* 13, (without charge.)
MAUGER, Eng., a sea-lion, rampant, az. *Pl.* 25, *cr.* 12.
MAUGHAM, and MAUGHAN, Eng., in lion's paw, erased, the hilt of a broken sword, in pale. *Pl.* 49, *cr.* 10.
MAUGHAN, Sco., the sun in splendour, or. *Resurgo. Pl.* 68, *cr.* 14.
MAUL, Eng., in hand an escutcheon, charged with a crescent, gu. *Pl.* 36, *cr.* 11, (crescent, *pl.* 141.)
MAUL, Sco., a wyvern with two heads, one at each end. *Pl.* 109, *cr.* 13.
MAULE, Eng., a phœnix in flames, ppr. *Vivit post funera virtus. Pl.* 44, *cr.* 8.
MAULE, Earl of Panmure. *See* PANMURE.
MAULE, Sco., a wyvern, vert, with two heads, vomiting fire at both ends, ppr., charged with a crescent, ar. *Clementia tecta rigore. Pl.* 109, *cr.* 13.
MAULE, Sco., a dragon, vert, with fire, ppr., out of mouth and tail. *Inest clementia forti. Pl.* 109, *cr.* 13.
MAULE, Sco., same crest. *Clementiâ et animus.*
MAULE, Kent, same crest.
MAULEVERER, Yorks., a greyhound, ar., (collared, or.) *Pl.* 104, *cr.* 1, (without chapeau.)
MAULEVERER, Yorks., a maple-branch, rising out of the trunk of a tree, ppr. *En Dieu ma foy. Pl.* 92, *cr.* 8.
MAULEVEREX, Yorks., a greyhound, current, ar., (collared, gu.) *Pl.* 28, *cr.* 7, (without charge.)
MAUNCELL, Iri., a lion, rampant, vert. *Pl.* 67, *cr.* 5.
MAUNCELL, a griffin's head, erased, per pale, indented, ar. and gu., a rose, counterchanged on neck, beaked, az. *Pl.* 48, *cr.* 6, (rose, *pl.* 141.)
MAUND, or MAUNDE, Eng., on a mount, a deer, (trippant,) ppr. *Pl.* 50, *cr.* 6.
MAUNDEFIELD, Eng., a comet-star, ppr. *Pl.* 39, *cr.* 9.
MAUNDRELL, in lion's gamb, couped and erect, a fleur-de-lis. *Pl.* 5, *cr.* 5, (fleur-de-lis, *pl.*141.)
MAUNDRELL, an arm, embowed, in fess, couped, vested, ar., in hand, ppr., a cross crosslet, fitched, sa. *Pl.* 88, *cr.* 7.
MAUNDUIT, Eng., out of a ducal coronet, or, a griffin's head, between wings, ar. *Pl.* 97, *cr.* 13, (without charge.)
MAUNELL, Eng., from the top of a tower, issuing from the weeath, an eagle, wings addorsed, in beak an acorn, slipped and leaved, ppr. *Pl.* 60, *cr.* 8.
MAUNSELL, GEORGE-MEARES, Esq., of Ballywilliam, Iri., a hawk, rising, ppr. *Honorantes me honorabo. Pl.* 105, *cr.* 4.
MAUNSELL, STANDISH-GRADY, Esq., co. Limerick: 1. A hawk, rising, ppr. *Pl.* 105, *cr.* 4. 2. A chapeau, inflamed at top, ppr. *Quod vult valde vult*—and—*Honorantes me honorabo. Pl.* 71, *cr.* 11.
MAURICE, Eng., a hawk, perching on stump of tree, or, armed and belled, gu. *Pl.* 78, *cr.* 8.
MAURICE, Wel., a unicorn's head, erased, sa., (winged, ar., in mouth a shamrock, ppr.) *Pl.* 67, *cr.* 1.

MAURICE, Wel., a lion, passant, sa. *Pl.* 48, *cr.* 8.
MAVER, on a rock, an eagle, ppr., wings close. *Pl.* 99, *cr.* 14, (eagle, *pl.* 7, *cr.* 11.)
MAW, Lanc. and Suff., (on a mount, vert,) a camel, couchant, ar., lump on back, and end of tail, or. *Pl.* 70, *cr.* 2.
MAWBEY, and MAWBREY, Eng., an eagle, displayed, az., charged on breast with a bezant. *Pl.* 12, *cr.* 7.
MAWBEY, Bart., of Botleyes, Surr., same crest. *Auriga virtutum prudentia.*
MAWBEY, Eng., an eagle, displayed. *Pl.* 48, *cr.* 11.
MAWBRAY, a young man's head, couped, affrontée. *Pl.* 19, *cr.* 1.
MAWDLEY, Somers., out of a ducal coronet, or, an eagle's head, ar. *Pl.* 20, *cr.* 12, (without pellet.)
MAWER, a lion's gamb, issuing, sa., resting on an escutcheon, erm. *Pl.* 43, *cr.* 12.
MAWGAWLEY, Iri., a horse's head, ar., in a waggon-harness, sa. *Pl.* 49, *cr.* 6.
MAWGYRON, Eng., a Catherine-wheel, sa., (embrued,) gu. *Pl.* 1, *cr.* 7.
MAWHOOD, Eng., a lion's head, erased, ar., gorged with a collar, gu., rimmed, studded, and ringed, or, charged on neck with a cross crosslet, fitched, gu. *Pl.* 7, *cr.* 10, (cross, *pl.* 141.)
MAWLE, Suff., on a chapeau, gu., turned up, erm, a (demi-)peacock, displayed, ar. *Pl.* 50, *cr.* 15.
MAWLEY, Eng., a cross crosslet, fitched, gu., and a palm-branch, in saltier. *Pl.* 98, *cr.* 11, (palm, *pl.* 123, *cr.* 1.)
MAWSON, Lond., a lion's head, or, collared, gobony, erm. and erminois. *Pl.* 7, *cr.* 10.
MAWSON, a greyhound, ar., passing a tree, vert. *Pl.* 27, *cr.* 2.
MAXEY, or MAXIE, Ess. and Suff., a talbot's head, erased, ar., collared and ringed, gu. *Pl.* 2, *cr.* 15.
MAXFIELD, Eng., on a ducal coronet, a dolphin naiant. *Pl.* 94, *cr.* 14.
MAXTON, JAMES, Esq., of Cultoquhey, Perth, a bee, volant, ppr. *Providus esto. Pl.* 100, *cr.* 3.
MAXTON, Sco., a cross crosslet, fitched, az. *Fides. Pl.* 16, *cr.* 10.
MAXWELL, a stag, rising from a holly-bush, ppr. *Viresco et surgo. Pl.* 82, *cr.* 8.
MAXWELL, Sco., a falcon, looking at the sun, ppr. *I'll bide broad Albine. Pl.* 43, *cr.* 5.
MAXWELL, Sco., a hart, couchant, (attires wreathed with holly-leaves, ppr.) *Semper viridis. Pl.* 67, *cr.* 2.
MAXWELL, an eagle, rising. *Reviresco. Pl.* 67, *cr.* 4.
MAXWELL, Iri., a buck's head, erased, ppr. *Je suis pret. Pl.* 66, *cr.* 9.
MAXWELL, Sco., a man's head, affrontée, ppr. *Think on. Pl.* 19, *cr.* 1.
MAXWELL, Sco., a moor's head, affrontée, within two laurel-branches, in orle, vert. *Think on. Pl.* 78, *cr.* 5.
MAXWELL, Eng., a griffin's head, or. *Pl.* 38, *cr.* 3.
MAXWELL, Sco., a stag's head, cabossed, ppr. *Propero, sed curo. Pl.* 36, *cr.* 1.
MAXWELL, Sco., a stag, couchant, under a thicket of holly. *Reviresco. Pl.* 95, *cr.* 10.

MAXWELL, Sco., a stag, lodged within two branches of laurel, in orle. *Curo dum quiesco.* Pl. 24, cr. 4.

MAXWELL, Iri., a buck's head, erased, ppr. Pl. 66, cr. 9.

MAXWELL, Sco., a savage's head, affrontée, from shoulders, within two branches of laurel, in orle, all ppr. *Think on.* Pl. 12, cr. 4.

MAXWELL, Sco., a deer's head, erased, ppr. *I am ready.* Pl. 66, cr. 9.

MAXWELL, Sco., a stag, lodged in a bush, all ppr. *Non dormio.* Pl. 82, cr. 8.

MAXWELL, Sco., a stag, lodged in a bush, all ppr. *Nunquam dormio.* Pl. 82, cr. 8.

MAXWELL, a buck's head. Pl. 91, cr. 14.

MAXWELL, a demi-eagle, wings extended, ppr. Pl. 52, cr. 8.

MAXWELL, Sco., in an eagle's talon, a pen, ppr. *Non sine usu.* Pl. 60, cr. 15.

MAXWELL, Sco., an eagle, rising, sa., beaked and membered, gu. *Reviresco.* Pl. 67, cr. 4.

MAXWELL, Yorks. and Sco., a stag, ppr., attired, ar., couchant before a holly-bush, ppr. Pl. 95, cr. 10.

MAXWELL, Sco., a man's head looking up, ppr. Pl. 121, cr. 2.

MAXWELL, Sco., a stag, rising from a holly-bush, ppr. Pl. 82, cr. 8.

MAXWELL, Sco., an eagle, issuing. Pl. 52, cr. 8.

MAXWELL, Sco., a falcon, looking at a (star.) Pl. 43, cr. 5.

MAXWELL, Sco., a hart, couchant, (his attires wreathed with holly-leaves, all ppr.) Pl. 67, cr. 2.

MAXWELL, Sco., a falcon, looking toward the sun. Pl. 43, cr. 5.

MAXWELL, Sco., a hand, issuing, ppr., holding up two eagles' heads, conjoined at neck, and erased, sa. *Revirescat.* Pl. 118, cr. 9, (heads, pl. 4, cr. 6.)

MAXWELL, Lord Herries: 1. A hedgehog, sa., quilled, or. Pl. 32, cr. 9. 2. On a helmet, a garb. Pl. 18, cr. 9, (garb, pl. 141.)

MAXWELL-GRAHAM, JAMES, Esq., Sco.: 1. An eagle, regardant, rising from the top of a rock, all ppr. *Souvenez.* Pl. 79, cr. 2. 2. A stag's head, cabossed, ppr. *Propero, sed curo.* Pl. 36, cr. 1.

MAXWELL-PERCEVAL, ROBERT, Esq., of Groomsport House, co. Down; and Moore Hill, co. Waterford, a stag's head and neck, erased, ppr. *Je suis prêt.* Pl. 66, cr. 9.

MAY, Iri., a triton, in sinister a trident. Pl. 35, cr. 10.

MAY, Sco., on a rock, a wild goose, statant, ppr. Pl. 94, cr. 3.

MAY, Eng., a leopard's head and neck, ppr. *Vigilo.* Pl. 92, cr. 13.

MAY, Suss. and Somers., out of a ducal coronet, per pale, or and gu., a tiger's head, gold, pellettée, maned, sa. Pl. 36, cr. 15.

MAY, an arm, in mail, embowed, in hand, all ppr., a truncheon, or, tipped, sa. Pl. 45, cr. 10, (truncheon, pl. 33, cr. 4.)

MAY, a leopard's head, ppr. Pl. 92, cr. 13.

MAY, Suff., out of a mural coronet, ar., a leopard's head, gu., billettée, or. Pl. 46, cr. 11, (without gorging).

MAY, Lond., out of a ducal coronet, or, a leopard's head, gu., bezantée. Pl. 36, cr. 15, (bezant, pl. 141.)

MAY, Hants and Kent, out of a ducal coronet, or, a leopard's head and neck, ppr. *Ib.*

MAY, Cornw., an eagle, (devouring a serpent.) Pl. 17, cr. 8.

MAY, Sir STEPHEN, Iri., out of ducal coronet, or, a leopard's head and neck, ppr. *Fortis et fidelis.* Pl. 36, cr. 15.

MAY, WALTER-BARTON, Esq., of Hadlow Castle, Kent, out of a ducal coronet, or, a leopard's head, ppr. *Nil desperandum.* Pl. 36, cr. 15.

MAYATS, a boar's head, (couped) and erect. Pl. 21, cr. 7.

MAYCE, Eng., a pestle in a mortar, ppr. Pl. 83, cr. 6.

MAYCE, Eng., a swan, wings addorsed, ar., ducally gorged and lined, sa. Pl. 111, cr. 10.

MAYCOTE, Kent, out of a mural coronet, gu., a buck's head, or. Pl. 112, cr. 5, (without arrow.)

MAYDWELL, Lond. and Northamp., out of a ducal coronet, or, a pyramid of laurel-leaves, vert. Pl. 61, cr. 13, (coronet, pl. 128, fig. 3.)

MAYER, an eagle, wings addorsed, ppr. Pl. 61, cr. 1.

MAYER, a demi-lion, rampant, regardant, in dexter a sword, ppr., hilt and pommel, or. Pl. 33, cr. 2, (sword, pl. 41, cr. 13.)

MAYERSBACH, or MAYERSBACK, out of a ducal coronet, two laurel-branches, erect, between two elephants' trunks, addorsed. Pl. 96, cr. 1, (coronet, *same plate*, cr. 8; laurel, pl. 123, cr. 5.)

MAYFIELD, Camb., a lion's head, couped, gu., (in mouth a may-flower, or.) Pl. 126, cr. 1.

MAYHEW, Eng., three roses, gu., stalked, leaved, and barbed, vert. Pl. 79, cr. 3.

MAYN, Eng., an oak-tree, ppr. Pl. 16, cr. 8.

MAYNARD, Leic., Devons., and Middx., a stag, trippant, or, attired, ppr. Pl. 68, cr. 2.

MAYNARD, St Albans, Herts., a buck, ppr. Pl. 88, cr. 9, (without arrow.)

MAYNARD, a stag, or. Pl. 68, cr. 2.

MAYNARD, Ess. and Iri., a stag, or, charged on breast with a crescent, sa. Pl. 61, cr. 15, (crescent, pl. 141.)

MAYNARD, Iri., in dexter hand a palm-branch, both ppr. Pl. 23, cr. 7.

MAYNARD, Leic., a stag, or, attired, ppr. Pl. 67, cr. 2.

MAYNARD, Derbs., a buck, passant, or, (gorged with a collar, invected, ar., fimbriated, sa.) Pl. 67, cr. 2.

MAYNARD, of Harsley Hall, Yorks.: 1. For *Maynard*, a stag, trippant, or, (gorged with a collar, invected, ar., fimbriated, sa.) Pl. 67, cr. 2. 2. For *Lax*, on a mount, vert, a Catherine-wheel, or. *Manus justa nardus.* Pl. 1, cr. 7, (mount, pl. 98, cr. 13.)

MAYNARD, Viscount and Baron, and a Bart., (Maynard,) a stag, statant, or. *Manus justa nardus.* Pl. 88, cr. 9, (without arrow.)

MAYNE, Iri., a human heart, gu., winged, or. Pl. 39, cr. 7.

MAYNE, Bucks., out of a mural coronet, or, a dragon's head, erm. Pl. 101, cr. 4.

MAYNE, Warw. and Yorks., out of a ducal coronet, or, a dragon's head, erm. Pl. 101, cr. 4, (coronet, pl. 128, fig. 3.)

MAYNE, Lond. and Devons., a cubit arm, (vested, az.,) in palm of hand an eye, all ppr. Pl. 99, cr. 13.

MAYNE, Bucks., a hand, ppr., between wings, erm. *Pl.* 79, *cr.* 6, (without coronet.)
MAYNE, a cubit arm, in pale, ppr., vested, sa., cuffed, ar., in hand a cross crosslet, gu. *Pl.* 75, *cr.* 3, (cross, *pl.* 141.)
MAYNE, Berks., a cubit arm, in armour, in pale, hand, ppr., holding a cross-flory, ar. *Pl.* 51, *cr.* 1, (cross, *pl.* 141.)
MAYNELL, Eng., a demi-savage, in dexter a dagger, in sinister a key, all ppr. *Pl.* 88, *cr.* 10.
MAYNER, Eng., in hand, erect, ppr., a lion's gamb, erased, ar. *Pl.* 94, *cr.* 13.
MAYNESTON, Lond., a hedgehog, or. *Pl.* 32, *cr.* 9,
MAYNEY, an arm, in armour, ar. and sa., wielding a battle-axe, of the second, handle, or. *Pl.* 121, *cr.* 14.
MAYNSTONE, a reindeer, passant, ppr. *Pl.* 12, *cr.* 8.
MAYO, Dors., out of a ducal coronet, or, a sinister hand, ppr., between wings, ar. *Pl.* 79, *cr.* 6.
MAYO, Earl of, and Viscount, and Baron of Naas, Iri., (Bourke,) a mountain-cat, sejant, gardant, ppr., (collared and chained, or.) *A cruce salus.* *Pl.* 24, *cr.* 6.
MAYOR, Eng., on a chapeau, ppr., an escallop, gu., between wings, or. *Pl.* 17, *cr.* 14.
MAYOW, Lestwithiel, Cornw., a Cornish chough, erm. *Pl.* 100, *cr.* 13.
MAYOW, an eagle, wings addorsed, preying on a serpent, nowed. *Pl.* 61, *cr.* 7, (serpent, *pl.* 1, *cr.* 9.)
MAYOW, a pelican, standing on a snake, nowed. *Pl.* 75, *cr.* 11, (pelican, *pl.* 109, *cr.* 15.)
MAYS, out of a ducal coronet, a dexter arm, vambraced, in hand a scimitar, ppr. *Pl.* 15, *cr.* 5.
MAYSEY, a lion, (current,) in a wood, ppr. *Pro libertate patriæ.* *Pl.* 125, *cr.* 14.
MAZA, Eng., on a lion's head, erased, az., a chapeau, or. *Pl.* 122, *cr.* 10.
MAZZINGHI, out of a foreign baronet's coronet, on a helmet, partially open, a demi-lion, holding a club, in pale. *Chilafa l'aspetti.*
MEACHAM, a falcon, wings extended, ppr., belled, or. *Pl.* 105, *cr.* 4.
MEAD, Eng., a reindeer, trippant, vert. *Pl.* 12, *cr.* 8.
MEAD, on a ducal coronet, an eagle, displayed. *Pl.* 9, *cr.* 6.
MEADE, Earl of Clanwilliam. See CLANWILLIAM.
MEADE, Iri., an eagle, displayed, with two heads, sa., armed, or. *Toujours prest.* *Pl.* 87, *cr.* 11, (without flame.)
MEADOWS, out of a ducal coronet, or, a demi-lion, displayed, sa. *Pl.* 45, *cr.* 7, (displayed, *pl.* 120, *cr.* 2.)
MEADOWS, Burgersh House, Suff., a pelican, vulned, ppr. *Mea dos virtus.* *Pl.* 109, *cr.* 15.
MEADOWS, Eng., out of a ducal coronet, or, a demi-eagle, wings expanded, sa. *Pl.* 9, *cr.* 6.
MEAGER, Eng., a buffalo's head, erased, or. *Pl.* 57, *cr.* 7.
MEAKIN, Worc., a unicorn's head, erased. *Pl.* 67, *cr.* 1.
MEALES, Eng., a stag, at gaze, sa. *Pl.* 81, *cr.* 8.
MEARA, Iri., a pelican, vulning. *Pl.* 109, *cr.* 15.
MEARE, Salop, Cambs., and Chesh., a mermaid, ppr., hair, or. *Pl.* 48, *cr.* 5.

MEARE, a bull's head, erased. *Pl.* 19, *cr.* 3.
MEARES, of Meares Court, Iri., a kingfisher, ppr. *Omnia providentiæ committo.*
MEARES, Eng., a bear's paw, (erased,) ar. *Pl.* 126, *cr.* 2.
MEARING, on a ducal coronet, or, a griffin, segreant, gu. *Pl.* 39, *cr.* 2.
MEARNS, Eng., a peacock, in pride, ppr. *Pl.* 92, *cr.* 11.
MEARS, Eng., a cock's head, ppr. *Pl.* 92, *cr.* 3.
MEASON-LAING, of Lindertis, Sco., a castle, ppr. *Firm.* *Pl.* 28, *cr.* 11.
MEASTER, Heastbury, Wilts., a cubit arm, couped, erect, vested, gu., purfled, ar., in hand a bunch of (honeysuckles,) all ppr. *Pl.* 64, *cr.* 7.
MEASTER, a dexter arm, in pale, vested, in hand a slip, triple-flowered. *Pl.* 64, *cr.* 7.
MEATH, Earl of, and Baron Brabazon, Iri., Baron Chaworth, U.K., (Brabazon;) on a mount, vert, a falcon, rising, or, belled, gold. *Vota vita mea.* *Pl.* 61, *cr.* 12, (without gorging.)
MEAUTYS, Ess., a unicorn, sejant, erminois. *Pl.* 100, *cr.* 15, (without tree.)
MEDCALF, Ess. and Yorks., a talbot, sejant, ppr., resting dexter on an escutcheon, ar. *Pl.* 19, *cr.* 2.
MEDDERBURN, in lion's gamb, erased and erect, a scimitar. *Pl.* 18, *cr.* 8.
MEDDOP, a boy, ppr. *Pl.* 17, *cr.* 5.
MEDDOWES, or MEDDUS, a cross formée, or, entwined with a snake, ppr. *Pl.* 112, *cr.* 6.
MEDEWE, DE, DANIEL-CHARLES, Esq., of Witnesham Hall; and Great Bealings, Suff., a pelican, vulned, ppr. *Mea dos virtus.* *Pl.* 109, *cr.* 15.
MEDFORD, Eng., a deer, lodged, ar. *Pl.* 67, *cr.* 2.
MEDGLEY, or MIDGLEY, on a mount, an heraldic-tiger, sejant, resting paw on a caltrap. *Pl.* 111, *cr.* 7, (without coronet; caltrap, *pl.* 7, *cr.* 4.)
MEDHURST, a martlet, (charged with a fleur-de-lis, in beak an acorn and oak-leaf.) *Pl.* 111, *cr.* 5.
MEDLAND, Cornw., a sea-gull, rising, ppr., on beast a crescent. *Pl.* 79, *cr.* 11, (crescent, *pl.* 141.)
MEDLEY, Suss., an heraldic-tiger, sejant, vert, tufted and maned, or. *Pl.* 111, *cr.* 7, (without chapeau.)
MEDLICOTT, Berks., Salop, and Lond., out of a mural coronet, gu., a demi-eagle, wings expanded, or. *Dat cura quietem.* *Pl.* 33, *cr.* 5.
MEDLYCOTT, out of a ducal coronet, a demi-eagle, displayed. *Pl.* 9, *cr.* 6.
MEDLYCOTT, Bart., Somers., out of a mural coronet, gu., a demi-eagle, wings elevated, or. *Pl.* 33, *cr.* 5.
MEDLYCOTT, the Rev. JOHN-THOMAS, of Rocketts Castle, co. Waterford, out of a mural coronet, gu., a demi-eagle, wings elevated, or. *Dat cura quietem.* *Pl.* 33, *cr.* 5.
MEE, Eng., a ram's head, erased, ar., armed, or. *Pl.* 1, *cr.* 12.
MEECH, Eng., a greyhound, current, ar. *Pl.* 28, *cr.* 7, (without charge.)
MEEK, Eng., a demi-wolf, ducally gorged and lined, between paws a mullet of six points. *Pl.* 65, *cr.* 4.

MEEK, Eng., a demi-lion, rampant, holding over his head a scimitar. *Pro recto. Pl.* 126 A, *cr.* 1.
MEEK, Sco., an increscent and decrescent. *Pl.* 99, *cr.* 4.
MEEKE, Ess., a lion, rampant, ar. *Pl.* 67, *cr.* 5.
MEEKINS, out of an antique earl's coronet, a wolf's head, erased, ar. *Pl.* 14, *cr.* 6, (coronet, *pl.* 80, *cr.* 11.)
MEER, Sherborn, Dors., an eagle's head, couped, or, (mouth embrued, gu.) *Pl.* 100, *cr.* 10.
MEER, Dors. and Durh., a demi-dogfish. *Pl.* 122, *cr.* 6.
MEEREHURST, Surr., a rose, ar., barbed, vert, between dragons' wings, gu. *Pl.* 105, *cr.* 7, (wings, *same plate, cr.* 11.)
MEERES, Linc., a peacock's tail, erect, ppr. *Pl.* 120, *cr.* 13, (without coronet.)
MEERS, Eng., in lion's paw, erased, a rose-branch, all ppr. *Pl.* 60, *cr.* 14.
MEERZA, ALI MAHOMED KHAN, Bombay, a demi-lion, banded twice, or, in dexter a (scimitar, sinister resting on a shield, thereon the sun in splendour.) *Pl.* 41, *cr.* 13.
MEESTED, on a broken tower, ar., a bird, or. *Pl.* 8, *cr.* 15.
MEETEKERKE, Herts., a unicorn's head, erased, ar., crined, tufted, and horned, or. *Pl.* 67, *cr.* 1.
MEGGES, a griffin, sejant, party per pale, gu. and or, winged, of the same, beaked, and gorged with a ducal coronet, gold. *Pl.* 100, *cr.* 11, (gorging, *same plate.*)
MEGGET, Sco., a square padlock, (therein the key.) *Lock sicker. Pl.* 18, *cr.* 7.
MEGGISON, Eng., on a mountain, a dove, all ppr. *Pl.* 104, *cr.* 8.
MEGGS, Lond., a griffin, sejant, per pale, gu. and or, beaked, legged, and ducally gorged, gold, wings addorsed. *Pl.* 100, *cr.* 11, (gorging, *same plate.*)
MEGG, Dors., a talbot's head, erased, ar., eared, sa., collared, or, under the collar two pellets, in fess, three acorns, erect, out of the top of the head, ppr. *Pl.* 2, *cr.* 15, (pellet, *pl.* 141; acorns, *pl.* 69, *cr.* 12.)
MEGGS, Cambs. and Kent, a greyhound's head, sa., eared, ar., (on neck a gemelle, or, between three bezants, one and two, head crowned with three oak-branches, ppr.) *Pl.* 14, *cr.* 4.
MEIGH, a lion, rampant, or, in dexter a cross pattée, fitched, az., sinister resting on an anchor, ppr., (pendent therefrom by a chain, gold, an escutcheon, gu., charged with a boar's head, erased, ar.) *Pl.* 125, *cr.* 2, (anchor, *same plate, cr.* 13.)
MEIGNELL, Eng., a rose-bush, ppr. *Pl.* 23, *cr.* 2.
MEIK, Sco., an increscent and decrescent, respecting and joining the one to the other, ppr. *Jungor ut implear. Pl.* 99, *cr.* 4.
MEIKLE, Sco., a deer's head, or. *Pl.* 91, *cr.* 14.
MEIN, Eng., in hand a vine-branch, ppr. *Pl.* 37, *cr.* 4.
MEIN, Sco., a dexter hand, erect, charged with an eye, ppr. *Deus providebit. Pl.* 99, *cr.* 13.
MELBOURNE, Viscount and Lord, Baron of Kilmorne, Iri., Baron Melbourne, U.K., and an English Baronet, (Lamb,) a demi-lion, rampant, gu., (between paws) a mullet, sa. *Virtute et fide. Pl.* 89, *cr.* 10.

MELBORNE, on a ducal coronet, a wyvern, sans legs, vert. *Pl.* 104, *cr.* 11.
MELDERS, Sco., a lion's head and neck, erased and erect, ppr. *Pl.* 81, *cr.* 4.
MELDERT, a dexter gauntlet, apaumée, az. *Pl.* 15, *cr.* 15.
MELDRUM, Sco., in dexter hand a book, ppr. *Mens immota manet. Pl.* 45, *cr.* 3.
MELES, on stump of tree, a martlet. *Pl.* 71, *cr.* 5, (martlet, *pl.* 111, *cr.* 5.)
MELHUISH, Somers., a cubit arm, in hand a pheon, in pale. *Pl.* 123, *cr.* 12.
MELHUISH, Eng., a pelican, in nest, ppr. *Pl.* 44, *cr.* 1.
MELL, Eng., on a chapeau, az., turned up, or, a martlet, wings addorsed, sa. *Pl.* 89, *cr.* 7.
MELLER, and MELLERS, Suff., a greyhound, passant, sa., collared, or, resting dexter on an escutcheon, sa. *Pl.* 104, *cr.* 1, (without chapeau; escutcheon, *pl.* 19, *cr.* 2.)
MELLES, a portcullis, sa., chains, or. *Pl.* 51, *cr.* 12.
MELLIS, Sco., the sun in splendour, or. *Pl.* 68, *cr.* 14.
MELLISH, Eng., out of a ducal coronet, a demi-ostrich, wings addorsed, ppr. *Pl.* 29, *cr.* 9.
MELLISH, Lond., Surr., and Notts., out of a ducal coronet, or, a swan's head and neck, ar. *Pl.* 83, *cr.* 1, (without wings.)
MELLISHIP, an ibex. *Sedulus et audax. Pl.* 115, *cr.* 13.
MELLO, Eng., a mullet, ar. *Pl.* 41, *cr.* 1.
MELLOR, Eng., a demi-leopard, issuing, ar., supporting an anchor, sa. *Pl.* 77, *cr.* 1.
MELTON, Eng., a serpent, nowed, az. *Pl.* 1, *cr.* 9.
MELTON, a lion's head, erased, az., guttée d'or, ducally gorged, of the last. *Pl.* 81, *cr.* 4, (gorging, *pl.* 128, *fig.* 3.)
MELVETON, Sco., a talbot's head and neck, erased. *Pl.* 90, *cr.* 6.
MELVETON, Sco., a talbot's head. *Denique cœlum. Pl.* 123, *cr.* 15.
MELVILE, or MELVILL, Sco., a crescent, ppr. *Denique cœlum. Pl.* 18, *cr.* 14.
MELVILE, of Balgarvie, a talbot's head and neck, erased and collared. *Pl.* 2, *cr.* 15.
MELVILE, Sco., a talbot's head. *Denique cœlum. Pl.* 123, *cr.* 15.
MELVILL, Sco., an eagle, rising, ppr. *Ultra aspicio. Pl.* 67, *cr.* 4.
MELVILL, Sco., a ratch-head, erased, ppr., collared, gu., charged with a crescent, ar. *Denique cœlo fruar. Pl.* 2, *cr.* 15, (crescent, *pl.* 141.)
MELVILL, Sco., a sloth-hound's head, couped, ppr. *Denique cœlum. Pl.* 123, *cr.* 15.
MELVILL, or MELVILLE, Sco., two eagles' wings, conjoined, ppr. *Denique cœlum. Pl.* 15, *cr.* 10.
MELVILLE, Eng. and Sco., a talbot's head, or. *Pl.* 123, *cr.* 15.
MELVILLE, Viscount, and Baron Duniera, (Saunders-Dundas,) a lion's head, affrontée, gu., struggling through an oak-bush, all ppr. *Essayez. Pl.* 119, *cr.* 5.
MELVILLE-WHYTE, Sco.: 1. An arm, embowed, holding up a laurel-wreath, all ppr. *Virtute parta. Pl.* 118, *cr.* 4. 2. A crescent. *Denique cœlum. Pl.* 18, *cr.* 14.
MELVINE, Sco., an eagle, rising. *Ultra aspicio. Pl.* 67, *cr.* 4.
MEMES, Lond. and Kent, an antelope's head, gu., tufted and armed, or, issuing from rays, gold. *Pl.* 24, *cr.* 7, (rays, *pl.* 116, *cr.* 13.)

MENDES, and MENDS, Wel., out of the top of a tower, an arm, in armour, embowed, wielding a battle-axe. *Pl.* 12, *cr.* 5, (arm, *pl.* 121, *cr.* 14.)

MENDORF, Eng., an oak-tree, fructed, ppr. *Pl.* 16, *cr.* 8.

MENELL, or MEYNELL, Eng., a demi-savage, in dexter a dagger, in sinister a key, all ppr. *Pl.* 88, *cr.* 10.

MENELL, a unicorn's head, couped, (gorged with a chaplet of laurel.) *Pl.* 20, *cr.* 1.

MENELL, a moor's head, in profile, couped at shoulders, wreathed, of and az. *Pl.* 36, *cr.* 3.

MENET, or MENETT, a demi-lion, rampant, az. *Pl.* 67, *cr.* 10.

MENIL, Eng., a boar, passant, between (two) trees, ppr. *Pl.* 57, *cr.* 12.

MENLES, a portcullis, sa., chain, or. *Pl.* 51, *cr.* 12.

MENTEATH, Sco. and Eng., in hand a dagger, erect, both ppr. *Dum vivo, spero.* *Pl.* 23, *cr.* 15.

MENTEITH, GRANVILLE-STUART, Bart., Closeburn, Dumfries, a lymphad, sails furled, a pennon, gu., attached to the mast, at either end a flag, charged with a saltier, az., all flowing to the dexter. *Dum vivo, spero.* *Pl.* 24, *cr.* 5.

MENYS, a lion's paw, erased, sa., charged with a cheveron, or. *Pl.* 88, *cr.* 3.

MENZIES, Sco., a book, expanded, ppr. *Spero.* *Pl.* 15, *cr.* 12.

MENZIES, Sco., a cherub, wings expanded, ppr. *Scopus vitæ Christus.* *Pl.* 126, *cr.* 10.

MENZIES, Eng., a savage's head, affrontée, couped at shoulders, sa. *Pl.* 19, *cr.* 1.

MENZIES, Sco., a savage's head, (erased,) ppr. *Will God, I shall.* *Pl.* 19, *cr.* 1.

MENZIES, Sco., a demi-eagle, wings expanded, ppr. *Malo mori quam fœdari.* *Pl.* 52, *cr.* 8.

MENZIES, Sco., a crescent, ppr. *Ut crescit clarescit.* *Pl.* 18, *cr.* 14.

MENZIES, Sco., a demi-lion, in dexter a baton, ppr. *Fortem fors juvat.* *Pl.* 84, *cr.* 7.

MEOLES, Chesh., a lion's head, erased, sa., winged, or. *Pl.* 73, *cr.* 3.

MERBURY, a camel's head, sa., ducally gorged, or.' *Pl.* 120, *cr.* 12.

MERBURY, Chesh., a mermaid, ppr., with mirror and comb, or. *Pl.* 48, *cr.* 5.

MERCAUNT, Suff., two lions' gambs, erased, in saltier, or; in each a battle-axe, ar., handles, gu. *Pl.* 32, *cr.* 12, (axe, *pl.* 26, *cr.* 7.)

MERCER, Sco., a heron's head and neck, in mouth an eel. *The grit poul.* *Pl.* 41, *cr.* 6.

MERCER, Sco., same crest.

MERCER, Sco., a dexter hand holding a Bible, expanded, ppr. *Jehova portio mea.* *Pl.* 126 A, *cr.* 9.

MERCER, Lond., a stork's head, erased, ppr., in mouth a snake, vert. *Pl.* 41, *cr.* 6.

MERCER, Sco., a cross pattée, fitched, gu. *Crux Christi mea corona.* *Pl.* 27, *cr.* 14.

MERCER, Sco., a naked arm, embowed, in hand a curtal-axe, ppr. *Pl.* 47, *cr.* 13, (axe, *pl.* 73, *cr.* 7.)

MERCHAND, and MERCHANT, Bucks., on a mount, vert, a moorcock, ppr. *Pl.* 10, *cr.* 1, (mount, *pl.* 98, *cr.* 13.)

MERCHANT COMPANY, Edinr., a celestial globe on its standard, ppr. *Terraque marique.* *Pl.* 81, *cr.* 1.

MERCHANT COMPANY, Leith, a globe on its standard, ppr. *Terraque marique.* *Pl.* 81, *cr.* 1.

MERCIER, Northumb., a demi-huntsman, winding a horn, ppr., vested, az. *Blow shrill.* *Pl.* 38, *cr.* 8.

MERCY, Eng., in dexter hand an olive-branch, ppr. *Pl.* 43, *cr.* 6.

MERE, MERES, and MEYRES, Salop, Cambs., and Chesh., a mermaid, ppr., hair, or. *Pl.* 48, *cr.* 5.

MEREDITH, Eng. and Wel., a lion's head, erased, ppr. *Pl.* 81, *cr.* 4.

MEREDITH, Chesh., a demi-lion, sa., collared, (chain reflexed over back, or.) *Pl.* 18, *cr.* 13.

MEREDITH, Chesh., on an Eastern coronet, or, a dragon, passant, gu., langued, az. *Pl.* 90, *cr.* 10, (coronet, *pl.* 57, *cr.* 5.)

MEREDITH, Devons. and Wel., a demi-lion, rampant, sa., ducally gorged and chained, or. *Pl.* 87, *cr.* 15.

MEREDITH, RICHARD, Esq., of Dick's Grove, co. Kerry, out of a ducal coronet, or, a griffin's head. *Sapere aude.* *Pl.* 54, *cr.* 14.

MEREDITH, Sir JOSHUA COLLES, Bart., of Greenhills, co. Kildare, on an Eastern coronet, or, a dragon, passant, gu., langued, az. *Fiat Dei voluntas.* *Pl.* 90, *cr.* 10, (coronet, *pl.* 79, *cr.* 12.)

MEREDITH, co. Kerry, out of a ducal coronet, or, a griffin's head. *Pl.* 54, *cr.* 14.

MEREDITH, Kent and Wel., on an Eastern coronet, a dragon, passant, wings expanded, gu. *Pl.* 90, *cr.* 10, (coronet, *pl.* 57, *cr.* 5.)

MEREDITH, Bucks., a demi-lion, rampant, per pale, or an ar., collared and lined, sa. *Pl.* 18, *cr.* 13.

MEREDITH-WARTER, HENRY, Esq., of Pentrebychan, Denbigh, Wel., a lion's head, erased, or. *Heb Dduw heb ddim, a Duw a digon.* *Pl.* 81, *cr.* 4.

MEREDYTH, Iri., a goat's head, erased, ar. *Pl.* 29, *cr.* 13.

MEREDYTH, Eng., a yew-tree, ppr. *Pl.* 49, *cr.* 13.

MEREDYTH, Bart., of Carlandstown, Iri., on an Eastern coronet, or, a dragon, passant, gu. *Fiat Dei voluntas.* *Pl.* 90, *cr.* 10, (coronet, *pl.* 79, *cr.* 12.)

MEREFIELD, Lond., a garb, or, banded, sa. *Pl.* 48, *cr.* 10.

MERES, Eng., in dexter hand a sword, in bend, ppr. *Sine metu.* *Pl.* 21, *cr.* 10.

MEREWEATHER, an arm, in armour, embowed, in hand a sword, ar., hilt and pommel, or, entwined with a serpent, vert. *Pl.* 116, *cr.* 2, (armour, *pl.* 2, *cr.* 8.)

MERICK, Eng., a cat's face, sa. *Pl.* 97, *cr.* 7.

MERICK, Lond. and Wel., a sea-horse, ppr., maned, or, holding in feet a mullet, pierced, az. *Pl.* 103, *cr.* 3, (mullet, *pl.* 45, *cr.* 1.)

MERICK, Somers., a water-spaniel, passant, ar. *Pl.* 58, *cr.* 9.

MERITON, Eng., a demi-savage, over shoulder a club, ppr. *Pl.* 14, *cr.* 11.

MERKS, an otter's head and neck, erased, sa. *Pl.* 126, *cr.* 14.

MERLAY, a hind's head, or, (gorged with a collar, sa.,) charged with three bezants. *Pl.* 21, *cr.* 9, (bezant, *pl.* 141.)

MERLE, a lion's tail, erased. *Pl.* 17, *cr.* 4.

MERLING, a lion's head, erased, gu. *Pl.* 81, *cr.* 4.
MERLYON, Eng., an eagle's head, or, between wings, vair. *Pl.* 81, *cr.* 10.
MERMYON, Eng., a unicorn's head, erased, sa. *Pl.* 67, *cr.* 1.
MERREY, Eng., a thistle and rose, stalked and leaved, in saltier, ppr. *Pl.* 57, *cr.* 10.
MERREY, or MERRY, Derbs., out of a ducal coronet, a demi-lion, gu., crowned, or. *Pl.* 90, *cr.* 9, (crown, *same plate, cr.* 4.)
MERRICK, Wel., on a tower, ar., a Cornish chough, ppr., holding a fleur-de-lis, gu. *Pl.* 84, *cr.* 3, (fleur-de-lis, *pl.* 141.)
MERRICK, a tower, ar. *Pl.* 12, *cr.* 5.
MERRIFIELD, Eng., the sun, rising, ppr. *Pl.* 67, *cr.* 9.
MERRILEES, Sco., in the sea, an open boat. *Pl.* 57, *cr.* 4.
MERRILL, Eng., a peacock's head, erased, ppr. *Pl.* 86, *cr.* 4.
MERRIMAN, Eng., a boar, passant, (collared) and bristled, vert. *Pl.* 48, *cr.* 14.
MERRIMAN, Lond., an arm, in armour, embowed, ppr., garnished, or, wielding a sword, ar., hilt and pommel, gold. *Pl.* 2, *cr.* 8.
MERRINGTON, a lion's head, collared. *Pl.* 7, *cr.* 10.
MERRITT, Eng., out of a ducal coronet, a demi-salmon, ppr. *Pl.* 36, *cr.* 13.
MERRY, a demi-lion, in paws an anchor, fluke upward. *Pl.* 19, *cr.* 6.
MERRY, Norf., the mast of a ship, rompu and erect, thereto a yard, with sail furled, in bend sinister, above it a round top, three arrows issuing therefrom on each side, in saltier, points upward, all ppr.
MERRY, Highlands, Berks., out of a mural coronet, a lion, rampant, ducally crowned, (between paws a chess-rook, charged on shoulder with a cross pattée.) *Pl.* 98, *cr.* 1, (coronet, *pl.* 128, *fig.* 18.)
MERRYTON, a pair of wings, ar. *Pl.* 39, *cr.* 12.
MERRYWEATHER, MERYWEATHER, or MERRIWEATHER, in hand, gauntleted, a sword, entwined with a serpent. *Pl.* 116, *cr.* 11. Another, an arm, in armour, embowed, in hand a sword, entwined with a serpent. *Pl.* 116, *cr.* 8, (armour, *pl.* 2, *cr.* 8.)
MERSAR, a cross pattée, or. *Crux Christi nostra corona*. *Pl.* 15, *cr.* 8.
MERSER, Linc., out of a mural coronet, gu., a demi-lion, or, in dexter a battle-axe, ar., handle, gold. *Pl.* 120, *cr.* 14.
MERTON, Eng., a demi-moor, in hand a scimitar, ppr. *Pl.* 82, *cr.* 2.
MERVIN, Eng., an escutcheon, per cross, or and gu. *Pl.* 36, *cr.* 11.
MERVYN, Iri., an ear of wheat and a palm-branch, in saltier, ppr. *Pl.* 63, *cr.* 3.
MERVYN, Wilts., a squirrel, sejant, cracking a nut, gu. *Pl.* 16, *cr.* 9.
MERYDALE, Bucks., an eagle's head, ar., erased, per fess, gu. *Pl.* 20, *cr.* 7.
MERYET, a porcupine's (head,) sa. *Pl.* 55, *cr.* 10.
MERYNG, Notts., a nag's head, erased, sa., bezantée, in mouth an annulet, or. *Pl.* 81, *cr.* 6, (annulet, *pl.* 141.)
MERYON, a bee, displayed, ppr. *Pl.* 100, *cr.* 3.
MERYWEATHER, Kent, in gauntlet, ppr., a sword, ar., hilted, or, (a snake, ppr.), entwining sword and gauntlet.) *Pl.* 125, *cr.* 5.

MESCHINES, Eng., a rose, ar., surmounted by a thistle, ppr. *Pl.* 73, *cr.* 6.
MESCHINES, DE, Eng., in hand a scimitar. *Pl.* 29, *cr.* 9.
MESCOW, Eng., a buck's head, erased, sa., attired, or. *Pl.* 66, *cr.* 9.
MESSENGER, Eng., a pegasus, current, (ducally gorged and chained.) *Pl.* 28, *cr.* 9.
MESSENT, out of a ducal coronet, gu., a demi-eagle, sa., winged, or. *Semper sursum*. *Pl.* 19, *cr.* 9.
MESSER, and MESSING, Eng., an eagle, displayed, gu. *Pl.* 48, *cr.* 11.
MESSYE, Worc., a dragon's head, quarterly, or and az. *Pl.* 87, *cr.* 12.
MESURIER, LE, an ostrich's head, between two feathers, ppr. *Pl.* 50, *cr.* 1.
METCALF, Eng., a talbot, sejant, resting dexter on an escutcheon, ar. *Pl.* 19, *cr.* 2.
METCALF, or METCALFE, Ess. and Yorks., a talbot, sejant, ar., spotted, liver-colour, resting dexter on an escutcheon, or. *Pl.* 19, *cr.* 2.
METCALFE, Bart., Berks., a talbot, sejant, sa., dexter supporting an escutcheon, or, charged with a hand, out of clouds on sinister, holding a pen, all ppr. *Conquiesco*. *Pl.* 19, *cr.* 2.
METCALFE, Lond., a talbot, sejant, pied, resting dexter on an escutcheon, or. *Pl.* 19, *cr.* 2.
METCALFE, HENRY-CHRISTOPHER, Esq., of Hawstead House, Suff., a talbot, sejant, ppr., in dexter an escutcheon, or. *Pl.* 19, *cr.* 2.
METGE, a dolphin, naiant. *Pl.* 48, *cr.* 9.
METHAM, Eng., a bull's head, barry of six, ar. and az. *Pl.* 63, *cr.* 11.
METHAM, Yorks. and Linc., a bull's head, barry of ten, ar. and az., attired, sa. *Pl.* 63, *cr.* 11.
METHEN, Sco., a cross pattée, or, within a crescent, ar. *Marte et clypeo*. *Pl.* 37, *cr.* 10.
METHEWEN, a wolf's head, (erased,) ppr., collared, vair. *Pl.* 8, *cr.* 4.
METHOULDE, or METHWOLD, Norf., a goat's head, erased, ar., attires and beard, sa. *Pl.* 29, *cr.* 13.
METHOULDE, oz METHWOLD, Norf., a goat's head, erased, or. *Pl.* 29, *cr.* 13.
METHUEN, Sco., a wolf's head, erased, ppr. *Fortis in arduis*. *Pl.* 14, *cr.* 6.
METHUEN, and METHVEN, Eng., a wolf's head, erased, ppr. *Virtus invidiæ scopus*. *Pl.* 14, *cr.* 6.
METHWOLD, a goat's head, erased, ar. *Pl.* 29, *cr.* 13.
METLEY, a mermaid, ppr. *Pl.* 48, *cr.* 5.
METTORD, Eng., a lion, rampant, supporting a garb, ppr. *Pl.* 63, *cr.* 14.
MEURS, Eng., a demi-savage, with a club over dexter shoulder, and a serpent entwined round sinister arm, wreathed round middle with leaves, all ppr. *Pl.* 92, *cr.* 10.
MEUX, Bart., Herts., two wings, inverted and addorsed, ar., (conjoined by a cord, with tassels, or.) *Pl.* 15, *cr.* 10.
MEVERELL, Staff., a demi-griffin, segreant, sa., beaked and legged, gu. *Pl.* 18, *cr.* 6.
MEVERELL, Derbs., in gauntlet a dagger, all ppr. *Pl.* 125, *cr.* 5.
MEWBERY, the emblem of plenty, with cornucopia, ppr. *Pl.* 91, *cr.* 4.
MEWESS, or MEWSSE, Beds., a demi-eagle, displayed, or, ducally gorged, gu., beaked, az. *Pl.* 22, *cr.* 11, (gorging, *pl.* 128, *fig.* 3.)
MEWIS, a dexter hand, couped, in fess, charged with an eye, ppr. *Pl.* 10, *cr.* 14.

MEXBOROUGH, Earl of, Viscount and Baron Pollington, (Saville,) an owl, ar. *Be fast. Pl.* 27, *cr.* 9.
MEY, a demi-savage, wreathed round loins with leaves, over dexter shoulder a club, ppr., round sinister arm a serpent, entwined, vert. *Pl.* 92, *cr.* 10.
MEYER, Eng., a lion, rampant, double-queued. *Pl.* 41, *cr.* 15.
MEYERS, Eng., a mermaid, (in dexter a comb, in sinister a mirror.) *Pl.* 48, *cr.* 5.
MEYMOTT, three mullets, in fess, gu., in front of a dexter arm, in armour, embowed, ppr., in hand a wreath of laurel, or. *Pl.* 68, *cr.* 1, (mullet, *pl.* 141.)
MEYNELL, GODFREY-FRANCEYS, Esq., of Meynell, Langley, Derbs., a horse's head, erased, ar. *Virtute vici. Pl.* 81, *cr.* 6.
MEYNELL, THOMAS, Esq., of North Kilvington and the Fryerage, Yorks. ; and Hartlepool, Durh., a negro's head, ppr., couped at shoulders, wreathed, or and az. *Deus non reliquit memoriam humilium. Pl.* 48, *cr.* 7.
MEYNELL, Derbs. and Staffs., a horse's head, ar. *Pl.* 81, *cr.* 5.
MEYRIC, or MEYRICK, Wel., on a tower, ar., a mount, vert, thereon, a Cornish chough, ppr., in dexter a fleur-de-lis, gu. *Heb Dduw heb ddim, Dhuw a digon. Pl.* 84, *cr.* 3.
MEYRICK, Eng., a tower. *Pl.* 12, *cr.* 5.
MEYRICK, Sir SAM., Knt., LL.D., &c., Heref. and Middx., a tower, per pale, ar. and erminois. *Stemmata quid faciunt. Pl.* 12, *cr.* 5.
MEYSEY, Worc., a dragon's head, quarterly, or and az. *Pl.* 87, *cr.* 12.
MIALL, a crane, in mouth a branch, ppr. *Pl.* 46, *cr.* 9.
MICHAEL, Eng., a garb, erect, or. *Pl.* 48, *cr.* 10.
MICHAEL, MICHALL, or MICHELL, Berks., a leopard's head, per pale, or and az. *Pl.* 92, *cr.* 13.
MICHEL, Eng., in dexter hand, a heron's head, erased. *Pl.* 29, *cr.* 4, (head, *pl.* 41, *cr.* 6.)
MICHEL, Eng., in dexter hand a crane's head, erased. *Nil conscire sibi. Pl.* 29, *cr.* 4, (head, *pl.* 20, *cr.* 9.)
MICHEL, an arm, in armour, embowed, ppr., garnished, or, in hand a broken spear, gold. *Pl.* 44, *cr.* 9.
MICHELBOURNE, Ess. and Suss., a tiger, or, mouth embrued, ppr. *Pl.* 67, *cr.* 15.
MICHELBOURNE, Suss., Hants., and Middx., a tiger, passant, sa. *Pl.* 67, *cr.* 15.
MICHELGROVE, a unicorn's head, erased, ar. *Pl.* 67, *cr.* 1.
MICHELL, Wilts., a cubit arm, erect, ppr., in hand a sword, ar., hilt and pommel, or, (seven flames issuing from the blade, ppr., three from each side, and one from the point.) *Pl.* 125, *cr.* 5.
MICHELL, Cornw., a pegasus, flying. *Pl.* 28, *cr.* 9.
MICHELL, Norf., an arm, in armour, embowed, in hand, all ppr., a cutlass, ar., on edge of blade, three spikes, hilt and pommel, or. *Pl.* 81, *cr.* 11.
MICHELL, Cornw., an arm, in armour, embowed, in hand a sword, (dropping blood.) *Pl.* 2, *cr.* 8.
MICHELSON, of Chester, a fleur-de-lis, ppr. *Pl.* 68, *cr.* 12.

MICHELSTON, MICHESTON, and MICHELSTANE, Eng., a banner, displayed, ar., charged with a cross, gu., between four torteaux, of the last. *Pl.* 8, *cr.* 3, (torteaux, *pl.* 141.)
MICHIE, Sco., a dexter hand, couped, in fess, holding a dagger, in pale, ppr., hilt and pommel, or. *Pro patriâ et libertate. Pl.* 56, *cr.* 6, (without garland.)
MICKLETHWAITE, Lond., on a chapeau, a talbot, sejant. *Pl.* 102, *cr.* 9.
MICKLETHWAITE, Yorks., a griffin's head, erased, ppr. *In cœlo spes mea est. Pl.* 48, *cr.* 6.
MICKLETHWAITE, Suss., a griffin's head, ar., erased, gu., gorged with a collar, componée, of the second and first. *Pl.* 69, *cr.* 13.
MICKLETHWAITE, or MICKLETHWAYT, Yorks., same crest. *In cœlo spes mea est.*
MICKLETHWYATT-PECKHAM, Bart., Suss., on a mount, vert, an ostrich, or, in mouth a horseshoe, sa., between two palm-branches, vert. *Favent numine. Pl.* 16, *cr.* 2, (branches, *pl.* 87, *cr.* 8; mount, *pl.* 98, *cr.* 13.)
MICO, Lond., out of clouds, a hand holding a sword, in pale, ppr., hilt and pommel, or, charged on blade with a moor's head, ppr., (point embrued, gu.) *Pl.* 76, *cr.* 6.
MIDDLECÒT, Linc., a demi-eagle, displayed, erm., (ducally gorged, or,) in beak an escallop, gold. *Pl.* 22, *cr.* 11, (escallop, *pl.* 141.)
MIDDLEMORE, or MIDLEMORE, Middx., Worc., and Warw., in grass and reeds, a moorcock, all ppr. *Pl.* 10, *cr.* 1, (grass, *pl.* 34, *cr.* 6.)
MIDDLETON, Ess., a dexter hand, apaumée, ppr. *Pl.* 32, *cr.* 14.
MIDDLETON, Ess. and Salop, a wolf's head, erased, ppr. *Pl.* 14, *cr.* 6.
MIDDLETON, Surr., a monkey, passant, ppr., ringed and lined, or. *Pl.* 101, *cr.* 11.
MIDDLETON, Camb., Lanc., and Westm., a hawk's head, ar., beaked, or. *Pl.* 99, *cr.* 10, (without wings.)
MIDDLETON, out of a tower, a demi-lion, rampant. *Fortis in arduis. Pl.* 42, *cr.* 4.
MIDDLETON, a tower, embattled, sa., on top a lion, rampant. *Fortis in arduis. Pl.* 121, *cr.* 5.
MIDDLETON, Sco., a boar's head, erased and erect, az. *Guard yourself. Pl.* 21, *cr.* 7.
MIDDLETON, Ess., in lion's paw, a branch of palm, ppr. *Sobrie, pie, juste. Pl.* 70, *cr.* 9.
MIDDLETON, Sco., on top of a tree, an ape, sejant, all ppr. *Arte et Marte.*
MIDDLETON, Lanc., on trunk of a tree, or, a monkey, sejant, ppr., ringed round loins, az.
MIDDLETON, Northumb., a savage, in dexter an oak-tree, erased, fructed, all ppr. *Lesses dire.*
MIDDLETON, Derbs. and Yorks.: 1. For *Middleton,* an eagle's head, erased, ar., (charged on neck with a saltier, engrailed, sa.) *Pl.* 20, *cr.* 7. 2. On a mount, vert, a cross (clechée,) or, charged on centre with a fleur-de-lis, sa. *Conjunctio firmat. Pl.* 58, *cr.* 6, (fleur-de-lis, *pl.* 141.)
MIDDLETON, PETER, Esq., of Middleton Lodge and Stockfield Park, Yorks., between wings, ar., a garb, or. *Pl.* 108, *cr.* 13.
MIDFORD, Durh., an owl, ar. *Pl.* 27, *cr.* 9.
MIDGLEY, an heraldic-tiger, sejant, (erect,) between paws a caltrap. *Pl.* 111, *cr.* 7, (without coronet ; caltrap, *pl.* 141.)

MIDGLEY, on a mount, an heraldic-tiger, sejant, resting dexter on a caltrap. *Pl.* 111, *cr.* 7, (caltrap, *pl.* 7, *cr.* 4.)
MIDGELEY, (two) keys, in saltier, az., wards down. *Pl.* 54, *cr.* 12.
MIDLEHAM, Eng., on a chapeau, vert, turned up, or, a wyvern, wings expanded, az. *Pl.* 80, *cr.* 8.
MIDWINTER, Devons., a dexter arm, embowed, per pale, sa. and or, in hand, ppr., a plume of feathers, two, sa., one, or. *Pl.* 47, *cr.* 13, (plume, *pl.* 12, *cr.* 9.)
MIKEN, Iri., a demi-black, in dexter an arrow, on back a quiver, ppr. *Pl.* 80, *cr.* 9.
MIKIESON, Sco., a decrescent, ppr. *Ut implear.* *Pl.* 16, *cr.* 15.
MIKIESON, Sco., a crescent, ppr. *Ut implear.* *Pl.* 18, *cr.* 14.
MILBANK, Yorks., a lion's head, erased, gu., (charged with a bend, erm.) *Pl.* 81, *cr.* 4.
MILBORNE, Eng., an eagle, wings expanded, ppr. *Pl.* 126, *cr.* 7.
MILBORNE, a griffin's head, erased. *Pl.* 48, *cr.* 6.
MILBURN, Eng., a bear's head, erased, sa., muzzled, or. *Pl.* 71, *cr.* 6.
MILBURNE, Eng., in hand a battle-axe, ppr. *Pl.* 73, *cr.* 7.
MILCHAM, Norf., a griffin's head, ppr. *Pl.* 38, *cr.* 3.
MILDMAY, Eng., a lion, rampant, gardant, or. *Pl.* 92, *cr.* 7.
MILDMAY, a chapeau, winged, the points of the wings surrounded by a band, therefrom pendent a mortar, in fess, the whole surmounted by an etoile.
MILDMAY, Ess. and Northamp., a leopard's head, erased, or, ducally gorged, gu., ringed and lined, of the last, on neck, beneath the coronet, three pellets. *Pl.* 116, *cr.* 8, (pellets, *pl.* 141.)
MILDMAY, Ess., a demi-stag, salient, ppr., attired, (and collared, or, wings addorsed, ar.) *Pl.* 55, *cr.* 9, (without rose.)
MILDMAY, ST JOHN, Bart., Ess., a lion, rampant, gardant, az., armed and langued, gu. *Alla ta Hara.* *Pl.* 92, *cr.* 7.
MILDRED, Eng., a bear, passant, struck through by the head of a broken spear, in bend, ppr. *Pl.* 82, *cr.* 14.
MILDWAY, Ess., a lion, rampant, gardant, az. *Pl.* 92, *cr.* 7.
MILEHAM, Norf., a griffin's head, erased. *Pl.* 48, *cr.* 6.
MILES, a dove, between two ears of wheat. *Pl.* 2, *cr.* 11, (wheat, *pl.* 9, *cr.* 13.)
MILES, a dove, between two laurel-branches, in orle. *Pl.* 2, *cr.* 11.
MILES, a griffin's head, erased. *Pl.* 48, *cr.* 6.
MILES, Eng., a demi-lion, supporting an anchor. *Pl.* 19, *cr.* 6.
MILES, Somers., an arm, in armour, embowed, garnished, supporting an anchor, all or. *Pl.* 122, *cr.* 8, (without coronet.)
MILES, Hants, on a mural coronet, gu., an escallop, ar, *Pl.* 20, *cr.* 10, (escallop, *pl.* 141.)
MILES, Lond., a boar's head and neck, couped, (transfixed by an arrow.) *Pl.* 2, *cr.* 7.
MILES, out of a ducal coronet, a lion's head, (gorged with a chaplet of laurel, murally crowned.) *Pl.* 90, *cr.* 9.

MILES, Leic., an eagle, rising, erminois, collared, therefrom a chain, reflexed over back, on breast a mill-rind, sa. *Sans crainte.* *Pl.* 126 B, *cr.* 10.
MILESON, Yorks., a tiger's head, sa., tufted, tusked, collared, and lined, or. *Pl.* 40, *cr.* 10.
MILFORD, in lion's gamb, a trefoil, ppr. *Pl.* 60, *cr.* 14, (trefoil, *pl.* 141.)
MILL, Sco., a Pallas's head, couped, helmeted, beaver, turned up and plumed, gu. *Tam arte quam Marte.* *Pl.* 33, *cr.* 14.
MILL, Sco., a galley, oars erect, in saltier, and flagged, ppr. *Dat cura commodum.* *Pl.* 77, *cr.* 11.
MILL, a greyhound's head, erazed. *Pl.* 89, *cr.* 2.
MILL, Suss., a demi-bear, salient, sa., muzzled, ringed, and lined, or. *Pl.* 104, *cr.* 10.
MILL, an eagle's head, erased, gu., beaked, or, in beak a cross moline, erect, sa. *Pl.* 22, *cr.* 1, (cross, *pl.* 141.)
MILL, a bloodhound's head, erased, ar. *Toujours fidele.* *Pl.* 90, *cr.* 6.
MILL, Kent, a demi-bear, salient, sa., muzzled, ringed, and lined, or, on shoulder three guttées, gold. *Pl.* 104, *cr.* 10.
MILL, Bart., Hants, a demi-bear, muzzled and chained, or. *Aides Dieu.* *Pl.* 104, *cr.* 10.
MILL, Sco., a greyhound's head, issuing, ar., collared, az., ringed, or. *Toujours fidele.* *Pl.* 43, *cr.* 11.
MILLAN, Sco., a dexter and sinister hand, issuing, supporting a sword, in pale, ppr. *Pl.* 59, *cr.* 10.
MILLAR, Eng., three ears of wheat, issuing, or. *Pl.* 102, *cr.* 1.
MILLAR, in dexter hand, a book, open, ppr. *Felicem reddit religio.* *Pl.* 126 A, *cr.* 9.
MILLAR, a demi-moor, drawing an arrow to the head in a bow, ppr. *Non eget Mauri jaculis.* *Pl.* 41, *cr.* 8.
MILLARD, Eng., on a mount, vert, a stag, feeding, ppr. *Pl.* 37, *cr.* 8.
MILLARD, Hants, a demi-lion, rampant, az., between paws, a mascle, or. *Pl.* 47, *cr.* 4, (mascle, *pl.* 141.)
MILLBANK, Eng., a hill, vert. *Pl.* 98, *cr.* 13.
MILLBURN, Eng., out of a ducal coronet, a demi-lion. *Pl.* 45, *cr.* 7.
MILLE, Eng., a unicorn's head. *Pl.* 20, *cr.* 1.
MILLER, Sco., a cross moline, sa. *Optima cœlo.* *Pl.* 89, *cr.* 8.
MILLER, Eng., a caltrap, or, the uppermost point, embrued, gu. *Pl.* 7, *cr.* 4.
MILLER, Eng., a hand, with two fingers pointing upward, ppr. *Manent optima cœlo.* *Pl.* 67, *cr.* 6.
MILLER, a demi-savage shooting an arrow from a bow. *Non eget Mauri jaculis.* *Pl.* 41, *cr.* 8.
MILLER, Iri., a pole-cat, sa. *Pl.* 119, *cr.* 7.
MILLER, Suss., a wolf's head, erased, ar., gorged with a fess, wavy, az. *Pl.* 14, *cr.* 6.
MILLER, Sco., a hand, in pale, with two fingers pointing up. *Pl.* 67, *cr.* 6.
MILLER, Sco., a dexter hand, pointing with two fingers. *Spei bonœ atque animi.* *Pl.* 67, *cr.* 6.

MILLER, Sco., two arms, their hands joined, ppr. *Unione augetur.* Pl. 1, cr. 2.

MILLER, Sco., a lion, rampant, sa., between paws a cross moline, gu. *Forward.* Pl. 65, cr. 6, (cross, pl. 141.)

MILLER, a griffin's head, erased, ar., ducally gorged and chained, az. Pl. 42, cr. 9, (without branch.)

MILLER, a wolf's head, erased, per pale, or and purp., collared, gold. Pl. 8, cr. 4.

MILLER, Lanc., a demi-wolf, erminois, (gorged with a collar, gobony, ar. and az., supporting with paws a spindle, erect, ppr.) Pl. 56, cr. 8.

MILLER, Kent., a wolf's head, erazed, az., collared, erm. Pl. 8, cr. 4.

MILLER, Devons. and Middx., a demi-lion, rampant, gardant, az., holding a mascle, or. Pl. 35, cr. 4, (mascle, pl. 141.)

MILLER, Warw. and Dors., a demi-lion, az., between paws a mascle, or. Pl. 47, cr. 4, (mascle, pl. 141.)

MILLER, Beds., a wolf's head, erased, per pale, erm. and purp., collared, or. Pl. 8, cr. 4.

MILLER, Bart., Sco., a hand, couped at wrist, the third and fourth fingers folded in the palm, ar. Pl. 67, cr. 6.

MILLER, Bart., Iri., a wolf's head, erased, ar. Pl. 14, cr. 6.

MILLER, Bart., Hants, a wolf's head, erased, (gorged with a fess, wavy, az.) Pl. 14, cr. 6.

MILLER, BOYD, Esq., of Collier's Wood, Surr., a hand, couped at wrist, third and fourth fingers folded in palm, ar. *Manent optima cœlo.* Pl. 67, cr. 6.

MILLER, OLIVER GOURLAY, of Ratho. Same crest.

MILLES, Eng., a cat, sejant, ppr. Pl. 24, cr. 6.

MILLES, a demi-bear, sa., muzzled, collared, and stringed, or. Pl. 104, cr. 10.

MILLES, a bear, passant, sa., muzzled and chained, or. Pl. 61, cr. 5.

MILLES, Suff., a hare, (sejant, ppr.), in mouth three ears of wheat, or.) Pl. 21, cr. 9.

MILLES, Kent and Norf., a lion, rampant, or, between paws a mill-rind, sa. Pl. 125, cr. 2, (mill-rind, pl. 141.)

MILLES, Lond., a paschal lamb, passant, ar., unguled, or, over dexter shoulder a banner of St George, double-pennoned. Pl. 48, cr. 13.

MILLETT, Middx. and Bucks., out of a mural coronet, an arm, erect, vested, or, in glove, ar., a dragon's head, erased, vert. Pl. 79, cr. 4, (head, pl. 107, cr. 10.)

MILLIGAN, Sco., a demi-lion, in dexter a sword. *Fide et fortitudine.* Pl. 41, cr. 13.

MILLIGAN, Sco., a demi-lion, rampant, gu., in dexter a sword, ppr. *Regarde bien.* Pl. 41, cr. 13.

MILLIKEN, Sco., a demi-lion, royally crowned, gu., in dexter a sword, ppr. *Regarde bien.* Pl. 41, cr. 13, (crown, pl. 127, fig. 2.)

MILLINGTON, Eng., an ass's head, ppr. Pl. 91, cr. 7.

MILLMAN, Eng., a cross moline, gu. Pl. 89, cr. 8.

MILLMAN, or MILMAN, a (sinister) gauntlet, or. Pl. 15, cr. 15.

MILLMAN, a stag, lodged, per pale, ar. and or, attired and hoofed, gold, charged on body with hurts, in fess. Pl. 67, cr. 2, (hurt, pl. 141.)

MILLMAN, Eng., a gauntlet, ppr., Pl. 15, cr. 15.

MILLNER, or MILNER, Yorks., a horse's head, sa., crined and bridled, or, charged on neck with a bezant. Pl. 92, cr. 1, (bezant, pl. 141.)

MILLOT, Durh., an arm, in armour, embowed, in glove of mail, a billet, sa. Pl. 2, cr. 8, (billet, pl. 28, cr. 8.)

MILLS, Surr. and Glouc., a lion, rampant, or. Pl. 67, cr. 5.

MILLS, a lion's paw, erased, sa. Pl. 126, cr. 9.

MILLS, on an earl's coronet, the sun shining. Pl. 68, cr. 14, (coronet, pl. 127, fig. 8.)

MILLS, Berks., a lion, rampant, or, in mouth a sinister hand, gu. Pl. 67, cr. 5, (hand, pl. 107, cr. 9.)

MILLS, Ess., a hart, charged with an etoile, or. Pl. 88, cr. 9, (etoile, pl. 141.)

MILLS, Hants., on a mural coronet, gu., an escallop, ar. Pl. 49, cr. 6, (escallop, pl. 141.)

MILLS, Kent, on a round chapeau, gu., turned up, erm., a mill-rind, sa., between two marlion's wings, of the second. Pl. 80, cr. 15, (mill-rind, pl. 141.)

MILLS, Middx., on a ducal coronet, a lion, rampant, gu. *Honor virtutis pretium.* Pl. 107, cr. 11, (lion, pl. 67, cr. 5.)

MILLS, Suff., a demi-bear, rampant, sa., muzzled, collared, and chained, or. Pl. 104, cr. 10.

MILLS, Ess., a demi-lion, rampant, regardant, or, between paws a mill-rind, sa. Pl. 33, cr. 2, (mill-rind, pl. 141.)

MILLS, Beds. and Herts., a wing, (barry of ten,) ar. and vert. Pl. 39, cr. 10.

MILLS, WILLIAM, Esq., of Saxham Hall, Suff., a lion, rampant, or. *Confido.* Pl. 67, cr. 5.

MILLWARD, Eng., a dexter arm, in armour, embowed, in hand a sabre, ppr. Pl. 81, cr. 11.

MILMEN, Devons., a stag, lodged, party per pale, ar. and or, charged with two roundles, counterchanged. Pl. 67, cr. 2, (roundle, pl. 141.)

MILN, Eng., a garb, erect, banded, ppr. Pl. 48, cr. 10.

MILNE, Sco., a martlet, volant, ar. *Prudenter qui sedulo.* Pl. 40, cr. 4.

MILNE, Sco., in dexter hand a folded book, ppr. *Efficiunt clarum studia.* Pl. 45, cr. 3.

MILNE, Sco., a Pallas's head, couped at shoulders, ppr., vested about neck, vert, on head a helmet, az., beaver turned up, and a plumash, gu. *Tam arte quam marte.* Pl. 33, cr. 14.

MILNE, Edinr., a martlet, volant, sa. *Ex industriâ.* Pl. 40, cr. 4.

MILNE, Sco., in the sea, ppr., a cross moline, sa., within two ears of wheat, in orle. *Clarum reddit industria.* Pl. 103, cr. 8, (cross, pl. 23, cr. 14.)

MILNE, Sco., a galley, oars erect, in saltier, ppr. *Dat cura commodum.* Pl. 77, cr. 11.

MILNER, Yorks.: 1. For *Milner*, a greyhound, current, sa., (collared and ringed, or.) Pl. 28, cr. 7. 2. For *Wheeler*, a lion's head, couped, ar., charged on breast with a Catherine-wheel, gu. Pl. 126, cr. 1, (wheel, pl. 141.)

MILNER, a horse's head, bridled, (with wings addorsed.) Pl. 92, cr. 1.

MILNER, Yorks., a horse's head, erased, sa., bridled, or, on neck a bezant. Pl. 92, cr. 1, (bezant, pl. 141.)

MILNER, Bart., Yorks., a horse's head, couped, sa., (bridled) and maned, or, charged on neck with a bezant, between wings, az. *Pl.* 19, *cr.* 13, (bezant, *pl.* 141.)

MILNES, Sco., a garb, ppr. *Pl.* 48, *cr.* 10.

MILNES, Bart., Leic., a garb, or, banded by a fess, dancettée, az., charged with three mullets, pierced, gold. *Pl.* 48, *cr.* 10, (mullet, *pl.* 45, *cr.* 1.)

MILNES, Derbs., a bear's head, couped at neck, sa., charged with a mill-rind, or. *Pl.* 2, *cr.* 8, (mill-rind, *pl.* 141.)

MILNES, Stubbing Edge, Derbs., a demi-lion, rampant, or, in paws a mill-rind, sa. *Pl.* 126, *cr.* 12, (mill-rind, *pl.* 141.)

MILNES, Beckingham Hall, Linc., an elephant's head, erased, ppr., gorged with a ducal coronet, or. *Pl.* 68, *cr.* 4, (gorging, *same plate*.)

MILNES, RICHARD-MONCKTON, Esq., of Fryston Hall, and Batry Hall, Yorks., a garb, or. *Scio cui credidi. Pl.* 48, *cr.* 10.

MILROY, Sco., a leopard's face, or. *Pl.* 66, *cr.* 14.

MILSOLM, a tiger's head, sa., tufted, collared, and lined, or. *Pl.* 40, *cr.* 10.

MILTON, Lond. and Oxon., in lion's gamb, erect, ar., an eagle's head, erased, gu. *Pl.* 58, *cr.* 7, (head, *pl.* 20, *cr.* 7.)

MILTON, Lond., an arm, in armour, ppr., scarfed, az., in hand a broken spear, gu., headed, ar. *Pl.* 44, *cr.* 9.

MILTOWN, Earl of, Viscount and Baron Russborough, Iri., (Leeson,) a demi-lion, rampant, gu., between paws (the sun,) or. *Clarior e tenebris. Pl.* 126, *cr.* 12.

MILWARD, Ess., out of a palisado coronet, or, a lion's gamb, sa., grasping a sceptre, gold. *Pl.* 16, *cr.* 1, (coronet, *pl.* 128, *fig.* 21.)

MILWARD, Ess., in lion's gamb, sa., a sceptre, or. *Pl.* 16, *cr.* 1.

MILWARD, Lechlade, Glouc., a bear's paw, erased, sa., claws, or, holding a sceptre, (in bend, sinister, gold entwined by a sprig of oak,) between wings, az. *Pl.* 16, *cr.* 1, (wings, *pl.* 1, *cr.* 15.)

MINCHIN, Eng., a lion's tail, erased. *Pl.* 17, *cr.* 4.

MINETT, Eng., a mermaid, in dexter a mirror, with sinister combing her hair, all ppr. *Pl.* 48, *cr.* 5.

MINGAY, or MINGEY, Norf., a lance, or, headed, ar., environed with a laurel-branch, ppr. *Pl.* 15, *cr.* 6, (lance, *pl.* 97, *cr.* 4.)

MINIET, Eng., an eagle, volant, over a ruined castle, ppr. *Pl.* 118, *cr.* 15, (eagle, *pl.* 94, *cr.* 1.)

MINNE, Ruts., a heathcock, ppr.

MINNETT, a wing, erect, ar., (charged with three bars, gu.) *Pl.* 39, *cr.* 10.

MINNIT, a helmet, beaver open, sa., garnished, or. *Pl.* 38, *cr.* 15.

MINORS, Lond., Herts., and Staffs., a naked cubit arm, ppr., in hand a lion's gamb, erased, sa. *Pl.* 94, *cr.* 13.

MINORS, a cubit arm, ppr., in hand a lion's gamb, erased, paw downward. *Pl.* 94, *cr.* 13.

MINORS, a wolf's head, erased, sa., devouring a sinister hand, ppr. *Pl.* 14, *cr.* 6, (hand, *pl.* 107, *cr.* 9.)

MINSHALL, Suff., Chesh., Devons., and Bucks., two lions' paws holding a crescent. *Pl.* 62, *cr.* 3.

MINSHALL, and MYNSHALL, Bucks., Chesh., Devons., Suff., and Suss., a Turk, kneeling on one knee, vested, gu., legs and arms, in mail, ppr., at his side a scimitar, sa., hilted, or, on his head a turban, with a crescent and feathers, ar., in dexter a crescent, of the last.

MINSHULL, two bears' paws, erased and erect, supporting a crescent. *Good deeds shine clear*—and—*In hoc plenius redibo. Pl.* 62, *cr.* 3.

MINSTER, Baron. *See* CONYNGHAM, Marquess.

MINTERNE, and MINTERN, Surr. and Dors., a bull's head, gu., ducally gorged and armed, or. *Pl.* 68, *cr.* 6.

MINTO, Earl of, Viscount Melgund and Baron Minto, Sco., and a Bart., N.S., (Elliot-Murray-Kynynmound,) a dexter arm, embowed, (out of clouds,) throwing a dart, all ppr. *Non eget arcu. Pl.* 92, *cr.* 14.

MIREHOUSE, an arm, in armour, embowed, in hand a sword, all ppr. *Pl.* 2, *cr.* 8.

MIRFIN, a demi-lion, ppr., holding a flag, ar., charged with a saltier, sa. *Pl.* 67, *cr.* 10, (flag, *pl.* 99, *cr.* 2.)

MIRRIE, or MIRRY, Eng., out of a ducal coronet, or, a demi-lion, gu. *Pl.* 45, *cr.* 7.

MIRTLE, a cubit arm, erect, ppr., (encircled with a chaplet of myrtle, vert,) in hand a scimitar. *Pl.* 29, *cr.* 8.

MISSENDEN, amongst flags, vert, a demi-swan, displayed, ar., (collared, gu.) *Pl.* 66, *cr.* 10.

MISSIRINEN, or MISSERINEN, Eng., a battle-axe, in pale, ppr. *Pl.* 14, *cr.* 8.

MITCHAEL, or MITCHELL, Sco., a stalk of wheat, bladed, ppr. *Cresco. Pl.* 85, *cr.* 6.

MITCHALL, a garb, or. *Pl.* 48, *cr.* 10.

MITCHELL, Yorks., a cross crosslet, fitched, gu. *Pl.* 16, *cr.* 10.

MITCHELL, Sco., three ears of barley, bladed, ppr. *In deo spes. Pl.* 102, *cr.* 1.

MITCHELL, Sco., a phœnix in flames, ppr., *Spernit humum. Pl.* 44, *cr.* 8.

MITCHELL, Sco., in hand a writing pen, ppr. *Favente Deo supero. Pl.* 26, *cr.* 13.

MITCHELL, Sco., a stalk of wheat, or, slipped and bladed, vert. *Sapiens qui assiduus. Pl.* 85, *cr.* 6.

MITCHELL, Sco., in hand a garland of laurel, both ppr. *Deo favente. Pl.* 86, *cr.* 1.

MITCHELL, Eng., a garb, vert. *Pl.* 48, *cr.* 10.

MITCHELL, Bart., of Bandeth and Westshore, (three) ears of barley on one stalk, ppr. *Sapiens qui assiduus. Pl.* 41, *cr.* 3.

MITCHELL, of Berry, same crest and motto.

MITCHELL, a demi-angel, (pointing upward with dexter, in sinister a sceptre.) *Pl.* 90, *cr.* 11.

MITCHELL, a cubit arm, vested, surrounded by wheat-ears, in hand a flag-staff, with flag downward, staff broken.

MITCHELL, a pelican, wings elevated and addorsed, vulned, ppr. *Pl.* 109, *cr.* 15.

MITCHELL, St Michael the archangel, in armour, ppr., face, neck, arms, and legs bare, wings, ar., hair, auburn, in dexter a spear, of the first. *Pl.* 90, *cr.* 1.

MITCHELL, a cubit arm, erect, gu., (cuffed, ar.,) in hand a crane's head, erased, ppr. *Pl.* 29, *cr.* 4, (crane, *pl.* 20, *cr.* 9.)

MITCHELL, Cornw., a demi-pegasus, or, winged, az., (charged on shoulder with a demi-rose, gu., divided fessways, rays issuing from the division, pendent, ar.) *Pl.* 57, *cr.* 15.

MITCHELL-FORBES, DUNCAN, Esq., of Thainston, Aberdeen: 1. For *Forbes*, a cock, ppr. *Watch. Pl.* 67, *cr.* 14. 2. For *Mitchell*, a phœnix in flames, all ppr. *Nullâ palescere culpâ. Pl.* 44, *cr.* 8.

MITCHELSON, Sco., an increscent, ar. *Crescam ut prosim. Pl.* 122, *cr.* 15.

MITCHELSON, Eng., a hawk, rising. *Virtute tutus. Pl.* 105, *cr.* 4.

MITCHENER, Eng., a dove, ar. *Pl.* 66, *cr.* 12.

MITFORD, Hants and Northumb., a dexter and sinister arm, one above the other, both in fess, holding a sword, in pale, ar., pommelled, or, on point a boar's head, sa., tusked, ppr., couped, in fess, ar. *God careth for us. Pl.* 10, *cr.* 2, (hands, *pl.* 3, *cr.* 5.)

MITFORD, of Mitford Castle, Northumb., a dexter and sinister arm, issuing in bend, couped, ppr., holding a sword, in pale, ar., pommelled, or, on point a boar's head, sa., tusked, ppr., couped, in fess, ar. *Pl.* 3, *cr.* 5, (head, *pl.* 10, *cr.* 2.)

MITFORD, on a mole, passant, sa., an escallop, or.

MITFORD, Baron Redesdale. *See* REDESDALE.

MITTLEWELL, an eagle's head, erased, ar. *Pl.* 20, *cr.* 7.

MITTON, Salop and Staffs., a demi-eagle, displayed, with two heads, per pale, or and az. *Pl.* 4, *cr.* 6, (without escutcheon.)

MITTON, Salop, a ram's head, couped, ar., armed, or. *Pl.* 34, *cr.* 12.

MITTON, a ram's head, couped, ar. *Pl.* 34, *cr.* 12.

MITTON, a demi-eagle, displayed, per pale, ar. and az. *Pl.* 22, *cr.* 11.

MITTON, Staffs., a bull's head, sa., armed, or, charged with three annulets, gold. *Pl.* 63, *cr.* 11, (annulet, *pl.* 141.)

MITTON, Oxon., in lion's gamb, couped and erect, ar., an eagle's head, erased, gu. *Pl.* 89, *cr.* 13, (head, *pl.* 20, *cr.* 7.)

MOBERLEY, MOBERLY, and MODBURLEY, Eng., a demi-lady in the character of Justice, in dexter a pair of scales. *Pl.* 57, *cr.* 1.

MOCKET, Kent., a tiger, sejant, az., collared, ar. *Pl.* 26, *cr.* 9.

MOCKLOW, Notts., a griffin's head, per pale, indented, ar. and gu., guttée-de-larmes, in beak a buck's foot, of the first. *Pl.* 9, *cr.* 12, (foot, *pl.* 66, *cr.* 7.)

MOCKLOW, Worc., a griffin's head, per pale, indented, gu. and ar., in beak an eagle's leg, erased, or. *Pl.* 38, *cr.* 3, (leg, *pl.* 103, *cr.* 4.)

MODA, Suff., a demi-lion, rampant, crowned, or. *Pl.* 61, *cr.* 4, (without branch.)

MODDER, Staffs., on a staff, couped, raguly, in fess, vert, a lion, sejant, or. *Pl.* 76, *cr.* 11.

MODERBY, Eng., in hand a thunderbolt, ppr. *Pl.* 21, *cr.* 8.

MODERN COLLEGE, Blackheath, a lion, rampant, gu. *Pl.* 67, *cr.* 5.

MODEY, out of a ducal coronet, or, a demi-lion, with wings displayed, gu. *Pl.* 17, *cr.* 9, (lion, *pl.* 45, *cr.* 7.)

MODYFORD, Devons., Kent., Jamaica, and Middx., a garb, or. *Pl.* 48, *cr.* 10.

MOESLER, Lond., a talbot, (statant,) collared. *Pl.* 65, *cr.* 2.

MOFFAT, Eng., a cat, sejant on hind legs, gardant, ppr. *Pl.* 53, *cr.* 5.

MOFFAT, Sco., a cross crosslet, fitched, gu. *Spero meliora. Pl.* 16, *cr.* 10.

MOFFAT, the sun in splendour, ppr. *Pl.* 68, *cr.* 14.

MOGG, Somers., a cock, ppr., (bearing a shield, ar., charged with a crescent, gu., pendent from neck, by a chain, gold.) *Curæ pii Diis sunt. Pl.* 112, *cr.* 12.

MOHUM, and MOHUN, Eng., a dexter arm, vested with a maunch, erm., in hand, ppr., a fleur-de-lis, or. *Pl.* 22, *cr.* 14, (cross, *pl.* 99, *cr.* 1.)

MOILE, or MOILL, Eng., on a winged globe, an eagle, rising, ppr. *Pl.* 34, *cr.* 2, (globe, *pl.* 50, *cr.* 7.)

MOIR, Sco., a moor's head. *Non sibi, sed cunctis. Pl.* 120, *cr.* 3.

MOIR, ROBERT-GRAHAM, Esq., of Leckie, Sco., a falcon, ppr., armed and belled, or, perching on a heron, lying on its back, ppr., beaked and membered, gu. *Ne oublie. Pl.* 17, *cr.* 8.

MOIR, Sco., a negro's head, couped, ppr. *Mediocriter*—or—*Sur esperance. Pl.* 120, *cr.* 3.

MOIR, Sco., a Mauritanian's head, couped, ppr. *Major opima ferat. Pl.* 120, *cr.* 3.

MOIR, Sco., a Mauritanian's head, couped, (guttée-de-sang, ppr.) *Major opima ferat. Pl.* 120, *cr.* 3.

MOIR, Sco., out of a cloud, an arm, from shoulder, in hand a branch of laurel, slipped. *Virtute non aliter. Pl.* 80, *cr.* 3, (laurel, *pl.* 43, *cr.* 6.)

MOIR, Sco., a mort-head, with two leg-bones, in saltier, ppr. *Non sibi, sed cunctis. Pl.* 62, *cr.* 12, (bone, *pl.* 25, *cr.* 11.)

MOIRA, Earl of. *See* HASTINGS, Marquess of.

MOISES, a tuft of reeds, vert. *Nisi virtus vilior algâ.*

MOLANT, a demi-mule, gu.

MOLCASTER, and MONCASTER, Eng., an old man's head, affrontée, ducally crowned, or. *Pl.* 28, *cr.* 3.

MOLDFORD, a buck's head, gu. *Pl.* 91, *cr.* 14.

MOLE, Devons., out of a ducal coronet, or, a snake, head erect, body entwined. *Pl.* 116, *cr.* 2.

MOLE, Beds. and Northamp., out of clouds, ppr., a cubit arm, in pale, vested, gu., hand open, of the first. *Pl.* 32, *cr.* 14, (cloud, *pl.* 22, *cr.* 6.)

MOLESWORTH, Bart., Cornw., an arm, in armour, embowed, ppr., in gauntlet a cross crosslet, or. *Sic fidem teneo. Pl.* 2, *cr.* 8, (cross, *pl.* 141.)

MOLESWORTH, Viscount and Baron Philipstown, Iri., (Molesworth,) an arm, in armour, embowed, ppr., in hand a cross crosslet, or. *Vincit amor patriæ. Pl.* 44, *cr.* 9, (cross, *pl.* 141.)

MOLFORD, Devons., out of a ducal coronet, or, a demi-swan, wings expanded, ar., beaked, gu. *Pl.* 83, *cr.* 1.

MOLINEAUX, Eng., a cross moline, lozenge-pierced, az. *Pl.* 91, *cr.* 10.

MOLINEUX, Hawkley, Lanc., a beaver, passant, ppr. *Pl.* 49, *cr.* 5.

MOLINEUX, a garb. *Pl.* 48, *cr.* 10.

MOLINEUX, Notts., a peacock's tail, ppr., in bend sinister, affixed to the side of a chapeau, gu., turned up, erm. *Pl.* 120, *cr.* 13, (chapeau, *same plate, cr.* 15.)

MOLINEUX, in a chapeau, gu., turned up, erm., a peacock's feather, in bend sinister, ppr. *Ib.*
MOLINEUX, Earl of Sefton. *See* SEFTON.
MOLINS, Lond., a water-wheel, or. *Pl.* 32, *cr.* 15.
MOLL, Sco., a phœnix in flames, ppr. *Post funera fœnus. Pl.* 44, *cr.* 8.
MOLLESON, Sco., a Saracen's head, erased, dropping blood, ppr. *Fax mentis honestæ gloria. Pl.* 23, *cr.* 1.
MOLLESONE, Sco., a hart's head, cabossed, ppr. *Fax mentis honestæ gloria. Pl.* 36, *cr.* 1.
MOLLING, and MOLYING, on a rock, a martlet, sa. *Pl.* 36, *cr.* 5.
MOLLINGTON, Eng., a demi-man, shooting an arrow from a bow, ppr. *Pl.* 41, *cr.* 8.
MOLLOY, Iri., out of a cloud, a hand, erect, holding a book, expanded, ppr. *Pl.* 82, *cr.* 5.
MOLLOY, Middx., a greyhound, current, ar., against a tree, vert. *Pl.* 27, *cr.* 2.
MOLLOY, on a ducal coronet, a lion, rampant, all or. *Pl.* 67, *cr.* 5, (coronet, *same plate.*)
MOLLOY, a sea-lion, sejant. *Pl.* 25, *cr.* 12.
MOLLOY, out of a ducal coronet, a demi-lion, rampant, or. *Pl.* 45, *cr.* 7.
MOLONY, an arm, in armour, embowed, in hand a scimitar, ppr. *Periissem, ni periissem. Pl.* 81, *cr.* 11.
MOLOWNEY, a stag, passant, (in mouth a branch.) *Pl.* 68, *cr.* 2.
MOLSON, a crescent, between wings, ar. *Pl.* 31, *cr.* 11, (without etoile.)
MOLTON, or MOULTON, Eng., a shark's head, regardant, issuing, swollowing a black-a-moor. *Pl.* 16, *cr.* 6.
MOLYNEAUX, Eng., a cock's head, between wings, ppr. *Pl.* 47, *cr.* 3, (without cross.)
MOLYNES, Berks. and Leic., a falcon's head, wings expanded. *Pl.* 99, *cr.* 10.
MOLYNES, Eng., a savage's head, couped, ppr. *Pl.* 81, *cr.* 15.
MOLYNEUX, a peacock's tail, erect, ppr., banded, or and az. *Pl.* 120, *cr.* 13, (without coronet.)
MOLYNEUX, Bart., Iri., an heraldic-tiger, passant, ar., in dexter a cross moline, or. *Patriæ infelici fidelis.*
MOLYNS, a savage's head, in profile, ppr. *Pl.* 81, *cr.* 15.
MOMPESSON, Norf., a plume of ostrich-feathers, ar. *Ma foy en Dieu seulement. Pl.* 12, *cr.* 9.
MOMPESSON, Wilts., a jug, or, stringed, az., tasselled, gold.
MOMPISSON, Wilts., a plume of ostrich-feathers, ar., the centre, sa., all turned, or. *Ma foy en Dieu seulement. Pl.* 12, *cr.* 9.
MONCK, Earl of Rathdown. *See* RATHDOWN.
MONCK, Bart., Northumb., (on a mount, vert,) a demi-griffin, az. *Pl.* 18, *cr.* 6.
MONCK, JOHN BLIGH, Esq., of Coley Park, Berks., a wyvern, ar. *Pl.* 63, *cr.* 13.
MONCKTON, or MONKETON, Yorks., Surr., and Linc., a martlet, or. *Pl.* 111, *cr.* 5.
MONCKTON; MONGTOWN, MONKTON, MONGDENE, and MONGTON, two arms, in armour, embowed, placing a Saracen's head, affrontée, on the point of a pheon, all ppr. *Pl.* 83, *cr.* 11.
MONCKTON, Viscount Galway. *See* GALWAY.
MONCRIEF, Sco., a gilliflower, ppr. *Diligentiâ cresco. Pl.* 22, *cr.* 9.
MONCRIEF, Sco., a gilliflower, ppr. *Firma spes. Pl.* 22, *cr.* 9.

MONCRIEF, Sco., a stork's head. *Virescit. Pl.* 32, *cr.* 5.
MONCRIEFF, Sco., three ears of rye, banded together, ppr. *Pl.* 102, *cr.* 1.
MONCRIEFF, or MONCRIEFFE, Sco., a demi-lion, rampant, gu., armed and langued, az. *Sur esperance. Pl.* 67, *cr.* 10.
MONCRIEFF, a demi-lion, rampant, gu. *Sur esperance. Pl.* 67, *cr.* 10.
MONCUR, in dexter hand a garland of roses, ppr. *Pl.* 41, *cr.* 7.
MONETON, Sco., a martlet, or. *Pl.* 111, *cr.* 5.
MONEY, on a mount, vert, a hedgehog, ppr. *Pl.* 32, *cr.* 9, (mount, *pl.* 98, *cr.* 13.)
MONEY, Ess., a bezant, between wings, az., semée of fleurs-de-lis, or. *Factis, non verbis. Pl.* 2, *cr.* 3.
MONEY, a cubit arm, erect, (vested,) in hand a battle-axe, in bend sinister. *Pl.* 73, *cr.* 7, (vested, *pl.* 64, *cr.* 7.)
MONEY, an eagle's head, in beak three roses, stalked, all ppr. *Pl.* 22, *cr.* 1; rose, *pl.* 23, *cr.* 2.
MONEY-KYRLE, of Much Marcle, Heref. : 1. For *Money*, an eagle's head, erased, sa., (collared, gemelle,) in mouth a fleur-de-lis, or. *Pl.* 121, *cr.* 7, 2. For *Kyrle*, on a mount, vert, a hedgehog, or. *Nil moror ictus. Pl.* 32, *cr.* 9, (mount, *pl.* 98, *cr.* 13.)
MONGREDIEN, (on a mount, vert,) an eagle's head, erased, or, between two palm-branches, ppr. *Sursum. Pl.* 20, *cr.* 7, (palm, *pl.* 87, *cr.* 8.)
MONHALT, in lion's gamb, erased, ar., an oak-branch, fructed, or, leaved, ppr. *Pl.* 68, *cr.* 10, (oak, *pl.* 32, *cr.* 13.)
MONHAULT, Yorks., a lion's head, gu., charged with a cross crosslet, fitched, or. *Pl.* 126, *cr.* 1, (cross, *pl.* 141.)
MONINGTON, Eng., a savage's head, in profile, ppr. *Pl.* 81, *cr.* 15.
MONINS, WILLIAM, Esq., of Waldershare, an increscent, or. *Mediocria maxima. Pl.* 122, *cr.* 15.
MONK, a wyvern, ppr. *Pl.* 63, *cr.* 13.
MONKE, Eng., an eagle, wings expanded, resting dexter on a small mount, ppr. *Pl.* 118, *cr.* 1.
MONKE, MONCK, or MUNCKE, Devons., a dragon, passant, vert. *Pl.* 90, *cr.* 10.
MONKHOUSE, Eng., a church, ppr. *Pl.* 45, *cr.* 6.
MONKHOUSE, Northumb., out of a tower, ppr., masoned, sa., an arm, in armour, in hand a (sword,) ppr. *Monachus salvabor. Pl.* 116, *cr.* 12.
MONMOUTH, a hawk's head, erased, vert, (charged on neck with a cheveron, or,) in mouth a trefoil, of the first. *Pl.* 34, *cr.* 11, (trefoil, *pl.* 55, *cr.* 12.)
MONMOUTH, an eagle's head, erased, or, charged on neck with a cheveron, in mouth a trefoil, or. *Pl.* 22, *cr.* 1, (trefoil, *pl.* 141.)
MONNOUX, Beds., a dove, in mouth an oak-sprig, fructed, all ppr. *Pl.* 48, *cr.* 15, (oak, *pl.* 32, *cr.* 13.)
MONNOUX, Beds., a turtle-dove, az., winged, or, membered and beaked, purp., in mouth an oak-stalk, vert, fructed, or. *Ib.*
MONNYNGS, three crescents, interlaced, ar. *Pl.* 119, *cr.* 10, (crescents, *pl.* 141.)
MONNYPENNY, on a dolphin, embowed, bridled, Neptune astride, holding with sinister, a trident over shoulder. *Pl.* 58, *cr.* 12, (trident, *pl.* 35, *cr.* 10.)

MONOX, MONNOX, or MONOUX, Ess., a dove, ar., in mouth three acorns, vert, fructed, or. *Pl.* 66, *cr.* 12, (acorns, *pl.* 69, *cr.* 12.)
MONRO, an eagle's head, erased, ppr. *Alis et animo. Pl.* 20, *cr.* 7.
MONRO, Sco., an eagle, perching, ppr. *Time Deum. Pl.* 67, *cr.* 4.
MONRO, Sco., an eagle, looking to the sun in glory, ppr. *Cœlestia sequor. Pl.* 43, *cr.* 5.
MONRO, Sco., an eagle, perched, or. *Non inferiora. Pl.* 7, *cr.* 11.
MONRO, Bart., an eagle, rising, ppr. *Dread God. Pl.* 67, *cr.* 4.
MONRO, K.B., Sco., an eagle, close, ppr. *Dread God. Pl.* 7, *cr.* 11.
MONRO, Sco., an eagle, rising, with a sword, ppr. *Alis et animo. Pl.* 87, *cr.* 5.
MONRO, an eagle, wings addorsed, ar. *Pl.*61, *cr.*1.
MONRO, Surr., an eagle, displayed, ppr. *Pl.* 48, *cr.* 11.
MONRO, HECTOR, Esq., of Ewell Castle, Surr., and Edmondsham, Dors., an eagle, displayed, ppr. *Non inferiora. Pl.* 48, *cr.* 11.
MONROSE, an eagle, rising, ppr. *Pl.* 67, *cr.* 4.
MONSELL, a lion, rampant, in paws a mullet. *Pl.* 125, *cr.* 2, (mullet, *pl.* 141.)
MONSON, of Preston, three Saracens' heads, conjoined in one neck, one to dexter and sinister, and one looking upward. *Pretio prudentia præstat. Pl.* 32, *cr.* 2.
MONSON, Eng., a lion, rampant, or, supporting a pillar, gold. *Prest pour mon pays. Pl.* 22, *cr.* 15, (pillar, *pl.* 33, *cr.* 1.)
MONSON, Baron, and a Bart., (Monson), a lion, rampant, or, sustained by a pillar, ar. *Prest pour mon pays. Pl.* 22, *cr.* 15, (pillar, *pl.* 33, *cr.* 1.)
MONTACUTE, DE, a griffin's head, between wings, or. *Pl.* 65, *cr.* 1.
MONTAGU, Eng., on a chapeau, a leopard, passant. *Pl.* 110, *cr.* 8.
MONTAGU, Wilts., a griffin's head, couped, wings expanded, or, gorged with a collar, ar., charged, with three lozenges, gu. *Disponendo me, non mutando me. Pl.* 22, *cr.* 2, (lozenge, *pl.* 141.)
MONTAGU, Baron, (Montagu-Scott,) a griffin's head, or. *Spectemur agendo. Pl.* 38, *cr.* 3.
MONTAGU, Duke of Manchester. *See* MANCHESTER.
MONTAGU, Earl of Sandwich. *See* SANDWICH.
MONTAGUE, Eng., a griffin's head, between wings, ppr. *Pl.* 65, *cr.* 1.
MONTAGUE, Duke of Montague, a griffin's head, couped, or, wings addorsed and beaked, sa. *Spectemur agendo. Pl.* 65, *cr.* 1.
MONTAGUE, a griffin's head, or, between wings, az. *Pl.* 65, *cr.* 1.
MONTAGUE, Glouc., a griffin's head, or, between wings, and beaked, sa. *Pl.* 65, *cr.* 1.
MONTAGUTA, a demi-lion, rampant, or. *Pl.* 67, *cr.* 10.
MONTALT, Eng., a dexter arm, embowed, issuing, throwing a dart, ppr. *Pl.* 92, *cr.* 14.
MONTCHANTSEY, and MOUNTCHANSEY, in hand a scimitar, in pale, ppr. *Pl.* 66, *cr.* 6.
MONTCHENCY, Eng., in the sea, a ship, all ppr. *Pl.* 109, *cr.* 8.
MONTEATH, Sco., in hand a dagger, in bend. *Dum vivo, spero. Pl.* 28, *cr.* 4.
MONTEFERIORE, a demi-lion, or, between paws a cross-moline, gu., issuing from a mount, vert, on which are three fleurs-de-lis. *Video meliora. Pl.* 72, *cr.* 13, (cross and fleur-de-lis, *pl.* 141.)
MONTEFIORE, Bart., Lond., out of trunk of oak-tree, sprouting fresh branches, a demi-lion, holding a flag-staff, pennon flotant to sinister, and inscribed with Hebrew, *Think and thank. Pl.* 10, *cr.* 6, (lion, *pl.* 36, *cr.* 11.)
MONTEITH, Sco., a galley, ppr., flagged, gu., (cantoned with the cross of St Andrew.) *Dum vivo, spero. Pl.* 34, *cr.* 5.
MONTEITH, Sco., an eagle, looking to the sun in glory. *Sub sole nihil. Pl.* 43, *cr.* 5.
MONTEITH, Sco., in hand a dagger, ppr. *Pl.* 28, *cr.* 4.
MONTEITH, Sco., a tree, ppr. *Viresco. Pl.* 100, *cr.* 14.
MONTEITH, Sco., a wolf's head, in mouth a rose. *Pl.* 92, *cr.* 15.
MONTEITH, Sco., a lymphad, oars in saltier, ppr., flagged, gu., (cantoned with St Andrew's cross.) *Dum vivo, spero. Pl.* 77, *cr.* 11.
MONTESEY, a sea-lion, supporting an anchor. *Pl.* 59, *cr.* 2, (anchor, *pl.* 42, *cr.* 12.)
MONTFORD, Yorks., a talbot head, sa., eared, or, gorged with a ducal coronet, gold. *Pl.* 123, *cr.* 15, (coronet, *pl.* 128, *fig.* 3.)
MONTFORD, Lord, Baron of Horseheath, Cambs., (Bromley,) out of a mural coronet, or, a demi-lion, rampant, sa., holding a standard, vert, charged with a griffin, passant, gold, staff, ppr., headed, ar. *Non inferiora secutus. Pl.* 86, *cr.* 11.
MONTGOMERIE, Sco., a lady, (or, figure of Hope,) in dexter an anchor, in sinister a savage's head, by the hair, couped. *Garde bien. Pl.* 107, *cr.* 2.
MONTGOMERIE, ALEXANDER, Esq., of Annick Lodge, Ayrs., a female figure, ppr., anciently attired, az., in dexter an anchor, or, in sinister a savage's head, couped, of the first. *Gardez bien. Pl.* 107, *cr.* 2.
MONTGOMERIE, Earl of Eglinton. *See* EGLINTON.
MONTGOMERY, JOHN, Esq., of Benvarden, co. Antrim, same crest and motto.
MONTGOMERY, Eng., an arm, in armour, in hand a broken spear, point falling down. *Garde bien. Pl.* 44, *cr.* 9.
MONTGOMERY, Iri., out of a ducal coronet, or, two laurel-branches, in orle, vert. *Pl.* 114, *cr.* 15.
MONTGOMERY, a fleur-de-lis, or. *An I may. Pl.* 68, *cr.* 12.
MONTGOMERY, Sco., a lady, ppr., vested, az., dexter supporting an anchor, in sinister a Saracen's head, erased, held by the hair, both ppr. *Garde bien. Pl.* 107, *cr.* 2.
MONTGOMERY, Eng., a Saracen's head, (erased) affrontée. *Pl.* 19, *cr.* 1.
MONTGOMERY, Sco., a branch of palm, ppr. *Procedamus in pace. Pl.* 23, *cr.* 7.
MONTGOMERY, an arm, in armour, embowed, in hand a dagger. *Pl.* 120, *cr.* 11.
MONTGOMERY, Sco., in hand a branch of palm, ppr. *Procedamus in pace. Pl.* 23, *cr.* 7.
MONTGOMERY, a cubit arm, in armour, erect, in hand a dagger, all ppr. *Pl.* 125, *cr.* 5.
MONTGOMERY, Norf.: 1. On a chapeau, gu., turned up, erm., a plume of peacock's feathers, pp. *Pl.* 120, *cr.* 13, (chapeau, *same plate, cr.* 15.) 2. A palm-branch, ppr. *Pl.* 123, *cr.* 1.

Y

MONTGOMERY, Grey Abbey, co. Down, out of a chapeau, an arm in armour, erect, in hand a sword. *Pl.* 115, *cr.* 14, (chapeau, *pl.* 127, *fig.* 13.)

MONTGOMERY, WILLIAM, Esq., of Milton, Northamp., a hind's head. *Pl.* 21, *cr.* 9.

MONTGOMERY, a merman, ppr., holding a target, or. *Pl.* 35, *cr.* 10.

MONTGOMERY, Sco., a cubit arm, in armour, in hand a broken spear, in bend dexter, the point falling. *Pl.* 23, *cr.* 9.

MONTGOMERY, Sco., a heart surmounted of an eye, ppr. *Pl.* 13, *cr.* 11, (eye, *pl.* 68, *cr.* 15.)

MONTGOMERY, Sco., an eagle, rising. *Pl.* 67, *cr.* 4.

MONTGOMERY, Bart., Iri., a dexter arm, in armour, embowed, in hand a broken spear, all ppr. *Pl.* 44, *cr.* 9.

MONTGOMERY, Bart., Sco., a female figure representing Hope, hair dishevelled, vested, az., trained, ar., supporting in dexter an anchor, and in sinister a Saracen's head, couped, all ppr. *Gardez bien. Pl.* 107, *cr.* 2.

MONTGOMERY, ROBERT-GEORGE, Esq., of Convoy House, co. Donegal, an arm, in armour, embowed, in hand a broken spear, head drooping, all ppr. *Patriæ infelici fidelis. Pl.* 44, *cr.* 9.

MONT HERMER, Eng., a griffin's head, between wings, ppr. *Pl.* 65, *cr.* 1.

MONT HERMER, DE, Eng., a gem-ring, or, stoned, vert. *Pl.* 35, *cr.* 3.

MONTLABY, a (demi)-fleur-de-lis, issuing. *Pl.* 68, *cr.* 12.

MONTMORENCY, DE, Viscount Mountmorres. *See* MOUNTMORRES.

MONTMORENCY, DE, Viscount Frankfort. *See* FRANKFORT.

MONTOLIEU, Lond., a fleur-de-lis, or between wings, erect, sa. *Pl.* 62, *cr.* 4, (fleur-de-lis, *pl.* 141.)

MONTON, Eng., a horse's head, or, maned, sa. *Pl.* 81, *cr.* 6.

MONTPENSTON, Wilts., three ostrich-feathers, two, ar., centre one, sa., turned over, or. *Pl.* 12, *cr.* 9.

MONTRESOR, Kent, a ducal helmet, ppr. *Pl.* 8, *cr.* 12.

MONTRESOR, HENRY-EDWARD, Esq., of Denne Hill, Kent, a royal helmet, or. *Mon Trésor. Pl.* 38, *cr.* 15.

MONTRIOU, Norf., a pheasant, ppr. *Pl.* 82, *cr.* 12, (without collar.)

MONTROSE, Duke, Marquess and Earl of, Marquess of Graham and Buchanan, Earl of Kincardine, Viscount Dundaff, Lord Graham, &c., Sco ; Earl and Baron Graham, U.K., (Graham,) an eagle, wings hovering, or, preying on a stork on its back, ppr. *Ne oubliez. Pl.* 17, *cr.* 8.

MONYNS, Walwarsher, Kent, an increscent, or. *Pl.* 122, *cr.* 15.

MONYPENNY, Sco., a dolphin, az., finned, gu. *Pl.* 48, *cr.* 9.

MONYPENNY, Kent and Sco., Neptune bestriding a dolphin, naiant, in the sea, in dexter, reins, in sinister his trident, all ppr. *Temperat æquor.*

MOODIE, Eng., a demi-pegasus, wings addorsed, body enfiled with a ducal coronet. *Pl.* 91, *cr.* 2.

MOODY, or MOODYE, Eng., two arms, embowed, in saltier, dexter vested, gu., sinister, vert, in each hand a cutlass, ar., hilt, or. *Pl.* 52, *cr.* 1.

MOODY, Sco., in lion's paw, a pennon, or, charged with a double-headed eagle, displayed, sa., and in an escroll above—*The reward of valour. Pl.* 7, *cr.* 7.

MOODY, or MOODYE, Wilts., a wolf's head, erased, ppr. *Pl.* 14, *cr.* 6.

MOODY, of Aspley, Beds., two falchions, in saltier, ppr., hilts and pommels, or, surmounted by a wolf's head, erased, per pale, ar. and az. *Pl.* 113, *cr.* 9, (head, *pl.* 96, *cr.* 11:)

MOONE, Eng., a bear, rampant, supporting a staff, in pale, ppr. *Pl.* 1, *cr.* 3.

MOOR, Berks., a griffin, sejant, regardant, or, winged, az., beaked and legged, gold. *Nihil utile quod non honestum. Pl.* 100, *cr.* 11, (regardant, *pl.* 4, *cr.* 9.)

MOOR, out of a ducal coronet, a moor's head, between two spears, points upward, in bend. *Pl.* 57, *cr.* 5, (coronet and spear, *same plate*.)

MOORE, Kent, a moor's head, in profile, ppr., wreathed about temples, or and sa., on neck, a crescent for difference. *Pl.* 36, *cr.* 3, (crescent, *pl.* 141.)

MOORE, Surr., a demi-bull, salient, erminois, attired, or. *Pl.* 63, *cr.* 6.

MOORE, Suff., a stag, passant, sa., platée, attired, or. *Pl.* 68, *cr.* 2.

MOORE, Berks., on a mount, vert, a moorcock, ppr. *Pl.* 10, *cr.* 1, (mount, *pl.* 98, *cr.* 13.)

MOORE, on a human heart, gu., an eagle's leg, erased at thigh, sa. *Pl.* 27, *cr.* 1.

MOORE, Eng., a demi-bull, erm., armed, or. *Pl.* 63, *cr.* 6.

MOORE, of Appleby, Parva, Leic., a moorcock, sa., guttée, or, wattles and legs, gu., (wings expanded, in beak a branch of heath, ppr.) *Non civium ardor. Pl.* 108, *cr.* 5.

MOORE, an eagle, preying on a rabbit, all ppr. *Pl.* 61, *cr.* 3.

MOORE, Iri., out of a ducal coronet, or, a moor's head, in profile, ppr., (wreathed, ar. and az.) *Fortis cadere, non cedere potest. Pl.* 120, *cr.* 3, (coronet, *same plate*.)

MOORE, Kent, out of a ducal coronet, or, a moor's head, ppr., (wreathed round the head, az. and or,) a jewel pendent in ears, ar. *Pl.* 120, *cr.* 3, (coronet, *same plate*.)

MOORE, Linc., a lion, passant, (gardant,) gu., ducally gorged and chained, ar. *Pl.* 121, *cr.* 4.

MOORE, Suff., a Cornish chough, ppr., guttée-d'or. *Pl.* 100, *cr.* 13.

MOORE, Surr., on a ducal coronet, an antelope, or. *Pl.*19, *cr.* 14, (antelope, *pl.* 63, *cr.* 10.)

MOORE, out of a ducal coronet, or, a moor's head and shoulders, in profile, sa., wreathed about head. *Pl.* 57, *cr.* 5, (coronet, *same plate*.)

MOORE, of Tara House, co. Meath, out of a ducal coronet, or, a moor's head, ppr., filletted round temples, az. and or, in the ear a jewel pendent, ar. *Durum patientiâ frango. Pl.* 120, *cr.* 3, (coronet, *same plate*.)

MOORE, a Cornish chough, rising, sa., in beak an ear of wheat, ppr. *Pl.* 6, *cr.* 11, (wheat, *pl.* 9, *cr.* 8.)

MOORE, a naked man, sa., holding a dart, or.

MOORE, a moor's head, couped at shoulders, ppr., wreathed about head, ar. *Pl. 63, cr. 3.*

MOORE, Kent, a moor's head, in profile, ppr., wreathed, or and sa., charged on neck with a crescent. *Pl. 36, cr. 3,* (crescent, *pl. 141.*)

MOORE, Devons., Hants, and Surr., out of a ducal coronet, az., a swan's neck, ar., beaked, gu. *Pl. 83, cr. 1.*

MOORE, Lond. and Herts., out of a demi-castle, ar., a demi-lion, rampant, gardant, or, holding a banner of the family arms, staff, sa.

MOORE, Lond. and Herts, out of a ducal coronet, gu., a demi-lion, rampant, gardant, or, holding a banner of the family arms, staff, sa.

MOORE, a moor's head, in profile, couped at shoulders, ppr., turban, ar. *Pl. 36, cr., 3.*

MOORE, Sir JOHN, (killed at Corunna,) a moor's head, couped at neck, turban, ppr. *Pl. 36, cr. 3.*

MOORE, Baron. *See* DROGHEDA, Marquess of.

MOORE, Earl of Mountcashel. *See* MOUNTCASHEL.

MOORE, a moor's head, affrontée, ppr., wreathed, a jewel pendent in ears, ar. *Pl. 97, cr. 2.*

MOORE, Westm., in front of bulrushes, ppr., a swan, wings elevated, ar., charged on breast with a pheon, sa. *Pl. 66, cr. 10,* (pheon, *pl. 141.*)

MOORE, STEPHEN, Esq., of Barn, co. Tipperary, a goshawk, seizing a coney, both ppr. *Vis unita fortior. Pl. 61, cr. 3.*

MOORES, Eng., an eagle, rising, ppr. *Juravi et adjuravi. Pl. 67, cr. 4.*

MOORHEAD, a negro's head, sa., banded, ar., *Pl. 48, cr. 7.*

MOORHOUSE, Yorks., a pelican, vulning, ppr. *Pl. 109, cr. 15.*

MOORMAN, Eng., in hand, (four) arrows, points downward. *Pl. 56, cr. 4.*

MOORSIDE, Eng., a tree, ppr. *Insiste firmater. Pl. 100, cr. 14.*

MOORSIDE, a demi-dragon, vert, in dexter, (an arrow, point downward, sa.) *Insiste firmater. Pl. 82, cr. 10.*

MOORSOM, on a mount, vert, a moorcock, in front, a banner, erect. *Ad astra.*

MOORTON, an eagle, preying on a hare, ppr. *Pl. 61, cr. 3.*

MOOTHAM, Eng., a cubit arm, in armour, in gauntlet the two ends of a broken spear. *Pl. 23, cr. 9.*

MORANT, Eng., out of a ducal coronet, a stag's head, cabossed. *Pl. 29, cr. 7.*

MORANT, Hants, a dove and olive branch. *Pl. 48, cr. 15.*

MORAR, Lond., a lion's head, erased, erm., collared, bendy, or and az. *Pl. 7, cr. 10.*

MORAY, of Abercairny, Sco., an earl's crown, surmounted of a star of twelve rays, ar. *Sans tache*—and—*Tanti talem genuere parentes.*

MORAY, Earl of, and Baron Doune, Sco.; Baron Stuart, U.K., (Stuart;) a pelican in nest, feeding her young, ppr. *Salus per Christum redemptorem. Pl. 44, cr. 3.*

MORBY, an eagle, displayed, or. *Pl. 48, cr. 11.*

MORCRAFT, Eng., out of a ducal coronet, gold, a bull's head, sa., attired, or. *Pl. 68, cr. 6.*

MORDANT, Viscount Mordant, Eng., a black's head, affrontée, couped at shoulders, sa., (vested, or,) banded round temples and tied, gu. and ar. *Pl. 97, cr. 2.*

MORDANT, Earl of Peterborough, same crest.

MORDANT, or MORDAUNT, Bart., of Massingham, Norf., out of an earl's coronet, or, the bust of a moorish prince, affrontée, couped below shoulders, ppr., vested, gold, wreathed about temples, ar. and sa. *Ferro comite. Pl. 80, cr. 11.*

MORDAUNT, Bart., Norf., a Saracen's head, in profile, ppr., wreathed, ar. and sa. *Pl. 36, cr. 3.*

MORDEN, Kent, a hawk, wings addorsed, ar., beaked, or, preying on a partridge, ppr. *Pl. 61, cr. 7.*

MORE, Sco., a black's head. *Major opima ferat. Pl. 120, cr. 3.*

MORE, Lond., Ess., Staffs., and Linc., a moor's head, ppr., wreathed, ar. and sa. *Pl. 36, cr. 3.*

MORE, Grantham, Linc., a lion, passant, regardant, gu., ducally gorged and chained, ar. *Pl. 121, cr. 4.*

MORE, Hants and Somers., a mermaid, ppr. *Pl. 48, cr. 5.*

MORE, Innernytie, an eye, eradicated, ppr. *Deus dedit. Pl. 68, cr. 15.*

MORE, Notts., on a moor's head, in profile, ppr., a chapeau, gu., turned up, erm. *Pl. 36, cr. 3,* (chapeau, *same plate, cr. 8.*)

MORE, Lond., a moorcock, ar., guttée-de-poix, beaked and legged, gu. *Pl. 10, cr. 1.*

MORE, of Linley, Salop, an eagle, ar., preying on a hare, sa. *Pl. 61, cr. 3.*

MORE, Wilts. and Somers., a tiger's head, erased, ar., pierced through neck by a broken spear, or, headed, of the first. *Pl. 94, cr. 10,* (spear, *pl. 79, cr. 9.*)

MORE, Suff., a wolf's head, erased, sa., gorged with a collar, dancettée, or. *Pl. 8, cr. 4.*

MORE, Yorks., a demi-moor, ppr., in both hands a sword, ar., hilt, or, reclining over sinister shoulder.

MORE, Yorks., a moor's head and shoulders, ppr., in ear a ring, or. *Pl. 120, cr. 3.*

MORE, Yorks., a moor's head, in profile, ppr., wreathed, or and sa., charged on neck with a crescent. *Pl. 36, cr. 3,* (crescent, *pl. 141.*)

MORE, on a tower, triple-towered, or, a moor's head, in profile, ppr. *Pl. 116, cr. 12,* (head, *pl. 120, cr. 3.*)

MORE, a moor's head, affrontée, sa. *Pl. 19, cr. 1.*

MORE, Lond., Beds., and Lanc., a moorcock, ar., wings expanded, guttée-de-poix, in beak an ear of wheat, or.

MORE, Devons., a naked arm, couped above elbow, ppr., in hand a sword, ar., hilt and pommel, or. *Pl. 21, cr. 4.*

MORE, Dors., a demi-lion, rampant, (gardant,) az., supporting a garb, vert, banded, gu. *Pl. 84, cr. 7.*

MORE, a dove, wings expanded, ppr. *Pl. 27, cr. 5.*

MORE, Lanc., a partridge, (wings expanded, in beak a stalk of wheat, all ppr.) *Comme je fus. Pl. 108, cr. 5.*

MOREAU, on a wreath, a coronet composed of fleurs-de-lis, or, therein a dexter arm, in armour, embowed, ppr., in hand a (scimitar,) ar., hilt and pommel, or. *Pl. 115, cr. 14,* (fleur-de-lis, *pl. 141.*)

MOREHEAD, Sco., two hands, conjoined, couped, supporting a sword, in pale. *Auxilio Dei. Pl. 75, cr. 8.*

MOREIDDIG, Wel., a boy's head, couped at shoulders, ppr., having a snake entwined about neck, vert. Another, crined, or.

MORELAND, Eng., a ship, in full sail, ppr. *Pl.* 109, *cr.* 8.

MORES, a demi-lion, rampant. *Deus nobis, quis contra. Pl.* 67, *cr.* 10.

MORES, Coxwell, Berks., a moor's head, erased, erminois, in profile, wreathed round temples, or and az. *Pl.* 36, *cr.* 3.

MORES-ROWE, Middx., a moor's head, ppr., wreathed, ar. and sa. "Ητοι τὸν λόγον ἄφετε ἢ καλῶς αὐτῳ πρόσστητε. *Either discard the word, or becomingly adhere to it. Pl.* 36, *cr.* 3.

MORET, a demi-griffin, gu., collared, or, supporting an anchor, az. *Pl.* 74, *cr.* 15.

MORETON, Chesh. and Suss., a wolf's head, (couped,) ar. *Pl.* 8, *cr.* 4.

MORETON, a cock's head, or, wings expanded, az., collared with a fess, cottised, gu., combed, of the last, in bill a trefoil, slipped, of the third. *Pl.* 47, *cr.* 3, (trefoil, *pl.* 55, *cr.* 12.)

MORETON, or MORTON, a demi-moorcock, displayed, sa., combed and wattled, gu. *Perseverando. Pl.* 90, *cr.* 13.

MORETON, Chesh., a greyhound's head, couped, collared, (with a twisted wreath, vert.) *Pl.* 43, *cr.* 11.

MORETON, Baron Ducie. *See* DUCIE.

MOREWOOD, Derbs., two arms., in armour, embowed, ppr., holding a chaplet, or. *Pl.* 10, *cr.* 9, (chaplet, *pl.* 54, *cr.* 10.)

MOREWOOD, Alfreton Hall, Derbs.: 1. On a torse, ar. and vert, two arms, in armour, embowed, ppr., supporting a chaplet of oak branches, of the second, fructed, or. *Pl.* 10, *cr.* 9, (oak, *pl.* 74, *cr.* 7.) 2. For *Palmer,* a greyhound, sejant, sa., (collared.) *Pl.* 66, *cr.* 15.

MORFYN, a blackamoor's head, couped at shoulders, vested, paly of six, erm., and ermines, pendents in ears, or, wreathed about temples, bat's wings to his head, sa., expanded. *Pl.* 115, *cr.* 11.

MORGAN, Eng., a reindeer's head, cabossed, ar. *Pl.* 114, *cr.* 7.

MORGAN, Lond., in dexter hand, ppr., a swan's head and neck, erased, ar. *Pl.* 29, *cr.* 4.

MORGAN, of Golden Grove, Flints., Wel.: 1. A Saxon's head, ppr. *Pl.* 81, *cr.* 15. 2. A Cornish chough, ppr. *Hheb Dhaw hheb dhim a Dhuw digon. Pl.* 100, *cr.* 13.

MORGAN, a savage's head, affrontée, wreathed. *Pl.* 97, *cr.* 2.

MORGAN, Eng., a reindeer's head, or. *Pl.* 2, *cr.* 13.

MORGAN, on a mount, an oak-tree, fructed, or, against it a wolf, ppr. *Pl.* 58, *cr.* 10.

MORGAN, Wel., a reindeer's head, or, attired, gu., (another, sa., attired, or.) *Pl.* 2, *cr.* 13.

MORGAN, an eagle's head, erased. *Pl.* 20, *cr.* 7.

MORGAN, a griffin, segreant. *Pl.* 67, *cr.* 13.

MORGAN, Wel., a reindeer's head, cabossed, or. *Pl.* 114, *cr.* 7.

MORGAN, Dors., a griffin's head, erased, or, (charged with two bends, sa.) *Pl.* 48, *cr.* 6.

MORGAN, out of a ducal coronet, two eagles' heads, addorsed, all or. *Pl.* 118, *cr.* 12, (coronet, *same plate.*)

MORGAN, Durh., out of a ducal coronet, a demi-eagle, displayed, with two heads. *Pl.* 4, *cr.* 6, (coronet, *pl.* 128, *fig.* 3.)

MORGAN, Ess. and Wel., a demi-eagle, displayed, or, (charged on body with a fess, wavy, sa.) *Pl.* 22, *cr.* 11.

MORGAN, Ess., a lion, rampant, sa. *Pl.* 67, *cr.* 5.

MORGAN, Norf., a reindeer's head, sa., attired, or, charged on neck with a mullet. *Pl.* 2, *cr.* 13, (mullet, *pl.* 141.)

MORGAN, Somers., a demi-griffin, segreant, (erased,) sa. *Pl.* 18, *cr.* 6.

MORGAN, Devons., Dors., and Worc., an heraldic-tiger, sejant, sa., crined and tufted, or, in dexter a battle-axe, in pale. *Pl.* 111, *cr.* 7, (axe, *pl.* 44, *cr.* 3.)

MORGAN, GOULD, Bart., Monm.: 1. For *Morgan,* a reindeer's head, (couped,) or, attired, gu. *Pl.* 2, *cr.* 13. 2. For *Gould,* an eagle, rising, ppr., (in beak a pine-cone.) *Pl.* 67, *cr.* 4.

MORGAN, Biddlesdon Park, Bucks., a demi-lion, rampant, regardant, ar. *Pl.* 33, *cr.* 2.

MORGAN, Suss., (on a fer-de-moline, in fess,) a griffin's head, erased, ppr. *Pl.* 48, *cr.* 6.

MORHAM, Eng., a talbot's head, erased, sa. *Pl.* 90, *cr.* 6.

MORIARTY, Iri., an eagle, wings addorsed, ppr. *Pl.* 61, *cr.* 1.

MORIARTY, Eng., on a ducal coronet, a griffin, sejant, supporting an escutcheon, gu. *Pl.* 42, *cr.* 8.

MORICE, Eng., in lion's gamb, a crescent. *Pl.* 91, *cr.* 1.

MORIER, a greyhound's head, ppr., between two roses, slipped and leaved. *Pl.* 84, *cr.* 13.

MORING, a greyhound, statant. *Pl.* 104, *cr.* 1, (without chapeau.)

MORIS, Suff., a talbot, gu., collared and lined, or. *Pl.* 65, *cr.* 2.

MORISKINES, Eng., a stork, or, legged and beaked, sa. *Pl.* 33, *cr.* 9.

MORISON, or MORRISON, three moors' heads, conjoined in one neck, ppr., the faces looking to the chief, dexter, and sinister. *Pretio prudentia præstat. Pl.* 32, *cr.* 2.

MORISON, MORRISON, or MORRYSON, Eng., a pegasus, or. *Pl.* 28, *cr.* 9.

MORISON, Herts., Linc., and Lanc., out of a ducal coronet, or, an eagle's head, between wings, ar. *Pl.* 66, *cr.* 5.

MORJARTY, Iri., an arm, in (armour,) embowed, in hand a dagger, blade entwined by a serpent. *Pl.* 116, *cr.* 11.

MORLAND, Eng., an arm, couped and embowed, in hand three stalks of wheat, ppr. *Pl.* 89, *cr.* 4.

MORLAND, a camel's head, erased, (charged with three bars, wavy.) *Pl.* 120, *cr.* 12, (without gorging.)

MORLAND, WILLIAM-COURTNEY, Esq., of The Court Lodge, Lamberhurst, Kent, a falcon, ppr., belled, or. *Pl.* 67, *cr.* 3.

MORLAND, Kent, a leopard's head, jessant-de-lis, or, between wings, erm. *Pl.* 123, *cr.* 9, (wings, *pl.* 1, *cr.* 15.)

MORLAND, a griffin's head, wings (addorsed,) az., semée of fleurs-de-lis and cross crosslets, or. *Pl.* 65, *cr.* 1, (charging, *pl.* 141.)

MORLAND, a dove and olive-branch, ppr. *Pl.* 48, *cr.* 15.

MORLAND, a tiger's head, jessant-de-lis, between wings. *Pl.* 123, *cr.* 9, (wings, *pl.* 1, *cr.* 15.)

MORLAND-BERNARD, Bart., Linc.: 1. For *Morland,* a griffin's head, wings addorsed, az., semée of cross crosslets and fleurs-de-lis, alternately, or. *Pl.* 65, *cr.* 1, (charging, *pl.* 141.) 2. For *Bernard*, a demi-bear, sa., muzzled and (collared, or.) *Bear and forbear. Pl.* 104, *cr.* 10.

MORLEIGH, Lanc., a unicorn's head, erased, or. *Pl.* 67, *cr.* 1.

MORLEY, Eng., a demi-griffin, wings (expanded.) *Pl.* 18, *cr.* 6.

MORLEY, Norwich, a wolf, sejant, sa., maned, tufted, (collared, and lined, or.) *Pl.* 110, *cr.* 4.

MORLEY, Suss., out of a ducal coronet, a griffin's head, between wings, all ar. *Pl.* 97, *cr.* 13.

MORLEY, Suss., a man, in armour, ppr., garnished, or, in dexter a baton, gold, across his body a sash, of the last. *Pl.* 60, *cr.* 2.

MORLEY, Hants., Herts., Suss., and Yorks., on a chapeau, gu., turned up, erm., a leopard's head, ar., jessant-de-lis, or. *Pl.* 123, *cr.* 9, (chapeau, *same plate, cr.* 6.)

MORLEY, out of a mural coronet, a griffin's head, between wing. *Pl.* 65, *cr.* 1, (coronet, *pl.* 128, *fig.* 18.)

MORLEY, a talbot, passant, (regardant,) ermines, collared, or. *Pl.* 65, *cr.* 2.

MORLEY, Earl of, Viscount and Baron Boringdon, (Parker,) an arm, erect, vested, az., slashed, and cuffed, ar., in hand the attire of a stag, gu. *Fideli certa merces. Pl.* 5, *cr.* 3.

MORLEY, out of a ducal coronet, a demi-talbot, or. *Pl.* 99, *cr.* 7, (talbot, *pl.* 97, *cr.* 9.)

MORLEY, FRANCIS, Esq., of Marrick Park, Yorks., out of a ducal coronet, a griffin's head, between wings, all ar. *S'ils te mordent, mord les. Pl.* 97, *cr.* 13.

MORNELL, out of a mural coronet, az., a dragon's head, vomiting flames, ppr. *Pl.* 101, *cr.* 4, (flames, *pl.* 37, *cr.* 9.)

MOROW, out of a ducal coronet, an eagle's head, between wings. *Pl.* 66, *cr.* 5.

MORPHEW, Eng., a crane, ppr. *Pl.* 111, *cr.* 9.

MORRALL, Salop: 1. A demi-griffin. *Pl.* 18, *cr.* 6. 2. A boar's head, erased, ducally gorged. *Norma tuta veritas. Pl.* 36, *cr.* 9.

MORRAL, EDWARD, Esq., of Plâs Yolyn, Salop, a demi-griffin. *Norma tuta veritas. Pl.* 18, *cr.* 6.

MORRELL, Eng., the horns of a bull, fixed to scalp, ppr. *Pl.* 9, *cr.* 15.

MORRELL, a harpy, ar., crined, or. *Pl.* 126, *cr.* 11.

MORRES, Eng., a demi-lion, rampant, ppr. *Deus nobiscum quis contra nos. Pl.* 67, *cr.* 10.

MORRES, Iri., a demi-lion, rampant, erminois. *Pl.* 67, *cr.* 10.

MORRES, a cock, entwined by a serpent. *Pl.* 18, *cr.* 5.

MORRICE, or MORRIS, Eng., a lion, rampant, or, charged on shoulder with a cross, gu. *Pl.* 67, *cr.* 5, (cross, *pl.* 141.)

MORRICE, Kent, on a rest, a falcon, ppr., beaked and belled, or. *Pl.* 10, *cr.* 7.

MORRICE, a lion, rampant, regardant, *Pl.* 10, *cr.* 15, (without brand.)

MORRICE, a hawk, ppr., belled and jessed, or. *Pl.* 67, *cr.* 3.

MORRICE, Lond., a lion, rampant, or, collared, gu., holding a pellet. *Pl.* 88, *cr.* 1, (pellet, *pl.* 141.)

MORRICE, or MORICE, Ess., a cock, gu., beaked, combed, and wattled, or, environed round neck by a snake, ppr. *Pl.* 67, *cr.* 14, (snake, *pl.* 53, *cr.* 14.)

MORRIS, Coxwell, Berks., a moor's head, (erased, erminois,) in profile, wreathed, ar. and az. *Pl.* 36, *cr.* 3.

MORRIS, Iri., a lion's head, ar., guttée-de-sang, *Pl.* 126, *cr.* 1.

MORRIS, a stag, passant, ppr. *Pl.* 68, *cr.* 2.

MORRIS, a lion, rampant. *Pl.* 67, *cr.* 5.

MORRIS, a fox's head, couped, ppr. *Pl.* 91, *cr.* 9.

MORRIS, a demi-lion, rampant, or, supporting a plate. *Pl.* 126, *cr.* 12.

MORRIS, a tower in flames, ppr. *Pl.* 118, *cr.* 15.

MORRIS, a castle, domed, ar. *Pl.* 42, *cr.* 10.

MORRIS, a cock, with a serpent enwrapped round body, the head in beak. *Pl.* 67, *cr.* 14, (serpent, *pl.* 53, *cr.* 12.)

MORRIS, Glouc., a demi-lion, rampant, or, charged on shoulder with a cross-fleury, sa., in paws an ear of wheat, ppr. *Pl.* 47, *cr.* 4, (cross, *pl.* 141 ; wheat, *pl.* 85, *cr.* 6.)

MORRIS, a tower, or, inflamed, gu. *Pl.* 118, *cr.* 15,

MORRIS, Ess., a lion, rampant, sa., bezantée, ducally gorged, or. *Pl.* 67, *cr.* 5, (gorging, *same plate.*)

MORRIS, Bart., Glams., a lion, rampant, or, charged on shoulder with a cross, couped, gu., within a chain in the form of an arch, gold. *Scuto fidei. Pl.* 67, *cr.* 5, (chain, *pl.* 28, *cr.* 12; cross, *pl.* 141.)

MORRIS, Yorks., a lion, rampant, regardant, or. *Marte et mare faventibus—Irrupta copula—*and—*Spectemur agendo. Pl.* 10, *cr.* 15, (without brand.)

MORRIS, PHILIP, Esq., of The Hurst, Salop, an eagle, displayed, sa. *Pl.* 48, *cr.* 11.

MORRISON, three men's faces conjoined in one neck, one affrontée, the others facing the dexter and sinister. *Pl.* 95, *cr.* 5.

MORRISON, Iri., an oak branch, fructed, ppr. *Pl.* 32, *cr.* 18.

MORRISON, Eng., a cubit arm, in armour, in hand a branch of oak, ppr. *Pl.* 55, *cr.* 6, (oak, *pl.* 32, *cr.* 13.)

MORRISON, Eng., a pegasus. *Pl.* 28, *cr.* 9.

MORRISON, two arms, dexter and sinister, in fess, couped, holding a two-handed sword, in pale. *Pl.* 75, *cr.* 8.

MORRISON, Lanc., on a ducal coronet, ppr., an eagle's head and neck, between wings, ar. *Pl.* 97, *cr.* 13.

MORRITT, or MORRIT, Eng., a griffin's head, erased, ppr., in beak a rose, gu., barbed and slipped, vert. *Pl.* 9, *cr.* 12, (rose, *pl.* 117, *cr.* 10.)

MORSE, Eng., a lion, rampant, supporting a plumb rule. *Pl.* 50, *cr.* 8.

MORSE, two battle-axes, in saltier, banded with a chaplet of roses, ppr. *Pl.* 52, *cr.* 10, (chaplet, *pl.* 20, *cr.* 11.)

MORSE, a battle-axe, erect. *Pl.* 14, *cr.* 8.

MORSHEAD, Cornw., a demi-griffin, regardant, (between feet an escutcheon, ar.) *Pl.* 125, *cr.* 12.

MORSHEAD, Bart., Cornw., a demi-wyvern, rampant, regardant, vert., collared, or, supporting an escutcheon, az., charged with a bezant. *Pl.* 46, *cr.* 1, (escutcheon, *pl.* 19, *cr.* 2.

MORSON, Lond., a lion's head, erased, per fess, erm. and gu. *Pl.* 81, *cr.* 4.

Morson, Lond., a lion's head, erased, per fess, erm. and gu., a pale, counterchanged. Pl. 81, cr. 4.

Mort, Astley, Lanc., a phœnix in flames, ppr. Pl. 44, cr. 8.

Mortimer, Eng., a rose, per pale, ar. and gu. Pl. 20, cr. 2.

Mortimer, Lond., a torteau, gu., between wings, or. Pl. 2, cr. 3.

Mortimer, Sco., a bull's head, cabossed, sa. *Acquirit qui tuetur.* Pl. 111, cr. 6.

Mortimer, Eng., in a ducal coronet, or, a pyramid of leaves, az. Pl. 61, cr. 13, (coronet, *pl.* 128, *fig.* 3.)

Mortimer, Eng., a buck's head, quarterly, or and gu., attired, or. Pl. 91, cr. 14.

Mortimer, Sco., a buck's head, cabossed, sa. *Acquirit qui tuetur.* Pl. 36, cr. 1.

Mortimer, Lond., a buck's head, erased, quarterly, or and gu. *Press forward.* Pl. 66, cr. 9.

Mortimore, on a chapeau, gu., turned up, erm., a stag's head. Pl. 108, cr. 14.

Mortinius, a sword, in pale, enfiled with a ducal coronet, all between two elephants' proboscies. Pl. 96, cr. 1, (sword and coronet, same plate.)

Mortlake, Surr., a lion, sejant, or, in dexter a cross pattée, fitched, az., on it a scroll with motto, *Hic labor;* resting sinister on a cone, ar., and on that another scroll, with *Hic opus,* Pl. 56, cr. 12

Mortlock, Eng., a lion's head, erased, sa. Pl. 81, cr. 4.

Mortoffe, and Mortoft, Norf., a stag's head, erased, sa., nose, ar., attired, or, gorged with a ducal coronet, of the second. Pl. 66, cr. 9, (coronet, same plate.)

Morton, Sco., a lion's paw, erect, sa. *A te, pro te.* Pl. 126, cr. 9.

Morton, Erbeck, Herts., an eagle, wings expanded, erm. Pl. 126, cr. 7.

Morton, Salop, Leic., and Staffs., a cock's head, or, between wings, az. Pl. 47, cr. 3, (without cross.)

Morton, Leic., same crest. *Perseverando.*

Morton, Chesh., a greyhound's head, ar., collared, vert, rimmed, of the first. Pl. 43, cr. 11.

Morton, a wolf's head, ar. Pl. 14, cr. 6.

Morton, Sco., an oak-tree, ppr. *Virtutis præmium.* Pl. 16, cr. 8.

Morton, Surr., Dors., and Kent, a goat's head, ar., attired, or. Pl. 105, cr. 14.

Morton, De, Eng., a griffin, segreant, sa. Pl. 67, cr. 13.

Morton, Sco., a tree, truncated, leaves sprouting therefrom, ppr. Pl. 92, cr. 8.

Morton, Earl of, Lord Dalkeith, Aberdour, and Douglas, Sco., (Douglas;) a wild boar, ppr., sticking between two clefts of an oaktree, a chain and lock holding the clefts together. *Lock sicker.* Pl. 57, cr. 12.

Mortymer, Norf., a buck's head, erased, quarterly, or and gu. Pl. 66, cr. 9.

Mortymer, Wilts. and Worc., a rose, per pale, ar. and gu. Pl. 20, cr. 2.

Morvile, a cat's head, affrontée, gu. Pl. 97, cr. 7.

Morwell, a demi-griffin. Pl. 18, cr. 6.

Moselay, Walter, Esq. of Buildwas, Salop, an eagle, displayed, erm. *Honorate, diligite, timete.* Pl. 48, cr. 11.

Moseley, Eng., an eagle, displayed, sa. Pl. 48, cr. 11.

Moseley, or Mosley, Eng., an eagle, displayed, erm. Pl. 48, cr. 11.

Moseley, or Mosley, Lond. and Staffs., out of a mural coronet, chequy, ar. and sa., a demi-lion, (in dexter a mill-pick, of the first.) Pl. 120, cr. 14.

Moses, Eng., a cock, regardant, ppr. Pl. 19, cr. 10.

Mosley, Lanc., Northumb., and Derbs., an eagle, displayed, erm. *Mos legem regit.* Pl. 48, cr. 11.

Mosman, of Aughtefardle, a hand, couped at wrist, erect, holding a closed book. Pl. 45, cr. 3.

Moss, T. Edwards, Esq., Roby Hall, Prescot, a rock, ppr., therefrom rising a dove, ar., holding in beak an olive branch, and surmounted by a rainbow, also ppr. *Peace with power.* Pl. 126 D, cr. 14.

Moss, or Mosse, out of a mural coronet, or, a griffin's head, erm., charged on neck with a bezant. Pl. 97, cr. 13.

Moss, a demi-sea-horse, ppr., (collared, vair, resting sinister on an escutcheon, ar., charged with a pine-apple, ppr.) *Non nobis solum.* Pl. 58, cr. 15.

Mossey, Lond., an eagle, displayed, erm. Pl. 48, cr. 11.

Mossman, Sco., a hand, couped at wrist, erect, holding a book. *Me meliora manent.* Pl. 45, cr. 3.

Moston, Eng., a lion's head, gu. Pl. 126, cr. 1.

Mostyn, Eng. and Wel., a lion, rampant, or. Pl. 67, cr. 5.

Mostyn, Wel., a lion, rampant, or. *Auxilium meum a Domino.* Pl. 67, cr. 5.

Mostyn, Baron, and a Bart., (Lloyd,) a stag, trippant, ppr. *Heb Dduw heb ddym, Dduw a dygon.* Pl. 68, cr. 2.

Motham, Suff., (on a mount, vert,) a talbot, couchant, erm. Pl. 32, cr. 7.

Motherwell, Sco., a crescent, or. Pl. 18, cr. 14.

Mott, Suff. and Ess., an etoile of eight points, ar. Pl. 83, cr. 3, (without coronet.)

Mott, a griffin's head, erased, between two fleurs-de-lis. Pl. 108, cr. 15.

Mottershed, stump of tree, ppr., with a branch sprouting, vert. Pl. 92, cr. 8.

Motteux, Norf., a lion, passant, gardant, gu., ducally crowned. *Quid vult valde vult.* Pl. 105, cr. 5, (without chapeau.)

Motton, Eng., a stag, statant, wounded by an arrow. Pl. 88, cr. 9.

Mouat, Eng., a lion, passant, gardant. Pl. 120, cr. 5.

Moubray, and Mubray, Sco., a demi-lion, rampant, gu. *Fortitudine.* Pl. 67, cr. 10.

Moubray, Sco., a heron's head and neck, issuing. *Let the dead shaw.* Pl. 32, cr. 5.

Moubray, or Mowbray, a falcon, rising, belled, *Sola nobilitat virtus.* Pl. 105, cr. 4.

Moubray, Sco., a man's head, affrontée. *Audentes fortuna javat.* Pl. 19, cr. 1.

Moubray, Knt. of Cockairny, Sco., a demi-lion, rampant, crowned. *Fortitudine.* Pl. 61, cr. 4, (without branch.)

Moul, or Moule, Eng., a lion, rampant, supporting a broad arrow, point downward, ppr. Pl. 22, cr. 15.

Mould, Eng., a demi-lion, rampant, gardant, or. Pl. 35, cr. 4.

Moulden, Kent, a griffin's head, erased. Pl. 48, cr. 6.

MOULE, Beds., out of clouds, ppr., a cubit arm, vested, gu., cuffed, ar., hand open and erect. *Pl.* 22, *cr.* 6, (hand, *pl.* 32, *cr.* 14.)

MOULSON, an elephant, ar., lifting with its proboscis a branch of laurel, ppr. *Pl.* 56, *cr.* 14, (laurel, *pl.* 123, *cr.* 5.)

MOULSON, a lion's head, erased, per pale, embattled, or and sa. *Pl.* 81, *cr.* 4.

MOULT, Eng., a fish, naiant, az., spotted, or. *Pl.* 85, *cr.* 7.

MOULT, Notts., on a mound, or, a pelican, ar., wings expanded, beaked and legged, sa., vulning, gu. *Pl.* 109, *cr.* 15, (mound, *pl.* 37, *cr.* 3.)

MOULTON, a shark's head, regardant, issuing, swallowing a blackamoor. *Pl.* 16, *cr.* 6.

MOULTON, a griffin, segreant, (regardant.) *Pl.* 67, *cr.* 13.

MOULTON, Devons., a cubit arm, erect, vested, gu., cuffed, erm., in hand, ppr., a chaplet of roses, of the first, leaved, vert. *Pl.* 44, *cr.* 13, (roses, *pl.* 41, *cr.* 7.)

MOULTON, Kent, Lond., Yorks., and Glouc., on a pellet, a falcon, rising, ar. *Pl.* 105, *cr.* 4, (pellet, *pl.* 141.)

MOULTON, Lond., a griffin, passant, per pale, gu. and az., resting dexter on a mullet, or. *Pl.* 39, *cr.* 8, (mullet, *pl.* 141.)

MOULTRIE, Sco., a mermaid, ppr. *Nunquam non fidelis. Pl.* 48, *cr.* 5.

MOULTRIE, GEORGE-AUSTIN, Esq., of Aston Hall, Salop, same crest and motto.

MOULTRIE, a mermaid, ppr. *Pl.* 48, *cr.* 5.

MOUNEHENSE, Eng., out of a ducal coronet, a phœnix in flames. *Pl.* 53, *cr.* 6.

MOUNSEY, Eng., an arm, in armour, in hand a sword. *Pl.* 2, *cr.* 8.

MOUNSEY, Castletown, Cumb., a demi-griffin, (wreathed round neck with oak, bearing with three claws a banner, erect.) *Pl.* 18, *cr.* 6.

MOUNSHER, Eng., a man's head, in profile, ppr. *Pl.* 81, *cr.* 15.

MOUNT, Eng., a demi-man, in armour, brandishing a scimitar, ppr. *Pl.* 27, *cr.* 11.

MOUNT, Kent, a fox, salient, supporting the trunk of a tree, raguled, ppr.

MOUNTAIGNE, a crane's head, or, out of (flames,) ppr. *Pl.* 116, *cr.* 13.

MOUNTAIN, Herts., a demi-lion, rampant, gardant, per fess, wavy, ar. and sa., between paws an escallop, gu., on breast a cross crosslet, fitched, of the second. *In cruce salus. Pl.* 35, *cr.* 4, (escallop and cross, *pl.* 141.)

MOUNTAINE, Middx., a stork's head, out of rays, or. *Pl.* 116, *cr.* 13, (head, *pl.* 32, *cr.* 5.)

MOUNTANEY, a wolf, sejant, (collared and lined, the line reflexed over back, ending with a ring.) *Pl.* 110, *cr.* 4.

MOUNTCASHELL, Earl of and Viscount, and Baron Kilworth, Iri., (Moore,) a goshawk seizing a cony, both ppr. *Vis unita fortior. Pl.* 61, *cr.* 3.

MOUNTCHANSEY, Eng., in hand a scimitar, in pale, ppr. *Pl.* 66, *cr.* 6.

MOUNT-EDGCUME, Earl of, Viscount Mount Edgecumbe and Valletort, and Baron Edgecumb, (Edgecumb,) a boar, passant, ar., gorged with a chaplet of oak-leaves, fructed ppr. *Au playsire fort de Dieu. Pl.* 29, *cr.* 10.

MOUNTFORD, Sco., a talbot's head. *Pl.* 123, *cr.* 15.

MOUNTFORD, and MOUNTFORT, Norf., a fleur-de-lis, gu. *Pl.* 68, *cr.* 12.

MOUNTFORD, Radwinter, Staffs. and Warw., a lion's head, couped, az. *Pl.* 126, *cr.* 1.

MOUNTFORD, Yorks., a talbot's head, sa., ducally gorged and eared, or. *Pl.* 68, *cr.* 12.

MOUNTJOY, Eng., a demi-sportsman firing his piece, ppr. *Pl.* 51, *cr.* 6.

MOUNTMORRES, Viscount, and Baron, and a Baronet, Iri., (De Montmorency ;) a peacock, in pride, ppr. *Dieu ayde. Pl.* 92, *cr.* 11.

MOUNTMORRIS, Earl of, and Baron, Viscount Valentia, Baron Altham, and a Bart., Iri., (Annesley;) a moor's head, in profile, couped, ppr., wreathed, ar. and az. *Virtutis amore. Pl.* 36, *cr.* 3.

MOUNTNEY, Norf., Ess., and Leic., a wolf, sejant, ar., (collared and lined, gu.) *Pl.* 110, *cr.* 4.

MOUNTNEY, Leic., a greyhound, sejant, collared, and lined. *Pl.* 66, *cr.* 15.

MOUNT-SANDFORD, Baron, Iri., (Sandford ;) out of a ducal coronet, gu., a boar's head and neck, or. *Cor unum, via una. Pl.* 102, *cr.* 14.

MOUNTSTEPHEN, Northamp. and Devons., a demi-griffin, salient, wings addorsed, sa. *Pl.* 18, *cr.* 6.

MOUNTSTEVEN, Devons. and Northamp., a demi-griffin, salient, wings addorsed, sa., armed, or. *Pl.* 18, *cr.* 6.

MOUSELL, a wolf, salient, sa. *Mos legem regit. Pl.* 126, *cr.* 13.

MOUTHWEY, Eng., a Doric pillar, entwined with ivy, on top a flame of fire, all ppr. *Pl.* 14, *cr.* 15, (flame, *pl.* 16, *cr.* 12.)

MOUTRIE, Sco., a talbot's head, ar. *Nunquam non fidelis. Pl.* 123, *cr.* 15.

MOUTRY, Sco., a mermaid, ppr. *Nunquam non fidelis. Pl.* 48, *cr.* 5.

Mow, Sco., a phœnix in flames, ppr. *Post funera fœnus. Pl.* 44, *cr.* 8.

MOWAT, Sco., an oak tree growing out of a mount, ppr. *Monte alto. Pl.* 48, *cr.* 4.

MOWATT, Eng., a demi-lion, or. *Pl.* 67, *cr.* 10.

MOWBRAY, DE, Eng., in hand a scimitar. *Pl.* 29, *cr.* 8.

MOWBRAY, DE, Eng., a fox, current, ppr. *Pl.* 80, *cr.* 5.

MOWBRAY, Sco., a female's head, affrontée, issuing, ppr. *Audentes fortuna juvat. Pl.* 45, *cr.* 5.

MOWBRAY, a dexter naked arm, erect, in hand a saw.

MOWBRAY, on a chapeau, gu., lined, erm., a lion, passant, ar., between the attires of a stag, or. *Pl.* 107, *cr.* 1, (attires, *pl.* 118, *cr.* 11.)

MOWBRAY, on a chapeau, gu., turned up, ar., a lion, passant, of the last, between the attires of a stag, or. *Ib.*

MOWBRAY, an oak-tree, ppr., pendent therefrom a shield, gu., (charged with a lion's head, erased.) *Suo stat robore virtus. Pl.* 75, *cr.* 2.

MOWBRAY, Northumb., a mulberry-tree, or. *Pl.* 105, *cr.* 13.

MOWER, Eng., a dove and olive-branch, ppr. *Pl.* 48, *cr.* 15.

MOWLES, out of a ducal coronet, a demi-savage, ppr. *Pl.* 14, *cr.* 11, (coronet, *pl.* 128, *fig.* 3.)

MOWNE, two arms, in armour, embowed, ppr., supporting a ball, sa. *Pl.* 6, *cr.* 8.

MOXON, Eng., a demi-eagle, displayed, az. *Pl.* 22, *cr.* 11.

MOYES, Canons, Surr., a dove, ar., in mouth a (laurel)-sprig, vert. *Pl.* 48, *cr.* 15.

MOYLE, two demi-dragons, addorsed, their necks, entwined round each other, one gu., the other, or.

MOYLE, a wyvern, wings (expanded, gu.,) platée. *Pl.* 63, *cr.* 13, (plate, *pl.* 141.)

MOYLE, Cornw., two demi-dragons, sans wings, the sinister, ar., the dexter, gu., addorsed, and necks interweven.

MOYNE, Somers., out of a ducal coronet, a tiger's head. *Pl.* 36, *cr.* 15.

MOYNES, Eng., a lion, rampant, in dexter a battle-axe. *Pl.* 64, *cr.* 2, (axe, *pl.* 109, *cr.* 7.)

MOYNLEY, Eng., a hind's head, couped. *Pl.* 21, *cr.* 9.

MOYSE, Eng., a leopard, rampant, ppr. *Pl.* 73, *cr.* 2.

MOYSEY, Somers., a dragon's head, vert, charged on neck with a cross-flory, or. *Pl.* 87, *cr.* 12, (cross, *pl.* 141.)

MUCHELL, a camel's head, ducally gorged. *Pl.* 120, *cr.* 12.

MUCKLE, Sco., a lion, passant, gu. *Pl.* 48, *cr.* 8.

MUCKLESTON, Salop, a greyhound's head (erased,) ppr., collared, gu. *Pl.* 43, *cr.* 11.

MUCKLEWAITE, a griffin's head, erased, ppr. *Pl.* 48, *cr.* 6.

MUDGE, a pheon, ar. *Pl.* 26, *cr.* 12.

MUDGE, LACHARY, Esq., of Sidney, Devons., a cockatrice. *All's well.* *Pl.* 63, *cr.* 15.

MUDIE, Sco., a pheon, ar. *Defensio non offensio.* *Pl.* 26, *cr.* 12.

MUDIE, JOHN, Esq., of Pitmuies, Forfars., same crest and motto.

MUDIE, Eng., a ship in full sail, or. *Pl.* 109, *cr.* 8.

MUILMAN, Ess. and Lond., a mullet of six points, or, between wings, ar. *Pl.* 1, *cr.* 15.

MUIR, Sco., a moor's head, in profile, couped at neck, ppr. *Duris non frangor.* *Pl.* 81, *cr.* 15.

MUIR, of Riccarton, Bart., a savage's head, from shoulders, in profile, wreathed about temples with laurel, ppr. *Duris non frangor.* *Pl.* 118, *cr.* 7.

MUIR, Sco., a savage's head, couped, ppr. *Durum patientiâ frango.* *Pl.* 81, *cr.* 15.

MUIRE, or MURE, Sco., in dexter hand a sword, all ppr. *Help at hand, brother.* *Pl.* 21, *cr.* 10.

MUIRHEAD, of Lauchop, two hands supporting a sword, in pale, ppr. *Auxilio Dei.* *Pl.* 59, *cr.* 10.

MUIRHEAD, Sco., two hands issuing, grasping a broadsword, in pale, all ppr. *Auxilio Dei.* *Pl.* 3, *cr.* 5.

MUIRSIDE, Eng., an oak-tree, ppr. *Insiste firmiter.* *Pl.* 16, *cr.* 8.

MULBERY, and MULBURY, Eng., a lion, passant, sa., holding a crescent, or. *Pl.* 77, *cr.* 3.

MULCASTER, Kent, a lion, rampant, erminois, in fore-dexter a (sword,) erect, hind-dexter resting on a bomb, fired, ppr. *Pl.* 64, *cr.* 2, (bomb, *pl.* 70, *cr.* 12.)

MULCASTER, Surr. and Cumb., a lion, rampant, az., (ducally gorged, or, holding a sword, erect, ar., hilt and pommel, gold, point embrued, gu.) *Pl.* 88, *cr.* 1.

MULES, Devons. and Somers., a mule, ppr.

MULGRAVE, Earl of and Baron, and Viscount Normanby, U.K., Baron Mulgrave, Iri., (Phipps,) in lion's gamb, erect, sa., a trefoil, slipped, ar. *Virtute quies.* *Pl.* 60, *cr.* 14, (trefoil, *pl.* 141.)

MULHOLLAND, ANDREW, Esq., of Springvale, co. Down, an escallop, gu. *Semper præcinctus.* *Pl.* 117, *cr.* 4.

MULLADY, Iri., on a ducal coronet, or, a greyhound, current, sa. *Pl.* 47, *cr.* 2, (coronet, same plate.)

MULLER, Eng., a swan, ppr. *Pl.* 122, *cr.* 13, (without mount.)

MULLINS, Baron Ventry. *See* VENTRY.

MULLOY, Iri., a greyhound, (gorged with a collar,) running by an oak-tree, all ppr. *Malo mori quam fœdari.* *Pl.* 27, *cr.* 2.

MULSHO, or MULSHOE, Bucks., a griffin, sejant, wings addorsed, gu., armed, or. *Pl.* 100, *cr.* 11.

MULTON, Eng., a savage's head, couped, wreathed with laurel, ppr. *Pl.* 118, *cr.* 7.

MULTRAIN, Iri., a griffin, segreant, gu., in sinister, a sword, in pale. *Pl.* 67, *cr.* 13, (sword, *pl.* 49, *cr.* 4.)

MUMBEE, Bristol, a Peruvian chief, affrontée, on head a plume of five ostrich-feathers, with beads round neck, all ppr. *Faut être.*

MUMBY, on a ducal coronet, a lion, sejant, ppr. *Pl.* 107, *cr.* 11, (lion, *pl.* 126, *cr.* 15.)

MUMFORD, Eng., a demi-cat, rampant, gardant, ppr. *Pl.* 80, *cr.* 7.

MUN, Middx. and Ess., a cubit erm., in (armour,) in hand a lion's gamb, erased, gu. *Pl.* 94, *cr.* 13.

MUNCASTER, Baron, Iri., and a Bart., G.B., (Pennington,) a mountain-cat, (passant,) ppr. *Vincit amor patriæ.* *Pl.* 119, *cr.* 7.

MUNDAY, or MUNDY, Derbs. and Cornw., a wolf's head, sa. *Pl.* 14, *cr.* 6.

MUNDAY, a leopard's head, erased, sa., flames issuing from mouth. *Pl.* 112, *cr.* 9.

MUNDAY, or MUNDEY, Derbs., a wolf's head, erased, sa., bezantée, (vomiting flames, ppr.) *Pl.* 14, *cr.* 6.

MUNDELL, Sco., an arm, in armour, embowed, striking with a dagger, ppr. *Strike.* *Pl.* 120, *cr.* 11.

MUNDELL, Sco., a globe rent, ppr. *Impavidum ferient ruinæ.* *Pl.* 79, *cr.* 1.

MUNDEN, Middx., (in a rostrell crown, or,) a leopard's head, sa., bezantée. *Pl.* 36, *cr.* 15.

MUNDS, and MUNS, Middx., Ess., and Kent, a cubit arm, (in armour,) erect, in hand a lion's gamb, erased, or. *Pl.* 94, *cr.* 13.

MUNDY, Derbs., a wolf's head, erased, sa., bezantée, (fire issuing from mouth, ppr.) *Pl.* 14, *cr.* 6.

MUNDY, Lond., Cornw., and Leic., a leopard's head, (erased,) sa., bezantée, fire issuing from mouth, ppr. *Pl.* 112, *cr.* 9.

MUNN, Sco., a lion's head, erased, ar. *Pl.* 81, *cr.* 4.

MUNN, Eng., a lion's head, ermine. *Pl.* 126, *cr.* 1.

MUNRO, Eng. and Sco., an eagle, close, ppr. *Dread God.* *Pl.* 7, *cr.* 11.

MUNRO, Sco., an eagle, rising, ppr. *Dread God.* *Pl.* 67, *cr.* 4.

MUNRO, an eagle, wings expanded. *Pl.* 126, *cr.* 7.

MUNRO, on a mural coronet, ar., an eagle, close, or. *Pl.* 7, *cr.* 11, (coronet, *pl.* 128, *fig.* 18.)

MUNRO, Bart., an eagle, close, ppr., (having a representation of a silver medal, presented by the East India Company to the first Baronet for his services at Seringapatam in 1799, pendent from his neck by a ribbon, dexter resting on an escutcheon, gu., charged with a representation of the first syllable of the word *Badamy*, in letters of gold, and in beak a sprig of laurel.) *Pl.* 7, *cr.* 11.

MUNSTER, Earl of, Viscount Fitzclarence, and Baron Tewkesbury, (Fitz-Clarence,) a lion, statant, gardant, or, imperially crowned, ppr. *Nec temere, nec timide. Pl.* 120, *cr.* 5. (crown, *pl.* 127, *fig.* 2.)

MUNT, Eng., a savage's head, couped, dropping blood, ppr. *Pl.* 23, *cr.* 1.

MUNTON, Eng., a cannon, mounted, ppr. *Pl.* 111, *cr.* 3.

MURDEN, a leopard, rampant, (gardant,) ppr. *Pl.* 73, *cr.* 2.

MURDOCH, Eng. and Sco., a sword, in pale, enfiled with a savage's head, couped, ppr. *Pl.* 27, *cr.* 3.

MURDOCH, Sco., a lion's head, erased, gu. *Omine secundo. Pl.* 81, *cr.* 4.

MURDOCH, Sco., a raven, rising, sa., pierced through breast by an arrow, gu. *Pl.* 110, *cr.* 13.

MURDOCH, JOHN BURN, Esq., of Gartincaber, Perths., a raven, rising, transfixed by an arrow, ppr. *Omnia pro bono. Pl.* 110, *cr.* 13.

MURDOCK, Sco., a raven, rising, sa., shot through breast by an arrow, gu., headed and feathered, ar. *Omnia pro bono. Pl.* 110, *cr.* 13.

MURDOCK, a raven, issuing, regardant, in dexter a sword, in pale.

MURE, Sco., a moor's head, in profile, wreathed with a garland, all ppr. *Duris non frangor. Pl.* 118, *cr.* 7.

MURE, Sco., a savage's head, from shoulders, wreathed with laurel, ppr. *Duris non franger. Pl.* 118, *cr.* 7.

MURE, WILLIAM, Esq., of Caldwell, Ayrs., a Saracen's head, ppr. *Duris non frangor. Pl.* 19, *cr.* 1.

MUREHEAD, two hands, ppr., issuing, grasping a two-handed sword, in pale, az., hilted and pommelled, or. *Auxilio Dei. Pl.* 3, *cr.* 5.

MURIELL, Eng., a lion, passant, gardant, tail extended, ppr. *Pl.* 120, *cr.* 5.

MURIELL, a demi-cat, per pale, ar. and sa., in claws a branch of roses, of the first, leaved, ppr., (gorged with a fess, counterchanged.) *Pl.* 80, *cr.* 7, (roses, *pl.* 23, *cr.* 2.)

MURISON, Sco., three moors' heads conjoined in one neck, ppr., banded, az. *Mediocriter. Pl.* 95, *cr.* 5.

MURPHY, Sco., a hawk's head, or. *Pl.* 34, *cr.* 11.

MURPHY, Iri., a lion, rampant, gu., between paws a garb, or. *Pl.* 63, *cr.* 14.

MURPHY, Eng., a lion, rampant, gu., in dexter a garb, or. *Pl.* 64, *cr.* 2, (garb, *pl.* 84, *cr.* 7.)

MURPHY, Iri., a demi-sportsman, firing his piece, ppr. *Pl.* 51, *cr.* 6.

MURRAY, Iri., on a ducal coronet, a martlet, ppr. *Pl.* 98, *cr.* 14.

MURRAY, Sco., a horse, ar., furnished, gu. *Virtute fideque. Pl.* 99, *cr.* 11.

MURRAY, Sco., a ship under sail, ppr. *Tutum te littore sistam. Pl.* 109, *cr.* 8.

MURRANT, Lond., a moor's head, ppr., wreathed, ar. and gu., between dragon's wings, or. *Pl.* 36, *cr.* 3, (wings, *pl.* 105, *cr.* 11.)

MURRAY, Sco., a mermaid, in dexter a mirror, in sinister a comb, all ppr. *Tout prest. Pl.* 48, *cr.* 5.

MURRAY, Sco., an olive-tree, ppr. *Ex bello quies. Pl.* 100, *cr.* 14.

MURRAY, an angel, ppr. *Noctesque diesque præsto. Pl.* 25, *cr.* 7.

MURRAY, Lord Elibank. *See* ELIBANK.

MURRAY, JOHN-DALRYMPLE, Esq., of Murraythwaite, Dumfries, a cherub, ppr., winged, or. *Noctes diesque præsto. Pl.* 126, *cr.* 10.

MURRAY, Earl of Mansfield. *See* MANSFIELD.

MURRAY, Eng., an eagle's head, erased, sa., in beak a fleur-de-lis. *Pl.* 121, *cr.* 7.

MURRAY, an eagle's head, ppr. *Tout prest. Pl.* 100, *cr.* 10.

MURRAY, Sco., a horse, salient, ppr. *Functa virtute fides. Pl.* 57, *cr.* 15, (without wings or gorging.)

MURRAY, Sco., a mermaid, in dexter a sword, ppr. *In utrumque paratus. Pl.* 88, *cr.* 12.

MURRAY, Sco., a greyhound, current, ppr. *Gloria, non præda. Pl.* 28, *cr.* 7, (without charge.)

MURRAY, Sco., a demi-man, vested in green, winding a hunting-horn, ppr. *Hinc usque superna venabor. Pl.* 38, *cr.* 8.

MURRAY, Sco., an escallop, gu. *Fidei signum. Pl.* 117, *cr.* 4.

MURRAY, Sco., in dexter hand a roll of parchment, ppr. *Deum time. Pl.* 27, *cr.* 4.

MURRAY, Sco., an olive-branch, issuing, vert. *Ex bello quies. Pl.* 98, *cr.* 8.

MURRAY, Sco., a dove, in mouth an olive-branch, ppr. *Pacis munera. Pl.* 48, *cr.* 15.

MURRAY, Sco., a mullet, or. *Sans tache. Pl.* 41, *cr.* 1.

MURRAY, Earl of Dunmore. *See* DUNMORE.

MURRAY, Duke of Atholl. *See* ATHOLL.

MURRAY, Baron Glenlyon. *See* GLENLYON.

MURRAY, JOHN, Esq., of Murrayshall, (Perth,) a buck's head, ppr. *Macte virtute. Pl.* 91, *cr.* 14.

MURRAY, Sco., a griffin, salient. *Impero. Pl.* 67, *cr.* 13.

MURRAY, Sco., a mermaid, in dexter a mirror, ppr. *Pl.* 48, *cr.* 5.

MURRAY, Sco., in dexter hand a roll of paper, all ppr. *Deum time. Pl.* 27, *cr.* 4.

MURRAY, Sco., a dexter arm, in armour, embowed, hand apaumée. *Pl.* 97, *cr.* 1.

MURRAY, Sco., a burning-lamp, ppr. *Placeam. Pl.* 40, *cr.* 7.

MURRAY, Sco., in hand, ppr., a fetterlock, or. *Inde securior. Pl.* 27, *cr.* 4, (fetterlock, *pl.* 122, *cr.* 12.)

MURRAY, Sco., a lion's head, erased, crowned with an antique crown. *Pl.* 81, *cr.* 4, (crown, *pl.* 79, *cr.* 12.)

MURRAY, Sco., in dexter hand a mirror. *Nosce teipsum.*

MURRAY, Sco., a demi-savage, with club over dexter shoulder, ppr. *Furth fortune. Pl.* 14, *cr.* 11.

MURRAY, a lion, rampant, gardant, gu., collared and chained, supporting an anchor, or. *Virtute fideque. Pl.* 92, *cr.* 7, (anchor, *pl.* 19, *cr.* 6.)

MURRAY, Warw., a telescope, on a stand, or. *They by permission shine.*
MURRAY, Sco., a swan's head, couped. *Malo mori quam fœdari.* Pl. 30, cr. 10, (without gorging.)
MURRAY, Sco., in lion's gamb, a sword, ppr. *Fortes fortuna adjuvat.* Pl. 47, cr. 14.
MURRAY, a demi-man, couped at thighs, ppr., wreathed about head and loins, vert, in dexter a sword, in sinister a key, all ppr. Pl. 88, cr. 10.
MURRAY, Sco., an eagle, ppr. *Noctesque diesque præsto.* Pl. 7, cr. 11.
MURRAY, a branch of laurel, erect, vert. *Paritur bello.* Pl. 123, cr. 5.
MURRAY, Sco., an olive-branch, ppr. *In bello quies.* Pl. 98, cr. 8.
MURRAY, MUNGO, Esq., of Lintrose, Perth, same crest and motto.
MURRAY, Sco., in dexter hand a flaming sword, ppr. *Deum time.* Pl. 21, cr. 10, (sword, pl. 58, cr. 11.)
MURRAY, JAMES WOLFE, Esq., of Cringletie, Peebles; and West Shields, Lanark; in dexter hand a roll. *Deum time.* Pl. 27, cr. 4.
MURRAY, JOHN, Esq., of Polmaise, Stirling, a mermaid, in dexter a mirror, in sinister a comb. *Tout prest.* Pl. 48, cr. 5.
MURRAY, ALEXANDER, Esq., of Eriswell Lodge, Suff., a demi-savage, ppr., wreathed about head and waist, vert, in dexter a dagger, also ppr., pommel and hilt, or, in sinister a key, gold. *Furth fortune and fill the fetters.* Pl. 88, cr. 10.
MURRELL, a griffin's head, wings addorsed. Pl. 65, cr. 1.
MURRELL, or MURRILL, a demi-lion, rampant, gardant, per pale, ar. and sa., (collared, counterchanged,) in dexter a bunch of flowers, ar., stalked, vert. Pl. 35, cr. 4, (flowers, pl. 86, cr. 15.)
MURRY, Eng., a demi-savage, wreathed about middle and temples, vert, in dexter a dagger, in sinister a key. Pl. 88, cr. 10.
MURRY, Eng., in hand a roll of parchment. Pl. 27, cr. 4.
MURRY, a branch of olive. Pl. 98, cr. 8.
MURRY, a demi-lion, in paws a battle-axe. Pl. 120, cr. 14, (without coronet.)
MUSARD, Eng., a savage's head, couped, dropping blood, ppr. Pl. 23, cr. 1.
MUSCHAMP, Durh., a lion, rampant, gu., in dexter a banner, ar. *Vulneror, non vincor.* Pl. 99, cr. 2.
MUSCHAMPE, Surr., a mastiff-dog, ar., collared. Pl. 65, cr. 2.
MUSCOVY, or RUSSIAN COMPANY OF MERCHANTS, Lond., a leopard's head, erased, gardant, ppr., ducally gorged, gu. *God be our guide.* Pl. 116, cr. 8.
MUSGRAVE, two arms, embowed, (erm., cuffed, or,) in hands, ppr., an annulet, gold, between arms, a human heart, gu. Pl. 6, cr. 8, (heart, pl. 55, cr. 13; annulet, pl. 141.)
MUSGRAVE, Bart., Iri., two arms, in armour, ppr., (gauntleted,) supporting the sun, or. *Sans changer.* Pl. 6, cr. 8, (sun, pl. 68, cr. 14.)
MUSGRAVE, Bart., Glouc., two arms, in armour, embowed, supporting the sun, ppr. *Ib.*
MUSGRAVE, Bart., Cumb., two arms, in armour, ppr., (gauntleted,) supporting an annulet, or. *Sans changer.* Pl. 6, cr. 8, (annulet, pl. 141.)

MUSGROVE, Bart., a demi-lion, ppr., gorged with a double collar, gemelle, sa., between paws a lozenge, az., charged with a cross crosslet, or. *Nil desperandum.* Pl. 18, cr. 13, (lozenge and cross, pl. 141.)
MUSHAT, and MUSHET, Eng., a mount, vert, semée of strawberries, ppr. Pl. 62, cr. 11.
MUSHET, Sco., a twig of rose, blooming, ppr. *Dabunt aspera rosas.* Pl. 105, cr. 7.
MUSHET, on the top of a Saracen's head, affrontée, a dove and olive-branch, ppr. Pl. 19, cr. 1, (dove, pl. 79, cr. 8.)
MUSICIANS, TRADE, Lond., a lyre, or. Pl. 104, cr. 15.
MUSKERRY, Baron, and a Bart., Iri., (Deane,) on a ducal coronet, or, (a crocodile, statant, ppr.) *Forti et fideli nihil difficile.* Pl. 17, cr. 15.
MUSKETT, Suff. and Norf., out of a ducal coronet, sa., a demi-antelope, or, chained and ringed, of the first. Pl. 34, cr. 8, (coronet, same plate, cr. 15.)
MUSNER, out of a ducal coronet, or, a camel's head, sa. Pl. 55, cr. 5, (without collar and crown.)
MUSSELL, Wilts., a wolf, salient, sa. Pl. 126, cr. 13.
MUSSENDEN, Linc., a Cornish chough, ppr., (in beak a sprig of laurel, vert.) Pl. 100, cr. 13.
MUSSENDEN, WILLIAM, Esq., of Larchfield, co. Down, a dove, in mouth an olive-branch, all ppr. *J'aime la liberté.* Pl. 48, cr. 15.
MUSTERS, Eng., a lion, sejant, on hind legs, (gardant,) supporting an escutcheon, charged with a bend. Pl. 22, cr. 13.
MUSTON, Eng., on a chapeau, ppr., a garb, or. Pl. 62, cr. 1.
MUTERER, Sco., a castle, triple-towered, ppr., door and windows, gu. *Patience and resolution.* Pl. 123, cr. 14.
MUTLOW, Glouc. and Worc., a griffin's head, couped, per pale, indented, ar. and gu., guttée, counterchanged, in beak a buck's foot, erased and erect, or. Pl. 48, cr. 6, (foot, pl. 66, cr. 7.)
MUTTLEBURY, Somers., a hare, current, ar.
MUTTON, Eng., a unicorn, rampant. Pl. 37, cr. 7.
MYALL, an eagle, wings addorsed, erminois, chained, collared, and charged on breast with a mill-rind, sa. Pl. 61, cr. 1, (mill-rind, pl. 141.)
MYDDLETON, Wel., out of a ducal coronet, or, a dexter hand, erect, ppr. Pl. 79, cr. 6, (without wings.)
MYDDLETON-WHARTON, of Old Park, Durh., and of Grinkle Park, Yorks.: 1. For *Myddleton*, a savage, wreathed about head with leaves, in dexter (an oak-tree, erased and fructed, all ppr.) Pl. 87, cr. 13. 2. For *Wharton*, a bull's head, erased, ar., charged with a trefoil, vert. *Lesses dire.* Pl. 19, cr. 3, (trefoil, pl. 141.)
MYDHOPE, Yorks., a demi-lion, rampant, az., holding a ducal coronet, or. Pl. 67, cr. 10, (coronet, pl. 9, cr. 7.)
MYERS, Eng., a ducal coronet, or, ensigned with three arrows, points downward, entwined with a serpent, ppr.
MYERS, a demi-horse, rampant, erased. Pl. 91, cr. 2, (without wings or coronet.)
MYERS, a boar's head, erased, in fess. Pl. 16, cr. 11.

MYERS, Bart., Eng., a mermaid, with (dexter) combing her hair, in (sinister) a mirror. *Pl.* 48, *cr.* 5.
MYGGS, a talbot's head, sa., eared, ar., collared, or. *Pl.* 2, *cr.* 15.
MYLBOURNE, a leopard's head, per pale, ar. and sa. *Pl.* 92, *cr.* 13.
MYLECENT, Yorks., out of an antique crown, or, a dragon's head, sa., collared (and chained.) *Pl.* 107, *cr.* 10, (crown, *pl.* 79, *cr.* 12.)
MYLES, Kent, a buzzard, ppr. *Pl.* 67, *cr.* 3.
MYLIE, Sco., a bull's head, erased, sa. *Pl.* 19, *cr.* 3.
MYLNE, Sco., a martlet, volant. *Ex industria.* *Pl.* 40, *cr.* 4.
MYLNE, THOMAS, Esq., of Mylnefield, Perths., a dexter hand holding a book, ppr. *Efficiunt clarum studia.* *Pl.* 45, *cr.* 3.
MYNDE, Salop, a heathcock, ppr. *Pl.* 67, *cr.* 3.
MYNN, a demi-pegasus, or. *Pl.* 91, *cr.* 2, (without coronet.)
MYNORDS, Heref., a naked cubit arm, ppr., in hand a lion's gamb, erased, sa. *Spero ut fidelis.* *Pl.* 94, *cr.* 13.
MYNORS, Weatherook, Worc., a dexter cubit arm, (in armour,) in hand a lion's paw, erased, all ppr. *Pl.* 94, *cr.* 13.

MYNSHULL, Chesh., two lions' gambs, gu., supporting a crescent, ar. *Pl.* 62, *cr.* 3.
MYRESON, Eng., a buck's head, erased, sa., attired, or. *Pl.* 66, *cr.* 9.
MYRETON, Sco., out of a cloud, a dexter hand, in fess, ppr., holding a cross formée, fitched, gu. *Pl.* 26, *cr.* 4.
MYRETON, Sco., two arms issuing from clouds, drawing up an anchor out of the water, ppr. *Pl.* 94, *cr.* 4.
MYRTOUN, Sco., out of a cloud, a dexter hand, in fess, ppr., holding a cross pattée, fitched, gu. *Pl.* 26, *cr.* 4.
MYRTOUN, Sco., a crescent, ar. *Pl.* 18, *cr.* 14.
MYSTERS, Lond., a griffin's head, erased, sa., charged with two bars-gemelle, or. *Pl.* 48, *cr.* 6.
MYTTON, Eng., an arm, in armour, embowed, in hand, by the blade, a sword, point downward, ppr. *Pl.* 65, *cr.* 8.
MYTTON, THOMAS, Esq., of Shipton Hall, Salop, a bull's head, erased, bezantée. *Pl.* 19, *cr.* 3.
MYTTON, RICHARD-HERBERT, Esq., of Garth, Montgomery, a ram's head, couped, ar., horned, or. *Pl.* 34, *cr.* 12.
MYTTON, of Halston, Salop, same crest.

N

NADLER, Eng., a cross crosslet, fitched, and a sword, in saltier. *Pl.* 89, *cr.* 14.
NAESMITH, Sco., in hand a broken hammer. *Non arte sed marte.* *Pl.* 93, *cr.* 5.
NAGLE, Eng., a unicorn's head, sa. *Pl.* 20, *cr.* 1.
NAGLE, Bart., Iri., a goldfinch, ppr. *Non vox sed votum.* *Pl.* 10, *cr.* 12.
NAGLE, Cloger House, co. Cork, on a coronet, ppr., an eagle, perched. *Pl.* 7, *cr.* 11, (coronet, *pl.* 128, *fig.* 3.)
NAGLE-CHICHESTER, JOSEPH, Esq., of Calverleigh Court, Devons.: 1. For *Nagle,* a gold finch, ppr. *Pl.* 10, *cr.* 12. 2. For *Chichester,* a heron, rising, in beak an eel, ppr. *Non vox, sed votum.* *Pl.* 59, *cr.* 11.
NAIL, a round buckle, gu., between wings, dexter, ar., sinister, of the first. *Pl.* 73, *cr.* 10, (wings, *pl.* 109, *cr.* 12.)
NAIRN, Sco., a globe and standard, ppr. *Spes ultra.* *Pl.* 81, *cr.* 1.
NAIRN, Sco., trunk of oak-tree, sprouting leaves, ppr. *Sero, sed serio.* *Pl.* 92, *cr.* 8.
NAIRN, Eng., a lion, rampant, supporting a garb, ppr. *Pl.* 63, *cr.* 14.
NAIRN, or NAIRNE, Sco., a globe, on a stand, ppr. *Spes ultra.* *Pl.* 81, *cr.* 1.
NAIRNE, Eng., the sun, in splendour, or. *Pl.* 68, *cr.* 14.
NAIRNE, Sco., a globe. *Spes ultra.* *Pl.* 14, *cr.* 1.
NAIRNE, Lord, Sco., (Murray-Nairne,) a sphere. *Plus ultra.* *Pl.* 114, *cr.* 6.
NAISH, Eng., in dexter hand a sword, in pale, ppr. *Pl.* 23, *cr.* 15.
NAISH, co. Limerick, a greyhound, sejant, ppr., (collared, ar.) *Pl.* 66, *cr.* 15.
NALDER, Berks., a griffin's head, erased. *Pl.* 48, *cr.* 6.
NALDER, Berks., a domed tower. *Pl.* 42, *cr.* 10.

NALLINGHURST, Eng., a wyvern, gu. *Pl.* 63, *cr.* 13.
NANBY, in lion's paw, sa., an ostrich feather, ar. *Pl.* 58, *cr.* 7.
NANDIKE, Yorks., a demi-griffin, wings addorsed, ar., supporting a spear, sa., headed, of the first. *Pl.* 18, *cr.* 6, (spear, *pl.* 97, *cr.* 4.)
NANFANT, a spaniel-dog, ar. *Pl.* 58, *cr.* 9.
NANFANT, three vine-hooks, or pruning-hooks, ar., one erect, two in saltier. *Pl.* 58, *cr.* 8.
NANFANT, three pruning-hooks, one in pale, two in saltier, or, environed in middle by a wreath. *Pl.* 58, *cr.* 8.
NANFANT, on a coronet, or, a bird, az. *Pl.* 41, *cr.* 10.
NANFAN, or NANPHAN, Eng., two dolphins, addorsed, az. *Pl.* 81, *cr.* 2.
NANGLE, Iri., a falcon, ppr., belled, or. *Pl.* 67, *cr.* 3.
NANGOTHAM, and NANGOTHAM, Sco. and Eng., a pole-cat, ar. *Pl.* 119, *cr.* 7.
NANNEY, Wel., a lion, rampant, az. *Pl.* 67, *cr.* 5.
NANPHAN, Worc., a water-spaniel, passant, ar. *Pl.* 58, *cr.* 9.
NANSOLYN, Eng., a cross pattée, fitched, az. *Pl.* 27, *cr.* 14.
NANSON, Eng., a peacock, in pride, ppr. *Pl.* 92, *cr.* 11.
NANTON, Suff., a cockatrice, close, ppr., wings, sa. *Pl.* 63, *cr.* 15.
NANTS, an etoile of (eight) points, or. *Pl.* 63, *cr.* 9.
NAPEAN, a goat, (passant.) *Pl.* 66, *cr.* 1.
NAPER, Devons., a demi-antelope, erased, or, attired, ar. *Pl.* 34, *cr.* 8, (without collar.)
NAPER, Iri., on a mount, vert, a falcon, ppr. *Pl.* 111, *cr.* 8.

NAPER, or NAPIER, Bucks., a dexter cubit arm, vested, gu., cuffed, ar., in hand a crescent, of the first. *Pl.* 110, *cr.* 7.

NAPER, JAMES-LENOX-WILLIAM, Esq., of Loughcrew, co. Meath, a dexter cubit arm, vested, gu., turned up, ar., in hand a crescent, ppr. *Pl.* 110, *cr.* 7.

NAPIER, Sco., in hand an eagle's leg, erased, ppr., talons expanded, gu. *Fides servata secundat. Pl.* 103, *cr.* 4.

NAPIER, Sco., two hands, conjoined, grasping a cutlass, in pale, ppr. *Absque dedecore. Pl.* 95, *cr.* 1.

NAPIER, Sco., a man's head, adorned with laurel, ppr. *Virtute gloria parta. Pl.* 118, *cr.* 7.

NAPIER, Sco., a dexter arm, in hand a crescent. *Sans tache. Pl.* 38, *cr.* 7.

NAPIER, Dors., a heron, ppr. *Pl.* 6, *cr.* 13.

NAPIER, Dors. and Beds., a dexter arm, erect, vested, gu., in hand, ppr., a crescent, ar. *Pl.* 110, *cr.* 7.

NAPIER, Beds. and Oxon., a greyhound, sejant, gu., collared and (lined,) or. *Pl.* 101, *cr.* 7.

NAPIER, Sco., in hand a couteau sword, ppr. *Sans tache. Pl.* 29, *cr.* 8.

NAPIER, Sco., in dexter hand an eagle's leg, erased, in bend, ppr., armed, gu. *Vincit veritas. Pl.* 103, *cr.* 4.

NAPIER, Sco., same crest. *Nil veritur veritas.*

NAPIER, Sco., an eagle's leg, erased, ppr., armed, gu., in fess. *Vincit veritas. Pl.* 60, *cr.* 15, (without feather.)

NAPIER, Sco., an eagle's leg, erased, in bend, ppr., armed, gu. *Usque fidelis. Pl.* 103, *cr.* 4, (without hand.)

NAPIER, a demi-antelope, (erased at flank,) or, armed, ar. *Pl.* 34, *cr.* 8, (without collar.)

NAPIER, two dexter hands, clasped in amity, holding a (dagger,) in pale, all ppr. *Absque dedecore. Pl.* 75, *cr.* 8.

NAPIER, Bart., Sco.: 1. For *Napier*, an arm, in hand an eagle's leg, ppr. *Pl.* 103, *cr.* 4. *Fides servata secundat.* 2. For *Milliken*, a demi-lion, rampant, gu., in dexter a dagger, or. *Regarde bien. Pl.* 41, *cr.* 13.

NAPIER, Baron, Sco., (Napier;) a dexter cubit arm, erect, in hand a crescent. *Sans tache* —and—*Ready, aye ready. Pl.* 38, *cr.* 7.

NAPIER, EDWARD-BERKELEY, Esq., of Pennard House, Somers., a dexter cubit arm, erect, in hand a crescent. *Fato providentia major. Pl.* 38, *cr.* 7.

NAPLETON, Eng., a griffin, statant. *Pl.* 66, *cr.* 13.

NAPPER, a demi-antelope, or, armed and maned, az. *Pl.* 34, *cr.* 8, (without collar.)

NAPPER, Lond., on a mount, vert, a falcon, close, ppr. *Pl.* 111, *cr.* 8.

NAPPIER, Beds., a dexter cubit arm, erect, vested, gu., cuffed, ar., in hand, ppr., a crescent of the second. *Pl.* 110, *cr.* 7.

NAPPIER, Beds., a demi-antelope, (erased,) or, attired, ar. (Another, az.) *Pl.* 34, *cr.* 8, (without collar.)

NAPTON, Eng., a lion, passant, tail extended, ppr. *Pl.* 118, *cr.* 10.

NARBON, Eng., a dove, volant, in mouth an olive-branch. *Pl.* 25, *cr.* 6.

NARBOON, or NARBOONE, Eng., the golden fleece, or, banded, az. *Pl.* 77, *cr.* 12.

NARES, Kent, two spears, in saltier, (banded) in middle, az. (Another, gu.) *Pl.* 53, *cr.* 14, (without pennons.)

NASH, a greyhound, sejant, ar. *Omnia vincit veritas. Pl.* 66, *cr.* 15.

NASH, Iri., a pelican, ppr. *Pl.* 109, *cr.* 15.

NASH, a wolf, regardant. *Pl.* 77, *cr.* 14, (without spear.)

NASH, Lond., a cubit arm, erect, vested, az., cuffed, ar., in hand an oak-branch, fructed, ppr. *Pl.* 32, *cr.* 6, (branch, *same plate, cr.* 13.)

NASH, Iri., a greyhound, sejant, sa., collared, ar., studded, or. *Omnia vincit veritas. Pl.* 66, *cr.* 15.

NASH, Worc.: 1. On a mount, vert, a greyhound, current, ar., charged on body with an ermine-spot, sa., (in mouth a sprig of ash, ppr.) *Pl.* 47, *cr.* 2, (mount, *pl.* 117, *cr.* 8.; ermine, *pl.* 141.) 2. Out of a ducal coronet, jewelled and turned up, erm., a greyhound's head, ar., (collared, sa.,) rim and ring, or. *Pl.* 70, *cr.* 5.

NASMYTH, Bart., Sco., in hand a hammer, or. *Non arte sed marte.*

NASMYTH, or NEASMITH, in hand a broken hammer. *Non arte sed marte. Pl.* 93, *cr.* 5.

NASSAU, Eng., in a coronet, composed of fleurs-de-lis and strawberry leaves, or, two single attires of a stag, gu. *Ne supra modum sapere. Pl.* 118, *cr.* 11.

NASSAU, out of a ducal coronet, or, the attires of a buck, gu. *Pl.* 118, *cr.* 11, (coronet, *pl.* 128, *fig.* 3.)

NATHALEY, NATHILEY, or NATHELEY, Eng., out of a ducal coronet, or, a demi-swan, sa., wings displayed. *Pl.* 100, *cr.* 7, (without collar.)

NATHAN, a heart, gu., pierced by an arrow, in bend sinister, sa. *Pl.* 16, *cr.* 14.

NAUGHTON, Sco., a (demi)-tower, gu. *I hope in God. Pl.* 12, *cr.* 5.

NAUGHTON, Eng., a demi-lion, rampant, gardant, in dexter a fleur-de-lis. *Pl.* 35, *cr.* 4, (fleur-de-lis, *pl.* 91, *cr.* 13.)

NAUNTON, an ostrich's head, ar., ducally gorged, az. *Pl.* 108, *cr.* 2, (without feathers.)

NAYLOR, Yorks., a lark, volant, or. *Pl.* 87, *cr.* 10.

NAYLOR, or NAYLOUR, Lond., Durh., Oxford, and Hunts., a lion's head, erased, sa., (charged on neck with a saltier, or.) *Pl.* 81, *cr.* 4.

NAYLORD, Glouc., a goat's head, or, attired, sa., in mouth a sprig of laurel, ppr. *Pl.* 105, *cr.* 14, (sprig, *pl.* 123, *cr.* 5.)

NAYLOUR, Kent, on a mount, vert, an eagle, rising, ppr. *Pl.* 61, *cr.* 1.

NEAGLE, a demi-griffin, segreant. *Pl.* 18, *cr.* 6.

NEAL, Eng., a ram, (statant,) ppr. *Pl.* 109, *cr.* 2.

NEAL, Eng., a mound, gu., banded and crossed, or. *Pl.* 37, *cr.* 3.

NEAL, an arm, in armour, in bend dexter, in hand a sword, in bend sinister. *Pl.* 2, *cr.* 8.

NEAL, or NEALE, Beds., Ess., and Northamp., a griffin's head, erased, ar. *Pl.* 48, *cr.* 6.

NEALE, Eng., a mascle, or. *Pl.* 54, *cr.* 1.

NEALE, Hants, out of a ducal coronet, or, a chaplet of laurel, vert. *Pl.* 114, *cr.* 15.

NEALE, Middx., a dragon's head, or, vulned in neck, gu. *Pl.* 121, *cr.* 9.

NEALE, a tower, gu., from battlements a pelican, rising, wings displayed, or, vulning, ppr. *Pl.* 12, *cr.* 5, (pelican, *pl.* 109, *cr.* 15.)

NEALE, on a mount, vert, a stag, statant. *Pl.* 50, *cr.* 6.

NEALE, Allesley Park, Warw. : 1. For *Neale*, out of a mural coronet, or, a demi-lion, rampant, per fess, erm. and gu., charged on shoulder with an escallop, counterchanged. *Pl.* 86, *cr.* 11, (escallop, *pl.* 141.) 2. On two crosses pattée, ar., a demi-eagle, displayed, sa. *Pl.* 117, *cr.* 15.

NEALE, or NELE, a fret, az. *Pl.* 82, *cr.* 7.

NEALE-BURRARD, Bart.: 1. *Of honourable augmentation*, granted in 1815, out of a naval coronet, or, a cubit arm, erect, encircled by a branch of oak, ppr., in hand, a trident, in bend sinister, point downward, gold. *Pl.* 93, *cr.* 1. 2. A dexter arm, in armour, embowed, in hand a sword, all ppr. *Pl.* 2, *cr.* 8.

NEARNS, Iri., a lion's head, erased. *Pl.* 81, *cr.* 4.

NEASMITH, Sco., in dexter hand a sword, all ppr. *Marte non arte*. *Pl.* 21, *cr.* 10.

NEAT, Eng., a horse's head, bridled, ppr. *Pl.* 92, *cr.* 1.

NEAT, Eng., a bull's head, between wings. *Pl.* 60, *cr.* 9.

NEAT, or NEATE, Lond. and Wilts., a bull's head, couped at neck, gu., armed and crined, ar., between dragon's wings, vert. *Pl.* 60, *cr.* 9, (dragon's wings, *pl.* 105, *cr.* 11.)

NEAVE, Lond., a demi-leopard, rampant, gardant, ppr., supporting an anchor, or. *Industriâ permanente*. *Pl.* 77, *cr.* 1.

NEAVE, Bart., Ess., out of a ducal coronet, gold, a lily, stalked and leaved, vert, flowered and seeded, or. *Sola proba quæ honesta*. *Pl.* 93, *cr.* 3.

NECHURE, Eng., in hand a rose-branch, ppr. *Pl.* 118, *cr.* 9.

NEDHAM, Herts., a dolphin, naiant, or. *Pl.* 48, *cr.* 9.

NEED, out of an Eastern crown, or, a griffin's head, sa., (charged with an etoile, gold.) *Pl.* 38, *cr.* 3, (crown, *pl.* 25, *cr.* 8.)

NEEDES, a buck's head, cabossed, (pierced through by an arrow,) all ppr. *Pl.* 36, *cr.* 1.

NEEDHAM, Viscount Kilmorey. *See* KILMOREY.

NEEDHAM, Derbs., a phœnix in flames, ppr., (charged on breast with a trefoil, slipped, or.) *Pl.* 44, *cr.* 8.

NEEDHAM, Chesh., Derbs., and Leic., on a mount, vert, a stag, lodged, sa., attired, or, charged with a crescent for difference. *Pl.* 22, *cr.* 5, (crescent, *pl.* 141.)

NEEDHAM, Leic., a phœnix in flames, ppr. *Nunc aut nunquam*. *Pl.* 44, *cr.* 8.

NEEDHAM, Herts., out of a palisado coronet, or, a buck's head, sa., attired, of the first. *Pl.* 91, *cr.* 14, (coronet, *pl.* 128, *fig.* 21.)

NEEDHAM, WILLIAM, Esq., of Lenton, Notts., out of flames, or, a demi-eagle, displayed. *Soyez ferme*. *Pl.* 44, *cr.* 8.

NEEDLE-MAKERS, London, a moor's head, couped at shoulders, in profile, ppr., wreathed about temples, ar. and gu., vested, of the second, in his ear a pearl. *Pl.* 126, *cr.* 8.

NEEFIELD, and NERFIELD, Eng., two anchors, in saltier, az. *Pl.* 37, *cr.* 12.

NEELE, Eng., out of a ducal coronet, a chaplet of laurel, vert. *Pl.* 114, *cr.* 15.

NEELE, Eng., a mound, gu., banded and crossed, or. *Pl.* 37, *cr.* 3.

NEEVE, out of a ducal coronet, a Narcissus, stalked and leaved, ppr. *Pl.* 93, *cr.* 3.

NEFIELD, and NESFIELD, a pillar, ar., supported by two lions' paws, ppr. *Pl.* 77, *cr.* 4.

NEFMENEILL, or NEFMENELL, Eng., a dexter hand, apaumée, ppr. *Pl.* 32, *cr.* 14.

NEGUS, Norf., a sea-mew, resting dexter on an escallop, or. *Pl.* 6, *cr.* 11, (escallop, *pl.* 141.)

NEIL, Sco., a lion, passant, gardant, sa. *Pl.* 120, *cr.* 5.

NEIL, Eng., a unicorn's head, erased, gu. *Pl.* 67, *cr.* 1.

NEILL, Eng., out of a cloud, a hand holding a club, all ppr. *Pl.* 37, *cr.* 13.

NEILL, Barnweill, Ayr : 1. A (sinister) arm, in armour, in hand a dagger, back-handed. *Pl.* 120, *cr.* 11. 2. In dexter hand, ppr., a sword. *Pl.* 21, *cr.* 10.

NEILSON, Sco., demi-man, over shoulder a hammer, all ppr. *Præsto pro patriâ*. *Pl.* 51, *cr.* 14.

NEILSON, Sco., in dexter hand a dagger, ppr. *Virtute et votis*. *Pl.* 28, *cr.* 4.

NEILSON, Eng., out of a mural coronet, az., a lion's head, or. *Pl.* 45, *cr.* 9.

NEILSON, Sco., in dexter hand a lance, (in pale,) ppr. *His regi servitium*. *Pl.* 99, *cr.* 8.

NEILSON, in dexter hand, a spear, ppr. *Præsto pro patriâ*. *Pl.* 99, *cr.* 8.

NEILSON, Sco., a dexter hand, ppr., pointing to a crescent, or. *His regi servitium*. *Pl.* 35, *cr.* 5, (crescent, *pl.* 17, *cr.* 10.)

NEISH, Cupid, with bow and arrow, ppr. *Amicitiam trahit amor*. *Pl.* 17, *cr.* 5.

NEKE, in lion's gamb, az., a lozenge, in pale, ar., charged with a cross crosslet, sa. *Pl.* 89, *cr.* 15.

NELL, Eng., a stag's head, erased, ar., attired, or. *Pl.* 66, *cr.* 9.

NELME, out of a ducal coronet, a demi-dragon, or, wings addorsed, az., (between claws a cross crosslet, fitched, gu.) *Pl.* 82, *cr.* 10, (coronet, *same plate*.)

NELSON, Iri., a dexter arm, in armour, in hand an oak-branch, ppr. *Pl.* 68, *cr.* 1, (branch, *pl.* 32, *cr.* 13.)

NELSON, Yorks., a cubit arm, quarterly, ar. and sa., in hand, ppr., a fleur-de-lis, per pale, ar. and sa. *Pl.* 95, *cr.* 9.

NELSON, a cubit arm, in armour, in hand a baton, all ppr. *Pl.* 33, *cr.* 4.

NELSON, Kent, a dexter arm, erect, in hand a tilting-spear, all ppr. *Pl.* 99, *cr.* 8.

NELSON, a lion's gamb, erect, ppr., holding an escutcheon, sa., charged with a cross patonce, or. *Pl.* 43, *cr.* 12, (cross, *pl.* 141.)

NELSON, Beeston, Norf., a cubit arm, ppr., in hand a scimitar, hilt and pommel, or. *Pl.* 29, *cr.* 8.

NELSON, a dexter hand, erect, ppr., the first finger and thumb pointing to a crescent, or, the others, clenched. *Pl.* 35, *cr.* 5, (crescent, *pl.* 141.)

NELSON, Devons., a dexter arm, in armour, couped and erect, ppr., in hand a fleur-de-lis, counterchanged. *Pl.* 95, *cr.* 9.

NELSON, Earl and Baron, Viscount Merton and Trafalgar, U.K., and Duke of Bronté, in Sicily, (Nelson) : 1. On a naval coronet, or, the chelengk, or plume of triumph, presented to the first Lord by the Grand Signior. 2. The stern of a Spanish line-of-battle-ship, flotant, upon waves, all ppr., inscribed under the gallery, "San Josef." *Faith and works*.

NELSON, Durh., out of a ducal coronet, or, a demi-lion, rampant, ar. *Pl.* 45, *cr.* 7.

NELTHORPE, Bart., Middx., out of clouds, an arm, couped, ppr., in fess, in hand a sword, in pale, hilt and pommel, or. *Pl.* 93, *cr.* 8.

NEMPHARTS, a (demi-)lamb, salient, over dexter shoulder the holy banner of the cross, all ppr. *Pax potior bello. Pl.* 48, *cr.* 13.

NEPEAN, Eng., a goat, (passant,) ppr. *Pl.* 66, *cr.* 1.

NEPEAN, Bart., Dors., on a mount, vert, a goat, (passant,) sa., charged on side with two ermine spots, in fess, or, collared and horned, gold. *Pl.* 11, *cr.* 14, (ermine, *pl.* 141.)

NERBERYE, and NERBURY, Eng., three organpipes, (two in saltier, and one in pale,) or, banded with leaves, vert. *Pl.* 50, *cr.* 12.

NEREFORD, a glowworm, ppr.

NERFIELD, Eng., two anchors, in saltier, az. *Pl.* 37, *cr.* 12.

NESBETT, an arm, in armour, couped below wrist, in gauntlet a baton. *Pl.* 33, *cr.* 4.

NESBITT, Eng., out of a mural coronet, a talbot's head, ppr. *Pl.* 91, *cr.* 15.

NESBITT, ALEXANDER, Esq., of Lismore House, co. Cavan, a dexter cubit arm, in armour, in hand a truncheon. *Je maintien drai. Pl.* 33, *cr.* 4.

NESHAM, Durh.: For *Nesham*, a demi-lion, rampant, in dexter a cross crosslet. *Pl.* 65, *cr.* 6. 2. For *Douthwaite*, on a rock, ppr., a fleur-de-lis, counterchanged, or and gu. *Spes, salus, decus. Pl.* 76, *cr.* 12.

NESMETH, an arm, (in bend dexter,) in hand a broken hammer, in bend sinister, top pendent. *Pl.* 93, *cr.* 5.

NESS, Sco., in dexter hand a laurel-branch, ppr. *Pl.* 43, *cr.* 6.

NETBY, in lion's gamb, a (bird-bolt,) sa. *Pl.* 85, *cr.* 13.

NETHERCOAT, Northamp., a wolf's head, erased. *Pl.* 14, *cr.* 6.

NETHERSALL, and NETHERSOLE, Kent, an arm, in armour, embowed, ppr., (girt with a scarf, flotant, vert,) in gauntlet a broken tiltingspear, or. *Pl.* 44, *cr.* 9.

NETHERSOLE, Eng., a stag, at gaze. *Pl.* 81, *cr.* 8.

NETTER, a unicorn's head, erased, gu., ducally gorged, armed and maned, or. *Pl.* 67, *cr.* 1, (gorging, *same plate, cr.* 7.)

NETTERVILLE, Viscount Netterville, Iri., a demi-lion, rampant, gardant, gu., bezantée. *Cruci, dum spiro, fido. Pl.* 35, *cr.* 4.

NETTERVILLE, Eng., a demi-lion, rampant, gu., bezantée. *Cruci, dum spiro, fido. Pl.* 67, *cr.* 10.

NETTLEFOLD, Eng., a water-bouget, gu. *Pl.* 14, *cr.* 12.

NETTLES, ROBERT, Esq., of Nettleville, co. Cork, a stag, statant, under a tree, ppr. *Nemo me impune lacessit. Pl.* 118, *cr.* 13.

NETTLESHIP, Eng., in dexter hand, ppr., a (nettle-branch,) vert. *Pl.* 36, *cr.* 6.

NETTLESHIP, a demi-bear, rampant, ar., muzzled, or. *Pl.* 104, *cr.* 10.

NETTLESHIP, Lond., a lion, passant, per pale, erm. and az., in dexter a buckle, or. *Pl.* 77, *cr.* 3, (buckle, *pl.* 73, *cr.* 10.)

NETTLETON, Eng., a bear's paw, (erased,) gu. *Pl.* 126, *cr.* 2.

NEVE, LE, Lond. and Norf., out of a ducal coronet, or, a lily, ar., leaved, vert. *Pl.* 93, *cr.* 3.

NEVELL, an anchor, sa., environed by a serpent, or. *Pl.* 35, *cr.* 14.

NEVEMENELL, Eng., a dexter hand, apaumée, ppr. *Pl.* 32, *cr.* 14.

NEVETT, Eng., an arm, in armour, embowed, in hand a battle-axe, all ppr. *Pl.* 121, *cr.* 14.

NEVITT, Birmingham, same crest.

NEVIL, Monm., out of a ducal coronet, or, a bull's head, pied, ppr., attired, of the first, charged on neck with a rose, gu., seeded, gold, barbed, vert. *Ne vile velis. Pl.* 68, *cr.* 6, (rose, *pl.* 141.)

NEVIL, Suss., same crest.

NEVILE, of Thorney, Notts.: 1. Out of a ducal coronet, a bull's head, ar. *Pl.* 68, *cr.* 6. 2. On a chapeau, turned up, erm., a ship, sa. *Ne vile velis. Pl.* 109, *cr.* 8, (chapeau, *same plate.*)

NEVILL, Ess., a demi-lion, rampant, ar., guttéede-sang, holding (in pale,) a sword, of the first, hilt and pommel, or. *Pl.* 41, *cr.* 13.

NEVILL, Northumb., Leic., and Notts., out of a ducal coronet, or, a bull's head, erm., armed, gold. *Pl.* 68, *cr.* 6.

NEVILL, Iri., a lion's head, az., royally crowned, ppr. *Pl.* 123, *cr.* 13, (crown, *pl.* 127, *fig.* 2.)

NEVILL, Staffs., a griffin, passant, or, charged on breast with a crescent. *Pl.* 61, *cr.* 14, (without gorging; crescent, *pl.* 141.)

NEVILL, Iri., a greyhound's head, erased, ar., collared, gu., charged with a harp, or. *Pl.* 43, *cr.* 11, (harp, *pl.* 104, *cr.* 15.)

NEVILL, Linc. and Yorks., a tiger, sejant, erm. *Pl.* 26, *cr.* 9.

NEVILL, Leic. and Yorks., a greyhound's head, erased, or, (charged on neck with a label of three points, vert, between as many pellets.) *Pl.* 89, *cr.* 2.

NEVILL, Earl of Abergavenny. See ABERGAVENNY.

NEVILL, Kent and Berks., a bull, passant, pied, (collared, lined,) and armed, or. *Pl.* 66, *cr.* 11.

NEVILLE, Eng., out of a cloud, a hand holding up a garb by the band, all ppr. *Pl.* 43, *cr.* 4.

NEVILLE, THOMAS, Esq., of Borrismore House, co. Kilkenny, out of a ducal coronet, or, a bull's head, pied, attired, gold. *Ne vile velis. Pl.* 68, *cr.* 6.

NEVINSON, Kent, a wolf, passant, ar., pellettée, (collared, lined, and ringed, or.) *Pl.* 46, *cr.* 6.

NEVOY, a pegasus, ppr. *Marte et arte. Pl.* 28, *cr.* 9.

NEW, Eng., a dexter arm, ppr., vested, per cheveron, or and gu., in hand a roll of parchment, ar. *Pl.* 95, *cr.* 7.

NEWALL, Eng., a cross crosslet, fitched, az. *Pl.* 16, *cr.* 10.

NEWARKE, Eng., a savage's head, in profile, looking up, ppr. *Pl.* 121, *cr.* 2.

NEWBALD, or NEWBOLD, Derbs. and Lond., a cross, flory, fitched, az. *Pl.* 65, *cr.* 9.

NEWBERRY, and NEWBERY, Eng., a dexter arm, ppr., vested, az., cuffed, or, in hand a truncheon, gu., tipped, gold. *Pl.* 18, *cr.* 1.

NEWBERY, Eng., an eagle's head, erased, ar. *Pl.* 20, *cr.* 7.

NEWBERY, Lond., a moor's head, in profile, ppr. *Pl.* 81, *cr.* 15.

NEWBIGGING, Sco., a stag's head, erased, ppr., between attires a cross crosslet, fitched, sa. *Cruce vincimus. Pl.* 24, *cr.* 9.

NEWBIGGING, Sco., an eagle, rising, ppr. *I'll try.* *Pl.* 67, *cr.* 4.
NEWBIGGING, Sco., a date-tree, fructed, ppr. *Fructu noscitur.* *Pl.* 18, *cr.* 12.
NEWBOLD, Eng., a griffin's head, erased. *Pl.* 48, *cr.* 6.
NEWBOLD, Yorks., a boar's head and neck, couped, in mouth a broken spear, in bend, ppr. *Pl.* 11, *cr.* 9.
NEWBOROUGH, Eng., a dexter arm, in armour, vambraced and embowed, in hand a sword, all ppr. *Pl.* 2, *cr.* 8.
NEWBOROUGH, Eng., an arm, in armour, embowed, in hand a fleur-de-lis, or. *Pl.* 24, *cr.* 14.
NEWBOROUGH, Eng., in hand a fleur-de-lis. *Pl.* 95, *cr.* 9.
NEWBOROUGH, Eng., a blackamoor's head, in profile, sa. *Pl.* 120, *cr.* 3.
NEWBOROUGH, Baron, Iri., and a Bart., Eng., (Wynn,) a dexter arm, in armour, in hand, ppr., a fleur-de-lis, or. *Suaviter in modo, fortiter in re.* *Pl.* 24, *cr.* 14.
NEWBURGH, Earl of, and Viscount, Visct. Kinnaird, and Baron Livingstone, Sco., (Eyre-Radcliffe-Livingstone,) a leg, erect, in armour, per pale, ar. and sa., couped at thigh, gu., knee-cap and spur, or. *Si je puis.* *Pl.* 81, *cr.* 5.
NEWBURY, Eng., a demi-eagle, displayed, or. *Pl.* 22, *cr.* 11.
NEWBURY, DE, Eng., a quatrefoil, vert. *Pl.* 65, *cr.* 7.
NEWBY, Eng., an arm, in armour, in hand a sword, ppr. *Pl.* 2, *cr.* 8.
NEWCASTLE-UNDER-LINE, Duke of, and Earl of Lincoln, (Frennes-Pelham-Clinton,) out of a ducal coronet, gu., a plume of five ostrich-feathers, ar., banded with a line, laid (cheveronwise, az. *Loyaulte n'a honte.* *Pl.* 106, *cr.* 11, (without chapeau.)
NEWCE, and NEWSE, Herts., Norf., and Surr., on a mount, vert, a garb, or, banded, gu. *Pl.* 13, *cr.* 2.
NEWCOM, NEWCOMBE, NEWCOME, and NEWCOMEN, Linc. and Lond., a lion's gamb, erased, sa. *Pl.* 126, *cr.* 9.
NEWCOME, Rev. HENRY-JUSTINIAN, Shenley, Herts., same crest.
NEWCOMB, Iri., out of a mural coronet, a demi-eagle, displayed. *Pl.* 33, *cr.* 5.
NEWCOMBE, Devons., a demi-horse, ar., gorged with a chaplet, vert.
NEWCOMBE, Devons., on a mural coronet, or, a raven, wings expanded, ppr. *Pl.* 8, *cr.* 5, (coronet, *pl.* 128, *fig.* 18.)
NEWCOME, Lond., out of a mural coronet, or, a Cornish chough, wings expanded, ppr. *Pl.* 8, *cr.* 5, (coronet, *pl.* 128, *fig.* 18.)
NEWCOURT, Devons., a demi-griffin, gu., guttée-d'or, beaked and legged, gold. *Pl.* 18, *cr.* 6.
NEWDEGATE, or NEWDIGATE, Eng., a fleur-de-lis, ar. *Confide recte agens.* *Pl.* 68, *cr.* 12.
NEWDEGATE, CHARLES-NEWDEGATE, Esq., of Arbury, Warw., and Harefield Place, Middx., same crest and motto.
NEWDICH, and NEWDICK, Worc., out of a mural coronet, or, a lion's head, gu. *Pl.* 45, *cr.* 9.
NEWDEGATE, Warw., Surr., and Middx., a swan, ar., beaked and membered, gu., gorged with a ducal coronet, or, thereto a chain affixed and reflexed over back, vert. *Pl.* 111, *cr.* 10, (without crown and rose.)

NEWDIGATE, Surr. and Derbs., a fleur-de-lis, ar. *Pl.* 68, *cr.* 12.
NEWDIGATE, Surr., a lion's gamb, erased, ar. *Pl.* 126, *cr.* 9.
NEWDIGATE, Surr., a horse, current, az., (flames issuing from nostrils, ppr.) *Pl.* 107, *cr.* 5, (without spear.)
NEWEKE, between two quills, ar., a mullet, az. *Pl.* 93, *cr.* 2.
NEWELL, Eng., out of a mural coronet, az., a lion's head, or. *Pl.* 45, *cr.* 9.
NEWELL, Oxon., an Italian greyhound, ppr., (collar dovetailed, or, charged on shoulder with a cinquefoil, ar.) *Pl.* 11, *cr.* 1, (without mount and trees.)
NEWELL, or NEWALL, Sco., a falcon, rising, in dexter a pen, all ppr. *Diligentia ditat.* *Pl.* 105, *cr.* 4, (pen, *pl.* 60, *cr.* 15.)
NEWENHAM, Iri., in the sea, an anchor, in pale, ensigned with a dove, in mouth an olive-branch. *Pl.* 3, *cr.* 10.
NEWENHAM, Rev. E. H., of Coolmore, between wings, gu., a demi-lion, rampant, ar., charged on shoulder with three guttées-de-sang. *Deo adverso, les vincitur.* *Pl.* 126 B, *cr.* 1. For *Worth,* an arm, in armour, embowed, holding a broken tilting-spear. *Crucem ferre dignum.* *Pl.* 126 D, *cr.* 8.
NEWENHAM, Notts. and Northamp., between wings, gu., a demi-lion, rampant, ar., charged on shoulder with three guttées-de-sang. *Pl.* 126 B, *cr.* 1.
NEWENHAM, Herts., a demi-lion, rampant, ar., (charged with a bend, vert.) *Pl.* 67, *cr.* 10.
NEWENHAM, and NEVENHAM, Eng., a pegasus, current, ppr. *Pl.* 28, *cr.* 9.
NEWENSON, Herts. and Kent, a wolf, passant, ar., pellettée, collared, (lined, and ringed, or.) *Pl.* 5, *cr.* 8, (without staff.)
NEWENTON, Eng., a sea-lion, rampant, or. *Pl.* 25, *cr.* 12.
NEWENTON, Ess. and Suss., on a chapeau, az., turned up, erm., a demi-eagle, displayed, ar. *Pl.* 96, *cr.* 9, (eagle, *pl.* 22, *cr.* 11.)
NEWFOUNDLAND COMPANY, Eng., a reindeer, trippant. *Pl.* 12, *cr.* 8.
NEWHOUSE, Eng., a squirrel, sejant, gu. *Pl.* 16, *cr.* 9.
NEWHOUSE, Lanc., an arm, erect, ppr., in hand a banner, az. *Pl.* 6, *cr.* 5.
NEWINGTON, Eng., a reindeer's head, cabossed, sa., attired, or. *Pl.* 114, *cr.* 7.
NEWINGTON, Suss., on a chapeau, gu., turned up, erm., a demi-eagle, displayed, or. *Pl.* 96, *cr.* 9, (eagle, *pl.* 22, *cr.* 11.)
NEWINGTON, Suss., on a chapeau, az., turned up, erm., a demi-eagle, displayed, ar. *Fac justa.* *Pl.* 96, *cr.* 9, (eagle, *pl.* 22, *cr.* 11.)
NEWLAND, Devons. and Hants, in lion's gamb, erect, ar., a cross formée, fitched, gu., charged with three bezants. *Pl.* 46, *cr.* 7, (bezant, *pl.* 141.)
NEWLAND, Herts., a tiger's head, erased, ar., maned and tufted, or, gorged with a collar, sa., (charged with three crescents, of the first, in mouth a broken spear, embrued, ppr.) *Pl.* 86, *cr.* 13.
NEWLANDS, Sco., a demi-lion, rampant. *Pro patriâ.* *Pl.* 67, *cr.* 10.
NEWLING, in lion's gamb, erased, ar., a cross pattée, fitched, gu. *Pl.* 46, *cr.* 7.

NEWMAN, Somers., Berks., and Dors., a martlet, volant, ppr. *Pl.* 40, *cr.* 4.
NEWMAN, Eng., a martlet, rising, ppr. *Lux mea Christus. Pl.* 107, *cr.* 6, (without tower.)
NEWMAN, Lond., on a plume of five feathers, three, az., two, or, a griffin's head, gold. *Pl.* 38, *cr.* 3, (plume, *pl.* 100, *cr.* 12.)
NEWMAN, Lond., on a mount, vert, (a man, jacket, az., breeches, sa., on head, ppr., a cap, gu., on a ladder, lighting) a beacon, all ppr. *Pl.* 89, *cr.* 9.
NEWMAN, a mermaid, (in the sea,) ppr., hair, or. *Pl.* 48, *cr.* 5.
NEWMAN, Glouc., a swallow, rising, ppr. *Lux mea Christus. Pl.* 40, *cr.* 4.
NEWMAN, Cornw., between wings, gu., a demi-lion, rampant, ar., guttée-de-sang. *Pl.* 73, *cr.* 3, (lion, *pl.* 67, *cr.* 10.)
NEWMAN, Bart., Devons., a lion, rampant, ar. *Ubi amor, ibi fides. Pl.* 67, *cr.* 5.
NEWMAN, JOHN, Esq., of Brands House, Bucks., a swallow, volant. *Ad te, Domine. Pl.* 40, *cr.* 4.
NEWMAN, Bart., Devons., a lion, rampant, per cheveron, az., guttée-d'eau, ar., and guttée-de-sang. *Probitas verus honos. Pl.* 67, *cr.* 5.
NEWMARCH, Eng., in the sea, an anchor, in pale, ensigned with a dove and olive-branch, all ppr. *Pl.* 3, *cr.* 10.
NEWMARCH, Yorks., a dove and olive-branch, ppr. *Pl.* 48, *cr.* 15.
NEWMARCH, Northumb., a demi-griffin, ppr. *Pl.* 18, *cr.* 6.
NEWMARCHE, Eng., a tower, triple-towered, ppr. *Pl.* 123, *cr.* 14.
NEWNHAM, Eng., a ram's head, erased, ar. *Pl.* 1, *cr.* 12.
NEWNHAM, a demi-lion, (charged with a pale.) *Pl.* 67, *cr.* 10.
NEWPORT, Eng., a dexter arm, in armour, embowed, garnished, or, in hand, ppr., a sword, ar., hilt and pommel, gold. *Pl.* 2, *cr.* 8.
NEWPORT, Salop, a unicorn's head, ar., armed and crined, or., erased, gu. *Pl.* 67, *cr.* 1.
NEWPORT, a fleur-de-lis, ar. *Pl.* 68, *cr.* 12.
NEWPORT, a stag, gu., (collared with a ducal coronet, stringed) and attired, or. *Pl.* 81, *cr.* 8.
NEWPORT, Salop, a unicorn's head, erased, ar., ducally gorged, or. *Pl.* 67, *cr.* 1, (gorging, *same plate, cr.* 7.)
NEWPORT, Herts. and Northamp., a buck, gu., attired, (gorged and chained,) or. *Pl.* 81, *cr.* 8.
NEWPORT, Worc., a bugle-horn, sa., stringed, az. *Pl.* 48, *cr.* 12.
NEWPORT, Bart., Iri., a unicorn's head, erased, ar., armed, maned, bearded, and ducally gorged, or. *Ne supra modum sapere. Pl.* 67, *cr.* 1, (gorging, *same plate, cr.* 1.)
NEWS, a demi-lion, holding a laurel-branch, all ppr. *Pl.* 39, *cr.* 14, (laurel, *pl.* 123, *cr.* 5.)
NEWSAM, Yorks., a sword, in pale, ar., enfiled with a thistle, ppr. *Pl.* 105, *cr.* 1, (thistle, *pl.* 100, *cr.* 9.)
NEWSHAM, Lanc., a boar's head, erased, or, charged with a cross crosslet, gu. *Pl.* 16, *cr.* 11, (cross, *pl.* 141.)
NEWSHAM, Eng., a dove and olive-branch, ppr. *Pl.* 48, *cr.* 15.
NEWSHAM, Eng., in lion's gamb, gu., a crescent, or. *Pl.* 91, *cr.* 1.
NEWSOM, Eng., in lion's paw, erased, sa., a bezant. *Pl.* 97, *cr.* 10.

NEWTE, a newt, ppr. *Pugilem claraverat. Pl.* 93, *cr.* 4, (without tree.)
NEWTON, Sco., a demi-lion, rampant, or, brandishing a scimitar, ppr. *Pro patriâ. Pl.* 126 A, *cr.* 1.
NEWTON, Eng., a bear's head, couped, ar., muzzled, gu. *Pl.* 111, *cr.* 4.
NEWTON, Yorks., Linc., and Derbs., a lion, rampant, ar. *Pl.* 67, *cr.* 5.
NEWTON, Kent and Warw., out of a ducal coronet; or, a boar's head, between two ostrich-feathers, ar. *Pl.* 102, *cr.* 14, (feathers, *pl.* 98, *cr.* 6.)
NEWTON, Northumb., an arm, embowed, vested, in hand a shin-bone. *Pl.* 120, *cr.* 1, (bone, *pl.* 25, *cr.* 11.)
NEWTON, Sco., a boar's head, erased and erect, ppr. *Pl.* 21, *cr.* 7.
NEWTON, Chesh., in lion's gamb, erect, a key, affixed to a chain, or. *Pl.* 5, *cr.* 5.
NEWTON, Chesh. and Salop, an eagle's leg, erased at thigh, sa., (environed by a snake, or.) *Pl.* 27, *cr.* 1, (without heart.)
NEWTON, Linc., Derbs., and Yorks., a wild man, kneeling on sinister knee, presenting a sword, all ppr.
NEWTON, Linc., Derbs., and Yorks., a man, in armour, crowned with an antique crown, kneeling on sinister knee, presenting a sword, ppr.
NEWTON, Beds., Bucks., and Devons., two arms, counter-embowed, dexter and sinister, (vested, az.,) supporting in hands ppr., a garb, or. *Pl.* 10, *cr.* 9, (garb, *pl.* 48, *cr.* 10.)
NEWTON, Cheadle Heath, Chester, a lion, rampant, per fess, erm. and gu., collared, of the last, between paws a cross, of the first, beurettée, or. *Pl.* 67, *cr.* 5.
NEWVILLE, Eng., a dove, in mouth an olive-branch, ppr. *Pl.* 48, *cr.* 15.
NEYLAN, Iri., in hand a sword. *Pl.* 21, *cr.* 10.
NIBBS, Eng., a buck's head, ppr. *Pl.* 91, *cr.* 14.
NIBBS, a buck's head, cabossed, gu., (pierced through by an arrow, or, feathered, ar.) *Pl.* 36, *cr.* 1.
NIBLET, an eagle, wings extended, or. *Pl.* 126, *cr.* 7.
NIBLETT, Glouc., an eagle, rising, quarterly, or and az. *Pl.* 67, *cr.* 4.
NIBLETT, Surr., a lion, couchant, mounted, vert, guarding a cross, gu. *Veritatis assertor.*
NIBLIE, Sco., in hand a scimitar, ppr. *Honor et amor. Pl.* 29, *cr.* 8.
NIBLOCK, a leopard, passant, in dexter a trefoil, slipped. *Pl.* 86, *cr.* 2, (trefoil, *pl.* 4, *cr.* 10.)
NICHELL, a demi-griffin, az., (in beak a pink, flowered, gu., leaved, vert.) *Pl.* 18, *cr.* 6.
NICHOL, or NICHOLL, Eng., in lion's paw, az., an olive-branch, ppr. *Pl.* 68, *cr.* 10.
NICHOL, or NICOL, Sco., a demi-lion, gu., armed and langued, or. *Generositate. Pl.* 67, *cr.* 10.
NICHOLAS, on top of a tower, issuing, a raven, wings expanded. *Pl.* 8, *cr.* 15.
NICHOLAS, Eng., a lion, passant, az., semée of etoiles, or. *Pl.* 48, *cr.* 8, (etoile, *pl.* 141.)
NICHOLAS, Wilts. and Lond., on a chapeau, az., turned up, erm., an owl, wings expanded, or. (Another, the chapeau, gu.) *Pl.* 123, *cr.* 6.
NICHOLAS, a lion, (statant,) or, semée of etoiles, az. *Pl.* 48, *cr.* 8, (etoile, *pl.* 141.)

NICHOLAS, and NICHOLLS, Glouc. and Wilts., a quatrefoil, on a stalk, raguly, or, charged with a martlet, sa. *Pl.* 65, *cr.* 7, (martlet, *pl.* 76, *cr.* 14.)

NICHOLAS, Glouc., Wilts., Devons., and Somers., a raven, wings elevated, sa., perched on battlements of a tower, ar. *Pl.* 84, *cr.* 3.

NICHOLAS, Cornw., out of a naval coronet, the word "Pilot" inscribed on the rim, a demi-eagle, displayed, sa. *Patria cara, carior fides. Pl.* 113, *cr.* 4, (demi-eagle, *pl.* 22, *cr.* 11.)

NICHOLL, JANE, of Tredunnock, Monmouth, on the battlements of a tower, a Cornish chough, wings addorsed. *Pl.* 84, *cr.* 3.

NICHOLL, Wel., on a mural coronet, a Cornish chough, wing addorsed, ppr. *Pl.* 84, *cr.* 3, (coronet, *pl.* 128, *fig.* 18.)

NICHOLLS, a squirrel. *Pl.* 16, *cr.* 9.

NICHOLLS, Bart., Eng., a wolf's head, erased, sa. *Pl.* 14, *cr.* 6.

NICHOLS, Cornw., in hand, couped above wrist, in fess, a bow, or, stringed, ar. *Pl.* 46, *cr.* 12, (bow, *pl.* 3, *cr.* 12.)

NICHOLLS, Cornw., a cubit arm, in fess, ppr., in hand a bow, strung, (and across it an arrow.) *Ib.*

NICHOLLS, a lion's head, erased, collared, charged with three martlets. *Pl.* 7, *cr.* 10, (martlet, *pl.* 111, *cr.* 5.)

NICHOLLS, Bucks., an eagle, rising, sustaining a cross crosslet, fitched, or. *Pl.* 65, *cr.* 3, (cross, *pl.* 141.)

NICHOLLS, Lond. and Salop., a dove, close, ppr. *Dum spiro, spero. Pl.* 66, *cr.* 12.

NICHOLS, a pheon, ar. *Pl.* 26, *cr.* 12.

NICHOLS, a demi-lion, rampant, between paws a human heart. *Pl.* 126, *cr.* 12, (heart, *pl.* 55, *cr.* 13.)

NICHOLS, out of a ducal coronet, or, a demi-lion, rampant, ar. *Pl.* 45, *cr.* 7.

NICHOLSON, Iri., a lion's head, erased, gu., (charged with a fess, or.) *Pl.* 81, *cr.* 4.

NICHOLSON, Sco., a unicorn's head, erased, sa. *Pl.* 67, *cr.* 1.

NICHOLSON, Eng., a stag, trippant, gu., armed, or. *Pl.* 68, *cr.* 2.

NICHOLSON, between two roses, gu., slipped and leaved, vert, a greyhound's head, ar. *Pl.* 84, *cr.* 13.

NICHOLSON, a demi-lion, rampant. *Pl.* 67, *cr.* 10.

NICHOLSON, a demi-man, vested in a close coat, az., buttons and cuffs of sleeves, turned up, or, face and hands, ppr., armed with a head-piece and gorget, ar., beaver open, in dexter a sword, in pale, ppr., hilt and pommel, gold, in sinister a Bible, open, clasps, of the fourth.

NICHOLSON, Bart., Glenbervie, Sco., a lion's head, erased, gu. *Nil sistere contra. Pl.* 81, *cr.* 4.

NICHOLSON, of East Court, Glouc.: 1. For *Nicholson*, a demi-lion, erased, charged with a bomb, fired, ppr., supporting a flag-staff, encircled by an eastern crown, with banner, gu., inscribed "Baroach." *Generositate.* 2. For *M'Innes*, out of a mural coronet, ppr., inscribed "Vittoria," a dexter arm embowed, vested, gu., entwined by a thistle, ppr., in glove, ar., a sword, also ppr., the Waterloo medal pendent from the guard. *Post prælia præmia.*

NICHOLSON, Waverley Abbey, in front of rays, a lion's head, erased. *Pl.* 81, *cr.* 4, (rays, *pl.* 117, *cr.* 11.)

NICHOLSON, Roundhay Park, Yorks., on branch of tree, in fess, ppr., a lion's head, erased at neck, or, charged with a cross pattée, gu. *Pl.* 81, *cr.* 4, (tree, *pl.* 10, *cr.* 1; cross, *pl.* 141.)

NICHOLSON, Lanc. and Cumb., out of a ducal coronet, gu., a lion's head, erm. *Pl.* 90, *cr.* 9.

NICHOLSON, Balrath, co. Meath, a leopard, sejant, ar., spotted sa., thrust through neck by a demi-lance, ppr.) *Pl.* 10, *cr.* 13.

NICHOLSON, Roe Park, Londonderry, out of a mural coronet, a demi-lion, rampant, all ppr. *Pl.* 17, *cr.* 7, (without branch.)

NICHOLSON-STEELE, of Ballow-House, co. Down.: 1. For *Nicholson*, out of a ducal coronet, gu., a lion's head, erm. *Pl.* 90, *cr.* 9. 2. For *Steele*, a demi-eagle, wings displayed, in beak, a snake, ppr. *Deus mihi sol. Pl.* 52, *cr.* 8, (snake, *pl.* 74, *cr.* 3.)

NICKELSON, Sco., a demi-lion, ppr. *Generositate. Pl.* 67, *cr.* 10.

NICKLIN, Eng., a griffin's head, erased, ar. *Pl.* 48, *cr.* 6.

NICKOLS, in hand, in armour, couped above wrist, in fess, an arrow, in pale, ppr., crossed at top by a bow, in fess, or, strung, ar.

NICKOLSON, Eng., a hawk's head, erased, sa. *Pl.* 34, *cr.* 11.

NICOL, Eng., a demi-lion, rampant, gu. *Pl.* 67, *cr.* 10.

NICOLAS, out of a count's coronet, a wolf's head. *Pl.* 14, *cr.* 6, (coronet, *pl.* 127, *fig.* 9.)

NICOLL, Eng., a sparrow-hawk, sa., beaked and legged, gu. *Pl.* 67, *cr.* 3.

NICOLL, or NICOLLS, Middx., a wolf's head, sa., charged with five ermine spots, in fess, or. *Pl.* 14, *cr.* 6, (ermine, *pl.* 141.)

NICOLL, a lion's head, erased, az., collared, ar., charged with three martlets, sa. *Pl.* 7, *cr.* 10, (martlet, *pl.* 111, *cr.* 5.)

NICOLLS, Norf., a squirrel, sejant, sa., collared, or, between fore-legs a water bouget, ar. *Pl.* 85, *cr.* 3, (bouget, *pl.* 14, *cr.* 12.)

NICOLLS, a cubit arm, ppr., in hand a bow, or, strung, ar. *Pl.* 3, *cr.* 12.

NICOLLS, or NYCOLLS, Lond., a demi-Cornish chough, ppr., in beak an ear of wheat, or.

NICOLSON, Iri., an arm in armour, ppr., in hand a holly-branch, vert. *Pl.* 55, *cr.* 6, (arm, *pl.* 68, *cr.* 1.)

NICOLSON, a lion's head, erased. *Generositate. Pl.* 81, *cr.* 4.

NICOLSON, Sco., same crest. *Nil sistere contra.*

NICOLSON, a demi-lion, or, armed and langued, gu. *Generositate. Pl.* 67, *cr.* 10.

NICOLSON, Lond., on a mount, vert, a leopard, sejant, ar., spotted sa., (pierced through breast by a lance, ppr., wound dropping blood.) *Pl.* 123, *cr.* 8.

NICOLSON, Middx., Kent, and Linc., in lion's gamb, gu., an anchor, or. *Pl.* 47, *cr.* 14, (anchor, *pl.* 25, *cr.* 15.)

NIELSON, Sco., on a mount, vert, a tower, with cupola and vane, ppr. *Murus ahenus. Pl.* 42, *cr.* 10, (mount, *pl.* 98, *cr.* 13.)

NIGELL, or NIGILL, an oak-tree, vert. *Pl.* 16, *cr.* 8.

NIGHTINGALE, Bart., Cambs. and Ess., an ibex, sejant, ar., tufted, armed and maned, or. *Pl.* 93, *cr.* 11, (without coronet.)

Z

NIGHTINGALE, Lond. and Warw., a greyhound, current, erm., charged with a crescent for difference. *Pl.* 28, *cr.* 7, (crescent, *pl.* 141.)
NIGHTINGALE, Kent, a greyhound, (passant,) ppr. *Mens conscia recti. Pl.* 104, *cr.* 1, (without chapeau.)
NIGHTINGALL, an ibex. *Pl.* 115, *cr.* 13.
NIGHTINGALL, of Brome Hall, Norf., on a mural coronet, or, an ibex, ar., horned, maned, and tufted, gold, gorged with a laurel-wreath, vert. *Pl.* 115, *cr.* 13, (coronet, same plate, *cr.* 14.)
NIGON, a leopard's face. *Pl.* 66, *cr.* 14.
NIMMO, Sco., out of a mural coronet, an arm, in armour, embowed to sinister, supporting in pale a pennon of two points. *I show, not boast. Pl.* 126 A, *cr.* 4.
NIND, Eng., a torteau, gu., charged with a pale indented, ar. *Pl.* 63, *cr.* 7.
NISBET, Eng., a stag's head, cabossed, or. *Pl.* 36, *cr.* 1.
NISBET, a castle, sa., growing beside it a thistle, ppr. *Hinc ducitur honos. Pl.* 8, *cr.* 7.
NISBET, Sco., out of a cloud, in fess, a dexter hand holding a balance and scales, all ppr. *Discite justitiam. Pl.* 43, *cr.* 4, (scales, *pl.* 26, *cr.* 8.)
NISBET, Sco., a boar's head, erased. *His fortibus arma. Pl.* 16, *cr.* 11.
NISBET: 1. An eagle, wings displayed, ppr. *Non tabes virtuti sors. Pl.* 126, *cr.* 7. 2. A boar, passant, sa. *I byde it. Pl.* 48, *cr.* 14.
NISBET, or NISBETT, Sco., a boar, passant, sa. *I byde it. Pl.* 48, *cr.* 14.
NISBET, Sco., a boar's head, erased, sa. *Vis fortibus arma. Pl.* 16, *cr.* 11.
NISBET, Sco., a boar's head, erased, (within a bordure), sa. *His fortibus arma. Pl.* 16, *cr.* 11.
NISBET, a torteau, charged with a pale indented, ar. *Pl.* 63, *cr.* 7.
NISBET, Sco., a cubit arm, in armour, erect, in hand a truncheon, ppr. *I byde it. Pl.* 33, *cr.* 4.
NISBET, Eng., a boar's head, erased, sa. *Pl.* 16, *cr.* 11.
NISBETT, JOHN-MORE, Esq., of Cairnhill, Lanark, a boar's head, erased, sa. *Vis fortibus arma. Pl.* 16, *cr.* 11.
NIVEN, Sco., a branch of palm, vert. *Vivis sperandum. Pl.* 26, *cr.* 3.
NIVEN, Eng., a holly-branch, vert. *Pl.* 99, *cr.* 6.
NIVISON, Sco., a wolf, passant, sa., collared and lined, or. *Exitus acta probat. Pl.* 5, *cr.* 8, (without staff.)
NIX, Eng., on a mount, a stag, lodged, ppr. *Pl.* 22, *cr.* 5.
NIXON, Eng., in dexter hand a sword, ppr. *Pl.* 21, *cr.* 10.
NIXON, Iri., on point of a sword, in pale, a cross pattée, ppr. *Pl.* 56, *cr.* 1.
NIXON, a moorcock, ppr. *Pl.* 10, *cr.* 1, (without stump.)
NIXON, Oxon., a leopard, rampant, gardant, ppr. *Pl.* 73, *cr.* 2, (gardant, *pl.* 77, *cr.* 1.)
NOBBES, on a chapeau, ppr., an eagle's head, az. *Pl.* 96, *cr.* 9, (head, *pl.* 100, *cr.* 10.)
NOBLE, Eng., an eagle, displayed, or. *Fide et fortitudine. Pl.* 48, *cr.* 11.
NOBLE, Iri., in lion's paw, sa., a cross pattée, fitched, or. *Pl.* 46, *cr.* 7.
NOBLE, Sco., in dexter hand a dagger. *Virtute et valore. Pl.* 28, *cr.* 4.
NOBLE, Leic., an eagle, displayed, or. *Pl.* 48, *cr.* 11.

NOBLE, Kent, Devons., and Cornw., a lion, passant, az. *Pl.* 48, *cr.* 8.
NOBLE, a demi-greyhound, ar., (pierced in breast by an arrow, ppr.) *Pl.* 48, *cr.* 3.
NOCK, Eng., in dexter hand a scimitar, ppr. *Pl.* 29, *cr.* 8.
NODES, two lions' gambs sa., holding a garb, or. *Pl.* 42, *cr.* 2, (garb, *pl.* 48, *cr.* 10.)
NODIN, Eng., a stag's head, couped, gu. *Pl.* 91, *cr.* 14.
NOEL, a buck, statant, ar., armed, or. *Pensez a bein. Pl.* 88, *cr.* 9, (without arrow.)
NOEL, Eng., a buck, ar., attired or. *Tout bien ou rien. Pl.* 88, *cr.* 9, (without arrow.)
NOEL, Leic. and Notts., same crest.
NOEL, Bart., Ruts., a buck, at gaze, ar., attired, or. *Tout bien ou rien. Pl.* 81, *cr.* 8.
NOEL, BERKELEY - PLANTAGENET - GUILDFORD - CHARLES, Esq., of Moxhul Park, Warw., same crest and motto.
NOEL, Baron Barham. See BARHAM.
NOGLE, a goldfinch, ppr. *Pl.* 10, *cr.* 12.
NOLAN, Iri., a hawk. *Pl.* 67, *cr.* 3.
NOLAN, Lond., a demi-lion, rampant, gu., holding a fleur-de-lis, or. *Pl.* 91, *cr.* 13.
NOLAND, or NOWLAND, Iri., a demi-lion, rampant, gu. *Pl.* 67, *cr.* 10.
NONE, Eng., an eagle, displayed, az., on breast a mullet, or. *Pl.* 12, *cr.* 7, (mullet, *pl.* 141.)
NONFANT, three vine-hooks, interlaced, ppr. *Pl.* 58, *cr.* 8.
NONWERS, NORWERS, and NOWERS, a pestle and mortar, or. *Pl.* 83, *cr.* 6.
NONWIKE, out of a plume of ostrich-feathers, ar., a demi-griffin, ppr. *Pl.* 11, *cr.* 6.
NOONE, Norf. and Suff., a bull's head, erased, per fess, ar. and gu., attired, of the last. *Pl.* 19, *cr.* 3.
NOONE, Leic., an eagle, displayed, with two heads, or, wings, vert. *Pl.* 87, *cr.* 11, (without flame.)
NORBERY, and NORBURY, Eng., a dove, or. *Pl.* 66, *cr.* 12.
NORBORNE, Wilts., a demi-lion, erm., between paws a ducal coronet, or. *Pl.* 126, *cr.* 12, (coronet, *pl.* 9, *cr.* 7.)
NORBURY, Iri., a fleur-de-lis. *Right can never die. Pl.* 68, *cr.* 12.
NORBURY, Chesh., out of a ducal coronet, or, a bull's head, sa. *Pl.* 68, *cr.* 6.
NORBURY, Earl of, and Baron, Viscount Glandine and Baron Norwood, Iri., (Toler ;) a fleur-de-lis, or. *Regi et patriæ fidelis. Pl.* 68, *cr.* 12.
NORCLIFFE, Eng., a buck's head, erased, az. *Pl.* 66, *cr.* 9.
NORCLIFFE, Yorks., a lion, passant, gu., (gorged with a chaplet, vert.) *Pl.* 48, *cr.* 8.
NORCLIFFE, of Langton, Yorks., a greyhound, sejant, or, collared, az., sustaining with dexter a mascle, ar. *Sine maculâ. Pl.* 66, *cr.* 15, (mascle, *pl.* 141.)
NORCOP, WILLIAM-CHURCH, Esq., of Betton Hall, Salop, a boar's head, sa. *Pl.* 48, *cr.* 2.
NORDEN, Lond., an arm, couped, erect, vested, az., cuff, ar., in hand, ppr., an escarbuncle, or. *Providentiâ tutamur. Pl.* 114, *cr.* 4.
NORDEN, Kent, a hawk, ar., belled, or, preying on a partridge, of the first, beaked, gold. *Pl.* 61, *cr.* 7.
NORDEN, a demi-beaver, sa., (in mouth a branch of five leaves, vert.) *Pl.* 9, *cr.* 9.
NORDET, Eng., between wings, ppr., a torteau, gu. *Pl.* 2, *cr.* 3.

NORFOLK, Eng., a lion, rampant, sa. *Pl.* 67, *cr.* 5.

NORFOLK, Duke of, Earl of Arundel, Surr. and Norf.; Baron Howard Fitz-Alan, Clun and Osweldestrie, and Maltravers; Earl Marshall and Hereditary Marshall of England; Premier Duke and Earl, (Howard,) on a chapeau, gu., turned up, erm., a lion, statant, gardant, tail extended, or, (gorged) with a ducal coronet, ar. *Solo virtus invicta. Pl.* 120, *cr.* 15.

NORGATE, a demi-wolf, salient, ar., charged on breast with an etoile, gu, *Pl.* 56, *cr.* 8, (without spear; etoile, *pl.* 141.)

NORHOPÉ, Kent and Notts., a cubit arm, vested, per pale, ar. and vert, in hand, ppr., a garland, of the second. *Pl.* 44, *cr.* 13, (without bird.)

NORIE, Sco., on point of a pheon, a negro's head, couped, between two arms, in armour, vambraced, all ppr. *Domi ac foris. Pl.* 83, *cr.* 11.)

NORIE, and NORRIE, Eng., a wolf's head, erased, sa. *Pl.* 14, *cr.* 6.

NORMAN, Iri., out of a ducal coronet, a bull's head. *Pl.* 86, *cr.* 6.

NORMAN, Eng., a spear, issuing, in pale, thrust through a savage's head, couped, ppr. *Pl.* 7, *cr.* 3.

NORMAN, Dencombe, Suss., a sea-horse, sejant, (resting dexter on an escutcheon.) *Pl.* 103, *cr.* 3.

NORMAND, Sco., a holy lamb and banner, ppr. *Auxilium ab alto. Pl.* 48, *cr.* 13.

NORMAN-LEE: 1. A lion, passant, gardant. *Pl.* 120, *cr.* 5. 2. A demi-lion, rampant. *Pl.* 67, *cr.* 10.

NORMANTON, Earl of, Viscount and Baron Somerton, Iri., (Agar,) a demi-lion, or. *Via trita, via tuta. Pl.* 67, *cr.* 10.

NORREYS-JACKSON, of Davyhulme Hall, Lanc., on a mount, vert, an eagle, wings elevated, sa. *Pl.* 61, *cr.* 1.

NORREYS-JEPHSON, Bart., of Mallow, co. Cork, on a mount, vert, a raven, rising, sa., charged on breast with a crescent, or. *Loyalment je deserts. Pl.* 50, *cr.* 5, (crescent, *pl.* 141; mount, *pl.* 98, *cr.* 13.)

NORRINGTON, Eng., a bat, displayed, ppr. *Pl.* 94, *cr.* 9.

NORRIS, Eng., an escarbuncle, gu. *Pl.* 51, *cr.* 10.

NORRIS, Iri., a virgin's head, couped at breast, ppr., vested, gu. *Pl.* 81, *cr.* 12.

NORRIS, Sco., a pelican, in nest. *Sic his qui diligunt. Pl.* 44, *cr.* 1.

NORRIS, Eng., a sea-lion, or, tail part, ppr., in dexter a cross flory, sa. *Pl.* 59, *cr.* 2.

NORRIS, Norf., a talbot, sejant, collared and ringed. *Fideliter serva. Pl.* 107, *cr.* 7.

NORRIS, Hants, on a mount, vert, an owl, (in dexter an arrow.) *Pl.* 27, *cr.* 9, (mount *pl.* 98, *cr.* 13.)

NORRIS, and NORREYS, Glouc., Somers., and Wel., a demi-stag, ar., attired, sa., pierced through body by an arrow, of the last, headed and feathered, of the first. *Pl.* 55, *cr.* 9, (arrow, *pl.* 56, *cr.* 11; without rose.)

NORRIS, and NORREYS, Berks. and Lanc., a raven, wings elevated, sa. *Pl.* 50, *cr.* 5.

NORSE, Sco., in dexter hand a pair of scales. *Pl.* 26, *cr.* 8.

NORTH, Earl of Guildford. *See* GUILDFORD.

NORTH, Cambs., a dragon's head, (erased,) sa., ducally gorged and chained, or. *Pl.* 36, *cr.* 7.

NORTH, Notts., a lion's head, erased, ar., collared, vair, or and az. *Pl.* 7, *cr.* 10.

NORTH, Eng., a dragon's head, (erased,) sa., purfled, or, gorged with a ducal coronet and chain, gold. *Pl.* 36, *cr.* 7.

NORTH, Middx., a cock's head, couped, wings, or, each charged with two cheverons, sa., collared, in beak a branch of holly, leaved and fructed, ppr. *Pl.* 47, *cr.* 3, (branch, *pl.* 99, *cr.* 6.)

NORTH, Rougham, Norf., a dragon's head, (erased,) sa., scaled, ducally gorged and chained, or, *Pl.* 36, *cr.* 7.

NORTHAGE, Lond., a stag's head and neck, affrontée, ppr. *Pl.* 111, *cr.* 13.

NORTHAM, Eng., a demi-wolf, gu. *Pl.* 56, *cr.* 8, (without spear.)

NORTHAMPTON, Marquess and Earl of, Earl Compton and Baron Wilmington, (Compton,) on a mount, vert, a beacon, or, inflamed on top, ppr., (on beacon a label, inscribed, *Nisi Dominus.) Je ne cherche que ung. Pl.* 89, *cr.* 9.

NORTHCOTE, Devons., on a chapeau, gu., turned up, erm., a stag, trippant, ar. *Christi crux est mea lux. Pl.* 63, *cr.* 8.

NORTHCOTE, of Crediton, Devons., same crest.

NORTHCOTE, Somerset Court, a stag, ar., (charged on body with two crosses botonnée, gu., resting dexter on an escutcheon, or charged with a pale, eng., bendy of six, of the first and az.) *Pl.* 68, *cr.* 2.

NORTHCOTT, Devons., a demi-unicorn, (erased,) or. *Pl.* 26, *cr.* 14.

NORTHEN, out of a mural coronet, a dragon's head, vomiting flames, ppr. *Pl.* 101, *cr.* 4, (flames, *pl.* 37, *cr.* 9.)

NORTHESK, Earl of, Baron Rosehill and Inglismaldie, Sco., (Carnegie:) 1. The stern of a line-of-battle ship, (on fire,) ppr. *Pl.* 109, *cr.* 8. 2. Out of a naval coronet, or, a demi-leopard, ppr. *Tache sans tache. Pl.* 32, *cr.* 8, (leopard, *pl.* 12, *cr.* 14.)

NORTHEVER, Somers., a lion's gamb, ar., supporting a lozenge, az., charged with a cross crosslet, or. *Pl.* 89, *cr.* 15.

NORTHEY, Eng., a demi-unicorn, ar. *Pl.* 26, *cr.* 14.

NORTHEY, Epsom, a cockatrice, (flames issuing from the mouth), ppr. *Pl.* 63, *cr.* 15.

NORTHFOLKE, or NORFOLK, Eng., a lion, rampant, sa. *Pl.* 67, *cr.* 5.

NORTHIN, Lond., on a ducal coronet, or, a talbot, passant, az., collared, of the last. *Pl.* 3, *cr.* 8.

NORTHLEIGH, Eng., three savages' heads, conjoined in one neck, one looking to dexter, one to sinister, and one upward. *Pl.* 32, *cr.* 2.

NORTHMORE, JOHN, Esq., of Cleve Hall, Exeter, a lion's head, erased, gu., crowned with radiant crown of five points, ar., charged on breast with a rose, of the second, barbed and seeded, ppr. *Nec elata, nec dejecta. Pl.* 126 B, *cr.* 14.

NORTHMORE, Devons., a lion's head, erased, charged with a cinquefoil, crowned with a radiant crown, ar. *Pl.* 126 B, *cr.* 14.

NORTHUMBERLAND, Duke and Earl of, Earl and Baron Percy, Baron Warkworth, and a Bart., (Percy,) on a chapeau, gu., turned up, erm., a lion, statant, az., (tail extended.) *Espérance en Dieu. Pl.* 107, *cr.* 1.

NORTHWICK, Baron, and a Bart., (Rushout,) a lion, passant, gardant, or. *Par ternis suppar.* *Pl.* 120, *cr.* 5.
NORTHWOOD, Eng., a demi-lion, az., armed and langued, or. *Pl.* 67, *cr.* 10.
NORTON, Kent, a wolf's head, erased. *Pl.* 14, *cr.* 6.
NORTON, Eng., a griffin's head, or. *Pl.* 38, *cr.* 3.
NORTON, Hants., Yorks., and Suff., a moor's head, couped at shoulders, ppr. *Pl.* 120, *cr.* 3.
NORTON, Beds., Herts., and Bucks., a griffin, sejant, ppr., winged, gu., beak and fore-legs, or. *Pl.* 100, *cr.* 11.
NORTON, Eng., a moor's head, in profile, ppr., bound about forehead with a fillet, wreathed and tied in a knot, ar., az., and gu. *Pl.* 23, *cr.* 3.
NORTON, Suff., a hare, sejant, gu., (in grass, vert.) *Pl.* 70, *cr.* 1.
NORTON, Iri., between wings, or, a spur rowel, az. *Pl.* 109, *cr.* 12, (rowel, *pl.* 54, *cr.* 5.)
NORTON, a maiden's head, ppr., garlanded, vert. *Pl.* 114, *cr.* 2.
NORTON, a buck's head, cabossed, or. *Pl.* 36, *cr.* 1.
NORTON, Bucks. and Cambs., a greyhound's head, or, gorged with a fess, engrailed, between two bars, gu., the fess ringed, gold. *Pl.* 43, *cr.* 11.
NORTON, Baron Grantley. *See* GRANTLEY.
NORTON, Norf., a halberd, ppr. *Pl.* 14, *cr.* 8.
NORTON, Berks., Kent, and Middx., out of a ducal coronet, az., a demi-lion, rampant, double-queued, ar. *Pl.* 120, *cr.* 10, (coronet, *same plate, cr.* 13.)
NORTON, Lond. and Salop, between wings, or, a wreath of laurel, vert, tied with a ribbon, gu. *Pl.* 54, *cr.* 10, (wings, *same plate, cr.* 6.)
NORTON, Worc., a tiger's head, erased, in mouth a broken spear, or. *Pl.* 94, *cr.* 10, (spear, *pl.* 11, *cr.* 9.)
NORVEL, an apple, in pale, stalked and leaved, ppr.
NORVILL, Sco., a martlet, rising, ppr. *Spem renovant alæ. Pl.* 107, *cr.* 6, (without tower.)
NORWICK, a lion's head, erased, (environed with a circle of peacock's feathers,) ppr. *Pl.* 81, *cr.* 4.
NORWICH, Ess., Norf., Northamp., and Suff., on a mount, vert, a cock, ar., combed, legged, and wattled, gu. *Pl.* 76, *cr.* 7.
NORWOOD, J. D., Esq., Ashford, Kent, on waves of the sea, ppr., a lion, sejant, holding between paws an anchor, fluxes upward. *Sub cruce vinces. Pl.* 126 c, *cr.* 14.
NORWOOD, Eng., an eagle, rising, ppr. *Pl.* 67, *cr.* 4.
NORWOOD, out of a ducal coronet, a boar's head and neck, all or. *Pl.* 102, *cr.* 14.
NORWOOD, and NORTHWOOD, a demi-lion, rampant, erased, ar., ducally crowned, or, in gambs a branch of palm, ppr. *Pl.* 61, *cr.* 4.
NORYS, out of an antique crown, or, a dragon's head, gu. *Pl.* 101, *cr.* 4, (crown, *pl.* 79, *cr.* 12.)
NORZAM, a lion's head, erased, (environed with a circle of peacocks' feathers,) ppr. *Pl.* 81, *cr.* 4.
NOSWARTH, Eng., out of a ducal coronet, or, a unicorn's head, sa., armed and crined, ar. *Pl.* 45, *cr.* 14.
NOTLEY, JAMES-THOMAS-BENEDICTUS, Esq., of Combe, Sydenham Hall, and Chillington House, Somers., out of a mural coronet, a lion's head. *Noli mentiri. Pl.* 45, *cr.* 9.

NOTMAN, an eagle, rising, ppr., sustaining a flag, gu., staff, sa. *Pl.* 65, *cr.* 3.
NOTON, Eng., a hind's head, or. *Pl.* 21, *cr.* 9.
NOTT, Eng., a stag's head, ppr. *Pl.* 91, *cr.* 14.
NOTT, Lond. and Kent., a martlet, ar., ducally crowned, or, in beak an olive-branch, ppr. *Pl.* 111, *cr.* 5, (branch, *pl.* 48, *cr.* 15 ; crown, *same plate.*)
NOTTAGE, Eng., a seax, ppr. *Pl.* 27, *cr.* 10.
NOTTAGE, Suff., a cross pattée, fitched. *Pl.* 27, *cr.* 14.
NOTTIDGE, Ess., a boar's head, couped at neck, gu., langued, az., crined and tusked, or, (collared, erminois.) *Pl.* 2, *cr.* 3.
NOTTINGHAM, Iri., in hand an escallop, ppr. *Pl.* 57, *cr.* 6.
NOTTINGHAM, Eng., in dexter hand, ppr., an annulet, or. *Pl.* 24, *cr.* 3.
NOUNE, and NUNNE, Eng., a bull's head, erased, per fess, ar. and gu., attired, of the last. *Pl.* 19, *cr.* 3.
NOURSE, Eng., a stag's head, or. *Pl.* 91, *cr.* 14.
NOURSE, Oxon., two bears' gambs, or, holding a fire-ball, ppr. *Pl.* 42, *cr.* 3, (ball, *pl.* 70, *cr.* 3.)
NOURSE, Bucks., Ess., and Oxon., an arm, embowed, vested, az., cuffed, ar., in hand, ppr., a snake, of the last, environed round arm. *Pl.* 91, *cr.* 6, (vesting, *pl.* 39, *cr.* 1.)
NOVE, Leic., an eagle, displayed, vert. *Pl.* 48, *cr.* 11.
NOVELL, Lond., a buck, trippant, ar. *Pl.* 68, *cr.* 2.
NOVELLE, Eng., a bat, displayed, sa. *Pl.* 94, *cr.* 9.
NOWELL, and NOEL, Leic., a stag, trippant, ar., attired, or. *Pl.* 68, *cr.* 2.
NOWELL, Middx., a cubit arm, in pale, ppr., in hand a snake, or. *Pl.* 91, *cr.* 6.
NOWELL, Kent, Middx., and Suss., an arm in armour, embowed, ppr., garnished, or, in hand a fire-ball, of the first. *Pl.* 62, *cr.* 9, (armour, *pl.* 120, *cr.* 11.)
NOWENHAM, a sturgeon, ppr.
NOWLAN, and NOWLAND, Eng., a cock, ar., combed and wattled, gu. *Pl.* 67, *cr.* 14.
NOWLAN, Iri., an arm, in armour, az., couped at shoulder, embowed, resting elbow on the wreath, in hand, ppr., a sceptre, or. *Pl.* 104, *cr.* 13.
NOWLAND, Iri., a demi-lion, rampant, gu. *Pl.* 67, *cr.* 10.
NOWNE, Eng., a lion, rampant, or, charged on shoulder with a crescent, gu. *Pl.* 67, *cr.* 5, (crescent, *pl.* 141.)
NOY, Eng., a fir-tree, vert. *Pl.* 26, *cr.* 10.
NOY, Iri., two daggers, in saltier, ppr. *Pl.* 24, *cr.* 2.
NOYE, Cornw., a dove, ar., in beak a sprig of (laurel,) vert. *Pl.* 48, *cr.* 15.
NOYE, Cornw., on a chapeau, gu., turned up, erm., a falcon, wings expanded, (in beak a branch of laurel,) ppr. *Pl.* 105, *cr.* 4, (chapeau, *same plate, cr.* 5.)
NOYE, Cornw., on a chapeau, gu., turned up, erm., a falcon, close, ar., in beak a laurel-branch, vert. *Pl.* 41, *cr.* 10, (chapeau, *pl.* 127, *fig.* 13.)
NOYES, a deer's head, erm. *Pl.* 91, *cr.* 14.
NOYES, East Mascall's, Suss., on a chapeau, a dove, in mouth an olive-branch, ppr. *Pl.* 48, *cr.* 15, (chapeau, *pl.* 127, *fig.* 13.)

NOYES, Eng., a deer's head, erased, erm. *Pl.* 66, *cr.* 9.
NUBURGH, Eng., on a mural coronet, a sheaf of (seven) arrows, points upward, banded. *Pl.* 75, *cr.* 7, (coronet, *pl.* 128, *fig.* 18.)
NUGENT, Ess., a cockatrice, vert, beaked, combed, wattled, and armed, gu. *Decrevi. Pl.* 126 B, *cr.* 11.
NUGENT, FITZGERALD, Bart., Iri., a griffin, vert, charged on breast with a martlet. *Decrevi. Pl.* 66, *cr.* 13, (martlet, *pl.* 111, *cr.* 5.)
NUGENT, Bart., Berks., a cockatrice, vert, (gorged with a plain collar, or, pendent therefrom an escutcheon, gu., charged with a dagger, in pale, ppr., hilt and pommel, or.) *Decrevi. Pl.* 63, *cr.* 15.
NUGENT, Bart., Iri., a cockatrice, ppr. *Decrevi. Pl.* 63, *cr.* 15.
NUGENT, Baron, Iri., (Grenville-Nugent-Temple.) 1. For *Grenville*, a garb, vert. *Pl.* 48, *cr.* 10. 2. For *Temple*, on a ducal coronet, a martlet, or. *Pl.* 98, *cr.* 14. *Templa quam dilecta.*
NUGENT, Earl. See BUCKINGHAM, Duke of.
NUGENT, Marquis of Westmeath. See WESTMEATH.
NUGENT, EDMOND-ROBERT, Esq., of Farren Connell, co. Cavan, a cockatrice, rising, ppr., tail, nowed, wattles, ppr. *Decrevi. Pl.* 126 B, *cr.* 11.
NUGENT, RICHARD, Lond. Same crest.
NUN, Eng., an arm, in armour, vambraced, in hand a hawk's lure, all or. *Pl.* 120, *cr.* 11, (lure, *pl.* 44, *cr.* 2.)
NUN, a bull's head, erased, per fess, vert and or. *Pl.* 19, *cr.* 3.
NUNN, Eng., an arm, in armour, embowed, in hand a battle axe. *Pl.* 121, *cr.* 14.

NUNN, and NUNNE, Iri., a bull's head, erased, per fess, ar. and gu., armed and crined, of the last. *Pl.* 19, *cr.* 3.
NUNN, EDWARD-WESTBY, Esq., of St Margaret's, co. Wexford, a bull's head, erased, per fess, ar. and gu., armed and crined, of the last. *Suaviter in modo, fortiter in re. Pl.* 19, *cr.* 3.
NURSE, Sco., a pair of balances, ppr. *Justitia. Pl.* 12, *cr.* 11.
NUSHAM, a monster, with a lion's head, fish's body, and bird's feet. *Pl.* 80, *cr.* 13.
NUTBROWNE, Ess., a lion, sejant, sa., in paws a (sword, ar., hilt, of the first, pommel and gripe, of the second.) *Pl.* 60, *cr.* 4.
NUTCOMBE, Wilts., on a mural coronet, or, a falcon, close, ppr., beaked and belled, or. *Pl.* 41, *cr.* 10, (coronet, *pl.* 128, *fig.* 18.)
NUTHALL, Chesh. and Lanc., a talbot, (statant,) ar., chained, or. *Pl.* 65, *cr.* 2.
NUTHALL, Chesh., a falcon, rising, ar., beaked and ducally gorged, or. *Pl.* 61, *cr.* 12.
NUTT, Eng., on a chapeau, a cock, crowing, ppr. *Pl.* 104, *cr.* 3.
NUTT, Glouc. and Suss., on a chapeau, gu., turned up, erm., a pheon, or, between wings, ar. (Another, between wings, vert, a pheon, ar.) *Pl.* 21, *cr.* 13, (pheon, *pl.* 141.)
NUTTALL, a martlet, sa. *Pl.* 111, *cr.* 5.
NUTTALL, ROBERT, Esq., of Kempsay House, Worc., a martlet, sa. *Serva jugum. Pl.* 111, *cr.* 5.
NUTTER, Eng., a dolphin, naiant, or. *Pl.* 48, *cr.* 9.
NYSSELL, Eng., a lion, rampant, per fess, ar. and az., in dexter a fleur-de-lis, or. *Pl.* 87, *cr.* 6.

O

OAKDEN, Stockwell Green, Surr., a wolf, rampant, ar., against an oak-tree, fructed, ppr. *Et, si ostendo non jacto. Pl.* 58, *cr.* 10.
OAKELEY, Bart., Salop: A dexter arm, in armour, embowed, ppr., charged with two fleurs-de-lis, or, each in a crescent, gu., in hand a scimitar, also ppr., hilt and pommel, gold. *Pl.* 81, *cr.* 11, (fleur-de-lis and crescent, *pl.* 141.) 2. A stag's head, erased, ar. *Non timeo, sed caveo. Pl.* 66, *cr.* 9.
OAKELEY, Salop and Wales, a dexter arm, in armour, embowed, ppr., in hand a scimitar, ppr., hilt and pommel, or. *Pl.* 81, *cr.* 11.
OAKELEY, the Rev. ARTHUR, of Oakeley, Salop, same crest.
OAKES, Eng., a cock's head, erased, gu. *Pl.* 92, *cr.* 3.
OAKES, within pailings, ppr., an oak-tree, vert. *Pl.* 16, *cr.* 8, (pailings, *pl.* 13, *cr.* 12.)
OAKES, a serpent, (erect) on tail, in mouth a sprig. *Pl.* 104, *cr.* 9.
OAKES, a demi-leopard, rampant, gorged with an antique crown, in paws an acorn-branch, fructed, ppr. *Pl.* 97, *cr.* 5, (crown, *pl.* 79, *cr.* 12.)
OAKES, or OKES, Northamp., an oak-tree, vert, fructed, or, supported by two lions, rampant, ar. *Pl.* 16, *cr.* 8, (lions, *pl.* 36, *cr.* 8.)

OAKEY, Eng., the rising sun, ppr. *Pl.* 67, *cr.* 9.
OAKLEY, Eng., an arm, in armour, embowed, charged with a crescent, in hand a scimitar. *Pl.* 81, *cr.* 11, (crescent, *pl.* 141.)
OAKLEY, Eng., a terrestrial globe, ppr. *Pl.* 14, *cr.* 1.
OATES, Eng., a boar's head, erased, ar. *Pl.* 16, *cr.* 11.
OATLY, Eng., a garb, ppr. *Pl.* 48, *cr.* 10.
O'BIERNE, Eng. a cockatrice, az., winged, or. *Pl.* 63, *cr.* 15.
O'BREANON, Iri., an arm, in armour, embowed, in hand a sword. *Pl.* 2, *cr.* 8.
O'BRIEN, Eng., a crane, ar., beaked and legged, gu. *Pl.* 111, *cr.* 9.
O'BRIEN-STAFFORD, Northamp., out of a cloud, a naked arm, in hand a sword, all ppr. *Vigueur de dessus. Pl.* 34, *cr.* 7, (cloud, *pl.* 124, *cr.* 12.)
O'BRIEN, Ess., out of a cloud, a naked arm, in hand a sword, all ppr. *Ib.*
O'BRIEN, Bart., Iri., out of clouds, a naked arm, embowed, in hand a sword, all ppr. *Lamh laidir an nachtar. Ib.*
O'BRYEN, Marquess of Thomond. See THOMOND.
O'BRYNE, and OBYRNE, Iri., a mermaid, in dexter a mirror, with sinister combing her hair. *Pl.* 48, *cr.* 5.

O'Cahane, Iri., a dexter arm, embowed, purp., in hand a sword, ppr. *Pl.* 34, *cr.* 7.

O'Cahill, Iri., an anchor, erect, cabled, ppr., issuing from dexter fluke an oak-branch, vert. *Pl.* 42, *cr.* 12, (branch, *pl.* 32, *cr.* 13.)

O'Callaghan, Viscount Lismore. *See* Lismore.

O'Callaghan, John, Esq., of Maryfort, co. Clare, a dexter arm, embowed, couped at shoulder, in hand a sword, thereon a snake, all ppr. *Fidus et audax. Pl.* 116, *cr.* 11.

O'Carol, Iri., an escutcheon, ar., (charged with three piles, gu., issuing from the chief.) *Pl.* 36, *cr.* 11.

O'Carrie, Iri., an arm, in armour, embowed, in hand a spear, all ppr. *Pl.* 44, *cr.* 9, (spear, *pl.* 19, *cr.* 5.)

O'Carrill, Iri., (between two sprigs,) a falcon, rising, belled, ppr. *Pl.* 105, *cr.* 4.

O'Carroll, Iri., on stump of tree a hawk, rising, ppr. *In fide et in bello fortis. Pl.* 78, *cr.* 8.

Ochterlonie, Sco., an eagle, displayed, az. *Deus mihi adjutor. Pl.* 48, *cr.* 11.

Ochterlony, Sco., a swan, rousant, ar., ducally crowned, or, collared and chained, gold, charged on breast with a rose, gu. *Pl.* 111, *cr.* 10.

Ochterlony, Bart., out of an Eastern crown, or, inscribed "Nepaul," a cubit arm, erect, in hand a scroll, entwined with laurel, all ppr. *Prudentiâ et animo. Pl.* 25, *cr.* 8, (laurel, *pl.* 93, *cr.* 1.)

Ockleshaw, Lanc., a flaming sword, erect, or. *Pl.* 58, *cr.* 11.

Ockley, Salop, in hand, two palm-branches, in orle, ppr. *Pl.* 16, *cr.* 5.

O'Cobthaigs, Iri., a naked boy, riding on back of a dolphin. *Pl.* 58, *cr.* 12.

O'Conarchy, Iri., on a ducal coronet, az., an eagle, displayed, gu. *Pl.* 9, *cr.* 6, (eagle, *pl.* 48, *cr.* 11.)

O'Connell, Iri., a stag, statant. *Pl.* 81, *cr.* 8.

O'Connell, Iri., a stag's head, erased, ar. *Pl.* 66, *cr.* 9.

O'Connell, Iri., on a ducal coronet, a stag, passant, ar. *Pl.* 68, *cr.* 2, (coronet, *same plate, cr.* 6.)

O'Connell, Daniel, Esq., of Darrinane Abbey, co. Kerry, a stag's head, erased. *Pl.* 66, *cr.* 9.

O'Connor, Iri., an arm, in armour, embowed, in hand a sword. *Pl.* 2, *cr.* 8.

O'Connor, Sco., a hand, gauntleted, throwing a javelin. *Pl.* 125, *cr.* 5, (javelin, *pl.* 95, *cr.* 14.)

O'Connor, Eng., a cock's head, or. *Pl.* 92, *cr.* 3.

O'Connor-Don, co. Roscommon, an arm, in armour, embowed, in hand a sword, ar., hilt and pommel, gold, entwined with a snake, ppr. *Pl.* 116, *cr.* 11, (armour, *pl.* 2, *cr.* 8.)

O'Conyers, Iri., a bull's head, couped, (pierced through neck by an arrow.) *Pl.* 120, *cr.* 7.

O'Cuilean, Iri., a pelican, vulning. *Pl.* 109, *cr.* 15.

O'Daniel, Iri., a bull, passant. *Pl.* 66, *cr.* 11.

O'Davoron, Iri., a hind, (statant,) ppr. *Pl.* 20, *cr.* 14.

Oddie, an otter's head, erased, in mouth a fish. *Pl.* 74, *cr.* 13.

Oddy, Eng., a goat's head, per pale, or and az., horns counterchanged. *Pl.* 105, *cr.* 14.

Odehull, and Odell, Eng., an eagle, displayed, gu. *Pl.* 48, *cr.* 11.

Odel, an arm, in armour, embowed, in hand a sword. *Pl.* 2, *cr.* 8.

Odell, Edward, Esq., of Carriglea, co. Waterford, an arm, in armour, embowed, in hand a sword, ppr. *Quantum in rebus inane. Pl.* 2, *cr.* 8.

Odiard, an arm, in armour, embowed, ppr., garnished, or, in gauntlet a covered cup, or. *Pl.* 39, *cr.* 1, (armour, *pl.* 2, *cr.* 8.)

Odingsell, or Odingsells, Notts. and Warw., a wolf, passant, gu. *Pl.* 46, *cr.* 6.

Odingsells, Eng., a wolf, passant, or, guttée on neck, gu. *Pl.* 46, *cr.* 6.

Odingsells, Warw., a naked arm, erect, in hand, ppr., a mullet, gu. *Pl.* 62, *cr.* 13.

O'Dogherty, and O'Doherty, Iri., in dexter hand a sword. *Pl.* 21, *cr.* 10.

O'Donavan, Iri., an eagle, rising. *Pl.* 67, *cr.* 4.

O'Donel, Bart.,Iri.,two armed arms, embowed, ppr., in saltier, in hand on dexter side a heart, in sinister a scimitar, all ppr. *In hoc signo vinces. Pl.* 93, *cr.* 14.

O'Donnel, or O'Donnell, Eng., on a ducal coronet, the attires of a stag, ppr. *Pl.* 118, *cr.* 11.

O'Donnoghue, Iri., on a mount, vert, a peacock, az., spotted, or, *Pl.* 9, *cr.* 1.

O'Donochoo, Iri., an arm, in armour, embowed, in hand a sword, entwined with a serpent, head toward handle. *Pl.* 116, *cr.* 11, (armour, *pl.* 2, *cr.* 8.)

O'Donovan, Morgan-William, co. Cork, on a chapeau, gu., turned up, erm., an eagle, rising, ppr. *Adjuvante Deo in hostes*—and —*Vis super hostem. Pl.* 114, *cr.* 13.

O'Dovanan, Iri., an eagle, rising. *Pl.* 67, *cr.* 4.

O'Duane, Iri., a wolf's head, erased. *Pl.*14,*cr.* 6.

O'Duane, Iri. a wolf's head and neck, couped. *Pl.* 92, *cr.* 15, (without rose.)

O'Dunn, Iri., a tree, ppr., at foot a lizard, passant, vert. *Pl.* 93, *cr.* 4.

O'Duire, or O'Dwire, Iri., in hand a sword. *Pl.* 21, *cr.* 10.

O'Dyearne, an arm, in armour, ppr., garnished, or, couped at shoulder, in fess, in hand, erect from elbow, of the first, a covered cup, gold. *Pl.* 114, *cr.* 9, (cup,*pl.* 35, *cr.* 9.)

O'Farrail, Iri., on a ducal coronet, a greyhound, current, sa. *Pl.* 47, *cr.* 2, (coronet, *same plate, cr.* 5.)

O'Farraill, Iri., on a ducal coronet, a greyhound, springing, sa.

O'Ferral-More, co. Kildare: 1. Out of a ducal coronet, a dexter hand, apaumée. *Pl.* 79, *cr.* 6, (without wings.) 2. A dexter arm, vested, couped, in fess, in hand, ppr., a sword, erect. *Spes mea Deus. Pl.* 102, *cr.* 5, (without head.)

Officer, Sco., in dexter hand a cutlass, ppr. *Deo juvante, vinco. Pl.* 66, *cr.* 6.

Offley, out of a ducal coronet, or, the attires of a stag affixed to scalp, sa. *Pl.* 86, *cr.* 10.

Offley, a demi-lion, per pale, or and az., collared (and lined,) in dexter a pink, ppr., stalked and leaved, vert. *Pl.* 18, *cr.* 13, (pink, *pl.* 45, *cr.* 13.)

Offley, Lond. and Surr., a demi-lion, rampant, or, collared, gu., between paws an olive-branch, stalked and leaved, ppr., fructed, gold. *Pl.* 18, *cr.*13, (branch, *pl.* 98, *cr.* 8.)

OFFLEY, Glouc., a demi-lion, rampant, per pale, or and az., collared, per pale, counterchanged, holding a branch of laurel, ppr. *Pl.* 39, *cr.* 14, (branch, *pl.* 123, *cr.* 5.)

O'FLAHERTIE, a lizard, passant, ppr. *Pl.* 93, *cr.* 4, (without tree.)

O'FLYNN, Iri., in hand, couped at wrist, a snake. *Pl.* 91, *cr.* 6.

OGDEN, a griffin's head, erased, in beak an oak-branch, fructed, ppr. *Pl.* 9, *cr.* 12, (branch, *pl.* 32, *cr.* 13.)

OGDEN, between two branches of oak, in orle, leaves, ppr., fructed, or, a stag's head, cabossed, ppr., attired, gold. *Pl.* 36, *cr.* 1, (branches, *pl.* 74, *cr.* 7.)

OGIE, Eng., a human heart, gu., pierced by a passion nail, in bend sinister, az. *Pl.* 81, *cr.* 3.

OGILBY, Eng., out of a ducal coronet, or, a cock's head, gu. *Pl.* 97, *cr.* 15.

OGILBY, Iri., a lion, rampant, gu., supporting a (tilting-spear, entwined with a string of trefoils, ppr.) *Pl.* 22, *cr.* 15.

OGILVIE, Sco., on a garb, in fess, or, a lion, passant, gardant, gu. *Quæ moderate, firma. Pl.* 59, *cr.* 15.

OGILVIE, a demi-lady, in hand a flower, ppr. *Pl.* 2, *cr.* 10.

OGILVIE, a lion's head, (erased,) gu., crowned with an imperial crown. *A fin. Pl.* 123, *cr.* 13.

OGILVIE, Sco., in dexter hand a branch of palm, ppr. *Secundat vera fides. Pl.* 23, *cr.* 7.

OGILVIE, Sco., a lion's gamb, ppr. *Ex ungui bus leonis. Pl.* 126, *cr.* 9.

OGILVIE, Sco., a sword, in bend, ppr. *Pro patriâ. Pl.* 22, *cr.* 7.

OGILVIE, Earl of Airlie and Lintrathen. See AIRLIE.

OGILVIE, Sco., a demi-lion, gu., unguled and armed, az. *Forward. Pl.* 67, *cr.* 10.

OGILVIE, Sco., a demi-man, armed at all points, ppr. *Præclarum regi et regno servitium. Pl.* 23, *cr.* 4.

OGILVIE, Sco., in dexter hand a sword, all ppr. *Pro patriâ. Pl.* 21, *cr.* 10.

OGILVIE, Sco., a lion, rampant, gardant, ppr. *Nil desperandum. Pl.* 92, *cr.* 7.

OGILVIE, Sco., a dexter arm, in hand a scimitar, all ppr. *Pro patriâ. Pl.* 92, *cr.* 5.

OGILVIE, Sco., a galley, ppr. *Cum periculo lucrum. Pl.* 34, *cr.* 5.

OGILVIE, Sco., a demi-lion, in dexter a sword, (in pale,) ppr. *Ex armis honos. Pl.* 41, *cr.* 13.

OGILVIE, Sco., a lady's dexter arm, hand apaumée, bracelet round wrist, ppr. *Pro salute. Pl.* 85, *cr.* 10.

OGILVIE, Sco., a lion's head, erased, gu. *Pl.* 81, *cr.* 4.

OGILVIE, Sco., a bull, issuant, sa., collared with a garland of roses, ppr. *Industria. Pl.* 73, *cr.* 8.

OGILVIE, Sco., a dexter arm, couped, in bend dexter, in hand a plumb-rule, in bend sinister, resting on the wreath.

OGILVIE, Sco., a talbot's head, ar. *Ad finem spero. Pl.* 123, *cr.* 15.

OGILVIE, Sco., a lion, rampant, ppr., armed and langued, gu., in dexter a rose, of the last, stalked and leaved, ppr. *Fortiter et suaviter. Pl.* 64, *cr.* 2, (rose, *pl.* 39, *cr.* 14.)

OGILVIE, Earl of Seafield. See SEAFIELD.

OGILVIE, Sco., a lion, rampant, ppr. *Nil desperandum. Pl.* 67, *cr.* 5.

OGILVIE, Sco., a naked cubit arm, in hand a sword, ppr. *Pro patriâ. Pl.* 21, *cr.* 10.

OGILVIE, Sco., a lion's head, erased, gu. *Forward. Pl.* 81, *cr.* 4.

OGILVY, Sco., a deer's head, couped, gu., attired, or. *Bene paratum dulce. Pl.* 91, *cr.* 14.

OGILVY, Eng., out of a ducal coronet, gu., a nag's head, ar. *Pl.* 50, *cr.* 13.

OGILVY, Sco., a sun-flower, ppr. *Quo duxeris adsum. Pl.* 105, *cr.* 15.

OGILVY, Sco., a lion's head, erased, gu. *Fideliter. Pl.* 81, *cr.* 4.

OGILVY, Sco., a demi-bull, sa., collared with a garland of roses, ppr. *Industria. Pl.* 73, *cr.* 8.

OGILVY, Sco., a demi-lion, in dexter a garb, ppr. *Marte et industriâ. Pl.* 84, *cr.* 7.

OGILVY, Sco., on a garb, in fess, or, a lion, passant, gardant. *Quæ moderata firma. Pl.* 59, *cr.* 15.

OGILVY, Sco., a sword, in bend, ppr. *Pugno pro patriâ. Pl.* 22, *cr.* 7.

OGILVY, Sco., in hand a palm-branch, ppr. *Secundat vera fides. Pl.* 23, *cr.* 7.

OGILVY, Sco., a lion, rampant, between paws a sword, in pale, ppr. *Ex armis honos. Pl.* 125, *cr.* 2, (sword, *same plate.*)

OGILVY, Sco., a demi-lion, gu., armed, az. *Forward. Pl.* 67, *cr.* 10.

OGILVY, JOHN, Esq., of Inshewan, Forfars., a stag's head, couped at neck, attired, or. *Bene paratum dulce. Pl.* 91, *cr.* 14.

OGLANDER, Hants, a bear's head, couped, or, (mouth embrued, gu.) *Servare munia vitæ. Pl.* 2, *cr.* 9.

OGLANDER, an antelope's head, erased. *Pl.* 24, *cr.* 7.

OGLANDER, a boar's head, couped, in fess. *Pl.* 48, *cr.* 2.

OGLE, Iri., a demi-tiger, rampant, ducally gorged, ppr. *Pl.* 125, *cr.* 4.

OGLE, Eng., a bull's head, erased, or, horned, gu. *Pl.* 19, *cr.* 3.

OGLE, Northumb., a bull's head, or, armed, az., ducally gorged, gu. *Pl.* 6, *cr.* 3, (without cross.)

OGLE, Northumb. and Northamp., out of a ducal coronet, or, a bull's head, ppr. *Pl.* 68, *cr.* 6.

OGLE, Sco., an arm, in armour, embowed, couped, resting on elbow, ppr., in hand an ancient mace, sa., studded, ar. *Pl.* 28, *cr.* 2.

OGLE, an antelope's head, erased. *Pl.* 24, *cr.* 7.

OGLE, Linc., a bull's head, erased, or, armed, gu., gorged with a chaplet, vert. *Pl.* 64, *cr.* 4, (without arrow.)

OGLE, Northumb., an antelope's head, erased, ar., tufts, mane, and horns, or. *Pl.* 24, *cr.* 7.

OGLE, Bart., Hants, an heraldic-antelope's head, (erased,) ar., tufted, maned, and horned, gu. *Prenez en gre. Pl.* 76, *cr.* 3.

OGLE, Eglingham, Northumb., an antelope's head, erased, horned, or, and an arm, armed in mail, issuing from a circle of gold, in hand a sword, broken in middle, edge bloody, hilt and pommel, gold.

OGLE, a demi-lion, or, in dexter a (truncheon,) gu. *Pl.* 11, *cr.* 2.

OGLETHORPE, Eng., a cock's head, or, between wings, gu. *Pl.* 47, *cr.* 3, (without cross.)

OGLETHORPE, Oxon., a boar's head, couped, gu., in mouth an oak-branch, vert, fructed, or. *Pl.* 125, *cr.* 7.

O'GORMAN, Iri., a cubit arm, couped, in hand a sword, all ppr. *Primi et ultimi in bello.* *Pl.* 21, *cr.* 10.

O'GRADY, Iri., a horse's head and neck, erased. *Pl.* 81, *cr.* 6.

O'GRADY, of Kilballyowen, Iri., a horse's head, ar. *Vulneratus, non victus.* *Pl.* 81, *cr.* 6.

O'HAHARTY, or O'FLARTY, Iri., a lizard, vert. *Pl.* 93, *cr.* 4, (without tree.)

O'HANLAN, Iri., on a mount, a lizard, erect, ppr. *Pl.* 93, *cr.* 6.

O'HARA, Eng., a crane's head, or, beak, gu. *Pl.* 20, *cr.* 9.

O'HARA, a demi-lion, rampant, pean, in dexter a chaplet of oak-leaves, vert, fructed, ppr. *Pl.* 39, *cr.* 14, (chaplet, *pl.* 74, *cr.* 7.)

O'HARA, Iri., a lion, rampant, in dexter a (sprig.) *Pl.* 64, *cr.* 2.

O'HARA, Iri., a demi-lion, rampant, erm., in dexter a chaplet of laurel, ppr., fructed, gu. *Pl.* 39, *cr.* 14, (chaplet, *pl.* 79, *cr.* 14.)

O'HICKIE, Iri., in hand, gauntleted, a baton. *Pl.* 33, *cr.* 4.

OKEBOURN, Eng., an eagle, rising from a globe, winged, all ppr. *Pl.* 34, *cr.* 2, (globe, *pl.* 79, *cr.* 8.)

OKEDEN, Eng., in bear's paw, sa., an oak-branch, ppr., fructed, or. *Pl.* 126, *cr.* 2, (branch, *pl.* 32, *cr.* 13.)

OKEDEN, Hants, between two oak-branches, in orle, a buck's head, cabossed, all ppr. *Pl.* 36, *cr.* 1, (branches, *pl.* 74, *cr.* 7.)

O'KEEFE, Iri., a dove, gu. *Pl.* 66, *cr.* 12.

O'KELLY, Iri., a demi-savage, hand-cuffed, wreathed about temples and middle, vert. *Pl.* 98, *cr.* 10.

O'KELLY, Iri., a greyhound, statant, ppr. *Pl.* 104, *cr.* 1, (without chapeau.)

O'KELLY, Iri., on a ducal coronet, or, a greyhound, current, or. *Pl.* 47, *cr.* 2, (coronet, same plate, *cr.* 5.)

O'KENNELLY, Iri., an arm, in armour, embowed, in hand a flaming sword, ppr. *Pl.* 2, *cr.* 8, (sword, *pl.* 58, *cr.* 11.)

O'KENNELLY, Iri., an arm, in armour, embowed, in hand a sword, ppr., blade wavy. *Pl.* 2, *cr.* 8, (sword, *pl.* 71, *cr.* 7.)

OKEOVER, Oxon. and Staffs., out of a ducal coronet, or, a demi-dragon, erm. *Pl.* 59, *cr.* 14.

OKEOVER, HAUGHTON-CHARLES, Esq., of Okeover, Staffs., and Oldbury Hall, Warw., out of a coronet, or, a demi-wyvern, erm., langued, gu. *Esto vigilans.* *Pl.* 104, *cr.* 11.

O'KERNEY, Iri., a swan's head, sa., between wings, or. *Pl.* 54, *cr.* 6.

OKES, a cockatrice, sa. *Pl.* 63, *cr.* 15.

OKETON, or OKTON, Eng., a fleur-de-lis, or. *Pl.* 68, *cr.* 12.

OKEWOLD, Glouc., a leopard's head, erased, or, between wings, vert. *Pl.* 94, *cr.* 10, (wings, same plate, *cr.* 2.)

OLD, a cluster of grapes, pendent, slipped and leaved, vert. *Pl.* 77, *cr.* 7.

OLDAKER, a griffin's head. *Observe.* *Pl.* 38, *cr.* 3.

OLDAKER, Kent, a bull's head, erased. *Pl.* 19, *cr.* 3.

OLDBEIFE, Eng., a spread eagle. *Pl.* 87, *cr.* 11, (without flames.)

OLDERBURY, Lond., out of an antique crown, or, a demi-lion, rampant, az. *Pl.* 45, *cr.* 7, (crown, *pl.* 79, *cr.* 12.)

OLDERSHAW, Suff., a pheon, sa., entwined by a snake, ppr. *Pl.* 93, *cr.* 7.

OLDES, Eng., a lion, sejant, (gardant,) ppr., supporting an antique shield, gu., charged with a fess, or. *Pl.* 22, *cr.* 13.

OLDESWORTH, Glouc., a lion, sejant, gu., supporting between paws a (scroll, or.) *Pl.* 22, *cr.* 13.

OLDFIELD, Chesh., a demi-eagle, displayed, ar. *Pl.* 22, *cr.* 11.

OLDFIELD, Oxon., Leic., and Linc., on a garb, or, a dove, ar., beaked and legged, gu., in beak an ear of wheat, gold. *Pl.* 112, *cr.* 10.

OLDFIELD, Linc., a dove, close, ar., in beak an ear of wheat, or. *Pl.* 108, *cr.* 8, (without key.)

OLDFIELD, Chesh., out of a ducal coronet, a demi-wyvern, wings displayed, ar. *Pl.* 59, *cr.* 14, (demi-wyvern, *pl.* 116, *cr.* 15.)

OLDGATE, out of a mural coronet, ar., a bull's head, sa., collared, gobony, ar. and gu. *Pl.* 68, *cr.* 6, (coronet, *pl.* 128, *fig.* 18.)

OLDHAM, Eng., a dove, sa., in mouth a sprig of (laurel,) vert. *Pl.* 48, *cr.* 15.

OLDHAM, Lond., an owl (in an ivy-bush,) both ppr. *Pl.* 27, *cr.* 9.

OLDMIXON, Somers., a battle-axe, erect, or, headed, ar., (in middle of handle a ribbon, tied, az.) *Pl.* 14, *cr.* 8.

OLDSWORTH, Glouc., a lion, sejant, gardant, gu., (resting dexter on a carved shield, or.) *Pl.* 101, *cr.* 8.

O'LEARIE, Iri., an arm, in armour, embowed, in hand a sword. *Pl.* 2, *cr.* 8.

OLIPHANT, Sco., a crescent, or. *What was may be.* *Pl.* 18, *cr.* 14.

OLIPHANT, Sco., the sun in glory, ppr. *Hinc illuminabimur.* *Pl.* 68, *cr.* 14.

OLIPHANT, Sco., an elephant's head, erased, ppr. *Quod agis fortiter.* *Pl.* 68, *cr.* 4.

OLIPHANT, Sco., a falcon, volant, ppr. *Altiora peto.* *Pl.* 94, *cr.* 1.

OLIPHANT, Sco., an eagle, regardant, wings expanded, ppr. *Altiora peto.* *Pl.* 87, *cr.* 5, (without sword.)

OLIPHANT, Eng., a camel, ppr. *Pl.* 17, *cr.* 2.

OLIPHANT, Sco., a falcon, perched, ppr. *A tout pourvoir.* *Pl.* 67, *cr.* 3.

OLIPHANT, an elephant's head, couped, ppr. *Quod agis fortiter.* *Pl.* 35, *cr.* 13.

OLIPHANT, Sco., an elephant's head, couped, ar. *Non mutat fortuna genus.* *Pl.* 35, *cr.* 13.

OLIPHANT, a unicorn's head, couped, ar., maned and horned, or. *Tout pourvoir.* *Pl.* 20, *cr.* 1.

OLIPHANT, Sco., a hand, issuing, pointing, ppr. *Hope and not rue.* *Pl.* 35, *cr.* 5.

OLIPHANT, Sco., a unicorn's head, erased, ar., maned and horned, or. *Tout pourvoir.* *Pl.* 67, *cr.* 1.

OLIPHANT, Sco., an elephant's trunk, ppr. *Pl.* 28, *cr.* 8.

OLIPHANT, Broadfield House, Cumb.: 1. For *Oliphant*, an elephant. *Pl.* 56, *cr.* 14. 2. For *Hewitt*, a falcon. *Pl.* 67, *cr.* 3.

OLIPHANT, LAURENCE, Esq., of Condie and Newton, Perth, a unicorn's head, couped, ar., armed and maned, or. *Altiora peto.* *Pl.* 20, *cr.* 1.

OLIVE, Lond., a cockatrice's head, erased, ppr., combed and wattled, gu. *Pl.* 76, *cr.* 9.

OLIVER, Iri., an heraldic-tiger's head, erased, or, collared, az. *Pl.* 113, *cr.* 3.

OLIVER, Sco., a dexter arm, ppr., vested, ar., turned up, gu., in hand an olive-branch, fructed, ppr. *Ad fœdera cresco. Pl.* 120, *cr.* 1, (branch, *pl.* 98, *cr.* 8.)

OLIVER, Exeter, Devons., a lion's head, erased, erminois, collared and ringed, ar. *Pl.* 7, *cr.* 10.

OLIVER, Sco., a dexter hand, couped, hurling a curling-stone, all ppr. *Pl.* 104, *cr.* 6.

OLIVER, Kent, a lion's head, erased, gu., collared, ar. *Non sine. Pl.* 7, *cr.* 10.

OLIVER, a dexter naked arm, in hand an olive-branch, fructed, ppr. *Pl.* 118, *cr.* 4, (branch, *pl.* 98, *cr.* 8.)

OLIVER, Cornw., an arm, in armour, embowed, in hand a sprig of oak, ppr., fructed, or. *Pl.* 68, *cr.* 1, (branch, *pl.* 32, *cr.* 13.)

OLIVER, Suss., a martlet, ar., (in beak a sprig, vert.) *Pl.* 111, *cr.* 5.

OLIVER, JOHN-DUDLEY, Esq., of Cherrymount, co. Wicklow, in hand a branch of olive, ppr. *Ito tu et fac similiter. Pl.* 43, *cr.* 6.

OLIVIER, HENRY-STEPHEN, Esq., of Potterne Manor House, Wilts., an esquire's helmet, ppr. *Sicut oliva virens lætor in æde Dei. Pl.* 109, *cr.* 5.

OLIVIER, Lond. and Beds., an esquire's helmet, ppr. *Pl.* 109, *pl.* 5.

OLLNEY, or OLNEY, Glouc. and Northamp., out of a ducal coronet, or, a phœnix's head in flames, in beak an olive branch, all ppr. *Pl.* 112, *cr.* 7, (coronet, *pl.* 53, *cr.* 6; branch, *pl.* 98, *cr.* 8.)

OLMIUS, Lond., between two laurel branches, vert, a demi-moor, in armour, ppr., garnished, or, wreathed round head, ar. and gu., on head a fess, counter-embattled.

O'LOGHLEN, Bart., Iri., on a ducal coronet, or, an anchor, erect, entwined with cable, ppr. *Anchora salutis. Pl.* 42, *cr.* 12, (coronet, same plate, *cr.* 8.)

O'LOGHLIN, Iri., an anchor, erect, and cable, ppr. *Pl.* 42, *cr.* 12.

O'MALLAHAN, Iri., a horse, at full speed. *Pl.* 107, *cr.* 5, (without spear.)

O'MALLEY, Bart., Iri., a horse, at full speed. *Terrâ marique potens. Ib.*

O'MALLEY, a hare, current.

O'MALY, Iri., a ship, in full sail, ppr. *Pl.* 109, *cr.* 8.

O'MANNIS, Iri., in hand, ppr., a long cross, in pale, purp. *Pl.* 23, *cr.* 15, (cross, *pl.* 141.)

O'MEAGHIR, Iri., a falcon, rising, ppr. *Pl.* 105, *cr.* 4.

O'MEARA, Iri., a pelican, vulning, ppr. *Pl.* 109, *cr.* 15.

O'MEARD, Iri., a pelican, ppr., vulning. *Pl.* 109, *cr.* 15.

OMER, Eng., a dove and olive-branch, ppr. *Pl.* 48, *cr.* 15.

OMMANEY, Surr., a cubit arm, erect, (per pale, ar. and sa., cuffed, of the first,) in hand a battle-axe, in bend sinister, ppr. *Pl.* 73, *cr.* 7.

OMOND, Sco., a cubit arm, in armour, erect, in hand a spear in fend, point downwards. *Pl.* 126 c, *cr.* 15.

O'MULLEN, Iri., out of a crescent, gu., a sword, erect, ppr. *Pl.* 93, *cr.* 12.

O'MULRIAN, OWNEY, Iri., a griffin, segreant, gu., (in sinister a dagger, in pale.) *Pl.* 67, *cr.* 13.

O'NEALE, Iri., out of a ducal coronet, a cubit arm, in hand a (sword.) *Pl.* 103, *cr.* 2.

O'NEILL, Iri., a dexter arm, in antique mail, embowed, in gauntlet a sword, all ppr. *Pl.* 2, *cr.* 8.

O'NEILL, out of a ducal coronet, or, a dexter arm, in armour, embowed, ppr., in hand a sword, blade waved, gold. *Pl.* 122, *cr.* 8, (sword, *pl.* 65, *cr.* 10.)

O'NEILL, Earl, Viscount, and Baron, and Viscount Reymond, Iri., (O'Neill,) an arm, in armour, embowed, ppr., garnished, or, in hand a sword, also ppr. *Lamh deary eirin. Pl.* 2, *cr.* 8.

O'NELEY, Northamp., out of a ducal coronet, or, an eagle's head, in flames, ppr., in beak a sprig, vert. *Pl.* 112, *cr.* 7, (coronet, *pl.* 53, *cr.* 6; sprig, *pl.* 98, *cr.* 8.)

O'NEYLAN, Iri., in hand a sword. *Pl.* 21, *cr.* 10.

O'NEYLAN, Iri., in dexter hand, couped below wrist, a sword, in pale, on point a boar's head, in fess. *Pl.* 71, *cr.* 9.

ONGLEY, Baron, Iri., (Henley-Ongley,) a phœnix in flames, in beak a fire-ball, all ppr. *Mihi cura futuri. Pl.* 61, *cr.* 6.

ONION, Eng., in dexter hand, gu., a spear, or. *Pl.* 99, *cr.* 8.

ONLEY, Northamp. and Suff., out of a ducal coronet, or, an eagle's head, in flames, ppr., in beak, a sprig, vert. *Pl.* 112, *cr.* 7, (coronet, *pl.* 53, *cr.* 6; sprig, *pl.* 98, *cr.* 8.)

ONLEY-SAVILL, Ess. and Middx. : 1. For *Onley*, out of a crown vallary, or, an eagle's head, issuing from flames, ppr., in beak a laurel-sprig, vert. *Pl.* 53, *cr.* 6, (crown, *pl.* 128, *fig.* 17.) 2. For *Savill*, (on a mount, vert,) an owl, ar., charged on body with three mullets, in bend, gu. *Pl.* 27, *cr.* 9, (mullet, *pl.* 141.) 3. For *Harvey*, a dexter cubit arm, hand apaumée, ppr., (charged from wrist with a pile, gu., above the fingers a crescent reversed, ar.) *Pl.* 32, *cr.* 14.

ONMANY, Iri., a gate, ppr. *Pl.* 67, *cr.* 4.

O'NOLAN, Iri., a hawk. *Pl.* 67, *cr.* 3.

ONSLOW, Surr. and Salop, a (falcon,) ppr., legged and belled, or, preying on a partridge, of the first. *Festina lente. Pl.* 61, *cr.* 7.

ONSLOW, Bart., Lanc., an eagle, sa., preying on a partridge, or. *Festina lente. Pl.* 61, *cr.* 7.

ONSLOW, Earl and Baron, Viscount Cranley, and a Bart., (Onslow,) an eagle, sa., preying on a partridge, or. *Festina lente*—and—*Semper fidelis. Pl.* 61, *cr.* 7.

OPENHEMER, or OPPENHEMER, a garland of laurel, surmounted by a trident, in bend dexter. *Pl.* 54, *cr.* 10, (trident, *pl.* 12, *cr.* 3.)

O'PHEALAN, and OFFEALAM, out of a ducal coronet, a morion, feathers issuant from top.

OPIE, Cornw., a demi-stag, rampant, in mouth an (arrow.) *Pl.* 55, *cr.* 9.

OPYE, Cornw., a demi-stag, erm., attired, or, pierced through neck by an arrow, sa., feathered and headed, ar., wound and head of arrow, guttée-de-sang. *Pl.* 55, *cr.* 9.

ORAM, Eng., a torteau, az., charged with a stag, standing on a mount, vert. *Pl.* 45, *cr.* 11.

ORANMORE, and BROWNE, Baron, Iri.,(Browne,) an eagle's head, erased. *Fortiter et fideliter. Pl.* 20, *cr.* 7.

ORAY, or OYRY, a pennon, per fess, gu. and or, staff, in bend, counterchanged. *Pl.* 8,*cr.* 8.
ORBY, an ox-yoke, (erect,) ar. *Pl.* 35, *cr.* 11.
ORBY, or ORREBY, on a chapeau, erm., a ram's head. *Pl.* 124, *cr.* 8, (chapeau, *pl.* 127, *fig.* 13.)
ORCHARD, Sco., in hand a sheaf of (four) arrows, points downward, ppr. *Pl.* 56, *cr.* 4.
ORCHARD, Eng., a crow, sa. *Pl.* 23, *cr.* 8.
ORD, Sco., a fish, haurient. *Pl.* 98, *cr.* 12.
ORD, Eng., a stag's head, erased, purp. *Pl.*.66, *cr.* 9.
ORD, Northumb., an elk's head, (erased,) ar., attired, or. *Pl.* 70, *cr.* 4.
ORD: 1. For *Ord*, an elk's head, couped, ppr. *Pl.* 70, *cr.* 4. 2. For *Craven*, on a chapeau, purp., turned up, erm., a griffin, statant, wings elevated and addorsed, of the second, beak, or. *Pl.* 122, *cr.* 11.
ORDE, Northumb., a demi-lion, or, in dexter a fleur-de-lis, gu. *Pl.* 91, *cr.* 13.
ORDE, Hants, an elk's head, erased, ppr. *Pl.* 70, *cr.* 4.
ORDE, Bart., Northumb., a demi-lion, in dexter a fleur-de-lis, or. *Pl.* 91, *cr.* 13.
ORDE, CHARLES-WILLIAM, Esq., of Nunny-kirk, Northumb, an elk's head, ppr. *Mitis et fortis. Pl.* 70, *cr.* 4.
ORDWAY, two wings, displayed, each charged with a mullet, pierced. *Pl.* 39, *cr.* 12, (mullet, *pl.* 45, *cr.* 1.)
O'REILLY, Iri., on a roundel, sa., (a cheveron, or.) *Pl.* 7, *cr.* 6.
O'REILLY, Eng., an acorn, slipped and leaved, vert. *Pl.* 81, *cr.* 7.
O'REILLY, East Brefney: 1. Out of a ducal coronet, or, an oak-tree, with a snake, entwined, (descendant,) ppr. *Pl.* 94, *cr.* 5, (serpent, *pl.* 84, *cr.* 4.) 2. A cubit arm, in armour, in gauntlet a dagger, all ppr. *Pl.* 28,*cr.* 4, (armour, *pl.* 125, *cr.* 5.)
ORENGE, Somers., a demi-talbot, erased, or. *Pl.* 97, *cr.* 9, (without arrow.)
ORFEUR, Cumb., a woman's head, couped at breasts, all ppr., on head a cross pattée, fitched, or. *Pl.* 45, *cr.* 5, (cross, *pl.* 27, *cr.* 14.)
ORFORD, Earl of, and Baron, (Walpole,) the bust of a man, in profile, couped, ppr., ducally crowned, or, from the coronet flowing a long cap, turned forward, gu., tasselled, gold, charged with a Catherine-wheel, of the last. *Fari quæ sentias. Pl.* 78, *cr.* 14, (wheel, *pl.* 141.)
ORGAINE, Berks. and Wilts., three organ-pipes, one in pale, (two in saltier,) or, bound, with a chaplet of laurel, vert. *Pl.* 50, *cr.* 12.
ORGAN, same crest.
ORIEL, Baron. *See* FERRARD, Viscount.
O'RILEY, Iri., out of a ducal coronet, an oak-tree, around stem a serpent, entwined, all ppr. *Pl.* 94, *cr.* 5, (serpent, *pl.* 84, *cr.* 4.)
ORKNEY, Earl of, Viscount Kirkwall, and Baron Dechmont, Iri., (Fitzmaurice,) a centaur, passant, ppr. *Pl.* 70, *cr.* 13.
ORLEBAR, Lond. and Beds., an eagle's head, between wings, erect, ar., (charged on neck with two barrulets, gu.) *Pl.* 81, *cr.* 10.
ORME, Sco., a griffin, passant, gu. *Pl.* 61, *cr.* 14, (without gorging.)
ORME, Sco., a demi-griffin, wings addorsed, ar. *Pl.* 18, *cr.* 6.

ORME, Northamp., a dolphin, naiant, ar., fins, tail, and tusk, or. *Pl.* 48, *cr.* 9.
ORME, Sco., a dragon, passant, wings addorsed, ppr. *Pl.* 90, *cr.* 10.
ORME, Abbey Town, co. Mayo, a dolphin, embowed, az., fins and tail, or, surmounted of a pole-axe, gold. *Pl.* 48, *cr.* 9, (axe, *pl.* 14, *cr.* 8.)
ORMEROD, Lond., Glouc., and Lanc., a wolf's head, couped at neck, barry of four, or and gu., in mouth an ostrich-feather, in pale, ppr. *Pl.* 92, *cr.* 15, (feather, *pl.* 12, *cr.* 9.)
ORMESBY, Linc., an arm, embowed, vested, sa., cuffed, or, in hand, ppr., a leg, in armour, couped at thigh, of the last, garnished, gold. *Pl.* 39, *cr.* 6, (arm, *same plate, cr.* 1.)
ORMSBY, Linc., an arm, couped at elbow, (vested, sa.,) in hand a leg, in armour, couped at thigh, all ppr. *Pl.* 39, *cr.* 6.
ORMISTONE, Sco., a cock, crowing, ppr. *In dubiis constans. Pl.* 67, *cr.* 14.
ORMISTONE, Sco., an anchor, ppr. *Felicior quo certior. Pl.* 25, *cr.* 15.
ORMONDE, Marquess of, Earl of Ormonde and Ossory, Viscount Thurles and Baron Arklow, Iri., Baron Ormonde, U.K., (Butler,) out of a ducal coronet, or, a plume of five ostrich-feathers, ar., therefrom a falcon, rising, of the last. *Comme je trouve*—and—*Depressus extollor. Pl.* 100, *cr.* 12, (falcon, *pl.* 54, *cr.* 8.)
ORMSBY, Iri., two globes, ppr. *Pl.* 85, *cr.* 9.
ORMSBY, Eng., a falcon, rising, or. *Pl.* 105, *cr.* 4.
ORMSBY, a dexter arm, in armour, embowed, in hand a leg, in armour, couped above knee, all ppr. *Fortis qui prudens. Pl.* 39, *cr.* 6, (armour, *pl.* 120, *cr.* 11.)
ORMSBY, co. Sligo and Salop, a dexter arm, in armour, embowed, ppr., (charged with a rose, gu.,) in hand a leg, in armour, couped above knee, also ppr. *Pl.* 39, *cr.* 6, (armour, *pl.* 120, *cr.* 11.)
O'ROURK, Iri., out of a ducal coronet, or, a gauntlet grasping a (sword,) ppr. *Pl.* 15, *cr.* 5.
ORPSEN, the Rev. EDWARD-CHATTERTON, co. Kerry, out of a ducal coronet, a demi-lion, rampant, or. *Vincit veritas. Pl.* 45, *cr.* 7.
ORPWOOD, Berks., a boar, passant, quarters, erm. and ermines, bristled, armed, and hoofed, or. *Pl.* 48, *cr.* 14.
ORR, Sir ANDREW, of Harvieston, Clackm., a cornucopia. *Virtuti fortuna comes. Pl.* 91, *cr.* 4.
ORR, Sco., a hand, issuing from a man's heart brandishing a (sword.) *True to the end. Pl.* 35, *cr.* 7.
ORR, Sco., a cornucopia, ppr. *Bonis omnia bona. Pl.* 91, *cr.* 4.
ORR, Sco., a cornucopia. *Virtuti fortuna comes. Pl.* 91, *cr.* 4.
ORR, a lion, passant, ppr., resting dexter on a torteau. *Pl.* 4, *cr.* 14, (torteau, *pl.* 141.)
ORR, Sco., out of a heart, a dexter hand grasping a scimitar. *True to the end. Pl.* 35, *cr.* 7.
ORRED, a hare, salient, ppr., in mouth three ears of corn, or.
ORRELL, Camb. and Chesh., a lion's head, erased, ar., powdered with torteaus, and ducally gorged, gu. *Pl.* 18, *cr.* 4, (gorging, *pl.* 87, *cr.* 15; torteau, *pl.* 141.)
ORROCK, Sco., a falcon, perching, ppr. *Solus Christus mea rupes. Pl.* 105, *cr.* 4.

ORROCK, United States, America, same crest and motto.
ORTON, and ORTUN, Eng., a tower, ppr., cupola and flag, gu. *Pl.* 42, *cr.* 10.
ORTON, a tower, ar. *Pl.* 12, *cr.* 5.
ORY, an arm, in armour, in hand a sword, all ppr. *Pl.* 2, *cr.* 8.
OSBALDESTON, Glou. : 1. A stag's head, erased, per pale, ar. and sa., guttée, counterchanged, attired, or. *Pl.* 66, *cr.* 9. 2. A man, in armour, on horseback, all ppr., in dexter a (sword,) ar., hilt, or. *Pl.* 28, *cr.* 5.
OSBALDESTON, of Osbaldeston, Lanc., same crests.
OSBALDESTON, of Humanby, Yorks., same crests.
OSBALDESTON, Heref., a stag's head, erased, per pale, ar. and sa., guttée, counterchanged, attired, or. *Pl.* 66, *cr.* 9.
OSBALDESTON, Heref., a man, in armour, on horseback, all ppr., in dexter a (sword,) ar., hilt, or. *Pl.* 28, *cr.* 5.
OSBALDESTON, of Oxon., a knight, in complete armour, on a white horse, (on his shield the family arms.) *Constance et ferme. Pl.* 28, *cr.* 5.
OSBORN, Iri., out of a mural coronet, gu., a lion's head, ar. *Pl.* 45, *cr.* 9.
OSBORN, Eng., an heraldic-tiger, passant, ppr. *Pl.* 7, *cr.* 5.
OSBORN, or OSBORNE, a lion's head, erased, ar., ducally crowned, or. *Pl.* 90, *cr.* 4, (without charging.)
OSBORNE, Eng., an heraldic-tiger, passant, ar., (with a label of three points for difference.) *Pax in bello. Pl.* 7, *cr.* 5.
OSBORNE, Duke of Leeds. *See* LEEDS.
OSBORNE, Norf. and Ess., out of a ducal coronet, or, a tiger's head, sa., armed and crined, gold. *Pl.* 36, *cr.* 15.
OSBORNE, Derbs., a pelican, in nest, feeding her young, or. *Pl.* 44, *cr.* 1.
OSBORNE, Yorks., a tiger, passant, ar., crested and tufted, sa. *Pax in bello. Pl.* 67, *cr.* 15.
OSBORNE, Bart., Beds., a lion's head, erased, ar., ducally crowned, or. *Quantum in rebus inane. Pl.* 90, *cr.* 4, (without charging.)
OSBORNE, Derbs., a demi-lion, rampant, gu. *Pl.* 67, *cr.* 10.
OSBORNE, Kent, a demi-leopard, rampant, (collared and lined.) *Pl.* 12, *cr.* 14.
OSBORNE, Lond., an heraldic-tiger, (statant,) ar., crested and tufted, sa. *Pl.* 7, *cr.* 5.
OSBORNE, Suff., a unicorn, passant, or, ducally gorged, ringed, lined, armed, and crined, sa. *Pl.* 106, *cr.* 3.
OSBORNE, Beds., a leopard's head, ppr., ducally crowned, or. *Pl.* 92, *cr.* 13, (coronet, *pl.* 128, *fig.* 3.)
OSBORNE, Bart., Iri., a sea-lion, sejant, in dexter a trident. *Pax in bello. Pl.* 25, *cr.* 12, (trident, *pl.* 12, *cr.* 3.)
OSBORNE, Eng., on a rock, a castle in flames, ppr. *Pl.* 59, *cr.* 8.
OSBOURNE, a unicorn, passant, or, ducally gorged and chained, sa., horned, of the second and first. *Pl.* 106, *cr.* 3.
OSBOURNE, Sco., a sword, erect, ppr. *Je gagnie. Pl.* 105, *cr.* 1.
O'SELBAC, Iri., a dexter hand pointing with one finger, gu. *Pl.* 35, *cr.* 5.

OSEVAIN, Eng., a horse, passant, saddled and bridled. *Pl.* 99, *cr.* 11.
OSGODBY, on a chapeau, a cross pattée, fimbriated. *Pl.* 56, *cr.* 9, (cross, *pl.* 141.)
O'SHANLY, Iri., a hand, in armour, grasping a broken sword. *Pl.* 23, *cr.* 9, (sword, *pl.* 22, *cr.* 6.)
O'SHAUGHNESSY, Iri., a nag's head, erased, sa., bridled, or. *Pl.* 92, *cr.* 1.
O'SHEE, Iri., a swan, rousant, sa., beaked and membered, gu. *Vincit veritas. Pl.* 54, *cr.* 4.
O'SLATTERIE, or SLATTERIE, Iri., a cock, crowing, ppr. *Pl.* 67, *cr.* 14.
OSMER, a buck's head, cabossed, ppr. *Pl.* 36, *cr.* 1.
OSMOND, Eng., an eagle, or. *Pl.* 7, *cr.* 11.
OSTLE, Eng., a horse's head. *Pl.* 81, *cr.* 6.
OSTLER, a nag's head, (issuing.) *Pl.* 81, *cr.* 6.
OSTRICH, an ostrich's head, erased, az., in mouth a horse-shoe, or. *Pl.* 99, *cr.* 12, (without feathers.)
O'SULLEVAN, Iri., on a ducal coronet, a bird, ppr. *Pl.* 98, *cr.* 14.
O'SULLIVAN-BEARRA, Iri., on a serpent, vert, a moorcock, ppr. *Pl.* 75, *cr.* 11, (moorcock, *pl.* 10, *cr.* 1.)
OSWALD, Sco., a star of six points, waved, ar. *Monstrant astra viam. Pl.* 63, *cr.* 9.
OSWALD, Eng., (on a mount,) a stag, lodged under a holly-bush, all ppr. *Pl.* 95, *cr.* 10.
OSWALD, out of a cloud, a dexter hand pointing toward a star of (eight) rays. *Forti favet cœlum. Pl.* 77, *cr.* 6.
OSWALD, Sco., the same crest. *Sequamur.*
OSWALD, a comet-star, or. *Monstrant astra viam. Pl.* 39, *cr.* 9.
OTGHER, a martlet, wings expanded, ar.
OTHWELL, Eng., a dove, volant, gu. *Pl.* 25, *cr.* 6.
OTLEY, Salop, in front of a garb, or, three arrows, two in saltier, one in pale, points downward, sa. *Dat Deus incrementum. Pl.* 43, *cr.* 14, (garb, *pl.* 48, *cr.* 10.)
OTTER, Hunts., a crescent, or. *Pl.* 18, *cr.* 14.
OTTLEY, Eng., a demi-lion, or, holding a (branch.) *Pl.* 39, *cr.* 14.
OTTLEY, Salop, a sheaf of oats, or, banded, vert. *Pl.* 48, *cr.* 10.
OTTO, an otter, ppr.
OTWAY, Eng., a demi-eagle, displayed, ppr. *Pl.* 22, *cr.* 11.
OTWAY, Yorks., out of a ducal coronet, or, two wings, expanded, sa. (Another, the wings, az.) *Pl.* 17, *cr.* 9.
OTWAY, Bart., Suss., out of a ducal coronet, or, two wings, in pale, sa. *Si Deus nobiscum, quis contra nos. Pl.* 17, *cr.* 9.
OUCHTERLONY, Sco., an eagle, displayed, party per pale. *Deus mihi adjutor. Pl.* 48, *cr.* 11.
OUCHTERLONY, a rock, ppr. *Jamais abattu. Pl.* 73, *cr.* 12.
OUGHTON, Eng., an eagle's head, or. *Pl.* 100, *cr.* 10.
OUGHTON, Sco., a tower, (the sinister side-battlement broken, all ppr., thereout a laurel-sprig, vert,) the tower charged on centre with a grenade, sa., fired, ppr. *Nescit abolere vetustas. Pl.* 12, *cr.* 5, (grenade, *pl.* 70, *cr.* 12.)
OUGHTON, a tower, (ruined on sinister top, therefrom a laurel-branch issuing, ppr.) *Nescit abolere vetustas. Pl.* 12, *cr.* 5, (branch, *pl.* 123, *cr.* 5.)

OULD, Iri., five arrows, in saltier, banded in middle. *Pl.* 54, *cr.* 15.
OULDESWORTH, a lion, sejant, gu., resting dexter on a shield. *Pl.* 126, *cr.* 15, (shield, *pl.* 19, *cr.* 2.)
OULDFIELD, Linc., on a garb, or, a dove, ar., in beak an ear of wheat, gold. *Pl.* 112, *cr.* 10.
OULDSWORTH, Eng., out of a ducal coronet, a plume of ostrich-feathers, ppr. *Pl.* 44, *cr.* 12.
OULDSWORTH, Glouc., a lion, sejant, gu., resting dexter on a carved shield, or. *Pl.* 126, *cr.* 15, (shield, *pl.* 19, *cr.* 2.)
OULRY, an owl, sa., between wings, dexter, or, sinister, sa. *Pl.* 27, *cr.* 9, (wings, *pl.* 1, *cr.* 15.)
OULTON, and OWLTON, Eng., a martlet, ar. *Pl.* 111, *cr.* 5.
OULTON, out of a ducal coronet, or, a demi-lion, rampant, ar. *Pl.* 45, *cr.* 7.
OUSELEY, Bart., Herts., out of a ducal coronet, or, a wolf's head, erased, sa., in mouth a dexter hand, couped at wrist, gu. *Mors lupi agnis vita.*
OUSELEY, Northamp., same crest.
OUTLAWE, Norf., a demi-wolf, ppr., (pierced through side by an arrow, or, feathered and headed, ar., the arrow in bend sinister.) *Pl.* 56, *cr.* 8, (without spear.)
OUTRAM, Eng., a goat's head, erased, per fess, or and sa. *Pl.* 29, *cr.* 13.
OVER, Middx. and Herts., a bird, rising, or, beaked and membered, gu., in beak an olive-branch, vert, fructed, or. *Pl.* 79, *cr.* 8, (without globe.)
OVERBERY, and OVERBURY, Glouc., a lion's gamb, erect, ar., encircled by a ducal coronet, or. *Pl.* 93, *cr.* 9.
OVEREND, Iri., a cherub's head, or. *Pl.* 126, *cr.* 10.
OVERMAN, Norf. and Suff., a leopard, sejant, ppr., in dexter a fleur-de-lis, or. *Pl.* 10, *cr.* 13, (fleur-de-lis, *pl.* 141.)
OVERTON, Ruts., a maiden's head, ppr., vested, gu., crined, or. *Pl.* 75, *cr.* 5, (without coronet.)
OVERTON, Eng., on a chapeau, a martlet, sa. *Pl.* 89, *cr.* 7.
OVERY, Eng., a bull's head, az. *Pl.* 120, *cr.* 7.
OWEN, Salop, a wolf, passant, ar. *Pl.* 46, *cr.* 6.
OWEN, Salop, a demi-dragon, gu., winged, or. *Pl.* 82, *cr.* 10.
OWEN, Wel., Lond., Kent, and Salop, two eagles' heads, conjoined at neck, erased, or. *Pl.* 94, *cr.* 12.
OWEN, Wel., a lion, rampant, or. *Honestas optima politia.* *Pl.* 67, *cr.* 5.
OWEN, Salop, two eagles' heads, conjoined in one neck, erased, party per fess, or and gu., membered, of the last.
OVERSTONE, Baron, (Jones Loyd,) a buck's head, ppr., attired, or, erased, sa., (charged on neck with a fess, engrailed, of the last, thereon three bezants.) *Non mihi sed patriæ.* *Pl.* 66, *cr.* 9.
OWEN-BULKELEY, of Tedsmore Hall, Salop : 1. For *Owen*, two eagles' heads, conjoined in one neck, erased, party per fess, or and gu., membered, of the last. 2. For *Hatchett*, the blade of a battle-axe, ppr., (edge upward.) *Pl.* 16, *cr.* 3. 3. For *Bulkeley*, in a ducal coronet, a bull's head, ar., armed, or. *Eryr Eryrod Eryri*—and—*Nec temere, nec timide.* *Pl.* 68, *cr.* 6.

OWEN, a hawk's lure, charged with a fleur-de-lis. *Pl.* 97, *cr.* 14, (fleur-de-lis, *pl.* 141.)
OWEN, Worc., an eagle's neck, with two heads, couped, ppr.
OWEN, an anchor, sa., on base thereof a lion, statant, gu.
OWEN, Iri., a cubit arm, vested, in hand a lizard. *Pl.* 58, *cr.* 4.
OWEN, Oxon., a cubit arm, erect, vested, az., cuffed, erm., in hand, ppr., a chaplet, vert. *Pl.* 44, *cr.* 13, (without bird.)
OWEN, Salop, a Cornish chough, ppr., in dexter a fleur-de-lis, ar. *Pl.* 100, *cr.* 13, (fleur-de-lis, *pl.* 141.)
OWEN, Ess., a demi-lion, rampant, gu. *Pl.* 67, *cr.* 10.
OWEN, Glouc., out of a mural coronet, or, a lion's gamb, sa., holding a fleur-de-lis, gold.
OWEN, Sir JOHN, Bart., Wel., a lion, rampant, or. *Honestas optima politia.* *Pl.* 67, *cr.* 5.
OWEN, Wel., a raven, ppr., (in beak a bait.) *Deus pascit corvos.* *Pl.* 123, *cr.* 2.
OWEN, Wel. : 1. A Cornish chough, ppr., in dexter a fleur-de-lis, ar. *Pl.* 100, *cr.* 13, (fleur-de-lis, *pl.* 141.) 2. Two eagles' heads, conjoined in one neck, erased, party, per fess, or and gu., membered, of the last.
OWEN, Garthynghared, Wel., a cock's head, erased, ar., in mouth a snake, az. *Pl.* 92, *cr.* 3, (snake, *pl.* 41, *cr.* 6.)
OWENS, Holastone, co. Antrim, a boar, passant, ppr., (collared and chained, or, to a holly-bush, also ppr.) *Pl.* 48, *cr.* 14.
OWENS, Eng., out of a ducal coronet, sa., a beech-tree, vert. *Pl.* 94, *cr.* 5.
OWERS, a lion passant, tail extended. *Sine timore.* *Pl.* 118, *cr.* 10.
OWERS, a snake, nowed. *Pl.* 1, *cr.* 9.
OWGAN, a cockatrice, (close,) gu., legged and beaked, sa., crested, or. *Pl.* 63, *cr.* 15.
OWSLEY, Leic., a lion, rampant, in dexter a holly-branch. *Pl.* 64, *cr.* 2, (branch, *pl.* 99, *cr.* 6.)
OXBOROUGH, and OXBURGH, Eng., on point of a sword, erect, ppr., a cross pattée, sa. *Pl.* 56, *cr.* 1.
OXBOROUGH, and OXBURGH, Norf., on a mount, vert, a lion, rampant, or, holding up a spear, gu., headed, ar., under the head two ribbons, flotant, one or, the other az. *Pl.* 93, *cr.* 10.
OXCLIFFE, Eng., on a mount, vert, a bull, passant, sa. *Pl.* 39, *cr.* 5.
OXENBRIDGE, Bart., Eng., a demi-lion, (tail forked,) ar., langued and armed, gu. *Pl.* 67, *cr.* 10.
OXENBRIDGE, Eng., out of a cloud, in fess, a hand holding a club, ppr. *Pl.* 55, *cr.* 4.
OXENDEN, Bart., (out of a ducal coronet) gu., a lion's head, affrontée, or. *Pl.* 1, *cr.* 5.
OXFORD, and MORTIMER, Earl of, and Baron Harley, (Harley,) a castle, triple-towered, ar., out of middle tower a demi-lion, gu. *Virtute et fide.* *Pl.* 101, *cr.* 1.
OXLEY, Eng., out of a ducal coronet, a peacock, ppr. *Pl.* 43, *cr.* 7.
OXMAN, Ruts., a demi-lion, rampant, regardant, gu. *Pl.* 33, *cr.* 2, (without spears.)
OXNAM, Cornw., an ox, sa. *Pl.* 66, *cr.* 11.
OXTOBY, Eng., in dexter hand a sword. *Pl.* 21, *cr.* 10.
OYKE, Eng., an ox-yoke, (erect,) sa., bows, or. *Pl.* 35, *cr.* 11.
OYRY, a pennon, in bend, waving toward sinister, per fess, gu. and or, staff counterchanged, *Pl.* 8, *cr.* 8.

P

PACE, Eng., an arm, in armour, embowed, in hand a sword, ppr. *Pl.* 2, *cr.* 8.

PACE, a boar's head, (couped) and erect, sa., eared, or, charged with an anchor, gold. *Pl.* 21, *cr.* 7, (anchor, *pl.* 25, *cr.* 15.)

PACE, Leic., a buck's head, cabossed, ar., attired, or, between attires a bird, wings expanded, sa. *Pl.* 58, *cr.* 13.

PACHNUM, Eng., out of a mural coronet, a demi-hawk, rising, ppr. *Pl.* 113, *cr.* 11, (coronet, *same plate, cr.* 6.)

PACK, or PACKE, Eng., a leg, in armour, couped, bent at knee, spurred, all ppr. *Pl.* 81, *cr.* 5.

PACK, out of a mural coronet, ar., a lion's head, gu., (gorged with a wreath, or.) *Pl.* 45, *cr.* 9.

PACKE, Norf., a lion's head, erased, or, collared, sa., charged with three cinquefoils, erm. *Pl.* 7, *cr.* 10, (cinquefoil, *pl.* 141.)

PACKE, Leic., a lion's head, erased, or, collared, sa., on collar three cinquefoils, with an ermine-spot on each leaf. *Libertas sub rege pio.* *Pl.* 7, *cr.* 10, (charging, *pl.* 141.)

PACKE, Northamp., a lion's head, erased, or, collared, sa., on collar three mullets, ar. *Pl.* 7, *cr.* 10, (mullet, *pl.* 141.)

PACKENHAM, Hants, a leopard, couchant. *Pl.* 111, *cr.* 11.

PACKER, Berks., a black's head, couped, sa., wreathed round temples, or and gu. *Pl.* 48, *cr.* 7.

PACKER, Ess., a pelican in her piety, ar. *Pl.* 44, *cr.* 1.

PACKINGTON, Surr. and Middx., a demi-lion, az., in dexter a (dagger,) ar. *Pl.* 41, *cr.* 13.

PACKINGTON, Worc. and Bucks., an elephant, passant, or. *Pl.* 56, *cr.* 14.

PACKINGTON, Worc., a demi-hare, rampant, az., charged with three plates. *Pl.* 58, *cr.* 14.

PACKINGTON, Beds. and Bucks., a demi-hare, az., charged with three bezants. *Pl.* 58, *cr.* 14.

PACKNAM, out of a mural coronet, an eagle, wings elevated. *Pl.* 33, *cr.* 5, (eagle, *pl.* 126, *cr.* 7.)

PACKWOOD, Warw., a demi-lion, rampant, ar., holding with dexter and supporting with sinister a bell, sa., with a canton, erm. *None is truly great but he that is truly good.* *Pl.* 47, *cr.* 4, (bell, *pl.* 73, *cr.* 15.)

PADDON, Eng., in dexter hand, ppr., a covered cup, or. *Pl.* 35, *cr.* 9.

PADDON, Surr. and Hants, a tower in flames, ppr. *Pl.* 118, *cr.* 15.

PADDON, WILLIAM-HUSBAND, Esq., of Thralesend, Beds., a tower, or, flammant, ppr. *Pl.* 118, *cr.* 15.

PADDON, Norf., a tower, ar., fire issuing from top. *Pl.* 12, *cr.* 5, (fire, *pl.* 71, *cr.* 11.)

PADDYE, Lanc., on a chapeau, gu., turned up, erm., a lion, passant, ar. *Pl.* 107, *cr.* 1.

PAGAN, Eng., in hand a dagger, erect, ppr. *Nec timeo, nec sperno.* *Pl.* 23, *cr.* 15.

PAGAN, Sco., out of a mural coronet, a demi-eagle, displayed, ppr. *Pl.* 33, *cr.* 5.

PAGANELL, and PAGNELL, Eng., in the sea, ppr., a column, sa. *Pl.* 14, *cr.* 3.

PAGE, out of a ducal coronet, per pale, or and gu., (another, gu. and ar.,) a demi-griffin, salient, per pale, counterchanged, beaked, of the second. *Pl.* 39, *cr.* 2.

PAGE, out of a mural coronet, or, a demi-griffin, gu. *Pl.* 18, *cr.* 6, (coronet, *pl.* 101, *cr.* 6.)

PAGE, ROBERT, Esq., of Holebrook, Somers., a demi-griffin. *Honneur pour objet.* *Pl.* 18, *cr.* 6.

PAGE, or PAIGE, Devons., an eagle, displayed, erm. *Pl.* 48, *cr.* 11.

PAGE, Middx., out of a mural coronet, gu., a lion's head, or. *Pl.* 45, *cr.* 9.

PAGE, Kent, a demi-griffin, erm., beaked and legged, gu. (Another, ar.) *Pl.* 18, *cr.* 6.

PAGE, Beds. and Kent, a demi-horse, per pale, dancettée, or and az. *Pl.* 91, *cr.* 2, (without wings and coronet.)

PAGE, Hants, a demi-seahorse, assurgent. *Pl.* 58, *cr.* 15.

PAGE, Camb., a demi-griffin, holding a ducal coronet. *Pl.* 19, *cr.* 15, (coronet, *same plate, cr.* 14.)

PAGELET, a morion, ppr. *Pl.* 18, *cr.* 9.

PAGENHAM, out of a mural coronet, or, a demi-eagle, gu., armed, gold. *Pl.* 33, *cr.* 5.

PAGET, Somers., a demi-(tiger,) rampant, sa., tufted and maned, ar., ducally gorged, or. *Diciendo y haciendo.* *Pl.* 125, *cr.* 4.

PAGET, Lond. and Staffs., a demi-(tiger,) rampant, sa., ducally gorged, tufted, and maned, ar. *Pl.* 125, *cr.* 4.

PAGET, Marquis of Anglesea. *See* ANGLESEA.

PAGET, CHARLES, Esq., of Ruddington Grange, Leic., a lion, rampant. *Honestas.* *Pl.* 67, *cr.* 5.

PAGET, Chipping Norton, a cubit arm, erect, vested, sa., cuffed, ar., in hand a scroll, of the second, bearing the inscription—*Deo Paget.* *Pl.* 32, *cr.* 4.

PAGETT, a demi-(tiger,) sa., ducally gorged and tufted, ar. *Pl.* 125, *cr.* 4.

PAGITT, Lond., Middx., and Northamp., a cubit arm, erect, vested, sa., cuffed, ar., in hand, ppr., a scroll, of the second, charged with motto—*Deo pagit*—a seal affixed thereto, pendent, gu. *Pl.* 32, *cr.* 4.

PAGRAVE, Eng., a greyhound's head, ar. *Pl.* 89, *cr.* 2.

PAGRAVE, a rhinoceros, or. *Pl.* 4, *cr.* 11.

PAIN, Iri., on a chapeau, ppr., a greyhound, sejant, or. *Pl.* 66, *cr.* 15, (chapeau, *pl.* 127, *fig.* 13.)

PAIN, Eng., a lion, rampant, ppr., supporting a garb, or. *Pl.* 63, *cr.* 14.

PAIN, Patcham Place, Suss., a stag's head, erased. *Pl.* 66, *cr.* 9.

PAINE, Eng., on a mount, vert, a lion, rampant, (collared,) in dexter an arrow. *Pl.* 59, *cr.* 5.

PAINTER, Eng., a goat, (passant,) ar., armed, bearded, and hoofed, or. *Pl.* 66, *cr.* 1.

PAINTER, Cornw., three pheons, ar., handled, or, two in saltier, one in pale, banded, gu.

PAITON, a griffin, or. *Pl.* 66, *cr.* 13.
PAKEMAN, a cockatrice, (close,) gu., combed and wattled, or. *Pl.* 63, *cr.* 15.
PAKENHAM, Earl of Longford. *See* LONGFORD.
PAKENHAM, Eng., in hand (three) arrows, points downward, all ppr. *Pl.* 56, *cr.* 4.
PAKENHAM, Iri. and Eng., a griffin, segreant, holding an escarbuncle, all ppr. *Pl.* 67, *cr.* 13, (escarbuncle, *pl.* 141.)
PAKENHAM, Lond., out of a ducal coronet, a demi-eagle, displayed. *Pl.* 9, *cr.* 6.
PAKINGTON, Middx. and Surr., a demi-lion, az., in dexter a dagger, ar. *Pl.* 41, *cr.* 13.
PAKINGTON, a demi-hare, az., bezantée. *Pl.* 58, *cr.* 14.
PAKINGTON, a demi-squirrel, erased, gu.
PAKINGTON, Bucks., an elephant, passant, or, armed, gu. *Pl.* 56, *cr.* 14.
PALEY, Eng., a hand, issuing from a heart, brandishing a scimitar, all ppr. *Pl.* 35, *cr.* 7.
PALEY, a boar's head, (couped,) in pale. *Pl.* 21 *cr.* 7.
PALEY, JOHN-GREEN, Esq., of Oatlands, Yorks., a stag's head, couped, ppr. *Pl.* 91, *cr.* 14.
PALK, Bart., Devons., on a (semi-)terrestrial globe, ppr., an eagle, rising, ar. *Pl.* 34, *cr.* 2.
PALLANT, Suff., an escutcheon, of the family arms, between wings, ppr. *Pl.* 14, *cr.* 7, (wings, *pl.* 1, *cr.* 15.)
PALLEY, a camel's head, sa. *Pl.* 109, *cr.* 9.
PALLISER, Bucks., out of a ducal coronet, gu., a demi-eagle, wings elevated, or. *Pl.* 19, *cr.* 9.
PALLISER, Bucks., out of a ducal coronet, gu., a demi-eagle, wings elevated, erminois, charged on breast with an anchor, in pale, az. *Pl.* 19, *cr.* 9, (anchor, *same plate*.)
PALLISER, WRAY, Esq., of Derryluskan, co. Tipperary; and Comragh, co. Waterford, out of a ducal coronet, gu., a demi-eagle, wings elevated, or. *Deo volente. Pl.* 19, *cr.* 9.
PALMER, Eng., a griffin, sejant, ar., beaked and legged, or, a crescent on breast. *Pl.* 100, *cr.* 11, (crescent, *pl.* 141.)
PALMER, Sco., a cat, sejant, ppr. *Pl.* 24, *cr.* 6.
PALMER, Beds., a greyhound, current, sa. *Pl.* 28, *cr.* 7, (without charge.)
PALMER, Northamp., a wyvern, or, armed and langued, gu. *Pour apprendre oblier ne puis. Pl.* 63, *cr.* 13.
PALMER, Iri., same crest.
PALMER, Northamp., a wyvern, wings addorsed, vert. *Pl.* 63, *cr.* 13.
PALMER, Warw. and Yorks., a griffin, sejant. *Pl.* 100, *cr.* 11.
PALMER, out of a ducal coronet, or, an elephant's head, sa. *Pl.* 93, *cr.* 13.
PALMER, of Holme Park, Berks., a talbot, sejant, erminois. *Pl.* 107, *cr.* 7.
PALMER, between two laurel-branches, vert, an escallop, ar. *Pl.* 86, *cr.* 9, (laurel, *same plate, cr.* 5.)
PALMER, a dragon's head, couped, or, collared and winged, vert, (on collar three plates, breast guttée-de-poix, wings fretty, ar., between the fret, trefoils, of the last.) *Pl.* 107, *cr.* 10.
PALMER, Herts., a wyvern's head, or, collared, gu., wings expanded, vert, fretty, semée of trefoils, slipped, ar. *Pl.* 107, *cr.* 10, (trefoil, *pl.* 141.)

PALMER, Kent, an ostrich, (volant,) ar. *Pl.* 9, *cr.* 3.
PALMER, Linc., a cubit arm, erect, vested, az., cuffed, ar., in hand, ppr., a (palmer's staff.) *Pl.* 18, *cr.* 1.
PALMER, Lond., a lion, rampant, or, holding a (palmer's staff, sa., head, end, and rest, or.) *Pl.* 22, *cr.* 15.
PALMER, Northamp., a wyvern, or, wings addorsed, vert. *Pl.* 63, *cr.* 13.
PALMER, out of a ducal coronet, a griffin's head. *Pl.* 54, *cr.* 14.
PALMER, Surr., a greyhound, sejant, sa., collared, or, on shoulder a trefoil, slipped, ar. *Pl.* 66, *cr.* 15, (trefoil, *pl.* 141.)
PALMER, Bucks. and Northamp., a cubit arm, (in mail, erect, ppr., in hand a halberd, sa., headed, ar.) *Pl.* 73, *cr.* 7.
PALMER, Bucks. and Northamp., out of rays, ppr., a griffin's head, ar. *Pl.* 84, *cr.* 9, (head, *pl.* 48, *cr.* 6.)
PALMER, Suss., a demi-panther, rampant, gardant, flames issuing from ears and mouth, ppr., holding a branch, vert, fructed, gu. *Pl.* 76, *cr.* 1.
PALMER, HENRY, Esq., of Clifton Lodge, Beds., same crest.
PALMER, Bart., Leic., a lion, couchant, or. *Pl.* 75, *cr.* 5, (without chapeau.)
PALMER, Bart., Iri., an arm, in armour, embowed, ppr., ornamented, or, in hand a spear, ppr. *In Deo est mihi omnis fides. Pl.* 44, *cr.* 9.
PALMER, Bart., Kent, a demi-panther, rampant, flames issuing from mouth and ears, holding a palm-branch, all ppr. *Palma virtuti. Pl.* 76, *cr.* 1.
PALMERSTON, Viscount, and Baron, Iri., (Temple,) a talbot, sejant, sa., collared and lined, or. *Flecti, non frangi. Pl.* 107, *cr.* 7.
PALMES, in hand a palm-branch. *Justus ut palma. Pl.* 23, *cr.* 7.
PALMES, Hants. and Yorks., a naked arm, erect, in hand (three) branches of palm, ppr. *Ut palma justus. Pl.* 118, *cr.* 7.
PALMES, the Rev. WILLIAM-LINDSAY, of Naburn Hall, Yorks., in hand a palm-branch. *Ut palma justus. Pl.* 23, *cr.* 7.
PALMES, out of a ducal coronet, gu., a dragon's head, sa., encompassed with flames, ppr. *Pl.* 93, *cr.* 15.
PALSHED, an arm, embowed, vested, bendy of eight, ar. and gu., in hand, ppr., three flowers, az., stalked and leaved, vert. *Pl.* 120, *cr.* 1, (flowers, *pl.* 23, *cr.* 2.)
PALTOCK, Surr., on a mount, vert, a greyhound, sejant, sa., spotted, ar., (collared, or.) *Pl.* 5, *cr.* 2.
PAMURE, a demi-lion, rampant, az., in dexter an heraldic-rose, stalked and leaved, or. *Pl.* 64, *cr.* 2, (rose, *pl.* 105, *cr.* 7.)
PANCEFOOTE, Eng., a fleur-de-lis, az. *Pl.* 68, *cr.* 12.
PANELLEE, Eng., out of a ducal coronet, or, an heraldic-tiger's head, gu. *Pl.* 98, *cr.* 4.
PANMURE, Baron, (Maule,) a wyvern, vert, spouting fire before and behind. *Clementia et animis. Pl.* 109, *cr.* 13.
PANNELL, Eng., out of an earl's coronet, a moor's head, from shoulders, ppr. *Pl.* 80, *cr.* 11.
PANTER, Eng., a talbot, passant, sa. *Pl.* 120, *cr.* 8.

PANTHER, Eng., a panther, passant, gardant, ppr. *Pl.* 51, *cr.* 7.

PANTON, Suss., a dolphin, haurient, or, between two wings, gu., each charged with as many bars, ar. *Pl.* 111, *cr.* 12.

PANTON, Wel., a sword, ppr., hilt and pommel, or, enfiled with a leopard's head, gold, *Pl.* 24, *cr.* 13.

PANTON, Sco., a spear-head, ppr. *Firmius ad pugnam.* *Pl.* 82, *cr.* 9.

PANTON, a lion, couchant, tail between hind legs, az., bezantée. *Pl.* 75, *cr.* 5, (without chapeau.)

PANTON, Durh., a sword, ppr., hilt and pommel, or, enfiled with a leopard's head, gold. *Semper eadem.* *Pl.* 24, *cr.* 13.

PAPE, Eng., in dexter hand, ppr., a clam-shell, or. *Pl.* 57, *cr.* 6.

PAPE, a falcon, wings expanded, ppr. *Pl.* 105, *cr.* 4.

PAPEWORTH, Eng., a fox's head, erased, gu. *Pl.* 71, *cr.* 4.

PAPILLON, THOMAS, Esq., of Acrise Place, Kent; and Crowhurst Place, Suss.; a crescent, ar. *Ditat servata fides.* *Pl.* 18, *cr.* 14.

PARAMORE, Kent, two arms, embowed, (vested, az.,) between hands, ppr., an etoile, or. *Pl.* 10, *cr.* 9, (etoile, *pl.* 141.)

PARAMOUR, Kent, a cubit arm, erect, (vested, az., cuffed ar.,) in hand, ppr., an etoile, or. *Pl.* 62, *cr.* 13, (etoile, *pl.* 141.)

PARAMOUR, Leic. and Salop, an antelope, sejant, or, attired, maned, and tufted, sa. *Pl.* 115, *cr.* 3, (without gorging.)

PARAVISIN, Lond., out of a tower, an arm, embowed, vested, in hand a tilting-spear. *Pl.* 5, *cr.* 1.

PARBURY, Lond., between two branches of (laurel,) in saltier, ppr., a pelican, or, semée of torteaux, in nest, also ppr., feeding her young. *Cras mihi.* *Pl.* 76, *cr.* 15.

PARDEO, a tower, gu. *Pl.* 12, *cr.* 5.

PARDOE, Eng., a griffin, sejant, az., winged, legged, and beaked, or. *Pl.* 100, *cr.* 11.

PARDOE, a demi-lion, rampant, gardant, ar., supporting an escallop, sa. *Pl.* 35, *cr.* 4, (escallop, *pl.* 141.)

PARDOE, Nash Court, Salop, a lion, passant, gardant. *Pl.* 120, *cr.* 5.

PARDOE, Herts., a tower, or. *Pl.* 12, *cr.* 5.

PARES, Eng., a greyhound, current, gu. *Pl.* 28, *cr.* 7, (without charge.)

PARES, THOMAS, Esq., of Hopwell Hall, Derbs.; and Ulverscroft Abbey and Kirkby Frith, Leic.; a demi-griffin, or. *Pares cum paribus.* *Pl.* 18, *cr.* 6.

PARGITER, Northamp., a dexter arm, embowed, ppr., vested, ar., in hand a covered cup, or. *Pl.* 39, *cr.* 1.

PARIS, Eng. and Sco., a quill, erect, ppr. *Pl.* 105, *cr.* 3.

PARIS, Hunts. and Herts., a sphinx, couchant, gu., face and breast, ppr., wings addorsed, or, crined, gold. *Pl.* 116, *cr.* 5, (without cinquefoil.)

PARIS, a sphinx, ppr., winged, or. *Pl.* 91, *cr.* 11.

PARISH, Eng., a unicorn's head, erased, ar. *Pl.* 67, *cr.* 1.

PARK, or PARKE, Eng., on a ducal coronet, a lion, passant, (ducally crowned, ppr.) *Pl.* 107, *cr.* 11.

PARK, Sco., a buck's head, cabossed. *Providentiæ me committo.* *Pl.* 36, *cr.* 1.

PARK, a stag, lodged, ppr. *Pl.* 67, *cr.* 2.

PARK, in dexter hand a book, closed, ppr. *Graviter et piè.* *Pl.* 45, *cr.* 3.

PARK, in (sinister) hand an open book, ppr. *Sapienter et piè.* *Pl.* 82, *cr.* 5, (without cloud.)

PARKE, (on a mount, vert, paled in, ar.,) a fox, paly of four, or and az. *Pl.* 126, *cr.* 5.

PARKE, a talbot's head, erased, ar., (pierced through by an arrow, barwise,) ppr. *Pl.* 90, *cr.* 6.

PARKE, Cambs., a talbot's head, gu., pierced in breast by a pheon, or. *Pl.* 123, *cr.* 15, (pheon, *pl.* 141.)

PARKER, Eng., a cock's head, gu., between wings, tawney, bill, ar. *Pl.* 47, *cr.* 3, (without cross.)

PARKER, Wales, a lion, rampant, or. *Pl.* 67, *cr.* 5.

PARKER, Eng., an elephant's head, ar., trunk and tusks, or, ears, gu. *Pl.* 35, *cr.* 13.

PARKER, Suss., on a chapeau, az., turned up, erm., a greyhound, or. *Pl.* 104, *cr.* 1.

PARKER, Suss., out of a ducal coronet, or, a bear's head, sa., muzzled, gold. *Pl.* 6, *cr.* 6.

PARKER, out of clouds ar., a dexter arm, ppr., vested, gu., in hand the hilt of a broken sword, ppr. *Pl.* 22, *cr.* 6.

PARKER, Kent, out of a ducal coronet, gu., a bull's head, or, armed, ar. *Pl.* 68, *cr.* 6.

PARKER, Linc., Derbs., and Staffs., a leopard's head, erased, gardant, or, ducally gorged, gu. *Pl.* 116, *cr.* 8.

PARKER, Eng., in hand, or, a falchion, blade, ar., hilt, gold. *Pl.* 21, *cr.* 10.

PARKER, Earl of Macclesfield. *See* MACCLESFIELD.

PARKER, Eng., a horse's head, (couped,) per pale, indented, ar. and az. *Pl.* 81, *cr.* 6.

PARKER, five darts, points downward, one in pale, four in saltier. *Pl.* 54, *cr.* 15.

PARKER, an arm, erect, vested, az., cuffed and puffed, ar., in hand, ppr., an attire of a stag, gu. *Pl.* 5, *cr.* 3.

PARKER, a stag's head, couped, ppr. *Pl.* 91, *cr.* 14.

PARKER, Yorks., a talbot's head, ar., eared and langued, gu., collared, ermines. *Pl.* 2, *cr.* 15.

PARKER, a talbot's head, ar., collared, pean, eared, gu. *Pl.* 2, *cr.* 15.

PARKER, on a mount, vert, a stag, (trippant,) ppr. *Pl.* 50, *cr.* 6.

PARKER, EDWARD, Esq., of Alkincoats, Lanc., a stag, trippant, ppr. *Non fluctu, nec flatu movetur.* *Pl.* 68, *cr.* 2.

PARKER, a buck's head, couped, ar., attired, or, (with an arrow through horns, of the first.) *Pl.* 91, *cr.* 14.

PARKER, on trunk of tree, couped at top, ppr., an eagle, preying on a bird. *Pl.* 5, *cr.* 4.

PARKER, Middx., a stag, trippant, ppr. *Pl.* 68, *cr.* 2.

PARKER, Norf., a demi-cock, (wings expanded,) gu., beaked, combed, and wattled, ar. *Pl.* 72, *cr.* 4.

PARKER, Norf., a demi-cock, wings addorsed, gu., combed and wattled, ar. *Pl.* 72, *cr.* 4.

PARKER, Suff., a talbot, passant, ar., resting dexter on a buck's head, cabossed, or. *Pl.* 120, *cr.* 8, (head, *pl.* 36, *cr.* 1.)

PARKER, Lanc., a buck, (trippant,) ppr., pierced by an arrow, in pale, point downward ar. *Pl.* 88, *cr.* 9.

PARKER, Lond., on a chapeau, az., a greyhound, (passant, or, collared, ringed, and lined, ar.) *Pl.* 104, *cr.* 1.

PARKER, Kent, a cubit arm, erect, in mail, or, in hand, ppr., a falchion, ar., hilt and pommel, gold. *Pl.* 125, *cr.* 5.

PARKER, Kent, a talbot, passant, ar., against an oak-tree, ppr., fructed, or. *Pl.* 120, *cr.* 8, (tree, *pl.* 16, *cr.* 8.)

PARKER, Kent, an elephant's head, couped, ar., (gorged with a collar, gu., charged with three fleurs-de-lis, or.) *Pl.* 35, *cr.* 13.

PARKER, Kent, out of a mural coronet, or, a horse's head, gu., maned, gold. *Pl.* 50, *cr.* 13, (coronet, *pl.* 128, *fig.* 18.)

PARKER, Chesh., a buck's head, erased, ppr. *Pl.* 66, *cr.* 9.

PARKER, Chesh., on a mount, vert, a talbot, sejant, ppr., collared, or, resting dexter on a buck's head, cabossed, gu. *Pl.* 19, *cr.* 2, (head, *pl.* 36, *cr.* 1.)

PARKER, Cumb., a cubit arm, erect, vested, vert, cuffed, ar., in hand, the attire of a stag, (and a bow and arrow, in saltier, ppr.) *Virtutis alimentum honos. Pl.* 5, *cr.* 3.

PARKER, Warw. and Devons., a cubit arm, erect, vested, sa., cuffed, ar., in hand, ppr., a stag's horn, gu. *Fideli certa merces. Pl.* 5, *cr.* 3.

PARKER, Ess., in lion's gamb, erased, or, an (arrow, gu., headed and feathered, ar.) *Pl.* 85, *cr.* 15.

PARKER, Bart., Warw., on a naval coronet, az., a stag, statant, ar., behind him a laurel-branch, issuant, in pale, ppr. *Pl.* 69, *cr.* 2.

PARKER, Bart., Ess., an elephant's head, couped, ar., (collared, gu., charged with three fleurs-de-lis, or.) *Try. Pl.* 35, *cr.* 13.

PARKER, Bart., Suff., a dexter arm, erect, vested, az., slashed and cuffed, ar., in hand, ppr., an attire of a stag, or, piece of coral, gu. *Pl.* 5, *cr.* 3.

PARKER, Earl of Morley. *See* MORLEY.

PARKER, MONTAGU-EDMUND, Esq., of Whiteway, Devons., an arm, erect, vested, az., cuff, ar., in hand the attire of a stag, ppr. *Fideli certa merces. Pl.* 5, *cr.* 3.

PARKER-ROBERT, BROCKHOLES, Esq., of Hareden, Yorks.: 1. For *Parker*, on a chapeau, a stag, trippant, ppr. *Pl.* 63, *cr.* 8. 2. For *Brockholes*, a brock, passant, sa. *Non fluctu, non flatu movetur. Pl.* 34, *cr.* 4.

PARKES, Eng., an escutcheon, party, per cheveron, gu. and or, between two branches of laurel, vert. *Pl.* 14, *cr.* 7.

PARKES, a talbot's head, erased, gu., on breast a pheon, or. *Pl.* 90, *cr.* 6, (pheon, *pl.* 141.)

PARKES, Staffs., in an oak-tree, ar., a squirrel, sejant, ppr. *Pl.* 5, *cr.* 6, (tree, *pl.* 16, *cr.* 8.)

PARKHOUSE, and PARKHURST, Lond., a stag, trippant, ppr. *Pl.* 68, *cr.* 2.

PARKHOUSE, Hants, a buck, ppr., charged on body with three mullets, az., fore-dexter, resting on a cross flory, vert. *The cross our stay. Pl.* 61, *cr.* 15, (cross and mullets, *pl.* 141.)

PARKHURST, Eng., a griffin, segreant, per fess, or and gu. *Pl.* 67, *cr.* 13.

PARKHURST, Surr., a demi-griffin, wings addorsed, sa., in dexter a cutlass, ar., hilt and pommel, or. *Pl.* 49, *cr.* 4.

PARKHURST, Lond., out of a palisado coronet, or, a buck's head, erased, ar., attired, gold. *Pl.* 66, *cr.* 9, (coronet, *pl.* 128, *fig.* 21.)

PARKIN, Eng., a fox, sejant, ppr. *Pl.* 87, *cr.* 4.

PARKINS, Iri., out of a ducal coronet, a demi-eagle, displayed. *Honesta audax. Pl.* 9, *cr.* 6.

PARKINS, out of a ducal coronet, a swan, wings expanded, collared and lined, in bill an acorn-slip. *Pl.* 100, *cr.* 7, (acorn, *same plate, cr.* 8.)

PARKINS, Lond., a bull, passant, az., (wings addorsed, or, ducally gorged, gold.) *Pl.* 66, *cr.* 11.

PARKINS, Notts., a pine-apple, ppr., stalked and leaved, vert.

PARKINSON, Eng., a griffin's head, erased, in beak a sword, ppr. *Pl.* 35, *cr.* 15.

PARKINSON, Heref., a cubit arm, erect, vested, erminois, cuffed, ar., in hand, ppr., an ostrich-feather, in pale, gu. *Pl.* 69, *cr.* 1.

PARKYNS, a bull, passant, az., winged, or, ducally gorged, gold, *Pl.* 66, *cr.* 11, (gorging, *same plate, cr.* 5.)

PARKYNS, two eagles' heads, conjoined in one neck, ppr.

PARKYNS, Baron Rancliffe. *See* RANCLIFFE.

PARLAR, Middx., a Cornish chough, sa., beaked and legged, gu. *Pl.* 100, *cr.* 13.

PARMINTER, Cornw., an eagle, displayed, ppr. *Pl.* 48, *cr.* 11.

PARNELL, Iri., out of a ducal coronet, or, a dexter arm, in hand a sheaf of arrows, ppr. *Pl.* 9, *cr.* 4.

PARNELL, Eng. and Iri., a griffin's head, sa., between wings, or. *Pl.* 65, *cr.* 1.

PARNELL, in lion's gamb., erect and erased, a key, in bend sinister, wards upward, pendent from a chain. *Pl.* 5, *cr.* 5.

PARNELL, Iri., a boar's head, erased, or. *Pl.* 16, *cr.* 11.

PARNELL, JOHN-HENRY, Esq., of Avondale, co. Wicklow, a boar's head, erased, or. *Pl.* 16, *cr.* 11.

PARNHAM, Eng., a leopard's head, erased, ar. *Pl.* 94, *cr.* 10.

PARNTHER, Eng., a dexter arm, in armour, ppr., in hand a cross crosslet, fitched, in pale, or. *Pl.* 51, *cr.* 1.

PAROISSIEN, Hardingham, Norf., on a ducal coronet, or, a dove, ppr. *Pl.* 66, *cr.* 12, (coronet, *same plate.*)

PARR, Eng., a lady's head, from shoulders, vested. *Pl.* 74, *cr.* 5, (without coronet.)

PARR, Eng., a hind, trippant, ppr. *Pl.* 20, *cr.* 14.

PARR, an arm, in armour, embowed, in hand a pair of compasses. *Pl.* 69, *cr.* 3.

PARR, Westm., Northamp., Leic., Staffs., and Derbs., a cubit arm, in armour, ppr., in hand a (bar, az.) *Pl.* 33, *cr.* 4.

PARR, Westm., Northamp., Leic., Staffs., and Derbs., a female's head, couped below shoulders, vested, az., (regally crowned, or, over neck and shoulders a rich chain, gold, set with rubies and sapphires.) *Pl.* 81, *cr.* 13.

PARR, Chesh., a demi-boar, rampant, az., bristled, or, (charged with a bend, gu., thereon three lozenges, gold.) *Pl.* 20, *cr.* 5.

PARR, the Rev. THOMAS, Salop, a female's head, couped below shoulders, vested, az., on head a wreath of roses, alternately ar. and gu. *Amour avec loyaulte. Pl.* 81, *cr.* 13.

PARR-CODRINGTON, out of a ducal coronet, or, a dragon's head, gu., between wings, chequy, or and az. *Pl.* 105, *cr.* 11, (coronet, *pl.* 128, *fig.* 3.)

PARRAM, in lion's paw, erased, or, (a mallet, erect, gu.) *Pl.* 126, *cr.* 9.

PARRE, Eng., a horse's head, gu., maned, or. *Pl.* 81, *cr.* 6.

PARRET, and PERROTT, Kent and Oxon., a parrot, close, ppr., beaked and legged, gu., (in dexter a pear, or,) on breast a mullet, gold. *Pl.* 25, *cr.* 2, (mullet, *pl.* 141.)

PARROT, or PARROTT, Eng., a parrot, gu. *Pl.* 25, *cr.* 2.

PARRY, Eng., a lamb, ar., bearing a banner, or. *Pl.* 48, *cr.* 13.

PARRY, Wel., a stag, at gaze, ppr. *Pl.* 81, *cr.* 8.

PARRY, Iri., an arrow, point (upwards,) enfiled with a ducal coronet, ppr. *Pl.* 55, *cr.* 1.

PERRY, a demi-lion, rampant, az., (on head) a garb, or. *Pl.* 84, *cr.* 7.

PARRY, Heref., three battle-axes, (erect,) ppr. *Pl.* 20, *cr.* 11.

PARRY, Berks., a cubit arm, ppr., hand grasping a snake, vert, (biting the hand.) *Pl.* 91, *cr.* 6.

PARRY, Lond., a griffin, sejant, ppr., (chained round loins.) *Pl.* 100, *cr.* 11.

PARRY, Salop, same crest. *Veritas odit morem.*

PARRY, Wel., on a chapeau, erm., turned up, gu., a boar's head, couped, sa., armed, or. *Vince fide. Pl.* 48, *cr.* 2, (chapeau, *pl.* 127, *fig.* 13.)

PARRY-SEGAR, Herts.: 1. For *Parry*, a buck's head, couped, ar., in mouth a sprig, ppr. *Pl.* 100, *cr.* 8. 2. For *Segar*, on a ducal coronet, or, two snakes, vert, entwined round a (sceptre,) gold, between wings, dexter, gold, sinister, ar. *Pl.* 69, *cr.* 7.

PARSCOE, Eng., a castle, triple-towered, ppr., from middle tower a demi-lion, rampant, az. *Pl.* 101, *cr.* 1.

PARSONS, Heref., a halberd, headed, ar., (embrued, gu.) *Pl.* 14, *cr.* 8.

PARSONS, Iri., out of a ducal coronet, or, a cubit-arm, erect, in hand a sprig of roses, all ppr. *Pl.* 60, *cr.* 1.

PARSONS, a tower, ar. *Pl.* 12, *cr.* 5.

PARSONS, Lond., on a leopard's head, gu., an eagle's leg, erased at thigh, or. *Pl.* 66, *cr.* 14, (leg, *pl.* 103, *cr.* 4.)

PARSONS, Suss., a garb of quatrefoils, vert, banded, or. *Pl.* 69, *cr.* 4.

PARSONS, Bucks., on a chapeau, az., turned up, erm., an eagle's head, erased, ar., (ducally crowned, or, charged on neck with a cross, gu.) *Pl.* 13, *cr.* 5.

PARSONS, Bucks., on a chapeau, gu., turned up, erm., an eagle's head, erased, ar., beaked, of the first. *Pl.* 13, *cr.* 5.

PARSONS, Bucks., on a chapeau, gu., turned up, erm., a griffin's head, erased, ar., beaked, gu. *Pl.* 13, *cr.* 5, (head, *pl.* 48, *cr.* 6.)

PARSONS, Earl of Rosse. *See* ROSSE.

PARTHERICHE, and PARTHERICKE, Middx., a dexter arm, in armour, embowed, couped, in hand a scimitar, ppr. *Pl.* 81, *cr.* 11.

PARTINGTON, Eng., an arm, ppr., vested, ar., in hand an anchor, of the first. *Pl.* 53, *cr.* 13.

PARTINGTON, a hawk, wings expanded, ppr. *Pl.* 105, *cr.* 4.

PARTIS, Northumb., a stag's head, cabossed. *Pl.* 36, *cr.* 1.

PARTRICH, a (partridge,) volant, or. *Pl.* 87, *cr.* 18.

PARTRICK, or PATRICK, an arm, in armour, embowed, hand apaumée, ppr. *Pl.* 97, *cr.* 1.

PARTRICKSON, Cumb., on a mount, vert, a stag, current, regardant, ppr., hoofed and attired, or. *Pl.* 3, *cr.* 2.

PARTRICKSON, and PATRICKSON, Camb., on a mount, vert, a stag, current, regardant, ppr., hoofed and attired, or. *Pl.* 3, *cr.* 2.

PARTRIDGE, Eng., a demi-lion, rampant, or, collared, gu., garnished, or. *Pl.* 18, *cr.* 13.

PARTRIDGE, Glouc. and Suff., out of a ducal coronet, or, a horse's head, sa. *Pl.* 50, *cr.* 13.

PARTRIDGE, Glouc. and Suff., a horse's head, sa., crined, or, erased, per fess, gu. *Pl.* 81, *cr.* 6.

PARTRIDGE, and PARTRICH, a lion's head, or, issuing from a rose, gu., stalked and leaved, vert. *Pl.* 69, *cr.* 6.

PARTRIDGE, HENRY-SAMUEL, Esq., of Hockham Hall, Norf., a partridge, wings displayed, or. *Dum spiro, spero. Pl.* 108, *cr.* 5.

PARTRIDGE, a partridge, rising, or, (in beak an ear of wheat, ppr.) *Pl.* 108, *cr.* 5.

PARTRIDGE, a demi-leopard, rampant, gardant, sa, (bezantée, gorged with a collar, gu., charged with three plates.) *Pl.* 1, *cr.* 10, (without anchor.)

PARTRIDGE, Middx., a partridge, rising, in beak an ear of wheat, all ppr. *Pl.* 108, *cr.* 5, (wheat, *same plate, cr.* 8.)

PARTRIDGE, Kent, an arm, embowed, (tied round elbow with a ribbon,) in hand, ppr., a fire-ball, of the last. *Pl.* 62, *cr.* 9.

PARTRIDGE, JOHN, Esq., of Bishop's Wood, in Heref. and Glouc.: 1. Out of a ducal coronet, or, a horse's head, sa. *Pl.* 50, *cr.* 13. 2. A leopard, ar., spotted, sa. *Pl.* 86, *cr.* 2.

PARVISE, Surr., a Cornish chough, rising, ppr. *Pl.* 50, *cr.* 5.

PASCALL, Eng., on a mount, a holy lamb, ppr., flag, sa. *Pl.* 101, *cr.* 9.

PASCALL, or PASCHALL, Ess., a demi-man, couped at breast, (vested, ppr., lined, erm.,) head, hair, and beard, of the first. *Pl.* 126, *cr.* 8.

PASCOE, (on a mount,) a wolf, statant, regardant. *Pl.* 77, *cr.* 14, (without spear.)

PASCOL, Eng., a paschal lamb, ar., flag, gu. *Pl.* 48, *cr.* 13.

PASHLEY, and PASLEY, Eng., a balance and scales, ar., beam, az. *Pl.* 12, *cr.* 11.

PASKE, a lion, rampant, ar., supporting a cross pattée, fitched, sa. *Pl.* 125, *cr.* 2.

PASLEW, Yorks. and Suff., a lion, rampant, gu. *Pl.* 67, *cr.* 5.

PASLEY, Bart., Sco., out of a ducal coronet, gold, a sinister arm, in armour, ppr., in hand a staff, thereon a flag, ar., charged with a cross, gu., and on a canton, az., a human leg, in pale, couped above knee, or. *Pro rege et patriâ pugnans.*

2 A

PASLEY, Sco., a dexter arm, from shoulder, in armour, in hand a dagger, point downward, all ppr. *Be sure.* Pl. 120, cr. 11.

PASMORE, out of a mural coronet, seven Lochaber axes, addorsed, ppr. Pl. 62, cr. 8.

PASMORE, Berks., a demi-sea-wolf, ppr.

PASS, Eng., the sun in splendour, or. Pl. 68, cr. 14.

PASSINGHAM, Eng., a demi-lion, rampant, party per fess, or and gu., each charged with a cinquefoil, counterchanged. Pl. 67, cr. 10, (cinquefoil, pl. 141.)

PASSINGHAM, a demi-lion, semée of cinquefoils, in dexter a sword, in pale. Pl. 41, cr. 13.

PASSMERE, Devons., a demi-sea-dog, az., finned, ar.

PASSMERE, Devons., a demi-leopard, az. Pl. 12, cr. 14.

PASSMORE, Eng., a stag, at gaze, ar. Pl. 81, cr. 8.

PASTON, Eng., a griffin, sejant, or. Pl. 100, cr. 11.

PASTON, a griffin, passant, or, (collared,) ar., lined, az. Pl. 61, cr. 14.

PASTON, Norf., a griffin, sejant, wings addorsed, or, (in beak,) a chaplet, gu. Pl. 56, cr. 10.

PASTON, Norf., a griffin, sejant, wings addorsed, or, (collared, in mouth a coil.) Pl. 100, cr. 11.

PATCH, Devons., a dexter arm, in armour, in fess, couped, ppr., in hand a cross crosslet, fitched, sa. Pl. 71, cr. 13.

PATE, Leic., a stag's head, cabossed, ar., attired, or, between attires, a raven, wings (expanded,) sa. Pl. 58, cr. 13.

PATE, Glouc., a demi-lion, rampant, vair, crowned, or. Pl. 61, cr. 4, (without branch.)

PATEIS, Eng., a greyhound, current towards a tree. Pl. 27, cr. 2.

PATER, Eng., a leopard's head and neck, erased, gardant, gu. Pl. 56, cr. 7.

PATERSON, Sco., in hand a sword, in pale, ppr. *Pro rege et grege.* Pl. 23, cr. 15.

PATERSON, Sco., a pelican's head, couped, ppr. *Pro rege et grege.* Pl. 41, cr. 4.

PATERSON, Sco., a branch of palm, ppr. *Virtute viresco.* Pl. 123, cr. 1.

PATERSON, of Bannockburn, in hand a quill, ppr. *Hinc orior.* Pl. 26, cr. 13.

PATERSON, GEORGE, Esq., of Castle Huntly, Perths., a pelican, in nest, feeding her young, ppr. *Mercie.* Pl. 44, cr. 1.

PATES, Glouc., a lion, vair, sa. and ar., crowned. Pl. 98, cr. 1.

PATESHALL, Heref., a demi-griffin, ar. Pl. 18, cr. 6.

PATESHALL, a peacock's head, sa., between wings, or, beaked, gold, on neck three bends, ar. Pl. 50, cr. 9, (without snake.)

PATESHALL-BURNAM, Heref., out of a ducal coronet, a pelican, ar., vulning, ppr. Pl. 64, cr. 1, (coronet, *same plate, cr. 5*.)

PATESON, Norf., a pelican, in nest, vulning, ppr. Pl. 44, cr. 1.

PATISHULL, and PATTISHALL, Eng., in hand a billet, az. Pl. 28, cr. 8.

PATISON, Sco., a pelican, in nest. *Hostis honori invidia.* Pl. 44, cr. 1.

PATMER, Eng., in hand an imperial crown, ppr. Pl. 97, cr. 12.

PATON, Sco., a sparrow-hawk, wings expanded, ppr. *Virtute adepta.* Pl. 105, cr. 4.

PATON, Sco., a sparrow-hawk, perched, ppr. *Virtus laudanda.* Pl. 78, cr. 8, (without stump.)

PATON, and PATOUN, Surr., a sparrow-hawk, close, ppr., (charged on breast with a trefoil, slipped or.) Pl. 78, cr. 8, (without stump.)

PATON, Sco., in dexter hand a rose-slip, leaved, ppr. *Virtute viget.* Pl. 118, cr. 9.

PATON, Sco., a sparrow-hawk, rising, ppr. *Virtute viget.* Pl. 105, cr. 4.

PATON, PATTON, and PATTONE, a sparrow-hawk, wings expanded, ppr. *Virtute adepta.* Pl. 105, cr. 4.

PATRIARCHE, a greyhound, (passant,) ar. *Honor et honestas.* Pl. 104, cr. 1.

PATRICK, W. RALSTON, Esq., of Roughwood, a dexter hand, erect, ppr., holding a saltier, sa. *Ora et labora.* Pl. 126 D, cr. 11. For *Ralston,* a falcon looking to the sinister. *Fide et marte.* Pl. 126 D, cr. 12.

PATRICK, Sco., a hand, erect, ppr. *Ora et labora.* Pl. 32, cr. 14.

PATRICK, Durh., an arm, in armour, embowed. Pl. 97, cr. 1.

PATRICK, a stag, trippant. Pl. 68, cr. 2.

PATRICK, Sco., in dexter hand, ppr. a saltier, sa. *Ora et labora.*

PATRICK, Kent, a stag, trippant. *Study quiet.* Pl. 68, cr. 2.

PATRICKSON, Cumb., on a mount, vert, a stag, current, regardant, ppr., hoofed and attired, or. Pl. 3, cr. 2.

PATRICKSON, HUGH, Esq., Kirklinton Park, Cumb., same crest. *Mente et manu.*

PATTE, Eng., a lion, rampant, az. Pl. 67, cr. 5.

PATTEN, Eng., a griffin's head, erased, vert. *Nullâ pallescere culpâ.* Pl. 48, cr. 6.

PATTEN, Linc. and Middx., a tower, or, issuing flames of fire, ppr., over which a label charged with this motto—*Mal au tour.* Pl. 12, cr. 5, (flames, pl. 16, cr. 12.)

PATTEN, Lanc., a tower, or, issuing flames of fire, ppr. *Ib.*

PATTEN, a griffin's head and neck, erased, vert, beaked, or. Pl. 48, cr. 6.

PATTEN-WILSON, of Bank Hall, Lanc.: 1. For *Patten,* a griffin's head, erased, vert. *Nullâ pallescere culpâ.* Pl. 48, cr. 6. 2. For *Wilson,* a demi-wolf, rampant. *Virtus ad sidera tollit.* Pl. 67, cr. 10.

PATTENSON, Yorks., out of a ducal coronet, a camel's head. Pl. 55, cr. 5, (without collar or crown.)

PATTENSON, Kent, a camel's head, (erased,) sa., bezantée. *Finem respice.* Pl. 109, cr. 9.

PATTERS, a cross crosslet, fitched, or, and a palm-branch, vert, in saltier. Pl. 102, cr. 3, (palm, pl. 123, cr. 1.)

PATTERSON, Eng., a cross crosslet, fitched, or, and palm-branch, vert, in saltier. Pl. 98, cr. 11, (palm, pl. 123, cr. 1.)

PATTERSON, Sco., a naked arm, erect, in hand a pen, ppr. Pl. 26, cr. 13.

PATTERSON, a talbot's, head, erased. Pl. 90 cr. 6.

PATTERSON, a pelican, in nest, (close,) vulning, all ppr. Pl. 44, cr. 1.

PATTISON, Iri., an arm, in armour, vambraced, az., in hand a hawk's lure, or. Pl. 44, cr. 2, (arm, pl. 120, cr. 11.)

PATTISON, Eng., a hind's head, couped, or. Pl. 21, cr. 9.

PATTISON, Sco., out of a ducal coronet, a camel's head, sa., gutée-d'or, gorged with a collar, crowned with an antique crown, both or. *Hostis honori invidia.* Pl. 55, cr. 5.

PATTISON, Sco., a pelican, feeding three young in a nest, all ppr. *Hostis honori invidia.* Pl. 44, cr. 1.

PATTISON, Sco., out of a ducal coronet, or, a camel's head, ar., guttee, sa., crowned with an antique crown, gold, collared, az., charged with three escallops, of the second. *Hostis honori invidia.* Pl. 55, cr. 5, (escallop, pl. 141.)

PATTLE, an eagle, displayed, ppr. Pl. 48, cr. 11.

PATTLE, an eagle, displayed, or. Pl. 48, cr. 11.

PATTON, Eng., on a rock, a swan, close, ppr. Pl. 122, cr. 13.

PATTON, Sco., a sparrow-hawk, perching, ppr. *Virtus laudanda.* Pl. 105, cr. 4.

PAUL, or PAULE, Lond., Surr., and Norf., a garb, vert, banded, ar. Pl. 48, cr. 10.

PAUL, Iri., a hand issuing from a cloud, in fess, holding a (torteau.) Pl. 104, cr. 4.

PAUL, Sco., two arms, in armour, placing a savage's head, affrontée, on a pheon. Pl. 83, cr. 11.

PAUL, Sco., a leopard's head. *Pro rege et republicâ.* Pl. 92, cr. 13.

PAUL, Surr. and Norf., on trunk of tree, (raguly,) in fess, sprigged and leaved, vert, a bird, close, ar. Pl. 10, cr. 1.

PAUL, Lond., an elephant, ar., on back a castle, gu., tied under belly, (on point of trunk a falchion, in pale, of the last.) Pl. 114, cr. 14.

PAUL, Bart., Glouc., a leopard's head, ppr., erased, per fess, gu. *Pro rege et republicâ.* Pl. 94, cr. 10.

PAUL, Iri., a cross pattée, fitched, or, between two swords, in pale, ar., pommels and hilts, gold. *Vana spes vitæ.* Pl. 27, cr. 14, (sword, pl. 105, cr. 1.)

PAUL, High Grove, Glouc., a leopard's head, per pale, or and az., on neck a cross crosslet, counterchanged. Pl. 94, cr. 10, (cross, pl. 141.)

PAULET, Marquess of Winchester. See WINCHESTER.

PAULET, Devons. and Glouc., an arm, in armour, embowed, in hand a sword, all ppr. Pl. 2, cr. 8.

PAULET, Bart., Southampton, a falcon, wings displayed and belled, or, ducally gorged, gu. *Aimez loyaulte.* Pl. 61, cr. 12, (without mount.)

PAULEY, within an annulet, an eagle, displayed. Pl. 88, cr. 2, (eagle, pl. 48, cr. 11.)

PAULI, a pillar, enfiled with a ducal coronet. Pl. 33, cr. 1, (coronet, pl. 55, cr. 1.)

PAULL, a leopard's head, erased at neck. Pl. 94, cr. 10.

PAUMIER, Devons., a hawk's leg, erased, jessed, and belled, ppr. Pl. 83, cr. 7.

PAUNCEFOTE, Sco., out of a ducal coronet, or, a plume of ostrich-feathers, ppr. Pl. 44, cr. 12.

PAUNCEFOTE, Notts., a lion, rampant, crowned with a ducal coronet. *Pensez forte.* Pl. 98, cr. 1.

PAVELEY, Eng., an anchor and a sword, in saltier, ppr. Pl. 25, cr. 1.

PAVER, Yorks., a tree, ppr. *Faded, but not destroyed.* Pl. 100, cr. 14.

PAVEY, Eng., a lion, rampant, gardant, sa. Pl. 92, cr. 7.

PAWLE, Eng., a leopard's head, erased, ppr. Pl. 94, cr. 10.

PAWLET, Somers., on a mount, vert, a falcon, rising, or, ducally gorged, gu. *Aimez loyaulte.* Pl. 61, cr. 12.

PAWLETT, Eng., a falcon, volant, or. Pl. 94, cr. 1.

PAWLETT, Middx., on a wreath, a terrestrial orb, or, thereon a falcon, rising, ppr., collared and belled, gold. Pl. 34, cr. 2.

PAWLETT, Middx., on a mount, vert, a falcon, rising, or. Pl. 81, cr. 12, (without gorging.)

PAWSON, Eng., a griffin's head, or. Pl. 38, cr. 3.

PAWSON, Northumb.: 1. For *Pawson*, a buck's head, erased, quarterly, idented, ar. and gu., attired, sa. Pl. 66, cr. 9. 2. For *Hargreave*, on a mount, vert, the sun in splendour, or. *Favente Deo.* Pl. 78, cr. 3.

PAXTON, Eng., on top of a tower, a (sea-pyot,) rising, ppr. Pl. 107, cr. 6.

PAXTON, Sco., a garb, ppr. *Industria ditat.* Pl. 48, cr. 10.

PAXTON, Herts. and Wel., an eagle's head, erased, az., (charged on neck with two cheverons, or,) between wings, ar., semée of mullets, gu. Pl. 81, cr. 10, (mullet, pl. 141.)

PAYLER, a lion, sejant, in dexter a saltier. Pl. 109, cr. 7.

PAYNE, Suss., a lion's head, erased, per fess, sa. and ar. Pl. 81, cr. 4.

PAYNE, Suss., a griffin, passant, wings addorsed, per pale, or and az. Pl. 61, cr. 14, (without gorging.)

PAYNE, Norf., an ostrich's head, erased, between wings, az., in beak a horse-shoe, ar. Pl. 28, cr. 13.

PAYNE, Norf., an ostrich's head, erased, or, between wings, sa., in beak a horse-shoe, of the first. Pl. 28, cr. 13.

PAYNE, Fulham, Middx., a griffin, passant, wings addorsed, or. Pl. 61, cr. 14, (without gorging.)

PAYNE, Middx., in lion's gamb, erect and erased, ar., a (tilting-spear,) rompée, gu. *Malo mori quam fœdari.* Pl. 1, cr. 4.

PAYNE, a lion's gamb, erased, ar., grasping a broken tilting spear, gu. *Malo mori quam fœdari.* Pl. 85, cr. 15.

PAYNE, Lond., out of clouds, ppr., two hands conjoined. Pl. 53, cr. 11.

PAYNE, a lion's head, erased, ppr., (ducally gorged, lined and ringed, or, in mouth a laurel-sprig, vert.) Pl. 95, cr. 6.

PAYNE, in lion's gamb, a cross pattée, sa. Pl. 46, cr. 7.

PAYNE, an ostrich's head, couped, or, between wings, sa. Pl. 28, cr. 13, (without horse-shoe.)

PAYNE, a demi-man, couped at loins, in profile, in dexter an (arrow.) Pl. 35, cr. 12.

PAYNE, a griffin, passant, az., feet and wings, or. Pl. 61, cr. 14, (without gorging.)

PAYNE, out of a plume of ostrich-feathers, a leopard's head, or. Pl. 92, cr. 13, (feathers, pl. 106, cr. 4.)

PAYNE, Leic., an heraldic-tiger, sejant, per pale, engrailed, az. and erm., surmounting a branch of oak, fructed, ppr., dexter resting on a mascle, gu. *Be just, and fear not.* Pl. 111, cr. 7, (without coronet; mascle, pl. 141.)

PAYNE, Hunts., among grass, ppr., an otter, passant, or, in mouth a fish, ar. Pl. 74, cr. 13.

PAYNE, in lion's gamb, erased, gu., a broken tilting-spear, or. *Pl.* 85, *cr.* 15.

PAYNE, Dors. and Leic., out of a ducal coronet, or, a woman's head, couped below shoulders, ppr., vested, erm., hair dishevelled, gold, (on head a chapeau, az.) *Pl.* 74, *cr.* 5.

PAYNE, Dors. and Wel., a leopard's head, or, gorged with a collar, az., rimmed, gold, charged with three bezants. *Pl.* 40, *cr.* 10, (bezant, *pl.* 141.)

PAYNE, Leic. and Suff., a wolf's head, erased, az., charged with five bezants, in saltier. *Pl.* 14, *cr.* 6, (bezant, *pl.* 141.)

PAYNE, Lond., an arm in armour, embowed, ar., in hand a sword, hilt and pommel, or, enfiled with a boar's head, sa., vulned, gu. *Pl.* 2, *cr.* 8, (head, *pl.* 10, *cr.* 2.)

PAYNE, Norf., an ostrich's head, or, out of a plume of feathers, ar. *Pl.* 50, *cr.* 1.

PAYNE, Suff., an arm, in armour, embowed, in gauntlet, a leopard's head, all or. *Pl.* 75, *cr.* 1, (head, *pl.* 92, *cr.* 13.)

PAYNE, Lond. and Berks., a demi-ostrich, wings addorsed, ar., in beak a key, or. *Pl.* 29, *cr.* 9, (without coronet ; key, *pl.* 9, *cr.* 12.)

PAYNE, Bart., Beds., in lion's gamb, erect, ar., a broken tilting-spear, gu. *Malo mori quam fœdari.* *Pl.* 85, *cr.* 15.

PAYNE, GEORGE, Esq., of Sulby Hall, Northamp., an ostrich's head, erased, or, in beak a horse-shoe, ar., between wings, sa. *Pl.* 28, *cr.* 13.

PAYNELL, Eng., a lion, passant, vert. *Pl.* 48, *cr.* 8.

PAYNELL, a lion, rampant, vert. *Pl.* 67, *cr.* 5.

PAYNELL, Linc., an ostrich's head, ppr. *Pl.* 50, *cr.* 1, (without feathers.)

PAYNTELL, Lond., an arm, erect, vested, gu., cuffed, ar., in hand, ppr., three lilies, or, leaved, vert. *Pl.* 101, *cr.* 5, (lily, *pl.* 81, *cr.* 9.)

PAYNTER, Eng., an old man's head, couped at shoulders, ppr., vested, gu., on head a long cap, az. *Pl.* 51, *cr.* 4.

PAYNTER, Norf., a lapwing, ar., environed with two branches, vert, tops in saltier. *Pl.* 3, *cr.* 13, (bird, *pl.* 10, *cr.* 12.)

PAYNTER, Kent, on stump of tree, erased, ppr., a wyvern, vert, sans wings, tail entwined round tree.

PAYNTER, THOMAS, Esq., of Boskenna, Cornw., three (broken) broad arrows, or, points downward, two in saltier, one in pale, knit with a lace and mantlet, gu., doubled, ar. *Pl.* 43, *cr.* 14.

PAYNTER, Surr., three (broken) arrows, or, points downward, two in saltier, one in pale, banded, gu. *Pl.* 43, *cr.* 14.

PAYTHERUS, Eng., a boar, passant, gu., bristled and hoofed, or. *Pl.* 48, *cr.* 14.

PAYTON, Suff., a griffin, sejant, wings addorsed, or. *Pl.* 100, *cr.* 11.

PEACE, Eng., a demi-lion, rampant, purp. *Pl.* 67, *cr.* 10.

PEACE, a dove, wings expanded, ar., in beak an olive-branch, vert. *Pl.* 27, *cr.* 5, (branch, *pl.* 48, *cr.* 15.)

PEACH, Kent, a lion's head, erm., crowned, or. *Pl.* 90, *cr.* 4, (without charging.)

PEACH, and PEACHE, Glouc., a demi-lion, rampant, per fess, erm. and gu., ducally crowned, or. *Pl.* 61, *cr.* 4, (without branch.)

PEACHE, Eng., a lion's head, erased, ducally crowned, or. *Pl.* 90, *cr.* 4, (without charging.)

PEACHEY, Eng., a dexter arm, in hand a sabre, ppr. *Pl.* 92, *cr.* 5.

PEACHEY, a demi-lion, rampant, ducally crowned, double-queued. *Pl.* 120, *cr.* 10, (crown, *same plate*, *cr.* 13.)

PEACHEY, a demi-lion, rampant, erminois, ducally crowned, or, holding a tower, ar. *Pl.* 61, *cr.* 4, (tower, *pl.* 12, *cr.* 5.)

PEACHEY, Suss., a demi-lion, rampant, doublequeued, erm., in dexter a sword, in pale, ar., hilt and pommel, or. *Ne quisquam serviat enses.* *Pl.* 120, *cr.* 10, (sword, *pl.* 41, *cr.* 13.)

PEACHEY, Baron Selsey. *See* SELSEY.

PEACOCK, Eng., a wyvern, wings addorsed, ppr. *Pl.* 63, *cr.* 15.

PEACOCK, Sco., a plume of peacock's feathers, ppr. *Naturæ donum.* *Pl.* 120, *cr.* 13, (without coronet.)

PEACOCK, Lond., a peacock's head and neck, or, wings expanged, az., a snake entwined about neck, of the last. *Pl.* 53, *cr.* 12.

PEACOCK, Durh., a peacock's head, erased, az., gorged with a mural coronet, or. *Pl.* 69, *cr.* 5.

PEACOCKE, Bart., Iri., a cockatrice, vert. *Vincit veritas.* *Pl.* 63, *cr.* 15.

PEACOCKS-BLIGH, a peacock's head, erased, az., gorged with a mural coronet, or. *Naturæ donum.* *Pl.* 69, *cr.* 5.

PEAK, Eng., a lion's head, issuing, or. *Pl.* 126, *cr.* 1.

PEAK, Linc., Northamp., and Lond., a lion's head, or, (pierced through side of head by an arrow, in fess, point coming out of mouth, gold,) feathered and headed, ar. *Pl.* 113, *cr.* 15.

PEAKE, Lond., a human heart, gu., winged, ar. *Pl.* 39, *cr.* 7.

PEAKE, a leopard's face, gu., (in mouth an arrow, ppr., headed and flighted, or.) *Pl.* 66, *cr.* 14.

PEAKE, Leic., a human heart, gu., between wings, ar. (Another, erm.) *Pl.* 52, *cr.* 2, (without coronet.)

PEAKE, Lond., a lion's head, or, erased, per fess, gu., on neck three gutteés-de-sang, one and two, (pierced through side of head by an arrow, ar., barbed and feathered, gold, the point issuing from mouth.) *Pl.* 113, *cr.* 15.

PEAKE, Kent, a cockatrice, (volant,) or, beaked, combed, legged, and wattled, gu. *Pl.* 63, *cr.* 15.

PEAL, a wolf's head, couped, gorged with a ducal coronet. *Pl.* 8, *cr.* 4, (gorging, *same plate*, *cr.* 5.)

PEARCE, Eng., a dexter arm, in hand a dagger, in pale, ppr. *Pl.* 23, *cr.* 15.

PEARCE, a leopard, sejant, gardant, ppr., dexter resting on an escutcheon, ar., charged with a bee, volant, sa.

PEARCE, a dexter arm, in armour, embowed, in hand a (lance,) pointing to dexter. *Pl.* 47, *cr.* 13.

PEARCE, Middx. and Norf., a demi-pelican, rising, or, vulned in breast, ppr., crowned, gu.

PEARCE, Yorks., out of a mural coronet, gu., a cross crosslet, fitched, or. *Pl.* 16, *cr.* 10, (coronet, *pl.* 128, *fig.* 18.)

PEARCE, Cornw., an arm, in armour, embowed, in hand an arrow, in pale, shaft resting on the wreath. *Pl.* 76, *cr.* 10, (without bow.)

PEARCE, Cambs., a Cornish chough, sa., beaked and membered, gu. *Pl.* 100, *cr.* 13.
PEARCE, Brecon, on rocks, ppr., a cross crosslet, fitched, transpiercing a mural coronet, az. *Celer et audax.*
PEARD, Eng., a demi-lion, rampant, erm., collared, sa. *Pl.* 18, *cr.* 13.
PEARD, Devons., a tiger's head, or, (pierced through neck by a broken spear, ppr., headed, ar., wound embrued, gu.) *Pl.* 94, *cr.* 10.
PEARETH, Durh., a leopard's head and neck, (erased,) ppr., in mouth a cross crosslet, fitched. *Pl.* 92, *cr.* 13, (cross, *pl.* 141.)
PEARKS, in an oak-tree, a squirrel, sejant, cracking a nut, all ppr. *Pl.* 5, *cr.* 6, (tree, *pl.* 16, *cr.* 8.)
PEARLE, Eng., in hand a thistle, ppr. *Pl.* 36, *cr.* 6.
PEARMAIN, a demi-lion, rampant. *Pl.* 67, *cr.* 10.
PEARS, Eng., a demi-lion, or. *Pl.* 67, *cr.* 10.
PEARSALL, Eng., a lion's head, erased, or. *Pl.* 81, *cr.* 4.
PEARSALL, DE, ROBERT LUCAS, Esq., of Willsbridge, Glouc., and of the Castle of Wartensee, Switzerland, out of a ducal coronet, a boar's head, gu., crined and tusked, or, langued, az. *Better deathe than shame.* *Pl.* 102, *cr.* 14.
PEARSE, Eng., a seax, az., hilt and pommel, or. *Pl.* 27, *cr.* 10.
PEARSE, Devons., a wyvern, gu., wings displayed, ar. *Pl.* 63, *cr.* 13.
PEARSE, Somers. and Devons., an arm, in armour, embowed, in hand a (lance) by the middle, point to the dexter, ppr. *Cadenti porrigo dextram.* *Pl.* 65, *cr.* 8.
PEARSE, GEORGE, Esq., of Harlington, Beds., a lion's head, erased, ar. *Vi divinâ.* *Pl.* 81, *cr.* 4.
PEARSON, Sco., an ostrich, in mouth a horseshoe, ppr. *Nil desperandum.* *Pl.* 16, *cr.* 2, (without gorging.)
PEARSON, Sco., a tower, ppr. *Rather die than be disloyal.* *Pl.* 12, *cr.* 5.
PEARSON, Sco., a dove, in mouth an olive-branch, ppr. *Dum spiro, spero.* *Pl.* 48, *cr.* 15.
PEARSON, Eng., three savages' heads, conjoined in one neck, one looking to dexter, one to sinister, and one upward. *Pl.* 32, *cr.* 2.
PEARSON, the sun in splendour. *Pl.* 68, *cr.* 14.
PEARSON, Yorks., out of a cloud, the sun in splendour. *Pl.* 67, *cr.* 9.
PEARSON, a parrot, ppr. *Pl.* 25, *cr.* 2.
PEARSON, an arm, in armour, embowed, in hand a rose-branch, slipped, ppr. *Pl.* 24, *cr.* 14, (rose, *pl.* 118, *cr.* 9.)
PEARSON, a cock's head, erased, az., combed and wattled, gu., (charged on neck with a sun, or, in beak a yellow flower, sprigged and leaved, vert,) between two branches of palm, ppr. *Pl.* 92, *cr.* 3, (branches, *pl.* 87, *cr.* 8.)
PEARSON, Surr., out of an Eastern coronet, or, a stag's head, erm. *Pl.* 91, *cr.* 14, (coronet, *pl.* 57, *cr.* 5.)
PEARSON, a cubit arm, erect, in hand a wreath of laurel, ppr. *Pl.* 86, *cr.* 1.
PEARSON, Lond., a demi-lion, rampant, gu., (in dexter a sun, or.) *Pl.* 89, *cr.* 10.
PEART, Eng., in dexter hand a sword, ppr. *Pl.* 21, *cr.* 10.
PEART, a lion, rampant, or. *Pl.* 67, *cr.* 5.

PEART, and PERT, Eng., out of an earl's coronet, or, a moor's head, from shoulders, affrontée, ppr. *Pl.* 80, *cr.* 11.
PEART, a stork, statant, ppr., between bulrushes, three on each side. *Pl.* 124, *cr.* 1.
PEASE, Yorks., an eagle's head, erased, in beak a (pea-stalk,) ppr. *Pl.* 34, *cr.* 1.
PEASE, Devons., a leopard's head, gardant, couped at neck, collared, az., in mouth a sword, barwise, ppr.
PEASE, Lond., on a mount, vert, a dove, rising, ar., in beak, gu., a pea-stalk, blossoms and pods, ppr., legs, of the third. *Pl.* 124, *cr.* 13, (without stump.)
PEASLEY, Iri., a dragon, sejant, vert, advancing a spear, or, headed, az.
PEAT, Sco., a deer's head, ppr. *Prospere si propere.* *Pl.* 91, *cr.* 14.
PEAT, Eng., a hand holding a fish, ppr. *Pl.* 105, *cr.* 9.
PEAT, of Sevenoaks, Kent, on a mount of bulrushes, ppr., a stork, ar., beaked and legged, gu., (in front of mount two mascles, interlaced, in fess, az.) *Ardens.* *Pl.* 124, *cr.* 1.
PEAT, Sco., a dexter hand holding a book, expanded. *Amicus certus.* *Pl.* 82, *cr.* 5, (without cloud.)
PEAT, Middx., out of a ducal coronet, or, a heron's head, ppr. *Pl.* 32, *cr.* 5, (coronet, *pl.* 128, *fig.* 3.)
PEATERSON, of Bannockburn, Sco., a pelican's head, erased, gu. *Pour le roy.* *Pl.* 26, *cr.* 1.
PECHE, or PECHEY, Eng., an astrolabe, or. *Pl.* 26, *cr.* 2.
PECHELL, Eng., a Cornish chough, ppr. *Pl.* 100, *cr.* 13.
PECHELL-BROOKE, Bart., Ess., a lark, ppr., (charged with two fleurs-de-lis, in fess, or.) *Pl.* 10, *cr.* 12.
PECHEY, a lion's head, erased, ar., ducally crowned, or. *Pl.* 90, *cr.* 4, (without charging.)
PECHEY, Kent, a lion's head, erm., crowned, or. *Pl.* 90, *cr.* 4, (without charging.)
PECK, Ess. and Norf., two lances, or, in saltire, headed, ar., pennons, gold, (each charged with a cross formée, gu.,) spears enfiled with a chaplet, vert. *Pl.* 125, *cr.* 8.
PECK, Lond., a demi-lion, rampant, ppr., holding an anchor, or. *Pl.* 19, *cr.* 6.
PECK, a cubit arm, vested, in pale, in hand, three flowers, stalked and leaved. *Pl.* 64, *cr.* 7.
PECK, a dexter arm, embowed, ppr., in hand a branch. *Pl.* 47, *cr.* 13.
PECK, out of a ducal coronet, a cubit arm, erect, vested and cuffed, in hand, ppr., a sprig of three roses. *Crux Christi salus mea.* *Pl.* 89, *cr.* 11, (roses, *pl.* 69, *cr.* 10.)
PECKE, Suss., a helmet, in profile, close, plumed, sa. *Pl.* 8, *cr.* 12.
PECKHAM, and PECKAM, a hand holding a scroll of paper, ppr. *Pl.* 27, *cr.* 4.
PECKHAM, Eng., a cubit arm, in hand a dagger, point downward, ppr. *Pl.* 18, *cr.* 3.
PECKHAM, Suss., an ostrich, ppr. *Tentanda via est.* *Pl.* 64, *cr.* 3, (without coronet.)
PECKOVER, Eng., a lion's head, erased, or. *Pl.* 81, *cr.* 4.
PECKSALL, Middx., a moor's head, couped, ppr. *Pl.* 120, *cr.* 3.

PECKSHALL and PESHALL, a wolf's head, (erased,) ar., collared, flory, gu. *Pl.* 8, *cr.* 4.
PECKWELL, a stag's head, cabossed, *Pl.* 36, *cr.* 1.
PECKWELL, Eng., a griffin's head, between wings, ppr. *Pl.* 65, *cr.* 1.
PEDDER, Lanc., two lions' heads, erased, addorsed, erminois, (gorged with one collar, gu.,) between two olive-branches, ppr. *Je dis la verité.* *Pl.* 28, *cr.* 10, (branches, *pl.* 79, *cr.* 14.)
PEDDER, two lions' heads, erased, addorsed, (each respectively collared and counterchanged.) *Pl.* 28, *cr.* 10.
PEDDER, Eng., two branches of palm, in orle, vert. *Pl.* 87, *cr.* 8.
PEDE, Suff., a chapeau, gu., turned up, erm., with an ostrich-feather on each side, dexter, or, sinister, az. *Pl.* 6, *cr.* 12.
PEDLER, Devons., a demi-lion, rampant, sa., crowned with an (Oriental) crown, or, between paws a lozenge, charged with a fleur-de-lis, (in mouth a red flag.) *Animo non astutiâ.* *Pl.* 61, *cr.* 4, (lozenge and fleur-de-lis, *pl.* 141.)
PEDLEY, a lion's head, gu. *Pl.* 126, *cr.* 1.
PEDLEY, Hunts., a demi-lion, rampant, in paws a lozenge, or, charged with a fleur-de-lis, gu. *Pl.* 47, *cr.* 4, (lozenge and fleur-de-lis, *pl.* 141.)
PEDYWARD, a cross crosslet, charged on centre and on each crosslet with a mullet. *Pl.* 69, *cr.* 8.
PEECH, Eng., a lion's head, erased, erm., crowned, or. *Pl.* 90, *cr.* 4, (without charging.)
PEEL, Eng., a lion, rampant. *Pl.* 67, *cr.* 5.
PEEL, Bart., Staffs., a demi-lion, rampant, ar., gorged with a collar, az., (charged with three bezants,) between paws a shuttle, or. *Industriâ.* *Pl.* 18, *cr.* 13, (shuttle, *pl.* 102, *cr.* 10.)
PEELE, Eng., a stag's head, erased, or. *Pl.* 66, *cr.* 9.
PEERES, or PERSE, Kent, a sphere, at north and south poles an etoile, all or. *Pl.* 114, *cr.* 6, (etoile, *pl.* 141.)
PEERES, or PEERS, Eng., (out of clouds, ppr.,) an arm, in armour, embowed, of the first, garnished, or, bound above elbow with a ribbon in a bow, gu., in gauntlet a spear, of the third, headed with a pheon. *Pl.* 47, *cr.* 15, (ribbon, *pl.* 28, *cr.* 2.)
PERRIS, a celestial sphere in a stand, (above it, on dexter side, an etoile, below it, on sinister, the same.) *Pl.* 81, *cr.* 1.
PEERMAN, a stag's head, couped, or, collared, sa. *Pl.* 125, *cr.* 6, (without roses.)
PEERS, Eng., on a chapeau, ppr., a lion's head, per cheveron, or and az. *Pl.* 99, *cr.* 9.
PEERS, Oxon., a demi-griffin, segreant, ar. *Pl.* 18, *cr.* 6.
PEERSON, Lond. and Cambs., a parrot, ppr. *Pl.* 25, *cr.* 2.
PEERSON, out of a mural coronet, chequy, ar. and az., a parrot's head, vert. *Pl.* 94, *cr.* 2, (without wings; coronet, *pl.* 112, *cr.* 5.)
PEGG, or PEGGE, Derbs., a demi-sun, issuing, or, rays alternately ar. and sa. *Pl.* 67, *cr.* 9.
PEGG, Eng., a lion's gamb, erased, az., armed, or. *Pl.* 126, *cr.* 9.
PEGLER, Halifax, a griffin's head, erased, ducally crowned. *Speranza e verita.* *Pl.* 100, *cr.* 15.
PEGRIS, Eng., two hands, holding up a broadsword, in pale, ppr. *Pl.* 59, *cr.* 10.

PEGRIZ, Eng., a dexter and sinister arm holding a two-handed sword, in pale, ppr. *Pl.* 59, *cr.* 10.
PEIRCE, a griffin, passant, or. *Pl.* 61, *cr.* 14, (without gorging.)
PEIRCE, Kent, a unicorn's head, couped, ar., armed and maned, or. *Pl.* 20, *cr.* 1.
PEIRCE, a stag's head, erased. *Pl.* 66, *cr.* 9.
PEIRSE, Lond., out of a mural coronet, a cross crosslet, fitched. *Pl.* 16, *cr.* 10, (coronet, *pl.* 128, *fig.* 18.)
PEIRSON, Sco., a lion's paw, az., holding a heart, gu. *Pl.* 23, *cr.* 13.
PEIRSON, Eng., a dear's head, issuing, or. *Pl.* 91, *cr.* 14.
PEIT, Sco., in dexter hand a book, expanded, ppr. *Amicus.* *Pl.* 82, *cr.* 5, (without cloud.)
PEITERE, Sco., in hand a dagger, in pale, ppr. *Pour mon Dieu.* *Pl.* 23, *cr.* 15.
PEITERS, or PETERS, Sco., a boar's head, between two (bay) branches, ppr. *Pl.* 19, *cr.* 8.
PEITON, a griffin, sejant, fore-dexter extended. *Pl.* 100, *cr.* 11.
PEKE, Linc., a lion's head, erased, or, guttée-de-sang, pierced through side of head by an arrow, gold, headed and feathered, ar., arrow (coming through mouth,) vulned, gu. *Pl.* 113, *cr.* 15.
PELHAM, Linc., Dors., and Suss., a peacock in pride, ar. *Pl.* 92, *cr.* 11.
PELHAM, Earl of Chichester. See CHICHESTER.
PELHAM, a cage.
PELHAM, Suss.: 1. A peacock in pride, ar. *Pl.* 92, *cr.* 11. 2. A buckle, ar. *Pl.* 73, *cr.* 10.
PELL, Eng., a pelican, ar., wings (addorsed,) vulning, ppr. *Pl.* 109, *cr.* 15.
PELL, on a mural coronet, or, a mullet, pierced, sa. *Pl.* 45, *cr.* 5, (coronet, *same plate, cr.* 9.)
PELL, Linc. and Norf., on a chaplet, vert, flowered, or, a pelican, gold, vulned, gu. *Pl.* 109, *cr.* 15, (chaplet, *pl.* 60, *cr.* 6.)
PELLAT, Eng., a lion, rampant, or. *Pl.* 67, *cr.* 5.
PELLEW, Cornw., a ship in distress, (on a rock,) ppr. *Deo juvante.* *Pl.* 21, *cr.* 11.
PELLEW, Viscount Exmouth. See EXMOUTH.
PELLOT, Suss., a lion, passant, ar., guttée, sa., in dexter an acorn, slipped, vert, fructed, or. *Pl.* 77, *cr.* 3, (acorn, *pl.* 81, *cr.* 7.)
PELLOTT, Eng., a lion, sejant, gu., holding an escutcheon of the arms. *Pl.* 22, *cr.* 13.
PELLY, out of a ducal coronet, or, an elephant's head, ar. *Pl.* 93, *cr.* 13.
PELLY, Bart., Ess., out of a naval coronet, an elephant's head. *Deo ducente, nil nocet.* *Pl.* 93, *cr.* 13, (coronet, *same plate, cr.* 1.)
PELTON, Eng., in hand a swan's head and neck, erased, ppr. *Pl.* 29, *cr.* 4.
PEMBERTON, Durh., a griffin's head, sa. *Pl.* 38, *cr.* 3.
PEMBERTON, Durh., a dragon's head, sa., couped, gu., ducally gorged, or. *Pl.* 36, *cr.* 7.
PEMBERTON, a wolf, regardant, in mouth an (arrow,) point downward. *Pl.* 77, *cr.* 14.
PEMBERTON, Lond., a dragon's head, vert, couped, gu. *Pl.* 87, *cr.* 12.
PEMBERTON, Herts., a dragon's head, erased, sa. *Pl.* 107, *cr.* 10, (without collar.)
PEMBERTON, Durh., a griffin's head, (couped,) gorged with a ducal coronet, all ppr. *Pl.* 42, *cr.* 9, (without branch.)

PEMBERTON, Lanc., on a coney, ar., an eagle, ppr. *Pl.* 61, *cr.* 3.

PEMBERTON, Durh., a griffin's head, erased, sa. *Sunt sua prœmia laudi. Pl.* 48, *cr.* 6.

PEMBERTON, Durh., a griffin's head, erased, sa. *Labore et honore. Pl.* 48, *cr.* 6.

PEMBERTON, LEIGH : 1. For *Leigh*, a demi-lion, rampant, in dexter a lozenge, ar., charged with a rose of York and Lancaster. *Pl.* 67, *cr.* 10, (lozenge, *pl.* 141.) 2. For *Pemberton*, a wyvern's head, neck transfixed by a dart. *Pl.* 121, *cr.* 9.

PEMBRIDGE, a bull's head, sa., between wings, or. *Pl.* 60, *cr.* 9.

PEMBROKE, Lond. and Herts., out of a ducal coronet, or, a wolf's head, gu. *Pl.* 14, *cr.* 6, (coronet, *pl.* 128, *fig.* 3.)

PEMBROKE, Earl of, Earl of Montgomery, Baron Herbert, Ross, Parr, Marmion, and St Quentin, (Herbert,) a wyvern, wings elevated, vert, in mouth a sinister hand, couped at wrist, gu. *Ung je serviray. Pl.* 61, *cr.* 8.

PEMBROOKE, Eng., a heart, gu., charged with a rose. *Pl.* 123, *cr.* 7, (rose, *pl.* 141.)

PENBAR, Eng., on a mount, vert, a moorcock, ppr., combed and wattled, gu. *Pl.* 10, *cr.* 1, (mount, *pl.* 98, *cr.* 13.)

PENDARVES, Lond., a lion, sejant, collared and lined. *Pl.* 21, *cr.* 3.

PENDARVES, Cornw., a demi-bear, erm., muzzled, (lined, and ringed, or.) *Pl.* 104, *cr.* 10.

PENDARVES-WYNNE, of Pendarves, Cornw. : 1. A lion, rampant, regardant, or. *Pl.* 10, *cr.* 15, (without brand.) 2. A demi-bear, erm., muzzled, (lined, and ringed, or.) *Pl.* 104, *cr.* 10. 3. A saltier, raguly, or.

PENDER, Sco., a demi-lion, or, holding a sabre, ppr. *Pl.* 41, *cr.* 13.

PENDLETON, Eng., in lion's paw, sa., a battle-axe, or. *Pl.* 51, *cr.* 13.

PENDLETON, Norf., on a chapeau, gu., turned up, erm., a demi-dragon, wings addorsed, or, holding an escallop, ar. *Pl.* 82, *cr.* 10, (chapeau, *pl.* 127, *cr.* 13; escallop, *pl.* 141.)

PENDOCK, Northamp., on top of a tower, gu., a demi-pelican, wings addorsed, or, vulning, of the first. *Pl.* 41, *cr.* 4, (tower, *pl.* 60, *cr.* 8.)

PENDRET, Eng., a fox, current, ppr. *Pl.* 80, *cr.* 5.

PENDRETH, Kent, a tiger, sejant, erm., tufted and maned, or, (ducally crowned, gold.) *Pl.* 26, *cr.* 9.

PENDRILL, Somers., a sword and sceptre, in saltier, (surmounted of a regal crown, ppr.) *Pl.* 124, *cr.* 6.

PENFOLD, Eng., a lion, rampant, double-queued, or. *Pl.* 41, *cr.* 15.

PENFOLD, Suss., out of park pales, alternately ar. and sa., charged with three escallops, in fess, or, a pine-tree, fructed, ppr. *Pl.* 26, *cr.* 10, (pales, *pl.* 13, *cr.* 12.)

PENGELLY, Cornw., in lion's paw, a palm-branch, ppr. *Pl.* 70, *cr.* 9.

PENGELLEY, Cornw., a wyvern, wings addorsed, vert, (devouring a dexter arm, ppr.) *Pl.* 61, *cr.* 8.

PENHALLOW, Cornw., a goat, (passant,) az., hoofed and attired, or. *Pl.* 66, *cr.* 1.

PENHELLEKE, Cornw., a Saracen's head, ppr. *Pl.* 19, *cr.* 1.

PENKEN, Worc., an antelope, sejant, sa., tufted, attired, and maned, ar. *Pl.* 115, *cr.* 3, (without gorging.)

PENKEVELL, or, PENKEVILL, Cornw., on a mount, vert, a lion, couchant, ppr. *Pl.* 75, *cr.* 5, (mount, *same plate, cr.* 6.)

PENLEAZE, Hants, a wyvern, wings elevated, ppr. *Pl.* 63, *cr.* 13.

PENLEY, or PENLY, Eng., a lion's head, erased, gu., ducally crowned, or. *Pl.* 90, *cr.* 14, (without charging.)

PENMAN, Eng., a hart's head, cabossed, or. (Another, sa.) *Pl.* 36, *cr.* 1.

PENMAN, out of clouds, a dexter arm, in hand a hammer over an anvil, all ppr.

PENMARCH, Eng., an ostrich, regardant, murally crowned, resting dexter on an escallop, ppr.

PENN, Bucks., a demi-lion, rampant, ar., gorged, with a collar, sa., charged with three plates. *Pl.* 18, *cr.* 13, (plates, *pl.* 141.)

PENN, Bucks., a demi-lion, rampant, ar., gorged with a collar, sa., charged with three plates. *Dum clarum, rectum teneam. Pl.* 18, *cr.* 13, (plate, *pl.* 141.)

PENNANT, out of a ducal coronet, ar., an heraldic antelope's head, of the last, maned, tufted, armed, and crined, or. *Pl.* 76, *cr.* 3, (coronet, *same plate, cr.* 8.)

PENNANT, Lond., out of a ducal coronet, an antelope's head, ar., armed, tufted, and maned, or. *Pl.* 24, *cr.* 7, (coronet, *same plate, cr.* 10.)

PENNANT, a lion, passant, gardant, gu. *Pl.* 120, *cr.* 5.

PENNANT, Wel. : 1. For *Pennant*, out of a ducal coronet, ar., an heraldic-antelope's head, of the last, tufted, horned, and crined, or. *Pl.* 76, *cr.* 3, (coronet, *same plate, cr.* 8.) 2. For *Dawkins*, a dexter arm, embowed, ppr., ensigned with a crescent, gu., in hand a battle-axe, ppr., blade, ar., charged with a rose, gu.

PENNECK, Cornw., an arm, embowed, sleeve, gu., cuffed, or, in hand a wren, ppr.

PENNEFATHER, MATTHEW, Esq., of New Park, co. Tipperary, a lion, sejant, ar., supporting an oval shield, per fess, or and gu., charged with a bend, erm., on shoulder a mullet. *I abide my time. Pl.* 22, *cr.* 13.

PENNEL, a griffin, sejant. *Pl.* 100, *cr.* 11.

PENNEL, or PENNELL, Eng., an arm, in armour, couped at shoulder, embowed, resting elbow on the wreath, in hand a scimitar, ppr. *Pl.* 107, *cr.* 15.

PENNELL, an ostrich's head, couped. *Pl.* 50, *cr.* 1, (without feathers.)

PENNEY, a demi-lion, rampant, ar., collared, sa. *Pl.* 18, *cr.* 13.

PENNEY, Herts., a demi-lion, rampant, gu., holding a (comb,) ar. *Pl.* 41, *cr.* 13.

PENNIECOOK, or PENNYCUICK, Sco., a stag, lodged under an oak-tree, ppr. *Ut resurgam. Pl.* 95, *cr.* 10.

PENNILL, a (demi)-heraldic antelope. *Pl.* 76, *cr.* 3.

PENNILL, a demi-wolf, rampant. *Pl.* 56, *cr.* 8, (without spear.)

PENNIMAN, out of a mural coronet, a lion's head, ppr. *Pl.* 45, *cr.* 9.

PENNINGTON, a talbot, passant, (in mouth a pen.) *Pl.* 120, *cr.* 8.

PENNINGTON, Devons., a man's head, couped below shoulders, in armour, affrontée, ppr., between wings. *Pl.* 53, *cr.* 8, (wings, *pl.* 1, *cr.* 15.)

PENNINGTON, Cumb., a mountain-cat, passant, gardant, ppr. *Vincit amor patriæ. Pl.* 119, *cr.* 7.

PENNINGTON, a man's head and shoulders, in armour, affrontée. *Pl.* 53, *cr.* 8.

PENNINGTON, Ess., a mountain-cat, passant, gardant, ppr. *Pl.* 119, *cr.* 7.

PENNINGTON, Baron Muncaster. See MUNCASTER.

PENNY, Eng., a porcupine, or. *Pl.* 55, *cr.* 10.

PENNY, Northamp., on a ducal coronet, ar., a lynx, or. *Pl.* 122, *cr.* 14, (coronet, *same plate, cr.* 8.)

PENNY, Sco., a demi-lion, or, holding a fleur-de-lis, gu. *Pl.* 91, *cr.* 13.

PENNY, Devons., on a crown vallary, gu., a lynx, statant, or, in mouth a fleur-de-lis, az. *Pl.* 122, *cr.* 14, (crown, *pl.* 128, *fig.* 17; fleur-de-lis, *pl.* 141.)

PENNYCOOCK, Sco., a man winding a horn. *Free for a blast. Pl.* 38, *cr.* 8.

PENNYCUICK, Sco., a demi-huntsman, winding a horn, ppr. *Free for a blast. Pl.* 38, *cr.* 8.

PENNYFATHER, Lond., a lion, sejant, ar., supporting an oval shield, per fess, or and gu., charged with a bend, erm., on shoulder a mullet. *Pl.* 22, *cr.* 13.

PENNYMAN, Bart., Yorks., out of a mural coronet, gu., a lion's head, erased, or; (pierced through neck by a broken spear, staves, or, headed, ar.) *Fortiter et fideliter. Pl.* 45, *cr.* 9.

PENREY, Eng., two hands, conjoined, couped at wrists, holding a sword, in pale, ppr. *Pl.* 75, *cr.* 8.

PENRICE, Norf. and Suff., a wing, elevated, surmounting another, ar., the former charged with two mullets of six points, in pale, gu. *Tuto et celeriter.*

PENRITH, a fox, current, ppr. *Pl.* 80, *cr.* 5.

PENROSE, Cornw., a fish, gu. *Pl.* 85, *cr.* 7.

PENROSE, Iri. and Berks., a lion's head, erased, or, collared, gu. *Pl.* 7, *cr.* 10.

PENRUDDOCK, or PENRUDDOCKE, Eng., a ram's head, erased, sa., armed, or. *Pl.* 1, *cr.* 12.

PENRUDDOCK, Cornw., Wilts., and Cumb., a demi-dragon, rampant, vert, (sans wings,) between eagle's wings, or. *Pl.* 82, *cr.* 10, (wings, *pl.* 1, *cr.* 15.)

PENTAGRASS, an antelope's head, erased, ar., attired, gu. *Pl.* 24, *cr.* 7.

PENTELAND, Sco., a talbot, passant, ar. *Pl.* 120, *cr.* 8.

PENTLAND, Iri., a lion's head, or, collared, az. *Pl.* 7, *cr.* 10.

PENTLAND, Sco., a lion's head, erased. *Pl.* 81, *cr.* 4.

PENTON, Eng., a lion's paw, erased. *Pl.* 126, *cr.* 9.

PENTON, a lion, couchant, gardant, (double-queued,) az., bezantée. *Pl.* 101, *cr.* 8.

PENWARNE, Cornw., a demi-lion, rampant, supporting with both paws the helm of a ship. *Pl.* 102, *cr.* 4.

PENWYN, Cornw., a stag's head, couped, per fess, indented, ar. and gu. *Pl.* 91, *cr.* 14.

PENYNG, Suff., a buck's head, erased, per fess, indented, ar. and gu., attired, of the last. *Pl.* 66, *cr.* 9.

PENYSTON, Oxon., on a ducal coronet, or, an eagle, displayed, sa. *Pl.* 9, *cr.* 6, (eagle, *pl.* 48, *cr.* 11.)

PENNYSTON, Suss. and Bucks., a griffin, passant, sa., armed, or. *Pl.* 61, *cr.* 14, (without gorging.)

PEOR, Iri., a mermaid, ppr., (in dexter a musket, or, in sinister a fleur-de-lis, az.) *Pl.* 125, *cr.* 3.

PEPE, a falcon, wings expanded, ppr. *Pl.* 105, *cr.* 4.

PEPERELL, out of a mural coronet, or, an arm, in armour, embowed, between two laurel-branches, ppr., (in hand a staff, thereon a flag, ar.) *Peperi. Pl.* 115, *cr.* 14, (branches, *pl.* 79, *cr.* 14.)

PEPERWELL, (on a mount, five) palm-trees. *Pl.* 18, *cr.* 12.

PEPLOE, Lanc., (on a wreath,) a ducal coronet, or, thereon a reindeer's head, gu., antlers, gold, (charged on neck with a human eye, shedding tears, ppr.) *Pl.* 60, *cr.* 3.

PEPLOE, Eng., out of a ducal coronet, a reindeer's head, all or. *Pl.* 60, *cr.* 3.

PEPPARD, in front of three ostrich-feathers, ar. and az., a greyhound, current, ppr. *Virtute et valore. Pl.* 28, *cr.* 7, (feathers, *pl.* 12, *cr.* 9.)

PEPPER, Iri., a demi-lion, rampant, gardant, or. *Pl.* 35, *cr.* 4.

PEPPER, Eng., a stag, trippant, ar. *Pl.* 68, *cr.* 2.

PEPPER, a greyhound's head, ar., between two roses, gu., stalked and leaved, ppr. *Pl.* 84, *cr.* 13.

PEPPER, Leic. and Yorks., a demi-lion, rampant, or. *Pl.* 67, *cr.* 10.

PEPPER, THOMAS, Esq., of Ballygarth Castle, co. Meath, a demi-lion, rampant, gardant, or. *Semper erectus. Pl.* 35, *cr.* 4.

PEPPERELL, a parrot, between two rose-slips. *Pl.* 25, *cr.* 2, (rose-slips, *pl.* 84, *cr.* 13.)

PEPPIN, a pegasus, current, wings addorsed, ar., (charged on shoulder with a cross avellane,) vert. *Pl.* 28, *cr.* 9.

PEPWALL, Glouc., a hawk, close, (between two carnations,) all ppr. *Pl.* 67, *cr.* 3.

PEPYS, Ess., Norf., Cumb., and Hants, a camel's head, erased, or, bribled, lined, ringed, gorged with a ducal coronet, sa. *Pl.* 120, *cr.* 12.

PEPYS, a camel's head, (muzzled.) *Pl.* 109, *cr.* 9.

PEPYS, Cambs. and Hunts., a camel's head, erased, ppr., ducally gorged and lined, or. *Pl.* 120, *cr.* 12.

PEPYS, Bart., Lond., a camel's head, erased, or, bridled, lined, ringed, and gorged with a ducal coronet, sa. *Mens cujusque, is est quisque. Pl.* 120, *cr.* 12.

PERBO, Middx., a tiger's head, ar., maned and langued, or, collared, vert, thereon three fleurs-de-lis, of the last. *Pl.* 40, *cr.* 10, (fleur-de-lis, *pl.* 141.)

PERCEHAY, Yorks., a bull's head, az., horns, per fess, az. and or. *Pl.* 120, *cr.* 7.

PERCEVAL, Earl of Egmont. See EGMONT.

PERCEVAL, Eng., a thistle, slipped and leaved, ppr. *Sub cruce candore. Pl.* 68, *cr.* 9.

PERCEVAL, Baron Arden. *See* ARDEN.
PERCEVAL, a squirrel, devouring a nut, ppr. *Pl.* 16, *cr.* 9.
PERCEY, a crescent, ar. *Pl.* 18, *cr.* 14.
PERCIVAL, a thistle, slipped and leaved, ppr. *Pl.* 68, *cr.* 9.
PERCIVAL, Somers., a thistle, slipped and leaved, ppr. *Sub cruce candida. Pl.* 68, *cr.* 9.
PERCIVALL, Eng., a demi-lion, gu. *Pl.* 67, *cr.* 10.
PERCIVALL, Hants, a nag's head, ar. *Pl.* 81, *cr.* 6.
PERCIVALL, Hants, a demi-lion, rampant, or. *Pl.* 67, *cr.* 10.
PERCY, Duke of Northumberland. *See* NORTHUMBERLAND.
PERCY, Dors., a demi-lion, rampant, az., collared, or, in dexter a spear, gold. *Pl.* 18, *cr.* 2, (spear, *pl.* 1, *cr.* 4.)
PERCY, Earl of Beverley. *See* BEVERLEY.
PERCY, Baron Prudhoe. *See* PRUDHOE.
PERIGAL, Lond. and Devons., a duke's helmet, full-faced, with five bars of gold, gorged with a collar and medal, or, bordered, of the same, lined, gu. *Peri—Gal. Pl.* 38, *cr.* 15.
PERIN, out of a ducal coronet, or, a peacock's head, ppr. *Pl.* 100, *cr.* 5, (coronet, *same plate.*)
PERKIN, Eng., a stag, lodged, ppr. *Pl.* 67, *cr.* 2.
PERKINS, Iri., a demi-eagle, displayed, sa. *Pl.* 22, *cr.* 11.
PERKINS, out of a five-leaved coronet, or, a unicorn's head, ar., maned and horned, gold. *Pl.* 45, *cr.* 14, (coronet, *pl.* 23, *cr.* 11.)
PERKINS, a lion, passant, sa., (holding) a fleur-de-lis, gu. *Pl.* 4, *cr.* 14.
PERKINS, Warw., a lion, passant, sa, (holding) a fleur-de-lis, gu. *Simplex vigilium veri. Pl.* 4, *cr.* 14.
PERKINS, the Rev. DUNCOMBE-STEELE, of Orton Hall, Leic., out of a ducal coronet, a unicorn's head. *Toujours loyale. Pl.* 45, *cr.* 14.
PERKINS, Berks. and Northamp., a pine-apple, ppr., stalked and leaved, vert.
PERKINSON, Eng., a unicorn's head, erased. *Pl.* 67, *cr.* 1.
PERKINSON, Durh., a falcon, ppr. *Pl.* 67, *cr.* 3.
PERKS, Eng., a lion's head, erased, or. *Pl.* 81, *cr.* 4.
PERNE, Cambs., out of a ducal coronet, ar., a pelican's head, or, vulned, gu. *Pl.* 41, *cr.* 4, (coronet, *same plate.*)
PEROTT, a bull's head, couped, sa., armed, or, (gorged with two bars, gold.) *Pl.* 120, *cr.* 7.
PEROTT, Eng., a stag's head, ppr. *Pl.* 91, *cr.* 14.
PERPOUND, in lion's gamb, erased, sa., a cinquefoil, gu. *Pl.* 60, *cr.* 14, (cinquefoil, *pl.* 141.)
PERREAU, Lond., out of a ducal coronet, or, a leopard's head, gardant, couped at neck, ar. *Pl.* 56, *cr.* 7, (coronet, *same plate, cr.* 2.)
PERRIER, out of a French ducal coronet, a lion's head, ppr. *Consilio et vi. Pl.* 126, *cr.* 1, (coronet, *pl.* 142, *fig.* 3.)
PERRIMAN, Eng., a wolf, passant, sa. *Pl.* 46, *cr.* 6.
PERRIN, Eng., a cock, crowing, ppr. *Pl.* 67, *cr.* 14.
PERRING, Eng., in dexter hand a sword, ppr. *Pl.* 21, *cr.* 10.

PERRING, Bart., Devons., a fir-pine, leaved, ppr. *Pl.* 84, *cr.* 12.
PERRINGS, Eng., three organ-pipes, (two in saltier,) surmounted by one in pale, az., banded, vert. *Pl.* 50, *cr.* 12.
PERRINGS, Devons., a fir-apple, erect, leaved, ppr. *Pl.* 84, *cr.* 12.
PERRIS, Lond., a demi-tiger, regardant, per cheveron, gu. and ar., in dexter an arrow, of the last.
PERROT, Eng., a lion's head, erased, sa. *Pl.* 81, *cr.* 4.
PERROT, or PERROTT, Berks., a parrot, vert, (in dexter, a pear, or.) *Pl.* 25, *cr.* 2.
PERROT, Wel., a parrot, (holding a pear,) ppr. *Pl.* 25, *cr.* 2.
PERROT, Oxon., a parrot, vert. *Pl.* 25, *cr.* 2.
PERROTT, Iri. : 1. On an ancient royal chapeau, a lion of Britain, (imperially) crowned. *Pl.* 105, *cr.* 5. 2. A parrot, vert, (in dexter a pear, or, with two leaves, of the first.) *Amo, ut invenio. Pl.* 25, *cr.* 2.
PERRY, Eng., a castle, ar., masoned, sa. *Pl.* 28, *cr.* 11.
PERRY, an arm, in armour, erect, ppr., issuing from the top of a tower, gu., in hand a dagger, sa. *Pl.* 63, *cr.* 5, (tower, *pl.* 60, *cr.* 8.)
PERRY, Lond., a hind's head, erased, ppr., (gorged with a ducal coronet, or, in mouth a pear-tree branch, vert, fructed, gold.) *Pl.* 6, *cr.* 1.
PERRY, Worc., a cubit arm, in armour, ppr., in gauntlet a sword, ar., hilt and pommel, or, strings and tassels flowing from the pommel, gu. *Pl.* 125, *cr.* 5.
PERRY, Glouc., a stag's head, ppr., pierced through neck by an arrow, or, feathered, ar., headed, sa. *Pl.* 91, *cr.* 14, (arrow, *pl.* 56, *cr.* 11.)
PERRY, Moor Hall, Ess. : 1. A demi-lion, ppr., (semée of spear-heads, sa.,) in dexter an escutcheon, of the last, charged with a saltier, double-parted and frettée, or. *Pl.* 69, *cr.* 14. 2. A lion's head, erased, or, semée of saltiers, ducally crowned, gu., (in mouth a pear, slipped, ppr.) *Pl.* 90, *cr.* 4.
PERRY, Devons., a hind's head, erased, or, (in mouth a sprig of pear-tree, vert, fructed, gold.) *Pl.* 6, *cr.* 1.
PERRYMAN, Eng., a wolf, passant, sa. *Pl.* 46, *cr.* 6.
PERRYMAN, Lond, out of clouds, ppr., two arms, vested, vert, cuffed, ar., holding a leopard's head, or.
PERRYN, Middx., Glouc., and Salop, a pine-apple, or, stalked and leaved, vert.
PERSHALL, and PESHALL, Eng., a wolf's head, sa., in mouth a marigold, ppr. *Pl.* 92, *cr.* 15, (marigold, *pl.* 105, *cr.* 15.)
PERSHOUSE, Staffs., a greyhound, sejant, ar., (collared, sa.,) resting dexter on a mullet, of the first. *Pl.* 66, *cr.* 15, (mullet, *pl.* 141.)
PERT, Eng., out of an earl's coronet, or, a moor's head, affrontée, ppr. *Pl.* 80, *cr.* 11.
PERT, Middx., a ram's head. *Pl.* 34, *cr.* 12.
PERT, Middx., a ram's head, erased, ar., armed, or, (on neck three bars-gemelle, gu.) *Pl.* 1, *cr.* 12.
PERT, Ess., a stork, ppr., beaked, or, statant, among bulrushes, gold, leaved, vert, bearing cats'-tails, sa. *Pl.* 124, *cr.* 1.

PERTON, Salop, (on a mount, vert,) a pear-tree, fructed, ppr. *Avi numerantur avorum.* Pl. 105, cr. 13.
PERWICHE, Eng., a crescent, per pale, or and gu. Pl. 18, cr. 14.
PERY, Eng., a spear-head, ppr. Pl. 82, cr. 9.
PERY, Earl of Limerick. *See* LIMERICK.
PERY, Iri., a unicorn's head, sa. Pl. 20, cr. 1.
PERYAN, Herts., a griffin's head, erased, gu., charged with three crescent, in pale, ar. Pl. 48, cr. 6, (crescent, pl. 141.)
PERYAN, Herts., a lion, rampant, ar., guttée-de-sang. Pl. 67, cr. 5.
PERYENT, Herts.: 1. A lion, rampant, ar., guttée-de-sang. Pl. 67, cr. 5. 2. A griffin's head, erased, gu., charged with three crescents, in pale, ar. Pl. 48, cr. 6, (crescent, pl. 141.)
PESHALL, Bart., Staffs., a boar's head, couped, gu., crined and tusked, or. Pl. 48, cr. 2.
PETER, Iri., a hand and (sword,) erect, ppr. Pl. 23, cr. 15.
PETER, Sco., in hand a dagger, point upward, ppr. *Pour mon Dieu.* Pl. 23, cr. 15.
PETER, Cornw., two lions' heads, erased, conjoined and addorsed, dexter, or, sinister, az., (collared, ringed, and counterchanged.) *Sans Dieu rien.* Pl. 28, cr. 10.
PETER, or PETRE, Ess. and Devons., two lions' heads, erased, conjoined, and addorsed, dexter, or, sinister, az., (collared, ringed, and counterchanged.) Pl. 28, cr. 10.
PETER, Clan Alpine House, Sco., out of a mural coronet, ar., masoned, sa., a lion's head, gu., crowned with an antique crown, ppr. *Eadhon dean agus na caomhain.* Pl. 45, cr. 9, (crown, pl. 79, cr. 12.)
PETER, and PETERS, Sco., same crest. *E'en do, and spare not.*
PETER, of Whitesleed, Sco.: 1. Out of an antique crown, a dexter hand holding a dagger, in pale, ppr. *Pour mon Dieu.* Pl. 23, cr. 15, (crown, pl. 79, cr. 12.) 2. A boar's head, couped, ar. *E'en do, and spare not.* Pl. 48, cr. 2.
PETER, of Cauterland, Sco.: 1. A dexter (arm, in bend,) in hand a dagger, both ppr. *Pour mon Dieu.* Pl. 28, cr. 4. 2. Out of a mural coronet, ar., masoned, sa., a demi-lion, gu., crowned with an antique crown, ppr. *Usque fac et non parcas*—and—*Turris fortis mihi Deus.* Pl. 120, cr. 14, (crown, pl. 79, cr. 12.)
PETER, of Cookston, Sco., between two laurel-branches, ppr., a boar's head, couped. *Usque fac et non parcas.* Pl. 19, cr. 8, (branches, pl. 79, cr. 14.)
PETERBOROUGH, a garb, ppr. Pl. 48, cr. 10.
PETERKIN, Sco., a unicorn's head, or. Pl. 20, cr. 1.
PETERKIN, or PETERKYN, Eng., a dove, ppr. Pl. 56, cr. 12.
PETERKIN, Sco., a unicorn's head. *Confido in Domino.* Pl. 20, cr. 1.
PETERS, Sco., out of a heart, a hand holding a (sword, in pale,) all ppr. *Verus ad finem.* Pl. 35, cr. 7.
PETERS, Sco., out of a cloud, a dexter hand holding a dagger, in pale, all ppr. *Dieu pour nous.* Pl. 76, cr. 6, (without head.)
PETERS, Sco., a boar's head, couped, ppr. Pl. 48, cr. 2.

PETERS, Lond., a buckle, ar. Pl. 73, cr. 10.
PETERS, Sco., a boar's head, erased, ar., in front of a laurel-branch, in pale, ppr. *Versus.* Pl. 16, cr. 11, (branch, pl. 123, cr. 5.)
PETERS, Sco., between two laurel-branches, vert, a boar's head, erased, ar. *Sit sine labe fines.* Pl. 19, cr. 8, (laurel, pl. 79, cr. 14.)
PETERS, Sco., between two laurel-branches, ppr., a boar's head, couped, erect. *Confido.* Pl. 21, cr. 7, (branches, pl. 79, cr. 14.)
PETERS, Middx., a griffin's head, couped, ppr., in mouth a bugle-horn, az., strung, gu. *Invidiâ major.* Pl. 9, cr. 12, (bugle, pl. 48, cr. 12.)
PETERS, Sco., a boar's head, couped, between two laurel-branches, ppr. *Deo adjuvante, non timendum.* Pl. 19, cr. 8, (branches, pl. 79 cr. 14.)
PETERS, Sco., out of a heart, a hand holding a (broadsword,) all ppr. *Rien sans Dieu.* Pl. 35, cr. 7.
PETERS, Sco., out of a heart, a hand, in pale, all ppr., holding a scimitar, hilt and pommel, or. Pl. 35, cr. 7.
PETERS, Sco., out of a heart, a hand grasping a couteau-sword, in pale, all ppr. *Rien sans Dieu.* (And another, *Verus ad finem.*) Pl. 35, cr. 7.
PETERS, Kent, an arm, in hand a rose-sprig, ppr. Pl. 118, cr. 9.
PETERS, Lond., a swan, regardant, ppr., gorged with a ducal coronet, sa., resting dexter on a mascle, or.
PETERS, Northumb., a lion's head, erased, erm., (charged with a bend, engrailed,) between two escallops, az. *Absque Deo nihil.* Pl. 81, cr. 4, (escallop, pl. 141.)
PETERSON, Sco., a pelican, ppr. *Nihil sine Deo.* Pl. 109, cr. 15.
PETERSON, Eng., a dexter hand brandishing a sabre, ppr. Pl. 21, cr. 10.
PETERSON, Sco., a pelican, or. Pl. 109, cr. 15.
PETHER, a rose, gu., barbed, vert, seeded, or. Pl. 52, cr. 11.
PETIT, Kent, in lion's gamb, erased and erect, or, a pellet. Pl. 97, cr. 10.
PETIT, of Hexstall, Staffs., a demi-wolf, salient. Pl. 56, cr. 8, (without spear.)
PETIT, in hand a hunting-horn, or. Pl. 89, cr. 3.
PETLEY, Eng., a horse's head, or. Pl. 81, cr. 6.
PETLEY, Kent, a cubit arm, in armour, erect, ppr., garnished, or, hand holding a (scimitar) by the blade, of the first, hilt, gold. *Toujours prêt.* Pl. 125, cr. 5, (scimitar, pl. 65, cr. 8.)
PETO, Eng., an ounce, sejant, ppr., collared, gu., resting dexter on a shield, az. Pl. 10, cr. 13, (shield, pl. 19, cr. 2.)
PETOE, and PEYTO, Warw., two wings, addorsed, or. Pl. 63, cr. 12.
PETOE, Warw., a sinister wing, or. Pl. 39, cr. 10.
PETRIE, Sco., an anchor, erect, az. *Spem fortuna alit.* Pl. 25, cr. 15.
PETRIE, Sco., a cross crosslet, fitched. *Fides.* Pl. 16, cr. 10.
PETRIE, Bart., an eagle, soaring aloft, ppr., looking to the sun in glory, or. *Fide, sed vide.* Pl. 114, cr. 10, (sun, pl. 43, cr. 5.)
PETRIE, Eng., a dove and olive-branch, ppr. Pl. 48, cr. 15.
PETRIE, a demi-eagle, displayed, ppr. *Fide, sed vide.* Pl. 22, cr. 11.

PETRIE, Sco., a demi-eagle, displayed, looking towards the sun, ppr. *Fide, sed vide.* *Pl.* 22, *cr.* 11, (sun, *pl.* 43, *cr.* 5.)
PETRIE, a cross crosslet. *Fides.* *Pl.* 66, *cr.* 8.
PETRIE, Baron, (Petrie,) two lions' heads, erased and addorsed, dexter, or, sinister, az., (each gorged with a plain collar, counterchanged.) *Sans Dieu rien.* *Pl.* 28, *cr.* 10.
PETT, Kent, out of a ducal coronet, or, a demi-pelican, wings expanded, ar.
PETT, Lond. and Surr., a demi-greyhound, sa., collared, (charged on body with two bendlets, between as many fern-branches.) *Pl.* 5, *cr.* 10.
PETTEGREW, Sco., an increscent, gu. *Sine sole nihil.* *Pl.* 122, *cr.* 15.
PETTET, or PETTIT, Kent, a leopard, passant. *Pl.* 86, *cr.* 2.
PETTIT, or PETYT, Eng., a bishop's mitre, gu. *Pl.* 12, *cr.* 10.
PETTUS, Norf., a hammer, erect, ar., handle, or.
PETTUS, Norf., out of a ducal coronet, or, a demi-lion, ar., holding a spear, gu., headed, of the first. *Pl.* 45, *cr.* 7, (spear, *pl.* 1, *cr.* 4.)
PETTUS, Norf., out of a ducal coronet, or, a demi-lion, erm., vulned, holding, in pale, a piece of a broken tilting-spear, ppr. *Pl.* 45, *cr.* 7, (spear, *pl.* 85, *cr.* 15.)
PETTY, of Shelburne, Iri., a bee-hive, beset with bees, diversely volant, ppr. *Virtute, non verbis.* *Pl.* 81, *cr.* 14.
PETTY, Eng., a bee-hive, beset with bees, diversely volant, ppr. *Ut apes geometricam.* *Pl.* 81, *cr.* 14.
PETTY, Iri., a bee-hive, or, fretty, az., bees, ppr. *Virtute, non verbis.* *Pl.* 81, *cr.* 14.
PETTY, out of a ducal coronet, or, an elephant's head, ar., trunked and eared, gu. *Pl.* 93, *cr.* 13.
PETTY, Hants, a centaur, per fess, ppr. and ar., drawing a bow, of the first. *Pl.* 70, *cr.* 13.
PETTY-FITZMAURICE, Marquess of Lansdowne. *See* LANSDOWNE.
PETTYT, Lond., a crane, ppr., in dexter a pebble-stone. *Pl.* 26, *cr.* 11.
PETTYT, Kent, in lion's gamb, erased and erect, or, a pellet. *Pl.* 97, *cr.* 10.
PETTYWARD, out of a ducal coronet, or, a demi-pelican, wings expanded, ar.
PETYE, Oxon. and Warw., out of a ducal coronet, or, an elephant's head, ar., armed and eared, gu. *Pl.* 93, *cr.* 13.
PETYT, Lond. and Yorks., a crane, erm., in dexter a pebble, sa. *Qui s'estime Petyt deviendra grand.* *Pl.* 26, *cr.* 11.
PETYTT, Suff., a demi-swan, displayed, ar., beaked, gu., between two battle-axes, in pale, vert. *Pl.* 54, *cr.* 6, (axes, *pl.* 14, *cr.* 13.)
PEUSAY, a pelican's head, vulning, ppr. *Pl.* 41, *cr.* 4.
PEVELESDON, Eng., a stag's head, erased, ppr. *Pl.* 66, *cr.* 9.
PEVENSEY, Linc., a demi-moor, ppr., in dexter a broken tilting-spear, or. *Pl.* 41, *cr.* 8, (spear, *pl.* 66, *cr.* 4.)
PEVENSEY, six laurel-leaves, vert, issuing from a castle, ar. *Pl.* 28, *cr.* 11, (leaves, *pl.* 123, *cr.* 5.)
PEVERELL, Eng., a plume of four ostrich-feathers, two, gu., two, az., enfiled with a ducal coronet, or. *Pl.* 44, *cr.* 12.
PEVERELL, Eng., in hand a dagger, point downward. *Hinc mihi salus.* *Pl.* 18, *cr.* 3.

PEW, Eng., a cock, in beak a rose, ppr. *Pl.* 55, *cr.* 12, (rose, *pl.* 117, *cr.* 10.)
PEXALL, Eng., a moor's head, couped, ppr. *Pl.* 120, *cr.* 3.
PEYRSE, Norf., a pelican, wings addorsed, ar., vulning, ppr. *Pl.* 109, *cr.* 15.
PEYTON, Eng., a griffin, sejant, or. *Pl.* 100, *cr.* 11.
PEYTON, Kent, a griffin, sejant, or. *Patior, potior.* *Pl.* 100, *cr.* 11.
PEYTON, GEORGE-HAMILTON-CONYNGHAM, Esq., of Driney House, co. Leitrim, same crest and motto.
PHAIRE, ROBERT-WILLIAM, Esq., of Killoughrum Forest, co. Wexford, a dove, in mouth an olive-branch, ppr. *Virtute tutus.* *Pl.* 48, *cr.* 15.
PHELAN, Iri., a stag's head, or. *Pl.* 91, *cr.* 14.
PHELIPS, Herts., a square beacon or chest, (on two wheels,) or, filled with fire, ppr. *Pro aris et focis.* *Pl.* 89, *cr.* 9.
PHELPS, Eng., a talbot's head, erased, ar., collared, or. *Pl.* 2, *cr.* 15.
PHELPS, Wilts., a demi-lion, erased, sa., (charged on shoulder with a cheveron, ar., in dexter a tilting-spear,) ppr., resting sinister on a cross pattée, sa. *Toujours prêt.* *Pl.* 41, *cr.* 13, (cross, *pl.* 141.)
PHELPS, Lond., a wolf's head, erased, az., collared, or, thereon a martlet, sa. *Pl.* 69, *cr.* 15, (head, *pl.* 14, *cr.* 6.)
PHENE, a lion, rampant, or, (gorged with a label of three points,) gu. *Pl.* 67, *cr.* 5.
PHESANT, Middx., a pheasant, close, or. *Pl.* 82, *cr.* 12.
PHESANT, a pheasant, ppr., in beak a rose, gu., stalked and leaved, vert. *Pl.* 64, *cr.* 14, (rose, *pl.* 117, *cr.* 10.)
PHESANT, Lond., a pheasant, close, or, in beak a gilliflower, ppr. *Pl.* 64, *cr.* 14, (flower, *pl.* 22, *cr.* 9.)
PHETOPLACE, Oxon. and Berks., a griffin's head, erased, vert. *Pl.* 48, *cr.* 6.
PHIBBS, Iri., a bear's paw, erect and erased, sa. *Pl.* 126, *cr.* 2.
PHILIMORE, on a tower, a bird, close. *Pl.* 113, *cr.* 14.
PHILIP, a talbot, ppr. *Vivis sperandum.* *Pl.* 120, *cr.* 8.
PHILIP, Suff. and Lond., out of a ducal coronet, az., three ostrich feathers, ar. *Pl.* 69, *cr.* 11, (without wings.)
PHILIPOE, out of a mural coronet, a demi-lion, rampant, ar. *Quod tibi vis fieri, facias.* *Pl.* 120, *cr.* 14, (without axe.)
PHILIPS, Iri., a lion, rampant, sa., (ducally) gorged and chained, or. *Ducit amor patriæ.* *Pl.* 88, *cr.* 1.
PHILIPS, Warw., a leopard, sejant, or. *Pl.* 10, *cr.* 13, (without flag.)
PHILIPS, Pemb. and Salop, a lion, rampant, sa., collared and chained, or. *Ducit amor patriæ.* *Pl.* 88, *cr.* 1.
PHILIPS, Staffs., Lanc., and Warw., a demi-lion, rampant, erminois, (collared, sa.,) ducally crowned, or, between paws a fleur-de-lis, az., within a mascle, gold. *Pl.* 61, *cr.* 4, (fleur-de-lis and mascle, *pl.* 141.) *Simplex munditiis.*
PHILIPS, in dexter hand, gauntleted, a sword, in pale, az., hilt and pommel, or. *Pl.* 125, *cr.* 5.
PHILIPS, ALEXANDER, of Montrose, a bear's head, erased, sa. *Bear and forbear.* *Pl.* 71, *cr.* 6.

PHILIPS, Somers., a lion, sejant, sa., collared and lined, or. *Pl.* 21, *cr.* 3.
PHILIPS, a horse, passant, (a wreath of laurel encircling its neck.) *Pl.* 15, *cr.* 14.
PHILIPS, Somers., a beacon, (on two wheels, or,) filled with fire, ppr. *Pl.* 89, *cr.* 9.
PHILIPS, Worc., on a chapeau, ar., turned up, erm., a demi-lion, rampant, gardant, of the first. *Pl.* 35, *cr.* 4, (chapeau, *pl.* 127, *fig.* 13.)
PHILIPS, or PHILLIPS, Lond., a rose-branch, vert, bearing three roses, gu., between wings, ar. *Pl.* 23, *cr.* 2, (wings, *pl.* 1, *cr.* 15.)
PHILIPS, Kent, on a mount, vert, a stag, (sejant,) erm., attired, or. *Pl.* 22, *cr.* 5.
PHILIPS-LAUGHARNE, Bart., Pemb., a lion, rampant, sa., (ducally) gorged and chained, or. *Pl.* 88, *cr.* 1.
PHILIPPS, Bart., Pemb., a lion, rampant, sa., (ducally) gorged and chained, or. *Ducit amor patriæ. Pl.* 88, *cr.* 1.
PHILIPSE, America, out of a coronet, a demi-lion, rampant. *Quod tibi vis fieri, facias. Pl.* 45, *cr.* 7.
PHILIPSON, Westm., out of a mural coronet, or, a (plume of seven) feathers, four, ar., three, gu. *Pl.* 125, *cr.* 11.
PHILLIMORE, Eng., an eagle, displayed, gu. *Pl.* 48, *cr.* 11.
PHILLIMORE, Oxon., on a tower, a falcon, wings elevated, ppr. *Fortem post animum. Pl.* 84, *cr.* 3.
PHILLIP and PHILFS, Sco., a bear's head, erased, sa. *Bear and forbear. Pl.* 71, *cr.* 6.
PHILLIP, Sco., a boar's head, erased, sa. *Pl.* 16, *cr.* 11.
PHILLIP, out of a flower, ar., stalked and leaved, vert, a greyhound's head, of the first, collared, or. *Pl.* 84, *cr.* 15.
PHILLIP, in lion's gamb, sa., three branches of flowers, az., leaved, vert. *Pl.* 86, *cr.* 15.
PHILLIP, out of a ducal coronet, a pyramid, ar. *Pl.* 8, *cr.* 10, (coronet, *same plate.*)
PHILLIPS, Iri., an eel, naiant, ppr. *Pl.* 25, *cr.* 13.
PHILLIPS, Eng., an eagle's head, erased, az. *Pl.* 20, *cr.* 7.
PHILLIPS, Warw., a garb, in fess, or, thereon a leopard, sejant, ppr., in mouth a trefoil, slipped, vert. *Mens conscia recti. Pl.* 10, *cr.* 13, (garb, *pl.* 59, *cr.* 15 ; trefoil, *pl.* 141.)
PHILLIPS, a tiger, sejant, (collared and chained.) *Pl.* 26, *cr.* 9.
PHILLIPS, a garb, banded, ppr. *Pl.* 48, *cr.* 10.
PHILLIPS, out of a ducal coronet, or, an arm, in armour, embowed, in hand, ppr., a broken spear, of the last, powdered with fleurs-de-lis, gold. *Pl.* 122, *cr.* 8, (spear, *pl.* 23, *cr.* 9; fleur-de-lis, *pl.* 141.)
PHILLIPS, a demi-lion, (crowned, or,) holding a fleur-de-lis, gold. *Pl.* 91, *cr.* 13.
PHILLIPS, a horse, passant, erm., (gorged with a chaplet, vert.) *Pl.* 15, *cr.* 14.
PHILLIPS, a dog, sejant, regardant, surmounted by a bezant, charged with a representation of a dog saving a man from drowning.
PHILLIPS, out of a ducal coronet, a bull's head. *Pl.* 68, *cr.* 6.
PHILLIPS, Salop, on trunk of tree, in fess, sprouting at dexter end, vert, a Cornish chough, ppr. *Pl.* 10, *cr.* 1, (chough, *pl.* 100, *cr.* 13.)
PHILLIPS, Bart., Worc., a demi-lion, rampant, ar., in paws a fleur-de-lis, or. *Deus, patria, rex. Pl.* 91, *cr.* 13.

PHILLIPS, Wel., a demi-lion, rampant, sa., collared and (chained,) or. *Pl.* 18, *cr.* 13.
PHILLIPS, Iri., an arm, in armour, embowed, ppr., purfled, or, in hand a broken spear, of the first, charged with a fleur-de-lis, gold. *Pl.* 44, *cr.* 9, (fleur-de-lis, *pl.* 141.)
PHILLIPS, LISLE-PHILLIPS, Leic. : 1. For *Phillips*, a demi-griffin, gu., ears, wings, and claws, or, (collared and chained, gold, holding a shield, az., thereon a lion, rampant, of the second.) *Pl.* 18, *cr.* 6. 2. For *March*, a demi-lion, rampant, quarterly, or and az., holding a cross, couped, sa., charged with a cross crosslet, fitched, or. *Pl.* 65, *cr.* 6. 3. For *Lisle*, a stag, trippant, ppr. *Quod justum, non quod utile. Pl.* 68, *cr.* 2.
PHILLIPS, Salop and Cornw., a lion, rampant, sa., collared and chained, or. *Pl.* 88, *cr.* 1.
PHILLIPS, Somers., a lion, sejant, sa., collared and lined, or. *Pl.* 21, *cr.* 3.
PHILLIPS, on a mount, a lion, rampant, (ducally crowned, in dexter a sword, in pale,) charged on neck with a fleur-de-lis. *Pl.* 59, *cr.* 5, (fleur-de-lis, *pl.* 141.)
PHILLIPS, a demi-lion, sa., collared and chained, between paws a leopard's face, jessant-de-lis, or. *Pl.* 18, *cr.* 13, (face, *pl.* 123, *cr.* 9.)
PHILLIPS, Wel., a boar's head, sa., langued, gu., ringed, or. *Spero meliora. Pl.* 48, *cr.* 2.
PHILLIPS, on a garb, in fess, or, a lion, rampant, sa., (ducally gorged and chained, gold, holding a cross crosslet, fitched, of the last.) *Pl.* 125, *cr.* 2, (garb, *pl.* 59, *cr.* 15.)
PHILLIPSON, Eng., a boar, sa. *Pl.* 48, *cr.* 14.
PHILLIPSON, a camel's head, couped, in mouth an acorn-branch, slipped, ppr. *Pl.* 109, *cr.* 9, (acorn, *pl.* 81, *cr.* 7.)
PHILLIPSON, out of a mural coronet, or, a (plume) of feathers, gu. *Pl.* 125, *cr.* 11.
PHILLIPSON, a greyhound's head, couped, in mouth a laurel-branch, all vert. *Pl.* 14, *cr.* 4, (branch, *pl.* 123, *cr.* 5.)
PHILLIPSON, Westm., out of a mural coronet, or, a (plume of seven) feathers, four, ar., three, gu. *Pl.* 125, *cr.* 11.
PHILLOTT, a unicorn's head, couped. *Pl.* 20, *cr.* 1.
PHILLPOT, Eng., a plume of ostrich-feathers, sa. *Pl.* 12, *cr.* 9.
PHILLPOTTS, Glouc. and Devons., a dexter arm, in armour, embowed, in hand a sword, all ppr. *Pl.* 2, *cr.* 8.
PHILLPOTTS, Rev. THOMAS, of Porthgwidden, Cornw., a dexter arm, in armour, embowed, in hand a sword, all ppr. *Semper paratus. Pl.* 2, *cr.* 8.
PHILPOT, Kent and Lond., a lion's head, erased, ar., between wings, sa., each charged with a bend, arm. *Pl.* 73, *cr.* 3.
PHILPOT, Eng., a porcupine, passant, or, charged with an annulet for difference. *Pl.* 55, *cr.* 10.
PHILPOT, Herts. and Kent, a porcupine, passant, or. *Pl.* 55, *cr.* 10.
PHIN, Sco., a phœnix in flames, ppr. *Perit ut vivat. Pl.* 44, *cr.* 8.
PHINE, Sco., a crane's head, (couped,) ppr. *Vigilantia securitas. Pl.* 20, *cr.* 9.
PHIPPS, two laurel-branches, issuing, ppr. *Pl.* 21, *cr.* 2.
PHIPPS, in lion's gamb, erect and erased, sa., a trefoil, slipped, ar. *Pl.* 126, *cr.* 9, (trefoil, *pl.* 141.)

PHIPPES, Lond., a demi-lion, rampant, ar., holding with both paws a palm-branch, ppr. *Pl.* 61, *cr.* 4, (without crown.)
PHIPPS, Earl of Mulgrave. *See* MULGRAVE.
PHIPPS, in lion's gamb, erased, sa., a mullet, ar. *Pl.* 126, *cr.* 9, (mullet, *pl.* 141.)
PHIPSON, Warw., a plume of (seven) feathers, alternately, ar. and gu. *Pl.* 12, *cr.* 9.
PHITTON, Eng., a lion, passant, ppr. *Pl.* 48, *cr.* 8.
PICARD, Eng., in dexter hand a sword, in pale, ppr. *Pl.* 23, *cr.* 15.
PICKARD, Eng., an eagle's head, erased, sa. *Pl.* 20, *cr.* 7.
PICKARD, a lion, sejant, ar., supporting an antique shield, charged with a canton. *Pl.* 22, *cr.* 13.
PICKARD, Lond., a lion, sejant, ar., (resting dexter on a shield, gu., within a carved bordure, or, charged with a fleur-de-lis, gold.) *Pl.* 126, *cr.* 15.
PICKAS, a demi-lion, rampant, gu., (supporting in paws a spear, ar., headed and garnished, or.) *Pl.* 69, *cr.* 14.
PICKEN, Sco., a demi-lion, ar. *Pl.* 67, *cr.* 10.
PICKERGET, (two) pomegranates on one slip, stalked and leaved, ppr. *Pl.* 67, *cr.* 8.
PICKERING, Eng., a fleur-de-lis, or. *Pl.* 68, *cr.* 12.
PICKERING, Eng., a lion's paw, erect, (couped,) az. *Pl.* 126, *cr.* 9.
PICKERING, Notts., a leopard's head, or. *Pl.* 92, *cr.* 13.
PICKERING, Hunts., Northamp., Cambs., Yorks., and Suss., a lion's gamb, erect and erased, az. *Pl.* 126, *cr.* 9.
PICKERING, Chesh., a demi-griffin, sa., beaked and membered, ar., grasping a garb, or. *Pl.* 18, *cr.* 6, (garb, *pl.* 84, *cr.* 7.)
PICKERING, Chesh., a lion's gamb, erect and erased, az., enfiled with a ducal coronet, or. *Pl.* 93, *cr.* 9.
PICKERING, Yorks., a lion's gamb, erect and erased, az., armed, or. *Pl.* 126, *cr.* 9.
PICKERING, Surr., a lion's gamb, erased, ar. *Pl.* 126, *cr.* 9.
PICKERING, Lond., a lion's gamb, erased, ppr. *Pl.* 126, *cr.* 9.
PICKERING, a sword, in pale, ppr., hilt and pommel, or, within two branches of laurel, in orle, vert. *Pl.* 71, *cr.* 3.
PICKERING, a lion's gamb, (coupsd,) az. *Pl.* 126, *cr.* 9.
PICKERNELL, Eng., a lion's head, erased, gu. *Pl.* 81, *cr.* 4.
PICKETT, Eng., a martlet, gu. *Pl.* 111, *cr.* 5.
PICKETT, an arm, embowed, vested, ar., cuffed, vert, charged with two bars, wavy, of the last, in hand a pick-axe, ppr. *Pl.* 113, *cr.* 10, (arm, *pl.* 39, *cr.* 1.)
PICKFORD, Eng., an arm, embowed, in hand an arrow, ppr. *Pl.* 92, *cr.* 14.
PICKFORD, a lion's head, erased. *Pl.* 81, *cr.* 4.
PICKWICK, Somers., between wings, az., a hart's head, couped, erm., attired, or, gorged with a collar, gu., (therefrom a chain reflexed over neck, gold.) *Pl.* 125, *cr.* 6, (without roses.)
PICTON, or PICKTON, Berks. and Chesh., a demi-lion, rampant, gu. *Pl.* 67, *cr.* 10.
PIDCOCK, (on a bar-shot, ppr.,) a griffin, segreant, sa., in claws a grenade, fired, ppr.

Seigneur, je te prie garde ma vie. Pl. 67, *cr.* 13, (grenade, *pl.* 70, *cr.* 12.)
PIDDLE, a hawk's head, ar. *Pl.* 34, *cr.* 11.
PIE, between wings, a cross crosslet, fitched. *Pl.* 34, *cr.* 14.
PIERCE, Eng., a parrot, in beak an annulet. *Pl.* 33, *cr.* 11.
PIERIE, Sco., a hunting-horn, az., garnished, or, and stringed, gu. *Vespere et mane. Pl.* 48, *cr.* 12.
PIERPONT, Salop, a lion, rampant, sa., between wings, ar. *Pl.* 29, *cr.* 5.
PIERPONT, Notts., same crest. *Pie repone te.*
PIERPONT, Hants, a fox, gu. (Another, ppr.) *Pl.* 126, *cr.* 5.
PIERREPOINT, Eng., a lion, rampant, sa., between wings, ar. *Pl.* 29, *cr.* 5.
PIERREPOINT, Hunts., a fox, passant, gu. *Pl.* 126, *cr.* 5.
PIERREPONT, a fox, passant, gu. *Pie repone te. Pl.* 126, *cr.* 5.
PIERREPONT, Earl Manvers. *See* MANVERS.
PIERRIE, Sco., a horse's head, between wings. *Pl.* 19, *cr.* 13.
PIERS, a griffin, or, winged, ar. *Pl.* 66, *cr.* 13.
PIERS, Bart., Iri., an arm, embowed, vested, az., cuffed, ar., in hand a flag, in pale, per fess, of the last and first, in chief, two torteaux, in base a plate. *Pl.* 99, *cr.* 3, (torteau and plate, *pl.* 141.)
PIERSON, Eng., three savages' heads, conjoined in one neck, one looking to dexter, one to sinister, and one upward. *Pl.* 32, *cr.* 2.
PIERSON, Eng., a parrot, vert, beaked and legged, gu. *Pl.* 25, *cr.* 2.
PIERSON, Herts. and Middx., out of a ducal coronet, or, an ostrich's head, between two ostrich-feathers, ar. *Pl.* 50, *cr.* 1, (coronet, same plate, *cr.* 13.)
PIERSON, Devons., out of a mural coronet, chequy, ar. and az., a parrot's head, ppr. *Pl.* 94, *cr.* 2, (coronet, *pl.* 112, *cr.* 5.)
PIERSON, Lond., a hind's head, couped, ar., (charged with two cheverons,az.) *Pl.*21,*cr.* 9.
PIERSON, Wilts., a demi-lion, ppr., in dexter a sun, or. *Pl.* 39, *cr.* 14, (sun, *pl.* 13, *cr.* 10.)
PIESSE, an eagle, displayed, ppr. *Per mare, per terras. Pl.* 48, *cr.* 11.
PIGEON, Kent., a demi-griffin, erm., beaked and legged, or. *Pl.* 18, *cr.* 6.
PIGEON, Lond., a demi-griffin. *Pl.* 18, *cr.* 6.
PIGEON, Middx. and Hants, on a chapeau, gu., turned up, erm., a buck's head, ppr. *Pl.* 108, *cr.* 14, (head, *pl.* 91, *cr.* 14.)
PIGEON, Norf., an elephant's head, erased, gu., eared, tusked, (collared, lined, and ringed, or.) *Pl.* 35, *cr.* 13.
PIGG, Eng., a demi-lion, purp. *Pl.* 67, *cr.* 10.
PIGGOT, Eng., a bull's head, erased, gu. *Pl.* 19, *cr.* 3.
PIGGOT, or PIGGOTT, Eng., an ostrich, in mouth a horse-shoe, all ppr. *Pl.* 16, *cr.* 2.
PIGGOT, a stag's head, erased, ppr. *Pl.* 66, *cr.* 9.
PIGOT, Eng., a greyhound, passant, per pale, sa. and erminois. *Pl.*104,*cr.*1,(without chapeau.)
PIGOT, a lion, rampant, supporting an ancient mace, in pale. *Pl.* 125,*cr.* 2, (mace,*pl.* 28,*cr.* 2.)
PIGOT, Bart., Staffs., a wolf's head, erased, ppr *Pl.* 14, *cr.* 6.
PIGOT, a martlet, gu. *Pl.* 111, *cr.* 5.
PIGOTT, J. SMYTH, of Brockley and Weston-super-Mare: 1. For *Smyth*, a wolf's head,

erased, sa., gorged, with a collar, ar., charged with three torteaux. *Qui capit capitur.* Pl. 126 o, cr. 7. For *Pigott*, a griffin's head, erased, gu., charged on neck with a bar gemel, beaked and eared, or. *Toujours prêt.* Pl. 126 o, cr. 13.

PIGOTT, of Pateshall, Staffs., and Queen's County, Iri., a wolf's head, erased, ar. Pl. 14, cr. 6.

PIGOTT, the Rev. JOHN-DRYDEN, of Edgmond, Salop, a wolf's head, erased, ar., langued, gu. Pl. 14, cr. 6.

PIGOTT, a dove and olive-branch, ppr. Pl. 48, cr. 15.

PIGOTT, Somers., on a wolf's head, erased, sa., three torteaux, ar. Pl. 116 o, cr. 7.

PIGOTT, Bucks. and Linc., a greyhound, couchant, ar., (charged on breast with three mill-picks, sa.) Pl. 6, cr. 7.

PIGOTT, Hants, a greyhound, statant, ppr. *Labore et virtute.* Pl. 104, cr. 1, (without chapeau.)

PIGOTT, a greyhound, couchant, ar., (collared, sa., charged on shoulder with three pick-axes, of the second.) Pl. 6, cr. 7.

PIGOTT, Berks., Bucks., Cambs., Beds., and Notts., a greyhound, (passant,) sa. Pl. 104, cr. 1, (without chapeau.)

PIGOTT, Bart., Iri., a wolf's head, erased, ppr., collared, or. Pl. 8, cr. 4.

PIGOU, Eng., a lion's head, erased, ppr. Pl. 81, cr. 4.

PIKE, Iri., a pike, naiant, ppr. Pl. 39, cr. 11.

PIKE, Eng., a pike, haurient, or. Pl. 98, cr. 12.

PIKE, a demi-moor, ppr., in the ears rings and drops, ar., in dexter a pike-staff, ar.

PIKE, a pike, naiant, or. Pl. 39, cr. 11.

PILCHER, Eng., on a chapeau, a cockatrice, wings addorsed, ducally crowned. Pl. 103, cr. 9.

PILFORD, Eng., an eagle, displayed, sa. Pl. 48, cr. 11.

PILE, on a ducal coronet, or, a pelican, wings addorsed, vulning, ppr. Pl. 64, cr. 1, (coronet, *same plate, cr. 5.*)

PILGRIM, an arm, in armour, embowed, ppr., garnished, or, in hand a cutlass, of the first, hilt and pommel, gold. Pl. 81, cr. 11.

PILGRIME, Eng., an escallop, or. Pl. 117, cr. 4.

PILKINGTON, Bart., Yorks, a husbandman, mowing, ppr. *Now thus, now thus.*

PILKINGTON, Linc., Northamp., Durh., Lanc., and Leic., a mower, with scythe, ppr., vested, quarterly, ar. and gu.

PILLAND, Eng., on a chapeau, gu., turned up, erm., a garb, or. Pl. 62, cr. 1.

PILLANS, Sco., in dexter hand a dagger, point upward, all ppr. *Virtute et robore.* Pl. 23, cr. 15.

PILLANS, Sco., in hand a sword, ppr. *Virtute et robore.* Pl. 21, cr. 19.

PILLETT, or PILLOTT, Eng., a lion, sejant, gu., between paws an escutcheon of the arms, ppr. Pl. 22, cr. 13.

PILLINER, Eng., a unicorn's head, gu. Pl. 20, cr. 1.

PILMUIRE, Cupar-Angus, Sco., a martlet, volant, az. *Honeste vivo.* Pl. 40, cr. 4.

PIM, Iri., in dexter hand a scimitar, ppr. Pl. 29, cr. 8.

PINCHYON, Ess., a tiger's head, erased, ar. Pl. 94, cr. 10.

PINCKARD, Lond., an arm, embowed, ppr., vested, az., charged with two bars, ar., cuffed, of the last, in hand a sword, ppr., point resting on the wreath, hilt and pommel, or.

PINCKENEY, Eng., the rising sun, or, clouds, ar. Pl. 67, cr. 9.

PINDALL, Lond. and Linc., a lion's head, erased, or, ducally crowned, az. Pl. 90, cr. 4, (without charging.)

PINDAR, or PINDER, Lond. and Linc., a lion's head, erased, ar., ducally crowned, az. Pl. 90, cr. 4, (without charging.)

PINDAR, Linc. and Lond., a lion's head, erased, ar., ducally crowned, az. Pl. 90, cr. 4, (without charging.)

PINDAR, Linc. and Lond., a stork, ar., ducally crowned, or. Pl. 33, cr. 9, (crown, pl. 128, fig. 3.)

PINDER, Earl of Beauchamp. *See* BEAUCHAMP.

PINE, Eng., a lion's head, ar. Pl. 126, cr. 1.

PINFOLD, Beds., a pine-tree, or, leaved, vert, fructed, ppr., inclosed with pales, ar. and sa. Pl. 26, cr. 10, (pales, pl. 13, cr. 12.)

PINFORD, Eng., a dove, in mouth a (honeysuckle,) slipped, all ppr. Pl. 48, cr. 15.

PINK, or PINCK, Eng., a mullet of six points, gu. Pl. 21, cr. 6.

PINK, or PINCK, Oxon., a cubit arm, erect, vested, az., cuffed, ar., in hand, ppr., in pale, a cross pattée, fitched, or. Pl. 75, cr. 3, (cross, pl. 99, cr. 15.)

PINKARD, a dexter arm, embowed, (vested, charged with three bars, in hand, by its blade, a sword, in pale, point upwards.) Pl. 65, cr. 8.

PINKER, Somers., on a mount, vert, a heathcock, rising, ppr.

PINKERTON, Lond. and Sco., a rose, gu., stalked and leaved, vert. *Post nubila sol.* Pl. 105, cr. 7.

PINKNEY, Surr., out of a ducal coronet, or, a griffin's head, ppr. Pl. 54, cr. 14.

PINKTON, Eng., in dexter hand, gauntleted, a sword, ppr. Pl. 125, cr. 5.

PINNER, a dexter arm, in armour, embowed, in hand a cross crosslet, fitched, in bend. Pl. 120, cr. 11, (cross, pl. 99, cr. 1.)

PINNER, Lond., a stork, passant, ar., ducally gorged, or. Pl. 33, cr. 9, (gorging, pl. 128, fig. 3.)

PINNEY, Eng., an eagle, displayed, gu. Pl. 48, cr. 11.

PINNOCK, an arm, embowed, vested, in hand a martlet. Pl. 39, cr. 1, (martlet, pl. 111, cr. 5.)

PIPARD, Eng., a lion, sejant, ppr., supporting an escutcheon (of the arms.) Pl. 22, cr. 13.

PIPE, Cambs., a camel's head, erased, or, bridled and ducally gorged, sa. Pl. 120, cr. 12.

PIPER, Eng., a unicorn's head, ar. Pl. 20, cr. 1.

PIPER, Ess., out of an Eastern crown, or, a demi-dove, ar., wings addorsed.

PIPER, Cornw., a magpie, sa. Pl. 100, cr. 13.

PIPER, Devons. and Kent, a cubit arm, (encircled with a wreath of laurel,) ppr., in hand a boar's head, erased, sa. *Feroci fortior.* Pl. 86, cr. 6.

PIPIS, Cambs. and Hunts., a camel's head, erased, or, bridled, lined, ringed, and ducally gorged, sa. Pl. 120, cr. 12.

PIRCE, Eng., a lion's head, ppr. Pl. 126, cr. 1.

PIRIE, Bart., Lond., an eagle's head, erased, sa., in beak an ostrich-feather, ar. Pl. 20, cr. 7, (feather, pl. 58, cr. 7.)

PIRRIE, Sco., a hawk's head, erased, az. *Pl.* 34, *cr.* 11.
PIRTON, a dragon. *Pl.* 90, *cr.* 10.
PISTER, Linc. and Surr., a cubit arm, erect, vested and cuffed, in hand, ppr., a baker's peel, sa., charged with three plates.
PITCAIRN, JOHN, Esq., of Pitcairn House, Perths., the sun in splendour, or. *Spes lucis æternæ. Pl.* 68, *cr.* 14.
PITCAIRN, an anchor, erect, az. *Sperabo. Pl.* 25, *cr.* 15.
PITCAIRN, Sco., the full moon, ar. *Refulget. Pl.* 43, *cr.* 8.
PITCAIRN, Sco., the moon in her compliment, ppr. *Plena refulget. Pl.* 43, *cr.* 8.
PITCAIRN, Sco., a star of six points, wavy, (with straight rays between each point,) within a circle of clouds. *Spes lucis æternæ. Pl.* 63, *cr.* 9, (clouds, *pl.* 16, *cr.* 13.)
PITCHER, Eng., a demi-man, in a military habit, in hand a flag, displayed, az. *Pl.* 2, *cr.* 12.
PITCHES, a man's head, in profile, bearded, ppr., wearing a long cap with tassel hanging down behind. *Pl.* 51, *cr.* 4.
PITES, a swan's neck, ar., wings expanded, gu., between two branches, vert, (in beak, a trefoil, slipped, or.) *Pl.* 54, *cr.* 6, (branches, same plate, *cr.* 9.)
PITFIELD, Dors. and Middx., a swan-royal, ar., ducally gorged and lined, (line reflexed over back,) or. *Pl.* 111, *cr.* 10, (without rose and crown.)
PITMAN, Eng., a Catherine-wheel, ppr. *Pl.* 1, *cr.* 7.
PITMAN, on a Catherine-wheel, a bird, statant, ppr. *Pl.* 1, *cr.* 7, (bird, *same plate, cr.* 13.)
PITMAN, Devons., on a shell, a martlet. *Pl.* 117, *cr.* 4, (martlet, *pl.* 111, *cr.* 5.)
PITMAN, Devons., (on a wrinkle-shell,) or, a Cornish chough, ppr. *Fortiter agendo. Pl.* 100, *cr.* 13.
PITSON, Surr., a peacock's head, erased, az. *Pl.* 86, *cr.* 4.
PITT, Lond., a dexter arm, ppr., vested, az., cuffed, ar., in hand two branches of laurel, in orle, vert, in centre a (martlet,) sa. *Pl.* 44, *cr.* 13.
PITT, Baron Rivers. *See* RIVERS.
PITT, Cornw. and Dors., a stork, ar., beaked, and legged, gu., supporting an anchor, or, cabled, ppr. *Pl.* 61, *cr.* 10.
PITT, Earl of Chatham. *See* CHATHAM.
PITT, Dors. and Cornw., a stork, beaked and legged, gu. *Pl.* 33, *cr.* 9.
PITT, a demi-horse, salient. *Pl.* 91, *cr.* 2, (without wings and coronet.)
PITT, Dors., a stork, ar., beaked and legged, ppr. *Pl.* 33, *cr.* 9.
PITT, Worc., on trunk of tree, in fess, raguly, vert, a stag, ppr., attired, or, between two acorn-branches sprouting from the tree, of the first, fructed, gold. *Pl.* 88, *or.* 9, (stump, *pl.* 14, *cr.* 14.)
PITT, Glouc., a stork, ppr. *Pl.* 33, *cr.* 9.
PITT, Salop, a cubit arm, erect, ppr., erased, at elbow, gu., in hand a banner, or, charged with a human heart, of the second.
PITT, Salop and Worc., a dove, wings expanded, ar., beaked and legged, gu., between two ears of wheat, or. *Pl.* 27, *cr.* 5, (wheat *pl.* 9, *cr.* 13.)

PITT, Somers., a stork, ppr., resting dexter on a bezant. *Pl.* 61, *cr.* 10, (bezant, *pl.* 141.)
PITT, Somers., a stork, ppr., in dexter a bezant. *Pl.* 122, *cr.* 7, (bezant, *pl.* 141.)
PITT, Cornw., a stork, ar., beaked and legged, or. *Pl.* 33, *cr.* 9.
PITTER, Middx., on two billets, erect, or, a stag's head, erased and attired, ppr., gorged with a collar and chain, gold. *Pl.* 125, *cr.* 6, (without roses.)
PITTILLO, a sword, erect, point upward, on point a fleur-de-lis. *Pl.* 55, *cr.* 15, (fleur-de-lis, *pl.* 141.)
PITTMAN, Eng., a rock, sa. *Pl.* 73, *cr.* 12.
PITTMAN, a moor's arm, ppr., escarroned of the colours, advancing a pole-axe, handle, or, headed, ar. *Pl.* 92, *cr.* 14, (axe, *pl.* 58, *cr.* 2.)
PITTS, Worc., a dove, ppr., enclosed by a wreath of wheat, or. *Pl.* 66, *cr.* 12, (wreath, *pl.* 23, *cr.* 14.)
PITTS, Lond. and Somers., a stork, ar., beaked and legged, gu., resting dexter on a bezant. *Pl.* 61, *cr.* 10, (bezant, *pl.* 141.)
PIVERNE, a cubit arm, vested, gu., cuffed, ar., in hand, ppr., a sword, in pale, enfiled with a leopard's head, of the second, hilt and pommel, or, point, guttée-de-sang. *Pl.* 71, *cr.* 9, (head, *pl.* 102, *cr.* 5.)
PIX, Eng., a tree, vert. *Pl.* 16, *cr.* 8.
PIX, Kent, on a round chapeau, gu., turned up, erm., a cross crosslet, fitched, or, between wings, az. *Pl.* 11, *cr.* 8, (cross, *pl.* 141.)
PIXT, Kent, on a chapeau, gu., turned up, erm., a cross crosslet, fitched, or, between wings, az. *Pl.* 11, *cr.* 8, (cross, *pl.* 141.)
PLACE, Eng., a palm-tree, vert, fructed, or. *Pl.* 18, *cr.* 12.
PLACE, Warw., out of a ducal coronet, or, a dexter arm, in armour, embowed, in hand a battle-axe, all ppr. *Pl.* 122, *cr.* 8, (axe, *pl.* 121, *cr.* 14.)
PLACETIS, DE, Eng., a lion's head, ppr., collared, gu. *Pl.* 7, *cr.* 10.
PLACETIS, Eng., a lion's head, ppr., collared, gu. *Pl.* 7, *cr.* 10.
PLAFAIR, Sco., an arm, ppr., armed and embowed, az., in hand a fleur-de-lis, or. *Pl.* 24, *cr.* 14.
PLAINE, Eng., the trunk of a tree, sprouting forth branches, ppr. *Pl.* 92, *cr.* 8.
PLAISTO, or PLAISTOW, out of a ducal coronet, a griffin's head, ppr. *Pl.* 54, *cr.* 14.
PLAITERS, or PLATERS, Eng., a falcon, ar., armed, beaked, and membered, or. *Pl.* 67, *cr.* 3.
PLAIZ, Eng., a lion's head, erased, vomiting flames, ppr. *Pl.* 20, *cr.* 3.
PLANK, or PLANKE, Eng., an olive-branch, ppr. *Pl.* 98, *cr.* 8.
PLANT, Eng., a stag, trippant, gu. *Pl.* 68, *cr.* 2.
PLANTA, Lond., out of a marquess's coronet, or, a bear's hind-leg, erect, couped at thigh, showing bottom of the foot, all ppr.
PLANTAGENET, Eng., a fleur-de-lis, or. *Pl.* 68, *cr.* 12.
PLANTAGENET, and PLANTAGINET, Eng., a rose, per pale, gu. and ar. *Pl.* 20, *cr.* 2.
PLANTNEY, Staffs., a tiger's head, erased, or, tufted and maned, gu. *Pl.* 94, *cr.* 10.
PLASKETT, Eng., a swan, ar. *Pl.* 122, *cr.* 13.
PLASTO, a lion's head, erased. *Pl.* 81, *cr.* 4.

PLATER, Eng., a pheon, az. *Pl.* 26, *cr.* 12.
PLATER, Suff., a hawk, regardant, (wings expanded,) ar., belled, or. *Pl.* 42, *cr.* 7, (without chaplet.)
PLATER, Suff., a vulture, regardant, wings expanded, ar. *Pl.* 87, *cr.* 8, (without sword.)
PLATT, Eng., a garb, or, banded, vert. *Pl.* 48, *cr.* 10.
PLATT, a bird, volant, ar., wings ar. and sa., in beak an escallop, of the first. *Pl.* 94, *cr.* 1, (escallop, *pl.* 141.)
PLATT, Lond. and Middx., a demi-lion, rampant, ppr., between paws a plate. *Pl.* 126, *cr.* 12.
PLATT, a duck, rising, ppr. *Pl.* 90, *cr.* 15.
PLATT, Ess., a shoveller, (wings expanded,) ppr. *Pl.* 90, *cr.* 15.
PLAUNCH, DE LA, Eng., a hunting-horn, sans strings, sa. *Pl.* 89, *cr.* 3.
PLAYDELL, Berks., a tiger's head, erased, or, charged with hurts, in mouth a cross pattée, fitched, of the first. *Pl.* 94, *cr.* 10, (cross, *pl.* 125, *cr.* 2.)
PLAYER, Middx., an arm, in armour, in fess, in hand a (broken) lance, all ppr. *Servitute clarior.* *Pl.* 57, *cr.* 3, (without chapeau.)
PLAYER, an arm, in armour, (in bend,) couped below elbow, hand supporting a broken spear, in pale, all ppr. *Pl.* 23, *cr.* 9.
PLAYFAIR, Eng., on a chapeau, a pelican, vulning, ppr. *Pl.* 21, *cr.* 5.
PLAYFAIR, Sco., a globe, ppr. *Sic te non vidimus olim.* *Pl.* 14, *cr.* 1.
PLAYFAIR, Sco., a pelican, feeding her young, ppr. *Pl.* 44, *cr.* 1.
PLAYFORD, Kent, Norf., and Suff., a leopard, sejant, ppr. *Pl.* 10, *cr.* 13, (without flag.)
PLAYNE, Suff., a dead tree, (erased) at root, and erect, ppr. *Pl.* 92, *cr.* 8.
PLAYSE, Eng., a lion's head, erased, issuing flames, ppr. *Pl.* 20, *cr.* 3.
PLAYSES, Eng., a gauntlet, in fess, ppr., holding, in pale, a broken tilting-spear, or, top hanging down, headed, ar. *Pl.* 23, *cr.* 9, (gauntlet, *pl.* 71, *cr.* 13.)
PLAYSTOW, Ess., out of a ducal coronet, or, a griffin's head, ppr. *Pl.* 54, *cr.* 14.
PLAYTERS, Suff., a hawk, regardant, or, winged, az., belled, gold. *Pl.* 42, *cr.* 7, (without garland.)
PLAYTERS, on a ducal coronet, a lion, rampant. *Pl.* 67, *cr.* 5, (coronet, *same plate.*)
PLEASANCE, Suff., a griffin, sejant, wings expanded, erm. *Pl.* 100, *cr.* 11.
PLEASAUNCE, Eng., a griffin, segreant, erm., legged, or. *Pl.* 67, *cr.* 13.
PLECKFORD, a demi-swan, rising, ar., wings addorsed, ducally gorged, or. *Pl.* 54, *cr.* 4, (gorging, *same plate.*)
PLEDGER, Cambs., a buck's head, erased, or, in mouth an oak-sprig, ppr., fructed, gold. *Pl.* 100, *cr.* 8.
PLEDGRED, Cambs., a stag's head, erased, or, in mouth an oak-branch, vert, fructed, gold. *Pl.* 100, *cr.* 8.
PLENDERLEITH, Sco., a hand holding a writ or scroll of paper almost rolled, ppr. *Promptu et consulto.* *Pl.* 27, *cr.* 4.
PLESANT, a bird, in beak two roses, stalked and leaved. *Pl.* 52, *cr.* 12, (roses, *pl.* 23, *cr.* 2.)
PLESHEY, Eng., a bull, passant, gu. *Pl.* 66, *cr.* 11.

PLESSEIS, Eng., a church with a spire, environed with trees, all ppr. *Pl.* 110, *cr.* 5.
PLEYDELL, a tiger's head, erased, sa., bezantée, devouring a cross pattée, fitched, gu. *Pl.* 94, *cr.* 10, (cross, *pl.* 27, *cr.* 14.)
PLEYDELL, Wilts. and Berks., a wolf's head, erased, gu., plattée, in mouth a cross formée, fitched, of the first. *Pl.* 14, *cr.* 6, (cross, *pl.* 27, *cr.* 14.)
PLEYDELL, Dors., a panther's head, erased, sa., bezantée, swallowing a cross pattée, fitched, gu. *Imitare quam invidere.* *Pl.* 92, *cr.* 13, (cross, *pl.* 27, *cr.* 14.)
PLOMER, Iri., a lion, sa., in dexter a dagger, gu. *Pl.* 64, *cr.* 2, (dagger, *pl.* 41, *cr.* 13.)
PLOMER, Eng., within an annulet, or, a shield, sa. *Pl.* 88, *cr.* 2, (without lion.)
PLOMER, a demi-lion, rampant, ar., in dexter a (sprig,) vert. *Pl.* 39, *cr.* 14.
PLOMER, Suss., a demi-lion, rampant, gu., holding a garb, or. *Pl.* 84, *cr.* 7.
PLOMPTON, Eng., a mortar, mounted on a carriage, ppr. *Pl.* 55, *cr.* 14.
PLOMPTON, or PLOMTON, Eng., a buck's head, couped, ar., attired, or. *Pl.* 91, *cr.* 14.
PLOMSTED, Norf., out of a ducal coronet, a griffin's head, ar., erased, sa., beaked, or. *Pl.* 54, *cr.* 14.
PLONCKETT, or PLONKETT, Eng. and Iri., a stag's head, affrontée, gorged with a ducal coronet, ppr. *Pl.* 55, *cr.* 2.
PLONCKETT, Iri., a wolf, sejant, ppr. *Pl.* 110, *cr.* 4.
PLONKET, Eng., in hand a lance, (in pale), ppr. *Pl.* 99, *cr.* 8.
PLONKET, and PLONKETT, a stag's head, affrontée, gorged with a ducal coronet, or. *Pl.* 55, *cr.* 2.
PLOTT, Berks. and Lond., an arm, in armour, embowed, sa., vambraced and garnished, or, in hand a scimitar, ppr. *Pl.* 81, *cr.* 11.
PLOTT, Devons. and Heref., a dexter arm, in armour, or, purfled, sa., in hand a falchion, ar., hilt and pommel, gold, (a scarf, flotant from the hilt, enfiling the wrist, and tied in a knot, of the first and second.) *Pl.* 2, *cr.* 8.
PLOWDEN, Eng., a hart's head, erased, az. *Pl.* 66, *cr.* 9.
PLOWDEN, or PLOWDON, Oxon. and Salop, on a mount, vert, a buck, (passant,) sa., attired, or. *Pl.* 50, *cr.* 6.
PLOWDEN, (on a mount, vert,) a stag, trippant, sa., horned and hoofed, or. *Pl.* 68, *cr.* 2.
PLOWMAN, Eng., a demi-savage, wreathed about middle, over dexter shoulder a club, round sinister arm a serpent, entwined. *Pl.* 92, *cr.* 10.
PLUM, and PLUME, Eng., out of a ducal coronet, a plume of ostrich-feathers, ppr. *Pl.* 44, *cr.* 12.
PLUM, Ess., a talbot, sejant, gu., collared and (lined,) or. *Pl.* 107, *cr.* 7.
PLUMBE, Leic., Norf., and Kent, a greyhound, sejant, ar., (collared, gu.) *Pl.* 66, *cr.* 15.
PLUMBE, Kent, Leic., and Norf., an otterhound, sejant, ar., collared, gu. *Pl.* 107, *cr.* 7.
PLUMTREE, a phœnix in flames, ppr. *Pl.* 44, *cr.* 8.
PLUME, Eng., out of a ducal coronet, or, a plume of ostrich-feathers, ar. *Pl.* 44, *cr.* 12.
PLUMER, or PLUMMER, a demi-lion, rampant, ar., in dexter a (sprig,) vert. *Pl.* 39, *cr.* 14.

PLUMERAGE, Eng., a demi-lion, rampant, ppr., langued, gu., in paw a fleur-de-lis, of the last. *Pl.* 91, *cr.* 13.
PLUMERAGE, a demi-lion, rampant, az., (between paws) a fleur-de-lis, gu. *Pl.* 91, *cr.* 13.
PLUMERDON, a magpie, ppr. *Pl.* 100, *cr.* 13.
PLUMETT, Iri., a horse, passant, ar. *Pl.* 15, *cr.* 14.
PLUMLEIGH, and PLUMLEY, Devons., an arm, embowed, vested, gu., cuffed, ar., in hand, ppr., an arrow, of the first, sans feathers, headed, of the second. *Pl.* 112, *cr.* 1, (without bow or pellets.)
PLUMMER, Eng., a water-bouget, or. *Pl.* 14, *cr.* 12.
PLUMPTON, Nottingham, a phœnix, or, among flames, ppr. *Pl.* 44, *cr.* 8.
PLUMSTOCK, on a goat's head, erased, ar., attired, or, a cheveron, gu. *Pl.* 29, *cr.* 13.
PLUMTRE, JOHN-PEMBERTON, Esq., of Fredville, Kent, a phœnix, or, in flames, ppr. *Sufficit meruisse.* *Pl.* 44, *cr.* 8.
PLUMTREE, Notts., a phœnix, or, in flames, ppr. *Pl.* 44, *cr.* 8.
PLUNKET, Baron, (Plunket,) a horse, passant, ar., charged on shoulder with a portcullis. *Festina lente.* *Pl.* 15, *cr.* 14, (portcullis, *pl.* 51, *cr.* 12.)
PLUNKET, or PLUNKETT, Iri., a horse, passant, ar. *Pl.* 15, *cr.* 14.
PLUNKETT, Eng., a wolf, sejant, ppr. *Pl.* 110, *cr.* 4.
PLUNKETT, a greyhound's head, between two rose slips. *Pl.* 84, *cr.* 13.
PLUNKETT, Baron Dunsany. *See* DUNSANY.
PLUNKETT, Baron Louth. *See* LOUTH.
PLUNKETT, Earl of Fingall. *See* FINGALL.
PLYMOUTH, Earl of, and Baron Windsor, (Andrews-Windsor,) a buck's head, affrontée, ar., couped at neck, attired, or. *Je me fie en Dieu.* *Pl.* 111, *cr.* 13.
POCHER, Eng., a harpy, gardant, wings expanded, ppr. *Pl.* 32, *cr.* 3.
POCHIN, Leic., a harpy, wings (addorsed,) or, face, ppr. *Pl.* 32, *cr.* 3.
POCHING, and POCHER, a harpy, wings (addorsed,) or, face, ppr. *Pl.* 32, *cr.* 3.
POCKLINGTON, Eng., a demi-leopard, rampant, ppr., in dexter an ostrich-feather, ar. *Pl.* 12, *cr.* 14, (feather, *pl.* 58, *cr.* 7.)
POCOCK, Westminster and Durh., out of a naval coronet, or, an antelope's head, ppr., attired, gold. *Regi regnoque fidelis.* *Pl.* 118, *cr.* 5.
POCOCK, an antelope's head, erased, ppr., attired, or. *Pl.* 24, *cr.* 7.
PODE, Devons., out of clouds, ppr., a demi-eagle, az., collared, or, wings elevated, ar., on breast, and on each wing, an etoile, counterchanged. *Pl.* 44, *cr.* 14, (clouds, same plate, *cr.* 4; etoile, *pl.* 141.)
PODMORE, Iri., out of a mural coronet, ar., a head holding a record, all ppr. *Pl.* 27, *cr.* 4, (coronet, *pl.* 128, *fig.* 18.)
POE, a stag's head, cabossed, ar., attired, or, between attires, a crucifix. *Per crucem ad coronam.* *Pl.* 124, *cr.* 14, (crucifix, *pl.* 141.)
POIGNDESTRE, Lond., an esquire's helmet, ppr. *Pl.* 109, *cr.* 5.
POINTER, Eng., a talbot, passant, ppr. *Pl.* 120, *cr.* 8.
POINTER, a pointer, or. *Pl.* 117, *cr.* 8.

POINTING, a horse's head, erased, or, on neck a cross pattée, sa. *Pl.* 11, *cr.* 12, (without trefoil.)
POINTS, an arm, couped above wrist, hand (clenched,) ppr. *Pl.* 67, *cr.* 6.
POLDEN, a buck, trippant, ppr., attired, or. *Clariores e tenebris.* *Pl.* 68, *cr.* 2.
POLE, Bart., Devons., a lion's gamb, erased, gu., armed, or. *Pollet virtus.* *Pl.* 126, *cr.* 9.
POLE, Devons., out of a ducal coronet, or, a griffin's head, az., beaked, or. *Pollet virtus.* *Pl.* 54, *cr.* 15.
POLE, Eng., an eagle, rising, ppr. *Pl.* 67, *cr.* 4.
POLE, Eng., a lion's gamb. *Pollet virtus.* *Pl.* 126, *cr.* 9.
POLE, a lion's gamb., sa. *Pl.* 126, *cr.* 9.
POLE, Derbs., a hawk, wings expanded and distended, ppr., belled and jessed, or. *Pl.* 105, *cr.* 4.
POLE, Bart., Hants., an eagle, rising, ppr., charged on breast with a mullet, az. *Pollet virtus.* *Pl.* 67, *cr.* 4, (mullet, *pl.* 141.)
POLE, WELLESLEY, Baron, Maryborough. *See* MARYBOROUGH.
POLE, CHANDOS: 1. A falcon, rising, ppr., belled and jessed, or. *Pl.* 105, *cr.* 4. 2. A knight's head, in (chain) armour. *Pl.* 33, *cr.* 14. 3. A goat, (passant,) ar. *Pl.* 66, *cr.* 1.
POLERHIL, a man's head, in profile, (erased,) at neck, ppr., wreathed round temples, (in mouth a sprig, vert.) *Pl.* 36, *cr.* 3.
POLEWHEELE, or POLWHILL, Cornw., a bull, passant, gu., armed, or. *Pl.* 66, *cr.* 11.
POLEY, of Boxted Hall, Suff., a lion, rampant, sa., collared and chained, or. *Fortior est qui se.* *Pl.* 88, *cr.* 1.
POLEY, a lion, rampant, per pale, or and sa., collared and chained, or. *Pl.* 88, *cr.* 1.
POLHILL, a bear, statant, muzzled, collared, and lined, line reflexed over back. *Pl.* 61, *cr.* 5.
POLHILL, or POLLHILL, Beds. and Lond., out of a mural coronet, or, a hind's head, ppr., between two acorn-branches, vert, fructed, gold. *Pl.* 13, *cr.* 9, (branches, *pl.* 74, *cr.* 7; coronet, *pl.* 128, *fig.* 18.)
POLKINGHORNE, Cornw., an arm, in armour, embowed, in hand a battle-axe. *Pl.* 121, *cr.* 14.
POLKINGTON, Lanc., a mower, with sythe, ppr., pole, or, vested, quarterly, gu. and ar., his cap, per pale, of the same.
POLLACK, Sco., a boar, passant, wounded in body by an arrow. *Pl.* 36, *cr.* 2.
POLLALION, out of a ducal coronet, or, a lion's head. *Pl.* 90, *cr.* 9.
POLLARCK, a boar, passant, pierced in side by an arrow, ppr. *Pl.* 36, *cr.* 2.
POLLARD, Oxon., Worc., Devons., and Cornw., a stag, trippant, ar., attired, or. *Pl.* 68, *cr.* 2.
POLLARD, Durh. and Yorks., a falchion, erect, ar., gripe, vert, hilt and pommel, or. *Pl.* 105, *cr.* 1.
POLLARD, a stag, trippant, ar. *Pl.* 68, *cr.* 2.
POLLARD, URQUHART: 1. For *Urquhart*, a demi-otter, rampant, ppr., (crowned with an antique crown, or, collared, gold, charged with three crescents, gu.) *Pl.* 74, *cr.* 13, (without fish.) 2. For *Pollard*, a stag, trip-

2 B

pant, ar., horned, or. *Pl.* 68, *cr.* 2. 3. For *Hampson*, out of a mural coronet, ar., a greyhound's head, sa., gorged with a collar, gu., charged with three plates. *Pl.* 113, *cr.* 6, (plate, *pl.* 141.)

POLLEN, Eng., a pelican, in nest, vulning, ppr. *Pl.* 44, *cr.* 1.

POLLEN, a pelican, with young ones, or, in a nest, ppr. *Pl.* 44, *cr.* 1.

POLLEN, Bart., Hants, a pelican, wings (expanded,) in nest, paly, ar. and az., vulning, ppr., charged on wing with a lozenge, ar., thereon an escallop, sa. *Pl.* 44, *cr.* 1, (charging, *pl.* 141.)

POLLEN, Surr., same crest. *Detout mon cœur.*

POLLENER, Eng., a pelican, in nest, vulning, ppr. *Pl.* 44, *cr.* 1.

POLLETT, an arm, in armour, embowed, in hand a sword, all ppr. *Pl.* 2, *cr.* 8.

POLLEY, or POOLEY, Suff., a lion, rampant, sa., collared and chained, or. *Pl.* 88, *cr.* 1.

POLLEYNE, Glouc. : 1. A hound couchant, or. *Pl.* 6, *cr.* 7. 2. On a mount, vert, a hound, current, ar., (collared and lined, line tied in a knot, sa.) *Pl.* 28, *cr.* 7, (mount, *pl.* 98, *cr.* 13.)

POLLOCK, an open book. *Delectatio mea. Pl.* 15, *cr.* 12.

POLLOCK, Eng., an etoile of eight points, or. *Pl.* 83, *cr.* 3, (without coronet.)

POLLOCK, Bart., Sco., a boar, passant, pierced by an arrow, ppr. *Audacter et strenue. Pl.* 36, *cr.* 2.

POLLOCK, a castle, triple-towered, ar. *Pl.* 123, *cr.* 14.

POLSTROD, out of a ducal coronet, or, a boar's head and neck, sa. *Pl.* 102, *cr.* 14.

POLTIMORE, Baron, and a Bart., (Bampfylde,) a lion's head, erased, sa., ducally crowned, or. *Delectare in Domino. Pl.* 90, *cr.* 4, (without charging.)

POLTON, Eng., in hand a swan's head and neck, erased, ppr. *Pl.* 29, *cr.* 4.

POLWARTH, Baron, Sco., (Scott,) a lady, richly attired, in dexter the sun, in sinister a half-moon. *Reparabit cornua Phœbe. Pl.* 107, *cr.* 14.

POLWHELE, Cornw. : 1. A negro's head, in mouth an olive-branch. *Pl.* 120, *cr.* 3, (branch, *pl.* 98, *cr.* 8.) 2. A bull, gu., horns, or. *Karenza wheelas Karenza. Pl.* 66, *cr.* 11.

POLWHILE, Cornw., a man's head, in profile, (erased,) ppr., in mouth an oak-branch, leaved, vert, fructed, or. *Pl.* 81, *cr.* 15, (branch, *same plate, cr.* 7.)

POMEROY, Eng., a lion's head, erased, charged with four bezants, ducally crowned, ppr. *Pl.* 90, *cr.* 4.

POMEROY, and POMERY, Devons. and Cornw., (out of a ducal coronet,) or, a lion's head, gardant, gu. *Pl.* 1, *cr.* 5.

POMEROY, Iri., a lion, rampant, gu., holding an (apple.) *Pl.* 84, *cr.* 7.

POMEROY, Bucks., a fir-cone, vert, charged with a bezant. *Pl.* 84, *cr.* 12.

POMEROY, Iri., a demi-lion, vert. *Pl.* 67, *cr.* 10.

POMEROY, Viscount Harberton. *See* HARBERTON.

POMERY, Devons. and Cornw., a lion, sejant, gu., (in dexter an apple, or.) *Pl.* 126, *cr.* 15.

POMFREE, an arm, in armour, in hand a sword. *Pl.* 2, *cr.* 8.

POMFRET, Earl of, Baron Lempster or Leominster, and a Bart., (Fermor,) out of a ducal coronet, or, a cock's head, gu., crested and wattled, gold. *Hora e sempre. Pl.* 97, *cr.* 15.

POMFRETT, Eng., in dexter hand a battle-axe, ppr. *Pl.* 73, *cr.* 7.

PONCHARDON, Eng., a unicorn's head, erased, gu., bezantée, and armed, or. *Pl.* 67, *cr.* 1.

PONDRELL, Eng., a fox, current, ppr. *Pl.* 80, *cr.* 5.

PONPONS, three pruning-hooks, two in saltier, one in pale, or, environed in middle with a wreath. *Pl.* 58, *cr.* 8.

PONSFORD, Devons., a lion, sejant, regardant, gu., crowned, ar., charged on neck with three escallops, or, between paws an anchor, gold.

PONSONBY, Iri., on a ducal coronet, az., a sheaf of arrows, entwined by a snake, ppr. *Pl.* 86, *cr.* 12.

PONSONBY, Iri. and Cumb., on a ducal coronet, or, three arrows, enveloped by a snake, ppr. *Pl.* 86, *cr.* 12.

PONSONBY, Earl of Besborough. *See* BESBOROUGH.

PONSONBY, Baron (Ponsonby,) on a ducal coronet, or, three arrows, one in pale, two in saltier, points downward, entwined by a snake, all ppr. *Pro rege, lege, grege. Pl.* 86, *cr.* 12.

PONT, Sco., a sphere, az., beautified with six of the celestial signs, environing the terrestrial globe, all ppr. *Perenne sub polo nihil. Pl.* 114, *cr.* 6.

PONTEN, a lion's paw, erased, sa., charged with an escallop, ar. *Pl.* 126, *cr.* 9, (escallop, *pl.* 141.)

PONTIFEX, Eng., a tower, ensigned with a crescent, gu. *Pl.* 85, *cr.* 1.

PONTON, Sco., a tree, ppr. *Stand sure. Pl.* 16, *cr.* 8.

POOL, or POOLE, Ess., Staffs., and Derbs., a hawk, wings expanded, ppr. *Pl.* 105, *cr.* 4.

POOL, Chesh. and Suss., a mermaid, in profile, ppr., in hands a Saxon coronet, or.

POOLE, Wilts., Glouc., and Devons., a stag's head, cabossed, gu., attires, barry of six, or and az. *Pl.* 36, *cr.* 1.

POOLE, Chesh. and Devons., out of a ducal coronet, or, a griffin's head, az., beaked, gold. *Pollet virtus. Pl.* 54, *cr.* 14.

POOLE, Chesh., in a ducal coronet, or, a griffin's head, ar., beaked, gold. *Pl.* 54, *cr.* 14.

POOLE, Eng., a stag's head, cabossed, gu., attired, one, or, the other, az. *Pl.* 36, *cr.* 1.

POOLE, a griffin's head, erased, az., (collared, or.) *Pl.* 48, *cr.* 6.

POOLE, Ess., a unicorn, passant, az., tufted, maned, and armed, or, ducally gorged, ar. *Pl.* 106, *cr.* 3.

POOLE, Chesh., a mermaid, ppr., crined, or, holding in (both) hands a naval crown, gold. *Pl.* 88, *cr.* 12, (coronet, *pl.* 128, *fig.* 10.)

POOLE, a hawk, rising, ppr. *Pl.* 105, *cr.* 4.

POOLE, Chesh. and Suss., out of a ducal coronet, or, a griffin's head, ar. *Pollet virtus. Pl.* 54, *cr.* 14.

POOLE, HEWITT, Esq., of Mayfield, co. Cork, out of a ducal coronet, a griffin's head, ar. *Pollet virtus. Pl.* 54, *cr.* 14.

POOLEY, Chesh. and Suff., a lion, rampant, or, collared and (lined,) sa. *Pl.* 88, *cr.* 1.

POOLEY, Chesh. and Suff., a lion, rampant, sa., collared and (lined,) or. *Pl.* 88, *cr.* 1.

POOR, Eng., a tower, sa., masoned, ar. *Pl.* 12, *cr.* 6.

POORE, Iri., a stag's head, cabossed, between attires, (our Saviour on the cross,) all ppr. *Pl.* 36, *cr.* 1, (cross, *pl.* 141.)

POORE, Bart., Wilts., a cubit arm, erect, (vested, sa., slashed, ar., cuffed, erm., charged with two mullets, in fess, or,) in hand an arrow, ppr. *From henceforth.* *Pl.* 42, *cr.* 13.

POPE, Eng., a demi-lion, vert. *Pl.* 67, *cr.* 10.

POPE, Oxon., two griffins' heads, erased and addorsed, or and az., ducally collared, counterchanged.

POPE, Oxon., two griffins' heads, erased and addorsed, or and az., collared with a plain collar.

POPE, Berks. and Iri., a tiger, passant, or, tufted, maned, (collared, ringed, and lined, sa.) *Pl.* 67, *cr.* 15.

POPE, Cornw., a griffin, passant, ppr., collared, gu. *Pl.* 61, *cr.* 14.

POPE, Lond., an heraldic-tiger, passant, or, (collared and lined, sa.) *Pl.* 7, *cr.* 5.

POPE, Salop, a cubit arm, erect, vested, gu., cuffed, ar., in hand, ppr., a pair of scales. *Mihi, tibi.* *Pl.* 26, *cr.* 8, (vesting, *pl.* 32, *cr.* 6.)

POPE, Salop, in hand, ppr., a pair of scales, or. *Pl.* 26, *cr.* 8.

POPHAM, Somers. and Wilts., a stag's head, couped, ppr. *Pl.* 91, *cr.* 14.

POPHAM, Hants, Middx., Somers., and Wilts., a stag's head, erased, ppr. *Pl.* 66, *cr.* 9.

POPHAM-LEYBORNE, of Littlecott, Wilts., a stag's head, erased, ppr. *Mens pristina mansit.* *Pl.* 66, *cr.* 9.

POPINGAY, Eng., a lion's head, per pale, or and az., ducally crowned, and powdered with roundles, all counterchanged. *Pl.* 90, *cr.* 4.

POPKIN, Sco., a hand holding a writing-pen, ppr. *Pl.* 26, *cr.* 13.

POPPLEWELL, Eng., a demi-lioness, rampant, ppr.

POPPLEWELL, a falcon, belled, vert, between two gilliflowers, ppr. *Pl.* 67, *cr.* 3, (flowers, *pl.* 22, *cr.* 9.)

PORCH, Somers., on a mount, vert, a wolf, passant, in mouth an arrow, barb downward, in dexter a bow, stringed, all ppr. *Cordi dat robora virtus.*

PORCHER, Norf., a lion, rampant, or, charged with three bars, gu., between paws a cinquefoil, erm. *Pro rege.* *Pl.* 125, *cr.* 2, (cinquefoil, *pl.* 141.)

PORDAGE, Kent, a dragon's head, (erased,) or, vomiting flames, ppr. *Pl.* 37, *cr.* 9.

PORT, or PORTE, Eng., in hand, erect, a pistol, ppr. *Pl.* 101, *cr.* 12.

PORT, an eagle's head, erased, in beak a cross pattée, fitched, or. *Pl.* 121, *cr.* 7, (cross, *pl.* 125, *cr.* 2.)

PORTAL, Hants, a castle, ar. *Pl.* 28, *cr.* 11.

PORTAL, Hants, a castellated portal, (each tower charged with a fleur-de-lis, in chief, az., and a wreath of laurel, in base, vert.) *Pl.* 8, *cr.* 7.

PORTAL, Eng., a lion's head, erased, ar. (Another, or.) *Pl.* 81, *cr.* 4.

PORTARLINGTON, Earl of, Viscount Carlow and Baron Dawson, Iri., (Dawson,) a cat's head, affrontée, erased near shoulders, ar., spotted, sa., in mouth a rat, of the last. *Vitæ vea virtus.* *Pl.* 108, *cr.* 4.

PORTE, a bird, in mouth a cross crosslet, fitched, or. *Pl.* 84, *cr.* 10.

PORTEEN, Eng., a pair of wings, expanded, dexter, or, sinister, gu. *Pl.* 39, *cr.* 12.

PORTEOUS, Sco., a turtle-dove, with olive-branch in beak, ppr. *I wait my time.* *Pl.* 48, *cr.* 15.

PORTEOUS, of Hawkshaw, Sco., a falcon, belled, ppr. *Let the hawk shaw*—and—*I byde my time.* *Pl.* 67, *cr.* 3.

PORTER, Sco., a dexter arm, in armour, embowed, in hand a sword, all ppr. *Vigilantiâ et virtute.* *Pl.* 2, *cr.* 8.

PORTER, Eng., a bull's head, couped, gu., armed, or. *Pl.* 120, *cr.* 7.

PORTER, Eng., a demi-antelope, or, spotted, collared, and attired, gu. *Pl.* 34, *cr.* 8.

PORTER, Dublin, a cherub's head, ppr. *Fear God, honour the King.* *Pl.* 126, *cr.* 10.

PORTER, Isle of Wight and Hants, a dragon's head, couped, gu. *Pl.* 87, *cr.* 12.

PORTER, Suss., Kent, and Linc., a portcullis, ar., chains, or. *Pl.* 51, *cr.* 12.

PORTER, a harrow, ppr. *Pl.* 7, *cr.* 2.

PORTER, a demi-squirrel, or, semée of hurts, holding an acorn-branch, vert, fructed, gold.

PORTER, an heraldic-antelope's head, (erased,) ducally gorged. *Pl.* 76, *cr.* 3, (gorging, *same plate, cr.* 8.)

PORTER, an heraldic-antelope's head, couped, ducally gorged. *Pl.* 76, *cr.* 3, (gorging, *same plate, cr.* 8.)

PORTER, a stag's head, erased, ar., attired, and (ducally gorged, or, between two laurel-branches, vert.) *Pl.* 66, *cr.* 9.

PORTER, between two pillars, roofed, spired, and flagged, or, a church-bell, ar.

PORTER, Worc., a squirrel, sejant, holding a (bell.) *Pl.* 2, *cr.* 4.

PORTER, Lond., an heraldic-antelope's head, (erased, ar., attired, or, gorged with a collar, gu., therefrom, on centre of neck, a bell pendent, sa., charged with an ermine-spot, of the first.) *Pl.* 76, *cr.* 3.

PORTER, Linc. and Suff., a portcullis, ar., nailed and chained, or, the chains cast over in fret. *Pl.* 51, *cr.* 12.

PORTER, Cornw., a demi-goat, erect. *Pl.* 11, *cr.* 4, (without gate.)

PORTERFIELD, Sco., a branch of palm, slipped, erect, vert. *Sub pondere sursum.* *Pl.* 123, *cr.* 1.

PORTERFIELD, Sco., a sloth-hound, ppr. *Gang warily.* *Pl.* 120, *cr.* 8.

PORTINGTON, Eng., in dexter hand a dart, point downward. *Pl.* 45, *cr.* 12, (without clouds.)

PORTLAND, Duke and Earl of, Marquess of Titchfield, Viscount Woodstock, and Baron Cirencester, (Cavendish-Scott-Bentinck): 1. For *Bentinck,* out of a marquess's coronet, two arms, counter-embowed, vested, gu., on hands, gloves, or, each holding an ostrich-feather, ar. *Pl.* 45, *cr.* 2, (coronet, *pl.* 127, *fig.* 4.) 2. For *Cavendish,* a snake, nowed, ppr. *Craignez honte.* *Pl.* 1, *cr.* 9.

PORTLOCK, an ostrich, in beak, (two) keys, ppr. *Pl.* 64, *cr.* 3, (key, *pl.* 9, *cr.* 12.)
PORTMAN, Somers., a talbot, sejant, or. *Pl.* 107, *cr.* 7, (without collar.)
PORTMAN, Somers., a leopard's head, or, with a cross crosslet, fitched, run through the skull and out of the mouth, between two snakes' heads, downward, ppr.
PORTMAN, Baron, (Berkeley-Portman,) of Bryanstone, Dors. ; and Orchard Portman, Somers.: 1. A talbot, sejant, or. *Pl.* 107, *cr.* 7. 2. A unicorn, gu. *A clean heart and a cheerful spirit. Pl.* 106, *cr.* 3.
PORTSMOUTH, Earl of, Viscount Lymington, and Baron Wallop, (Wallop,) a mermaid, with mirror and comb, all ppr. *En suivant la verité. Pl.* 48, *cr.* 5.
POSINGWORTH, POSSINGWORTH, and POSYNGWORTH, Eng., out of a ducal coronet, or, a plume of ostrich-feathers, ppr. *Pl.* 44, *cr.* 12.
POSTLETHWAITE, on a ducal coronet, or, a boar's head, sa., couped, gu. *Pl.* 102, *cr.* 14.
POSTON, a demi-lion, or, supporting an (arch,) gu. *Pl.* 19, *cr.* 6.
POSYNWORTH, Eng., a lion's head, erased, gu., collared, or. *Pl.* 7, *cr.* 10.
POTKIN, Herts., Kent, and Cambs., a stag's head, erased, sa., attired, or, nose, ar. *Pl.* 66, *cr.* 9.
POTT, Eng., on top of a tower, ppr., a crescent, ar. *Pl.* 85, *cr.* 1.
POTT, and POTTS, Lond. and Norf., a leopard, sejant, ppr., (collared, lined, and ringed, az.) *Pl.* 10, *cr.* 13, (without flag.)
POTT, and POTTS, Land., Durh., and Norf., on a mount, vert, an ounce, sejant, ppr., (collared and chained, or.) *Pl.* 123, *cr.* 8.
POTT, Chesh., a wild cat, sejant, (collared and chained, or.) *Pl.* 24, *cr.* 6.
POTT, Chesh. and Derbs., on a mount, vert, a greyhound, couchant, gu., (collared and ringed, or. *Pl.* 6, *cr.* 7, (mount, *pl.* 98, *cr.* 13.)
POTTER, Devons., Oxon., Kent, and Somers., a seahorse, ppr. *Pl.* 103, *cr.* 3.
POTTER, Somers., Devons., Oxon., and Kent, a seahorse, or. *Pl.* 103, *cr.* 3.
POTTER, a star of (twelve) rays, or, between wings, ar. *Pl.* 1, *cr.* 15.
POTTMAN, Eng., a fleur-de-lis, gu. *Pl.* 68, *cr.* 12.
POTTS, Eng., a lion's head, erased, az. *Pl.* 81, *cr.* 4.
POTTS, (on a mount, vert,) a greyhound, couchant, ar. *Pl.* 6, *cr.* 7.
POULAIN, Eng., an eagle, displayed, gu. *Pl.* 48, *cr.* 11.
POULDEN, Eng., a hand, issuing from a cloud, holding a book, expanded. *Pl.* 82, *cr.* 5.
POULET, a hawk, wings elevated, ducally gorged and belled. *Pl.* 81, *cr.* 12, (without mount.)
POULETT, Earl and Baron, Viscount Hinton, (Poulett,) Eng., an arm, in armour, embowed, in hand a sword, all ppr. *Garde la foy. Pl.* 2, *cr.* 8.
POULETT, Eng., a unicorn's head, vert. *Pl.* 20, *cr.* 1.
POULEY, Ess., within an annulet, or, an eagle, displayed, az. *Pl.* 77, *cr.* 9, (eagle, *pl.* 48, *cr.* 11.)
POULTER, Eng., a ship in full sail, ppr. *Pl.* 109, *cr.* 8.

POULTNEY, Leic. and Yorks., a leopard's head, gardant, erased, sa., gorged with a ducal coronet, or. *Pl.* 116, *cr.* 8.
POULTNEY, Leic. and Yorks., a leopard's head, gardant, erased, sa. *Pl.* 56, *cr.* 7.
POULTON, Eng., an anchor and cable, sa. *Pl.* 42, *cr.* 12.
POUND, Hants, a castle, ppr. *Pl.* 28, *cr.* 11.
POUNT, Sco., a buck's head, cabossed, ppr., attired, or. *Dum spiro, spero. Pl.* 36, *cr.* 1.
POUNTNEY, Eng., a leopard's head and neck, erased. *Pl.* 94, *cr.* 10.
POURIE, POWRIE, and PURIE, Sco., a hunting-horn, az., garnished, gu. *Vespere et mane. Pl.* 89, *cr.* 3.
POVEY, Eng., a bugle-horn, sa., or, stringed, gu. *Pl.* 48, *cr.* 12.
POVEY, Lond., out of a mural coronet, a griffin's head, (charged with an annulet.) *Pl.* 101, *cr.* 6, (without gorging.)
POWE, a crescent, az. *Pl.* 18, *cr.* 14.
POWEL, and POWELL, Eng., a demi-savage, in dexter, a club. *Pl.* 14, *cr.* 11.
POWEL, Heref., a lion's gamb, erased, or. *Pl.* 126, *cr.* 9.
POWELL, Herts., out of a ducal coronet, or, a demi-griffin. *Pl.* 39, *cr.* 2.
POWELL, Surr., a lion, rampant, ar., holding a garb, vert. *Pl.* 63, *cr.* 14.
POWELL, Lanc., a lion's head, erased, ar., gorged with a collar, flory, counterflory, gu. *Anima in amicis una. Pl.* 7, *cr.* 10.
POWELL, Suss., a lion, passant, or, in dexter the (broken shaft of a spear, in pale,) ppr. *Pl.* 106, *cr.* 5.
POWELL, Wilts., a lion's gamb, erect and erased, gu. *Spes mea Christus erit. Pl.* 126, *cr.* 9.
POWELL, a lion, (statant,) regardant, (pierced through chest by an arrow, in bend, point downward.) *Pl.* 100, *cr.* 6.
POWELL, Wel., a Saracen's head, affrontée, couped at shoulders, ppr., wreathed about temples, ar. and sa. *Pl.* 97, *cr.* 2.
POWELL, (two) broken spears, in saltier, ppr., within two laurel-branches, in orle, vert. *Pl.* 33, *cr.* 3, (branches, *pl.* 71, *cr.* 3.)
POWELL, a boar, passant, sa., (collared and lined, or.) *Pl.* 48, *cr.* 14.
POWELL, Somers., a lion, passant, resting dexter on a broken tilting-spear, ar. *Pl.* 48, *cr.* 8, (spear, *pl.* 107, *cr.* 5.)
POWELL, Lond., out of a ducal coronet, or, a demi-griffin, sa. *Pl.* 39, *cr.* 2.
POWELL, Heref., out of a ducal coronet, or, a demi-griffin, sa., beaked and legged, gold. *Pl.* 39, *cr.* 2.
POWELL, Wel., a boar's head, cabossed.
POWELL, Wel., a talbot's head, ppr. *Pl.* 123, *cr.* 15.
POWELL, Wel., a talbot's head, (couped,) ar., collared and ringed, or. *Pl.* 2, *cr.* 15.
POWELL, a demi-lion, rampant. *Pl.* 67, *cr.* 10.
POWELL, Lanc., a lion, rampant, sa., gorged with a (double chain, or, therefrom pendent a pheon, ar., fore-sinister resting on a shield, gold, charged with an eagle's head, erased, az.) *Omne bonum Dei donum. Pl.* 88, *cr.* 1.
POWER, Iri., an antelope's head, erased, neck transfixed by a spear, ppr. *Pl.* 79, *cr.* 9.
POWER, Sco., a stag's head, between attires a cross pattée. *Per crucem ad coronam. Pl.* 9, *cr.* 10.

POWER, Eng., a dexter hand, ppr., holding a close helmet, az. *Pl.* 37, *cr.* 15.

POWER, Oxon., a buck's head, couped, sa., attired, or. *Pl.* 91, *cr.* 14.

POWER, a stag's head, cabossed, ppr., attired, or, on top of a scalp a cross, brown. *Pl.* 115, *cr.* 1, (cross, *pl.* 141.)

POWER, Bart., of Kilfane, Iri., a stag's head, erased, ppr. *Pro patriâ semper. Pl.* 66, *cr.* 9.

POWERS, a stag's head, couped, ppr., on neck a trefoil, vert. *Pl.* 91, *cr.* 14, (trefoil, *pl.* 141.)

POWERSCOURT, Viscount, and Baron Wingfield, Iri., (Wingfield,) a demi-eagle, rising, wings expanded, ar., looking at the sun in his glory. *Fidelite est de Dieu. Pl.* 52, *cr.* 8, (sun, *pl.* 43, *cr.* 5.)

POWERTON, Eng., a hand, ppr., holding a spur, or. *Pl.* 34, *cr.* 9.

POWIS, Eng., in lion's paw, erased, sa., a sceptre, or. *Pl.* 16, *cr.* 1.

POWIS, Salop, a lion's gamb, erased, gu., grasping a sceptre, or, on top a fleur-do-lis, gold. *Pl.* 16, *cr.* 1.

POWIS, Earl of, and Baron, Viscount and Baron Clive, and Baron Herbert, U.K.; also, Baron Clive, Iri., (Clive,) a griffin, passant, ar., ducally gorged, gu. *Audiciter et sincere. Pl.* 61, *cr.* 14.

POWIS, Baron Lilford. *See* LILFORD.

POWLE, Eng., a demi-savage, brandishing a sabre, ppr. *Pl.* 82, *cr.* 2.

POWLE, Ess., a unicorn, passant, az., horned and maned, or. *Pl.* 106, *cr.* 3.

POWLETT, Hants, a sphinx, (statant,) wings expanded, ppr. *Pl.* 91, *cr.* 11.

POWLETT, Baron Bayning. *See* BAYNING.

POWLETT-OORDE, Baron Bolton. *See* BOLTON.

POWNALL, Eng., a unicorn's head, erm. *Pl.* 20, *cr.* 1.

POWNALL, Lond., a lion's gamb, erect and erased, sa., charged with two roses, ar., holding a key, or, from which a chain is reflexed, gold. *Grace me guide. Pl.* 5, *cr.* 5, (rose, *pl.* 141.)

POWNALL, Lanc., a Lion's gamb, erect and erased, ppr., holding a key, or, from which a chain is reflexed, gold. *Officium præsto. Pl.* 5, *cr.* 5.

POWNEY, Berks., a demi-eagle, wings expanded, sa., on breast a mascle, ar. *Pl.* 44, *cr.* 14, (mascle, *pl.* 141.)

POWTRELL, Eng., a Saracen's head, issuing, ppr. *Pl.* 19, *cr.* 1.

POWTRELL, a porcupine, gu., (collared and corded, or.) *Pl.* 55, *cr.* 10.

POWTRELL, Derbs., a hedgehog, (chained.) *Pl.* 32, *cr.* 9.

POWYS, Northamp., in lion's gamb, erased, gu., a sceptre, or. *Parta tuere. Pl.* 16, *cr.* 1.

POWYS, in lion's gamb, erect, gu., a sceptre, (in bend,) or. *Pl.* 16, *cr.* 1.

POWYS, HENRY-PHILIP, Esq., of Hardwick, Oxon., and Broomfield, Middx., in lion's gamb, erased, a sceptre. *Pl.* 16, *cr.* 1.

POWYS, Salop, in lion's gamb, erased, erect, gu., a fleur-de-lis, or. *Pl.* 5, *cr.* 5, (fleur-de-lis, *pl.* 141.)

POYLE, a hemp-hackle, or.

POYNDER, out of a demi-tower, ar., charged with a cross patonce, gu., a cubit arm, erect, vested, sa., cuffed, or, in hand, ppr., a cross pattée, fitched, of the first.

POYNER, Salop, a demi-buck, ppr., attired, or, between feet a chaplet of laurel, vert. *Pl.* 55, *cr.* 9, (chaplet, *pl.* 56, *cr.* 10.)

POYNES, Eng., a demi-leopard, ducally gorged, ppr. *Pl.* 125, *cr.* 4.

POYNES, Ess. and Glouc., a hand, issuing from clouds, ppr. *Pl.* 32, *cr.* 14, (clouds, *pl.* 67, *cr.* 12.)

POYNINGS, Eng., a pomegranate, ppr. *Pl.* 67, *cr.* 8.

POYNINGS, a key, ar., crowned, or, and a demi-wyvern, on a wreath.

POYNINGS, Dors., a dragon's head, wings displayed. *Pl.* 105, *cr.* 11.

POYNTEN, Eng., a pelican's nest, with young birds, ppr. *Pl.* 56, *cr.* 5.

POYNTER, Middx., a cubit arm, vested, sa., cuff, ar., in hand, ppr., a baton, in bend, ensigned with a cross formée, or. *Pl.* 18, *cr.* 1, (cross, *pl.* 141.)

POYNTER, Eng., a hand holding a baton. *Pl.* 18, *cr.* 1.

POYNTER, an arm in bend, vested, sa., cuffed, or, (pointing with fore-finger, ppr.) *Pl.* 39, *cr.* 1.

POYNTON, Eng., a stag's head, vert. *Pl.* 91, *cr.* 14.

POYNTZ, Eng., a sword, erect, ppr. *Pl.* 105, *cr.* 1.

POYNTZ, and POYNES, Berks., a cubit arm, fist clenched, ppr., vested in a shirt-sleeve, ar. *Pl.* 32, *cr.* 6.

POYNTZ, Suss. and Berks., a cubit arm, erect, vested, ar., fist clenched, ppr. *Pl.* 64, *cr.* 7.

POYSER, Lond., a stag's head, erased, gu., attired, or, in mouth an olive-branch, fructed, ppr., on neck an Eastern crown, gold. *Pl.* 66, *cr.* 9, (crown, *pl.* 79, *cr.* 12; branch, *pl.* 98, *cr.* 8.)

PRAED, Eng., a demi-lion, az. *Pl.* 67, *cr.* 10.

PRAED, Bucks. and Oxon., out of a five-leaved ducal coronet, or, a unicorn's head, ar., maned and horned, gold. *Pl.* 45, *cr.* 14, (coronet, *pl.* 23, *cr.* 11.)

PRANCE, VAUGHAN, a plume of five ostrich-feathers, surmounted on a scroll. *Muthig Vorwarts. Pl.* 106, *cr.* 11, (without chapeau.)

PRANELL, or PRANNELL, Lond. and Hants, issuing from rays, ppr., an eagle's head, sa. *Pl.* 84, *cr.* 9.

PRANNELL, Herts., issuing from rays, an eagle's head, all or. *Pl.* 84, *cr.* 9.

PRATER, Eng., a pegasus, current, sa., ducally gorged, or. *Pl.* 28, *cr.* 9, (gorging, *pl.* 57, *cr.* 15.)

PRATER, under a palm-tree, vert, a lion, couchant, gardant. *Pl.* 101, *cr.* 8, (tree, *pl.* 18, *cr.* 12.)

PRATT, Eng. and Iri., a caltrap, embrued, gu. *Pl.* 7, *cr.* 4.

PRATT, Eng., a wolf's head, erased, per cross, ar. and sa., counterchanged. *Pl.* 14, *cr.* 6.

PRATT, Kent, an elephant's head, erased, ar. *Judicium parium aut lex terræ. Pl.* 68, *cr.* 4.

PRATT, Norf., a wolf's head, per pale, ar. and sa. *Pl.* 92, *cr.* 15, (without rose.)

PRATT, Suff., a lizard, vert, (ducally gorged and lined, or.) *Pl.* 93, *cr.* 4, (without tree.)

PRATTE, Eng., a lion's head, erased, vert. *Pl.* 81, *cr.* 4.

PRATT, Leic. and Surr., a demi-unicorn, salient, or, holding a mascle, az. *Pl.* 26, *cr.* 14, (mascle, *pl.* 141.)

PRATT, Norf., a wolf's head, langued and erased, gu., charged with a fess, between two branches, one oak, (the other pine,) fructed, ppr. *Rident florentia prata. Pl.* 14, *cr.* 6, (branches, *pl.* 74, *cr.* 7.)

PRATT, Hunts. and Norf., a wolf's head, per pale, ar. and sa., gorged with a collar, (charged with three roundles,) all counterchanged. *Pl.* 8, *cr.* 4.

PRATT, Marquess Camden. *See* CAMDEN.

PRATTER, a horse's head, charged with a caltrap. *Pl.* 46, *cr.* 4.

PRATTMAN, Durh.: 1. Two lions' gambs, erased, holding a mullet, or. *Pl.* 42, *cr.* 3, (mullet, *pl.* 141.) 2. A demi-lion, rampant, holding a cross (pattée,) fitched, gu. *Labor omnia vincit. Pl.* 65, *cr.* 6.

PREADEAUX, Eng., a cutlass and caduceus, in saltier, and, in chief, Mercury's cap, all ppr. *Pl.* 17, *cr.* 13, (without head.)

PRELATE, Eng., a garb, in fess, ppr. *Pl.* 12, *cr.* 15.

PRENDERGAST, co. Tipperary, a cockatrice, wings expanded, ppr. *Pl.* 63, *cr.* 15.

PRENDERGAST, an antelope's head, couped, ppr., attired, gu. *Pl.* 79, *cr.* 9, (without spear.)

PRENDERGAST, Eng., a man's head, couped at neck, ppr. *Pl.* 81, *cr.* 15.

PRENTICE, Sco., a wolf's head, erased, or. *Pl.* 14, *cr.* 6.

PRENTICE, Eng., an eagle, displayed, in dexter a dagger, in sinister a (pistol.) *Pl.* 99, *cr.* 5.

PRENTIS, Eng., a leopard's face, gu., spotted, or. *Pl.* 66, *cr.* 14.

PRENTYS, Norf., a demi-greyhound, rampant, or, collared, (ringed and lined, sa., line coiled at end.) *Pl.* 5, *cr.* 10.

PRESCOD, out of a ducal coronet, or, a boar's head and neck, ar. *Pl.* 102, *cr.* 14.

PRESCOP, Eng., a horse's head, ar. *Pl.* 81, *cr.* 6.

PRESCOT, or PRESCOTT, Eng., a dexter hand, apaumée, gu. *Pl.* 32, *cr.* 14.

PRESCOT, Linc., out of a ducal coronet, or, a boar's head and neck, ar., bristled, gold. *Pl.* 102, *cr.* 14.

PRESCOTT, Hants, on a mural coronet, a buck, sejant. *Pl.* 101, *cr.* 3.

PRESCOTT, Bart., Herts., a cubit arm, erect, (vested, gu., cuffed, erm., in hand a handbeacon, sa., fired,) ppr. *Pl.* 2, *cr.* 6.

PRESLAND, and PRESTLAND, Eng., a man's head, couped at shoulders, affrontée, sa., ducally crowned, or. *Pl.* 28, *cr.* 3.

PRESSLY, Wilts., Hants, and Lond., a cockatrice, sejant, ppr. *Pl.* 63, *cr.* 15.

PREST, Sheffield, a semi-terrestrial globe, ppr., thereon a demi-pegasus, regardant, erm., semée of mullets, gu., supporting an anchor, erect, sa. *Toujours prest. Pl.* 109, *cr.* 11.

PRESTAGE, Eng., a porcupine, ppr. *Pl.* 55, *cr.* 10.

PRESTLEY, Lond. and Herts., a cockatrice, ar., standing on a broken lance, or, top in mouth, headed, of the first. *Pl.* 63, *cr.* 15, (spear, *pl.* 75, *cr.* 12.)

PRESTON, Sco., out of a ducal coronet, a unicorn's head. *Præsto, ut præstem. Pl.* 45, *cr.* 14.

PRESTON, Sco., a good angel, ppr. *Præsto, ut præstem. Pl.* 25, *cr.* 7.

PRESTON, an angel, affrontée, dexter on breast, (sinister elevated,) ppr., vested, ar. *Præsto, ut præstem. Pl.* 25, *cr.* 7.

PRESTON, Lanc., Cumb., and Westm., over a ruined tower, a falcon, volant, both ar., beaked, legged, and belled, or. *Pl.* 94, *cr.* 1, (tower, *pl.* 118, *cr.* 15.)

PRESTON, out of a marquess's coronet, a unicorn's head, ppr. *Præsto, ut præstem. Pl.* 45, *cr.* 14, (coronet, *pl.* 127, *fig.* 4.)

PRESTON, Iri., on a ducal coronet, per pale, or and gu., a griffin, sejant, gold, resting dexter on a shield, of the last. *Pl.* 42, *cr.* 8.

PRESTON, an arm, in armour, embowed, in hand a dagger, all ppr., hilted, or. *Pl.* 120, *cr.* 11.

PRESTON, Iri. and Lanc., on a chapeau, gu., turned up, erm., a fox, passant, ppr. *Pl.* 126, *cr.* 5, (chapeau, *pl.* 127, *fig.* 13.)

PRESTON, Suff. and Iri., between wings, az., a crescent, or. *Pl.* 31, *cr.* 11, (without etoile.)

PRESTON, Herts. and Beds., out of a mural coronet, or, a demi-fox, rampant, sa., (gorged with a collar, erm.) *Pl.* 30, *cr.* 9, (coronet, same plate, *cr.* 15.)

PRESTON, of West Derby, Lower House, Lanc.: 1. On a (ruined) tower, or, a falcon, wings expanded and elevated, ppr., beaked, legged, and belled, gold. *Pl.* 8, *cr.* 15. 2. On a chapeau, gu., turned up, erm., a wolf, or. *Si Dieu veult. Pl.* 46, *cr.* 6, (chapeau, *pl.* 127, *fig.* 13.)

PRESTON, Devons. and Durh., on a chapeau, gu., turned up, erm., a wolf, or. *Ib.*

PRESTON, Yorks., on a tower, or, a falcon, wings expanded and elevated, ppr., beaked, legged, and belled, gold. *Pl.* 8, *cr.* 15.

PRESTON, Bart., Norf., a crescent, ar. *Pristinum spero lumen. Pl.* 18, *cr.* 14.

PRESTON, Bart., Sco., out of a ducal coronet, a unicorn's head. *Præsto, ut præstem. Pl.* 45, *cr.* 14.

PRESTON, Viscount Gormanston. *See* GORMANSTON.

PRESTWICK, Eng., a leopard's face, jessant-delis, or. *Pl.* 123, *cr.* 9.

PRESTWICK, or PRESTWICH, Eng., a porcupine, ppr. *In te, Domine, speravi. Pl.* 55, *cr.* 10.

PRESTWICK, Eng., a hedgehog, sa. *Pl.* 32, *cr.* 9.

PRESTWOLD, Eng., a demi-lion, rampant, ducally gorged. *Pl.* 87, *cr.* 15.

PRESTWOOD, Devons., a griffin's head, sa., beaked, or, between wings, gold, pellettée. *Pl.* 65, *cr.* 1.

PRETOR, an eagle's head, couped, or, wings, addorsed, sa., (gorged with a collar, ar.) *Pl.* 19, *cr.* 9, (without coronet.)

PRETTYMAN, Suff., two lions' gambs, supporting a mullet, all or. *Pl.* 42, *cr.* 3, (mullet, *pl.* 141.)

PREVOST, Bart., Hants, a demi-lion, rampant, az., charged on shoulder with a mural coronet, or. *Pl.* 67, *cr.* 10, (coronet, *pl.* 128, *fig.* 18.)

PRICE, Iri., a mortar, mounted, ppr. *Pl.* 55, *cr.* 13.

PRICE, Bucks, a leopard's head, or. *Pl.* 92, *cr.* 13.

PRICE, a lion, rampant, sa. *Pl.* 67, *cr.* 5.

PRICE, a demi-griffin, segreant, (collared.) *Pl.* 18, *cr.* 6.

PRICE, a garb, banded, or. *Pl.* 48, *cr.* 10.

PRICE, Iri., a lion's head, erased, or. *Pl.* 81, *cr.* 4.

PRICE, out of a mural coronet, a lion's head. *Pl.* 45, *cr.* 9.

PRICE, Lond., a griffin's head, erased, ar., in beak a thistle, gu., stalked and leaved, vert, between wings, ppr. *Virtus præ numina. Pl.* 65, *cr.* 1, (thistle, *pl.* 68, *cr.* 9.)

PRICE, of Castle Madoc, Wel.: 1. For *Price*, a dragon's head, vert, erased, gu., in mouth a sinister hand, erect, couped at wrist, dropping blood, all ppr. *Pl.* 106, *cr.* 13. 2. For *Powell*, a boar's head, erased, in fess. *Pl.* 16, *cr.* 11.

PRICE, a holy lamb, passant, bearing a banner, charged with a cross. *Pl.* 48, *cr.* 13.

PRICE, Lond., a horse's head, couped, in mouth a spear, ar. *Pl.* 110, *cr.* 6.

PRICE, Surr., on a mural coronet, or, a lion, rampant, regardant, sa., (between paws a fleur-de-lis,) gold. *Pl.* 10, *cr.* 15, (coronet, *pl.* 128, *fig.* 18.)

PRICE, Wel., a lion, rampant, or, holding a rose, gu., stalked and leaved, vert. *Pl.* 64, *cr.* 2, (rose, *pl.* 39, *cr.* 14.)

PRICE, Bart., Heref., a lion, rampant, ar., in dexter a rose, slipped, ppr. *Auxilium meum a Domino. Ib.*

PRICE, Bart., Cornw., a dragon's head, vert, erased, gu., in mouth a sinister hand, erect, couped at wrist, dropping blood, all ppr. *Pl.* 106, *cr.* 13.

PRICE, Bart., Surr., a lion, rampant, ar., in dexter a sprig of roses, ppr. *Vive, ut vivas. Pl.* 64, *cr.* 2, (roses, *pl.* 86, *cr.* 15.)

PRICE, JOHN-BULKELEY, Esq., of Plas Cadnant, Anglesey, a falcon, rising, az. *Na fynno Duw ni fydd. Pl.* 105, *cr.* 4.

PRICE, Birkenhead, a cock, in mouth a (peapod.) *In vigila sic vinces. Pl.* 55, *cr.* 12.

PRICE, Glangwilley, a wolf, (rampant,) ar. *Spes tutissima cœlis. Pl.* 126, *cr.* 13.

PRICHARD, Lanc., a dragon's head, erased, at neck, vert. *Pl.* 107, *cr.* 10, (without collar.)

PRICKETT, Eng., a heart, gu., within a fetterlock, az. *Pl.* 59, *cr.* 6.

PRICKETT, a hind. *Auxilium ab alto. Pl.* 20, *cr.* 14.

PRICKLEY, Lond., (on a chapeau, gu.,) a mural coronet, ar., thereon an arm, in armour, embowed, ppr., vambraced, or, in hand a battle-axe, gold, armed, sa. *Pl.* 115, *cr.* 14. (axe, *pl.* 73, *cr.* 7.)

PRIDDLE, Eng., a demi-lion, or. *Pl.* 67, *cr.* 10.

PRIDEAULX, Eng., a horse's head, erased, per fess, or and gu. *Pl.* 81, *cr.* 6.

PRIDEAUX, Devons., an (eagle,) volant, ar., beaked and legged, gu. *Pl.* 94, *cr.* 1.

PRIDEAUX, Devons. and Cornw., on a chapeau, a Saracen's head, in profile, couped at shoulders, ppr. *Pl.* 81, *cr.* 15, (chapeau, *pl.* 127, *fig.* 13.)

PRIDEAUX, Devons. and Cornw., an old man's head, couped at shoulders, ppr., hair and beard, or (on head a chapeau, gu.,) turned up, ar. *Pl.* 126, *cr.* 8.

PRIDEAUX, Sco. and Eng., a man's head, in profile, couped at shoulders, (on head a chapeau, az., turned up, ar.) *Pl.* 126, *cr.* 8.

PRIDHAM, Eng., a hand, ppr., holding a chapeau, az., turned up, erm., between two branches of laurel, vert, in orle. *Pl.* 59, *cr.* 4.

PRIESE, a unicorn's head, gu., collared, vert. *Pl.* 78, *cr.* 1.

PRIEST, Eng., a martlet, sa. *Pl.* 111, *cr.* 5.

PRIESTLEY, Eng., a demi-lion, sa. *Pl.* 67, *cr.* 10.

PRIESTLEY, Yorks., a cockatrice, ar., standing on lower part of a broken spear, in fess, or, other part in mouth. *Respice finem. Pl.* 63, *cr.* 15, (spear, *pl.* 75, *cr.* 12.)

PRIGION, or PRUJEAN, Eng., a greyhound's head, erased, sa., (gorged with three roses, in fess, between two bars, ar.) *Pl.* 89, *cr.* 2.

PRIME, out of a ducal coronet, or, a lion's gamb, holding a (tilting)-spear, ppr. *Pl.* 120, *cr.* 6.

PRIME, Suss., an owl., ppr, (in mouth a scroll, inscribed, *Nil, invitâ Minervâ*, collared, on collar, two mullets.) *Pl.* 27, *cr.* 9.

PRIMEROSE, Sco., a demi-lion, rampant, ppr., armed and langued, gu. *Primus tametsi virilis. Pl.* 67, *cr.* 10.

PRIMOUT, and PRIMOUTH, Surr., a demi-buck, sa., attired, or. *Pl.* 55, *cr.* 9, (without rose.)

PRIMROSE, Sco., a demi-lion, gu., in dexter a primrose, ppr. *Fide et fiduciâ. Pl.* 39, *cr.* 14.

PRIMROSE, Eng., in dexter hand a sword, in pale, ppr. *Pl.* 23, *cr.* 15.

PRIMROSE, Eng. and Sco., a lion, rampant, gu., in dexter a (primrose,) ppr. *Pl.* 64, *cr.* 2.

PRIMROSE, a demi-lion, gu., in dexter a primrose, or. *Pl.* 39, *cr.* 14.

PRIMROSE, Earl of Roseberry. *See* ROSEBERRY.

PRIN, Eng., out of a ducal coronet, or, a demieagle, volant, sa. *Pl.* 19, *cr.* 9.

PRINCE, Salop, out of a ducal coronet, or, a cubit arm, vested, gu., cuffed, erm., (in hand, ppr., three pine-apples, gold, stalked and leaved, vert.) *Pl.* 89, *cr.* 11.

PRINCEP, an eagle's head, erased, ppr. *Pl.* 20, *cr.* 7.

PRING, Eng., out of a ducal coronet, or, a demieagle, displayed, sa. *Pl.* 9, *cr.* 6.

PRING, Eng., a dagger, in pale, ppr. *Pl.* 73, *cr.* 9.

PRINGLE, Eng. and Sco., an escallop, or. *Amicitia reddit honores. Pl.* 117, *cr.* 4.

PRINGLE, Sco., a serpent, nowed, ppr. *Nosce te ipsum. Pl.* 1, *cr.* 9.

PRINGLE, an escallop, between two palmbranches, in orle. *Spero et progredior. Pl.* 86, *cr.* 9.

PRINGLE, Sco., an escallop, between two branches of palm, in orle. *Prompte et consel. Pl.* 86, *cr.* 9.

PRINGLE, Sco., a man's heart, ppr., winged, or. *Sursum. Pl.* 39, *cr.* 7.

PRINGLE, Sco., an anchor, within a garland of bay-leaves, ppr. *Semper spero meliora. Pl.* 84, *cr.* 11.

PRINGLE, Bart., Sco., a (saltier), within a garland of bay-leaves, ppr. *Coronat fides. Pl.* 84, *cr.* 11.

PRINGLE, ALEXANDER, Esq., of Whytbank, Selkirk, a man's heart, ppr. *Sursum. Pl.* 55, *cr.* 13.

PRINNE, out of a ducal coronet, or, a demi-eagle, displayed, ppr., beaked, sa. *Pl.* 9, *cr.* 6.

PRIOR, Eng., in dexter hand a crosier, ppr. *Pl.* 17, *cr.* 12.

PRIOR, a bird, in beak a slip. *Pl.* 48, *cr.* 15.
PRIOR, an escallop, ar. *Pl.* 117, *cr.* 4.
PRIOR, Iri., a star of eight points, wavy, or. *Pl.* 83, *cr.* 3, (without coronet.)
PRISETT, or PROSSET, Eng., a hand holding a torteau, gu. *Pl.* 24, *cr.* 3, (torteau, *pl.* 141.)
PRITCHARD, Eng., a dexter arm, ppr., in hand a battle-axe, az., handle, gu. *Pl.* 73, *cr.* 7.
PRITCHARD, a horse's head, bridled. *Pl.* 92, *cr.* 1.
PRITCHARD, a goat's head, erased. *Pl.* 29, *cr.* 13.
PRITTIE, Baron Dunalley. *See* DUNALLEY.
PROBERT, Eng., an arm, in armour, embowed, in hand a sword, ppr. *Pl.* 2, *cr.* 8.
PROBY, and PROBYN, Hunts., Chesh., and Salop, an ostrich's head, erased, ar., ducally gorged, or, in mouth a key, gold. *Pl.* 108, *cr.* 2, (key, *pl.* 9, *cr.* 12.)
PROBY, Earl of Carysfort. *See* CARYSFORT.
PROCTOR, Sco., a greyhound, sejant, ppr. *Toujours fidele. Pl.* 66, *cr.* 15.
PROCTOR, Cambs. and Middx., a martlet. *Pl.* 111, *cr.* 5.
PROCTOR, Eng., on a chapeau, ppr., a martlet, or. *Pl.* 89, *cr.* 7.
PROCTOR, Middx. and Lond., on a mount, vert, a greyhound, sejant, ar., spotted, brown, (collared, or.) *Pl.* 5, *cr.* 2.
PROCTOR, Bart., Norf., same crest. *Toujours fidele.*
PRODGERS, in front of a cross Calvary, or, a wyvern, wings addorsed, vert, in mouth a sinister hand, gu., (gorged with a collar and line, reflexed over back,) gold, dexter resting on a cross pattée, of the first. *Devouement sans bornes. Pl.* 61, *cr.* 8, (crosses, *pl.* 141.)
PROMOLI, Liverpool, out of a ducal coronet, a long cross, between two ostrich-feathers. *Nil desperandum. Pl.* 98, *cr.* 6.
PROSSER, Eng., on a mount, a horse, bridled, at full speed, ppr. *Pl.* 57, *cr.* 9.
PROSSER, a wolf's head, erased, in mouth a sword, in bend sinister, point upward, all ppr. *Pl.* 14, *cr.* 6, (sword, *pl.* 28, *cr.* 14.)
PROTHER, Eng., on a tower, sa., a crescent, or. *Pl.* 85, *cr.* 1.
PROTHEROE, a raven, ppr. *Pl.* 123, *cr.* 2.
PROTHERS, Eng., a bird, volant, purp. *Pl.* 87, *cr.* 10.
PROUD, Eng., a buffalo's head, erased, vair. *Pl.* 57, *cr.* 7.
PROUD, Middx. and Salop, a cross formée, fitched, or, (charged with five pellets, a chaplet of laurel, entwined round cross, vert.) *Pl.* 27, *cr.* 14.
PROUDE, Eng., in hand a club. *Pl.* 28, *cr.* 6.
PROUDE, Kent, an otter's head, erased, or, in mouth a fish, ar. *Pl.* 74, *cr.* 13.
PROUDFOOT, Iri., an arm, in armour, embowed, in hand an arrow, all ppr. *Pl.* 96, *cr.* 6.
PROUSE, Eng., a demi-lion, or. *Pl.* 67, *cr.* 10.
PROUT, Middx., issuant from grass, ppr., a lion, rampant, gardant, ar., collared and ringed, or, supporting between paws a lighted taper, ppr.
PROUZE, Devons., an ibex, sejant, or, armed, tufted, and maned, ar. *Pl.* 93, *cr.* 11, (without coronet.)
PROVAN, Sco., a plough, ppr. *Pl.* 28, *cr.* 15.
PROVAN, Sco., same crest. *Pro patriâ.*
PROVEN, Sco., an arm, from shoulder, couped, in fess, in hand a cross crosslet, fitched, gu., vested, az., cuffed, or. *Pl.* 88, *cr.* 7.

PROVENDER, Wilts., a squirrel, (current), quarterly, or and gu. (Another, or and sa.) *Pl.* 85, *cr.* 3.
PROVIS, Eng., on a rock, a wild duck, ppr. *Pl.* 94, *cr.* 3.
PROVOST, Eng., a buckle, or. *Pl.* 73, *cr.* 10.
PROWSE, Eng., the golden fleece, ppr. *Pl.* 77, *cr.* 12.
PROWSE, Somers., an ibex's head, erased, sa., eared, or, armed, (collared, and lined, gold.) *Pl.* 73, *cr.* 9.
PROWZE, a dexter hand throwing a dart. *Pl.* 42, *cr.* 13.
PROWZE, Glouc., Somers., and Devons., out of a ducal coronet, ar., a demi-lion, rampant, gardant, of the first, (collared and ringed, or.) *Pl.* 35, *cr.* 4, (coronet, *pl.* 34, *cr.* 15.)
PRUDHOE, Baron, (Percy,) on a chapeau, gu., turned up, erm., a lion, (statant,) az., tail extended. *Espérance en Dieu. Pl.* 118, *cr.* 10, (chapeau, *pl.* 127, *fig.* 13.)
PRUDHOME, and PRIDHAM, Devons., a lion's paw, erased, ppr. *Pl.* 126, *cr.* 9.
PRUDOW, a lion's paw. *Pl.* 126, *cr.* 9.
PRUEN, Glouc., a demi-eagle, displayed, sa., (charged on breast with a fess, ar., thereon three crosses pattée, gu., in beak a sprig of olive, ppr.) *Pl.* 22, *cr.* 11.
PRYCE, Cambs., a lion, rampant, regardant, in dexter a trefoil. *Pl.* 10, *cr.* 15, (trefoil, *pl.* 11, *cr.* 12.)
PRYCE, Wel., a lion, rampant, regardant, or. *Pl.* 10, *cr.* 15, (without brand.)
PRYCE, Herts., a cock, gu., combed, wattled, and legged, or, (in beak a violet, az., stalked and leaved, vert.) *Pl.* 55, *cr.* 12.
PRYDEUX, Eng., a dexter cubit arm, ppr., in hand a billet, (in pale,) az. *Pl.* 28, *cr.* 8.
PRYDEUX, Devons., a dove, volant, ar., membered and beaked, gu. *Pl.* 25, *cr.* 6.
PRYER, or PRYOR, Eng., an escallop, ar. *Pl.* 117, *cr.* 4.
PRYNNE, Eng., in a coronet, or, an eagle, displayed, ppr., beaked, sa. *Pl.* 9, *cr.* 6, (eagle, *pl.* 48, *cr.* 11.)
PRYSE, Wel. and Berks., a lion, rampant, regardant, sa., in paws a fleur-de-lis, ar. *Duw au bendithis. Pl.* 10, *cr.* 15, (fleur-de-lis, *pl.* 141.)
PRYTHERCH, Wel., a stag's head, cabossed, between attires an imperial crown, ppr. *Duw a digon. Pl.* 36, *cr.* 1, (crown, *pl.* 127, *cr.* 2.)
PUCKERING, Herts. and Warw., a buck, (rampant.) *Pl.* 65, *cr.* 14.
PUCKERING, Herts. and Warw., a buck, current, or. *Pl.* 3, *cr.* 2.
PUCKLE, Eng., a cubit arm, erect, in hand a spear, in bend. *Pl.* 99, *cr.* 8.
PUCKLE, Graffham, Hunts., a dexter hand, open, in palm an heraldic rose, both ppr. *Pl.* 32, *cr.* 14, (rose, *pl.* 141.)
PUDDESEY, Yorks., a leopard, passant, ppr. *Pl.* 86, *cr.* 2.
PUDDESEY, Yorks., a cat, (passant,) ppr. *Pl.* 119, *cr.* 7.
PUDSEY, Warw., Yorks., Oxon., Lanc., Staffs., and Beds., a cat, (passant,) ppr. *Pl.* 119, *cr.* 7.
PUDSEY, Beds., Yorks., Oxon., Lanc., and Staffs., a leopard, passant, ppr. *Pl.* 86, *cr.* 2.
PUDSEY, DE, Eng., an eagle's head, in beak an acorn, stalked and leaved. *Pl.* 22, *cr.* 1.

PUELESDON, or PULLESTON, Chesh. and Wel., a buck, trippant, ppr., attired, or. *Pl.* 68, *cr.* 2.
PUGET, Eng., a dove, holding an olive-branch, flying over the sea, ppr. *Pl.* 46, *cr.* 13.
PUGGES, Eng., a dexter hand, ppr., holding up a covered cup, or. *Pl.* 35, *cr.* 9.
PUGH, Eng., a cross moline, lozenge pierced, erm. *Pl.* 91, *cr.* 10.
PUGH, a lion, rampant, ar., holding a fleur-de-lis, gu. *Pl.* 87, *cr.* 6.
PUGH, a dolphin, naiant, ppr. *Pl.* 48, *cr.* 9.
PUGH, a lion, passant, gardant, sa. *Pl.* 120, *cr.* 5.
PUGHE, Wel., a lion's head, erased, in mouth a trefoil, slipped, ppr. *Nid meddyg ond meddyg cniad. Pl.* 95, *cr.* 6, (trefoil, *pl.* 11, *cr.* 12.)
PUJOLAS, Middx., a hind, (at gaze,) ppr., about neck a bugle-horn, or, string, gu. *Pl.* 106, *cr.* 10, (horn, *pl.* 98, *cr.* 2.)
PUKRING, Bart., Eng., a buck, salient. *Pl.* 65, *cr.* 14.
PULESDON, Chesh., Salop, and Wel., a stag, trippant, ppr. *Pl.* 68, *cr.* 2.
PULESTON, Wel., a stag, trippant, ppr. *Pl.* 68, *cr.* 2.
PULESTON, Bart., Wel.: 1. An oak-tree, ppr., pendent therefrom by a band, az., an escutcheon, gu., charged with three ostrich-feathers. *Pl.* 75, *cr.* 2, (feathers, *pl.* 12, *cr.* 9.) 2. On a chapeau, turned up, erm., a buck, (statant,) ppr., attired, or. *Clariores e tenebris. Pl.* 63, *cr.* 8.
PULLEINE, JAMES, Esq., of Crake Hall, Yorks., a pelican, feeding her young. *Nullâ pallescere culpâ. Pl.* 44, *cr.* 1.
PULLEN, or PULLEYN, Yorks., a pelican, in nest, all or. *Pl.* 44, *cr.* 1.
PULLER, Eng., in dexter hand a trident, in bend. *Pl.* 12, *cr.* 3.
PULLER, on a chapeau, gu., turned up, erm., a dove, in mouth a laurel-branch, both ppr. *Pl.* 109, *cr.* 10, (branch, *pl.* 29, *cr.* 15.)
PULLEY, Eng., a palm-tree, vert. *Pl.* 18, *cr.* 12.
PULLEYN, or PULLEN, Yorks., a pelican, in nest, all ppr. *Pl.* 44, *cr.* 1.
PULLING, a demi-eagle, displayed, gu., charged on each wing with a cross pattée, fitched, or, and on breast with a mill-rind, gold. *Pl.* 22, *cr.* 11, (cross and mill-rind, *pl.* 141.)
PULTENEY, Eng., a leopard's head, erased, sa., gorged with a ducal coronet, or. *Pl.* 116, *cr.* 8.
PULTENEY, Eng., a lion's head, erased, sa. *Pl.* 81, *cr.* 4.
PULTNEY, a leopard's head, gardant, erased. *Pl.* 56, *cr.* 7.
PULTS, an eagle's head, erased, ar., beaked, or, holding a trefoil, vert. *Pl.* 22, *cr.* 1, (trefoil, *pl.* 141.)
PUNCHARDON, Eng., a unicorn's head, erased, gu., bezantée and armed, or. *Pl.* 67, *cr.* 1.
PUNSHON, Northumb., a lion, passant, erm., (charged with a pallet, wavy, az.,) between two oval buckles, or, tongues pointing upward. *Pl.* 48, *cr.* 8, (buckle, *pl.* 73, *cr.* 10.)
PURCELL, Salop, a boar's head, erased, in fess, ar. *Pl.* 16, *cr.* 11.
PURCELL, Salop, out of a ducal coronet, or, a boar's head, ar., guttée-de-sang. *Pl.* 102, *cr.* 14.

PURCELL, Iri., in hand, couped above wrist, erect, (sleeve, az., turned up, ar.,) a sword, ppr., hilt and pommel, or, pierced through the jaw of a boar's head, couped, sa., vulned, dropping blood. *Pl.* 71, *cr.* 9.
PURCHAS, Eng., a dexter hand, ppr., holding up a cushion, sa., tasselled, or. *Pl.* 83, *cr.* 9.
PURCHAS, a demi-lion, sa., supporting a bezant. *Pl.* 126, *cr.* 12.
PURCHON, Yorks., in front of a demi-woman, vested, az., (mantle, gu., flowing over left shoulder, in dexter a palm-branch,) ppr., two anchors, in saltier, or. *Prudentia et vigilantia. Pl.* 20, *cr.* 6, (anchors, *pl.* 37, *cr.* 12.)
PURDIE, or PURDY, Eng., a peacock's head, erased, gu. *Pl.* 86, *cr.* 4.
PURDIE, Sco., a dexter hand holding a roll of parchment, ppr. *Fidelitas. Pl.* 27, *cr.* 4.
PURDON, Cumb., a dexter arm, in armour, in hand, ppr., a banner, gu., fringed, or, (charged with a leopard's face, ar., staff broken.) *Pl.* 6, *cr.* 5.
PUREFEY, Eng., a demi-talbot, rampant, sa., ducally gorged, or. *Pl.* 15, *cr.* 2.
PUREFOY, and PUREFEROY, Eng., in dexter hand a garland of flowers, ppr. *Pl.* 41, *cr.* 7.
PUREFOY, Leic., in dexter gauntlet, or, inside, az., a broken tilting-spear, of the second. *Pl.* 23, *cr.* 9.
PUREFOY-BAGWELL, EDWARD, Esq., of Greenfield, co. Tipperary, in hand, in armour, a broken lance, all ppr. *En bonne foy. Pl.* 23, *cr.* 9.
PURFIELD, Eng., on a ducal coronet, sa., a martlet, ar. *Pl.* 98, *cr.* 14.
PURKIS, Eng., out of a ducal coronet, or, a greyhound's head, ppr. *Pl.* 70, *cr.* 5.
PURLAND, Norf., a demi-eagle, wings displayed. *Pl.* 52, *cr.* 8.
PURLING, Eng., in dexter hand a grenade, fired. *Pl.* 2, *cr.* 6.
PURLING, out of a mural coronet, sa., an ostrich's head and neck, ppr. *Pl.* 50, *cr.* 1, (coronet, *pl.* 128, *fig.* 18.)
PURLING, a lion, sejant, or, crowned with an Eastern coronet, resting dexter on an anchor, sa. *Pl.* 109, *cr.* 7, (anchor, *pl.* 19, *cr.* 6; crown, *pl.* 66, *cr.* 13.)
PURLING, Lond., a lion, sejant, or, crowned with a naval coronet, ar., between paws an anchor, sa. *Pl.* 60, *cr.* 4, (coronet, *pl.* 128, *fig.* 19; anchor, *pl.* 19, *cr.* 6.)
PURNELL, Glouc., out of a mural coronet, ar., (another, or,) a demi-griffin, segreant, erminois, in dexter a thunder-bolt, ppr. *Pl.* 39, *cr.* 2, (coronet, *pl.* 128, *fig.* 18; thunderbolt, *pl.* 110, *cr.* 3.)
PURNELL, King's Hill, out of a mural coronet, ar., (charged with three lozenges, in fess,) gu., a demi-falcon, rising, ppr., in beak a cinquefoil, slipped, vert. *Pl.* 103, *cr.* 6, (coronet, *same plate, cr.* 11; cinquefoil, *pl.* 141.)
PURRIER, a dolphin, naiant, sa., under a peartree, ppr., fructed, or. *Pl.* 48, *cr.* 9, (tree, *pl.* 105, *cr.* 13.)
PURSE, Eng., a demi-bull, per fess, or and gu. *Pl.* 63, *cr.* 6.
PURSER, Eng., a fox's head, erased, or. *Pl.* 71, *cr.* 4.
PURSLOW, Salop, a hare, sejant, erm. *Pl.* 70, *cr.* 1.

PURTON, Eng., an eagle, displayed, gu. *Pl.* 48, *cr.* 11.

PURTON, Salop, (on a mount, vert,) a pear-tree, fructed, ppr. *Pl.* 105, *cr.* 13.

PURVIS, Sco., the sun issuing from a cloud, ppr. *Clarior e tenebris. Pl.* 67, *cr.* 9.

PURVIS, Lieut-Col. CHARLES, of Dursham, Suff., same crest and motto.

PURVIS, Sco., the sun issuing from a cloud, ppr. *Post nubila Phœbus. Pl.* 67, *cr.* 9.

PURY, Eng., on a ducal coronet, or, a martlet, gu. *Pl.* 98, *cr.* 14.

PUSEY, SIDNEY-EDWARD-BOUVERIE, of Pusey, Berks., a cat, (passant,) ar. *Pl.* 119, *cr.* 7.

PUSEY, Eng., a leopard, passant, ppr. *Pl.* 86, *cr.* 2.

PUT, a demi-lion, rampant, ar., holding a mascle, sa. *Pl.* 39, *cr.* 14, (mascle, *pl.* 141.)

PUTTINGER, on stump of tree, couped at top, and sprouting a fresh branch on either side, a stag's head, cabossed, ppr. *Pl.* 36, *cr.* 1, (stump, *pl.* 30, *cr.* 5.)

PUTLAND, an elephant's head, sa. *Pl.* 35, *cr.* 13.

PUTNAM, Bucks. and Beds., a wolf's head, gu. *Pl.* 92, *cr.* 15, (without rose.)

PUTT, Eng., out of a mural coronet, a leopard's head, ducally gorged, all ppr. *Pl.* 46, *cr.* 11.

PUTTEMAN, two bears' gambs, erased and erect, supporting a caltrap, ar. *Pl.* 42, *cr.* 3, (caltrap, *pl.* 141.)

PUTTENHAM, Bucks., Beds., and Hants, a wolf's head, gu. *Pl.* 14, *cr.* 6.

PUXTY, Yorks, a pelican's head, vulning, ppr. *Pl.* 41, *cr.* 4.

PYBUS, Herts, an elephant, (carrying on trunk some sugar-canes,) all ppr. *Pl.* 56, *cr.* 14.

PYCHARD, and PYCHOW, Eng., in hand a club, (in pale,) ppr. *Pl.* 28, *cr.* 6.

PYCOMBE, an arm, in armour, embowed, in hand a scythe, in bend sinister. *Pl.* 120, *cr.* 11, (scythe, *pl.* 106, *cr.* 2.)

PYCROFT, Eng., a hand, couped, in fess, apaumée, charged with an eye, ppr., lying on the wreath. *Pl.* 10, *cr.* 14.

PYE, Berks., Northamp., and Worc., a cross crosslet, fitched, gu., between wings, ar. *In cruce glorior. Pl.* 34, *cr.* 14.

PYE, HENRY-JOHN, Esq., of Clifton Hall, Staffs.; and Pinner, Middx., same crest and motto.

PYE, Devons., on a mount, vert, a talbot's head, couped, ar., (charged with a saltier, wavy, az. *Pietatis causâ. Pl.* 123, *cr.* 15, (mount, *pl.* 98, *cr.* 13.)

PYE, Lond., a demi-lion, rampant, az., gorged with a ducal coronet, or, holding an escallop, gold. *Pl.* 87, *cr.* 15, (escallop, *pl.* 141.)

PYE, Middx., a cross crosslet, fitched, between wings, gu. *Pl.* 34, *cr.* 14.

PYGOTT, Beds., a cubit arm, vested, bendy of six, ar. and vert, in hand, ppr., a pick-axe, of the first. *Pl.* 113, *cr.* 10, (vesting, *pl.* 95, *cr.* 7.)

PYKE, Eng., a boar, passant, ar., gorged with a garland of (laurel,) vert. *Pl.* 29, *cr.* 10.

PYKE, a lamb, couchant, ppr.

PYKIN, Eng., a savage's head, couped, sa. *Pl.* 19, *cr.* 1.

PYLBOROW, an eagle's head, erased, (bendy of six, ar. and az., five bezants thereon,) in beak a branch of three roses, gu., leaved, ppr. *Pl.* 22, *cr.* 1, (roses, *pl.* 23, *cr.* 2.)

PYM, Eng., a lion's gamb, holding up a human heart, ppr. *Pl.* 23, *cr.* 13.

PYM, Heref., a lamb's head and neck, erased, ppr., in mouth a sprig, or.

PYNCOMBE, Devons., an arm, in armour, embowed, ppr., purfled, in hand, of the first, a Polish mace, ar., fastened to arm with a scarf, gu. *Pl.* 28, *cr.* 2.

PYNDAR, Worc., a lion's head, erased, erminois, crowned, ar. *Pl.* 90, *cr.* 4, (without charging.)

PYNDE, in lion's gamb, erased, ar., three (pines, or, fructed,) vert. *Pl.* 86, *cr.* 15.

PYNE, Eng., a demi-pegasus, rampant, enfiled round body with a ducal coronet. *Pl.* 91, *cr.* 2.

PYNE, Bucks., Devons., Cornw., Somers., and Dors., a pine-branch, with three pine-apples, or, leaved, vert.

PYNE, Eng., a pine-tree, ppr. *Pl.* 26, *cr.* 10.

PYNE, a goat's head, couped, ppr. *Pl.* 105, *cr.* 14.

PYNE, Somers., an antelope's head, or, horned and maned, sa. *Pl.* 79, *cr.* 9, (without spear.)

PYNELL, Eng., a demi-eagle, with two heads, displayed, gu., winged, or. *Pl.* 7, *cr.* 8, (without flame.)

PYNSON, Eng., on a chapeau, az., turned up, or, an eagle, wings (expanded,) ppr. *Pl.* 114, *cr.* 13.

PYNSON, three leaves, or, issuing from an etoile of sixteeen points, gu.

PYOT, Lond., a demi-lion, gu., on shoulders three bezants, two and one. *Pl.* 67, *cr.* 10, (bezant, *pl.* 141.)

PYRKE, Eng., in hand a sickle. *Pl.* 36, *cr.* 12.

PYRRY, Eng., a hind's head. *Pl.* 21, *cr.* 9.

PYRRY, Wilts., a stag's head, erased, ar., attired, or, (in mouth a pear-branch, vert, fructed, gold.) *Pl.* 66, *cr.* 9.

PYRTON, Eng., on a chapeau, gu., turned up, erm., a wyvern, vert. *Pl.* 104, *cr.* 5, (without crown.)

PYRTON, a wyvern, wings (expanded,) vert. *Pl.* 63, *cr.* 13.

PYRTON, Ess., on a chapeau, ar., turned up, erm., a wyvern, wings (expanded,) vert. *Pl.* 104, *cr.* 5, (without crown.)

PYSCENT, a wing, erect, ppr., (surmounted by an escutcheon, charged with three mullets, ar., two in chief, one in base, parted by a cheveron, engrailed, az.) *Pl.* 38, *cr.* 10.

PYTTS, of Kyre, Eng., within a chaplet, a dove. *Pl.* 2, *cr.* 11.

PYTTS, a dove, wings elevated, between two laurel-branches, in orle, ppr. *Pl.* 2, *cr.* 11, (dove, *pl.* 124, *cr.* 7.)

Q

QUADERING, Linc., a blackamoor's head. *Pl.* 120, *cr.* 3.

QUADRING, Linc., a moor's head, affrontée, ppr., couped below shoulders, wreathed about head, ar. and gu. *Pl.* 97, *cr.* 2.

QUANTOCK, out of the battlements of a tower, gu., charged with two annulets, or, a demi-eagle, with two heads, wings, per pale, erminois and erm. *Non immemor beneficii.* *Pl.* 12, *cr.* 5, (eagle, *pl.* 7, *cr.* 8; annulet, *pl.* 141.)

QUAPLOD, Eng., a boar, passant, ppr. *Pl.* 48, *cr.* 14.

QUAPLOD, on a mount, vert, a boar, passant, ppr. *Pl.* 48, *cr.* 14, (mount, *pl.* 108, *cr.* 9.)

QUARLES, Ess. and Beds., out of a ducal coronet, or, a demi-eagle, displayed, vert. *Pl.* 9, *cr.* 6.

QUARTON, a hand, ppr., in a maunch, ar. *Pl.* 8, *cr.* 11.

QUASH, Devons., a demi-griffin, or, wings addorsed, sa., legged, of the last, supporting a fleur-de-lis, gold. *Pl.* 44, *cr.* 3, (fleur-de-lis, *pl.* 141.)

QUATERMAYNE, Eng., in hand a sickle, ppr. *Pl.* 36, *cr.* 12.

QUATHERINE, Eng., a ship in full sail, ppr., flagged, gu. *Ad littora tendit.* *Pl.* 109, *cr.* 8.

QUEADE, Eng., an arm, embowed, in hand a dagger, ppr. *Pl.* 34, *cr.* 7.

QUEENSBERRY, Marquess and Earl of, Viscount Drumlanrig, and Lord Douglas, Sco., and a Bart., N.S., (Douglas,) a human heart, gu., ensigned with an imperial crown, between wings, or. *Forward.* *Pl.* 52, *cr.* 2.

QUELCH, Berks, an elephant's head, erased, az., (charged with a castle, ar., fired,) ppr. *Pl.* 68, *cr.* 4.

QUELCH, Eng., a stag's head, at gaze, erased, ppr. *Pl.* 8, *cr.* 6.

QUERLETON, or QUERLTON, Eng., an acorn, stalked and leaved, ppr. *Pl.* 81, *cr.* 7.

QUERONALLE, Eng., a dagger and (sword,) in saltier, ppr. *Pl.* 24, *cr.* 2.

QUESTED, Eng., out of a mural coronet, a garb, thereon a blackbird, ppr. *Pl.* 14, *cr.* 5.

QUICK, Bucks., Somers., and Devons., a demi-antelope, ar., armed, attired, tufted, and maned, gu., collared, sa., lined, or. *Pl.* 34, *cr.* 8.

QUICKE, Devons., a tent, ar., flag, gu. *Pl.* 111, *cr.* 14.

QUILTER, Kent, an armed arm, embowed, in hand a battle-axe, all ppr., a scarf round wrist, ar. *Pl.* 121, *cr.* 14.

QUIN, Iri., a wolf's head, erased, ar. *Quo sursum volo videre.* *Pl.* 14, *cr.* 6.

QUIN, Eng., an arm, in armour, embowed, in hand a sword, ppr. *Pl.* 2, *cr.* 8.

QUIN, Sco., a pheon, reversed, ppr. *Pl.* 56, *cr.* 15.

QUIN-WYNDHAM, Earl of Dunraven. *See* DUNRAVEN.

QUINEY, Staffs., a cubit arm, erect, (vested, or, with three slashes in sleeve,) in hand, ppr., a scimitar, hilted, gold, blade embrued. *Pl.* 29, *cr.* 8.

QUINTIN, Eng., out of a ducal coronet, or, a lion's paw, sa., holding a cross crosslet, fitched, or. *Pl.* 65, *cr.* 5.

QUINTON, Eng., an arm, in armour, couped, embowed, in hand a sword, ppr. *Pl.* 2, *cr.* 8.

QURRELL, Eng., a wolf, current, ppr. *Pl.* 111, *cr.* 1.

QUYXLEY, Eng., an antelope's head, erased, gu. *Pl.* 24, *cr.* 7.

QYRE, Lond., an ass's head, ar., (gorged with a chaplet, vert.) *Pl.* 91, *cr.* 7.

R

RABAN, on a mural coronet, or, charged with three fire-balls, sa., a boar's head, erased, in fess, of the last, in mouth a sword, in pale, ppr. *Pl.* 6, *cr.* 2.

RABETT, a demi-rabbit, rampant, sa., guttée-d'or. *Superabit omnia virtus.* *Pl.* 58, *cr.* 14.

RABY, Eng., a greyhound's head, erased, in mouth a stag's foot, erased. *Pl.* 66, *cr.* 7.

RACKHAM, Eng., a lion's head, erased, ar. *Pl.* 81, *cr.* 4.

RACKHAM, a griffin's head, erased, ducally gorged. *Pl.* 42, *cr.* 9, (without branch.)

RADBORNE, Eng., a horse's head, between wings, ar. *Pl.* 19, *cr.* 13.

RADCLIFF, Eng., a bull's head, erased, sa., attired, ar., points, or, ducally gorged, of the second, (lined and ringed, gold.) *Pl.* 68, *cr.* 6.

RADCLIFF, a bull's head, erased, gu., gorged with a ducal coronet, or. *Pl.* 68, *cr.* 6.

RADCLIFF, Durh., Northumb., Warw., and Beds., on a ducal coronet, or, a bull's head, erased, sa., horned, gold. *Pl.* 68, *cr.* 6.

RADCLIFF, a dragon, (sans legs and wings,) az. *Pl.* 90, *cr.* 10.

RADCLIFF, Lanc., in a mural coronet, ar., a bull's head, sa., armed and crined, or. *Pl.* 120, *cr.* 7. (coronet, *same plate, cr.* 14.)

RADCLIFF, Devons., on a mural coronet, a bull's head. *Cœteris major qui melior.* *Pl.* 120, *cr.* 7, (coronet, *same plate, cr.* 14.)

RADCLIFF-DELME, FREDERICK-PETER, Esq., of Hitchin Priory, Herts., a bull's head, sa., armed and gorged with a ducal coronet, or, in mouth a cross crosslet, fitched. *Pl.* 6, *cr.* 3.

RADCLIFFE, Lanc., Derbs., and Northumb., a bull's head, erased, sa., armed, ar., ducally gorged and (lined,) or. *Pl.* 68, *cr.* 6.

RADCLIFFE, Devons., a battle-axe, erect, ppr. *Pl.* 14, *cr.* 8.

RADCLIFFE, Bart., Yorks., a bull's head, erased, sa., horns, ar., tipped, or, gorged with a ducal coronet, of the second, and charged with a crescent. *Virtus propter se.* *Pl.* 68, *cr.* 6, (crescent, *pl.* 141.)

RADCLYFFE, out of a ducal coronet, or, a bull's head, sa. *Pl.* 68, *cr.* 6.

RADFORD, Iri., an arm, in armour, embowed, holding a dagger, ppr. *Pl.* 120, *cr.* 11.

RADFORD, Eng., an escutcheon, per pale, ar. and sa., between two laurel-branches, in orle, vert. *Pl.* 14, *cr.* 7.

RADFORD, Derbs., a bird, in beak an ear of wheat, ppr. *Pl.* 112, *cr.* 10, (without garb.)

RADLEY, Eng., a phœnix, in flames, ppr. *Pl.* 44, *cr.* 8.

RADNOR, Eng., a cross crosslet, fitched, az. *Pl.* 16, *cr.* 10.

RADNOR, Earl of, Viscount Folkestone, Baron Longford and Pleydell-Bouverie, and a Bart., (Bouverie,) a demi-eagle, with two heads, displayed, sa., (ducally gorged, or,) charged on breast with a cross crosslet, ar. *Patria cara, carior libertas.* *Pl.* 4, *cr.* 6, (cross, *pl.* 141.)

RADSTOCK, Baron, Iri., (Waldegrave,) out of a ducal coronet, or, five ostrich-feathers, per pale, ar. and gu., a crescent for difference. *St Vincent.* *Pl.* 100, *cr.* 12.

RAE, Eng., a lion's paw, ppr. *Pl.* 126, *cr.* 9.

RAE, Eng., a mountain-cat, current, gardant, ppr. *Pl.* 119, *cr.* 7.

RAE, Sco., a hand holding an open book. *Hinc laus et honos.* *Pl.* 126 A, *cr.* 9.

RAE, Sco., a stag, at gaze. *In omnia promptus.* *Pl.* 81, *cr.* 8.

RAE, Sco., a stag, at gaze, ppr. *Ever ready.* *Pl.* 81, *cr.* 8.

RAE, a buck, at gaze, ppr. *Pl.* 21, *cr.* 8.

RAE, Bart., Sco., a stag, statant, ppr. *Pl.* 88, *cr.* 9, (without arrow.)

RAEBURN, Sco., a pheon, az. *Pl.* 26, *cr.* 12.

RAEBURN, Sco., a hand, issuing, holding a club, ppr. *Tutus, si fortis.* *Pl.* 28, *cr.* 6.

RAFFLES, Lanc., out of an Eastern coronet, or, a griffin's head, purp., beaked and gorged with a (collar, gemelle,) gold. *Pl.* 181, *cr.* 6, (coronet, *pl.* 57, *cr.* 5.)

RAGLAN, Baron, Somers., a portcullis, or, nailed, az., chains pendent, gold. *Mutare vel timere sperno.* *Pl.* 51, *cr.* 12.

RAGON, Eng., a hind's head, erased, ar. *Pl.* 6, *cr.* 1.

RAGOUT, a leopard, passant, gorged with a ducal coronet, (and chained, the chain reflexed over back.) *Pl.* 120, *cr.* 9.

RAIKES, Eng., a stag's head, erased, or. *Pl.* 66, *cr.* 9.

RAIKES, Yorks., a griffin's head. *Honestum præferro utili.* *Pl.* 38, *cr.* 3.

RAIKES, Lond. and Herts., a griffin's head, erased, sa. *Pl.* 48, *cr.* 6.

RAILTON, Eng., a hind's head, ppr. *Pl.* 21, *cr.* 9.

RAIN, or RAINE, Eng., a leg, erased at middle of thigh, ppr. *Pl.* 73, *cr.* 5.

RAINES, Yorks., a lion, rampant. *Judicium parium.* *Pl.* 67, *cr.* 5.

RAINES, WILLIAM, Esq., of Wyton, Yorks., out of a ducal coronet, or, two rows of ostrich-feathers, ppr. *Vici.* *Pl.* 64, *cr.* 5.

RAINS, Eng., a dexter hand, brandishing a sword, ppr. *Pl.* 21, *cr.* 10.

RAINSFORD, a reindeer's head, erased, ppr. *Pl.* 60, *cr.* 3, (without coronet.)

RAISON, Eng., a boar's head, erased and erect, sa. *Pl.* 21, *cr.* 7.

RAIT, Sco., an anchor, ppr. *Spero meliora.* *Pl.* 25, *cr.* 15.

RAIT, Sco., a lily, ppr. *Sperandum.* *Pl.* 81, *cr.* 9.

RAIT, Sco., an anchor, ppr., ensigned on top with a crescent, ar. *Meliora spero sequorque.* *Pl.* 62, *cr.* 15, (crescent, *pl.* 141.)

RAIT, JAMES, Esq., of Anniston House, Forfars., an anchor, ppr. *Spero meliora.* *Pl.* 25, *cr.* 15.

RAITT, Eng., a dolphin, naiant, or. *Pl.* 48, *cr.* 9.

RAKE, Eng., an arm, in armour, embowed, brandishing a club, all ppr., at shoulder a beau of ribbons gu. *Pl.* 45, *cr.* 10.

RALEGH, Eng., a boar's head, couped and erect. *Pl.* 21, *cr.* 7.

RALEIGH, Devons., a roe-buck, ppr. *Pl.* 68, *cr.* 2.

RALEIGH, Warw., a boar's head, erect, gu. *Pl.* 21, *cr.* 7.

RALEY, a lion, rampant, ppr. *Pl.* 67, *cr.* 5.

RALPH, Eng., a naked arm, in hand, a book, expanded, both ppr. *Fideliter.* *Pl.* 126 A, *cr.* 9.

RALPH, a griffin's head, couped, or, in beak a serpent, entwined round neck, ppr. *Pl.* 5, *cr.* 7.

RALPHSTON, Iri., a griffin's head, erased, gu., ducally gorged, or. *Pl.* 42, *cr.* 9, (without branch.)

RALSTON, Sco., a falcon, looking (at the sun.) *Fide et Marte.* *Pl.* 126 D, *cr.* 12.

RALSTON, Sco., a hawk, regardant, ppr. *Fide et Marte.* *Pl.* 42, *cr.* 7, (without garland.)

RALSTON, Sco., a falcon, ppr. *Fide et Marte.* *Pl.* 67, *cr.* 3.

RAM, Eng., on a chapeau, or, turned up, gu., a fox, sejant, ppr. *Pl.* 57, *cr.* 14.

RAM, Ess. and Iri., a ram's head, erased, ar., armed, or, (charged with a cheveron, az.) *Pl.* 1, *cr.* 12.

RAMADGE, Lond., a unicorn's head, erased, ar., armed and crined, or. *Consilio et animis.* *Pl.* 67, *cr.* 1.

RAMAGE, Sco., an increscent, ar. *Poco a poco.* *Pl.* 122, *cr.* 15.

RAMPSTON, Eng., a caltrap, embrued, ppr. *Pl.* 7, *cr.* 4.

RAMSAY, Iri., a beech-tree, ppr. *Pl.* 100, *cr.* 14.

RAMSAY, Sco., a unicorn's head, couped, ar., horned and maned, or. *Nil temere.* *Pl.* 20, *cr.* 1.

RAMSAY, Earl of Dalhousie. *See* DALHOUSIE.

RAMSAY, Sco., a unicorn's head, couped, ar., armed, or, within two branches of laurel, in orle, ppr. *Pl.* 54, *cr.* 9.

RAMSAY, an eagle, rising, regardant, sa., armed and membered, or. *Migro et respicio.* *Pl.* 35, *cr.* 8.

RAMSAY, Sco., a unicorn's head, couped, ppr., armed, or, and charged with a crescent, ar. *Dum varior.* *Pl.* 20, *cr.* 1, (crescent, *pl.* 141.)

RAMSAY, CHARLES-WILLIAM-RAMSAY, Esq., of Barnton House, Mid-Lothian; and Sauchie, Stirling, a unicorn's head, couped, ar., armed and maned, or. *Ora et labora.* *Pl.* 20, *cr.* 1.

RAMSAY, a star of six rays, issuing from a crescent, ar. *Superiora sequor.* Pl. 111, cr. 15.
RAMSAY, Sco., a unicorn's head, couped, ar., horned and maned, or. *Spernit pericula virtus.* Pl. 20, cr. 1.
RAMSAY, Bart., Sco., a unicorn's head, couped, ar., charged with a cinquefoil, gu. *Semper victor.* Pl. 20, cr. 1, (cinquefoil, pl. 141.)
RAMSAY, Bart., a demi-eagle, displayed, sa. *Aspiro.* Pl. 22, cr. 11.
RAMSAY, Bart., an eagle, displayed, sa. *Probando et approbando.* Pl. 48, cr. 11.
RAMSAY, Sco., a horse's head, ar., maned, or. *Avance.* Pl. 81, cr. 6.
RAMSAY, GEORGE-ANTOINE, Esq., of Hill Lodge, Enfield, Middx., a unicorn's head, couped, ar., horned, maned, and tufted, or. *Ora et labora.* Pl. 20, cr. 1.
RAMSAY, Eng., a parrot, vert, breast, gu., in beak an annulet, or. Pl. 33, cr. 11.
RAMSAY, Sco., a griffin's head, couped, ppr. *Ora et labora.* Pl. 38, cr. 3.
RAMSAY, Sco., a unicorn's head, erased, ar., charged with a rose, gu. *Semper victor.* Pl. 67, cr. 1, (rose, pl. 141.)
RAMSAY, Sco., a horse's head, sa., bridled, gu. Pl. 92, cr. 1.
RAMSAY, Sco., a unicorn's head, couped, ar., horned and maned, or, charged with a crescent. *Dum vario.* Pl. 21, cr. 1, (crescent, pl. 141.)
RAMSAY, Bart., of Banff House, Sco., a unicorn's head. *Spernit pericula virtus.* Pl. 20, cr. 1.
RAMSAY, Sco., a demi-eagle, displayed, sa. *Aspiro.* Pl. 22, cr. 11.
RAMSBOTTOM, Berks., a ram's head, couped, ppr., in mouth a trefoil, vert, (gorged with a collar, engrailed, az.,) charged with a fleur-de-lis, between two plates. Pl. 34, cr. 12, (charging, pl. 141.)
RAMSBOTTOM, Lond., out of a (ducal) coronet, or, a ram's head, couped, ppr. Pl. 124, cr. 8.
RAMSBOTTON, Eng., an eagle's head, erased, gu. Pl. 20, cr. 7.
RAMSDEN, Bart., Yorks., an armed arm, couped at elbow and erect, ppr., in (gauntlet) a fleur-de-lis, sa. Pl. 95, cr. 9.
RAMSEY, Sco., a dexter hand, holding a covered cup, ppr. Pl. 35, cr. 9.
RAMSEY, Eng., a sea lion, sejant, ppr. Pl. 80, cr. 13.
RAMSEY, a unicorn's head, couped, ar., armed and maned, or. Pl. 20, cr. 1.
RAMSEY, a unicorn's head, erased, ar., crined and armed, or. Pl. 67, cr. 1.
RAMUS, Middx., on a ducal coronet, or, an owl, ppr. Pl. 27, cr. 9, (coronet, *same plate.*)
RANCLIFFE, Baron, Iri., and an Eng. Baronet, (Parkyns,) out of a ducal coronet, or, a demi-eagle, displayed, az., (billettée, or, each billet charged with an ermine-spot.) *Honeste audax.* Pl. 9, cr. 6.
RANDS, and RANDES, Eng., a marigold, stalked and leaved, ppr. Pl. 105, cr. 15.
RAND, Lond. and Durh., issuing from a coronet, a boar's head, erect. Pl. 102, cr. 14.
RANDAL, Kent, an antelope's head, or. Pl. 79, cr. 9.
RANDALL, Iri., a demi-griffin, gu., winged, or. Pl. 18, cr. 6.

RANDALL, Warw. and Northamp., a bat, displayed, sa. Pl. 94, cr. 9.
RANDALL, Sco., an arm, in armour, embowed, brandishing a scimitar, all ppr., (the hilt affixed by a chain to the wrist of the armour, or.) Pl. 81, cr. 11.
RANDALL, a dove, volant, ppr. Pl. 25, cr. 6.
RANDALL, a buck, statant, pierced in back by an arrow. Pl. 88, cr. 9.
RANDALL, and RANDOLPH, Eng., an antelope's head, couped, or. Pl. 79, cr. 9, (without spear.)
RANDALL, Wilts., an antelope's head, couped, or, charged on breast with four mullets in cross, and in mouth a rose, gu., slipped and leaved, vert. Pl. 24, cr. 7, (charging, pl. 141.)
RANDALL, Lond., a buck's head, erased, az., (ducally gorged, lined, and ringed, or.) (Another, erased, ppr.) Pl. 66, cr. 9.
RANDALL, out of a ducal coronet, an antelope's head, ar., attired, or. Pl. 24, cr. 7, (coronet, *same plate,* cr. 10.)
RANDALL, Devons., a staff, couped and raguly, in fess, vert, thereon a wolf, passant, az., collared, or. Pl. 5, cr. 8.
RANDE, Northamp., on a ducal coronet, a boar's head, couped, all ar. Pl. 102, cr. 14.
RANDELL, and RANDLE, Eng., an arm, in armour, couped at shoulder, embowed, and resting elbow on the wreath, hand holding a spiked club. Pl. 28, cr. 2.
RANDES, Eng., out of a ducal coronet, or, a lion's paw, gu., holding a cross crosslet, fitched, ar. Pl. 65, cr. 5.
RANDES, Linc., two lions' gambs, erect, sa., supporting a sword, ar., hilt and pommel, or. Pl. 106, cr. 12, (sword, *same plate.*)
RANDES, Linc., two lions' gambs, erect, ppr., holding up a sword. *Ib.*
RANDILL, of Northamp., a martlet, volant, or. Pl. 40, cr. 4.
RANDOLFE, Eng., a bat, ar., wings expanded. Pl. 94, cr. 9.
RANDOLFE, a bat, wings expanded, ppr. Pl. 94, cr. 9.
RANDOLL, Eng., a garb, or. Pl. 48, cr. 10.
RANDOLPH, Sco., a demi-lion, az., in dexter a thistle, ppr. *Per aspera belli.* Pl. 45, cr. 15, (without fleur-de-lis.)
RANDOLPH, Eng., a greyhound's head, ar., semée of torteaux, gu. Pl. 14, cr. 4.
RANDOLPH, an antelope's head, erased, or. Pl. 24, cr. 7.
RANDULPH, an antelope's head, ar., attired, or. Pl. 79, cr. 9, (without spear.)
RANELAGH, Viscount, and Baron Jones, Iri., (Jones,) a dexter arm, in armour, embowed, hand holding an arrow, all ppr. *Cœlitus mihi vires.* Pl. 96, cr. 6.
RANFURLY, Earl of, Viscount Northland, and Baron Wells, Iri., and Baron Ranfurly, U.K., (Knox,) a falcon, perched, ppr. *Moveo et propitior.* Pl. 67, cr. 3.
RANKEN, Sco., an ostrich, in mouth a horse-shoe, all ppr. Pl. 16, cr. 2.
RANKIN, Eng., a spear, erect. Pl. 97, cr. 4.
RANKIN, Lond. and Sco., a lance, issuing. *Fortiter et recte.* Pl. 97, cr. 4.
RANKINE, a broken lance and a palm-branch, slipped, in saltier, surmounted by a crescent. *Utrius auctus auxilio.* Pl. 5, cr. 11.

RANKINE, Sco., a ship, ppr. *Prudentiâ et virtute.* Pl. 109, cr. 8.

RANSON, Eng., an eagle, displayed, per fess, az. and or. Pl. 48, cr. 11.

RANSON, Suff., a hawk's head, erased, az., in beak an annulet, or. Pl. 34, cr. 11, (annulet, pl. 141.)

RANT, on a ducal coronet, ar., a lion, sejant, or, tail between hind legs. Pl. 126, cr. 15, (coronet, pl. 128, fig. 3.)

RANTT, Norf., a tiger, sejant, or, tufted and maned, sa., ducally gorged,. gold. Pl. 26, cr. 9, (gorging, pl. 128, fig. 3.)

RAPARIIS, a griffin's head, erased, sa. Pl. 48, cr. 6.

RAPARUS, Eng., a griffin's tail, erased, sa. Pl. 17, cr. 4.

RAPER, Yorks. and Lond., an antelope's head, per fess, wavy and erased, or and az. Pl. 24, cr. 7.

RAPER, Eng., a buck's head. Pl. 91, cr. 14.

RAPER, Lond., an antelope, ppr., (collared, or.) Pl. 63, cr. 10.

RAPHAEL, Surr., out of an Eastern coronet, or, a demi-eagle, with two heads, displayed, sa., beaked, and charged on breast with a cross moline, gold. Pl. 4, cr. 6, (cross, pl. 141; coronet, pl. 57, cr. 5.)

RASDALL, two arms, in armour, embowed, supporting in hands a heart, inflamed, ppr., charged with a tower, ar. Pl. 64, cr. 11.

RASHLEIGH, Eng., a dexter hand holding a sword. Pl. 21, cr. 10.

RASHLEIGH, Cornw., a Cornish chough, ppr. Pl. 100, cr. 13.

RASPER, on a chapeau, an etoile of six points. Pl. 63, cr. 9, (chapeau, *same plate.*)

RASYN, and RASYNGE, Eng., an arm, erect, vested, paly of (four,) or and gu., cuffed, ar., in hand, ppr., a bunch of lavender, vert, flowered, az. Pl. 94, cr. 15.

RATCHETT, Chesh., on a chapeau, gu. and erm., a lion, passant, parted, per pale, gu. and or, (charged with a label, ar.,) dexter resting on an escutcheon. Pl. 107, cr. 1, (escutcheon, pl. 42, cr. 8.)

RATCLIFF, Bart., Kent, a crane, ppr. Pl. 111, cr. 9.

RATCLIFFE, Sir JOHN, F.S.A., a bull's head, erased, sa., armed, or, charged with three escallops, and gorged with a coronet. *Fide et fortitudine.* Pl. 126 A, cr. 3.

RATCLIFFE, Lanc. and Yorks., a bull's head, erased, per pale, ar. and sa., armed and ducally gorged, or. Pl. 68, cr. 6.

RATCLIFFE, Bucks., a bull's head. Pl. 120, cr. 7.

RATCLIFFE, Derbs. and Lanc., a bull's head, erased, sa., armed, or, ducally gorged, (lined and ringed,) ar. Pl. 68, cr. 6.

RATCLIFFE, Yorks., on a mount, vert, a Cornish chough, sa. Pl. 34, cr. 13.

RATFORD, Eng., a man holding a banner, ar., charged with a saltier. Pl. 2, cr. 12.

RATHBONE, Eng., a dove and olive-branch, ppr. Pl. 48, cr. 15.

RATHBONE, the Roman fasces, in fess, in front of a lion's head, ppr., gorged with a collar, ar., (charged with two roses, gu.) *Suaviter et fortiter.* Pl. 7, cr. 10, (fasces, pl. 65, cr. 15.)

RATHDOWNE, Earl of, Viscount and Baron Monck, Iri., (Monck,) a wyvern. *Fortiter, fideliter, feliciter.* Pl. 63, cr. 13.

RATHLOW, Eng., a martlet, or. Pl. 111, cr. 5.

RATSEY, Eng., a dragon's head, vert, transfixed by a spear-head, (in fess.) Pl. 121, cr. 9.

RATTARY, and RATTRAY, Sco., a dexter hand, ppr., holding a cross crosslet, or. *Ex hoc victoria signo.* Pl. 99, cr. 1.

RATTRAY, Eng., an arm, in armour, embowed, holding a battle-axe, all ppr. Pl. 121, cr. 14.

RATTRAY, Sco., a mullet, ensigned by a flaming heart, all ppr. Pl. 5, cr. 14.

RATTRAY, Sco., a mullet, ar., ensigned by a flaming heart, ppr. *Super sidera votum.* (Another, mullet, or.) Pl. 5, cr. 14.

RATTRAY, Sco., a demi-huntsman, winding a horn, ppr., vested, vert. *Free for a blast.* Pl. 38, cr. 8.

RATTRAY, Sco., a cubit arm, in armour, in hand a battle-axe, ppr. *Ex hoc victoria signo.* Pl. 73, cr. 7, (armour, pl. 125, cr. 5.)

RAULEIGH, Eng., a boar's head, (couped) and erect. Pl. 21, cr. 7.

RAVEN, Lond. and Norf., a raven, ppr. Pl. 123, cr. 2.

RAVEN, a demi-dragon, vert, winged, gu. Pl. 82, cr. 10.

RAVEN, Lond., on a mount, vert, a caltrap, or. Pl. 7, cr. 4, (mount, pl. 98, cr. 13.)

RAVENCROFT, on a chapeau, a lion, statant, gardant. Pl. 7, cr. 14.

RAVENHILL, a demi-lion, rampant, ar., supporting a cross crosslet, fitched, sa. Pl. 65, cr. 6.

RAVENSHOLME, Eng., a demi-lion, rampant, gu. Pl. 67, cr. 10.

RAVENSCROFT, Wel., Suss., Lanc., and Chesh., on a chapeau, gu., turned up, erm., a lion, (passant,) gardant, ar. Pl. 7, cr. 14.

RAVENSWORTH, Baron, and a Baronet, (Liddell,) a lion, rampant, sa., billettée, or, ducally crowned, gold. *Fama semper vivit*—and—*Unus et idem.* Pl. 98, cr. 1.

RAVIS, Eng., a lion's head, erased, per fess, ar. and gu., within a chain, in orle, or. Pl. 28, cr. 12.

RAW, Lond. and Yorks., an arm, in armour, embowed, sa., garnished, or, in hand, ppr., an escallop. Pl. 24, cr. 14, (escallop, pl. 57, cr. 6.)

RAWDEN, Yorks. and Iri., on a mural coronet, ar., a pheon, sa., with a laurel-branch issuing therefrom, ppr. Pl. 26, cr. 12, (laurel, pl. 123, cr. 5; coronet, pl. 128, fig. 18.)

RAWDON, Eng., on a mount, vert, a wyvern, sejant, or. Pl. 33, cr. 13.

RAWE, Kent, a dexter arm, in armour, embowed, sa., garnished, or, in hand, ppr., a spiked club, ar. Pl. 83, cr. 2, (armour, pl. 120, cr. 11.)

RAWES, Eng., an arm in armour, embowed, holding a spiked club, all ppr. Pl. 83, cr. 2, (armour, pl. 120, cr. 11.)

RAWLE, Corn., an arm, in armour, embowed, ppr., in gauntlet, a sword, ar., hilt, or. Pl. 2, cr. 8.

RAWLES, Dors., a demi-lion, rampant, gu., supporting a battle-axe, or. Pl. 101, cr. 14, (without charging.)

RAWLEY, Devons., a roebuck, ppr. Pl. 68, cr. 2.

RAWLINGS, Eng., a ram, passant, sa., attired, or. Pl. 109, cr. 2.

RAWLINGS, Corn., an arm, in armour, embowed, elbow resting on the wreath, in gauntlet a (falchion,) ar., hilt, or. *Cognosce teipsum et disce pati.* Pl. 107, cr. 15.

RAWLINS, Eng., an arm, in armour, embowed, ppr., in gauntlet a falchion, ar., hilt, or. *Pl.* 2, *cr.* 8.
RAWLINS, Ess., a bear's head, couped, or. *Pl.* 2, *cr.* 9.
RAWLINS, Iri., a lion's head, erased, gu. *Pl.* 81, *cr.* 4.
RAWLINS, Heref., an arm, in armour, embowed, ppr., brandishing a sword, ar., hilted, or. *Nec mutandys nec metus. Pl.* 2, *cr.* 8.
RAWLINS, or RAWLYNS, Lond. and Heref., a bull's leg, couped near body, sa., covered to fetlock, ar., on top an eagle's head, erased, gu.
RAWLINSON, Eng., an eagle's head, couped. *Pl.* 100, *cr.* 10.
RAWLINSON, Lanc., a drake, ppr., in beak an escallop, ar. *Pl.* 90, *cr.* 15, (escallop, *pl.* 141.)
RAWSON, Yorks., a falcon, sa., rising from a tower, or. *Pl.* 84, *cr.* 3.
RAWSON, Yorks. and Lanc., a raven's head, (couped,) sa., in beak an annulet, or. *Pl.* 27, *cr.* 13, (annulet, *pl.* 39, *cr.* 11.)
RAWSON, a castle, sa., flagged, gu. *Pl.* 123, *cr.* 14.
RAWSON, a quadrangular castle, ppr. *Pl.* 28, *cr.* 11.
RAWSON, issuing from clouds, ppr., a cubit arm, erect, vested and cuffed, gu., (charged with a rose, ar.,) hand, az., grasping an anchor, (in fess,) or. *Pl.* 41, *cr.* 5, (vesting, *pl.* 32, *cr.* 6.)
RAWSON, Yorks., an eagle's head, erased, sa., charged on neck with three guttes, or, one and two, in beak an annulet, gold. *Pl.* 121, *cr.* 7, (annulet, *pl.* 33, *cr.* 11.)
RAWSTON, Eng., a lion, passant, or. *Pl.* 48, *cr.* 8.
RAWSTON, out of a ducal coronet, a demi-lion, rampant, supporting a tower, triple-towered. *Pl.* 45, *cr.* 7, (tower, *pl.* 123, *cr.* 14.)
RAWSTORNE, Lanc., a lion, passant, or. *Pl.* 48, *cr.* 8.
RAY, Suff., an ostrich, or, in mouth a horse-shoe, az. *Pl.* 16, *cr.* 2.
RAY, Eng., the bust of a man, in profile, couped, ppr., ducally crowned, or, with a long cap turning forward, gu., thereon a Catherine-wheel, gold. *Pl.* 78, *cr.* 14, (wheel, *pl.* 141.)
RAY, Ess. and Glouc., an eagle's head, couped, with wings addorsed and elevated, ppr. *Pl.* 19, *cr.* 9, (without coronet.)
RAY, Linc., an ostrich. *Pl.* 16, *cr.* 2.
RAYCE, Eng., out of a ducal coronet, a phœnix's head in flames, in beak a branch of palm. *Pl.* 53, *cr.* 6, (branch, *pl.* 123, *cr.* 1.)
RAYE, Eng., a lion's paw, per cheveron, gu. and or. *Pl.* 88, *cr.* 3.
RAYLEY, Eng., a savage's head, affrontée. *Pl.* 19, *cr.* 1.
RAYMENT, Eng., a boar's head, erased and erect, ar. *Pl.* 21, *cr.* 7.
RAYMOND, ANTHONY, Esq. of Kilmurray, Kerry, an eagle, displayed, ppr. *Renovatur ætas ejus sicut aquilæ. Pl.* 48, *cr.* 11.
RAYMOND, Eng., a leopard, sejant, per fess, or and sa., spotted, counterchanged. *Pl.* 10, *cr.* 13, (without flag.)
RAYMOND, Devons., on a mount, vert, a leopard, sejant, per fess, or and sa., spotted counterchanged. *Pl.* 123, *cr.* 8.

RAYMOND, Lond., out of a mural coronet, a demi-eagle, displayed, erm., beaked, sa., (charged on breast with three ogresses, two and one.) *Pl.* 33, *cr.* 5.
RAYMOND, a dragon's head, (erased, or, ducally gorged, gu.) *Pl.* 36, *cr.* 7.
RAYMOND, Kent, Devons., and Ess., a dexter arm, in armour, embowed, hand grasping a battle-axe, all ppr. *Pl.* 121, *cr.* 14.
RAYMOND, Cornw., out of an earl's coronet, a demi-dragon. *Pl.* 82, *cr.* 10, (coronet, *pl.* 80, *cr.* 11.)
RAYMOND, Lond., out of a mural coronet, a demi-eagle, displayed, erm., beaked, sa., charged on breast with three torteaux. *Pl.* 33, *cr.* 5, (torteau, *pl.* 141.)
RAYMOND, out of a mural coronet, a demi-eagle, displayed, or, charged on body with three torteaux, in pale. *Pl.* 33, *cr.* 5, (torteau, *pl.* 141.)
RAYMONT, Eng., an antelope's head, erm., (collared, or.) *Pl.* 24, *cr.* 7.
RAYNER, Eng., a dexter hand, holding (three) arrows, points downward, ppr. *Pl.* 56, *cr.* 4.
RAYNES, Eng., an arm, embowed, hand holding a club, ppr. *Pl.* 123, *cr.* 10.
RAYNEY, Lond., out of a mural coronet, ar., a lion's head, or, pellettée. *Pl.* 45, *cr.* 9.
RAYNEY, Yorks., out of a mural coronet, ar., a lion's head, ppr., pellettée. *Pl.* 45, *cr.* 9.
RAYNOLDS, a fox's head, (couped,) sa., collared with two bars-gemelle, or, and between them three bezants. *Pl.* 69, *cr.* 15.
RAYNOR, Eng., two winged hands conjoined, all ppr. *Pl.* 14, *cr.* 9.
RAYNOR, on a mount, vert, a leopard, passant, or. *Pl.* 86, *cr.* 2, (mount, *pl.* 9, *cr.* 14.)
RAYNSFORD, Ess., a greyhound, current, dark russet colour, (collared and ringed, or.) *Pl.* 28, *cr.* 7, (without charge.)
RAYNSFORD, a roebuck's head, erased, sa., attired, or. *Pl.* 66, *cr.* 9.
RAYNSFORD, Oxon., Northamp., Middx., and Warw., a reindeer, erm., attired, or. *Pl.* 12, *cr.* 8.
RAYNSFORD, Eng., a deer's head, cabossed, az., attired, or. *Pl.* 36, *cr.* 1.
RAYNTON, Middx., a griffin's head, couped, sa., beaked, or, (charged on neck with a cinquefoil, gold.) *Pl.* 38, *cr.* 3, (cinquefoil, *pl.* 141.)
RAYSON, Eng., a hart's head, erased, gu. *Pl.* 66, *cr.* 9.
REA, and REE, Worc. and Lond., out of a mural coronet, ar., a dragon's head, az. *Pl.* 101, *cr.* 4.
REABURN, Sco., a hand, issuing, holding a Hercules' club, all ppr. *Tutus si fortis. Pl.* 28, *cr.* 6.
READ, Eng., a buck's head, erased, sa., bezantée. *Pl.* 66, *cr.* 9.
READ, Eng., an eagle, displayed. *Pl.* 48, *cr.* 11.
READ, Iri., a leg, couped above knee, erect, (vested, az.,) spurred, or. *Pl.* 38, *cr.* 14.
READ, a greyhound's head, couped, ar., between two roses, gu., slipped and leaved, ppr. *Pl.* 84, *cr.* 13.
READ, a demi-lion, rampant. *Pl.* 67, *cr.* 10.
READ, Hayton, in lion's gamb, erect, a cross moline, erminois. *Pl.* 46, *cr.* 7, (cross, *pl.* 141.)

READ, a shoveller, bendy of six, ar. and sa., beaked, or. *Pl.* 90, *cr.* 15.

READ, Herts., a buck's head, erased, sa., attired, or, between two balm-branches, vert, charged on neck with two bars-gemelle, gold. *Pl.* 125, *cr.* 6, (branches, *pl.* 87, *cr.* 8.)

READ, Bucks., a falcon, wings expanded. *Pl.* 105, *cr.* 4.

READ, or READE, Berks. and Herts., a falcon, wings expanded, ppr., belled, or, (statant on a reed, in fess, vert.) *Pl.* 105, *cr.* 4.

READ-CREWE: 1. For *Read*, an eagle, displayed, sa. *Pl.* 48, *cr.* 11. 2. For *Crewe*, out of a ducal coronet, or, a lion's gamb, ar., (charged with a crescent.) *Pl.* 67, *cr.* 7.

READE, PHILIP, Esq., of The Wood Parks, co. Galway and co. Clare, out of clouds, an arm, erect, in hand an open book. *Amor sine timore*—and—*Cedant arma togæ*. *Pl.* 82, *cr.* 5.

READE, Iri., a leg, couped above knee, (vested, az.,) spurred, or. *Pl.* 38, *cr.* 14.

READE, Somers., Herts., Cambs., Kent, and Wel., an eagle, displayed, sa., beaked and legged, or. *Pl.* 48, *cr.* 11.

READE, Lond., a griffin's head, erased, az., purfled, or. *Pl.* 48, *cr.* 6.

READE, Lond., a griffin's head, erased, az. *Pl.* 48, *cr.* 6.

READE, Eng., on trunk of tree, vert, a falcon, rising, ppr. *Pl.* 78, *cr.* 8.

READE, Norf., a stag's head, erased, sa., bezantée, attired, or. *Pl.* 66, *cr.* 9.

READE, Norf., a goat's head, sa., ducally gorged, attired, ar. *Pl.* 105, *cr.* 14, (gorging, *pl.* 90, *cr.* 12.)

READE, Linc., a shoveller, close, sa. *Pl.* 90, *cr.* 15.

READE, Bart., Oxon., on stump of tree, vert, a falcon, (rising,) ppr., belled and jessed, or. *Cedant arma togæ.* *Pl.* 78, *cr.* 8.

READER, Iri., a leopard's head, (erased,) az., collared, or. *Pl.* 40, *cr.* 10.

READERS, Eng., a dexter hand, brandishing a sabre, ppr. *Pl.* 21, *cr.* 10.

READING, or REDING, Eng., a griffin, sejant, in dexter a garland of laurel, all ppr. *Pl.* 56, *cr.* 10.

READING, Lond., a griffin's head, erased, or. *Pl.* 48, *cr.* 6.

READSHAW, Lanc., a hind's head, ar., (collared, sa.) *Pl.* 21, *cr.* 9.

REAMAN, a cushion, charged with a dragon's head, couped.

REANOLDS, Somers. and Devons., out of a mural coronet, ar., a talbot's head, az., bezantée, and eared, or. *Pl.* 91, *cr.* 15.

REARDON, Iri., a dolphin, naiant, az. *Pl.* 48, *cr.* 9.

REASON, Eng., a boar's head, erased and erect, sa. *Pl.* 21, *cr.* 7.

REASON, Eng., a fox's head, erased, ppr. *Pl.* 71, *cr.* 4.

REASTON-RODES, of Barlborough Hall, Derbs.: 1. For *Rodes*, a cubit arm, in hand an (oak)-branch, fructed, all ppr. *Pl.* 43, *cr.* 6. 2. For *Reaston*, a demi-lion, collared, ppr., (collared, or, between paws a spear, of the last, headed, ppr., therefrom a banner, gu., charged with a cinquefoil, gold,) and also supporting a rudder, az. *Pl.* 102, *cr.* 4.

REATH, Sco., a garb, or. *Industria ditat.* *Pl.* 48, *cr.* 10.

REAVE, Suss., a dragon's head, ar., charged on breast with three escallops, az. *Pl.* 87, *cr.* 12, (escallop, *pl.* 141.)

REAY, Eng., a griffin's head. *Pl.* 38, *cr.* 3.

REAY, Northumb., out of a mural coronet, ar., a griffin's head, or. *Pl.* 101, *cr.* 6, (without gorging.)

REAY, Durh., a griffin's head, erased, ppr. *Pl.* 48, *cr.* 6.

REAY, Lord, and a Bart., Sco., (MacKay,) a dexter arm, from elbow, erect, hand holding a dagger, in pale, all ppr., hilt and pommel, or. *Manu forti*. *Pl.* 23, *cr.* 15.

REBEIRO, (five) tulips, in pale. *Pl.* 64, *cr.* 2.

REBOW, Ess., out of a mural coronet, or, a demi-eagle, displayed, sa., (on breast a bezant, charged with a fleur-de-lis, az., in beak an arrow, of the second, headed and feathered, ar.) *Pl.* 85, *cr.* 5.

REDCOMYN, Eng., a phœnix in flames, ppr. *Pl.* 48, *cr.* 8.

REDDIE, Eng., an arm, in armour, couped at shoulder, embowed, and resting on elbow, in hand a scimitar, all ppr. *Pl.* 107, *cr.* 15.

REDDINGFIELD, Eng., on point of sword, erect, ppr., a cross pattée, ar. *Pl.* 56, *cr.* 1.

REDDISH, Dors., Wilts., and Lanc., a cock's head, erased, sa., combed and wattled, gu., (ducally gorged, or.) *Pl.* 92, *cr.* 3.

REDE, Suff. and Norf., a buck's head, erased, ar., attired, or, between two palm-branches, gold, charged on neck with three bars-gemelle, of the second. *Pl.* 125, *cr.* 6, (branches, *pl.* 87, *cr.* 8.)

REDE, Suff., a stag's head, erased. *Pl.* 66, *cr.* 9.

REDE, or REED, Kent. and Worc., a garb, or, banded, gu. *Pl.* 48, *cr.* 10.

REDEGE, Eng., a hand, apaumée, thereon an eye, ppr. *Pl.* 99, *cr.* 13.

REDESDALE, Baron, (Mitford,) a dexter hand, in fess, couped, ppr., supporting a (sword,) in pale, ar., hilt and pommel, or, pierced through a boar's head, sa., tusked, of the first, couped, gu. *Æqualibiter et diligenter.* *Pl.* 85, *cr.* 12.

REDFERN, Eng., a birch-tree, ppr. *Pl.* 18, *cr.* 10.

REDFORD, Eng., a quatrefoil, gu. *Pl.* 65, *cr.* 7.

REDHAM, Eng., a cross crosslet, fitched, gu. *Pl.* 16, *cr.* 10.

REDHEAD, Eng., an eagle's head, az. *Pl.* 100, *cr.* 10.

REDHEAD, a sinister arm, in armour, ppr., embowed to sinister, in gauntlet a sword, point downward, ar., hilt and pommel, or, charged above wrist with a crescent, gold.

REDING, Eng., a gilliflower, stalked and leaved, ppr. *Pl.* 22, *cr.* 9.

REDINGHAM, Eng., a salmon, naiant, az. *Pl.* 85, *cr.* 7.

REDINGTON, Sir THOMAS-NICHOLAS, K.C.B., of Kilcornan, co. Galway, a lion, rampant. *Pro rege sæpe, pro patriâ semper.* *Pl.* 67, *cr.* 5.

REDLEY, Eng., on a chapeau, a salamander in flames, ppr. *Pl.* 86, *cr.* 14.

REDMAN, Eng., out of a ducal coronet, gu., a horse's head, ar. *Pl.* 50, *cr.* 13.

REDMAN, out of a mural coronet, or, a horse's head, ar., maned, gu. *Pl.* 50, *cr.* 13, (coronet, *pl.* 128, *fig.* 18.)

REDMAN, on a cushion, gu., a horse's head, couped, ar. *Pl.* 5, *cr.* 9.
REDMAN, Yorks., on a cushion, gu., tasselled, or, a horse's head, couped, ar., crined, gold. *Pl.* 5, *cr.* 9.
REDMOND, HENRY-THOMSON, Esq., of Killoughter House, co. Wicklow, a beacon, ppr. *Pie vivere et Deum et patriam deligere. Pl.* 88, *cr.* 6.
REDPATH, Sco., an ostrich, in mouth a key, ppr. *Pl.* 16, *cr.* 2, (key, *pl.* 9, *cr.* 12.)
REDWOOD, (on a rock,) an eagle, rising, ppr., charged on each wing with a mullet of six points, in beak a staff, raguly, or. *Lumen servimus antique. Pl.* 67, *cr.* 4, (staff, *pl.* 11, *cr.* 2; mullet, *pl.* 21, *cr.* 6.)
REECE, Eng., a galley, with oars in action. *Pl.* 34, *cr.* 5.
REECE, Wel., a wyvern, sejant, vert, wings elevated, in mouth a spear-head, ar., embrued, gu. *Respice futurum. Pl.* 63, *cr.* 13, (spear-head, *pl.* 75, *cr.* 12.)
REED, Eng., a griffin, segreant. *Pl.* 67, *cr.* 13.
REED, a tower. *Pl.* 12, *cr.* 5.
REED, Northumb., a demi-griffin, or, holding an oak-branch, ppr. *In Deo omnia. Pl.* 19, *cr.* 15, (branch, *same plate.*)
REED, Northumb., a griffin, segreant. *Memor et fidelis. Pl.* 67, *cr.* 13.
REED, STEPHEN, Esq., of East and West Cragg, Northumb., and of Newcastle-upon-Tyne, a dragon. *Memor et fidelis. Pl.* 90, *cr.* 10.
REEDE, Eng., a hand holding a lance, (in pale,) ppr. *Pl.* 99, *cr.* 8.
REEDE, Eng., a garb, or, banded, gu., the anns, ar. *Pl.* 48, *cr.* 10.
REEDE, a fleur-de-lis, ar. *Pl.* 68, *cr.* 12.
REES, Eng., a lion, rampant, supporting a plumb-rule, all ppr. *Pl.* 50, *cr.* 8.
REES, JOHN-HUGHES, Esq., Killymaenllwyd, Carmarthen, a talbot, ppr. *Spes melioris ævi. Pl.* 120, *cr.* 8.
REEVE, Suff., a tiger's head, erased, ar., armed, maned, and collared, or. *Pl.* 86, *cr.* 13.
REEVE, Linc., a horse's head, erased, per fess, nebulée, ar. and gu., (charged on neck with two mullets, in pale, ar.) *Pl.* 46, *cr.* 4.
REEVE, an eagle's head, erased, or, (collared, sa.) *Pl.* 70, *cr.* 4.
REEVE, between wings, a caduceus. *Pl.* 69, *cr.* 7.
REEVE, Suff., a griffin's head, erased, gu. *Pl.* 48, *cr.* 6.
REEVES, Eng., a demi-griffin. *Pl.* 18, *cr.* 6.
REEVES, Eng., out of a ducal coronet, a griffin's head. *Pl.* 54, *cr.* 14.
REEVES, an eagle, displayed. *Pl.* 48, *cr.* 11.
REEVES, a greyhound, sejant, sa., bezantée, (collared and ringed, or.) *Pl.* 66, *cr.* 15.
REEVES, Vartersberg, Cork, a dragon's head, erased, or, collared, az. Above an escroll, with words, "Animum rege." *Virtute et fidelitate. Pl.* 107, *cr.* 10.
REGAN, Iri., a demi-griffin, per fess, or and az. *Pl.* 18, *cr.* 6.
REGNOLD, a wolf's head, erased, sa., (charged on neck with three bezants between two bars,) or. *Pl.* 8, *cr.* 4.
REICHENBERG, Cornw., a naked arm, embowed and couped, in hand a laurel-(branch.) *Pl.* 118, *cr.* 4.

REID, a hand, holding an open book. *Pl.* 126 A, *cr.* 9.
REID, Iri., a sheaf of rye, gu. *Pl.* 48, *cr.* 10.
REID, Sco., a demi-eagle, issuant, gu., beaked, az. *Fortitudine et labore. Pl.* 52, *cr.* 8.
REID, Sco. and Lond., an eagle, rising, ppr. *In sublime. Pl.* 67, *cr.* 4.
REID, Eng., a lion, passant, tail extended, ppr. *Pl.* 118, *cr.* 10.
REID, Sco., out of a cloud, a hand holding a book, expanded, ppr. *Pro virtute. Pl.* 82, *cr.* 5.
REID, Iri., a cock-pheasant, ppr. *Semper eadem. Pl.* 82, *cr.* 12.
REID, Lond., an eagle, rising, ppr. *Fortitudine et labore. Pl.* 67, *cr.* 4.
REID, Lond. and Herts., out of a cloud, a cubit arm, in hand the Holy Bible, open at Job xix., all ppr., leaved, or. *Pl.* 82, *cr.* 5.
REID, Bart., Surr., a castle, ar., surmounted by two spears, in saltier, ppr., points upward. *Firm. Pl.* 69, *cr.* 9.
REID, Bart., Sco., a pelican in nest, feeding her young, ppr. *Nihil amanti durum. Pl.* 44, *cr.* 1.
REIDHEUGH, Sco., two turtle-doves, respecting each other, az. *Nil nequit amor. Pl.* 68, *cr.* 13.
REIELLY, Iri., an archer, shooting an arrow from a bow, ppr. *Pl.* 90, *cr.* 3.
REIGNOLDS, Somers. and Devons., out of a mural coronet, ar., a talbot's head, az., bezantée, eared, or. *Pl.* 91, *cr.* 15.
REILLY, Iri., an archer, shooting an arrow from a bow, ppr. *Pl.* 60, *cr.* 5.
REILLY, Iri., the sun, gu. *Pl.* 68, *cr.* 14.
REISELEY, a young man's head, couped at shoulders, sa., ear-rings, or, crowned with a chaplet of flowers, ar. *Pl.* 118, *cr.* 7.
RELF, Worc. and Suss., an opiman's head, or, in beak a snake, vert, environed round neck.
RELFE, Lond., a peacock, ppr., (collared, gu.,) wings erect, ar., charged with several mascles, of the second. *Pl.* 54, *cr.* 13, (mascle, *pl.* 141.)
RELHAM, three ostrich-feathers. *Pl.* 12, *cr.* 9.
RELHAN, Eng., three ostrich-feathers, ar. *Naturæ minister. Pl.* 12, *cr.* 9.
REMINGTON, Yorks., a hand holding a broken tilting-spear, all ppr. *Pl.* 66, *cr.* 4.
REMINGTON, HENRY, Esq., of The Crow Trees, Melling, Lanc., in hand, erect, a tilting-spear, all ppr. *Pl.* 99, *cr.* 8.
REMMINGTON, between two laurel-branches, in orle, a fleur-de-lis. *Pl.* 68, *cr.* 12, (branches, *pl.* 79, *cr.* 14.)
REMNANT, Sco., a dolphin, naiant, ppr. *Mind your own business. Pl.* 48, *cr.* 9.
REMNANT, Eng., an eagle, displayed, sa. *Pl.* 48, *cr.* 11.
REMPSTON, Eng., a caltrap, embrued, ppr. *Pl.* 7, *cr.* 4.
RENDLESHAM, Baron, Iri., (Thelusson,) a demi-greyhound, couped, ar., collared, sa., between wings, of the last, each charged with a trefoil, slipped, or. *Labore et honore. Pl.* 5, *cr.* 10.
RENNEY, Sco., two wings, conjoined and inverted, erm. *Pl.* 87, *cr.* 1.
RENNIE, Eng. and Sco., a parrot, gu., feeding on a bunch of cherries, ppr. *Pl.* 49, *cr.* 3.
RENNIE, Lond. and Sco., a dexter hand wielding a scimitar, ppr. *Probitate. Pl.* 29, *cr.* 8.
RENNY, a dexter hand, issuing, holding a balance and scales, or. *Probitate. Pl.* 26, *cr.* 8.

RENNY, Sco., a dexter hand, (in fess,) couped, suspending a pair of scales. *Probitate consilium perficitur.* *Pl.* 26, *cr.* 8.

RENNY, a dexter hand holding a scimitar, ppr. *Probitate.* *Pl.* 29, *cr.* 8.

RENOLDS, a portcullis, chained. *Pl.* 51, *cr.* 12.

RENOUS, Eng., a demi-griffin, segreant, regardant, erminois, supporting a banner, or, flotant from him, charged with a (mullet,)az. *Pl.* 46, *cr.* 1.

RENSHAW, Eng., a decrescent, ar., and increscent, or, (addorsed.) *Pl.* 99, *cr.* 4.

RENWICK, a lion's head, erased. *Pl.* 81, *cr.* 4.

REOCH, Sco., a rock, ppr. *Dieu est ma roche.* *Pl.* 73, *cr.* 12.

REOCH, Sco., a dexter hand holding a dagger, in pale, ppr. *Stand.* *Pl.* 23, *cr.* 15.

REPINGTON, of Armington Hall, Warw., a demi-antelope, gu., maned, bearded, tusked, and hoofed, or, billettée, ar. *Virtus propter se.* *Pl.* 34, *cr.* 8.

REPLEY, Surr., a demi-lion, rampant, or. *Pl.* 67, *cr.* 10.

REPLEY, Eng., a lion's head, erased, az., collared, or. *Pl.* 7, *cr.* 10.

REPPES, out of a ducal coronet, a plume of feathers, ar., quills, or, between wings, gold. *Pl.* 69, *cr.* 11.

REPPLEY, a lion, rampant, az., collared, ar. *Pl.* 88, *cr.* 1.

REPPS, or REPPES, Norf., out of a ducal coronet, or, a plume of ostrich-feathers, erm., between wings, gold. *Pl.* 69, *cr.* 11.

RERESBY, on a chapeau, vert, turned up, erm., a goat, ar. *Pl.* 66, *cr.* 1, (chapeau, *pl.* 127, *fig.* 13.)

RERESBY, on a chapeau, purp., turned up, erm., a goat, passant, or. *Pl.* 66, *cr.* 1, (chapeau, *pl.* 127, *fig.* 13.)

RERESBY, Hunts. and Yorks., on a chapeau, gu., turned up, erm., a goat, ar. *Pl.* 66, *cr.* 1, (chapeau, *pl.* 127, *fig.* 13.)

RESBYE, Suff., an arm, a wolf, couped at shoulder, embowed and erect from elbow, vested, az., in hand, ppr., (four) ears of wheat, or, stalked, vert. *Pl.* 89, *cr.* 4, (arm, *pl.* 62, *cr.* 7.)

RESKINNER, Cornw., a wolf, passant. *Pl.* 46, *cr.* 6.

RESKYMER, Cornw., a lion, rampant, sa., holding a branch of laurel, vert. *Pl.* 64, *cr.* 2, (branch, *pl.* 123, *cr.* 5.)

RESLEY, Bucks., a greyhound, erm., (collared, az., ringed, or,) resting fore-dexter on an escutcheon, ar. *Pl.* 104, *cr.* 1, (without chapeau; escutcheon, *pl.* 19, *cr.* 2.)

RESON, Eng., a fox's head, erased, ppr. *Pl.* 71, *cr.* 4.

REST, Eng., a dove, az., winged, or, gu., in mouth a branch, vert. *Pl.* 38, *cr.* 15.

REUCE, a greyhound, (passant,) per pale, ar. and ppr. *Pl.* 104, *cr.* 1, (without chapeau.)

REVE, a tiger's head, erased, ar., collared and maned, or. *Pl.* 86, *cr.* 13.

REVE, Suff., a dragon's head, erased, ar., collared, or. *Pl.* 107, *cr.* 10.

REVEL, Yorks. and Warw., a cubit arm, in armour, ppr., hand holding a lion's paw, erased, of the last. *Pl.* 94, *cr.* 13, (armour, *pl.* 23, *cr.* 9.)

REVELEY, Wel., an etoile of (twelve) points, az. *Optima revelatio stella.* *Pl.* 63, *cr.* 9.

REVELEY, an etoile of (sixteen) points, az. *Pl.* 63, *cr.* 9.

REVELL, and REVELLEY, Derbs., a cubit arm, in armour, erect, garnished, or, in hand, all ppr., a lion's gamb, erased. *Pl.* 94, *cr.* 13, (armour, *pl.* 23, *cr.* 9.)

REVETT, Suff., a dove, az., winged, or and gu., in mouth a branch, vert. *Pl.* 48, *cr.* 15.

REVETT, Camb. and Suff., an arm, erect, (bendy of four, ar. and sa.,) in hand, ppr., a broken sword, of the first, hilt and pommel, or. *Pl.* 22, *cr.* 6.

REVETT, Camb. and Suff., an arm, hand holding a battle-axe. *Pl.* 73, *cr.* 7, (arm, *pl.* 123, *cr.* 10.)

REWSE, Middx., a demi-lion, erm., holding a laurel-branch, vert. *Pl.* 39, *cr.* 14, (branch, *pl.* 123, *cr.* 5.)

REWTOURE, Eng., a seax, erect, ppr. *Pl.* 27, *cr.* 10.

REYE, Eng., an ostrich-feather, enfiled with a ducal coronet. *Pl.* 8, *cr.* 9.

REYGNALES, and REYNOLDS, Suff., a wolf's head, erased, sa., collared, or, charged with three guttes-de-poix. *Pl.* 8, *cr.* 4.

REYMES, and REYNES, Norf., out of a ducal coronet, or, a plume of two rows of ostrich-feathers, purp. *Pl.* 64, *cr.* 5.

REYNALL, Lond. and Beds., on a mount, vert, a fox, sejant, regardant, ppr., (collared, ar.,) resting dexter on a lozenge, or. *Pl.* 5, *cr.* 12.

REYNARDSON, on a mount, a fox, sejant, regardant, resting dexter on a lozenge. *Pl.* 5, *cr.* 12.

REYNARDSON, Lond. and Devons., a lion's head, erminois, crowned with a mural coronet, chequy, ar. and gu. *Pl.* 126, *cr.* 1, (coronet, *pl.* 112, *cr.* 5.)

REYNELL, Eng., a martlet, gu. *Pl.* 111, *cr.* 5.

REYNELL, a fox, current, ppr. *Pl.* 80, *cr.* 5.

REYNELL, Devons., a fox, passant, ppr. *Pl.* 126, *cr.* 5.

REYNELL, Middx. and Devons., a fox, passant, or. *Pl.* 126, *cr.* 5.

REYNELL, Bart., a wolf, (statant,) or, tail extended. *Murus aheneus esto.* *Pl.* 46, *cr.* 6.

REYNELL, RICHARD-WINTER, Esq., of Killynon, co. Westmeath, a fox, passant, or. *Murus aheneus esto—and—Indubituta fides.* *Pl.* 126, *cr.* 5.

REYNES, Suss., a bird, breast, ar., back, az., in beak a rose, ppr. *Pl.* 10, *cr.* 12, (rose, *pl.* 55, *cr.* 9.)

REYNES, Notts., an arm out of clouds, hand holding three roses, all ppr. *Pl.* 69, *cr.* 10.

REYNETT, a cubit arm, erect, in hand an anchor, in bend. *Pl.* 53, *cr.* 13.

REYNHAM, Norf., a morion, (between two mallets.) *Pl.* 18, *cr.* 9.

REYNHOUSE, Middx., a demi-griffin, segreant, regardant, erminois, holding a banner, or, the point, staff, and tassels, of the last, charged with a (mullet,) az. *Pl.* 46, *cr.* 1.

REYNOLD, Eng., an eagle, close. *Pl.* 7, *cr.* 11.

REYNOLD, Warw., a fox's head, erased, or. *Pl.* 71, *cr.* 4.

REYNOLDS, Ess., a griffin's head, erased, per pale, or and ar. *Pl.* 48, *cr.* 6.

REYNOLDS, Iri., a globe, mounted, ppr. *Pl.* 81, *cr.* 1.

REYNOLDS, Eng., out of a crescent, an etoile. *Pl.* 111, *cr.* 15.

REYNOLDS, an eagle, close, ar., (ducally gorged and lined, or.) *Pl.* 7, *cr.* 11.

REYNOLDS, Eng., a dove, ar. *Pl.* 66, *cr.* 12.
REYNOLDS, a fox, (statant,) ppr. *Jus meum tuebor.* *Pl.* 126, *cr.* 5.
REYNOLDS, Suff., a wolf's head, erased, sa., collared, or. *Pl.* 8, *cr.* 4.
REYNOLDS, a dexter arm, in armour, embowed, in hand a garb, all ppr. *Pl.* 3, *or.* 3, (arm, *pl.* 120, *cr.* 11.)
REYNOLDS, Suff., a fox's head, erased, sa., gorged with a collar, or, charged with three torteaux, on neck a martlet. *Pl.* 69, *cr.* 15.
REYNOLDS, Surr., out of a mural coronet, or, a demi-talbot, ar., eared, gu., collared and lined, line ending in a knot, or. *Pl.* 5, *or.* 13.
REYNOLDS, Lond., on a mount, vert; a panther, couchant, gardant, ar., spotted various colours, fire issuing from mouth and ears, ppr., gorged with a collar and lined, gu., ringed, or. *Pl.* 9, *cr.* 14.
REYNOLDS, Norf., a cat, couchant, ppr., collared and lined, or.
REYNOLDS, Hants., a cock's head, erased, gu., beaked, or. *Pl.* 92, *cr.* 3.
REYNOLDS, Lond., a wyvern, wings elevated, in dexter a sword, in pale. *Fide, sed cui vide.* *Pl.* 63, *cr.* 13, (sword, *pl.* 87, *cr.* 5.)
REYNOLDS, Lond., a wyvern, ar., wings elevated, in dexter a sword, in pale, ppr., hilt and pommel, or. *Pl.* 63, *cr.* 13, (sword, *pl.* 87, *cr.* 5.)
REYNOLDS, a wyvern, (passant,) gu. *Pl.* 63, *cr.* 13.
REYNOLDS, Sir JOSHUA, Knt., out of a mural coronet, or, a demi-talbot, ar., collared and lined, gold. *Pl.* 5, *cr.* 13.
REYNOUS, Middx., a demi-griffin, segreant, regardant, erminois, holding a banner by the staff, point and tassels of the last charged with a (mullet,) az. *Pl.* 46, *cr.* 1.
RHAN, Middx., a sprig of three acorns. *Pl.* 69, *cr.* 12.
RHODES, Notts. and Derbs., a hand holding a bunch of acorns, ppr. *Pl.* 118, *cr.* 9, (acorns, *pl.* 69, *cr.* 12.)
RHODES, a griffin's head, erased, tied round neck with a ribbon. *Pl.* 69, *cr.* 13.
RHODES, an eagle, displayed, per pale, or and sa., on breast a cross pattée, counterchanged. *Pl.* 12, *cr.* 7, (cross, *pl.* 141.)
RHODES, Yorks., a leopard, sejant, or, spotted, sa., (collared and ringed, ar. *Pl.* 10, *cr.* 13.
RHODES, Devons., a hand holding an (oak)-branch, all ppr. *Cœlum non animum.* *Pl.* 43, *cr.* 6.
RIALL, a lion's head, erased, or, (charged with an escallop, gu.,) in mouth a trefoil, vert. *Pl.* 95, *cr.* 6, (trefoil, *pl.* 11, *cr.* 12.)
RIBLESDALE, Baron, (Lister) a stag's head, erased, per fess, ppr. and gu., attired, or, charged with a crescent. *Retinens vestigia famæ.* *Pl.* 61, *cr.* 9.
RIBTON, Eng., out of an Eastern crown, or, a demi-lion, rampant, gu. *Pl.* 45, *cr.* 7, (coronet, *pl.* 57, *cr.* 5.)
RIBTON, Bart., Iri., a dove, close, az., in mouth a (laurel)-branch, ppr. *J'aime la liberté.* *Pl.* 48, *cr.* 15.
RICARD, Lond., a man's head, couped at shoulders, ppr. *Pl.* 81, *cr.* 15.
RICARDO, Glouc., a bird, bearing in dexter a flag-staff with flag, the latter charged with a cross. *Pl.* 65, *cr.* 3.

RICCAAD, Lond., two lions' heads, erased and addorsed. *Pl.* 28, *cr.* 10.
RICE, Iri., an arm, in armour, embowed, in hand a scimitar, all ppr. *Pl.* 81, *cr.* 11.
RICE, Suff., a raven's head, erased, or. *Pl.* 27, *cr.* 13.
RICE, Wel., a raven, ppr. *Pl.* 123, *cr.* 2.
RICE, Baron Dynevor, on a chapeau, gu., turned up, erm., a lion, (statant), or. *Secret et hardi.* *Pl.* 107, *cr.* 1. See DYNEVOR, Baron.
RICE, Wel., a lion, rampant, (holding a doubleheaded shot, ppr.) *Pl.* 67, *cr.* 5.
RICE, a spear-head, issuing, embrued. *Pl.* 82, *cr.* 9.
RICH, Suff., a wyvern. *Pl.* 63, *cr.* 13.
RICH, on a mount, vert, a wyvern, ar. *Garde la foy.* *Pl.* 33, *cr.* 13.
RICH, Bart., Ess., on a mount, vert, a wyvern, ar. *Pl.* 33, *cr.* 13.
RICH, Lond., Ess., Surr., Norf., and Herts., on a mount, vert, a wyvern, rising, ar. *Pl.* 33, *cr.* 13.
RICH, Eng., a wyvern, ar. *Pl.* 63, *cr.* 13.
RICH, Iri., a (demi)-sea-lion, gu., armed and langued, az., finned, or. *Pl.* 80, *cr.* 13.
RICH, Berks., an armed arm and hand, ppr., holding a cross crosslet, fitched, gu. (Another, embowed.) *Pl.* 51, *cr.* 1.
RICH, Ess., on stump of tree, couped and erased, or, a hawk, wings addorsed, ar., preying on a (pheasant,) ppr. *Pl.* 5, *cr.* 4.
RICH, Kent, a demi-lion, rampant, sa., between two spears, erect, ar. *Pl.* 69, *cr.* 14.
RICH, Bart., Hants, a wyvern, wings (expanded.) *Pl.* 63, *cr.* 13.
RICHARD, Sco., a mountain cat, current, ppr. *Pl.* 119, *cr.* 7.
RICHARDS, Norf., a fleur-de-lis, per pale, erm. and ar. *Pl.* 68, *cr.* 12.
RICHARDS, Hants, a griffin's head, erased, ar. *Pl.* 48, *cr.* 6.
RICHARDS, Eng., a fox's head, couped, gu. *Pl.* 91, *cr.* 9.
RICHARDS, Devons., Middx., and Somers., a paschal lamb, passant, ar., staff and banner, ppr. *Pl.* 48, *cr.* 13.
RICHARDS, Bart., Suss., a lion, rampant, az. *Honore et amore.* *Pl.* 67, *cr.* 5.
RICHARDS, Hants, an eagle, wings expanded, ppr. *Pl.* 126, *cr.* 7.
RICHARDS, an eagle's head, couped, ppr. *Pl.* 100, *cr.* 10.
RICHARDS, an arm, in armour, embowed, ppr., garnished, or, in gauntlet, a staff, raguly, sa., the end (burning.) *Pl.* 45, *cr.* 10, (staff, *pl.* 11, *cr.* 2.)
RICHARDS, Middx., on a chapeau, gu., (another, sa.,) turned up, erm., a lamb, passant, ar., resting dexter on a lozenge, or. *Pl.* 116, *cr.* 1, (lozenge, *pl.* 141; chapeau, *pl.* 127, *fig.* 13.)
RICHARDS, Middx., on a chapeau, gu., turned up, erm., a lamb, passant, ar., resting dexter on an escutcheon. *Pl.* 116, *cr.* 1, (chapeau, *pl.* 127, *fig.* 13; escutcheon, *pl.* 42, *cr.* 8.)
RICHARDS, Suss., a lion, passant, az. *Honore et amore.* *Pl.* 48, *cr.* 8.
RICHARDS, RICHARD, Esq., of Caerynwch, Merioneth, a dexter arm, in hand a scimitar, all ppr. *Pl.* 92, *cr.* 5.

RICHARDS, Yorks., out of a mural coronet, gu., a talbot's head, ar., (collared, vert, ringed, or.) *Pl.* 91, *cr.* 15.

RICHARDSON, Surr., out of a mural coronet, or, a demi-lion, rampant, gu., (between paws a guidon, ar., charged with a slip of oak, ppr., fructed, gold, the staff and tassels, of the last.) *Pl.* 120, *cr.* 14.

RICHARDSON, Sco., a unicorn's head, couped, erm., horned, or. *Virtute acquiritur honos. Pl.* 20, *cr.* 1.

RICHARDSON, a bull's head, couped, ppr. *Virtute et robore. Pl.* 120, *cr.* 7.

RICHARDSON, Sco., out of a ducal coronet, or, a unicorn's head, ppr. *Virtute acquiritur honos. Pl.* 45, *cr.* 14.

RICHARDSON, a hand, in armour, holding a sword, in pale, all ppr. *Virtute acquiritur honos. Pl.* 125, *cr.* 5.

RICHARDSON, Iri., a hind's head, couped, or. *Pl.* 21, *cr.* 9.

RICHARDSON, Eng., on a ducal coronet, a unicorn's head, couped, erm., horned, or. *Virtute acquiritur honos. Pl.* 45, *cr.* 14.

RICHARDSON, on a chapeau, a wyvern, wings addorsed. *Pl.* 104, *cr.* 5, (without crown.)

RICHARDSON, a lion, rampant, between paws two oak-slips, fructed, ppr. *Pl.* 125, *cr.* 2, (oak, *pl.* 32, *cr.* 13.)

RICHARDSON, Yorks., a demi-lion, holding a thistle, ppr. *Firmus infirmis. Pl.* 45, *cr.* 15, (without fleur-de-lis.)

RICHARDSON, of Pitfour, Sco., a dexter cubit arm, in armour, in hand a sword, in pale, ppr. *Virtute acquiritur honos. Pl.* 125, *cr.* 5.

RICHARDSON, HENRY, Esq., of Aber-Hirnant, Merioneth, on a ducal coronet, or, a unicorn's head, couped, erm., horned, or. *Virtute acquiritur honos. Pl.* 45, *cr.* 14.

RICHARDSON, Worc., an armed arm, hand holding a sword, enfiled with a chaplet of roses, ppr., hilt and pommel, sa. *Pl.* 125, *cr.* 5, (chaplet, *pl.* 56, *cr.* 6.)

RICHARDSON, Suss. and Yorks., an arm, in armour, couped at elbow, (wielding) a falchion, ar., the gripe, vert, hilt and pommel, or. *Pl.* 125, *cr.* 5.

RICHARDSON, WILLIAM-WESTBROOKE, Esq., of Finden Place, Suss., out of a mural coronet, or, a cubit arm, in armour, in gauntlet a falchion, ar., gripe, vert, hilt and pommel, or. *Pl.* 115, *cr.* 14.

RICHARDSON, Durh., on a mural coronet, or, a lion's head, erased, ermines, langued, gu., crowned with an earl's coronet, gold. *Pl.* 45, *cr.* 9, (coronet, *pl.* 127, *fig.* 8.)

RICHARDSON, Glouc., a dexter cubit arm, in armour, erect, in hand, ppr., a falchion. *Pl.* 125, *cr.* 5.

RICHARDSON, Glouc., a cubit arm, ar., in hand, ppr., a broken sword, blade, of the first, hilt and pommel, or. *Pl.* 22, *cr.* 6, (without cloud.)

RICHARDSON, Ess., a cubit arm, (in armour, erect, ppr., in gauntlet) a broken sword, ar., hilt and pommel, or. *Pl.* 22, *cr.* 6, (without cloud.)

RICHARDSON, Norf. and Worc., on a marquess's coronet, a dexter arm, in armour, couped at elbow, in fess, in gauntlet a sword, erect, all ppr. *Pl.* 96, *cr.* 11, (coronet, *pl.* 127, *fig.* 4.)

RICHARDSON, Sco., a dexter arm, in armour, hand holding a broadsword, in pale, all ppr. *Virtute acquiritur honos. Pl.* 125, *cr.* 5.

RICHARS, Norf., a fleur-de-lis, per pale, erm., and sa. *Pl.* 68, *cr.* 12.

RICHES, Eng., a hand, erect, issuing from a cloud, holding a garb, in bend sinister. *Pl.* 67, *cr.* 12.

RICHMOND, Eng., the sun in glory. *Pl.* 68, *cr.* 14.

RICHMOND, Sco., between two palm-branches, in orle, vert, a mullet, gu. *Pl.* 3, *cr.* 9.

RICHMOND, Norf., on a mount, vert, an eagle, wings expanded, erm., the beak and feathers on back of head and tip of tail, or. *Pl.* 126, *cr.* 7.

RICHMOND, Wilts. and Bucks., a tilting-spear, ar., headed, or, broken in three parts, one piece erect, the other two in saltier, enfiled with a ducal coronet, of the last. *Pl.* 33, *cr.* 3, (coronet, *pl.* 51, *cr.* 1.)

RICHMOND, Duke of, Earl of March, and Baron Settrington, Eng.; Duke of Lennox, Earl of Darnley, and Baron Methuen, Sco.; and Duke of Aubigny, in France, (Gordon-Lennox;) on a chapeau, gu., turned up, erm., a lion, statant, gardant, or, ducally crowned, gu., and gorged with a collar, compony, ar. and gu. *En la rose je fleurie. Pl.* 105, *cr.* 5.

RICHTER, Lond., an eagle, displayed, sa., in dexter an olive-branch, vert, and in sinister a thunderbolt, ppr. *Pl.* 99, *cr.* 5, (branch, *pl.* 98, *cr.* 8; thunderbolt, *pl.* 110, *cr.* 3.)

RICHTIE, a cubit arm, in hand a cross moline. *Pl.* 99, *cr.* 15, (moline, *pl.* 141.)

RICKARD, Sco., a grey cat, sejant, gardant. *Prenez garde. Pl.* 24, *cr.* 6.

RICKARDS, Wel., from a tower, ppr., a talbot's head, ar., collared, vert, ringed, or. *Pl.* 2, *cr.* 15, (tower, *pl.* 105, *cr.* 10.)

RICKARDS, Eng., a lion, passant, gardant, ppr. *Pl.* 120, *cr.* 5.

RICKART, of Rickartown, Sco., a grey cat, (passant.) *Prenez garde* — and — *Præmonitus præmunitus. Pl.* 119, *cr.* 7.

RICKETS, and RICKETTS, Eng., a demi-lion, rampant, gardant in dexter a battle-axe, all ppr. *Pl.* 26, *cr.* 7.

RICKETTS, Heref., an arm, embowed, vested, erminois, charged on arm with two roses, gu., cuffed, az., hand, ppr., holding a (scimitar,) ar., hilt and pommel, or. *Quid verum atque decens. Pl.* 12, *cr.* 1, (rose, *pl.* 141.)

RICKETTS, Bart., Glouc., out of a naval coronet, or, a dexter arm, embowed, vested, az., charged on sleeve with two roses, ar., in hand a scimitar, the arm in front of an anchor, in bend sinister, sa. *Prend moi tel que je suis.*

RICKFORD, Bucks., a hawk's lure, winged, ppr. *Pl.* 97, *cr.* 14, (wings, *pl.* 39, *cr.* 7.)

RICKTHORNE, or RYKTHORNE, Lond. and Somers., a buck, trippant, ppr., attired, or, in mouth a rose, gu., stalked and leaved, vert. *Pl.* 68, *cr.* 2, (rose, *pl.* 55, *cr.* 9.)

RICROFT, Lanc., a griffin's head, erased. *Pl.* 48, *cr.* 6.

RIDALL, RIDDALL, and RIDDELL, Durh. and Northumb., a demi-lion, erminois, supporting (between paws,) a garb, az. (Another, or,) *Pl.* 84, *cr.* 7.

RIDDEL, Sco., a dexter hand, ppr., holding an ear of rye, slipped and bladed, or. *Virtus maturat.* Pl. 71, cr. 15.

RIDDELL, Sco., a demi-greyhound, ar. *Right to share.* Pl. 48, cr. 3.

RIDDELL, a greyhound, issuing, ppr. *Row and retake.* Pl. 48, cr. 3.

RIDDELL, a greyhound, issuing, ppr. *Hab shar,* or *Hope to share.* Pl. 48, cr. 3.

RIDDELL, or RIDELL, Norf., a martlet, ar. Pl. 111, cr. 5.

RIDDELL, a demi-lion, rampant. Pl. 67, cr. 10.

RIDDELL, Bart., Sco., a hand issuing from the coronet of a French count, holding a baton, all ppr. *Utile et dulce.*

RIDDELL, of Riddell, Bart., Sco., a demi-greyhound, ar. *I hope to share.* Pl. 48, cr. 3.

RIDDLE, Eng., a demi-greyhound. Pl. 48, cr. 3.

RIDDOCK, Sco. and Iri., a hind's head, erased. *Tu ne cede malis.* Pl. 6, cr. 1.

RIDELL, Sco., a demi-greyhound, (salient, ar., ducally gorged, or.) Pl. 48, cr. 3.

RIDELL, a talbot's head, (couped,) ar., collared, az. Pl. 2, cr. 15.

RIDEOUT, or RIDOUT, Suss., a trotting horse, ar., bridled, gu. *Toutz Foitz Chevalier.* Pl. 99, cr. 11.

RIDER, Middx., out of a ducal coronet, or, a dragon's head, ar. Pl. 59, cr. 14.

RIDER, an eagle, displayed, ppr., in dexter a laurel-branch, in sinister a thunderbolt, of the first. Pl. 99, cr. 5, (branch, pl. 123, cr. 5; thunderbolt, pl. 110, cr. 3.)

RIDER, Middx., Surr., and Staffs., out of a mural coronet, or, a dragon's head, ar. Pl. 101, cr. 4.

RIDER, Warw., out of a mural coronet, per pale, or and az., a snake, in pale, ppr., in mouth a trefoil, slipped, vert. Pl. 116, cr. 2, (trefoil, pl. 141; coronet, pl. 103, cr. 11.)

RIDER, Lanc., a crescent, ar. *Dum cresco, spero.* Pl. 18, cr. 14.

RIDGE, Eng., a hand, apaumée, thereon an eye, ppr. Pl. 99, cr. 13.

RIDGE, Sco., out of a mural coronet, two arms embowed, hands holding an escutcheon. Pl. 30, cr. 15.

RIDGE, Suss., a peacock in pride, ar. Pl. 92, cr. 11.

RIDGEWAY, Devons., a hawk, ppr. Pl. 67, cr. 3.

RIDGEWAY, Earl of Londonderry, a dromedary, couchant, ar., bridle and trappings, or, saddle, chequy, sa., and of the second. Pl. 70, cr. 2.

RIDGEWAY, a demi-lion, gu., (holding an eagle's wing, ar.) Pl. 84, cr. 7.

RIDGEWAY, on a mount, vert, a hawk, ppr., wings addorsed, beaked and legged, or. Pl. 81, cr. 12, (without coronet.)

RIDGLEY, Staffs. and Salop, a buck's head, erased, or. Pl. 66, cr. 9.

RIDGWAY, Bart., Devons., a dromedary, couchant, ar., mane, sa., bridle and trappings, or. Pl. 70, cr. 2.

RIDING, a griffin's head, erased, ar. Pl. 48, cr. 6.

RIDLEY, Northumb., a bull, passant, gu. *Constans fidei.* Pl. 66, cr. 11.

RIDLEY, Eng., a greyhound, current, ar., (collared, or.) Pl. 28, cr. 7.

RIDLEY, Salop, a greyhound, (passant, ar., collared, gu.) Pl. 101, cr. 4.

RIDLEY, Chesh. and Northumb., a greyhound, current, ar. Pl. 28, cr. 7.

RIDLEY, Lond., a bull, passant, gu. Pl. 66, cr. 11.

RIDLEY, JOHN, Esq., of Parkend, Northumb., a bull, passant, tail turned over the back, gu. *Constans fidei.* Pl. 66, cr. 11.

RIDLEY, Sir MATTHEW WHITE, Bart., Heaton Hall, same crest and motto.

RIDOUT, and RIDEOUT, Eng., a savage's head, issuing, ppr. Pl. 19, cr. 1.

RIDOUT, Eng., a demi-lion, gu. Pl. 67, cr. 10.

RIDOUT, on a mount, vert, a horse, passant, ar., bridled, or. Pl. 99, cr. 11, (mount, pl. 57, cr. 9.)

RIDPATH, Sco., a demi-boar, gu., bristled and armed, or. Pl. 20, cr. 5.

RIDSDALE, Yorks., a lion's head, az. Pl. 126, cr. 1.

RIDSDALE, Wakefield Hall, Yorks., a lamb. *Deus est spes.* See BURKE'S ARMOURY.

RIG, Sco., a cock, sa., beaked and armed, gu. *Virtute et labore.* Pl. 67, cr. 14.

RIGAUD, Eng., a buck's head, erased, az. Pl. 66, cr. 9.

RIGBY, Lanc., an antelope's head, erased, or, guttée-de-sang. Pl. 24, cr. 7.

RIGBY, Lanc., a goat's head, sa., bezantée, attires and beard, or. Pl. 105, cr. 14.

RIGBYE, Lanc., an antelope's head, erased, sa., armed, bearded, and crined, or. Pl. 24, cr. 7.

RIGDON, Linc., a cock's head, ppr., combed and wattled, gu., beaked, ar. Pl. 92, cr. 3.

RIGG, a cock, sa., beaked and armed, gu. *Virtute et labore.* Pl. 67, cr. 14.

RIGG, a cock, ppr. *Virtute et labore.* Pl. 67, cr. 14.

RIGG, Eng., a cock, sa., combed, legged, and wattled, gu. Pl. 67, cr. 14.

RIGGE, Eng., a human heart, or, charged with a rose, gu. Pl. 123, cr. 7, (rose, pl. 141.)

RIGGE, Lanc., a drake, ppr., in beak an escallop, ar. *Festina lente.* Pl. 90, cr. 15, (escallop, pl. 141.)

RIGGELEY, Staffs., a buck's head, erased, or. Pl. 66, cr. 9.

RIGGES, Surr., Suss., and Hants., a talbot, passant, gu., eared, or, (in mouth a bird-bolt, or, plumed, ar.) Pl. 120, cr. 8.

RIGGS, and RYGGES, Middx. and Linc., a talbot, passant, gu., eared, or, (in mouth a bird-bolt, gold.) Pl. 120, cr. 8.

RIGHTON, Kent, a tree. Pl. 16, cr. 8.

RIGMAIDEN, Lanc., a buck's head, erased, sa. Pl. 66, cr. 9.

RIGMAYDEN, Eng., a buck's head, erased, sa., attired, or. Pl. 66, cr. 9.

RIGNOUS, Eng., a demi-griffin, segreant, regardant, erm., holding a banner, or, the staff, point, and tassels, of the last, charged with a (mullet,) sa. Pl. 46, cr. 1.

RIKY, Iri., a dexter hand holding a sword, ppr. Pl. 21, cr. 10.

RILEY, Berks., an oak-tree, a snake clinging to the trunk, ppr. Pl. 84, cr. 4.

RILEY, a dragon's head, or, pellettée. Pl. 87, cr. 12.

RILEY, a dragon's head, erased, sa., charged with a plate and two bezants. Pl. 107, cr. 10, (charging, pl. 141.)

RILEY, Lanc., a dragon's head, erased, sa., charged with three bezants. Pl. 107, cr. 10, (bezants, pl. 141.)

RILEY, Lanc. and Linc., a dragon's head, erased, gu., bezantée. Pl. 107, cr. 10.

RIMMER, Eng., a dolphin, naiant, ppr. *Pl.* 48, *cr.* 9.

RING, Eng., a hand, vested, sa., cuffed, or, holding a roll of paper. *Pl.* 32, *cr.* 6.

RING, a dragon, wings elevated. *Pl.* 90, *cr.* 10.

RINGELEY, a wolf's head, erased, paly of four, or and sa., ducally gorged, ar., devouring a fish, gu.

RINGER, Norf., a unicorn's head, couped, or, semée-de-lis, az., between two branches of laurel, vert. *Pl.* 54, *cr.* 9, (fleur-de-lis, *pl.* 141.)

RINGEWOOD, or RINGWOOD, Eng., a goat running towards a tree, ppr. *Pl.* 70, *cr.* 3.

RINGLEY, a wolf's head, paly, or and sa., enfiled round neck with a coronet, ar., in mouth a fish, gu.

RINTOUL, Sco., an elm-tree, ppr. *Pl.* 18, *cr.* 10.

RIPINGHAM, of Armington, Warw., a demi-antelope, gu., billettée, ar. *Pl.* 34, *cr.* 8.

RIPINGTON, Eng., a demi-antelope, gu., billettée, ar. *Pl.* 34, *cr.* 8.

RIPLEY, Eng., a demi-Bengal (tiger,) ducally gorged, ppr. *Pl.* 125, *cr.* 4.

RIPLEY, Lond., Middx., Wilts., and Yorks., a demi-lion, rampant, regardant, vert, collared, ar., supporting between paws an escutcheon, per cheveron, or and az. *Pl.* 33, *cr.* 2, (escutcheon, *pl.* 75, *cr.* 10.)

RIPON, Earl of, and Viscount Goderich, (Robinson,) out of a coronet composed of fleurs-de-lis, a buck at gaze, or. *Foi est tout. Pl.* 19, *cr.* 14.

RIPPON, Eng., an antelope's head, erased, or. *Pl.* 24, *cr.* 7.

RIPPON, Northumb., a lion, sejant, ducally gorged, in dexter a cross (pattée-fleury,) fitched, sa. *Our hope is on high*—and—*Frangas, non flectas. Pl.* 65, *cr.* 6.

RISDON, Devons., an elephant's head, erased, erm., eared and armed, or. *Pl.* 68, *cr.* 4.

RISDON, Eng., an elephant's head, erased, erm. *Pl.* 68, *cr.* 4.

RISHTON, Lanc., on a chapeau, gu., turned up, erm., a demi-lion, erminois. *Pl.* 46, *cr.* 8.

RISHTON, Lanc., a demi-lion, rampant, gu. *Pl.* 67, *cr.* 10.

RISHTON, on a chapeau, gu., turned up, erm., a demi-lion, rampant, of the first. *Pl.* 46, *cr.* 8.

RISHTON, Lanc., a lion, passant, sa. *Pl.* 48, *cr.* 8.

RISING, Eng., a pelican, vulning, ppr. *Pl.* 109, *cr.* 15.

RITCHIE, Eng., a demi-Bengal (tiger,) ppr., ducally gorged, gu. *Pl.* 53, *cr.* 10.

RITCHIE, Sco., a unicorn's head. *Virtute acquiritur honos. Pl.* 20, *cr.* 1.

RITCHIE, Sco., a dexter hand holding a cross flory, gu. *Ostendo non ostento. Pl.* 75, *cr.* 3.

RITCHIE, Lond., out of a ducal coronet, or, a unicorn's head, ar. *Pl.* 45, *cr.* 14.

RITSON, Eng., a lion, rampant. *Pl.* 67, *cr.* 5.

RIVEL, Eng., a gem-ring, or, stoned, gu. *Pl.* 35, *cr.* 3.

RIVERS, Eng., a griffin's tail, erased, sa. *Pl.* 17, *cr.* 4.

RIVERS, an arm, in armour, embowed, hand grasping a dart. *Pl.* 96, *cr.* 6.

RIVERS, DE, Eng., a land-tortoise, ppr. *Pl.* 12, *cr.* 13.

RIVERS, DE, Sco., a land-tortoise, ppr. *Pl.* 12, *cr.* 13.

RIVERS, Bart., Kent, on a mount, vert, a bull, passant, ar., (collared, ringed, lined, and armed, or.) *Secus rivos aquarum. Pl.* 39, *cr.* 5.

RIVERS, Baron, of Sudley Castle, (Beckford,) a stork, ppr., beaked and membered, or, dexter resting on an anchor, erect, cabled, of the last. *Æquam servare mentem. Pl.* 61, *cr.* 10.

RIVERSDALE, Baron, Iri., (Tonson,) out of a mural coronet, or, a (cubit) arm, in pale, in armour, in hand a sword, all ppr. *Manus hæc inimica tyrannis. Pl.* 115, *cr.* 14.

RIVES, Dors., a greyhound, sejant, sa. *Pl.* 66, *cr.* 15.

RIVES, Dors., a greyhound, sejant, sa., bezantée, (collared, or.) *Pl.* 66, *cr.* 15.

RIVETT, Camb., an arm, in hand a battle-axe, ppr. *Pl.* 73, *cr.* 7.

RIVETT, of Crettinge, Suff.: 1. An arm, erect, (bendy of four, ar. and sa.,) hand, ppr., grasping a broken sword, of the first, hilt and pommel, or. *Pl.* 22, *cr.* 6, (without cloud.) 2. An arm, in hand a battle-axe. *Pl.* 73, *cr.* 7.

RIVETT, Hants, a cubit arm, in armour, erect, in hand a sword, ppr. *Pl.* 125, *cr.* 5.

RIVINGTON, Eng., on a ducal coronet, a hawk, belled, ppr. *Pl.* 41, *cr.* 10.

RIX, Eng., a demi-griffin, ppr. *Pl.* 18, *cr.* 6.

RIXON, Eng., out of a mural coronet, a tiger's head, ducally gorged. *Pl.* 5, *cr.* 15.

ROACH, Eng., a horse's head, (erased,) ar., bridle, gu. *Pl.* 92, *cr.* 1.

ROACH, on a mount, vert, (a pelican, preying on a roach, all ppr.) *Pl.* 84, *cr.* 8.

ROACH, on a rock, a stork, wings elevated, in dexter a fish, all ppr. *Pl.* 122, *cr.* 7, (fish, *pl.* 84, *cr.* 8.)

ROACHEAD, Sco., a savage's arm, erect, ppr. *Pro patriâ. Pl.* 87, *cr.* 7.

ROAD, and ROADES, Eng., an eagle, displayed, in dexter a dagger, ppr. *Pl.* 107, *cr.* 4.

ROAED, and ROALD, in a ducal coronet, two dragons' wings, expanded, or, with a chapeau between them, ar. *Pl.* 17, *cr.* 9, (chapeau and wings, *pl.* 105, *crs.* 5 and 11.)

ROANE, a stag's head, (erased,) ppr., attired, or, in mouth an acorn, gold, leaved, vert. *Pl.* 100, *cr.* 8.

ROBARTES-AGAR, of Llanhyderock, Cornw.: 1. A lion, rampant, or, holding a flaming sword, in pale, ppr., hilt and pommel, gold. *Pl.* 64, *cr.* 2, (sword, *pl.* 58, *cr.* 11.) 2. A demi-lion, rampant, or. *Pl.* 67, *cr.* 10.

ROBARTS, Eng., out of a maunch, per pale, ar. and gu., cuff, of the second, a hand clenched, ppr. *Pl.* 22, *cr.* 14.

ROBARTS, a stag, lodged, regardant, ppr., attired, or. *Pl.* 67, *cr.* 2.

ROBARTS, Lond., a stag's head, erased, per fess, erminois and gu., attired, or, gorged with a collar, (invected, per fess, az. and ar., thereon a cross pattée, between two annulets, gold.) *Pl.* 125, *cr.* 6, (without roses.)

ROBARTS, Lond., a stag, lodged, ppr., attired, or. *Pl.* 67, *cr.* 2.

ROBB, Sco., a hand holding a chapeau, between two branches of laurel, in orle, ppr. *Pl.* 59, *cr.* 4.

ROBE, Lond., Somers., and Sco, an ermine, ar. *Candore. Pl.* 9, *cr.* 5.

ROBE, Lond., a cross crosslet, fitched, or. *Pl.* 16, *cr.* 10.

ROBERTON, an anchor, erect, ppr. *Securitate.* *Pl.* 25, *cr.* 15.

ROBERTON, Sco., an anchor, ppr. *For security.* *Pl.* 25, *cr.* 15.

ROBERTS, Eng., a demi-lion, rampant, az., holding a mullet, sa. (Another, mullet, ar.) *Pl.* 89, *cr.* 10.

ROBERTS, Iri., an antelope's head, erased, per fess, ar. and gu. *Pl.* 24, *cr.* 7.

ROBERTS, Glouc., Bristol, Leic., Salop, and Iri., a stag's head. *Pl.* 91, *cr.* 14.

ROBERTS, Leic., a leopard's head, gardant, erased, ar., semée of torteaux. *Pl.* 56, *cr.* 7.

ROBERTS, Lond., Linc., Worc., and Cornw., a demi-lion, az., holding a mullet, ar., (pierced,) sa. *Pl.* 89, *cr.* 10.

ROBERTS, Glouc., Bristol, Salop, Somers., Leic., and Iri., an antelope's head, erased, parted per fess, or and gu. *Pl.* 24, *cr.* 7.

ROBERTS, Middx. and Ess.: 1. Out of a ducal coronet, or, a demi-greyhound, sa. *Pl.* 70, *cr.* 5, (demi, *pl.* 48, *cr.* 3.) 2. A leopard's head, gardant and erased, ar., charged with torteaux. *Pl.* 56, *cr.* 7.

ROBERTS, on a chapeau, az., turned up, erm., a lion, sejant, gardant. *Pl.* 113, *cr.* 8.

ROBERTS, a stag, trippant, sa. *Successus a Deo est. Pl.* 68, *cr.* 2.

ROBERTS, Kent and Suss., an eagle, displayed, ar., beaked and legged, or, gorged with a chaplet of laurel, vert., charged with a crescent. *Pl.* 84, *cr.* 14, (without mount; crescent, *pl.* 141.)

ROBERTS, Kent, an eagle, displayed, ar., gorged with a chaplet, vert. *Pl.* 84, *cr.* 14, (without mount.)

ROBERTS, Middx., a greyhound, ar., (gorged, gu.) *Pl.* 104, *cr.* 1, (without chapeau.)

ROBERTS, Salop, on a mount, vert, a buck, (trippant, sa., attired, or, ducally gorged and chained, gold.) *Pl.* 50, *cr.* 6.

ROBERTS, a griffin's head, couped. *Pl.* 38, *cr.* 3.

ROBERTS, an eagle's head, couped. *Pl.* 100, *cr.* 10.

ROBERTS, a demi-lion, rampant, az., (charged on breast) with a mullet, or. *Pl.* 89, *cr.* 10.

ROBERTS, Middx. and Cornw., a lion, rampant, or, in dexter a sword, the blade wavy, ar., hilt and pommel, of the first. *Pl.* 64, *cr.* 2, (sword, *pl.* 71, *cr.* 7.)

ROBERTS, Middx., Ess., and Leic., out of a ducal coronet, or, a demi-greyhound, sa. *Pl.* 70, *cr.* 5, (demi, *pl.* 48, *cr.* 3.)

ROBERTS, Middx., Ess., and Leic., a leopard's head, gardant, erased, ar., charged with torteaux. *Pl.* 56, *cr.* 7.

ROBERTS, Bart., co. Cork, on a mount, vert, an eagle, displayed, az., wreathed round neck with ivy, ppr. *Pl.* 84, *cr.* 14.

ROBERTSON, Sco., a wolf's head, (erased.) ar., in mouth a rose, gu. *Robore et sapore. Pl.* 92, *cr.* 15.

ROBERTSON, Sco., a hand holding a crescent, ppr. *Quæque favilla micat. Pl.* 38, *cr.* 7.

ROBERTSON, a sleeping dog. *Dinna waken sleeping dogs. Pl.* 29, *cr.* 3.

ROBERTSON, a dexter hand holding up an imperial crown, all ppr., a crescent, ar., for difference. *Virtutis gloria merces. Pl.* 97, *cr.* 12, (crescent, *pl.* 141.)

ROBERTSON, a dexter hand, issuing from a cloud, holding a garb, ppr. *Perseveranti dabitur. Pl.* 67, *cr.* 12.

ROBERTSON, a swan, ppr. *Vitæ faciendo nemini timeas. Pl.* 122, *cr.* 13, (without mount.)

ROBERTSON, DAVID, Esq., of Ladykirk, Berwick, a dexter hand holding up an imperial crown, all ppr. *Virtutis gloria merces. Pl.* 97, *cr.* 12.

ROBERTSON, Hoe Place, Surr., same crest and motto.

ROBERTSON, a phœnix in flames, ppr. *Post funera virtus. Pl.* 44, *cr.* 8.

ROBERTSON, Eng., a triton, in sinister a trident, ppr. *Pl.* 35, *cr.* 10.

ROBERTSON, Sco., a dexter hand, holding two laurel branches, slipped, ppr. *Hac virtus mercede digna. Pl.* 86, *cr.* 1.

ROBERTSON, Sco., a savage's arm, erect and erased, ppr. *Intemerata fides. Pl.* 87, *cr.* 7.

ROBERTSON, Sco., a cubit arm, erect, hand holding a falchion, enfiled with an antique crown, all ppr. *Ramis miscat radix. Pl.* 21, *cr.* 10, (crown, *pl.* 79, *cr.* 12.)

ROBERTSON, Lond., a dagger, erect, ensigned on point with a regal crown, ppr. *Intemerata fides. Pl.* 73, *cr.* 9, (crown, *pl.* 97, *cr.* 12.)

ROBERTSON, Linc., a stag, trippant, or. *Pl.* 68, *cr.* 2.

ROBERTSON, Sco., in dexter hand a sword, in pale, ensigned with a royal crown. *Virtutis gloria merces. Pl.* 23, *cr.* 15, (crown, *pl.* 97, *cr.* 12.)

ROBERTSON, WILLIAM, Esq., of Kinlochmoidart, Inverness, out of a cloud, a dexter hand holding up a wheat-sheaf, ppr. *Pl.* 67, *cr.* 12.

ROBIN, Chesh. and Derb., a robin, ppr. *Vivit post funera virtus. Pl.* 10, *cr.* 12.

ROBINS, Lond., a talbot's head, ar. *Pl.* 123, *cr.* 15.

ROBINS, a fleur-de-lis between two dolphins, embowed. *Pl.* 81, *cr.* 2, (fleur-de-lis, *pl.* 141.)

ROBINSON, Eng., a stag, trippant, or, charged on side with an (ermine-spot,) sa. *Pl.* 61, *cr.* 15.

ROBINSON, Iri., a buck, trippant, or, pellettée. *Non nobis solum, sed toti mundo nati. Pl.* 68, *cr.* 2.

ROBINSON, Yorks., a buck, trippant, or, pellettée. *Pl.* 68, *cr.* 2.

ROBINSON, Yorks., in a coronet, composed of fleurs-de-lis, or, a mount, vert, thereon a buck at gaze, gold. *Virtute, non verbis. Pl.* 19, *cr.* 14.

ROBINSON, Bart., Eng., a buck, trippant, or, (collared and lined, vert.) *Pl.* 68, *cr.* 2.

ROBINSON, a dog, couchant, gardant. *Pl.* 29, *cr.* 3.

ROBINSON, a buck, or, pellettée. *Pl.* 88, *cr.* 9, (without arrow.)

ROBINSON, on a ducal coronet, or, a mount, vert, thereon a buck, gold. *Pl.* 46, *cr.* 2.

ROBINSON, Linc., a buck, trippant, sa., bezantée. *Pl.* 68, *cr.* 2.

ROBINSON, Lond. and Yorks., a stag, trippant, vert., attired, or, bezantée. *Pl.* 68, *cr.* 2.

ROBINSON, of Tottenham, Middx., a buck, ppr., resting dexter on an escutcheon, charged with a trefoil, vert. *Pl.* 68, *cr.* 2, (escutcheon, *pl.* 75, *cr.* 2.)

ROBINSON, Lond. and Staffs., a goldfinch, ppr., standing on the sun in splendour, or. *Pl.* 10, *cr.* 12, (sun, *pl.* 68, *cr.* 14.)

ROBINSON, out of a mural coronet, per pale, gu. and or, a demi-stag, per pale, of the last and first, horns counterchanged. *Pl.* 55, *cr.* 9, (coronet, *pl.* 101, *cr.* 3.)

ROBINSON, out of a cloud, a dexter arm, erect, hand holding up a garb. *Pl.* 67, *cr.* 12.

ROBINSON, Northamp. and Northumb., out of a mural coronet, chequy, ar., and gu., a demi-buck, or, attired, ppr. *Pl.* 112, *cr.* 5, (buck, *pl.* 55, *cr.* 9.)

ROBINSON, Earl of Ripon. *See* RIPON.

ROBINSON, Somers., on a mural coronet, gu., a buck at gaze, or. *Pl.* 19; *cr.* 14, (coronet, same plate, *cr.* 7.)

ROBINSON, Suff., a buck, trippant, or. *Pl.* 68, *cr.* 2.

ROBINSON, Suff., a stag's head, erased, or. *Pl.* 66, *cr.* 9.

ROBINSON, Yorks., a roebuck, trippant, or. *Virtute, non verbis. Pl.* 68, *cr.* 2.

ROBINSON, Bucks., on a mural coronet, chequy, ar. and az., a stag's head, cabossed, ppr. *Vincum malum bono. Pl.* 112, *cr.* 5, (head, *pl.* 36, *cr.* 1.)

ROBINSON, Cornw., a buck's head, erased. *Pl.* 66, *cr.* 9.

ROBINSON, Durh., a stag, trippant, or. *Pl.* 68, *cr.* 2.

ROBINSON, Lond., a buck, statant, ppr. *Pl.* 88, *cr.* 9, (without arrow.)

ROBINSON, Haveringate Bower, Ess., a stag, trippant, ppr. *Pl.* 68, *cr.* 2.

ROBINSON, Bart., Somers., a buck, trippant, or, in front of park pales, ppr. *Pl.* 68, *cr.* 2, (pales, *pl.* 13, *cr.* 12.)

ROBINSON, Bart., Iri., a buck, trippant, or. *Pl.* 68, *cr.* 2.

ROBISON, Sco., a hand, holding a royal crown, ppr. *Tute tua tuta. Pl.* 97, *cr.* 2.

ROBLEY, Eng., a mount, semée of (cinquefoils.) *Pl.* 62, *cr.* 11.

ROBLEY, a goat's head, erased, ar., attired, ppr. *Pl.* 29, *cr.* 13.

ROBOTHAM, a demi-griffin, az., guttée, ar., ducally gorged, or. *Pl.* 18, *cr.* 6.

ROBOTTOM, and ROBOTHAM, Eng., an eagle, or, pellettée, preying on a wing, ar., vulned, gu. *Pl.* 114, *cr.* 5.

ROBSERT, Eng., a fish's head, erased, in fess, ppr. *Pl.* 79, *cr.* 10.

ROBSON, Eng., a boar's head, erect, or. *Pl.* 21, *cr.* 7.

ROBSON, out of a mural coronet, az., a boar's head, erminois. *Pl.* 6, *cr.* 2, (without sword.)

ROBSON, Durh., a boar's head, erased, and erect, or. *Justus esto et non metue. Pl.* 21, *cr.* 7.

ROBSON, Northumb., a boar's head, erased and erect, or. *Pl.* 21, *cr.* 7.

ROBSON, Somers. and Durh., out of a mural coronet, az., a boar's head, erminois, crined, of the last. *Pl.* 6, *cr.* 2, (without sword.)

ROBY, Eng., a garb, vert. *Pl.* 48, *cr.* 10.

ROBYNS, Staffs. and Worc., between two dolphins, haurient, (respecting each other,) or, a fleur-de-lis, per pale, ar. and sa. *Pl.* 81, *cr.* 2, (fleur-de-lis, *pl.* 141.)

ROBYNSONE, or ROBYSON, a cubit arm, vested, bendy-wavy of six, or and az., cuffed, ar., hand holding a Saracen's head by the beard, ppr.

ROCH, Iri., on a rock, a (rook,) in dexter a fish all ppr. *Pl.* 84, *cr.* 8.

ROCHE, Iri., out of a ducal coronet, or, the attires of a stag affixed to scalp, gu. *Pl.* 86, *cr.* 10.

ROCHE, Eng., a rock. *Mon Dieu est ma roche. Pl.* 73, *cr.* 12.

ROCHE, Eng., a lion's head, erased, per fess, or and sa., within a chain, issuing, in orle, az. *Pl.* 28, *cr.* 12.

ROCHE, of Granagh Castle, co. Kilkenny, a rock, ppr., thereon a fish-eagle, wings displayed, ar., membered, or, in dexter a roach. *Mon Dieu est ma roche. Pl.* 84, *cr.* 8.

ROCHE, Iri., on a rock, ppr., an eagle, purp., wings diaplayed. *Mon Dieu est ma roche. Pl.* 126, *cr.* 7, (rock, *pl.* 79, *cr.* 2.)

ROCHEAD, Sco., a savage's head, in profile, couped, ppr. *Fide et virtute. Pl.* 81, *cr.* 15.

ROCHEAD, Sco., a savage's head, affrontée, couped, ppr., wreathed, vert. *Fide et virtute. Pl.* 97, *cr.* 2.

ROCHEFORT, Eng., on a ducal coronet, a bird, wings expanded. *Pl.* 8, *cr.* 5.

ROCHEFORT, Eng., a unicorn's head, between two laurel-branches, in orle. *Pl.* 54, *cr.* 9.

ROCHESTER, Ess., a crane, ar. *Pl.* 111, *cr.* 9.

ROCHESTER, Ess. and Suss., a cubit arm, in armour, erect, out of clouds, ppr., in gauntlet a marigold, a rose, and a pomegranate, all ppr., leaved, vert, and environed with a ducal coronet, or.

ROCHFORD, Eng., a cock, gu. *Pl.* 67, *cr.* 14.

ROCHFORT, Iri., a robin-redbreast, ppr. *Candor dat viribus alas. Pl.* 10, *cr.* 12.

ROCHFORT, Eng., a rose-branch, bearing roses, ppr. *Pl.* 23, *cr.* 2.

ROCHFORT, HORACE-WILLIAM-NOEL, Esq., of Clogrenane, co. Carlow, a robin, ppr. *Vi vel suavitate. Pl.* 10, *cr.* 12.

ROCK, Eng., a demi-lion, az. *Pl.* 67, *cr.* 10.

ROCKE, Salop, on a rock, ppr., a martlet, or. *Pl.* 36, *cr.* 5.

ROCKLEY, Yorks., a stag's head, ppr., attired, or. *Pl.* 91, *cr.* 14.

ROCKWOOD, Suff., a lion, sejant, supporting a spear, erect, ar. *Pl.* 60, *cr.* 4.

ROCKWOOD, Norf., a lion, sejant, gardant, ar., (supporting a spear, sa., headed, of the first.) *Pl.* 113, *cr.* 8, (without chapeau.)

ROCLAY, Eng., a dolphin, haurient, ppr. *Pl.* 14, *cr.* 10.

RODANTY, Eng., a rose-branch, flowered and leaved, ppr. *Pl.* 117, *cr.* 10.

RODATZ, Eng., a rose-tree, ppr. *Pl.* 23, *cr.* 2.

RODBER, a demi-heraldic-antelope, erased.

RODD, a colossus astride, his head rayonnée, a bow thrown across his shoulders, ppr., in dexter an arrow, in sinister a beacon, fired.

RODD, Cornw., out of a ducal coronet, a double plume of ostrich-feathers, five and (three.) *Pl.* 64, *cr.* 5.

RODD, Cornw., a naked man with a bow on his shoulder, an arrow in dexter, the sinister hand finger pointing upward, rays round his head.

RODDAM, Eng., a savage's head, couped, ppr., distilling blood, gu. *Pl.* 23, *cr.* 1.

RODDAM, a cross moline. *Pl.* 89, *cr.* 8.

RODDAM, of Roddam Hall, Northumb., the stump of an oak, couped, sprouting a young branch, ppr. *Nec deficit alter. Pl.* 92, *cr.* 8.

RODDAM, on a mount, vert, trunk of tree, sprouting fresh branches, all ppr. *Pl.* 124, *cr.* 13, (without bird.)

RODE, Chesh., a wolf's head, sa., gorged with a ribbon, ar. *Pl.* 8, *cr.* 4.

RODEN, Earl of, Viscount Jocelyn, and Baron Newport, Iri.; Baron Clanbrassil, and a Bart., Eng., (Jocelyn,) a falcon's leg, erased at thigh, ppr., belled, or. *Faire mon devoir.* *Pl.* 83, *cr.* 7.

RODES, Eng., an arm, couped at elbow, ar., in hand an (oak)-branch, or, fructed, az. *Pl.* 43, *cr.* 6.

RODES, Yorks., a leopard, sejant, or, spotted, sa., (collared and ringed,) ar. *Pl.* 86, *cr.* 8, (without coronet.)

RODES-REASTON. *See* REASTON.

RODGER, Sco., a demi-lady, ppr., attired, az., in dexter a pair of scales, or. *Pl.* 57, *cr.* 1.

RODICK, Eng., two doves, respecting each other, ppr. *Pl.* 60, *cr.* 13.

RODIE, Eng., a roebuck, trippant, ppr. *Spero meliora.* *Pl.* 68, *cr.* 2.

RODNEY, Devons., a boar's head, sa., couped, gu. *Pl.* 48, *cr.* 2.

RODNEY, Devons., on a ducal coronet, or, an eagle, wings expanded, purp. *Pl.* 126, *cr.* 7, (coronet, *pl.* 128, *fig.* 3.)

RODNEY, Bart., Hants, in a ducal coronet, or, a demi-eagle, displayed, purp. *Pl.* 9, *cr.* 6.

RODNEY, out of a ducal coronet, a demi-eagle, displayed. *Pl.* 9, *cr.* 6.

RODNEY, Baron, and a Bart., (Rodney,) on a ducal coronet, or, an eagle, rising, purp. *Non generant aquilæ columbas.* *Pl.* 67, *cr.* 4, (coronet, *same plate.*)

RODWAY, Lond., a buck, trippant, ppr. *Pl.* 68, *cr.* 2.

RODWELL, Eng., the sun, per fess, sa. and or. *Pl.* 68, *cr.* 14.

ROE, Iri., a roebuck, springing, ppr. *Pl.* 65, *cr.* 14.

ROE, Middx. and Ess., a buck's head, erased, gu. *Pl.* 66, *cr.* 9.

ROE, or Roo, Lond. and Kent, a stag's head, gu., on neck three bezants. *Pl.* 91, *cr.* 14, (bezant, *pl.* 141.)

ROE, Iri., a demi-lion, rampant, erm., supporting a crescent, gu. *Pl.* 19, *cr.* 6, (crescent, *pl.* 141.)

ROE, a roebuck's head, gu. *Pl.* 91, *cr.* 14.

ROE, Bart., Suff., on a mount, vert, a roebuck, statant, gardant, attired and hoofed, or, (between attires a quatrefoil, gold.) *Tramite recta.* *Pl.* 19, *cr.* 14, (without coronet; quatrefoil, *pl.* 141.)

ROE, HENRY-RICHARD, Esq., of Gnaton Hall, Devons., a stag's head, erased, gu. *Pl.* 66, *cr.* 9.

ROEBUCK, Somers., a lion, passant, gardant, gu. *Pl.* 120, *cr.* 5.

ROEBUCK, Kent., a stork, ar., beaked and membered, gu. *Pl.* 33, *cr.* 9.

ROFEY, or ROFY, an eagle, displayed, or. *Pl.* 48, *cr.* 11.

ROFFEY, on a mural coronet, a serpent, nowed, ppr. *Pl.* 103, *cr.* 11.

ROFY, an eagle, displayed, ppr. *Pl.* 48, *cr.* 11.

ROGER, Sco., out of a ducal coronet, a dexter hand, ppr., holding a crosier, in bend, or. *Le Roy et l'Eglise.* *Pl.* 17, *cr.* 12, (coronet, *same plate, cr.* 15.)

ROGERS, Dors. and Glouc., a fleur-de-lis, or. *Pl.* 68, *cr.* 12.

ROGERS, Kent, a man's head, in armour, in profile, ppr., helmet, or, feathers, ar. *Pl.* 33, *cr.* 14.

ROGERS, Iri., an eagle, displayed, or. *Pl.* 48, *cr.* 11.

ROGERS, a griffin's head, couped. *Pl.* 38, *cr.* 3.

ROGERS, on a mount, vert, a buck, sa., (ducally gorged, ar., over back a string reflexed, attired, or.) *Pl.* 50, *cr.* 6.

ROGERS, Somers., a stag, sa., bezantée, (ducally gorged and attired, or.) *Pl.* 88, *cr.* 9.

ROGERS, The Home, Salop, a buck's head, sa., (charged with three ermine-spots, or,) erased, gu., attired, gold. *Celeriter et jucunde.* *Pl.* 66, *cr.* 9.

ROGERS, Rainscombe, Wilts., a stag, sa., (chained) and spotted, or. *Nil conscire sibi.* *Pl.* 88, *cr.* 9.

ROGERS, FRANCIS, Esq., of Yarlington Lodge, Somers., a stag's head, couped, sa., attired, or, in mouth an acorn, gold, stalked and leaved, vert. *Justum perficito, nihil timeto.* *Pl.* 100, *cr.* 8.

ROGERS, Salop, on a mount, vert, a buck, trippant, sa., attired, ar., (ducally gorged, ringed and lined, of the last.) *Pl.* 50, *cr.* 6.

ROGERS, Norf., a demi-stag, sa., platée, attired, or, (ducally gorged, per pale, or and ar.) *Pl.* 55, *cr.* 9.

ROGERS, Lond., a (cubit) arm, in coat of mail, in hand, ppr., a banner, staff and flag, or. *Pl.* 6, *cr.* 5.

ROGERS, Glouc., a stag's head, (erased,) ppr., in mouth an acorn, or, stalked and leaved, vert. *Pl.* 100, *cr.* 8.

ROGERS, Glouc., Ess., Kent, and Worc., a buck's head, sa., attired, or, in mouth an acorn, gold, stalked and leaved, vert. *Pl.* 100, *cr.* 8.

ROGERS, a man's head, ppr., in a helmet, or. *Pl.* 33, *cr.* 14.

ROGERS, Kent and Wilts., a stag, trippant, sa., bezantée, (ducally gorged and attired, or.) *Pl.* 68, *cr.* 2.

ROGERS, Cornw., a buck, trippant, ar. *Pl.* 68, *cr.* 2.

ROGERS, JOHN-JOPP, Esq., of Treassowe, and Penrose, Cornw., a stag, trippant, sa. *Pl.* 68, *cr.* 2.

ROGERS, Bart., Devons., on a mount, vert, a roebuck, current, ppr., attired and gorged with a ducal coronet, or, between two branches of laurel, vert. *Nos nostraque Deo.* *Pl.* 84, *cr.* 5.

ROGERS-COXWELL, RICHARD-ROGERS, Esq., of Ablington Manor and Dowdeswell, Glouc., a fleur-de-lis. *Vigila et ora.* *Pl.* 68, *cr.* 12.

ROGERSON, a demi-lion, rampant, per fess, or and purp. *Pl.* 67, *cr.* 10.

ROHAN, Eng., a dexter arm, embowed, couped, resting on elbow, vested and cuffed, in hand a cross crosslet, fitched. *Pl.* 88, *cr.* 7.

ROHDE, Middx., an eagle, displayed, per pale, or and purp., charged on breast with a cross pattée, counterchanged. *Pl.* 48, *cr.* 11, (cross, *pl.* 141.)

ROKEBY, Eng., a dexter hand holding an escutcheon, ar., charged with a (crescent,) gu. *Pl.* 21, *cr.* 12.

ROKEBY, Baron, Irl., and a Bart., Eng., (Montague,) a roebuck, trippant, or. *Sola in Deo salus.* Pl. 68, cr. 2.

ROKEBY, the Rev. HENRY-RALPH, of Arthingworth Manor House, Northamp., a rook, ppr. Pl. 123, cr. 2.

ROKESTON, Eng., an arm, in armour, embowed, in hand a sword, ppr. Pl. 2, cr. 8.

ROKLEY, Yorks., a stag's head, couped. Pl. 91, cr. 14.

ROKWOOD, Eng., a lion's head, vert, collared, ar. Pl. 42, cr. 14.

ROLESLEY, Derbs., a demi-lion, rampant, per pale, ar. and gu., holding a rose, of the last, stalked and leaved, vert. Pl. 39, cr. 14.

ROLF, Wilts., on a staff, couped and raguly, in fess, and (sprouting at dexter end, vert,) a raven, close, sa. Pl. 123, cr. 2, (staff, pl. 5, cr. 8.)

ROLFE, Middx. and Kent, a raven, close, sa., in beak a trefoil, slipped, vert. Pl. 123, cr. 2, (trefoil, pl. 11, cr. 12.)

ROLFE, Norf., (on a mount,) a crescent, issuing therefrom a rose, slipped. Pl. 118, cr. 12, (rose, *same plate, cr.* 9.)

ROLFE, Norf., a lion's head, erased. Pl. 81, cr. 4.

ROLLAND, a hand issuing, holding a dagger, ppr. *Spes juvat.* Pl. 28, cr. 4.

ROLLAND, Sco., a fleur-de-lis, ar. *Immutabile durabile.* Pl. 68, cr. 12.

ROLLAND, Sco., a lymphad, her sails furled and oars in action, ppr., flagged, gu. *Sustentatus providentiâ.* Pl. 34, cr. 5.

ROLLE, Oxon., a cubit arm, erect, ppr., vested, az., charged with a fess, indented, doublecottised, or, in hand a roll of paper, gold. *Nec rege, nec populo, sed utroque.* Pl. 95, cr. 7.

ROLLE, Baron, (Rolle,) a cubit arm, erect, vested, az., charged with a fess, indented, double-cottised, or, in hand a (flint-stone,) ppr. *Nec rege, nec populo, sed utroque.* Pl. 95, cr. 7.

ROLLE, Dors. and Devons., same crest and motto.

ROLLES, Devons., an arm, (charged with a fess, indented and cottised, or,) in hand a baton, sa. Pl. 18, cr. 10.

ROLLESTON, Notts., Staffs., and Derbs., an eagle's head, ppr. Pl. 100, cr. 10.

ROLLESTON, LANCELOT, Esq., of Watnall Hall, Notts., an eagle's head, erased, ppr. *Ainsi, et peut este meilleur.* Pl. 20, cr. 7.

ROLLO, Eng., a stag's head, couped, ppr. *La fortune passe par tout.* Pl. 91, cr. 14.

ROLLO, a boar, passant, ppr. *Valor et fortuna.* Pl. 48, cr. 14.

ROLLS, Eng., out of a ducal coronet, an arm, in armour, brandishing a sabre, all ppr. Pl. 15, cr. 5.

ROLLS, The Hendre, Monm., out of a wreath of oak, a dexter cubit arm, vested, or, cuffed, sa., arm charged with a fess dancettée, double-cottised, of the second, charged with three bezants, in hand, ppr., a roll of parchment, ar. Pl. 32, cr. 6, (wreath, pl. 74, cr. 7.)

ROLLSTON, an eagle's head, ppr. Pl. 100, cr. 10.

ROLPH, a raven, ppr., in beak a trefoil, slipped, vert. Pl. 123, cr. 2, (trefoil, pl. 11, cr. 12.)

ROLT, or ROLTE, of Deptford, Kent : 1. For *Rolt*, on a broken tilting-spear, ar., a griffin, sejant, gu., in mouth the head of the spear. *Cuspis fracta causa coronæ.* Pl. 74, cr. 10. 2. For *Pett*, out of a ducal coronet, a demi-pelican, vulning, ar. Pl. 19, cr. 9, (pelican, pl. 41, cr. 4.)

ROMAINE, Eng., an arrow, point downward. Pl. 56, cr. 13.

ROMANES, Sco., a dexter hand holding a sword, ppr. Pl. 21, cr. 10.

ROMAYNE, Eng., a deer's head, erased, ppr. Pl. 66, cr. 9.

ROME, Sco., a slip of a rose-tree, bearing roses, ppr. *Pungit, sed placet.* Pl. 23, cr. 2.

ROME, Eng., a lion, passant, ppr. Pl. 48, cr. 8.

ROMERA, DE, Eng., a stag's head, at gaze, ppr. Pl. 111, cr. 13.

ROMERLEY, and ROMILLY, Eng., a crescent. Pl. 18, cr. 14.

ROMNEY, Lond., two cubit arms, erect, vested, az., cuffed, ar., hands, ppr., holding an escallop, gu. Pl. 113, cr. 12, (escallop, pl. 141.)

ROMNEY, Kent, an arm, in armour, embowed, ppr., vambraced, or, hand holding a pennon of (two streamers,) gu., thereon three leopards' heads, crowned, of the third, staff, ppr. Pl. 6, cr. 5, (head, pl. 84, cr. 1.)

ROMNEY, Earl of, and Baron, Viscount Marsham, and a Bart., (Marsham,) a lion's head, erased, gu. *Non sibi, sed patriæ.* Pl. 81, cr. 4.

ROMPNEY, and RUMPNEY, Worc., on a mount, vert, a lion, gardant, gu., standing against a tree, ppr. Pl. 82, cr. 4, (tree, pl. 48, cr. 4.)

RONALD, Sco., an oak-tree, acorned and (eradicated,) ppr. *Sic virescit virtus.* Pl. 16, cr. 8.

RONALD, Sco., an oak-tree, fructed, ppr. *Sic virescit virtus.* Pl. 16, cr. 8.

RONALDSON, Sco., a greyhound's head, erased, in mouth a deer's foot, erased. Pl. 66, cr. 7.

RONE, Salop, a buck's head, erased, ppr., attired, or. Pl. 66, cr. 9.

RONNE, Middx., a buck's head, erased, ppr., attired, or. Pl. 66, cr. 9.

ROOE, Eng., a buck's head, couped, gu., attired, or. Pl. 91, cr. 14.

ROOE, Eng., a swan, wings addorsed, swimming in water, ppr. Pl. 66, cr. 9.

ROOK, Lond., on a garb, or, a rook in a feeding posture, ppr. Pl. 51, cr. 8, (garb, pl. 112, cr. 10.)

ROOK, Eng., a rook, ppr. Pl. 123, cr. 2.

ROOK, and ROOKES, Eng., on a trumpet, in fess, a rook, ppr. Pl. 123, cr. 2, (trumpet, pl. 2, cr. 1.)

ROOKBY, a rook, ppr. Pl. 123, cr. 2.

ROOKE, Eng., a rook, feeding. Pl. 51, cr. 8.

ROOKE, Cumb., on a garb, or, a rook, feeding, ppr. Pl. 51, cr. 8, (garb, pl. 112, cr. 10.)

ROOKE, on a rock, ppr., a martlet, or. Pl. 36, cr. 5.

ROOKE, Kent, an arm, in armour, embowed, ppr., garnished, in gauntlet a pistol, of the last, (the arm environed with a trumpet, ar.) Pl. 96, cr. 4.

ROOKE, a demi-eagle, displayed, ar., charged on breast with a chess-rook, gu. Pl. 44, cr. 14, (chess-rook, pl. 40, cr. 11.)

ROOKE, Cumb., on a garb, or, a rook preying, ppr. *Efflorescent cornices, dum micat sol.* Pl. 51, cr. 8, (garb, pl. 112, cr. 10.)

ROOKEWOOD, Norf., a dragon's head, gu. Pl. 87, cr. 12.

ROOKWOOD, Suff., a lion, sejant, supporting a spear, in pale, ar. *Pl.* 60, *cr.* 4.

ROOPE, Eng., a demi-antelope, sa., collared, or. *Pl.* 34, *cr.* 8.

ROOPER, BONFOY, Esq., of Abbott's Ripton, Hunts., on a chapeau, gu., turned up, erm., a blazing star, or. *Lux Anglis, crux Francis. Pl.* 30, *cr.* 13.

ROOS, Notts., Linc., Suss., and Derbs., on a chapeau, gu., turned up, erm., a peacock in pride, ppr. *Pl.* 50, *cr.* 15.

Roos, Eng., three slips of roses, ar., leaved, vert. *Pl.* 79, *cr.* 3.

Roos, and ROSSE, (now ROSE,) Dors., a rose, gu., slipped, seeded, or, barbed, vert, between wings, erm. *Sursum*—and—*En la rose je fleurie. Pl.* 105, *cr.* 7, (wings, *pl.* 4, *cr.* 10.)

Roos, or Ros, Yorks., a falcon's head, az. *Pl.* 34, *cr.* 11.

ROOTS, Eng., a tree, ppr. *Pl.* 16, *cr.* 8.

ROPE, Chesh. and Devons., a lion, rampant, or, in dexter a pheon, sa. *Pl.* 87, *cr.* 6, (pheon, *pl.* 123, *cr.* 12.)

ROPER, Yorks. and Lond., an antelope's head, erased, per fess, wavy, or and az. *Pl.* 24, *cr.* 7.

ROPER, Kent, a lion, rampant, sa., in (dexter) a ducal coronet, or. *Spes mea in Deo. Pl.* 64, *cr.* 2, (coronet, *same plate, cr.* 5.)

ROPER, Eng., a lion, rampant, gu., holding up a ducal coronet, or. *Spes mea in Deo. Pl.* 9, *cr.* 7.

ROPER, Durh., a roebuck's head, erased, gorged with a branch, ppr. *Pl.* 38, *cr.* 1.

ROPER, Norf., a buck's head, erased, or, attired, sa., (in mouth a pear, gold, stalked and leaved, vert.) *Pl.* 66, *cr.* 9.

ROPER, Derbs., on a chapeau, gu., turned up, erm., a blazing star, or. *Pl.* 30, *cr.* 13.

ROPER, a goat's head, erased, (gorged with a branch,) ppr. *Pl.* 29, *cr.* 13.

ROPER, West Dereham, Norf., a stag's head, erased, ppr. *Pl.* 66, *cr.* 9.

ROPER-CURZON, Baron Teynham. *See* TEYNHAM.

RORIE, Eng., a cinquefoil, gu. *Pl.* 91, *cr.* 12.

RORIE, Sco., a galley, oars in action, ppr. *Pl.* 34, *cr.* 5.

RORKE, Iri., an eagle's head, erased, or. *Pl.* 20, *cr.* 7.

ROSCARROCK, Cornw., a lion, rampant, ppr., ducally (gorged,) ar. *Pl.* 98, *cr.* 1.

ROSCOE, two elephants' trunks, gu. *Pl.* 24, *cr.* 8.

ROSCOMMON, Earl of, Lord Dillon, Baron of Kilkenny, (Dillon,) a falcon, ar. *Auxilium ab alto. Pl.* 67, *cr.* 3.

ROSCRUGE, Cornw., a demi-lion, rampant, or, in dexter a rose, slipped, gu., stalked and leaved, vert. *Pl.* 39, *cr.* 14.

ROSE, Bucks., a roebuck, trippant, ar. *Pl.* 68, *cr.* 2.

ROSE, Bucks., a stag, ar. *Pl.* 88, *cr.* 9, (without arrow.)

ROSE, Eng., a rose, gu., slipped and bladed, vert. *Armat spina rosas. Pl.* 105, *cr.* 7.

ROSE, Sco., a harp, az. *Constant and true. Pl.* 104, *cr.* 15.

ROSE, Lond., a dexter hand, issuing, ppr., holding a rose, gu., slipped, vert. *Constant and true. Pl.* 118, *cr.* 9.

ROSE, a pheasant. in beak a rose, slipped and leaved, ppr. *Pl.* 82, *cr.* 12, (rose, *pl.* 55, *cr.* 9.)

ROSE, between wings a rose. *Pl.* 117, *cr.* 16, (wings, *pl.* 4, *cr.* 10.)

ROSE, a rose, slipped and leaved, ppr. *Pl.* 105, *cr.* 7.

ROSE, Hants, a hart, az., figure, or. *Pl.* 104, *cr.* 15.

ROSE, an antelope's head, erased. *Pl.* 24, *cr.* 7.

ROSE, or ROSSE, Bucks., a buck, trippant, ar. *Pl.* 68, *cr.* 2.

ROSE, a lion, rampant, sa. *Pl.* 67, *cr.* 5.

ROSE, Eng., a cubit arm, erect, vested, sa., cuffed, ar., in hand a rose, slipped and leaved, ppr. *Pl.* 64, *cr.* 7, (rose, *pl.* 118, *cr.* 9.)

ROSE, Kilravock, Nairn, a hawk, ppr. *Audeo. Pl.* 67, *cr.* 3.

ROSE, of Innish, Sco., an etoile, az. *Constant and true. Pl.* 63, *cr.* 9.

ROSE, JOHN-NUGENT, Esq., of Holme, Inverness, a hawk, ppr. *Constant and true. Pl.* 67, *cr.* 3.

ROSEBERRY, Earl of, and Viscount, Visct. Inverkeithing, Baron Primrose and Dalmeny, Sco.; Baron Roseberry, U.K.; and a Bart., N.S., (Primrose,) a demi-lion, gu., in dexter a primrose, within a double tressure, flory counter-flory, or. *Fide et fiducia. Pl.* 39, *cr.* 14.

ROSEVEAR, a dove, in mouth a rosebud, all ppr. *Pl.* 66, *cr.* 12, (rose, *pl.* 55, *cr.* 9.)

ROSEWARNE, a lion's head, erased, gu., pierced in neck by (an arrow,) ppr. *Pl.* 113, *cr.* 15.

ROSHER, Eng., an eagle's head, sa. *Pl.* 100, *cr.* 10.

ROSIER, Eng., a pelican in nest, ppr. *Pl.* 44, *cr.* 1.

ROSINGTON, Derbs., a griffin's head, erased, gu., beaked, or. *Pl.* 48, *cr.* 6.

ROSKELL, Lanc., issuing from a wreath of oak, or, a dexter cubit arm, in armour, ppr., (charged with a martlet, gu.,) in hand a cross crosslet, fitched, of the third. *Ros coeli. Pl.* 51, *cr.* 1, (wreath, *pl.* 74, *cr.* 7.)

Ross, Baron. *See* GLASGOW, Earl of.

Ross, Sco., a dexter hand plucking a rose, all ppr. *Constant and true. Pl.* 48, *cr.* 1.

Ross, a harp, az. *Constant and true. Pl.* 104, *cr.* 15.

Ross, a hawk's head, erased, ppr. *Think on. Pl.* 34, *cr.* 11.

Ross, an eagle, displayed. *Pl.* 48, *cr.* 11.

Ross, a dexter arm, in armour, in hand a sword, (in fess,) ppr. *Floret qui laborat. Pl.* 2, *cr.* 8.

Ross, of Rossie, Sco., a falcon's head, erased, ppr. *Think on. Pl.* 34, *cr.* 11.

Ross, Rosstrevor, co. Down: 1. An arm, in armour, embowed, hand grasping a dagger, all ppr. *Pl.* 120, *cr.* 11. 2. Out of a mural coronet, an arm, in general's uniform, hand grasping broken staff of the Standard of the United States.

Ross, Sco., a rose-tree, bearing roses, ppr. *Floret qui laborat. Pl.* 23, *cr.* 2.

Ross, a water-bouget, sa. *Agnoscar eventu. Pl.* 14, *cr.* 12.

Ross, Sco., a lymphad, oars in action, sa., flagged, gu. *Pro patriâ. Pl.* 34, *cr.* 5.

Ross, Sco., a spear and rose, in saltier, ppr. *Per aspera virtus.* Pl. 57, cr. 10, (spear, same plate, cr. 3.)

Ross, Sco., a rose, gu., stalked and barbed, vert. *Magnes et adamas.* Pl. 105, cr. 7.

Ross, Sco., a dexter hand holding a slip of rose-bush, ppr. *Quo spinosior, fragrantior.* Pl. 118, cr. 9.

Ross, Sco., a fox's head, couped, ppr. *Spes aspera levat.* Pl. 91, cr. 9.

Ross, Eng., three slips of roses, ar., leaved, vert. Pl. 79, cr. 3.

Ross, Sco., a laurel in flower, ppr. *Agnoscar eventu.* Pl. 123, cr. 5.

Ross, a dexter hand, issuing, holding a garland of laurel, all ppr. *Spem successus alit.* Pl. 86, cr. 1.

Ross, Sco., a lion's head, erased, ppr. *Per aspera virtus.* Pl. 81, cr. 4.

Ross, Iri., an arm, in armour, brandishing a sword, ppr. *Constant and true.* Pl. 2, cr. 8.

Ross, Sco., a rose, gu., stalked and barbed, vert. Pl. 105, cr. 7.

Ross, Sco., (of Craigie,) K.C.H., &c., a lion's head, erased, ppr. *Per aspera virtus.* Pl. 81, cr. 4.

Ross, Sco., a fox, passant. *Caute non astute.* Pl. 126, cr. 5.

Ross, Sco., a fox, issuant, with a rose in his mouth, ar. *Rosam ne rode.* Pl. 30, cr. 9, (rose, pl. 92, cr. 15.)

Ross, Herts., a laurel branch, erect, ppr. Pl. 123, cr. 5.

Ross, Eng., an eagle's head, couped, az. Pl. 100, cr. 10.

Ross-Lewin, Rev. George, of Ross Hill, co. Clare, on a chapeau, gu., turned up, erm., a peacock, in pride, ppr. *Consilio ac virtute.* Pl. 50, cr. 15.

Rosse, of Waddesden, Bucks., a roebuck, trippant, ar. Pl. 68, cr. 2.

Rosse, Sco., a harp, stringed, or. *Constant and true.* Pl. 104, cr. 15.

Rosse, Derbs., on a chapeau, gu., turned up, erm., a peacock in his pride, ppr. Pl. 50, cr. 15.

Rosse, Somers., a demi-leopard, rampant, gardant, gu., eared, vert. Pl. 77, cr. 1, (without anchor.)

Rosse, Earl of, Baron Oxmantown, and a Bart., Iri., (Parsons,) out of a ducal coronet, or, a cubit arm, in hand a sprig of roses, all ppr. *Pro Deo et rege.* Pl. 60, cr. 1.

Rosseline, or Rosselyne, Eng., a spur-rowel, az., between wings, or. Pl. 109, cr. 12, (rowel, pl. 54, cr. 5.)

Rossell, Eng., an arm, in armour, couped at shoulder, and resting on elbow, hand holding a club, ppr. Pl. 65, cr. 13.

Rosselyne, Eng., a cross moline, or. Pl. 89, cr. 8.

Rosser, Suff., an arm, embowed, erect from elbow, vested, or, cuffed, erm., in hand (four leaves,) vert. Pl. 62, cr. 7.

Rosseter, Eng., a spear-head, ppr. Pl. 82, cr. 9.

Rosseter, Linc., a leopard, passant, or. Pl. 86, cr. 2.

Rossie, Sco., a cross pattée, gu. Pl. 15, cr. 8.

Rossie, Baron. See Kinnaird, Lord.

Rossington, Derbs., a griffin's head, erased, gu. Pl. 48, cr. 6.

Rosslyn, Earl of, Baron Loughborough, Eng., and a Bart., N.S., (St Clair-Erskine :) 1. A phœnix in flames, ppr., and over it the device—*Rinasce piu glorioso.* Pl. 44, cr. 8. 2. An eagle's head, erased, ppr., with the words—*Illæso lumine solem.* Pl. 20, cr. 7.

Rossmore, Baron, Iri., (Westenra,) a lion, rampant. *Post prœlia prœmia.* Pl. 67, cr. 5.

Rosson, Eng., a demi-griffin, gu. *Fight.* Pl. 18, cr. 6.

Roster, Eng., a spear-head, ppr. Pl. 82, cr. 9.

Rotchford, a bird, close. Pl. 10, cr. 12.

Rote, Eng., a stork, or. Pl. 33, cr. 9.

Rotham, Kent, a bird, rising, sa., between two spears, or, headed, ar. Pl. 79, cr. 13.

Rotherham, Eng., a stag's head. Pl. 91, cr. 14.

Rotherham, Sco., a sword, erect, thrust through a savage's head, affrontée, ppr. Pl. 42, cr. 6.

Rotheram, Ess., Beds., and Somers., a stag's head, or. Pl. 91, cr. 14.

Rotheram, between two brenches, vert, a buck's head, couped, or. Pl. 91, cr. 14, (branches, pl. 79, cr. 14.)

Rotherfield, Eng., a lion's gamb, erect, sa. Pl. 126, cr. 9.

Rothery, Eng., on a tower, a demi-lion, rampant. Pl. 42, cr. 4.

Rothery, Littlethorpe, Yorks., a tower, ar., charged with two bendlets, indented, out of battlements a demi-lion, gu., in dexter three arrows, one in pale and two in saltier, ppr. *Festina lente.* Pl. 42, cr. 4, (arrows, pl. 9, cr. 4.)

Rothes, Earl of, and Baron Leslie, (Leslie,) a demi-griffin, ppr. *Grip fast.* Pl. 18, cr. 6.

Rothings, Eng., a lion's paw, erased, holding a spear, tasselled, ppr. Pl. 1, cr. 4.

Rothschild : 1. A star of six points, or, between two elephants' trunks, erect and reflexed, quarterly, counterchanged, or and sa. Pl. 96, cr. 1, (star, pl. 21, cr. 6.) 2. An eagle, displayed, sa. Pl. 48, cr. 11. 3. A plume of three feathers, the middle one az., the others, ar. Pl. 12, cr. 9. All three crests issuing from a marquess's coronet, pearled and jewelled, ppr. *Concordia, integrita, industria.* Pl. 127, fig. 4.

Rothwell, Hants., out of a mural coronet, a stag's head, ar., attired, or, in mouth a rose, ppr., leaved, vert. Pl. 112, cr. 5, (rose, pl. 55, cr. 9.)

Rotland, Surr., a nag's head, or, erased, per fess, gu., maned, of the last. Pl. 81, cr. 6.

Rotten, between wings, a sinister arm, embowed, vested, hand holding a bow, stringed, ppr. Pl. 52, cr. 5, (wings, same plate, cr. 2.)

Rotton, Eng., an oak-tree, and pendent therefrom an escutcheon, ppr. Pl. 97, cr. 2.

Roudon, Eng., a bezant, or. Pl. 7, cr. 6, (see pl. 141.)

Roughead, Sco., a Saracen's head, affrontée. *Fide et virtute.* Pl. 19, cr. 1.

Roughsedge, a demi-lion. *Res, non verba.* Pl. 67, cr. 10.

Round, Eng., cupid with his attributes, ppr. Pl. 17, cr. 5.

Round, Ess., a lion, couchant, ar. Pl. 75, cr. 5, (without chapeau.)

Roundel, Eng., an arm, in armour, embowed, in fess, ppr., in hand a mace, gu., studded, or, tied at shoulder with a scarf, ar. Pl. 28, cr. 2.

ROUNDELL, Eng., a sword, erect, ar., hilt and pommel, or, the gripe, gu. *Pl.* 105, *cr.* 1.

ROUNDELL, the Rev. DANSON-RICHARDSON, of Gledstone, Yorks., same crest.

ROUPELL, Suss., a demi-African, (wreathed round middle with feathers, in dexter a bow, and in sinister three arrows, ppr.) *Fidele. Pl.* 80, *cr.* 9.

ROURK, Iri., out of a ducal coronet, a hand holding a (dagger.) *Pl.* 65, *cr.* 10.

ROUS, or ROUSE, Worc. and Norf., a man's head, ar., beard, hair, and whiskers, sa., having on a (cap,) of the last, tied with ribbons, of the first. *Pl.* 23, *cr.* 3.

ROUS, or ROUSE, Lond., a demi-lion, rampant, az., between paws a bezant. *Pl.* 126, *cr.* 12.

ROUS, Ess., a pyramid of laurel-leaves, counterchanged, vert and ar. *Pl.* 61, *cr.* 13.

ROUS, Wel., Devons., and Cornw., a dove, ar. *Vescitur Christo. Pl.* 66, *cr.* 12.

ROUS, Wel., a dove, ppr., (supporting an escutcheon, lozenge-shaped, charged with an eagle's head, erased, az.) *Pl.* 66, *cr.* 12.

ROUS, Devons., a demi-eagle, regardant, wings displayed, ppr. *Pl.* 27, *cr.* 15, (displayed, *pl.* 52, *cr.* 8.)

ROUS, Earl of Stradbroke. *See* STRADBROKE.

ROUSE, Eng., a demi-lioness, ppr., collared, or.

ROUSE, a stork's head, erased, in bill an eel, ppr. *Pl.* 41, *cr.* 6.

ROUSE, Leic., a demi-lion, rampant, per pale, indented, gu. and erm., between paws a crescent, ar. *Pl.* 126, *cr.* 12, (crescent, *pl.* 141.)

ROUSHLAND, Surr., a nag's head, or, erased, per fess, gu., maned, of the last. *Pl.* 81, *cr.* 6.

ROUSHOUT, Ess., Worc., and Middx., a lion, passant, gardant, or. *Pl.* 120, *cr.* 5.

ROUTH, Eng., the sun, or. *Pl.* 68, *cr.* 14.

ROUTH, out of a mural coronet, a talbot's head. *Pl.* 91, *cr.* 15.

ROUTLEDGE, Eng., a garb, vert. *Pl.* 48, *cr.* 10.

ROW, Devons., a stag's head, erased, gu., attired, or. *Pl.* 66, *cr.* 9.

ROW, Sco., an arm, in armour, issuing, in hand a sword, ppr. *Non desistam. Pl.* 63, *cr.* 5.

ROWAN, Sco., a garb, ppr. *Per industriam. Pl.* 48, *cr.* 10.

ROWAN, Iri., a garb, ppr. *Hæc lucra laborum. Pl.* 48, *cr.* 10.

ROWAN, on a mount, vert, a holy lamb, ppr., holding a banner, per fess, or and gu. *Pl.* 101, *cr.* 9.

ROWAN, a demi-antelope, salient, (affrontée, ar., attired, or, charged on breast with a human heart, gu.) *Pl.* 38, *cr.* 8.

ROWAN, the Rev. ROBERT-WILSON, of Mount Davys, co. Antrim, a naked cubit arm, in hand a dagger, ppr. *Cresco per crucem. Pl.* 28, *cr.* 4.

ROWAND, Iri., a garb, or. *Hæc lucra laborum. Pl.* 48, *cr.* 10.

ROWBACHE, Herts., on a wing, ar., a bend, gobony, or and gu. *Pl.* 39, *cr.* 10.

ROWCHE, Eng., a rock, ppr. *Mon Dieu est ma roche. Pl.* 73, *cr.* 12.

ROWDON, Eng., a cock crowing, ppr. *Pl.* 68, *cr.* 14.

ROWDON, Suff., a bezant. *Pl.* 7, *cr.* 6, (*see pl.* 141.)

ROWE, Eng., a hand, issuant, ppr., holding a cross crosslet, fitched, az. *Auspice Christo. Pl.* 99, *cr.* 1.

ROWE, Eng., a buck's head, couped, gu., attired, or. *Pl.* 91, *cr.* 14.

ROWE, Derbs. and Bristol, a dexter arm, ppr., vested, erm., in hand a trefoil, vert. *Pl.* 78, *cr.* 6.

ROWE, Middx. and Lond., a stag's head, ppr. *Pl.* 91, *cr.* 14.

ROWE, Devons., a holy lamb, staff, cross, and banner, ar. *Pl.* 48, *cr.* 13.

ROWE, Suss., out of a ducal coronet, or, a demi-lion, gu., in dexter a Polish mace, in pale, sa., spiked and pointed, ar. *Pl.* 45, *cr.* 7, (mace, *pl.* 28, *cr.* 2.)

ROWE, Suss., a stag's head, erased, gu., attired, or, on neck a crescent, ar. *Pl.* 61, *cr.* 9.

ROWE, Northamp., a stag's head, gu., attired, or. *Pl.* 91, *cr.* 14.

ROWE, Yorks. and Devons., a holy lamb, staff, cross, and banner, ar. *Innocens, non timidus. Pl.* 48, *cr.* 13.

ROWE, Wexford, an arm, in armour, embowed, ppr., round wrist a scarf, gu., in hand a sword, ar., hilted, or, holding up a wreath, vert, arm charged with a cross pattée, fitched, also gu. *Pl.* 21, *cr.* 4, (wreath, *pl.* 56, *cr.* 6; cross, *pl.* 141.)

ROWED, Eng., a hand holding a lion's paw, erased, ppr. *Pl.* 94, *cr.* 13.

ROWELL, Eng., a hand, couped, in fess, holding a cross crosslet, fitched. *Pl.* 78, *cr.* 9.

ROWELL, a hind, passant, in mouth a rose, leaved, ppr. *Pl.* 20, *cr.* 14, (rose, *pl.* 55, *cr.* 9.)

ROWLAND, Sco., a demi-lion, rampant, gu., holding a sword (by the blade, in pale,) hilt, or. *Pl.* 41, *cr.* 13.

ROWLAND, two ducks, issuing, wings elevated and addorsed, respecting each other.

ROWLAND, a lion's head, erased. *Pl.* 81, *cr.* 4.

ROWLAND, Salop, out of a ducal coronet, or, a demi-talbot, ar. *Pl.* 99, *cr.* 7, (talbot, *pl.* 5, *cr.* 13.)

ROWLANDS, Eng., a fleur-de-lis, gu., entwined with a serpent, or. *Pl.* 15, *cr.* 13.

ROWLATT, Eng., a demi-lion, ar., maned, or. *Pl.* 67, *cr.* 10.

ROWLES, Eng., a horse, current, in mouth the point of a broken spear, all ppr. *Pl.* 107, *cr.* 5.

ROWLES, Surr., out of a ducal coronet, a demi-griffin, segreant. *Pl.* 39, *cr.* 2.

ROWLESLEY, Derbs., a demi-lion, rampant, per pale, ar. and gu., holding a rose, of the last, stalked and leaved, vert. *Pl.* 39, *cr.* 14.

ROWLEY, Salop, an etoile of (eight points, pierced.) *Pl.* 63, *cr.* 9.

ROWLEY, a wolf's head, collared. *Bear and forbear. Pl.* 8, *cr.* 4.

ROWLEY, a sword, in bend, ar., hilted, or, through a mullet, sa.

ROWLEY, Salop, a mullet, ar., pierced, sa. *Pl.* 45, *cr.* 1.

ROWLEY, Bart., Berks., a mullet, pierced, or. *Ventis secundis. Pl.* 45, *cr.* 1.

ROWLEY, Bart., Suff., same crest and motto.

ROWLEY, co. Meath, a wolf's head, (erased,) sa., collared and langued, gu. *La vertue surmonte tout obstacle. Pl.* 8, *cr.* 4.

ROWLEY, Baron Langford. *See* LANGFORD.
ROWLEY, a mullet, pierced, or. *Pl.* 45, *cr.* 1.
ROWNTREE, Eng., a tree, ppr. *Pl.* 16, *cr.* 8.
ROWSEWELL, and ROWSWELL, of Devons., Norf., and Somers., a lion's head, couped, ar. *Pl.* 126, *cr.* 1.
ROWSEWELL, Wilts., a lion's head, erased, ar. *Pl.* 81, *cr.* 4.
ROXBURGH, Duke, and Earl of, Marquess of Beaumont, and Cessford, Earl of Kelso, Viscount Broxmouth, Baron Ker, all Sco.; Earl of Innes, U.K., and a Bart., (Innes-Ker,) a unicorn's head, erased, ar., armed and maned, or. *Pro Christo et patriâ dulce periculum.* *Pl.* 67, *cr.* 1.
ROXBY, Blackwood, Yorks.: 1. For *Roxby*, a wolf's head, erased, per pale, ar. and vert, gorged with a collar, counterchanged, (in mouth a branch of hop, ppr.) *Pl.* 8, *cr.* 4. 2. For *Maude*, (issuing from a wreath of laurel, vert,) a lion's head, gu., charged on neck with a cross crosslet, fitched, or. *Pl.* 126, *cr.* 1, (cross, *pl.* 141.)
ROY, Eng. and Sco., a lymphad, sails furled and oars in action, sa., in the sea, ppr. *Quâ tendis.* *Pl.* 34, *cr.* 5.
ROYCROFT, Lanc., a griffin's head, erased. *Pl.* 48, *cr.* 6.
ROYDEN, or ROYDON, Devons., out of a ducal coronet, or, a demi-griffin, per pale, ar. and gu. *Pl.* 39, *cr.* 2.
ROYDES, Lanc., a leopard, sejant, ppr., bezantée, resting dexter on a pheon. *Semper paratus.* *Pl.* 10, *cr.* 13, (pheon, *pl.* 141.)
ROYDHOUSE, Lond., a demi-archer, ppr., vested, vert, in dexter an arrow, ar., in sinister a bow, or. *Pl.* 60, *cr.* 5.
ROYDON, Eng., out of a ducal coronet, a demi-griffin. *Pl.* 39, *cr.* 2.
ROYER, Middx., a dove, ar., wings expanded, or, gorged with an Eastern coronet, gold, (in mouth an olive-branch, vert.) *Pl.* 27, *cr.* 5, (coronet, *pl.* 79, *cr.* 12.)
ROYLE, Eng., on a chapeau, ppr., a lion's head, erased, gu., ducally crowned, or. *Pl.* 34, *cr.* 10.
ROYS, Leic., a demi-griffin, ar., holding a rose, gu., barbed, vert. *Pl.* 18, *cr.* 6, (rose, *pl.* 39, *cr.* 14.)
ROYSE, Kent, a demi-lion, gardant, ar. *Pl.* 35, *cr.* 4.
ROYSTON, Eng., out of a ducal coronet, or, two lions' paws, in saltier, ppr. *Pl.* 110, *cr.* 2.
RUBRIDGE, Eng., a dove, or, in mouth an olive-branch, vert. *Pl.* 48, *cr.* 15.
RUCK, Eng., an old man's head, ppr., bound round temples with laurel, vert. *Pl.* 118, *cr.* 7.
RUDALL, or RUDDALL, Eng., a hawk's head, erased, or. *Pl.* 34, *cr.* 11.
RUDALL, Eng., a falcon, ppr. *Pl.* 67, *cr.* 3.
RUDD, or RUDDE, Wel., an arm, erect, vested, az., (charged with a cheveron, erm.,) in hand a scroll, all ppr. *Pl.* 32, *cr.* 6.
RUDD, a griffin's head, couped, ppr., (collared, ar.) *Pl.* 38, *cr.* 3.
RUDD, Worc., a maiden's head, affrontée, couped below shoulders, ppr. *Pl.* 45, *cr.* 5.
RUDD, Northamp. and Wel., a lion, rampant, or, holding an escutcheon, az., (charged with a canton, or.) *Pl.* 125, *cr.* 2, (escutcheon, *pl.* 22, *cr.* 13.)

RUDD, and RUDDE, Ess. and Linc., a cross botonée, or. *Pl.* 89, *cr.* 8, (*see plate* 141.)
RUDDE, Lond., between wings, ar., a cross crosslet, fitched, gu. *Pl.* 34, *cr.* 14.
RUDDIMAN, Sco., a spur, ppr. *Vis viri fragilis.* *Pl.* 15, *cr.* 3.
RUDGE, Eng., a pelican, in nest, ppr. *Pl.* 44, *cr.* 1.
RUDGE, Evesham, out of a mural coronet, or, two arms, erect, sleeves, gu., hands and cuffs, ppr., supporting a shield, ar. *In cruce fides.* *Pl.* 113, *cr.* 12, (coronet, *pl.* 30, *cr.* 15.)
RUDGE, out of a mural coronet, two arms, in armour, embowed, holding an escutcheon charged with a cross, engrailed. *Pl.* 30, *cr.* 15, (armour, *pl.* 10, *cr.* 9.)
RUDGER, a Saracen's head, affrontée, ppr., wreathed, ar. and sa. *Pl.* 97, *cr.* 2.
RUDGERD, Eng., a Saracen's head, affrontée, ppr., banded, ar. and sa. *Pl.* 97, *cr.* 2.
RUDHALL, Eng., a falcon, ppr. *Pl.* 67, *cr.* 3.
RUDHALL, Heref., a cubit arm, erect, (in armour, ppr., cuff, barry-lozengy, counterchanged, of two rows, ar. and az., hand holding three roses, gu., stalked, ppr.) *Pl.* 69, *cr.* 10, (without cloud.)
RUDIARD, Leic. and Staffs., a lion's head, gardant and erased, or. *Pl.* 1, *cr.* 5, (without crown.)
RUDIERD, Berks., Hants, and Somers., a lion's head, gardant, ar. *Pl.* 1, *cr.* 5, (without crown.)
RUDING, Eng., a cross moline, pierced, az. *Pl.* 91, *cr.* 10.
RUDING, Lond., a wyvern's head, erased, ppr., collared and chained, or, holding in fangs a bear's paw, erased, ppr. *Pl.* 107, *cr.* 10, (paw, *pl.* 126, *cr.* 2.)
RUDINGE, and RUDINGS, Leic. and Worc., a dragon's head, sa., collared and chained, or, in mouth a lion's gamb, erased, gold. *Pl.* 107, *cr.* 10, (gamb, *pl.* 126, *cr.* 9.)
RUDSTON, Yorks. and Cambs., a bull's head, sa. *Pl.* 120, *cr.* 7.
RUFF, Eng., a stag, statant, transfixed by an arrow, ppr. *Pl.* 88, *cr.* 9.
RUFFORD, Bucks., an eagle, wings expanded, in mouth a trefoil, slipped, all sa. *Pl.* 126, *cr.* 7, (trefoil, *pl.* 11, *cr.* 12.)
RUFFY, Eng., a demi-archer, shooting an arrow from a bow. *Pl.* 60, *cr.* 5.
RUFUS, Eng., an antique crown, or. *Pl.* 79, *cr.* 12.
RUGELEY, or RUGELLY, Staffs. and Warw., a tower, or, (flames issuant, ppr., against four arrows, in saltier, ar.) *Pl.* 69, *cr.* 9.
RUGGE, Norf., a talbot, passant, ar., collared, ringed, and eared, sa. *Pl.* 65, *cr.* 2.
RUGGE, Norf., an ibex's head sa., armed, maned, and tufted, or. *Pl.* 72, *cr.* 9.
RUGGLES, Ess. and Suff., a tower, or, (flames issuing from the top, ppr., behind the tower four arrows, in saltier,) ar. *Pl.* 69, *cr.* 9.
RULE, Eng., an arm, in armour, embowed, in hand a sword, all ppr. *Pl.* 2, *cr.* 8.
RUMBOLD, Herts., a demi-lion, rampant, or. *Pl.* 67, *cr.* 10.
RUMBOLD, a greyhound's head, ar., between two roses, gu., slipped and leaved, ppr. *Pl.* 84, *cr.* 13.
RUMBOLD, Bart., Yorks., a demi-lion, rampant. *Pl.* 67, *cr.* 10.

RUMFORD, Eng., a hand holding a leg, in armour, couped at thigh, embowed and spurred, ppr. *Pl.* 39, *cr.* 6.

RUMNEY, a lion, (statant,) gardant, ppr. *Pl.* 120, *cr.* 5.

RUMP, a demi-lion, rampant, regardant, ppr., between paws a shield, az., (charged with the sun, or.) *Pl.* 33, *cr.* 2, (shield, *pl.* 22, *cr.* 13.)

RUMSEY, Eng., a horned owl, gu. *Pl.* 1, *cr.* 8.

RUMSEY, a horned owl, ppr. *Pl.* 1, *cr.* 8.

RUMSEY, Wel., a talbot, passant, az., collared, or. *Pl.* 65, *cr.* 2.

RUNDLE, Cornw. and Devons., (on a mount, vert,) a squirrel, sejant, ppr., collared, az., chained, or, in mouth an oak-branch, fructed, ppr. *Laus Deo. Pl.* 2, *cr.* 4.

RUNDLE, Cornw. and Devons., a wolf's head, ppr. *Pl.* 92, *cr.* 15, (without rose.)

RUNDLE, Iri., a sword, in pale, ar., gripe, gu., pommel and hilt, or. *Pl.* 105, *cr.* 1.

RUPE, out of a ducal coronet, five ostrich-feathers. *Pl.* 100, *cr.* 12.

RUSH, an arm, in armour, embowed to the sinister, in (hand a Saracen's head by the beard.) *Pl.* 83, *cr.* 11.

RUSH, a bear's head, couped, bezantée, muzzled, in mouth an ear of wheat. *Pl.* 2, *cr.* 9, (wheat, *pl.* 108, *cr.* 8; bezant, *pl.* 141.)

RUSH, a wolf's head, erased, erm. *Pl.* 14, *cr.* 6.

RUSH, Ess., a wolf's head, (erased,) vert, langued, gu., guttée-d'or, collared, of the last, on the collar three torteaux. *Dieu, un roi une foi. Pl.* 8, *cr.* 4, (torteau, *pl.* 141.)

RUSHBROOK, Eng., a Catherine-wheel, sa., (embrued,) gu. *Pl.* 1, *cr.* 7.

RUSHBROOK, Suff., a lion, sejant, in dexter a rose, slipped and leaved. *Pl.* 126, *cr.* 15, (rose, *pl.* 39, *cr.* 14.)

RUSHBROOKE, Eng., a rose, or. *Pl.* 20, *cr.* 2.

RUSHBROOKE, Suff., a lion, sejant, in mouth a rose, or. *Pl.* 126, *cr.* 15, (rose, *pl.* 39, *cr.* 14.)

RUSHE, Eng., a wolf's head, erased, vert, guttée, ar., langued, gu. *Pl.* 14, *cr.* 6.

RUSHE, Suff., a fox's head, erased, ar., guttée, vert. *Pl.* 71, *cr.* 4.

RUSHE, a horse's head, erased, vert, guttée, ar. *Pl.* 81, *cr.* 6.

RUSHE, Ess., an arm, in armour, embowed, garnished, or, (hand holding by the hair a man's head, neck dropping blood,) all ppr. *Pl.* 83, *cr.* 11.

RUSHOUT, Baron Northwick. See NORTHWICK.

RUSHOUT, Eng., a lion, passant, gardant, or. *Paternis suppar. Pl.* 120, *cr.* 5.

RUSHTON, Lanc., on a chapeau,-gu., turned up, erm., a demi-lion, of the last. *Pl.* 46, *cr.* 8.

RUSPENI, or RUSPINI, on a serpent, nowed, a dove and olive-branch, ppr. *Pl.* 3, *cr.* 4, (branch, *same plate, cr.* 10.)

RUSSEL, Worc., on a wreath, ar. and sa., a demi-lion, of the first, (collared, of the second, studded, or,) holding a cross crosslet, (botonnée,) fitched, sa. *Pl.* 65, *cr.* 6.

RUSSELL, Sco. and Cumb., a goat, (passant,) ar., attired, or. *Pl.* 66, *cr.* 1.

RUSSELL, JAMES, Esq., Blackbraes, Stirling, a goat, passant, in mouth a thistle, both ppr. *Che sara, sara. Pl.* 126 D, *cr.* 7.

RUSSELL, Sir JAMES, K.C.B., of Ashiesteel, Selkirk, a fountain, ppr. *Agitatione purgatur. Pl.* 49, *cr.* 8.

RUSSELL, Sco., same crest and motto.

RUSSELL, Worc. and Heref., a demi-lion, rampant, ar., holding a cross crosslet, fitched, sa. *Pl.* 65, *cr.* 6.

RUSSELL, Sco., a goat, (passant,) ppr. *Pl.* 66, *cr.* 1.

RUSSELL, Iri., a phœnix in flames, ppr. *Pl.* 44, *cr.* 8.

RUSSELL, a goat, (passant,) ar., armed, or. *Che sara, sara. Pl.* 66, *cr.* 1.

RUSSELL, of Meiklour, Sco., out of a cloud, a dexter arm, in fess, in hand a sword, in pale. *Pl.* 93, *cr.* 8.

RUSSELL, Killough, co. Down, a demi-lion, rampant, gu. *Che sara, sara. Pl.* 67, *cr.* 10.

RUSSELL, Worc., a demi-lion, rampant, or, holding a cross crosslet, fitched, sa. *Pl.* 65, *cr.* 6.

RUSSELL, a bezant, charged with three bars, wavy. *Pl.* 95, *cr.* 15.

RUSSELL, a dexter hand, sustaining on the point of a sword a pair of balances, all ppr. *Virtus sine macula. Pl.* 44, *cr.* 10, (hand, *pl.* 23, *cr.* 15.)

RUSSELL, on a bezant, a Cornish chough, sa., wings expanded, beaked and legged, gu. *Pl.* 8, *cr.* 5, (bezant, *pl.* 141.)

RUSSELL, a pyramid, of leaves, az. *Pl.* 61, *cr.* 13.

RUSSELL, Derb.: 1. For *Russell*, on a mount, vert, a goat, (passant,) erm., attired, ppr., collared, gu. *Pl.* 11, *cr.* 14. 2. A demi-lion, or, charged with a cross pattée, az., in mouth an oak-branch, ppr., fructed, gold, between paws an escutcheon, az., charged with a fess, erminois, between three fleurs-de-lis in chief, and a cross pattée in base, or, from the escutcheon a scroll bearing motto—*A mice*—and under arms—*Memor*.

RUSSELL, Dors., a demi-Indian goat, rampant, ar., attires, ears, hoofs, and beard, sa. *Pl.* 90, *cr.* 12, (without gorging.)

RUSSELL, of Brancepeth Castle, Durh., a goat (passant,) ar. *Pl.* 66, *cr.* 1.

RUSSELL, Duke of Bedford. See BEDFORD.

RUSSELL, Surr., Ess., and Northamp., a demi-lion, rampant, ar., collared, gu., (charged on body with a cheveron, sa., thereon au escallop), or, between paws a cross crosslet, fitched, of the third. *Pl.* 18, *cr.* 13, (cross, *pl.* 65, *cr.* 6.)

RUSSELL, Ess. and Suss., an adder's head, erased, ppr., (collared, gu., ringed, or.) *Pl.* 58, *cr.* 5.

RUSSELL, Norf., a demi-goat, ar., attired, or. *Pl.* 11, *cr.* 4, (without gate.)

RUSSELL, Worc., a talbot, passant, ar. *Pl.* 120, *cr.* 8.

RUSSELL, Bucks., a goat, (passant,) ppr., unguled and horned, or, (murally collared, gold.) *Pl.* 66, *cr.* 1, (collar, *pl.* 74, *cr.* 1.)

RUSSELL, Bucks., a demi-griffin, segreant, vert. *Pl.* 18, *cr.* 6.

RUSSELL, Bart., Lond., a fountain. *Agitatione purgatur. Pl.* 95, *cr.* 15.

RUSSELL, Bart., Bucks., a goat, ar., attired and gorged with a mural coronet, or. *Che sara, sara. Pl.* 66, *cr.* 1, (gorging, *pl.* 74, *cr.* 1.)

RUSSELL, Camb. and Berks, a goat, ar., attired and (gorged with a mural coronet, or.) *Pl.* 66, *cr.* 1, (gorging, 74, *cr.* 1.)

RUSSIA MERCHANT COMPANY, Lond., a leopard's head, gardant, erased, ppr., ducally gorged, gu. *God be our guide. Pl.* 116, *cr.* 8.

RUST, Suff., a demi-lion, rampant. *Pl.* 67, *cr.* 10.

RUST, Eng., a wyvern, gu. *Pl.* 63, *cr.* 13.
RUSTED, Eng., an olive-branch, slipped, vert. *Pl.* 98, *cr.* 8.
RUTHALL, Bucks. and Northamp., a demi-eagle, rising, ar., the inside of wings, gu., each wing charged with three guttes-d'or, in beak a rose, of the second, slipped, vert. *Pl.* 52, *cr.* 8, (rose, *pl.* 55, *cr.* 9.)
RUTHERFORD, a horse's head, issuant, bridled, gu. *Sedulus et audax. Pl.* 92, *cr.* 1.
RUTHERFORD, Sco., a martlet, sa., beaked, gu. *Nec sorte nec fato. Pl.* 111, *cr.* 5.
RUTHERFORD, Eng., on a rock, a wild goose, ppr. *Pl.* 94, *cr.* 3.
RUTHERFORD, a martlet, sa. *Amico fidus ad aras. Pl.* 111, *cr.* 5.
RUTHERFORD, Sco., a mermaid, ppr. *Per mare, per terras. Pl.* 48, *cr.* 5.
RUTHERFORD, or RUTHERFURD, Sco., a horse's head and neck. *Sedulus et audax. Pl.* 81, *cr.* 6.
RUTHERFURD, a mermaid, in dexter a mirror, in sinister a comb, all ppr. *Per mare, per terras. Pl.* 48, *cr.* 5.
RUTHERFURD-OLIVER, WILLIAM, Esq., of Edgerston, Roxburgh, a martlet, sa. *Nec sorte, nec fato. Pl.* 111, *cr.* 5.
RUTHVEN, a goat's head, ar., attired and maned, or. *Deeds shaw. Pl.* 105, *cr.* 14.
RUTHVEN, Iri., a goat's head, erased, ppr. *Deeds shaw. Pl.* 29, *cr.* 13.
RUTHVEN, a goat's head, erased, ar., horned, or. *Deeds shaw. Pl.* 29, *cr.* 13.
RUTHVEN, Sco., a ram's head, couped, ppr. *Pl.* 34, *cr.* 12.
RUTHVEN, a goat's (head,) couped, affrontée. *Pl.* 113, *cr.* 1.
RUTHVEN, Baron, Sco., (Ruthven,) a ram's head, couped, ar. horned, or. *Deeds show. Pl.* 34, *cr.* 12.
RUTLAND, Surr., a nag's head, ar., erased, per fess, gu., maned, of the last. *Pl.* 81, *cr.* 6.
RUTLAND, Duke and Earl of, Marquess of Granby, and Baron Manners, (Manners ;) on a chapeau, gu., turned up, erm., a peacock in pride, ppr. *Pour y parvenir. Pl.* 50, *cr.* 15.
RUTLEDGE, Iri., an antique crown, or. *Pl.* 79, *cr.* 12.
RUTSON, Yorks., a griffin's head, couped, per bend, sa. and or, entwined by a serpent, ppr. *Spectemur agendo. Pl.* 5, *cr.* 7.
RUTT, Bucks, the sun, or. *Pl.* 68, *cr.* 14.
RUTTER, Devons., an eagle, ar. *Pl.* 7, *cr.* 11.
RUTTER, a greyhound's head, between two roses, slipped and leaved. *Pl.* 84, *cr.* 13.
RUTTER, Devons., an eagle, ar., perched on trunk of tree, erased, sa. *Pl.* 1, *cr.* 11.
RUTTLEDGE, an oak-tree, ppr., pendent from a branch on dexter, by a ribbon, az., an escutcheon, or. *Verax atque probus. Pl.* 23, *cr.* 6.
RUXTON, Iri., a hand, gauntleted, holding an arrow, ppr. *Pl.* 33, *cr.* 4, (arrow, *pl.* 96, *cr.* 6.)
RUXTON, Broad Oak, Kent, a bull's head, sa., armed, or, charged with a crescent, ar. *Pl.* 63, *cr.* 11, (crescent, *pl.* 141.)
RUXTON, WILLIAM, Esq., of Ardee House, co. Louth, a bull's head, sa., armed, or. *I am, I am. Pl.* 120, *cr.* 7.
RYAN, Eng., a hand, ppr., vested, az., cuffed, ar., holding a baton, gu., veruled, or. *Pl.* 18, *cr.* 1.
RYAN, Iri., a griffin's head, erased, ppr. *Pl.* 48, *cr.* 6.
RYAN, Eng., the sun, rising from behind a hill, ppr. *Pl.* 78, *cr.* 3.
RYAN, a griffin, segreant, az., holding a sword, in pale, ppr. *Pl.* 67, *cr.* 13, (sword, *pl.* 49, *cr.* 4.)
RYCROFT, Yorks., a griffin's head, erased and erect, ar. *Pl.* 48, *cr.* 6.
RYCROFT, Bart., Surr., a griffin's head, erased, per bend, or and az. *Pl.* 48, *cr.* 6.
RYDER, out of a mural coronet, or, a dragon's head, ar., (on neck an ermine-spot, sa.) *Servata fides cinere. Pl.* 101, *cr.* 4.
RYDER, Earl of Harrowby. *See* HARROWBY.
RYE, Eng., an ostrich-feather, enfiled with a ducal coronet, ppr. *Pl.* 8, *cr.* 9.
RYE, a hand, ppr., sleeve, purp., holding (three) ears of wheat, or. *Pl.* 63, *cr.* 1.
RYECROFT, a griffin's head, erased, erm. *Pl.* 48, *cr.* 6.
RYED, or RYEDE, Eng., a lion, couchant, gardant, ppr. *Pl.* 101, *cr.* 8.
RYLAND, Eng., a portcullis, sa. *Pl.* 51, *cr.* 12.
RYLE, Eng., a lion's head, erased, per pale, or and gu. *Pl.* 81, *cr.* 4.
RYLEY, Eng., a crane's head, erased, ar. *Pl.* 20, *cr.* 9.
RYLEY, a demi-dragon, or, holding a cross pattée, fitched, sa. *Pl.* 82, *cr.* 10, (cross, *pl.* 125, *cr.* 2.)
RYMER, Sco., a hand, holding a sword, in pale, all ppr. *Ense animus major. Pl.* 23, *cr.* 15.
RYNELL, Eng., a hand holding an eagle's leg, erased, ppr. *Pl.* 103, *cr.* 4.
RYPON, Lanc. and Lond., a lion, sejant, ar., (ducally gorged, or,) holding in paws a cross flory, fitched, sa. *Pl.* 14, *cr.* 2, (cross, *pl.* 65, *cr.* 9.)
RYTHE, a hawk, ppr. *Pl.* 67, *cr.* 3.
RYTHRIE, DE, WILLIAM, Esq., of Riverstown House, co. Kildare, out of a mural coronet, a dragon's head, or. *Pl.* 101, *cr.* 4.
RYTON, Eng., a dolphin, naiant, az. *Pl.* 48, *cr.* 9.
RYVELL, Eng., a buck's head, couped, ppr., attired, or. *Pl.* 91, *cr.* 14.
RYVES, Iri., an escutcheon, quarterly, or and gu., between two cypress-branches, in orle, vert. *Pl.* 14, *cr.* 7, (branches, *pl.* 119, *cr.* 8.)
RYVES, a greyhound, sejant, sa., (collared, or.) *Pl.* 66, *cr.* 15.
RYVETT, Lond., Cambs., Somers., and Suff., an arm, erect, (bendy of four, ar. and sa.,) hand ppr., grasping a broken sword, of the first, hilt and pommel, or. *Pl.* 22, *cr.* 6, (without cloud.)
RYVETT, Suff., an arm, erect, couped at elbow, per pale, ar. and sa., in hand, ppr., a broken sword, of the first, hilt and pommel, or. *Pl.* 22, *cr.* 6, (without cloud.)
RYVETT, Lond., Cambs., Somers., and Suff., an (arm,) in hand a battle-axe. *Pl.* 73, *cr.* 7.

S

SABBE, Lond. and Norf., an arm, embowed, in coat of mail, in hand, ppr., a pennon, ar., fringed, ar. and sa., charged with a cross, of the last, staff, of the first, headed, of the second. *Pl.* 6, *cr.* 5.

SABBEN, Eng., a demi-savage, ppr. *Pl.* 14, *cr.* 11.

SABINE, Eng., out of a ducal coronet, or, a hand holding a fleur-de-lis, gu. *Pl.* 120, *cr.* 4.

SABLE, an arm, purp., hand, ppr., holding a streamer, staff, ar., (on the flag, in an escutcheon, of the last, a cross, sa.) *Pl.* 99, *cr.* 3.

SACHEVERELL, Warw., Notts., Derb., Leic., and Devons., a goat (passant,) ar., attired, or. *Pl.* 66, *cr.* 1.

SACHEVERELL, Derb., on a water-bouget, or, a lure, gu., the top, az., thereon a falcon, belled, ar. *Pl.* 14, *cr.* 2.

SACKFORD, Eng., a savage's head, ppr., banded, gu. *Pl.* 36, *cr.* 3.

SACKVILL, a ram's head, erased, sa., attired, or. *Pl.* 1, *cr.* 12.

SACKVILE, or SACKVILL, Eng., a ram's head, erased, sa., attired, or., charged on breast with a cinquefoil, ar. *Pl.* 1, *cr.* 12, (cinquefoil, *pl.* 141.)

SACKVILE, on a ducal coronet, an etoile of eight points, ar. *Aut nunquam tentes, aut perfice. Pl.* 83, *cr.* 3.

SACKVILE, Suss., same crest. *Toujours loyal.*

SACKVILE, or SACKVIL, Eng., on a coronet of fleurs-de-lis, or, an etoile of eight points, ar. *Pl.* 83, *cr.* 3.

SACKVILLE, Eng., the morning-star in its splendour. *Pl.* 21, *cr.* 6.

SACKVILLE-GERMAIN, Duke of Dorset. *See* DORSET.

SACKWILLE, Eng., on a coronet, composed of fleurs-de-lis, an etoile of eight rays. *Pl.* 83, *cr.* 3.

SACRE, Kent, an elephant, or, in a wood, ppr. *Pl.* 56, *cr.* 14, (wood, *pl.* 125, *cr.* 14.)

SADLER, Middx., an eagle's head, between wings, sa., beaked, ar. *Pl.* 81, *cr.* 10.

SADLER, Wilts., a tilting-spear, erect, or, charged in middle with an escutcheon, gu. *Pl.* 31, *cr.* 1.

SADLER, Herts. and Warw., a demi-lion, az., ducally crowned, gu. (Another, or.) *Pl.* 61, *cr.* 4, (without branch.)

SADLEYR, a beaver, or. *Pl.* 49, *cr.* 5.

SAFFIN, Somers., on a mural coronet, an etoile of (sixteen) rays, or. *Pl.* 83, *cr.* 3, (coronet, *pl.* 128, *fig.* 18.)

SAGE, Eng., a stag's head, erased and erect, ppr. *Non sibi. Pl.* 66, *cr.* 9,

SAGE, an old man's head, affrontée, couped at neck, and dropping blood. *Pl.* 19, *cr.* 1, (blood, *pl.* 23, *cr.* 1.)

SAGE, a sage's head, ppr., affrontée, vested in a close cap, sa. *Pl.* 31, *cr.* 2.

SAGE, a sage's head, (erased at neck,) ppr., vested with a skull-cap, sa. *Pl.* 31, *cr.* 2.

SAGRENOR, Eng., a cross moline, lozenge-pierced, gu. *Pl.* 91, *cr.* 10.

SAINSBURY, Eng., a hand holding a ducal coronet, caped, between two branches of laurel, in orle, ppr. *Pl.* 95, *cr.* 11.

SAINSBURY, Hants, a demi-antelope, ppr., collared, or, (charged on body with three lozenges conjoined, in bend, erminois.) *Pl.* 34, *cr.* 8.

ST ALBANS, (Beauclerk,) Duke of, Earl of Burford, Baron Heddington and Vere, on a chapeau, gu., turned up, erm., a lion, (statant,) gardant, or, ducally crowned, per pale, ar. and gu., gorged with a collar, gu., thereon three roses, ar., seeded and barbed, ppr. *Auspicium melioris ævi. Pl.* 120, *cr.* 15.

ST ALBYN, a wolf, sejant, erm., (collared, ringed, and line reflexed over back, or.) *Deus meus dux meus. Pl.* 110, *cr.* 4.

ST AMOND, Sco., an arm, in armour, brandishing a scimitar, ppr. *Pl.* 81, *cr.* 11.

ST AMOND, Eng., out of a ducal coronet, gu., an ass's head, ar. *Pl.* 80, *cr.* 6.

ST AMOND, a mule's head, couped, az., (collared, or, between three bezants, one and two, on neck a martlet, or.) *Pl.* 91, *cr.* 7.

ST ANDREA, or ST ANDREW, Eng., a dolphin, haurient, az. *Pl.* 14, *cr.* 10.

ST ANDREW, a cinquefoil. *Pl.* 91, *cr.* 12.

ST AUBIN, Somers., a wolf, sejant, erm., (collared, lined, and ringed, or.) *Pl.* 110, *cr.* 4.

ST AUBYN, Eng., an eagle, rising, ppr. *Pl.* 67, *cr.* 4.

ST AUBYN, Cornw., a falcon, rising, ppr. *Pl.* 105, *cr.* 4.

ST AUBYN, Bart., Cornw., on a rock, a Cornish chough, rising, ppr. *Pl.* 8, *cr.* 5, (rock, *pl.* 38, *cr.* 10.)

ST AWBYNE, Cornw., on a rock, ppr., an eagle, rising, ar., beaked and legged, gu. *Pl.* 61, *cr.* 1.

ST BARBE, Hants, a wyvern, sa. *Pl.* 63, *cr.* 13.

ST CLAIR, Sco., a phœnix in flames, ppr. *Rinasci piu gloriosa. Pl.* 44, *cr.* 8.

ST CLAIR, Sco., a dove, in mouth an olive-branch, all ppr. *Credo. Pl.* 48, *cr.* 15.

ST CLAIR-ERSKINE, Earl of Rosslyn. *See* ROSSLYN.

ST CLERE, Eng., a fox, current, ppr. *Pl.* 80, *cr.* 5.

ST DENOUAC, Eng., a vol, ppr. *Pl.* 15, *cr.* 10.

ST GEORGE, Bart., Iri., a demi-lion, rampant, gu., ducally crowned, or, armed and langued, az. *Firmitas in cœlo. Pl.* 61, *cr.* 4, (without branch.)

ST GEORGE, Lond., Cambs., and Iri., a demi-lion, rampant, gu., ducally crowned, or. *Pl.* 61, *cr.* 4, (without branch.)

ST GERMANS, Earl of, and Baron Eliot, (Eliot:) 1. For *Eliot*, an elephant's head, couped, ar., (collared, gu.) *Pl.* 35, *cr.* 1. 2. For *Craggs*, a dexter and sinister hand and arm, couped at elbows, (armed, or, garnished, ar.,) grasping a sword, of the last, hilt and pommel, gold. *Occurrent nubes. Pl.* 3, *cr.* 5.

ST GERMYN, Eng., a demi-otter. *Pl.* 9, *cr.* 9.

2 D

ST HELENS, Baron, U.K., and Iri., (Fitz-Herbert,) a hand in a gauntlet, erect, ppr. *Intaminatis honoribus. Pl.* 15, *cr.* 15.

ST HILL, Devons., issuing through a ducal coronet, or, two wyverns' heads erased (and respecting each other,) vert, langued, gu. *Tout fin fait. Pl.* 6, *cr.* 4.

ST HILL, Devons., out of a ducal coronet, or, two wyverns' heads, addorsed, vert, langued, gu. *Pl.* 6, *cr.* 4.

ST JOHN, Northamp., Hunts., and Wilts., on a mount, vert, a falcon, rising, or, belled, gold, ducally gorged, gu. *Pl.* 81, *cr.* 12.

ST JOHN, on a mount, vert, a falcon, rising, or, belled, gold, ducally gorged, gu. *Data fata secutus. Pl.* 81, *cr.* 12.

ST JOHN, Eng., a monkey, passant, ppr. *Pl.* 105, *cr.* 11.

ST JOHN, Iri., a long cross, gu., upon three grieces, ar. *Pl.* 49, *cr.* 2.

ST JOHN, Viscount Bolingbroke. *See* BOLINGBROKE.

ST JOHN, a falcon, wings expanded, or, ducally gorged, gu. *Data fata secutus. Pl.* 61, *cr.* 12.

ST JOHN, a falcon, (volant,) or, (ducally gorged; gu.) *Pl.* 94, *cr.* 1.

ST JOHN, Hants. and Worc., on a mount, ppr., a falcon, rising, or, belled, gold, ducally gorged, gu. *Pl.* 81, *cr.* 12.

ST JOHN, a monkey, passant, or. *Pl.* 101, *cr.* 11.

SAINT JOHN, Hants, a falcon, rising, or. *Pl.* 105, *cr.* 4.

ST JOHN THE BAPTIST COLLEGE, Oxford, a stork, ppr. *Pl.* 33, *cr.* 9.

ST LAWRENCE, Earl of Howth. *See* HOWTH.

ST LEGER, Eng., a mullet of (five) points, pierced, gu. *Pl.* 45, *cr.* 1.

ST LEGER, Iri., a mullet, ar., between two palm-branches, vert. *Pl.* 3, *cr.* 9.

ST LEGER, Eng., a griffin, passant, or. *Pl.* 61, *cr.* 14, (without gorging.)

ST LEGER, an eagle, displayed, sa., issuing from a plume of feathers, ar. *Pl.* 54, *cr.* 8.

ST LEGER, Viscount Doneraile. *See* DONERAILE.

ST LEONARDS, Baron, a leopard's head, (erased, or, ducally gorged, az.) *Pl.* 40, *cr.* 10.

ST LIZE, Eng., a globe in its stand, ppr. *Pl.* 81, *cr.* 1.

ST LOE, Eng., a blackamoor's head, in profile, wreathed on forehead, ar. and sa. *Pl.* 48, *cr.* 7.

SAINT LO, a moor's head, ppr., affrontée. *Pl.* 19, *cr.* 1.

ST LOW, Eng., a water-bouget, sa. *Pl.* 14, *cr.* 12.

ST LYZ, Eng., a demi-lion, rampant, or, holding a mullet, sa. *Pl.* 89, *cr.* 10.

ST MAUR, Eng., a falcon's leg and wing conjoined, ppr., jessed and belled, or. *Pl.* 101, *cr.* 15.

ST MAURE, Eng., a branch of oak, fructed and leaved, ppr. *Pl.* 32, *cr.* 13.

ST MICHAEL, or ST MICHELL, Eng., out of a ducal coronet, a bear's head, muzzled. *Pl.* 6, *cr.* 6.

ST OWEN, Eng., an escallop, or, between wings, gu. *Pl.* 62, *cr.* 4.

ST OWEN, Eng., a demi-savage, holding a club. *Pl.* 14, *cr.* 11.

SAINT OWEN, Eng., a lion's paw, surmounted of a cheveron, and thereon a mullet, sa. *Pl.* 88, *cr.* 3.

ST PAUL, Linc., an elephant and castle, ppr. *Esse quam videri. Pl.* 114, *cr.* 14.

ST PAUL, a plume of five ostrich-feathers, alternately ar. and gu., crowned at the quills with a ducal coronet, or. *Pl.* 100, *cr.* 12.

ST PAUL, Bart., Northumb., out of a ducal coronet, or, a plume of five ostrich-feathers, ar. and gu., alternately. *Esse quam videri. Pl.* 100, *cr.* 12.

ST PERE, or ST PIERRE, Ess., a spear, erect, or, headed, ar., on point a dolphin, naiant, ppr. *Pl.* 49, *cr.* 14.

ST PHILIBERT, Eng., out of a mural coronet, a leopard's head, ducally gorged. *Pl.* 46, *cr.* 11.

ST QUENTIN, Yorks., out of a ducal coronet, gu., a pea-rise, ppr., on the top of a fluted column, between two horns, or.

ST QUENTON, Devons., a Cornish chough, ppr. *Pl.* 100, *cr.* 13.

ST QUINTIN, Yorks., an eagle's head, erased, vair. *Pl.* 20, *cr.* 7.

ST VINCENT, Viscount, (Jervis-Rickets,) out of a naval coronet, or, enwrapped by a wreath of laurel, vert, a demi-pegasus, ar., maned and hoofed, of the first, winged, az., charged on the wing with a fleur-de-lis, gold. *Thus. Pl.* 76, *cr.* 2.

SAKER, or SACKER, Kent, a bull's head, erased, or, between two laurel-branches, vert. *Pl.* 31, *cr.* 5.

SALE, Eng., a demi-chevalier, brandishing a sword. *Pl.* 23, *cr.* 4.

SALES, on a ducal coronet, or, a wyvern, sejant, vert. *Pl.* 104, *cr.* 11.

SALISBURY, Lanc., a demi-lion, rampant, couped, ar., crowned, or, in paws a crescent of the first. *Pl.* 61, *cr.* 4, (crescent, *pl.* 141.)

SALISBURY, Leic., a lion, rampant, ar., charged on shoulder with a crescent, sa., in dexter a crescent, or. *Pl.* 64, *cr.* 2, (crescent, *pl.* 141.)

SALISBURY, Devons., two lions, rampant, combatant, ar., ducally crowned, or, supporting a crescent, of the last. *Pl.* 117, *cr.* 2.

SALISBURY, or SALUSBURY, Wel., a demi-lion, rampant, ar., ducally crowned, or, holding a crescent, of the last. *Pl.* 61, *cr.* 4, (crescent, *pl.* 141.)

SALISBURY, Marquess and Earl of, Viscount Cranbourne and Baron Cecil (Gascoyne-Cecil,) six arrows in saltier, or, barbed and flighted, ar., girt together by a belt, gu., buckled and garnished, gold, over the arrows a morion-cap. *Sero, sed serio. Pl.* 101, *cr.* 13.

SALKELD, Northumb., a demi-dragon, rampant, (sans wings,) vert, charged with a mullet. *Pl.* 82, *cr.* 10, (mullet, *pl.* 141.)

SALKYNS, Lond., a lynx, sa. *Pl.* 122, *cr.* 14.

SALL, a pheon, sa. *Pl.* 26, *cr.* 12.

SALLOWAYE, Eng., a Saracen's head, ppr., banded about temples, or. *Pl.* 36, *cr.* 3.

SALMAN, and SALMON, Middx. and Chesh., issuing from a cloud, ppr., an armed arm, sa., purfled, or, in hand a falchion, of the first. *Pl.* 85, *cr.* 4.

SALMON, Iri., a dexter hand, brandishing a sword. *Pl.* 21, *cr.* 10.

SALMON, Cumb., an armed arm, sa., in hand a falchion, or. *Pl.* 2, *cr.* 8.

SALMON, a lion, passant, or, (collared, with a line reflexed over back, sa., supporting with dexter an escutcheon, az., charged with a cross pattée, gold.) *Pl.* 4, *cr.* 14.
SALMON, an etoile, ar. *Pl.* 63, *cr.* 9.
SALMON, a lion, sejant, gu. *Pl.* 126, *cr.* 15.
SALMOND, Eng., a salmon, haurient, ppr. *Pl.* 98, *cr.* 12.
SALMOND, a dexter arm, embowed, in hand an eel-spear, in bend. *Pl.* 39, *cr.* 15.
SALMOND, a salmon, naiant, ppr. *Pl.* 85, *cr.* 11.
SALOMONS, Lond., (on a mount, vert,) out of a crown of five palisadoes, or, a demi-lion, rampant, double-queued, gu., (between paws a bezant, charged with an ermine-spot.) *Deo adjuvante. Pl.* 120, *cr.* 10, (coronet, *pl.* 128, *fig.* 21.)
SALT, Yorks., on a rock, an alpaca, statant, ppr. *Quid non, deo juvante.*
SALT, (on a chapeau, gu., turned up, erm.,) a demi-ostrich, wings displayed, or, in mouth a horse-shoe, sa. *Pl.* 29, *cr.* 9, (horse-shoe, *pl.* 28, *cr.* 13.)
SALT, Lond. on a chapeau, az., turned up, erm., a demi-ostrich, wings expanded, ar., in mouth a horse-shoe, sa. *Ib.*
SALT, a dove and olive-branch, ppr. *Pl.* 48, *cr.* 15.
SALT, Staffs., an eagle, displayed, sa. *Pl.* 48, *cr.* 11.
SALTER, Iri., a dexter hand, holding a (salter or saltseller.) *Pl.* 35, *cr.* 9.
SALTER, an eagle's head, couped, gu., billettée, or. *Pl.* 100, *cr.* 10.
SALTER, a falcon's head, gu., (on neck three billets, or.) *Pl.* 34, *cr.* 11.
SALTER, Bucks., Northamp., and Suff., a cock's head, (couped,) gu., combed and wattled, or, charged on neck with four billets, of the last. *Pl.* 92, *cr.* 3, (billet, *pl.* 141.)
SALTERSFORD, Baron. *See* COURTOWN, Earl of.
SALTHOUSE, Eng., a dexter hand holding an open book. *Pl.* 126 A, *cr.* 9.
SALTIRE, Salop, a cock's head, az., combed and wattled, gu., charged on neck with four billets, or, one, two, and one. *Pl.* 92, *cr.* 3, (billet, *pl.* 141.)
SALTMARSH, a rudder, or. *Pl.* 60, *cr.* 10.
SALTMARSHE, PHILIP, Esq., of Saltmarshe, Yorks., a rudder, or. *Ad astra virtus. Pl.* 60, *cr.* 10.
SALTONSTALL, and SALTONSTON, Lond. and Yorks., out of a ducal coronet, or, a pelican's head, az., vulning, gu. *Pl.* 41, *cr.* 4, (coronet, *same plate.*)
SALTOUN, Baron, Sco., (Fraser,) an ostrich, in mouth a horse-shoe, all ppr. *In God is all. Pl.* 16, *cr.* 2.
SALTREN, Cornw., a lion, rampant. *Pl.* 67, *cr.* 5.
SALUSBURY, Bart., Monm., a demi-lion, rampant, couped, ar., crowned, or, in dexter a crescent, gold. *Satis est prostrasse leoni. Pl.* 61, *cr.* 4, (crescent, *pl.* 141.)
SALVIN, Durh., a wyvern, vert, wings elevated and addorsed, ppr. *Pl.* 63, *cr.* 13.
SALVIN, GERARD, Esq., of Croxdale, Durh., a dragon, vert, wings elevated and addorsed, ppr. *Je ne change qu' en mourant. Pl.* 90, *cr.* 10.
SALWAY, Worc., a Saracen's head, couped at shoulders, affrontée, ppr., wreathed about temples, ar. and sa. *Pl.* 97, *cr.* 2.

SALWAY, Worc., a demi-moor, sa., wreathed about head, ar. and sa., a belt from sinister shoulder to dexter hip, az.
SALWEY, Salop, a Saracen's head. *Fiat voluntas Dei. Pl.* 19, *cr.* 1.
SALWEY, Salop, a Saracen's dead. *Pl.* 19, *cr.* 1.
SAMBADGE, Kent and Chesh., a reindeer's head, erminois, attired, or. *Pl.* 60, *cr.* 3, (without coronet.)
SAMBORNE, Eng., a dexter hand holding a sheaf of arrows, ppr. *Pl.* 56, *cr.* 4.
SAMBY, Eng., a winged heart, or. *Pl.* 39, *cr.* 7.
SAMFORD, Eng., an escallop, or, marled, gu. *Pl.* 117, *cr.* 4.
SAMLER, Eng., an arm, in armour, embowed, ppr., in hand a battle-axe, or. *Pl.* 121, *cr.* 14.
SAMLER, a unicorn's head, erased, ar., horned, and (ducally) gorged, or. *Pl.* 73, *cr.* 1.
SAMMES, or SAMS, Ess., a man's head in a (helmet,) ppr., garnished, or, on top a plume of feathers, sa. *Pl.* 105, *cr.* 2.
SAMMES, Eng., a lion, rampant, ar., collared and chained, or. *Pl.* 88, *cr.* 1.
SAMPAYE, Portugal, a demi-unicorn, ar., armed, or, mane, ppr. *Pl.* 26, *cr.* 14.
SAMPSON, Eng., a demi-lion, az., in dexter a sword, in pale, ppr. *Deo juvante. Pl.* 41, *cr.* 13.
SAMPSON, Suff., a demi-lion, az., in dexter a sword, in pale, ar., hilt and pommel, or. *Pl.* 41, *cr.* 13.
SAMS, Ess., a leopard, salient, sa., spotted, or, ducally gorged, ringed, and lined, gold. *Pl.* 125, *cr.* 4.
SAMSON, Sco., a dexter hand, issuing, grasping a Hercules' club, all ppr. *If God will. Pl.* 28, *cr.* 6.
SAMUEL, and SAMWELL, Yorks., a wolf, current, sa., (pierced in breast by an arrow, or, feathered, ar.) *Pl.* 111, *cr.* 1.
SAMWAYES, Devons. and Wilts., a lion's gamb, erect and erased, or, holding a mullet, gu. *Pl.* 126, *cr.* 9, (mullet, *pl.* 141.)
SAMWELL-WATSON, of Upton Hall, Northamp. : 1. For *Samwell*, on stump of tree, couped, or, sprouting on each side, vert, a squirrel, sejant, gu., cracking a nut, gold, stalked and leaved, of the second. *Christus sit regula vitæ. Pl.* 5, *cr.* 6. 2. For *Watson*, a griffin, ducally gorged, or. *Spero meliora. Pl.* 61, *cr.* 14.
SAND, Sco., a dove and olive-branch. *Virtute duce. Pl.* 48, *cr.* 15.
SAND, Eng., a dove, in mouth a (laurel)-branch. *Virtute duce. Pl.* 48, *cr.* 15.
SANDBACH, a reindeer's head, erased, per fess, ar. and or, attired, gold, (gorged with a wreath of oak, in mouth an ear of wheat, vert.) *Virtutis gloria merces. Pl.* 2, *cr.* 13.
SANDBACH, Chesh., a garb, or. *Pl.* 48, *cr.* 10.
SANDBY, Eng., an antelope, passant, or. *Pl.* 63, *cr.* 10.
SANDBY, a griffin's head, erased, ar., (collared, az., thereon a fret, of the first.) *Pl.* 69, *cr.* 13.
SANDELAND, Eng., a crescent, ensigned with an etoile of six points. *Pl.* 111, *cr.* 15.
SANDELL, Eng., a flag, issuant, charged with a cross, sa. *Pl.* 8, *cr.* 3.
SANDEMAN, Sco., a rock, ppr. *Stat veritas. Pl.* 73, *cr.* 12.

SANDERS, Surr., Staffs., Lond., and Derbs., a demi-bull, rampant, gu., armed, or. *Pl.* 63, *cr.* 6.
SANDERS, Bucks. and Northamp., an elephant's head, erased, per cheveron, sa. and ar., armed, or. *Pl.* 68, *cr.* 4.
SANDERS, Bucks. and Northamp., an elephant's head, erased, sa., eared and armed, ar. *Pl.* 68, *cr.* 4.
SANDERS, Bucks. and Northamp., an elephant's head, erased, sa. *Pl.* 68, *cr.* 4.
SANDERS, Sco., an antelope's head, erm., (collared, gu.) *Pl.* 79, *cr.* 9, (without spear.)
SANDERS, Iri., a boar's head, erased, or. *Pl.* 16, *cr.* 11.
SANDERS, Derbs., a demi-bull, sa. *Non bas in lingua. Pl.* 63, *cr.* 6.
SANDERS, Middx., out of a ducal coronet, or, an elephant's head, ar., eared, gold. *Pl.* 93, *cr.* 13.
SANDERSON, Sco., a talbot, passant, ppr. *Paratus et fidelis. Pl.* 120, *cr.* 8.
SANDERSON, Eng., same crest.
SANDERSON, West Jesmond, Northumb., a wolf's head, ar., erased, gu., collared, and a chain reflexed behind neck, or, between a branch of palm, and another of laurel, ppr., (for distinction, on neck a saltier, humettée, gu.) *Clarior ex obscuro. Pl.* 8, *cr.* 4, (branches, *pl.* 116, *cr.* 9.)
SANDERSON, Eng., a talbot, passant, ar., eared and spotted, sa. *Pl.* 120, *cr.* 8.
SANDERSON, Northamp., on a mount, vert, a talbot, sa., eared, ar., spotted, of the last. *Pl.* 120, *cr.* 8, (mount, *pl.* 98, *cr.* 13.)
SANDERSON, Linc., a wolf's head, sa., devouring a man, ppr., the body, from the small of the back downward, hanging out of his mouth.
SANDERSON, Durh. and Northumb., a talbot, passant, spotted, sa. *Sans Dieu rien. Pl.* 120, *cr.* 8.
SANDES, Surr. and Kent, a griffin, segreant, per fess, or and gu. *Pl.* 67, *cr.* 13.
SANDES, Somers. and Westm., same crest. *Probum non pœnitet. Pl.* 67, *cr.* 13.
SANDES, Surr. and Cumb., an heraldic-tiger, az., tufted, maned, (collared and lined, or, the line twisted round body four times, and falling behind hind-legs.) *Pl.* 7, *cr.* 5.
SANDFORD, Iri., a martlet, sa. *Pl.* 111. *cr* 5.
SANDFORD, Baron, Mount Sandford. *See* MOUNT SANDFORD.
SANDFORD, Westm., a boar's head, couped, ar. *Pl.* 48, *cr.* 2.
SANDFORD, THOMAS-HUGH, Esq., of Sandford, Salop, a falcon, wings addorsed, ppr., belled, or, preying on a partridge, of the first. *Nec temeré, nec timidé. Pl.* 61, *cr.* 7.
SANDFORD, HUMPHREY, Esq., of the Isle of Rossall, Salop, a boar's head, or. *Pl.* 48, *cr.* 2.
SANDFORD, Herts., an arm, in armour, embowed, ppr., within the gauntlet a broken tilting-spear, sa., (and a laurel-branch, vert.) *Pl.* 44, *cr.* 9.
SANDFORD, Ess., Glouc., and Salop, a boar's head, couped, or, with a kroken spear, az., headed, ar., thrust into the mouth. *Pl.* 11, *cr.* 9.
SANDFORD, Cambs., out of a ducal coronet, gu., a boar's head and neck, or. *Pl.* 102, *cr.* 14.
SANDIFORD, a boar's head, couped, in fess, in mouth a dagger, thrust hilt foremost. *Pl.* 28, *cr.* 14.
SANDILANDS, an eagle, displayed, ppr. *Spero meliora. Pl.* 48, *cr.* 11.
SANDILANDS, Sco., a palm-tree, ppr. *Pl.* 18, *cr.* 12.
SANDILANDS, an (eagle,) volant, ppr. *Victoria, non præda. Pl.* 94, *cr.* 1.
SANDILANDS, a star, issuing from a crescent, ar. *Justi ut sidera fulgent. Pl.* 111, *cr.* 15.
SANDILANDS, Sco., an eagle, displayed, or. *Pl.* 48, *cr.* 11.
SANDILANDS, Eng., a mullet, between the horns of a crescent, or, between two palm-branches, environed with clouds, ppr. *Pl.* 118, *cr.* 2.
SANDILANDS, Baron Torphichen. *See* TORPHICHEN.
SANDOM, Eng., a boar, passant, or. *Pl.* 48, *cr.* 14.
SANDON, out of a ducal coronet, a phœnix in flames, ppr. *Pl.* 53, *cr.* 6.
SANDS, Surr., Kent, Somers., and Westm., a griffin, segreant, per fess, or and gu. *Probum non pœnitet. Pl.* 67, *cr.* 13.
SANDS, Sco., out of a ducal coronet, or, a lion's gamb, erect, sa. *Audaces juvat. Pl.* 67, *cr.* 7.
SANDWELL, or SANDWILL, Kent, a lion's gamb, erect and erased, gu., enfiled with a ducal coronet, erm. *Pl.* 93, *cr.* 9.
SANDWICH, Earl of, Viscount Hinchinbroke, and Baron Montagu, (Montagu,) a griffin's head, couped, or, beaked, sa., wings addorsed, of the last. *Post tot naufragia portus. Pl.* 65, *cr.* 1.
SANDY, Eng., a griffin, segreant. *Pl.* 67, *cr.* 13.
SANDY, a demi-antelope, (erased,) at flank, or, armed, ar. *Pl.* 34, *cr.* 8, (without collar.)
SANDY, a demi-antelope, or, armed and maned, az. *Pl.* 34, *cr.* 8, (without collar.)
SANDYS, Eng., a griffin, segreant. *Pl.* 67, *cr.* 13.
SANDYS, Eng., a griffin, parted per fess, or and gu. *Probum non pœnitet. Pl.* 66, *cr.* 13.
SANDYS, Lanc., a griffin, segreant, per fess, or and gu. *Probum non pœnitet. Pl.* 67, *cr.* 13.
SANDYS, Worc., a griffin, per fess, or and gu. *Pl.* 66, *cr.* 13.
SANDYS, Cornw., a griffin, segreant, gu., between feet a cross crosslet, fitched, of the last. *Pl.* 13, *cr.* 10, (cross, *pl.* 141.)
SANDYS, BAYNTUN, Bart. : 1. For *Sandys*, a griffin, segreant, per fess, or and gu. *Pl.* 67, *cr.* 13. 2. For *Bayntun*, a griffin's head, erased, sa., charged with a cross crosslet, fitched, or. *Pl.* 48, *cr.* 6, (cross, *pl.* 141.)
SANFORD, Eng., a bull's head, gu. *Pl.* 120, *cr.* 7.
SANFORD, EDWARD-AYSHFORD, Esq., of Nynehead Court, Somers.; and Lynton, Devons., a martlet, ppr. *Ferme en foy. Pl.* 111, *cr.* 5.
SANGSTER, Eng., on a rock, a blackbird, ppr. *Pl.* 31, *cr.* 3.
SANGSTER, and SONGSTER, Sco., a blackbird, ppr. *Providentia divina. Pl.* 10, *cr.* 12.
SANKEY, Iri., a peacock's head, couped, ppr. *Pl.* 100, *cr.* 5.
SANKEY, Coolmore, co. Tipperary, a cubit arm, vested, sa., cuffed, ar., in hand a fish, ppr. *Pl.* 105, *cr.* 9, (vesting, *pl.* 32, *cr.* 6.)
SANSON, Eng., a demi-talbot, az. *Pl.* 15, *cr.* 2, (without gorging.)

SANSUN, Eng., a lion's head, erased, in mouth a cinquefoil, vert. *Pl.* 95, *cr.* 6, (cinquefoil, *pl.* 141.)

SANTON, Eng., a swan, ppr. *Pl.* 122, *cr.* 13, (without mount.)

SAPCOT, Eng., a demi-lion, rampant, az., in dexter a sword, ppr. *Pl.* 41, *cr.* 13.

SAPCOTES, Cornw., Hunts., Herts., and Linc., a goat's head, erased, ar., attired, or. *Pl.* 29, *cr.* 13.

SAPCOTT, Eng., a goat's head, erased, sa., armed, or. *Pl.* 29, *cr.* 13.

SAPHAR, Eng., a beacon on fire, ppr. *Pl.* 88, *cr.* 6.

SAPIE, Eng., a bezant, ar., charged with a lion's head, erased, gu. *Pl.* 50, *cr.* 10, (without collar.)

SAPTE, Herts., a dove, in mouth a sprig of (laurel,) ppr. *Pl.* 48, *cr.* 15.

SAPY, or SAPYE, Eng., a falcon's wing and leg, conjoined, ppr., jessed and belled, or. *Pl.*101, *cr.* 15.

SARE, Kent, an arm, embowed, vested with leaves, vert, in hand, ppr., a dragon's head, erased, of the first. *Pl.* 83, *cr.* 2, (head,*pl.* 87, *cr.* 12.)

SARE, Kent, an elephant, or, in a wood, ppr. *Pl.* 56, *cr.* 14, (wood, *pl.* 125, *cr.* 14.)

SAREBRUCHE, Eng., a horse's head, or, couped and bridled, gu. *Pl.* 92, *cr.* 1.

SARESBERY, Eng., a fish, haurient. *Pl.* 98, *cr.* 12.

SARGANT, and SARGEANT, Eng., two eagles' wings, conjoined and inverted, ppr. *Pl.* 87, *cr.* 1.

SARGANT, Bucks., a dolphin, naiant, or, guttée, az. *Pl.* 48, *cr.* 9.

SARGANT, SARGEANT, or SARGENT, Staffs., a dolphin, naiant, sa., between wings, ar. *Pl.* 111, *cr.* 12, (dolphin, *pl.* 48, *cr.* 9.)

SARGENT, Eng., a goat's head, erased, or. *Pl.* 29, *cr.* 13.

SARJEANTSON, a cherub's head and wings, ppr. *Pl.* 126, *cr.* 10.

SARMON, Eng., an elephant, passant, ar. *Pl.* 56, *cr.* 14.

SARSFIELD, THOMAS-RONAYNE, Esq., of Doughcloyne, co. Cork, a leopard's face, ppr. *Virtus non veritur. Pl.* 66, *cr.* 14.

SARSON, Eng., a wolf, collared and lined, in dexter a fleur-de-lis. *Pl.* 5, *cr.* 8, (fleur de-lis, *pl.* 4, *cr.* 14.)

SATHERTHWAYTE, Lanc., a lion's head, erased, or, gorged with a collar, sa., charged with three roses, ar. *Pl.* 7, *cr.* 10.

SATTERTHWAITE, Eng., a greyhound, sejant, az. *Pl.* 66, *cr.* 15.

SAUL, and SAULE, Eng., a swan, ar., collared and lined, gu. *Fideli certa merces. Pl.* 73, *cr.* 14.

SAULT, Eng., on a ducal coronet, gu., a wyvern, sans legs, or. *Pl.* 104, *cr.* 11.

SAULTON, an ostrich, in mouth a horse-shoe. *Pl.* 16, *cr.* 2.

SAUMAREZ, an eagle, rising, ppr. *In Deo spero. Pl.* 67, *cr.* 4.

SARMAREZ, Eng., an eagle, displayed, ppr. *Orbe circum cincto. Pl.* 48, *cr.* 11.

SAUNDERS, Northamp., an elephant's head, erased, per cheveron, counterchanged, ar. and sa. *Pl.* 68, *cr.* 4.

SAUNDERS, Sco., a spur-rowel, az. *Pl.* 54, *cr.* 5.

SAUNDERS, Surr., Derbs., a demi-bull, erased, gu., on shoulder a rose, ar., mane, of the last. *Pl.* 63, *cr.* 6, (rose, *pl.* 141.)

SAUNDERS, Oxon., Warw., and Leic., an elephant's head, erased, per cheveron, ar. and sa. *Pl.* 68, *cr.* 4.

SAUNDERS, Leic., Warw., and Oxon., an elephant's head, erased, sa., eared, ar. *Pl.* 68, *cr.* 4.

SAUNDERS, Bucks. and Northamp., an elephant's head, erased, per cheveron, sa. and ar., armed, or. *Pl.* 68, *cr.* 4.

SAUNDERS, Bucks., Herts., and Northamp., an elephant's head, erased, sa. *Pl.* 68, *cr.* 4.

SAUNDERS, Bucks., Northamp., and Northumb., an elephant's head, erased, sa., armed and eared, ar. *Pl.* 68, *cr.* 4.

SAUNDERS, a tree, from the branches on either side, pendent, a hawk's lure. *Pl.* 117, *cr.* 1.

SAUNDERS, a bull's head, erased, ar. *Pl.* 19, *cr.* 3.

SAUNDERS, a demi-bull, salient, (erased) at loins, ar., charged on neck with a rose, gu. *Pl.* 63, *cr.* 6, (rose, *pl.* 141.)

SAUNDERS, out of a naval coronet, ar., a demi-bull, rampant, gu., armed and hoofed, or. *Pl.* 63, *cr.* 6, (coronet, *pl.* 128, *fig.* 19.)

SAUNDERS, Lond., out of a mural coronet, an elephant's head, ar., (charged on breast with an ogress.) *Pl.* 93, *cr.* 13, (coronet, *pl.* 128, *fig.* 18.)

SAUNDERS, Hants, a demi-bull, gu. *Pl.* 63, *cr.* 6.

SAUNDERSON, Eng., a greyhound's head, erm. *Pl.* 84, *cr.* 13, (without roses.)

SAUNDERSON, a hound, statant, ppr. *Pl.* 104, *cr.* 1, (without chapeau.)

SAUNDERSON, an arm, in armour, embowed, in hand a scimitar. *Pl.* 81, *cr.* 11.

SAUNDERSON, ALEXANDER, Esq., of Castle Saunderson, co. Cavan, a talbot-dog, passant, spotted, sa. *Je suis veillant à plaire. Pl.* 120, *cr.* 8.

SAVAGE, Eng., a lion's gamb, erect and erased, sa. *Pl.* 126, *cr.* 9.

SAVAGE, Derbs. and Chesh., a unicorn's head, ar., erased, gu. *Pl.* 67, *cr.* 1.

SAVAGE, Worc., out of a ducal coronet, or, a lion's gamb, erect, sa., charged with a rose, ar. *Pl.* 67, *cr.* 7, (rose, *pl.* 141.)

SAVAGE, Salop, Kent, Glouc., Hants, and Chesh., out of a ducal coronet, or, a lion's gamb, erect, sa. *Pl.* 67, *cr.* 7.

SAVAGE, Lond., a pheon, point upward, az. *Pl.* 56, *cr.* 15.

SAVAGE, Sco., out of a ducal coronet, a lion's gamb, erect, sa. *Fortis atque fidelis. Pl.* 67, *cr.* 7.

SAVAGE, Iri., a savage's head, ppr. *Pl.* 19, *cr.* 1.

SAVAGE, Eng., out of a ducal coronet, or, a lion's gamb, sa. *Te pro te. Pl.* 67, *cr.* 7.

SAVAGE, Norelands, co. Kilkenny, (rising from the waves,) a mermaid, ppr. *Fortis atque fidelis. Pl.* 48, *cr.* 5.

SAVAGE, FRANCIS, Esq., of Ballymadun, co. Dublin, out of a ducal coronet, or, a lion's gamb, erect, sa. *Fortis atque fidelis. Pl.* 67, *cr.* 7.

SAVAGE, a lion's paw, erect, sa. *A te pro te. Pl.* 126, *cr.* 9.

SAVAGE, a female's head, couped at breasts, hair dishevelled, affrontée. *Pl.* 45, *cr.* 5.

SAVAGE, a unicorn's head, erased, per fess, ar. and gu., horned and crined, and in mouth a fleur-de-lis, az. *Pl.* 117, *cr.* 3.

SAVARY, Lond., a cubit arm, in armour, in hand, all ppr., a sword, in pale, ar., hilt and pommel, or, enfiled on blade with a boar's head, erased, ppr. *Noscentes prosequor. Pl.* 71, *cr.* 9, (armour, *pl.* 125, *cr.* 5.)

SAVELL, SAVILL, and SAVIL, Eng., an owl, ar. *Pl.* 27, *cr.* 9.

SAVELL, SAVILL, or SAVILE, Linc. and Notts., an owl, ar. *Be fast. Pl.* 27, *cr.* 9.

SAVERY, Devons., an eagle's head, erased, ar., between wings, sa., in beak an olive-branch, vert. *Pl.* 81, *cr.* 10, (branch, *pl.* 98, *cr.* 8.)

SAVIGNAC, a lion's head, erased, devouring a man, the body from the small of the back hanging out of mouth. *Pl.* 117, *cr.* 5.

SAVILE, Notts., an owl, ar., (ducally gorged,) or. *Pl.* 27, *cr.* 9.

SAVILE, Oaklands, Devons., an eagle, rising, per bend sinister, or, and sa., in beak a fleur-de-lis, az. *Nil conscire sibi. Pl.* 67, *cr.* 4, (fleur-de-lis, *pl.* 121, *cr.* 7.)

SAVILE, Notts., out of a ducal coronet, or, a pelican's head, vulned, ppr. *Pl.* 41, *cr.* 4, (coronet, *same plate, cr.* 10.)

SAVILL, Notts., an owl, ar., on breast a fleur-de-lis, gu. *Pl.* 27, *cr.* 9, (fleur-de-lis, *pl.* 141.)

SAVILLE, Eng., the rising sun, or, clouds, ar., tinged, gu. *Pl.* 67, *cr.* 9.

SAVILLE, Earl of Mexborough. *See* MEXBOROUGH.

SAVORY, Eng., a hand holding a chapeau, between two branches of laurel, in orle. *Pl.* 59, *cr.* 4.

SAWBRIDGE, Lond. and Kent, a demi-lion, az., supporting a (saw,) in pale, or. *Pl.* 41, *cr.* 13.

SAWBRIDGE, a demi-lion, az., charged on breast with an ermine-spot, or, supporting a (saw,) in pale, gold. *Pl.* 47, *cr.* 4, (ermine-spot, *pl.* 141.)

SAWERS, Sco., a dexter hand holding a scimitar, all ppr., the last hilted and pommelled, or. *Virtute, non verbis. Pl.* 29, *cr.* 8.

SAWERS, Eng., a mullet, pierced, gu. *Pl.* 45, *cr.* 1.

SAWLL-GRAVES, Bart., of Penrice, Cornw.; and Barley, Devons., an eagle, displayed, or, supporting in dexter a staff, erect, ppr., thereon a forked pennon, flowing to sinister, gu., with this inscription—*Per sinum Codanum. Pl.* 107, *cr.* 4, (pennon, *pl.* 65, *cr.* 3.)

SAWREY, Lanc., on a Roman fasces, an arm, in armour, embowed, in hand an arrow, all ppr. *Dictis factisque simplex. Pl.* 65, *cr.* 15, (arm, *pl.* 96, *cr.* 6.)

SAWYER, Northamp., on a mural coronet, gu., a parrot's head, erased, vert, beaked, of the first. *Pl.* 94, *cr.* 2, (coronet, *pl.* 128, *fig.* 18.)

SAWYER, Eng., in a mural coronet, gu., a falcon's head, erased, vert, beaked, of the first. *Pl.* 24, *cr.* 10, (coronet, *same plate.*)

SAWYER, Berks., a talbot, (gardant,) ppr. *Pl.* 120, *cr.* 8.

SAWYER, Cambs. and Norf., on a mount, vert, a hound on scent, ar., spotted, liver-colour. *Pl.* 117, *cr.* 8.

SAXBY, Kent, on a mount, vert, a lion, rampant, erminois, collared, dove-tailed, with a line thereto, reflexed over back, and terminating in a knot, az., in dexter a dart, sa., feathered, ar., headed, or. *Sit saxum firmum. Pl.* 121, *cr.* 15.

SAXON, Eng., a talbot, passant, sa. *Pl.* 120, *cr.* 8.

SAXTON, Chesh., out of a ducal coronet, or, a nag's head, ar., between wings, gu. *Pl.* 50, *cr.* 13, (wings, *pl.* 17, *cr.* 9.)

SAXTON, Bart., Berks., on a mount, vert, a griffin's head, erased, sa., (ducally gorged, or,) between wings, ar. *Pl.* 65, *cr.* 1, (mount, *pl.* 98, *cr.* 13.)

SAY, Eng., a goat's head, gu. *Pl.* 105, *cr.* 14.

SAY, a buck's head, couped, or, on a wreath of thorns, az. and gu. *Pl.* 91, *cr.* 14, (wreath, *pl.* 78, *cr.* 7.)

SAY, out of a ducal coronet, or, a bull's head, sa., armed, ar. *Pl.* 68, *cr.* 6.

SAYE, and SELE, Baron, (Eardley-Twiselton-Fiennes,) an arm, embowed, vested, sa., cuffed, ar., in hand, ppr., a mole-spade, or, headed and armed, of the second. *Fortem posce animum. Pl.* 89, *cr.* 6, (vesting, *pl.* 39, *cr.* 1.)

SAYER, Eng., a dexter hand, ppr., vested and tied at cuff, holding up a griffin's head, erased. *Pl.* 94, *cr.* 6, (vesting, *pl.* 32, *cr.* 6.)

SAYER, a (sinister) arm, in armour, embowed, hand grasping a flag-staff, with pennon flotant to sinister, (ensigned with a cap of liberty.) *Pl.* 6, *cr.* 5.

SAYER, a cubit arm, erect, ppr., in hand a dragon's head, erased, ar. *Pl.* 29, *cr.* 4, (head, *pl.* 107, *cr.* 10.)

SAYER, Kent, an arm, in armour, embowed, ppr., garnished, or, hand grasping a griffin's head, erased, of the second. *Pl.* 75, *cr.* 1, (head, *pl.* 94, *cr.* 6.)

SAYER, Cornw., on a mount, vert, a leopard, couchant, (regardant,) ppr. *Pl.* 9, *cr.* 14, (without crown.)

SAYERS, Eng., a hand holding a scroll of paper, between two branches of laurel, vert. *Pl.* 86, *cr.* 5.

SAYVELL, or SAYVILL, the head and shoulders of an Indian king, ppr., ducally crowned, or, crined, and necklace, of the last, out of the coronet, a plume of feathers, vert, charged with three cinquefoils, ar. *Pl.* 28, *cr.* 3, (feathers, *pl.* 105, *cr.* 2; cinquefoil, *pl.* 141.)

SCAIFE, Northumb., an escallop, reversed, ppr. *Pl.* 53, *cr.* 3.

SCALES, Sco., a lion's paw, holding a branch of palm, ppr. *Pl.* 70, *cr.* 9.

SCALES, Eng., out of a ducal coronet, or, a swan's head, between wings, sa. *Pl.* 83, *cr.* 1.

SCALES, Norf., out of a ducal coronet, or, a plume of ostrich-feathers, ar. *Pl.* 44, *cr.* 12.

SCALES, Sco., a chevalier, in complete armour, scaling a ladder, ppr. *Paulatim.*

SCAMBLER, Norf., a garb, or, banded, gu. *Pl.* 48, *cr.* 10.

SCAMBLER, Norf., a garb, or, encircled by a ducal coronet, gu. *Pl.* 76, *cr.* 13.

SCARBOROUGH, Norf., out of a mural coronet, gu., a demi-lion, or, holding upon the point of a lance, of the first, a Saracen's head, ppr., wreathed, az. *Pl.* 120, *cr.* 14, (head, *pl.* 88, *cr.* 15.)

SCARBOROUGH, Earl of, Viscount and Baron Lumley, Eng., and Viscount Lumley, Iri.,

(Lumley-Saville,) a pelican, in nest, feeding her young, all ppr. *Murus œneus conscientia sana.* *Pl.* 44, *cr.* 1.

SCARBROW, Lond., a demi-lion, or, billettée, gu., supporting a spear, erect, ppr., encircled by a mural coronet, gold. *Pl.* 69, *cr.* 14, (coronet, *pl.* 55, *cr.* 1.)

SCARDLOW, Eng., an oak-tree, vert. *Pl.* 16, *cr.* 8.

SCARGELL, or SKARGILL, Cumb. and Yorks., a plume of three feathers, ar., (confined with a bend, or.) *Pl.* 12, *cr.* 9.

SCARISBRICK, CHARLES, Esq., of Scarisbrick, Lanc.: 1. For *Scarisbrick*, a dove, sa., beaked and legged, gu., in mouth an olive-branch, ppr. *Pl.* 48, *cr.* 15. 2. For *Eccleston*, a magpie, ppr. *Pl.* 100, *cr.* 13.

SCARLET, Ess., two lions' gambs, erased, erm., supporting a pillar, gobony, or and gu., capital and base, of the second. *Pl.* 77, *cr.* 4.

SCARLETT, Eng., out of a ducal coronet, or, a demi-eagle, displayed, sa. *Pl.* 9, *cr.* 6.

SCARLETT, Baron Abinger. *See* ABINGER.

SCARROW, Eng., a naked arm, embowed, brandishing a scimitar, all ppr. *Pl.* 92, *cr.* 5.

SCARSBOROUGH, Eng., a rock, ppr. *Pl.* 73, *cr.* 12.

SCARSDALE, Baron, and a Bart., (Curzon,) a popinjay, rising, or, (collared, gu.) *Pl.* 25, *cr.* 2. (Another crest, a cockatrice, wings elevated, or, tail nowed, with a head at the end thereof.) *Recte et suaviter.* *Pl.* 63, *cr.* 15.

SCARTA, Sco., on stump of tree, couped, sprouting a branch from dexter side, and environed with a serpent, head to the sinister, an eagle, rising, all ppr. *Volando reptilia sperno.* *Pl.* 1, *cr.* 11, (serpent, *pl.* 84, *cr.* 4.)

SCARTH, Sco., a dexter hand holding a dagger, ppr. *Pax aut bellum.* *Pl.* 28, *cr.* 4.

SCATCHARD, Eng., a torteau, or, charged with a stag, ppr., on a mount, vert. *Pl.* 45, *cr.* 11.

SCAWEN, Cornw., a cubit arm, vested, gu., cuffed, ar., hand holding the trunk of a tree, eradicated, near the top a branch issuing, all ppr.

SCEPTER, Eng., a demi-lion, rampant, ppr., langued, gu., in dexter a scimitar, of the first. *Fac et spera.* *Pl.* 126 A, *cr.* 1.

SCHANK, Sco., an eagle, rising, gu. *Spero.* *Pl.* 67, *cr.* 4.

SCHANK, Devons. and Sco., an eagle, wings expanded, ppr. *Pl.* 126, *cr.* 7.

SCHANK, JOHN-MACKELLAR-SKEENE-GRIEVE, Esq., of Barton House, Dawlish, Devons., an eagle, rising, ppr. *Spero.* *Pl.* 67, *cr.* 4.

SCHAPMAR, Sco., a tower, ar., masoned, sa. *Pl.* 12, *cr.* 5.

SCHARDELOW, Eng., a ship in full sail. *Pl.* 109, *cr.* 8.

SCHAW, Sco., a covered cup, or. *Pl.* 75, *cr.* 13, (without swords.)

SCHAW, Eng., a rose, gu., barbed, vert. *Pl.* 20, *cr.* 2.

SCHELLEY, Eng., an escallop, gu. *Pl.* 117, *cr.* 4.

SCHERLIS, Eng., a castle, or. *Pl.* 28, *cr.* 11.

SCHINDLER, Eng., an anchor and cable, ppr. *Pl.* 42, *cr.* 12.

SCHNEIDER, Eng., from a round turret, a Cornish chough, volant. *Pl.* 84, *cr.* 3.

SCHOFFIELD, or SCHOFIELD, Eng., a fleur-de-lis, or. *Pl.* 68, *cr.* 12.

SCHOLES, Eng., a cross crosslet, sa. *Pl.* 66, *cr.* 8.

SCHOLEY, Eng., a dexter hand brandishing a sword. *Pl.* 21, *cr.* 10.

SCHOLEY, Lond., an arm, in armour, erect, ppr., gauntlet holding a hurt, on the arm a bend, charged with a swan, sa., between two hurts.

SCHOLTON, or SCHOLTEN, an antelope's head, couped, ppr. *Pl.* 79, *cr.* 9, (without spear.)

SCHOMBERG, Eng., on a winged globe, a dove, rising, ppr. *Pl.* 50, *cr.* 7.

SCHRIEBER, JOHN-CHARLES, Esq., of Henhurst, Kent, an arm, in armour, embowed, ppr., garnished, or, hand holding a dagger, point towards the dexter, also ppr., hilt and pommel, of the second. *Deutlich und wahr.* *Pl.* 120, *cr.* 11.

SCHRODER, Eng., a castle, triple-towered, ppr. *Pl.* 123, *cr.* 14.

SCHULTZ, or SCHULTZE, Eng., on the top of an old castle, (in ruins,) an eagle, volant. *Pl.* 90, *cr.* 2.

SCIAUALUGA, an esquire's helmet, ppr., garnished, or. *Pl.* 109, *cr.* 5.

SCLATER, Eng., a hunting-horn, stringed, or. *Pl.* 48, *cr.* 12.

SCLATER, Hants, out of a ducal coronet, or, an eagle, rising, wings displayed, sa. *Pl.* 9, *cr.* 6.

SCLATER, Sco., a lion, passant, gardant, ppr. *Vi et virtute.* *Pl.* 120, *cr.* 5.

SCOBELL, Cornw., a dexter hand holding up a bomb, inflamed, ppr. *Pl.* 2, *cr.* 6.

SCOBELL, Cornw., a demi-lion, rampant, in dexter a fleur-de-lis. *Pl.* 91, *cr.* 13.

SCOBIE, Eng., a sword, erect, ppr. *Pl.* 105, *cr.* 1.

SCOFFIELD, Lanc., a bull's head, or. *Pl.* 120, *cr.* 7.

SCOFIELD, or SCOFFIELD, Lanc., a bull's head, gu., collared, ar. *Pl.* 63, *cr.* 11.

SCOFIELD, Kent, a bull's head, gu., collared, ar., attired, or. *Pl.* 63, *cr.* 11.

SCOLLAY, Sco., a hand pointing with one finger, ppr. *Pl.* 35, *cr.* 5.

SCOPHAM, Eng., an archer shooting an arrow from a bow. *Pl.* 90, *cr.* 3.

SCOPHOLME, Sco., an eagle, displayed, ppr. *Spero meliora.* *Pl.* 48, *cr.* 11.

SCOPYN, Eng., an archer shooting an arrow from a bow, ppr. *Pl.* 90, *cr.* 3.

SCOREY, Eng., out of a ducal coronet, a demi-eagle, all or. *Pl.* 19, *cr.* 9.

SCORY, Herts., out of a ducal coronet, a demi-eagle, displayed, all or. *Pl.* 9, *cr.* 6.

SCOT, Eng., out of a ducal coronet, a phœnix in flames, ppr. *Pl.* 53, *cr.* 6.

SCOT, Kent and Lond., an eagle, or, preying on a bittern, ppr. *Pl.* 17, *cr.* 8.

SCOT, Kent, Hants, and Suss., a demi-griffin, segreant, sa., beaked and legged, or. *Pl.* 18, *cr.* 6.

SCOT, a dexter hand holding a lance, all ppr. *I am ready.* *Pl.* 99, *cr.* 8.

SCOT, Sco., out of a mural coronet, six horsemen's lances or spears, (with pennons thereat,) three and three, disposed in saltier. *Ready, aye ready.* *Pl.* 95, *cr.* 8.

SCOT, or SCOTT, Sco., a stag, trippant, ppr. *Pacem amo.* *Pl.* 68, *cr.* 2.

SCOT, a hart, couchant, ppr. *Amo probos.* *Pl.* 67, *cr.* 2.

SCOT, Sco., a stag's head, erased, ppr. *Ardenter amo.* *Pl.* 66, *cr.* 9.

Scot, Sco., a boar's head, couped, or, in mouth (four) arrows, gu., feathered and headed, ar. *Do well, and let them say.* Pl. 8, cr. 14.

Scot, a stag, trippant, ppr., charged on neck with a crescent, or. *Amo.* Pl. 61, cr. 15, (crescent, *same plate*, cr. 9.)

Scot, Sco., an eagle, (rising, or, and looking up to the sun, appearing from under a cloud,) ppr. *Amo inspici.* Pl. 43, cr. 5.

Scot, Sco., the head of a lance, ppr. *Pro aris et focis.* Pl. 82, cr. 9.

Scot, Sco., a hand, issuing, holding a broken spear, gu. *Pro amor patriæ.* Pl. 66, cr. 4.

Scot, Sco., a stag, trippant, armed with ten tynes, ppr. *Pacem amo.* Pl. 68, cr. 2.

Scot, Sco., a dexter hand holding a scroll of paper, ppr. *Facundia felix.* Pl. 27, cr. 4.

Scot, Sco., a lion's paw holding a thistle, ppr. *Reddunt aspera fortem.* Pl. 109, cr. 4.

Scot, Sco., a hand, erect, holding a (pole)-axe, ppr. *Trusty and true.* Pl. 73, cr. 7.

Scot, or Scott, a lion's head, erased, gu., langued, az. *Me fortem reddit Deus.* Pl. 81, cr. 4.

Scot, Sco., an anchor, erect, enwrapped with a cable, ppr. *Sperandum.* Pl. 42, cr. 12.

Scot, a star, or. *Lucet.* Pl. 21, cr. 6.

Scot, Sco., a dexter hand, erect, holding an annulet, therein an escarbuncle, ppr. *In tenebris lux.* Pl. 24, cr. 3, (escarbuncle, pl. 141.)

Scot, a boar's head, couped, or, in mouth (four) arrows, gu., feathered and headed, ar. *Do well, and let them say.* Pl. 8, cr. 14.

Scot, a star of six points. *Potior origine virtus.* Pl. 21, cr. 6.

Scot, or Scott, Sco., a lion's head, erased, in mouth a cinquefoil, ppr. *Aut tace, aut face.* Pl. 95, cr. 6, (cinquefoil, pl. 141.)

Scot, a nymph, in dexter the sun, and in sinister the moon, ppr. *Reparabit cornua Phœbe.* Pl. 107, cr. 14.

Scot, a crescent, or. *Crescendo prosim.* Pl. 18, cr. 14.

Scot, Sco., an arm, hand holding a book (half-opened,) ppr. *Fidelitus.* Pl. 45, cr. 3.

Scot, Sco., a hand holding a ring, ppr. *Do well, and let them say.* Pl. 24, cr. 3.

Scot, Sco., a demi-lion, ppr., in dexter a rose, gu., slipped and leaved, vert. *Fortis et placabilis.* Pl. 39, cr. 14.

Scot, a stalk of wheat, ppr. *I increase.* Pl. 85, cr. 6.

Scot, or Scott, Sco., a demi-lion, brandishing a (scimitar,) ppr. *Aut tace, aut face.* Pl. 41, cr. 13.

Scot, or Scott, Sco., a demi-lion, gardant. *Aut tace, aut face.* Pl. 35, cr. 4.

Scot, or Scott, Sco., a ship, the sails bent and flags displayed, all ppr. *Mihi lucra.* Pl. 109, cr. 8.

Scot, or Scott, Sco., a demi-lion, ppr. *Aut tace, aut face.* Pl. 67, cr. 10.

Scot, Sco., a lion's head, erased, langued, az. *Spes vires augentur.* Pl. 81, cr. 4.

Scot, or Scott, Sco., a dexter hand holding up a gem-ring, carbuncled, ppr. *In tenebris lux.* Pl. 24, cr. 3, (gem-ring, pl. 35, cr. 3.)

Scot, or Scott, Sco., a stag, lodged, ppr. *Amo probis.* Pl. 67, cr. 2.

Scot, a lion's head, erased, gu. *Tace, aut face.* Pl. 81, cr. 4.

Scot, Sco., a demi-lady, richly attired, in dexter a (rose,) ppr. *Prudenter amo.* Pl. 2, cr. 10.

Scot, or Scott, Sco., a lady richly attired, in dexter the sun, in sinister the moon. *Reparabit cornua Phœbe.* Pl. 107, cr. 14.

Scot, Eng., a cherub's head, ppr., wings in saltier, or. Pl. 67, cr. 11.

Scot, Sco., a demi-lion, ppr., in dexter a rose, gu., slipped and leaved, vert. *Fortis et placabilis.* Pl. 39, cr. 14.

Scot, Sco., a hand holding an annulet, ppr. *Nescit amor fines.* Pl. 24, cr. 3.

Scot, or Scott, a lion's head, erased, per cheveron, or and ar., charged with a cheveron, az., thereon five bezants. Pl. 42, cr. 4.

Scot, or Scott, Surr., a boar's head, couped, ar., a pheon stuck, in fess, in neck, sa. Pl. 2, cr. 7, (pheon, pl. 141.)

Scot, or Scott, Surr., a cup of fire, ppr. Pl. 31, cr. 8.

Scot, Lond., out of a ducal coronet, or, an eagle's head, sa., charged with an escallop, ar. Pl. 20, cr. 12, (escallop, pl. 141.)

Scote, Cumb., a stag, trippant, ppr., attired and unguled, or. *Amo.* Pl. 68, cr. 2.

Scotland, Sco., a lion's head, erased, ppr. Pl. 81, cr. 4.

Scott, Staffs., a beacon, fired, ppr. Pl. 88, cr. 6.

Scott, Sco., a boar's head, couped, gu., in mouth a sheaf of arrows, ppr. *Do well, and let them say.* Pl. 8, cr. 14.

Scott, Eng., a griffin's head and wings, sa. Pl. 65, cr. 1.

Scott, Yorks., a monkey, passant, collared, round waist and lined. Pl. 101, cr. 11.

Scott, Eng., a buck's head. Pl. 91, cr. 14.

Scott, Sco., a lion's head, erased, ppr. *Pro patria.* Pl. 18, cr. 4.

Scott, a stag, statant, ppr. *Amo.* Pl. 88, cr. 9, (without arrow.)

Scott, Robert, Esq., of Raeburn, Dumfres, a lady, richly attired, in dexter the sun, in sinister the moon, all ppr. *Reparabit cornua Phœbe.* Pl. 107, cr. 14.

Scott, a lion's head, erased, langued, az. *Tace aut face.* Pl. 81, cr. 4.

Scott, Sco., a lion's head, erased, gu., langued, az. *Spe vires augentur.* Pl. 81, cr. 4.

Scott, a dove, in mouth an olive-branch, all ppr. ΕΤΡΑΚΑ, (*I have found it.*) Pl. 48, cr. 15.

Scott, Sco., a stag's head, ar. Pl. 91, cr. 14.

Scott, Sco., a buck's head, erased, ppr., collared, az., (charged with a star between two crescents, or, all within an orle of laurel-branches, vert.) *In rectu decus*—and—*Nemo sibi nascitur.* Pl. 125, cr. 6, (without roses.)

Scott, Sco., a hand holding a book, shut, ppr. *Fidelitas.* Pl. 45, cr. 3.

Scott, Worc. and Staffs., a stag, couchant, ppr., dexter resting on a billet, or, charged on shoulder with a cross crosslet, gold. *Nunquam libertas gratior.* Pl. 67, cr. 2.

Scott, Iri., a buck, trippant, ppr. Pl. 68, cr. 2.

Scott, an owl, ppr. Pl. 27, cr. 9.

Scott, a female figure, ppr., vested in a white dress, showing the bottom of an under one, blue, her arms extended, in dexter the sun, in sinister a crescent. Pl. 107, cr. 14.

SCOTT, of Vogrie, a dexter hand holding a ring, ppr. *Nescit amor fines*. *Pl.* 24, *cr.* 3.
SCOTT, a star of six points. *Potior origine virtus*. *Pl.* 21, *cr.* 6.
SCOTT, a demi-griffin, segreant, ppr. *Pl.* 18, *cr.* 6.
SCOTT, a hand holding up a human heart. *Pl.* 59, *cr.* 12.
SCOTT, a hand holding a pen. *Vive la plume*. *Pl.* 26, *cr.* 13.
SCOTT, Salop and Wel., a demi-griffin, segreant, sa., membered, gu. *Recte faciendo neminem timeas*. *Pl.* 18, *cr.* 6.
SCOTT, Ess., out of pales, or, an arm, erect, vested, az., cuffed, ar., in hand a truncheon, of the last. *Pl.* 18, *cr.* 1, (pales, *pl.* 13, *cr.* 12.)
SCOTT, Ess. and Hants, an arm, erect, couped at elbow, vested, gu., cuffed, erm., in hand a roll of paper, ar., environed with park-pales, or. *Pl.* 32, *cr.* 6, (pales, *pl.* 13, *cr.* 12.)
SCOTT, Middx., in pales, a dexter arm, vested, az., cuffed, ar., in hand a roll of paper, ppr. *Pl.* 32, *cr.* 6, (pales, *pl.* 13, *cr.* 12.)
SCOTT, Surr., a stag's head, couped, ppr., gorged with a collar, az., (thereon a mullet, ar., between two crescents, or.) *Pl.* 125, *cr.* 6, (without roses.)
SCOTT, Bart., Dors., out of park-pales, erm., an arm, erect, vested, per pale, indented, ar. and gu., cuffed, az., in hand a scroll, ppr. *Pl.* 32, *cr.* 6, (pales, *pl.* 13, *cr.* 12.)
SCOTT, late Sir WALTER, Bart., of Abbotsford, Sco., a female figure, ppr., (couped above knees,) vested, gu., with az. waist, and laced stomacher, or, cuffs and ruffs, ar., in dexter the sun, gold, in sinister a crescent, of the fifth. *Reparabit cornua Phœbe*—and—*Watch weel*. *Pl.* 107, *cr.* 14.
SCOTT-HOPE, JAMES-ROBERT, Esq., of Abbotsford, Roxburgh; 1. For *Scott*, same as above. 2. For *Hope*, a globe, fructed at top, under a rainbow, with clouds at each end, all ppr. *Reparabit cornua Phœbe*—and—*At spes non fracta*. *Pl.* 79, *cr.* 1.
SCOTT, Sco., a lion's head, erased, gu. *Domini factum est*—and—*Spe vires augentur*. *Pl.* 81, *cr.* 4.
SCOTT, Bart., Derbs., a crescent, above it an etoile of six points, gu., between eagle's wings, or. *Sidus adsit amicum*. *Pl.* 31, *cr.* 11.
SCOTT, Bart., Staffs., on a mount, vert, a beacon, fired, ppr., ladder, or. *Pl.* 89, *cr.* 9, (ladder, *pl.* 88, *cr.* 6.)
SCOTT, Earl of Clonmel. *See* CLONMEL.
SCOTT, Earl of Eldon. *See* ELDON.
SCOTT, Berks., out of a ducal coronet, ar., a wheat-sheaf, between two sickles, ppr. *Domini factum est*—and—*Spe vires agentur*. *Pl.* 62, *cr.* 1, (sickle, *pl.* 31, *cr.* 12; coronet, *pl.* 128, *fig.* 3.)
SCOTT, Yorks., a stag's head, erased. *Pl.* 66, *cr.* 9.
SCOTT, Sco., a lion's head, erased, gu. *Tace aut face*. *Pl.* 81, *cr.* 4.
SCOTT, DOUGLAS, Duke of Buccleuch. *See* BUCCLEUCH.
SCOTT, MONTAGUE, Baron Montague. *See* MONTAGUE.
SCOTT, of Abbethune, Sco., a lion's head, erased, gu., over it a rainbow, ppr. *Spe versus*. *Pl.* 81, *cr.* 4, (rainbow, *pl.* 79, *cr.* 1.)
SCOTT, Sco., a demi-lion, gu. *Spe vires augenter*. *Pl.* 67, *cr.* 10.

SCOTT, Sco., a stag's head. *Amo*. *Pl.* 91, *cr.* 14.
SCOTT, Sco., a lion, rampant, gu., wielding a scimitar, az., hilt and pommel, or. *Aut tace, aut face*. *Pl.* 64, *cr.* 2, (scimitar, *pl.* 18, *cr.* 8.)
SCOTT, GEORGE-JONATHAN, Esq., of Betton Strange, Salop, and Peniarthuchaf, Merioneth, a demi-griffin, segreant, sa., membered, gu. *Recte faciendo neminem timeas*. *Pl.* 18, *cr.* 6.
SCOTT, CARTERET-GEORGE, Esq., of Malleny, Mid-Lothian, a stag, lodged, ppr. *Amo probos*. *Pl.* 67, *cr.* 2.
SCOUGAL, Sco., a crescent, ar. *Tandem implebitur*. *Pl.* 18, *cr.* 14.
SCOUGALL, Sco., a writing-pen, ppr. *Hac ornant*. *Pl.* 26, *cr.* 13.
SCOWLES, Berks., a demi-lion, erm., in dexter an escallop, ar. *Pl.* 126 A, *cr.* 13.
SCRACE, a Cornish chough, ppr., between wings, gu. *Pl.* 100, *cr.* 13, (wings, *pl.* 1, *cr.* 15.)
SCRACE, on trunk of tree, entwined by a serpent, a falcon, (wings expanded.) *Pl.* 78, *cr.* 8, (serpent, *pl.* 84, *cr.* 4.)
SCRAS, Suss., a falcon, wings addorsed, ppr., beaked, membered, and belled, or, standing on the stock of a tree, round the last, a snake, entwined, all ppr. *Volando reptilia sperno*. *Pl.* 55, *cr.* 11, (snake, *pl.* 84, *cr.* 4.)
SCREVENER, SCRIVENER, SCRIVENOR, Suff. and Norf., an arm, couped at elbow and erect, holding between the thumb and finger a pen, all ppr. *Pl.* 26, *cr.* 13.
SCRIMSHAW, and SCRIMSHIRE, Staffs., a demi-man, couped at knees, in armour, in dexter a sword, (reclining on his shoulder, ar., hilt and pommel, or, on sinister arm a shield, ppr.) *Pl.* 23, *cr.* 4.
SCRIMZEOR, or SCRYMZEOR, Sco., in lion's paw, erect, a cutlass, ppr. *Dissipate*. *Pl.* 18, *cr.* 8.
SCRIVEN, Salop, Camb., and Worc., a buck, passant, ppr., attired, or. *Pl.* 68, *cr.* 2.
SCRIVENOR, Suff., a stag, erm., attired, or, ducally gorged, gu. *Pl.* 88, *cr.* 9, (gorging, *same plate*.)
SCRIVINGTON, Hants, a tun, in fess, or, issuing from the bung-hole an apple-tree, vert, fructed, gold, the root erased and through the tun. *Pl.* 31, *cr.* 14.
SCROGGS, and SCRUGGES, Eng., a pewit's head, ar., collared, sa., wings addorsed, bendy of four, or and sa.
SCROGGS, or SCREGGS, an eagle's head erased, or. *Pl.* 20, *cr.* 7.
SCROGIE, Sco., trunk of oak-tree, sprouting leaves and branches, ppr. *Ero quod eram*. *Pl.* 92, *cr.* 8.
SCROOP, Eng., out of a ducal coronet, a triple plume of ostrich-feathers, five, four, and three. *Pl.* 114, *cr.* 8.
SCROOPE, or SCROPE, Hants, out of a ducal coronet, or, a triple plume of ostrich-feathers, az. *Pl.* 114, *cr.* 8.
SCROOPE, Heref., out of flames, ppr., a demi-eagle, displayed, or, (fire, of the first, issuing from mouth.) *Pl.* 44, *cr.* 8.
SCROOPE, Heref., out of flames, ppr., a dragon's head, or, between wings, az. *Pl.* 105, *cr.* 11, (flames, *pl.* 64, *cr.* 6.)

SCROOPE, a plume of feathers, az., on a crown, or. *Pl.* 44, *cr.* 12.

SCROOPE, Yorks., out of a ducal coronet, a plume of ostrich feathers. *Devant si je puis.* *Pl.* 44, *cr.* 12.

SCROPE, GEORGE-POULETT, Esq., of Castle-Combe, Wilts., out of a ducal coronet, gu., a plume of feathers, ar. *Non hæc sed me.* *Pl.* 44, *cr.* 12.

SCRUTEVILL, Durh., an arm, embowed, vested, erminois, cuffed, ar., in hand, ppr., a large pistol, stock, sa., barrel, of the second, firing, of the third. *Pl.* 96, *cr.* 4, (vesting, *pl.* 39, *cr.* 1.)

SCRYMZEOR, Sco., a lion's paw holding a sword, ppr. *Dissipate.* *Pl.* 47, *cr.* 14.

SCUDAMORE, Heref., out of a ducal coronet, or, a lion's gamb, in pale, sa. *Scuto amoris divini.* *Pl.* 67, *cr.* 7.

SCUDAMORE, Heref., out of a ducal coronet, a bear's gamb, in pale, sa., armed, gu. *Pl.* 67, *cr.* 7, (gamb, *pl.* 126, *cr.* 2.)

SCUDAMORE, JOHN-LUCY, Esq., of Kentchurch Court, Heref., out of a ducal coronet, or, a bear's paw, ppr. *Scuto amoris divini.* *Pl.* 67, *cr.* 7.

SCURFIELD, a hand, gauntleted, ppr., holding a large pistol. *Vidi vici.* *Pl.* 101, *cr.* 12, (gauntlet, *pl.* 33, *cr.* 4.)

SCURFIELD, an arm, embowed, vested, erminois, cuffed, ar., in hand, ppr., a large pistol, stock, sa., barrel, of the second, firing, of the third. *Pl.* 96, *cr.* 4, (vesting, *pl.* 39, *cr.* 1.)

SCURFIELD, Durh., a cubit arm, (in armour, erect, ppr., encircled by a wreath of oak, or, in hand a carbine, erect, also ppr.) *Vidi vici.* *Pl.* 101, *cr.* 12.

SCUTTE, Dors., a crane, wings elevated, az., beaked and legged, gu., (in beak a rose, ppr.) *Pl.* 6, *cr.* 13.

SEA, two lobster's claws, in pale, in each claw a fish. *Pl.* 116, *cr.* 6.

SEABRIGHT, or SEBRIGHT, Worc., an heraldic-tiger, sejant, ar., maned and crowned, or. *Pl.* 111, *cr.* 7.

SEABRIGHT, or SEBRIGHT, Worc., a lion, ar. *Pl.* 48, *cr.* 8.

SEABROOK, Eng., in hand, erect, a cross cross-let, fitched, in pale, gu. *Pl.* 99, *cr.* 1.

SEABRY, or SEBRY, a bird, wings addorsed, sa., supporting with dexter a quill, enflamed and environed with a serpent, all ppr.

SEAFIELD, Earl of, Viscount Reidhaven, Baron Ogilvie, and a Bart., Sco., (Grant-Ogilvie :) 1. For *Ogilvie*, a lion, rampant, gu., between paws a plumb-rule, in pale, ppr. *Pl.* 50, *cr.* 8. 2. For *Grant*, a mountain in flames, ppr. *Stand fast.* *Pl.* 92, *cr.* 9.

SEAFORD, Baron, (Ellis,) (on a mount, vert,) a goat's head, erased, ar. *Non quo, sed quomodo.* *Pl.* 29, *cr.* 13.

SEAGAR, or SEAGER, Eng., a dolphin, haurient, devouring a fish, ppr. *Pl.* 71, *cr.* 1.

SEAGRAVE, and SEAGROVE, Eng., in dexter hand a palm-branch, ppr. *Pl.* 23, *cr.* 7.

SEAGRAVE, Northamp. six arrows, fretways, and (three) in pale, points downward, all ppr., interlaced, and bound with a wreath of the colours. *Pl.* 110, *cr.* 11.

SEAGRIM, Eng., a long cross, gu. *Pl.* 7, *cr.* 13.

SEAL, Eng., a wolf's head, or, embrued at nose and mouth, gu. *Pl.* 14, *cr.* 6.

SEALE, Northumb., out of a ducal coronet, or, a wolf's head, ar., embrued at nose and mouth.

SEALE, Bart., of Mount Boone, Devons., out of a crown vallary, or, a wolf's head, ar., neck encircled with a wreath of oak, vert. *Pl.* 14, *cr.* 6, (crown, *pl.* 2, *cr.* 2.)

SEALY, co. Cork, out of a ducal coronet, or, a wolf's head, sa. *Concipe spes certes.* *Pl.* 70, *cr.* 5, (head, *pl.* 14, *cr.* 6.)

SEALY, Eng., a quatrefoil, gu. *Pl.* 65, *cr.* 7.

SEALY, a talbot, sejant, ppr., collared and (chained,) or. *Pl.* 107, *cr.* 7.

SEALY, out of a ducal coronet, or, a wolf's head, sa. *Pl.* 14, *cr.* 6, (coronet, *pl.* 70, *cr.* 5.)

SEAMAN, a demi-seahorse, salient, ar. *Pl.* 58, *cr.* 15.

SEAMAN, Lond., out of a crescent, erminois, a demi-seahorse, barry-wavy of six, ar. and az. *Pl.* 58, *cr.* 15, (crescent, *pl.* 84, *cr.* 1.)

SEAMARK, Eng., a yew-tree, ppr. *Pl.* 49, *cr.* 13.

SEARLE, Eng., a lion, rampant, or, (holding the mast of a ship, on the top a flag, ar., charged with a cross, gu.) *Pl.* 22, *cr.* 15.

SEARLE, Cornw., on a mount, vert, a grey-hound, sejant, ar., (ducally gorged, gu.) *Pl.* 5, *cr.* 2.

SEARLES, Eng., a gem-ring, stoned, or. *Pl.* 35, *cr.* 3.

SEATON, Sco., a swan, swimming, ppr. *Cum progressu euntis.* *Pl.* 66, *cr.* 10.

SEATON, a gauntlet, ppr. *Majorum vestigia premo.* *Pl.* 15, *cr.* 15.

SEATON, a boar's head, couped, or. *Forward ours.* *Pl.* 48, *cr.* 2.

SEATON, Sco., a wolf's head, erased. *Forward ours.* *Pl.* 14, *cr.* 6.

SEATON, Sco., a soldier, from middle, bearing up the (royal banner,) in bend, and displayed, all ppr. *Sustento sanguine signa.* *Pl.* 2, *cr.* 10.

SEATON, Sco., a Cornish chough, on the face of a rock. *Hazard warily.* *Pl.* 70, *cr.* 11.

SEATON, Sco., a star of six points, in its splen-dour, or. *Habet et suam.* *Pl.* 21, *cr.* 6.

SEATON, Eng., a dexter hand brandishing a sabre. *Pl.* 21, *cr.* 10.

SEATON, Sco., a crescent, gu. *Semper.* *Pl.* 18, *cr.* 14.

SEATON, or SETON, Sco., a crescent, flaming. *Habet et suam.* *Pl.* 29, *cr.* 2.

SEATON, Sco., a buck's head, couped, ppr., at-tired, or. *Bydand.* *Pl.* 91, *cr.* 14.

SEATON, an arm, in armour, (embowed,) in fess from elbow, in hand a sword, enfiled with a savage's head, couped. *Pl.* 36, *cr.* 10.

SEATON, on a ducal coronet, a wyvern, wings addorsed. *Pl.* 104, *cr.* 11.

SEATON, a dragon, vert, emitting fire, ppr. *Pl.* 90, *cr.* 10, (fire, *pl.* 37, *cr.* 9.)

SEATON, Durh., a lion, rampant, or. *Dieu de-fende le droit.* *Pl.* 67, *cr.* 5.

SEATON, Baron, (Colborne,) out of a mural coro-net, or, a reindeer's head, ar., attired, gold, between two branches, laurel on dexter, palm on sinister, both ppr. *Sperat infestis.* *Pl.* 60, *cr.* 3, (branches, *pl.* 116, *cr.* 9; coronet, *pl.* 128, *fig.* 18.)

SEBORNE, Heref., an eagle, close, vert, in beak a hawk's lure, lined and ringed, gu. *Pl.* 7, *cr.* 11, (lure, *pl.* 141.)

SEBRIGHT, Eng., a demi-lion, rampant, or. *Pl.* 67, *cr.* 10.

SEBRIGHT, Bart., Worc., an heraldic-tiger, sejant, ar., maned and (crowned,) or. *Pl.* 111, *cr.* 7, (without coronet.)

SECHION, Oxon., out of a mural coronet, or, a bull's head, couped, az., attired, gold. *Pl.* 120, *cr.* 7, (coronet, *same plate, cr.* 14.)

SECKFORD, or SECKFORDE, Suff., a cock's head, erased, vert, combed, and wattled, gu. *Pl.* 92, *cr.* 3.

SECRETAN, (on a mount, vert,) an eagle, regardant, or, semée of hurts, gu., in beak a laurel-wreath, of the first. *Pl.* 77, *cr.* 13, (wreath, *pl.* 56, *cr.* 10.)

SEDDON, Lanc., two lions' gambs, erased and erect, sa., supporting a cinquefoil, or. *Pl.* 42, *cr.* 3, (cinquefoil, *pl.* 141.)

SEDDON, Durh., two bears' gambs, reversed, sa., holding a cinquefoil, or. *Non sono, sed dono.*

SEDGEWICK, or SEDGEWICKE, two ears of rye, in saltier, or. *Pl.* 9, *cr.* 8.

SEDGEWICK, a sun-flower. *Pl.* 84, *cr.* 6.

SEDLEY, or SIDLEY, Kent, out of a ducal coronet, a goat's head, ar., attired, or. *Pl.* 72, *cr.* 2.

SEDLEY, or SIDLEY, Kent, out of a ducal coronet, a goat's head, or. *Pl.* 72, *cr.* 2.

SEE, Eng., in hand, az., an arrow, point downward. *Pl.* 43, *cr.* 13.

SEE, two lobsters' claws, in pale, gu., each holding a fish, ar. *Pl.* 116, *cr.* 6.

SEED, Eng., a demi-lion, holding a cross crosslet. *Pl.* 65, *cr.* 6.

SEEDS, Lond. and Lanc., a demi-cock, wings (expanded,) az. *Pl.* 72, *cr.* 4.

SEERES, a martlet, in beak a serpent, all ppr. *Pl.* 111, *cr.* 5, (serpent, *pl.* 53, *cr.* 12.)

SEFTON, Earl of, Viscount Molyneux, Iri., Baron Sefton, and a Bart., Eng., (Molyneux,) a chapeau, gu., turned up, erm., adorned with a plume of peacock's feathers, ppr. *Vivere sat vincere. Pl.* 120, *cr.* 13, (chapeau, *same plate, cr.* 15.)

SEGAR, Kent and Lanc., (on a mount, vert,) an eagle, rising, regardant, ppr. *Pl.* 35, *cr.* 8.

SEGAR, on a ducal coronet, or, two snakes, vert, entwined round a sceptre, of the first, between wings, the dexter, or, the sinister, ar. *Pl.* 27, *cr.* 8.

SEGAR, a demi-lion, ar., crowned, or, between paws a mascle, gold. *Pl.* 61, *cr.* 4, (mascle, *pl.* 141.)

SEGAR, Norf., a demi-lion, ar., out of the top of a tower, gu., between paws a fire-brand, or, fired, ppr. *Pl.* 53, *cr.* 2, (brand, *pl.* 10, *cr.* 15.)

SEGRAVE, Eng., five arrows, wreathed and bound, ar. and sa., headed and barbed, ar., sticks, or, banded, gold. *Pl.* 54, *cr.* 15.

SEGRAVE, Dublin, a demi-lion, rampant, ar., between paws a branch of oak, ppr., fructed, or. *Pl.* 125, *cr.* 2, (branch, *pl.* 32, *cr.* 13.)

SEGRAVE, Leic., six arrows in saltier, banded. *Pl.* 110, *cr.* 11.

SEGRAVE, Baron, (Fitzhardinge-Berkeley,) a mitre, gu., labelled and garnished, or, charged with a cheveron, (and ten crosses pattée, six in chief, and four in base, ar.) *Dieu avec nous. Pl.* 12, *cr.* 10.

SEGRAVE, DE, Eng., a lion's paw, holding a branch of laurel, vert. *Pl.* 68, *cr.* 10.

SEGROVE, a lion, rampant, or, holding an oak-sprig, ppr. *Pl.* 64, *cr.* 2, (oak, *pl.* 81, *cr.* 7.)

SELBY, Northumb. and Durh., a Saracen's head, ppr., wreathed, or and sa. *Pl.* 36, *cr.* 3.

SELBY, of Earle and Biddleston, Northumb., a Saracen's head, couped at shoulders, ppr., wreathed, tied in a knot behind, or and sa. *Semper sapit suprema. Pl.* 23, *cr.* 3.

SELBY, Durh., same crest.

SELBY, THOMAS, Esq., of Whitley and Wimbish Hall, Ess., a Saracen's head, ppr. *Fort et loyal. Pl.* 81, *cr.* 15.

SELDON, an arm, embowed, vested with leaves, vert, in hand, ppr., a swan's head, erased, or, ducally gorged, gu. *Pl.* 29, *cr.* 4, (arm, *pl.* 83, *cr.* 2.)

SELENGER, a griffin's head, between wings. *Pl.* 65, *cr.* 1.

SELKIRK, Earl of, and Baron Daer and Shortclouch, Sco., (Douglas,) on a chapeau, gu., turned up, erm., a salamander in flames, ppr. *Jamais arriere. Pl.* 86, *cr.* 14.

SELLERS, Eng., a demi-swan, wings addorsed, ar. *Pl.* 54, *cr.* 4.

SELSEY, Baron, and a Bart., (Peachey,) a demi-lion, double-queued, erm., in dexter a mullet, pierced, gu. *Memor et fidelis. Pl.* 120, *cr.* 10, (mullet, *pl.* 45, *cr.* 1.)

SELWARD, Wilts. and Warw., an eagle's head, erased, sa., (collared, or.) *Pl.* 20, *cr.* 7.

SELWYN, Suss. and Ess., a demi-lion, rampant, ppr. *Pl.* 67, *cr.* 10.

SELWYN, Ess. and Suss., two lions' gambs, erased, or, holding a beacon, in pale, fired, ppr. *Pl.* 77, *cr.* 4, (beacon, *pl.* 89, *cr.* 9.)

SELYOCKE, Herts. and Derbs., out of a mural coronet, or, a cubit arm, vested, ar., in hand, ppr., an oak-branch, vert, fructed, gold. *Pl.* 79, *cr.* 4, (branch, *pl.* 32, *cr.* 13.)

SEMPILL, a buck's head, erased. *Pl.* 66, *cr.* 9.

SEMPILL, Sco., a stag's head, couped, ducally gorged, ppr., charged on neck with a cross crosslet. *Pl.* 91, *cr.* 14, (gorging, *pl.* 55, *cr.* 2.)

SEMPLE, Eng., a stag's head, ppr., attired, ar. *Diligentia et vigilantia. Pl.* 91, *cr.* 14.

SEMPLE, a stag's head, ppr., attired, ar. *Keep tryste. Pl.* 91, *cr.* 14.

SEMPLE, a stag's head, ar., attired, az., charged with a crescent, gu. *Diligentia et vigilantia. Pl.* 61, *cr.* 9.

SEMPLE, in hand a pistol, ppr. *In loyaltie. Pl.* 101, *cr.* 12.

SEMPLE, Iri., out of a ducal coronet, a broken battle-axe, all ppr. *Pl.* 24, *cr.* 15, (coronet, *same plate, cr.* 10.)

SEMPLE, Sco., a stag's head, erased. *Keep tryste. Pl.* 66, *cr.* 9.

SEMPLE, Sco., a stag's head, couped, ppr., attired, ar., (gorged with a royal coronet, or, charged with a gilliflower. *Keep tryste. Pl.* 91, *cr.* 14.

SENHOUSE, Cumb., a parrot, ppr. *Pl.* 25, *cr.* 2.

SENHOUSE, of Nether Hall, Cumb., a popinjay, ppr., (with a label in its beak, inscribed, "Deo gratias.") *Væ victis. Pl.* 33, *cr.* 11.

SENIOR, Herts., on a mount, vert, a leopard, couchant, gardant, ppr., crowned with a Saxon coronet, or. *Medio tutissimus ibis. Pl.* 9, *cr.* 14.

SENLIZE, DE, Eng., a lion, passant, gardant, tail extended, gu. *Pl.* 120, *cr.* 5.

SENNICOTS, a rose-branch, bearing (six) roses, ppr. *Pl.* 23, *cr.* 2.

SENTHILL, two dragons' heads, erased, (respecting each other,) enfiled with a ducal coronet. *Pl.* 6, *cr.* 4.

SENTLEGER, Iri., a griffin, passant, or. *Haut et bon. Pl.* 61, *cr.* 14, (without gorging.)

SENTON, Eng., out of a mural coronet, a lion's head, az. *Pl.* 45, *cr.* 9.

SENT-PIER, Eng., on a spear, or, pointed, ar., a dolphin, naiant, gold. *Pl.* 49, *cr.* 14.

SEORN, a cubit arm, in pale, vested and cuffed, hand grasping the trunk of a tree, erased at bottom, couped at top, and sprouting a fresh branch.

SEPHAM, Kent and Surr., a mermaid, ppr., ducally crowned, crined, finned, and comb, or, (in sinister sea-weeds, vert.) *Pl.* 88, *cr.* 12, (crown, *same plate.*)

SEPTUANS, Kent, a dolphin, naiant, ppr. *Pl.* 48, *cr.* 9.

SERANS, an esquire's helmet, (on top a fish.) *Pl.* 109, *cr.* 5.

SERELL, or SERRELL, Eng., a covered cup, gu. *Pl.* 75, *cr.* 13, (without swords.)

SERGEANT, Bucks., a dolphin, naiant, or, guttée, az. *Pl.* 48, *cr.* 9.

SERGISON, Suss., a dolphin, naiant, sa., (pierced by an arrow, ar., transversely vulned, gu.) *Pl.* 48, *cr.* 9.

SERMON, Eng., a crescent, sa., issuing from between the horns, a cross crosslet, fitched, gu. *Pl.* 43, *cr.* 3.

SEROCOLD, Cherryhinton, Camb. : 1. For *Serocold*, a castle, or, with a fleur-de-lis issuing from battlements, az. *Pl.* 28, *cr.* 11, (fleur-de-lis, *pl.* 141.) 2. In front of a rose, gu., a Cornish chough, ppr. *Pl.* 100, *cr.* 13, (rose, *pl.* 20, *cr.* 2.)

SERRES, Sco., an arm, in armour, in hand a sword, all ppr. *Pl.* 2, *cr.* 9.

SERVANTE, Eng., a demi-bull, gu. *Pl.* 63, *cr.* 6.

SERVINGTON, Devons., a pine-tree, erased, vert, fructed, or, enfiled with a tun, gold. *Pl.* 31, *cr.* 14.

SETH, Eng., a hand, ppr., holding up a cannon-ball, sa. *Pl.* 33, *cr.* 6.

SETON, a crescent, gu. *Set on. Pl.* 18, *cr.* 14.

SETON, Sco., a demi-man, in a military habit, holding the banner of Scotland, with the motto on a scroll above, "Sustento sanguine signa." *Merces hæc certa laborum. Pl.* 2, *cr.* 12.

SETON, Sco., a boar's head, couped, or. *Forward ours. Pl.* 48, *cr.* 2.

SETON, a wyvern, vert. *Hazard it forward. Pl.* 63, *cr.* 13.

SETON, Sco., a man, in armour, on horseback, at full speed, (holding on the point of a sword, an imperial crown.) *Inclytus perditæ recuperator coronæ. Pl.* 28, *cr.* 5.

SETON, Sco., a star of six points. *Habet et suam. Pl.* 21, *cr.* 6.

SETON, Sco., on a ducal coronet, a dragon, vert, (spouting fire, ppr., wings elevated and charged with a star, ar.) "Hazard it forward," above the crest. *Invia virtuti via nulla. Pl.* 93, *cr.* 15, (dragon, *pl.* 90, *cr.* 10.)

SETON, Sco., a Cornish chough, on the face of a rock, ppr. *Hazard warily. Pl.* 70, *cr.* 11.

SETON, Eng., a hawk's head, az. *Pl.* 34, *cr.* 11.

SETON, Sco., a crescent, gu. *Semper. Pl.* 18, *cr.* 14.

SETON, Hants., a crescent, gu., on a scroll above the crest the motto, "Set on." *Virtus durat avorum. Pl.* 18, *cr.* 14.

SEVANS, Kent, on a helmet, (a fish.) *Pl.* 109, *cr.* 5.

SEVERN, and SEVERNE, Worc., a cinquefoil, or. *Pl.* 91, *cr.* 12.

SEVERN, CHEESMENT-SEVERN, a demi-horse, salient, pierced in breast by an arrow.

SEVERNE-AMY, of Wallop Hall, Salop, and of Northamp. and Wales, a cinquefoil, or. *Virtus præstantior auro. Pl.* 91, *cr.* 12.

SEWARD, Eng., out of a ducal coronet, or, a horse's leg, foot upward. *Pl.* 38, *cr.* 11.

SEWELL, an arm, in armour, in bend dexter, (grasping a staff in bend sinister, crowned with a cap of liberty.) *Pl.* 6, *cr.* 5.

SEWELL, in a chaplet of roses, ar., leaved, vert, a bee, volant, of the first. *Pl.* 100, *cr.* 3, (chaplet, *pl.* 41, *cr.* 7.)

SEWELL, Hants., an arm, in armour, embowed, ppr., garnished, or, in hand an acorn, of the first. *Pl.* 68, *cr.* 1, (acorn, *pl.* 81, *cr.* 7.)

SEXTON, Iri., a leopard's face, ppr. *Pl.* 66, *cr.* 14.

SEXTON, Eng., a woman, couped at waist, ppr., vested, gu., hair flowing, or, in dexter a chaplet, vert. *Pl.* 87, *cr.* 14.

SEXTON, Lond., out of a ducal coronet, or, a dexter arm, in armour, embowed, ppr., garnished, in gauntlet an anchor, sa., fluke and cable or. *Pl.* 122, *cr.* 8.

SEXTON, Iri., a leopard's face, az. *Pl.* 66, *cr.* 14.

SEYMER, Eng., a hawk's leg, in fess, erased, holding a quill. *Pl.* 60, *cr.* 15.

SEYMER-KER, of Handford, Dors., on a chapeau, gu., turned up, erm., two wings, or. *Pl.* 80, *cr.* 15.

SEYMOR, a swan's neck, couped, bendy wavy of six, ar. and gu., beaked, or. *Pl.* 30, *cr.* 10, (without gorging.)

SEYMOUR, Eng., a branch of oak, fructed and leaved, ppr. *Pl.* 32, *cr.* 13.

SEYMOUR, of Bury, Pomeray, Devons., out of a ducal coronet, or, a phœnix in flames, ppr. *Pl.* 53, *cr.* 6.

SEYMOUR, Duke of Somerset. *See* SOMERSET.

SEYMOUR, Iri., a hind, passant, ppr. *Pl.* 20, *cr.* 14.

SEYMOUR, a negro's head. *Fide et amore. Pl.* 120, *cr.* 3.

SEYMOUR, HENRY-DANBY, Esq., of Knoyle House, Wilts.; and Northbrook Lodge, Devons., out of a ducal coronet, or, a phœnix, gold, in flames, ppr. *Foy pour devoir. Pl.* 53, *cr.* 6.

SEYMOUR, a phœnix, or, in flames, ppr. *Pl.* 44, *cr.* 8.

SEYMOUR, Somers., two wings conjoined in leure, surmounted by a ducal coronet, all or. *Pl.* 87, *cr.* 1, (coronet, *pl.* 128, *fig.* 3.)

SEYMOUR, Dors., on each side of a chapeau, gu., turned up, erm., a wing, or. *Pl.* 80, *cr.* 15.

SEYMOUR, Bart., Devons., on a naval coronet, or, two brands, in saltier, inflamed at the ends, ppr., thereon an eagle, rising, also ppr., looking at the sun, gold.

SEYMOUR-CROSSLEY, of Castletown, Iri., out of a ducal coronet, or, a phœnix in flames, ppr., wings expanded, gold. *Foy pour devoir.* *Pl.* 53, *cr.* 6.

SEYS, Wel., a demi-lion, rampant. *Crescit sub pondere virtus.* *Pl.* 67, *cr.* 10.

SHACKLETON, Eng., a poplar-tree, vert. *Pl.* 95, *cr.* 2.

SHAD, Norf., out of a ducal coronet, or, a nag's head, ar., between wings, sa. *Pl.* 50, *cr.* 13, (wings, *pl.* 17, *cr.* 9.)

SHADEGROVE, a wood or grove, the sun shining thereon. *Pl.* 123, *cr.* 3, (wood, *pl.* 125, *cr.* 14.)

SHADFORD, the sun shining on stump of oak-tree, sprouting fresh branches. *Pl.* 123, *cr.* 3.

SHADFORD, on a staff, raguly, in fess, or, a lion, passant, reposing fore-dexter on an hour-glass, erect, (in mouth a trefoil, slipped.) *Pl.* 48, *cr.* 8, (staff, *pl.* 5, *cr.* 8; hour-glass, *pl.* 32, *cr.* 11.)

SHADFORD, Northumb., a lion, passant, gardant, ppr., fore-dexter resting on an hour-glass, ar., in mouth a trefoil, slipped, vert. *Fugit irrevocabile tempus.* *Pl.* 120, *cr.* 5, (hour-glass, *pl.* 32, *cr.* 11; trefoil, *pl.* 11, *cr.* 12.)

SHADFORTH, Eng., the sun shining on stump of oak-tree, sprouting anew. *Pl.* 123, *cr.* 3.

SHADWELL, Eng., a demi-griffin, ppr. *Pl.* 18, *cr.* 6.

SHAEN, Ess., a greyhound, statant, regardant, erm., collared, gu.

SHAFTESBURY, Earl of, Baron Ashley and Cooper, and a Bart., (Ashley-Cooper,) on a chapeau, gu., turned up, erm., a bull, passant, sa., gorged with a ducal coronet, or, attired and hoofed, ar. *Love, serve.* *Pl.* 65, *cr.* 11, (gorging, *pl.* 68, *cr.* 6.)

SHAFTO, Durh., Cum., and Northumb., a salamander, (regardant,) vert, in the midst of flames, ppr. *Pl.* 20, *cr.* 15.

SHAFTO, ROBERT·DUNCOMBE, Esq., of Whitworth Park, Durh., same crest.

SHAFTOW, Northumb., a salamander, vert, in flames, ppr. *Pl.* 20, *cr.* 15.

SHAIRP, NORMAN, Esq., of Houstoun, Linlithgow, a steel helmet, in profile, with a plumage of feathers, ppr. *Vivit post funere virtus.* *Pl.* 8, *cr.* 12.

SHAIRP, a demi-lion, erased, ppr., gorged with a collar, nebulée, az., (between paws a wreath of oak, ppr., encircling an escallop, or.) *Pl.* 18, *cr.* 13.

SHAKELTON, Eng., a poplar-tree, vert. *Pl.* 95, *cr.* 2.

SHAKERLEY, a demi-hare, rampant, ar., supporting a garb, or. *Pl.* 58, *cr.* 14, (garb, *pl.* 63, *cr.* 14.)

SHAKERLEY, Chesh. and Berks., a hare, sa., supporting a garb, or. *Antiquum obtinens.*

SHAKESPEARE, the Poet, an eagle, volant. *Pl.* 94, *cr.* 1.

SHAKESPEARE, Warw., a falcon, displayed, ar., holding a (spear, in pale, or.) *Pl.* 107, *cr.* 4.

SHALCROSS, Lond. and Derbs., a martlet, or, in beak a cross pattée, fitched, gu., charged on breast with a mullet. *Pl.* 111, *cr.* 5, (cross and mullet, *pl.* 141.)

SHALES, Eng., a goat's head, erased, ar., attired, or. *Pl.* 29, *cr.* 13.

SHANAN, Iri., a dove and olive-branch. *Virtute duce.* *Pl.* 48, *cr.* 15.

SHAND, Sco. and Eng., a dove, in mouth an olive branch, all ppr. *Virtute duce.* *Pl.* 48, *cr.* 15.

SHAND, Sco., a dove, volant, above the waters, in mouth a branch of olive, ppr. *Virtute duce, comite fortuná.* *Pl.* 46, *cr.* 13.

SHANK, Sco., an eagle, rising, or. *Spero.* *Pl.* 67, *cr.* 4.

SHANK, HENRY, Esq., of Castlerig and Gleniston, Fife; and of the Villa, Laurencekirk, Forfars., an eagle, rising, ar. *Spero.* *Pl.* 67, *cr.* 4.

SHANKE, Norf., on a ducal coronet, or, a lion's head, erased, per fess, ar. and gu. *Pl.* 90, *cr.* 9.

SHANNON, Eng., a demi-talbot, sa. *Pl.* 97, *cr.* 9, (without arrow.)

SHANNON, Earl of, Viscount Boyle, and Baron Castle-Martyr, Iri.; Baron Carlton, G.B., (Boyle,) out of a ducal coronet, or, a lion's head, erased, per pale, crenellée, ar. and gu. *Vivit post funera virtus*—and—*Spectemur agendo.* *Pl.* 90, *cr.* 9.

SHAPLEIGH, Devons. and Cornw., an arm, vested, gu., turned up, ar., in hand, ppr., a chaplet, vert, garnished with roses, of the last. *Pl.* 41, *cr.* 7, (arm, *pl.* 39, *cr.* 1.)

SHARD, Surr, a lion, passant, per pale, or and sa., guttée, counterchanged, resting foredexter on a bugle-horn, of the second. *Pl.* 4, *cr.* 14, (horn, *pl.* 89, *cr.* 3.)

SHARDELOU, a plume of feathers, ar. *Pl.* 12, *cr.* 9.

SHARNBORNE, Norf., a lion's gamb, couped and erect, grasping a griffin's head, erased, sa. *Pl.* 58, *cr.* 7, (head, *pl.* 94, *cr.* 6.)

SHARP, Sco., a branch of oak, acorned, ppr. *Progredior.* *Pl.* 32, *cr.* 13.

SHARP, Sco., a pheon, ppr. *Progredere, ne regredere.* *Pl.* 26, *cr.* 12.

SHARP, a steel cap with a plume of feathers. ppr. *Vivit post funera virtus.* *Pl.* 8, *cr.* 12.

SHARP, a griffin's head, erased, per pale. *Pl.* 48, *cr.* 6.

SHARP, out of a ducal coronet, per pale, or and sa., a wolf's head, counterchanged. *Pl.* 14, *cr.* 6, (coronet, *pl.* 99, *cr.* 9.)

SHARP, Durh., an eagle's head, erased, az., ducally gorged, or, in mouth a pheon, ar. *Dum spiro, spero.* *Pl.* 39, *cr.* 4.

SHARP, or SHARPE, Yorks., same crest.

SHARPE, Sco., a celestial crown, or. *Pro mitrá coronam.* *Pl.* 128, *fig.* 1.

SHARPE, on a ducal coronet, or, a peacock, (sejant,) ppr. *Pl.* 43, *cr.* 7.

SHARPE, a wolf's head, erased, per pale, sa. and or. *Pl.* 14, *cr.* 6.

SHARPE, a wolf's head, erased, per pale, or and sa., (gorged with a ducal coronet, counterchanged.) *Pl.* 14, *cr.* 6.

SHARPE, a wolf's head, erased, or, (ducally gorged, az.) *Pl.* 14, *cr.* 6.

SHARPE, Leic. and Cumb., a peacock, (sejant,) ppr., in a ducal coronet, or, in beak an ear of wheat, of the second, leaved, vert. *Pl.* 43, *cr.* 7, (wheat, *pl.* 94, *cr.* 7.)

SHARPE, a hand holding a dagger, in pale, dropping blood. *I make sure.* *Pl.* 23, *cr.* 15.

SHARPEY, an arm, ppr., vested, az., in hand three javelins. *Pl.* 39, *cr.* 1, (javelin, *pl.* 39, *cr.* 15.)

SHARPEY, Kent, a cubit arm, vested, az., with

three puffs, ar., in hand, ppr., (three) spears, two in saltier, one in pale, headed, of the second, staves, or. *Pl.* 99, *cr.* 8, (vesting, *pl.* 18, *cr.* 1.)

SHARPLES, Eng., a dexter hand brandishing a sword, ppr. *Pl.* 21, *cr.* 10.

SHATTOCK, Wilts., in dexter hand a lion's paw, erased, ppr. *Pl.* 94, *cr.* 13.

SHAW, Yorks., a talbot, passant, erminois, eared, ar. *Pl.* 120, *cr.* 8.

SHAW, Sco., a phœnix, or, in flames, ppr. *Pl.* 44, *cr.* 8.

SHAW, Sco., a demi-savage. *I mean well. Pl.* 14, *cr.* 11.

SHAW, Lond., issuing from the rays of the sun, or, an arm, ppr., vested, sa., hand holding up a mort-head, ppr. *Pl.* 37, *cr.* 6.

SHAW, Wel., on a bugle-horn, in fess, a swan, wings elevated, ppr. *Lætitiæ et spe immortalitatis. Pl.* 4, *cr.* 7.

SHAW, Arrowe Park, Chesh.: 1. For *Shaw*, a dove, bendy sinister, of six, ar. and sa., in beak an olive-branch, ppr., (dexter resting on a lozenge.) *Pl.* 48, *cr.* 15. 2. For *Nicholson*, out of a ducal coronet, gu., a lion's head, erm. *Pl.* 90, *cr.* 9.

SHAW, Sco., a demi-lion, rampant, armed and langued, az. *Mens immota manet. Pl.* 67, *cr.* 10.

SHAW, Sco., a hand holding up a covered cup, ppr. *I mean well. Pl.* 35, *cr.* 9.

SHAW, Sco., a demi-savage, wreathed about middle, ppr. *I mean well. Pl.* 14, *cr.* 1

SHAW, a demi-lion, gu., in dexter a sword, ppr. *Fide et fortitudine. Pl.* 41, *cr.* 13.

SHAW, Iri., a cock's head, issuing, gu. *Pl.* 92, *cr.* 3.

SHAW, a lion, rampant, gu., armed and langued, az. *Mens immota. Pl.* 67, *cr.* 5.

SHAW, Lond. and Ess., a hind's head, or, pierced through by an arrow, gold, headed and feathered, ar. *Pl.* 56, *cr.* 11, (without coronet.)

SHAW, Lond., an arrow, in pale, or, feathered and headed, ar., passing through a mascle, sa. *Pl.* 56, *cr.* 13, (mascle, *pl.* 141.)

SHAW, Salop, Chesh., and Surr., six arrows, interlaced in saltier, or, flighted, headed, and tied together by a belt, gu., buckle, and pendent, gold. *Pl.* 101, *cr.* 13, (without cap.)

SHAW, a hawk, wings expanded, ppr. *Pl.* 105, *cr.* 4.

SHAW, a falcon, wings expanded and belled, ppr. *Pl.* 105, *cr.* 4.

SHAW, Staffs., a hind's head, quarterly, ar. and or, pierced through neck by an arrow, headed, az., (the feather broken and drooping, ar.) *Pl.* 56, *cr.* 11, (without coronet.)

SHAW, Yorks., a talbot, passant, ermines, eared, ar. *Pl.* 120, *cr.* 8.

SHAW, Yorks., a talbot, (statant), sa. *Pl.* 120, *cr.* 8.

SHAW, Bart., Sco., a demi-savage, affrontée, wreathed about head and waist, ppr., in (dexter) a key, or, the sinister resting on a club reversed, also ppr. *I mean well. Pl.* 88, *cr.* 10.

SHAW, Bart., Kent, six arrows, interlaced in saltier, or, flighted, headed, and tied together by a belt, gu., buckle and pendent, gold. *Vincit qui patitur. Pl.* 101, *cr.* 13, (without cap.)

SHAW, Bart., Iri., a hind's head, couped, az., neck transpierced by an arrow, in bend, or, flighted, ar. *Teipsum nosce. Pl.* 56, *cr.* 11, (without coronet.)

SHAWE, ROBERT-NEWTON, Esq., of Kesgrave Hall, Suff., a falcon, volant. *Pl.* 94, *cr.* 1.

SHAWE, five arrows, one in pale, and four in saltier, bound by a ribbon. *Pl.* 43, *cr.* 14.

SHAXTON, Norf., out of a ducal coronet, gu., a talbot's head, sa., (collared,) eared, and ringed, or. *Pl.* 99, *cr.* 7.

SHAYER, on the top of a tree, a pelican, wings elevated and addorsed, in a nest, feeding her young. *Pl.* 76, *cr.* 15, (tree, *pl.* 16, *cr.* 8.)

SHEAFFE, Bart., out of a mural coronet, ar., a cubit arm, vested, gu., cuffed, vert, hand grasping a sword, in bend sinister, ppr., hilt and pommel, or, between a branch of laurel and another of oak, also ppr.

SHEARER, Sco., on a chapeau, a dexter hand, (holding up by the band) a garb, all ppr. *Pl.* 3, *cr.* 3, (chapeau, *pl.* 62, *cr.* 1.)

SHEARS, Eng., a talbot's head, erased, collared, or, and lined. *Pl.* 2, *cr.* 15.

SHEARWOOD, Eng., a raven, sa. *Pl.* 123, *cr.* 2.

SHEATH, a lion, passant. *Pl.* 48, *cr.* 8.

SHED, Eng., a tent, or. *Pl.* 111, *cr.* 14.

SHEDDAN, Sco., a dove, volant, or, in mouth an olive-branch, vert. *Pl.* 25, *cr.* 6.

SHEDDEN, a hermit's head and shoulders, affrontée, vested in russet, his hood thrown back. *Fidem meam observabo. Pl.* 31, *cr.* 2.

SHEE, Eng., out of a ducal coronet, or, a mount, vert, thereon a stag, at gaze, ppr. *Pl.* 19, *cr.* 14.

SHEE, Iri., a swan, rising, ppr. *Pl.* 54, *cr.* 4.

SHEE, out of a ducal coronet, or, (on a mount, vert,) a swan, wings addorsed, ppr. *Pl.* 100, *cr.* 7, (mount, *pl.* 122, *cr.* 13.)

SHEE, Knt., a swan, rousant, wings addorsed. *Cruce salus. Pl.* 4, *cr.* 7, (without trumpet.)

SHEE, Bart., Iri., a swan, wings addorsed, sa., beak, gu. *Vincit veritas. Pl.* 46, *cr.* 5.

SHEEN, Eng. and Iri., a sword, erect, blade enfiled with a rebel's head, all ppr. *Pl.* 27, *cr.* 3.

SHEEN, Eng., out of a mural coronet, a staff, raguly, vert. *Pl.* 78, *cr.* 15, (coronet, *pl.* 128, *fig.* 18.)

SHEEPSHANKS, Yorks., (on a mount, vert,) a lamb, passant, ar. *Pl.* 116, *cr.* 1.

SHEERE, out of a ducal coronet, a swan, wings addorsed. *Pl.* 100, *cr.* 7.

SHEFFIELD, Linc., a boar's head and neck, (erased,) gu. *Pl.* 2, *cr.* 7.

SHEFFIELD, Bart., Linc. and Ess. a boar's head and neck, (erased,) or. *Pl.* 2, *cr.* 7.

SHEFFIELD, Earl of, and Baron, and Viscount Pevensey, Iri. ; Baron Sheffield, U.K., (Holroyd,) a demi-griffin, segreant, wings addorsed, sa., between feet a ducal coronet, or. *Quem te Deus esse jussit. Pl.* 13, *cr.* 10, (coronet, *pl.* 9, *cr.* 7.)

SHEFFIELD, Eng., three ears of rye, or. (Another, ar.) *Pl.* 102, *cr.* 1.

SHEFFIELD, a tiger's head, erased, or. *Pl.* 94, *cr.* 10.

SHEIL, Iri., out of a ducal coronet, or, a triple-plume of twelve ostrich-feathers, three, four, and five. *Pl.* 114, *cr.* 8.

SHEILS, Sco., a boar's head, couped. *Be traist. Pl.* 48, *cr.* 2.

SHEIRCLIFF, Yorks., a cutlass, in pale, ar., hilt and pommel, or, enfiled on the blade with a leopard's head, gold, vulned at mouth, gu. *Pl.* 24, *cr.* 13.

SHEKELL, THOMAS, Esq., of Pebworth, Glouc., an esquire's helmet, ppr. *Pl.* 109, *cr.* 5.

SHELBERY, or SHELBURY, Lond., Surr., and Ess., a lion's head, erased, gobony of four, ar. and gu. *Pl.* 81, *cr.* 4.

SHELBURNE, Earl. *See* LANSDOWNE.

SHELDON, Warw. and Worc., a swan, ar. *Pl.* 122, *cr.* 13, (without mount.)

SHELDON, HENRY-JAMES, Esq., of Brailes House, Warw., a sheldrake, ppr. *Optimum pati.* *Pl.* 90, *cr.* 15.

SHELDON, Sir JOSEPH, Bart., Lond.: 1. A (goose,) ar. *Pl.* 90, *cr.* 15. 2. Out of a mural coronet, az., a demi-monkey, or. *Pl.* 24, *cr.* 12.

SHELDON, Middx., a swan, ar., beaked, gu., in beak a rose, of the last, seeded, or, slipped and leaved, vert. *Pl.* 122, *cr.* 13, (rose, *pl.* 55, *cr.* 9.)

SHELDON, Warw., Staffs., Worc., and Glouc., a swan, ppr. (Another, ar.) *Pl.* 122, *cr.* 13, (without mount.)

SHELDRAKE, Eng., a swan, ppr. *Pl.* 122, *cr.* 13, (without mount.)

SHELLETOE, a lion, rampant, ar., ducally crowned, or, (in flames of fire, ppr.) *Pl.* 98, *cr.* 1.

SHELLEY, or SHELLY, Suss., a griffin's head, erased, ar., ducally gorged, or. *Pl.* 42, *cr.* 9, (without branch.)

SHELLEY, a wolf's head, couped, tawny, bezantée, between wings, or, charged with as many bars, gu. *Pl.* 92, *cr.* 15, (wings, *pl.* 1, *cr.* 15.)

SHELLEY, Suss., a griffin's head, erased, ar., beaked and ducally gorged, or. *Pl.* 42, *cr.* 9, (without branch.)

SHELLY, Suff., a griffin's head, erased, ar., ducally gorged, or. *Ib.*

SHELTON, Eng., a Saracen's head, ppr. *Pl.* 19, *cr.* 1.

SHELTON, Notts. and Yorks., a lion, passant, gu., (gorged with a chaplet of laurel, vert.) *Pl.* 60, *cr.* 6.

SHENTON, Eng., a dexter hand holding an open book, ppr. *Pl.* 82, *cr.* 5, (without cloud.)

SHEPARD, or SHEPHERD, Devons., on a mount, vert, a stag, lodged, regardant, ar., (vulned on shoulder, gu.) *Pl.* 51, *cr.* 9.

SHEPARD, or SHEPPARD, Bucks., two battle-axes, in saltier, or. *Pl.* 52, *cr.* 10.

SHEPARD, Suff. and Suss., a lion's head, sa., issuing from a tower, or. *Pl.* 42, *cr.* 4, (head, *pl.* 126, *cr.* 1.)

SHEPARD, Surr. and Suss., on a mount, vert, a stag, current, regardant, ppr., attired, ar. *Pl.* 3, *cr.* 2.

SHEPARD, or SHEPHERD, Kent and Suss., a stag, couchant, regardant, ar. *Pl.* 51, *cr.* 9, (without mount.)

SHEPARD, or SHEPPERD, Oxon., a ram, passant, ar., attired, or, between two branches of laurel, vert. *Pl.* 109, *cr.* 2, (branches, *pl.* 79, *cr.* 14.)

SHEPARD, Suss. and Suff., a talbot's head, sa., issuing from a tower, or. *Pl.* 42, *cr.* 4, (head, *pl.* 123, *cr.* 15.)

SHEPERD, Eng., two halberds, in saltier, ppr. *Pl.* 52, *cr.* 10.

SHEPHERD, Eng., a cock, gu., in beak a cinquefoil, stalked, vert. *Pl.* 55, *cr.* 12, (cinquefoil, *pl.* 141.)

SHEPHEARD, and SHEPPARD, Eng., a dexter hand, ppr., holding up a cross crosslet, fitched, sa. *Pl.* 99, *cr.* 1.

SHEPHERD, Suff., a ram, passant, ppr. *Pl.* 109, *cr.* 2.

SHEPHERD, Lond., a buck, couchant, regardant, or, (wreathed round neck with laurel, vert.) *Pl.* 51, *cr.* 9, (without mount.)

SHEPHERD, on a mural coronet, a wyvern, wings expanded, in mouth a broken spear. *Pl.* 75, *cr.* 12, (coronet, *pl.* 128, *fig.* 18.)

SHEPLEY, Eng., a lion, sejant, or, collared, gu. *Pl.* 21, *cr.* 3.

SHEPLEY, Surr. and Yorks., a buck's head, erased, ppr. *Pl.* 66, *cr.* 9.

SHEPPARD, Iri., a bull's head, erased, az. *Pl.* 19, *cr.* 3.

SHEPPARD, Eng., on a mount, vert, a stag in full chase, regardant, or. *Pl.* 3, *cr.* 2.

SHEPPARD, Frome Selwood, Somers., a ram, passant, ppr., between two olive-branches, vert. *Pl.* 109, *cr.* 2, (branches, *pl.* 75, *cr.* 9.)

SHEPPARD-COTTON, Bart., Bucks.: 1. For *Sheppard*, a lamb, passant, ar., between two laurel-branches, vert. *Pl.* 116, *cr.* 1, (branches, *pl.* 79, *cr.* 14.) 2. For *Cotton*, on a mount, vert, a falcon, wings expanded, and belled, or. *Nec timeo, nec sperno.* *Pl.* 61, *cr.* 12, (without gorging.)

SHEPPERD, Norf., a demi-buck, regardant, ppr., attired, or. *Pl.* 55, *cr.* 9, (regardant, *pl.* 51, *cr.* 9.)

SHERAR, Salop, on a chapeau, gu., turned up, erm., a cubit arm, in pale, vested, az., cuffed, of the second, in hand, ppr., a garb, or. *Pl.* 3, *cr.* 3, (chapeau, *pl.* 62, *cr.* 1.)

SHERARD, Baron. *See* HARBOROUGH.

SHERARD, or SHERRARD, Eng., out of a ducal coronet, or, a peacock's tail, in pale, ppr. *Hostis honori invidia.* *Pl.* 120, *cr.* 13.

SHERBORNE, Lanc., a unicorn's head, ar., crined and armed, or. *Pl.* 20, *cr.* 1.

SHERBORNE, Baron, (Dutton,) a plume of (five) ostrich-feathers, ar., az., or, vert, and gu. *Servabo fidem.* *Pl.* 12, *cr.* 9.

SHEREROOKE, Eng., a fleur-de-lis. *Vi si non consilio.* *Pl.* 68, *cr.* 12.

SHERBROOKE, Notts., a horse's head, (couped, ar., charged with three bars, gu.) *Pl.* 81, *cr.* 6.

SHERBURNE, Eng., a unicorn's head, (couped, ar., attired, or.) *Pl.* 20, *cr.* 1.

SHERD, a bugle-horn, ar., strung and garnished, sa. *Pl.* 48, *cr.* 12.

SHERFEILD, Eng., on a rock, sa., a fire-beacon, or, flammant, gu. *Pl.* 89, *cr.* 9.

SHERFELD, Wilts., a lion, couchant, ar., supporting with the fore-legs a ducal coronet over his head, or.

SHERFIELD, Eng., on the top of a tower, a Cornish chough, rising, all ppr. *Pl.* 84, *cr.* 3.

SHERGOLD, a demi-lion, rampant, gu., holding an escallop, az. *Pl.* 89, *cr.* 10, (escallop, *pl.* 141.)

SHERIDAN, Eng., a dexter hand, gu., holding a cross crosslet, fitched, or. *Pl.* 99, *cr.* 1.

SHERIDAN, Iri., an angel, in a praying posture, between two laurel-branches, all ppr. *Pl.* 94, *cr.* 11.

SHERIDAN, RICHARD-BRINSLEY, Esq., of Frampton Court, Dors., out of a ducal coronet, a stag's head, ppr. *Cervus lacessitus leone*. *Pl.* 29, *cr.* 7.

SHERIDAN, or SHERIDEN, Eng., on a chapeau, gu., turned up, erm., a lion's head, erased. *Pl.* 99, *cr.* 9.

SHERIDAN, Middx., out of a ducal coronet, a stag's head. *Pl.* 29, *cr.* 7.

SHERIFF, or SHERIVE, Warw., a lion's paw, erased, or, holding a branch of dates, the fruit, gold, in the pods, ar., the stalk and leaves, vert. *Pl.* 70, *cr.* 9.

SHERIFF, Sco., a lion's paw, erased, or, holding a laurel-branch, vert. *Esse quam videri*. *Pl.* 68, *cr.* 10.

SHERIFF, SHERIVE, and SHERRIFF, Warw., a demi-lion, rampant, in dexter a laurel-branch, ar., fructed, or. *Pl.* 39, *cr.* 14, (branch, *pl.* 68, *cr.* 10.)

SHERIFFE, Lond., a dragon, segreant, gu., holding between paws a chaplet, of the last, leaved, vert. *Pl.* 13, *cr.* 10, (chaplet, *pl.* 56, *cr.* 10.)

SHERINGTON, Lond., a talbot, passant, erm., sa. *Pl.* 120, *cr.* 8.

SHERINGTON, Lond., a talbot, sa., eared, ar. *Pl.* 120, *cr.* 8.

SHERINGTON, Wilts., Worc., and Norf., a scorpion, in pale, or, tail in chief, between two elephant's teeth, the upper part chequy, ar. and az., the bottom, gu., each charged with a cross formée, sa.

SHERLAND, Eng., a bull's scalp, ar. *Pl.* 9, *cr.* 15.

SHERLAND, Kent and Norf., a griffin, segreant, ar., in dexter a fleur-de-lis, or. *Pl.* 67, *cr.* 13, (fleur-de-lis, *pl.* 141.)

SHERLAND, Devons., a sea-horse, ar., charged with an anchor, sa. *Pl.* 103, *cr.* 3, (anchor, *pl.* 25, *cr.* 15.)

SHERLEY, Eng., a crosier, or. *Pl.* 7, *cr.* 15.

SHERLOCK, Iri., among flags, vert, a duck, az. *Pl.* 34, *cr.* 6.

SHERLOCK, Lond., a dolphin, haurient, arondée, az. *Pl.* 14, *cr.* 10.

SHERMAN, a lion's head, regardant, erased. *Pl.* 35, *cr.* 2.

SHERMAN, Cambs. and Surr., a demi-lion, rampant, sa., holding a sprig of holly, vert. *Pl.* 39, *cr.* 14, (holly, *pl.* 99, *cr.* 6.)

SHERMAN, Suff., a sea-lion, sejant, per pale, or and ar., guttée-de-poix, finned, of the first. *Pl.* 80, *cr.* 13.

SHERMAN, Devons. and Lond., a sea-lion, sejant, per pale, or and ar., guttée-de-poix, finned, of the first, on shoulders a crescent for difference. *Pl.* 80, *cr.* 13, (crescent, *pl.* 141.)

SHERMAN, a lion's head, erased, gardant, erm. *Pl.* 1, *cr.* 5, (without crown.)

SHERMAN, Suff., a sea-lion, sejant, sa., charged on shoulder with three bezants, two and one. *Pl.* 80, *cr.* 13, (bezant, *pl.* 141.)

SHERRARD, Linc. and Leic., out of a ducal coronet, or, a peacock's tail, erect, ppr. *Hostis honori invidia*. *Pl.* 120, *cr.* 13.

SHERRIF, Sco., a lion's paw, erased, or, holding a branch of laurel, vert. *Esse quam videri*. *Pl.* 68, *cr.* 10.

SHERSHALL, a lion, sejant, sa. *Pl.* 126, *cr.* 15.

SHERWIN, Hants, an eagle, or, pellettée, wings expanded, az. *Pl.* 126, *cr.* 7.

SHERWIN, or SHIRWIN, Eng., a demi-man, in dexter a sword, in sinister a staff, all ppr. *Pl.* 121, *cr.* 8.

SHERWOOD, Eng., a dexter hand, ppr., holding a branch of a rose-tree, ar., leaved, vert. *Pl.* 118, *cr.* 9.

SHETTOW, Eng., a cubit arm, erect, in hand an etoile of eight points. *Pl.* 62, *cr.* 3, (etoile, *pl.* 83, *cr.* 3.)

SHEVILL, Durh., out of a naval coronet, or, a demi-lion, rampant, gu., (holding between the paws a ship's sail, ar., charged with an anchor, sa.) *Mon privilege et mon devoir*. *Pl.* 86, *cr.* 11, (coronet, *pl.* 128, *fig.* 19.)

SHEWEN, Eng., an antelope, passant, vert. *Pl.* 63, *cr.* 10.

SHEWERSDEN, Ess., a demi-talbot, ar., eared, sa., collared, gu., between paws a lozenge, of the second. *Pl.* 97, *cr.* 9.

SHIEL, Iri., an eagle's head, between wings, ppr. *Pl.* 81, *cr.* 10.

SHIELD, Northumb., a buck, passant, ppr., (on breast an escutcheon, sa., charged with an escallop, ar.) *Pl.* 61, *cr.* 15.

SHIELDS, Eng., a demi-leopard, rampant, or. *Pl.* 12, *cr.* 14.

SHIELDS, Eng., an escutcheon, az. *Pl.* 36, *cr.* 11.

SHIELDS, Iri., a demi-lion, rampant, or, holding with fore-paws an anchor, az. *Pl.* 19, *cr.* 6.

SHIELDS, or SHIELLS, Sco., a dexter hand, gu., holding a shield, az. *Pl.* 21, *cr.* 12.

SHIELDS, a demi-lion, rampant, or. *Pl.* 67, *cr.* 10.

SHIELDS, Sco., a dexter hand, gu. *Pl.* 32, *cr.* 14.

SHIELS, Sco., a boar's head, couped, ppr. *Be traist*. *Pl.* 48, *cr.* 2.

SHIELS, Eng., a mullet, pierced, or. *Pl.* 45, *cr.* 1.

SHIERCLIFFE, Ecclesfield Hall, a falchion, erect, enfiled with a leopard's head, or. *Pl.* 24, *cr.* 13.

SHIERS, Eng., a dexter hand holding a palm-branch, ppr. *Pl.* 23, *cr.* 7.

SHIERS, Surr., a demi-lion, rampant, sa., supporting an escallop, or. *Pl.* 126 A, *cr.* 13.

SHIFFNER, Eng., a greyhound's head, erased, gu. *Pl.* 89, *cr.* 2.

SHIFFNER, Barf., Suss., an etoile, or, between the rays six annulets, sa. *Pl.* 63, *cr.* 9, (annulet, *pl.* 141.)

SHIKLEWORTH, a garb, or, banded, sa., in the band a sickle, ar. *Pl.* 48, *cr.* 10, (sickle, *pl.* 36, *cr.* 12.)

SHILLINGLAW, Sco., a bee-hive, with bees, volant and counter-volant, ppr. *Pl.* 81, *cr.* 14.

SHILTON, Eng., on a ducal coronet, or, a dolphin, naiant, az. *Pl.* 94, *cr.* 14.

SHINGLEHURST, Lond., a battle-axe, erect, ppr. *Pl.* 14, *cr.* 8.

SHIPEY, or SHIPPEY, Eng., on a chapeau, sa., turned up, erm., an escallop, of the first, between wings, or. *Pl.* 17, *cr.* 14.

SHIPHAM, a demi-reermouse, wings expanded, gu. and ar., ducally crowned, or, vulned, of the first. *Pl.* 108, *cr.* 6.

SHIPLEY, out of an earl's coronet, a moor's head, affrontée, couped at shoulders, vested, (forehead banded.) *Pl.* 80, *cr.* 11.

SHIPLEY, Eng., in hand, ppr., an (olive)-branch, vert. *Pl.* 43, *cr.* 6.

SHIPMAN, Notts., a leopard, sejant, ar., spotted, sa., resting dexter on a ship's rudder, az. *Pl.* 10, *cr.* 13, (rudder, *pl.* 102, *cr.* 4.)

SHIPMAN, Heref., a demi-ostrich, wings expanded, ar., ducally gorged and beaked, or, in mouth a key, az., and vulned on breast, gu. *Pl.* 29, *cr.* 9, (key, *pl.* 9, *cr.* 12.)

SHIPPARD, Eng., out of a ducal coronet, a peacock's tail, all ppr. *Pl.* 120, *cr.* 13.

SHIPTON, Eng., an eel, naiant, ppr. *Pl.* 25, *cr.* 13.

SHIPTON, Yorks., a lion, rampant. *Pl.* 67, *cr.* 5.

SHIRBORNE, Lanc., a unicorn's head, ar., crined and armed, or. *Pl.* 20, *cr.* 1.

SHIRLEY, Earl Ferrers. *See* FERRERS.

SHIRLEY, Sco., a crozier, or. *Pl.* 7, *cr.* 15.

SHIRLEY, Eng., a moor's head, couped at shoulders, sa. *Pl.* 120, *cr.* 3.

SHIRLEY, Derbs., Leic., and Warw., a Saracen's head, in profile, couped, ppr., wreathed, or and az. *Pl.* 36, *cr.* 3.

SHIRLEY, EVELYN-PHILIP-JOHN, Esq., of Lower Eatington Park, and Houndshill, Warw.; and Lough Fea, co. Monaghan, a Saracen's head, couped at neck, ppr., wreathed, or and az., on a torse of the same colour. *Honor virtutis præmium*—and—*Loyal suis je*. *Pl.* 81, *cr.* 15.

SHIRLEY, Lond., three broad arrows, two in saltier, one in pale, or, plumed, ar., (enfiled with a garland of laurel, vert.) *Pl.* 43, *cr.* 14.

SHIRLEY, Suss., out of a ducal coronet, a stag's head, all ar. *Pl.* 91, *cr.* 14, (coronet, *pl.* 29, *cr.* 7.)

SHIRREFF, Eng., a lion, rampant, double-queued, az., armed and langued, or. *Pl.* 41, *cr.* 15.

SHIRT, Eng., a griffin's head, between wings. *Pl.* 65, *cr.* 1.

SHIVEZ, a demi-cat, ppr. *Virtute non vi*. *Pl.* 80, *cr.* 7.

SHONE, Eng., a dolphin, naiant, gu. *Pl.* 48, *cr.* 9.

SHOOBRIDGE, Suss., a leopard's head, affrontée, or, between wings, sa. *Pl.* 66, *cr.* 14, (wings, *pl.* 1, *cr.* 15.)

SHORE, a stork, in dexter a stone, ppr. *Perimus licitis*. *Pl.* 122, *cr.* 7, (without mount.)

SHORE, Derbs., a (stork,) regardant, ar., resting dexter on a pellet. *Pl.* 77, *cr.* 15.

SHORE, Derbs., a crane, ppr., resting dexter on a mullet, sa. *Pl.* 111, *cr.* 9, (mullet, *pl.* 141.)

SHORE, Baron Teignmouth. *See* TEIGNMOUTH.

SHORT, Kent, a griffin's head, or, between two wings, az., charged with etoiles, gold. *Pl.* 65, *cr.* 1, (etoile, *pl.* 141.)

SHORT, Sco., a ship (in flames,) ppr. *Spes in extremum*. *Pl.* 21, *cr.* 11.

SHORT, a griffin's head, ar., in beak a trefoil, slipped, vert. *Pl.* 9, *cr.* 12, (trefoil, *pl.* 11, *cr.* 12.)

SHORT, a griffin's head, collared, erm., between wings. *Pl.* 22, *cr.* 2.

SHORT, Ess., a griffin's head, between wings. *Pl.* 65, *cr.* 1.

SHORTE, Eng., a griffin's head, or, winged, az., charged with etoiles, ar. *Pl.* 65, *cr.* 1, (etoile, *pl.* 141.)

SHORTER, Lond., a griffin's head, sa., between wings, collared and beaked, or. *Pl.* 22, *cr.* 2.

SHORTHOSE, Eng., a wyvern, az. *Pl.* 63, *cr.* 13.

SHORTHOSE, in hand a dagger, in pale, point downward, all ppr. *Pl.* 18, *cr.* 3.

SHORTLAND, Eng., a sea-horse, az., ducally gorged, ar. *Pl.* 103, *cr.* 3, (gorging, *same plate*, *cr.* 2.)

SHORTLAND, a sea-horse, (rampant, az.,) ducally gorged, or.) *Pl.* 103, *cr.* 3.

SHORTREED, Sco., in dexter hand a scimitar, ppr. *Pro aris et focis*. *Pl.* 29, *cr.* 8.

SHORTSEY, a wolf, passant, in mouth a fish. *Pl.* 46, *cr.* 6, (fish, *pl.* 74, *cr.* 13.)

SHOTTER, Surr., a demi-lion, rampant, erminois, (charged on shoulder with two arrows, in saltier, gu.,) flighted, ppr., in paws a slip of oak-leaves and acorns, also ppr. *Pl.* 47, *cr.* 4, (oak, *pl.* 32, *cr.* 13.)

SHOVEL, out of a naval coronet, or, a demi-lion, gu., holding a sail, ar., charged with an anchor, sa.

SHOYSWELL, Suss., a horse's head, erased, ar., (gorged with a collar,) sa., charged with three horse-shoes, of the first. *Pl.* 81, *cr.* 6, (horse-shoe, *pl.* 52, *cr.* 4.)

SHRAWLEY, Lond., a hind's head, ar., pierced through by an arrow, in bend, or. *Pl.* 56, *cr.* 11, (without coronet.)

SHREWSBURY, Earl of, Eng., and Earl of Waterford, Iri., (Talbot,) on a chapeau, gu., turned up, erm., a lion, statant, or, (tail extended.) *Prest d'accomplir*. *Pl.* 107, *cr.* 1.

SHRIGLEY, Eng., a hand holding a bull's head, erased, ppr. *Pl.* 29, *cr.* 4, (head, *pl.* 19, *cr.* 3.)

SHRIMPTON, a leopard, passant, ppr. *Pl.* 86, *cr.* 2.

SHRUB, Surr., on an acorn-branch, in fess, vert, fructed, ppr., an eagle, close, (regardant, of the last, charged on breast with a rose, gu.) *Pl.* 7, *cr.* 11, (branch, *pl.* 81, *cr.* 7.)

SHRUBSOLE, Kent, a cubit arm, erect, vested, gu., cuffed, ar., in hand, ppr., a (cherry-tree-branch, fructed, of the first.) *Pl.* 64, *cr.* 7.

SHUCKBURGH, Bart., Warw., a blackamoor, couped at waist, ppr., in hand a dart, or. *Hæc manus ob patriam*.

SHUCKBURGH, Wilts., a demi-moor, wreathed about head, in dexter (an arrow, in bend sinister, ppr.) *Hæc manus ob patriam*. *Pl.* 20, *cr.* 4.

SHUCKFORTH, Norf., an eagle's head, erased, ppr. *Pl.* 20, *cr.* 7.

SHUGBOROUGH, Warw., a demi-moor, ppr., wreathed about head, or, in dexter an (arrow,) of the first. *Pl.* 20, *cr.* 4.

SHUGBOROUGH, and SHUCKBURGH, Warw. and Northamp., a demi-moor, ppr., wreathed about head, or, vested, ar., with an under vestment, of the second, in dexter an arrow, of the same.

SHULDHAM, Eng. and Iri., a griffin, passant, ar. *Post nubili Phœbus*. *Pl.* 61, *cr.* 14, (without gorging.)

SHUM, Eng., a cock, regardant. *Pl.* 19, *cr.* 10.

SHUM, a cock, regardant, ppr., (collared,) or, from the collar a bugle-horn, pendent, of the last. *Pl.* 19, *cr.* 10, (bugle-horn, *pl.* 98, *cr.* 2.)

SHUM-STOREY, Surr.: 1. A falcon, sa., within a chaplet of laurel, ppr., (charged on breast

2 E

with an Eastern crown, or, also charged with a saltier, gu., for difference.) *Pl.* 67, *cr.* 3, (chaplet, *pl.* 2, *cr.* 11.) 2. A cock, regardant, ppr., (collared,) or, from collar a bugle-horn, pendent, gold. *Pl.* 19, *cr.* 10, (bugle-horn, *pl.* 98, *cr.* 2.)

SHURMER, out of a ducal coronet, or, an arm, in armour, in hand a cross crosslet, fitched. *Pl.* 122, *cr.* 8, (cross, *pl.* 99, *cr.* 1.)

SHURY, out of a ducal coronet, or, a dexter arm, in armour, embowed, ppr., garnished, gold, in hand, also ppr., a cross crosslet, fitched, sa. *Pl.* 122, *cr.* 8, (cross, *pl.* 99, *cr.* 1.)

SHUTE, Hants., a griffin, sejant, or, pierced through breast by a broken spear, ppr. *Pl.* 74, *cr.* 10.

SHUTE, Cumb. and Yorks., a griffin, sejant, or, pierced in breast by a broken (sword-blade,) ar., vulned, gu. *Pl.* 74, *cr.* 10.

SHUTER, Wilts., on a mount, vert, a leopard, sejant, ppr., (ducally gorged and lined, or.) *Pl.* 123, *cr.* 8.

SHUTTLEWORTH, Lanc. and Durh., a bear, passant, ar. *Pl.* 61, *cr.* 5.

SHUTTLEWORTH, Lond., a cubit arm, in armour, ppr., in gauntlet a weaver's shuttle, sa. *Pl.* 33, *cr.* 4, (shuttle, *pl.* 102, *cr.* 10.)

SHUTTLEWORTH, of Great Bowden, and Market Haddington, same crest. *Æquanimiter.*

SHUTTLEWORTH, a cubit arm, vested, in hand a shuttle, sa., tipped, and furnished with quills of yarn, threads pendent, or. *Pl.* 18, *cr.* 1, (shuttle, *pl.* 102, *cr.* 10.)

SHYER, a tower, domed. *Pl.* 42, *cr.* 10.

SIBBALD, Sco., a hand, erect, apauméé, ppr., *Ora et labora. Pl.* 32, *cr.* 14.

SIBBALD, Sco., two laurel-branches, in orle, ppr. *Sae bauld. Pl.* 79, *cr.* 14.

SIBBALD, THOMAS, Esq., of Westcott, Cornw., in hand, erect, ppr., a sword. *Sae bauld. Pl.* 21, *cr.* 10.

SIBBALD, a mort-head, ppr. *Me certum mors certa facit. Pl.* 62, *cr.* 12.

SIBBALD, a cross moline, gu. *Justitia. Pl.* 89, *cr.* 8.

SIBBALD, Sco., two laurel-branches, in orle, vert. *Pl.* 79, *cr.* 14.

SIBBALD, Sco., a hand holding a book shut, ppr. *Ora et labora. Pl.* 45, *cr.* 3.

SIBBALD, Berks., (out of a ducal coronet, ar.,) a garb, between two sickles, ppr. *Domini factum. Pl.* 62, *cr.* 1, (sickle, *pl.* 31, *cr.* 12.)

SIBTHORPE, WALDO-SIBTHORPE, Linc.: 1. For *Sibthorpe,* a demi-lion, (erased, ar., collared, sa.,) in dexter a fleur-de lis, of the last. *Pl.* 91, *cr.* 13. 2. A demi-leopard, gardant, ppr., (debruised, with two bendlets, az.) *Pl.* 1, *cr.* 10, (without anchor.)

SICKLEMORE, Suff., a garb, banded. *Pl.* 48, *cr.* 10.

SIDDONS, two lions' gambs, erased, sa., holding up a cinquefoil, or. *Pl.* 42, *cr.* 3, (cinquefoil, *pl.* 141.)

SIDELEY, out of a ducal coronet, a goat's head. *Pl.* 72, *cr.* 2.

SIDESERF, or SIDSERF, Sco., an eagle's head, issuing, gu. *Virtute promoves. Pl.* 100, *cr.* 10.

SIDESERF, or SIDSERF, Sco., a cornucopia, ppr. *Industria ditat. Pl.* 91, *cr.* 4.

SIDESERF, Sco., an eagle's head, couped, az. *Semper virtute vivo. Pl.* 100, *cr.* 10.

SIDEY, a tiger, sejant, (regardant, ar., maned, sa., holding an arrow, of the same.) *Pl.* 10, *cr.* 13.

SIDMOUTH, Viscount, (Addington,) a mountain-cat, sejant, gardant, ppr., (bezantée,) resting dexter on a shield, az., charged with a mace, in pale, with a regal crown, or, for Speaker of the House of Commons, within a bordure engrailed, ar. *Libertas sub rege pio. Pl.* 24, *cr.* 6.

SIDNEY, a boar, passant, or. *Quo fata vocant. Pl.* 48, *cr.* 14.

SIDNEY, a bear and raguled staff, ppr. *Pl.* 1, *cr.* 3.

SIDNEY, Cowpen Hall, Northumb., a porcupine, ppr., (with chain reflexed over back, or.) *Pl.* 55, *cr.* 10.

SIDNEY-SHELLEY, Bart., Kent: 1. For *Sidney,* a porcupine, passant, az., armed, (collared, and chained,) or. *Pl.* 65, *cr.* 10. 2. For *Shelley,* a griffin's head, erased, ar., beaked and ducally gorged, or. *Quo fata vocant. Pl.* 42, *cr.* 9, (without branch.)

SIER, upon a staff, raguly, or, a pelican in her piety, sa., semée of mullets, in the nest, ppr. *Virtus in actione consistit. Pl.* 44, *cr.* 1, (staff, *pl.* 5, *cr.* 8.)

SIEVEWRIGHT, or SIEVWRIGHT, Sco., a hand holding a thunderbolt, ppr. *Pl.* 21, *cr.* 8.

SIKES, of the Chantry House, Notts.: 1. A bull, passant. *Ferox inimicis. Pl.* 66, *cr.* 11. 2. Out of a ducal coronet, a wyvern. *Quod facis, valdè facis. Pl.* 104, *cr.* 11.

SILCHESTER, Baron. *See* LANGFORD, Earl of.

SILK, Eng., a greyhound, current, ar., (collared, az.) *Pl.* 28, *cr.* 7.

SILL, Northamp., a demi-griffin, ppr., (collared, ar.) *Pl.* 18, *cr.* 6.

SILLESDEN, a bird's head, az., beaked and collared, or, between wings, gu. *Pl.* 99, *cr.* 10.

SILLIFANT, at foot of a cross Calvary, or, a lizard, ppr. *Mens conscia recti. Pl.* 93, *cr.* 4, (cross, *pl.* 7, *cr.* 13.)

SILLY, Cornw., a lion, sejant. *Pl.* 126, *cr.* 15.

SILVER, Eng., a hand holding a vine-branch. *Pl.* 37, *cr.* 4.

SILVER, a lion, rampant, between paws a battle-axe. *Pl.* 125, *cr.* 2, (axe, *pl.* 26, *cr.* 7.)

SILVER, of Netherley, Sco., a unicorn's head, erased, ar., (charged with a cheveron, gu.) *Nil desperandum. Pl.* 73, *cr.* 1.

SILVERTHORN, Bristol, a dove alighting on a sheaf of barley, all ppr. *Pl.* 124, *cr.* 13, (barley, *pl.* 112, *cr.* 10.)

SILVERTOP, Northumb., a wolf's head, erased, ar., langued, gu., pierced (with a broken spear, cruented,) ppr. *Pl.* 40, *cr.* 12.

SILVERTOP, Northumb., a tiger's head, erased, ar., pierced through neck by a broken lance, ppr. *Pl.* 94, *cr.* 10.

SILVESTER, Eng., a lion's head, erased, vert. *Pl.* 81, *cr.* 4.

SILVESTER-CARTERET, Ess.: 1. For *Silvester,* a lion, couchant, gu. *Pl.* 75, *cr.* 15, (without chapeau.) 2. For *Carteret,* (on a mount, vert,) a squirrel, sejant, cracking a nut, ppr. *Pl.* 16, *cr.* 9.

SIM, SIMM, or SIME, Sco., a lion's head, erased, ppr. *Pl.* 81, *cr.* 4.

SIMCOE, Middx., an arm, in armour, embowed, in hand a sword, all ppr. *Pl.* 2, *cr.* 8.

SIMDEN, Eng., a savage's head, from shoulders, on head a cap. *Pl.* 51, *cr.* 4.

SIMEON, Eng., out of a mural coronet, erm., a lion's head, sa. *Pl.* 45, *cr.* 9.

SIMEON, Bart., Berks., a fox, passant, (regardant, ppr., in mouth a trefoil, slipped, vert.) *Nec temerè, nec timidè. Pl.* 126, *cr.* 5.

SIMEON, Cambs., stump of tree, eradicated, two laurel-branches crossing it, in saltier, all ppr.

SIMMER, Sco., a stag, couchant, ppr. *Pl.* 67, *cr.* 2.

SIMMINGES, a raven, sa., (in dexter a rose, gu., leaved and slipped, vert.) *Pl.* 123, *cr.* 2.

SIMMINGES, Lond., a lion, sejant, gu., holding under dexter an escutcheon, or. *Pl.* 126, *cr.* 15, (escutcheon, *pl.* 19, *cr.* 2.)

SIMMONDS, Eng., a lion's gamb, wielding a battle-axe, all or. *Pl.* 51, *cr.* 13.

SIMMONS, Rochester, a greyhound's head, (erased,) collared. *In recto decus. Pl.* 43, *cr.* 11.

SIMMONS, Eng., a dolphin, naiant. *Pl.* 48, *cr.* 9.

SIMMONS, Eng., a stag's head, erased. *Pl.* 66, *cr.* 9.

SIMMONS, Iri., a sea-lion, rampant, gu. *Pl.* 25, *cr.* 12.

SIMMONS, a greyhound's head, gorged with a plain collar, charged with a mullet of five points. *Pl.* 43, *cr.* 11, (mullet, *pl.* 141.)

SIMMONS, Kent, a beaver, passant, in mouth an olive-branch, all ppr. *Pl.* 49, *cr.* 5, (branch, *pl.* 98, *cr.* 8.)

SIMMS, Eng., a gad-fly, ppr.

SIMON, Perth, in lion's gamb a battle-axe. *God giveth the victory. Pl.* 51, *cr.* 13.

SIMON, Eng., a pegasus, current, ar., winged, gu. *Pl.* 28, *cr.* 9.

SIMON, Lond., a cock, ar., combed, beaked, and legged, gu. *Pl.* 67, *cr.* 14.

SIMONDS, Eng., on a mount, vert, an ermine, passant, ppr., (in mouth a trefoil, slipped, or.) *Pl.* 87, *cr.* 3.

SIMONS, Eng., a wing, erect, per pale, ar. and or. *Pl.* 39, *cr.* 10.

SIMPSON, Sco., a dexter hand pointing with the thumb and fore-finger. *Confido. Pl.* 35, *cr.* 5.

SIMPSON, a crescent, or. *Tandem implebitur. Pl.* 18, *cr.* 14.

SIMPSON, of Easter Ogil, Sco., same crest and motto.

SIMPSON, Iri., a lion's gamb, issuing, erm., holding a branch of (olive,) vert. *Pl.* 68, *cr.* 10.

SIMPSON, Sco. and Lond., falcon, volant, ppr. *Alis nutrior. Pl.* 94, *cr.* 1.

SIMPSON, Eng., a snake, nowed in a love-knot, vert. *Pl.* 1, *cr.* 9.

SIMPSON, on a tower, (ruined on sinister side,) a bird, rising. *Pl.* 84, *cr.* 3.

SIMPSON, on a demi-tower, (ruined,) a bird, wings elevated, in beak a sprig. *Pl.* 60, *cr.* 8.

SIMPSON, a cross, raguly, suspended thereon an escutcheon, per bend sinister, charged with a lion, rampant. *Regi regnoque fidelis.*

SIMPSON, out of a mural coronet, a demi-lion, rampant, in dexter a sword, (in pale.) *Pl.* 41, *cr.* 13.

SIMPSON, Middx. and Surr., a lion, rampant, or. *Pl.* 67, *cr.* 5.

SIMPSON, an eagle, wings expanded, ppr. *Pl.* 126, *cr.* 7.

SIMPSON, JOSEPH, Esq., of Whitburn, Westhouse, Durh., a naked arm, in hand a wreath of laurel. *Perseveranti dabitur. Pl.* 118, *cr.* 4.

SIMPSON, Knaresborough, a demi-lion, rampant. *Nil desperandum. Pl.* 67, *cr.* 10.

SIMPSON, Yorks., out of a mural coronet, ar., a demi-lion, rampant, gardant, per pale, or and sa., in dexter a (sword, erect,) ppr. *Pl.* 120, *cr.* 14, (lion, *pl.* 35, *cr.* 4.)

SIMPSON, Lond., an eagle's head, erased, ppr. *Je suis prêt. Pl.* 20, *cr.* 7.

SIMPSON, Yorks., out of a tower, az., a demi-lion, rampant, (gardant, per pale, or and sa., in dexter a sword, ar., hilt and pommel, of the second.) *Pl.* 42, *cr.* 4.

SIMPSON, Kent, an ounce's head, pean, (erased,) gu., gorged with a collar-gemelle, ar. *Nunquam obliviscar. Pl.* 40, *cr.* 10.

SIMPSON, Bucks., out of a tower, a demi-lion, rampant, (between paws a scimitar, ppr.) *Pl.* 42, *cr.* 4.

SIMS, Sco., a demi-lion, in dexter a battle-axe, ppr. *Ferio, tego. Pl.* 101, *cr.* 14, (without charging.)

SIMSON, Sco., an eagle's head, erased, ppr. *Profundo cernit. Pl.* 20, *cr.* 7.

SIMSON, Eng., a lion's head, erased, ducally crowned, or. *Pl.* 90, *cr.* 4.

SIMSON, GEORGE, Esq., of Brunton and Pitcorthie, Fife, a falcon, volant, ppr. *Alis nutrior. Pl.* 94, *cr.* 1.

SINCLAIR, Sco., a demi-soldier, displaying a banner, ppr. *Te duce gloriamur. Pl.* 2, *cr.* 12.

SINCLAIR, a cross pattée, within a circle of stars, ar. *Via crucis via lucis. Pl.* 33, *cr.* 10.

SINCLAIR, a man displaying a banner, ppr. *Te duce gloriamur. Pl.* 79, *cr.* 5.

SINCLAIR, Sco., a man on horseback, ppr. *Promptus ad certamen. Pl.* 115, *cr.* 5.

SINCLAIR, an arrow and branch of palm, in saltier, ppr. *Detur forti palma. Pl.* 50, *cr.* 11.

SINCLAIR, a phœnix, in flames, ppr. *Fides. Pl.* 44, *cr.* 8.

SINCLAIR, Bart., Sco., a star, issuing out of a cloud, ppr. *Aspera virtus. Pl.* 16, *cr.* 13.

SINCLAIR, a griffin's head, erased, (wings addorsed.) *Candide, sed caute. Pl.* 65, *cr.* 1.

SINCLAIR, a griffin's head, erased, ppr. *Candide, sed caute. Pl.* 48, *cr.* 6.

SINCLAIR, an otter, issuing, ppr. *Quocunque ferar. Pl.* 9, *cr.* 9.

SINCLAIR, Eng., a pole-cat, ar.

SINCLAIR, Sco., a dove, in mouth an olive-branch, ppr. *Credo. Pl.* 48, *cr.* 15.

SINCLAIR, Bart., Sco., a dove, ppr. *Credo. Pl.* 66, *cr.* 12.

SINCLAIR, Sco., a demi-man, (holding in one hand a sea-cat, and in the other a pair of pencils, all ppr.) *Sic rectius progredior. Pl.* 121, *cr.* 8.

SINCLAIR, Sco., a savage, (resting his club on the wreath,) ppr. *Per ardua virtus. Pl.* 87, *cr.* 13.

SINCLAIR, Sco., a cross, engrailed, sa. *Cruce delector. Pl.* 7, *cr.* 13.

SINCLAIR, Sco., a naked arm, issuing from a cloud, hand grasping a small sword, (with another lying by,) all ppr. *Me vincit, ego mereo.* Pl. 76, cr. 6, (without head.)

SINCLAIR, Bart., of Longformacus, Sco., a man bearing a flag. *Te duce gloriamur.* Pl. 79, cr. 5.

SINCLAIR, Bart., of Dunbeath, Sco., a cock, ppr. *Commit thy work to God.* Pl. 67, cr. 14.

SINCLAIR, JAMES, Esq., of Holy Hill, co. Tyrone, same crest.

SINCLAIR, Baron, Sco., (Sinclair,) a swan, ar., ducally collared and chained, or. *Fight.* Pl. 111, cr. 10.

SINCLAIR, Earl of Caithness. *See* CAITHNESS.

SINCLAIRE, Sco., a swan, ar., ducally collared and chained, or. Pl. 111, cr. 10.

SINGE, Salop, out of a ducal coronet, or, an eagle's foot, ar. Pl. 96, cr. 7.

SINGLETON, Iri., a lion's head, affrontée, between wings, ppr. Pl. 87, cr. 2.

SINGLETON, Eng., an eagle, rising, regardant, in dexter a sword, in pale, all ppr. Pl. 87, cr. 5.

SINGLETON, Yorks., a camel, passant, erm., bridled, or. Pl. 17, cr. 2.

SINGLETON, Lanc. and Norf., a demi-antelope, sa., plattée, crined and attired, ar., pierced through breast by a broken spear, or, headed, of the second, vulned and guttée-de-sang. Pl. 75, cr. 10, (spear, pl. 79, cr. 9.)

SINGLETON, Lanc. and Norf., an arm, in armour, embowed, ppr., hand grasping a sceptre, or, (on the top an etoile.) Pl. 65, cr. 8, (sceptre, pl. 82, cr. 3.)

SINIOR, Sco., on a mount, vert, a leopard, couchant, gardant, crowned with an (Eastern) coronet, or. *Medio tutissimus ibis.* Pl. 9, cr. 14.

SINNOTT, a swan, sa., wings elevated. Pl. 46, cr. 5.

SIPLING, Yorks., a leopard's head, or, (gorged with a chaplet, vert.) Pl. 92, cr. 13.

SIBRINGES, an eagle, (holding a rose-branch, gu., leaved, vert.) Pl. 7, cr. 11.

SISSON, Eng., a stag, trippant, ar. Pl. 68, cr. 2.

SISSONS, Penrith, a griffin's head, erased. *Hope for the best*—and—*Si monent tubæ, paratus.* Pl. 48, cr. 6.

SITLINGTON, Cumb., a holy lamb, (regardant, erm., accoled with a laurel-branch, vert,) holding a banner, ppr. *Have mercy on us, good Lord.* Pl. 48, cr. 13.

SITSILL, a thistle, ppr. Pl. 68, cr. 9.

SITWELL, Derbs., a demi-lion, rampant, erased, sa., holding between paws an escutcheon, per pale, or and ar. Pl. 19, cr. 6, (escutcheon, pl. 22, cr. 13.)

SITWELL, Bart., Derbs., a demi-lion, rampant, erased, sa., holding between paws an escutcheon, per pale, or and vert. Pl. 19, cr. 6, (escutcheon, pl. 22, cr. 13.)

SITWELL-WILMOT, Stainsby, Derbs.: 1. A demi-lion, rampant, erased, sa., between paws an escutcheon, per pale, or and ar. Pl. 19, cr. 6, (escutcheon, pl. 22, cr. 13.) 2. An eagle's head, couped, ar., in beak an escallop, gu. Pl. 100, cr. 10, (escallop, pl. 141.)

SIVEDALE, a demi-eagle, wings expanded, or. Pl. 52, cr. 8.

SKAE, Sco., a buck, lodged, gu. Pl. 67, cr. 2.

SKARLETT, Norf., two lions' gambs, erased, erm., supporting a pillar, gobony, or and gu., capital and base, of the second. Pl. 77, cr. 4.

SKEA, Sco., an arm, erect, grasping a club, ppr. Pl. 123, cr. 10.

SKEARNE, Eng., on a tower, a lion, rampant, both ar. Pl. 121, cr. 5.

SKEARNE, or SKERNE, Linc. and Yorks., on a tower, or, a lion, couchant, ar. Pl. 96, cr. 5, (tower, pl. 121, cr. 5.)

SKEEN, Sco., a dexter arm, from shoulder, issuing from a cloud, holding forth a triumphal crown or garland, ppr. *Virtutis regia merces.* Pl. 80, cr. 3.

SKEEN, Sco., a dexter hand, ppr., holding a dagger, ar., hilt and pommel, or. *Virtutis.* Pl. 28, cr. 4.

SKEEN, Sco., a garb, ppr. *Assiduitate.* Pl. 48, cr. 10.

SKEEN, Sco., a birch-tree, environed with stalks of oats, all growing out of a mount, ppr. *Sub montibus altis.* Pl. 4, cr. 5, (birch, pl. 18, cr. 10.)

SKEEN, a wolf's head, (couped.) *Virtutis regia merces.* Pl. 14, cr. 6.

SKEEN, Sco., a hand holding a dagger, ar., hilt and pommel, or, surmounted of a wolf's head. *Virtutis regia merces.* Pl. 96, cr. 11.

SKEEN, Sco., a dexter hand holding a garland, ppr. *Gratis a Deo data.* Pl. 41, cr. 7.

SKEEN, Sco., a hand holding a laurel-crown, ppr. *Sors mihi grata cadet.* Pl. 86, cr. 1.

SKEEN, Sco., a hand holding a sword, in pale, on the point a wolf's head, couped close by the scalp, all ppr. *Virtutis regia merces.* Pl. 96, cr. 11.

SKEFFINGHAM, Eng. and Iri., a mermaid, ppr. *Augusta ad augusta.* Pl. 48, cr. 5.

SKEFFINGTON, Lanc., a mermaid, ppr., the mirror, comb, hair, and tip of the tail, or. Pl. 48, cr. 5.

SKEFFINGTON, Eng., a mermaid, with comb and mirror, all ppr. Pl. 48, cr. 5.

SKEFFINGTON, Bart., Leic., a mermaid, ppr., comb, mirror, and fins, or. Pl. 48, cr. 5.

SKEFFINGTON-FOSTER, Viscount Massareene. *See* MASSAREENE.

SKEFFINGTON-FOSTER, Viscount Ferrard. *See* FERRARD.

SKEGES, Hunts., a demi-peacock, az., (wings expanded,) or, beaked and combed, gold. Pl. 53, cr. 12, (without serpent.)

SKELMERSDALE, Baron, (Bootle-Wilbraham :) 1. For *Wilbraham*, a wolf's head, erased, ar. Pl. 14, cr. 6. 2. For *Bootle*, a demi-lion, rampant, regardant, ppr., (holding between paws an antique oval shield, gu., rimmed, or, charged with a cross patonce, ar.) *In portu quies.* Pl. 33, cr. 2.

SKELTON, Cambs., Cumb., and Yorks., a bird's head, erased, sa., in beak an acorn, or, stalked and leaved, vert. Pl. 22, cr. 1.

SKELTON, Devons., out of a ducal coronet, az., a horse's head, ar. Pl. 50, cr. 13.

SKENE, Sco., a dexter arm, embowed, issuing from a cloud, hand holding a triumphal crown, ppr. *Virtutis regia merces.* Pl. 80, cr. 3.

SKENE, JAMES, Esq., of Rubislaw, Aberdeen, out of a cloud, a dexter arm, from shoulder, in hand a garland, ppr. *Gratis a Deo data.* Pl. 80, cr. 3.

SKENE, Sco., out of a cloud, a naked arm, in pale, hand holding a garland of laurel, all ppr. *Virtutis regia merces.* *Pl.* 88, *cr.* 13.

SKENE, Eng., a hart's head, couped, or. *Pl.* 91, *cr.* 14.

SKEPPER, Durh., a lion's gamb, erect, or, grasping three roses, gold, stalked and leaved, vert. *Pl.* 86, *cr.* 15.

SKERES, Yorks., a demi-lion, rampant, sa., in dexter (three oak-leaves, vert.) *Pl.* 39, *cr.* 14.

SKEENE, Eng., on a tower, ar., a lion, rampant, of the last. *Pl.* 121, *cr.* 5.

SKERRET, Eng., an heraldic-tiger, passant, gu. *Pl.* 7, *cr.* 5.

SKERRITT, WILLIAM-JOSEPH, Esq., of Finavara, co. Clare, a squirrel, sejant, ppr. *Primus ultimusque in acie.* *Pl.* 16, *cr.* 9.

SKETTEW, a cubit arm, erect, hand holding up an etoile. *Pl.* 62, *cr.* 13, (etoile, *pl.* 141.)

SKEVINGTON, Eng., a mermaid, ppr., comb and mirror, or. *Pl.* 48, *cr.* 5.

SKEWSE, Cornw., a wolf, passant, ppr., collared, (on body six stars, or.) *Pl.* 5, *cr.* 8, (without staff.)

SKEY, Eng., a dove, regardant, in mouth an olive-branch. *Pl.* 77, *cr.* 2.

SKIDDY, Iri., out of a ducal coronet, a bull's foot, hoof upward. *Pl.* 38, *cr.* 11, (foot, *pl.* 6, *cr.* 14.)

SKIDDY, Iri., out of a ducal coronet, a horse's leg and foot, in pale. *Pl.* 38, *cr.* 11.

SKIDDY, out of a ducal coronet, a bear's paw, (middle toe, couped.) *Pl.* 67, *cr.* 7, (paw, *pl.* 126, *cr.* 2.)

SKIDMORE, Eng., a unicorn's head, erased, sa., plattée. *Pl.* 67, *cr.* 1.

SKIFFINGTON, Eng., a mermaid. *Pl.* 48, *cr.* 5.

SKILLICOME, Eng., a raven's head, erased, ppr. *Pl.* 27, *cr.* 13.

SKILLING, Wilts. and Hants, a greyhound, current, or, (collared and lined, sa.) *Pl.* 28, *cr.* 7.

SKINNER, a griffin's head, erased, ar., in mouth a dexter hand, couped at wrist, gu. *Pl.* 48, *cr.* 6, (hand, *pl.* 106, *cr.* 13.)

SKINNER, Devons., out of a ducal coronet, or, a demi-talbot, gu., collared and lined, ar. *Pl.* 3, *cr.* 8, (demi, *pl.* 15, *cr.* 2.)

SKINNER, Heref., a griffin's head, erased, ar., in mouth a hand, couped, gu., (charged on breast with a mullet.) *Pl.* 48, *cr.* 6, (hand, *pl.* 106, *cr.* 13.)

SKINNER, Sco., a lion's head, erased, crowned with an antique crown, ppr. *Nunquam non paratus.* *Pl.* 81, *cr.* 4, (crown, *pl.* 79, *cr.* 12.)

SKIPPE, Heref., a demi-lion, or, in dexter a rose, gu. *Pl.* 39, *cr.* 14.

SKIPTON, Eng., on a mural coronet, a stag, sejant, ppr. *Pl.* 101, *cr.* 3.

SKIPTON, of Ballyshasky, Iri., an armed arm, embowed, in hand, naked, a dagger, all ppr. *Pl.* 34, *cr.* 7.

SKIPWITH, Norf., Linc., Warw., and Leic., a turnpike, or. *Pl.* 73, *cr.* 4.

SKIPWITH, a griffin's head, erased, per fess, gu. and or, guttée, counterchanged, in beak a lion's paw, couped, erm. *Pl.* 9, *cr.* 12, (paw, *pl.* 94, *cr.* 13.)

SKIPWITH, on a mount, vert, a turnpike, ar. *Pl.* 73, *cr.* 4.

SKIPWITH, Bart., Leic., a reel, ppr.

SKIPWORTH, a reel, or turn-stile, ppr. *Sans Dieu je ne puis.*

SKIRVIN, Sco., a hand holding a buckle, ppr. *Fit inde firmior.* *Pl.* 38, *cr.* 9.

SKORY, Cornw. and Heref., out of a ducal coronet, a demi-eagle, wings expanded, or. *Pl.* 9, *cr.* 6.

SKOTTOW, Lond., a lion's head, erased, ar., collared, gu. *Pl.* 7, *cr.* 10.

SKOTTOWE, Eng., a wolf's head, erm. *Pl.* 14, *cr.* 6.

SKRIMPSHIRE, a demi-man, in armour, in dexter a sword, (in sinister a shield.) *Pl.* 23, *cr.* 4.

SKRINE, Somers. and Suss., a tower, ar., on the battlements a lion, couchant, erm., ducally crowned, or. *Pl.* 121, *cr.* 5.

SKULL, an heraldic-tiger, passant, per pale, gu. and erm. *Pl.* 7, *cr.* 5.

SKYNNER, Lond., Warw., and Worc., a griffin's head, erased, ar., (another, ppr.,) in mouth a gauntlet, or. *Pl.* 48, *cr.* 6, (gauntlet, *pl.* 61, *cr.* 8.)

SKYNNER, of Thornton and Boston, Linc., on a ducal coronet, ar., a falcon, of the last, beaked and legged, gu. *Pl.* 41, *cr.* 10.

SKYRME, Eng., a deer's head, cabossed, or. *Pl.* 36, *cr.* 1.

SKYRNE, Eng., on a tower, ar., a lion, rampant, of the last. *Pl.* 121, *cr.* 5.

SLACK, Eng., a bridge of three arches, ppr. *Pl.* 38, *cr.* 4.

SLADDEN, Eng., a unicorn's head, az. *Pl.* 20, *cr.* 1.

SLADE, Eng., a hart, at gaze, ppr. *Pl.* 81, *cr.* 8.

SLADE, or SLADER, Beds., Hunts., and Northamp., a horse's head, erased, sa. *Pl.* 81, *cr.* 6.

SLADE, Iri., a lion's head, erased, gu., pierced by (an arrow,) ppr. *Pl.* 113, *cr.* 15.

SLADE, Cornw., a lion's gamb, erased, holding (three) ostrich-feathers. *Pl.* 58, *cr.* 7.

SLADE, Bart., Somers., on a mount, vert, a horse's head, erased, sa., encircled by a chain in the form of an arch, gold. *Fidus et audax.* *Pl.* 81, *cr.* 4, (chain, *pl.* 28, *cr.* 12.)

SLADEN, a mount, vert, thereon, between two branches of palm, ppr., a lion's gamb, erect and erased, sa., holding a plume of five ostrich-feathers, gu. *Vive ut vivas.*

SLADER, Kent, a lion's gamb, erect and erased, or, holding (five) ostrich-feathers, three ar. and two az. *Pl.* 58, *cr.* 7.

SLANING, Devons., a demi-lion, rampant, as., collared, or. *Pl.* 18, *cr.* 13.

SLANNING, a demi-lion, az., collared, gu. *Pl.* 18, *cr.* 13.

SLANY, Lond. and Staffs., a griffin's head, ppr., (wings addorsed,) or, beaked, gold. *Pl.* 65, *cr.* 1.

SLANY, or SLANEY, Lond. and Staffs., a griffin's head, ppr., (wings addorsed,) or, beaked, gold. *Pl.* 65, *cr.* 1.

SLATER, Middx., a lion, passant, gardant, ppr. *Pl.* 120, *cr.* 5.

SLATER, out of a ducal coronet, a demi-eagle, wings expanded. *Pl.* 9, *cr.* 6.

SLATER, a cubit arm, in armour, erect, in gauntlet a dagger, all ppr. *Pl.* 125, *cr.* 5.

SLATER, Eng., a cock, crowing, gu. *Pl.* 67, *cr.* 14.

SLATER, an arm, in armour, couped below wrist, in gauntlet, a sword, all ppr., hilt and pommel, or. *Pl.* 125, *cr.* 5.

SLATER, ADAM-BARKER, of Durant Hall, Chesterfield, a gauntlet, ppr. *Crescit sub pondere virtus. Pl.* 15, *cr.* 15.

SLAUGHTER, Glouc., out of a ducal coronet, or, an eagle's head, between wings, az., beaked, gold. *Pl.* 66, *cr.* 5.

SLAUGHTER, Worc., a falcon, wings expanded. *Pl.* 105, *cr.* 4.

SLAUGHTER, Heref., out of a ducal coronet, or, an eagle's head, ar., wings addorsed, sa. *Pl.* 19, *cr.* 9.

SLAUTER, a monkey's head, ppr. *Pl.* 11, *cr.* 7.

SLAYER, Somers, a stag's head, erased, or, (in mouth an arrow, ar.) *Pl.* 66, *cr.* 9.

SLEATH, Eng., a crane, or. *Pl.* 111, *cr.* 9.

SLEE, Eng. a chapeau, sa., with a plume of three ostrich-feathers in front. *Pl.* 28, *cr.* 1.

SLEFORD, Linc., a mermaid, ppr. *Pl.* 48, *cr.* 5.

SLEGGE, Cambs., a demi-griffin, segreant, erm., wings addorsed, or, legs, ar., holding a sceptre, of the first. *Pl.* 49, *cr.* 4, (sceptre, *pl.* 82, *cr.* 3.)

SLEGGS, Hunts., a demi-peacock, displayed, az. *Pl.* 50, *cr.* 9, (without snake.)

SLEIGH, Sco., an eagle's head, erased, sa., beaked, gu. *Unalterable. Pl.* 20, *cr.* 7.

SLEIGH, a demi-lion, rampant, ar., holding a cross crosslet, fitched, or, (ducally crowned, gold.) *Pl.* 65, *cr.* 6.

SLEIGH, Derbs. and Lond., an arm, erect, vested, vert, in hand, ppr., a cinquefoil, slipped. *Pl.* 101, *cr.* 5.

SLESSER, Sco., a dexter arm, brandishing a spear, all ppr. *Spectemur agendo. Pl.* 99, *cr.* 8.

SLEY, Iri., a cubit arm, vested, erm., in hand a broken sword. *Pl.* 22, *cr.* 6, (without cloud.)

SLEY, Derbs., a demi-lion, rampant, erm., (ducally crowned, or,) holding a cross crosslet, fitched, gold. *Pl.* 65, *cr.* 6.

SLIGO, Marquess of, Earl of Altamont, Viscount Westport, and Baron Monteagle, Iri., and Baron Monteagle, U.K., (Browne,) an eagle, displayed, vert. *Suivez la raison. Pl.* 48, *cr.* 11.

SLINGSBY, Yorks. and Bucks., a lion, passant, vert. *Pl.* 48, *cr.* 8.

SLINGSBY, Eng., a Cornish chough, ppr. *Pl.* 100, *cr.* 13.

SLINGSBY, Bart., Yorks., a lion, passant, vert. *Veritas liberavit. Pl.* 48, *cr.* 8.

SLOAN, Sco., a lion, rampant, ppr. *Vi et veritate. Pl.* 67, *cr.* 5.

SLOAN, Eng., an eagle, displayed, ppr. *Pl.* 48, *cr.* 11.

SLOANE, Middx. and Iri., a lion's head, erased, or, collared, (with mascles interlaced,) sa. *Pl.* 7, *cr.* 10.

SLOCOMBE, Somers., a griffin's head, gu., between wings, or. *Pl.* 65, *cr.* 1.

SLOPER, Kent, on (two) snakes, entwined together, ppr., a dove, statant, ar., bearing an olive-branch, vert. *Pl.* 3, *cr.* 4, (branch, *pl.* 48, *cr.* 15.)

SLOPER, Wilts., over a rock, ppr., a dove, volant, ar., guttée-de-sang, in beak an olive-branch, vert. *Pacis. Pl.* 85, *cr.* 14, (dove, *pl.* 25, *cr.* 6.)

SLOPER, a boar's head, or, (pierced through neck by a dart.) *Pl.* 2, *cr.* 7.

SLOUGH, Eng., a stork's head, erased. *Pl.* 32, *cr.* 5.

SLY, Eng., a dove, az. *Pl.* 66, *cr.* 12.

SMACHEY, a lion, rampant, erm., (crowned, or,) holding a cross pattée, fitched. *Pl.* 125, *cr.* 2.

SMAIL, Sco., an eagle, rising, ppr. *Pl.* 67, *cr.* 4.

SMALE, and SMALLEY, on a chapeau, gu., turned up, erm., a unicorn, couchant, ar., (another, the unicorn, sejant.)

SMALL, Sco., a branch of palm, ppr. *Ratione, non ira. Pl.* 123, *cr.* 1.

SMALL, on a chess-rook, ar., a wren, ppr.

SMALLBONES, Eng., a Cornish chough, ppr. *Pl.* 100, *cr.* 13.

SMALLBROOK, Eng., a cock's head, erased, or. *Pl.* 92, *cr.* 3.

SMALLBROOK, a martlet, wings displayed. *Pl.* 111, *cr.* 5.

SMALLMAN, Eng., a hand, gauntleted, holding a sword, in pale, ppr. *Pl.* 125, *cr.* 5.

SMALLMAN, Herts., Heref., and Salop, an heraldic-antelope, sejant, (holding up dexter paw,) sa., horns and tail, or, gorged with a ducal coronet and line, of the last. *Pl.* 115, *cr.* 3.

SMALLMAN, Salop, same crest. *My word is my bond.*

SMALLPAGE, Lond. and Yorks., an antelope, ar., supporting a broken spear, or, the head downward. *Pl.* 63, *cr.* 10, (spear, *pl.* 60, *cr.* 4.)

SMALLPECE, SMALPECE, or SMALLPIECE, Eng., a wolf's head, erased, per fess, embattled, ar. and sa. *Pl.* 14, *cr.* 6.

SMALLPIECE, Salop and Norf., an eagle, rising, ar. *Pl.* 67, *cr.* 4.

SMALLWOOD, a cubit arm, vested, chequy, ar. and sa., in hand, ppr., a chaplet of oak, vert, fructed, or. *Pl.* 44, *cr.* 13, (oak, *pl.* 74, *cr.* 7.)

SMART, Sco., a pheon, sa. *Pl.* 26, *cr.* 12.

SMART, Eng., an ostrich's head, between two palm-branches, ppr. *Pl.* 49, *cr.* 7.

SMART, Sco., a hand throwing a dart. *Ettle weel. Pl.* 42, *cr.* 13.

SMART, Sco., a boar's head, erased, sa. *Vincet virtute. Pl.* 16, *cr.* 11.

SMART, Lond. and Sco., a demi-eagle, rising, wings displayed, ar., (in beak a flower of the burdock,) ppr. *Pl.* 52, *cr.* 8.

SMART, Lond. and Sco., an eagle's head, between wings, or, (in beak a thistle, slipped and leaved, ppr.) *Pl.* 81, *cr.* 10.

SMART, Lond., a hawk's head, between wings, ar., (in beak a thistle, ppr.) *Pl.* 99, *cr.* 10.

SMEDLY, Eng., an eagle's head, erased, sa. *Pl.* 20, *cr.* 7.

SMELLET, Sco., stump of oak-tree shooting a green branch, on each side, ppr. *Viresco. Pl.* 92, *cr.* 8.

SMELLIE, Lond. and Sco., a dexter hand holding a crescent, ppr. *Industria, virtus, et fortitudine. Pl.* 38, *cr.* 7.

SMERDON, Devons., in lion's paw, erased, a battle-axe, or. *Vincit qui patitur. Pl.* 51, *cr.* 13.

SMERT, Cornw., a beaver's head, erased, ar., (collared, in mouth a branch, vert.) *Pl.* 126, *cr.* 14.

SMETHAM, out of a ducal coronet, or, a demi-dragon, rampant, ppr. *Pl.* 59, *cr.* 14, (demi, *pl.* 82, *cr.* 10.)

SMITHWICKE, Chesb., an arm, embowed, vested, ar., charged with two bars, wavy, vert, cuffed, of the first, in hand, ppr., a tulip, or, leaved, of the second. *Pl.* 39, *cr.* 1, (tulip, *pl.* 64, *cr.* 2.)

SMIGHT, Bart., Ess., a salamander in flames, ppr. *Pl.* 20, *cr.* 15.

SMINEEN, Leic. and Staffs., a boar's head, couped, sa. *Pl.* 48, *cr.* 2.

SMINFEN, Leic. and Staffs., a boar's head, couped, sa. *Pl.* 48, *cr.* 2.

SMIRKE, on an antique steel helmet, mantled, as the arms, fringed and tasselled, or, a wreath of the colours encircling the head-piece, thereon a falcon, wings addorsed and distended, preying on a serpent, all ppr.

SMITH, an eagle, rising, ppr. *Pl.* 67, *cr.* 4.

SMITH, Surr., a stag's head, erased, gu., attired, ar. *Pl.* 66, *cr.* 9.

SMITH, Derbs., an escallop, party per fess, or and az. *Pl.* 117, *cr.* 4.

SMITH, Lanc., an ostrich, or, in mouth a horse-shoe, ar. *Pl.* 16, *cr.* 2.

SMITH, Eng. and Sco., an arm, couped below wrist, hand holding a pen between the finger and thumb, all ppr. *Pl.* 26, *cr.* 13.

SMITH, Lond., a talbot, passant, party per pale, or and sa. *Pl.* 120, *cr.* 8.

SMITH, Notts., an elephant's head, couped, or. *Tenax in fide.* *Pl.* 35, *cr.* 15.

SMITH, Sco., a dolphin, haurient, ppr. *Mediis tranquillus in undis.* *Pl.* 14, *cr.* 10.

SMITH, Somers., a griffin's head, erased, gu., charged on neck with two bars, or, beaked and eared, gold. *Quid capit, capitur.* *Pl.* 48, *cr.* 6.

SMITH, Notts., an elephant's head, couped, or, charged on neck with three fleurs-de-lis, sa., two and one. *Tenax in fide.* *Pl.* 35, *cr.* 13, (fleur-de-lis, *pl.* 141.)

SMITH, Sco., an anchor, erect, or, the stock, sa. *Sine sanguine victor.* *Pl.* 25, *cr.* 15.

SMITH, Sco., a dexter hand holding a writing-pen, ppr. *Ex usu commodium.* *Pl.* 26, *cr.* 13.

SMITH, Sco., a minerva's head, ppr. *Non in vita.* *Pl.* 92, *cr.* 12.

SMITH, Sco., a flame, between two twigs of palm, ppr. *Luceo, non uro.* *Pl.* 62, *cr.* 6.

SMITH, Sco., a crescent, az. *Cum plena magis.* *Pl.* 18, *cr.* 14.

SMITH, Eng., two arms, armed, couped above elbow, ppr., holding a sword in both hands, crossways, ar., pommel, or. *Pl.* 3, *cr.* 5, (armour, *pl.* 41, *cr.* 2.)

SMITH, Eng., an eagle's head, or, (depressed with two bends, vert,) winged, one ar., the other, sa., beaked, gu. *Pl.* 100, *cr.* 10.

SMITH, Sco., a sword and pen in saltier, ppr. *Marte et ingenio.* *Pl.* 49, *cr.* 12.

SMITH, Lond., an ostrich's head, ppr., quarterly, ar. and sa., between two ostrich-feathers, of the first, in mouth a horse-shoe, or. *Pl.* 99, *cr.* 12.

SMITH, a hand grasping a dagger. *Ready.* *Pl.* 28, *cr.* 4.

SMITH, Sco., an anchor, ppr. *Hold fast.* *Pl.* 25, *cr.* 15.

SMITH, Sco., a dolphin, haurient. *Mediis tranquillus in undis.* *Pl.* 14, *cr.* 10.

SMITH, an elephant's head. *Tenax et fidelis.* *Pl.* 35, *cr.* 13.

SMITH, Iri., a martlet, sa. *Pl.* 111, *cr.* 5.

SMITH, a dolphin, haurient, arondée, ppr. *Mediis tranquillus in undis.* *Pl.* 14, *cr.* 10.

SMITH, Wilts., a greyhound, current. *Pl.* 28, *cr.* 7, (without charge.)

SMITH, Sco. and Lond., an arm from shoulder, in armour, brandishing a sword, ppr. *Carid nam fecham.* *Pl.* 2, *cr.* 8.

SMITH, a heron's head, erased, in beak a (fish,) ppr. *Pl.* 41, *cr.* 6.

SMITH, Sco., a dexter hand holding a hammer, ppr. *Semper paratus.* *Pl.* 93, *cr.* 5.

SMITH, Sco., a dexter hand, in fess, issuing from a cloud in sinister, and holding a pen, all ppr. *Floret qui vigilat.* *Pl.* 73, *cr.* 11, (pen, *pl.* 26, *cr.* 13.)

SMITH, Sco., a (broken) sword and pen, in saltier, all ppr. *Pl.* 49, *cr.* 12.

SMITH, a peacock's head, erased, (ducally) gorged, or. *Pl.* 69, *cr.* 5.

SMITH, a leopard's head, (erased,) ar., spotted, sa., collared, lined, and ringed, or. *Pl.* 40, *cr.* 10.

SMITH, out of a ducal coronet, or, a dove, rising, ar. *Pl.* 55, *cr.* 11, (coronet, *same plate.*)

SMITH, a stag's head, erased, gu. *Pl.* 66, *cr.* 9.

SMITH, a phœnix's head, or, in flames, ppr. *Pl.* 112, *cr.* 7.

SMITH, a plume of (five) feathers. *Pl.* 12, *cr.* 9.

SMITH, out of a mural coronet, an ostrich's head, ar. *Pl.* 64, *cr.* 3, (head, *pl.* 49, *cr.* 7.)

SMITH, a fleur-de-lis, per pale, or and gu. *Pl.* 68, *cr.* 12.

SMITH, a hand, ppr., vested, chequy, ar. and az., holding three arrows, two in saltier and one in pale, or, feathered and headed, ar. *Pl.* 95, *cr.* 9, (arrows, *pl.* 9, *cr.* 4.)

SMITH, a dragon's head, erased, or, pellettée. *Pl.* 107, *cr.* 10.

SMITH, (on a mount, vert,) a talbot, sejant, erm., collared. *Pl.* 107, *cr.* 7.

SMITH, Worc., a demi-ostrich, ar., wings expanded, gu., in mouth a horse-shoe, or. *Pl.* 29, *cr.* 9, (shoe, *pl.* 28, *cr.* 13.)

SMITH, Yorks., out of a ducal coronet, or, a boar's head, az., tusked and crined, of the second, langued, gu. *Pl.* 102, *cr.* 14.

SMITH, Norf., an eagle, regardant, wings elevated, ppr., beaked, membered, and (crowned with a naval coronet, or, resting dexter on a quadrant, of the last, the string and plummet, az.) *Pl.* 87, *cr.* 5.

SMITH, Notts., an elephant's head, erased, or, eared, gu., charged on neck with three fleurs-de-lis, az., two and one. *Pl.* 68, *cr.* 4, (fleur-de-lis, *pl.* 141.)

SMITH, Northumb., an elephant, ppr. *Pl.* 56, *cr.* 14.

SMITH, Somers., a heron's head, per fess, or and gu., in beak a (dart, gold, flighted, ppr., barbed, of the second.) *Pl.* 41, *cr.* 6.

SMITH, Suff., a dexter arm, in armour, ppr., garnished, or, in hand, of the first, a chaplet, vert. *Pl.* 68, *cr.* 1.

SMITH, or SMYTH, Suss. and Suff., out of a mural coronet, an ostrich's head, or. *Pl.* 64, *cr.* 3, (head, *pl.* 49, *cr.* 7.)

SMITH, Suss., a demi-unicorn, gu., maned, horned, unguled, and tufted, ar., holding a lozenge, or. *Pl.* 128, *cr.* 3.

SMITH, Surr., a greyhound, couchant, or, collared and lined, sa. *Pl.* 6, *cr.* 7.

SMITH, Surr., out of a ducal coronet, a demi-bull. *Pl.* 63, *cr.* 6.

SMITH, Suss., an arm, in armour, embowed, ppr., charged with an escallop, or, in hand, of the first, a sword, ar., hilt and pommel, of the second, the blade environed with a chaplet of laurel, vert. *Pl.* 2, *cr.* 8, (garland, *pl.* 56, *cr.* 6.)

SMITH, Leic., Linc., and Middx., out of a ducal coronet, or, an Indian goat's head, ar., eared, sa., beard and attires, gold. *Pl.* 72, *cr.* 2.

SMITH, Lond., two arms, embowed, vested, az., cuffed, ar., holding in the hands, ppr., a pheon, or. *Pl.* 10, *cr.* 9, (pheon, *pl.* 26, *cr.* 12.)

SMITH, Lond., a tiger, sejant, ar., tufted and maned, or, (resting dexter on a broken pillar, gold.) *Pl.* 26, *cr.* 9.

SMITH, Lond., an arm, in pale, vested, az., cuffed, ar., in hand, ppr., three acorn-branches, vert, fructed, or. *Pl.* 64, *cr.* 7, (acorns, *pl.* 69, *cr.* 12.)

SMITH, Lond., an ostrich, ar., in mouth a horse-shoe, all ppr. *Pl.* 16, *cr.* 2.

SMITH, or SMYTH, Lond., an ostrich's head, couped, in mouth a horse-shoe, all ppr. *Pl.* 99, *cr.* 12, (without wings.)

SMITH, Middx., a sword, in pale, point upward, (entwined with an ivy-branch,) ppr. *Pl.* 105, *cr.* 1.

SMITH, Kent and Northamp., a talbot's head, couped, gu., charged on neck with a cinquefoil, erm. *Pl.* 123, *cr.* 15, (cinquefoil, *pl.* 141.)

SMITH, a demi-lion, rampant, supporting a (smith's hammer,) all ppr. *Pl.* 47, *cr.* 4.

SMITH, a talbot, statant, ppr., collared, (a chain reflexed over back,) or. *Pl.* 65, *cr.* 2.

SMITH, Glouc., a saltier, gu., surmounted of a fleur-de-lis. *Pl.* 68, *cr.* 12, (saltier, *pl.* 25, *cr.* 5.)

SMITH, Glouc., a cross, gu., surmounted of a fleur-de-lis, ar. *Ib.*

SMITH, Herts., an elephant's head, erased, or, on neck three fleurs-de-lis, sa., one and two. *Pl.* 68, *cr.* 4, (fleur-de-lis, *pl.* 141.)

SMITH, Lond. and Lanc., out of a mural coronet, ar., an ostrich's head, of the last. *Pl.* 64, *cr.* 3, (head, *pl.* 49, *cr.* 7.)

SMITH, Ess., a talbot, statant, sa., collared, and chain reflexed over back, or. *Pl.* 65, *cr.* 2.

SMITH, Derbs., an escallop, per fess, or and az. *Pl.* 117, *cr.* 4.

SMITH, Devons., a greyhound, sejant, gu., (collared, and line reflexed over back,) or. *Pl.* 66, *cr.* 15.

SMITH, Durh., a dexter arm, embowed, erminois, cuffed, ar., hand grasping a broken sword, ppr., hilt, or. *Pl.* 44, *cr.* 4, (without rays.)

SMITH, Durh., a stork, ar., (rising from a mount, vert,) beaked and legged, gu., in beak a serpent, ppr. *Pl.* 59, *cr.* 11.

SMITH, Ess., an arm, couped at elbow, and erect, vested, gu., cuffed, ar., in hand, p. r., a cross formée, sa. *Pl.* 75, *cr.* 3, (cross, *pl.* 15, *cr.* 8.)

SMITH, of Rowchester, Kent, a sword, in pale, hilted, or, (entwined with two ivy-branches, gold.) *Rapit ense triumphos. Pl.* 105, *cr.* 1.

SMITH, Bucks., a heron's head, erased, in beak a (fish,) ppr. *Pl.* 32, *cr.* 5.

SMITH, Bart., Northumb., a sinister hand, erect, apaumée, couped at wrist, gu., the wrist encircled with a wreath of oak, or, (the palm charged with a trefoil, slipped, ar.,) on an escroll, above, the word, "Canada." *Pro rege et patria. Pl.* 74, *cr.* 8, (wreath, *pl.* 93, *cr.* 1.)

SMITH, Bart., Herts., between a pen, in bend, or, feathered, ar., surmounted by a sword, ppr., hilt and pommel, gold, (an escutcheon, az., charged with an escallop, of the first, pendent by a ribbon, gu.) *Marte et ingenio. Pl.* 49, *cr.* 12.

SMITH, Bart., Worc., a greyhound, couchant, sa., (collared, and line reflexed over back, or,) the body charged with a cross crosslet, of the last, dexter resting on a cross flory, gold. *Pl.* 6, *cr.* 7, (crosses, *pl.* 141.)

SMITH, Bart., Middx., a falcon, wings addorsed, ppr., belled, or, in beak an acorn, slipped and leaved, also ppr. *Spes, decus, et robur. Pl.* 60, *cr.* 8.

SMITH, Bart., Iri., in a ducal coronet, a unicorn's head, az., armed, gold. *En Dieu est mon espoir. Pl.* 45, *cr.* 14.

SMITH, Bart., Dors., a greyhound, sejant, gu., (collared, and line reflexed over back, or,) charged on shoulder with a mascle, ar. *Semper fidelis. Pl.* 66, *cr.* 15, (mascle, *pl.* 141.)

SMITH, Baron Carrington. *See* CARRINGTON.

SMITH, CHARLES-HERVEY, Esq., of Aspley House, Beds., an oak-tree, ppr., fructed, gold. *Non deficit alter. Pl.* 16, *cr.* 8.

SMITH, HENRY-JEREMIAH, Esq., of Beabeg, co. Meath, a demi-bull, salient, az., armed and unguled, or. *Delectat amor patriæ. Pl.* 63, *cr.* 6.

SMITH, Lieut.-General Sir LIONEL, Bart.: 1. *Of augmentation*, a representation of the ornamental centre-piece of the service of plate presented to Sir Lionel by his European and native friends at Bombay, all ppr. 2. Out of an Eastern crown, or, a dexter arm, in armour, embowed, encircled by a wreath of laurel, in hand a broken sword, all ppr. *Mea spes est in Deo.*

SMITH, Lanc., on a mount, vert, a squirrel, sejant, ar., (in paws a marigold, slipped, charged on body with a fountain, ppr.) *Pl.* 2, *cr.* 4, (mount, *pl.* 98, *cr.* 13.)

SMITH, of Ryhope, Durh.; and Carrowborough, Northumb., (on a mount, vert,) a stork, wings elevated, ar., charged on breast and on either wing with a cross crosslet, gu., in beak a snake, ppr. *Pl.* 59, *cr.* 11, (cross, *pl.* 141.)

SMITH, of Holesowen Grange, Salop, a unicorn, ar., guttée-de-poix, gorged with a double tressure, fleury, and counter-fleury, gu. *Pl.* 106, *cr.* 3.

SMITH, Jordan Hill, Renfrew, an eagle's head, erased, ducally gorged, ppr. *Pl.* 39, *cr.* 4, (without pheon.)

SMITH, TAYLOR-SMITH, of Colpike Hall, Durh.: 1. For *Smith*, a stag, lodged, ar., (semée of etoiles, az., attired and gorged with an Eastern crown, chain reflexed over back, or.) *Pl.* 67, *cr.* 2. 2. For *Taylor*, a horse's head, couped, sa., gorged with a plain collar, pendent therefrom a shield, ar., charged with a cinquefoil, vert. *Vigilans.*

SMITH, Chesh., an ostrich, ar., in mouth a horse-shoe, or. *Pl.* 16, *cr.* 2.
SMITHER, Eng., a hawk's head, erased, ppr. *Pl.* 34, *cr.* 11.
SMITHERMAN, a stork, or, (charged on neck with two bars-gemelle, sa., and gorged with a ducal coronet, gu.) *Pl.* 33, *cr.* 9.
SMITHERS, Eng., an eagle's head, gu. *Pl.* 100, *cr.* 10.
SMITHESBY, Iri., a wolf's head, (erased,) ar., collared with a belt, gu., buckle, or. *Pl.* 8, *cr.* 4.
SMITHSON, a squirrel, sejant, cracking a nut, ppr. *Pl.* 16, *cr.* 9.
SHITHWICK, Herts., an arm, embowed, vested, (bendy of six,) engrailed, vert and ar., cuffed, of the last, in hand a rose, all ppr. *Pl.* 39, *cr.* 1, (rose, *pl.* 118, *cr.* 9.)
SMOLLET, stump of oak-tree, shooting young branches, ppr. *Viresco. Pl.* 92, *cr.* 8.
SMOLLETT, ALEXANDER, Esq., of Bonhill, Dumbarton, an oak-tree, ppr. *Viresco. Pl.* 16, *cr.* 8.
SMYLY, Iri., out of a mural coronet, or, a dexter arm, in armour, embowed, ppr., holding a pheon, in pale, gu. *Pl.* 115, *cr.* 14, (pheon, *pl.* 123, *cr.* 12.)
SMYTH, Ess., out of a ducal coronet, per pale, or and gu., a plume of feathers, ar. and vert. *Pl.* 44, *cr.* 12.
SMYTH, Hants and Ess., a demi-wild man, ppr., (in hand a bunch of barley, vert, and wreathed round temples, of the same.) *Pl.* 35, *cr.* 12.
SMYTH, Kent, out of a ducal coronet, per pale, or and gu., a plume of five ostrich-feathers, three vert and two ar. *Pl.* 100, *cr.* 12.
SMYTH, Wilts. and Somers., a stag, or, attired, ar. *Pl.* 88, *cr.* 9.
SMYTH, Yorks., out of a ducal coronet, or, a demi-bull, salient, ar., attired, gold. *Pl.* 63, *cr.* 6, (coronet, *pl.* 128, *fig.* 3.)
SMYTH, Yorks., a unicorn's head, erased, az. *Pl.* 67, *cr.* 1.
SMYTH, Linc., a talbot, passant, or. *Pl.* 120, *cr.* 8.
SMYTH, Northamp. and Middx., a cubit arm, erect, (vested, per pale, or and gu.,) hand, ppr., grasping a griffin's head, erased, az. *Pl.* 94, *cr.* 6.
SMYTH, Eng., an arm, erect, (vested, per pale, or and az., cuff, ar.,) in hand, ppr., a griffin's head, erased, of the second. *Pl.* 94, *cr.* 6.
SMYTH, Norf., a peacock's head, erased, ppr. *Pl.* 86, *cr.* 4.
SMYTH, of Newcastle-under-Line, a tiger, passant, ar., (vulned on shoulder, ppr.) *Pl.* 67, *cr.* 15.
SMYTH, Lond. and Chesh., an ostrich, ar., in mouth a horse-shoe, or. *Pl.* 16, *cr.* 2.
SMYTH, Lond., a pegasus, az., wings, gu., ducally gorged and lined, or. *Pl.* 57, *cr.* 15.
SMYTH, Lond., a tiger, erm., armed, maned, and tufted, or. *Pl.* 67, *cr.* 15.
SMYTH, Salop, Notts., Herts., and Heref., a horse's head, sa., bridled, or. *Pl.* 92, *cr.* 1.
SMYTH, Salop, Herts., Notts., and Heref., a horse's head, roan colour, mane, sa., bridle, or. *Pl.* 92, *cr.* 1.
SMYTH, Ess., a salamander in flames, all ppr. *Pl.* 20, *cr.* 15.

SMYTH, Worc. and Ess., an ostrich's head, quarterly, sa. and ar., between wings, gu., in mouth a horse-shoe, or. *Pl.* 28, *cr.* 13.
SMYTH, Iri., a wolf, current, gu. *Pl.* 111, *cr.* 1.
SMYTH, Iri., a dove, regardant, az., in mouth an olive-branch, vert. *Pl.* 77, *cr.* 2.
SMYTH, Sco., a dexter arm, embowed, vambraced, hand holding a sword, ppr. *Carid nam fecham. Pl.* 2, *cr.* 8.
SMYTH, Eng., in a coronet, per pale, or and purp., a plume of feathers, ar. and vert. *Pl.* 44, *cr.* 12.
SMYTH, Iri., a demi-peacock, ppr., (charged with a trefoil, or.) *Pl.* 53, *cr.* 12.
SMYTH, on the top of a pillar, ppr., a sphere, or. *Pl.* 122, *cr.* 4, (sphere, *pl.* 114, *cr.* 6.)
SMYTH, a lion's head, erased, or. *Pl.* 81, *cr.* 4.
SMYTH, on a ducal coronet, vert, two swords, in saltier, ar., hilts, or. *Pl.* 110, *cr.* 2, (swords, *pl.* 75, *cr.* 13.)
SMYTH, Surr., a demi-stag, salient, erm., attired, sa. *Pl.* 55, *cr.* 9, (without rose.)
SMYTH, Suff., a wolf's head, erased, ar., (ducally gorged, or.) *Pl.* 14, *cr.* 6.
SMYTH, Suff., a demi-unicorn, gu., armed and crined, or, supporting a lozenge, gold. *Pl.* 26, *cr.* 14, (lozenge, *pl.* 141.)
SMYTH, Wilts., a peacock's head, ppr., (ducally) gorged, or. *Pl.* 69, *cr.* 5.
SMYTH, Yorks., out of a ducal coronet, gu., a demi-bull, salient, ar., armed, or. *Pl.* 63, *cr.* 6, (coronet, *pl.* 128, *fig.* 3.)
SMYTH, Lond., a tiger, erm., armed, tufted, and maned, or. *Pl.* 67, *cr.* 15.
SMYTH, Lond. and Suss., a dragon's head, erased, or, pellettée. *Pl.* 107, *cr.* 10.
SMYTH, Norf., a horse's head, erased, per cheveron, nebulée, or and sa. *Pl.* 81, *cr.* 6.
SMYTH, Norf., an arm, embowed, ppr., (round wrist a ribbon, az.,) in hand a broken tilting-spear, or. *Pl.* 44, *cr.* 9.
SMYTH, Norf., on a chapeau, gu., turned up, erm., two wings, expanded, az., (each charged with the arms.) *Pl.* 80, *cr.* 15.
SMYTH, Norf., an antelope's head, erased, sa., (collared, gu., rimmed, studded, lined, and ringed, or.) *Pl.* 24, *cr.* 7.
SMYTH, Surr., an arm, in armour, embowed, ppr., in gauntlet a broken tilting-spear, ar. *Pl.* 44, *cr.* 9.
SMYTH, Staffs., a griffin's head, erased, per fess, sa. and gu., (collared, ar.) *Pl.* 69, *cr.* 13.
SMYTH, Staffs., a tiger, passant, ar., (vulned on shoulder, ppr.) *Pl.* 67, *cr.* 15.
SMYTH, Suff., on a chapeau, gu., turned up, erm., two wings, az., billettée, or, on each a bend, erm. *Pl.* 80, *cr.* 15.
SMYTH, Glouc. and Linc., a falcon's head, erased, sa., guttée, or, (in beak a fish, ppr.) *Pl.* 34, *cr.* 11.
SMYTH, Glouc. and Linc., a heron's head, erased, az., in beak a (fish,) ar. *Pl.* 32, *cr.* 5.
SMYTH, Herts. and Heref., an eagle's head, between wings, a., beaked, sa., charged on neck with three pellets. *Pl.* 81, *cr.* 10, (pellet, *pl.* 141.)
SMYTH, Kent, a leopard's head, erased, ar., spotted, sa., collared (and lined,) or. *Pl.* 86, *cr.* 13.
SMYTH, Linc. and Northamp., out of a ducal coronet, or, a demi-falcon, ppr., wings expanded, ar. *Pl.* 103, *cr.* 6.

SMYTH, Devons., an eagle, close, regardant, ppr., beaked and legged, or. *Pl.* 77, *cr.* 13.

SMYTH, Bucks. and Cornw., on a chapeau, gu., turned up, erm., a griffin's head, bezantée, beaked, or. *Pl.* 54, *cr.* 14, (chapeau, *pl.* 127, *fig.* 13.)

SMYTH, Lond., Berks., and Leic., out of a ducal coronet, or, an Indian goat's head, ar., eared, sa., attired, gold. *Pl.* 72, *cr.* 2.

SMYTH, Beds., Ess., Leic., and Warw., a peacock's head, erased, ppr., (ducally) gorged, or. *Pl.* 69, *cr.* 5.

SMYTH, Beds., a leopard's head, ar., pellettée, (murally gorged, lined, and ringed, gu.) *Pl.* 92, *cr.* 13.

SMYTH, Beds., a stag's head, erased, or, on neck three mullets. *Pl.* 66, *cr.* 9, (mullet, *pl.* 141.)

SMYTH, Derbs., on a mount, vert, a tower, triple-towered, or, (on sinister side of the mount a laurel-branch, pendent over the tower, ppr.) *Pl.* 123, *cr.* 14, (mount, *same plate, cr.* 8.)

SMYTH, Bart., Somers., a griffin's head, erased, gu., beak and ears, or, (charged on neck with two bars, gold.) *Qui capit capitur.* *Pl.* 48, *cr.* 6.

SMYTH, ROBERT, Esq., of Gaybrook, co. Westmeath, out of a ducal coronet, or, a unicorn's head, az. *Exaltabit honore.* *Pl.* 45, *cr.* 14.

SMYTH, Herts., a falcon, volant, wings expanded, ppr. *Pl.* 94, *cr.* 1.

SMYTH-BARTELOT, Suss., a swan, ar., couchant, wings expanded. *Pl.* 114, *cr.* 3.

SMYTH-CARMICHAEL, Bart., Surr., a cubit arm, erect, in armour, in hand a broken tilting-lance, the point falling, all ppr. *Toujours pret.* *Pl.* 23, *cr.* 9.

SMYTHE, WILLIAM, Esq., of Methven Castle, Perths., a dolphin, haurient. *Mediis tranquillus in undis.* *Pl.* 14, *cr.* 10.

SMYTHE, of Hilton, Salop, a buffalo's head, ppr. *Pl.* 57, *cr.* 7.

SMYTHE, Eng., three holly-leaves, vert, banded, gu. *Pl.* 78, *cr.* 12.

SMYTHE, Surr., a demi-stag, salient, erm., attired, sa. *Pl.* 55, *cr.* 9.

SMYTHE, Kent, on a mount, vert, a talbot, sejant, erm., eared and collared, sa., ringed, or, (on dexter side of the mount a laurel-branch, of the first.) *Pl.* 107, *cr.* 7, (mount, *pl.* 98, *cr.* 13.)

SMYTHE, Hants., a stag's head, erased, ppr., attired, or, gorged with a chaplet of laurel, vert. *Pl.* 38, *cr.* 1.

SMYTHE, Bart., Durh., a stag's head, gorged with a garland of laurel. *Regi semper fidelis.* *Pl.* 38, *cr.* 1.

SMYTHE, Viscount Strangford. *See* STRANGFORD.

SMYTHIES, Ess., a demi-arm, az., in hand, ppr., an (oak)-branch, leaved and fructed, or. *Pl.* 43, *cr.* 6.

SMYTHSON, Kent, an arm, embowed, vested, ar., hand, ppr., holding a battle-axe, of the first, handle, or. *Pl.* 39, *cr.* 1, (axe, *pl.* 73, *cr.* 7.)

SNAFFORD, Eng., an elephant, passant, or, on back a castle, triple-towered, ar. *Pl.* 114, *cr.* 14.

SNAGG, or SNAGGE, Herts., a demi-goat, erm., attired, or. *Pl.* 11, *cr.* 4, (without gate.)

SNAGG, or SNAGGE, Herts., a demi-antelope, ppr. *Pl.* 75, *cr.* 10.

SNAPE, Eng., between wings, an escallop, ppr. *Pl.* 62, *cr.* 4.

SNAPE, SNAPPE, or SNEPP, Oxon., a buck's head, per pale, or and vert, attires, counterchanged. *Pl.* 91, *cr.* 14.

SNELL, Eng., on a chapeau, ppr., an owl, wings expanded, ar. *Pl.* 123, *cr.* 6.

SNELL, Devons., Glouc., and Wilts., a demi-talbot, rampant, gu., (collared and lined, or.) *Pl.* 15, *cr.* 2.

SNELL, Devons., Glouc., and Wilts., a wolf, preying on a lamb, behind them a cross Calvary, in pale, gu.

SNELLGROVE, Eng., an anchor, sa., entwined with a serpent, vert. *Pl.* 64, *cr.* 9.

SNELLING, Surr., a demi-eagle, displayed, ar. *Pl.* 22, *cr.* 11.

SNELLING, Surr., Suss., and Suff., a griffin's head, or, (collared, gu., studded, gold.) *Pl.* 69, *cr.* 13.

SNELLING, Surr., a demi-dog, rampant, with dragon's wings, addorsed, or.

SNELLING, Dors. and Suss., an arm, embowed, vested, vert, in hand, ppr., a (cutlass, of the second, hilt, or, from the pommel a line round arm tied to wrist, of the last.) *Pl.* 120, *cr.* 1.

SNEPP, Eng., between wings, an escallop, ppr. *Pl.* 62, *cr.* 4.

SNEYD, Staffs., a lion, passant, gardant, sa. *Nec opprimere, nec opprimi.* *Pl.* 120, *cr.* 5.

SNIGG, or SNIGGE, Somers., a demi-stag, salient, erased, or. *Pl.* 55, *cr.* 9, (without rose.)

SNIGG, or SNIGGE, Eng., a swallow, volant, ppr. *Pl.* 40, *cr.* 4.

SNODGRASS, Sco., a phœnix in flames, ppr. *Pl.* 44, *cr.* 8.

SNOOKE, Suss., a rock, ppr., thereon an eagle, regardant, wings (elevated, or, dexter resting on an escutcheon, ar., charged with a fleur-de-lis, gu.) *Pl.* 77, *cr.* 13.

SNOTHERLEY, SNOTTERLEY, and SOTHERLEY, Eng., a crane, (asleep, with head under his wings,) holding under dexter a stone, ppr. *Pl.* 77, *cr.* 15.

SNOW, Beds. and Surr., an antelope's head, erased, per pale, nebulée, ar. and az. *Pl.* 24, *cr.* 7.

SNOWBALL, Berks. and Northamp., on a plate, a horse's head, erased, sa. *Pl.* 81, *cr.* 6, (plate, *pl.* 141.)

SNOWDEN, and SNOWDON, Eng., a peacock in pride, ppr. *Pl.* 92, *cr.* 11.

SNOWDON, Eng., on a mount, vert, a horse, current, bridled, sa. *Pl.* 57, *cr.* 9.

SNUGGS, Eng., a salamander in flames, ppr. *Vive ut vivas.* *Pl.* 20, *cr.* 15.

SOAME, HERNE-BUCKWORTH, Bart., Surr.: 1. For *Soame*, a lure, gu., garnished and stringed, ar., thereon a falcon, or, beaked and legged, of the second. *Pl.* 10, *cr.* 7. 2. For *Buckworth*, a man's head, affrontée, armed with a helmet, beaver up, all ppr. *Pl.* 53, *cr.* 8.

SOAME, Lond. and Suff., an arm, embowed, vested, gu., in hand a mullet, or. *Pl.* 39, *cr.* 1, (mullet, *pl.* 62, *cr.* 13.)

SOAME, Lond. and Suff., on a lure, ar., garnished and lined, gu., a hawk, close, or. *Pl.* 10, *cr.* 7.

SOAMES, Eng., a demi-eagle, regardant, in dexter a sword, ppr. *Pl.* 87, *cr.* 5.

SOAPER, a demi-lion, rampant, gu., holding a (billet,) sa. *Pl.* 11, *cr.* 2.

SOCKWELL, on a ducal coronet, or, an eagle, displayed, ar. *Pl.* 9, *cr.* 6, (eagle, *pl.* 48, *cr.* 11.)

SODEN, Eng., a parrot, gu., in beak an annulet, or. *Pl.* 33, *cr.* 11.

SODEN, and SODEY, a stag, lodged, at gaze, between two laurel-branches, ppr. *Pl.* 24, *cr.* 4.

SODON, Iri., a stag, lodged, at gaze, between two laurel-branches, ppr. *Pl.* 24, *cr.* 4.

SOLAY, Eng., a dolphin, naiant, az. *Pl.* 48, *cr.* 9.

SOLE, Lond., out of a mural coronet, or, a demi-lion, sa., langued and armed, gold. *Pl.* 120, *cr.* 14, (without axe.)

SOLERS, Eng., on a ducal coronet, a phœnix in flames, ppr. *Pl.* 53, *cr.* 6.

SOLEY, Eng., a dolphin, naiant, az. *Pl.* 48, *cr.* 9.

SOLEY, on a crescent, a salmon. *Pl.* 18, *cr.* 14, (salmon, *pl.* 85, *cr.* 7.)

SOLLEY, and SOLLY, Eng., in a lake, a swan, swimming, wings addorsed, ppr. *Pl.* 66, *cr.* 10.

SOLOMON, Eng., a heron, devouring a fish. *Pl.* 121, *cr.* 13.

SOLOMON, a demi-wolf, in dexter a rose, slipped and leaved, ppr. *Pl.* 56, *cr.* 8.

SOLOMONS, Eng., a clam-shell, or. *Pl.* 117, *cr.* 4.

SOLSBY, a boar's head, (couped) and erect, sa. *Pl.* 21, *cr.* 7.

SOLTAN, a demi-lion, ar., between two branches of roses, ppr. *Miseris succurrere disco. Pl.* 69, *cr.* 14, (roses, *pl.* 125, *cr.* 6.)

SOMER, and SOMNER, on a mount, a peacock, ppr. *Pl.* 9, *cr.* 1.

SOMER, Kent, a stork, per pale, gu. and az., (ducally gorged, or.) *Pl.* 33, *cr.* 9.

SOMERFORD, Eng., on a mount, vert, a palm-tree, ppr. *Pl.* 52, *cr.* 6.

SOMERHILL, Baron. See CLANRICARDE, Marquess of.

SOMERS, Kent, a lion's head, erased, or, charged with a fess dancettée, erm. *Pl.* 81, *cr.* 4.

SOMERS, Dors., a coat of mail hanging on a laurel-tree, all ppr.

SOMERS, Earl and Lord, Viscount Eastnor, Baron of Evesham, and a Bart., (Cocks,) on a mount, ppr., a stag, lodged, regardant, ar. *Prodesse quam conspici. Pl.* 51, *cr.* 9.

SOMERSET, Glouc., a portcullis, or, nailed, az., chained, gold. *Mutare vel timere sperno. Pl.* 51, *cr.* 12.

SOMERSET, Duke of Beaufort. See BEAUFORT.

SOMERSET, Suff., a panther, ar., spotted of various colours, (fire issuing from mouth and ears, ppr.) *Pl.* 86, *cr.* 2.

SOMERSET, Lond., out of a naval coronet, or, a hippocampus, erect, ar.

SOMERSET, Duke of, Baron Seymour, and a Bart., (Seymour,) out of a ducal coronet, or, a phœnix, gold, in flames, ppr. *Foy por devoir. Pl.* 53, *cr.* 6.

SOMERSET, Somers., a dove, ppr., between two oak-branches, stalked and leaved, vert, fructed, or. *Pl.* 15, *cr.* 11.

SOMERVALE, Sco., a wheel, or, surmounted of a dragon, vert, (spouting fire before and behind.) *Fear God in life. Pl.* 122, *cr.* 2.

SOMERVILE, or SOMERVILLE, Eng., two dexter hands, conjoined, the first in armour, holding a branch of laurel and a thistle, in orle, all ppr. *Pl.* 23, *cr.* 10.

SOMERVILE, two leopards' faces, in fess, both crowned with one ducal coronet.

SOMERVILE, Warw., two leopards' heads, in fess, or, ducally crowned, gu.

SOMERVILL, two leopards' heads, ar., both ducally crowned with one coronet, gu.

SOMERVILLE, Eng., a wyvern, ppr. *Pl.* 63, *cr.* 13.

SOMERVILLE, Dinder House, Somers.: 1. For *Somerville*, a wyvern, wings raised, vert, langued, gu., on a wheel, erect, ar. *Pl.* 122, *cr.* 2. 2. For *Fownes*, a stump of oak-tree, erased at top, sprouting a branch on each side, ppr. *Fear God in life. Pl.* 92, *cr.* 8.

SOMERVILLE, Baron, Sco., (Somerville,) a dragon, vert, (sprouting fire before and behind, ppr.,) standing on a wheel, of the first. *Fear God in life. Pl.* 122, *cr.* 2.

SOMERY, a sword and ear of wheat, in saltier. *Pl.* 50, *cr.* 4.

SOMERY, an olive-branch, ppr. *Pl.* 98, *cr.* 8.

SOMESTER, or SOMMASTER, Devons., a portcullis, with lines, ar. *Pl.* 51, *cr.* 12.

SOMIM, and SOMIN, a demi-wolf, sa., guttée-d'or, holding in the feet a cross formée, fitched, in pale, or. *Pl.* 56, *cr.* 8, (cross, *pl.* 125, *cr.* 2.)

SOMMER, Dublin, Iri., a harvest-fly, or, speckled, sa.

SOMMERS, Sco., a lion, rampant, or. *Pl.* 67, *cr.* 5.

SOMMERS, a coat of mail, ensigned with an oak-branch, acorned, all ppr.

SOMMERVILLE, a crescent, ppr. *Donec rursus impleat orbem. Pl.* 18, *cr.* 14.

SOMMERVILLE, and SOMMERVIL, a hand holding a crescent, ppr. *Donec rursus impleat orbem. Pl.* 38, *cr.* 7.

SOMMERVILLE, Sco., a dexter hand throwing a hand-grenade, ppr. *Audacem juvant fata. Pl.* 2, *cr.* 6.

SOMNER, Eng., an eagle's head, erased, or. *Pl.* 20, *cr.* 7.

SOMNER, a sun-flower. *Pl.* 84, *cr.* 6.

SOMNER, Kent, a crane, per pale, gu. and az., (ducally gorged,) beaked and legged, or. *Pl.* 111, *cr.* 9.

SONDES, Baron, (Milles,) a griffin's head, erased, ar., ducally gorged, or. *Esto quod esse videris. Pl.* 42, *cr.* 9, (without branch.)

SONE, or SOONE, Derbs. and Suff., a demi-lion, rampant, ar., guttée-de-sang, in dexter a (baton,) or, tipped at end, sa. *Pl.* 11, *cr.* 2.

SONIBANCK, Oxon., out of a ducal coronet, or, two wings, expanded, az., (each charged with a sun, gold.) *Pl.* 17, *cr.* 9.

SOPER, Eng., a demi-cupid, holding a hymenial torch, all ppr. *Pl.* 70, *cr.* 14.

SOPER, a demi-lion, rampant, gu., holding a (billet, sa.) *Pl.* 84, *cr.* 7.

SOPER, Cumb., a demi-lion, rampant, between paws a (billet,) all sa. *Pl.* 47, *cr.* 4.

SOROCOLD, Lond., on top of a tower, or, a fleur-de-lis, az. *Pl.* 12, *cr.* 5, (fleur-de-lis, *pl.* 141.)

SORRELL, Eng., on a ducal coronet, a peacock, ppr. *Pl.* 43, *cr.* 7.

SOTHEBY, Eng., the sun in splendour, or. *Pl.* 68, *cr.* 14.

SOTHEBY, Ess., a lion, rampant, or, in dexter an (apple,) gu. *Pl.* 64, *cr.* 2.

SOTHERAM, Eng., a crane, in dexter a flint-stone, all ppr. *Pl.* 26, *cr.* 11.

SOTHERON, Notts., an eagle, with two heads, displayed, party per pale, ar. and gu., wings, (semée of cross crosslets, counterchanged, murally crowned,) beaked and membered, or. *Pl.* 87, *cr.* 11.

SOTHERTON, Eng., a leg, couped above knee, gu., spurred, ppr. *Pl.* 38, *cr.* 14.

SOTWELL, Berks. and Wilts., out of a mural coronet, gu., a lion's head, or, (pierced through neck by an arrow, headed, sa., feathered, ar.) *Pl.* 45, *cr.* 9.

SOUCH, Wilts., an ass's head, tied round mouth with a cord, az., charged on neck with a fleur-de-lis, vert. *Pl.* 91, *cr.* 7, (fleur-de-lis, *pl.* 141.)

SOUCHAY, an eagle, displayed. *Pl.* 48, *cr.* 11.

SOULSBY, Yorks. and Northumb., a boar's head, in fess, erased. *Pl.* 16, *cr.* 11.

SOUTER, Eng., a harpy, gardant, wings displayed, ppr. *Pl.* 32, *cr.* 3.

SOUTER, Sco., a crescent, or. *Donec impleat.* *Pl.* 18, *cr.* 14.

SOUTH, Eng., a griffin's head, erased. *Pl.* 48, *cr.* 6.

SOUTH, a lion, rampant, (ducally gorged, or,) in dexter a mullet, ar., pierced, sa. *Pl.* 87, *cr.* 6, (mullet, *pl.* 45, *cr.* 1.)

SOUTH, Wilts., a dragon's head, ppr., ducally gorged, per pale, or and az., issuing from mouth flames of fire, of the last. *Pl.* 36, *cr.* 7, (flame, *pl.* 37, *cr.* 9.)

SOUTH, Wilts., a dragon's head, per pale, or and vert, ducally gorged, az., vomiting flames, ppr. *Ib.*

SOUTH SEA COMPANY, a ship in full sail, ppr. *A gradibus usque Auroram.* *Pl.* 109, *cr.* 8.

SOUTHALL, Eng., a rock, sa. *Pl.* 73, *cr.* 12.

SOUTHAM, Eng., a thistle and rose, in saltier, ppr. *Pl.* 57, *cr.* 10.

SOUTHAMPTON, Baron, (Fitzroy,) on a chapeau, gu., turned up, erm., a lion, statant, gardant, or, ducally crowned, az., and gorged with a collar counter-compony, ar., and of the fourth. *Et decus et pretium recti.* *Pl.* 105, *cr.* 5.

SOUTHBEY, or SOUTHEBYE, Suff. and Yorks., a demi-talbot, purp. *Pl.* 15, *cr.* 2.

SOUTHBEY, or SOUTHBY, Berks., a lion, rampant, or, in dexter an (apple,) gu. *Pl.* 64, *cr.* 2.

SOUTHBY Eng., a demi-peacock, issuing, ppr. *Pl.* 53, *cr.* 12.

SOUTHCOMB, a dove, in mouth an olive-branch, all ppr. *Pl.* 48, *cr.* 15.

SOUTHCOTE, Eng., a star, rising from a cloud, ppr. *Pl.* 16, *cr.* 13.

SOUTHERN, Eng., a serpent, nowed, vert. *Pl.* 1, *cr.* 9.

SOUTHERN, a bull's head, erased at neck. *Pl.* 19, *cr.* 3.

SOUTHERNE, Salop and Lond., an eagle with two heads, displayed, per pale, ar. and az., each head crowned, or. *Pl.* 63, *cr.* 2.

SOUTHERTON, Norf., a goat's head, sa., (powdered with plates, ducally gorged) and armed, or. *Pl.* 105, *cr.* 14.

SOUTHEY, Eng., an oak-tree, vert. *Pl.* 16, *cr.* 8.

SOUTHLAND, Kent, a lion's gamb, erect, or, grasping a spear-(head,) ar. *Pl.* 1, *cr.* 4.

SOUTHOUSE, Eng., out of a ducal coronet, a talbot's head, *Pl.* 99, *cr.* 7.

SOUTHWELL, a demi-Indian goat, ar., eared, hoofed, and ducally gorged, gu., on body three annulets, sa. *Pl.* 90, *cr.* 12.

SOUTHWELL, Viscount, and Baron, and a Bart., all Iri., (Southwell,) a demi-Indian goat, armed, eared, and ducally gorged, gu., charged on body with three annulets, in pale, of the last. *Nec male notus eques.* *Pl.* 90, *cr.* 12.

SOUTHWERTH, Iri., out of a ducal coronet, ar., a bull's head, sa. *Pl.* 68, *cr.* 6.

SOUTHWERTH, or SOUTHWORTH, Lanc., a bull's head, erased, sa., attired, ar. *Pl.* 19, *cr.* 3.

SOUTHWORTH, Lanc. and Somers., a bull's head, erased, sa., the horn, ar., tips, of the first, on neck a crescent for difference. *Pl.* 19, *cr.* 3, (crescent, *pl.* 141.)

SOUTHWORTH, Eng., a bull's head, erased, ar. *Pl.* 19, *cr.* 3.

SOUTHY, Eng., a stag's head, at gaze, ducally gorged, ppr. *Pl.* 55, *cr.* 2.

SOWDON, Eng., a lion's head, couped, ar., collared, az., (charged with three mullets,) or. *Pl.* 42, *cr.* 14.

SOWERBY, Eng., a peacock's head, erased, ppr. *Pl.* 86, *cr.* 4.

SOWERBY, Durh., Northumb., Cumb., and Herts., a lion, rampant, ar., langued, gu. *Pl.* 67, *cr.* 5.

SPAIGHT, a jay, ppr. *Vi et virtute.* *Pl.* 100, *cr.* 13.

SPALDING, Sco. and French, a cross crosslet, fitched, or. *Hinc mihi salus.* *Pl.* 16, *cr.* 10.

SPALDING, Eng., a bishop's mitre, or, banded, gu., charged with a cheveron, ar., and thereon three bezants, gold. *Pl.* 12, *cr.* 10.

SPALDING, an elephant's head, or, (crowned, gu.) *Pl.* 56, *cr.* 14.

SPAN, Eng., on a mount, an apple-tree, fructed, ppr. *Pl.* 48, *cr.* 4.

SPANGE, an arm, in armour, embowed, brandishing a sword, ppr. *Fata viam invenient.* *Pl.* 2, *cr.* 8.

SPANKIE, a lion, rampant, az., holding an escutcheon, or. *Pl.* 125, *cr.* 2, (escutcheon, *pl.* 22, *cr.* 13.)

SPARCHFORD, Lond. and Bucks., a demi-dragon, (sans wings, tail entwined round neck,) or. *Pl.* 82, *cr.* 10.

SPARHAWK, Eng., a hawk, close, belled, ppr. *Pl.* 67, *cr.* 3.

SPARK, Eng., a swan, wings addorsed, devouring a fish, ppr. *Pl.* 103, *cr.* 1.

SPARK, or SPARKE, a demi-panther, ppr. *Pl.* 12, *cr.* 14.

SPARKE, and SPARKES, Lond., Ess., and Devons., out of a ducal coronet, or, a demi-panther, rampant, gardant, ar., spotted, of various colours, fire issuing from ears and mouth, ppr. *Pl.* 76, *cr.* 1, (coronet, *same plate, cr.* 8.)

SPARKE, Eng., a swan, wings addorsed, swallowing a fish, ppr. *Pl.* 103, *cr.* 1.

SPARKES, Eng., a fleur-de-lis. *Pl.* 68, *cr.* 12.

SPARKES, Devons. and Cornw., out of a ducal coronet, or, a demi-lion, guttée-de-sang. *Pl.* 45, *cr.* 7.

SPARKLING, Kent, a tiger's head, erased, ar., gorged with a ducal coronet, maned and armed, or. *Pl.* 116, *cr.* 8.

SPARKS, and SPARKES, out of a ducal coronet, a demi-tiger. *Pl.* 53, *cr.* 10, (coronet, *same plate.*)

SPARLING, Salop, a cubit arm, in pale, (vested, az., cuffed, ar.,) in hand a dagger, both ppr. *Pl.* 23, *cr.* 15.

SPARROW, Iri., a rose, ar., barbed, vert. *Pl.* 20, *cr.* 2.

SPARROW, Eng., a yew-tree, ppr. *Pl.* 49, *cr.* 13.

SPARROW, Staffs., out of a ducal coronet, or, a unicorn's head, ar. *Pl.* 45, *cr.* 14.

SPARROW, Ess., out of a mural coronet, or, a unicorn's head, ar., mane and horns, gold. *Pl.* 45, *cr.* 14, (coronet, *same plate, cr.* 9.)

SPARROW, 'Wel., a sparrow-hawk, with spurs, belled. *Honestas optima politia. Pl.* 67, *cr.* 3.

SPARROW, Staffs., out of battlements of a tower, ppr., a unicorn's head, ar., horned and crined, or, semée of pheons, az. *In Deo solo salus est. Pl.* 12, *cr.* 5, (head, *pl.* 67, *cr.* 1.)

SPARSHOTT, Eng., a palm-tree, vert, fructed, or. *Pl.* 18, *cr.* 12.

SPATEMAN, Derbs., out of a mural coronet, ar., a griffin's head, erminois. *Pl.* 101, *cr.* 6, (without gorging.)

SPAYNE, Norf., a bull's head, ar., horns, gobonated, or and sa. *Pl.* 120, *cr.* 7.

SPEAKE, Somers., a hedgehog, ar., armed, sa. *Pl.* 32, *cr.* 9.

SPEAKE, and SPEKE, Wilts., Somers., and Devons., a hedgehog, passant, ppr. *Pl.* 32, *cr.* 9.

SPEALT, Devons., out of a ducal coronet, or, a (demi-)dragon, wings addorsed, az. *Pl.* 59, *cr.* 14.

SPEAR, Eng., a dolphin, haurient, devouring a fish, ppr. *Pl.* 71, *cr.* 1.

SPEAR, Iri., a rose, gu., barbed, stalked, and leaved, vert, and a spear, or, in saltier. *Pl.* 104, *cr.* 7.

SPEARING, Eng., on a globe, a ship under sail, ppr. *Pl.* 41, *cr.* 12.

SPEARMAN, Bart., a lion, rampant, ppr., gorged with a collar, gemelle, or, (supporting a tilting-spear, also ppr., enfiled with a mural coronet, gold.) *Dum spiro, spero. Pl.* 88, *cr.* 1.

SPEARMAN, Salop, a demi-lion, rampant, (in mouth a spear,) ppr. *Dum spiro, spero. Pl.* 69, *cr.* 14.

SPEARMAN, out of a ducal coronet, a demi-lion (grasping a spear.) *Pl.* 45, *cr.* 7.

SPEARNAN, Durh. and Northumb., a lion, rampant, grasping a (spear,) ppr. *Dum spiro, spero. Pl.* 22, *cr.* 15.

SPEARNAN, Northumb., a lion, rampant, ppr., gorged with a collar, ar., (pendent therefrom a bell, sa., and supporting a tilting-spear, ar., headed, or, the spear entwined by a laurel-branch, ppr.) *Pl.* 88, *cr.* 1.

SPECCOTT, Cornw., an eagle, displayed. *Pl.* 48, *cr.* 11.

SPEDDING, Eng., a cornucopia, or, flowers and fruit, ppr. *Pl.* 91, *cr.* 4.

SPEDDING, Summer Grove, Cumb., out of a mural coronet, or, a dexter arm, in armour, embowed, in hand, a (scimitar, arm charged with three acorns, one and two,) and entwined by a branch of oak, all ppr. *Utile dulci. Pl.* 115, *cr.* 14, (oak, *pl.* 93, *cr.* 1.)

SPEEDE, Lond., a swallow, (wings expanded,) ppr. *Pl.* 111, *cr.* 5.

SPEGHT, a dexter arm, vested, sa., cuffed, ar., in hand, ppr., a pheon, of the second. *Pl.* 123, *cr.* 12, (arm, *pl.* 39, *cr.* 1.)

SPEIR, an arm, in armour, embowed, in hand (a lance,) ppr. *Forward. Pl.* 44, *cr.* 9.

SPEIRS, same crest. *Salvet me Deus.*

SPEKE, WILLIAM, Esq., of Jordans, Somers., a porcupine. *Pl.* 55, *cr.* 10.

SPELMAN, Eng., a torteau, gu. *Pl.* 7, *cr.* 6.

SPENCE, Sco., a bear's head, erased, sa. *Bold —or—Do good. Pl.* 71, *cr.* 6.

SPENCE, Sco., two hands, from wrist, issuing from clouds, letting down an anchor into the sea, ppr. *Visa per invisa firma. Pl.* 94, *cr.* 4.

SPENCE, Sco., a hart's head, erased, ppr. *Si Deus, quis contra. Pl.* 66, *cr.* 9.

SPENCE, Sco., an anchor. *Visa per invisa firma. Pl.* 25, *cr.* 15.

SPENCE, Sco., out of a ducal coronet, a demi-lion, rampant. *Virtus auget honorem. Pl.* 45, *cr.* 7.

SPENCE, Sco., a boar's head, erased, ppr. *Felix qui pacificus. Pl.* 16, *cr.* 11.

SPENCE, Sco., (three) palm-branches, slipped, vert, banded, or. *Felix qui pacificus. Pl.* 123, *cr.* 1.

SPENCE, Sco., a demi-lion, rampant, gu. *Pl.* 67, *cr.* 10.

SPENCE, Sco., a stag's head, couped, ppr. *Pl.* 91, *cr.* 14.

SPENCE, a maltster, vested about loins with a plaid skirt, sustaining with both hands a malt-shovel, in pale, ppr.

SPENCE, out of a mural coronet, ar., three palm-branches, in pale, vert, each encircled by an annulet, and respectively interlaced, ar.

SPENCE, a demi-lion, gu. *Virtute acquiritur honos. Pl.* 67, *cr.* 10.

SPENCE, Suss., out of a mural coronet, ar., three palm-branches, vert, tied with a ribbon, az.

SPENCER, Norf., out of a ducal coronet, per pale, ar. and gu., a griffin's head, of the first, (gorged with a collar, of the second,) charged with three plates, all within wings, or. *Pl.* 97, *cr.* 13.

SPENCER, Norf. and Suff., out of a ducal coronet, per pale, or and gu., a griffin's head, ar., eared and beaked, of the second, (gorged with a collar, per pale, gu. and or,) between wings, the dexter, gu., and sinister, ar., on each a mullet. *Pl.* 97, *cr.* 13, (mullet, *pl.* 141.)

SPENCER, Suff., Beds., and Oxon, out of a ducal coronet, per pale, or and ar., a griffin's head, between wings, of the second, (collared,) gu. *Pl.* 97, *cr.* 13.

SPENCER, Notts., out of a ducal coronet, or, a griffin's head, between wings, in pale, ar., (collared, gu.,) beaked, of the first. *Dieu defendit le droit. Pl.* 97, *cr.* 13.

SPENCER, Eng., an arm, or, thereon a bend, az., in hand a chaplet of roses, gu., leaved, vert. *Pl.* 41, *cr.* 7.

SPENCER, Iri., on a ducal coronet, a star of (twelve) rays, or. *Pl.* 83, *cr.* 3.

SPENCER, DE, Eng., two wings, conjoined, ppr. *Pl.* 15, *cr.* 10.

SPENCER, out of a mural coronet, an arm, erect, vested, charged with two bars-gemelle, hand grasping a sword. *Pl.* 79, *cr.* 4, (sword, *pl.* 21, *cr.* 10.)

SPENCER, an arm, erect, or, (charged with two cheverons, gu., fist clenched.) *Pl.* 87, *cr.* 7.

SPENCER, an arm, (vested, or,) thereon a bend, az., holding a chaplet of roses, gu., leaved, vert. *Pl.* 41, *cr.* 7.

SPENCER, (on trunk of tree, in fess, raguly, and at dexter end a branch, erect, vert,) a talbot, sejant, gu., eared, ar., collared, or. *Pl.* 107, *cr.* 7.

SPENCER, War., a moor-hen, ppr. *Pl.* 10, *cr.* 1.

SPENCER, Yorks., on a rock, a sea-mew, all ppr. *Pl.* 79, *cr.* 11.

SPENCER, Northumb., an antelope's head, couped, or, gorged with a collar, engrailed, az., between wings, ar., each charged with a fret, gu.

SPENCER, Herts., out of a ducal coronet, per pale, ar. and or, a griffin's head of the first, eared, gu., (collared, per pale, of the third and gold,) between wings, of the second, charged with three fleurs-de-lis, in fess, sa., one on each wing, and one on neck. *Pl.* 97, *cr.* 13, (fleur-de-lis, *pl.* 141.)

SPENCER, Lond. and Kent, a panther's head, or, erased at neck, gu., fire issuing from mouth and ears, ppr. *Pl.* 94, *cr.* 10, (fire, *pl.* 76, *cr.* 1.)

SPENCER, Leic. and Northamp., an antelope's head, erased, or, attired, sa., (collared, gu., lined and ringed, of the second.) *Pl.* 24, *cr.* 7.

SPENCER, Earl, Viscount and Baron, and Viscount Althorp, (Spencer,) out of a ducal coronet, or, a griffin's head, ar., gorged with a bar-gemelle, gu., between wings, of the second. *Dieu defendit le droit. Pl.* 97, *cr.* 13.

SPENDLUFF, Linc., a Saracen's head, in profile, couped at shoulders, ppr., beard, sa., hair of the head, ar., wreathed about temples, or and gu. *Pl.* 126, *cr.* 8.

SPENEY, Norf., a bull's head, ar., horns gobonated, or and sa. *Pl.* 120, *cr.* 7.

SPENS, Sco., a hart's head, erased, ppr. *Si Deus qui contra. Pl.* 66, *cr.* 9.

SPENS, NATHANIEL, Esq., of Craigsanquhar, Fife, same crest.

SPERLING, Herts., on a chapeau, az., turned up, erm., a greyhound, sejant, or. *Pl.* 66, *cr.* 15, (chapeau, *pl.* 127, *fig.* 13.)

SPERLING, of Dynes Hall, Esq., between wings, conjoined and displayed, ar., a mullet, (suspended,) or. *Sapiens quis assiduus. Pl.* 1, *cr.* 15.

SPERT, Glouc., a broken mainmast, or, shrouds, sa., in round top six spears, in saltier, on top a flag, ar., thereon the cross of St George, ppr.

SPICER, Eng., a round tower, embattled, and cupola, ar. *Pl.* 42, *cr.* 10.

SPICER, Devons., out of a viscount's coronet, ppr., a cubit arm, (vested, gloved, of the first,) holding a fire-ball. *Pl.* 2, *cr.* 6, (coronet, *pl.* 72, *cr.* 11.)

SPIED, of Ardovie, Sco., a demi-man, in armour, (resting dexter on his sword-hilt, in sinister the scabbard, point downwards.) *Speed well*—and—*Auspice Deo. Pl.* 23, *cr.* 4.

SPIERS, Eng., a sheaf of arrows, or, banded, az. *Pl.* 43, *cr.* 14.

SPIERS, Sco., a dexter hand, issuing, holding a sword, all ppr. *Salvet me Deus. Pl.* 21, *cr.* 10.

SPIERS, Eng. and Sco., an arm, in armour, embowed, wielding a (lance,) ppr. *Advance. Pl.* 44, *cr.* 9.

SPIGERNELL, Eng., a hand, issuing from a cloud, in pale, shedding forth rays, holding a mort-head. *Pl.* 37, *cr.* 6.

SPILLER, Wilts., a falcon, wings expanded, ar., standing on a snake, nowed, vert. *Pl.* 75, *cr.* 11.

SPILLER, Middx., Surr., and Bucks., a bird, (a sacre,) ppr., beaked and legged, or. *Pl.* 67, *cr.* 3.

SPILLER, Staffs., an eagle, ar., winged, or, standing on a snake, nowed, vert. *Pl.* 75, *cr.* 11, (eagle, *pl.* 7, *cr.* 11.)

SPILMAN, a hand, issuing from a cloud, in pale, holding a garland of laurel, ppr. *Pl.* 88, *cr.* 13.

SPILMAN, Norf. and Staffs., a savage, ppr., wreathed about loins and temples, vert, in dexter a club, of the last. *Pl.* 14, *cr.* 11.

SPILSBURIE, Worc., a unicorn's head, gorged with a band of four pearls. *Pl.* 73, *cr.* 1.

SPILSBURY, Eng., a garb, az. *Pl.* 48, *cr.* 10.

SPILSBURY, Eng., a garb, or, thereon a dove, ppr. *Pl.* 112, *cr.* 10.

SPINKES, Northamp., a talbot, passant, gu., bezantée, gorged with three fusils, ar. *Pl.* 120, *cr.* 8, (fusil, *pl.* 141.)

SPINKS, Eng., a pheon, az. *Pl.* 26, *cr.* 12.

SPITTAL, Sco., two battle-axes, in saltier, or, hafted, gu. *Pl.* 52, *cr.* 10.

SPITTY, Ess., out of a ducal coronet, or, a plume of two rows of ostrich-feathers, ar. *Pl.* 64, *cr.* 5.

SPLIDT, on water, a man rowing in a boat to the sinister, all ppr. *Pl.* 57, *cr.* 4.

SPODE, a demi-griffin, wings elevated, gu., between paws a shield, per bend, indented, sa. and erminois, a bend, between two mullets, counterchanged. *Sub tutelâ Domini. Pl.* 18, *cr.* 6.

SPOFFORTH, a chess-rook, gu. *Tempus meæ opes. Pl.* 40, *cr.* 11, (without wings.)

SPONER, or SPOONER, Worc., a boar's head, couped, or, (pierced through neck, by a spear, ar., embrued, ppr.) *Pl.* 2, *cr.* 7.

SPOOKS, a swan, wings expanded, standing on a trumpet. *Pl.* 4, *cr.* 7.

SPOONER, Eng., on a chapeau, a pelican, ppr. *Pl.* 21, *cr.* 5.

SPOONER-LILLINGSTON, Warw., a demi-griffin, wings elevated, in dexter a battle-axe, all ppr. *Pl.* 44, *cr.* 3.

SPORHART, Lond., out of a mural coronet, or, a demi-lion, rampant, sa., supporting a (spear, of the first, headed, ar.) *Pl.* 86, *cr.* 11.

SPOTSWOOD, Sco., an eagle, displayed, gu., looking toward the sun in splendour. *Patior ut potior. Pl.* 115, *cr.* 7, (eagle, *pl.* 117, *cr.* 15.)

SPUTSWOOD, or SPOTTISWOOD, Sco., a wolf's head, couped, ppr. *Patior ut potior. Pl.* 92, *cr.* 15, (without rose.)

SPOTTISWOOD, Sco., two globes, ppr. *Utriusque auxilio. Pl.* 85, *cr.* 9.

SPOURE, or SPOOR, Durh., a demi-antelope, erm., (erased, per fess, gu., crined and attired, or, in mouth a broken spear, sa., headed, ar., the head downward.) *Constans et fidelis. Pl.* 75, *cr.* 10.

SPOURE, Cornw., a demi-antelope, erm., (erased, per fess, gu., crined and attired, or, in mouth a broken spear, sa., headed, ar., the head downward.) *Ib.*

SPOUSE, Cornw., a demi-buck, couped, in mouth an (arrow.) *Pl.* 55, *cr.* 9.

SPRACKLING, Kent, a wolf's head, erased, sa., tufted, armed, and (ducally gorged,) or. *Pl.* 14, *cr.* 6.

SPRAGG, Eng., a sword, erect, ppr., on point a crown of (olive,) suspended, or. *Pl.* 15, *cr.* 6.

SPRAGGS, a talbot, passant, ar., resting dexter on a fleur-de-lis, gu. *Pl.* 120, *cr.* 8, (fleur-de-lis, *pl.* 4, *cr.* 14.)

SPRAKLING, a griffin's head, ducally gorged, or. *Pl.* 42, *cr.* 9, (without branch.)

SPRANGER, Eng., a cinquefoil, erm. *Pl.* 91, *cr.* 12.

SPRANGER, Ess., on a ducal coronet, per pale, or. and az., a fleur-de-lis, per pale, of the first and second, between wings, the dexter, az., the sinister, or. *Pl.* 17, *cr.* 6, (fleur-de-lis, *pl.* 141.)

SPRATLEY, out of a ducal coronet, a dragon's head. *Pl.* 59, *cr.* 14.

SPRATT, Eng., two battle-axes, in saltier, ppr. *Pl.* 52, *cr.* 10.

SPRENCHEAUX, Eng., a Cornish chough, wings addorsed, between two spear-heads, in pale, sa. *Pl.* 79, *cr.* 13.

SPREVELL, Sco., a book, displayed, with seals, all ppr. *Manet in æternum. Pl.* 15, *cr.* 12.

SPREWELL, Sco., a book, expanded. *Manet in æternum. Pl.* 15, *cr.* 12.

SPRIGG, Eng., a laurel-branch, vert. *Pl.* 123, *cr.* 5.

SPRIGNELL, Yorks., and Highgate, Middx., a demi-lion, rampant, or, in dexter a battle-axe, ar., handle, gold. *Pl.* 101, *cr.* 14.

SPRING, Suff., a demi-stag, quarterly, ar. and or, in mouth some flowers, of the first. *Pl.* 55, *cr.* 9.

SPRING, a stag's head. *Pl.* 91, *cr.* 14.

SPRING, Suff., a demi-antelope, quarterly, ar. and or, horns counterchanged. *Pl.* 34, *cr.* 8.

SPRINGE, Suff., a stag's head, ppr. *Non mihi, sed patriæ. Pl.* 91, *cr.* 14.

SPRINGET, or SPRINGETT, Kent and Suss., an eagle, displayed, ar., membered and crowned, gu., standing on a serpent, nowed, in fret, ppr. *Pl.* 85, *cr.* 11, (serpent, *pl.* 75, *cr.* 11.)

SPRINGETT, Suss., a spread eagle. *Pl.* 87, *cr.* 11, (without flames.)

SPRINGHAM, Iri., a demi-lion, rampant, ar., holding a book, displayed, ppr., garnished, or, ribbons, vert. *Pl.* 72, *cr.* 13, (without mount and charge.)

SPRINGHOSE, Eng., a Cornish chough, wings addorsed, between two spear-heads, erect, sa. *Pl.* 79, *cr.* 13.

SPROTT, Eng., a pelican's head, erased, vulning, ppr. *Pl.* 26, *cr.* 1.

SPROUL, Sco., a water-bouget, or. *Pl.* 14, *cr.* 12.

SPROULE, Somers., a falcon, belled, devouring a partridge, ppr. *Pl.* 61, *cr.* 7.

SPRY, a greyhound's head, ar. *Pl.* 14, *cr.* 4.

SPRYE, Cornw. and Devons., a dove, standing on a snake, nowed, all ppr. *Pl.* 66, *cr.* 12, (snake, *pl.* 75, *cr.* 11.)

SPURCOCK, a cock, (volant,) ar., crested, gu. *Pl.* 76, *cr.* 7.

SPURDENS, Norf., in lion's gamb, ppr., a cross moline, counterchanged. *Denuo fortasse lutescat. Pl.* 46, *cr.* 7.

SPURLING, Ess., between wings, conjoined and displayed, ar., a mullet of six points, (suspended,) or. *Pl.* 1, *cr.* 15.

SPURLING, Herts., on a chapeau, az., turned up, erm., a greyhound, sejant, or. *Pl.* 66, *cr.* 15, (chapeau, *pl.* 127, *fig.* 13.)

SPURRIER, Eng., a long cross, or, on three steps, sa., ar. and gu. *Pl.* 49, *cr.* 2.

SPURSELL, a cross-bow, erect. *Pl.* 58, *cr.* 3, (without wings.)

SPURSTOW, and SPURSTOWE, Chesh. and Lond., a demi-woman, couped (below) breasts, hair flotant, all ppr. *Pl.* 45, *cr.* 5.

SPURWAYE, Devons., a garb, or. *Pl.* 48, *cr.* 10.

SPYCER, Warw., a tower with a dome on top, ar. *Pl.* 42, *cr.* 10.

SPYCER, out of a mural coronet, a cubit arm, in armour, in hand a fire-ball. *Pl.* 2, *cr.* 6, (coronet, *pl.* 115, *cr.* 14.)

SPYER, Berks. and Oxon., a garb, per fess, or and vert, banded, ar. *Pl.* 48, *cr.* 10.

SPYGERNELL, Eng., a hand, issuing from a cloud, erect, shedding forth rays, holding a mort-head. *Pl.* 37, *cr.* 6.

SPYLMAN, Eng., a torteau, gu. *Pl.* 7, *cr.* 6.

SPYNGOURNE, Eng., a hand issuing from a cloud, erect, shedding forth rays, holding a mort-head. *Pl.* 37, *cr.* 6.

SPYRE, Eng., a garb, or, banded, vert. *Pl.* 48, *cr.* 10.

SQUAREY, Eng., a cross crosslet, or. *Pro cruce audax. Pl.* 66, *cr.* 8.

SQUIB, Eng., on a chapeau, a pelican in (flames,) ppr. *Pl.* 21, *cr.* 5.

SQUIBB, Eng., a swan, in pride, crowned with an antique crown, ppr. *Pl.* 111, *cr.* 10.

SQUIRE, Eng., an antelope's head, erased, pierced through neck by a spear, the handle broken off. *Pl.* 79, *cr.* 9.

SQUIRE, Ess. and Lond., an elephant's head, ar., (ducally gorged) and eared, or. *Pl.* 35, *cr.* 13.

SQUIRE, of Barton Place, Suff., in bear's paw, erect, a plume of (three) ostrich-feathers, ppr. *Tiens ferme. Pl.* 58, *cr.* 7.

SQUIRES, Ess., on a wheel, a wyvern, wings addorsed, (spouting fire at both ends,) ppr. *Pl.* 122, *cr.* 2.

SRABONNE, Eng., an arrow, point downwards. *Pl.* 56, *cr.* 13.

STABLE, Eng., a castle, ar., thereon a flag of St George. *Pl.* 123, *cr.* 14.

STABLE, Eng., a demi-lion, rampant, gu., holding a mullet, ar. *Pl.* 89, *cr.* 10.

STABLES, Eng., a tower, or. *Pl.* 12, *cr.* 5.

STACE, Kent, a cubit arm, erect, charged with three caltraps, in hand a fleur-de-lis. *Pl.* 95, *cr.* 9, (caltrap, *pl.* 141.)

STACEY, Eng., a sword, erect, supporting a balance and scales, equally poised. *Pl.* 44, *cr.* 10.

STACEY, Kent, an antelope's head, erased, ar., attired, or. *Pl.* 24, *cr.* 7.

STACK, Sco., a dexter hand, issuing, holding by the horn a bull's head, erased, ar., dropping blood. *Fortiorum fortia facta. Pl.* 26, *cr.* 8, (head, *pl.* 19, *cr.* 3.)

STACKHOUSE, Eng., a ship, in full sail. *Pl.* 109, *cr.* 8.

STACKHOUSE, Cornw., a saltire, raguly, or.

STACKPOLE, on a ducal coronet, a pelican in a nest, feeding her young. *Pl.* 44, *cr.* 1, (coronet, *same plate, cr.* 12.)

STACKPOOLE, Eng., on a rock, a fort in flames, ppr. *Pl.* 59, *cr.* 8.

STACYE, Bucks., out of a marquess's coronet, or, a demi-pegasus, az., (charged with three etoiles, winged and attired, gold, in mouth a pansy, gu., stalked and leaved, vert.) *Pl.* 76, *cr.* 2, (coronet, *pl.* 127, *cr.* 4.)

STACYE, Bucks., a cubit arm, (vested, az., cuffed, ar.,) in hand, ppr., a fleur-de-lis, or, charged on arm with three bezants. *Pl.* 95, *cr.* 9, (bezant, *pl.* 141.)

STAFF, Kent, a demi-lion, rampant, ppr., supporting a staff, raguly, vert. *Pl.* 11, *cr.* 2.

STAFFERTON, Berks. and Hants, a buck's head, erased, ppr., (pierced through neck by a spear, or.) *Pl.* 66, *cr.* 9.

STAFFORD, Eng., in a ducal coronet, a tiger's head, couped, maned. *Pl.* 36, *cr.* 15.

STAFFORD, a griffin's head, couped, ppr. *Pl.* 38, *cr.* 3.

STAFFORD, in a mural coronet, gu., a swan's neck, with wings expanded, ar., ducally gorged, of the first. *Pl.* 83, *cr.* 1, (coronet, *pl.* 128, *fig.* 18.)

STAFFORD, on a ducal coronet, per pale, sa. and gu., a swan, rising, ar., beaked, sa. *Pl.* 100, *cr.* 7.

STAFFORD, Berks., Bucks., Glouc., Staffs., and Northamp., out of a ducal coronet, per pale, or and gu., a boar's head and neck, sa. *Pl.* 102, *cr.* 14.

STAFFORD, Durh., a demi-lion, rampant, in dexter a dagger, in pale. *Pl.* 41, *cr.* 13.

STAFFORD, Baron, and a Bart., (Stafford-Jerningham,) out of a ducal coronet, or, a demi-falcon, wings expanded, ppr. *Abstulit qui dedit. Pl.* 103, *cr.* 6.

STAFFORD, Marquess of. *See* SUTHERLAND, Duke of.

STAFFORD, Blathenwick, Northamp., out of clouds, a naked arm, embowed, in hand a sword, all ppr. *The strongest arm uppermost. Pl.* 34, *cr.* 7, (cloud, *pl.* 30, *cr.* 6.)

STAGG, Eng., a stag's head, (collared, or,) between the horns a cross pattée. *Pl.* 9, *cr.* 10.

STAGG, a stag's head, cabossed, or, between the attires a cross pattée. *Pl.* 115, *cr.* 1, (cross, *pl.* 9, *cr.* 10.)

STAHLSCHMIDT, Surr., a demi-warrior, couped at thighs, in armour, an open helmet on head, face affrontée, in dexter a (battle-axe,) all ppr., a label upon a label for difference. *Deo inspirante, rege favente. Pl.* 23, *cr.* 4.

STAHLSCHMIDT, Surr., same crest, (with a crescent on a label for difference.) *Ib.*

STAINBANK, Lond., in a ducal coronet, or, a demi-dragon, regardant, az., wings expanded, guttée-d'eau, charged on neck with a bezant.

STAINES, Eng., a castle, sa. *Pl.* 28, *cr.* 11.

STAINES, and STAINS, Eng., a dexter hand, issuing from a cloud, ppr., holding up a garland, vert. *Pl.* 88, *cr.* 13.

STAINES, Kent, out of a naval coronet, or, a buck's head, quarterly, ar. and ppr., attired, gu. *Pl.* 118, *cr.* 5, (head, *pl.* 91, *cr.* 14.)

STAINFORTH, a dexter arm, in armour, erect, in hand, ppr., a broken sword, ar., hilt and pommel, or. *Pl.* 63, *cr.* 5, (sword, *pl.* 22, *cr.* 6.)

STAINFORTH, Eng., an anchor, az. *Pl.* 25, *cr.* 15.

STAINFORTH, a cubit arm, in hand a broken sword, in pale, all ppr. *Pl.* 22, *cr.* 6, (without cloud.)

STAINSBURY, Eng., a demi-lion, rampant, gu., crusuly, or. *Pl.* 67, *cr.* 10.

STAINTON, Eng., a covered cup, gu. *Pl.* 75, *cr.* 13, (without swords.)

STAIR, a cubit arm, ppr., hand holding an arrow. *Pl.* 43, *cr.* 13.

STAIR, Earl and Baron, Viscount Stair and Dalrymple, all Sco., and a Bart., N.S., (Dalrymple;) a rock, ppr. *Firm. Pl.* 73, *cr.* 12.

STALEY, Eng., a globe on a stand, ppr. *Pl.* 81, *cr.* 1.

STALLER, Eng., a stork's head, or. *Pl.* 32, *cr.* 5.

STALTON, Eng., a lion's paw, erased, holding a rose-branch, slipped and leaved, ppr. *Pl.* 60, *cr.* 14.

STAMER, Bart., Iri., a stag's head, erased, gorged with a mural coronet, or. *Jubilee*—and —*Virtute et valore. Pl.* 66, *cr.* 9, (gorging, *pl.* 74, *cr.* 1.)

STAMFIELD, Sco., a goat's head, erased, ar., armed, or, within two laurel-branches, ppr. *Pl.* 29, *cr.* 13, (branches, *pl.* 79, *cr.* 14.)

STAMFORD, Middx. and Staffs., a gauntlet, or, grasping a (broken) sword, ar., hilt and pommel, sa. *Pl.* 125, *cr.* 5.

STAMFORD, Staffs., a stag's head, ar., attired, of the last, guttée-de-sang, (charged on neck with a bar-gemelle, gu.) *Pl.* 91, *cr.* 14.

STAMFORD, Earl of, Earl of Warrington, Baron Grey, of Groby, and Baron Delamere, (Grey,) a unicorn, (salient,) erm. *A ma puissance. Pl.* 37, *cr.* 7.

STAMP, Berks. and Oxon., a demi-colt, ar.

STAMPART, a gauntlet, or, grasping a (broken) sword, ar., hilt and pommel, sa. *Pl.* 125, *cr.* 5.

STAMPS, Eng., on a ducal coronet, a swan, wings addorsed, ducally gorged, all ppr. *Pl.* 111, *cr.* 10, (coronet, *same plate, cr.* 7.)

STANARD, Lond., an arm, in antique mail, ppr., in hand a battle-axe, sa., headed and armed, ar. *Pl.* 41, *cr.* 2.

STANBURY, Cornw., a lion, rampant. *Pl.* 67, *cr.* 5.

STANDARD, Oxon., a cubit arm, erect, vert, cuffed, ar., in hand, ppr., a bow, strung, ppr. *Pl.* 3, *cr.* 12, (vesting, *pl.* 32, *cr.* 6.)

STANDBRIDGE, Suss. and Birm., a demi-lion, rampant, or, holding an escallop, ar. *Pl.* 126 A, *cr.* 13.

STANDEN, Eng., an angel, ppr. *Pl.* 25, *cr.* 7.

STANDISH, Berks., Lanc., and Leic., a cock, ar., armed and crested, gu. *Pl.* 67, *cr.* 14.

STANDISH, a cock, crowing, ppr. *Pl.* 67, *cr.* 14.

STANDISH, a griffin, sejant, erect, on hind legs, holding with fore-feet a battle-axe, in pale. *Pl.* 74, *cr.* 10, (axe, *pl.* 44, *cr.* 3.)

STANDISH, Berks., Leic., and Lanc., an owl, ar., beaked and legged, or, statant on a rat, sa. *Pl.* 27, *cr.* 9, (rat, *pl.* 121, *cr.* 10.)

STANDISH, Lanc., an owl, ar., statant on a rat, sa. *Pl.* 27, *cr.* 9, (rat, *pl.* 121, *cr.* 10.)

STANDISH-CARR, WILLIAM STANDISH, ESQ., of Duxbury Park, Lanc., and Cocken Hall, Durh., a cock, ar. *Constant en tout. Pl.* 67, *cr.* 14.

STANDISH-STRICKLAND, of Standish Hall, Lanc.: 1. For *Standish*, an owl, (with a rat in its talons,) ppr. *Pl*. 27, *cr*. 9. 2. For *Strickland*, a holly-bush, ppr. *Pl*. 99, *cr*. 6.

STANDLEY, Eng., a stag's head, erased. *Pl*. 66, *cr*. 9.

STANDON, Eng., on stump of oak-tree, shooting new branches, a stork, ppr. *Pl*. 23, *cr*. 5.

STANE-BRAMSTON : 1. For *Stane*, a cubit arm, erect, ppr., in hand a battle-axe, ar., headed, or. *Pl*. 73, *cr*. 7. 2. For *Bramston*, a lion, sejant, or, collared, sa., charged with three plates. *Pl*. 21, *cr*. 3.

STANESBY, Durh., a hand holding a horse-lock.

STANFIELD, Suss., on a mount, a vine, (fructed,) all vert. *Pl*.117, *cr*. 12, (without escutcheon.)

STANFORD, Eng., a buck's head, couped, attired, or. *Pl*. 91, *cr*. 14.

STANFORD, a lion's head, erased, gu. *Pl*. 81, *cr*. 4.

STANGER, Eng., a lion, rampant, gu. *Pl*. 67, *cr*. 5.

STANHOP, five bell-flowers, erect, ppr., leaved, vert.

STANHOPE, Yorks. and Notts., a tower, az., with a demi-lion, rampant, issuing from the battlements, or, (ducally crowned, gu.,) between paws a grenade, fired, ppr. *Pl*. 53, *cr*. 2.

STANHOPE, Earl of, and Baron Stanhope, (Stanhope,) Chesterfield, same crest. *Exitus acta probat*—and—*A Deo et rege*. *Pl*. 53, *cr*. 2.

STANHOPE, Earl of Harrington. *See* HARRINGTON.

STANHOPE, out of a mural coronet, a dragon's head, (vomiting flames.) *Pl*. 101, *cr*. 4.

STANHOPE, Earl and Baron, and Viscount Stanhope, of Mahon, (Stanhope,) a tower, az., thereon a demi-lion, rampant, or, (ducally crowned, gu.,) between paws a grenade, ppr. *A Deo et rege*. *Pl*. 53, *cr*. 2.

STANHOPE-SCUDAMORE, Bart., Middx., same crest.

STANHOPE-SPENCER, of Cannon Hall, Yorks. : 1. For *Stanhope*, a tower, az., thereon a demi-lion rampant, or, (ducally crowned, gu.,) between paws a grenade, fired, ppr. *A Deo et rege*. *Pl*. 53, *cr*. 2. 2. For *Spencer*, a sea-mew, ppr. *Dieu defend le droit*.

STANIER, out of a ducal coronet, or, a griffin's head, ppr. *Pl*. 54, *cr*. 14.

STANLEY, Norf., a stag's head, erased, ar., attired, or. *Pl*. 66, *cr*. 9.

STANLEY, Kent and Lanc., on a chapeau, gu., turned up, erm., a cradle, or, containing a child, swaddled, of the first, thereon an eagle, preying. *Sans changer*. *Pl*. 121, *cr*. 6.

STANLEY, Chesh., a stag's head, couped, ar., attired, or. *Pl*. 91, *cr*. 14.

STANLEY, Baron, U.K., (Stanley,) on a chapeau, gu., turned up, erm., an eagle, wings expanded, or, preying on an infant, ppr., swaddled, of the first, banded, ar. *Sans changer*. *Pl*. 121, *cr*. 6.

STANLEY, Northamp., an eagle, az., preying on a child, ppr., swaddled in a basket, gu. *Pl*. 121, *cr*. 6, (without chapeau.)

STANLEY, Earl of Derby. *See* DERBY.

STANLEY, Eng., a stag's head, ppr. *Pl*. 91, *cr*. 14.

STANLEY, a griffin's head, erased. *Pl*. 48, *cr*. 6.

STANLEY, a griffin's head, erased, ar., (charged with three ogresses), in mouth a lion's gamb, erased. *Pl*. 9, *cr*. 12, (gamb, *pl*. 94, *cr*. 13.)

STANLEY, a griffin's head, erased, sa., (on breast three bezants, in triangle,) in mouth a lion's gamb, erased, gu. *Pl*. 9, *cr*. 12, (gamb, *pl*. 94, *cr*. 13.)

STANLEY, a stag's head, couped, or. *Pl*. 91, *cr*. 14.

STANLEY, a stag's head, couped, ar., attired, or, gorged with a mural coronet, gold. *Pl*. 91, *cr*. 14, (gorging, *pl*. 74, *cr*. 1.)

STANLEY, Lond., Suss., and Derbs., an eagle's head, couped, ar., (charged with three ogresses, one and two,) in beak an eagle's leg, erased at thigh, gu. *Pl*. 100, *cr*. 10, (leg, *pl*. 103, *cr*. 4.)

STANLEY, an eagle's head, erased, or, in beak an eagle's leg, erased at thigh, gu. *Pl*. 100, *cr*. 10, (leg, *pl*. 103, *cr*. 4.)

STANLEY, Kent, a demi-heraldic-wolf, erased, ar., tufted, or.

STANLEY, Cumb., a stag's head, ar., attired, or, collared, vert. *Sans changer*. *Pl*. 125, *cr*. 6, (without roses.)

STANLEY, Suss. and Lanc., a stag's head, erased, ar., attired, or, collared, gu. *Ib*.

STANLEY, MASSEY-STANLEY, Bart., Chesh., a stag's head and neck, couped, ar., attired (and collared, or, the tongue hanging out,) gu. *Pl*. 91, *cr*. 14.

STANMER, Ess. and Chesh., a stag's head, erm., attired, or, gorged with a fess dancettée. *Pl*. 91, *cr*. 14.

STANNARD, Iri., an eagle, displayed, per pale, or and sa. *Pl*. 48, *cr*. 11.

STANNARD, Eng., on a ducal coronet, a dolphin, naiant, ppr. *Pl*. 94, *cr*. 14.

STANNOW, Norf., a demi-eagle, displayed, erm., (on breast three guttes-de-sang, two and one, in beak a holly-leaf, vert.) *Pl*. 22, *cr*. 11.

STANNUS, Carlingford, co. Louth, a talbot's head, (couped,) ar., collared, sa., lined, and catching a dove, volant, of the first. *Et vi et virtute*. *Pl*. 2, *cr*. 15.

STANSFIELD-CROMPTON, of Esholt Hall, Yorks. : 1. For *Stansfield*, a lion's head, erased, encircled by a wreath. *Nosce teipsum*. *Pl*. 22, *cr*. 3. 2. For *Crompton*, a demi-horse, sa., vulned in chest by an arrow, ppr. *Love and loyalty*.

STANTON, Norf., Warw., and Suff., a wolf, sejant, ar., guttée-de-sang, (collared and lined, or.) *Pl*. 110, *cr*. 4.

STANTON, Eng., an ermine, gu. *Pl*. 9, *cr*. 5.

STANTON, Beds. and Leic., a demi-lion, rampant, vairé, sa. and erm., ducally crowned, or. *Pl*. 61, *cr*. 4, (without branch.)

STAPERS, Lond., a lion, sejant, ar., in dexter an etoile, sa. *Pl*. 126, *cr*. 15, (etoile, *pl*. 141.)

STAPILFORD, a boar's head, couped, or, in mouth a (flower-branch,) vert. *Pl*. 125, *cr*. 7.

STAPLE, Eng., a ram, ar., armed and unguled, or. *God be our friend*. *Pl*. 109, *cr*. 2.

STAPLE, Eng., a lion, passant, ppr. *Pl*. 48, *cr*. 8.

STAPLE, Middx., a lion, rampant, collared. *Pl*. 88, *cr*. 1.

STAPLES, Norwood and Boughton Gifford, out of a crown vallary, ar., a lion's head, affrontée, gu., semée-de-lis, ducally crowned, or. *Pl* 1, *cr*. 5, (crown, *pl*. 2, *cr*. 2.)

2 F

STAPLES, Iri., a dexter arm, couped and embowed, hand holding up a fire grenade, fired, ppr. *Pl.* 62, *cr.* 9.
STAPLES, Eng., on a ducal coronet, a swan, in pride, ducally gorged, ppr. *Pl.* 111, *cr.* 10, (coronet, *same plate, cr.* 7.)
STAPLES, Bart., Iri., a demi-negro, affrontee, holding a bolt-staple, or.
STAPLES-BROWNE, Lauton, Oxon.: 1. Same as above. 2. An eagle, displayed, sa., wings, fretty, resting each claw on a mullet, or. *Pl.* 117, *cr.* 15, (mullet, *pl.* 141.)
STAPLETON, of Milton and Carleton, Yorks., out of a ducal coronet, a man's head, couped at shoulder, in profile, ppr., wreathed about temples, ar. and sa. *Pl.* 118, *cr.* 7, (coronet, *pl.* 128, *fig.* 3.)
STAPLETON, Ess., same crest. *Fide, sed cui vide.*
STAPLETON, Eng., a talbot, ar., on shoulders six guttes, gu. *Pro magnâ chartâ. Pl.* 120, *cr.* 8.
STAPLETON, Baron Le Despencer. *See* LE DESPENCER.
STAPLETON, Ess. and Yorks., a man's head, couped at shoulders, in profile, ppr., wreathed about head, ar. and sa. *Pl.* 126, *cr.* 8.
STAPLETON, Ess. and Yorks., a unicorn's head, erased, armed and attired, or. *Pl.* 67, *cr.* 1.
STAPLETON, Yorks., a Saracen's head, in profile, ppr. *Pl.* 81, *cr.* 15.
STAPLETON, Bart., Leeward Islands, out of a ducal coronet, a Saracen's head, affrontée, wreathed about temples, ar. and sa. *Pl.* 97, *cr.* 2, (coronet, *same plate, cr.* 13.)
STAPLETON-COTTON, Lord Combermere. *See* COMBERMERE.
STAPLEY, Suss., on a mount, vert, a buck, ar. *Pl.* 50, *cr.* 6.
STAPLEY, Suff., (on a mount, vert,) a stag, at gaze, ar., attired, or. *Pl.* 81, *cr.* 8.
STAPLEY, Suss., a demi-hairy-savage, girt round body with a belt, gu., rimmed and studded, or, thereon a chain, gold, in hands a staple, or, points downward.
STAPYLTON, Eng., a Saracen's head, affrontée, couped at shoulders, ppr. *Pl.* 19, *cr.* 1.
STAPYLTON, of Norton, Durh., out of a ducal coronet, or, a Saracen's head, affrontée, ppr. *Fide, sed cui vide. Pl.* 19, *cr.* 1, (coronet, *same plate, cr.* 9.)
STAPYLTON-MARTIN, of Myton, Yorks., in a ducal coronet, ar., a Saracen's head, affrontée, wreathed, ar. and sa. *Fide, sed cui vide. Pl.* 97, *cr.* 2, (coronet, *same plate, cr.* 13.)
STARK, Sco., a bull's head, erased, ar. *Fortiorum fortia facta.* (Another, sa.) *Pl.* 19, *cr.* 3.
STARK, Sco., a dexter hand holding by the horn a bull's head, erased, ar., and (dropping blood, ppr.) *Fortiorum fortia facta. Pl.* 26, *cr.* 8, (head, *pl.* 19, *cr.* 3.)
STARK, Sco. and America, a bull's head, erased, ar., (dropping blood,) ppr. *Fortiorum fortia facta. Pl.* 19, *cr.* 3.
STARK, and STARKE, Eng., out of a ducal coronet, or, a stag's head, gardant, gu., armed, of the first. *Pl.* 29, *cr.* 7.
STARKEY, Chesh. and Derbs., a stork's head, erased, per pale, ar. and sa., in beak, gu., a snake, vert. *Pl.* 41, *cr.* 6.
STARKEY, or STARKIE, Lond. and Lanc., a stork, sa. *Pl.* 33, *cr.* 9.

STARKEY, on a five-leaved coronet, a stork, sa., beaked and membered, gu. *Pl.* 33, *cr.* 9, (coronet, *pl.* 23, *cr.* 11.)
STARKEY, Lond., a stork's head, erased, per pale, ar. and sa., in beak a snake, vert. *Pl.* 41, *cr.* 6.
STARKEY, Derbs. and Chesh., a stork's head, per pale, ar. and sa., in beak, gu., a snake, vert. *Pl.* 41, *cr.* 6.
STARKEY, Chesh., two others, the same, the one with a mullet, and the other a crescent, for difference, (mullet and crescent, *pl.* 141.)
STARKIE, LE-GENDRE-NICHOLAS, Esq., of Huntroyde, Lanc., a stork, ppr. *Pl.* 33, *cr.* 9.
STARKY, a heron's head, erased, per pale, ar. and sa., in beak a snake, vert. *Pl.* 41, *cr.* 6.
STARLING, Eng., a lion's head, ppr., collared, az. *Pl.* 42, *cr.* 14.
STARLING, Norwich, a starling, wings addorsed, sa., resting dexter on an etoile of eight points. *Pl.* 6, *cr.* 11, (etoile, *pl.* 83, *cr.* 3.)
STARR, of Halifax, Nova Scotia, a lion, rampant, ppr. *Vive en espoir. Pl.* 67, *cr.* 5.
STARR, Eng., a demi-lion, ppr., holding a mullet, or. *Pl.* 89, *cr.* 10.
STARR, Kent, a lion, couchant, or, charged with an etoile, gu. *Pl.* 75, *cr.* 5, (without chapeau; etoile, *pl.* 141.)
STASAM, Eng., a bell, az. *Pl.* 73, *cr.* 15.
STATHAM, Eng., a lion's head, erased, within a fetterlock, ppr. *Pl.* 90, *cr.* 14.
STATHUM, Eng., a greyhound's head, erased, gu. *Pl.* 89, *cr.* 2.
STATIONERS TRADE, Lond., an open Bible, ppr., garnished, or. *Verbum, Domine, manet in æternum. Pl.* 15, *cr.* 12.
STAUNTON, Norf., Warw., and Suff., a wolf, sejant, ar., guttée-de-sang, (collared and lined, or.) *Pl.* 110, *cr.* 4.
STAUNTON, Warw., a fox, ppr. *Moderata durant. Pl.* 126, *cr.* 5.
STAUNTON, Linc., a lion, passant, or, in dexter a cross formée, fitched, gu. *Pl.* 106, *cr.* 5, (cross, *pl.* 125, *cr.* 2.)
STAUNTON, HENRY CHARLTON, Esq., of Staunton Hall, Notts., a fox, passant, ppr. *Pl.* 126, *cr.* 5.
STAUNTON, Bart., Iri., (on a mount,) a fox, statant, all ppr. *Pl.* 126, *cr.* 5.
STAVELEY, Eng., an oak-branch, and cross crosslet, fitched, in saltier. *Pl.* 98, *cr.* 11.
STAVELEY, a stag's head, cabossed. *Pl.* 36, *cr.* 1.
STAVERTON, a stag's head, erased, sa., (pierced through neck by an arrow, feathered and armed, or.) *Pl.* 66, *cr.* 9.
STAWELL, on a chapeau, a hawk, wings displayed, in beak a label, or. *Pl.* 105, *cr.* 4, (chapeau, *same plate, cr.* 5.)
STAWELL, Somers., out of a ducal coronet, gu., a demi-buck, or, attired, sa. *Pl.* 55, *cr.* 9, (coronet, *same plate.*)
STAWTON, Berks., a roebuck's head. *Pl.* 91, *cr.* 14.
STAYLEY, Eng., a globe on a stand, ppr. *Pl.* 81, *cr.* 1.
STAYLTON, Eng., a lion's paw, erased, holding a rose-branch, slipped and leaved, ppr. *Pl.* 60, *cr.* 14.
STAYNINGS, Somers., a bull. *Pl.* 66, *cr.* 11.
STEAD, Eng., on a chapeau, a salamander in flames, all ppr. *Pl.* 86, *cr.* 14.

STEAD, Sco., a nag's head. *Pl.* 81, *cr.* 6.
STEADE, PEGGE-BURNELL, of Beauchieff Abbey, Derbs., a stag, trippant, ar. *Pl.* 68, *cr.* 2.
STEADMAN, Eng., a demi-griffin, or. *Pl.* 18, *cr.* 6.
STEAVENSON, Northumb. and Sco., on a rock, ppr., a lion, couchant, gardant, or. *Cœlum, non solum. Pl.* 101, *cr.* 8, (rock, *pl.* 94, *cr.* 3.)
STEBBING, Norf., Suff., and Lond., a lion's head, erased, ar. *Pl.* 81, *cr.* 4.
STEDDERT, Sco., a star, issuing from a cloud, ppr. *Post nubes lux. Pl.* 16, *cr.* 13.
STEDMAN, Sco., a horse's head, or. *Pl.* 81, *cr.* 6.
STEDMAN, Eng., a peacock's head, between wings, in beak an adder, ppr. *Pl.* 50, *cr.* 9.
STEDMAN, Glouc., a demi-virgin, ppr., hair dishevelled, in dexter a cross crosslet, vert. *Pl.* 2, *cr.* 10, (cross, *pl.* 141.)
STEDMAN, a chevalier, in complete armour, on horseback, at speed, tilting with a lance, all ppr. *Pl.* 43, *cr.* 2.
STEDMAN, an anchor, ppr. *Pl.* 25, *cr.* 15.
STEDMAN, an anchor and cable, ppr. *Cuncta mea mecum. Pl.* 42, *cr.* 12.
STEED, Eng., a horse's head, erased, ar. *Pl.* 81, *cr.* 6.
STEEDE, Kent, a stag, trippant, ar. *Pl.* 68, *cr.* 2.
STEEDE, Kent, a reindeer, ar., attired, or. *Pl.* 12, *cr.* 8.
STEEDE, Kent, a reindeer, (current,) ar., attired, or. *Pl.* 12, *cr.* 8.
STEEDE, Kent, a castle, (environed with a laurel-branch.) *Pl.* 28, *cr.* 11.
STEEDMAN, Sco., an anchor, az. *For security. Pl.* 25, *cr.* 15.
STEEL, Sco., a horse, passant, sa. *Pl.* 15, *cr.* 14.
STEEL, and STEELE, Eng., out of a ducal coronet, or, a demi-ostrich, wings addorsed, gu. *Pl.* 29, *cr.* 9.
STEEL, Somers. and Suff., a stork, ar. *Pl.* 33, *cr.* 9.
STEEL, and STEELE, a cubit arm, (in armour,) hand holding up an esquire's helmet. *Pl.* 37, *cr.* 15.
STEELE, Eng., a lion's head, erased, gu. *Pl.* 81, *cr.* 4.
STEELE, or STEELL, Sco., a lion's head, erased, gu. *Prudentiâ et animis. Pl.* 81, *cr.* 4.
STEELE, Bart., Iri., a demi-eagle, displayed, in beak a snake, all ppr. *Pl.* 22, *cr.* 11, (snake, *pl.* 41, *cr.* 6.)
STEER, Eng., an arm, in armour, embowed, with a shield buckled on, ppr. *Pl.* 98, *cr.* 5.
STEER, Eng., two oars, in saltier, ppr. *Pl.* 7, *cr.* 9.
STEER, Eng., an eagle, wings addorsed, devouring a land-tortoise, ppr. *Pl.* 70, *cr.* 8.
STEERE, Surr., a dexter arm, vested, gu., hand holding a sword, (in pale,) ppr., hilt and pommel, or, the blade entwined by a serpent, head downward, also ppr. *Pl.* 116, *cr.* 11, (vesting, *pl.* 39, *cr.* 1.)
STEERE, Surr. : 1. For *Steere*, out of a (mural) coronet, per pale, gu. and sa., a lion's gamb, erect, ar., armed, of the first. *Pl.* 67, *cr.* 7. 2. An arm, embowed, vested, gu., cuffed, ar., in hand, ppr., a sword, erect, of the second, hilt, or, on blade a snake, entwined, vert. *Tu ne cede malis. Pl.* 116, *cr.* 11, (vesting, *pl.* 39, *cr.* 1.)
STEERES, Surr., out of a mural coronet, a lion's gamb, erect. *Tu ne cede malis. Pl.* 67, *cr.* 7, (coronet, *pl.* 128, *fig.* 18.)
STEERR, and STEERRS, Eng., a horse's head, sa., maned, or. *Pl.* 81, *cr.* 6.
STEERS, Iri., on a chapeau, a wyvern, sans legs, wings expanded, ppr. *Pl.* 80, *cr.* 8.
STEERS, Eng., a griffin, sejant, or. *Pl.* 100, *cr.* 11.
STEIN, Sco., an eagle's head, between wings. *Ad diem tendo. Pl.* 81, *cr.* 10.
STEINMAN, a demi-ibex, rampant, ar., armed, or, charged on shoulder with a cross pattée, az. *Ante expectatam diem.*
STEINMETZ, Eng., two elephants' trunks, addorsed, sa. *Pl.* 24, *cr.* 8.
STELTON, Eng., a yew-tree, ppr. *Pl.* 49, *cr.* 13.
STEMPE, Hants, a greyhound's head, couped, sa., guttée-d'eau, (ducally gorged, ringed, and lined, or.) *Pl.* 43, *cr.* 11.
STENHOUSE, a talbot's head, collared, (in mouth a martlet,) ppr. *Fortes fideles. Pl.* 2, *cr.* 15.
STENNETT, or STENNITT, out of a ducal coronet, a stag's head, or. *Pl.* 91, *cr.* 14, (coronet, *pl.* 29, *cr.* 7.)
STENT, Suss., a colt's head, in mouth a banner.
STENYNGE, Somers. and Suff., a ram, passant, gu., attired, or. *Pl.* 109, *cr.* 2.
STEPHEN, Sco., a leopard's head, affrontée, or. *Pl.* 66, *cr.* 14.
STEPHEN, Middx., an eagle, displayed, with two heads, sa., beaked and legged, or. *Pl.* 87, *cr.* 11, (without flame.)
STEPHEN, Glouc., out of a ducal coronet, a dolphin's head, ar. *Pl.* 112, *cr.* 8, (coronet, *pl.* 128, *fig.* 3.)
STEPHENS, a demi-eagle, wings addorsed. *Pl.* 19, *cr.* 9, (without coronet.)
STEPHENS, Wilts., between wings, or, a raven's head, erm. *Pl.* 27, *cr.* 13, (wings, *same plate, cr.* 8.)
STEPHENS, Ess., an eagle, or, preying on a (lion's gamb, erased,) gu. *Pl.* 61, *cr.* 3.
STEPHENS, Cornw., on a rock, ppr., a salmon, in fess, ar., (in mouth a rose, gu., stalked and leaved, vert.) *Pl.* 85, *cr.* 7, (rock, *pl.* 31, *cr.* 3.)
STEPHENS, HENRY-LEWIS, Esq., of Tregenna Castle, Cornw., a lion, rampant, ar., guttéede-sang. *Virtutis amore. Pl.* 67, *cr.* 5.
STEPHENS, Salop and Cornw., a demi-eagle, displayed, or, beaked and winged, sa. *Pl.* 22, *cr.* 11
STEPHENS, Ess., a demi-eagle, displayed, or. *Pl.* 22, *cr.* 11.
STEPHENS, Eng., an eagle's head, or, between wings, erm. *Pl.* 81, *cr.* 10.
STEPHENS, of Waterford, Iri., a cock, gu. *Pl.* 67, *cr.* 14.
STEPHENS, Rev. RICHARD-RUDING, of Little Sodbury, Glouc., a demi-eagle, displayed, or. *Deus intersit. Pl.* 22, *cr.* 11.
STEPHENSON, a ship in full sail, ppr. *Pl.* 109, *cr.* 8.
STEPHENSON, Parish of St Luke's, Lond., an eagle, displayed, in dexter a sword, in pale, (in sinister a pistol,) all ppr. *For right. Pl.* 99, *cr.* 5.

STEPHENSON, a leopard's head and shoulders, ppr., fire issuing from mouth. *Pl.* 112, *cr.* 9.
STEPHENSON, Berks., Lond., Yorks., Linc., Cumb., and Derb., a garb, or. *Pl.* 48, *cr.* 10.
STEPHENSON, Middx., a hawk's head, erased, or. *Pl.* 34, *cr.* 11.
STEPKINS, Middx., a stag's head, couped, ar., attired, or. *Pl.* 91, *cr.* 14.
STEPNEY, Wel., a talbot's head, erased, gu., eared, or, gorged with a collar, chequy, gold and az., in mouth a buck's horn, of the second. *Fide et vigilantiâ*. *Pl.* 2, *cr.* 15, (horn, *pl.* 5, *cr.* 3.)
STEPPLE, a sword and laurel-branch in saltier, ppr. *Pl.* 50, *cr.* 4, (branch, *pl.* 123, *cr.* 5.)
STERLING, Iri., on point of sword, erect, ppr., a maunch, gu. *Pl.* 78, *cr.* 1.
STERLING, Herts, a lion, passant, ppr. *Pl.* 48, *cr.* 8.
STERN, Eng., a griffin, segreant, ppr. *Pl.* 67, *cr.* 13.
STERNE, Norf., Herts., Cambs., Bucks., and York, a falcon, rising, ppr. *Pl.* 105, *cr.* 4.
STERNE, Norf., Herts., Cambs., Bucks., and York, a cock-starling, ppr.
STERRY, Eng., a fir-branch, fructed, or. *Pl.* 80, *cr.* 1.
STERRY, Eng., a sword, in bend, ppr. *Pl.* 22, *cr.* 7.
STERT, Devons., a cross formée, sa., between wings, ar. *Pl.* 29, *cr.* 14.
STEUART, of Allanton, a dexter hand holding a thistle, both ppr. *Juvant aspera fortes—* and—*Virtutis in bello præmium*. *Pl.* 36, *cr.* 6.
STEUART, Sco., a demi-lion, rampant. *Hinc orior*. *Pl.* 67, *cr.* 10.
STEUART, Sco., a dexter and sinister hand holding up a heart, ppr. *Corde et manu*. *Pl.* 43, *cr.* 15.
STEUART, Sco., a pelican, in nest, feeding her young, ppr. *Salus per Christum Redemptorem*. *Pl.* 44, *cr.* 1.
STEUART, Earl of Castle-Steuart. *See* CASTLE-STEUART.
STEUART, Sco., a lion's head, erased, gu. *Stat felix, amice Domino*. *Pl.* 81, *cr.* 4.
STEUART, Bart., Sco., a thistle, and a full-blown rose, in saltier, ppr. *Juvant aspera probum*. *Pl.* 57, *cr.* 10.
STEUART, WILLIAM-RICHARD, Esq., of Stewart's Lodge, co. Carlow, a pelican, ar., winged, or, in nest, feeding her young, ppr. *Pl.* 44, *cr.* 1.
STEVENS, of St Ives, Cornw., a lion, rampant, ar., guttée-de-sang. *Pl.* 67, *cr.* 5.
STEVENS, Gloucester, an eagle, issuing, wings displayed, or, charged on breast with a mullet, sa. *Ad diem tendo*. *Pl.* 44, *cr.* 14.
STEVENS, Edinr., an eagle, (rising,) looking at the sun, ppr. *Ad diem tendo*. *Pl.* 43, *cr.* 5.
STEVENS, an eagle, wings addorsed, preying on a (talon.) *Pl.* 61, *cr.* 3.
STEVENS, out of a ducal coronet, a cubit arm, vested and cuffed, hand holding a book, expanded. *Pl.* 89, *cr.* 11, (book, *pl.* 82, *cr.* 5.)
STEVENS, out of a ducal coronet, a demi-lion, holding a flag. *Pl.* 45, *cr.* 7, (flag, *pl.* 99, *cr.* 2.)
STEVENS, Sco., a dexter hand holding a mason's chisel, ppr. *Vi et arte*.
STEVENS, a garb, or, banded. *Pl.* 48, *cr.* 10.

STEVENS, Berks, a demi-falcon, displayed, or. *Pl.* 103, *cr.* 6, (without coronet.)
STEVENS, Cornw., a demi-lion, rampant, ar., guttée-de-sang. *Pl.* 67, *cr.* 10.
STEVENSON, Cumb. and Lond., a garb, erminois. *Pl.* 48, *cr.* 10.
STEVENSON, a dexter hand, issuing from a cloud, holding a laurel garland, all ppr. *Cœlum, non solum*. *Pl.* 88, *cr.* 13.
STEVENSON, a hand holding a scroll, rolled up, ppr. *Fidus in arcanis*. *Pl.* 27, *cr.* 4.
STEVENSON, Chesh., a rose-tree, bearing, ppr. *Virtus ubique sedem*. *Pl.* 23, *cr.* 2.
STEVENSON, a griffin's head, couped. *Pl.* 38, *cr.* 3.
STEVENSON, out of a ducal coronet, an eagle's head, between wings. *Pl.* 66, *cr.* 5.
STEVENSON, an antelope's head, erased. *Pl.* 24, *cr.* 7.
STEVENSON, on the top of a hollow rock, a lion, couchant.
STEVENSON, Uffington, Linc.: 1. For *Stevenson*, a demi-lion, regardant, gu., charged on shoulder with a cross crosslet, fitched, between paws, a mullet, or. *Pl.* 33, *cr.* 2, (cross and mullet, *pl.* 141.) 2. For *Bellairs*, a lion's gamb, per pale, gu. and sa. *Virtus tutissima cassis*. *Pl.* 126, *cr.* 9.
STEVENSON, a demi-lion, ar. *Pl.* 67, *cr.* 10.
STEVENSON, Sco., a dexter hand holding a laurel crown, ppr. *Cœlum, non solum*. *Pl.* 86, *cr.* 1.
STEVENSON, Sco., a dexter hand holding a scroll of vellum, ppr. *Fidus in arcanum*. *Pl.* 27, *cr.* 4.
STEVENSON, Derb. and Linc., a garb, or. *Pl.* 48, *cr.* 10.
STEVENSTONE, Sco., a dexter hand, issuing from a cloud, holding a garland of laurel, ppr. *Cœlum, non solum*. *Pl.* 88, *cr.* 13.
STEVENTON, Salop, a stag's head, couped. *Pl.* 91, *cr.* 14.
STEVENTON, Salop, a stag's head, cabossed, ppr. *Pl.* 36, *cr.* 1.
STEVYNSON, Derbs. and Linc., a garb, or. *Pl.* 48, *cr.* 10.
STEWARD, RICHARD-OLIVER-FRANCIS, Esq., of Nottington House, Dors., a pelican, vulning, ppr. *Pl.* 109, *cr.* 15.
STEWARD, on a griffin's head, erased, gu., beaked, ar., (a bend, raguly, or, between three bezants, one and two.) *Pl.* 48, *cr.* 6.
STEWARD, a stag, ppr., (ducally gorged) and attired, or. *Pl.* 50, *cr.* 6, (without mount.)
STEWARD, a griffin's head, couped, gu. *Pl.* 38, *cr.* 3.
STEWARD, Cambs., Suff., and Norf., a stag, passant, ppr., attired, ar., ducally gorged, gu. *Pl.* 68, *cr.* 2, (gorging, *same plate*, *cr.* 6.)
STEWARD, Cambs., Suff., and Norf., a lion, rampant, gu., (ducally) collared, or. *Pl.* 88, *cr.* 1.
STEWARD, Northamp., a stag, ppr., (gorged with a collar, chequy, ar. and az.) *Pl.* 50, *cr.* 6, (without mount.)
STEWART, Sco., a unicorn's head, between two branches of laurel, in orle, ppr. *Pl.* 54, *cr.* 9.
STEWART, Sco., a pelican, feeding her young, in a nest, all ppr. *Virescit*. *Pl.* 44, *cr.* 1.
STEWART, Sco., a lion's head. *Pl.* 126, *cr.* 1.

STEWART, Baron. *See* LONDONDERRY, Marquess of.
STEWART, Baron Blantyre. *See* BLANTYRE.
STEWART, a hand, issuing, holding a scimitar, all ppr. *Avant. Pl.* 29, *cr.* 8.
STEWART, a unicorn's head and neck, issuing. *Quhidder will ye. Pl.* 20, *cr.* 1.
STEWART, Sco., a bee, erect, wings expanded, ppr. *God will provide. Pl.* 100, *cr.* 3.
STEWART, Sco., a man's head, affrontée, armed with a helmet, ppr. *Pro rege et patriâ. Pl.* 53, *cr.* 8.
STEWART, a demi-lion, rampant, gu. *Nobilis ira*—and—*Avito viret honore. Pl.* 67, *cr.* 10.
STEWART, a garb, or, surmounted of a crow, ppr. *Judge nought. Pl.* 112, *cr.* 10.
STEWART, WILLIAM, Esq., of Ardvorlich, Perth, a dexter naked arm, in hand a sword, in bend sinister, ppr., hilt and pommel, or. *Deo juvante, vinco. Pl.* 34, *cr.* 7.
STEWART, HENRY, Esq., of St Fort, Fife, a dexter cubit arm, in hand a dagger, in pale, both ppr. *Never fear. Pl.* 23, *cr.* 15.
STEWART, Glenormiston, Peebles, a branch of olive and Indian palm, in saltier. *Pax copia virtus. Pl.* 63, *cr.* 3, (olive, *pl.* 98, *cr.* 8.)
STEWART, a pelican, feeding her young, or, in nest, vert. *Salus per Christum redemptorem. Pl.* 44, *cr.* 1.
STEWART, Sco., a unicorn's head and neck, ar., maned, or, horned, gu. *Quhidder will zie. Pl.* 20, *cr.* 1.
STEWART, Sco., a unicorn's head, issuing, ar., maned, horned, and beaked, or. *Quhidder will zie. Pl.* 20, *cr.* 1.
STEWART, Sco. and Eng., a thistle and sprig of rose-tree, in saltier, ppr. *Juvant aspera probum. Pl.* 57, *cr.* 10.
STEWART, Sco., a savage's head, couped, ppr. *Reddunt commercia mitem. Pl.* 81, *cr.* 15.
STEWART, JOHN, Esq., of Belladrum, Inverness, two hands, conjoined, holding a man's heart, ppr. *Corde et manu. Pl.* 43, *cr.* 15.
STEWART, Sco., a man's head, couped, ppr. *Pro rege et patriâ. Pl.* 81, *cr.* 15.
STEWART, Sco., a bee, volant, in arriere, ppr. *Providentiæ fido. Pl.* 100, *cr.* 3.
STEWART, Sco., a gilliflower, slipped, ppr. *Viresco. Pl.* 22, *cr.* 9.
STEWART, Sco., a greyhound, couchant, within two branches of bay, ppr. *Fide et operâ. Pl.* 102, *cr.* 13.
STEWART, Sco., a dexter hand grasping a sword, ppr. *Avant. Pl.* 21, *cr.* 10.
STEWART, Sco., a boar's head, couped, or. *Virtute orta. Pl.* 48, *cr.* 2.
STEWART, Sco., a unicorn's head, issuing, ar., horned, or. *Pass forward. Pl.* 20, *cr.* 1.
STEWART, Sco., a pelican, in nest, feeding her young. *Salus per Christum redemptorem. Pl.* 44, *cr.* 1.
STEWART, Sco., a dexter hand holding a dagger, erect, ppr., hilt and pommel, or. *Never fear. Pl.* 23, *cr.* 15.
STEWART, Sco., a pelican, in her nest, ppr. *Salus per Christum redemptorem Pl.* 44, *cr.* 1.
STEWART, Sco., a unicorn's head, ar., maned, and horned, or. *Whadder. Pl.* 20, *cr.* 1.
STEWART, Sco., a demi-lion, rampant, gu., in dexter a dagger, in pale, ppr. *Hinc orior. Pl.* 41 *cr.* 12.

STEWART, Sco., a lion's head, erased, gu. *Nil sistere contra. Pl.* 81, *cr.* 4.
STEWART, Sco., a pelican, vulning, ppr. *Virescit vulnere. Pl.* 109, *cr.* 15.
STEWART, Sco., a demi-lion, rampant, gu. *Hinc orior. Pl.* 67, *cr.* 10.
STEWART, Sco., a lion's head, erased, ppr. *Semper fidelis. Pl.* 81, *cr.* 4.
STEWART, Sco., a dexter hand holding a thistle, slipped, both ppr. *Aspera juvant. Pl.* 36, *cr.* 6.
STEWART, Sco., a demi-lion, ppr. *Nobilis ira. Pl.* 67, *cr.* 10.
STEWART, Sco., a demi-lion, rampant, gu., langued and armed, az. *Nobilis ira. Pl.* 67, *cr.* 10.
STEWART, Sco., a bee, volant, ppr. *Parat et curat. Pl.* 100, *cr.* 3.
STEWART, Sco., a phœnix in flames, ppr. *Virtute fortuna comes. Pl.* 44, *cr.* 8.
STEWART, of Lorn, a hand holding a key, in bend. *Pl.* 41, *cr.* 11.
STEWART, Sco., a unicorn's head. *Quhidder will zie. Pl.* 20, *cr.* 1.
STEWART, Sco., a dragon's head, vert. *Pass forward. Pl.* 87, *cr.* 12.
STEWART, a lion's head, erased. *Spero meliora. Pl.* 81, *cr.* 4.
STEWART, Sco., a lion's head, erased, gu. *Stat felix, amice Domino. Pl.* 81, *cr.* 4.
STEWART, Bart., Sco.: 1. On the dexter side, a lion's head, erased, gu., armed and langued, az. *Spero meliora. Pl.* 81, *cr.* 4. 2. And on the sinister side, a demi-savage, holding a club over shoulder, ppr., wreathed about head and middle with laurel, vert. *I mean well. Pl.* 14, *cr.* 11.
STEWART, Sco., a dexter hand holding a dagger, ppr. *Pro rege, et lege. Pl.* 28, *cr.* 4.
STEWART, Sco., a lion's head, erased, gu. *Lædere noli. Pl.* 81, *cr.* 4.
STEWART, Iri., a dexter hand, couped below elbow, holding a heart, in pale, all ppr. *Nil desperandum. Pl.* 59, *cr.* 12.
STEWART, a dexter hand, in pale, grasping a rose and thistle, in saltier. *Pl.* 118, *cr.* 9, (thistle, *pl.* 57, *cr.* 10.)
STEWART, a griffin, passant. *Pl.* 61, *cr.* 14.
STEWART, Sco., trunk of old oak-tree sprouting a branch on the dexter side, acorned, ppr. *Resurgam. Pl.* 92, *cr.* 8.
STEWART, Sco., a lion's paw, and a palm-branch, in saltier, ppr. *Christus mihi lucrum. Pl.* 63, *cr.* 3, (paw, *pl.* 126, *cr.* 9.)
STEWART, Sco., a king enthroned, holding in dexter hand a sword, and in sinister a falcon. *Sic fuit, est, et erit.*
STEWART, Sco., in hand a thistle, ppr. *Virtutis præmium. Pl.* 36, *cr.* 6.
STEWART, Sco., a demi-lion, gu., in dexter a buckle, or. *Suffibulatus majores sequor. Pl.* 39, *cr.* 14, (buckle, *same plate, cr.* 8.)
STEWART, Sco., an anchor, erect, az., ensigned with a man's heart, ppr. *Fixus ac solidus. Pl.* 62, *cr.* 15, (heart, *pl.* 55, *cr.* 13.)
STEWART, Sco., a demi-savage, wreathed round loins, chequy, az. and ar., on head an antique crown, holding over dexter shoulder a club, and in sinister a heart, between wings, imperially crowned. *Dant priscæ decorem. Pl.* 14, *cr.* 11, (heart, *pl.* 52, *cr.* 2.)
STEWART, Earl of Galloway. *See* GALLOWAY.

STEWART, Sco., a civet-cat, couchant, ppr. *Semper paratus.*
STEWART, Sco., two bees, in saltier, ppr. *Providentiæ fido.* Pl. 13, cr. 1.
STEWART, Sco., a demi-lion, gardant, ppr., in dexter a mullet, sa. *Suffibulatus majores sequor.* Pl. 89, cr. 10.
STEWART, Sco., a pelican, ar., winged, or, in nest, feeding her young, ppr. *Virescit.* Pl. 44, cr. 1.
STEWART, Sco., a demi-lion, in dexter a sword, and in sinister a pair of scales, all ppr. *Honestate vetustas stat.* Pl. 41, cr. 13, (scales, pl. 57, cr. 1.)
STEWART, Sco., a holly-leaf, slipped, vert. *Sic virescit industria.* Pl. 78, cr. 12.
STEWART, Sco., a hand holding a plumb-rule, ppr. *Candide.* Pl. 28, cr. 6, (rule, pl. 13, cr. 3.)
STEWART, Sco., a sovereign in a chair of state, in armour, regally crowned, and robed, in dexter a dagger, in sinister an owl, all ppr. *Sic fuit, est erit.*
STEWART, a griffin's head, couped, gu. Pl. 38, cr. 3.
STEWART, a dragon, (statant,) or. Pl. 90, cr. 10.
STEWART, Bart., Iri., a unicorn's head, couped, ar., horned and crined, or, between two (olive)-branches, ppr. *Forward.* Pl. 54, cr. 9.
STEWART, Bart., Sco., two bees, counter-volant, ppr. *Provide.* Pl. 13, cr. 1.
STEWART, Bart., Iri., a dexter hand in armour, ppr., holding a heart, gu. *Nil desperandum est.* Pl. 59, cr. 12, (armour, pl. 33, cr. 4.)
STEWART-VANE, Marquess of Londonderry. *See* LONDONDERRY.
STEWEKLEY, Somers., a triple plume of ostrich-feathers, intermixed, one, ar., the others, sa. Pl. 114, cr. 8, (without coronet.)
STEWINS, Eng., a cross moline, lozenge-pierced, gu. Pl. 91, cr. 10.
STIBBERT, a castle, (ruined in sinister tower,) with flag displayed. Pl. 123, cr. 14.
STIBBERT, Lond., out of an Eastern crown, or, doubled, erm., the second and fourth points, vert, an arm, in armour, embowed, gold, grasping a Persian scimitar, hilt and pommel, or. *Per ardua.* Pl. 81, cr. 11, (coronet, pl. 25, cr. 8.)
STIDDOLPH, Surr., a wolf's head, erased, per fess, or and gu. Pl. 14, cr. 6.
STIDDOLPH, Surr., a wolf's head, erased, ar. Pl. 14, cr. 6.
STILES, a wolf's head, (erased,) sa., collared, or, the neck below the collar fretty, gold. Pl. 8, cr. 4.
STILES, Berks., an arm, hand grasping a head, all ppr., the elbow tied with a scarf, az.
STILL, Wilts., Somers., and Suff., a stork, ar. Pl. 33, cr. 9.
STILL, a kingfisher, ppr.
SLILLINGFLEET, a leopard's head and neck, ppr., collared and chained, gu. *Magna est veritas.* Pl. 40, cr. 10.
STILLINGTON, Eng., on a ducal coronet, a mullet, between two branches of laurel, in orle. Pl. 82, cr. 6.
STIRLIN, Eng., a griffin's head, erased, ar. Pl. 48, cr. 6.
STIRLING, Sco., a lion, passant, ppr. *Fides servata secundat.* Pl. 48, cr. 8.

STIRLING, Sco., a ship under sail, ppr. *Faven tibus auris.* Pl. 109, cr. 8.
STIRLING, Sco., a dexter hand pointing a lancet, ppr. *By wounding I cure.* Pl. 29, cr. 6.
STIRLING, Sco., an eagle, displayed, in dexter, a sword, (in sinister a pistol,) ppr. *For right* —and—*Noctesque diesque præsto.* Pl. 99, cr. 5.
STIRLING, WILLIAM, Esq., of Keir, Perths., a moor's head, couped, ppr. *Gang forward.* Pl. 120, cr. 3.
STIRLING, JOHN, Esq., of Kippendavie, Perths., a Saracen's head, in profile, wreathed. *Gang forward.* Pl. 36, cr. 3.
STIRLING, Bart., Sco., a demi-moor, issuing, at his back a quiver of arrows, (dexter arm stretched out, holding an arrow in fess,) all ppr. *Forward.* Pl. 80, cr. 9.
STIRLING, Sco., same crest.
STIRLING, Bart., Sco., a lion, passant, gu. *Semper fidelis.* Pl. 48, cr. 8.
STIRLING, Bart., Sco., a moor's head, couped, ppr. *Gang forward.* Pl. 120, cr. 3.
STIRLING, Sco., a black's head, couped, sa. *Gang forward.* Pl. 120, cr. 3.
STIRLING, Sco., a lady, issuing, from breasts upward, ppr., attired and winged, or, ensigned on head with a cross, gu. Pl. 90, cr. 11.
STIRLING, Sco., a boar's head, couped, ppr. Pl. 48, cr. 2.
STIRLING, Sco., a lion's gamb, holding an (oak)-branch, fructed, ppr. *Hic fidus et robore.* Pl. 68, cr. 10.
STIRLING, Sco., a stag's head, erased, ppr. *Hic fidus et robore.* Pl. 66, cr. 9.
STIRLING, Sco., out of a ducal coronet, or, a stag's head, ppr. *Forward.* Pl. 91, cr. 14, (coronet, pl. 29, cr. 7.)
STIRLING, Sco., out of a ducal coronet, or, a buck's head, az., attired, gold. *Ib.*
STIRLING, Bart., of Faskine, Sco., a dexter armed arm, issuing from a ducal coronet, hand grasping a dagger, in fess, all ppr., hilt and pommel, or. Pl. 120, cr. 11, (coronet, *same plate*, cr. 13.)
STIRROP, an arm, in armour, embowed to sinister, garnished, or, in gauntlet a tilting-lance, ppr., thereon a forked pennon, flowing to sinister, per fess, ar. and sa., fringed and tasselled, gold, charged with an escutcheon, bearing the arms of the Holy Trinity.
STIVEN, Sco., a crescent, gu. *Cresco.* Pl. 18, cr. 14.
STOBART, Durh., a cubit arm, in hand a dagger, point upward. Pl. 23, cr. 15.
STOCK, Eng., a domed tower, with a flag displayed from top. Pl. 42, cr. 10.
STOCK, Iri., a pheon, ppr., point upward. Pl. 56, cr. 15.
STOCK, a hawk, ppr., wings displayed, belled, and (in beak a laurel-branch, or.) Pl. 105, cr. 4.
STOCKBRIDGE, Eng., out of a cloud, two dexter hands, in armour, conjoined, holding up a heart inflamed, all ppr. Pl. 52, cr. 13.
STOCKDALE, Eng., out of a ducal coronet, or, a triple plume of ostrich-feathers, ppr. Pl. 114, cr. 8.
STOCKDALE, Yorks., out of a mural coronet, or, a griffin's head, ar. Pl. 101, cr. 6, (without gorging.)
STOCKDALE, Yorks., a talbot, passant, ppr. Pl. 120, cr. 8.

STOKEN, Iri., an arm, from shoulder, hand holding a garland of laurel, ppr. *Pl.* 118, *cr.* 4.

STOCKENSTROM, Bart., of Masstrom, Cape of Good Hope, in front of stump of tree, with (one) branch sprouting from dexter side, two swords, in saltier, points upward, ppr., hilts and pommels, or. *Fortis, si jure fortis. Pl.* 75, *cr.* 13, (stump, *pl.* 92, *cr.* 8.)

STOCKER, Eng., an old man's head, in profile, (vested, gu.,) wreathed about temples, ar. and sa. *Pl.* 126, *cr.* 8.

STOCKES, Eng., a demi-lion, rampant. *Fortis, non ferox. Pl.* 67, *cr.* 10.

STOCKET, Lond. and Kent, on stump of tree, couped and eradicated, ar., a lion, sejant, sa. *Pl.* 76, *cr.* 11.

STOCKHAM, a demi-eagle, displayed, or, on breast a thistle, ppr. *Pl.* 22, *cr.* 11.

STOCKLEY, Eng., a hind's head, ppr. *Pl.* 21, *cr.* 9.

STOCKOE, Eng., a horse's head, erased, or, bridled, sa. *Pl.* 92, *cr.* 1.

STOCKS, or STOKES, Eng., out of a ducal coronet, or, a plume of ostrich feathers, ar., in a case, gu. *Pl.* 106, *cr.* 11, (without chapeau.)

STOCKTON, Eng., a lion, rampant, supporting an Ionic pillar, ppr. *Pl.* 22, *cr.* 15, (pillar, *pl.* 33, *cr.* 1.)

STOCKTON, a wolf's head, erased, collared and tied behind. *Pl.* 8, *cr.* 4.

STOCKWELL, Kent, (against the stock of a tree, couped and leaved, ppr.,) a lion, sejant, sa., collared, or, supporting between paws a bezant, charged with a cross formée, gu. *Pl.* 14, *cr.* 2, (charging, *pl.* 141.)

STOCKWOOD, Eng., out of a mural coronet, a demi-lion, rampant, supporting a flag, gu. *Pl.* 86, *cr.* 11.

STODART, Sco., out of a cloud, ppr., a star of six points, waved, ar. *Post nubes lux. Pl.* 16, *cr.* 13, (star, *pl.* 63, *cr.* 9.)

STODDARD, Suff., a demi-horse, erm, environed round body with a ducal coronet, or. *Pl.* 91, *cr.* 2, (without wings.)

STODDART, Sco., a star, issuing from a cloud, ppr. *Post nubes lux. Pl.* 16, *cr.* 13.

STODDART, Sco., a mullet, issuing from a cloud. *Denique decus. Pl.* 16, *cr.* 13.

STODDYR, Eng., a fleur-de-lis, issuant, gu. *Pl.* 68, *cr.* 12.

STOKE, Eng., a (stork), regardant, ar., resting dexter on a pellet. *Pl.* 77, *cr.* 15, (pellet, *pl.* 141.)

STOKELY, Eng., an esquire's helmet, az. *Pl.* 109, *cr.* 5.

STOKES, Devons., a demi-lion, rampant, double-queued, erm. *Pl.* 120, *cr.* 10.

STOKES, a tiger, sejant, ar., guttée-de-sang, (collared and chained, or.) *Pl.* 26, *cr.* 9.

STOKES, Cambs., out of a ducal coronet, or, an arm, embowed, vested, gu., cuffed, ar., in hand, ppr., a staff, of the second, thereon an imperial crown, gold. *Pl.* 39, *cr.* 1, (coronet, *same plate, cr.* 2; staff, *pl.* 121, *cr.* 8.)

STOKEWOOD, Eng., out of a mural coronet, a demi-lion, rampant, supporting a flag, gu. *Pl.* 86, *cr.* 1.

STOKOG, Eng., a horse's head, (erased,) or, bridled, sa. *Pl.* 92, *cr.* 1.

STOLYON, Suss., a stag's head, (erased sa., on neck a bezant,) in mouth an acorn, or, stalked and leaved, vert. *Pl.* 100, *cr.* 8.

STOMPE, Berks. and Oxon., a demi-mule, ar.

STONARD, Eng., a leopard's head and neck, erased, gardant, ppr. *Pl.* 56, *cr.* 7.

STONE, Suff., a demi-lion. *Pl.* 67, *cr.* 10.

STONE, Ess., out of a ducal coronet, or, a griffin's head, between wings, gu., bezantée. *Pl.* 97, *cr.* 13.

STONE, Lond., out of a ducal coronet, a griffin's head, erm., between wings, or. *Pl.* 97, *cr.* 13.

STONE, Wilts., on a mount, vert, a horse, current, sa., bridled, crined, and hoofed, or. *Pl.* 57, *cr.* 9.

STONE, Eng., out of a ducal coronet, or, a demi-griffin, erm., winged and beaked, of the last. *Pl.* 39, *cr.* 2.

STONE, Lond., a unicorn's head, sa., issuing from rays, or, maned and armed, gold, (between wings,) of the first. *Pl.* 67, *cr.* 1, (rays, *pl.* 84, *cr.* 9; wings, *pl.* 1, *cr.* 15.)

STONE, Lond., a sea-horse, or, crined, gu., tail, ppr., between fore-feet an escallop, of the first. *Pl.* 103, *cr.* 3, (escallop, *pl.* 141.)

STONE, Suff. and Lond., out of a ducal coronet, a demi-peacock, wings (expanded,) or. *Pl.* 53, *cr.* 12, (coronet, *same plate.*)

STONE, Suss., a demi-cockatrice, wings expanded, or. *Pl.* 77, *cr.* 5, (without coronet.)

STONE, Suss., a demi-cockatrice, rising, ar., winged and crested, or. *Ib.*

STONE, Kent, a spaniel, passant, ar. *Pl.* 58, *cr.* 9.

STONE, Cornw., on a rock, paly-wavy of six, ar. and az., a salmon, ppr., (in mouth a rose, of the last, stalked and leaved, vert.) *Pl.* 85, *cr.* 7, (rock, *pl.* 31, *cr.* 3.)

STONEHEWER, out of a ducal coronet, or, an eagle's head, erased, ppr., on neck an escallop, ar. *Pl.* 20, *cr.* 12, (escallop, *pl.* 141.)

STONEHOUSE, Bart., Berks., a talbot's head, (couped,) ar., collared, sa., lined and catching a dove, volant, of the first. *Sublimiora petamus. Pl.* 2, *cr.* 15, (dove, *pl.* 25, *cr.* 6.)

STONER, Hants., out of a ducal coronet, sa., a demi-eagle, displayed, or. *Pl.* 9, *cr.* 6.

STONER, Eng., on a rock, ppr., a bird, ar., in mouth a stone. *Pl.* 99, *cr.* 14.

STONES, Eng., an eagle, displuming a wing, ppr. *Pl.* 114, *cr.* 5.

STONES, Derbs., a demi-dragon, pean, (holding a cross humettée, vert, gorged with a collar, ar., charged with three roses, gu.) *Pl.* 82, *cr.* 10.

STONES, Middx. and Lanc., a demi-dragon, vert, (collared, ar.,) supporting between paws a cross crosslet, sa. *Pl.* 82, *cr.* 10, (cross, *pl.* 141.)

STONESTREET, a bull's head, cabossed, ar., between wings, sa. *Pl.* 111, *cr.* 6, (wings, *pl.* 60, *cr.* 9.)

STONOR, Oxon, on a rock, ppr., charged with spots, gu. and az., a dove, ar., with a (stone) in beak. *Pl.* 85, *cr.* 14.

STOPFORD, Earl of Courtown. *See* COURTOWN.

STOPFORD, Iri., a lamb, ar., bearing a banner, gu. *Pl.* 48, *cr.* 13.

STOPFORD, WILLIAM-BRUCE, Esq., of Drayton House, Northamp., a wyvern, wings addorsed, vert. *Patriæ infelici fidelis. Pl.* 63, *cr.* 13.

STOPHAM, an escutcheon, sa. *Pl.* 36, *cr.* 11.

STORAR and STORER, a crane, ppr. *Pl.* 111, *cr.* 9.
STORER, ANTHONY-MORRIS, Esq., of Purley Park, Berks., a crane, ppr. *Dum spiro, spero. Pl.* 111, *cr.* 9.
STORER, the Rev. JOHN, M.A., of Combe Court, Surrey, a stork, ppr. *Pl.* 33, *cr.* 9.
STOREY, Eng., an escallop, or, between eagle's wings, ppr. *Pl.* 62, *cr.* 4.
STOREY, a heron. *Pl.* 6, *cr.* 13.
STOREY, on a garland of laurel, a raven, ppr. *Pl.* 54, *cr.* 10, (raven, *pl.* 123, *cr.* 2.)
STOREY, Dors., a stork, ppr. *Pl.* 33, *cr.* 9.
STORIE, two branches of olive, in saltier, ppr. *Mœret qui laborat. Pl.* 19, *cr.* 12, (olive, *pl.* 98, *cr.* 8.
STORIE, of Springfield Lodge, Surr., a demi-lion, rampant, double-queued, gu. *Courage et esperance. Pl.* 120, *cr.* 10.
STORK, Sco., a bull's head, erased, sa. *Fortiorum fortia facta. Pl.* 19, *cr.* 3.
STORKS, Eng., a buffalo's head, erased, gu. *Pl.* 57, *cr.* 7.
STORMONT, Viscount. *See* MANSFIELD, Earl of.
STORMYN, Eng., a bear, sejant, ppr. *Pl.* 1, *cr.* 1.
STORR, Eng., a cubit arm, in armour, couped, in fess, in hand a cross crosslet, fitched. *Pl.* 71, *cr.* 13.
STORY, Eng., a cupid, in dexter an arrow, (in sinister a bow, and at back a quiver,) ppr. *Pl.* 17, *cr.* 5.
STORY, a stork's head, erased, in beak a serpent, nowed. *Pl.* 41, *cr.* 6.
STORY, Durh., a stork's head, erased, gorged with a mural coronet. *Pl.* 32, *cr.* 5, (gorging, *pl.* 74, *cr.* 1.)
STOTE, a demi-lion, rampant, double-queued. *Pl.* 120, *cr.* 10.
STOTE, Northumb., a demi-lion, rampant, erminois, supporting a mullet, (pierced,) or. *Pl.* 89, *cr.* 10.
STOTEVILLE, Cambs., a plume of feathers, paly of six, ermine and ermines. *Pl.* 12, *cr.* 9.
STOTHART, in a cloud, a mullet of (six) points, ar. *Post nubes lux. Pl.* 16, *cr.* 13.
STOTHER, Eng., a camel's head, sa. *Pl.* 109, *cr.* 9.
STOTT, Sco., a martlet, az. *Alta petit. Pl.* 111, *cr.* 5.
STOTT, Eng., on a mount, a peacock, ppr. *Pl.* 9, *cr.* 1.
STOUGHTON, Warw., a redbreast, ppr. *Hoc signum non onus, sed honor. Pl.* 10, *cr.* 12.
STOUGHTON, Surr., a robin-redbreast, ppr. *Pl.* 10, *cr.* 12.
STOUGHTON, THOMAS-ANTHONY, Esq., of Owlpenn, Glouc.; Ballyhorgon, co. Kerry; and Gortugrennan, co. Cork, same crest.
STOURTON, Eng., a demi-greyfriar, ppr., vested in russet, girt, or, in dexter a scourge of three lashes, with knots, and in sinister a cross, both gold. *Loyal je serai durant ma vie. Pl.* 83, *cr.* 15, (cross, *pl.* 141.)
STOUT, Eng., a talbot, passant, or. *Pl.* 120, *cr.* 8.
STOVEN, or STOVIN, a bow, in fess, gu., transfixed by an arrow, erect and flighted, of the same, headed, ar. *Pl.* 76, *cr.* 10, (without arm.)
STOVIN, Eng., a dragon's head, vert. *Pl.* 87, *cr.* 12.

STOWE, Linc., on a ducal coronet, a leopard's head, or, between wings, vert. *Pl.* 17, *cr.* 9, (head, *pl.* 92, *cr.* 13.)
STOWERS, a rose, gu., seeded and barbed, ppr. *Pl.* 20, *cr.* 2.
STOWNE-LOWNDES, Brightwell Park, Oxon.: 1. Out of a ducal coronet, or, a griffin's head, ar., (charged with two bars-gemelle, gu.,) between wings, gold. *Pl.* 97, *cr.* 13. 2. A leopard's head, erased at neck, or, gorged with a laurel-branch, ppr. *Pl.* 94, *cr.* 10.
STRABANE, Viscount. *See* ABERCORN, Marquess of.
STRACEY, Bart., Norf., a lion, rampant, erminois, ducally crowned, gu., supporting a cross pattée, fitched, of the last. *Pl.* 125, *cr.* 2, (crown, *pl.* 98, *cr.* 1.)
STRACHAN, Sco., a hart, at gaze, attired, and unguled, gu. *Non timeo, sed caveo. Pl.* 81, *cr.* 8.
STRACHAN, Eng., on a ducal coronet, or, a wyvern, sans legs, vert. *Pl.* 104, *cr.* 11.
STRACHAN, Sco., a ship in full sail, ppr. *Juvat Deus impigros. Pl.* 109, *cr.* 8.
STRACHAN, a stag's head, erased. *Pl.* 66, *cr.* 9.
STRACHAN, or STRAUCHAN, Sco., a demi-stag, springing, or, in mouth a (thistle,) ppr. *Non timeo, sed caveo. Pl.* 55, *cr.* 9.
STRACHEY, Somers., an eagle displayed, gu., charged on breast with a cross pattée, fitched, ar. *Pl.* 12, *cr.* 7, (cross, *pl.* 125, *cr.* 2.)
STRACHEY, Somers., an eagle, displayed, gu., on breast a cross crosslet, fitched. *Pl.* 12, *cr.* 7, (cross, *pl.* 141.)
STRACHEY, Bart., Somers., a lion, rampant, erm., ducally crowned, or, supporting a cross pattée, fitched, gold. *Pl.* 125, *cr.* 2, (crown, *pl.* 98, *cr.* 11.)
STRACHEY, Ess. and Ruts., same crest.
STRADBROKE, Earl of, Viscount Dunwich, Baron Rous, and a Bart., (Rous;) a bunch of bay-leaves, piled in the form of a cone, vert. *Je vive en espoir. Pl.* 61, *cr.* 13.
STRADLING, Heref., a stag, trippant, ar., attired, or, collared. *Heb a hyw heb I him dyne a digon. Pl.* 68, *cr.* 2.
STRADLING, Heref., same crest.
STRADLING, Wel., a stag, at gaze, ar. *Pl.* 81, *cr.* 8.
STRAFFORD, Eng., an elephant, statant, sa. *Pl.* 56, *cr.* 14.
STRAFFORD, Baron, (Byng:) 1. An (heraldic-antelope, statant,) erm., horned, tusked, maned, and hoofed, or. *Tuebor. Pl.* 115, *cr.* 13. 2. *Of augmentation*, out of a mural coronet, an arm, embowed, vested, in hand a banner. *Pl.* 115, *cr.* 14, (arm, *pl.* 99, *cr.* 3.)
STRAHAN, Eng., on a ducal coronet, a wyvern, sans legs, ppr. *Pl.* 104, *cr.* 11.
STRAHAN, a dexter arm, embowed, wielding a scimitar, both ppr., hilt and pommel, or. *Pl.* 92, *cr.* 5.
STRAITON, Sco., a mortar, and therein a pestle, ppr. *Ardus vinco. Pl.* 83, *cr.* 6.
STRAITON, Captain, Sco., a falcon, rising, ppr. *Resurgere tento. Pl.* 105, *cr.* 4.
STRAKER, Durh., a horse at full speed, ppr. *Deus est super domo. Pl.* 107, *cr.* 5, (without spear.)
STRANG, Lond., a cluster of wine grapes, ppr. *Dulce quod utile. Pl.* 77, *cr.* 7.

STRANGE, Lanc. and Lond., a lion, passant, ar. *Pl.* 48, *cr.* 8.
STRANGE, Lond., two hands, clasped, ppr., couped at wrists. *Pl.* 1, *cr.* 2.
STRANGE, Glouc. and Norf., a lion, passant, gardant, the tail extended, or. *Pl.* 120, *cr.* 5.
STRANGE, Glouc. and Wilts., out of clouds, two hands, clasped, all ppr. *Pl.* 53, *cr.* 11.
STRANGE, a demi-lion, rampant. *Pl.* 67, *cr.* 10.
STRANGE, Earl. *See* ATHOLL, Duke of.
STRANGEBOW, Eng., a bull's head, cabossed, between two flags, (charged with a cross.) *Pl.* 118, *cr.* 8.
STRANGER, Eng., a fox, current, ppr. *Pl.* 80, *cr.* 5.
STRANGEWAYES, or STRANGWAYS, Lanc., Dors., and Yorks., a lion, passant, paly of six, ar. and gu. *Pl.* 48, *cr.* 8.
STRANGEWAYS, Dors., Lanc., and Yorks., a lion, passant, paly of six, ar. and gu. *Pl.* 48, *cr.* 8.
STRANGEWAYS, Sco., a lion, sa. *Pl.* 118, *cr.* 10.
STRANGEWICHE, Yorks., Dors., and Lanc., a lion, passant, paly of six, ar. and gu. *Pl.* 48, *cr.* 8.
STRANGFORD, Viscount, Iri., and Baron Penshurst, U.K., (Smythe,) a leopard's head, (erased,) ar., collared and chained, sa. *Virtus incendit vires*. *Pl.* 40, *cr.* 10.
STRANGFORTH, an arm, in armour, embowed, in hand a scimitar. *Pl.* 81, *cr.* 11.
STRANGWAYS, Yorks., a lion, passant, ar., paled, gu. *Ystoyeau et ne doublero*. *Pl.* 48, *cr.* 8.
STRANGWAYS, of Alne, Yorks.: 1. A lion, passant, paly of six, ar. and gu. *Pl.* 48, *cr.* 8. 2. Out of a ducal coronet, or, a boar's head, sa., between wings, az., pellettée, or. *Ystoyeau et ne doublero*. *Pl.* 102, *cr.* 14, (wings, *pl.* 27, *cr.* 8.)
STRANGWAYS, Earl of Ilchester. *See* ILCHESTER.
STRANSHAM, Kent, a demi-ostrich, in mouth a horse-shoe. *Pl.* 29, *cr.* 9, (shoe, *pl.* 99, *cr.* 12.)
STRATFORD, of Coventry, an arm, in armour, embowed, ppr., grasping a falchion, hilt and pommel, or. *Pl.* 2, *cr.* 8.
STRATFORD, Earl of Aldborough. *See* ALDBOROUGH.
STRATFORD, Eng., an arm, bent, ar., in hand a scimitar, blade, of the first, pommel, or, hand, ppr. *Pl.* 92, *cr.* 5.
STRATFORD, Iri., a goat's head, erased, ppr. *Pl.* 29, *cr.* 13.
STRATFORD, Glouc., an arm, in armour, embowed, in hand a scimitar, ppr. *Pl.* 81, *cr.* 11.
STRATFORD, Glouc. and Warw., a dexter arm, embowed, vested, ar., in hand a scimitar, or. *Pl.* 92, *cr.* 5, (vesting, *pl.* 120, *cr.* 1.)
STRATFORD DE REDCLIFFE, Viscount, a demi-griffin, az., guttée-d'or. *Ne cede malis, sed contra*. *Pl.* 18, *cr.* 6.
STRATHALLAN, Viscount, Baron Drummond, and Maderty, Sco., (Drummond,) a goshawk, wings expanded, ppr. *Prias mori quam fidem fallere*—and— *Virtutem coronat honos*. *Pl.* 105, *cr.* 4.
STRATHMORE and KINGHORN, Earl of, Viscount Lyon, Baron Glammis, Tannadyce, Seidlaw, and Stradichtie, Sco., (Lyon-Bowes,) within two branches of laurel, a lady to the girdle, vested, in dexter the royal thistle, all ppr., in allusion to the alliance of Sir John Lyon with Jean, daughter of Robert II. *In te, Domine, speravi*. *Pl.* 2, *cr.* 10, (branches, same plate, *cr.* 11; thistle, *pl.* 36, *cr.* 6.)
STRATON, Sco., a falcon, belled, ppr., wings expanded and inverted. *Surgere tento*. *Pl.* 105, *cr.* 4.
STRATON, Sco., an eagle, wings expanded, standing on a man's hand, in armour, couped, at wrist. *Surgere tento*. *Pl.* 126, *cr.* 7, (hand, *pl.* 83, *cr.* 13.)
STRATOUN, Sco., a pelican's head, erased, vulning, ppr. *Pl.* 26, *cr.* 1.
STRATTLE, a swan, wings addorsed and distended, ar. *Pl.* 46, *cr.* 5.
STRATTON, Eng., out of mural coronet, or, an eagle's head, ppr. *Pl.* 121, *cr.* 11.
STRATTON, Suff., a hawk, belled and jessed, ppr. *Pl.* 67, *cr.* 3.
STRAUNGE, Eng., two hands, couped at wrists, clasped together, the dexter, or, the sinster, ar. *Pl.* 1, *cr.* 2.
STRAUNGE, a wolf, az., (devouring a child, ppr.) *Pl.* 46, *cr.* 6.
STRAY, Eng., an eagle, regardant, or, wings expanded and inverted, ar., holding a sword, ppr. *Pl.* 87, *cr.* 5.
STRAY, an owl, or, wings displayed, gu., (charged on breast with three hurts, between two palets, gu.) *Pl.* 123, *cr.* 6, (without chapeau.)
STREATFIELD, a bunch of quills, one in bend (sinister,) ppr. *Pl.* 86, *cr.* 7.
STREATFIELD, Suss., a mailed arm and banner, *Pl.* 6, *cr.* 5.
STREET, an esquire's helmet, ppr., garnished, or. *Pl.* 109, *cr.* 5.
STREET, Middx., (on a mount, vert,) a Catherine-wheel, or, charged with a cup. *Pl.* 1, *cr.* 7, (cup, *pl.* 42, *cr.* 1.)
STREET, Lond., an arm, embowed, vested, hand holding a bell, pendent. *Pl.* 39, *cr.* 1, (bell, *pl.* 73, *cr.* 15.)
STREETE, a lion, rampant, or, supporting, between fore-paws a Catherine-wheel, gu. *Pl.* 125, *cr.* 2, (wheel, *pl.* 141.)
STREETER, Kent, a bird, wings expanded, ar., beaked and legged, gu. *Pl.* 126, *cr.* 7.
STRELLEY, Notts., a Saracen's head, ppr. *Pl.* 19, *cr.* 1.
STRELLEY, Notts., an old man's head, couped, affrontée, ppr., on his head a cap, or, turned up, sa. *Pl.* 31, *cr.* 2.
STRELLEY, Notts., a cock's head, ar., combed and wattled, gu., (gorged with two bars-nebulée, az.) *Pl.* 92, *cr.* 3.
STRELLEY, Eng., an old man's head, in profile, couped at neck, sa., (round the forehead five bells, or.) *Pl.* 118, *cr.* 7.
STRETCHLEY, a demi-lion, rampant, crowned, or, supporting between paws a cinquefoil. *Pl.* 61, *cr.* 4, (cinquefoil, *pl.* 141.)
STRETFIELD, or STREATFIELD, of Chiddingstone, Kent, a dexter arm, couped at shoulder, embowed, in armour, ppr. garnished, or, supporting in gauntlet a pennon, flotant to dexter, and returning behind the staff to sinister side, gu., top of pennon, ar., thereon a cross, of the third, on the back, (towards the point, three bezants, the staff, of the fourth, round arm, near wrist, a sash, tied with bows, gu.) *Data fata secutus*. *Pl.* 6, *cr.* 5.
STRETTELL, a swan in pride, ppr. *Pl.* 111, *cr.* 10.

STRETTON, Eng., a demi-eagle, issuing, in dexter a laurel-branch, ppr. *Pl.* 59, *cr.* 13.

STREVELING, Eng., the sun shining on stump of oak-tree, ppr. *Pl.* 123, *cr.* 3.

STRICKLAND, a turkey-cock, sa., membered and wattled, gu.

STRICKLAFD, a bundle of holly, vert, fructed, gu., (banded round middle with a wreath, ar. and sa.) *Pl.* 99, *cr.* 6.

STRICKLAND, Yorks., a full-topped holly-bush, ppr. *Pl.* 99, *cr.* 6.

STRICKLAND, Bart., Yorks., a turkey-cock in pride, ppr. *A la volonté de Dieu.*

STRICKLAND, Dors., an escallop, ppr. *Pl.* 117, *cr.* 4.

STRICKSON, from a mural coronet, or, a dragon, issuing, gu., wings addorsed, in dexter a thunderbolt, also gu. *Pl.* 82, *cr.* 10, (coronet, *pl.* 128, *fig.* 18.)

STRINGER, Eng., a martlet, erminois. *Celeriter nil crede.* *Pl.* 111, *cr.* 5.

STRINGER, Middx., a griffin's head, or. *Pl.* 38, *cr.* 3.

STRINGER, an eagle's head, sa., ducally collared and lined, or. *Pl.* 39, *cr.* 4, (without pheon.)

STRINGFELLOW, Yorks., a cock's head, erased, or, combed and wattled, gu., (gorged with a ducal coronet, and lined, sa.) *Pl.* 92, *cr.* 3.

STRODE, Newnham Park, Devons., on a mount, a (savan)-tree, vert, fructed, gu. *Hyeme viresco.* *Pl.* 52, *cr.* 6.

STRODE-CHETHAM, of South Hill, Somers.: 1. For *Strode*, a demi-lion, couped, or. *Pl.* 67,*cr.*10. 2. For *Chetham*, a demi-griffin, holding a cross patonce, ar. *Malo mori quam fœdari.* *Pl.* 44, *cr.* 3.

STROODE, or STROUD, Dors. and Lond., a demi-lion, or. *Pl.* 67, *cr.* 10.

STROODE, Devons., on a mount, a tree, vert, fructed, gu. *Pl.* 48, *cr.* 4.

STRONG, Eng., an eagle, with two heads, wings expanded. *Pl.* 87, *cr.* 11, (without flame.)

STRONG, Iri., a lion, rampant, az., supporting a pillar, ar. *Pl.* 50, *cr.* 8, (pillar, *pl.* 33, *cr.* 1.)

STRONG, Sco., a cluster of grapes, stalked and leaved. *Pl.* 77, *cr.* 7.

STRONG, Eng., out of a mural coronet, or, a demi-eagle, wings displayed, gold. *Pl.* 33, *cr.* 5.

STRONG, an eagle, displayed, or. *Pl.* 48, *cr.* 11.

STRONGBOW, Eng., a bull's head, cabossed, between two flags, (charged with a cross. *Pl.* 118, *cr.* 8.

STRONGE, Bart., Iri., an eagle, displayed, with two heads, sa., beaked and legged, az., langued, gu. *Tentanda via est.* *Pl.* 87, *cr.* 11, (without flame.)

STRONGE, Heref.,an eagle, displayed, or. *Pl.*48, *cr.* 11.

STROTHER,Sco.,a martlet, sa. *Ad alta.* *Pl.* 111, *cr.* 5.

STROTHER, Eng., a greyhound, sejant, or. *Pl.* 66, *cr.* 15.

STROUDE, a demi-lion, rampant. *Pl.* 67, *cr.* 10.

STROVER, Eng., a scaling ladder, sa. *Pl.* 98, *cr.* 15.

STRUT, or STRUTT, Middx., a dexter arm, erect, couped at elbow, vested, sa., cuffed, erminois, charged on sleeve with a cross crosslet, fitched, or, in hand, ppr., a roll of parchment, of the last. *Pl.* 32. *cr.* 6, (cross, *pl.* 141.)

STRUTHERS, Sco., an eagle, displayed, az *Pl.* 48, *cr.* 11.

STRUTT, Eng., a falcon, standing on a glove, ppr. *Pl.* 1, *cr.* 13.

STUART, Eng., a demi-lion, rampant, gu. *Nobilis ira.* *Pl.* 67, *cr.* 10.

STUART, of Inchbreck, Kincardine, a civet cat, couchant, ppr. *Semper apparatus.*

STUART, Fettercairn, Sco., on a chapeau, gu., turned up, erm., a dexter cubit arm, in hand a scimitar, ppr. *Avant.* *Pl.* 29, *cr.* 8, (chapeau, *pl.* 127, *fig.* 13.)

STUART, Sco., a dexter hand grasping a sword, ppr. *Avant.* *Pl.* 21, *cr.* 10.

STUART, Sco., a pelican, in her nest, ppr. *Salus per Christum redemptorem.* *Pl.* 44, *cr.* 1.

STUART, a unicorn's head, between two laurel-branches, in orle. *Forward.* *Pl.* 54, *cr.* 9.

STUART, Bart., Sco., a dexter hand holding a scimitar, all ppr. *Avant.* *Pl.* 29, *cr.* 8.

STUART, a demi-lion, rampant, ppr. *Avito viret honore.* *Pl.* 67, *cr.* 10.

STUART, Sco., a bird, standing on a wheat-sheaf, or. *Judge nought.* *Pl.* 14, *cr.* 5, (without coronet.)

STUART, Sco., a pelican, feeding her young, all ppr. *Pl.* 44, *cr.* 1.

STUART, Beds., a demi-lion, rampant, gu. *Avito viret honore.* *Pl.* 67, *cr.* 10.

STUART, Bart., Hants, a roebuck, statant, ppr., attired and hoofed, ar., (ducally gorged, gu.) *Pl.* 88, *cr.* 9, (without arrow.)

STUART, Earl of Moray. *See* MORAY.

STUART, Earl of Traquair. *See* TRAQUAIR.

STUART DE DECIES, Baron, (Villiers-Stuart:) 1. For *Stuart*, a demi-lion, rampant, gu., over it the motto, *Nobilis ira*, charged on shoulder with a martlet for distinction. *Pl.* 67, *cr.*10, (martlet, *pl.* 69, *cr.* 15.) 2. For *Villiers*, a lion, rampant, ar., ducally crowned, or, charged with a crescent for distinction. *Pl.* 67, *cr.* 5, (crescent, *pl.* 141.)

STUART, DE ROTHSAY, Baron, Sco., (Stuart,) a demi-lion, rampant, gu. *Avito viret honore.* *Pl.* 67, *cr.* 10.

STUBB, on a mural coronet, a stag's head, cabossed, ppr., between attires a pheon, ar. *Pl.* 124, *cr.* 14, (pheon, *pl.* 141.)

STUBBE, Norf., a bull's head, cabossed, between horns a pheon. *Pl.* 30, *cr.* 12.

STUBBE, Suff., a stag's head, ppr., between horns a pheon, ar. *Pl.* 9, *cr.* 10, (pheon, *pl.* 30, *cr.* 12.)

STUBBER, on top of a mural coronet, gu., a martlet, ar. *Gladio et arcu.* *Pl.* 98, *cr.* 14, (coronet, *pl.* 128, *fig.* 18.)

STUBBES, Ess., an arm, embowed, vested, barry of ten, ar. and az., in hand, ppr., a lighted match, of the first, fire, of the third. *Pl.* 39, *cr.* 1, (match, *pl.* 70, *cr.* 14.)

STUBBEY, out of a ducal coronet, sa., a tiger's head, or, tufted, maned, and horned, gold. *Pl.* 36, *cr.* 15.

STUBBING, Derb., a lamb, (sejant, ppr., collared, gu., resting dexter on a trefoil, slipped, vert.) *Pl.* 116, *cr.* 1.

STUBBS, or STUBBES, Eng., a tiger, passant, party, per pale, ar. and sa. *Pl.* 67, *cr.* 15.

STUBBS, Linc., a demi-eagle, displayed, or, in beak a laurel-branch, vert. *Pl.* 27, *cr.* 7, (branch, *pl.* 59, *cr.* 13.)

STUBBS, Eng., an eagle, regardant, issuing, ppr. *Pl.* 27, *cr.* 15.
STUBBS, Durh., on a mural coronet, sa., a pheon, ar. *Pl.* 19, *cr.* 7, (pheon, *pl.* 141.)
STUBS, a demi-eagle, displayed, or, in beak an oak-branch, ppr. *Pl.* 22, *cr.* 11, (branch, *same plate, cr.* 1.)
STUCKEY, Devons., a demi-lion, rampant, double-queued, erm. *Pl.* 120, *cr.* 10.
STUCKEY, Somers., a demi-lion, rampant, erm., charged with a mascle, az. *Pl.* 67, *cr.* 10, (mascle, *pl.* 141.)
STUDDART, or STUDDERT, Iri., a demi-horse, rampant, body environed by a ducal coronet, or. *Refulgent in tenebris. Pl.* 91, *cr.* 2, (without wings.)
STUDDERT, Eng., a bull's head, erased, erm. *Pl.* 19, *cr.* 3.
STUDELEY, Baron, (Hanbury-Tracey:) 1. For *Tracey*, on a chapeau, gu., turned up, erm., an escallop, sa., between wings, or. *Pl.* 17, *cr.* 14. 2. For *Hanbury*, out of a mural coronet, sa., a demi-lion, rampant, or, in paws a battle-axe, of the first, helved, gold. *Memoriâ pii æternâ. Pl.* 120, *cr.* 14.
STUDHOLME, Cumb., a horse's head, couped, ar., bridled, or. *Pl.* 92, *cr.* 1.
STUDLEY, Eng., an eagle, devouring a turtle, ppr. *Pl.* 70, *cr.* 8.
STUDLEY, Kent, a stag's head, cabossed, or, (pierced through scalp by an arrow, in bend sinister, vert, feathered, ar., headed, sa.) *Pl.* 36, *cr.* 1.
STUDLEY, Dors., a stag's head, cabossed, or. *Pl.* 36, *cr.* 1.
STUKELEY, Devons., a demi-lion, rampant, ar., in dexter a battle-axe, or, headed, of the first, (the battle-axe lying behind the head as if carried on the shoulder.) *Pl.* 101, *cr.* 14.
STUMP, Wilts., a griffin's head, erased, per cheveron, ar. and sa. *Pl.* 48, *cr.* 6.
STUPART, Sco., a rock, ar., thereon an eagle, regardant, wings (displayed,) ppr., beaked and membered, or. *Pl.* 79, *cr.* 2.
STURDY, Eng., an arm, in armour, (issuing,) embowed, and tied at shoulder, in hand a spiked club, ppr. *Pl.* 28, *cr.* 2.
STURGEON, Suff., a sturgeon, or, fretty, gu.
STURGES, Eng., a talbot, sejant, ar., collared, az. *Pl.* 107, *cr.* 7.
STURROCK, out of a ducal coronet, or, two elephants' proboscis, sa., issuing from each side, to the dexter and sinister five flags, per fess, gu. and or, staves, sa.
STURT, Lond., a demi-lion, gu., holding a banner, also gu., charged with a (rose,) ar., staff, or. *Pl.* 19, *cr.* 6, (banner, *pl.* 99, *cr.* 2.)
STURTON, Dors., Lond., and Notts., a sledge, ar.
STURTON, a demi-friar, ppr., vested in russet gown, holding a lash, or, thongs bloody. *Pl.* 83, *cr.* 15.
STURTON, Lond., Notts., and Dors., a demi-friar, vested in russet, girt, or, in dexter a (whip of three lashes,) in the sinister a cross. *Pl.* 90, *cr.* 5.
STURTON, Leic., a demi-friar, vested in russet, girt, or, in dexter a whip of three lashes, ppr., (laying the sinister on a church, or, port, ar.) *Pl.* 83, *cr.* 15.
STUTVILE, Eng., a camel's head, couped, ppr. *Pl.* 109, *cr.* 9.

STYCH, Chesh., Ess., and Salop, an eagle, displayed, ar., (collared, az.,) in beak a laurel-sprig, vert. *Pl.* 48, *cr.* 11, (sprig, *pl.* 59, *cr.* 13.)
STYLE, a wolf's head, (erased,) sa., fretted on lower part of neck, and gorged with a collar, or, charged with a mullet for difference. *Pl.* 8, *cr.* 4, (mullet, *pl.* 141.)
STYLE, Kent, Suff., and Ess., a wolf's head, couped, sa., collared, or, the lower part of neck from the collar fretty, gold. *Pl.* 8, *cr.* 4.
STYLE, Suff., Norf., and Linc., a wolf's head, (erased,) sa., collared, or, below the collar fretty, of the last. *Pl.* 8, *cr.* 4.
STYLE, WILLIAM, Esq., of Bicester House, Oxon., same crest.
STYLES, Eng., on a chapeau, an eagle, rising, ppr. *Pl.* 114, *cr.* 13.
STYLES, Lond., a lion's gamb, erased, in fess, ar., holding a fleur-de-lis, sa.
STYLMAN, Wilts., a camel's head, erased, az., billettée, muzzled, (collared, lined, and ringed, or, on collar, three hurts.) *Pl.* 120, *cr.* 12.
STYSTED, Suff., a palm-tree. *Pl.* 18, *cr.* 12.
SUBLET, Eng., a mortar-piece on its stand, mouth elevated, ppr. *Pl.* 55, *cr.* 14.
SUCKLING, Eng., an escallop, charged with a cross moline, between wings. *Pl.* 80, *cr.* 2, (cross, *pl.* 141.)
SUCKLING, Norf., a buck, current, or, in mouth a sprig of honeysuckle, ppr. *Mora trahit periculum.*
SUDELL, a long-cross, or, (lozenge-pierced, the top encompassed with a circle of laurel, ppr.) *Pl.* 7, *cr.* 13.
SUDELL, Lanc. and Yorks., a long-cross, or, (the top encompassed with a circle of laurel, ppr. *Pl.* 7, *cr.* 13.
SUETING, Eng., a spur-rowel, between wings. *Pl.* 54, *cr.* 5, (wings, *pl.* 1, *cr.* 15.)
SUFFIELD, Baron, and a Bart., (Harbord,) on a chapeau, gu., turned up, erm., a lion, couchant, ar. *Æquanimiter. Pl.* 75, *cr.* 5.
SUFFOLK, Earl of, and Earl of Berkshire, Viscount Andover, and Baron Howard, (Howard,) on a chapeau, gu., turned up, erm., a lion, statant, gardant, tail extended, or, ducally gorged, ar. *Nous maintiendrons*—and—*Non quo, sed quomodo. Pl.* 7, *cr.* 14.
SUGDEN, Eng., a dragon's head, or, vomiting flames. *Pl.* 37, *cr.* 9.
SUGDEN, Knt., Suss., a leopard's head, erased, or, ducally gorged, az. *Pl.* 116, *cr.* 8.
SULBY, Eng., the scalp of an ox, gu. *Pl.* 9, *cr.* 15.
SULLIARD, Suff. and Ess., a stag's head, ppr., attired, or. *Pl.* 91, *cr.* 14.
SULLIVAN, Eng., out of an antique crown, gu., a demi-lion, rampant, or. *Pl.* 45, *cr.* 7, (crown, *pl.* 79, *cr.* 12.)
SULLIVAN, Iri., out of a ducal coronet, gu., two arms, in saltier, ppr., vested, az., each holding a (sabre,) of the second. *Pl.* 52, *cr.* 1, (coronet, *pl.* 57, *cr.* 8.)
SULLIVAN, on a ducal coronet, a dove, statant. *Pl.* 66, *cr.* 12, (coronet, *same plate, cr.* 5.)
SULLIVAN, of Richings Lodge, Bucks., on a ducal coronet, or, a robin, in beak a laurel-sprig, ppr. *Lamh foisdineah an vachter. Pl.* 41, *cr.* 10, (robin, *pl.* 10, *cr.* 12; sprig, *pl.* 29, *cr.* 15.)

SULLIVAN, Bart., Surr., on a ducal coronet, or, a robin, in beak a laurel-sprig, ppr. *Ib.*

SULLY, Eng., a goat, (passant,) ar. *Pl.* 66, *cr.* 1.

SULYARD, Bart., Suff., a stag's head, cabossed, ppr. *Pl.* 36, *cr.* 1.

SUMMERS, on a globe of the world, winged, ppr., an eagle, rising, or. *Pl.* 50, *cr.* 7, (eagle, *pl.* 34, *cr.* 2.)

SUMNER, Eng., a crosier, erect, az. *Pl.* 7, *cr.* 15.

SUMNER, of Puttingham Priory, Surr., a lion's head, erased, ar., (ducally) gorged, or. *Pl.* 7, *cr.* 10.

SUMNER, Surr., a lion's head, erased, erm., (ducally) gorged, or. *Pl.* 7, *cr.* 10.

SUMNER-HOLME, of Hatchlands, Surr.: 1. For *Sumner*, a lion's head, erased, ar. *Pl.* 81, *cr.* 4. 2. For *Holme*, a hawk, wings elevated, ppr. *Pl.* 105, *cr.* 4.

SUNDRIDGE, Baron. *See* ARGYLE, Duke of.

SUNGER, on a ducal coronet, or, two bears' paws, to the dexter and sinister, sa., ensigned with a plume of ostrich-feathers, two, gu., one, ar.

SUPPLE, a cubit arm, erect, armed, ppr., in hand an anchor, az., (flukes upward.) *Pl.* 53, *cr.* 13, (arm, *pl.* 33, *cr.* 4.)

SURKAS, Durh., out of a ducal coronet, or, a plume of five ostrich-feathers, ar. *Pl.* 100, *cr.* 12, (without crescent.)

SURMAN, Eng., an eagle, regardant, wings expanded and inverted, holding a sword, in pale, ppr. *Pl.* 87, *cr.* 5.

SURMAN, JOHN-SURMAN, Esq., of Swindon Hall, and Lay Court, Glouc., a lion's head, erased, sa. *Yet in my flesh shall I see God.* *Pl.* 81, *cr.* 4.

SURRIDGE, Eng., a greyhound, sejant, gu. *Pl.* 66, *cr.* 15.

SURTEES, Durh., out of a ducal coronet, or, five ostrich-feathers, ar. *Pl.* 100, *cr.* 12, (without crescent.)

SURTEES, Eng., out of a mural coronet, gu., a wyvern's head, or. *Pl.* 101, *cr.* 4.

SURTEES, of Redworth House, Durh., out of a five-leaved ducal coronet, or, three ostrich-feathers, ar. *Malo mori quam fœdari.* *Pl.* 12, *cr.* 9, (coronet, *pl.* 23, *cr.* 11.)

SURTEES, Northumb., a lion, passant. *Pl.* 48, *cr.* 8.

SURTES, out of a five-leaved coronet, or, a plume of three feathers, ar. *Pl.* 12, *cr.* 9, (coronet, *pl.* 23, *cr.* 11.)

SUSFIELD, Norf., on a mount, vert, a lion, couchant, gardant, erminois. *Pl.* 101, *cr.* 8, (mount, *pl.* 9, *cr.* 14.)

SUTCLIFF, a demi-man, armed in antique mail, or, in dexter a (spear in pale, of the last, over the shoulder a belt, gu.) *Pl.* 23, *cr.* 4.

SUTCLIFFE, Eng., a dexter hand holding up a (baptismal) cup, ppr. *I mean well.* *Pl.* 35, *cr.* 9.

SUTER, Eng., out of a ducal coronet, a hand grasping a swan's neck, erased, ppr. *Pl.* 29, *cr.* 4, (coronet, *same plate, cr.* 7.)

SUTHERLAND, Sco., a cat, salient, ppr. *Still without fear.* *Pl.* 70, *cr.* 15.

SUTHERLAND, Eng., a camel's head, couped, or. *Pl.* 109, *cr.* 9.

SUTHERLAND, Sco., a cat, sitting, ppr. *Without fear.* *Pl.* 24, *cr.* 6.

SUTHERLAND, Sco., a cat, sejant, erect. *Sans peur.* *Pl.* 53, *cr.* 5.

SUTHERLAND, Sco., a cat, sejant, sa. *Sans peur.* *Pl.* 24, *cr.* 6.

SUTHERLAND, Duke of, Marquess of Stafford, Earl and Baron Gower, Viscount Trentham, and a Bart., (Leveson-Gower,) a wolf, passant, ar., (collared and lined, or.) *Frangas, non flectes.* *Pl.* 46, *cr.* 6.

SUTHILE, Linc., a lion, rampant, vert, supporting a staff, raguly, or. *Pl.* 22, *cr.* 15, (staff, *pl.* 11, *cr.* 2.)

SUTTER, Sco., a fox's head, ppr. *Pl.* 91, *cr.* 9.

SUTTER, on a mount, vert, a leopard, sejant, ducally gorged, ppr. *Pl.* 123, *cr.* 8.

SUTTIE, Sco., the hull of a ship, with one mast, tackling, ppr. *Nothing hazard, nothing have.*

SUTTIE, Sco., a hive of bees, ppr. *Sponte favos ægre spicula.* *Pl.* 81, *cr.* 14.

SUTTIE, Bart., a ship, under sail, flagged and rigged, ppr. *Mini lucra pericula.* *Pl.* 109, *cr.* 8.

SUTTIE, Bart., Sco., a ship, under sail, all ppr. *Nothing hazard, nothing have.* *Pl.* 109, *cr.* 8.

SUTTON, Lond., a demi-figure, the emblem of love, in dexter hand the hymenial torch, all ppr. *Tuto, celeritur, et jucunde.* *Pl.* 70, *cr.* 14.

SUTTON, Norf., same crest.

SUTTON, Linc. and Derbs., a greyhound's head, couped, erm., collared, gu., garnished, and ringed, or, on collar three annulets, gold. *Pl.* 43, *cr.* 11, (annulet, *pl.* 141.)

SUTTON, Lond. and Staffs., a demi-lion, rampant, double-queued, vert. *Pl.* 120, *cr.* 10.

SUTTON, Bart., Notts., a wolf's head, erased, gu. *Touts jours prest.* *Pl.* 14, *cr.* 6.

SUTTON, Eng., a lion's paw, (erased,) holding a branch, ar., leaved, vert. *Pl.* 68, *cr.* 10.

SUTTON, Eng., a lion's head, erased, per pale, ar. and vert, collared, gu. *Pl.* 7, *cr.* 10.

SUTTON, Iri., an elephant's head, erased, ar. *Pl.* 68, *cr.* 4.

SUTTON, Eng., on a chapeau, a peacock in pride, ppr. *Pour y parvenir.* *Pl.* 50, *cr.* 15.

SUTTON, Eng., a harpy, gardant, ppr. *Pl.* 32, *cr.* 3.

SUTTON, Sco., three annulets, conjoined in triangle, or, one in chief, and two in base. *Pl.* 119, *cr.* 10.

SUTTON, Chesh., out of a ducal coronet, or, a demi-lion, rampant, vert. *Pl.* 45, *cr.* 7.

SUTTON, Linc., out of a ducal coronet, a demi-lion, double-queued, vert. *Pl.* 120, *cr.* 10, (coronet, *same plate.*)

SUTTON, Derbs., three annulets, interwoven, or. *Pl.* 119, *cr.* 10.

SUTTON, of Elton House, near Durham, on a mount, vert, a stork, ppr., (charged on breast with a cross pattée, gu., the dexter foot supporting a rose, of the last, surmounted of another, ar.) *Fidelis usque ad mortem.* *Pl.* 122, *cr.* 7.

SUTTON, Middx., a crescent, ar., charged with an anchor, between horns of the crescent a griffin's head, erased, collared, in beak an eagle's leg, erased at thigh.

SUTTON, Nots., on a chapeau, gu., turned up, erm., a peacock in pride, ppr. *Pl.* 50, *cr.* 15.

SUTTON, a wolf's head, erased, gu. *Pl.* 14, *cr.* 6.

SUTTON, in a ducal coronet, or, a lion's head, az. *Pl.* 90, *cr.* 9.

SUTTON, a lion's gamb, erect and erased, az., charged with three bezants, holding a demi-slip of leaves, ar. *Pl.* 68, *cr.* 10, (bezant, *pl.* 141.)

SUTTON, ROBERT, Esq., of Rossway, Herts., a griffin's head, erased. *Prend moi tel que je suis. Pl.* 48, *cr.* 6.

SUTTON-MANNERS. See MANNERS, Baron.

SUTTON-MANNERS, Viscount Canterbury. See CANTERBURY.

SWABEY, Bucks., a swan, regardant, ar., beaked and membered, sa., wings elevated, also sa., murally crowned, gu., resting dexter on an escallop, or. *Pl.* 44, *cr.* 15.

SWABY, same crest.

SWAIL, a greyhound, current, erminois, (collared, az.) *Pl.* 28, *cr.* 7.

SWAIN, and SWAINE, Eng., a fetterlock, az. *Pl.* 122, *cr.* 12.

SWAINSON, Lanc., a stag's head, couped, ar., charged with a mullet of eight points, in mouth (two ears of barley,) or. *Pro ecclesiâ Dei. Pl.* 100, *cr.* 8, (mullet, *pl.* 16, *cr.* 13.)

SWAINSON, or SWAYNSON, Yorks., Lanc., and Salop, a stag's head, attired, ar., charged with an etoile of eight points, gu., in mouth (two ears of barley.) *Ib.*

SWAINSON, or SWAYNSON, Yorks., Lanc., and Salop, on a ducal coronet, an etoile of (sixteen) points, ppr. *Pl.* 83, *cr.* 3.

SWAINSTON, Eng., same crest.

SWALE, Bart., Yorks., a greyhound, current, erm., (collared, az.) *Jesu esto mihi Jesus. Pl.* 28, *cr.* 7.

SWALE, Yorks., on a mount, vert, a greyhound, current, erm., (collared, az.) *Pl.* 47, *cr.* 2, (mount, *pl.* 5, *cr.* 2.)

SWALLMAN, Kent, a swan's neck, between wings, or, ducally gorged, gu.) *Pl.* 30, *cr.* 10, (wings, *pl.* 54, *cr.* 6.)

SWALLOW, Eng., a stag, standing beside a tree, ppr. *Pl.* 118, *cr.* 13.

SWALLOW, issuing from a whale's mouth, a mast, rigging, &c., of a ship.

SWAN, of Baldwinstown Castle, co. Wexford, a swan, ppr., displayed, unguled, and crowned, or, charged with a trefoil, vert. *Sit nomen decus. Pl.* 33, *cr.* 7, (trefoil, *pl.* 141.)

SWAN, Sco., a hand holding a spear, in bend, all ppr. *Pl.* 99, *cr.* 8.

SWAN, Sco., a cockatrice's head, erased, ppr., ducally gorged, or. *Pl.* 106, *cr.* 15, (without wings.)

SWAN, Kent, a demi-talbot, salient, gu., collared, or. *Pl.* 15, *cr.* 2.

SWAN, a cockatrice's head, erased, ppr., ducally gorged, (ringed and lined, ar.) *Pl.* 106, *cr.* 15, (without wings.)

SWANLEY, Middx., a unicorn's head, erased. *Pl.* 67, *cr.* 1.

SWANN, Eng., out of a ducal coronet, gu., a swan's head, ar., between wings, or. *Pl.* 83, *cr.* 1.

SWANS, Eng., a sword, erect, ppr., between two cross crosslets, fitched, sa. *Pl.* 117, *cr.* 14, (cross, *pl.* 141.)

SWANSON, Eng., two branches of laurel (in saltier,) ppr. *Pl.* 21, *cr.* 2.

SWANSTON, Sco., a wolf's head, issuing. *Gesta verbis prævenient. Pl.* 92, *cr.* 15, (without rose.)

SWAYNE, Somers., a maiden's head, couped, ppr., crined, or, between wings, gold. *Pl.* 45, *cr.* 5, (wings, *pl.* 1, *cr.* 15.)

SWAYNE, Dors., a demi-griffin, erm., legs, or. *Pl.* 18, *cr.* 6.

SWAYNE, Sco., a ram's head, erased, sa. *Pl.* 1, *cr.* 12.

SWAYNE, Lond., a demi-dragon, supporting an arrow, ar., armed, or. *Pl.* 82, *cr.* 10, (arrow, *pl.* 22, *cr.* 15.)

SWEET, Eng., on the top of a tower, issuing, ppr., an eagle, wings addorsed, or, in beak an oak-branch, vert. *Pl.* 60, *cr.* 8.

SWEET, Devons., between two gilliflowers, ppr., a mullet, or, pierced, az. *Pl.* 30, *cr.* 14.

SWEETING, Kent, a goat's head, erased, ar., at tired, or. *Pl.* 29, *cr.* 13.

SWEETINGHAM, Chesh., a porcupine's head, erased, az., guttée-d'or, quills, gold, collared and lined, or.

SWEETENHAM, Chesh., same crest.

SWEETLAND, Devons., a cubit arm, in armour, couped, ppr., garnished, or, in gauntlet, two stalks of wheat, bladed and eared, and a vine branch, fructed, also ppr. *Pl.* 71, *cr.* 15, (branch, *pl.* 47, *cr.* 13 ; armour, *pl.* 33, *cr.* 4.)

SWEETLAND, same crest, with the difference of a rose, ar., barbed and seeded, ppr. *Ib.*

SWEETMAN, a griffin, sejant. *Pl.* 100, *cr.* 11.

SWEETNAM, Iri., an eagle, wings expanded, ppr., standing on a plume of ostrich-feathers, or. *Pl.* 54, *cr.* 8.

SWEETNAM, Eng., an eagle, wings expanded, ppr., holding up a banner, gu., tasselled, or. *Pl.* 65, *cr.* 3.

SWELLINGTON, a friar's head, in profile, ppr., couped at shoulder, vested, grey. *Pl.* 51, *cr.* 4.

SWERTCHOFF, out of a coronet, a plume of ostrich-feathers. *Pl.* 44, *cr.* 12.

SWETENHAM, of Somerford Booths, Chesh., a hedgehog's head, erased, az., guttée, ar., chained and collared, or.

SWETTENHAM, of Swettenham Hall, Chesh., a tree, vert, on the sinister side of it a lion, rampant, gu. *Ex sudore vultus. Pl.* 58, *cr.* 10, (lion, *pl.* 67, *cr.* 5.)

SWETTENHAM, a porcupine's head, erased, az., guttée, ar., armed and collared, or. *Ex sudore vultus.*

SWIFT, Lond., a pegasus at full speed, vert, wings addorsed, or. *Pl.* 28, *cr.* 9.

SWIFT, Blandford, Dors., a demi-lion, rampant, or, between paws a helmet, gold. *Pl.* 47, *cr.* 4, (helmet, *pl.* 19, *cr.* 15.)

SWIFT, Iri., on a chapeau, a flame of fire, ppr. *Pl.* 71, *cr.* 11.

SWIFT, a dexter hand, gauntleted, throwing a dart, all ppr. *Pl.* 42, *cr.* 13, (gauntleted, *pl.* 33, *cr.* 4.)

SWIFT, Yorks., a cubit arm, vested, ar., charged with two bendlets, az., in hand a laurel-wreath, vert, encircling a (martlet,) or. *Pl.* 44, *cr.* 13.

SWIFT, Heref. and Yorks., a demi-buck, rampant, in mouth a (honeysuckle,) ppr., stalked and leaved, vert. *Pl.* 55, *cr.* 9.

SWIFT, RICHARD, Esq., of Lynn, near Mulingar, co. Westmeath, same crest. *Festina lente.*

SWIFT, a dexter arm, embowed, in hand (three arrows, one in fess and two in saltier.) *Pl.* 92, *cr.* 14.

SWINBORNE, Hewthwayt, Cumb., a boar's head, (couped) and erect, ar. *Pl.* 21, *cr.* 7.

SWINBURN, Chopwell, Durh., out of a ducal coronet, or, a demi-boar, ar., crined and armed, gold. *Pl.* 20, *cr.* 5, (coronet, *same plate, cr.* 12.)

SWINBURNE, Sir JOHN-EDWARD, Bart., Capheaton, Northumb., out of a ducal coronet, or, a demi-boar, rampant, ar., crined, gold, langued, gu. *Semel et semper. Pl.* 20, *cr.* 5, (coronet, *same plate, cr.* 12.)

SWINBURNE, THOMAS-ROBERT, Esq., F.R.S., of Pontop Hall, Durh., and Marcus Lodge, Forfar, Sco., same crest and motto.

SWINBURNE, Edlingham and Nafferton, Northumb., same crest.

SWINEY, Eng., a fox's head, ppr. *Pl.* 91, *cr.* 9.

SWINFEN, Swinfen Hall, Staffs., a boar's head, erased, or. *Pl.* 16, *cr.* 11.

SWINFORD, Eng., a weaver's shuttle, threaded, ppr. *Pl.* 102, *cr.* 10.

SWINHOE, a boar's head, erased and erect, or. *Pl.* 21, *cr.* 7.

SWINNEE, or SWINEY, Iri., a talbot, passant, ar., spotted, sa. *Pl.* 120, *cr.* 8.

SWINNERTON, Lond., and of Butterton Hall, Staffs.: 1. On a mount, vert, a boar, passant, sa. *Pl.* 48, *cr.* 14, (mount, *pl.* 108, *cr.* 9.) 2. A boar's head, erased, per pale, sa., (collared, ar.) *Avauncez et archez bien. Pl.* 2, *cr.* 7.

SWINNY, Kent, a boar, passant, ppr. *Pl.* 48, *cr.* 14.

SWINTON, Sco., an ear of wheat, issuing. *Dum sedulo prospero. Pl.* 85, *cr.* 6.

SWINTON, or SWYNTON, Eng., a dove, between two branches of laurel, in orle. *Pl.* 2, *cr.* 11.

SWINTON, JOHN-EDULPHUS, Esq., of Swinton Bank, Peebles, a boar, chained to a tree, above, "J'espère." *Je pense. Pl.* 57, *cr.* 12.

SWINTON-CAMPBELL, JOHN, Esq., of Kimmerghame, Berwick, a boar, chained to an oaktree, fructed, all ppr. *J'espère. Pl.* 57, *cr.* 12.

SWIRE, the Rev. JOHN, of Dowgill Hall, Yorks., a swan's head and neck, couped, ar., ducally gorged, or. *Esse quam videri. Pl.* 30, *cr.* 10.

SWORD, or SWOURD, a sword, in pale, ppr., between wings, or. *Paratus. Pl.* 117, *cr.* 14.

SWORDER, Eng., a demi-lion, rampant, gu., in dexter a sword, ar., hilt and pommel, or. *Pl.* 41, *cr.* 13.

SWOURD, Eng., a sword, in pale, ppr., hilted, or, between wings, gold. *Pl.* 117, *cr.* 14.

SWYMMER, a demi-lion, rampant, gu., between paws a bell, or. *Pl.* 47, *cr.* 4, (bell, *pl.* 73, *cr.* 15.)

SWYNERTON, Lond., out of a ducal coronet, or, a goat's head, ar. *Pl.* 72, *cr.* 2.

SWYNERTON, Eng., on a chapeau, a dove, wings addorsed, all ppr. *Pl.* 109, *cr.* 10.

SWYTHAM, SWYNGHAM, or SWITHAM, Herts., out of a ducal coronet, a demi-dragon. *Pl.* 82, *cr.* 10, (coronet, *pl.* 104, *cr.* 11.)

SYBELLS, (five) halberds, in pale, ar., corded together, of the first, and gu. *Pl.* 62, *cr.* 8, (without coronet.)

SYBSEY, Westbarssam, Norf., a griffin's head, erased, gu. *Pl.* 48, *cr.* 6.

SYBTHORP, St Alban's, Herts.; and Ladham, Norf., a demi-lion, rampant, (erased,) ar., collared, sa., in dexter a fleur-de-lis, of the last. *Pl.* 18, *cr.* 13, (fleur-de-lis, *pl.* 91, *cr.* 13.)

SYBYLE, Eng., out of a ducal coronet, or, a swan's head, between wings. *Pl.* 83, *cr.* 1.

SYDENHAM, Winford-Eagle, Dors.; Brimpton, Combe, Sidenham, and Whitstow, Somers., a ram's head, erased, sa., attired, ar. *Sit Deus in studiis. Pl.* 1, *cr.* 12.

SYDENHAM, Somers., a pegasus, ar., (charged on shoulder with a cross, vert.) *Pl.* 28, *cr.* 9.

SYDNEY, Sir WILLIAM-ROBERT, Knt., of The Bourne, near Maidenhead, Berks., a pheon, az. *Quo fata vocant Pl.* 26, *cr.* 12.

SYDNEY, Richmond, Surr.; and Tamworth, Warw., a porcupine, az., quills, or, (collared and chained, gold, chain reflexed over back.) *Pl.* 55, *cr.* 10.

SYDNEY, a hedgehog, az., (collared and stringed, or.) *Pl.* 32, *cr.* 9.

SYDNEY, Viscount and Baron, (Townshend,) a buck, trippant, sa., attired, ppr., charged on shoulder with an escallop, ar. *Pl.* 61, *cr.* 15.

SYDSERFE, of Recklaw, an eagle's head, couped, gu. *Virtute promoveo. Pl.* 100, *cr.* 10.

SYDSERFE, an eagle's head, couped, az. *Semper virtute vivo. Pl.* 100, *cr.* 10.

SYDSERFE, Sco., a cornucopia, ppr. *Industria ditat. Pl.* 91, *cr.* 4.

SYER, Eng., a cock, az., in mouth a (cinquefoil,) slipped, or. *Pl.* 55, *cr.* 12.

SYKES, an ox, passant, charged on shoulder with an heraldic-fountain, ppr. *Pl.* 66, *cr.* 11, (charging, *pl.* 141.)

SYKES, out of weeds, vert, a swan, wings addorsed, ar., ducally gorged, or. *Pl.* 111, *cr.* 10, (weeds, *pl.* 34, *cr.* 6.)

SYKES, Eng., a swan, among flags. *Pl.* 66, *cr.* 10.

SYKES, Sir TATTON, Bart., Sledmere, Yorks., out of flags or reeds, a demi-Triton, blowing a shell, wreathed about temples with flags or reeds, all ppr. *Pl.* 35, *cr.* 10.

SYKES, Sir FRANCIS-WILLIAM, Bart., Basildon, Berks.; and Bucks., a swan, (rising from a tuft of reeds, ppr.) *Pl.* 66, *cr.* 10.

SYKES, a demi-lady, in profile, vested as a nun, in dexter a rose, in sinister a rosary, suspended round neck.

SYLVER, co. Cork, a unicorn's head, erased, gu., (charged with a cheveron, or.) *Pl.* 67, *cr.* 1.

SYLVESTER, or SILVESTER, Eng., a crow, wings expanded, transfixed by an arrow, ppr. *Pl.* 110, *cr.* 13.

SYM, Sco., in hand a pen, ppr. *Fortunâ et labore. Pl.* 26, *cr.* 13.

SYM, Sco., a spur-rowel, or. *Pl.* 54, *cr.* 5.

SYMCOATS, Linc. and Lond., a pheon, sa., within a chaplet, vert, flowered, or. *Pl.* 30, *cr.* 11.

SYMCOT, SYMCOTT, or SYMCOCK, Notts., Somers., and Staffs., a beaver, passant, erm. *Pl.* 49, *cr.* 5.

SYME, Eng., an eagle's head. *In recto decus. Pl.* 100, *cr.* 10.

SYME, Sco., a demi-lion, rampant, between paws a battle-axe. *Ferio, tego. Pl.* 120, *cr.* 14, (without coronet.)

SYMEON, Eng., out of a crown vallary, an arm, in hand an oak-branch, acorned and leaved, vert. *Pl.* 2, *cr.* 2.

SYMES, or SYMMES, Somers. and Devons., a demi-hind, erased, or.

SYMINGES, Eng., a lion, sejant, (gardant,) supporting an escutcheon, or. *Pl.* 22, *cr.* 13.

SYMINGTON, Sco., a cross moline, lozenge-pierced, or. *Pl.* 91, *cr.* 10.

SYMMER, Sco., a stag, lodged, or, attired, gu. *Tandem tranquillus*. *Pl.* 67, *cr.* 2.

SYMMES, Daventry, Northamp., a head, helmeted, or, plumed, az., beaver up, face, ppr. *Pl.* 33, *cr.* 14.

SYMONDS, of Pengethly, the Rev. THOMAS-POWELL, Pengethly, near Ross, a dolphin, embowed, in mouth a fish, ar. *Pl.* 71, *cr.* 1.

SYMONDS, or SYMONDES, Heref., same crest.

SYMONDS, White Lady Aston, a vine-tree, with grapes, ppr. *Pl.* 89, *cr.* 1.

SYMONDS, a (goose,) ar. *Pl.* 90, *cr.* 15.

SYMONDS, out of a mural coronet, chequy, ar. and az., a boar's head, of the first, crined, sa. *Pl.* 102, *cr.* 14, (coronet, *pl.* 112, *cr.* 5.)

SYMONDS, or SYMMONDS, Norf., a dolphin, naiant, ppr., finned, or. *Pl.* 48, *cr.* 9.

SYMONDS, Heref., a dolphin, ar. *Pl.* 48, *cr.* 9.

SYMONDS, Coleby, Suffield, Cley by the Sea, Great Ormsby, and Runham Hall, Norf.: 1. A demi-swan, wings expanded, ar., in mouth a trefoil, slipped, az. *Pl.* 54, *cr.* 4, (trefoil, *pl.* 141.) 2. For the *Ormsby* branch, a dolphin, (naiant,) devouring a fish, both ppr. *Rectus in curvo*—and—*Dum spiro, spero.* *Pl.* 71, *cr.* 1.

SYMONDS, Lond., a pansy-flower, ppr. *Pl.* 30, *cr.* 1.

SYMONDS, Lond., on a mount, vert, an ermine, ppr., (in mouth a cinquefoil, gu., slipped, of the first.) *Pl.* 87, *cr.* 3.

SYMONDS, on a mount, vert, a wolf, (statant,) in mouth a rose, slipped, leaved, and stalked, all ppr. *Simplex munditiis*. *Pl.* 5, *cr.* 8, (rose, *pl.* 92, *cr.* 15.)

SYMONDS, Glouc., an arm, embowed, sa., (tied at elbow with ribbons, ar. and az.,) in hand a fire-ball, ppr. *Pl.* 62, *cr.* 9.

SYMONDS, Lyme-Regis and Colesden, Dors.; and Taunton, Somers., on a mount, vert, an ermine, ppr., (in mouth a cinquefoil, or.) *Pl.* 87, *cr.* 3.

SYMONDS, or SYMMONDS, Exeter, Devons., a cubit arm, erect, ppr., in hand a (pole)-axe, ar., handle, sa. *Pl.* 73, *cr.* 7.

SYMONDS, of Woodsford Castle, and Pilsdon, Dors.; and Dowlish Wake, Somers.: 1. On a chapeau, gu., turned up, erm., a moor's arm, embowed, ppr. tied at elbow with ribbons, ar. and az., in hand a fire-ball, ppr. *Pl.* 62, *cr.* 9, (chapeau, *same plate*, *cr.* 9.) 2. On a mount, vert, an ermine, passant, ppr., (in mouth a cinquefoil, of the first.) *Simplex munditiis*. *Pl.* 87, *cr.* 3.

SYMONS, THOMAS-GEORGE, Esq., of Mynde Park, Hereford, on a mount, vert, a wolf, statant, in mouth a rose, slipped, leaved, and stalked, all ppr. *Simplex munditiis.* *Pl.* 5, *cr.* 8, (rose, *pl.* 92, *cr.* 15.)

SYMONS, St John's College, Camb., an otter, (passant, in mouth a trefoil, slipped.) *Fideliter.* *Pl.* 9, *cr.* 9.

SYMONS, Whiteflord, Camb., on a mural coronet, gu., three arrows, or, feathered, ar., two in saltier, one in pale, tied in middle with a ribbon, az., flotant. *Pl.* 43, *cr.* 14, (coronet, *pl.* 128, *fig.* 18.)

SYMONS - SOLTAU, GEORGE - WILLIAM - CULME, Esq., of Chaddlewood, Devons., on a mount, vert, an ermine, ppr., in mouth a trefoil, slipped, ar. *Simplex munditiis.* *Pl.* 87, *cr.* 3.

SYMPSON, Kent, a lion's head, erased, erm., per fess, gu., ducally crowned, or. *Pl.* 90, *cr.* 4.

SYMPSON, WALCOTT, Winkton, near Ringwood, Hants., an ounce's head, ar., erased, gu., ducally crowned, or. *Pl.* 94, *cr.* 10, (crown, *same plate*.)

SYMPSON, Polton, Beds., on a mural coronet, ar., a demi-lion, rampant, gardant, per pale, undée, or and sa., in dexter a (sword, erect,) of the first, hilted, gold. *Pl.* 26, *cr.* 7, (coronet, *pl.* 128, *fig.* 18.)

SYMS, Eng., a demi-leopard, ppr. *Pl.* 12, *cr.* 14.

SYMSON, Peddinghall Garth, Durh., out of a moral coronet, az., a demi-lion, regardant, per pale, or and sa., (in dexter a sword, ppr., pommel, or.) *Pl.* 33, *cr.* 2, (coronet, *same plate*, *cr.* 5.)

SYNGE, FRANCIS, Esq., of Glenmore Castle, Ashford, co. Wicklow, out of a ducal coronet, or, an eagle's claw, ppr. *Cœlestia canimus.* *Pl.* 96, *cr.* 7.

SYNNOT, Iri., a swan, sejant, sa., ducally gorged, or, (pierced in breast by an arrow, gold.) *Ama Deum, et serva mandata.* *Pl.* 114, *cr.* 3, (gorging, *pl.* 30, *cr.* 10.)

SYSELEY, a buck's head, erased, gu., guttée, collared and attired, or, (in mouth a branch of fir, vert.) *Pl.* 125, *cr.* 6, (without roses.)

SYSINGTON, Eng., a dexter arm, ppr., in hand a covered cup, az. *Pl.* 88, *cr.* 5.

SYWARD, Eng., a sand-glass, gu., winged, az. *Pl.* 32, *cr.* 11.

T

TAAFE, Viscount, and Baron Ballymote, Iri., a dexter arm, in armour, embowed, in hand a sword, ppr., hilt and pommel, or. *In hoc signo, spes mea.* *Pl.* 2, *cr.* 8.

TAAFFE, MYLES, Esq., of Smarmore, co. Louth, same crest and motto.

TAAP, or TAPP, on point of sword, erect, ppr., a mullet, or. *Pl.* 55, *cr.* 15.

TABER, Ess., a griffin's head, erased, ppr. *Pl.* 48, *cr.* 6.

TABERS, Ess., a lion's head, erased, pierced by (a dart.) *Pl.* 113, *cr.* 15.

TABOR, Eng., in hand a sealed letter, ppr. *Pl.* 33, *cr.* 8, (without cloud.)

TACKLE, Eng., two halberds, addorsed, or, environed by a snake, vert. *Pl.* 14, *cr.* 13.

TADCASTER, Baron. *See* THOMOND, Marquess of.

TADDY, a fleur-de-lis, ar. *Pl.* 68, *cr.* 12.

TADDY, Eng., issuing from a cloud, ppr., the morning-star, or. *Pl.* 16, *cr.* 13.

TADWELL, or TEDWELL, Middx., on a piece of battlement, ar., an arm, (in armour,) embowed, ppr., garnished, or, in hand a javelin, all ppr. *Pl.* 95, *cr.* 14.

TAEMAYNE, an old man's face, affrontée, ar., hat, sa., supported by two arms, of the first.

TAGG, Eng., on a mount, vert, an ermine, (collared.) *Pl* 87, *cr.* 3.

TAILBOIS, or TAILBOYS, Durh., a bull's head, couped, ar. *Pl.* 120, *cr.* 7.

TAILBOYS, Linc., a bull, passant, ar. *Pl.* 66, *cr.* 11.

TAILEFER, Sco., trunk of oak-tree, sprouting, ppr. *Viresco.* *Pl.* 92, *cr.* 8.

TAILOUR, Canada, a dexter arm, issuing, ppr., in hand a cross pattée, fitched, in pale, az. *Per ardua.* *Pl.* 99, *cr.* 15.

TAILYOUR, Sco., in dexter hand, ppr., a passion cross, gu. *In cruce salus.* *Pl.* 99, *cr.* 1, (cross, *pl.* 7, *cr.* 13.)

TAIT, Sco., a horse's head, (couped,) sa. *Ægre de tramile.* *Pl.* 81, *cr.* 6.

TAIT, Sco., the rising sun. *God give grace.* *Pl.* 67, *cr.* 9.

TAIT, Eng., stump of tree, couped and eradicated, in fess, vert, between the branches a fleur-de-lis, or. *Pl.* 14, *cr.* 14.

TAIT, Middx., a horse's head, (couped,) ppr. *Pl.* 81, *cr.* 6.

TAIT, Lanc., an arm, embowed, vested, quarterly, or and sa., in hand, ppr., a bunch of flowers, gu., leaved, vert. *Toujours la meme.* *Pl.* 39, *cr.* 1, (flowers, *pl.* 69, *cr.* 10.)

TALBOT, Mount Talbot, co. Roscommon : 1. For *Talbot,* on a chapeau, az., turned up, erm., a lion, passant, gu. *Pl.* 107, *cr.* 1. 2. For *Crosbie,* three swords, one in pale, point upward, two in saltier, points downward, entwined by a serpent, all ppr. *Prent d'accomplir.*

TALBOT, a talbot, passant, sa. *Pl.* 120, *cr.* 8.

TALBOT, Devons., a talbot, ar., collared, gu. *Pl.* 65, *cr.* 2.

TALBOT, Dors., a talbot, passant, collared and chained. *Pl.* 65, *cr.* 2.

TALBOT, Norf., Suff., and Devons., a demi-ostrich, wings expanded, ar., (ducally gorged, gu.) *Pl.* 29, *cr.* 9, (without coronet.)

TALBOT, Bart., Iri., on a chapeau, ppr., a lion, (statant, tail extended,) or. *Humani nihil alienum.* *Pl.* 107, *cr.* 1.

TALBOT, WILLIAM-HENRY-FOX, Esq., of Lacock Abbey, Wilts., a lion, or, tail extended. *Pl.* 118, *cr.* 10.

TALBOT, Earl and Baron, and Viscount Ingestrie, (Chetwynd-Talbot,) on a chapeau, gu., turned up, erm., a lion, (statant, or, tail extended.) *Humani nihil alienum.* *Pl.* 107, *cr.* 1.

TALBOT, Earl of Shrewsbury. *See* SHREWSBURY.

TALBOT DE MALAHIDE, Baron, Iri., (Talbot,) on a chapeau, gu., a lion, passant, tail extended, erminois. *Forte et fidele.* *Pl.* 118, *cr.* 10, (chapeau, *pl.* 107, *cr.* 1.)

TALBY, Leic., on a mount, vert, a bull, passant, or, (gorged with a wreath of laurel, ppr.,) sinister resting on an escallop, gold. *Pl.* 39, *cr.* 5, (escallop, *pl.* 141.)

TALCOTT, a demi-griffin, rampant, sa., (gorged with a collar, ar., thereon three pellets.) *Pl.* 18, *cr.* 6.

TALCOTT, Ess., a demi-griffin, erased, ar., (gorged with a collar, sa., charged with three roses, of the first.) *Pl.* 18, *cr.* 6.

TALLANT, a hind's head, couped, ppr. *Pl.* 21, *cr.* 9.

TALLANTIRE, two arms, in armour, embowed, ppr., supporting a bezant. *Pl.* 6, *cr.* 8.

TALLERTON, Lond., a boar's head, couped, in fess. *Pl.* 48, *cr.* 2.

TALLIS, Iri., a dove, ar., in mouth an ear of wheat, ppr. *Pl.* 108, *cr.* 8, (without key.)

TALMACH, Suff., a horse's head, erased, ar., between wings, or, pellettée. *Pl.* 19, *cr.* 13.

TAME, a wolf's head, erased, gu., (ducally gorged, or.) *Pl.* 14, *cr.* 6.

TAME, a plume of feathers. *Pl.* 12, *cr.* 9.

TAME, Eng., a cock, regardant, ppr. *Pl.* 19, *cr.* 10.

TAMWORTH, Lond. and Linc., a cock, gu., combed, wattled, and legged, or. *Pl.* 67, *cr.* 14.

TANCRED, Bart., Yorks., an olive-tree, fructed, ppr. *Pl.* 18, *cr.* 10.

TANDY, Eng., on a ducal coronet, a martlet, sa. *Pl.* 98, *cr.* 14.

TANE, Eng., a plough, ppr. *Labor et industria.* *Pl.* 28, *cr.* 15.

TANEY, or TANY, Eng., a demi-eagle, with two heads, gu., (ducally gorged, or.) *Pl.* 4, *cr.* 6.

TANFIELD, and TANSFIELD, Ess., a maiden's head, ppr. *Pl.* 45, *cr.* 5.

TANFIELD, Ess., Northamp., and Yorks., a woman's head, couped at shoulders, ppr., crined, or, wreathed about head with roses, ar. and sa. *Pl.* 45, *cr.* 5, (wreath, *pl.* 81, *cr.* 13.)

TANKARD, Yorks., an olive-tree, vert, fructed, or, environed with a ducal coronet, gold. *Pl.* 94, *cr.* 5.

TANKARD, Yorks., an olive-tree, vert. *Pl.* 18. *cr.* 10.

TANKARDE, a holly-tree, erased, vert. *Pl.* 22, *cr.* 10.

TANKARDE, five holly-branches, vert, (flowered, gu.) *Pl.* 99, *cr.* 6.

TANKE, out of a ducal coronet, or, two wings, az. *Pl.* 17, *cr.* 9.

TANKERVILLE, Earl of, and Baron Ossulston, (Bennett :) 1. For *Grey,* a double scaling-ladder, or. *Pl.* 59, *cr.* 7. 2. Out of a mural coronet, or, a lion's head, gu., charged on neck with a bezant. *De bon vouloir servir le roi.* *Pl.* 45, *cr.* 9, (bezant, *pl.* 141.)

TANNER, Wilts. and Cornw., a moor's head, couped, sa., banded, gu. (Another, banded, ar. and gu.) *Pl.* 48, *cr.* 7.

TANNER, Cornw., a demi-talbot, or, eared, ar. *Pl.* 97, *cr.* 9, (without arrow.)

TANNER, Surr., a demi-antelope, rampant, regardant, erm.

TANNER, Somers., a talbot's head, erased. *Pl.* 90, *cr.* 6.

TANQUERAY, Beds., out of a mount, vert, in front of two battle-axes, in saltier, (a pine-apple, ppr.) *Pl.* 52, *cr.* 10, (mount, *pl.* 98, *cr.* 13.)

TANSLEY, Sco., in hand a branch of laurel, all ppr. *Virtutis laus actio.* *Pl.* 43, *cr.* 6.

TANY, a greyhound's head, erased, az., (ducally gorged, or.) *Pl.* 89, *cr.* 2.

TANY, Eng., a demi-eagle, with two heads, gu., (ducally gorged,) or. *Pl.* 4, *cr.* 6.

TAPLEN, Eng., a boar's head, erased, ppr. *Pl.* 16, *cr.* 11.

TAPP, Eng., on point of sword, erect, ppr., a mullet, or. *Pl.* 55, *cr.* 15.

TAPPER, Eng., a lion's head, erased, regardant. *Pl.* 35, *cr.* 2.

TAPPER, Eng., in hand, erect, out of a cloud, a garb, in bend. *Pl.* 67, *cr.* 12.

TAPPIN, Eng., a lion, rampant, ar. *Pl.* 67, *cr.* 5.

TAPPS, Hants., a griffin, passant. *Pl.* 61, *cr.* 14, (without gorging.)

TAPPS-GERVIS, Bart., Hants., a greyhound, couchant, per pale, ar. and sa., charged on body with two escallops, in fess, counterchanged. *Pl.* 6, *cr.* 7, (escallop, *pl.* 141.)

TARBOCK, a popinjay, close, vert, beaked and (collared,) gu. *Pl.* 25, *cr.* 2.

TARBOCK, Staffs. and Yorks., a parrot, vert, beaked and legged, gu. *Pl.* 25, *cr.* 2.

TARELL, Eng., out of a cloud, a hand, in pale, holding an arrow, point downwards. *Pl.* 45, *cr.* 12.

TARLETON, between two ostrich-feathers, ar., a leopard's head, affrontée, ppr. *Pl.* 31, *cr.* 7.

TARLETON, Heref., between two ostrich-feathers, ar., a mural coronet, thereon a leopard's head, affrontée, ppr. *Post nubila Phœbus.* *Pl.* 31, *cr.* 7, (coronet, *pl.* 128, *fig.* 18.)

TARLEY, Eng., a boar's head, couped, sa., in fess, armed, ar., (charged with a pale, of the last.) *Pl.* 48, *cr.* 2.

TARPLEY, Northamp., a dove, wings displayed, (in mouth an olive-branch,) all ppr. *Pl.* 27, *cr.* 5.

TARRANT, Lond., a demi-eagle, displayed, gu. *Pl.* 22, *cr.* 11.

TASELL, Suff., a hawk's head, erased, az., in beak a pine-branch, vert, fructed, gu. *Pl.* 31, *cr.* 4.

TASH, Lond., a demi-greyhound, or, (collared, gu,) between feet an escallop, of the last. *Pl.* 6, *cr.* 9.

TASKER, Eng., a boar's head, ar., couped, gu. *Pl.* 48, *cr.* 2.

TASSIE, Sco. and Eng., out of a tower, ppr., a demi-griffin, segreant, or. *Pl.* 68, *cr.* 11.

TASWELL, a demi-lion, rampant, ar. *Pl.* 67, *cr.* 10.

TATAM, Eng., within a fetterlock, or, a heart, gu. *Pl.* 59, *cr.* 6.

TATE, Eng., on point of sword, erect, ppr., a maunch, erm. *Pl.* 78, *cr.* 1.

TATE, Notts., an arm, embowed, couped at shoulder, vested, per pale, gu. and or, in hand, ppr., a pine-branch, gold. *Pl.* 39, *cr.* 1, (branch, *pl.* 80, *cr.* 1.)

TATENHALL, Chesh., a buck's head, ppr. *Pl.* 91, *cr.* 14.

TATHAM, Somerfield House, Lanc., a williegoat, (trippant,) pp. *Veritatem.* *Pl.* 66, *cr.* 1.

TATHAM, Eng., out of a ducal coronet, a plume of ostrich-feathers, ppr. *Pl.* 44, *cr.* 12.

TATHAM, Lond., on a trumpet, or, a swan, wings displayed, sa. *Pl.* 4, *cr.* 7.

TATLER, a demi-eagle, displayed, with two heads, in each beak a cross crosslet, fitched. *Pl.* 31, *cr.* 9.

TATLOCK, Lond. and Surr., a demi-lion, rampant, or. *Pl.* 67, *cr.* 10.

TATLOCK, Eng., out of a mural coronet, az. an arm, embowed, in hand a sword, ppr. *Pl.* 115, *cr.* 14.

TATNALL, and TATTALL, a cutlass, in pale, ar., hilt and pommel, or, (a ribbon tied round the gripe, gu.) *Pl.* 27, *cr.* 10.

TATTERSALL, Eng., a dove and olive-branch, ppr. *Good news.* *Pl.* 48, *cr.* 15.

TATTON, Chesh., a greyhound, sejant, ar., collared and tied by a hand, or, to a hawthorntree, ppr. *Pl.* 66, *cr.* 15, (tree, *pl.* 18, *cr.* 10.)

TATTON, Eng., a sword and garb, in saltier, ppr. *Pl.* 70, *cr.* 7.

TATUM, Eng., an eagle, displayed, crowned with an (antique) coronet. *Pl.* 85, *cr.* 11.

TATUM, a dexter arm, in armour, embowed, ppr., garnished, or, in hand three arrows, all ppr. *Pl.* 31, *cr.* 10.

TAUNTON, WILLIAM-ELIAS, Esq., of Freeland Lodge, Oxon., a Cornish chough, ppr. *Pl.* 100, *cr.* 13.

TAUNTON, Eng., out of a ducal coronet, a dexter arm, in hand a slip of rose-tree, ppr. *Pl.* 60, *cr.* 1.

TAUNTON, Dors., a greyhound, sejant, ar., collared, gu., tied to an oak-tree, ppr. *Pl.* 66, *cr.* 15, (tree, *pl.* 16, *cr.* 8.)

TAVERNER, Ess., Kent, and Herts., out of a ducal coronet, gu., an oak-tree, fructed, ppr. *Pl.* 94, *cr.* 5, (oak, *pl.* 16, *cr.* 8.)

TAVERNER, Ess., Kent, and Herts., a dove, wings expanded, ar., beaked and legged, gu., in mouth a branch of laurel, vert. *Pl.* 27, *cr.* 5, (branch, *pl.* 42, *cr.* 9.)

TAWKE, Eng., in dexter hand a lion's paw, ppr. *Pl.* 94, *cr.* 13.

TAWSE, Sco., a lion's head, erased, sa. *Deo juvante.* *Pl.* 81, *cr.* 4.

TAY, Eng., on point of sword, a garland of laurel, ppr. *Pl.* 15, *cr.* 6.

TAY, two pruning-hooks, in saltier, az. *Pl.* 31, *cr.* 12.

TAYLER, or TAYLOR, Lond., a demi-otter, rampant, or. *Pl.* 9, *cr.* 9.

TAYLER, a leopard, passant, ar., spotted, sa., charged with a pheon, or. *Pl.* 86, *cr.* 2, (pheon, *pl.* 141.)

TAYLER, Lond., a unicorn's head, erased, ar., armed and maned, or, collared, sa., (thereon three annulets, gold.) *Pl.* 21, *cr.* 1.

TAYLER, Lond., a greyhound's head, quarterly, ar. and sa., collared, counterchanged. *Pl.* 43, *cr.* 11.

TAYLER, Oxon., a lion's head, erased, ar., (ducally gorged, or.) *Pl.* 81, *cr.* 4.

TAYLEUR, Salop, out of a ducal coronet, or, a dexter arm, in armour, in hand a (sword.) *Pl.* 15, *cr.* 5.

TAYLOR, PIERCE-GILBERT-EDWARD, Esq., of West Ogwell House, Devons., a leopard, passant, ppr. *Pl.* 86, *cr.* 2.

TAYLOR, PRINGLE, Esq., of Pennington House, Southamp., a dexter arm, in armour, embowed in hand, gauntleted, a javelin, all ppr. *Consequitur quodcunque petit.* *Pl.* 47, *cr.* 15.

TAYLOR, WILLIAM, Esq., of Radcliffe-on-Trent, Notts., an oak-tree. *Pl.* 16, *cr.* 8.

TAYLOR, a dexter arm, in hand, ppr., a (broken) sword, ar., hilt and pommel, or. *Pl.* 34, *cr.* 7.

2 G

TAYLOR, Strensham Court, Worc., a demi-lion, rampant, ppr., (semée of escallops, sa., between paws a saltier, of the last surmounted by an escallop, ar.) *Fidelisque ad mortem.* Pl. 39, cr. 14.

TAYLOR, Ardgillan Castle, Dublin, a naked arm, embowed, in hand an arrow, ppr. *Consequitur quodcunque petit.* Pl. 92, cr. 14.

TAYLOR, Moreton Hall, Yorks., a demi-lion, sa., semée of mullets, or, between paws an acorn, gold, slipped, vert. *Annoso robore quercus.* Pl. 47, cr. 4, (acorn, pl. 81, cr. 7.)

TAYLOR, Todmorden Hall, Lanc., a demi-lion, rampant, az., (charged on shoulder with a bezant,) between paws an escutcheon, or, charged with a tau, gu. *Natale solum dulce.* Pl. 47, cr. 4, (escutcheon, pl. 22, cr. 13.)

TAYLOR, Kirktonhill, Sco., out of a marquess's coronet, or, a dexter hand ppr., holding a cross crosslet, fitched, gu. *In hoc signo vinces.* Pl. 99, cr. 1, (coronet, pl. 127, fig. 4.)

TAYLOR, CHARLES-WILLIAM, Bart., Suss., a demi-lion, erminois, (charged on body with two escallops,) and between paws an escallop, sa. Pl. 126 A, cr. 13.

TAYLOR, a dexter arm, in armour, in hand a spear, all ppr. Pl. 44, cr. 9.

TAYLOR, Lond., a demi-talbot, in mouth a buck's horn. Pl. 97, cr. 9, (horn, pl. 5, cr. 3.)

TAYLOR, a cock, wings displayed, (standing on a fish,) ppr. Pl. 76, cr. 7, (fish, pl. 29, cr. 11.)

TAYLOR, in hand, issuing, ppr., a cross crosslet, fitched, az. *Victoriæ signum.* Pl. 99, cr. 1.

TAYLOR, Sco., an arm, from elbow, in armour, in hand a dagger, both ppr. *Semper fidelis.* Pl. 28, cr. 4.

TAYLOR, Sco., in hand, ppr., a cross crosslet, fitched, sa. *Semper fidelis.* Pl. 99, cr. 1.

TAYLOR, a demi-lion, rampant, sa., between paws a ducal coronet, or. Pl. 67, cr. 10, (coronet, pl. 9, cr. 7.)

TAYLOR, or TAYLOUR, Lond., Suss., and Surr., a demi-greyhound, az., (ringed and collared, or, in dexter an annulet, gold.) Pl. 6, cr. 9.

TAYLOR, Cambs., a unicorn's head, erased, or, (ducally) gorged and armed, az. Pl. 73, cr. 1.

TAYLOR, Derbs., a stork, resting dexter on an anchor, ppr. Pl. 61, cr. 10.

TAYLOR, Glouc. and Lond., a lion, passant, gu. Pl. 48, cr. 8.

TAYLOR, out of a ducal coronet, or, a cubit arm, erect, ppr., in hand a cross crosslet, in pale, gu. *In hoc signo vinces.* Pl. 65, cr. 10, (cross, same plate, cr. 6.)

TAYLOR, Northumb. and Sco., same crest.

TAYLOR, Lond. and Lanc., a demi-lion, rampant, erm., between paws an escallop, or. Pl. 126 A, cr. 13.

TAYLOR, Lond., a lion's head, erased, erm., collared, gu., (thereon three roses, ar.) Pl. 7, cr. 10.

TAYLOR, Lond., a tiger's head, erased, sa., ducally gorged, or. Pl. 116, cr. 8.

TAYLOR, Hants, an ounce, sejant, or, collared, az., supporting with dexter a plain shield, sa., charged with two etoiles, in chief, ar., and in base an escallop, gold. Pl. 10, cr. 13, (shield, pl. 19, cr. 2; charging, pl. 141.)

TAYLOR, Middx., a greyhound's head, quarterly, ar. and sa., gorged with a collar, or, (charged with a ducal coronet, gu.) Pl. 43, cr. 11.

TAYLOR, Beds., a leopard, passant, ppr., resting dexter on a shield. Pl. 86, cr. 2, (shield, pl. 19, cr. 2.)

TAYLOR, Yorks., a demi-talbot, or, in mouth an arrow, erect. Pl. 97, cr. 9.

TAYLOR-DOMVILLE, MASCIE-DOMVILLE, Esq., of Lymme Hall, Chester, a buck's head, cabossed, ppr. Pl. 36, cr 1.

TAYLOR-WATSON, Wilts.: 1. For *Taylor*, out of a ducal coronet of five leaves, or, a cubit arm, erect, ppr., (charged with a heart, gu.,) in hand a cross crosslet, fitched, of the last. *In hoc signo vinces.* Pl. 99, cr. 1, (coronet, pl. 23, cr. 11.) 2. For *Watson*, trunk of a tree, erased at top, a branch sprouting from each side. Pl. 92, cr. 8.

TAYLOR, Iri., a naked arm, in hand a bolt-arrow, ppr. Pl. 92, cr. 14.

TAYLOUR, Northamp. and Lanc., a lion's head, erased, sa., ducally gorged, or. Pl. 81, cr. 4.

TAYLOUR, Lond., and Salop, a cubit arm, erect, vested, vair, in hand, ppr., three roses, gu., stalked and leaved, vert. Pl. 64, cr. 7, (roses, pl. 69, cr. 10.)

TAYLOUR, Middx., a leopard's head, erminois. Pl. 92, cr. 13.

TAYLOUR, Beds. and Derbs., a buck's head, cabossed, ppr., (pierced through by) two arrows, in saltier, gu., headed and feathered, ar. Pl. 124, cr. 14.

TAYLOUR, Hants, Cambs., and Glouc., a leopard, passant, ppr. Pl. 86, cr. 2.

TAYLOUR, Kent, a martin, passant, or. Pl. 119, cr. 15.

TAYLOUR, Marquess of Headfort. See HEADFORT.

TAYLOURE, a talbot's head, erased, ar., eared, sa. Pl. 90, cr. 6.

TAYTE, an arm, embowed, vested, quarterly, or. and sa., in hand, ppr., a branch of flowers, gu., leaved, vert. Pl. 39, cr. 1, (flowers, pl. 64, cr. 7.)

TEALE, Lond., a spaniel, sejant, ppr., resting dexter on an antique shield, ar., charged with a teal, of the first.

TEASDALE, Eng., an arm, in armour, embowed, in fess, in hand a sceptre, ppr. Pl. 104, cr. 13.

TEASDALE, Eng., an arm, in armour, embowed, in hand, by the blade, a sword, point downward, ppr. Pl. 65, cr. 8.

TEDWELL, out of a demi-tower, (ruined in the sinister,) an arm, embowed, vested, in hand a spear, (in bend.) Pl. 95, cr. 14.

TEGART, Eng., a fire-beacon, ppr. Pl. 89, cr. 9.

TEIGNMOUTH, Baron, Iri., and a Bart., G.B., (Shore,) a stork, ppr., beaked and legged, sa., in dexter a mullet. *Perimus licitis.* Pl. 61, cr. 10, (mullet, pl. 141.)

TELFER, in a ducal coronet, or, a tree, vert. Pl. 94, cr. 5.

TELLAU, Eng., out of a ducal coronet, a griffin's head. Pl. 54, cr. 14.

TEMMES, an Indian goat's head, erased, guttée. Pl. 29, cr. 13.

TEMPEST, Bart., Boughton Hall, Yorks., a griffin's head, erased, per pale, ar. and sa., beaked, gu. *Loyowf as thow fynds.* Pl. 48, cr. 6.

TEMPEST, Durh., a martlet, sa. Pl. 111, cr. 5.

TEMPEST, a griffin's head, couped. *Pl.* 38, *cr.* 3.

TEMPEST-PLUMBE, of Tong Hall, Yorks., and Aughton, Linc.: 1. For *Tempest*, a griffin's head, erased, per pale, ar. and sa., beaked, gu. *Loyowf as thow finds. Pl.* 48, *cr.* 6. 2. A greyhound, sejant, ar., spotted, gu., (collared, or.) *Pl.* 66, *cr.* 15.

TEMPLAR, or TEMPLER, Devons., on a mount, vert, a holy lamb, ar., in dexter a pennon, of the second, charged with the cross of St George, (the streamers wavy, az. and gu.,) staff, or, under an oak-tree, ppr., fructed, gold. *Nihil sine labore. Pl.* 101, *cr.* 9, (tree, *pl.* 48, *cr.* 4.)

TEMPLAR, or TEMPLER, Eng., a crane's head, (issuing,) ppr. *Pl.* 20, *cr.* 9.

TEMPLE, WILLIAM, Esq., of Bishopstron, Wilts., a talbot. *Pl.* 120, *cr.* 8.

TEMPLE, Sco., a pillar, wreathed about with woodbine ppr. *Te stante virebo. Pl.* 14, *cr.* 15.

TEMPLE, Bucks. and Warw., on a ducal coronet, a martlet, all or. *Pl.* 98, *cr.* 14.

TEMPLE, Bart., Bucks., same crest. *Templa quam dilecta.*

TEMPLE, Bucks. and Warw., (on a mount, vert,) a talbot, sejant, sa. *Pl.* 107, *cr.* 7.

TEMPLE, Bucks., Leic., Warw.; and Kent, a talbot, sejant, sa., collared and ringed, or. *Pl.* 107, *cr.* 7.

TEMPLE, Lond., on a ducal coronet, or, a martlet, sa. *Pl.* 98, *cr.* 14.

TEMPLE, Baron Nugent. *See* NUGENT, Baron.

TEMPLE, Viscount Palmerston. *See* PALMERSTON, Viscount.

TEMPLE. *See* BUCKINGHAM, Duke of.

TEMPLEMAN, Dors., on a chapeau, a phœnix in flames, ppr. *Pl.* 83, *cr.* 12.

TEMPLEMAN, Dors. and Hants, a cubit arm, erect, vested, az., cuffed, gu., in hand, ppr., a rose, of the second, stalked and leaved, vert. *Pl.* 118, *cr.* 9, (vesting, *pl.* 64, *cr.* 7.)

TEMPLEMORE, Baron, (Chichester,) a stork, ppr., wings expanded, in mouth a snake, ar., head, or. *Invitum sequitur honor. Pl.* 59, *cr.* 11.

TEMPLER, Devons., a bee-hive,' semée of bees. *Pl.* 81, *cr.* 14.

TEMPLETON, a holy lamb, (regardant,) ar., supporting a banner, gu. *Pl.* 48, *cr.* 13.

TEMPLETON, Sco., a tree, ppr. *Pl.* 16, *cr.* 8.

TEMPLETOWN, Viscount, and Baron, Iri., (Upton,) on a ducal coronet, or, a war-horse, passant, sa., saddled, without stirrups, bridled, and accoutred, gold. *Virtutis avorum præmium. Pl.* 76, *cr.* 8.

TENCH, Derbs. and Lond., a stag, statant. *Pl.* 81, *cr.* 8.

TENCH, Iri., a lion, rampant, sa., supporting a battle-axe, or. *Pl.* 125, *cr.* 2, (axe, *pl.* 120, *cr.* 14.)

TENCHE, Lond., an arm, vested, gu., turned up, ar., in hand a tench, all ppr. *Pl.* 105, *cr.* 9, (vesting, *pl.* 18, *cr.* 1.)

TENDERING, or TENDRING, Eng., a ship under sail, ppr. *Pl.* 109, *cr.* 8.

TENISON, EDWARD-KING, Esq., of Kilronan Castle, co. Roscommon, a leopard's face, jessant-de-lis. *Pl.* 123, *cr.* 9.

TENISON, Iri., a mitre, charged with a cheveron. *Pl.* 12, *cr.* 10.

TENNANT, Eng., on a chapeau, ppr., a unicorn's head, erased, or. *Pl.* 102; *cr.* 7.

TENNANT, Chapel House, Yorks., a winged heart, gu., pierced by a dagger, ppr., hilted, or. *Tenax et fidelis. Pl.* 39, *cr.* 7, (pierced, *pl.* 21, *cr.* 15.)

TENNANT, Staffs., a lion, passant, gardant, gu., fore-dexter resting on an escutcheon, erm., (thereon two bars charged with bezants.) *Pl.* 120, *cr.* 5, (escutcheon, *pl.* 19, *cr.* 2.)

TENNANT, Sco., a sail, ppr. *Dabut Deus vela. Pl.* 22, *cr.* 12.

TENNENT-EMERSON, of Tempo, Iri.: 1. For *Tennent*, a boar's head, gu. *Pl.* 48, *cr.* 2. 2. For *Emerson*, a demi-lion, rampant, vert, bezantée, grasping a battle-axe, gu., headed, ar. *Deus protector noster. Pl.* 101, *cr.* 14, (without charging.)

TENNYSON D'EYNCOURT: 1. For *D'Eyncourt*, a lion, passant, gardant, ar., on head a crown of fleurs-de-lis, or, (fore-dexter supporting a shield, quarterly, first and fourth, az., a fess dancettée between ten billets, four and six, or.) *Pl.* 105, *cr.* 5, (without chapeau.) 2. For *Tennyson*, a dexter arm, in armour, in hand, gauntleted, or, a broken tilting-spear, (enfiled with a garland of laurel, ppr.) *Pl.* 44, *cr.* 9.

TENTERDEN, Baron, (Abbot,) a fox, passant, per pale, sa. and ar., charged on shoulder with a water-bouget, or. *Labore. Pl.* 126, *cr.* 5, (water-bouget, *pl.* 14, *cr.* 12.)

TENYSON, a dexter arm, in armour, embowed, in hand a tilting-spear, in bend sinister, enfiled with a garland. *Pl.* 44, *cr.* 9, (garland, *pl.* 15, *cr.* 6.)

TERELL, Eng., a sword and key, in saltier, ppr. *Pl.* 54, *cr.* 12.

TERINGHAM, a talbot, gu., billettée, or. *Pl.* 120, *cr.* 8.

TERNE, Lond., a demi-seahorse, ppr., finned, or, in paws an anchor, gold. *Pl.* 58, *cr.* 15, (anchor, *pl.* 19, *cr.* 6.)

TERRELL, a leopard's face, gu. *Pl.* 66, *cr.* 14.

TERRY, Eng., on a rock, a swan, ppr. *Pl.* 122, *cr.* 13.

TERRICK, a lion, (salient,) or. *Pl.* 67, *cr.* 5.

TERY, Iri., a boar's head, erased and erect, *Pl.* 21, *cr.* 7.

TERRY, Lond., a dragon's head, erased, vert, vomiting flames, ppr., collared, erm., ringed and lined, or. *Pl.* 37, *cr.* 9, (collared, *pl.* 107, *cr.* 10.)

TERRY, a dragon's head, (couped,) collared. *Pl.* 107, *cr.* 10.

TERRY, Eng., a demi-lion, ppr., holding a fleur-de-lis, gu. *Pl.* 91, *cr.* 13.

TERVISE, Eng., (on a mount,) a stag, rising from under a bush, ppr. *Pl.* 82, *cr.* 8.

TETLEY, Norf., a boar's head and neck, issuant, sa. *Pl.* 2, *cr.* 7.

TETLOW, Lanc., on a book, erect, gu., clasped and ornamented, or, a silvery penny, thereon the Lord's Prayer, on the top of the book, a dove, ppr, in mouth a crow-quill pen, sa. *Præmium virtutis honor. Pl.* 117, *cr.* 7.

TEULON, Eng., a cross pattée, gu., within an orle of seven stars, ppr. *Pl.* 33, *cr.* 10.

TEW, Eng., between wings, a spur-rowel, az. *Pl.* 1, *cr.* 15, (spur-rowel, *pl.* 54, *cr.* 5.)

TEWYDALL, Middx., an eagle's head, couped, sa., in beak an ear of wheat, or. *Pl.* 100, *cr.* 10, (wheat, *pl.* 108, *cr.* 8.)

TEYNHAM, Baron, (Roper-Curzon:) 1. For *Roper*, a lion, rampant, sa., between paws a ducal coronet, or. *Pl. 9, cr. 7.* 2. For Curzon, a popinjay, (rising, or, collared,) gu. *Spes mea in Deo. Pl. 25, cr. 2.*

TEYS, Ess., out of a ducal coronet, or, a tiger's head, ar., maned az. *Pl. 36, cr. 15.*

THACKER, Eng., out of clouds, a dexter and sinister arm, (in armour,) embowed, holding up the sun, ppr. *Pl. 107, cr. 8.*

THACKERAY, Cambs., a falcon, (in mouth an arrow.) *Nobilitas est sola virtus. Pl. 67, cr. 3,* (arrow, *pl. 117, cr. 9.*)

THACKERAY, or THACKERY, Ess., an eagle, wings elevated, on breast a cherub's head, ppr., in beak an arrow, in pale, sa., barbed and feathered, ar. *Pl. 117, cr. 9.*

THACKWELL, within a wreath of oak, ppr., a dragon's head, erased, paly of six, or and gu., (behind it an arrow,) also ppr. *Pl. 107, cr. 10,* (wreath, *pl. 74, cr. 7.*)

THAKER, Derbs., between two laurel-branches, vert, a stork's head, ppr. *Pl. 32, cr. 5,* (branches, *pl. 79, cr. 14.*)

THAKER, Derbs., a heron, in reeds, ppr. *Pl. 124, cr. 1.*

THANET, Earl of, Baron Tufton, and a Bart., (Tufton,) a sea-lion, sejant, ar. *Fiel pero desdichado*—and—*A les volat propriis. Pl.80, cr. 13.*

THARROLD, on the top of a Corinthian pillar, ar., a trefoil, vert. *Ex merito. Pl. 31, cr. 13.*

THATCHER, Eng., a Saxon sword, or, seax, ppr. *Pl. 27, cr. 10.*

THAYER, Ess., a talbot's head, erased, per fess, erm. and gu. *Pl. 90, cr. 6.*

THEED, Bucks., an eagle's head, erased, or. *Pl. 20, cr. 7.*

THELLUSSON, between wings a demi-greyhound, rampant. *Pl. 5, cr. 10.*

THELUSON, Baron Rendlesham. See RENDLESHAM.

THELWALL, on a mount, vert, a stag, lodged, ppr., attired, or, (pierced in breast by an arrow, ar., vulned, gu.) *Pl. 22, cr. 5.*

THEOBALD, Kent, a phœnix, sa., flames, ppr. *Pl. 44, cr. 8.*

THEOBALD, Suff., a cock, wings addorsed. *Pl. 76, cr. 7,* (without mount.)

THEOBALD, Suff., on a chapeau, a cock, gu. *Pl. 104, cr. 3.*

THEOBALD, Ess., out of clouds, ppr., rays issuing, or, a demi-lion, (wings displayed, sa.) *Pl. 117, cr. 11.*

THESHMAKER, Eng., between wings, ar., an eagle's head. *Pl. 81, cr. 10.*

THESTLETHWAYTE, Wilts., on a ducal coronet, or, an eagle, displayed, ar. *Pl. 9, cr. 6,* (eagle, *pl. 48, cr. 11.*)

THETFORD, Eng., a dagger, erect, ppr. *Pl. 73, cr. 9.*

THETFORD, Norf., a tiger, sejant, or, maned and tufted, sa. *Pl. 26, cr. 9.*

THICKNESSE, Staffs., a cubit arm, erect, vested, paly of six, or and gu., in hand a scythe, ppr., blade downwards. *Pl. 106, cr. 2.*

THICKNESSE-TOUCHET, Baron Audley. See AUDLEY.

THIMBLEBY, Linc., a boar's head, or, couped, gu. *Pl. 43, cr. 2.*

THIMBLETHORP, Norf., an ostrich's head, erased, or, between wings, in mouth a horse-shoe, ar. *Pl. 28, cr. 13.*

THIMBLETHORP, Glouc., between wings, ar., a greyhound's head, erased, or. *Pl. 89, cr. 2,* (wings, *pl. 1, cr. 15.*)

THIN, Sco., a boar's head, couped, sa. *Pl. 48, cr. 2.*

THIRKE, a lion, couchant, between two laurel-branches, in orle. *Pl. 75, cr. 5,* (without chapeau; branches, *pl. 102, cr. 13.*)

THIRWELL, two daggers, in saltier, ppr. *Pl. 24, cr. 2.*

THIRWELL, out of a ducal coronet, lined, erm., a boar's head and neck, or. *Pl. 102, cr. 14.*

THIRWELL, Northumb., on a chapeau, gu., turned up, ar., a boar's head, couped at neck, of the second. *Pl. 102, cr. 14,* (chapeau, same plate, cr. 7.)

THISTLETHWAYTE, of Southwick Park, Hants, a demi-lion, az., supporting a pheon, or. *Pl. 19, cr. 6,* (pheon, *pl. 141.*)

THOM, Sco., in hand a sword, ppr. *Dum vivo spero. Pl. 21, cr. 10.*

THOMAS, RESS-GORING, Esq., of Gellywernew, Carmarthen, a heron's head, erased, gorged with a garland of roses, gu. *A Deo et patre. Pl. 31, cr. 6.*

THOMAS, a dragon's head, erased, ppr., in mouth a hand, couped at wrist, gu. *Pl. 106, cr. 13.*

THOMAS, Welfield House, Radnor, out of a mural coronet, ar., a demi-seahorse, gu., crined, or, charged on shoulder with a cinquefoil, of the first, in paws an anchor, erect, sa., resting on coronet. *Pl. 58, cr. 15,* (coronet, *pl. 128, fig. 18.*)

THOMAS, Heref., a dragon's head, erased, ppr. *Pl. 107, cr. 10,* (without collar.)

THOMAS, a greyhound's head, ar., between two roses, gu., slipped and leaved, vert. *Pl. 84, cr. 13.*

THOMAS, three arrows, two in saltier, and one in pale, ppr., banded, gu. *Pl. 43, cr. 14.*

THOMAS, between two spears, erect, or, a Cornish chough, rising, ppr. *Pl. 79, cr. 13.*

THOMAS, out of a ducal coronet, a demi-lion, rampant, (holding a flag.) *Pl. 45, cr. 7.*

THOMAS, a heron's head, erased, gorged with a chaplet of roses. *Pl. 31, cr. 6.*

THOMAS, a buck, trippant. *Pl. 68, cr. 2.*

THOMAS, (on a cross aiguise, ar., the foot trunked, and the middle stem raguled,) a bird, sa. *Pl. 10, cr. 12.*

THOMAS, Kent, a demi-leopard, rampant, ppr., supporting a baton, erect, or. *Pl. 12, cr. 14.*

THOMAS, Kent, between two spears, erect, or, headed, ar., a Cornish chough, sa., wings expanded, beaked and legged, gu. *Pl. 79, cr. 13.*

THOMAS, Lond., on the branch of a tree, in fess, at dexter end sprigs, vert, a raven, wings expanded, sa. *Pl. 50, cr. 5,* (tree, *pl. 14, cr. 14.*)

THOMAS, Wel., out of a ducal coronet, a demi-seahorse, salient. *Pl. 58, cr. 15,* (coronet, same plate, cr. 2.)

THOMAS, Suss.: 1. A talbot, sejant, spotted, ar. and sa., eared, of the last. *Pl. 107, cr. 7.* 2. A talbot, passant, spotted, ar. and sa., eared, of the last. *Pl. 120, cr. 8.*

THOMAS, Bart., Wel., a demi-unicorn, erm., armed, crined, and unguled, or, (supporting a shield, sa.) *Virtus invicta gloriosa. Pl. 26, cr. 14.*

THOMAS, Suss., a demi-lion, rampant, gu., (charged on shoulder with an ermine spot, ar.) *Pl.* 67, *cr.* 10.

THOMAS, Bart., Suss., a demi-lion, rampant, gu. *Honesty is the best policy. Pl.* 67, *cr.* 10.

THOMASON, Eng., a demi-talbot, ar., ducally gorged, or. *Pl.* 15, *cr.* 2.

THOMKINS, Eng. a dove, within an adder, in orle, ppr. *Pl.* 92, *cr.* 6.

THOMLINSON, Lond. and Yorks., out of a ducal coronet, or, a griffin's head, ar. *Pl.* 54, *cr.* 14.

THOMLINSON, Northumb., a greyhound, per pale, wavy, ar. and vert. *Pl.* 104, *cr.* 1, (without chapeau.)

THOMOND, an arm, embowed, ppr., in hand a sword, ar., hilt and pommel, or. *Pl.* 34, *cr.* 7.

THOMOND, Marquess of, Earl and Baron of Inchquin, and Baron of Burren, Iri.: Baron Tadcaster, U.K., (O'Bryen,) an arm, embowed, in hand a sword, ar., hilt and pommel, or. *Vigueur de desus. Pl.* 34, *cr.* 7.

THOMSON, WILLIAM, of Clements, Weymouth, on a cramp, sa., a falcon, close, belled, ppr., in beak a teazel, vert. *Patria cara, carior fides carior. Pl.* 126 D, *cr.* 4.

THOMPSON, Northumb., an arm, erect, vested, gu., cuffed, ar., in hand, ppr., five ears of wheat, or. *In lumine luce. Pl.* 63, *cr.* 1.

THOMPSON, Clonfin, Longford, an arm, in armour, embowed, in hand, all ppr., five ears of wheat, or, arm charged with a trefoil, vert. *In lumine luce. Pl.* 89, *cr.* 4, (armour, *pl.* 120, *cr.* 11.)

THOMPSON, a demi-griffin, segreant. *Pl.* 18, *cr.* 6.

THOMPSON, out of a naval coronet, or, a buck's head, gu., attired, gold, on breast a cross crosslet, fitched, of the first, in mouth an oak-branch, ppr., fructed, of the third. *Pl.* 100, *cr.* 8, (coronet, *pl.* 118, *cr.* 5; cross, *pl.* 141.)

THOMPSON, a buck's head, cabossed, ppr. *Pl.* 36, *cr.* 1.

THOMPSON, a lion, rampant, gu., ducally (gorged,) or. *Pl.* 98, *cr.* 1.

THOMPSON, a palm-branch, ppr. *Patientiâ vinco. Pl.* 123, *cr.* 1.

THOMPSON, of Scarborough, Yorks., a demi-man rising from water, in dexter a flaming sword, on sinister arm a shield with the arms of Hotham, all ppr. *Certum pete finem.*

THOMPSON, Kent, out of a ducal coronet, ar., an ostrich's head, in mouth a horse-shoe, all or. *Pl.* 28, *cr.* 13, (coronet, *pl.* 29, *cr.* 9.)

THOMPSON, Kent, a greyhound, sejant, (collared and lined.) *Pl.* 66, *cr.* 15.

THOMPSON, Lond., a lion, rampant, gu. *Pl.* 67, *cr.* 5.

THOMPSON, Lond., a hawk, wings expanded, ppr., beaked and legged, or, between two spears, erect, staves, gold, headed, ar. *Pl.* 105, *cr.* 4, (spear, *pl.* 79, *cr.* 13.)

THOMPSON, Lond., between two palm-branches, in orle, a flaming heart, all ppr. *Pl.* 88, *cr.* 11.

THOMPSON, Surr., a lion, sejant, or, (holding a saltier, ar.) *Pl.* 126, *cr.* 15.

THOMPSON, Yorks., a demi-ounce, erminois, (collared, ringed, and lined,) az. *Pl.* 12, *cr* 14.

THOMPSON, Bart., Herts., out of a naval coronet, or, an arm, in armour, embowed, ppr., garnished, gold, the hand supporting a (lance, erect,) also ppr. *Pl.* 115, *cr.* 14, (coronet, *pl.* 93, *cr.* 1.)

THOMPSON, Lond., Herts., Bucks., and Cambs., same crest.

THOMPSON, Lond., Durh., and Yorks., a lion, rampant, gu., ducally gorged, or. *Go on, and take care. Pl.* 67, *cr.* 5, (gorging, *pl.* 87, *cr.* 15.)

THOMPSON, Durh., an arm, in armour, embowed, quarterly, or and az., in gauntlet, ppr., a tilting-spear, (erect.) *Pl.* 44, *cr.* 9.

THOMPSON, Durh., an arm, in armour, embowed, quarterly, or and az., in gauntlet, ppr., a broken lance, gold. *Dum spiro, spero. Pl.* 44, *cr.* 9.

THOMPSON, Lond., Suff., and Yorks., same crest.

THOMPSON, Northumb., same crest. *Je veux bonne guerre.*

THOMPSON, Bart., Suss., on a naval coronet, az., (charged on rim with three crosses, pattée, ar.,) a unicorn, passant, of the last, gorged with a (laurel-wreath,) ppr. *Pl.* 106, *cr.* 3, (coronet, *pl.* 76, *cr.* 2.)

THOMS, Eng., on a mount, an oak-tree, fructed, ppr. *Pl.* 48, *cr.* 4.

THOMSON, Banchory, Sco., a rose, gu., barbed, vert, seeded, or. *Christus providebit. Pl.* 20, *cr.* 2.

THOMSON, Kenfield, Kent: 1. On a mount, vert, a greyhound, sejant, ar., (gorged with a collar, az., studded, or, therefrom, reflexed over back, a leash, gold,) charged on shoulder, for distinction, with a cross crosslet, gu. *Pl.* 5, *cr.* 2, (cross, *pl.* 141.) 2. A heart, gu., (encircled) by a ducal coronet, ar., between two palm-branches, ppr. *Providentia tutamen. Pl.* 52, *cr.* 2, (branches, *pl.* 87, *cr.* 8.)

THOMSON, a cubit arm, erect, vested, in hand five ears of wheat. *Pl.* 63, *cr.* 1.

THOMSON, a martlet. *Pl.* 111, *cr.* 5.

THOMSON, Sco., a dexter hand, couped, in fess, ppr., holding a cross crosslet, fitched, az. *Honesty is good policy. Pl.* 78, *cr.* 9.

THOMSON, Sco., in hand a (bunch) of flowers, ppr. *Industria murus. Pl.* 118, *cr.* 9.

THOMSON, a cubit arm, erect, vested, gu., cuffed, ar., in hand, ppr., a sprig, or. *Pl.* 113, *cr.* 5.

THOMSON, a lion, rampant, or, ducally (gorged,) az. *Pl.* 98, *cr.* 1.

THOMSON, an arm, couped below elbow, in hand a cross crosslet, fitched. *Optima est veritas. Pl.* 99, *cr.* 1.

THOMSON, a crane, in mouth a palm-branch, all ppr. *Curæ cedit fatum*—and—*Secum cuique. Pl.* 46, *cr.* 9, (palm, *pl.* 123, *cr.* 1.)

THOMSON, Ess. and Linc.: 1. A lion, rampant, ducally (gorged,) or. *Pl.* 98, *cr.* 1. 2. A demi-lion, rampant, gardant, or. *Pl.* 35, *cr.* 4.

THOMSON-ANSTRUTHER, Fife: 1. For *Anstruther*, two arms, in armour, holding a battle-axe, all ppr. *Pl.* 41, *cr.* 2. 2. For *Thomson*, a naked arm, couped at elbow, ppr., in hand a cross crosslet, gu. *Pl.* 99, *cr.* 1, (cross, *pl.* 141.) 3. For *Sinclair*, a swan, ar., ducally collared and chained, or. *Pl.* 111, *cr.* 10.

THORBURN, Sco., a hawk, (in dexter an olive-branch, ppr.) *We live in hope. Pl.* 94, *cr.* 7.

THORBURN, a leopard, sejant, (gardant,) ppr. *We live in hope. Pl.* 10, *cr.* 13.

THORLBY, and THORLEY, Sco., a tower, ppr. *Fide et fiduciâ.* *Pl.* 12, *cr.* 5.
THORLEY, Eng., a lion's gamb, erect, ar., fretty, sa. *Pl.* 126, *cr.* 9.
THORLEY, a demi-lion, rampant, or, supporting a cinquefoil, sa. *Pl.* 35, *cr.* 4, (cinquefoil, *pl.* 141.)
THORN, or THORNE, Eng., an owl, gardant, ppr. *Pl.* 27, *cr.* 9.
THORNAGH, Notts., a tiger's head, maned, armed, and tufted, sa., gorged with a collar, wavy, az. *Pl.* 86, *cr.* 13.
THORNBOROUGH, and THORNBURY, Hants, Middx., and Yorks., a tiger, sejant, or, pellettée. *Pl.* 26, *cr.* 9.
THORNBROUGH, Devons., on a naval coronet, or, a fox, passant, ppr. *Spectemur agendo.* *Pl.* 126, *cr.* 5, (coronet. *pl.* 128, *fig.* 19.)
THORNDICK, Linc., a demi-lion, rampant, gardant, supporting a chaplet of laurel, vert. *Pl.* 39, *cr.* 14, (chaplet, *pl.* 56, *cr.* 10.)
THORNDIKE, Linc., a damask rose, ppr., leaves and thorns, vert, at the bottom of the stalk a beetle, or, scarabæus, ppr. *Pl.* 117, *cr.* 10.
THORNE, Suff. and Devons., a lion, rampant, sa. *Pl.* 67, *cr.* 5.
THORNE, Suff., out of a ducal coronet, or, a mermaid, ppr., crined, gold, conjoined to a dolphin, haurient, of the same, devouring her sinister hand.
THORNES, Salop, in hand a club, ppr. *Pl.* 28, *cr.* 6.
THORNEX, on a mount, vert, a greyhound, couchant, or, (gorged with a label of three points, gu.) *Pl.* 6, *cr.* 7, (mount, *pl.* 117, *cr.* 8.)
THORNEY, Lond., a demi-lion, rampant, ppr., (extending his paw, wounded by a thorn.) *Pl.* 67, *cr.* 10.
THORNEYCROFT, or THORNICROFT, Lond., Chesh., and Oxon., over a mural coronet, gu., a falcon, volant, ppr., jessed, membered, and beaked, or, between two palmbranches, gold. *Fortis qui se vincit.* *Pl.* 94, *cr.* 1, (coronet, *pl.* 128, *fig.* 18; branches, *pl.* 87, *cr.* 8.)
THORNHILL, Derby, on a mount, a thorn-tree, ppr. *Pl.* 50, *cr.* 3, (without bells.)
THORNHILL, Derby, out of a crown vallary, gu., a demi-eagle, displayed, or, pendent from neck a bugle-horn, stringed, sa. *Pl.* 44, *cr.* 14, (horn, *pl.* 96, *cr.* 2; crown, *pl.* 2, *cr.* 2.)
THORNHILL, on a mount, an oak-tree, all ppr. *Pl.* 48, *cr.* 4.
THORNHILL, out of a ducal coronet, a hawthorn-tree, ppr. *Pl.* 94, *cr.* 5.
THORNHILL, Linc., a woman's head, couped at shoulders, affrontée, vested, crined, and (ducally crowned,) all or. *Pl.* 74, *cr.* 5. (Another, with a hawthorn-bush surmounting the coronet.)
THORNHOLME, Yorks., on a mount, vert, a tower, ar. *Pl.* 31, *cr.* 15.
THORNHULL, Wilts., Bucks., and Dors., a bird, sa., legged, or. *Pl.* 10, *cr.* 12.
THORNLEY, Lond., a wolf's head, erased, ar., (charged on neck with a bar-gemelle, gu.) *Pl.* 14, *cr.* 6.
THORNTHWAITE, Cumb., a lion's head, erased, gu., in mouth a (thorn-sprig, vert, fructed, ppr.) *Pl.* 95, *cr.* 6.

THORNTON, of Brock Hall, Northamp.: 1. A demi-lion, rampant, gu., (charged on shoulder) with an escarbuncle, or. *Pl.* 113, *cr.* 2. 2. Out of a ducal coronet, or, a dragon's head, wings elevated. *Pl.* 59, *cr.* 14.
THORNTON, out of a mural coronet, a demi-lion, rampant, in dexter a slip. *Pl.* 17, *cr.* 7.
THORNTON, Sco., a maiden's head, from shoulders, affrontée, vested, az. *Vincit pericula virtus.* *Pl.* 74, *cr.* 5, (without coronet.)
THORNTON, Linc., a leopard's head, erased at neck, gardant, or. *Pl.* 56, *cr.* 7.
THORNTON, Middx., a griffin's head, erased, sa., beaked, or, charged on neck with an escarbuncle, gold. *Pl.* 48, *cr.* 6, (escarbuncle, *pl.* 141.)
THORNTON, Northumb., a fountain, or, playing, ppr. *Pl.* 49, *cr.* 8.
THORNTON, Yorks., out of a ducal coronet, a cockatrice's head, combed and wattled, gu., between dragon's wings, ar. *Pl.* 77, *cr.* 5.
THORNTON, Linc., out of a ducal coronet, gold, a maiden's head, or, vested, gu. *Pl.* 74, *cr.* 5.
THORNTON, Chesh., out of the top of a tower, an arm, in armour, embowed, all ppr., in hand a pennon of St George. *Pl.* 6, *cr.* 5, (tower, *pl.* 95, *cr.* 14.)
THORNTON, a lion's head, erased, ppr., (gorged) with a ducal coronet, or. *Pl.* 90, *cr.* 9.
THORNTON, Surr., out of a ducal coronet, or, a lion's head, ppr. *Pl.* 90, *cr.* 9.
THORNTON, Cambs., Norf., and Yorks., out of a ducal coronet, or, a dragon's head, (between wings,) ar. *Pl.* 59, *cr.* 14.
THORNTON, Northamp. and Yorks., a demi-lion, rampant, ar., (on shoulder) an escarbuncle, cr. *Pl.* 113, *cr.* 2.
THOROGOOD, Ess., a wolf's head, ar. *Pl.* 92, *cr.* 15, (without rose.)
THOROLD, Lond., Linc., and Cambs., a roebuck, erm., attired, or. *Pl.* 88, *cr.* 9, (without arrow.)
THOROLD, Bart., Linc., a roe-buck, trippant, ar., attired, or. *Pl.* 68, *cr.* 2.
THOROTON, Notts., a lion, rampant, per fess, gu. and sa., supporting a bugle-horn, of the last. *Pl.* 125, *cr.* 2, (horn, *pl.* 47, *cr.* 4.)
THOROUGHGOOD, and THROWGOOD, Lond.: 1. A demi-lion, or. *Pl.* 67, *cr.* 10. 2. A demi-greyhound, salient, ar., (collared, gu.) *Pl.* 48, *cr.* 3.
THORP, Durh., a lion, rampant, gu., in dexter a fleur-de-lis, az., (gorged with a plain collar, pendent therefrom an escutcheon, or, charged with a cross pattée quadrate, gu.) *Pl.* 87, *cr.* 6.
THORP, Headingly, near Leeds, a demi-lion, gu., (resting sinister on an escutcheon, ar., charged with a fess, gu., thereon another fess, nebuly, or.) *Comme à Dieu playra.* *Pl.* 19, *cr.* 6.
THORP, a (demi)-lady, representing Hope, with anchor, &c., all ppr. *Pl.* 107, *cr.* 2.
THORP, an arrow and palm-branch, in saltier, ppr. *Pl.* 50, *cr.* 11.
THORPE, Suff. and Norf., on a chapeau, gu., turned up, erm., a stag, sa. *Pl.* 3, *cr.* 14.
THORPE, Lond., two lions' gambs, erect, dexter, or, sinister, ar., supporting a fleur-de-lis, az. *Pl.* 106, *cr.* 12, (fleur-de-lis, *pl.* 141.)

THORPE, Lond. and Northamp., a cock, gu., beaked, combed, legged, and wattled, or. *Pl.* 67, *cr.* 14.

THORPE, Leic., a bull's head, couped at neck, quarterly, or and sa., horns counterchanged. *Pl.* 120, *cr.* 7.

THORPE, Linc., a lion, sejant, or, between paws a (lozenge, ar., charged with a maunch, sa.) *Pl.* 22, *cr.* 13.

THOYTS, Lond. and Berks., a heath-cock, rising, ppr., charged on breast with a character of the planet Venus, or.

THRALE, out of a ducal coronet, an oak-tree, fructed, ppr. *Pl.* 94, *cr.* 5.

THRALE, Eng., a cross crosslet, fitched, gu. *In cruce confido*. *Pl.* 16, *cr.* 10.

THRALE, or THREELE, Surr. and Suss., an oak-tree, ppr., fructed, or. *Pl.* 16, *cr.* 8.

THREIPLAND, Bart., Sco., a hart's head, erased, ppr. *Animis et fato*. *Pl.* 66, *cr.* 9.

THRELLE, out of a ducal coronet, or, an oak-tree, ar. *Pl.* 94, *cr.* 5.

THRING, Eng., a cock. *Pl.* 67, *cr.* 14.

THROCKMORTON, of Molland, Devons., an elephant's head. *Pl.* 35, *cr.* 13.

THROCKMORTON, or THROGMORTON: 1. A falcon, rising, ar., jessed, or. *Pl.* 105, *cr.* 4. 2. An elephant's head, erased, sa., eared, or. *Pl.* 68, *cr.* 4.

THROCKMORTON, Bart., Warw.: 1. An elephant's head. *Pl.* 35, *cr.* 13. 2. A falcon, volant, ppr., belled and jessed, or. *Virtus sola nobilitas*—and—*Moribus antiquis*. *Pl.* 94, *cr.* 1.

THROUGHSTON, Worc., a pelican in her piety, ar. *Pl.* 44, *cr.* 1.

THROUGHTON, Bucks., a lion's head, erased, per cheveron, ar. and sa., (charged on neck with three roundles, counterchanged.) *Pl.* 81, *cr.* 4.

THROWGOOD, or THROGOOD, Eng., a wolf's head, ar., (charged on neck with a buckle, its tongue in fess, az.) *Pl.* 92, *cr.* 15, (without rose.)

THRUXTON, Worc., a pelican, ar., in nest, feeding her young, ppr., beaked, legged, and vulned, gu. *Pl.* 44, *cr.* 1.

THUNDER, a cubit arm, ppr., in hand a (trumpet,) sa. *Certavi et vici*. *Pl.* 109, *cr.* 3.

THURCLE, a cubit arm, erect, ppr., vested, gu., cuffed, ar., in hand a fleur-de-lis, or. *Pl.* 95, *cr.* 9, (vesting, *pl.* 18, *cr.* 1.)

THURGRYN, Eng., a pelican, feeding her young, or, in nest, ar. *Pl.* 44, *cr.* 1.

THURKETTLE, Ess., a cubit arm, erect, vested, ar., (charged with a fleur-de-lis, gu.,) in hand, ppr., a fleur-de-lis, or. *Pl.* 95, *cr.* 9, (vesting, *pl.* 64, *cr.* 7.)

THURKILL, Lond., an arm, erect, vested, gu., (charged with three fleurs-de-lis, ar.,) in hand, ppr., a fleur-de-lis, or. *Pl.* 24, *cr.* 14, (vesting, *pl.* 39, *cr.* 1.)

THURLAND, Surr. and Yorks., a capuchin friar's head, ppr., couped at shoulders, vested, ar. *Pl.* 51, *cr.* 4.

THURLEY, Lond. and Northamp., a demi-dragon, segreant, vert, wings addorsed, sa., supporting an escallop, ar. *Pl.* 82, *cr.* 10.

THURLOW, Baron, (Thurlow,) a greyhound, couchant, or, (collared and lined, sa.) *Justitiæ soror fides*—and—*Quo fata vocant*. *Pl.* 6, *cr.* 7.

THURLOW, Eng., a crow, ppr. *Justitiæ soror fides*. *Pl.* 23, *cr.* 8.

THURLOW, Suff., a raven, ppr., a portcullis, hanging round neck, ar. *Pl.* 123, *cr.* 2, (portcullis, *pl.* 101, *cr.* 2.)

THURSBY, Eng., seven arrows, one in pale, and six in saltier, ppr. *Pl.* 110, *cr.* 11.

THURSBY-HARVEY, of Abbington Abbey, Northamp., a lion, rampant, sa., holding a battle-axe, erect, or. *Pl.* 125, *cr.* 2, (axe, *pl.* 14, *cr.* 8.)

THURSTON, a thrush, ppr. *Pl.* 10, *cr.* 12.

THURSTON, a woodpecker, ppr. *Pl.* 10, *cr.* 12.

THURSTON, Kent, a demi-griffin, segreant, issuing from a plum of (five) ostrich-feathers. *Pl.* 11, *cr.* 6.

THURSTON, Suff., a stork, ar., legged, az. *Pl.* 33, *cr.* 9.

THURSTONE, Hunts., a wolf's head, or, pierced through neck by an arrow, gu., headed and feathered, ar., vulned, of the second. *Pl.* 40, *cr.* 12.

THWAITES, Iri., a chevalier on horseback, at full speed, holding a broken spear, ppr. *Pl.* 43, *cr.* 2.

THWAITES, Yorks., a cock, wings addorsed, ppr., combed, wattled, and legged, gu. *Pl.* 76, *cr.* 7.

THWAITES, Derbs., a hind's head, *Pl.* 21, *cr.* 9.

THWAITES, Bucks. and Ess., a cock, wings elevated, sa., combed, wattled, and legged, gu. *Pl.* 76, *cr.* 7.

THWAITS, Eng., on a mural coronet, a bunch of seven arrows, ppr., banded, gu. *Pl.* 62, *cr.* 8, (arrows, *pl.* 110, *cr.* 11.)

THWENG, a pelican, in nest, feeding her young, ppr. *Pl.* 44, *cr.* 1.

THYLY, Norf., an escallop, or. *Pl.* 117, *cr.* 4.

THYNNE, Salop, a reindeer, or. *J'ai bonne cause*. *Pl.* 12, *cr.* 8.

THYNNE, Baron Carteret. *See* CARTERET.

THYNNE, Marquess of Bath. *See* BATH.

THYNNE, Beds., a squirrel, sejant, feeding on a nut, all ppr. *Loyal devoir*. *Pl.* 16, *cr.* 9.

TIBBET, Eng., a demi-lion, ppr. *Vincere vel mori*. *Pl.* 67, *cr.* 10.

TIBBETT, a demi-cat, (rampant,) gardant, az. *Pl.* 70, *cr.* 15.

TIBBITTS, Eng., a bee, in pale, sa. *Per industriam*. *Pl.* 100, *cr.* 3.

TIBBS, an oak-branch, vert. *Pl.* 32, *cr.* 13.

TICHBONE, an ass's head, between wings. *Pl.* 91, *cr.* 7, (wings, *pl.* 1, *cr.* 15.)

TICHBORNE, Kent, Hants, and Norf., on a chapeau, a wing, erect, per fess, or and vair. *Pl.* 83, *cr.* 8.

TICHBORNE, Bart., Hants, a hind's head, couped, ppr., between wings, gu. *Pugno pro patriâ*. *Pl.* 13, *cr.* 9, (wings, *pl.* 1, *cr.* 15.)

TICHBORNE, Kent, same crest and motto.

TICHBOURNE, Eng., a hind's head. *Pugno pro patriâ*. *Pl.* 21, *cr.* 7.

TICHBURNE, on a chapeau, a wing, erect, charged with three pellets. *Pl.* 83, *cr.* 8, (pellet, *pl.* 141.)

TICKEL, or TICKELL, Eng., an eagle, displayed, ppr. *Pl.* 48, *cr.* 11.

TICKHILL, a cubit arm, erect, vested, gu., charged with three fleurs-de-lis, ar., in hand, ppr., a fleur-de-lis, or. *Pl.* 95, *cr.* 9, (vesting, *pl.* 64, *cr.* 7.)

TIDBURY, Eng., the point of a spear, in pale, shaft and hilt, in saltier, ppr., banded, gu. *Pl.* 33, *cr.* 3.

TIDCASTLE, Lond., a leopard, statant, ppr., resting dexter on an escutcheon, or. *Pl.* 86, *cr.* 2, (escutcheon, *pl.* 19, *cr.* 2.)

TIDCOMBE, Wilts., a dexter cubit arm, in armour, ppr., garnished, or, in hand a broken lance, gu. *Pl.* 23, *cr.* 9.

TIDDEMAN, or TIDEMAN, Eng., a savage's head, couped, dropping blood, ppr. *Pl.* 23, *cr.* 1.

TIDMARSH, Eng., a broken lance, head turned toward the sinister, ppr. *Pl.* 3, *cr.* 6.

TIERNEY, Eng., an oak-tree, ppr. *Pl.* 16, *cr.* 8.

TIERNEY, Bart., Lond. and Suss., on a mount, vert, a pheasant, ppr., (ducally) gorged, or. *Pl.* 82, *cr.* 12, (mount, *same plate, cr.* 4.)

TIFFIN, Eng., a greyhound's head, erased, in mouth a stag's foot, erased, ppr. *Pl.* 66, *cr.* 7.

TIFFIN, Cumb., a demi-lion, rampant, gu., (gorged with a collar, flory counterflory,) or, supporting a battle-axe, ppr. *Patria fidelis. Pl.* 101, *cr.* 14.'

TIGHE, Mitchelstown, co. Westmeath: 1. For *Tighe*, a wolf's head, (erased,) ppr., gorged with a collar, ar., charged with a cross crosslet, sa. *Pl.* 8, *cr.* 4, (cross, *pl.* 141.) 2. For *Morgan*, a stag's head. *Pl.* 91, *cr.* 14.

TIGHE, Iri., a wolf's head, erased, ppr., gorged with a collar, ar., charged with a cross crosslet, sa. *Summum nec metuam diem nec optem. Pl.* 8, *cr.* 4, (cross, *pl.* 141.)

TIGHE, Iri., a galley, oars in saltier, sa. *Pl.* 77, *cr.* 11.

TILL, Eng., an ounce, sejant, ppr., resting fore-dexter on a shield, az. *Pl.* 10, *cr.* 13, (shield, *pl.* 19, *cr.* 2.)

TILLARD, Street End House, Kent: *Originally*, a mort-head. *Pl.* 62, *cr.* 12. *Now, usually*, out of a ducal coronet, or, a griffin's head, az., ears and beak, gold. *Pl.* 54, *cr.* 14.

TILLARD, Kent, an esquire's helmet, ppr., garnished, or. *Pl.* 109, *cr.* 5.

TILLER, Eng., on a mural coronet, six spears in saltier, ppr. *Pl.* 19, *cr.* 7.

TILLER, Middx., a demi-cat, rampant. *Pl.* 80, *cr.* 7.

TILLET, or TILLETT, Eng., six arrows, in saltier, ppr., banded, gu., ensigned with a round hat, of the first. *Pl.* 101, *cr.* 13.

TILLEY, Eng., the head of a battle-axe. *Pl.* 16, *cr.* 3.

TILLNEY, a griffin's head, erased, gu., eared, or, in beak, a gem-ring, gold. *Pl.* 48, *cr.* 6.

TILLOTSON, Yorks. and Kent, out of a mural coronet, a greyhound's head. *Pl.* 113, *cr.* 6.

TILLOTSON, a pelican's head, erased, ppr. *Pl.* 26, *cr.* 1.

TILLY, Eng., a rose-tree, vert, bearing roses, ar. *Pl.* 23, *cr.* 2.

TILNEY, Cambs. and Norf., a griffin's head, erased, gu. *Pl.* 48, *cr.* 6.

TILSON, and TILSTON, Chesh., out of a mural coronet, a boar's head, *Pl.* 6, *cr.* 2.

TILSON, Eng., a dexter hand plucking a rose, ppr. *Pl.* 48, *cr.* 1.

TILSON, and TILSTON, an arm, embowed, vested, ar., ruffled, of the last, in hand, ppr., a crosier, gu., head and point, or. *Pl.* 120, *cr.* 1, (crosier, *pl.* 17, *cr.* 12.)

TILYARD, Norf., a lion's head, erased, collared, vert, rimmed, or, on collar five ermine-spots, ar. *Pl.* 7, *cr.* 10.

TIMBRELL, Eng., a phœnix in flames, ppr. *Pl.* 44, *cr.* 8.

TIMEWELL, a demi-eagle, gu., wings expanded, erm., ducally crowned and gorged with a chaplet, or. *Pl.* 52, *cr.* 8.

TIMINS, Eng., a rose, gu., barbed, vert. *Pl.* 43, *cr.* 10.

TIMMINS, Eng., a dexter cubit arm, in hand a pair of scales, all ppr. *Pl.* 26, *cr.* 8.

TIMMINS, on a mural coronet, ar., six spears, in saltier, sa. *Pl.* 19, *cr.* 7.

TIMPORIN, Herts., on a mount, vert, a greyhound, couchant, ar., resting fore-paws on an escutcheon, of the first, charged with a fess, wavy, az., thereon three etoiles, or. *Pl.* 6, *cr.* 7, (escutcheon, *pl.* 19, *cr.* 2.)

TIMPSON, Devons. and Iri., on a piece of battlement, ar., an eagle, rising, ppr., in beak an oak-slip, vert, fructed, or. *Pl.* 60, *cr.* 8.

TIMS, a goat's head, couped. *Pl.* 105, *cr.* 14.

TIMSON, Eng., a horse's head, gu., bridled, or. *Pl.* 92, *cr.* 1.

TINDAL, Eng., in dexter hand a writing-pen. *Pl.* 26, *cr.* 13.

TINDALL, a demi-lion, rampant, (supporting) a garb. *Pl.* 84, *cr.* 7.

TINDALL, out of a ducal coronet, or, five pales, erm., banded, gold.

TINDALL, Norf., in lion's gamb, erect, or, a (cross of five mascles, gu.) *Pl.* 46, *cr.* 7.

TINDALL, and TINDALE, Suff. and Norf,, out of a ducal coronet, or, a plume of five ostrich-feathers, ar. *Pl.* 100, *cr.* 12.

TINDALL, Suss., out of a ducal coronet, or, a plume of feathers, erm., (within a basket, gu.) *Pl.* 44, *cr.* 12.

TINKER, Eng., a cross crosslet, az. *Pl.* 66, *cr.* 8.

TINKLER, a griffin, passant. *Pl.* 61, *cr.* 14, (without gorging.)

TINKLER, Eng., a cross moline, az. *Pl.* 89, *cr.* 8.

TINLING, Eng., an ear of wheat, or, bladed, vert, and a palm-branch, of the last, in saltier. *Pl.* 63, *cr.* 3.

TINNEY, Wilts., a griffin's head, couped, wings elevated, sa., beaked, gu. *Pl.* 65, *cr.* 1.

TIPPER, Eng., in hand, couped, in fess, a sword, erect, on point a garland of laurel. *Pl.* 56, *cr.* 6.

TIPPET, Eng., a garb, or, banded, vert. *Pl.* 48, *cr.* 10.

TIPPET, Cornw., a cubit arm, vested, charged with a cross crosslet, ar., in hand an anchor, by middle of shank. *Non robore sed spe. Pl.* 53, *cr.* 13.

TIPPETS, Eng., a squirrel, sejant, gu., cracking a nut, or. *Pl.* 16, *cr.* 9.

TIPPETTS, Devons., an eagle's claw, erased, ppr. *Pl.* 27, *cr.* 1, (without heart.)

TIPPING, Oxon., an antelope's head, erased, vert, ducally gorged and armed, or. *Pl.* 24, *cr.* 7, (gorging, *pl.* 55, *cr.* 2.)

TIPPING, Oxon., out of a ducal coronet, or, an antelope's head, vert, attired and maned, gold. *Pl.* 24, *cr.* 7, (coronet, *same plate, cr.* 10.)

TIPPING, a cubit arm, in armour, erect, ppr., garnished, or, in hand a truncheon, sa., tipped, gold. *Pl.* 33, *cr.* 4.

TIPTOFT, Eng., a stag's head, erased, or, gorged with a garland of (roses), gu., leaved, vert. Pl. 38, cr. 1.

TIRRELL, Surr., Bucks., Suff., and Ess., a boar's head, erect, ar., out of mouth a peacock's tail, ppr. Pl. 108, cr. 1, (tail, pl. 120, cr. 13.)

TIRREY, Lond., out of a mural coronet, or, a dragon's head, vert, vomiting flames, ppr., (collared and lined, gold.) Pl. 101, cr. 4, (flames, pl. 37, cr. 9.)

TIRREY, or TIRRY, Lond., Herts., and Heref., a demi-roebuck, ppr., attired and unguled, or, in mouth (three ears of corn, bladed, of the first.) Pl. 55, cr. 9.

TIRRINGHAM, Bucks., a talbot's head, gu., billettée, or. Pl. 123, cr. 15.

TIRWHIT, Linc., a savage, ppr., wreathed about head and loins, vert, holding over dexter shoulder a club, or. *Me stante, virebunt.* Pl. 14, cr. 11.

TIRWHIT, Hunts., a lapwing's head and neck, or.

TISDALL, Charlesfort, co. Meath, out of a ducal coronet, or, an armed hand, erect, ar., charged with a pellet, holding an arrow, ppr. *Tutantur tela coronam.* Pl. 122, cr. 8, (arrow, pl. 43, cr. 13.)

TISDALE, or TISDALL, Eng., a peacock's head, couped, ppr. Pl. 100, cr. 5.

TISON, or TYSON, Glouc., a (sinister) arm, in mail, or, hand, ppr., defended by an antique shield, gold, lined, vert, with straps, gu. Pl. 98, cr. 5.

TITCHBURNE, Eng., on a chapeau, gu., turned up, erm., a wing, per fess, or and vair. Pl. 83, cr. 8.

TITFORD, a demi-lion, rampant. Pl. 67, cr. 10.

TITLEY, and TITTELEY, Salop, between two laurel-branches, vert, an escallop, or. Pl. 86, cr. 9, (laurel, same plate, cr. 5.)

TITTERTON, Eng., an oak-tree, ppr. Pl. 16, cr. 8.

TITUS, Herts., a moor's head, (couped at shoulders,) ppr., temples wreathed, ar. and az. Pl. 48, cr. 7.

TIVITOE, Lond., a demi-Turk, affrontée, vested ppr., in dexter a (scimitar,) ar., hilt and pommel, or. Pl. 72, cr. 8.

TIZARD-HAWKINS, Dors.: 1. On a ducal coronet, or, between wings, gu., a bugle-horn, stringed, gold. Pl. 98, cr. 2, (coronet, same plate.) 2. Out of a mural coronet, a cubit arm, erect, vested, az., cuffed, gu., charged with a fleur-de-lis, or, in hand, ppr., a baton, gold, tipped, sa. *Ne timeas recte faciendo.* Pl. 18, cr. 1, (coronet, pl. 79, cr. 4.)

TOBIN, Eng., two battle-axes, in pale, environed by a serpent, ppr. Pl. 14, cr. 13.

TOBY, Eng., a perch's head, issuing, ppr. Pl. 122, cr. 6.

TOD, Sco., a fox's head, ppr. *Vigilantia.* Pl. 91, cr. 9.

TODCASTLE, Lond., a leopard, statant, ppr., resting dexter on an escutcheon, or. Pl. 86, cr. 2, (escutcheon, pl. 19, cr. 2.)

TODD, a fox, statant, ppr., collared, chain reflexed over back, or, supporting with dexter an escutcheon, sa., charged with an etoile, gold. Pl. 126, cr. 5, (escutcheon, pl. 19, cr. 2.)

TODD, a fox, current, (with a goose over back,) all ppr. Pl. 80, cr. 5.

TODD, a fox, sejant, ppr. Pl. 87, cr. 6.

TODD, a fox's head, couped, gu. *Oportet vivere.* Pl. 91, cr. 9.

TODD, of Tranby, near Hull, Yorks., on a chapeau, gu., turned up, erm., a fox, sejant, ppr. *Oportet vivere.* Pl. 57, cr. 14.

TODD, Northumb., a fox's head, erased, ppr. Pl. 71, cr. 4.

TODD, Berks., a wolf's head, or, collared, flory, counter-flory, gu. Pl. 8, cr. 4.

TODD, Ess., a wolf, sejant, ppr. Pl. 110, cr. 4.

TODMAN, Eng., a cannon, mounted, ppr. Pl. 111, cr. 3.

TODRICK, Sco., a griffin's head, erased, gu. Pl. 48, cr. 6.

TODRIG, Sco., a sword, in pale, ppr. Pl. 105, cr. 1.

TOFT, or TOFTE, Eng., a phœnix in flames, ppr. Pl. 44, cr. 8.

TOKE, Kent, a fox, current, (regardant,) or. Pl. 80, cr. 5.

TOKE, Goddington, Kent: 1. A griffin's head, erased, per cheveron, ar. and sa., guttée, counterchanged, in beak a tuck, ppr., hilt and pommel, or. Pl. 35, cr. 15. 2. *By augmentation,* a fox, current, regardant, ppr. Pl. 80, cr. 5.

TOLCARNE, Cornw., a wolf, sejant, ar., (gorged with a spiked collar, lined,) and legged, or. Pl. 110, cr. 4.

TOLER, Earl of Norbury. *See* NORBURY, Earl of.

TOLL, HENRY-LIMBREY, Esq., of Perridge House, Devons., a boar's head, erect. Pl. 21, cr. 7.

TOLL, or TOLLE, Eng., in hand, couped, a dagger, erect, ppr. Pl. 23, cr. 15.

TOLLEMACHE, JOHN, Esq., of Helmingham Hall, Suff., and Peckforton Castle, Chester, a horse's head, between wings. *Confido, conquiesco.* Pl. 19, cr. 13.

TOLLER, Eng., a mullet, gu., (charged with an ermine-spot, or.) Pl. 41, cr. 1.

TOLLER, Cornw., between wings, or, a cinquefoil, ar. Pl. 91, cr. 12, (wings, pl. 1, cr. 15.)

TOLLET, of Betley Hall, Staffs., a pyramid on a (pedestal, ar., the top entwined by a serpent, descending, ppr.) *Prudentia in adversis.* Pl. 8, cr. 10.

TOLLEY, or TOLLYE, a demi-tiger, vert, (collared, ar., and pellettée, the body bezantée.) Pl. 53, cr. 10.

TOLLEY, Eng., an acorn, stalked and leaved, vert. Pl. 81, cr. 7.

TOLLIOTT, a lion, rampant, per pale, ar. and gu. Pl. 67, cr. 5.

TOLMAN, Eng., two arms, in armour, embowed, wielding a battle-axe, all ppr. Pl. 41, cr. 2.

TOLSON, of Woodland Lodge, Somers., and Bridekirke, Cumb., out of a ducal coronet, or, a lion's gamb, holding (two) ostrich-feathers, vert, the other, az. *Ferro comite.* Pl. 58, cr. 7, (coronet, pl. 88, cr. 8.)

TOM, a Cornish chough, ppr., in mouth an escallop. Pl. 100, cr. 13, (escallop, pl. 141.)

TOMB, Eng., between wings, a pegasus' head. Pl. 19, cr. 13.

TOMES, or TOMS, Eng., a Cornish chough, volant, ppr. Pl. 87, cr. 10.

TOMKINS, Eng., out of a ducal coronet, a broken battle-axe, all ppr. Pl. 24, cr. 15, (coronet, same plate, cr. 10.)

TOMKINS, Heref., a lion, rampant, or, holding a broken tilting-spear, ar. *Pl.* 22, *cr.* 15, (spear, *pl.* 60, *cr.* 4.)

TOMLIN, Dane Court, Kent, two battle-axes, in saltier, ppr., (surcharged with a dexter hand, couped at wrist, also ppr.) *Quondam his vicimus armis. Pl.* 52, *cr.* 10.

TOMLIN, out of a mural coronet, a martlet, ar., (in mouth an oak-branch, vert, fructed, or.) *Pl.* 98, *cr.* 14, (coronet, *pl.* 128, *fig.* 18.)

TOMLIN, Eng., a peacock's head, erased, az., beaked, or. *Pl.* 86, *cr.* 4.

TOMLINE-PRETYMAN, Bart., N.S., two lions' gambs, erased, or, supporting a mullet, gold. *Pl.* 62, *cr.* 3, (mullet, *pl.* 141.)

TOMLINS, Middx. and Suss., on a mount, vert, a vine-stem, couped at top, and leaved, ppr., on stem an escutcheon, ar. *Pl.* 117, *cr.* 12.

TOMLINS, Eng., out of a mural coronet, seven Lochaber-axes, turned outward, ppr. *Pl.* 62, *cr.* 8.

TOMLINSON, Eng., out of a ducal coronet, ar., a griffin's head. *Non sibi, patriæ. Pl.* 54, *cr.* 14.

TOMLINSON, Yorks., a savage, wreathed about loins, ppr., (holding in both hands a spear, headed at each end, or.) *Pl.* 109, *cr.* 1, (without serpent.)

TOMPKINS, Eng., a ship, under sail, ppr. *Pl.* 109, *cr.* 8.

TOMPKINS, Heref., a unicorn's head, erased, per fess, ar. and or, armed and maned, gold, (gorged with a laurel-wreath, vert.) *Pl.* 67, *cr.* 1.

TOMPKINSON, Lanc., a wolf's head, erased, ar., ducally gorged, or. *Pl.* 14, *cr.* 6, (gorging, *pl.* 65, *cr.* 4.)

TOMPSON, Witchingham Hall, Norf., on a mount, vert, a demi-lion, rampant, gardant, or. *Pl.* 35, *cr.* 4, (mount, *pl.* 72, *cr.* 13.)

TOMPSON, Eng., a palm-branch, slipped, ppr. *Pl.* 123, *cr.* 1.

TOMS, Middx., a Cornish chough, ppr., charged on breast with a bezant. *Pl.* 100, *cr.* 13, (bezant, *pl.* 141.)

TONCKS, or TONKES, Eng., two arms, (in armour,) embowed, issuing from clouds, supporting the sun, ppr. *Pl.* 107, *cr.* 8.

TONG, or TONGE, Eng., a shield, quarterly, or and sa. *Pl.* 36, *cr.* 11.

TONG, Kent, on a rock, ppr., a martlet, rising, or. *Pl.* 36, *cr.* 5.

TONGE, AUGUSTUS-HENRY, Esq., of Highway, Wilts., and Victoria House, Cheltenham, same crest. *Steady.*

TONGE, in hand a grappling-iron, all ppr.

TONGUE, Iri., on an oak-tree, (a nest with three young ravens, fed with the dew of heaven, distilling from a cloud,) all ppr. *Pl.* 16, *cr.* 8.

TONGUE, Eng., a shield, or, between two (myrtle)-branches, in orle, ppr. *Pl.* 14, *cr.* 7.

TONKIN, Cornw., a Cornish chough, ppr. *Pl.* 100, *cr.* 13.

TONKIN, Devons., an eagle's head, erased. *Pl.* 20, *cr.* 7.

TONKIN, Devons., a dragon's head, couped. *Kensol Tra Tonkein Ouna Dieu Mathern yn. Pl.* 87, *cr.* 12.

TONSON, Iri., out of a mural coronet, or, a (cubit) arm, in armour, in hand, ppr., a sword, also ppr., hilt and pommel, or. *Pl.* 115, *cr.* 14.

TONSON, Baron Riversdale. *See* RIVERSDALE Baron.

TONYN, Eng., in dexter hand a sword, in pale, ppr. *Pl.* 23, *cr.* 15.

TOOK, or TOOKE, Eng., a griffin's head, erased, per cheveron, ar. and sa., guttée, counterchanged, eared, or, in beak a sword, (erect, ar., hilt, gu., pommel, or, hilt resting on wreath.) *Pl.* 35, *cr.* 15.

TOOKE, Hurston Clays, Suss., a griffin's head, erased, in beak a tuck sword, ppr. *Pl.* 35, *cr.* 15.

TOOKE, Eng., a griffin's head, erased, sa., in beak by middle of blade, a sword, ar., pommel downwards. *Pl.* 35, *cr.* 15.

TOOKER, a human heart, (enfiled) with a ducal coronet. *Pl.* 52, *cr.* 2, (without wings.)

TOOKER, Somers., a whale's head, haurient, erased, sa., (charged with a mascle, ar.) *Mirabile in profundis. Pl.* 96, *cr.* 8, (without gorging.)

TOOKER, Eng., a spur-rowel, or. *Pl.* 54, *cr.* 5.

TOOKY, Northamp. and Ruts., a demi-seahorse, rampant, quarterly, gu. and or, (gorged with a ducal coronet,) counterchanged. *Pl.* 58, *cr.* 15.

TOOLE, Iri., a lion's head, erased, gu. *Spero. Pl.* 81, *cr.* 4.

TOOLEY, or TOWLEY, Eng., within an annulet, or, a shield, sa. *Pl.* 88, *cr.* 2.

TOONE, Eng., a lion's head, erased, in mouth a hand, (couped,) ppr. *Pl.* 107, *cr.* 9.

TOOVEY, Oxon., on a mount, vert, a stag, current, ar., pierced through neck by an arrow, in fess, pheon to dexter, ppr., vulned, gu.

TOPHAM, Yorks., (two) serpents, entwined round a cross pattée, fitched. *Cruce non prudentiâ. Pl.* 112, *cr.* 6, (fitched, *pl.* 27, *cr.* 14.)

TOPHAM, Eng., an anchor, with cable, and a sword, in saltier, ppr. *Pl.* 25, *cr.* 1.

TOPLIFFE, and TOPLIS, Linc., a talbot, sejant, ar., collared, or. *Pl.* 107, *cr.* 7.

TOPP, Wilts., Devons., and Glouc., a (gauntlet) grasping a hand, couped at wrist, all ppr. *Pl.* 42, *cr.* 15.

TOPPER, Eng., an old man's head, issuing, in profile, ppr., banded, or and gu., tied of the colours. *Pl.* 23, *cr.* 3.

TOPPING, Eng., two lions' gambs., sa., supporting a roundle, vair. *Pl.* 42, *cr.* 3.

TOPSFIELD, Suff. and Norf., a talbot, couchant, gardant, (against a tree,) all ppr. *Pl.* 106, *cr.* 8.

TORBOCK, Staffs. and Lanc., an eagle, close, ppr., beaked and legged, gu., on breast a mullet. *Pl.* 7, *cr.* 11, (mullet, *pl.* 141.)

TORIANO, Lond., an arm, in armour, from shoulder, in fess, and from elbow, in pale, in hand a helmet. *Pl.* 114, *cr.* 9.

TORIN, Eng., an eagle's head, erased, ar. *Pl.* 20, *cr.* 7.

TORINGS, a martlet, between two laurel-branches, in orle. *Pl.* 111, *cr.* 5, (branches *pl.* 79, *cr.* 14.)

TORKINGTON, Eng., between wings, or, a spur-rowel. *Pl.* 54, *cr.* 5, (wings, *pl.* 1, *cr.* 15.)

TORLESSE, Berks., a stork, ppr. *Pl.* 33, *cr.* 9.

TORLESTE, a heron, or, between two branches, vert. *Pl.* 111, *cr.* 9, (branches, *pl.* 79, *cr.* 14.)

TORLEY, Eng., a boar's head, couped, sa., in fess, armed, ar., (charged with a pale, of the last.) *Pl.* 48, *cr.* 2.

TORNEY, Kent, a bull's head, erased, ar., attired (and collared,) or. *Pl.* 19, *cr.* 3.
TORPHICHEN, Baron, Sco., (Sandilands,) an eagle, displayed, or. *Spero meliora. Pl.* 48, *cr.* 11.
TORR, Linc., upon a headland, ppr., a tower, ar. *Altiora spero. Pl.* 31, *cr.* 15.
TORR, a griffin, passant, wings addorsed, ppr. *Pl.* 61, *cr.* 14, (without gorging.)
TORRANCE, Sco., a bull's head, erased. *I saved the king. Pl.* 19, *cr.* 3.
TORRE, Snydale, Yorks., a griffin, passant, per pale, or and ar. *Turris fortissima Deus. Pl.* 61, *cr.* 14, (without gorging.)
TORRE, Yorks., a tower. *Pl.* 12, *cr.* 5.
TORRE, a lily, ar., leaved, vert. *Pl.* 81, *cr.* 9.
TORRELL, Eng., a boar's head, erased, or. *Pl.* 16, *cr.* 11.
TORRENCE, Eng., two laurel-branches, in saltier, vert. *Pl.* 82, *cr.* 11, (without axe.)
TORRENS, a martlet, or. *Pl.* 111, *cr.* 5.
TORRENS, a martlet, sa., (round neck a blue ribbon, pendent therefrom, on breast, a medal.) *Pl.* 111, *cr.* 5.
TORRIE, a horse's head, ar. *Pl.* 81, *cr.* 6.
TORRINGS, Eng., a dove, between two branches of laurel, fructed, ppr. *Pl.* 2, *cr.* 11.
TORRINGTON, Viscount, Baron Byng, and a Bart., (Byng,) an heraldic-antelope, statant, erm., horned, tusked, maned, and hoofed, or. *Tuebor.*
TORVERS, a griffin, passant. *Pl.* 61, *cr.* 14, (without gorging.)
TORY, or TORRY, Eng., a horse, passant, ppr., furnished, gu. *Pl.* 99, *cr.* 11.
TOSH, and TOSE, Sco., a thistle, ppr. *Ad finem. Pl.* 68, *cr.* 9.
TOSH, Sco., a withered branch of holly, sprouting new leaves, ppr. *Pl.* 99, *cr.* 6.
TOSHANCH, on a sinister hand, issuing, a falcon, rising, all ppr. *Pl.* 7, *cr.* 1.
TOT, a demi-lion, ppr. *Pl.* 67, *cr.* 10.
TOTHILL, Devons., on a mount, vert, a turtle-dove, ppr., (in mouth a sprig, vert, fructed, or.) *Pl.* 104, *cr.* 8.
TOTHILL, Eng., an olive-branch, erect, ppr. *Pl.* 98, *cr.* 8.
TOTTENHAM, CHARLES, Esq., of Ballycurry, Wicklow, a lion, rampant, gu. *Ad astra sequor. Pl.* 67, *cr.* 5.
TOTTENHAM, Iri., a crescent, erm. *Pl.* 18, *cr.* 14.
TOUCHET, Eng., out of a ducal coronet, a swan, rising, ar., (ducally) gorged, or. *Je le tiens. Pl.* 100, *cr.* 7.
TOUCHET, Ess. and Iri., an old man's head, couped, ppr., wreathed, ar. and gu. *Pl.* 126, *cr.* 8.
TOUGH, Sco., a dexter hand, pointing with two fingers, gu. *Pl.* 67, *cr.* 6.
TOUKE, Worc., a leopard's head, couped, az., spotted, or. *Pl.* 92, *cr.* 13.
TOULMIN, a dexter arm, in armour, embowed, in hand a sabre, all ppr. *Pl.* 2, *cr.* 8.
TOULMIN, Eng., a garb, in fess, ppr. *Pl.* 12, *cr.* 15.
TOUNSON, Northamp. and Wilts., three cross crosslets, fitched, gu., (two in saltier,) one in pale, on centre an escallop, or. *Pl.* 42, *cr.* 5, (escallop, *pl.* 141.)
TOURES, Sco., a lion, rampant, ppr. *Pl.* 67, *cr.* 5.

TOURNAY, Eng., a tower, ar. *Pl.* 12, *cr.* 5.
TOURNAY-BARGRAVE, Kent, a bull's head, erased, ar., armed, or, (collared, az., charged with three bezants.) *Pl.* 19, *cr.* 3.
TOURNEMINE, Eng., an arm, in armour, embowed, ppr., in hand a fleur-de-lis. *Pl.* 24, *cr.* 14.
TOURNER, Sco., a flaming heart, ppr. *Tu ne cede malis. Pl.* 68, *cr.* 13.
TOUT, on a chapeau, an angel, in dexter a sword, in pale, supporting with sinister an escutcheon.
TOVEY, Sco., an eagle displayed. *In Deo confido. Pl.* 48, *cr.* 11.
TOVEY, Eng., an eagle, displayed, with two heads, on breast a saltier, ppr. *Pl.* 25, *cr.* 5.
TOWER, of Weald Hall, Ess., a griffin, passant, per pale, or and az., wings addorsed, gold. *Love and dread. Pl.* 61, *cr.* 14, (without gorging.)
TOWERS, Sco., a stag, lodged, ppr. *Pl.* 67, *cr.* 2.
TOWERS, Berks. and Northamp., a griffin, passant, per pale, or and ar., wings addorsed, gold, (charged on breast with a mullet, sa.) *Pl.* 61, *cr.* 14, (without gorging.)
TOWERS, Eng., a tower. *Bon accord. Pl.* 12, *cr.* 5.
TOWERS, Cambs., a griffin, passant, per pale, or and az., wings addorsed, gold. *Pl.* 61, *cr.* 14, (without gorging.)
TOWERS, Lond., an antelope's head, az., armed and maned, or. *Pl.* 24, *cr.* 7.
TOWGOOD, Devons., an arm, vested in russet grey, cuffed, erm., in hand, ppr., a wallet, ar., buckles and buttons, or.
TOWLE, Sco. and Eng., a dove and olive-branch, ppr. *Amo pacem. Pl.* 48, *cr.* 15.
TOWN, or TOWNE, Eng., on a rock, a tree, growing, ppr. *Pl.* 48, *cr.* 4.
TOWN, or TOWNE, Eng., a spear, in pale, ppr. *Pl.* 97, *cr.* 4.
TOWNELEY, of Towneley Hall, Lanc., on a perch, or, a hawk, close, ppr., beaked and belled, gold, (round perch a ribbon, gu.) *Tenez le vraye. Pl.* 10, *cr.* 7.
TOWNRAWE, and TOWNROE, Derbs. and Linc., a tiger, sejant, per pale, erm. and sa. *Pl.* 26, *cr.* 9.
TOWNSEND-STEPHENS, the Rev. MAURICE FITZGERALD, of Castle Townsend, co. Cork, a stag, trippant. *Hæc generi incrementa fides. Pl.* 68, *cr.* 2.
TOWNSEND, Lord CHARLES, of Rainham Hall, Norf.: 1. Out of a ducal coronet, or, a demi-swan, wings addorsed, (in mouth an ostrich-feather, or., ducally gorged and chained, gu.) *Pl.* 100, *cr.* 7. 2. A stag, trippant, ppr. *Pl.* 68, *cr.* 2. 3. Out of a ducal coronet, or, a plume of peacock's feathers, ppr. *Pl.* 120, *cr.* 13.
TOWNSEND, Eng., an eye, ppr. *Pl.* 68, *cr.* 15.
TOWNSEND, Honnington Hall, Warw., a stag, gorged with a wreath of oak, ppr., resting fore-sinister on two annulets, interlaced, or. *Vitâ posse priore frui. Pl.* 68, *cr.* 2, (annulet, *pl.* 119, *cr.* 10.)
TOWNSEND, out of a ducal coronet, a demi-swan, (ducally gorged, line reflexed over back.) *Pl.* 100, *cr.* 7.
TOWNSEND, Norf., a stag, trippant, ppr. *Pl.* 68, *cr.* 2.

TOWNSEND, Surr.: 1. A salamander, ar., in flames, ppr. *Pl.* 20, *cr.* 15. 2. A phœnix, ar., in flames, ppr. *Pl.* 44, *cr.* 8.

TOWNSHEND, of Hem and Trevallyn, Wel., a roebuck's head, attired, or, gorged with a collar, az., charged with three (escallops,) ar. *Huic generi incrementa fides*—and—*Vince malum patientia*. *Pl.* 125, *cr.* 6, (without roses.)

TOWNSHEND, Ess., on a mount, vert, a buck, (sejant, ppr., attired, or, supporting with dexter a lance, erect, gu., headed, gold.) *Pl.* 22, *cr.* 5.

TOWNSHEND, Marquess, Viscount, and Baron, Earl of Leicester, Baron Ferrars and Compton, and a Bart., (Townshend,) a buck, trippant, ppr. *Hœc generi incrementa fides*. *Pl.* 68, *cr.* 2.

TOWNSHEND, Viscount Sydney. *See* SYDNEY.

TOWRY, Eng., a griffin, passant, per pale, or and az. *Pl.* 61, *cr.* 14, (without gorging.)

TOWSE, Lond. and Somers., an eagle's head, erased, or, (pierced through neck by a sword, ar., hilt and pommel, gold.) *Pl.* 20, *cr.* 7.

TOY, or TOYE, Glouc., on a mural coronet, gu., a martlet, ar. *Pl.* 98, *cr.* 14, (coronet, *pl.* 128, *fig.* 18.)

TRABY, Eng., a demi-lion, rampant, sa. *Pl.* 67, *cr.* 10.

TRACEY, on a chapeau, gu., turned up, erm., an escallop, ar. *Pl.* 17, *cr.* 14, (without wings.)

TRACY, Devons., on a chapeau, gu., turned up, erm., an escallop, ar., between wings, or. *Pl.* 17, *cr.* 14, (without wings.)

TRAFFORD, a man holding a flail, handle part, ar., the other, or, legs of the first, coat, gu., cap, ppr.

TRAFFORD, Ess. and Lanc., a thrasher, ppr., hat and coat, per pale, ar. and gu., sleeves counterchanged, breeches and stockings, of the second and third, flail, of the first, on the flail a scroll, with motto—*Now thus.*

TRAFFORD, Chesh., a demi-pegasus, wings expanded, ar. *Pl.* 91, *cr.* 2, (without coronet.)

TRAHERNE, Wel., on a ducal coronet, a goat's head, erased, ppr., (charged on neck with three plates, one and two.) *Pl.* 72, *cr.* 2.

TRAIL, a column, in the sea, ppr. *Pl.* 14, *cr.* 3.

TRANCKMORE, Devons., a demi-heraldic-antelope, transpierced through neck by an arrow, in bend.

TRANSOME, or TRANSAM, Salop, a leopard's head, erased, in profile, (transpierced through mouth by an arrow.) *Pl.* 94, *cr.* 10.

TRANT, Eng., a demi-lion, supporting an anchor, ppr. *Pl.* 19, *cr.* 6.

TRANT, Iri., a demi-eagle, (in mouth a rose-sprig,) all ppr. *Pl.* 59, *cr.* 13.

TRAPNELL, Eng., a griffin's head, couped, az., beaked, or. *Pl.* 38, *cr.* 3.

TRAPPES, of Nidd, Yorks., a man's head, couped at shoulders, on head a steel cap, garnished with a plume of feathers, all ppr. *Pl.* 33, *cr.* 14.

TRAQUAIR, Earl of, Baron Stuart, Linton and Carbaston, Sco., (Stuart,) on a garb, in fess, a crow, wings expanded and addorsed, ppr. *Judge nought*. *Pl.* 50, *cr.* 5, (garb, *pl.* 112, *cr.* 10.)

TRAQUAIR, Sco., the sun shining on the stump of an old tree, sprouting new branches, ppr. *Pl.* 123, *cr.* 3.

TRASHER, Cornw., a demi-talbot, rampant, (regardant,) ar., eared, gu. *Pl.* 97, *cr.* 9, (without arrow.)

TRAVELL, Northamp. and Warw., a greyhound's head, sa., charged with (three mullets,) or, two and one. *Pl.* 14, *cr.* 4.

TRAVERS, Cork, a wolf, passant. *Nec timide, nec temere*. *Pl.* 46, *cr.* 6.

TRAVERS, Iri., the sun shining on stump of broken tree, sprouting new branches. *Pl.* 123, *cr.* 3.

TRAVERS, Eng., a rock, in the sea, ppr. *Pl.* 91, *cr.* 5.

TRAVERS, a griffin's head, erased, or, in mouth an eft, az. *Pl.* 48, *cr.* 6, (eft, *pl.* 93, *cr.* 4.)

TRAVES, Eng., a leopard's head, erased, gardant. *Pl.* 56, *cr.* 7.

TRAVESS, Eng., a bird, ar., in mouth a branch, vert. *Pl.* 48, *cr.* 15.

TRAVIS, Eng., a bear's head, erased, gu. *Pl.* 71, *cr.* 6.

TRAYTON, or TRETON, Eng., a horse, dapple-grey. *Pl.* 15, *cr.* 14.

TREACHER, Eng., a griffin's head, erased, ppr. *Pl.* 48, *cr.* 6.

TREACY, Eng., out of a tower, a demi-lion, rampant, all ppr. *Pl.* 42, *cr.* 4.

TREADWAY, Eng., a dexter hand, couped below wrist, in armour, ppr., holding a sword, of the last, hilt, or, on point a Turk's head, couped at neck, ppr. *Pl.* 36, *cr.* 10.

TREBA, a demi-lion, ar., collared, vairé, az. and erm. *Pl.* 18, *cr.* 13.

TREDCROFT, EDWARD, Esq., of Warnham Court, Suss., a cock's head, erased, ppr. *Vigilando quiesco*. *Pl.* 92, *cr.* 3.

TREDCROFT, a cock's head, erased, ppr. *Vigilando quiesco*. *Pl.* 92, *cr.* 3.

TREDEGAR, Baron, a reindeer's head, couped, or, attired, gu. *Pl.* 60, *cr.* 3, (without coronet.)

TREDENNICK, a buck's head and neck, couped. *Pl.* 91, *cr.* 14.

TREE, an oak-tree, fructed, ppr. *Pl.* 16, *cr.* 8.

TREFRY, Cornw., a Cornish chough's head, erased, sa., (in mouth a sprig of laurel, vert.) *Pl.* 27, *cr.* 13.

TREFUSIS, Baron Clinton. *See* CLINTON.

TREGENT, Eng., a Triton, in (dexer) a trident. *Pl.* 35, *cr.* 10.

TREGONWELL, Cornw., same crest, but in mouth a gold ring. *Pl.* 27, *cr.* 13, (ring, *pl.* 33, *cr.* 11.)

TREGONWELL-ST-BARBE, of Anderson, Dors. and Cornw., a Cornish chough, head and neck, sa., in mouth a chaplet, erm. and sa. *Nosce teipsum*. *Pl.* 27, *cr.* 13, (chaplet, *pl.* 56, *cr.* 10.)

TREGORE, or TREGOUR, Cornw., out of a ducal coronet, or, a unicorn's head, erm., maned and attired, gold. *Pl.* 45, *cr.* 14.

TREGOS, Eng., a crescent, ensigned with a buckle, or. *Pl.* 25, *cr.* 3.

TREGOS, Eng., an arm, in armour, embowed, in hand a scimitar, both ppr. *Ferro consulto*. *Pl.* 81, *cr.* 11.

TREHERON, Cornw., a demi-griffin, (erased,) ar., gorged with two bars, az., between claws a fleur-de-lis, of the last. *Pl.* 18, *cr.* 6, (fleur-de-lis, *pl.* 141.)

TRELAWNEY, a wolf's head, erased, ppr. *Pl.* 14, *cr.* 6.

TRELAWNEY, Eng., an acorn, ppr. *Pl.* 81, *cr.* 7.
TRELAWNEY-SALUSBURY, Bart., Cornw. : 1. For *Trelawney*, a wolf, (statant,) ppr. *Pl.* 46, *cr.* 6. 2. For *Salusbury*, a demi-lion, (per bend sinister, ar. and erminois, in paws a shield, or, charged with a bear's head, sa., muzzled, of the first.) *Sermoni consona facta* —and—*Virtus patrimonio nobilior.* *Pl.* 67, *cr.* 10.
TRELAWNY, CHARLES, of Coldrinick, Cornw., a wolf, passant, ppr. *Pl.* 46, *cr.* 6.
TREMAYNE, Eng., an escutcheon, erm., between two (myrtle)-branches, in orle, ppr. *Pl.* 14, *cr.* 7.
TREMAYNE, Cornw. and Devons., two arms, embowed, vested, or, between hands a man's head, ppr., on head a high-crowned hat, sa.
TREMENHEERE, HUGH SEYMOUR, Esq., of Tremenheere, Cornw., a Saracen's head, in profile. *Thysrscrysough ne Dieu a nef.* *Pl.* 81, *cr.* 15.
TREMENHEERE, Cornw., a demi-man, naked, in profile, wreathed about head. *Nil desperandum.*
TREMINELL, or TREMYNELL, an eagle rising, ppr. *Pl.* 67, *cr.* 4.
TREMYNELL, Eng., an eagle, rising, ppr. *Pl.* 67, *cr.* 4.
TRENANCE, Cornw., on a chapeau, gu., turned up, erm., a unicorn's head, of the last, maned, armed, and (ducally crowned, or.) *Pl.* 102, *cr.* 7.
TRENCH, HENRY, Esq., of Cangort Park, King's County, an arm, in armour, embowed, in hand a sword, all ppr. *Virtutis fortuna comes.* *Pl.* 2, *cr.* 8.
TRENCH, Sir FREDERICK-WILLIAM, K.C.H., of Heywood, Iri., same crest. *Consilio et prudentiâ.*
TRENCH, a cubit arm, in armour, ppr., garnished, or, in hand a scimitar, ar., hilt and pommel, gold. *Pl.* 81, *cr.* 11.
TRENCH, Baron Ashtown. *See* ASHTOWN.
TRENCH-LA POER, Earl of Clancarty. *See* CLANCARTY.
TRENCHARD, Dors., a cubit arm, erect, vested, az., cuffed, ar., in hand, ppr., a sword, of the second, hilt and pommel, or. *Pl.* 21, *cr.* 10, (vesting, *pl.* 18, *cr.* 1.)
TRENCHARD, of Weymouth and Poxwell, Dorset : 1. For *Trenchard*, a dexter arm, embowed, vested, az., cuffed, or, in hand a (trenching-knife,) in bend sinister, ppr. *Pl.* 47, *cr.* 15. 2. For *Pickard*, a lion sejant, ar., charged on shoulder with an ermine-spot, and gorged with a collar gemelle, sa., fore-dexter supporting an escutcheon, gu., charged with a fleur-de-lis, within a bordure, or. *Pl.* 21, *cr.* 3, (escutcheon, *pl.* 19, *cr.* 2.)
TRENCHARD-ASHFORDLY, Wilts. . 1. For *Trenchard*, a dexter arm, embowed, vested, az., cuffed, or, in hand a (trenching-knife, in bend sinister, the point depressed, ppr.) *Pl.* 120, *cr.* 1. 2. For *Ashfordley*, an ass's head, erased, or, (gorged with a collar, sa., thereon three mullets, gold.) *Pl.* 91, *cr.* 7.
TRENCHARDE, in hand ppr., vested, az;, a (knife, ar., handled, or.) *Pl.* 18, *cr.* 1.
TRENFIELD, a demi-antelope, (transpierced through neck by an arrow, in bend.) *Pl.* 34, *cr.* 8.

TRENT, an arm, in armour, embowed, in hand a scimitar. *Pl.* 81, *cr.* 11.
TRENT, Eng., a crescent, erm. *Augeo.* *Pl.* 18, *cr.* 14.
TRENT, a demi-eagle, wings, expanded, or, in beak a laurel-branch, ppr. *Pl.* 52, *cr.* 8, (branch, *pl.* 29, *cr.* 15.)
TRENTHAM, Staffs., a griffin's head, erased, sa. *Pl.* 48, *cr.* 6.
TRENWITH, Cornw., a falcon, rising, (in beak a branch.) *Pl.* 105, *cr.* 4.
TRESHAM, Eng., a bezant, or, charged with a talbot's head, az. *Pl.* 38, *cr.* 2.
TRESHAM, a boar's head, ducally gorged, or, in mouth a trefoil, slipped, vert, in fess.
TRESHAM, Bucks., a boar's head, erased at neck, sa., ducally gorged, or, in mouth a trefoil, slipped, vert. *Pl.* 36, *cr.* 9, (trefoil, *pl.* 141.)
TRESSE, Kent, an eagle's head, couped, erm., (ducally crowned,) and beaked, or, between wings, erect, ermines. *Pl.* 81, *cr.* 10.
TRESSON, on a mount, a lion, passant, (ducally crowned, supporting with dexter an arrow, in pale.) *Pl.* 48, *cr.* 8, (mount, *pl.* 59, *cr.* 5.)
TRESWELL, Eng., on a rock, a wild goose, ppr. *Pl.* 94, *cr.* 3.
TREUNWITH, Cornw., a hawk, or, wings expanded, ar., (in mouth three ashen keys, vert.) *Pl.* 105, *cr.* 4.
TREVANION-BETTESWORTH, JOHN CHARLES, Esq., of Cærhayes Castle, Cornw., a stag, trippant, ppr. *En Dieu est mon espoir.* *Pl.* 68, *cr.* 2.
TREVELYAN, Raleigh, Esq., of Netherwitton, Northumb., two arms, in armour, embowed, in hands, ppr., a bezant. *Time trieth troth.* *Pl.* 6, *cr.* 8.
TREVELYAN, Cornw., two arms, in armour, embowed, hands, ppr., supporting a bezant, thereon a parrot, statant, ppr. *Pl.* 6, *cr.* 8, (parrot, *pl.* 25, *cr.* 2.)
TREVELYAN, Northumb., a tower, encircled by water. *Pl.* 12, *cr.* 5.
TREVELYAN, Bart., Somers., two arms, counter-embowed, ppr., (vested, az.,) supporting in hands a bezant. *Time trieth troth.* *Pl.* 6, *cr.* 8.
TREVENYON, and TREVANION, Cornw., a stag, quarterly, gu. and ar. *Pl.* 88, *cr.* 9, (without arrow.)
TREVES, Eng., a demi-griffin, in dexter a sword, ppr. *Pl.* 49, *cr.* 4.
TREVET, or TREVETT, Eng., a castle, ar., masoned, sa. *Pl.* 28, *cr.* 11.
TREVILIAN, Somers. and Devons., two arms, embowed, (vested, az.,) in hands, ppr., a bezant. *Pl.* 6, *cr.* 8.
TREVITHICK, Cornw., a unicorn's head, couped. *Pl.* 20, *cr.* 1.
TREVOR, Norf., on a chapeau, gu., turned up, erm., a wyvern, wings addorsed, sa. *Pl.* 104, *cr.* 5.
TREVOR-HILL, Viscount Dungannon. *See* DUNGANNON.
TREW, Eng., a demi-chevalier, in armour, in dexter a sword, ppr. *Pl.* 23, *cr.* 4.
TREWARTHEN, Eng., in lion's gamb, sa., a sceptre, in pale, or. *Pl.* 16, *cr.* 1.
TREWARTHER, Eng., a pillar, in the sea, ppr. *Pl.* 14, *cr.* 3.
TREWENT, out of a ducal coronet, or, an eagle's head, between wings. *Pl.* 66, *cr.* 5.

TREWSDALE, Linc., a dragon's head, (in mouth) a broken spear. *Pl.* 121, *cr.* 9.
TREYS, Eng., two hands, couped, conjoined, in fess, supporting a scimitar, ppr. *Pl.* 95, *cr.* 1.
TRICE, Hunts., a phœnix in flames, ppr. *Pl.* 44, *cr.* 8.
TRICKEY, a lion's head, couped, sa., in mouth a man by the middle, his legs in chief, and head in base, embrued, ppr. *Pl.* 117, *cr.* 5.
TRIGG, a demi-talbot, salient. *Pl.* 97, *cr.* 9, (without arrow.)
TRIGGS, Eng., the sun, rising, ppr. *Pl.* 67, *cr.* 9.
TRIMLESTOWN, Baron, Iri., (Barnewall,) from a plume of (five) ostrich-feathers, or, gu., az., vert, and ar., a falcon, rising, gold. *Malo mori quam fœdari. Pl.* 54, *cr.* 8.
TRIMMER, Eng., a dove, in mouth an olive-branch, ppr. *Pl.* 48, *cr.* 15.
TRIMNEL, or TRIMNELL, Eng., a harpy, close, ppr. *Pl.* 126, *cr.* 11.
TRIMWELL, a lion's head, erased. *Pl.* 81, *cr.* 4.
TRINDER, Eng., a hawk, jessed and belled, standing on a fish, naiant, all ppr. *Pl.* 29, *cr.* 11.
TRINDER, Oxon., out of a ducal coronet, or, a stag's head, ppr., attired, gold. *Pl.* 29, *cr.* 7.
TRINGHAM, Eng., on a chapeau, a dexter wing, charged with a cheveron. *Pl.* 83, *cr.* 8.
TRINLING, Eng., a crescent. *Pl.* 18, *cr.* 14.
TRIPCONIE, and TRIPONIA, Cornw., a cock's head, couped, ar., combed, beaked, and wattled, gu., in beak a snake, ppr., environed round neck. *Pl.* 92, *cr.* 3, (snake, *pl.* 50, *cr.* 9.)
TRIPP, the Rev. CHARLES, D.D., Devons., an eagle, close. *Pl.* 7, *cr.* 11.
TRIPP, Lond. and Kent, out of rays, or, an eagle's head, gu. *Pl.* 84, *cr.* 9.
TRIPP, Yorks., an eagle, close, ppr. *Pl.* 7, *cr.* 11.
TRIST, Eng., on a serpent, nowed, a falcon, ppr. *Pl.* 75, *cr.* 11.
TRIST, Cornw., a falcon, ppr., (in mouth a fish.) *Nec triste, nec trepidum. Pl.* 67, *cr.* 3.
TRISTHAM, a wolf's head, couped. *Pl.* 92, *cr.* 15, (without rose.)
TRISTRAM, Cumb., a stag's head, ppr., attired, or, in mouth a (trefoil,) ar., stalked and leaved, vert. *Pl.* 100, *cr.* 8.
TRISTRAM, Eng., on a chapeau, ar., turned up, gu., a martlet, (wings addorsed,) sa. *Pl.* 98, *cr.* 14.
TRITE, or TRITON, crowned with an Eastern coronet, holding over shoulder with sinister hand a trident. *Pl.* 35, *cr.* 10, (crown, *pl.* 79, *cr.* 12.)
TRITE, Eng., a Triton, in sinister a trident. *Pl.* 35, *cr.* 10.
TRITTON, a horse, passant, ar. *Pl.* 15, *cr.* 14.
TRITTON, Eng., a cross pattée, erm. *Fortiter gerit crucem. Pl.* 15, *cr.* 8.
TRIVETT, Suss. and Suff., a leopard's head, couped at neck, ppr. *Salvus in igne. Pl.* 92, *cr.* 13.
TRIVETT, or TRYVETT, Eng., an ostrich, wings addorsed, ar., in mouth a horse-shoe, az. *Pl.* 16, *cr.* 2.
TRIVETT, an eagle, rising, ppr. *Pl.* 67, *cr.* 4.
TROGOOD, Dors., an arm, in armour, embowed, in hand a caltrap. *Pl.* 120, *cr.* 11, (caltrap, *pl.* 22, *cr.* 4.)

TROLLOP, Eng., a buck, or, pellettée. *Pl.* 88, *cr.* 9, (without arrow.)
TROLLOP, Durh., a buck, passant, ar., armed, or. *Audio, sed taceo. Pl.* 68, *cr.* 2.
TROLLOPE, Bart., Linc., on a mount, vert, a buck, trippant, ar., attired, or, (in mouth an oak-leaf, ppr.) *Pl.* 68, *cr.* 2.
TROOGOOD, Eng., on a wolf's head, couped, ar., a buckle, az. *Pl.* 92, *cr.* 15, (buckle, *pl.* 73, *cr.* 10.)
TROSSE, Cornw., a demi-lion, rampant, or, supporting a shield. *Pl.* 47, *cr.* 4, (shield, *pl.* 22, *cr.* 13.)
TROTMAN, Eng., out of a ducal coronet, or, a demi-ostrich, wings addorsed, sa. *Pl.* 29, *cr.* 9.
TROTMAN, a garb, ar., banded, az., between two ostrich-feathers, of the first. *Pl.* 48, *cr.* 10, (feathers, *pl.* 13, *cr.* 7.)
TROTMAN, Glouc., a garb, erect, or, banded, ar. and az., between two ostrich-feathers, of the second, quilled, gold. *Ib.*
TROTTER, RICHARD, Esq., of Mortonhall, Mid-Lothian, a man holding a horse, ppr., furnished, gu. *In promptu. Pl.* 37, *cr.* 11.
TROTTER, ROBERT-KNOX, Esq., of Ballindean, Perth, a horse, trotting, ar. *Festina lente. Pl.* 15, *cr.* 14.
TROTTER, Bart., Linc., same crest and motto.
TROTTER, an heraldic-antelope's head, couped, *Pl.* 76, *cr.* 3.
TROTTER, a galley, oars in action. *Pl.* 34, *cr.* 5.
TROTTER, a horse, passant, ar. *Pl.* 15, *cr.* 14.
TROTTER, Morpeth, Northumb., a boar, passant, ppr. *Nec timidus, nec ferus. Pl.* 48, *cr.* 14.
TROTTER, Yorks., a lion's head, erased, ar., collared, erm. *Pl.* 7, *cr.* 10.
TROTTER, Glenkens, Galloway, a horse, trotting, ppr., furnished, gu. *Festina lente. Pl.* 99, *cr.* 11.
TROUBRIDGE, Eng., a bridge of three arches, gu., masoned, sa. *Pl.* 38, *cr.* 4.
TROUGHTON, Bucks., Lanc., and Northamp., a lion's head, erased, (per cheveron, ar. and sa., charged with three roundles, counter-changed.) *Pl.* 81, *cr.* 4.
TROUP, Eng., a buck, trippant, ar. *Pl.* 68, *cr.* 2.
TROUP, Sco., a hind's head, erased, ppr. *Pl.* 6, *cr.* 1.
TROUT, Devons., on a mount, vert, an ostrich, close, ar. *Pl.* 65, *cr.* 3, (mount, *pl.* 122, *cr.* 7.)
TROUTBACK, and TROUTBECK, Eng., a wolf's head, erased, ppr. *Pl.* 14, *cr.* 6.
TROVE, Eng., a wolf's head, erased, erm. *Pl.* 14, *cr.* 6.
TROWART, an eagle, displayed, with two heads, wings expanded and (inverted.) *Pl.* 87, *cr.* 11, (without flame.)
TROWBRIDGE, Bart., Devons., a dexter arm, embowed, ppr., in hand a flag, erect, thereon a broad pennant, az., (charged with two keys, in saltier, wards upward, gold.) *Pl.* 6, *cr.* 5.
TROWBRIDGE, a bridge of (two arches, ruined on the dexter side.) *Pl.* 38, *cr.* 4.
TROWELL, Eng., a beaver, passant, ppr. *Pl.* 49, *cr.* 5.
TROWER, a lion, passant, gardant, per pale, or and az. charged on body with three crosses, pattée, counterchanged, (in dexter a spear, ppr.) *Pl.* 120, *cr.* 5, (cross, *pl.* 141.)

TROWER, Eng., stump of oak-tree, ppr., sprouting new leaves, vert. *Pl.* 92, *cr.* 8.

TROWER, out of a ducal coronet, or, a demi-eagle, displayed, with two heads, gu. *Pl.* 4, *cr.* 6, (coronet, *pl.* 66, *cr.* 5.)

TROWTBACK, Eng., a scaling-ladder, sa. *Pl.* 98, *cr.* 15.

TROWTBECK, a naked man, sa., (in dexter a dart, or.) *Pl.* 109, *cr.* 1.

TROWTEBACK, Eng., out of a ducal coronet, or, a lion's gamb, ppr., supporting a cross crosslet, fitched, gold. *Pl.* 65, *cr.* 5.

TROYHIN, Eng., a lion's head, erased. *Pl.* 81, *cr.* 4.

TROYHIN, Iri., a griffin's head, erased, ppr. *Pl.* 48, *cr.* 6.

TROYS, Eng., a tree, erect and raguled, out of the top, couped, three acorn-branches, fructed, or, leaved, vert. *Pl.* 5, *cr.* 6, (acorns, *pl.* 69, *cr.* 3.)

TROYTE, an eagle's wing, sa., charged with five etoiles, or, environed by a snake, ppr.

TRUBSHAW, Middx., a mullet, per pale, gu. and sa. *Pl.* 41, *cr.* 1.

TRUELL, a heart, gu., between two palm-branches, vert. *Semper fidelis.* *Pl.* 88, *cr.* 11, (without flame.)

TRUEMAN, or TRUMAN, Eng., on a ducal coronet, or, a wyvern, vomiting fire at both ends, ppr. *Pl.* 109, *cr.* 13, (coronet, *pl.* 104, *cr.* 11.)

TRUESDALE, Eng., a boar's head, (couped) and erect, ppr. *Pl.* 21, *cr.* 7.

TRUMAN, or TRUEMAN, Lond. and Yorks., a human heart, ducally crowned, or. *Pl.* 52, *cr.* 2, (without wings.)

TRUMBULL, Berks., a bull's head, erased, sa., (breathing fire, ppr.) *Pl.* 19, *cr.* 3.

TRUMP, a cock's head, (couped, az., billettée,) or. *Pl.* 92, *cr.* 3.

TRUMPETER, Eng., a demi-savage, ppr. *Pl.* 14, *cr.* 11.

TRUMWYN, and TRUWILL, Worc., a Saracen's head, ppr., wreathed, or and sa., (vested on shoulders, also sa., round neck a sash, tied in a bow behind, vert.) *Pl.* 26, *cr.* 8.

TRUSBUT, Eng., a hand issuing from a cloud, lifting a garb, in fess, ppr. *Pl.* 43, *cr.* 4.

TRUSCOAT, or TRUSCOTT, Eng., an arrow and a palm-branch, in saltier, ppr. *Pl.* 50, *cr.* 11.

TRUSSELL, Northamp. and Leic., an ass's head, ar., (gorged with a collar and bell, ppr.) *Pl.* 91, *cr.* 7.

TRUSTON, on a mount, vert, a lion, party per pale, gu. and sa., holding an arrow, point resting on the wreath, or. *Pl.* 48, *cr.* 8, (arrow, *pl.* 22, *cr.* 15.)

TRYE, the Rev. CHARLES-BRANDON, of Leckhampton, Gloucester, a buck's head, cabossed, gu. *Pl.* 36, *cr.* 1.

TRYGOTT, Yorks., a lion's head, couped, sa., in mouth a man (by the waist, ppr., his legs in chief and head in base, embrued on body, gu.) *Pl.* 117, *cr.* 5.

TRYON, Eng., an ostrich's head, between two ostrich-feathers, ar., in mouth a horse-shoe, ppr. *Pl.* 99, *cr.* 12.

TRYON, Lond. and Ess., a bear's head, sa., powdered with etoiles, or. *Pl.* 2, *cr.* 9, (etoile, *pl.* 141.)

TUBB, Cornw., a beaver, passant, ppr., (in mouth a gurnet, gu.) *Pl.* 49, *cr.* 5.

TUBERWILLE, Eng., a bomb, inflamed, ppr. *Pl.* 70, *cr.* 12.

TUCHFIELD, Devons., a hawk, (supporting an arrow,) ppr. *Pl.* 67, *cr.* 3.

TUCK, Eng., three mullets, in cheveron. *Pl.* 46, *cr.* 15.

TUCKER, of Welling, Kent, in (bear's) paw, erect and erased, gu., a battle-axe, in bend, head, ar., handle, or. *Pl.* 51, *cr.* 13.

TUCKER, Devons., in lion's gamb, erect and erased, gu., (charged with three billets, in pale, or,) a battle-axe, ar., handle, gold. *Nil desperandum.* *Pl.* 51, *cr.* 13.

TUCKER, and TUCKIE, Eng., in lion's gamb, erased, gu., a battle-axe, handle, or, head, ar. *Pl.* 51, *cr.* 13.

TUCKER, Kent and Dors. : 1. In lion's gamb, erect and erased, gu., (charged with three billets, in fess, or,) a battle-axe, ar., handle, gold. *Pl.* 51, *cr.* 13. 2. A demi-seahorse, supporting a trident, all ppr. *Pl.* 58, *cr.* 15, (trident, *pl.* 35, *cr.* 10.)

TUCKER-EDWARDES, of Sealyham, Pembroke, in (bear's) paw a battle-axe, ar. *Vigilate*—and—*Gardez la foi.* *Pl.* 51, *cr.* 13.

TUCKEY, Iri., a crane, wings expanded, in mouth a serpent. *Pl.* 59, *cr.* 11.

TUCKIE, Eng., in lion's gamb, erased, gu., a battle-axe, handle, or, headed, ar. *Pl.* 51, *cr.* 13.

TUDA-TREVOR, Wel., on a chapeau, gu., turned up, erm., a wyvern, sa., ducally (gorged,) or. *Pl.* 104, *cr.* 5.

TUDMAN, a demi-fox, ppr. *Pl.* 30, *cr.* 9, (without cross.)

TUDOR, Eng., on a mural coronet, or, a serpent, vert. *Pl.* 103, *cr.* 11.

TUDWAY, a demi-lion, rampant, gu., holding a rose, az., slipped, ppr. *Pl.* 39, *cr.* 14.

TUDWAY, Somers., an ostrich-feather, sa., enfiled with a ducal coronet, or. *Pl.* 8, *cr.* 9.

TUFFNAL, and TUFTNELL, Lond. and Middx., a dexter arm, in armour, embowed, ppr., in gauntlet, a cutlass, ar., hilt, or. *Pl.* 81, *cr.* 11.

TUFNELL, JOHN-JOLLIFFE, Esq., of Langleys, Ess., an arm, in armour, embowed, ppr., in gauntlet a cutlass, ar., hilt, or. *Pl.* 81, *cr.* 11.

TUFTON, Surr. and Kent, a sea-lion, ar. *Pl.* 80, *cr.* 13.

TUFTON, Earl of Thanet. *See* THANET.

TUGWELL, Somers., a stag's head, erased, ppr., (in mouth a trefoil, slipped, vert.) *Pl.* 66, *cr.* 9.

TUITE, Iri., a dexter arm, embowed, throwing a dart, all ppr. *Pl.* 92, *cr.* 14.

TUITE, Bart., Iri., an angel, vested, ar., in dexter a flaming sword, ppr., sinister resting on a shield of the arms. *Alleluiah.* *Pl.* 25, *cr.* 7.

TUKE, a demi-lion, rampant, gu., ducally crowned, or. *Pl.* 61, *cr.* 4, (without branch.)

TUKE, Kent, a griffin's head, erased, per cheveron, ar. and sa., guttée, counterchanged, in beak a sword, ppr., hilt and pommel, or. *Pl.* 35, *cr.* 15.

TULLOCH, a mitre, gu., garnished and rimmed, or, jewelled, ppr. *Pl.* 12, *cr.* 10.

TULLOCK, Eng., two wings, in leure, or. *Pl.* 87, *cr.* 1.

TULLY, Iri., on a chapeau, a serpent, nowed in a love-knot, all ppr. *Pl.* 123, *cr.* 4.

TULLY, Cumb., Cupid with bow and quiver, all ppr. *Pl.* 17, *cr.* 5.

TUNNADINE, Iri., the top of a halberd, issuing ppr. *Pl.* 16, *cr.* 3.

TUNNARD, Linc., a swan, wings elevated, erm., beaked, or, legged, sa., dexter resting on a bugle-horn, of the last, stringed, gu. *Pl.* 16, *cr.* 3.

TUNSTALL, Durh., Northumb., Westm., and Yorks., a cock, ar., beaked, gu., combed, wattled, and membered, or, charged with a mullet. *Pl.* 67, *cr.* 14, (mullet, *pl.* 141.)

TUNSTALL, Durh., a cock, ar., combed, wattled, and legged, or, in beak a (scroll, inscribed, *Droit.*) *Pl.* 55, *cr.* 12.

TUNSTALL, Lanc. and Yorks., a cock, ar., armed, or, beaked and wattled, gu. *Pl.* 67, *cr.* 14.

TURBERVILE, Berks., an eagle, displayed, sa. *Pl.* 48, *cr.* 11.

TURBERVILE, Dors., a castle, ar., portcullis, or. *Pl.* 28, *cr.* 11.

TURBERVILL, GERVAS-POWELL, Esq., of Ewenny Abbey, Glam., an eagle, displayed, sa. *Avi numerantur avorum.* *Pl.* 48, *cr.* 11.

TURBOTT, or TURBUTT, Yorks., a naked arm, in hand, ppr., a trident, or, armed and headed, ar. *Pl.* 12, *cr.* 3.

TURBUTT, of Arnold Grove, Notts., a naked dexter arm, in hand a trident. *Pl.* 12, *cr.* 3.

TURGEIS, (in a knot of rope,) a talbot's head, or, eared, sa. *Pl.* 123, *cr.* 15.

TURING, Bart., N.S., a hand holding up a knight's helmet, all ppr. *Audentes fortuna juvat.* *Pl.* 37, *cr.* 15.

TURISDEN, between wings, a griffin's head, in beak, a palm-branch, ppr. *Pl.* 105, *cr.* 6.

TURNBULL, of Stickathrow, Sco., a bull's head, erased, sa., armed, vert. *Audaces fortuna juvat.* *Pl.* 19, *cr.* 3.

TURNBULL, Sco., a bull's head, cabossed, sa., armed, vert. *Courage.* *Pl.* 111, *cr.* 6.

TURNBULL, Sco., a bull's head, erased. *Audaci favet fortuna.* *Pl.* 19, *cr.* 3.

TURNBULL, a cubit arm, erect, couped below wrist, in hand a sword, erect, ppr., enfiled with a bull's head, erased, sa. *Pl.* 71, *cr.* 9, (head, *pl.* 19, *cr.* 3.)

TURNER, a sword and a trident, in saltier, enfiled with an Eastern coronet. *Pl.* 124, *cr.* 6, (coronet, *pl.* 79, *cr.* 12; trident, *pl.* 12, *cr.* 3.)

TURNER, Surr., two wings conjoined, in saltier, ar., charged in middle with a trefoil, slipped, vert.

TURNER, a lion, passant, gardant, ar., (regally crowned, ppr., in dexter a fer-de-moline, sa.) *Pl.* 105, *cr.* 5, (without chapeau.)

TURNER, on a mill-rind, in fess, or, a Cornish chough, sa. *Pl.* 100, *cr.* 13, (mill-rind, *pl.* 141.)

TURNER, Eng. and Sco., a flaming heart, ppr. *Tu ne cede malis.* *Pl.* 68, *cr.* 13.

TURNER, GEORGE, Esq., of Menie, Aberdeen, same crest and motto.

TURNER, a wolf's head, erased, sa., guttée, ar., in mouth a tulip-branch, vert. *Pl.* 14, *cr.* 6, (tulip, *pl.* 64, *cr.* 2.)

TURNER, a demi-lion, rampant, gu., between paws (a fer-de-moline, ar.) *Pl.* 47, *cr.* 4.

TURNER, on a chapeau, gu., turned up, erm., a greyhound, statant, sa., (collared, ar.) *Pl.* 104, *cr.* 1.

TURNER, on a tower, ar., (with broken battlements,) an eagle, regardant, sa., in dexter a mill-rind, of the last. *Pl.* 87, *cr.* 5, (tower, *pl.* 12, *cr.* 5; mill-rind, *pl.* 141.)

TURNER, Salop, a tower, ar., (with broken battlements.) *Pl.* 12, *cr.* 5.

TURNER, Norf., a lion, passant, gu. *Pl.* 48, *cr.* 8.

TURNER, Suss., a lion, couchant, ar., in dexter a mill-rind, or. *Pl.* 75, *cr.* 5, (mill-rind, *pl.* 141.)

TURNER, Norf., a lion, passant, gu., (in dexter a laurel-branch, vert.) *Pl.* 48, *cr.* 8.

TURNER, a lion, passant, (ducally crowned.) *Pl.* 48, *cr.* 8.

TURNER, Lond., an antelope, sejant, erm., attired, or, resting dexter on an escutcheon, gold. *Pl.* 115, *cr.* 3, (escutcheon, *pl.* 19, *cr.* 2.)

TURNER, Lanc., Ess., Glouc., Hunts., and Suff., a lion, passant, gardant, ar., in dexter a mill-rind, sa. *Pro patriâ.* *Pl.* 120, *cr.* 5, (mill-rind, *pl.* 141.)

TURNER, Hunts. and Suff., a lion, passant, gardant, sa., in dexter a mill-rind, ar. *Pl.* 120, *cr.* 5, (mill-rind, *pl.* 141.)

TURNER, Ess., a demi-tiger, salient, or, tufted and maned, sa., armed, gold. *Pl.* 53, *cr.* 10.

TURNER, Linc., a lion, passant, ar., (gorged with a plain collar, or,) in dexter a mill-rind, sa. *Pl.* 4, *cr.* 14, (mill-rind, *pl.* 141.)

TURNER, Ess., a demi-wolf, gu., collared, or, between paws a mill-rind, gold. *Pl.* 65, *cr.* 4, (mill-rind, *pl.* 141.)

TURNER-PAGE, Bart., Oxon.: 1. For *Turner*, a lion, passant, gardant, ar., ducally crowned, or, (in dexter a fer-de-moline, pierced, sa.) *Pl.* 105, *cr.* 5, (without chapeau.) 2. For *Page*, a demi-horse, per pale, dancettée, or and az. *Pl.* 91, *cr.* 2, (without wings or coronet.)

TURNEY, Eng., a cross pattée, fitched, or. *Pl.* 27, *cr.* 14.

TURNEY, a tower, sa., towered, ar. *In hoc signo vinces.* *Pl.* 12, *cr.* 5.

TURNLY, on a mount, vert, an oak-tree, ppr., pendent on (sinister side) a shield, gu., charged with a cross pattee, or. *Perseverando.* *Pl.* 75, *cr.* 2, (cross, *pl.* 141.)

TURNOR, Linc., a lion, passant, ar., (crowned, or, in dexter a fer-de-moline.) *Pl.* 4, *cr.* 14.

TURNOUR, Earl of Winterton. *See* WINTERTON.

TURNOUR, Eng., between two laurel-branches, ppr., a shield, gu. *Pl.* 14, *cr.* 7.

TURPIN, Lond., Camb., and Leic., a griffin, passant, ar., guttée-de-sang, wings addorsed, or. *Pl.* 61, *cr.* 14, (without gorging.)

TURPIN, and TURPYNE, French, same crest.

TURSTALL, a cock. *Pl.* 67, *cr.* 14.

TURTLE, between wings, or, a parrot's head, gu. *Pl.* 94, *cr.* 2.

TURTON, Yorks. and Staffs., out of a mural coronet, ar., a cubit arm, vested, vert, cuffed, of the first, in hand, ppr., a banner, per fess, ar. and vert, the fringe counterchanged. *Pl.* 79, *cr.* 4, (banner, *pl.* 6, *cr.* 5.)

TURTON, Bart., Surr., out of a mural coronet, ar., a cubit arm, erect, vested, vert, cuffed, of the first, in hand, ppr., a banner, per pale, ar., and of the second, fringed, gold, staff, of the first, headed, or. *Ib.*

TURVILE, Leic., a gate, ppr., charged with a crescent, or. *Pl.* 73, *cr.* 4, (crescent, *pl.* 141.)

TURVILE, GEORGE-FORTESCUE, Esq., of Husband's Bosworth Hall, Leic., a dove, close, in mouth an olive-branch, all ppr. *Virtus semper eadem. Pl.* 48, *cr.* 15.
TURVILE, Eng., a gate, ppr. *Pl.* 73, *cr.* 4.
TURYN, Iri. and Eng., a demi-lady, in dexter a garland of laurel, ppr., vested, gu. *Pl.* 87, *cr.* 14.
TUSON, a lion's head, erased, ar. *Pl.* 81, *cr.* 4.
TUSON, Eng., a gad-fly, ppr.
TUSSER, Ess., a lion's gamb, erased, or, armed, gu., holding a battle-axe, az., purfled, gold. *Pl.* 51, *cr.* 13.
TUTHILL, Eng., a bee, volant, in pale, ppr. *Pl.* 100, *cr.* 3.
TUTIN, Eng., a bridge, of three arches, or, (water flowing underneath, az.) *Pl.* 38, *cr.* 4.
TUTT, Eng., out of a ducal coronet, a griffin's head, in beak a key, all ppr. *Pl.* 89, *cr.* 5.
TUTT, Devons., Wilts., Suss., and Hants, a talbot, sejant, or, collared and lined, ar. *Pl.* 107, *cr.* 7.
TWEDDALE, a lion's head, erased, gu. *Pl.* 81, *cr.* 4.
TWEDDELL, Eng., a pelican's head, couped, vulning, ppr. *Pl.* 41, *cr.* 4.
TWEDIE, Sco., a demi-lion, in paws an anchor, ppr. *Pl.* 19, *cr.* 6.
TWEDY, Eng., a bird, volant, ar., legged, or. *Pl.* 94, *cr.* 1.
TWEDDALE, Marquess and Earl of, Earl of Gifford, Viscount Walden, and Baron Hay, (Hay,) a goat's head, erased, ar., armed, or. *Spare nought. Pl.* 29, *cr.* 13.
TWEEDIE, Lond., a palm, and a laurel-branch, in saltier, vert. *Aut pax, aut bellum. Pl.* 63, *cr.* 3, (laurel, *pl.* 123, *cr.* 5.)
TWEMLOW, THOMAS, Esq., of Peatswood, Staffs., a parrot, perched on the stump of a tree, ppr. *Pl.* 30, *cr.* 5.
TWEMLOW, of Hatherton, Chesh., on stump of oak-tree, erect, a parrot, perched, ppr. *Teneo, tenuere majores. Pl.* 30, *cr.* 5.
TWEMLOW, of Peatswood, Staffs., same crest.
TWENTYMAN, Eng., a horse's head, ar., bridled, gu. *Pl.* 92, *cr.* 1.
TWICKET, Eng., a lion's head, erased, sa., in mouth a rose, gu. *Pl.* 95, *cr.* 6.
TWIGG, or TWIGGE, Eng., an esquire's helmet, ppr. *Pl.* 109, *cr.* 5.
TWINIHAW, and TWINIEA, Dors., a lapwing, wings expanded, ar.
TWINING, a cubit arm, hand grasping two snakes, each entwined round arm, all ppr. *Pl.* 30, *cr.* 2.
TWINING, Eng., stump of oak-tree, sprouting new branches, ppr., thereon pendent an escutcheon, gu. *Pl.* 23, *cr.* 6.
TWINNELL, Northamp., in lion's gamb, a lozenge, ar., charged with a cross crosslet, gu. *Pl.* 89, *cr.* 15.
TWISDEN, Lond. and Kent, a cockatrice, wings (expanded,) az., beaked, wattled, legged, and winged, or. *Pl.* 63, *cr.* 15.
TWISDEN, Bart., Kent, a cockatrice, az., wings (displayed,) or. *Prævisa mala pereunt. Pl.* 63, *cr.* 15.
TWISLETON, Yorks., a dexter arm, embowed, vested, sa., turned up, ar., in hand, ppr., a mole-spade, or, headed and armed, of the second. *Vidi, vici. Pl.* 89, *cr.* 6, (vesting, *pl.* 39, *cr.* 1.)

TWISLETON, Kent, on a mount, vert, a hind, statant, or, (ducally) gorged, gu. *Pl.* 75, *cr.* 6.
TWISLETON-FIENNES, Baron Say and Sele. See SAY and SELE.
TWISS, Eng., an etoile, rays, or. *Pl.* 63, *cr.* 9.
TWISS, a cockatrice. *Pl.* 63, *cr.* 15.
TWISS, a demi-griffin, ppr. *Pl.* 18, *cr.* 6.
TWIST, Eng., a wyvern, sejant, or. *Pl.* 63, *cr.* 13.
TWYFORD, Leic. and Lanc., a demi-lion, rampant, double-queued, sa., holding, a cinquefoil, or. *Pl.* 120, *cr.* 10, (cinquefoil, *pl.* 141.)
TWYFORD, Suss., a demi-lion, double-queued, sa., guttée-d'or, in dexter a trefoil, slipped, vert. *Pl.* 120, *cr.* 10, (trefoil, *pl.* 141.)
TWYRE, Eng., a hawk's head, vair. *Pl.* 34, *cr.* 11.
TWYSDEN, Bart., Kent, a cockatrice, az., winged, beaked, wattled, and legged, or. *Pl.* 63, *cr.* 15.
TWYSDEN, Eng., a cockatrice, or. *Pl.* 63, *cr.* 15.
TYAS, and TYES, Lond., a griffin's head, erased, ar., beaked, gu. *Pl.* 48, *cr.* 6.
TYAS, of Bolton-upon-Dearne, same crest. Try.
TYE, Ess., out of a ducal coronet, or, a tiger's head, tufted and armed, ar. *Pl.* 36, *cr.* 15.
TYERS, Eng., a demi-lion, rampant, gu. *Pl.* 67, *cr.* 10.
TYLDEN, Kent, a broken spear, erect, or, environed by a snake, vert. *Pl.* 30, *cr.* 3.
TYLDEN, Sir JOHN MAXWELL, Knt., of Milsted, Kent, (a battle-axe,) erect, environed by a snake, ppr. *Truth and liberty. Pl.* 14, *cr.* 13.
TYLDESLEY, Lanc., a pelican in nest, feeding her young, all or. *Pl.* 44, *cr.* 1.
TYLER, a tiger, salient, gardant, ppr., navally crowned, or, in dexter a flag-staff, with the French tri-colour flag flowing, depressed and reversed.
TYLER, Eng., a hind's head, erased, or. *Pl.* 6, *cr.* 1.
TYLER, a demi-cat, rampant and (erased,) or, charged on side with a cross crosslet, fitched, gu., in a crescent, of the last. *Pl.* 80, *cr.* 7, (charging, *pl.* 141.)
TYLGHAM, Kent, a demi-lion, sa., crowned, or. *Pl.* 61, *cr.* 4, (without branch.)
TYLLEY, Somers., a demi-lion, rampant, gardant, ar., pellettée, supporting a crescent, gu. *Pl.* 35, *cr.* 4, (crescent, *pl.* 141.)
TYLLIOT, Suff. and Yorks., a greyhound, passant, gu., collared, or. *Pl.* 104, *cr.* 1, (without chapeau.)
TYLNEY, Suff. and Norf., out of a ducal coronet, or, a griffin's head, erased, gu., armed, gold. *Pl.* 54, *cr.* 14.
TYLSON, a dexter arm, couped, vested, sa., cuffed, ar., in hand, ppr., a crosier, or. *Pl.* 17, *cr.* 12, (vesting, *pl.* 39, *cr.* 1.)
TYMEWELL, Lond., a demi-eagle, gu., wings displayed, erm., (crowned, armed, and gorged with a garland, or.) *Pl.* 52, *cr.* 8.
TYNDERNE, an ox-yoke, (in fess.) *Pl.* 35, *cr.* 11.
TYNEDALE, Lond. and Somers., out of a ducal coronet, of five leaves, or, a plume of five ostrich-feathers, ar., charged with a (fess,) erm. *Confido, non confundor. Pl.* 100, *cr.* 12, (coronet, *pl.* 23, *cr.* 11.)
TYNINGHAM, Bucks., a talbot's head, couped, gu., charged with three billets, or, one and two. *Pl.* 123, *cr.* 15, (charging, *pl.* 141.)

2 H

TYNTE-KEMEYS, Somers.: 1. For *Tynte*, (on a mount, vert,) a unicorn, sejant, az., armed, crined, and unguled, or. *Pl.* 110, *cr.* 15, (without tree.) 2. For *Kemeys*, out of a ducal coronet, a demi-griffin, or. *Dyw Dy Ras. Pl.* 39, *cr.* 2.

TYRCONEL, Earl of, Viscount Carlingford, and Baron Carpenter, Iri., (Carpenter,) a globe, in a stand, all or. *Per acuta belli. Pl.* 81, *cr.* 1.

TYRELL, Bart., Ess., a boar's head, erect, ar., out of the mouth a (peacock's tail,) ppr. *Sans crainte. Pl.* 108, *cr.* 1.

TYRON, Eng., an esquire's helmet, az., garnished, or. *Pl.* 109, *cr.* 5.

TYRONE, Baron. *See* WATERFORD, Marquess.

TYRRELL, Eng., a lion's head, az., royally crowned, or. *Pl.* 126, *cr.* 1, (crown, *pl.* 127, *fig.* 2.)

TYRRELL, Iri., a lion's head, erased, or, within a chain, in orle, issuing from the wreath, az. *Pl.* 28, *cr.* 12.

TYRRELL, Staffs., a boar's head, erect, ar., out of the mouth a (peacock's tail,) ppr. *Pl.* 108, *cr.* 1.

TYRWHIT, Linc.: 1. A lapwing's head, erased. 2. A wild man, holding a club, ppr. *Pl.* 14, *cr.* 11.

TYRWHITT, of Nantyr, Denbigh, Wel., a savage man, ppr., tinctured and wreathed, vert, holding in both hands a club. *Me stante, virebunt.*

TYRWHITT, a lapwing's head, couped, or.

TYSON, a demi-lion, rampant, or, ducally crowned, gu., (between paws an escutcheon, az., thereon an etoile, gold.) *Pl.* 61, *cr.* 4.

TYSSEN, Lond. and Middx., same crest.

TYTHERLEY, Hants, a wolf, passant, gu. *Pl.* 46, *cr.* 6.

TYTLER, Sco., two laurel-branches, in orle, vert. *Virtutis gloria crescit. Pl.* 54, *cr.* 10.

TYTLER, Sco., the rays of the sun, issuing from a cloud, ppr. *Occultus, non extinctus. Pl.* 25, *cr.* 14.

TYZARD, Eng., a boar's head, couped, or. *Pl.* 48, *cr.* 2.

TYZDALE, Iri., out of a ducal coronet, or, a dexter arm, in armour, charged with an etoile, in hand an arrow, all ppr. *Pl.* 122 *cr.* 8, (arrow, *pl.* 43, *cr.* 13 ; etoile, *pl.* 141.)'

U

UARBON, Eng., an etoile of eight points. *Pl.* 63, *cr.* 9.

UDNEY, Sco., a fleur-de-lis. *All my hope is in God. Pl.* 68, *cr.* 12.

UDNIE, Sco., a fleur-de-lis, or. *Pl.* 68, *cr.* 12.

UDWARD, Sco., a torteau, ppr. *Nec flatu, nec fluctu. Pl.* 7, *cr.* 6.

UFFLEET, or UFFLET, Eng., in lion's paw, erased, sa., the hilt of a broken sword, erect, ppr. *Pl.* 49, *cr.* 10,

UFFLEETE, Eng., on top of a Doric pillar, a heart, gu. *Pl.* 122, *cr.* 4.

UFFORD, a talbot, passant, charged on shoulder with three guttes, gu. *Pl.* 120, *cr.* 8.

UFFORD, DE, Eng., a demi-eagle, displayed, sa. *Pl.* 22, *cr.* 11.

UFFORD, Eng., an anchor, or, in the sea, vert. *Pl.* 62, *cr.* 10.

UGLETREIGHT, out of a ducal coronet, a buck's head. *Pl.* 91, *cr.* 14, (coronet, *pl.* 29, *cr.* 7.)

UHTHOFF, a yew-tree, ppr. *Pl.* 49, *cr.* 13.

UMFREVILE, Bucks. and Northumb., out of a mural coronet, or, an eagle's head, erm. *Pl.* 121, *cr.* 11.

UMFREVILE, Ess. and Linc., out of a ducal coronet, or, an eagle's head, ar. *Pl.* 20, *cr.* 12.

UMFREVILLE, Eng., in lion's paw, erased, gu., a sceptre, in pale, or. *Pl.* 16, *cr.* 1.

UMFREVILLE, Lond., Ess., Bucks., Middx., Surr., Northumb., and Suff., out of a mural coronet, gu., a griffin's head, erm. *Pl.* 101, *cr.* 6, (without gorging.)

UMPHRAY, an open boot, ppr. *Pax tua, Domine, est requies mea. Pl.* 15, *cr.* 12.

UMPHREVILLE, Eng., out of a mural coronet, or, an eagle's head, ar. *Pl.* 121, *cr.* 11.

UMPTON, Berks. and Oxon., on a chapeau, a griffin. *Pl.* 122, *cr.* 11.

UMPTON, a demi-greyhound, sa., (in mouth a spear, or.) *Pl.* 48, *cr.* 3.

UMPTON, a demi-greyhound, sa., (collared and ringed, in mouth a spear-head, or.) *Pl.* 48, *cr.* 3.

UMPTON, Eng., on a chapeau, az., turned up, erm., a griffin, (passant,) ar. *Pl.* 122, *cr.* 11.

UNDALL, Dors., a serpent, vert, entwined round two halberds, addorsed, ppr. *Pl.* 14, *cr.* 13.

UNDERHILL, Middx., Staffs., and Warw., on a mount, vert, a (hind,) lodged, or. *Pl.* 22, *cr.* 5.

UNDERWOOD, Eng., a hind's head. *Pl.* 21, *cr.* 9.

UNDERWOOD, Iri., a lion, passant, az. *Noli irritare leonem. Pl.* 48, *cr.* 8.

UNDERWOOD, Iri., in lion's gamb, a thistle, ppr. *Pl.* 109, *cr.* 4.

UNDERWOOD, Heref., a hind's head, erased. *Pl.* 6, *cr.* 1.

UNDERWOOD, Norf., a hind's head, or, (gorged with a chaplet, vert.) *Pl.* 21, *cr.* 9.

UNETT, of Woodlands, Harborne, Staffs., a lion's head, erased. *Pl.* 81, *cr.* 4.

UNETT, Eng., on a chapeau, a cockatrice, sejant, wings addorsed, and ducally crowned, all ppr. *Pl.* 103, *cr.* 9.

UNETT, Salop, out of a ducal coronet, or, a griffin's head, sa. *Pl.* 54, *cr.* 14.

UNIACKE, or UNIAKE, Eng., a dexter arm, in armour, gauntleted, ppr., in hand a hawk's lure, or. *Pl.* 44, *cr.* 2, (armour, *same plate, cr.* 9.)

UNSWORTH, Lanc., a lion, rampant, (bendy of six, or and az.,) in paws a cross pattée, fitched, gold. *Pl.* 125, *cr.* 2.

UNTERCOMBE, Eng., a sword, erect, enfiled with a man's head, couped, (wreathed.) *Pl.* 27, *cr.* 3.

UNTON, Berks, a demi-greyhound, sa., (collared, or, in mouth a broken spear.) *Pl.* 48, *cr.* 3.

UPHILL, Lond. and Devons., on a mount, charged with trefoils, slipped, vert, a bird, volant, in beak a trefoil, slipped, also vert.
UPJOHN, a stork, ppr. *Pl.* 33, *cr.* 9.
UPPLEBY, a buck's head, ppr., collared. *Metuo secundis. Pl.* 125, *cr.* 6, (without roses.)
UPTON, Eng., in lion's gamb, az., a crescent, or, *Pl.* 91, *cr.* 1.
UPTON, LEWIS, Esq., of Clyde Court, co. Louth, and Stanstead Bury, Herts., on a ducal coronet, or, a war-horse, current, sa., caparisoned, gold. *Semper paratus. Pl.* 76, *cr.* 8.
UPTON, Eng., on a chapeau, az., turned up, erm., a griffin, passant, ar. *Pl.* 122, *cr.* 11.
UPTON, Devons. and Worc., on a ducal coronet, or, a horse, passant, sa., furnished, gold. *Pl.* 76, *cr.* 8.
UPTON, Lanc., a demi-wolf, rampant, ar. *Pl.* 56, *cr.* 8, (without spear.)
UPTON, Suss., two dolphins, in saltier, or, finned, az. *Pl.* 125, *cr.* 1.
UPTON, Viscount Templeton. See TEMPLETON.
URBY, Eng., a man's head, (couped at shoulders,) in profile, ppr. *Pl.* 81, *cr.* 15.
URE, Sco., a lion's paw, erect and erased, gu. *Sans tache. Pl.* 126, *cr.* 9.
URMESTONE, Lanc. and Yorks., a dragon's head, erased, vert. *Pl.* 107, *cr.* 10.
URQUHART, Sco., a boar's head, erased, or. *Mean, speak, and doe well. Pl.* 16, *cr.* 11.
URQUHART, Sco., same crest. *Per mare et terras.*
URQUHART, Eng., in lion's paw, a human heart, ppr. *Pl.* 23, *cr.* 13.
URQUHART, Sco., a boar's head, couped, gu. *Per actum intentio. Pl.* 48, *cr.* 2.
URQUHART, Sco., a palm-branch and sword, in saltier, ppr. *Weigh well. Pl.* 50, *cr.* 4, (palm, *pl.* 26, *cr.* 3.)
URQUHART, Sco.: 1. A (dagger) and branch of palm, slipped, in saltier, ppr. *Weigh well. Pl.* 50, *cr.* 4, (palm, *pl.* 26, *cr.* 3.) 2. A demi-otter, sa., crowned with an antique crown, or, (between paws a crescent, gu.) *Per mare, per terras. Pl.* 9, *cr.* 9, (crown, *pl.* 79, *cr.* 12.)
URREN, Wel., a Cornish chough, rising, wings overt, ppr., resting dexter on an escutcheon, sa., charged with a leopard's head, or. *Pl.* 6, *cr.* 11.
URRIE, a lion's paw, erased, gu. *Sans tache. Pl.* 126, *cr.* 9.
URRY, Eng., a lioness, ppr. *Pl.* 103, *cr.* 13.
URRY, Sco., a lion's paw, erased, sa. *Sans tache. Pl.* 126, *cr.* 9.
URRY, a demi-lioness, ppr.
URSWICKE, Eng., a lion, passant, ar. *Pl.* 48, *cr.* 8.
USHER, Eng., a Doric pillar, ar., winged, or. *Pl.* 33, *cr.* 12.
USHER, Iri., a swan, wings addorsed, regardant, ar., murally crowned, or, dexter resting on an escallop, gu. *Pl.* 44, *cr.* 15.
USSHER, CHRISTOPHER, Esq., of Eastwell House, co. Galway, a cubit arm, vested, az., cuffed, ar., in hand a baton, of the last. *Ne vele veles. Pl.* 18, *cr.* 1.
UTBER, and UTKER, Norf., an arrow, erect, sa., headed and feathered, ar., to shaft, wings expanded, or, the barb of an arrow, in base. *Pl.* 6, *cr.* 10.
UTREIGHT, Eng., out of a ducal coronet, a bull's head, couped, az., armed, or. *Pl.* 120, *cr.* 7, (coronet, *pl.* 43, *cr.* 9.)
UVEDALE, Hants, Suss., and Dors., on each side of a chapeau, az., turned up, erm., an ostrich-feather, within the turning up. *Pl.* 6, *cr.* 12.
UVEDALL, on each side of a chapeau, az., turned up, ar., a bugle-horn, gu. *Pl.* 6, *cr.* 12, (horn, *pl.* 89, *cr.* 3.)
UVEDELL, Eng., a pheasant, vert, crested, armed, and gorged with a (chaplet,) gu. *Pl.* 82, *or.* 12.
UVERY, Eng., an elephant's head, bendy of six, ar. and gu. *Pl.* 35, *cr.* 13.
UXBRIDGE, Earl of. See ANGLESEY, Marquess.

V

VACH, Sco., a cow's head, affrontée, sa. *Famam extendimus factis. Pl.* 103, *cr.* 15.
VACHELL, a bull, passant, ar., armed and (collared, or, a bell pendent from collar, gold.) *Pl.* 66, *cr.* 11.
VACHELL, a bull's leg, embowed, couped at thigh, erm., hoof upward. *Pl.* 6, *cr.* 14.
VACHELL, Berks., Beds., and Bucks., a bull's gamb, in pale, couped, ar., hoof in base, or, *Pl.* 91, *cr.* 3.
VAIR, Sco., a boar's head and neck, couped, ar. *Cura atque industria. Pl.* 2, *cr.* 7.
VAIRE, a fret, gu. *Pl.* 82, *cr.* 7.
VALANGE, Sco., a rose surmounted by a thistle, ppr. *In utroque. Pl.* 73, *cr.* 6.
VALE, Lond., on a mount, vert, a swan's head, couped at neck, guttee-de-poix, surmounting two crosses, pattée, fitched in saltier, gu. *In te, Domine, speravt.*
VALE, Eng., on a tower, sa., a crescent, gu. *Pl.* 85, *cr.* 1.
VALENCE, and VALOMESS, Eng., between wings, or, each charged with a rose, gu., a cross fleury, fitched, az., charged on centre with the sun, and ensigned with a demi-fleur-de-lis, gold. *Pl.* 26, *cr.* 6.
VALENCE, a greyhound's head, gu. *Pl.* 14, *cr.* 4.
VALENTINE, Heref., a demi-pegasus, salient, erm., enfiled on body with a ducal coronet, or. *Pl.* 91, *cr.* 2.
VALENTINE, Suff., an ostrich, wings addorsed, in mouth a horse-shoe, ppr. *Pl.* 16, *cr.* 2.
VALLACK, Eng., a dove, rising, ppr. *Pl.* 27, *cr.* 5.
VALLANCE, Sco., a garb, gu. *Pl.* 48, *cr.* 10.
VALLANCE, Eng., out of a ducal coronet, a demi-ostrich, wings addorsed, all ppr. *Pl.* 29, *cr.* 9.
VAMPAGE, Eng., a demi-lion, rampant, or. *Pl.* 67, *cr.* 10.
VAMPAGE, Eng., a bridge of three arches, ar. *Pl.* 38, *cr.* 4.
VAN, Eng., a stag, lodged, ppr. *Pl.* 67, *cr.* 2.
VAN, Wel., a heron, wings expanded, ar. *Pl.* 6, *cr.* 13.

VAN JUCKEN, two wings, expanded, ppr. *Pl.* 39, *cr.* 12, (without charge.)

VAN STRAUBENZEE, Yorks., out of a ducal coronet, or, two wings, per fess, ar. and gu., counterchanged. *Pl.* 17, *cr.* 9.

VAN STRAUBENZEE, of Spennithorne, Yorks., an ostrich, in mouth a horse-shoe. *Pl.* 16, *cr.* 2.

VAN STREYAN, a demi-lion, rampant, sa. *Pl.* 67, *cr.* 10.

VAN VOORST, Lond., a demi-mermaid, in dexter a drinking cup, in sinister a jug. *Pl.* 125, *cr.* 3.

VANAM, or VANNAM, Lond., a bundle of five arrows, sa., (points upward,) bound by a belt, gu., and buckle, or. *Pl.* 54, *cr.* 15.

VANBRUG, and VANBURGH, Foreign and Eng., out of a bridge of three arches, (reversed,) a demi-lion, or. *Pl.* 38, *cr.* 4, (lion, *pl.* 67, *cr.* 10.)

VANCE, Iri., an old man's head, ppr., helmet, az., garnished, ar. *Pl.* 33, *cr.* 14.

VANDELEUR, CROFTON-MOORE, Esq., of Kilrush, co. Clare, a martlet, ppr. *Virtus astra petit.* *Pl.* 111, *cr.* 5.

VANDELEUR, Iri., five arrows, in saltier, entwined by a serpent, all ppr. *Pl.* 21, *cr.* 14.

VANDEPUT, a dolphin, haurient, az. *Pl.* 14, *cr.* 10.

VANDEPUT, Lond., between wings, or, a dolphin, haurient, az. *Pl.* 111, *cr.* 12.

VANDERGUCHT, Lond., an etoile, ar. *Pl.* 63, *cr.* 9.

VANDERPLANK, Eng., a garb, or. *Industria ditat.* *Pl.* 48, *cr.* 10.

VANDYK, or VANDYKE, an eagle's head and neck in a tun, dexter wing elevated, sinister cut off and lying on wreath. *Pl.* 6, *cr.* 15.

VANE, Duke of Cleaveland. *See* CLEAVELAND.

VANE, an arm, in armour, embowed, in hand a sabre. *Pl.* 2, *cr.* 8.

VANE, Durh. and Kent, in dexter gauntlet, ppr., garnished, or, a sword, of the first, hilt and pommel, gold. *Pl.* 125, *cr.* 5.

VANE-FLETCHER, Bart., Cumb., in dexter gauntlet, erect, a sword, all ppr., hilt and pommel, or. *Pl.* 125, *cr.* 5.

VANE-STEWART, Marquess of Londonderry. *See* LONDONDERRY.

VAN-HAGEN, between wings, ar., a trefoil, vert. *Pl.* 4, *cr.* 10.

VANHECK, Lond., a rose, gu., barbed, stalked, and leaved, ppr. *Pl.* 105, *cr.* 7.)

VANHITHESON, out of a ducal coronet, or, a dragon's head, gold, wings addorsed, ar., each wing charged with three bars, gu. *Pl.* 59, *cr.* 14.

VAN-MILDERT, Durh., out of a ducal coronet, a bishop's mitre. *Pl.* 12, *cr.* 10, (coronet, *pl.* 128, *fig.* 3.)

VANNECK, Baron Huntingfield. *See* HUNTINGFIELD.

VANNECK, Eng., between wings, a hunting-horn, stringed. *Pl.* 98, *cr.* 2.

VAN-NECK, Surr. and Suff., between wings, ar., a bugle-horn, gu., stringed, or. *Pl.* 98, *cr.* 2.

VANORT, Dutch and French, on a terraqueous globe, a ship, ppr. *Pl.* 41, *cr.* 12.

VANSITTART, Baron Bexley. *See* BEXLEY.

VANSITTART, Berks., between two crosses pattée, ar., an eagle, displayed, sa. *Pl.* 117, *cr.* 15.

VAN-SITTART, Lond., same crest.

VAN-SITTART, Shottesbrook Park, Berks, an eagle's head, (couped at neck,) between wings, sa., all resting on two crosses pattée, ar. *Fata viam invenient.* *Pl.* 117, *cr.* 15.

VYN-WHALFF, Eng., a demi-wolf. *Pl.* 56, *cr.* 8, (without spear.)

VARDON, Eng., in dexter hand a sheaf of arrows, ppr. *Pl.* 56, *cr.* 4.

VARLEY, Eng., out of a ducal coronet, or, a staff, raguly, sa. *Pl.* 78, *cr.* 15.

VARLO, Eng., a cross moline, gu., between two ears of wheat, bladed, ppr. *Pl.* 23, *cr.* 14.

VARNHAM, an eagle, wings elevated, preying on a coney. *Pl.* 61, *cr.* 3.

VASS, Eng., an ostrich's head, between two feathers, ar., in mouth, gu., a horse-shoe, az. *Pl.* 99, *cr.* 12.

VASSALL, SPENCER-LAMBERT-HUNTER, of Milford, Hants ; and Newfound River, Jamaica : 1. On a mount, vert, a breached fortress, ppr., thereon a flag, gu., inscribed, "Monte-Video," in letters of gold. 2. A ship with masts and shrouds, all ppr. *Sæpe pro rege, semper pro republicâ*—and—*Every bullet has its billet.*

VASSALL, Baron Holland. *See* HOLLAND.

VAUGHAN, JOHN, Esq., of Penmaen, Marioneth., a demi-lion, rampant. *Pl.* 67, *cr.* 10.

VAUGHAN, Eng., a lion, rampant, ppr. *Pl.* 67, *cr.* 5.

VAUGHAN, Salop, a boar's head, gu., couped, or. *Pl.* 48, *cr.* 2.

VAUGHAN, Chilton Grove, near Shrewsbury, a lion, rampant, az. *Pl.* 67, *cr.* 5.

VAUGHAN, on a five-leaved coronet, or, a demi-lion, rampant, per fess, ar. and sa., ducally crowned, or. *Pl.* 61, *cr.* 4, (without branch ; coronet, *pl.* 23, *cr.* 11.)

VAUGHAN, three hand-guns, erect, or, and two serpents, az., entwined about the barrels, of the last.

VAUGHAN, Eng., in lion's paw, or, a torteau. *Pl.* 97, *cr.* 10.

VAUGHAN, Middx., in lion's paw, or, a human heart, gu. *Pl.* 23, *cr.* 13.

VAUGHAN, Wel., a demi-lion, rampant, per fess, or, and gu., between paws a scroll, inscribed, " Immaculate Gens." *Pl.* 126, *cr.* 12.

VAUGHAN, Wel., a man, erect, ppr., arms, extended, vested in a jacket, ar., breeches, sa., hair flotant, in dexter a large knife, of the second.

VAUGHAN, Wel., a maiden's head, hair dishevelled, couped (below breasts,) all ppr. *Pl.* 45, *cr.* 5.

VAUGHAN, Yorks., Heref., and Wel., a boy's head, couped at shoulders, ppr., with snakes entwined about neck, vert.

VAUGHAN, Wilts., Dors., and Glouc., an arm, erect, hand grasping a snake, entwined round arm, all ppr. *Pl.* 91, *cr.* 6.

VAUGHAN, Wilts. and Heref., on a plume of three ostrich-feathers, gu., a griffin's head, or. *Pl.* 12, *cr.* 9, (head, *pl.* 38, *cr.* 3.)

VAUGHAN, Bart., Wel., a lion, rampant, az., gorged with an antique coronet, or. *Pl.* 67, *cr.* 5, (coronet, *pl.* 79, *cr.* 12.)

VAUGHAN, Earl of Lisburne. *See* LISBURNE.

VAUGHAN, Heref., on a mount, vert, a hound, sejant, ar., (collared,) gu. *Pl.* 5, *cr.* 2.

VAUGHAN-CHAMBER, of Burlton Hall, near Shrewsbury, Salop: 1. For *Vaughan*, on a chapeau, gu., turned up, erm., a boar's head, couped, in fess, gu., armed, or, langued, az. *Afrad pob afraid. Pl.* 48, *cr.* 2, (chapeau, *pl.* 127, *fig.* 13.) 2. For *Chamber*, out of a (garland of roses,) a greyhound's head and neck, ar., collared, az., chained, or. *Pl.* 84, *cr.* 15. 3. For *Bolas*, a demi-boar, rampant, ppr., armed, bristled, and unguled, or, (pierced in shoulder by an arrow, gold, feathered, ar., embrued, gu.) *Pl.* 20, *cr.* 5.

VAULT, a demi-ape, couped at shoulders, ppr. *Pl.* 24, *cr.* 12, (without coronet.)

VAULX, Eng., a falcon's head, couped, sa., beaked, or. *Pl.* 99, *cr.* 10, (without wings.)

VAULX, an eagle's head, erased, sa., ducally gorged, or. *Pl.* 39, *cr.* 4, (without pheon.)

VAULX, a cubit arm, erect, vasted, checky, or and gu., in hand ppr., a chaplet, vert, fructed. *Pl.* 44, *cr.* 13, (without bird.)

VAULX, and VAUS, Wilts., Yorks., and Cumb., an eagle's head, erased, sa., ducally gorged and beaked, or. *Pl.* 39, *cr.* 4, (without pheon.)

VAULX, and VAUS, Beds., an eagle's head sa., beaked, or. *Pl.* 100, *cr.* 10.

VAUX, Baron, Mostyn: 1. On a mount, vert, a lion, rampant, or. *Pl.* 59, *cr.* 5, (without dart.) 2. A trefoil, (slipped,) vert. *Morte leonis vita. Pl.* 4, *cr.* 10, (without wings.)

VAUX, Eng., on a ducal coronet, a peacock, statant, ppr. *Pl.* 43, *cr.* 7.

VAUX, a griffin's head, erased. *Pl.* 48, *cr.* 6.

VAUX, Baron. See BROUGHAM and VAUX.

VAVASOUR, Eng., a squirrel, cracking a nut, gu. *Pl.* 16, *cr.* 9.

VAVASOUR, of Weston Hall, Yorks., a cock, gu., combed and wattled, or. *Pl.* 67, *cr.* 14.

VAVASOUR, Northamp. and Yorks., a goat's head, or, (gorged with a collar, dancettée, sa.) *Pl.* 105, *cr.* 14.

VAVASOUR, Bart., Spaldington, Yorks., a cock, gu., combed, wattled, and legged, or, charged on breast, with a fleur-de-lis, ar. *Pl.* 67, *cr.* 14, (fleur-de-lis, *pl.* 141.)

VAVASOUR, Bart., of Hazelwood, Yorks.: 1. For *Vavasour*, a cock, gu., charged with a fountain. *Pl.* 67, *cr.* 14, (fountain, *pl.* 141.) 2. For *Stourton*, a demi-friar, vested, ppr., in dexter a scourge, in sinister an open book. *Pl.* 83, *cr.* 15, (book, *pl.* 82, *cr.* 5.)

VAVAZOR, Cambs., a squirrel, sejant, (on a hazel-branch, turned up behind back,) and feeding on a slip of the same, all ppr. *Pl.* 2, *cr.* 4.

VAWDREY, Chesh., a swallow, ppr. *Pl.* 111, *cr.* 5.

VAWDREY, of Tushingham Hall, Chesh., a cock, statant, ar., armed, combed, and legged, gu. *Pl.* 67, *cr.* 14.

VAZIE, Oxon., an arm, couped at shoulder, in fess, embowed at elbow, vested, gu., cuffed, erm., in hand a bunch of laurel, vert. *Pl.* 62, *cr.* 7, (laurel, *pl.* 123, *cr.* 5.)

VEALE, Eng., a chevalier standing in front of his horse, leaning on the saddle, ppr. *Pl.* 37, *cr.* 11.

VEELE, Glouc., a demi-calf, or, pallettée.

VEALE, or VELE, Glouc., a garb, or, enfiled, with a ducal coronet, gu. *Pl.* 76, *cr.* 13.

VEITCH, Sco., a bull's head, affrontée, sa. *Famam extendimus factis. Pl.* 18, *cr.* 15.

VEITCH, JAMES, Esq., of Eliock, Dumfries, same crest and motto.

VENABLES, of Woodhill, near Oswestry, Salop, a wyvern, wreathed, gu. *Venabulis vinco. Pl.* 63, *cr.* 13.

VENABLES, Chesh., a wyvern, gu., issuing from a whilk-shell, ar. *Pl.* 117, *cr.* 13.

VENABLES, Chesh., a wyvern, wings addorsed, gu., on a fish-weir, devouring a child, and pierced through neck by an arrow, all ppr.

VENABLES, Hants, a dragon, gu., issuing from a shell, in fess, ar. *Pl.* 117, *cr.* 13.

VENABLES-VERNON, Lord Vernon. See VERNON.

VENANT, Eng., a bull's head, cabossed. *Pl.* 111, *cr.* 6.

VENN, Freston Lodge, Suff., on a mount, vert, a lion, passant, erminois, (dexter resting on an escutcheon,) az., charged with a fleur-de-lis, or. *Fide et integritate. Pl.* 4, *cr.* 14, (mount, *pl.* 98, *cr.* 13.)

VENN, Eng., out of a ducal coronet, an eagle's head, ppr. *Pl.* 20, *cr.* 12.

VENNER, Eng., an eagle, displayed, or, winged, ar. *Pl.* 48, *cr.* 11.

VENNOR, Eng., a boar's head, couped, or. *Pl.* 48, *cr.* 2.

VENOR, or VENOUR, Lond., Kent, and Warw., an eagle, displayed, ar., on breast a cross formée, gu. *Pl.* 12, *cr.* 7, (cross, *pl.* 141.)

VENOUR, Eng., an eagle, displayed, ppr. *Pl.* 48, *cr.* 11.

VENTRIS, Cambs., between wings, az., a sword, erect, ar., hilt and pommel, or. *Pl.* 117, *cr.* 14.

VENTRY, Baron, Iri., (Mullins,) a Saracen's head, affrontée, couped below shoulders, ppr., wreathed about temples. *Vivere sat vincere. Pl.* 97, *cr.* 2.

VERDELIN, Eng., a Roman lictor's rod and axe, ppr. *Pl.* 65, *cr.* 15.

VERDIER, Eng., on a mount, vert, a peacock, ppr. *Pl.* 9, *cr.* 1.

VERDON, Eng., out of a tower, sa., a demi-lion, gu. *Pl.* 42, *cr.* 4.

VERE, JOHN, Esq., M.A., of Carlton House, Notts., on a chapeau, gu., turned up, erm., a boar, az., bristled and armed, or. *Vero nihil verius. Pl.* 22, *cr.* 8.

VERE, Suff., a hind's head, pierced through neck by an arrow. *Pl.* 56, *cr.* 11, (without coronet.)

VERE, Eng., on a chapeau, gu., turned up, erm., a boar, az., armed and bristled, or. *Pl.* 22, *cr.* 8.

VERE, Suff., a boar, passant, az., armed, or. *Pl.* 48, *cr.* 14.

VERE-HOPE, of Craigie Hall, Sco.: 1. For *Hope*, a broken globe, surmounted by a rainbow, all ppr. *At spes non fracta. Pl.* 79, *cr.* 1. 2. For *Vere*, a demi-horse, rampant, ar., saddled and bridled, gu. *Vero nihil verius.*

VEREKER, Viscount Gort. See GORT.

VERNEY, Lond., Herts., and Bucks., a phoenix in flames, ppr. *Un tout seul. Pl.* 44, *cr.* 8.

VERNEY, Baron Willoughby de Broke. See WILLOUGHBY.

VERNEY, Bart., Bucks.: 1. For *Verney*, a

phœnix in flames, ppr., (charged with five mullets, in cross, or, and gazing at the sun.) *Pl.* 44, *cr.* 8. 2. For *Calvert*, out of a ducal coronet, ar., two spears, erect, with pennons flowing towards the dexter, one erminois, the other pean. *Servata fides cineri.*

VERNON, Salop, a lion, rampant, gu. *Pl.* 67, *cr.* 5.

VERNON, Ess. and Notts.: 1. A boar's head, erased, per fess, sa. and gu., ducally gorged, or. *Pl.* 36, *cr.* 9. 2. A tiger's head, erased, gu., ducally gorged, or, (charged on neck with a martlet, gold.) *Pl.* 116, *cr.* 8.

VERNON, Derbs. and Salop, a boar's head, erased, sa., tusked, ar., ducally gorged, or. *Pl.* 36, *cr.* 9.

VERNON, Worc., a demi-female, ppr., vested, or and purp., hair, gold, wreathed about head, gu. *Pl.* 81, *cr.* 13.

VERNON, Chesh. and Yorks., a demi-female, ppr., vested, az., in dexter a sickle, (under sinister arm, a garb, or, wreathed about head with wheat, gold.) *Pl.* 101, *cr.* 2, (sickle, *pl.* 36, *cr.* 12.)

VERNON, Chesh., a demi-female, vested, vert, under sinister arm a garb, or, in dexter hand a sickle, gold, headed, ppr. *Ib.*

VERNON, Baron, (Venables-Vernon,) a boar's head, erased, sa., ducally gorged and bristled, or. *Vernon semper viret. Pl.* 36, *cr.* 9.

VERNON-GRAHAM, of Hilton Park, Staffs., same crest.

VERNON-WENTWORTH, of Wentworth Castle, Yorks.: 1. For *Vernon*, a boar's head, erased, sa., ducally gorged and bristled, or. *Vernon semper viret. Pl.* 36, *cr.* 9. 2. For *Wentworth*, a griffin, passant. *En Dieu est tout. Pl.* 61, *cr.* 14, (without gorging.)

VERNOR, co. Armagh, a boar's head, couped, sa. *Pro Christo et patriâ. Pl.* 48, *cr.* 2.

VERSCHOYLE, a boar's head, erased, gu. *Pl.* 16, *cr.* 11.

VERST, a horse's head, erased, ar. *Virtus ubique. Pl.* 81, *cr.* 6.

VERTHON, Eng., an arm, in armour, embowed, in hand a battle-axe. *Pl.* 2, *cr.* 8, (axe, *pl.* 121, *cr.* 14.)

VERULAM, Earl of, and Baron, and Viscount Grimston, U.K., Viscount Grimston and Baron Dunboyne, Iri., Baron Forrester, Sco., and a Baronet, G.B., (Grimston,) a stag's head, erased, ppr., attired, or. *Mediocra firma. Pl.* 66, *cr.* 9.

VESEY, Derrebard House, co. Tyrone, a hand, in armour, holding a laurel-branch, all ppr. *Pl.* 55, *cr.* 6, (laurel, *pl.* 123, *cr.* 5.)

VESEY, Viscount de Vesci. *See* DE VESCI.

VESSEY, Camb., a griffin's head, erased, or, per fess, gu., ducally gorged, ar. *Pl.* 42, *cr.* 9, (without branch.)

VESSEY, Suff., Norf., Oxon., and Ess., an arm, embowed, couped at shoulder, erect from elbow, vested, gu., cuffed, erm., in hand, ppr., four leaves, vert. *Pl.* 62, *cr.* 7.

VEZAY, or VEZEY, Eng., on a ducal coronet, a wyvern, sans legs, vert. *Pl.* 104, *cr.* 11.

VIALLS, Middx., a demi-leopard, ppr., (without tail,) ducally gorged, or. *Pl.* 125, *cr.* 4.

VICARY, or VIKARY, Devons., a peacock, close, or. *Pl.* 54, *cr.* 13.

VICARY, of Warminster, Wilts., a peacock, close, or. *Probitas veras honos. Pl.* 54, *cr.* 13.

VICKERS, Eng., a cubit arm, ppr., vested, gu., in hand a mill-rind, az. *Pl.* 34, *cr.* 3.

VICKERY, Eng., two dolphins, haurient, addorsed, ppr. *Pl.* 81, *cr.* 2.

VICTOR, Eng., on a ducal coronet, gu., a wyvern, sans legs, or. *Pl.* 104, *cr.* 11.

VIDLER, Eng., out of a ducal coronet, a demi-griffin, all ppr. *Pl.* 39, *cr.* 2.

VIEL, and VIELER, Eng., out of a tower, ppr., a leopard's head, gu., collared, or. *Pl.* 51, *cr.* 11.

VIELL, Glouc., a demi-lion, rampant, gu., holding a baton, gobonated, ar., and of the first. *Pl.* 11, *cr.* 2.

VIGNE, Eng., a rose, ar., barbed, between two laurel-branches, in orle, slips, in saltier, vert. *Pl.* 3, *cr.* 13.

VIGNOLES, Eng., a unicorn's head, per fess, gu. and or, erased, of the first. *Pl.* 67, *cr.* 1.

VIGORS, HENRY-RUDKIN, Esq., of Erindale, co. Carlow, a stag's head, erased at neck, ar., attired, or. *Spectamur agendo. Pl.* 66, *cr.* 9.

VIGURES, Eng., a peacock's head, erased, az., head feathers, or. *Pl.* 86, *cr.* 4.

VIGURS, a mullet, ar. *Pl.* 41, *cr.* 1.

VILANT, Sco., an arm, in armour, embowed, in hand a spear, ppr. *Firma nobis fides. Pl.* 44, *cr.* 9.

VILE, Eng. an arm, in hand a scimitar, ppr. *Pl.* 92, *cr.* 5.

VILLAGES, Eng., a unicorn's head, erased, az. *Pl.* 67, *cr.* 1.

VILLEBOIS, a tiger, salient, ppr.

VILLEBOIES, Eng., a leopard, rampant. *Pl.* 73, *cr.* 2.

VILLERS, or VILLIERS, Eng. and Iri., a lion, rampant, ar., ducally crowned, or. *Pl.* 98, *cr.* 1.

VILLIERS, Leic. and Staffs., the same crest, but the lion charged with a crescent. Crescent, *pl.* 141.

VILLET, Lond., a tiger's head, erased, erm., ducally gorged, or. *Pl.* 116, *cr.* 8.

VILLETTES, Somers., out of a ducal coronet, an elephant's head, all or. *Pl.* 93, *cr.* 13.

VILLIERS, Earl of Clarendon. *See* CLARENDON.

VILLIERS-CHILD, Earl of Jersey. *See* JERSEY.

VINCENT, out of a ducal coronet, a boar's head. *Pl.* 102, *cr.* 14.

VINCENT, Iri., on a chapeau, a pelican, vulning, ppr. *Pl.* 21, *cr.* 5.

VINCENT, Leic., a demi-ram, ar.

VINCENT, a demi-ram, sa., armed, or, collared.

VINCENT, Northamp., out of a ducal coronet, or, a bear's head, ar., (collared with a belt, sa.) *Pl.* 6, *cr.* 6.

VINCENT, Staffs. and Worc., a talbot, ar., eared, sa., collared and lined, gu., (the end of the line tied in a bunch.) *Pl.* 65, *cr.* 2.

VINCENT, Surr., a bull's head, cabossed, ar., guttée-de-poix, armed, or. *Pl.* 111, *cr.* 6.

VINCENT, Yorks., out of a ducal coronet, or, a bear's head, gu. *Pl.* 6, *cr.* 6.

VINCENT, Bart., Surr., out of a ducal coronet, ppr., a bear's head, or. *Vincenti dabitur. Pl.* 6, *cr.* 6.

VINE, Eng., out of a ducal coronet, an heraldic-tiger's head, all ppr. *Pl.* 98, *cr.* 4.

VINER, a dexter arm, in armour, embowed, ppr., garnished, or, in hand a mullet of six points, gold. *Pl.* 24, *cr.* 14, (mullet, *pl.* 21, *cr.* 6.)

VINER, ELLIS-VINER, of Badgeworth, Glouc., 1. For *Viner*, a dexter arm, in armour, or, embowed, (encircled at elbow by a wreath of vine,) in hand a gem-ring. *Pl*. 24, *cr*. 14, (ring, *pl*. 35, *cr*. 3.) 2. For *Ellis*, a horse's head, erased, erm., (gorged with a plain collar, ar., charged with a cinquefoil, between two crescents, sa.,) in mouth a trefoil, slipped, ppr. *Labore et honore*. *Pl*. 11, *cr*. 12.

VINEY, Eng., on a chapeau, a phœnix in flames, ppr. *Pl*. 83, *cr*. 12.

VINEY, Kent, an arm, couped at shoulder, in hand a bunch of grapes by the stalk, all ppr. *Pl*. 47, *cr*. 13, (grapes, *pl*. 37, *cr*. 4.)

VINICOMBE, Eng., a greyhound's head, sa., bezantée, or. *Pl*. 14, *cr*. 4.

VINTRIS, Eng., a sword, erect. *Pl*. 105, *cr*. 1.

VIPONT, or VIPOUNT, Eng., out of a ducal coronet, a swan's head, between wings, all ppr. *Pl*. 83, *cr*. 1.

VIRNEY, a maiden's head, couped at shoulders, affrontée, vested and crowned with an Eastern coronet. *Pl*. 81, *cr*. 13, (coronet, *pl*. 79, *cr*. 12.)

VIRTUE, a lion's head, erased, ar. *Pl*. 81, *cr*. 4.

VIRTUE, Sco., a pomegranate, stalked and leaved, ppr. *Pl*. 67, *cr*. 8.

VIVIAN, Eng., on a chapeau, a serpent, nowed, ppr. *Pl*. 123, *cr*. 4.

VIVIAN, HENRY HUSSEY, Esq., of Singleton, Swansea, issuing from a bridge of one arch, embattled, at each end a tower, a demi-hussar, of the 18th Regiment, in dexter a sabre, in sinister a pennant, flying to sinister, gu. *Vive revictmus*. *Pl*. 126 B, *cr*. 6.

VIVIAN, Bart., of Truro, Cornw. *Cor nobyle, cor immobile*. Same crest.

VIVIAN, of Pencalnenick, Cornw.: For *Vivian*, between two roses, gu., slipped, vert, a dexter cubit arm, vested, az., (charged with five plates, in saltier,) cuffed, ar., in hand, ppr., an anchor, in fess, flukes toward the dexter, sa. *Vive ut vivas*. *Pl*. 53, *cr*. 13, (roses, *pl*. 84, *cr*. 13.) For *Tippet*, *Non robore sed spe*.

VIVIAN, Eng., a lion's head, erased, ppr., collared (and chained,) or. *Pl*. 7, *cr*. 10.

VIVIAN, a lion's head, erased, gorged with a naval coronet. *Pl*. 42, *cr*. 14, (gorging, *pl*. 128, *fig*. 19.)

VIVIAN, Cornw., a horse, passant, furnished, ppr. *Pl*. 99, *cr*. 11.

VIVIAN, French, an etoile, or. *Pl*. 63, *cr*. 9.

VIVIAN, French, a spur-rowel, or. *Pl*. 54, *cr*. 5.

VOASE, Yorks., an eagle's head, erased, sa., beaked and ducally gorged, or. *Pl*. 39, *cr*. 4, (without pheon.)

VOLLER, Eng., a demi-antelope, ar., collared, gu. *Pl*. 34, *cr*. 8.

VOWE, of Hallaton, Leic., a lion, rampant, gu. *Vows should be respected*. *Pl*. 67, *cr*. 5.

VOWELL, Devons., out of a mural coronet, gu., an antelope's head, ar., armed, of the first. *Pl*. 24, *cr*. 7, (coronet, *same plate, cr*. 12.)

VOWELL, Eng., between two palm-branches, vert, a mullet, gu. *Pl*. 3, *cr*. 9.

VOWILL, out of a mural coronet, an heraldic-antelope's head. *Pl*. 76, *cr*. 3, (coronet, *pl*. 128, *fig*. 18.)

VYCHAN, Wel., out of clouds, a dexter arm, in armour, embowed, in gauntlet a sword, erect, all ppr., on point a moor's head, couped, in profile, sa., (dropping blood.) *Pl*. 30, *cr*. 6, (head, *pl*. 27, *cr*. 3.)

VYEL, Cornw., a greyhound, passant, ppr., (head towards the sinister.) *Pl*. 104, *cr*. 1, (without chapeau.)

VYGOR, a demi-lion, sa., (between paws,) a staff, raguly, ar. *Pl*. 11, *cr*. 2.

VYLGUS, Sco., a lion's head, erased, ppr. *Pl*. 81, *cr*. 4.

VYNALL, Suss., a demi-lion, (erased,) sa., holding a bezant. *Pl*. 126, *cr*. 12.

VYNER, Lond. and Salop, an arm, in armour, ppr., garnished, or, in hand, of the first, a gem-ring, gold. *Pl*. 24, *cr*. 14, (ring, *pl*. 35, *cr*. 3.)

VYNOR, and VYNORS, Wilts., an arm, in armour, embowed, ppr., garnished, or, in gauntlet, a round buckle, tongue, erect, gold. *Pl*. 24, *cr*. 14, (buckle, *pl*. 73, *cr*. 10.)

VYVYAN, Bart., of Trelowarren, Cornw., a horse, passant, furnished, ppr. *Pl*. 99, *cr*. 11.

W

WACKETT, Eng., a stag's head, erased, ar., attired, or. *Pl*. 66, *cr*. 9.

WADDEL, a battle-axe, in pale, ppr. *Pl*. 14, *cr*. 8.

WADDELL, Eng., two battle-axes, in saltier, ppr. *Pl*. 52, *cr*. 10.

WADDELL, Kent, a lamb, couchant, ppr., surmounted by a demi-eagle, displayed, ppr.

WADDELL, Sco., a lion's head, erased, gu. *Orna verum—or—Adorn the truth*. *Pl*. 81, *cr*. 4.

WADDINGTON, an arm, in hand a hatchet, ppr. *Pl*. 73, *cr*. 7.

WADDINGTON, Lond., a martlet, gu. *Pl*. 111, *cr*. 5.

WADDY, a naked arm, embowed, ppr., hand grasping a sword, ar., hilted and pommelled, or. *Ob ducem, ob patriam*. *Pl*. 34, *cr*. 7.

WADE, Eng., a dove and branch. *Vincit qui patitur*. *Pl*. 48, *cr*. 15.

WADE, Eng., an arm, in armour, embowed, in hand a sword. *Pro fide et patriâ*. *Pl*. 2, *cr*. 8.

WADE, Northamp., (on a mount, vert,) a rhinoceros, ar. *Pl*. 4, *cr*. 11.

WADE, Oxon., a boar, salient, sa., (collared, or.) *Pl*. 20, *cr*. 5.

WADE, a griffin's head, erased, or, (in beak a pink, ppr.) *Pl*. 48, *cr*. 6.

WADE, Durh., Quebec, and Iri., a dove and olive-branch, all ppr., charged on breast with a cross crosslet, sa. *Pl*. 48, *cr*. 15, (cross, *pl*. 141.)

WADE, Middx., Yorks., and Ess., a rhinoceros, passant, ar. *Pl*. 4, *cr*. 11.

WADESON, Eng., two lions' gambs, erased, ppr., supporting a crescent, or. *Pl*. 62, *cr*. 3.

WADHAM, the scalp of a buck, or, between the horns a boar's head, (couped) and erect. *Pl*. 33, *cr*. 15.

WADHAM, Somers. and Devons., the scalp of a buck, or, between the horns a rose, ar. *Pl.* 50, *cr.* 14.

WADHAM, Dors., a stag's head, erased, or, gorged with a collar, charged with three bezants, all between two rose-branches, erect, flowered, ar., stalked and leaved, vert. *Pl.* 125, *cr.* 6.

WADMAN, Wilts., a demi-eagle, displayed, erm., wings, gu. *Pl.* 22, *cr.* 11.

WADMAN, Lond., an eagle, displayed, ppr. *Rosa sine spinâ. Pl.* 48, *cr.* 11.

WADSWORTH, Eng., on a terrestrial globe, winged, ppr., an eagle, rising, or. *Pl.* 34, *cr.* 2, (globe, *pl.* 50, *cr.* 7.)

WAGER, Eng., a dexter arm, in hand an annulet, or. *Pl.* 24, *cr.* 3.

WAGNER, Eng., in water, a swan, naiant, in pride, all ppr. *Pl.* 66, *cr.* 10.

WAGS, Eng., an eagle, displayed. *Pl.* 48, *cr.* 11.

WAGSTAFF, Warw., a demi-lion, ar., holding a staff raguly, sa. *Pl.* 11, *cr.* 2.

WAGSTAFF, Derbs., out of a ducal coronet, or, a staff, couped and raguly, in pale, sa. *Pl.* 78, *cr.* 15.

WAILES, Eng., between wings, a spur, all ppr. *Pl.* 109, *cr.* 12.

WAINWRIGHT, Worc., a lion, rampant, ar., holding an ancient battle-axe, handle and head, of the first. *Pl.* 101, *cr.* 14, (without charging.)

WAIT, WILLIAM-SAVAGE, Esq., of Woodbrough, Somers., a bugle-horn, stringed, sa., garnished, or. *Pro aris et focis. Pl.* 48, *cr.* 12.

WAITE, and WAITH, Eng., a bugle-horn, sa., garnished, or, strung. *Pl.* 48, *cr.* 12.

WAITHMAN, WILLIAM, Esq., of Westville, Lanc., a demi-eagle, displayed, sa. *Pl.* 22, *cr.* 11.

WAKE, Eng., a lion, passant. *Pl.* 48, *cr.* 8.

WAKE, Northamp. and Somers., a lion, passant, tail extended, sa., (ducally gorged, ar.) *Pl.* 118, *cr.* 10.

WAKE, Bart., Somers., a wake's knot. *Vigila et ora. Pl.* 11, *cr.* 5.

WAKEFIELD, Eng., a bat, displayed, ar. *Pl.* 94, *cr.* 9.

WAKEFIELD, Eng., on a ducal coronet, a wyvern, sans legs, ppr. *Pl.* 104, *cr.* 11.

WAKEHAM, on a mount, between two trees, a greyhound, ar., spotted, sa., (collared.) *Pl.* 11, *cr.* 1.

WAKEHAM, Devons., on a mount, vert, a greyhound, ar., between two trees, ppr. *Pl.* 11, *cr.* 1.

WAKEHURST, Eng., a buckle, or. *Pl.* 73, *cr.* 10.

WAKELING, Eng., a wyvern, wings addorsed, in mouth a hand, couped, ppr. *Pl.* 61, *cr.* 8.

WAKELYN, Northamp. and Derbs., a lion, rampant, or, in dexter a tulip, gu., slipped, vert. *Pl.* 64, *cr.* 2.

WAKEMAN, THOMAS, Esq., of The Graig, near Monmouth, a lion's head, erased, vomiting smoke and flames. *Ora et labora. Pl.* 20, *cr.* 3.

WAKEMAN, Glouc., a lion's head, (couped,) or, out of mouth, flames, ppr. *Pl.* 20, *cr.* 3.

WAKEMAN, Bart., Worc. and Salop, between two palm-branches, ppr., a lion's head, erased, ar., vomiting flames, gorged with a collar, engrailed and cottised, vert, and charged with three ermine-spots, or. *Nec temere, nec timide. Pl.* 11, *cr.* 3.

WAKEMAN, Eng., a lion's head, erased, ar. *Pl.* 81, *cr.* 4.

WAKERING, Ess., on a mural coronet, or, a pelican, gold, vulning, ppr. *Pl.* 64, *cr.* 1.

WAKERLEY, Eng., two daggers, in saltier, ppr. *Pl.* 24, *cr.* 2.

WALCHER, Eng., a talbot's head, gu. *Pl.* 123, *cr.* 15.

WALCOT, or WALCOTT, Eng., a bull's head, erased, ar., ermed, or, ducally gorged, gold. *Pl.* 68, *cr.* 6.

WALCOTT, Bitterley Court, Salop, out of a ducal coronet, or, a buffalo's head, erased, ar., armed, and ducally gorged, or. *Pl.* 57, *cr.* 7, (coronet, *pl.* 128, *fig.* 3.)

WALCOT, or WALCOTT, Oxon., an eagle's head, or, guttée-de-sang, in beak, az., a fleur-de-lis, gold. *Pl.* 121, *cr.* 7.

WALCOTT, a bull's head, erased, erm., armed, or, gorged with a wreath of trefoil, vert, in mouth an arrow, in bend, gold. *Pl.* 64, *cr.* 4.

WALDEGRAVE, Earl of, and Baron, Viscount Chewton, and a Bart., (Waldegrave,) out of a ducal coronet, or, a plume of five ostrich-feathers, per pale, ar. and gu. *Cœlum, non animum. Pl.* 100, *cr.* 12, (without charging.)

WALDEGRAVE, Suff., Norf., Ess., and Northamp., out of a ducal coronet, or, a double plume of feathers, per pale, ar. and gu. *Pl.* 64, *cr.* 5.

WALDEGRAVE, Baron Radstock. *See* RADSTOCK.

WALDEN, Eng., a winged spur, rowel upward, ppr. *Pl.* 59, *cr.* 1.

WALDESHESCHEFF, WALDESHEFF, and WALDSHEFF, two spears, in saltier, pendent thereto two flags, quarterly, gu. and or, surmounted by a garland of laurel, all ppr. *Pl.* 125, *cr.* 8.

WALDIE, JOHN, Esq., of Hendersyde Park, Roxburghe, a dove, in mouth an olive-branch, all ppr. *Fidelis. Pl.* 48, *cr.* 15.

WALDO, or WALDOE, Eng., a griffin's head, erased, vert. *Pl.* 48, *cr.* 6.

WALDOURE, Eng., a wolf's head, erased, or. *Pl.* 14, *cr.* 6.

WALDREN, on a mural coronet, an heraldic-tiger, sejant. *Pl.* 111, *cr.* 7, (coronet, *pl.* 128, *fig.* 18.)

WALDRON, Iri., a lion, rampant, gardant, or. *Pl.* 92, *cr.* 7.

WALDRON, Eng., two laurel-branches, in saltier, ppr. *Pl.* 82, *cr.* 11.

WALDRON, and WALDROND, Devons., a tiger, sejant, ar., armed, tufted, and maned, or. *Pl.* 26, *cr.* 9.

WALDY, out of a mural coronet, a demi-lion, rampant, az., holding a cross crosslet, fitched, or. *Fidelis. Pl.* 65, *cr.* 6, (coronet, *pl.* 128, *fig.* 18.)

WALDY, Durh., out of a mural coronet, a dove, in mouth an olive-branch, all ppr. *Fidelis. Pl.* 48, *cr.* 15, (coronet, *pl.* 128, *fig.* 18.)

WALE, Eng., a yew-tree, ppr. *Pl.* 49, *cr.* 13.

WALE, Northumb., a greyhound, current, ar. *Pl.* 28, *cr.* 7.

WALE, Ess., a lion, rampant, or, supporting a long cross, sa. *Pl.* 22, *cr.* 15, (cross, *pl.* 82, *cr.* 4.)

WALFORD, Eng., two palm-branches, in orle, vert. *Pl.* 87, *cr.* 8.

WALFORD, Ess., a dem-lion, rampant, in dexter a cross crosslet, fitched, gu. *Pl.* 65, *cr.* 6.

WALFORD, Ess., out of a mural coronet, or, an ostrich-feather, ar. *Nosce teipsum.* Pl. 125, cr. 11.

WALGRAVE, Suff., out of a ducal coronet, or, a plume of feathers, per pale, ar. and gu. Pl. 44, cr. 12.

WALKER, H. B., Esq., New Romney, on a lion's gamb, erect and erased, gu., a mural coronet, or. *Gänger.* Pl. 126 D, cr. 2.

WALKER, JAMES, Esq., of Dalry, Mid-Lothian, a cornucopia, ppr. *Cura et industria.* Pl. 91, cr. 4.

WALKER, Eng., a stag, at gaze, under a nut-tree, ppr. *In omnes casus.* Pl. 118, cr. 13.

WALKER, of Redland, near Bristol, on a mount, vert, a falcon, close, or, (collared, gu., resting dexter on an escutcheon, charged with a bezant.) *Nec temere, nec timide.* Pl. 111, cr. 8.

WALKER, of Blythe Hall, Notts., and Clifton House, Yorks., a dove, within a serpent in a circle. Pl. 92, cr. 6.

WALKER, a dove and olive-branch, ppr. Pl. 48, cr. 15.

WALKER, out of a mural coronet, an arm, in armour, embowed, in hand a lizard. Pl. 115, cr. 14, (lizard, pl. 58, cr. 4.)

WALKER, a demi-wolf, between paws a branch of trefoil, slipped, vert. Pl. 56, cr. 8, (trefoil, pl. 141.)

WALKER, Iri., a cherub's head, wings in saltier, ppr. Pl. 67, cr. 11.

WALKER, Sco., a greyhound, sejant, (collared and chained, or.) Pl. 66, cr. 15.

WALKER, Sco., a rock, ppr. *Per varios casus.* Pl. 73, cr. 12.

WALKER, Sco., a rock, ppr. *Cura et industria.* Pl. 73, cr. 12.

WALKER, a greyhound's head, erased, sa., collared and cottised, ar., on collar three crescents, of the first. Pl. 43, cr. 11.

WALKER, a greyhound, (passant, ar., collared, gu., rimmed and ringed, or, collar charged with three ducal coronets, of the first. Pl. 104, cr. 1.

WALKER, a stag's head, erased, ppr. Pl. 66, cr. 9.

WALKER, a dragon's head, vert, issuing from flames, ppr., crowned, or. Pl. 64, cr. 6.

WALKER, on a mount, a dove, statant, within a wreathed serpent, all ppr. Pl. 92, cr. 6, (mount, pl. 104, cr. 6.)

WALKER, a demi-tiger, per pale, indented, ar. and sa., holding a rose branch, or, slipped, vert. Pl. 53, cr. 10, (branch, pl. 60, cr. 14.)

WALKER, Suss., a greyhound, sejant, ar., (collared, charged on shoulder with a cinquefoil, sa.) Pl. 66, cr. 15.

WALKER, Sco., a stag, standing before a tree, ppr. *Semper vigilans.* Pl. 118, cr. 13.

WALKER, Yorks., a demi-tiger, per pale, indented, ar. and az., tufted, or, holding a rose-branch, vert, flowered, gu. Pl. 53, cr. 10, (branch, pl. 60, cr. 14.)

WALKER, Yorks., a demi-heraldic tiger, per pale, indented, ar. and sa., armed, langued, and tusked, gu., mane and tail purfled, or. Pl. 57, cr. 13, (without gorging.)

WALKER, Yorks., on a hen, a dunghill cock, sa., beaked, legged, combed, and wattled, gu.

WALKER, Yorks., a greyhound's head, couped, ar., collared, sa. Pl. 43, cr. 11.

WALKER, Yorks., out of a ducal coronet, or, a greyhound's head, couped, ar., (collared, sa.) Pl. 70, cr. 5.

WALKER, Camb., a lion in a wood, all ppr. Pl. 125, cr. 14.

WALKER, Herts., an ostrich, az., in dexter a caltrap, or. Pl. 64, cr. 3, (without coronet; caltrap, pl. 141.)

WALKER, Kent and Staffs., on a lion's gamb, erect and erased, gu., a mural coronet, or. Pl. 126 D, cr. 2.

WALKER, Lanc., the sun rising, in clouds, all ppr. Pl. 67, cr. 9.

WALKER, a garb, issuing from a crown of a King of Arms, supported by a lion, ar., and a dragon, gu.

WALKER, Middx., on a mount, vert, a greyhound, sejant, (per pale, ar. and sa., the ar. powdered with crescents, az., the sa. with bezants, collared, or.) Pl. 5, cr. 2.

WALKER, Ruts., a pilgrim's head, affrontée, couped at shoulders, vested in a (slouched) hat and gown, on the hat and cope of the gown three escallops, all ppr. Pl. 31, cr. 2, (escallop, pl. 141.)

WALKER, West Indies, in the sea a rock, thereon the waves beating, all ppr. *Per varios casus.* Pl. 91, cr. 5.

WALKER, Lond. and Beds., out of flames, gold, a dragon's head, vert, crowned with an (Eastern crown,) or. Pl. 64, cr. 6.

WALKER, Northumb. and Sco., a swan, swimming in a loch, ppr. *Non sine periculo.* Pl. 66, cr. 10.

WALKER, Bart., on a mural coronet, or, encircled by a wreath of laurel, an ostrich, ppr. *Nil desperandum.* Pl. 64, cr. 3.

WALKER, Lieut.-Gen., K.C.B., K.T.S., same crest and motto.

WALKFARE, Eng., a branch of thistle, in pale, ppr. Pl. 68, cr. 9.

WALKFARE, a holly-branch, in pale, ppr. Pl. 99, cr. 9.

WALKINGSHAW, Sco., a dove and olive-branch, ppr. Pl. 48, cr. 15.

WALKINGSHAW, Sco., a martlet, ppr. *In season.* Pl. 111, cr. 5.

WALKINGTON, Eng., a mullet of six points, or. Pl. 21, cr. 6.

WALKINGTON, Middx., a stag, trippant, gu. Pl. 68, cr. 2.

WALL, Iri., an arm, in armour, embowed, in hand a sword, ppr. Pl. 2, cr. 8.

WALL, Eng., a demi-boar, rampant, sa. Pl. 20, cr. 5.

WALL, a demi-eagle, az., wings addorsed, ar. Pl. 19, cr. 9, (without coronet.)

WALL, of Worthy Park, Hants, out of a mural coronet, or, a demi-wolf, ar., charged on neck with a fess, embattled, counter embattled, gu. *Firm.* Pl. 56, cr. 8, (coronet, pl. 128, fig. 18.)

WALL, out of a ducal coronet, a swan's head and neck. Pl. 83, cr. 1, (without wings.)

WALL, Lanc., a boar's head, couped, sa., in mouth an acorn, erect, or, stalked and leaved, vert. Pl. 125, cr. 7.

WALL, Middx., a demi-lion, rampant, gardant, az., holding a battle-axe, headed, ar., handled, gu. Pl. 26, cr. 7.

WALL, Kent, a cubit arm, erect, (in mail,) hand presenting a pistol, all ppr. Pl. 101, cr. 12.

WALL, Somers., an arm, embowed, ppr., tied below elbow by a ribbon, vert, in hand a lion's gamb, erased, or. *Pl. 47, cr.* 13, (gamb, *pl.* 94, *cr.* 13.)

WALL, Worc., out of a mural coronet, or, a demi-wolf, salient, ppr., collared, embattled and counter-embattled, gold. *Pl.* 56, *cr.* 8, (coronet, *pl.* 182, *fig.* 18.)

WALL, Salop and Heref., out of a mural coronet, or, a wolf's head, ar., charged on neck with a fess, embattled and counter-embattled, gu. *Pl.* 8, *cr.* 4.

WALL, or WALLE, Suff., Glouc., Ruts., Norf., and Ess., a lion, rampant, gardant, or, supporting a long cross, sa. *Pl.* 82, *cr.* 4, (without mount.)

WALLACE, of Kelly, Sco., a dexter arm, in armour, embowed, in hand a sword, ppr. *Pro libertate. Pl.* 2, *cr.* 8.

WALLACE, a boar's head, erased. *Pl.* 16, *cr.* 11.

WALLACE, out of a ducal coronet, a swan's head and neck. *Pl.* 83, *cr.* 1, (without wings.)

WALLACE, Iri., a sword, erect, enfiled with a Saracen's head, affrontée, ppr. *Pl.* 42, *cr.* 6.

WALLACE, Sco., an ostrich, ppr., in mouth a horse-shoe, az. *Sperandum est. Pl.* 16, *cr.* 2.

WALLACE, Eng., a lion's head, ppr., collared, ar. *Pl.* 42, *cr.* 14.

WALLACE, Ayrs., two eagles' heads and necks conjoined. *Pl.* 94, *cr.* 12.

WALLACE, Sco., an ostrich, in full flight, ppr. *Sperandum est. Pl.* 9, *cr.* 3.

WALLACE, Sco., an ostrich's head, couped, ar. *Esperance. Pl.* 49, *cr.* 7, (without branches.)

WALLACE, on a rock, a martlet, or. *Pl.* 36, *cr.* 5.

WALLACE, Cumb., out of a ducal coronet, or, an ostrich's head, ar., in mouth a horse-shoe, az. *Pl.* 29, *cr.* 9, (shoe, *pl.* 99, *cr.* 12.)

WALLACE, Baron, (Wallace,) out of a ducal coronet, or, an ostrich's head and neck, ppr., in mouth a horse-shoe. *Pl.* 29, *cr.* 9, (shoe, *pl.* 99, *cr.* 12.)

WALLACE-DUNLOP, Bart., N.S., an ostrich, ppr., wings expanded. *Sperandum est. Pl.* 16, *cr.* 2.

WALLANGE, a rose, surmounted by a thistle, both ppr. *In utroque. Pl.* 73, *cr.* 6.

WALLER, a demi-griffin, segreant. *Pl.* 18, *cr.* 6.

WALLER, a goat's head, ppr. *Pl.* 105, *cr.* 44.

WALLER, Eng., a dexter-arm, couped, embowed, resting on elbow, in hand a sword, erect, enfiled with a Saracen's head, dropping blood, all ppr., (wreathed about head, ar. and az.) *Pl.* 102, *cr.* 11.

WALLER, Middx., Kent, Hants, and Devons., on a mount, vert, an oak-tree, ppr., on the sinister side, pendent, an escutcheon, ar., charged with three fleurs de-lis, or, two and one. *Pl.* 48, *cr.* 4, (escutcheon, *pl.* 23, *cr.* 6; fleur-de-lis, *pl.* 141.)

WALLER, Suff., a fox's head, az. *Pl.* 91, *cr.* 9.

WALLER, Bart., Iri., out of a ducal coronet, a plum of five ostrich-feathers, the second and fourth, az., the first, third, and fifth, ar., surmounted by an eagle's claw, gu. *Honor et veritas. Pl.* 100, *cr.* 12, (claw, *pl* 27, *cr.* 1.)

WALLER, Bart., Berks., on a mount, vert, a walnut-tree, ppr., on the sinister side an escutcheon pendent, (charged with the arms of France, with a label of three points, ar.) *Hic fructus virtutis*—and—*Agincourt. Pl.* 48, *cr.* 4, (escutcheon, *pl.* 23, *cr.* 6.)

WALLES, Devons. and Cornw., a flame, ppr. *Pl.* 16, *cr.* 12.

WALLEY, Eng., an eagle, preying on an infant, ppr. *Nihil desperandum. Pl.* 123, *cr.* 11.

WALLEYS, Eng., a helmet, close, ppr. *Pl.* 109, *cr.* 5.

WALLFORD, or WALFORD, Eng., two palm-branches, in orle, vert. *Pl.* 87, *cr.* 8.

WALLFORD, a griffin's head, ermines, beaked and ducally gorged, or. *Pl.* 42, *cr.* 9, (without branch.)

WALLINGER, Ess., Beds., and Bucks., out of a ducal coronet, or, a falcon's head between wings, gold. *Pl.* 103, *cr.* 6.

WALLINGHAM, out of a ducal coronet, or, an antelope's head, erm. *Pl.* 24, *cr.* 7, (coronet, same plate, *cr.* 10.)

WALLINGTON, Eng., on a ducal coronet, a peacock, ppr. *Pl.* 43, *cr.* 7.

WALLINGTON, Glouc., a buck's head, ppr., erased, gu., collared, sa., charged with a cinquefoil, or, between two lozenges, ar. *Pl.* 125, *cr.* 6, (without roses.)

WALLIS, Eng., a fire, ppr. *Pl.* 16, *cr.* 12.

WALLIS, Iri., a talbot's head, erased, or, collared, az., studded, gold. *Pl.* 2, *cr.* 15.

WALLIS, a Cornish chough, ppr. *Pl.* 100, *cr.* 13.

WALLIS, out of a ducal coronet, an ostrich's head, all ar. *Pl.* 29, *cr.* 9, (head, *pl.* 50, *cr.* 1.)

WALLISCOURT, Baron, Iri., (Blake,) a leopard, passant, ppr. *Virtus sola nobilitat. Pl.* 86, *cr.* 2.

WALLOP, Earl of Portsmouth. *See* PORTSMOUTH.

WALLOP, and WALLOPI, Eng., a mermaid, with mirror and comb, all ppr. *Pl.* 48, *cr.* 5.

WALLOP, a mermaid, (with two tails expanded, ppr., hair, or, holding the tails in her hands.) *Pl.* 88, *cr.* 12.

WALLPOOL, Kent, an arm, in hand a royal coronet. *Pl.* 97, *cr.* 12.

WALLPOOL, or WALPOLE, Norf., a Saracen's head and neck, couped at shoulders, ppr., ducally crowned, or, with a long cap turned forward, and tasselled, gold, thereon a Catherine-wheel, of the same. *Fari quæ sentiat. Pl.* 78, *cr.* 14, (wheel, *pl.* 141.)

WALLPOOL, or WALPOLE, Linc., a stag's head, gardant, couped at neck, ppr., attired, or. *Pl.* 111, *cr.* 13.

WALMESLEY, Lanc., a lion, statant, gardant, ducally crowned, gu. *En Dieu est mon esperance. Pl.* 105, *cr.* 5, (without chapeau.)

WALMESLEY, Lanc., a lion, passant, gardant, erm., ducally crowned, or. *Pl.* 120, *cr.* 15, (without chapeau.)

WALMOUTH, Lanc., a leopard's head, or, cut through on the sinister side to the eye by a cutlass, ar., hilt and pommel, or, the hilt resting on the wreath. *Pl.* 125, *cr.* 9.

WALMSLEY, Eng., in dexter hand a sabre. *Pro patriâ. Pl.* 21, *cr.* 10.

WALMSLEY, Derbs., a lion, statant, gardant, erm., ducally crowned, or, on body a trefoil, slipped, vert. *Pl.* 105, *cr.* 5, (without chapeau.)

WALPOLE, a lion, passant, az. *Pl.* 48, *cr.* 8.

WALPOLE, Earl of Orford. *See* ORFORD.

WALPOLE, VADE-WALPOLE, Norf. : 1. For *Walpole*, a Saracen's head, in profile, couped, ppr., ducally crowned, or, from the coronet a long cap, turned forward, gu., tasselled, or, and charged with a Catherine-wheel, gold. *Pl.* 78, *cr.* 14, (wheel, *pl.* 141.) 2. For *Vade,* a dexter arm, in armour, embowed, garnished, or, in hand a dagger, ppr., hilt and pommel, gold. *Pl.* 120, *cr.* 11.

WALROND, Eng., a leopard's face, or. *Pl.* 66, *cr.* 14.

WALROND, JOHN, Esq., of Bradfield and Knightshayes, Devons., an heraldic-tiger, sa., pellettée. *Sic vos non vobis. Pl.* 7, *cr.* 5.

WALROND, a leopard's head, affrontée, or. *Pl.* 66, *cr.* 14.

WALROUND-BETHELL, of Dulford House, Devons.: 1. An heraldic-tiger, sa., pellettée. *Pl.* 7, *cr.* 5. 2. On a mural coronet, an heraldic-tiger, sa., pellettée. *Nec beneficii immemor, nec injuriæ. Pl.* 7, *cr.* 5, (coronet, *pl.* 128, *fig.* 18.)

WALSAM, and WALSHAM, Eng., a fir-tree, issuing, ppr. *Pl.* 26, *cr.* 10.

WALSHAM, Bart., Heref., out of a ducal coronet, or, a demi-eagle, with two heads, displayed, sa., pendent from neck an escutcheon, ar., (charged with a Saracen's head, couped at neck, ppr., temples wreathed, az.) *Sub libertate quietem. Pl.* 4, *cr.* 6, (coronet, *pl.* 128, *fig.* 3.)

WALSH, Bart., Iri.: 1. A griffin's head, erased, ar., langued, gu. *Pl.* 48, *cr.* 6. 2. A tower, ar., thereon a cock, ppr., langued, ar. *Firm. Pl.* 113, *cr.* 14.

WALSH, an arm, the part below the elbow in bend dexter, elbow on the wreath, in hand a scimitar, in bend sinister. *Pl.* 107, *cr.* 15.

WALSH, Iri., a cubit arm, in hand a tilting-spear, ppr. *Pl.* 99, *cr.* 8.

WALSH, Berks., a griffin's head, erased, ar. *Pl.* 48, *cr.* 6.

WALSH-BENN, Bart., Cumb., a griffin's head, erased, per fess, wavy, ar. and erm., beak and ears, or. *Pl.* 48, *cr.* 6.

WALSHE, a goat's head, erased, az., attired, or, on top of horns two hawks' bells, ar., on neck three bezants, two and one. *Pl.* 29, *cr.* 13, (charging, *pl.* 141.)

WALSHE, Eng., out of a ducal coronet, or, a demi-lion, rampant, ar. *Pl.* 45, *cr.* 7.

WALSHE, Worc. and Heref., a griffin's head, erased, ar. *Pl.* 48, *cr.* 6.

WALSHE, Somers., an antelope's head, erased az., attired, or, on end of each horn a bell, ar., charged on neck with a fess gobony, ar. and gu., between three bezants, one and two. *Pl.* 24, *cr.* 7, (charging, *pl.* 141.)

WALSINGHAM, Surr., Kent, and Warw., out of a mural coronet, gu., a tiger's head, or, ducally gorged, az. *Pl.* 5, *cr.* 15.

WALSINGHAM, Baron, (De Grey,) a wyvern's head, ppr. *Excitari, non hebescere. Pl.* 87, *cr.* 12.

WALSTENHOLME, on a snake, nowed, an eagle, with two heads displayed. *Pl.* 87, *cr.* 11, (snake, *pl.* 75, *cr.* 11.)

WALSTONECROFT, out of a naval coronet, a demi-mermaid, in dexter a (purse,) in sinister a comb. *Pl.* 32, *cr.* 8.

WALTER, Yorks., an arm, vested, gu., turned up, ar., in hand, ppr., a chess-rook, sa. *Pl.* 39, *cr.* 1, (rook, *pl.* 40, *cr.* 11.)

WALTER, a cubit arm, in hand an anchor. *Pl.* 53, *cr.* 13.

WALTER, Devons., a stork, ppr., (dipping beak into a whilk-shell, erect, or.) *Pl.* 121, *cr.* 13.

WALTER, Lond. and Salop, a lion's gamb, erased, ar. *Pl.* 126, *cr.* 9.

WALTERS, a lion's head, erased, ar. *Pl.* 81, *cr.* 4.

WALTERS, Eng., a dove and olive-branch, ppr. *Pl.* 48, *cr.* 15.

WALTHALL, Chesh., an arm, embowed, vested, gu., cuffed, erm., (hand clenched,) thereon a falcon, close, ppr., beaked, or. *Pl.* 7, *cr.* 1, (arm, *pl.* 39, *cr.* 1.)

WALTHAM, Eng., a peacock's head, az. *Pl.* 100, *cr.* 5.

WALTHEW, Kent, out of a mural coronet, or, a demi-lion, sa., supporting the lower part of a tilting-spear, of the last. *Pl.* 120, *cr.* 14.

WALTON, Glouc., a griffin's head, erased, ar., semée of buckles, az., (pierced through mouth by a spear, in bend sinister, point upward, or.) *Murus aeneus virtus. Pl.* 48, *cr.* 6.

WALTON, on a chapeau, ar., turned up, gu., a bugle-horn, of the last, stringed, or. *Pl.* 48, *cr.* 12, (chapeau, *pl.* 127, *fig.* 13.)

WALTON, a wild man, striding forward, in sinister the branch of a tree, resting on the shoulder, wreathed round temples with a chaplet of laurel, all vert.

WALTON, Ess., an antelope's head, (couped at neck, gu., armed, or, gorged with a collar, ar., thereon three fleurs-de-lis, gu.,) in mouth a trefoil, ppr. *Pl.* 24, *cr.* 7, (trefoil, *pl.* 11, *cr.* 12.)

WALTON, Somers., a dragon's head, couped, or, flames issuing from mouth, ppr., on neck a cross pattée, sa. *Pl.* 37, *cr.* 9, (cross, *pl.* 141.)

WALTON, Durh., a buck, current, ar., charged on shoulder with three torteaux, attired, or, pierced through neck by an arrow, gold, feathered, of the first.

WALTON, Wilts. and Lanc., a wild man, wreathed about loins and head, ppr., in dexter a trefoil, slipped, or, in sinister a tree, eradicated, ppr., reclining on his shoulder.

WALTON, Wilts. and Lanc., a wild man, wreathed about loins and head, ppr., holding a spiked club, or.

WALWORTH, out of a ducal coronet, or, two arms, embowed, vested, gu., in hands, ppr., (a cake of bread, ar.) *Pl.* 45, *cr.* 2.

WALWYN, Eng., a pheasant, ppr. *Pl.* 82, *cr.* 12.

WALWYN, of Longworth, Wel., on an embattled wall, ar., masoned, sa., a wyvern, wings expanded, vert, scaled, or, (pierced through head by a javelin, ppr.) *Non deficit alter*—and—*Drwy Rynwedd Gwaed. Pl.* 75, *cr.* 12, (wall, *pl.* 90, *cr.* 7.)

WALWYN, out of a battlement, ar., a wyvern, wings expanded, vert, (pierced through mouth by an arrow, or.) *Pl.* 75, *cr.* 12, (battlement, *pl.* 90, *cr.* 7.)

WALWYN, Heref., on part of a tower, ar., a dragon, wings expanded, vert, (pierced through mouth by a spear, sa., headed, of the first, vulned, gu.) *Pl.* 90, *cr.* 10, (tower, same plate, *cr.* 7.)

WALWYN, Suss., on a mural coronet, gu., a dragon, wings expanded, vert, (pierced through mouth by an arrow, or.) *Pl.* 90, *cr.* 10, (coronet, *pl.* 128, *fig.* 18.)

WANDESFORD, and WANDFORD, Yorks., a church, ppr., spire, az. *Pl.* 45, *cr.* 6.

WANDESFORD, Eng., a cathedral church and spire, ppr. *Pl.* 45, *cr.* 6.

WANKFORD, Ess., a lion, rampant, gardant, between paws a hurt. *Pl.* 92, *cr.* 7, (hurt, *pl.* 141.)

WANLEY, a cross, (surmounted) by a crescent, or. *Pl.* 43, *cr.* 3.

WANTON, Norf., a trefoil, slipped, sa., (charged with another, ar.) *Pl.* 82, *cr.* 1.

WANTON, Hunts., a plume of (seven) ostrich-feathers, three, ar., two, sa., and two, vert. *Pl.* 12, *cr.* 9.

WARBERTON, or WARBURTON, Chesh., Cumb., Suff., and Notts., a Saracen's head, ppr., couped at shoulders, wreathed about head, ar. and gu., on head a plume of feathers, of the second. *Pl.* 105, *cr.* 2.

WARBURTON-EGERTON-ROWLAND-EYLES, of Warburton and Arley, Chesh.: 1. For *Warburton*, a man's head, affrontée, couped at shoulders, ppr., temples wreathed, ar. and gu., issuing therefrom three ostrich-feathers, or, on breast a cross crosslet, sa. *Pl.* 105, *cr.* 2, (cross, *pl.* 141.) 2. For *Egerton*, three arrows, two in saltier, one in pale, or, headed and feathered, sa., bound by a ribbon, gu. *Pl.* 43, *cr.* 14.

WARBURTON, Iri., a mermaid, with mirror and comb, ppr. *Pl.* 48, *cr.* 5.

WARCOP, WARCUP, and WARCUPP, Oxon., Yorks., and Cumb., a boar's head, couped, ar. *Pl.* 48, *cr.* 2.

WARCOP, Eng., in dexter hand a cross crosslet, gu. *Pl.* 99, *cr.* 1.

WARD, or WARDE, Suff., on a mount, vert, a hind, conchant, ar. *Pl.* 1, *cr.* 14, (mount, *pl.* 22, *cr.* 5.)

WARD-LUCAS-TOUCH, of Guilsborough, and Great Addington Hall, Northamp., a wolf's head, erased. *Sub cruce salus.* *Pl.* 14, *cr.* 6.

WARD-PLUMER, of Gilston Park, Herts., and of Bucks. and Suff.: 1. For *Ward*, a wolf's head, erased and langued, ppr., in mouth a key. *Pl.* 14, *cr.* 6, (key, *pl.* 9, *cr.* 12.) 2. For *Plumer*, a demi-lion, gu., in (paws) a garb. *Pl.* 84, *cr.* 7.

WARD, a dove and olive-branch, ppr. *Pl.* 48, *cr.* 15.

WARD, Iri., a wolf's head, erased, ar. *Pl.* 14, *cr.* 6.

WARD, a doe, trippant, (collared and lined, line reflexed over back.) *Pl.* 20, *cr.* 14.

WARD, an heraldic-antelope, sejant.

WARD, a wolf's head. *Pl.* 92, *cr.* 15, (without rose.)

WARD, a griffin's head, erased. *Pl.* 48, *cr.* 6.

WARD, out of a mural coronet, gu., a wolf's head, or. *Pl.* 14, *cr.* 6, (coronet, *same plate, cr.* 5.)

WARD, Norf., a buck, trippant, ppr., (collared, lined, and ringed, or.) *Pl.* 68, *cr.* 2.

WARD, Ess., Kent, Durh., and Yorks., a wolf's head, erased, per fess, or and az. *Pl.* 14, *cr.* 6.

WARD, Ess., Warw., and Yorks., a wolf's head, erased, or, charged on breast with a mullet, sa. *Pl.* 14, *cr.* 6, (mullet, *pl.* 141.)

WARD, Lond., out of a mural coronet, or, a wolf's head, per fess, gold and az. *Pl.* 14, *cr.* 6, (coronet, *same plate, cr.* 5.)

WARD, Lond., a wolf's head, erased, ppr. *Pl.* 14, *cr.* 6.

WARD, Lond., out of a ducal coronet, or, a wolf's head, ppr. *Pl.* 14, *cr.* 6, (coronet, *pl.* 70, *cr.* 5.)

WARD, Berks. and Warw., an Indian goat, ppr., (collared, ringed, lined,) and armed, or. *Pl.* 66, *cr.* 1.

WARD, Lond., Kent, and Chesh., a wolf's head, erased, or. *Pl.* 14, *cr.* 6.

WARD, Durh., same crest. *Sub cruce salus.*

WARD, of Troyford, Hants., a Saracen's head, affrontée, couped below shoulders, and plumed, ppr. *Pl.* 105, *cr.* 2.

WARD, Baron: 1. Out of a ducal coronet, or, a lion's head, az. *Pl.* 90, *cr.* 9. 2. A lion, sejant, gardant, az. *Comme je fus.* *Pl.* 113, *cr.* 8, (without chapeau.)

WARD, Bangor Castle, Down, a Saracen's head, affrontée, couped below shoulders, ppr. *Sub cruce salus.* *Pl.* 28, *cr.* 3, (without crown.)

WARD, Willey Place, Surr., a martlet, sa., guttée-d'or, in beak a fleur-de-lis, or. *Sub cruce salus.* *Pl.* 111, *cr.* 5, (fleur-de-lis, *pl.* 141.)

WARD, Upton Park, Bucks., a wolf's head, (erased,) or, gorged with a collar, and thereon an escallop, az., between two bezants. *Garde la croix.* *Pl.* 8, *cr.* 4, (escallop and bezant, *pl.* 141.)

WARD, Sallhouse Hall, Norf., a dexter arm, erect, couped at elbow, vested, quarterly, or and vert, cuff, ar., in hand, ppr., a pheon, of the third. *Usque ad mortem fidus.* *Pl.* 123, *cr.* 12, (vesting, *pl.* 95, *cr.* 9.)

WARD, Viscount Bangor. *See* BANGOR.

WARDALL, Eng., a boar's head and neck, or. *Pl.* 2, *cr.* 7.

WARDE, Eng., a wolf's head, erased, sa., eared and nosed, or, charged with a cheveron, paly of six, or and ar. *Pl.* 14, *cr.* 6.

WARDE, Eng., a goat's head, erased, attired, or. *Pl.* 29, *cr.* 13.

WARDE, Norf., on a mount, vert, an eagle, displayed, erm. *Pl.* 84, *cr.* 14.

WARDE, Beds., a wolf's head, erased, or. *Pl.* 14, *cr.* 6.

WARDE, CHARLES-THOMAS, Esq., of Clopton House, and Rhine Hill, Warw., same crest.

WARDE, Devons., a martlet, wings overt, gu., rising from the battlements of a tower, ar. *Pl.* 107, *cr.* 6.

WARDELL, or WARDLE, Eng., in lion's gamb a spear, ppr., tasselled, or. *Pl.* 1, *cr.* 4.

WARDELL, Lond., a hawk, ar., charged on breast with three torteaux, in bend. *Pl.* 96, *cr.* 10, (torteau, *pl.* 141.)

WARDEN, a peacock's feather and two ostrich-feathers, in pale, all enfiled by a ducal coronet. *Pl.* 44, *cr.* 12, (peacock's feather, *pl.* 120, *cr.* 13.)

WARDEN, Sco., a fleur-de-lis, or. *Industriâ et spe.* *Pl.* 68, *cr.* 12.

WARDEN, Eng., out of a crescent, ra., an arrow, sa., pointed and feathered, or. *Pl.* 82, *cr.* 15.

WARDLAW, Bart., Sco., an etoile, or. *Familias firmat pietas.* *Pl.* 63, *cr.* 9.

WARDMAN, Lond., a ram's head, attired, or. *Pl.* 34, *cr.* 12.

WARDON, a pellet, charged with a lion's head, erased, ar., collared, gu. *Pl.* 50, *cr.* 10.

WARDOR, a fleur-de-lis. *Pl.* 68, *cr.* 12.

WARDOR, Hants, a fleur-de-lis, ar., enfiled by a ducal coronet, or. *Pl.* 47, *cr.* 7.

WARDROP, Sco., issuing from an antique crown, a demi-eagle, wings expanded, all ppr. *Superna sequor. Pl.* 52, *cr.* 8, (crown, *pl.* 79, *cr.* 12.)

WARDROP, or WARDROPE, Sco., a husbandman, issuing, bonnet and vestments, az., holding a ploughshare over his dexter shoulder, ppr. *Revertite. Pl.* 122, *cr.* 1.

WARE, a demi-lion, (between paws) a mullet of five points. *Pl.* 89, *cr.* 10.

WARE, Eng., a boar, passant, ar. *Pl.* 48, *cr.* 14.

WARE, Ess., Devons., and Iri., a dragon's head, or, pierced through neck by a (broken swordblade,) ppr. *Pl.* 121, *cr.* 9.

WAREING, and WARINGE, Lanc., a wolf's head, couped at neck, in mouth an ostrich-feather, all ppr. *Pl.* 92, *cr.* 15, (feather, *pl.* 58, *cr.* 7.)

WARHAM, Hants. and Dors., an arm, in armour, in hand a sword. *Pl.* 2, *cr.* 8.

WARING, Eng., a boar's head, erased, gu. *Pl.* 16, *cr.* 11.

WARING, Waringstown, co. Down, a crane's head and neck, ppr. *Nec vi, nec astutia. Pl.* 20, *cr.* 9.

WARING-MAXWELL, a stork's head, (couped,) ar. *Pl.* 32, *cr.* 5.

WARING, Salop, an arm, erect, (vested, gu., cuffed, ar.,) in hand, ppr., a lure, of the first, garnished, or, lined and ringed, vert. *Cavendo tutus. Pl.* 44, *cr.* 2, (vesting, *same plate, cr.* 4.)

WARINGE, Iri., a rose, or, barbed, vert. *Pl.* 20, *cr.* 2.

WARLEY, Eng., a tree, ppr. *Pl.* 16, *cr.* 8.

WARLEY, Lond., out of a mural coronet, az., a dexter arm, in armour, embowed, garnished, or, in hand, ppr., a falchion, ar., hilt and pommel, gold. *Pl.* 115, *cr.* 14.

WARMOUTH, Northumb., a demi-lion, rampant, erm., armed, or, supporting a mullet of (six) points, gold. *Pl.* 89, *cr.* 10.

WARNE, Eng., a horse-shoe, or, between wings, ppr. *Pl.* 17, *cr.* 3.

WARNECOMBE, Heref., a caltrap, or, environed by a serpent, vert. *Pl.* 7, *cr.* 4, (serpent, *pl.* 112, *cr.* 6.)

WARNER, Iri., a badger, passant, sa. *Pl.* 34, *cr.* 4.

WARNER-LEE, Norf., a squirrel, sa., sitting between two hazel-branches, cracking a nut, or. *Non nobis tantum nati. Pl.* 5, *cr.* 6.

WARNER, Kent, same crest.

WARNER, Lond., Norf., and Northamp., a double plume of feathers, or. *Pl.* 64, *cr.* 5, (without coronet.)

WARNER, Suff., a lizard, vert. *Pl.* 93, *cr.* 4, (without tree.)

WARNER, Warw., a horse's head, erased, per fess, erm. and gu., maned, of the last. *Pl.* 81, *cr.* 6.

WARNER, PATRICK, Esq., of Ardeer, Sco., an open Bible. *Manet in æternum. Pl.* 15, *cr.* 12.

WARNER, Ess., Lond., and Suss., a man's head, ppr., couped below shoulders, vested, chequy, or and az., temples wreathed, gold and gu., on head a cap, ar. *Pl.* 31, *cr.* 2.

WARNER, Yorks., a Saracen's head, affrontée, ppr., temples wreathed, or and gu. *Pl.* 97, *cr.* 2.

WARNER, Kent, a double plume of feathers. *Pl.* 64, *cr.* 5, (without coronet.)

WARNFORD, Wilts. and Hants, a garb, ppr. *Pl.* 48, *cr.* 10.

WARR, an ostrich's head, wings elevated, ar., in beak a key, or. *Pl.* 28, *cr.* 13, (key, *pl.* 9, *cr.* 12.)

WARR, Eng., a cross fleury, fitched, gu., fleurs, or. *Pl.* 65, *cr.* 9.

WARRAND, Somers., a dexter arm, in armour, in hand a sword, all ppr., hilted and pommelled, or. *Fortiter. Pl.* 2, *cr.* 8.

WARRAND, out of a ducal coronet, az., a demi-lion, erm. *Pl.* 45, *cr.* 7.

WARRE, out of a ducal coronet, a griffin's head, ar., in beak the attires and scalp of a stag, ppr. *Pl.* 54, *cr.* 14, (attires, *pl.* 86, *cr.* 10.)

WARRE, Somers., out of a ducal coronet, or, a griffin's head, ar. *Pl.* 54, *cr.* 14.

WARREN, Iri., an arm, in armour, embowed, ppr., in hand a dart, sa., feathered, ar., barbed, or. *Fortuna sequatur. Pl.* 96, *cr.* 6.

WARREN, a coney, sejant (in a fern-bush.) *Pl.* 70, *cr.* 1.

WARREN, on a chapeau, gu., turned up., erm., a wyvern, ar., wings expanded, chequy, or and az. *Pl.* 104, *cr.* 5, (without crown.)

WARREN, Eng., a talbot, ppr. *Pl.* 120, *cr.* 8.

WARREN, on a mount, vert, a lion, rampant, or, in dexter a (spear,) ppr. *Pl.* 59, *cr.* 5.

WARREN, Lond., a dragon's head, couped, gu. *Pl.* 87, *cr.* 12.

WARREN, Herts., in a ducal coronet, or, an eagle's leg, sa., out of a plume of feathers, ar. *Pl.* 96, *cr.* 7, (feathers, *pl.* 106, *cr.* 4.)

WARREN, Herts., a wyvern, ar., tail nowed, wings expanded, chequy, or and az. *Pl.* 63, *cr.* 13.

WARREN, Herts., a lion's gamb, erased, ar., grasping an eagle's leg, erased at thigh, or. *Pl.* 89, *cr.* 13.

WARREN, Lond., out of a ducal coronet, or, a leopard's head, gold, spotted, sa. *Pl.* 36, *cr.* 15.

WARREN, Middx. and Lond., in a mural coronet, ar., charged with three torteaux, an eagle's leg, couped at knee and erect, or, between two laurel-branches, vert. *Omne tulit punctum qui miscuit utile dulci.*

WARREN, Middx., a wyvern, ar., wings expanded, chequy, or and az. *Virtus mihi scutum. Pl.* 63, *cr.* 13.

WARREN, Suff., out of a ducal coronet, gu., a pyramid of leaves, ar. *Pl.* 61, *cr.* 13, (coronet, *pl.* 128, *fig.* 3.)

WARREN, Suff., a demi-greyhound, erm., (collared, chequy, or and az.) *Pl.* 48, *cr.* 3.

WARREN, Chesh., out of a ducal coronet, a plume of five ostrich-feathers, ar., in the middle of them a griffin's claw, or. *Pl.* 100, *cr.* 12, (claw, *pl.* 96, *cr.* 7.)

WARREN, Lond. and Devons., a greyhound, sa., seizing a hare, ppr.

WARREN, Glouc., a demi-greyhound, rampant, erm., (gorged with a collar, chequy, or and az.) *Pl.* 48, *cr.* 3.

WARREN, on a chapeau, gu., turned up, erm., a wyvern, ar., wings expanded, chequy, or and az. *Tenebo. Pl.* 104, *cr.* 5, (without crown.)

WARREN-BORLASE, Bucks., on a cheapeau, gu., turned up, erm., a wyvern, ar., wings expanded, chequy, or and gu. *Pl.* 104, *cr.* 5, (without crown.)

WARRENDER, Bart., Sco., a hare, sejant, ppr. *Industriâ.* Pl. 70, cr. 1.

WARRINGTON, out of a ducal coronet, az., a demi-eagle, displayed, or. Pl. 9, cr. 6.

WARTER, or WARTUR, Eng., a fox, sejant, ppr. Pl. 87, cr. 4.

WARTUR, Lond. and Salop, a lion, rampant, sa., collared, ar., between paws a chess-rook, of the last. Pl. 2, cr. 14, (chess-rook, pl. 40, cr. 11.)

WARTERTON, Walton Hall, Yorks., a bear, passant, (in mouth a fish,) all ppr. Pl. 82, cr. 14, (without spear.)

WARTNABY, a lion's head, erased, or. Pl. 81, cr. 4.

WARTON, Eng., a winged spur, ppr. Pl. 59, cr. 1.

WARTON, an arm, in armour, erect, ppr., supporting a battle-axe, (in pale,) ar. Pl. 73, cr. 7, (armour, pl. 125, cr. 5.)

WARWICK, Eng., a leopard's head, or. Pl. 92, cr. 13.

WARWICK, Cumb., a dexter arm, in armour, couped at shoulder, in gauntlet a battle-axe, all ppr. Pl. 73, cr. 7, (armour, pl. 125, cr. 5.)

WARWICK, Earl of. *See* BROOKE and WARWICK.

WASE, Lond. and Leic., on a wreath, clouds, ppr., issuing rays, or, thereon an arm, (in armour, embowed, of the first, garnished gold,) supporting a battle-axe, headed, ar., staff, gu., garnished, of the second. Pl. 44, cr. 4, (axe, pl. 121, cr. 14.)

WASE, Suss., a demi-lion, rampant, ar., ducally gorged, az., on shoulder a pellet, thereon a crescent, or. Pl. 87, cr. 15, (pellet and crescent, pl. 141.)

WASEY, Eng., a sinister arm and a dexter hand shooting an arrow from a bow. Pl. 100, cr. 4.

WASEY, Berks., a falcon, rising, or, beaked, membered, and (collared, sa.) belled, gold, collar charged with three bezants. Pl. 105, cr. 4, (bezant, pl. 141.)

WASHBORNE, Eng., in hand a dagger, ppr. Pl. 28, cr. 4.

WASHBOURNE, Berks, Heref., and Worc., on a wreath, a coil of flax, ar., surmounted by another wreath, of the same, and gu., thereon flames, ppr.

WASHBOURNE, Lond. and Glouc., same crest. *Industriâ et probitate.*

WASHINGTON, Eng., on a ducal coronet, or, a martlet, sa. Pl. 98, cr. 14.

WASHINGTON, Kent, Bucks., Northamp., and Warkw., out of a ducal coronet, or, a raven, wings addorsed, ppr. Pl. 6, cr. 11, (coronet, same plate, cr. 6.)

WASHINGTON, Kent, Bucks., Northamp., and Warw., out of a ducal coronet, or, an eagle, wings addorsed, sa. Pl. 19, cr. 9.

WASTELL, Northamp. and Westm., a cubit arm, erect, vested, gu., charged with three guttés-d'or, cuffed, ar., holding on hand, ppr., (a dove, az., collared, of the third.) Pl. 44, cr. 13, (without branches.)

WASTER, within a ring, or, gemmed, sa., (two snakes, entwined and erect, ppr.) Pl. 35, cr. 3.

WASTFIELD, Lond., Somers., and Wilts., a lamb, passant, sa., holding a banner, ar., charged with a Catherine-wheel, of the first. Pl. 48, cr. 13, (wheel, pl. 141.)

WASTLEY, Eng., in dexter hand, gu., an annulet, or. Pl. 24, cr. 3.

WASTNEYS, Notts., Chesh., and Leic., a demi-lion, rampant, ar., collared, gu. Pl. 18, cr. 13.

WASTOILE, or WASTOYLE, Eng., in hand a grenade, sa., fired, ppr. Pl. 2, cr. 6.

WATERFORD, Marquess of, Earl and Viscount Tyrone, Baron Beresford, Baron De-la-Poer, and a Bart., all Iri.; Baron Tyrone, G.B., (De-la-Poer Beresford:) 1. For *Beresford*, a dragon's head, erased, ar., pierced through neck by a broken spear, or, point, ar., (thrust through upper jaw.) Pl. 121, cr. 9. 2. For *La Poer*, a stag's head, cabossed, ppr., attired, or, (between the horns a crucifix, gold, thereon the resemblance of Jesus,) ppr. *Nil nisi cruce.* Pl. 36, cr. 1.

WATERFORD and WEXFORD, Earl of. *See* SHREWSBURY, Earl.

WATERHOUSE, a demi-swan, wings expanded, murally crowned. Pl. 54, cr. 4, (crown, Pl. 44, cr. 15.)

WATERHOUSE, Lond. and Yorks., the dexter side of an eagle, divided palewise, without head, sa.

WATERHOUSE, Middx., Herts., and Linc., an eagle's leg, erased at thigh, thigh, sa., leg and claws, or. Pl. 27, cr. 1, (without heart.)

WATERHOUSE, Middx., Herts., and Linc., a demi-wolf. Pl. 56, cr. 8, (without spear.)

WATERHOUSE, Herts., a demi-talbot, erm., (collared,) gu., eared, sa. Pl. 15, cr. 2.

WATERLOW, WALTER BLANDFORD, 5 Storey's Gate, St James's Park, Lond., a demi-eagle, displayed, ppr., langued, gu., in beak a cross crosslet, fitched, or, charged on breast with a mullet of five points, gold. *Per ardua ad alta.* Pl. 44, cr. 14.

WATERPARK, Baron, Iri., and a Bart., G.B., (Cavandish;) on a ducal coronet, or, a snake, nowed, ppr. *Cavendo tutus.* Pl. 116, cr. 2.

WATERS, THOMAS, Esq., of Sarnau, Carmarthen, a demi-griffin, az. *Honor pietas.* Pl. 18, cr. 6.

WATERS, Iri., an eagle, rising, regardant, ppr. *Spero.* Pl. 35, cr. 8.

WATERS, Eng. and Sco., a demi-talbot, ar., in mouth an arrow, gu. *Toujours fidele.* Pl. 97, cr. 9.

WATERTON, Eng., a goat's head, erased, or, (collared, gu.) Pl. 29, cr. 13.

WATFORD, two arms, in armour, embowed, hands grasping a battle-axe. Pl. 41, cr. 2.

WATHE, Herts. and Northamp., a dragon's head, (erased,) sa. Pl. 87, cr. 1.

WATKENS, Wilts. and Wel., a griffin's head, gu. Pl. 38, cr. 3.

WATKIN, Eng., a cock's head, ar., combed and wattled, gu. Pl. 92, cr. 3.

WATKINS, JAMES, Esq., of Shotton Hall, Salop, a leopard's face, jessent-de-lis, or. *Vitæ via virtus.* Pl. 123, cr. 9.

WATKINS, CHARLES-WILLIAM, Esq., of Badby House, Northamp., a griffin's head, erased. *In portu quies.* Pl. 48, cr. 6.

WATKINS, Yorks., a lion, rampant, gu., in dexter a fleur-de-lis, or. *Virtute avorum.* Pl. 87, cr. 6.

WATKINS, Lloegyn, Brecon, a wolf, rampant, regardant, ar., langued and unguled, gu. *Primum tutare domum.* Pl. 10, cr. 3.

WATKINS, Woodfield, Worc., a talbot's head, erased, ar., gorged with a collar (of cinquefoils,) gu. *Pl.* 2, *cr.* 15.

WATKINS, Pennoyre, Brecknock: 1. A dragon's head, erased, vert, in mouth a dexter hand, couped at wrist, gu. *Pl.* 106, *cr.* 13. 2. On a ducal coronet, a lion, rampant. *Peri aur y chalon wir. Pl.* 67, *cr.* 5, (coronet, *pl.* 45, *cr.* 7.)

WATKINS, Eng., a cubit arm, erect, hand grasping a tilting-spear, in bend sinister, ppr. *Pl.* 99, *cr.* 8.

WATKINS, out of an Eastern coronet, or, a griffin's head, gu. *Pl.* 54, *cr.* 14, (coronet, *pl.* 79, *cr.* 12.)

WATKINS, Heref., a cubit arm, in armour, erect, in hand the broken shaft of a tilting-spear, in bend sinister, all ppr. *Pl.* 23, *cr.* 9.

WATKINS, Wel., a dragon's head, erased, vert, in mouth a dexter hand, couped at wrist, gu. *Pl.* 106, *cr.* 13.

WATKINS, Yorks. and Notts., a lion, rampant, gu., in dexter a fleur-de-lis, or. *Pl.* 87, *cr.* 6.

WATKINSON, Eng., an hour-glass, winged, ppr. *Pl.* 32, *cr.* 11.

WATKYNS, Eng., a lion, rampant, in dexter a battle-axe, all ppr. *Pl.* 64, *cr.* 2, (axe, *pl.* 26, *cr.* 7.)

WATLING, Eng., out of a heart, a dexter hand grasping a sabre, all ppr. *Corde manuque. Pl.* 35, *cr.* 7.

WATLINGTON, PERRY-WATLINGTON, Moor Hall, Ess., a lion's head, ppr., ducally crowned, or. *Pl.* 90, *cr.* 4.

WATLINGTON, Herts., a demi-lion, rampant, in dexter a sword, ppr., hilt and pommel, or. *Pl.* 41, *cr.* 13.

WATMAN, Kent, a demi-lion, between paws a pheon. *Pl.* 47, *cr.* 4, (pheon, *pl.* 141.)

WATMOUGH, or WATMOUGHE, Eng., a ferret, passant, sa., collared, or, lined, gu. *Pl.* 12, *cr.* 2.

WATSON, T. EDWARDS, Low Hall, Shrops., an ermine, passant, ppr., vulned on shoulder, gu. *Pl.* 126 c, *cr.* 8.

WATSON, Eng., an arm, from shoulder, erect, out of the sea, ppr., in hand an anchor, az., cable, or. *Pl.* 27, *cr.* 6.

WATSON, of Turin, Sco., a lily of the Nile, ppr. *Sine injuriâ. Pl.* 81, *cr.* 9.

WATSON, a sprig of (five) leaves. *Pl.* 98, *cr.* 8.

WATSON, Sco., a dexter hand, erect, ppr. *Confisus veribus. Pl.* 32, *cr.* 14.

WATSON, Sco., a griffin's head, erased, ar., gorged with a collar, sa., in beak a (flower,) gu., leaved, vert. *Pl.* 42, *cr.* 9.

WATSON, Sco., a ship under sail, ppr. *Ad littora tendo. Pl.* 109, *cr.* 8.

WATSON, Sco., two hands, issuing from clouds, in fess, grasping trunk of an oak-tree, in pale, branches sprouting. *Insperata floruit. Pl.* 126, *cr.* 4.

WATSON, an eagle's head, erased, in beak (three flowers.) *Pl.* 22, *cr.* 1.

WATSON, a griffin's head, erased, ar., on neck two cheverons, sa., in mouth a (rose-branch,) gu., leaved, vert. *Pl.* 42, *cr.* 9.

WATSON, Kent and Suff., on a mount, vert, a demi-dragon, rampant. *Pl.* 82, *cr.* 18, (mount, *pl.* 33, *cr.* 13.)

WATSON, Middx. and Yorks., an ermine, passant, ar., (collared, ringed, and lined, or.) *Pl.* 9, *cr.* 5.

WATSON, Salop, an ermine, passant, ppr., vulned on shoulders, gu. *Pl.* 126 c, *cr.* 8.

WATSON, Westm., two arms, issuing from clouds, hands grasping stump of tree, fructed at top, with branches on each side, all ppr. *Pl.* 55, *cr.* 8.

WATSON, Yorks., a griffin's head, erased, ar., in beak a sprig, leaved, vert. *Pl.* 29, *cr.* 15, (without gorging.)

WATSON, Yorks., a griffin's head, erased, ar., ducally gorged, or. *Mea gloria fides. Pl.* 42, *cr.* 9, (without branch.)

WATSON, Durh., same crest. *Esto quod esse videris.*

WATSON, Cambs., a griffin's head, erased, sa., (gorged with two bars-gemelle, ar.) *Pl.* 48, *cr.* 6.

WATSON, Cumb., an arm, in armour, embowed, ppr., garnished, or, in gauntlet a palm-branch, vert. *Pl.* 68, *cr.* 1, (palm, *pl.* 23, *cr.* 7.)

WATSON, Lond., Kent, and Cumb., on a mount, vert, a palm-tree, or. *Pl.* 52, *cr.* 6.

WATSON, Bart., Bucks., a griffin's head, erased, ar., ducally gorged, or. *Pl.* 42, *cr.* 9, (without branch.)

WATT, Eng., a crescent. *Pl.* 18, *cr.* 14.

WATT, out of a mural coronet, or, a wolf's head, sa., charged with a fess, embattled, ar. *Pl.* 8, *cr.* 4, (coronet, *same plate*, *cr.* 5.)

WATT, Sco., a falcon, ppr., hooded and belled, or. *Fide et fiducid. Pl.* 38, *cr.* 12.

WATT, Sco., a hawk, ppr. *Pl.* 67, *cr.* 3.

WATT, Eng., a talbot's head, erased, ar., collared, gu. *Pl.* 2, *cr.* 15.

WATT, Heref., out of a mural coronet, or, a demi-wolf, salient, ar., charged on neck with a fess, embattled, az., between paws a garb, in pale, ppr.

WATTE, a cubit arm, in armour, erect, in hand a pistol, all ppr. *Pl.* 101, *cr.* 12, (armour, *pl.* 33, *cr.* 4.)

WATTERTON, Linc. and Yorks., a beaver, passant, (in mouth a fish,) all ppr. *Pl.* 49, *cr.* 5.

WATTERTON, Linc. and Yorks., an otter, (passant,) ppr., in mouth a fish, ar. *Pl.* 74, *cr.* 15.

WATTES, Wilts., Somers., and Devons., a greyhound, sejant, ar., (collared, az., studded, or, supporting a broad arrow, gold, plumed, of the first.) *Pl.* 66, *cr.* 15.

WATTS, Northamp., a lozenge, gu., between wings, or. *Pl.* 4, *cr.* 10, (lozenge, *pl.* 141.)

WATTS, a seal's head, couped, ar. *Pl.* 97, *cr.* 11.

WATTS, a griffin's head, erased, in beak an annulet. *Pl.* 48, *cr.* 6, (annulet, *pl.* 33, *cr.* 11.)

WATTS, a demi-lion, or, charged with a cross pattée, az., in mouth an oak-branch, ppr., fructed, gold, supporting a shield, of the first, charged with a fess, erminois, between three fleurs-de-lis, in chief, and a cross pattée, in base, of the fourth, from the shield an escroll, inscribed, "Amice."

WATTS, of Hawkesdale Hall, Cumb. : 1. A dexter arm, in armour, embowed, ppr., in gauntlet an amphisbæna or snake, (with a head at each extremity,) or, langued, gu. *Pl.* 96, *cr.* 6, (serpent, *pl.* 91, *cr.* 6.) 2. A lozenge, or, between wings, gu. *Pl.* 4, *cr.* 10, (lozenge, *pl.* 141.)

WATTS, Sir JAMES, of Abney Hall, Chesh., a demi-griffin, sa., wings extended, chequy, or and sa., in dexter a garb, or. *Fide, sed cui vide. Pl.* 19, *cr.* 15, (garb, *pl.* 84, *cr.* 7.)

WATTS, a greyhound, sejant, ar., (supporting with dexter an arrow, or, headed and barbed, of the first.) *Pl.* 66, *cr.* 15.

WATTS, Norf., a lion's gamb, (erased,) gu., supporting a shield, or. *Pl.* 43, *cr.* 12.

WATTS, Cumb. and French.: 1. A dexter arm, in armour, embowed, ppr., in gauntlet a two-headed snake, or. *Pl.* 120, *cr.* 11, (snake, *pl.* 91, *cr.* 6.) 2. A cross crosslet, gu., surmounted by an escallop, ar., all between wings, or. *Pl.* 62, *cr.* 4, (cross, *pl.* 141.)

WATUR, Eng., a garb, per pale, or and ar., banded, gu. *Pl.* 48, *cr.* 10.

WAUCH, Sco., a greyhound, sejant, sa. *Pl.* 66, *cr.* 15.

WAUCH, or WAUGH, Eng., out of a ducal coronet, a dexter hand holding a sword, erect, blade wavy, all ppr. *Pl.* 65, *cr.* 10.

WAUCHOP, Sco., a wheat-sheaf, or. *Industria ditat. Pl.* 48, *cr.* 10.

WAUCHOPE, ANDREW, Esq., of Niddrie Marischall, Mid-Lothian, same crest and motto.

WAUD, a martlet, ppr. *Sola virtus invicta. Pl.* 111, *cr.* 5.

WAUTON, Eng., a trefoil, slipped and voided, sa. *Pl.* 4, *cr.* 10, (without wings.)

WAY, an eagle, displayed, gu. *Pl.* 48, *cr.* 11.

WAY, Bucks., an arm, embowed, in mail, in hand, ppr., a baton, or. *Pl.* 120, *cr.* 11, (baton, *pl.* 33, *cr.* 4.)

WAY, a dexter arm, embowed, in (chain) mail, in hand, ppr., a baton, or, ends, sa. *Fit via vi. Ib.*

WAYER, Eng., the attires of a stag, or. *Pl.* 71, *cr.* 8.

WAYLAND, Eng., two hands conjoined, in fess, couped at wrists, ppr. *Pl.* 1, *cr.* 2.

WAYNEMAN, Oxon., a cock's head, erased, az., combed, wattled, and beaked, or. *Pl.* 92, *cr.* 3.

WAYNEWRIGHT, Eng., a lion, rampant. ar., in dexter a battle-axe, handle of the last, headed, or. *Pl.* 64, *cr.* 2, (axe, *pl.* 26, *cr.* 7.)

WAYNFLETE, Eng., a griffin's head, erased. *Nullâ pallescere culpâ. Pl.* 48, *cr.* 6.

WAYTE, Hants, a bugle-horn, stringed, sa., garnished, or. *Pl.* 48, *cr.* 12.

WEALE, Eng., a boar's head, erased and erect, az. *Pl.* 21, *cr.* 7.

WEAR, or WEARE, Eng., a stag, trippant, ppr. *Pl.* 68, *cr.* 2.

WEARE, Berks. and Wilts., on a lure, in fess, gu., a falcon, wings addorsed, ppr. *Pl.* 10, *cr.* 7.

WEATHERALL, Eng., a cup, or. *Pl.* 42, *cr.* 1.

WEATHERBY, an arm, embowed, hand grasping a dagger, ppr. *Pl.* 120, *cr.* 11.

WEATHERHEAD, Eng., a pelican, ppr. *Pl.* 109, *cr.* 15.

WEATHERSTON, Eng., a lion's head, erased, ppr. *Pl.* 81, *cr.* 4.

WEAVER, Eng., a ram's head, erased, ar., armed, or. *Pl.* 1, *cr.* 12.

WEBB, demi-eagle, displayed, in beak a cross crosslet, fitched. *Pl.* 22, *cr.* 11, (cross, *pl.* 31, *cr.* 9.)

WEBB, a demi-stag, ar., ducally gorged, or. *Pl.* 55, *cr.* 9, (without rose.)

WEBB, Iri., a wolf, sejant, ppr. *Pl.* 110, *cr.* 4.

WEBB, a demi-stag, springing, ar., attired, or. *Pl.* 55, *cr.* 9, (without rose.)

WEBB, a phœnix, az., in flames, ppr., winged, ar., (collared, or, pendent therefrom a cross gold.) *Pl.* 44, *cr.* 8.

WEBB, a spread eagle. *Pl.* 87, *cr.* 11, (without flames.)

WEBB, a demi-eagle, displayed, ar., wings pellettée, (ducally gorged, gu.) *Pl.* 22, *cr.* 11.

WEBB, a broken spear, in three pieces, head piece in pale, others in saltier, ppr., enfiled with a ducal coronet, or. *Pl.* 33, *cr.* 3, (coronet, *pl.* 55, *cr.* 1.)

WEBB, Heref., out of a mural coronet, a demi-eagle, displayed, or. *Pl.* 33, *cr.* 5.

WEBB, Glouc. and Kent, a hind's head, erased, ppr., (vulned in neck, gu.) *Pl.* 6, *cr.* 1.

WEBB, Glouc., an eagle, displayed, sa. *Pl.* 48, *cr.* 11.

WEBB, Kent, a dexter arm, embowed, in hand an oak-branch, ppr. *Pl.* 118, *cr.* 4, (branch, *pl.* 32, *cr.* 13.)

WEBB, Lond., out of an Eastern coronet, or, a dexter arm, erect, couped at elbow, (vested, az.,) in hand a slip of laurel, all ppr. *Pl.* 25, *cr.* 8, (branch, *pl.* 43, *cr.* 6.)

WEBB, Dors. and Wilts., out of a ducal coronet, a demi-eagle, displayed, or. *Pl.* 9, *cr.* 6.

WEBB, Bart., Wilts., same crest.

WEBB, Somers., a demi-stag, (erased,) salient, ar. *Pl.* 55, *cr.* 9, (without rose.)

WEBB, W. F., Esq., Cowton, Yorks., an elephant's head, surmounted by a griffin, with wings chequy. *In hoc signo vinces. Pl.* 126 B, *cr.* 8.

WEBB, RICHARD, Esq., of Donnington Hall, Heref., a stag, lodged. *Pl.* 67, *cr.* 2.

WEBB, CHARLES - DANIEL - HENRY, Esq., of Woodville, co. Tipperary, a demi-eagle, displayed, gu., wings elevated, erminois, in beak a cross crosslet, or. *Quid prodest. Pl.* 22, *cr.* 11, (cross, *pl.* 31, *cr.* 9.)

WEBB, Eng., a hind's head, (vulned, gu.) *Pl.* 21, *cr.* 9.

WEBBE, Cambs., a griffin's head, erased, or, ducally gorged, ar. *Pl.* 42, *cr.* 9, (without branch.)

WEBBE-WESTON, THOMAS, Esq., of Sarnesfield Court, Heref.: 1. For *Weston*, a Saracen's head. *Pl.* 19, *cr.* 1. 2. Out of a ducal coronet, or, a demi-eagle, displayed, gu. *Pl.* 9, *cr.* 6.

WEBBER, Sco., a hawk, jessed and belled, ppr. *Pl.* 67, *cr.* 3.

WEBBER, Eng., a demi-lion, gardant, or, holding a fleur-de-lis, az. *Pl.* 26, *cr.* 7, (fleur-de-lis, *pl.* 91, *cr.* 13.)

WEBBER, on a ducal coronet, an eagle, displayed, or. *Pl.* 9, *cr.* 6, (eagle, *pl.* 48, *cr.* 11.)

WEBBER, Cornw., a wolf's head, per pale, ar. and gu. *Pl.* 92, *cr.* 15, (without rose.)

WEBBES, in hand, couped at elbow, an (oak)-branch, fructed and leaved, ppr. *Pl.* 23, *cr.* 7.

WEBLEY, Ess. and Surr., out of a ducal coronet, az., a griffin's head, or, (gorged with a collar, of the first, fretty gold.) *Pl.* 54, *cr.* 14.

WEBLEY, Eng., an antelope, trippant, ppr. *Pl.* 63, *cr.* 10.

WEBSTER, Eng., a weaver's shuttle, in pale. *Pl.* 102, *cr.* 10.

WEBSTER, Sco., the son rising (from the sea,) ppr. *Emergo. Pl.* 67, *cr.* 9.

WEBSTER, Chesh., a dragon's head, erased, quarterly, ar. and vert. *Pl.* 107, *cr.* 10, (without collar.)

WEBSTER, an eagle's head. *Pl.* 100, *cr.* 10.
WEBSTER, a swan's head and neck, erased, ar., beaked, gu., in beak an annulet, or. *Pl.* 54, *cr.* 6, (without wings ; annulet, *pl.* 33, *cr.* 11.)
WEBSTER, Lond., a leopard's head, affrontée, erased, crowned with an antique crown, in mouth a shuttle, gu., tipped, and furnished with quills of yarn, or. *Pl.* 56, *cr.* 7, (coronet, *pl.* 79, *cr.* 12 ; shuttle, *pl.* 102, *cr.* 10.)
WEBSTER, Bart., Suss., a dragon's head, couped, regardant, quarterly, per fess, embattled, vert and or, flames issuing from mouth, ppr.
WEBSTER, of Murlingden, Sco., a wyvern's head, erased, vert. *Vincit veritas. Pl.* 107, *cr.* 10, (without collar.)
WEDDALL, Middx., on the battlements of a castle, az., a demi-lion, or, (fixing the banner of St George.) *Pl.* 121, *cr.* 5.
WEDDELL, a hawk, hooded and belled, or. *Pl.* 38, *cr.* 12.
WEDDELL, Sco., a horse's head, ar. *Pl.* 81, *cr.* 6.
WEDDELL, a lion's head, erased, gu. *Orna verum. Pl.* 81, *cr.* 4.
WEDDEL, or WEDDELL, Eng., a battle-axe, in pale, ppr. *Pl.* 14, *cr.* 8.
WEDDERBOURNE, or WEDDERBURN, an eagle's head, erased, ppr. *Illæso lumine solem. Pl.* 20, *cr.* 7.
WEDDERBURN, Bart., Sco., an eagle's head, erased, ppr. *Aquila non captat muscas—*and—*Non degener. Pl.* 20, *cr.* 7.
WEDDERBURN, Lond., same crest.
WEDDERBURN, Sco., same crest. *Non degener.*
WEDDERBURN-COLVILE, Sir JAMES WILLIAM, Knt., of Ochiltree and Crombie, a talbot's head, ppr. *Ad finem fidelis. Pl.* 123, *cr.* 15.
WEDDERBURN-SCRYMGEOUR : 1. In lion's gamb, erect, a scimitar, all ppr. *Pl.* 18, *cr.* 8. 2. For *Scrymgeour*, an eagle's head, erased, ppr. *Aquila non captat muscas. Pl.* 20, *cr.* 7.
WEDGEWOOD, Eng., two hands, conjoined, ppr., issuing from clouds. *Pl.* 53, *cr.* 11.
WEDGEWOOD, Staffs., on a ducal coronet, a lion, passant, ar. *Pl.* 107, *cr.* 11.
WEDSON, Notts., out of a ducal coronet, or, a flame, ppr. *Pl.* 71, *cr.* 11, (coronet, *pl.* 128, *fig.* 3.)
WEEDON, Bucks., Dors., and Lanc., a hedgehog, sa. *Pl.* 32, *cr.* 9.
WEEDON, Bucks., Dors., and Lanc., a martlet, sa. *Pl.* 111, *cr.* 5.
WEEKES, Suss., a dexter arm, in armour, embowed, in hand a battle-axe, gu. *Cari Deo nihilo carent. Pl.* 2, *cr.* 8, (axe, *pl.* 81, *cr.* 11.)
WEEKS, Eng., in dexter hand, a scimitar, ppr. *Pl.* 29, *cr.* 8.
WEEKS, Eng., out of a marquess's coronet, a demi-eagle, displayed, ppr. *Pl.* 9, *cr.* 6, (coronet, *pl.* 127, *fig.* 4.)
WEEMS, Sco., a swan, ppr. *Je pense. Pl.* 122, *cr.* 13.
WEEMS, Sco., a cross crosslet, or, within two palm-branches, in orle, vert. *Virtus, dum patior, vincit. Pl.* 86, *cr.* 9, (cross, *pl.* 141.)
WEEMS, Sco., a demi-swan, wings expanded, ppr. *Cogito. Pl.* 54, *cr.* 4.
WEEVER, Surr., an antelope, passant, erm., supporting with dexter an escutcheon, or. *Pl.* 63, *cr.* 10, (escutcheon, *pl.* 19, *cr.* 2.)

WEGERTON, or WEIGERTON, Eng., the sun shining on a sun-flower. *Pl.* 45, *cr.* 13, (flower, *pl.* 84, *cr.* 6.)
WEGG, Eng., a mullet, vair. *Pl.* 41, *cr.* 1.
WEGG, Northumb., an armed hand, clenched, ppr. *Hostis honori invidia. Pl.* 125, *cr.* 5, (without sword.)
WEGG, same crest. *Vigilanter.*
WEGG, or WEGGE, Middx., a sinister gauntlet, erect, ppr., fist clenched. *Nil conscire sibi.*
WEGGE, Eng., a hand, from wrist, in gauntlet. *Pl.* 15, *cr.* 15.
WEGGET, Eng., a dove, regardant, in mouth an olive-branch, all ppr. *Pl.* 77, *cr.* 2.
WEIR, Sco., a demi-horse, in armour, ppr., bridled and sadled, gu. *Nihil verius.*
WEIR, Lond. : 1. A demi-horse, in armour, ppr., plumed, bridled and saddled, gu. *Pl.* 126 B, *cr.* 2. 2. A boar, passant. *Pl.* 48, *cr.* 14. *Vero nihil verius*, and *Band weel theyither.*
WELBORE, Lond. and Camb., a (spear,) in pale, or, headed, ar., enfilled with a boar's head, couped, of the second, vulned, gu. *Pl.* 10, *cr.* 2.
WELBORNE, Dors., in hand (three) darts. *Pl.* 56, *cr.* 4.
WELBY, Berks., Ruts., and Lanc., a naked arm, embowed, issuing from flames, ppr., in hand a sword, ar., hilt and pommel, or. *Pl.* 34, *cr.* 7, (flames, *pl.* 64, *cr.* 12.)
WELBY, Bart., Linc., an arm, in armour, embowed, issuing from clouds, in fess, in hand a sword, all ppr., hilt and pommel, or, (flames issuing from the wreath, also ppr.) *Per ignem, per gladium. Pl.* 85, *cr.* 4.
WELBY, Linc., same crest.
WELCH, or WELSH, Eng., a demi-wolf, rampant, gu. *Pl.* 56, *cr.* 8, (without spear.)
WELCH, Sco., on three grieces a long cross, az. *Pl.* 49, *cr.* 2.
WELCH, GEORGE-ASSER-WHITE, Esq., of Arle House, Glouc., an antelope's head, erased, billettée, in mouth a cross crosslet, fitched. *Pl.* 24, *cr.* 7, (cross, *pl.* 84, *cr.* 10.)
WELCH, an antelope's head, erased, az., bezantée, (gorged with a collar, gobony, ar. and gu., on the top of each horn, a ring, or.) *Pl.* 24, *cr.* 7.
WELCHMAN, a (dexter) wing, or. *Pl.* 39, *cr.* 10.
WELCOME, Linc., on stump of tree, ppr., branches, vert, a bird, close, ar., beaked, or. *Pl.* 78, *cr.* 8.
WELCOME, Linc., a pewit, wings expanded, ar., in beak a laurel branch, vert.
WELD, out of a ducal coronet, or, a wyvern's head, wings addorsed, gu., (collared and lined.) *Pl.* 59, *cr.* 14.
WELD, Lond. and Chesh., a wyvern, wings, (expanded, sa., guttée-d'or, collared and lined, or.) *Pl.* 63, *cr.* 13.
WELD, Dors., out of a ducal coronet, ppr., a wyvern, sa., guttée of ermine. *Nil sine numine. Pl.* 104, *cr.* 11.
WELD, Chesh., a wyvern, sa., guttée, (ducally gorged and chained, or.) *Pl.* 63, *cr.* 13.
WELDISH, Kent, a demi-fox, erased, guttéed'eau. *Pl.* 30, *cr.* 9, (without cross.)
WELDON, Iri., a cross moline, erm. *Pl.* 89, *cr.* 8.
WELDON, Northumb., a demi-lion, rampant, ar. *Pl.* 67, *cr.* 10.

2 I

WELDON, Kent, the bust of Queen Elizabeth in her usual costume. *Bene factum.*

WELDONE, a blackamoor's head, couped at shoulders, ppr., bells in ears, wreathed about temples, or and az., stringed, of the last. *Pl.* 97, *cr.* 2.

WELDY, Eng., a horse's head, issuing, gu., furnished with waggon harness, or. *Pl.* 49, *cr.* 6.

WELFITT, a buck's head, couped, (charged on neck with two bends, invected.) *Servata fides cineri. Pl.* 91, *cr.* 14.

WELFORD, or WELSFORD, Heref., a leopard's head, per pale, or and gu. *Sic fidem teneo. Pl.* 92, *cr.* 13.

WELLAN, a demi-lion, in dexter an etoile, sinister resting on the wreath. *Pl.* 96, *cr.* 3, (etoile, *pl.* 141.)

WELLER, a demi-lion, rampant, in dexter an etoile. *Pl.* 89, *cr.* 10, (etoile, *pl.* 141.)

WELLER, Eng., a laurel-branch, fructed, ppr. *Pl.* 123, *cr.* 5.

WELLER, Kent, a greyhound's head, erased, sa., in mouth a rose, slipped, gu., leaves, vert. *Steady. Pl.* 30, *cr.* 7, (rose, *pl.* 92, *cr.* 15.)

WELLES, DE, an ostrich's head and wings, ar., ducally gorged, gu., in beak a horse-shoe, az. *Pl.* 28, *cr.* 13.

WELLES, Cornw., on a chapeau, az., turned up, erm., a (horse's head, ar., maned, or, ducally gorged, gu.) *Pl.* 102, *cr.* 7.

WELLES, Suss., a talbot, passant, ar., collared, sa., garnished, or. *Pl.* 65, *cr.* 2.

WELLES, or WELLS, Eng., a well, ppr. *Pl.* 70, *cr.* 12.

WELLES, Camb., a unicorn's head, erased, az., crined, armed, and ducally crowned, or, between wings, gold.

WELLESLEY, Marquess and Viscount, Earl of and Baron Mornington, all Iri.; and Baron Wellesley, G.B., (Wellesley): 1. A cubit arm, erect, vested gu., enfiled with a ducal coronet, or, in hand a staff, in bend, on top thereof the Union standard of Great Britain and Ireland, and underneath the Mysore standard, all ppr. 2. Out of a ducal coronet, or, a demi-lion, gu., holding a banner, purp., charged with an etoile, radiated, wavy, between eight spots of the royal tiger, in pairs, in saltier, or, staff, gold, surmounted by a pennon, ar., charged with a cross of St George. A motto over the crest in Hindustan characters. *Virtutis fortuna comes*—and—*Porro unum est necessarium.*

WELLESLEY, Baron Cowley. *See* COWLEY.

WELLESLEY, Duke of Wellington. *See* WELLINGTON.

WELLESLEY-LONG-TYLNEY, of Draycot, Wilts. ;
1. For *Wellesley*, out of a ducal coronet, or, a demi-lion, rampant, gu., holding a (forked) pennon. *Pl.* 86, *cr.* 11, (coronet, *same plate, cr.* 10.) 2. For *Long*, out of a ducal coronet, or, a demi-lion, rampant, ar. *Pl.* 45, *cr.* 7. 3. Also for *Long*, a lion's head, ar., in mouth a hand, erased. *Pl.* 107, *cr.* 9.

WELLESLEY-POLE, Baron Maryborough. *See* MARYBOROUGH.

WELLEY, Durh., out of a ducal coronet, a reindeer's head. *Pl.* 60, *cr.* 3.

WELLINGTON, Duke, Marquess, Earl of, and Viscount, Marquess of, and Baron Douro,

(Wellesley,) out of a ducal coronet, or, a demi-lion, rampant, gu., holding a (forked pennon, of the last, flowing to sinister, one third per pale, from the staff, ar., charged with the cross of St George.) *Virtutis fortuna comes. Pl.* 86, *cr.* 11, (coronet, *same plate, cr.* 10.)

WELLS, EDMUND-LIONEL, Esq., of The Grange, West Molesley, Surr.: 1. A demi-lion, rampant. *Pl.* 67, *cr.* 10. 2. A sword, erect, ar., hilt and pommel, or. *Semper paratu. Pl.* 105, *cr.* 1.

WELLS, a demi-lion, rampant, sa. *Pl.* 67, *cr.* 10.

WELLS, Devons., out of an embattlement, ppr., a demi-lion, (double-queued, sa., between paws two annulets interlaced, or.) *Virtute et honore. Pl.* 101, *cr.* 1.

WELLS, Holm-House, a demi-ostrich, wings displayed, ar., ducally gorged, or, on breast an escallop, sa., in mouth a horse-shoe, gold. *Pl.* 29, *cr.* 9, (without coronet.)

WELLS, Wel., a fire-beacon, ppr. *Pl.* 88, *cr.* 6.

WELLWOOD, of Garvock, Sco., trunk of an oak, sprouting branches, ppr. *Reviresco. Pl.* 92, *cr.* 8.

WELMAN-NOEL, of Poundsford Park, Somers., a demi-lion, rampant, ar., langued, gu., (between paws) a mullet, or. *Dei providentia juvat. Pl.* 89, *cr.* 10.

WELSH, Sco., trunk of oak-tree, on a branch thereof a hawk, all ppr. *Auspice numine. Pl.* 78, *cr.* 8.

WELSH, an antelope, sejant, ar., collared and chained, or, attired and unguled, gold. *Pl.* 115, *cr.* 3.

WELSH, on branch of a tree, an eagle, close, all ppr. *Pl.* 1, *cr.* 11, (eagle, *pl.* 7, *cr.* 11.)

WELSH, Worc., a griffin's head, erased, ar. *Pl.* 48, *cr.* 6.

WELSTEAD, Eng., out of a mural coronet, gold, a dexter hand, ppr., vested, sa., holding a sword, blade wavy, of the second. *Pl.* 65, *cr.* 10, (coronet, *pl.* 79, *cr.* 4.)

WELSTEAD, or WELSTED, Eng., a hind, trippant, ar. *Pl.* 20, *cr.* 14.

WELSTED, RICHARD, Esq., of Ballywalter, co. Cork, a hind, trippant. *Tutus prompto animo. Pl.* 20, *cr.* 14.

WELSTOD, a hind, trippant, ppr. *Pl.* 20, *cr.* 14.

WELTDEN, Northumb., a moor's head. *Pl.* 120, *cr.* 3.

WEMYSS, Bart., Sco., a sword, ppr. *Je pense. Pl.* 105, *cr.* 1.

WEMYSS, Earl of, and Baron Elcho, Earl of March, Viscount Peebles, and Baron Douglas, all Sco., (Wemyss-Charteris-Douglas,) a swan, ppr. *Je pense. This our charter*—and—*Forward. Pl.* 122, *cr.* 13, (without mount.)

WEMYSS, Bart., N.S., same crest. *Je pense.*

WEMYSS, Eng., an antelope's head, erased, gu. *Pl.* 24, *cr.* 7.

WEMYSS, Eng., a dexter hand grasping a scimitar, both ppr. *Nec viribus, nec numero. Pl.* 29, *cr.* 8.

WEMYTS, a swan, wings elevated. *Pl.* 46, *cr.* 5.

WENARD, Eng., a mullet, pierced, gu. *Pl.* 45, *cr.* 1.

WENDESLEY, Eng., an old man's head, in profile, couped at neck, ppr. *Pl.* 81, *cr.* 15.

WENDEY, Camb., a lion's head, erased, az., gorged with a collar, dancettée, or. *Pl.* 7, *cr.* 10.

WENDOVER, Wilts., a demi-lion, or, between paws an eagle's claw, sa., erased, gu., claws in base. *Pl.* 126, *cr.* 12, (claw, *pl.* 89, *cr.* 13.)

WENHAM, Suss., on a chapeau, gu., turned up, erm., a greyhound, sa., (collared, or.) *Pl.* 104, *cr.* 1.

WENINGTON, a still, ar.

WENLOCK, Baron, (Belby-Lawley-Thompson :) 1. For *Thompson*, an arm, embowed, quarterly, or and az., gauntlet, ppr., grasping the truncheon of a tilting-spear, or. *Pl.* 44, *cr.* 9. 2. For *Lawley*, a wolf, (statant,) sa. *Je veux bonne guerre. Pl.* 46, *cr.* 6.

WENLOCK, Salop, a griffin, passant, wings addorsed, or. *Pl.* 61, *cr.* 14, (without gorging.)

WENMAN, Iri., a cock's head, erased, az., crested and wattled, or. *Omnia bona bonis. Pl.* 92, *cr.* 3.

WENMAN, Oxon., same crest.

WENSLEY, a man's head, in profile, couped at (shoulders,) ppr. *Pl.* 81, *cr.* 15.

WENSLEYDALE, Baron, (Parke,) a talbot's head, couped, gu., eared and (gorged with a collar gemmelle, or, pierced in breast by a pheon, gu.) *Institutœ tenax. Pl.* 123, *cr.* 15.

WENTWORTH, Eng., out of a ducal coronet, or, a unicorn's head, ar., horned and maned, gold. *Pl.* 45, *cr.* 14.

WENTWORTH, Ess., Linc., Northamp., Suff., and Yorks.: 1. A griffin, passant, wings expanded, ar. *Pl.* 61, *cr.* 14, (without gorging.) 2. A griffin's head, erased, ar., ducally gorged, or, in beak a lily, ppr. *Pl.* 29, *cr.* 15, (lily, *pl.* 81, *cr.* 9.)

WENTWORTH, Suff., a leopard, sejant, erm., (ducally gorged, ringed and lined, or.) *Pl.* 10, *cr.* 13, (without flag.)

WENTWORTH, Yorks., a griffin, passant, wings addorsed, ar. *Pl.* 61, *cr.* 14, (without gorging.)

WENTWORTH, Bart., Linc., (on a mount, vert,) a griffin, passant, per pale, or and sa., (charged with two antique keys,) erect, per fess, counterchanged. *En Dieu est tout. Pl.* 61, *cr.* 14, (mount, *pl.* 98, *cr.* 13.)

WENTWORTH-FITZWILLIAM. See FITZWILLIAM, Earl.

WENTWORTH-VERNON. See VERNON.

WENWARD, Eng., a mullet, pierced, gu. *Pl.* 45, *cr.* 1.

WEOLEY, Glouc., on a chapeau, az., turned up, erm., a cockatrice, (close,) ar., combed and wattled, of the first. *Pl.* 103, *cr.* 9.

WERDEN, Chesh., a pegasus' head, gu., between wings, or. *Pl.* 19, *cr.* 13.

WERDEN, Lond., Lanc., and Chesh., a horse's head, between wings. *Pl.* 19, *cr.* 13.

WERDMAN, Bucks., a bear's head, erased, ar., muzzled and (collared, sa., lined and ringed,) or. *Pl.* 71, *cr.* 6.

WERE, Eng., a dexter arm, hand holding up a gem-ring, ppr., stoned, gu. *Pl.* 24, *cr.* 3, (ring, *pl.* 35, *cr.* 3.)

WERGE-EDWARDS, of Hexgrave Park, Notts., a demi-lion, rampant, gu., in dexter a pheon, purp., charged with three torteaux. *Pl.* 39, *cr.* 14, (pheon, *pl.* 141.)

WERGMAN, a dove, wings expanded, (in mouth an olive-branch, ppr., charged on body with an anchor, and on each wing with an etoile, sa.) *Pl.* 27, *cr.* 5.

WERKESLY, or WERKESLEY, Eng., a wyvern, az., sting and ears, or. *Pl.* 63, *cr.* 13.

WESCOMBE, Somers., out of a mural coronet, a griffin's head, or. *Pl.* 101, *cr.* 6, (without gorging.)

WESCOMBE, Linc., on the top of a rock, ppr., a bird, close, ar. *Pl.* 99, *cr.* 14.

WESCOPE, or WESTCOPE, Eng., two hands, issuing from clouds, conjoined, in fess, ppr. *Pl.* 53, *cr.* 11.

WESLEY, a cubit arm, enfiled with a ducal coronet, in hand, (two flags, in saltier, in bend sinister, each charged with a cross.) *Pl.* 47, *cr.* 8.

WESLEY, a wyvern, ppr. *God is love. Pl.* 63, *cr.* 13.

WEST, out of a ducal coronet, a wolf's head. *Pl.* 14, *cr.* 6, (coronet, *pl.* 128, *fig.* 3.)

WEST, a demi-dragon, ppr., (without tail, collared, or,) in dexter a sword, also ppr. *Pl.* 49, *cr.* 4.

WEST, Lond., out of a mural coronet, or, a griffin's head, ar., charged with a fess dancettée, sa. *Pl.* 101, *cr.* 6, (without gorging.)

WEST, Lond., (on a coronet, composed of ears of wheat, or,) an eagle, displayed, gu. *Pl.* 48, *cr.* 11.

WEST, Lond., a griffin's head, erased, per fess, erm. and gu., on the first a fess dancettée, sa. *Pl.* 48, *cr.* 6.

WEST, Lond., out of a mural coronet, or, an eagle's head, ar., gorged with a fess dancettée, sa. *Pl.* 121, *cr.* 11.

WEST, Bucks. and Suss., out of a ducal coronet, a griffin's head, all or. *Pl.* 54, *cr.* 14.

WEST, Northamp., out of a ducal coronet, or, a griffin's head, az., beaked and eared, gold, charged with a fleur-de-lis. *Pl.* 54, *cr.* 14, (fleur-de-lis, *pl.* 141.)

WEST, Suss., a griffin's head, erased, per pale, wavy, or and az. *Pl.* 48, *cr.* 6.

WEST, Warw., out of a ducal coronet, or, a griffin's head, pean, beaked and eared, or. *Pl.* 54, *cr.* 14.

WEST, Earl of Delaware. See DELAWARE.

WEST-ROBERTS, JAMES, Esq., of Alscot Park, Glouc., same crest. *Dux vitæ ratio.*

WESTALL, Eng., a buck's head, *Pl.* 91, *cr.* 14.

WESTBROOK, Surr., Suss., and Kent, an armed leg, couped above knee, ppr., purfled, or, spur, gold. *Pl.* 81, *cr.* 5.

WESTBY, JOSCELYN-TATE, Esq., of Whitehall, Upper Rawcliffe, Lanc., a martlet, sa., in beak three ears of wheat, or, stalked, vert. *Nec volenti, nec volanti. Pl.* 111, *cr.* 5, (wheat, *pl.* 102, *cr.* 1.)

WESTBY, of Thornhill, Iri., a martlet, sa., (in beak a sprig, or.) Same motto. *Pl.* 111, *cr.* 5.

WESTBY, Eng., an elephant's head, ppr. *Pl.* 35, *cr.* 13.

WESTCOMBE, out of a mural coronet, a griffin's head, both or. *Festina lente. Pl.* 101, *cr.* 6, (without gorging.)

WESTCOTE, Eng., a moor's head, couped, ppr., wreathed about temples, ar. and sa. *Renovato nomine. Pl.* 48, *cr.* 7.

WESTCOTT, or WESTCOT, Eng., two hands, issuing from clouds, conjoined, in fess, ppr. *Pl.* 53, *cr.* 11.

WESTELL, Berks., a cubit arm, erect, vested, and slashed, on hand, clenched, ppr., a falcon. *Pl.* 44, *cr.* 13, (falcon, *pl.* 67, *cr.* 3.)

WESTENRA, Iri., a lion, rampant, ar. *Pl.* 67, *cr.* 5.
WESTERNA, Baron Rossmore. *See* ROSSMORE.
WESTERDALE, Eng., two anchors, in saltier. *Pl.* 37, *cr.* 12.
WESTERN, Baron, (Western,) a demi-lion, rampant, in dexter a trefoil, slipped, vert *Nec temere, nec timide*. *Pl.* 39, *cr.* 14, (trefoil, *pl.* 141.)
WESTERNE, Lond., a demi-lion, rampant, in dexter a trefoil, slipped, vert. *Ib.*
WESTHORP, Yorks., an eagle's head, erm., beaked, or. *Pl.* 100, *cr.* 10.
WESTLEMORE, Eng., a tent, ar., flagged and garnished, gu. *Pl.* 111, *cr.* 14.
WESTLY, Eng., out of a ducal coronet, or, a hand, gu., holding a fleur-de-lis, az. *Pl.* 120, *cr.* 4.
WESTMEATH, Marquess and Earl of, Iri., (Nugent,) a cockatrice, rising, ppr., tail nowed, combed and wattled, gu. *Decrevi*. *Pl.* 63, *cr.* 15.
WESTMINSTER, Marquess of, Earl and Baron Grosvenor, Viscount Belgrave, and a Bart., (Grosvenor,) a talbot, (statant,) or. *Nobilitatis virtus, non stemma, character*. *Pl.* 120, *cr.* 8.
WESTMORE, Lanc., a lion, passant, gardant. *Pl.* 120, *cr.* 5.
WESTMORELAND, Eng., a wolf, passant, sa. *Pl.* 46, *cr.* 6.
WESTMORELAND, Eng., a fox, sejant, or. *Pl.* 87, *cr.* 4.
WESTMORELAND, Earl of, and Baron Burghersh, (Fane,) out of a ducal coronet, or, a bull's head, ar., pied, sa., armed, gold, on neck a rose, gu., barbed and seeded, ppr. *Ne vile fano*. *Pl.* 68, *cr.* 6, (rose, *pl.* 141.)
WESTON, a demi-lion, in dexter a trefoil, vert. *Pl.* 39, *cr.* 14, (trefoil, *pl.* 141.)
WESTON, a camel, sa., (collared,) or. *Pl.* 17, *cr.* 2.
WESTON, Surr., a wolf, passant, ar., (ducally gorged, or.) *Pl.* 46, *cr.* 6.
WESTON, Surr., a wolf's head, couped, sa. *Pl.* 92, *cr.* 15, (without rose.)
WESTON, Dors., an eagle, rising, regardant, sa., beaked and membered, or. *Craignez honte*. *Pl.* 35, *cr.* 8.
WESTON, Suff., an eagle's head, erased, beaked, gu., charged on breast with a crescent. *Pl.* 20, *cr.* 7, (crescent, *pl.* 141.)
WESTON-WEBBE, Swarsfield Court, Heref.: 1. For *Weston*, a Saracen's head. *Pl.* 19, *cr.* 1. 2. Out of a ducal coronet, or a demi-eagle, displayed, gu. *Pl.* 9, *cr.* 6.
WESTRIPP, a griffin's head. *Pl.* 38, *cr.* 3.
WESTROPE, Norf., out of a ducal coronet, or, a stag's head, ppr. *Pl.* 91, *cr.* 14, (coronet, *pl.* 29, *cr.* 7.)
WESTROPP, Eng., a dragon's head, gu. *Pl.* 87, *cr.* 12.
WESTROPP, JOHN, Esq., of Attyflin Park, co. Limerick, out of a ducal coronet, an eagle's head. *Je me tourne vers l'occident*. *Pl.* 20, *cr.* 12, (without pellet.)
WESTWOOD, Lond., a (cubit) arm, vested with leaves, vert, in hand, ppr., a club, gu., spiked, ar. *Pl.* 83, *cr.* 2.
WESTWOOD, Worc., a wild man's arm, vert, in hand a club, in bend, gu., spiked at end, or, the thicker part, ar. *Pl.* 123, *cr.* 10.

WETHERALL, or WETHERELL, Linc., a demi-lion, rampant, sa., holding a covered cup, or. *Pl.* 47, *cr.* 4, (cup, *pl.* 35, *cr.* 9.)
WETHERED, Herts., a goat's head, erased. *Pl.* 29, *cr.* 13.
WETHERELL, a lion's gamb, erased, sa., holding up a (covered) cup, or. *Pl.* 30, *cr.* 4.
WETHERTON, Eng., a lion's paw, ppr. *Pl.* 126, *cr.* 9,
WETHERTON, Northumb., a lion's gamb, erased, gu., charged with a cheveron, ar. *Pl.* 88, *cr.* 3.
WETHERTON, Eng., a lion's head, erased. *Pl.* 81, *cr.* 4.
WETNALL, Chesh., out of a ducal coronet, or, a goat's head, ar. *Pl.* 72, *cr.* 2.
WETTENHALL, Chesh., out of a ducal coronet, gold, an antelope's head, ar., attired, or. *Pl.* 24, *cr.* 7, (coronet, *same plate, cr.* 10.)
WETTYN, and WETTYNG, Eng., a lion's head, erased, or, vomiting flames, ppr. *Pl.* 20, *cr.* 3.
WEVER, Eng., a garb, in fess, or. *Pl.* 12, *cr.* 15.
WEY, a mailed arm, embowed, hand grasping a (baton.) *Pl.* 45, *cr.* 10.
WEYKES, a greyhound's head, erased, or, gorged with a bar-gemelle, gu., in mouth a man's leg, couped above knee, ar. *Pl.* 30, *cr.* 7.
WEYLAND, Eng., a dolphin, naiant, az. *Pl.* 48, *cr.* 9.
WEYLAND, Norf., a lion, rampant, sa. *Pl.* 67, *cr.* 5.
WEYMOUTH, a dexter arm, in armour, embowed, (cuffed, paly of six, ar. and gu., in hand three arrows, ppr., one in fess, and two in in saltier.) *Pl.* 96, *cr.* 6.
WEYMOUTH, Viscount. *See* BATH, Marquess of.
WHALE, Eng., a lion, rampant, per fess, gu. and ar. *Pl.* 67, *cr.* 5.
WHALEY, Eng., two anchors, in saltier, az. *Pl.* 37, *cr.* 12.
WHALLEY, a whale's head, erased and erect, sa. *Pl.* 96, *cr.* 8, (without gorging.)
WHALLEY, Hants and Leic., a whale's head, erased, in fess, sa.
WHANNELL, Sco., a dove and olive-branch, ppr. *Nuncia pacis*. *Pl.* 48, *cr.* 15.
WHARNCLIFFE, Baron, (Stuart-Wortley-Mackenzie:) 1. For *Mackenzie*, an eagle, rising from a rock, ppr. *Pl.* 61, *cr.* 1, (rock, *pl.* 79, *cr.* 2.) 2. For *Wortley*, an eagle's leg, plumed on thigh with three feathers, ar. 3. For *Stuart*, a demi-lion, rampant, gu. *Avito viret honore*. *Pl.* 67, *cr.* 10.
WHARTON, Durh., a bull's head, erased, ar., horned, or, charged with a trefoil, vert. *Pl.* 19, *cr.* 3, (trefoil, *pl.* 141.)
WHARTON, Eng., a bull's head, erased, per pale, ar. and sa., ducally gorged, per pale, gu. and ar. *Pl.* 68, *cr.* 6.
WHARTON, Yorks., on stump of tree, erased, a squirrel, sejant, both ppr., (collared, or, cracking a nut, gold.) *Pl.* 5, *cr.* 6.
WHARTON, Yorks., a bull's head, erased, or. *Pl.* 19, *cr.* 3.
WHARTON, Westm.: 1. A moor, kneeling, in coat of mail, all ppr., crowned, or, stabbing himself with a sword, of the first, hilt and pommel, gold. 2. A bull's head, erased, ar., attired, or, gorged with a ducal coronet, per pale, gold and gu. *Pl.* 68, *cr.* 6.
WHARTON, Cumb., Yorks., and Durh., a bull's head, erased, sa., armed, or. *Pl.* 19, *cr.* 3.

WHARTON, Westm., a bull's head, erased, ar., armed, or. *Pl.* 19, *cr.* 3.

WHARTON-MYDDLETON. *See* MYDDLETON.

WHARTON-SMITH, Devonport, on a wreath, ar. and sa., a lion, sejant, of the first, armed, of the second, langued, gu., (in mouth a battle-spear, reversed, ppr., charged on neck with a plain label of three points, or.) *Pl.* 126, *cr.* 15.

WHATELY, Eng., a stag's head, ppr. *Pl.* 91, *cr.* 14.

WHATLEY, Eng., a lion, rampant, or, in dexter a fleur-de-lis, sa. *Pl.* 87, *cr.* 6.

WHATMAN, Kent, a demi-lion, rampant, ppr., between paws a pheon. *Pl.* 47, *cr.* 4, (pheon, *pl.* 141.)

WHATTON, out of a ducal coronet, ar., an eagle, rising, sa., beaked, or. *Pl.* 19, *cr.* 9.

WHEAT, or WHEATE, Glouc., a stag's head, couped, or, in mouth (three ears of wheat,) ppr. *Pl.* 100, *cr.* 8.

WHEATHILL, Eng., a sword and ear of wheat, bladed, vert, in saltier. *Pl.* 50, *cr.* 4.

WHEATHILL, two arms, az., in hands, ppr., a garb, or. *Pl.* 113, *cr.* 12, (garb, *pl.* 48, *cr.* 10.)

WHEATLEY, Eng., on a rock, a fire-beacon, ppr. *Pl.* 89, *cr.* 9.

WHEATLEY, Somers., a stag's head, cabossed. *Pl.* 36, *cr.* 1.

WHEATLEY, Suss., two arms, embowed, vested, az., between hands, ppr., a garb, or. *Pl.* 45, *cr.* 2, (garb, *pl.* 48, *cr.* 10.)

WHEATLING, three garbs, erect, banded. *Pl.* 96, *cr.* 14.

WHEELER, or WHELER, Eng., a camel's head. *Pl.* 109, *cr.* 9.

WHEELER, Lond., a goat's herd, erased, vert, attired, or, in mouth a fleur-de-lis, gold. *Pl.* 29, *cr.* 13, (fleur-de-lis, *pl.* 117, *cr.* 3.)

WHEELER, on a ducal coronet, a demi-eagle, displayed with two heads. *Pl.* 4, *cr.* 6.

WHEELER, Iri., a rose-branch, ppr., flowered, gu. *Pl.* 23, *cr.* 2.

WHEELER, Surr., a camel's head, erased, vert, bezantée. *Pl.* 120, *cr.* 12, (without gorging.)

WHEELER, or WHELER, Worc. and Warw., on a ducal coronet, or, an eagle, displayed, gu. *Pl.* 48, *cr.* 11, (coronet, *pl.* 9, *cr.* 6.)

WHEELER, or WHELER, Worc. and Warw., on a five-leaved coronet, or, an eagle, displayed, sa. *Pl.* 48, *cr.* 11, (coronet, *pl.* 23, *cr.* 11.)

WHEELER, Middx., out of a mural coronet, or, a griffin's head, ar. *Pl.* 101, *cr.* 6, (without gorging.)

WHEELER, Salop, a lion's head, couped, ar., on neck a Catherine-wheel, gu. *Pl.* 126, *cr.* 1, (wheel, *pl.* 141.)

WHEELTON, Lond. and Surr., out of a crown vallary, or, a demi-lion, ppr., (gorged with a collar gemelle, sa., between paws a Catherine-wheel, or.) *Deo duce, sequor.* *Pl.* 126, *cr.* 12, (crown, *pl.* 2, *cr.* 2.)

WHELAN, Kent, on a mount, vert, a stag, lodged, regardant, erm., attired, ar., fore-dexter resting on an escallop, az., in mouth a trefoil, ppr. *Pl.* 51, *cr.* 9, (escallop and trefoil, *pl.* 141.)

WHELDALE, Eng., an open book, ppr. *Pl.* 15, *cr.* 12.

WHELER, Rev. CHARLES, of Otterden Place, Kent, and Ledstone Hall, Yorks.: 1. For *Medhurst*, a martlet, (charged with a fleur-de-lis, in beak an oak-leaf and acorn.) *Pl.* 111, *cr.* 5. 2. For *Wheler*, out of a mural coronet, or, a griffin's head, erased, ar. *Pl.* 101, *cr.* 6, (without gorging.)

WHELER, a camel's head, erased, az. *Pl.* 120, *cr.* 12.

WHELER, Ess. and Linc., a dove, wings addorsed, ar., (in mouth a branch, vert, fructed, or.) *Pl.* 55, *cr.* 11, (without stump.)

WHELER, Bart., Warw., out of a ducal coronet, or, a spread eagle, gu. *Facie tenus.* *Pl.* 87, *cr.* 11, (coronet, *pl.* 128, *fig.* 3.)

WHELLING, Iri., a cross crosslet, ar., surmounted by a sword, in bend sinister, ppr. *Pl.* 66, *cr.* 8, (sword, *pl.* 89, *cr.* 14.)

WHELPDALE, Eng., in hand a hawk's lure, ppr. *Pl.* 44, *cr.* 2.

WHETCROFT, Suss., a garb, or, charged with a martlet, sa. *Pl.* 48, *cr.* 10, (martlet, *pl.* 69, *cr.* 15.)

WHETE, or WHEATE, Warw. and Staffs., a stag's head, ppr., (on neck three bars, or, in mouth three ears of wheat, gold.) *Pl.* 100, *cr.* 8.

WHETENHALL, Kent, out of a ducal coronet, gu., an ibex's head, ar. *Pl.* 72, *cr.* 9.

WHETERTON, Eng., a lion's head, erased. *Pl.* 81, *cr.* 4.

WHETERTON, Eng., a lion's paw, ppr. *Pl.* 126, *cr.* 9.

WHETHAM, Eng., an eagle, displayed, sa. *Pl.* 48, *cr.* 11.

WHETHAM, Eng., a cubit arm, in armour, in hand a sword, all ppr., hilt and pommel, or. *Pl.* 63, *cr.* 5.

WHETLEY, Norf., a leopard's head, erased, gardant, or, flames issuing from ears and mouth, (collared, lined, and ringed, az.) *Pl.* 112, *cr.* 9.

WHETNALL, Eng., out of a cup, or, a nosegay, ppr. *Pl.* 102, *cr.* 12.

WHETTELL, Suff., a talbot's head, erased, or, eared, collared, and ringed, ar., the collar studded. *Pl.* 2, *cr.* 15.

WHETSTONE, Ess., an arm, in armour, embowed, sa., garnished, or, in hand a broken tilting-spear, gold, head, ar., (streamers, gu.) *Pl.* 44, *cr.* 9.

WHETSTONE, Ess., a bugle-horn, sa., stringed, or. *Pl.* 48, *cr.* 12.

WHETWELL, Eng., in hand a sword, ppr. *Pl.* 21, *cr.* 10.

WHICHCOTE, Bart., Lond., a boar's head, erased and erect, gu., langued, az., armed, or. *Juste et droit.* *Pl.* 21, *cr.* 7.

WHICHCOTT, Linc., a boar's head, erased, in pale, gu., langued, ar., armed, or, *Pl.* 21, *cr.* 7.

WHICKER, a lion, rampant, holding a cross pattée, fitched, or, *Pl.* 125, *cr.* 2.

WHIELDON, GEORGE, Esq., of Springfield House, Warw., and of the Grove, Hants, on a mount, vert, between two branches of oak, ppr., a fer-de-moline, in fess, sa., thereon a parrot, perched, vert, collared, gu., in dexter a pear, stalked and leaved. *Virtus præstantior auro.*

WHIGHT, out of a ducal coronet, or, a dragon's head, vert. *Pl.* 93, *cr.* 15, (without flames.)

WHINFIELD, Eng., a horse's head, couped, gu., furnished, or. *Pl.* 92, *cr.* 1.

WHIPPY, a horse's head, erased. *Pl.* 81, *cr.* 6.
WHIRPLE, Norf., an elephant, (passant,) erm. *Pl.* 56, *cr.* 14.
WHISHAW, Eng., an eagle's head, couped, per fess, sa. and or. *Pl.* 100, *cr.* 10.
WHISTLER, Eng., a harp, or, stringed, sa. *Pl.* 104, *cr.* 15.
WHITACRE, Warw. and Yorks., a cubit arm, erect, in hand a sword, all ppr. *Pl.* 21, *cr.* 10.
WHITACRE, Wilts., a horse, passant, or. *Pl.* 15, *cr.* 14.
WHITAKER, out of a ducal coronet, a stag's head. *Pl.* 91, *cr.* 14, (coronet, *pl.* 29, *cr.* 7.)
WHITAKER, THOMAS-HORDERN, Esq., of The Holme, Lanc., an arm, in mail armour, hand grasping a flaming-sword, ppr. *Pl.* 2, *cr.* 8, (sword, *pl.* 58, *cr.* 11.)
WHITAKER, the Rev. CHARLES, of Symonstone Hall, Lanc., a dexter arm, hand grasping a flaming-sword, sleeve, or. *Robur atque fides. Pl.* 120, *cr.* 1, (sword, *pl.* 58, *cr.* 11.)
WHITAKER, Eng., a tent, gu., furnished, or, pennon, az. *Pl.* 111, *cr.* 14.
WHITAKER, Heref., a horse, passant, ar. *Pl.* 15, *cr.* 14.
WHITBREAD, Eng., a water-bouget, az. *Pl.* 14, *cr.* 12.
WHITBREAD, Beds., a hind's head, erased, gu. *Pl.* 6, *cr.* 1.
WHITBREAD, WILLIAM-HENRY, Esq., of Southill, Beds., and Purfleet, Ess., same crest.
WHITBREAD, JACOB-WILLIAM-CAREY, Esq., of Loudham Park, Suff., same crest. *Virtute non astutiâ.*
WHITBREAD, Lond., a fox's head, couped, gu. *Pl.* 91, *cr.* 9.
WHITBRED, Ess., a hind's head, erased, gu. *Pl.* 6, *cr.* 1.
WHITBROKE, Hunts., a bull's head, erased, ar., armed and ducally gorged, or. *Pl.* 68, *cr.* 6.
WHITBROKE, Salop, a bull's head, cabossed, ar., attires, az., tipped, or. *Pl.* 111, *cr.* 6.
WHITBY, THOMAS-EDWARD, Esq., of Cresswell Hall, Staffs., a pheon, in pale, piercing a serpent. *Pl.* 93, *cr.* 7.
WHITBY, Eng., a talbot's head, erased, collared and lined, or. *Pl.* 2, *cr.* 15.
WHITBY, an arrow, in pale, barb downward, environed by a serpent. *Pl.* 30, *cr.* 3, (arrow, *pl.* 56, *cr.* 13.)
WHITCHURCH, Eng., a lion's head, erased, ppr. *Pl.* 81, *cr.* 4.
WHITCOMB, Eng., out of a ducal coronet, ar., a demi-eagle, per pale, sa. and ar., wings counterchanged. *Pl.* 19, *cr.* 9.
WHITE, WILLIAM-LOGAN, Esq., of Kellerstain, Mid-Lothian, an arm, supporting a garland of laurel. *Virtute parta. Pl.* 118, *cr.* 4.
WHITE, in hand a rose-branch. *Pl.* 118, *cr.* 9.
WHITE, Eng., on a ducal coronet, an eagle, displayed, ppr. *Pl.* 48, *cr.* 11, (coronet, *pl.* 9, *cr.* 6.)
WHITE, a demi-wolf, sa., (gorged with a wreath of vine-leaves, charged on shoulder with three ermine-spots, two and one, or.) *Pl.* 56, *cr.* 8, (without spear.)
WHITE, MATTHEW-ESMONDE, Esq., of Scarnagh, co. Wexford, three arrows, one (in fess,) and two in saltier, ppr. *Sis justus, et ne timeas. Pl.* 43, *cr.* 14.
WHITE, a garb. *Pl.* 48, *cr.* 10.

WHITE, SAMUEL-WHITE, Esq., of Charlton Marshall, Dors., a dexter arm, embowed, couped above elbow, vested, or, cuff, ar., hand holding by the legs an eagle, volant, ppr., beaked, gold, between two roses, gu., slipped, ppr. *Virtus omnia vincit.*
WHITE, an arm, from elbow, in bend sinister, hand grasping a sword.
WHITE, an arm, embowed, vested, on the hand, clenched, an ostrich, statant, wings expanded. *Pl.* 39, *cr.* 1, (ostrich, *pl.* 16, *cr.* 2.)
WHITE, Iri., a cubit arm, erect, in hand a sprig, all ppr., bearing three roses, gu. *Pl.* 69, *cr.* 10, (without cloud.)
WHITE, Iri., a dexter arm, in armour, in hand a sword, all ppr. *Pl.* 2, *cr.* 8.
WHITE, a demi-lion, rampant, gu., holding a flag, ar., (charged with a cross,) of the first, staff, ppr. *Pl.* 86, *cr.* 11, (without coronet.)
WHITE, out of a ducal coronet, or, a bear's head, muzzled, sa. *Pl.* 6, *cr.* 6.
WHITE, a wolf, sejant, ppr. *Pl.* 110, *cr.* 4.
WHITE, out of a ducal coronet, per pale, or and gu., a camel's head, az., eared, gold, (charged on neck with a wreath, of the first and second.) *Pl.* 55, *cr.* 5, (without collar or crown.)
WHITE, Eng., a popinjay's head, vert, between wings, the dexter, or, the sinister, ar., (in beak a rose-branch, ppr.) *Pl.* 94, *cr.* 2.
WHITE, an eagle, preying on a pea-hen, both ppr. *Pl.* 61, *cr.* 7.
WHITE, Yorks., an ostrich, ar. *Pl.* 64, *cr.* 3, (without coronet.)
WHITE, Lond., a lion's head, erased, quarterly, or and az. *Pl.* 81, *cr.* 4.
WHITE, Lond., Middx., and Yorks., out of a mural coronet, gu., a boar's head, ar., crined, or. *Pl.* 102, *cr.* 14, (coronet, *pl.* 6, *cr.* 2.)
WHITE, Northamp., an olive-branch, issuing from a mount, thereon a dove, (in mouth a narcissus-flower, slipped and leaved,) all ppr. *Pl.* 104, *cr.* 6, (branch, *pl.* 98, *cr.* 8.)
WHITE, Middx., a lion's head, erased. *Pl.* 81, *cr.* 4.
WHITE, Surr., out of a ducal coronet, a dragon's head. *Pl.* 93, *cr.* 15, (without flames.)
WHITE, Dors., Derbs., and Hants, a goat's head, gu., attired, az., in mouth an acorn, of the last, leaved, vert. *Pl.* 105, *cr.* 14, (acorn, *pl.* 22, *cr.* 1.)
WHITE, Dors., an arm, embowed, vested, or, charged with two bends wavy, gu., hand holding a stork by the legs, wings expanded, ppr., beaked and legged, gold.
WHITE, Dors., (on a mount, vert,) a curlew, close, ar. *Pl.* 52, *cr.* 12.
WHITE, Cornw., a griffin's head, erased, sa. *Pl.* 48, *cr.* 6.
WHITE, Cornw., an ermine, (sejant,) ppr. *Pl.* 9, *cr.* 5.
WHITE, Devons., an eagle, preying on a pheasant, all ppr. *Pl.* 61, *cr.* 7, (pheasant, *pl.* 76, *cr.* 6.)
WHITE, Derbs., an ermine, ppr. *Pl.* 9, *cr.* 5.
WHITE, Durh., Yorks., and Northumb., a cock's head, erased, sa., combed and wattled, gu. *Pl.* 92, *cr.* 3.
WHITE, Lond. and Glouc., a lion's head, erased, or, collared, vairé, gold and vert. *Pl.* 7, *cr.* 10.
WHITE, Berks. and Hants, an ostrich, ar., beaked and legged, or. *Pl.* 64, *cr.* 3, (without coronet.)

WHITE, Bucks, a lion's head, couped, or, (vulned in neck, gu.) *Pl.* 126, *cr.* 1.
WHITE, Cambs. and Suss., a talbot. *Pl.* 120, *cr.* 8.
WHITE, Bart., Yorks., out of a ducal coronet, ar., a demi-eagle, wings expanded, sa. *Pl.* 9, *cr.* 6.
WHITE, Earl of Bantry. *See* BANTRY.
WHITE-CORRANCE, of Parham and Londham Hall, Suff.: 1. For *White*, a wolf's head, erased, sa. *Pl.* 14, *cr.* 6. 2. A raven supporting with dexter an escutcheon, sa., charged with a leopard's face, or. *Pl.* 6, *cr.* 11.
WHITEBALL, Derbs., a large plume of feathers, consisting of two rows, ar. and az., banded, counter-componée, sa. and gu. *Pl.* 64, *cr.* 5.
WHITEBALL, Derbs., out of a mural coronet, chequy, gu., and sa., a demi-lion, ar., collared, of the first, in dexter a (broken) falchion, ppr. *Pl.* 41, *cr.* 13, (coronet, *pl.* 112, *cr.* 5.)
WHITEBALL, Staffs., out of a mural coronet, ar., a demi-lion, rampant, or, in dexter an ostrich-feather, of the first. *Pl.* 17, *cr.* 7, (feather, *pl.* 58, *cr.* 7.)
WHITEBREAD, Ess., a hind's head, gu. *Pl.* 21, *cr.* 9.
WHITEFOORD, a garb, gu., banded, or. *Ubique aut nusquam*. *Pl.* 48, *cr.* 10.
WHITEFOORD, Sco., on a garb, a pigeon, statant, all ppr. *D'en haut*. *Pl.* 112, *cr.* 10.
WHITEFOORD, on a garb, a dove. *Pl.* 112, *cr.* 10.
WHITEFORD, CHARLES-COLLEY, Esq., of Thornhill, Devons., a garb, az., banded, or, (therefrom suspended an escutcheon, ar., charged, with a bend, sa., cottised, az.) *Virtute superanda fortuna*. *Pl.* 48, *cr.* 10.
WHITEHEAD, a cross crosslet, gu. *Ad finem fidelis*. *Pl.* 66, *cr.* 8.
WHITEHEAD, Hants, a wolf, sejant, ar. *Pl.* 110, *cr.* 4.
WHITEHORN, five spears, sa., headed, or, one in pale, and four in saltire. *Pl.* 54, *cr.* 15, (spears, *pl.* 95, *cr.* 8.)
WHITEHOUSE, Eng., a lion's paw, erect and erased, ppr. *Pl.* 126, *cr.* 9.
WHITEHURST, Eng., a cross crosslet, fitched, sa., between two (palm)-branches, vert. *Pl.* 37, *cr.* 14.
WHITELAW, Sco., a bee, erect, ppr. *Solertia ditat*. *Pl.* 100, *cr.* 3.
WHITELING, a salmon, naiant, or, (in mouth a rose, gu., stalked and leaved, vert.) *Pl.* 85, *cr.* 7.
WHITELOCK, on a castle, ar., a bird, wings displayed, or. *Pl.* 90, *cr.* 2, (bird, *pl.* 124, *cr.* 13.)
WHITELOCK, Eng., in dexter hand a dagger, ppr. *Pl.* 28, *cr.* 4.
WHITELOCKE, Berks., on a mural coronet, vair, an eagle, wings expanded, or. *Pl.* 126, *cr.* 7, (coronet, *pl.* 33, *cr.* 5.)
WHITELOCKE, Eng., between two swords, in saltire, ppr., a cross crosslet, fitched, sa. *Pl.* 42, *cr.* 5.
WHITEMAN, a tower, gu., masoned, or. *Pl.* 12, *cr.* 5.
WHITEMAN, (on stump of tree), a buck. *Pl.* 88, *cr.* 9.
WHITENHALL, a crescent, gu., charged with three bezants, between the points a garb, or. *Pl.* 84, *cr.* 1, (garb, *pl.* 48, *cr.* 10.)

WHITERAGE, a talbot's head, couped, gu., (collared, or,) between six fern slips, ar. *Pl.* 123, *cr.* 15, (fern, *pl.* 80, *cr.* 1.)
WHITEWAY, Eng., out of a tower, ppr., a demi-lion, gu. *Pl.* 42, *cr.* 4.
WHITEWAY, Iri., in hand a sword, ppr. *Dum vivo, spero*. *Pl.* 21, *cr.* 9.
WHITEWAY, Dors., on a ducal coronet, or, a lion's gamb, erased, (in fess,) gu. *Pl.* 67, *cr.* 7.
WHITFIELD, Eng., an anchor, az., entwined by a serpent, or. *Pl.* 35, *cr.* 14.
WHITFIELD, Lond., Surr., Kent, Northamp., and Northumb., out of a palisado coronet, ar., a stag's head, or. *Pl.* 91, *cr.* 14, (coronet, *pl.* 128, *fig.* 21.)
WHITFORD, Eng., a cross Calvary, on three grieces, or. *Pl.* 49, *cr.* 2.
WHITFORD, Sco., on a garb, or, a dove, ar., beaked, gu. *Tout est d'en haut*. *Pl.* 112, *cr.* 10.
WHITGIFT, Surr., out of a ducal coronet, or, a lion's gamb, ar., holding a (chaplet, vert.) *Pl.* 88, *cr.* 8.
WHITGRAVE, Ess. and Staffs., out of a ducal coronet, gu., a demi-antelope, or. *Pl.* 34, *cr.* 8, (coronet, *same plate, cr.* 15.)
WHITGREAVE, GEORGE-THOMAS, Esq., of Moseley Court, Staffs.: 1. Out of a ducal coronet, gu., a demi-antelope, or. *Pl.* 34, *cr.* 8, (coronet, *same plate, cr.* 15.) 2. *Of augmentation*, out of a ducal coronet, a sceptre, in pale, or, surmounted by a branch of oak, ppr., and a rose, gu., slipped, in saltier, also ppr. *Regem defendere victum*.
WHITHAM, Eng., a rose, or, stalked and leaved, vert. *Pl.* 105, *cr.* 7.
WHITHERING, or WITHERING, Staffs., a raven, wings expanded, sa., beaked, and ducally gorged, or. *Pl.* 44, *cr.* 11, (raven, *pl.* 110, *cr.* 13.)
WHITHERS, Wilts., out of a ducal coronet, or, a staff, raguly, sa. *Pl.* 78, *cr.* 15.
WHITING, a demi-eagle, with two heads, displayed, ppr. *Pl.* 4, *cr.* 6, (without charge.)
WHITINGHAM, Lanc. and Yorks., a cubit arm, erect, (vested, ar.,) in hand, ppr., an open book, of the first, garnished, or. *Pl.* 82, *cr.* 5, (without cloud.)
WHITINGHAM, Eng., a tower, ppr. *Pl.* 12, *cr.* 5.
WHITINGTON, a wyvern's head, bezantée, (in mouth the point of a spear, in bend, embrued.) *Pl.* 121, *cr.* 9.
WHITINGTON, Eng., a dolphin, haurient, ar. *Pl.* 14, *cr.* 10.
WHITINGTON, Staffs., out of a ducal coronet, gold, a goat's head, ar., armed, or. *Pl.* 72, *cr.* 2.
WHITINGTON, Glouc., a lion's head, couped, sa. *Pl.* 126, *cr.* 1.
WHITINGTON, Glouc., a lion's head, erased, sa. *Pl.* 81, *cr.* 4.
WHITLEY, or WHITLIE, Eng., between two swords, in saltier, ppr., a cross crosslet, fitched, gu. *Pl.* 42, *cr.* 5.
WHITLOCK, Eng., a cross pattée, between wings, gu. *Pl.* 29, *cr.* 14.
WHITLOCK, on a castle, ar., a bird, wings displayed, or. *Pl.* 90, *cr.* 2, (bird, *pl.* 124, *cr.* 13.)
WHITMARSH, Eng., a lion's gamb, erased, ppr. *Pl.* 126, *cr.* 9.

WHITMORE, Lond., an arm, erect, couped at elbow, vested, or, turned up, az., in hand, ppr., a cinquefoil, gold, leaved, vert, all between wings, of the fourth. Pl. 11, cr. 11, (cinquefoil, pl. 101, cr. 5.)

WHITMORE, Chesh., out of a ducal coronet, or, a lion's head, ar., (gorged with a plain collar, az., tied behind with a bow.) Pl. 90, cr. 9.

WHITMORE, THOMAS-CHARLTON, Esq., of Apley, Salop: 1. A falcon, on stump of tree, with a branch springing from dexter side, all ppr. Pl. 78, cr. 8. 2. An arm, couped at elbow and erect, vested, or, turned up, az., in hand, ppr., a cinquefoil, gold, leaved, vert, all between wings, of the fourth. Pl. 11, cr. 11, (cinquefoil, pl. 101, cr. 5.)

WHITMORE, Lond., Chesh., and Salop, same as crest 1 above.

WHITNEY, THOMAS-ANNESLEY, Esq., of Merton, Wexford, a bull's head, couped, sa., armed, ar., points, gu. Pl. 120, cr. 7.

WHITNEY, Chesh. and Glouc., same crest.

WHITNEY, Heref., same crest. Magnanimiter crucem sustine.

WHITNEY, Iri., a Roman soldier's head, helmeted, ppr. Pl. 33, cr. 14.

WHITNEY, a bull's head, couped, sa., armed, or, points, gu. Pl. 120, cr. 7.

WHITSHED-HAWKINS, Bart., Iri., a demi-lion, per pale, indented, ar. and gu., (in dexter a trefoil, slipped, vert.) Pl. 39, cr. 14.

WHITSHED, Iri., same crest.

WHITSON, Parkhill, Sco., a dexter arm, in armour, embowed, hand grasping a broken lance, (round point a "favour," ppr.) Cœlitus vires. Pl. 44, cr. 9.

WHITSON, Sco., an arm, in armour, embowed, ppr., in hand a tilting-spear, broken in middle, or, (ribbons waving at top, gu.) Pl. 45, cr. 10.

WHITTAKER, Dors. and Wilts., same crest.

WHITTAKER, JOHN-ABRAHAM, Esq., of Newcastle Court, Radnor, a horse, passant, ar. Pl. 15, cr. 14.

WHITTAKER, a sea-gull, wings (expanded,) ppr. Pl. 79, cr. 11.

WHITTAKER, Kent, a horse, passant, or. Pl. 15, cr. 14.

WHITTELEY, three garbs, gu., banded, or. Pl. 96, cr. 14.

WHITTELL, or WHITTELLE, and WHITTLE, Lanc., two arms, embowed, vested, az., cuffed, erm., in hands, ppr., a garb, or. Pl. 10, cr. 9, (garb, pl. 48, cr. 10; vesting, pl. 39, cr. 1.)

WHITTELL, Lond., a talbot's head, erased, or, collared, eared, and ringed, ar. Pl. 2, cr. 15.

WHITTER, Suss., an arm, in armour, embowed, hand grasping a battle-axe, ppr. Pl. 121, cr. 14.

WHITTEWRONGE, a Saracen's head, affrontée, wreathed, ppr. Pl. 97, cr. 2.

WHITTINGHAM, a lion's head, couped. Pl. 126, cr. 1.

WHITTINGHAM, a dexter cubit arm, (vested, or, cuffed, gu.,) in hand, ppr., an open book, sa., leaved and tasselled, vert, and on the first page, a pomegranate, gold. Pl. 82, cr. 5, (without cloud; pomegranate, pl. 67, cr. 8.)

WHITTINGHAM, Durh., a cubit arm, erect, ppr., vested, ar., cuffed, az., in hand an open book, of the second, edges of the leaves and clasps, or. Pl. 82, cr. 5, (without cloud; vesting, pl. 32, cr. 6.)

WHITTINGTON, a dragon's head, sa., bezantée, issuing from a rose, gu., (in mouth) a spear, head, ar., the point in chief, guttée-de-sang. Pl. 121, cr. 9, (rose, pl. 69, cr. 6.)

WHITTINGTON, Staffs., a goat's head, erased, ar., (ducally gorged,) and armed, or. Pl. 29, cr. 13.

WHITTINGTON, Linc., an antelope's head, erased, ar., (ducally gorged) and armed, or. Pl. 24, cr. 7.

WHITTINGTON, Eng., a dove and olive-branch, ppr. Pl. 48, cr. 15.

WHITTLE, Eng., a bear's head and neck, sa., muzzled, gu. Pl. 2, cr. 9.

WHITTLEBURY, Eng., a fountain, throwing up water, ppr. Pl. 49, cr. 8.

WHITTON, Eng., in the sea, a ship in full sail, ppr. Pl. 109, cr. 8.

WHITTUCK, JOSEPH-WHITTUCK, Esq., of Hanham Hall, Glouc., a boar's head, erased, or. Messis ab alto. Pl. 16, cr. 11.

WHITTUCK, Bristol, a hand holding a pen, all ppr. Pl. 26, cr. 13.

WHITWANGE, Northumb., a hedgehog, ppr. Pl. 32, cr. 9.

WHITWELL, Eng., a lion's head, erased, or. Pl. 81, cr. 4.

WHITWELL, Northamp., a griffin's head, erased, or. Pl. 48, cr. 6.

WHITWICK, a demi-tiger, ar., crined, sa., holding a pheon, or. Pl. 53, cr. 10, (pheon, pl. 141.)

WHITWICKE, Berks. and Staffs., same crest.

WHITWIKE, Staffs., a demi-lion, or, gorged with a mural coronet, holding a pheon, gu. Pl. 87, cr. 15, (pheon, pl. 141.)

WHITWONG, a hedgehog, or, bristled, sa. Pl. 32, cr. 9.

WHITWORTH, out of a ducal coronet, or, a garb, gu. Pl. 62, cr. 1, (coronet, pl. 128, fig 3.)

WHORWOOD, Eng., a demi-griffin, issuing from a tower, all ppr. Pl. 68, cr. 11.

WHORWOOD, Oxon. and Staffs., a buck's head, cabossed, sa., (in mouth an acorn-branch, vert, fructed, or.) Pl. 36, cr. 1.

WHYDON, Devons., out of a ducal coronet, ar., a demi-swan, sa., wings expanded, or, beaked, gold. Pl. 100, cr. 7.

WHYT, Sco., a boar's head, ppr. Per ardua fama. Pl. 48, cr. 2.

WHYT, Eng., a boar's head, couped at shoulders, ar., bristled and unguled, or. Pl. 20, cr. 5.

WHYTE, JOHN-JAMES, Esq., of Newtown Manor, co. Leitrim, a dexter arm, hand holding a long straight sword. Fortiter sed feliciter. Pl. 34, cr. 7.

WHYTE, JOHN, Esq., of Loughbrickland, co. Down, a demi-lion, rampant, holding a flag, (ensigned with a cross.) Echel Coryg. Pl. 86, cr. 11, (without coronet.)

WHYTE, Eng., a lion's head, couped, gu. Pl. 126, cr. 1.

WHYTEHEAD, HENRY-YATES, Esq., of Crayke, Yorks., a fox, sejant, ar. Pl. 87, cr. 4.

WHYTING, Eng., a boar's head. Pl. 48, cr. 2.

WHYTOCK, Sco., a dexter hand holding a pen. Pl. 26, cr. 13.

WHYTT, Sco., a dexter arm, embowed, in hand a wreath of laurel, ppr. Virtute parta. Pl. 118, cr. 4.

WHYTT, Sco., a dexter hand, erect, holding a heart, ppr. Candidiora pectora. Pl. 59, cr. 12.

WIBERD, Ess., a demi-lion, rampant, or, ducally crowned, gold. *Pl.* 61, *cr.* 4, (without branch.)

WICHINGHAM, and WITCHINGHAM, Suff., an arm, erect, in hand an escallop. *Pl.* 57, *cr.* 6.

WICHLAFE, or WICHLAFFE, Devons., a goat's head, erased, per pale, ar. and sa., (charged with two crescents, in fess, counterchanged,) in mouth a rose-branch, stalked and leaved, vert, fructed, or. *Pl.* 29, *cr.* 13, (rose, *pl.* 92, *cr.* 15.)

WICKENDEN, Eng., a dexter hand holding a cross crosslet, fitched, az. *Pl.* 99, *cr.* 1.

WICKENS, a talbot, current, ar., spotted, sa., between two trees, vert, fructed, or.

WICKHAM, Kent, Berks., and Oxon., a bull's head, sa., armed, or, (charged on neck with two cheverons, ar.) *Pl.* 63, *cr.* 11.

WICKHAM, JAMES-ANTHONY, Esq., of North Hill House, Frome, Somers., same crest. *Manners maketh man.*

WICKHAM, of Chatham and Stroud, Kent, a bull's head, erased, sa., armed, or. *Manners makyth man.* *Pl.* 19, *cr.* 3.

WICKHAM, a bull's head, couped, sa., armed, or, (gorged on neck with two bars, gold.) *Pl.* 120, *cr.* 7.

WICKHAM, Eng., out of a tower, sa., a martlet, volant, or. *Pl.* 107, *cr.* 6.

WICKLIFF, or WYCKLIFFE, a buck's head, ppr., between horns a cross crosslet, fitched. *Pl.* 24, *cr.* 9.

WICKLIFFE, Eng., an anchor and cable, ppr. *Pl.* 42, *cr.* 12.

WICKLOW, Earl of, and Viscount, Baron Clonmore, (Howard,) on a chapeau, gu., turned up, erm., a lion, statant, gardant, or, (ducally gorged, gu., in mouth an arrow, ppr.) *Inservi Deo et lœtare*—and—*Certum pete finem.* *Pl.* 105, *cr.* 5, (without crown.)

WICKS, Eng., on a chapeau, a garb, ppr. *Pl.* 62, *cr.* 1.

WICKSTEAD, or WICKSTED, Eng., two anchors, in saltier, sa. *Pl.* 37, *cr.* 12.

WICKSTED, Cambs., two snakes, ppr., entwined round a garb, or. *Pl.* 36, *cr.* 14.

WICKSTED, CHARLES, Esq., of Betley Hall, Staffs., and Shakenhurst, Worc.: 1. Two serpents, ppr., issuing from and round a garb, or. *Pl.* 36, *cr.* 14. 2. A pyramid, erected on a pedestal of one degree, ar., the top entwined by a serpent descending, ppr., respecting escrol with motto, *Prudentia in adversis.*

WICKSTED, of Nantwich, Chesh., two serpents, vert, surrounding and issuing from a garb, or. *Pl.* 36, *cr.* 14.

WIDDEVIL, Eng., an ear of (rye,) and a palmbranch, in saltier, all ppr. *Pl.* 63, *cr.* 3.

WIDDRINGTON, SHALLCROSS-FITZHERBERT, Esq., of Newton Hall and Hauxley, Northumb.: 1. On a chapeau, a bull's head, sa. *Pl.* 120, *cr.* 7, (chapeau, *same plate, cr.* 15.) 2. A garb, or. *Pl.* 48, *cr.* 10.

WIDDRINGTON, Linc. and Northumb., a bull's head, sa., platée. *Pl.* 120, *cr.* 7.

WIDEVILE, Eng., on a chapeau, ppr., a wyvern, vert. *Pl.* 104, *cr.* 5, (without crown.)

WIDOPE, or WYDOP, Westm., three horse-shoes, interlaced, ar. *Pl.* 52, *cr.* 4, (interlacing, *pl.* 119, *cr.* 10.)

WIDSON, Notts., out of a ducal coronet, or, flames, ppr. *Pl.* 16, *cr.* 12, (coronet, *pl.* 128, *fig.* 3.)

WIDVILE, Eng., a demi-man, in armour, ppr., wielding a scimitar. *Pl.* 27, *cr.* 11.

WIDWORTHY, Devons., an eagle, rising, ppr. *Pl.* 67, *cr.* 4.

WIFIELD, Eng., a cinquefoil. *Pl.* 91, *cr.* 12.

WIGAN, Baron. *See* BALCARRES, Earl of.

WIGGE, a dexter gauntlet, erect, fist clenched, ppr. *Pl.* 125, *cr.* 5, (without sword.)

WIGGETT, Norf., a dove, regardant, in mouth an olive-branch, all ppr. *Pl.* 77, *cr.* 2.

WIGGANS, a talbot, statant, ar., spotted, sa., between two trees, in perspective, ppr.

WIGGINS, Eng., a spur, or, between wings, ppr. *Pl.* 109, *cr.* 12.

WIGGON, Eng., a martlet, ppr. *Pl.* 111, *cr.* 5.

WIGHT, ALBERT, Esq., of Brabœuf Manor, Surr., out of a mural coronet, a bear's head, ar., muzzled, sa. *Pl.* 6, *cr.* 6, (coronet, *same plate, cr.* 2.)

WIGHT, Sco., a dexter hand grasping a dagger, point downward. *Fortiter.* *Pl.* 18, *cr.* 3.

WIGHT, Eng., an acorn, or, stalked and leaved, vert. *Pl.* 81, *cr.* 7.

WIGHTMAN, Middx., a stork, ar., winged, sa., membered, gu., (in mouth a snake, vert, winding round body.) *Pl.* 33, *cr.* 9.

WIGHTMAN, Sco., a demi-savage, wreathed round temple and loins, holding over dexter shoulder a club, ppr. *A Wightman never wanted a weapon.* *Pl.* 14, *cr.* 11.

WIGHTON, Sco., same crest.

WIGHTWICK, Staffs., a demi-heraldic, tiger, sa., (holding a pheon, or.) *Pl.* 57, *cr.* 13, (without gorging.)

WIGLESWORTH, Eng., a pheon, az. *Pl.* 56, *cr.* 15.

WIGLEY, Derbs. and Leic., a tiger's head, ar., maned and tufted, sa., issuing from flames, ppr., gorged with a collar, embattled, gu. *Pl.* 86, *cr.* 13, (flames, *pl.* 16, *cr.* 12.)

WIGMORE, Eng., an esquire's helmet, az., garnished, or. *Pl.* 109, *cr.* 5.

WIGMORE, Linc., a greyhound, sejant, ar., (collared, gu., ringed and garnished, or.) *Pl.* 66, *cr.* 15.

WIGMORE, Norf., on a mount, vert, a greyhound, sejant, ar., (collared, gu., garnished and ringed, or.) *Pl.* 5, *cr.* 2.

WIGMORE, Heref., on a mount, vert, a greyhound, sejant, ar., (collared, gu., garnished, or.) *Pl.* 5, *cr.* 2.

WIGOTT, a griffin's head, or, winged, gu., on each wing an escallop, ar. *Pl.* 65, *cr.* 1, (escallop, *pl.* 141.)

WIGRAM, Ess., on a mount, vert, a hand, (in armour,) couped at wrist, in fess, ppr., charged with an escallop, holding a fleur-de-lis, or. *Pl.* 46, *cr.* 12, (mount, *pl.* 98, *cr.* 13.)

WIGRAM, Eng., Bart., a hand, couped, in fess, holding a fleur-de-lis. *Amor dulcis patriæ.* *Pl.* 46, *cr.* 12.

WIGSTON, Eng., a lion's head, erased, per pale, gu. and az., guttée-d'or. *Pl.* 81, *cr.* 4.

WIGTON, a stag's head, in mouth an (adder,) all ppr. *Rl.* 100, *cr.* 8.

WIKES, Eng., a demi-lion, rampant, in dexter a scimitar, ppr. *Pl.* 41, *cr.* 13.

WILBERFORCE, Middx., an eagle, displayed, sa., beaked, and legged, ppr. *Pl.* 48, *cr.* 11.

WILBERFORCE, and WILBERFOS, Yorks., same crest.
WILBRAHAM-BOOTLE, Baron Skelmersdale. *See* SKELMERSDALE.
WILBRAHAM, Chesh., a wolf's head, erased, ar. *Par fluctus portui.* Pl. 14, cr. 6.
WILBRAHAM, Chesh., a wolf's head, ar. Same motto. Pl. 8, cr. 4.
WILBY, Eng., on the point of a sword, a garland of laurel, all ppr. Pl. 15, cr. 6.
WILCOCKS, Lond., Middx., Ess., and Salop: 1. Out of a mural coronet, or, a demi-lion, rampant, sa. Pl. 17, cr. 7, (without branch.) 2. An eagle's leg, erased at thigh, or, between wings, az.
WILCOCKS, Leic., a demi-lion, rampant, az. Pl. 67, cr. 10.
WILCOTTS, a demi-eagle, wings displayed, ar., beaked, sa. Pl. 52, cr. 8.
WILCOX, Eng., on a mount, a dove, ppr. Pl. 104, cr. 8.
WILCOX, Leic., a demi-eagle, wings displayed, ar., ducally gorged, or. Pl. 22, cr. 11, (gorging, *pl.* 39, cr. 4.)
WILCOXON, a lion's gamb, erect, bendy, ar. and sa., in paw a fleur-de-lis, or, encircled by a wreath of oak, ppr. Pl. 46, cr. 7, (fleur-de-lis, *pl.* 141.)
WILD, a lion, passant, gu., resting dexter on an escutcheon, ar. Pl. 4, cr. 14, (escutcheon, *pl.* 19, cr. 2.)
WILD, Kent: 1. An eagle, displayed, or, beaked and membered, sa. Pl. 48, cr. 11. 2. On a chapeau, gu., turned up, erm., a stag, couchant, ppr. Pl. 67, cr. 2, (chapeau, *pl.* 3, cr. 14.) 3. A lion, sejant, gardant, gu., (between paws an escutcheon, ar.) Pl. 101, cr. 8.
WILD, Notts., a demi-stag, couped, (ducally gorged, or.) Pl. 55, cr. 9, (without rose.)
WILDBORE, Eng., a sanglier, sa., bristled, or. Pl. 48, cr. 14.
WILDBORE, Dors. and Yorks., (the upper part of a spear, ppr.,) through a boar's head, erased, ar., (dropping blood, gu.) Pl. 10, cr. 2.
WILDE, Lond., a wyvern, sa., guttée-d'or, (collared and lined, gold.) Pl. 63, cr. 13.
WILDE, Notts., a demi-stag, salient, sa., attired and (ducally gorged,) or. Pl. 55, cr. 9, (without rose.)
WILDE, Eng., a lion, passant, gardant. Pl. 120, cr. 5.
WILDER, Berks., a savage's head, affrontée, couped at shoulders, wreathed with (woodbines,) all ppr. *Virtuti mœnia cedant.* Pl. 97, cr. 2.
WILDER, a demi-griffin, between claws a garland of laurel. Pl. 18, cr. 6, (laurel, *pl.* 56, cr. 10.)
WILDER, Camb., a man's bust, affrontée, wreathed round temples, ar. and az. Pl. 97 cr. 2.
WILDGOOSE, Ess. and Suss., a wild man, ppr., wreathed round temples and loins, vert. Pl. 14, cr. 11.
WILDING, Eng., an oak-tree, ppr. Pl. 16, cr. 8.
WILDING, Middx., a dragon's head, erased, vert. Pl. 107, cr. 10, (without collar.)
WILDMAN, THOMAS, Esq., of Newstead Abbey, Notts., out of a mural coronet, chequy, or and az., a demi-lion, rampant, ar., supporting a battle-axe, gold, blade, ppr., dropping blood. *Tentanda via est.* Pl. 120, cr. 14, (wing, *pl.* 39, cr. 10.)

WILDMAN, a griffin's head, or, charged with a plate. Pl. 38, cr. 3, (plate, *pl.* 141.)
WILDMAN, Berks., out of a mural coronet, ar., a demi-lion, ppr., holding a battle-axe, or, headed, of the first. Pl. 120, cr. 14.
WILDMAN, Kent, out of a mural coronet, chequy, or and az., a demi-lion, ar., supporting a battle-axe, gold, headed, of the first, dropping blood. Pl. 120, cr. 14.
WILES, Eng., a sheaf of arrows, gu., pointed, az., feathered and banded, or. Pl. 43, cr. 14.
WILEY, Eng., a rose-bush, vert, bearing roses, ar. Pl. 23, cr. 2.
WILFOORD, Worc., a stag's head, gorged with a laurel crown. Pl. 38, cr. 1.
WILFORD, Middx., a bundle of swans' quills, banded, ar. Pl. 86, cr. 7.
WILK, on a mount, vert, a cross-bow, erect, or, round it a scroll, inscribed—*Arcui mei non confido.* Pl. 56, cr. 3, (without wings; mount, *pl.* 98, cr. 13.)
WILKES, Eng., a holly-branch, vert. Pl. 99, cr. 6.
WILKES, a cubit arm, vested, gu., cuffed, ar., hand holding a cross-bow, or. Pl. 18, cr. 1, (bow, *pl.* 56, cr. 5.)
WILKES, Cambs. and Yorks., a tiger, sejant, gu., tufted and maned, or, (ducally gorged, ringed, and lined, gold.) Pl. 26, cr. 9.
WILKIE, Eng., a primrose, ppr. Pl. 109, cr. 6.
WILKIE, West Indies, a demi-negro, wreathed about head, or and gu., girt round waist, vert, ear-rings, pendent, ar., in dexter a bill, in sinister a sugar-cane, couped, all ppr. *Favente Deo.*
WILKIN, Kent, a dragon's head, per pale, ar. and vert. Pl. 87, cr. 12.
WILKINS, Leic., a demi-griffin, segreant, regardant, gu., (in dexter a sword, in pale, ar.,) hilt and pommel, or. Pl. 125, cr. 12.
WILKINS, Wel., a wyvern's head, erased, vert. Pl. 107, cr. 10.
WILKINS, Kent, a boar, passant, (regardant,) pierced through shoulder by an arrow, ar., (in bend sinister, the boar biting the arrow.) Pl. 36, cr. 2.
WILKINS-CANN, of Clifton, Glouc., a wyvern, ppr. *Syn ar du hun.* Pl. 63, cr 13.
WILKINSON, Iri., a fire-beacon, inflamed, ppr. Pl. 89, cr. 9.
WILKINSON, Sco., a demi-talbot, ar. Pl. 97, cr. 9, (without arrow.)
WILKINSON, a demi-eagle, wings expanded, per pale, or and ar., (in beak a rose, gu., barbed, leaved, and stalked, vert.) Pl. 52, cr. 8.
WILKINSON, an arm, vested, embowed to dexter, holding between the thumb and forefinger an annulet. Pl. 39, cr. 1, (annulet, *pl.* 24, cr. 3.)
WILKINSON, THOMAS-CLIFTON, Esq., of Winterburn Hall, Yorks., a unicorn's head. *Tenez le droit.* Pl. 20, cr. 1.
WILKINSON, on a mount, vert, a talbot, sejant, ar., (among rushes,) ppr. Pl. 102, cr 9, (mount, *pl.* 98, cr. 13.)
WILKINSON, a wolf's head, per pale, vert and or, in mouth a wing, ar., (charged on neck with a trefoil, slipped, gu.) Pl. 92, cr. 15.
WILKINSON, Yorks., a stag's head, erased, az., attired, ar., on neck a sun, or. Pl. 62, cr. 14.
WILKINSON, Norf. and Westm., a unicorn's head, erased, per cheveron, or and gu., armed, gobony, gold and sa. Pl. 67, cr. 1.

WILKINSON, HENRY-COX, Esq., of White Webbs Park, Middx., a demi-talbot, sa., holding a rose-branch, vert. *Early and late.* *Pl.* 97, *cr.* 9, (branch, *pl.* 39, *cr.* 14.)

WILKINSON, Durh., out of a mural coronet, gu., a demi-unicorn, rampant, erminois, erased, of the first, armed and maned, or. *Pl.* 26, *cr.* 14, (coronet, *pl.* 128, *fig.* 18.)

WILKINSON, Durh., same crest. *Nec rege, nec populo, sed utroque.*

WILKINSON, Durh., out of a mural coronet, gu., a unicorn's head, ar. *Pl.* 45, *cr.* 14, (coronet, *same plate, cr.* 9.)

WILKINSON, Kent, on a mount, vert, a greyhound, sejant, ar., (gorged with a collar, sa., rimmed and ringed, or, on the dexter side of the mount a laurel-branch, of the first.) *Pl.* 5, *cr.* 2.

WILKINSON, Kent, on a mount, vert, a bird, close, sa., (in dexter a banner, gu. and az., bearing, ar., a cross, gu., staff, or.) *Pl.* 104, *cr.* 8.

WILKINSON, Durh., a demi-talbot, sa., eared, erm., charged with three billets, or, two and one, between paws a branch, vert, thereon three daisies, sa., seeded, gold. *Incepta persequor.* *Pl.* 97, *cr.* 9.

WILKINSON, Bucks. and Yorks.: 1. A pelican's head, vulned, ppr. *Pl.* 41, *cr.* 4. 2. A tiger's head, erased, per pale, vert and or, in mouth a wing, ar. *Pl.* 94, *cr.* 10, (wing, *pl.* 39, *cr.* 10.)

WILKS, Eng., an arm, couped and embowed, hand holding up a grenade, fired, all ppr. *Pl.* 62, *cr.* 9.

WILKS, an heraldic-tiger, (rampant.) *Pl.* 57, *cr.* 13.

WILLAN, Lond. and Yorks., a demi-lion, rampant, or, in dexter a mullet of (six) points, sa. *Pl.* 89, *cr.* 10.

WILLANS, Yorks., a griffin's head, with wings expanded, ppr., collared, or. *Pl.* 22, *cr.* 2.

WILLARD, Suss., a griffin's head, erased, or. *Pl.* 48, *cr.* 6.

WILLASON, Heref., a demi-lion, rampant, or, charged with three pellets, holding a (chaplet, vert.) *Pl.* 84, *cr.* 7, (pellet, *pl.* 141.)

WILLAUME, Beds., on a mount, vert, a pineapple, or, stalked and crowned, of the first.

WILLCOCKS, Eng., a fleur-de-lis, az. *Pl.* 68, *cr.* 12.

WILLEIGH, or WILLELEY, Eng., a salmon, naiant, az. *Pl.* 85, *cr.* 7.

WILLES, or WILLIS, a hawk, wings displayed, ppr. *Pl.* 105, *cr.* 4.

WILLET, or WILLETT, Eng., out of a ducal coronet, a plume of ostrich-feathers, all ppr. *Pl.* 44, *cr.* 12.

WILLET, Ess.: 1. On a ducal coronet, or, a moorcock, wings expanded, sa., combed and wattled, gu. 2. Out of a ducal coronet, or, a cockatrice, sa., wings expanded, combed, wattled, beaked, and legged, gu. *Pl.* 77, *cr.* 5.

WILLETT, a heathcock, ppr.

WILLETT, Yorks., on a ducal coronet, or, a heathcock, ppr., combed and wattled, gu. *Noli me tangere.*

WILLEY, or WILLY, Northumb., out of a ducal coronet, or, a reindeer's head, erminois, attired, ar. *Pl.* 60, *cr.* 3.

WILLIAM, Lond., a demi-lion, rampant, or, in dexter an (etoile,) sa. *Pl.* 89, *cr.* 10.

WILLIAMS, out of a ducal coronet, a demi-eagle, wings expanded, ppr., in beak a trefoil, sa. *Pl.* 9, *cr.* 6, (trefoil, *pl.* 55, *cr.* 12.)

WILLIAMS, out of a ducal coronet, a hand holding a sword, in pale, blade waved, ppr. *Pl.* 65, *cr.* 10.

WILLIAMS, Eng., a boar's head, couped, gu. *Ne cede malis.* *Pl.* 48, *cr.* 2.

WILLIAMS, DAVID, Esq., Dundraeth, Merioneths., a griffin, segreant, gu., beaked and armed, or. *Nid da onid Duw.* *Pl.* 67, *cr.* 13.

WILLIAMS, BENJAMIN, Esq., of The Lodge, Hillingdon, and Cowley Grove, Middx., a cubit arm, vested, or, (charged with a pile, sa., thereon three spear-heads, ar., cuff, also ar.,) hand holding an oak-branch, fructed and slipped, ppr. *Deo adjuvante, non timendum.* *Pl.* 64, *cr.* 7, (branch, *pl.* 32, *cr.* 13.)

WILLIAMS, THOMAS-PEERS, Esq., of Temple House, Berks.; and Craig-y-Don, Anglesey; a Cornish chough, ppr., in dexter a fleur-de-lis. *Duw a ddarpar i'r Brain—(God feedeth the ravens.)* *Pl.* 100, *cr.* 3, (fleur-de-lis, *pl.* 141.)

WILLIAMS, FRANCIS-EDWARD, Esq., of Malvern Hall, Warw.; and of Pitmaston and Doddenham, Worc.; between two spears, erect, ppr., a talbot, passant, per pale, ermine and ermines. *Pl.* 120, *cr.* 8, (spears, *pl.* 69, *cr.* 14.)

WILLIAMS, of Greenwich and Boons, Kent, a cook, ppr. *Deus hæc otia fecit.* *Pl.* 67, *cr.* 14.

WILLIAMS, a garb, in fess. *Pl.* 12, *cr.* 15.

WILLIAMS, a ring-dove, ppr., in dexter a fleur-de-lis, ar. *Pl.* 66, *cr.* 12, (fleur-de-lis, *pl.* 141.)

WILLIAMS, a demi-griffin, gu., wings, erm., on body three bezants, in pale, between claws the rudder of a ship, sa. *Pl.* 18, *cr.* 6, (rudder, *pl.* 102, *cr.* 4.)

WILLIAMS, a lion, rampant, regardant. *Pl.* 10, *cr.* 15, (without brand.)

WILLIAMS, a lion's head, erased. *Pl.* 81, *cr.* 4.

WILLIAMS, a boar's head, couped, gu. *Pl.* 48, *cr.* 2.

WILLIAMS, a cubit arm, erect, vested, sa., (charged with a cross crosslet, or, cuffed, gold, in hand two oak-sprigs, in saltier, ppr., fructed, of the second, on hand a Cornish chough, statant, ppr.) *Pl.* 44. *cr.* 13.

WILLIAMS, of Langibby Castle, Monm., Wel.: 1. For *Williams*, a talbot, passant, per pale, ermine and ermines. *Pl.* 120, *cr.* 8. 2. For *Adams*, a griffin's head, erased, erm., beaked, gu., charged on neck with a cheveron, vairé, or and az. *En suivant la verité.* *Pl.* 48, *cr.* 6.

WILLIAMS, a savage's head, affrontée, bearded, ppr. *Pl.* 19, *cr.* 1.

WILLIAMS; a greyhound, passant, (collared and ringed.) *Pl.* 104, *cr.* 1, (without chapeau.)

WILLIAMS, an arm, vested, ar., cuffed, sa., charged with a cross pattée, az., between four bezants, in hand, ppr., an oak-branch, leaved, vert, fructed, or. *Pl.* 64, *cr.* 7, (branch, *pl.* 32, *cr.* 13.)

WILLIAMS, Eng., out of a mural coronet, or, a demi-lion, rampant, gold, holding a battle-axe, sa., head, ar. *Pl.* 120, *cr.* 14.

WILLIAMS, a bull's head, erased, sa. *Pl.* 19, *cr.* 3.

WILLIAMS, a bull's head, couped, sa. *Pl.* 120, *cr.* 7.

WILLIAMS, Kent, a tower, ar., out of the battlements, an arm, in mail, embowed, in hand, ppr., a broken lance, point downward, guttée-de-sang. *Virtus incumbit honori.* Pl. 12, cr. 5, (arm, pl. 44, cr. 9.)

WILLIAMS, Linc., a cubit arm, erect, vested, erm., cuffed, ar., hand holding, erect, ppr., a long cross, gu. Pl. 75, cr. 3, (cross, pl. 7, cr. 13.)

WILLIAMS, Wel., a talbot, passant, per pale, erm. and or, eared, gold. Pl. 120, cr. 8.

WILLIAMS, an arm, embowed, vested, sa., in hand, ppr., (three) laurel sprigs, vert. Pl. 118, cr. 4, (vesting, pl. 39, cr. 1.)

WILLIAMS, America, an eagle, wings expanded, ppr., resting dexter on a mound, or. Pl. 118, cr. 1.

WILLIAMS, Salop, on a mount, vert, a stag, statant, ar., attired, sa. Pl. 50, cr. 6.

WILLIAMS, Suss., a dragon's head, ar., emitting flames, ppr. Pl. 37, cr. 9.

WILLIAMS, Wel., a buck, (statant,) ar., collared, or. Pl. 88, cr. 9, (without arrow.)

WILLIAMS, Hants, a goat, (passant,) ppr. Pl. 66, cr. 1.

WILLIAMS, Wel., a fox's head, erased, gu. Pl. 71, cr. 4.

WILLIAMS, Devons., a falcon. Pl. 67, cr. 3.

WILLIAMS, Dors. and Oxon., a cubit arm, erect, vested, sa., (charged with a cross formée, or, between four bezants,) cuffed, gold, in hand, ppr., an acorn-branch, vert, fructed, of the second. Pl. 64, cr. 7, (branch, pl. 32, cr. 13.)

WILLIAMS, Wel., a cock, gu., combed and legged, or. Pl. 67, cr. 14.

WILLIAMS, Wel., a cock, gu. *Deus hæc otia fecit.* Pl. 67, cr. 14.

WILLIAMS, Berks. and Oxon., a fish-weir.

WILLIAMS, Kent, an eagle, displayed, or. Pl. 48, cr. 11.

WILLIAMS, Cambs., a bustard, close. Pl. 30, cr. 8.

WILLIAMS, Devons., Suss., and Linc., a lion, rampant, ppr. Pl. 67, cr. 5.

WILLIAMS, Bart., Wel., an eagle, displayed, or. *Cadam ar cyfrwys.* Pl. 48, cr. 11.

WILLIAMS, Bart., Devons., a swan, ar., wings addorsed, beaked and legged, or, (collared, gu., in beak a bird-bolt, sa.) *Meâ virtute me involvo.* Pl. 4, cr. 7, (without trumpet.)

WILLIAMS-BULKELEY, Bart. *See* BULKELEY.

WILLIAMS-GRIFFIES, Bart.: 1. For *Williams*, a bull's head, erased at neck, pean, armed, or, in mouth a spear, staff broken, ppr. Pl. 19, cr. 3, (spear, pl. 11, cr. 9.) 2. For *Griffies*, a griffin, segreant, az., beaked and armed, or, wings elevated, erm., the claws supporting a scaling-ladder, gold. Pl. 67, cr. 13, (ladder, pl. 98, cr. 15.)

WILLIAMS LLOYD, EDWARD, Esq., of Gwernant Park, Cardigan: 1. A lion, rampant, regardant, or. Pl. 10, cr. 15, (without brand.) 2. A scaling-ladder. *Of nwn yr Arglwydd* —(Let us fear the Lord.) Pl. 98, cr. 15.

WILLIAMSON, Sco., a garb, in fess, (unbound,) ppr. *Mod.ce augetur modicum.* Pl. 12, cr. 15.

WILLIAMSON, Lanc., a demi-eagle, displayed, or, in beak a trefoil, slipped, sa. *Murus æneus conscientia sana.* Pl. 22, cr. 11, (trefoil, pl. 55, cr. 12.)

WILLIAMSON, DAVID-ROBERTSON, Esq., of Lawers, Perth, a hand, erect, holding a dagger. Pl. 28, cr. 4. Also, issuing from clouds, a cubit arm, ppr., hand holding a garb, over it the motto — "Perseveranti dabitur." *In defence.* Pl. 67, cr. 12.

WILLIAMSON, a lion's head, ducally crowned, between two ostrich-feathers. Pl. 90, cr. 4, (feathers, pl. 108, cr. 2.)

WILLIAMSON, out of a mural coronet, a dragon's head, (vomiting flames.) Pl. 101, cr. 4.

WILLIAMSON, a buck's head, erased, az., attired, ar., charged on neck with the sun, or. Pl. 62, cr. 14.

WILLIAMSON, Durh., Oxon., and Yorks.: 1. Out of a ducal coronet, or, a griffin's head, gu. Pl. 54, cr. 14. 2. Out of a ducal coronet, gu., a demi-dragon, ar., collared, of the first. Pl. 82, cr. 10, (coronet, pl. 59, cr. 14.)

WILLIAMSON, Linc. and Notts., out of a ducal coronet, gu., a dragon's head, wings addorsed, or. Pl. 59, cr. 14.

WILLIAMSON, Middx. and Northamp., out of a ducal coronet, gu., a demi-wyvern, wings addorsed, or. Pl. 116, cr. 15, (coronet, pl. 104, cr. 11.)

WILLIAMSON, Cumb., a falcon's head, or, between wings, az., (charged on each wing with a sun, gold.) Pl. 99, cr. 10.

WILLIAMSON, Notts., out of a ducal coronet, gu., a dragon's head, or. Pl. 93, cr. 15, (without flames.)

WILLIAMSON, Bart., Notts., on a mural coronet, gu., a wyvern's head, between wings, or. Pl. 105, cr. 11, (coronet, pl. 128, fig. 18.)

WILLIMOT, a demi-leopard, gardant, ppr. Pl. 77, cr. 1, (without anchor.)

WILLIMOT, Derbs., an eagle's head, couped, ar., in beak an escallop, gu. Pl. 100, cr. 10, (escallop, pl. 141.)

WILLINGHAM, a demi-savage, wreathed about temples and loins with laurel-leaves, all ppr. Pl. 14, cr. 11.

WILLINGTON, Warw., a pine-tree, ppr. Pl. 26, cr. 10.

WILLIS, RICHARD, Esq., of Halsnead Park, and of Hall-of-the-Hill, Lanc., two lions' paws, erect and erased, holding a human heart, gu. *Virtus tutissima cassis.* Pl. 42, cr. 3, (heart, pl. 23, cr. 13.)

WILLIS, on a chapeau, gu., turned, up, erm., a unicorn's head, (couped, ar., ducally gorged, or.) Pl. 102, cr. 7.

WILLIS, Cambs. and Herts., two lions' gambs, erased, the dexter, ar., the sinister, gu., supporting an escutcheon, or. Pl. 78, cr. 13.

WILLIS, Lond., a hind, trippant, ppr., in mouth an oak-branch, ar., fructed, or, (on shoulder a cross formée,) gold. Pl. 20, cr. 14, (branch, pl. 100, cr. 8.)

WILLIS, Berks., a falcon, wings expanded, ppr., belled, or. Pl. 105, cr. 4.

WILLIS, Lond., a hind, passant, ppr., in mouth an oak-branch, vert, fructed, or, (on shoulder a mullet, gold.) Pl. 20, cr. 14, (branch, pl. 100, cr. 8.)

WILLISON, out of flames, ppr., a crescent, or. Pl. 29, cr. 2.

WILLMOTT, an eagle's head, ar., gorged with a (collar, engrailed, az., in beak an escallop, gu.) Pl. 39, cr. 4.

WILLMOTT, a demi-leopard, rampant, gardant, ar., (spotted with hurts and torteaux,) in paws an oak-branch, fructed, or. *Pl.* 77, *cr.* 1, (branch, *pl.* 32, *cr.* 13.)

WILLMOTT, in dexter hand a palm-branch, ppr. *Pl.* 23, *cr.* 7.

WILLMOTT, Berks., a demi-panther, rampant, gardant, ppr., holding a battle-axe, or. *Pl.* 77, *cr.* 1, (axe, *pl.* 26, *cr.* 7.)

WILLMOTT, Oxon., a demi-leopard, rampant, ar., spotted with hurts and torteaux, holding an acorn-branch, vert, fructed, or. *Pl.* 12, *cr.* 14, (branch, *pl.* 32, *cr.* 13.)

WILLOCK, a demi-lion, rampant, ar., (holding in paws a spear inverted, gu.) *Pl.* 69, *cr.* 14.

WILLOCK, a griffin's head and neck, erased, ppr. *Pl.* 48, *cr.* 6.

WILLOUGHBY, Kent, Linc., Devons., Derbs., and Wilts., an old man's head, couped at shoulders, ppr., ducally crowned, or. *Pl.* 28, *cr.* 3.

WILLOUGHBY, Derbs., Notts., Northamp., and Staffs., an owl, ar., (ducally crowned, collared, chained,) beaked and legged, or. *Pl.* 27, *cr.* 9.

WILLOUGHBY, Bart., Oxon., a Saracen's head, couped, ppr., ducally crowned, or. *Verite sans peur. Pl.* 28, *cr.* 3.

WILLOUGHBY, Baron Middleton. *See* MIDDLETON.

WILLOUGHBY, Notts., an owl, ar., (crowned, or.) *Pl.* 27, *cr.* 9.

WILLOUGHBY-DE BROKE, Baron, (Verney,) a Saracen's head, affrontee, couped at shoulders, ppr., ducally crowned, or. *Vertue vaunceth. Pl.* 28, *cr.* 3.

WILLOUGHBY-DE ERESBY, Baron, and Baron Gwidir, (Drummond-Burrell :) 1. A naked arm, embowed, in hand a laurel-branch, ppr. *Pl.* 118, *cr.* 4. 2. On a ducal coronet, a sloth-hound, ppr., collared, gu. *Animus non deficit æquus. Pl.* 3, *cr.* 8.

WILLS, Iri., a harp, or. *Pl.* 104, *cr.* 15.

WILLS, Cornw., a demi-griffin, salient, between claws a battle-axe. *Pl.* 44, *cr.* 3.

WILLS-SANDFORD, THOMAS GEORGE, Esq., of Willsgrove and Castlerea, Roscommon : 1. Out of a ducal coronet, a boar's head and neck, or, langued, gu. *Pl.* 102, *cr.* 14. 2. A demi-griffin, segreant, sa., holding in claws a battle-axe, ppr. *Cor unum, via una. Pl.* 44, *cr.* 3.

WILLSON, a cannon, sa., stock, or. *Pl.* 111, *cr.* 3.

WILLSON, Glouc., a wolf's head, erased, erminois, collared, sa., charged with three mullets, ar. *Pl.* 8, *cr.* 4, (mullet, *pl.* 141.)

WILLY, or WILLEY, Eng., in dexter hand a battle-axe, ppr. *Pl.* 73, *cr.* 7.

WILLYAMS, HUMPHRY, Esq., of Carnanton, Cornw., on a ducal coronet, a falcon, close, ppr., belled, or. *In Domino confido.* Cornish motto, *Meor ras tha Dew. Pl.* 41, *cr.* 10.

WILLYAMS, Cornw., on a ducal coronet, or, a falcon, close, ppr. *Pl.* 41, *cr.* 10.

WILLYMOT, Heref., on a chapeau, sa., turned up, or, an eagle, displayed, ar., winged, gold, membered and beaked, gu. *Pl.* 48, *cr.* 11, (chapeau, *pl.* 127, *fig.* 13.)

WILMER, Northamp. and Warw., an eagle's head, or, between wings, vair. *Pl.* 81, *cr.* 10.

WILMOT, out of a mural coronet, an eagle's head. *Pl.* 121, *cr.* 11.

WILMOT, Bart., Derbs., an eagle's head, couped, ar., gorged with a mural coronet, sa., (in beak an escallop, gu.) *Pl.* 74, *cr.* 1.

WILMOT, Eng., a portcullis, az., chained, or. *Pl.* 51, *cr.* 12.

WILMOT-EARDLEY, Bart., Warw. : 1. For *Wilmot*, an eagle's head, couped, ar., in beak an escallop, gu. *Pl.* 100, *cr.* 10, (escallop, *pl.* 141.) 2. For *Eardley*, a buck, current, gu., attired and unguled, or.

WILMOT-SITWELL, Derbs. : 1. For *Sitwell*, a demi-lion, rampant, (erased, sa., in dexter an escutcheon, per pale, or and ar.) *Pl.* 84, *cr.* 7. 2. For *Wilmot*, an eagle's head, couped, ar., in beak an escallop, gu. *Pl.* 100, *cr.* 10, (escallop, *pl.* 141.)

WILNEY, Eng., a lion's gamb, erect. *Pl.* 126, *cr.* 9.

WILSEY, a demi-griffin, wings elevated, in claws a garland. *Pl.* 18, *cr.* 6, (garland, *pl.* 56, *cr.* 10.)

WILSFORD, Kent, a leopard's head, per pale, or and gu. *Pl.* 92, *cr.* 13.

WILSHERE, Herts., a cup, or. *Pl.* 42, *cr.* 1.

WILSHERE, Herts., a lion, rampant, gu., maned, ppr. *Pl.* 67, *cr.* 5.

WILSON, of Beckenham, Kent : 1. A demi-wolf, rampant, or. *Pl.* 56, *cr.* 8, (without spear.) 2. Out of a ducal coronet, or, a plume of five ostrich-feathers, half, az., half, ar. *Pl.* 100, *cr.* 12, (without charge.) 3. A squirrel, sejant, cracking a nut, all ppr. *Facta, non verba. Pl.* 16, *cr.* 9.

WILSON, HENRY, Esq., of Stowlangtoft Hall, Suff., a demi-wolf, or, sinister resting on a pellet, charged with a fleur-de-lis, gold. *Wil sone wil. Pl.* 56, *cr.* 8, (pellet and fleur-de-lis, *pl.* 141.)

WILSON, Eng., a crescent, or, flammant, ppr. *Pl.* 29, *cr.* 2.

WILSON, GEORGE-EDWARD, Ess., of Dallam Tower, Westm., same crest.

WILSON, a lion's gamb, erect and erased. *Pl.* 126, *cr.* 9.

WILSON, a (globe,) inflamed at top, ppr. *Pl.* 70, *cr.* 12.

WILSON, Iri., a water-bouget, or. *Pl.* 14, *cr.* 12.

WILSON, Sco., a wolf, salient, or. *Expecta cuncta superne. Pl.* 126, *cr.* 13, (without collar.)

WILSON, Sco., a demi-lion, gu. *Semper vigilans. Pl.* 67, *cr.* 10.

WILSON, Sco., a talbot's head, erased, ar. *Semper vigilans. Pl.* 90, *cr.* 6.

WILSON, Eng., a lion's head, erased, ar., guttée, gu. *Pl.* 81, *cr.* 4.

WILSON, an eagle, displayed, sa. *Pl.* 48, *cr.* 11.

WILSON, out of a marquess's coronet, or, jewelled, ppr., a demi-wolf, between paws, a (crescent, sa.) *Pl.* 65, *cr.* 4, (coronet, *pl.* 127, *fig.* 4.)

WILSON, an arm, in armour, embowed, issuing from clouds, and resting on battle-axe, the rising sun breaking the clouds, all ppr.

WILSON, Northumb., a demi-wolf, rampant, per fess, erm. and erminois. *Pl.* 56, *cr.* 8, (without spear.)

WILSON, Cumb. and Linc., a lion's head, ar., guttée-de-sang. *Pl.* 126, *cr.* 1.

WILSON, Herts., a demi-wolf, or, (charged with a crescent.) *Pl.* 56, *cr.* 8, (without spear.)

WILSON, Kent, a talbot's head, erased, ppr. *Semper vigilans. Pl.* 90, *cr.* 6.

WILSON, Northumb., Suss., Linc., and Yorks., a demi-wolf, salient, or. *Res, non verba. Pl.* 56, *cr.* 8, (without spear.)

WILSON, Berks., Yorks., and Lond., a demi-wolf, salient. *Res, non verba*—and—*Pro legibus ac regibus. Ib.*

WILSON, Bart., Suss., same crest and motto.

WILSON, Westm., a crescent, or, (issuing from fire, ppr.) *Pl.* 29, *cr.* 2.

WILSON, Suss., a demi-wolf. *Pl.* 56, *cr.* 8, (without spear.)

WILSON, Westm., a demi-wolf, rampant, vert. *Ib.*

WILSON, Yorks., a talbot's head, erased, az., (on neck three ingots of gold, in fess, crossed by another in bend,) ppr. *Pl.* 90, *cr.* 6.

WILSON-CARUS, Westm. : 1. For *Wilson*, a crescent, or, (issuing from flames,) ppr. *Pl.* 29, *cr.* 2. 2. For *Carus*, a hawk, rising, sa., beaked, belled, and (collared, or, from the collar an escutcheon, pendent, ar., charged with a wolf's head, sa., vulned, ppr.) *Non nobis solum. Pl.* 105, *cr.* 4.

WILSON-FOUNTAYNE, of Melton Hall, Yorks. : 1. A demi-wolf, sa., (holding a shield.) *Pl.* 56, *cr.* 8. 2. (On a mount,) an elephant. *Pl.* 53, *cr.* 14.

WILTON, Wilts., an arm, in armour, embowed, in hand a dagger, ppr., hilt and pommel, or. *Pl.* 21, *cr.* 4.

WILTON, Eng., a dexter arm, in hand a bludgeon, ppr. *Pl.* 123, *cr.* 10.

WILTON, Ess., an owl, ppr., (gorged with a collar, or, affixed thereto by a ribbon, az., a perpendicular gold line and plumb, sa.) *Pl.* 27, *cr.* 9.

WILTON, Earl of, and Viscount Grey-de-Wilton, (Egerton,) three arrows, one in pale, and two in saltier, or, headed, and feathered, sa., tied together by a ribbon, gu. *Virtuti, non armis fido. Pl.* 43, *cr.* 14.

WILTSHIRE, Bart., a Caffre, in dexter an assaygay, in bend sinister, point downward, supporting with sinister three assaygays, points upward, all ppr.

WILTSHIRE, Eng., a horse's head, erased, bridled, ppr. *Pl.* 92, *cr.* 1.

WIMBERLEY, Linc., a buck's head, ppr., attired, or, issuing from a garland of bay-leaves, of the first. *Pl.* 38, *cr.* 1.

WIMBLE, Suss., a demi-lion, chequy, or and az., (supporting with paws an antique shield, gu., thereon the chemical character of Mars, gold.) *Pl.* 67, *cr.* 10.

WIMBOLT, Eng., a dagger, erect, ppr. *Pl.* 73, *cr.* 9.

WIMBOLTS, a dexter arm, embowed, vested, gu., slashed, ar., in hand, ppr., a falcon, of the second, belled, or, all between wings, sa.

WIMBUSH, a friar, vested in russet gown, his paternoster, &c., all ppr., supporting himself on a crutch.

WIMPEY, Eng., an arm, in armour, in gauntlet, a dagger, ppr. *Pl.* 21, *cr.* 4.

WINALL, on a mural coronet, gu., a mullet, or. *Pl.* 41, *cr.* 1, (coronet, *pl.* 128, *fig.* 18.)

WINCH, or WINCHE, Eng., in dexter hand a spear. *Pl.* 99, *cr.* 8.

WINCH, out of a ducal coronet, or, a lion's head, affrontée, ar., between two spears, gold, headed, ppr.

WINCHELSEA, Earl of, Earl of Nottingham, Viscount Maidstone, Baron Finch, and a Bart., (Finch-Hatton,) a pegasus, current, ar., winged, maned, hoofed, and ducally gorged, gold. *Nil conscire sibi*—and—*Virtus tutissima cassis. Pl.* 28, *cr.* 9.

WINCHESTER, Sco., a hand holding a cluster of grapes, ppr. *Hoc ardua vincere docet. Pl.* 37, *cr.* 4.

WINCHESTER, Lond. and Kent, in front of a cross crosslet, fitched, or, a lion, passant, az., fore-dexter supporting a (mascle, gu., and pendent from mouth a double chain, gold.) *Pl.* 77, *cr.* 3, (cross, *pl.* 16, *cr.* 10.)

WINCHESTER, Surr., same crest, but without chain.

WINCHESTER, Marquess of, Earl of Wiltshire, and Baron St John, (Paulet;) on a mount, vert, a falcon, rising, or, gorged with a ducal coronet, gu. *Aymez loyaulté. Pl.* 61, *cr.* 12.

WINCKWORTH, Eng., a cinquefoil, ppr. *Pl.* 91, *cr.* 12.

WINCOLD, and WINCOLL, Leic. and Suff., an arm, in armour, embowed, couped at shoulder, erect from elbow, ppr., garnished, or, in hand, also ppr., a spear, gold, headed, ar. *Pl.* 114, *cr.* 9, (spear, *pl.* 99, *cr.* 8.)

WINDE, Norf., a griffin's head, erased. *Pl.* 48, *cr.* 6.

WINDER, Cumb., out of a ducal coronet, or, a bull's head, erm., (in mouth a cherry-branch, slipped and fructed, all ppr.) *Pl.* 68, *cr.* 6.

WINDER, Eng., a dexter hand throwing a dart, ppr. *Pl.* 42, *cr.* 13.

WINDHAM, WILLIAM-FREDERICK, Esq., of Felbrigg Hall, Norf., a lion's head, erased, or, within a fetterlock, gold, the bow compony, counter-compony, of the first and az. *Au bon droit. Pl.* 90, *cr.* 14.

WINDHAM-SMIJTH, JOSEPH, Esq., (Smijth-Windham,) of Waghen, Yorks., same crest.

WINDLE, Eng., a stag's head, cabossed, ppr. *Pl.* 36, *cr.* 1.

WINDLOVE, WINLOVE, and WINDLOWE, Eng., a bunch of leaves, vert, encircled in a ducal coronet, or. *Pl.* 61, *cr.* 13, (coronet, *pl.* 128, *fig.* 3.)

WINDOUTE, Herts., a cubit arm, vested, ar., gloved, gu., (hand holding a falcon,) ppr., beaked and belled, or, the whole between wings, of the third. *Pl.* 11, *cr.* 11.

WINDOW, Glouc., a lion's gamb, erect and erased, az., paw holding a (cross crosslet, fitched,) or. *Pl.* 46, *cr.* 7.

WINDSOR, Eng., a sheaf of (seven) arrows, enfiled by a ducal coronet, all ppr. *Pl.* 37, *cr.* 5.

WINDSOR, Berks. and Warw., a stag's head, gardant, couped at neck, ar. *Pl.* 111, *cr.* 13.

WINDSOR, Earl of Plymouth. *See* PLYMOUTH.

WINDUS, a plume of three feathers, ar. *Pl.* 12, *cr.* 9.

WINDUS, Eng., on a ducal coronet, or, a serpent, entwining a sheaf of arrows, ppr. *Pl.* 21, *cr.* 14, (coronet, *pl.* 116, *cr.* 2.)

WINFORD, Eng., a dexter hand holding a sheaf of arrows, all ppr. *Pl.* 56, *cr.* 4.

WINFORD, Worc., on a ducal coronet, a man's head, in profile, (erased.) *Pl.* 81, *cr.* 15, (coronet, *pl.* 74, *cr.* 5.)

WING, between wings, or, a maunch, per pale, ar. and vert. *Pl.* 78, *cr.* 1, (wings, *pl.* 1, *cr.* 15.)

WINGAM, Eng., out of a ducal coronet, a broken halberd. *Pl.* 24, *cr.* 15, (coronet, *same plate, cr.* 10.)

WINGATE, Beds., a gate, or. *Pl.* 73, *cr.* 4.

WINGATE, Beds., a gate, or, (over it the word, "Win.") *Pl.* 73, *cr.* 4.

WINGATE, Beds., a hind's head, couped, ppr. *Pl.* 21, *cr.* 9.

WINGATE, Sco., an arm, in armour, embowed, in hand a scimitar, ppr. *Suum cuique. Pl.* 81, *cr.* 11.

WINGATE, on a rock, a palm-tree, ppr. *Per ardua surgo. Pl.* 52, *cr.* 6.

WINGFIELD, Iri., a cap, per pale, ermines and ar., charged with a fess, gu., between wings, the dexter, of the second, sinister, of the first. *Pl.* 126, *cr.* 3, (wings, *pl.* 1, *cr.* 15.)

WINGFIELD, Eng., an eagle, (rising, wings expanded,) ar., looking at the sun in splendour. *Fidelité est de Dieu. Pl.* 43, *cr.* 5.

WINGFIELD, Eng., a hawk's lure, ar. *Pl.* 97, *cr.* 14.

WINGFIELD, Eng., a swan's neck, or, with wings, gu. *Pl.* 54, *cr.* 6.

WINGFIELD, Worc., two wings, elevated, ar. *Pl.* 39, *cr.* 12.

WINGFIELD, Viscount Powerscourt. *See* POWERSCOURT.

WINGFIELD, of Tickencote, Ruts., a cap, per pale, sa. and ar., the first guttée-d'eau, charged with a fess, gu., between wings, the dexter, of the second, sinister, of the first. *Posse, nolle, nobile. Pl.* 126, *cr.* 3, (wings, *pl.* 1, *cr.* 15.)

WINGFIELD, of Onslow, Salop, and of Suff., a high bonnet or cap, per pale, sa. and ar., banded, gu., between wings, all guttée, counterchanged, on the cap a fess, gu. *Ib.*

WINGHAM, Eng., a sword and feather, in saltier, ppr. *Pl.* 106, *cr.* 9.

WINGOAK, (two) oaks, between wings. *Pl.* 16, *cr.* 8, (wings, *pl.* 1, *cr.* 15.)

WINGROVE, Eng., a phœnix in flames, ppr. *Pl.* 44, *cr.* 8.

WINN, Yorks. and Lond., a demi-eagle, displayed, or, (ducally gorged, erm.) *Tout pour Dieu et ma patrie. Pl.* 22, *cr.* 11.

WINN-ALLANSON, Baron Headley. *See* HEADLEY.

WINNINGTON, Bart., Worc., a Saracen's head, affrontée, couped at shoulders, ppr., wreathed about temples, ar. and sa. *Gratâ sume manu. Pl.* 97, *cr.* 1.

WINSLOE, a dragon, passant, wings elevated, (in dexter a dagger, in pale.) *Pl.* 90, *cr.* 10.

WINSTANLEY, JAMES-BEAUMONT, Esq., of Braunston House, Leic., a cockatrice, displayed, or, crested and wattled, gu. *Pl.* 102, *cr.* 15.

WINSTANLEY, Lanc., an arm, embowed, vested, gu., cuffed, ar., in hand, ppr., a sword, of the first, hilt and pommel, or. *Pl.* 120, *cr.* 1.

WINSTANTON, Eng., a boar's head, couped, sa. *Pl.* 48, *cr.* 2.

WINSTON, or WINSTONE, Eng., a dexter hand holding (four) arrows, ppr. *Pl.* 56, *cr.* 4.

WINTER, SAMUEL, Esq., of Agher, co. Meath, a martlet. *Pl.* 111, *cr.* 5.

WINTER, Leic., a hawk, ar., in dexter a fish, erect, or. *Pl.* 47, *cr.* 3, (fish, *pl.* 66, *cr.* 3.)

WINTER, a demi-griffin, gu., winged, per pale, ar. and az., (gorged with a ducal coronet, gold,) in dexter a garb, of the last. *Pl.* 19, *cr.* 15, (garb, *pl.* 84, *cr.* 7.)

WINTER, Surr., Glouc., and Worc., a cubit arm, erect, vested, or, in hand, ppr., (three) ostrich-feathers, middle one, sa., others, gold. *Pl.* 69, *cr.* 1.

WINTER, the same, but out of a ducal coronet. Coronet, *same plate, cr.* 11.

WINTER, Glouc., Worc., and Norf., a hind, trippant, ar., (ducally gorged, lined, and ringed, or.) *Pl.* 20, *cr.* 14.

WINTER, Kent, on a mount, vert, a hind, gu., (ducally gorged, lined,) and charged on shoulder with an annulet, or. *Pl.* 75, *cr.* 6, (annulet, *pl.* 141.)

WINTERBOTHAM, a demi-mountain cat, rampant, gardant, per pale, or and gu., guttée, counterchanged. *Prævisa mala pereunt. Pl.* 80, *cr.* 7.

WINTERBOTTOM, Eng., out of a mural coronet, ar., a spear, between two palm-branches, in saltier. *Pl.* 97, *cr.* 8.

WINTERSELLS, Eng., a tower, ar. *Pl.* 12, *cr.* 5.

WINTERTON, Earl of, and Baron, and Viscount Turnour, Iri., (Turnour;) a lion, passant, gardant, ar., (in dexter a fer-de-moline, sa.) *Esse quam videri. Pl.* 120, *cr.* 5.

WINTHORP, two wings, expanded, ppr. *Pl.* 39, *cr.* 12.

WINTHORP, on a mount, vert, a hare, current, ppr.

WINTLE, Eng., two wings, expanded, ppr. *Pl.* 39, *cr.* 12.

WINTON, Sco., a garb, or. *Pl.* 48, *cr.* 10.

WINTOUN, Sco., a dove, volant, ppr. *Pl.* 25, *cr.* 6.

WINTOUR, Hants and Worc.: 1. a cock pheasant, close, ppr. *Pl.* 82, *cr.* 12, (without collar.) 2. Out of a ducal coronet, or, a cubit arm, in armour, erect, ppr., garnished, gold, in gauntlet three ostrich-feathers. *Pl.* 15, *cr.* 5, (feathers, *pl.* 12, *cr.* 9.)

WINTRINGHAM, Lond., a demi-lion, rampant, az. *Fortis esto, non ferox. Pl.* 67, *cr.* 10.

WINWOOD, Bucks., out of a ducal coronet, or, an eagle's head, between wings, sa., (in beak a chaplet of laurel, vert.) *Pl.* 66, *cr.* 5.

WINYARD, Eng., a buck's head, cabossed, ppr. *Pl.* 36, *cr.* 1.

WINZIET, Sco., a tower, ar., with copula and flag, gu. *Pl.* 42, *cr.* 10.

WIRDNAM, Berks., a bear's head, erased, ar., muzzled, or, (collared, sa., ringed and lined, gold.) *Pl.* 71, *cr.* 6.

WIRE, Woodcote, Warw., a demi-lion, rampant, ar., a snake coiling round him, in paws a rose-branch, ppr. *Pl.* 39, *cr.* 14, (snake, *pl.* 124, *cr.* 5.)

WIRGMAN, Lond., a dove and olive-branch, all ppr. *Veritas. Pl.* 48, *cr.* 15.

WISE, a demi-lion, rampant, ar., holding a rose, ppr. *Pl.* 39, *cr.* 14.

WISE, of Ford-Ayshford, Devons., a demi-lion, rampant, gu., guttée, ar., in dexter a (regal mace, or.) *Sapere aude. Pl.* 41, *cr.* 13.

WISE, Warw., same crest.

WISE, Cambs., out of a ducal coronet, sa., a lion's head, ar., pellettée. *Pl.* 90, *cr.* 9.

WISE, Glouc., a duck, ar., beaked, gu., amongst flags, vert. *Pl.* 34, *cr.* 6.

WISEMALE, Eng., the point of a spear, ppr. *Pl.* 82, *cr.* 9.

WISEMAN, out of a tower, a demi-man, armed in male, ppr., in dexter a dart, on sinister arm a shield, temples wreathed, ar. and sa.

WISEMAN, Ess., a demi-dragon, sa., wings addorsed, or, holding a broken staff, gold. *Pl.* 82, *cr.* 10.
WISEMAN, Ess. and Berks., a tower, or, port, ar., on top a demi-moor, in mail, all ppr., temples wreathed, ar. and sa., in dexter a dart, of the first, plumed and headed, of the second, in sinister a Roman shield, gold.
WISEMAN, Ess., a sea-horse, sejant, sa., fins, or. *Pl.* 100, *cr.* 1.
WISEMAN, Bart., Ess., a castle, triple-towered, or, port open, ar., from top a demi-moor, issuing, armed, ppr., in dexter a dart of the second, barbed and flighted, gold, in sinister a Roman target, of the last.
WISHAM, Eng., a demi-lion, or. *Pl.* 67, *cr.* 10.
WISHART, of Brechin, Sco., an eagle, displayed, gu. *Mercy is my desire. Pl.* 48, *cr.* 11.
WITFORD, eight pens, in saltier, four and four, banded.
WITHAM, Eng., a cubit arm, erect, vested, az., cuffed, ar., in hand, ppr., a cinquefoil, stalked, or. *Pl.* 101, *cr.* 5.
WITHAM, Linc., out of a ducal coronet, or, a demi-peacock, (displayed,) or. *Pl.* 53, *cr.* 12, (coronet, *same plate, cr.* 4.)
WITHAM, Rev. THOMAS, of Lartington Hall, Yorks., out of a ducal coronet, or, a demi-woman, hair dishevelled, ppr., (in dexter a gem-ring, gold.) *Optime merenti. Pl.* 53, *cr.* 4.
WITHAM, Ess., same crest.
WITHER, a demi-hare, quarterly, gu. and az., (in mouth three ears of wheat, or.) *Pl.* 58, *cr.* 14.
WITHER-BIGG, the Rev. LOVELACE, of Manydown, and of Tangier Park, Hants.: 1. A demi-hare, erect, az., (in mouth three ears of ripe corn, on shoulder a mullet, or.) *Pl.* 58, *cr.* 14. 2. A rhinoceros, ppr. *Pl.* 4, *cr.* 11.
WITHERING, Ess. and Staffs., a raven, wings expanded, sa., beaked, ar., (gorged with a coronet, or.) *Pl.* 50, *cr.* 5.
WITHERINGTON, Eng., a bull's head, couped, sa., platée, horned, ar. *Pl.* 120, *cr.* 7.
WITHERS, a demi-hare, salient, az., (in mouth three ears of wheat, or.) *Pl.* 58, *cr.* 14.
WITHIE, Wilts., out of a ducal coronet, or, a cross, gu., between wings, erect, ar. *Pl.* 17, *cr.* 9, (cross, *pl.* 7, *cr.* 13.)
WITHIE, on a ducal coronet, a cross Calvary, between wings, (conjoined,) ar. *Ib.*
WITHIE, Lond. and Devons., issuing from a ducal coronet, or, a cross Calvary, between wings, ar. *Ib.*
WITHYPOULE, Suff., a demi-mountain cat, rampant, gardant, per pale, or and gu., guttée, counterchanged. *Pl.* 80, *cr.* 7.
WITLEY, Salop, a buck's head, ar., attired, or, (holding the end of a scroll, inscribed, "Live to live.") *Pl.* 91, *cr.* 14.
WITMORE, out of a ducal coronet, a cock's head. *Pl.* 97, *cr.* 15.
WITT, Eng., a dexter hand, couped, in fess, apaumée. *Pl.* 32, *cr.* 4.
WITTEWRONG, Bucks. and Herts., a Saracen's head, couped below shoulders, ppr., wreathed round temples, and tied in bows, or and gu. *Pl.* 23, *cr.* 3.
WITTINGHAM, Eng., a lion's head. *Pl.* 126, *cr.* 1.

WITTON, Yorks., an owl, ar., ducally gorged, or. *Pl.* 27, *cr.* 9.
WITTS, Lond., an eagle, wings elevated, sitting on a mount (of corn, springing,) in beak a sprig of bloom, all ppr. *Pl.* 61, *cr.* 1, (bloom, *pl.* 94, *cr.* 15.)
WITTS, a greyhound, current. *Pl.* 28, *cr.* 7, (without charge.)
WITTY, Eng., out of a ducal coronet, or, a dexter hand, ppr., holding a sword, wavy, in pale, gu., hilt, or. *Pl.* 65, *cr.* 10.
WIX, Eng., on a rock, ppr., a wyvern, sejant, gu. *Pl.* 33, *cr.* 13.
WMPHREY, Eng., a book, expanded, ppr. *Pax tua, Domine, et requies mea. Pl.* 15, *cr.* 12.
WODDERSPOON, Sco., a dexter hand holding a garland of laurel, all ppr. *Deo juvante. Pl.* 86, *cr.* 1.
WODEHOUSE, Baron, and a Bart., (Wodehouse,) a dexter hand, issuing from clouds, ppr., holding a club, with this motto over it— "*Frappez fort.*" *Azincourt. Pl.* 37, *cr.* 13.
WODEHOUSE, Eng., out of a cloud, a dexter hand holding a club. *Frappe forte. Pl.* 37, *cr.* 13.
WODEHOUSE, WILLIAM-HERBERT, Esq., of Woolmer's Park, Herts., on a coronet, a cross crosslet, ar. *In hoc signo. Pl.* 66, *cr.* 8, (coronet, *same plate, cr.* 5.)
WODNESTER, an eagle's head, erased, ar., gorged with a ducal coronet, or. *Pl.* 39, *cr.* 4, (without pheon.)
WODON, an eagle, wings addorsed, ar., preying on a (fox,) ppr. *Pl.* 61, *cr.* 3.
WODRINGTON, Eng., a bull's head, couped, sa., platée, horned, or. *Pl.* 120, *cr.* 7.
WODRINGTON, Eng., a wyvern, with (two) heads, ar., winged, or. *Pl.* 63, *cr.* 13.
WOLCOTT, JOHN-MARWOOD, Esq., of Knowle House, Salcombe Regis, Devons., a hawk's head, gu., guttée-d'or, (in beak a fleur-de-lis, gold.) *Pl.* 34, *cr.* 11.
WOLF, or WOLFE, Eng., a wolf, current, erm. *Pl.* 111, *cr.* 1.
WOLF, a wolf, passant, gray, against an oak, vert. *Pl.* 46, *cr.* 6, (oak, *pl.* 58, *cr.* 10.)
WOLF, Salop, a demi-wolf, rampant, or, supporting between paws (a regal crown, ppr.) *Pl.* 56, *cr.* 8.
WOLFALL, Eng., out of a ducal coronet, a dexter hand, ppr., holding a rose, of the first, stalked and leaved, vert. *Pl.* 60, *cr.* 1.
WOLFALL, Lond., a wolf's head, erased, sa., (ducally gorged, or.) *Pl.* 14, *cr.* 6.
WOLFE, a wolf passant, (collared, line reflexed over back.) *Pl.* 46, *cr.* 6.
WOLFE, Chesh., out of a ducal coronet, a demi-wolf, rampant. *Pl.* 56, *cr.* 8, (without spear; coronet, *same plate, cr.* 2.)
WOLFE, Iri., a wolf's head, erased, sa., (ducally gorged, or.) *Pro patriæ amore. Pl.* 14, *cr.* 6.
WOLFERSTAN-PIPE-STANLEY, of Statfold Hall, Staffs. : 1. For *Wolferstan*, a wolf, under a tree, all ppr. *Pl.* 58, *cr.* 10. 2. For *Pipe*, a leopard's head, erased, or. *Pl.* 94, *cr.* 10.
WOLFF, a wolf, regardant, in mouth an (arrow,) in bend, barb downward. *Pl.* 77, *cr.* 14.
WOLFF, Bart., Hants, an imperial baron's coronet, with five pearls fixed on a circle of gold, surmounted with three full-faced helmets, ppr., thereon as many crests, viz. : on

the centre helmet, out of a ducal coronet, or, a demi-wolf, salient, ppr. On the dexter helmet, a ducal coronet, or, thereon a fleur-de-lis, ar., between two imperial eagle's wings, displayed, tawny. On the sinister helmet, a ducal coronet, or, thereon an eagle displayed, sa., ducally crowned, gu. *Dante Deo.*

WOLGAR, Hants., on a mount, vert, a pewit, ppr.

WOLIN, Eng., a lion's head, erased, sa. *Favente Deo.* *Pl.* 81, *cr.* 4.

WOLLACOMBE, Devons., a spur, with leathers, or, (the rowel-points bloody.) *Pl.* 15, *cr.* 3.

WOLLACOMBE, Devons., a falcon, ppr., wings expanded, (charged with three bars, gu.,) belled, or. *Pl.* 105, *cr.* 4.

WOLLASTON, FREDERICK, Esq., of Shenton Hall, Leic., out of a mural coronet, or, a demi-griffin, salient, ar., holding a mullet, pierced, sa. *Ne quid falsi.* *Pl.* 39, *cr.* 2, (coronet, *pl.* 101, *fig.* 6; mullet, *pl.* 45, *cr.* 1.)

WOLLCOTE, Devons., an eagle's head, or, guttée-de-sang, beaked, az., in beak a fleur-de-lis, gold. *Pl.* 100, *cr.* 10, (fleur-de-lis, *pl,* 141.)

WOLLEN, a demi-lion, between paws a cushion, tasselled. *Pl.* 47, *cr.* 4, (cushion, *pl.* 83, *cr.* 9.)

WOLLEY, Eng., a cubit arm, erect, vested, paly of four, ar. and az., in hand, ppr., a (bunch of leaves,) vert. *Pl.* 113, *cr.* 5.

WOLLEY, Salop, a lion, rampant, erminois. *Pl.* 67, *cr.* 5.

WOLLEY, Derbs., a man's head, couped, in coat of mail, all ppr. *Pl.* 33, *cr.* 14.

WOLLEY, Linc., on a mount, vert, a lion, couchant, ar. *Pl.* 75, *cr.* 5, (mount, *same plate, cr.* 6.)

WOLLEY, Linc., a lion, couchant, sa. *Pl.* 75, *cr.* 5, (without chapeau.)

WOLLSTONECRAFT, Lond. and Ess., issuing from a naval coronet, or, a demi-mermaid, in dexter a mirror, ppr., in sinister a comb, gold. *Pl.* 32, *cr.* 8.

WOLMER, Eng., a dexter arm, embowed, ppr., vested, vert, cuffed, or, in hand a covered cup, gold. *Pl.* 39, *cr.* 1.

WOLMER, Linc., two lobsters' claws, erect, or, supporting an escallop, ar. *Pl.* 116, *cr.* 6, (escallop, *pl.* 141.)

WOLMER, Worc., between wings, or, a wolf's head, erased, sa. *Pl.* 14, *cr.* 6, (wings, *pl.* 1, *cr.* 15.)

WOLMER, Worc., a griffin's head, erased, between wings, or. *Pl.* 65, *cr.* 1.

WOLRICH, Eng., a demi-royal-tiger, ppr. *Pl.* 53, *cr.* 10.

WOLRIDGE, or WOLRIGE, Eng., between wings, ppr., a horse's head, or. *Pl.* 19, *cr.* 13.

WOLSELEY, out of a ducal coronet, a wolf's head. *Pl.* 14, *cr.* 6, (coronet, *pl.* 128, *fig.* 3.)

WOLSELEY, Iri. and Eng., out of a ducal coronet, a talbot's head, ppr. *Pl.* 99, *cr.* 7.

WOLSELEY, Bart., Suff., out of a ducal coronet, or, a talbot's head, (erased,) ppr. *Homo homini vulpes.* *Pl.* 99, *cr.* 7.

WOLSEY, Norf., a beast in shape of a beaver, az., with long ears, erect, finned down back, or, web-footed.

WOLSTANHOLME, Derbs., an eagle, displayed, or, (seizing a serpent, nowed, in fret, az.) *Pl.* 119, *cr.* 1.

WOLSTANHOLME, Middx., an eagle, displayed, or, standing on a snake, nowed, vert. *Pl.* 48, *cr.* 11, (snake, *pl.* 75, *cr.* 11.)

WOLSTENHOLME, Lond., an eagle, displayed, or, standing on a snake, nowed, vert. *In ardua virtus.* *Pl.* 48, *cr.* 11, (snake, *pl.* 75, *cr.* 11.)

WOLSTON, or WOLSTONE, Eng., an arm, in armour, embowed, wielding a sword, ppr. *Pl.* 2, *cr.* 8.

WOLSTONECRAFT, Eng., out of a mural coronet, or, a demi-mermaid, (in dexter a purse, ppr., in sinister a comb.) *Vigilans.* *Pl.* 125, *cr.* 3, (coronet, *pl.* 128, *fig.* 18.)

WOLTON, on a bezant, a martlet, ar. *Pl.* 111, *cr.*.5, (bezant, *pl.* 38, *cr.* 2.)

WOLVERSTONE, Eng., a minerva's head, affrontée, ppr. *Pl.* 92, *cr.* 12.

WOLVERSTONE, Suff. and Staffs., against a tree, ppr., a wolf, passant, or. *Pl.* 46, *cr.* 6, (tree, *pl.* 58, *cr.* 10.)

WOMBELL, a dragon's head, erased, or, on neck a (chaplet, vert.) *Pl.* 107, *cr.* 10.

WOMBWELL, Kent, a tiger's head, erased, or, gorged, with a (garland of laurel, vert.) *Pl.* 86, *cr.* 13.

WOMBWELL, Bart., a unicorn's head, couped, ar. *In well beware.* *Pl.* 20, *cr.* 1.

WOMBWELL, Yorks., same crest.

WONDESFORD, Eng., a cross crosslet, gu., surmounted by a sword, in bend sinister, point, downward, ppr. *Pl.* 66, *cr.* 8, (sword, *pl.* 50, *cr.* 4.)

WOOD, Eng., a wolf's head, sa., collared, or. *Pl.* 8, *cr.* 4.

WOOD, FREDERICK-HENRY, Esq., of Hollin Hall, Yorks., an oak-tree, ppr., acorned, or. *Pro patriâ.* *Pl.* 16, *cr.* 8.

WOOD, of Swanwick Hall, Derbs., same crest.

WOOD, WILLIAM-SEWARD, Esq., of the Whitehouse, Heref., a cubit arm, erect, vested, or, cuffed, ar., in hand, ppr., a cross (crosslet), gu. *Credo cruce Christi.* *Pl.* 75, *cr.* 3.

WOOD, WILLIAM-MARK, Esq., of Bishop's Hall, Ess.: 1. An oak-tree, (eradicated,) ppr. *Pl.* 16, *cr.* 8. 2. A martlet, ppr., on stump of oak-tree, branched, ppr. *Tutis in undis.* *Pl.* 111, *cr.* 5, (stump, *pl.* 1, *cr.* 11.)

WOOD, Iri., a cherub's head. *Pl.* 126, *cr.* 10.

WOOD, Sco., an oak-slip, fructed, ppr. *Die virescit.* *Pl.* 32, *cr.* 13.

WOOD, Sco., a savage, from loins upward, in dexter a club, erect, wreathed about temples and loins with laurel, all ppr. *Defend.* *Pl.* 87, *cr.* 13.

WOOD, a dexter arm, in armour, embowed, in hand a sword, (enfiled with a human heart.) *Pl.* 2, *cr.* 8.

WOOD, on an Eastern coronet, or, a leopard, passant, regardant, ppr., in dexter a banner, gu., staff and spear-head, also ppr.

WOOD, a demi-wild man, on shoulder a club, (in dexter an oak-branch,) all ppr., wreathed about loins, vert. *Pl.* 14, *cr.* 11.

WOOD, an arm, embowed, vested in green leaves, in hand a spear, broken in three pieces, (one in pale,) and two in saltire, all ppr. *Pl.* 88, *cr.* 4, (arm, *pl.* 57, *cr.* 2.)

WOOD, on a ducal coronet, an eagle, per pale, or and sa. *Pl.* 7, *cr.* 11, (coronet, *pl.* 128, *fig.* 3.)

WOOD, Devons., a woodman, (in dexter an oak-slip,) in sinister a club, resting on shoulder, all ppr. *Pl.* 14, *cr.* 11.

2 K

Wood, a wolf's head, sa., collared, or. *Pl.* 8, *cr.* 4.
Wood, Durh., on a mount, vert, an oak-tree, fructed, ppr. *Irrideo tempestatem. Pl.* 48, *cr.* 4.
Wood, William-Rayner, Esq., of Singleton Lodge, Lanc., a boar, passant, regardant, sa., collared, chained, and hoofed, or, before a tree, ppr. *Civil and religious liberty.*
Wood, a lion's head, erased, ducally crowned. *Pl.* 90, *cr.* 4, (without charge.)
Wood, Middx., on a lure, ar., caped and lined, or, a falcon, close, gold. *Pl.* 10, *cr.* 7.
Wood, Glouc., an arm, in pale, vested, chequy, or and sa., cuffed, ar., in hand, ppr., a fleur-de-lis, gu. *Pl.* 95, *cr.* 9.
Wood, Kent and Suss., a dexter gauntlet, gu., erect, purfled, or, between two ostrich-feathers, ar. *Pl.* 15, *cr.* 15, (feathers, *pl.* 13, *cr.* 7.)
Wood, Lanc., out of a mural coronet, ar., a demi-man, wreathed about loins and head, vert, (in dexter, a griffin's head, erased, sinister holding a club over sinister shoulder.) *Pl.* 14, *cr.* 11, (coronet, *same plate, cr.* 5.)
Wood, Middx., a hawk, close, ar., jessed and belled, or, standing on a lure, ppr. *Pl.* 10, *cr.* 7.
Wood, Lond., a wolf's head, erased, sa., collared, gu., rimmed, or. *Pl.* 88, *cr.* 4.
Wood, Middx. and Yorks., on a mount, vert, an oak-tree, ppr., fructed, or. *Pl.* 48, *cr.* 4.
Wood, Middx., out of a mural coronet, gu., a wolf's head, sa., collared, ar. *Pl.* 8, *cr.* 4, (coronet, *pl.* 91, *cr.* 15.)
Wood, Middx., a gauntlet, erect, gu., garnished, or, between two branches of laurel, vert. *Pl.* 15, *cr.* 15, (branches, *pl.* 79, *cr.* 14.)
Wood, Norf., a martlet, wings (expanded,) ar., in beak a tulip, ppr., stalked and leaved, vert. *Pl.* 111, *cr.* 5, (tulip, *pl.* 64, *cr.* 2.)
Wood, Notts., an oak-tree, ppr., fructed, or. *Pl.* 16, *cr.* 8.
Wood, Oxon., a squirrel, sejant, between paws a (honeysuckle,) ppr. *Pl.* 2, *cr.* 4.
Wood, Salop, Surr., and Oxon., a demi-woodman, ar., holding a club over dexter shoulder, or. *Pl.* 14, *cr.* 11.
Wood, Somers., a demi-lion, rampant, holding an (acorn, or, the cup, vert.) *Pl.* 39, *cr.* 14.
Wood, Staffs., a demi-lion, rampant, purp., holding (an acorn-branch, vert, fructed, or.) *Ib.*
Wood, Suff., a demi-lion, rampant, or, holding a wreath of laurel, vert. *Pl.* 84, *cr.* 7, (wreath, *pl.* 56, *cr.* 10.)
Wood, Staffs. and Yorks., a wolf's head, erased, sa., collared and ringed, or. *Pl.* 8, *cr.* 4.
Wood, Staffs. and Yorks., a demi-lion, rampant, ar. *Pl.* 67, *cr.* 10.
Wood, Suff., on a ducal coronet, or, an eagle, wings expanded, per pale, or and sa. *Pl.* 126, *cr.* 7, (coronet, *pl.* 9, *cr.* 6.)
Wood, Yorks., an oak-tree, fructed, ppr. *Pl.* 16, *cr.* 8.
Wood, Cambs. and Kent, a demi-lion, rampant, or, (gorged with a wreath, az. and gu., tied behind with two bows.) *Pl.* 18, *cr.* 13.
Wood, Devons., a demi-man, ppr., (in dexter an oak-slip, vert, fructed, or, holding over sinister shoulder a club, gold.) *Pl.* 14, *cr.* 11.

Wood, Devons., a woodman, ppr., wreathed about head and loins, vert, in dexter an (olive-branch,) of the last. *Pl.* 35, *cr.* 12.
Wood, Surr., a ship in full sail, ppr. *Tutis in undis. Pl.* 109, *cr.* 8.
Wood, Sir M., Bart., Lond., out of a mural coronet, a demi-savage, affrontée, (in dexter a tree, eradicated and erased, in sinister a club, reclining on shoulder.) *Defend. Pl.* 14, *cr.* 11, (coronet, *same plate, cr.* 5.)
Wood, Bart., Yorks., a naked savage, ppr., (in dexter a shield, sa., charged with a griffin's head, erased, ar., in sinister a club, resting on shoulder,) also ppr. *Perseverando.*
Woodall, Eng., a Cornish chough, (wings expanded,) and ducally gorged. *Pl.* 44, *cr.* 11.
Woodbridge, a chaplet of roses, ppr. *Pl.* 41, *cr.* 7, (without hand.)
Woodburgh, Eng., a bundle of five arrows, banded round middle by a serpent, ppr. *Pl.* 21, *cr.* 14.
Woodburn, out of a ducal coronet, an eagle's head, all ppr. *Pl.* 20, *cr.* 12.
Woodburne, Eng., a camel's head, sa. *Pl.* 109, *cr.* 9.
Woodcock, Eng., an arm, from shoulder, ppr., vested, gu., cuff vandyked, ar., wielding a sword, ppr. *Pl.* 120, *cr.* 1.
Woodcock, a demi-lion, rampant, gu., supporting a cross crosslet, fitched, or. *Pl.* 65, *cr.* 6.
Woodcock, Ess., a demi-lion, rampant, or, collared, az., studded, and holding a cross pommée, gold. *Pl.* 18, *cr.* 13, (cross, *pl.* 141.)
Woodcock, Salop, a pelican, or, in nest, ppr., feeding her young, ar. *Pl.* 44, *cr.* 1.
Woodcock, Bucks., two lions' gambs, erect and (addorsed,) the dexter, ar., sinister, sa. *Pl.* 106, *cr.* 12.
Woodcock, Lond., Suss., and Warw., (out of rays, issuing from the wreath,) or, a demi-peacock, displayed, ar. *Pl.* 50, *cr.* 9, (without snake.)
Woodd, Basil-George, Esq., of Hillfield, Hampstead, Middx., a demi-savage, ar., holding a club over dexter shoulder, or. *Non nobis. Pl.* 14, *cr.* 11.
Woodd, Middx., a demi-woodman, with club over dexter shoulder, all ppr. *Pl.* 14, *cr.* 11.
Woodeson, Middx., out of a ducal coronet, or, flames, ppr. *Pl.* 16, *cr.* 11, (coronet, *pl.* 128, *fig.* 3.)
Woodford, a savage, holding across him with both hands the stump of a tree, eradicated, all ppr.
Woodford, a demi-woodman, sa., wreathed about temples, or, in (sinister) a club, vert. *Pl.* 14, *cr.* 11.
Woodford, Leic., two lions' gambs, erased, or. *Pl.* 42, *cr.* 3.
Woodford, Linc., a naked savage, wreathed about temples and loins, in dexter a club, in sinister a palm-branch, in bend, all ppr. *Libertate quietum.*
Woodforde, William-Heighes, Esq., of Ansford House, Somers., and of Slaten Island, New York, U.S., a woodman, ppr., holding a club, ar., crowned and girt with oak-leaves. *Pro aris et focis.*
Woodgate, a squirrel, sejant, ppr., holding a nut. *Pl.* 16, *cr.* 9.

WOODGATE, a dexter arm, in armour, embowed, in hand a sword, by the blade, (in fess, surmounted by a sprig of laurel.) *Pl.* 65, *cr.* 8.
WOODHALL, Beds., Northamp., and Chesh., out of a ducal coronet, or, two wings, addorsed, gu. *Pl.* 63, *cr.* 12, (coronet, *pl.* 17, *cr.* 9.)
WOODHALL, Ess., a cubit arm, (vested, per pale, or and sa., cuff, counterchanged,) in hand, ppr., a sword, ar., hilt and pommel, gold. *Pl.* 21, *cr.* 10.
WOODHAM, Eng., an arm, in armour, embowed, hand holding a sword by the blade, (point upward,) ppr. *Pl.* 65, *cr.* 8.
WOODHAM, Cornw., between two sprigs of roses, a buck's head, erased, all ppr. *Pl.* 125, *cr.* 6, (without collar.)
WOODHEAD, Eng., a vol, or. *Pl.* 15, *cr.* 10.
WOODHEAD, Eng., a buck's head, erased. *Pl.* 66, *cr.* 9.
WOODHOUSE, Norf.: 1. Issuing from clouds, ppr., an arm, couped at elbow, and erect, (vested, ar., charged with four sinister bendlets, sa.,) in hand, ppr., a club, also sa., over it this inscription—"Frappe fort." *Pl.* 37, *cr.* 13. 2. A savage, (couped at knees,) ppr., crined, or, holding a club, erect, sa., wreathed about loins, ar. and sa. *Pl.* 87, *cr.* 13.
WOODHOUSE, Norf., a griffin, segreant, or. *Pl.* 67, *cr.* 13.
WOODING, Eng., a goat, (passant,) ar., in mouth a slip of ivy, ppr. *Pl.* 15, *cr.* 9.
WOODLEY, an owl, ar. *Pl.* 27, *cr.* 9.
WOODMAN, Eng., a stork, regardant, sa., resting dexter on a (torteau.) *Pl.* 77, *cr.* 15.
WOODMAN, a buck's head, erased, ppr. *Pl.* 66, *cr.* 9.
WOODNESTER, Heref., an eagle's head, erased, ar., ducally gorged, or. *Pl.* 39, *cr.* 4, (without pheon.)
WOODNOTH, Chesh. and Cornw., a squirrel, sejant, erect, cracking a nut, ppr. *Pl.* 16, *cr.* 9.
WOODHOUSE-HERBERT, of Eastville, Linc., on a coronet, a cross crosslet, fitched. *In hoc signo.* *Pl.* 16, *cr.* 10, (coronet, *pl.* 128, *fig.* 3.)
WOODRIFF, Eng., a hind's head, ppr. *Pl.* 21, *cr.* 9.
WOODROF, and WOODROW, a bull's head, erased, gu. *Pl.* 19, *cr.* 3.
WOODROF, and WOODROW, Yorks., a woodcock, close, ppr.
WOODROFFE, and WOODRUFF, Lond and Surr., a dexter arm, embowed, vested with leaves, vert, in hand a (branch of honeysuckle,) all ppr. *Pl.* 57, *cr.* 2, (without coronet.)
WOODROFFE, Eng., a demi-lady, ppr., vested, ar., in dexter a civic crown, or. *Pl.* 87, *cr.* 14.
WOODROFFE, Suff., a dexter arm, embowed, vested, ermines, cuffed, ar., in hand, ppr., a buck's head, of the last. *Pl.* 39, *cr.* 1, (head, *pl.* 91, *cr.* 14.)
WOODROFFE, Derbs. and Yorks., a woodcock, ppr.
WOODS, GEORGE, Esq., of Milverton, and Winter Lodge, co. Dublin, a demi-woodman, in dexter an (oak-slip.) *Fortis in procellâ.* *Pl.* 35, *cr.* 12.
WOODS, Iri., an arm, in armour, vambraced, hand holding two pieces of a broken spear, in saltier, ppr. *Pl.* 88, *cr.* 4.

WOODS, HENRY, Esq., of Wigan, Lanc., a staff, raguly, in fess, sa., thereon a martlet, wings elevated, of the last, guttée-d'eau. *Labore et perseverantiâ.* *Pl.* 107, *cr.* 6, (staff, *pl.* 5, *cr.* 8.)
WOODS, Lanc., a martlet, sa., wings (addorsed,) in beak a tulip, ppr. *Pl.* 111, *cr.* 5, (tulip, *pl.* 64, *cr.* 2.)
WOODS, Suss., between two ostrich-feathers, erect, ar., a gauntlet, ppr. *Pl.* 15, *cr.* 15, (feathers, *pl.* 13, *cr.* 7.)
WOODS, Norf., a martlet, sa., wings (addorsed,) guttée-d'or. *Pl.* 111, *cr.* 5.
WOODSTOCK, Town, Oxon., out of a ducal coronet, or, an oak-tree, vert, fructed, gold. *Pl.* 94, *cr.* 5.
WOODSTOCK, Eng., a sand-glass, ppr. *Pl.* 43, *cr.* 1.
WOODTHORPE, Eng., a camel's head, ppr. *Pl.* 109, *cr.* 9.
WOODVILE, and WOODVILL, Northamp., a demi-man, ppr., vested, or, on head a cap, sa., (in dexter a cutlass, of the first.) *Pl.* 122, *cr.* 1.
WOODVILLE, Eng., an ear of rye and a palm-branch, in saltier, ppr. *Pl.* 63, *cr.* 3.
WOODWARD, Eng., a squirrel, sejant, ppr., in paws a nut, or. *Pl.* 16, *cr.* 9.
WOODWARD, a tiger's head, erased, ar., maned, or. *Pl.* 94, *cr.* 10.
WOODWARD, a wolf's head, couped, ar., collared, sa., thereon three bezants, between two oak-branches, vert, fructed, or. *Pl.* 8, *cr.* 4.
WOODWARD, Worc., a demi-lion, rampant, sa., supporting between paws a pheon, or. *Pl.* 47, *cr.* 4, (pheon, *pl.* 141.)
WOODWARD, Norf., a buck's head, erased, ppr., attired, (and on neck three billets, or, in mouth a mulberry-leaf, vert.) *Pl.* 66, *cr.* 9.
WOODWARD, Warw., on a ducal coronet, or, a greyhound, sejant, ar. *Pl.* 66, *cr.* 15, (coronet, *same plate.*)
WOODWARD, Lond., on a ducal coronet, a boar's head, couped, ar. *Pl.* 102, *cr.* 14.
WOODWARD, Bucks., a wolf's head, couped, ar., gorged with a collar, sa., charged with three plates. *Pl.* 8, *cr.* 4.
WOODWARD, Beds. and Bucks., a wolf's head, ar., collared, sa., studded, or, between an acorn-branch and a (branch of fern,) ppr. *Pl.* 8, *cr.* 4, (branches, *pl.* 74, *cr.* 7.)
WOODWARD, Kent, a demi-woman, couped at knees, vested, gu., hair dishevelled, or, in dexter a honeysuckle, of the first, stalked and leaved, vert. *Pl.* 2, *cr.* 10.
WOODYEARE, Yorks., a demi-griffin, regardant, per pale, gu. and sa., semée-de-lis, or. *Pl.* 125, *cr.* 12.
WOODYEARE, the Rev. JOHN-FOUNTAIN-WOOD-YEARE, of Crookhill, Yorks., on a wreath, or and sa., a demi-griffin, segreant, regardant, wings inverted, sa., beaked, membered, and semée-de-lis, or. *Pl.* 125, *cr.* 12.
WOOLASTON, Lond., Leic., and Staffs., out of a mural coronet, or, a demi-griffin, segreant, ar., between claws a mullet, sa., pierced, of the second. *Pl.* 39, *cr.* 2, (coronet, *pl.* 101, *cr.* 6; mullet, *pl.* 45, *cr.* 1.)
WOOLCOMBE, Devons., a falcon, ppr., wings expanded and inverted, charged with three bars, gu., beaked, belled, and legged, or. *Pl.* 105, *cr.* 4.
WOOLCOT, Devons., an eagle's head, erased,

ar., on neck three guttes, gu., in beak a fleur-de-lis, of the last. *Pl.* 121, *cr.* 7.

WOOLRIDGE, Eng., out of a ducal coronet, ar., an ass's head, gu. *Pl.* 80, *cr.* 6.

WOOLER, Durh., a demi-lion, rampant, ppr., between paws a (tassel, or.) *Pl.* 126, *cr.* 12.

WOOLEY, Eng., a hind's head, erased, erm. *Pl.* 6, *cr.* 1.

WOOLFE, a wolf's head, ppr., (ducally gorged, or.) *Pl.* 8, *cr.* 4.

WOOLHOUSE, Derbs., an eagle's head, erased, erminois, ducally collared, ar. *Pl.* 39, *cr.* 4, (without pheon.)

WOOL, Warw., a lion, couchant, or. *Pl.* 75, *cr.* 5, (without chapeau.)

WOOLLEY, Eng., an eagle, ppr. *Pl.* 7, *cr.* 11.

WOOLRYCH, HUMPHREY-WILLIAM, Esq., of Croxley House, Herts., an oak-tree, ppr. *Pl.* 16, *cr.* 8.

WOOLSEY, Suff., a naked arm, embowed, in hand a shin-bone, all ppr. *Pl.* 123, *cr.* 10, (bone, *pl.* 25, *cr.* 11.)

WOORLEY, or WORLEY, Kent, out of a mural coronet, az., an arm, in armour, embowed, ppr., garnished, or, hand holding a cutlass, ar., hilt and pommel, gold. *Pl.* 115, *cr.* 14.

WOOTON, or WOOTTON, Eng., out of a ducal coronet, ar., a greyhound's head, gu. *Pl.* 70, *cr.* 5.

WOOTTON, a blackamoor's head, (in profile,) sa., forehead wreathed, and bat's wings to head, az. *Pl.* 115, *cr.* 11.

WORDEN, Eng., on a chapeau, gu., turned up, erm., an eagle, rising, ppr. *Pl.* 114, *cr.* 13.

WORDESWORTH, a stag, trippant, ar. *Pl.* 68, *cr.* 2.

WORDIE, Sco., a sword, in pale, surmounted by two laurel-sprigs, in orle, ppr. *Nil indigne.* *Pl.* 71, *cr.* 3.

WORDSWORTH, Cambs., an antelope's head, erased, ar. *Pl.* 24, *cr.* 7.

WORGE, Suss., a lion's head, erased, ar. *Pl.* 81, *cr.* 4.

WORHEAD, a buck's head, cabossed, sa. *Pl.* 36, *cr.* 1.

WORKESLEY, Eng., a wyvern, passant, az., wings addorsed. *Pl.* 63, *cr.* 13.

WORKLYCH, Suss. and Suff., an arm, in armour, embowed, erect from elbow, in hand, all ppr., a battle-axe, or. *Pl.* 121, *cr.* 14.

WORKMAN, out of a crescent, quarterly, sa. and ar., a lictor's fasces. *Non pas l'ouvrage, mais l'ouvrier.* *Pl.* 93, *cr.* 12, (fasces, *pl.* 65, *cr.* 15.)

WORLEY, Eng., a griffin, sejant, per fess, or and gu. *Pl.* 100, *cr.* 11.

WORLEY, an eagle's leg, erased at thigh, surmounted by three ostrich-feathers. *Pl.* 27, *cr.* 1, (feathers, *pl.* 12, *cr.* 9.)

WORLINGHAM, Baron, (Acheson,) Earl Gosford, Iri. *See* GOSFORD.

WORME, Northamp., a bull, sejant, or, armed and attired, sa.

WORMINGTON, Iri., a wolf's head, (erased,) sa., collared, or. *Pl.* 8, *cr.* 4.

WORMLEIGHTON, Lond. and Leic., an eagle, displayed, or, on breast a (cross,) vair. *Pl.* 12, *cr.* 7.

WORRALL, Eng., a lion's gamb, erect and erased, sa. *Pl.* 126, *cr.* 9.

WORRELL, Eng., in lion's gamb, erect and erased, ar., a (cross crosslet,) of the same. *Pl.* 46, *cr.* 7.

WORRELL, in lion's gamb, erect and erased, sa. a (covered) cup, or. *Pl.* 30, *cr.* 4.

WORSELEY, Surr., Hants., and Lanc., a wolf's head erased, or. *Ut sursum desuper.* *Pl.* 14, *cr.* 6.

WORSELEY, Northamp., trunk of tree, in fess, couped and raguled, ar., at dexter end an acorn-branch, ppr., thereon a pheasant, of the first, combed and wattled, or. *Pl.* 14, *cr.* 14, (pheasant, *pl.* 82, *cr.* 12.)

WORSLEY, Bart., of Holvingham, Yorks., a wyvern, vert. *Quam plurimis prodesse.* *Pl.* 63, *cr.* 13.

WORSLEY, Hants., a wyvern, wings addorsed, az., armed and legged, gu. *Ut sursum desuper.* *Pl.* 63, *cr.* 13.

WORSLEY, a wolf's head, erased, or. *Pl.* 14, *cr.* 6.

WORSLEY, Derbs., out of a mural coronet, or, a wyvern, gu. *Pl.* 63, *cr.* 13, (coronet, *pl.* 128, *fig.* 18.)

WORSLEY, Durh. and Yorks., an eagle's leg, plumed on thigh with feathers. *Pl.* 27, *cr.* 1, (without heart.)

WORSLEY, and WORTLEY, Eng., a lion, rampant, ppr., in dexter a fleur-de-lis. *Pl.* 87, *cr.* 6.

WORSOLLEY, Eng., a wolf's head, or. *Pl.* 91, *cr.* 15, (without rose.)

WORSTER, Eng., a griffin, segreant, gu. *Pl.* 67, *cr.* 13.

WORSYCKE, a bundle of three arrows, points downward, banded, ppr. *Pl.* 43, *cr.* 14.

WORTH, Somers., an arm, erect, vested and gloved, ermine, hand holding an eagle's leg, couped at thigh, or. *Pl.* 103, *cr.* 2.

WORTH, and DE WORTHE, Somers. and Devons., same crest.

WORTHINGTON, EDWARD, Esq., of The Bryn, Chesh., a goat, statant, ar., armed or. *Virtute dignus avorum.* *Pl.* 66, *cr.* 1.

WORTHINGTON, a goat, statant, (on dexter side of the wreath a laurel-slip, erect.) *Pl.* 66, *cr.* 1.

WORTHINGTON, Suff., Lanc., Linc., and Yorks., a goat, (passant, ar., attired, or, in mouth an acorn-branch, vert, fructed, gold.) *Pl.* 15, *cr.* 9.

WORTHOM, Eng., a lion, rampant, double queued, per fess, gu. and ar. *Pl.* 41, *cr.* 15.

WORTHY, and WORPHY, Eng., a griffin, passant, wings addorsed, or. *Pl.* 67, *cr.* 14, (without gorging.)

WORTLEY-STUART, Baron Wharncliffe. *See* WHARNCLIFFE.

WORTLING, a greyhound's head, ar., between two roses, gu., leaved and slipped, ppr. *Pl.* 84, *cr.* 13.

WORYNDON, Eng., on a ducal coronet, a martlet. *Pl.* 98, *cr.* 14.

WOTTON, Eng., out of a mural coronet, az., a lion's head, or. *Pl.* 45, *cr.* 9.

WOTTON, Kent, a satyr's head, in profile, couped at shoulders, sa., wings to the side of the head, az.

WOTTON, Somers., an ostrich's head, or, on neck a cross formée, sa. *Pl.* 49, *cr.* 7, (cross, *pl.* 141.)

WOWAN, Eng., a hawk's lure. *Pl.* 97, *cr.* 14.

WOWEN, Lond., a hawk's lure, feathers, ar., garnished, or, charged with a fleur-de-lis, sa., the string and tassel erect and nowed, gu. *Pl.* 97, *cr.* 14, (fleur-de-lis, *pl.* 141.)

WRAGG, Eng., a mullet, pierced, erm. *Pl. 45, cr.* 1.

WRANGHAM, Eng., four ostrich-feathers, gu., enfiled with a ducal coronet, or. *Pl. 44, cr.* 12.

WRANGHAM, Yorks.: 1. A dove, volant, in mouth an olive-branch, ppr. *Pl. 25, cr.* 6. 2. A lion, passant, paly of six, ar. and gu. *Hyeme exsuperatâ. Pl. 48, cr.* 8.

WRAXALL, Bart., Somers., a buck's head, gardant, erased, gu., charged on breast with two lozenges, in fess, between attires an etoile, or. *Pl.* 8, *cr.* 6, (lozenge and fleur-de-lis, *pl.* 141.)

WRAY, a parrot's head and neck. *Pl.* 94, *cr.* 2, (without wings.)

WRAY, Durh., an ostrich, or. *Pl.* 64, *cr.* 3, (without coronet.)

WRAY, Linc., an ostrich, or. *Et juste et vray. Ib.*

WREAHOKE, Suff., a talbot, passant, sa., (ducally gorged, or.) *Pl.* 65, *cr.* 2.

WREN, Eng., on a chapeau, ppr., a lion's head, erased, gu. *Pl.* 99, *cr.* 9.

WREN, Durh., a lion's head, erased, ar., collared, gu., (pierced through neck by a broken spear, of the last, headed, of the first, vulned, of the second.) *Pl.* 7, *cr.* 10.

WRENCH, Eng., a stag, trippant, ppr. *Pl.* 68, *cr.* 2.

WRENCH, a slip of three acorns, ppr., leaved, vert. *Pl.* 69, *cr.* 12.

WREY, Bart., Cornw.: 1. An arm, embowed, vested, sa., hand, ppr., holding a hatchet, ar., helved, gu. *Pl.* 120, *cr.* 1, (hatchet, *pl.* 73, *cr.* 7.) 2. A man's head, in profile, couped at shoulders, on head a ducal coronet, thereon a cap, turned forward and tasselled, ppr., charged with a Catherine-wheel, gold. *Le bon temps viendra. Pl.* 78, *cr.* 14, (wheel, *pl.* 141.)

WREY, a lion's head, erased. *Pl.* 81, *cr.* 4.

WREY, Eng., a Saracen's head, ducally crowned, or., issuing therefrom a long cap, gu., falling forward. *Pl.* 78, *cr.* 14.

WRIGHT, FRANCIS, Esq., of Osmaston Manor, Derbs., a unicorn's head, ar., erased, gu., armed and maned, or. *Ad rem. Pl.* 67, *cr.* 1.

WRIGHT, a naked arm, couped at shoulder, and embowed, elbow on the wreath, hand holding a sword, in pale, enfiled with a leopard's head, cabossed. *Pl.* 102, *cr.* 11, (head, *same plate, cr.* 5.)

WRIGHT, Iri., out of a ducal coronet, a broken battle-axe, all ppr. *Pl.* 24, *cr.* 15, (coronet, *same plate, cr.* 10.)

WRIGHT, ICHABOD, Esq., of Mapperley, Notts., out of a crescent, or, a unicorn's head, ar., erased, gu., armed and maned, gold. *Pl.* 74, *cr.* 2, (head, *pl.* 67, *cr.* 1.)

WRIGHT, Sco., an arm, in armour, embowed, hand grasping a battle-axe, both ppr. *Marte et ingenio. Pl.* 2, *cr.* 8, (axe, *pl.* 73, *cr.* 7.)

WRIGHT Eng., a dragon's head, ar. *Pl.* 87, *cr.* 12.

WRIGHT, Sco., an arm, in armour, embowed, issuing from a cloud, in gauntlet a (sabre,) ppr. *Pro rege sæpe. Pl.* 30, *cr.* 6.

WRIGHT, a bull's head, cabossed. *Pl.* 111, *cr.* 6.

WRIGHT, Sco., an arm, in armour, embowed, resting on elbow, in hand a battle-axe, all ppr. *Pl.* 121, *cr.* 14.

WRIGHT, two arms, embowed, hands holding a battle-axe, all ppr. *Pl.* 41, *cr.* 2.

WRIGHT, Sco., a dexter arm, in hand a battle-axe, ppr. *Tam arte quam marte. Pl.* 73, *cr.* 7.

WRIGHT, Eng., out of a ducal coronet, or, a bull's head, ar., attired, gold. *Pl.* 68, *cr.* 6.

WRIGHT, a dragon's head, couped, erm. *Pl.* 87, *cr.* 12.

WRIGHT, Suff., out of a mural coronet, vert, a dragon's head, ar. *Pl.* 101, *cr.* 4.

WRIGHT, Surr., a lion's head, erased, gardant, or, ducally crowned, az. *Pl.* 1, *cr.* 5.

WRIGHT, of Bolton-on-Swale, Yorks., a unicorn, passant, regardant, quarterly, ar. and az., armed, or. *Pl.* 106, *cr.* 3, (regardant, *same plate, cr.* 1.)

WRIGHT, Ess., out of a ducal coronet, or, a dragon's head, vert, (collared, gold.) *Pl.* 93, *cr.* 15, (without flames.)

WRIGHT, Lond. and Hants., (on a mount, vert,) a tiger, passant, or, tufted and maned, sa., resting dexter on an escutcheon, ar. *Pl.* 86, *cr.* 2, (escutcheon, *pl.* 19, *cr.* 2.)

WRIGHT, Hants., out of a ducal coronet, an eagle. *Pl.* 7, *cr.* 11, (coronet, *pl.* 128, *fig.* 3.)

WRIGHT, Kent and Suff., a stag's head, erased, gu., guttée-d'or, attired, gold. *Pl.* 66, *cr.* 9.

WRIGHT, Kent and Suff., a stag's head, erased, or, (charged with three guttes, in cross, gu.) *Pl.* 66, *cr.* 9.

WRIGHT, Kent, a lion's head, erased, gardant, or, ducally crowned, sa. *Pl.* 1, *cr.* 5.

WRIGHT, Lond., a pelican, in nest, feeding her young, all ppr. *Pl.* 44, *cr.* 1.

WRIGHT, Linc., on a mount, vert, a unicorn, passant, (regardant, ar., semée of etoiles, az., armed, maned, and hoofed, or, gorged with a collar, of the third, dexter resting on a cross pattée, gold.) *Pl.* 106, *cr.* 3, (mount, *pl.* 122, *cr.* 5.)

WRIGHT, Lond., a martlet, ar., gorged with a bar-gemelle, counter-flory, az. *Pl.* 111, *cr.* 5.

WRIGHT, Lond. and Surr., a falcon's head, erased, ppr. *Pl.* 34, *cr.* 11.

WRIGHT, Lond. and Surr., a camel's head, couped, (bridled,) or, in mouth three ostrich-feathers. *Pl.* 109, *cr.* 9, (feathers, *pl.* 12, *cr.* 9.)

WRIGHT, of Kilverstone, Norf., a dragon's head, erased, ar., pellettée. *Pl.* 107, *cr.* 10, (without collar.)

WRIGHT, Oxon., out of a mural coronet, chequy, or and gu., a dragon's head, vert, scaled, or, (charged on neck with three leopards' heads, of the second, between two bars-gemelle, ar.) *Pl.* 101, *cr.* 4.

WRIGHT, Chesh., a dexter arm, embowed, vested, az., in hand, ppr., a sword, point downward, ar., hilt and pommel, or, enfiled with a leopard's head, of the third.

WRIGHT, Staffs. and Derbs., a cubit arm, erect, in coat of mail, ppr., in hand a spear, or, headed, az. *Pl.* 23, *cr.* 9.

WRIGHT, Durh., a dragon's head, couped, gu., semée of cross crosslets, ar. *Pl.* 87, *cr.* 12.

WRIGHT, Durh., an (eagle's) head, erminois, ducally crowned, az. *Pl.* 100, *cr.* 15.

WRIGHT, Ess., a wheat-sheaf, or, environed by an antique crown, sa. *Pl.* 76, *cr.* 13.

WRIGHT, Ess., a dexter arm, couped and embowed, vested, az., purfled, or, cuffed, ar., in hand a sword, both ppr., hilt and pommel, gold, enfiled with a leopard's head, affrontée, of the last. *Pl.* 102, *cr.* 5.

WRIGHT, Ess., out of a ducal coronet, or, a dragon's head, ppr. *Pl.* 101, *cr.* 4.

WRIGHT, Bart., South Carolina, on a mount, vert, and within an annulet, or, a dragon's head, couped at neck, ar., semée of annulets, sa., and murally gorged, gu. *Mens sibi conscia recti.*

WRIGHTSON, Northumb., a unicorn, (salient,) or. *Pl.* 37, *cr.* 7.

WRIGHTSON, of Cusworth, Yorks., a unicorn, (salient,) ar., armed, crined, tufted, and unguled, or. *Pl.* 37, *cr.* 7.

WRIGHTSWORTH, a crane, ppr., in beak a (fish,) ar. *Pl.* 46, *cr.* 9.

WRIOTHESLEY, or WRIOTHSLEY, a bull, passant, sa., armed and (crowned, or, in nose an annulet, with line reflexed over back.) *Pl.* 66, *cr.* 11.

WRITINGTON, a demi-fox, holding a cross crosslet fitched, az. *Pl.* 30, *cr.* 9.

WRITINGTON, Eng., a stag, at gaze, or. *Pl.* 81, *cr.* 8.

WROTESLEY, Eng., a boar's head, couped, erm., armed, or. *Pl.* 48, *cr.* 2.

WROTH, or WROTHE, Kent, Ess., Herts., and Suff., a lion's head, erased, gardant, ar., crowned, or. *Pl.* 1, *cr.* 5.

WROTTESLEY, Eng., a boar's head, erased and erect. *Pl.* 21, *cr.* 7.

WROTTESLEY, Baron, (Wrottesley,) out of a ducal coronet, a boar's head, erm., crined and tusked, or. *Pl.* 102, *cr.* 14.

WROTTESLEY, Bart., Staffs., out of a ducal coronet, or, a boar's head, erm., armed and crined, gold. *Pl.* 102, *cr.* 14.

WROTTESLEY, out of a ducal coronet, or, a boar's head, ar., on neck an ermine-spot. *Pl.* 102, *cr.* 14.

WROUGHTON, Berks. and Wilts., an ibex's head, ar., pellettée, collared, ringed, and armed, or. *Pl.* 105, *cr.* 12.

WROUGHTON, Eng., a stag, lodged, ppr. *Pl.* 67, *cr.* 2.

WRYNE, a talbot, ar., guttée, sa., collared, gu., (between two holly-branches, leaved, vert, fructed, gu.) *Pl.* 65, *cr.* 2.

WYAT, a buck, (sejant,) regardant. *Pl.* 51, *cr.* 9.

WYATT, a boar's head, couped, in fess. *Pl.* 48, *cr.* 2.

WYATT, out of a mural coronet, ar., a demi-lion, rampant, sa., charged on shoulder with an etoile, of the first, and holding (an arrow,) ppr. *Pl.* 120, *cr.* 14, (etoile, *pl.* 141.)

WYATT, an ostrich, gu., the tail, bezantée, in mouth a horse-shoe, sa. *Pl.* 16, *cr.* 2.

WYATT, Somers., a demi-lion, per pale, crenellée, or and sa., in dexter an arrow, gu., headed and feathered, ar. *Pl.* 41, *cr.* 13, (arrow, *pl.* 59, *cr.* 5.)

WYATT, Ess., a demi-lion, rampant, sa., guttéed'or, holding an arrow, gold. *Ib.*

WYATT, Ess. and Kent, a demi-lion, rampant, sa., holding an arrow, or, plumed and barbed, ar. *Ib.*

WYATT, Devons. and Kent, an ostrich, ppr., in mouth a horse-shoe, ar. *Pl.* 16, *cr.* 2.

WYBERG, an eagle's head, erased, ppr. *Pl.* 20, *cr.* 7.

WYBERGH, WILLIAM, Esq., of Clifton Hall, Westm., a griffin's head, erased, or. *Hominem te esse memento.* *Pl.* 48, *cr.* 6.

WYBORN, Kent, a swan, ar., membered, gu. *Fama perennis erit.* *Pl.* 122, *cr.* 15, (without mount.)

WYBRANTS, Eng., a buck's head, erased, ppr. *Pl.* 66, *cr.* 9.

WYCH, a dexter arm, embowed, vested, gu., cuffed, or, in hand, ppr., a trefoil, slipped, vert. *Pl.* 39, *cr.* 1, (trefoil, *pl.* 78, *cr.* 6.)

WYCH, or WYCHE, Chesh., a dexter arm, embowed, vested, gu., cuffed, or, in hand, ppr., a (sprig, vert.) *Pl.* 39, *cr.* 1.

WYCHCOMBE, a buck's head, erased. *Pl.* 66, *cr.* 9.

WYCHERLEY, Salop, an eagle, displayed, sa., (ducally gorged, ar.) *Pl.* 48, *cr.* 11.

WYCOMB, Eng., (two) arrows, in pale, ppr., points upward. *Pl.* 75, *cr.* 7.

WYCOMBE, Salop, out of a ducal coronet, ar., a demi-eagle, displayed, per pale, or and sa., (gorged with a collar, counterchanged.) *Pl.* 33, *cr.* 5.

WYDENT, an arm, gu., hand, ppr., between wings, sa., thereon a bird, az. *Pl.* 11, *cr.* 11, (bird, *pl.* 44, *cr.* 13.)

WYDNELL, Surr., a stork, or, (wings expanded,) sa., bezantée, beaked, of the second. *Pl.* 33, *cr.* 9.

WYDOPE, and WYDROPE, three horse shoes, interlaced, ppr. *Pl.* 52, *cr.* 4, (interlacing, *pl.* 119, *cr.* 10.)

WYE, Eng., on a mount, a stag, passant, ppr. *Pl.* 61, *cr.* 15, (mount, *pl.* 50, *cr.* 6.)

WYE, Glouc. and Suff., a griffin's (head,) wings addorsed, az., issuing from a plume of ostrich-feathers, two, ar., and three, or. *Pl.* 11, *cr.* 6.

WYER, Eng., an arm, ppr., vested, az., in hand a holly-branch, vert. *Pl.* 64, *cr.* 7, (holly, *pl.* 4, *cr.* 15.)

WYGHTWYCK, WYGTWYCKE, or WYGHTWICK, Staffs., a demi-heraldic-tiger, ar., mane and tail crined, and in dexter a pheon, or. *Aut viam inveniam aut faciam.* *Pl.* 57, *cr.* 13, (pheon, *pl.* 141.)

WYKE, Eng., a demi-savage, in dexter an arrow, at his back a sheaf of arrows, ppr.

WYKEHAM, PHILIP-THOMAS-HERBERT, Esq., of Tythrop House, Oxon., a bull's head, sa., horned, or, (charged on neck with two chevronels, ar,) *Manners maketh man.* *Pl.* 63, *cr.* 11.

WYKEHAM-MARTIN. *See* MARTIN.

WYKES, Eng., a cock, gu. *Pl.* 67, *cr.* 14.

WYKES, Glouc., a greyhound's head, erased, or, collared, gu., in mouth a man's leg, couped at thigh, ar. *Pl.* 30, *cr.* 7.

WYLDBORE, a (spear-head,) in pale, guttée-desang, thrust through a boar's head, erased, in fess. *Pl.* 10, *cr.* 2.

WYLDE, Worc., a lion, passant, gardant, gu., resting dexter on an escutcheon, ar. *Pl.* 120, *cr.* 5, (escutcheon, *pl.* 19, *cr.* 2.)

WYLDE, JOHN-CHARLES, Esq., of Southwell, Notts., a demi-buck, couped, sa., (with a crown and ring about neck,) horned and hoofed, gold. *Confide recte agens.* *Pl.* 55, *cr.* 9, (without rose.)

WYLDE, an eagle, displayed, or. *Pl.* 48, *cr.* 11.
WYLDE, Worc., a stag's head, erased, erm. *Pl.* 66, *cr.* 9.
WYLIDON, Eng., a dexter hand, couped, in fess, holding a cross crosslet, in pale. *Pl.* 78, *cr.* 9.
WYLIE, Eng., on a rock, a fort in flames, ppr. *Pl.* 59, *cr.* 8.
WYLIE, Bart., a (cossack, mounted,) and in the act of charging at full speed, ppr. *Labore et scientiâ. Pl.* 115, *cr.* 5.
WYLLIE, of Forfar, Sco., a talbot, passant, white, spotted liver colour. *Fides. Pl.* 120, *cr.* 8.
WYMAN, Eng., on a garb, in fess, or, a cock, gu. *Pl.* 122, *cr.* 3.
WYMOND, Suss., a cubit arm, erect, (in coat of mail,) in hand, ppr., a fire-ball, or, fired, also ppr. *Pl.* 2, *cr.* 6.
WYMOND, Eng., a demi-eagle, displayed, vert. *Pl.* 22, *cr.* 11.
WYNALL, Eng., an owl, sa. *Pl.* 27, *cr.* 9.
WYNCHCOMBE, Berks., a buck's head, erased, quarterly, az. and or, (in mouth a laurel-branch, ppr.) *Pl.* 66, *cr.* 9.
WYNCHE, Ess., out of a naval coronet, a lion's head, erased, gardant, ar., between two spears, or, headed, of the first. *Pl.* 118, *cr.* 5, (spears, *pl.* 69, *cr.* 14; head, *pl.* 1, *cr.* 5.)
WYNCHE, Ess., a lion's head, erased, gardant, ar., ducally crowned, between two spears, or, headed, of the first. *Pl.* 1, *cr.* 5, (spears, *pl.* 69, *cr.* 14.)
WYNDHAM, Earl of Egremont. *See* EGREMONT.
WYNDHAM, WILLIAM, Esq., of Dinton, Wilts., a lion's head, erased, within a fetterlock, or. *Au bon droit. Pl.* 90, *cr.* 14.
WYNDHAM, of Cromer, Norf., same crest and motto.
WYNDHAM, a fetterlock, chain archwise, gold, (thereon an escutcheon,) charged with a lion's head, erased, or, the chain counterchanged, of the first and az. *Pl.* 90, *cr.* 14.
WYNDHAM, Lond., Somers., Devons., Suff., and Norf., a lion's head, erased, or, within a fetterlock, gold, the bow compony, counter-compony, of the first and az. *Pl.* 90, *cr.* 14.
WYNDHAM-QUIN, Earl of Dunraven. *See* DUNRAVEN.
WYNFORD, Baron, (Best,) out of a ducal coronet, or, a demi-swan, wings displayed, ar. *Pl.* 100, *cr.* 7.
WYNGATE, Beds., a hind's head, or, (gorged with a bar-gemelle, sa.) *Pl.* 21, *cr.* 9.
WYNGATE, Beds., a gate, or. *Pl.* 73, *cr.* 4.
WYNILL, Yorks., a wyvern, wings elevated, ar., vomiting flames, ppr. *Par la volonté de Dieu. Pl.* 51, *cr.* 12, (without crown.)
WYNILL, Durh., a wyvern, wings addorsed, ar., vomiting flames, ppr. *Pl.* 51, *cr.* 12, (without crown.)
WYNN, a cubit arm, vested, sa., in hand, ppr., a fleur-de-lis, ar. *Pl.* 95, *cr.* 9.
WYNN, a unicorn's head, erased, ar., maned, horned, and crined, ppr. *Pl.* 67, *cr.* 1.
WYNN, Salop, a boar's head, gu., couped, or. *Pl.* 48, *cr.* 2.

WYNN, Baron Newborough. *See* NEWBOROUGH.
WYNN-WILLIAMS, Bart., Wel., an eagle, displayed, or. *Pl.* 48, *cr.* 11.
WYNNE, WILLIAM-WATKIN-EDWARD, Esq., of Peniarth, Merioneth, Wel., on a chapeau, a boar, passant, ar., fretty, gu. *Pl.* 22, *cr.* 8.
WYNNE, the Right Hon. JOHN-ARTHUR, of Haslewood, co. Sligo, a wolf's head, erased, ar. *Non sibi, sed toto. Pl.* 14, *cr.* 6.
WYNNE, BROWNLOW-WYNNE, Esq., of Garthewin, Denbigh, Wel., a stag, trippant. *Pl.* 68, *cr.* 2.
WYNNE, Middx., an arm, (in armour,) erect, ppr., in gauntlet a fleur-de-lis, ar. *Pl.* 95, *cr.* 9.
WYNNE, Wel., a dolphin, haurient, ar. *Pl.* 14, *cr.* 10.
WYNNE, Yorks. and Wel., an eagle displayed, or. *Pl.* 48, *cr.* 11.
WYNNIATT, the Rev. REGINALD, of Guiting Grange, Glouc., a lion's head, ducally crowned. *Pl.* 90, *cr.* 4, (without charging.)
WYNNINGTON, Lond. and Chesh., a still, ar.
WYNSTON, Glouc. and Heref., a garb, erect, or, sustained on either side by two lions, rampant, dexter, ar., sinister, az. *Pl.* 36, *cr.* 8, (without chapeau.)
WYNSTONE, Wel., same crest.
WYNTER, Wel., a heath-cock, ppr.
WYRALL, Eng., a cock's head, erased, gu. *Pl.* 92, *cr.* 3.
WYRLAY, or WYRLEY, out of a ducal coronet, or, two wings, addorsed, ppr. *Pl.* 63, *cr.* 12, (coronet, *pl.* 17, *cr.* 9.)
WYRLEY, Staffs., a wing, erect. *Pl.* 39, *cr.* 10.
WYRRALD, Glouc., in lion's gamb, erect, gu., a cross (crosslet,) fitched, ar. *Pl.* 46, *cr.* 7.
WYRRALL, Glouc., an arm, in armour, in hand a sword, all ppr. *Pl.* 2, *cr.* 8.
WYRRALL, Yorks., in lion's gamb, erased, sa., a cup, or. *Pl.* 30, *cr.* 4.
WYTHENS, Kent, Lond., and Berks, on a ducal coronet, gu., a talbot. *Pl.* 3, *cr.* 8, (without collar and line.)
WYTHENS, Kent, Lond., and Berks., a leopard, sejant, erm., (collared and lined, or, holding out the line with the dexter paw.) *Pl.* 86, *cr.* 8, (without coronet.)
WYTHERNEWYKE, Linc., a bustard, close, ar., winged, or. *Pl.* 30, *cr.* 8.
WYTHERS, Eng., a demi-eagle, displayed, with two heads, ppr. *Pl.* 4, *cr.* 6.
WYTHERS, Ess. and Hants, a demi-hare, ppr., (in mouth three stalks of wheat, or.) *Pl.* 58, *cr.* 14.
WYVELL, Eng., on a mount, a peacock, ppr. *Pl.* 9, *cr.* 1.
WYVELL, Surr. and Yorks., a wyvern, wings addorsed, ar., vomiting fire, ppr. *Pl.* 51, *cr.* 2, (without crown.)
WYVILL, MARMADUKE, Esq., of Constable Burton, Yorks., a wyvern, ar. *Par la volonté de Dieu. Pl.* 63, *cr.* 13.
WYSE, the Right Hon. Sir THOMAS, K.C.B., of the Manor of St John, co. Waterford, and of Cuddagh, in the Queen's County, a demi-lion, rampant, gu., guttée, ar. *Sapere aude. Pl.* 67, *cr.* 10.

Y

YABSLEY, Devons., a demi-lion, rampant, holding in paws a serpent, ppr. *Industriâ et spe.* *Pl.* 124, *cr.* 5.

YALDWYN, Suss., on a chapeau, sa., turned up, erm., a sword, in pale, ar., hilt and pommel, or, between wings, gold. *Pl.* 11, *cr.* 8.

YALE, Salop, on a chapeau, a boar, in a net. *Pl.* 64, *cr.* 8.

YARBOROUGH, Linc., a falcon, (close;) or, belled, gold, preying on a cock-pheasant, ppr. *Pl.* 61, *cr.* 7, (pheasant, *pl.* 72, *cr.* 6.)

YARBOROUGH, Earl of, and Baron, and Baron Dursley, (Anderson-Pelham :) 1. For *Pelham*, a peacock, in pride, ppr. *Pl.* 92, *cr.* 11. 2. For *Anderson*, a water-spaniel, or. *Pl.* 58, *cr.* 9.

YARBURGH, GEORGE-JOHN, Esq., of Heslington Hall, Yorks., a falcon, (close, or, belled, gold, preying on a duck, ppr.) *Non est sine pulvere palma.* *Pl.* 61, *cr.* 7.

YARD, an arrow, in pale, point (upwards,) enfiled with a ducal coronet, ppr. *Pl.* 55, *cr.* 1.

YARDELEY, or YARDLEY, a stag, in full course, or. *Pl.* 3, *cr.* 2.

YARDELEY, Eng., a hind, passant, ppr. *Pl.* 20, *cr.* 14.

YARDLEY, Wel., a buck, springing. *Pl.* 65, *cr.* 14.

YARDLEY, Kent and Staffs.: 1. A buck, current, gu., attired, or. *Pl.* 3, *cr.* 2. 2. A goat, salient, ppr. *Pl.* 32, *cr.* 10, (without tree.)

YARDLY, or YARDLEY, Eng., a hind's head, or. *Pl.* 21, *cr.* 9.

YARKER, Eng., a greyhound, current, ppr. *Pl.* 28, *cr.* 7, (without charging.)

YARKER, HENRY-JOHN-FORSTER, Esq., of Leyburn Hall, Yorks., a stork, (rising, ar., collared, beaked, and legged, gu., resting dexter on a human heart, of the second,) in beak an oak-branch, fructed, ppr. *La fin couronne les œuvres.* *Pl.* 33, *cr.* 9, (branch, *pl.* 46, *cr.* 9.)

YARMOUTH, Norf. and Suff., a pheasant, close, ppr. *Pl.* 82, *cr.* 12.

YARROW, Eng., a buck, trippant, gu., attired and unguled, or. *Pl.* 68, *cr.* 2.

YARWORTH, Wilts. and Devons., an arm, erect, ppr., hand grasping a snake, environed round arm, vert. *Pl.* 91, *cr.* 6.

YARWORTH, Suff., a hawk, ppr., belled, or. *Pl.* 67, *cr.* 3.

YATE, Glouc., an elephant's head, ar., tusked, or. *Quo virtus vocat.* *Pl.* 35, *cr.* 13.

YATE, Glouc., a falcon, volant, or. *Quod pudet, hoc pigeat.* *Pl.* 94, *cr.* 1.

YATE, Eng., a horse's head, gu. *Pl.* 81, *cr.* 6.

YATE, Warw., out of a ducal coronet, or, a goat's head, sa., armed, ar. *Pl.* 72, *cr.* 2.

YATE, Berks., out of a ducal coronet, ar., a goat's head, sa., bearded and attired, of the first. *Pl.* 72, *cr.* 2.

YATE, Wilts., a demi-goat, rampant, per pale sa. and ar., attired, counterchanged, holding between paws a gate, or. *Pl.* 11, *cr.* 4.

YATES, out of a ducal coronet, or, a goat's head, sa., attired and bearded, ar. *Pl.* 72, *cr.* 2.

YATES, Eng., a demi-lion, rampant, az. *Pl.* 67, *cr.* 10.

YATES, an antelope's head, ppr. *Pl.* 24, *cr.* 7.

YATES, Sco., a gate, ppr. *Securus.* *Pl.* 73, *cr.* 4.

YAWKINS, Sco., a naked arm, embowed, wielding a scimitar, all ppr. *Præsto et persisto.* *Pl.* 92, *cr.* 5.

YAXLEY, an heraldic-antelope, sa., (bezantée,) attired, maned, and tufted, or *Pl.* 115, *cr.* 13.

YAXLEY, Suff., a demi-unicorn, collared, gobony. *Pl.* 21, *cr.* 1.

YAXLEY, Suff., an Indian goat, ar., pellettée, attired, or. *Pl.* 66, *cr.* 1.

YEA, a ram, passant, ar. *Pl.* 109, *cr.* 2.

YEA, Bart., Somers., a talbot, passant, ar. *Esto semper fidelis.* *Pl.* 120, *cr.* 8.

YEARDS, Eng., an arrow, in pale, point (upwards,) enfiled with a ducal coronet, ppr. *Pl.* 55, *cr.* 1.

YEATES, or YEATS, Eng., a lion's head, erased, ar. *Pl.* 81, *cr.* 4.

YEATES, Iri., a shark, issuing, regardant, swallowing a man, all ppr. *Pl.* 16, *cr.* 6.

YEATMAN, the Rev. HARRY FARR, LL.B., of Stock House, Dors., a goat's head, erased, sa., horned, bearded, and (charged with a gate,) or. *Propositi tenax.* *Pl.* 29, *cr.* 13.

YELDHAM, or YILDHAM, Ess., a bezant, thereon a lion's head, erased, az., collared with a bargemelle, flory counter-flory, ar. *Fides culpari metuens.* *Pl.* 50, *cr.* 10.

YELLOWLEY, Eng., a bat, displayed, sa. *Pl.* 94, *cr.* 9.

YELVERTON, Viscount Avonmore. See AVONMORE.

YELVERTON, a lion, passant, gardant, gu. *Foy en tout.* *Pl.* 120, *cr.* 5.

YELVERTON, a lion, passant, regardant, gu. *Foy en tout.* *Pl.* 100, *cr.* 6.

YELVERTON, Norf., a lion, passant, regardant, gu. *Pl.* 100, *cr.* 6.

YENN, Lond., a lion, passant, az. *Pl.* 48, *cr.* 8.

YEO, Devons., a peacock, ppr. *Pl.* 54, *cr.* 13.

YEOMAN, a hand throwing a dart. *Shoot thus.* *Pl.* 42, *cr.* 13.

YEOMAN, a dexter arm, in armour, embowed, in hand a spear, both ppr. *Pl.* 44, *cr.* 9.

YEOMANS, Glouc. and Somers., a dexter arm, in hand a spear, ppr. *Pl.* 99, *cr.* 9.

YER, Eng., a wolf, sejant, sa. *Pl.* 110, *cr.* 4.

YERBINE, Glouc. and Wilts., a lion's head, per fess, or and ar. *Pl.* 81, *cr.* 4.

YERBURY, Glouc. and Wilts., same crest.

YESTER, a ram's head, ar., crowned, or. *Pl.* 125, *cr.* 10.

YETSWORTH, Middx., out of a ducal coronet, a buck's head, both or, in mouth a rose, (gu.,) stalked and leaved, vert. *Pl.* 100, *cr.* 8, (coronet, *pl.* 29, *cr.* 7.)

YETTS, Sco., a greyhound's head, ar. *Pl.* 14, *cr.* 4.

YEVEREY, Eng., an elephant's head, bendy of six, ar. and gu. *Pl.* 35, *cr.* 13.
YLES, Sco., a stag's head, erased. *Pl.* 66, *cr.* 9.
YOE, Eng., an anchor, sa. *Pl.* 25, *cr.* 15.
YON, Linc., a cubit arm, erect, vested, purp., cuffed, ar., in hand, ppr., a bunch of marigolds, of the third, stalked and leaved, vert. *Pl.* 64, *cr.* 7.
YONG, Suss., a demi-griffin, segreant, regardant, az., beaked and legged, or, charged with a crescent. *Pl.* 125, *cr.* 12.
YONGE, the Rev. JOHN, of Puslinch and Combe, Devons., a buck's head, couped, (between two fern-branches, all ppr.) *Qualis vita, finis ita.* *Pl.* 91, *cr.* 14.
YONGE, or YOUNG, Berks., out of a mural coronet, gu., a goat's head, or. *Pl.* 72, *cr.* 2, (coronet, *pl.* 128, *fig.* 18.)
YONGE, Eng., a (stork,) ar., wings expanded, az., in beak a snake, ppr. *Pl.* 59, *cr.* 11.
YONGE, Lond., a dragon's head, (erased,) or, ducally gorged, ar. *Pl.* 36, *cr.* 7.
YONGE, Rev. VERNON-GEORGE, of Charnes Hall, Staffs., an antelope's head, erased, or, guttée-de-sang. *Et servata fides perfectus amorque ditabunt.* *Pl.* 24, *cr.* 7.
YONGE, Salop, a wolf, passant, sa. *Pl.* 46, *cr.* 6.
YONGE, Somers., a lion's head, erased, per fess, or and gu., ducally crowned, gold. *Pl.* 90, *cr.* 4, (without charging.)
YONGE, Berks. and Devons., a boar's head, erased, vert, armed and bristled, or. *Fortitudine et prudentiâ.* *Pl.* 16, *cr.* 11.
YORK, EDWARD, Esq., of Wighill Park, Yorks., a demi-lion, per fess, wavy, the upper part, gu., the lower barry wavy of four, erminois and az., supporting a (wool pack, erect, ppr., on the breast a gold key, barways.) *Pl.* 84, *cr.* 7.
YORK, out of a ducal coronet, a dragon's head. *Pl.* 93, *cr.* 15, (without flames.)
YORK, or YORKE, Yorks., a monkey's head, erased, ppr. *Pl.* 11, *cr.* 7.
YORK, Eng., a thistle, ppr. *Pl.* 68, *cr.* 9.
YORKE, SIMON, Esq., of Erddig, Denbigh, Wel., a lion's head, erased, ppr., collared, gu., (charged with a bezant.) *Nec cupias, nec metuas.* *Pl.* 7, *cr.* 10.
YORKE, Glouc. and Linc., same crest and motto.
YORKE, Glouc., a lion's head, erased, per pale, ppr., collared, gu., (charged with a bezant.) *Pl.* 7, *cr.* 10.
YORKE, Linc., Yorks., and Northamp., a monkey's head, ppr. *Pl.* 11, *cr.* 7.
YORKE, JOHN, Esq., of Bewerley Hall and Halton Place, Yorks., same crest.
YORKE, Earl of Hardwicke. *See* HARDWICKE.
YORKS, Eng., a lion's head, erased, collared, (charged with a roundle.) *Pl.* 7, *cr.* 10.
YORSTONE, Sco., a rose, stalked and leaved, ppr. *Pl.* 105, *cr.* 7.
YOUL, Sco., a garb, or. *Per vim et virtutem.* *Pl.* 48, *cr.* 10.
YOUNG, Bart., Bucks., a cubit arm, erect, hand grasping an arrow, all ppr. *Press through.* *Pl.* 43, *cr.* 13.
YOUNG, Bart., an arm, from shoulder, issuing, hand grasping a spear, ppr. *Press through.* *Pl.* 34, *cr.* 7, (spear, *pl.* 99, *cr.* 8.)
YOUNG, Iri., a stag's head, erased, or. *Pl.* 66, *cr.* 9.

YOUNG, Wel., a demi-lion, or, collared, per pale, ermine and ermines. *Pl.* 18, *cr.* 13.
YOUNG, Sco., a dolphin, naiant, ppr. *Every point.* *Pl.* 48, *cr.* 9.
YOUNG, Sco., an anchor, placed in the sea, surmounted of a dove, in mouth an olive-branch, all ppr. *Sperando spiro.* *Pl.* 3, *cr.* 10.
YOUNG, Sco., a dexter hand holding a pen, ppr. *Pl.* 26, *cr.* 13.
YOUNG, Sco., a dexter arm, embowed, in hand a lance, in bend, ppr. *Pl.* 89, *cr.* 6, (lance, *pl.* 99, *cr.* 8.)
YOUNG, out of a ducal coronet, a buck's head, between two palm-branches. *Pl.* 91, *cr.* 14, (branches, *pl.* 87, *cr.* 8; coronet, *pl.* 128, *fig.* 3.)
YOUNG, a buck's head, bezantée, between two palm-branches. *Pl.* 91, *cr.* 14, (branches, *pl.* 87, *cr.* 8.)
YOUNG, a boar's head, couped at neck, ppr. *Pl.* 48, *cr.* 2.
YOUNG, Sco., a demi-lion, gu., in dexter a sword, erect, ppr. *Robere prudentia præstat.* *Pl.* 41, *cr.* 13.
YOUNG, a lion, rampant, gardant, per fess, or and gu., supporting a battle-axe, gold. *Pl.* 92, *cr.* 7, (axe, *pl.* 26, *cr.* 7.)
YOUNG, a squirrel, sejant, gu., (charged on body with a cheveron, compony, or and az.,) holding a nut-branch, vert., fructed, gold. *Pl.* 2, *cr.* 4.
YOUNG, Yorks., out of a ducal coronet, or, an ibex's head, armed and tufted, gold. *Pl.* 72, *cr.* 9, (coronet, *same plate, cr.* 2.)
YOUNG, Surr., from water, ppr., an anchor, erect, sa., stock and ring, or, the stem entwined by a serpent, also ppr. *Pl.* 64, *cr.* 9.
YOUNG, Chesh. and Wel., a demi-lion, or, collared, per pale, ermine and ermines. *Pl.* 18, *cr.* 13.
YOUNG, a sword and pen, in saltier, ppr. *Pl.* 49, *cr.* 12.
YOUNG, Kent, a griffin's head, erased, per fess, charged with two escallops, counterchanged. *Pl.* 48, *cr.* 6, (escallop, *pl.* 141.)
YOUNG, Kent, a lion's head, gardant, or, between wings, ar., each charged with a fleur-de-lis, az. *Pl.* 87, *cr.* 2, (fleur-de-lis, *pl.* 141.)
YOUNG, Northumb., out of a ducal coronet, or, an ibex, ar., attired, gold. *Pl.* 115, *cr.* 13, (coronet, *same plate, cr.* 8.)
YOUNG, Bart., Iri., a demi-lion, rampant, (charged on shoulder with a trefoil, slipped,) in dexter a dagger, erect. *Robori prudentia præstat.* *Pl.* 41, *cr.* 13.
YOUNG, Bart., Bucks., a demi-unicorn, couped, erm., armed, crined, and unguled, or, gorged with a naval coronet, az., supporting an anchor, erect, sa. *Be right, and persist.* *Pl.* 125, *cr.* 13.
YOUNG, Sco., a dexter hand holding a pen, ppr. *Scripta manent.* *Pl.* 26, *cr.* 13.
YOUNG, ALLEN-ALLICOCKE, Esq., of Orlingbury, Northamp., a boar's head. *Pl.* 48, *cr.* 2.
YOUNG, Roscommon, out of a ducal coronet, or, a dragon's head, erect, ppr. *Pl.* 93, *cr.* 15, (without flames.)
YOUNG, JAMES, Esq., of Kingerby, Linc.: 1. A wolf, sejant, regardant, sa., between paws a human head. 2. A lion, rampant, or. *Toujours jeune.* *Pl.* 67, *cr.* 5.

YOUNG, Bart., Bucks., a dexter arm, throwing a dart, ppr. *Press through.* *Pl.* 92, *cr.* 14.

YOUNGE, Dors., a sea-unicorn, ar., finned and horned, gu. *Pl.* 125, *cr.* 15.

YOUNGE, Ess., within a chaplet, vert, a griffin's head, erased, or. *Pl.* 38, *cr.* 3, (chaplet, *pl.* 54, *cr.* 10.)

YOUNGE, Middx. and Wilts., a demi-greyhound. *Pl.* 48, *cr.* 3.

YOUNGE, Dors., a demi-sea-unicorn, ar., armed and finned, gu. *Pl.* 125, *cr.* 15.

YOUNGE, Hants., a stag's head, erm., erased, per fess, gu. *Pl.* 66, *cr.* 9.

YOUNGE, Lond. and Staffs., on a rock, a Cornish chough, all ppr. *Pl.* 38, *cr.* 10.

YOUNGER, Northamp. and Heref., a stag's head, or. *Pl.* 91, *cr.* 14.

YOUNGER, Sco., an armed leg, couped above the thigh, az., spurred, or. *Pl.* 81, *cr.* 5.

YOUNGRAVE, Heref. and Northamp., a buck's head, or. *Pl.* 91, *cr.* 14.

YPRES, Eng., an eagle, wings expanded. *Pl.* 126, *cr.* 7.

YUILLE, Lond., an ear of wheat, ppr., leaved, vert. *Pl.* 85, *cr.* 6.

YUILLE, ANDREW-BUCHANAN, Esq., of Darleith, Dumbarton, same crest. *Numine et virtute.*

YULE, Sco., a stalk of wheat, bladed. *Per vim et virtutem.* *Pl.* 85, *cr.* 6.

YVAIN, Eng., out of a ducal coronet, a dexter hand holding a rosebranch, all ppr. *Pl.* 84, *cr.* 2.

Z

ZACHERT, and ZACHET, on stalks, vert, three roses, the middle one, ar., the others, gu. *Pl.* 79, *cr.* 3.

ZAMOYSKA, a demi-Indian goat, rampant. *Pl.* 90, *cr.* 12, (without gorging.)

ZEPHANE, or ZEPHANI, Surr., a demi-man, representing Surajud Dowla Subah, of Bengal, in his complete dress, sinister resting on the head of a tiger, enraged, dexter wielding a scimitar in the attitude of striking, (the blade broken,) all ppr. *Miserrima vidi—* and—*Scuto divino.* *Pl.* 62, *cr.* 2.

ZETLAND, Earl of, Baron Dundas, (Dundas,) a lion's head, gardant, ppr., crowned with an antique crown, or, struggling through an oak-bush, also ppr., fructed, or. *Essayez.* *Pl.* 119, *cr.* 5.

ZINZAN, Eng., a dove, wings expanded, az. *Pl.* 27, *cr.* 5.

ZORKS, Eng., an eagle, with two heads, displayed, surmounted of a saltier, gu. *Pl.* 25, *cr.* 5.

ZORNLIN, Surr., an arm, (embowed,) bare to the elbow, in hand a barbel. *Fai bien crain rien.* *Pl.* 105, *cr.* 9.

ZOUCH, Eng., out of a ducal coronet, gu., a mule's head, ar., (bridled,) grey. *Pl.* 80, *cr.* 6.

ZOUCH, Wilts. and Somers., on a staff, couped and raguly, or, (sprouting at dexter point,) a raven, wings expanded, ar. *Pl.* 123, *cr.* 2, (staff, *pl.* 5, *cr.* 8.)

ZOUCH, Eng., an ass's head, couped, or. *Pl.* 91, *cr.* 7.

ZOUCH, Wilts., an ass's head, ar., (muzzled with cord,) charged on neck with a fleur-de-lis, vert. *Pl.* 91, *cr.* 7, (fleur-de-lis, *pl.* 141.)

ZOUCH, Eng., an ass's head, (tied round mouth by a cord,) all ar. *Pl.* 91, *cr.* 7.

ZOUCHE, Eng., an ass's head, couped, erm. *Pl.* 91, *cr.* 7.

ZURICH, Eng. on a ducal coronet, or, a lion, passant, gardant, gu., ducally crowned, gold. *Pl.* 120, *cr.* 15, (coronet, 107, *cr.* 11.)

ZYMON, Eng., a cross crosslet and sword, (point downward,) in saltier. *Pl.* 89, *cr.* 14.

GLOSSARY.

A

ACCOLED, collared.
ACORNED, an oak-tree, fructed. *Pl.* 16, *cr.* 8.
ADDORSED, ADOSSED, or ADOSÉE, two animals, birds, fish, &c., placed back to back. *Pl.* 62, *cr.* 5.
AFFRONTÉE, full-faced; it is often used in the same sense as *gardant*. *Pl.* 19, *cr.* 1.
ALLERION, an eagle, displayed, without beak or feet.
ANNULET, a ring. *Pl.* 141.
ANTELOPE, an animal of the deer kind, with two straight taper horns. *Pl.* 63, *cr.* 10.
ANTELOPE, HERALDIC, fabled, with the body of the stag, tail of a unicorn, tusk at tip of nose, tufts down back part of neck, and on his tail, chest, and thighs. *Pl.* 115, *cr.* 13.
APAUMÉE, front view of the hand. *Pl.* 32, *cr.* 13.
ARGENT, silver, or white; when engraved, left plain.
ARM, or CUBIT ARM, unless otherwise described, is always from the elbow. *Pl.* 91, *cr.* 6.
ARM, EMBOWED, issuing from the shoulder. *Pl.* 87, *cr.* 7.
ARM EMBOWED AND COUPED, always resting on the elbow. *Pl.* 89, *cr.* 4.
ARMED, when the horns, claws, or teeth of any beast, and the beak or talons of any bird, are in colour different from the body, it is said to be *armed* of that colour.
ASSURGENT, rising out of the sea. *Pl.* 100, *cr.* 1.
ASTROID, a small star.
ASTROLABE, an instrument for taking the altitude of the sun or stars.
ATTIRED, HORNED, used when speaking of the horns of a stag, hart, or buck.
ATTIRES, horns of a stag. *Pl.* 118, *cr.* 11.
AURE, drops of gold.
AYLET, sea-swallow or Cornish chough. *Pl.* 100, *cr.* 13.
AZURE, blue; when engraved, horizontal lines.

B

BAND, the fillet, or bandage, by which a garb, arrows, &c., are bound.
BANDED, when the band of a garb, &c., is of a colour different from the garb itself, it is said to be *banded*, and the colour described.
BAR, a diminutive of the *fess*.
BAR-GEMELLE, a double bar, or two bars placed near and parallel to each other.
BARBED, the five green leaves on the outside of a full-blown rose are the barbs.
BARBED-ARROW, an arrow with head pointed and jagged.
BARBED-HORSE, a horse, barbed at all points; a war-horse, completely accoutred.
BARNACLE, a water-fowl resembling a goose.
BARRULET, a diminutive of the bar—one fourth.
BARRULY, divided into several equal parts, fessways.
BARRY, a transverse division into several equal parts, fessways, of two or more tinctures interchangeably disposed; the number of divisions are always specified as barry of six, eight, ten, or twelve. *Pl.* 52, *cr.* 9.
BASILISK, an imaginary animal like a wyvern, with the head of a dragon at the end of its tail.
BAT, always displayed. *Pl.* 94, *cr.* 9.
BATON, a staff or truncheon.
BATTLE-AXE, an ancient warlike weapon. *Pl.* 14, *cr.* 8.
BATTLED, in form of a battlement.
BATTLED, EMBATTLED, one battlement upon another.
BATTLEMENT, upper works of a castle or tower.
BEACON, a fire-beacon, used as a signal. *Pl.* 89, *cr.* 9.
BEAK, the bill of a bird; in birds of prey, termed *arms*.
BELLED, when a hawk or falcon has bells attached to its legs.
BEND, one of the nine ordinaries; it occupies one-third part of the field or crest, and is drawn diagonally from the dexter chief to the sinister base.
BENDLET, a diminutive of the bend, one-half of its breadth. See *Per Bend*.
BENDWAYS, obliquely, or in bend.
BENDY, divided into an equal number of pieces in a slanting direction from dexter to sinister.
BEZANT, a round flat piece of metal representing money. *Pl.* 141.
BEZANTÉE, strewed with bezants.
BILLETS, oblong square figures. *Pl.* 141.
BILLETTE, BILLETTÉE, strewed with billets. *Pl.* 115, *cr.* 3.
BLADED, when the stalk or blade of grain is of a tincture different from the ear or fruit; thus, an ear of wheat, or, *bladed*, vert. *Pl.* 85, *cr.* 6.
BLAZING STAR or COMET, is represented with an illuminated tail streaming from it. *Pl.* 39, *cr.* 9.
BLOODHOUND, like the talbot, and generally drawn on scent. *Pl.* 117, *cr.* 8.

BOAR, always the wild boar. *Pl.* 43, *cr.* 14.
BOAT, various kinds are used.
BOOK, always the Bible.
BOUGET. See *Water-Bouget*.
BRISTLED, the hair on the neck and back of the boar.
BROAD-ARROW differs from the pheon by having the inside of the barbs plain.
BUCKLES, are borne of various forms, oval, round, lozengy, and masculy.
BUGLE-HORNS are generally stringed and garnished, or veruled; when unstrung they are always described so.
BURGANET, or BURGONET, a steel cap or helmet, anciently worn by infantry. *Pl.* 18, *cr.* 9.
BUSH, or BRUSH, the tail of a fox.
BUSTARD, a kind of wild turkey, of a brownish colour. *Pl.* 30, *cr.* 8.

C

CABLE, a rope, affixed to an anchor. *Pl.* 41, *cr.* 12.
CABOSSED, a head, full-faced, no part of the neck visible. *Pl.* 111, *cr.* 6.
CADUCEUS, or MERCURY'S MACE, a slender staff, entwined by two serpents, heads meeting at top, and tails at base or handle. *Pl.* 69, *cr.* 7.
CALTRAPS, or GALTRAPS, an instrument anciently used in war to wound the horses' feet, having four points, and, when placed on the ground, one point was always erect. *Pl.* 141.
CANNET, a duck without beak or feet, with larger and more curvating neck than the martlet, and, unlike the allerion, by having its head in profile.
CAP OF DIGNITY OR MAINTENANCE, of crimson velvet, turned up with ermine, with two points turned to the back; also called a *chapeau*, and borne by some families under the crest, instead of the wreath. *Pl.* 127, *fig.* 13.
CAPARISONED, a horse completely armed.
CARTOUCHE, an oval shield.
CARBUNCLE, or ESCARBUNCLE, a gem, or precious stone. *Pl.* 141.
CASQUE, a helmet. *Pl.* 18, *cr.* 9.
CASTLES have always two towers, joined by an intervening wall; when the cement is different in colour from the stones, it is said to be *masoned* of that particular colour. *Pl.* 8, *cr.* 7.
CAT, generally understood to be the wild or mountain cat, and is always gardant. *Pl.* 24, *cr.* 6.
CATHERINE-WHEEL, that on which St Catherine is supposed to have suffered martyrdom. *Pl.* 141.
CENTAUR, or SAGITTARIUS, fabled, half-man, half-horse. *Pl.* 70, *cr.* 13.
CHALICE, a communion cup. *Pl.* 42, *cr.* 1.
CHAPEAU, a cap, hat, or bonnet. See *Cap of Dignity*.
CHAPLET, a garland, or wreath of flowers, laurel, olive, oak, &c. *Pl.* 128.
CHAPLET OF ROSES, composed of four roses only, the other part of leaves.
CHECKY, CHEQUY, a field, &c., divided into equal parts or squares, of different tinctures.
CHERUB, a child's head between two wings. *Pl.* 126, *cr.* 10.

CHESS-ROOK, used in the game of chess. *Pl.* 40, *cr.* 11.
CHEVALIER, a knight on horseback, completely armed. *Pl.* 28, *cr.* 5.
CHEVERON, CHEVRON, resembling two rafters, meeting at top. *Pl.* 71, *cr.* 12.
CINQUEFOIL, five-leaved grass, with the leaves issuing from a ball or centre-point. *Pl.* 141.
CIVIC CROWN, among the Romans, was a garland of oak-leaves and acorns. *Pl.* 128, *fig.* 7.
CLARION, a shrill trumpet.
CLENCHED, the hand closed. *Pl.* 87, *cr.* 7.
CLOSE, a bird, addicted to flight, is *close* when the wings are kept close to the body; also, a helmet, with the vizor down. *Pl.* 7, *cr.* 11.
COCKATRICE, fabled, differs from the wyvern, being combed, wattled, and spurred like the dunghill-cock. *Pl.* 63, *cr.* 15.
COCK, generally represented crowing. *Pl.* 17, *cr.* 1.
COLLARED, or GORGED, when a collar, coronet, &c., is round the neck of any animal. *Pl.* 74, *cr.* 1.
COLUMNS, generally of the Doric order. *Pl.* 33, *cr.* 1.
COMBATANT, two lions, fronting each other. *Pl.* 117, *cr.* 2.
COMBED, when the comb or crest is of a colour different from the body.
COMET, a blazing star, streaming light. *Pl.* 39, *cr.* 9.
COMPLEMENT, applied to the moon, to denote her being full. *Pl.* 43, *cr.* 8.
COMPONÉE, or COMPONY, squares formed by two different colours.
CONEY, or CONY, a rabbit.
CONFRONTÉE, fronting each other.
CONJOINED, when charges are linked together. *Pl.* 119, *cr.* 10.
COOTE, a water-fowl. *Pl.* 90, *cr.* 15.
CORBIE, a crow, or raven. *Pl.* 123, *cr.* 2.
CORNISH CHOUGH, a species of crow or raven, black, with legs and beak red; common in Cornwall. *Pl.* 100, *cr.* 13.
CORNUCOPIA, or HORN OF PLENTY, filled with fruits, corn, &c. *Pl.* 91, *cr.* 4.
CORONET, DUCAL, if not otherwise described, should exhibit three leaves only. *Pl.* 128, *fig.* 3.
CORONET, EASTERN, or ANTIQUE, represented with five points. *Pl.* 128, *fig.* 2.
CORONET, MURAL, embattled, also called a *mural crown*. *Pl.* 128, *fig.* 18.
CORONET, NAVAL, also called a *naval crown*; a circle, chaced; on the edge four masts, each with top-sail, and as many sterns of vessels, placed alternately. *Pl.* 128, *fig.* 19.
CORONET, PALISADO, also called a *palisado crown*; a circle, with pales or palisadoes fastened to the rim. *Pl.* 128, *fig.* 21.
CORONET, Vallarie, Vallor, Vallary. See *Vallary Crown*.
COUCHANT, COUCHÉ, or COUCHED, lying, with head upright, to distinguish from *dormant*. *Pl.* 67, *cr.* 2.
COULTER, knife of a plough.
COUPED, cut clean off. *Pl.* 120, *cr.* 7.
COUNTERCHANGED, an alternate changing of the colours.
COURANT, CURRENT, CURSANT, running at full speed. *Pl.* 8, *cr.* 2.

COUTEAU, a knife, cutlass, or sword.
CRENELLÉE, embattled.
CRESCENT, a half-moon, horns turned upwards. *Pl.* 141.
CRESTED, applied to the comb of a cock, or other bird.
CRINED, the hair of man or animal, when of a colour different from that of the body, is *crined* of that colour.
CROSS AVELANE, or AVELLANE, resembles four filberts or hazel nuts, stalk to stalk.
CROSS CALVARY, or THE CROSS, generally mounted on three steps, grieces, or degrees. *Pl.* 49, *cr.* 2.
CROSS CAPITAL, corniced at each extremity.
CROSS CROSSLET, ending in little crosses at each extremity. *Pl.* 141.
CROSS CROSSLET, FITCHED, lower part sharpened to a point. *Pl.* 141.
CROSS FLORY, or FLEURY, a fleur-de-lis at each extremity. *Pl.* 141.
CROSS FORMÉE, or PATTÉE, spreading like dove-tails at each extremity. *Pl.* 141.
CROSS MILL-RIND, resembling a mill-rind.
CROSS MOLINE, same as the mill-rind, but not perforated in the centre.
CROSS CLECHÉE, spreads from the centre towards the extremities, and ends in an angle.
CROSS PATTÉE. See *Cross Formée*.
CROSSWAYS, figures in form of a cross.
CRUSILY, strewed with cross crosslets.
CUP. See *Chalice*.
CUPOLA, dome of a building. *Pl.* 42, *cr.* 10.
CURLEW, a waterfowl. *Pl.* 52, *cr.* 12.
CURVED, CURVAL, CURVANT, bowed.
CYGNET, a young swan. *Pl.* 122, *cr.* 13.

D

DANCETTÉE, when the teeth or indents of a zigzag line are large and wide.
DECRESCENT, the half-moon looking to the sinister. *Pl.* 141.
DEMI, one half. *Pl.* 48, *cr.* 3.
DEVOURING, fish borne feeding are termed *devouring*, because they swallow without chewing.
DEXTER, right-hand side.
DISPLAYED, wings when expanded. *Pl.* 39, *cr.* 12.
DOLPHIN, a sea-fish, very straight, but generally drawn embowed. A dolphin, *naiant*. *Pl.* 48, *cr.* 9.
DORMANT, sleeping, with head resting upon forepaws. *Pl.* 29, *cr.* 3.
DRAGON, fabled, differs from the wyvern by having four feet. *Pl.* 90, *cr.* 10.
DOUBLE-QUEUED, having two tails. *Pl.* 41, *cr.* 15.
DUCAL CORONET, frequently used instead of a wreath, or as a collar; it should have three leaves. *Pl.* 128, *fig.* 3.

E

EAGLE, a bird of prey. *Pl.* 7, *cr.* 11.
EAGLE DISPLAYED, when the wings and legs are extended on each side of the body. *Pl.* 117, *cr.* 15.
EAGLE RISING, about to take wing, or, wings expanded and inverted. *Pl.* 67, *cr.* 4.
EAGLE PERCHING, or alighting, with wings expanded. *Pl.* 126, *cr.* 7.
EARED, when the ears are in colour different from the body, they are *eared* of such colour.
ELEPHANTS are represented with and without castles on their backs. *Pl.* 114, *cr.* 14.
EMBATTLED, like the battlements of a castle.
EMBOWED, arm from the shoulder, bent at the elbow. *Pl.* 118, *cr.* 4.
EMBRUED, dipt in blood; any weapon, bloody, or mouths bloody with devouring prey.
ENDORSED. See *Addorsed*.
ENFILED; when a head, or any other charge, is placed on the blade of a sword, it is *enfiled* with whatever is borne upon it. *Pl.* 10, *cr.* 2.
ENGRAILED, when the edge of a border, bend, fess, &c., is composed of semicircular indents.
ENSIGNED, crowns, coronets, and other things, borne on or over charges: As, a heart *ensigned* with a crown. *Pl.* 52, *cr.* 2; or *pl.* 13, *cr.* 11.
ENTWINED, generally round the neck with a snake; sometimes a sword with a branch of laurel. *Pl.* 53, *cr.* 12.
ENVELOPED, animals entwined by snakes. *Pl.* 119, *cr.* 1.
ENWRAPPED. See *Entwined*.
ERASED, forcibly torn off, leaving the separated parts jagged and uneven. *Pl.* 20, *cr.* 7.
ERECT, upright. A sword, *erect*. *Pl.* 105, *cr.* 1.
ERMINE, white, with black spots or tufts.
ERMINES, black, with white spots.
ERMINOIS, ground, yellow, powdered, black.
ESCALLOP-SHELL, bearings for those who have made long voyages, or who have had important naval commands, and gained great victories; much used by pilgrims. *Pl.* 141.
ESCARBUNCLE. See *Carbuncle*.
ESCROL, a slip on which crests were formerly placed; now used to receive mottoes.
ESCUTCHEON, the original shield used in war, and on which arms were borne; the surface is termed the *field*, because it contains such marks of honour as were assumed or worn in the field. *Pl.* 36, *cr.* 11.
ETOILE, a star with six waved rays or points. *Pl.* 141.
ETOILE of eight points, four waved and four straight; of sixteen points, eight waved and eight straight.
EXPANDED. See *Displayed*.
EYE. See *pl.* 68, *cr.* 15.
EYED, the variegated spots in the peacock's tail.

F

FALCHION, a kind of broadsword.
FALCON, large species of sporting hawk.
FEATHERS, always those of the ostrich. *Pl.* 12, *cr.* 9.
FER-DE-MOLINE, a mill-rind. *Pl.* 141.
FESS, two horizontal lines drawn across the field, giving a space nearly a third part of the escutcheon.
FESSWAYS, in fess; in a horizontal line.
FIMBRIATED, a garment charged or bordered all round.
FIRE-BALL, or BALL FIRED, ppr., has always the fire issuing from the top.

FIRE-BEACON, formerly used to give notice of the approach of an enemy. *Pl.* 89, *cr.* 9.
FITCHED, or FITCHÉE, sharpened to a point. *Pl.* 141.
FLAMANT, flaming. *Pl.* 31, *cr.* 8.
FLEUR-DE-LIS, flower of the lily. *Pl.* 141.
FLEURY, FLORY, any bearing ending with a fleur-de-lis.
FLOTANT, floating, or flying in the air.
FORMÉE, or PATTÉE, small at the centre, and widening, till very broad at the ends. *Pl.* 141.
FOUNTAIN, a waved roundle. *Pl.* 141.
FRASIER, a strawberry-plant, a *cinquefoil*. *Pl.* 141.
FRET, two long pieces in saltier, extending to the extremity of the field, and interlaced within a mascle in the centre. *Pl.* 82, *cr.* 7.
FRETTY, eight, ten, or more pieces interlacing each other. *Pl.* 82, *cr.* 7.
FRUCTED, bearing fruit. *Pl.* 105, *cr.* 13.
FULGENT, having rays. *Pl.* 25, *cr.* 14.
FUMENT, emitting smoke.
FURCHÉ, FOURCHÉE, also FOURCHI, forked or fitched.
FURNISHED, a horse when completely caparisoned; also applied to other things; as, the attire of a stag, *furnished* with six antlers, &c.
FURS, are six in number, Ermine, Ermines, Erminois, Pean, Potent, and Vair.

G

GAD, a plate of steel or iron.
GAD-FLY, a fly that so stings the cattle as to make them gad or run madly about.
GALLEY, a vessel with oars. *Pl.* 34, *cr.* 5.
GALTRAP. See *Caltrap*.
GAMB, the fore-leg of a lion or other beast, from the knee joint; if couped or erased near the middle joint, it is called a *paw*.
GARB, a sheaf of corn, or wheat. *Pl.* 48, *cr.* 10.
GARDANT, looking right forward. *Pl.* 56, *cr.* 7.
GAUNTLET, an iron glove. *Pl.* 15, *cr.* 15.
GAZE, AT, the hart, stag, buck, or hind, when affrontée, or full-faced; all other beasts in this attitude are gardant.
GOLDEN-FLEECE, a ram stuffed and suspended by a collar round his middle. *Pl.* 77, *cr.* 12.
GOLPES, purple-coloured roundles. *Pl.* 141.
GOBONY. See *Componée*.
GORGED. See *Collared*.
GOS-HAWK, used in falconry.
GRIECES, steps, or degrees on which crosses are placed. *Pl.* 23, *cr.* 12.
GRIFFIN, fabled, half-eagle and half-lion, to express swiftness and strength. *Pl.* 61, *cr.* 14.
GULES, red; when engraved, perpendicular lines.
GUTTÉE, liquid drops, varying in colour, according to what is intended to be represented, and are named as follows:—
GUTTÉE-D'EAU, drops of water, *azure*.
GUTTÉE-DE-HUILE, or GUTTÉE-D'OLIVE, drops of oil.
GUTTÉE-DE LARMES, tear drops, *argent*.
GUTTEÉ-D'OR, drops of gold, *or*.
GUTTÉE-DE-POIX, drops of pitch, *sable*.
GUTTÉE-DE-SANG, drops of blood, *gules*.

GUTTÉE-REVERSED, drops, contrary to the natural position.
GWYES, roundles of a sanguine colour.
GYRON, two straight lines from the dexter fess and chief points, meeting in an acute angle in the fess point.

H

HABITED, clothed, vested.
HAND, couped at the wrist. *Pl.* 32, *cr.* 14.
HARPY, fabled, head and breasts of a woman, and body of a vulture. *Pl.* 126, *cr.* 11.
HARROW, used in husbandry, triangular. *Pl.* 7, *cr.* 2.
HAURIENT, a fish, erect. *Pl.* 14, *cr.* 10.
HEDGEHOG, or URCHIN. *Pl.* 32, *cr.* 9.
HAWK'S LURE, used by falconers; a decoy. *Pl.* 141.
HELMET, an esquire's, when used as a crest. *Pl.* 128, *fig.* 14.
HILT, the handle of a sword.
HIND, female stag, generally trippant. *Pl.* 20, *cr.* 14.
HOODED, when borne with a hood. A hawk, *hooded*. *Pl.* 38, *cr.* 12.
HOOFED, when the hoofs are of a tincture different from the body.
HORNED, when the horns are of a tincture different from the body.
HORSE, *passant*, when walking. *Pl.* 15, *cr.* 14.
HUNTING-HORN, borne strung and unstrung. Strung, *pl.* 48, *cr.* 12. Unstrung, *pl.* 89, *cr.* 3.
HURT, HEURT, HUEURT, blue roundles, like the hurtle-berry. *Pl.* 141.
HURTY, strewed with hurts.
HYDRA, fabled, like a dragon with seven heads. *Pl.* 38, *cr.* 5.

I

IBEX, fabled, like the heraldic-antelope, but with two straight horns, teethed like a saw.
IMBATTLED. See *Embattled*.
IMPERIAL CROWN, royal crown of Britain. *Pl.* 127, *fig.* 2.
IN BEND. See *Bendways*.
INCRESCENT, the moon in her increase, horns to the right. *Pl.* 141.
INDENTED, notched like a saw.
INDORSED, INDORSÉE. See *Addorsed*.
IN FESS, horizontal. *Pl.* 32, *cr.* 4.
INGRAILED. See *Engrailed*.
IN ORLE, nearly a circle; used to express two branches encompassing any bearing. See *pl.* 4, *cr.* 3.
IN PALE, upright; borne in the centre of the field. *Pl.* 105, *cr.* 1.
INVECTED, the reverse of engrailed.
INVERTED, upside down.
INVEXED, arched.
ISSUANT, coming up.

J

JAMBE, see GAMB, generally of the lion or bear.
JELLOPED, or JOWLOPED, the comb of a cockatrice or cock, when borne of a tincture different from the head.

JESSANT, shooting forth; applied to lions or other beasts, issuing from the middle of the fess.

JESSANT-DE-LIS, a fleur-de-lis shooting through any charge. *Pl.* 123, *cr.* 9.

JESSES, leather thongs, with which the bells are tied to the legs of hawks.

K

KIDD, young goat; a roe in its first year.

KINGFISHER, a rapacious little bird that feeds on fish.

KITE, bird of prey.

L

LABEL, a figure of three points to distinguish the eldest son during the life of the father; also given to the ribbons that hang from a mitre or coronet.

LANCE, a spear, to thrust or tilt with.

LANGUED, the tongue of beasts or birds, when borne of a colour different from the body.

LEASH, small leather thong used by falconers; the line attached to the collar of a dog.

LEASHED, lined.

LEOPARD, borne in all the positions of the lion. *Pl.* 86, *cr.* 2.

LION, unless expressed differently, is always understood to be rampant. *Pl.* 67, *cr.* 5.

LODGED, the buck, hart, hind, &c., when at rest, or lying; beasts of chase are *lodged*, those of prey in the same position are couchant. *Pl.* 67, *cr.* 2.

LOZENGE, a diamond square. *Pl.* 141.

LOZENGÉE, or LOZENGY, covered with lozenges. *Pl.* 39, *cr.* 11.

LUCY, a fish called a pike. *Pl.* 39, *cr.* 11.

LURE, or LEURE, a decoy. *Pl.* 141. Wings conjoined, with their tips downward, are *in leure*. *Pl.* 87, *cr.* 1.

LYMPHAD, antique ship, with mast and oars. *Pl.* 34, *cr.* 5.

LYRE, a musical instrument.

M

MACE, a club, or emblem of dignity.

MAIDEN'S HEAD, head and neck of a woman couped below the breasts.

MAIL, defensive armour.

MANED, when the main is of a colour different from the body, it is *maned* of that colour.

MAN'S HEAD, unless differently expressed, is always in profile and bearded; if without a beard, it is a young man's head.

MANTLET, a wide and short cloak.

MANTLING, an eagle when stretching out both legs and wings.

MARTLET, a bird without feet, representing the martin. *Pl.* 111, *cr.* 5.

MASCLE, in form of a lozenge, always perforated, or voided. *Pl.* 141.

MASONED, represents the cement or mortar in stone buildings.

MAUNCH, antique sleeve, with long hangers. *Pl.* 22, *cr.* 14.

MEMBERED, when the legs or beak of a bird are of a colour different from the body, they are *beaked* and *membered* of that colour.

MERMAID, half-woman, half-fish, generally with a comb in one hand, and a mirror in the other. *Pl.* 48, *cr.* 5.

MERMAN, half-man, half-fish. *Pl.* 35, *cr.* 10.

MILL-RIND, or FER-DE-MOLINE, the iron in the centre of the mill-stone, by which it is turned. *Pl.* 141.

MINERVA, goddess of wisdom and the arts.

MIRROR, oval and handled.

MOOR'S HEAD, a black's head, generally in profile, and frequently banded. *Pl.* 120, *cr.* 3.

MORION, antique helmet worn by infantry. *Pl.* 18, *cr.* 9.

MOUND, a ball or globe, forming part of the regalia of sovereigns. *Pl.* 37, *cr.* 3.

MOUNT, a rising, on which frequently crests are represented. *Pl.* 98, *cr.* 13.

MOUNTAIN, larger in proportion to the bearing placed upon it.

MOUNTAIN CAT. See *Cat*.

MULLET, British, a star. *Pl.* 141. French, a spur rowel. *Pl.* 54, *cr.* 5.

MURAL, walled.

MURAL CROWN, battlemented on the edge of the circle. *Pl.* 128, *fig.* 18.

MURREY COLOUR, dark brown; a dun sanguine.

MUZZLED, banded, to prevent biting. *Pl.* 111, *cr.* 4.

MYRTLE, an oval garland, for the victors at the Julian Games.

N

NAIANT, swimming. *Pl.* 66, *cr.* 10.

NAISSANT. See *Issuant*.

NARCISSUS, flower with six petals, like the leaf of the cinquefoil.

NEBULÉE, or NEBULY, waved lines to represent clouds.

NOWED, knotted. *Pl.* 1, *cr.* 9.

O

OGRESSES, sable-coloured roundles. *Pl.* 141.

OR, yellow or gold colour; when engraved, small points or dots are spread over the field or bearing.

ORLE, to encompass.

OUNCE, the upper part of the body is tawny white, and the lower part ash-colour, and sprinkled with numerous black spots.

OSTRICH-FEATHERS, generally borne in a plume; ostrich is often, but improperly, omitted. *Pl.* 12, *cr.* 9.

OTTER, an amphibious animal, something like a dog.

OWL, always full-faced. *Pl.* 27, *cr.* 9.

P

PALE, divided from top to bottom into three equal parts by two lines.

PALISADO CORONET. See *Coronet, Palisado*.

PALY, when, by perpendicular lines, a field is divided into any equal number of pieces, it is *paly* of so many parts.

PARROT or POPINGJAY, in colour, green, generally red feet and collar. *Pl.* 25, *cr.* 2.

PARTY PER PALE. See *Per pale*.

PASCHAL LAMB, passant, carrying a banner, generally charged with a cross, called the banner of St George. *Pl.* 48, *cr.* 13.
PASSANT, passing, walking. *Pl.* 118, *cr.* 10.
PASSION CROSS. See *Cross Calvary*.
PATTÉE. See *Formée*.
PAW, same to gamb as hand is to cubit arm.
PEACOCK, IN PRIDE, tail expanded, affrontée. *Pl.* 92, *cr.* 11.
PEAN, a sable fur, powdered with spots of gold.
PEGASUS, fabled horse with wings. *Pl.* 28, *cr.* 9.
PELLETÉE, strewed with pellets.
PELLETS. See *Ogresses*.
PELICAN, like an eagle, with long neck, wings addorsed, always pricking her breast, whence issue drops of blood. *Pl.* 76, *cr.* 15.
PENDENT, hanging.
PENNED, when the stem or quill of a feather is of a colour different from the feather.
PENNON, an oblong flag, terminating sometimes in one, and sometimes in two sharp points, carried on the point of a spear. *Pl.* 8, *cr.* 8.
PER, signifies by or *with*.
PER BEND, divided into two equal parts of different colours, by a diagonal line.
PER CHEVERON, divided by two lines placed in cheveron.
PER FESS, divided into two equal parts of different colours by a horizontal line.
PER PALE, divided into two equal parts of different colours by a perpendicular line.
PER SALTIER, two diagonal lines crossing each other.
PEWIT, a bird.
PHEON, barbed head of a dart or arrow, pointing down, unless expressed otherwise. *Pl.* 141.
PHŒNIX, fabled, always in flames, about half of the body seen. *Pl.* 44, *cr.* 8.
PIERCED, an ordinary or charge, perforated, and showing the field under it.
PIKE, a fish, the lucy. *Pl.* 39, *cr.* 11.
PILE, an ordinary with a sharp point, like the piles driven into the ground to strengthen the foundations of buildings.
PINE APPLE, cone or fruit of the pine-tree.
PINE APPLE STALKED AND LEAVED, with part of a branch attached to it.
PLATE, a round flat piece of silver, without any impression. *Pl.* 141.
PLATÉE, charged with plates. *Pl.* 95, *cr.* 4.
PLOUGH, an implement of husbandry. *Pl.* 28, *cr.* 15.
POMEGRANATE, generally stalked and leaved, and the side of the fruit burst. *Pl.* 67, *cr.* 8.
POMEIS, roundles painted green, like apples.
POMMEL, the rounded knob of the sword's handle.
POPINJAY. See *Parrot*.
PORTCULLIS, for the defence of the gateway of a city, castle, or other fortress. *Pl.* 51, *cr.* 12.
POWDERED, strewed, same as semée.
PREYING, a ravenous beast or bird, standing on, and in a proper position for devouring its prey. *Pl.* 61, *cr.* 7.
PROPER, borne in the proper or natural colours.
PURFLE, or PURFLEW, a kind of bodkin-work or embroidery made of gold thread, &c.
PURFLED, the golden studs and rims of armour.
PURFLEW, a border of fur.
PURPURE, purple; engraved by diagonal lines, drawn from the sinister chief to the dexter base.

PYRAMID, a building or figure coming to a point. *Pl.* 8, *cr.* 10.
PYTHON, a winged serpent or dragon.

Q

QUARTERLY, divided into four equal parts.
QUATREFOIL, four-leaved grass, properly clover. *Pl.* 141.
QUEUE, the tail.
QUIVER OF ARROWS, a case filled with arrows. *Pl.* 19, *cr.* 4.

R

RABBIT. See *Coney*.
RAGULÉE, RAGULED, or RAGULY, any bearing jagged or notched in an irregular manner.
RAINBOW, an arch of various colours, rising from clouds. *Pl.* 79, *cr.* 1.
RAMPANT, standing erect on sinister hind-leg. *Pl.* 67, *cr.* 5.
REFLEXED, curved, or turned round.
REGARDANT, looking behind. *Pl.* 100, *cr.* 6.
REINDEER, a stag, with double attires, two of them turning down. *Pl.* 12, *cr.* 8.
RESPECTING, placed upright, one against the other.
REVERSED, contrary to each other, or to the usual position.
RISING, preparing to fly.
ROSE, consisting of five principal leaves with small ones in the centre, between each leaf a petal or barb, sometimes of a different colour, and when blazoned proper, the rose is red and the barbs green. *Pl.* 141.
ROSE, SLIPPED, has only a small stem attached to it.
ROSE, SLIPPED AND LEAVED. *Pl.* 105, *cr.* 7.
ROSE BRANCH, divested of the stiffness of the heraldic rose, and drawn more natural. *Pl.* 117, *cr.* 10.
ROUNDLES, when of metal, as bezants and plates, are flat; and when of colours, as torteaux, pellets, hurts, pomeis, golpes, &c., round, though not always so, torteaux being frequently flat. By some their names are changed according to the different metal or colour of which they are composed. *Pl.* 141.
RUSTRE, a square figure like a mascle, only the mascle is pierced square, and the rustre round. *Pl.* 141.
RYE, EAR OF, is always drawn bent downwards.

S

SABLE, black; engraved by perpendicular and horizontal lines crossing each other.
SAGITTARIUS, the archer or bowman, the ninth sign in the order of the Zodiac. *Pl.* 70, *cr.* 13.
SAIL OF A SHIP, only a small portion of the mast and yard-arm should be shown. *Pl.* 25, *cr.* 15.
SALAMANDER, fabled, is represented green, surrounded with flames, ppr. *Pl.* 20, *cr.* 15.
SALIENT, leaping or springing, hind feet down. *Pl.* 126, *cr.* 13.

SALTANT, refers to the squirrel, weasel, rat, and all vermin, and to the cat, greyhound, ape, and monkey, when springing forward.

SALTIER, in form of St Andrew's Cross. *Pl.* 25, *cr.* 5.

SALTIERWAYS, when oblong figures are in the position of the saltier. *Pl.* 106, *cr.* 9.

SANGLIER, a wild boar. *Pl.* 84, *cr.* 14.

SARACEN'S HEAD, same as SAVAGE'S HEAD. *Pl.* 19, *cr.* 1.

SAVAGE, a wild man, always naked, with beard, affrontée.

SCALING-LADDER, hooked at top to affix it to the wall. *Pl.* 98, *cr.* 15.

SCROGS, term applied by Scotch heralds in blazoning a small branch of a tree.

SCROLL. See *Escrol*.

SEAX, a sword or scimitar, much hollowed out in the back of the blade.

SEA-HORSE, upper part like the horse, but with webbed feet, hinder without legs, tail of a fish, generally couchant. *Pl.* 103, *cr.* 3.

SEA-LION, upper part like a lion, and lower part like the tail of a fish. *Pl.* 80, *cr.* 13. They are sometimes placed erect on their tails. *Pl.* 25, *cr.* 12.

SEGREANT, applied only to the griffin when rampant. *Pl.* 67, *cr.* 13.

SEJANT, sitting. *Pl.* 66, *cr.* 15.

SEMI, one half.

SEMÉ, or SEMÉE, strewed or powdered.

SERRATED, cut like a saw.

SHIP IN FULL SAIL, never in a sea, unless so expressed. *Pl.* 109, *cr.* 8.

SHOVELLER, a water-fowl, somewhat like a duck; in heraldry, drawn with a tuft on breast and back of head. *Pl.* 90, *cr.* 15.

SINISTER, left-hand side.

SINOPLE, vert, or green.

SLIPPED, stems or slips of plants. *Pl.* 123, *cr.* 1.

SNAIL, always the shell-snail, and shown as moving along. *Pl.* 105, *cr.* 8.

SPEAR, generally tilting-spear. *Pl.* 97, *cr.* 4.

SPHERE, a globe. *Pl.* 14, *cr.* 1.

SPHINX, fabled, body of a lion, wings of an eagle, face and breasts of a woman. *Pl.* 91, *cr.* 11.

SPIRED, raised points.

SPLENDOUR, applied to the sun when represented as a human face, encircled with rays. *Pl.* 68, *cr.* 14.

SPREAD EAGLE, an eagle, displayed, with two heads. *Pl.* 87, *cr.* 11.

SPRINGING. See *Salient*.

STAR. See *Etoile*.

STATANT, standing. *Pl.* 88, *cr.* 9.

STEEL CAP. See *Morion*.

STRINGED, applied to the bugle-horn when borne with strings. *Pl.* 48, *cr.* 12.

STRINGING, applied to a purse of state and a harp.

SURMOUNTED, when a bearing is placed over or upon another. *Pl.* 5, *cr.* 11.

SWAN, to prevent mistakes, the position should always be mentioned. *Pl.* 122, *cr.* 13.

SWORD, always two-edged. *Pl.* 105, *cr.* 1.

T

TALBOT, a species of hound. *Pl.* 120, *cr.* 8.

TASSELLED, adorned with tassels. *Pl.* 112, *cr.* 14.

TEAL, a water-fowl.

TIARA, triple or Papal crown.

TIGER, *heraldic*; is represented with hooked talon at the nose, and mane formed of tufts. *Pl.* 119, *cr.* 9.

TILTING SPEAR, used at tilts and tournaments. *Pl.* 97, *cr.* 4.

TINCTURE, colour, including the two metals.

TORCE or TORSE, the French term for *wreath*.

TORQUED, resembling the letter S, a dolphin haurient or *torqued*. *Pl.* 14, *cr.* 10.

TORTEAU, roundle painted red. *Pl.* 141.

TORTOISE or TURTLE, full back displayed, and the four legs, two on each side.

TREFOIL, three-leaved grass. *Pl.* 141.

TRIDENT, Neptune's emblem, with three barbed prongs. *Pl.* 35, *cr.* 10.

TRIPPANT or TRIPPING, a beast of chase, with right foot lifted up, as if walking briskly. *Pl.* 68, *cr.* 2.

TRITON. See *Merman*.

TRUNCHEON, a marshall's staff; a baton.

TRUNKED, when the main stem of a tree is borne of a tincture different from the branches.

TURRETED, a tower or wall having small towers upon it. *Pl.* 12, *cr.* 5.

TYNES, the branches of the horns of beasts of chase, borne of a tincture different from that of the body.

U

UNDÉE, same as wavy.

UNGULED, the hoofs of a colour different from the body.

UNICORN, fabled, with head, neck, and body of a horse, legs of a buck, tail of a lion, and long horn projecting from the forehead. *Pl.* 106, *cr.* 3.

URCHIN. See *Hedgedog*.

V

VAIR, a fur white and blue, unless described otherwise.

VAIRÉE, formed the same as vair, with this difference, it may be any number of colours, which must be expressed in the blazon.

VALLARY CROWN, a kind of palisado crown. *Pl.* 128, *cr.* 17.

VAMBRACED, hand or arm covered with armour. *Pl.* 120, *cr.* 11.

VANDYKE. See *Dancettée*.

VELLOPED, a cock is armed, crested, and *velloped*, when his spurs, comb, and wattles are borne of a tincture different from the body.

VERT, green, engraved by diagonal lines from the dexter chief to the sinister base.

VERVELLED, in falconry, leather thongs with rings at the ends.

VERVELS, in falconry, small rings to which the jesses of the hawk are fastened.

VERULED, ornamental rings round hunting-horns.

VESTED, clothed or habited.

VOL, two wings conjoined. *Pl.* 15, *cr.* 10.

VOLANT, flying. *Pl.* 94, *cr.* 1.

VULNED, wounded and bleeding. *Pl.* 74, *cr.* 10.

2 L

VULNING, wounding, particularly applied to the pelican, which is always depicted wounding her breast. *Pl.* 41, *cr.* 4.

W

WALLET, a pilgrim's pouch.
WATER-BOUGET, an antique vessel used for carrying water by soldiers. *Pl.* 14, *cr.* 12.
WATTLED, applied to the gills of a cock.
WAVED, called also *Undée*, formed like waves.
WAVY. See *Waved*.
WHEEL-CATHERINE. See *Catherine Wheel*.
WREATH, a garland. The wreath upon which the crest is usually borne is composed of two bands of silk interwoven, the one tinctured of the principal metal, the other of the principal colour in the arms; but, if there be no metal in the coat armour, the bands which compose the wreath are of the two principal colours in the arms. Wreaths upon which crests are placed, show six folds in front, three of metal and three of colour, beginning with metal and ending with colour. Crests are upon wreaths, when not expressed as borne upon a cap, or chapeau, or out of a coronet.
WREATH, sometimes applied to the tail of a boar.
WREATHED, twisted in the form of a wreath.
WYVERN, or WIVERN, fabled, upper part like a dragon, with only two legs, and the lower part like that of a serpent, always drawn with wings up and addorsed, unless otherwise described. *Pl.* 63, *cr.* 13.

Y

YOKE, for oxen. *Pl.* 35, *cr.* 11.

Z

ZULIS, a German bearing, resembling a chess-rook.

MOTTOES.

A

Abest timor	Avaunt fear	Ewart, Ker.
Ab origine fidus	Faithful from the first	Maclaurin.
Absit ut glorier nisi in cruce..	God forbid that I should glory save in the cross	Clarke.
Absque dedecore	Without stain	Napier.
Absque Deo nihil	Nothing without God	Peters.
Absque labore nihil	Nothing without labour	Steele.
Absque metu	Without fear	Dalmahoy.
Abstulit qui dedit	He who gave has taken away	Jerningham-Stafford.
Accendit cantu	Music excites	Cockburn.
Accipiter prædam nos gloriam	The hawk wins prey, we glory	Hawker.
A clean heart and a cheerful spirit		Portman.
Acquirit qui tuetur	He obtains who maintains	Mortimer.
A cruce salus	Salvation from the cross	Bourke, Burgh, Burke, Græme.
A cuspide corona	From the spear a crown	Brodrick.
Ad admissum	About to be accepted	Cunningham.
Ad alta	To things high	Cairnie, Strother.
Ad ardua tendit	He attempts difficult things	M'Olum.
Ad arma paratus	Prepared for arms	Johnston, Johnstone.
Ad astra	To the stars	Moorsom.
Ad astra per ardua	To the stars, by high deeds	Drummond.
Ad astra sequor	I follow to the stars	Tottenham.
Ad astra virtus	Virtue leads to heaven	Saltmarshe.
Ad cœlos volans	Flying to the heavens	Clavering.
Addicunt aves	The omen is favourable	Loutfuttes, Lutefoot, Lutefoote.
Ad diem tendo	I long for day	Stein, Stevens.
Addunt robor	They give strength	Hamilton.
A Deo et patre	From God and my father	Thomas.
A Deo et rege	From God and the king	Stanhope.
A Deo lumen	Light from God	Ker, Kerr.
A Deo victoria	Victory from God	Graham, Græme.
Ad escam et usum	For food and use	Garden, Gardin.
Adest et visum	Present to the sight	Greiden.
Adest prudenti animus	Courage belongs to prudence	Hamilton.
Ad finem	To the end	Tosh, Tose.
Ad finem fidelis	Faithful to the end	Colvil, Colville, Gilroy, Horsfall, Howson, Wedderburn, Scrymgeour, Whitehead.
Ad finem spero	I hope to the last	Ogilvie.
Ad fœdera cresco	I gain by treaty	Oliphant, Oliver.
Adhæreo virtute	I cling to virtue	Kennedy.
Adjuvante Deo	With God's assistance	Acton.
Adjuvante Deo in hostes	With the assistance of God against our enemies	Donovan, O'Donovan.
Ad littora tendit	It makes for the shore	Jamaieson, Jamieson, Quatherine.

Ad littora tendo	I make for the shore	Watson.
Ad metam	To the goal	Bower, Combrey, Comrie, Comry, M'Leurg.
Ad mortem fidelis	Faithful unto death	Caudler.
Adorn the truth		Waddell.
Ad rem	To the purpose	Wright.
Adsit Deus non demovebor	God with me, I shall not be banished	Baird.
Adsit Deus	God with me	Balfour.
Ad summa virtus	Courage to the last	Bruce.
Ad te, Domine	To thee, O Lord	Newman.
Advance		Brand, Ferrier, Spiers.
Advance with courage		Majoribanks, Marjoribanks.
Adversa virtute repello	I repel adversity with fortitude	Dennistoun, Londesborough.
Adversis major, par secundis	Greater than adversity, a match for prosperity	Bulwer, Forbes.
Ægis fortissima virtus	Virtue is the strongest shield	Aspinall.
Ægre de tramite	Having passed a rough path	Tait.
Ægre de tramite recto	Having safely passed through a rough path	Horseburgh.
Æ necastu		Brook.
Æquabiliter et diligenter	Constantly and carefully	Mitford.
Æquam servare mentem	To preserve a steady mind	Beckford, Green, Pitt.
Æquanimiter	With equanimity	Shuttleworth.
Æquo adeste animo	Be ready with constancy	Cope, Copland.
Æquo pede propera	Proceed with a steady pace	East.
Affectat Olympo	Aspires to heaven	Bell.
A fin	To the end	Griffith, Ogilvie, Ogilvy.
Afrad pob afraid	All unnecessary things waste	Vaughan-Chamber.
A fyn Duw a fydd	What God wills, will be	Mathew.
A fynno Dwy y fydd	Let what God wills be	Matthew.
A fynno Duw deued	Let God's will be done	Edwards.
Age aut perfice	Act or achieve	M'Millan.
Age omne bonum	Do all good	Algood, Allgood.
Agitatione purgatur	It is purfied by motion	Russel, Russell.
Agnoscar eventu	I am known by the issue	Ross.
A Home, a Home, a Home		Home.
Aides, Dieu!	Help, O God	Mill.
Aimez loyauté	Love loyalty	Paulet, Pawlet, Orde-Powlet.
Ainsi et peut-être meilleur	Thus and perhaps better	Rolleston.
A jamais	For ever	James.
A la vérité	Certainly	Bremer.
A la volonté de Dieu	At the will of God	Strickland.
Ales reposita	The bird replaced	Cant.
Ales volat propriis	The bird flies to its own	Tufton.
Algiers		Pellew.
Alis aspicit astra	Flying, he looks to the stars	Carnagie.
Alis et animo	With wings and mind	Monro.
Alis nutrior	I am fed by birds	Simpson, Simson.
Alla corona fidissimo	Most faithful to the crown	Leche.
Alla ta Hara		Mildmay.
Alleluiah		Tuite.
All is in God		Clovile, Clovyle.
All my hope is in God		Fraser, Frazer, Udney.
All's well		Mudge.
Alta pete	Aim at high things	Glen, Glenn.
Alta petit	He seeks high deeds	Marshall, Stott.
Altera merces	Another reward	Maclaine, M'Lean, Maclean.
Alteri, si tibi	To another, if to thee	Harvey.
Alterum non lædere	Not to the injury of our neighbour	Keir.
Altiora in votis	Desire greater things	Des Vœux.
Altiora pete	Seek greater things	Gordon.
Altiora peto	I seek greater things	Oliphant, Drummond.
Altiora spero	I cherish loftier hopes	Torr.
Altius ibunt qui ad summa nituntur	They will rise higher, who aim at the greatest things	Forbes, Fordyce.
Altius tendo	I reach higher	Kinloch, Kinlock.
Always faithful		M'Kenzie.
Always helping		Garvine.
Always the same		Freebairn.
Ama Deum, et sarva mandata	Love God, and obey his commandments	Synnot.
A ma puissance	To the utmost of my power	Grey.

Amat victoria curam............	*Success is gained by careful attention*	Clerk.
A ma vie.........................	*For my life*......................	Lievre.
Amice.............................	*In friendship*.....................	Russel, Russell, Watts.
Amicitia reddit honores.......	*Friendship gives honours*.........	Pringle.
Amicitia sine fraude...........	*Friendship without guile*.........	Allardice.
Amicitiæ virtutisque fœdus...	*The league of friendship and virtue*................................	Hippisley.
Amicitiam trahit amor.........	*Love draws friendship*............	Neish.
Amicta vitibus ulmo............	*The elm being covered with vines*	Elmsall, Greaves.
Amico fidus ad aras.............	*Faithful to your friend and your religion*......................	Rutherford, Rutherfurd.
Amicus............................	*Friendly*	Peit.
Amicus amico....................	*Friendly to a friend*...............	Bellingham.
Amicus certus	*A trusty friend*.....................	Peat.
Amo.................................	*I love*................................	Douglas, Hoops, Montagu Scott, Scott, Scote.
Amo, inspicio.....................	*I love, I look*	Scot.
Amo pacem........................	*I love peace*........................	Towle.
Amo probos.......................	*I love the virtuous*................	Blair, Scot, Scott, Towle.
Amor Dei et proximi summa beatitudo	*The love of God and our neighbour the greatest blessing*........	Dobbs.
Amor dulcis patriæ..............	*The sweet love of country*..........	Wigram.
Amore pataiæ.....................	*By the love of our country*.........	Scot.
Amor et pax......................	*Love and peace*....................	Ireland.
Amore vici........................	*I conquered by love*................	M'Kenzie, Mackenzie.
Amore vinci......................	*Vincible by love*...................	M'Kenzie.
Amor patitur moras.............	*Love endures delays*	Lumisden.
Amor sine timore................	*Love without fear*.................	Reade.
Amour avec loyauté.............	*Love with loyalty*..................	Parr.
Amo, ut invenio.................	*I love, when I find*................	Perrott.
Anchora salutis...................	*The anchor of salvation*...........	O'Loghlen.
Anchor fast......................	....	Groat.
Anchor, fast anchor............	....	Gray.
Angusta ad augusta............	*Dangers to honour*	Sheffinham.
Anima in amicis una............	*A single soul in friends*............	Powell.
An I may..........................	....	De Lyle, Lyle, Montgomery.
Animo et fide.....................	*With resolution and fidelity*.......	Guilford, North.
Animo non astutiâ...............	*By courage, not by stratagem*.....	Gordon, M'Nish, Pedler.
Animum fortuna sequitur......	*Fortune follows courage*...........	Craik.
Animum prudentia firmat.....	*Prudence strengthens courage*.....	Brisbane.
Animum rege.....................	*Govern your mind*..................	Keith, Reeves.
Animus et fata...................	*Courage and fortune*...............	Thriepland.
Animus non deficit æquus.....	*Composure does not desert me*.....	Burrell.
Animus tamen idem............	*A mind yet unchanged*.............	Cuffe, Wheeler.
Animus valet.....................	*Courage prevails*...................	Bosworth.
Annoso robore quercus.........	*An oak in full strength*	Aikenhead, Taylor.
Ante expectatem diem..........	*Before the wished-for day*.........	Steinman.
Ante honorem humilitas.......	*Humility before honour*...........	Battersby.
Antiquum assero decus........	*I claim ancient honour*............	Arrot.
Antiquum obtinens..............	*Possessing antiquity*................	Bagot, Cotgreave, Shakerley.
Aperto vivere voto...............	*To live without a principle concealed*.............................	Aylesford, Finch.
Apparet quod.....................	*It appears that*.....................	Edgar.
Appetitus rationi pareat.......	*Let reason govern desire*...........	Custance, Fitzwilliam.
Appropinquat dies...............	*Day dawns*.........................	Johnson.
Apto cum lare....................	*With a fit abode*....................	Elliot.
Aquila petit solem...............	*The eagle soars to the sun*	Kendall.
Aquila non captat muscas.....	*The eagle is no fly-catcher*	Buller, Bedingfield, Chinn Drake, Flounders, Graves Gothard, Wedderburn.
Aquilæ vitem pocula............	....	Boteler.
Arcui meo non confido.........	*I trust not to my bow*..............	Wilk.
Arcus, artes, astra...............	*The bow, arts, and stars*...........	Birney, Burmey.
Ard choille........................	*The woody hill*.....................	MacConachie, M'Gregor.
Ardens.............................	*Burning*............................	Peat.
Ardenter amo.....................	*I love fervently*	Scot.
Ardenter prosequor alis........	*On wings I ardently pursue*.......	Græme.
Ardet virtus non urit...........	*Valour burns but consumes not*...	Fyres.
Ardua petit ardea................	*The heron seeks high places*.......	Heron.
Ardua tendo......................	*I attempt difficult things*..........	Malcolm.

Ardua vinco	I conquer difficulties	Straiton.
Arduo vinco	I overcome by hardihood	Straiton.
A rege et victoriâ	From the king and conquest	Ligonier, Barry.
Ariverette		Cameron.
Arma parata fero	I carry arms in readiness	Campbell, MacGuffie.
Armat et ornat	For defence and ornament	Brown.
Armat spina rosas	The thorn is the rose's arms	Rose.
Armis et animis	By arms and courage	Carnagie, Carnegie, Gilfillan, Gilfillian.
Armis et diligentiâ	By arms and diligence	Baskenford, Baskin.
Armis et fide	By arms and fidelity	Campbell.
Armis et industriâ	By arms and industry	Cochran.
Armis potentius æquum	Justice is more powerful than arms	Falconer.
Arte et animo	By stratagem and courage	Ferguson.
Arte et industriâ	By art and industry	Baynes.
Arte et marte	By art and force	Adair, Drummond, Hunter, Middleton.
Artes honorabit	He shall honour the arts	Hanger.
Arte vel marte	By art or force	Deans.
Artis vel martis	Of skill or force	Eastoft.
Aspera ad virtutem est via	Rough is the path to virtue	Edwardes.
Aspera juvant	Dangers delight	Stewart.
Aspera me juvant	Sharp prickles help me	Low.
Aspera virtus	Rugged valour	Sinclair.
Aspira	Aspire unto	Feld.
Aspire		Edward.
Aspiro	I aspire unto	M'Fell, Ramsay.
Assaye	Try	Dundas.
Assiduitate	By constant care	Buist, Johnston, Skeen.
Assiduitate non desidiâ	By constant care, not by sloth	Loch, Lock.
Ast necas tu	Ah! certainly thou killest	Lindsay.
Astra, castra, numen, lumen	The stars, the camp, God, and light	Brooke.
Astra, castra, numen, lumen, munimen	The stars my camp, God my light and protection	Balcarres, Lindsay.
Atalanta		Hardinge.
At all tymes God me defend		Lyell.
A te, pro te	From thee, for thee	Savage.
A tout pourvoir	Provide for all	Oliphant.
At spes infracta	But hope is undaunted	Dick, Hood.
At spes non fracta	But hope is not lost	Hope-Johnstone, Scott-Hope, Leckie.
At spes solamen	But hope is comfort	Hope.
Attamen tranquillus	But yet quiet	Maitland.
Attendez vous	Give attention	Boyes.
Au bon droit	Not without cause	Lecaufield, Wyndham.
Auctor pretiosa facit	The author stamps the value	Hampden, Hobert.
Audacem juvant fata	The fates assist the bold	Sommerville.
Audaces fortuna juvat	Fortune favours the brave	Baron, Burroughs, Carpenter, Costello, Flanagan, King, Turnbull.
Audaces juvat	She favours the brave	Campbell, Cleveland, Googe, Sands.
Audaces juvo	I favour the brave	Buchanan, Campbell, MacCausland.
Audacia	Daring deeds	Grant.
Audaciâ et industriâ	By boldness and diligence	Buchanan.
Audaci favet fortuna	Fortune favours the brave	Turnbull.
Audaciter	Boldly	Euen, Ewan, Ewing.
Audaciter et sincere	Boldly and sincerely	Clive.
Audaciter et strenue	Boldly and readily	Pollock.
Audax	Bold	Erthe.
Audax et promptus	Bold and ready	Douglas.
Audax omnia perpeti	Bold to endure all things	Harding.
Aude et prevalebis	Dare and you will prevail	Frend.
Audentis fortuna juvat	Fortune assists the daring	Burroughs, Mackinnon, Moubray, Mowbray, Turing, Twing.
Audeo	I dare	Rose.
Audio, sed taceo	I hear, but say nothing	Trollop.
Augeo	I increase	Trent.

Audito et gradito...............	*Listen and go......................*	Cruickshank, Cruikshanks.
Augeor dum progredior.........	*I increase as I proceed...............*	Durham.
Au plaisir for de Dieu	*At the good pleasure of God.......*	Edgcombe, Edgcume, Edgecumb.
Auriga virtutum prudentia...	*Prudence is the charioteer of the virtues......................................*	Mawbey.
Ausim et confido................	*I dare, and I trust..................*	Areskine, Erskin, Erskine.
Auspice Christo..................	*Under the guidance of Christ.....*	Davie, Lawley, Rowe.
Auspice Deo.......................	*Under the guidance of God........*	Spied.
Auspice numine.................	*Under divine direction............*	Welsh.
Auspice summo Numine	*Under direction of the great God*	Irvine.
Auspicium melioris avi........	*The token of a better age..........*	Beauclerc.
Aut homo aut nullus...........	*Either a man or none...............*	Atkinson.
Aut mens aut vita Deus.......	*God is either life or mind..........*	Gordon.
Aut mors aut vita decora......	*Either death or an honourable life..*	Gordon.
Aut mors aut vita Deus........	*Or death or life is of God.........*	Gordon.
Aut nunquam tentes, aut perfice..................................	*Either do not attempt, or complete...*	Bennet, Creswell, Germain, Sackville, Sackvill,
Aut pax, aut bellum............	*Either peace or war.................*	Donaldson.
Aut tace, aut face...............	*Either be silent, or act.............*	Scot, Scott, Tweedie.
Aut viam inveniam aut faciam	*I shall either find or make a path..*	Wyhtwyck.
Auxiliante resurgo...............	*I arise through help..................*	Graham.
Auxilio ab alto.	*By aid from above..................*	Martin.
Auxilio Dei......................	*By the help of God.................*	Erisby, Morehead, Muirhead, Murehead.
Auxilio divino	*By divine assistance................*	Drake.
Auxilium ab alto.................	*Aid from above......................*	Dillon, Kallet, Machin, Martin, Normand, Prickett.
Auxilium meum ab alto........	*My help is from above............*	Blakeney.
Auxilium meum a Domino....	*My help is from the Lord.........*	Mostyn, Price.
Avance...............................	*Advance..................................*	Colyear, Collyer, Ramsay.
Avancez............................	*Advance..................................*	Chalmers, Chambers, Hill, Rowland-Hill.
Avant................................	*Forward..................................*	Stewart, Stuart.
Avauncez et archez bien	*Advance and shoot well..........*	Swinnerton.
Avi numerantur avorum.......	*The generations of our forefathers are numbered..............*	Norton, Perton, Grantley, Turbervill.
Avis la fin.........................	*Consider the end....................*	Kennedy, Keydon.
Avito viret honore...............	*He flourishes by ancestral honours ....*	Stewart, Stuart, Creighton-Stuart, Mackenzie-Wortley-Stuart, M'Kenzie.
Avonno div dervid...............	*The all-sufficient God will send...*	Lloyd.
A Wightman never wanted a weapon		Wightman, Wighton.
Aye forward.......................		Brand.
Ayez prudence...................	*Have prudence........................*	Biss.
Aymez loyauté....................	*Love loyalty............................*	Paulet, Bolton.
Azincourt..........................		Billan, Lenthall, Waller, Wodehouse.

B.

Badamy.............................		Munro.
Baroach.............................		Nicholson.
Basis virtutum constantia......	*Steadiness is the foundation of the virtues.............................*	Devereux.
Bear and forbear		Barwis, Bernard, Morland, Bernard, Macevoy, Rowley, Philip, Philips, Phillip, Philps.
Beare and forbeare...............		Langley.
Bear up.............................		Fulford.
Beati pacifici......................	*Blessed are the peace-makers......*	Stewart, Finlay.
Be bolde, be wyse...............		Gollop, Tilly.
Be ever mindful..................		Campbell.
Be fast..............................		Savill, Saville.
Be firm.............................		Coats, Cotes, Ferrie.
Be hardie..........................		Edmonston, Edmonstone.

Be hardy		Edminston.
Be it fast		Ashby, Atkins, Fotheringham.
Be just and fear not		Hewitt, Payne.
Bella! horrida bella	*Wars! horrid wars!*	Lysaght.
Bello ac pace paratus	*Prepared in peace and in war*	Braikenridge.
Be mindful		Brodie, Calder, Campbell.
Benedictus qui tollit crucem	*He is blessed who bears the cross*	Bennet.
Bene factum	*Well done*	Weldon.
Beneficiorum memor	*Mindful of favours*	Nicholson.
Bene paratum dulci	*Well prepared for good fortune*	Ogilvy.
Bene præparatum pectus	*A heart well prepared*	Blake-Jex.
Bene qui pacifici	*Blessed are the peace-makers*	Allardice.
Bene qui sedula	*He who acts diligently acts well*	Arkley.
Bene tenax	*With noble tenacity*	Bennet.
Benigno numine	*Under propitious influence*	Bentley, Horsford, Pitt.
Be not wanting		Baillie, Bazilie, Bazley.
Be right, and persist		Young.
Be sure		Pasley.
Be traist		Innes, Sheils.
Be true		Bruce, M'Guarie.
Better deathe than shame		Pearsall.
Beware in time		Lumisden, Lumsdean.
Be watchful		Daroch.
Bi 'se mac an t-slaurie	*Be thou the son of the crook*	Beacher-Wrixon, M'Laurin.
Bis ti ici		Kincaid.
Blow, hunter, thy horn		Forrester.
Blow shrill		Mercier.
Bold		Spence.
Bon accord	*Good harmony*	Towers.
Bon fin	*A good end*	Graham.
Bon fortune	*Good luck*	Ferrier.
Bonis omnia bona	*All is good to the good*	Orr.
Bonne et belle assez	*Good and handsome enough*	Belasis, Bellasyse.
Bono vince malum	*Overcome evil with good*	Finch, Gerard.
Boulogne et Cadiz	*Boulogne and Cadiz*	Heygate.
Boutez en avant	*Put forward*	Barry, Barry-Garrett-Standish, Barry-Smith.
Boyne		Kidder.
Breyrgrod Eryri	*The Barons of North Wales*	Wynn-Williams.
Byand	*Remain*	Gordon, Seaton.
Bydand	*Remaining*	Gordon.
Bydand to the last	*Remaining for ever*	Gordon.
Byde		
Byde be		Gordon.
By degrees		Brey.
Byde together		Gordon.
By faith we are saved		Cathcart.
By industry we prosper		Gavin.
By the providence of God		Mac Sween.
By these we shine		MacCouach.
By valour		Herin, Heron.
By wounding I cure		Stirling.

C

Cada uno es higo de sub obras	*Every man according to his works*	Boss.
Cadam a 'r cyfrwys	*Mighty and cunning*	Williams.
Cadenti porrigo dextram	*I extend my right hand to the falling*	Pearse.
Cælitus mihi vires	*My strength is from Heaven*	Jones.
Cælitus vires	*Strength from Heaven*	Whitson.
Cæteris major qui melior	*He is greater who is better than the rest*	Radcliff.
Calcar honeste	*A spur with honour*	Crawford.
Callide et honeste	*With skill and honour*	Calley.
Calm		Macadam, M'Adam.
Campo fero præmia belli	*I bear off the rewards of war from the field*	Campbell.
Canada		Brock, Prevost.

Latin	Translation	Names
Candide	With candour	Stewart.
Candide et caute	With candour and caution	Elliot, Elliott, Grieve.
Candide et constanter	Candidly and steadily	Coventry, Irvine.
Candide et secure	Openly and fearlessly	Graham.
Candide, sed caute	Openly, but cautiously	Sinclair.
Candidiora pectora	Purer hearts	Whytt.
Candor dat viribus alas	Candour gives wings to strength	Hogarth, Howgart, Rochfort.
Candore	By candour	Robe.
Capta majora	Employed in greater things	Geddes.
Cara Deo nihilo carent	God's beloved are in want of nothing	Weekes.
Caraid 'an àm feum	A friend in time of need	Smith, Smyth.
Carn na cuimhne	The rock of remembrance	Farquharson.
Carpe diem	Enjoy to-day	Cullen.
Cassis tutissima virtus	Virtue is the safest helmet	Armour, Cholmondely, Delamare.
Cause caused it		Elphinstone.
Caute et sedulo	Cautiously and carefully	Brown, Johnston.
Caute, non astute	Cautiously, not treacherously	Ross.
Caute, sed strenue	Cautiously, but vigorously	Hamlyn.
Cautus a futuro	Cautious for the future	Bowen.
Cave	Beware	Cave.
Cave, adsum	Beware, I am here	Jardin, Jardine.
Cave, Deus videt	Beware, God sees	Cave.
Cave lupum	Beware of the wolf	Huband.
Cavendo tutus	Safe by waring	Candlish, Cavendish, Cruikshank, Cruckshanks, M'Candlish, Waring.
Cave paratus	Be prepared, and beware	Johnston.
Cedant arma togæ	Arms must give place to the gown	Reade.
Celer atque fidelis	Swift and faithful	Duine.
Celer et audax	Swift and bold	Jackson, Pearce.
Celer et vigilans	Swift and watchful	Douce.
Celeriter et jucunde	Quickly and pleasantly	Rogers.
Celeriter nil crede	Believe nothing hastily	Stringer.
Certa cruce salus	Sure salvation by the cross	Garritte, Kinnaird.
Certamine parata	Prepared for the contest	Cairncross.
Certamine summo	In the midst of the battle	Brisbon, Brisbane, M'Onoghuy.
Certavi et vici	I have fought and conquered	Byrne, Thunder.
Certior dum cerno	While I discern more surely	Lundin.
Certior in cœlo domus	A surer habitation in heaven	Adams.
Certum pete finem	Aim at a sure end	Bissland, Corse, Crosse, Howard, Thompson.
Cervus lacessitus leo	The stag harassed by the lion	Sheridan.
Cervus, non servus	A stag, not a slave	Goddard.
Chacun le sien	Each his own	Bourke.
Chase		Geary.
Che sara sara	What must be, must be	Chatfeild, Chatfield, Russell.
Chi la fa l' aspetti	As a man does, so let him expect to be done by	Mazzinghi.
Chi senimi vertu raccoglia fama	He who sows virtue shall reap fame	Coore.
Christi crux est mea lux	Christ's cross is my light	Northcote.
Christi pennatus sidera morte peto	Through the death of Christ, on wings I seek the sky	Fetherston.
Christo duce feliciter	Happily, Christ being my conductor	Binning.
Christus mihi lucrum	Christ is my reward	Stewart.
Christus providebit	Christ will provide	Thomson.
Christus sit regula vitæ	Let Christ be the rule of life	Samevell-Watson.
Civil and religious liberty		Wood.
Cio che Dio vuole is voglio	What God will, I will	Dormer.
Clariora sequor	I pursue more illustrious objects	Buchanan.
Clarior e tenebris	Brighter after obscurity	Leeson, Lightbody, Purves, Purvis.
Clarior ex obscuro	More glorious from obscurity	Sanderson.
Clariores e tenebris	Brighter after the darkness	Polden, Puleston.
Clarior hinc honos	Hence the greater honour	Buchanan.
Clarum reddit industria	Industry renders illustrious	Milne.
Clementiâ et animis	By clemency and courage	Maule.
Clementia tecta rigore	Clemency tempering rigour	
Cœlestia canimus	We sing of heavenly things	Synge.

Cœlestia sequor	I follow heavenly things	M'Donald, Monro.
Cœlis exploratis	Having searched the heavens	Herschel.
Cœlitus datum	Granted by heaven	Borthwick, Finlason, Finlay.
Cœlitus mihi vires	My strength is from heaven	Jones.
Cœlitus vires	Strength from the sky	Mallet.
Cœlum, non animum	Heaven, not courage	Ashworth, Finlayson, Rhodes, Waldegrave, Waldgrave.
Cœlum, non solum	Heaven, not the earth	Steavenson, Stevenson, Stevenstone.
Cœlum quid quærimus ultra...	What seek we more than heaven...	Godman.
Cœlum versus	Heavenward	Dickson.
Cœur fidele	Faithful heart	Hart.
Cogadh na sith	Peace or war	M'Crummin.
Cogit amor	Love compels	Joass.
Cogito	I think	Weems.
Cognosce teipsum, et disce pati	Know thyself, and learn to suffer	Rawlings.
Colens Deum et regem	Worshipping God and the king	Collins.
Color fidesque perennis	Beauty and everlasting faith	Irton.
Comme à Dieu playra	When to God I cry	Thorp.
Comme je fus	As I was	More, Ward.
Comme je trouve	As I find it	Butler.
Commit thy work to God		Sinclair.
Commodum, non damnum	A gain, not a loss	Backie.
Compositum jus fasque animi	Law and equity	Law, Laws.
Conamine augeor	I am enriched by the effort..	Leslie, Lesly.
Concipe spescertes	Indulge sure hopes	Sealy.
Concordant nomini facta	Deeds suiting our name	Grace.
Concordiâ et sedulitate	With harmony and diligence	Goldsmid.
Concordia, integrita, industria	Concord, integrity, and industry	Rothschild.
Concordia præsto	Concord at hand	Forbes.
Concordiâ res crescunt	Riches increase by concord	Bromhead.
Concordia vincit	Unanimity overcomes	Cochran, Cochrane, Cochrin.
Concussus surgit	Rises though shaken	Garrioch.
Concussus surgo	I arise from the shock	Garriock, Garriocks.
Condide	Be secret	Stewart.
Confide recté agens	Trust in fair dealing	Broadhead, Newdegate, Newdigate, Wooler, Wylde.
Confido	I trust	Bell, Boyd, Le Bon, Mills, Peters, Simpson.
Confido, conquiesco	I trust, I am content	Dysart, Dysert, Hodgetts, Tollemache.
Confido in Deo	I trust in God	Backhouse.
Confido in Domino	I trust in the Lord	Peterkin.
Confido, non confundor	I trust; I am not put to shame...	Tyndale, Tynedale.
Confisus veribus	Expecting the spring	Watson.
Conjuncta virtuti fortuna	Fortune is joined to bravery	M'Beth.
Conjunctio firmat	Union strengthens	Middleton.
Conquiesco	I am at rest	Metcalfe.
Consequitur quodcunque petis	Whatever you seek is obtained	Taylor, Taylour.
Consequitur quodcunque petit	He obtains whatever he seeks	Drummond, Taylor.
Consilio ac virtute	By wisdom and valour	Rose-Lewin.
Consilio et animis	With prudence and courage	Maitland, Ramadge.
Consilio et impetu	By wisdom and valour	Agnew.
Consilio et prudentiâ	By policy and prudence	Le Poer Trench, Trench.
Consilio et vi	By wisdom and might	Perrier.
Consilio, non impetu	By wisdom, not by rashness	Agnew, Agnew-Vans.
Constance et ferme	Perseverance and decision	Osbaldeston, Osboldeston.
Constans contraria spernit	Firmly spurns opposition	Edgeworth.
Constans et fidelis	Constant and faithful	Spoure, Spoor.
Constans et prudens	Firm and prudent	Campbell.
Constans fidei	Constant to honour	Coggan, Cogan, Colborne, Ridley.
Constans justitiam moniti	Persevering in justice with moderation	Russell.
Constant		Gray.
Constant and true		Rose, Ross, Rosse.
Constant en tout	Constant in all	Standish-Carr.
Constanter	With constancy	Hore.
Constanter et prudentiâ	Steadily and with prudence	Campbell.
Constantiâ et virtute	By constancy and virtue	Amherst.
Constancy		M'Kowan.
Contentement passe richesse..	Contentment surpasses riches	Bowyer.

Copiose et opportune............	*Plentifully, and in time............*	Bunten.
Corda serata fero................	*I carry a heart shut up..........*	} Lockhart.
Corda serata pando..............	*I lay open a heart shut up........*	
Corde et animo...................	*With heart and soul..............*	Clayhills.
Corde et manu....................	} *With heart and hand.............*	} Gordon, Steuart, Stewart, Watling.
Corde manuque		
Cordi dat robora virtus..........	*Virtue strengthens the heart.......*	Porch.
Cor nobyle, cor immobyle......	} *A heart noble, and a heart immovable......................*	} Vivian.
Corona mea Christus.............	*Christ is my crown.................*	Chetwoode, Lapsley, Lapslie.
Coronat fides.....................	*Fidelity crowns....................*	Dall, Pringle.
Cor unum, via una...............	*One heart, one way................*	Cecil, Sandford.
Cor vulneratum...................	*A wounded heart..................*	Mack.
Courage...........................	....	{ Arrol, Cuming, Cumming, Cummin, Cumınyng, Dounie, Downie, Hillson, Turnbull.
Courage et esperance............	*Hope and courage.................*	Storie.
Courage sans peur................	*Courage without fear ....*	{ Anesworth, Ainsworth, Aynesworth, Gage.
Court no friend, dread no foe.		Mallock.
Craggan an fhithich..............	*The rock of the raven..............*	M'Donnel, MacDonnell.
Craig elachie......................	*The rock of alarm..................*	Grant.
Craignez honte....................	*Dread shame ....*	Bentinck, Dillwyn, Weston.
Craig dhubh......................	*The black rock....................*	Farquharson.
Cras mihi.........................	*To-morrow for me................*	Parbury.
Creag dhubh chloinn Chatain	*The black rock of clan Chattan...*	Macpherson.
Crede Byron......................	*Trust Byron ....*	Biron, Byron.
Crede cornu.......................	*Trust in horn......................*	Hornby.
Crede Deo	*Trust in God......................*	Atkinson.
Crede et vince....................	*Believe and conquer...............*	Toash.
Credo..............................	*I believe..........................*	Sinclair.
Credo, amo et regno	*I believe, love, and rule............*	Clive.
Credo cruci Christi	*Trust in the cross of Christ........*	Wood.
Credo et videbo..................	*I believe, and I shall see..........*	Cheslie, Chiesly.
Crescam ut prosim...............	*I will increase, that I may do good*	Mitchelson.
Crescat Deo promotore.........	{ *Let him prosper under the guidance of God...................*	} Leslie.
Crescendo prosim	*Let me do good by increasing.....*	Scot.
Crescit sub pondere virtus.....	*Virtue thrives under oppression...*	Alison, Chapman, Fielding, Seys, Slater.
Crescitur cultu	*Is increased by culture..............*	Barton.
Crescitque virtute................	*And grows by virtue ....*	Mackenzie, M'Kenzie.
Cresco	*I increase..........................*	Mitchael, Mitchell, Stiven.
Cresco et spero	*I increase, and I hope..............*	Hannay.
Cresco per crucem...............	*I grow through the cross............*	Rowan.
Crom-a-boo (an Irish watchword)............................	} *I will burn.........................*	Bodkin, Fitzgerald.
Cruce delector....................	*I joy in the cross...................*	Sinclair.
Cruce glorior......................	*I glory in the cross.................*	Pye.
Crucem ferre dignum...........	*Bear your cross with dignity......*	Newenham, Worth.
Cruce, non leone fides	{ *My trust is in the cross, not in the lion..............................*	} Mathew.
Cruce, non prudentiâ............	*By the cross, not by wisdom........*	Topham.
Cruce salus.......................	*Salvation in the cross...............*	Shee.
Cruce spes mea...................	*In the cross is my hope.............*	Bird.
Cruce vincimus...................	*We conquer by the cross...........*	Newbigging.
Cruci, dum spiro, fido	{ *While I breathe, my trust is in the cross..........................*	} Arundel, Netterville.
Cruciata cruce junguntur......	{ *Troubles are connected with the cross..............................*	} Gairden, Gardyne.
Crux Christi nostra corona....	*The cross of Christ is our crown..*	Barclay, Mercer, Mersar.
Crux Christi mea corona.......	*Christ's cross my crown...........*	Mercer.
Crux Christi salus mea.........	*My salvation is the cross of Christ*	Peck.
Crux dat salutem	*The cross gives salvation...........*	Sinclair.
Crux mihi grata quies	*The cross gives me welcome rest...*	{ Adam, Adie, Edie, Macadam, M'Adam.
Crux salutem confert............	*The cross brings salvation........*	Barclay.
Cubo, sed curo...................	*I lie down, but am on my guard..*	Dickson.
Cubo, ut excubo.................	*I rest while I watch ....*	Græme, Graham.
Cui debeo fidus..................	{ *Faithful to whom I am under an obligation........................*	} Craw.

Cuidich an rìgh	*Assist the king*	M'Donnel, M'Kenzie.
Cuidich in rhi		
Cuimhnich bas Alpin	*Remember the death of Alpin*	M'Alpin, Alpin, Macalpin.
Cuislean mo chridhe	*The pulsation of my heart*	M'Donnel.
Cum corde	*With the heart*	Drummond.
Cum periculo lucrum	*Gain with danger*	Ogilvie.
Cum plena magis	*When more full*	Smith.
Cum progressu euntis	*Moving with progress*	Seation.
Cum prudentiâ sedulus	*Careful, with prudence*	Beatson, Betson.
Cuncta mea mecum	*All my property is with me*	Stedman.
Cunctanter, tamen fortiter	*Leisurely, yet resolutely*	Hutchinson.
Curâ atque industriâ	*By care and industry*	Vair.
Cura cedit fatum	*Carefulness is a substitute for fortune*	Thomson.
Cura dat victoriam	*Foresight gives victory*	Denham.
Curæ cedit fato	*Destiny yields to care*	Thomson.
Curâ et candore	*By prudence and sincerity*	Cunningham, Forbes.
Cura et constantia	*Care and constancy*	Cunninghame, Cunningham.
Cura et industria	*Care and industry*	Walker.
Curæ pii Diis sunt	*The pious are the care of the gods*	Mogg.
Cura quietem	*Regard your repose*	Hall.
Cu re bu	*I have broken my hold*	Farrell.
Curo dum quiesco	*I am on my guard while I rest*	Maxwell.
Currit qui curat	*He runs who takes care*	Fuller.
Cursum perficio	*I accomplish my course*	Hunter.
Cuspis fracta causa coronæ	*The broken spear the cause of the coronet*	Rolt, Rolte.

D

Dabit Deus vela	*God will fill the sails*	Tennant.
Dabit otia Deus	*God will give repose*	Brisbane-M'Dougall.
Dabunt aspera rosas	*Difficulties will produce pleasure*	Mushet.
Dakyns, the devil's in the hempe		Dakyns.
Dante Deo	*By the bounty of God*	Wolff.
Dant Deo	*They give for God*	Wood.
Dant priscæ decorum	*Ancient things give renown*	Stewart.
Dant vires gloriam	*Strength gives glory*	Hog.
Darcen		Knight.
Dare quam accipere	*To give rather than to receive*	Guy.
Data fata secutus	*Following the fates allotted to me*	Archdale, Archdall, Duthie, St John, Streatfield, Stretfield.
Dat cura commodum	*Prudence gives profit*	Mill, Milne.
Dat cura quietem	*Prudence gives rest*	Medlicott, Medlycott.
Dat Deus incrementum	*God gives increase*	Crofton, Otley.
Dat Deus originem	*God gives high birth*	Hamilton.
Dat et sumit Deus	*God gives and God takes away*	Ethelston.
Dat gloria vires	*A good name gives strength*	Hog, Hogg, Hogue.
Debonnair	*Kind or gracious*	Bethune, Lindsay.
De bon valoir servir le roi	*To serve the king with good will*	Bennet, Gray, Grey.
Deccan		Hislop.
Decens et honestum	*Becoming and honourable*	Fyfe, Fyffe.
Decerptæ dabunt odorem	*Roses plucked will give sweet smell*	Aiton.
Decide and dare		Dyce.
Decori decus addit avito	*He adds honour to that of his ancestors*	Erskine.
Decrevi	*I have determined*	Nugent.
Decus summum virtus	*Virtue the chief ornament*	Holburn, Holeburne, Hulburn.
De Dieu tout	*From God is everything*	Mervyn, Beckford.
Deeds show		Ruthven.
Deeds shaw		
Defend		Grassick, Wood.
Defend, and spare not		MacConachie.
Defendendo vinco	*I conquer by defending*	Graham.
Defensio, non offensio	*Defence, not offence*	Mudie.
Defend the fold		Cartwright.
De hirundine	*Of the swallow*	Arundel.

Dei dono sum quod sum	By the grace of God I am what I am	Lumisden, Lumsden, Lundin.
Dei donum	The free gift of God	Darling.
Dei memor, gratus amicis	Mindful of God, grateful to friends	Antrobus.
Dei providentia juvat	God's providence assists	Welman-Noel.
Delectare in Domino	To rejoice in the Lord	Bampfylde.
Delectat amor patriæ	The love of native land delights	Smith.
Delectat et ornat	It delights and adorns	Brown, Cree, Harvie, Harvey, M'Crae, M'Crea, M'Cree, M'Crie.
Delectatio mea	My delight	Pollock.
Del fugo I avola		Berners.
Delhi		Ochterlony.
Deliciæ mei	My delight	Dalgleish.
Demeure par la vérité	Keep fast by the truth	Mason.
De monte alto	From a lofty mountain	Maude.
D'en haut	From above	Whitefoord.
Denique cœlo fruar	I will enjoy heaven at last	Melville.
Denique cœlum	Heaven at last	Beswick, Bonar, Melveton, Melvile, Melville, Melvill.
Denique decus	Honour at last	Stoddart.
Denuo fortasse lutescat	May again perchance become obscure	Spurdens.
Deo adjuvante	God assisting me	Pellew, Solomons.
Deo adjuvante, non timendum	When God assists there is nothing to fear	Fitzwilliam, Peters, Williams.
Deo adverso, leo vincitur	God opposing, the lion is conquered	Newenham.
Deo data	Given to God	Arundel.
Deo donum	A gift from God	Darling.
Deo duce	Under the conduct of God	Hennidge.
Deo duce, ferro comitante	God my leader, and my sword accompanying me	Caulfield.
Deo duce, decrevi	Under the guidance of God, I have resolved	Harnage.
Deo ducente, nil nocet	When God leads, nothing hurts	Pelly.
Deo duce, sequor	I follow, God being my guide	Wheelton.
Deo et principe	For God and my prince	Lamb.
Deo et regi fidelis	Faithful to God and the king	Atkinson.
Deo et regi	For God and king	Stanhope.
Deo favente	By God favouring me	Alves, Mitchell.
Deo favente, florebo	By the favour of God I shall prosper	Blenshell, Blinshall.
Deo gloria	Glory to God	Bennet, Gennys.
Deo gratias	Thanks to God	Senhouse.
Deo inspirante, rege favente	God inspiring me, and the king favouring me	Stahlschmidt, Strahlschmidt.
Deo juvante	God assisting	Groze, Maitland, Pellew, Sampson, Tawse, Wodderspoon.
Deo juvante, vinco	I conquer by the help of God	Stewart, Officer.
Deo, non fortuna	Through God, not by chance	Digby, Gardiner, Harrison, Pellew.
Deo pagit	He promises to God	Pagit, Pagitt.
Deo patriæ amicus	A friend to God and my country	Abbot, Granville.
Deo, patriæ, tibi	For God, my native land, and thee	Lambard.
Deo, regi, et patriæ	To God, my king, and my country	Irvine.
Deo, regi, patriæ		Duncombe.
Deo regique debeo	I owe it to God and the king	Johnson.
Deo volente	If God will	Campbell, Palliser.
Depechez	Make haste	Govan.
Depressus extollor	I am exalted by depression	Butler.
Despicio terrena	I contemn earthly things	Bedingfield, M'Crobie.
Despicio terrena et solem contemplor	I gaze on the sun, and spurn the earth	Bedingfield.
De tout mon cœur	With all my heart	Boleau, Pollen.
Detur forti palma	Let the reward be given to the brave	Sinclair.
Deum cole, regem serva	Worship God, obey the king	Cole.
Deum et regem	God and king	Collins.
Deum time	Fear God	Murray.
Deum timete		Carnegie.
Deus adesto	Let God be present	Brown.
Deus adjuvat nos	God assists us	Booth.

Latin/Motto	Translation	Bearer
Deus alit eos	God feeds them	Croker.
Deus clypeus meus	God is my shield	Biddell, Biddle, Biddelle.
Deus dabit	God will give	More.
Deus dabit vela	God will fill the sails	Albertus de Alasco, Campbell.
Deus est super domo	God is	Straker.
Deus evehit pios	God exalts the pious	Brown.
Deus gubernat navem	God steers the vessel	Leckie.
Deus hæc otia fecit	God hath given this tranquillity	Williams.
Deus incrementum dabit	God will give increase	Firth.
Deus intersit	Let God be in the midst	Stephens.
Deus juvat	God assists	Duff, M'Duff.
Deus major columna	God the greater support	Henniker, Major.
Deus me sustinet	God sustains me	Arbuthnot.
Deus meum solamen	God is my comfort	Keir.
Deus mihi adjutor	God is my helper	Auchterlonie, Aughterlony, Ochterlonie, Ouchterlony.
Deus mihi providebit	God will provide for me	Goold.
Deus mihi sol	God is my sun	Nicholson-Steele.
Deus nobiscum, quis contra nos	If God be with us, who can be against us	Morres.
Deus nobis hæc otio fecit	God hath given us these things in tranquillity	Bolger.
Deus nobis, quis contra?	God is for us, who can be against us?	Bolgar, Burrow, De Montmorency, Morres, Mores.
Deus non reliquit memoriam humilium	God hath not forgotten the humble	Meynell.
Deus pascit corvos	God feeds the ravens	Jones, Owen, Corbet.
Deus pastor meus	God is my shepherd	Boggie, Bogie.
Deus, patria, rex	God, native land, and king	Phillips.
Deus prosperat justos	God prospers the just	Heathcote.
Deus protector noster	God our protector	Sweden, Tennent.
Deus providebit	God will provide	Burton, Drummond, Lesly, Mein, Marshall, Mather.
Deus solamen	God my comfort	Ker, Kerr.
Deutlich und wahr	Distinct and true	Schrieber.
Devant, si je puis	Foremost, if I can	Jackson, Mainwaring, Mainwarring, Mainwairing, Scroope.
Devouement sans bornes	Devotion without bounds	Prodgers.
Deus et libertas	God and liberty	Godfrey.
Duw yd ein cryfdur	God, that is our strength	Edwards.
Dextra cruce vincit	My right hand conquers by the cross	Hurley.
Dextrâ fideque	By my right hand and faith	Bell.
Dh' aindheoin co theireadh e	In spite of who would gainsay	M'Donald.
ΔΙΑ ΤΗΣ ΣΤΕΝΗΣ	Through the narrow way	Clarke.
Diciendo y haciendo		Paget.
Dictis factisque simplex	Simple in words and deeds	Sawrey.
Dieppe		Harvey.
Dieu aidant	God assisting	Balfour.
Dieu avec nous	God with us	Berkeley, Burroughs.
Dieu ayde	May God help	De Montmorency.
Dieu defend le droit	God defends the right	Blenkinsopp, Churchill, Leaton, Seaton, Spencer.
Dieu donne	God gives	Colpoys.
Dieu est ma roche	God is my rock	Reoch.
Dieu est mon aide	God is my help	Band.
Dieu et ma foi	God and my faith	Favil.
Dieu et mon droit	God and my right	Guelp.
Dieu et mon pays	God and my country	M'Kirdy.
Dieu me conduise	God guide me	Delaval.
Dieu pour la Tranchée, qui contre	God for the trenches, whoever may oppose	La Poer Trench.
Dieu pour nous	God for us	Fletcher, Peters.
Dieu, une voi, une foi	God, one king, one faith	Rush.
Die virescit	It flourishes by day	Wood.
Difficilia quæ pulchra	What is honourable is difficult	Elford.
Dilectatio	Delight	Forbes.
Diligentia	Diligence	Dickman.
Diligentiâ cresco	I increase by diligence	Moncrief.
Diligentia ditat	Diligence enriches	Ferrier, Newall, Newell.
Diligentiâ et honore	With diligence and honour	Garnett.

Diligentiâ et vigilantiâ..........	*By diligence and vigilance*........	Semple.
Diligentiâ fit ubertas	*Diligence causes plenty*.............	Hay.
Dinna waken sleeping dogs...	....	Robertson, Forbes.
Disce ferenda pati...............	*Learn to suffer what must be borne*	De Hollyngworthe.
Disce pati..........................	*Learn to bear*.......................	Donkin, Duncan.
Disciplinâ, fide, perseverentiâ	*By discipline, faith, and perseverance*................................	Duckworth.
Discite justitiam.................	*Learn justice*.........................	Nisbet.
Disponendo me, non mutando me......................................	*By disposing, not by changing me*.......................................	Montagu.
Dissipate	*Disperse*...............................	Scrimzeor, Scrymzeor.
Ditat Deus........................	*God enriches*.........................	Fortun, M'Taggart.
Ditat et alit......................	*It enriches and nourishes*..........	Guthrie.
Ditat servata fides...............	*Faith kept enriches*................	Archibald, Innes, Papillon.
Divina gloria roris...............	*The beauty of the country is from God*..	Foster.
Divina sibi canit	*To herself she chants divine strains*...............................	Lachlan, Lauchlan, Lawchlan, Loghlan.
Divino robore......	*By divine strength*.................	Galiez, Galliez, Gellie, Gelly.
Divisa conjungo..................	*I heal divisions*.....................	Gordon.
Docendo disce....................	*Learn by teaching*.................	Brown.
Do good............................	....	Spence.
Doluére dente lacessiti	*Bitten, they felt pain*..............	Arden.
Domat omnia virtus............	*Virtue overcomes all things*.......	Ffarrington.
Domi ac foris.....................	*At home and abroad*...............	Norie.
Domine, dirige nos	*O Lord, direct us*...................	Brome.
Domine, speravi..................	*O Lord, I have hoped*.............	Lloyd.
Domini factum	*The work of the Lord*.............	Sibthorpe.
Domini factum est..............	*It is the work of the Lord*.........	Sibbald, Scott.
Domino quid reddam...........	*What shall I render to the Lord?*	Blofeld.
Dominus dedit...................	*The Lord gave*......................	Harries, Harris, Herns, Herries.
Dominus fecit....................	*The Lord made*.....................	Baird, Jackson.
Dominus fortissima turris......	*God is a most strong tower*........	Haviland.
Dominus ipse faciet........	*The Lord himself will do it*......	Adam.
Dominus providebit.............	*The Lord will provide*.............	Anderson, Boyle, Burton, Glasgow, Lawson, MacLaws, M'Laws, M'Vicar, Mason.
Domum antiquam redintegrare	*To restore an ancient house*.......	Hepburn.
Donec impleat....................	*Until it fill*...........................	Souter, Kidd, Kydd.
Donec impleat orbem..........	*Until it fill the world*..............	Hay, Kidd, Kyd.
Donec rursus impleat orbem	*Until it again fill the world*.......	Somervil, Sommerville.
Do no yll, quoth D'Oyle.......	....	D'Oyley.
Do, or die..........................	....	Douglas.
Do well, and doubt not.........	....	Blakiston, Brice, Bryce.
Do well, and let them say......	....	Bruce, Elphingston, Gordon, Scot, Scott.
Do well, doubt not...............	....	Kingsmill.
Do well, doubt nought..........	....	Bruce.
Dread God.......................	....	Carnagie, Carnaghi, Gordon, Hay-Macdougall, Hodgson, Monro, Munro.
Dread shame.....................	....	Leighton.
Droit................................	*Right*	Tunstall.
Droit à chacun...................	*Right to each*	Dobede.
Droit et avant....................	*Right and forward*.................	Townshend.
Droit et loyal.....................	*Upright and loyal*.................	Vanneck.
Droit et loyauté...	*Right and loyalty*...................	Vannock.
Drwy Rynwedd Gwaed.........	....	Walwyn.
Ducit amor patriæ...............	*The love of my country leads me on*.................................	Lechmere, Philips.
Ducit Dominus..................	*The Lord leads*.....................	Dezom.
Ducitur honus honos...........	*Hence honour is drawn*...........	Buchanan.
Ducitur, non trahitur...........	*He is led, not drawn*..............	Alexander.
Dulcedine capior.................	*I am captivated with pleasantness*.....................................	Houlatsone.
Dulce periculum.................	*Danger is sweet*.....................	M'Alla, M'Call, M'Aulay, Mackauly.
Dulce pro patriâ periculum...	*Danger for our country is sweet*	Ker.
Dulce quod utile.................	*That is sweet which is useful*......	Strang.
Dulces ante omnia musœ......	*The sweetness of music is before all things*.........................	Lowes.

Dulcidine....................	By sweetness....................	Bogle.
Dulcis amor patriæ..............	Sweet is the love of country.......	Clifford, Fitz-Wygram.
Dulcis pro patriâ labor........	Labour for our country is sweet...	M'Kerrel, McKerrell.
Dulcius ex asperis...............	Sweeter after difficulties............	Ferguson, Fergusson.
Dum clarum, rectum teneam	While I hold to glory, let me hold to right........................	Penn.
Dum cresco, spero...............	While I grow, I hope...............	Rider.
Dum in arborem...................	While in the tree....................	Hamilton.
Dum memor ipse mei..........	While he himself is mindful of me	Irvine.
Dum vigilo, paro............	While I watch, I prepare.........	Gordon.
Dum sedulo prospero...........	As yet I prosper by assiduity......	Swinton.
Dum sisto, vigilo.................	While I stand, I watch	Gordon.
Dum spiro, cœlestia spero......	While I breathe, I hope for heavenly things........................	Innes.
Dum spiro, spero..................	While I breathe, I hope............	Anderson, Asscoti, Asscotti, Auchmuty, Aylmer, Bannatyne, Brook, Colquhoun, Compton, Coriton, Coryton, Dearden, Dillon, Drummond, Elrick, Gaunt, Glazebrook, Greaves, Hoare, Hunter, Learmonth, Nicholls, Partridge, Pearson, Pount, Sharp, Spearman, Stover, Symonds, Taylor, Thompson.
Dum varior......................	Until I am changed.................	Ramsay.
Dum vigilo tutus.................	While I watch, I am safe..........	Gordon.
Dum vivo, spero.................	While I live, I hope	Menteath, Monteith, Thom, Whiteway.
Dum vivo, vireo..................	While I live, I flourish.............	Latta.
Durat, ditat, placet..............	It sustains, it enriches, it pleases	Ged, Geddes, Geddies.
Durate	Be lasting.............................	Evelyn.
Duris non frangor	I am not broken by hardships.....	Muir, Mure.
Durum patientiâ frango........	I overcome difficulty by patience	Crawford, Crawfurd, Moore, Muir, Mure.
Durum sed certissimum........	Hard, but very sure.................	Gillanders.
Duw a ddarpar i'r brain	God feedeth the ravens............ ..	Williams.
Duw a digon......................	God and enough....................	Prytherch.
Duw au bendithi.................	God bless them......................	Pryse.
Duw vde ein cryfdwr...........	God, thou art my strength.........	Edwards.
Dux mihi veritas.................	Truth is my guide..................	Haggard.
Dux vitæ ratio...................	Reason is the guide of my life.....	Bennet, West-Roberts.
Duw dy ras.......................	God, thy grace.................... ...	Kemeys-Tynte.

E

Eadhon dean agus na caomhain	Even do, and spare not............	Macgregor, Peter.
Eamus quo ducit fortuna......	Let us go where fortune leads.....	Atty.
Echel Coryg....	The Axle of Coryg..................	White.
E'en do.............................	....	M'Hud.
E'en do, and spare not.........	....	Greg, Gregorson, Macgregor. MacPeter, Mallock, Peter. Peters.
E'en do, bait spair nocht......	....	M'Gregor.
E'en do, but spare not.........	....	Gregorson.
Efficiunt clarum studio.........	They make it clear by study......	Milne, Mylne.
Effloresco........................	I flourish.............................	Boyle, Cairnes, Cairns.
Efflorescent cornices dum micat sol...:..............	Crows will abound while the sun shines.............................	Rooke.
E labore dulcedo................	Pleasure arises from labour.......	Bogle, Innes, M'Innes.
Elvenaca floreat vitis............	Let the vine of Elvine flourish.....	Elvin.
Emergo.............................	I come up...........................	Glass, Webster.
En bonne foy.....................	In good faith........................	Chadwick, Purefoy-Bagwell.
En caligine veritas...............	Truth in darkness...................	Calverley.
En Dieu est ma fiance..........	In God is my trust.................	Luttrell-Olmius.
En Dieu est ma foy.............	On God is my reliance.............	Staunton.
En Dieu est mon esperance...	In God is my hope.................	Gerard, Walmesley.

En Dieu est mon espoir	In God is my hope	Trevanion-Bettesworth, Smith
En Dieu est tout	In God is all	Conolly, Dawes, Wentworth.
En Dieu ma foi	On God is my reliance	Favill.
Endure fort	Suffer bravely	Lindsay.
En esperanza	In hope	Mack.
En grace affie	Engrafted into grace	Brudenell, Grace.
En la rose je fleurie	I flourish in the rose	Lenox, Roos, Roose.
Enough in my hand		Cunninghame.
En parole je vis	I live by the word	Legge.
Ense animus major	Courage is greater than the sword	Rymer.
Ense et animo	With sword and courage	Grant.
En suivant la verité	By following the truth	Wallop, Williams.
En vain espere, qui ne craint Dieu	They hope in vain who fear not God	Janssen.
Er cordiad y cæra	Notwithstanding the agreement of the fortification	Heaton.
Erectus, non electus	Exalted, not chosen	Beaumont.
Ero quod eram	I will be what I was	Landen, Scrogie.
Errantia lumina fallunt	Wandering lights deceive	Kinnaird.
Eryr Eryrod Eryri	The eagle of the eagles of North Wales	Owen.
Esperance	Hope	Ffytche, Wallace.
Esperance en Dieu	Hope in God	Beverley, Bullock, Percy.
E spinis	From the thorns	Dunlop.
Essayez	Try	Dundas, Saunders.
Essayez hardiment	Try boldly	Dundas.
Esse quam videri	To be, rather than to seem	Boevey, Boevy, Bourne, Bower, Bunbury, Couts, Croft, Deline, Maitland, Mathie, Sheriff, Sherrif, St Paul, Swire, Turnour, Woodcock.
Est meruisse satis	It is enough to have deserved	Massingberd.
Est modus	There is a mean	Lister.
Est nulla fallacia	There is no deception	Car-Standish.
Est pii Deum et patriam diligere	It is the duty of a pious man to love God and his native country	Atkinson.
Est voluntas Dei	It is the will of God	Baldwin.
Esto quod esse videris	Be what you seem to be	Aufrere, Cole, Milles, Southerne, Watson.
Esto semper fidelis	Be always faithful	Yea.
Esto, sol, testis	Sun, be thou a witness	Jones.
Esto vigilans	Be watchful	Okeover.
Et arma et virtus	Both arms and valour	Hamilton.
Et arte, et marte	Both by art and force	Bain, Bayne.
Et custos et pugnax	Both a keeper and champion	Majorebanks, Majoribanks, Marjoribanks.
Et decerpta dabunt odorem	And plucked, they will give forth an odour	Aiton.
Et decus et pretium recti	Both the glory and reward of worth	Fitzroy, Grafton.
Et Dieu mon appuy	And God my support	Hungerford.
Et domi et foris	Both at home and abroad	Callander, Livingstone, Mack.
E tenebris lux	Light out of darkness	Alston, Aston, Lightbody.
Eternitatem cogita	Think on eternity	Boyd.
Et juste et vray	Both just and true	Wray.
Et loquor et taceo	I both speak and hold my tongue	Keith.
Et manu et corde	With hand and heart	Bates.
Et marte, et arte	Both by strength and art	Bain, Bayn, Drummond.
Et mea messis erit	My harvest also will come	Denny.
Et neglecta verescit	It flourishes, even when neglected	Hamilton.
Et nos quoque tela sparsimus	And we also throw darts	Hastings, Rawdon.
Et patribus et posteritati	Both for forefathers and posterity	Lydal, Lydall, Lyddall.
Et servata fides perfectus amorque ditabunt	Both faith preserved and perfect love will enrich	Yonge.
Ettle weel	Purpose well	Smart.
Et suavis et fortis	Pleasant and brave	Harper.
Et suives moy	And follow me	Hawley.
Et, si ostendo, non jacto	And if I show, I do not boast	Oakden.
Et vi et virtute	Both by strength and valour	Borrowes, Stannus.

2 M

Et vitam impendere vero	To sacrifice life for truth	Fox-Vassel, Holland.
Ever faithful		Gordon.
Ever ready		Bryson, Burn.
Evertendo fœcundat	It becomes fruitful by turning over	Imbrie, Imrie.
Every bullet has its billet		Vassall.
Every point		Young.
Ewch yn uchae	Go well	Wynn-Williams.
Exaltabit honore	He will exalt with honour	Smyth.
Exaltavit humiles	He hath exalted the humble	Holt.
Ex armis honos	Honour from arms	Ogilvies, Ogilvy.
Ex bello quies	Rest from war	Murray.
Ex campo victoriæ	From the field of victory	Campbell.
Ex candore decus	Honour from sincerity	Keith.
Excitari, non hebescere	To be alive, not to grow dull	De Grey.
Excitari, non hebescere	To be refreshed, not to decay	De Grey.
Excitat	Arouses	Ford.
Exegi	I have tried	Lees.
Exempla suorum	The examples of our countrymen	Innes.
Ex fide fortis	Brave from trust	Beauchamp, Lygon, Pindar.
Ex flammâ lux	Light is from flame	Ingledew.
Ex hoc victoria signo	Victory by this sign	Rattary, Rattray.
Ex industriâ	From industry	Milne, Mylne.
Exitus acta probat	The end proves actions	Biset, Nivison, Stanhope.
Ex merito	By desert	Cheston, Tharrold.
Expecta cuncta superne	Expect all things from above	Wilson.
Expecto	I wait	Hepburn.
Expedite	Extricate	Hunter.
Expertus fidelem	Having found thee faithful	Lewis.
Expugnare	To conquer	Crawfurd.
Ex recto decus	Honour is from rectitude	Durno.
Ex se ipso renascens	Coming again from himself	Fraser.
Ex solâ virtute honos	Honour springs from virtue alone	Johnston.
Ex sudore voluptas	Beauty is produced by labour	Swettenham.
Extant recte factis præmia	Rewards await right actions	Coffin.
Extinguo	I extinguish	Dundas.
Ex undis aratra	Ploughs from the waters	Downie.
Ex unguibus leonis	From the claws of the lion	Ogilvie.
Ex unitate incrementum	Increase comes from unity	Guthrie, Guthry.
Ex usu commodum	Convenient from use	Smith.
Ex virtute honos	Honour comes from virtue	Jarden, Jardin.
Ex vulnere salus	Health comes from a wound	Borthwick.

F

Fac et spera	Do and hope	Arthur, Askew, Ayscough, Campbell, Crommelin, De la Cherios, Donald, Fea, Hyatt, Ledsam, Littledale, Matheson, Macknight, M'Gee, Scepter.
Facies qualis, mens talis	As the countenance is, so is the mind	Blair.
Facie tenus	Even to the face	Wheeler.
Facta, non verba	Deeds, not words	Deedes, De Rinzy, Lewis, Wilson, Yarde.
Factis, non verbis	With deeds, not with words	Money.
Facundia felix	Happy eloquence	Scot.
Faded, but not destroyed		Paver.
Famæ studiosus honestæ	Zealous of honourable fame	Brown.
Famæ vestigia retinens	Keeping to the footsteps of fame	Ennishowen.
Fai bien, crain rien	Do good, fear nothing	Zornlin.
Faire mon devoir	To do my duty	Jocelyn.
Faire sans dire	To do, and be silent	Blamire, Fox-Strangeways.
Faith and hope		Lindsey.
Faith and works		Nelson.
Faithful in adversity		Hamilton.
Faithful to an unhappy country		Molyneux.

Faitz proverount		Grimston.
Fal y gallo	As he can	Lyle, Greenly.
Famam extendimus factis	We extend our reputation by deeds	Vach, Veitch.
Fama perennis erit	Fame will be everlasting	Wyborn.
Fama semper vivit	Fame lives always	Liddell.
Familias firmat pietas	Religion strengthens families	Wardlaw.
Fari fac	Make him speak out	Fairfax.
Fari quæ sentias	To speak what you think	Walpole.
Fari quæ sentiat	To speak what he feels	Barkas, Wallpool, Walpole.
Fari qui sentient	To speak what they shall feel	Bretargh.
Fast		Gray.
Fata viam invenient	The fates will find a way	Spange, Van-Sittart.
Fato providentia major	Providence is greater than fate	Napier.
Fato prudentia major	Wisdom is greater than fate	Cheney.
Faugh-a-ballagh	Clear the way	Gough.
Faut être	Must be	Numbee.
Faveat fortuna	May fortune favour	Heyland.
Favente Deo	By God's favour	Pawson, Wilkie, Wolin.
Favente Deo, supero	By the favour of God I succeed	Mitchell.
Favente numine	By the favour of Providence	Micklethwyatt-Peckham.
Faventibus auris	With favouring breeze	Stirling.
Fax mentis honesta gloria	Honest fame is the torch of the mind	Lauder, Molleson.
Fax mentis incendium gloriæ	The torch of the mind is the incitement to glory	Brunton, Forbes, Grammer.
Fear God		Crumbie, Gordon, M'Andrew, M'Dowall, M'Dowell, M'Dougal.
Fear God and fight		M'Clambroch.
Fear God and spare nought		Grassick.
Fear God, honour the king		Porter.
Fear God in life		Somervale, Somerville.
Fear God in love		Somerville.
Fear to transgress		Scott.
Fecunditate afficior	I am blessed with fruitfulness	Hunter.
Felicem reddet religio	Religion will render man happy	Millar.
Felicior quo certior	The happier, the surer	Ormistone.
Feliciter floret	Flourishes prosperously	Crawfurd.
Felix qui pacificus	Happy is the peace-maker	Spence.
Ferendo et feriendo	By bearing and striking	Harrison.
Ferendo feres	You will gain by enduring	Irvine.
Ferendum et sperandum	Enduring and hoping	Mackenzie, M'Kenzie.
Feret ad astra	It shall carry to heaven	Kellet.
Feret ad astra virtus	Virtue shall bear to the stars	Kellet.
Ferio, tego	I strike, I cover	Howdon.
Ferio, tego	I strike and defend	Hawdon, Howdon, M'Aul, M'Call, Sims, Syme.
Ferme en foy	Strong in faith	Chichester, Sanford.
Feroci fortior	More brave than fierce	Lockhart, Piper.
Feror unus et idem	I am borne along one and the same	Collingwood.
Feros ferio	I strike the fierce	Chisholm.
Ferox inimicis	Bold against enemies	Sikes.
Ferré va Ferme		Farrar.
Ferro comite	The sword my companion	Mordant, Tolson.
Ferro consulto	I appeal to the sword	Tregose.
Fert lauream fides	Faith bears the laurel	Hay.
Fertur discrimine fructus	Profit is gained by peril	Gordon.
Fest		Delafield.
Festina lente	Diligently, but not hurriedly	Blaauw, Blaw, Campbell, Colquhon, Colquhoun, Onslow, Plunket, Plunkett, Rigge, Trotter, Westcombe.
Ffyddylon at y gorfin		James.
Fiat Dei voluntas	Let God's will be done	Meredith, Meredyth.
Fiat justitia	Let justice be done	Bryce, Coker.
Fiat justitia, ruat cœlum	Let justice be done, though heaven should fall in ruins	Lloyd.
Fiat voluntas Dei	Let God's will be done	Salway.
Fide et amore	By fidelity and love	Carden, Conway, Dicey, Heart, Seymour.

Fide et armis	By fidelity and arms	Fairquhar.
Fide et constantia	By fidelity and constancy	Dixon.
Fide et diligentiâ	With fidelity and diligence	Crawford.
Fide et fiduciâ	By fidelity and confidence	Blackman, Gilchrist, James-Grevis, Primrose, Thorlby, Thorley, Watt.
Fide et firme	With fidelity and steadiness	Fairholm.
Fide et fortitudine	By fidelity and fortitude	Aubert, Barton, Capel-Coningsby, Cooper, Cox, Farquharson, Hickson, Higgans, M'Farquhar, Milligan, Noble, Ratcliff, Shaw.
Fide et integritate	With fidelity and integrity	Venn.
Fide et labore	With fidelity and labour	Allan.
Fide et marte	With fidelity and bravery	Ralston.
Fide et operâ	By fidelity and labour	M'Arthur, Stewart.
Fide et sedulitate	With fidelity and diligence	Elwood.
Fide et spe	With faith and hope	Borthwick.
Fide et vigilantiâ	With fidelity and vigilance	Stepney.
Fide et virtute	With faith and valour	Brandling, Gladstanes, Glaidstanes, Gledstanes, Gooch, Goodwin, Rochead, Roughead.
Fidei coticula crux	The cross is the touchstone of faith	Baker, Villiers.
Fidei signum	The sign of my faith	Murray.
Fide laboro	I labour with fidelity	Borrer, Geddes, Geddies.
Fidele	Trusty	Halyburton, Roupell.
Fideli certa merces	There is a sure reward to the faithful	Parker.
Fideli certe merces	Certainly there is a reward to the faithful	Saul, Saule.
Fideli quid obstat	What stands in the way of the faithful	Firebrae.
Fideli quod obstat	What hinders the faithful	Firebrace.
Fidelis	Trusty	Blaikie, M'Vean, Waldie, Waldy.
Fidelis ad urnam	Faithful to death	Malone.
Fidelis et constans	Faithful and constant	Bragge.
Fidelis et in bello fortis	Trusty and brave in war	Gillespie.
Fidelis et suavis	Faithful and pleasant	Emery.
Fidelisque ad mortem	And faithful to death	Taylor.
Fidelis usque ad mortem	Faithful even to death	Sutton.
Fidelitas	Fidelity	M'Invoy, Purdie, Scot, Scott.
Fidelitas vincit	Fidelity overcomes	Cotton.
Fidelitate	With faithfulness	Elphinston.
Fidelite est de Dieu	Faithfulness is from God	Wingfield.
Fideliter	Faithfully	Bow, Havelock, Henrie, Ogilvy, Ralph, Symons.
Fideliter et diligenter	Faithfully and diligently	Graham.
Fideliter serva	Persevere faithfully	Norris.
Fidem meam observabo	I will keep my plighted word	Shedden.
Fidem parit integritas	Integrity produces confidence	Kay, Kaye.
Fidem rectumque colendo	By cultivating fidelity and rectitude	Hibbert.
Fidem servo	I keep faith	Alexander.
Fide, non armis	By fidelity, not by arms	Gambier.
Fide parta, fide aucta	Acquired by fidelity, increased by fidelity	M'Kenzie.
Fide parta, fide aucta	By faith obtained, by faith increased	Mackenzie, M'Kenzie.
Fideque perennant	And they endure by faith	Irvine.
Fides	Faith	Forbes-Leith, Maxton, Petree, Petrie, Wylie.
Fides culpari metuens	Fidelity fearful of being blamed	Yeldham, Yildham.
Fide, sed cui vide	Have confidence, but be cautious in whom you place it	Astley, Bankes, Beaumont, Birbeck, Greensugh, Reynolds, Stapleton, Stapyltou, Watts.
Fide, sed vide	Trust, but observe	Petrie, Reynolds.
Fides præstantior auro	Fidelity is better than gold	Clapperton, Gibb.
Fides probata coronat	Approved faith crowns	Campbell, Laidlaw.
Fides servata ditat	Tried fidelity enriches	Baillie.

Fides servata secundat	Faith being preserved, renders prosperous	Napier, Stirling.
Fides sufficit	Faith is sufficient	Hacket, Halket, Halkett-Craigie-Inglis.
Fides unit	Faith unites	M'Kenzie.
Fiduciâ et labore	By confidence and industry	Jockel.
Fidus ad extremum	Faithful to the end	Leith.
Fidus amicus	A trusty friend	Campbell.
Fidus et audux	Faithful and bold	O'Callaghan, Slade.
Fidus in arcanis	Faithful in secret affairs	Stevenson.
Fidus in arcanum	Faithful in a secret	Stevenson.
Fiel però disdichado	Faithful though unfortunate	Churchill, Spencer, Tufton.
Fier sans tache		Goff.
Fight		Ashe, Erskine, Sinclair, St Clair.
Filicior quo certior	The surer, the happier	Ormiston.
Finem respice	Consider the end	Bligh, Pattenson.
Finis coronat opus	The end crowns the work	Baker.
Finis dat esse	Death gives life	Brograve.
Firm		Dalrymple, Meason, Reid, Walch, Walsh, Wall.
Firma durant	Solid bodies endure	Lesly.
Firma et ardua	Bold and dangerous	Mackenzie.
Firma nobis fides	Our faith is constant	Vilant.
Firmâ spe	By sure hope	Leslie, Lesly.
Firma spes	Firm hope	Moncrief, Moncriff.
Firme	Firmly	Dalrymple, Elphistone, Hay.
Firme, dum fide	Steadfastly while in trust	Heignie.
Firmior quo paratior	More steady, because better equipped	Dunbar.
Firmitas et sanitas	Strength and health	Griffiths.
Firmitas in cœlo	Stability in heaven	Macnamara, Maher, St George.
Firmiter maneo	I steadfastly remain	Lindsay.
Firmius ad pugnam	More strongly for battle	Panton.
Firmor ad fidem	I am true to my faith	Chippendall.
Firm to my trust		Glyn.
Firmum in vitâ nihil	Nothing in life is permanent	Bunbury, Dolphin.
Firmus in Christo	Steadfast in Christ	Firmin.
Firmus infirmis	Strong to the feeble	Richardson.
Firmus maneo	I remain constant	Breek, Breck, Lindsay
Firrinneach gus a chrich	Faithful to the last	Macgregor.
Fisus et fidus	Trusted and faithful	Maitland.
Fit inde firmior	Thence it becomes stronger	Skirvin.
Fit via vi	The way is made by labour	Campbell.
Fixus ac solidus	Fixed and solid	Stewart.
Fixus adversa sperno	Resolute I scorn adversity	Hamerton.
Flecti, non frangi	To be bent, not broken	Temple.
Floreant lauri	Let the laurels flourish	Lowry.
Floreat majestas	Let majesty flourish	Braid, Brown.
Flores curat Deus	God cares for the flowers	Flowers.
Floret qui laborat	He prospers who labours	Ross.
Floret qui vigilat	He prospers who watches	Smith.
Floret virtus vulnerata	Virtue though wounded flourishes	Floyer.
Fluctus fluctu	Wave on wave	Maitland.
Follow me		Campbell.
Force avec vertu	Strength with virtue	Leigh.
Force d'en haut	Strength from above	Mallet.
Foresight is all		Lidderdale.
Foreget not		Campbell.
Forma, flos ; fama, flatus	Beauty a flower, fame a breath	Bagshaw.
Formosa quæ honesta	Things honourable alone are worthy	Tarton.
For my country		Jobling.
For my Duchess		Grant.
For right		Stephenson, Stirling.
For right and reason		Graham.
For security		Roberton, Robertoun, Steedman.
For sport		Cleiland, Cleilland, Cleland.
For true liberty		Renwick.
Forte en loyauté	Brave in my loyalty	Dacre.
Forte et fidèle	Bravely and faithfully	Ellis, Furnival, Talbot.

Fortem fors juvat...............	Fortune assists the brave............	Menzies.
Fortem posce animum	Wish for a brave soul...............	Fynney, Heriot, Twisleton-Fiennes, Phillimore, Saye, Sele.
Fortem post animum...........	After a brave mind.................	Heriot.
Forte non ignave	Bravely not cowardly...............	Lee.
Forte scutum salus ducem....	A strong shield is the safeguard of a general.....................	Fortescue.
Fertes fortuna adjuvat.........	Fortune assists the brave...........	Blennerhassett, Dickson, Murray, Bloomfield.
Fortes fortuna juvat.............		
Fort et loyal	Brave and loyal.....................	Selby.
Forti et fideli nihil difficile....	Nothing is difficult to the brave and faithful......................	Deane, M'Carthy.
Forti favet cœlum	Heaven favours the brave..........	Oswald.
Forti, non ignavo	To the brave, not to the dastardly	Lyell, Lyle.
Fortior est qui se ?...............	Who is braver than himself ?......	Poley.
Fortior leone justus.............	The just is braver than a lion	Goodricke.
Fortior qui melior	He is the braver who is the better man............................	Buchan.
Fortiorum fortia facta	The brave deeds of brave men.....	Stark, Stack, Stork.
Fortiorum fortia facta	The brave actions of the brave	Stark.
Fortis atque fidelis..............	Brave and faithful.................	Savage.
Fortis cadere,non cedere potest	The brave can die, not yield......	Moore.
Fortis esto, non ferox...........	Be brave, not ferocious.............	Wintringham.
Fortis est veritas.................	Strong is the truth	Angus, Barton, Hutchon.
Fortis et æquus	Brave and just.....................	Livingstone.
Fortis et fide	Brave and with faithfulness......	Carfrae.
Fortis et fidelis...................	Brave and faithful	Beton, Close, Douglas, Dumbar, Dunbar, Finlay, Findlay, Fletcher, Lalor, May, Middleton.
Fortis et fidus....................	Brave and trusty	Innes, Loughman, M'Clauchlan, M'Lachlan, M'Lauchlan, MacLaughlan.
Fortis et lenis.....................	Brave and gentle	Curry.
Fortis et placabilis	Brave, and easily appeased	Scot.
Fortis et stabilis..................	Brave and steadfast	Killikelley.
Fortis fidelis......................	Brave, faithful	Stenhouse.
Fortis in arduis..................	Brave in difficulties.................	Beton, Betton, Beaton, Findlay, Findley, Fletcher, Ford, MacDowall, M'Dougall, MacDougall, Methuen, Middleton.
Fortis in procellâ................	Brave in the storm.................	Woods.
Fortis non ferox..................	Brave, not fierce...................	Stockes.
Fortis que se vincit	Brave is he who conquers himself	Thorneycroft, Thornicroft.
Fortis qui prudens	He is brave who is prudent........	Ormsby.
Fortis, si jure fortis	Brave, if justly brave...............	Stockenstrom.
Fortissima veritas................	Truth is the strongest.............	Kirkaldie, Kirkaldy.
Fortis sub forte...................	Brave under the brave.............	Fitzpatrick, Fitz-Patrick.
Fortis sub forte fatiscet........	The brave will yield to the brave	Fitzpatrick.
Fortis valore et armis..........	Brave by valour and arms.........	Hatch.
Fortiter	Boldly.............................	Allan, Allen, Balmanno, Balmano, Beauman, Boswell, Clipsham, Elliot, Longbottom, Macalaster, Macalister, M'Alaster, M'Alister, Maclachlan, M'Lachlan, M'Cray, Warrand, Wight.
Fortiter agendo...................	By acting bravely	Pitman.
Fortiter et celeriter.............	Boldly and quickly	Mather.
Fortiter defendit.................	Defends bravely	Andrews.
Fortiter et fide	Boldly and with fidelity	Bontein, Briggs, Bunten.
Fortiter et fideliter..............	Boldly and faithfully...............	Brown, Browne, Cox, Goodsir, Pennyman, Peperell.
Fortiter et honeste..............	Bravely and honourably..........	Abney.
Fortiter et recte..................	Boldly and rightly	Allot, Elliot, Fuller, Keay, Lomelying, Rankin.
Fortiter et strenue................	Boldly and strenuously	Dempster, M'Lean.
Fortiter et suaviter	Boldly and with suavity	Ogilvie.

Motto	Translation	Names
Fortiter, fideliter, feliciter	Boldly, faithfully, and happily	Bottomley, Monck, Rathdowne.
Fortiter gerit crucem	He bears the cross patiently	Allan, Hutchinson, M'Hutcheon, Tritton.
Fortiter qui fide	Those who act faithfully act bravely	Hamilton.
Fortiter qui sedulo	Those who act diligently act bravely	Keith.
Fortiter sed apte	Boldly, but to the purpose	Falconer.
Fortiter sed feliciter	Bravely but fortunately	White.
Fortitudine	With fortitude	Barr, Barry, Boyle, Cuninghame, Cunningham, Duerryhouse, Erskin, Erskine, Grant, Hoste, M'Rach, Macrae, M'Crae, Moubray.
Fortitudine crevi	I have gained strength by fortitude	Craven.
Fortitudine Deo	By trust in God	Hobson.
Fortitudine et ense	By fortitude and the sword	Crossdell.
Fortitudine et labore	By fortitude and labour	Reid, Yonge.
Fortitudine et prudentiâ	With fortitude and prudence	Hargreaves, Lighton, Stuart, Yonge.
Fortitudine et velocitate	With courage and celerity	Balnaves, Balneaves.
Fortitudine vincit	He conquers by fortitude	Doyle.
Fortitudini	To fortitude	Hoste.
Fortuna audaces juvat	Fortune assists the daring	Cregoe, Barron, Cleveland.
Fortunâ et labore	By fortune and labour	Sym.
Fortunâ favente	By the favour of fortune	Falkiner.
Fortuna parcet labori	Good luck saves much trouble	Buchanan.
Fortuna sequatur	Let fortune follow	Gordon, Hunter, Warren.
Fortuna viam ducit	Fortune leads the way	Hassard.
Fortuna virtute	Fortune is from virtue	Beath, Beith, Bieth.
Fortune de guerre	Chance of war	Chute.
Fortune helps the forward		Carmichael.
Fortune le veut	Fortune attends him	Chaytor.
Forward		Balfour, Curl, Currel, Currell, Douglas, Howales, Ker, Maclaren, Millar, Miller, Ogilvie, Ogilvy, Strachan, Stuart, Stewart, Speir, Stirling.
Forward, kind heart		Bell.
Forward, non temere	Forward, not rashly	Balfour.
Forward ours		Seaton, Seton.
Forward without fear		Gordon.
Foy	Fidelity	Gilpin.
Foy en tout	Fidelity in all things	Grey, Yelverton.
Foy est tout	Fidelity is everything	Babington, Robinson.
Foy pour devoir	Fidelity for duty	Seymour.
Fractum non abjicio ensem	I throw not away the broken sword	Armitage.
Fragrat, delectat, et sanat	It smells sweet, and delights, and it cures	Clelland.
Fragrat post funera virtus	Virtue smells sweet after death	Chesly, Cheisly, Chiesly.
Française	French woman	Harris.
Franco leale toge	Free and loyal is to thee	Dolphin.
Frangas, non flectes	You may break, not bend	Gower, Granville, Jones, Kimber, Rippon, Sutherland.
Frango	I break	M'Laren.
Frappez fort	Strike hard	Wodehouse, Woodhouse.
Free for a blast		Clark, Clerk, Pennycook, Pennycoock, Pennycuick, Rattray.
Friendship		Carr.
From henceforth		Poore.
Fructum habet caratis	Charity hath fruit	Luckston.
Fructu noscitur	It is known by the fruit	Newbigging.
Fugit hora	The hour flies	Forbes.
Fugit irrevocabile tempus	Time flies beyond recall	Shadford, Shadforth.
Fulget virtus	Virtue shines forth	Bell.
Fulget virtus intaminata	Virtue shines unspotted	Belches.

Fuimus............................	We have been......................	Bruce-Brudenell, Bruce, Kennedy, Llewellin.
Fuimus, et sub Deo erimus...	We have been, and shall be, under God......................................	Coham.
Functa virtute fides............	Faith having exhibited valour.....	Murray.
Furor arma ministrat...........	Fury supplies arms..................	Baynes.
Furth fortune.....................		Murray.
Furth fortune and fill the fetters.............................		Aynsley, Glenlyon, Murray, Stewart.
Futurum invisibile	The future is unknown	Bevill.

G

Galea spes salutis................	Hope is the helmit of salvation...	Cassells.
Gänger.............................		Walker.
Gang forrit........................		Haly, Kennedar.
Gang forward.....................		Stirling.
Gang warily		Drummond, Porterfield.
Garde..............................		M'Kenzie.
Garde bien	Guard well............................	Carrick, Montgomerie, Montgomery.
Gardez bien......................		
Garde le roy.....................	Guard the King	Lane.
Garde l'honneur.................	Keep fast honour...................	Hanmer.
Gardez............................	Keep...................................	Cave.
Gardez la foy	Keep faith	Edwardes, Poulett, Rich.
Gaudeo	I rejoice..............................	Brown, Browne.
Gaudet luce videri..............	Rejoices to be seen in the light.....	Galton, Howard.
Gaudet tentamine virtus.......	Virtue exults in the trial...........	Legge.
Gaudium adfero..................	I bring joy...........................	Campbell.
Gauge and measure..............		Edminston.
Generositate.....................	By generosity.......................	Nicol, Nicolson, Nichol, Nicholson, Nickelson.
Genti æquus utrique............	Just to both nations................	Booth.
Gesta verbis prævenient........	Actions will be preferable to words	Harcourt, Swanston.
Give and forgive.................		Anderson, Andrew.
Giving and forgiving............		Biggar.
Gladio et arcu	With sword and bow................	Stubber.
Gladio et virtute	With sword and valour............	Ganstin, Garstin.
Gloria Deo	Glory to God........................	Henn.
Gloria in excelsis Deo	Glory to God on high...............	Kellock.
Gloria, non præda	Glory, not plunder..................	Murray.
Gloria patri.......................	Glory to the Father.................	Dewar.
Gloria virtutis umbra...........	Glory is the shadow of virtue......	Pakenham.
Gnaviter..........................	Actively..............................	Anderson.
God be guide		Kennedy.
God be my guide.................		Blair, Butler.
God be our friend		Staple.
God careth for us................		Mitford.
God feeds the crows		Crawford, Crawfurd.
God for us........................		Douglas.
God give grace...................		Tait.
God gives increase		Balfour.
God giveth the victory..........		Simon.
God guide all.....................		Lesly.
God is all.........................		Fraser.
God is love.......................		Wesley.
God is my defender..............		Bream, Breame.
God is my safety.................		Craw.
God me guide		Crichton.
God save the right...............		Crawford.
God send grace...................		Creighton, Chrichton.
God shaw the right..............		Crawford, Craufurd.
God will provide.................		Stewart.
God with my right		Bryson, Buchanan.
God with us.......................		Gordon.
Gogoniant yr clethaf............	Glory to the sword	Gwyn.
Good friend......................		Godfrey.
Good deeds shine clear.........		Minshull.

Good God increase...............	....	Goodale, Goodalle.
Good news......................	....	Tattersall.
Go on, and take care............	....	Thompson.
Go thou and do likewise.......	....	Colston.
Go through......................	....	Brenton.
Grace me guide.................	....	Forbes, Pownall.
Grace my guide.................	....	Forbes.
Gradatim..........................	By degrees	Anderson, Hopwood, Kilgour, MacNicol.
Gradatim plena...................	Full by degrees..................	Burnside, Gordon.
Gradatione vincimus............	We conquer step by step	Curtis.
Gradu diverso via una..........	The same way, by different steps..	Calthorpe.
Grandescunt aucta labore....	What is increased by labour grows great......................................	A'Court.
Gratâ manu......................	With a grateful hand............	Call.
Grata quies.....................	Welcome rest	Vansittart.
Gratâ sume manu	Take with a grateful hand........	Winnington.
Gratia naturam vincit...........	Grace overcomes nature............	Edwardes.
Gratis a Deo data..............	Given freely by God...............	Skeen, Skene.
Gratitudo........................	Gratitude........................	Bigland.
Graviter et pie..................	Gravely and piously...............	Park.
Grip fast.........................	....	Leslie, Lesly.
Gronwi hil Gwerninion.........	Goronwy, a descendant of the Gwerninion	Gronow.
Growing.........................	....	Fergusson.
Guarde la foy...................	Preserve our fidelity.............	Rich.
Guard yourself..................	....	Middleton.
Guardez vous....................	Guard yourself..................	Lidiard.
Gwell angau nachywilydd......	Rather death than shame...........	Basset, Mackworth.

H

Habet et suam....................	He has also his own...............	Seaton, Seton.
Hab shar..........................	Without offence or a share	Riddell.
Hac ornant.......................	In this way they adorn	Scougall.
Hactenus invictus................	Hitherto unconquered................	Crawford, Crawfurd, Gallightly, Gellatly.
Hac virtus mercede digna......	Virtue is worthy of this reward...	Robertson.
Hæc fructus virtutis............	These things are the fruits of virtue	Waller.
Hæc generi incrementa.........	These things are gains to the race	Townsend-Stephens.
Hæc generi incrementa fides..	Faith has bestowed these honours on the family......................	Townshend.
Hæc generi incrementa fides..	Ennobled for fidelity...............	Townshend.
Hæc lucra laborum..............	These are the advantages of industry................................	Rowan, Rowand.
Hæc manus ob patriam.........	This hand for my country.........	Mactier, Shuckburgh.
Hæc olim meminisse juvabit.	In future, it will delight us to remember these things.............	Lewis.
Hæc omnia transeunt..........	All these things pass away........	Bourne.
Hæc origo	This origin	Balnaves.
Hæc prestat militia............	This warfare excels...............	Bannerman.
Hallelujah........................	....	Aylmer.
Ha persa la fide, ha perso l'honore	He who hath lost his faith hath lost his honour...................	Lewis.
Hastings.........................	....	Heron, Horn.
Haud ullis labentia ventis.....	Yielding under no winds..........	Irving, Irvine, Irwin.
Haut et bon......................	High and good	Sentleger, St Leger.
Have at all.....................	....	Drummond.
Have faith in Christ...........	....	Glendoning, Glendowing
Have mercy on us, good Lord	....	Sitlington.
Hazard warily...................	....	Seaton, Seton.
Hazard zet forward.............	....	Seton.
Heb nevoe nerth nid sier saeth	Without heavenly strength the arrow is not sure...................	Jones.
Help at hand, brother..........	....	Muire, Mure.
Heb Dhuw, heb ddim, Duw a digon................................	Without God, without anything, God and enough.................	Davies, Lloyd, Edwards, Hughes, Meredith-Warter, Meyric, Meyrick, Morgan, Mostyn, Stradling, Williams.

Hic fidus et robore	He is faithful and courageous	Stirling.
Hic fructus virtutis	This is the fruit of virtue	Waller.
Hic labor	This labour	Dee, Mortlake.
Hic murus aheneus	This is a brazen wall	M'Leod.
Hic opus	Here is the work	Mortlake.
Higher		Galloway.
Hinc ducitur honos	Honour is derived hence	Nisbet.
Hinc fortior et clarior	Hence braver and more illustrious	Martin, Martine.
Hinc garbæ nostræ	Hence our sheaves	Cumine, Cummin, Cumming.
Hinc honor et opes	Hence honour and wealth	Hay.
Hinc illuminabitur	Hence it shall be enlightened	Oliphant.
Hinc incrementum	Hence comes increase	Hay.
Hinc laus et honos	Hence springs glory and honour	Rae.
Hinc mihi salus	Hence comes my salvation	Spalding, Peverell.
Hinc odor et sanitas	Hence is perfume and health	Liddel.
Hinc origo	Hence our origin	Balnaves.
Hinc orior	Hence I arise	Cameron, Howie, Paterson, Steuart, Stewart.
Hinc spes effulget	Hence beams forth our hope	Aberdour.
Hinc usque superna venabor	Henceforward I will seek after heavenly things	Murray.
His fortibus arma	Arms to these brave men	Nisbet.
His gloria reddit honores	Glory renders honours to them	Drummond.
His nitimur et munitur	We rely on and are strengthened by these things	Maconochie.
His regi servitium	With these we render service to the king	Neilson.
His securitas	Safety from these	Barsane, Bartane, Barton.
Hoc ardua vincere docet	This teaches us to overcome difficulties	Winchester.
Hoc in loco Deus rupes	Here God is a rock	Hockin.
Hoc majorum opus	This is the work of my ancestors	Eliot, Elliot.
Hoc majorum virtus	This is the valour of my ancestors	Logan.
Hoc opus	This work	Dee, Mortlake.
Hoc securior	More secure by this	Greson, Grier, Grierson, Grieve, Lockhart.
Hoc signum non onus, sed honor	This banner is no burden, but an honour	Stoughton.
Hoc vinco	This I conquer	Hay.
Hoc virtutis opus	This is the work of virtue	Collison.
Hold fast		Ancram, Dowine, Leslie, Lesly, M'Leod, MacLeod, Macloide, M'Loud, Smith.
Holme semper viret	Holme always is green	Holme.
Hominem te esse memento	Remember you are a man	Wybergh.
Homo homini vulpes	Man a fox to man	Wolseley.
Homo sum	I am the man	Homan.
Honesta peto	I seek honourable things	Oliphant.
Honesta quam splendida	Honourable acquisitions rather than splendid	Barrington.
Honestas	Honesty	Goldie, Goudie, Faal, Fall, Paget.
Honestas optima politia	Honesty is the best policy	Goff-Davies, Granger, Owen, Sparrow.
Honestate vetustas stat	Ancestry is established by honour	Stewart.
Honeste audax	Honestly bold	Edingtoun, Parkins, Parkyns.
Honeste vivo	I live honestly	Craige, Craigg, Pilmuire.
Honesto vivo	I live by honesty	Halket.
Honestum præfero utili	I prefer what is honourable to what is useful	Raikes.
Honestum prætulit utili	He has preferred honesty to advantage	Emline, Emlyn.
Honestum utili præfero	I prefer honesty to profit	M'Gell.
Honesty is good policy		Thomson.
Honesty is the best policy		Anderson, Kinnear, Thomas.
Honneur pour objet	Honour for aim	Page.
Honneur sans repos	Honour without rest	Montgomery.
Honorantes me honorabo	I will honour those who honour me	Atthill, Hastings, Maunsell.
Honorate, diligite, timete	Honour, love, fear	Moselay.
Honorat mors	Death confers honour	Bragge, Broge, Brogg, Broig.
Honor et amor	Honour and love	Dowglas, Niblie.
Honore et amore	With honour and love	Grantham, Richards.

Honor et honestas	Honour and honesty	Patriarche.
Honor et veritas	Honour and truth	Waller.
Honor et virtus	Honour and virtue	Atkins.
Honore et virtute	With honour and virtue	Gilleanks, MacDermot.
Honor fidelitatis præmium	Honour, the reward of fidelity	Fielding, Irby.
Honor me guide		Lusado.
Honor, pietas	Honour, piety	Waters.
Honor potestate honorantis	Honour with the power of honouring	Kynaston.
Honor probataque virtus	Honour and approved virtue	Fitzgerald.
Honor sequitur fugientem	Honour follows the fleeing	Chichester.
Honor, virtus, probitas	Honour, virtue, and probity	Barrett.
Honor virtutis præmium	Honour is the reward of virtue	Boyle, Ferrers, Hawtin, Hawtyn, Shirley.
Honor virtutis pretium	Honour is the price of virtue	Mills.
Honos alit artes	Honour cherishes the arts	Greenhill.
Honos vitâ clarior	Honour more glorious than life	Innes.
Hope and not rue		Oliphant.
Hope for the best		Sissons.
Hope to come		Foliot, Foliott.
Hope to share		Riddell.
Hope well and have well		Bower.
Hora e sempre	Now and for ever	Denys.
Hora et semper		Farmer, Fermor.
Hos gloria reddit honores	Glory has given these honours	Drummond.
Hostis honori invidia	Envy is an enemy to honour	Dickens, Patison, Pattison, Sherard, Sherrard, Wegg.
Ητοι τὸν λόγον ἄφετε ἢ καλῶς ταύτῳ πρόσστητε	Either discard the word, or becomingly adhere to it	Mores-Rowe.
Huad nomine tantum	Not in name alone	Best.
Humani nihil alienum	Nothing concerning man is indifferent to me	Hanrott, Talbot.
Hyeme exsuperata	When the winter was predominant	Wrangham.

I

I abide my time		Pennefather.
I am alone		Lone.
I am ever prepared		MacBreid, M'Breid.
I am, I am		Ruxton.
I am readie		Fraser.
I am ready		Fairlie, Fairly, Fraser, Frazer, Maxwell, Scott.
I beare in minde		Campbell.
I beir the bel		Macdonald.
I burn weil, I see		M'Leod.
I byde		Gordon.
I byde it		Nisbet.
I byde my time		Campbell, Loudon, Porteous.
Ich dien	I serve	Prince of Wales.
I conquer or die		Lumisden.
I dare		Adair, Dalsiel, Dalziel, Dalziell, Dalzell.
I desire not to want		Cranston.
I die for those I love		Forbes-Leith.
If God will		Samson.
If I can		Colquhoun.
I gain by hazard		Hamilton.
Igne constricto vita secura	Fire restrained, our lives are secure	Davy.
I hope		Forrest, Gordon, Ogle.
I hope for better		Boswell.
I hope in God		M'Naughtan, Macnaghten, M'Naughton, Naughten.
I hope to share		Nisbet.
I hope to speed		Cathcart, Gilchrist.
I increase		Scot.
I live in hope		Kennear.

Illæso lumine solem	I can, unhurt, behold the sun	Kebble, Sharpe, St Clair-Erskine, Wedderburn, Wedderburn.
I'll be wary		Finlay.
I'll bide broad Albine		Maxwell.
I'll deceive no man		Hamilton.
I'll stand sure		Grant.
I'll try		Newbigging.
Illumino	I give light	Farquharson.
Il suffit	It is enough	Darker.
Il tempo passa	Time passes	Boynton.
I make sure		Kilpatrick, Kirkpatrick.
I mean well		Callendar, Callender, Shaw, Stewart, Sutcliffe.
Imitare quam invidere	To imitate, rather than to envy	Child, Pleydell.
Immaculata gens	An unspotted race	Vaughan.
Immersabilis	Unconquerable	Hamilton.
Immersabilis est vera virtus	True virtue cannot be conquered	Codrington.
Immobile	Steadfast	Grant.
Immotus	Unmoved	Alston.
Immutabile, durabile	Unchangeable, durable	Rolland.
Impavidum ferient ruinæ	Ruin shall strike me unappalled	Mundell.
Impegerit fidus	The faithful man has made fast	Constable.
Impelle obstantia	Subdue obstacles	Arthur.
Impendam, expendar	I will spend and be spent	Burket, Burkett.
Imperio	By command	Murray.
Imperio regit unus æquo	One governs with just sway	Gunning.
In altum	Toward heaven	Alston, Alstone.
In ardua nitor	I endeavour in difficulties	Halkerston.
In ardua petit	Aims at lofty things	Malcolm.
In ardua tendit	He has attempted difficult things	M'Allam M'Callum, Malcolm.
In arduâ virtus	Virtue in distress	Wolstenholme.
In arduis fortis	Brave in difficulties	Fordyce, Dingwall.
In arduis fortitudo	Firmness in dangers	Hamilton.
In arduis viget virtus	Virtue flourishes in danger	Gurdon.
In bello quies	Repose in war	Murray.
In cælo confidemus	We trust in heaven	Hill.
In caligine lucit	It shines in the dark	Baillie.
In candore decus	Honour in purity	Chadwick.
In canopo ut ad canopum	In canopus as to canopus	Louis.
Incepta persequor	I prosecute my undertakings	Wilkinson.
In certâ salutis anchorâ	Upon a sure anchor of safety	Gillespie.
In Christo salus	Salvation is in Christ	Abernethy.
Incidendo sano	I cure by cutting	Kincaid.
Inclinata resurgo	Though abased, I rise again	Cooper.
Inclyte perdide recuperator corona	The famous recoverer of a lost crown	Seton.
Inclytus perditæ recuperator coronæ	The glorious recoverer of a lost crown	Seton.
In cœlo quies	Rest is in heaven	Bewick, Boscowen.
In cœlo spes mea est	My hope is in heaven	Micklethwaite.
Inconcussa virtus	Unshaken virtue	Benson.
In cornua salutem spero	I hope for safety against the horns	Hunter.
Incorrupta fides nudaque veritas	Uncorrupted faith and unvarnished truth	Forde.
In cruce confido	I trust in the cross	Thrale.
In cruce et lacrymis spes est	In the cross and tears there is hope	Hincks.
In cruce glorior	I glory in the cross	Cliffe, Pye.
In cruce mea fides	In the cross is my faith	Billairs.
In cruce salus	Salvation from the cross	Abercrombie, Abercromby, Adams, Aitkin, Aitkine, Bourke, Brigham, Carse, Carss, Langholme, Marr, Tailour, Tailyour.
In cruce spero	I hope in the cross	Barclay.
In cruce vinco	I conquer by the cross	Copley.
In crucifixo gloria mea	My glory is in the cross	Knatchbull.
In defence		Williamson.
In defence of the distressed		Allardice, Allerdice, Barclay.
In Deo confido	I trust in God	Kirkman, Tovey, Tovy.
In Deo est mihi omnis fides	In God is all my faith	Palmer.

Motto	Translation	Names
In Deo omnia	All things are in God	Bluett, Huxley, Reed.
In Deo rober meus	In God is my strength	Armstrong.
In Deo solo spes mea	In God alone is my hope	Kay, Key.
In Deo spero	I hope in God	Saumarez.
In Deo spes	Hope in God	Mitchell.
In Deo spes mea	In God is my hope	Beers.
Inde securior	Thence the more secure	Murray.
Indignante invidia florebit justus	Despising envy, the just shall flourish	Crosbie.
In Domino confido	I trust in the Lord	Asheton, Ashton, Areskine, Cargill, Erskin, Erskine, M'Gill, Willyams.
In dubiis constans	Steady in doubtful affairs	Cockburn, Cockburne, Ormistone.
Indubitata fides	Undoubted faith	Reynell.
Indulge not		Edwards.
Industriâ	With industry	Crierie, Crisie, Deas, Ferguson, Fettes, Fiddes, Gentle, Keltie, Kelty, Ogilvie, Ogilvy, M'Crire, Peel, Warrender.
Industria atque fortuna	Industry and fortune	Lawrie.
Industria ditat	Industry enriches	Paxton, Reath, Sideserf, Sydserfe, Vanderplank, Wauchop.
Industriæ manus	The gift of industry	Leechman, Leishman, Leeshman.
Industriâ et labore	By industry and labour	M'Gallock, M'Gassock, MacGuffock, M'Guffock.
Industriâ et probitate	By industry and probity	Washbourne.
Industriâ et spe	With industry and hope	Fenouillet, Warden, Yabsley.
Industria murus	Industry is a protection	Thomson.
Industriâ permanente	With unremitting industry	Neave.
Industria, virtus, et fortitudo	Industry, bravery, and fortitude	Smellie.
Industry and liberality		Jejeebhoy.
Inêbranlable	Unshaken	Acland.
Inest clementia forti	Mercy is inherent in the brave	Fort, Forte, Gent, Maule.
Inest jucunditas	Mirth is therein	Elliot, Elliott.
In fide et in bello fortes	Firm in faith and in war	Bagwell, Carroll, O'Carroll.
Ingenio et veribus	By the force of genius	Huddleston.
Ingenio innumerato habe	Possess by immense genius	Lawrie.
Ingenium innumerata habi...	Justly esteemed a man of genius	Lawrie.
Ingenium vires superat	Genius surpasses power	Alexander.
Ingenuas suscipit artes	Undertakes noble arts	Farnborough.
In God is all		Fraser, Frazer.
In God is all my trust		Grant.
In God I trust		Frazer.
Ingratis servire nefas	It is wrong to provide for the ungrateful	Martin.
In hoc plenius redibo	In this I shall return more full	Minshull.
In hoc signo	In this token	Wodehouse, Woodhouse.
In hoc signo spes mea	In this sign is my hope	Taaffe.
In hoc signo vinces	Under this sign you shall conquer	Aiscough, Arran, Berrie, Berry, Booth, Burke, Glasham, Gore, Ironside, Macadam, M'Carlie, M'Kerlie, O'Donel, O'Donnel, Newling, Stanhope, Taafe, Taylor, Turney, Webb.
In hoc spes mea	In this is my hope	Gordon.
Initium sapientiæ est timor Domini	The fear of the Lord is the beginning of wisdom	Martin.
Injussi virescunt	They grow green unbidden	Greenfield.
In labore quies	Repose in labour	Helyar.
In libertate sociorum defendenda	In defending the liberty of allies	Macgregor.
In lumine luce	Shine in light	Thompson.
In malos cornu	My horn against the bad	Dadley.
In memoriam majorum	In remembrance of our ancestors	Farquharson.
In moderation placing all my glory		Fitzhugh.

In multis, in magnis, in bonis expertus	Tried in many great and good exploits	Bowes.
Innocence surmounts		Gulland.
Innocens non timidus	Innocence is not afraid	Rowe.
Innocent and true		Arburthnot.
Innocue ac provide	Harmless and with foresight	Aberbuthnet, Arbuthnot, Lapington, Newbigging.
In omnes casus	For all chances	Walker.
In omnia paratus	Prepared for all things	Layton, Prittie.
In omnia promptus	Ready for everything	Rae.
In periculis audax	Bold in danger	Maher.
In portu quies	Rest in the haven	Wilbraham, Watkins.
In pretium persevero	I abide my reward	Jenoure, Jenoyre.
In promptu	In readiness	Dunbar, Trotter.
In recte decus	Honour in rectitude	Ferrier, Simmons.
In recto decus	There is honour in the right path	Hoseason, Scott, Syme.
In recto fides	Faith in rectitude	Dixon.
In season		Walkingshaw.
Inservi Deo et lætare	Serve God and rejoice	Howard.
Insignia fortunæ paria	The equal badges of fortune	Delafield.
Insiste firmiter	Stand to it stoutly	Moorside, Muirside.
In solitos docuere nisus	Unusual efforts have been resorted to	Babington.
In solo Deo salus	Safety is in God alone	Harewood, Lascelles.
Insontes ut columbæ	Harmless as doves	Francis.
In spe et labore transigo vitam	I pass life in hope and labour	Mack.
Insperata floruit	It has flourished beyond expectation	Cleghorn, Watson.
Instaurator ruinæ	A repairer of ruin	Forsyth.
Instituæ tenax	Holding by the arrangement	Parke.
In sublime	Aloft	Reid.
Insult me not		M'Kenzie.
Intaminatis fulget honoribus	It shines with unstained honours	Seton.
Intaminatis honoribus	With unstained honours	Fitz-Herbert.
In te, Domine, confido	In thee, Lord, I confide	Knyfton.
In te, Domine, speravi	In thee, O Lord, I have placed my hope	Bowes, Greenhill, Haine, Lyon, Prestwich, Prestwick, Vale.
In te, Domine, spes nostra	In thee, Lord, is our hope	Gill.
In te fido	I trust in thee	M'Larty.
Integra mens augustissima possessio	Integrity is the most glorious possession	Blaney.
Integritas semper tutamen	Integrity is a constant defence	Harries.
Integritas tuta virus non capit	Cautious integrity excites not bitterness	Holl.
Integritate stabis ingenuus	You will stand free by integrity	Stewart.
In the Lord is all our trust		Masons.
Intemerata fides	Uncorrupted faith	Aberdeen, Robertson.
In tempestate floresco	I flourish in the tempest	Coffin.
In tenebris lucidior	Brighter in darkness	Inglis.
In tenebris lux	Light in darkness	Scot, Scott.
Inter cruces triumphans in cruce	Amid crosses triumphing in the cross	Dalton.
Inter lachrymas micat	Shines amid tears	Blundell, Blunt.
Interna præstant	Internal things stand fast	Arburthnet.
Inter primos	Among the first	Hopkins.
In the defence of the destroyed		Allardice.
In time		Hauston, Houston.
Intrepidus et benignus	Intrepid and benign	Mackannel, Mackennal.
In utramque fortunam paratus	Prepared for either fortune	Stapleton-Cotton.
In utrâque fortunâ paratus	Prepared in all situations	Cotton.
In utroque	In both	Valange, Wallange.
In utroque fidelis	Faithful in both	Carey, Cary.
In utrumque paratus	Prepared for both	Heylyn.
In utrumque utroque paratus	Prepared for both and in both	Deacon, Elphingston, Mackenzie, Murray.
In veritate	In truth	Hastings.
In veritate victoria	Victory in truth	Hastings.
Invia virtuti pervia	Virtue finds a way where there is none	Hamilton.
Invia virtuti via nulla	No path is too hard to virtue	Seton.
Invicta labore	Unconquered by fatigue	Armstrang, Armstrang, Armstrong.

Invicta veritate	With invincible truth	Abell.
Invictus maneo	I remain unvanquished	Armstrang, Armstrang, Armstrong, Inglis.
Invidiâ major	Above envy	Drago, Inwards, Peters.
In vigiliâ sic vinces	In watchfulness thus will you conquer	Price.
In virtute et fortunâ	In valour and fortune	Fraser, Frazer.
Invita sortem fortuna	Seek the aid of lucky events	Knightley.
Invitum sequitur honor	Honour follows, though unsought for	Chichester.
In well beware		Wombwell.
Ipse amicus	He is a friend	Baron.
Iram leonis noli timere	Fear not the rage of the lion	Long.
I renew my age		Garshore, Gartshore.
I rise by industry		Foulis.
I rise with the morning		Cockburn.
Irrevocabile	Irrevocable	Bennitt, Bruce.
Irrideo tempestatem	I deride the storm	Wood.
Irrupta copula	An unbroken bond	Morris.
I saved the king		Torrance.
I show not boast		Nimmo.
I soar		Ellidge.
It is fortified		MacConach.
It is good to be blown		Forrester.
Ito tu et fac similiter	Go thou and do likewise	Oliver.
I wait my time		Porteous.

J

J'ai bonne cause	My cause is good	Thynne.
J'ai bonne esperance	I have good hope	Craig, M'Kean.
J'ai la clef	I have the key	Greive, Grive.
J'aime à jamais	I love always	James.
Jamais arriére	Never behind	Douglas.
J'amais abattu	Never cast down	Ouchterlony.
J'aime la liberté	I love freedom	Ribton, Mussenden.
J'aspire	I aim	Devizmes.
J'avance	I advance	Bartram, Clayton, East, Ker.
J'ay bonne cause	I have good cause	Boteville, Boteville, Bouteville, Botfield.
J'ay espere mieux avoir	I have hoped for the best	Dine, Dive.
J'ay ma foy tenu à ma puissance	I have kept my faith in my power	Croker.
Je dis la verite	I speak truth	Pedder.
Je gagne	I gain	Osbourne.
Jehovah-Jireh	The Lord will regard it	Grant.
Jehova portio mea	The Lord is my portion	Mercer.
Je le feray durant ma vie	I shall do it while I live	Fairfax.
Je le tiens	I hold it	Touchet, Tuchet.
Je maintiendrai	I will support	Harris.
Je maintien devrai	I maintain the right	Nesbitt.
Je me fie en Dieu	I trust in God	Blois, Windsor.
Je me tourne vers l'occident	I turn towards the west	Westropp.
Je mourrai pour ceux que j'aime	I would die for those I love	Coulthart.
Je ne change qu'en mourant	I only change in death	Salvin.
Je ne cherche que ung	I seek but one	Compton.
Je ne puis	I cannot	Delves.
Je n'oublierai jamais	I will never forget	Hervey.
Je pense	I think	Charteris, Jennoway, Swinton, Weems, Wemyss, Wiems.
Je pense plus	I think more	Areskine, Arsking, Erskin, Erskine.
Je reçois pour donner	I acquire, that I may distribute.	Innes.
J'espere	I hope	Swinton.
Jesu, esto mihi Jesus	Jesus, be my Jesus	Swale.
Jesu seul bon et bel	Jesus alone good and beautiful	Brearey, Breary.

Je suis prêt........................	I am ready...........................	Fraser, Maxwell-Barry, Maxwell-Perceval, M'Kimmie, Simpson.
Je suis veillant à plaire.........	I am watching to please	Saunderson.
Jesus...............................		Chipman, Chippengham.
Jesus hominum salvator.......	Jesus the saviour of men............	Legat, Legatt.
Je trouve bien....................	I find good...........................	Barnardiston.
Je veux bonne guerre..........	I would prefer war..................	Thompson.
Je veux le droit...................	I will have my right...............	Duckett.
Je vive en espoir.................	I live in hope........................	Rous.
Je vive en esperance............	I live in hope........................	Akers.
Je voy..............................	I have seen.........................	Jossey.
Jour de ma vie!...................	Day of my life!......................	West.
Jouir en bien......................	To enjoy innocently.................	Beckwith.
Jova confido......................	I confide in Jove....................	Gairdner.
Jovis omnia plena................	All things are full of Jove........	Goodden.
Jubilee	The year of joy.......................	Stamer.
Judge not..........................		Erskine, Stuart.
Judge nought.....................		Erskine, Stewart, Stuart.
Judicium parium................	The judgment of our peers.......	Raines.
Judicium parium, aut leges terræ	The judgment of my peers, or the laws of the land......................	Pratt.
Juncta arma decori..............	Arms united to glory...............	M'Gouan, M'Gowan.
Juncta virtuti fides..............	Faithfulness joined to courage....	Murray.
Jungor ut implear................	I am joined that I may be complete....................................	Meik.
Juravi et adjuravi................	I have solemnly sworn	Moores.
Jure, non dono...................	By right, not by gift.................	Ffoulkes.
Jus meum tuebor................	I will look after my right.........	Reynolds.
Jussu regis India subacta......	India subdued by the king's command............................	Munro.
Justa sequor......................	I will follow just things............	Keith.
Juste et droit......................	Just and right	Whichcote.
Justitia.............................	Justice.................................	Lunden, Nurse, Sibbald.
Justitiæ et veritas................	Justice and truth....................	Lauriston.
Justitiæ soror fides..............	Fidelity is the sister of justice.....	Justice, Thurlow.
Justi ut sidera fulgent.........	The righteous shine as the stars..	M'Coll, Sandilands.
Justum et tenacem..............	Just and persevering................	Colthurst, Macknight, M'Knight.
Justum perficito, nihil timeto	Do justly and fear not	Rogers.
Justus esto et non metue......	Be just, and fear not...............	Charley, Chorley, Robson.
Justus et propositi tenax......	Just and resolute..............,......	Ferrand, How.
Justus ut palma..................	The righteous flourish as the palm-tree............................	Palmes.
Juvant arva parentum	The field of our ancestors' delight	Cassan.
Juvant aspera forteis............	Dangers delight the brave.........	Steuart.
Juvant aspera probum.........	Hardships are profitable to the good man............................	Denham, Steuart, Stewart.
Juvante Deo......................	By the help of God.................	Layard.
Juvat Deus impigros............	God assists the diligent............	Strachan.
Juxta Salopiam...................	Near to Shropshire...................	Chadwick.

K

Kar Duw...........................	For God..............................	Harris.
Kar Duw, res pub. trap........	For God and the commonwealth	Harris.
Keep fast...........................		Lesly.
Keep traist.........................		Hepburn.
Keep tryst.........................		Belches, Hepburn.
Keep tryste........................		Belshes, Semple.
Keep watch.......................		Bryden.
Kynd kynn knawne kepe......	Keep your own kin kind...........	Kaye-Lister.

L

Labes pejus morte	A stain is worse than death	Durrant.
Labora	Endeavour	Mackie, M'Kie.
Laboranti numen adest	God is with him that endeavours	Macfarlane.
Labora ut æternum vivas	Strive for eternal life	Aprece, Apreece.
Labore	By labour	Abbot.
Labore et diligentiâ	With labour and diligence	Binns.
Labore et fiduciâ	By labour and prudence	Litster.
Labore et honore	By industry and honour	Pemberton, Thelusson, Viner.
Labore et perseverantiâ	With labour and perseverance	Woods.
Labore et scientiâ	By labour and science	Wylie.
Labore et virtute	By labour and virtue	Gardner, Pigott, Thelusson.
Labor et industriâ	Labour and industry	Tane.
Labor improbus omnia vincit	Excessive labour overcomes every difficulty	Mitchell.
Labor ipse voluptus	Labour itself is a pleasure	King.
Labor omnia superat	Labour overcomes all things	Campbell, Laing.
Labor omnia vincit	Labour conquers all things	Brown, Chaplin, Cromie, Edington, M'Nair, Pratman.
Lædere noli	Injure no man	Stewart.
Lætavi	I have rejoiced	Jolly.
Lætitia per mortem	Joy through death	Luther.
Lætitiæ et spe immortalitatis	In the hope of joy and immortality	Shaw.
La fin couronne les œuvres	The end crowns the works	Yarker.
La fortune passe par tout	The vicissitudes of fortune are common to all	Rollo.
La liberté	Liberty	Ackers.
Lamh laidir an uachdar	The strong hand uppermost	O'Brien.
Lamh dhearg Eirin	The red hand of Ireland	O'Neill.
Lamh foistinneach an uachdar	The gentle hand uppermost	Sullivan.
L'antiquité ne peut pas l'abolir	Antiquity cannot abolish it	Conroy.
Lassez dire	Let them speak	Middleton, Myddleton.
Latet anguis in herba	A snake lies hid in the grass	Anguish.
Laudes cano heroum	I sing the praises of heroes	Daile, Dailie.
Laugh ladur an aughtur	The strong hand uppermost	Kennedy.
Lauro scutoque resurgo	I rise again by the shield and the laurel	Loraine, Lorraine.
Laus Deo	Praise to God	Arbuthnot, Rundle.
La vertu est la seule noblesse	Virtue is the only nobility	Guilford, North.
La vertu surmonte tout obstacle	Virtue surmounts every obstacle	Rowley.
La vie durante	During life	Amyand, Cornewall, Cornwall.
Lead on!		Botham, Hotham.
Le bon temps viendra	Good times will come	Farrington, Farring, Harcourt, Wray, Wrey.
Leges arma tenent sanctas	Arms keep the laws sacred	Benson.
Leges juraque serva	Get your right, and keep it	Grant.
Legibus antiquis	By ancient laws	Leigh.
Legibus et armis	According to law and arms	Gordon.
Le jour viendra	The day will come	Lambton.
Lente, sed opportune	Slowly, but suitably	Campbell.
Leo de Juda est robur nostrum	The Lion of Judah is our strength	Borlace, Warren.
Leoni, non sagittis, fido	I trust to the lion, and not to my arrows	Egerton.
Le roi et l'etat	The king and country	Ashburnham, Sherard.
Le roi le veut	It is the king's pleasure	Clifford.
Le roy et l'eglise	The king and the church	Roger.
L'esperance me comfort	Hope comforts me	Nairn.
L'esperance me console	Hope consoles me	De Cardonnel.
L'esperance du salut	Hope of safety	Grabham.
Let Curzon hold what Curzon held		Curzon.
Let Curzon holde what Curzon helde		Pen-Curzon-Howe.

Let the hawk shaw	....	Porteous.
Let the deed shaw...............	....	Addison, Fleeming, Fleming, Flemming, Moubray.
Let them talk	....	Hewetson.
Leve et reluis	*Arise and re-illumine*	Lawson.
Levius fit patientiâ	*Patience makes difficulties light*....	Burgess.
L'homme vrai aime son peys...	*The true man loves his country*....	Homfray.
Liberalitas........................	*Liberality*	Furlong.
Libera terra, liberque animus	*A free land and a free soul*	Frankland.
Libertas.....	*Liberty*.................................	Bailey, Birch, Evans, Evans-A'Arcy, Evans-Freke.
Libertas et natale solum.......	*Liberty and our native soil*	Adams.
Libertas sub rege pio	*Liberty under a pious king*........	Addington, Packe.
Libertate extinctâ nulla virtus	*There is no virtue when liberty is dead*	Fletcher.
Libertate quietem	*Ease in liberty*	Woodford.
Liberté toute entière............	*Full liberty*	Butler-Danvers.
Librum cum lampade trado...	*I yield the book with the lamp*....	Hill.
Light on	....	Leighton, Lighton.
Littore sistam....................	*I shall take my stand on the shore*	Hamilton.
Littora specto....................	*I view the shores*	Hamilton.
Live, but dread..................	....	Lindsay.
Live in hope	....	Coldstream.
Live to live.......................	....	Sutton, Witley.
Lock sick..........................	*Be sure*................................	Erwin.
Lock sicker		Douglas, Megget.
Loisgim agus soilleirghim......	*I burn and I shine*..................	M'Leod.
Loquendo placet	*He pleases when he speaks*........	Fairfowl.
Lord, have mercy	....	Drummond.
Love	....	M'Cleish, M'Clesh.
Love and dread..................	....	Baker, Tower.
Love and loyalty	....	Crompton.
Love as you find................	....	Tempest.
Love, serve......................	....	Ashley-Cooper.
Loyal à la mort	*Faithful unto death*................	Adair, Barnwell, Chatterton, Drummond, Hepworth, Laforey, Loftus, Lyster.
Loyal devoir	*Honest duty*	Thynne.
Loyal en tout....................	*Loyal in everything*................	Browne.
Loyal je serai durant ma vie...	*I shall be loyal during life*........	Stourton.
Loyal secret......................	....	Lawson.
Loyal suis je.....................	*Am I loyal*	Shirley.
Loyallement je desers	*Loyally I leave*	Norreys.
Loyauté me lie	*Loyalty binds me*...................	Margesson.
Loyauté m' oblige...............	*Loyalty binds me*	Bertie, Bertue.
Loyauté n'a honte...............	*Loyalty is not ashamed*............	Clinton.
Loyauté sans tache	*Loyalty without spot*	Dare.
Loyowf as thou fynds.........	....	Tempest.
Lucem spero	*I hope for light*	Kemp.
Luceo boreale	*I shine in the north*	Seton.
Luceo et terreo...................	*I shine and terrify*.................	Allan.
Luceo, non uro...................	*I shine, but not burn*	Mackenzie, Mackinzie, Macleod, M'Hardie, M'Kenzie, M'Leod, Smith.
Lucet...	*It is light*	Scot.
Luctor, at emérgam	*I contend, but I shall recover*....	Maitland.
Luctor, non mergor	*I struggle, but I am not overwhelmed*	Glass.
Lumen accipe et imperti.......	*Receive the light, and communicate it*	Hollingsworth.
Lumen cœleste sequamur......	*Let us follow heavenly light*.......	Beatie, Beattie, Beatleys.
Lumen servamus antiquum...	*We preserve the ancient light*......	Redwood.
Lux Anglis, crux Francis	*Light to the English, a cross to the French*	Rooper.
Lux in tenebris...................	*Light in darkness*	Fullarton, Fullerton.
Lux mea Christus	*Christ is my light*	Newman.
Lux mihi laurus	*Light is a laurel to me*............	Chambers.
Lux tua vita mea	*Thy light is my life*................	Blount, Blunt.
Lux venit ab alto................	*Light cometh from on high*	Dallas.

M

Macte virtute	Blessings on your valour	Murray.
Ma force d'en haut	My strength is from above	Malet.
Mæret qui laborat	The labourer is worthy of his hire	Storie.
Ma foy en Dieu seulement	My faith is in God alone	Mompesson.
Magistratus indicat virum	The magistrate shows the man	Lowther.
Magna est veritas	Great is truth	Stillingfleet.
Magnanimiter crucem sustine	Sustain the cross bravely	Kenyon, Whitney.
Magnanimus esto	Be magnanimous	Ingram.
Magnes et adamas	The magnet and adamant	Ross.
Magnum in parvo	Much in little	Congalton, Congilton, Little.
Magnus et animus	And a great mind	Ross.
Magnus Hippocrates; Tu nobis major	Great Hippocrates; Thou art greater than we	Dimsdale.
Maintien le droit	Support the right	Bridges, Brydges, Leatham.
Majora sequor	I follow greater things	Halibuton, Halyburton.
Majores sequor	I follow our ancestors	Gordon.
Major optima ferat	Let the worthier carry off the prize	Moir, More.
Majorum vestigia premo	I follow close on the footsteps of my ancestors	Seaton.
Major virtus quam splendor	Virtue is greater than splendour	Auld, Baillie.
Mal au tour	Unaccustomed to artifice	Patten.
Malgré le tort	In spite of wrong	Hoghton-Bold, Houghton.
Malim esse probus quam haberi	I would rather be honest than merely be considered so	Kennedy.
Mallem mori quam mutare	I prefer death to change	Gilbert.
Malo mori quam fœdari	Death rather than disgrace	Adams, Athlone, Barnewall, Barnewell, Beale, Doeg, Ffrench, French, Ginkell, Harty, Higginson, Jackson, Lister, Menzies, Mulloy, Murray, Payne, Strode, Surtees.
Malo pati quam fœdari	I prefer suffering to disgrace	Duckett.
Malum bono vince	Overcome evil with good	Hay.
Man do it		Edgar.
Manent optima cœlo	The best await us in heaven	Miller.
Maneo et muneo	I wait and defend	Dalrymple.
Maneo, non fugio	I remain, I do not fly	Gordon.
Manes non fugio	I do not shun death	Gordon.
Manet in æternum	It remains for ever	Sprevell, Sprewell, Warner.
Manners maketh man		Wickham, Wykeham.
Manners makyth man		Wickham, Martin-Wykeham.
Manu et corde	With hand and heart	Bates.
Manu forti	With a strong hand	Clinkscales, Geoghan, Mackay, M'Can, M'Casker, M'Caskill, M'Quie.
Manuque	And by strength	Jossey, Proby, Tonson.
Manus hæc inimica tyrannis	This hand is an enemy to tyrants	Jossey, Proby, Tonson.
Manus justa nardus	A just hand is a jewel	Maynard.
Mar bu mhiann leinn	As we would desire	Campbell.
Marack-gu	Pretty Marack	Lyons.
Marte et arte	By strength and art	Drumond, Ferguson, Nevoy, Jones.
Marte et clypeo	By offensive and defensive warfare	Methen.
Marte et industriâ	By bravery and industry	Ogilvy.
Marte et ingenio	By war and wit	Smith, Wright.
Marte et labore	By war and toil	Hewgill.
Marte et mari faventibus	War and the sea favouring	Morris.
Marte non arte	By strength, not art	Neasmith.
Marte suo tutus	Safe by his own exertions	Byers.
Martis non cupidinis	By war, not by love	Fletcher.
Mature	Maturely	
Mea dos virtus	Virtue is my dowry	Meadows, Medewe.

Mea fides in sapientiâ............	My faith is in wisdom........	Fryer.
Mea gloria fides..................	Fidelity is my glory...............	Addagh, Ainsworth, Gilchrist, Watson.
Meæ memor originis............	Mindful of my descent............	Manson.
Mean, speak, and do well......	....	Urquhart.
Mea spes est in Deo..................	My hope is in God....................	Smith.
Meâ virtute me involvo........	I wrap myself up in my integrity......................................	Williams.
Me certum mors certa facit...	Sure death makes me determined	Sibbald.
Mecum habita.....................	Dwell with me...........................	Dun.
Mediis tranquillus in undis...	Calm amid the waves...............	Smythe, Smith.
Mediocria firma..................	Mediocrity is stable...............	Bacon, Grimston, Lawder, Lowndes-Stone.
Mediocria maxima................	Moderate things are the greatest	Monins.
Mediocriter........................	With moderation....................	Moir, Murison.
Medio tutissimus ibis............	The middle path is safest..........	King, Senior.
Me fortem reddit Deus.........	God renders me brave..............	Scot, Scott.
Me meliora manent...............	Better fortune awaits me...........	Mossman.
Meliora sperando.................	Hoping for better things............	Douglas, Douglass.
Meliora spero sequorque.......	I hope for better things, and follow them.....................................	Rait.
Meliore fide quam fortunâ.....	With better fidelity than fortune......................................	Greseley, Gresley.
Memento Creatorem............	Remember thy Creator.............	Keith.
Memini...............................	I remember............................	Campbell.
Memor................................	Mindful	Russell.
Memorare novissima............	An unchangeable mind............	Hopkirk.
Memor esto........................	Be mindful.............................	Campbell, Graham, Green, Hutchinson, Hutchison, M'Fell, M'Phaill.
Memor et fidelis..................	Mindful and faithful...............	Reed, Peachey.
Memoriâ pii æternâ............	The pious of eternal memory......	Hanbury-Tracey.
Mens æqua rebus in arduis...	An equal mind in difficulties......	Hardinge.
Mens conscia recti...............	A mind conscious of rectitude.....	Ashbrook, Chrisp, Collis, Flower-Macartney, Maccartney, Nightengale, Phillips, Silifant, Wright.
Mens cujusque is est quisque	The mind is the man................	Leslie, Pepys.
Mens et manus.....................	Intelligence and activity...........	Duncanson.
Mens flecti nescia.................	Remember the last....................	Hulton.
Mens immota......................	An unmoved mind....................	Shaw.
Mens immota manet............	My mind remains immovable.....	Meldrum, Shaw.
Mens pristina mansit............	The former mind remained.......	Popham.
Mens sibi conscia recti.........	A mind conscious of its own rectitude.......................................	De Crispigny, Wright.
Mente et manu....................	With heart and hand...............	Glassford, Patrickson.
Mente manuque..................		Benshaw, Bonshaw, Borthwick, Farquhar.
Mente manuque præsto........	I perform with resolution and diligence............................	Foulis.
Meor ras tha Duw...............	The great grace of God who is good.......................................	Willyams.
Merces hæc certa laborum.....	The sure reward of our labours...	Seton.
Mercie................................	Mercy....................................	Paterson.
Mercy is my desire...............	....	Abercrombie, Laing, Lang, Wishart.
Mérite................................	Deserve..................................	Currer.
Merito	Deservedly.............................	Delap, Delop, Dunlop.
Messis ab alto .....:.............	Our harvest is from the deep......	Whittuck.
Me stante, virebunt.............	While I stand they will flourish..	Tirwhit, Tyrwhitt.
Metuenda corolla draconis.....	Fear the dragon's crest.............	Vane, Stewart.
Metuo secundis	I fear in prosperity...................	Hodgson, Uppleby.
Me vincit; ego mereo...........	He hath conquered me—I am the gainer...................................	Sinclair.
Micat inter omnis................	Is illustrious among all.............	Haggard.
Mieux être que paraitre........	Better to be than to seem...........	Barclay.
Migro et respicio..................	I go away, and look back..........	Ramsay.
Mihi cœlum portus...............	Heaven is my haven.................	Brages, Bruges.
Mihi cura futuri...................	I am careful for the future.........:	Ongley.
Mihi lucra...........................	My gain..................................	Scot, Scott.
Mihi lucra pericula...............	My dangers are profitable.........	Suttie.
Mihi robore robor	I have power with strength........	Cunninghame.

Mihi terraque lacusque	*I have lands and waters*	Fullerton.
Mihi, tibi	*To me and you*	Pope.
Mind your own business		Remnant.
Min, sicker, reag		Connor.
Mirabile in profundis	*Wonderful in depth*	Tooker.
Miseris succurrere disco	*I learn to succour the unfortunate*	MacMillan, Soltan, Hinde-Hodgson.
Miserrima vidi	*I saw most miserable things*	Zephane, Zephani.
Misneach	*Courage*	Campbell.
Mitis et fortis	*Mild but brave*	Orde.
Mitis sed fortis		
Moderata durant	*Moderate things are permanent*	Bushe, Irvine, Staunton.
Modico angetur modicum	*The smaller, the less exposed to danger*	Williamson.
Modicum modico erit magnum	*A little will be much, with moderation*	Williamson.
Moeret qui laborat	*He is sad who labours*	Storie.
Monachus salvabor	*Being a monk, I shall be saved*	Monkhouse.
Mon Dieu, mon roi, et ma patrie	*My God, my king, and my country*	Broadley, Kirwan.
Mon Dieu est ma roche	*My God is my rock*	Fermoy, Roche, Rowche.
Moneo et munio	*I warn, and I protect*	Dalrymple, Elphinstone.
Moniti meliora sequamur	*Being warned, let us follow better fortune*	Mahon.
Monitus munitus	*He who is warned is fortified*	Horn.
Mon privilége et mon devoir	*My privilege and duty*	Shevill.
Monte alto	*On a high mountain*	Mowat.
Monstrant astra viam	*The stars show the way*	Oswald.
Mon trésor	*My treasure*	Montresor.
Montjoye et St Dennis		France.
Mora trahit periculum	*Delay causes danger*	Suckling.
Mores meliore metallo	*Morals of a better character*	Smith.
Moribus antiquis	*With ancient manners*	Throckmorton.
Moriens, sed invictus	*Dying, but unconquered*	Gammell.
Mors aut vita decora	*Death or a life of honour*	Dempster.
Mors Christi mors mortis mihi	*Christ's death is to me the death of death*	Boothby.
Mors lupi agnis vita	*The death of the wolf is the life of the lamb*	Ouseley, Ousley.
Mors mihi lucrum	*Death is gain to me*	Jones.
Mors patior maculà	*Death rather than disgrace*	Chamberlayne.
Mort dessus	*Death is hanging over us*	Bunney, Bunny.
Morte leonis vita	*Life by the death of the lion*	Vaux.
Mortem aut triumphum	*Death or triumph*	Clifton.
Mort en droit	*Death in right*	Drax.
Mortua vivescunt	*The dead shall become alive*	Lindsay.
Mos legem regit	*Custom regulates the law*	Mosley, Mousell.
Mot pour mot	*Word for word*	Harries.
Moveo et profitior	*I proceed and am more prosperous*	Knox.
Mowe warilie		Mather.
Mallahar a boo	*Victory to Mallahar*	Fitzgerald.
Multá tuli fecique	*I have borne and done many things*	Arkwright.
Multum in parvo	*Much in little*	Congalton, Congilton.
Munifice et fortiter	*Bountifully and bravely*	Handyside.
Murus aheneus	*A brazen wall*	Macleod, M'Leod, Nielson.
Murus œneus esto	*Be thou a wall of brass*	Reynell.
Murus œneus virtus	*Virtue is a wall of brass*	Walton.
Murus œneus conscientia sana	*A sound conscience is a wall of brass*	Lumley, Williamson.
Mutare vel timere sperno	*I scorn to change or fear*	Beauford, Raglan, Somerset.
Muthig vorwartz	*Forward with courage*	Prance.
Mutuo amore cresco	*I increase by mutual love*	Lindsay.
Mutus inglorias artis	*Deceitful silence is mean*	Halford.
Mutus inglorius	*The dumb is inglorious*	Halford.
My defence		Allardice, Allerdice.
My hope is constant in thee		Crammond, Donaldson, Gardiner, M'Donald, Macdonald.
My hope is in God		Middleton.
My prince and my country		Harris
My word is my bond		Smallman.

N

Nafragus in portum............	*Shipwrecked, brought to harbour*	Heard.
Na fynno Duw ni fydd.........	*What God wishes not will not be..*	Price.
Natale solum dulce	*Sweet is our native soil............*	Taylor.
Nativum retinet decus.........	*He retains his native honour......*	Livingston, Livingstone.
Naturæ donum....................	*The gift of nature...................*	Peacock, Peacocks.
Naturæ minister.................	*A servant of nature................*	Relham, Relhan.
Nec abest jugum.................	*There is always some yoke ....*	Hay.
Nec beneficii immemor, nec injuriæ...........................	*Unmindful neither of benefits nor injuries.........................*	Walround-Bethel.
Ne cadem insidiis	*Let me not fall into snares........*	Cleland, Clelland.
Nec careo, nec curo	*I have neither want nor care......*	Craw.
Nec cede malis....................	*Yield not to adversity..............*	Doig, Keppel, Stratford, Williams.
Ne cede malis, sed contra......	*Do not yield to difficulties, but bear up ....*	Canning, Garvagh.
Nec cito, nec tardo	*Neither fast nor slow..............*	Ballantyne, Bannatyne.
Nec cupias, nec metuas.........	*Neither desire nor fear............*	Crowhall, Hardwicke, Yorke.
Nec deficit alter..................	*Another succeeds...................*	Gregory, Roddam.
Nec deerit operi dextra.........	*His hand shall not be wanting to his work ....*	Borthwick.
Nec elata, nec dejecta	*Neither elated nor depressed.....*	Northmore.
Nec ferro, nec igne..............	*Neither by sword nor fire........*	M'Kaile.
Nec flatu, nec fluctu............	*Neither with wind nor tide........*	Edward, Udward.
Nec fluctu, nec flatu............	*Neither with tide nor wind........*	Burnet, Burnett.
Nec male notus eques	*A knight well known..............*	Southwell.
Nec me qui cætera vincit......	*Nor does he who conquers all other things conquer me.................*	Bruce.
Nec metuas nec optes...........	*Neither fear nor wish............*	Coddington.
Nec minus fortiter...............	*Not the less bravely..............*	Cuthbert, Cuthbertson.
Nec mireris homines mirabiliores..............................	*Do not wonder at wonderful men*	Lambert.
Nec mutandus, nec metus.....	*Neither confusion nor fear........*	Rawlins.
Nec mons, nec substrahit aer	*The mountain is not moved, nor does the blast subside............*	Forbes.
Nec parvis sisto..................	*Neither do I hesitate at trifles....*	De Bath, De Burgh.
Nec placidâ contenta quiete est	*No content in soft repose.........*	Mordaunt.
Nec obscura, nec ima...........	*Neither obscure nor low............*	Law.
Nec opprimere, nec opprimi...	*Neither to oppress nor to be oppressed ....*	Sneyd.
Nec prece, nec pretio...........	*Neither by entreaty nor bribery...*	Bateman.
Nec quærere, nec spernere honorem..........................	*Neither to seek nor despise honour*	Boughey, St John.
Nec rege, nec populo, sed utroque...........................	*Neither for king nor people, but for both..........................*	Rolle, Rolley, Wilkinson.
Nec sinit esse feros..............	*Nor doth he allow them to be fierce.............................*	Langham.
Nec sorte, nec fato..............	*Neither by chance nor fate........*	Rutherford.
Nec sperno, nec timeo	*I neither despise nor fear.........*	Ellames.
Nec tempore, nec fato..........	*Neither by time nor fate............*	M'Donald, MacDonald.
Nec timeo, nec sperno...........	*I neither fear nor despise............*	Greene, Hamilton, Pagan, Pagen, Shepphard-Cotton, Shippard.
Nec temere, nec timide.........	*Neither rashly nor timidly........*	Aldworth, Arabin, Beadnell, Bent, Blair, Blosse, Bradford, Bridgman, Bulkeley, Chinnery, Chinning, Fitz-Clarence, Forbes, Graham, Guest, Holden, Sandford, Simeon, Vane, Walker, Wakeman, Western.
Nec timide, nec temere.........	*Neither timidly nor rashly........*	Barne, Buckley, Bulkeley-Williams, Forbes, Macsagan, Rashleigh, Travers.
Nec timidus, nec ferus.........	*Neither timid nor fierce............*	Trotter.
Nec triste, nec trepidum	*Neither sad nor fearful... ....*	Trist.

Ne cuiquam serviant enses....	Let not your swords be the slaves of every one.......................	Peachy.
Nec vi, nec astutiâ...............	Neither by violence nor cunning..	Waring.
Nec viribus, nec numero.......	Neither by power nor numbers....	Wemyss.
Nec volenti, nec volanti	Neither to me wishing nor flying.	Westby.
Nemo me impune lacesset.....	No one shall provoke me with impunity	Irwin, Nettles.
Nemo sibi nascitur................	No one is born for himself.........	Scott.
Nemo sine cruce beatus........	None is happy but by the cross....	Baker.
Ne m' oubliez	Forget not.............................	Carsain, Corsair.
Ne nimium..........................	Not too much	Hamilton-Gordon.
Ne obliviscaris.....................	Forget not.............................	Colvil, Colville.
Ne obliviscaris.....................	You must not forget	Campbell, Lorn, M'Tavish.
Ne parcas, nec spernas	Neither spare nor despise	Lamond, Lamont.
Ne quid falsi........................	Nothing false.........................	Wollaston.
Ne quid nimis	Not too much of anything	Austen, Fouler.
Nescit abolere vestutas.........	Antiquity cannot abolish it........	Oughton.
Nescit amor fines.................	Love knows no end	Scot, Scott.
Nescitur Christo..................	He is not known by Christ.........	Rous.
Nescit vox missa reverti.......	A word once uttered cannot be re-called..............................	Halsey.
Ne supra.............................	Not beyond	Catsnellage, Catznellage.
Ne supra modum sapere.......	Be not over wise.....................	Nassu, Newport.
Ne tentes, aut perfice...........	Either do not attempt, or accomplish	Daris, Faunce, Hill.
Ne te quæsiveris extra.........	Seek nothing beyond your sphere.	Hewit, Hewitt, Hewett.
Ne timeas recte faciendo	Fear not to do what is right.......	Hadderwick, Tizard-Hawkins.
Never fear...........................	....	Stewart.
Ne vile fano........................	Nothing to disgrace the altar.....	Fane, Stapleton.
Ne vile velis........................	Form no vile wish...................	Griffin, Nevil, Neville, Ussher.
Nid cyfœth and boddlondeb..	Not wealth but contentment........	Garnons.
Nid da onid Duw.................	No good but God....................	Williams.
Nid meddyg, ond meddyg enaid.............................	Not a physician, but a soul-physician............................	Fraser, Pughe.
Nihil alienum	Nothing strange.....................	Rice.
Nihil amanti durum.............	Nothing hard to a lover...........	Reid.
Nihil desperandum	Nothing to be despaired of........	Walley.
Nihil humani alienum..........	Nothing human is alien...........	Hutchinson.
Nihilo nisi cruce	With nothing but the cross.........	Barbour.
Nihil quod obstat virtute......	Nothing which obstructs virtue....	Higgins.
Nihil sine cruce...................	Nothing without the cross..........	Beresford, Hillocks.
Nihil sine Deo.....................	Nothing without God...............	Peterson.
Nihil sine labore..................	Nothing without labour.............	Berry, Cator, Templar, Templer.
Nihil utile quod non honestum	Nothing dishonest is useful........	Moor.
Nihil verius	Nothing more truly..................	Weir.
Nil admirari........................	To be astonished at nothing	Fitzgibbon, Shapland-Carew, Johnson.
Nil arduum.........................	Nothing dangerous..................	Cumming, Gordon.
Nil certum est.....................	Nought is certain....................	M'Min, M'Minn, M'Myne.
Nil clarius astris..................	Nothing clearer than the stars....	Baillie.
Nil conscire sibi	Having no remorse..................	Anderson, Biss, Carew, Collingwood, Finch-Hatton, French, Michel, Rogers, Savile, Saville, Wegg.
Nil desperandum.................	Never despairing....................	Anson, Arnold, Bullock, Carr, Chard, Chawner, Coddington, Cookson, Crosbie-Gardiner, Gradwell, Hawkins, Hawxwell, Hay, Horn, Heron, Imrey, May, Musgrove, Ogilvie, Ogilvy, Pearson, Promoli, Silver, Simpson, Stewart, Tremenheere, Tucker, Walker, Walley.
Nil desperandum, auspice Deo	Nothing is to be despared of, under God's guidance............	Anderson.
Nil desperandum est.............	Nothing is to be despaired of......	Stewart.
Nil impossibile....................	Nothing impossible..................	Du Bisson, Dubisson.
Nil indigne.........................	Nothing unworthily.................	Wordie.
Nil invitâ Minervâ...............	Nothing in spite of genius.........	Prime.
Nil magnum, nisi bonum......	Nothing great unless it be good...	Cooper.

Nil moror ictus	I delay not, when struck	Money-Kyrle.
Nil nequit amor	Love is all-powerful	Reidheugh.
Nil nisi cruce	Depend only in the cross	Beresford.
Nil nisi patria	Nothing but one's country	Hindmarsh, Hyndmarsh.
Nil obliviscar	I shall forget nothing	Collvile.
Nil penna, sed usus	Not the pen, but custom	Gilmer, Gilmour.
Nil sine cruce	Nothing without the cross	Gully.
Nil sine Deo	Nothing without God	Awdry.
Nil sine numine	Nothing without the Deity	Weld.
Nil sistere contra	Nothing to stand against	M'Nicoll, Nicolson, Nicholson, Stewart.
Nil solidum	Nothing is permanent	Goldie.
Nil tibi	Nothing for you	Campbell.
Nil time	Fear nothing	Man.
Nil timeo	I fear nothing	Drummond.
Nil timere	Nothing rashly	Balfour, Ramsay.
Nil timere, neque timore	Nothing either rashly or in fear	Berney.
Nil timere tenta nil timide	Try nothing rashly or timidly	Buckle.
Nil veretur veritas	Truth fears nothing	Napier.
Nisi Dominus	Unless the Lord	Compton.
Nisi Dominus frustra	It is in vain without the Lord	Inglis.
Nisi paret, imperat	Unless he obeys, he commands	Bernard.
Nisi virtus vilior algâ	Viler than the sea-weed without virtue	Moises.
Nitor in adversum	I strive against	Bredel, Horner.
Nobilis est ira leonis	The lion's anger is noble	Buchanan, Ingles, Inglis.
Nobilis ira	Noble ardour	Creighton-Stuart, Stewart, Villers-Stuart.
Nobilitas est sola virtus	Virtue is the sole nobility	Thackeray.
Nobilitatis virtus, non stemma, character	Virtue, not lineage, is the mark of nobility	Grosvenor.
Nocentes prosequor	I prosecute the guilty	Dumbreck, Savary.
Noctes diesque præsto	I perform night and day	Murray, Stirling.
Nodo firmo	In a firm knot	Harrington.
No heart more true		Hamilton.
Noli irritare leonem	Be unwilling to vex the lion	Abbs, Underwood.
Noli irritare leones	Do not irritate lions	Lyons.
Noli mentiri	Do not lie	Noteley.
Noli me tangere	Beware of injuring me	Græme, Graham, Willett.
Non abest virtuti sors	Good fortune follows virtue	Nisbet.
Non aliunde pendere		Coke.
Non arbitrio popularis auræ	Not at the will of the popular breath	Dale.
Non arte, sed marte	Not by art, but strength	Nasmyth, Naesmith, Neasmith.
Non cauta sed actu	Not by singing but by acting	Gillman.
Non civium ardor	Not the ardour of the citizens	Moore.
Non crux, sed lux	Not the cross, but the light	Black, Blair, Cramer, Griffeth, Griffiths.
Non deerit alter aureus	Another golden branch will succeed	Don.
Non deest spes	Hope is not wanting	Forbes.
Non deficit	He does not fail	Foulis, Hamilton.
Non deficit alter	Another succeeds	Aljoy, Hamilton, Smith, Walwyn.
Non degener	Not degenerate	Grindlay, Kinloch, Kinloch, Wedderburn.
Non desistam	I will not desist	Row.
Non dormio	I do not sleep	Maxwell.
Non dormit qui custodit	The guardian does not sleep	Cramer, Coghill, Gulliver, Lothian, Loudon, Louthian, Lowthian, M'Kellip, M'Killop.
Non eget arcu	He needs not the bow	Kynynmound, Elliot, Elliott.
Non eget Mauri jaculis	He needs not the Moorish javelins	Miller.
None is truly great, but he that is truly good		Packwood.
Non est sine pulvere palma	The prize is not won without dust	Yarburgh.
Non extinguar	I shall not be extinguished	Frazer.
Non fallor	I am not deceived	Kennedy.
Non fecimus ipsi	We have not done it ourselves	Duncombe.
Non fluctu, non flatu movetur	Is moved neither by wind nor wave	Brockholes-Parker, Parker.
Non fraude, sed laude	Not with deceit, but praise	Gordon.

Non frustra...............	*Not in vain............,............*	Barron
Non generant aquilæ columbas	*Eagles do not bring forth doves...*	Lempriere, Rodney.
Non gladio, sed gratiâ............	*Not with the sword, but kindness...*	Charters.
Non hæc, sed me...............	*Not these, but me...............*	Scrope.
Non hæc sine numine	*These things are not without the Deity*	Ellis.
Non immemor	*Not forgetful............*	Graham.
Non immemor beneficii	*Not unmindful of kindness ......*	Broadley, Fitzgerald, Graham, Quantock.
Non inferiora	*Not inferior things...............*	Monro.
Non inferiora secutus	*Not following meaner things ......*	Bromley, Buchan, Grant, Hepburn.
Non invita...............	*Not by constraint ....*	Smith.
Non in vita...............	*Not in life............*	Smith.
Non metuo...............	*I fear not............,......*	Hamilton.
Non mihi, sed Deo et regi	*Not for myself, but for God and the king*	Booth.
Non mihi, sed patriæ............	*Not for myself, but for my country*	Hippisley, Jones-Loyd, Springe.
Non minima sed magna prosequor............	*I follow not small but great things*	Dobie, Dobbie.
Non moritur cujus fama vivat	*He does not die whose fame may survive............*	Congreve.
Non mutat fortuna genus......	*Fortune does not change the race*	Oliphant.
Non mutat genus solum......	*The country does not alter the race*	Hamilton
Non nobis nascimur............	*We are not born for ourselves.....*	Lucy.
Non nobis solum...............	*Not for ourselves alone............*	Drayton, Eardley, Fardell, Lawless, Moss, Wilson.
Non nobis solum nati sumus..	*We are not born for ourselves alone ....*	Bradshaw.
Non nobis tantum nati.........		Warner.
Non nobis, sed omnibus........	*Not for us, but for all ..*	Ash, Ashe.
Non nobis solum, sed toti mundo nati............	*Born not for ourselves but for the whole world. ......*	Robinson.
Non sine periculo	*Not without danger............*	Freer.
Non nobis	*Not for us............*	Wood.
Non obliviscar............	*I shall not forget............*	Colvil, Colville.
Non obstante Deo...............	*If God oppose not............*	Cunningham.
Non omnibus nati	*We are not born for all......*	Frank.
Non opes, sed ingenium	*Not wealth, but mind............*	Ross.
Non pas l'ouvrage, mais l'ouvrier............	*Not the work, but the workman...*	Workman.
Non præda, sed victoria........	*Not the spoil, but victory............*	Chambers.
Non quo, sed quomodo.........	*Not by whom, but by what means*	Ellis, Howard.
Non rapui, sed recepi...	*I stole not, but received ....*	Cotterell.
Non revertar inultus............	*I will not return unrevenged......*	Vaughan.
Non robore, sed spe	*Not with strength, but with hope...*	Tippet.
Non semper sub umbrâ	*Not always under the shade.......*	Farquharson.
Non servit sed laborat...........	*Does not serve but labours............*	Innes.
Non sibi...............	*Not for himself ....*	Aillen, Cleland, Connell, Cullen, Lyde, Sage.
Non sibi, cunctis...............	*For all, not for himself ....*	Moir.
Non sibi, patriæ...............	*For his country, not for himself..*	Tomlinson.
Non sibi, sed patriæ		Heppesley, Marsham, Baker.
Non sibi, sed cunctis............	*Not for self, but for all............*	Moir.
Non sibi, sed patriæ natus	*Not born for himself, but for his country............*	Joddrell, Jodrell.
Non sibi, sed toti	*Not for self, but for the whole....*	Wynne.
Non sine...............	*Not without............*	Oliver.
Non sine anchorâ............	*Not without an anchor......,......*	Drysdale.
Non sine causâ	*Not without cause............*	Justice.
Non sine Deo...............	*Not without God............*	Eliot.
Non sine numine...............	*Not without authority............*	Gifford.
Non sine periculo...............	*Not without danger............*	Freer, M'Kenzie, Walker.
Non sine prædâ............	*Not without prey ....*	Echlin.
Non sine usu............	*Not without use............*	Maxwell.
Non sino, sed dono	*I do not permit, but I give............*	Seddon.
Non solum armis...............	*Not by arms only ....*	Lindsay.
Non terrâ, sed aquis............ ..	*Not by land, but by water ....*	Dunnet.
Non timeo, sed caveo	*I do not fear, but am careful......*	Oakeley, Strachan, Strauchan.
Non temere..	*Not rashly ....*	Forbes.
Non tua, te moveant, sed publica voto	*Neither thy affairs, nor thyself, but the public wish ....*	Alleyne.

Non vi, sed voluntate	Not by force but good will	Boucher.
Non vox, sed votum	Not a voice, but a wish	Nagle.
Norma tuta veritas	Truth is the safe rule	Morrall.
Nos aspera juvant	Difficulties are useful to us	Louis, Lowis.
Nosce teipsum	Know thyself	Buck, Fraser-Allan, Fraazer, Murray, Pringle, Stanfield, Tregonwell, Walford.
No sine periculo	I swim without danger	Walker.
Nos nostraque Deo	We and ours to God	Rogers.
Nothing hazard, nothing have		Suttie.
Nothing venture, nothing have		Boswell.
Not in vain		Aylett, Branfill.
Not rashly, nor with fear		Harrison.
Not too much		Mackinlay, M'Kinlay.
N' oublié	Not forgotten	Graham, Moir, Mour.
Nous maintiendrons	We will maintain	Howard.
Nous travaillerons en l'esperance	We will labour in hope	Blacket, Blackett.
Now thus		Trafford.
Now thus, now thus		Pilkington.
Nullâ pallescere culpâ	To turn pale at no crime	Farrand, Mitchell, Patten, Pulleine, Waynflete.
Nulla salus bello	No safety in war	Lorimer.
Nulli inimicus ero	I will be an enemy to none	Donaldson.
Nulli præda	A prey to none	Arundel, M'Aben, M'Cabin.
Nulli præda sumus	We are a prey to none	Marley.
Nullis fraus tuta latebris	Fraud is safe in no place of concealment	Ellacombe, Ellicombe.
Nullius in verba	Nothing upon trust	Banks.
Numen et lumen effugio	I shun the Deity and light	Hewson.
Numen et omnia	Authority and all things	Graham.
Numine et virtute	With authority and virtue	Yuille, Yule.
Numine et patria asto	I stand by God and my country	Aston.
Nunc aut nunquam	Now or never	Hampson, Needham.
Nuncia pacis	Tidings of peace	Buchanan, Whannell.
Nunc mihi grata quies	Now is there pleasant repose for me	Gordon.
Nunc ut olim	Now as before	Longcroft.
Nunquam deorsum	Never down	Graham.
Nunquam dormio	I never sleep	Maxwell.
Nunquam nisi honorificentissime	Never, unless most honourably	Freeling.
Nunquam non fidelis	Never unfaithful	Montrie, Moultrie, Moutrie, Moutry.
Nunquam non paratus	Never unprepared	Betton, Fairholm, Johnston, Johnstone, Johnstoun, Kerrick, Knight, Skinner.
Nunquam obliviscar	I will never forget	Campbell, M'Iver, Simpson.
Nunquam senescit	Never grows old	Gloag.
Ny dessux ny dessoux	Neither above nor beneath	Grove.

O

Ob ducem ob patriam	On account of our leader and country	Waddy.
Obdurum adversus urgentia	Not yielding to provocations	Bothwell.
Obey and rule		Loades.
Oblier ne puis	I cannot forget	Colville.
Obliviscar	I shall forget	Colvil, Colville.
Obliviscaris	Forget	Campbell.
Ob patriam vulnera passi	Having suffered wounds for our country	Burnes.
Obsequio, non viribus	By gentle management, not by force	Hamilton.
Observe		Achieson, Aitchison, Atcheson, Oldaker.
Occultus, non extinctus	Hidden, not lost	Tytler.
Occurrent nubes	Clouds will intervene	Eliot.

Odi profanum	I hate whatever is profane	Hare.
Odor vitæ	The sweet breath of life	Hutton.
Officium præsto	I perform my duty	Pownall.
Of nwn yr Arglwydd	Let us fear the Lord	Williams-Lloyd.
Olet et sanat	It smells and cures	Dunbar.
Olim sic erat	Thus it was formerly	Hood.
Omine secundo	Under favourable auspices	MacMurdoch, Murdoch.
Omne bonum Dei donum	Every good thing is from God	Boughton, Powell.
Omne bonum desuper	All good is from above	Burney, Honywood.
Omne solum forti patria	Every land is a native country to a brave man	Balfour.
Omne solum vivo patria est	Every land is a living man's country	Matthews.
Omne tulit punctum qui miscuit utile dulci	He has gained every point, who has mixed the useful with the sweet	Warren.
Omnia bona bonis	All things are good to the good	Wenman.
Omnia bona desuper	All good things are above	Goodlake.
Omnia debeo Deo	I owe all things to God	Grenehalgh.
Omnia Deo juvant	All things help under God	Crawfurd.
Omnia fert ætas	Age brings all things	Cheese.
Omnia firmat	He strengthens all things	Colquhoun.
Omnia fortunæ committo	I commit all things to fortune	Duff, M'Knight, M'Naught.
Omnia pro bono	All things for the good	Murdoch, Murdock.
Omnia providentiæ committo	I commit all things to God	Meares.
Omnia recte	All things rightly	M'Cracken.
Omnia superat diligentia	Diligence overcomes all difficulties	Mitchell.
Omnia superat virtus	Virtue conquers all	Gardiner.
Omnia vincit amor	Love conquers all things	Bruce.
Omnia vincit veritas	Truth conquers all	Munn, Nash.
Omni liber metu	Free from all fear	Birley.
Omni secundo	I do good to every one	Murdock.
Omnium rerum vicissitudo	All things are subject to change	Ford.
Omni volentiâ major	Greater than all violence	Donelan.
On things transitory resteth no glory		Isham.
Onus sub honore	Burden under honour	Johnston.
Opera Dei mirifica	The works of God are wonderful	Garmston, Hustwick.
Opera illius mea sunt	His works are mine	Cust.
Opera mundi	The works of the world	Sanderson.
Ope solis et umbræ	By the power of the sun and shadow	Irvine.
Opiferque per orbem dicor	I am called an assistant throughout the world	Kadie, Keddie.
Opitulante Deo	With the aid of God	Brereton.
Oportet vivere	It is necessary to live	Todd.
Optima cœla	Conceal what is best	Millar.
Optima est veritas	Truth is best	Thompson, Thomson.
Optima revelatio stella	A star the best revelation	Reveley.
Optime merenti	To the most meritorious	Witham.
Optime quod opportune	What is done opportunely is best	Campbell.
Optimum pati	To suffer is best	Sheldon.
Optimum quod primum	The best first	Kirk.
Optimus est qui optime facit	Best is he who does best	Best.
Optivo cognomine crescit	He becomes great by the wished-for name	Larpent.
Ora et labora	Pray and labour	Alexander, Holmes, Mure, Patrick, Ramsay, Sibbald, Wakeman.
Orbe circum cincto	The world being girt around	Saumarez.
Ore lego, corde credo	I speak with the mouth, I believe with the heart	Hamilton.
Ornat fortem prudentia	Prudence adorns the brave man	Dunbar.
Ornatur radix fronde	The root is adorned with foliage	Innes.
Orna verum	Adorn the truth	Waddell, Weddell.
Ostendo, non ostento	I show, not boast	Betts, Isham, Ritchie.
Otium cum dignitate	Repose with dignity	Kelso.
Oublier ne puis	I cannot forget	Colvil, Colville.
Our hope is on high		Rippon.
Over fork over		Conyngham, Cuninghame, Cunningham, Dick.

P

Pace et bello paratus	*Prepared for peace and war*	Fraser, Frazer.
Pacem amo	*I love peace*	Columball, Scot, Scott.
Pacis nuncia	*The messenger of peace*	Murray.
Paix et peu	*Peace and a little*	Maitland.
Pallodia fama	*Palæadian report*	Inchbold.
Palmam qui meruit ferat	*Let him who merits bear the palm*	Nelson.
Palma non sine pulvere	*I have with difficulty gained the palm*	Archibald, Doughty, Jenkinson, Lamb,
Palma virtuti	*The palm is for virtue*	Acland, Fuller, Palmer.
Pandite	*Open*	Gibson.
Pandite, cœlestes portæ	*Open, O ye heavenly gates*	Gibson, Gibsone.
Parat et curat	*He prepares and cures*	Stewart.
Paratus	*Prepared*	Fraser, Sword, Swourd.
Paratus ad æthera	*Prepared for heaven*	Falconer.
Paratus ad arma	*Prepared for war*	Johnson.
Paratus et fidelis	*Ready and faithful*	Carruthers, Hamond, Sanderson.
Paratus sum	*I am prepared*	Fairlie, Fairly, Maclure, M'Lure.
Parcere prostratis	*To spare the fallen*	Le Hunte.
Parcere subjectis	*To spare the vanquished*	Grant, Longfield.
Par commerce	*By commerce*	French.
Parere subjectus	*To appear obedient*	Glasgow.
Pares cum paribus	*Equals with equals*	Pares.
Par fluctus portui	*The wave equal to the haven*	Wilbraham.
Pariter pax bello	*Peace equally with war*	Blane.
Paritur bello	*He is prepared for war*	Murray.
Par la volonté de Dieu	*By the will of God*	Wynill, Wyvill.
Par sit fortuna labori	*Let the reward equal the labour*	Buchanan, Palmer.
Parta labore quies	*Rest obtained by labour*	Fulton.
Parta tueri	*I will defend what I have won*	Haddon, Powys, Jacob.
Par ternis suppar	*The two are equal in antiquity to the three*	Rushout.
Parva contemninus	*We despise small things*	Gernon.
Pass forward		Stewart.
Paternis suppar	*Nearly equal to ancestral glory*	Rushout.
Patience		Dow, Dowie.
Patience and resolution		Muterer.
Patience makes every thing light		Lamb.
Patience passe science	*Patience surpasses knowledge*	Boscowen.
Patientia casus exsuperat omnes	*Patience overcomes all misfortunes*	Askew.
Patientiâ et spe	*By patience and hope*	Duguid, Duiguid, Duniguid, Dwigwid.
Patientiâ vinces	*You will conquer by patience*	Alvanley, Arden.
Patientia vincit	*Patience conquers*	Chein, Cheine, Chéyne, Gall, Lindesay, Lindesey, Nafleur.
Patientiâ vinco	*I conquer by patience*	Thompson.
Patior et spero	*I suffer and hope*	Baillie.
Patior, potior	*I suffer, I obtain*	Peyton.
Patior ut potiar	*I suffer that I may obtain*	Spottiswood, Spotswood.
Patitur qui vincit	*He who conquers, suffers*	Kinnaird.
Patria cara, carior fides	*My country is dear, but my religion is dearer*	Nicholas.
Patria cara, carior fides	*Dear is our country, dearer is faith*	Nicholas, Thompson.
Patria cara, carior libertas	*My country is dear, but liberty is dearer*	Bouverie, Cay, Lindon.
Patriæ infelici fidelis	*Faithful to an unhappy country*	Molyneux, Montgomery, Stopford.
Patria fidelis	*A faithful country*	Tiffin.
Patriam hinc sustinet	*Hence he sustains his country*	Higgins.
Patriis virtutibus	*With his father's virtues*	Clements.
Paulatim	*By little and little*	Scales.
Pax	*Peace*	Foulis, Hutton, Almack.

Pax alma redit....................	*Bountiful peace returns*...........	Domville.
Pax armis acquiritur............	*Peace is acquired by arms*	Arnot, Arrat, Arrot.
Pax aut bellum...................	*Peace or war*	Belean, Blain, Blaine, Blane, Blean, Scarth.
Pax aut defensio..................	*Peace or defence*....................	Landale.
Pax, copia, sapientia............	*Peace, plenty, wisdom*	Fleming, West.
Pax et amor.......................	*Peace and love*	Jessop.
Pax et libertas....................	*Peace and liberty*...................	Gordon.
Pax in bello.......................	*Peace in war*	Osborne.
Pax potior bello...................	*Peace is better than war*...........	Bastard, Nempharts.
Pax quæritur bello...............	*Peace is sought by war*............	Cromwell.
Pax tua, Domine, est requies mea.................................	*Thy peace, O Lord, is my rest*....	Umphray, Wmphrey.
Peace	....	Higga.
Peace and grace...................	....	Graham.
Peace and plenty.................	....	Barns.
Peace with power.................	....	Moss.
Pedetentim	*Step by step*..........................	Foote.
Pejus letho flagitium............	*Disgrace is worse than death*......	Martin.
Pensez à bien......................	*Think of good*	Noel.
Pensez comment..................	*As you think*.........................	Davell, Deyvelle.
Pensez forte.......................	*Think much*	Pauncefote.
Peperi..............................	*I have brought forth*...............	Peperell.
Per acuta belli....................	*By the strategems of war*	Carpenter.
Per actum intentio	*The intention is judged of by the act*	Urquhart.
Peradventure......................	....	Cockburn, Eliot, Elliott, Fogg.
Per adversa virtus.........	*Virtue through difficulties*..........	Leghton, Lighton.
Per augusta ad augusta.........	*Through dangers to honour*........	Christall, Skeffington.
Per ardua...........................	*Through difficulties*.................	Berry, Bervy, Clarkson, Crookshank, Curtis, Fuller, M'Entire, M'Intyre, Stibbert, Tailour.
Per ardua ad alta.................	*Through difficulties to heaven*......	Achanye, Ahanny, Hall, Hanman, Hannay, Waterlow.
Per ardua fama...................	*Fame through difficulties*...........	Whyte.
Per ardua stabilis.................	*Steady in difficulties*.................	Mann.
Per ardua surgo...................	*I rise through difficulties*...........	Fenton, Mahon, Wingate.
Per ardua virtus..................	*Virtue through difficulties*..........	Sinclair.
Per aspera belli...................	*Through the hardships of war*...	Hopkins, Randolph.
Per aspera virtus.................	*Virtue through hardships*..........	Ross.
Per bellum qui providet........	*He who provides through war*.....	Lidderdale.
Per callem collem	*Over a mountain road*..............	Collins.
Per cœli favorem.................	*By the favour of heaven*............	Cowie.
Per crucem ad coronam	*By the cross to the crown*...........	Poe, Power.
Per crucem ad stellas...........	*By the cross to heaven*..............	Legard.
Percussus resurgo	*When struck down I rise again*...	Jordan.
Per Deum et ferrum obtinui..	*By God and my sword I have obtained*................................	Hill.
Perenne sub polo nihil	*Nothing is everlasting under heaven*.................................	Pont.
Peri aur y chalon wir	*A true heart will make gold*.......	Watkins.
Periculum fortitudine evasi...	*Fortitude preserved me from the dungeon*.............................	Mahon.
Peri-Gal.............................	....	Perigal.
Per ignem, per gladium	*By fire and sword*	Welby.
Periimus licitis....................	*Death in a good cause*.............	Teignmouth, Shore.
Periissem, ni perstitissem......	*I would have perished, had I not persisted*.............................	Anstruther, Molony.
Periissemus, nisi perstitissemus.................................	*We had perished, had we not persisted*................................	Anstruther.
Periit ut vivat	*He looses his life that he may gain it*.....................................	Fenwick, Phin.
Per il suo contrario..............	*By its reverse*........................	Paget.
Per industriam....................	*By industry*..........................	Rowan.
Per juga, per fluvios.............	*Through precipices and torrents*..	Harland.
Per mare	*By sea*.................................	Anderson.
Per mare, per terras	*By sea and land*.....................	Alexander, Drummond, Dupré, Lamb, M'Alister, Macelester, Macdonald, M'Donald, Piessf, Rutherford, Rutherfurd, Urquhart.

Permitte cætera divis	Leave the rest to the care of the gods	M'Crummen, M'Crummin.
Perseverance		Hume.
Perseverando	By persevering	Abbot, Broadhead, Brooks, Drake, Flower, Hanrott, Henley, Larkworthy, M'Kellar, Morton, Moreton, Turnly, Wood.
Perseverantia	Perseverance	Crichton.
Perseverantia vincit	Perseverance conquers	Burness.
Perseveranti dabitur	It will be given to the persevering	Gilmore, Gilmour, Robertson, Williamson.
Persevere		Congreve, Fordyce, Gardiner, Greig, Hall, Oakes, Simpson.
Per sinum Codanum	Through the Baltic Sea	Sawll-Graves.
Perspicax, audax	Active, bold	Erskine.
Per tela, per hostes	By arrows, by enemies	Bremner, Brymer.
Per varios casus	By various fortunes	Douglas, Drysdale, Hamilton, Lammie, L'Amy, Walker.
Per vias rectas	By right ways	Blackwood.
Per vim et virtutem	By strength and courage	Youl, Yule.
Per virtutem scientiam	By courage and knowledge	MacNeil, McNeil.
Pestis patriæ pigrities	Sloth is the plague of one's country	Dugdale.
Petit alta	He aims at high things	Abercrombie.
Petit ardua virtus	Courage aims at hard things	Douglas.
Phœbo lux	Light from the sun	Kinnaird.
Phœbus, lux in tenebris	Phœbus, light in darkness	Jeffrey.
Piedmontaise	The inhabitants of Piedmont	Hardinge.
Pie repone te	In pious confidence	Mordey, Pierpoint, Pierrepont.
Pietas et frugalitas	Piety and carefulness	Guthry.
Pietas tutissima virtus	Piety is the chief virtue	Ainsley, Ainslie.
Pietatis causâ	For the sake of piety	Pye.
Pieux quoique preux	Pious though valiant	Long.
Pie vivere et Deum et patriam diligere	To live piously, and live God and our country	Redmond.
Pignus amoris	The pledge of love	Graham.
Pille mise gu muier	I will return to sea	M'Laurin.
Placeam	I shall pacify	Murray.
Plena refulget	The full moon shines	Pitcairn.
Plus ultra	More beyond this	Nabbs, Nairne, Elliott.
Plutot rompe que plie	Break rather than bend	De Ponthieu.
Poco a poco	Little by little	Ramage.
Pollet virtus	Virtue excels	Pole, Poole.
Porro unum est necessarium	Moreover, one thing is needful	Wellesley.
Portanti spolia palma	The prize is to him that carries off the booty	Feltham.
Posce teipsum	Ask thyself	Hodges.
Posse, nolle, nobile	To have the power without the wish is noble	Wingfield.
Possunt qui posse videntur	They conquer who believe they can	Goodere, Keightley.
Posterâ laude recens	New with future praise	Hardinge.
Post est occasio calva	Afterwards is a bald occasion	Chapman.
Post funera fœnus	An interest after death	Moll, Mow.
Post funera virtus	Virtue survives death	Robertson.
Post nubes	Light after clouds	Steddert, Stodart, Stothart, Blunstone.
Post nubes lux	Light after clouds	Blunstone, Blundestone, Steddert, Stodart, Stoddart, Stothart.
Post nubila	After clouds	Jack.
Post nubila Phœbus	After clouds sunshine	Ahrends, Cranworth, Jack, Jaffray, Jaffrey, Jeffrey, Purvis, Shuldham, Tarleton.
Post nubila sol	After clouds sunshine	Pinkerton.
Post prælia præmia	Reward after battle	Nicholson, Westenra.
Post tenebras lux	Light after darkness	Hewat, Hewatt.
Post tot naufragia portum	After so many dangers I find a port	Montagu.
Post virtutem curro	I run after virtue	Blome, Briscoe.
Petior origine virtus	Virtue rather than lineage	Scot, Scott.

Potius ingenio quam vi..........	Rather by genius than strength...	Edgar.
Potius ingenio quam vi..........	By skill rather than by force......	Edgar.
Potius mori quam fœdari......	Death rather than disgrace........	Gifford.
Pourapprendre oublier ne puis	I cannot learn to forget............	Palmer.
Pour bien désirer................	To wish well........................	Bolden, Brand, Leonard, Leonard-Barrett.
Pour jamais......................	For ever.............................	Gorwood.
Pour le roy.......................	For the king........................	Macaul.
Pour ma patrie...................	For my country	Cooper.
Pour mon Dieu...................	For my God.........................	Macpeter, Peitere, Peter.
Pour Dieu, pour terre..........	For God, for earth.................	Leigh.
Pour Dieu et mon roi...........	For God and my king.............	Bagot.
Pour y parvenir...................	In order to accomplish............	Manners, Sutton.
Poussez en avant................	Push forward......................	Barry, Barrow.
Practise no fraud................	....	Henderson.
Præcedentibus insta.............	Urge your way among the leaders	Eliot-Craggs.
Præcipitatus, attamen tutus..	Among the headstrong, yet in safety................................	Dunbar.
Præclarior, quo propinquior...	The more illustrious, the nearer...	Constable.
Præclarum regi et regno servitium...............................	Honourable service to king and country	Ogilvie.
Præclarius quo difficilius......	The harder, the more honourable	Fountain.
Prædæ memor.....................	Mindful of the prize................	Graham.
Præmium, virtus, gloria........	Reward, courage, glory............	Corsane.
Præmium, virtus, honor........	Reward, courage, honour.........	Boreland, Brown, Cox.
Præmium virtutis honor.......	Honour is the reward of virtue...	Cheere, Chere, Corsane, Tetlow.
Præmonitus præmunitus......	Forwarned, forearmed.............	Rickart.
Præstando, præsto................	Having taken the precedence, I hold it................................	Hamilton.
Præstat auro virtus	Virtue is better than gold..........	Cunningham.
Præsto et persisto................	I excel and persist	Hamilton, Yawkins.
Præsto et persto...................	I undertake and persevere.........	Coe, Crawhall, Hamilton.
Præsto et præsto..................	I undertake and perform..........	Yawkins.
Præsto pro patriâ.................	I undertake for my country......	Neilson.
Præsto ut præstem	I undertake that I may perform..	Preston.
Prævisa mala pereunt...........	Foreseen misfortunes die away...	Hodges, Twisden, Twysden, Winterbotham.
Prato et pelago...................	By sea and land....................	Killingworth.
Prend moi tel que je suis......	Take me such as I am.............	Bell, Loftus, Ricketts, Sutton.
Prenez en gré.....................	Willingly.............................	Ogle.
Prenez garde......................	Be on your guard..................	Elmsley, Elmslie, Elmsly, M'Intosh, Macintosh, Macritchie, Rickard, Rickart.
Prenez haleine trez fort........	Take full strong breath............	Giffard.
Press forward.....................	....	Mortimer.
Press through.....................	....	Boreland, Borelands, Cockburn, Young.
Prêt.................................	Ready.................................	Aston.
Prêst d'accomplir................	Ready to accomplish...............	Aston, Talbot.
Pretio prudentia præstat......	Prudence excels reward...........	Monson, Morison.
Pretiosum quod utile...........	What is useful is valuable........	Affleck, Auchinleck.
Pretium et causa laboris.......	The reward and cause of labour	Frederick.
Prêt pour mon pays	Ready to serve my country........	Monson.
Primâ voce salutat...............	Salutes with the first voice........	Boucherett.
Primi et ultimi in bello........	First and last in war...............	O'Gorman.
Primum tutare demum........	First defend home..................	Watkins.
Primus tametsi virilis..........	First although manly..............	Primerose.
Primus ultimusque in acie....	First and last in battle.............	Sherritt.
Principiis obsta...................	Oppose beginnings..................	Folkes, M'Laggan.
Pristinum spero lumen.........	I wait the early dawn.............	Preston.
Prius frangitur quam flectitur	Is sooner broken than bent........	Dykes-Ballantine.
Prius mori quam fidem fallere	Yield to death rather than betray trust................................	Drummond.
Pro amore patriæ................	For love of country................	Scot.
Pro aris et focis..................	For our homes and altars.........	Campbell, Hasilrigge, Hesilrigge, Kirkland, M'Naught, Phelips, Scot, Shortland, Shortreed, Wait, Woodforde.
Pro arte non marte..............	For art not strength................	Blagrave.
Probando et approbando.......	To be tried and approved.........	Ramsay.

Pro bello vel pace	For war or peace	Anderson, Anderton.
Probitas et firmitas	Honesty and firmness	Lesly.
Probitas verus honos	Probity is true honour	Bateson, Chetwynd, Hansard, Lacon, Newman, Vicary.
Probitate	By honour	Rennie, Renny.
Probitate consilium perficitur	An undertaking is achieved by honesty	Renny.
Probitate et labore	By probity and labour	Gould.
Probitatem quam divitias	Probity rather than riches	Claydan, Claydon, Clayton.
Pro bonis ad meliora	From good to better	Goodwright.
Probum non pœnitet	We do not repent of what is good	Sands, Sandes, Sandys.
Procedamus in pace	Let us proceed in peace	Montgomery.
Pro Christo et patriâ	For Christ and our country	Ker, Vernon.
Pro Christo et patriâ dulce periculum	For Christ and our country danger is sweet	Ker.
Pro Deo et ecclesiâ	For God and the Church	Bisshopp.
Pro Deo et rege	For God and the king	Bickerton, Blacker, Masterton, Mastertown, Parsons.
Pro Deo, patriâ, et rege	For our God, our country, and king	James, Beugo.
Pro Deo, rege, et patriâ	For our God, our king, and country	Beuga, Bickerton, Blaydes, Blaydes-Marvel, M'Dowall.
Prodesse quam conspici	To do good rather than be conspicuous	Chamberlayne, Cocks, Coxs, Grote, Leigh.
Prodesse civibus	To do good to one's countrymen	Beckett.
Prodigiose qui laboriose	Who acts laboriously acts marvellously	Innes.
Pro ecceslia Dei	For the Church of God	Swainson.
Pro fide et patriâ	For our faith and country	Wade.
Profunda cernit	He penetrates deep things	Gourlay, Gourley, Simson.
Progredere, ne regrede	Go forward, not back	Honnyman, Honyman, Sharp.
Progredior	I go forward	Sharp.
Projeci	I have thrown away	Main.
Pro legibus et regibus	For laws and kings	Wilson.
Pro libertate	For liberty	Wallace.
Pro libertate patriæ	For the liberty of my country	Massey, Massy, Maysey.
Pro lusu et prædâ	For sport and plunder	MacMoran, M'Morran.
Pro magnâ chartâ	For the Magna Charta	Dashwood, Stapleton.
Pro mitrâ coronam	A mitre for a crown	Sharpe.
Prompte et consel	Quickly and advisedly	Pringle.
Prompte et consulto	Quickly and with advice	Plenderleith.
Promptus	Ready	Donaldson, Kemp, Kempt.
Promptus ad certamen	Ready for the contest	Sinclair.
Promptus et fidelis	Ready and faithful	Carruthers, Chalmers, Croudace.
Pro patriâ	For my country	Bannerman, Betson, Borrowman, Bullman, Bulman, Douglas, Gregor, Groseth, Hamilton, Hastie, Hay, Higgins, Innes, Newlands, Newton, Ogilvie, Provan, Roachead, Rochead, Ross, Scott, Turner, Walmsley, Wood.
Pro patriæ amore	For the love of my country	Wolfe.
Pro patriâ, auxilio Dei	For my country, by the aid of God	Grossett.
Pro patria ejusque libertate	For my country and its liberty	Joy.
Pro patriâ et libertate	For our country and liberty	Michie.
Pro patriâ non timidus perire	Not afraid to die for my country	Champneys, Champreys.
Pro patriâ semper	For my country always	Collow, Power.
Pro patriâ uro	I burn for my country	Costerton.
Propositi tenax	Tenacious of my resolve	Yeatman.
Proprio vos sanguine pasco	I feed you with kindred blood	Cantrell.
Propter obedientem	Because of obedience	Hay.
Pro recto	Because of right	Meek.
Pro rege	For the king	Aberkirdor, Burnaby, Christie, Graham, Macfie, M'Phie, Porcher.
Pro rege Dimico	For King Dimicus	Dymoke.
Pro rege et grege	For the king and people	Grieve, Paterson.

Pro rege et lege...............	For the king and law...............	Horton, Kidson, Maudit, Stewart.
Pro rege et limite...............	For the king and his dominions..	Elliot, Elliott.
Pro rege et patriâ...............	For our king and country.........	Aberherdour, Aberkerdour, Ainsley, Ainslie, Bell, Cameron, Carr, Franklyn, Hammond, Licester, Leslie, Lyon, M'Cubbin, Smith, Stewart.
Pro rege et patriâ pugnans....	Fighting for king and country...	Pasley.
Pro rege et populo...............	For king and people...............	Basset.
Pro rege et republicâ...........	For king and state...............	Paul.
Pro rege in tyrannos...........	For the king against tyrants......	Macdonald, M'Dowall.
Pro rege, lege, et grege........	For king, law, and people........	Besborough.
Pro rege, lege, grege...........	For the king, law, people...........	Brougham, Ponsonby.
Pro rege sæpe.....................	For the king often..................	Wright.
Pro rege sæpe, pro patriâ semper..............................	For our king often, for our country always........................	Eyre, Redington.
Pro republicâ semper...........	For my country always............	Hellier.
Pro salute	For safety........................	Ogilvie.
Prosequor alis....................	I pursue with wings...............	Graham.
Prospere qui sedulo............	The diligent prosper..............	Cunninghame.
Prospere, si propere............	Prosperously if speedily............	Peat.
Prospero, sed curo...............	I make haste, but am cautious....	Graham, Maxwell.
Pro utilitate.......................	For utility	Tennant.
Pro veritate	For truth	Keith.
Provide.............................		Stewart.
Providence........................		Craick.
Providence with adventure ...		Hawkins.
Providentiâ........................	By Providence	Anderson.
Providentiâ Dei stabiliuntur familiæ...........................	Families are established by the providence of God..................	Lamplugh.
Providentiâ divinâ...............	By divine providence..............	Keating, Keching, Sangster.
Providentiæ fido.................	I trust to Providence..............	Stewart.
Providentiæ me committo.....	I commit myself to Providence...	Kyle, Park.
Providentia et virtute...........	By providence and virtue	Hepburn, Rankin, Rankine.
Providentia in adversis........	Providence in adversity............	Tollet.
Providentia tutamen............	Providence is our protection	Thomson.
Providentiâ tutamur.............	We are protected by Providence...	Beardmore, Norden.
Providus esto.....................	Be careful........................	Maxton.
Pro virtute........................	For virtue........................	Reid.
Prudens, fidelis, et audax......	Prudent, faithful, and bold.......	Legh.
Prudens qui patiens.............	He who is patient is prudent......	Leicester, Lushington.
Prudens sicut serpens	Wise as the serpent...............	Pole.
Prudenter amo....................	I love wisely......................	Scot.
Prudenter qui sedulo...........	He who acts diligently acts prudently..............................	Milne.
Prudenter vigilo..................	I watch prudently.................	Donaldson.
Prudentiâ et animo..............	With prudence and courage	Antram, Ochterlony, Steele, Steell.
Prudentiâ et constantiâ.........	By prudence and constancy	Denmark, Tichbourne.
Prudentia et honor..............	Prudence and honour............	M'Kinna.
Prudentiâ et simplicitate......	By prudence and simplicity.......	Denman, Lant.
Prudentiâ et vi....................	By prudence and might	Innes.
Prudentia et vigilantia.........	Prudence and vigilance............	Purchon.
Prudentia in adversis...........	Prudence in adversity............	Tollet, Wicksted.
Prudentia me sustinet...........	Prudence holds me up............	Boyd.
Prudentia præstat...............	Prudence excels....................	Morison, Morrison, Morryson.
Publica salus mea merces......	The public safety is my reward...	Dick.
Pugilem claraverat	He hath ennobled the champion...	Newte.
Pugna pro patriâ.................	Fight for your country............	Tichborne, Tichbourne.
Pugno pro patriâ.................	I fight for my country............	Ogilvy.
Pulchrior ex arduis	More illustrious from difficulties	Mackenzie, M'Kenzie.
Pungit sed placet................	It is painful but pleasing	Rome.

Q

Quæ amissa salva...............	What was lost is safe...............	Falconer, Keith.
Quæ fecimus ipsi................	What we ourselves have performed	Fulton.
Quæ juncta firma................	Union is strength	Lesly.
Quæ moderata firma...........	Moderate things are permanent..	Ogilvie, Ogilvy.
Quæque favilla micat	Every spark shines...............	Robertson.
Quæ recta sequor	I follow the things which are right...............................	Campbell.
Quærere verum...................	To seek the truth...............	Carleton.
Quæ serata secura...............	The things which are locked are safe...............................	Douglas.
Quæ supra	Which things are above............	Hobart.
Quæ sursum volo................	I wish those things which are above...............................	M'Quinn.
Quæ sursum volo videre.......	I wish to see the things which are above...............................	Quin, Macqueen, M'Queen.
Quæ vernant crescent...........	The things which are growing shall yield increase	Burnet.
Quâ fidem servasti...............	Where you have kept faith.........	Grieve.
Qualis ab incepto................	The same as from the beginning...	De Grey, Majendie, Weddell.
Qualis vita, finis ita...	As life, so its end	Yong.
Quam plurimis prodesse	To do good to as many as possible	Worsley.
Quam sibi sortem	Any condition to him	Fraser.
Quantum in rebus inane	What vanity in human affairs...	Osborn, Osborne.
Quarta saluti	A fourth to salvation...............	Halliday.
Qua tendis	Wherever you go	Roy.
Que je surmonte	That I may overcome	Chanceler.
Quem te Deus esse jussit.	What God commands you to be...	Holroyd, Holroyde.
Que pensez?........................	What do you think ?...............	Lawrence.
Quhidder will ye .... Quhidder will zie................	Whither will ye	Stewart.
Qui capit, capitur	He who takes is taken...............	Smyth.
Qui conducit......................	He who leads	Borthwick.
Quicquid crescit, in cinere perit	Whatever grows, perishes in ashes	Aserburne, Ashburne, Asherburne, Ashburner.
Quid capit, capitur...............	What takes, is taken	Smith.
Quid clarius astris ?.............	What is brighter than the stars ?..	Baillie, Bayly.
Quid leone fortis?...............	What is braver than the lion ?....	Clayton.
Quidni prod sodali?.............	Why not for a companion ?.......	Burnet.
Quid non, Deo juvante ?.......	What may not be performed under the favour of God ?.........	Chalmers, Salt.
Quid non pro patriâ ?............	What will a man not undergo for his country ?	Campbell, Mathew.
Quid prodest?.....................	What advantage is it ?...............	Webb.
Quid utilius?.....................	What is more useful ?...............	Gouldie.
Quid utilius?.....................	What more useful ?...............	Goldie.
Quid verum atque decens	What is true and honourable......	Rickets, Trevor.
Quid vult, valde vult...........	What he wishes, he wishes well....	Motteux.
Quiescam	I shall rest	Dalrymple.
Quiescens et vigilans............	Resting and watching............	Fairnie, Fernie.
Qui honeste, fortiter............	Who acts honestly acts bravely....	Anderson.
Qui invidet minor est...........	He that envies is less	Cadogan.
Qui me tangit pœnitebit	He who touches me will repent it..	Macpherson.
Qui nos vincet ?...................	Who shall conquer us ?............	Beugo.
Qui nucleum vult, nucem frangat	Whoso wishes the kernel must crack the nut	Haslen.
Qui patitur, vincit	He who endures patiently, conquers	Kinaird, Kinnaird.
Qui pense ?.........................	Who thinks ?...............	Lawrence, St Lawrence.
Qui potest capere, capiat......	Let him take who can take.........	Gleg.
Quis accursabit	Who shall run up to...............	Hamilton.
Qui sera sera	What will be will be...............	Betenson, Bettenson, Bettinson, Bettison, Edgell, Folkes.
Qui s'estime petyt deviendra grand	Who esteems himself little, will become great......................	Petyt.
Quis similis tui in fortibus, Domine ?........................	Who is like to Thee among the mighty. O Lord ?	Goldsmid.

Qui uti scit ei bona	It is good to him who knows how to use it	Berwick, Hill.
Qui vit content tient assez.....	He that lives content, has got enough	Bradshagh, Bradshaigh, Bradshaw.
Qui vult capere, capiat.........	Who wishes to take, let him take...	Gloag.
Quocunque ferar	Whithersoever I may be led.......	Sinclair.
Quocunque jeceris stabit......	Wherever you shall have thrown, it shall stand.....................	M'Leod.
Quod adest	What is present......................	Marsham.
Quod agis fortiter	Which you do bravely..............	Oliphant.
Quod Deus vult fiat	God's will shall be done............	Chetwynd.
Quod dixi, dixi	What I have said, I have said....	Dixie, Dixon.
Quod ero, spero	I hope that I shall be	Barton, Booth, Bough, Gowans, Haworth.
Quod facio, valde facio..........	What I do, I do well...............	Holmes.
Quod facit, valde facit..........	What he does, he does with all his might	Sikes.
Quod honestum utile	What is honest is useful	Annand, Annandale, Lawson.
Quod justum, non quod utile	Justice not utility	Phillips.
Quod non pro patriâ ?..........	What not for your country ?......	Bowie, Bowrie, Campbell.
Quod potui, perfici	What I could, I have done	Dundas.
Quod sors fert, ferimus........	What fate requires, we bear......	Clayton.
Quod sursum volo videre......	I am resolved to look upwards....	Quin.
Quod tibi, hoc alteri.............	That is for thee; this, for the other	Crawford, Crawfurd, Hesketh.
Quod tibi, id alii	What for thee, that for another...	Lopas.
Quod tibi, ne alteri..............	That is for thee, not for the other	Alexander.
Quod tibi vis fieri, facias.......	What you wish done, do yourself	Philipoe, Philipse.
Quod utilis.......................	That which is useful................	Bell, Goldie, Gouldie.
Quo duxeris, adsum............	Whither you shall lead, I am ready	Ogilvy.
Quod verum atque decens.....	What is true is honourable	Trevor.
Quo virtus vocat.................	Where virtue calls...................	
Quod pudet, hoc pigeat.........	That which causes shame is irksome..................................	Yate.
Quod vult, valde vult	What he wishes, he fervently wishes	Holt, Mansel, Mansell, Maunsell.
Quo fas et gloria	Where right and glory.............	Glasgow.
Quo fata vocant	Wherever fate may summon me...	Bland, Shelley, Sidney, Thurlow.
Quo major, eo utilior	By how much he is greater he is more useful..........................	Neilson.
Quo me cunque vocat patria..	Wherever my country calls me....	Arden.
Quondam his vicimus armis...	Formerly we conquered with these arms..................................	Carleton, Tomlin.
Quos dedit arcus amor	The bows which love hath given...	Hamilton.
Quo spinosior fragrantior......	The more thorns, the greater fragrance............................	Ross.
Quo virtus et fata vocant......	Where virtue and destiny call ...	Ffolliott.
Quo virtus ducit scando	I climb where virtue leads.........	Follett.

R

Radicem firmant frondes	Leaves bind the root.................	Grant.
Radii omnia lustrant	The rays illuminate all things....	Brownhill.
Ramis micat radix	The root moves with the branches	Robertson.
Rapit ense triumphos...........	Wins triumphs with the sword.....	Smith.
Rara avis in terris................	A rare bird in the world	Kett.
Rara bonitas	Goodness is scarce....................	Bennet.
Rather die than be disloyal...		Pearson.
Ratione, non irâ..................	By reason, not by rage	Small.
Ready..............................		Archever, Fraser, Smith.
Ready, aye ready		Napier, Scot.
Reason contents me..............		Graham.
Recreat et alit	It refreshes and cherishes..........	Duddingstoun.
Recreation.........................		Forrester.
Recta pete	Seek what is right....................	Fletcher.
Recta sursum	Things are right which are above	Graham.
Recta vel ardua..................	Right or difficult.....................	Evelick, Lindsay.
Recta ad ardua	Act rightly in difficulties...........	Mackenzie, M'Kenzie.

Recte et fideliter	Rightly and faithfully	Gibson.
Recte et suaviter	Justly and mildly	Curzon.
Recte faciendo neminem timeo	I fear none in doing right	Cairncross, Scott.
Recte faciendo securus	Safe in doing right	Inglis.
Recte quod honeste	Rightly, which is honestly	Anderson.
Recte sequor	I follow rightly	Campbell, Keith.
Recte vel ardua	Rightly or difficult	Lindsay.
Recto cursu	In a right course	Corsar, Corser.
Rectus in curvo	Right in bending	Symonds.
Redde diem	Restore the day	Foster.
Reddunt aspera fortem	Dangers render brave	Scot.
Reddunt commercia mitem	Commercial intercourses render man sociable	Stewart.
Redeem time		Hancocks.
Redoutable et fougueux	Formidable and fiery	Harvey.
Re é merito	This through merit	Gildea, Vassal-Fox.
Refero	I call to mind	Campbell.
Refulgent in tenebris	They glitter in the dark	Stodart, Studdart.
Refulget	Is resplendent	Pitcairn.
Regard bien	Regard well	Milligan, Milliken.
Regardez mon droit	Regard my right	Middleton.
Regem defendere victum	To defend a conquered king	Whitgreave.
Regi et patriæ fidelis	Faithful to king and country	Toler.
Regi patriæque fidelis	Faithful to king and country	Scott.
Regi regnoque fidelis	Faithful to the king and kingdom	Pocock, Simpson.
Regi semper fidelis	Ever true to the king	Smythe.
Regulier et vigoreux	Regular and vigorous	Ker.
Remember		Allen, Gavin, Home.
Remember and forget not		Hall.
Remember thy end		Keith.
Renascentur	We shall rise again	Skiffington, Yelverton.
Renovate animos	Renew your courage	Drummond, Hay.
Renovato nomine	The name renewed	Westcote.
Renovatur ætas ejus sicut aquilæ	His youth is renewed like the eagle's	Raymond.
Reparabit cornua Phœbe	The moon shall fill again her horns	Hope, Scot, Scott.
Repetens exempla suorum	Pursuing the examples of his ancestors	Grenville.
Republique	The state	Harris.
Repullulat	It buds anew	Bisset, Lauder, Laurie, Lawder.
Requiesco sub umbrâ	I rest under the shade	Hamilton.
Rerum sapientia custos	Wisdom is the guardian of things	Affleck, Auchinleck.
Res, non verba	Deeds, not words	Duberley, Freeland, Heely, Jarrett, Macrorie, M'Rorie, Roughsedge, Wilson.
Resolute and firm		Milbanke.
Resolutio cauta	Prudent resolution	Bethune.
Respice finem	Consider the end	Lucas, Priestley.
Respice futurum	Regard the future	Reece.
Respice, prospice	Look behind, look before	Hardress, Lloyd.
Resurgam	I shall rise again	Crosbie, Crosby, Stewart.
Resurgere tento	I strive to rise again	Straiton.
Resurgo	I rise again	Cooper, Haxton, M'Fall, Maughan.
Retinens vestigia famæ	Retracing the deeds of honourable ancestors	Lister, Lyster.
Revertite	Return ye	Wardrop.
Revirescimus	We grow green again	Glenelg.
Revirescit	He revives	Belches, Belshes, Bisset, Maxwell.
Reviresco	I grow green	Bisset, M'Ewan, Mackenan, Mackeuan, Mackewan, Maxwell, Wellwood.
Revocate animos	Rouse your courage	Hay.
Rex, non verba	The king, not words	Wilson.
Rident florentia prata	The flourishing meadows smile	Pratt.
Ride through		Hamilton.
Rien sans Dieu	Nothing without God	Kerrison, Peters.
Right and reason		Graham.
Right own never die		Norbury, Toler.

Right to share................	....	Riddell.
Rinasce piu gloriosa............	*To be renewed more gloriously....*	Erskine, St Clair.
Rise and shine.................	....	Lawson.
Robore et sapore................	*With strength and taste...........*	Robertson.
Robori prudentia præstat......	*Prudence excels strength..........*	Young.
Robur atque fides................	*Strength and faith..................*	Whitaker.
Robur in vitâ Deus..............	*God is the strength of life........*	Jadewine.
Rosam ne rode..................	*Do not speak ill of the rose.......*	Cashen, Ross.
Rosario............................	*In a bed of roses..................*	Harvey.
Rosas coronat spina.............	*Thorns encompass the roses........*	Forbes.
Rosa sine spina................	*A rose without the thorn..........*	Wadman.
Row and retake................	....	Riddell.
Rule be ours....................	....	Byres.
Rumeur acerbe, tace...........	*Unpleasant rumour, be silent.....*	Echlin.
Rupto robore nati..............	*We are born in a weak condition*	Aikenhead, Aitkenhead, Sibbald.

S

Sae bauld......................	*So bold............................*	Sibbald.
Sæpe pro rege, semper pro republicâ........................	*Often for the king, always for the state............................*	Vassall.
Sævumque tridentem servamus............................	*Let us preserve the fierce trident..*	Broke.
Sagesse sans tache..............	*Wisdom without spot..............*	Concanon.
Sail through....................	....	Hamilton.
Salamanca......................	....	Cotton.
Salus in fide....................	*Salvation by faith.................*	Magrath.
Salus mea Christus.............	*Christ is my salvation............*	Forbes.
Salus per Christum.............	*Salvation through Christ........*	Abernethy, Forbes, Christian.
Salus per Christum Redemptorem...........................	*Salvation through Christ the Redeemer...........................*	Steuart, Stewart, Stuart.
Salutem disponit Deus.........	*God administers salvation.......*	Edgar.
Salve me Deus..................	*God save me......................*	Spiers.
Salvus in igne..................	*Safe in the fire....................*	Trivett.
San Josef.......................	....	Nelson.
Sans changer...................	*Without changing.................*	Musgrave.
Sans charger...................	*Without overloading..............*	Eddisbury, Enery, Stanley.
Sans crainte	*Without fear......................*	Gordon-Cumming, Petre, Sanderson, Tyrel, Tyrell.
Sans Dieu, je ne puis...........	*Without God I cannot............*	Skipworth.
Sans Dieu rien..................	*Nothing without God.............*	Godley, Hodgkinson, Peter, Petrie, Sanderson.
Sans heur.......................	*Without good luck................*	Arncell.
Sans peur	*Without fear......................*	Arneel, Arneil, Arnied, Hagart, Hogart, Karr, Sutherland.
Sans reculla jamais..............	*Without ever drawing back.......*	Brackenbury.
Sans tache......................	*Without stain....................*	Hurry, Le Blanc, Moray, Murray, Napier, Preston, Ure, Urie, Urrie, Urry.
Sans variance et mon droit....	*Without change, and for my right*	Bowes.
Sans varier.....................	*Without change..................*	Charlton, Cunningham.
Sapere aude....................	*Dare to be wise..................*	Amos, Meredith, Parker, Wise, Wyse.
Sapere aude et tace.............	*Be wise, and say nothing.........*	Hesse.
Sapere aude, incipe.............	*Dare to be wise, begin............*	Birney, Burnie, Burney, Claxson.
Sapiens non eget	*The wise man wanteth not........*	Dunbar.
Sapiens qui assiduus............	*He is wise who is assiduous......*	Mitchell, Sperling.
Sapienter et pié................	*Wisely and piously...............*	Park.
Sapienter si sincere.............	*Wisely, if sincerely................*	Davidson.
Sapienter uti bonis	*Wisely to enjoy blessings..........*	Butler.
Sapientia et veritas.............	*Wisdom and truth...............*	Douglas.
Sapit qui laborat................	*He who labours is wise............*	Dunbar.
Sapit qui reputat...............	*He who considers is wise..........*	M'Clellan, M'Clelland, Macklellan, M'Lellan.
Sat amico si mihi felix.........	*Enough for a friend, if he be kind to me........................*	Law.

Sat cito, si sat tuto	Quick enough, if safe enough	Clerk.
Satis est prostrasse leoni	It is enough to have overcome the lion	Salusbury.
Save me, Lord		Corbet.
Say and do		Everard.
Scienter utor	I use skilfully	Forbes.
Scio cui credidi	I know in whom I have believed	Milnes.
Scopus vitæ Christus	Christ is the end of life	Menzies.
Scripta manent	What is written remains	Young.
Scite, citissime certe	Skilfully, quickly, surely	Havergal.
Scuto amoris divini	By the shield of divine love	Jackson, Scodamore.
Scuto divino	With the divine shield	Kay, Zephane, Zephani.
Scuto fidei	With the shield of faith	Morris.
Secum cuique	To every one with himself	Thomson.
Secundat vera fides	Real fidelity prospers	Ogilvie, Ogilvy.
Secundis dubiisque rectus	Upright in prosperity and in perils	Duncan, Lippincott.
Secundo, curo	I am prosperous, I am careful	Buchanan.
Secura frugalitas	Frugality is secure	Mitchell.
Securior quo paratior	The better prepared, the more secure	Johnston.
Securis fecit securum	The axe makes secure	Luxmore.
Securitate	By security	Roberton, Robertstown.
Securum præsidium	The fortress is secure	Craigdailie, Craigie.
Securus	Secure	Yates.
Secus rivos aquarum	By rivers of waters	Rivers.
Se defendendo	By defending himself	Eccles, Ecles, Ekles.
Sedulitate	By diligence	Divie, Divvie, Elphingston.
Sed sine labe decus	Honour, but without stain	Scott.
Sedulo et honeste	Carefully and honestly	Lyal, Lyall, Lyle.
Sedulo et honeste tutela	Guardianship with honour and diligence	Lyell.
Sedulo numen adest	The Deity is present watching	Cunninghame, Harrower.
Sedulus et audax	Diligent and resolute	Melliship, Rutherford, Rutherfurd, Seaton.
Seigneur je te prie, garde ma vie	Lord, I beseech thee, save my life	Pidcock, Tyzack.
Semel et semper	Once and always	Allcard, Swinburne.
Semper	Always	Seaton, Seton.
Semper ad paratus	Always prepared	Stuart.
Semper constans et fidelis	Always constant and faithful	Irton, Spoor.
Semper eadem	Always the same	Carrol, Colamore, Collmore, Fairbairn, Forester, Gouch, Harvey, Hornsey, Panton, Reid.
Semper erectus	Always erect	Pepper.
Semper fidelis	Always faithful	Broadmead, Bruce, Cairns, Dick, Formby, Houlton, Lynch, Onslow, Smith, Stewart, Stirling, Taylor, Truell.
Semer fidus	Always true	Leitch, Leith.
Semper parati	Always prepared	Fraser, Frazer.
Semper paratus	Always ready	Armitage, Clifford, Constable, Dallas, Elphinstone, Johns, Johnston, Johnstone, Knowles, Macreadie, Macready, Phillpots, Roydes, Smith, Stewart, Upton, Welles, Wells.
Semper paratus pugnare pro patriâ	Always ready to fight for my country	Lockhart.
Semper præcinctus	Always girt	Mulholland.
Semper pugnare paratus	Always ready to fight	Litchfield.
Semper sapit suprema	Is always supremely wise	Selby.
Semper sic	Always thus	Johnson.
Semper sitiens	Always thirsty	Drought.
Semper spero meliora	I always hope for better things	Pringle.
Semper sursum	Always upward	Graham, Messent.
Semper verus	Always true	Home, Howe.
Semper victor	Always a conqueror	Ramsay.

Semper vigilans..................	Always watchful..................	Bourne, Walker, Williams, Wilson.
Semper virens....................	} Always flourishing..................	Broadwood.
Semper virescens................		Hamilton.
Semper viridis...................		Green, Maxwell.
Semper virescet virtus.........	Virtue will always flourish.........	Marishall, Marshall.
Semper virescit virtus.........	Virtue always flourishes...........	Lind.
Semper virtute constans.......	Always constant in virtue..........	Beaven.
Semper virtute vivo.............	I always live by virtue.............	Sideserf, Sydserfe.
Sepultos viresco.................	I grow green when buried..........	Graham, Messent.
Sequamur........................	Let us follow......................	Oswald.
Sequitando si giunge...........	By pursuing we become united....	Lambert.
Sequitur patrem, non passibus æquis.............................	{ He follows his father with unequal steps............................. }	Wilson.
Sequitur vestigia patrum......	He follows the steps of his fathers	Irvine.
Sequitur victoria forteis........	Victory follows the brave...,......	Campbell.
Sequor.............................	I follow...........................	Campbell, MacInroy.
Sequor, nec inferior............	I follow, yet not inferior...........	Crewe.
Sera deshormais hardi..........	Be always courageous...............	Hardie.
Sermoni consona facta.........	Deeds answering to words.........	Collins, Trelawney.
Sermoni consona facta.........	{ Actions in harmony with our words .... }	Trelawney.
Sero, sed serie...................	Late, but in earnest...............	Cecil, Ker, Nairn.
Serpentes velut et columbæ...	Like serpents and doves............	Enys.
Servabit me semper Jehova...	Jehovah will always preserve me	Barclay.
Servabo fidem.....................	I will keep the faith...............	Dutton, Johnston.
Serva jugum.....................	Keep the yoke.....................	Hay, Nuttall.
Serva jugum sub jugo..........	Keep the yoke under the yoke......	Hay.
Servare modum..................	To observe the golden mean........	Folke.
Servare munia vitæ.............	To observe the duties of life.......	Oglander.
Servata fides cinere.............	{ The promise made is faithfully kept............................. }	Ryder, Verney, Welfitt, Wellfitt.
Serve the king....................	....	Bennet.
Serviendo........................	By serving........................	Simeon.
Servire Deo regnare est........	To serve God is to rule............	Middleton.
Servitute clarior.................	More illustrious by serving........	Player.
Set on.............................	....	Campbell, Seton.
Shanet a boo.....................	Victory to Shanet..................	{ Fitzgerald, Fitz-Gerald, Vesey, Fitzgerald. }
Shenichun Erin..................	The tradition of Ireland...........	M'Carthy.
Sherwoode......................	....	Hood.
Shoot thus.......................	....	Yeoman.
Sic cuncta caduca................	All things are thus fading.........	Henderson.
Sic cuncta nobilitat..............	Thus he ennobles all...............	Henderson.
Sic donec.........................	Thus until........................	Egerton, Jobb, Jopp.
Sic fidem teneo..................	Thus I keep my faith...............	{ Molesworth, Welford, Welsford. }
Sic fidus et robor................	Thus true and strong...............	Stirling.
Sic fuit, est, et erit.............	Thus it was, is, and shall be......	Stewart.
Sic his qui diligunt..............	Thus to those who are in love......	Norris.
Sic itur ad astra..................	Thus they go to heaven.............	{ Ballenden, Carnac-Rivett, Day, Martin, Martyn, Mackinzie, M'Kenzie. }
Sic itur in altum.................	Thus they go into the deep.........	Cowan.
Sic, nos sic sacra tuemur......	Thus, thus we keep holy things....	Macmahon, M'Mahon.
Sic paratior......................	Thus more ready...................	Johnston.
Sic parvis magna................	Thus great things by small........	Drake.
Sic rectius progredior.........	Thus I go more honourably........	Sinclair.
Sic te non videmus olim........	We did not see thee thus formerly	Playfair.
Sic tutus..........................	Thus safe...........................	Gordon.
Sicut oliva virens, lætor in æde Dei...........................	{ Like the green olive-tree, I rejoice in the house of God............. }	Oliver.
Sicut quercus....................	As the oak.........................	Challoner.
Sic virescit industria...........	Thus industry flourishes...........	Stewart.
Sic virescit virtus..............	Thus virtue flourishes..............	Ronald.
Sic viresco.......................	Thus I flourish.....................	Christie.
Sic vita human..................	Such is life........................	Capel.
Sic vivere, vivetis	Thus to live, ye shall live.........	Bunce.
Sic vos, non vobis..............	So you, not for yourselves.........	Walpole.
Si Deus nobiscum, quis contra nos?...............................	{ If God be for us, who can be against us?...................... }	Mairis, Otway.

Si Deus, quis contra?	If God is for us, who is against us	Spence, Spens.
Si Dieu veult	God willing	Preston.
Sidus adsit amicum	Let my friendly star be present	Bateman, Scott.
Si fractus fortis	If broken, brave	Foster.
Signum pacis amor	Love is the token of peace	Bell.
Si je n'estoy	If I were not	Curwen.
Si je pouvois	If I can	Cleland.
Si je puis	If I can	Cahun, Colquhoun, Eyre, Livingston, Livingstone, Radcliffe.
Silentio et spe	With silence and hope	Brander.
S'ils te mordent mord les	If they bite you, bite them	Morley.
Similis frondescit virga metallo	The twig grows covered with leaves like metal	Calmady.
Si monent tubæ, paratus	Prepared when the trumpets warn	Sissons.
Simplex munditiis	Plain and neat	Symonds, Symons-Soltan, Philips.
Simplex vigilia veri	The simple defence of truth	Perkins.
Sinceritate	With sincerity	Francklin.
Sine crimine fiat	It may be done	Innes.
Sine Deo nihil	Nothing without God	Litster.
Sine fine	Without end	M'Gill.
Sine fraude fides	Faith without deceit	Johnston.
Sine injuriâ	Without injury	Watson.
Sine labe fides	Faith without dishonour	Lockhart.
Sine labe lucebit	He shall shine without dishonour	Crawford.
Sine labe nota	Known without dishonour	Crawford, Crawfurd, M'Kenzie.
Sine maculâ	Without stain	Cary, Clough, Flint, Mackenzie, M'Culloch, Norcliffe.
Sine metu	Without fear	Jameson, Meres.
Sine sanguine victor	A conqueror without blood	Smith.
Sine sole nihil	Nothing without the sun	Pettegrew.
Sine stet viribus	Can stand with power	Abinger.
Sine timore	Without fear	Cormack, M'Cormack, Owers.
Si possem	If I could	Livingstone.
Sis fortis	Be thou brave	Lindsay.
Si sit prudentia	If there be prudence	Auckland, Brown, Eden, Henley.
Sis justus nec timeas	Be just, and fear not	Garvey.
Sis justus, et ne timeas		White.
Sis pius in primis	Be pious at the beginning	Barlow.
Sit Deus in studiis	Let God be amid my studies	Sydenham.
Sit laus Deo	Let praise be to God	Arburthnot.
Sit nomen decus	Let the name be a glory	Swan.
Sit saxum firmum	Let the stone be firm	Saxby.
Sit sine labe fides	Let faith be without stain	Lockhart, Peters.
Sit sine labe fines	May my end be without stain	Peters.
Sit sine spinâ	Let it be thornless	Cay.
Sit vita nomini congrua	May our life be like our name	Christie.
Sobrie, pie, juste	Soberly, piously, righteously	Middleton.
Sobrii este vigilantes	Be well advised by watching	Geekie.
So fork forward		Cunninghame.
Sola bona quæ honesta	These things alone are good which are honest	Archer, Colebrook, Colebrooke.
Sola in Deo salus	Safety in God alone	Robinson, Montague.
Sola juvat virtus	Virtue alone assists	Stewart.
Sola nobilitat virtus	Virtue alone ennobles	Hamilton, Moubray, Mowbray
Sola proba quæ honesta	The things which are honourable alone are good	Neave.
Sola, salus servire Deo	Safety is in serving God, and there alone	Gore.
Sola virtus invicta	Virtue alone is invincible	Haige, Howard, Waud.
Sola virtus nobilitat	Virtue alone ennobles	Henderson.
Sola virtus triumphat	Virtue alone triumphs	Carvile.
Solem fero	I bear the sun	Aubrey.
Solertia ditat	Skill enriches	Whitelaw.
Soli Deo gloria	Glory to God alone	Bontein, Bonteine, Lesly.
Soli Deo honor et gloria	Honour and glory to God alone	Huddleston.
Solus Christus mea rupes	Christ alone is my rock	Orrock.
Solus inter plures	I am alone among many	Forbes.

Sola cruce salus	Salvation by the cross alone	Barclay.
Sola salus servire Deo	To serve God is the only safety	Magenis.
Solem ferre possum	I can endure the sun	Davies.
Solem contemplor, despicio terram	I gaze on the sun, and spurn the earth	Bedingfield.
Sol, mi, re, fa		Bull.
Sors mihi grata cadet	A pleasant lot shall fall to me	Skeen.
Sorte suâ contentus	Let him be content with his condition	Hartwell.
Sorti æquus utrique	Equal to each condition	Maclean.
So run that you may obtain		Baker.
Souvenez	Remember	Graham.
Soyez ferme	Be steadfast	Butler, Needham.
Spare not		Giffard, Macgregor.
Spare nought		Hay.
Spare when you have nought		Gifford.
Spe	By hope	Horrocks.
Spe aspera levat	He eases difficulties by hope	Ross.
Spectemur agendo	Let us be judged by our actions	Agar, Boyle, Browne, Drumson, Elles, Elvin, M'Leur, M'Lure, Montagu-Scott, Montague, Morris, Rutson, Slesser, Thornbrough, Vigors.
Speed		Garnock.
Speed well		Spied.
Spe et amore	With hope and love	Fisher.
Spe et labore	By hope and labour	Jebb.
Spe expecto	I wait in hope	Forbes, Livingstone.
Spei bonæ atque animi	Of good hope and courage	Millar, Miller.
Spe meliore vehor	I am borne along by a better hope	Bogle.
Spem fortuna alit	Fortune nourishes hope	Kinnear, Petree, Petrie.
Spem renovat	He renews hope	Grierson.
Spem renovant alæ	Its wings renew its hope	Norvill.
Spem successus alit	Success nourishes hope	Ross.
Spe posteri temporis	In the hope of the future	Atchely.
Sperabo	I will hope	Annand, Pitcairn.
Sperando spiro	I breathe by hoping	Young.
Sperandum	To be hoped for	Rait, Scot.
Sperandum est	We must hope	Wallace.
Sperans	Hoping	Ellis.
Sperans pergo	I go hoping	Fletcher.
Speranza é verita	Hope and truth	Pegler.
Sperare timere est	To hope is to fear	Ratcliff.
Sperat infestis	Hopes against hostility	Seaton.
Speratum et completum	Hope, and realise	Arnet, Arnot; Arnott, Arnut.
Speravi in Domino	I have hoped in the Lord	Hay.
Spernit humum	He despises the earth	Forbes, M'Kindley, Mackinlay, Mitchell.
Spernit pericula virtus	Valour despises dangers	Forrester, Ramsay.
Sperno	I despise	Elleis.
Spero	I hope	Brown, Calderwood, Forbes, Gib, Gordon, Hunter, Hutton, Langlands, Learmont, Learmonth, Menzies, Schank, Shank, Waters.
Spero dum spiro	I hope while I breathe	Chambers.
Spero et progredior	I hope and advance	Pringle.
Spero in Deo	I hope in God	Blackie.
Spero infestis, metuo secundis	I hope in adversity, and fear in prosperity	Ludlow, Stewart.
Spero meliora	I hope for better things	Ainsworth, Baillie, Blyth, Douglas, Fairholm, French, Greaves, Kirkwood, Laird, Lowe, Maxwell, Moffat, Murray, Rait, Philips, Rhet, Rodie, Roper-Curzon, Samwell-Watson, Sandilands, Shaw, Stewart, Torphichen.
Spero procedere	I hope to prosper	Hopkirk.
Spero donec suspiro	While I breathe I hope	Hope.
Spero ut fidelis	I hope as faithful	Baskerville-Mynors, Mynords.

Spes	Hope	Gaskell.
Spes alit	Hope nourishes	Child.
Spes anchora tuta	Hope is a safe anchor	Dunmure.
Spes anchora vitæ	Hope is the anchor of life	M'Leay.
Spes aspera levat	Hope lightens dangers	Ross.
Spes audaces adjuvat	Hope assists the brave	Hollis.
Spes dabit auxilium	Hope will give help	Dunbar.
Spes, decus, et robor	Hope, honour, and strength	Smith.
Spes durat avorum	The hope of my ancestors subsists	Nassau.
Spes est in Deo	Hope is in God	Bagge.
Spes et fides	Hope and faith	Chamberlain.
Spes et fortuna	Hope and fortune	Chelmsford.
Spes in extremum	Hope in extremity	Short.
Spes juvat	Hope delights	Kollands, Rolland.
Spes lucis æternæ	The hope of eternal life	Pitcairn.
Spes mea Christus	Christ is my hope	Bingham.
Spes mea Christus erit	Christ will be my hope	Powell.
Spes mea Deus	God is my hope	O'Ferral.
Spes mea in cœlis	My hope is in Heaven	Boyd.
Spes mea in Deo	My hope is in God	Blewitt, Brooke, Dewhurst, Goskar, Lethbridge, Roper,
Spes mea, res mea	My hope, my estate	Drummond.
Spes mea superné	My hope is from above	Bruce.
Spes melioris ævi	The hope of a better age	Rees.
Spes meum solatium	Hope is my consolation	Cushney.
Spes, salus, decus	Hope, safety, honour	Nesham.
Spes tamen infracta	Yet hope is unbroken	Hope.
Spes tutissima cœlis	The safest hope is in Heaven	King, Price.
Spes ultra	Hope is beyond	Nairn, Nairne.
Spes vitæ melioris	The hope of a better life	Broughton, Hobhouse.
Spe tutiores armis	Safer with hope than with arms	Lewis, Lewys.
Spe verus	True in hope	Scott.
Spe vires augentur	Strength is increased by hope	Black, Scott.
Spe vivitur	Lives on hope	Dobree, Dorrel.
Spiritûs gladius	The sword of the Spirit	Hutton.
Splendeo tritus	I shine by being rubbed	Ferrers.
Sponti favus, ægro spicula	Honey to the willing, thorns to the unwilling	Suttie.
S'rioghal mo dhream	My race is royal	Greg, M'Alpin, Macgregor, M'Gregor.
Stabit	He shall stand	Grant.
Stabo	I shall stand	Accorne, Hawthorne, Kinnimond.
Standard		Kidder.
Stand fast		Grant, Grant-Ogilvie.
Stand sure		Adson, Anderson, Crechton, Glenelg, Grant, Ponton.
Stans cum rege	Standing with the king	Chadwick.
Stant cætera tigno	The rest stand on a beam	Gordon.
Stant innixa Deo	They stand depending upon God	Crawford, Crawfurd.
Stare super vias antiquas	To pursue the track of my ancestors	Bayning, Powlett, Townshend.
Stat felix amico Domino	His happiness is established under the favour of the Lord	Steuart, Stewart.
Stat fortuna domûs	The good fortune of the house stands	Guy, Howes, Howse.
Stat promissa fides	Promised faith abides	Leslie, Lesly.
Stat religione parentum	Stands in the religion of parents	Lucas.
Stat veritas	Truth stands	Sandeman.
St Domingo		Louis.
Steady		Aylmer, Dalrymple, Hood, MacAdam, M'Adam, Weller, Yonge.
Steer steady		Donaldson.
Stemmata quid faciunt?	What value is pedigree?	Meyrick.
Stet	Stand	Standbridge.
Still bydand		Gordon.
Still without fear		Sutherland.
Stimulat, sed ornat	It stimulates, but it adorns	MacCartney, M'Cartnay, Mackartney.
Strength		Armstrong.
Strength is from heaven		Grubb.

Strenue et prospere	Strenuously and prosperously	Eamer.
Strenue insequor	I follow strenuously	Luke.
Strike		Hawke, Mundell.
Strike alike		Lauder.
Strike, Dakyns, the devil's in the hempe		Dakyns.
Strike sure		Grieg.
Sto, cado fide et armis	I stand by faith, and fall by arms	Farquhar, Farquhar-Gray.
Sto mobilis	I stand movable	Drummond.
Sto pro fide	I stand on account of faith	MacFarquhar.
Sto pro veritate	I stand on account of truth	Guthrie, Guthry.
Struggle		Brise-Ruggles.
Studendo et contemplando inde fessus	Wearied by study and contemplation	Cardale.
Studiis et rebus honestis	By learning and virtue	Dunning.
Study quiet		Head, Patrick.
St Vincent		Waldgrave.
Sue præmia virtus	Virtue is its own reward	M'Cartney.
Suaviter et fortiter	Mildly and firmly	Elliot, Elliott, Kynynmound.
Suaviter in modo, fortiter in re	Mildly in manner, boldly in action	Nunn, Rathbone, Wynn.
Suaviter sed fortiter	Mildly but firmly	Busk.
Sub cruce candidâ	Under the white cross	Arden, Perceval, Percival.
Sub cruce candor	Sincerity under the cross	Perceval.
Sub cruce glorior	I glory under the cross	Astell.
Sub cruce salus	Salvation by the cross	Bangor, Fletcher, Ward.
Sub cruce veritas	Truth under the cross	Adams.
Sub cruce vinces	Under the cross you shall conquer	Norwood.
Subditus fidelis regis et salus regni	A subject faithful to his king is the safety of the kingdom	Carlos.
Sub hoc signo vinces	Under this sign you shall conquer	Vassey.
Subito	Hastily	Cringan, Crinan.
Sub libertate quietem	Rest under liberty	Burrell, Cay, Kay, Keay, Walsham.
Sublime petimus	We ask for heaven	Cleghorn.
Sublimia cures	Care for high things	Bowman.
Sublimiora petamus	Let us aim at loftier things	Biddulph, Stonehouse.
Sublimiora peto	I seek higher things	Jackson.
Sub montibus altis	Under high mountains	Skeen.
Sub pace, copia	In peace, plenty	Francklyn, Franco.
Sub pondere cresco	I increase under weight	Fleeming.
Sub pondere sursum	In difficulty I look upward	Porterfield.
Sub robore virtus	Virtue under strength	Aikman.
Sub sole nihil	All below the sun is nothing	Monteith.
Sub sole patebit	He shall be exposed under the sun	Ellies.
Sub sole, sub umbrâ, crescens	Increasing both in sunshine and in shade	Irvine, Irving.
Sub sole, sub umbrâ, virens	Flourishing both in sunshine and in shade	Irvine, Irving, Irwine.
Sub sole viresco	I increase under the sun	Irvine.
Sub spe	In hope	Cairns, Dunbar.
Sub tegmine	Under covert	Gordon.
Sub tegmine fagi	Under the covert of the beech	Beech.
Sub tutelâ Domini	Under the protection of God	Spode.
Sub umbrâ alarum tuarum	Under the shadow of thy wings	Lauder, Lawder.
Sub umbrâ quiescam	I will rest under the shade	Fairn.
Successus a Deo est	Success comes from God	Roberts.
Suffer		Gleneagles, Hadden, Haldane, Halden.
Suffibulatus majores sequor	Harnessed I imitate my ancestors	Hathorn, Stewart.
Sufficit meruisse	It is enough to have deserved	Plumtree.
Sui oblitus commodi	Forgetful of his own interest	Asgile, Asgill.
Suivez la raison	Let reason be your guide	Armistead, Barberie, Barberrie, Brown, Browne.
Suivez moi	Follow me	Borough.
Summum nec metuam diem nec optem	Let me neither fear nor wish for the last day	Tighe.
Sum quod sum	I am what I am	Coldicott, Foresight.
Sunt aliena	They are foreign	Fust.
Sunt sua præmia laude	His rewards are with praise	Barberrie, Brown, Pemberton
Suo se robore firmat	He strengthens himself by his own might	Grant.

Suo stat robore virtus	Virtue stands in its own strength	Mowbray.
Superabit omnia virtus	Virtue will conquer all	Rabett.
Supera audi et tace	Hear celestial things and keep silence	Hesse.
Superb		Keats.
Superba frango	I humble the proud	Macklellan, MacLagan, M'Lagan.
Superiora sequor	I follow higher things	Ramsay.
Superna sequor	I follow heavenly things	Ramsay, Wardrop.
Super sidera votum	My desires extend beyond the stars	Rattray.
Supra spem spero	I hope against hope	Jeffreys.
Suprema quæro	I seek the highest	Greaves.
Sure		Macdonald.
Sure and steadfast		Martin.
Sur espérance	Upon hope	Moir, Moncrief, Moncrieff, Moncrieffe.
Surgam	I shall rise	Hutchison.
Surgere tento	I strive to rise	Straton.
Surgite, lumen adest	Arise, the light is near	Glover.
Surgit post nubila Phœbus	After clouds, sunshine arises	Constable.
Surgo, lumen adest	I arise, light is here	Lawson.
Sursum	Upward	Alston, Calandrine, Douglas, Hutcheson, Hutchison, Kilner, Pringle, Roos, Rosse.
Sursum corda	Hearts upward	Howison.
Sustentatus Providentiâ	Upheld by providence	Rolland.
Sustento sanguine signa	I bear the standards with blood	Seaton.
Sustine, abstine	Sustain, forbear	Gairden.
Sustineatur	Let him be sustained	Cullum.
Sustineo sanguine signum	I keep the standard in the midst of blood	Seton.
Suum cuique	To every one his own	Bickersteth, Don, Every, Grant, Wingate.
Syn ar dy hûn	Wonder at thyself	Dewing.
Syn ar du hun		Wilkins-Cann.

T

Tace	Keep silence	Abercromby.
Tace aut face	Keep silence, or act	Scot, Scott.
Tache sans tache	Spot without spot	Carnagie, Carnegie, Carnegy-Watson, Patterson.
Tak tent	Take heed	Crockat, Crockatt.
Tam animo quam mente sublimis	Exalted in soul as in mind	Forteath.
Tam arte, quam marte	As well by art as strength	Mill, Milne, M'Lea, Wright.
Tam fidus, quam fixus	As well faithful as firm	Stewart.
Tam genus, quam virtus	Lineage as well as virtue	Lunden.
Tam in arte, quam marte	Both in skill and in force	Milne.
Tam interna, quam externa	As well internal as external	Arburthnet, Arbuthnot.
Tam virtus, quam honos	As well virtue as honour	Hamilton.
Tam virtute, quam labore	As well by virtue as labour	
Tandem	At length	Cunningham, Cunninghame, Finnie.
Tandem fit arbor	At length it becomes a tree	Hamilton.
Tandem fit surculus arbor	At length the sprig becomes a tree	Burnet, Douglas.
Tandem implebitur	At length he shall be filled	Scougal, Simpson.
Tandem licet sero	It is allowed at length, but late	Campbell.
Tandem tranquillus	Tranquil at length	Symmer.
Tanquam despicatus sum, vinco	Though I am despised, I conquer	Grant.
Tanti talem gentrere parentes	So mighty parents produced such a noble man	Moray.
Tant que je puis	Such as I can	Hilton, Joliffe, Lawson.
Tantum in superbos	Only against the proud	Jacob.
Te Deum laudamus	We praise thee, O God	Harper, M'Whirter.

Te duce, gloriamur...............	*We glory under thy guidance* ...	Sinclair.
Te duce, libertas	*Liberty under thy guidance*	Crosby.
Te favente, virebo...............	*I shall flourish, thou favouring me*..	Grant.
Teg. Yw. Hedwsh	*Peace is pleasing*.....................	Gilbert.
Teipsum nosce....................	*Know thyself*	Shaw.
Téméraire...........................	*Rash*......................................	Harvey.
Temperat æquor	*The sea is calm*	Monypenny.
Templa quam delecta...........	*How beloved are the temples*.......	Brydges, Grenville, Temple.
Tempore candidior...............	*Become fairer by time*...............	Mair.
Tempus meæ opes................	*Time is my wealth*	Spofforth.
Tempus omnia monstrat.......	*Time shows all*.......................	Lovell.
Tenax in fide	*Steadfast in the faith*...............	Smith.
Tenax et fide	*Persevering and with faith*........	Smith.
Tenax et fidelis	*Persevering and faithful*	Abdy, Smith, Tennant.
Tenax prepositi...................	*Be firm to your purpose*............	Gibbes, Gibbs, Gilbert.
Tenax propositi, vinco...........	*Firm in resolve, I conquer*.........	Grimshaw.
Tendens ad æthera virtus......	*Virtue tending to the sky*..........	Lewthwaite.
Tendimus...........................	*We push forward*.....................	Craik.
Tendit ad astra....................	*He goes towards heaven*.............	Maxwell.
Tendit ad astra fides.............	*Faith extends to heaven*............	Burn, Burne.
Teneat, luceat, floreat, vi, virtute, et valore...............	*Let it hold, shine, and flourish, by strength, courage, and valour*...	Kenney.
Tenebo	*I will hold*	Warren.
Tenebris lux.......................	*Light in darkness*...................	Scot.
Teneo, tenuere majores.........	*I maintain, my ancestors have maintained*	Twemlow.
Tenes le vraye	*Keep the truth*........................	Townley.
Tenez le droit	*Keep the right*.	Clifton, Wilkinson.
Tentanda via est	*The way is to be tried*..............	Peckham, Stronge, Wildman.
Tentando superabis	*You will conquer by trying*.......	Kingdom.
Tenuimus...........................	*We have held*.........................	Lockett,
Te pro te............................	*Thee for thee*.........................	Savage.
Terra, aqua, ignis, sal, spiritus, sulphur, Sol, Venus, Mercurius.........................	*Land, water, fire, salt, spirit, sulphur, Sun, Venus, Mercury*	Irvine.
Terrâ, mare, fide.................	*By the earth, sea, and faith*.......	Campbell.
Terra marique fides..............	*Faith by land and sea*...............	Campbell.
Terrâ marique potens	*Valiant by sea and land*............	O'Malley.
Terrena pericula sperno	*I despise earthly dangers*...........	Ogilvy.
Terrena per vices sunt aliena	*Earthly things change hands*......	Fust.
Terrere nolo, timere nescio...	*I will not affright, and know not to fear*	Dering.
Te splendente.....................	*Thou being illustrious*...............	Carstairs.
Te stante virebo..................	*I shall flourish, while you remain*	Temple.
The cross our stay		Parkhouse.
The grit poul......................		Mercer.
The noblest motive is the public good		Bantry, White.
The reward of valour............		Moodie, Moody.
The strongest arm uppermost		Stafford.
The strongest hand uppermost		Kennedy.
They by permission shine		Murray.
Think and thank		Ailesbury, Brudenell, M'Lellan, Montefiore.
Think on		Macklellan, M'Lellan, Maxwell, Ross.
Think well.........................		Erskine.
This I'll defend..................		Dorward, Durnard, Macfarlane, MacPharlane, M'Farlin, M'Pharlin.
This is our chart		Charteris.
This is our charter..............		Chartres, Wemyss-Charteris Douglas.
Thou shalt want ere I want...		Cranstoun.
Through............................		Beckford, Hamilton.
Through God revived...........		Hamilton.
Thure et jure	*By frankincense and right*........	Foulis.
Thurst on		Thurston.
Thus.................................		Jervis-Ricketts.
Thus far		Campbell.

Motto	Translation	Names
Thysrscrysough ne Dieu a nef		Tremenheere.
Tien le droit	Maintain the right	Clench.
Tiens à la vérité	Stick to the truth	Blaquier, De Blaquiere, Hoffman, Lewthwait, Lewthwaite.
Tiens ferme	Hold fast	Squire.
Tien ta foy	Keep thy faith	Bathurst, Giberne.
Time Deum	Fear God	Monro, Ross.
Timet pudorem	He dreads shame	Burton, Dawnay.
Time tryeth troth		Trevelyan.
Timor Domini fons vitæ	The fear of the Lord is the fountain of life	Butler.
Timor omnis abest	All fear is absent	Craigie.
Timor omnes abesto	Let fear be far from all	Craigge, Craigie, Craigy, Macnab, M'Nab.
Touch not the cat, bot the glove		Gillies, MacPherson, M'Gilleray.
Touch not the cat, but a glove		Gillespie, Mackintosh, M'Bean, M'Combie, M'Crombie, M'Intosh.
Touch not the cat without a glove		M'Gilevray.
Toujours ferme	Always firm	Heneage.
Toujours fidèle	Always faithful	Bladen, Garde, Gillis, Goodall, Grant-Macpherson, Hairstanes, Harestans, Hickman, Holford, Macbean, M'Bean, Mercier, Mill, Proctor-Beauchamp, Waters.
Toujours gai	Always lively	Gay.
Toujours jeune	Always young	Young.
Toujours le même	Always the same	Tait.
Toujours loyal	Always loyal	Sackville, Perkins.
Toujours prêt	Always ready	Donald, Hawkins, Macdonald, M'Connell, Meade, Petley, Phelps, Pigott, Smyth.
Toujours prest		Carmichael, MacDonel, Meade, Prest.
Toujours propice	Always propitious	Dawson.
Tous jours loyal	Always loyal	Fenwick.
Tout bien ou rien	The whole good, or none	Barham, Noel.
Tout d'enhaut	All from above	Bellew, Bellew-Dillon, Whitford.
Tout droit	All right	Carling, Carre, Ker.
Tout en bonne heure	All in good time	Hicks.
Tout est d'en haut	All is from above	Whilford.
Tout fin fait	Every contrivance serves	St Hill.
Tout foitz chevalier	Always a knight	Rideout.
Tout hardi	Quite bold	Hardie, M'Hardie.
Tout jour	Always	Ogilvie.
Tout jours prest	Always ready	Anstruther, Carmichael, Donald, Sutton.
Tout pour Dieu et ma patrie	All for God and my country	Winn.
Tout pourvoir	To provide for everything	Oliphant.
Tout prest	Quite ready	Murray.
Tout ung durant ma vie	All one during my life	Barrington.
Tout vient de Dieu	All from God	Leigh, Trefusis.
Traditus, non victus	Yielded not conquered	Cardoc, Cradock.
Traducere ævum leniter	To pass life gently	Browne.
Tramite recto	By a right path	Roe.
Transfigam	I shall pierce	Colt, Coult.
Trial by jury		Erskine.
Triumpho morte tam vita	I triumph in death as well as in life	Allen.
Troimh chrudal	Through hardships	M'Intyre.
Trop hardi	Too bold	Hardie.
True		Bruce, Home-Everard.
True as the dial to the sun		Hyndman.
True to the end		Campbell, Ferguson, Foreman, Forman, Home, Hume, Orr.
Trustie and bydand		Leith.

Trust in God		Hardness, Husdell.
Trusty and true		Scot.
Trusty to the end		Leith.
Truth and liberty		Tylden.
Truth prevails		Gordon.
Truth will prevail		M'Kenzie, Mackenzie.
Try		Gethin, O'Hara, Parker.
Try and tryst		Clark.
Tu digna sequere	Follow thou worthy things	Knight.
Tu Domine gloria mea	Thou, O Lord, art my glory	Leicester.
Tuebor	I will defend	Bying.
Tuemur	We can defend	Higgins.
Tueris tutissime virtus	Thou, Virtue, defendest me most safely	Carlyon.
Tulloch ard	The high hill	M'Kenzie.
Tum pace, quam prælio	As well in peace as in war	Gordon.
Tu ne cede malis	Yield not to misfortunes	Amery, Damer, Riddock, Steere, Tourner, Turner.
Tu ne cede malis, sed contra audentior ito	Yield not thou to misfortunes, but march boldly against them	Cooke.
Turpiter desperatur	Despair is base	Hall.
Turris fortis mihi Deus	God is a strong tower to me	Clugstone, M'Guarrie, Macquaire, Peter.
Turris fortissima Deus	God is a most strong tower	Torre.
Turris fortitudinis	The tower of fortitude	Mansfield.
Turris prudentia custos	Prudence is the sentinel of a tower	Lauder.
Tutantur tela coronam	Weapons protect the crown	Tisdall.
Tutamen Deus	God is a defence	Bent.
Tutela	Protection	Lyle.
Tutemur	Let us defend	Higgins.
Tute tua tuta	Your safe things safely	Robison.
Tuto, celeriter, et jucunde	Safely, quickly, and pleasantly	Sutton.
Tuto et celeriter	Safely and quickly	Penrice.
Tutum te robore reddam	I will give you safety by strength	Crauford, Crawford, Hinde, Murray.
Tutum te littore robore sistam		
Tutum refugium	A safe refuge	Gillon, Gullon.
Tutum monstrat iter	He showeth a safe road	Cook.
Tutus in undis	Safe amid the waves	Wood.
Tutus prompto animo	Safe by a ready mind	Welsted.
Tutus si fortis	Safe, if brave	Fairborne, Raeburn, Reaburn.
Tuum est	It is thine	Cowper.
Tyde what may		Haig, Haige.
Tyme proveth truth		Adlam.
Tyrii tenuere coloni	It was possessed by Tyrian colonists	M'Lauren.

U

Ubi amor, ibi fides	Where there is love there is fidelity	Duckenfield, Newman.
Ubi lapsus? Quid feci?	Where have I fallen? What have I done?	Courtenay.
Ubi libertas, ibi patria	Where there is liberty, there is my country	Beverley, Dinwiddie, Hugar, Huger.
Ubique aut nusquam	Everywhere or nowhere	Whitefoord.
Ubique fidelis	Everywhere faithful	Hamilton.
Ubique paratus	Everywhere prepared	Fraser, Frazer.
Ubique patriam reminisci	To remember your country everywhere	Harris.
Ulterius	Farther	Durham.
Ultra aspicio	I look farther	Melville, Melvine.
Ultra fert animus	My mind carries me farther	Durham.
Ultra pergere	To advance farther	Copley.
Unalterable		Sleigh.
Un Dieu, un roi	One God, one king	D'Arcy, Lyttleton.
Un Dieu, un roy, un cœur	One God, one king, one heart	Lake.
Un Dieu, un roy, un foy	One God, one king, one faith	Curle.
Un durant ma vie	The same while I live	Barrington.
Un tout seul	One alone	Verney.

Une pure foy	One pure faith	Hewett.
Une stay	A barrier	Lang.
Une foy mesme	One and the same faith	Gilpin.
Ung Dieu et ung roy	One God and one king	Littleton, Lyttleton.
Ung je serviray	I will serve one	Fitz-Herbert, Herbert.
Ung roy, ung foy, ung loy	One king, one faith, one law	Burke, De Burgh, De Burgho, De Burgo.
Uni æquus virtuti	Friendly to virtue alone	Grenville, Murray.
Unica spes mea Christus	Christ is my only hope	Dishington.
Unica virtus necessaria	Virtue alone is necessary	Colley.
Unione augetur	It is increased by union	Miller.
Unite		Brodie, Brody.
Unus et idem	One and the same	Liddell.
Usque ad aras	Even at the altars	Campbell.
Usque ad mortem fidus	Faithful even to death	Ward.
Usque fac et non parcas	E'en do and spare not	Peter.
Usque fidelis	Everywhere faithful	Napier.
Ut amnis vita labitur	Life glides away like a river	Brooks.
Ut apes, geometricam	As bees, geometry	Petty.
Ut crescit, clarescit	As it increases, it becomes famous	Anderson, Menzies.
Utcunque placuit Deo	Howsoever God pleases	How, Howe.
Ut deficiar	That I may be destitute	Auchinleck.
Utile dulci	The useful to the pleasant	Spedding.
Utile et dulce	Useful and agreeable	Riddell.
Ut implear	That I may be filled	Mikieson.
Utitur ante quæsitis	He uses former acquisitions	Draghorn, Dreghorn.
Ut migraturus habita	As if about to remove my possessions	Lauder.
Ut olim	As formerly	Kinloch, Kinlock.
Ut palma justus	The just like a palm	Palmes.
Ut possim	That I can	Livingston.
Ut prosim	That I may be of use	Foley, Greenwood.
Ut prosim aliis	That I may profit others	Clerke-Jennings, Greenwood.
Ut quocunque paratus	As everywhere prepared	Lambart, Lambert.
Utráque pallade	By each art	Bendyshe.
Ut reficiar	That I may be refreshed	Archibald.
Ut resurgam	That I may rise again	Penniecook, Pennycook, Pennycuick.
Utrius auctus auxilio	Increasing by the help of both	Rankine.
Utriusque auxilio	By the help of both	Spottiswood.
Ut sanem vulnero	I wound in order to heal	Holt.
Ut se crescit, clarescit	He grows illustrious as he increases	Anderson.
Ut sim paratior	That I may be the more ready	Clepan, Clepham, Clephan.
Ut sursum desuper	Descend to ascend	Worseley, Worsley.
Ut tibi sic aliis	As to thee so to others	Hussey.
Ut tibi sic alteri	As I do to thee, so will I do to others	Bowles, Pemberton-Leigh.

V

Vade ad formicam	Go to the ant	Anketell.
Væ victis	Woe to the conquered	Senhouse.
Vaillance avance l'homme	Valour advances the man	Acton.
Valebit	Shall prevail	Lysons.
Valens et volens	Able and willing	Fetherstonhaugh.
Valet anchora virtus	Virtue is a sheet anchor	Gardner.
Valet et vulnerat	It heals and wounds	Hay.
Valor et fortuna	Valour and fortune	Rollo.
Valor et lealdade	Valour and loyalty	Croft.
Vana spes vitæ	Vain hope of life	Paul.
Vanus est honor	Honour is vain	Bowdon.
Vectis	A lever	Holmes.
Vel arte vel marte	Either by art or by strength	Baines.
Velle bene facere	To wish to do well	Curtis.
Vellera fertis oves	You sheep carry fleeces	Elliot, Elliott.
Vellient et vaillant	Wise and valiant	Erskine.
Velocitate	With velocity	Carse.
Vel pax, vel bellum	Either peace or war	Fraser, Frazer, Gordon, Gunn
Venabulis vinco	I conquer with hunting spears	Venables.

Venale nec auro	Not to be bribed	Jervis-White.
Venit ab astris	He came from heaven	Keith.
Venit hora	The hour has come	Hoare.
Ventis secundis	By favourable winds	Hood, Rowley.
Venture and gain		Hay, Wilson.
Venture forward		Bruce.
Verax atque probus	Truthful and honest	Ruttledge.
Veritas	Truth	Eiston, Wirgman.
Veritatis assertor	Assertor of truth	Niblett.
Veritas ingenio	Truth with wit	Gordon.
Veritas liberabit	Truth shall make free	Bodenham.
Veritas liberavit	Truth has made free	Slingsby.
Veritas magna est	Truth is great	Jephson.
Veritas me dirigat	Let truth direct me	Brocklehurst.
Veritas odit mos	Truth hates	Parry.
Veritas omnia vincit	Truth conquers all things	Kedslie, Kidslie.
Veritas prematur, non oppramitur	Truth may be kept down, but not entirely overwhelmed	Calderwood.
Veritas superabit	Truth shall prevail	Hill.
Veritas superabit montes	Truth shall cross mountains	Hill.
Veritas vincit	Truth conquers	French, Geddes, Geddies, Keith.
Veritatem	Truth	Tatham.
Verite sans peur	Truth without fear	Gunning, Hemans, Willoughby.
Vernon semper viret	Vernon always flourishes	Vernon.
Vero nihil verius	Truth, nothing but truth	Devere, Hunt, Vere, Weir.
Versus	Towards	Peters.
Vertitur in diem	It is changed into day	Farquhar.
Vertitur in lucem	It is changed into light	Baillie.
Vertue vauncet	Virtue prevails	Verney.
Verum atque decorus	True and decent	Browne, Lee.
Verus ad finem	True to the end	Deuchar, Lizars, Peters.
Verus amor patriæ	True love of country	Hughes.
Verus et fidelis semper	Always true and faithful	Aylward.
Vescitur Christo	Feeds on Christ	Rous.
Vespere et mane	In the evening and morning	Pierie, Pourie, Powrie, Purie.
Vestigia nulla restrorsum	There is no going back	Baily, Hampden, Levinge.
Via crucis via lucis	The way of the cross is the way of light	Sinclair.
Via trita via tuta	The beaten way is the safe way	Agar.
Via una, cor unum	One way, one heart	Hart, M'Corda.
Vici	I have conquered	Raines.
Vicisti et vivimus	Thou hast conquered, and we live	Johnson.
Vicit, pepercit	He conquered, he spared	Draper.
Victor	Conqueror	James, Linskill.
Victoria	Victory	Conqueror.
Victoriam concordia crescit	Concord insures victory	Amherst.
Victoriam coronat Christus	Christ crowns victory	Campbell.
Victoria non præda	Victory, not booty	Durham, Sandilands.
Victoria signum	Victory is the sign	Taylor.
Victoria vel mors	Victory or death	Macdonald, M'Donall, M'Dowall, M'Dowgal.
Victor in arduis	A conqueror in arduous things	M'Connel.
Victrix fortunæ sapientia	Wisdom the conqueror of fortune	Andrew, Calthorp.
Victrix patientia	Patience is victorious	Gordon.
Victus in arduis	Conquered in difficulties	Harrison.
Video alta sequorque	I see and follow high things	Carnagie.
Video et taceo	I see and hold my peace	Fox.
Video meliora	I see better things	Montefiore.
Viditque Deus hanc lucem esse bonam	And God saw the light that it was good	Rundle.
Vidi, vici	I have seen, I have conquered	Seurfield, Twiselton, Twiselton.
Vi divinâ	By divine force	Pearse.
Vi et armis	By force and arms	Armstrong.
Vi et animo	By strength and courage	Hankinson, M'Culloch.
Vi et arte	By strength and art	Chisholm, Ferguson, Stevens.
Vi et fide	By force and faith	Campbell.
Vi et industriâ	By strength and industry	Falconer.
Vi et veritate	By force and by truth	Sloan.

Vi et virtute	By strength and valour	Baird, Bolton, Brown, Chisholme, Hunt, M'Taggart, Smart, Spraight.
Viget in cinere virtus	Virtue survives death	Davidson, Gray.
Viget sub cruce	He flourishes under the cross	Colquhoun.
Vigila et ora	Watch and pray	Wake, Rogers.
Vigilance		Laing.
Vigilando	By watching	M'Leod.
Vigilando quiesco	I rest by watchfulness	Tredcorft, Tredcroft.
Vigilans	Watchful	Kadwell, Mathisson, Smith, Taylor, Wolstonecraft.
Vigilans et audax	Watchful and bold	Cockburn, Currie, Currie, Dunn.
Vigilans non cadit	Watching, he does not fall	Calder.
Vigilant		Laing.
Vigilante salus	Safety by watching	Cochran, Cochrane.
Vigilanter	Vigilantly	Wegg.
Vigilantia	Vigilance	Aird, Ard, Carfrae, Tod.
Vigilantiâ et virtute	By vigilance and valour	Porter.
Vigilantiâ non cadet	By watching he shall not fall	Cadell.
Vigilantia, robur, voluptas	Vigilance, strength, pleasure	Blair, Hunter.
Vigilantibus	By the watchful	Acheson, Aitcheson, Aitchison, Atchison, Briston, Gosford.
Vigilantiâ securitas	Security by watching	Phine.
Vigilate	Watch ye	Alcock, Edwardes, Gael, Leeds.
Vigilate et orate	Watch and pray	Hancock, Handcock.
Vigilat et orat	He watches and prays	Fennison.
Vigilo	I watch	Desse, Gregson, May, M'Haddo, M'Hado.
Vigilo et spero	I watch and hope	Daunt, Galbraith, Tivitoe.
Vigueur de dessus	Strength from above	Braidwood, O'Brien, O'Bryen.
Vigueur l'amour de croix	The love of the cross gives strength	Darnel.
Vim vi repellere licet	May repel force by force	Gwyn.
Vincam vel moriar	Conquest or death	Benyor, M'Dowal, M'Dowall.
Vince fide	Conquer by faith	Parry.
Vince malum bono	Overcome evil with good	Robinson, Johnes, Jones.
Vince malum patentiâ	Overcome evil by patience	Townshend.
Vincendo victus	Conquered in conquering	Ley.
Vincenti dabitur	It shall be given to the conqueror	Vincent.
Vincere	To conquer	M'Coul.
Vincere vel mori	To conquer or die	Macneil, M'Dowall, M'Dowal, M'Dougal, M'Gougan, M'Lea, M'Neil, M'Nelly, M'Oul, M'Owl, Tibbet.
Vincet virtute	Shall conquer by virtue	Smart.
Vincit amor patriæ	The love of my country prevails	Gun, Molesworth, Pelham, Pennington, James.
Vincit cum legibus arma	He shall repress violence with laws	Atkins, Atkyns.
Vincit labor	Labour overcomes	Campbell.
Vincit omnia veritas	Truth overcomes all things	De Courcy, Eaton, Goodchild, Laffan.
Vincit pericula virtus	Virtue overcomes dangers	Thornton, Maine.
Vincit qui curat	He overcomes who is cautious	White.
Vincit qui patitur	He conquers who endures	Ashurst, Chester, Colt, Gildea, Harrison, Homfrey, Llewellyn, Llewellen Shaw, Smerdon.
Vincit qui se vincit	He conquers who conquers himself	Ackworth, Ellis, Holland.
Vincit veritas	Truth prevails	Alison, Allison, Burn, Coote, Dickin, Gort, Hastings, Napier, Orpsen, O'Shee, Peacock, Shee, Vereker, Ward, Warde, Webster.
Vincit vigilantia	Watchfulness overcomes	Wright.
Vinculo temno	I despise bonds	Sinclair.
Virebo	I will become strong	Hamilton.
Vires agminis unus habet	One has the power of a regiment	Grylls.

Vires animat virtus............	*Virtue enlivens strength*............	Garden, Gairden.
Virescit...........................	*He flourishes*.....................	Moncrief, Stewart.
Virescit in arduis virtus........	*Virtue grows by means of hardships*.....................	Keir.
Virescit virtus...................	*Virtue increases*...................	Jackson.
Virescit vulnere.................	*He grows strong by being wounded*	Stewart.
Virescit vulnere virtus.........	*Virtue, when wounded, flourishes.*	Brownrigg, Burnet, Burnett, Foot, Galloway, Ker, Stewart.
Viresco...........................	*I become green*.....................	Greenless, Monteith, Smellet, Smollet, Stewart, Tailefer.
Viresco et surgo.................	*I flourish and revive*..............	Maxwell.
Vires in arduis...................	*Strength in difficulties*............	MacBain.
Vires veritas.....................	*Truth is power*.....................	Kennedy.
Viridis et fructifera.............	*Flourishing and bearing fruit*...	Hamilton.
Viridis semper....................	*Always green*......................	Mathison.
Virtue.............................		Ferguson.
Virtue mine honour..............		Maclean, M'Clean, M'Clen.
Virtus acquirit honorem........	*Virtue procures honour*............	Spence.
Virtus ad æthera tendit........	*Virtue tends towards heaven*......	Balfour, Cairns.
Virtus ad astra...................	*Virtue to the sky*...................	Innes.
Virtus ad sidera tollit	*Virtue exalts to the stars*	Wilson.
Virtus ariete fortior	*Virtue is stronger than a battering-ram*....................	Bertie.
Virtus astra petit................	*Virtue seeks the sky*	Vandeleur.
Virtus auget honorem..........	*Virtue increases honour*............	Edmonstone, Spence.
Virtus basis vitæ.................	*Virtue is the support of life*.......	Jerningham.
Virtus castellum meum........	*Virtue is my fortress*...............	Bence.
Virtus curâ servabit.............	*Virtue shall preserve by care*......	Browne.
Virtus dabit, cura servabit....	*Virtue shall give, care shall preserve*.....................	Brown.
Virtus dedit, cura servabit ...	*Virtue has given, discretion will preserve*...................	Browne.
Virtus dum patior vincit......	*Virtue overcomes, while I suffer*...	Weems.
Virtus durat avorum............	*The virtue of ancestry remains*...	Seton.
Virtus durissima ferret.........	*Virtue sustains the most severe trials*.......................	M'Lean.
Virtus est Dei....................	*Virtue is God-like*.................	Briggs, Brooke.
Virtus et industria..............	*Virtue and industry*...............	Browne.
Virtus et nobilitas...............	*Virtue and nobility*................	Henvill.
Virtus in actione consistit.....	*Virtue consists in action*...........	Clayton, Craven, Sier.
Virtus in arduis..................	*Valour in difficulties*	Cockain, Cokaine, Cokayne, Gammon, Macqueen.
Virtus in caducis.................	*Virtue in adversity*	M'Dowal.
Virtus incendit vires...........	*Valour exerts strength*.............	Smythe.
Virtus incumbet honori........	*Virtue will rest upon honour*......	Williams.
Virtus insignat audentes.......	*Virtue distinguishes the bold*.....	Beamish-Bernard.
Virtus invecta gloriosa.........	*Unconquered virtue is glorious*....	Thomas.
Virtus invidiæ scopus	*Virtue a mark for envy*............	Methuen, Methven.
Virtus laudanda..................	*Virtue is praiseworthy*.............	Paton, Patton.
Virtus, laus, actio...............	*Virtue, praise, exploit*.............	Frazer.
Virtus maturat...................	*Virtue ripens*......................	Riddel, Riddell.
Virtus mihi scutum	*Virtue, be thou my shield*.........	Warren.
Virtus mille scuta...............	*Virtue is a thousand shields*	Howard, Dayrel.
Virtus nobilitat...................	*Virtue ennobles*	Boyd, Henderson.
Virtus omnia nobilitat	*Virtue ennobles all*................	Herrick.
Virtus omnia vincit.............	*Virtue conquers all*................	White.
Virtus non veritur...............	*Virtue does not fear*...............	Sarsfield.
Virtus patrimonio nobilior....	*Virtue is more noble than patrimony*......................	Salusbury.
Virtus parit robur...............	*Virtue yields strength*..............	Richardson.
Virtus post facta.................	*Virtue after exploits*...............	Borthwick.
Virtus præ numina..............	*Virtue is preferable to power*......	Price.
Virtus præstantior auro	*Virtue more excellent than gold*..	Severene, Whieldon.
Virtus probata florebit.........	*Proved virtue will flourish*........	Bernard, Bernard-Beamish.
Virtus propter se.................	*Virtue for its own sake*............	Radcliffe, Repington.
Virtus Pyramidis.................	*Virtue of the Pyramid*............	Kinchant.
Virtus repulsæ nescia sordidæ	*Virtue that knows not mean repulse*.......................	Cuffe, Laurie.
Virtus semper eadem...........	*Virtue always the same*............	Turvile.
Virtus semper viridis...........	*Virtue is always flourishing*......	Corry, France, Green, Laurie, Lowry.

Virtus sibi præmium............	Virtue is its own reward............	Calderwood.
Virtus sine dote................	Virtue without a dowry............	Davies.
Virtus sine macula................	Virtue without a stain	Russell.
Virtus sola invicta................	Virtue alone unconquered	Eyre.
Virtus sola nobilitas...............	Virtue is the only nobility.........	Blake, Throckmorton.
Virtus sola nobilitat............	Virtue alone ennobles...............	Blake, Blakes, Henrieson, Henrison.
Virtus sub cruce crescit	Virtue grows under the cross......	Bury.
Virtus sub cruce crescit ad æthera tendens..............	Virtue increases under trial, and tends towards heaven.............	Bury.
Virtus triumphat................	Virtue triumphs......................	Church.
Virtus tutissima cassis.........	Virtue is the safest helmet.........	Barker, Finch-Hatton, Raymond, Stevenson, Willis.
Virtus ubique	Virtue everywhere	Stevenson, Verst.
Virtus vera nobilitas............	Virtue is true nobility...............	Henville.
Virtus vincit invidiam..........	Virtue overcomes envy...........,...	Clebborn, Cornwallis.
Virtus virtutis præmium......	Virtue is its own reward............	MacMoran, Macmorran, M'Moran.
Virtute.............................	By virtue.............................	Burnet, Burnett, Church, Cooper, Couper, Dick, Ferguson, Keane.
Virtute adepta.....................	Acquired by virtue..................	Paton.
Virtute acquiritur honos......	Honour is acquired by virtue......	Richardson, Richie, Ritchie, Spence.
Virtute avorum.....................	By the virtue of ancestors..........	Watkins.
Virtute cresco	I increase by virtue..................	Burnet, Forbes, Leask.
Virtute decoratus	Adorned with virtue...............	Glasscott.
Virtute dignus avorum.........	Worthy of the virtue of our ancestors.....................	Worthington.
Virtute doloque	By courage and policy............	Binning.
Virtute duce......................	Under the guidance of valour....	Elder, Sand, Shanan, Shand, Shannon.
Virtute duce, comite fortunâ	Under the guidance of valour, accompanied by good fortune...	Shand.
Virtute et amore................	By virtue and love.................	M'Kenzie.
Virtute et constantiâ	By courage and perseverance......	Auld.
Virtute et fide...................	By bravery and faith................	Harley, Lamb, Marriot.
Virtute et fidelitate.............	By bravery and fidelity.............	Beauvale, Blackie, Blaikie, Crofts, Goodsir, Reeves.
Virtute et fortunâ................	By virtue and fortune.......... ..	Andrew, Andrews, Gardner.
Virtute et honore...............	By virtue and honour...............	Baird, Blair, Wells.
Virtute et labore.................	By bravery and labour.............	Allanson, Cochran, Cochrane, Cunningham, Downfield, Heddle, M'Clintock, M'Lintock, Rig, Rigg, Winn.
Virtute et numine...............	By bravery and divine aid........	Lawless.
Virtute et operâ..................	By virtue and deeds	Bennie, Benny, Benzie, Bernie, Binnie, Binny, Duff, Harris.
Virtute et probitate............	By virtue and honesty	Magan.
Virtute et prudentiâ...........	By virtue and prudence............	Hepburn.
Virtute et robore................	By virtue and strength............	Pillans, Richardson.
Virtute et valore..................	By virtue and valour...............	Batt, Mackenzie, M'Kenzie, Noble, Peppard, Stamer.
Virtute et veritate............ ..	By virtue and truth.................	Blathwayt.
Virtute et votis..................	By virtue and vows...............	Neilson.
Virtute excerptæ	Conspicuous for virtue............	Cary.
Virtute fideque..................	By bravery and faith	M'Murray, Murray.
Virtute gloria parta.............	Renown is obtained by bravery...	Napier.
Virtutem coronat honos.......	Honour crowns virtue.............	Drummond.
Virtutem extendere fac........	Act so as to encourage virtue......	Fisher.
Virtute nihil invium............	No way is impassable to virtue...	Chamberlayne, Hillary.
Virtute, non aliter..............	By virtue, not otherwise............	Moir.
Virtute, non astutiâ	By bravery, not stratagem........	Clements, Pery, Whitbread.
Virtute, non ferociâ............	By bravery, not by cruelty.........	Forbes.
Virtute, non sanguine.........	By virtue, not by blood	Hayman, Hayward-Curtis.
Virtute, non verbis..............	By virtue, not by words............	Baxter, Coulthart, Fitz-Maurice, Petty, Robinson, Sawers.
Virtute, non vi..................	By virtue, not by force.............	Barneby, Berkeley, Chivas, Coppinger, Shivez.

Virtute, non viribus	By virtue, not by force	Derrick.
Virtute orta	Sprung from virtue	Stewart.
Virtute orta occidunt rarius	What is sprung from virtue rarely fails	Aiton.
Virtute parata	Prepared by virtue	Melville, Whytt.
Virtute parta	Produced by virtue	Haliday, Halliday, Hallyday, Melville - Whyte, White, Whytt.
Virtute parta tuemini	You defend what is obtained by valour	Blackwood, Peperpell.
Virtute promoveo	I prevail by virtue	Sideserf, Sydserfe.
Virtute promoves	You effect advancement by virtue	Sideserf, Sidserf.
Virtute quies	Rest through valour	Phipps.
Virtute securus	Secure by virtue	Maude.
Virtute sibi præmium	Let his reward be in virtue	Fenwick.
Virtute superanda fortuna	Fortune is to be overcome by virtue	Whiteford.
Virtute tutus	By virtue safe	Blair, Marshall, Mitchelson, Phaire.
Virtute vici	I have conquered by virtue	Meynell.
Virtute viget	He flourishes by virtue	Keirie, Paton.
Virtute vincit invidium	He overcomes calumny by virtue	Mann.
Virtute viresco	I flourish by virtue	Paterson.
Virtuti comes invidia	Envy companion to virtue	Cunninghame, Devereux.
Virtuti damnosa quies	Inactivity inimical to virtue	Brisbane.
Virtuti fido	I trust in virtue	Ap-Eynions.
Virtuti inimica quies	Inactivity is an enemy to virtue	Forbes.
Virtuti mœnia cedant	Fortifications may yield to bravery	Wilder.
Virtuti nihil invium	Nothing is inaccessible to virtue	Hillary.
Virtuti nihil obstat et armis	Nothing withstands virtue and arms	Stratford.
Virtuti, non armis fido	I trust to virtue, not to arms	Egerton.
Virtutis	Of virtue	Skeen.
Virtutis alimentum honos	Honour is the aliment of virtue	Parker.
Virtutis amore	By the love of virtue	Annesley, Stephens.
Virtutis avorum præmium	The reward of my ancestors' valour	Upton.
Virtutis comes invidia	Envy accompanies virtue	Devereux.
Virtutis fortuna comes	Fortune the companion of virtue	Ashtown, Ferguson, Gyll, Orr, Pomeroy, Stewart, Trench, Wellesley.
Virtutis gloria crescit	The glory of virtue increases	Tytler.
Virtutis gloria merces	Glory is the recompense of valour	Deuchar, Lorimer, M'Donagh, M'Donegh, M'Donogh, M'-Robertson, Robertson, Sandbach.
Virtutis in bello præmium	The reward of bravery in war	Robertson, Steuart.
Virtutis laus actio	Deeds are the praise of virtue	MacDougall, Rumbold, Tansley.
Virtutis præmium	Virtue's reward	Morton, Stewart.
Virtutis præmium honor	Honour is the reward of virtue	Hapsburgh, Percy-Fielding.
Virtutis regia merces	A palace the reward of bravery	Alpin, Feilden, Macgregor, Skeen, Skene.
Virtutis regio merces	A country the recompense of bravery	Blackadder, Duff.
Virtutis robore robor	Strong in virtue's strength	Dackcombe, Fielding.
Visa per invisa firma	Seen things established by unseen	Spence.
Vise à la fin	Aim at the end	Blackader, Home.
Vis et fides	Power and fidelity	Campbell.
Vis et virtus	Strength and courage	Chisalme.
Vis fortibus arma	Vigour is arms to brave men	Barton, Cruikshanks, Nisbett.
Vi si non consilio	By force, if not by contrivance	Sherbrooke.
Vis in vita Deus	God the strength in life	M'Connel.
Vis super hostem	Power over the enemy	O'Donovan.
Vis unita fortior	Power increased by union	Brooke, Flood, Hales, Hosken, Moore.
Vis viri fragilis	Weak is the strength of man	Lilborne, Lilburne, Ruddiman.
Vitæ faciendo nemini timeas	Fear no one in performing the duties of life	Robertson.
Vitæ via virtus	Virtue is the way of life	Dawson, Watkins.
Vitâ posse priore frui	To be able to enjoy the former part of life	Townsend.

Vittoria		Nicholson.
Vivat rex	Long life to the king	M'Corquodall, M'Corquodell, M'Corquodill.
Vivat veritas	May truth continue	Duncan.
Vive Deo ut vivas	Live to God, that you may have life	Craig.
Vive en espoir	Live in hope	Hassard, Starr.
Vive et vivas	Live and let live	Abercromby.
Vive la plume	Live the pen	Scott.
Vive le roi	Long life to the king	Gairden.
Vi vel suavitate	By violence or mildness	Rochfort.
Vivere sat vincere	To live enough is to conquer	Molyneaux, Mullins.
Vive revicturus	Live as to live again	Vivian.
Vive ut postea vivas	Live, that you may hereafter live	Fraser, Frazer, Johnston.
Vive ut semper vivas	Live so that you may live for ever	Hopson.
Vive ut vivas	Live, that you may have life	Abercrombie, Abercromby, Bathgate, Falconer, Faulkner, Johnston, M'Kenzie, Sladen, Snuggs, Price.
Vive valeque	Live and farewell	Green.
Vivis sperandum	While there is life there is hope	Niven, Philip.
Vivit post funera virtus	Virtue lives after death	Boyle, Maule, Robin, Shairp, Sharp.
Vivitur ingenio	He lives by ingenuity	Copen, Darley.
Vivunt dum virent	They live as long as they are green	Forrest.
Vix ea nostra voco	I scarce call these deeds of our ancestors ours	Campbell, Foster, Fountaine, Greville.
Vixi liber, et moriar	I have lived free, and will die so	Ibbetson, Ibetson.
Vix labora ut in æternum vivas	Strive that you may have eternal life	Apreece.
Volabo ut requiescam	I will make haste, that I may have rest	Collens, Collins.
Volando, reptilia sperno	Flying, I despise reptiles	Scarta, Scarth, Scras, Seras.
Volens et valens	Willingly and powerfully	Fetherston.
Volenti nil difficile	Nothing is grievous to a willing mind	Creech.
Volo, non valeo	I am willing, but not able	Greystock, Howard.
Volonté de Dieu	The will of God	Fyler.
Volvitur et ridet	He despises dangers	Fairwether.
Vota vitamea	Vows are my life	Brabazon.
Votis et conamine	With prayers and strenuous exertion	Kirk.
Votis tune velis	Then mayest thou be favourable to my prayers	Edmunds.
Vows should be respected		Vowe.
Vraye foy	True faith	Boswell.
Vulnere sano	I cure by a wound	Balderston, Balderstone.
Vulneror, non vincor	I am wounded, but not vanquished	Homfrey, Muschamp.

W

Watch		Forbes, Gordon.
Watch and pray		Forbes.
Watchful and bold		Coats, Cotes.
Watch well		Halliburton, Halyburton, Hallyburton.
Watch wiel		Scott.
Waterloo		Nicholson.
We big you sae warily		Cornwall.
Weigh well		Urquhart.
We live in hope		Thorburn.
Wer gutes u böses nit kan ertragan wirt kein grose ehre erjagen	Who cannot bear good and evil shall obtain no great honours	Brander.
We rise		Martinson.
West Indies		Provost.
We stoop not		Anderton.
Whadder		Stewart.
What was may be		Oliphant.

Whyll God wyll...............	....	Treffry.
Will God, and I shall............	....	Ashburnham, Menzies.
Wise and harmless............	....	Grant.
With heart and hand............	....	Dudgeon.
Without fear	....	Campbell, Sutherland.
Without help from above the arrow flies in vain............	....	Jones.
With truth and diligence......	....	Lucy.
Wrth ein ffrwythau yn hadna bydder........................	By our fruits we are known.......	Ellis.

Y

Y Cadarn a'r cyprwyns.........	The mighty and cunning...........	Wynn-Williams.
Yet higher.......................	....	Kinloch, Kinlock.
Yet in my flesh shall I see God	....	Surman.
Y gwir yn erbyn y byd........	The truth against the world.......	Edwards.
Ystoyeau et ne doublero.......	....	Strangeways.
Yvery.............................	....	Perceval, Percival.

Z

Zealous.............................	....	Hood.

PRINTED BY BALLANTYNE, ROBERTS, AND CO., PAUL'S WORK, EDINBURGH.

www.ingramcontent.com/pod-product-compliance
Lightning Source LLC
Chambersburg PA
CBHW071933220426
43662CB00009B/897